The Good Pub Guide 2009

Edited by

Alisdair Aird and Fiona Stapley

Managing Editor: Karen Fick
Associate Editor: Tim Locke
Editorial Assistance: Fiona Wright

EBURY PRESS
LONDON

Please send reports on pubs to

The Good Pub Guide
FREEPOST TN1569
WADHURST
East Sussex
TN5 7BR

or contact our website:
www.thegoodpubguide.co.uk

Good Guide publications are available at special discounts for bulk purchases
or for sales promotions or premiums. Special editions, including personalised
covers, excerpts of existing Guides and corporate imprints, can be created in
large quantities for special needs. Enquiries should be sent to the Sales
Development Department, Random House, 20 Vauxhall Bridge Road, London
SW1V 2SA (020 7840 8400).

Published in 2008 by Ebury Press, an imprint of Ebury Publishing

A Random House Group Company

Copyright © 2008 Random House Group Ltd
Maps copyright © 2008 Perrott Cartographics
Cover design by Two Associates
Cover photograph of the Kings Head in Aston Cantlow, Warwickshire © Rowan Isaac

Alisdair Aird and Fiona Stapley have asserted their right to be identified as the authors of
this Work in accordance with the Copyright, Designs and Patents Act 1988

The Random House Group Limited Reg. No. 954009

Addresses for companies within the Random House Group can be found at
www.randomhouse.co.uk

A CIP catalogue record for this book is available from the British Library

Mixed Sources
Product group from well-managed
forests and other controlled sources
www.fsc.org Cert no. TT-COC-2139
© 1996 Forest Stewardship Council
FSC

Typeset from authors' files by Clive Dorman
Edited by Pat Taylor Chalmers
Project managed by Nicky Thompson

Printed in the UK by CPI Cox & Wyman, Reading, RG1 8EX

ISBN 9780091922511

To buy books by your favourite authors and register for offers visit www.rbooks.co.uk

Contents

Introduction

The big pub companies or 'pubcos' which dominate Britain's pub scene have taken a battering on the stock market in the past few months, seeing their share prices nose-dive. Shares in Punch, the biggest, lost over three-quarters of their value in the year to July. This was largely because of the huge amounts of money that the company had borrowed to pay for building its pub empire – over seven times the value of its annual income. Just like home-owners who had borrowed over seven times their salary to get their mortgage, then faced having to renew the mortgage when interest rates are going up, credit is in short supply, and property prices are falling, so the over-borrowed pubcos are not in an enviable position. What's more, pub beer sales – one of pubcos' main sources of income – have fallen sharply in the last year, by around 10%.

Does this mean that the pubs themselves are in trouble? There is no doubt that having to fund these pubcos' debts puts an extra burden on pubs' finances. We believe that it has been a major factor behind the remorseless rise in pub food and drink prices over the last decade or so. As we warned last year, customers have started resisting high prices. So now, pubcos and individual pub owners facing higher costs – which they certainly do, with rising raw materials, energy and wages bills – are finding it almost impossible to resort to their usual response of simply putting up their own prices. Our survey of meal prices in over 1,000 pubs, comparing what each of those pubs is charging this year for a range of snacks, starters, main dishes and puddings with what it charged last year, shows that on average pub food prices have risen by only just over 2% – far less than the increase in the cost of running the pub and producing that food.

So it's clear that at last customers are holding pub food prices down successfully, by spending on pub meals which they do think worth the money – but not on ones which seem overpriced.

The squeeze between higher costs and lower income has of course been putting pubs out of business for years. Until very recently, the pubs which have been affected have tended to be the traditional locals, relying largely on male drinkers, often smokers, and often coming by car. Many such places have closed over the years, and the smoking ban was the final straw for many more. By contrast, pubs serving food, and catering to a wider mix of customers, have until now flourished.

In the last few months we have seen the first signs of real trouble for some of the country's top food pubs. The West Country has been the first area to feel the squeeze badly, with two of its best pubs either closing or facing something of a hiatus. Here, distance is probably a factor: with good dining pubs scattered over what is after all a very large area, and drawing their customers from far and wide, the cost of getting there becomes more of an obstacle when fuel prices rise steeply – as they have done. We fear that there will be more trouble over this coming year. Even the best pubs in remote areas without local regular support are now at risk. In more populated areas, pubs giving poorer value than their local competitors will be the ones to suffer.

The lesson for us has been clear. This year, we have concentrated even more on value – not just in the one in 12 main entries whose commendably low prices have earned our Bargain Award, but right through the range. So we do include pubs where the prices are very much on a 'special occasion' level, but where sheer quality justifies them. As always, though, the bulk of our good pubs are the places which give honest value – all-round enjoyment at sensible prices.

The pubs which work hardest and most flexibly to give customers what they want are the pubs which will survive and flourish. This, of course, is all good news for customers. As one of our top landlords who opens at 10am told us, as he and his staff are there anyway cleaning up and getting organised, it would be senseless to keep his doors closed to people wanting to drop in for an early coffee. Other pubs open even earlier, for breakfast.

Although some pubs still close for the afternoon, all-day opening has now become widespread. Moreover, this year we have found that one in seven pubs now serves food all day at least on some days, and we expect this proportion to grow substantially.

BABY LAGER LOUTS

Most pubs now allow children, many doing cut-price smaller food helpings for them. A great many readers really appreciate this, enjoying being able to go to the pub as a family treat. Occasionally, though, children don't behave decently, and this can spoil things for everyone else.

This year more readers than ever before have complained to us about pub visits being spoilt for them by badly behaved children running around unchecked. As one said: 'Far too many pubs let children run around playing near the bar like they are at play school.' Another: 'They completely spoil it for aficionados like myself who love "proper pubs"... I am sick of going into a pub and feeling I am at play school.' Another: 'No longer can one enjoy an adult evening without feeling that one is dining in a crèche.' As one pointed out: 'It's not the kids' fault, it's the b****y stupid parents who let their kids run riot in a place where hot food and drink is being served.' Another agreed: 'I find it very helpful to be able to take children to the pub on special occasions. The moment any of them cause a problem to adult drinkers we remove them from the pub without ceremony. Surely any problem is entirely the fault of ill-disciplined parents. I feel so sorry for hard-working landlords who have to deal with bad manners from parents who ought to know better. It is so often the parents who should be asked to leave!' But take care about that: one of our readers, a solicitor in his sixties, asked a doting father if there was any possibility of his keeping his obviously sick baby quiet – the father suggested that they resolved the matter outside!

This is a peculiarly british problem: in continental restaurants and cafés it's normal to see families with children, not normal to see kids spoil things for grown-ups. So we have considerable sympathy with the landlord of one charming Sussex pub who told us that he had decided it 'just didn't suit children', as he didn't want to do plates of chips or burgers and didn't want to have to look after customers' children while they had a meal and a few drinks. However, over 90% of the pubs in this *Guide* do allow children (an increase of about 10% in just the last four years). And there are plenty of pub-going families whose well-behaved children cause no problem.

We confess that we can't see an easy solution. It's easy to say that we could start treating parents who let their children run riot with the disdain normally reserved for lager louts. But would that have any impact on people who think they are entitled to a thoroughly relaxed family day out? And you can imagine the retort when a publican asks a badly behaved family to quieten their children: 'We've just spent over 50 quid here, do you want us to leave without paying?'

SENSIBLE SIZES FOR WINE GLASSES

Three years ago we started a campaign for pubs to sell wine in standard-sized glasses. As we pointed out then, many pubs use a 175ml glass as standard – that's nearly quarter of a bottle. To them, a large glass is 250ml, or a third of a bottle. This isn't generosity, it's just a way of getting more money into their tills. And it leaves many customers drinking more than they want to – and perhaps more than is safe. We proposed that pubs should revert to the original 'standard' 125ml glass size.

Since then, others including the Royal College of Physicians, an increasing number of politicians, and a report published in July 2008 by the Department of Health, have backed us up. So we repeat the call. We would like to see all pubs selling wine use the 125ml glass as their standard size. They should call 175ml glasses 'large', and 250ml glasses 'giant'. And proportionate pricing must be a part of this, as it is with beer pricing. If a pub charges £4 for a 175ml glass, it should charge only £2.85 for the 125ml standard size (and £5.70 for the 250ml giant size).

SOFT DRINKS BUT HARD PRICING

One couple wrote to us recently to say that they were shocked to the core when a Yorkshire pub charged them £2.20 each for the children's apple juices. Our own records over the last few months show that £1.80 is now typical for a standard soft drink, and that £2 is not uncommon.

We know all the usual arguments about how it's not just the drink you are paying for, it's the service, the furnishings, and so forth. But pubs make no friends for themselves by charging so much for drinks that people are used to paying 40p or so in the shops – and that some pubs (such as those in the Tynemill group) charge a much more pocket-friendly price for.

THE COST OF THE SMOKING BAN

Some of the effects of the ban are already obvious – pubs that are cleaner as well as not smoky, big pub chains putting more energy into selling food, more people (an estimated 400,000) giving up smoking. Undoubtedly, the ban has added to the problems of many marginal pubs, and could be the last straw for them; one estimate is that over the next five years it could contribute to 7 or 8% closing.

There are also less obvious effects. Pub-goers haven't needed so much dry cleaning – to the extent that one dry cleaning group nearly went out of business. On the other hand, through the prices pubs charge us for our food and drink, we now have to pay for the massive investment many pubs have been making in outdoor awnings and heaters, and even smokers' shelters. The bill for heaters and other such external embellishments has climbed to over £85 million – money that will eventually come out of pub users' pockets.

We asked a number of our readers what they thought about the outdoor changes, which do at least help to eliminate the gloomy sight of a huddle of shivering smokers decorating the pub doorway. One or two said the heaters added to conviviality. One was a bit disheartened when two of his friends sitting smoking in what he called the Sin Bin found that people eating 20 yards away had complained to the landlord. Several, with no prompting from us, said that they objected to the heaters on environmental grounds – pumping enormous quantities of carbon dioxide out, trying to heat the open air. One remembered an open-air meal some years ago, when someone at another table lit a cigarette. Immediately a woman, dressed as a man complete with stiff collar, tie and monocle, jumped up waving her arms to dispel the virtually non-existent smoke, and moved pointedly to a more distant table. At which point the smoker's companion went over to her and said: 'How kind of you to move, madam. Your aftershave was becoming rather dominant.'

Finally, one reader was mildly nostalgic for the old pre-ban days – when at least the smoke hid other things, like cooking smells: 'we were glad of a stroll on the pier afterwards to blow away the grease'.

LIVE MUSIC – VERY MUCH ALIVE

When the licensing laws were amended in 2003, many people feared that the new requirements for licensing musical entertainment would be a problem for small-scale live music sessions. At least in pubs, live music is still thriving. A hundred and fifty of our main entries – one in seven or eight – and hundreds more of the small-print Lucky Dip entries have regular live music sessions.

Juke boxes, incidentally, are dying out rapidly in pubs. Just four years ago, we noted the decline, saying that by then only one in 25 of the pubs in the *Guide* had one. Now, the proportion has dropped to one in 37. If you are desperate to find a juke box, head north: pubs in Scotland are four times as likely to have one.

PUB FOOD – MUCH CHEAPER IN SOME AREAS THAN OTHERS

In our national survey of pub food prices, we take seven prices for each of the main entries: the price of their most popular dish, and the prices of their cheapest and most expensive snack or starter, main dish, and pudding.

Of course, there are enormous variations from pub to pub. And the most popular dish varies from pub to pub. Nationally, the three favourite pub meals are steak pie in one of its many forms (steak and ale, steak and mushroom, steak and kidney etc), fish and chips, and steak. In a top-notch dining pub, a really good piece of rare-breed steak could easily set you back £17 or even more, and it's nearly impossible now to find any steak anywhere for under £10. We found fish and chips varied from a bargain £4.49 to £13.75, and steak and ale pie might cost anything from £4.50 to £13.50. The cheaper slow-cooked cuts of meat which are becoming more fashionable seem to vary rather less in price, by the time they reach your plate, with lamb shank or pork belly typically costing from around £9.50 to £14.95.

In a good pub, the average price of a main dish is now around £11. Allowing for all the variations mentioned above, pubs' most popular dishes averaged £10.88 in price; taking instead the middle price-point on each pub's main dish menu gives a national average of £11.51.

Taking all pub food prices – starter or snack, main dish, pudding, most popular dish – there are striking variations from area to area, as follows. Each group starts with the cheapest area in the group, working on up through the more expensive ones. Within a group, there's often little or no price difference between adjacent entries, but there is a noticeable difference – up to a pound or so for a meal – between the cheapest and the most expensive in that group.

Remarkably cheap: West Midlands
Cheap: Derbyshire, London, Scotland, Lancashire, Nottinghamshire, Northumbria
Below average: Devon, Staffordshire, Worcestershire, Hertfordshire, Wales, Isle of Wight, Cumbria, Lincolnshire, Essex, Somerset, Cornwall, Shropshire, Northamptonshire, Dorset
Above average: Norfolk, Leicestershire and Rutland, Suffolk, Wiltshire, Hampshire, Cambridgeshire, Sussex, Herefordshire, Oxfordshire, Yorkshire
Expensive: Buckinghamshire, Bedfordshire, Gloucestershire, Warwickshire, Kent, Berkshire, Surrey.

HOW TO SAVE £££ ON YOUR PINTS
Our national price survey shows that the average price of a pint has now reached £2.58 – up a crushing 7% since last year. Only about a quarter of the increase is accounted for by the last Budget's excise duty rise.

One way of cutting the price you pay for a pint is to go to a pub brewing its own beers. Typically, that now saves about 35p a pint. Individual breweries whose beers our price survey showed giving comparable or better savings included – in order, starting with the cheapest – Wyre Piddle, Holts, Sam Smiths, Springhead, Clarks, Titanic, Hydes, Castle Rock, fff, Highwood/Tom Woods, Ballards, Breconshire, Butts, Cumbrian, Lees, Loweswater, Rockingham, Donnington, Hadrian & Borders, Three Tuns, York, Bathams and Burton Bridge. All these are small or smallish independent brewers. Because the small independent brewers give good value, as well as producing good interesting drinks, their sales have actually been increasing recently, while the big breweries have seen a decline.

If you have just one pub pint a week and normally buy at the national average price, buying one of these good value beers instead, or a pub's own brew, saves you £18 by the end of a year. And if you normally buy a pricy beer (some cost much more than the £2.58 average), you save much more by switching.

Where you drink also has a major effect on your pocket. Pubs in some areas set much lower prices than others, as the Table (opposite) shows.

To put this in perspective, that pint-a-week pub-goer in Surrey has to shell out over £30 a year more than someone in the West Midlands.

AWARDS
Best pubs for beer
Good beer seems to taste even better in good company, in a really nice interesting pub. Some places which stand out for beer lovers are the Engineers Arms in Henlow (Bedfordshire), the floating pub Charters in Peterborough (Cambridgeshire), the Bhurtpore at Aston (Cheshire), the Watermill at Ings (Cumbria), the Brunswick in Derby (Derbyshire), the Bridge Inn just outside Topsham (Devon), the Old Spot in Dursley (Gloucestershire), the Marble Arch in Manchester and Stalybridge Station Buffet

HOW BEER PRICES VARY   £/pint

extraordinarily cheap
West Midlands   2.25

very cheap
Nottinghamshire   2.33
Lancashire   2.34
Staffordshire   2.35
Cheshire   2.38
Cumbria   2.41

quite cheap
Derbyshire   2.44
Herefordshire   2.45
Yorkshire   2.46
Worcestershire   2.47
Northumbria, Lincolnshire, Shropshire   2.48
Cornwall   2.49
Channel Islands   2.52
Devon   2.53

average
Cambridgeshire, Gloucestershire, Somerset   2.56
Wales   2.57
Leicestershire and Rutland, Wiltshire   2.59
Northamptonshire   2.60
Dorset, Essex   2.63

quite expensive
Isle of Wight   2.65
Scotland   2.66
Hampshire, Hertfordshire, Norfolk   2.67
Bedfordshire, Kent   2.69
Sussex   2.70
Oxfordshire   2.71
Suffolk, Warwickshire   2.72

very expensive
Buckinghamshire   2.76
Berkshire   2.78
London   2.81
Surrey   2.88

(Lancashire chapter), the Crown Posada in Newcastle (Northumbria), the Victorian in Beeston and Lincolnshire Poacher (Nottinghamshire), the Crown at Churchill (Somerset), the Griffin at Shustoke (Warwickshire), the Nags Head in Malvern (Worcestershire), the New Barrack in Sheffield (Yorkshire), the Market Porter in south London, and the Guildford Arms in Edinburgh and Bon Accord in Glasgow (Scotland). All of these are committed to interesting real ales, often changing quickly, with publicans or staff who enjoy talking informatively about them.

Many other pubs keep a few real ales in excellent condition, but only a very few manage the tricky task of keeping lots of them really well. Masters of this craft are the Tom Cobley at Spreyton (a new *Guide* entry, in Devon), the Fat Cat in Norwich (Norfolk), and the Fat Cat in Ipswich (Suffolk). The friendly Tom Cobley in Spreyton is **Beer Pub of the Year 2009**.

OWN BREW BEER
The dozens of pubs which now brew their own beer all bring the immediate reward of cheaper pints. Some also bring a real quality advantage, so good that pubs elsewhere want to stock them too. Prime examples are the Brewery Tap in Peterborough with its 'Oakham' beers (Cambridgeshire), the Brunswick in Derby (Derbyshire), the Flower Pots at Cheriton (Hampshire), the Grainstore in Oakham (Leicestershire and Rutland), the Keelman in Newburn with its Big Lamp beers (Northumbria), the Six Bells and the Three Tuns, both in lucky old Bishop's Castle (Shropshire), the Burton Bridge Inn in Burton upon Trent (Staffordshire), the St Peters Brewery in South Elmham (Suffolk), the Gribble Inn at Oving (Sussex), the Beacon in Sedgley (Warwickshire), and the Fox & Hounds in Houston (Scotland). The excellent and extremely popular Oakham beers earn the Brewery Tap in Peterborough the title of **Own Brew Pub of the Year 2009**.

WHICH PUBS ARE BEST FOR WINE?
For our top wine award, we look for quality, choice and value, particularly in wines by the glass. Outstanding are the French Horn at Steppingley (Bedfordshire), the Culm Valley at Culmstock and Harris Arms at Portgate (Devon), the Rose at Peldon (Essex), the Wykeham Arms in Winchester (Hampshire), the Olive Tree at Clipsham (Leicestershire and Rutland), the George of Stamford (Lincolnshire), Woods in Dulverton (Somerset), the Crown in Southwold and Crown at Stoke-by-Nayland (Suffolk), the Howard Arms at Ilmington (Warwickshire), and the Vine Tree at Norton (Wiltshire). With its exceptional cellar and a well informed landlord who takes real interest in his wines, Woods at Dulverton is **Wine Pub of the Year 2009**.

SOME OUTSTANDING MALT WHISKY COLLECTIONS
From the many pubs which offer dozens of single malt whiskies, we have shortlisted four as being particularly notable. The Britons Protection in Manchester (Lancashire chapter) with its wonderful collection of well over 200 is exceptional for England. The other three are all in Scotland. The Bow Bar in Edinburgh, just the right sort of chatty atmosphere in which to try at least one or two of their 160; the Stein Inn on Skye, a beautiful spot, perfect for any malt whisky lover; and a new entry to the *Guide*, the Port Charlotte Hotel on Islay. With its remarkable array of rare Islay whiskies, the Port Charlotte Hotel is **Whisky Pub of the Year 2009**.

THE TOP DINING PUBS
The best dining pubs now do superb food, almost all using local produce, often organic and free range. Nearly one in four main entries now holds our Food Award, giving plenty of choice for top-quality pub meals. At this elevated level, prices, matching the quality, are often high; many of these places are great choices for a special meal out, rather than everyday eating. However, this year we have been pleased to see more and more special deals, especially two- and three-course menus, often at lunchtime. Many of these offer exceptional value, given the quality.

The pubs holding their County Dining Pub of the Year titles all serve excellent food, as do the pubs we mention as runners-up in the chapter introductions, in those areas where the competition is high. Here, we name the very best: the Anchor at Sutton Gault (Cambridgeshire), the Stagg at Titley (Herefordshire), the Olive Branch at Clipsham (Leicestershire and Rutland), the George of Stamford (Lincolnshire), the Hoste Arms in

Burnham Market (Norfolk), the Queens Head at Bulwick (Northamptonshire), the Lord Poulett Arms at Hinton St George (Somerset), the Crown in Southwold (Suffolk), the Jolly Sportsman at East Chiltington (Sussex), the Vine Tree at Norton (Wiltshire), the Durham Ox at Crayke (Yorkshire), the Applecross Inn (Scotland), and the Duke of Cambridge (north London). Three of these earn particular praise for sheer value: the Anchor at Sutton Gault (special lunch deals), the Queens Head at Bulwick and the Applecross Inn. A fourth pub, the Lord Poulett Arms at Hinton St George, can't quite match these on price but does have the edge for a really special meal out: it is **Dining Pub of the Year 2009.**

All these pubs take great care to fuel their kitchens with tip-top produce. Two of them take it a stage further. Geetie Singh of the north London pub, the Duke of Cambridge, won't use anything unless it's organic (even the beers), and seasonal; she is the local recycling queen, and her pub uses solar and wind power. Steve and Nicola Reynolds in the Stagg at Titley grow their own veg, and keep free-range chickens and pigs.

Quite a few other good pubs are doing likewise. The European at Piddletrenthide (Dorset), Anchor at Nayland (Suffolk) and Parrot at Forest Green (Surrey) all use meat and produce from their own farms; the Anchor's adjacent farm is full of heritage breeds. Others grow their own vegetables, herbs and fruit, and – perhaps in return for a pint or two – get extra supplies from neighbours and friends: notable examples are the Pot Kiln at Frilsham (Berkshire), the Horse & Groom at Bourton-on-the-Hill (Gloucestershire), the Riverside Inn at Aymestrey and Three Horseshoes at Little Cowarne (Herefordshire), the Bricklayers Arms at Flaunden (Hertfordshire), the Inn on the Green at Ingham (Lincolnshire), the Kings Arms at Farthingstone (Northamptonshire), the Nut Tree at Murcott (Oxfordshire), the Golden Key at Snape and Anchor at Walberswick (Suffolk), the Star at Harome and Appletree at Marton (Yorkshire), and the Griffin at Felinfach (Wales).

BARGAIN PUBS
It's not hard to find cheap food in good pubs; as we have said, prices at one in 12 of the main entries qualify for the Bargain Award. What is rarer is food that's both cheap and interesting – proper home cooking. Value champions are the Old Poets Corner in Ashover (Derbyshire), the Adam & Eve in Norwich (Norfolk), the Lincolnshire Poacher and Olde Trip to Jerusalem in Nottingham (Nottinghamshire), the Queens Head in Lichfield (Staffordshire), the Basketmakers Arms in Brighton and Six Bells at Chiddingly (Sussex), the Fat Cat in Sheffield (Yorkshire), the Four Marys in Linlithgow (Scotland), and the Pen-y-Gwryd near Llanberis (Wales). Engagingly idiosyncratic and refreshingly unsmart, the Six Bells at Chiddingly's homely food at nicely old-fashioned prices earns it the title of **Bargain Pub of the Year 2009.**

UNSPOILT PUBS
There are dozens of genuinely unspoilt traditional pubs in the *Guide* – so many, and with so much individuality, that it has been quite a task selecting a shortlist of favourites. Our top ten are the Bell at Aldworth (Berkshire), the Cock at Broom (Bedfordshire), the Queens Head at Newton (Cambridgeshire), the White Lion at Barthomley (Cheshire), the Bridge Inn at Topsham (Devon), the Square & Compass at Worth Matravers (Dorset), the Boat at Ashleworth Quay (Gloucestershire), the Harrow at Steep (Hampshire), the Tuckers Grave at Faulkland (Somerset), and the Case is Altered at Five Ways (Warwickshire chapter). The Square & Compass above the sea at Worth Matravers, with good beer as well as the splendid farm ciders from its serving hatch, is **Unspoilt Pub of the Year 2009.**

Anybody who enjoys unspoilt pubs will have a special treat in visiting three pubs, each quite unique in its idiosyncratic way: the Yew Tree at Cauldon (Staffordshire), for its rare polyphons, longcase clocks, and all sorts of other amazing collections – bargain drinks, too; the Monkey House near Defford (Worcestershire), a cider house so old-fashioned that you can scarcely believe it's survived; and the Tafarn Sinc at Rosebush (Wales), a corrugated iron oddity like a railway-halt inn tucked away in some dim past.

THE CLASSIC COUNTRY PUB
Most of the pubs in this *Guide* are country pubs, in the sense that they are pubs in the countryside, or in country villages. But a few are just the sort of places you imagine, when you try to conjure up the ideal country pub. Classic examples are the White Horse

at Hedgerley (Buckinghamshire), the Vine at Pamphill (Dorset), the Mole Trap at Stapleford Tawney (Essex), the Golden Heart near Brimpsfield (Gloucestershire), the Flower Pots at Cheriton and Royal Oak at Fritham (Hampshire), the Live & Let Live on Bringsty Common, a new entry, and Carpenters Arms at Walterstone (Herefordshire), the Gate at Boyden Gate (Kent), the Lower Buck at Waddington, another new entry (Lancashire), the London at Molland (Somerset), the Olde Royal Oak at Wetton (Staffordshire), the Queens Head at Icklesham (Sussex), the Cross Keys at Upper Chute (Wiltshire), and the Farmers Arms at Birtsmorton (Worcestershire). Part of a New Forest working farm, the Royal Oak at Fritham is **Country Pub of the Year 2009**.

TOWN-CENTRE GEMS
A dozen of the very best town pubs are the Albion in Chester (Cheshire), Adam & Eve in Norwich (Norfolk), the Victoria in Durham and Crown Posada in Newcastle (Northumbria), the Turf in Oxford (Oxfordshire), the Armoury in Shrewsbury (Shropshire), the Old Green Tree in Bath (Somerset), the Nutshell in Bury St Edmunds (Suffolk), the Nags Head in Malvern (Worcestershire), the Olde White Hart in Hull and Maltings in York (Yorkshire), the Jerusalem Tavern in central London, and the Café Royal in Edinburgh (Scotland). The Jerusalem Tavern is something really special for London and is **Town Pub of the Year 2009**.

WARM-HEARTED HOTEL BARS
It's often a surprising pleasure to find a thriving proper bar, used by locals, at the heart of a sizeable hotel: places such as the George in Buckden (Cambridgeshire), the Pheasant at Bassenthwaite Lake (Cumbria), the Port Gaverne Inn near Port Isaac (Cornwall), the Feathers in Ledbury (Herefordshire), the Seaview Hotel (Isle of Wight), the George of Stamford (Lincolnshire), the Hoste Arms in Burnham Market and Crown in Wells-next-the-Sea (Norfolk), the Ravenwood Hall at Rougham and Crown in Southwold (Suffolk), the Mermaid in Rye (Sussex), the Golden Lion at Easenhall (Warwickshire), the Castle Inn in Castle Combe (Wiltshire), the White Swan in Middleham, Boars Head at Ripley and Sportsmans Arms at Wath in Nidderdale (Yorkshire), and the George in Inveraray (Scotland). With great atmosphere in its bars (not to mention the summer bonus of a charming courtyard), the civilised old George of Stamford takes the title of **Hotel Bar of the Year 2009**.

NEW FINDS
There are 1,931 new Lucky Dip entries in this edition of the *Guide*, and 122 newcomers to the main entries. The most memorable of these new main entries are the Hole in the Wall at Little Wilbraham (Cambridgeshire), the Duke of Portland in Lach Dennis (Cheshire), the European at Piddletrenthide (Dorset), the Tunnel House at Coates (Gloucestershire), the Bakers Arms in Droxford (Hampshire), the Live & Let Live on Bringsty Common (Herefordshire), the Tally Ho at Barkway (Hertfordshire), the Inn at Wray (Lancashire), the Pigs at Edgefield (Norfolk), the Barrasford Arms (Northumbria), the Rock at Waterrow (Somerset), the Golden Key in Snape (Suffolk), the Butchers Arms at Eldersfield (Worcestershire), the Crown at Roecliffe (Yorkshire), the Laurie Arms at Haugh of Urr and Meikleour Hotel (Scotland), and the Hardwick near Abergavenny (Wales). A proper pub with a relaxing little bar, a dining area of real individuality, good food and drink, and genuine personality, the Tally Ho at Barkway is **New Pub of the Year 2009**.

INN OF THE YEAR
More than one in three main entries have bedrooms. About half of these have qualified for our Stay Award. Some are quite simple, though enjoyable. Others are places for a special few days away. Among these, top treats are the Port Gaverne Inn near Port Isaac (Cornwall), the Pheasant at Bassenthwaite Lake (Cumbria), the Inn at Whitewell (Lancashire), the Olive Branch at Clipsham (Leicestershire and Rutland), the George of Stamford (Lincolnshire), the Hoste Arms in Burnham Market (Norfolk), the Rose & Crown at Romaldkirk (Northumbria), the Castle Combe Inn (Wiltshire), the Star at Harome and White Swan in Pickering (Yorkshire), the Applecross Inn (Scotland), the Groes at Ty'n-y-Groes (Wales), and the Fleur du Jardin in King's Mills (Channel Islands). Overlooking the Vale of Conwy and the peaks of Snowdonia, the Groes at Ty'n-y-groes is **Inn of the Year 2009**.

LANDLORD OF THE YEAR

At the heart of every good pub is a good publican. The best have a wonderful gift for making everyone feel welcome and at home, even on a first visit – as well as making sure everything works well. Outstanding landlords and landladies are Aubrey Sinclair Ball in the Blue Bell at Helpston (Cambridgeshire), Suzy Turner, the newish landlady of the Red Lion in Litton (Derbyshire), Jill and Michael Dyson at the Dodbrooke Inn in Kingsbridge (a new Devon entry), John Ford, Karen Trimby, Ron Hobson and Cherry Ball in the Greyhound at Sydling St Nicholas (Dorset), Trevor Oliver at the Cricketers in Clavering (Essex), John Barnard of the Red Lion at Ampney St Peter, Assumpta and Peter Golding in the Chequers at Churchill, Jo and Jon Carrier of the Five Mile House at Duntisbourne Abbots and Paul Davidson and Pat LeJeune of the Bell at Sapperton (Gloucestershire), Mark and Sue Watts in the Rising Sun at Swanmore and Hassan Matini in the Trooper near Petersfield (Hampshire), Chris Smith in the Gate at Boyden Gate (Kent), Pip Wilkinson at the Buckinghamshire Arms, Blicking (Norfolk), Maggie Chandler at the George in Kilsby (Northamptonshire), Peter and Veryan Graham at the George in Croscombe (Somerset), Emily Hammond at the George, Alstonefield (Staffordshire), Nick Attfield, the newish tenant of the Golden Key in Snape (Suffolk) and Judith Fish up at the Applecross Inn (Scotland). Welcoming, cheerful and always on the go, Mark and Sue Watts of the Rising Sun in Swanmore are **Licensees of the Year 2009.**

PUB OF THE YEAR

Pubs which have really hit the spot with a very wide range of readers this year are the Pheasant at Bassenthwaite Lake and Three Shires at Little Langdale (Cumbria), the John Thompson near Melbourne (Derbyshire), the Golden Heart near Brimpsfield, Five Mile House at Duntisbourne Abbots and Bell at Sapperton (all in Gloucestershire), the Royal Oak at Fritham and Wykeham Arms in Winchester (Hampshire), the Hoste Arms in Burnham Market (Norfolk), the Queens Head at Bulwick (Northamptonshire), the Crown in Southwold (Suffolk), the Queens Head at Icklesham (Sussex), the Bell in Welford-on-Avon (Warwickshire), the Nags Head in Malvern (Worcestershire), the Durham Ox at Crayke and Blue Lion at East Witton (Yorkshire), and the Moulin in Pitlochry (Scotland). With affordable food, good beers, welcoming atmosphere and a series of rooms each with its own character, the Golden Heart near Brimpsfield – as readers say, 'a little gem' – is **Pub of the Year 2009.**

What is a Good Pub?

The main entries in this *Guide* have been through a two-stage sifting process. First of all, some 2,000 regular correspondents keep in touch with us about the pubs they visit, and double that number report occasionally. We also get a flow of sent to us at **feedback@thegoodpubguide.co.uk**. This keeps us up to date about pubs included in previous editions – it's their alarm signals that warn us when a pub's standards have dropped (after a change of management, say), and it's their continuing approval that reassures us about keeping a pub as a main entry for another year. Very important, though, are the reports they send us on pubs we don't know at all. It's from these new discoveries that we make up a shortlist, to be considered for possible inclusion as new main entries. The more people that report favourably on a new pub, the more likely it is to win a place on this shortlist – especially if some of the reporters belong to our hard core of about 600 trusted correspondents whose judgement we have learned to rely on. These are people who have each given us detailed comments on dozens of pubs, and shown that (when we ourselves know some of those pubs too) their judgement is closely in line with our own.

This brings us to the acid test. Each pub, before inclusion as a main entry, is inspected anonymously by one of the editorial team. They have to find some special quality that would make strangers enjoy visiting it. What often marks the pub out for special attention is good value food (and that might mean anything from a well made sandwich, with good fresh ingredients at a low price, to imaginative cooking outclassing most restaurants in the area). The drinks may be out of the ordinary – maybe several hundred whiskies, remarkable wine lists, interesting ciders, or a wide range of well kept real ales possibly with some home-brewed, or bottled beers from all over the world. Perhaps there's a special appeal about it as a place to stay, with good bedrooms and obliging service. Maybe it's the building itself (from centuries-old parts of monasteries to extravagant Victorian gin-palaces), or its surroundings (lovely countryside, attractive waterside, extensive well kept garden), or what's in it (charming furnishings, extraordinary collections of bric-a-brac).

Above all, though, what makes the good pub is its atmosphere – you should be able to feel at home there, and feel not just that *you're* glad you've come but that *they're* glad you've come. A good landlord or landlady makes a huge difference here – they can make or break a pub.

It follows from this that a great many ordinary locals, perfectly good in their own right, don't earn a place in the *Guide*. What makes them attractive to their regular customers (an almost clubby chumminess) may even make strangers feel rather out-of-place.

Another important point is that there's not necessarily any link between charm and luxury. A basic unspoilt village tavern, with hard seats and a flagstone floor, may be worth travelling miles to find, while a deluxe pub-restaurant may not be worth crossing the street for. Landlords can't buy the Good Pub accolade by spending thousands on thickly padded banquettes, soft music and elaborate menus – they can only win it, by having a genuinely personal concern for both their customers and their pub.

Using the *Guide*

THE COUNTIES

England has been split alphabetically into counties. Each chapter starts by picking out the pubs that are currently doing best in the area, or are specially attractive for one reason or another.

The county boundaries we use are those for the administrative counties (not the old traditional counties, which were changed back in 1976). We have left the new unitary authorities within the counties that they formed part of until their creation in the most recent local government reorganisation. Metropolitan areas have been included in the counties around them – for example, Merseyside in Lancashire. And occasionally we have grouped counties together – for example, Rutland with Leicestershire, and Durham with Northumberland to make Northumbria. If in doubt, check the Contents.

Scotland, Wales and London have each been covered in single chapters. Pubs are listed alphabetically (except in London which is split into Central, East, North, South and West), under the name of the town or village where they are. If the village is so small that you probably wouldn't find it on a road map, we've listed it under the name of the nearest sizeable village or town. The maps use the same town and village names, and additionally include a few big cities that don't have any listed pubs – for orientation.

We list pubs in their true county, not their postal county. Just once or twice, when the village itself is in one county but the pub is just over the border in the next-door county, we have used the village county, not the pub one.

STARS ★

Really outstanding pubs are awarded a star, and in a few cases two: these are the aristocrats among pubs. The stars do NOT signify extra luxury or specially good food – in fact some of the pubs which appeal most distinctively and strongly of all are decidedly basic in terms of food and surroundings. The detailed description of each pub shows what its particular appeal is, and this is what the stars refer to.

FOOD AWARD ⑪

Pubs where food is quite outstanding.

STAY AWARD ⇨

Pubs that are good as places to stay at (obviously you can't expect the same level of luxury at £60 a head as you'd get for £100 a head). Pubs with bedrooms are marked on the maps as a dot within a square.

WINE AWARD ♀

Pubs with particularly enjoyable wines by the glass – often a good choice.

BEER AWARD ◖

Pubs where the quality of the beer is quite exceptional, or pubs which keep a particularly interesting range of beers in good condition.

BARGAIN AWARD £

Pubs with decent snacks at £3.75 or less, or worthwhile main dishes at under £7.

RECOMMENDERS

At the end of each main entry we include the names of readers who have recently recommended that pub (unless they've asked us not to).

Important note: the description of the pub and the comments on it are our own and not the recommenders'; they are based on our own personal inspections and on later verification of facts with each pub. A good pub which has no reader recommenders, or one that we judge deserves to stay in the main entries despite a very recent management includes the acronym BOB (buyer's own brand) as a recommender.

LUCKY DIPS

The Lucky Dip section at the end of each county chapter includes brief descriptions of pubs that have been recommended by readers in the year before the *Guide* goes to print and that we feel are worthy of inclusion. We do not include a pub unless readers' descriptions make the nature of the pub quite clear, and give us good grounds for trusting that other readers would be glad to know of the pub. A bare mention that food is served shouldn't be taken to imply a recommendation of the food. The same is true of accommodation and so forth. At the end of the entry we print the recommenders' names. BB means we have inspected a pub and found nothing against it and LYM means the pub was a main entry in a previous edition of the *Guide*. In both these cases, the description is our own; in others, it's based on the readers' reports. This year, we have deleted many previously highly rated pubs from the *Guide* simply because we have no very recent reports on them. This may well mean that we have left out some favourites – please tell us if we have!

LUCKY DIPS WITH ☆

Roughly speaking these pubs are as much worth considering as some of the main entries themselves.

All the Lucky Dips, but particularly the starred ones, are under consideration for inspection for a future edition so please let us have any comments you can make on them using the report forms in this *Guide*, by writing to us at The Good Pub Guide, FREEPOST TN1569, WADHURST, East Sussex TN5 7BR or by emailing us at **feedback@thegoodpubguide.co.uk**.

LOCATING PUBS

To help readers who use digital mapping systems we include a **postcode** for every pub.

Pubs outside London are given a British Grid four-figure **map reference**. Where a pub is exceptionally difficult to find, we include a six-figure reference in the directions. The map number (main entries only) refers to the map in our *Guide*.

MOTORWAY PUBS

If a pub is within four or five miles of a motorway junction we give special directions for finding it from the motorway. The Special Interest Lists at the end of the book include a list of these pubs, motorway by motorway.

PRICES AND OTHER FACTUAL DETAILS

The *Guide* went to press during the summer of 2008, after each pub was sent a checking sheet to get up-to-date food, drink and bedroom prices and other factual information. By the summer of 2009 prices are bound to have increased, but if you find a significantly different price please let us know.

Breweries or independent chains to which pubs are 'tied' are named at the beginning of the italic-print rubric after each main entry. That generally means the pub has to get most if not all of its drinks from that brewery or chain. If the brewery is not an independent one but just part of a combine, we name the combine in brackets. When the pub is tied, we have spelled out whether the landlord is a tenant, has the pub on a lease, or is a manager. Tenants and leaseholders of breweries generally have considerably greater freedom to do things their own way, and in particular are allowed to buy drinks including a beer from sources other than their tied brewery.

Free houses are pubs not tied to a brewery. In theory they can shop around but in practice many free houses have loans from the big brewers, on terms that bind them to sell those breweries' beers. So don't be too surprised to find that so-called free houses may be stocking a range of beers restricted to those from a single brewery.

Real ale is used by us to mean beer that has been maturing naturally in its cask. We do not count as real ale beer which has been pasteurised or filtered to remove its natural yeasts. If it is kept under a blanket of carbon dioxide to preserve it, we still generally mention it – as long as the pressure is too light for you to notice any extra fizz, it's hard to tell the difference. (For brevity, we use the expression 'under light blanket pressure' to cover such pubs; we do not include among them pubs where the blanket pressure is high enough to force the beer up from the cellar, as this does make it unnaturally fizzy.)

Other drinks: we've also looked out particularly for pubs doing enterprising non-alcoholic drinks (including good tea or coffee), interesting spirits (especially malt whiskies), country wines, freshly squeezed juices, and good farm ciders.

Bar food usually refers to what is sold in the bar, we do not describe menus that are restricted to a separate restaurant. If we know that a pub serves sandwiches we say so – if you don't see them mentioned, assume you can't get them. Food listed is an example of the sort of thing you'd find served in the bar on a normal day and we try to indicate any difference we know of between lunchtime and evening.

Children If we don't mention children at all, assume that they are not welcome. All but one or two pubs allow children in their garden if they have one. 'Children welcome' means the pub has told us that it lets them in with no special restrictions. In other cases we report exactly what arrangements pubs say they make for children. However, we have to note that in readers' experience some pubs make restrictions that they haven't told us about (children only if eating, for example). If you come across this, please let us know, so that we can clarify with the pub concerned for the next edition. The absence of any reference to children in a Lucky Dip entry means we don't know either way. Children's Certificates exist, but in practice children are allowed into some part of most pubs in this *Guide* (there is no legal restriction on the movement of children over 14 in any pub). Children under 16 cannot have alcoholic drinks. Children aged 16 and 17 can drink beer, wine or cider with a meal if it is bought by an adult and they are accompanied by an adult.

Dogs If main entry licensees have told us they allow dogs in their pub or bedrooms we say so. Absence of reference to dogs means dogs are not welcome. If you take a dog into a pub you should have it on a lead. We also mention in the text any pub dogs or cats (or indeed other animals) that we've come across ourselves, or heard about from readers.

Parking If we know there is a problem with parking we say so; otherwise assume there is a car park.

Credit cards We say if a pub does **not** accept them; some which do may put a surcharge on credit card bills, to cover charges made by the card company. We also say if we know that a pub tries to retain customers' credit cards while they are eating. This is a reprehensible practice, and if a pub tries it on you, please tell them that all banks and card companies frown on it – and please let us know the pub's name, so that we can warn readers in future editions.

Telephone numbers are given for all main entries that are not ex-directory.

Opening hours are for summer; we say if we know of differences in winter, or on particular days of the week. In the country, many pubs may open rather later and close earlier than their details show (if you come across this, please let us know – with details). Pubs are allowed to stay open all day if licensed to do so. However, outside cities many english and welsh pubs close during the afternoon. We'd be grateful to hear of any differences from the hours we quote.

Bedroom prices normally include full english breakfasts (if available), VAT and any automatic service charge. If we give just one price, it is the total price for two people sharing a double or twin-bedded room for one night. Otherwise, prices before the / are for single occupancy, prices after it for double. A capital B against the price means that it includes a private bathroom, a capital S a private shower. As all this coding packs in quite a lot of information, some examples may help to explain it:

£70	on its own means that's the total bill for two people sharing a twin or double room without private bath; the pub has no rooms with a private bath, and a single person might have to pay that full price.
£70B	means exactly the same – but all the rooms have a private bath
£65(£70B)	means rooms with private baths cost £5 extra
£40/£65(£70B)	means the same as the last example, but also shows that there are single rooms for £40, none of which has a private bathroom

If there's a choice of rooms at different prices, we normally give the cheapest. If there are seasonal price variations, we give the summer price (the highest). During the winter, many inns, particularly in the country, will have special cheaper rates. And at other times, especially in holiday areas, you will often find prices cheaper if you stay for several nights. On weekends, inns that aren't in obvious weekending areas often have bargain rates for two- or three-night stays.

Meal times Bar food is commonly served from 12-2 and 7-9, at least from Monday to Saturday. If we don't give a time against the *Bar food* note at the bottom of a main entry you should be able to get bar food at those times. However, we do spell out the times if we know that bar food service starts after 12.15 or after 7.15; if it stops before 2 or before 8.45; or if food is served for significantly longer than usual (say, till 2.30 or 9.45).

Though we note days when pubs have told us they don't do food you should play safe on Sundays, and check before you visit. Please let us know if you find anything different from what we say!

Disabled access Deliberately, we do not ask pubs about this, as their answers would not give a reliable picture of how easy access is. Instead, we depend on readers' direct experience. If you are able to give us help about this, we would be particularly grateful for your reports.

SAT NAV AND ELECTRONIC ROUTE PLANNING
A digital version of *The Good Pub Guide* is now available for Garmin sat-nav systems. Available on an SD card, the sat-nav guide will tell you the nearest pubs to your current location (including Lucky Dips), or you can get it to track down a particular pub, and it will direct you to your choice.

For more information visit **www.thegoodpubguide.co.uk/satnav**.

Computer users may also like to know of a route-finding programme, Microsoft® AutoRoute™, which shows the location of *Good Pub Guide* pubs on detailed maps, works out the quickest routes for journeys, adds diversions to nearby pubs – and shows our text entries for those pubs on screen.

OUR WEBSITE (www.thegoodpubguide.co.uk)
This year has seen the launch of our completely redesigned website. It includes virtually all the material in *The Good Pub Guide*, with sophisticated search options. We are excited about also being able to include far more material than we can in a manageable-sized book.

CHANGES DURING THE YEAR – PLEASE TELL US
Changes are inevitable during the course of the year. Landlords change, and so do their policies. We very much hope that you will find everything just as we say but if not please let us know, using the tear-out card in the middle of the book, the report forms at the back of the book, or just a letter. You don't need a stamp: the address is The Good Pub Guide, FREEPOST TN1569, WADHURST, East Sussex TN5 7BR. You can also send us reports at **feedback@thegoodpubguide.co.uk**.

Ack...

This *Guide* would be impossible ...
thousands of readers who report to ...
the special help they have given us m...
Bryant, Guy Vowles, Reg Fowle, Helen Ric...
Angela Buckell, LM, Michael Doswell, Tracey ...
Michael Dandy, Phil and Jane Hodson, Michael ...
Alan Thwaite, Ian Phillips, Dr and Mrs M E Wilson, ...
Keith and Sue Ward, Jeremy King, Susan and John D...
Michel Hooper-Immins, JJW, CMW, Ann and Colin Hunt, ...
Gordon and Margaret Ormondroyd, Dennis Jenkin, Roger a...
Martin, Val and Alan Green, Phyl and Jack Street, Steve Wha...
Kevin Thorpe, Donna and Roger, Ewan and Moira McCall, Tom M...
Murdoch, Comus and Sarah Elliott, Phil and Sally Gorton, David an...
Butler, Andy and Jill Kassube, Catherine and Rob Dunster, Brian and A...
Evans, Keith and Chris O'Neill, Michael and Alison Sandy, Bruce Bird, Joh...
and Sylvia Stephenson, Pete Baker, Edward Mirzoeff, Tom Evans, Martin and ...
John Saville, Joe Green, Brian and Janet Ainscough, Ray and Winifred Halliday, ...
and Pauline Jennings, John Beeken, Dr Kevan Tucker, MB, Charles and Pauline Str...
and Anita Christopher, Paul A Moore, R T and J C Moggridge, Bob and Margaret Holde...
Peter F Marshall, Valerie Baker, Dr and Mrs C W Thomas, JCW, MDN, Tom and Jill Jones,
Torrens Lyster, Margaret Dickinson, Howard Dell, Neil Powell, Dennis Jones, J F M and
M West, Dave Braisted, Anthony Longden, Mrs Margo Finlay, Jörg Kasprowski, MLR, Ross
Balaam, Colin Moore, Dr and Mrs J Temporal, Paul and Ursula Randall, Sara Fulton, Roger
Baker, Dr and Mrs A K Clarke, Mr and Mrs Maurice Thompson, Mike Gorton, Simon and
Sally Small, Mike and Eleanor Anderson, Barry and Anne, Tony and Jill Radnor, Sheila
Topham, B and M Kendall, Bruce and Sharon Eden, David M Smith, Heather and Dick
Martin, Howard and Margaret Buchanan, Mike and Sue Loseby, Dr and Mrs Jackson, WW,
Eric Larkham, Les and Sandra Brown, Eithne Dandy, Sue and Mike Todd, KC, Ian Malone,
C and R Bromage, Simon Collett-Jones, Julian and Janet Dearden, Roy Hoing, Paul and
Gail Betteley, Mr and Mrs P D Titcomb, Mark Farrington, Denys Gueroult, Marianne Welsh,
Tina and David Woods-Taylor, Ryta Lyndley, Karen Eliot, Roger Thornington, Len Beattie,
Mike and Mary Carter, Adrian Johnson, P and D Carpenter, Gwyn and Anne Wake, John
Branston, Dr Phil Putwain, Joyce and Maurice Cottrell, R C Vincent, Mark, Amanda, Luke
and Jake Sheard, Robert Watt, Dr and Mrs Michael Smith, Peter and Audrey Dowsett, D...
and Madeleine Brown, Ron and Sheila Corbett, and Michael and Maggie Betton.

Warm thanks, too, to John Holliday of Trade Wind Technology, who built and ...
our database. And to Pat Taylor Chalmers, who has checked every word of ...
edition of the *Guide* with such scrupulous care.

Alisdair Ai...

England

Bedfordshire

For quite a small county, this has its fair share of good pubs – and they're a nice cross section, notching up a decent batch of Awards. One old favourite is the Cock at Broom, a charmingly unspoilt place, straightforward and friendly, with very good value pubby food and beers tapped straight from the cask. The lovely Crown at Northill and the Red Lion at Milton Bryan both have a proper traditional atmosphere in their old bars, and both offer enjoyable food. Food takes centre stage at the comfortably civilised Hare & Hounds in Old Warden, with its emphasis on fine dining; it's doing particularly well these days. Right at the top of the tree is the Plough at Bolnhurst, with its really charming staff, and imaginative food, prepared from carefully sourced ingredients – it is our Bedfordshire Dining Pub of the Year. New to us this year, the neatly contemporary Prince of Wales in Ampthill offers imaginative food, backed up by traditional lunchtime bar snacks. And we look forward to readers' reactions to the new Jean-Christophe Novelli regime (and some quite eye-catching menu items) at the stylishly refurbished French Horn in Steppingley. Among the Lucky Dip entries at the end of the chapter, four gaining particularly warm approval recently are the Black Horse at Ireland, Live & Let Live near Pegsdon, Sow & Pigs in Toddington and Black Horse in Woburn. A local brewery to look out for is Potton, started a decade or so ago; its beers are gaining ground in the area. Wells & Youngs ales, brewed in Bedford, are widely available.

AMPTHILL
TL0338   MAP 5

Prince of Wales
Bedford Street (B540 N from central crossroads); MK45 2NB

Civilised lunch pub with contemporary décor and menu

This open-plan L-shaped bar-brasserie has big leather deco-style armchairs and sofas on wood strip flooring as you come in, then it angles around past a slightly sunken flagstoned bit, with a brick fireplace, to a comfortable partly ply-panelled dining area with sturdy pine tables. They have Wells & Youngs Bombardier and Eagle on handpump, good coffee, and brisk helpful service; good lighting, nicely framed modern prints on mainly cream walls (dark green and maroon accents at either end), quite well reproduced piped music. There are picnic-sets out on a nicely planted two-level lawn, and a terrace by the car park. We have not yet had reports on the five newish bedrooms.

🍴 As well as a lunchtime snack menu with sandwiches, tortilla wraps, burgers, chilli and battered cod, pie of the day and so on, other changing dishes might include grilled mushrooms filled with pancetta and brie, grilled tiger prawns, artichoke salad with feta, pine nuts and beetroot pesto, mediterranean vegetable penne with a creamy pesto sauce, roast rack of lamb with redcurrant and rosemary jus and steaks. *Starters/Snacks: £5.00 to £7.00. Main Courses: £12.00 to £22.00. Puddings: £5.00*

Charles Wells ~ Tenants Richard and Neia Heathorn ~ Real ale ~ Bar food (12-2.30(3 Sun), 7-9.30) ~ Restaurant ~ (01525) 840504 ~ Children welcome ~ Dogs welcome ~ Open 12-3, 6-11; 12-midnight Fri, Sat; 12-4 Sun; closed Sun evening ~ Bedrooms: £55S/£70S
Recommended by Stephen Cavender, Michael Dandy

BIDDENHAM   TL0249   MAP 5

Three Tuns

Village signposted from A428 just W of Bedford; MK40 4BD

Extended thatched village pub with fairly priced straightforward food, and good children's play area in big garden

The traditional pleasant low-beamed lounge here has wheelback chairs round dark wood tables, window seats and pews on a red turkey carpet, and country paintings. The green-carpeted oak panelled public bar has photographs of the local football team, darts, skittles, cards and dominoes; piped music. On handpump, Greene King Abbot is well kept alongside a guest such as Ruddles. There are seats in the attractively sheltered spacious garden, lots of picnic-sets on a big decked terrace, and swings and a climbing frame.

🍽 Served in generous helpings, enjoyable food runs from soup, sandwiches and ploughman's, to steak and kidney pie, good battered haddock, lamb shank in red wine and mint sauce and steaks, with puddings such as mandarin cheesecake and chocolate fudge cake. *Starters/Snacks: £4.50 to £8.50. Main Courses: £8.00 to £16.50. Puddings: £4.50*

Greene King ~ Lease Kevin Bolwell ~ Real ale ~ Bar food (not Sun evening) ~ Restaurant ~ (01234) 354847 ~ Children in dining room ~ Dogs allowed in bar ~ Open 11.30-2.30, 6-11; 12-3, 7-10.30 Sun

Recommended by John Saville, John Taylor, Colin and Janet Roe, Stuart Turner, Revd R P Tickle, M and GR

BLETSOE   TL0157   MAP 5

Falcon ♀

Rushden Road (A6 N of Bedford); MK44 1QN

Thoughtfully cared for beamed old place with cheerful attentive service, good value imaginative food, a decent range of drinks, and extensive riverside garden

The welcoming carpeted bar here is comfortably traditional with low beams and joists, a pleasant mix of sturdy dark tables, seating that ranges from cushioned wall/window seats to high-backed settles, and in winter a couple of open fires – in summer the brick inglenook on the left is instead decorated with copperware and fat church candles. A little side snug on the right has a couple of chairs and stools, and through on the left there's a quietly comfortable beamed and timbered dining room. They have Wells & Youngs Eagle and Bombardier on handpump, with a guest such as Wadworths 6X, a decent choice of around 16 wines by the glass, and good coffee; daily papers and unobtrusive piped music. French doors lead out onto a sheltered terrace and a big grassed area, which works its way down to the slow River Ouse and has plenty of trees and shrubs, perhaps strolling peafowl, at least one stone table and seats, and a couple of teak seats on a lower stretch of grass.

🍽 The pleasing lunchtime menu might include deli plates, imaginative sandwiches such as tuna with purple basil jam, black olives and tomato, interesting salads, linguini with roasted sweet pepper, cheshire cheese, pine nuts and basil, sausage with cheddar mash, chargrills, and fish specials such as baked mahi mahi with spring onion risotto and parsley butter; good value two- or three-course menu. The evening menu is a slightly more serious affair, with perhaps duck breast with black cherry and honey sauce or garlic glazed pork belly with caraway seed and mustard cream sauce. Puddings are fairly traditional, and they've a thoughtfully annotated english cheeseboard. *Starters/Snacks: £3.95 to £6.95. Main Courses: £9.75 to £15.50. Puddings: £4.35 to £6.95*

Charles Wells ~ Tenants Jonathan Seaton-Reid and Lianne Poole ~ Real ale ~ Bar food (12-2, 6.30-9; 12-8.30 Sun) ~ Restaurant ~ (01234) 781222 ~ Children welcome ~ Jazz bank hol Mons ~ Open 12-3, 6-11; 12-11 Sat; 12-10.30 Sun

Recommended by Michael Dandy, Lucy Rhodes, Ryta Lyndley

We say if we know a pub allows dogs.

BOLNHURST

TL0858 MAP 5

Plough 🍴 ☒

Kimbolton Road; MK44 2EX

BEDFORDSHIRE DINING PUB OF THE YEAR

Stylish conversion of ancient building; thriving atmosphere, charming staff, top-notch food and drinks, and lovely garden

This striking old building has been beautifully restored: impressive old timbers are set off nicely by the light and airy contemporary décor, and you can see into the smart kitchen. It's a well run ship, with helpful staff coping happily with the chatty crowd. Sourced with care, the range of drinks here includes local Potton Village Bike and a couple of guests such as Batemans XB and Caledonian Deuchars IPA on handpump, a very good wine list (inluding organic vintages), with well over a dozen by the glass, home-made lemonade (in summer) and tomato juice, and local apple juice. The attractive tree-shaded garden overlooks a pond, where you can still see the remains of the moat that used to surround the pub.

🍴 **Beautifully presented inventive food, from a well balanced changing menu, is prepared using carefully sourced ingredients, many of which come from local named producers. Served with complimentary home-made bread, dishes work their way up from tasty canapés such as devils on horseback, to starters such as carpaccio of local venison, potted shrimp risotto with chilli and lemon. Main courses range from sausage and mash to spinach, mascarpone and black truffle lasagne, roast brill with roast fennel and tapenade, and osso bucco; vegetable sides are extra. Imaginative puddings might include red fruit soup with prosecco sorbet and sticky toffee pudding, and they've a very good cheese platter; a reasonably priced set lunch menu too.** *Starters/Snacks: £4.95 to £6.95. Main Courses: £9.95 to £18.50. Puddings: £5.25 to £6.50*

Free house ~ Licensees Martin and Jayne Lee and Michael Moscrop ~ Real ale ~ Bar food (12-2, 6.30-9.30) ~ Restaurant ~ (01234) 376274 ~ Children welcome ~ Dogs allowed in bar ~ Open 12-3, 6.30-11; closed Sun evening, Mon, 31 Dec, 1 Jan, and first two weeks in Jan

Recommended by Michael Sargent, John Saul, Susan and Jeremy Arthern, Eithne Dandy, Ryta Lyndley, Dr Brian and Mrs Anne Hamilton

BROOM

TL1743 MAP 5

Cock ★ £

High Street; from A1 opposite northernmost Biggleswade turn-off follow Old Warden 3, Aerodrome 2 signpost, and take first left signposted Broom; SG18 9NA

Friendly traditional village green pub with straightforward tasty food, beers tapped straight from the cask; garden, and caravanning and camping facilities

Readers enjoy the unspoilt simplicity of this little old-fashioned house. There's no bar counter, so the Greene King IPA, Abbot and Ruddles County are tapped straight from casks by the cellar steps off a central corridor. Original latch doors lead from one quietly cosy little room to the next (four in all). You'll find warming winter fires, low ochre ceilings, stripped panelling, and farmhouse tables and chairs on antique tiles; piped (perhaps classical) music, darts and board games. There are picnic-sets and flower tubs on the terrace by the back lawn.

🍴 **Well liked generously served bar food includes sandwiches, soup, ploughman's, scampi, vegetarian curry and filled yorkshire pudding.** *Starters/Snacks: £3.65. Main Courses: £6.00 to £9.00. Puddings: £3.50*

Greene King ~ Tenants Gerry and Jean Lant ~ Real ale ~ Bar food ~ Restaurant ~ (01767) 314411 ~ Children welcome ~ Dogs allowed in bar ~ Open 12-3(4 Sat, Sun), 6-11; closed Sun evening

Recommended by Andy Lickfold, Pete Baker, R T and J C Moggridge, Laurence Milligan, the Didler, Michael B Griffith, Michael Dandy

HENLOW   TL1738   MAP 5

Engineers Arms 🍺 £
A6001 S of Biggleswade; High Street; SG16 6AA

Good choice of drinks including fabulous range of up to nine beautifully kept guest ales at charmingly spick and span village pub; snacks (all day)

They get through about 25 different real ales a week at this traditional local. Besides their house beer (Timothy Taylors Landlord) real ales come from a tremendous range of smaller, often far-flung brewers such as Batemans, Buntingford, Cottage, Newby Wyke, Potton, Southport and Stonehenge. They also stock four ciders and a perry, and many belgian bottled beers. Helpful staff are very knowledgeable about the range, and the pub holds quarterly bank holiday beer festivals, and a bigger one in mid-October. They also keep decent wines by the glass and Tyrrells crisps, and serve good coffee. The comfortable green-carpeted front room has lots of old local photographs on its green fleur-de-lys wallpaper, tidily kept and interesting bric-a-brac collections, traditional green-cushioned wall seats, settles and other dark seats, armchair-style bar stools, daily papers and a good log fire. A small tiled inner area has wide-screen TV, and beyond is a step up to another comfortable carpeted area, with a second TV, juke box, silenced fruit machine, board games and other games such as table football; the good-natured spaniel is called Chico. The back terrace has picnic-sets and heaters and the garden is now no smoking; more reports please.

🍴 Light snacks, including sausage rolls, pies and pizzas, are served most of the time they are open. *Starters/Snacks: £1.60 to £6.00*

Free house ~ Licensees Kevin Machin and Claire Sturgeon ~ Real ale ~ Bar food (snacks most of the time) ~ (01462) 812284 ~ Children welcome in back room till 8pm ~ Dogs allowed in bar ~ Live blues Fri ~ Open 12-midnight (1 Fri, Sat)

Recommended by Bruce Bird, Michael Dandy

HOUGHTON CONQUEST   TL0441   MAP 5

Knife & Cleaver 🍽 ♀
Between B530 (old A418) and A6, S of Bedford; MK45 3LA

Comfortably civilised attractive 17th-c dining pub with thoughtfully prepared food, and a good range of drinks including lots of wines by the glass

---

Nearby ruined Houghton House is said to be the source of the rather lovely dark panelling in the bar here. Maps, drawings and old documents on the walls, as well as lamps, comfy seating and a blazing winter fire lend a cosy clubby feel. An airy white-walled conservatory restaurant has rugs on the tiled floor, and lots of hanging plants. There's also a family room, and tables on a terrace alongside a neatly kept attractive garden; unobtrusive piped music. Batemans XB and Potton Village Bike are on handpump alongside Stowford Press farm cider. They've around two dozen good wines by the glass, and a dozen well aged malt whiskies.

🍴 With emphasis on carefully sourced good quality ingredients, food here is all carefully prepared from scratch – they even make their own bread. You may have to book, and do be aware that they may not serve bar meals if the restaurant is full on Saturday evenings and Sunday lunchtimes. The seasonally changing menu might include rabbit and pork terrine, steak baguettes, oysters, battered fish, sausage and mash and caesar salad. Good specials might be rabbit and venison pie, bass with caramelised red onions and thyme and pigeon breast with celeriac rösti and blackberry sauce. As well as home-made ice-creams, puddings could be baked cheesecake with blueberry sauce or marmalade bread and butter pudding; very good cheese platter. *Starters/Snacks: £4.00 to £7.95. Main Courses: £7.50 to £9.50. Puddings: £4.75*

Our website is: www.thegoodpubguide.co.uk

Free house ~ Licensees David and Pauline Loom ~ Real ale ~ Bar food (12-2.30(2 Sat), 7-9.30; no bar food Sat, Sun lunchtime if busy) ~ Restaurant ~ (01234) 740387 ~ Children welcome ~ Dogs allowed in bedrooms ~ Open 12-2.30(2 Sat, 3 Sun), 7-11; closed 27-31 Dec and possibly Sun evening ~ Bedrooms: £59B/£74B

Recommended by Roger and Lesley Everett, Lyndsey Millar, Michael Dandy

KEYSOE   TL0763   MAP 5

Chequers

Pertenhall Road, Brook End (B660); MK44 2HR

Down-to-earth village local with good value simple but tasty food, and garden with play area

One reader tells us that the welcoming couple at this yellow and cherry-brown painted house have just marked their thirtieth year as licensees here. Usually fairly quiet at lunchtime (unless a group is in), two simple beamed rooms are divided by a stone-pillared fireplace. Piped local radio or music lends a homely 1960s air – the carpets and furnishings appear to have rather marked out the years here too. A changing beer (maybe Black Sheep) is served from a handpump on the stone bar counter, they've a few malt whiskies and the short wine list is very reasonably priced. Tables and chairs on the back terrace look over the garden, which has a play tree and swings.

 Straightforward bar food takes in pub standards such as sandwiches, ploughman's, chilli and steaks, and a few blackboard specials. *Starters/Snacks: £4.00 to £5.00. Main Courses: £7.00 to £12.00. Puddings: £4.75*

Free house ~ Licensee Jeffrey Kearns ~ Real ale ~ Bar food ~ No credit cards ~ (01234) 708678 ~ Children welcome ~ Open 12-2.30, 6.30-11; 12-2.30, 7-10.30 Sun; closed Mon evening, Tues

Recommended by Michael and Jenny Back, R T and J C Moggridge, JJW, CMW

MILTON BRYAN   SP9730   MAP 4

Red Lion ♀

Toddington Road, off B528 S of Woburn; MK17 9HS

Beamed pub quite near Woburn Abbey and Safari Park with good food, attentive staff and pretty views from garden

The immaculately kept beamed bar area at this attractive old pub has cream-coloured walls, some exposed brickwork, polished wood and part flagstoned floors, and cheery fresh flowers on round wooden tables. Greene King IPA, Abbot and Old Speckled Hen are kept under light blanket pressure, and ten wines and a local apple juice are sold by the glass. In summer, a plethora of carefully tended hanging baskets makes a spectacular show, and there are plenty of tables, chairs and picnic-sets out on the terrace and lawn, which looks across to a delightful row of thatched black and white timbered cottages.

 Using some thoughtfully sourced ingredients, bar food includes sandwiches, thai fishcakes, ploughman's, caramelised onion and cherry tomato tartlet with taleggio cheese, toulouse sausage and crème fraîche mash, steak and kidney pudding, smoked haddock fillet on cabbage with poached egg and butter sauce, and puddings such as summer fruit pudding or warm chocolate fudge brownie with preserved cherries and mascarpone cream. *Starters/Snacks: £4.95 to £7.95. Main Courses: £9.50 to £14.50. Puddings: £4.95 to £5.50*

Greene King ~ Lease Paul Ockleford ~ Real ale ~ Bar food (12-2.30(3 Sun), 7-9.30) ~ Restaurant ~ (01525) 210044 ~ Children welcome lunchtimes if eating ~ Open 11.30-3, 6-11; 12-4 Sun; closed Mon in winter, Sun evening

Recommended by Malcolm and Sue Scott, Michael Dandy, Andrea and Guy Bradley, John Saville, Mike and Jennifer Marsh, Mrs Nading Ridgeway, B R and M F Arnold, Catherine and Rob Dunster

Tipping is not normal for bar meals, and not usually expected.

NORTHILL   TL1446   MAP 5

Crown

Ickwell Road; village signposted from B658 W of Biggleswade; SG18 9AA

Prettily situated village pub with nice old interior, warmly relaxed atmosphere, enjoyable food, and big child-friendly garden

You can choose between the cosy bar or more formal restaurant at this thoughtfully run place. The smallish bar is snugly traditional with a big open fire, flagstones, heavy low beams and comfortable bay window seats. Greene King IPA and Abbot and a couple of guests from brewers such as Bath and Hydes are served on handpump from the copper-topped counter. On the left is a small dining area, while on the right, the light walled main dining room has elegantly laid tables on bare boards, with steps up to a smaller more intimate side room. The atmosphere throughout is warm and relaxed with friendly service and fairly unobtrusive piped music. This attractive old building is situated just across from the church, in a green and peaceful village, and has big tables under cocktail parasols out in front looking over the village pond. A sheltered side terrace (with picnic-sets) opens up into a very large back garden with widely spaced canopied tables, plenty of trees and shrubs, a good play area, and masses of room for children to run around.

⊞ **The nicely traditional bar menu includes a good range of sandwiches, tortillas and ciabattas (lunchtimes only), as well as ploughman's, sausage and mash, chilli, burger, scampi, chicken caesar salad and beef stew and dumplings, and there's a more elaborate restaurant menu.** *Starters/Snacks: £3.99 to £5.95. Main Courses: £7.95 to £16.95. Puddings: £4.50*

Greene King ~ Tenant Kevin Blois ~ Real ale ~ Bar food (12-2.30, 6.30-9.30; 12-9 Sun) ~ Restaurant ~ (01767) 627337 ~ Children welcome away from main bar ~ Dogs allowed in bar ~ Open 11.30-3, 6-11; 11.30-midnight Fri, Sat in summer; 12-11 Sun

Recommended by Malcolm and Sue Scott, Pete Baker, Michael Dandy

OLD WARDEN   TL1343   MAP 5

Hare & Hounds

Village signposted off A600 S of Bedford and B658 W of Biggleswade; SG18 9HQ

Popular but comfortably elegant dining pub with emphasis on good food served by thoughtful well turned out staff; lovely gardens

Four beautifully kept beamed rooms, with dark standing timbers, work their way round the central servery here. Cleverly blending contemporary styling with the attractive old structure, décor is in cosy reds and creams, with upholstered armchairs and sofas on stripped flooring, light wood tables and coffee tables, a woodburning stove in an inglenook fireplace and fresh flowers on the bar. Prints and photographs displayed on the walls depict historic aircraft in the famous Shuttleworth Collection just up the road. Wells & Youngs Eagle and Bombardier are on handpump, with eight or so wines by the glass including some from a local vineyard; piped music. The village and pub form part of the Shuttleworth Estate which was built about 200 years ago in a swiss style, and the glorious sloping garden (with tables on a terrace) which stretches up to pine woods behind the pub dates back to the same period, and was designed in the same style. Though there's an ample car park, you may need to use the village hall parking as an overflow. There are some substantial walks nearby.

⊞ **Food here is beautifully prepared and presented. They make an effort to use local and even organic ingredients (such as pork from the Shuttleworth Estate), the breads and ice-cream are home made, and they sell a small range of home-made larder goods. The changing menus might include whitebait, battered haddock, pie of the day, salmon tagliatelle, baked tomato tart, crab, lime and chilli risotto and sirloin steak with rocket and basil salad, with puddings such as warm bakewell tart or caramelised lemon tart, and british cheeses.** *Starters/Snacks: £5.00 to £7.00. Main Courses: £10.00 to £11.00. Puddings: £6.00 to £7.00*

Charles Wells ~ Lease Jane Hasler ~ Real ale ~ Bar food (12-2(3 Sun), 6.30-9; not Sun evening) ~ (01767) 627225 ~ Children welcome in family room ~ Dogs allowed in bar ~ Open 12-3, 6-11; 12-10.30 Sun; closed Mon except bank hols

Recommended by Geoff and Carol Thorp, Michael Dandy, Peter and Margaret Glenister, David and Ruth Shillitoe, Mr and Mrs D S Price, Roger and Lesley Everett, P Waterman, Alain and Rose Foote

RISELEY   TL0462   MAP 5

Fox & Hounds

High Street; village signposted off A6 and B660 N of Bedford; MK44 1DT

Cheery bustling old pub with decent food including good steaks; pleasant garden

The longstanding licensees here run a sound and welcoming establishment. Traditional pub furniture is spread among timber uprights under heavy low beams, and a relaxing clubby lounge area has comfortable leather chesterfields, low tables and wing chairs; unobtrusive piped classical or big band piped music. A decent range of drinks takes in Wells & Youngs Eagle and Bombardier with a guest such as Hook Norton Old Hooky on handpump, bin-end wines and a range of malts and cognacs. Service is normally very attentive and friendly, but it does get busy; they don't take bookings on Saturday night, so you may have to wait for your table and food. An attractively decked terrace with wooden tables and chairs has outside heating, and the pleasant garden has shrubs and a pergola.

🍴 You get to choose your own piece of steak here (you pay by weight), and you can then watch it cooked on an open grill. Other good food (listed on blackboards) might include parsnip and ginger soup, ploughman's, steak and stilton pie, salmon in champagne sauce, and puddings such as jam roly-poly or spotted dick and custard. Even if you don't see anything you fancy, it's worth asking as they're very obliging and will try to cope with particular food requests. *Starters/Snacks: £2.95 to £6.25. Main Courses: £7.95 to £14.25. Puddings: £3.75*

Charles Wells ~ Lease Jan and Lynne Zielinski ~ Real ale ~ Bar food (11.30-1.45, 6.30-9.30(10 Sat); 12-2, 7-9 Sun) ~ Restaurant ~ (01234) 708240 ~ Children welcome ~ Dogs allowed in bar ~ Open 11.30-2.30, 6.30-11; 12-3, 7-10.30 Sun

Recommended by Michael Dandy, Michael Sargent, Tim and Mark Allen

STEPPINGLEY   TL0135   MAP 5

French Horn ♀

Village signposted off A507 just N of Flitwick; Church End; MK45 5AU

Gastropub newly converted by Jean-Christophe Novelli; pubby food in bar, elaborate meals in smart restaurant

This is the second pub to be transformed by Jean-Christophe Novelli. Contemporary furniture and artworks contrast inspiringly with traditional inglenook fireplaces and flagstone floors. The bar has high stools round high tables and cosy nooks with armchairs at low tables and co-ordinating cushions arranged along bench seats. Smartly uniformed staff serve Greene King IPA and Old Speckled Hen and a guest, and ten wines by the glass from a very good list; piped music (which one reader found too loud). The smart restaurant is minimalist with sparklingly set tables.

🍴 The strongly seasonal menu might include scallops with butternut mousse and pickled girolle mushrooms, steak tartare, lemon sole with clam chowder, fried gnocchi with summer vegetables and parmesan cream, fried monkfish with pork belly and smoked paprika potatoes, 28-day aged sirloin steak, and puddings such as apple tart with calvados cream and organic toffee ice-cream and baked jaffa fondant with Grand Marnier ice-cream. *Starters/Snacks: £4.95 to £6.95. Main Courses: £7.50 to £14.95. Puddings: £6.50 to £7.50*

Greene King ~ Lease Philip Kelly ~ Real ale ~ Bar food (12-2.30, 6-9.30; 12-4.30 Sun) ~
Restaurant ~ (01525) 712051 ~ Open 12-11; 12-midnight Sat; 12-10.30 Sun
Recommended by Geoff and Carol Thorp, Michael Dandy

WOBURN   SP9433   MAP 4

Birch ♀

*3.5 miles from M1 junction 13; follow Woburn signs via A507 and A4012, then in village
turn right and head out on A5130 (Newport Road); MK17 9HX*

**Well run dining establishment right in Woburn with focus on good imaginative food, good
wines and attentive service**

White liming on the servery, rough wall planking and some white-painted chairs contrast
effectively with good dark hardwood flooring and soft brown leather sofas, bar stools and
deep armchairs here. Modern prints on cream walls, deeply coloured ceilings and
handsome flower arrangements further reflect the distinctive thinking that has gone into
the décor. The carefully lit back part consists of an extensive but well divided and
comfortable dining area, the central part of which is given an airy conservatory feel by
its ceramic tile floor, light panelling and glazed pitched roof, with a step up either side
to carpeted or bare-boards sections with attractive artwork on their soft canary walls;
unobtrusive piped music and daily papers. They keep a good range of interesting wines by
the glass as well as Adnams and Fullers London Pride on handpump. Service by neatly
dressed staff is helpful and efficient. There are tables out on a sheltered deck.

🍴 **The changing menu might include lunchtime dishes such as ciabatta, battered fish,
caesar salad and steaks, with evening dishes such as ham hock terrine, mushroom risotto
with gruyère, peppered venison steak with apricot chutney, trout fillets steamed with
leeks, ginger, lemon grass and garlic, and puddings such as pistachio nut crème brûlée
and warm treacle tart.** *Starters/Snacks: £4.95 to £7.50. Main Courses: £5.95 to £9.95.
Puddings: £3.95 to £5.95*

Free house ~ Licensee Mark Campbell ~ Real ale ~ Bar food ~ Restaurant ~ (01525) 290295 ~
Children welcome ~ Open 11.30-3, 6-11; 12-5 Sun; closed Sun evening
Recommended by Gerry and Rosemary Dobson, Michael Sargent, Michael Dandy, Howard Dell, Mr and Mrs C Prentis

LUCKY DIP

Besides the fully inspected pubs, you might like to try these Lucky Dips recommended to us and
described by readers (if you do, please send us reports: feedback@thegoodpubguide.co.uk).

BEDFORD [TL0550]
Park MK40 2PF [Park Ave/Kimbolton Rd]:
Large modernised pub with mix of
furnishings inc leather sofas in partly
flagstoned linked areas, enjoyable food,
Wells & Youngs Bombardier and Eagle, good
coffee and wine by the glass, daily papers,
conservatory eating area (best to book Sun
lunch); piped music; garden with tables on
decking, open all day *(Bruce and
Sharon Eden, Eithne Dandy)*
BROOM [TL1742]
White Horse SG18 9NN [Southill Rd]:
Comfortable, with three real ales, enjoyable
reasonably priced simple food, welcoming
staff; back camp site *(Geoff and Carol Thorp)*
CARDINGTON [TL0847]
Kings Arms MK44 3SP [The Green; off A603
E of Bedford]: Comfortably refurbished
Vintage Inn dining pub, their well thought-
through menu, good choice of wines by the
glass, Fullers London Pride and Timothy

Taylors Landlord, friendly staff, nice mix of
varying-sized tables in attractive linked
areas, interesting local airship photographs;
good tables and chairs out on peaceful front
terrace, open all day *(Eithne Dandy,
Michael Dandy)*
CHALTON [TL0326]
Star LU4 9UJ [Luton Rd (B579 3 miles from
M1 junction 12, via Toddington)]: Big
comfortable Chef & Brewer with four well
kept mainstream and guest ales, all-day
food, main dining area separate from bar;
big garden, good for families *(Michael and
Alison Sandy)*
CLOPHILL [TL0838]
Stone Jug MK45 4BY [N on A6 from A507
roundabout, after 200 yds 2nd turn on right
into Back St]: Secluded stone-built local,
cosy and welcoming, with bargain pubby
lunchtime food from sandwiches up, well
kept ales such as Everards Beacon, Fullers
London Pride and Shepherd Neame Spitfire,

pleasantly unpretentious comfortable bar with family area and darts in small games extension; piped music; small pretty back terrace, roadside picnic-sets *(Michael Dandy, Geoff and Carol Thorp)*

EVERSHOLT [SP9832]

Green Man MK17 9DU [Church End]: Some settees and open fire, part of carpeted bar screened off for eating, second dining room, Banks's, Hook Norton and Wadworths 6X, reasonably priced pubby food from baguettes up; back terrace tables with trees and shrubs, pretty village handy for Woburn Abbey *(Michael Dandy)*

GREAT BARFORD [TL1351]

Anchor MK44 3LF [High St; off A421]: Open-plan bar with real ales such as Fullers/Gales and Wells & Youngs, friendly staff, usual food from sandwiches up, back restaurant; piped music; picnic-sets overlooking River Ouse by medieval bridge and church, bedrooms *(Michael Dandy)*

HARROLD [SP9456]

Muntjac MK43 7BJ [High St]: Some booth seating in long carpeted front bar, changing ales such as Black Sheep and Timothy Taylors Landlord, pubby bar lunches from sandwiches and toasted panini up, quick helpful service, contemporary back restaurant; pavement tables, bedrooms, cl Mon-Thurs lunchtimes *(Michael Dandy)*

Oakley Arms MK43 7BH [between A6 and A428, E of Northampton; High St]: Cosy refurbished beamed pub with several linked areas around central bar, well kept Wells & Youngs Eagle, limited good value changing food; piped music; quiet garden tables, bedrooms *(Revd R P Tickle, Michael Dandy)*

HENLOW [TL1738]

Crown SG16 6BS [High St]: Small inviting pub with good choice of all-day food and of wines by the glass, Adnams Broadside and Greene King IPA, good coffee, nice log fire, daily papers; piped music, games machine; terrace and small garden, open all day *(Michael Dandy)*

HOUGHTON CONQUEST [TL0342]

☆ *Chequers* MK45 3JP [B530 towards Ampthill]: Roomy and pleasantly contemporary, nice and airy, with good choice of reasonably priced food, Black Sheep, Caledonian Deuchars IPA and Fullers London Pride, good choice of wines by the glass, quick helpful service; plenty of courtyard tables, garden with play area, open all day *(Dudley and Moira Cockroft, Michael Dandy)*

IRELAND [TL1341]

☆ *Black Horse* SG17 5QL [off A600 Shefford—Bedford]: Picturesque dining pub recently stylishly refurbished and extended, good food from ciabattas and interesting light dishes up, wider evening menu, welcoming helpful staff, comfortable mix of furniture and plenty of space, Fullers London Pride, Greene King IPA and a local guest beer, good range of wines and good coffee; plenty of tables on attractive terracing, play area,

cottage bedrooms – nice peaceful rural setting *(Giles Barr, Eleanor Dandy, BB, Eithne Dandy, Jill and Julian Tasker, John Saul, Malcolm Clydesdale)*

KEMPSTON [TL0247]

King William IV MK42 7AL [High St]: Welcoming and attentive new licensees in attractive old beamed pub now concentrating well on the food side inc traditional favourites, Wells & Youngs and a guest beer, good-sized bar and restaurant; good garden *(Richard Keogh, S Holder)*

Slaters Arms MK43 8RS [Box End Rd (A5134, off A4218 W of Bedford)]: Comfortably modern carpeted bar and family restaurant area, enterprising choice of pub food from generous sandwiches up using some local and organic ingredients, Greene King ales, speciality coffees; picnic-sets in big back tree-shaded garden with plenty for children inc well equipped fenced-off play area, pets corner, summer barbecues and ice-cream bar, open all day *(Michael Dandy)*

KEYSOE [TL0860]

White Horse MK44 2JA [Kimbolton Rd (B660), Keysoe Row E]: Beamed and flagstoned Tudor pub nicely cleaned up by friendly new licensees, cheerful service, Wells & Youngs Eagle, good choice of food, conservatory; good-sized garden *(Michael and Jenny Back)*

LANGFORD [TL1840]

Plough SG18 9QA [Church St]: Simple comfortable two-bar pub, Batemans XXXB and Greene King IPA and good choice of wines by the glass from central servery, bargain food from good sandwiches up, quick service, pool; piped music, TV; good-sized garden, bedrooms *(Michael Dandy)*

LINSLADE [SP9126]

Globe LU7 2TA [off A4146 nr bridge on outskirts]: Newly refurbished 19th-c pub very popular for nice setting below Grand Union Canal, lots of rooms, beams and flagstones, log and coal fires, several well kept Greene King ales, good winter hot drinks, usual food (all day wknds), pleasant service; piped music; children welcome in eating areas, disabled access and facilities, tables up on embankment and in garden, open all day *(Charles and Pauline Stride, Mike and Jennifer Marsh, LYM)*

MAULDEN [TL0538]

Dog & Badger MK45 2AD [Clophill Rd]: Attractive thatched family pub with enormous helpings of decent pubby food from lunchtime sandwiches up, real ales such as Flowers IPA and Fullers London Pride, friendly willing staff, refurbished bare-boards bar, steps down to two carpeted areas and restaurant; piped music; children welcome, tables in front garden *(Michael Dandy, Paul Goldman)*

White Hart MK45 2DH [Ampthill Rd]: Thatch and low beams, big fireplace dividing bar, good value pubby food from baguettes up, friendly helpful service, Greene King IPA and Timothy Taylors Landlord, good choice of wines by the glass, large well divided dining area; piped music; plenty of tables in sizeable gardens with pleasant back decking, open all day wknds *(Michael Dandy)*

MILLBROOK [TL0138]

Chequers MK45 2JB: Two-room village pub opp golf club, log fire and plate collection in small low-beamed carpeted bar, changing seasonal ales such as Tring, good coffee, reasonably priced food inc lunch deals, chatty landlord and quick service, back restaurant; piped music *(Michael Dandy)*

PEGSDON [TL1130]

☆ *Live & Let Live* SG5 3JX [B655 W of Hitchin]: Neatly kept dining pub with wide choice of generous enjoyable food, friendly staff, well kept Adnams, Flowers IPA, Fullers London Pride and Marstons Pedigree, good wine choice, snug traditional tiled and panelled core; piped music; nice terrace and garden below Deacon Hill, great show of hanging baskets and flower tubs, open all day *(David and Ruth Shillitoe, LYM, Michael Dandy, Mr and Mrs John Taylor)*

RADWELL [TL0057]

Swan MK43 7HS [Felmersham Rd]: This small thatched Charles Wells pub, an appealing main entry in the last edition, was closed as we went to press; news please *(LYM)*

RAVENSDEN [TL0754]

☆ *Horse & Jockey* MK44 2RR [Church End]: Welcoming village pub with good enterprising food using local organic sources, well kept Wells & Youngs and guest ales, upscale wines by the glass, willing service, modern sofas etc in bar, clean-cut contemporary restaurant (lively acoustics); tables out on decking, small garden, open all day Fri-Sun *(Eithne Dandy, Michael Sargent, D C Poulton, Michael Dandy)*

RIDGMONT [SP9736]

Rose & Crown MK43 0TY [2 miles from M1 junction 13: A507, follow Ampthill signs – High St]: Useful off-motorway standby with open fire in neat comfortable lounge, traditional public bar, well kept Adnams Broadside, Theakstons Best and Wells & Youngs Eagle, usual food at good prices (not Sun evening), darts; piped music and machines; children and dogs allowed, good wheelchair access, sheltered back garden, camp site, open all day wknds *(LYM, Michael Dandy)*

SHILLINGTON [TL1234]

Crown SG5 3LP [High Rd, S end]: Small flagstoned bar and attractive lounge area, Greene King and a guest beer, good choice of wines by the glass, good value generous pubby food from baguettes up, quick friendly service; pleasant garden with heaters *(Michael Dandy)*

SILSOE [TL0835]

☆ *Star & Garter* MK45 4DR [High St]: Large comfortably redecorated bar and raised dining area, wide choice of usual bar food from sandwiches up, separate evening menu, quick service and reasonable prices, well kept Adnams, B&T Two Brewers, Brakspears

and Greene King IPA, good choice of wines by the glass, open fire, darts; piped music; good-sized attractive terrace, nice spot by village church *(Craig Turnbull, Michael Dandy, John Saul)*

SLIP END [TL0818]

Frog & Rhubarb LU1 4BJ [Church Rd (B4540), not far from M1, junction 10]: Local bar, steps down to roomy contemporary dining area, very wide food choice, Greene King ales; partly covered terrace *(Michael and Alison Sandy)*

SOULDROP [SP9861]

Bedford Arms MK44 1EY [High St; off A6 Rushden—Bedford]: Rambling beamed village pub pleased to see its previous popular licensees back, friendly atmosphere, good value food and Greene King ales, large central stone fireplace and several bright and cheerful linked areas; children welcome, good garden with play area *(BB, D C Poulton)*

SOUTHILL [TL1441]

White Horse SG18 9LD [off B658 SW of Biggleswade]: Well run and comfortable country pub with extensive eating area, wide range of good value generous pubby food from baguettes up, welcoming staff, changing well kept ales such as Adnams and Potton, good wine choice; piped music; lots of tables in large pleasant neatly kept garden with good play area *(LYM, Michael Dandy)*

STANBRIDGE [SP9623]

☆ *Five Bells* LU7 9JF [Station Rd/A505]: New licensees for roomy and attractive dining pub in old coaching inn, comfortable contemporary interior with low-beamed bar and airy dining area, Fullers London Pride and ESB, all-day food from baguettes up; children welcome, large well tended garden, open all day *(LYM, Michael Dandy)*

STANFORD [TL1541]

Green Man SG18 9JD [Southill rd]: L-shaped bar with big fireplace, adjoining games area with pool, reasonably priced bar food from generous sandwiches up, restaurant extension with beams and stripped brick, Courage Best and Theakstons; terrace with barbecue, big garden with play area, 11 bedrooms in chalet block *(Michael Dandy)*

TEMPSFORD [TL1652]

Wheatsheaf SG19 2AN [Church St]: 18th-c village pub with open fire in cosy lounge, Special Operations Executive memorabilia (nearby World War II base), friendly service, wide choice of bargain simple pub food from sandwiches up, small helpings available, Adnams Broadside and Theakstons, pleasant restaurant; may be piped music; tables on decking and in big garden (some traffic noise) *(Michael Dandy)*

TODDINGTON [TL0128]

Angel LU5 6DE [Luton Rd]: Contemporary furnishings inc a log-fire area with sofas and comfortable seats, Greene King and a guest beer, good coffee and choice of wines by the glass, wide range of food from sandwiches up, quick helpful service, daily papers, pub games; tables in garden with terrace and heaters, overlooking village pond and green *(Michael Dandy)*

☆ **Sow & Pigs** LU5 6AA [Church Sq]: Quaint 19th-c pub named after carving on church opp, lots of pig decorations, also old books and knick-knacks, mixed bag of furnishings inc pews, two armchairs and a retired chesterfield, friendly chatty landlady, well kept Greene King ales, good coffee, home-made lunchtime food from good cheap rolls up (not Sun; back Victorian-style dining room can be booked for parties), two log fires, games; children allowed, picnic-sets in small garden, bedrooms, open all day *(Mel Smith, Conor McGaughey)*

TURVEY [SP9452]

Three Cranes MK43 8EP [off A428 W of Bedford]: Two-level pub with quickly served pub food all day, helpful attentive staff, four Greene King ales, log fire, darts and games; two TVs; children in restaurant area, secluded tree-shaded garden, bedrooms *(LYM, Michael Dandy, George Atkinson)*

☆ **Three Fyshes** MK43 8ER [A428 NW of Bedford; Bridge St, W end of village]: Early 17th-c beamed pub with plenty of character, big inglenook log fire, mix of easy chairs and upright chairs around tables on carpet or ancient flagstones, good friendly service, four ales such as Black Sheep, Fullers ESB, Greene King IPA and Timothy Taylors Landlord, good coffee, low-priced usual food, daily paper; piped music; decking and canopy in charming garden overlooking bridge and mill on Great Ouse *(Michael Dandy, George Atkinson, LYM, Michael Tack)*

WESTONING [SP0332]

Chequers MK45 5LA [Park Rd (A5120 N of M1 junction 12)]: Multi-gabled thatched pub with black bargeboards, well kept Fullers London Pride and Greene King IPA, good choice of wines by the glass, good coffee, enjoyable pub food from panini up, helpful service, cask tables in small low-beamed front bar, good-sized back bar inc some settees, big stables restaurant; piped music; courtyard tables, open all day *(Dudley and Moira Cockroft, Michael Dandy)*

WOBURN [SP9433]

Bell MK17 9QJ [Bedford St]: Small beamed bar area, longer bare-boards dining lounge up steps, pleasant décor and furnishings, generous all-day food from sandwiches to some interesting dishes, friendly helpful service, a couple of Greene King ales, good choice of wines by the glass, good coffee; piped music, games; children welcome at lunchtime, tables on back terrace, hotel part

across busy road, handy for Woburn Park *(Paul Humphreys, George Atkinson, Michael Dandy)*

☆ **Black Horse** MK17 9QB [Bedford St]: Warm friendly atmosphere in stylishly updated 18th-c dining pub with cheerful staff, all-day food inc deli board and wide choice of other dishes, Greene King ales, good choice of wines by the glass, several bare-boards areas ranging from bar with old leather settles and coal fire through more contemporary furnishings, steps down to pleasant back restaurant; piped music; children in eating areas, summer barbecues in attractive sheltered back courtyard, open all day *(Martyn and Sue Smith, LYM, Paul Humphreys, Michael Dandy, Mr and Mrs John Taylor, John and Joyce Snell)*

Flying Fox MK17 9HD [Sheep Lane (actually A5 Bletchley—Hockcliffe, well away from village)]: Well run Vintage Inn dining pub with pictures and artefacts in well arranged linked beamed areas, reasonably priced food from sandwiches to steaks, good choice of wines by the glass, Greene King IPA and Old Speckled Hen and Wadworths 6X; piped music, pub games; tables out on lawn *(Michael Dandy)*

Inn at Woburn MK17 9PX [George St]: Attractive Georgian hotel with sofas and high-backed leather seats in beamed bar, Wells & Youngs Bombardier and Eagle, friendly service, up-to-date all-day bar food inc baguettes, good choice of wines by the glass, brasserie-style restaurant; nice bedrooms, open all day *(Michael Dandy)*

Magpie MK17 9QB [Bedford St]: Small low-ceilinged traditional bar, sofas in small lounge, Marstons Pedigree and Thwaites Lancaster Bomber, sensible food from sandwiches and pubby things to popular restaurant dishes; TV; tables in neatly kept back courtyard, bedrooms, open all day *(Michael Dandy)*

Royal Oak MK17 9PY [George St]: Nicely refurbished thatched pub, bare boards and flagstones, simple décor, mix of modern furniture in various small alcoves, all-day food, Greene King ales, good choice of wines by the glass, good service; piped music; tables on terrace and back walled garden *(Michael Dandy)*

WRESTLINGWORTH [TL2547]

Chequers SG19 2EP [High St]: Redecorated for friendly new licensees, good value simple bar lunches, Greene King ales from central servery, open fire, daily papers, side dining area, pool and darts in games end; garden tables *(Michael Dandy)*

Post Office address codings confusingly give the impression that some pubs are in Bedfordshire, when they're really in Buckinghamshire or Cambridgeshire (which is where we list them).

Berkshire

This county gives an interesting sample of different pub styles, from the beautifully unspoilt Bell up on the downs at Aldworth, through that fine no-frills town pub the Hobgoblin in Reading, with its great range of eight changing real ales, all the way up to the Hinds Head in Bray, an exemplary civilised dining pub in a handsome old building. Other pubs on splendid form here include the Pot Kiln at Frilsham, still with strong country roots despite some emphasis on the dining side, the stylish Little Angel near the Thames at Remenham, the warmly welcoming Winterbourne Arms at Winterbourne, and the Chequers, an appealing new main entry in Cookham Dean – all three with excellent food. It's the Hinds Head in Bray, with its simple traditional english food done with the best possible ingredients and care, that wins the Award as Berkshire County Dining Pub of the Year for the second year in a row. In the Lucky Dip section at the end of the chapter, pubs doing notably well in recent months (all of them already inspected and approved by us – how we wish we had more pages, to described them in more detail) are the Flower Pot at Aston, Watermans Arms in Eton, Dew Drop near Hurley, Swan at Inkpen, restauranty Royal Oak at Knowl Hill, Fox & Hounds at Peasemore, Sweeney & Todd in Reading, Bell at Waltham St Lawrence, Wheelwrights Arms in Winnersh and Royal Oak at Yattendon. Look out for West Berkshire's rather charmingly named good beers, stocked at quite a few pubs in this chapter (including most of those with Beer Awards). They use local supplies as much as possible, including hops from the area's only surviving hop garden, at Kingston Bagpuize. Other good local brews are Butts, and Loddon (from just over the Oxfordshire border outside Reading).

ALDERMASTON   SU5865   MAP 2
Hinds Head
Wasing Lane; RG7 4LX

Welcoming licensee at comfortable pub with enjoyable food and drink, and nice bedrooms

This creeper-clad red brick 17th-c inn is at the heart of a rather attractive old village. The spacious but homely bar is traditionally furnished with a busy red patterned carpet, wooden pews, old tables, a big comfy red sofa, and brasses over the fireplace. Neatly turned out staff serve Fullers ESB and London Pride and a guest such as Gales Festival Mild from handpump, a good choice of wines by the glass and quite a collection of malt whiskies; piped music and board games. There are seats outside in the fine garden, and the bedrooms have been attractively redone.

🍴 Generous helpings of deliberately pubby food include sardines on toast, mussels, chilli, steak, ale and mushroom pie, battered fish, roast vegetable lasagne and duck breast. *Starters/Snacks: £3.95 to £6.95. Main Courses: £7.15 to £14.95. Puddings: £3.50 to £6.25*

Fullers ~ Manager Louis Thacker ~ Real ale ~ Bar food (12-2.30(3 Sun), 6-9.15(8 Sun)) ~ Restaurant ~ (0118) 971 2194 ~ Children welcome if eating ~ Open 11.30-11; 12-10.30 Sun ~ Bedrooms: £75S/£90B

Recommended by Wendy Arnold, Sara Fulton, Roger Baker, Dr and Mrs A K Clarke, Angus and Rosemary Campbell

ALDWORTH   SU5579   MAP 2

Bell ★ ♀ ◀ £

A329 Reading—Wallingford; left on to B4009 at Streatley; RG8 9SE

Exceptional unspoilt pub, super value snacks, very well kept beers, good quality house wines, lovely friendly atmosphere, and nice garden; can be busy

'One of the best pubs I've been to', 'worth many many stars' and 'still the benchmark' are just a few of the comments delighted readers have sent us about this unpretentious gem of a pub. It's been run by the same family for over 250 years and remains a favourite with the wide mix of customers who love the fact that mobile phones, piped music and games machines are banned. Quite unspoilt and unchanging, the rooms have benches around the panelled walls, an ancient one-handed clock, beams in the shiny ochre ceiling, and a woodburning stove. Rather than a bar counter for service, there's a glass-panelled hatch from which they serve the very well kept Arkells BBB and Kingsdown, local West Berkshire Old Tyler and Mild and a monthly guest from West Berkshire; also Upton farm cider, good house wines and spiced porter at Christmas; no draught lager. As you might expect, the pub games here are traditional: darts, shove-ha'penny and dominoes. The quiet, old-fashioned cottagey garden is by the village cricket ground, and behind the pub there's a paddock with farm animals. In summer there may be occasional morris dancers, while at Christmas local mummers perform in the road by the ancient well-head (the shaft is sunk 365 feet through the chalk). It tends to get very busy at weekends; dogs must be kept on leads.

🍴 **Excellent value bar food is limited to filled hot crusty rolls and a variety of ploughman's; in winter they also do home-made soup.** *Starters/Snacks: £2.60 to £6.00*

Free house ~ Licensee H E Macaulay ~ Real ale ~ Bar food (11-2.45, 6-9.30; 12-2.45, 7-9 Sun) ~ No credit cards ~ (01635) 578272 ~ Children welcome ~ Dogs welcome ~ Open 11-3, 6-11; 12-3, 7-10.30 Sun; closed Mon and Mon bank hol evenings

Recommended by Thomas Lane, I H G Busby, Mike Vincent, Pete Baker, Mark and Diane Grist, Dick and Madeleine Brown, N R White, Edward Bainton, the Didler, Anthony Longden, Catherine Pitt, Martin and Marion Vincent, Tracey and Stephen Groves, Ray J Carter, Roger Wain-Heapy, Mr and Mrs H J Langley, Phil and Sally Gorton, Fred and Kate Portnell, Pam and John Smith

ASHMORE GREEN   SU4969   MAP 2

Sun in the Wood ♀

B4009 (Shaw Road) off A339, then right on to Kiln Road, then left on to Stoney Lane. Pub one mile on left; RG18 9HF

Cheery family pub with a genuine mix of customers, plenty of room, tasty food, beer and wine, and friendly licensees

The enthusiastic hard-working licensees (well backed by an attentive team of staff) at this popular country pub offer a genuinely warm welcome to all. Comfortable and unimposing, the high-beamed front bar has bare boards on the left, carpet on the right, and a mix of nice old chairs, padded dining chairs and stripped pews around sturdy tables. It opens into a big back dining area which has the same informal feel, candles on tables, and some interesting touches like the big stripped bank of apothecary's drawers. There's a small conservatory sitting area by the side entrance. Wadworths 6X and IPA are well kept on handpump, and they offer a fine choice of wines by the glass. Outside, the decked terrace has heaters, plenty of flowers, and old-fashioned street lights. A big woodside garden with lots of picnic-sets, and a small child-free area; the nine-hole woodland crazy golf pitch is a big hit with families. It's hard to believe the pub is only a few minutes away from the centre of Newbury.

🍽 Enjoyable bar food such as good freshly baked filled baguettes (Tuesday-Saturday lunchtimes), smoked haddock and salmon fishcake on pea purée, mushroom and vegetable lasagne, pork escalope with a pumpkin seed crumb on provençale sauce, chicken, bacon and blue cheese pie and beef wellington with creamy stilton and port sauce. Puddings might include bread and butter pudding, lemon curd cheesecake and local ice-creams, and they've a british cheeseboard; two- and three-course Sunday lunches. *Starters/Snacks: £4.00 to £8.00. Main Courses: £7.00 to £12.00. Puddings: £3.95 to £5.00*

Wadworths ~ Tenant Philip Davison ~ Real ale ~ Bar food (12-2, 6-9.30; 12-4 Sun) ~ Restaurant ~ (01635) 42377 ~ Children welcome ~ Open 12-2.30, 6-11; 12-11 Sat; 12-6 Sun; closed Mon, Sun evening

Recommended by Stephen Moss, Dr and Mrs A K Clarke, Martin and Karen Wake

BRAY   SU9079   MAP 2

Crown

1.75 miles from M4 junction 9; A308 towards Windsor, then left at Bray signpost on to B3028; High Street; SL6 2AH

Low-beamed, busy pub with roaring log fires in knocked-through rooms, enjoyable food

Though there are tables for drinkers, this bustling 14th-c pub is mainly set out for eating. To be sure of a place it's best to arrive early or book in advance. Some of its heavy old beams are so low you may have to mind your head, and there are plenty of timbers handily left at elbow height where walls have been knocked through. In winter three roaring log fires are deliciously cosy. The partly panelled main bar has oak tables and leather-backed armchairs, and one dining area has photographs of WWII aeroplanes. Courage Best and Directors on handpump are served alongside a guest such as Wadworths 6X and a decent choice of wines. There are tables and benches out in a sheltered flagstoned front courtyard (which has a flourishing grape vine), and in the large back garden.

🍽 Popular (if not cheap) food such as home-made soup, goats cheese on peppered pineapple, moules marinières and chips, good beef and Guinness pie, warm oriental chicken salad, tagliatelle carbonara, wild boar sausages and sirloin steak. *Starters/Snacks: £5.25 to £10.95. Main Courses: £9.90 to £16.95. Puddings: £3.00 to £4.50*

Scottish Courage ~ Lease John and Carole Noble ~ Real ale ~ Bar food (not Sun or Mon evenings) ~ Restaurant ~ (01628) 621936 ~ Children in restaurant ~ Open 11-3, 6-11; 12-3, 7-10.30 Sun; closed 25 and 26 Dec, 1 Jan

Recommended by Tom and Ruth Rees, Julia Morris, Ray J Carter, Stephen Moss, Susan and John Douglas, Dr and Mrs A K Clarke, Michael Dandy, Dr Kevan Tucker

Hinds Head 🍽 ♀

High Street; car park opposite (exit rather tricky); SL6 2AB
BERKSHIRE DINING PUB OF THE YEAR

Top-notch gastropub with outstanding classic british food in traditional surroundings, a fine choice of drinks, and efficient service

This handsome old pub is under the same ownership as the nearby renowned Fat Duck restaurant. It's no surprise then that most customers are here to experience the excellent (though not cheap) food, which is prepared in a simpler style and served in a more relaxed and informal atmosphere than at its more sophisticated parent. The thoroughly traditional L-shaped bar has dark beams and panelling, polished oak parquet, blazing log fires, red-cushioned built-in wall seats and studded leather carving chairs around small round tables, and latticed windows. They've a dozen interesting wines by the glass (including two champagnes) from an extensive list, Greene King and Rebellion IPA and a couple of guests such as Ruddles County on handpump, 24 malt whiskies, an excellent bloody mary, Sheppy's farm cider and a fine choice of tea and coffee. They may ask to retain your credit card.

🍴 Superbly executed, the delicious bar food includes pea and ham soup, dandelion salad with bacon and quails eggs, oysters, rabbit and bacon terrine, lancashire hotpot, oxtail and kidney pudding, sausage and mash, salmon and pollack fishcakes and rump steak, with puddings such as treacle sponge, eton mess and quaking pudding. *Starters/Snacks: £1.95 to £12.00. Main Courses: £11.95 to £19.95. Puddings: £5.50 to £7.95*

Free house ~ Licensee Steven Holland ~ Real ale ~ Bar food (12-2.30, 6.30-9.30; Sun 12-4) ~ Restaurant ~ (01628) 626151 ~ Children welcome ~ Dogs allowed in bar ~ Open 11-11; 12-8.30 Sun

Recommended by Simon Collett-Jones, David and Sue Smith, Dr Kevan Tucker, Ray J Carter, John Urquhart, Dr and Mrs A K Clarke, Minda and Stanley Alexander, David Tindal, Mandy and Simon King, Humphry and Angela Crum Ewing, P Waterman, Howard Dell

COOKHAM DEAN   SU8785   MAP 2

Chequers 🍴 ⏛

Dean Lane; from Cookham follow signpost Cookham Dean, Marlow (unsuitable for heavy vehicles); SL6 9BQ

Restauranty dining pub with good food, friendly staff and cosy bar

Cheerful welcoming service and the comfortable old sofas in the compact bar give this beamed and flagstoned pub a warm heart. They do good coffee, as well as some 16 good value wines by the glass, Greene King IPA and Marlow Rebellion Smuggler on handpump and a good range of spirits. Fresh flowers and crisp white linen grace the mixed dining tables on either side of the bar; there may be piped music. The area on the left, with an open stove in its big brick fireplace, flows back into a conservatory looking up the lawn's neat slope. There are picnic-sets outside, some on a front terrace.

🍴 A handful of quite pubby lunchtime dishes, such as battered haddock and sausage and mash, is a simpler alternative to the main menu which might include roast pepper and tomato soup, seared scallops with chorizo, asparagus and parmesan, braised lamb shank with redcurrant and rosemary jus and smoked garlic mash, cod fillet on creamy brown shrimp risotto and rib-eye steak with béarnaise sauce, and puddings such as blackcurrant and mascarpone cheesecake and sticky toffee pudding. *Starters/Snacks: £3.95 to £9.95. Main Courses: £9.50 to £17.95. Puddings: £4.75*

Free house ~ Licensee Peter Roehrig ~ Real ale ~ Bar food (12-2.30, 6.30-9.30(10 Fri, Sat); 12-9.30 Sun) ~ Restaurant ~ (01628) 481232 ~ Children welcome ~ Open 11-3, 5.30-12; 11-12 Fri-Sun

Recommended by Ron and Kathy Durnford, Fred and Kate Portnell, P Farrar, P Waterman

FRILSHAM   SU5573   MAP 2

Pot Kiln 🍴

From Yattendon take turning S, opposite church, follow first Frilsham signpost, but just after crossing motorway go straight on towards Bucklebury ignoring Frilsham signposted right; pub on right after about half a mile; RG18 0XX

Traditional pub dishes up to imaginative modern cooking in country dining pub with good choice of ales and suntrap garden

Two or three readers have had to persevere in finding this isolated dining pub but all report that it was well worth the effort. Surprisingly, given its tucked away location, it's still essential to book to be sure of a table. Emphasis is very much on the imaginative restaurant food, though friendly locals do still gather in the little bar where they offer West Berkshire Brick Kiln Bitter, Mr Chubbs Lunchtime Bitter and Maggs Magnificent Mild with a guest on handpump. The main bar area has dark wooden tables and chairs on bare boards, and a good winter log fire, and the extended lounge is open plan at the back and leads into a large, pretty dining room with a nice jumble of old tables and chairs, and an old-looking stone fireplace; darts and cards. This is a charming rural spot, and seats in the big suntrap garden have good views of the nearby forests and meadows; plenty of nearby walks.

🍴 Bread, pasta and gnocchi are made here every morning, some salads and vegetables come from the pub's own garden, and most of the venison on the menu is stalked by the landlord and Sassy. The menu includes pubby staples such as filled rolls, beef and venison burger, ploughman's and sausage casserole, and more elaborate dishes such as warm salad of wood pigeon, potted cornish crab, vegetable tortilla and organic salmon and confit pork belly with butter bean purée and cider reduction; puddings such as vanilla and cardamom rice pudding, apple and berry crumble, treacle tart with marmalade ice-cream, and a good cheeseboard; good value weekday lunchtime set menu (service may be added to the bill). *Starters/Snacks: £3.20 to £4.95. Main Courses: £6.50 to £10.00. Puddings: £6.00*

Free house ~ Licensees Mr and Mrs Michael Robinson ~ Real ale ~ Bar food (12-2, 7-9; 12-3, 6-9 Sun) ~ Restaurant ~ (01635) 201366 ~ Children welcome ~ Dogs allowed in bar ~ Open 12-3, 6-11; 12-11 Sat; 12-10.30 Sun

Recommended by I H G Busby, Dr and Mrs A K Clarke, the Didler, G Coates, Robert Watt, A J Bowen, Andrew Given, Robert Jamieson, Graham and Toni Sanders

HOLYPORT   SU8977   MAP 2

Belgian Arms
Handy for M4 junction 8/9, via A308(M) and A330; SL6 2JR

Popular dining pub with friendly staff, good food and waterside garden terrace

The low-ceilinged bar at this bustling place has well spaced tables and chairs on a stripped wooden floor, interesting cricketing memorabilia on the walls, a china cupboard in one corner, a log fire and a discreetly placed TV; piped music. The old cellar room is now a dining area, and a spacious conservatory opens on to a terrace with good quality wooden furniture and views overlooking the village pond. Friendly, humorous staff serve Brakspears Bitter and a guest beer on handpump, and there are quite a few wines by the glass.

🍴 The well balanced menu includes sandwiches, caesar salad, scallops with black pudding and cauliflower purée, roast butternut and feta risotto, fish and chips, sausage and mash, beef, Guinness and mushroom pie, catch of the day, a full range of steaks and puddings such as pistachio crème brûlée and sticky toffee pudding. *Starters/Snacks: £5.50 to £6.95. Main Courses: £6.95 to £15.00. Puddings: £4.50 to £5.50*

Brakspears ~ Tenant Jamie Sears ~ Real ale ~ Bar food (12-2.30(3.30 Sun), 7-9) ~ Restaurant ~ (01628) 634468 ~ Children welcome ~ Dogs allowed in bar ~ Open 11-3, 5.30-11; 11-11 Fri, Sat; 12-10.30 Sun

Recommended by David and Sue Smith, Simon Collett-Jones

HURST   SU8074   MAP 2

Green Man
Hinton Road, off A321 just outside village; RG10 0BP

An interesting mix of bars in bustling pub with decent food, and plenty of space outside on terrace and in big garden

The old-fashioned bar at this partly 17th-c pub has black standing timbers and dark oak beams around cosy alcoves, cushioned wall seats and built-in settles around copper-topped and other pub tables, and attractive prints, Edwardian enamels and decorative plates on cream or terracotta walls; it's warmed by a hot little fire in one fireplace and a nice old iron stove in another. Beyond is a light and airy dining room and the appealing cellar room has just four tables and lots of pictures on its cream-painted brickwork; well kept Brakspears, Wychwood Hobgoblin, and a guest such as Wychwood Dirty Tackle on handpump, and half a dozen wines by the glass. The sheltered, heated terrace has tables under giant umbrellas, there are picnic-sets under big oak trees in the large garden, and there's a good sturdy children's play area.

🍴 Reasonably priced bar food includes lunchtime sandwiches and baked potatoes, as well as lamb tagine, fish pie, butternut and beetroot parcel, chicken, gammon and leek pie, with specials such as grilled bass with rocket salad, pork fillet stuffed with mushroom and onion on creamy wholegrain mustard sauce *Starters/Snacks: £3.50 to £4.95. Main Courses: £7.95 to £15.95. Puddings: £3.95 to £4.50*

Brakspears ~ Tenants Simon and Gordon Guile ~ Real ale ~ Bar food (12-2.30, 6-9.30; 12-9 Sun (roasts until 4)) ~ Restaurant ~ (0118) 934 2599 ~ Children welcome ~ Open 11-3, 5.30-11; 12-10.30 Sun

Recommended by Ian Phillips, Fred and Kate Portnell, Nina Randall, Kevin Thomas, Priscilla Sandford, D J and P M Taylor, M G Hart, Mark and Diane Grist, Dr and Mrs A K Clarke, June and Robin Savage

INKPEN   SU3764   MAP 2

Crown & Garter 🍺 🛏

Inkpen Common: Inkpen signposted with Kintbury off A4; in Kintbury turn left into Inkpen Road, then keep on into Inkpen Common; RG17 9QR

Remote-feeling pub with appealing layout, lovely garden and nearby walks, local ales and tasty food in nicely lit bars, and friendly licensee

This attractive old 16th-c brick pub is run by a welcoming landlady, and is surprisingly substantial for somewhere so remote-feeling. The appealing low-ceilinged and relaxed panelled bar keeps West Berkshire Mr Chubbs Lunchtime Bitter and Good Old Boy and Timothy Taylors Landlord plus a guest such as Arkells Moonlight on handpump, decent wines by the glass and several malt whiskies. Three areas radiate from here; our pick is the parquet-floored part by the raised log fire which has a couple of substantial old tables and a huge old-fashioned slightly curved settle. Other parts are slate and wood with a good mix of well spaced tables and chairs, and nice lighting; piped music. There's a front terrace for outside eating, a lovely long side garden with picnic-sets, and plenty of good downland walks nearby. In a separate single-storey building, the bedrooms form an L around a pretty garden. James II is reputed to have used the pub on his way to visit his mistress locally.

🍽 **Enjoyable bar food might include mushroom soup, red onion and goats cheese tart, hake and chips, leek, tomato and cheese tart, roast lamb shank, steak and kidney pudding, crab lasagne, and puddings such as Tia Maria and fresh fruit brûlée or profiteroles.** *Starters/Snacks: £4.95 to £6.95. Main Courses: £9.95 to £19.95. Puddings: £4.95 to £6.75*

Free house ~ Licensee Gill Hern ~ Real ale ~ Bar food (not Sun evening) ~ Restaurant ~ (01488) 668325 ~ Children over 7 in evenings and in bedrooms ~ Dogs allowed in bar ~ Open 12-3, 5.30-11; 12-5, 7-10.30 Sun; closed Mon and Tues lunchtimes ~ Bedrooms: £59.50B/£90B

Recommended by Alun Jones, C R Crofton, Jeff and Wendy Williams, Sue Demont, Tim Barrow, Michael Dallas, Mr and Mrs H J Langley, Paul A Moore

READING   SU7173   MAP 2

Hobgoblin 🍺

2 Broad Street; RG1 2BH

No-frills backstreet pub with small panelled rooms, cheerful atmosphere and eight quickly changing ales

Real ales at this cheerfully basic pub include three from the West Berkshire Brewery alongside five well kept guests from interesting smaller brewers such as Church End, Hampshire, Fuzzy Duck, Itchen Valley, Spinning Dog or Woodlands. Pump clips cover practically every inch of the walls and ceiling of the simple bare-boards bar – a testament to the enormous number of brews that have passed through the pumps over the past few years (now well over 5,000). They've also lots of different bottled beers, czech lager on tap, Weston's farm cider and perry and country wines. Up a step is a small seating area, but the best places to sit are the three or four tiny panelled rooms reached by a narrow corridor leading from the bar; cosy and intimate, each has barely enough space for one table and a few chairs or wall seats, but they're very appealing if you're able to bag one; the biggest also manages to squeeze in a fireplace. It does get very busy, especially at weekends; piped music (very much in keeping with the rough and ready feel of the place), and TV.

🍴 **No food.**

Community Taverns ~ Manager Rob Wain ~ Real ale ~ No credit cards ~ (0118) 950 8119 ~ Open 11-11; 12-10.30 Sun

Recommended by Martin and Marion Vincent, Catherine Pitt, Mark and Diane Grist, Mike Vincent, the Didler, Dr and Mrs A K Clarke

REMENHAM
SU7682 MAP 2

Little Angel 🍴 ♟

A4130, just over bridge E of Henley; RG9 2LS

Relaxed linked contemporary areas plus attractive conservatory, good modern bar food, helpful service, and a dozen wines by the glass

The interior of this attractive pub has been cleverly opened up so you can feel tucked away in your own individually charactered area, but still feel part of the buzzy atmosphere. There are well spaced seats and tables on the bare boards or ochre tiles, and soft furnishings are mainly in pale fabrics or suede, running from comfortable bar seats through tub chairs to deep sofas, with new artwork on the walls. In one corner a case of art books and the like help to set the tone; conservatory. The attractive curved bar counter has a good choice of a dozen wines by the glass (plus champagne), smoothies and cocktails, and Brakspears Bitter and a guest on handpump; board games, unobtrusive piped music, TV, and friendly and efficient young staff. A sheltered floodlit back terrace has tables under cocktail parasols, looking over to the local cricket ground.

🍴 **Very good food using local estate game and organic fruit and vegetables includes lunchtime food such as interesting sandwiches, pie of the day, port and stilton on toast with fries, and a plate of mixed antipasti, plus soup, eggs benedict, scallops and king prawns on parma ham salad, cauliflower, broccoli and dolcelatte lasagne, calves liver, mushy pea mash and pancetta, slow-roast shoulder of lamb with chorizo, baby onion and potato cassoulet, and puddings like treacle apple sponge with vanilla crumble ice-cream.** *Starters/Snacks: £6.50 to £7.50. Main Courses: £8.50 to £15.00. Puddings: £5.50 to £6.50*

Brakspears ~ Lease Douglas Green ~ Real ale ~ Bar food (12-3, 7-10; 12-4, 7-9 Sun) ~ Restaurant ~ (01491) 411008 ~ Well behaved children welcome, some restrictions on buggies etc ~ Dogs allowed in bar ~ Open 11-midnight; 12-11 Sun

Recommended by Chris Glasson, Ray J Carter, Andy and Claire Barker, Tom and Ruth Rees, Simon Rodway, Michael Dandy, Stephen P Edwards, Ian Phillips

RUSCOMBE
SU7976 MAP 2

Royal Oak

Ruscombe Lane (B3024 just E of Twyford); RG10 9JN

Wide choice of popular food at welcoming pub with interesting furnishings and paintings and adjoining antiques and collectables shop

It's the genuine personal touches that lend such a welcoming atmosphere to this bustling village pub. The open plan carpeted interior is well laid out so that each bit is fairly snug, yet it keeps the overall feel of a lot of people enjoying themselves. A good variety of furniture runs from dark oak tables to big chunky pine ones, with mixed seating to match – the two sofas facing one another are popular. Contrasting with the old exposed ceiling joists, mostly unframed modern paintings and prints decorate the walls – mainly dark terracotta over a panelled dado. Drinks include Brakspears Bitter, Fullers London Pride and maybe a guest on handpump, and half a dozen nicely chosen wines including a local vintage. Picnic-sets are ranged around a venerable central hawthorn in the garden behind (where there are ducks and chickens); summer barbecues. A pleasing new distraction is the landlady's antiques and collectables shop, which is open during pub hours.

🍴 **Bar food is popular and as well as lunchtime snacks such as sandwiches and panini, ploughman's, beer-battered fish, stilton and bacon burger and bangers and mash, there's soup, king prawns in garlic citrus butter, lamb shank with rosemary jus, spinach and leek pasta, and daily specials like smoked salmon and scrambled eggs, red thai chicken and prawn on noodles, and home-made steak in ale pie.** *Starters/Snacks: £4.25 to £9.95. Main Courses: £9.95 to £18.00. Puddings: £3.50 to £5.50*

Enterprise ~ Lease Jenny and Stefano Buratta ~ Real ale ~ Bar food (12-2.30, 6.30-9.30; 12-3 Sun) ~ Restaurant ~ (0118) 934 5190 ~ Children welcome ~ Dogs welcome ~ Open 12-3, 6-11; 12-4 Sun; closed Sun and Mon evenings

Recommended by Tracey and Stephen Groves, Mr and Mrs C R Little, Fred and Kate Portnell, Paul Humphreys

SHINFIELD
SU7367   MAP 2

Magpie & Parrot 🍺

2.6 miles from M4 junction 11, via B3270; A327 just SE of Shinfield – heading out on Arborfield Road, keep eyes skinned for small hand-painted green Nursery sign on left, and Fullers 'bar open' blackboard; RG2 9EA

Unusual homely little roadside cottage with warm fire, lots of bric-a-brac in cosy small bars, and hospitable landlady

This is a charmingly relaxed place to while away a winter's afternoon beside the warm open fire. You go in through the lobby (with its antiquated telephone equipment), and find a cosy and inviting high-raftered room with a handful of small polished tables – each with a bowl of peanuts (they don't do any food) – and a comfortable mix of individualistic seats from Georgian oak thrones to a red velveteen sofa, not to mention the armchair with the paw-printed cushion reserved for Aitch the pub dog. Everything is spick and span, from the brightly patterned carpet, to the plethora of interesting bric-a-brac covering the walls: miniature and historic bottles, dozens of model cars, veteran AA badges and automotive instruments, and mementoes of a pranged Spitfire (do ask about its story – they love to chat here). Well kept Fullers London Pride and a changing guest such as Timothy Taylors are on handpump at the small corner counter. There are teak tables on the back terrace and an immaculate lawn beyond; hog roasts and morris men at various summer events and two beer festivals in June and December with 22 real ales; Aunt Sally. Note the unusual opening hours.

🍴 **No food.**

Free house ~ Licensee Mrs Carole Headland ~ Real ale ~ No credit cards ~ (0118) 988 4130 ~ Open 12-7; 12-3 Sun; closed evenings

Recommended by Tracey and Stephen Groves, Dr and Mrs A K Clarke, Phil and Sally Gorton, R T and J C Moggridge, Mark and Diane Grist, Jeremy Woods

STANFORD DINGLEY
SU5771   MAP 2

Old Boot

Off A340 via Bradfield, coming from A4 just W of M4 junction 12; RG7 6LT

Neat pub with emphasis on imaginative food; country furnishings and rural garden views

Good food is very much the draw at this stylish 18th-c pub – not surprising given that the kitchen is staffed by a team of well trained french chefs. Most tables are laid for dining and to be sure of a place you must book in advance, especially at weekends. The beamed bar has two welcoming fires (one in an inglenook), fine old pews, settles, old country chairs, and polished tables. There are some striking pictures and hunting prints, boot ornaments in various sizes, and fresh flowers. Three real ales might include West Berkshire Good Old Boy, Batemans and Fullers London Pride on handpump and around half a dozen wines by the glass. There are seats in the quiet sloping back garden or on the terrace, and pleasant rural views; more tables out in front.

🍴 As well as tasty bar food such as filled baguettes, fresh cod and chips, game stew and risotto, there are more elaborate dishes too: deep-fried brie with red fruit compote, moules marinières, seared scallops, gressingham duck breast with blackcurrant sauce, venison in port wine and chestnuts, winter casseroles, best end of lamb, and steak with a stilton and mushroom sauce. *Starters/Snacks: £5.50 to £11.50. Main Courses: £10.50 to £14.50. Puddings: £5.50*

Free house ~ Licensees John and Jeannie Haley ~ Real ale ~ Bar food ~ Restaurant ~ (0118) 974 4292 ~ Children welcome ~ Dogs allowed in bar ~ Open 11(12 Sun)-3, 6-11
Recommended by A J Bowen, I H G Busby

WHITE WALTHAM   SU8477   MAP 2

Beehive 🍺

Waltham Road (B3024 W of Maidenhead); SL6 3SH

Honest bar food and welcoming staff at traditional village pub

This solidly run country local quietly does what it says on the box. To the right, several comfortably carpeted spacious areas have country kitchen chairs around sturdy tables and a conservatory. The neat bar to the left is brightened up by cheerful scatter cushions on its comfortable seats – built-in wall seats, captain's chairs and a leather wing armchair. Brakspears, Fullers London Pride, Greene King Abbot and a changing guest such as Rebellion Prime Suspect are well kept on handpump, with a good choice of soft drinks, nuts and so forth; piped music, games machine, and board games. Picnic-sets and teak seats out in front on the recently extended terrace take in the pub's rather fine topiary, and look over the village cricket field, and there's more seating on a good-sized sheltered back lawn; good disabled access and facilities.

🍴 Honest bar food includes sandwiches, ploughman's, salads, soup, calamari in lemon batter, ham and eggs, spicy beanburger, thai-style fishcakes, steak and kidney pie, braised lamb shank, and puddings like belgian chocolate mousse. *Starters/Snacks: £2.00 to £7.95. Main Courses: £6.95 to £19.95. Puddings: £4.95*

Enterprise ~ Lease Guy Martin ~ Real ale ~ Bar food (12-2.30, 5.30-9.30; 12-9.30 Sat; 12-8.30 Sun) ~ Restaurant ~ (01628) 822877 ~ Children welcome ~ Dogs welcome ~ Open 11-3, 5-11; 11-12 Sat; 12-10.30 Sun
Recommended by Paul Humphreys, Dr and Mrs A K Clarke, June and Robin Savage, Alan and Carolin Tidbury

WINTERBOURNE   SU4572   MAP 2

Winterbourne Arms ♀

3.7 miles from M4 junction 13; at A34 turn into Chievley Services and follow Donnington signs to Arlington Lane, then follow Winterbourne signs; RG20 8BB

Charming country pub with enjoyable bar food, lots of wines by the glass and large landscaped garden

You can be sure of a warm welcome and rather good meal at this pretty black and white village house. There's also a good wine list with 20 offered by the glass (served in elegant glasses and including sparkling and sweet wines), and Fullers London Pride, Ramsbury Gold and Winterbourne Whistle Wetter on handpump. The traditional bars have stools along the counter, a collection of old irons around the big fireplace (log fire), and early prints and old photographs of the village on very pale washed pink, or exposed stone walls; piped music. Big windows take in peaceful views over rolling fields – the surrounding countryside here is lovely, with nearby walks to Snelsmore Common and Donnington Castle, and there are seats outside in the large landscaped side garden and pretty flowering tubs and hanging baskets.

🍴 The nicely varied menu includes filled baguettes and ploughman's, garlic mushrooms in white wine cream sauce on toasted brioche, goats cheese and red onion tartlet, organic sausages and mash, gammon and eggs, wild mushroom and spinach risotto and slow-roast pork belly, daily specials such as wild boar terrine and grilled bass on crushed citrus

potatoes with walnut and garlic butter, and puddings such as apple and blackberry crumble or lemon posset with shortbread fingers; popular Sunday lunch *Starters/Snacks: £3.95 to £8.55. Main Courses: £7.95 to £19.95. Puddings: £3.95 to £5.95*

Free house ~ Licensee Frank Adams ~ Real ale ~ Bar food (12-2.30, 6-9.30; 12-3.30, 6-9 Sun) ~ (01635) 248200 ~ Children welcome ~ Dogs allowed in bar ~ Open 12-3, 6-11; 12-10.30 Sun

Recommended by Martin and Pauline Jennings, Mike and Heather Watson, Mr and Mrs J P Blake, Mike and Sue Loseby, Mark and Ruth Brock, Paul A Moore

LUCKY DIP

Besides the fully inspected pubs, you might like to try these Lucky Dips recommended to us and described by readers (if you do, please send us reports: feedback@thegoodpubguide.co.uk).

ASTON [SU7884]
☆ *Flower Pot* RG9 3DG [small signpost off A4130 Henley—Maidenhead at top of Remenham Hill]: Roomy country pub with roaring log fire, array of stuffed fish and fishing prints on dark green walls of attractively done airy country dining area, good value food from sandwiches to fish and game, Brakspears, Hook Norton and Wychwood ales, quick friendly service, snug traditional bar with more fishing memorabilia; very busy with walkers and families wknds; lots of picnic-sets giving quiet country views from nice big dog-friendly orchard garden, side field with chickens, ducks and guinea fowl *(P Waterman, Susan and John Douglas, Michael Dandy, BB, Roy Hoing, David and Sue Smith)*

BEECH HILL [SU6964]
Elm Tree RG7 2AZ [3.3 miles from M4 junction 11: A33 towards Basingstoke, turning off into Beech Hill Rd after about 2 miles]: Five carefully furnished and decorated rooms, one with dozens of clocks, Hollywood photographs and blazing fire, nice views especially from simply furnished more modern barn-style restaurant and conservatory, quick friendly staff, enjoyable if not cheap food (all day wknds) from hearty baguettes up inc some unusual dishes, well kept Fullers London Pride, Greene King IPA and Old Speckled Hen and a guest beer, amazing ladies'; children welcome away from bar, benches and tables on front decking in nice setting, open all day *(David and Sue Smith, LYM)*

BINFIELD [SU8470]
Roebuck RG42 4AJ [St Marks Rd]: Friendly new licensees doing good value generous food, good local atmosphere; garden *(Martin Kerby)*

BRACKNELL [SU8566]
Golden Retriever RG12 7PB [Nine Mile Ride (junction A3095/B3430)]: Clever Vintage Inn pastiche of olde-worlde beamed, tiled and thatched pub, comfortable farmhouse-style décor in maze of linked rooms, decent food all day, Bass and Fullers London Pride, plenty of wines by the glass, lots of young attentive staff, log fires, daily papers; ample seating outside, open all day *(R Lake, Ian*

Phillips, P J Ridley, David and Sue Smith)
BURGHFIELD [SU6870]
Cunning Man RG30 3RB [Burghfield Bridge]: Comfortable Vintage Inn using some local produce for their usual good value food choice, Greene King Old Speckled Hen and Hancocks HB, efficient staff; plenty of good tables outside *(Reg Fowle, Helen Rickwood, Bob and Laura Brock)*
CHADDLEWORTH [SU4177]
Ibex RG20 7ER [Main St]: Homely village pub with friendly attentive staff, enjoyable food from good baguettes up, good choice of beers and soft drinks, good coffee, games in public bar, PO in back room; wheelchair access, dogs and walkers welcome, tables out on sheltered lawn and floodlit terrace *(Tony Winckworth, LYM, Paul Humphreys, Guy Vowles)*
CHEAPSIDE [SU9469]
☆ *Thatched Tavern* SL5 7QG [off A332/A329, then off B383 at Village Hall sign]: Civilised dining pub with a good deal of character, interesting up-to-date food, friendly service, good choice of wines by the glass and farm cider as well as a couple of well kept ales, daily papers, big inglenook log fire, low beams and polished flagstones in cottagey core, three smart carpeted dining rooms off; children in restaurant, rustic tables on attractive sheltered back lawn, open all day wknds, handy for Virginia Water *(Chris Sale, LYM)*
COOKHAM [SU8985]
☆ *Bel & the Dragon* SL6 9SQ [High St (B4447)]: Smart old dining pub with panelling and heavy Tudor beams, log fires, bare boards and simple country furnishings in two-room front bar and dining area, more formal back restaurant, helpful friendly staff, enjoyable food at prices you might expect for the area, real ales such as Brakspears and Fullers London Pride, good choice of wines; this is the original Bel – the small group which owns it has now also given the name to a handful of other home counties dining pubs; children welcome, garden with terrace tables, Stanley Spencer Gallery almost opposite, open all day *(LYM, Phil Bryant)*
Ferry SL6 9SN [Sutton Rd]: Splendidly placed riverside pub with relaxing modern décor, decent if not cheap food (very popular Sun

lunchtime), obliging staff, Loddon ale, some interesting lagers and good wine range, contemporary artwork, solid teak furnishings in light and airy Thames-view dining areas upstairs and down, dark décor and small servery in beamed core; piped music; children welcome, extensive decking overlooking river *(Roy Hoing, BB, David Tindal, Susan and John Douglas)*

COOKHAM DEAN [SU8785]

☆ *Jolly Farmer* SL6 9PD [Church Rd, off Hills Lane]: Traditional pub owned by village consortium, old-fashioned unspoilt bars with open fires, friendly staff and black labrador (called Czar), prompt service, well kept ales, farm cider, decent wines and coffee, sensibly priced food from sandwiches up, good-sized more modern eating area and small dining room, old local photographs, pub games, no music or machines; well behaved children welcome, tables out in front and in good garden with play area *(Chris Sale, John Saville, Paul Humphreys, LYM)*

CRAZIES HILL [SU7980]

Horns RG10 8LY [Warren Row Rd off A4 towards Cockpole Green, then follow Crazies Hill signs]: Comfortable and individual beamed pub, Brakspears ales, good choice of wines by the glass, upscale bar snacks and restaurant meals (can take a while, veg extra, and nothing really cheap and cheerful for kids), stripped furniture and open fires, prints for sale on warm-coloured walls, raftered barn dining room; pleasant seats in large informal garden with civilised barbecues and play area *(LYM, Paul Humphreys, David and Sue Smith)*

EAST ILSLEY [SU4981]

☆ *Crown & Horns* RG20 7LH [just off A34, about 5 miles N of M4 junction 13; Compton Road]: Bustling pub in horse-training country, lots of interesting racing pictures, well worn in rambling beamed rooms, blazing log fire, well kept Adnams Regatta, Brakspears and Timothy Taylors Landlord, massive whisky choice, bar food and four dining rooms; piped music, TV and games machine; children and dogs allowed, comfortable tables in pretty courtyard, modern bedroom extension, open all day *(LYM, Tom and Ruth Rees, David Coleman)*

ETON [SU9677]

☆ *Gilbeys* SL4 6AF [High St]: Not a pub, but well worth knowing for imaginative home-made bar meals, nice house wines inc one from their own vines (bottled beers), cheerful helpful family service; can be very busy if there's an event at the school, best to book for light and airy back restaurant down long corridor *(Peter Smith, Judith Brown, Mike and Sue Richardson, Alistair Forsyth, BB)*

☆ *Watermans Arms* SL4 6BW [Brocas St]: Large friendly dark-panelled pub facing Eton College boat house, horseshoe servery with well kept Brakspears, Fullers London Pride, Hogs Back TEA and Wychwood Hobgoblin, prompt helpful foreign staff, good usual food (all day Fri/Sat, not Sun eve) from sandwiches to fresh fish, bargain prices, roomy back dining area, overhead Thames map and lots of old river photographs; children welcome, covered tables outside *(LYM, Phil Bryant, Bruce Bird, Ian Phillips, Derek and Sylvia Stephenson)*

FIFIELD [SU9076]

Fifield Inn SL6 2NX [just off B3024 W of Windsor; Fifield Rd]: Neat and attractively refurbished stone-built village local with friendly staff, enjoyable fresh restaurant and bar food (no snacks on Sun), reasonable prices, Greene King ales, lots of wines by the glass, daily papers, flame-effect fire; live jazz Sun evening; children welcome, picnic-sets in lovely garden *(June and Robin Savage)*

FINCHAMPSTEAD [SU7963]

Queens Oak RG40 4LS [Church Lane, off B3016]: Relaxed well worn in country local, largely open plan, with good mix of simple seats and tables, some in airy parquet-floored area on right, well kept ale such as Hook Norton Dark, friendly attentive staff, separate dining room where children allowed; picnic-sets, some sheltered, in good-sized garden with aunt sally, play area, Sun lunchtime barbecues; open all day at least in summer *(BB, Dr and Mrs Jackson, David and Sue Smith)*

GREAT SHEFFORD [SU3875]

☆ *Swan* RG17 7DS [2 miles from M4 junction 14 – A338 towards Wantage (Newbury Rd)]: Low-ceilinged bow-windowed pub reopened after floods, good welcoming service, pleasant furnishings, good log fire, enjoyable baguettes and hot dishes inc pubby favourites, real ales inc local Butts and Fullers London Pride, good wine choice, daily papers, nice river-view dining room; soft piped music; good wheelchair access, children in eating areas, tables on attractive waterside lawn and terrace *(Simon Collett-Jones, Colin and Janet Roe, LYM, Henry Snell)*

HARE HATCH [SU8078]

Queen Victoria RG10 9TA [Blakes Lane; just N of A4 Reading—Maidenhead]: Two low-beamed and panelled bars recently redecorated in black and white, good value food, well kept Brakspears, conservatory; children in eating area, one or two tables outside *(LYM, Paul Humphreys)*

HERMITAGE [SU5072]

White Horse RG18 9TB [Newbury Rd]: Comfortably refurbished, attractive and interesting, with enjoyable traditional food (freshly made so may be a wait), well kept ales and decent wines, friendly caring licensees; well behaved dogs welcome *(Dr and Mrs A K Clarke)*

HUNGERFORD [SU3368]

Bear RG17 0EL [3 miles from M4 junction 14; town signed at junction]: Minimalist neo-scandinavian décor, a useful stop for all-day bistro food inc good range of sandwiches, restaurant; bedrooms comfortable and attractive

(Roger Wain-Heapy, LYM)
Downgate RG17 0ED [Down View, Park St]:
Prettily placed and relaxing country local,
decent food inc good Sun roast, friendly
efficient licensees, well kept Arkells, two
linked areas overlooking common, small
lower room with open fire, coin/currency
collection, model aircraft overhead
(John Grist, J Woolf)
☆ **Plume of Feathers** RG17 0NB [High St]: Big
well run open-plan family pub, lots of tables
around central bar, bare boards and lack of
fabrics giving a slight brasserie feel, good
food from soup, well made sandwiches and
pubby favourites to more adventurous
dishes, friendly staff, Greene King ales, good
coffee and wines by the glass, sofas, old
beams and cosy fire; garden tables,
bedrooms *(JCW)*

HUNGERFORD NEWTOWN [SU3571]
Tally Ho RG17 0PP [A338 just S of M4
junction 14]: Good cooking from home-
baked bread to interesting dishes under new
landlord in roomy and well appointed red
brick pub with well kept Wadworths and
decent house wines; children welcome,
picnic-sets outside *(John and
Penelope Massey Stewart)*

HURLEY [SU8281]
☆ **Dew Drop** SL6 6RB [small yellow sign to pub
off A4130 just W]: Nice rustic setting,
popular food from good baguettes up,
welcoming landlord and good service (free
transport for local customers), Brakspears
ales, enjoyable house wine, traditional
games, two friendly pub dogs (not at meal
times); children in eating area, french
windows to courtyard and attractive sloping
garden with barbecue, good walks
(Paul Humphreys, LYM, David Tindal)
Red Lyon SL6 5LH [A4130 SE, just off A404]:
Several warmly traditional linked low-
beamed and partly quarry-tiled areas, two
log fires, attractive medley of seating, lots
of pewter and bric-a-brac, friendly helpful
service, enterprising food from sandwiches
up, Greene King Old Speckled Hen, Marlow
Rebellion and Timothy Taylors Landlord,
good wine and coffee choice; piped music
(can be turned down for your table);
children welcome, picnic-sets in good-sized
garden behind, open all day *(Michael Dandy,
Susan and John Douglas)*

INKPEN [SU3564]
☆ **Swan** RG17 9DX [Lower Inkpen; coming from
A338 in Hungerford, take Park St (first left
after railway bridge, coming from A4)]:
Rambling beamed country pub with strong
organic leanings in its wines as well as the
food from sandwiches and pubby things to
more upscale dishes (farming owners have
interesting organic shop next door), cosy
corners, three log fires, friendly helpful staff,
good Butts and West Berkshire ales, local
farm cider, pleasant restaurant, flagstoned
games area; piped music; well behaved
children welcome in eating areas, picnic-sets
out in front, small quiet garden, good

bedrooms, open all day in summer
*(Guy Vowles, LYM, M J Daly, Pete Baker,
D Nightingale, N R White)*

KINTBURY [SU3866]
☆ **Dundas Arms** RG17 9UT [Station Rd]: Fine
summer pub, with tables out on deck above
Kennet & Avon Canal and pleasant walks;
well kept Adnams Best, West Berkshire Mr
Chubbs and a couple of changing guest
beers, good coffee and wines by the glass
(but pricy soft drinks), generally enjoyable
home-made pub food (not Sun), evening
restaurant; they may try to keep your credit
card while you eat outside; comfortable
bedrooms with own secluded waterside
terrace, good breakfast, cl Sun evening
*(Mrs J H S Lang, Brian and Janet Ainscough,
Colin Wood, Jeff and Wendy Williams, LYM,
Julia and Richard Tredgett, Philip and
June Caunt)*

KNOWL HILL [SU8178]
☆ **Bird in Hand** RG10 9UP [A4, quite handy for
M4 junction 8/9]: Relaxed, civilised and
roomy, with cosy alcoves, heavy beams,
panelling and splendid log fire in tartan-
carpeted main area, enjoyable home-made
straightforward food even Sun evening from
sandwiches up (children allowed in buffet),
well kept Brakspears and interesting local
guest beers, good choice of other drinks,
polite prompt staff, much older side bar,
smart restaurant; soft piped music; tables
out on front terrace, tidy modern bedrooms
*(Mark and Diane Grist, LYM, Simon Collett-
Jones, Paul Humphreys)*
Old Devil RG10 9UU [A4]: Roomy refurbished
roadhouse, sofas in bar, dining areas each
side, friendly service, decent food, good
range of wines by the glass; pleasant
verandah above attractive lawn
(Paul Humphreys)
☆ **Royal Oak** RG10 9YE [pub signed off A4]:
More bistro-with-bar than pub, French
chef/landlord doing good imaginative bistro-
style food (not Sun evening or Mon), Loddon
ales, interesting wines by the glass,
comfortably modern softly lit pale wood
dining tables, simple contemporary décor,
one fireside sofa; well reproduced piped
music; children welcome, good-sized
informal garden, meadow with sturdy play
installation *(Brian England, Paul Humphreys,
Susan and John Douglas, Simon Collett-Jones,
LYM, Julia and Richard Tredgett, Mr and
Mrs John Taylor)*

LAMBOURN [SU3180]
Malt Shovel RG17 8QN [Upper Lambourn]:
Décor reflecting race-stables surroundings,
traditional locals' bar, smart modern dining
extension (good Sun carvery), good choice
of wines by the glass, real ales, helpful staff
(Michael Sargent)

LITTLE SANDHURST [SU8362]
Bird in Hand GU47 8LQ [High St]: Friendly
unpretentious local with enjoyable
attractively served food inc thai and
seafood, Greene King Morlands, short
reasonably priced wine choice, neat pleasant

dining room, front public bar with pool and TV; large outdoor area *(David and Sue Smith)*

LITTLEWICK GREEN [SU8379]

Cricketers SL6 3RA [not far from M4 junction 9; A404(M) then left on to A4 – village signed on left; Coronation Rd]: Proper old-fashioned pub with friendly service and local atmosphere, well kept Badger ales, good choice of wines by the glass, good value simple food from good lunchtime sandwiches up, daily papers, darts, lots of cricketing prints; piped music; charming spot opp cricket green, bedrooms, open all day wknds *(Paul Humphreys, Susan and John Douglas, LYM)*

Novello SL6 3RX [A4, W of A404(M)]: Former Ring o' Bells, renamed for local 'We'll Gather Lilacs' song writer, friendly helpful service, enjoyable pub food (all day wknds) inc good sandwiches and light dishes and proper pies, real ales such as Loddon and Marlow Rebellion from horseshoe bar, comfortable sofas, pleasant décor; tables outside, open all day *(Paul Humphreys)*

MAIDENHEAD [SU8683]

Lemon Tree SL6 6NW [Golden Ball Lane, Pinkneys Green – off A308 N]: Low-beamed linked rooms and good-sized smart airy dining area, pubby food inc some interesting dishes, Marlow Rebellion, good coffee and choice of wines by the glass, good service; picnic-sets out on grass behind, open all day *(Michael Dandy)*

Robin Hood SL6 6PR [Furze Platt Rd, Pinkneys Green (A308N)]: Recently reworked as dining pub, choose your own meat or fish to be cooked how you want (not Sun evening), friendly helpful service, modern furnishings in neat carpeted areas off small bar with Greene King ales and very good range of wines by the glass; piped music; front terrace, open all day *(Eithne Dandy)*

MIDGHAM [SU5566]

☆ *Coach & Horses* RG7 5UX [Bath road (N side)]: Comfortable main-road pub doing well under current management, cheerful helpful service even when busy, wide choice of good value generous food inc good Sun roasts and lots of puddings, Fullers and West Berkshire ales; garden behind, cl Mon *(BB, Dr and Mrs R E S Tanner, Angus and Rosemary Campbell)*

NEWBURY [SU4766]

King Charles RG14 5BX [Cheap St]: Enjoyable food inc good Sun roast, friendly landlord and staff, real ale, imaginative décor; children welcome *(Simon and Philippa Hughes)*

NORTH STREET [SU6372]

Thatchers Arms RG7 5EX [just N of Theale]: Small pub tucked quietly in countryside, well kept Brakspears, reasonably priced food inc good fish, friendly enthusiastic staff *(Prof Chris Bucke, Julia and Richard Tredgett)*

OAKLEY GREEN [SU9276]

Greene Oak SL4 5UW [Dedworth Rd (B3024 just W of Windsor)]: Smart Greene King dining pub with upmarket food, good choice of wines by the glass, well kept IPA and Abbot, pleasant service, traditional country furnishings with a modern slant, fresh flowers and woodburner; good-sized attractive terrace (some traffic noise), open all day, cl Sun evening *(Simon Collett-Jones, Susan and John Douglas)*

☆ *Olde Red Lion* SL4 4PZ [4 miles from M4 junctions 8 and 6; B3024]: Popular dining pub, particularly busy at wknds, low-ceilinged bar with brown leather sofa and coal-effect fire, Adnams and Brakspears, decent range of wines by the glass, generous good value food (all day Sun), extensive carpeted dining area; piped music; children and dogs welcome, good-sized sheltered back garden, comfortable bedrooms, open all day *(June and Robin Savage, Susan and John Douglas, LYM)*

PALEY STREET [SU8675]

Bridge House SL6 3JS: Extended cottage with comfortably refurbished traditional beamed bar, Brakspears and Fullers London Pride, decent straightforward home-made food from lunchtime baguettes up, friendly long-serving landlady, cheerful service, darts, pleasant back dining room; soft piped music, TV; children welcome, big garden *(June and Robin Savage, Simon Collett-Jones, Paul Humphreys)*

PANGBOURNE [SU6376]

☆ *Cross Keys* RG8 7AR [Church Rd, opp church]: Linked beamed rooms and open fires, new oak floors in dining rooms, enjoyable bar food (not Sun evening) from good baguettes to steaks, own-baked bread, interesting restaurant menu, Greene King and guest ales, good wine choice; good back terrace with heated pergola and decorative japanese bridge over little River Pang, open all day *(Paul Humphreys)*

Swan RG8 7DU [Shooters Hill]: Attractive Thames-side pub dating from 17th c, good choice of wines by the glass, Greene King ales, friendly staff, lounge with open fire, river-view dining balcony and conservatory (food all day); piped music, sports TV; picnic-sets on terrace overlooking weir and moorings, open all day *(Bob and Angela Brooks, June and Robin Savage)*

PEASEMORE [SU4577]

☆ *Fox & Hounds* RG20 7JN [off B4494 Newbury—Wantage]: Proper old-fashioned village local tucked away in racehorse country, good honestly priced home cooking such as fresh asparagus, trout, rabbit, pheasant, particularly good house wines, well kept West Berkshire ales, good service, welcoming log fire *(Rachel Poole, LYM, Stan Edwards, Mark and Ruth Brock)*

READING [SU7273]

☆ *Fishermans Cottage* RG1 3DW [Kennet Side – easiest to walk from Orts Rd, off Kings Rd]: Friendly local in nice spot by canal lock and towpath, good value lunches esp sandwiches (very busy then but service quick), full Fullers beer range, small choice of wines, modern furnishings, pleasant stone snug behind woodburning range, light and airy conservatory, small darts room; SkyTV; dogs allowed (not in garden), waterside tables, lovely big back garden (the Didler, Susan and John Douglas)

Griffin RG4 7AD [Church Rd, Caversham]: Roomy good value dining pub with Courage Best and Directors and Wadworths 6X, cafetière coffee, good friendly service, separate areas with several log fires; tables in attractive courtyard garden, beautiful spot on Thames overlooking swan sanctuary (Tony Hobden)

☆ *Sweeney & Todd* RG1 7RD [Castle St]: Cross between café and pub with exceptional value home-made pies all day, also ploughman's, casseroles and roasts, in warren of private little period-feel alcoves and other areas on various levels, prompt cheery service, small well stocked bar with several real ales, children welcome in restaurant area, open all day (cl Sun and bank hols) (JCW, Susan and John Douglas, LYM, the Didler)

SHEFFORD WOODLANDS [SU3673]

☆ *Pheasant* RG17 7AA [less than ½ mile from M4 junction 14 – A338 towards Wantage then 1st left on to B4000]: Tucked-away horse-racing pub with enjoyable regularly changing traditional food, welcoming old-school landlord and friendly staff, well kept ales, log fires, four neat rooms inc end dining area with burgundy décor and bistro atmosphere, public bar with games inc ring the bull; attractive views from pleasant garden (LYM, I H G Busby, John Urquhart, Tony and Tracy Constance)

SONNING [SU7575]

☆ *Bull* RG4 6UP [off B478, by church; village signed off A4 E of Reading]: Unchanging old-world inn in pretty setting nr Thames, low heavy beams, cosy alcoves, cushioned antique settles and low-slung chairs, inglenook log fires, well kept Fullers, food from grand baguettes to steaks (remember this is a pricy area), neat waistcoated staff, back dining part (children allowed); large TV in small public bar; charming courtyard, five attractive bedrooms, open all day summer wknds (Simon Collett-Jones, John and Joan Nash, Mike and Heather Watson, Susan and John Douglas, LYM)

SOUTHEND [SU6072]

Queens Head RG7 6EY [Cock Lane/Southend Rd]: Comfortable pub with new licensees doing enjoyable food from good chunky sandwiches to restaurant meals (David Edelman)

STANFORD DINGLEY [SU5771]

☆ *Bull* RG7 6LS [off A340 via Bradfield]: Nice 15th-c building, much enjoyed as proper two-bar village pub of some character, with good choice of ales and wines and well liked food, but closed as we went to press, awaiting new licensees; plenty of seating in big side garden, comfortable bedroom block; reports on new regime, please (LYM)

STREATLEY [SU5980]

Swan RG8 9HR [High St]: Hotel not pub, but

has real ales and well made bar food in welcoming riverside bar; children welcome, tables on terrace and in colourful Thames-side grounds, bedrooms, many with river views and own terraces (LYM, Susan and John Douglas)

SUNNINGHILL [SU9568]

Belvedere Arms SL5 7SB [London Rd]: Thoughtfully modernised as more restaurant than pub, friendly helpful staff, enjoyable smart food (good platters), well kept real ale, fancy furnishings; large split-level garden with stream (David Sizer, Piotr Chodzko-Zajko)

SWALLOWFIELD [SU7364]

☆ *George & Dragon* RG7 1TJ [Church Rd, towards Farley Hill]: Restauranty pub, relaxed and cottagey, with thriving atmosphere, enjoyable food, hearty and interesting, several real ales, good reasonably priced wines, big log fire, stripped beams, red walls, rugs on flagstones and plenty of character; very popular with business diners, piped music; well-behaved children welcome, open all day (David and Sue Smith, LYM, R and H Fraser, Fred and Kate Portnell)

THATCHAM [SU4968]

Taste of England RG18 3AP [Lower Henwick Farm, Turnpike rd]: Simple relaxed country pub in farm's converted barn, low-priced food from sandwiches up (just carvery roasts, Sun), real ale, friendly staff and pub dog, darts, some live music; terrace with aviary (anon)

THEALE [SU6471]

Fox & Hounds RG7 4AA [Station Rd, Sunnyside]: Large neatly kept pub, friendly and busy, with good range of well kept ales, decent wines and coffee, welcoming staff, enjoyable food from baguettes up, well spaced tables (David and Sue Smith)

☆ *Winning Hand* RG7 5JB [A4 W, opp Sulhamstead turn; handy for M4 junction 12]: Enjoyable reasonably priced food from sandwiches up inc particularly good fish and chips, good friendly service, Arkells and Hook Norton, varied wine list, restaurant; quiet piped music; bright gardens, four bedrooms (Bob and Margaret Holder)

TIDMARSH [SU6374]

Greyhound RG8 8ER [A340 S of Pangbourne]: Prettily restored thatched pub, warm and friendly, with enjoyable food slightly more adventurous than usual, pleasant service, Fullers ales, woodburner, back dining extension; good walks nearby (Nigel and Sue Foster, DWAJ, Dr and Mrs A K Clarke)

WALTHAM ST LAWRENCE [SU8376]

☆ *Bell* RG10 0JJ [B3024 E of Twyford; The Street]: Heavy-beamed and timbered village local with cheerful landlord and chatty regulars, good log fires, efficient friendly service, good value pubby bar food (not Sun evening) from good sandwich range up inc interesting pizzas, small choice of main dishes, well kept changing local ales such as Loddon and West Berkshire, plenty of malt whiskies, good wine, daily papers, compact panelled lounge; children and dogs welcome, tables in back garden with extended terrace, open all day wknds *(Tracey and Stephen Groves, LYM, Paul Humphreys, Geoff and Teresa Salt, Mark and Diane Grist, Fred and Kate Portnell)*

Star RG10 0HY [Broadmoor Rd]: Neat old pub with enjoyable food from good if not cheap sandwiches and substantial starters to restaurant dishes, friendly licensees, beams, brasses, daily papers, open fire, Wadworths ales *(Paul Humphreys)*

WARGRAVE [SU7878]

Bull RG10 8DE [off A321 Henley—Twyford; High St]: Good friendly atmosphere in olde-worlde low-beamed two-bar pub with interesting choice of enjoyable food inc bargain lunches, helpful smiling staff, Brakspears, reasonably priced wines, good log fires, lots of brasses, separate dining room; tables on neat partly covered terrace, bedrooms *(David and Sue Smith, LYM)*

St George & Dragon RG10 8HY [High St]: Large smartly refurbished M&B dining pub, decent food from tapas to traditional dishes; attractive decking overlooking Thames *(N B Vernon)*

WARREN ROW [SU8180]

Old House RG10 8QS: Attractive old pub with friendly landlady, enjoyable food inc Sun roasts, real ales inc Loddon *(Fred and Kate Portnell)*

WEST ILSLEY [SU4782]

Harrow RG20 7AR [signed off A34 at E Ilsley slip road]: Appealing country pub in peaceful spot overlooking cricket pitch and pond, Victorian prints in deep-coloured knocked-through bar, some antique furnishings, log fire, Greene King ales, good choice of wines by the glass; children in eating areas, dogs allowed in bar, picnic-sets in big garden, more seats on pleasant terrace, cl Sun evening *(I H G Busby, Tony and Wendy Hobden, J and F Gowers, LYM, Henry Snell)*

WINDSOR [SU9676]

51 SL4 1DE [Peascod St]: Modern bar with up-to-date pubby food from sandwiches up, continental lagers, daily papers; nice sheltered side courtyard *(Michael Dandy)*

☆ *Carpenters Arms* SL4 1PB [Market St]: Town pub ambling around central servery with particularly well kept changing ales such as Everards, Greene King Abbot, Marlow Rebellion and Theakstons Old Peculier, good value pubby food all day from sandwiches up (can take a while when busy), good choice of wines by the glass, sturdy pub furnishings and Victorian-style décor inc two pretty fireplaces, family areas up a few steps, also downstairs beside former tunnel entrance with suits of armour; piped music, no nearby parking; tables out on cobbled pedestrian alley opp castle, handy for Legoland bus stop, open all day *(Pete Coxon, Michael Dandy, David and Sue Smith, Derek and Sylvia Stephenson, BB, Tracey and Stephen Groves)*

Duke of Connaught SL4 1RZ [Arthur Rd]: Traditional Victorian pub, home-made food, Greene King ales, good choice of wines, log fires; secluded courtyard with smokers' shelter, open all day *(M Collinge)*

Three Tuns SL4 1PB [Market St]: Courage Best, Fullers London Pride and Greene King Abbot from central servery, kind helpful service, sensibly priced pubby food from sandwiches up, lots of games; piped music, TV; tables out on pedestrianised street *(Pete Coxon, Michael Dandy)*

☆ *Two Brewers* SL4 1LB [Park St]: Three compact bare-board rooms, Fullers London Pride and Wadworths 6X, good choice of wines by the glass, friendly staff and thriving old-fashioned pub atmosphere, daily papers, enjoyable food (not wknd evenings); no children inside; tables out by pretty Georgian street next to Windsor Park's Long Walk, open all day *(Michael Dandy, Mr and Mrs J P Blake, Ian Phillips, John Saville, LYM, Ron and Sheila Corbett)*

Windsor Castle SL4 2AP [Kings Rd]: Pleasant informal atmosphere, four changing ales such as Brakspears, Courage Best, Marlow Rebellion and Timothy Taylors Landlord, good choice of wines by the glass, helpful staff, reasonably priced usual food from sandwiches up, log fire; piped music, sports TV; dogs very welcome (handy for the Park with view over Royal Paddocks to Frogmore House), good parking, small outside deck *(Jeremy Woods, Michael Dandy)*

WINNERSH [SU7871]

☆ *Wheelwrights Arms* RG10 0TR [off A329 Reading—Wokingham at Winnersh crossroads by Sainsburys, signed Hurst, Twyford; then right into Davis Way]: Cheerfully bustling beamed local with bargain food from huge lunchtime sandwiches up, quick friendly service, Wadworths IPA, 6X and guest beers, good value wines, big woodburner, bare black boards and flagstones, cottagey dining area; children welcome, disabled parking and facilities, picnic-sets in smallish garden with terrace, open all day wknds *(Paul Humphreys, BB)*

WOOLHAMPTON [SU5766]

Rowbarge RG7 5SH [Station Rd]: Big canalside pub now in Blubeckers chain, good if rather pricy fresh food all day, helpful friendly service, well kept West Berkshire ales, good log fire in neatly modernised beamed bar, panelled side room, large water-view conservatory; children welcome, tables out by water and in roomy garden *(Angus and Rosemary Campbell, LYM, Bob and Laura Brock, Charles and Pauline Stride, Roy and Jean Russell)*

YATTENDON [SU5574]

☆ *Royal Oak* RG18 0UG [The Square; B4009 NE from Newbury; turn right at Hampstead Norreys, village signposted on left]: Appealing civilised old-world inn with panelled and prettily decorated brasserie/bar (quite expensive, no food Sun evening), nice log fire and striking flower arrangements, West Berkshire beers, several wines by the glass, friendly unhurried service; well behaved children welcome, tables in lovely walled garden, more in front by peaceful village square, attractive bedrooms, open all day *(Gerald and Gabrielle Culliford, the Didler, Graham and Toni Sanders, Bob and Margaret Holder, LYM, Dr and Mrs A K Clarke, Roy Hoing)*

Post Office address codings confusingly give the impression that some pubs are in Berkshire, when they're really in Buckinghamshire, Oxfordshire or Hampshire (which is where we list them).

Buckinghamshire

There are some very smart dining pubs here, and you can also find unspoilt little country gems – often in lovely scenery, with good nearby walks. If it's a good meal you are after, head for the Royal Oak, Bovingdon Green (a super pub with a good mix of customers and drinking space too), the civilised White Hart in Chalfont St Giles (interesting modern dishes, and with four real ales too), the Swan in Denham (in the same little group as the Royal Oak, with the same high values and a warm atmosphere), the Mole & Chicken at Easington (new licensees and refurbished bedrooms), and the Polecat in Prestwood (chintzy and smart, with tasty homely cooking). We have high hopes too for the food at the stylishly reworked Old Queens Head on the edge of Penn – a newcomer to the Royal Oak's good little group, and a new main entry. It is in fact the Royal Oak at Bovingdon Green which this year takes our Dining Pub of the Year Award for Buckinghamshire. For simple charm it's hard to beat some of the places in this county: the Farmers Bar in the National Trust's Kings Head in Aylesbury (15th-c building, including an arts and craft shop and coffee shop), the Red Lion in Chenies (quite unpretentious, with long-serving licensees), the Chequers at Fingest (in quiet countryside with fine views), the Full Moon on Hawridge Common (quite a few real ales and nice nearby walks), the White Horse in Hedgerley (happily unchanging and with a good mix of customers), and the Crown in Little Missenden (in the same family for over 90 years). Back in these pages is the transformed Red Lion in Great Kingshill; lost to us for some years, as virtually a fish restaurant, it's now much more pubby, with contemporary furnishings and décor and enthusiastic new owners. The Lucky Dip section at the end of the chapter has over a hundred more possibilities, nearly half of them new to this edition. Ones notching up strong support recently include the Nags Head in Great Missenden, Stag & Huntsman at Hambleden, Horseshoe at Lavendon, Rising Sun at Little Hampden, Queens Head at Little Marlow, Two Brewers in Marlow, Red Lion at Marsworth, Lamb at Stoke Goldington, Old Swan at The Lee and Cowpers Oak at Weston Underwood (we have already inspected almost all of these, so can vouch for them ourselves). The local beers you are most likely to find here are Rebellion, with Vale also quite widely available, and one or two of our recommended pubs stocking Chiltern.

Post Office address codings confusingly give the impression that some pubs are in Buckinghamshire, when they're really in Bedfordshire or Berkshire (which is where we list them).

AYLESBURY
SP8113   MAP 4

Kings Head ◖

Kings Head Passage (narrow passage off Bourbon Street), also entrance off Temple Street; no nearby parking except for disabled; HP20 2RW

Handsome and carefully restored town centre pub with civilised atmosphere, good local ales (used in the food, too), and friendly service

This is a real surprise and tucked away in a modern town centre. It's a 15th-c National Trust-owned building and only the Farmers Bar is used as a pub. Other parts include a coffee shop, arts and craft shop, and conference rooms. Besides striking early Tudor window lighting, the former Great Hall has even more ancient stained-glass showing the Royal Arms of Henry VI and Margaret of Anjou. The three rooms have been restored with careful and unpretentious simplicity – stripped boards, cream walls with little decoration, gentle lighting, a variety of seating which includes upholstered sofas and armchairs, cushioned high-backed settles and little dove-grey café chairs. Most of the bar tables are of round glass, supported on low cask tops; the left-hand room has simple modern pale dining tables and chairs. It's all nicely low-key – not smart, but thoroughly civilised. The neat corner bar has Chiltern Ale, Beechwood Bitter, 300s Old Ale, and a guest on handpump (there will be several beer festivals during the summer with pig roasts and jazz), and some interesting bottled beers. Service is friendly and there's no piped music or machines; disabled access and facilities. The original cobbled courtyard has teak seats and tables, some under cover of a pillared roof, and there's a florist and (in the old panelled dining room) Aylesbury Tourist Information. No children inside.

🍴 Their beer is included in some of the food: soup, sandwiches, ploughman's with ale chutney, steak in ale pie, broccoli and blue cheese bake, sausages made with different ales, home-made burger cooked in old ale, wild rabbit in creamy beer and garlic mustard sauce, and puddings such as apple crumble and barley wine fruitcake. *Starters/Snacks: £3.95 to £5.95. Main Courses: £5.50 to £12.00. Puddings: £3.95 to £4.95*

Chiltern ~ Manager Claire Bignell ~ Real ale ~ Bar food (12-2(3 Sat), 6-9; 1-4 Sun; not Sun or Mon evenings) ~ (01296) 718812 ~ Open 11-11; 12-10.30 Sun; closed 25 Dec, Easter Sun

Recommended by Roger Shipperley, Mr and Mrs A Hetherington, Tim and Ann Newell, Adam F Padel, Ann Griffiths, Gordon Davico, Ryta Lyndley

BENNETT END
SU7897   MAP 4

Three Horseshoes

Horseshoe Road; from Radnage follow unclassified road towards Princes Risborough and turn left into Bennett End Road, then right into Horseshoe Road; HP14 4EB

Several seating areas in quietly set country pub with quite an emphasis on interesting meals

There are several separate seating areas in this friendly old country inn. To the left of the entrance (mind your head) is the flagstoned and darkly-lit snug bar with a log fire in the raised stone fireplace and original brickwork and bread oven. To the right of the entrance are two further sitting areas, one with a long wooden winged settle and the other enclosed by standing timbers with wooden flooring and a woodburning stove. The two-part light and airy dining room overlooks the garden and valley beyond. Rebellion IPA and a guest beer on handpump, 13 wines by the glass, summer Pimms and winter mulled wine, all served by smart uniformed staff. Seats in the garden and a rather endearing red telephone box that is gradually sinking into one of the duck ponds. More reports please.

🍴 Good bar food at lunchtime includes sandwiches, soup, chicken liver parfait with home-made piccalilli, warm salad of seared scallops and chorizo with avocado purée and mango salsa, cumberland sausages with onion gravy, home-made burger with cheese and red onion compote and grilled ham with local eggs, with evening choices such as confit duck leg salad with poached egg, thai crab cakes, roast guinea fowl with wild mushroom and tarragon risotto and butternut squash purée, rump of veal with lemon sauce and organic scottish salmon supreme with chive butter sauce. Puddings like hot bitter chocolate

fondant with pistachio ice-cream and iced griottine cherry parfait with cherry syrup.
Starters/Snacks: £4.50 to £8.50. Main Courses: £9.50 to £15.50. Puddings: £5.75

Free house ~ Licensee Simon Crawshaw ~ Real ale ~ Bar food (12-2.30, 7-9.30; 12-4 Sun; not Sun evening) ~ Restaurant ~ (01494) 483273 ~ Dogs allowed in bar ~ Live jazz first Mon of month ~ Open 12-2.30, 6-11; 12-11 Sat; 12-6 Sun; closed Sun evening, Mon lunchtime and Tues after bank hol ~ Bedrooms: /£120S(£110B)

Recommended by Tracey and Stephen Groves, Colin and Janet Roe, Howard Dell, Roy Hoing, Mrs Ann Gray, Stephen Moss, John Silverman

BOVINGDON GREEN

SU8386   MAP 2

Royal Oak ⑪ 𝚈

.75 miles N of Marlow, on back road to Frieth signposted off West Street (A4155) in centre; SL7 2JF

BUCKINGHAMSHIRE DINING PUB OF THE YEAR

Fantastic choice of european wines by glass and popular food in civilised and attractively decorated pub

This is an extremely well run and civilised old pub with a genuinely warm welcome for all and a really good mix of customers. Several attractively decorated areas open off the central bar, the half-panelled walls variously painted in pale blue, green or cream: the cosiest part is the low-beamed room closest to the car park, with three small tables, a woodburner in an exposed brick fireplace, and a big pile of logs. Throughout there's a mix of church chairs, stripped wooden tables and chunky wall seats, with rugs on the partly wooden, partly flagstoned floors, co-ordinated cushions and curtains, and a very bright, airy feel; thoughtful extra touches set the tone, with a big, square bowl of olives on the bar, carefully laid out newspapers and fresh flowers or candles on the tables. Brakspears Bitter, Fullers London Pride, and local Rebellion IPA on handpump, 19 wines and nine pudding wines by the glass and quick, helpful service; board games, and piped music. A terrace with good solid tables leads to an appealing garden with plenty more, and there's a smaller garden at the side as well. The pub is part of a little group which comprises the Alford Arms in Frithsden (see Hertfordshire main entries), the Old Queens Head in Penn (Buckinghamshire), and the Swan at Denham (see Buckinghamshire main entries). Sheltered area next to bar for smokers.

🍴 **Good, interesting bar food includes soup, steamed scottish mussels with cumin cream sauce, grain mustard potted ham with griddled soda bread and pickles, a tapas plate, roast sweet potato and wensleydale filo parcel with pickled grape, chicory and mizuna salad, home-made local venison sausage with port wine jus, shepherd's pie with braised lamb shoulder and chanterelle mushroom sauce, free-range pork chop on boxty potato with sticky parsnips, onion, pork belly faggot and calvados jus, chicken supreme with fried chicken liver and fennel broth and truffle boudin, and puddings such as banana and walnut whip ripple cheesecake and plum and blackberry cobbler with honeycomb ice-cream. A good few tables may have reserved signs (it's worth booking ahead, especially on Sundays).** *Starters/Snacks: £3.75 to £6.75. Main Courses: £10.75 to £15.75. Puddings: £4.25 to £6.75*

Salisbury Pubs ~ Lease Trasna Cryer ~ Real ale ~ Bar food (12-2.30(3 Sat, 4 Sun), 7-10) ~ Restaurant ~ (01628) 488611 ~ Children welcome ~ Dogs allowed in bar ~ Open 11-11; 12-10.30 Sun; closed 25 and 26 Dec

Recommended by Mrs Ann Gray, Tracey and Stephen Groves, Michael Dandy, M E and J R Hart, Geoff Simms, David Tindal

---

'Children welcome' means the pub says it lets children inside without any special restriction. If it allows them in, but to restricted areas such as an eating area or family room, we specify this. Places with separate restaurants often let children use them, hotels usually let them into public areas such as lounges. Some pubs impose an evening time limit – let us know if you find one earlier than 9pm.

CHALFONT ST GILES   SU9893   MAP 4

White Hart 🍽

Three Households (main street, W); HP8 4LP

Bustling place with quite an emphasis on food, modern but comfortable furnishings, neatly dressed staff

It's the imaginative modern cooking that draws customers to this civilised dining pub though they do keep Greene King IPA, Morlands Original, Old Speckled Hen and a guest beer on handpump. The bar has chocolate leather seats and sofas and contemporary artwork on the mushroom coloured walls. The extended, spreading dining room (similarly furnished to the bar) is mainly bare boards – the bright acoustics make for a lively medley of chatter – and it can be on the noisy side when very busy. Several wines by the glass, broadsheet daily papers, piped music, and neatly dressed young staff. A sheltered back terrace has squarish picnic-sets under cocktail parasols, with more beyond in the garden. Please note, no under-21s (but see below for children). More reports please.

🍴 As well as sandwiches and daily specials, the menu might include **baked avocado and crab gratin with smoked applewood cheese sauce, potted foie gras and chicken liver with port glaze and quince marmalade, wild mushroom and chive risotto with parmesan shavings, poached paupiettes of plaice, crayfish mousse and fines herbes Noilly fish cream, chicken supreme with sun-dried tomato and olive farce, whole roasted garlic thyme new potatoes and chorizo jus, calves liver with pancetta wafers, spring onion mash and peppered red cabbage, and duck in a garlic and orange marinade with honey-roast potatoes.** *Starters/Snacks: £4.50 to £8.50. Main Courses: £7.95 to £17.50. Puddings: £5.25 to £5.75*

Greene King ~ Lease Scott MacRae ~ Real ale ~ Bar food (12-2(2.30 Sat and Sun), 6.30-9.30) ~ Restaurant ~ (01494) 872441 ~ Well behaved children allowed in bar and restaurant ~ Dogs allowed in bar and bedrooms ~ Open 11.30-2.30, 5.30-11(11.30 Sat); 12-10.30 Sun ~ Bedrooms: £77.50S/£97.50S

Recommended by Kevin Thomas, Nina Randall, Howard Dell, Roy Hoing

CHENIES   TQ0298   MAP 3

Red Lion ★ 🍺

2 miles from M25 junction 18; A404 towards Amersham, then village signposted on right; Chesham Road; WD3 6ED

Traditional pub with long-serving licensees, a bustling atmosphere, and very well liked food

By adding a small extension to this much loved village pub, the long-serving and friendly licensees will be able to create extra seating space where they will take bookings (a first for them). They were also hoping, as we went to press, to redecorate the whole pub. The bustling, unpretentious L-shaped bar has comfortable built-in wall benches by the front windows, other traditional seats and tables, and original photographs of the village and traction engines; there's also a small back snug. Well kept Rebellion Lion Pride (brewed for the pub), Vale Best Bitter, Wadworths 6X, and a guest beer on handpump, several wines by the glass and some nice malt whiskies. The hanging baskets and window boxes are pretty in summer, and there are picnic-sets on a small side terrace. No children, games machines or piped music.

🍴 As well as lunchtime filled baps, baguettes and baked potatoes, the very reasonably priced and tasty bar food includes **soup, home-made pâté, chicken satay with peanut dip, mushroom and mixed pepper stroganoff, their incredibly popular lamb pie, bangers with red wine gravy and surprise mash, a curry of the day, fishcakes with horseradish and beetroot dip, roast pork belly with crackling and apple sauce, and home-made puddings.** *Starters/Snacks: £4.95 to £5.95. Main Courses: £7.50 to £12.95. Puddings: £3.95 to £4.50*

Free house ~ Licensee Mike Norris ~ Real ale ~ Bar food (12-2, 7-10(9.30 Sun) ~ Restaurant ~ (01923) 282722 ~ Dogs allowed in bar ~ Open 11-2.30, 5.30-11; 12-3, 6.30-10.30 Sun; closed 25 Dec

Real ale is used by us to mean beer that has been maturing naturally in its cask. We do not count as real ale beer which has been pasteurised or filtered to remove its natural yeasts. If it is kept under a blanket of carbon dioxide to preserve it, we still generally mention it – as long as the pressure is too light for you to notice any extra fizz, it's hard to tell the difference. (For brevity, we use the expression 'under light blanket pressure' to cover such pubs; we do not include among them pubs where the blanket pressure is high enough to force the beer up from the cellar, as this does make it unnaturally fizzy.)

Other drinks: we've also looked out particularly for pubs doing enterprising non-alcoholic drinks (including good tea or coffee), interesting spirits (especially malt whiskies), country wines, freshly squeezed juices, and good farm ciders.

Bar food usually refers to what is sold in the bar, we do not describe menus that are restricted to a separate restaurant. If we know that a pub serves sandwiches we say so – if you don't see them mentioned, assume you can't get them. Food listed is an example of the sort of thing you'd find served in the bar on a normal day and we try to indicate any difference we know of between lunchtime and evening.

Children If we don't mention children at all, assume that they are not welcome. All but one or two pubs allow children in their garden if they have one. 'Children welcome' means the pub has told us that it lets them in with no special restrictions. In other cases we report exactly what arrangements pubs say they make for children. However, we have to note that in readers' experience some pubs make restrictions that they haven't told us about (children only if eating, for example). If you come across this, please let us know, so that we can clarify with the pub concerned for the next edition. The absence of any reference to children in a Lucky Dip entry means we don't know either way. Children's Certificates exist, but in practice children are allowed into some part of most pubs in this *Guide* (there is no legal restriction on the movement of children over 14 in any pub). Children under 16 cannot have alcoholic drinks. Children aged 16 and 17 can drink beer, wine or cider with a meal if it is bought by an adult and they are accompanied by an adult.

Dogs If main entry licensees have told us they allow dogs in their pub or bedrooms we say so. Absence of reference to dogs means dogs are not welcome. If you take a dog into a pub you should have it on a lead. We also mention in the text any pub dogs or cats (or indeed other animals) that we've come across ourselves, or heard about from readers.

Parking If we know there is a problem with parking we say so; otherwise assume there is a car park.

Credit cards We say if a pub does **not** accept them; some which do may put a surcharge on credit card bills, to cover charges made by the card company. We also say if we know that a pub tries to retain customers' credit cards while they are eating. This is a reprehensible practice, and if a pub tries it on you, please tell them that all banks and card companies frown on it – and please let us know the pub's name, so that we can warn readers in future editions.

Telephone numbers are given for all main entries that are not ex-directory.

Opening hours are for summer; we say if we know of differences in winter, or on particular days of the week. In the country, many pubs may open rather later and close earlier than their details show (if you come across this, please let us know – with details). Pubs are allowed to stay open all day if licensed to do so. However, outside cities many english and welsh pubs close during the afternoon. We'd be grateful to hear of any differences from the hours we quote.

Bedroom prices normally include full english breakfasts (if available), VAT and any automatic service charge. If we give just one price, it is the total price for two people sharing a double or twin-bedded room for one night. Otherwise, prices before the / are for single occupancy, prices after it for double. A capital B against the price means that it includes a private bathroom, a capital S a private shower. As all this coding packs in quite a lot of information, some examples may help to explain it:

£70	on its own means that's the total bill for two people sharing a twin or double room without private bath; the pub has no rooms with a private bath, and a single person might have to pay that full price.
£70B	means exactly the same – but all the rooms have a private bath
£65(£70B)	means rooms with private baths cost £5 extra
£40/£65(£70B)	means the same as the last example, but also shows that there are single rooms for £40, none of which has a private bathroom

If there's a choice of rooms at different prices, we normally give the cheapest. If there are seasonal price variations, we give the summer price (the highest). During the winter, many inns, particularly in the country, will have special cheaper rates. And at other times, especially in holiday areas, you will often find prices cheaper if you stay for several nights. On weekends, inns that aren't in obvious weekending areas often have bargain rates for two- or three-night stays.

Meal times Bar food is commonly served from 12-2 and 7-9, at least from Monday to Saturday. If we don't give a time against the *Bar food* note at the bottom of a main entry you should be able to get bar food at those times. However, we do spell out the times if we know that bar food service starts after 12.15 or after 7.15; if it stops before 2 or before 8.45; or if food is served for significantly longer than usual (say, till 2.30 or 9.45).

Though we note days when pubs have told us they don't do food you should play safe on Sundays, and check before you visit. Please let us know if you find anything different from what we say!

Disabled access Deliberately, we do not ask pubs about this, as their answers would not give a reliable picture of how easy access is. Instead, we depend on readers' direct experience. If you are able to give us help about this, we would be particularly grateful for your reports.

SAT NAV AND ELECTRONIC ROUTE PLANNING
A digital version of *The Good Pub Guide* is now available for Garmin sat-nav systems. Available on an SD card, the sat-nav guide will tell you the nearest pubs to your current location (including Lucky Dips), or you can get it to track down a particular pub, and it will direct you to your choice.

For more information visit **www.thegoodpubguide.co.uk/satnav**.

Computer users may also like to know of a route-finding programme, Microsoft® AutoRoute™, which shows the location of *Good Pub Guide* pubs on detailed maps, works out the quickest routes for journeys, adds diversions to nearby pubs – and shows our text entries for those pubs on screen.

OUR WEBSITE (www.thegoodpubguide.co.uk)
This year has seen the launch of our completely redesigned website. It includes virtually all the material in *The Good Pub Guide*, with sophisticated search options. We are excited about also being able to include far more material than we can in a manageable-sized book.

CHANGES DURING THE YEAR – PLEASE TELL US
Changes are inevitable during the course of the year. Landlords change, and so do their policies. We very much hope that you will find everything just as we say but if not please let us know, using the tear-out card in the middle of the book, the report forms at the back of the book, or just a letter. You don't need a stamp: the address is The Good Pub Guide, FREEPOST TN1569, WADHURST, East Sussex TN5 7BR. You can also send us reports at **feedback@thegoodpubguide.co.uk**.

Authors' Acknowledgements

This *Guide* would be impossible to produce without the great help we have from the many thousands of readers who report to us on the pubs they visit, often in great detail. For the special help they have given us this year, we are deeply grateful to the Didler, Phil Bryant, Guy Vowles, Reg Fowle, Helen Rickwood, Paul Humphreys, N R White, Chris and Angela Buckell, LM, Michael Doswell, Tracey and Stephen Groves, George Atkinson, Michael Dandy, Phil and Jane Hodson, Michael and Jenny Back, Tony and Wendy Hobden, Alan Thwaite, Ian Phillips, Dr and Mrs M E Wilson, Peter Meister, Alan and Eve Harding, Keith and Sue Ward, Jeremy King, Susan and John Douglas, Nick Holding, Joan and Michel Hooper-Immins, JJW, CMW, Ann and Colin Hunt, Richard Fendick, Terry Buckland, Gordon and Margaret Ormondroyd, Dennis Jenkin, Roger and Lesley Everett, Pat and Tony Martin, Val and Alan Green, Phyl and Jack Street, Steve Whalley, Mr and Mrs W W Burke, Kevin Thorpe, Donna and Roger, Ewan and Moira McCall, Tom McLean, Dave Irving, Rona Murdoch, Comus and Sarah Elliott, Phil and Sally Gorton, David and Sue Smith, Michael Butler, Andy and Jill Kassube, Catherine and Rob Dunster, Brian and Anna Marsden, Chris Evans, Keith and Chris O'Neill, Michael and Alison Sandy, Bruce Bird, John Wooll, Derek and Sylvia Stephenson, Pete Baker, Edward Mirzoeff, Tom Evans, Martin and Karen Wake, John Saville, Joe Green, Brian and Janet Ainscough, Ray and Winifred Halliday, Martin and Pauline Jennings, John Beeken, Dr Kevan Tucker, MB, Charles and Pauline Stride, Neil and Anita Christopher, Paul A Moore, R T and J C Moggridge, Bob and Margaret Holder, Peter F Marshall, Valerie Baker, Dr and Mrs C W Thomas, JCW, MDN, Tom and Jill Jones, Torrens Lyster, Margaret Dickinson, Howard Dell, Neil Powell, Dennis Jones, J F M and M West, Dave Braisted, Anthony Longden, Mrs Margo Finlay, Jörg Kasprowski, MLR, Ross Balaam, Colin Moore, Dr and Mrs J Temporal, Paul and Ursula Randall, Sara Fulton, Roger Baker, Dr and Mrs A K Clarke, Mr and Mrs Maurice Thompson, Mike Gorton, Simon and Sally Small, Mike and Eleanor Anderson, Barry and Anne, Tony and Jill Radnor, Sheila Topham, B and M Kendall, Bruce and Sharon Eden, David M Smith, Heather and Dick Martin, Howard and Margaret Buchanan, Mike and Sue Loseby, Dr and Mrs Jackson, WW, Eric Larkham, Les and Sandra Brown, Eithne Dandy, Sue and Mike Todd, KC, Ian Malone, C and R Bromage, Simon Collett-Jones, Julian and Janet Dearden, Roy Hoing, Paul and Gail Betteley, Mr and Mrs P D Titcomb, Mark Farrington, Denys Gueroult, Marianne Welsh, Tina and David Woods-Taylor, Ryta Lyndley, Karen Eliot, Roger Thornington, Len Beattie, Mike and Mary Carter, Adrian Johnson, P and D Carpenter, Gwyn and Anne Wake, John Branston, Dr Phil Putwain, Joyce and Maurice Cottrell, R C Vincent, Mark, Amanda, Luke and Jake Sheard, Robert Watt, Dr and Mrs Michael Smith, Peter and Audrey Dowsett, Dick and Madeleine Brown, Ron and Sheila Corbett, and Michael and Maggie Betton.

Warm thanks, too, to John Holliday of Trade Wind Technology, who built and looks after our database. And to Pat Taylor Chalmers, who has checked every word of almost every edition of the *Guide* with such scrupulous care.

Alisdair Aird and Fiona Stapley

Recommended by Danielle and Simon, Howard Dell, Joan York, Tracey and Stephen Groves, Mr and Mrs Paul Ridgeway, Jarrod and Wendy Hopkinson, Kevin Thorpe, Stuart and Doreen Ritchie, Roy Hoing, Charles Gysin, Sue Demont, Tim Barrow

DENHAM   TQ0487   MAP 3

Swan

0.75 miles from M40 junction 1 or M25 junction 16; follow Denham Village signs; UB9 5BH

So popular, it's best to book in advance – civilised dining pub with a fine choice of wines and interesting food

In May when the wisteria is flowering, this civilised dining pub and the other old tiled village buildings here are a very pretty sight. The rooms are stylishly furnished with a nice mix of antique and old-fashioned chairs and solid tables, individually chosen pictures on the cream and warm green walls, rich heavily draped curtains, inviting open fires, newspapers to read, and fresh flowers. A smashing choice of 19 european wines plus nine pudding wines by two sizes of glass, and Courage Best, Rebellion IPA, and Wadworths 6X on handpump; piped music. The extensive garden is floodlit at night, and leads from a sheltered terrace with tables to a more spacious lawn. It can get busy at weekends, and parking may be difficult. The pub is part of a little group which comprises the Royal Oak, Bovingdon Green and the Old Queens Head in Penn (also in Buckinghamshire) and the Alford Arms in Frithsden (see Hertfordshire main entries).

🍴 Impressive bar food includes soup, crayfish and cornish crab vol au vent with bloody mary jelly, oak-smoked bacon on bubble and squeak with hollandaise and poached egg, toad-in-the-hole with red onion gravy, coriander marinated halloumi burger with roast tomato and pumpkin seed pesto, roast corn-fed chicken with fried root vegetable terrine, shallot cream and bay leaf jus, slow-roast lamb shoulder on turnip gratin with spinach purée and puy lentil jus, and puddings such as sticky toffee and apple pudding with vanilla custard and hazelnut and praline roulade with chantilly cream. Best to book to be sure of a table. *Starters/Snacks: £3.75 to £7.25. Main Courses: £11.25 to £15.75. Puddings: £4.25 to £6.75*

Salisbury Pubs ~ Lease Mark Littlewood ~ Real ale ~ Bar food (12-2.30(3 Sat, 4 Sun), 7-10) ~ Restaurant ~ (01895) 832085 ~ Children welcome ~ Dogs allowed in bar ~ Open 11-11; 12-10.30 Sun; closed 25 and 26 Dec

Recommended by Philip Clouts, Richard and Sissel Harris, Mrs Hazel Rainer, Mrs Margo Finlay, Jörg Kasprowski, Kevin Thomas, Nina Randall, Phil and Gill Wass, Evelyn and Derek Walter, John Silverman, Susan and John Douglas

DORNEY   SU9279   MAP 2

Pineapple 🍺

2.4 miles from M4 junction 7; turn left on to A4, then left on B3026 (or take first left off A4 at traffic lights, into Huntercombe Lane S, then left at T junction on main road – shorter but slower); Lake End Road; SL4 6QS

Fantastic choice of interesting sandwiches in unpretentious pub

Even when really busy – which this nicely old-fashioned and unpretentious pub usually is – the staff remain pleasant and helpful. There are low shiny Anaglypta ceilings, black-panelled dados and sturdy country tables – one very long, another in a big bow window. There is a woodburning stove at one end, a pretty little fireplace in a second room and china pineapples join the decorations on a set of shelves in one of three cottagey carpeted linked rooms on the left. It's bare boards on the right where the bar counter has Black Sheep Bitter, Fullers London Pride and Wells & Youngs Bombardier on handpump and several wines by the glass; friendly staff and piped music. A roadside verandah has some rustic tables, and there are plenty of round picnic-sets out in the garden, some on fairy-lit decking under an oak tree; the nearby motorway makes itself heard out here.

🍴 A remarkable choice of up to 1,000 varieties of sandwiches in five different fresh breads that come with your choice of hearty vegetable soup, salad or chips, run from cream cheese with beetroot, smoked salmon and cream cheese to chicken, avocado, crispy

bacon and lettuce with a honey and mustard dressing; well liked Sunday roasts.
Starters/Snacks: £6.95

Punch ~ Lease Stuart Jones ~ Real ale ~ Bar food (12-9) ~ (01628) 662353 ~ Children welcome
~ Dogs welcome ~ Open 11-11; 12-10.30 Sun

*Recommended by Priscilla Sandford, Dr and Mrs A K Clarke, Bob and Laura Brock, Michael Dandy, Ian Phillips,
Tracey and Stephen Groves, Paul Humphreys, B J Harding*

EASINGTON   SP6810   MAP 4

Mole & Chicken ⊕ ☺ ⊨

*From B4011 in Long Crendon follow Chearsley, Waddesdon signpost into Carters Lane
opposite the Chandos Arms, then turn left into Chilton Road; HP18 9EY*

**Lovely views and sunsets from decked area and garden, nice open-plan layout and
enjoyable food**

The terrace of this bustling pub has been extended this year and extra tables and chairs
added giving more customers the chance to enjoy the fine views over the rolling open
countryside. As we went to press one of the new licensees told us they were hoping to
add some children's play equipment out here too. Inside, the open-plan layout is cleverly
done, so that all the different parts seem quite snug and self-contained without being
cut off from what's going on, and the atmosphere is relaxed and sociable. The beamed
bar curves around the serving counter in a sort of S-shape, and there are oak and pine
tables on flagstones, lots of big antique prints, lit candles and good winter log fires. A
thoughtful choice of wines, over 40 malt whiskies, and Hook Norton Bitter and a guest
beer on handpump; piped music. The bedrooms have been refurbished.

⊞ **As well as a lighter lunch menu, the enjoyable bistro-style food includes sandwiches,
soup, devilled kidneys, moules marinières, smoked haddock rarebit with a poached egg,
butternut, wild mushroom and parmesan risotto, grilled free-range pork cutlet with
bubble and squeak and cider cream, wok-fried tiger prawns with calamari and satay sauce,
and puddings such as hazelnut praline and blueberry pavlova or warm chocolate fondant
with caramel ice-cream.** *Starters/Snacks: £4.95 to £6.95. Main Courses: £10.95 to £14.95.
Puddings: £5.00*

Free house ~ Licensees A Heather and Steve Bush ~ Real ale ~ Bar food (12-2.30, 6-9.30;
all day Sun) ~ Restaurant ~ (01844) 208387 ~ Children welcome ~ Open 12-3, 6-11; 12-10 Sun
~ Bedrooms: £65B/£85B

*Recommended by Dennis and Doreen Haward, Karen Eliot, John Tyrle, Gordon Davico, Julia and Richard Tredgett,
Graham Oddey, Andy Dale, K S Whittaker, Dr A McCormick, Dr David C Price*

FINGEST   SU7791   MAP 2

Chequers

Village signposted off B482 Marlow—Stokenchurch; RG9 6QD

Friendly, spotlessly kept old pub with big garden, good food and sunny dining extension

Although there is a smart back dining extension, the licensees are keen to emphasise
that this 15th-c place is a proper pub with a warm and friendly atmosphere and an
unaffected public bar with real rural charm. Several spotless old-fashioned rooms have
pewter tankards, horsebrasses and pub team photographs on the walls, large open fires,
Brakspears Bitter and Oxford Gold and Wychwood Hobgoblin and Mad Hatter on
handpump, a dozen wines by the glass, jugs of Pimms, and several malt whiskies; helpful,
welcoming service. Board games. French doors from the dining extension open out onto
the terrace where there are plenty of picnic-sets and this leads on to the big garden with
fine views over the Hambleden valley; beyond here, quiet pastures slope up to beech
woods. Over the road is a unique Norman twin-roofed church tower – probably the nave
of the original church.

⊞ **Enjoyable, honest bar food includes sandwiches, soup, venison pâté, local venison and
bacon pie with port and redcurrant sauce, local rabbit pie with wild mushrooms and garlic,**

their own sausages with onion gravy, chicken curry, steak in red wine casserole and puddings like spotted dick and custard or apple crumble; the fresh local eggs for sale over the bar counter are said to be very good. *Starters/Snacks: £4.75 to £5.95. Main Courses: £7.95 to £14.95. Puddings: £2.95 to £5.95*

Brakspears ~ Tenants Ray Connelly and Christian Taubert ~ Real ale ~ Bar food (not Mon evening or winter Sun evening) ~ Restaurant ~ (01491) 638335 ~ Children welcome ~ Dogs allowed in bar ~ Open 12-3, 6-11; 12-10.30 Sun; closed winter Sun evening

Recommended by Richard Endacott, Anthony and Marie Lewis, Paul Humphreys, Martin and Karen Wake, Roy Hoing, Howard Dell, Tracey and Stephen Groves, John and Sharon Hancock, the Didler, Andy and Jill Kassube, Susan and John Douglas

FORTY GREEN   SU9291   MAP 2

Royal Standard of England 🍺

3.5 miles from M40 junction 2, via A40 to Beaconsfield, then follow sign to Forty Green, off B474. 0.75 mile N of New Beaconsfield; keep going through village; HP9 1XT

Ancient place with fascinating antiques in rambling rooms and good choice of drinks

Full of history and interest, this old inn evolved from a Saxon dwelling into an alehouse – it's been trading for nearly 900 years. There's certainly lots to look at – both in the layout of the building itself and in the fascinating collection of antiques which fills it. The rambling rooms have huge black ship's timbers, finely carved old oak panelling, and roaring winter fires with handsomely decorated iron firebacks. There's a massive settle apparently built to fit the curved transom of an Elizabethan ship; you can also see rifles, powder-flasks and bugles, ancient pewter and pottery tankards, lots of brass and copper, needlework samplers, and stained-glass. Brakspears Bitter, Chiltern Ale, Hop Back Entire Stout, Marstons Pedigree, and Rebellion IPA and Mild on handpump, quite a range of bottled beers, Old Rosie scrumpy, Weston's perry, several wines by the glass and Somerset brandy; shove-ha'penny. Seats outside in a neatly hedged front rose garden or under the shade of a tree. They may insist on keeping your credit card behind the bar.

🍴 Bar food includes lunchtime sandwiches, soup, devilled lamb's kidneys, moules marinières, cauliflower and aubergine moussaka, ham and egg, mutton shepherd's pie, smoked haddock with spinach and poached egg, pork belly with bubble and squeak, and puddings such as treacle tart or spotted dick; Sunday roasts. *Starters/Snacks: £3.95 to £12.00. Main Courses: £8.00 to £18.00. Puddings: £4.00 to £5.50*

Free house ~ Licensee Matthew O'Keeffe ~ Real ale ~ Bar food (all day every day) ~ Restaurant ~ (01494) 673382 ~ Children welcome ~ Dogs welcome ~ Open 11-11; 12-10.30 Sun

Recommended by the Didler, Anthony Longden, Chris Smith, D and M T Ayres-Regan, Susan and John Douglas, Tracey and Stephen Groves, Howard Dell, John Silverman

GREAT KINGSHILL   SU8798   MAP 4

Red Lion 🍷

A4128 N of High Wycombe; HP15 6EB

Carefully refurbished pub with contemporary décor, brasserie-style pub food, local beers and friendly licensees

Since it was last in these pages, this bustling pub has been completely refurbished by the hard-working and friendly licensees. The entrance is now a small bar with brown leather sofas and armchairs, low tables and an open log fire. To the left is a spacious dining room with a contemporary brown colour scheme and dining chairs and tables on the oak flooring. There are modern paintings on the stripey brown wallpaper, candles on tables, and some original flagstones. The atmosphere is relaxed and the service attentive. Rebellion IPA and Prime Suspect on handpump and a good wine list.

🍴 Good, brasserie-style food includes filled baguettes, soup, ham hock terrine with piccalilli and pea shoots, devilled kidneys on toast, smoked haddock fishcakes, lamb burger with goats cheese, mussels and chips, wild mushroom risotto, pie, mash and gravy, skate wing with beurre noisette, free-range chicken with butterbeans, chorizo and cavalo nero cabbage, and puddings such as bakewell tart with blueberry compote and vanilla ice-cream and crème brûlée with white raspberry chocolate. There's also a two- and three-course set menu. *Starters/Snacks: £5.00 to £7.00. Main Courses: £9.00 to £18.00. Puddings: £5.00*

Pubmaster ~ Managers Kim and Chris O'Brien ~ Real ale ~ Bar food (12-2.30, 6-9.30) ~ Restaurant ~ (01494) 711262 ~ Well behaved children welcome ~ Open 12-3, 6-11.30; 12-4 Sun; closed Sun evening, Mon

Recommended by Tracey and Stephen Groves

GROVE   SP9122   MAP 4

Grove Lock ♀ ◖

Pub signed off B488, on left just S of A505 roundabout (S of Leighton Buzzard); LU7 0QU

By Grand Union Canal and usefully open all day, with plenty of room inside and lots of seats overlooking the water

---

New licensees have taken over this modern, open-plan pub and it's been refurbished this year. There are squishy brown leather sofas, an eclectic mix of tables and chairs, a couple of butcher's block tables by the bar, diagonal oak floor boarding, a lofty high-raftered pitched roof, a big open-standing winter log fire and artwork to do with canal life. Steps take you up to a further three-room restaurant area (the original lock keeper's cottage) which is partly flagstoned, has more winter log fires and looks down on the narrow canal lock. Fullers London Pride, ESB and Discovery on handpump and several wines by the glass; piped music. There are plenty of seats and picnic-sets in the terraced waterside garden and on the canopied decking area overlooking the Grand Union Canal. More reports on the new regime, please.

🍴 Bar food includes sandwiches, toasties, ploughman's, home-made crab and haddock cakes, home-cooked ham with free-range eggs, burgers, a pie of the week, beer-battered cod, lots of summer salads and daily specials; there's a smaller menu for outside eating. *Starters/Snacks: £3.95 to £5.95. Main Courses: £7.95 to £15.00. Puddings: £4.50 to £4.95*

Fullers ~ Managers Gregg and Angela Worrall ~ Real ale ~ Bar food (12-9(8 in winter)) ~ Restaurant ~ (01525) 380940 ~ Children welcome ~ Open 11-11(10.30 Sun)

Recommended by Michael Dandy, Charles and Pauline Stride, Chris Smith

HAWRIDGE COMMON   SP9406   MAP 4

Full Moon ◖

Hawridge Common; left fork off A416 N of Chesham, then follow for 3.5 miles towards Cholesbury; HP5 2UH

Attractive country pub with outside heaters and awning, six real ales, and enjoyable food; plenty of nearby walks

---

This is a nice pub with a good welcome. The low-beamed rambling bar is the heart of the building, with oak built-in floor-to-ceiling settles, ancient flagstones and flooring tiles, hunting prints and an inglenook fireplace. They keep half a dozen real ales on handpump such as Adnams Best, Bass, Brakspears Bitter, Fullers London Pride, Timothy Taylors Landlord, and a changing guest like Hopback GFB and there are several wines by the glass; pleasant service. On fine days, you can sit outside in the garden or on the heated and covered terrace and gaze over the fields or windmill behind; lots of walks over the common.

🍴 Popular bar food includes ciabattas and bagels, soup, potted shrimps, lamb kebab, pork and leek sausages with red wine and onion gravy, pasta with cherry tomatoes, mozzarella, pine nuts and capers, ham and eggs, chicken bourguignon, steak and kidney pudding and citrus-crusted bass fillet with a white wine and dill cream sauce; puddings like rhubarb and black cherry crumble and bread and butter pudding; Sunday roasts. *Starters/Snacks: £4.50 to £6.50. Main Courses: £9.95 to £13.95. Puddings: £4.95 to £5.25*

Enterprise ~ Lease Peter and Annie Alberto ~ Real ale ~ Bar food ~ Restaurant ~ (01494) 758959 ~ Well supervised children welcome ~ Dogs welcome ~ Open 12-11; 12-10.30 Sun; closed 25 Dec

Recommended by Richard and Sissel Harris, Malcolm and Sue Scott, Tracey and Stephen Groves, Maggie Atherton, D J and P M Taylor, Roy Hoing, Susan and John Douglas

HEDGERLEY   SU9687   MAP 2

White Horse ★ 🍺

2.4 miles from M40 junction 2; at exit roundabout take Slough turn-off then take Hedgerley Lane (immediate left) following alongside M40; after 1.5 miles turn right at T junction into Village Lane; SL2 3UY

Old-fashioned drinkers' pub with lots of beers, regular beer festivals and a jolly mix of customers

'Just what a village pub ought to be' is how one reader describes this unchanging country local. The cottagey main bar has plenty of character, with lots of beams, brasses and exposed brickwork, low wooden tables, some standing timbers, jugs, ballcocks and other bric-a-brac, a log fire, and a good few leaflets and notices about future village events. There is a little flagstoned public bar on the left. Tapped from the cask in a room behind the tiny hatch counter, there's Greene King IPA and Rebellion IPA and at least five daily changing guests from anywhere in the country, with good farm cider and perry, and belgian beers as well. On the way out to the garden, which has tables and occasional barbecues, they have a canopy extension to help during busy periods. The atmosphere is cheerful with warmly friendly service from the chatty staff. In front are lots of hanging baskets and a couple more tables overlooking the quiet road. There are good walks nearby, and the pub is handy for the Church Wood RSPB reserve. It can get crowded at weekends.

🍴 **Lunchtime bar food such as sandwiches, ploughman's, cold meats and quiches, and changing straightforward hot dishes.** *Starters/Snacks: £3.95. Main Courses: £5.75 to £8.95. Puddings: £3.50*

Free house ~ Licensees Doris Hobbs and Kevin Brooker ~ Real ale ~ Bar food (lunchtime only) ~ (01753) 643225 ~ Children in canopy extension area ~ Dogs allowed in bar ~ Open 11-2.30, 5-11; 11-11 Sat; 12-10.30 Sun

Recommended by Roger Shipperley, Piotr Chodzko-Zajko, Simon Rodway, Anthony Longden, Mrs Ann Gray, N R White, Roy Hoing, Stephen Moss, the Didler, Susan and John Douglas, Bob and Laura Brock, LM

LACEY GREEN   SP8201   MAP 4

Pink & Lily ♀ 🍺

From A4010 High Wycombe—Princes Risboro follow Loosley sign, then Gt Hampden, Gt Missenden one; HP27 0RJ

Friendly, extended pub with several real ales, good choice of wines, seasonal food and big garden

The little tap room in this extended and modernised dining pub has been preserved very much as it used to be, with built in wall benches on the red flooring tiles, an old wooden ham-rack hanging from the ceiling and a broad inglenook with a low mantelpiece (there's always a fire in winter). The airy main bar has traditional pub tables and chairs, an open fire and some cosier side areas, and there's a conservatory-style extension with big arches decorated in various shades of browns, beiges and creams. Batemans Valiant, Brakspears Bitter, Fullers London Pride, Vale Gravitas, and Westerham British Bulldog on handpump, 27 wines by the glass including organic and Fairtrade ones and polite, friendly staff; piped music, dominoes and cribbage. The big garden has lots of wooden tables and seats. Rupert Brooke liked the pub so much that he wrote about it at the start of one of his poems; the result is framed on the wall (and there's a room dedicated to him).

🍴 Good food from a seasonally changing menu includes sandwiches, filled ciabattas and baked potatoes, hot open flat breads with various toppings, ploughman's and platters, fried halloumi with roasted figs, pecan nuts and basil infused oil, grilled whole plaice with crayfish meunière, breast of guinea fowl with red wine gravy and chargrilled venison steak in real ale sauce. *Starters/Snacks: £4.25 to £8.50. Main Courses: £8.00 to £17.50. Puddings: £4.25 to £6.50*

Enterprise ~ Lease Shakira Englefield ~ Real ale ~ Bar food (12-2.30, 6.15-9; 12-8 Sun(till 3 winter Sun)) ~ Restaurant ~ (01494) 488308 ~ Children welcome ~ Dogs welcome ~ Open 11-11; 12-8 Sun; 12-4 Sun in winter; closed winter Sun evening

Recommended by Roy Hoing, Jennifer Banks, Chris Maunder, Jarrod and Wendy Hopkinson, Mel Smith, the Didler

LEY HILL   SP9901   MAP 4

Swan 🍺

Village signposted off A416 in Chesham; HP5 1UT

Charming, old-fashioned pub with chatty customers and decent food

This charming little timbered 16th-c pub is run by friendly, enthusiastic licensees who keep everything spic and span and the atmosphere is relaxed and chatty. The main bar has black beams (mind your head) and standing timbers, an old range, a log fire and a collection of old local photographs; there's a cosy snug. Adnams Bitter, Brakspears Bitter, Fullers London Pride, Timothy Taylors Landlord and a guest such as Archers Golden on handpump, and several wines by the glass. In front of the pub amongst the flower tubs and hanging baskets are some picnic-sets, with more in the large back garden. There's a cricket pitch, a nine-hole golf course, and a common opposite.

🍴 Well liked bar food includes sandwiches, baked brie wrapped in filo pastry with cranberry sauce, beer-battered haddock and chips, wild mushroom risotto, fillet steak with a blue cheese crust, and puddings; also, a two-course set menu. *Starters/Snacks: £4.50 to £6.95. Main Courses: £8.50 to £9.50. Puddings: £4.95*

Punch ~ Lease Nigel Byatt ~ Real ale ~ Bar food (12-2.30, 7-9.30; not Sun or Mon evenings) ~ Restaurant ~ (01494) 783075 ~ Children welcome ~ Various jazz and blues evenings monthly ~ Open 12-3, 5.30-11; 12-10.30 Sun

Recommended by Richard and Sissel Harris, Roy Hoing, Angela and Ray Seger, Wilma Hooftman

LITTLE MISSENDEN   SU9298   MAP 4

Crown ★ 🍺 £

Crown Lane, SE end of village, which is signposted off A413 W of Amersham; HP7 0RD

Long-serving licensees and a cheerful pubby feel in little brick cottage; attractive garden

A good mix of customers, including a loyal bunch of regulars, adds to the cheerfully chatty atmosphere in this small brick cottage. It's been in the same family for over 90 years and the friendly landlord keeps things spotless. Adnams Bitter, Hook Norton Gold, St Austells Tribute, and Woodfordes Wherry on handpump or tapped from the cask, farm cider and several malt whiskies. There are old red flooring tiles on the right, oak parquet on the left, built-in wall seats, studded red leatherette chairs, and a few small tables; darts and board games. The large attractive sheltered, garden behind has picnic-sets and other tables; the interesting church in the pretty village is well worth a visit. They hope to have opened bedrooms by the time this book is published.

🍴 Straightforward bar food such as winter soup, good fresh sandwiches, buck's bite (a special home-made pizza-like dish), filled baked potatoes, ploughman's, and steak and kidney pie. *Starters/Snacks: £3.50 to £7.00*

Free house ~ Licensees Trevor and Carolyn How ~ Real ale ~ Bar food (lunchtime only, not Sun) ~ No credit cards ~ (01494) 862571 ~ Children over 12 allowed ~ Open 11-2.30(3 Sat), 6-11; 12-3, 7-11 Sun

Recommended by Dr W I C Clark, Anthony Longden, Tracey and Stephen Groves

OVING

SP7821 MAP 4

Black Boy

Village signposted off A413 out of Whitchurch, N of Aylesbury; HP22 4HN

Extended 16th-c pub with lots of room, plenty of fresh flowers and candles, quite a choice of popular food, and impressive garden

Run by particularly nice licensees, this distinctive 16th-c pub is tucked away in a small village. The old front parts perhaps have the most atmosphere – especially the cosy red and black-tiled area around the enormous inglenook. The low heavy beams have quotes and witticisms chalked on them and, up a couple of steps, another snug corner has a single table, some exposed stonework, and a mirror over a small brick fireplace. The long, light wooden bar counter is covered with posters advertising sales of agricultural land. Brakspears Bitter and Rebellion Mutiny on handpump, and a dozen wines by the glass; piped music. Opposite the bar counter, two big comfortable leather armchairs lead into the lighter, more modern dining room with good-sized country kitchen pine tables set for eating and picture windows offering the same view of the gardens. Throughout are plenty of candles and fresh flowers. The impressive garden has tables on its spacious sloping lawns and terrace with remarkable views down over the Vale of Aylesbury. The licensees breed and train chocolate labradors.

🍴 Well liked bar food includes soup, lunchtime sandwiches, deli boards (good for sharing), smoked duck salad with pine nuts and balsamic glaze, smoked salmon and crayfish cocktail, ham and free-range eggs, pasta arrabiatta with parmesan shavings and garlic bread, pork loin on mustard mash, garlic, corn-fed chicken supreme on leeks and bacon, rosemary roast shoulder of lamb, and whole bass with cabbage and bacon and dauphinoise potatoes. *Starters/Snacks: £4.75 to £7.50. Main Courses: £7.75 to £15.75. Puddings: £5.25*

Free house ~ Licensees Sally and David Hayle ~ Real ale ~ Bar food (12-2, 6.30-9; 12-3.30 Sun; not Sun evening or all day Mon) ~ Restaurant ~ (01296) 641258 ~ Well behaved children welcome ~ Dogs welcome ~ Open 12-3, 6-11; 12-4.30 Sun; closed Sun evening and all day Mon (exc bank hols)

Recommended by P and J Shapley, Malcolm Ward, Gordon Davico, David and Sue Smith, Mel Smith, Gerry and Rosemary Dobson, John Faircloth

PENN

SU9093 MAP 4

Old Queens Head

Hammersley Lane/Church Road, off B474 between Penn and Tylers Green; HP10 8EY

Smartly updated rambling pub with flourishing food side

This has been well reworked as one of a small local group of other good dining pubs such as the Swan in Denham. Airy and open plan, it has well spaced tables in a variety of linked areas, with a modicum of old prints, and comfortably varied seating on flagstones or broad dark boards. Stairs take you up to an attractive two-level dining room, part carpeted, with stripped rafters. The active bar side has Greene King IPA and Ruddles County on handpump, good fresh juices, and a good choice of old-world wines by the glass; the turntable-top bar stools let you swivel to face the log fire in the big nearby fireplace. The young staff are pleasant and efficient; lots of daily papers; well reproduced piped music. The L-shaped lawn, sheltered by shrubs, has picnic-sets, some under cocktail parasols; St Margaret's church is just across the quiet road.

🍴 Enjoyable modern food includes weekday lunchtime sandwiches, soup, pigeon with sherried raisin gravy, chestnut mushroom gnocchi with a spring onion dressing, crispy pollock and crayfish fishcake with roast lemon and an apple and celery slaw, sausage and mash with onion gravy, manchego flat bread pizza with slow-roast tomato, wild garlic, asparagus, rocket and truffle oil, brie and rosemary stuffed chicken kiev on borlotti bean and tomato ragoût, pork fillet with beetroot and celeriac fondant, rhubarb compote and sage jus, duck breast on sweet potato dauphinoise with creamy french-style peas, and puddings like warm chocolate brownie with chocolate sauce and malt ice-cream and lemon and thyme panna cotta with ginger snap biscuits. *Starters/Snacks: £4.25 to £7.50. Main Courses: £10.75 to £16.75. Puddings: £4.75 to £5.50*

Salisbury Pubs ~ Lease Becky and David Salisbury ~ Real ale ~ Bar food ~ Restaurant ~ (01494) 813371 ~ Children welcome ~ Dogs allowed in bar ~ Open 11-11; 12-10.30 Sun; closed 26 Dec
Recommended by Tracey and Stephen Groves, John Faircloth

PRESTWOOD   SP8799   MAP 4

Polecat 🍴

170 Wycombe Road (A4128 N of High Wycombe); HP16 0HJ

Enjoyable food in several smallish civilised rooms, chatty atmosphere, and attractive sizeable garden

The atmosphere here is always very congenial and with its slightly chintzy appearance, rather civilised too. Opening off the low-ceilinged bar are several smallish rooms with an assortment of tables and chairs, various stuffed birds as well as the stuffed white polecats in one big cabinet, small country pictures, rugs on bare boards or red tiles, and a couple of antique housekeeper's chairs by a good open fire. Brakspears Bitter, Flowers IPA, Greene King Old Speckled Hen and Marstons Pedigree on handpump, quite a few wines by the glass, and 20 malt whiskies; piped music. The garden is most attractive with lots of spring bulbs and colourful summer hanging baskets, tubs, and herbaceous plants; quite a few picnic-sets under parasols on neat grass out in front beneath a big fairy-lit pear tree, with more on a big well kept back lawn; in good weather these seats get snapped up fast.

🍴 Tasty, popular food includes lunchtime sandwiches, filled baked potatoes and ploughman's, as well as soup, baked avocado with smoked bacon rarebit, waldorf salad and toasted walnut bread, smoked salmon terrine with lime crème fraîche and melba toast, chickpea, sweet potato and apricot tagine with coriander couscous and toasted almonds, home-made steak and kidney pie, braised lamb shank and daily specials like stilton soufflé with red onion marmalade and grilled king prawns with smoked haddock kedgeree and a creamy curry sauce; puddings such as chocolate torte with cherry coulis and sherry trifle. *Starters/Snacks: £3.90 to £5.00. Main Courses: £9.50 to £13.80. Puddings: £4.60*

Free house ~ Licensee John Gamble ~ Real ale ~ Bar food (not Sun evening) ~ (01494) 862253 ~ Children in Gallery Room and Drovers Bar only ~ Dogs allowed in bar ~ Open 11.30-2.30, 6-11; 12-3 Sun; closed Sun evening, evenings 24 and 31 Dec, all day 25 and 26 Dec and 1 Jan
Recommended by Roy Hoing, Phil Bryant, Tracey and Stephen Groves, Gordon Davico, Howard Dell

SKIRMETT   SU7790   MAP 2

Frog 🍷 🛏

From A4155 NE of Henley take Hambleden turn and keep on; or from B482 Stokenchurch—Marlow take Turville turn and keep on; RG9 6TG

Bustling, brightly decorated pub with a good mix of locals and visitors, modern cooking and wide choice of drinks; lovely garden and nearby walks

You can be sure of a friendly welcome from both the licensees and their staff in this well run country pub. The neatly kept beamed bar area has a mix of comfortable furnishings, a striking hooded fireplace with a bench around the edge (and a pile of logs sitting beside it), big rugs on the wooden floors and sporting and local prints around the salmon painted walls. The function room leading off is sometimes used as a dining overflow. Although brightly modernised, there is still something of a local feel with leaflets and posters near the door advertising raffles and so forth; piped music. Lodden Hoppit, Rebellion IPA and Sharps Doom Bar on handpump, 16 wines by the glass (including champagne), and 24 malt whiskies. A side gate leads to a lovely garden with a large tree in the middle, and the unusual five-sided tables are well placed for attractive valley views. Plenty of nearby hikes, Henley is close by, and just down the road is the delightful Ibstone windmill. There's a purpose-built outdoor heated area for smokers. The breakfasts are very good.

🍴 As well as much liked daily specials, the popular food includes sandwiches, soup, a tapas plate, smoked venison with pickled vegetables and redcurrant dressing, watercress pancake filled with smoked haddock and chive sauce, pasta with courgettes, chilli and fresh parmesan, confit of duck on baked field mushroom with a confit of red onions, roast fillet of pork in port with banana crème sauce, twice-cooked chicken breast with sun-dried tomatoes wrapped in parma ham, and poached fillet of halibut on spinach with a light saffron sauce. *Starters/Snacks: £4.95 to £7.50. Main Courses: £10.95 to £14.95. Puddings: £5.50*

Free house ~ Licensees Jim Crowe and Noelle Greene ~ Real ale ~ Bar food (12-2.30, 6.30-9.30; not winter Sun evening) ~ Restaurant ~ (01491) 638996 ~ Children welcome ~ Dogs allowed in bar ~ Occasional live entertainment ~ Open 11-3, 6-11; 12-4, 6-10.30 Sun; closed Sun evening Oct-May ~ Bedrooms: £60B/£80B

Recommended by Mike and Sue Richardson, David Collison, Andy and Claire Barker, T R and B C Jenkins, Fred and Kate Portnell, Martin and Karen Wake, J and F Gowers, Michael Dandy, Andy and Jill Kassube

TURVILLE   SU7691 MAP 2

Bull & Butcher ♀

Off A4155 Henley—Marlow via Hambleden and Skirmett; RG9 6QU

Timbered pub, a handy all-day stop in this lovely village

Enjoyed by a very wide mix of customers, this remains a well run pub that can get packed at weekends. There are two low-ceilinged, oak-beamed rooms both with inglenook fireplaces, and the bar, with cushioned wall settles and a tiled floor, has a deep well incorporated into a glass-topped table. Brakspears Bitter, Oxford Gold and a seasonal guest, and Hook Norton Hooky Dark on handpump, Addlestone's cider and 16 wines by the glass; piped music and TV. There are seats on the lawn by fruit trees in the attractive garden, and plenty of walks in the lovely Chilterns valley. The village is popular with television and film companies; *The Vicar of Dibley*, *Midsomer Murders* and *Chitty Chitty Bang Bang* were all filmed here.

🍴 Bar food includes soup, chicken liver parfait with onion jam, ploughman's, beer-battered cod with mushy peas, a pie of the day, vegetable hotpot, bangers and mash and pork fillet with mustard crust. *Starters/Snacks: £4.95 to £7.95. Main Courses: £9.95 to £15.95. Puddings: £4.95 to £5.95*

Brakspears ~ Tenant Lydia Botha ~ Real ale ~ Bar food (12-2.30(4 Sat), 6.30-9.30; 12-4, 7-9 Sun and bank hol Mon; no food winter Sun evening) ~ (01491) 638283 ~ Children allowed but away from bar ~ Dogs allowed in bar ~ Live music monthly ~ Open 11-11(12 Sat); 12-10.30 Sun

Recommended by Gordon Davico, Andy and Claire Barker, Ross Balaam, Mark Farrington, Martin and Karen Wake, Tracey and Stephen Groves, Andy and Jill Kassube, Susan and John Douglas, Tim Maddison

WOOBURN COMMON   SU9187 MAP 2

Chequers

From A4094 N of Maidenhead at junction with A4155 Marlow road keep on A4094 for another 0.75 mile, then at roundabout turn off right towards Wooburn Common, and into Kiln Lane; if you find yourself in Honey Hill, Hedsor, turn left into Kiln Lane at the top of the hill; OS Sheet 175 map reference 910870; HP10 0JQ

Sizeable wine list and bustling bar as well as busy hotel and restaurant side

---

Although there's a thriving hotel and restaurant side to this place, the bar remains busy and friendly and has a good mix of local customers. Standing timbers and alcoves break up the low-beamed room that is furnished with comfortably lived-in sofas (just right for settling into) on its bare boards, a bright log-effect gas fire, and various pictures, plates, a two-man saw, and tankards. They offer a sizeable wine list (with champagne and good wines by the glass), a fair range of malt whiskies and brandies, and Greene King Abbot, IPA, Old Speckled Hen and a guest such as Rebellion Smuggler on handpump; piped music. The spacious garden, set away from the road, has cast-iron tables. The bedroom rate given below is for a weekend stay; the weekly rate is quite a bit more expensive.

🍴 **Good bar food includes sandwiches, filled ciabatta and baguettes, chicken caesar salad, home-made burger with cheese and bacon, salmon and crayfish risotto, thai chicken curry, slow-roasted lamb shank, fish and chips, and puddings such as chocolate brownie with chocolate sauce and rhubarb crumble.** *Starters/Snacks: £3.95 to £8.95. Main Courses: £8.95 to £15.95. Puddings: £4.50 to £5.25*

Free house ~ Licensee Peter Roehrig ~ Real ale ~ Bar food (12-2.30, 6.30-9.30; all day Sat and Sun) ~ Restaurant ~ (01628) 529575 ~ Children welcome ~ Dogs allowed in bar ~ Open 11-11(midnight Sat); closed evenings 25 Dec and 1 Jan ~ Bedrooms: £82.50B/£87.50B

Recommended by Paul Humphreys, Roy Hoing, Kevin Thomas, Nina Randall, David Tindal, Mrs Deborah Chalmers, W K Wood, Mike and Heather Watson, Stewart Bingham

---

LUCKY DIP

Besides the fully inspected pubs, you might like to try these Lucky Dips recommended to us and described by readers (if you do, please send us reports: feedback@thegoodpubguide.co.uk).

AKELEY [SP7037]
Bull & Butcher MK18 5HP [just off A413 Buckingham—Towcester]: Cheery village pub with good log fires each end of long open-plan beamed and stripped stone bar, red plush banquettes and lots of old photographs, welcoming efficient service, well kept Fullers ales, good house wines, separate areas for wide choice of reasonably priced food and for traditional games; children allowed in eating area, tables in pleasant small back garden, handy for Stowe Gardens *(C J Pratt, LYM)*

AMERSHAM [SU9597]
Crown HP7 0DH [Market Sq]: Small modernised hotel bar, leather, polished wood and beams, interesting 16th-c features in comfortable lounge, pleasant formal dining area, short choice of bar food (not cheap) from sandwiches to some interesting dishes, young helpful staff, Bass, good range of wines by the glass; attractive split-level outside seating area with cobbled courtyard and plant-filled garden, comfortable bedrooms *(BB, Tracey and Stephen Groves, Michael Dandy)*
Eagle HP7 0DY [High St]: Rambling low-beamed pub with decent pubby food from sandwiches up, quick friendly service, Adnams and Fullers London Pride, good choice of wines by the glass, log fire, simple décor with a few old prints, pub games; pleasant streamside walled back garden *(Michael Dandy)*
Pheasant HP6 6HL [Plantation Rd]: Reopened after impressive up-to-date rich-textured refurbishment, good value pubby food all day, Fullers London Pride and Greene King IPA, Tues quiz night *(D and M T Ayres-Regan)*
☆ *Saracens Head* HP7 0HU [Whielden St (A404)]: Neat and friendly 17th-c beamed local, massive inglenook with log fire in ancient decorative fire-basket, interesting décor, good fresh food from sandwiches up, Greene King ales, good choice of wines by the glass, pleasant staff, cheery chatty landlord; soft piped music; little back

courtyard, bedrooms *(Phil Bryant, LYM, Michael Dandy)*
Swan HP7 0ED [High St]: Vintage Inn refurbished in their latest comfortably contemporary style of cream and brown, with pale pastel décor, enterprising food all day, good choice of wines by the glass, Timothy Taylors Landlord, more tables upstairs; picnic-sets in pleasant garden behind, open all day *(Michael Dandy)*

ASTON CLINTON [SP8811]
Duck In HP22 5HP [London Rd]: Relaxed, roomy and warm Vintage Inn with reasonably priced quickly served food inc good value Sun roasts, good choice of wines by the glass and real ales, nice variety of furnishings with flagstones and dark brown and dark cream paintwork; picnic-sets under trees in garden, bedrooms, open all day *(Mrs Margaret Peacock)*
☆ *Oak* HP22 5EU [Green End St]: Cosy and attractive beamed pub, Fullers ales and good choice of wines by the glass, friendly efficient staff, enjoyable home-made food (not Sun pm) cooked to order inc good value lighter lunches, real fire, no music or machines *(Mel Smith)*

ASTWOOD [SP9547]
☆ *Old Swan* MK16 9JS [Main Rd]: Stylish low-beamed pub with helpful friendly service, Fullers Chiswick, Shepherd Neame Bishops Finger and Timothy Taylors Landlord, enjoyable interesting food, fair prices, flagstones, inglenook woodburner, nice china collection, two attractive dining areas, warm cosy atmosphere; large garden *(Michael Dandy, LYM)*

AYLESBURY [SP7510]
Bottle & Glass HP17 8TY [A418 some miles towards Thame, beyond Stone]: Rambling low-beamed pub reopened 2007, completely renovated following fire four years earlier, nice modern layout and décor, enjoyable food from sandwiches up using local supplies, neat friendly staff *(LYM, Mel Smith)*
Broad Leys HP21 9LB [Wendover Rd]: Recently renovated, enjoyable home-made food using local supplies, friendly service,

Fullers London Pride and Hook Norton, simple décor with beams and stripped brick, leather armchairs in snug, bar eating area, big plain tables in restaurant beyond; good-sized garden with attractive terrace, open all day *(anon)*

Hop Pole HP19 9AZ [Bicester Rd]: Open-plan pub tied to Vale, their Best and lots of guest beers, good value food; open all day *(Roger Shipperley)*

BLEDLOW [SP7702]

Lions of Bledlow HP27 9PE [off B4009 Chinnor—Princes Risboro; Church End]: Great views from bay windows of relaxed take-us-as-you-find-us Chilterns pub with low 16th-c beams, ancient floor tiles, inglenook log fires and a woodburner, real ales such as Marlow Rebellion and Wadworths 6X, good value bar food from sandwiches up, games room; well behaved children allowed, picnic-sets out in attractive sloping garden with sheltered terrace, nice setting, good walks *(LYM, the Didler, Mel Smith)*

BOURNE END [SU8887]

Spade Oak SL8 5PS [Coldmoorholme Lane (off A4155 towards Thames)]: Rambling M&B pub/restaurant well refurbished in current neo-70s rustic style, three comfortable linked area inc proper bar with real ales such as Adnams Best, Marlow Rebellion and Timothy Taylors Landlord, good choice of wines by the glass or carafe, decent food from mezze and dips up; tables outside, peaceful setting *(D and M T Ayres-Regan, Fred and Kate Portnell, Susan and John Douglas, Simon Collett-Jones)*

BRADENHAM [SU8297]

☆ *Red Lion* HP14 4HF [on corner of Walters Ash turn off A4010]: Neatly refurbished, with enjoyable pubby food inc good pies, well kept real ales such as Adnams, Black Sheep and Brakspears, good friendly service, simple carpeted bar one side, good-sized rather smart cheerfully tiled dining room the other, unspoilt National Trust village; no under-10s; cl Mon lunchtime *(Alan and Anne Driver, Ross Balaam)*

BUCKINGHAM [SP6933]

Woolpack MK18 1EP [Well St]: Refreshingly light and airy, with well kept Black Sheep, Timothy Taylors Landlord and two changing guest beers, pubby lunchtime food (not Mon), a couple of sofas and easy chairs; popular with young people evenings *(Guy Vowles)*

CADMORE END [SU7793]

Blue Flag HP14 3PF [B482 towards Stokenchurch]: Comfortable beamed bar (civilised atmosphere influenced by separate modern hotel wing), well kept ales such as Marstons, decent wines, wide choice of good value food, lots of proper big dining tables, attractive little restaurant; 14 bedrooms *(BB, Roy Hoing)*

Old Ship HP14 3PN [B482 Stokenchurch—Marlow (Marlow Road)]: Tiny, carefully restored old cottage with new licensees, two

little low-beamed rooms separated by standing timbers, simple furnishings (one chair still has a hole for game called five-farthings), coal fire, Black Sheep, Sharps Doom Bar and Youngs tapped straight from the cask down in cellar, wines by glass, bassett hound and great dane; children and dogs welcome, cl Sun pm and Mon, seats in sheltered garden and on terrace; parking on other side of road *(Mark Farrington, Pete Baker, the Didler, LYM)*

CALVERTON [SP7939]

Shoulder of Mutton MK19 6ED [just S of Stony Stratford]: Friendly open-plan L-shaped pub, usually several well kept ales, good choice of other drinks, enjoyable food from sandwiches up inc wkdy bargain lunches, friendly service, brasses and pewter on beams, stripped brickwork, decorative plates in pleasant dining area, darts; piped music, TV, games machines; picnic-sets in big attractive back garden with nice view and play area, well equipped bedrooms, open all day wknds *(JJW, CMW, George Atkinson)*

CHACKMORE [SP6835]

Queens Head MK18 5JF [Main St]: Comfortable village pub by Stowe Gardens, prompt friendly service, enjoyable lunchtime food, real ales, good house wines, Stowford Press cider, nice local feel in bar, small dining room *(Guy Vowles)*

CHALFONT ST GILES [SU9895]

☆ *Ivy House* HP8 4RS [A413 S]: Open-plan dining pub now tied to Fullers, their ales inc Gales, good if not cheap food, friendly young staff, good wines by the glass, espresso coffee, comfortable fireside armchairs in carefully lit and elegantly cosy L-shaped tiled bar, lighter flagstoned dining extension; pleasant terrace and sloping garden (can be traffic noise), five bedrooms *(Tracey and Stephen Groves, BB, Roy Hoing)*

CHESHAM [SP9604]

Black Horse HP5 3NS [Hawridge/Colesbury rd, off A416 towards Berkhamsted]: Neatly extended black-beamed country pub with enjoyable food inc OAP lunch Weds, real ales, decent wines, good service; well spaced tables on back grass *(LYM, Roy Hoing)*

CHICHELEY [SP9045]

☆ *Chester Arms* MK16 9JE [quite handy for M1 junction 14]: Cosy and pretty, with low-beamed rooms off semicircular bar, log fire, comfortable settles and chairs, helpful service, wide choice of good popular home-made meals, children's helpings, Greene King ales, decent wines, good coffee, daily papers, interesting back dining room down steps; picnic-sets in small back garden and out in front *(BB, Michael Dandy)*

COLESHILL [SU9594]

Mulberry Bush HP7 0LU [Magpie Lane/A355]: Modern family-friendly roadside dining pub with wide range of generous pubby food all day from sandwiches up, staff cheerful and helpful even when busy, Fullers London Pride, good choice of wines and hot drinks; piped music; children welcome, disabled facilities, large fenced garden with terrace and good play area, walking country, open all day *(Michael Dandy)*

☆ *Red Lion* HP7 OLH [Village Rd]: Small well worn in local with helpful welcoming long-serving licensees, wide choice of good value pubby food (not Sun eve) from sandwiches up, changing ales such as Wells & Youngs Bitter and Vale Wychert, quick service, two open fires, thriving darts and dominoes teams; TV for racing, games machine; front and back gardens, sturdy climbing frames, good walks, open all day wknds *(BB, Roy Hoing, Michael B Griffith, Michael Dandy)*

CUDDINGTON [SP7311]

☆ *Crown* HP18 0BB [village signed off A418 Thame—Aylesbury; Spurt St]: Small convivial thatched village pub, olde-worlde charm, candles, low beams, good tables, nicely cushioned settles, pleasant décor and inglenook log fires, efficient friendly service, unusual choice of good food inc interesting hot sandwiches and specials, well kept Adnams and Fullers; appealing small terrace, open all day Sun *(Craig Turnbull, Roger Edward-Jones)*

DENHAM [TQ0487]

Falcon UB9 5BE [Village Rd]: Cheery open-plan local, several well kept ales, enjoyable food, bare boards and quarry tiles, old painted woodwork, coal-effect gas fires with inglenook fireside seats below ancient cupboards, lower back dining area; sports TV; teak tables out on terrace, comfortable new character bedrooms *(Graham and Glenis Watkins)*

DINTON [SP7610]

Chouette HP17 8UW [High St]: Pub/restaurant with entertaining Belgian chef/landlord, small bar with belgian beers, enjoyable if not cheap food in two dining rooms, good value lunch deals *(E Seymour)*

Seven Stars HP17 8UL [signed off A418 Aylesbury—Thame, nr Gibraltar turn-off; Stars Lane]: Pretty pub with inglenook bar, comfortable beamed lounge and spacious dining room, real ales such as Fullers London Pride, good choice of reasonably priced food; tables under cocktail parasols in sheltered garden with terrace, pleasant village *(LYM, David Lamb)*

DORNEY [SU9279]

☆ *Palmer Arms* SL4 6QW [2.7 miles from M4 junction 7, via B3026; Village Rd]: Smartly modernised extended dining pub in attractive conservation village, lots of wines by the glass, Greene King ales, open fires, daily papers, civilised front bar, elegant back dining room allowing children; soft piped music; stylish terrace overlooking mediterranean-feel garden, open all day, cl Sun evening *(Dr and Mrs A K Clarke, Ian Phillips, Susan and John Douglas, Mike and Sue Richardson, Gerald and Gabrielle Culliford, Michael Dandy, LYM)*

DOWNLEY [SU8495]

☆ *Le De Spencers Arms* HP13 5YQ [The Common]: Unpretentious and softly lit

18th-c Fullers local hidden away from High Wycombe on Chilterns common, their good beers, prompt cheerful service, low-priced bar food, big pine tables, pictures and bric-a-brac, some stripped masonry, low ceilings; fairy-lit loggia overlooking lawn with picnic-sets, woodland walks to nearby Hughenden Manor *(Roy Hoing, LYM)*

EVERSHOLT [SP9832]

Green Man MK17 9DU [Church End]: Welcoming early Victorian building, fresh pubby food, picturesque village; dogs welcome, big terrace *(Alexandra Upton)*

FLACKWELL HEATH [SU8889]

Crooked Billet SL7 3SG [off A404; Sheepridge Lane]: Cosily old-fashioned 16th-c pub with lovely views (beyond road) from suntrap front garden, low beams, good choice of reasonably priced food, eating area spread pleasantly through alcoves, prompt friendly service, well kept Brakspears, good open fire *(BB, Roy Hoing)*

FORD [SP7709]

☆ *Dinton Hermit* HP17 8XH [SW of Aylesbury]: Extended 16th-c stone building with scrubbed tables and comfortable chairs on old tiled floor, huge inglenook, Adnams, Batemans XB and Brakspears, decent choice of wines and food, back dining area, church candles, wine-bottle décor; well behaved children allowed, garden picnic-sets, nice bright bedrooms in good barn conversion, open all day *(LYM, J Sugarman, Gordon Davico, Mr and Mrs J Jennings)*

FRIETH [SU7990]

Prince Albert RG9 6PY [off B482 SW of High Wycombe]: Friendly cottagey Chilterns local with low black beams and joists, high-backed settles, big black stove in inglenook, big log fire in larger area on the right, good value pubby food from sandwiches up, Brakspears; children and dogs welcome, nicely planted informal side garden with views of woods and fields, open all day *(the Didler, Paul Humphreys, Pete Baker, LYM)*

FULMER [SU9985]

Black Horse SL3 6HD [Windmill Rd]: Nooks and crannies in small traditional bar areas, friendly and cheerful, beams, woodburner and some sofas, some emphasis on more modern dining area, popular Sun lunch, Greene King ales with a guest such as Brains Rev James, decent wines; garden with play area, attractive village, bedrooms next door, open all day wknds *(R K Phillips, N R White)*

GREAT HAMPDEN [SP8401]

☆ *Hampden Arms* HP16 9RQ [off A4010 N and S of Princes Risborough]: Nicely placed dining pub opp village cricket pitch, good range of enjoyable reasonably priced food made by landlord from lunchtime sandwiches to substantial main dishes, speedy civilised service, Adnams, a seasonal Vale ale and Addlestone's cider from small corner bar, good choice of wines by the glass, big woodburner in more spacious back room; children and dogs welcome, tree-sheltered garden, good walks nearby *(LYM, Mel Smith,*

Charles Gysin, Roy Hoing)

GREAT HORWOOD [SP7630]

Swan MK17 0QN [B4033 N of Winslow]: Well modernised old coaching inn, low beams, pictures and good log fires (one in a big inglenook) in open-plan lounge/dining area, Wells & Youngs Eagle and guest beers, pubby food from sandwiches up inc OAP wkdy lunches, friendly landlord and staff, back bar with darts and pool; TV; nice side garden, open all day wknds *(George Atkinson, Michael Dandy)*

GREAT LINFORD [SP8442]

Black Horse MK14 5AJ [from Newport Pagnell take Wolverton Rd towards Stony Stratford]: Large pub rambling through different levels, sensibly priced food in bar and upstairs restaurant, interesting nooks and crannies devoted to Grand Union Canal alongside – drinks can be taken out on the towpath (good walks along here), and sizeable lawn with well spaced picnic-sets; children welcome *(Charles and Pauline Stride, LYM)*

GREAT MISSENDEN [SP8901]

☆ *Cross Keys* HP16 0AU [High St]: Relaxed and unspoilt beamed bar divided by standing timbers, bric-a-brac, traditional furnishings inc high-backed settle and open fire in huge fireplace, Fullers ales, good wines, interesting modern food from tasty baguettes up, attractive and spacious beamed restaurant (children allowed here), cheerful helpful staff; back terrace *(Roy Hoing, LYM, Mrs Ann Gray)*

☆ *Nags Head* HP16 0DG [old London rd, E – beyond abbey]: Civilised and neatly revamped by licensees of Bricklayers Arms, Flaunden (see Herts main entries), similar good food using local produce and own smoked fish and meat, Black Sheep, Fullers London Pride and Timothy Taylors Landlord, good armagnac range and wines by the glass, unusual bar counter (windows behind face road), carpet throughout, low beams on left, loftier on right, log fire; garden tables, seven comfortably redone bedrooms, open all day *(BB)*

White Lion HP16 0AL [High St]: Pleasantly refurbished, with comfortable atmosphere and furniture, good choice of enjoyable food using local produce, nice wines by the glass, quick efficient service, good coffee; children welcome, cl Sun evening *(John Millwood)*

HADDENHAM [SP7408]

Green Dragon HP17 8AA [Churchway]: Formerly good dining pub, closed as we go to press (and being used for BBC TV *Restaurant* series), but due to reopen under new ownership – news please *(LYM)*

HAMBLEDEN [SU7886]

☆ *Stag & Huntsman* RG9 6RP [off A4155 Henley—Marlow]: Handsome brick and flint pub in pretty Chilterns village, congenial old-fashioned front public bar with masses of beer mats, big fireplace in low-ceilinged partly panelled lounge bar, Marlow Rebellion IPA and Wadworths 6X, Thatcher's farm cider,

good wines, friendly efficient staff, tasty pubby food (not Sun evening), traditional games, secluded dining room; piped music; provision for children and dogs, good garden with some raised areas and decking, nice walks, bedrooms *(LYM, Michael Dandy, Roy Hoing, Klaus and Elizabeth Leist, Susan and John Douglas)*

HAWRIDGE [SP9505]

☆ *Rose & Crown* HP5 2UG [signed from A416 N of Chesham; The Vale]: Roomy open-plan pub dating from 18th c, good value home-made food from sandwiches up (popular lunchtime with OAPs), well kept Fullers London Pride and guest beers, good range of wines, friendly efficient staff, big log fire, peaceful country views from upper restaurant area; children welcome, broad terrace with lawn dropping down beyond, play area, open all day wknds *(LYM, Ross Balaam, Roy Hoing)*

HYDE HEATH [SU9300]

Plough HP6 5RW [off B485 Great Missenden—Chesham]: Prettily placed pub with good value food in bar and evening restaurant extension, friendly landlord, real ales such as Adnams, Fullers London Pride and Wells & Youngs, open fires *(LYM, Roy Hoing)*

ICKFORD [SP6407]

Rising Sun HP18 9JD [E of Thame; Worminghall Rd]: Cosy low-beamed bar in pretty thatched local reopened after careful restoration of 2006 fire damage, friendly staff and locals, good value food made to order, two Adnams ales *(David Lamb)*

LACEY GREEN [SP8200]

Black Horse HP27 0QU [Main Rd]: Friendly little beamed country local very popular for good value home-made food (not Mon or Sun evening), real ale, good choice of wines by the glass, big open fire; sports TV; picnic-sets in garden with play area, cl Mon lunchtime, open all day Fri-Sun *(Mel Smith)*

LANE END [SU8091]

Grouse & Ale HP14 3JG [High St]: Former Clayton Arms, enjoyable food, great range of wines by the glass, four or five changing ales, friendly helpful staff *(Christopher Turner)*

Old Sun HP14 3HG [B482 Marlow—Stokenchurch]: Nicely laid out and refitted old pub with two Tring ales, good value food inc popular Sun lunch, log fires; pretty garden *(Andy and Jill Kassube)*

LAVENDON [SP9153]

Green Man MK46 4HA [A428 Bedford—Northampton]: Handsome 17th-c thatched pub in pretty village, friendly attentive staff, generous standard food from soup and sandwiches up, Greene King ales, good choice of wines by the glass, good coffee, roomy and relaxed open-plan wood-floored bar with beams, lots of stripped stone and open woodburner, big carpeted evening/wknd restaurant; piped music; children welcome, tables and heaters outside, open all day *(Michael Dandy, George Atkinson)*

☆ *Horseshoe* MK46 4HA [A428 Bedford—Northampton; High St]: Immaculate low-beamed village pub with log fire and plush banquettes, airy dining extension, enjoyable food from baguettes to great range of fish (ex-fisherman landlord), Fullers ESB and Wells & Youngs Eagle, good value small but interesting wine list, quick cheerful service, skittles in public bar, steps between levels; piped music; appealing good-sized garden behind with terrace, decking and play area, cl Sun evening (*Jack Pridding, BB, Michael Dandy, Howard and Margaret Buchanan, George Atkinson*)

LITTLE BRICKHILL [SP9029]

George MK17 9NB [Watling St, off A5 SE of Milton Keynes]: Settees, pine tables and woodburner in roomy front bar, L-shaped restaurant opening into big back conservatory with striking ceiling canopy, friendly service, Fullers London Pride and Greene King IPA, good choice of wines by the glass, enjoyable up-to-date food (not Sun evening or Mon lunchtime) from wkdy sandwiches up, daily papers; quiet piped music, TV; heated terrace, play equipment in large mature garden (*Michael Dandy*)

Old Green Man MK17 9LU [just off A5 SE of Milton Keynes]: Large tastefully refurbished good value dining pub, unusual sandwiches too, Greene King ales, decent wines by the glass, neat friendly staff, log fire (*Mel Smith*)

LITTLE HAMPDEN [SP8503]

☆ *Rising Sun* HP16 9PS [off A4128 or A413 NW of Gt Missenden; OS Sheet 165 map ref 856040]: Comfortable beamed dining pub in delightful out-of-the-way setting, opened-up bar with woodburner and log fire, good food inc interesting dishes and popular Sun lunch (can be busy wknds), friendly service, Adnams and Shepherd Neame Spitfire, good short wine list, winter mulled wine and spiced cider; piped music; terrace tables, lovely walks, appealing bedrooms, cl Sun evening and Mon (*Mark Farrington, Roy Hoing, LYM*)

LITTLE HORWOOD [SP7930]

Old Crown MK17 0PA [Mursley Rd]: Friendly thatched and beamed village pub, good choice of pubby food, real ales, small bar, dining area with small room off; front and side garden (*David Lamb*)

LITTLE KINGSHILL [SU8999]

Full Moon HP16 0EE [Hare Lane]: Picturesque country pub with friendly staff, enjoyable generous pub food, Adnams, Fullers London Pride and Wells & Youngs, good choice of wines by the glass, pleasantly traditional front bar and bigger carpeted side room, some *Carry On* memorabilia, buoyant atmosphere evenings and wknds; neat attractive garden (*Barney Drake, Steve Langbridge, Roy Hoing*)

LITTLE MARLOW [SU8788]

☆ *Kings Head* SL7 3RZ [A4155 about 2 miles E of Marlow; Church Rd]: Long flower-covered pub with open-plan low-beamed bar, wide blackboard choice of good value food from plenty of sandwiches to popular Sun roasts, smart dining room, Adnams Broadside, Fullers London Pride and Timothy Taylors Landlord, quick cheerful service even though busy, log or coal fires, Sun bar nibbles, cricket memorabilia; children welcome; big attractive walled garden behind popular with families, nice walk down to church (*D and M T Ayres-Regan, BB, Roy Hoing, Paul Humphreys*)

☆ *Queens Head* SL7 3RZ [Church Rd/Pound Lane; cul de sac off A4155 nr Kings Head]: Civilised refurbished local with good value food from chunky rolls to some interesting main dishes (not Sun-Tues evenings) and popular Sun lunch, quick friendly service, real ales and good choice of wines by the glass, cosy lighter dining room and biggish back extension, lots of books in saloon; darts and TV in public bar on left, no dogs; appealing cottagey front garden, a couple more tables on secluded terrace across lane – short walk from Thames (*BB, Roger and Lesley Everett, Roy Hoing, Simon Collett-Jones, D J and P M Taylor, Susan and John Douglas*)

LITTLE MISSENDEN [SU9298]

☆ *Red Lion* HP7 0QZ: Small 15th-c local reopened after restoration of fire damage, still charmingly unpretentious, with two coal fires, friendly retriever, well kept ales, decent wines, generous good value standard food inc nice fairly priced proper sandwiches; tables and busy aviary in sunny side garden by river with ducks, swans and fat trout (*Dr W I C Clark, Roy Hoing*)

LITTLEWORTH COMMON [SP9386]

☆ *Blackwood Arms* SL1 8PP [3 miles S of M40 junction 2; Common Lane, OS Sheet 165 map ref 937864]: Lovely spot on edge of beech woods with good walks, sturdy furniture, cream and mulberry décor, dark woodwork and blinds, welcoming service, well kept Brakspears and a guest beer, some emphasis on the food side (very wide standard choice), roaring log fire; children and dogs welcome, good garden (*LYM, LM*)

Jolly Woodman SL1 8PF [2 miles from M40 junction 2; off A355]: Brightened up in simple country style under friendly new licensees, changing ales inc Fullers London Pride, St Austell Tribute and Wychwood Hobgoblin, fresh blackboard food, rambling beamed and timbered linked areas inc new armchair snug, log fire, central woodburner; picnic-sets outside, good site by Burnham Beeches, open all day (*Michael Dandy, LYM, Peter and Eleanor Kenyon, Susan and John Douglas*)

LOUDWATER [SU9090]

Derehams HP10 9RH [off A40 E of High Wycombe, almost opp village turnoff]: Three linked low-ceilinged old-fashioned areas, thriving atmosphere, well kept beers, enjoyable pubby food, pleasant service, log fire (*Anthony Longden*)

LUDGERSHALL [SP6617]
Bull & Butcher HP18 9NZ [off A41
Aylesbury—Bicester; The Green]: Gently
updated beamed country pub, good value
food (not Tues lunchtime), Greene King IPA
and Vale VPA, back dining room, exemplary
ladies'; nice front garden, attractive setting,
cl Mon (*David Lamb, Lucien Perring*)
MAIDS MORETON [SP7035]
Wheatsheaf MK18 1QR [Main St, just off
A413 Towcester—Buckingham]: Attractive
thatched and low-beamed local, cheery staff
and atmosphere, wide choice of good value
food from good sandwiches up, Tring ales,
farm cider, decent choice of wines, lots of
pictures and bric-a-brac in old part, two
inglenooks, settles and chairs, conservatory
restaurant with woodburner; unobtrusive
piped music; hatch service for pleasant quiet
enclosed garden behind (*George Atkinson,
Michael Clatworthy*)
MARLOW [SU8486]
Chequers SL7 1BA [High St]: Attractive pub
with large air-conditioned front bar, bare
boards and heavy beams, leather settees,
Brakspears ales, good choice of wines by the
glass, friendly service, good food range in
bright and pleasant back restaurant area,
daily papers; piped music, TV, games –
popular with young people (stays open late
wknds); children welcome, pavement tables,
bedrooms (*Michael Dandy*)
☆ *Two Brewers* SL7 1NQ [St Peter St, first right
off Station Rd from double roundabout]:
Busy low-beamed pub with shiny black
woodwork, nautical pictures, gleaming
brassware and interesting layout, most
tables inc upstairs and downstairs overflows
set for good food (wide evening choice),
Brakspears, Fullers London Pride, Hop Back
Summer Lightning and Marlow Rebellion,
nice wines and coffee, good friendly service,
relaxed atmosphere; children in eating area,
may be unobtrusive piped music; tables in
sheltered back courtyard with covered area,
front seats with glimpse of the Thames –
pub right on Thames Path (*Paul Humphreys,
Michael Dandy, LYM, Phil Bryant*)
MARLOW BOTTOM [SU8588]
Three Horseshoes SL7 3RA [signed from
Handy Cross roundabout, off M40 junction
4]: Tied to nearby Rebellion, with half a
dozen of their good ales, though main
emphasis is on popular food (not Sun
evening) from baguettes up inc speciality
sizzlers, good value wines by the glass; open
all day Fri/Sat (*Tracey and Stephen Groves,
Alan and Anne Driver*)
MARSWORTH [SP9114]
☆ *Red Lion* HP23 4LU [village signed off B489
Dunstable—Aylesbury; Vicarage Rd]: Low-
beamed partly thatched village pub with real
ales such as Batemans, Crouch Vale, Tring
and Vale, cheerful old-fashioned service,
good value food from enterprising baguettes
up, decent wines, leather sofas and open
fires in lounge, steps up to snug parlour and
games area, nice variety of seating inc

traditional settles; sheltered garden, not far
from impressive flight of canal locks (*LYM,
Roy Hoing, Andrew Scarr, Paul Humphreys,
Ross Balaam, Tracey and Stephen Groves*)
MILTON KEYNES [SP9137]
Wavendon Arms MK17 8LJ [not far from M1
junctions 13 and 14]: Pleasant front bar with
mix of modern furniture, airy contemporary
tiled-floor restaurant, Timothy Taylors
Landlord, good choice of wines by the glass,
popular up-to-date food, good service;
tables out in back garden with terrace, more
in front (*Michael Dandy*)
MOULSOE [SP9141]
Carrington Arms MK16 0HB [1.25 miles from
M1, junction 14: A509 N, first right signed
Moulsoe; Cranfield Rd]: Wide food choice inc
chargrilled meats and fish sold by weight
from refrigerated display, Greene King ales,
helpful staff, open-plan layout with
comfortable mix of wooden chairs and
cushioned banquettes; children allowed,
long pretty garden behind, decent bedrooms
in adjacent block (*Alan Sutton, LYM,
Michael Dandy*)
OAKLEY [SP6312]
Chandos Arms HP18 9QB [The Turnpike]:
Small peaceful 16th-c village pub with
current chef/landlord doing enjoyable food
in bar and end restaurant, friendly service
(*Andrew Finn, David Lamb*)
Royal Oak HP18 9QY [Worminghall Rd]:
Large village pub with reasonably priced
food, real ales, several linked areas (*David
Lamb*)
OLNEY [SP8851]
Bull MK46 4EA [Market Pl/High St]: Sofas
and other seats in two smallish front rooms,
big airy bare-boards eating area on the
right, friendly staff and chatty landlord,
popular quickly served food from sandwiches
up inc imaginative vegetarian board, well
kept Wells & Youngs and guest ales,
flourishing Aug bank hol beer festival, good
coffee, log-effect gas fires, lots of games;
small courtyard (no dogs), big back garden
with big climbing frame; HQ of the famous
Shrove Tuesday pancake race (*R T and
J C Moggridge, Ted George, George Atkinson*)
☆ *Swan* MK46 4AA [High St S]: Friendly
beamed and timbered linked rooms, wide
choice of good value generous food from
sandwiches up, Shepherd Neame and guest
ales, good value wines by the glass, quick
helpful service, daily papers; attractive
flowers, rather close-set pine tables, log
fires, small back bistro dining room (booking
advised for this); back courtyard tables,
some cover (*BB, Michael Dandy*)
PENN [SU9193]
☆ *Crown* HP10 8NY [B474 Beaconsfield—High
Wycombe]: Busy Chef & Brewer opp 14th-c
church on high ridge with distant views,
quick friendly service, interesting décor and
attractive furnishings in linked areas around
low-ceilinged medieval core, wide range of
generous food all day from sandwiches up,
good choice of real ales and wines by the

glass, two roaring log fires; piped music, games machine; children very welcome, lots of tables in attractive gardens with good play area, open all day *(Tracey and Stephen Groves, Roy Hoing, Mrs Ann Gray, LYM)*

Red Lion HP10 8LF [Elm Rd]: Attractive low-ceilinged traditional bar with vast log fire and plenty of bric-a-brac, choice choice of generous well priced food, five real ales, friendly efficient service, games room; piped music; children welcome, nice spot opp green and duck pond *(Roy Hoing)*

PENN STREET [SU9295]

☆ *Hit or Miss* HP7 0PX [off A404 SW of Amersham, then keep on towards Winchmore Hill]: Well laid out low-beamed pub with own cricket ground, enjoyable food (freshly made so can take a while when busy), well kept Badger ales, decent wines, friendly attentive young staff, cheerful atmosphere in three clean linked rooms, log fire, charming décor, candles on tables, interesting cricket and chair-making memorabilia; piped music may obtrude; picnic-sets out in front, pleasant setting, open all day *(Kevin Thomas, Nina Randall, Tracey and Stephen Groves, Mrs Ann Gray, LYM, D and M T Ayres-Regan)*

Squirrel HP7 0PX: Friendly open-plan bar with flagstones, log fire, comfortable sofas as well as tables and chairs, good value home-made traditional food from baguettes up (not Sun evening), good children's meals, well kept changing ales, good service, free coffee refills, bric-a-brac and cricketing memorabilia, darts; big garden with good play area, handy for lovely walks (and watching cricket), open all day wknds *(Ross Balaam, Roy Hoing, Mel Smith)*

POUNDON [SP6425]

Sow & Pigs OX27 9BA [Main St]: Small quaint village local, warm and friendly, now doing bargain lunches as well as good sandwich range, several real ales *(David Lamb)*

PRESTON BISSETT [SP6529]

White Hart MK18 4LX [off A421 or A4421 SW of Buckingham; Pound Lane]: Thatched, timbered and low-beamed 18th-c village pub with three cosy rooms, log fire, home-made food from sandwiches up, real ales, good choice of wines by the glass; some seats outside *(LYM, E A and D C T Frewer)*

PRINCES RISBOROUGH [SP8104]

Red Lion HP27 0LL [Whiteleaf, off A4010; OS Sheet 165 map ref 817043]: Simple comfortably worn in village pub with good generous home-made food, well kept ales, log fire, traditional games; garden tables, charming village, good Chilterns walks *(LYM, Roy Hoing)*

SHERINGTON [SP8946]

White Hart MK16 9PE [off A509; Gun Lane]: Good changing ales such as Archers Village, Greene King IPA, Purity Gold and Rebellion Defector, helpful landlord and friendly staff, good pub food (not Sun evening) from sandwiches and tapas up, bright fire, two-

room bar, contemporary flagstoned dining room; children and dogs welcome, picnic-sets in garden with terrace, pretty hanging baskets, bedrooms in adjacent building *(George Atkinson, Michael B Griffith, Michael Dandy)*

SOULBURY [SP8826]

☆ *Boot* LU7 0BT [High Rd (B4032 W of Leighton Buzzard)]: In administration as we go to press, though still open (all day), and has been smart and civilised, with pleasant staff, super choice of wines, several real ales, separate restaurant, light and sunny red-tiled bar; children welcome, small garden and terrace overlooking peaceful fields; news please *(LYM)*

ST LEONARDS [SP9107]

White Lion HP23 6NW [Jenkins Lane, by Buckland Common; off A4011 Wendover—Tring]: Neat open-plan pub, highest in the Chilterns, with old black beams, well kept ales such as Batemans and Greene King, good value pub food, friendly service, log-effect gas fire; children and dogs welcome, attractive sheltered garden, good walks *(BB, Roy Hoing)*

STOKE GOLDINGTON [SP8348]

☆ *Lamb* MK16 8NR [High St (B526 Newport Pagnell—Northampton)]: Chatty village pub with friendly helpful licensees, three or four interesting changing ales, Weston's farm cider, decent wines by the glass, good generous home-made food (all day Sat, not Sun evening) from baguettes to bargain Sun roasts, good public bar with table skittles, two small pleasant dining rooms, quiet lounge with log fire and sheep decorations; may be quiet piped music, TV; dogs welcome, terrace and sheltered garden behind, open all day wknds *(JJW, CMW, BB, Elizabeth Whelan)*

STOKE MANDEVILLE [SP8310]

☆ *Woolpack* HP22 5UP [Risborough Rd (A4010 S of Aylesbury)]: Management changes in stylish partly thatched M&B pub with beams, timbers, massive inglenook fireplace, comfortable knocked-through front bar, big busy dining room, Fullers London Pride and Timothy Taylors Landlord, decent wines; piped music; well behaved children allowed, neat back garden, heated front terrace, open all day *(Adam F Padel, Mel Smith, Gordon Davico, John Silverman, LYM)*

STOKE POGES [SU9885]

Fox & Pheasant SL2 4EZ [Gerrards Cross Rd (B416, Stoke Common)]: Reasonably priced carvery, usual other food too, quick friendly service, small quiet bar with Wells & Youngs Bombardier *(David Lamb)*

STONE [SP7912]

Bugle Horn HP17 8QP [Oxford Rd, Hartwell (A418 SW of Aylesbury)]: Long low 17th-c stone-built family dining pub, friendly and comfortable linked rooms, good choice of modestly priced home-made food from good daytime sandwiches up, friendly service (can slow in fine weather), Brakspears and Hook Norton Old Hooky, lots of wines by the glass, several log fires, prettily planted well furnished conservatory; tables on attractive terrace, lovely trees in large pretty garden, pastures beyond, open all day *(Mel Smith, Tim and Ann Newell, David Lamb)*

STONY STRATFORD [SP7840]

Old George MK11 1AA [High St]: Attractive and lively beamed and timbered inn, cosily pubby, with good value food at any time inc roast of the day, quick friendly staff, real ales such as Fullers London Pride and Greene King IPA, good coffee, small dining room up at the back; piped music, lavatories up rather awkward stairs; tables in courtyard behind, bedrooms *(Dr and Mrs A K Clarke, George Atkinson)*

SWANBOURNE [SP8027]

Betsy Wynne MK17 0SH [Mursley Rd]: Newish pub with good choice of real ales, enjoyable food, great service, thriving atmosphere, bare-boards L-shaped contemporary layout; tables outside *(Gill and Keith Croxton)*

TAPLOW [SU9182]

Oak & Saw SL6 0ET [Rectory Rd]: Cosy open-plan local opp attractive village green, well kept Brakspears, enjoyable fresh pubby food, efficient friendly service, interesting pictures *(Ross Balaam)*

THE LEE [SP8904]

☆ *Cock & Rabbit* HP16 9LZ [back roads 2.5 miles N of Great Missenden, E of A413]: Warmly welcoming italian-run dining pub, stylish and comfortable, with reasonably priced home-made food (not Sun or Mon evenings) inc good fresh fish, pasta, real ales such as Fullers and Greene King, decent wines, good lively staff, panelled locals' bar, charming back dining areas welcoming children; big garden with tables on verandah, terraces and lawn *(Paul Humphreys, LYM, Roy Hoing)*

☆ *Old Swan* HP16 9NU [Swan Bottom, back rd 0.75 mile N of The Lee]: Long-serving landlord doing good well priced interesting food esp seafood in well worn in tucked-away 16th-c dining pub, three simply but attractively furnished linked rooms, low beams and flagstones, cooking-range log fire in inglenook, well kept Brakspears and a guest beer, decent wines, relaxed service, TV etc tucked nicely away; lovely big back garden with play area, good walks *(LYM, Gordon Davico, Mel Smith, R K Phillips, Susan and John Douglas)*

WADDESDON [SP7316]

Bell HP18 0JF [High St]: Welcoming new licensees, new chef doing good value pubby food from huge sandwiches up, quick friendly service, nice eating area by small bar; tables out front and back *(Gill and Keith Croxton, Mel Smith)*

WENDOVER [SP8607]

Shoulder of Mutton HP22 6EJ [Pound St]: Chef & Brewer with welcoming well divided layout and medley of furnishings, their usual food with good value specials, good choice of wines by the glass, Courage Best and Directors; attractive setting *(Phil Bryant)*

WEST WYCOMBE [SU8394]

George & Dragon HP14 3AB [High St; A40 W of High Wycombe]: In preserved Tudor village, dark rambling bar with massive beams and sloping walls, big log fire, Adnams, Courage Best and Wells & Youngs Bombardier, fairly priced food from interesting starters to some exotic specials, friendly staff, small family dining room; garden with fenced play area, character bedrooms (magnificent oak staircase), handy for West Wycombe Park *(Alan and Anne Driver, LYM, Martin and Karen Wake)*

WESTON UNDERWOOD [SP8650]

☆ *Cowpers Oak* MK46 5JS [signed off A509 in Olney; High St]: Wisteria-covered beamed pub in pretty thatched village, warmly welcoming, with generous good value interesting food (all day wknds) using local supplies, even their own pigs, five well kept changing ales, nice medley of old-fashioned furnishings, woodburners, dark red walls, dark panelling and some stripped stone, back restaurant (best to book Sun), good traditional games room, daily papers; piped music, TV; children very welcome, dogs in main bar, small suntrap front terrace, more tables on back decking and in big orchard garden (no dogs) with play area and farm animals, bedrooms, open all day wknds *(LYM, George Atkinson, David Campbell, Vicki McLean)*

WHEELER END [SU8093]

☆ *Chequers* HP14 3NH [off B482 NW of Marlow]: Neatly kept 17th-c pub with inglenook log fire in convivial low-ceilinged little bar, bigger back dining room, candlelit tables and hunting prints, enjoyable bar food (not Sun evening) using their garden herbs, good fish choice and local game, well kept Fullers, reasonably priced wines, brisk friendly service, dominoes and cribbage; can get crowded Sat in rugby season; children welcome in eating areas, dogs in bar, two charmingly kept gardens (M40 noise), open all day *(Martin and Karen Wake, LYM)*

WOBURN SANDS [SP9235]

Swan MK17 8RL [High St (A5130)]: Large Vintage Inn nicely refurbished in modern style with mixed furnishings in separate areas (we don't know if the Green Lady who used to haunt it has been driven away), their usual food all day from open sandwiches up, good choice of wines by the glass, Fullers London Pride and Timothy Taylors Landlord; children welcome, open all day *(Michael Dandy)*

WOOBURN COMMON [SU9387]

☆ *Royal Standard* HP10 0JS [3.4 miles from M40 junction 2]: Good choice of well kept changing ales in busy low-ceilinged local with good value pubby food from baguettes up, welcoming helpful staff, well chosen wines, lots of daily papers, open fire, daily papers and crossword reference books, neat dining area; picnic-sets on pretty roadside terrace and in back garden, open all day *(Roy Hoing, LYM)*

Cambridgeshire

At one end of the spectrum here are some very civilised pubs, with much emphasis on high-quality, restaurant-style food, while at the other are some genuinely unspoilt places that seem little changed for decades. Of these simple pubs, prime examples are the city of Cambridge main entries, the Cambridge Blue, the Free Press and the Live & Let Live, the genteel little Fountain in Ely, and the Queens Head at Newton, which has been in the same family for three generations. For a special meal out, try the imaginative cooking at the Chequers in Fowlmere (some refurbishment this year), at the Cock in Hemingford Grey (as well as a smart restaurant they have a proper drinkers' bar, too), at the Old Bridge in Huntingdon (this civilised hotel in a lovely waterside spot also has a chatty bar for drinkers), at the Pheasant in Keyston (they also stock four real ales and have a smashing wine list), at the Three Horseshoes in Madingley (almost a restaurant really), at the Bell in Stilton (a fine old coaching inn with informal bars too), and at the Anchor at Sutton Gault (it does keep a pubby atmosphere as well as serving first-class food). Our Cambridgeshire Dining Pub of the Year is the Anchor at Sutton Gault. One of our new main entries, the Hole in the Wall at Little Wilbraham, might well give the Anchor a close run for its money; another really nice place for a special meal out. Our other newcomer, the stylishly reworked George in Buckden, also comes straight in with a Food Award (and it's a nice place to stay in). Real ales feature strongly in the county, with the aforementioned Cambridge pubs riding high on the list, as well as the Blue Bell at Helpston (which, despite its very popular food, always has some surprisingly interesting beer choices), the Brewery Tap and Charters, both in Peterborough (featuring their own Oakham beers as well as lots of guests), and the Dyke's End at Reach with its own-brewed beers and guest ales. There are several other good local breweries, such as Elgoods, City of Cambridge, Milton, and Isle of Ely Fenland. In the Lucky Dip section at the end of the chapter, pubs to note particularly include the Kingston Arms in Cambridge (a great beer pub), Cutter near Ely, Exhibition in Godmanchester, and Blue Ball and Green Man in Grantchester.

BARNACK
TF0704   MAP 5

Millstone ◀

Off B1443 SE of Stamford, via School Lane into Millstone Lane; PE9 3ET

Stone-built pub in a picturesque village, with new licensees, good range of drinks and pubby food

New licensees again for this pub, built of the same local stone as most of Cambridge University and Ely Cathedral. There are welcoming fires and cosy corners in the timbered bar, some bold oil paintings by local artists and a clean, contemporary feel. Adnams

Bitter, Greene King Old Speckled Hen, and Everards Tiger and Original on handpump and several wines by the glass. There's a lovely enclosed courtyard for outside dining. Burghley House, home of the famous horse trials, is nearby. More reports on the new regime, please.

🍴 Lunchtime bar food now includes sandwiches, ploughman's, soup, chicken liver pâté with chutney, home-made pork pie with piccalilli, pollack in beer batter, a proper burger with home-made tomato ketchup and shepherd's pie, with evening extras such as crispy bacon and black pudding salad with poached egg, roast onion and goats cheese tart and beef and kidney pudding; puddings like warm treacle tart with home-made vanilla ice-cream or warm chocolate brownie with home-made Snickers ice-cream. *Starters/Snacks: £3.00 to £6.00. Main Courses: £7.50 to £13.50. Puddings: £3.50 to £5.95*

Everards ~ Tenants Luke Marsh and Lauren Mackintosh ~ Real ale ~ Bar food (12-2.30(3 Sun), 6.30-9.30) ~ Restaurant ~ (01780) 740296 ~ Children welcome ~ Dogs allowed in bar ~ Open 12-3, 5.30-11; 12-midnight Sat and Sun; closed evenings 25 and 26 Dec and 1 Jan

Recommended by Roy Bromell, Ian Stafford

BUCKDEN   TL1967   MAP 5

George 🍴 ♀ 🛏
High Street; PE19 5XA

Modern stylish refurbishment of handsome coaching inn, friendly staff, first-rate modern cooking, fine choice of wines and lovely bedrooms

This handsome Georgian-faced former coaching inn has been stylishly and elegantly refurbished with contemporary furnishings, but making the most of its medieval origins. The bar with its leather and chrome bar chairs and log fire is still well used by regulars. It has some wonderful fan beamwork, Adnams Best and Iceni Elveden Forest Gold on handpump from a chrome-topped counter, 20 wines (including champagne) by the glass and good coffee, served by hospitable staff. The bustling brasserie has smart cream dining chairs around carefully polished tables set with proper white napkins and pretty foliage arrangements, and this leads out on to the pretty sheltered terrace with box hedging and flowering plants and seats under large parasols. The charming bedrooms are all named after a famous George.

🍴 Excellent food includes sandwiches (the steak sandwich with chips is well liked), interesting soups, pork, smoked bacon and roasted red onion terrine, dorset crab and saffron tart, twice-baked aubergine and parmesan ricotta torte, roast red peppers with garlic oil dressing and rocket salad, risotto of braised rabbit, rosemary, black olives, vermouth and parmesan shavings, breast of chicken with roasted butternut squash, cottechino sausage, cherry vine tomatoes, pancetta and smoked paprika feta pesto, rare grilled ahi tuna niçoise salad, and puddings such as peanut butter and chocolate cheesecake with strawberry jelly and orange and cinnamon rice pudding with armagnac prunes. *Starters/Snacks: £5.50 to £8.50. Main Courses: £6.50 to £20.00. Puddings: £4.50 to £8.50*

Licensee Cynthia Schaeffer ~ Real ale ~ Bar food ~ Restaurant ~ (01480) 812300 ~ Children welcome ~ Dogs allowed in bedrooms ~ Open 12-11(11.30 Sat; 10.30 Sun) ~ Bedrooms: £80S/£100B

Recommended by Mr and Mrs Staples, Michael Dandy, H Bramwell, Paul Humphreys, Michael Sargent, Gerry and Rosemary Dobson

CAMBRIDGE   TL4658   MAP 5

Cambridge Blue 🍺 £
85 Gwydir Street; CB1 2LG

Friendly backstreet pub, simply decorated with lots to look at, and interesting ales

The new licensees in this friendly backstreet pub keep up to 17 real ales on handpump or tapped from the cask: City of Cambridge Hobsons Choice, Nethergate Dewdrop,

Woodfordes Wherry and lots of changing guests. Quite a choice of bottled beers and malt whiskies as well. There's an attractive little conservatory and two peaceful rooms that are simply decorated with old-fashioned bare-boards style furnishings, candles on the tables, and a big collection of breweriana; board games, cards and dominoes. The big back garden is surprisingly rural feeling. It does get very busy at weekends.

Ⓜ **Straightforward bar food includes home-made soup, filled ciabatta rolls and baked potatoes, nut roast, chilli, daily specials and Sunday roast.** *Starters/Snacks: £1.50 to £5.00. Main Courses: £6.25 to £8.50. Puddings: £2.95 to £3.50*

Free house ~ Licensees Jethro and Terri Scotcher-Littlechild ~ Real ale ~ Bar food (12-2(12-4 Sun), 6-9) ~ (01223) 361382 ~ Children and dogs allowed in conservatory ~ Open 12-2.30, 5.30-11; 12-11(10.30 Sun) Sat

Recommended by Jerry Brown, Ben Guy, the Didler, John Saville

Free Press £
Prospect Row; CB1 1DU

Quiet and unspoilt with some interesting local décor, and good value food

The quiet, unspoilt atmosphere in this little pub is undisturbed by mobile phones, piped music or games machines and you can sit peacefully reading a paper by the warm log fire. In a nod to the building's history as home to a local newspaper, the walls of its characterful bare-board rooms are hung with old newspaper pages and printing memorabilia, as well as old printing trays that local customers are encouraged to top up with little items. Greene King IPA, Abbot and Mild and a guest or two such as Bath Ales Gem or Hydes Jekyll Gold on handpump, around 20 malt whiskies and up to nine wines by the glass; quite a few assorted board games. In fine weather, there are seats in the suntrap sheltered and paved back garden.

Ⓜ **Monthly changing bar food such as filled ciabattas, soup, ploughman's, stuffed peppers, gammon with bubble and squeak and lamb shank; good value Monday and Tuesday lunch and evening set menus.** *Starters/Snacks: £1.50 to £3.75. Main Courses: £5.25 to £10.95. Puddings: £3.25 to £3.75*

Greene King ~ Tenant Craig Bickley ~ Real ale ~ Bar food (12-2(2.30 Sat and Sun), 6-9; not Sun evening) ~ (01223) 368337 ~ Children welcome ~ Dogs welcome ~ Open 12-2.30, 6-11; 12-11 Sat; 12-3, 7-10.30 Sun

Recommended by Virginia Williams, John Wooll, the Didler, Michael Dandy

Live & Let Live ◖ £
40 Mawson Road; off Mill Road SE of centre; CB1 2EA

Fine real ales in popular local, a relaxed atmosphere, and pubby food

The eight real ales on handpump or tapped from the cask in this busy old local are the main draw here: Everards Tiger, Nethergate Umbel Magna, and five changing guests that might include B&T Black Dragon Mild, Buntingford Robin Hood, and Tring Brock Bitter. There are also 40 Belgian bottled beers, a guest draught, and local ciders. The atmosphere is relaxed and friendly, and the heavily timbered brickwork rooms have sturdy varnished pine tables with pale wood chairs on bare boards, and sometimes, real gas lighting. An assortment of collectables takes in lots of interesting old country bric-a-brac and some steam railway and brewery memorabilia, and posters advertise local forthcoming events; cribbage and dominoes.

Ⓜ **Straightforward food might include sandwiches and filled baked potatoes, soup, ploughman's, chilli, and steak in ale stew.** *Starters/Snacks: £3.50 to £5.00. Main Courses: £6.50 to £7.50*

Burlison Inns ~ Lease Peter Wiffin ~ Real ale ~ Bar food ~ (01223) 460261 ~ Children welcome ~ Dogs welcome ~ Open 11.30-2.30, 5.30(6 Sat)-11; 12-3, 7-11 Sun

Recommended by Dr David Cockburn, Revd R P Tickle, Richard J Stanley, Giles and Annie Francis

ELSWORTH   TL3163   MAP 5

George & Dragon
Off A14 NW of Cambridge, via Boxworth, or off A428; CB3 8JQ

Busy dining pub with quite a choice of interesting food served by efficient staff

With enjoyable food and courteous staff, it's not surprising that this bustling brick-built dining pub is so popular; to be sure of a table it is best to book in advance. A pleasant panelled main bar, decorated with a fishy theme, opens on the left to a slightly elevated dining area with comfortable tables and a good woodburning stove. From here, steps lead down to a garden room behind with tables overlooking attractive garden terraces. On the right is a more formal restaurant. Greene King IPA and Old Speckled Hen and a guest beer on handpump and decent wines.

🍽 **As well as their weekday set menus, there might be sandwiches, filled baguettes and ploughman's, soup, gammon and eggs, vegetarian dishes, scottish steaks, plenty of fish such as bass, red snapper, gurney, large skate wings, haddock and seasonal lobsters and crabs, and daily specials.** *Starters/Snacks: £4.50 to £8.00. Main Courses: £10.00 to £18.50. Puddings: £5.25*

Free house ~ Licensees Paul and Karen Beer ~ Real ale ~ Bar food (12-2, 7-9; 12-3.30 Sun) ~ Restaurant ~ (01954) 267236 ~ Children welcome ~ Dogs allowed in bar ~ Open 11-3, 6-11; 12-3.30, 6-10.30 Sun; closed Sun evening in Jan and Feb; 25 and 26 Dec

Recommended by Michael and Jenny Back, J Jennings, Simon Watkins, Keith and Janet Morris

ELTON   TL0893   MAP 5

Black Horse ♀
B671 off A605 W of Peterborough and A1(M); Overend; PE8 6RU

Well run dining pub with country furnishings and super views from big garden

Regulars do still drop into this handsome honey brick dining pub for a chat and a pint of Adnams Bitter, Black Sheep, Digfield Barnwell Bitter or Everards Tiger on handpump, but many people are here to eat. There are roaring log fires, hop-strung beams, a homely and comfortable mix of furniture (no two tables and chairs seem the same), antique prints, and lots of ornaments and bric-a-brac including an intriguing ancient radio set. Dining areas at each end of the bar have parquet flooring and tiles, and the stripped stone back lounge towards the restaurant has an interesting fireplace; 15 wines by the glass. The big garden has super views across to Elton Hall park and the village church, there are seats on the terrace, and a couple of acres of grass for children to play.

🍽 **They do offer some bar snacks like sandwiches, soup, dressed crab, chicken liver pâté with red onion chutney, bangers and mash, and a pie of the day, but most of the not particularly cheap dishes are more restauranty: carpaccio of beef with beetroot, green bean and parmesan salad, salad of toasted goats cheese with a spicy roasted red pepper dressing, chargrilled chicken breast with honey and mustard roasted carrots, roasted partridge with beetroot and parsnip purée, fillet of bass with tiger prawns in a thai green curry sauce, and puddings.** *Starters/Snacks: £4.50 to £7.95. Main Courses: £9.95 to £16.95. Puddings: £4.95*

Free house ~ Licensee John Clennell ~ Real ale ~ Bar food (12-2, 6-9; all day April-Oct) ~ Restaurant ~ (01832) 280240 ~ Children welcome ~ Dogs allowed in bar ~ Open 12-11(midnight Sat)

Recommended by Dave Braisted, M and GR, Oliver and Sue Rowell, Justin and Emma King, Dr D J and Mrs S C Walker

---

Post Office address codings confusingly give the impression that some pubs are in Cambridgeshire, when they're really in Bedfordshire, Lincolnshire, Norfolk or Northamptonshire (which is where we list them).

ELY   TL5380   MAP 5

Fountain 🍺

Corner of Barton Square and Silver Street; CB7 4JF

Happily escaping tourists but close to cathedral

Simple yet genteel, this 19th-c corner pub is very neatly kept and has no music, fruit machines or even food. There's a good mix of chatty customers, old cartoons, local photographs, regional maps and mementoes of the neighbouring King's School on the elegant dark pink walls, and tied-back curtains hanging from gold-colour rails over the big windows. Above one fireplace is a stuffed pike in a case, and there are a few antlers dotted about. An extension at the back provides much needed additional seating. Adnams Bitter and Broadside, Woodfordes Wherry and a guest such as Fullers London Pride on handpump. Note the limited opening times below. More reports please.

🍽 **No food served.**

Free house ~ Licensees John and Judith Borland ~ Real ale ~ No credit cards ~ (01353) 663122 ~ Children welcome away from bar until 8pm ~ Dogs welcome ~ Open 5-11; 12-2, 6-11.30 Sat; 12-2, 7-10.30 Sun; closed weekday lunchtimes
Recommended by Mrs Hazel Rainer, the Didler, Dr Andy Wilkinson

FEN DITTON   TL4860   MAP 5

Ancient Shepherds

Off B1047 at Green End, The River signpost, just NE of Cambridge; CB5 8ST

Beamed and comfortable with coal fires and homely food

Although many customers come to this solidly beamed old pub to enjoy the generously served food, the friendly staff will make you just as welcome if you only want a pint and a chat. Perhaps the nicest room is the softly lit central lounge where you can't fail to be comfortable on one of the big fat dark red button-back leather settees or armchairs which are grouped round low dark wood tables. The warm coal fire and heavy drapes around the window seat with its big scatter cushions add to the cosiness. Above a black dado, the walls (and ceiling) are dark pink, and decorated with comic fox and policeman prints and little steeplechasing and equestrian ones. On the right the smallish more pubby bar, with its coal fire, serves Adnams Bitter and Greene King IPA and Old Speckled Hen on handpump, while on the left is a pleasant restaurant. The licensee's west highland terrier, Billie, might be around outside food service times.

🍽 As well as lunchtime filled baguettes, the well liked bar food includes soup, smoked salmon pâté, popular smoked haddock and spring onion fishcakes, wild mushroom lasagne, shepherd's pie, chicken breast baked with stilton in an asparagus sauce, venison mixed grill, and fillet of plaice stuffed with prawns in a parsley sauce. *Starters/Snacks: £4.50 to £6.95. Main Courses: £8.95 to £16.95. Puddings: £4.75*

Punch ~ Tenant J M Harrington ~ Real ale ~ Bar food (12-2(2.30 Sun), 6-9; not Sun or Mon evenings) ~ Restaurant ~ (01223) 293280 ~ Children allowed until 9pm ~ Dogs allowed in bar ~ Open 12-2.30, 6-11; 12-5 Sun; closed Sun and Mon evenings, 1 Jan
Recommended by Mrs M K Matthews, Alan and Eve Harding, R T and J C Moggridge, Gordon Tong, Mrs Carolyn Dixon, John Marsh, Catherine and Rob Dunster, John Saville

FORDHAM   TL6270   MAP 5

White Pheasant 🍷

A142 (may be bypassed now) at junction with B1102 to Burwell, north of Newmarket; Market Street; CB7 5LQ

Unassuming from outside but with simple, stylish rooms, a restaurant feel but with relaxed friendliness, and interesting food

You can be sure of a friendly welcome from the knowledgeable licensees at this bustling dining pub. It's open plan and light and airy with pastel paintwork, an attractive mix of well spaced big farmhouse tables and chairs on bare boards, some stripped brickwork, and a cheery log fire at one end. One or two steps lead down to a small similarly furnished but carpeted room; piped music. Brandon Rusty Bucket and Nethergate Azza Parrot on handpump, quite a few malt whiskies and a dozen carefully chosen wines (including champagne) by the glass served from the horseshoe bar that faces the entrance.

🍴 **Good, enjoyable food at lunchtime includes sizeable sandwiches such as minute steak or chargrilled merguez sausage, duck liver parfait with red onion marmalade, a deli board, ham with free-range eggs, various sausages and free-range chicken breast with barbecue sauce, bacon and cheddar, whilst evening choices might be organic goats cheese and sweet potato terrine with piperade dressing, a plate of local game, chargrilled sardines, aromatic duck breast with crispy duck hash, asian greens, rhubarb and crispy sage sauce, and roasted saddle of wild rabbit stuffed with spinach and onion jam, beetroot cakes and rosemary jus; puddings such as lemon grass panna cotta with coconut ice-cream and sweet chilli syrup, and warm chocolate mousse with rum raisin ice-cream; two- and three-course set Sunday lunches.** *Starters/Snacks: £4.95 to £8.95. Main Courses: £7.95 to £16.95. Puddings: £4.95 to £6.25*

Free house ~ Licensee Elizabeth Trangmar ~ Real ale ~ Bar food (12-2.30, 6-9.30(7-9 Sun)) ~ (01638) 720414 ~ Well behaved children welcome until 8pm ~ Open 12-3, 6-11; 12-3, 7-10 Sun; closed 26 Dec, 1 Jan

Recommended by John Saville, Ryta Lyndley, George Atkinson, B A Lord, Sally Anne and Peter Goodale

FOWLMERE
TL4245 MAP 5

Chequers 🍴 ♈
B1368; SG8 7SR

First-rate food in lovely coaching inn, comfortable bars, and lots of wines by the glass

The dining terrace here has smart new dark green furniture this year and it overlooks the flowers and shrub roses in the neatly kept floodlit garden. Inside this 16th-c country pub there's also been some gentle refurbishment with new comfortable brown leather banquettes and new dining chairs and tables. It's all very attractive and civilised and whilst many customers do come here for a special meal out, they do keep Adnams Bitter and a couple of guests like Adnams Spindrift and Sharps Doom Bar on handpump; also, 21 wines by the glass and 30 malt whiskies. Two comfortably furnished downstairs rooms are warmed by an open log fire, and upstairs there are beams, wall timbering and some interesting moulded plasterwork above the fireplace. The airy conservatory overlooks the terrace. Historic aeroplanes from Duxford fly over here during the summer months.

🍴 **As well as starters and light meals such as soup, moules normande, scallops with curly endive and mange tout salad with ginger dressing, and baked smoked haddock with chopped chives and sliced tomatoes and cheese, imaginative meals might include a fish of the day and daily specials, freshwater prawn and mango curry with wonton crisp and rice infused with cinnamon, cloves and sultanas, calves liver with wholegrain mustard mash, chargrilled leeks topped with pancetta and red wine and thyme gravy, roasted free-range chicken breast stuffed with basil and wrapped in parma ham, and steamed steak and kidney suet pudding with ale gravy; puddings like hot date sponge with hot toffee sauce or honeycomb cheesecake with ginger syrup.** *Starters/Snacks: £4.95 to £8.50. Main Courses: £10.95 to £22.95. Puddings: £4.95 to £6.00*

Free house ~ Licensee Paul Beaumont ~ Real ale ~ Bar food (12-2, 7-9.30(9 Sun) ~ Restaurant ~ (01763) 208369 ~ Children in conservatory only ~ Open 12-3, 6-11(7-10.30 Sun); closed 25 Dec, evenings 26 Dec and 1 Jan

Recommended by Mrs Jane Kingsbury, Roy Hoing, Virginia Williams, Alan and Eve Harding, David and Ruth Shillitoe, Peter and Jean Hoare, D E Ball, K S Whittaker

---

Pubs with outstanding views are listed at the back of the book.

HELPSTON

TF1205   MAP 5

Blue Bell ◀

Woodgate; off B1443; PE6 7ED

Bustling and friendly, fine choice of beers, and tasty food including good value lunches

Particularly well run by a knowledgeable, hard-working landlord and his cheerful staff, this bustling, friendly pub remains as popular as ever. Comfortable cushioned chairs and settles, plenty of pictures, ornaments, mementoes and cart-wheel displays give a homely atmosphere to the lounge, parlour and snug. The dining extension is light and airy with a sloping glass roof. Grainstore Cooking Bitter, Ten Fifty and (exclusive to this pub) John Clare, and a quickly changing guest such as Black Dog Mild, Exmoor Gold or Tydd Steam Swedish Blond on handpump and Weston's cider in summer; pool and TV. A sheltered and heated terrace has plastic seats and garden tables and an awning; pretty hanging baskets and wheelchair access.

🍴 **As well as a very good value two-course lunch (not Sunday), the popular food includes doorstep sandwiches, ploughman's, soup, sausage or home-cooked ham and eggs, smoked salmon salad, steak in ale pie, liver and bacon hotpot, lasagne, chicken breast in creamy tarragon sauce, smoked trout fishcakes, and steaks.** *Starters/Snacks: £3.95 to £6.95. Main Courses: £6.95 to £13.95. Puddings: £2.50 to £4.75*

Free house ~ Licensee Aubrey Sinclair Ball ~ Real ale ~ Bar food (12-2, 6.30-9; 12-4 Sun) ~ Restaurant ~ (01733) 252394 ~ Children in snug and dining areas but no under-16s after 9pm ~ Dogs allowed in bar ~ Open 11.30-2.30, 5(6 Sat)-11; 12-6 Sun; closed 1 Jan

Recommended by Michael and Jenny Back, Gordon and Margaret Ormondroyd, Ian Stafford, Eddie and Lynn Jarrett, Ben and Helen Ingram, Carolyn Browse

HEMINGFORD GREY

TL2970   MAP 5

Cock 🍽 🍷 ◀

Village signposted off A14 eastbound, and (via A1096 St Ives road) westbound; High Street; PE28 9BJ

Imaginative food in pretty pub, extensive wine list plus other drinks, bustling atmosphere, and smart restaurant

More seating, improved lighting and additional stone troughs and flowers have made the neat garden of this pretty little pub even more attractive. Inside, the traditional public bar on the left is still sensibly kept for drinkers only. There's an open woodburning stove on the raised hearth, bar stools, wall seats and a carver, steps that lead down to more seating below black beams, and Buntingford Highwayman IPA, Elgoods Black Dog, Nethergate Azza Parrot, and Wolf Golden Jackal on handpump, 16 wines by the glass and Weston's cider. In marked contrast, the stylishly simple spotless restaurant on the right – you must book to be sure of a table – has clattery pale bare boards, canary walls above a powder-blue dado, and another woodburning stove. There's a friendly, bustling atmosphere and a good mix of locals and visitors.

🍴 **As well as a very useful two- and three-course lunch menu (not Sunday), changing dishes might include sandwiches, soup, potted ham hock with fennel salad, duck parcel with sweet and sour cucumber, clam, back bacon and leek risotto, a fine choice of home-made sausages such as pork, spring onion and ginger with a selection of sauces and mash, prawn, squid and crayfish linguine with chilli and cucumber, slow-cooked pork belly, seared foie gras and rhubarb and red wine sauce, roast saddle of lamb with apricot, almond and raisin stuffing, puy lentils, goats cheese mousse and port sauce, and puddings such as crème brûlée and warm chocolate tart with chocolate sauce.** *Starters/Snacks: £4.00 to £7.00. Main Courses: £11.00 to £14.00*

Free house ~ Licensees Oliver Thain and Richard Bradley ~ Real ale ~ Bar food (12-2.30(3 Sun), 6.30-9(6.15-9.30 Fri and Sat; 8.30 Sun)) ~ Restaurant ~ (01480) 463609 ~ Children in restaurant only but must be over 5 in evening ~ Dogs allowed in bar ~ Open 11.30-3, 6-11; 12-4, 6.30-10.30 Sun; closed 26 Dec

Recommended by Michael Sargent, Christopher Turner, Howard and Margaret Buchanan, Gordon and Margaret Ormondroyd, Chris Bell, R T and J C Moggridge, Jim and Sheila Prideaux, Sally Anne and Peter Goodale, Barry Collett, Mrs B Barwick, Alison and Pete

HEYDON   TL4339   MAP 5

King William IV
Off A505 W of M11 junction 10; SG8 8PW

Rambling rooms with fascinating rustic jumble, quite a few vegetarian dishes on sizeable menu, and pretty garden

The rambling beamed rooms in this neatly kept dining pub are warmed by a winter log fire and filled with ploughshares, yokes and iron tools, cowbells, beer steins, samovars, brass or black wrought-iron lamps, copper-bound casks and milk ewers, harness, horsebrasses, and smith's bellows – as well as decorative plates, cut-glass and china ornaments. Adnams Best, Fullers London Pride, Greene King IPA and Timothy Taylors Landlord on handpump and helpful staff; piped music. There are teak seats and tables and outdoor heaters on the terrace as well as more seats in the pretty garden.

🍴 Well liked bar food includes filled ciabattas and paninis, quite a few vegetarian choices like goats cheese and mediterranean vegetable wellington with sunblush tomato and roasted garlic sauce or cauliflower and date tagine with tunisian pilau rice as well as home-made burgers, steak and kidney pudding, beer-battered cod, mixed chicken supreme filled with gorgonzola wrapped in parma ham on linguini with chorizo and sunblush tomatoes, game pie with bubble and squeak, and puddings such as apple and pear strudel and white chocolate and raspberry torte with a shot of tequila. *Starters/Snacks: £5.95 to £7.25. Main Courses: £10.95 to £17.95. Puddings: £5.95 to £6.95*

Free house ~ Licensee Elizabeth Nicholls ~ Real ale ~ Bar food (12-2(2.15 Sun), 6.30-9.30) ~ Restaurant ~ (01763) 838773 ~ Children over 12 in restaurant ~ Dogs allowed in bar ~ Open 12-3, 6(7 Sun)-11

Recommended by R T and J C Moggridge, Virginia Williams, M S Pizer, Richard Siebert, Mrs M K Matthews

HINXTON   TL4945   MAP 5

Red Lion
2 miles off M11 junction 9 northbound; take first exit off A11, A1301 N, then left turn into village – High Street; a little further from junction 10, via A505 E and A1301 S; CB10 1QY

Pink-washed and handy for Duxford and M11, friendly staff, and neat, big garden

With its twin gables and pink-washed walls, this carefully extended 16th-c inn is most attractive. The mainly open-plan beamed bar is bustling and convivial and has leather chesterfields on wooden floors, an old wall clock, a dark green fireplace, and Adnams Bitter, Greene King IPA, Woodfordes Wherry and a guest such as Nethergate Augustinian Ale on handpump, 12 wines by the glass, and Aspall's cider; there are some unusual foreign insects in glass cases. An informal dining area has high-backed settles and the smart restaurant is decorated with various pictures and assorted clocks. The neatly kept big garden has a pleasant terrace with picnic-sets, a dovecote and views of the village church. By the time this book is published they hope to have opened eight bedrooms.

🍴 As well as a popular monthly Pudding Club (warm chocolate brownie, poached apricot mille-feuille with brandy and cinnamon cream, rhubarb crème brûlée and so forth), the good bar food might include sandwiches, filled baguettes and baked potatoes, soup, chargrilled or cold ham with a free-range egg, spinach and cherry tomato lasagne with gorgonzola, steak and mushroom in ale pie, chicken breast stuffed with ham duxelle and wholegrain mustard sauce, mint-glazed lamb chops with rosemary and red wine reduction and fresh fish dishes. *Starters/Snacks: £3.95 to £6.50. Main Courses: £7.50 to £17.50. Puddings: £3.50 to £5.50*

Free house ~ Licensee Alex Clarke ~ Real ale ~ Bar food (12-2, 6.45-9; 12-2.30, 6.45-9.30 Fri and Sat; 12-2.30, 7-9 Sun) ~ Restaurant ~ (01799) 530601 ~ Well-behaved children welcome ~ Dogs allowed in bar ~ Open 11-3, 6-11; 12-4, 7-10.30 Sun; closed evenings 25 and 26 Dec and 1 Jan

Recommended by Charles Gysin, R T and J C Moggridge, David Cosham, Keith Widdowson, Mrs Hazel Rainer, Kevin Thorpe, Paul Humphreys, Anthony Barnes, Mrs Margo Finlay, Jörg Kasprowski

HUNTINGDON   TL2471   MAP 5

Old Bridge Hotel ★ ⑪ ♀ ⇌

1 High Street; ring road just off B1044 entering from easternmost A14 slip road; PE29 3TQ

Georgian hotel with smartly pubby bar, splendid range of drinks, and excellent food

In fine weather, this civilised ivy-covered Georgian hotel is just the place to be – right by the River Great Ouse with its own landing stage and tables on waterside terraces. Inside, the quietly chatty bar with its good log fire and comfortable sofas and low wooden tables on polished floorboards remains a relaxing place for a drink: Adnams Bitter, City of Cambridge Hobsons Choice, and a guest beer on handpump, 18 wines by the glass, ten sweet ones and two champagnes. Most customers are here though to enjoy the imaginative food served by excellent staff which can be eaten in the big airy Terrace (an indoor room, but with beautifully painted verdant murals suggesting the open air) or in the slightly more formal panelled restaurant. This is a very nice place to stay.

⑪ **Carefully presented, the modern dishes might include various nibbles, sandwiches (hot or cold), interesting soups, a daily changing terrine and pasta, thai squid salad with coriander, mint, cashews and lime, smoked sausage with pickled potato, poached egg and frisée salad, deep-fried haddock with tartare sauce and smashed peas, vegetable biryani with red pepper tikka, madai masala, lime pickle, cucumber raita and poppadom, roast saddle of wild boar with polenta and buttered spinach, corn-fed chicken breast with wild mushroom and potato cake, leeks and morel mushroom and cream sauce, steaks using Aberdeenshire beef and puddings such as sticky toffee pudding and vanilla panna cotta with rhubarb; there's also a two- and three-course set lunch (not Sunday). They do list some of their favourite suppliers.** *Starters/Snacks: £4.95 to £9.95. Main Courses: £9.95 to £25.00. Puddings: £5.50 to £7.50*

Huntsbridge ~ Licensee John Hoskins ~ Real ale ~ Bar food (12-2, 6.30-9.30) ~ Restaurant ~ (01480) 424300 ~ Children welcome ~ Dogs welcome ~ Open 11-11 ~ Bedrooms: £95B/£135B

Recommended by Bruce and Sharon Eden, Mrs Margo Finlay, Jörg Kasprowski, Michael Sargent, Leslie and Barbara Owen, Martin and Pauline Jennings, Jeremy King, Mrs Hazel Rainer, Michael Dandy, John and Helen Rushton, Mrs B Barwick

KEYSTON   TL0475   MAP 5

Pheasant ⑪ ♀

Just off A14 SE of Thrapston; village loop road, off B663; PE28 0RE

Essentially a restaurant but with a relaxed bar, highly thought-of modern food and excellent range of drinks

This most attractive long, low thatched dining pub is just the place for an excellent meal out but they do keep four real ales on handpump from breweries such as Adnams, Cottage, Grainstore and Nethergate. The immaculately kept spacious oak-beamed bar has a comfortably civilised atmosphere, open fires, simple wooden tables and chairs and country paintings on the pale walls; there are three distinct dining areas as well. 16 wines by the glass (plus eight sweet wines and two champagnes), and fine port and sherry; very good service. There are seats out in front of the building and on a back terrace.

⑪ **As well as daily specials, the delicious food might include chunky sandwiches, various nibbles like stuffed bell peppers or warm marinated olives, soup, braised pig cheeks with sauce gribiche and crisp pig's ear salad, local beef bresaola with spring onion and mustard dressing, line caught cod with puy lentils, salt cod ravioli and garlic greens, wild mushroom ragoût with poached morels and lemon butter sauce, calves liver with chorizo, roast tomato, basil and crème fraîche, brace of quail with creamed onions, onion rings and crisp potato, and puddings such as pineapple charlotte, pineapple carpaccio and lime sorbet, blackberry fool and chocolate pot with lemon polenta biscuits. They have helpful notes about some of their ingredients and list their preferred suppliers.** *Starters/Snacks: £5.00 to £6.00. Main Courses: £9.00 to £15.00. Puddings: £4.50 to £5.50*

Free house ~ Licensee Taffeta Scrimshaw ~ Real ale ~ Bar food (12-2.30, 6.30-9.30) ~ Restaurant ~ (01832) 710241 ~ Children welcome ~ Dogs allowed in bar ~ Open 12-11(till 6 on Sun); closed Sun evening and all day Mon

Recommended by Paul and Margaret Baker, J F M and M West, Michael Sargent, Ryta Lyndley, Oliver and Sue Rowell, M and GR, J C M Troughton

KIMBOLTON   TL0967   MAP 5

New Sun ♀

High Street; PE28 0HA

Several interesting bars and rooms, tapas menu plus other good food, and pleasant back garden

In a lovely village high street, this is a nice old pub. The cosiest room is perhaps the low-beamed front lounge with a couple of comfortable armchairs and a sofa beside the fireplace, standing timbers and exposed brickwork, and books, pottery and brasses. This leads into a narrower locals' bar with Wells & Youngs Bombardier and Eagle, and a weekly changing guest such as Hook Norton Old Hooky on handpump, and there's about a dozen wines (including champagne) by the glass; piped music and games machine. The dining room opens off here. The conservatory has doors opening on to the terrace where there are smart seats and tables under giant umbrellas. Do note that some of the nearby parking spaces have a 30-minute limit.

🍴 As well as lunchtime sandwiches, filled baked potatoes, home-cooked ham with a free-range egg and daily specials, the well liked food includes popular hot and cold tapas, king prawns in hot garlic and chilli oil, grilled goats cheese with local honey and parsnip crisp salad, caesar salad with or without chicken, home-made steak and kidney pudding, vegetable moussaka, chargrilled chicken breast with leek and bacon mash and burgundy braised baby onions, bass with champ potato cake, wilted spinach and pesto sauce, and puddings such as baked lemon tart, blood orange compote and crème fraîche and sticky toffee pudding with butterscotch sauce and banana ice-cream; roast Sunday lunch.
Starters/Snacks: £3.25 to £6.25. Main Courses: £9.25 to £21.00. Puddings: £3.75 to £6.25

Charles Wells ~ Lease Stephen and Elaine Rogers ~ Real ale ~ Bar food (12-2.15(2.30 Sun), 7-9.30; not Sun or Mon evenings) ~ Restaurant ~ (01480) 860052 ~ Children allowed in front bar and eating areas ~ Dogs allowed in bar ~ Open 11.30-2.30, 6-11; 12-10.30 Sun
Recommended by Peter Dandy, Charles Mear, Mrs Margo Finlay, Jörg Kasprowski

LITTLE WILBRAHAM   TL5458   MAP 5

Hole in the Wall 🍽 ♀ 🍺

Taking Stow cum Quy turn off A14, turn off A1303 Newmarket Road at The Wilbrahams signpost, then right at Little Wilbraham signpost; High Street; CB1 5JY

Charming tucked-away dining pub – quite a find

Run by the friendly and thoughtful team who put the Lough Pool over in Herefordshire so firmly on our map, this interesting place scores highly in every way. Whatever your drinks tastes, you'll be pleased: well kept Woodfordes Wherry and Nelsons Revenge and a changing guest like Isle of Ely Fenland Rabbit Poacher on handpump, a good choice of wines by the glass, unusual soft drinks such as pomegranate and elderflower pressé. Service is friendly and unfailingly helpful. The carpeted ochre-walled bar on the right is a cosy place for a robust no-nonsense pub lunch, with its logs burning in the big brick fireplace, 15th-c beams and timbers, snug little window seats and other mixed seating around scrubbed kitchen tables. For more of an occasion, either the similar middle room (with another fire in its open range) or the rather plusher main dining room (yet another fire here) fill the bill well. The neat side garden has good teak furniture, and a little verandah. It's a very quiet hamlet, with an interesting walk to nearby unspoilt Little Wilbraham Fen.

🍴 From a modern menu, the beautifully presented food might include their lovely home-made bread and lunchtime specials such as ham and cheese ploughman's or pork sausages with dijon mustard mash, but the emphasis is on the more refined dishes like asparagus with poached organic salmon and a watercress and citrus butter sauce, carpaccio of aberdeen angus beef with braised leek and shallot salad, risotto of broad beans with garlic and globe artichoke velouté, free-range pork cheek slow cooked in local apple juice, cornish plaice in breadcrumbs with sea salt and rosemary potato wedges and a crayfish tail and spinach salad, baked stuffed aubergine with courgettes, pine nuts, basil and a chilled gazpacho dressing, leg of lamb with pea purée, anya potatoes, and a roast garlic cream sauce, and puddings such as set vanilla cream with poached rhubarb and an orange tuile biscuit and pear, elderflower and ginger crumble with locally milled oats and honeycomb ice-cream. *Starters/Snacks: £3.75 to £8.50. Main Courses: £11.00 to £16.50. Puddings: £5.75*

Free house ~ Licensees Stephen Bull, Jenny Chapman and Chris Leeton ~ Real ale ~ Bar food ~ (01223) 812282 ~ Well behaved children welcome ~ Dogs allowed in bar ~ Open 11.30-3, 6.30-11; closed Sun evening, all day Mon

Recommended by K C Watson, P and D Carpenter, Mark Farrington, Dr Phil Putwain

MADINGLEY   TL3960   MAP 5

Three Horseshoes 🍽 🍷

Off A1303 W of Cambridge; High Street; CB3 8AB

Sophisticated italian cooking in civilised dining pub, outstanding wine list, and efficient service

The italian cooking in this civilised thatched dining pub is so popular that you must book to be sure of a table. The pleasantly relaxed little airy bar (which can be a bit of a crush at busy times) has an open fire, simple wooden tables and chairs on bare floorboards, stools at the bar counter and pictures on green walls; there's also a pretty conservatory restaurant. Adnams Bitter and a guest such as City of Cambridge Boathouse Bitter handpump and an outstanding wine list with over 16 by the glass, plus sweet wines and ports. More reports please.

🍽 Carefully prepared, the good (if not cheap) food might include nibbles like chicken liver crostini, marcona almonds and warm amalfi olives, seared and peppered tuna carpaccio with shaved fennel, celery, radish and parsley salad, gnocchi with beef ragu, courgette risotto with mint, marjoram, garlic, crème fraîche, wine and parmesan, salmon with brown shrimps, clams and mussels with swiss chard, borlotti beans, tomato, garlic and rosemary, and puddings like chocolate nemesis with stracciatella ice-cream and panna cotta with prunes in grappa; there's usually a good value two- and three-course set menu. *Starters/Snacks: £7.00 to £9.00. Main Courses: £9.00 to £23.00. Puddings: £6.00 to £7.00*

Free house ~ Licensee Richard Stokes ~ Real ale ~ Bar food (12-2, 7-9; 12-2.30, 6.30-9.30 Sat, 12-2.30, 6-8 Sun) ~ Restaurant ~ (01954) 210221 ~ Children welcome ~ Open 11.30-3, 6-11; 12-3, 7-11 Sun; closed 1 and 2 Jan

Recommended by Dave Braisted, Sally Anne and Peter Goodale, B and M Kendall, John and Joan Calvert, Michael Dandy

NEWTON   TL4349   MAP 5

Queens Head ★ 🍺 £

2.5 miles from M11 junction 11; A10 towards Royston, then left on to B1368; CB2 5PG

Lovely traditional old pub in the same family for many years, simple popular food and fair choice of drinks

For those who like their pubs traditional, comfortably worn and definitely low key, this is a gem. It's been run by the same genuinely welcoming family for three generations and has changed little during that time. The peaceful main bar has a low ceiling and crooked beams, bare wooden benches and seats built into the cream walls, paintings, and bow windows. A curved high-backed settle stands on yellow tiles, a loudly ticking clock marks the unchanging time, and a lovely big log fire crackles warmly. The little carpeted saloon is similar but even cosier. Adnams Bitter and Broadside and seasonal guest tapped from the cask, farm cider and several wines by the glass. Darts, shove-ha'penny, table skittles, dominoes, cribbage and nine men's morris. There are seats in front of the pub, with its vine trellis. This is a popular place so you will need to get here early for a seat during peak times, and there may be a queue of people waiting for the doors to open on a Sunday.

🍴 **A limited range of basic but well liked food, which comes in hearty and very fairly priced helpings: toast and beef dripping, lunchtime sandwiches (including things like banana with sugar and lemon or herb and garlic), a mug of their famous home-made soup and filled Aga-baked potatoes; evening and Sunday lunchtime plates of excellent cold meat, smoked salmon, cheeses and pâté.** *Starters/Snacks: £2.90 to £5.80*

Free house ~ Licensees David and Robert Short ~ Real ale ~ Bar food (12-2.15, 7-9.30) ~ No credit cards ~ (01223) 870436 ~ Very well behaved children welcome in games room ~ Dogs welcome ~ Open 11.30-2.30, 6-11; 12-2.30, 7-10.30 Sun; closed 25 and 26 Dec

Recommended by Conor McGaughey, Mr and Mrs W Mills, Steve Williamson, Louise Gibbons, C Galloway, R T and J C Moggridge, Mrs Margo Finlay, Jörg Kasprowski, Tom and Ruth Rees, Pat and Tony Martin, Tim Maddison

PETERBOROUGH   TL1899   MAP 5

Brewery Tap 🍺 £

Opposite Queensgate car park; PE1 2AA

Fantastic range of real ales including its own brews and popular thai food in huge conversion of old labour exchange

There's a vast two-storey-high glass wall in this striking modern conversion of an old labour exchange that divides the bar and the brewery, giving fascinating views of the massive copper-banded stainless brewing vessels. From here they produce their own Oakham beers (Bishops Farewell, JHB, and White Dwarf) but also keep nine guests from thoughtfully chosen countrywide brewers as well; also, a good number of bottled belgian beers and quite a few wines by the glass. There's an easy going relaxed feel to the open-plan contemporary interior, with an expanse of light wood and stone floors for drinkers and blue-painted iron pillars holding up a steel-corded mezzanine level. It's stylishly lit by a giant suspended steel ring with bulbs running around the rim, and steel-meshed wall lights. A band of chequered floor tiles traces the path of the long sculpted light wood bar counter, which is boldly backed by an impressive display of bottles in a ceiling-high wall of wooden cubes. A sofa seating area downstairs provides a comfortable corner for a surprisingly mixed bunch of customers from young to old; there's a big screen TV for sporting events, piped music and games machines and DJs or live bands at the weekends. It gets very busy in the evening. The pub is owned by the same people as Charters (see below).

🍴 **The thai food is very good and extremely popular and runs from snacks such as chicken satay or tempura vegetables to soups like aromatic crispy duck noodle or tom yum and to main courses such as curries, noodle and rice dishes, salads and stir fries.** *Starters/Snacks: £1.99 to £3.99. Main Courses: £5.99 to £6.99. Puddings: £3.99*

Own brew ~ Licensee Jessica Loock ~ Real ale ~ Bar food (12-2.30, 6-9.30; 12-10.30 Fri, Sat) ~ Restaurant ~ (01733) 358500 ~ Children welcome until 9pm ~ Dogs allowed in bar ~ Two live bands per month ~ Open 12-11(till 2am, Fri and Sat); closed 25 and 26 Dec, 1 Jan

Recommended by Pat and Tony Martin, Ben and Helen Ingram, the Didler, Mike and Sue Loseby, Ian Stafford, Joe Green, Rona Murdoch

Charters 🍺 £

Town Bridge, S side; PE1 1FP

Remarkable conversion of dutch grain barge with impressive real ales and good value oriental-style food

As well as having one of the biggest pub gardens in the city, this unusual place was once a barge working on the rivers and canals of Holland, Belgium and Germany. It is now moored on the River Nene and houses a sizeable timbered bar on the lower deck and an oriental restaurant on the upper deck. Old wooden tables and pews provide plenty of seating, and there's an impressive range of real ales including four Oakham beers and around nine quickly changing guests from an interesting variety of brewers. They also keep around 30 foreign bottled beers, and hold regular beer festivals; piped music, games machines and darts. More reports please.

⌂ Good value oriental-style food includes filled pitta bread, various starters like tempura prawns, spring rolls or dim sum. *Starters/Snacks: £3.00 to £5.00. Main Courses: £5.00 to £8.00. Puddings: £2.00 to £5.00*

Free house ~ Licensee Paul Hook ~ Real ale ~ Bar food (12-2.30, 5.30-10.30) ~ Restaurant ~ (01733) 315700 ~ Children welcome ~ Dogs allowed in bar ~ Live bands Fri and Sat after 11pm ~ Open 12-11(later Fri, Sat; 10.30 Sun); closed 25 and 26 Dec, 1 Jan

Recommended by Joe Green, the Didler, Ben and Helen Ingram, Barry Collett, Rona Murdoch

REACH   TL5666   MAP 5
Dyke's End 🍺

From B1102 E of A14/A1103 junction, follow signpost to Swaffham Prior and Upware – keep on through Swaffham Prior (Reach signposted from there); Fair Green; CB5 0JD

Candlelit rooms in former farmhouse, enjoyable food, and own-brewed beer

Built around a 17th-c farmhouse, this popular pub is next to the church and the charming village green. A high-backed winged settle screens off the door and the simply decorated ochre-walled bar has stripped heavy pine tables and pale kitchen chairs on dark boards and one or two rugs. In a panelled section on the left are a few rather smarter dining tables, and on the right there's a step down to a red-carpeted part with the small red-walled servery and sensibly placed darts at the back. All the tables have lit candles in earthenware bottles, and there may be a big bowl of lilies to brighten up the serving counter. As well as their own-brewed Devils Dyke Bitter, No 7 Pale Ale and No 8 Ale, they keep a couple of guests such as Adnams Bitter and Milton Pegasus on handpump alongside a decent wine list, and Old Rosie cider. There are picnic-sets under big green canvas parasols out in front on the grass and Banger and Butter, the dachshunds, may have pride of place on a rug spread out on the lawn. The very close relationship which the pub has with the village does mean that when it's busy with cheerful regulars at the weekend, outsiders may feel a little left out.

⌂ Tasty bar food includes sandwiches and filled baked potatoes, soup, local sausages with onion gravy, home-cooked ham and egg, pasta with wild mushrooms and parmesan, rack of lamb with parsley crust, smoked haddock with spinach and poached egg, and puddings like rich chocolate pot and zesty lemon posset; best to book at weekends. *Starters/Snacks: £6.00 to £9.00. Main Courses: £9.00 to £15.00. Puddings: £5.00 to £6.50*

Free house ~ Licensee Simon Owers ~ Real ale ~ Bar food (not Sun evening or Mon lunchtime) ~ Restaurant ~ (01638) 743816 ~ Children allowed but no small children after 7.30pm ~ Dogs allowed in bar ~ Folk 1st and 3rd Sun ~ Open 12-2.30, 6-11; 12-11(10.30 Sun) Sat; closed Mon lunchtime

Recommended by Bettye Reynolds, Sally Anne and Peter Goodale, M and GR, Chris Bell, Marion and Bill Cross, R T and J C Moggridge, John Saville, P and D Carpenter, Ryta Lyndley, John and Elisabeth Cox

ST NEOTS   TL1859   MAP 5
Chequers
St Marys Street, Eynesbury (B1043 S of centre); PE19 2TA

Pleasant old pub with a fair choice of food and drink

This 16th-c village pub is run by friendly people. The small carpeted bar has lots of traditional character with its dark heavy beams, an appealing mix of seats including an unusually shaped rocking chair, and a log fire in a big inglenook fireplace. Archers IPA and Thwaites Original on handpump. The busy communicating back restaurant area has attractively set tables, fresh flowers throughout, and rugs on its brick floor; piped music. There are tables out in the sheltered garden behind and more on a terrace.

⌂ Tasty bar food includes sandwiches, soup, nachos with spicy tomato, sour cream, guacamole and melted cheese, salmon fishcakes with sweet chilli sauce, vegetable lasagne, steak and kidney pie, local sausages with onion gravy, beer-battered haddock, and rogan josh lamb shank. Two-course OAP lunch weekdays (not Mon). *Starters/Snacks: £4.25 to £6.95. Main Courses: £9.25 to £10.95. Puddings: £4.50 to £5.75*

Free house ~ Licensee Stephen Lamb ~ Real ale ~ Bar food (not Sun evening or Mon) ~ Restaurant ~ (01480) 472116 ~ Children in restaurant ~ Open 12-2.30, 6.30-11; 12-2.30 Sun; closed Sun evening and all day Mon

Recommended by Mrs Jane Kingsbury, Michael Dandy, R T and J C Moggridge

STILTON   TL1689   MAP 5

Bell (🍴) 🍷 🛏

High Street; village signposted from A1 S of Peterborough; PE7 3RA

Fine coaching inn with several civilised rooms including a residents' bar, well liked food, and very pretty courtyard

Even though this is a civilised and elegant 17th-c coaching inn, the two neatly kept bars have an informal and relaxed atmosphere and a good mix of both locals and visitors. There are bow windows, sturdy upright wooden seats on flagstone floors as well as plush button-back built-in banquettes, and a good big log fire in one handsome stone fireplace; one bar has a large cheese press. The partly stripped walls have big prints of sailing and winter coaching scenes, and there's a giant pair of blacksmith's bellows hanging in the middle of the front bar. Fullers London Pride, Greene King IPA and Abbot, Oakham JHB and a changing guest such as Crouch Vale Brewers Gold or Hop Back Crop Circle on handpump or tapped from the cask and a dozen wines by the glass. Also, a bistro, restaurant and residents' bar. Through the fine coach arch is a very pretty sheltered courtyard with tables, and a well which dates back to Roman times. Super breakfasts.

🍴 **Very good bistro-style food includes sandwiches, stilton, roast parsnip and apple soup, potted crab and brown shrimp with a caper and dijon mustard mayonnaise, pigeon and rabbit pâté with cumberland jam, chickpea, spinach and feta cheese bake with herb oat topping, corn-fed chicken with bacon dauphinoise potatoes and stilton and mushroom sauce, steamed fillet of salmon on roast pumpkin and sweet potato with lemon butter sauce, pork belly with sage and onion mash, braised red cabbage and caramelised apple jus, and puddings such as sticky toffee pudding with toffee sauce and clotted cream and classic lemon tart.** *Starters/Snacks: £3.25 to £7.95. Main Courses: £9.75 to £17.95. Puddings: £4.75*

Free house ~ Licensee Liam McGivern ~ Real ale ~ Bar food (12-2.15, 6-9.30; 12-2.30, 7-9 Sun) ~ Restaurant ~ (01733) 241066 ~ Children allowed away from main bar ~ Open 12-2.30(3 Sat), 6-11(midnight Fri and Sat); 12-3, 7-11 Sun; closed 25 and 26 Dec, 1 Jan ~ Bedrooms: £73.50B/£100.50B

Recommended by Mrs Hazel Rainer, John Robertson, Jerry Brown, John Saville, Paul and Marion Watts, Martin and Karen Wake, Dr A McCormick, John Roots, Paul Humphreys, Pete Coxon

SUTTON GAULT   TL4279   MAP 5

Anchor (🍴) 🍷

Village signed off B1381 in Sutton; CB6 2BD
CAMBRIDGESHIRE DINING PUB OF THE YEAR

Tucked away inn with charming candlelit rooms, good modern food, and thoughtful wine list

Although we had worried about this charming pub becoming rather too restauranty, readers have been quick to point out that although there is quite an emphasis on the particularly good modern cooking, drinkers are warmly welcomed and the place still has the layout and informal atmosphere of a pub. City of Cambridge Hobsons Choice or Boathouse Bitter tapped from the cask and a dozen wines by the glass (including champagne); meticulous but welcoming service. The four heavily timbered rooms are stylishly simple with two log fires, antique settles and well spaced candlelit scrubbed pine tables on gently undulating old floors, and good lithographs and big prints on the walls. There are nice walks along the high embankment by the river and the bird-watching is said to be good. Seats outside.

▥ As well as a very reasonably priced two- and three-course weekly set lunch menu, the first-class food might include soup, grilled dates wrapped in bacon in a mild grain mustard cream sauce, thai crab salad with sweet chilli dressing, baked field mushroom topped with chestnut stuffing and vintage cheddar, local sausages with rich onion gravy, fillet of cod topped with welsh rarebit on saffron mash and creamed leeks with roasted red pepper sauce, moroccan-style chicken tagine with couscous, gingerbread stuffed pork tenderloin wrapped in parma ham, and puddings such as warm double chocolate brownie with vanilla ice-cream and mulled wine poached pear in vanilla and honey rice pudding. *Starters/Snacks: £4.95 to £7.00. Main Courses: £9.50 to £18.50. Puddings: £4.95 to £6.00*

Free house ~ Licensees Carlene Bunten and Adam Pickup ~ Real ale ~ Bar food (12-2, 7-9 (6.30-9.30 Sat evening; 6.30-8.30 Sun evening)) ~ (01353) 778537 ~ Children welcome ~ Open 12-2.30, 7-10(6.30-11 Sat); 12-3, 6.30-10 Sun ~ Bedrooms: £59.50S/£75(£79.50S)(£115B)

Recommended by John Wooll, Sally Anne and Peter Goodale, Stephen Woad, Anthony Longden, John Saville, M and GR, Mike and Shelley Woodroffe, David Johnson, Ryta Lyndley, Michael Jefferson

THRIPLOW

TL4346   MAP 5

Green Man

3 miles from M11 junction 10; A505 towards Royston, then first right; Lower Street; SG8 7RJ

Comfortable and cheery with homely food and changing ales

You can't really miss this Victorian pub as the exterior is painted a striking dark blue – the window boxes and potted plants look particularly nice against this strong background. It's comfortably laid out with modern tables and attractive high-backed dining chairs and pews, and there are some small pictures on deeply coloured walls; two arches lead through to a restaurant on the left. Four regularly changing real ales are likely to be from brewers such Cottage, Eccleshall, Oldershaw and Nethergate; darts. There are tables and an outdoor heater outside. The pub is handy for Duxford.

▥ Hearty helpings of homely bar food served by friendly staff include lunchtime baguettes, home-made burger and sausage and mash, evening chicken, duck, salmon or stuffed pepper with a choice of sauces, and daily specials like pork loin with cider gravy or roast lamb shoulder with minted gravy. *Starters/Snacks: £5.00 to £7.00. Main Courses: £7.00 to £14.50. Puddings: £4.50 to £5.50*

Free house ~ Licensee Ian Parr ~ Real ale ~ Bar food (Sun evening or Mon) ~ (01763) 208855 ~ Children welcome away from the bar ~ Open 12-3, 6-11; closed Sun evening, all day Mon

Recommended by Christine and Phil Young, KC, Paul Humphreys, Stan Edwards, Mr and Mrs John Taylor, Gerry and Rosemary Dobson, Louise Gibbons

LUCKY DIP

Besides the fully inspected pubs, you might like to try these Lucky Dips recommended to us and described by readers (if you do, please send us reports: feedback@thegoodpubguide.co.uk).

ALWALTON [TL1396]
Cuckoo PE7 3UP [Oundle Rd, just off A1 at A605 junction]: Attractively refurbished well divided Vintage Inn with well kept beer, good wine choice, food all day, some nice cosy corners *(Gordon and Margaret Ormondroyd)*
ARRINGTON [TL3250]
☆ *Hardwicke Arms* SG8 0AH [Ermine Way (A1198)]: Handsome 18th-c coaching inn with 13th-c origins and 1792 work by Sir John Soane, enjoyable food from sandwiches and up-to-date snacks to game and fish, Greene King IPA and two interesting guest beers, good friendly service, dark-panelled dining room, huge central fireplace, daily papers; piped music; 12 bedrooms, handy for

Wimpole Hall, open all day *(LYM, Michael Dandy, Marion and Bill Cross)*
BABRAHAM [TL5150]
☆ *George* CB2 4AG [High St; just off A1307]: Restaurantly beamed and timbered dining pub, interesting and good value if not cheap food from lunchtime ciabattas up, friendly waitresses, warm relaxed atmosphere, comfortably refurbished lounge and attractive dining areas; heated terrace tables, nice setting on quiet road *(Mrs P J Pearce, David Rule)*
BARRINGTON [TL3849]
Royal Oak CB2 5RZ [turn off A10 about 3.75 miles SW of M11 junction 11, in Foxton; West Green]: Rambling thatched Tudor pub

with tables out overlooking classic village green, heavy low beams and timbers, mixed furnishings inc leather sofa, friendly helpful service, enjoyable if not cheap food from ciabattas to steak, children's helpings, Adnams, Greene King IPA and Morlands Original and Wells & Youngs Special, good coffee, light and airy dining conservatory; children welcome, open all day Sun *(Michael Dandy, LYM)*

BOURN [TL3256]

Willow Tree CB3 7SQ [High St]: Attractively fitted out dining pub with good unpretentious food, friendly efficient staff, good wines by the glass and soft drinks choice, Black Sheep, Fullers London Pride, Greene King IPA and Shepherd Neame Spitfire, log fire, medley of furnishings from plain pine tables and chairs to leather sofas on tiled floors; children welcome, back decking and play area *(Richard Atherton, John Wooll, Michael Dandy)*

BOXWORTH [TL3464]

☆ *Golden Ball* CB3 8LY [High St]: Attractive partly thatched building, open-plan contemporary bar with pine tables, three-part restaurant in original core, was under serious consideration for a main entry but changing management as we go to press – has had friendly helpful staff, enjoyable generous food from sandwiches and interesting light dishes up, reasonably priced wines, Wells & Youngs ales, good coffee; piped music; nice garden and heated terrace, pastures behind, 11 good quiet bedrooms in adjacent block *(J Jennings, Bruce and Sharon Eden, Michael Dandy, BB)*

BUCKDEN [TL1967]

☆ *Lion* PE19 5XA [High St]: Partly 15th-c coaching inn, black beams and big inglenook log fire in airy and civilised bow-windowed entrance bar with plush bucket seats, wing armchairs and settees, decent bar food inc good value lunchtime sandwiches, good choice of wines, Greene King ales, friendly staff, no music or machines, panelled back restaurant beyond latticed window partition; children welcome, bedrooms *(Michael Dandy, BB, Gerry and Rosemary Dobson, Nigel and Sue Foster)*

CAMBRIDGE [TL4458]

Anchor CB3 9EL [Silver St]: Well laid out if touristy pub in beautiful riverside position by a punting station, fine river views from upper bar and suntrap terrace, well kept beer, bar lunches from sandwiches up, evening baguettes; children in eating areas, open all day *(LYM, Ian and Jane Haslock)*

Bath CB2 3QN [Bene't St]: Unpretentious panelled pub with Black Sheep and Greene King, sensibly priced food (as Eagle next door); sports TV, piped music, games machine *(Giles and Annie Francis, Michael Dandy)*

Burleigh Arms CB5 8EG [Newmarket Rd]: Two well furnished bars, good food choice, prompt service, good wines by the glass; terrace *(John Marsh)*

Castle CB3 0AJ [Castle St]: Large airy bare-boards bar, several simple and pleasantly

decorated rooms, full Adnams ale range and lots of guest beers, wide range of good value quick pubby food from sandwiches up, friendly staff, peaceful upstairs (downstairs can be noisy, with piped pop music – live jazz Sun night); picnic-sets in good walled back courtyard *(the Didler, Michael Dandy)*

Clarendon Arms CB1 1JX [Clarendon St]: Partly flagstoned, with interesting wall hangings and other collectables, friendly attentive service, bustling local atmosphere, Greene King ales, reasonably priced food, carpeted dining area, books and daily papers, darts, cribbage; piped music, TV; simple good value bedrooms, open all day *(P and D Carpenter, Tony and Jill Radnor, Michael Dandy, John Marsh)*

☆ *Eagle* CB2 3QN [Bene't Street]: The star is for this rambling and interesting ancient building's striking architectural features (even one ceiling left unpainted since World War II to preserve airmen's signatures worked in with Zippo lighters, candle smoke and lipstick; Greene King ales, bar food; attractive cobbled and galleried courtyard, open all day *(John Saville, Peter and Pat Frogley, Ian and Jane Haslock, Barry Collett, Giles and Annie Francis, Simon Watkins, the Didler, Michael Dandy, D P and M A Miles, LYM, Catherine and Rob Dunster)*

Fleur CB4 1JD [Humberstone Rd]: Reopened (after long closure) as contemporary bar and bistro, reasonably priced food from mezze and wraps up, stylish dark furniture, pale boards and pastel walls; nice terrace, open all day *(anon)*

Flying Pig CB2 1LQ [Hills Rd]: Individual small local with pig emblems everywhere, young friendly staff, well kept Adnams, Fullers London Pride and Greene King, daily papers, back games room with pool; eclectic piped music, seats outside front and back *(Colin McKerrow, Jerry Brown)*

Green Dragon CB4 1NZ [Water St, Chesterton]: Attractive late medieval beamed and timber-framed building, well kept Everards Tiger and Greene King ales, substantial bargain basic food all day, comfortable linked areas, huge inglenook fireplace with secondhand books and videos; waterside green *(Catherine and Rob Dunster)*

☆ *Kingston Arms* CB1 2NU [Kingston St]: Well kept interesting changing ales from a dozen or so handpumps, enjoyable lunchtime food freshly made from good ingredients, companionably big plain tables and basic seating, thriving chatty largely studenty atmosphere, good choice of wines by the glass, friendly service, no music or children inside, two internet points; small pretty back yard, torch-lit, heated and partly covered, open all day Fri-Sun *(James Crouchman, BB, Jerry Brown)*

Mill CB2 1RX [Mill Lane]: Sturdy scrubbed wooden tables and high-backed settles, short choice of enjoyable sensibly priced lunchtime food, quick pleasant service, several well kept ales, farm cider; piped music; children in eating area, open all day, overlooks mill pond where punts can be hired – very popular waterside garden *(John Wooll, LYM)*

Mitre CB2 1UF [Bridge St, opp St Johns Coll]: Welcoming M&B pub with soft lighting and old-fashioned tavern décor, tasty bargain food, friendly service, well priced wines by the glass, Wadworths 6X and Wells & Youngs, farm cider, log-effect fire *(Michael Dandy, Maggie Atherton)*

☆ *Old Spring* CB4 1HB [Ferry Path; car park on Chesterton Rd]: Extended Victorian pub, roomy and airy, with smartly old-fashioned scrubbed-wood décor, bare boards, gas lighting, lots of old pictures, enjoyable food inc enterprising dishes and Sun roasts, quick pleasant service, well kept Greene King IPA and Abbot, good coffee and choice of wines by the glass, two log fires, long back conservatory; no under-21s evenings; large heated well planted terrace, summer barbecues *(Simon Watkins, LYM, Keith and Janet Morris, John Wooll)*

Pickerel CB3 0AF [Magdelene St]: Nicely old-fashioned low-beamed local with welcoming staff, well kept ales, limited good value lunchtime food, good choice of wines by the glass; heated courtyard *(Tony and Glenys Dyer, P and D Carpenter)*

Punter CB3 0AE [Pound Hill]: Former Rose & Crown, Town & Gown, Rope & Twine then Sino Tap, now stylishly reworked as dining pub with enterprising food from burgers to good changing continental dishes, prompt friendly service, good choice of wines by the glass, real ale, continental lagers, Addlestone's cider, leather sofas as well as tables and chairs, log fire, several areas inc adjoining barn; courtyard *(P and D Carpenter)*

CASTOR [TL1298]

Prince of Wales Feathers PE5 7AL [off A47]: Cheerful stone-built local with well kept Woodfordes and interesting guest beers, landlady doing limited choice of good lunchtime food (not Tues or Sun), farm cider and perry, darts, dominoes, pool, friendly setter called Maddy; games machine, Sat live music; children welcome, garden tables, open all day *(Ian Stafford)*

CHITTERING [TL4969]

Travellers Rest CB25 9PH [Ely Rd (A10)]: Roomy open-plan roadside dining pub, neat and comfortable, friendly helpful staff, wide choice of good generous fresh food from filled rolls to Sun carvery, proper coffee, family area, spotless lavatories; may be soft piped music; easy wheelchair access, picnic-sets among fruit trees behind, well fitted new bedroom block *(Mr and Mrs A H Young, BB, P M Newsome)*

CLAYHITHE [TL5064]

☆ *Bridge Hotel* CB5 9HZ [Clayhithe Rd]: Popular Chef & Brewer dining pub with friendly staff, plenty of tables (even so, get there early), small bar area, beams and timbers; picturesque spot by River Cam with

pretty waterside garden, comfortable bedroom extension *(LYM, Dr and Mrs T C Dann, Simon Watkins, Paul Humphreys)*

CONINGTON [TL3266]

☆ *White Swan* CB3 8LN [signed off A14 (was A604) Cambridge—Huntingdon; Elsworth Rd]: Attractive and quietly placed Victorian country local with friendly helpful staff, fairly priced pubby food from baps up, well kept Batemans XXXB and Greene King ales, cheerful simple bar, neat eating areas; good big front garden with terrace, play area and play house, open all day *(Michael Dandy, Keith and Janet Morris, David Campbell, Vicki McLean)*

CROYDON [TL3149]

☆ *Queen Adelaide* SG8 0DN [off A1198 or B1042; High St]: Spreading open-plan turkey-carpeted local with wide range of enjoyable food inc Mon-Weds OAP lunches, friendly prompt service, real ales such as Church End and Greene King, lots of spirits, big low-beamed main area with standing timbers dividing off part with settees, banquettes and stools, games area with pool, conservatory extension; faint piped music (even in gents' – a shrine to Marilyn Monroe), TV, machines; heated terrace with smokers' shelter, lawn with play area, new bedrooms, open all day Fri-Sun *(R T and J C Moggridge, Michael Dandy, Simon Watkins, P and D Carpenter, BB)*

DUXFORD [TL4746]

John Barleycorn CB2 4PP [handy for M11 junction 10; signed off A505 E at Volvo junction]: Thatch, shutters, low beams, charming old-world furnishings, prints and china, gentle lighting, good generous reasonably priced food from open sandwiches up all day (cooked to order, so may be a wait), nice staff, well kept Greene King IPA and Abbot, decent wines; may be piped music; tables out among flowers, open all day, pleasantly simple beamed bedrooms *(Philip Denton, LYM)*

EATON SOCON [TL1658]

Crown PE19 8EN [Gt North Rd (B4128, nr A1/A428 interchange)]: Chef & Brewer with linked low-beamed areas, moderately priced food from sandwiches and baked potatoes up, Courage Directors, Theakstons and Wells & Youngs Bombardier, good coffee, two coal-effect gas fires; games machine, piped music; garden, comfortable bedroom block *(Michael Dandy)*

☆ *White Horse* PE19 8EL [Gt North Rd (B4128)]: Rambling, comfortable and interestingly furnished low-beamed rooms dating from 13th c, nice high-backed traditional settles around big inglenook log fire in end room, relaxing atmosphere, good value food from baked potatoes up, good value Sun lunch, Flowers Original, Greene King and Fullers London Pride, decent wines, quick friendly service, daily papers, pub games; play area in back garden, children in eating areas, refurbished bedrooms, open all day Fri-Sun *(Michael Dandy, Marion and Bill Cross, LYM)*

ELSWORTH [TL3163]

Poacher CB3 8JS [Brockley Rd]: 17th-c thatched and beamed pub with pews, settles, bare boards and a couple of sofas, lots of carving inc deftly done birds on bar front, nice pictures, Black Sheep, Greene King IPA, Shepherd Neame Spitfire and Wells & Youngs Bombardier, cheerful staff, popular traditional food from baguettes up; piped music; plenty of tables in pretty garden with play area and barbecues, good walks *(Keith and Janet Morris, BB, Simon Watkins, Michael Dandy)*

ELTISLEY [TL2759]

☆ ***Eltisley*** PE19 6TG [signed off A428; The Green]: Former Leeds Arms, reopened under new name by people from Hare & Hounds, Old Warden (good Beds dining pub), smart contemporary refit keeping bar's beams and big woodburner, cool décor in attractive dining areas inc stylish barn room, enjoyable carefully sourced food, friendly service, Wells & Youngs ales, good choice of wines by the glass; children welcome, nice garden *(LYM, Michael Dandy)*

ELY [TL5479]

☆ ***Cutter*** CB7 4BN [Annesdale, off Station Rd (or walk S along Riverside Walk from Maltings)]: Beautifully placed contemporary riverside pub with reasonably priced generous food from sandwiches up inc good value Sun roasts in carpeted dining bar and smart contemporary dining bar, Greene King, Shepherd Neame Spitfire and Woodfordes Wherry, good coffee and wines by the glass; plenty of tables outside *(Dr Andy Wilkinson, LYM, Mrs Hazel Rainer, Ryta Lyndley, Michael Dandy)*

Hereward CB7 4LZ [Market St]: Long lively modern pub, plenty of tables, low-priced beers, wines and pubby food, pleasant staff, busy with young people at night, more mixed lunchtime; disabled facilities, big-screen sports TVs *(John Wooll)*

High Flyer CB7 4PQ [Newnham St]: Good service, enjoyable fresh food inc all-afternoon Sun carvery in restaurant (where children allowed); bedrooms *(Peter Snow)*

Lamb CB7 4EJ [Brook St (Lynn rd)]: Enjoyable lunchtime food from sandwiches up in panelled lounge bar, friendly staff, good choice of wines by the glass, Greene King ales; bedrooms *(Michael Dandy)*

FEN DITTON [TL4860]

Plough CB5 8SX [Green End]: Big recently refurbished M&B dining pub with helpful staff, good choice of promptly served all-day food, well kept ales, rowing décor; lots of tables on decking and riverside lawns, nice walk from town *(LYM, P M Newsome, Paul Humphreys)*

FEN DRAYTON [TL3468]

☆ ***Three Tuns*** CB4 5SJ [off A14 NW of Cambridge at Fenstanton; High St]: Well preserved thatched pub in charming village, heavy Tudor beams and timbers, inglenook fireplaces, tiled-floor bar, comfortable settles and other seats, well laid out dining end

(children welcome), Greene King ales, sensibly placed darts, good value usual bar food (not Sun evening) from lunchtime sandwiches to steaks; piped music; tables on covered terrace and neat back lawn, good play area, open all day *(Barry and Anne, LYM)*

GODMANCHESTER [TL2470]

☆ ***Exhibition*** PE29 2HZ [London Rd]: Attractive choice of rooms inc main bar with re-created shop-fronts on walls, complete with doors and stock in windows; cosy, with big flagstones, traditional furnishings, fairy lights, enjoyable food, Fullers London Pride and Greene King IPA; picnic-sets on back lawn (a couple in front, too), open all day *(Elizabeth Lester, Michael Dandy, Virginia Williams, R T and J C Moggridge, Christopher Turner, Alan and Eve Harding, Mick Miller, LYM)*

GRANTCHESTER [TL4355]

☆ ***Blue Ball*** CB3 9NQ [Broadway]: Particularly well kept Adnams and a guest such as Timothy Taylors Landlord in character bare-boards village local, said to be the area's oldest, proper hands-on landlord, good log fire, Aspall's cider, cards and traditional games inc shut the box and ring the bull, lots of books; dogs welcome, tables on small terrace with lovely views to Grantchester meadows, nice village *(Conor McGaughey, Oliver J Brown, Pete Baker, Jerry Brown)*

☆ ***Green Man*** CB3 9NF [High St]: Friendly and genuine, dating from 16th c, bare boards, log fire, heavy beams and scrubbed tables, leather chairs in lower room, enjoyable good value food, well kept ales inc Black Sheep, separate dining room; disabled facilities, tables out behind *(Jerry Brown, Simon Watkins, Adrian Johnson, LYM, DC)*

Rupert Brooke CB3 9NQ [Broadway; junction Coton rd with Cambridge—Trumpington rd]: Tidy open-plan pub with enjoyable food from good lunchtime sandwiches and light dishes up, well kept Adnams, Harveys and Woodfordes Wherry, good choice of wines by the glass, friendly young staff, central log fire in small comfortable bar, simple extended family dining area; piped music *(MJB, Jerry Brown)*

GREAT STAUGHTON [TL1264]

☆ ***Tavern on the Green*** PE19 5DG [aka Snooty Tavern; The Green (B645/B661)]: Comfortably up-to-date and bright uncluttered open-plan layout, in same small group as Snooty Fox, Lowick (Northants) – see main entries; good and not over-generous fresh food from sandwiches, ploughman's and appealing light dishes up, good range of wines by the glass, several real ales, friendly service; children welcome, some picnic-sets outside, open all day *(Michael Dandy, Fr Robert Marsh, BB)*

HEMINGFORD ABBOTS [TL2870]

Axe & Compass PE28 9AH [High St]: Appealing 15th-c two-bar thatched pub with flagstones and inglenook, friendly staff, Adnams and Greene King IPA, good choice of wines by the glass, good value fresh pubby lunchtime food from baguettes up inc OAP meals, wider evening menu, contemporary extension dining areas, pool and bar billiards; piped music, TV, quiz or live music nights; children and dogs welcome, garden tables and separate menu, quiet pretty village, open all day *(JJW, CMW, Paul Humphreys, Ian Blake, Michael Dandy)*

HILDERSHAM [TL5648]

☆ *Pear Tree* CB1 6BU [off A1307 N of Linton]: New team keeping up standards in friendly Victorian pub, good value home-made food, well kept Greene King ales, daily papers, board games, odd crazy-paved floor and plenty of curios; children welcome, garden behind, picturesque thatched village, cl Mon lunchtime *(BB, Jane Elliott, Simon Watkins)*

HISTON [TL4363]

Red Lion CB4 9JD [High St]: Cheery and friendly, with half a dozen well kept changing ales (spring and early autumn beer festivals), lots of bottled belgian beers, good value generous pub lunches, proper character landlord, lots of pubby memorabilia, log fire in well used lounge, games in extended public bar; big garden, open all day Sat *(Jerry Brown)*

HOLYWELL [TL3370]

☆ *Old Ferry Boat* PE27 4TG [signed off A1123]: Partly thatched Greene King pub in lovely peaceful setting, low beams, open fires and interesting side areas, window seats overlooking Great Ouse, real ales, decent wines by the glass, good coffee, reasonably priced food (all day in summer – service well organised to cope with crowds); quiet piped music, games; children welcome, plenty of tables and cocktail parasols on front terrace and riverside lawn, moorings, seven good bedrooms, open all day wknds *(Ian Phillips, Ian Blake, LYM, Mrs Hazel Rainer, Ross Balaam)*

HORSEHEATH [TL6147]

Old Red Lion CB1 6QF [Linton Rd]: Well refurbished and neatly kept Greene King pub, sensibly priced food, hard-working staff; 12 comfortable bedroom cabins *(Simon Watkins, Mr and Mrs T B Staples)*

HOUGHTON [TL2872]

Three Horseshoes PE28 2BE [The Green]: Cosy village pub with low black beams and inglenook, good-sized L-shaped eating area with conservatory, Greene King and a guest beer, fine choice of wines by the glass, pubby lunchtime food inc lots of fish, different evening menu, pool in small second bar, darts; quiet piped music; tables outside, next to Houghton watermill (NT) and Ouse walks, bedrooms, open all day *(LYM, Mrs Hazel Rainer)*

HUNTINGDON [TL2371]

☆ *George* PE29 3AB [George St]: Relaxed, friendly and comfortable hotel lounge bar, generous reasonably priced sandwiches and bar and brasserie meals, Greene King IPA and Abbot, good choice of wines by the glass, good coffee (or tea and pastries); piped music; magnificent galleried central

courtyard, comfortable bedrooms *(LYM, Michael Dandy)*

LEIGHTON BROMSWOLD [TL1175]

☆ *Green Man* PE28 5AW [signed off A14 Huntingdon—Kettering]: Enjoyable real food in neatly modernised open-plan village pub, real ales such as Timothy Taylors Landlord, pleasant staff, heavy low beams, inglenook log fire, pool *(LYM, Ryta Lyndley)*

LONGSTOWE [TL3154]

☆ *Red House* CB3 7UT [Old North Road; A1198 Royston—Huntingdon, S of village]: Creeper-covered pub with dark red décor and sporting theme, red-tiled bar with big log fire, lower part with chintzy easy chairs and settees, well kept ales such as Church End and Woodfordes, several wines by glass, straightforward food; piped music; children and dogs welcome, sheltered little garden with picnic-sets, open all day wknds *(Russell and Alison Hunt, Michael Dandy, Simon Watkins, LYM, O K Smyth, Jeremy King)*

LONGTHORPE [TL1698]

Fox & Hounds PE3 6NB [just W of Peterborough]: Popular rambling dining pub with welcoming landlady, generous enjoyable blackboard food, well kept Shepherd Neame Spitfire; piped music turned down on request *(Tom Evans)*

NEEDINGWORTH [TL3571]

☆ *Pike & Eel* PE27 4TW [pub signed from A1123; Overcote Rd]: Marvellous peaceful riverside location with spacious lawns and small marina; plush bar opening into room with easy chairs, settees and big open fire, civilised eating area (also separate smart restaurant) in light and airy glass-walled block overlooking water, boats and swans, immaculate service, Adnams Broadside, Greene King IPA and Woodfordes Wherry, good coffee and wines; children welcome, clean simple bedrooms, good breakfast *(LYM, Mrs Hazel Rainer)*

PAMPISFORD [TL4948]

Chequers CB2 4ER [Town Lane, off A505 E of M11 junction 10]: Picturesque, low-beamed and civilised, with friendly hard-working newish landlord, good value food, Greene King ales, no piped music; lovely window boxes and hanging baskets, tables in pleasant garden, open all day *(D and M T Ayres-Regan, Roy and Lindsey Fentiman, Charles Gysin)*

PERRY [TL1466]

Wheatsheaf PE28 0BX [nr Grafham Water sailing club]: Clean and pleasant, with full menu inc good baguettes, cheerful helpful staff, Greene King ales, good value coffee, flagstoned bar, dining area; dogs welcome, plenty of picnic-sets in big pleasant garden with terrace, bedrooms *(Ian Phillips)*

PETERBOROUGH [TL1897]

Coalheavers Arms PE2 9BH [Park St, Woodston]: Friendly old-fashioned flagstoned local, well kept Milton and guest beers, farm cider, good range of continental imports and malt whiskies; pleasant garden, cl Mon-Weds lunchtimes, open all day wknds *(Ben and*

Helen Ingram, the Didler, Joe Green)
Goodbarns Yard PE1 5DD [St Johns St,
behind Passport Office]: Dark two-room local
popular for its changing real ales tapped
from the cask, some food all day wkdys, big
conservatory; big-screen sports TV; open all
day *(the Didler)*
Palmerston Arms PE2 9PA [Oundle Rd]:
Recently refurbished open-plan pub, partly
17th-c, Batemans and lots of guest ales
tapped from the cask, good choice of malt
whiskies, good pork pies, welcoming service,
no music or machines; picnic-sets in small
garden, open all day wknds *(Joe Green,
P Dawn, the Didler)*
Wortley Almshouses PE1 1QA [Westgate]:
Attractive conversion of old stone-built
almshouses (among modern buildings), with
well kept bargain Sam Smiths, appropriately
robust furnishings and simple décor in
several appealing rooms off corridor; open
all day *(the Didler)*
SPALDWICK [TL1372]
☆ **George** PE28 0TD [just off A14 W of
Huntingdon]: Friendly 16th-c pub with good
individual up-to-date food, cool stylish
décor, sofas in bar, larger bistro area, lots of
wines by the glass, local real ales, good
coffee; children welcome *(J Roberts,
D Vigers, LYM, P Berry)*
STAPLEFORD [TL4751]
Longbow CB2 5DS [Church St]: Welcoming
bright local, simple and roomy, with five well
kept changing ales, local Cassels' cider, good
thai food, well chosen reasonably priced
wines, pleasant staff, darts and pool; some
live music; open all day Fri *(Jerry Brown)*
Rose CB22 5DG [London Rd]: Good value
family-friendly dining pub, prompt smiling
service, tap room on left of small bar with
well kept Adnams and Fullers London Pride,
reasonably priced wines, nicely decorated
lounge with low beams, big inglenook log
fire and roomy adjacent dining area; picnic-
sets out on grass *(Revd R P Tickle)*
STILTON [TL1689]
Stilton Cheese PE7 3RP [signed off A1;
North St]: Enjoyable food from sandwiches
up inc lots of fish, good guest beers, decent
wines, welcoming staff, interesting old
interior with log fire in unpretentious central
bar, good tables in two rooms off, separate
two-room restaurant; tables out in back
garden with sheltered decking, bedrooms
(Oliver and Sue Rowell)
STRETHAM [TL5072]
Lazy Otter CB6 3LU [Elford Closes, off A10 S
of Stretham roundabout]: Big rambling
nicely furnished family pub on Great Ouse,
good views from waterside conservatory and
big garden, good value food, good wine
choice, interesting guest ales such as Bull
Box, cheerful staff, warm fire; piped music;
bedroom annexe, open all day *(LYM, R M
Chard, Ryta Lyndley)*
SWAFFHAM PRIOR [TL5663]
Red Lion CB5 0LD [B1102 NE of Cambridge;
High St]: Attractive and spotless ancient

building, nice range of good moderately
priced food from sandwiches up, friendly
efficient staff, good value house wines,
Greene King Old Speckled Hen and Abbot,
comfortably divided dining area, interesting
old local photographs; tables in big back
courtyard *(Stephen Wood, R Halsey)*
THOLOMAS DROVE [TF3906]
Chequers PE13 4SL [High Rd]: Old pub with
well kept Elgoods ales, wide choice of sensibly
priced food, small cosy bar, larger dining room
(Gordon and Margaret Ormondroyd)
UFFORD [TF0904]
☆ **White Hart** PE9 3BH [back rd
Peterborough—Stamford, just S of B1443;
Main St]: 17th-c village pub with enjoyable
food all day using local organic supplies and
their own free range eggs, good coffee and
wines by the glass, welcoming service, guest
beers and Ufford ales brewed here, leather
sofas, log fire and railway memorabilia in
busy stripped stone and flagstoned bar,
rustic back dining area and conservatory;
children welcome, big garden with terrace
and play area, newish bedroom block, open
all day *(the Didler, Tom Evans, Roy Bromell,
Jeff and Wendy Williams, LYM)*
WANSFORD [TL0799]
Haycock PE8 6JA [just off A1 W of
Peterborough]: Big hotel and conference
centre, useful break for bar food all day from
sandwiches and tapas up, Bass and Black
Sheep, good wine choice, variety of seating
areas with plenty of character, big log fire,
restaurant with airy conservatory; may
expect you to pay full price in advance if
you book meals on special days; children in
eating areas, attractive courtyard and garden
near river, dogs allowed in bar and
comfortable bedrooms, open all day *(LYM,
Eithne Dandy, Derek Thomas, Pete Coxon)*
WATERBEACH [TL4965]
White Horse CB5 9HP [Greenside]: Spacious
comfortable two-bar pub with authentic thai
food in dining area, some pub food and Sun
roasts too, open fire, impressive range of
beers on tap; discreet piped music; terrace
with barbecue and play area
(P and D Carpenter)
WICKEN [TL5670]
Maids Head CB7 5XR [High St]: Neat
thatched dining pub with freshly made food
(may take a while), friendly local
atmosphere, real ales such as Adnams, fair-
priced wines, restaurant; tables outside,
village-green setting, handy for Wicken Fen
nature reserve (NT) *(P and D Carpenter)*
WOODDITTON [TL6558]
Three Blackbirds CB8 9SQ [signed off B1063
at Cheveley]: Pretty thatched pub with low
beams and flagstones, second bar opening
into large dining area with more tables
upstairs, enterprising food inc local game,
good service, Greene King IPA and Old
Speckled Hen, racing photographs and
cartoons; TV; children welcome, pretty
garden; cl first Tues of month *(Stephen
Wood, Simon Watkins, LYM)*

Cheshire

Brunning & Price, owners of just over a dozen pubs, have a strong foothold in this, their home county. Now that one of their long-serving managers is to be found as landlord of his own pub, the Fox & Barrel at Cotebrook, an astonishing quarter of the main entries here bear the Brunning & Price stamp, in one form or another. Let's hope the group's new owners keep up its great track record for good food, a fine range of drinks and friendly service, all served up in really nice interiors. Without listing them all, it's fair to say that all the Brunning & Price main entries in this chapter (including the Sutton Hall Hotel near Macclesfield, formerly a main entry but reopened in 2008 after complete reworking as a newcomer to the group) are doing very well. But don't let that make you think that Cheshire is a one-horse county, as far as pubs are concerned. The Bhurtpore in Aston is hugely popular – really friendly, with good value food and a terrific range of changing beers. Another favourite is the White Lion at Barthomley, full of character, and one of only three Cheshire pubs to qualify for our Bargain Award this year. The other two are both newcomers to the *Guide*: the Mill at Chester, not quite our usual style, but with its 16 real ales certainly worth a look; and the friendly Swan in a choice spot at Marbury. Other new main entries are the stylish Duke of Portland at Lach Dennis, and the Smoker at Plumley (an impressive Robinsons pub, quite handy for the M6, back in the *Guide* after a break). The Duke of Portland joins Cheshire's elite squad of top-notch dining pubs. Six now carry our Food Award, and among these the top title of Cheshire Dining Pub of the Year goes to the intimate but chatty Dysart Arms in Bunbury. Front-runners among the Lucky Dip entries at the end of the chapter are the Poachers in Bollington, White Lion at Childer Thornton, Bulls Head in Frodsham, George & Dragon at Great Budworth, Swan at Kettleshulme, Davenport Arms at Marton, Plough & Flail in Mobberley and Ryles Arms at Sutton. The county has several thriving small breweries, led by Weetwood; other good local ales we found in several pubs here were Coach House, Woodlands, Spitting Feathers, Storm and Station House.

ALDFORD   SJ4259   MAP 7

Grosvenor Arms ★

B5130 Chester—Wrexham; CH3 6HJ

Spacious place with buoyantly chatty atmosphere, impressive range of drinks, well balanced sensibly imaginative menu, good service; lovely big terrace and gardens

Cream-painted areas are sectioned by big knocked-through arches and a variety of wood, quarry tile, flagstone and black and white tiled floor finishes – some good richly coloured turkey rugs look well against these natural materials. Good solid pieces of traditional furniture, plenty of interesting pictures and attractive lighting keep it all intimate enough. A big panelled library room has tall bookshelves lining one wall, and lots of substantial tables well spaced on its handsomely boarded floor. Lovely on summer evenings, the airy terracotta-floored conservatory has lots of gigantic low hanging flowering baskets and chunky pale wood garden furniture. This opens out to a large elegant suntrap terrace, and a neat lawn with picnic-sets, young trees and an old tractor. The rather fine-looking bar counter stocks a comprehensive range of drinks including around 16 wines (all served by the glass), an impressive range of whiskies (including 100 malts, 30 bourbons, and 30 irish whiskeys) as well as Caledonian Deuchars IPA, Weetwood Eastgate, Thwaites and three interesting guests from brewers such as Beartown, Station House and Osset. Attentive service is friendly and reliable, and they keep a good selection of board games.

🍴 **Food is very good, and the well balanced changing menu includes something to please most tastes. As well as sandwiches, there might be mushroom and stilton tart, duck rillette, ham, egg and chips, aubergine, spinach and lentil moussaka, fried bass with crab and chorizo linguini, duck breast with red wine sauce, kidney and mushroom pie and fillet steak, with puddings such as bread and butter pudding and raspberry and lemon cheesecake.** *Starters/Snacks: £4.50 to £6.95. Main Courses: £8.95 to £19.95. Puddings: £5.25*

Brunning & Price ~ Manager Tracey Varley ~ Real ale ~ Bar food (12-9.30) ~ (01244) 620228 ~ Children welcome till 7pm ~ Dogs allowed in bar ~ Open 11.30-11; 12-10.30 Sun

Recommended by Phil and Gill Wass, Alex and Claire Pearse, J S Burn, Mr and Mrs J Palmer, Clive Watkin, Maurice and Gill McMahon, David and Katharine Cooke, Revd D Glover, M G Hart, Bruce and Sharon Eden, Paul Boot, Don Bryan

ASTBURY   SJ8461   MAP 7

Egerton Arms 🛏

Village signposted off A34 S of Congleton; CW12 4RQ

Cheery village pub with decent straightforward bar food, good value OAP lunches, large garden and nice bedrooms

This welcoming family-run place is in a pretty spot overlooking an attractive old church. Rambling around the bar, its cream-painted rooms are decorated with the odd piece of armour and shelves of books. Mementoes of the Sandow Brothers who performed as 'the World's Strongest Youths' are particularly interesting as one of them was the landlady's father. In summer dried flowers replace the fire in the big fireplace. Robinsons Double Hop, Tempus Fugit and Unicorn are well kept on handpump; piped music, fruit machine, TV. You'll find a few well placed tables out in front, and a play area with a wooden fort. Despite the large car park you might struggle for a place Sunday lunchtime. More reports please.

🍴 **The traditional menu includes sandwiches, sausage and chips, chicken and leek pudding, battered haddock and lemon, roast loin of pork with apple sauce and thyme and mushroom risotto.** *Starters/Snacks: £3.65 to £4.95. Main Courses: £8.50 to £14.95. Puddings: £3.75 to £3.95*

Robinsons ~ Tenants Alan and Grace Smith ~ Real ale ~ Bar food (11.30-2, 6(6.30 Sat, Sun)-9) ~ Restaurant ~ (01260) 273946 ~ Children welcome ~ Open 11.30-11; 11.30-3, 6.30-10.30 Sun ~ Bedrooms: £45S/£65B

Recommended by Neil Kellett, Ross Balaam, Dr D J and Mrs S C Walker, Chris Brooks, Paul J Robinshaw

ASTON   SJ6146   MAP 7

Bhurtpore ★ ♀ 🍺

Off A530 SW of Nantwich; in village follow Wrenbury signpost; CW5 8DQ

Fantastic range of drinks (especially real ales) and tasty curries in warm-hearted pub with some unusual artefacts; big garden

With its full complement of 11 real ales, you're likely to find beers from anywhere in the country at this very enthusiastically run red brick free house, though they do try to give preferential treatment to local brews. Other than Salopian Shropshire Gold, which tends to be on most of the time, they usually get through over 1000 different superbly kept real ales in a year. They also stock dozens of unusual bottled beers and fruit beers, a great many bottled ciders and perries, over 100 different whiskies, carefully selected soft drinks; good wine list. If you're a very keen real ale enthusiast it's worth going during their summer beer festival. The pub takes its unusual name from the town in India where a local landowner, Lord Combermere, won a battle; it also explains why a collection of exotic artefacts in the carpeted lounge bar has an indian influence – look out for the turbaned statue behind the counter, proudly sporting any sunglasses left behind by customers; also good local period photographs, and some attractive furniture. Tables in the comfortable public bar are reserved for people not eating; darts, dominoes, cribbage, pool, TV and games machine. At lunchtime and early weekday evenings the atmosphere is cosy and civilised, and on weekends, when it gets packed, the cheery staff cope superbly.

🍴 **The enjoyable menu has sandwiches and paninis (not Friday or Saturday night), a choice of five tasty curries, traditional dishes such as sausage, egg and chips, cheese and leek cakes with creamy dijon sauce, steak and kidney pie and steaks. Daily changing specials might include pork and black pudding patties with mustard and apple sauce and roast monkfish wrapped in bacon with cheese sauce, and puddings such as chocolate and raspberry brownie.** *Starters/Snacks: £3.75 to £7.50. Main Courses: £8.50 to £13.50. Puddings: £3.95 to £4.25*

Free house ~ Licensee Simon George ~ Real ale ~ Bar food (12-9 Sun) ~ Restaurant ~ (01270) 780917 ~ Children welcome ~ Dogs allowed in bar ~ Open 12-2.30(3 Sat), 6.30-11.30(midnight Sat); 12-11 Sun

Recommended by Selwyn Roberts, Dave Webster, Sue Holland, Malcolm Pellatt, the Didler, Ann and Tony Bennett-Hughes

BARTHOMLEY
SJ7752   MAP 7

White Lion ★ £

A mile from M6 junction 16; from exit roundabout take B5078 N towards Alsager, then Barthomley signposted on left; CW2 5PG

Charming 17th-c thatched village tavern with classic period interior and good value straightforward tasty lunchtime food

Unchanging and forever warmly welcoming, the main bar here has a timelessly informal feel, with its blazing open fire, heavy low oak beams (dating back to Stuart times), attractively moulded black panelling, cheshire history and prints on the walls, latticed windows and thick wobbly old tables. Up some steps, a second room has another welcoming open fire, more oak panelling, a high-backed winged settle, a paraffin lamp hinged to the wall, and shove-ha'penny, cribbage and dominoes; local societies make good use of a third room – and look out for the cat here – one reader told us it is totally mad! Five real ales include Marstons Bitter and Pedigree and Mansfield and a couple of guests – usually Jennings Cocker Hoop and Snecklifter. Outside, seats and picnic-sets on the cobbles have a charming view of the attractive village, and the lovely early 15th-c red sandstone church of St Bertiline across the road, where you can learn about the Barthomley massacre, is well worth a visit.

🍴 **The short traditional menu includes enjoyable sandwiches, staffordshire oakcakes with cheese, onions, tomatoes and beans, ploughman's, sausage and mash, hotpot and beef and mushroom pie.** *Starters/Snacks: £3.95 to £7.95. Main Courses: £3.95 to £7.95. Puddings: £2.95*

Marstons ~ Tenant Laura Condliffe ~ Real ale ~ Bar food (lunchtime only) ~ (01270) 882242 ~ Children welcome away from bar until 9pm ~ Dogs welcome ~ Open 11.30-11; 12-10.30 Sun

Recommended by Dave Webster, Sue Holland, Edward Mirzoeff, Pauline and Philip Darley, I A Herdman, David Green, Maurice and Gill McMahon, Tracey and Stephen Groves, John R Ringrose, Louise English, the Didler, Patricia Walker, MLR, Dr and Mrs A K Clarke, Piotr Chodzko-Zajko

Pubs close to motorway junctions are listed at the back of the book.

BICKLEY MOSS   SJ5550   MAP 7

Cholmondeley Arms ♀

Cholmondeley; A49 5.5 miles N of Whitchurch; the owners would like us to list them under Cholmondeley Village, but as this is rarely located on maps we have mentioned the nearest village which appears more often; SY14 8HN

Imaginatively converted high-ceilinged schoolhouse with decent range of real ale and wines, jolly nice food, and sizeable gardens

The fact that Clarissa Dickson Wright listed the breakfast fried bread here as one of the ten best things she had ever eaten seems oddly fitting. It's something to do with this having been a schoolhouse once upon a time – the cross-shaped lofty bar, high gothic windows, huge old radiators and old school desks on a gantry above the bar all leave no doubt that that's what it was. Well used chairs in all shapes and forms – some upholstered, some bentwood, some with ladderbacks and some with wheelbacks – are set in groups round an equally eclectic mix of tables, all on comfy carpets. There's a stag's head over one of the side arches, an open fire and lots of Victorian portraits and military pictures on colour-washed walls. Adnams and Marstons Pedigree and a couple of guests from brewers such as Weetwood and Woodlands are served from a pine clad bar, alongside around eight interesting, and reasonably priced wines by the glass, all listed on a blackboard. There are seats outside on the sizeable lawn, and more in front overlooking the quiet road. The pub is handy for Cholmondeley Castle Gardens.

🍽 **Readers very much enjoy the food here, which runs from lunchtime sandwiches and steak baguettes, hot crab pâté, devilled kidneys on toast, fish and chips, lasagne and steaks, to daily specials such as duck breast with cranberry and port sauce, lamb shank with red wine gravy, madras beef curry and roast peppers stuffed with couscous and vegetables; puddings such as bakewell tart, syrup tart and chocolate banana split and lots of ice-creams.** *Starters/Snacks: £3.95 to £7.25. Main Courses: £7.25 to £18.00. Puddings: £3.95 to £4.95*

Free house ~ Licensee Carolyn Ross-Lowe ~ Real ale ~ Bar food ~ (01829) 720300 ~ Children welcome ~ Dogs welcome ~ Open 11-3, 6-11(10.30 Sun) ~ Bedrooms: £55B/£80B

Recommended by Denys Gueroult, M Thomas, George and Maureen Roby, Ray and Winifred Halliday, K S Whittaker, Edward Leetham, Mr and Mrs J Freund

BUNBURY   SJ5658   MAP 7

Dysart Arms 🍽 ♀ 🍺

Bowes Gate Road; village signposted off A51 NW of Nantwich; and from A49 S of Tarporley – coming this way, coming in on northernmost village access road, bear left in village centre; CW6 9PH

CHESHIRE DINING PUB OF THE YEAR

Civilised chatty dining pub attractively filled with good furniture in thoughtfully laid out rooms; very enjoyable food, lovely garden with pretty views.

The meandering series of knocked-through rooms at this well run country pub gives rise to an intimate and homely but still very social-feeling atmosphere. They are immaculately kept and ramble gently around the pleasantly lit central bar. Cream walls keep it light, clean and airy, with deep venetian red ceilings adding cosiness, and each room (some with good winter fires) is cleverly furnished with an appealing variety of well spaced sturdy wooden tables and chairs, a couple of tall filled bookcases and just the right amount of carefully chosen bric-a-brac, properly lit pictures and plants. Flooring ranges from red and black tiles, to stripped boards and some carpet. Service is efficient and friendly. Thwaites and Weetwood Eastgate and a couple of guests such as Spitting Feathers Farmhouse Ale and Youngs Special are very well kept on handpump, alongside a good selection of 16 wines by the glass, just over 20 malts and fresh apple juice. Sturdy wooden tables on the terrace and picnic-sets on the lawn in the neatly kept slightly elevated garden are lovely in summer, with views of the splendid church at the end of the pretty village, and the distant Peckforton Hills beyond.

🍴 From a changing menu, food is tasty, just imaginative enough, attractively presented, and fairly priced. As well as sandwiches, there might be ham hock terrine, smoked duck, bacon and mango salad, steak burger, sausage and mash, wild mushroom and truffle risotto, fish and chips with mushy peas, cajun salmon fillet, braised beef with dumplings and spiced red cabbage, grilled rib-eye steak, and puddings such as lemon and ginger cheesecake, sticky toffee pudding, ice-creams and a British cheeseboard. *Starters/Snacks: £4.25 to £8.50. Main Courses: £6.45 to £16.50. Puddings: £4.25 to £5.45*

Brunning & Price ~ Manager Greg Williams ~ Real ale ~ Bar food (12-9.30(9 Sun)) ~ (01829) 260183 ~ Children welcome ~ Dogs allowed in bar ~ Open 11.30-11; 12-10.30 Sun

Recommended by Mrs P J Carroll, R T and J C Moggridge, Derek and Sylvia Stephenson, J S Burn, Pam and John Smith, Dave Webster, Sue Holland, Maurice and Gill McMahon, Mr and Mrs J Palmer, Roger Yates, Dr D Scott, Revd D Glover, Richard and Maria Gillespie

BURLEYDAM   SJ6042   MAP 7

Combermere Arms

A525 Whitchurch—Audlem; SY13 4AT

Roomy and attractive beamed pub successfully mixing good drinking side with imaginative all-day food; garden

Much as at the previous main entry, the attractive interior of this popular 18th-c place has been cleverly opened up to give a light and roomy impression while still feeling cosy in its many different areas. Trademark Brunning & Price furnishings and décor take in their usual eclectic mix of dark wood furniture and rugs on wooden (some old and some new oak) or stone floors, cream walls filled with prints, deep red ceilings, and open fires. Friendly staff extend an equally good welcome to drinkers and diners, with both aspects of the business seeming to do well here. Half a dozen real ales are usually from smaller brewers such as Cotleigh, Sharps, Thwaites, Timothy Taylor and Weetwood. They also stock three ciders, 100 whiskies and 15 wines by the glass from an extensive list; a few board games. During summer evenings, they put candles on tables in the pretty, well tended garden.

🍴 A well as interesting sandwiches and ploughman's, enjoyable food, often giving a contemporary twist to a traditional dish, might include starters such as salt beef hash cake with poached egg or blue cheese fritter with walnut and apple salad, main courses such as sausage and spring onion mash, battered haddock with mushy peas, roast bass with fennel and lemon butter, pork fillet and apricot stuffing wrapped in parma ham with sage sauce, and rump steak with peppercorn salad; puddings such as apple pie with cinnamon ice-cream, crème brûlée and raspberry bakewell tart and local ice-creams; english cheeseboard. *Starters/Snacks: £4.50 to £5.75. Main Courses: £6.50 to £15.95. Puddings: £5.00*

Brunning & Price ~ Manager John Astle Rowe ~ Real ale ~ Bar food (12-9(10 Fri, Sat)) ~ (01948) 871223 ~ Children welcome ~ Dogs allowed in bar ~ Open 12-11(10.30 Sun)
Recommended by Philip Hesketh, Alun Jones, Ann and Tony Bennett-Hughes

BURWARDSLEY   SJ5256   MAP 7

Pheasant

Higher Burwardsley; signposted from Tattenhall (which itself is signposted off A41 S of Chester) and from Harthill (reached by turning off A534 Nantwich—Holt at the Copper Mine); follow pub's signpost on up hill from Post Office; OS Sheet 117 map reference 523566; CH3 9PF

Fantastic views, local beer and good range of very enjoyable food at heavily beamed and roomily fresh conversion of old inn

The nicely beamed interior of this half-timbered sandstone 17th-c pub has an airy modern feel, with wooden floors and well spaced furniture, including comfy leather armchairs and some nice old chairs. They say the see-through fireplace houses the largest log fire in the county, and there's a pleasant restaurant. Three local Weetwood beers and a guest from a brewer such as Beartown are served on handpump alongside a selection of bottled beers, nine wines by the glass and around 20 malts; piped music, daily newspapers. On a clear day the telescope on the terrace (with nice hardwood furniture) lets you make out the pier head and cathedrals in Liverpool, while from inside you can see right across the Cheshire plain. A big side lawn has picnic-sets, and on summer weekends they sometimes have barbecues. Popular with walkers, the pub is well placed for the Sandstone Trail along the Peckforton Hills.

🍽 Besides sandwiches, the changing menu might include prawn pil pil, potted ham hock with onion marmalade, a fish, cheese or charcuterie board, mushroom risotto, hotpot, chicken with fried leeks, baked cod with pease pudding, confit tomatoes and orange butter, penne with mushroom and madeira sauce, steak, ale and mushroom pie, rib-eye steak, and puddings such as lemon possett with fresh raspberries, bread and butter pudding, and local ice-creams; cheeseboard. They only take bookings for tables of six or more. *Starters/Snacks: £4.00 to £8.00. Main Courses: £8.00 to £18.00. Puddings: £4.00 to £6.00*

Free house ~ Licensee Andrew Nelson ~ Real ale ~ Bar food (12-3, 6-9.30 Mon; 12-9.30 (10 Fri, Sat, 8.30 Sun)) ~ (01829) 770434 ~ Children welcome till 6pm ~ Dogs welcome ~ Open 12-11 ~ Bedrooms: £65B/£85B

Recommended by Rita and Keith Pollard, Alan and Eve Harding, Mark and Ruth Brock, Peter Craske, Adrian and Dawn Collinge

CHESTER   SJ4066   MAP 7

Albion ★ 🍺

Albion Street; CH1 1RQ

Strongly traditional pub with comfortable Edwardian décor and captivating World War I memorabilia; hearty food and good drinks

Tucked away on a quiet street corner in the shadow of the Roman Wall, this unspoilt Victorian pub is said to be the last surviving place in the city in its original layout. Uniquely, its homely interior is entirely dedicated to the Great War of 1914-18, and most unusually it's the officially listed site of four war memorials to soldiers from the Cheshire Regiment. Throughout its tranquil rooms (no games machines or children here) you'll find an absorbing collection of World War I memorabilia, from big engravings of men leaving for war, and similarly moving prints of wounded veterans, to flags, advertisements and so on. The post-Edwardian décor is appealingly muted, with dark floral William Morris wallpaper (designed on the first day of World War I), a cast-iron fireplace, appropriate lamps, leatherette and hoop-backed chairs, a period piano and cast-iron-framed tables; there's an attractive side dining room too. Service is friendly, though this is a firmly run place (the landlord has been here 37 years now): groups of race-goers are discouraged (opening times may be limited during meets), and they don't like people rushing in just before closing time. Beers come from Batemans, Black Sheep and Timothy Taylor, with a guest such as Coach House Cheshire Gold. They also stock new world wines, fresh orange juice, over 25 malt whiskies and a good selection of rums and gins. We'd very much like to hear about the new bedrooms here as we are sure they will be immaculate and possibly deserving of a stay award.

🍽 Served in generous helpings, wholesome good value bar food includes doorstep sandwiches, filled staffordshire oatcakes, cottage pie, creamy coconut chicken and rice, lambs liver, bacon and onions in cider gravy, curries, stews, casseroles, and puddings such as chocolate torte or bread and butter pudding with marmalade. *Main Courses: £5.20 to £8.90. Puddings: £4.20*

Punch ~ Lease Michael Edward Mercer ~ Real ale ~ Bar food (12-2, 5-8(6-8.30 Sat); not Sun evening) ~ Restaurant ~ No credit cards ~ (01244) 340345 ~ Dogs allowed in bar ~ Open 12-3, 5(6 Sat, 7 Sun)-11(10.30 Sun) ~ Bedrooms: £65B/£75B

Recommended by Roger and Anne Newbury, Mrs Philippa Wilson, Dave Webster, Sue Holland, Graham Findley, Maurice and Gill McMahon, J S Burn, Gwyn and Anne Wake, Joe Green, Chris and Heather Street, J and F Gowers, the Didler, Catherine and Rob Dunster, Ann and Tony Bennett-Hughes, Derek and Sylvia Stephenson, Pam and John Smith

Mill ◧ £

Milton Street; CH1 3NF

Big hotel with huge range of real ales, good value food and cheery service in sizeable bar

They carry an astonishing range of up to 16 real ales in the comfortable cruiser-style bar at this modern canalside hotel. Mill Premium and Cornmill are brewed especially for them by Coach House and Phoenix, respectively, and are well kept alongside Theakstons XB and a dozen guests that change on a daily basis; also a dozen wines by the glass and a farm cider. Service here is very friendly and you'll find a real mix of customers. The very neatly kept bar has new stripped light wood flooring by the bar and dark green patterned carpeting elsewhere, red leather and blue cushioned chairs at marble topped tables, some exposed brickwork and supporting pillars (this is an old converted mill) and local photographs and cigarette cards framed on cream papered walls; quiet piped music and unobtrusively placed big-screen sports TV. Readers say the bedrooms are comfortable and make a handy base for exploring the city.

🍴 **Very reasonably priced pubby food includes sandwiches, ciabattas and enjoyable hot dishes such as curry and rice, fish and chips, steak and ale pie and mushroom stroganoff, with mainly cold puddings such as cheesecake, fresh fruit and profiteroles.** *Starters/Snacks: £2.25 to £2.75. Main Courses: £5.50. Puddings: £2.95*

Free house ~ Licensees Gary and Gordon Vickers ~ Real ale ~ Bar food (11.30(12 Sun)-10 (sandwiches only Mon-Sat afternoon)) ~ Restaurant ~ (01244) 350035 ~ Children welcome, not in bar after 8pm ~ Open 11am-midnight; 12-11.30 Sun ~ Bedrooms: £73B/£91B
Recommended by Colin Moore

Old Harkers Arms ♀ ◧

Russell Street, down steps off City Road where it crosses canal – under Mike Melody antiques; CH3 5AL

Well run spacious canalside building with great range of drinks (including lots of changing real ales) and good value tasty food

Lofty ceilings and tall windows (you can watch canal and cruise boats glide past) make for an appealingly light and airy interior at this big early Victorian warehouse. Huge brick pillars and cleverly divided off areas create some intimate places, and cheery staff spread a happy bustle. Mixed dark wood furniture is grouped on stripped wood floors, walls are covered with frame to frame old prints, and the usual Brunning & Price wall of bookshelves is to be found above a leather banquette at one end. Attractive lamps add cosiness, and the bar counter is apparently constructed from salvaged doors; board games. The very well stocked bar carries a great choice of around nine real ales on handpump, including Thwaites Original, Weetwood Cheshire Cat and Wadworths 6X, with regularly changing guests from brewers such as Brimstage, Coniston, Moorhouses and Titanic; also around 100 malt whiskies, 65 well described wines (with around 40 by the glass), farmhouse ciders and local apple juice.

🍴 **As well as a good range of sandwiches, nicely presented bar food includes snacks and starters such as hot beef and onion bap, ploughman's, teriyaki chicken with satay sauce, and breaded tiger prawns with pineapple salsa, main courses such as spicy meatballs and tomato sauce with linguini, sausages with spring onion mash, moroccan lamb chump chop with couscous and chickpeas, sweet potato and spinach curry and braised shoulder of lamb, and puddings such as sticky toffee pudding, raspberry crème brûlée and local ice-creams.** *Starters/Snacks: £4.25 to £7.95. Main Courses: £7.95 to £15.50. Puddings: £5.00 to £5.25*

Brunning & Price ~ Manager Paul Jeffery ~ Real ale ~ Bar food (12-9.30) ~ (01244) 344525 ~ Dogs allowed in bar ~ Open 11.30-11; 12-10.30 Sun
Recommended by Dave Webster, Sue Holland, Joe Green, Simon J Barber, the Didler, Graham Findley, Steve Whalley, Mrs Hazel Rainer, Roger Yates, Maurice and Gill McMahon, Don Bryan

COTEBROOK   SJ5765   MAP 7

Fox & Barrel

A49 NE of Tarporley; CW6 9DZ

Good new licensee revamping menu and décor as we went to press

Though it was closed as we went to press, we have high hopes for this pretty white
cottage as the licensee is well known to us from his days at the helm of the Grosvenor
Arms in Aldford – a longstanding and several times award winning main entry.
Redecorations are planned but roughly speaking the original snug bar is still sure to be
dominated by a big log fireplace and a bigger uncluttered dining area will have attractive
rugs and rustic tables on bare boards and will keep its extensive panelling. Real ales will
probably include Black Sheep, Caledonian Deuchars IPA and Timothy Taylors Landlord.

🍴 **Bar food is likely to include imaginative snacks and sandwiches, with main courses
ranging from pubby standards to more imaginative dishes.** *Starters/Snacks: £0.50 to £6.95.
Main Courses: £7.00 to £15.95. Puddings: £5.25*

Punch ~ Lease Gary Kidd ~ Real ale ~ Bar food ~ (01829) 760529 ~ Children welcome ~
Dogs allowed in bar ~ Open 12-11(10.30 Sun)
Recommended by BOB

HAUGHTON MOSS   SJ5855   MAP 7

Nags Head 🍴 🍷

Turn off A49 S of Tarporley into Long Lane, at 'Beeston, Haughton' signpost; CW6 9RN

**Spotlessly kept with nice traditional décor, log fires, popular tasty food including good
value lunchtime buffet, and big garden**

'No problem' is virtually the staff motto at this traditional old black and white pub which
is clearly run with loving pride and a desire to put customers first. It has gleaming black
and white tiles by the serving counter, pews, and a heavy settle by the fire in a small
quarry-tiled room on the left, and button-back wall banquettes in the carpeted room on
the right, which also has logs burning in a copper-hooded fireplace. Below heavy black
beams are shelves of pewter mugs, attractive Victorian prints and a few brass ornaments,
and the front window of the pub is full of charmingly arranged collector's dolls. An oak-
beamed conservatory extension serves as a dining room; maybe very quiet piped music,
and board games. Drinks include a well chosen wine list (with 15 by the glass), a dozen
malts, and Charles Wells Bombardier, Flowers and a guest such as Coachhouse Old Wharf
on handpump. A big immaculately kept garden has well spaced picnic-sets and a bowling
green.

🍴 **The generously served tasty bar food does draw the crowds, particularly between
12 and 2 on weekdays when they run the bargain-priced self-service buffet. Other dishes
include soup, sandwiches, ploughman's, whitebait, half a roast chicken, pork medallions
with cider and cream sauce, creamy mixed seafood tagliatelle, mushroom stroganoff, all
day breakfast, steaks and specials such as black pudding salad or curry, a pudding trolley,
and various ice-cream sundaes.** *Starters/Snacks: £3.60 to £7.95.
Main Courses: £4.75 to £15.25. Puddings: £3.25 to £4.45*

Free house ~ Licensees Rory and Deborah Keigan ~ Real ale ~ Bar food (12-10) ~ Restaurant ~
(01829) 260265 ~ Children welcome ~ Open 11am-midnight
Recommended by Maurice and Gill McMahon, David A Hammond, J Roy Smylie, M Thomas

---

Post Office address codings give the impression that some pubs are in Cheshire, when
they're really in Derbyshire (and therefore included in this book under that chapter) or in
Greater Manchester (see the Lancashire chapter).

LACH DENNIS
SJ7072   MAP 7

Duke of Portland ⊕ ⏛ ◖

Holmes Chapel Road (B5082, off A556 SE of Northwich); CW9 7SY

Good food in stylish upscale dining pub which doesn't neglect the beer side

Given its emphasis on the food side, we like the careful way this smartly refurbished L-shaped pub looks after people who are just in for a drink or a coffee. A civilised bar area, gently decorated in beige, grey and cream, has comfortable leather armchairs, square pouffes and sofas around chunky low tables, with nicely framed prints above its panelled dado. More importantly, its handsomely carved counter serves a fine range of half a dozen well kept ales from handpump, including Banks's Original, Marstons Pedigree and Old Empire, with three guests from brewers such as Moorhouses, Okells and Weetwood. The interesting changing choice of about a dozen wines by the glass is fairly priced. The young staff are attentive and helpful; daily papers, TV. The main dining room, with its lofty ceiling, sturdy balustrades and big pictures, gives quite a sense of occasion, but keeps a fairly relaxed feel – perhaps because of the friendly mixture of styles in the comfortable dining chairs on its floorboards; piped music, TV. Outside, a neat new terrace has alloy tables and chairs among modernist planters. The family, long famous locally for their Belle Epoque restaurant in Knutsford, have recently opened another pub, the George & Dragon in Tarvin.

⑪ They take great care over sourcing really good ingredients from named local suppliers, showing justifiable pride in their meats and cheeses; even the chips come in for admiration. Starters might include fishcake with aïoli, lamb terrine with rosemary, cumin and hot mint jelly, or you can build your own antipasto platter to share. Main courses might be red pepper and crispy leek risotto, fish and chips, saddle of lamb stuffed with mushrooms and lemon thyme, and 21-day hung sirloin steak. They also do a good value two-course lunchtime and early evening menu. Readers have been particularly enthusiastic about the puddings, such as crème brûlée and sticky toffee pudding. *Starters/Snacks: £3.95 to £7.95. Main Courses: £10.95 to £17.95. Puddings: £5.50*

Free house ~ Licensees David and Matthew Mooney ~ Real ale ~ Bar food (12-2.30, 5.30-10; 12-8 Sun) ~ Restaurant ~ (01606) 46264 ~ Children welcome ~ Dogs allowed in bar ~ Open 12-11(10.30 Sun)

Recommended by Mrs P J Carroll, Mr and Mrs John Taylor, Jonathon Reed, Tom and Jill Jones, Brian Scanlon, Malcolm Pellatt

LANGLEY
SJ9569   MAP 7

Hanging Gate ⏛

Meg Lane, Higher Sutton; follow Langley signpost from A54 beside Fourways Motel, and that road passes the pub; from Macclesfield, heading S from centre on A523 turn left into Byrons Lane at Langley, Wincle signpost; in Sutton (0.5 miles after going under canal bridge, ie before Langley) fork right at Church House Inn, following Wildboarclough signpost, then 2 miles later turning sharp right at steep hairpin bend; OS Sheet 118 map reference 952696; SK11 0NG

Remotely set old place with fires in traditional cosy rooms, helpful licensees, lovely views from airy extension and terrace

Clinging to the top of a Peak District ridge, this welcoming old drover's inn commands panoramic views across the Cheshire plains and beyond. Still in their original layout, its three cosy little low-beamed rooms are simply furnished. The tiny little snug bar, at its pubbiest at lunchtime, has a welcoming log fire in a big brick fireplace, a single table, plain chairs and cushioned wall seats (though there's barely room in here to sit), and a few old pub pictures and seasonal photographs on its creamy walls. Beers served in here include well kept Hydes Original, Jekylls Gold and a Hydes and a guest such as Saddleworth St George on handpump, quite a few malt whiskies and ten wines by the glass. The second room, with a section of bar counter in the corner, has only fives tables, and a third appealing little oak beamed blue room has a little chaise longue. Down some stone steps, an airy dining extension has terrific views over a patchwork of valley pastures to distant moors and the tall Sutton Common transmitter – seats out on the crazy-paved terrace also have great views; piped music. It does get busy so it's best to book on weekends.

▥ **Bar food from the menu and changing specials board could include sandwiches (home-made bread), soup, wild salmon steak with crayfish tails, steak and ale pie, grilled vegetables with goat's cheese and home-made puddings such as warm bakewell tart or hot chocolate pudding.** *Starters/Snacks: £3.95 to £6.95. Main Courses: £7.95 to £19.95. Puddings: £3.50 to £4.95*

Hydes ~ Tenants Ian and Luda Rottenbury ~ Real ale ~ Bar food (12-2.30(4 Sun), 6.30(6 Sun)-9.30) ~ Restaurant ~ (01260) 252238 ~ Children welcome with restrictions ~ Dogs welcome ~ Open 11.30-3, 5-10.30; 11-11 Sat; 12-10.30 Sun

Recommended by Pam and John Smith, Alun Jones, the Didler

MACCLESFIELD   SJ9271   MAP 7

Sutton Hall Hotel

Leaving Macclesfield southwards on A523, turn left into Byrons Lane signposted Langley, Wincle, then just before canal viaduct fork right into Bullocks Lane; OS Sheet 118 map reference 925715; SK11 0HE

Newly refurbished historic building set in attractive grounds; good range of drinks and good food

Though it was closed as we went to press, we are pretty confident that new owners Brunning & Price will turn this fine old place into a success story. We have yet to be disappointed by one of their ventures, and being well acquainted with the superb potential of this fabulous old building, we felt reluctant to deprive readers of the opportunity for a visit. The 16th-c baronial hall which forms the heart of the building is beautifully impressive, particularly in the entrance space. The bar is divided into separate areas by tall oak timbers, and has some antique squared oak panelling, lightly patterned art nouveau stained-glass windows, broad flagstones and a raised open fire. A good range of changing real ales and very decent wines, with plenty by the glass, are sure to be on offer. Lovely grounds have tables on a tree-sheltered lawn, and ducks and moorhens swimming in the pond. Bedrooms are being completely refurbished and are sure to be very comfortable.

▥ **Bar food is likely to follow the usual Brunning & Price policy (the chef is given guided free range) and include imaginative sandwiches, interestingly turned out pub staples, a few other more creative dishes, all fairly priced to reflect the good quality of the ingredients.**

Brunning & Price ~ Real ale ~ Bar food ~ (01260) 253211 ~ Bedrooms

Recommended by BOB

MARBURY   SJ5645   MAP 7

Swan ◨ £

NNE of Whitchurch; OS Sheet 117 map reference 562457; SY13 4LS

Charmingly set proper country pub with good value food and drinks

Since long-serving licensees retired a decade ago, this prettily set village-green pub has been through quite a string of licensees, but has now firmly found its feet under a welcoming publican (with his new wife and chocolate labrador Cally) who takes as much care of its warm-hearted atmosphere as he does of its beers. These he calls 'my lads': Adnams and a couple of changing guests such as Weetwoods Cheshire Cat (from nearby Wrenbury) and Woodlands Bees Knees. All 16 of the reasonably priced wines on the list are available by the glass. The roomy partly panelled lounge has upholstered easy chairs and other country furniture, a copper-canopied fireplace with a good winter log fire (masses of greenery in summer), daily papers, board games, quiet piped music and discreet lighting.

The cottagey turkey-carpeted dining room, candlelit at night, has another inglenook fireplace, and a magnificent sculpture of a swan, carved from a pear tree blown down in the pub's garden in 2007 storms. The garden itself is good-sized, with well spaced picnic-sets and big shrubs. Rebuilt in 1884, the pub is in a quiet and attractive village, a half-mile's country walk from the Llangollen Canal, Bridges 23 and 24. Showing a lovely generosity of spirit, the licensees are quite happy for you to use his car park if walking, even if you aren't popping in for a drink. The nearby lakeside church dates from the 1400s.

⚉ **The Bargain Award is for their very popular two-course lunch deals, when they offer a handful of pubby dishes such as stilton cheese mushroom, warm black pudding and smoked bacon salad, steak and ale pie and battered cod. The more elaborate evening menu might include hake fillet en papillote with dill and tomatoes, roast loin of venison with yam fritters and thyme and redcurrant sauce, vegetable gateaux with creamy stilton sauce. Puddings could be warm bread and butter pudding or cranachan – which the licensee tells us is a traditional scottish dish with cream, honey, raspberry and rolled oats. Their fortnightly Wednesday supper club (welcoming visitors too) is good value as well as good fun.** *Starters/Snacks: £4.50 to £6.00. Main Courses: £6.00 to £14.50. Puddings: £3.70*

Oxford Hotels ~ Lease Rob and Clarissa Adam ~ Real ale ~ Bar food (12-2, 6.30-9) ~ (01948) 662220 ~ Children welcome ~ Dogs allowed in bar ~ Open 12-3, 6.30-11; 12-11 Sat, Sun in summer; closed Mon except bank hols

Recommended by John and Joyce Farmer, Edward Leetham

MOBBERLEY   SJ7879   MAP 7

Roebuck ♀

Mill Lane; down hill from sharp bend on B5085 at E edge of 30mph limit; WA16 7HX

Stylish and airy country interior, warm welcome and very helpful service, very good food, good wine list, courtyard and garden.

There's a gently civilised dining atmosphere (with capable friendly service) at this popular white-painted pub. Old tiled and boarded floors carry a comfortable mix of relaxed country furnishings, from cushioned long wood pews (rescued from a welsh chapel) to scrubbed pine farmhouse tables and a mix of old chairs. The wine list is short but well chosen and very reasonably priced, with just over a dozen by the glass; also Greene King Old Speckled Hen, Tetleys, Timothy Taylors Landlord and a guest such as Jennings Cumberland; piped music. A cobbled courtyard has benches and tables and there are picnic-sets in an enclosed and well manicured beer garden (and more by the car park).

⚉ **The enjoyable food is thoughtfully prepared and includes traditional dishes with an appealing twist. As well as interesting sandwiches (not evenings), dishes might include soup, fried pigeon breast with rosemary crumpet, steak, ale and mushroom pie, aubergine and tomato tagine, battered haddock with mushy peas, fried chicken breast with thyme cream and mushroom and leek risotto, steak, and puddings such as poached vanilla figs with mascarpone ice-cream, lemon and lime tart, ice-creams and a british cheeseboard. Side orders are extra so you might want to add a couple of pounds to the prices below, and you will probably need to book.** *Starters/Snacks: £3.95 to £6.25. Main Courses: £8.95 to £13.95. Puddings: £3.95 to £5.25*

Free house ~ Licensee Jane Marsden ~ Real ale ~ Bar food (12-2.30, 6-9.30; 12-9.30(9 Sun) wknds) ~ (01565) 873322 ~ Children welcome ~ Open 12-3, 5-11(12-11 Sat, Sun)

Recommended by Mrs P J Carroll, Steve Whalley, Catherine and Rob Dunster

---

Bedroom prices normally include full english breakfast, VAT and any inclusive service charge that we know of. Prices before the '/' are for single rooms, after for two people in double or twin (B includes a private bath, S a private shower). If there is no '/', the prices are only for twin or double rooms (as far as we know there are no singles). If there is no B or S, as far as we know no rooms have private facilities.

PEOVER HEATH

SJ7973   MAP 7

Dog 🍺

Off A50 N of Holmes Chapel at the Whipping Stocks, keep on past Parkgate into Wellbank Lane; OS Sheet 118 map reference 794735; note that this village is called Peover Heath on the OS map and shown under that name on many road maps, but the pub is often listed under Over Peover instead; WA16 8UP

Homely pub with interesting range of beers and generous traditional food

The neatly kept bar here is gently old fashioned with a comfortably cottagey feel. Neat tied back floral curtains hang at its little windows, a curved cushioned banquette is built into a bay window and mixed furnishings, mostly traditional dark wheelbacks, are arranged on a patterned carpet. A coal fire, copper pieces and pot plants dotted around add to the homely feel; games machine, darts, pool, dominoes, board games, TV and piped music. The five reasonably priced and very well kept real ales here will probably be Copper Dragon Scotts 1816, Hydes Bitter and Dark Mild, Weetwood and a guest. They also have Addlestone's cider, 35 different malt whiskies and eight wines by the glass. There are picnic-sets beneath colourful hanging baskets on the peaceful lane, and more out in a pretty back garden. It's a pleasant walk from here to the Jodrell Bank Centre and Arboretum; recently refurbished bedrooms.

🍽 Bar food includes many pub standards, such as soup, sandwiches, hot baguettes, ploughman's, curry or sausage of the day and mash, steak and ale pie, oatcakes stuffed with leeks, mushrooms and cheese, giant cod with chips and mushy peas and roast beef, with puddings such as strawberry pavlova or pecan and lemon cheesecake. *Starters/Snacks: £3.50 to £8.50. Main Courses: £9.75 to £15.00. Puddings: £3.95*

Free house ~ Licensee Steven Wrigley ~ Real ale ~ Bar food (12-2.30, 6-9; 12-8.30 Sun) ~ Restaurant ~ (01625) 861421 ~ Dogs allowed in bar ~ Live music monthly Fri, also Weds and Fri in Dec ~ Open 11.30-3, 4.30-11; 11.10-11 Sat; 12-10.30 Sun ~ Bedrooms: £60B/£80B

Recommended by Susan and Nigel Brookes, John Saville, Brian and Janet Ainscough, Anne and Steve Thompson, P J and R D Greaves, Gerry and Rosemary Dobson

PLUMLEY

SJ7075   MAP 7

Smoker

2.5 miles from M6 junction 19: A556 towards Northwich and Chester; WA16 0TY

400-year-old pub with spotlessly kept comfortable lounges, welcoming staff and good food

Named after a favourite racehorse of the Prince Regent, this relaxing 16th-c thatched pub has dark panelling, open fires in impressive period fireplaces, deep sofas, and other comfortable seats and settles in its three connecting rooms. Look out for the Edwardian print of a hunt meeting outside (tucked in amongst the military prints), which shows how little the pub's appearance has changed over the centuries. The collection of copper kettles is sweet; piped music. Very helpful staff serve a good choice of wines and whiskies, with Robinsons Unicorn and a couple of guests such as Hartleys XB and Tempus Fugit on handpump. The sizeable garden has roses, flower beds and a children's play area.

🍽 Very enjoyable food includes chicken liver pâté with onion marmalade, crispy duck pancake, battered haddock and mushy peas, steak and ale pie, ham hock with apricot and brandy sauce, poached salmon with watercress sauce, puddings such as lemon tart with raspberry coulis, crème brûlée, and meringue nest with whipped cream and butterscotch sauce, and local cheeses. *Starters/Snacks: £3.95 to £5.95. Main Courses: £7.95 to £15.95. Puddings: £4.95*

Robinsons ~ Tenants John and Diana Bailey ~ Real ale ~ Bar food (10-2.30, 6-9.30; 10-9 Sun) ~ Restaurant ~ (01565) 722338 ~ Children welcome ~ Open 10-3, 6-11; 10am-10.30pm Sun

Recommended by Paul and Margaret Baker, K C and B Forman, Piotr Chodzko-Zajko, Alan Bulley, Pam and John Smith

PRESTBURY

SJ8976   MAP 7

Legh Arms 🛏

A538, village centre; SK10 4DG

Comfortable and immaculately kept inn with good food, appealingly individual bar, terraced garden, and beautiful bedrooms

The relaxing bar areas here are smartly traditional, very much smart-hotel-lounge, with plenty of elegant soft furnishings. Though opened up, it is well divided into several intimate areas, with muted tartan fabric over a panelled dado on the right, ladderback dining chairs, good solid dark tables, stylish french steam train prints, italian costume engravings and a glass case of china and books. On the left there are brocaded bucket seats around more solid tables, antique steeplechase prints, and staffordshire dogs on the stone mantelpiece, all warmed by a good coal fire; a snug panelled back part has cosy wing armchairs and a grand piano, and a narrow side offshoot has pairs of art deco leather armchairs around small granite tables, and antique costume prints of french tradesmen. The bar, towards the back on the left, has well kept Robinsons Unicorn and Hatters Mild on handpump and nice house wines (eight by the glass), a good range of malts and cognacs, good coffee, and maybe genial regulars perched on the comfortable leather bar stools; this part looks up to an unusual balustraded internal landing. There are daily papers on a coffee table, and magazines on an antique oak dresser; piped music. A garden behind has a terrace with outdoor heating, tables and chairs.

🍽 **Very tasty bar food might include soup, spicy fishcakes with sweet chilli sauce, pea, leek and mint risotto with goats cheese, thai chicken curry, fish and chips, slow roast pork belly with apple sauce, steak, Guinness and cheese pie, roast trout with rosemary and white wine sauce, and puddings such as chocolate torte and sticky toffee pudding. The pricier menu in the sumptuous restaurant is more elaborate.** *Starters/Snacks: £3.95 to £8.00. Main Courses: £8.00 to £20.00. Puddings: £3.50*

Robinsons ~ Tenant Peter Myers ~ Real ale ~ Bar food (12-10(9.30 Sun)) ~ Restaurant ~ (01625) 829130 ~ Children welcome if seated ~ Open 11-11(midnight Sat) ~ Bedrooms: /£95B

Recommended by Mrs P J Carroll, Ian Legge, Revd D Glover, Malcolm Pellatt, Howard Dell, Chris Brooks, Pam and John Smith

TARPORLEY

SJ5562   MAP 7

Rising Sun

High Street; village signposted off A51 Nantwich—Chester; CW6 0DX

Friendly, bustling and quaint, with wide range of generously served homely food

The nice old interior at this family-run pub completely lives up to its appealingly aged brick frontage. It's cosily furnished with well chosen tables surrounded by eye-catching old seats (including creaky 19th-c mahogany and oak settles), an attractively blacked iron kitchen range, and sporting and other old-fashioned prints on the walls. There are one or two seats in a tiny side bar where they might put on a portable TV for major sporting events; piped music. Happy to please staff serve Robinsons Double Hop, Hartleys XB and Unicorn from handpumps.

🍽 **A very extensive menu lists pub standards such as soup, sandwiches, toasties, filled baked potatoes, half a dozen tasty pies, fish and chips, poached salmon with prawn and tomato sauce, a dozen spicy dishes such as fruit beef curry, over a dozen vegetarian dishes such as vegetable stroganoff, and 12oz sirloin.** *Starters/Snacks: £2.95 to £5.25. Main Courses: £7.35 to £16.00. Puddings: £3.75 to £3.95*

Robinsons ~ Tenant David Robertson ~ Real ale ~ Bar food (11.30-2, 5.30-9.30; 12-9 Sun) ~ Restaurant (evening) ~ (01829) 732423 ~ Children welcome ~ Open 11.30-3, 5.30-11; 11.30-11 Sat; 12-10.30 Sun

Recommended by the Didler, Denys Gueroult, Bob Broadhurst, Derek and Sylvia Stephenson

WILLINGTON

SJ5367 MAP 7

Boot

Boothsdale, off A54 at Kelsall; CW6 ONH

Friendly dining pub (you may need to book at weekends) with suntrap terrace, charming restaurant

This lovely old place is a careful conversion of a row of attractive sandstone cottages. The interior has been opened up around the central bar, leaving small unpretentiously furnished room areas, with lots of original features, and there's a woodburning stove. The charming flagstoned restaurant (with a roaring log fire) has wheelback chairs around plenty of tables. Friendly staff serve Greene King IPA, Tetleys and a guest from the local Weetwood brewery from handpumps, and 30 malt whiskies; they keep a decent wine list. An extension with french windows overlooks the garden (the three donkeys, and Sooty and Sweep the cats, are popular with children), and picnic-sets in front on the raised stone terrace are an idyllic suntrap in summer.

🍴 **Besides regularly changing specials such as spicy crab fishcakes, bass, smoked haddock with rarebit topping or pork belly, other dishes could include soup, olives and bread, sandwiches, steak and ale or fisherman's pie, fillet steak, and puddings such as sticky toffee pudding or rhubarb crumble.** *Starters/Snacks: £3.75 to £6.95. Main Courses: £9.50 to £16.95. Puddings: £3.90 to £4.95*

Punch ~ Lease Mike and Jon Gollings ~ Real ale ~ Bar food (11-2.30, 6-9.30; 11-9.30 Fri-Sun and bank hols) ~ Restaurant ~ (01829) 751375 ~ Well-behaved children welcome, no pushchairs ~ Open 10am-midnight

Recommended by Roger and Anne Newbury, Mrs Jane Kingsbury, Pamela and Alan Neale, Ann and Tony Bennett-Hughes, Derek and Sylvia Stephenson

WINCLE

SJ9665 MAP 7

Ship

Village signposted off A54 Congleton—Buxton; SK11 0QE

Popular sandstone 16th-c village pub in good walking country, thoughtful staff, Lees beers, good inventive food, and little garden

Durable flagstone floors and a warming coal fire in two simple little tap rooms make this stone walled pub the perfect refreshment stop after a walk in the lovely surrounding countryside – they even sell their own book of local walks, £3. The carpeted and gently lit lounge bar and restaurant provide a comfier alternative, and the sympathetically designed extension into the old stables, with flagstone floors, beams and woodburning stove, helps ease the weekend bustle. Three or four real ales come from the J W Lees portfolio and they've a few foreign bottled beers. A small garden has wooden tables.

🍴 **As well as imaginative generously served sandwiches, tasty bar food could include starters such as winter vegetable soup, fried lamb kidneys with brandy and pine nuts on black pudding, scallops in coconut sauce, main courses such as steak and ale pie, trout topped with basil pesto and almonds, mediterranean vegetable and goats cheese filo parcel with provençal sauce and roast chicken breast stuffed with stilton mousse on smoked bacon and leek carbonara, and puddings such as crème brûlée or banoffi pie.** *Starters/Snacks: £3.50 to £7.50. Main Courses: £9.95 to £17.95. Puddings: £4.95 to £6.95*

Lees ~ Tenant Christopher Peter Knights ~ Real ale ~ Bar food (12-2.30(3 Sat, Sun), 6.30-9) ~ Restaurant ~ (01260) 227217 ~ Children welcome but not in bar after 8pm ~ Dogs allowed in bar ~ Open 12-3, 6.30(5 Fri)-11; 5-11 Mon; 12-11 Sat; 12-10.30 Sun; closed Mon lunchtime

Recommended by Gwyn and Anne Wake, DC, Brian and Anna Marsden

---

Looking for a pub with a really special garden, or in lovely countryside, or with an outstanding view, or right by the water? They are listed separately, at the back of the book.

WRENBURY   SJ5947   MAP 7

Dusty Miller

Village signposted from A530 Nantwich—Whitchurch; Cholmondeley Road; CW5 8HG

Generous food and views of busy canal from bars and terrace of big mill conversion

Sitting right next to the Shropshire Union Canal, this substantial brick pub is a neatly converted 19th-c corn mill – you can still see the old lift hoist up under the rafters. The River Weaver runs in an aqueduct under the canal at this point, and it was the river that once powered the millrace. These days a constant stream of boats slipping through the striking counter-weighted canal drawbridge outside, provides entertainment if you're sitting at picnic-sets among rose bushes on the gravel terrace, or at one of the tables inside by a series of tall glazed arches. The atmosphere is low-key restaurant, with some emphasis on the generously served food, though drinkers are welcome, and in summer the balance may even tip. The very spacious modern feeling main bar area is comfortably furnished with a mixture of seats (including tapestried banquettes, oak settles and wheelback chairs) round rustic tables. Further in, a quarry-tiled part by the bar counter has an oak settle and refectory table. Friendly staff serve three well kept Robinsons beers on handpump; eclectic piped music.

🍴 **The monthly changing menu might include soup, creamed garlic and horseradish mushrooms, smoked salmon and halibut salad, roast vegetable lasagne, steak, kidney and Guinness pie, blackened salmon fillet with horseradish cream, beer braised chuck steak, puddings such as syrup sponge and warm chocolate brownie and rhubarb and honey crumble; british cheeses.** *Starters/Snacks: £4.25 to £5.95. Main Courses: £9.95 to £15.95. Puddings: £4.50 to £4.95*

Robinsons ~ Tenant Mark Sumner ~ Real ale ~ Bar food (12-2(2.30 Sun), 6.30-9.30(7-9 Sun)) ~ Restaurant ~ (01270) 780537 ~ Children welcome ~ Dogs allowed in bar ~ Folk last Fri of month ~ Open 12-3, 6.30(7 Sun)-11; closed Mon lunchtime in winter

Recommended by Paul and Gail Betteley, Meg and Colin Hamilton, A Darroch Harkness

LUCKY DIP

Besides the fully inspected pubs, you might like to try these Lucky Dips recommended to us and described by readers (if you do, please send us reports: feedback@thegoodpubguide.co.uk).

ACTON BRIDGE [SJ5974]
Hazel Pear CW8 3RA [Hill Top Rd]:
Welcoming country pub with good value home cooking, OAP discounts, pleasant attentive service, Marstons Pedigree and Timothy Taylors Landlord, good wine choice; children welcome, open all day *(Mr and Mrs John Taylor)*
ALPRAHAM [SJ5759]
Travellers Rest CW6 9JA [A51 Nantwich—Chester]: Unspoilt four-room country local with friendly staff and veteran landlady (same family for three generations), well kept Caledonian Deuchars IPA and Tetleys Bitter and Mild, low prices, leatherette, wicker and Formica, some flock wallpaper, fine old brewery mirrors, darts and dominoes, back bowling green; no machines, piped music or food (apart from crisps and nuts), cl wkdy lunchtimes *(Dave Webster, Sue Holland, the Didler, Pete Baker)*
ALTRINCHAM [SJ7688]
☆ *Victoria* WA14 1EX [Stamford St]: Civilised dining pub, airy and uncluttered, with panelling and chunky tables, lots of wood, slate and exposed brick, comfortable fireside settees on right, sensibly short choice of

generous local seasonal food such as herdwick mutton hotpot and pink veal and mushroom pudding, good Sun roasts, mainstream real ales, friendly service; some outside seating, open all day *(Siobhan Pollitt, Dave and Shirley Shaw)*
ANDERTON [SJ6475]
Stanley Arms CW9 6AG [just NW of Northwich; Old Rd]: Busy friendly local by Trent & Mersey Canal in pleasant surroundings overlooking amazing restored Anderton boat lift, wide choice of good value generous pubby food, well kept John Smiths and Tetleys, nice family dining area; tables in attractive yard with grassy play area, overnight mooring *(Tony Hobden, Ben Williams)*
AUDLEM [SJ6543]
Shroppie Fly CW3 0DX [Shropshire St]: Three-room former warehouse by Locks 12/13 of Shrops Union Canal, welcoming staff, five ales, good value pub food, bar made from original barge, canal memorabilia, mainly modern furnishings, central fire, pool in public bar; piped music, live music Mon (folk) and wknds, they may try to keep your credit card while you eat; children welcome,

waterside terrace, cl winter lunchtimes, open almost all day summer (David and Sue Smith, LYM)

BARBRIDGE [SJ6156]
Barbridge Inn CW5 6AY [just off A51 N of Nantwich]: Open-plan family dining pub by lively marina at junction of Shropshire Union and Middlewich canals, well kept Greene King, Boddingtons and Wells & Youngs ales, enjoyable pub food, friendly staff, tiled floors, faded woodwork, country prints and artefacts, flagstoned conservatory with washtub tables, games room; play area in busy riverside garden, good disabled facilities, open all day (LYM, Tim and Rosemary Wells)

BEESTON [SJ5559]
Beeston Castle Hotel CW6 9NJ [A49 S of Tarporley]: Comfortable pub below castle, friendly efficient staff, wide choice of good food inc bargain OAP lunches, small wing chairs and nicely placed tables in spacious bar, well kept Black Sheep and Timothy Taylors Landlord, short well chosen wine list, restaurant; children till 8, comfortable bedrooms, good walking country, open all day Sun (Alan and Eve Harding)

BICKERTON [SJ5254]
Bickerton Poacher SY14 8BE [A534 E of junction with A41]: Rambling 17th-c poacher-theme pub, linked beamed rooms with open fires, glass-covered well, copper-mining memorabilia and talkative parrot, reasonably priced food inc wknd carvery, Greene King Old Speckled Hen, Theakstons and Wells & Youngs Bombardier, selection of wines, skittle alley; sheltered partly covered courtyard, play area (LYM, Edward Leetham)

BOLLINGTON [SJ9477]
☆ *Poachers* SK10 5BU [Mill Lane]: Friendly stone-built village local prettily set in good walking area, wide choice of good food (not Mon) inc bargain lunches and Sun menu, well kept Copper Dragon, Timothy Taylors Landlord and three guest beers, decent wines, dining room (best to book wknds); attractive secluded garden and terrace behind, cl Mon lunchtime (Brian and Anna Marsden)
Vale SK11 0AW [heading N off B5091 by railway viaduct]: Pleasantly modernised one-room local doing well under friendly and enthusiastic new licensees, five well kept changing ales inc Storm Tornado, Timothy Taylors Landlord and Weetwood Cheshire Cat, good value home-made food (all day Sat) from baguettes up, log fire; children welcome till 7, garden overlooking cricket pitch, canal walks nearby, open all day wknds (Brian and Anna Marsden, LYM, G D K Fraser)

BROWNLOW [SJ8360]
Brownlow Inn CW12 4TH [Brownlow Heath Lane, off A34 S of Congleton]: Tucked-away (but busy) traditional country dining pub, wide choice of good value food from baguettes to daily roasts (should book for popular Sun lunch), choice of beers, good

value house wine, good friendly service, log fire, conservatory (Annette and John Derbyshire)

CHESTER [SJ4065]
☆ *Bear & Billet* CH1 1RU [Lower Bridge St]: Handsome timbered 17th-c Okells pub with four changing guest ales such as Copper Dragon Best Bill, belgian and US imports, nice range of wines by the glass and of reasonably priced home-cooked pubby food, interesting features and some attractive furnishings in friendly and comfortable open-plan bar with fire, sitting and dining rooms upstairs; plasma sport TV; pleasant courtyard, open all day (Dave Webster, Sue Holland, the Didler, BB)
Dublin Packet CH1 2HA [Northgate St]: Comfortable pastiche of old-style town pub, etched windows, plenty of old-world prints, real ales such as Theakstons and Wells & Youngs Bombardier, good value pubby food, friendly staff; quiet piped music, big-screen TV; open all day (BB, Tim and Rosemary Wells)
Falcon CH1 1RS [Lower Bridge St]: Striking ancient building with handsome beams and brickwork, good value bar food (not Sun) from sandwiches to enterprising specials, friendly helpful staff, bargain Sam Smiths; piped music, games machine; children allowed lunchtime (not Sat) in airy attractive upstairs room; open all day Sat, interesting vaults tours (LYM, Colin Moore)
Olde Boot CH1 1LQ [Eastgate Row N]: Cosy pub in lovely 17th-c Rows building, heavy beams, dark woodwork, oak flooring, flagstones, some exposed Tudor wattle and daub, old kitchen range in lounge beyond, old-fashioned settles and oak panelling in upper area popular with families, enjoyable good value food, bargain Sam Smiths OB, good service; piped music (the Didler, Joe Green, LYM, Ian Legge, Colin Moore)
Pied Bull CH1 2HQ [Upper Northgate St]: Roomy open-plan carpeted bar, wide choice of generous reasonably priced food all day inc afternoon teas, well kept Adnams Broadside, attentive welcoming staff, attractive mixed furnishings, divided inner area with china cabinet and lots of pictures, nice snug by pillared entrance, imposing fireplace; games machines, may be piped music; open all day, handsome Jacobean stairs to bedrooms (BB, Catherine and Rob Dunster)
Ship Victory CH1 3EQ [George St]: Welcoming old local, low beams and simple décor, well kept Tetleys and changing guest beers, music nights (the Didler)
Telfords Warehouse CH1 4EZ [Tower Wharf, behind Northgate St nr rly]: Well kept interesting ales in large converted canal building, generous fresh up-to-date food, efficient staff, bare brick and boards, high pitched ceiling, big wall of windows overlooking water, massive iron winding gear in bar, some old enamelled advertisements, good photographs for sale, steps to heavy-

beamed area with sofas, more artwork and restaurant; late-night live music; tables out by water, open all day *(BB, the Didler, Colin Moore, Catherine and Rob Dunster)*

☆ **Union Vaults** CH1 3ND [Francis St/Egerton St]: Friendly old-fashioned street-corner local, well kept Caledonian Deuchars IPA and two changing guest ales, three separate dining areas, friendly staff, old local photographs, back games room; piped music, sports TV; open all day *(Dave Webster, Sue Holland, the Didler, Joe Green)*

CHILDER THORNTON [SJ3678]

☆ **White Lion** CH66 5PU [off A41 S of M53 junction 5; New Rd]: Low two-room whitewashed country pub, old-fashioned and unpretentiously welcoming, good value sensible lunches (not Sun) from good hot filled rolls up, well kept Thwaites ales, open fire, framed matchbooks, no music or machines (small TV for big matches); children welcome, tables out in covered front area and secluded back garden, play area, open all day *(MLR)*

CHRISTLETON [SJ4565]

Plough CH3 7PT [Plough Lane]: Welcoming 18th-c country local, three linked areas, up to nine ales inc Spitting Feathers and Theakstons, home-cooked local food (not Sun); garden with play area *(the Didler, Alan and Eve Harding)*

CHURCH LAWTON [SJ8255]

Red Bull ST7 3AJ [Congleton Rd S (A34), by Trent & Mersey Canal]: Welcoming pub by Trent & Mersey Canal lock, several rooms inc upstairs lounge and eating area, open fires, good value home-made food, well kept Robinsons; no credit cards *(Richard and Karen Holt)*

CHURTON [SJ4156]

White Horse CH3 6LA [Chester Rd (B5130)]: Warm friendly village pub, three attractive and comfortable linked areas, good fresh food (not Mon, all day Sun), good value midweek fixed-price menu, Adnams and Jennings, good choice of well priced wines; children welcome, garden, cl Mon lunchtime *(Mr and Mrs J Palmer, Barry Hayes)*

CONGLETON [SJ8663]

Beartown Tap CW12 1RL [Willow St (A54)]: Tap for small nearby Beartown brewery, their interesting beers well priced and perhaps a guest microbrew, changing farm cider, bottled belgians, bare boards in friendly down-to-earth bar and two light airy rooms off, no food, games or music; upstairs lavatories; open all day Fri-Sun *(Tony Hobden, the Didler)*

Queens Head CW12 3DE [Park Lane]: Friendly licensees, good choice of well kept ales, limited choice of basic food; by Macclesfield Canal, steps up from towpath to large garden with play area, bedrooms, open all day *(Ben Williams, Tony and Wendy Hobden)*

CREWE [SJ7055]

Borough Arms CW1 2BG [Earle St]: Popular and friendly, nine changing ales and own microbrewery, great range of belgian beers,

friendly enthusiastic landlord, two small rooms off central bar and downstairs lounge, no machines; occasional sports TV, no under-21s; picnic-sets on back terrace and lawn, cl wkdy lunchtimes, open all day wknds from 12 *(Dave Webster, Sue Holland, Selwyn Roberts, the Didler)*

British Lion CW2 6AL [Nantwich Rd]: Cosy traditional local known as the Pig, genuine and friendly, comfortable partly panelled bar, back snug, well kept Tetleys and guest beer, darts, dominoes; no food; cl wkdy lunchtimes *(John Tav, Dave Webster, Sue Holland)*

Hops CW1 2DF [Prince Albert St]: Relaxed family-run belgian café-bar with huge range of continental bottled beers, three local real ales, interesting snacks and light meals, real tea and coffee *(Edward Leetham)*

DARESBURY [SJ5782]

Ring o' Bells WA4 4AJ [B5356, handy for M56 junction 11]: Chef & Brewer with wide choice of food all day, several real ales, lots of wines by the glass, comfortable library-style areas and part more suited to walkers (canal is not far); young staff (service can slow); children in eating areas, good disabled access, tables in long partly terraced garden, pretty village, church with *Alice in Wonderland* window, open all day *(LYM, Glenwys and Alan Lawrence, Mrs Hazel Rainer, Revd D Glover, Pat and Tony Martin)*

DEAN ROW [SJ8781]

Unicorn SK9 2LN [Adlington Rd]: Large well run local with several rooms off main bar, Black Sheep, Fullers London Pride, Timothy Taylors Landlord and Wells & Youngs Bombardier, bar food and separate restaurant; outside heated seating *(Malcolm Pellatt)*

EATON [SJ8765]

☆ **Plough** CW12 2NH [A536 Congleton—Macclesfield]: 17th-c family pub with beams, stripped brickwork, log fires, well kept Hydes and Moorhouses, ten wines by the glass, pubby food (all day Sun) inc sandwiches, attractive raftered back barn restaurant, occasional live music; piped music, TV; Peak views from big attractive garden, good bedroom block (dogs welcome), open all day *(LYM, Catherine and Rob Dunster, Mrs P J Carroll, David and Ros Hanley)*

FRODSHAM [SJ5277]

☆ **Bulls Head** WA6 6BS [Bellemonte Rd, Overton – off B5152 at Parish Church sign; M56 junction 12 not far]: Charming early 17th-c pub renamed by new licensees (was Ring o' Bells), bargain food inc good Sun lunch, friendly staff and cats, little rambling rooms, beams, dark oak panelling and stained glass, changing ales from central servery, games room; children in eating areas, lovely secluded back garden with pond *(Ann and Tony Bennett-Hughes, LYM)*

FULLERS MOOR [SJ4954]

Copper Mine CH3 9JH [A534]: Comfortable bustling dining pub, light and airy, with wide choice of enjoyable food from big lunchtime sandwiches to good Sun lunches, well kept ale, friendly staff, pine furnishings, cosy coal fire, pretty nooks and crannies, interesting copper-mining memorabilia and lots of copper kettles and warming pans; children welcome, spacious garden with barbecues and lovely views, handy for Sandstone Trail *(Rita and Keith Pollard, LYM)*

GAWSWORTH [SJ8869]

☆ *Harrington Arms* SK11 9RJ [Church Lane]: Rustic 17th-c farm pub with two small basic rooms (children allowed in one), bare boards and panelling, fine carved oak bar counter, Robinsons Best and Hatters Mild, simple bar snacks such as pork pies (may be more food); Fri folk night; sunny benches on small front cobbled terrace *(LYM, the Didler)*

GRAPPENHALL [SJ6386]

Parr Arms WA4 3EP [nr M6 junction 20; A50 towards Warrington, left after 1.5 miles; Church Lane]: Charming pub in picture-postcard setting with tables out by church, good smiling service, enjoyable fresh food from sandwiches up, well kept Thwaites and a guest such as Spitting Feathers, several different areas of central bar *(Alan and Eve Harding, Julian and Janet Dearden, Edward Mirzoeff)*

GREAT BUDWORTH [SJ6677]

☆ *George & Dragon* CW9 6HF [signed off A559 NE of Northwich; High St]: Attractive 17th/18th-c building, doing well under friendly current licensees, good value pubby food inc good Sun lunch, three good changing ales inc local Weetwood, farm cider, decent coffee, rambling beamed and panelled lounge, interesting old pictures, red plush button-back banquettes and older settles, upstairs restaurant and family dining area, back games room; delightful village, open all day Fri-Sun *(Mark Bannister, LYM, Tony Hobden, Alan and Eve Harding)*

HANKELOW [SJ6645]

White Lion CW3 0JA [A529 Audlem–Nantwich]: Pleasantly refurbished traditional pub opp village green and pond, two roomy bars and restaurant, open fires, Wells & Youngs Bombardier and two guest ales (often local), interesting menu (not Mon), good value Sun lunches, small varied wine list, efficient attentive service; garden picnic-sets and play area *(Edward Leetham)*

HASSALL GREEN [SJ7858]

Romping Donkey CW11 4YA: Picturesque black-and-white pub by Trent & Mersey Canal locks, bevelled beams and ledged doors in bustling bar neatly furnished to match appearance, several real ales, good wines by the glass, pub food; garden with terrace and play area *(LYM, Ben Williams)*

HIGH LEGH [SJ7084]

Bears Paw WA16 0RT [Warrington Rd (A50 E of M6 junction 20)]: Comfortable and welcoming old roadside pub, two carpeted dining rooms offer a wide, enjoyable food cooked to order (so may take a while), Marstons Pedigree; tables out behind *(Steve and Sarah Eardley)*

HUXLEY [SJ5061]

Farmers Arms CH3 9BG [off A51 SE of Chester]: Friendly local with two fires, bric-a-brac and real ales, smallish separately run restaurant with good food esp steaks, Sun lunches, well priced wines; tables outside *(J Bittlestone)*

KELSALL [SJ5268]

Morris Dancer CW6 0RS [Chester Rd]: Friendly efficient new licensees reworking this as traditional village pub, good simple home-made food, local Weetwood ales, good wines by the glass, reopened restaurant (may restore old name – the Globe) *(Su Titchner)*

Royal Oak CW6 0RR [Chester Rd]: Impressive building with some emphasis on enjoyable all-day food, Sun carvery, several changing ales, welcoming staff; children welcome, courtyard tables, six bedrooms, camping, open all day *(Maartin Allcock)*

KETTLESHULME [SJ9879]

☆ *Swan* SK23 7QU [Macclesfield Rd (B5470)]: Thriving little stone-built beamed 16th-c pub run by consortium of locals inc former main-entry landlord of Oddfellows in Mellor, smartly renovated, well kept Marstons and two interesting guest beers, farm cider, good food from sandwiches to great fish range, popular Sun lunch inc very rare beef, log fires, old settles and pews, Dickens prints; children welcome, large garden with stream, good walks, cl Mon lunchtime, open all day wknds *(Annette and John Derbyshire, Roger Yates, Dr Peter Crawshaw, Brian and Anna Marsden, Dennis Jones)*

KNUTSFORD [SJ7578]

Cross Keys WA16 6DT [King St]: Ancient building, well kept ale inc guests, good bar menu inc well served steaks, very pleasant service *(Dr D Scott)*

Lord Eldon WA16 6AD [Tatton St, off A50 at White Bear roundabout]: Old coaching inn with friendly staff and chatty locals, four comfortable rooms, beams and brasses, large open fire, well kept local ales; music nights *(Roger Wain-Heapy, Tom and Jill Jones)*

LANGLEY [SJ9471]

☆ *Leathers Smithy* SK11 0NE [off A523 S of Macclesfield, OS Sheet 118 map ref 942715]: Isolated pub up in fine walking country, Theakstons, Wells & Youngs and guest ales, lots of whiskies, enjoyable bar food from sandwiches up, good cheerful service, pleasant relaxing atmosphere, log fire, flagstoned bar and dining room, interesting local prints and photographs; unobtrusive piped music; no dogs, picnic-sets in garden behind and on grass opposite, open all day wknds *(Michael Butler, LYM, David Crook, Edward Leetham)*

LITTLE BUDWORTH [SJ5867]

Cabbage Hall CW6 9ES [Forest Rd (A49)]: Smart dining pub handy for Cheshire Polo Club (has a helipad), good wines by the glass and top-drawer list, beautifully presented restaurant food, good value early suppers, friendly staff, squashy sofas and plush chairs in bar still used by drinkers, thriving atmosphere; garden tables *(Mrs P J Carroll)*

Red Lion CW6 9BY [Vicarage Lane]: Traditional local in unspoilt spot, good choice of generous food from sandwiches up, well kept Robinsons, bright interior with nice fire; good bedrooms, country walks *(John Andrew)*

LOWER PEOVER [SJ7474]

Bells of Peover WA16 9PZ [just off B5081; The Cobbles]: Chef & Brewer in charming spot, lovely wisteria-covered building with plenty of old-fashioned character, panelling, antiques and good coal fire, well kept Timothy Taylors Landlord and Wells & Youngs Bombardier; piped music, no children unless eating full meal in dining room; terrace tables, big side lawn with trees, rose pergolas and little stream, on quiet cobbled lane with fine black and white 14th-c church, open all day *(Dr Phil Putwain, the Didler, Ann and Tony Bennett-Hughes, LYM, Pam and John Smith)*

LOWER WHITLEY [SJ6178]

Chetwode Arms WA4 4EN [just off A49, handy for M56 junction 10; Street Lane]: Rambling low-beamed family dining pub, good generous food in side and other rooms from lunchtime baguettes up inc bargain meals, pleasant efficient service, solid furnishings all clean and polished, friendly local front bar, warm coal fires, four real ales, good wines by the glass; immaculate bowling green, play area, has been open all day Sat *(LYM, Oliver Richardson)*

LOWER WITHINGTON [SJ8268]

Black Swan SK11 9EQ [Trap St]: Pleasantly refurbished country pub popular for its restaurant (worth booking), bar snacks too, friendly staff *(Mrs P J Carroll)*

LYMM [SJ7087]

Barn Owl WA13 0SW [Agden Wharf, Warrington Lane (just off B5159 E)]: Comfortably extended building in picturesque setting by Bridgewater Canal, good value fresh food all day inc OAP bargains, Marstons Bitter and Pedigree and guest beers, decent wines by the glass, friendly atmosphere, pleasant service even though bay canal trips, open all day *(Ben Williams)*

MACCLESFIELD [SJ9272]

Railway View SK11 7JW [Byrons Lane (off A523)]: Pair of 1700 cottages knocked into roomy pub with attractive snug corners, six or more changing ales inc Storm, farm cider, good value simple home-made food, friendly service, remarkably shaped gents'; music nights and beer festivals; back terrace overlooking railway, open all day wknds *(the Didler)*

Waters Green Tavern SK11 6LH [Waters Green, opp stn]: Quickly changing and interesting largely northern ales in roomy L-shaped open-plan local, good home-made lunchtime food (not Sun), friendly staff and locals, back pool room *(the Didler)*

MARTON [SJ8568]

☆ *Davenport Arms* SK11 9HF [A34 N of

Congleton]: Comfortable, roomy and tasteful, good fresh food from ciabattas and baguettes up in bar and refurbished dining room inc their speciality venison and black pudding salad, good value Sun lunch, friendly obliging service, Courage Directors, Theakstons Best and a more or less local guest beer; no dogs; nr ancient half-timbered church and Europe's widest oak tree) *(Dr D J and Mrs S C Walker)*

MOBBERLEY [SJ8079]

☆ *Bird in Hand* WA16 7BW [Knolls Green; B5085 towards Alderley]: Well run low-beamed traditional pub, good plain fairly priced food, bargain Sam Smiths OB, lots of malt whiskies, decent house wines, linked rooms with comfortably cushioned heavy wooden seats, warm coal fires, small pictures on Victorian wallpaper, little panelled snug, good top dining area, pub games; children allowed, pleasant sunny front terrace with awning, open all day *(Noel Grundy, LYM, Dr Phil Putwain, Pam and John Smith)*

☆ *Plough & Flail* WA16 7DB [Paddock Hill; small sign off B5085 towards Wilmslow]: Light and airy family pub with consistently good unpretentious home-made food, attentive cheerful service, good wines by the glass, real ales; good garden with play area *(Mrs P J Carroll, John and Barbara Hirst, P J and R D Greaves)*

MOORE [SJ5784]

Red Lion WA4 6UD [Runcorn Rd]: Beamed pub with two homely rooms off main bar, good range of bar food, local Coach House ales, interesting wines by the glass, separate sports bar with big-screen TV; outside picnic-sets, back play area *(Edward Leetham)*

MOULDSWORTH [SJ5170]

Goshawk CH3 8AJ [Station Rd (B5393)]: Comfortable family dining pub with masses of pictures and nice mix of largely pine furniture in extensive series of rooms inc small 'library' area, large double-sided log fire, attentive uniformed staff, good food from sandwiches to upscale restaurany dishes (all day wknds); free rail travel from Chester if you eat), enterprising wines by the glass, real ales such as Greene King, Timothy Taylors Landlord and Wells & Youngs Bombardier; piped music; good spot nr Delamere Forest with big outdoor area inc good play area and bowling green *(Tom and Jill Jones, Robin and Yvonne Calvert)*

NANTWICH [SJ6452]

☆ *Black Lion* CW5 5ED [Welsh Row]: Three little rooms alongside main bar, Titanic White Star and local Weetwood ales, farm cider, friendly locals and lots of dogs, old-fashioned nooks and crannies, beams, bare floors and timbered brickwork, big grandfather clock, coal fire, chess; open all day from 4 (1 Fri-Sun) *(the Didler, BB, Pete Baker, Edward Leetham)*

Globe CW5 7EA [Audlem Rd]: Now tied to nearby Woodlands with five of their ales and guest beers, good range of home-made reasonably priced pubby food, friendly helpful staff, comfortable seating inc some small room areas; garden tables *(Dave Webster, Sue Holland, Edward Leetham)*

NESTON [SJ2976]

☆ *Harp* CH64 0TB [Quayside, SW of Little Neston; keep on along track at end of Marshalls Rd]: Tucked-away two-room country local, well kept interesting changing ales, good malt whiskies, basic good value home-made lunchtime food, woodburner in pretty fireplace, pale quarry tiles and simple furnishings; children allowed in room on right, picnic-sets up on grassy front sea wall facing Dee marshes and Wales, glorious sunsets with wild calls of wading birds; open all day *(BB, MLR)*

NORLEY [SJ5772]

Tigers Head WA6 8NT [Pytchleys Hollow]: Refurbished 17th-c inn nr Delamere Forest under new friendly management, good value no-nonsense food inc giant yorkshire puddings, well kept Mild and other changing ales *(J S Burn)*

OVER PEOVER [SJ7674]

Whipping Stocks WA16 9EX [Stocks Lane]: Several neat rooms, good oak panelling and fittings, solid furnishings, well kept cheap Sam Smiths, neat friendly staff, big log fire, wide choice of low-priced popular food all day; children in eating area, picnic-sets in good-sized garden with safe play area, easy parkland walks *(Pam and John Smith, LYM)*

PARKGATE [SJ2778]

Boathouse CH64 6RN [village signed off A540]: Black and white timbered pub with well spaced tables in attractively refurbished linked rooms, enjoyable food from bar food to restaurant meals, cheerful staff, good value wines, Timothy Taylors Landlord, big conservatory with great views to Wales over silted Dee estuary *(Paul Humphreys, Alan and Eve Harding)*

☆ *Red Lion* CH64 6SB [The Parade (B5135)]: Comfortable neatly kept Victorian local with views over silted grassy estuary to Wales, typical pub furnishings, shiny brown beams hung with china, copper and brass, standard food inc sandwiches, OAP lunches and other bargain offers, Adnams, Tetleys and Wells & Youngs Bombardier, decent wines by the glass, flame-effect fire in pretty fireplace, good games room off public bar; picnic-sets on small front terrace, open all day *(BB, Keith and Sue Campbell)*

Ship CH64 6SA [The Parade]: Bow-window estuary views from long cheery bar of large hotel, good changing beers inc locals, good value bar food inc local fish (and afternoon teas), quick pleasant service, armchairs by open fire, restaurant; tables outside, 24 bedrooms, open all day *(Derek and Sylvia Stephenson, Paul Humphreys, MLR)*

PLUMLEY [SJ7275]

☆ *Golden Pheasant* WA16 9RX [Plumley Moor Lane (off A556 by the Smoker)]: Civilised, friendly and well extended, well kept Lees

Bitter and Mild and decent food in comfortable lounge areas, wider menu in roomy restaurant and conservatory; children welcome, spacious gardens inc play area and bowling green, good bedrooms *(LYM, Paul and Margaret Baker, Pam and John Smith)*

RAINOW [SJ9678]

☆ *Highwayman* SK10 5UU [A5002 Whaley Bridge—Macclesfield, NE of village]: Warmly welcoming 17th-c moorside pub with good value food from unusual sandwiches to good local steaks, Thwaites ales, cosy low-beamed rooms with lovely log fires, separate restaurant; outside seating, grand views *(LYM, the Didler)*

RODE HEATH [SJ8057]

Broughton Arms ST7 3RU [Sandbach Rd (A533)]: By Trent & Mersey Canal, bar food, Burton Bridge and Marstons Pedigree; picnic-sets on heated terrace and waterside lawn *(Tony and Wendy Hobden, Ben Williams)*

SHOCKLACH [SJ4349]

Bull SY14 7BL [off B5069 W of Malpas]: Recently reopened village pub with contemporary feel, beams and open fire, unusual furniture on stone and wood floors, good range of interesting fresh food and of wines, five ales inc Marstons Pedigree, friendly informal service, conservatory; back terrace and garden *(N Woods)*

SMALLWOOD [SJ7861]

☆ *Legs of Man* CW11 2UG [A50 S of Sandbach]: Good home-made food inc some imaginative dishes, good friendly family service, Robinsons ales, carefully matched comfortable chairs, banquettes, carpet, curtains and wallpaper, fin de siècle tall white nymphs on columns, lush potted plants, separate restaurant; children truly welcome, well spaced tables in attractive garden with play area *(BB, John Trevor and Susan Rispin)*

STOAK [SJ4273]

Bunbury Arms CH2 4HW [Little Stanney Lane; a mile from M53 junction 10, A5117 W then first left]: Small snug and big but cosy beamed lounge with interesting antique furniture, pictures and books, enjoyable and interesting food (all day Sun) from sandwiches up, good changing real ales, jovial landlord and friendly staff, open fires, board games; can get busy; garden tables (some M-way noise), short walk for canal users from bridge 136 or 138, handy for Cheshire Oaks shopping outlet, open all day *(Ann and Tony Bennett-Hughes, MLR)*

STRETTON [SJ6181]

Hollow Tree WA4 4LX [Tarporley Rd (A49 just off M56 junction 10)]: Large pub, part of group specialising in two-for-one meal deals, several attractive areas and different levels, Timothy Taylors Landlord and Theakstons Old Peculier, young staff *(Jeremy King)*

SUTTON [SJ9469]

☆ *Ryles Arms* SK11 0NN [Hollin Lane, Higher Sutton]: Popular dining pub in fine countryside, good generous food (all day wknds) from sandwiches to more elaborate dishes, well kept ales inc local Storm, decent priced wines, good choice of whiskies, pleasant décor, hill-view dining room, no music or games; french windows to terrace, bedrooms in converted barn, open all day wknds *(Catherine and Rob Dunster, LYM)*

SWETTENHAM [SJ7967]
☆ *Swettenham Arms* CW12 2LF [off A54 Congleton—Holmes Chapel or A535 Chelford—Holmes Chapel]: Attractive old country pub in pretty setting by scenic Quinta wildlife arboretum, imaginative choice of good food from sandwiches up in immaculate line of individually furnished rooms from sofas and easy chairs to dining area (must book Sun) with well spaced tables, fine range of well kept changing real ales, good wine choice, efficient friendly service, log fires; children welcome, picnic-sets on quiet side lawn, open all day Sun *(LYM, Selwyn Roberts, Mrs P J Carroll, Debbie Hiom)*

TARVIN [SJ4966]
George & Dragon CH3 8EE [High St]: Very promising newcomer, reopened by the restaurateur family who have made such a success of the Duke of Portland at Lach Dennis, good country food, nice wines by the glass, real ales inc Marstons, fresh proper bar with clean-cut contemporary décor, log fire in comfortable restaurant; six thoroughly up-to-date bedrooms *(anon)*

WARRINGTON [SJ6389]
Dog & Partridge WA1 3TZ [Manchester Rd, Paddington]: Now privately owned, with enjoyable locally sourced food, six ales; garden with play area *(Phil Holland)*

WETTENHALL [SJ6261]
☆ *Boot & Slipper* CW7 4DN [Long Lane]: Low-beamed knocked-through country pub with straightforward furnishings, log fire, unusual trio of back-lit arched pseudo-fireplaces forming one stripped-brick wall, Bass and Tetleys, darts, pubby food (all day Sun), attractive back restaurant with big country pictures; piped music; children welcome, picnic-sets on front cobbles, play area, bedrooms, open all day wknds *(Ann and Tony Bennett-Hughes, Dr A McCormick, LYM)*

WILDBOARCLOUGH [SK0071]
Cat & Fiddle SK11 0AR [A537 Macclesfield—Buxton]: Britain's 2nd-highest pub, surrounded by spectacular moorland (though on a trunk road), with magnificent views; otherwise an ordinary roadside pub, with Robinsons ales, generous food, second walkers' and bikers' bar with pool *(LYM, David Abbot)*

Crag SK11 0BD: Old stone-built pub, straightforward and spacious, in charming little sheltered valley below moors (good walk up Shutlingsloe for great views), good home cooking using local ingredients, well kept Worthington and a guest beer such as Marstons Pedigree, help-yourself coffee; walkers welcome (boot covers available), pretty terrace *(Maurice and Gill McMahon, Malcolm Pellatt, LYM)*

WYBUNBURY [SJ6949]
Swan CW5 7NA [Main Rd (B5071)]: Bow-windowed pub with nooks and crannies in comfortable rambling lounge, pleasant public bar, plenty of bric-a-brac, log fires, Robinsons ales, food, darts; piped music, TV, games machine; tables in garden by beautiful churchyard, bedrooms, open all day (cl Mon lunchtime) *(Dave Webster, Sue Holland, LYM, Martin Grosberg)*

Post Office address codings give the impression that some pubs are in Cheshire, when they're really in Derbyshire (and therefore included in this book under that chapter) or in Greater Manchester (see the Lancashire chapter).

Cornwall

New entries here this year include the Angarrack Inn (a fascinating collection of bric-a-brac and good Aga-cooked homely food), the Heron at Malpas (a lovely creekside spot for this light and airy pub, with popular food), the Beach Hut at Watergate Bay (a trendy but friendly and relaxed beach bar overlooking a great surfing beach), and the Bay View at Widemouth (a family-run sea-view hotel with informal, laid-back bars and bistro-style food). There are quite a few other waterside pubs in this county which do get extremely busy in good weather (best to arrive early): the Old Ferry at Bodinnick (just across the river from Fowey), the Cadgwith Cove (at the bottom of a little fishing village), the 5 Degrees West in Falmouth (the marina is across the road just by the car park), the Ship in Mousehole (views of the nearby harbour from the bars), the Pandora near Mylor Bridge (an idyllic waterfront spot), the Rashleigh at Polkerris (it overlooks a stunning beach and bay beyond), the Blue Peter in Polperro (windows in the bar have views of the harbour and sea), the Port Gaverne Inn near Port Isaac (just back from the sea and with lovely cliff walks all around), the Ship at Porthleven (built into the cliffs and looking down on the harbour), Blue at Porthtowan (right by a fantastic beach and popular with surfers), and the New Inn out on Tresco (handy for the quay and ferries). Other pubs doing well include the Blisland Inn (seven real ales in this cheerful pub), the Halzephron at Helston (a very popular dining pub, but it is up for sale), the Crown at Lanlivery (quite a few changes this year, most enjoyable), the Globe in Lostwithiel (bustling little town pub with good food), and the Kings Head at Ruan Lanihorne (in a little hamlet, with enjoyable drink and food). With our choice of Dining Pub of the Year in Cornwall, we have been stung for the last two years running. Our choice in each of those years has almost immediately changed, and not for the better. So we have had cold feet this year – fearing that our choice might again be the kiss of death for food quality. On current showing, our short list might have included the Rising Sun at Altarnun, Heron at Malpas, Blue at Porthtowan, Kings Head at Ruan Lanihorne and New Inn on Tresco. Some great picks in the Lucky Dip section at the end of the chapter include the Queens Arms at Botallack, Trengilly Wartha near Constantine, Smugglers Den at Cubert, King of Prussia in Fowey, Blue Anchor in Helston (for its own-brewed beers, and one might say own-brewed atmosphere), Ship at Lerryn, Cornish Arms at Pendoggett, Punch Bowl & Ladle at Penelewey, Crumplehorn Mill in Polperro, Who'd Have Thought It at St Dominick, Ship at Portloe, Springer Spaniel at Treburley, Driftwood Spars at Trevaunance Cove, New Inn at Veryan, and out in the Isles of Scilly the Turks Head on St Agnes and Atlantic Inn on St Mary's. The main local beers are Sharps (now the most widely available in good pubs), St Austell and Skinners; you may also come across beers from several smaller Cornish breweries such as Ales of Scilly and Organic.

ALTARNUN   SX2083   MAP 1

Rising Sun 🍴 ◖

Village signposted off A39 just W of A395 junction; pub itself NW of village, so if coming instead from A30 keep on towards Camelford; PL15 7SN

Welcoming pub with adventurous food and a good choice of real ales and wines

This is a chatty, friendly pub on the edge of Bodmin Moor with first-class food and several real ales. The low-beamed, L-shaped main bar has plain traditional furnishings, bare boards and polished delabole slate flagstones, some stripped stone, and a couple of coal fires. Greene King IPA and Skinners Betty Stogs and three guests on handpump from breweries such as St Austells, Sharps and Shepherd Neame; seven wines by the glass and local cider. Pool, games machine, darts and maybe piped music. Outside, there are seats on a terrace with more in the garden opposite. There's a field for camping (and a new shower block) screened off by high evergreens. The village itself is well worth a look and the church is beautiful. Dogs are allowed in the bar outside food times.

🍴 Using local produce, the well executed, imaginative bar food might include sandwiches using their home-made bread (the crab or the hot braised shredded beef rib tip with horseradish cream and gravy for dipping are both very good), ploughman's or fisherman's (local fresh, smoked and pickled fish), wild mushrooms on toast with a duck egg and pesto, pork and venison pâté with savoury jelly, sweet pickled vegetables and olive oil toast, goujons of plaice with tartare sauce, saddleback sausages with sage and onion gravy, ham with a honey-mustard glaze and eggs, roasted root vegetable and potato fritatta with herb crème fraîche, roast free-range chicken with sautéed wild mushrooms and leeks, cod in parsley sauce, large lunch salads like chicory, blue cheese and pear or crab, mango and avocado, popular steaks, and puddings such as molten-centred chocolate pudding with raspberry sauce and lemon meringue syllabub. There's a more elaborate restaurant menu. *Starters/Snacks: £3.95 to £5.25. Main Courses: £6.95 to £17.50. Puddings: £4.25*

Free house ~ Licensee Andy Mason ~ Real ale ~ Bar food ~ Restaurant ~ (01566) 86636 ~ Well behaved children welcome (but must be over 12 in restaurant) ~ Open 11-11; 12-10.30 Sun; 11-3, 5.30-11 Mon-Sat in winter

Recommended by Klaus and Elizabeth Leist, the Didler, P J Checksfield, Richard and Patricia Jefferson, Lynda Bentley, John and Bernadette Elliott, Di and Mike Gillam

ANGARRACK   SW5838   MAP 1

Angarrack Inn

Steamers Hill; off A30 at Hayle E roundabout; TR27 5JB

Amazing collection of bric-a-brac in friendly little village pub, real ales and proper home cooking

In a quiet village tucked below a railway viaduct, this little pub comes as quite a surprise. It's run by chatty and friendly licensees who are avid collectors of amazing bric-a-brac. The well divided rooms are stuffed full of plates and platters, measuring jugs, unusual black and white cigarette cards, stuffed owls, stag's head and a squirrel, a model plane and a seagull hanging from the green ceiling, various instruments such as bagpipes, a trumpet, trombone and bugle, a wicker pram filled with old-fashioned dolls, bone-handled cutlery in a butler's tray and several clocks and bellows. There are also several large cages with cockatiels and golden mantled rosellas (the cat coexists happily), a warm coal fire, and from a rather fine bar counter (with whisky boxes on the gantry above it) St Austell HSD, Tinners and Tribute on handpump; darts. Comfortable cushioned wall seats have homely cushions, and some tables are covered with lace cloths. The porch has soft toys and dried flowers and there are some picnic-sets outside. The tortoise is called Stanley.

🍴 Enjoyable Aga-cooked country food (using customers' home-grown produce) includes soups and broths, omelettes, mushroom risotto, steak in Guinness pie, trout caught by the landlord with parsley butter, chicken in stilton sauce, various stroganoffs, pork loin with a honey and mustard glaze, and puddings such as popular cherry pie and fruit crumbles; also, lunchtime sandwiches and ploughman's. *Starters/Snacks: £4.95 to £6.95. Main Courses: £6.95 to £12.50. Puddings: £3.95 to £5.50*

St Austell ~ Tenants David and Jackie Peake ~ Real ale ~ Bar food (12-2, 6(7 Sun)-9; not Mon or Tues lunchtime) ~ (01736) 752380 ~ Children welcome ~ Dogs welcome ~ Open 12-3, 6-11.30; closed Mon and Tues lunchtime

Recommended by Stanley and Annie Matthews

BLISLAND
SX1073   MAP 1

Blisland Inn 🍺
Village signposted off A30 and B3266 NE of Bodmin; PL30 4JF

Super choice of real ales and beer-related memorabilia in welcoming local; home-made food, and cheerful service

In a pretty village, this chatty local is a friendly place with a cheerful atmosphere and some fine real ales. Every inch of the beams and ceiling is covered with beer badges (or their particularly wide-ranging collection of mugs), and the walls are similarly filled with beer-related posters and memorabilia. Up to eight real ales are kept at any one time, tapped from the cask or on handpump. Two are brewed for the pub by Sharps – Blisland Special and Bulldog – and there's Exmoor Ale and four constantly changing guests from all over the country. They also have a changing farm cider, fruit wines, and real apple juice; good service. The carpeted lounge has a number of barometers on the walls, a rack of daily newspapers for sale, and a few standing timbers, and the family room has pool, table skittles, euchre, cribbage and dominoes; piped music. Plenty of picnic-sets outside. The popular Camel Trail cycle path is close by – though the hill up to Blisland is pretty steep. As with many pubs in this area, it's hard to approach without negotiating several single-track roads.

🍴 **Tasty, pubby food includes filled lunchtime baps, soup, burgers, fish and chips, and scampi with daily specials like steak and mushroom pie, stuffed peppers, lasagne, and moussaka, and puddings such as spotted dick and sticky toffee pudding.** *Starters/Snacks: £3.75 to £5.25. Main Courses: £6.95 to £14.95. Puddings: £3.95 to £5.75*

Free house ~ Licensees Gary and Margaret Marshall ~ Real ale ~ Bar food ~ (01208) 850739 ~ Children in family room only ~ Dogs welcome ~ Live music Sat evening ~ Open 11.30-11; 12-10.30 Sun

Recommended by Rona Murdoch, Barry and Sue Pladdys, R J Herd, John and Bernadette Elliott, W F C Phillips, Dr and Mrs M W A Haward, R K Phillips, Lynda Bentley, Mrs M K Matthews, Chris Glasson, Andrea Rampley, Pauline and Philip Darley, the Didler

BODINNICK
SX1352   MAP 1

Old Ferry
Across the water from Fowey; coming by road, to avoid the ferry queue turn left as you go down the hill – car park on left before pub; PL23 1LX

Bustling local across the water from Fowey, simple little rooms with nautical bits and pieces, and lots of summer customers

At its best (and least crowded) outside the peak holiday season, this popular old inn is a friendly place and best reached by parking in the public car park in Fowey and taking the small ferry across the water. The lane beside the pub, in front of the ferry slipway, is extremely steep and parking is limited. This is a splendid position and seats on the front terrace or in the homely little restaurant make the most of the pretty river views. Three simply furnished small rooms have quite a few bits of nautical memorabilia, a couple of half model ships mounted on the wall, and several old photographs, as well as wheelback chairs, built-in plush pink wall seats, and an old high-backed settle; there may be several friendly cats and a dog. The family room at the back is actually hewn into the rock; piped music. Sharps Own and in summer Sharps Coaster, on handpump, several wines by the glass and a farm cider. Lovely circular walks. Mobile phones are banned and a 50p fine goes to the RNLI.

🍴 **Bar food includes sandwiches, pasties, ploughman's, soup, filled baked potatoes, home-cooked ham and egg, steak and kidney in ale pie, battered cod, omelettes, evening** specials like duck liver and orange pâté, vegetable lasagne and scallop and monkfish au gratin, and puddings. *Starters/Snacks: £4.95 to £6.50. Main Courses: £7.50 to £9.95. Puddings: £4.25 to £5.00*

Free house ~ Licensees Royce and Patricia Smith ~ Real ale ~ Bar food (12-3, 6-9; 12-2.30, 6.30-8.30 in winter) ~ Restaurant ~ (01726) 870237 ~ Children welcome ~ Dogs allowed in bar and bedrooms ~ Open 11-11; 12-10 in winter; closed 25 Dec ~ Bedrooms: £80S/£85B

Recommended by Dave Webster, Sue Holland, Mrs Margo Finlay, Jörg Kasprowski, Peter Salmon, David Crook, Patrick Barber, Phil and Sally Gorton, Chris Glasson, MB, Francis Vernon, Canon Michael Bourdeaux, Nick Lawless

CADGWITH
SW7214   MAP 1

Cadgwith Cove Inn
Down very narrow lane off A3083 S of Helston; no nearby parking; TR12 7JX

Fine walks in either direction from old-fashioned inn at the bottom of fishing cove

This is a genuine community local but friendly to visitors too. It's in a fishing cove setting at the bottom of a charming village and whilst it's best to park at the top and meander down through the thatched cottages, it is quite a steep hike back up again. The two snugly dark front rooms have plain pub furnishings on their mainly parquet flooring, a log fire in one stripped stone end wall, lots of local photographs including gig races, cases of naval hat ribands and of fancy knot-work and a couple of compass binnacles. Some of the dark beams have ships' shields and others have spliced blue rope hand-holds. Flowers IPA, Sharps Doom Bar, Skinners Betty Stogs and a guest beer on handpump. A back bar has a huge and colourful fish mural and the left-hand room has a games machine and piped music. There are green-painted picnic-sets on the good-sized front terrace, some under a fairy-lit awning, looking down to the fish sheds by the bay. Fine coastal walks in either direction. The bedrooms look over the sea.

🍴 **Bar food includes sandwiches (the crab are well liked), soup, lasagne, spinach and feta pie, daily specials such as braised supreme of pheasant stuffed with pork and hazelnuts, seasonal lobster, monkfish with pancetta and garlic and local fish casserole, and puddings; best to check food times in winter.** *Starters/Snacks: £3.50 to £6.50. Main Courses: £6.00 to £10.00. Puddings: £4.95*

Punch ~ Lease David and Lynda Trivett ~ Real ale ~ Bar food ~ (01326) 290513 ~ Well supervised children welcome away from main bar ~ Dogs welcome ~ Live folk Tues evening, cornish singers Fri evening ~ Open 12-3, 6-11.30; midday-1am Sat; 12-10.30 Sun ~ Bedrooms: £30.25(£47.50S)/£60.50(£82.50S)

Recommended by Dave Webster, Sue Holland, Derek and Heather Manning, Barry and Anne

EGLOSHAYLE
SX0071   MAP 1

Earl of St Vincent
Off A389, just outside Wadebridge; PL27 6HT

Lots of interest including 200 antique clocks in tucked away local

It's worth popping into this pretty pub to look at the 200 antique clocks, all in working order. Other interesting collections include golfing memorabilia, art deco ornaments, and all sorts of rich furnishings. St Austell HSD, Tinners and Tribute on handpump; piped music. The flowering baskets and tubs are quite a sight in summer and you can enjoy them from the picnic-sets in the lovely garden.

🍴 **Bar food specialises in steaks but also has sandwiches, ploughman's, soup, mushroom and broccoli au gratin, ham and egg, various fish dishes like trout cleopatra, and puddings such as treacle tart.** *Starters/Snacks: £3.50 to £8.50. Main Courses: £5.00 to £16.00. Puddings: £4.00*

St Austell ~ Tenants Edward and Anne Connolly ~ Real ale ~ Bar food (not Sun evening) ~ Restaurant ~ (01208) 814807 ~ Well behaved children allowed at lunchtime ~ Open 11-3, 6.30-11; 12-3, 7-10.30 Sun

Recommended by John Tyrle, Mrs Angela Graham, Jacquie Jones, the Didler, Ian Phillips, Andrea Rampley

FALMOUTH   SW8132   MAP 1

5 Degrees West ♀

Grove Place, by the main harbourside car park; TR11 4AU

Modern, airy open-plan bar with décor to match, a fine choice of drinks, enjoyable food, and friendly young staff

You can be sure of a friendly welcome from the neatly dressed young staff in this light and airy modern bar. It's all open-plan but with several different areas, a spreading expanse of stripped wood flooring, and a relaxed and informal atmosphere. There are squashy sofas around low tables, some contemporary leatherette cushioned dining chairs around chunky pine tables, a few leather-topped high steel benches and stools dotted about (one table has a nice metal fish leg), and a log fire in a driftwood-effect fireplace. The artwork and photographs are local, there's a lot of steel and etched glass, and good lighting. From the long bar counter they serve St Austell Tribute on handpump and bottle conditioned beers, 14 good wines by the glass (local ones and fizz), lots of coffees and teas, and hot chocolate with marshmallows and a flake. A back dining area is similar in style with long built-in side pews and a couple of little semi-open booths; doors lead to an attractive and sheltered back terraced area with picnic-sets under umbrellas. A side ramp gives good wheelchair access; disabled facilities. Across the road by the marina is a useful short-term car park.

🍴 Well liked food includes filled toasted ciabattas (from midday to 6pm), soup, chicken liver and whisky pâté, a plate of tapas, a cornish cheese platter with bread, celery and an apple, moroccan-style spicy mixed bean and vegetable casserole, a trio of cumberland sausages with red wine and onion gravy, popular burger with bacon, mozzarella and an organic egg, chicken breast in a ginger and lemon marinade with white wine and basil sauce, local scallops and king prawns with white wine and garlic, daily specials and puddings such as a crumble of the day and chocolate brownie, both with clotted cream. *Starters/Snacks: £4.50 to £7.50. Main Courses: £8.95 to £13.95. Puddings: £3.95 to £5.45*

St Austell ~ Manager Justine Stevens ~ Real ale ~ Bar food (all day) ~ (01326) 311288 ~ Children welcome but must be supervised by an adult ~ Dogs welcome ~ Open 12-11(11.30 Sat, 10.30 Sun); closed 25 Dec

Recommended by Dr and Mrs M E Wilson, Andy and Claire Barker, Joan York

HELSTON   SW6522   MAP 1

Halzephron ♀ 🛏

Gunwalloe, village about 4 miles S but not marked on many road maps; look for brown sign on A3083 alongside perimeter fence of RNAS Culdrose; TR12 7QB

Popular inn, possibly under new licensees, well liked food, local beers, and bedrooms; lovely nearby walks

It is with some trepidation that we include this extremely popular inn in this year's *Guide* as we heard – just as we went to press – that Mrs Thomas was to sell the pub. We're keeping our fingers crossed that things will not change too much. It's a lovely place (though it does get packed at peak times) so you must book to be sure of a table. Seating is comfortable, the rooms are neatly kept with copper on the walls and mantelpiece, and there's a warm winter fire in the woodburning stove. What was the family room is now the newly refurbished Gallery which seats up to 30 people. Organic Halzephron Gold, St Austell Tribute and Sharps Own and Doom Bar on handpump, eight wines by the glass, and 40 malt whiskies; darts, cards and board games. There are lots of fine surrounding unspoilt walks with views of Mount's Bay. Gunwalloe fishing cove is just 300 yards away and Church Cove with its sandy beach is a mile away – as is the church of St Winwaloe (built into the dunes on the seashore). More reports on any changes, please.

🍴 Using local produce, the popular bar food has included lunchtime sandwiches, ploughman's, soup, locally smoked fish with avocado and mixed leaves, mushroom stroganoff, roast free-range chicken with herb stuffing, roast cod steak on seafood chowder topped with aïoli, lamb curry, italian braised beef with olives and fresh pappardelle, and crab salad (when available). Starters/Snacks: £4.60 to £7.95. Main Courses: £8.50 to £17.50. Puddings: £4.75 to £5.50

Free house ~ Licensee Angela Thomas ~ Real ale ~ Bar food ~ Restaurant ~ (01326) 240406 ~ Children in family room ~ Open 11-2.30, 6-11; 12-2.30, 6-10.30 Sun; 6.30 opening time in winter ~ Bedrooms: £50B/£90B

Recommended by Dave Webster, Sue Holland, Nick Lawless, Michael and Ann Cole, Dr Phil Putwain, Revd R P Tickle, Andy and Claire Barker, John Brough, Susie Symes, Steve Kirby, Andrea Rampley, John and Gloria Isaacs, Marianne Welsh, Simon Donan, Paul Boot, Barry andAnne, Jacquie Jones

LANLIVERY
SX0759 MAP 1

Crown 🍺

Signposted off A390 Lostwithiel—St Austell (tricky to find from other directions); PL30 5BT

Chatty atmosphere in nice old pub, old-fashioned rooms, and well liked food and drink; the Eden Project is close by

This year, there have been quite a few changes and substantial restoration work carried out in this fine old pub. A woodburning stove has been installed into the opened up fireplace of the main bar, there are now flagstones throughout the bars, the terrace has been extended and improved and they have bedrooms in a granite outbuilding; a huge old well was found beneath the pub and this has been topped with a glass lid and lit. The pub dates from the 12th c and has quite a bit of real character – our readers enjoy their visits very much. The small public bar has heavy beams and a mix of tables and chairs, and a lighter room leads off, with beams in the white boarded ceiling, cushioned black settles, and a little fireplace with an old-fashioned fire; another little room is similarly furnished. Sharps Doom Bar and Skinners Betty Stogs and Ginger Tosser on handpump, nine wines by the glass, and local cider; board games. There's also a restaurant and a sun room. The Eden Project is only ten minutes away.

🍴 At lunchtime, as well as sandwiches and ciabattas, ploughman's, pasties, and ham and free-range eggs, the reasonably priced food includes soup, smoked mackerel pâté, a charcuterie plate, a ravioli of the day, leek and mushroom or steak in ale pies, a good burger with melted cheese and red onion chutney, venison, hazelnut and burgundy sausages with wholegrain mustard mash and red wine gravy, fresh crab gratin, slow-roasted pork belly with roasted root vegetables, and daily specials such as local mussels in white wine and mixed fish grill. They list their local suppliers. *Starters/Snacks: £3.50 to £8.95. Main Courses: £7.95 to £16.95. Puddings: £4.00 to £5.00*

Wagtail Inns ~ Licensee Andrew Brotheridge ~ Real ale ~ Bar food (12-2.30(3 summer), 6.30-9(9.30 summer); not 25 Dec) ~ Restaurant ~ (01208) 872707 ~ Children welcome but must be away from bar ~ Dogs allowed in bar and bedrooms ~ Occasional live music Sun ~ Open 12-11(10.30 Sun) ~ Bedrooms: /£79.95S

Recommended by Andrea Rampley, Dennis Jenkin, Tom and Rosemary Hall, P and J Shapley, Nick Lawless, Colin and Peggy Wilshire, Brian and Anita Randall, Phil and Jane Hodson, Brian and Bett Cox, Mrs P Bishop, P R Waights, Jean and Douglas Troup

LOSTWITHIEL
SX1059 MAP 1

Globe 🍷 🍺

North Street (close to medieval bridge); PL22 0EG

Unassuming bar in traditional local, interesting food and drinks and friendly staff; suntrap back courtyard with outside heaters

You can be sure of a friendly welcome in this traditional, bustling town local. The cheerfully relaxed and unassuming bar is long and somewhat narrow with a good mix of pubby tables and seats, customers' photographs on pale green plank panelling at one end, nice more or less local prints (for sale) on canary walls above a coal-effect stove at the snug inner end, and a small red-walled front alcove. The ornately carved bar counter, with comfortable chrome and leatherette stools, dispenses well kept Greene King Ruddles County, Hydes 1863, Sharps Doom Bar and Skinners Betty Stogs from handpump, with 11 reasonably priced wines by the glass, several whiskies, and perry. Piped music, darts, board games and TV. The sheltered back courtyard, with a dogs' water bowl, is not large, but has some attractive and unusual pot plants, and is a real suntrap (with an extendable awning and outside heaters). You can park in several of the nearby streets. The 13th-c church is worth a look and the ancient river bridge a few yards away is lovely.

🍽 As well as lunchtime sandwiches, filled baguettes and baked potatoes and ploughman's, the enjoyable bar food might include soup, moules marinières, scallops and bacon, vegetarian roast with a red onion, port and mushroom sauce, pasta carbonara, sausage and mash with onion gravy, liver and bacon, game pie, salmon and monkfish roulade with lobster and brandy sauce, beef in Guinness with horseradish dumplings, popular roast shoulder of lamb, and puddings; Sunday roasts. *Starters/Snacks: £4.00 to £6.95. Main Courses: £8.95 to £16.95. Puddings: £3.50 to £4.95*

Free house ~ Licensee William Erwin ~ Real ale ~ Bar food ~ Restaurant ~ (01208) 872501 ~ Children welcome ~ Dogs allowed in bar ~ Live music Weds evening ~ Open 12-11(midnight Fri and Sat) ~ Bedrooms: /£70B

Recommended by B and M Kendall, Dave Webster, Sue Holland, PL, Peter Salmon, Evelyn and Derek Walter, Phil and Jane Hodson

MALPAS   SW8442   MAP 1

Heron ♀
Trenhaile Terrace, off A39 S of Truro; TR1 1SL

Lovely creekside spot, attractively decorated pub, friendly service and good food

If you are able to get one of the window tables here (or in fine weather, one of the seats on the terrace), you can enjoy the idyllic creekside position of this friendly pub. Inside, the bar is long and narrow with several areas leading off and a raised part at one end – it's all very light and airy with blue and white décor and furnishings throughout. There are two gas fires, mainly wooden floors with flagstones by the bar, modern yacht paintings on the wood-planked walls, some brass nautical items, heron pictures and a stuffed heron in a cabinet, and a chatty atmosphere. St Austell IPA and Tribute and summer HSD on handpump and 10 good wines by the glass. Parking is difficult, especially at peak times.

🍽 As well as lunchtime filled rolls, the much liked bar food includes ploughman's, local pork in ale sausages with onion gravy, spicy crab cakes, ham and egg, haddock in beer batter, vegetable and chickpea curry, grilled chicken breast with creamy mushroom sauce and crispy pancetta, a trio of local fish with lemon, black pepper and parsley butter, grilled lamb cutlets with buttery minted mash and redcurrant and wine sauce, and daily specials such as soup, beef and blue cheese burgers, cajun chicken, and seafood gratin. *Starters/Snacks: £5.75 to £7.25. Main Courses: £6.95 to £14.25. Puddings: £5.25*

St Austell ~ Tenant F C Kneebone ~ Real ale ~ Bar food ~ (01872) 272773 ~ Children welcome ~ Open 11-11(11.30 Sat and Sun); 11-3, 6-11 Mon-Sat and 12-4, 7-10.30 Sun in winter

Recommended by Peter Salmon, Andy and Claire Barker, Mrs Brenda Calver, Ian Phillips, Glenwys and Alan Lawrence

MITCHELL   SW8554   MAP 1

Plume of Feathers 🛏
Just off A30 Bodmin—Redruth, by A3076 junction; take the southwards road then turn first right; TR8 5AX

New public bar, several other bars with modern décor, real ales, and quite a choice of daily specials; comfortable bedrooms

An extension is being added to this busy dining pub to create a new public bar which will give space for a pool table and for special events. The other bars have appealing and contemporary décor with Farrow & Ball pastel-coloured walls, paintings by local artists, stripped old beams, painted wooden dado, and two fireplaces. Courage Directors, Sharps Doom Bar and a couple of guests like Fullers London Pride and Sharps Eden on handpump and several wines by the glass; piped music, games machine and TV. The well planted garden areas have plenty of seats, and the bedrooms are comfortable.

🍴 As well as sandwiches and greek mezze, bar food includes soup, grilled mackerel fillet with potato salad and wholegrain mustard and honey dressing, crispy pork belly with sweet chilli sauce, beef curry, corn-fed chicken breast with walnut pesto, roast salmon fillet with wild mushroom cream sauce, grilled bass fillets with a moroccan vegetable tagine and couscous, and lamb rump with gravy. *Starters/Snacks: £3.95 to £6.95. Main Courses: £8.25 to £14.50. Puddings: £4.25 to £4.95*

Free house ~ Licensee Joe Musgrove ~ Real ale ~ Bar food (10(for breakfast)-10) ~ (01872) 510387/511125 ~ Children welcome but must be away from bar ~ Dogs allowed in bar and bedrooms ~ Open 10-midnight ~ Bedrooms: £48.75S(£56.25B)/£65S(£75B)

Recommended by Phil and Sally Gorton, Mrs B J Pugh, Bernard Stradling, Marcus Mann, Phil and Jane Hodson, Gerry and Rosemary Dobson, John Marsh, Norman and Sarah Keeping, Stephen Moss, Dr Peter Andrews, Bettye Reynolds, Lesley and Peter Barrett

MITHIAN   SW7450   MAP 1
Miners Arms
Just off B3285 E of St Agnes; TR5 0QF

Cosy pub with open fires in several smallish rooms and friendly staff

In its 400 years, this old pub has been a court, a chapel and a smugglers' lair. Several cosy little rooms and passages are warmed by winter open fires, and the small back bar has an irregular beam and plank ceiling, a wood block floor and bulging squint walls (one with a fine old wall painting of Elizabeth I). Another small room has a decorative low ceiling, lots of books and quite a few interesting ornaments. Sharps Doom Bar and a guest beer on handpump served by cheerful staff; piped music and darts. There are seats outside on the back terrace with more on the sheltered front cobbled forecourt. More reports please.

🍴 Bar food under the new licensee includes lunchtime sandwiches, ploughman's, soup, breadcrumbed brie with cranberry sauce, steak in ale pie, vegetable lasagne, gammon and egg, lamb shank in minted gravy, and puddings like chocolate fudge brownie and lemon roulade. *Starters/Snacks: £4.00 to £6.00. Main Courses: £7.00 to £15.00. Puddings: £4.75 to £4.95*

Punch ~ Lease Anouska House ~ Real ale ~ Bar food (12-2, 6-9) ~ Restaurant ~ (01872) 552375 ~ Children allowed away from bar ~ Dogs allowed in bar ~ Pub quiz every 3rd Thurs ~ Open 12-midnight

Recommended by Mick and Moira Brummell, Michael Saunders, David and Sue Smith, Lynda Bentley, Mrs Angela Graham, Andrea Rampley, Tim and Joan Wright

MOUSEHOLE   SW4626   MAP 1
Ship
Harbourside; TR19 6QX

Bustling harbourside local in pretty village

Just across the road from the harbour in a lovely village, this is a bustling local with a welcoming, pubby atmosphere. The opened-up main bar has fishermen and other regulars enjoying the St Austell IPA, HSD, Tinners and Tribute on handpump, black beams and panelling, and built-in wooden wall benches and stools around the low tables; also, photographs of local events, sailors' fancy ropework, granite flagstones, and a cosy open fire. Ten wines by the glass, piped music, TV, games machine and darts. The elaborate harbour lights at Christmas are worth a visit; best to park at the top of the village and walk down (traffic can be a bit of a nightmare in summer).

🍴 Tasty bar food includes sandwiches and ciabattas, filled baked potatoes, ploughman's, hearty soup, smoked mackerel and cider pâté, steak in ale and fish pies, a trio of local sausages with onion gravy, vegetarian lasagne, chilli con carne, and salmon fishcakes with lime mayonnaise. *Starters/Snacks: £3.95 to £5.95. Main Courses: £6.95 to £13.95. Puddings: £4.25*

St Austell ~ Managers Colin and Jackie Perkin ~ Real ale ~ Bar food (12-2.30, 6-8.30; 12-3, 6-9 in summer) ~ Restaurant ~ (01736) 731234 ~ Children welcome ~ Dogs allowed in bar and bedrooms ~ Live music monthly weekends ~ Open 11am-11.30pm; 12-11 Sun ~ Bedrooms: £50S/£70S

Recommended by Alan Johnson, Carole Hall, JCW, the Weirs, the Whites, Julie Russell-Carter, Michael B Griffith, Stuart Turner, Tony and Jill Radnor

MYLOR BRIDGE   SW8137   MAP 1

Pandora ★★ ♀

Restronguet Passage: from A39 in Penryn, take turning signposted Mylor Church, Mylor Bridge, Flushing and go straight through Mylor Bridge following Restronguet Passage signs; or from A39 further N, at or near Perranarworthal, take turning signposted Mylor, Restronguet, then follow Restronguet Weir signs, but turn left down hill at Restronguet Passage sign; TR11 5ST

Beautifully placed waterside inn with seats on long floating pontoon, lots of atmosphere in beamed and flagstoned rooms, and some sort of food all day

On a fine day particularly, this is an idyllic spot. You can sit at picnic-seats on the long floating pontoon in front of this lovely medieval thatched pub and watch children crabbing and visiting dinghies pottering about in the sheltered waterfront. Inside is special too: several rambling, interconnecting rooms have low wooden ceilings (mind your head on some of the beams), beautifully polished big flagstones, cosy alcoves with leatherette benches built into the walls, old race posters, model boats in glass cabinets, and three large log fires in high hearths (to protect them against tidal floods). St Austell HSD, Tinners and Tribute and a guest such as Bass on handpump, and a dozen wines by the glass. It does get very crowded and parking is difficult at peak times.

🍴 **Popular bar food at lunchtime includes sandwiches (the crab are good), filled baked potatoes, ploughman's, moules marinières, beer-battered cod, cornish pasty, local sausages with sage mash and onion gravy, and roasted organic pumpkin and pistachio risotto, with evening dishes such as seared local scallops with crispy pancetta and leek purée, local smoked haddock and poached organic egg with smoked fish crème, a plate of vegetarian specialities, and roast saddle of lamb with boulangère potatoes, crispy sage and rosemary beurre blanc; puddings like warm bakewell tart with sweet mint yoghurt and sticky toffee pudding with caramel sauce, and afternoon teas.** *Starters/Snacks: £4.75 to £6.50. Main Courses: £8.50 to £15.95. Puddings: £5.75 to £8.25*

St Austell ~ Tenant John Milan ~ Real ale ~ Bar food (all day; sandwiches and afternoon tea between 3-6) ~ Restaurant ~ (01326) 372678 ~ Children welcome away from bar area ~ Dogs allowed in bar ~ Open 10.30am-midnight (11 in winter)

Recommended by Neil Whitehead, Victoria Anderson, David Rule, John and Bernadette Elliott, Clive Watkin, Andrea Rampley, John Marsh, D R Robinson, Dennis Jenkin, M P Mackenzie, Bruce and Sharon Eden, John and Fiona McIlwain, Kalman Kafetz, David Crook, Andy and Claire Barker, Steve Kirby, the Didler, Joan York, Julie Russell-Carter, M Bryan Osborne

PENZANCE   SW4730   MAP 1

Turks Head

At top of main street, by big domed building (Lloyds TSB), turn left down Chapel Street; TR18 4AF

Cheerfully run pub, the oldest in town, with a good, bustling atmosphere, and decent food and beer

There's always a good mix of visitors and locals in this friendly old town pub. The bustling bar has old flat irons, jugs and so forth hanging from the beams, pottery above the wood-effect panelling, wall seats and tables, and a couple of elbow-rests around central pillars; piped music. Courage Directors, Sharps Doom Bar, and Skinners Betty Stogs on handpump, and helpful service. The suntrap back garden has big urns of flowers. There has been a Turks Head here for over 700 years – though most of the original building was destroyed by a Spanish raiding party in the 16th c.

🍽 **Bar food includes lunchtime sandwiches, baps and ciabattas, filled baked potatoes, ploughman's, ham and egg, and omelettes, as well as soup, chicken liver pâté with red onion marmalade, moules marinières, beef stew with herb dumplings, vegetable moussaka, local beer-battered cod, and steaks.** *Starters/Snacks: £3.75 to £6.95. Main Courses: £7.99 to £13.99. Puddings: £4.99*

Punch ~ Lease Jonathan and Helen Gibbard ~ Real ale ~ Bar food ~ Restaurant ~ (01736) 363093 ~ Children welcome ~ Dogs welcome ~ Open 11am-midnight

Recommended by Tony and Jill Radnor, Andrea Rampley, Clifford Blakemore, Paul and Shirley White, Alan Johnson

PERRANWELL   SW7739   MAP 1

Royal Oak ♀
Village signposted off A393 Redruth—Falmouth and A39 Falmouth—Truro; TR3 7PX

Welcoming and relaxed with quite an emphasis on well presented food, and thoughtful wines

A back decking area should have been added on to this pretty and quietly set village pub by the time this *Guide* is published; you will be able to enjoy tapas and drinks while watching the sun going down. They may open bedrooms, too, but we heard that the pub was up for sale as we went to press so this may be on hold. The roomy, carpeted bar has a gently upmarket atmosphere, horsebrasses and pewter and china mugs on its black beams and joists, plates and country pictures on the cream-painted stone walls, and cosy wall and other seats around candlelit tables. It rambles around beyond a big stone fireplace (with a good log fire in winter) into a snug little nook of a room behind, with just a couple more tables. Skinners Betty Stogs and Greene King Old Speckled Hen on handpump from the small serving counter, good wines by the glass, scrumpy cider, summer sangria and winter mulled wine; piped music and board games.

🍽 **Popular bar food includes sandwiches, soup, field mushrooms filled with stilton, fried scallops with chorizo, a terrine of the day, a mezze platter, beer-battered cod, duck confit, rack of lamb, a trio of haddock, sole and monkfish, and steaks with pepper brandy sauce or port and stilton sauce.** *Starters/Snacks: £3.60 to £7.25. Main Courses: £7.25 to £15.75. Puddings: £5.25*

Free house ~ Licensee Richard Rudland ~ Real ale ~ Bar food (12-2.30, 7-9.30) ~ Restaurant ~ (01872) 863175 ~ Children in dining areas only ~ Dogs allowed in bar ~ Open 11-3, 6-midnight; 12-4, 6-11 Sun

Recommended by J K and S M Miln, John and Fiona McIlwain, Dr David Smith, Julie Russell-Carter, John Marsh, Mrs M K Matthews

POLKERRIS   SX0952   MAP 1

Rashleigh
Signposted off A3082 Fowey—St Austell; PL24 2TL

Popular pub by splendid beach with outside heaters on sizeable sun terrace, and well liked food and beer

As the big front terrace has heaters and an awning, you can make the best of this pub's lovely position even in cool weather. There's a splendid beach with a restored jetty only a few steps away and fine views towards the far side of St Austell and Mevagissey bays. Inside, the bar is cosy and the front part has comfortably cushioned seats and four real ales on handpump: Otter Bitter, Sharps Doom Bar, Timothy Taylors Landlord and a guest such as Cotleigh Sea Hawk or Skinners Betty Stogs. They also have a couple of farm ciders, several wines by the glass, and organic soft drinks. The more basic back area has local photographs on the brown panelling and a winter log fire, and the restaurant – every table has a sea view – has been redecorated to give a lighter feel. There's plenty of parking either at the pub's own car park or the large village one. The local section of the Cornish Coast Path is renowned for its striking scenery.

🍴 Using carefully sourced local ingredients, the well liked bar food includes sandwiches, ploughman's, soup, crab and prawn cocktail, mushrooms stuffed with pâté with roast garlic mayonnaise, mackerel and kiln roasted salmon with horseradish cream, lamb, apricot and chickpea curry, beer-battered cod, vegetable lasagne, steak and stilton pie, beef goulash, bass with lime and parsley butter, and puddings like rhubarb and ginger crumble and Baileys crème brûlée *Starters/Snacks: £3.60 to £5.75. Main Courses: £5.95 to £12.95. Puddings: £2.50 to £3.25*

Free house ~ Licensees Jon and Samantha Spode ~ Real ale ~ Bar food (12-2, 6-9; cream teas and snacks during the afternoon) ~ Restaurant ~ (01726) 813991 ~ Children welcome ~ Piano player Sat evening ~ Open 11-11; 12-10.30 Sun

Recommended by Paul Walmsley, Phil and Jane Hodson, Francis Vernon, the Didler, Andrew York, Darren and Kirstin Arnold, Dave Webster, Sue Holland, B and M Kendall, David Crook, Mr and Mrs B Hobden, Mrs Angela Graham, Colin and Peggy Wilshire, C Sale, Bob and Margaret Holder

POLPERRO   SX2050   MAP 1
Blue Peter
Quay Road; PL13 2QZ

Friendly pub overlooking pretty harbour, fishing paraphernalia, and paintings by local artists

Up narrow steps above the pretty working harbour, this busy and friendly little pub has a good mix of customers. The cosy low-beamed bar has fishing regalia, photographs and pictures by local artists for sale on the walls, traditional furnishings including a small winged settle and a polished pew on the wooden floor, candles everywhere, a solid wood bar counter, and a simple old-fashioned local feel despite being in such a touristy village. One window seat looks down on the harbour, another looks out past rocks to the sea. St Austell Tribute and guests such as Otter Ale, Shepherd Neame Spitfire, and Skinners Heligan Honey on handpump, and local cider. A few seats outside on the terrace and more in an upstairs amphitheatre-style area. The pub is quite small, so it does get crowded at peak times.

🍴 Enjoyable bar food includes filled baguettes (the crab is popular), tomato and pesto toasties, crab and oriental parcels, vegetarian quiche, pies such as chicken and mushroom or steak and plum, popular jambalaya (a creole rice dish with a mix of meats), tiger prawns in coconut breadcrumbs, fresh tuna on a vegetable stir fry, daily specials, evening choices, and puddings such as peanut butter and nougat cheesecake and crème brûlée; Sunday roasts. *Starters/Snacks: £3.95 to £6.95. Main Courses: £5.95 to £16.95. Puddings: £3.75 to £4.25*

Free house ~ Licensees Steve and Caroline Steadman ~ Real ale ~ Bar food (12-2.30, 6.30-9) ~ Restaurant ~ (01503) 272743 ~ Children in upstairs family room ~ Dogs welcome ~ Live music Fri and Sat and Sun lunch ~ Open 10.30am-11.30pm; 12-11 Sun

Recommended by Steve Kirby, Mrs Margo Finlay, Jörg Kasprowski, Dr and Mrs M E Wilson, the Didler, Lawrence Pearse

PORT ISAAC   SX0080   MAP 1
Port Gaverne Inn ♀ 🛏
Port Gaverne signposted from Port Isaac, and from B3314 E of Pendoggett; PL29 3SQ

Lively bar with plenty of chatty locals in popular small hotel close to sea and fine cliff walks

Balancing a clever act between the hotel side and the bustling bar, this popular 17th-c inn is the sort of place where customers come back over the years. The cheerful bar has a happy mix of locals and visitors, low beams, flagstones as well as carpeting, a big log fire, some exposed stone, and helpful staff. In spring, the lounge is usually filled with pictures from the local art society's annual exhibition, and at other times there are interesting antique local photographs. You can eat in the bar or the 'Captain's Cabin' – a little room where everything is shrunk to scale (old oak chest, model sailing ship, even the prints on the white stone walls. St Austell Tribute, Sharps Doom Bar and Cornish Coaster and a guest beer on handpump, a good wine list and several whiskies; cribbage and dominoes. There are seats in the terraced garden and splendid clifftop walks all around.

🍴 **Bar food includes sandwiches, soup, smoked mackerel pâté, ploughman's with home-made rolls, ham and eggs, seafood pie, beef in ale pie, fishcakes, more elaborate evening choices, and puddings.** *Starters/Snacks: £4.95 to £7.95. Main Courses: £7.00 to £13.95. Puddings: £4.95*

Free house ~ Licensee Graham Sylvester ~ Real ale ~ Bar food ~ Restaurant ~ (01208) 880244 ~ Children allowed away from bar area ~ Dogs welcome ~ Open 11-11; 12-10.30 Sun ~ Bedrooms: £60B/£100B

Recommended by Darren and Kirstin Arnold, David J Cooke, Dave Lowe, Peter and Margaret Glenister, Adrian Johnson, David Tindal, John and Bernadette Elliott, Bill and Marian de Bass, John and Gloria Isaacs, Sue Demont, Tim Barrow, John and Alison Hamilton, Gerry and Rosemary Dobson, Geoff and Brigid Smithers, R G Glover, Conor McGaughey, John and Sharon Hancock

PORTHLEVEN   SW6225   MAP 1

Ship

Village on B3304 SW of Helston; pub perched on edge of harbour; TR13 9JS

Fisherman's pub built into cliffs, fine harbour views from seats on terrace, and tasty bar food

On a stormy night, this friendly old fisherman's pub is just the place to sit in snug warmth and watch the boats and birds blowing across the harbour. In kinder weather, there are tables in the terraced garden that make the most of the sea view, and the harbour is interestingly floodlit. The knocked-through bar has a relaxed atmosphere, welcoming log fires in big stone fireplaces and some genuine individuality. The family room is a conversion of an old smithy with logs burning in a huge open fireplace; the candlelit dining room also looks over the sea. Courage Best and Sharps Doom Bar and a couple of summer guests on handpump; piped music and board games.

🍴 **Good bar food includes sandwiches or toasties, filled baked potatoes, ploughman's, moules marinières, smoked haddock fishcake with sweet chilli salsa, grilled goats cheese on pesto croûtons with gooseberry sauce, mediterranean vegetable bake, chicken in a rich barbecue sauce, minted leg of lamb casserole in rosemary and red wine sauce, king prawns with garlic mayonnaise, and puddings like syrup sponge and Baileys cheesecake.** *Starters/Snacks: £3.10 to £6.75. Main Courses: £6.95 to £20.95. Puddings: £4.50 to £4.95*

Free house ~ Licensee Colin Oakden ~ Real ale ~ Bar food ~ (01326) 564204 ~ Children in family room only ~ Dogs allowed in bar ~ Open 11.30-11; 12-10.30 Sun

Recommended by the Didler, Stuart Turner, Andrea Rampley, Peter Salmon, Lynda Bentley, Michael Saunders, Michael and Ann Cole, Revd R P Tickle, Comus and Sarah Elliott, Barry and Anne, Dr and Mrs Ellison, Phil and Jane Hodson, Clifford Blakemore, Paul and Shirley White, Andy and Claire Barker, Donna and Roger, Susie Symes, John Marsh, M Bryan Osborne

PORTHTOWAN   SW6948   MAP 1

Blue

Beach Road, East Cliff; use the car park (fee in season), not the slippy sand; TR4 8AW

Informal, busy bar – not a traditional pub – right by wonderful beach with modern food and drinks, and lively staff and customers

Certainly not a traditional pub (but it does now serve real ale which they tell us is incredibly popular), this light and airy bar, with its easy, informal atmosphere, is usually packed. Right by a fantastic beach – huge picture windows look across the terrace to the grand expanse of sand and sea – there's a genuinely interesting range of customers (and dogs) of all ages. The front bays have built-in pine seats and throughout are chrome and wicker chairs around plain wooden tables on the stripped wood floor, quite a few high-legged chrome and wooden bar stools, and plenty of standing space around the bar counter; powder blue painted walls, ceiling fans, some big ferny plants, two large TVs showing silent surfing videos, and fairly quiet piped music; pool table. Several wines by the glass, cocktails and shots, and giant cups of coffee; perky, helpful young staff.

🍴 Good modern bar food using local, seasonal produce includes lunchtime filled baps, soup, risotto of prawns with asparagus and mint, tasty burgers, nice pizzas, beer-battered pollock, mussels steamed with bacon, leeks, cider and cream, chargrilled mackerel with tomato, black olives and red onion salad, and grilled wild bass with crushed new potatoes and lemon oil. *Starters/Snacks: £4.50 to £6.00. Main Courses: £7.50 to £13.00. Puddings: £4.00 to £6.00*

Free house ~ Licensees Tara Roberts, Luke Morris and Alexandra George ~ Real ale ~ Bar food (12-9; limited menu in afternoon) ~ (01209) 890329 ~ Children welcome ~ Dogs welcome ~ Live bands Sat evening (and Fri also, in summer) ~ Open 10am-11pm(midnight Sat); 10am-10.30pm Sun; closed 2 weeks in Jan

Recommended by Tim and Ann Newell, David Crook, Andy and Claire Barker, Steve Pocock

RUAN LANIHORNE   SW8942   MAP 1

Kings Head
Off A3078; TR2 5NX

Friendly country pub with good popular food and beer, and welcoming licensees

In a little hamlet down country lanes and just a stroll from an interesting church, this attractive, neatly kept pub is run by friendly licensees and their helpful staff. The main bar has high bar chairs, comfortable sofas and seats around a low table, a winter log fire, and locals enjoying a chat and a pint of Skinners Betty Stogs, Cornish Knocker and a beer named for the pub on handpump; several malt whiskies and wines by the glass, and farm cider. Off to the right are two dining rooms with lots of china cups hanging from ceiling joists, plenty of copper and brass, old cigarette cards in picture frames, built-in planked seats with attractive cushions and pubby tables and chairs; there are also some hunting prints, a glass cabinet filled with interesting old glass bottles, and fish in an aquarium. The restaurant is to the left of the main door; piped music. Across the road is a sunken terrace with seats and tables under trees, and outdoor heaters.

🍴 Enjoyable food includes sandwiches (the crab are lovely), ploughman's, soup, chicken liver pâté with home-made walnut bread, a plate of antipasti, chicken caesar salad, a trio of local sausages with celeriac and apple mash and red onion marmalade, and roasted and sun-dried tomato risotto, with evening dishes such as roasted pork fillet with garlic and rosemary on fennel, cider and mascarpone and roast rump of lamb with herb sauce; puddings like hot apple and gingerbread pudding with ginger wine and brandy sauce and clotted cream and chocolate folly (dark chocolate, amaretti biscuits, raisins and rum), and Sunday roasts. *Starters/Snacks: £4.75 to £6.85. Main Courses: £8.95 to £18.50. Puddings: £4.75*

Free house ~ Licensees Andrew and Niki Law ~ Real ale ~ Bar food (12.30-2, 6.30-9; not winter Sun evening or Mon) ~ Restaurant ~ (01872) 501263 ~ Well behaved children welcome in dining areas only ~ Dogs allowed in bar ~ Open 12-2.30, 6-11(10.30 Sun); closed Mon in winter

Recommended by Michael Saunders, M Bryan Osborne, Christopher Wright, Chris and Angela Buckell, Guy Vowles, Andrew Clive, John Marsh, Richard Hussey

ST KEW   SX0276   MAP 1

St Kew Inn
Village signposted from A39 NE of Wadebridge; PL30 3HB

New licensees for this grand-looking 15th-c pub with neat bar, dining areas, and big garden

New licensees have taken over this sizeable stone building and have changed the menus, done substantial work to the garden and added a new outside kitchen for fine weather dining. The neatly kept bar has beams, stone walls, winged high-backed settles and wheelback chairs around varnished rustic tables on the tartan carpet, and a stove in the stone fireplace. There are three dining areas, one with pine tables and chairs on the delabole flagstones, various prints on the bright orangey/red walls, and another stove. St Austell HSD, IPA, Tinners and Tribute tapped from wooden casks behind the counter, a farm cider, and several wines by the glass. The flowering tubs and baskets are very pretty in summer. More reports please.

🍴 Bar food at lunchtime now includes sandwiches, platters, soup, steak and kidney or smoked haddock and bacon pies, a stir fry of the day, and steakburger with salad and fries, with evening choices such as smoked mackerel pâté, deep-fried camembert with a raspberry dressing, lamb curry, a trio of fish, burgundy beef, local steaks, and home-made puddings such as hot chocolate sponge with hot chocolate sauce and lemon meringue roulade. *Starters/Snacks: £4.50 to £7.50. Main Courses: £6.95 to £10.30. Puddings: £4.95*

St Austell ~ Tenants Philip and Lanie Calvert ~ Real ale ~ Bar food ~ Restaurant ~ (01208) 841259 ~ Children welcome in dining rooms ~ Open 11(11.30 Sun)-11; 11-2.30, 6-11 in winter

Recommended by Edna Jones, Paul Smurthwaite, the Didler, Andrea Rampley, Michael B Griffith, Tony Allwood, Conor McGaughey, Geoff and Brigid Smithers, Mick and Moira Brummell, David Rule, Barry and Sue Pladdys, Bill and Marian de Bass, John and Bernadette Elliott

TREGADILLETT
SX2983   MAP 1

Eliot Arms

Village signposted off A30 at junction with A395, W end of Launceston bypass; PL15 7EU

Interesting collection of antique clocks and snuffs in creeper-covered pub

The interesting collections in the series of small rooms here are well worth a look: 72 antique clocks (including seven grandfathers), 400 snuffs, hundreds of horsebrasses, old prints, old postcards or cigarette cards grouped in frames on the walls, quite a few barometers, and shelves of books and china. Also, a fine old mix of furniture on the delabole slate floors, from high-backed built-in curved settles, through plush Victorian dining chairs, armed seats, chaise longues and mahogany housekeeper's chairs, to more modern seats; open fires. Courage Best, Sharps Doom Bar and a guest like Sharps Own on handpump; piped music, games machine and darts. There are seats in front of the pub and at the back of the car park.

🍴 Bar food includes filled baguettes and baked potatoes, ploughman's, straightfoward pubby meals, and Sunday roasts. *Starters/Snacks: £4.95 to £6.45. Main Courses: £6.95 to £15.95. Puddings: £3.95*

S&N ~ Lease Chris Hume ~ Real ale ~ Bar food (12-2, 6-9) ~ (01566) 772051 ~ Children in front two bars ~ Dogs allowed in bar ~ Open 11.30-11(midnight Sat); 12-10.30 Sun; 11.30-3, 5-11 in winter ~ Bedrooms: £45B/£70S(£65B)

Recommended by John and Bernadette Elliott, Peter Salmon, Joan York, Comus and Sarah Elliott, Michael Saunders, Mr and Mrs H J Stephens, Nick Lawless, Chris Glasson, Rod and Chris Pring, Pauline and Philip Darley, the Didler

TRESCO
SV8815   MAP 1

New Inn ♀ 🍺 🛏️

New Grimsby; Isles of Scilly; TR24 0QG

Close to quay and very attractive with chatty bar and light dining extension, enjoyable food and drinks, and sunny terrace

As the island's only pub – it's handy for the ferries – this well run and attractive inn does get busy during the holiday season. There is a little locals' bar but visitors tend to head for the main bar room or the light, airy dining extension: comfortable old sofas, banquettes, planked partition seating, and farmhouse chairs and tables, a few standing timbers, boat pictures, a large model sailing boat, a collection of old telescopes, and plates on the delft shelf. The Pavilion extension has cheerful yellow walls and plenty of seats and tables on the blue wooden floors and looks over the flower-filled terrace with its teak furniture, huge umbrellas and views of the sea. Ales of Scilly Firebrand, St Austells Tribute and Skinners Tresco Tipple on handpump, a dozen good wines by the glass and several coffees; piped music, darts, and pool.

🍴 Good bar food includes lunchtime sandwiches, soup, pasta with mixed wild mushrooms and toasted pine nuts, salmon fishcakes with chive fish cream, chicken caesar salad, mushroom and brie or beef burgers, evening calves liver with mustard mash, crispy pancetta and onion gravy and confit duck leg with mixed bean casserole, daily specials such as grilled scallops with garlic butter, ray wing with nut brown butter, and brill fillets with chive mash and green thai fish sauce, and puddings such as baked alaska and walnut and dark chocolate brownie with clotted cream. *Starters/Snacks: £3.50 to £7.50. Main Courses: £9.00 to £18.00. Puddings: £5.00 to £8.00*

Free house ~ Licensee Robin Lawson ~ Real ale ~ Bar food (in summer, some sort of food all day) ~ Restaurant ~ (01720) 422844 ~ Children welcome ~ Live music every few weeks ~ Open 11-11; 12-10.30 Sun; 11-2.30, 6-11 weekdays and Sat in winter ~ Bedrooms: £165B/£200B

Recommended by Bernard Stradling, Michael Sargent, C J Fletcher, R J Herd

WATERGATE BAY   SW8464   MAP 1

Beach Hut

B3276 coast road N of Newquay; TR8 4AA

Bustling, informal beach bar with cheerful young staff, good mix of customers, decent drinks and popular food

Right on the beach and a short walk down from the public car park, this is one of those new breeds of beach bars. It's modern and relaxed, with a cheerful, bustling atmosphere, a good mix of customers of all ages, and friendly, helpful young staff. Big new windows and doors open out onto a new glass-fronted decking area and look across the sand to the sea which on our visit had a lone kite boarder battling with huge waves in a storm – quite extraordinary to watch. To set the scene inside there are surfing photographs on the planked walls, a large surfboard above a sizeable leatherette wall seat by one big table, and another above the bar counter. Wicker and cane armchairs with blue or pink cushions around green and orange painted tables sit on the nicely weathered stripped wooden floor, there's plenty of mushroom and cream paintwork, orange blinds, and an unusal sloping bleached-board ceiling. Decent wines by the glass, lots of coffees and teas and hot chocolate; piped soft rock music. An end room is slightly simpler, and outside on decking are some picnic-sets. They also run an extreme sports academy.

🍽 **Generous helpings of popular food includes clam chowder, fowey mussels in cider and cream, pea and basil fritters with sour cream, ham, chicken and pistachio terrine with home-made piccalilli, good proper burgers (meaty or vegetarian), grilled pollock with saffron aïoli, white beans, tomato and fennel, free-range chicken satay with a salad of snap peas, bean shoots, cucumber and peanut sauce, rib-eye steak, and puddings such as warm chocolate sponge with chocolate sauce and toasted almonds and crème brûlée flavoured with wild flower honey; their cakes are home made.** *Starters/Snacks: £4.95 to £7.50. Main Courses: £8.95 to £16.50. Puddings: £4.75*

Free house ~ Licensee Mark Williams ~ Bar food (all day) ~ (01637) 860877 ~ Children welcome ~ Dogs welcome ~ Open 8.30am-11pm; 10.30-dusk in winter

Recommended by Ryta Lyndley

WIDEMOUTH   SS1902   MAP 1

Bay View 🛏

Village signposted (with Bude Coastal Route) off A39 N of Pounstock; Marine Drive; EX23 0AW

Sizeable hotel, wonderful views of Widemouth Bay, real ales and bistro food, and relaxed atmosphere; bedrooms

Contemporary picnic-sets on decking in front of this sizeable, family-run hotel look across the road and dunes to a magnificent stretch of sand; the sunsets can be lovely. Inside are several spreading, interestingly decorated areas, and on our visit a good mix of customers. As well as some modern seaside paintings and large sea and sunset photographs, there are rugs on stripped wooden floors, some flagstones, comfortable leather sofas with cushions, low chunky tables with lit church candles, and several fireplaces with log-effect gas fires or decorative pebbles. A front part has pale wooden tables and chairs and a dresser with little wooden beach huts and china plates. Sharps Doom Bar, Skinners Betty Stogs and a beer named for them on handpump, some unusual bottled beers, several wines by the glass (and a notice for a 'fun and free wine tasting quiz'), and cheerful young staff; piped pop. Outside, there's an equipped children's play area with good, solid picnic-sets on grass beside it.

🍴 **Bistro-style food includes interesting baps, soup, toasted flat bread topped with garlic, rosemary and cheese with a trio of home-made dips, tian of crab with lime mayonnaise topped with a tiger prawn, a pie of the day (their fish is popular), beer-battered fish, a changing vegetarian tart, moules marinières, a good proper burger, corn-fed chicken with creamy leek and smoked bacon sauce, and puddings; they may offer a late afternoon bargain dish of the day and cream teas.** *Starters/Snacks: £3.50 to £8.00. Main Courses: £7.00 to £19.00. Puddings: £5.00 to £7.00*

Free house ~ Licensees Dave and Cherylyn Keene ~ Real ale ~ Bar food (12-2.30, 6-9; 12-8 Sun) ~ Restaurant ~ (01288) 361273 ~ Children welcome ~ Dogs allowed in bar ~ Open 10am-midnight(1am Sat); closed evening 25 Dec ~ Bedrooms: £38S/£76S

Recommended by John Urquhart, John and Sharon Hancock, the Didler, Carrie Wass

ZENNOR   SW4538   MAP 1

Tinners Arms
B3306 W of St Ives; TR26 3BY

Good mix of customers, friendly atmosphere, and tasty food

Our readers enjoy this well run and popular pub and there's always a good mix of locals and visitors. It's a friendly old place with low wooden-ceilings, cushioned settles, benches, and a mix of chairs around wooden tables on the stone floor, antique prints on the stripped plank panelling, and a log fire in cool weather. Sharps Own and a beer named for the pub, and St Austell Tinners on handpump. There are some fine nearby coastal walks and in good weather you can sit on benches in the sheltered front courtyard or at tables on a bigger side terrace. The pub was built in 1271 to house the masons who constructed St Senara's Church.

🍴 **Tasty bar food at lunchtime includes sandwiches, good soup, ploughman's, home-cooked ham and egg, and a vegetarian dish of the day, with evening choices like slow braised pork belly with thyme sauce, roasted pigeon with parsley and capers and supreme of halibut with a fish velouté, daily specials such as cottage pie and duck breast salad with a sweet orange dressing, and puddings like warm chocolate cake or treacle tart.** *Starters/Snacks: £4.95 to £7.50. Main Courses: £7.50 to £14.50. Puddings: £3.75 to £4.75*

Free house ~ Licensees Grahame Edwards and Richard Motley ~ Real ale ~ Bar food (12-2.30, 6.30-9) ~ (01736) 796927 ~ Children welcome away from main bar ~ Dogs welcome ~ Maybe live music Thurs evening ~ Open 11-11; 12-10.30 Sun; 11.30-3.30, 6.30-11 in winter ~ Bedrooms: £45/£80S

Recommended by Steve Kirby, Dr and Mrs M W A Haward, Alan Johnson, Mrs Angela Graham, Paul and Shirley White, Mrs M K Matthews, Terry and Linda Moseley, Steve Pocock, the Didler, David and Sue Smith, Roger and Anne Newbury, Joan York, Stuart Turner, Steve Crick, Helen Preston

LUCKY DIP

Besides the fully inspected pubs, you might like to try these Lucky Dips recommended to us and described by readers (if you do, please send us reports: feedback@thegoodpubguide.co.uk).

ALTARNUN [SX2280]
Kings Head PL15 7RX [Five Lanes]: Old beamed pub with good choice of well priced food, guest beers, ciders, traditional lounge with big log fire, simple public bar; open all day *(John Marsh)*
BOLVENTOR [SX1876]
☆ *Jamaica Inn* PL15 7TS [signed, just off

A30 on Bodmin Moor]: Genuinely 18th-c bar with oak beams, stripped stone, massive log fire and well kept Sharps Doom Bar, (easy to ignore the big all-day cafeteria, games machines, souvenir shop and tourist coaches), young enthusiastic staff, bar food, plaque commemorating murdered landlord Joss Merlyn, great Daphne du Maurier connection; pretty secluded garden with play area, bedrooms, moorland setting *(David Crook, Phil and Jane Hodson, J F M and M West)*

BOSCASTLE [SX0991]

☆ *Cobweb* PL35 0HE [B3263, just E of harbour]: Cosily dim-lit two-bar pub with plenty of character, hundreds of old bottles hanging from heavy beams, two or three high-backed settles, flagstones and dark stone walls, log fire, St Austell ales, generous popular blackboard food at good prices, quick friendly service, decent wine choice, pub games, sizeable family room with second fire; dogs welcome, open all day *(LYM, Lynda Bentley, Gerry and Rosemary Dobson, Ted George, the Didler, Di and Mike Gillam, R K Phillips)*

☆ *Napoleon* PL35 0BD [High St, top of village]: Good atmosphere in low-beamed 16th-c pub with good value generous blackboard bar food, St Austell ales tapped from the cask, decent wines, good coffee, friendly service, log fires, interesting Napoleon prints, slate floors and cosy rooms on different levels inc small evening bistro, traditional games; piped music; children welcome, small covered terrace and large sheltered garden, steep climb up from harbour (splendid views on the way), open all day *(LYM, the Didler, Gordon Stevenson, Peter and Margaret Glenister)*

BOTALLACK [SW3632]

☆ *Queens Arms* TR19 7QG: Unpretentious pub little changed under new owners, good food choice inc local seafood, all meat sourced within 3 miles, well kept Sharps Doom Bar, a Skinners ale brewed for the pub and guest beers, cheerful staff, log fire in unusual granite inglenook, dark wood furniture, tin mining and other old local photographs on stripped stone walls, attractive family extension; tables out in front and pleasant back garden with chickens, wonderful clifftop walks nearby, open all day *(Jeff Davies, Brian and Jenny Salmon)*

BREAGE [SW6128]

Queens Arms TR13 9PD [3 miles W of Helston]: L-shaped local with friendly landlord, Caledonian Deuchars IPA, Sharps Doom Bar and up to four guest beers, farm cider, decent wines by the glass, good value food from baguettes with cornish brie and ham up, daily papers, good coal fires, plush banquettes, restaurant area, back games area with pool; piped music; dogs welcome, some picnic-sets outside, bedrooms, medieval wall paintings in church opp, open all day Sun *(Dennis Jenkin, BB, David and Sue Smith)*

BUDE [SS2006]

Brendon Arms EX23 8SD: Canalside, with two big friendly pubby bars, back family room, well kept ales inc Sharps, enjoyable bargain food inc good crab sandwiches and interesting specials, good coffee;

juke box, pool and darts; picnic-sets on front grass, bedrooms *(Ryta Lyndley)*

CALLINGTON [SX3569]

Bulls Head PL17 7AQ [Fore St]: Ancient unspoilt local with handsome black timbering and stonework, well kept St Austell HSD, landlady nearing her 100th birthday *(Giles and Annie Francis)*

CALSTOCK [SX4368]

Tamar PL18 9QA [Quay]: Spotless comfortable bars in lovely setting yards from the river, good generous straightforward food at bargain prices, well kept changing ales inc Sharps and St Austell, impressive helpful service, darts and pool, separate dining room; shiny tables and chairs on sunny decking, hilly walk or ferry to Cotehele (NT) *(Barry Gibbs, David Crook)*

CAWSAND [SX4350]

☆ *Cross Keys* PL10 1PF [The Square]: Pretty pub in picturesque square opp boat club, friendly and simple-smart, with wide range of enjoyable generous food esp seafood (worth booking in season) in small bar and large attractive stripped-pine dining room, reasonable prices, changing ales such as Archers, Dawlish and Skinners, flexible service; pool, may be piped music, no nearby parking; children and dogs welcome, seats outside, pleasant bedrooms *(Dennis Jenkin, Andrew Gardner)*

CHAPEL AMBLE [SW9975]

☆ *Maltsters Arms* PL27 6EU [off A39 NE of Wadebridge]: More busy country restaurant than pub, enterprising proper cooking (sandwiches too), welcoming attentive staff, thriving atmosphere, Sharps and St Austell Tribute, splendid fire, beams, panelling, stripped stone and partly carpeted flagstones, upstairs family room, attractive restaurant; picnic-sets out in sheltered sunny corner *(M Hosegood, Jacquie Jones, Peter and Margaret Glenister, David Eberlin, Mrs Angela Graham, LYM)*

CHARLESTOWN [SX0351]

Rashleigh Arms PL25 3NX [Quay Rd]: Roomy pub with nautical touches, well kept St Austell ales and guest, good wine choice and coffee, quick friendly service, waterside family room; piped music, on the coach circuit – all-day carvery etc; lots of terrace tables (dogs allowed here) and garden above little harbour, good value bedrooms, open all day *(David and Katharine Cooke, Mick and Moira Brummell)*

CONSTANTINE [SW7229]

☆ *Trengilly Wartha* TR11 5RP [Nancenoy; off A3083 S of Helston, via Gweek then forking right]: Popular tucked-away inn with cheerful helpful staff, good reasonably priced food inc plenty of fish from bar or new bistro, good choice for children, Sharps, Skinners and perhaps a guest, good wines by the glass, long low-beamed main bar with woodburner and built-in high-backed settles boxing in heavy wooden tables, bright family conservatory; dogs welcome, pretty garden with boules, surrounding walks, bedrooms, open all day wknds *(Dennis Jenkin, Dr A McCormick, the Weirs, the Whites, Mrs M S Tadd, David Rule, Mrs M Godolphin, Brian and Anita Randall, Eamonn and Natasha Skyrme, LYM, Brian and Bett Cox, Michael Lamm, Paul Boot, Robin and Joyce Peachey, Andy and Claire Barker, Dr and Mrs M E Wilson)*

CRANTOCK [SW7960]
☆ *Old Albion* TR8 5RB [Languroc Rd]: Picture-postcard thatched village pub, low beams, flagstones and open fires, old-fashioned small bar with brasses and low lighting, larger more open room with local pictures, informal atmosphere, generous if not cheap basic home-made bar lunches inc good sandwiches and giant ploughman's, Sharps and Skinners, farm cider, decent house wines, pool and darts at back of lounge; staff may look dressed ready for beach and surf, loads of summer visitors, souvenirs sold; dogs welcome, tables out on small terrace, open all day *(LYM, Phil and Jane Hodson)*

CREMYLL [SX4553]
☆ *Edgcumbe Arms* PL10 1HX: Super setting by Plymouth foot-ferry, good Tamar views, picnic-sets out by water; attractive layout and décor, with slate floors, big settles, comfortably old-fashioned furnishings inc fireside sofas, old pictures and china, plentiful food from sandwiches up, St Austell ales, good wines by the glass, cheerful staff, good family room/games area; pay car park some way off; children in eating area, dogs allowed in one bar, bedrooms, open all day *(Dennis Jenkin, Shirley Mackenzie, Mr and Mrs W W Burke, LYM)*

CRIPPLES EASE [SW5036]
Engine TR20 8NF [B3311 St Ives—Penzance]: Family-friendly former tin-mine counting house in superb moorland location, sea views on all sides from nearby hill (very popular summer evenings), cheerful landlady, decent food from sandwiches up, well kept mainstream ales and Sharps Doom Bar, pool; good value bedrooms *(Stuart Turner, Steve Crick, Helen Preston)*

CROWN TOWN [SW6330]
Crown TR13 0AD [B3303 N of Helston]: Open-plan roadside local with particularly well kept Skinners ales tapped from stillroom casks and a guest beer, welcoming licensees, good value food running up to duck and steaks, side eating area, fine collection of brassware and jugs hanging from beams, giant Jenga (great fun) and pool; bedrooms in lodges, cl lunchtime exc Sun *(Donna and Roger, Tom McLean)*

CUBERT [SW7857]
☆ *Smugglers Den* TR8 5PY [village signed off A3075 S of Newquay, then brown sign to pub (and Trebellan holiday park) on left]: Big welcoming open-plan 16th-c thatched pub, neat ranks of tables (worth booking), dim lighting, stripped stone and heavy beam and plank ceilings, west country pictures and seafaring memorabilia, small barrel seats, steps down to further area with enormous inglenook woodburner, another step to big side family dining room; neat helpful staff, fresh generous enjoyable food inc local seafood, well kept Sharps, Skinners and St Austell, well lit pool area, darts; piped music, games machine; dogs welcome, small courtyard and lawn with climbing frame; has been cl winter Mon-Weds lunchtime *(Adrian Johnson, Steve Pocock, the Didler, Paul and Shirley White, BB, John and Jan Parkinson, Chris Reading, Carole Hall)*

DEVORAN [SW7938]
☆ *Old Quay* TR3 6NE [Quay Rd – brown sign to pub off A39 Truro—Falmouth]: Welcoming pub with two light and fresh rooms off bar, enjoyable good value food inc nice lunchtime sandwiches and enterprising specials, well kept ales, interesting wines by the glass, good friendly young staff, big coal fire, daily papers, boating bric-a-brac, some attractive prints, evening restaurant; they may try to keep your credit card while you eat; imaginatively terraced suntrap garden behind making the most of the idyllic spot – peaceful creekside village, lovely views, walks nearby, and this ends a coast-to-coast cycle way; dogs welcome, open all day summer *(Norman and Sarah Keeping, Betty Rose, Dr and Mrs M E Wilson, BB, Roger E F Maxwell)*

DULOE [SX2358]
☆ *Olde Plough House* PL14 4PN [B3254 N of Looe]: Long-serving licensees who made this neat pub's reputation left in spring 2008 (too late for us to get a proper handle on their successors); three linked rooms all with woodburners and restrained décor, dark polished slate floors, turkey rugs, a mix of pews and other seats, Fullers, Sharps and Skinners, small more modern restaurant; piped music; children welcome, dogs in bar, picnic-sets out by road *(LYM)*

EDMONTON [SW9672]
☆ *Quarryman* PL27 7JA [off A39 just W of Wadebridge bypass]: Welcoming three-room beamed bar, part of a small holiday courtyard complex; interesting decorations inc old sporting memorabilia, Sharps, Skinners and a couple of good guest beers, some good individual cooking besides generous pubby lunchtime food inc good baguettes, salads and fish and chips, good curry

night Tues, attentive staff, pool, cribbage and dominoes, no machines, piped music or mobiles; well behaved dogs and children welcome, open all day *(Dave Lowe, Mrs Jill Silversides, Barry Brown, Lynda Bentley, LYM)*

FALMOUTH [SW8132]

☆ *Chain Locker* TR11 3HH [Custom House Quay]: Fine spot by inner harbour with window tables (pub dog likes the seats here) and lots outside, Sharps and Skinners ales, generous bargain food from sandwiches and baguettes to fresh local fish, bargains for two, quick cheery service, masses of nautical bric-a-brac, darts alley; games machine, piped music; well behaved children welcome, self-catering accommodation, open all day *(Dr and Mrs M E Wilson, LYM, Rona Murdoch)*

Quayside Inn & Old Ale House TR11 3LH [ArwenackSt/Fore St]: Brightly lit bare-boards panelled bar with ales inc Sharps and Skinners, decent wines, efficient service, good value food (all day in summer) from doorstep sandwiches to Sun roasts, friendly helpful staff, tall tables, upstairs harbour-view lounge with armchairs and sofas one end; lots of pub games, piped music, big-screen TV, busy with young people evenings – esp Fri/Sat for live music; children welcome, plenty of waterside picnic-sets, open all day *(Barry Collett, LYM, Dr and Mrs M E Wilson)*

Seaview TR11 3EP [Wodehouse Terr]: Convivial maritime local above 111-step Jacob's Ladder, stunning harbour and dockyard view from picture windows and a few tables outside, lots of dark oak and appropriate bric-a-brac, warm fires, affable landlord, local beers; big-screen sports TV; bedrooms *(Dr and Mrs M E Wilson)*

☆ *Seven Stars* TR11 3QA [The Moor (centre)]: Quirky 17th-c local, unchanging and unsmart, with long-serving and entertaining vicar-landlord, no gimmicks, machines or mobile phones, warm welcome, Bass, Sharps and Skinners tapped from the cask, home-made rolls, chatty regulars, big key-ring collection, quiet back snug; corridor hatch serving roadside courtyard *(the Didler, Dr and Mrs M E Wilson, BB)*

FLUSHING [SW8033]

Seven Stars TR11 5TY [Trefusis Rd]: Well kept ales inc Skinners, welcoming local atmosphere, enjoyable food, darts, pool, separate dining room; pavement tables, great views of Falmouth with foot ferry across *(Chris and Mike Granville-Edge)*

FOWEY [SX1251]

Galleon PL23 1AQ [Fore St; from centre follow Car Ferry signs]: Superb spot by harbour and estuary, good ale range inc local microbrews, generous food from good sandwiches to plenty of fish,

reasonable prices, good wine choice, fast service, fresh modern nautical décor, lots of solid pine, dining areas off; pool, jazz Sun lunchtime, evenings can get loud with young people; children welcome, disabled facilities, attractive extended waterside terrace and sheltered courtyard with covered heated area, estuary-view bedrooms *(Dave Webster, Sue Holland, Mr and Mrs W W Burke, Colin and Peggy Wilshire, Andrew York, Mick and Moira Brummell, LYM)*

☆ *King of Prussia* PL23 1AT [Town Quay]: Handsome quayside building with good welcoming service in roomy neat upstairs bar, bay windows looking over harbour to Polruan, good pubby bar food, St Austell ales kept well, sensibly priced wines, splendid local seafood in side family restaurant; piped music may be loud; seats outside, open all day in summer, six pleasant bedrooms *(B and M Kendall, Chris Glasson, Michael and Alison Sandy, LYM, Phil and Sally Gorton, Dave Webster, Sue Holland, Alan Johnson, Liz Hryniewicz, Nick Lawless)*

Lugger PL23 1AH [Fore St]: Friendly family pub, good mix of locals and visitors in unpretentious bar, comfortable small candlelit back dining area, well kept St Austell ales, generous food inc good simply prepared fish specials (crab salad particularly good), big waterfront mural; piped music; children welcome, pavement tables *(BB, Dave Webster, Sue Holland, the Didler, Mr and Mrs W W Burke)*

Safe Harbour PL23 1BP [Lostwithiel St]: Relaxing homely local with home-cooked bargain food, St Austell ales, welcoming landlord, horsebrasses and old local prints *(Liz Hryniewicz, Dave Webster, Sue Holland, Ash Waller, Phil and Sally Gorton)*

☆ *Ship* PL23 1AZ [Trafalgar Sq]: Bustling local with friendly staff, good choice of good value generous food from sandwiches up inc fine local seafood, well kept St Austell ales, coal fire and banquettes in tidy bar with lots of yachting prints and nauticalia, steps up to family dining room with big stained-glass window, pool/darts room; piped music, small sports TV; dogs allowed, comfortably old-fashioned bedrooms, some oak-panelled *(Phil and Sally Gorton, LYM, Mike and Heather Watson, Dave Webster, Sue Holland, Nick Lawless, Margaret and Roy Randle, Michael and Alison Sandy)*

FRADDON [SW9157]

Blue Anchor TR9 6LS: Unpretentious friendly pub, well kept St Austell ales, enjoyable food; dogs welcome *(Chris Glasson)*

GORRAN HAVEN [SX0141]

☆ *Llawnroc* PL26 6NU [Chute Lane]: Comfortable and relaxed family-friendly granite hotel (try reading its name backwards), home-made food inc good fish and big Sun lunch in good-sized dining area, St Austell beers and one brewed for them by Sharps, good wine choice, friendly dedicated service, some refurbishment in progress; big garden overlooking cove and quiet fishing village, barbecues, good value bedroom block, open all day *(Phil and Jane Hodson)*

GULVAL [SW4831]

Coldstreamer TR18 3BB: Busy welcoming local with comfortable dining atmosphere, attractive restaurant with military prints, enjoyable food, well kept ales and decent wines, unusual high ceilings; quiet pleasant village very handy for Trengwainton Gardens, and for Scillies heliport – turn right opp entrance *(Kalman Kafetz)*

GURNARDS HEAD [SW4337]

☆ ***Gurnards Head Hotel*** TR26 3DE [B3306 Zennor—St Just]: Although this was Cornwall's Dining Pub in 2008, things seem to have gone awry, with some reports of indifferent service and food; it's 500 yards from Atlantic in outstanding bleak National Trust scenery, plenty of walks inland and along cliffy coast; bar rooms painted in bold, strong colours, interesting mix of furniture, pictures by local artists, open fires, St Austell and Skinners ales, several wines by glass, darts and board games; piped music; large garden *(LYM, Darren and Kirstin Arnold, Susie Symes, M Bryan Osborne)*

HARROWBARROW [SX4069]

Cross House PL17 8BQ [off A390 E of Callington; School Rd – over towards Metherell]: Substantial stone building, spreading carpeted bar with some booth seating, cushioned wall seats and stools around pub tables, decent pubby bar food, well kept Sharps and Skinners, friendly service, good coal fire, darts area, restaurant; children welcome, plenty of picnic-sets on good-sized lawn, good play area *(BB, Ted George)*

HELFORD [SW7526]

Shipwrights Arms TR12 6JX [off B3293 SE of Helston, via Mawgan]: Thatched pub of great potential by beautiful wooded creek, at its best at high tide, terraces making the most of the view, plenty of surrounding walks, and summer foot ferry from Helford Passage; nautical décor, winter open fire, separate dining area; has had real ale, decent wine list, bar food inc summer barbecues and lunchtime buffet platters, but up for sale as we go to press, as it's been for a year or so – news please; quite a walk from nearest car park, has been cl winter Sun and Mon evenings *(LYM, the Didler, Andrea Rampley, Michael and Ann Cole, Paul and Shirley White, Ian Phillips)*

HELSTON [SW6527]

☆ ***Blue Anchor*** TR13 8EL [Coinagehall St]: Many (not all) love this 15th-c no-

nonsense, highly individual, thatched local; quaint rooms off corridor, flagstones, stripped stone, low beams and well worn furniture, traditional games, family room, limited bargain lunchtime food (perhaps best time for a visit), ancient back brewhouse still producing their own distinctive and very strong Spingo IPA, Middle and specials; seats out behind, bedrooms, open all day *(Donna and Roger, Ian and Nita Cooper, Ian Barker, Joan and Michel Hooper-Immins, David Uren, LYM, Tom McLean, Clifford Blakemore, Dave Webster, Sue Holland)*

HESSENFORD [SX3057]

Copley Arms PL11 3HJ [A387 Looe—Torpoint]: Emphasis on good food from baguettes to popular Sun lunch and restaurant dishes using local produce in modernised linked areas, St Austell ales, nice wine choice, variety of teas and coffee, log fires, one part with sofas and easy chairs; piped music, dogs allowed in one small area, big plain family room; sizeable and attractive streamside garden and terrace (but by road), play area, bedrooms *(Jean and Douglas Troup, John and Joan Calvert, Evelyn and Derek Walter)*

KINGSAND [SX4350]

☆ ***Halfway House*** PL10 1NA [Fore St, towards Cawsand]: Attractive well sited inn with simple mildly Victorian bar around huge central fireplace, low ceilings and soft lighting, Sharps Doom Bar and guest beers, decent wines, bar food from crab sandwiches up, pleasant service, morning coffee, perhaps summer afternoon teas, restaurant; car park not close; children and dogs warmly welcome, picturesque village, marvellous walks, bedrooms, open all day summer *(W F C Phillips, Shirley Mackenzie, LYM)*

LAMORNA [SW4424]

Lamorna Wink TR19 6XH [off B3315 SW of Penzance]: Great collection of warship mementoes, sea photographs, nautical brassware, hats and helmets in proper no-frills country local with particularly well kept Sharps ales, nice house wine, enormous lunchtime sandwich platters (good crab) and the like from homely kitchen area (perhaps not out of season), swift service, coal fire, pool table, books and perhaps local produce for sale; children in eating area, picnic-sets outside, short stroll above beautiful cove with good coast walks *(Donna and Roger, LYM, Michael and Ann Cole, Thomas Lane)*

LANDS END [SW3425]

Lands End TR19 7AA: Hotel bar with big picture windows overlooking terrace and sea beyond, airy family conservatory, St Austell Tinners, standard food (can be pricy); car parking charge in season, bedrooms *(Joan and Michel Hooper-Immins)*

LANNER [SW7339]

☆ *Fox & Hounds* TR16 6AX [Comford; A393/B3298]: Cosily comfortable rambling low-beamed pub with top-notch friendly service, good choice of generous fresh food from sandwiches to massive steaks, St Austell ales tapped from the cask, good house wines, warm fires, high-backed settles and cottagey chairs on flagstones, stripped stone and dark panelling; pub games, piped music; children welcome in dining room, dogs in bar, disabled facilities, great floral displays in front, neat back garden with pond and play area, open all day wknds *(John Marsh, Paul and Shirley White, David Crook, LYM, Michael Saunders)*

LELANT [SW5436]

☆ *Old Quay House* TR27 6JG [Griggs Quay, Lelant Saltings; A3047/B3301 S of village]: Large neatly kept modern pub in marvellous spot by bird sanctuary estuary, good value food inc good salad bar, real ales such as Bass, Sharps Doom Bar and St Austell Tribute, good service, dining area off well divided open-plan bar, children allowed upstairs; garden with views over saltings, decent motel-type bedrooms, open all day summer *(Lesley and Peter Barrett, Mr and Mrs C R Little)*

LERRYN [SX1356]

☆ *Ship* PL22 0PT [signed off A390 in Lostwithiel; Fore St]: Lovely spot esp when tide's in (boats from Fowey then, can radio your order ahead), ales such as Bass, Skinners and Sharps Eden, local farm cider, good wines, country wines and whiskies, huge woodburner, attractive adults-only dining conservatory (booked quickly evenings and wknds), games room with pool; dogs on leads and children welcome, picnic-sets and pretty play area outside, nr famous stepping-stones and three well signed waterside walks, decent bedrooms in adjoining building *(David Crook, Nick Lawless, Mike and Heather Watson, Peter Salmon, Dave Webster, Sue Holland, LYM)*

LIZARD [SW7012]

Top House TR12 7NQ [A3083]: Neat pub with lots of good local sea pictures, fine shipwreck relics and serpentine craftwork (note the handpumps), good log fire, well kept ales, good range of food, friendly staff (can be overstretched when busy); sheltered terrace, interesting nearby serpentine shop *(BB, Dave Webster, Sue Holland, Paul and Shirley White)*

LOSTWITHIEL [SX1059]

☆ *Royal Oak* PL22 0AG [Duke St]: Fine choice of bottled beers from around the world in nice town local dating from 13th c, Bass, Fullers London Pride and Sharps Doom Bar, spacious neat lounge with log-effect gas fire, beamed and flagstoned back public bar, darts and board games, restaurant; games

machines, TV, juke box; children welcome, dogs in bar, picnic-sets on raised terrace by car park, open all day *(Simon Fox, Mrs Angela Graham, LYM, Colin and Peggy Wilshire, John and Pat Morris)*

LUDGVAN [SW5033]

☆ *White Hart* TR20 8EY [off A30 Penzance—Hayle at Crowlas]: Appealing old-fashioned 19th-c pub under enthusiastic new licensees (who also run the Turks Head in Penzance), small beamed rooms with woodburners; should be good – reports please *(LYM)*

LUXULYAN [SX0458]

Kings Arms PL30 5EF [Bridges]: Open-plan village pub by bridge, simple décor with light oak fittings and beams, friendly helpful staff, good range of good value home-made food, well kept St Austell ales, back games area with pool; small front terrace and back garden, handy for Eden Project, open all day *(Robert Watt)*

MANACCAN [SW7624]

New Inn TR12 6HA [down hill signed to Gillan and St Keverne]: Simple thatched pub in attractive setting above sea and popular with sailing folk, two distinct areas, beam and plank ceiling, comfortably cushioned wall seats and other chairs, fire, friendly staff, real ales inc Sharps Doom Bar, local apple juice and cordials, good simple home-cooked food, cribbage, dominoes; children and dogs welcome, picnic-sets in rose-filled garden, bedrooms *(Steve Pocock, LYM, Susie Symes, Nick Lawless, Ian and Deborah Carrington, the Didler, Michael and Ann Cole)*

MARAZION [SW5130]

Godolphin Arms TR17 0EN [West End]: Great views across beach and Mounts Bay towards St Michael's Mount, real ales inc Sharps, informal lower bar with pool table, upper lounge bar and dining room, Sun carvery, family room with play area; decked terrace, ten brightly painted bedrooms, most with sea view, good breakfast *(Ian Phillips, Donna and Roger)*

Kings Arms TR17 0AP [The Square]: Old one-bar pub in small square, friendly landlord, good value fresh food, well kept St Austell; picnic-sets out in front *(Giles and Annie Francis, David and Sue Smith)*

MAWGAN [SW7025]

Ship TR12 6AD: Recently nicely reworked, with convivial helpful landlord, well kept Sharps Doom Bar and Skinners Betty Stogs in welcoming L-shaped bar, stone fireplace and end snug, enjoyable bar food and good more ambitious restaurant (Old Court House); garden with picnic-sets *(Peter Holmes, Michael and Ann Cole)*

MAWNAN SMITH [SW7728]

☆ *Red Lion* TR11 5EP [W of Falmouth, off former B3291 Penryn—Gweek; The Square]: Homely old thatched pub with cosy series of carpeted and softly lit linked beamed rooms, open-view kitchen doing wide choice of good reasonably priced food esp seafood (should book summer evening), quick friendly service, lots of wines by the glass, Greene King and Sharps kept well, good coffee, daily papers, fresh flowers, woodburner, dark woodwork, country pictures, plates and bric-a-brac; piped music, TV; children welcome, picnic-sets outside, handy for Glendurgan and Trebah Gardens *(LYM, Dr and Mrs M E Wilson)*

MEVAGISSEY [SX0144]

Fountain PL26 6QH [Cliff St, down alley by Post Office]: Unpretentious and interesting fishermen's pub, low beams, slate floor, some stripped stone, good coal fire, old local pictures, small fish tank, well kept St Austell, enjoyable food from simple lunchtime menu (maybe not Sat), back locals' bar with glass-topped cellar (and pool, games machine and sports TV), good value upstairs restaurant, friendly staff; occasional sing-songs; dogs welcome, bedrooms, pretty frontage, open all day summer *(Ted George, Christopher Wright, Alan Bulley, David and Sue Smith, BB, the Didler, Andy and Claire Barker)*

☆ *Ship* PL26 6UQ [Fore St, nr harbour]: Lively yet relaxed 16th-c pub with interesting alcove areas in big open-plan bar, low beams and flagstones, nice nautical décor, open fire, cheerful uniformed staff, good range of generous pubby food esp fresh fish, small helpings available, full St Austell range kept well, back pool table; games machines, piped music, occasional live; dogs allowed, children welcome in two front rooms, comfortable bedrooms, open all day summer *(Ted George, Phil and Jane Hodson, Rona Murdoch, Christopher Wright, Chris Glasson, Michael and Alison Sandy, R K Phillips)*

MORVAL [SX2657]

Snooty Fox PL13 1PR: Enjoyable food inc bargain lunches in well decorated modern building, divided beamed bar, real ales inc Sharps, good short wine list, welcoming service; bedrooms, campsite *(Canon Michael Bourdeaux)*

MORWENSTOW [SS2015]

Bush EX23 9SR [signed off A39 N of Kilkhampton; Crosstown]: Beautifully placed beamed pub near interesting village church and great cliff walks, updated pastel décor with light and tidy contemporary dining room and conservatory, but keeping the bar's massive flagstones and fireplace (in fact it's partly Saxon and one of Britain's most ancient pubs, with a serpentine Celtic basin in one wall), well kept Skinners and St Austells, friendly service; garden with good views and solid wooden play things, big new car park, two new bedrooms *(John Lane, Conor McGaughey,*

Ryta Lyndley, Nigel Long, LYM, the Didler, Rona Murdoch, D P and M A Miles)

MULLION [SW6719]

Old Inn TR12 7HN [Churchtown – not down in the cove]: Extensive thatched and beamed family food pub with central servery doing generous good value food (all day Jul/Aug) from doorstep sandwiches to pies and evening steaks, fast service in linked eating areas with lots of brasses, plates, clocks, nautical items and old wreck pictures, big inglenook fireplace, two or more real ales, lots of wines by the glass; children welcome, picnic-sets on terrace and in pretty orchard garden, good bedrooms, open all day wknds and Aug *(LYM, David and Alison Walker, Comus and Sarah Elliott)*

NEWLYN [SW4629]

Tolcarne TR18 5PR [Tolcarne Pl]: Well kept traditional 17th-c quayside pub, open fire, local fishing photos, wide choice of good value home-made food inc good seafood, friendly staff, well kept Brakspears and Sharps; terrace (harbour wall cuts off view), good parking *(Chris and Mike Granville-Edge)*

NEWLYN EAST [SW8256]

Pheasant TR8 5LJ [Churchtown]: Friendly traditional village pub in quiet back street serving generous reasonably priced food, good service; not far from Trerice Gardens *(Muriel and John Hobbs)*

PADSTOW [SW9175]

Golden Lion PL28 8AN [Lanadwell St]: Cheerful black-beamed snug locals' bar, high-raftered back lounge with plush banquettes, well kept ales inc Sharps Doom Bar, reasonably priced simple bar lunches inc good crab sandwiches, evening steaks and fresh seafood, prompt friendly service, coal fire; pool in family area, piped music, games machines, sports TV; terrace tables, bedrooms, open all day *(Conor McGaughey, Dr and Mrs M W A Haward, Michael B Griffith, the Didler, Dave Lowe, BB)*

☆ *London* PL28 8AN [Llanadwell St]: Down-to-earth fishermen's local with lots of pictures and nautical memorabilia, jolly atmosphere, good staff, well kept St Austell ales, decent choice of malt whiskies, wknd lunchtime bar food inc good crab sandwiches, fresh local fish, more elaborate evening choice (small back dining area – get there early for a table), great log fire; can get very busy, games machines but no piped music – home-grown live music Sun night; dogs welcome (if the resident collies approve), open all day, good value bedrooms *(Sue and Dave Harris, Tim and Ann Newell, LYM, Ted George, Conor McGaughey, Lynda Bentley)*

PAR [SX0553]

Britannia PL24 2SL [Tregrehan (A390 St Austell—Lostwithiel, just E of A3092 roundabout)]: Modern refurbishment of 16th-c pub with log-effect fire in comfortable partly stripped stone nautical-theme lounge bar (only over-21s here), wide choice of enjoyable bar food (snacks all day in summer), changing ales inc Sharps and Skinners, good choice of wines by the glass, attentive friendly staff, family room and neat modern restaurant; big-screen sports TVs in bright main bar; plenty of picnic-sets in good-sized neatly kept enclosed garden with terrace and play area *(Mick and Moira Brummell, Peter and Audrey Dowsett)*

☆ *Royal* PL24 2AJ [Eastcliffe Rd (close to station, off A3082)]: Light and airy open-plan refurbishment, solid pale country furniture on flagstones and bare boards, some stripped stone, log-effect fire, restaurant opening into slate-floored conservatory, enjoyable food, well kept Sharps Doom Bar and St Austell Tribute, good choice of wines by the glass, welcoming landlord, darts, pool, exuberant Mon card night; piped music, big-screen TV, games machine; disabled access, small heated terrace, comfortable bedrooms *(BB, Sally and Tom Matson)*

PELYNT [SX2054]

☆ *Jubilee* PL13 2JZ [B3359 NW of Looe]: 16th-c beamed inn with well kept St Austell Tribute, good wines by the glass, wide food choice from good sandwiches up, interesting Queen Victoria mementoes, some handsome antique furnishings, log fire in big stone fireplace, separate bar with darts, pool and games machine; children and dogs welcome, inner courtyard with pretty flower tubs, good play area, 11 comfortable bedrooms, open all day wknds *(LYM, Dennis Jenkin, Evelyn and Derek Walter)*

PENDOGGETT [SX0279]

☆ *Cornish Arms* PL30 3HH [B3314]: Picturesque friendly old coaching inn with traditional oak settles on civilised front bar's handsome polished slate floor, fine prints, above-average food from good soup and sandwiches to fresh fish, splendid steaks and great Sunday lunch, particularly welcoming service, well kept Bass and Sharps Doom Bar, good wines by the glass, comfortably spaced tables in small dining room, proper back locals' bar with woodburner and games; provision for children, disabled access (staff helpful), terrace with distant sea view, bedrooms, open all day *(M A Borthwick, Mrs Angela Graham, Michael B Griffith, LYM, Tony Allwood)*

PENELEWEY [SW8140]

☆ *Punch Bowl & Ladle* TR3 6QY [B3289]: Thatched olde-worlde dining pub in picturesque setting handy for Trelissick Gardens, big settees, rustic bric-a-brac, several room areas, wide choice of generous sensibly priced home-made food

from good sandwiches to local steaks (Thurs very popular with elderly lunchers), children's helpings, efficient helpful service, St Austell ales, good wine choice; unobtrusive piped music; children and dogs on leads welcome, small back sun terrace, open all day summer *(LYM, Comus and Sarah Elliott, Clifford Blakemore, Tony Allwood, Paul and Shirley White, Dennis Jenkin, M Bryan Osborne)*

PENTEWAN [SX0147]

Ship PL26 6BX [just off B3273 St Austell—Mevagissey; West End]: 17th-c beamed pub opp tiny village's harbour, comfortable and clean with three separate areas and dining room, lots of dark tables and open fire, four St Austell ales, good value food inc plenty of fish and Sun carvery; pool room, piped music; views from tables outside, nr good sandy beach and big caravan park *(Hector Speight, Fi Exton)*

PENZANCE [SW4730]

Admiral Benbow TR18 4AF [Chapel St]: Well run rambling pub, full of life and atmosphere and packed with interesting nautical gear, friendly thoughtful staff, good value above-average food inc local fish, real ales such as Sharps, Skinners and St Austell, cosy corners, downstairs restaurant, upper floor with pool, pleasant view from back room; children welcome, open all day summer *(LYM, Kalman Kafetz, David Tindal)*

☆ *Dolphin* TR18 4EF [The Barbican; Newlyn road, opp harbour after swing-bridge]: Roomy and welcoming, part old-fashioned pub and part bistro, attractive nautical décor, good harbour views, good value food from good lunchtime sandwiches to steaks and fresh fish (landlady's husband is a fisherman), St Austell ales, good wines by the glass, helpful service, great fireplace, dining area a few steps down, cosy family room; big pool room with juke box etc, no obvious nearby parking; pavement picnic-sets, open all day *(Peter Salmon, Tony and Jill Radnor, LYM, the Didler)*

PERRANUTHNOE [SW5329]

☆ *Victoria* TR20 9NP [signed off A394 Penzance—Helston]: Comfortable low-beamed bar and good-sized dining room, good interesting food from freshly baked lunchtime baguettes through enterprising main dishes to great puddings, fully fledged dining pub evenings, friendly efficient service, well kept Bass and Sharps, nice wine choice, coal fire, some stripped stonework, old photographs; quiet piped music; dogs welcome, picnic-sets in pretty sunken garden, handy for Mounts Bay, good bedrooms *(Nigel Long, Dennis Jenkin, Bruce and Sharon Eden, LYM)*

PHILLACK [SW5638]

Bucket of Blood TR27 5AE [Churchtown Rd]: Welcoming bustle in traditional low-beamed thick-walled village pub, sturdy stripped pine tables, enjoyable generous fresh food (not Mon/Tues), low prices, well kept St Austell Tinners and HSD, gruesome ghost stories, locals' back snug; tables outside *(LYM, Adrian Johnson)*

PILLATON [SX3664]

☆ *Weary Friar* PL12 6QS [off Callington—Landrake back road]: Pretty tucked-away 12th-c pub, friendly and family-run, good food in bar and big back restaurant, well kept ales such as Bass and Sharps Eden, farm cider, four spotless and civilised knocked-together rooms, appealing tastefully updated décor, comfortable seating, log fire; children in eating area (no dogs inside), tables outside, Tues evening bell-ringing in church next door, comfortable bedrooms *(LYM, Ted George)*

POLPERRO [SX2051]

☆ *Crumplehorn Mill* PL13 2RJ [top of village nr main car park]: Converted mill keeping beams, flagstones and some stripped stone, snug lower beamed bar leading to long attractive main room with cosy end eating area, very welcoming, good choice of enjoyable food, well kept St Austells and Sharps, log fire; families welcome, outside seating, good value bedrooms, self catering *(Ted George, Allan and Janice Webb, BB, Lawrence Pearse)*

☆ *Three Pilchards* PL13 2QZ [Quay Rd]: Welcoming low-beamed fishermen's local behind fish quay, good value food from baguettes to nicely cooked local fish, real ales, quick service, lots of black woodwork, dim lighting, simple furnishings, open fire in big stone fireplace, regulars' photographs; piped music, can get very busy; tables on upper terrace (no sea view) up steep steps, open all day *(Lawrence Pearse, BB)*

POLRUAN [SX1250]

Lugger PL23 1PA [The Quay; back roads off A390 in Lostwithiel, or passenger/bicycle ferry from Fowey]: Beamed waterside local with high-backed wall settles, big model boats etc, open fires, good views from upstairs rooms, good bar food from sandwiches to generous fish and chips, friendly service, well kept St Austell ales, reasonably priced wines, restaurant; children welcome, good walks, open all day *(LYM, Dave Webster, Sue Holland, Brian and Bett Cox)*

Russell PL23 1PJ [West St]: Fishermen's local, lively yet relaxing, with sensibly priced straightforward food using local produce from good sandwiches up, enjoyable Sun lunch, St Austell beers, friendly staff, log fire, large bar with interesting photographs *(Dave Webster, Sue Holland)*

PORT ISAAC [SW9980]

☆ *Golden Lion* PL29 3RB [Fore Street]: Bustling local atmosphere in simply furnished old rooms, open fire in back one, window seats and three balcony tables looking down on rocky harbour and lifeboat slip far below, straightforward food inc good fish range, St Austell ales, darts, dominoes, cribbage; piped music, games machine; children in eating areas, dramatic cliff walks, open all day *(LYM, John and Alison Hamilton, David Tindal, Sue Demont, Tim Barrow, the Didler)*

PORTLOE [SW9339]

☆ *Ship* TR2 5RA: Unspoilt comfortably bright L-shaped local with reasonably priced straightforward food inc good crab sandwiches, well kept St Austell ales, farm cider, decent wines, prompt friendly service, interesting nautical and local memorabilia and photographs; piped music; disabled access to main bar, sheltered and attractive streamside picnic-sets over road, pretty fishing village with lovely cove and coast path above, open all day Fri-Sun summer *(Chris and Angela Buckell, Barry Collett, BB, Christopher Wright, David J Cooke, Guy Vowles, Comus and Sarah Elliott)*

PORTSCATHO [SW8735]

Plume of Feathers TR2 5HW [The Square]: Cheerful largely stripped stone pub in pretty fishing village, well kept St Austell and other ales, Healey's cider, pubby food from sandwiches up, bargain fish night Fri, sea-related bric-a-brac in comfortable linked room areas, side locals' bar (can be very lively evenings), restaurant; very popular with summer visitors, warm local atmosphere out of season; dogs welcome, disabled access, lovely coast walks, open all day summer (other times if busy) *(Chris and Angela Buckell, Tim and Joan Wright, Comus and Sarah Elliott, Paul and Shirley White, David J Cooke, LYM)*

SENNEN COVE [SW3526]

☆ *Old Success* TR19 7DG [Off A30 Land's End road]: The star's for the glorious Whitesand Bay view, from the terraced garden or inside this traditional seaside hotel; unpretentious bar with lifeboat memorabilia, ship's lanterns, black and white photographs, big ship's wheel used as coat stand, well kept Sharps and Skinners, local cider, food all day in hols, darts, restaurant; piped music, TV; children welcome, dogs in bar, basic decent bedrooms, four self-catering flats, open all day *(Dr and Mrs M W A Haward, Darren and Kirstin Arnold, Julie Russell-Carter, Christine and Phil Young, LYM, Gaynor Gregory, David and Sue Smith, Joan York)*

ST DOMINICK [SX4067]

☆ *Who'd Have Thought It* PL12 6TG [off A388 S of Callington]: Large comfortable country pub doing very well under current management, wide choice of good food inc blackboard specials (more tables for eating now), efficient friendly staff, well kept St Austell ales, superb Tamar views esp from conservatory, cosily plush lounge areas with open fires; dogs allowed in public bar, garden tables, handy for Cotehele (NT) *(Ted George, Jacquie Jones, LYM, Mr and Mrs E L Fortin)*

ST EWE [SW9746]

☆ *Crown* PL26 6EY [off B3287]: Low beams and flagstones, traditional furnishings, lovely log fire, voluble parrot and some nice decorative touches, full St Austell beer range kept well, good house wines, helpful attentive licensees, generous if pricy food (can take a while) from crab sandwiches up, large back dining room up steps (heavily booked in season); outside gents'; children in eating areas, dogs allowed in bar but not garden with its ducks, geese and stone tables, handy for Lost Gardens of Heligan, one bedroom, open all day summer *(George Murdoch, LYM, David Eberlin, Jack Pridding, Dr and Mrs M W A Haward, Nick Lawless, David Crook, Christopher Wright)*

ST ISSEY [SW9272]

Pickwick PL27 7QQ [Burgois, signed off A389 at St Issey]: Rambling old hillside pub with estuary views, generous all-day food inc good local meats, three St Austell ales, decent wines, friendly helpful staff, log fire, Dickensian kitsch and dark oak beams, two bars (one allowing older children) and pretty candlelit restaurant; quiet piped music, pool, machines; picnic-sets in sizeable garden with sea views and good play area, bowling green and tennis, bedrooms *(Ian Downes)*

ST IVES [SW5140]

Golden Lion TR26 1RS [High St]: Lively and welcoming with snug front bar and more room at back, standard lunchtime food inc filling pasties, well kept beers such as Courage Best and Sharps Doom Bar; sports TV *(Giles and Annie Francis)*

Lifeboat TR26 1LF [Wharf Rd]: Thriving quayside pub, wide choice of good value all-day food, three St Austell ales, friendly helpful staff, well spaced harbour-view tables and cosier corners, nautical theme; sports TV; dogs welcome, good disabled access and facilities, open all day *(Alan Johnson, Michael Saunders)*

☆ *Sloop* TR26 1LP [The Wharf]: Busy low-beamed, panelled and flagstoned harbourside pub with bright St Ives School pictures and attractive portrait drawings in front bar, booth seating in back bar, good value food from sandwiches and interesting baguettes to lots of fresh local fish, quick friendly service even though busy, Greene King, Ruddles and Sharps, good coffee; piped music, TV; children in eating area, a few beach-view seats out on cobbles, open all day (breakfast from 9am), cosy bedrooms, handy for Tate Gallery *(LYM, Klaus and Elizabeth Leist, Bruce and Sharon Eden,*

the Didler, Alan Johnson, Jarrod and Wendy Hopkinson, Adrian Johnson, Tim and Ann Newell)

Union TR26 1AB [Fore St]: Friendly low-beamed pub, roomy but cosy, with good value food worth waiting for from good soup and filled baguettes to local seafood specials, real ales inc Bass and Sharps, decent wines, friendly cheery, daily papers, small hot fire, dark woodwork and masses of old local photographs; piped music *(Alan Johnson)*

ST JUST IN PENWITH [SW3731]

Wellington TR19 7HD [Market Sq]: Unpretentious, busy and friendly, with good ample food, well kept St Austell beers, polite cheerful service, good local atmosphere, decent wines; bedrooms, good breakfast *(John and Gloria Isaacs)*

ST MAWES [SW8433]

Rising Sun TR2 5DJ [The Square]: Nicely placed pub under new management, main bar (being refurbished as we went to press) with prized bow-window seat and good coal fire, sizeable carpeted left-hand bar with dark wood furniture, well kept St Austell ales, wood-floored conservatory overlooking sunny terrace with picnic-sets just across road from harbour wall; piped music; bedrooms *(Comus and Sarah Elliott, LYM)*

Victory TR2 5DQ [Victory Hill]: Locals' bare-boards bar on left, carpeted dining area on right with partitions (may be upstairs dining room in season), Otter and Sharps, decent pubby food, log fires, plain wooden seating, board games; piped music; one or two picnic-sets outside, good value bedrooms, open all day *(LYM, Mr and Mrs A H Young, Dennis Jenkin, Barry Collett, Julie and James Horsley, Comus and Sarah Elliott, Gordon Tong)*

ST MAWGAN [SW8765]

☆ *Falcon* TR8 4EP [NE of Newquay, off B3276 or A3059]: New licensees took over this attractive old stone inn in Sept 2008, too late for us to gauge the changes; big bar with log fire, large antique coaching prints and falcon pictures, St Austell ales, darts and pool; children welcome, front cobbled courtyard and peaceful back garden with wishing well, pretty village, bedrooms, has been open all day in summer *(LYM)*

STICKER [SW9750]

Hewas PL26 7HD [signed just off A390]: Ivy-covered pub in pleasant village, flower-filled heated front terrace, good-sized bar with dining area each end, popular reasonably priced home-made food with some more unusual specials, St Austell beers; back pool room, weekly entertainment and quiz *(Comus and Sarah Elliott)*

STITHIANS [SW7640]

Cornish Arms TR4 8RP [Frogpool, which is not shown on many roadmaps but is NE of

A393 – ie opp side to Stithians itself]:
Welcoming comfortable village pub with
long beamed bar, fires either end, good
value generous food inc OAP bargain
lunches, local ales; good bedrooms *(BB,
John Marsh)*

STRATTON [SS2306]

☆ *Tree* EX23 9DA [just E of Bude; Fore St]:
Rambling and softly lit 16th-c beamed
local with interesting old furniture and
colourful décor, friendly relaxed
atmosphere, great log fires, well kept
Sharps and St Austell, good coffee, good
value generous home-made food using
local supplies, character Elizabethan-style
evening restaurant with old paintings;
big-screen sports TV; children welcome in
back bar, seats alongside unusual old
dovecot in ancient coachyard, bedrooms
*(Ryta Lyndley, Rona Murdoch,
Mrs M Etherington, BB)*

TREBARWITH [SX0585]

Port William PL34 0HB [Trebarwith
Strand]: Lovely seaside setting with
glorious views and sunsets, waterside
picnic-sets across road and on covered
terrace, fishing nets, fish tanks and
maritime memorabilia inside, gallery with
local artwork, well kept St Austell Tinners
and HSD, farm cider; pool and other
games, piped music; children in eating
area, well equipped comfortable
bedrooms, open all day *(LYM,
John Coatsworth, Mrs A Taylor)*

TREBURLEY [SX3477]

☆ *Springer Spaniel* PL15 9NS [A388
Callington—Launceston]: Doing well
under current licensees, good locally
sourced food inc sandwiches with choice
of interesting breads, well kept fairly
priced Sharps and Skinners, good wine
choice, friendly service, clean décor with
high-backed settle by woodburner, high-
backed farmhouse chairs and other seats,
olde-worlde prints, further cosy room with
big solid teak tables, attractive restaurant
up some steps; dogs very welcome in bar,
children in eating areas, covered terrace
*(Giles and Annie Francis, Barry and
Sue Pladdys, Mrs M S Tadd, Drs J and
J Parker, Simon J Barber, Dennis Jenkin,
Lynda Bentley, LYM)*

TREEN [SW3923]

Logan Rock TR19 6LG [just off B3315
Penzance—Lands End]: Low-beamed
traditional bar with inglenook seat by hot
coal fire, St Austell HSD and other ales,
courteous service, wide choice of standard
food all day in summer from sandwiches
up, smaller more enterprising choice out
of season, lots of games in family room,
small back snug with excellent cricket
memorabilia – landlady eminent in
county's cricket association; may be piped
music, no children inside; tables in small
pretty garden with covered area, good
coast walks *(JCW, LYM, Kalman Kafetz,
Dr and Mrs M W A Haward)*

TREGONY [SW9244]

Kings Arms TR2 5RW [Fore St (B3287)]:
Light and airy 16th-c pub with long
traditional main bar, St Austell ales, good
value food using local produce, keen
welcoming service and chatty landlord,
woodburners in two beamed and panelled
front rooms, one for families, back games
room; tables in pleasant garden,
charming village *(R K Phillips,
Christopher Wright, Tim and Joan Wright,
Comus and Sarah Elliott, Stephen and
Jean Curtis)*

TREMATON [SX3960]

☆ *Crooked Inn* PL12 4RZ [off A38 just W of
Saltash]: Down a long drive among free-
roaming farm animals, this laid-back and
decidedly not smart place has an open-
plan bar with lower lounge leading to a
conservatory with doors on to decking
overlooking the garden and valley; beams,
straightforward furnishings, open fire,
well kept ales such as Sharps and
Skinners, decent wines by the glass,
cheerful service, wide food choice;
children and dogs welcome, play area,
bedrooms overlooking courtyard, nice
breakfast, open all day *(J F M and
M West, LYM, Ted George, Roger and
Anne Newbury, Richard May)*

TRESILLIAN [SW8646]

Wheel TR2 4BA [A39 Truro—St Austell]:
Thatched roadside pub locally very
popular for good value food, steps
between two compact main areas with
plush seating, timbering, stripped stone
and low ceiling joists, spotless bric-a-
brac, well kept real ales, welcoming staff;
piped music; children welcome, play area
in neat garden down to tidal inlet
(Mr and Mrs M J Matthews, BB)

TREVAUNANCE COVE [SW7251]

☆ *Driftwood Spars* TR5 0RT [off B3285 in St
Agnes; Quay Rd]: Big nautical-theme pub
just up from beach and dramatic cove,
doing well under new owners; slate,
granite and massive timbers, lots of
nautical and wreck memorabilia, log fires,
good choice of ales and ciders, friendly
young staff, enjoyable food from bar and
restaurant; children and dogs welcome,
garden tables across road, great coastal
walks, good bedrooms and breakfast
*(Chris Reading, LYM, Gaye and Simon,
Chris Glasson)*

TREWARMETT [SX0686]

Trewarmett PL34 0ET [B3263]:
Welcoming early 18th-c pub with thick
stone walls and plenty of atmosphere,
popular with locals, good carvery
(Klaus and Elizabeth Leist)

TRURO [SW8244]

☆ *Old Ale House* TR1 2HD [Quay St]: Up for
sale as we went to press, long a readers'
favourite for its eight well kept ales,
great atmosphere and really good mix of
customers; dimly lit bar has had an
engaging diversity of furnishings,

interesting 1920s bric-a-brac, beer mats pinned everywhere, matchbox collections and daily papers, games room upstairs; our hope is that new tenants will run it in much the same way as its previous exceptional landlord, in which case it will remain a firm recommendation; open all day *(LYM)*
Try Dower TR1 2LW [Lemon Quay]: Bustling Wetherspoons in former newspaper offices on the quay, eight real ales at bargain prices, their usual meal deals, efficient service, pastel décor, sofas, family tables and quiet areas; TV news *(Tim and Ann Newell, David Crook)*
TYWARDREATH [SX0854]
New Inn PL24 2QP [off A3082; Fore St]: Relaxed timeless local, Bass tapped from the cask and St Austell ales on handpump, caring friendly landlord, games and children's room; large secluded garden behind, nice village setting, bedrooms *(Dave Webster, Sue Holland, the Didler, BB)*
VERYAN [SW9139]
☆ *New Inn* TR2 5QA [village signed off A3078]: Neat and comfortably homely one-bar beamed local, good generous food using local produce inc lots of fish, must book Sun lunch, well kept St Austell ales, Rattler's cider, good value house wines and good coffee, inglenook woodburner, polished brass and old pictures, friendly licensees, quick service even when very busy; piped music, nearby parking unlikely in summer, Sun quiz; disabled front access, quiet garden behind the pretty house, charming comfortable bedrooms, good breakfast, interesting partly thatched village not far from nice beach *(Guy Vowles, Michael Lamm, Norman and Sarah Keeping, Chris and Angela Buckell,*

Comus and Sarah Elliott, the Didler, BB, Nick Lawless)

ISLES OF SCILLY

ST AGNES [SV8808]
☆ *Turks Head* TR22 0PL [The Quay]: One of the UK's most beautifully placed pubs, idyllic sea and island views from garden terrace, good food from pasties up, friendly licensees and good service, well kept ales and cider; has been cl winter, open all day other times *(Shirley Sandilands, Michael Sargent, Mr and Mrs S Wilson, LYM, R J Herd)*
ST MARY'S [SV9010]
☆ *Atlantic Inn* TR21 0HY [The Strand; next to but independent from Atlantic Hotel]: Spreading and hospitable dark bar with well kept St Austell ales, good range of sensibly priced food, sea-view restaurant, friendly efficient service, low beams, hanging boat and other nauticalia, flowery-patterned seats, mix of locals and tourists – busy evenings, quieter on sunny lunchtimes; darts, pool, games machines; nice raised verandah with wide views over harbour, good bedrooms in adjacent hotel side *(Richard Tosswill, Gwyn and Anne Wake, BB, C J Fletcher)*
Mermaid TR21 0HY [The Bank]: Picture-window views across town beach and harbour from all-day back restaurant extension (not Tues), strong nautical theme in unpretentious bar with ceiling flags, lots of seafaring relics, rough timber, stone floor, dim lighting, big stove, Ales of Scilly and Skinners Betty Stogs, simple inexpensive bar food; packed Weds and Fri when the gigs race; cellar bar with boat counter, pool table, TV and music for young people (live wknds) *(C J Fletcher)*

Virtually all pubs in this book sell wine by the glass. We mention wines if they are a cut above the average.

Cumbria

The county has a terrific choice of pubs, many surrounded by glorious scenery and therefore popular with walkers and climbers – often with their dogs. These range from pretty basic taverns right up to civilised hotels, but the common theme running through them all is a genuine friendliness to all, whether regulars or visitors. Real ales feature strongly too, with many places offering a lot of local beers, some even brewing their own. No less than half the main entries hold one of our Beer Awards. If it's own-brewed real ales you are after, head for the Bitter End in Cockermouth, the Drunken Duck up above Hawkshead, the Old Crown in Hesket Newmarket, the Watermill at Ings, and the Kirkstile Inn at Loweswater. There's also some excellent food using fantastic local produce, especially the fell-bred lamb, cumberland sausages, and cheeses, and prices for the hearty fare that walkers yearn for are very reasonable, compared with many other areas. For an enjoyable meal, head for the Pheasant at Bassenthwaite Lake (a civilised hotel with a charming pubby bar), the Punch Bowl at Crosthwaite (early reports are that the new licensee is settling in well), the Highland Drove in Great Salkeld (the licensees have just taken on another pub, the Cross Keys in Carleton – yet to make it into these pages), the Drunken Duck near Hawkshead (pubby at lunchtime but rather sophisticated with meals to match in the evening), in or near Ulverston both the Bay Horse (this smart little hotel's bar is relaxed and informal at lunchtime) and the Farmers Arms (very much the heart of the village), and the Gate Inn at Yanwath (extremely popular for its innovative food). Our Cumbrian Dining Pub of the Year is the Gate Inn at Yanwath, not just for its first-class food but because it is such a well run and friendly place, too. New entries this year include the stylishly reworked Mardale at Bampton (a nice place to stay, with good beer and enjoyable local food), the ancient Hole in t' Wall in Bowness-on-Windermere, doing well under its new licensee and very popular in high season, and the Black Swan in Ravenstonedale, a family-run small hotel with a thriving bar, several real ales and enjoyable food. In the Lucky Dip section at the end of the chapter, pubs which have been winning warm praise in the last few months include the Royal Oak in Appleby, Barbon Inn, the Black Bull and the Sun in Coniston, Sun at Crook, Royal Oak at Lindale, Fat Lamb high above Ravenstonedale, Eagles Head at Satterthwaite, Greyhound in Shap, Church House at Torver, Queens Head at Tirril and Brown Horse at Winster. The Coniston Brewery behind the Black Bull produces Bluebird (perhaps the area's best beer), among others. Jennings, now part of the Marstons brewing empire, is Cumbria's main brewery, and smaller local breweries we found in at least some good pubs here included (in a rough order of availability) Hesket Newmarket, Dent, Barngates, Tirril, Keswick, Yates, Ulverston, Geltsdale, Cumbrian and Derwent.

AMBLESIDE   NY3704 MAP 9

Golden Rule

Smithy Brow; follow Kirkstone Pass signpost from A591 on N side of town; LA22 9AS

Simple town local with cosy, relaxed atmosphere, and real ales

Popular locally and with walkers and dogs, this is a no frills and quite unchanging town pub. The bar area has built-in wall seats around cast-iron-framed tables (one with a local map set into its top), horsebrasses on the black beams, assorted pictures on the walls, a welcoming winter fire, and a relaxed atmosphere. Robinsons Cumbria Way, Double Hop, Hartleys XB, Hatters, Unicorn, and a seasonal ale on handpump. A brass measuring rule hangs above the bar. There's also a back room with TV (not much used), a left-hand room with darts and a games machine, and a further room down a couple of steps on the right with lots of seating. The back yard has benches and a covered heated area, and the window boxes are especially colourful.

🍴 **Maybe snacks (but don't count on them) like pork pies, jumbo scotch eggs and (at weekends) filled rolls.** *Starters/Snacks: £0.95 to £2.00*

Robinsons ~ Tenant John Lockley ~ Real ale ~ Bar food ~ No credit cards ~ (015394) 32257 ~ Children welcome away from bar until 9pm ~ Dogs welcome ~ Open 11am-midnight; 12-midnight Sun

Recommended by David and Sue Smith, Bob Broadhurst, Mike and Sue Loseby, Edward Leetham, Michael Butler, Mr and Mrs Maurice Thompson, Dr and Mrs Jackson

ARMATHWAITE   NY5046 MAP 10

Dukes Head 🛏

Off A6 S of Carlisle; CA4 9PB

Interesting food in comfortable lounge, heated outside area and day fishing tickets; good value bedrooms

Not only is this an enjoyable place to stay with hearty breakfasts, but it is good value too – and dogs are allowed in some bedrooms. The comfortable lounge bar has oak settles and little armchairs among more upright seats, oak and mahogany tables, antique hunting and other prints, and some brass and copper powder-flasks above the open fire. Black Sheep and Jennings Cumberland on handpump and sometimes home-made lemonade and ginger beer; the separate public bar has darts, table skittles and board games. There are seats on a heated area outside with more on the lawn behind; boules. Day tickets for fishing are available.

🍴 **Good, popular bar food includes sandwiches, ploughman's, soup, chicken liver pâté with cumberland sauce, hot potted solway shrimps, a meat platter of smoked duck, venison pastrami and air-dried cumbrian ham with apricot preserve, chicken breast wrapped in bacon with a sage, mushroom and white wine sauce, filo parcels filled with strips of roasted red pepper, red onion and goats cheese, baked salmon on a bed of leeks with dry vermouth and prawns, super roast duckling with apple sauce, daily specials such as steak and mushroom in ale pie, nut cutlets with tomato sauce, and moroccan-style lamb, and puddings like strawberry and Pimms cheesecake.** *Starters/Snacks: £3.75 to £6.75. Main Courses: £8.95 to £14.95. Puddings: £3.25 to £3.95*

Punch ~ Tenant Henry Lynch ~ Real ale ~ Bar food ~ Restaurant ~ (016974) 72226 ~ Children welcome ~ Dogs allowed in bar and bedrooms ~ Open 11.30am-11.30pm; closed 25 Dec ~ Bedrooms: £38.50S/£62.50S

Recommended by Comus and Sarah Elliott, Lee and Liz Potter, Richard J Holloway, J M Renshaw, Michael Lamm, T Walker, Alastair Stevenson, B I Mason, Bill and Sheila McLardy

---

If you have to cancel a reservation for a bedroom or restaurant, please telephone or write to warn them. You may lose your deposit if you've paid one.

ASKHAM

NY5123 MAP 9

Punch Bowl 🛏

4.5 miles from M6 junction 40; village signposted on right from A6 4 miles S of Penrith; CA10 2PF

Well furnished inn in lovely spot with choice of different seating areas, log fires, imaginative food and good service

This attractive inn manages to offer imaginative food as well as keeping its role as a country local – and regulars do gather around the bar for a pint of Copper Dragon Best Bitter and Hawkshead Bitter on handpump. They also have 10 wines by the glass and 40 malt whiskies; kind, attentive service. The spreading main bar has good-sized round and oblong tables with spindle-back chairs and comfortable leather tub chairs on its turkey carpet, an antique settle by the log fire in its imposing stone fireplace, local photographs and prints, and coins stuck into the cracks of the dark wooden beams (periodically taken out and sent to charity). The lively locals' area has sturdy wooden stools, wall benches and window seats, with games machine, pool and TV; piped music. A snug separate lounge has button-back leather settees and easy chairs, and the attractive beamed formal dining room has regency striped wallpaper. There are tables out on a flower-filled terrace, and a marquee. Dogs are not allowed in the restaurant.

🍴 **Good, changing, seasonal food includes lunchtime filled baps, soup, roasted pepper, sunblush tomato and brie tartlet, spicy lamb samosas with lime crème fraîche and coriander and beansprout salad, cumberland sausage with black pudding, sage mash and rich red wine gravy, steak in ale pie, calves liver seared on to corned beef hash with a ball of caramelised onion and sage, red wine sauce and parsnip crisps, wild mushroom, chickpea and banana korma, lancashire lamb hotpot, and puddings such as cherry bakewell tart and Tia Maria crème brûlée; also, winter game dishes, fresh fish specials and a take-away service for home-made pizzas and fish and chips (3.30-10.30 Tuesday-Saturday). Starters/Snacks: £4.25 to £6.25. Main Courses: £9.50 to £25.00. Puddings: £5.50**

Enterprise ~ Lease Louise and Paul Smith ~ Real ale ~ Bar food ~ Restaurant ~ (01931) 712443 ~ Children welcome ~ Dogs welcome ~ Live music some weekends ~ Open 10.30-midnight(1am Sat) ~ Bedrooms: £59.50B/£85B

Recommended by Robert Turnham, Phil Bryant, Cedric Robertshaw, Graham and Elizabeth Hargreaves, Michael Doswell

BAMPTON

NY5118 MAP 10

Mardale 🍺 🛏

7.1 miles from M6, J39. A6 through Shap, then left at Post Office, signed to Bampton. After 3.5m cross river in Bampton Grange then next right. In Bampton turn left over bridge by post office; CA10 2RQ

Appealing country dining pub, with relaxed welcoming feel and spotless up-to-date furnishings

Formerly the St Patrick's Well, this pretty and attractively placed beamed pub has been completely reworked for its friendly and helpful new landlord. The décor is clean-cut and contemporary, with chunky modern country tables and chairs on newly laid flagstones, one or two big lakeland prints and a modicum of rustic bygones on pastel walls (and in one big brick fireplace), and a log fire in a second stylish raised fireplace. Coniston Bluebird, Hesket Newmarket Sca Fell Blonde, Timothy Taylors Landlord and maybe a summer guest on handpump, and 40 european bottled beers. Dogs will find a water bowl (and maybe even a biscuit) in the nicely lit bar, which is welcoming to walkers and has comfortable backed stools. There are good walks straight from the door, for example to the nearby Haweswater nature reserve.

🍴 **Using local produce, the enjoyable bar food at lunchtime might include soup and sandwiches and a very good value Farmers Lunch for two such as cumberland sausage and mash or chargrilled minted leg of lamb steak; evening choices such as smoked haddock in a creamy white wine sauce topped with cheese, crispy twice-cooked pork belly with sage and black pepper on bubble and squeak with cumberland sauce, popular half pound lamb** burgers with minted mayonnaise, roasted butternut squash filled with creamy leeks and mushrooms, chargrilled chicken marinated in lemon and thyme, salmon and dill fishcakes with herb mayonnaise, and puddings such as sticky toffee pudding with caramel sauce and key lime pie. *Starters/Snacks: £3.25 to £5.00. Main Courses: £7.50 to £15.50. Puddings: £5.00*

Free house ~ Licensee Sebastian Hindley ~ Real ale ~ Bar food (12-2, 6-9) ~ (01931) 713244 ~ Well-behaved children welcome ~ Dogs welcome ~ Open 11-11(10.30 Sun) ~ Bedrooms: £45S/£70S

Recommended by David and Katharine Cooke, Jane Rostron

BASSENTHWAITE
NY2332   MAP 9

Sun
Off A591 N of Keswick; CA12 4QP

Bustling old pub with tasty, good value food, real ales, and cheerful service

In a charming village, this is a white-rendered slate house with lattice windows and friendly licensees. The rambling bar has low 17th-c black oak beams, two good stone fireplaces with big winter log fires, built-in wall seats and plush stools around heavy wooden tables and areas that stretch usefully back on both sides of the servery. Jennings Bitter, Cumberland Ale, and Sneck Lifter and a guest like Hook Norton 303 on handpump, with some interesting whiskies. A huddle of white houses looks up to Skiddaw and other high fells, and you can enjoy the view from the tables in the front yard by the rose bushes and honeysuckle. The pub is handy for osprey viewing at Dodd Wood. Dogs are not allowed between 6 and 9pm. More reports please.

🍽 **Generous helpings of fairly priced food include sandwiches, steak in ale pie, thai fishcakes with sweet chilli dressing, aubergine and tomato bake topped with cheese, cumberland sausage with egg, half a roast chicken with gravy and stuffing, lamb shank in a red wine and berry sauce, and Sunday roast lunch.** *Starters/Snacks: £3.00 to £5.50. Main Courses: £7.95 to £12.95. Puddings: £3.50 to £3.95*

Jennings (Marstons) ~ Lease Ali Tozer ~ Real ale ~ Bar food (12-2, 6-8.45; not Mon lunch) ~ Restaurant ~ (017687) 76439 ~ Children welcome ~ Dogs allowed in bar ~ Live music monthly Mon ~ Open 12-11.30(10.30 Sun); closed until 4pm Mon (except bank hols)

Recommended by Sylvia and Tony Birbeck, W K Wood, D Miller, B I Mason

BASSENTHWAITE LAKE
NY1930   MAP 9

Pheasant ★ 🍽 ♀ 🛏
Follow Pheasant Inn sign at N end of dual carriageway stretch of A66 by Bassenthwaite Lake; CA13 9YE

Charming, old-fashioned bar in smart hotel with enjoyable bar food and fine range of drinks; excellent restaurant, and attractive surrounding woodlands; comfortable bedrooms

Much loved by many of our readers, this is a particularly well run, civilised hotel with comfortable bedrooms and excellent restaurant food. So it comes as a surprise to find a pubby and pleasantly old-fashioned little bar that has remained quite unchanged over many years. It's just the place to enjoy a quiet pint or informal lunch and the staff are friendly and knowledgeable. There are mellow polished walls, cushioned oak settles, rush-seat chairs and library seats, hunting prints and photographs, and Bass, Jennings Cumberland and Theakstons Best on handpump; 12 good wines by the glass and over 60 malt whiskies. Several comfortable lounges have log fires, beautiful flower arrangements, fine parquet flooring, antiques, and plants. Dogs are allowed in the residents' lounge at lunchtime and they do let them into the bar during the day too, unless people are eating. There are seats in the garden, attractive woodland surroundings, and plenty of walks in all directions.

🍽 **Enjoyable lunchtime bar food includes very good freshly made soup with home-made bread, chicken liver or stilton, walnut and apricot pâté, open sandwiches, ploughman's, their own potted silloth shrimps, baked goats cheese tartlet with red onion marmalade,** shepherd's pie, naturally smoked haddock on buttered spinach with light cheese sauce and poached egg, daily specials and puddings such as dark chocolate mousse and crème caramel with caramelised orange slices; excellent breakfasts. *Starters/Snacks: £4.35 to £8.25. Main Courses: £10.75 to £12.95. Puddings: £5.35*

Free house ~ Licensee Matthew Wylie ~ Real ale ~ Bar food (not in evening – restaurant only then) ~ Restaurant ~ (017687) 76234 ~ Children in eating area of bar if over 8 ~ Dogs allowed in bar and bedrooms ~ Open 11.30-2.30, 5.30-10.30(11 Sat); 12-2.30, 6-10.30 Sun; closed 25 Dec ~ Bedrooms: £85B/£160B

Recommended by Mr and Mrs W W Burke, Julian and Janet Dearden, John and Sylvia Harrop, Pat and Stewart Gordon, Paul Humphreys, Dr and Mrs S G Barber, Jane and Alan Bush, K S Whittaker, Alison and Pete, Mike and Sue Loseby, Chris Maunder, B I Mason, Neil Ingoe, Tina and David Woods-Taylor, Mr and Mrs J Roberts, Gordon and Margaret Ormondroyd, G D K Fraser

BEETHAM   SD4979   MAP 7

Wheatsheaf ♀ 🛏

Village (and inn) signposted just off A6 S of Milnthorpe; LA7 7AL

17th-c inn with handsome timbered cornerpiece, lots of beams, interesting food and quite a choice of drink

As there are good walks nearby, it's useful that this neatly kept old coaching inn serves food all day at weekends. There's an opened-up front lounge bar with lots of exposed beams and joists, and the main bar (behind on the right) has an open fire, Jennings Cumberland and a couple of guest beers like Thwaites Lancaster Bomber and Tirril Charles Gough's Old Faithful on handpump, a dozen wines by the glass, and quite a few malt whiskies. Two upstairs dining rooms are open only at weekends; piped music. The 14th-c church opposite is pretty.

🍴 **Bar food includes sandwiches, ploughman's, soup, potted shrimps, a salad of fruits marinated in kirsch, sausage and mash, steak and mushroom in ale pie, wild mushroom, tomato and goats cheese bread and butter pudding with sweet chilli oil, gammon with an orange and honey glaze, halibut loin with hot buttered prawns and a light scallop cream, and puddings like roast pear parcel with ginger caramel sauce and rich chocolate pot.** *Starters/Snacks: £4.25 to £7.70. Main Courses: £8.00 to £17.50. Puddings: £4.00 to £6.50*

Free house ~ Licensees Mr and Mrs Skelton ~ Real ale ~ Bar food (12-2, 6-9; all day weekends) ~ Restaurant ~ (015395) 62123 ~ Children welcome ~ Open 11-11; 12-10.30 Sun ~ Bedrooms: £65B/£75B

Recommended by Pam and John Smith, Ray and Winifred Halliday, Jo Lilley, Simon Calvert, Brian and Janet Ainscough, Mr and Mrs W W Burke, Maurice and Gill McMahon, Michael Doswell

BOUTH   SD3285   MAP 9

White Hart 🍺

Village signposted off A590 near Haverthwaite; LA12 8JB

A fine range of well kept real ales, tasty bar food, and plenty of bric-a-brac in cheerful Lakeland inn; good surrounding walks

With half a dozen real ales and a friendly atmosphere, it's not surprising that this well run inn is so popular. Kept well on handpump, there might be Black Sheep Best Bitter, Coniston Bluebird, Hesket Newmarket Blencathra Bitter, Jennings Cumberland, Slaters Queen Bee, and Ulverston Lonesome Pine; 30 malt whiskies and 12 wines by the glass. The sloping ceilings and floors show the building's age, and there are lots of old local photographs and bric-a-brac – farm tools, stuffed animals, a collection of long-stemmed clay pipes – and two woodburning stoves. The games room (where dogs are allowed) has a games machine, pool, TV and juke box; piped music. Some seats outside and fine surrounding walks.

🍴 **Good bar food, using local meat, includes sandwiches, soup, steak in Guinness pie, halibut steak in garlic and parsley butter, cumberland sausage with rich onion and cranberry gravy, rare breed sirloin steak, nice daily specials and a decent children's menu.** *Starters/Snacks: £4.25 to £6.25. Main Courses: £9.25 to £14.95. Puddings: £4.75*

Free house ~ Licensee Nigel Barton ~ Real ale ~ Bar food (12-2, 6-8.45; not Mon or Tues lunchtime except bank hols) ~ Restaurant ~ (01229) 861229 ~ Children in bar until 9pm ~ Dogs allowed in bedrooms ~ Live music every other Sun April-Dec ~ Open 12-2, 6-11; 12-11(10.30 Sun) Sat; closed Mon and Tues lunchtimes (except bank hols) ~ Bedrooms: £47.50S(£37.50B)/£80S(£60B)

Recommended by Michael Doswell, JDM, KM, Dr Peter Crawshaw, Alain and Rose Foote, Lee and Liz Potter, Michael Lamm, Mr and Mrs Maurice Thompson

BOWNESS-ON-WINDERMERE   SD4096   MAP 9

Hole in t' Wall ◖
Lowside; LA23 3DH

Bustling old pub with split-level rooms, country knick-knacks, real ales, and tasty food

This fine, unchanging old pub does get very busy during the tourist season but it's a friendly place with efficient staff. The two split-level rooms have beams, stripped stone and flagstones, lots of country bric-a-brac and old pictures, and there's a splendid log fire under a vast slate mantelpiece (in summer the logs are replaced with fresh flowers); the upper room has attractive plasterwork. Robinsons Double Hop, Hartleys XB, and Unicorn on handpump and several wines by the glass; juke box. The small flagstoned front courtyard has sheltered picnic-sets under a large umbrella and outdoor heaters.

🍴 Decent bar food includes sandwiches, ploughman's, soup, chicken liver pâté with cumberland sauce, caesar salad, cumberland sausage with onion gravy and apple sauce, beef in Guinness, fish pie, lasagne, a daily changing vegetarian dish, lamb henry and puddings like lemon mousse and chocolate sponge. *Starters/Snacks: £3.50 to £6.25. Main Courses: £7.95 to £10.50. Puddings: £3.00*

Robinsons ~ Tenant Susan Burnett ~ Real ale ~ Bar food (12-2.30, 6-8.30; 12-7 Fri and Sat; not Sun evening) ~ (015394) 43488 ~ Children welcome ~ Live music every Fri evening March-Dec and every alternate summer Sun lunchtime ~ Open 11-11; 12-10.30 Sun

Recommended by Margaret Whalley, Lindsley Harvard, Michael Butler, Kerry Law

BROUGHTON MILLS   SD2190   MAP 9

Blacksmiths Arms
Off A593 N of Broughton-in-Furness; LA20 6AX

Good food, local beers and open fires in charming small pub liked by walkers

The walks surrounding this charming little pub are superb – and the warm log fires in the bars very welcome. The staff are cheerful and friendly, and three of the four simply but attractively decorated small rooms have straightforward chairs and tables on ancient slate floors, Dent Aviator, Jennings Cumberland, and Tirril Thomas Slee's Academy Ale on handpump, eight wines by the glass, and summer farm cider. There are three smallish dining rooms, and darts, board games, dominoes and cribbage. The hanging baskets and tubs of flowers in front of the building are pretty in summer.

🍴 Using local produce, the good, often interesting bar food includes lunchtime sandwiches or ciabattas, ploughman's, and salads such as chargrilled cajun chicken and shredded confit of duck with plum sauce; there's also soup, ham hock and black pudding terrine with apricot chutney, home-made potted crab with caper dressing, deep-fried breaded brie with a vodka and cranberry sauce, cumberland sausage with black pudding mash and red onion gravy, butternut squash and butter bean crumble with roasted cherry tomatoes, partridge wrapped in pancetta with baby onion glaze and parsnip mash, fillets of bass with fennel, orange, beetroot and green bean salad with a mustard dressing, and puddings such as lime and ginger crème brûlée with raspberry coulis and sticky lemon sponge with custard. *Starters/Snacks: £3.65 to £5.35. Main Courses: £8.25 to £14.35. Puddings: £2.50 to £4.25*

Free house ~ Licensees Mike and Sophie Lane ~ Real ale ~ Bar food (12-2, 6-9; not Mon lunchtime) ~ Restaurant ~ (01229) 716824 ~ Children welcome ~ Dogs welcome ~ Open 12-11(5pm-11 Mon); 12-10.30 Sun; 12-2.30, 5-11 Tues-Fri in winter; closed Mon lunchtime

Recommended by Julie and Bill Ryan, Tina and David Woods-Taylor, Maurice and Gill McMahon, Peter F Marshall, Tim Maddison, V and E A Bolton, the Didler

CARTMEL   SD3778   MAP 7

Kings Arms

The Square, off Causeway; LA11 6QB

Timbered pub in ancient village with seats facing lovely village square

Seats outside this little black and white pub look over the lovely village square and there's a fine medieval stone gatehouse nearby. Inside, the neatly kept, rambling bar has a friendly atmosphere and is liked by both drinkers and diners. There are small antique prints on the walls, a mixture of seats including old country chairs, settles and wall banquettes, fresh flowers on the tables, and tankards hanging over the bar counter. Barngates Cat Nap, Bass, Hawkshead Red, and Marstons Pedigree on handpump and ten wines by the glass; good service, piped music.

🍴 **Well liked bar food includes lunchtime sandwiches, fresh hake in beer batter, cumberland sausage on bubble and squeak with onion gravy, gammon and egg, vegetable curry, local salt marsh lamb chops with minted butter, steak in Guinness pie, daily specials, and puddings such as sticky toffee pudding and bread and butter pudding.** *Starters/Snacks: £3.45 to £5.95. Main Courses: £8.95 to £12.95. Puddings: £3.95*

Enterprise ~ Lease Richard Grimmer ~ Real ale ~ Bar food (12-2.30(3 Sat and Sun), 5.30-8.30(8.45 Fri and Sat)) ~ Restaurant ~ (01539) 536220 ~ Children welcome ~ Dogs allowed in bar ~ Open 11-11(10.30 Sun); closed 25 Dec

Recommended by Pat and Graham Williamson, Dr John R and Hazel Allen, A and B D Craig, Alain and Rose Foote, Margaret Dickinson, Michael Lamm, Dr Kevan Tucker, N R White

CARTMEL FELL   SD4189   MAP 9

Masons Arms 🍺

Strawberry Bank, a few miles S of Windermere between A592 and A5074; perhaps the simplest way of finding the pub is to go uphill W from Bowland Bridge (which is signposted off A5074) towards Newby Bridge and keep right then left at the staggered crossroads – it's then on your right, below Gummer's How; OS Sheet 97 map reference 413895; LA11 6NW

Plenty of character in beamed bar, good food, real ales plus many foreign bottled beers, and fine views from terrace

A favourite with quite a few of our readers, this well run pub has stunning views down over the Winster Valley to the woods below Whitbarrow Scar – rustic benches and tables on the terrace make the most of this. The main bar has plenty of character with low black beams in the bowed ceiling and country chairs and plain wooden tables on polished flagstones. A small lounge has oak tables and settles to match its fine Jacobean panelling, there's a plain little room beyond the serving counter with pictures and a fire in an open range, a family room with an old-parlourish atmosphere, and an upstairs dining room; piped music and board games. Copper Dragon Best Bitter, Dent Aviator, Theakstons Best Bitter, and Timothy Taylors Landlord on handpump, a wide range of foreign bottled beers, several wines by the glass and quite a few malt whiskies. Comfortable self-catering cottages and apartments behind.

🍴 **Good, enjoyable bar food includes sandwiches, filled ciabattas and wraps, soup, brie and cherry tomato tart, black pudding, soft poached egg and crispy bacon on mash with a wholegrain mustard sauce, pork and damson sausages, steak in ale pie, fresh haddock in batter with home-made tartare sauce, popular ribs in their famous sticky sauce, chicken wrapped in bacon with a creamy wild mushroom sauce, a brace of pheasants with red wine, honey and mustard sauce, and puddings such as clotted cream baked cheesecake with Drambuie soaked soft fruits and chocolate fudge cake with chocolate sauce and cream.** *Starters/Snacks: £3.95 to £7.95. Main Courses: £9.95 to £13.95. Puddings: £5.25*

Individual Inns ~ Managers John and Diane Taylor ~ Real ale ~ Bar food (12-2.30, 6-9; all day weekends) ~ Restaurant ~ (015395) 68486 ~ Children welcome ~ Dogs allowed in bar ~ Open 11.30-11; 12-10.30 Sun

Recommended by Tina and David Woods-Taylor, Tony and Jill Radnor, Maurice Ricketts, Helen and Brian Edgeley, Ewan and Moira McCall, Mary McSweeney, Alistair and Kay Butler, Jo Lilley, Simon Calvert, Mr and Mrs Richard Osborne, Walter and Susan Rinaldi-Butcher, Nick Lawless

CASTERTON   SD6379   MAP 7

Pheasant ♀

A683 about 1 mile N of junction with A65, by Kirkby Lonsdale; OS Sheet 97 map reference 633796; LA6 2RX

Neat beamed rooms in pleasant inn, and seats in attractive garden with fell views

Customers tend to return to this traditional 18th-c inn again and again. It's very well run and neatly kept and the staff are attentive and charming. The beamed rooms of the main bar are attractively modernised, with wheelback chairs, cushioned wall settles, a nicely arched oak framed fireplace (gas-effect fires), and Copper Dragon Best Bitter, Dent Aviator, and Theakstons Best Bitter on handpump; 19 malt whiskies and several wines by the glass. Piped music and board games. There are some tables under cocktail parasols outside by the road, with more in the pleasant garden. The nearby church (built for the girls' school of Brontë fame here) has some attractive pre-Raphaelite stained-glass and paintings.

🍴 **Generous helpings of popular bar food include sandwiches, soup, ploughman's, smoked mackerel mousse, cannelloni stuffed with chopped mushrooms and asparagus spears topped with parsley cream sauce, cumberland sausage with onion rings and a fried egg, battered haddock with mushy peas, steak in ale pie, supreme of fresh salmon wrapped in smoked salmon and baked in butter and poppy seeds, roast crispy duckling with sage and onion stuffing and apple sauce, and puddings; daily specials and Sunday roasts.** *Starters/Snacks: £3.85 to £6.15. Main Courses: £8.65 to £19.35. Puddings: £4.45 to £5.00*

Free house ~ Licensee the Dixon family ~ Real ale ~ Bar food (12-2, 6-9) ~ Restaurant ~ (015242) 71230 ~ Children welcome ~ Open 12-3, 6-11(10.30 Sun); closed 2 weeks Jan ~ Bedrooms: £39B/£90B

Recommended by Mr and Mrs Ian King, William and Ann Reid, Tom and Jill Jones, Bill Gallon, John and Sylvia Harrop

CHAPEL STILE   NY3205   MAP 9

Wainwrights ◀

B5343; LA22 9JH

Fine choice of beers, lovely views, and surrounding walks

The fine range of seven real ales in this white-rendered Lakeland house is quite a draw after enjoying one of the good surrounding walks. On handpump there might be Black Sheep Best Bitter, Dent Ramsbottom Strong Ale, Moorhouses Black Cat and Blond Witch, Thwaites Lancaster Bomber, York Stonewall, and a beer named for the pub; quick, friendly service. They also have 16 wines by the glass and some malt whiskies.The slate-floored bar has plenty of room and it is here that walkers and their dogs are welcomed. There's a relaxed atmosphere, an old kitchen range, cushioned settles and piped music, TV and games machine. Picnic-table sets out on the terrace have fine views.

🍴 **Quickly served, reasonably priced bar food includes sandwiches, filled baked potatoes, soup, cottage or fish pie, cumberland sausage, lasagne, venison casserole, their popular lamb shoulder, and puddings such as apple pie and chocolate fudge cake.** *Starters/Snacks: £3.75 to £5.25. Main Courses: £8.00 to £11.00. Puddings: £3.75*

Free house ~ Licensee Mrs C Darbyshire ~ Real ale ~ Bar food (12-2(2.30 Sun), 6-9) ~ (015394) 38088 ~ Children welcome ~ Dogs welcome ~ Open 11.30-11; 12-11 Sun

Recommended by John Saville, Irene and Derek Flewin, Glenn and Julia Smithers, Louise English, Ewan and Moira McCall, John and Helen Rushton, Julie and Bill Ryan

COCKERMOUTH   NY1230   MAP 9

Bitter End ◀

Kirkgate, by cinema; CA13 9PJ

Own-brewed beers and lots of bottled beers in three interesting bars

This is a delightful little pub with friendly staff and a smashing range of real ales. As well as brewing their own beers such as Cockermouth Pride and Gold Pale Ale, they have six guests from all over the country: Fullers Summer Ale, Legendary Dicky Doodle, Leyden Nanny Flyer, O'Hanlons Gold Blade, Strathaven Claverhouse, and Titanic Iceberg. Quite a few bottled beers from around the world and eight wines by the glass. The three cosy main rooms have a different atmosphere in each – from quietly chatty to sporty, with the décor reflecting this, such as unusual pictures of a Cockermouth that even Wordsworth might have recognised, to more up-to-date sporting memorabilia, various bottles, jugs and books, and framed beer mats; welcoming log fire, piped music and quiz night on Tuesdays. The public car park round the back is free after 7pm.

🍴 **Good value traditional bar food includes sandwiches, steak in ale pie, cumberland sausage with caramelised onion sauce, goats cheese, tomato, red onion and garlic in puff pastry with home-made tomato sauce, fish in beer batter, lasagne, steaks, and puddings.** *Starters/Snacks: £3.95 to £4.50. Main Courses: £8.50 to £12.95. Puddings: £3.95*

Own brew ~ Licensee Susan Askey ~ Real ale ~ Bar food ~ (01900) 828993 ~ Children welcome ~ Open 12-2.30, 6-11; 12 noon-midnight Sat; 12-3, 6-11 Sun; closed 25 Dec

Recommended by Edward Mirzoeff, Peter Smith, Judith Brown, Pat and Stewart Gordon, GSB, Kevin Flack, the Didler, Julia Morris

CROSTHWAITE   SD4491   MAP 9

Punch Bowl 🍴 ☖ 🛏

Village signposted off A5074 SE of Windermere; LA8 8HR

Stylish dining pub, fine choice of drinks, impressive food, good wines and real ales, and seats on terrace overlooking valley; lovely bedrooms

A new licensee has taken over this stylish place and the food served by attentive and friendly staff is very good – they've got a fair range of real ales too, and enough life to still call it a pub. Barngates Cracker, Tag Lag and Westmorland Gold (brewed at their sister pub, the Drunken Duck near Hawkshead), and Coniston Bluebird on handpump, 16 wines by the glass and a dozen malt whiskies. The raftered and hop-hung bar has a couple of eye-catching rugs on flagstones and bar stools by the slate-topped counter, and this opens on the right into two linked carpeted and beamed rooms with well spaced country pine furnishings of varying sizes, including a big refectory table. The walls, painted in restrained neutral tones, have an attractive assortment of prints, with some copper objects, and there's a dresser with china and glass; winter log fire and daily papers. On the left, the wooden-floored restaurant area (also attractive) has comfortable leather seating. Throughout, the pub feels relaxing and nicely uncluttered. There are some tables on a terrace stepped into the hillside, overlooking the lovely Lyth Valley. This is a nice place to stay.

🍴 **Good, often unusual food includes lunchtime filled baguettes, soup, baked cheddar cheese and spring onion soufflé with a parmesan cream, toad in the hole with onion gravy, wild mushroom and spinach risotto, and steamed steak and kidney suet pudding, with evening choices such as braised pig's trotter with seared scallops and quail egg, confit duck and foie gras roulade with spiced plum and vanilla brioche, daube of beef with garlic mash, slow-cooked belly pork with confit of root vegetables and apple jus, halibut fillet poached in duck fat with oxtail, carrot purée and turnips, and puddings like frozen white chocolate mousse with damson compote and hazelnut tuile and pear poached in red wine with vanilla cheesecake.** *Starters/Snacks: £4.00 to £8.00. Main Courses: £10.95 to £18.95. Puddings: £2.95 to £7.50*

Free house ~ Licensee Paul Spencer ~ Real ale ~ Bar food (12-3, 6-9.30) ~ Restaurant ~ (015395) 68237 ~ Children welcome ~ Dogs allowed in bar ~ Open 12-11(10.30 Sun) ~ Bedrooms: £93.75B/£125B

Recommended by Margaret and Jeff Graham, Revd D Glover, Richard Greaves, Brian and Pat Wardrobe, W K Wood, Michael Doswell, Glenn and Julia Smithers, Dr Kevan Tucker, Simon and Mandy King, David Thornton

ELTERWATER

NY3204 MAP 9

Britannia

Off B5343; LA22 9HP

Well run and extremely popular inn surrounded by wonderful walks and scenery, six real ales and enjoyable food; bedrooms

Due to its glorious location in the heart of the beautiful southern Lake District, this well run pub is extremely popular – particularly with walkers as there are walks of every gradient right from the front door. It's friendly and old-fashioned and there's a small, traditionally furnished back bar plus a front one with a couple of window seats looking across to Elterwater itself through the trees; winter coal fires, oak benches, settles, windsor chairs, a big old rocking chair, and Caledonian Deuchars IPA, Coniston Bluebird, Fullers Sunchaser, Hawkshead Jennings Bitter, and a beer named for the pub on handpump. Quite a few malt whiskies and maybe winter mulled wine. The lounge is comfortable and there's a hall and dining room. Plenty of seats outside and summer morris and step garland dancers.

Usefully serving tasty bar food all day, there might be lunchtime cold and hot filled rolls and ploughman's, as well as soup, cumberland pâté with port sauce, wild mushroom and button mushroom stroganoff, popular lamb henry (lamb shoulder marinated in mint and spices), steak in ale pie, cumberland sausage with onion gravy, beer-battered fresh haddock, daily specials such as salmon fillet with home-made pesto sauce, pheasant, honey and mustard sausage with sweet plum jam, and duck breast with black pudding, crispy pancetta and a rich port and redcurrant jus, and puddings like white chocolate and Baileys bread and butter pudding and lemon brûlée. *Starters/Snacks: £3.80 to £5.75. Main Courses: £8.75 to £15.50. Puddings: £4.50 to £5.50*

Free house ~ Licensee Clare Woodhead ~ Real ale ~ Bar food (all day) ~ Restaurant ~ (015394) 37210 ~ Children welcome ~ Dogs allowed in bar and bedrooms ~ Open 10am-11.30pm ~ Bedrooms: £94S(£84B)/£114S(£104B)

Recommended by Mr and Mrs Maurice Thompson, Peter and Eleanor Kenyon, Arthur Pickering, Tina and David Woods-Taylor, John and Jackie Walsh, Margaret Dickinson, Paul Humphreys, Jarrod and Wendy Hopkinson, N R White, Ewan and Moira McCall, James and Helen Read, John and Helen Rushton, Peter and Liz Holmes, Dr Kevan Tucker

GREAT SALKELD

NY5536 MAP 10

Highland Drove 🍴

B6412, off A686 NE of Penrith; CA11 9NA

Bustling place with a cheerful mix of customers, good food in several dining areas, fair choice of drinks, and fine views from upstairs verandah

Neatly kept and genuinely friendly, this is a well run country pub liked by both drinkers and diners. The chatty main bar has sandstone flooring, stone walls, cushioned wheelback chairs around a mix of tables and an open fire in a raised stone fireplace. The downstairs eating area has cushioned dining chairs around wooden tables on the pale wooden floorboards, stone walls and ceiling joists and a two-way fire in a raised stone fireplace that separates this room from the coffee lounge with its comfortable leather chairs and sofas. There's also an upstairs restaurant. Best to book to be sure of a table. Theakstons Black Bull and a couple of guests such as Batemans Maypole Dancer and Hesket Newmarket Haystacks Refreshing Ale on handpump, several wines by the glass and around 25 malt whiskies. Piped music, TV, juke box, darts, pool, games machine and board games. The lovely views over the Eden Valley and the Pennines are best enjoyed from seats on the upstairs verandah. There are more seats on the back terrace.

Enjoyable food in the downstairs bar might include sandwiches, soup, chicken liver pâté with cumberland sauce, sausage and black pudding platter with pickled onion,

beetroot, and apple salad (lunchtime only), a proper burger, steak in ale pie, pasta with olives, peppers, onion and garlic in a tomato sauce, gammon and egg, large beer-battered haddock, and puddings such as chocolate brownie with rich chocolate sauce and baked blackcurrant and cassis cheesecake with blackcurrant compote and red berry coulis. *Starters/Snacks: £2.95 to £7.95. Main Courses: £7.95 to £14.95. Puddings: £4.75 to £5.25*

Free house ~ Licensees Donald and Paul Newton ~ Real ale ~ Bar food (12-2, 6-9; not Mon lunchtime except bank hols) ~ Restaurant ~ (01768) 898349 ~ Children welcome ~ Dogs allowed in bar ~ Open 12-3, 6-midnight; 12-midnight Sat; 12-3, 6-midnight Sun in winter; closed Mon lunchtime except bank hols; 25 Dec ~ Bedrooms: £35B/£65B

Recommended by Karen Eliot, Richard J Holloway, Phil Bryant, Kevin Tea, Henry Snell, J Crosby, John and Jackie Walsh, Peter Craske, R Macfarlane, K S Whittaker, B I Mason, Mr and Mrs Maurice Thompson, Comus and Sarah Elliott, Peter Tanfield, Lee and Liz Potter

HAWKSHEAD   NY3501   MAP 9

Drunken Duck 🍴 ♀ 🍺 🛏

Barngates; the hamlet is signposted from B5286 Hawkshead—Ambleside, opposite the Outgate Inn; or it may be quicker to take the first right from B5286, after the wooded caravan site; OS Sheet 90 map reference 350013; LA22 0NG

Stylish small bar, several restaurant areas, own-brewed beers and bar meals as well as innovative restaurant choices; lovely bedrooms, stunning views

There's no doubt that this civilised inn is at its most pubby during the day when walkers drop in for a pint of the own-brewed beers and a sandwich or bar meal. The small, smart bar has seating for around thirty on leather-topped bar stools by the slate-topped bar counter and leather club chairs, beams and oak floorboards, photographs, coaching prints and hunting pictures on the walls, and some kentish hop bines. From their Barngates brewery, there might be Cat Nap, Cracker, Moth Bag, Pride of Westmorland, and Westmorland Gold on handpump as well as 18 wines plus three pudding wines by the glass, a fine choice of spirits, and belgian and german draught beers. In the evening, the emphasis is definitely on the imaginative (and pricy) modern cooking in the three restaurant areas. Beautifully appointed bedrooms. Outside, wooden tables and benches on the grass bank opposite the building offer spectacular views across the fells, and there are thousands of spring and summer bulbs.

🍴 Good bar food (up till 4pm) includes sandwiches (which you can take away as well), ploughman's, soup or seafood chowder, sausage with mash and onion gravy, macaroni cheese, lamb hotpot, gammon and egg, and pork, chicken and stuffing pie, with puddings such as sticky toffee pudding and bakewell tart; there's also an interesting two- and three-course set lunch menu and afternoon tea. Some restaurant dishes might include rabbit ballotine with candied red cabbage, peppered beef fillet with potato galette and caramelised fig and apple, loin of herdwick lamb with spring onion croquette, roasted turnip, rosemary and shallot jus, black bream with shrimp, wilted baby gem, jerusalem artichoke and truffle ravioli and sauce gribiche. *Starters/Snacks: £4.50 to £7.95. Main Courses: £6.95 to £25.95. Puddings: £6.50 to £8.25*

Own brew ~ Licensee Steph Barton ~ Real ale ~ Bar food (12-4(2.30 restaurant), 6-9.30) ~ Restaurant ~ (015394) 36347 ~ Children allowed until 7pm ~ Dogs allowed in bar ~ Open 11.30-11; 12-10.30 Sun ~ Bedrooms: £90B/£120B

Recommended by Mike and Sue Loseby, David and Sue Atkinson, David Field, Tina and David Woods-Taylor, John Saville, Mrs Sheila Stothard, Peter and Lesley Yeoward, Richard Cole, Maurice and Gill McMahon, P Briggs, K S Whittaker, N R White, Richard Hennessy, John and Sylvia Harrop, Howard Kissack, Roger Yates, Dr Kevan Tucker

Kings Arms

The Square; LA22 0NZ

Some fine original features in 16th-c inn, decent drinks, pubby food, and free fishing permits for residents

If you want to bag a table on the terrace and enjoy the view over the central square of this lovely Elizabethan village, you must get here early. Inside this busy 16th-c inn there are some fine original features, traditional pubby furnishings, and an open log fire; Coniston Bluebird, Hawkshead Bitter and Red, and Moorhouses Pride of Pendle on handpump, 50 malt whiskies, a decent wine list, and summer farm cider. There's an overflow dining area to the side of the bar which is useful but perhaps doesn't have quite the same atmosphere. Piped music, games machine, and board games. As well as bedrooms, they offer self-catering cottages. There are free fishing permits for residents.

🍴 **Decent bar food includes lunchtime sandwiches and ploughman's, soup, ham hock terrine with red onion chutney, fresh beer-battered haddock, lancashire and mozzarella cheese sausages on mash with vegetarian gravy, steak in ale pie, chicken with creamy pancetta and parsley sauce, and slow-roasted lamb shank with caramelised onion gravy.** *Starters/Snacks: £3.25 to £5.75. Main Courses: £5.50 to £11.95. Puddings: £4.25 to £5.00*

Free house ~ Licensee Edward Johnson ~ Real ale ~ Bar food (12-2.30, 6-9.30) ~ Restaurant ~ (015394) 36372 ~ Children welcome ~ Dogs allowed in bar and bedrooms ~ Live music third Thurs in month ~ Open 11am-midnight; closed evening 25 Dec ~ Bedrooms: £47S/£84S

Recommended by Peter and Liz Holmes, Mr and Mrs Maurice Thompson, Margaret Whalley, Lindsley Harvard, Ewan and Moira McCall, Robert Wivell

Queens Head
Main Street; LA22 0NS

Lovely timbered pub with friendly bustling atmosphere; bedrooms

In summer, the window boxes at the front of this lovely black and white timbered pub are very pretty and there are plenty of seats out there too. The low-ceilinged bar has heavy bowed black beams, red plush wall seats and plush stools around heavy traditional tables, lots of decorative plates on the panelled walls, and an open fire; a snug little room leads off. Robinsons Cumbria Way, Double Hop, and Unicorn on handpump, quite a choice of whiskies and several wines by the glass; TV. As well as bedrooms in the inn, they have two holiday cottages to rent in the village. Residents can get a parking pass from the inn for the public car park about 100 yards away.

🍴 **Meals can be eaten either in the bar or the more formal restaurant: sandwiches, soup, duck liver pâté, leek and blue cheese tart, beer-battered haddock, monkfish and scottish salmon in a light curry cream sauce, slow-roasted shoulder of lamb, local pheasant with huntsman's sauce, and steaks.** *Starters/Snacks: £3.25 to £6.50. Main Courses: £10.25 to £22.50. Puddings: £5.75*

Robinsons ~ Tenants Mr and Mrs Tony Merrick ~ Real ale ~ Bar food (12-2.30, 6.15-9.30; 12-5, 6.15-9.30 Sun) ~ Restaurant ~ (015394) 36271 ~ Children welcome ~ Open 11am-midnight; 12-12 Sun; may close Jan ~ Bedrooms: £60B/£90B

Recommended by Jarrod and Wendy Hopkinson, David and Ros Hanley, Arthur Pickering, Christine and Phil Young, Mr and Mrs W W Burke, Tracey and Phil Eagles, Peter and Liz Holmes

HESKET NEWMARKET   NY3438   MAP 10
Old Crown 🍺
Village signposted off B5299 in Caldbeck; CA7 8JG

Straightforward local with own-brewed beers in attractive village

The own-brewed real ales remain the strong draw to this unpretentious local (still owned by a co-operative of 147 local people). On handpump, there might be Hesket Newmarket Blencathra Bitter, Doris's 90th Birthday Ale, Great Cockup Porter, Haystacks, Helvellyn Gold, Skiddaw Special Bitter, Old Carrock Strong Ale, Catbells Pale Ale and Sca Fell Blonde. The little bar has a few tables, a log fire, bric-a-brac, mountaineering kit and pictures, and a friendly atmosphere; darts, pool, and juke box. There's also a dining room and garden room. The pub is in a pretty setting in a remote, attractive village. You can book up tours to look around the brewery, £10 for the tour and a meal.

We say if we know a pub has piped music.

🍴 Bar food at lunchtime includes sandwiches and staffordshire oatcakes and a hot daily dish, and there are evening choices such as a meaty or vegetarian curries, cumberland sausage, steak in ale pie, and breaded haddock, with puddings like apple crumble and bakewell tart; Sunday roast beef. *Starters/Snacks: £3.50 to £5.50. Main Courses: £6.00 to £12.00. Puddings: £3.95*

Own brew ~ Tenants Pat and Malcolm Hawksworth ~ Real ale ~ Bar food (12-2, 6-9; not Mon-Thurs lunchtimes) ~ Restaurant ~ (016974) 78288 ~ Children welcome ~ Dogs allowed in bar ~ Live folk first Sun and northumbrian pipes 3rd Mon of month ~ Open 5.30-11; 12-2.30, 5.30-11(10.30 Sun) Fri and Sat; closed Mon-Thurs lunchtimes (open bank hol Mon)

Recommended by B I Mason, Tina and David Woods-Taylor, Dr Kevan Tucker, Mike and Sue Loseby, Adam F Padel, Comus and Sarah Elliott, V and E A Bolton

INGS
SD4498   MAP 9

Watermill

Just off A591 E of Windermere; LA8 9PY

Busy, cleverly converted pub with fantastic range of real ales including own brew

With a fantastic range of 16 real ales on handpump, it's not surprising that this chatty place is so popular. As well as their own-brewed Watermill Collie Wobbles, A Bit'er Ruff and W'Ruff Night (and maybe their guests such as Blackbeard and Dog'th Vader), there might be Coniston Bluebird, Hambleton Giddy Up, Hawkshead Bitter, Jennings Cumberland, Keswick Thirst Flight, Phoenix White Monk, Saltaire Pale Bitter, Theakstons Old Peculier, Ulverston Laughing Gravy, York Guzzler, and Youngs Special. Also, 60 foreign bottled beers and over 50 whiskies. The building has plenty of character and is cleverly converted from a wood mill and joiner's shop and the bars have a friendly, bustling atmosphere, a happy mix of chairs, padded benches and solid oak tables, bar counters made from old church wood, open fires and interesting photographs and amusing cartoons by a local artist. The spacious lounge bar, in much the same traditional style as the other rooms, has rocking chairs and a big open fire. Darts and board games. Seats in the gardens, and lots to do nearby. Dogs may get free biscuits and water.

🍴 Served all day, bar food includes lunchtime sandwiches, filled baguettes and filled baked potatoes, as well as soup, garlic mushrooms, solway potted shrimps, vegetable chilli, beer-battered fresh haddock, cumberland sausage with beer and onion gravy, lasagne, beef in ale pie, chicken in rosemary, english mustard and cream sauce, and puddings such as banoffi cheesecake and lemon tart with raspberry coulis. *Starters/Snacks: £3.75 to £5.50. Main Courses: £8.50 to £15.95. Puddings: £4.75*

Free house ~ Licensee Brian Coulthwaite ~ Real ale ~ Bar food (12-9) ~ (01539) 821309 ~ Children welcome ~ Dogs allowed in bar and bedrooms ~ Storytelling first Tues of month, folk third Tues ~ Open 11.45-11; 12-10.30 Sun; closed 25 Dec ~ Bedrooms: £42S/£78S

Recommended by Adrian Johnson, Mike and Sue Loseby, Ian and Sue Wells, David and Ruth Shillitoe, Mr and Mrs Maurice Thompson, the Didler, Pam and John Smith, Dennis Jones, Julian and Janet Dearden, Michael Butler, N R White, Margaret Whalley, Lindsley Harvard, Pauline and Philip Darley, Gwyneth and Salvo Spadaro-Dutturi, Neil Ingoe, Alain and Rose Foote, Paul Boot, Kerry Law, Tim Maddison, Lee and Liz Potter, Tom and Jill Jones, Jo Lilley, Simon Calvert, Tony and Maggie Harwood, J S Burn, Maurice and Gill McMahon, Andrew and Christine Gagg, Ray and Winifred Halliday, Arthur Pickering, Mr and Mrs W W Burke, Brian and Anita Randall

KESWICK
NY2623   MAP 9

Dog & Gun

Lake Road; CA12 5BT

Bustling and friendly unpretentious town pub with popular food and drink

Although a new landlord has taken over this no-nonsense pub, readers have been quick to voice their enthusiasm. It's popular with a good mix of customers – and dogs are genuinely welcomed too – and even though it can get crowded, the atmosphere is always good natured and friendly. The homely bar has low beams, a partly slate floor (the rest are carpeted or bare boards), some high settles, a fine collection of striking mountain photographs by the local firm G P Abrahams, brass and brewery artefacts, and coins (which go to the Mountain Rescue Service) in beams and timbers by the fireplace. The beers are from local breweries and might include Coniston Bluebird, Keswick Thirst Rescue, Theakstons Best and Old Peculier, and a couple of guests on handpump.

🍴 **Tasty bar food includes sandwiches and filled baked potatoes (lunchtime only), soup, a pie of the day, lasagne, sausage and mash, liver and onions, barbecue chicken, three-bean chilli, their not-to-be-missed famous goulash, daily specials, and puddings.** *Starters/Snacks: £3.00 to £5.00. Main Courses: £5.00 to £9.00. Puddings: £3.00 to £5.00*

Orchid ~ Manager Peter Welsh ~ Real ale ~ Bar food (all day) ~ (017687) 73463 ~ Children welcome only if dining and before 9pm ~ Dogs welcome ~ Open 12-11

Recommended by Mary McSweeney, Louise English, Mr and Mrs Maurice Thompson, Peter and Mary Burton, Mike and Sue Loseby, Nick Lawless, Chris and Maggie Kent, Fred and Lorraine Gill, N R White, Adrian Johnson, Andrew and Kathleen Bacon, Brian and Anna Marsden

KIRKBY LONSDALE   SD6178   MAP 7

Sun ♀ 🛏

Market Street (B6254); LA6 2AU

Nice contrast between mellow bar and stylish contemporary restaurant, good interesting food and several real ales; comfortable bedrooms

---

With a cheerful landlord and genuinely friendly, helpful staff, this 17th-c inn is an enjoyable place. The attractive rambling bar has a two log fires, and seats of some character, from cosy window seats and pews to armchairs; also, beams, flagstones and stripped oak boards, nice lighting, and big landscapes and country pictures on the cream walls above its handsome panelled dado. There's a back lounge with a leather sofa and comfortable chairs, too. Jennings Cumberland Ale, Hawkshead Bitter, Marstons Pedigree, Timothy Taylors Landlord, and guest beers on handpump, eleven wines by the glass (plus some organic ones) and plenty of malt whiskies; piped music and board games. The back dining room is very up to date: comfortable tall-backed seats and tables on woodstrip flooring, a clean-cut cream and red décor with a modicum of stripped stone, and attractive plain modern crockery (you can eat in any part of the establishment). It's an interesting looking building with its upper floors supported by three sturdy pillars above the pavement and a modest front door.

🍴 **Good bar food includes sandwiches, ploughman's, soup, goats cheese and fig tartlet, pork and leek sausages with crispy leeks, chicken caesar salad, lambs liver and bacon with mustard mash and red onion gravy, home-cooked honey-roast ham with a free-range egg, braised leeks and home-made pasta topped with dried mushroom and parmesan breadcrumb, organic salmon poached in chicken stock with toasted beetroot, fennel and apple, and puddings such as mulled wine plum crumble and baked chocolate and orange cheesecake with vanilla pod ice-cream.** *Starters/Snacks: £3.95 to £7.95. Main Courses: £5.95 to £11.95. Puddings: £4.50 to £5.95*

Free house ~ Licensee Mark Fuller ~ Real ale ~ Bar food ~ Restaurant ~ (015242) 71965 ~ Children welcome ~ Dogs allowed in bar and bedrooms ~ Open 10am-11pm ~ Bedrooms: /£90S(£110B)

Recommended by Pat Crabb, Alun and Stephanie Llewellyn, Michael Doswell, Eilidh Renwick, Mary McSweeney, Ian Stafford, John and Yvonne Davies, Paul Davies

LANGDALE   NY2806   MAP 9

Old Dungeon Ghyll 🍺

B5343; LA22 9JY

Straightforward place in lovely position with real ales and fine walks

---

This is the perfect place to come when you are dripping wet. It's a friendly, straightforward local, popular with fell walkers and climbers, and is at the heart of the Great Langdale Valley and surrounded by fells – including the Langdale Pikes flanking the

Dungeon Ghyll Force waterfall. The whole feel of the place is basic but cosy and there's no need to remove boots or muddy trousers – you can sit on seats in old cattle stalls by the big warming fire and enjoy well kept Harviestoun Truly Scrumptious, Hawkshead Lakeland Gold, Moorhouses Blond Witch, and guest beers on handpump; up to 30 malt whiskies, and farm cider. Darts and board games. It may get lively on a Saturday night (there's a popular National Trust campsite opposite).

🍴 **Good helpings of traditional food such as soup, lunchtime sandwiches, curries, stews, lasagne or pie of the day.** *Starters/Snacks: £3.45 to £5.50. Main Courses: £7.00 to £8.50. Puddings: £3.75 to £4.00*

Free house ~ Licensee Neil Walmsley ~ Real ale ~ Bar food (12-2, 6-9) ~ Restaurant ~ (015394) 37272 ~ Children welcome ~ Dogs allowed in bar and bedrooms ~ Folk first Weds of month ~ Open 11-11(10.30 Sun); closed Christmas ~ Bedrooms: £50/£100(£110S)

Recommended by Russell and Alison Hunt, the Didler, Mary McSweeney, John and Helen Rushton, Mr and Mrs Maurice Thompson, Irene and Derek Flewin, Jarrod and Wendy Hopkinson, Tim Maddison

LEVENS
SD4987   MAP 9

Strickland Arms ♀ 🍺

4 miles from M6 junction 36, via A590; just off A590, by Sizergh Castle gates; LA8 8DZ

Friendly, open-plan place, popular for home-made food and local ales

The staff here are always friendly and obliging – and the food, very good. It's a largely open plan dining pub with a light and airy modern feel, and the bar on the right has oriental rugs on the flagstones, a log fire, Thwaites Original and Lancaster Bomber and a couple of guests such as Coniston Bluebird and Dent Aviator on handpump, 30 malt whiskies and 11 wines by the glass. On the left are polished boards and another log fire, and throughout there's a nice mix of sturdy country furniture, candles on tables, hunting scenes and other old prints on the walls, heavy fabric for the curtains and some staffordshire china ornaments; there's a further dining room upstairs, piped music and board games, and seats out in front on a flagstone terrace. The Castle, in fact a lovely partly medieval house with beautiful gardens, is open in the afternoon (not Friday or Saturday) from April to October. They have disabled access and facilities. The pub is owned by the National Trust.

🍴 **As well as lunchtime sandwiches and salads such as a platter of meat and cheese with chutney or tuna niçoise, the popular food includes soup, potted duck with cranberries, chicken, leek and tarragon pie, lancashire cheese and onion pasty, beer-battered fish, lamb hotpot, gammon and a free-range egg, and puddings like raspberry and vanilla cheesecake and rich chocolate mousse with kendal mint cake; fish night is every Thursday and there's a well-thought-of two-course set lunch menu during the week.** *Starters/Snacks: £4.25 to £6.95. Main Courses: £8.95 to £15.95. Puddings: £5.00*

Free house ~ Licensees Kerry Parsons and Martin Ainscough ~ Real ale ~ Bar food (12-2(2.30 Sat), 6-9; all day Sun) ~ (015395) 61010 ~ Children welcome ~ Dogs welcome ~ Open 11.30-11(10.30 Sun); 11.30-3, 5.30-11 weekdays in winter

Recommended by Margaret and Jeff Graham, Susan Street, Dr Kevan Tucker, Mr and Mrs Maurice Thompson, Pam and John Smith, Ray and Winifred Halliday, Bruce Braithwaite, Revd D Glover, Cedric Robertshaw, Tony and Maggie Harwood, Michael Doswell, Paul Boot, Louise English

LITTLE LANGDALE
NY3103   MAP 9

Three Shires 🛏

From A593 3 miles W of Ambleside take small road signposted The Langdales, Wrynose Pass; then bear left at first fork; LA22 9NZ

Friendly inn with valley views from seats on terrace, good lunchtime bar food with more elaborate evening meals; comfortable bedrooms

Mr and Mrs Stephenson have been running this friendly, stone-built inn for 25 years now and it's been a main entry in this book for all of that time – quite a record. There's a good mix of customers and a genuine welcome for walkers, and with warm winter fires and lovely views from seats on the terrace over the valley to the partly wooded hills below Tilberthwaite Fells, it's popular all year round; there are more seats on a well kept lawn behind the car park, backed by a small oak wood. Inside, the comfortably extended back bar has a mix of green lakeland stone and homely red patterned wallpaper (which works rather well), stripped timbers and a beam-and-joist stripped ceiling, antique oak carved settles, country kitchen chairs and stools on its big dark slate flagstones, and lakeland photographs. An arch leads through to a small, additional area and there's a front dining room. Black Sheep Best and Jennings Cumberland and a couple of guests like Coniston Old Man and Hawkshead Red on handpump, over 50 malt whiskies and a decent wine list; darts and board games. The three shires are the historical counties Cumberland, Westmorland and Lancashire, which meet at the top of the nearby Wrynose Pass. The award-winning summer hanging baskets are very pretty.

🍴 At lunchtime, the well liked food includes sandwiches and filled baguettes, ploughman's, soup, cumberland sausage with onion rings, beef in ale pie, and scampi, with evening choices such as baked brie with honey and thyme, grilled fillet of bass on basil couscous with chilled vine tomato sauce, fresh tagliatelle with wild mushrooms in a rich parmesan cream and truffle sauce, pheasant breasts with a rich madeira cream sauce, lambs liver with pancetta, thyme, red wine and wasabi mash, roast cod loin wrapped in air-dried ham with a hot salsa of basil, black olives and cherry tomatoes, and puddings such as apple and cinnamon parfait with sultanas poached in vanilla syrup and lime and ginger crème brûlée. *Starters/Snacks: £4.25 to £6.95. Main Courses: £9.95 to £15.95. Puddings: £4.95 to £5.95*

Free house ~ Licensee Ian Stephenson ~ Real ale ~ Bar food (12-2, 6-8.45; not 24 or 25 Dec) ~ Restaurant ~ (015394) 37215 ~ Children welcome until 9pm ~ Dogs allowed in bar ~ Open 11-10.30(11 Fri and Sat); 12-10.30 Sun; 11-3, 6-10.30 in winter; closed 24 and 25 Dec ~ Bedrooms: /£88B

Recommended by JDM, KM, Irene and Derek Flewin, John and Helen Rushton, Tina and David Woods-Taylor, Simon and Mandy King, Arthur Pickering, Dr Kevan Tucker, T Walker, Ewan and Moira McCall, Stuart Turner, David and Sue Atkinson, Mr and Mrs Maurice Thompson, Paul Humphreys, Louise English

LOWESWATER   NY1421   MAP 9

Kirkstile Inn 🍺 🛏

From B5289 follow signs to Loweswater Lake; OS Sheet 89 map reference 140210; CA13 0RU

Busy bar in popular inn surrounded by stunning peaks and fells; own-brewed beers and tasty food

As this friendly 16th-c inn is situated between Loweswater and Crummock Water, it's not surprising that many of its customers are walkers. The fine view can be enjoyed from picnic-sets on the lawn, from the very attractive covered verandah in front of the building and from the bow windows in one of the rooms off the bar. The bustling main bar is low-beamed and carpeted, with a good mix of customers, a roaring log fire, comfortably cushioned small settles and pews and partly stripped stone walls; there's a slate shove-ha'penny board. As well as their own-brewed Loweswater Grasmere Dark Ale, Kirkstile Gold and Melbreak Bitter on handpump, they keep a couple of guest beers, too; ten wines by the glass.

🍴 As well as filled baguettes and baked potatoes, bar food includes soup, thai crabcakes, lakeland sausages, pasta carbonara, asparagus, feta and roasted pepper tart, steak in ale pie, game pudding, lamb shoulder in honey and mint, daily specials and puddings like fruit crumble and lemon tart. *Starters/Snacks: £3.50 to £5.25. Main Courses: £7.95 to £16.95. Puddings: £4.50*

Own brew ~ Licensee Roger Humphreys ~ Real ale ~ Bar food (12-2, 6-9) ~ (01900) 85219 ~ Children welcome ~ Dogs allowed in bar ~ Occasional jazz ~ Open 11-11(10.30 Sun); closed 25 Dec ~ Bedrooms: £59.50B/£87B

Recommended by Sylvia and Tony Birbeck, Dr and Mrs Michael Smith, Mike and Sue Loseby, David Morgan, Dr Kevan Tucker, Richard Tosswill, Comus and Sarah Elliott, the Didler, Pat and Stewart Gordon, Marcus Byron, Peter Smith, Judith Brown, GSB, Christopher Turner, Glenwys and Alan Lawrence, N R White, Gordon and Margaret Ormondroyd, Tim Maddison

MUNGRISDALE

NY3630   MAP 10

Mill Inn

Off A66 Penrith—Keswick, 1 mile W of A5091 Ullswater turn-off; CA11 0XR

Bustling pub in fine setting with marvellous surrounding walks, real ales, and interesting food cooked by new landlord; bedrooms

An amiable new Irish chef/landlord has taken over this partly 16th-c inn and early reports from our readers are very warm and enthusiastic. The neatly kept bar has a wooden bar counter with an old millstone built into it, traditional dark wooden furnishings, hunting pictures on the walls, an open log fire in the stone fireplace, Robinsons Cumbria Way, Dizzy Blonde, Hartleys XB, and Top Tipple on handpump, and up to 30 malt whiskies; good service, even when busy. Piped music, winter pool and darts, and an active dominoes team. In the lea of the Blencathra fell range, the pub is surrounded by stunning scenery and spectacular walks, and there are seats in the garden by the little river. Please note that there's a quite separate Mill Hotel here.

🍴 **Mr Carroll sources his local ingredients carefully and his good, enjoyable food might include sandwiches, soup, grilled black pudding with red onion marmalade and pepper sauce, asparagus wrapped in air-dried local ham with garlic butter, chicken and duck liver pâté with redcurrant jelly, spicy butter bean casserole, bass fillets with tomato and garlic butter, local red deer venison casserole and venison haunch steak with port and stilton mash, and puddings such as sticky toffee pudding and lemon meringue pie; there's also a lighter lunch menu with interesting toppings for their speciality rarebits, cumberland sausage, fresh fish in beer batter and gammon and egg, and they do dishes for coeliacs.** *Starters/Snacks: £3.10 to £4.95. Main Courses: £8.35 to £13.50. Puddings: £3.95 to £4.50*

Robinsons ~ Tenant Adrian Carroll ~ Real ale ~ Bar food (12-2, 6-9) ~ Restaurant ~ (017687) 79632 ~ Children welcome ~ Dogs welcome ~ Open 11-11 ~ Bedrooms: £47.50S/£75S

Recommended by Mike and Penny Sutton, J Crosby, Dr Kevan Tucker, Dr and Mrs Michael Smith, Dennis Jones, John and Jackie Walsh, Mike and Sue Loseby, Tina and David Woods-Taylor, Glenwys and Alan Lawrence, Jack and Rosalin Forrester

NEAR SAWREY

SD3795   MAP 9

Tower Bank Arms 🍺

B5285 towards the Windermere ferry; LA22 0LF

Backing on to Beatrix Potter's farm with a good range of ales; bedrooms

Many illustrations in the Beatrix Potter books can be traced back to their origins in this village, including this little country pub which features in *The Tale of Jemima Puddleduck*. The low-beamed main bar has plenty of rustic charm, seats on the rough slate floor, game and fowl pictures, a grandfather clock, a woodburning stove, and fresh flowers. Barngates Cat Nap, Hawkshead Bitter and Brodie's Prime, Keswick Thirst Blossom, and Hesket Newmarket Sca Fell Blonde on handpump (in winter the choice may be smaller); board games. There are pleasant views of the wooded Claife Heights from seats in the garden.

🍴 **Lunchtime bar food includes sandwiches, soup, cumberland sausage with rich onion gravy, beer-battered haddock, and beef in ale stew with dumplings; in the evening there might be chicken liver pâté, mussels in chilli, lime and lemon grass, mushroom stroganoff, pork tenderloin stuffed with black pudding mousse and fresh sage and wrapped in dry-cured bacon with a calvados and apple sauce, smoked haddock in cheese sauce, and puddings such as rhubarb and ginger teacup trifle and mixed berry meringue.** *Starters/Snacks: £3.95 to £7.50. Main Courses: £10.50 to £13.50. Puddings: £4.00 to £4.50*

Free house ~ Licensee Anthony Hutton ~ Real ale ~ Bar food (12-2, 6-9(8 Sun and bank hols) ~ Restaurant ~ (015394) 36334 ~ Children welcome until 9pm ~ Dogs allowed in bar and bedrooms ~ Open 11-11; 12-10.30 Sun; 11(12 Sun)-3, 5.30-11(10.30 Sun) in winter; closed one week in Jan ~ Bedrooms: £50B/£80B

Recommended by Arthur Pickering, Peter F Marshall, Peter Herridge, N R White, David S Clark, Noel Grundy, R E McEleney

RAVENSTONEDALE   NY7203   MAP 10

Black Swan 🛏

Just off A685 SW of Kirkby Stephen; CA17 4NG

Bustling hotel with thriving bar, several real ales, enjoyable food, and comfortable bedrooms; good surrounding walks

Doing very well since it was taken over by the Dinnes family, this is an attractively refurbished lakeland stone, Victorian hotel in excellent walking country at the foot of the Howgill Fells; they have leaflets describing the walks, their length and their difficulty (or easiness). There are original period features throughout and the thriving U-shaped bar has stripped stone walls, plush bar stools by the bar counter, a comfortable green button-back banquette, various dining chairs and little plush stools around a mix of tables, fresh flowers, Black Sheep Ale and Best Bitter and a couple of guests like Hesket Newmarket Doris's 90th Birthday Ale and Lancaster Red on handpump, and ten wines by the glass; service is genuinely friendly and helpful. There are picnic-sets in the tree-sheltered streamside garden over the road. The village is charming and the licensees of this little hotel have opened a village shop with outside café seating.

🍴 Good bar food includes sandwiches, toasties and panini, filled baked potatoes, soup, chicken liver pâté with cumberland sauce, trout or salmon fishcake with home-made tartare sauce, black pudding with apple, bacon and a creamy pepper sauce, fresh haddock in beer batter, four-cheese and spinach pasta bake with pine nuts, cumberland sausage with colcannon mash and rich onion gravy, caramelised local lamb steak, a pie of the day, gammon and egg, chicken satay with a spicy sauce, and puddings. *Starters/Snacks: £3.95 to £5.95. Main Courses: £8.95 to £14.95. Puddings: £3.95 to £4.95*

Free House ~ Licensee Louise and Alan Dinnes ~ Real ale ~ Bar food (12-2, 6-9) ~ Restaurant ~ (015396) 23204 ~ Children welcome ~ Dogs allowed in bar and bedrooms ~ Open 8am(9am Sun)-midnight(1am Sat); closed 25 Dec and one week after New Year ~ Bedrooms: £42B/£70B

Recommended by David Lowe, Stuart Paulley, Margaret Dickinson

SANDFORD   NY7316   MAP 10

Sandford Arms 🛏

Village and pub signposted just off A66 W of Brough; CA16 6NR

Neat little former farmhouse in tucked away village with enjoyable food and ale

This year there's a new garden in front of this neat and friendly little inn and the courtyard now has covered seating. Inside, the L-shaped carpeted main bar has stripped beams and stonework, a collection of Royal Doulton character jugs and some Dickens ware, Black Sheep Best Bitter and a beer from Hesket Newmarket and Tirril on handpump. The compact and comfortable, newly furnished dining area is on a slightly raised balustraded platform at one end, there's a more formal separate dining room, and a second bar area with broad flagstones, charming heavy-horse prints, and an end log fire; piped music, darts, TV, and board games.

🍴 Cooked by the landlord using local produce, the good bar food includes sandwiches, soup, chicken liver pâté with real ale chutney, thai salmon fishcakes with salsa, cumberland sausage, eggs and tomatoes, stuffed aubergine with vegetables in a cheese sauce, steak in ale pie, daily specials such as moules marinières, chicken breast wrapped in smoked bacon and topped with a blue cheese sauce, duck breast in orange sauce, and puddings like raspberry cheesecake and sticky toffee pudding. *Starters/Snacks: £4.25 to £5.75. Main Courses: £8.75 to £17.95. Puddings: £3.95 to £4.25*

Free house ~ Licensee Steven Porter ~ Real ale ~ Bar food (all day weekends; not winter Tues) ~ Restaurant ~ (017683) 51121 ~ Children welcome ~ Dogs allowed in bar ~ Open 11-3, 6-11; 11(12 Sun)-11 Sat; closed Tues in winter ~ Bedrooms: £45B/£65B

Recommended by Stephen Bennett, Tim and Liz Sherbourne

There are report forms at the back of the book.

SANTON BRIDGE
NY1101 MAP 9

Bridge Inn

Off A595 at Holmrook or Gosforth; CA19 1UX

A good choice of drinks and well liked food, cheerful atmosphere, and plenty of surrounding walks

As we went to press, we heard that this bustling and friendly black and white hotel was up for sale. It is nicely placed in a quiet riverside spot with fell views so we are keeping our fingers crossed that the new people won't change things too much. The turkey-carpeted bar is popular with locals and has stripped beams, joists and standing timbers, a coal and log fire, and three rather unusual timbered booths around big stripped tables along its outer wall. Bar stools line the long concave bar counter, which has Jennings Bitter, Cocker Hoop, Cumberland Ale, and Sneck Lifter and a couple of guest beers like Marstons Pedigree and York Guzzler on handpump; good big pots of tea, speciality coffees, and six wines by the glass. Piped music, games machine, darts and board games. As well as an italian-style bistro, there's a small reception hall with a rack of daily papers and a comfortable more hotelish lounge on the left. There are seats out in front by the quiet road and plenty of surrounding walks; more reports please.

🍴 **Well liked bar food includes filled baguettes, soup, moules marinières, cumberland sausage, a curry of the day, steak and kidney pie, goats cheese chilli, lamb shoulder in Jennings, salmon fillet with hollandaise, and daily specials.** *Starters/Snacks: £3.95 to £6.95. Main Courses: £8.95 to £14.95. Puddings: £4.10*

Marstons ~ Lease John Morrow and Lesley Rhodes ~ Real ale ~ Bar food (12-2.30, 5.30-9) ~ Restaurant ~ (01946) 726221 ~ Children welcome ~ Dogs allowed in bar and bedrooms ~ Open 11-11(midnight Sat) ~ Bedrooms: £65B/£85B

Recommended by R N and M I Bailey, J S Burn, Helen Rowett

SEATHWAITE
SD2295 MAP 9

Newfield Inn 🏮

Duddon Valley, near Ulpha (ie not Seathwaite in Borrowdale); LA20 6ED

Climbers' and walkers' cottagey inn with genuine local feel and hearty food

Food is usefully served all day for the walkers and climbers who crowd into this cottagey 16th-c inn – but there's still a relaxed and genuinely local atmosphere. The slate-floored bar has wooden tables and chairs, some interesting pictures and Jennings Cumberland Ale and Snecklifter and Tirril Thomas Slee's Academy Ale on handpump; several malt whiskies. There's a comfortable side room and a games room with board games. Tables outside in the nice garden have good hill views. The pub owns and lets the next-door self-catering flats and there's a large area for children to play and fine walks from the doorstep.

🍴 **Good value homely food includes filled rolls, lunchtime snacks like beans on toast and home-cooked ham and eggs, cumberland sausage, steak pie, battered cod, spicy bean casserole, lasagne, steaks and puddings such as apple pie and pear and chocolate crumble.** *Starters/Snacks: £3.00 to £5.00. Main Courses: £5.00 to £15.00. Puddings: £4.00 to £5.00*

Free house ~ Licensee Paul Batten ~ Real ale ~ Bar food (12-9; not 25 Dec) ~ Restaurant ~ (01229) 716208 ~ Children welcome ~ Dogs allowed in bar ~ Open 11-11; closed evenings 25 and 26 Dec

Recommended by Julie and Bill Ryan, Mr and Mrs Maurice Thompson, David Field, Tim Maddison

---

Bedroom prices normally include full english breakfast, VAT and any inclusive service charge that we know of. Prices before the '/' are for single rooms, after for two people in a double or twin (B includes a private bath, S a private shower). If there is no '/', the prices are only for twin or double rooms (as far as we know there are no singles).

STAVELEY   SD4797   MAP 9

Eagle & Child 🍺 🛏

Kendal Road; just off A591 Windermere—Kendal; LA8 9LP

Welcoming inn with warming log fires, a good range of beers and enjoyable food; bedrooms

Our readers are fond of this friendly, bustling inn and it's a popular place to stay overnight. The roughly L-shaped flagstoned main area has a good pubby atmosphere, plenty of separate parts to sit in, a welcoming fire under an impressive mantelbeam, and pews, banquettes, bow window seats and some high-backed dining chairs around polished dark tables. Also, police truncheons and walking sticks, some nice photographs and interesting prints, a few farm tools, a delft shelf of bric-a-brac and another log fire. The five real ales on handpump come from breweries like Barngates, Black Sheep, Hawkshead, Jennings, and Yates; several wines by the glass and farm cider. An upstairs barn-theme dining room (with its own bar for functions and so forth) doubles as a breakfast room. There are picnic-sets under cocktail parasols in a sheltered garden by the River Kent, with more on a good-sized back terrace, and second garden behind.

🍴 **As well as lunch for a fiver (not Sundays), the enjoyable bar food includes sandwiches, soup, chicken liver and port pâté, warm crispy bacon, sausage and black pudding salad with wholegrain mustard dressing, thai green vegetable curry, local cumberland sausage with red wine and onion gravy, beef and mushroom in ale pie, chicken supreme stuffed with goats cheese with a basil cream, roasted salmon with fresh spinach and lemon grass sauce, and local venison steak with a red wine and fresh thyme reduction.** *Starters/Snacks: £4.00 to £5.50. Main Courses: £8.50 to £14.95. Puddings: £4.95 to £5.95*

Free house ~ Licensees Richard and Denise Coleman ~ Real ale ~ Bar food (12-2.45, 6-9) ~ Restaurant ~ (01539) 821320 ~ Children welcome ~ Dogs allowed in bar ~ Open 11-11 ~ Bedrooms: £40B/£60B

Recommended by Michael Doswell, Dennis Jones, Tony and Maggie Harwood, Mr and Mrs Maurice Thompson, Julian and Janet Dearden, Jo Lilley, Simon Calvert, the Didler, John and Joan Nash, N R White, John Andrew, Janet and Peter Race, Roger and Carol Maden, Brian and Anita Randall, John and Helen Rushton, Pam and John Smith

STONETHWAITE   NY2513   MAP 9

Langstrath 🍺 🛏

Off B5289 S of Derwent Water; CA12 5XG

Civilised little place in lovely spot with interesting food and drink

The restaurant in this civilised little inn has been moved into what was the residents' lounge; it's been refurbished, and has fine views up the Langstrath Valley. The neat and simple bar (at its pubbiest at lunchtime) has a welcoming coal and log fire in a big stone fireplace, just a handful of cast-iron-framed tables, plain chairs and cushioned wall seats, and on its textured white walls maybe quite a few walking cartoons and attractive lakeland mountain photographs. Black Sheep and Jennings Bitter and a couple of guests such as Hawkshead Bitter and Hesket Newmarket Doris's 90th Birthday Ale on handpump, 30 malt whiskies and eight wines by the glass; quite a few customers also drop in for tea and coffee. Board games. A little oak-boarded room on the left is a bit like a doll's house living room in style – this is actually the original cottage built around 1590. Outside, a big sycamore shelters a few picnic-sets and there are fine surrounding walks as the pub is in a lovely spot in the heart of Borrowdale and en route for the Cumbrian Way and the Coast to Coast Walk. Please note, if they are very busy with diners in the evening, they may not serve those only wanting a drink – probably best to phone beforehand.

🍴 **Good food includes soup, wild boar terrine with chutney, chorizo and black pudding salad with a honey and mustard dressing, steak in ale pie, salmon and smoked haddock fishcakes with tartare sauce, courgette and hazelnut roast with a rich tomato sauce, slow-cooked herdwick lamb on olive oil mash with red wine gravy, chicken breast with bacon and wholegrain mustard sauce, specials such as suckling pig and caramelised apple, and puddings like lemon and raspberry crème brûlée and sticky toffee pudding with butterscotch sauce.** *Starters/Snacks: £3.95 to £5.50. Main Courses: £9.95 to £14.75. Puddings: £3.75 to £4.75*

Free house ~ Licensees Sara and Mike Hodgson ~ Real ale ~ Bar food (12-2.15, 6-9; not Mon, winter Sun and Tues, Dec/Jan) ~ Restaurant ~ (017687) 77239 ~ Children allowed lunchtime only; no children under 6 in bedrooms ~ Dogs allowed in bar ~ Open 12.30-10.30(10 Sun); closed Mon all year and winter Sun and Tues; all Dec/Jan ~ Bedrooms: /£85S(£90B)

Recommended by Steve Kirby, J and F Gowers, Mrs Sheila Stothard, Arthur Pickering, Tracey and Stephen Groves, Tina and David Woods-Taylor

TALKIN
NY5457   MAP 10

Blacksmiths Arms ♀ 🛏
Village signposted from B6413 S of Brampton; CA8 1LE

Neatly kept and welcoming, and a nice place to stay

After enjoying one of the surrounding walks, this well run and friendly inn is just the place to head for. There's a cheerful, bustling atmosphere and a good mix of customers and the neatly kept, warm lounge on the right has a log fire, upholstered banquettes, tables and chairs, and country prints and other pictures on the walls. The restaurant to the left is pretty, there's a long lounge opposite the bar with smaller round tables, and a well lit garden room. Geltsdale Brampton Bitter and Yates Bitter with a couple of guests such as Black Sheep Best Bitter and Copper Dragon Golden Pippin on handpump, 20 wines by the glass and 25 malt whiskies; piped music and darts. There are a couple of picnic-sets outside the front door with more in the back garden.

🍽 **As well as lunchtime sandwiches, toasties and filled baked potatoes, the reasonably priced, homely food might include soup, chicken and pistachio pâté, fresh haddock in beer batter, steak and kidney pie or mushroom stroganoff, chicken curry, beef stroganoff, daily specials, and Sunday roast.** *Starters/Snacks: £2.20 to £5.95. Main Courses: £5.95 to £16.95. Puddings: £2.95 to £4.85*

Free house ~ Licensees Donald and Anne Jackson ~ Real ale ~ Bar food (12-2, 6-9) ~ Restaurant ~ (016977) 3452 ~ Children welcome ~ Open 12-3, 6-11(midnight Sat) ~ Bedrooms: £40B/£60B

Recommended by Dr Kevan Tucker, Roy and Lindsey Fentiman, Di and Mike Gillam, Alistair and Kay Butler, Barry and Anne, Ian and Sue Wells, David and Katharine Cooke, Alun and Stephanie Llewellyn, Ian and Jane Irving, John and Sylvia Harrop

THRELKELD
NY3225   MAP 9

Horse & Farrier ◀
A66 Penrith—Keswick; CA12 4SQ

Well run 17th-c fell-foot dining pub with good food and drinks; bedrooms

A happy mix of locals and tourists can be found in this civilised Lakeland inn, enjoying the real ales and hearty food. The neatly fitted out, mainly carpeted bar has sturdy farmhouse and other nice tables, and seats from comfortably padded ones to pubby chairs and from stools to bigger housekeeper's chairs and wall settles, with country pictures on its white walls, one or two stripped beams, and some flagstones. Jennings Bitter, Cumberland, and Sneck Lifter, and a couple of seasonal guests, a good range of wines by the glass, and winter open fires; efficient service. The partly stripped stone restaurant is smart and more formal, with quite close-set tables. They have good disabled access and facilities, and a few picnic-sets outside, with inspiring views up to Blease and Gategill fells behind the pretty white-painted inn, or over to Clough Head behind the houses opposite; good walks straight from this attractive village.

🍽 **Bar food includes sandwiches and baguettes, soup, mediterranean vegetable lasagne, home-made burger, steak and kidney pie in rich ale gravy, a curry of the day, and puddings such as ginger and citrus sponge and white chocolate and apricot ice-cream parfait, with more elaborate choices such as a trio of tiger prawns in a lime and coriander sauce, duck liver pâté with fig chutney, lamb shoulder slowly braised in beer with redcurrant and mint sauce, and seared yellowfin tuna steak with a basil and saffron butter.** *Starters/Snacks: £4.95 to £6.45. Main Courses: £7.95 to £12.95. Puddings: £3.95*

Jennings (Marstons) ~ Lease Ian Court ~ Real ale ~ Bar food (12-3, 5.30-9; all day weekends) ~ Restaurant ~ (017687) 79688 ~ Children welcome ~ Dogs allowed in bar and bedrooms ~ Open 11am–midnight ~ Bedrooms: £35B/£70B

Recommended by David Morgan, Gordon and Margaret Ormondroyd, Dr Kevan Tucker, Fred and Lorraine Gill, Steve Godfrey, Ian and Jane Irving, Peter and Mary Burton

ULVERSTON
SD3177   MAP 7

Bay Horse
Canal Foot signposted off A590 and then you wend your way past the huge Glaxo factory; LA12 9EL

Civilised waterside hotel at its most relaxed at lunchtime, with super food, wine and beer, and a nice, smart place to stay

Once a staging post for coaches crossing the sands of Morecambe Bay to Lancaster, this smart and civilised hotel is at its most informal at lunchtime.The bar has a relaxed atmosphere despite its smart furnishings: attractive wooden armchairs, some pale green plush built-in wall banquettes, glossy hardwood traditional tables, blue plates on a delft shelf, a huge stone horse's head and black beams and props with lots of horsebrasses. Magazines are dotted about, there's an open fire in the handsomely marbled green granite fireplace, and decently reproduced piped music; board games, TV, and cards. Jennings Cumberland, Marstons Pedigree and Wadworths 6X on handpump, a dozen wines by the glass (champagne, too) from a carefully chosen and interesting wine list, and several malt whiskies. The conservatory restaurant has fine views over Morecambe Bay (as do the bedrooms) and there are some seats out on the terrace. More reports please.

Good lunchtime bar food might include sandwiches, chicken liver pâté with cranberry and ginger purée and a tomato and orange salad, deep-fried chilli prawns with a sweet and sour sauce, button mushrooms in a tomato, cream and brandy sauce on a peanut butter croûton, fresh crab and salmon fishcakes on a white wine and fresh herb cream sauce, hazelnut pancakes filled with fresh wild mushrooms with a garlic and chive cream sauce, grilled lambs liver with black and white puddings and a rich madeira sauce, Aberdeen Angus minced beef with red kidney beans, ginger and chilli with a white pudding mash, and puddings such as rhubarb with baked egg custard and russe biscuits and profiteroles with hot chocolate sauce; cakes with tea and coffee are served all day. *Starters/Snacks: £3.95 to £8.95. Main Courses: £12.95 to £14.50. Puddings: £2.50 to £5.95*

Free house ~ Licensee Robert Lyons ~ Real ale ~ Bar food (12-6(2 in conservatory restaurant, 4 Mon), 7.30-9) ~ Restaurant ~ (01229) 583972 ~ Children in eating area of bar but must be over 9 in evening ~ Dogs allowed in bar and bedrooms ~ Open 11-11; 12-10.30 Sun; closed 3 and 4 Jan ~ Bedrooms: £80B/£120B

Recommended by Dave Braisted, BOB, K S Whittaker

Farmers Arms
Market Place; LA12 7BA

Attractively modernised town pub with quickly changing real ales, a dozen wines by the glass, and good food

It's quite a surprise to find that the inside of this straightforward looking town pub has been so appealingly modernised. The original fireplace and timbers blend in well with the more contemporary furnishings in the front bar – mostly wicker chairs on one side, comfortable sofas on the other; the overall effect is rather unusual, but somehow it still feels like a proper village pub. A table by the fire has newspapers, glossy magazines and local information, and a second smaller bar counter leads into a big raftered eating area. Black Sheep, Courage Directors, Hawkshead Bitter, Thwaites Wainwright, and Yates bitter on handpump, a dozen wines by the glass, and piped music. In front is a very attractive terrace with outdoor heaters, plenty of good wooden tables looking on to the market cross and lots of colourful plants in tubs and hanging baskets. If something's happening in town, the pub is usually a part of it, and they can be busy on Thursday market day. More reports please.

🍽 Good food includes lunchtime hot and cold sandwiches, soup, crispy duck spring rolls on shredded salad with hoisin sauce, wooden plates with meats and cheeses (for sharing), stir-fried cashew nuts with fresh vegetables and sweet chilli sauce, cumberland sausage with dark onion gravy, prawn caesar salad, cajun chicken, beef and mushroom in ale pie, and daily specials such as pizzas with various toppings, kebab of monkfish and king prawns, and slow-roasted brisket of beef. *Starters/Snacks: £3.00 to £10.00. Main Courses: £5.00 to £15.00. Puddings: £4.25*

Free house ~ Licensee Roger Chattaway ~ Real ale ~ Bar food (11.30(11 Sun)-3, 5-8.30) ~ Restaurant ~ (01229) 584469 ~ Children allowed in restaurant ~ Open 9.30am-11pm(midnight Sat); 10am-11pm Sun

Recommended by Jo Lilley, Simon Calvert, Maurice and Gill McMahon, BOB

YANWARTH
NY5128   MAP 9

Gate Inn 🍽 ♟

2.25 miles from M6 junction 40; A66 towards Brough, then right on A6, right on B5320, then follow village signpost; CA10 2LF

CUMBRIA DINING PUB OF THE YEAR

Emphasis on imaginative food but with local beers and thoughtful wines, a pubby atmosphere, and warm welcome from helpful staff

Although there is quite an emphasis on the particularly good food, the atmosphere in this very well run 17th-c inn remains relaxed and pubby and customers do drop in for just a drink. Cumbrian Dickie Doodle, Hesket Newmarket Doris's 90th Birthday Ale, Keswick Thirst Run, and Tirril Old Faithful on handpump, a dozen wines by the glass, quite a few malt whiskies, and Weston's Old Rosie cider; friendly, helpful staff. The cosy bar has country pine and dark wood furniture, lots of brasses on the beams, church candles on all the tables and a good log fire in the attractive stone inglenook. Two restaurant areas have oak floors, panelled oak walls and heavy beams; piped music. There are seats on the terrace and in the garden.

🍽 At lunchtime, the excellent food includes soup, pork, herb and bacon terrine with pear chutney, mussels with white wine, garlic, shallots and parsley cream sauce, a platter of meat, fish and cheese with pickles and chutney, mixed local game burger, beer-battered fish with home-made tartare sauce, and cumberland sausage with roast tomato and black pudding, with evening choices such as duck liver pâté, native oysters, crevettes with garlic butter, butternut squash and parmesan risotto cake with cherry tomato compote and wild mushrooms, wild rabbit with cumbrian honey and mustard dumplings and watercress sauce, and crispy saddleback pork belly, black pudding, goats cheese mash and thyme gravy; puddings like sticky date pudding with toffee sauce and brandy and raisin ice-cream and white chocolate, hazelnut and raspberry bread and butter pudding. *Starters/Snacks: £4.50 to £8.00. Main Courses: £9.95 to £17.95. Puddings: £5.50 to £6.50*

Free house ~ Licensee Matt Edwards ~ Real ale ~ Bar food (12-2.30, 6-9) ~ Restaurant ~ (01768) 862386 ~ Children welcome ~ Dogs allowed in bar ~ Open 12-11; closed 25 Dec

Recommended by J S Burn, John Watson, Lucien Perring, Bill and Pauline Critchley, Dr J R Norman, Philip and Jude Simmons, David J Cooke, Richard J Holloway, David and Katharine Cooke, Nick Holding, Phil Bryant, Marcus Byron, Sylvia and Tony Birbeck, Mrs M Cohen, John Urquhart, Pauline and Philip Darley, Dr and Mrs A K Clarke, Barry and Anne, Comus and Sarah Elliott, Dr Kevan Tucker, Maurice and Gill McMahon, Walter and Susan Rinaldi-Butcher, C and H Greenly, Tina and David Woods-Taylor

---

Please tell us if the décor, atmosphere, food or drink at a pub is different from our description. We rely on readers' reports to keep us up to date: feedback@thegoodpubguide.co.uk or (no stamp needed) The Good Pub Guide, FREEPOST TN1569, Wadhurst, E Sussex TN5 7BR.

LUCKY DIP

Besides the fully inspected pubs, you might like to try these Lucky Dips recommended to us and described by readers (if you do, please send us reports: feedback@thegoodpubguide.co.uk).

ALSTON [NY7146]
Angel CA9 3HU [Front St]: 17th-c pub on steep cobbled street of charming small Pennine market town, Black Sheep and Greene King Old Speckled Hen, good choice of wines, reasonably priced food all day from sandwiches to roasts, big log and coal fire, beams, timbers, traditional furnishings, pleasant local atmosphere; children welcome in eating area, tables in sheltered back garden, bedrooms *(Pat and Stewart Gordon, LYM)*
Cumberland CA9 3HX [Townfoot]: Bustling local with three changing ales, friendly staff, enjoyable pub food; terrace with great views from picnic-sets, quoits pitch, good value bedrooms *(Mr and Mrs Maurice Thompson, R T and J C Moggridge)*
AMBLESIDE [NY4008]
☆ *Kirkstone Pass Inn* LA22 9LQ [A592 N of Troutbeck]: Lakeland's highest pub, in grand scenery, hiker-friendly décor of flagstones, stripped stone and simple furnishings with lots of old photographs and bric-a-brac, two log fires, friendly staff, cheap standard food all day from 9.30, changing ales such as Hawkshead and Hesket Newmarket, daily papers, games and books; piped music, pool room; dogs welcome, tables outside, three bedrooms, open all day *(Tina and David Woods-Taylor, Di and Mike Gillam, LYM, N R White)*
Queens LA22 9BU [Market Pl]: Roomy bar with dining area, Black Sheep, Jennings and Robinsons all helpfully described, inexpensive generous food; bedrooms *(Mr and Mrs Maurice Thompson, Dr and Mrs Jackson)*
Unicorn LA22 9DT [North Rd]: Bustling backstreet beamed local with plenty of atmosphere, excellent staff, Robinsons ales, bar food, coal fire; live music Sat; dogs welcome in bar, six good value bedrooms (two sharing bath), good breakfast *(Dr and Mrs Jackson, V and E A Bolton)*
☆ *Wateredge* LA22 0EP [Borrans Rd]: Lovely spot with sizeable garden running down to the edge of Windermere, lots of tables out here, same splendid view through big windows in much-modernised bar, cheerful staff, real ales inc Coniston Bluebird, several wines by the glass, quickly served generous food most of the day, cosy beamed area down steps with fireside sofa; piped music; children welcome in eating areas, open all day, comfortable bedrooms *(Michael Butler, Julia Morris, LYM, Margaret and Jeff Graham, John and Sylvia Harrop, Neil Ingoe, Dennis Jones, John Butterfield)*

APPLEBY [NY6819]
☆ *Royal Oak* CA16 6UN [B6542/Bongate]: Attractive old beamed and timbered coaching inn with promptly served popular bar food (all day Sun), well kept ales such as Hawkshead, Jennings and John Smiths, friendly young staff, log fire in panelled bar, armchair lounge with carved settle, traditional snug, nicely refurbished dining room; piped music; children and dogs welcome, terrace tables, good-sized bedrooms, good breakfast, open all day *(LYM, Ian and Jane Irving, Michael Lamm, Chris Smith, Jane and Martin Bailey)*
ARNSIDE [SD4578]
Albion LA5 0HA [Promenade]: Reliable generous fresh pubby food from hot and cold sandwiches up in spotless extended pub with great estuary and mountain views, quick friendly uniformed staff, Thwaites ales; pleasant verandah decking *(Mr and Mrs Ian King, Julia and Richard Tredgett)*
BAMPTON GRANGE [NY5218]
☆ *Crown & Mitre* CA10 2QR: Comfortable and welcoming, with enjoyable local food (steaks particularly good), friendly helpful staff, Black Sheep and local guest beers, fresh modern décor with some leather chairs, sofas and log fire, smaller bar with pool, stripped wood furniture in cheerful red-walled dining room; eight well refurbished bedrooms *(David and Katharine Cooke)*
BARBON [SD6282]
☆ *Barbon Inn* LA6 2LJ [off A683 Kirkby Lonsdale—Sedbergh]: Charmingly set fell-foot village inn, civilised and comfortable, with welcoming landlord and chatty staff, good value food from baguettes up, changing ales such as Barngates Westmorland Gold and Marstons Pedigree, good wine choice, log fire, some sofas, armchairs and antique carved settles, attractive restaurant; children welcome, sheltered pretty garden, good walks, bedrooms being refurbished *(LYM, Dr Kevan Tucker, Chris and Meredith Owen, Michael Doswell, John and Joan Nash)*
BLENCOW [NY4630]
Clickham CA11 0BP [on B5288; off A66 between Penrith & Keswick]: Comfortably cottagey two-bar local with real fires, quaint alcoves, warmly welcoming efficient service, good value wholesome food in small pretty dining room, real ale, pool room with darts *(V Gladden)*
Crown CA11 0DG: Friendly local with newish licensees gaining reputation for good value food, beer and wine; cl wkdy lunchtime *(Mike and Penny Sutton)*

BOOT [NY1701]

Boot Inn CA19 1TG [aka Burnmoor; signed just off the Wrynose/Hardknott Pass rd]: Comfortable beamed pub with ever-burning fire, Black Sheep, Jennings and a guest beer, decent wines and malt whiskies, friendly staff, reasonably priced home-made lunchtime bar food from sandwiches up, restaurant and dining conservatory; games room with pool and TV; children and dogs welcome, sheltered front lawn with play area, good walks, lovely surroundings, open all day *(N R White, LYM, Kevin Flack)*

☆ *Brook House* CA19 1TG: Converted small Victorian hotel with good views and walks, friendly family service, wide choice of good generous home-made food inc some interesting dishes, great whisky choice, well kept ales such as Black Sheep, Coniston, Theakstons and Yates, decent wines, log fires, small plushly modernised bar, comfortable hunting-theme lounge, peaceful separate restaurant; tables outside, seven good value bedrooms, good breakfast (for nearby campers too), excellent drying room, open all day *(Kevin Flack, the Didler, David and Katharine Cooke, J S Burn)*

BORROWDALE [NY2617]

Borrowdale Hotel CA12 5UY [B5289, S end of Derwentwater]: A hotel, but enjoyable lunchtime bar food from sandwiches up in conservatory, smart, friendly and roomy bar, well kept Jennings Cumberland, pleasant service, good value restaurant; garden tables, lovely fell-foot scenery, good bedrooms *(Mary McSweeney)*

BOTHEL [NY1839]

Greyhound CA7 2HS: Enjoyable food (proper shortcrust pies, great real chips), Jennings Cumberland, good wine choice, hard-working landlord *(Helen Clarke)*

BOWNESS-ON-WINDERMERE [SD4096]

Royal Oak LA23 3EG [Brantfell Rd]: Handy for steamer pier, split-level bar with well kept ales such as Coniston Bluebrd, Everards Tiger, Greene King Abbot and Jennings Cumberland, reasonably priced food, friendly efficient service, games room; children welcome, tables out in front, bedrooms *(Mr and Mrs Maurice Thompson, Dennis Jones)*

BRAITHWAITE [NY2324]

Middle Ruddings CA12 5RY: Friendly family-run hotel, enjoyable food in bar or carpeted dining conservatory with Skiddaw views, three well kept local ales; children and dogs welcome, garden with terrace picnic-sets, bedrooms *(Mike and Penny Sutton)*

Royal Oak CA12 5SY: Bustling local atmosphere, good choice of enjoyable food (best to book evenings) inc children's helpings, prompt helpful service, well kept Jennings, well worn in flagstoned bar; dogs welcome exc at mealtimes *(Brian and Anna Marsden, Dr and Mrs Michael Smith, Neil Tribe)*

BRANTHWAITE [NY0524]

Riverside CA14 4SZ: Enjoyable local food, good service, well kept Jennings, stone fireplace in nice bar area, river-view restaurant *(David Bennett)*

BRIGSTEER [SD4889]

☆ *Wheatsheaf* LA8 8AN: Attractive dining pub with good sensibly priced food from interesting sandwiches up, nice breads baked here, takeaways some nights, cheerful attentive staff, real ales such as Dent, Hesket Newmarket and Jennings, good choice of wines by the glass, neat minimalist décor in linked rooms off central bar; pretty village *(Paul Boot, Ray and Winifred Halliday, Alan and Carolin Tidbury, Tony and Maggie Harwood)*

BROUGHTON-IN-FURNESS [SD2187]

Black Cock LA20 6HQ [Princes St]: Hard-working newish licensees in cosy low-beamed pub dating from 15th c, Theakstons and a guest beer such as Butcombe or McMullens, friendly efficient service, usual bar food and restaurant menu; tables out in front and in attractive courtyard, pleasant bedrooms *(Clive Flynn, Angus Lyon)*

High Cross LA20 6ES [A595 towards Millom]: Nicely placed low-beamed inn reopened under new owners proud of their food, open fire, Lakeland pictures and soft lighting, separate estuary-view restaurant; disabled access (one small step), picnic-sets on front terrace and in garden, bedrooms overlooking Duddon fells *(BOB)*

BURTON-IN-KENDAL [SD5376]

Kings Arms LA6 1LR [Main St]: Friendly village pub with masses of old local memorabilia and advertisements, good value substantial food inc local dishes in bar or two knocked-through dining rooms, popular Mon steak night and Sun roasts, good atmosphere, five or six real ales, separate locals' area with pool and TV; comfortable bedrooms *(Mr and Mrs Ian King, Bruce Braithwaite, Tony and Maggie Harwood)*

BUTTERMERE [NY1716]

☆ *Bridge Hotel* CA13 9UZ [just off B5289 SW of Keswick]: Popular with walkers (but no dogs), with lakeside and other walks for all levels nearby; hotely feel but with traditional beamed bar, Coniston Bluebird, Hawkshead Bitter, Theakstons Old Peculier and a guest beer, straightforward bar food, plush dining room; may debit your card with a steep voidable deposit if you eat outside; children welcome, flagstoned terrace, bedrooms, self catering, open all day *(Dr and Mrs Michael Smith, the Didler, Sylvia and Tony Birbeck, Comus and Sarah Elliott, N R White, Alistair and Kay Butler, Paul and Margaret Baker,*

Margaret Whalley, Lindsley Harvard, LYM, Louise English, Clive Watkin)

Fish CA13 9XA: Spacious, fresh and airy former coaching inn on NT property between Buttermere and Crummock Water, fine views, changing ales inc Jennings, wide range of good value food, good staff, pleasant atmosphere; terrace tables, bedrooms (BB, the Didler, J and F Gowers)

CALDBECK [NY3239]

☆ **Oddfellows Arms** CA7 8EA [B5299 SE of Wigton]: Friendly split-level pub with particularly well kept Jennings, generous good value home cooking from lunchtime sandwiches up, good choice of wines by the glass, affable landlord, quick pleasant service, fine old photographs and woodburner in bustling comfortable front bar, big back dining room, exemplary lavatories; piped music, games area with darts, pool and TV; children and muddy walkers welcome, open all day Fri-Sun and summer, low-priced bedrooms, nice village (B I Mason, Helen Clarke, Adam F Padel, Piotr Chodzko-Zajko)

CARLISLE [NY4056]

Kings Head CA3 8RF [pedestrianised Fisher St]: Heavy beams, lots of old local prints, drawings and black and white photographs, friendly service, bargain pub lunches, well kept Yates and a recherché guest beer, raised dining area; piped music, TV; interesting historical plaque outside, partly covered courtyard, open all day (the Didler, Nick Holding, Jeremy King)

Woodrow Wilson CA1 1QS [Botchergate]: Wetherspoons with fine range of local ales inc two from Geltsdale, their usual bargain food, pleasant raised side booth area; attractive terrace, open all day (Nick Holding, the Didler)

CARTMEL [SD3778]

Royal Oak LA11 6QB [The Square]: Low beams and flagstones, cosy nooks, pleasant décor, generous good value food from baguettes to fresh local fish, good choice of real ales, decent wines, welcoming helpful staff, log fire; modern public bar with games, TV and piped music; nice big riverside garden, bedrooms (Michael Lamm, BB)

COCKERMOUTH [NY1230]

1761 CA13 9NH [Market Pl]: Friendly newish pub, upscale yet without pretension, in carefully refurbished old building, real ales such as Black Sheep, Jennings Cumberland and Yates, continental beers, good choice of wines by the glass, lots of board games, occasional music nights; smart terrace tables (Peter Marrs)

CONISTON [SD3097]

☆ **Black Bull** LA21 8DU [Yewdale Rd (A593)]: Lively welcoming atmosphere in range of linked bars popular for simple food from good sandwiches up, friendly attentive staff, well kept Coniston

Bluebird, XB and Old Man brewed here, farm ciders, interesting bottled beers and malt whiskies, cheering fire, lots of Donald Campbell water-speed memorabilia, separate restaurant; children and dogs welcome, tables out in suntrap former coachyard, bedrooms, open all day (Nick Lawless, Irene and Derek Flewin, Arthur Pickering, Stephen R Holman, David and Sue Smith, Christine and Phil Young, Maurice and Gill McMahon, Tony and Maggie Harwood, LYM, Jill Littlewood, Christopher Joinson)

Ship LA21 8HB [Bowmanstead, tucked away off A593 S]: Quiet local out of season, more popular in summer with walkers and campers for good-sized helpings of good value food, well kept Robinsons Hartleys XB; children and dogs welcome (Russell and Alison Hunt, Tony and Maggie Harwood)

☆ **Sun** LA21 8HQ: 16th-c pub in terrific setting below dramatic fells, interesting Donald Campbell and other lakeland photographs in old-fashioned back bar with beams, flagstones, good log fire in 19th-c range, cask seats and old settles, well kept Coniston Bluebird, Hawkshead and three good guest beers, good choice of wines by the glass, has had good interesting food (was a foodless spell last Feb), darts, cribbage, dominoes, big conservatory restaurant off carpeted lounge; children and dogs welcome, great views from pleasant front terrace, big tree-sheltered garden, comfortable bedrooms, good hearty breakfast, open all day (Jarrod and Wendy Hopkinson, Ewan and Moira McCall, Margaret Whalley, Lindsley Harvard, Tim Maddison, Arthur Pickering, Christine and Phil Young, Catherine and Rob Dunster, Maurice and Gill McMahon, LYM, M Thomas, Michael J Caley)

COWGILL [SD7686]

Sportsmans LA10 5RG [nr Dent Station, on Dent—Garsdale Head rd]: Beautifully placed dentdale local with good nearby walks, substantial food from sandwiches up, Black Sheep and Copper Dragon, decent wine, log fires, straight-talking landlord, simple bar/lounge with darts in snug at one end and pool room at the other, no piped music; tidy river-view bedrooms, camp site, cl wkdy lunchtimes out of season (anon)

CROOK [SD4695]

☆ **Sun** LA8 8LA [B5284 Kendal—Bowness]: Good bustling atmosphere in low-beamed bar with two dining areas off, good varied traditional food (all day wknds) from unusual sandwiches to enterprising hot dishes, winter game and lovely puddings, reasonable prices, prompt cheerful helpful service, well kept Coniston Bluebird and Hawkshead, good value wines, roaring log fire, fresh flowers (Janet and Peter Race, Ray and Winifred

Halliday, Mr and Mrs Maurice Thompson, Hugh Roberts, LYM, Julian and Janet Dearden)

CULGAITH [NY6029]

Black Swan CA10 1QW [off A66 E of Penrith]: 17th-c inn prettily set in quiet Eden Valley village handy for Acorn Bank (NT), enjoyable local food, attractive dining area, may be real ales such as Black Sheep and Tetleys, dynamic young licensees, open fire, plenty of brasses and old photographs, folk nights; pleasant bedrooms *(Joan York)*

DENT [SD7086]

George & Dragon LA10 5QL [Main St]: Comfortable flagstoned bar welcoming walkers, open fire, dark panelling (but bright lights), partitioned tables, good generous food inc reasonably priced evening restaurant meals, helpful service, separate dining room; bedrooms comfortable, lovely village *(Ann and Tony Bennett-Hughes)*

☆ ***Sun*** LA10 5QL [Main St]: Lively and friendly old-fashioned local with four good Dent ales brewed nearby, enjoyable walkers' food from sandwiches up, beamed and flagstoned traditional bar with coal fire and darts, lots of local events; children welcome, open all day in summer *(LYM, John Coatsworth, Margaret Dickinson, David and Sue Smith, Ann and Tony Bennett-Hughes)*

DOCKRAY [NY3921]

Royal CA11 0JY [A5091, off A66 or A592 W of Penrith]: Friendly new management in former coaching inn with bright open-plan bar, well kept Black Sheep, Jennings Cumberland and Tom Fool and a guest beer, straightforward food from bargain sandwiches up, two dining areas, walkers' part with stripped settles on flagstones; picnic-sets in large peaceful garden, great setting, open all day, comfortable bedrooms *(David J Cooke, Mr and Mrs Maurice Thompson, LYM, John and Gloria Isaacs)*

ESKDALE GREEN [NY1200]

☆ ***Bower House*** CA19 1TD [0.5 mile W]: Civilised old-fashioned stone-built inn extended around beamed and alcoved core, helpful friendly staff, Coniston, Dent Aviator and Kamikazi and Marstons Pedigree, good value pubby food, good fires, biggish restaurant; nicely tended sheltered garden by cricket field, charming spot with great walks, bedrooms, open all day *(David and Sue Smith, Tina and David Woods-Taylor, Mr and Mrs Maurice Thompson, LYM)*

FOXFIELD [SD2085]

☆ ***Prince of Wales*** LA20 6BX [opp stn]: Cheery bare-boards pub with half a dozen good changing ales inc bargain beers brewed here and at their associated Tigertops brewery, bottled imports, farm cider, enjoyable home-made food inc lots of unusual pasties, hot coal fire, pub

games inc bar billiards, daily papers and beer-related reading matter; children very welcome, games for them, reasonably priced bedrooms, opens mid-afternoon wkdys, open all day Fri-Sun *(the Didler, BB)*

GLENRIDDING [NY3816]

Travellers Rest CA11 0QQ [back of main car park, top of road]: Friendly unpretentious low-beamed and panelled two-bar pub with big helpings of usual food for hungry walkers (all day in summer, from breakfast on), Greene King Old Speckled Hen and Jennings, yet comfortable pubby décor; Ullswater views from terrace picnic-sets; open all day Sun and summer *(Phil Bryant)*

GRASMERE [NY3406]

Travellers Rest LA22 9RR [A591 just N]: Comfortable and cheery, with settles, banquettes, upholstered armchairs and log fire, local watercolours, old photographs, suggested walks, friendly staff, Jennings ales, bar food (all day in summer) from sandwiches up; piped music, big games end; provision for children and dogs, good quiet bedrooms, good breakfast, open all day *(Mr and Mrs Maurice Thompson, Tina and David Woods-Taylor, John and Joan Nash, John and Sylvia Harrop, Ian and Sue Wells, Arthur Pickering, LYM)*

☆ ***Tweedies*** LA22 9SW [part of Dale Lodge Hotel]: Lively properly pubby atmosphere in big square bar, warm and cosy, with enjoyable food from pizzas and lunchtime baguettes to some imaginative dishes and Sun roast (which is free for under-8s), four or five changing ales and good tasting 'bat' (helpful advice from friendly staff), farm cider, wide choice of wines by the glass, attractively updated traditional décor, sturdy furnishings in adjoining flagstoned family dining room; children, walkers and dogs welcome, picnic-sets out in large pleasant garden, bedrooms *(Mr and Mrs Maurice Thompson, Malcolm and Lynne Jessop, Alice English)*

GREAT CLIFTON [NY0429]

Old Ginn House CA14 1TS [Moor Rd; just off A66 E of Workington]: Plenty of character in unusual spanish-feel place with circular bar and wide choice of reasonably priced food in two-level restaurant, welcoming relaxing atmosphere, helpful young staff; good value peaceful bedrooms *(A S Wickes)*

GREYSTOKE [NY4430]

Boot & Shoe CA11 0TP: New licensees doing tasty generous reasonably priced food inc popular theme nights, small pub in pretty village on national cycle route *(Mike and Penny Sutton)*

HARTSOP [NY4113]

Brothers Water CA11 0NZ [A592]: Walkers' and campers' pub in magnificent setting at the bottom of Kirkstone Pass, Barngates Pride of Westmorland and

Jennings Bitter and Mountain Man
(Mr and Mrs Maurice Thompson)
HAVERTHWAITE [SD3284]
Anglers Arms LA12 8AJ [just off A590]:
Busy split-level pub with up to ten real
ales, friendly helpful staff, good choice of
fairly priced generous fresh food from
sandwiches to steak, sports memorabilia,
separate upstairs dining room, lower area
with pool; handy for steam railway
*(Mr and Mrs Maurice Thompson,
Dennis Jones)*
HAWKSHEAD [SD3598]
Sun LA22 0NT [Main St]: Lively family
pub with lots of brass, brickwork and
beams, helpful obliging staff, Hawkshead,
Jennings Cumberland and Timothy Taylors
Landlord, enjoyable food, sizeable
restaurant; children and dogs welcome,
tables out in front by small courtyard,
eight bedrooms *(Mr and Mrs Maurice
Thompson)*
KENDAL [SD5192]
Burgundys Wine Bar LA9 4DH [Lowther
St]: Small attractive three-level bistro bar
with (despite the name) interesting
changing ales such as Hawkshead Red,
Keswick Thirst Pitch and Oakham JHB,
enthusiastic landlord happy to talk about
them, bottled imports, ciders and unusual
wines too, helpful staff, lunchtime food
from sandwiches to light hot dishes; cl
Mon evening and Sun-Weds lunchtimes
(Mr and Mrs Maurice Thompson)
Castle LA9 7AD [Castle St]: Well run
bustling local by River Kent and nr castle,
well kept Jennings, Tetleys and guests
such as Black Sheep and Dent, good value
popular bar lunches from sandwiches up,
cheerful service; big-screen TV and games
in separate public bar; roadside tables
(David and Sue Smith)
Riflemans Arms LA9 4LD [Greenside]:
Village-green setting on edge of town,
welcoming locals and staff, real ales such
as Greene King Abbot, Tetleys and
Wychwood Hobgoblin *(Mr and Mrs Maurice
Thompson)*
KESWICK [NY2623]
Square Orange CA12 5AS [St Johns St]:
Two local real ales, good choice of wines
by the glass, good tapas and pizzas, nice
coffee, alternative customers, interesting
piped music, some live, lots of board
games *(Fred and Lorraine Gill)*
☆ *Swinside Inn* CA12 5UE [Newlands Valley,
just SW]: Brilliant peaceful valley setting,
long brightly busy bar with Jennings
Cumberland, Theakstons Best and a guest
beer, friendly staff, quick generous basic
food at popular prices, games area
beyond central log fire (two more
elsewhere – best atmosphere in original
south-end core); piped music; children
and dogs welcome, tables in garden and
on upper and lower terraces giving fine
views across to the high crags and fells
around Grisedale Pike, bedrooms, open all

day *(Sylvia and Tony Birbeck,
David J Cooke, J S Burn, Tina and
David Woods-Taylor, Edward Mirzoeff, LYM,
Stephen R Holman, Brian and
Anna Marsden)*
LANGDALE [NY2906]
Stickle Barn LA22 9JU [by car park for
Stickle Ghyll]: Lovely views from roomy
and busy café-style walkers' and climbers'
bar (boots welcome), half a dozen real
ales, good value generous food inc
packed lunches, quick friendly service,
mountaineering photographs; games
machines, TV, piped music (live Sat); big
pleasant terrace with inner verandah,
open all day; bunkhouse accommodation
*(Adrian Johnson, Mr and Mrs Maurice
Thompson)*
LANGWATHBY [NY5633]
Shepherds CA10 1LW [A686 Penrith—
Alston]: Welcoming open-plan beamed
village pub with good quickly served
reasonably priced food, friendly efficient
service, well kept ales such as Black
Sheep, decent wine choice, comfortable
banquettes, bar down steps from lounge,
games room; tables and chairs on big
back terrace, attractive spot on huge
green of Pennines village, play area
(Len Beattie, Mr and Mrs Maurice Thompson)
LINDALE [SD4180]
☆ *Royal Oak* LA11 6LX: Roomy open-plan
village pub popular for good gently
upscale food using local ingredients,
wider evening choice, welcoming helpful
staff, modestly priced wines, Robinsons
ales such as Hartleys XB; blue banquettes
and padded chairs in carpeted bar, wood-
floored dining areas either side,
restrained décor with a few modern
prints, pleasant atmosphere *(Mr and
Mrs Maurice Thompson, Michael Lamm,
Michael Doswell)*
MELMERBY [NY6137]
Shepherds CA10 1HF [A686 Penrith—
Alston]: Friendly split-level country pub
with comfortable heavy-beamed dining
room off flagstoned bar, spacious end
room with woodburner, generous food
served promptly, Black Sheep, Jennings
and a guest, quite a few malt whiskies,
games area with darts and pool; children
welcome, terrace tables *(Mr and
Mrs Maurice Thompson, John Saville, LYM)*
NEWBY BRIDGE [SD3686]
Swan LA12 8NB [just off A590]:
Substantial hotel in fine setting below
fells next to river with waterside picnic-
sets under cocktail parasols by old stone
bridge, extensive well used contemporary
bar with snacks and brasserie meals (all
day wknds), friendly staff, real ales, good
coffee; piped music; children in eating
areas, open all day, comfortable bedrooms
(Michael Doswell, LYM)
OUSBY [NY6134]
Fox CA10 1QA: Friendly pleasantly
updated pub with good value generous

pubby food, well kept Tirril ale, open fire, darts, pool, dining room; dogs welcome, bedrooms, caravan site, has been cl lunchtime exc Sun *(Bill and Sheila McLardy)*

OUTGATE [SD3599]

☆ *Outgate Inn* LA22 0NQ [B5286 Hawkshead—Ambleside]: Neatly kept country pub with three pleasantly modernised rooms, good value fresh simple food from sandwiches up, well kept Robinsons ales, attentive friendly staff, cheerful log fire; trad jazz Fri (very busy then); terrace picnic-sets, three bright comfortable bedrooms, good breakfast, nice walks, open all day summer wknds (restricted hours winter Mon/Tues) *(BB, Richard Hennessy, Mr and Mrs M Wall)*

PAPCASTLE [NY1131]

Belle Vue CA13 0NT [Belle Vue]: Unpretentious pub with well kept local ale, good value food and friendly helpful service *(Dr and Mrs S G Barber)*

PATTERDALE [NY3915]

Patterdale Hotel CA11 0NN: Large hotel's bar popular with locals, residents and walking parties for its generous food, Hesket Newmarket Helvellyn Gold and Scafell Blonde, helpful staff; bedrooms *(Mr and Mrs Maurice Thompson)*

PENRUDDOCK [NY4227]

☆ *Herdwick* CA11 0QU [off A66 Penrith—Keswick]: Current management settled in well in attractively cottagey and sympathetically renovated 18th-c inn, warm atmosphere, enjoyable food from lunchtime sandwiches up, Jennings and summer guest beers from unusual curved bar, decent wines, friendly efficient service, good open fire, stripped stone and white paintwork, nice dining room with upper gallery, games room with pool and darts; children in eating areas, five good value bedrooms *(LYM, Pauline and Philip Darley)*

RAVENSTONEDALE [NY7401]

☆ *Fat Lamb* CA17 4LL [Crossbank; A683 Sedbergh—Kirkby Stephen]: Isolated in great scenery (good walks), with pews in relaxing and cheerfully unsmart bar, coal fire in traditional black inglenook range, good local photographs and bird plates, friendly helpful staff, wide choice of good proper food from filled baguettes to enjoyable restaurant meals, well kept Tetleys, decent wines; facilities for disabled, children welcome, tables out by nature-reserve pastures, bedrooms, open all day *(BB, Mrs Ann Gray, Yvonne and Mike Meadley)*

☆ *Kings Head* CA17 4NH [Pub visible from A685 W of Kirkby Stephen]: Quaint country inn with friendly helpful staff, well kept Black Sheep, Dent and two guest ales, farm cider, enjoyable food using local produce from good sandwiches up, comfortable carpeted lounge and bar,

hot log fires, sizeable dining room with shelves of whisky-water jugs, lower games room; children and dogs welcome, picnic-sets out in front, by stream across lane, and in garden with red squirrel feeders, three comfortable bedrooms, open all day *(Christopher Beadle, Simon Marley, Adam F Padel, Margaret Dickinson)*

ROSTHWAITE [NY2514]

Scafell CA12 5XB [B5289 S of Keswick]: Big plain slate-floored back bar useful for walkers, weather forecast board, well kept ales such as Barngates, Copper Dragon, Keswick and Theakstons, blazing log fire, sandwiches, afternoon teas; piped music, pool; dogs welcome, tables out overlooking beck, hotel with appealing cocktail bar/sun-lounge and dining room, bedrooms not big but good *(Dr D J and Mrs S C Walker, Mr and Mrs Maurice Thompson, BB, J and F Gowers, Phil Bryant, Brian and Anna Marsden)*

SATTERTHWAITE [SD3392]

☆ *Eagles Head* LA12 8LN: Unpretentious and attractive beamed pub in pretty village on edge of Grizedale Forest (beautiful scenery), particularly welcoming and obliging landlord, good fairly priced pubby food (not Mon) inc notable filled rolls, wider evening choice, well kept local ales inc Barngates and one brewed for the pub, big log fire, lots of local photographs and maps; children welcome, picnic-sets outside, comfortable bedrooms *(Tina and David Woods-Taylor, Roger and Carol Maden)*

SCALES [NY3426]

☆ *White Horse* CA12 4SY [A66 W of Penrith]: Traditional Lakeland pub, warm fires in comfortable beamed bar, little snug and another room with butter churns, kettles, marmalade slicer and black range; Camerons Castle Eden and perhaps a beer brewed for them, straightforward food; piped music; children welcome, garden tables, pretty flowering tubs, lovely setting below Blencathra (leave muddy boots outside), open all day in summer *(LYM)*

SEDBERGH [SD6592]

☆ *Dalesman* LA10 5BN [Main St]: Vibrant linked rooms with good range of well kept ales, quickly served good value hearty food (all day Sun) from sandwiches to aberdeen angus steaks, log fire, modern furnishings alongside the sporting prints, stripped stone and beams; piped music; children welcome, picnic-sets out in front, bedrooms, open all day *(Mr and Mrs Ian King, John and Yvonne Davies, David and Sue Atkinson, LYM, David and Sue Smith, Nick and Meriel Cox)*

☆ *Red Lion* LA10 5BZ [Finkle St (A683)]: Cheerful family-run beamed local, down to earth and comfortable, with good value generous comfort food, full Jennings range kept well, friendly staff, splendid coal fire; sports TV, very busy wknds, no dogs *(BB, Arthur Pickering, John and Yvonne Davies, Dr D J and Mrs S C Walker)*

SHAP [NY5614]

☆ *Greyhound* CA10 3PW [A6, S end]: Good value former coaching inn, hearty sensible food in open-plan bar and two restaurants from sandwiches through particularly good carefully cooked local meats to imaginative puddings (chefs happy to share their recipes), well kept Jennings and up to half a dozen guest beers, good reasonably priced house wines, cheerful bustle and friendly helpful young staff; may be unobtrusive piped classical music, dogs welcome; nine comfortable bedrooms, good breakfast, popular with coast-to-coast walkers *(Mr and Mrs Maurice Thompson, Michael Doswell)*

SILLOTH [NY1053]

Golf CA7 4AB [Criffel St]: Substantial well run hotel with portraits of young Queen Elizabeth II and Churchill and comfortable deco chairs in time-warp bar, local Derwent ale, good choice of wines by the glass, decent food, restaurant, games and snooker rooms; 22 bedrooms, open all day *(Helen Clarke)*

SKELWITH BRIDGE [NY3403]

Talbot LA22 9NJ [part of Skelwith Bridge Hotel; A593 W of Ambleside]: Roomy oak-panelled bar in well run 17th-c hotel nr River Brathay, smart staff, Thwaites real ale, quickly served lunchtime bar food from sandwiches up, smart restaurant; 28 tidy modernised bedrooms *(Margaret Dickinson)*

STAVELEY [SD4798]

Hawkshead Brewery Bar LA8 9LR [Staveley Mill Yard, Back Lane]: Spacious modern span-roof beer hall, tap for Hawkshead beer range, local farm cider, good wine and soft drinks choice, friendly staff, long tables and benches and groups of leather sofas on new oak boards, view down into brewery, food from adjoining café, T-shirts etc for sale; brewery tours available, open 12-6, occasionally later *(the Didler)*

TEBAY [NY6104]

Cross Keys CA10 3UY: Friendly chatty atmosphere in comfortable beamed former coaching inn handy for M6 junction 38, promptly served usual food inc good local steaks, Black Sheep and Tetleys, decent wine, coal fire, separate eating area, games room with darts and pool; picnic-sets in back garden, good value bedrooms *(John and Bryony Coles)*

THIRLSPOT [NY3118]

Kings Head CA12 4TN [A591 Grasmere—Keswick]: Long modernised bar with wide food choice, well kept Jennings, close-set tables in eating area with inglenook fire; games room with pool, big-screen TV, piped music; walkers and children welcome, garden tables, comfortable

bedrooms (separate hotel part), attractive surroundings *(LYM, David and Pam Wilcox)*

THRELKELD [NY3225]

Salutation CA12 4SQ [old main rd, bypassed by A66 W of Penrith]: Friendly low-beamed village pub below Blencathra (busy wknds), well kept Jennings Cumberland, quite a few malt whiskies, good value pubby food from sandwiches and baguettes up, good coal or log fire, padded wall seats in three areas divided by standing timbers, back games room; piped music, TV; dogs welcome, spacious upper children's room, tables out on decking in pleasant outside area *(Tina and David Woods-Taylor, LYM, Fred and Lorraine Gill)*

TIRRIL [NY5026]

☆ *Queens Head* CA10 2JF [B5320, not far from M6 junction 40]: Thriving atmosphere, friendly attentive staff, well kept Robinsons, enjoyable fairly priced food, attractively old-fashioned linked bars with low beams, black panelling, flagstones, bare boards, high-backed settles and four open fireplaces inc a roomy inglenook, restaurant; piped music and pool in back bar; children welcome in eating areas, bedrooms, open all day Fri-Sun *(Michael and Maggie Betton, Peter Herridge, John Roots, Rona Murdoch, Phil Bryant, Tracey and Stephen Groves, LYM, Mr and Mrs Ian King, B I Mason)*

TORVER [SD2894]

☆ *Church House* LA21 8AZ [A593/A5084 S of Coniston]: Good individual food of restaurant quality at sensible prices in attractive rambling building dating from 14th c, lots of low beams, warmly welcoming hands-on landlady, Adnams, Barngates Tag Lag and Hawkshead, good choice of wines, fine log fire in cheerful locals' slate-floored bar with Lakeland bric-a-brac, another in comfortable lounge with dark red walls, separate dining room, splendid hill views (if weather allows); children and dogs welcome, big well tended garden with rabbits and guinea-pigs, six good bedrooms, has been open all day at least in summer *(David and Sue Smith, John and Hilary Penny, Christine and Phil Young, Dennis Jones, John Arnold, Maurice and Gill McMahon)*

Wilson Arms LA21 8BB: Comfortable, with good log fires, polished brass, some antiques, Coniston real ales, limited lunchtime menu and wider evening choice, pleasant dining room; children welcome, hill views from tables outside, bedrooms *(Tony and Maggie Harwood)*

TROUTBECK [NY4103]

☆ *Mortal Man* LA23 1PL [A592 N of Windermere; Upper Rd]: New management doing interesting food from good substantial sandwiches up in immaculate beamed lounge bar with comfortable armchairs and sofas as well as dining tables, simpler adjoining area, swift service by neat foreign staff, real ales such as Jennings, John Smiths and Theakstons Best, big log fire, picture-window restaurant; children welcome, great views from sunny garden, lovely village, comfortable bedrooms, open all day *(Paul Humphreys, Michael Doswell, Bruce Braithwaite, LYM)*

☆ *Queens Head* LA23 1PW [A592 N of Windermere]: Now a Robinsons pub, with expert new tenants; interestingly furnished and decorated rambling beamed and flagstoned bar, great log fire in raised stone fireplace, another coal fire, real ales from counter based on finely carved Elizabethan four-poster, all-day popular food, newer dining rooms similarly decorated to main bar; piped music; children welcome, dogs in bar, seats outside with fine view over Troutbeck valley to Applethwaite moors, bedrooms, open all day; more reports on new regime, please *(LYM, J Crosby, V and E A Bolton)*

UNDERBARROW [SD4692]
Punchbowl LA8 8HQ: Small friendly open-plan village local, homely beamed bar with button-back banquettes and good log fire, good value fresh food from sandwiches up, well kept Black Sheep and Jennings Cumberland, good service; handy for walkers *(Margaret Dickinson)*

WASDALE HEAD [NY1807]
Wasdale Head Inn CA20 1EX [NE of Wast Water]: Mountain hotel worth knowing for its stunning fellside setting and the interesting Great Gable beers it brews, available in taster glasses; roomy walkers' bar with side hot food counter (all day in summer, may be restricted winter), decent choice of wines and malt whiskies, striking mountain photographs, traditional games, old-fashioned residents' bar, lounge and restaurant; children welcome, dogs allowed in bar, open all day *(the Didler, LYM, Tim Maddison)*

WATERMILLOCK [NY4523]
Brackenrigg CA11 0LP [A592, Ullswater]: Worth knowing for spectacular Ullswater and mountain views, particularly from terrace; pleasant open-plan bar with real ales such as Coniston Bluebird, Copper

Dragon and Tirril Broughton, log fire, food that's somewhat pricy for what you get (service can be slow), good-sized dining room; no dogs inside, no children after teatime; ten bedrooms, self-catering *(BB, Tracey and Stephen Groves, David Morgan, Richard J Holloway, Tina and David Woods-Taylor, Mrs A J Robertson, Dave and Sue Mitchell)*

WEST CURTHWAITE [NY3248]
Royal Oak CA7 8BG: Simple and comfortable, with young chef/landlord doing wide choice of good fresh food using local produce, Jennings ales, good choice of wines with strong australian leanings, friendly landlady, efficient service, family dining area; terrace picnic-sets, open all day wknds *(B I Mason, Helen Clarke)*

WINDERMERE [SD3801]
Langdale Chase LA23 1LW: Victorian country-house hotel doing good bar lunches inc unusual sandwiches in conservatory with stunning Windermere views; extensive lakeside grounds, 37 bedrooms *(Mary McSweeney)*

WINSTER [SD4193]
☆ *Brown Horse* LA23 3NR [A5074 S of Windermere]: Warmly friendly open-plan pub nicely balancing local feel of traditional log-fire bar with comfortably elegant and up-to-date dining area, enjoyable food using good ingredients interestingly, helpful efficient service, Jennings and Timothy Taylors ales, decent wines; big-screen sports TV; children and walkers welcome, tables outside (lovely valley), handy for Blackwell Arts & Crafts House, reasonably priced bedrooms with good breakfast, has been cl wkdy lunchtimes out of season *(Kevin Flack, Jane and Alan Bush, LYM)*

WREAY [NY4349]
Plough CA4 0RL: Pretty village's heavy-beamed pub carefully restored in current style of sturdy pine tables on flagstones with a couple of leather settees, enjoyable reasonably priced usual food, well kept changing ales inc Theakstons Best, buoyant relaxed atmosphere; cl Mon/Tues *(Colin and Anne Glynne-Jones, N Tunstall, Dr Kevan Tucker)*

Derbyshire

A great Derbyshire speciality is its rich range of unpretentious pubs of real solid character. Their often fairly simple interiors are buoyed up by a warm homely feel and genuinely friendly welcome. You can often be sure of a good (if simple) meal, and many of them stock an interesting range of real ales. Their other strong feature is value for money. Many of these pubs offer traditional home-made bar meals at appealing prices. The Old Poets Corner in Ashover and John Thompson near Melbourne are prime examples. Both have real individuality, with the characters of their cheery hands-on licensees shining through, both brew their own beer, and both win Bargain Awards. You'll find a fine choice of real ales at our two Derby main entries, the Alexandra and the Brunswick. The Alexandra is part of Tynemill, a good small chain of real ale pubs, and the Brunswick carries an impressive 16 real ales – not bad for a tied pub. One of the most embracing welcomes is in the Red Lion at Litton where the fairly new landlady obviously cares deeply for her pub. The Quiet Woman at Earl Sterndale, a lovely historical gem, deserves a mention, as does the handsome old Barley Mow at Kirk Ireton with its beers straight from the cask behind the counter. These pubs are treasures to be experienced while they are still around. One thing you won't find much of here is the seriously food-oriented pub, challenging restaurants as a place for a swish meal out (we haven't named a dining pub of the year in this county). To us though this isn't necessarily a bad thing. The good value and good homely cooking you'll find at so many of the pubs here more than compensates. Some of the Lucky Dip entries at the end of the chapter have been winning special praise recently, too, most notable the Bulls Head in Ashford in the Water, Old Sun in Buxton, Abbey Inn in Derby, Barrel near Foolow, Chequers on Froggatt Edge, Hardwick Inn near Hardwick Hall, Red Lion at Hognaston and Ladybower Inn near the Ladybower Reservoir (we have inspected almost all of these and can therefore vouch for them ourselves). The area has a dozen or so good small breweries. The main ones we found were Whim and the newish Chatsworth-based Peak Ales (already gaining ground rapidly here), and others we found in at least some good pubs were Thornbridge, Headless, Spire, Howard Town, Ashover, Brampton (another newcomer), Leadmill, Derby and Falstaff.

'Children welcome' means the pub says it lets children inside without any special restriction. If it allows them in, but to restricted areas such as an eating area or family room, we specify this. Some pubs may impose an evening time limit. We do not mention limits after 9pm as we assume children are home by then.

ALDERWASLEY   SK3153   MAP 7

Bear ★ ♀

Village signposted with Breanfield off B5035 E of Wirksworth at Malt Shovel; inn 0.5 miles SW of village, on Ambergate—Wirksworth high back road; DE56 2RD

Country inn with plenty of character in low-beamed cottagey rooms; five real ales, peaceful garden and bedrooms

We're keeping our fingers crossed for the star award this lovely old country inn carries, as new licensees took over just as we went to press – they've assured us no changes are planned. With warming open fires in winter, the dark, low-beamed rooms have a cheerful miscellany of antique furniture including high-backed settles and locally made antique oak chairs with derbyshire motifs. Other characterful décor includes Staffordshire china ornaments, old paintings and engravings, and a trio of grandfather clocks. One little room is filled right to its built-in wall seats by a single vast table. Bass, Greene King Old Speckled Hen, Timothy Taylors Landlord, Whim Hartington Bitter and a guest such as Black Sheep are on handpump, with several wines by the glass. Well spaced picnic-sets out on the side grass have peaceful country views. There's no obvious front door – you get in through the plain back entrance by the car park.

🍴 There's a large choice of food: **sandwiches, soup, prawn cocktail, battered haggis with whisky sauce, chicken caesar salad, steak and potato pie, pork with scrumpy and wholegrain mustard sauce, chicken strips in creamy thyme and white wine sauce, battered haddock, brie and spinach tartlet and steaks. You must book to be sure of a table.** *Starters/Snacks: £3.95 to £5.50. Main Courses: £3.95 to £6.95. Puddings: £4.50*

Free house ~ Licensee Pete Buller ~ Real ale ~ Bar food (12-9.30) ~ Restaurant ~ (01629) 822585 ~ Children welcome in designated areas ~ Dogs allowed in bar ~ Open 12-midnight ~ Bedrooms: £55S/£75S(£95B)

Recommended by Richard Cole, Tony and Tracy Constance, Richard, Peter F Marshall, Maurice and Gill McMahon, Cathryn and Richard Hicks, Gerald and Gabrielle Culliford, David and Carole Sayliss, Annette Tress, Gary Smith, Paul and Margaret Baker, the Didler, Jim Farmer, Alex Harper, Ken and Barbara Turner, Dean Rose, John and Enid Morris, Graeme Askham

ASHOVER   SK3462   MAP 7

Old Poets Corner 🍺 £ 🛏

Butts Road (B6036, off A632 Matlock—Chesterfield); S45 0EW

A fine range of interesting real ales and ciders in simple village pub with enthusiastic owners

One of the appeals of this comfortably unpretentious village pub is its very genuine individual character. Readers also praise the friendly welcome, and it's in lovely countryside for walkers. Another big attraction is the award winning range of ciders and perries and very good choice of perfectly kept real ales – never fewer than six and often running to eight. These typically include beers from the pub's own microbrewery, which produces Ashover Light Rail and Poet's Tipple, as well as Greene King Abbot, Timothy Taylors Landlord and quickly changing guests from brewers such as Abbeydale, Phoenix and Titanic. Other carefully chosen drinks include a dozen bottled belgian beers and a good choice of malt whiskies and fruit wines; regular beer festivals. The enthusiastic landlord is very keen on music and holds acoustic, folk and blues sessions once or twice a week – posters around the walls list the range of what's coming up, including weekly quiz nights, occasional poetry evenings and morris dancers. We visited on a quieter winter Saturday night, when there was a steady murmur of laid-back chat, and candles in bottles flickering on the tables. With a cosy, lived-in feel, the bar has a mix of chairs and pews with well worn cushions, a pile of board games by a piano, a big mirror above the fireplace, plenty of blackboards, and lots of hops around the counter; piped music; there's also a simple dining room. A small room opening off the bar has another fireplace, a stack of newspapers and vintage comics and a french door leading to a tiny balcony with a couple of tables. The bedrooms are attractive, and they also have a holiday cottage for up to eight people.

🍴 Good honest bar food, very reasonably priced and served in very generous helpings, includes soup, hot baguettes, meat pie, a good choice of vegetarian dishes like butternut squash and ginger bake, haddock and chips, a Sunday carvery and specials such as steak or sausage platter; good helpings of nice breakfasts. *Starters/Snacks: £3.25 to £5.25. Main Courses: £3.95 to £11.95. Puddings: £1.50 to £3.95*

Own brew ~ Licensees Kim and Jackie Beresford ~ Real ale ~ Bar food (12-2(3 Sun), 6.30-9) ~ (01246) 590888 ~ Children welcome in dining area ~ Dogs welcome ~ Live music Sun and Tues evenings ~ Open 12-11 ~ Bedrooms: /£70S

Recommended by the Didler, Pete Coxon, Tony Mills, Keith and Chris O'Neill, Peter F Marshall, Dr and Mrs M W A Haward, B and M Kendall, Derek and Sylvia Stephenson

BARLOW   SK3474   MAP 7

Old Pump

B6051 (Hackney Lane) towards Chesterfield; S18 7TD

Dining pub with chatty atmosphere and a garden

There's a reddish hue to the long, narrow beamed bar, which has fresh flowers, quite a few dark tables and stools, and a tiny alcove with a single table tucked beside the neatly curtained windows. It's book-ended by the dining room and two comfortably traditional little rooms, the first with big cushioned wall-benches, the other with salmon-painted walls and more substantial wooden tables for larger groups; tables are candlelit at night; piped music. Two monthly changing real ales on handpump come from brewers such as Everards and Roosters; also several malt whiskies. There are a few tables outside in front and some in the side garden which is sheltered by hedges but overlooks fields. Barlow is well known for its traditional August well-dressing festivities, and there are good walks nearby. More reports please.

🍴 Popular bar food (you do need to book at weekends) includes sandwiches, soup, prawn and smoked salmon parcels, sausage and mash, chicken breast stuffed with chicken liver pâté and wrapped in puff pastry, fish, chips and mushy peas, bass on tagliatelle with garlic and herb sauce and steaks. *Starters/Snacks: £1.50 to £6.25. Main Courses: £4.95 to £14.95. Puddings: £3.95*

Union Pub Company ~ Lease Ken Redfearn ~ Real ale ~ Bar food (12-2, 7-9(12-7 Sun)) ~ (0114) 289 0296 ~ Children welcome ~ Quiz night Mon ~ Open 12-3, 6-11; 12-11 Sun ~ Bedrooms: /£55B

Recommended by Keith and Chris O'Neill

BEELEY   SK2667   MAP 7

Devonshire Arms 🍷 🍺 🛏️

B6012, off A6 Matlock—Bakewell; DE4 2NR

Contemporary twist to lovely old interior; local beers, good wine list, interesting carefully sourced food, attractive comfortable bedrooms

Bold contemporary colours are used in stimulating contrast to attractive traditional features at this handsome old stone building. Between black beams, flagstones, stripped stone, traditional settles and cheerful log fires you will find light brightly coloured modern furnishings, prints and floral arrangements. Five changing real ales will most likely include Black Sheep, Thornbridge Jaipur IPA, Peak Ales Chatsworth Gold and Swift Nick and Theakstons, and they've 15 wines by the glass from a well chosen list and a good range of malt whiskies. It's in a pretty village, within strolling distance of Chatsworth and its huge park, and surrounded by attractive rolling scenery. Good modish new bedrooms are comfortable.

🍴 All dishes are cooked to order, and some of the produce used in the kitchens comes from the Chatsworth Estate. The short but very well balanced changing menu might include warm salad of crispy pork belly, leek and stilton tart, sausage and mash, ploughman's, shoulder and leg of lamb with chilli, ginger, potato curry and coriander and salmon with baby onions and red wine and grain mustard and puddings such as coconut panna cotta, warm rice pudding with raisins and orange marmalade and praline brûlée with gingerbread ice-cream. *Starters/Snacks: £4.95 to £10.00. Main Courses: £10.95 to £20.00. Puddings: £4.95 to £5.95*

Free house ~ Licensee Alan Hill ~ Real ale ~ Bar food (12-9.30) ~ Restaurant ~ (01629) 733259 ~ Children welcome ~ Dogs allowed in bedrooms ~ Open 12-11 ~ Bedrooms: /£145B

Recommended by Roger Hobson, Roger Yates, D F Clarke, John and Enid Morris, Stephen Wood, Bruce and Sharon Eden, Susan and John Douglas, Keith and Chris O'Neill, Dr D J and Mrs S C Walker, Paul and Margaret Baker, Maurice and Janet Thorpe, Mike and Sue Loseby, A Darroch Harkness

BRASSINGTON   SK2354 MAP 7

Olde Gate ★

Village signposted off B5056 and B5035 NE of Ashbourne; DE4 4HJ

Lovely old interior, candlelit at night, country garden

After a good number of years under the same licensee this ancient tavern has recently changed hands. It's a listed building so we are sure that the recent opening up of an unused Georgian panelled room will be a gentle improvement. It's still full of lovely old furnishings and features, from a fine ancient wall clock to rush-seated old chairs and antique settles, including one ancient black solid oak one. Log fires blaze away, gleaming copper pots sit on a 17th-c kitchen range, pewter mugs hang from a beam, and a side shelf boasts a collection of embossed Doulton stoneware flagons. To the left of a small hatch-served lobby, another cosy beamed room has stripped panelled settles, scrubbed-top tables, and a blazing fire under a huge mantelbeam. Marstons Pedigree and a couple of guests from brewers such as Hook Norton and Jennings are on handpump, and they keep a good selection of malt whiskies; board games. Stone-mullioned windows look out across lots of tables in the pleasant garden to idyllic little silvery-walled pastures, and there are some benches in the small front yard; maybe Sunday evening boules in summer and Friday evening bell-ringers. Carsington Water is a few minutes' drive away.

🍴 Under the new licensee, lunchtime bar food might include smoked salmon with fennel, orange and rocket salad, chilli beef, mushroom and pepper stroganoff, and in the evening there might be salmon and crab terrine, monkfish with wild mushrooms and cream, chicken breast with white wine and avocado sauce and beef fillet with pâté and port sauce. *Starters/Snacks: £3.95 to £4.95. Main Courses: £7.95 to £14.50. Puddings: £4.10 to £5.10*

Marstons ~ Lease Peter Scragg ~ Real ale ~ Bar food (not Mon) ~ (01629) 540448 ~ Children over 10 welcome ~ Dogs welcome ~ Open 12-2.45(3.30 Sat), 6(6.30 Sun, 7 Sun in winter)-11

Recommended by the Didler, Richard, Derek and Heather Manning, John and Enid Morris, Maurice and Gill McMahon

DERBY   SK3635 MAP 7

Alexandra 🍺

Siddals Road, just up from station; DE1 2QE

Railway-themed paraphernalia in a town pub well liked for its range of drinks

The two simple rooms here have a buoyantly chatty atmosphere, good heavy traditional furnishings on dark-stained floorboards, shelves of bottles, breweriana, and lots of railway prints and memorabilia about Derby's railway history; darts, fruit machine and piped music. As well as three or four beers from Castle Rock (brewed in Nottingham and owned by Tynemill who own this pub), constantly changing guests – sometimes bringing the complement up to as many as nine – are sourced nationally from breweries such as Peak Ales and Sharps. They also keep a big range of continental bottled beers, belgian and german beers on tap and quite a few malt whiskies. A yard has plants in pots and in borders, and Derby station is just a few minutes away.

🍴 **Bar food is confined to tasty filled rolls, available during opening times.** *Starters/Snacks: £2.00*

Tynemill ~ Licensee Alan Yates ~ Real ale ~ (01332) 293993 ~ Children welcome ~ Dogs welcome ~ Open 11-11; 12-3, 7-10.30 Sun ~ Bedrooms: £35S/£40S

Recommended by the Didler, R T and J C Moggridge, C J Fletcher, P Dawn, MP, Pam and John Smith, David Carr, Bob

Brunswick 🍺 £

Railway Terrace; close to Derby Midland station; DE1 2RU

One of Britain's oldest railwaymen's pubs, now something of a treasure trove of real ales, with its own microbrewery adjacent

Seven or eight of the 16 or so beers on handpump or tapped straight from the cask at this Victorian pub come from their own purpose built microbrewery – if you're interested you can do a tour for £7.50 (price includes a meal and a pint). As well as a couple of beers from Everards, changing guests might be from Burton Bridge, Oakham, Sharpes and Timothy Taylors. The welcoming high-ceilinged bar has heavy well padded leather seats, whisky-water jugs above the dado, and a dark blue ceiling and upper wall with squared dark panelling below. Another room is decorated with little old-fashioned prints and swan's neck lamps, and has a high-backed wall settle and a coal fire; behind a curved glazed partition wall is a chatty family parlour narrowing to the apex of the triangular building. Informative wall displays tell you about the history and restoration of the building, and there are interesting old train photographs; TV, games machines and darts. There are two outdoor seating areas, including a terrace behind. They'll gladly give dogs a bowl of water.

🍴 **Straightforward lunchtime bar food includes toasties, home-made soup, home-made quiche and home-made beef stew (filled baguettes only on Sunday and Monday).** *Starters/Snacks: £1.70 to £5.50*

Everards ~ Tenant Graham Yates ~ Real ale ~ Bar food (11.30-2.30 Mon-Thurs; 11.30-5 Fri and Sat) ~ No credit cards ~ (01332) 290677 ~ Children in family parlour ~ Dogs welcome ~ Open 11-11; 12-10.30 Sun

Recommended by C J Fletcher, Pam and John Smith, Bob, Brian and Rosalie Laverick, John Honnor, Andrew Birkinshaw, MP, the Didler, Rona Murdoch, P Dawn, David Carr

EARL STERNDALE   SK0966   MAP 7

Quiet Woman

Village signposted off B5053 S of Buxton; SK17 0BU

Unspoilt, friendly and splendidly unpretentious rural local in lovely Peak District countryside

Unchanged places like this old farm pub seem thin on the ground these days – worth taking in before they disappear completely. You can buy free-range eggs, local poetry books and even silage here, and sometimes local dry-cured bacon and raw sausages. The interior is very simple, with hard seats, plain tables (including a sunken one for dominoes or cards), low beams, quarry tiles, lots of china ornaments and a coal fire. There's a pool table in the family room (where you may be joined by a friendly jack russell eager for a place by the fire), darts, bar skittles and board games. Jennings Dark Mild and Marstons Best and Pedigree, and a guest such as Archers Best, are on handpump. They also sell gift packs of their own-label bottled beers which are Quiet Woman Old Ale, Quiet Woman Headless and Nipper Ale – the latter named after one of their previous jack russells (you can also buy Nipper or Quiet Woman woollen sweaters and polo shirts). There are picnic-sets out in front, and the budgies, hens, turkeys, ducks and donkeys are great entertainment for children. It's a popular place with walkers, with some very rewarding hikes across the nearby Dove valley towards Longnor and Hollinsclough. They have a caravan for hire in the garden, and you can arrange to stay at the small campsite next door.

🍴 **Bar food is limited to locally made pork pies.**

Free house ~ Licensee Kenneth Mellor ~ Real ale ~ Bar food ~ No credit cards ~ (01298) 83211 ~ Children allowed in pool room ~ Dogs welcome ~ Open 12-3(Sat 4, Sun 5), 7-11

Recommended by the Didler, Barry Collett, John Dwane, M J Winterton

FENNY BENTLEY   SK1750   MAP 7

Coach & Horses

A515 N of Ashbourne; DE6 1LB

Cosy former coaching inn with pretty country furnishings and roaring open fires

This 17th-c rendered stone house has a gently civilised atmosphere, with most people here for the enjoyable food. The main part of the building is quite traditional, with flagstone floors, black beams hung with horsebrasses and wagon wheels, and pewter mugs and prints, hand-made pine furniture that includes flowery-cushioned wall settles and exposed brick hearths. There's also a conservatory dining room; quiet piped music, cards, board games and dominoes. Marstons Pedigree and a couple of guests such as Abbeydale Moonshine or Timothy Taylors Landlord are on handpump, and the landlord is knowledgeable about malt whiskies (he stocks about three dozen). Outside, there are views across fields from tables in the side garden by an elder tree, and modern tables and chairs under cocktail parasols on the front terrace. The ever-popular Tissington Trail is a short stroll away.

Ⅱ **Served by efficient uniformed staff, the well liked bar food might include lunchtime sandwiches, baguettes and ploughman's, soup, smoked salmon with citrus, dill and peppercorn dressing, roast mediterranean vegetable tart, rabbit and bacon puff pastry pie, barnsley chop with redcurrant, thyme and red wine gravy, sirloin steak, and puddings such as hot cross bun bread and butter pudding and spotted dick and custard; they also do fish specials such as fried tuna with tomato salsa and balsamic syrup on Fridays, and Sunday roasts.** *Starters/Snacks: £3.75 to £4.95. Main Courses: £8.25 to £15.00. Puddings: £4.25 to £4.75*

Free house ~ Licensees John and Matthew Dawson ~ Real ale ~ Bar food (12-9) ~
No credit cards ~ (01335) 350246 ~ Children welcome ~ Open 11-11; 12-10.30 Sun

Recommended by the Didler, Dudley Newell, Brian and Rosalie Laverick, M J Winterton, Mrs Tessa Hibbert, Ken and Barbara Turner, Glenwys and Alan Lawrence, Phil and Jane Hodson, Maurice and Gill McMahon, Mr and Mrs John Taylor

FOOLOW   SK1976   MAP 7

Bulls Head

Village signposted off A623 Baslow—Tideswell; S32 5QR

A cheerfully run inn by a village green, with well kept ales and decent food

'Dogs, muddy boots and children on leads' are all welcome at this friendly village pub. It's in an enjoyable area for a good country walk – from here you can follow paths out over rolling pasture enclosed by dry-stone walls, and the plague village of Eyam is not far away, or you can just stroll round the green and duck pond. The simply furnished flagstoned bar has interesting photographs including a good collection of Edwardian naughties, and well kept Adnams, Black Sheep, Peak Ale Swift Nick and a guest beer from a brewer such as Caledonian on handpump and they've just over two dozen malts; piped music, board games and darts. A step or two takes you down into what may once have been a stables with its high ceiling joists, stripped stone and woodburning stove. On the other side, a sedate partly panelled dining room has more polished tables and plates arranged around on delft shelves. The west highland terriers are called Holly and Jack. Picnic-sets at the side have nice views.

Ⅱ **Tasty bar food includes lunchtime snacks such as sandwiches and hot filled baps, as well as soup, thai fishcakes with sweet chilli sauce, sausages with yorkshire pudding, steak and ale pie and cajun chicken. The evening menu is slightly more restaurant, with dishes such as warm salad of black pudding and chorizo sausage, duck and mango salad, roast bass with fennel and beef wellington. They do a good value OAP two-course lunch menu during the week, and on Tuesday and Wednesday nights good value steak and chicken deals.** *Starters/Snacks: £3.75 to £5.25. Main Courses: £7.50 to £13.95. Puddings: £4.25 to £4.50*

Free house ~ Licensee William Leslie Bond ~ Real ale ~ Bar food (12-2, 6.30-9(5-8 Sun)) ~
Restaurant ~ (01433) 630873 ~ Children welcome ~ Dogs allowed in bar and bedrooms ~
Live music Fri evening ~ Open 12-3, 6.30-11; 12-10.30 Sun; closed Mon except bank hols ~
Bedrooms: £50S/£70S

Recommended by Eddie Edwards, Richard, David and Carole Sayliss, Peter F Marshall, Sean A Smith

HASSOP   SK2272   MAP 7

Eyre Arms

B6001 N of Bakewell; DE45 1NS

Neatly kept comfortable creeper-covered pub, with pretty views from the garden and decent food

Cheery log fires warm the low ceilinged oak beamed rooms at this 17th-c stone former farmhouse, the dining room of which is dominated by a painting of the Eyre coat of arms above the stone fireplace. Other traditional furnishings include cushioned oak settles, comfortable plush chairs, a long-case clock, old pictures and lots of brass and copper. The small public bar has an unusual collection of teapots, as well as Black Sheep, Marstons Pedigree and Theakstons Black Bull on handpump, and several wines by the glass; piped classical music, darts, board games. A fountain gurgles in the pretty small garden, where tables look out over beautiful peak district countryside.

⑪ The fairly standard bar menu includes lunchtime sandwiches, soup, thai-style crab cakes, fried garlic mushrooms, breaded plaice, steak and kidney pie, mushroom stroganoff, steaks, and puddings such as pear and almond tart and bread and butter pudding. *Starters/Snacks: £4.00 to £6.75. Main Courses: £7.95 to £14.95. Puddings: £4.45*

Free house ~ Licensee Lynne Smith ~ Real ale ~ Bar food (12-2, 6.30-9) ~ (01629) 640390 ~ Children welcome ~ Open 11-3, 6.30-11(10.30 Sun); closed Mon evenings Nov-Easter

Recommended by Susan and John Douglas, DC, Malcolm Pellatt, A N Duerr, B and M Kendall, Chris Brooks

HATHERSAGE   SK2380   MAP 7

Plough ⑪ 🍷 🛏

Leadmill; B6001 towards Bakewell, OS Sheet 110 map reference 235805; S32 1BA

Comfortable dining pub usefully placed for exploring the Peak District with good food and wine, waterside garden and bedrooms

With emphasis very much on the comfortable accommodation and upmarket dining, this is a popular place for a short stay. The fairly traditional neatly kept bar has dark wood tables (all laid for dining), a big log fire at one end and a woodburning stove at the other; quiet piped music. They've a good wine list (with a dozen by the glass), 25 malt whiskies, and three changing real ales that might include as Batemans, Fullers London Pride and Youngs. The pretty suntrap garden goes right down to the River Derwent.

⑪ As well as lunchtime pubby standards such as fish and chips, ploughman's and pie of the day, the changing menu might include escabeche of sardines, ham, fig and almond salad, baked pollack with samphire and cockle beurre blanc, medallions of home-smoked venison with beetroot jus, tempura vegetables with stir fried spring vegetables and peanut sauce, saddle of rabbit wrapped in pancetta with prune compote and rib-eye steak with hand-cut chips. Food is not cheap. *Starters/Snacks: £4.50 to £7.95. Main Courses: £9.95 to £13.95. Puddings: £4.50 to £6.95*

Free house ~ Licensees Bob, Cynthia and Elliott Emery ~ Real ale ~ Bar food (11.30-2.30, 6-9.30 Mon-Fri; 11.30-9.30 Sat; 12-9 Sun) ~ Restaurant ~ (01433) 650319 ~ Children welcome ~ Open 11-11; 12-10.30 Sun ~ Bedrooms: £60B/£90B

Recommended by Kevin Thomas, Nina Randall, Richard Marjoram, Barry and Anne, Tom and Ruth Rees, Susan and Nigel Brookes, Richard and Emily Whitworth, Paul and Gail Betteley, DC, Roger Yates, Mrs R A Cartwright, Bruce and Sharon Eden, John Robertson, Darren and Kirstin Arnold, Mr and Mrs W W Burke, Brian and Jacky Wilson

---

Scotsmans Pack 🛏

School Lane, off A6187; S32 1BZ

A perennially popular inn that strikes just the right note for food, service, beer and general attitude

This spotlessly kept and civilised place ticks many boxes. Walkers are made to feel very welcome (you can get a good sandwich here), it's a good place to stay and the enjoyable food is sensibly priced. Perhaps the nicest area is on the left as you enter, with a fireplace, and patterned wallpaper somewhat obscured by a splendid mass of brasses, stuffed animal heads and the like. Elsewhere there's plenty of dark panelling, lots of hanging tankards, plates on delft shelving and other knick-knacks arranged around the bar, and a good few tables, many with reserved signs (it's worth booking ahead, particularly at weekends). Five real ales, kept under light blanket pressure, might be from Hook Norton and Marstons; service remains prompt and cheery even when busy; piped music, games machine, TV, board games and darts. Outside is a small but very pleasant terrace, next to a trout-filled stream (one reader was sceptical about the idea that a stream could be filled with trout, but his scepticism was confounded after watching it for five minutes). This is close to the church where Little John is said to be buried.

🍴 **Good food includes sandwiches, thai fishcakes, button mushrooms in a peppercorn, cream and brandy sauce, feta cheese, parma ham and plum salad, lasagne, steak in ale pie, gammon with pineapple and egg, chicken with lemon and thyme sauce, fried bass fillet with crayfish tails and garlic butter and sirloin steak.** *Starters/Snacks: £3.75 to £5.95. Main Courses: £8.95 to £17.50. Puddings: £4.25*

Marstons ~ Lease Nick Beagrie, Steve Bramley and Susan Concannon ~ Real ale ~ Bar food ~ Restaurant ~ (01433) 650253 ~ Children welcome ~ Open 11.30-3, 5.30-11; 11.30-11 Fri, Sat; 11.30-10.30 Sun ~ Bedrooms: £45S/£75B

Recommended by Dr D J and Mrs S C Walker, David Crook, Bruce and Sharon Eden, Carole Hall, John Branston, Keith and Chris O'Neill, David Carr, Malcolm Pellatt, Peter F Marshall, K Almond, Richard Marjoram, Barry and Anne, Susan and Nigel Brookes, Dennis Jones

HAYFIELD   SK0388   MAP 7

Lantern Pike 🛏

Glossop Road (A624 N) at Little Hayfield, just N of Hayfield; SK22 2NG

Friendly retreat from the surrounding moors of Kinder Scout with reasonably priced food and bedrooms

The traditional red plush bar at this cheerfully run pub proudly displays photos of the original *Coronation Street* cast, many of whom were regulars here, along with Terry Warren, one of its earlier script writers and Arthur Lowe of *Dad's Army* fame. It's quite possible that the interior, with its warm fire, brass platters in numbers, china and toby jugs, fresh flowers on the tables and counter lined with red plush stools (Black Sheep and Timothy Taylors Landlord, a guest such as Howard Town Wrens Nest, and several malt whiskies) hasn't changed much since those days – certainly its homely feel can't have; TV and piped music. Tables on a stonewalled terrace look over a big-windowed weaver's house towards the hill of Lantern Pike, and there are plenty of challenging walks on to the moors of Kinder Scout.

🍴 **As well as sandwiches, the changing blackboard menu might include soup, spicy chicken wings, vegetarian dish of the day, chilli, braised lamb cutlets with mint gravy, sausage and mash, curries and puddings such as sherry trifle and fruit crumble.** *Starters/Snacks: £3.50 to £4.25. Main Courses: £7.95 to £11.50. Puddings: £3.75*

Enterprise ~ Lease Stella and Tom Cunliffe ~ Real ale ~ Bar food (12-2(not Mon lunchtime), 5-8(8.45 Fri); 12-8.45(5.45 Sun) Sat) ~ Restaurant ~ (01663) 747590 ~ Children welcome ~ Dogs welcome ~ Open 12-11; 5-11 Mon in winter ~ Bedrooms: £40B/£60B

Recommended by Chris Brooks, John and Helen Rushton, Bob Broadhurst, David and Sue Atkinson, Len Beattie, Malcolm Pellatt

Royal
Market Street, just off A624 Chapel-en-le-Frith—Buxton; SK22 2EP

Bustling old-fashioned hotel

On fine days, drinkers spill out on to the sunny terrace in front of this traditional old place. Inside, some nice old dark panelling recalls the building's former life as a vicarage. Separate feeling areas work their way round a counter and have several fireplaces, bookshelves, brasses and house plants, newspapers to read, board games and piped music. Friendly staff serve Hydes and four guest ales from brewers such as Everards and Roosters on handpump, and they keep around 16 malts and a farm cider; October beer festival.

🍴 **The good value very traditional bar menu includes sandwiches, soup, spinach and mushroom pancake, cod and chips, chicken madras, gammon, egg and pineapple, roast beef, and sirloin steak.** *Starters/Snacks: £3.50 to £4.95. Main Courses: £4.50 to £9.50. Puddings: £1.50 to £3.95*

Free house ~ Licensee David Ash ~ Real ale ~ Bar food (12-2.15, 6-8.30; 12-9(6 Sun and bank hols) Sat) ~ Restaurant ~ (01663) 742721 ~ Children welcome ~ Open 11-11(midnight Sat); 12-10.30 Sun ~ Bedrooms: £45B/£60B

Recommended by the Didler, Gwyn Wake, P Dawn

HOLBROOK   SK3645   MAP 7

Dead Poets 🍺 £
Village signposted off A6 S of Belper; Chapel Street; DE56 0TQ

Reassuringly pubby and unchanged, with an excellent range of real ales and simple cottagey décor

Readers enjoy the unpretentious and cheerfully chatty atmosphere at this unspoilt place. Although there's a range of basic snacks, beer is the thing, with eight well kept real ales on handpump or served in jugs from the cellar: Greene King Abbot and Marstons Pedigree with guests from breweries such as Abbeydale, Caledonian, Exmoor, Hartington, Hop Back and Theakstons. They also serve Old Rosie farm cider and country wines. It's quite a dark interior with low black beams in the ochre ceiling, stripped stone walls and broad flagstones, although there is a lighter conservatory at the back. There are candles on scrubbed tables, a big log fire in the end stone fireplace, high-backed winged settles forming snug cubicles along one wall, and pews and a variety of chairs in other intimate corners and hideaways. The décor makes a few nods to the pub's present name (it used to be the Cross Keys) including a photo of W B Yeats and a poem dedicated to the pub by Les Baynton, and there are old prints of Derby; piped music. Behind is a sort of verandah room with lanterns, heaters, fairy lights and a few plants, and more seats out in the yard.

🍴 **Alongside cobs (nothing else on Sundays), bar food is limited to a few good value hearty dishes such as home-made soup and chilli con carne or casserole.** *Starters/Snacks: £2.00 to £4.25*

Everards ~ Tenant William Holmes ~ Real ale ~ Bar food (12-2 only) ~ No credit cards ~ (01332) 780301 ~ Children welcome in conservatory till 8pm ~ Dogs welcome ~ Open 12-2.30, 5-12; 12-midnight Fri, Sat; 12-11 Sun

Recommended by Kerry Law, Rona Murdoch, the Didler, Richard, JJW, CMW

HOPE   SK1783   MAP 7

Cheshire Cheese 🛏
Off A6187, towards Edale; S33 6ZF

Cosy up-and-down old stone pub in attractive Peak District village; bedrooms

The three very snug oak-beamed rooms at this 16th-c pub are arranged on different levels, each with its own coal fire. It's a very popular place, with a true local following and at certain times plenty of tourists, so as parking is limited it might be worth arriving on foot: there is a glorious range of local walks, taking in the summits of Lose Hill and Win Hill, or the cave district of the Castleton area, and the village of Hope itself is worth strolling around. Black Sheep Bitter and Whim Hartington plus guests from brewers such as Adnams and Timothy Taylor and Peak Ales are on handpump, and they've a good range of spirits and several wines by the glass; piped music. The pub was recently taken over by Enterprise so we're very much keeping our fingers crossed for its unspoilt atmosphere; please do send us your feedback.

🍴 As well as lunchtime snacks such as sandwiches and salads, food includes grilled black pudding with mustard sauce, steak and kidney suet pudding, mixed grill, cream cheese and broccoli bake and roast fried cod with prawn and dill sauce, lamb shank in minted gravy, a few changing specials, and puddings such as spotted dick or chocolate pudding in chocolate sauce. *Starters/Snacks: £3.50 to £5.45. Main Courses: £8.95 to £12.95. Puddings: £3.95 to £4.50*

Enterprise ~ Lease Craig Oxley ~ Real ale ~ Bar food (12-2(3.30 Sat), 6.30-9; 12-5 Sun) ~ Restaurant ~ (01433) 620381 ~ Dogs allowed in bar ~ Open 12-3, 6.30-11; 12-11.30 Sat; 12-7 Sun; closed Sun evening ~ Bedrooms: £50S/£65S(£75B)

Recommended by Virginia Williams, Malcolm Pellatt, Dr and Mrs J Temporal, David and Carole Sayliss, Chris Brooks, Pete Baker, the Didler, Alan Sutton, Peter F Marshall

KIRK IRETON   SK2650   MAP 7

Barley Mow 🍺 🛏

Village signed off B5023 S of Wirksworth; DE6 3JP

Character-laden old inn that focuses on real ale and conversation rather than food

The dimly lit passageways, narrow stairwells and rooms tucked inside this striking three-storey 17th-c Jacobean house are timeless and unchanging. With a good mix of customers of all ages and a very kindly landlady, it's a place to sit and chat. The small main bar has a relaxed very pubby feel, with antique settles on the tiled floor or built into the panelling, a roaring coal fire, four slate-topped tables and shuttered mullioned windows. Another room has built-in cushioned pews on oak parquet and a small woodburning stove, and a third room has more pews, a tiled floor, low beams and big landscape prints. In casks behind a modest wooden counter are five well kept, often local, changing real ales from brewers such as Abbeydale, Burton Bridge, Peak Ales, Sharps and Storm; farm cider too. There's a good-sized garden, a couple of benches out in front and a shop in what used to be the stable; the hilltop village is very pretty, and within walking distance of Carsington Water. Bedrooms are comfortable and readers enjoy the good breakfasts served in the stone-flagged kitchen.

🍴 Very inexpensive lunchtime filled rolls are the only food; the decent evening meals are reserved for those staying here. *Starters/Snacks: £1.25*

Free house ~ Licensee Mary Short ~ Real ale ~ No credit cards ~ (01335) 370306 ~ Children welcome away from bar ~ Dogs allowed in bar and bedrooms ~ Open 12-2, 7-11(10.30 Sun) ~ Bedrooms: £35S/£55B

Recommended by David Martin, Simon Fox, Pete Baker, Mavis Devine, the Didler

LADYBOWER RESERVOIR   SK2084   MAP 7

Yorkshire Bridge 🛏

A6013 N of Bamford; S33 0AZ

Comfortably old-fashioned hotel close to the Upper Derwent Valley Reservoirs

This pleasantly genteel inn sits in dramatic country, beneath forested and moorland slopes just south of the Ladybower Reservoir dam. Inside, one area has a country cottage feel with floral wallpaper, sturdy cushioned wall settles, staffordshire dogs and toby jugs above a big stone fireplace, china on delft shelves, and a panelled dado. Another extensive area, also with a fire, is lighter and more airy with pale wood furniture, good big black and white photographs and lots of polished brass and decorative plates on the walls. The Bridge Room (with yet another fire) has oak tables and chairs, and the Garden Room gives views across a valley to steep larch woods. Black Sheep, Copper Dragon Best Bitter and Golden Pippin and Theakstons Old Peculier are on handpump; darts, dominoes, games machine and piped music; disabled lavatories.

🍴 Well liked bar food includes soup, salads, quiche, battered haddock, pot-roasted lamb with minted gravy, steak and kidney pie, and sirloin steak. *Starters/Snacks: £4.25 to £5.75. Main Courses: £8.25 to £14.00. Puddings: £4.50*

Free house ~ Licensees Trevelyan and John Illingworth ~ Real ale ~ Bar food (12-2, 6-9 (9.30 Fri, Sat); 12-8.30 Sun) ~ (01433) 651361 ~ Children welcome ~ Open 10-11(10.30 Sun) ~ Bedrooms: £60B/£96B

Recommended by Mike and Sue Loseby, Bruce and Sharon Eden, Bob, Brian and Jean Hepworth, Malcolm Pellatt, James A Waller, Hilary Forrest, Cedric Robertshaw, Brian and Anna Marsden, David and Carole Sayliss

LITTON   SK1675   MAP 7

Red Lion
Village signposted off A623, between B6465 and B6049 junctions; also signposted off B6049; SK17 8QU

Convivial all-rounder with unspoilt charm, prettily placed by village green

The landlady at this 18th-c village pub caringly oversees a particularly welcoming and enjoyable establishment. The two homely linked front rooms have low beams and some panelling, and blazing log fires. There's a bigger back room with good-sized tables, and large antique prints on its stripped stone walls. The small bar counter has very well kept Oakwell Barnsley and a couple of guests such as Abbeydale Absolution and Whim Hartington, with a good choice of decent wines and several malt whiskies; darts, board games and piped music. Outdoor seating is on the pretty village green, which is covered in daffodils in early spring. A particularly interesting time to visit this village is during the annual well-dressing carnival (usually the last weekend in June), when locals create a picture from flower petals, moss and other natural materials.

🍴 Well liked bar food includes filled baguettes, soup, cock-a-leekie pie, steak, ale and mushroom casserole, cumberland or vegetarian sausage and mash, and specials such as garlic and rosemary lamb shank and trout fillet with cream and herb sauce. *Starters/Snacks: £3.50 to £4.95. Main Courses: £6.95 to £9.95. Puddings: £3.95 to £4.50*

Enterprise ~ Lease Suzy Turner ~ Real ale ~ Bar food (12-2, 6-8; 12-8.30 Thurs-Sun) ~ (01298) 871458 ~ Children over 6 welcome ~ Dogs allowed in bar ~ Open 12-11(midnight Fri, Sat); 12-10.30 Sun

Recommended by Peter F Marshall, Hazel Matthews, Gary Rollings, Debbie Porter, Mrs Jordan, Richard, B and M Kendall, WAH, Chris Brooks, Paul and Margaret Baker, the Didler, Susan and John Douglas, Alan Thwaite, Phil Taylor, Sian Watkin, Dr and Mrs J Temporal, Maurice and Janet Thorpe

MELBOURNE   SK3427   MAP 7

John Thompson 🍴 £
Ingleby, which is NW of Melbourne; turn off A514 at Swarkestone Bridge or in Stanton by Bridge; can also be reached from Ticknall (or from Repton on B5008); DE73 7HW

Own-brew pub that strikes the right balance between attentive service, roomy comfort and good value food

This much enjoyed pub (it's named after its owner) has featured in every edition of this *Guide*. Everything ticks along in a perfectly relaxed way, with plenty of readers enthusing about the quality of the beer brewed out back here, the tasty good value food, and the friendly efficient staff. Simple but comfortable, the big modernised lounge has ceiling joists, some old oak settles, button-back leather seats, sturdy oak tables, antique prints and paintings and a log-effect gas fire; piped music. A couple of smaller cosier rooms open off; piano, games machine, board games, TV, and pool in the conservatory. They usually serve three of their own beers but may supplement a guest such as Black Sheep or Greene King IPA. Surrounded by pretty countryside and near the Trent river, there are lots of tables by flowerbeds on the neat lawns, or you can sit on the partly covered terrace. Six detached chalet lodges have recently been built in the grounds – we'd love to know what you think if you stay here.

🍴 **The short menu includes sandwiches, soup, beef, ham or cheese salads, beef carvery, and puddings like crumble or dark chocolate and pecan fudge brownie.** *Starters/Snacks: £2.50 to £3.80. Main Courses: £5.75 to £6.75. Puddings: £2.50 to £2.75*

Own brew ~ Licensee Nick Thompson ~ Real ale ~ Bar food (lunchtime only) ~ (01332) 862469 ~ Children welcome in conservatory ~ Dogs welcome ~ Open 11-2.30, 6-11; 11-11 Sat; 12-10.30 Sun; closed Mon lunchtime ~ Bedrooms: /£55S

Recommended by the Didler, N R White, Pete Baker, Michael Lamm, Annette Tress, Gary Smith, Pat and Peter Grove, Gwyn and Anne Wake, Mr and Mrs J T Clarke, Theo, Anne and Jane Gaskin, Rona Murdoch, Paul J Robinshaw, Mr and Mrs T Wilkinson, Barbara Parker, P and I Gowan, Ian and Jane Irving

MONSAL HEAD
SK1871 MAP 7

Monsal Head Hotel 🍺 🛏
B6465; DE45 1NL

Popular hilltop inn with good food, beer and friendly staff; worth seeking out for the view alone

---

You'll find the best selection of real ales and most relaxing atmosphere (and maybe muddy walkers and their dogs) in the cosy stable bar. In days gone by the stables here gave shelter to the horses that used to pull guests and their luggage up from the station at the other end of the steep valley – stripped timber horse-stalls, harness and brassware, and lamps from the disused station itself, all hint at those days. There are cushioned oak pews around the tables on the flagstone floor, and the big warming open fire is quite a feature. Lloyds Monsal Bitter and Theakstons Best are kept alongside four guests from local brewers such as Thornbridge or Whim, a good choice of german bottled beers and at least a dozen wines by the glass; board games. One of Derbyshire's most classic views is from this very spot, looking down to a bend in steep-sided Monsal Dale with its huge railway viaduct, which is now crossed by the Monsal Trail. The best places to admire this terrific view are from the big windows in the smarter lounge, four of the seven bedrooms and the extensive garden.

🍴 **Under new licensees, the well liked bar food includes lunchtime sandwiches, as well as butternut and roquefort double baked soufflé, several interesting salads, battered cod, chicken breast filled with stilton and wrapped in smoked bacon with white wine cream sauce, roast bacon with honey roast vegetables and mustard sauce, and a couple of specials such as roast duck breast with red wine sauce; puddings such as lemon posset with a ginger biscuit topping.** *Starters/Snacks: £3.00 to £6.00. Main Courses: £5.00 to £15.00. Puddings: £3.00 to £6.00*

Free house ~ Licensee Sarah Belfield ~ Real ale ~ Bar food (12-9.30(9 Sun)) ~ Restaurant ~ (01629) 640250 ~ Children welcome ~ Dogs allowed in bar ~ Open 11.30-midnight ~ Bedrooms: £65B/£90B

Recommended by Bruce and Sharon Eden, Pam and John Smith, Greta and Guy Pratt, Gary Rollings, Debbie Porter, N R White, Mike and Sue Loseby, the Didler, Peter F Marshall, Susan and John Douglas, Paul and Margaret Baker, Rona Murdoch, Keith and Chris O'Neill, Mark and Diane Grist, P Dawn, Cathryn and Richard Hicks

MONYASH
SK1566 MAP 7

Bulls Head
B5055 W of Bakewell; DE45 1JH

Unpretentious local with very tasty home cooking

Good traditional food is served at this very friendly village inn. Its high-ceilinged rooms are quite simple with a good log fire, straightforward furnishings, horse pictures and a shelf of china. A small back bar room has darts, games machine, juke box and pool; may be quiet piped music. Burton Ale, John Smiths and a guest such as Bradfield Farmers Blonde are on handpump. A gate from the pub's garden leads into a nice new village play area, and this is fine walking country.

🍴 **Bar food (very sensibly priced) includes sandwiches, ploughman's, salads, garlic mushrooms, steak and kidney pie, casseroles, breaded fish and puddings such as fresh fruit pavlova and banoffi pie.** *Starters/Snacks: £4.50 to £6.00. Main Courses: £8.00 to £14.00. Puddings: £4.00 to £4.50*

Free house ~ Licensee Sharon Barber ~ Real ale ~ Bar food (12-2.30, 6.30-9; 12-9 Sun) ~ (01629) 812372 ~ Children welcome ~ Dogs welcome ~ Live music alt Sats ~ Open 12-3, 6(6.30 winter)-midnight; 12-1am Fri, Sat; 11.30am-midnight Sun ~ Bedrooms: £25/£45

Recommended by Mrs Deborah Chalmers, Mike Wass, Ian Stafford, S P Watkin, P A Taylor, Pam and John Smith, Eddie and Lynn Jarrett, Mrs M Shardlow

OVER HADDON   SK2066   MAP 7

Lathkil 🍺

Village and inn signposted from B5055 just SW of Bakewell; DE45 1JE

Traditional pub well placed for Lathkill Dale with super views, good range of beers and decent food

Little changes from year to year at this well liked country inn where Robert Grigor-Taylor has been licensee for more than a quarter of a century. It's popular with a varied clientele, from day trippers to hikers (dogs are welcome but muddy boots must be left in the lobby) and can get very busy. The walled garden is a good place to sit and soak in the views over the bewitchingly secretive surroundings of Lathkill Dale, and there are great views from the pub windows too. The airy room on the right as you go in has a nice fire in the attractively carved fireplace, old-fashioned settles with upholstered cushions and chairs, black beams, a delft shelf of blue and white plates, original prints and photographs, and big windows. On the left, the sunny spacious dining area doubles as an evening restaurant. They keep Everards Tiger and Whim Hartington, three guests from brewers such as Bradfield, Cottage and Peak Ales on handpump, a reasonable range of wines and a decent selection of soft drinks; piped music, darts, shove-ha'penny and dominoes.

🍴 **The popular buffet-style lunch menu includes simple filled rolls, mediterranean vegetable and pine nut pie, several salads, shepherd's pie and venison and blackberry casserole. The evening menu is a little different, with chicken satay, battered cod, roast duck breast with cumberland sauce; good puddings such as blackberry and apple crumble.** *Starters/Snacks: £4.25 to £5.25. Main Courses: £7.00 to £11.50. Puddings: £3.50 to £4.00*

Free house ~ Licensee Robert Grigor-Taylor ~ Real ale ~ Bar food (12-2(2.30 Sat, Sun), 6(7 Fri, Sat)-8) ~ Restaurant ~ (01629) 812501 ~ Children welcome ~ Dogs welcome ~ Open 11.30-3, 6-10.30 Sun; 11.30-3, 6-11 Mon-Fri in winter ~ Bedrooms: £45B/£65S(£80B)

Recommended by Hilary Forrest, Roderick Braithwaite, Dr and Mrs R G J Telfer, Peter F Marshall, Richard, Gwyn and Anne Wake, Malcolm Pellatt, Chris Brooks, Guy Vowles, the Didler, Mrs Jordan, Brian and Anna Marsden, R M Chard

SHELDON   SK1768   MAP 7

Cock & Pullet £

Village signposted off A6 just W of Ashford; DE45 1QS

Well run village local with an appealingly unpretentious atmosphere and good value bar food

A collection of 30 clocks, various representations of poultry (including some stuffed) and a cheerful assembly of deliberately mismatched furnishings greets you from the cosy little rooms at this family-run pub. With its low beams, exposed stonework, flagstones, scrubbed oak tables, pews and open fire it looks like it's been a pub for hundreds of years, but surprisingly it was only converted some dozen years ago. A plainer public bar has pool, darts, dominoes, board games and a TV; piped music. Black Sheep and Timothy Taylors Landlord are on handpump with one guest. At the back a pleasant little terrace has tables and a water feature, and as this pretty village is just off the Limestone Way it's a popular all year round stop with walkers.

🍴 **Very reasonably priced bar food includes soup, sandwiches, fish pie, a curry of the day, a vegetarian dish, steak in ale pie, minted lamb casserole and specials; Sunday roast.** *Starters/Snacks: £2.75. Main Courses: £6.25. Puddings: £2.75*

Free house ~ Licensees David and Kath Melland ~ Real ale ~ Bar food (12-2.30, 6-9) ~ No credit cards ~ (01629) 814292 ~ Children welcome ~ Dogs welcome ~ Open 11-11; 12-10.30 Sun ~ Bedrooms: /£60B

Recommended by Chris Brooks, Jo Lilley, Simon Calvert, J and E Dakin, Dave Webster, Sue Holland, Peter F Marshall, Martin Peters, S P Watkin, P A Taylor, Brian and Anna Marsden, DC

WOOLLEY MOOR
SK3661   MAP 7

White Horse
Badger Lane, off B6014 Matlock—Clay Cross; DE55 6FG

Enthusiastic young licensee couple offering very good food at attractive old stone building in pretty countryside

This lovely old inn was built on the original pack horse route from the toll bar cottage at Stretton to Woolley Moor toll bar. The sign in front of the pub depicts a horse and cart carrying a badger (a measure of salt) down the toll road. Inside there's a buoyantly chatty feel to the tap room, with Black Sheep and a couple of guests such as Greene King Abbot and Peak Ales Bakwell Best on handpump, and great views of Ogston Reservoir from the conservatory; piped music. The garden has a boules pitch, picnic-sets, and a children's play area with a wooden train, boat, climbing frame and swings. More reports please.

🍴 **Good bar food includes smoked haddock and salmon fishcakes, mussels in coconut, lime and chilli sauce, tomato, goats cheese and basil tart, battered cod, duck breast with black cherry jus and steaks** *Starters/Snacks: £4.95 to £5.75. Main Courses: £9.95 to £14.95. Puddings: £4.95*

Free house ~ Licensees David and Melanie Boulby ~ Real ale ~ Bar food (12-2(3 Sun), 5.30-9; not Sun evening) ~ Restaurant ~ (01246) 590319 ~ Children welcome ~ Open 12-2.30, 5.30-11; 12-3, 6-10.30 Sun

Recommended by Phil and Jane Hodson, MP, Robert F Smith

LUCKY DIP

Besides the fully inspected pubs, you might like to try these Lucky Dips recommended to us and described by readers (if you do, please send us reports: feedback@thegoodpubguide.co.uk).

ASHBOURNE [SK1846]
Olde Vaults DE6 1EU [Market Pl]: Imposing and attractive building, cheerful staff, generous bargain food, well kept Bass, Caledonian Deuchars IPA and Marstons Pedigree, farm cider, good local atmosphere in simple open-plan bar; seats out in front, bedrooms, huge breakfast, open all day wknds and summer *(George Atkinson)*
ASHFORD IN THE WATER [SK1969]
☆ *Bulls Head* DE45 1QB [Church St]: Comfortable two-bar beamed pub dating from 16th c and well run by welcoming old-school landlord, well kept Banks's and Robinsons, good proper food from lunchtime sandwiches up inc some unusual dishes, reasonable prices, cheery

fire, daily papers; may be piped music; overshoes for walkers, tables out behind and in front, lovely village *(Martin Peters, Justin and Emma King, Peter F Marshall, David and Carole Sayliss, Mr and Mrs Staples, Richard Farmer)*
ASHOVER [SK3463]
Black Swan S45 0AB [Church St]: Good value food inc good range of sandwiches in open-plan bar, prompt cheerful service, well kept ales; popular with younger people wknds, may be live music *(the Didler)*
Crispin S45 0AB [Church St]: Well run carefully extended old building with very welcoming staff, reasonably priced enjoyable food, well kept Marstons-related real ale, log fires, several

attractive areas from beamed original core to back conservatory *(Jennifer Little, Darryl Wall, Barry Steele-Perkins)*

BASLOW [SK2772]

Robin Hood DE45 1PQ [A619/B6050]: Fairly modern, well decorated and comfortable, with tidy banquettes, good reasonably priced food from sandwiches up, well kept Marstons-related ales, friendly landlord, big uncarpeted back bar for walkers, climbers and dogs; bedrooms, good walking country nr Baslow Edge *(Dr D J and Mrs S C Walker)*

BELPER [SK3547]

Cross Keys DE56 1FZ [Market Pl]: Friendly two-room pub with well kept Bass, Batemans and a guest beer, bar food, coal fire in lounge, bar billiards; open all day *(the Didler)*

Fishermans Rest DE56 2JF [Broadholme Lane]: Recently refurbished, with well kept Marstons Pedigree and a related guest beer, enjoyable food, great view; garden with play area, pleasant surroundings *(John and Carol Shepherd)*

Queens Head DE56 1FF [Chesterfield Rd]: Simple three-room pub with well kept ales such as Caledonian Deuchars IPA, Jennings Cumberland, Tetleys and Timothy Taylors Landlord, nourishing rolls, constant coal fire, local photographs; good upstairs wknd band nights, beer festivals; good views from terrace tables, open all day Fri-Sun *(the Didler)*

BIRCH VALE [SK0186]

☆ *Sycamore* SK22 1AB [Sycamore Rd; from A6015 take Station Rd towards Thornsett]: Extensively reworked four-room dining pub, wide choice of good value up-to-date food (all day Sun), well kept John Smiths and Timothy Taylors Landlord, good choice of wines by the glass, genuinely welcoming service, contemporary furnishings; may be piped music; children welcome, spacious streamside gardens with good play area and summer bar, handy for Sett Valley trail, five comfortable bedrooms *(Rob Watson, Doug Christian, LYM)*

Waltzing Weasel SK22 1BT [New Mills Rd (A6015 E of New Mills)]: Civilised nicely furnished wine-bar-style pub with well kept Marstons, decent wines, friendly efficient staff, bar food, cosy fire, daily papers, some Thurs live jazz; children and dogs welcome, disabled access, bedrooms with nice views *(Dennis Jones, LYM, David Hoult, Brian and Anita Randall)*

BONSALL [SK2758]

☆ *Barley Mow* DE4 2AY [off A6012 Cromford—Hartington; The Dale]: Friendly tucked-away pub with well kept Whim Hartington, Greene King Abbot and a guest beer, fresh sandwiches and other decent plain food, character furnishings, coal fire, tiny pool room; live music Sat inc landlord playing

accordion or keyboards, runs local walks and idiosyncratic special events; small front terrace, cl wkdy lunchtimes and Mon, open all day wknds *(Richard, Rona Murdoch, the Didler)*

BUXTON [SK1266]

☆ *Bull i' th' Thorn* SK17 9QQ [Ashbourne Rd (A515) 6 miles S of Buxton, nr Flagg and Hurdlow]: Fascinating medieval hall doubling as straightforward roadside dining pub, handsome panelling, old flagstones and big log fire, armour, longcase clocks and all sorts of antique features, good value food all day from baguettes to restaurant dishes, well kept Robinsons Unicorn, jovial landlord, plain games room and family room; children and dogs welcome, terrace and big lawn, rare breeds farm behind, bedrooms, big breakfast, open all day from 9.30 am, may be cl Mon *(Brian and Jacky Wilson, the Didler, Dennis Jones, Mr and Mrs John Taylor)*

Old Hall SK17 6BD [The Square, almost opp Opera House]: Character bar in large hotel, well kept Timothy Taylors Landlord, good choice of wines by the glass, good value food inc generous panini, cock paintings and models; bedrooms *(Catherine and Rob Dunster)*

☆ *Old Sun* SK17 6HA [High St]: Charming old building with friendly helpful landlady, well kept Marstons-related ales with a guest such as Wychwood Hobgoblin, good choice of wines by the glass, farm cider, bargain food from good sandwiches and baked potatoes up served till 10, several cosy and interesting traditional linked areas, low beams and soft lighting, open fires, bare boards or tiles, stripped wood screens, old local photographs; piped music, TV; children in back bar, open all day *(Barry Collett, M G Hart, Bruce and Sharon Eden, the Didler, Catherine and Rob Dunster, LYM)*

BUXWORTH [SK0282]

☆ *Navigation* SK23 7NE [S of village towards Silkhill, off B6062]: Popular well worn in pub by restored canal basin, good attractively priced changing ales, summer farm ciders, winter mulled wine, generous pubby food all day from nice sandwiches up, cheery young staff, linked rooms with coal and log fires, flagstones and low ceilings, canalia and brassware, games room; quiet piped music; tables on sunken flagstoned terrace, play area and pets corner, open all day *(Ben Williams, J and E Dakin, LYM)*

CALVER [SK2474]

Bridge Inn S32 3XA [Calver Bridge, off A623 N of Baslow]: Unpretentious two-room stone-built village pub, short choice of good value plain food (not Mon evening or winter Sun evening), well kept Greene King ales, quick friendly service, cosy comfortable corners, coal fires, bank notes on beams, local prints and bric-a-brac inc old fire-fighting equipment, small separate eating area; picnic-sets in nice big garden by River Derwent *(Barry Collett, Malcolm Pellatt)*

Derwentwater Arms S32 3XQ [Low Side]: Neat simple local, plenty of room, courteous efficient attentive staff, good freshly cooked food (best to book); raised garden (but disabled access), bedrooms next door *(Richard Farmer)*

CASTLETON [SK1582]

☆ *Bulls Head* S33 8WH [Cross St (A6187)]: Roomy and attractively decorated, with good reasonably priced food, helpful friendly service, well kept Robinsons, log fire; four bedrooms *(Carole Hall, Paul McQueen)*

Castle Hotel S33 8WG [High St/Castle St]: Roomy Vintage Inn useful for sensibly priced all-day food (can take a while), good choice of real ales and of wines by the glass, friendly staff, log fires, stripped-stone walls, beams and some ancient flagstones; piped music; children welcome, heated terrace, comfortable bedrooms, open all day *(J and E Dakin, LYM, Jonathan Evans, John and Sharon Hancock, David Carr)*

☆ *George* S33 8WG [Castle St]: Busy but relaxed, good value food from hearty sandwiches to imaginative main dishes, four well kept ales, two good-sized rooms, one mainly for eating, ancient beams and stripped stone, no music; children and dogs welcome, wide forecourt with lots of flower tubs, good walks, may be cl Mon lunchtime *(Gwyn and Anne Wake, David Carr, Jenny, Keith and Chris O'Neill)*

CHELMORTON [SK1170]

☆ *Church Inn* SK17 9SL [between A6 and A515 SW of Buxton]: Convivial flagstoned bar, dining area with lots of bric-a-brac and woodburner, good range of good value generous food, four Marstons-related ales and a guest beer, prompt cheerful service, friendly golden labrador, games room with pool; piped music; nice spot at top of village with pleasant sloping garden and terrace tables, bedrooms, superb walking country, open all day *(Gwyn and Anne Wake, Malcolm Pellatt, Barry Collett, Peter F Marshall)*

CHESTERFIELD [SK3871]

Barley Mow S40 1JR [Saltergate]: Recently knocked-through L-shaped bar with wide choice of enjoyable food from sandwiches up, bargains for two early evening and Sat/Mon lunchtime, well kept Black Sheep and John Smiths, good hot drinks, original Wards stained-glass; sunny picnic-sets outside *(Keith and Chris O'Neill)*

Industry S40 4SF [Queen St]: Friendly relaxed local, well kept changing ales inc local Spire, home-made food; some live music *(the Didler)*

Portland S40 1AY [New Sq]: Well laid out Wetherspoons in handsome building, their usual food, good range of changing ales; nice terrace, 24 bedrooms, open all day *(Keith and Chris O'Neill)*

Rutland S40 1XL [Stephenson Pl]: Uncomplicated pub next to crooked-spire church, thriving atmosphere, Badger Best, Timothy Taylors Landlord, local Brampton and several other interesting changing ales, Weston's farm cider, low-priced pub food all day from sandwiches up, friendly polite service even when busy, rugs and assorted wooden furniture on bare boards, old photographs, darts; piped music; children welcome, open all day *(Keith and Chris O'Neill, Alan Johnson)*

CHINLEY [SK0484]

Lamb SK23 6AL [just off A624 S of Hayfield]: Profusely decorated three-room stone-built pub tucked below road, good range of beers and wines, good value generous food (all day wknds and bank hols) from lunchtime sandwiches up, welcoming service; children welcome, lots of tables out in front with good views *(Rob Watson, BB)*

CHURCH BROUGHTON [SK2033]

Holly Bush DE65 5AS [off A50 E of Uttoxeter, via same exit as A511; Main St]: Neat and attractive village pub doing well under current licensees, enjoyable food inc changing contemporary dishes, well kept Marstons Pedigree and guest beers, good wine choice *(Mark Henderson)*

COMBS [SK0378]

☆ *Beehive* SK23 9UT: Roomy, neat and comfortable, very popular for good pubby food (all day Sun) from huge baguettes to steaks, well kept ales such as Black Sheep, good choice of wines by the glass, bargain coffee, log fire, heavy beams and copperware; quiet piped jazz, live music Fri, quiz night Tues; bedrooms, plenty of tables out in front, by lovely valley tucked away from main road *(Malcolm Pellatt, Bruce and Sharon Eden, J and E Dakin)*

COXBENCH [SK3643]

Fox & Hounds DE21 5BA [off B6179 N of Derby; Alfreton Rd]: Friendly village pub nicely set by Trent & Mersey Canal, wide choice of good interesting fresh food (not Sat evening), reasonable prices, well kept Banks's and Marstons Pedigree, recent gentle refurbishment of long partly flagstoned beamed and panelled bar, attractive raised restaurant area, family room; can get very busy; waterside picnic-sets, lovely hanging baskets and flower tubs *(K E and B Billington, John Beeken, John Lowe)*

CRICH [SK3454]

Cliff DE4 5DP [Cromford Rd, Town End]: Cosy and unpretentious two-room pub with Greene King ales, reliable straightforward food, friendly staff, open fire; children welcome, great views, handy for National Tramway Museum *(the Didler)*

CROMFORD [SK2956]

Boat DE4 3QF [Scarthin, off Mkt Pl]: Traditional 18th-c pub with real ales such as Black Sheep, Derby, Falstaff, Springhead and Whim Hartington, relaxed atmosphere, coal fire, long narrow low-beamed bar with stripped stone and bric-a-brac, darts and pool area, cool cellar bar (used for easter and Nov beer festivals); TV; children and dogs welcome, back garden, open all day wknds *(Paul J Robinshaw, the Didler, Rona Murdoch, BB)*

CROWDECOTE [SK1065]

Packhorse SK17 0DB: Enjoyable food from sandwiches up in small 16th-c two-bar pub in lovely setting, three real ales inc local Hartington; tables out behind, beautiful views, popular walking route *(Richard, E A Eaves)*

CUTTHORPE [SK3273]

Gate S42 7BA [Overgreen; B6050 W of village]: Picture-window views from chatty area around bar, neat glass-fronted dining lounge down steps, enjoyable food inc local buffalo, well kept Black Sheep, Fullers London Pride and a guest beer, good choice of wines by the glass; terrace tables *(Keith and Chris O'Neill)*

DENBY [SK4047]

Bulls Head DE5 8PW [Denby Common, between A609 and A6007 S of Ripley]: Reopened after fire damage well restored, decent family food, smart service by young efficient staff, real ales such as Greene King Abbot, contemporary décor with white panelling, tiled floor and modern bar stools; pleasant garden behind *(Phyl and Jack Street)*

DERBY [SK3538]

☆ *Abbey Inn* DE22 1DX [Darley St, Darley Abbey]: A treasure, former abbey gatehouse opp Derwent-side park (pleasant riverside walk from centre), massive 15th-c or older stonework remnants, brick floor, studded oak doors, coal fire in big stone inglenook, stone spiral stair to upper bar (open Sun afternoon) with oak rafters and tapestries, pleasant service, bargain Sam Smiths and lunchtime bar food; the lavatories with their beams, stonework and tiles are worth a look too; piped music; children welcome, open all day wknds *(the Didler, LYM, Rona Murdoch, R T and J C Moggridge)*

Babington Arms DE1 1TA [Babington Lane]: Large well run open-plan Wetherspoons with massive bank of handpumps for great real ale choice, good welcoming service, well priced food, comfortable seating with steps up to relaxed back area; attractive verandah, open all day *(C J Fletcher, David Carr, the Didler)*

Falstaff DE23 6UJ [Silver Hill Rd, off Normanton Rd]: Basic unsmart local aka the Folly, brewing its own good value ales, guest beers too; left-hand bar with games, right-hand lounge with coal fire usually quieter; open all day *(the Didler)*

☆ *Flower Pot* DE1 3DZ [King St]: Extended real ale pub with glazed panel showing its own new Headless microbrewery and great choice of reasonably priced changing beers from small breweries (up to 20 at wknds), friendly staff, three linked rooms inc comfortable back bar with lots of books, side area with old Derby photographs and brewery memorabilia, good value basic bar food, daily papers, pub games; piped music/juke box, separate concert room – good live bands Thurs-Sat and busy then; disabled access and facilities, tables on small cherry-tree terrace, open all day *(the Didler, Pam and John Smith)*

☆ *Olde Dolphin* DE1 3DL [Queen St]: Quaint 16th-c timber-framed pub, four small dark unpretentious rooms, big bowed black beams, shiny panelling, opaque leaded windows, lantern lights and coal fires, well kept ales such as Adnams, Bass, Black Sheep, Caledonian Deuchars IPA, Greene King Abbot, Jennings Cumberland, and Marstons Pedigree, bargain simple food all day, good value upstairs steak bar (not always open); no children; terrace tables, open all day *(LYM, the Didler, Brian and Rosalie Laverick, Pam and John Smith)*

Rowditch DE22 3LL [Uttoxeter New Rd (A516)]: Welcoming two-bar local with well kept Marstons Pedigree and guest beers, country wines, Mon cheese night, attractive small snug on right, coal fire, Sat piano-player, occasional downstairs cellar bar; small pleasant back garden *(the Didler)*

☆ *Smithfield* DE1 2BH [Meadow Rd]: Friendly and comfortable bow-fronted local with big bar, snug, back lounge with traditional settles, old prints, curios and breweriana, up to ten well kept changing ales, filled rolls and hearty lunchtime meals, real fires, daily papers; piped music, games room with table skittles, board games, TV and machines (children welcome here), quiz and band nights; riverside terrace with wknd barbecues, open all day *(the Didler, C J Fletcher)*

☆ *Standing Order* DE1 3GL [Irongate]: Spacious Wetherspoons in grand and lofty-domed former bank, central bar, booths down each side, elaborately painted plasterwork, pseudo-classical torsos, high portraits of mainly local notables; usual popular food all day, good range of real ales, reasonable prices, daily papers, quick service even when very busy; good disabled facilities, open all day *(Dave Braisted, the Didler, BB)*

Station Inn DE1 2SN [Midland Rd, below station]: Friendly local, simple and neatly kept, with particularly well kept Bass (in jugs from cellar), Black Sheep and Caledonian Deuchars IPA, good food lunchtime and early evening in large back lounge and dining area, long panelled and quarry-tiled bar, side room with darts, pool and TV, ornate façade; piped music; open all day Fri (the Didler)

DRONFIELD [SK3479]

Coach & Horses S18 2GD [Sheffield Rd (B6057)]: Comfortably refurbished tap for Thornbridge microbrewery's interesting beers, friendly staff informative about them, enjoyable home-made food using fresh local ingredients, decent wines by the glass, pleasant civilised furnishings inc sofas; open all day (the Didler)

EDALE [SK1285]

Old Nags Head S33 7ZD [off A625 E of Chapel-en-le-Frith; Grindsbrook Booth]: Relaxed well used traditional pub at start of Pennine Way, good friendly staff, four real ales, log fire, flagstoned area for booted walkers, airy back family room with board games, pubby food; TV; front terrace and garden, open all day, cl Mon/Tues lunchtimes out of season (C J Fletcher, LYM, Jonathan Evans, Andrew Whitney, Edward Leetham)

ELTON [SK2260]

☆ *Duke of York* DE4 2BW [village signed off B5056 W of Matlock; Main St]: Old-fashioned local kept spotless by very long-serving friendly landlady, well kept Adnams Broadside, Bradford Farmers Blonde and Marstons Pedigree, low prices, welcoming regulars, lovely little quarry-tiled back tap room with coal fire in massive fireplace, glazed bar and hatch to flagstoned corridor, nice prints and more fires in the two front ones – one like private parlour with piano and big table, the other with pool, darts, dominoes; outside lavatories; in charming village, open 8.30-12, and Sun lunchtime (Pete Baker, the Didler)

FOOLOW [SK2078]

☆ *Barrel* S32 5QD [Bretton, N of village]: Outstanding views from stone-roofed turnpike inn's front terrace, old-fashioned low-beamed knocked-through bar with modern extension, well kept Greene King ales, decent bar food, friendly young staff, lots of pictures and end log fire; piped music, may be live Weds; children and dogs welcome, courtyard garden, good walking, four neat simple bedrooms, good breakfast, open all day wknds (Keith and Margaret Kettell, Susan and John Douglas, Malcolm Pellatt, Richard, LYM, Mrs M E Mills, Fiona Salvesen, Ross Murrell, Darren and Kirstin Arnold, Eddie Edwards, Robin M Corlett, Eddie and Lynn Jarrett, Alan Thwaite, Sean A Smith)

FROGGATT EDGE [SK2476]

☆ *Chequers* S32 3ZJ [A625, off A623 N of Bakewell]: Well run smart dining pub with good if not cheap interesting food (all day wknds) from unusual sandwiches up,

solid country furnishings in civilised and cosily attractive dining bar with woodburner, antique prints and longcase clock, changing ales such as Black Sheep and Greene King IPA, good choice of wines by the glass; unobtrusive piped music; children welcome, peaceful back garden with Froggatt Edge just up through the woods behind, comfortable bedrooms (quarry lorries use the road from 6am wkdys), very good breakfast, open all day wknds (LYM, Richard, Dr and Mrs J Temporal, Matt Waite, Phil and Gill Wass, Malcolm Pellatt, James A Waller)

Grouse S11 7TZ [Longshaw, off B6054 NE of Froggatt]: Plush front bar, log fire and wooden benches in back bar, big dining room, good home cooking from sandwiches to imaginative dishes, good value smaller helpings, well kept Caledonian Deuchars IPA, Banks's and Marstons Pedigree, friendly service, handsome views; verandah and terrace, neat bedrooms, good moorland walking country, open all day (Mr and Mrs Staples, C J Fletcher)

GLOSSOP [SK0294]

Globe SK13 8HJ [High St W]: Good changing ales inc its own microbrew and local guest beers, farm cider, vegetarian food, friendly licensees, comfortable relaxed atmosphere, old fittings and photographs, frequent live music upstairs; cl lunchtime and Tues, open till early hours (the Didler)

Star SK13 7DD [Howard St]: Good changing real ales such as local Howard Town, Pictish, Shaws and Whim and farm cider in friendly bare-boards alehouse opp station, interesting layout inc tap room with hatch service, helpful staff, old local photographs; piped music; bedrooms, open all day wknds (Dennis Jones, the Didler)

GREAT HUCKLOW [SK1777]

Queen Anne SK17 8RF: Comfortable and friendly 17th-c stone-built pub, low beams, big log fire and gleaming brass and copper, Adnams and changing guest beers, good soft drinks choice, good simple food (may be just soup and sandwiches, winter lunchtimes), walkers' bar, pub games; piped music; dogs welcome, french windows to small back terrace and charming garden with picnic-sets and lovely views, two quiet bedrooms, good walks, cl Mon in winter and Tues lunchtime (the Didler)

GREAT LONGSTONE [SK1971]

☆ *Crispin* DE45 1TZ [Main St]: Spotless pub increasingly popular for enjoyable generous food inc OAP lunches, four well kept Robinsons ales, welcoming and particularly obliging landlord, buoyant atmosphere, log fire; picnic-sets out in front, nice spot at top of *Peak Practice* village (David and Carole Sayliss, Peter F Marshall)

GRINDLEFORD [SK2478]
Maynard Arms S32 2HE [Main Rd]:
Spacious high-ceilinged hotel bar with
enjoyable food from sandwiches up, two
local ales, decent wines by the glass, dark
panelling, comfortable seats inc leather
sofa, local and autographed cricketing
photographs, restaurant overlooking
gardens with water feature; piped music;
walkers welcome, children in eating areas,
comfortable bedrooms, nice setting, open
all day Sun *(C J Fletcher, LYM)*

HARDSTOFT [SK4463]
Shoulder of Mutton S45 8AE [B6039]:
Attractively refurbished country inn with
comfortable linked areas, well kept
Greene King ales, lots of pictures and
plates, soft lighting; handy for Hardwick
Hall and Five Pits Trail *(Robert F Smith)*

☆ *Hardwick Inn* S44 5QJ [quite handy for
M1, junction 29; Doe Lea]: Busy 17th-c
golden stone building in parkland, good
atmosphere in several linked rooms, fine
range of some 220 malt whiskies and of
wines by the glass, well kept Black
Sheep, Greene King Old Speckled Hen,
Theakstons XB and Old Peculier and Wells
& Youngs Bombardier, log fire, generous
all-day food operation; unobtrusive
piped music, they may try to keep your
credit card while you eat; children
allowed, pleasant back garden, more
tables out in front, open all day
*(Rosemary K Germaine, D C Leggatt,
Peter F Marshall, Joan York, John and
Helen Rushton, LYM, the Didler,
Alan Thwaite, Stephen Woad, Ellen Weld,
David London, Mike Turner,
Michael Dandy)*

HARTINGTON [SK1260]
☆ *Devonshire Arms* SK17 0AL [Market Pl]:
Attractive old pub with good choice of
well kept ales, good if not cheap food in
lounge bar (nice if you can sit away from
the doors) and smart daytime
teashop/evening restaurant, friendly
helpful staff, log fire, flagstoned public
bar welcoming walkers and dogs; children
welcome, tables out in front facing
village duck pond, more in small garden,
good walks *(Hugh Stafford, Susan and
Nigel Brookes, Chris Reading, Richard,
Alan Johnson)*

HATHERSAGE [SK2381]
Millstone S32 1DA [Sheffield Rd (A6187
E)]: Good generous food in bar and side
brasserie with interesting menu, friendly
staff, adventurous choice of real ales,
wines and whiskies, lots of knick-knacks
and antiques (many for sale); tables
outside with excellent Hope Valley views,
nice bedrooms *(Cathy Robinson,
Ed Coombe)*

HAYFIELD [SK0486]
Sportsman SK22 2LE [Kinder Rd]: Wide
choice of enjoyable food in roomy and
neatly kept traditional pub, friendly staff,

Thwaites beers, decent wines, lots of malt
whiskies, two coal fires; handy for Kinder
Scout walks *(anon)*

HEATH [SK4467]
Elm Tree S44 5SE [just off M1 junction
29; A6175 towards Clay Cross, then first
right]: Large panelled lounge/dining
room, good value food (all day wknds),
generous Sun carvery, Jennings and a
guest beer, darts in bar; children
welcome, attractive garden with play area
and views to Bolsover and beyond
(but traffic noise) *(JJW, CMW)*

HOGNASTON [SK2350]
☆ *Red Lion* DE6 1PR [off B5035
Ashbourne—Wirksworth]: Open-plan
beamed bar with three open fires,
attractive mix of old tables, old-fashioned
settles and other comfortable seats on
ancient flagstones, friendly licensees,
home-made food inc imaginative dishes
in bar and conservatory restaurant, nice
wines by the glass, real ales such as
Marstons Pedigree; piped music;
boules, handy for Carsington Water,
bedrooms, big breakfast *(LYM, Jan and
Alan Summers, John Robertson,
Colin McKerrow)*

HOLYMOORSIDE [SK3369]
Lamb S42 7EU [Loads Rd, just off
Holymoor Rd]: Small cheerful village pub
kept spotless, up to half a dozen or so
particularly well kept ales such as
Adnams, Black Sheep, Fullers London
Pride, John Smiths and Timothy Taylors
Landlord, charming lounge, coal fire, pub
games; tables outside, leafy spot, cl wkdy
lunchtimes *(the Didler)*

HOPE [SK1683]
Woodroffe Arms S33 6SB [Castleton Rd]:
Several friendly rooms inc conservatory,
generous good value food inc good home-
made pies, well kept ales, real fire,
cheerful service; garden tables, bedrooms
(Lucy Wragg)

HORSLEY WOODHOUSE [SK3944]
Old Oak DE7 6AW [Main St (A609
Belper—Ilkeston)]: Attractively basic
two-bar beamed pub tied to Leadmill,
their interesting ales and guest beers,
farm cider, bar snacks, low prices,
friendly staff and locals, candles and coal
fires, back family area with toys, games
and pool, no piped music (occasional
live); children and dogs welcome,
hatch to covered courtyard tables,
cl wkdy lunchtimes, open all day wknds
*(Rona Murdoch, the Didler, A and
P Lancashire)*

HULLAND WARD [SK2647]
Black Horse DE6 3EE [Hulland Ward; A517
Ashbourne—Belper]: 17th-c pub with
good fresh food at sensible prices inc
local game in low-beamed quarry-tiled
bar or back country-view dining room,
popular Sun carvery, Bass, Harviestoun
Bitter & Twisted and two changing ales,
friendly licensees; children welcome,

garden tables, comfortable bedrooms, nr Carsington Water, open all day Fri-Sun *(the Didler)*

IDRIDGEHAY [SK2848]

Black Swan DE56 2SG [B5023 S of Wirksworth]: Attractive and relaxed bistro-style restaurant pub with enjoyable food from daily roast lunches to contemporary dishes, friendly obliging staff, Marstons Pedigree, decent wines; children welcome, pleasant garden views across valley, cl Sun evening *(LYM, Tony and Tracy Constance)*

ILKESTON [SK4643]

Bridge Inn DE7 8RD [Bridge St, Cotmanhay; off A609/A6007]: Welcoming pub by Erewash Canal, popular with fishermen and boaters for early breakfast and sandwich lunches, well kept Greene King ales, friendly service, interesting railway photographs in lounge, darts and dominoes in locals' bar; TV; well behaved children allowed, nice back garden with play area, open all day *(the Didler)*

Ilford DE7 5LJ [Station Rd]: Welcoming roadside pub with well kept interesting changing small-brewery ales, bottled imports, wknd rolls, darts and dominoes; TV, some live music; tables on pleasant terrace, open all day Sun, cl wkdy lunchtimes *(the Didler)*

Spanish Bar DE7 5QJ [South St]: Busy café-bar with interesting sensibly priced changing ales, bottled belgians, friendly efficient service even when busy, log fire, Tues quiz night, popular Sun lunchtime card games with free nibbles; video juke box; small garden, skittle alley, open all day *(the Didler)*

LADYBOWER RESERVOIR [SK1986]

☆ *Ladybower Inn* S33 0AX [A57 Sheffield—Glossop, junction with A6013]: Fine views of attractive reservoir from open-plan stone-built pub, clean and spacious, with friendly staff, good interesting food using prime local produce, Barnsley, Bradfield Farmer, Greene King Ruddles County and Wentworth Best, decent wines by the glass, red plush seats; can get crowded in summer, and parking across road – take care; children welcome, low stone seats and tables outside, good walks, good value bedrooms in recently converted annexe, good breakfast *(Richard, Mrs Jane Kingsbury, Derek Stapley, Sean A Smith)*

LULLINGTON [SK2513]

☆ *Colvile Arms* DE12 8EG [off A444 S of Burton; Main St]: Neatly preserved 18th-c village pub with high-backed settles in simple panelled bar, cosy comfortable beamed lounge, pleasant atmosphere, friendly staff, four well kept ales inc Bass, Marstons Pedigree and a Mild, good value food; may be piped music; picnic-sets on small sheltered back lawn overlooking bowling green, cl wkdy lunchtimes *(LYM, the Didler)*

MAKENEY [SK3544]

☆ *Holly Bush* DE56 0RX [from A6 heading N after Duffield, take 1st right after crossing R Derwent, then 1st left]: Down-to-earth two-bar village pub with three blazing coal fires (one in old-fashioned range by snug's curved high-backed settle), flagstones, beams, black panelling and tiled floors, lots of brewing advertisements, half a dozen or so well kept changing ales (some brought from cellar in jugs), cheap food inc rolls and pork pies, may be local cheeses for sale; games lobby; children allowed in basic hatch-served back conservatory, picnic-sets outside, dogs welcome, open all day Fri-Sun *(the Didler, Rona Murdoch, BB)*

MARSHLANE [SK4079]

Fox & Hounds S21 5RH [Main Rd]: Friendly open-plan pub with two interesting real ales, good soft drinks choice, good value food inc Sun roast, dark beams, open fire; piped music; children welcome, picnic-sets and big play area outside, open all day Sun *(JJW, CMW)*

MATLOCK BATH [SK2958]

Temple DE4 3PG [Temple Walk]: 18th-c hotel with wonderful Derwent valley views, comfortable bar, dining area and restaurant, two well kept changing ales from more or less local small breweries, enjoyable food; children welcome, tables outside, summer barbecues, bedrooms *(the Didler)*

MELBOURNE [SK3825]

Blue Bell DE73 8EJ [Church St]: Friendly chatty two-bar pub with full range of good local Shardlow ales, substantial bar food inc wide range of hot rolls, sporting pictures, games in public bar; sports TV in both bars; terrace tables *(Pete Baker, N R White)*

MILLERS DALE [SK1473]

Anglers Rest SK17 8SN [just down Litton Lane; pub is PH on OS Sheet 119, map ref 142734]: Spotless two-bar dining pub in lovely quiet riverside setting on Monsal Trail, enjoyable food, well kept real ales, efficient service, log fires, dining room; wonderful gorge views and riverside walks, though it's by no means a rough-and-ready ramblers' stop now; children welcome, attractive village *(Peter F Marshall, the Didler, Matthew Shackle)*

MILLTOWN [SK3561]

☆ *Miners Arms* S45 0HA [off B6036 SE of Ashover; Oakstedge Lane]: Good properly sensible home cooking (best to book) in appealing L-shaped pub, clean and bright, with friendly staff, Archers, Greene King and a guest beer, warm local atmosphere, quieter eating area further back; may be quiet piped classical music; children welcome, attractive country walks right from the door, cl Sun evening, Mon/Tues, winter Weds, and 10 days Aug *(the Didler, LYM)*

Nettle S45 0ES [Fallgate, Littlemoor]: Interesting old pub with coal fire in quiet traditional bar, linked areas behind, well kept Bradfield Farmers Blonde and Greene King ales, good value bar food, pub games; open all day Sun *(the Didler)*

NEW MILLS [SJ9886]

Fox SK22 3AY [Brookbottom; OS Sheet 109 map ref 985864]: Tucked-away unmodernised country local with friendly long-serving landlord, particularly well kept Robinsons, good value basic food (not Tues evening) inc good sandwiches, log fire, darts and pool; children welcome, lots of tables outside, good walking area (can get crowded wknds – open all day then) *(David Hoult, the Didler, John Fiander, Bob Broadhurst)*

Pack Horse SK22 4QQ [Mellor Rd]: Popular and friendly family-run country pub with lovely views across broad Sett valley to Kinder Scout, good choice of well kept real ales, plentiful good value food in bar and restaurant, sensibly priced wine, warm atmosphere; bedrooms, open all day *(Jan and Roger Ferris, Richard and Ruth Dean)*

OAKERTHORPE [SK3856]

Amber DE55 7LL [Furnace]: Charming old-fashioned pub with friendly landlady, good pubby food, well kept ales such as Abbeydale, Cropton or Timothy Taylors Landlord, blazing winter fires, lots of antiques inc a piano, well worn seating; good walks from the back terrace *(Derek and Sylvia Stephenson)*

Anchor DE55 7LP: Good relaxed service and food choice (not Sun/Mon evenings) inc bargain Sun carvery in comfortable partly 18th-c dining pub with linked rooms and bookable back restaurant extension, Cropton ales (unique around here); open all day wknds (can be busy then) *(Derek and Sylvia Stephenson)*

OCKBROOK [SK4236]

☆ *Royal Oak* DE72 3SE [village signed off B6096 just outside Spondon; Green Lane]: Quiet 18th-c village local run by same friendly family for half a century, bargain honest food (not wknd or Tues evenings) from super lunchtime cobs to steaks, Sun lunch and OAP meals, Bass and three interesting guest beers, good soft drinks choice, tiled-floor tap room, turkey-carpeted snug, inner bar with Victorian prints, larger and lighter side room, nice old settle in entrance corridor, open fires, darts and dominoes, charity book sales; sheltered cottage garden and cobbled front courtyard, separate play area *(Pete Baker, the Didler, BB, JJW, CMW)*

OLD GLOSSOP [SK0494]

Queens SK13 7RZ [Shepley St]: Open-plan dining pub with quick service even when busy, small bar area with well kept Black Sheep, upstairs restaurant; front picnic-sets *(John Fiander, Len Beattie)*

PARWICH [SK1854]

Sycamore DE6 1QL: Chatty old country pub with cheerful and welcoming young landlady, super log fire in neat comfortable main bar, generous wholesome food lunchtimes and most Weds-Sat evenings, Robinsons beers inc seasonal, lots of old local photographs, hatch-served tap room with games; tables out in front and on grass by car park, quiet village, good walks *(Malcolm Pellatt, the Didler, Pete Baker, Paul J Robinshaw)*

PEAK FOREST [SK1179]

Devonshire Arms SK17 8EJ [Hernstone Lane (A623)]: Friendly, attractive and relaxed, beams and panelling, enjoyable and imaginative reasonably priced evening restaurant meals (best to book); may be piped music; walkers welcome, tables on back lawn, bedrooms *(J S Hurst)*

PENTRICH [SK3852]

☆ *Dog* DE5 3RE [Main Rd (B6016 N of Ripley)]: Extended traditional pub, cosy and smartly fitted out, very popular wknds for its fresh up-to-date food (best to book), reasonable prices, Bass, Marstons Pedigree and a guest beer, nice wines by the glass, friendly efficient staff, beams and panelling; tables in attractive garden behind, quiet village, good walks *(P Dawn, the Didler)*

RIDDINGS [SK4352]

Moulders Arms DE55 4BX [off B6016 S of Alfreton; Church St]: Pretty 17th-c thatched pub with good value straightforward food inc Mon-Sat OAP lunches, Marstons Pedigree and a guest such as St Austell Tribute, two small beamed bars and immaculate cosy candlelit dining room, darts, gleaming brasses, no music or TV; no dogs; children welcome, elaborate heated smokers' shelter, usually open all day *(Phil and Jane Hodson)*

RIPLEY [SK3950]

Pear Tree DE5 3HR [Derby Rd (B6179)]: Well kept and priced Greene King ales inc a Mild, friendly chatty staff, blazing coal fires in both rooms, darts and dominoes; open all day *(the Didler)*

ROSLISTON [SK2416]

Plough DE12 8JL [off A38 SW of Burton]: Welcoming traditional country pub with pleasant landlady, friendly cat, log fires, well kept Marstons ales, generous home-made food (not Mon) inc bargain wkdy lunches; smokers' shelter *(B M Eldridge)*

ROWSLEY [SK2565]

Grouse & Claret DE4 2EB [A6 Bakewell—Matlock]: Attractive family dining pub in old stone building, spacious and comfortable, with friendly helpful staff, enjoyable food (all day wknd) from sandwiches and pubby things to more enterprising dishes, decent wines, open fires, tap room popular with walkers; tables outside, good value bedrooms *(Stuart Paulley, David Carr, Malcolm Pellatt)*

SHARDLOW [SK4430]

☆ *Malt Shovel* DE72 2HG [3.5 miles from M1 junction 24, via A6 towards Derby; The Wharf]: Busy old-world beamed pub in 18th-c former maltings, interesting odd-angled layout with cosy corners, Marstons Pedigree and a related guest beer, quick friendly service, bargain food (not Sat evening) from baguettes up, good central open fire, farm tools and bric-a-brac; lots of tables out on terrace by Trent & Mersey Canal, pretty hanging baskets and boxes *(Richard and Jean Green, Patricia Walker, the Didler, LYM, Rona Murdoch)*

☆ *Old Crown* DE72 2HL [off A50 just W of M1 junction 24; Cavendish Bridge, E of village]: Good value pub with wide choice of pubby food (not Fri/Sun evenings) from sandwiches and baguettes up, half a dozen or more well kept Marstons and related ales, nice choice of malt whiskies, friendly service and atmosphere, beams with masses of jugs and mugs, walls covered with other interesting bric-a-brac and breweriana, big inglenook fireplace; children and dogs welcome, simple good value bedrooms (with videos inc children's ones), good breakfast, open all day *(John and Enid Morris, the Didler, John Cook, LYM, P J Holt)*

Shakespeare DE72 2GP [London Rd (old A6)]: Cheerful service, good value pubby lunchtime food, good real ale range, evening restaurant (not Sun/Mon) *(Patricia Walker)*

SOUTH WINGFIELD [SK3755]

Old Yew Tree DE55 7NH [B5035 W of Alfreton; Manor Rd]: Convivial local with friendly obliging staff, good value food esp steaks and big Sun lunch, four well kept changing ales, log fire, panelling, kettles and pans hanging from beams, separate restaurant area *(Adrian Johnson)*

SPONDON [SK3935]

☆ *Malt Shovel* DE21 7LH [off A6096 on edge of Derby, via Church Hill into Potter St]: Unspoilt traditional pub with decent cheap food, well kept Bass and a guest beer from hatch in tiled corridor with cosy panelled and quarry-tiled or turkey-carpeted rooms off, old-fashioned décor, huge inglenook, steps down to big games bar with full-size pool table; lots of picnic-sets, some under cover, in big well used back garden with good play area *(the Didler, BB)*

STANTON IN PEAK [SK2364]

☆ *Flying Childers* DE4 2LW [off B5056 Bakewell—Ashbourne; Main Rd]: Cosy beamed right-hand bar with fireside settles and lots of character, larger comfortable lounge, well kept Black Sheep, Wells & Youngs Bombardier and interesting local guest beers, friendly licensees and chatty regulars, good value lunchtime soup and rolls, dominoes and cribbage; in delightful steep stone village overlooking rich green valley, good walks, cl Mon/Tues lunchtimes *(the Didler)*

STONEY MIDDLETON [SK2375]

Moon S32 4TW [Townend (A623)]: Sensibly priced food inc generous sandwiches and OAP lunchtime bargains, Marstons and related changing ales, reasonably priced wines, friendly staff, nice décor with old photographs; picnic-sets outside, handy for dales walks *(Gwyn and Anne Wake, Richard)*

SUDBURY [SK1632]

Vernon Arms DE6 5HS [off A50/A515; Main Rd]: 17th-c inn with enjoyable reasonably priced pubby food inc good carvery sandwiches, Marstons Pedigree and a couple of interesting guest beers, pleasant décor; piped music, games machine; good big garden *(Michael Dandy, Paul Newberry)*

THULSTON [SK4031]

Harrington Arms DE72 3EY [B5010, off A6 or A50 towards Elvaston Castle; Grove Cl]: Low-beamed pub with good value food inc bargain generous filled cobs *(Brian and Jean Hepworth)*

TICKNALL [SK3523]

Staff of Life DE73 1JH [High St (Ashby Rd)]: Spacious main bar with smaller room off, emphasis on simple pubby food inc popular Sun lunch, Timothy Taylors Landlord and a guest beer, friendly staff, open fire; unobtrusive piped music; bedrooms, handy for Calke Abbey *(N R White, David Barnes)*

☆ *Wheel* DE73 7JZ [Main St (A514)]: Attractive new contemporary décor in bar and restaurant, enjoyable home-made food, well kept Marstons Pedigree; children welcome, tables outside, nr entrance to Calke Abbey *(Paul McQueen)*

TIDESWELL [SK1575]

George SK17 8NU [Commercial Rd (B6049, between A623 and A6 E of Buxton)]: Unpretentiously comfortable L-shaped bar/lounge and linked dining room, well kept ales, modestly priced wines, good value food, log fires, paintings by local artists, separate bar with darts and pool; piped music; children and dogs welcome, by remarkable church, tables in front overlooking pretty village, sheltered back garden, pleasant walks *(BB, Alan Johnson, Hugh Stafford, the Didler)*

Star SK17 8LD [High St]: Friendly good value pub with several unspoilt rooms, three real ales, pubby bar food, decent wines, brisk cheerful service, local paintings (most for sale) and old photographs, restaurant; public bar with TV and games machine; bedrooms *(Alan Johnson, Phil Taylor, Sian Watkin)*

TUPTON [SK3966]

Britannia S42 6XP [Ward St, New Tupton]: Reopened as tap for Spire brewery (can arrange tours), four of theirs kept well and up to four guest beers, good bottled range, farm cider, chatty licensees, lively bar with sports TV, quieter lounge; open all day *(the Didler)*

WARDLOW [SK1875]
☆ **Three Stags Heads** SK17 8RW [Wardlow Mires; A623/B6465]: Basic no-frills farm pub of great individuality, flagstoned floors (often muddied by boots and dogs in winter), old country furniture, cast-iron kitchen range, Abbeydale ales inc Black Lurcher (brewed for the pub at a hefty 8% ABV), lots of bottled beers, hearty seasonal food on hardy home-made plates; no credit cards; children and dogs welcome, hill views from front terrace, cl Mon-Thurs and Fri lunchtimes, open all day wknds *(Mark and Diane Grist, the Didler, Rona Murdoch, LYM, Pete Baker, P Dawn)*

WENSLEY [SK2661]
Red Lion DE4 2LH [Main Rd (B5057 NW of Matlock)]: Friendly unspoilt farm pub run by chatty brother and sister, assorted 1950s-ish furniture, piano in main bar (landlord likes sing-songs), unusual tapestry in second room (usually locked, so ask landlady), no games or piped music, just bottled beer, soft or hot drink, filled sandwiches or home-baked rolls perhaps using fillings from the garden – may be their fruit for sale, too; outside gents'; open all day (may close if quiet) *(Pete Baker, the Didler)*

WHATSTANDWELL [SK3354]
Derwent DE4 5HG [Derby Rd (A6)]: Pleasant riverside pub with good value usual food from hot cobs to Sun lunch, quick friendly service even when busy, Greene King ales *(Paul J Robinshaw)*
Homesford Cottage DE4 5HJ [Homesford; A6 towards Cromford]: Friendly and comfortable, fair-priced food from good lunchtime snacks to really exotic dishes (worth the wait), Greene King ales, decent wines by the glass, separate restaurant; open all day *(John and Helen Rushton, Derek and Sylvia Stephenson)*

WHITTINGTON [SK3875]
Cock & Magpie S41 9QW [Church Street N, Old Whittington, behind museum]: Good value old stone-built dining pub, sandwiches and OAP bargains too, friendly well organised family service, well kept Marstons and related ales, good soft drinks choice, conservatory, separate public bar with games room; piped music, no dogs; children welcome in dining areas, next to Revolution House museum *(Keith and Chris O'Neill)*

WHITTINGTON MOOR [SK3873]
☆ **Derby Tup** S41 8LS [Sheffield Rd; B6057 just S of A61 roundabout]: Spotless no-frills Tynemill pub with up to ten good interesting changing ales from long line of gleaming handpumps, good choice of other drinks inc farm cider, pleasant service, simple furniture, coal fire and lots of standing room as well as two small side rooms (children allowed here), daily papers, good value basic bar lunches; can get very busy wknd evenings; dogs welcome, open all day at least Fri-Sun *(P Dawn, the Didler, LYM, Peter F Marshall, Keith and Chris O'Neill)*
Red Lion S41 8LX [Sheffield Rd (B6057)]: Simple friendly two-room 19th-c stone-built local tied to Old Mill with their real ales, hard-working landlady, thriving atmosphere, old local photographs; juke box, sports TV; open all day *(P Dawn, the Didler)*

WINSTER [SK2360]
Miners Standard DE4 2DR [Bank Top (B5056 above village)]: Simply furnished 17th-c local, relaxed at lunchtime and livelier evenings, with real ales such as Boddingtons, Flowers IPA and Marstons Pedigree, generous basic bar food inc huge pies, big woodburner, lead-mining photographs and minerals, ancient well, restaurant; children allowed away from bar, attractive view from garden, interesting stone-built village below, open all day wknds *(Reg Fowle, Helen Rickwood, the Didler, Malcolm Pellatt)*

WIRKSWORTH [SK2854]
Royal Oak DE4 4FG [North End]: Small chatty backstreet local with proper friendly licensees, well kept changing ales inc Bass, Timothy Taylors Landlord and Whim Hartington (may let you taste first), dominoes, may be good filled cobs, key fobs, old copper kettles and other bric-a-brac, interesting old photographs; opens 8, cl lunchtime exc Sun *(the Didler)*

YOULGREAVE [SK2064]
Farmyard DE45 1UW [Main St]: Welcoming comfortable low-ceilinged local, good well priced food, friendly staff, well kept ales, fire in impressive stone fireplace, old farm tools, big upstairs restaurant; children, walkers and dogs welcome, TV, tables in garden *(Jill Richards, Mr and Mrs R Duys)*
☆ **George** DE45 1WN [Alport Lane/Church St]: Handsome 17th-c stone-built inn opp Norman church, comfortably worn inside, with friendly service, wide range of good value home-made food all day inc game, well kept John Smiths, Theakstons Mild and a local guest beer, flagstoned tap room (walkers and dogs welcome), games room; attractive village handy for Lathkill Dale and Haddon Hall, roadside tables, simple bedrooms, open all day *(Paul J Robinshaw, Pete Baker)*

Post Office address codings confusingly give the impression that a few pubs are in Derbyshire, when they're really in Cheshire (which is where we list them).

Devon

About a quarter of the main entry pubs in last year's Devon chapter have this year dropped to the Lucky Dip section. In the *Guide*'s long history we have never before lost so many entries – in Devon or in any other county. Close analysis shows that Devon pubs seem to have been hurt particularly badly by the trends which have been making life more difficult for pubs throughout the country – rising costs on the one hand, and customers' reluctance to pay high prices on the other (exacerbated, in Devon's case, by the large distances involved, and the soaring cost of car fuel). These pressures have in some cases had an all too evident effect on standards; in others, such pressures have played a part in publicans' decisions to move on. We have even lost one or two stars, most notably the Drewe Arms at Broadhembury and the Nobody Inn at Doddiscombsleigh, both of which have faced difficulties despite their excellence. Obviously, all this has made us double our efforts to track down the Devon pubs which are still offering really good experiences. And we have even managed to find nine good new main entries. These are the Normandy Arms at Blackawton (run by a keen young couple – he does the cooking), the Cadeleigh Arms in Cadeleigh (civilised and relaxed, with good wines and innovative food), the Drewe Arms in Drewsteignton (back in these pages after a break, doing very well these days), the Fortescue Arms at East Allington (the Canadian landlord is very friendly, and his Austrian partner is a super cook), the Hour Glass in Exeter (a nice little backstreet pub with surprisingly interesting food and good wines), the Dodbrooke Inn in Kingsbridge (a bustling, homely local, enjoyed by a good mix of customers), the Half Moon at Sheepwash (run by friendly people, and loved by fishermen for its 12 miles of River Torridge), the Blue Ball in Sidford (open again after a complete rebuild following a devastating fire), and the Tom Cobley in Spreyton (up to nearly two dozen real ales in a friendly little village pub). Food has always played a major role in pubs here, and, with so much fantastic local produce from the land and sea, it's not surprising that chefs are keen to source ingredients as close to home as possible. For an especially good meal, head for the Merry Harriers at Clayhidon (friendly and popular, with interesting choices), the Culm Valley at Culmstock (innovative food using tip-top free-range and organic produce in an idiosyncratic pub), the Rock at Haytor Vale (at its pubbiest and most informal at lunchtime, with more elaborate meals in the evening), the Church House in Marldon (a civilised place with enjoyably modern dishes), the Jack in the Green at Rockbeare (very much a dining pub, and extremely busy), and the Rose & Crown at Yealmpton (contemporary food in both bar and restaurant, and all very stylish). The title of Devon Dining Pub of the Year goes to the Rose & Crown in Yealmpton. The Lucky Dip section at the end of the chapter has a good many promising entries, including the Quarrymans Rest at Bampton, Dolphin in Beer, Lazy Toad at Brampford Speke, Poltimore Arms at Brayford, Rockford Inn near Brendon, California at California Cross, Royal Castle in Dartmouth, Lower House at Georgeham, Luppitt Inn, Dartmoor Inn at Lydford, Olde Cider Bar in Newton Abbot, Beer Engine at Newton St Cyres, China House in Plymouth, Stag at Rackenford, Ness House in Shaldon, Queens Arms in Slapton, Oxenham Arms at South Zeal, Lighter in Topsham, Royal Seven Stars in Totnes, Cridford Inn at Trusham and Otter at Weston. The county has around two dozen independent brewers, many producing notable beers. By far the most popular is Otter, now very widely available. Other easily found good beers are from Dartmoor Brewery (the former Princetown brewery, now renamed – rather confusingly, as St Austell over in Cornwall also call one of their beers Dartmoor), O'Hanlons, Branscombe Vale, Teignworthy and Exe Valley; and we came across Summerskills, Topsham & Exminster, Country Life, South Hams, Warrior, Barum and Blackdown in a number of good pubs.

AVONWICK   SX6958   MAP 1
Turtley Corn Mill ♀
0.5 mile off A38 roundabout at SW end of S Brent bypass; TQ10 9ES

Careful conversion of tall mill house with interestingly furnished spreading areas, local beers, well liked food, and huge gardens

The spreading series of linked areas inside this careful conversion of a large, tall mill house (with a working waterwheel) are decorated with some individuality. There are bookcases, fat church candles and oriental rugs in one area, dark flagstones by the bar, a strategic woodburning stove dividing one part, a side enclave with a modern pew built in around a really big table, and so on. Throughout, lighting is good, with plenty of big windows looking out over the grounds, a pleasant array of prints, a history of the mill and some other decorations (framed 78rpm discs, elderly wireless sets, house plants), pastel walls, and a mix of comfortable dining chairs around heavy baluster-leg tables in a variety of sizes. They have a commendable range of wines and sherries including good french house wines, Dartmoor Brewery Jail Ale and Summerskills Tamar, with a guest or two such as Otter Bright and St Austell Tribute on handpump, up to 50 malt whiskies, and decent coffee; board games. The extensive gardens, leading down to a lake, have well spaced picnic-sets and a giant chess set. They will keep your credit card if you eat outside. More reports please.

🍴 Enjoyable food includes sandwiches, soup, ploughman's, a trio of smoked salmon, smoked trout and prawns, chicken liver pâté with red onion marmalade, a tapas plate to share, steak burger topped with gruyère cheese and bacon, vegetarian moussaka, pork and pepper sausages with crispy sage leaves and onion gravy, creamy chicken and ham pie, thai marinated salmon fillet with coconut rice and chilli dipping sauce, gammon with colcannon potatoes and parsley sauce, bass on crab and chorizo linguini, and puddings such as apple steamed pudding with sticky toffee sauce and clotted cream and rhubarb and ginger crumble with custard. *Starters/Snacks: £4.50 to £8.50. Main Courses: £10.00 to £17.50. Puddings: £5.95*

Free house ~ Licensees Lesley and Bruce Brunning ~ Real ale ~ Bar food (12-9.30(9 Sun)) ~ (01364) 646100 ~ Children welcome until 7.30pm ~ Dogs welcome ~ Open 11-11; 12-10.30 Sun ~ Bedrooms: £100S/£110S

Recommended by John Evans, Andrew York, Dr and Mrs A K Clarke, Dudley and Moira Cockroft, Mr and Mrs C R Little, Andy and Claire Barker

Waterside pubs are listed at the back of the book.

BEESANDS

SX8140   MAP 1

Cricket

About 3 miles S of A379, from Chillington; in village turn right along foreshore road; TQ7 2EN

Welcoming small pub by beach with enjoyable food (especially fish) and beer

Just over the sea wall in front of this friendly little pub is Start Bay beach; there are picnic-sets by the wall and the pub is popular with South Devon Coastal Path walkers. Inside, it's neatly kept and open-plan with dark traditional pubby furniture (carpeted in the dining part and with a stripped wooden floor in the bar area), some nice, well captioned photographs of local fisherpeople, knots and fishing gear on the walls and a couple of small fireplaces. Fullers London Pride and Otter Bitter on handpump, a dozen wines by the glass and local cider; piped music. The cheerful black labrador is called Brewster. The bedrooms have fine sea views; good wheelchair access. More reports please.

🍴 As well as very good fresh local fish and shellfish, the well liked bar food includes lunchtime sandwiches and salads, super crab soup, smoked mackerel on toast, a pie of the day, home-cooked ham with free-range eggs, seafood pancake, daily specials, and evening steaks. *Starters/Snacks: £5.00 to £10.00. Main Courses: £8.50 to £20.00. Puddings: £2.50 to £6.00*

Heavitree ~ Tenant Nigel Heath ~ Real ale ~ Bar food ~ Restaurant ~ (01548) 580215 ~ Children welcome ~ Dogs allowed in bar ~ Open 11-11; 11-3, 6-11 in winter ~ Bedrooms: /£65S

Recommended by M G Hart, Phil and Anne Nash, Jenny and Brian Seller, Roger Wain-Heapy

BLACKAWTON

SX8050   MAP 1

Normandy Arms

Off A3122 W of Dartmouth; TQ9 7BN

Interesting food cooked by chef/patron in friendly, refurbished pub

This friendly pub is now run by an enthusiastic couple – Mr Alcroft is also the chef and has returned to his home town. It's been carefully refurbished and there's a front drinkers' area with tub leather chairs and sofas in front of the woodburning stove, St Austell Dartmoor Best Bitter and a guest such as Brains Rev James or Shepherd Neame Spitfire on handpump and several wines by the glass; piped music. The two main dining areas have high-backed leather dining chairs around wooden tables on the grey slate floors and pictures of the village and the pub over the years. There are some benches outside in front of the building and picnic-sets in a small garden across the lane.

🍴 Good bar food at lunchtime includes filled focaccia rolls, soup, ham and eggs, pork and leek sausages with wholegrain mustard sauce, beer-battered haddock with home-made tartare sauce and thai green chicken curry, with evening choices like crab and spring onion fritters with slow-roasted tomatoes and citrus dressing, chicken liver and foie gras parfait with onion marmalade and truffle oil, baked red pepper stuffed with chickpea, spinach and spring onion with a pepper coulis, rump of lamb with pea and mint purée, fondant potato and roasted tomato jus, and gressingham duck breast with rhubarb compote, rösti potato and wild mushroom jus; puddings and two-course themed evenings. *Starters/Snacks: £4.00 to £7.95. Main Courses: £9.95 to £17.95. Puddings: £4.95 to £5.50*

Free house ~ Licensees Sharon Murdoch and Peter Alcroft ~ Real ale ~ Bar food (12-2, 7-9; not winter Sun evening, Mon, Tues-Thurs lunchtimes) ~ (01803) 712884 ~ Children welcome ~ Dogs welcome ~ Open 7-11 Tues-Thurs; 12-2.30, 7-11 Fri and Sat; 12-3, 7-10.30 summer Sun; closed Sun winter evening, all day Mon, lunchtimes Tues-Thurs; 1 week Jan, 1 week Nov

Recommended by Mike Ambrose, Roger Wain-Heapy

Though we don't usually mention it in the text, most pubs will now make coffee or tea – always worth asking.

BRANSCOMBE   SY1888   MAP 1

Fountain Head 🍺

Upper village, above the robust old church; village signposted off A3052 Sidmouth—
Seaton, then from Branscombe Square follow road up hill towards Sidmouth, and after
about a mile turn left after the church; OS Sheet 192 map reference SY188889; EX12 3BG

**Old-fashioned stone pub with unspoilt rooms, own-brewed beers and reasonably priced
food**

Happily unchanging and with a welcome for visitors as well as locals, this is an old-
fashioned and unspoilt stone pub brewing its own beers. These include Branscombe Vale
Branoc, Jolly Geff and Summa That – their annual beer festival is held in June. The room
on the left (formerly a smithy) has forge tools and horseshoes on the high oak beams, a
log fire in the original raised firebed with its tall central chimney, and cushioned pews
and mate's chairs. On the right, an irregularly shaped, more orthodox snug room has
another log fire, white-painted plank ceiling with an unusual carved ceiling-rose, brown-
varnished panelled walls, and rugs on its flagstone-and-lime-ash floor. Paintings (and
greeting cards) painted by local artists for sale. Darts and board games. There are seats
out on the front loggia and terrace, and a little stream rustling under the flagstoned
path; pleasant nearby walks.

🍴 As well as lunchtime sandwiches and ploughman's, the reasonably priced bar food
includes soup, chicken liver pâté, beer-battered cod, home-cooked ham and eggs, home-
made beefburger, chargrilled chicken breast with lime and ginger, cumberland sausages
with mash, vegetarian mixed bean chilli, and rack of lamb with a mint and garlic crust.
Starters/Snacks: £4.20 to £5.50. Main Courses: £7.50 to £10.50. Puddings: £3.95 to £5.25

Free house ~ Licensees Jon Woodley and Teresa Hoare ~ Real ale ~ Bar food ~ Restaurant ~
(01297) 680359 ~ Children welcome away from bar area ~ Dogs welcome ~ Regular live music
in summer ~ Open 11-3, 6-11; 12-3, 6-10.30 Sun

Recommended by JP, PP, the Didler, Laurence Milligan, Revd R P Tickle, Mike Gorton, Kerry Law, Lynne James,
Jill Healing, Phil and Sally Gorton

Masons Arms 🍷 🍺 🛏️

Main Street; signed off A3052 Sidmouth—Seaton, then bear left into village; EX12 3DJ

**Rambling low-beamed rooms, woodburning stoves, good choice of real ales and wines,
popular food, and seats in quiet terrace and garden; bedrooms**

The heart of this 14th-c longhouse is the rambling main bar with its ancient ships'
beams, massive central hearth in front of the roaring log fire (where spit-roasts are held)
and comfortable seats and chairs on slate floors. The Old Worthies bar also has a slate
floor, a fireplace with a two-sided woodburning stove and woodwork that has been
stripped back to the original pine. There's also the original restaurant (warmed by one
side of the woodburning stove) and another beamed restaurant above the main bar.
Branscombe Vale Branoc and Summa That, Otter Bitter, St Austell Tribute, and a guest
such as Timothy Taylors Landlord on handpump, 14 wines by the glass and 33 malt
whiskies; darts, shove-ha'penny, cribbage, and dominoes. Outside, the quiet flower-filled
front terrace has tables with little thatched roofs, extending into a side garden. You may
have to leave your credit card behind the bar.

🍴 Good bar food includes lunchtime sandwiches, panini and ploughman's, wild boar and
apple sausages with roasted balsamic onions, baked garlic field mushrooms with a stilton
glaze and port reduction, wilted spinach and brie gnocchi, steamed steak and kidney
pudding, salmon, mussel, haddock and leek stew, beef, thyme and marsala casserole, and
puddings such as dark chocolate crème brûlée and raspberry crème fraîche torte with
raspberry coulis. *Starters/Snacks: £3.95 to £6.50. Main Courses: £9.95 to £13.50. Puddings:
£3.95 to £4.50*

Free house ~ Licensees Colin and Carol Slaney ~ Real ale ~ Bar food ~ Restaurant ~
(01297) 680300 ~ Children in bar with parents but not in restaurant ~ Dogs allowed in
bar and bedrooms ~ Open 11-11; 12-10.30 Sun; 11-3, 6-11 weekdays in winter ~
Bedrooms: /£80S(£85B)

Recommended by Mike and Shelley Woodroffe, Dr Ian Mortimer, Barry Steele-Perkins, Andrew Shore, Maria Williams, Kerry Law, Lee and Liz Potter, Simon Donan, the Didler, Dennis Jenkin, John and Fiona McIlwain, Peter Craske, MB, Mrs L Aquilina, Pat and Roger Davies, Michael Doswell, Mr and Mrs P D Titcomb

BRIXHAM
SX9256 MAP 1

Maritime
King Street (up steps from harbour – nearby parking virtually non-existent); TQ5 9TH

Informal little one-bar pub with friendly landlady and lots to look at

As well as details of this very informal and relaxed little pub's history as a hideout for 18th-c pirates, the one bar here is crammed full of interest: hundreds of key fobs and chamber-pots hang from the beams, there's a binnacle by the door, cigarette cards and pre-war ensigns from different countries, toby jugs and horsebrasses, mannequins, pictures of astronomical charts and plenty of mugs and china jugs. Both the african grey parrot (mind your fingers) and the lively terrier may be around, and there are two warming coal fires, cushioned wheelback chairs and pink-plush cushioned wall benches, flowery swagged curtains. The small TV might be on if there's something the landlady wants to watch; darts, piped music and board games. Otter Bitter, St Austell Tribute and a changing guest beer on handpump (though only one in winter) and 78 malt whiskies. Fine views down over the harbour and almost non-existent nearby parking. More reports please.

🍴 **No food.**

Free house ~ Licensee Mrs Pat Seddon ~ Real ale ~ No credit cards ~ (01803) 853535 ~ Well behaved children allowed ~ Dogs allowed in bar ~ Open 11-3, 6.30-midnight ~ Bedrooms: £20/£40
Recommended by R T and J C Moggridge, BOB

BUCKLAND BREWER
SS4220 MAP 1

Coach & Horses
Village signposted off A388 S of Monkleigh; OS Sheet 190 map reference 423206; EX39 5LU

Friendly old village pub with a mix of customers, open fires, and real ales; good nearby walks

Handy after a visit to the RHS garden Rosemoor, this friendly old thatched village pub is liked by regulars as well as visitors. The heavily beamed bar has comfortable seats (including a handsome antique settle) and a woodburning stove in the inglenook – there's also a good log fire in the big stone inglenook of the cosy lounge. A small back room has darts and pool; several cats. Cotleigh Golden Seahawk, Shepherd Neame Spitfire, and Skinners Betty Stogs on handpump, and around eight wines by the glass; games machine, skittle alley (that doubles as a function room), piped music, and occasional TV for sports. There are picnic-sets on a front terrace and in the side garden, and walks on the nearby moorland and along the beaches of Westward Ho!

🍴 **Bar food includes sandwiches, filled baguettes and baked potatoes, home-made pasties, soup, home-made burgers, beef in ale pie, liver and bacon in red wine gravy, pork in apples and local cider, chicken breast stuffed with local brie with an orange and redcurrant sauce, salmon, prawn and cheddar pasta bake, and daily specials.**
Starters/Snacks: £3.95 to £6.95. Main Courses: £6.50 to £12.95. Puddings: £3.25 to £4.25

Free house ~ Licensees Oliver Wolfe and Nicola Barrass ~ Real ale ~ Bar food ~ Restaurant ~ (01237) 451395 ~ Well behaved children welcome ~ Dogs allowed in bar ~ Open 12-3, 5.30(6 Sun)-midnight
Recommended by Bob and Margaret Holder, the Didler, John Marsh, Ryta Lyndley

---

It's very helpful if you let us know up-to-date food prices when you report on pubs.

BUCKLAND MONACHORUM   SX4968 MAP 1

Drake Manor ◀

Off A386 via Crapstone, just S of Yelverton roundabout; PL20 7NA

Nice little village pub with snug rooms, popular food, quite a choice of drinks, and pretty back garden

The upstairs here has been converted into a very attractive self-catering apartment which is proving very popular with customers. It's a charming, friendly little pub and the long-serving landlady offers a warm welcome to both locals and visitors – she is keen that this should remain a proper village pub whilst offering good food, too. The heavily beamed public bar on the left has brocade-cushioned wall seats, prints of the village from 1905 onwards, some horse tack and a few ship badges on the wall, and a really big stone fireplace with a woodburning stove; a small door leads to a low-beamed cubbyhole. The snug Drakes Bar has beams hung with tiny cups and big brass keys, a woodburning stove in an old stone fireplace, horsebrasses and stirrups, a fine stripped pine high-backed settle with a hood, and a mix of other seats around just four tables (the oval one is rather nice). On the right is a small, beamed dining room with settles and tables on the flagstoned floor. Shove-ha'penny, darts, games machine and euchre. Courage Best, Greene King Abbot and Sharps Doom Bar on handpump, around 30 malt whiskies, and eleven wines by the glass. The sheltered back garden – where there are picnic-sets – is prettily planted, and the floral displays in front are very attractive all year round.

🍽 **As well as some interesting daily specials such as button scallops on spinach and rocket with coriander and lime dressing, crab cakes, local venison steak with blackcurrant red wine sauce, and grilled whole local lemon sole with lemon and parsley butter, the popular bar food might include lunchtime filled baguettes and ploughman's, a pâté of the day, soup, yorkshire pudding with vegetable korma filling, sausages with garlic mayo, steak and kidney pie, cajun chicken, gammon with pineapple and cheese, lentil cakes with spicy salsa and mozzarella glaze, and puddings such as hot chocolate sponge with chocolate sauce and butter crêpes with hot cherries and kirsch.** *Starters/Snacks: £3.75 to £5.50. Main Courses: £6.95 to £13.75. Puddings: £3.75*

Punch ~ Lease Mandy Robinson ~ Real ale ~ Bar food (12-2, 7-10(9.30 Sun)) ~ Restaurant ~ (01822) 853892 ~ Children in restaurant and cellar bar if eating ~ Dogs allowed in bar ~ Open 11.30-2.30(3 Sat), 6.30-11(11.30 Fri and Sat); 12-10.30 Sun
Recommended by Joan and Michel Hooper-Immins, Emma Kingdon, Mike Gorton, Dr Peter Andrews, Alec and Sheelagh Knight

CADELEIGH   SS9107 MAP 1

Cadeleigh Arms ♀

Village signposted off A3072 just W of junction with A396 Tiverton—Exeter in Bickleigh; EX16 8HP

Attractively refurbished and civilised pub in rolling countryside, carefully chosen wines, high quality food, and relaxed atmosphere

This is a well run and civilised pub in a farming community surrounded by rolling hills. It's been attractively refurbished by its present owners, who have placed quite an emphasis on the innovative cooking in relaxed surroundings. To the left of the door are high-backed farmhouse, church and blonde chairs around wooden tables (one is a barrel table) on the grey carpet, a bay window seat, an ornamental stove in the stone fireplace, and rather striking hound paintings; darts. This part leads to a flagstoned room with a high-backed settle to one side of the log fire in its big sandstone fireplace, and similar chairs and tables. Down a couple of steps is a light and airy dining room with country landscapes, pale wooden chairs and tables, and views over the valley. Otter Bitter on handpump, farm cider, a carefully chosen little wine list; friendly, efficient service; and unobtrusive piped music. On a gravel terrace are some picnic-sets, with more on a sloping lawn.

🍽 **Attractively presented and very good, the high quality food includes open sandwiches, soup, ham hock terrine with celeriac remoulade, salmon and dill fishcake with creamed leeks, ham and organic eggs, sautéed lambs kidneys with creamy mustard sauce, bangers** and mash with onion gravy, tian of mediterranean vegetables with goats cheese, beef in ale pie, smoked haddock with spinach and saffron risotto and a poached egg, and puddings such as warm treacle tart and dark chocolate mousse. *Starters/Snacks: £4.25 to £5.95. Main Courses: £7.95 to £15.95. Puddings: £4.95*

Free house ~ Licensee Jane Dreyer ~ Real ale ~ Bar food (not winter Sun evening or Mon) ~ Restaurant ~ (01884) 855238 ~ Children welcome ~ Dogs allowed in bar ~ Open 12-2.30-ish, 6-11; 12-3.30-ish, 7-10.30 Sun; closed winter Sun evening, all day Mon; 25 Dec

Recommended by Martin and Sue Hopper, Pam Dingley, R J Walden

CHERITON BISHOP   SX7792   MAP 1

Old Thatch Inn
Village signposted from A30; EX6 6JH

Welcoming old pub, handy for the A30 with good food and beer, and a pretty garden

Our readers enjoy their visits to this old-fashioned, thatched place very much. There's a happy, bustling atmosphere and the warmly welcoming licensees are very hands-on, cheerful and chatty. The traditionally furnished lounge and rambling beamed bar are separated by a large open stone fireplace (lit in the cooler months) and they keep O'Hanlons Royal Oak and Yellowhammer, Otter Ale, Sharps Doom Bar and a changing guest on handpump, and ten wines by the glass. The sheltered garden has lots of pretty flowering baskets and tubs.

🍴 **Good bar food includes lunchtime sandwiches, soup, seared pigeon breast on steamed fennel with a raspberry balsamic dressing, mussels in white wine, garlic and cream, gateau of cornish crab and cucumber with lemon mayonnaise, beer-battered cod with home-made tartare sauce, braised duck leg with a coconut, sweet chilli and coriander cream sauce, guinea fowl supreme with tarragon cream and wild mushroom risotto, and daily specials such as wild boar steak with a green peppercorn and curried peach sauce and apple fritter, goats cheese and asparagus filo tartlet with tomato coulis, and fillet of pork with a honey, mustard glaze.** *Starters/Snacks: £4.50 to £7.50. Main Courses: £8.50 to £18.50. Puddings: £5.95*

Free house ~ Licensees David and Serena London ~ Real ale ~ Bar food (12-2(2.30 Fri and Sat), 6.30-9(9.30 Fri and Sat); 12-3, 7-9 Sun) ~ Restaurant ~ (01647) 24204 ~ Children welcome away from bar area ~ Dogs allowed in bar ~ Open 11.30-3, 6-11; 12-4 Sun; closed Sun evening; 25 and 26 Dec ~ Bedrooms: £50B/£65B

Recommended by Comus and Sarah Elliott, David and Sue Smith, Mr and Mrs A H Young, Roger and Carol Maden, M Bryan Osborne, Mrs M N Grew, Dr and Mrs M E Wilson, Ray and Winifred Halliday, Norman and Sarah Keeping

CLAYHIDON   ST1817   MAP 1

Merry Harriers
3 miles from M5 junction 26: head towards Wellington; turn left at first roundabout signposted Ford Street and Hemyock, then after a mile turn left signposted Ford Street; at hilltop T junction, turn left towards Chard – pub is 1.5 miles on right; EX15 3TR

Bustling dining pub with imaginative food, several real ales and quite a few wines by the glass; sizeable garden

Run by a friendly landlord, this is a popular dining pub with a fair choice of drinks, too. There are several small linked green-carpeted areas with comfortably cushioned pews and farmhouse chairs, candles in bottles, a woodburning stove with a sofa beside it and plenty of horsey and hunting prints and local wildlife pictures. Two dining areas have a brighter feel with quarry tiles and lightly timbered white walls. Cotleigh Harrier Lite and Otter Head and a guest like Exmoor Fox or Yeovil Stargazer on handpump, 14 wines by the glass, two local ciders, 25 malt whiskies and a good range of spirits. There are picnic-sets on a small terrace, with more in a sizeable garden (which they hope to extend) sheltered by shrubs and the skittle alley; this is a good walking area. As we went to press, we heard that the Gatlings may be thinking of a change of scene, but they've made no decisions yet.

⑪ Using very carefully sourced local ingredients (they name all their suppliers on a special sheet), the good, interesting food includes lunchtime sandwiches, filled baguettes and ploughman's, as well as soup, diver-caught scallops with lemon butter sauce and crispy parma ham salad, potted chicken liver pâté with an apricot and stem ginger chutney, home-made organic pork and apple sausages with onion gravy and wholegrain mustard mash, sweet potato and aubergine green curry, aromatic duck on braised spring cabbage with cherry sauce, herb-crusted salmon fillet with brie sauce, daily specials such as steak and kidney pie with ale gravy and game casserole, and puddings like chocolate and coffee tart and passion fruit and vanilla crème brûlée. *Starters/Snacks: £4.00 to £5.50. Main Courses: £6.50 to £13.00. Puddings: £4.00 to £5.00*

Free house ~ Licensees Peter and Angela Gatling ~ Real ale ~ Bar food (not Sun evening or Mon) ~ Restaurant ~ (01823) 421270 ~ Children welcome ~ Dogs allowed in bar ~ Open 12-3, 6.30-11; 12-3.30 Sun; closed Sun evening, all day Mon; 25 and 26 Dec

Recommended by Philip and Jude Simmons, Mike Gorton, PLC, Bob and Margaret Holder, Piotr Chodzko-Zajko, Sue Ruffhead, C T Baker, I H G Busby, Heather Coulson, Neil Cross, Bruce and Sharon Eden, Gerry and Rosemary Dobson

CLYST HYDON
ST0201 MAP 1

Five Bells
West of the village and just off B3176 not far from M5 junction 28; EX15 2NT

Attractive thatched pub with several distinctive areas, well liked food and drink, and carefully planted cottagey garden

The immaculate cottagey garden in front of this attractive thatched pub is a fine sight in spring and summer with its thousands of flowers, big window boxes and pretty hanging baskets. Inside, the bar is divided at one end into different seating areas by brick and timber pillars: china jugs hang from big horsebrass-studded beams, there are many plates lining the shelves, lots of copper and brass, and a nice mix of dining chairs around small tables, with some comfortable pink plush banquettes on a little raised area. Past the inglenook fireplace is another big (but narrower) room they call the Long Barn, with a series of prints on the walls, a pine dresser at one end, and similar furnishings. Cotleigh Tawny, O'Hanlons Royal Oak, and Otter Bitter on handpump, local farm cider and several wines by the glass; piped music and board games. Up some steps outside is a sizeable flat lawn with picnic-sets, a play frame, and pleasant country views.

⑪ Popular bar food includes soup, mussels with garlic, wine and cream, chicken and pheasant terrine, roasted vegetable tart, lasagne, steak and kidney suet pudding, fish pie, chicken with bacon in a red wine sauce, a curry of the week, duck breast with honey, lime and ginger on stir-fried vegetables and noodles, and puddings such as raspberry fool and butterscotch sticky meringue with cream, ice-cream and roasted almonds. *Starters/Snacks: £4.25 to £7.50. Main Courses: £7.95 to £16.95. Puddings: £4.95 to £5.50*

Free house ~ Licensees Mr and Mrs R Shenton ~ Real ale ~ Bar food (11.30(12 Sun)-2, 6.30-9; not Mon lunchtime, 25 Dec, 1 Jan) ~ (01884) 277288 ~ Children welcome ~ Live jazz second Weds of the month and folk duo fourth Weds of month ~ Open 11.30-3, 6.30-11; 12-3, 6.30-10.30 Sun; closed Mon lunchtime; 25 Dec

Recommended by Peter Burton, Philip and Jude Simmons, Mike and Mary Carter, Roger and Carol Maden, Alistair Forsyth, D F Clarke

COCKWOOD
SX9780 MAP 1

Anchor ♀ ◀
Off, but visible from, A379 Exeter—Torbay; EX6 8RA

Extremely popular dining pub specialising in seafood (other choices available), with six real ales too

A new quirky extension has been added to this extremely popular place, which will provide much needed extra dining space. It's been constructed using mainly reclaimed timber and decorated with over 300 ship emblems, brass and copper lamps and nautical knick-knacks. The other small, low-ceilinged, rambling rooms have black panelling, good-sized tables in various alcoves, and a cheerful winter coal fire in the snug – and despite the emphasis on food, there's still a pubby atmosphere. The six real ales on handpump might include Adnams Broadside, Bass, Fullers London Pride, Greene King Abbot, Otter Ale, and Timothy Taylors Landlord, and there's a fine wine list of 300 (bin ends and reserves and 12 by the glass), 20 brandies and 20 ports, and 130 malt whiskies; lots of liqueur coffees too. Piped music and games machine. From the tables on the sheltered verandah you can look across the road to the inlet. There's often a queue to get in but they do two sittings in the restaurant on winter weekends and every evening in summer to cope with the crowds.

⊞ Fantastic fish dishes include 27 different ways of serving River Exe mussels, nine ways of serving local scallops and five ways of serving oysters, as well as crab and brandy soup, and various platters to share. Non-fishy dishes feature as well such as sandwiches, ploughman's, stilton and Guinness pâté, mushroom and asparagus wellington, chicken wrapped in bacon stuffed with garlic and herb cheese, lamb cutlets with port and redcurrant sauce, steak and kidney pudding, daily specials and puddings such as crumble and various differing kinds of treacle tart. *Starters/Snacks: £3.75 to £8.95. Main Courses: £5.95 to £9.95. Puddings: £4.25*

Heavitree ~ Tenants Mr Morgan and Miss Sanders ~ Real ale ~ Bar food (all day) ~ Restaurant ~ (01626) 890203 ~ Children welcome if seated and away from bar ~ Dogs allowed in bar ~ Jam session last Thurs in month and themed nights monthly ~ Open 11-11; 12-10.30 Sun; closed evening 25 Dec

Recommended by Robert Blake, Michael and Lynne Gittins, N R White, Hugh Roberts, Tom Evans, John and Fiona McIlwain, D F Clarke, the Didler, Mr and Mrs P D Titcomb, Richard Fendick, Roger and Carol Maden

COLEFORD   SS7701   MAP 1

New Inn ♀ 🛏

Just off A377 Crediton—Barnstaple; EX17 5BZ

New licensees for thatched 13th-c inn with interestingly furnished areas, inventive food and real ales

New licensees have taken over this 600-year-old inn but as they've just come from one of our Main Entry pubs in Dorset, the Cricketers at Shroton, we are confident that things will go from strength to strength here. They have lots of enthusiasm and as we went to press, had many plans for subtle improvements. It's an L-shaped building with the servery in the 'angle', and interestingly furnished areas leading off it: ancient and modern settles, cushioned stone wall seats, some character tables – a pheasant worked into the grain of one – and carved dressers and chests; also, paraffin lamps, antique prints and old guns on the white walls and landscape plates on one of the beams, with pewter tankards on another. Captain, the chatty parrot, has stayed on and will greet you with a 'hello' or even a 'goodbye'. Greene King IPA, and Otter Ale with a couple of guests such as Gales HSB and Skinners Heligan Honey on handpump, local cider and ten wines by the glass; good, cheerful service, piped music, games machine, darts, and board games. There are chairs and tables on decking under the willow tree by the babbling stream and more on the terrace and lawn.

⊞ Using good local produce, the bar food now includes sandwiches, seared scallops on garlic bruschetta with mustard oil, polenta, ratatouille and goats cheese stack, bacon-wrapped monkfish with Pernod cream sauce, grilled pork loin with cider sauce and caramelised apples, home-cured gin and fresh dill gravadlax with horseradish apple cream, ruby red steak with a wholegrain mustard and port sauce, and puddings such as white chocolate and champagne cheesecake and banana and toffee meringue roulade. *Starters/Snacks: £3.95 to £5.95. Main Courses: £8.50 to £12.95. Puddings: £3.50 to £4.95*

Free house ~ Licensees Carole and George Cowie ~ Real ale ~ Bar food ~ Restaurant ~ (01363) 84242 ~ Children welcome ~ Dogs allowed in bar ~ Open 12-3, 6-11; 12-3, 7-10.30 Sun; closed 25 and 26 Dec ~ Bedrooms: £65B/£85B

Recommended by Paul and Gail Betteley, Peter Burton, Bob and Angela Brooks, Tom Evans, Di and Mike Gillam, Peter Craske, Mike and Mary Carter

COMBEINTEIGNHEAD   SX9071 MAP 1

Wild Goose ♀ ◗

Just off unclassified coast road Newton Abbot—Shaldon, up hill in village; TQ12 4RA

Fine choice of real ales in well run, friendly pub with seats in attractive garden

With seven real ales on handpump, this bustling pub is, not surprisingly, very popular: Otter
Bright and Skinners Betty Stogs and five constantly changing guests, and they've two farm
ciders and ten wines by the glass as well. The back beamed spacious lounge has a mix of
wheelbacks and red plush dining chairs, a decent collection of tables, and french windows to
the garden, with nice country views beyond. The front bar has seats in the window
embrasures of the thick walls, flagstones in a small area by the door, some beams and
standing timbers, and a step down on the right at the end, with dining chairs around the
tables and a big old fireplace with an open log fire. There's a small carved oak dresser with a
big white goose, piped music, shove-ha'penny and board games, and also a cosy section on
the left with an old settee and comfortably well used chairs. The sheltered and walled back
garden – beneath the 14th-c church tower – has plenty of seats around outdoor heaters.

🍴 **Straightforward bar food includes sandwiches, ploughman's, garlic mushrooms, baked
whole camembert with cranberry jelly, sausages and egg, spinach and ricotta cannelloni,
herb-battered haddock, beef in ale with stilton, barbecued ribs, and puddings like hot
chocolate fudge cake.** Starters/Snacks: £2.35 to £6.25. Main Courses: £5.75 to £17.50.
Puddings: £4.50 to £7.25

Free house ~ Licensees Jerry and Kate English ~ Real ale ~ Bar food ~ Restaurant ~
(01626) 872241 ~ Children welcome ~ Dogs allowed in bar ~ Open 11-2.30(3 Sat),
5.30-11(midnight Sat); 12-3, 7-11 Sun

Recommended by Mike Gorton, Mike and Mary Carter, Gerry and Rosemary Dobson, J D O Carter

CULMSTOCK   ST1013 MAP 1

Culm Valley ⊗ ♀ ◗

B3391, off A38 E of M5 junction 27; EX15 3JJ

**Quirky dining pub with imaginative food, quite a few real ales, a fantastic wine list, and
outside seats overlooking River Culm**

'Determinedly free-spirited' is a rather nice way to describe this idiosyncratic and even
scruffy pub and it's certainly not the place for those who like everything neat and tidy.
But the lively atmosphere and the cheerful and friendly, slightly off-beat landlord are part
of the appeal to most customers. The salmon-coloured bar has a hotch-potch of modern
and unrenovated furnishings, a big fireplace with some china above it, newspapers, and a
long elm bar counter; further along is a dining room with a chalkboard menu, a small
front conservatory, and leading off here, a little oak-floored room with views into the
kitchen. A larger back room has paintings by local artists for sale. Board games and a
small portable TV for occasional rugby, rowing and racing events. The landlord and his
brother import wines from smaller french vineyards, so you can count on a few of those
(they offer 40 wines by the glass), as well as some unusual french fruit liqueurs, somerset
cider brandies, vintage rum, good sherries and madeira, local farm ciders, and real ales
such as Bath Ales Gem Bitter, Blackawton Saltash Sunrise, Box Steam Dark and
Handsome, Downton Chimera Dark Delight, Otter Bright, and Stonehenge Danish Dynamite
tapped from the cask; they may hold a beer festival over the late spring bank holiday
weekend. Outside, tables are very attractively positioned overlooking the bridge and the
River Culm. The gents' is in an outside yard.

🍴 **Imaginative food using as much free-range and organic local produce as possible might
include lunchtime sandwiches, interesting soups, a popular selection of tapas, sautéed
duck livers with raspberry vinaigrette, chicken, bacon and broad bean salad, hand-dived
scallops with sweet chilli and crème fraîche, chicken breast with white pudding and a
sweet white wine sauce, rack of spring lamb with redcurrant sauce, their own venison and
port sausages, rare breed steaks, shellfish platter, and puddings such as chocolate layer
cake with three different liqueurs and a white chocolate topping, and spicy apple
pudding.** Starters/Snacks: £5.00 to £8.00. Main Courses: £8.00 to £16.00. Puddings: £5.00

Free house ~ Licensee Richard Hartley ~ Real ale ~ Bar food (not Sun evening) ~ Restaurant ~
No credit cards ~ (01884) 840354 ~ Children allowed away from main bar ~ Dogs welcome ~
Live impromptu piano every two weeks or so ~ Open 12-3, 6-11; 11-11 Sat; 12-10.30 Sun ~
Bedrooms: £35B/£60B

*Recommended by MB, John and Fiona Merritt, FJS and DS, Brian and Anita Randall, David Collison,
S G N Bennett, Peter Craske, John and Hilary Penny, Michael Cleeve, Michael and Ann Cole, Dennis and Gill Keen,
Adrian and Dawn Collinge, Simon Watkins, John and Fiona McIlwain, Tony and Tracy Constance, John Urquhart,
Adrian Johnson, Comus and Sarah Elliott*

DARTMOUTH
SX8751   MAP 1

Cherub
Higher Street; TQ6 9RB

**Handsome old building with bustling bar and plenty of atmosphere; can get busy at peak
times**

This striking old inn has shown a resilient attitude to the progress of time: it survived an
1864 fire which destroyed the southern end of the street, and the World War Two
bombing which destroyed the north side – hence it's the oldest building around here.
Perhaps best enjoyed outside peak season (when locals certainly prefer it), the bustling
bar has tapestried seats under creaky heavy beams, leaded lights, a big stone fireplace
with a woodburning stove, and Sharps Doom Bar, a beer named for the pub and a
changing guest on handpump; quite a few malt whiskies and 14 wines by the glass.
Upstairs is the fine, low-ceilinged restaurant; piped music. The building is a fine sight
with each of the two heavily timbered upper floors jutting further out than the one
below; the hanging baskets are very pretty. No children inside.

🍴 **Good bar food might include sandwiches, soup, local scallops roasted with shredded
leeks, butter and muscat on a brioche, flaked smoked haddock in a saffron and herb sauce
topped with cheese, pasta with langoustines, basil, pancetta, sunblush tomatoes and
parmesan, bangers and mash, beer-battered cod, peppered steak pudding, lambs liver
with crispy smoked bacon and onion gravy, salmon fishcakes with a tomato and butter
sauce, and maize-fed chicken with morel mushrooms, a fine herb broth, and truffle oil.
Starters/Snacks: £4.95 to £7.95. Main Courses: £7.95 to £10.95. Puddings: £4.95**

Free house ~ Licensee Laurie Scott ~ Real ale ~ Bar food ~ Restaurant ~ (01803) 832571 ~
Dogs allowed in bar ~ Open 11(12 Sun)-11

*Recommended by Terry and Linda Moseley, Dr Ian Mortimer, Emma Kingdon, Hazel Morgan, Bernard Patrick,
Mr and Mrs W W Burke, Mike Batchelor, P Dawn, Dr and Mrs M E Wilson, Tom and Jill Jones, John Day, Jenny and
Brian Seller*

DREWSTEIGNTON
SX7390   MAP 1

Drewe Arms
Off A30 NW of Moretonhampstead; EX6 6QN

**Pretty thatched village pub, warmly welcoming, proper basic bar plus dining rooms, well
liked food and real ales; bedrooms and bunk house (for walkers)**

Although there have been quite a few changes to this thatched and friendly village pub
over the last few years, the small room on the left remains as unspoilt as ever with its
serving hatch and basic wooden wall benches, stools and tables. There are three dining
areas now, Mabel's Kitchen with its original Raeburn and a history of Aunt Mable
(Britain's longest serving and oldest landlady, whom both editors of this *Guide* remember
well), the Card Room which has a woodburning stove, and the back Dartmoor Room which
is ideal for a private party: high-backed, wooden slatted dining chairs around a mix of
wooden tables, lots of prints and pictures on the walls, and an array of copper saucepans.
Otter Ale, Bright and Druid Ale (made by Otter exclusively for the pub) and Dartmoor
Brewery Jail Ale tapped from casks in the original tap room; skittle alley. There are seats
under umbrellas along the front terrace surrounded by lovely flowering tubs and hanging
baskets, with more in the terraced garden. The bedrooms have been refurbished and

they've also converted some stables into bunk rooms which are ideal for walkers. The inn is handy for Castle Drogo.

🍽 Enjoyable bar food includes soup, mushrooms, bacon and tarragon baked in a creamy brie sauce, king prawns in garlic butter, lunchtime platters, 100% pure meat lamb and beef burgers, pies such as spicy lamb with chickpea and chorizo, venison with roasted squash and caramelised red onion, and mixed bean in fennel and carrot sauce, a curry of the day, beer-battered cod, sausages with wholegrain mustard mash and rich gravy, daily specials and puddings like raspberry and white chocolate cheesecake and warm coconut and treacle tart. *Starters/Snacks: £4.95 to £7.75. Main Courses: £7.45 to £19.50. Puddings: £3.95 to £4.95*

Enterprise ~ Lease Fiona Newton ~ Real ale ~ Bar food (all day in summer; 12-2.30, 6-9.30 in winter) ~ Restaurant ~ (01647) 281224 ~ Children welcome ~ Dogs allowed in bar and bedrooms ~ Live music in Long Room every two weeks ~ Open 11am-midnight; 11-3, 6-midnight Mon-Fri in winter ~ Bedrooms: /£80B

Recommended by Glenwys and Alan Lawrence, Tom and Rosemary Hall, Dr and Mrs A K Clarke, Dr Ian Mortimer, Mrs Angela Graham, Andrea Rampley, Colin and Peggy Wilshire, David Crook

EAST ALLINGTON   SX7648   MAP 1

Fortescue Arms

Village signposted off A381 Totnes—Kingsbridge, S of A3122 junction; TQ9 7RA

Pretty village pub, interesting modern food cooked by Austrian chef, good choice of drinks, attractive outside seating areas; bedrooms

Run by an Austrian chef and his Canadian business partner, this is a pretty village pub with a good mix of drinkers and diners. The main part of the two-roomed bar has a nice mix of wooden tables and cushioned dining chairs on the black slate floor, an open log fire, a dark green dado under cream walls, church candles and some brewery memorabilia, and attractive tartan curtains. The second room is more set for eating with similar furniture, a few old local photographs and red carpeting; darts, games in a little nook and very quiet piped music. There's also a stylish, contemporary restaurant. Butcombe Bitter and St Austell Dartmoor IPA on handpump, a carefully chosen wine list with helpful notes and nine by the glass, a fair choice of spirits, and two local ciders; friendly, attentive service. Outside are some picnic-sets in a sheltered courtyard, and a terrace has teak steamer chairs under a pair of small pointy marquees. We have not yet heard from readers who have stayed here, but would expect the bedrooms to be comfortable.

🍽 Interesting modern food with some austrian touches includes lunchtime sandwiches, soup, game terrine with waldorf salad and cumberland sauce, goats cheese tartlet with sun-dried tomatoes, roasted peppers and basil and topped with a chilli, honey and garlic dressing, scallops wrapped in black forest ham with a broad bean and celeriac purée, austrian potato goulash with rice and crème fraîche, roe deer on parsnip purée tartlet coated with damson wine sauce, beef or venison stew, bass fillet with saffron cream sauce, and puddings such as apple strudel with crème pâtissière and chocolate pot with fruit garnish and home-made biscuits; Sunday roasts. *Starters/Snacks: £4.00 to £5.25. Main Courses: £7.50 to £17.60. Puddings: £5.25*

Free house ~ Licensees Tom Kendrick and Werner Rott ~ Real ale ~ Bar food (12-2.30, 6-9.30; not Mon lunchtime) ~ Restaurant ~ (01548) 521215 ~ Children in own area; no children under 6 in restaurant ~ Dogs allowed in bar ~ Open 12-2.30, 6-11; 12-2.30, 6-10.30 Sun; closed Mon lunchtime ~ Bedrooms: £40S/£60S

Recommended by Mike and Shelley Woodroffe, Roger Wain-Heapy, MP

A very few pubs try to make you leave a credit card at the bar, as a sort of deposit if you order food. They are not entitled to do this. The credit card firms and banks which issue them warn you not to let them out of your sight. If someone behind the counter used your card fraudulently, the card company or bank could in theory hold you liable, because of your negligence in letting a stranger hang on to your card. Suggest instead that if they feel the need for security, they 'swipe' your card and give it back to you. And do name and shame the pub to us.

EXETER   SX9292   MAP 1

Hour Glass ◖

Melbourne Street, off B3015 Topsham Road (some nearby parking); EX2 4AU

Inventive food in old-fashioned local, friendly service, and good choice of real ales and wines by glass

Run by cheerful, welcoming people, this is a traditional, old-fashioned local in a little side street. There are beams, a mix of pub chairs and tables on the bare boards, dark red walls, an open fire in a small brick fireplace and a relaxed, chatty atmosphere; resident cats. Well kept Branscombe Vale Branoc, Otter Ale, and Topsham & Exminster Ferryman on handpump served from the island bar, and a fine choice of 16 wines including sparkling and rosé, by the glass.

🍴 **Good proper bar food with some interesting daily specials and nice tapas and nibbles might include soup, game terrine with pickles, dartmouth smoked eel with fennel, orange and chilli, cauliflower risotto with green herbs and spanish ham, grilled tuna with mussels, irish stew, bass with fenugreek and tahini, slow-cooked squid with Guinness and chorizo, and puddings such as rhubarb fool and chocolate and Amaretto truffle cake.** *Starters/Snacks: £4.00 to £6.00. Main Courses: £8.50 to £13.50. Puddings: £4.00 to £6.00*

Enterprise ~ Lease J Slade ~ Real ale ~ Bar food (not Mon lunchtime) ~ Restaurant ~ (01392) 258722 ~ Children allowed away from bar ~ Dogs allowed in bar ~ Open 12-3, 5-11; 12-11(10.30 Sun) Sat; closed Mon lunchtime, 25 and 26 Dec, 1 Jan

Recommended by the Didler, Dr and Mrs M E Wilson, Mike Gorton

Imperial ◖ £

New North Road (St David's Hill on Crediton/Tiverton road, above St David's station); EX4 4AH

19th-c mansion in own grounds with interesting seating areas and cheap food and drink

There's a good mix of customers in this early 19th-c mansion (though it's especially popular with students) and a cheerful, bustling atmosphere. The setting is impressive as it stands in its own six-acre hillside park and is reached along a sweeping drive, and there are plenty of picnic-sets in the grounds and elegant garden furniture in the attractive cobbled courtyard; a covered smoking area, too. Inside, the light and airy former orangery has an unusual lightly mirrored end wall, and there are various different areas including a couple of little clubby side bars, a left-hand bar that looks into the orangery, and a fine ex-ballroom filled with elaborate plasterwork and gilding brought here in the 1920s from Haldon House (a Robert Adam stately home that was falling on hard times). The furnishings give Wetherspoons' usual solid well spaced comfort, and the walls are hung with plenty of interesting pictures and other things to look at. Up to 14 real ales on handpump such as Exmoor Stag, Greene King IPA, Abbot and Wexford Irish Ale, Marstons Pedigree, O'Hanlons Yellowhammer, Otter Bright, and seven guests.

🍴 **Very reasonably priced bar food includes filled panini, meaty or vegetarian burgers (the price also includes a pint), battered cod, beef in ale pie, pasta with tomato and basil sauce, a decent curry, and sausages and mash.** *Starters/Snacks: £2.49 to £3.99. Main Courses: £5.59 to £6.99. Puddings: £1.49 to £2.89*

Wetherspoons ~ Manager Paul Dixey ~ Real ale ~ Bar food (all day) ~ (01392) 434050 ~ Children welcome ~ Open 9am-midnight(1am Sat)

Recommended by Henry Snell, the Didler, Dr and Mrs A K Clarke, Donna and Roger, Mike Gorton, Dr and Mrs M E Wilson, Ben Williams

---

Stars after the name of a pub show exceptional quality. One star means most people (after reading the report to see just why the star has been won) would think a special trip worth while. Two stars mean that the pub is really outstanding – for its particular qualities it could hardly be bettered.

EXMINSTER   SX9686   MAP 1

Turf Hotel ★

Follow the signs to the Swan's Nest, signposted from A379 S of village, then continue to end of track, by gates; park, and walk right along canal towpath – nearly a mile; there's a fine seaview out to the mudflats at low tide; EX6 8EE

Remote but very popular waterside pub with fine choice of drinks, super summer barbecues and lots of space in big garden

This place is great fun and extremely popular, especially on a sunny day when you must arrive early to be sure of a seat (the tables in the bay windows are much prized). You can't get here by car – you must either walk (which takes about 20 minutes along the ship canal) or cycle or catch a 60-seater boat which brings people down the Exe estuary from Topsham quay (15-minute trip, adult £4, child £2); there's also a canal boat from Countess Wear Swing Bridge every lunchtime. Best to phone the pub for all sailing times. For those arriving in their own boat there is a large pontoon as well as several moorings. Inside, the end room has a slate floor, pine walls, built-in seats, lots of photographs of the pub, and a woodburning stove; along a corridor (with an eating room to one side) is a simply furnished room with wood-plank seats around tables on the stripped wooden floor. Otter Ale and Bitter, O'Hanlons Yellowhammer and Royal Oak, and Topsham & Exminster Ferryman on handpump, local Green Valley cider, local juices, 20 wines by the glass (and local wine too), and jugs of Pimms. The outdoor barbecue is much used in good weather (as are the cook-your-own barbecues), and there are plenty of picnic-sets spread around the big garden. The children's play area was built using a lifeboat from a liner that sank off the Scilly Isles around 100 years ago; it was rebuilt last winter. Although the pub and garden do get packed in good weather and there are inevitable queues, the staff remain friendly and efficient. The sea and estuary birds are fun to watch at low tide.

🍴 **Interesting bar food using organic and local produce includes lunchtime sandwiches and toasties, soup, hummus with roasted garlic and sun-dried tomatoes, smoked mackerel pâté with beetroot chutney, beer-battered fish of the day with tartare sauce, hungarian pork goulash, mussels in white wine, herbs and garlic with frites, vegetable tart, salmon and dill fishcakes with béarnaise sauce and watercress salad, daily specials, and puddings.** *Starters/Snacks: £4.50 to £5.50. Main Courses: £7.50 to £15.50. Puddings: £1.95 to £4.50*

Free house ~ Licensees Clive and Ginny Redfern ~ Real ale ~ Bar food (12-2(3 Fri-Sun), 7-9(9.30 Fri and Sat); not Sun evening) ~ (01392) 833128 ~ Children welcome ~ Dogs welcome ~ Open 11-11(10.30 Sun); open only weekends Oct, Nov, March; closed Dec-Feb

Recommended by Dr and Mrs M E Wilson, Barry Steele-Perkins, J D O Carter, Richard Mason, Phyl and Jack Street, Peter Salmon, R T and J C Moggridge, the Didler, John and Helen Rushton, FJS and DS, Mr and Mrs P D Titcomb

HAYTOR VALE   SX7777   MAP 1

Rock ★

Haytor signposted off B3387 just W of Bovey Tracey, on good moorland road to Widecombe; TQ13 9XP

Civilised Dartmoor inn at its most informal at lunchtime; super food, comfortable bedrooms, and pretty garden

Very well run and genuinely welcoming, this is a civilised and neatly kept place on the edge of Dartmoor National Park. It's at its most informal at lunchtime when there's a nod towards pubbiness as walkers pop in for a pint of Dartmoor Brewery Jail Ale or St Austell Dartmoor Best on handpump and a relaxed meal. In the evening though, it becomes a restaurant-with-rooms with all space given over to the excellent food. The two communicating, partly panelled bar rooms have lots of dark wood and red plush, polished antique tables with candles and fresh flowers, old-fashioned prints and decorative plates on the walls, and warming winter log fires (the main fireplace has a fine Stuart fireback. There are seats in the large, pretty garden opposite the inn, with tables and chairs on a small terrace next to the pub itself. The bedrooms are comfortable with good facilities but some are up steep stairs, and breakfasts are very good. There is a car park at the back.

⑪ At lunchtime, the enjoyable food includes soup, ham hock terrine with piccalilli, mussels in white wine, shallots and garlic, smoked fish platter, pork and leek sausages with red wine gravy, chicken and pancetta caesar salad, seafood tagliatelle, steak in ale pie, thai-style chicken curry, and puddings like pear and frangipane tart with clotted cream and rhubarb crème brûlée with shortbread biscuit; evening dishes such as fillet of wild bass with parsnip purée, herb-crushed potatoes and lemon oil and fillet steak with thyme fondant potato and wild mushroom jus. *Starters/Snacks: £5.95 to £6.95. Main Courses: £11.95 to £16.95. Puddings: £4.95 to £5.95*

Free house ~ Licensee Christopher Graves ~ Real ale ~ Bar food ~ Restaurant ~ (01364) 661305 ~ Children welcome ~ Dogs allowed in bedrooms ~ Open 10.30am-11pm(11.30pm Sat); 12-11 Sun; closed 25 and 26 Dec ~ Bedrooms: £66.95B/£76.95S(£95.95B)

Recommended by Mike Gorton, Robert Watt, Mr and Mrs D J Nash, Roger and Carol Maden, Barry Steele-Perkins, Cathryn and Richard Hicks, Paul and Gail Betteley, Barry and Anne, James and Ginette Read, Dr Ian Mortimer, Lisa Robertson, Tom and Ruth Rees

HOLNE   SX7069 MAP 1

Church House
Signed off B3357 W of Ashburton; TQ13 7SJ

Medieval inn on Dartmoor, plenty of surrounding walks, log fires, real ales, and tasty bar food; comfortable bedrooms

Surrounded by fine walks and with open moorland just ten minutes away, this medieval inn is popular with walkers – especially at lunchtime – though there are plenty of cheerful locals, too. A hard-working new landlord has taken over and has refurbished throughout, adding fresh flowers and lit candles. The lower bar has stripped pine panelling and an 18th-c curved elm settle, and is separated from the lounge bar by a 16th-c heavy oak partition; open log fires in both rooms. Butcombe Bitter and Teignworthy Reel Ale with a guest like Otter Ale on handpump, and several good wines by the glass; darts, dominoes and board games. The bedrooms are comfortable and clean. Charles Kingsley (of *Water Babies* fame) was born in the village. The church is well worth a visit.

⑪ Well liked bar food now includes lunchtime sandwiches and filled baguettes, soup, devilled kidneys, greek salad, scallops with smoked bacon and salad, goats cheese on a herb croûton, home-cooked ham and eggs, local pasties, egg pasta in a creamy garlic, mushroom and basil sauce, steak in ale pie, liver and bacon casserole, popular seafood platter, and puddings such as sticky toffee pudding with butterscotch sauce and poached pears in red wine with a hot chocolate sauce. *Starters/Snacks: £4.95 to £6.95. Main Courses: £7.50 to £12.95. Puddings: £4.50*

Free house ~ Licensee Steve Ashworth ~ Real ale ~ Bar food (12-2.30, 7-8.30-ish) ~ Restaurant ~ (01364) 631208 ~ Children welcome ~ Dogs welcome ~ Open 12-3, 6-11(midnight Fri and Sat, 10.30 Sun); winter evening opening Mon-Sat 7pm, Sun 9pm ~ Bedrooms: £35S/£70S

Recommended by Mr and Mrs A Scadding, P and J Shapley, Gerry and Rosemary Dobson, Mike Gorton

HORNDON   SX5280 MAP 1

Elephants Nest 🍺 🛏

If coming from Okehampton on A386 turn left at Mary Tavy Inn, then left after about 0.5 mile; pub signposted beside Mary Tavy Inn, then Horndon signposted; on the Ordnance Survey Outdoor Leisure Map it's named as the New Inn; PL19 9NQ

Isolated old inn surrounded by Dartmoor walks, some interesting original features, real ales, and popular food

Surrounded by walks, this 400-year-old inn has plenty of picnic-sets under umbrellas in the spreading, attractive garden, and from here you look over dry-stone walls to the pastures of Dartmoor's lower slopes and the rougher moorland above. Inside, the main bar has lots of beer pump clips on the beams, bar chairs by the bar counter, and Palmers IPA, Dartmoor Brewery Jail Ale, Sharps Doom Bar, and a guest like O'Hanlons Yellowhammer on handpump, farm cider and several wines by the glass. There are two other newly refurbished rooms with nice modern dark wood dining chairs around a mix of tables, and throughout there are bare stone walls, flagstones, and three woodburning stoves; darts and maybe piped music. The bedrooms are comfortable and attractive.

🍴 Good, popular bar food at lunchtime includes filled baguettes and wraps, an antipasti plate, chicken liver parfait with cumberland sauce, king prawns sizzling in lemon, garlic, chilli and parsley butter, cumberland sausage with onion gravy, burgers with red onion marmalade, and caesar and niçoise salads, with evening choices such as duck teriyaki with figs, toasted walnuts and raspberry dressing, seafood salad, ravioli with taleggio cheese and watercress sauce, chinese pork belly with pak choi and rice noodles, fish pie, and puddings such as lemon posset and chocolate marquise. *Starters/Snacks: £4.50 to £6.95. Main Courses: £8.95 to £19.95. Puddings: £4.95*

Free house ~ Licensee Hugh Cook ~ Real ale ~ Bar food ~ (01822) 810273 ~ Children welcome ~ Dogs welcome ~ Open 12-3, 6.30-11 ~ Bedrooms: £65B/£75B

Recommended by John and Bernadette Elliott, Mr and Mrs M J Matthews, Emma Kingdon, FJS and DS, Dr and Mrs M E Wilson

IDDESLEIGH   SS5608   MAP 1

Duke of York ★ ♀

B3217 Exbourne—Dolton; EX19 8BG

Unfussy and exceptionally friendly pub with simply furnished bars, popular food, fair choice of drinks, and quirky bedrooms

'Everything a country pub should be' is used by several of our readers to describe this friendly, informal inn. It's run by a hospitable, genuinely welcoming landlord and there may well be chatty locals in their wellies (with maybe a dog or two) sitting around a roaring log fire, and flower posies on the tables. The enjoyably unspoilt bar has a lot of homely character: rocking chairs, cushioned wall benches built into the wall's black-painted wooden dado, stripped tables and other simple country furnishings. Well kept Adnams Broadside, Cotleigh Tawny, and Sharps IPA tapped from the cask, and quite a few wines by the glass. It does get pretty cramped at peak times; darts. There's also a dining room. Through a small coach arch is a little back garden with some picnic-sets. The bedrooms are quirky and in some cases very far from smart, so their appeal is very much to people who enjoy taking the rough with the smooth.

🍴 Good, honest, fairly priced bar food – using the landlord's own rare-breed beef – includes sandwiches, ploughman's, soup, chicken liver pâté, sausage or ham with eggs, liver and bacon, leek and parsnip cakes, game pie, steak and kidney pudding, chicken korma, local faggots with mash, double lamb chop with rosemary and garlic gravy, and puddings like chocolate parfait with chocolate sauce and orange sponge pudding with orange syrup and custard; there's a three-course evening menu in the dining room. *Starters/Snacks: £3.00 to £6.00. Main Courses: £5.00 to £15.00. Puddings: £3.50 to £4.00*

Free house ~ Licensees Jamie Stuart and Pippa Hutchinson ~ Real ale ~ Bar food (all day) ~ Restaurant ~ (01837) 810253 ~ Children welcome ~ Dogs welcome ~ Open 10am-11pm; 12-10.30 Sun ~ Bedrooms: £40B/£70B

Recommended by the Didler, Stephen Moss, Anthony Longden, John and Fiona McIlwain, Rona Murdoch, John Marsh, Steve Crick, Helen Preston, John Urquhart, Peter Craske, Paul and Ursula Randall, Sara Fulton, Roger Baker, P and J Shapley, Mrs Susan Clifford, Mike Gorton, Conor McGaughey, Mayur Shah, Maurice Ricketts, Ken and Janet Bracey, R J Walden, FJS and DS

KINGSBRIDGE   SX7344   MAP 1

Dodbrooke Inn 🍺

Church Street, Dodbrooke (parking some way off); TQ7 1DB

Chatty, bustling local, genuinely welcoming licensees, good mix of customers and honest food and drink

Up a steep side street, this bustling and quaint little local has a comfortably traditional feel, and on our evening visit, quite a mix of happy, chatting regulars: a table of customers enjoying a game of cards, a group of gents chatting over their pints, several younger customers gathered around the bar. The busy and efficient landlady managed to make us feel really welcome in the bar at the same time as serving food to the small, simply furnished dining room. There are bow windows, plush stools and built-in simple cushioned stall seats around straightforward pub tables (and an interesting barrel one), a patterned carpet, ceiling joists, some horse harness, old local photographs and china jugs, and coal-effect gas fires. Well kept Bass, Dartmoor IPA and Jail Ale and Sharps Cornish Jack on handpump, and local farm cider.

🍴 **As well as fish and chips to take away, the good, honest food includes sandwiches, ploughmans', garlic mushrooms, chicken liver, garlic and brandy pâté, a sausage or scampi basket, gammon with egg or pineapple, smoked haddock and spring onion fishcakes, daily specials such as scallops with bacon, baked bass with red onions, fresh lemon sole, and fillet steak with a cream, pepper and brandy sauce, and puddings like raspberry and almond tart and hot chocolate fudge cake with vanilla ice-cream.** *Starters/Snacks: £4.50 to £5.65. Main Courses: £5.75 to £14.25. Puddings: £3.95*

Free house ~ Licensees Michael and Jill Dyson ~ Real ale ~ Bar food (12-1.30, 6-9(7-8.30 Sun) ~ (01548) 852068 ~ Children welcome if over 5 ~ Open 12-2, 6(7 Sun)-11; closed Mon and Tues lunchtimes; evenings 25 and 26 Dec

Recommended by J Iorwerth Davies, Neil Robertson, MP

KINGSTON
SX6347 MAP 1

Dolphin 🛏

Off B3392 S of Modbury (can also be reached from A379 W of Modbury); TQ7 4QE

Peaceful old pub with walks down to the sea, cheerful atmosphere and decent drinks and food

The cheerful landlady in this peaceful little 16th-c inn offers a warm welcome to both visitors and locals.There are several knocked-through beamed rooms with cushioned wall settles, wheelback chairs and stools around a mix of wooden tables on the red patterned carpet, amusing drawings and photographs on the stone walls, and an open fire as well as a woodburning stove. Courage Best, Sharps Doom Bar and maybe Teignworthy Springtide on handpump, and summer farm cider. There are some seats and tables outside, and nice surrounding walks down to the sea. The gents' is across the road.

🍴 **Well liked bar food includes sandwiches, ploughman's, soup, steak in ale or fish pie, various curries, vegetarian lasagne, belly pork slow-cooked in cider, daily specials such as crab bisque, gammon steak and cod and chips, and puddings such as bread and butter pudding.** *Starters/Snacks: £5.95 to £7.95. Main Courses: £8.95 to £16.95. Puddings: £1.95 to £5.25*

Punch ~ Lease Janice Male ~ Real ale ~ Bar food (12-2.30, 6-9; not winter Sun evening or some winter Mon evenings) ~ (01548) 810314 ~ Children welcome ~ Dogs allowed in bar ~ Open 12-3, 6-11; 12-3, 7-10.30 Sun ~ Bedrooms: £42.50B/£68B

Recommended by Chris and Libby Allen, Alan and Anne Driver, Keith and Margaret Kettell, MB, Roger Wain-Heapy

MARLDON
SX8663 MAP 1

Church House 🍴 🍷

Just off A380 NW of Paignton; TQ3 1SL

Spreading bar plus several other rooms in pleasant inn, well liked drinks and bar food, and seats on three terraces

This is an attractive inn with friendly, efficient staff and well liked food and drink. The spreading bar has several different areas that radiate off the big semicircular bar counter with interesting windows, some beams, dark pine chairs around solid tables on the turkey carpet, and yellow leather bar chairs. Leading off here is a cosy little candlelit room with just four tables on the bare-board floor, a dark wood dado and stone fireplace. There's also a restaurant with a large stone fireplace and at the other end of the building, a similarly interesting room is split into two parts with a stone floor in one bit and a wooden floor in another (which has a big woodburning stove). The old barn holds yet another restaurant with art displays by local artists. Bass, Bays Gold, Fullers London Pride, and St Austell Dartmoor Best on handpump, and ten wines by the glass; piped music. There are picnic-sets on three carefully maintained grassy terraces behind the pub.

🍴 Good bar food includes sandwiches, soup, chicken liver pâté with tomato chutney, creamed leek and goats cheese tartlet with walnut dressing, carrot and rosemary roulade filled with spinach and cornish yarg with a spring onion and white wine sauce, corn-fed chicken in a bacon, spinach and sherry velouté, loin of pork with cider sauce and glazed pear, cajun-spiced bass with guacamole and sour cream, and king prawns in garlic butter. *Starters/Snacks: £5.50 to £9.00. Main Courses: £9.00 to £18.95. Puddings: £4.95 to £5.95*

Enterprise ~ Lease Julian Cook ~ Real ale ~ Bar food ~ Restaurant ~ (01803) 558279 ~ Children welcome ~ Dogs allowed in bar ~ Open 11-2.30, 5-11(11.30 Sat); 12-3, 5.30-10.30 Sun

Recommended by Pat Crabb, Chris and Jenny Howland-Harris, Andrea Rampley, Simon Fox

MEAVY   SX5467   MAP 1
Royal Oak
Off B3212 E of Yelverton; PL20 6PJ

Pleasant old pub with country furnishings and decent food and drink

Friendly new licensees have taken over this partly 15th-c pub, but apart from some re-painting, thankfully little has changed. The heavy-beamed L-shaped bar has pews from the church, red plush banquettes, and old agricultural prints and church pictures on the walls; a smaller bar – where the locals like to gather – has flagstones, a big open hearth fireplace and side bread oven. Dartmoor Brewery Jail Ale and IPA, and Sharps Doom Bar, with a guest such as St Austell Tribute or Skinners Betty Stogs on handpump. This is a pretty Dartmoor-edge village and the pub has seats on the green in front and by the building itself. The ancient oak from which the pub gets its name is just close by.

🍴 Decent bar food includes lunchtime sandwiches or filled baguettes and ploughman's as well as soup, farmhouse pâté, salmon and roasted pepper fishcakes with sweet chilli dip, home-cooked ham and eggs, local sausages with onion gravy, mushroom and goats cheese tartlets, steak in ale pie, cajun chicken, and puddings like fruit crumble and Bailey's cheesecake. *Starters/Snacks: £3.50 to £7.50. Main Courses: £7.95 to £10.95. Puddings: £3.95 to £4.50*

Free house ~ Licensee Steve Earp ~ Real ale ~ Bar food ~ Restaurant ~ (01822) 852944 ~ Children in lounge bar only ~ Dogs allowed in bar ~ Open 11-3, 6-11; 11am-midnight Sat; 11-11 Sun

Recommended by Wendda Johnson, John Branston, MB, Jacquie Jones

MOLLAND   SS8028   MAP 1
London 🍺
Village signposted off B3227 E of South Molton, down narrow lanes; EX36 3NG

A proper Exmoor inn with customers and their dogs to match, a warm welcome from the new licensees, honest food, farm cider and real ales

New licensees have taken over this old-fashioned inn but happily, have every intention of keeping the place as it always has been – a traditional Exmoor pub with the local farmers and gamekeepers (and their working dogs) being very much the focal part of things. The two small linked rooms by the old-fashioned central servery have hardly changed in 50 years and have lots of local stag-hunting pictures, tough carpeting or rugs on flagstones, cushioned benches and plain chairs around rough stripped trestle tables, a table of shooting and other country magazines, ancient stag and otter trophies, and darts and board games. On the left an attractive beamed room has accounts of the rescued stag which lived a long life at the pub many years ago, and on the right, a panelled dining room with a great curved settle by its fireplace has particularly good hunting and gamebird prints, including ones by McPhail and Hester Lloyd. A small hall with stuffed birds and animals and lots of overhead baskets has a box of toys. Cotleigh Tawny and Exmoor Ale, farm cider, and several wines by the glass; winter mulled wine and cider. The low-ceilinged lavatories are worth a look, with their Victorian mahogany and tiling (and in the gents' a testament to the prodigious thirst of the village cricket team). The garden is to be spruced up and they hope to use another garden opposite the pub for extra outdoor seating space. Don't miss the next-door church, with its untouched early 18th-c box pews – and in spring, a carpet of tenby daffodils in the graveyard.

🍴 Using local, seasonal produce, the honest bar food includes snacks with their own pork crackling, beef dripping on toast, pork pies and so forth, as well as soup, potted shrimps, mackerel and horseradish pâté, wild mushroom and goats cheese tart, venison sausages with bubble and squeak and gravy, steak and kidney suet pudding, rabbit pie, ling with brown shrimp sauce, and puddings such as chocolate roulade and various fruit crumbles. *Starters/Snacks: £3.20 to £4.50. Main Courses: £5.20 to £10.80. Puddings: £3.50 to £3.80*

Free house ~ Licensees Deborah See and Toby Bennett ~ Real ale ~ Bar food (not winter Sun evening) ~ Restaurant ~ No credit cards ~ (01769) 550269 ~ Children welcome ~ Dogs allowed in bar ~ Open 12-3, 6-11; 12-11 Sun and Sat ~ Bedrooms: /£60B

Recommended by Mr and Mrs P D Titcomb, MB, the Didler, Mrs J C Pank, Tony Winckworth, Keith and Sue Ward, Angus and Rosemary Campbell, Tom Evans, Bob and Margaret Holder, Martin and Pauline Jennings, Conor McGaughey, FJS and DS

NEWTON FERRERS   SX5447   MAP 1
Dolphin
Riverside Road East – follow Harbour dead end signs; PL8 1AE

Terraces looking down over the River Yealm, a simply furnished bar, traditional food and local ales

From the two terraces across the lane from this 18th-c pub, there's a grandstand view of the boating action on the busy tidal River Yealm. Inside, the L-shaped bar has a few low black beams, slate floors, some white-painted plank panelling, and simple pub furnishings including cushioned wall benches and small winged settles. It can get packed in summer. Badger Tanglefoot, First Gold and a seasonal beer on handpump and ten wines by the glass; euchre Monday evenings and winter Tuesday evening quiz nights. Parking by the pub is very limited, with more chance of a space either below or above. You can walk along the waterfront to the west end of the village.

🍴 Bar food includes chunky sandwiches, ploughman's, soup, garlic and thyme mixed wild mushrooms on toast, local seafood pie, seasonal mussels, proper burgers, honey and mustard baked ham with free-range eggs, daily specials like lamb curry, fresh beer-battered fish, and steak and kidney pie, and puddings such as sticky toffee pudding with toffee sauce and chocolate and orange baked cheesecake. *Starters/Snacks: £3.25 to £5.50. Main Courses: £8.50 to £11.50. Puddings: £2.95 to £4.95*

Badger ~ Tenants Jackie Cosens and Adrian Jenkins ~ Real ale ~ Bar food (12-2.30, 6-9; cream teas all day) ~ (01752) 872007 ~ Children welcome as long as seated and with adults ~ Dogs welcome ~ Open 10am-11pm(10.30pm Sun); 10-2.30, 6-11 Mon-Thurs in winter; closed winter Sun evening

Recommended by David M Cundy, M G Hart

NOMANSLAND   SS8313   MAP 1
Mount Pleasant
B3137 Tiverton—South Molton; EX16 8NN

Three fireplaces and a mix of furnishings in long bar, decent bar food, fair choice of drinks, and friendly service

Informal and friendly, this is a pleasant place for a drink or meal. The long bar is divided into three with huge fireplaces each end, one with a woodburning stove under a low dark ochre black-beamed ceiling, the other with a big log fire, and there are tables in a sizeable bay window extension. A nice mix of furniture on the patterned carpet includes an old sofa with a colourful throw, old-fashioned leather dining chairs, pale country kitchen chairs and tables all with candles in attractive metal holders; country prints and local photographs including shooting parties, and magazines and daily papers to read. The public bar, with plenty of bar stools, has Cotleigh Tawny and Sharps Doom Bar on handpump, several wines by the glass and Weston's Old Rosie cider. On the left, a high-beamed stripped stone dining room was once a smithy and still has the raised forge fireplace. Piped music, darts and board games. There are some picnic-sets in the neat back garden and some in front of the building.

🍽 **Bar food includes filled baguettes, soup, potato shells filled with creamy garlic mushrooms, ham and eggs, mushroom stroganoff, bangers and mash, steak and kidney pie, lamb shank with a redcurrant and orange sauce, seafood pasta, chicken breast with garlic, mushrooms, spring onions, brie, Benedictine and cream, and puddings such as chocolate brownie and apple pie.** *Starters/Snacks: £3.95 to £5.95. Main Courses: £5.50 to £14.95. Puddings: £4.95*

Free house ~ Licensees Anne, Karen and Sarah Butler ~ Real ale ~ Bar food (all day) ~ Restaurant ~ (01884) 860271 ~ Well behaved children welcome ~ Dogs allowed in bar ~ Open 11.30-11; 12-10.30 Sun; closed 25 and 26 Dec, 1 Jan

Recommended by Bob and Margaret Holder, A C Powell, Conor McGaughey, Ken and Janet Bracey, Rona Murdoch

NOSS MAYO   SX5447   MAP 1

Ship ♀ 🍴

Off A379 via B3186, E of Plymouth; PL8 1EW

Busy pub, seats overlooking inlet and visiting boats, thick-walled bars with log fires, west country beers, popular food, and friendly atmosphere

---

The front terrace here is extremely popular in fine weather – you can sit at the octagonal wooden tables under parasols and look over the inlet, and visiting boats can tie up alongside (with prior permission); there are outdoor heaters for cooler evenings. Inside, it's very attractively furnished and the two thick-walled bars have a happy mix of dining chairs and tables on the wooden floors, log fires, bookcases, dozens of local pictures, newspapers and magazines to read, and a chatty atmosphere; board games, dominoes and cards. Dartmoor Brewery IPA, Summerskills Tamar and a changing guest on handpump, lots of malt whiskies, and quite a few wines by the glass. Parking is restricted at high tide.

🍽 **Well liked bar food includes filled baguettes, ploughman's, soup, duck liver pâté with red onion marmalade, tempura king prawns with sweet chilli sauce, bubble and squeak topped with smoked salmon, poached egg and hollandaise sauce, sausage and mash, steak and kidney pie, wild mushroom and blue cheese pancakes, cajun-style salmon with roasted vine tomatoes, roast duck breast with port and redcurrant sauce, and puddings such as warm chocolate brownie with warm chocolate sauce and crème brûlée.** *Starters/Snacks: £4.75 to £6.00. Main Courses: £7.50 to £12.00. Puddings: £5.25 to £5.75*

Free house ~ Licensees Charlie and Lisa Bullock ~ Real ale ~ Bar food (all day) ~ Restaurant ~ (01752) 872387 ~ Children welcome ~ Dogs allowed in bar ~ Open 11-11; 12-10.30 Sun

Recommended by Graham Oddey, John Evans, MB, Lynda and Trevor Smith, David Rule, Gary Rollings, Debbie Porter, FJS and DS, John Smart, Gerry and Rosemary Dobson

---

Real ale to us means beer which has matured naturally in its cask – not pressurised or filtered. We name all real ales stocked. We usually name ales preserved under a light blanket of carbon dioxide too, though purists – pointing out that this stops the natural yeasts developing – would disagree (most people, including us, can't tell the difference!).

PETER TAVY   SX5177   MAP 1

Peter Tavy Inn ♀

Off A386 near Mary Tavy, N of Tavistock; PL19 9NN

Old stone inn with pretty garden, bustling bar with beams and big log fire, and good choice of food and drink

This is a very well run and friendly pub with an enjoyably bustling atmosphere and helpful, efficient staff. The low-beamed bar has high-backed settles on the black flagstones by the big stone fireplace (a fine log fire on cold days), smaller settles in stone-mullioned windows, and Blackawton Original Bitter, Dartmoor Brewery Jail Ale, Sharps Doom Bar and maybe Cotleigh 25 on handpump; local cider, 30 malt whiskies and several wines by the glass. There's also a snug dining area and restaurant; maybe piped music. From the picnic-sets in the pretty garden there are peaceful views of the moor rising above nearby pastures.

🍴 Good, popular food at lunchtime might include filled ciabatta and baguettes, ploughman's, soup, stilton and pear pâté, an antipasti plate, ham and egg, pork cobbler, vegetable chilli, and chicken and bacon tartlet, with evening choices such as chicken liver and mushroom pâté with chutney, king prawns with lemon mayonnaise, mexican fajita with a choice of meat, venison steak with blackberry and juniper sauce, and duck breast with a plum, star anise and orange sauce. *Starters/Snacks: £4.25 to £6.55. Main Courses: £6.25 to £14.95. Puddings: £3.75 to £4.50*

Free house ~ Licensees Chris and Joanne Wordingham ~ Real ale ~ Bar food (not 25 Dec, evenings 24-26 Dec and 1 Jan) ~ (01822) 810348 ~ Children welcome ~ Dogs welcome ~ Open 12-3, 6-11(10.30 Sun)

Recommended by Helen and Brian Edgeley, Dennis Jenkin, David and Katharine Cooke, Dr and Mrs M W A Haward, R and H Fraser, Dr Ian Mortimer, George Murdoch, Jacquie Jones, Peter Craske, Ted George, Irene and Derek Flewin, Andrea Rampley

PORTGATE   SX4185   MAP 1

Harris Arms ♀

Turn off A30 E of Launceston at Broadwoodwidger turn-off (with brown Dingle Steam Village sign), and head S; Launceston Road (old A30 between Lewdown and Lifton); EX20 4PZ

Enthusiastic, well travelled licensees in roadside pub with exceptional wine list and popular food

When it comes to wine, the friendly licensees here say, 'It is one of our lifetime passions.' They are both qualified award-winning wine-makers and are more than happy to help you through their eclectic wine list. With helpful notes and 22 of their favourites by the glass, there are plenty of gems to choose from – and you can buy them to take home, too. The bar has burgundy end walls and cream ones in between, some rather fine photographs, a huge table at one end (brought back from New Zealand), a long red-plush built-in wall banquette and a woodburning stove; afghan saddle-bag cushions are scattered around a mixture of other tables and dining chairs. On the left, steps lead down to the dining room with elegant beech dining chairs (and more afghan cushions) around stripped wooden tables, and some unusual paintings on the walls collected by the Whitemans on their travels. Sharps Doom Bar and Exe Valley Devon Spring on handpump, Luscombe organic soft drinks, and summer cider; there may be a pile of country magazines. Outside under outdoor heaters there are seats on a decked area amongst pots of lavender, and plenty of picnic-sets in the sloping back garden looking out over the rolling wooded pasture hills. They are growing 24 vines.

🍴 Enjoyable bar food using produce from Devon and Cornwall includes soup, home-cured gravadlax with lemon and caper mayonnaise, king prawns piri-piri, ham and free-range eggs, beef in ale, free-range chicken breast with wild mushroom and brandy cream and truffled potatoes royale, asparagus and pecorino ravioli with white wine, cream, and parmesan, battered haddock with tartare sauce, slow-roasted confit of pork belly with celeriac fondant and apple sauce, and puddings such as chocolate torte and crème brûlée. *Starters/Snacks: £4.50 to £7.50. Main Courses: £8.95 to £13.95. Puddings: £4.00 to £5.50*

Free house ~ Licensees Andy and Rowena Whiteman ~ Real ale ~ Bar food ~ Restaurant ~
(01566) 783331 ~ Children welcome ~ Dogs allowed in bar ~ Open 12-3, 6-11; 12-3 Sun;
evening opening 6.30 in winter; closed Sun evening, all day Mon

Recommended by Sue Ruffhead, Lesley and Peter Barrett, Lynne Carter

POSTBRIDGE   SX6780   MAP 1

Warren House

B3212 0.75 mile NE of Postbridge; PL20 6TA

Straightforward old pub, relaxing for a drink or snack after a Dartmoor hike

Friendly and with plenty of atmosphere, this straightforward place is most welcome after
a hike on Dartmoor. One of the fireplaces in the cosy bar is said to have been kept alight
almost continuously since 1845, and there are simple furnishings like easy chairs and
settles under the beamed ochre ceiling, old pictures of the inn on the partly panelled
stone walls, and dim lighting (fuelled by the pub's own generator); a family room also.
Otter Ale, Ringwood Old Thumper, St Austell Tribute and a guest beer on handpump, local
farm cider and malt whiskies; piped music, darts and pool. The picnic-sets on both sides
of the road have moorland views.

🍴 **Decent bar food includes filled baguettes and baked potatoes, ploughman's with
cornish yarg, tasty pasties, local jumbo sausage, mushroom stroganoff, rabbit pie, steak
in ale pie, breaded plaice, daily specials and puddings like sticky toffee pudding with
toffee sauce.** *Starters/Snacks: £3.50 to £5.95. Main Courses: £6.75 to £10.25. Puddings: £4.95*

Free house ~ Licensee Peter Parsons ~ Real ale ~ Bar food (all day but more restricted winter
Mon and Tues) ~ (01822) 880208 ~ Children in family room ~ Dogs allowed in bar ~
Open 11-11; 12-10.30 Sun; 11-5 Mon and Tues during Nov-Feb

*Recommended by Anthony Longden, Paul and Margaret Baker, Steve Derbyshire, Andrea Rampley,
Roger E F Maxwell, Phil and Sally Gorton*

POUNDSGATE   SX7072   MAP 1

Tavistock Inn

B3357 continuation; TQ13 7NY

Friendly old pub with some original features; lovely scenery and plenty of walkers

There are plenty of moorland hikes that start and finish at, or pass, this family-run and
picturesque old pub, so many customers are walkers (often with their dogs). There are
tables on the front terrace and pretty flowers in stone troughs, hanging baskets and
window boxes and more seats (and ducks) in the quiet back garden; lovely scenery.
Inside, some original features include a narrow-stepped granite spiral staircase, original
flagstones, ancient log fireplaces, and beams, and there's a friendly atmosphere and a
good mix of locals and visitors. Courage Best, Otter Ale, and Wychwood Hobgoblin Best
on handpump, and several malt whiskies.

🍴 **Traditional bar food includes filled baguettes and baked potatoes, pies like game,
chicken and ham or steak in ale, vegetarian pasta bake, and local trout.** *Starters/Snacks:
£4.10 to £4.55. Main Courses: £6.20 to £12.50. Puddings: £4.25*

Punch ~ Lease Peter and Jean Hamill ~ Real ale ~ Bar food (all day in summer) ~ Restaurant ~
(01364) 631251 ~ Children welcome away from bar ~ Dogs allowed in bar ~ Open 11-11;
12-10.30 Sun; 11-3, 6-11 winter

Recommended by Simon Rodway, JHW, Steve Derbyshire, Bob and Angela Brooks, FJS and DS, Mrs S Wallis

---

We accept no free drinks, meals or payment for inclusion. We take no advertising,
and are not sponsored by the brewing industry – or by anyone else.
So all reports are independent.

RATTERY   SX7461   MAP 1

Church House

Village signposted from A385 W of Totnes, and A38 S of Buckfastleigh; TQ10 9LD

One of Britain's oldest pubs with some fine original features and peaceful views

As this is one of Britain's oldest pubs, it's worth a visit to see some of the fine original features – notably the spiral stone steps behind a little stone doorway on your left as you come in that date from about 1030. There are massive oak beams and standing timbers in the homely open-plan bar, large fireplaces (one with a little cosy nook partitioned off around it), windsor armchairs, comfortable seats and window seats, and prints on the plain white walls; the dining room is separated from this room by heavy curtains and there's also a lounge area too. Otter Ale, Dartmoor Brewery Jail Ale, St Austell Dartmoor Best, and a guest such as Teignworthy Reel Ale on handpump, quite a few malt whiskies and several wines by the glass. The garden has picnic-sets on the large hedged-in lawn, and peaceful views of the partly wooded surrounding hills. More reports please.

🍴 **Bar food includes sandwiches, toasties, filled baguettes and baked potatoes, ploughman's, soup, vegetable and stilton crumble, a fry-up, sausages with onion gravy, battered cod, chicken in whisky cream sauce, steak and kidney pie, daily specials, and puddings like lemon meringue pie or syrup sponge pudding.** *Starters/Snacks: £4.50 to £6.50. Main Courses: £6.75 to £13.95. Puddings: £4.25 to £5.25*

Free house ~ Licensee Ray Hardy ~ Real ale ~ Bar food ~ Restaurant ~ (01364) 642220 ~ Children welcome ~ Dogs allowed in bar ~ Open 11-2.30, 6-11; 12-2.30, 6-10.30 Sun

Recommended by Hugh Roberts, Dudley and Moira Cockroft, Bob and Angela Brooks, Rona Murdoch, JT, B J Harding

ROCKBEARE   SY0195   MAP 1

Jack in the Green 🍴 ♀

Signposted from new A30 bypass E of Exeter; EX5 2EE

Neat dining pub with traditionally furnished bars and imaginative meals

There's no doubt that most customers are here to enjoy the good, carefully presented food in this big, neatly kept roadside dining pub. It's a friendly place and the comfortable good-sized bar has wheelback chairs, sturdy cushioned wall pews and varying-sized tables on its dark blue carpet, a dark carved oak dresser, and sporting prints and nice decorative china; piped music. The larger dining side is similarly traditional in style: some of its many old hunting and shooting photographs are well worth a close look and there are button-back leather chesterfields by the big woodburning stove. A couple of real ales on handpump such as Butcombe Bitter, O'Hanlons Yellowhammer or Otter Ale, and 12 wines by the glass. There are some tables out behind the building.

🍴 **Using seasonal, local produce, the top quality – not cheap – food includes bar snacks like ploughman's, soup, smoked salmon and prawns with dill and crème fraîche, honey and mustard sausages, beer-battered fish, thai green chicken curry and steak and kidney pie, as well as ham hock terrine with pickled vegetables, seared peppered tuna with wasabi cream sushi, ginger and rocket, free-range chicken breast with tarragon potato purée, duck breast with apples and calvados, and puddings such as rhubarb brûlée with shortbreads and chocolate mousse with lime ice-cream; fair value two- and three-course Sunday lunch.** *Starters/Snacks: £4.95 to £6.50. Main Courses: £8.50 to £19.50. Puddings: £5.75 to £7.75*

Free house ~ Licensee Paul Parnell ~ Real ale ~ Bar food (all day Sun) ~ Restaurant ~ (01404) 822240 ~ Well behaved children in one bar only ~ Open 11-3, 5.30(6 Sat)-11; 12-10.30 Sun; closed 25 Dec-6 Jan

Recommended by Hugh Roberts, Mike and Heather Watson, Cathryn and Richard Hicks, Henry Snell, Robert Blake, Oliver and Sue Rowell, John and Julie Moon, John and Dinah Waters, Rod Stoneman, Gene and Tony Freemantle, Dr D and Mrs B Woods, Mrs C Osgood, Barry Steele-Perkins, John and Fiona McIlwain, Andy and Claire Barker

SANDY PARK   SX7189   MAP 1

Sandy Park Inn 🛏

A382 Whiddon Down—Moretonhampstead; TQ13 8JW

Busy little thatched inn with snug bars, enjoyable food, and attractive bedrooms

With no intrusions from machines or music, the atmosphere in this little thatched inn is relaxed and chatty. The small bar on the right has rugs on the black-painted composition floor, black beams in the cream ceiling, varnished built-in wall settles forming separate areas around nice tables, and high stools by the chatty bar counter with Otter Ale, St Austell Tribute and guests such as Exe Valley Bitter and O'Hanlons Yellowhammer on handpump, and a decent choice of wines by the glass. The back snug has one big table that a dozen people could just squeeze around, stripped stone walls, and a cream-painted bright-cushioned built-in wall bench. On the left is a small dining room with golfing and other prints on the red walls and an inner private dining room with lots of prints, and one big table. There are seats by outdoor heaters in the large garden with fine views.

🍴 **Attractively presented bar food includes sandwiches, soup, crumbed tiger prawns with sweet chilli dip, pasta with gorgonzola, artichokes and walnuts, local sausages with mustard mash and parsnip crisps, beer-battered cod, chicken schnitzel with napoli sauce, honey-glazed ham and melted cheese, roasted halibut with mango, spring onion and coriander salsa, and puddings such as treacle tart and chocolate brownie with dark chocolate sauce.** *Starters/Snacks: £5.00 to £8.00. Main Courses: £7.00 to £12.00. Puddings: £5.00*

Free house ~ Licensee Nic Rout ~ Real ale ~ Bar food (12-2.30(4 Sun), 6.30-9) ~ Restaurant ~ (01647) 433267 ~ Children welcome ~ Dogs allowed in bar and bedrooms ~ Open 11(12 Sun)-11 ~ Bedrooms: £55B/£96B

Recommended by Roger and Carol Maden, FJS and DS, Donna and Roger, Bettye Reynolds, Andrea and Guy Bradley, Dr Ian Mortimer, Julie Russell-Carter

SHEEPWASH   SS4806   MAP 1

Half Moon 🍷 🛏

Off A3072 Holsworthy—Hatherleigh; EX21 5NE

Ancient inn loved by fishermen with 12 miles of River Torridge and fishing facilities; real ales, enjoyable food and newly refurbished bedrooms

Much loved by fishermen, this 15th-c inn has 12 miles of the River Torridge available for salmon, brown trout and sea trout fishing. They have a rod room, good drying facilities and a small tackle shop for basic necessities, and can issue rod licences. The main bar is simply furnished with solid old furniture and there's a wealth of beams and a large log fireplace fronted by flagstones. Brains Rev James, St Austell Dartmoor Best Bitter and Tinners, and Sharps Doom Bar on handpump, 11 wines by the glass from a good list, and a decent choice of malt whiskies. There's an attractive separate dining room with black oak woodwork polished to perfection; bar billiards. The bedrooms have been recently refurbished and there are four in a converted stable – ideal for guests with dogs.

🍴 **Good bar food includes sandwiches, filled baked potatoes, ploughman's, soup, smoked venison pâté with gooseberry and coriander chutney, pork, chilli and apricot balls with a cashew nut centre and peking sauce dip, home-cooked ham and eggs, proper home-made burger, wild mushroom stroganoff, fresh local game pie, lamb and coconut curry, daily specials such as crab flan, beef and Guinness stew, a trio of fish (plaice, haddock and red mullet) with dill and lemon butter, chicken in a tomato and wine sauce with garlic, rosemary and mushrooms, and puddings like chocolate and marshmallow cheesecake and eton mess.** *Starters/Snacks: £3.95 to £5.95. Main Courses: £7.50 to £14.95. Puddings: £3.25 to £4.25*

Free house ~ Licensees Chris and Tony Green ~ Real ale ~ Bar food ~ Restaurant ~ (01409) 231376 ~ Well behaved children welcome ~ Dogs allowed in bar and bedrooms ~ Open 11-3, 6-11; 12-10.30 Sun ~ Bedrooms: £45B/£90B

Recommended by Dr A McCormick, Ryta Lyndley, S G N Bennett

SIDBURY

SY1496   MAP 1

Hare & Hounds ◗

3 miles N of Sidbury, at Putts Corner; A375 towards Honiton, crossroads with B3174;
EX10 0QQ

Large well run roadside pub with log fires, beams and attractive layout, popular daily
carvery, efficient staff, and big garden

As this extremely popular and very well run roadside pub serves food all day, you could
avoid the lunchtime crowds by eating a little earlier or a little later (though the carvery
is at mealtimes only). It's much bigger inside than you could have guessed from outside
and there are two good log fires (and rather unusual wood-framed leather sofas complete
with pouffes), heavy beams and fresh flowers throughout, some oak panelling, plenty of
tables with red leatherette or red plush-cushioned dining chairs, window seats and well
used bar stools too; it's mostly carpeted, with some bare boards and stripped stone walls.
At the opposite end, on the left, another big dining area has huge windows looking out
over the garden. Branscombe Best Bitter and Otter Bitter and Ale tapped from the cask,
local farm cider and several wines by the glass; a side room has a big-screen sports TV
and games machine. The big garden, giving nice valley views, has picnic-sets, a children's
play area and a marquee, and there may be a small strolling flock of peafowl.

🍴 **Under the new licensees and using local produce, the enjoyable food includes the**
particularly good carvery (lunchtime and evening and all day on Sunday), as well as
sandwiches, filled baguettes and baked potatoes, soup, a pie and a curry of the day,
spinach and ricotta cannelloni, fishcakes with a lime and coriander salsa, salad platters,
garlic chicken with garlic and sherry, gammon with egg or pineapple, steaks, and daily
fish specials. *Starters/Snacks: £3.95 to £5.75. Main Courses: £8.25 to £14.95. Puddings: £2.50*
to £4.50

Free house ~ Licensees Graham Cole and Lindsey Chun ~ Real ale ~ Bar food (all day) ~
Restaurant ~ (01404) 41760 ~ Children welcome ~ Dogs allowed in bar ~ Open 10am-11pm;
12-10.30 Sun

Recommended by Dr and Mrs M E Wilson, FJS and DS, Richard Wyld, Mrs P Bishop, Rod Stoneman

SIDFORD

SY1389   MAP 1

Blue Ball ◗

A3052 just N of Sidmouth; EX10 9QL

Reincarnated after dreadful fire

Completely rebuilt after a terrible fire, this friendly place is now up and running again –
all that looked so good and special about the old pub has been more or less reincarnated
here. The central bar covers three main areas: light beams, bar stools and a nice mix of
wooden dining chairs around circular tables on the patterned carpet, three log fires,
prints, horsebrasses and plenty of bric-a-brac on the walls, and Bass, Greene King Abbot,
Otter Bitter, St Austell Tribute, and a guest such as Sharps Doom Bar on handpump. The
public bar has darts, a games machine, and board games; piped music. A new function
room has been opened. There are seats on a terrace and in the flower-filled garden.

🍴 **Popular bar food includes sandwiches, filled baked potatoes, ploughman's, soup,**
chicken liver parfait with red onion marmalade, beef or vegetarian lasagne, honey-roast
ham with fried eggs, specials such as tagliatelle with cherry tomatoes, peas and
courgettes, slow-roast pork belly on sweet potato mash with red wine sauce, and pepper
crusted salmon fillet with braised endive and parsley butter sauce, and puddings such as
chocolate and walnut sponge pudding and crème brûlée of the day. *Starters/Snacks: £3.95*
to £5.95. Main Courses: £7.25 to £13.95. Puddings: £3.95 to £4.50

Punch ~ Lease Roger Newton ~ Real ale ~ Bar food (all day) ~ Restaurant ~ (01395) 514062 ~
Children in dining areas only ~ Dogs allowed in bar ~ Open 8am-11pm ~ Bedrooms:
£30(£60B)/£95B

Recommended by Dr and Mrs M E Wilson

SPREYTON   SX6996   MAP 1

Tom Cobley ◖

*From A30 Whiddon Down roundabout take former A30 (opposite A382), then first left,
turning left at crossroads after 1.1 miles; in village centre turn left; can also be reached
from A3124; EX17 5AL*

**Up to 22 real ales well kept on handpump, cheerful licensees and home-made food in busy
village pub**

It's the splendid choice of real ales kept in top condition by the particularly cheerful and
welcoming landlord that draw customers to this bustling village pub. The six regulars on
handpump from the thatched bar might be Cotleigh Tawny, Clearwater Cavalier, Sharps
Doom Bar, and St Austell Proper Job, Tribute and HSD, and they often have up to
18 guests – all from the West Country on our visit. The comfortable little bar has
straightforward pubby furnishings, an open fire in the brick fireplace, local photographs,
country scenes and some old jokey west country bumpkin prints, and sporting trophies;
no music or games machines. The 20-year-old pub cat is called Daz. There's a large back
restaurant with beamery. Seats in the tree-shaded garden, with more out in front by the
quiet street. Big breakfasts.

🍴 Generous helpings of good value lunchtime bar food include sandwiches and toasties,
filled baked potatoes, ploughman's, soup, home-made pasties, home-made pies such as
steak and mushroom and chicken, ham, leek and tarragon, home-cooked ham and eggs,
omelettes, suet puddings like cherry tomato and mozzarella, liver, bacon and onion, and
lamb and mint, liver and onions, and puddings; the evening restaurant menu is more
elaborate. *Starters/Snacks: £3.95 to £5.95. Main Courses: £6.95 to £7.25. Puddings: £3.95*

Free house ~ Licensees Roger and Carol Cudlip ~ Real ale ~ Bar food ~ Restaurant ~
(01647) 231314 ~ Children welcome ~ Dogs allowed in bar ~ Open 12-3, 6-midnight(1am Sat);
12-3, 7-11.30 Sun; closed Mon lunchtime ~ Bedrooms: £24.50(£40S)/£50(£80S)

Recommended by Dave Lowe, Mike Gorton

STOCKLAND   ST2404   MAP 1

Kings Arms ♀

*Village signposted from A30 Honiton—Chard; and also, at every turning, from N end of
Honiton High Street; EX14 9BS*

Pleasant old inn with elegant bar, cosy restaurant, and local beers and cider

One of the partners who ran this 16th-c inn for around 20 years has returned, and the head
chef for the last four years now becomes joint licensee with him; as we went to press there
was no news of any major changes. The dark beamed, elegant Cotley Bar has solid refectory
tables and settles, attractive landscapes, a medieval oak screen (which divides the room
into two), and a great stone fireplace across almost the whole width of one end. The cosy
restaurant has a huge inglenook fireplace and bread oven; piped music. Branscombe Vale
Branoch, Exmoor Ale and Otter Ale on handpump and several wines by the glass. At the
back, a flagstoned bar has cushioned benches and stools around heavy wooden tables;
there's also a darts area, a room with more tables, a game machine, pool, and a neat skittle
alley. There are tables under parasols on the terrace in front of the white-faced thatched
pub and a lawn enclosed by trees and shrubs. More reports on any changes, please.

🍴 Bar food now includes sandwiches, soup, king scallops flamed in whisky with a cream
sauce, duck liver pâté with cranberry sauce, steak in ale pie, calves liver and bacon with
sherry jus, beer-battered cod, seared rack of lamb topped with a garlic and rosemary
sauce, beef stroganoff, and half a roast duck; also, daily specials and puddings.
Starters/Snacks: £4.00 to £6.00. Main Courses: £8.00 to £17.50. Puddings: £5.00 to £6.00

Free house ~ Licensees Shaun Barnes and John O'Leary ~ Real ale ~ Bar food ~ Restaurant ~
(01404) 881361 ~ Children welcome but not in bar areas after 9pm ~ Dogs allowed in bar and
bedrooms ~ Open 11.30-3, 6-11; 12-3, 6.30-10.30 Sun ~ Bedrooms: £45S/£70S

*Recommended by John Evans, Michael B Griffith, Jeremy and Jane Morrison, Gene and Tony Freemantle,
D Restarick, Mike Gorton, John and Julie Moon, Bob and Margaret Holder, Malcolm and Jane Levitt*

STOKE GABRIEL   SX8457   MAP 1

Church House

Village signposted from A385 just W of junction with A3022, in Collaton St Mary; can also be reached from nearer Totnes; TQ9 6SD

Busy local with fine medieval ceiling and huge fireplace, little public bar, and honest pubby food

There's a friendly welcome and plenty of chatty regulars in this early 14th-c pub. The lounge bar has an exceptionally fine medieval beam-and-plank ceiling, as well as a black oak partition wall, window seats cut into the thick butter-coloured walls, decorative plates and vases of flowers on a dresser, and a huge fireplace still used in winter to cook the stew; darts. The mummified cat in a case, probably about 200 years old, was found during restoration of the roof space in the verger's cottage three doors up the lane – one of a handful found in the West Country and believed to have been a talisman against evil spirits. Bass, Coors (Brains) Hancocks HB, and a guest such as Dartmoor Brewery Jail Ale on handpump and 20 malt whiskies. Euchre in the little public locals' bar. There are picnic-sets on the small terrace in front of the building. The church is very pretty, and relations with the Church of England and this pub go back a long way – witness the priest hole, dating from the Reformation, visible from outside. Parking is very limited. No children.

🍴 Straightforward, good value bar food includes sandwiches and toasties, filled baked potatoes, ploughman's, soup, sausage and mash with onion gravy or baked beans, beef stew with dumplings, a good steak, kidney and ale pie, wild mushroom ravioli, chicken curry and lamb shank. *Starters/Snacks: £3.25 to £5.95. Main Courses: £7.50 to £8.95. Puddings: £4.25*

Free house ~ Licensee T G Patch ~ Real ale ~ Bar food (11-2.30, 6-9.30; 12-3, 7-9.30 Sun) ~ (01803) 782384 ~ Dogs allowed in bar ~ Open 11-11; 12-4, 7-11 Sun

Recommended by Donna and Roger, R T and J C Moggridge, Simon Fox

STOKENHAM   SX8042   MAP 1

Church House ♀

Opposite church, N of A379 towards Torcross; TQ7 2SZ

Unspoilt pub, real ales and decent food, pretty surrounding countryside

Popular with locals, this spacious pub has three rambling, low-beamed open-plan areas connected by archways. There's usually a bustling atmosphere, Brakspears Bitter, Greene King Abbot, Otter Ale and a guest such as Wadworths 6X on handpump, local apple juice and cider, several wines by the glass and quite a few bourbons; piped music and darts. The attractive garden has some seats and the surrounding countryside is lovely. The pub looks out on to a common where sheep graze and is next to the ancient Norman church – which it has been associated with for centuries.

🍴 Well liked bar food includes sandwiches, soup, a good cheese platter, a daily changing tartlet, local crab cocktail, herby local sausages with caramelised onions, lambs liver with watercress and orange sauce, salmon fillet with oyster sauce and coriander, steak and kidney in Guinness pie, and puddings such as chocolate tart with ginger ice-cream or plum frangipane with clotted cream. *Starters/Snacks: £2.80 to £4.95. Main Courses: £7.50 to £13.95. Puddings: £3.95*

Heavitree ~ Tenants Richard Smith and Simon Cadman ~ Real ale ~ Bar food (12-2, 6-9) ~ Restaurant ~ (01548) 580253 ~ Children welcome ~ Dogs allowed in bar ~ Open 11-2.30, 6-11; 12-2.30, 6-10.30 Sun

Recommended by Mr and Mrs G Owens, Mr and Mrs H J Stephens, Jennifer Sheridan, Paul Hagan, Dennis Jenkin, Mrs D Shoults, Roger Wain-Heapy, B J Harding

---

If we know a pub has an outdoor play area for children, we mention it.

TIPTON ST JOHN   SY0991   MAP 1

Golden Lion
Signed off B3176 Sidmouth—Ottery St Mary; EX10 0AA

A good mix of diners and drinkers in friendly village pub; attractive garden with evening jazz summer Sundays

Well run and friendly, this attractive village pub has a good mix of both diners and drinkers, and the cheerful licensees even keep a few tables reserved for those just wanting a chat and a pint. There's a relaxed, comfortable atmosphere in the main bar area (which is split into two), and in the back snug, and throughout there are paintings from west country artists, art deco prints, tiffany lamps, and hops, copper pots and kettles hanging from the beams. Bass, Greene King IPA and Otter Ale on handpump, 11 wines by the glass and local organic soft drinks; efficient service, piped music. There are seats on the terracotta-walled terrace with outside heaters and grapevines and more seats on the grass edged by pretty flowering borders; summer Sunday evening jazz out here.

🍴 Good bar food at lunchtime includes sandwiches, ploughman's, soup, salads such as goats cheese with italian ham or smoked duck with onion marmalade, home-cooked ham and egg, moules frites, and steak and kidney pudding, with evening dishes like creamy garlic mushrooms, home-cured gravadlax with mustard and dill dressing, chicken with a light creamy, sherry sauce, lamb kebab in rosemary and garlic, and duck breast with a plum and balsamic sauce; daily specials, puddings, and Sunday roasts. *Starters/Snacks: £4.50 to £8.00. Main Courses: £8.50 to £16.00. Puddings: £4.50 to £5.50*

Heavitree ~ Tenants François and Michelle Teissier ~ Real ale ~ Bar food ~ (01404) 812881 ~ Children welcome ~ Jazz Sun evening (May–end Aug) every 2 weeks ~ Open 12-2.30(3 Sat), 6-11; 12-3, 7-10.30 Sun; closed Sun evening Sept–May

Recommended by Mike Gorton, Dr and Mrs M E Wilson, Michael and Lynne Gittins, Julie Cox, Colin Wright, John Kent

TOPSHAM   SX9688   MAP 1

Bridge Inn ★ ◀
2.25 miles from M5 junction 30: Topsham signposted from exit roundabout; in Topsham follow signpost (A376) Exmouth on the Elmgrove Road, into Bridge Hill; EX3 0QQ

Wonderful old drinkers' pub with eight real ales, in the landlady's family for five generations

Quite often a queue forms outside this marvellous old place waiting for the doors to open. It's a gem and much loved by a wide mix of customers for the utterly old-fashioned character and layout. The very friendly landlady is the fifth generation of her family to run it and the atmosphere is chatty and relaxed with no noisy games machines, music or mobile phones to spoil that. Of course, the perfectly kept eight real ales are a big draw too and are helpfully described on the daily changing list. Tapped from the cask, these might include Bays Gold, Branscombe Vale Branoc and 111 Not Out!, Cotleigh Kookaburra, Palmers 200, RCH Santa Fe, Teignworthy Harveys, and Warrior Sitting Bull; organic cider, country wines, non-alcoholic pressés, and decent wines by the glass. There are fine old traditional furnishings (true country workmanship) in the little lounge partitioned off from the inner corridor by a high-backed settle; log fire; a bigger lower room (the old malthouse) is open at busy times. Outdoors, riverside picnic-sets overlook the weir.

🍴 Simple, tasty bar food such as well filled pasties, sandwiches, a hearty winter soup and various ploughman's; the gooseberry and elderflower chutney is said to be good. *Starters/Snacks: £3.95 to £4.25. Main Courses: £6.50 to £6.95*

Free house ~ Licensee Mrs C Cheffers-Heard ~ Real ale ~ Bar food (lunchtime only) ~ No credit cards ~ (01392) 873862 ~ Children in two rooms ~ Dogs allowed in bar ~ Open 12-2, 6-10.30(11 Fri and Sat); 12-2, 7-10.30 Sun

Recommended by Richard and Anne Ansell, Donna and Roger, Philip and Jude Simmons, the Didler, Pete Baker, Terry and Linda Moseley, Mr and Mrs A H Young, Peter Craske, Dr and Mrs M E Wilson, Ian Barker, Phil and Sally Gorton, FJS and DS, Mark and Heather Williamson, Stephen Moss, Adrian and Dawn Collinge, Mr and Mrs P D Titcomb, Barry Steele-Perkins

TORBRYAN   SX8266   MAP 1

Old Church House

Most easily reached from A381 Newton Abbot—Totnes via Ipplepen; TQ12 5UR

Ancient inn with lovely original features, neat rooms, friendly service and well liked tasty food

Much enjoyed by both locals and visitors, this is a cheerfully run old pub with bags of atmosphere. The particularly attractive bar on the right of the door is neatly kept and bustling and has benches built into the fine old panelling as well as a cushioned high-backed settle and leather-backed small seats around its big log fire. On the left there is a series of comfortable and discreetly lit lounges, one with a splendid deep Tudor inglenook fireplace with a side bread oven; piped music. Skinners Betty Stogs and Cornish Knocker on handpump, 30 malt whiskies, and several wines by the glass; friendly service. Plenty of nearby walks.

🍴 **Generous helpings of good bar food include soup, sandwiches, filled baguettes, ploughman's, mushroom risotto, lasagne, beef in ale pie, haddock mornay and rack of lamb.** *Starters/Snacks: £4.00 to £6.00. Main Courses: £7.00 to £15.00. Puddings: £4.00*

Free house ~ Licensees Kane and Carolynne Clarke ~ Real ale ~ Bar food ~ Restaurant ~ (01803) 812372 ~ Children welcome ~ Dogs allowed in bar and bedrooms ~ Live music Sun evenings ~ Open 11-11 ~ Bedrooms: £54B/£79B

Recommended by Ronnie Jones, Mike Gorton, Dr and Mrs M E Wilson, Kevin and Jane O'Mahoney, Jane and Martin Headley

TORCROSS   SX8242   MAP 1

Start Bay

A379 S of Dartmouth; TQ7 2TQ

Fresh local fish dishes in exceptionally popular, straightforward dining pub; seats outside overlooking the beach

The cheerful licensees and their staff take great care sourcing the fresh fish and shellfish here. They dress their own cock crabs and shell their hand-picked scallops (and sell the shells for the Lifeboat and Air Ambulance charities), and take delivery of the fish caught off the beach in front of the pub. Queues often form even before the doors open and the straightforward main bar is always packed. It is very much set out for eating with wheelback chairs around plenty of dark tables or (round a corner) back-to-back settles forming booths; country pictures and some photographs of storms buffeting the pub on the cream walls, and a winter coal fire. A small chatty drinking area by the counter has a brass ship's clock and barometer and there's more booth seating in a family room with sailing boat pictures. Pool and darts in the winter. Bass, Flowers Original and Otter Ale on handpump, local Heron Valley cider, and local wine from the Sharpham Estate. They do warn of delays in food service at peak times but the staff remain friendly and efficient. There are seats (highly prized) outside that look over the three-mile pebble beach, and the freshwater wildlife lagoon of Slapton Ley is just behind the pub.

🍴 **Their speciality is fish in light batter: cod or haddock (medium, large or jumbo), plaice, lemon sole and other fish dishes as available; also, sandwiches, filled baked potatoes, ploughman's, vegetable lasagne, steaks, puddings like spotted dick and treacle sponge pudding, and gateaus (on display in the family room).** *Starters/Snacks: £4.10 to £6.95. Main Courses: £5.50 to £16.90. Puddings: £2.70 to £4.00*

Heavitree ~ Tenant Stuart Jacob ~ Real ale ~ Bar food (11.30-2.15, 6-9.30(10 Sat); not 25 Dec) ~ (01548) 580553 ~ Children in large family room ~ Open 11.30-2.15, 6-10(9.30 in winter)

Recommended by P and J Shapley, Jenny and Brian Seller, M Thomas, Eamonn and Natasha Skyrme, Steve Derbyshire, Roger and Carol Maden, Mr and Mrs G Owens

TOTNES

SX8059 MAP 1

Steam Packet

St Peters Quay, on W bank (ie not on Steam Packet Quay); TQ9 5EW

Seats outside overlooking the quay, as well as an interesting inside layout, and decent food and drink

A new licensee for this bustling pub overlooking the River Dart. There are plenty of seats and tables under outdoor heaters on the front terrace and attractive flowering tubs. Inside, it's interestingly laid out with stripped wood floors throughout. The end part has an open coal fire, a squashy leatherette sofa with lots of cushions against a wall of books, a similar seat built into a small curved brick wall (which breaks up the room), and a flat screen TV above the fireplace. The main bar has built-in wall benches and plenty of stools and chairs around traditional pubby tables, and a further section with another small fire and plain dark wooden chairs and tables leads into the conservatory restaurant. Courage Best, Otter Bright, and Dartmoor Brewery Jail Ale on handpump and several wines by the glass; piped music. More reports please.

🍴 Bar food now includes lunchtime sandwiches, soup, crab and chilli cakes with pepper sauce and spring onion salad, moroccan-spiced lamb kofta with chilli and cucumber dressing, beer-battered haddock, chicken and mango curry, goats cheese, wild mushroom and butternut squash risotto, and teriyaki salmon fillet with sweet and sour peppers, with daily specials such as game terrine and slow-cooked ham hock with cheese and parsley sauce. *Starters/Snacks: £4.95 to £5.95. Main Courses: £9.25 to £15.95. Puddings: £5.50*

Buccaneer Holdings ~ Manager Richard Cockburn ~ Real ale ~ Bar food ~ Restaurant ~ (01803) 863880 ~ Children welcome ~ Dogs allowed in bar and bedrooms ~ Open 11-11; 12-10.30 Sun; closed evenings 25 Dec and 1 Jan ~ Bedrooms: £59.50B/£79.50B

Recommended by P Dawn, Mrs M Tee, Mike Gorton, Dr and Mrs M E Wilson, John and Alison Hamilton

TUCKENHAY

SX8156 MAP 1

Maltsters Arms ♀

Take Ashprington road out of Totnes (signed left off A381 on outskirts), keeping on past Watermans Arms; TQ9 7EQ

Lovely spot by wooded creek with tables by the water, a good choice of drinks and varied food

In fine weather, you can really appreciate this pub's lovely position by a peaceful wooded creek; there are tables by the water, summer barbecues and regular live music concerts on the quayside. Inside, the long, narrow bar links two other rooms – a small snug one with an open fire and plenty of bric-a-brac and another with red-painted vertical seats and kitchen chairs on the wooden floor; there are nautical charts and local photographs on the walls. Adnams Explorer, Batemans XB Bitter, Dartmoor Brewery IPA and maybe a guest beer on handpump, 20 wines by the glass, seven kinds of kir, and local farm cider and perry; they keep several varieties of snuff. Darts, board games and maybe TV for sports.

🍴 As well as lunchtime sandwiches, bar food includes soup, smoked chicken and duck pâté with elderberry and apple jelly, oysters, local mussels with garlic, white wine and herbs, platters of meats, cheeses, fish and dips, whole grilled local plaice with lemon and chive butter, pasta with mediterranean vegetables, olives and parmesan, sausages with redcurrant gravy and mustard mash, local game pie, and puddings like vanilla crème brûlée and banoffi bread and butter pudding. *Starters/Snacks: £4.75 to £7.50. Main Courses: £8.95 to £19.95. Puddings: £4.50 to £4.95*

Free house ~ Licensees Denise and Quentin Thwaites ~ Real ale ~ Bar food (12-3, 7-9.30) ~ Restaurant ~ (01803) 732350 ~ Children welcome (not in bar or main part of restaurant) ~ Dogs welcome ~ Open 11-11; closed evening 25 Dec ~ Bedrooms: /£75S(£95B)

Recommended by Michael B Griffith, Gaye and Simon, Peter Burton, MP, John Day, Mike Gorton, Gerry and Rosemary Dobson, Alan and Anne Driver, John Chambers

WIDECOMBE   SX7276   MAP 1

Rugglestone
Village at end of B3387; pub just S – turn left at church and NT church house, OS Sheet 191 map reference 720765; TQ13 7TF

Unspoilt local near busy tourist village with just a couple of bars, cheerful customers and homely food

The small bar in this unspoilt local has a strong country atmosphere and plenty of cheerful customers. There are just four tables, a few window and wall seats, a one-person pew built into the corner by the nice old stone fireplace, and a rudimentary bar counter dispensing Bays Gold, Butcombe Bitter, St Austell Dartmoor Best, and a guest beer tapped from the cask; local farm cider and a decent little wine list. The room on the right is a bit bigger and lighter-feeling with another stone fireplace, beamed ceiling, stripped pine tables, and a built-in wall bench. There's also a small room which is used for dining. The pub is in rural surroundings – though just up the road from the bustling tourist village – and if you sit outside in the field, across the little moorland stream, where there are lots of picnic-sets, you might be joined by some wild dartmoor ponies. Tables and chairs in the garden, too. They now have a holiday cottage for rent.

🍴 **Well liked bar food includes filled baguettes, baps and baked potatoes, ploughman's, soup, chicken liver and cranberry pâté, steak and kidney or chicken and leek pies, cheese and spinach cannelloni with garlic, tomato and herb sauce, lambs liver with bacon and onion gravy, beer-battered haddock, gammon and egg, and trout baked with lemon and garlic.** *Starters/Snacks: £3.50 to £7.95. Main Courses: £7.95 to £11.95. Puddings: £3.95 to £4.50*

Free house ~ Licensees Richard Palmer and Vicky Moore ~ Real ale ~ Bar food ~ (01364) 621327 ~ Children allowed but must be away from bar area ~ Dogs welcome ~ Open 11.30-3, 6-midnight; 11.30am-midnight Sat; 12-11 Sun

Recommended by J D O Carter, the Didler, W K Wood, Lynne Carter, JHW, Michael and Ann Cole, Peter Craske, Geoff and Carol Thorp, Hazel Morgan, Bernard Patrick, Roger and Carol Maden, Dr Ian Mortimer

WINKLEIGH   SS6308   MAP 1

Kings Arms
Village signposted off B3220 Crediton—Torrington; Fore Street; EX19 8HQ

Friendly pub with woodburning stoves in beamed bar and popular pubby food served all day

On the edge of the little village square, this is a friendly thatched pub with a happy mix of customers. The attractive beamed main bar has some old-fashioned built-in wall settles, scrubbed pine tables and benches on the flagstones and a woodburning stove in a cavernous fireplace; another woodburning stove separates the bar from the dining rooms (one has military memorabilia and a mine shaft). Butcombe Bitter and Sharps Cornish Coaster and Doom Bar on handpump, local cider and several wines by the glass; darts and board games. There are seats out in the garden.

🍴 **Popular bar food includes sandwiches and filled baguettes, ploughman's, filled baked potatoes, burgers in a bun, soup, mushrooms in creamy garlic sauce, sweet and sour vegetables with rice, ham and egg, haddock and chips, chicken stir fry with oriental vegetables, lambs liver with bacon and onion gravy, and steak and kidney parcel, with puddings such as marmalade bread and butter pudding and chocolate mousse with chocolate sauce; cream teas all day.** *Starters/Snacks: £2.25 to £6.25. Main Courses: £6.50 to £13.95. Puddings: £3.95 to £4.75*

Enterprise ~ Lease Chris Guy and Julia Franklin ~ Real ale ~ Bar food (all day) ~ Restaurant ~ (01837) 83384 ~ Children welcome ~ Dogs allowed in bar ~ Open 11-11; 12-10.30 Sun

Recommended by R J Walden, Mayur Shah, John Lane, Mark Flynn, Tom Evans, Stephen Moss

---

Pubs with outstanding views are listed at the back of the book.

WOODBURY SALTERTON   SY0189   MAP 1

Diggers Rest

3.5 miles from M5 junction 30: A3052 towards Sidmouth, village signposted on right about 0.5 mile after Clyst St Mary; also signposted from B3179 SE of Exeter; EX5 1PQ

Bustling village pub with emphasis on good food (welcome for drinkers too), and lovely views from terraced garden

A cheerful antipodean landlord has taken over this thatched village pub but happily not much has changed. There are usually plenty of customers and the main bar has antique furniture, local art on the walls, and a cosy seating area by the open fire with its extra large sofa and armchair. The modern extension is light and airy and opens on to the garden which has contemporary garden furniture under canvas parasols on the terrace and lovely countryside views. Otter Ale and Bitter on handpump and 15 wines by the glass; piped music.

🍴 **Bar food now includes lunchtime sandwiches and ploughman's, chicken liver parfait, haddock fishcakes with a crème fraîche and dill tartare sauce, free-range pork sausages with onion gravy, beer-battered fresh fish with mushy peas, spinach tagliatelle in a mushroom, garlic and cream sauce, chargrilled mackerel with tomato and basil salad, steak in ale pie, and puddings such as chocolate brownie with chocolate sauce and crème brûlée.** *Starters/Snacks: £4.75 to £6.75. Main Courses: £7.50 to £15.95. Puddings: £4.75*

Free house ~ Licensee Mike Boyd ~ Real ale ~ Bar food (all day weekends and afternoon cream teas all week in summer) ~ Restaurant ~ (01395) 232375 ~ Children in certain dining areas ~ Dogs allowed in bar ~ Open 11-11; 12-10.30 Sun

Recommended by Michael and Lynne Gittins, DWT, Gene and Tony Freemantle, Dr and Mrs M E Wilson, John Evans, Emma Kingdon, Roger and Carol Maden, Joan and Michel Hooper-Immins, Richard Wyld

YEALMPTON   SX5851   MAP 1

Rose & Crown

A379 Kingsbridge—Plymouth; PL8 2EB
DEVON DINING PUB OF THE YEAR

Smart modern place, plenty of dark wood and heavy brass, neat staff, enjoyable bar food plus attractive adjacent seafood restaurant

Whether you are after a meal or just a drink, this is a civilised and stylish place for either. The big central bar counter, all dark wood and heavy brass with good solid leather-seated bar stools, has Otter Ale, St Austell Tribute and Sharps Doom Bar on handpump, quite a few wines by the glass and a fine choice of other drinks too; quick, friendly service by neatly aproned black-dressed staff. There's an attractive mix of tables and old dining chairs, good lighting, and some leather sofas down on the left. With its stripped wood floor and absence of curtains and other soft furnishings, the open-plan bar's acoustics are lively; beige carpeting keeps the two dining areas on the right rather quieter and here smart leather high-backed dining chairs, flowers on the tablecloths and framed 1930s high-life posters take you a notch or two upscale. They also have an attractive adjacent seafood restaurant with super big fishing photographs, lobster pots and nets on decking, and high-backed powder blue cushioned dining chairs around white clothed tables.

🍴 **Good bar food includes sandwiches, soup, venison and cranberry sausage with wholegrain mustard, green thai vegetable curry, popular fish goujons with pea purée, tartare sauce and skinny chips, spaghetti carbonara, ham and poached egg, and lamb shank with red wine jus; the more elaborate menu might have smoked salmon mousse with crayfish salad and anchovy stick, foie gras and ham hock terrine with pears, rack of local lamb with sweet thyme sauce, honey-glazed salmon fillet with pak choi and toasted sesame seeds, and puddings such as duo of chocolate and cappuccino crème brûlée; there's a good value two- and three-course set menu (not Sunday lunch or Friday or Saturday evenings).** *Starters/Snacks: £5.00 to £12.00. Main Courses: £8.00 to £15.00. Puddings: £4.00 to £6.00*

Enterprise ~ Lease Simon Warner ~ Real ale ~ Bar food ~ Restaurant ~ (01752) 880223 ~ Children welcome ~ Dogs allowed in bar ~ Open 12-3, 6.30-11; 12-10.30 Sun

Recommended by H Paulinski, Gary Rollings, Debbie Porter, J Crosby, Richard Beharrell, Richard and Deborah Morisot, John Evans

LUCKY DIP

Besides the fully inspected pubs, you might like to try these Lucky Dips recommended to us and described by readers (if you do, please send us reports: feedback@thegoodpubguide.co.uk).

ABBOTSHAM [SS4226]
Thatched Inn EX39 5BA: Extensively refurbished family pub popular at lunchtime for good value pubby food from sandwiches and baked potatoes to fresh fish and Sun lunch, helpful staff, Fullers London Pride and Greene King Old Speckled Hen, mix of modern seating and older features (dates from 15th c); garden tables, handy for the Big Sheep *(Mark Flynn)*
ABBOTSKERSWELL [SX8568]
☆ *Court Farm* TQ12 5NY [Wilton Way; look for the church tower]: Attractive neatly extended 17th-c longhouse tucked away in picturesque hamlet, various rooms off long crazy-paved main beamed bar, good mix of furnishings, big helpings of well presented food from sandwiches to steaks and bargain Sun lunch, half helpings for children and OAP specials, friendly helpful staff, several ales inc Otter, farm cider, decent wines and wide choice of other drinks, woodburners; piped music; children in eating area, picnic-sets in pretty lawned garden, open all day *(Dr and Mrs M E Wilson, LYM, D and S Price)*
APPLEDORE [SS4630]
Royal George EX39 1RY [Irsha St]: Good beer choice inc local Country Life, thriving narrow bar (dogs allowed) with attractive pictures and well worn in front room, simple fresh food inc local fish, decent wines, dining room with superb estuary views; disabled access (but no nearby parking), picnic-sets outside, picturesque street sloping to sea *(Tony and Wendy Hobden, Tom Evans)*
ASHBURTON [SX7570]
Victoria TQ13 7QH [North St]: Recently refurbished street-facing Georgian pub, carpeted bar with exposed stone wall, log fire with dimpled canopy, dark wheelbacks, brasses, stools at counter, good Bass and Otter, good value food inc local fish and game, restaurant, newspapers; picnic-sets in riverside garden, smoking shelter, three bedrooms *(JHW)*
ASHPRINGTON [SX8157]
☆ *Durant Arms* TQ9 7UP [off A381 S of Totnes]: Sale negotiations under way as we went to press, so this attractive Victorian gabled inn may have new owners later in 2008; has been more small country hotel than pub, but very

popular, with decent food, St Austell ales and local wines in three comfortable linked and turkey-carpeted areas, one with small corner bar counter; piped music; children welcome in top lounge, flagstoned back courtyard, comfortable bedrooms *(LYM)*
BAMPTON [SS9622]
Quarrymans Rest EX16 9LN [Briton St]: Recently refurbished, big beamed and carpeted lounge, inglenook woodburner, leather sofas, comfortable stripped stone dining room with heavy pine tables and leather chairs, imaginative good value food from top-notch new chef/landlord, well kept ales inc Butcombe and Wells & Youngs Bombardier, locals' bar, games room; picnic-sets out in front and in pretty secluded back garden, smoking shelter, three simple bedrooms *(Peter and Jan Humphreys, John Davies)*
White Horse EX16 9ND [Fore St]: Charming old-fashioned inn in pretty town *(Giles and Annie Francis)*
BANTHAM [SX6643]
Sloop TQ7 3AJ [off A379/B3197 NW of Kingsbridge]: Popular updated beamed and flagstoned pub in great spot across dunes from lovely beach, character bar with woodburner and sofa, relaxed atmosphere with friendly young staff, well kept St Austell ales, Rattler's cider, enjoyable bar food inc good crab sandwiches, sturdy tables in ship-shaped dining room, lots of children; dogs welcome, seats outside, bedrooms, surrounding walks *(MP, Lynda and Trevor Smith, David Crook, Mike Gorton, David Barnes, M Thomas, Jay Bohmrich, MB, Theocsbrian, Jo Rees, LYM)*
BEAFORD [SS5515]
Globe EX19 8LR: Newly refurbished village coaching inn, good traditional pub food and up using local ingredients, Fullers London Pride and Sharps Doombar, friendly staff; children and dogs welcome, disabled access, garden, bedrooms *(Katie Squire)*
BEER [ST2289]
Anchor EX12 3ET [Fore St]: Newly refurbished sea-view dining pub with sandwiches and good local fish, Otter and decent wines, good helpful service (can take a while when busy), rambling open-plan layout with old local photographs, large eating area; sports TV, piped music;

reasonably priced bedrooms, lots of tables in attractive clifftop garden over road, delightful seaside village – parking may not be easy *(Rod and Chris Pring, Mr and Mrs P D Titcomb, Penny Simpson, Mr and Mrs P A Stevens, LYM, Neil and Anita Christopher)*

☆ *Dolphin* EX12 3EQ [Fore St]: Friendly open-plan local quite near sea, comfortable old-fashioned décor, oak panelling, nautical bric-a-brac and interesting nooks inc marvellous old distorting mirrors and antique boxing prints, huge range of good value food inc fresh local fish, large back restaurant, well kept Cotleigh ales, decent wine; piped music; children and dogs welcome, back picnic-sets, bedrooms *(Joan and Michel Hooper-Immins, Mike Gorton, B and F A Hannam, LYM)*

BELSTONE [SX61293]
Tors EX20 1QZ [a mile off A30]: Austere granite building in ancient Dartmoor-edge village, enjoyable generous food from sandwiches up, friendly local licensees, well kept Flowers IPA, Sharps Doom Bar and Timothy Taylors Landlord, decent wines, 50 whiskies, old settles nicely dividing bar; dogs and well behaved children welcome, wheelchair access, picnic-sets outside, bedrooms *(Mike Gorton, Chris and Angela Buckell)*

BERRYNARBOR [SS5546]
Olde Globe EX34 9SG [off A399 E of Ilfracombe]: Rambling dim-lit rooms geared to family visitors (cutlasses, swords, shields and rustic oddments), with reasonably priced straightforward food, real ales, games area – and genuine age behind the trimmings, with ancient walls and flagstones, high-backed oak settles and antique tables, lots of old pictures; piped music; dogs and children welcome, crazy-paved front terrace, play area, pretty village *(Lisa Robertson, John and Alison Hamilton, Lynda and Trevor Smith, Bob and Margaret Holder, B M Eldridge, LYM)*

BICKLEIGH [SS9307]
Fishermans Cot EX16 8RW: Greatly extended thatched Marstons chain pub, enjoyable food in raised dining area, their real ales, lots of round tables on stone and carpet, pillars, plants and some panelled parts, fishing bric-a-brac and fairy lights in willow, charming view over shallow rocky race below 1640 Exe bridge; piped music, can get busy esp wknds; terrace and waterside lawn, 19 good bedrooms, open all day *(Adrian and Dawn Collinge, BB)*
Trout EX16 8RJ [A396, N of junction with A3072]: Useful touristy thatched pub with very spacious comfortable bar and dining lounge, real ales, nice coffee, decent pubby food inc good value Sun roasts, cheerful service; children welcome, tables on pretty lawn, well equipped

bedrooms, good breakfast *(LYM, Bob and Margaret Holder)*

BISHOP'S TAWTON [SS5629]
☆ *Chichester Arms* EX32 0DQ [signed off A377 outside Barnstaple; East St]: Friendly 15th-c cob and thatch pub, well priced good generous food from home-made soup and sandwiches to fresh local fish and seasonal game (all meat from named farms), quick obliging service even when crowded, Exmoor ales and Marstons Pedigree, decent wines, heavy low beams, large stone fireplace, restaurant; children welcome, disabled access not good but staff very helpful, picnic-sets on front terrace and in back garden, open all day *(Mrs Angela Graham, LYM, E J Sayer, B M Eldridge)*

BOLBERRY [SX6939]
Port Light TQ7 3DY: Set back from dramatic NT clifftop, right on the coast path, bright, clean, spacious and busy, real ales such as Blackdown Devons Pride, friendly efficient eager-to-please service, interesting memorabilia of its time as a radar station, conservatory, decent lunchtime bar food in oversized helpings, evening functions more as a restaurant; children and dogs welcome (they host dog wknds), picnic-sets on quiet terrace and in garden with splendid fenced play area, nr fine beaches, five bedrooms *(Theocsbrian)*

BRAMPFORD SPEKE [SX9298]
☆ *Lazy Toad* EX5 5DP [off A377 N of Exeter]: Former Agricultural Inn just reopened under top-notch licensees, after careful restoration; beams and flagstones, settles and woodburner, separate eating area, food from locally sourced ingredients and own smokery, home-grown herbs and soft fruits, may rear own meat in future; disabled facilities, walled garden, reports please *(anon)*

BRATTON CLOVELLY [SX4691]
Clovelly EX20 4JZ: Lively locals' pub with large helpings of enjoyable wholesome food, Fullers London Pride and guest beers, good fire, cheerful staff; pool table *(David and Katharine Cooke)*

BRAYFORD [SS7235]
☆ *Poltimore Arms* EX36 3HA [Yarde Down; 3 miles towards Simonsbath]: Unspoilt 17th-c two-bar beamed local, so remote it generates its own electricity, friendly landlord and cheerful efficient staff, enticing good value blackboard food from local produce inc good Sun lunches, ales such as Adnams, Cotleigh and Greene King tapped from the cask, good wines by the glass, basic traditional furnishings, fine woodburner in inglenook, interesting ornaments, two attractive restaurant areas; children welcome, also dogs on leads (pub has own dogs), picnic-sets in side garden, has been cl winter lunchtimes *(LYM, B M Eldridge, John and Jackie Walsh)*

BRENDON [SS7547]
☆ *Rockford Inn* EX35 6PT [Rockford; Lynton—Simonsbath rd, off B3223]: Warmly welcoming, unspoilt and interesting 17th-c beamed inn by East Lyn river, limited low-priced freshly cooked food from sandwiches to cottage pie, Cotleigh Barn Owl tapped from the cask, Thatcher's and North Devon ciders, interesting wines; small linked rooms with mix of padded settles and chairs around sturdy tables, woodburners, restaurant, soft piped jazz; children in eating areas, quiet dogs on leads welcome, good walks, five bedrooms sharing two bathrooms, cl Mon and Tues in winter (Lora Raffael, Sheila Topham, B M Eldridge, LYM)

BROADHEMBURY [ST1004]
Drewe Arms EX14 3NF [off A373 Cullompton—Honiton]: Charming old building that has been one of Devon's top food pubs, but closed as we went to press (licensees retiring - building owned by local estate, so fingers crossed that it may reopen with food at least approaching its past glory) (LYM)

BUCKFAST [SX7467]
☆ *Abbey Inn* TQ11 0EA [just off A38 at A384 junction; Buckfast Rd]: New licensees for sizeable riverside inn, partly panelled walls, mixed seating inc a couple of settees, woodburner in ornate fireplace, big panelled river-view dining room with another woodburner, St Austell ales, several wines by glass; piped music; children and dogs welcome, verandah over water, bedrooms, open all day Fri-Sun and summer (LYM, Norman and Sarah Keeping)

BUDLEIGH SALTERTON [SY0681]
Feathers EX9 6LE [High St]: Good bustling atmosphere, well kept ales, nice mix of customers (Dr and Mrs M E Wilson, Roger and Carol Maden)
☆ *Salterton Arms* EX9 6LX [Chapel St]: Light open-plan layout with mixed seating inc sofas and high tables and chairs, enjoyable reasonably priced food in bar and roomy upstairs gallery restaurant, thriving friendly atmosphere, three well kept real ales, farm cider, darts; games machine; children welcome, open all day wknds (Dr and Mrs M E Wilson, LYM)

BUTTERLEIGH [SS9708]
Butterleigh Inn EX15 1PN [off A396 in Bickleigh]: Small-roomed heavy-beamed country pub, pleasant friendly place for a drink, with O'Hanlons, Otter and guest ales, reasonably priced food, nice pictures, big fireplace, pine dining chairs around country kitchen tables in one room, darts in another; attractive gardens, comfortably up-to-date bedrooms (LYM, G and P Vago)

CALIFORNIA CROSS [SX7053]
☆ *California* PL21 0SG [brown sign to pub off A3121 S of A38 junction]: Neatly

modernised 18th-c or older pub with beams, panelling, stripped stone and log fire, wide choice of good sensibly priced food from sandwiches to steaks in dining bar and family area, good restaurant menu, sofa in small separate snug, efficient staff, Coachmans Best, Fullers London Pride and Greene King Abbot, decent wines, local farm cider; piped music; children and dogs welcome, good tables for attractive garden and back terrace, open all day (BB, Pam Williams, Bob and Margaret Holder, Steve and Miriam Jones)

CHAGFORD [SX7087]
☆ *Ring o' Bells* TQ13 8AH [off A382]: New licensees again for ancient black and white pub, Butcombe and Teignworthy ales, good service, beamed and panelled bar, log fire in big fireplace, pub dogs; dogs and well behaved children welcome, sunny walled garden behind, bedrooms, nearby moorland walks, open all day (LYM, Dr and Mrs A K Clarke)

CHALLACOMBE [SS6941]
☆ *Black Venus* EX31 4TT [B3358 Blackmoor Gate—Simonsbath]: Low-beamed 16th-c pub with good varied food from sandwiches up, friendly staff, two changing ales, Thatcher's farm cider, pews and comfortable chairs, woodburner and big open fire, roomy and attractive dining area; garden tables, grand countryside (B M Eldridge, BB)

CHITTLEHAMPTON [SS6325]
Bell EX37 9QL [signed off B3227 S Molton—Umberleigh]: Cheerful family-run village local, tasty local food from huge filled rolls to bargain hot dishes, Bass and guest beers, outstanding range of malt whiskies; children and dogs welcome, nice quiet garden, bedrooms (J Stickland, John and Gloria Isaacs, A C Powell)

CHRISTOW [SX8384]
Artichoke EX6 7NF: Pretty thatched local with small comfortable open-plan rooms stepped down hill, low beams, some black panelling, flagstones, reliable food inc fish and game, lovely log fire (2nd one in dining room), Otter tapped from cask, welcoming helpful service; tables on back terrace, pretty hillside village nr Canonteign Waterfalls and Country Park (BB, Peter and Helen Loveland)

CHUDLEIGH [SX8679]
Bishop Lacey TQ13 0HY [Fore St, just off A38]: Quaint partly 14th-c low-beamed church house with cheerful obliging landlady and staff, good choice of changing largely local ales, enjoyable food using local produce cooked by landlord, good strong coffee, two log fires, dark décor, dining room; live bands in next-door offshoot; children welcome, garden tables, winter beer festival, bedrooms, open all day (the Didler)

CHURCHSTOW [SX7145]
Church House TQ7 3QW [A379 NW of Kingsbridge]: Much refurbished pub dating

from 13th c, heavy black beams and stripped stone, helpful staff, home-cooked food inc busy Sun carvery, well kept St Austell Tribute, decent wines, back conservatory with floodlit well feature; well behaved children welcome, tables outside *(David Barnes, LYM, B J Harding, MP)*

CLAYHIDON [ST1615]

Half Moon EX15 3TJ: Pretty village pub with warm friendly atmosphere, good choice of enjoyable home-made food, real ales, tasteful furniture and inglenook fireplace in comfortable bar; children and dogs welcome, delightful calming views from picnic-sets in tiered garden over road *(John and Fiona Merritt)*

CLOVELLY [SS3225]

New Inn EX39 5TQ [High St (car-free village, visitors charged £5.50 each to enter)]: Friendly 17th-c inn halfway down the steep cobbled street, Arts & Crafts décor, simple easy-going lower bar with flagstones and bric-a-brac (narrow front part has more character than back eating room), well kept Sharps Cornish Coaster and a beer brewed for the pub by local Country Life, good value bar food, upstairs restaurant; great views, small garden, good bedrooms *(S P Watkin, P A Taylor, Bruce Bird)*

Red Lion EX39 5TF [The Quay]: Rambling 18th-c building in lovely position on curving quay below spectacular cliffs, beams, flagstones and interesting local photographs in character back bar, well kept Sharps Doom Bar and a beer from local Country Life, bar food and upstairs restaurant; great views, 11 simple attractive bedrooms *(S P Watkin, P A Taylor, Bruce Bird)*

CLYST ST GEORGE [SX9888]

St George & Dragon EX3 0QJ: Spaciously extended open-plan Vintage Inn, fresh and cheerful décor, with careful lighting, low beams and some secluded corners, log fires, welcoming and helpful young staff, real ales, good choice of wines by the glass, good value; bedrooms in adjoining Innkeepers Lodge, open all day *(Dr and Mrs M E Wilson)*

CLYST ST MARY [SX9791]

☆ *Half Moon* EX5 1BR [under a mile from M5 junction 30 via A376]: Attractive genuine old pub next to disused multi-arched bridge (Devon's oldest) over Clyst, enjoyable reasonably priced home-made food, cheerful attentive service, Bass, Fullers London Pride and Otter, friendly unpretentious local atmosphere, red plush seating, log fire; wheelchair access, bedrooms *(Dr and Mrs M E Wilson, Mr and Mrs A Green)*

COCKWOOD [SX9780]

Ship EX6 8RA [off A379 N of Dawlish]: Comfortable 17th-c pub overlooking estuary and harbour, partitioned beamed bar with big log fire and ancient oven, decorative plates and seafaring

memorabilia, small restaurant, generous reasonably priced food from open crab sandwiches up inc good evening fish dishes and puddings (freshly made so takes time), Butcombe and Sharps Doom Bar, friendly helpful staff; piped music; children and dogs welcome, good steep-sided garden *(Roger and Carol Maden)*

COLATON RALEIGH [SY0787]

Otter EX10 0LE [A376 Newton Poppleford—Budleigh Salterton]: Much-modernised café-style family pub with well priced food inc popular carvery in long airy bar and restaurant, welcoming efficient service, several real ales, fireside leather sofa, tall window bar tables, modern artwork; dogs welcome, lovely big garden with play area, May beer festival, handy for Bicton Park' *(Laurence Milligan)*

COLYTON [SY2494]

Gerrard Arms EX24 6JN [St Andrews Sq]: Unpretentious open-plan local with Bass, Branscombe Vale Branoc and a guest beer tapped from the cask, skittle alley, lunchtime food inc Sun roasts; tables in courtyard and informal garden *(the Didler)*

☆ *Kingfisher* EX24 6NA [off A35 and A3052 E of Sidmouth; Dolphin St]: Low-beamed village pub with well kept Badger ales, farm cider, good wines by the glass, big open fire, food from popular baguettes to local crab, stripped stone, plush seats and elm settles, pub games, upstairs family room, skittle alley; parking can be a problem, outside gents'; tables out on terrace, garden with water feature *(the Didler, LYM, Neil and Anita Christopher, LM)*

COMBE MARTIN [SS5747]

Dolphin EX34 0AW [Seaside]: Well placed pub long in same family, enjoyable fresh food inc local fish, good friendly staff, well kept beer, lots of whiskies and liqueurs, log fire, upstairs restaurant; bedrooms *(B M Eldridge, Mr and Mrs C Gulvin)*

COMBEINTEIGNHEAD [SX9072]

☆ *Coombe Cellars* TQ12 4RT [Shaldon rd, off A380 opp main Newton Abbot roundabout]: Big bustling Brewers Fayre, roomy, comfortable and particularly good value for families, with lots for children inc indoor play area, their own menu, fun days and parties with entertainment, outside play galleon and fenced-in playground; friendly efficient staff, very wide choice of good food all day, real ales, lots of wines by the glass, plenty of sporting and nautical bric-a-brac, lovely estuary views, various events; good disabled facilities, tables out on pontoons, jetties and big terraces, water sports, open all day *(LYM, D Restarick)*

CORNWORTHY [SX8255]

☆ *Hunters Lodge* TQ9 7ES [off A381 Totnes—Kingsbridge]: New licensees for village pub with small low-ceilinged two-roomed bar, traditional seating around heavy elm tables, cottagey dining room, log fire in big 17th-c fireplace, Teignworthy and Exe Valley ales, summer farm cider, food cooked by landlady; children and dogs welcome, big lawn with terrace and extensive views, cl Mon lunch *(LYM)*

COUNTISBURY [SS7449]

Blue Ball EX35 6NE [A39, E of Lynton]: Beautifully set rambling heavy-beamed pub doing well under friendly new management, handsome log fires, good range of food in bar and restaurant, decent wines, three ales inc one brewed for the pub, Addlestone's and Thatcher's ciders, reasonable prices; piped music; children in eating area, dogs and walkers welcome (two pub dogs), views from terrace tables, good nearby cliff walks (pub provides handouts of four circular routes), comfortable bedrooms, open all day *(LYM, Steve Ryman, Judith Coles)*

CULLOMPTON [ST0207]

Weary Traveller EX15 1BQ [Station Rd; M5 Junction 28]: Good value and popular with locals esp for OAP lunches, pleasant efficient service, tables in garden *(J S Hurst)*

DALWOOD [ST2400]

☆ *Tuckers Arms* EX13 7EG [off A35 Axminster—Honiton]: Pretty thatched old inn, beams, flagstones and inglenook log fire, Greene King Old Speckled Hen, Otter and Wadworths 6X, decent wines by the glass; food and service have been inconsistent recently; children in front dining part, skittle alley, seats outside, bedrooms *(LYM)*

DARTINGTON [SX7861]

Cott TQ9 6HE [Cott signed off A385 W of Totnes, opp A384 turn-off]: Long 14th-c thatched pub with heavy beams, flagstones and fire, Greene King IPA, dining area with close-set tables, enjoyable food from sandwiches up; children and dogs on leads welcome, picnic-sets in garden and on pretty terrace, seven bedrooms, open all day at least in summer *(B J Harding, MB, LYM)*

White Hart Bar TQ9 6EL [Dartington Hall]: Light bright modern décor and open fires in the college's bar (open to visitors), good low-priced food here and in baronial hall, well kept Otter ales, matter-of-fact service; special atmosphere sitting out in the famously beautiful grounds *(Giles and Annie Francis)*

DARTMOUTH [SX8751]

☆ *Royal Castle Hotel* TQ6 9PS [the Quay]: Rambling 17th-c or older hotel behind Regency façade overlooking inner harbour, traditional bar on right with dining area for all-day food from sandwiches to good steaks, perhaps winter lunchtime spit-roasts from their 300-year-old Lidstone range, bustling more contemporary bar on left (TV, piped music may be loud, dogs

welcome – no children), pleasant efficient staff, Bass, Courage, St Austell and Whitbread, new upstairs restaurant; 25 comfortable bedrooms with secure parking, open all day *(Keith and Margaret Kettell, Gerry and Rosemary Dobson, Mr and Mrs W W Burke, LYM)*

DENBURY [SX8268]

Union TQ12 6DQ [The Green]: Comfortable and welcoming stone-built pub by village green in quiet pretty village, low beams and exposed stonework, well kept Fullers London Pride, wide choice of enjoyable reasonably priced food inc lots of fish, children's menu, two eating areas, good service, may be live folk music in bar; tables out at front *(Jonathan and Gillian Shread, BB, Ray Crabb)*

DODDISCOMBSLEIGH [SX8586]

☆ *Nobody Inn* EX6 7PS [off B3193]: A big question-mark over what has been a favourite for many years: as we went to press there was no clear management structure – its buyers are clearly keen to get a proper return on their investment, so we hope the pub will be back on track by the time this book is published; some refurbishment, but two-room beamed lounge keeping handsomely carved antique settles among other seats, guns and hunting prints by big inglenook; has had fine wine list with 20 by the glass, 260 whiskies, Cotleigh Barn Owl, Exe Valley, Sharps Doom Bar and a guest beer, local ciders; children and dogs welcome, terrace, bedrooms, exceptional medieval stained-glass in nearby church; more reports please *(LYM)*

DOUSLAND [SX5368]

Burrator Inn PL20 6NP: Big cheerful Victorian pub with newish licensees doing good value food in bar and restaurant, real ales, games room, some live music; children welcome away from bar, eight good value bedrooms (some sharing bath) *(anon)*

DREWSTEIGNTON [SX7489]

☆ *Fingle Bridge Inn* EX6 6PW [E of village; OS Sheet 191 map ref 743899 – may be shown under its former Anglers Rest name]: Idyllic wooded Teign valley spot by 16th-c pack-horse bridge, lovely walks and a magnet for summer visitors; much extended former tea pavilion, tourist souvenirs and airy café feel, west country real ales, reliable food from baguettes and good local cheese ploughman's up, Sun carvery, friendly helpful service, log fire; children and dogs welcome, waterside picnic-sets, has been cl winter evenings *(Adrian and Dawn Collinge, Robert Gomme, Dr and Mrs M E Wilson, LYM)*

DUNSFORD [SX8189]

Royal Oak EX6 7DA [signed from Moretonhampstead]: Well worn in village inn with good generous food cooked to order, good choice of changing ales inc Dartmoor and Sharps, local farm cider, friendly landlord, light and airy lounge bar with woodburner and view from small sunny dining room, simple dining room, steps down to games room with pool; quiz nights, piped music; children welcome, sheltered tiered garden, good value bedrooms in converted barn *(the Didler, LYM)*

☆ **EAST BUDLEIGH** [SY0684]
Sir Walter Raleigh EX9 7ED [High St]: Quiet low-beamed village local, books on shelves, Adnams Broadside, Otter and St Austell Tribute, restaurant down step; no children, parking some way off; dogs welcome, wonderful medieval bench carvings in nearby church, handy too for Bicton Park gardens *(FJS and DS, LYM, Dr and Mrs M E Wilson, Mrs Jordan, Steve Whalley)*

EAST PRAWLE [SX7836]
Pigs Nose TQ7 2BY [Prawle Green]: Relaxed three-room inn with low beams and flagstones, ales tapped from the cask, enjoyable if limited food from good ploughman's and sandwiches up, open fire, easy chairs and sofa, interesting bric-a-brac and pictures, jars of wild flowers and candles on tables, bird log, darts, small family area with small box of unusual toys, nice dogs, laid-back service can be slow; unobtrusive piped music, hall for live bands (landlord was 60s tour manager); tables outside, nice spot on village green *(W K Wood, MB, the Didler, Roger Wain-Heapy)*

EXETER [SX9390]
Double Locks EX2 6LT [Canal Banks, Alphington, via Marsh Barton Industrial Estate; OS Sheet 192 map ref 933901]: Unsmart pub by ship canal, remote yet busy, Youngs and guest ales, Gray's farm cider in summer, wide variety of good value plain home-made bar food all day; piped music, live wknds, service can get swamped; children and dogs welcome, seats out on decking with distant view to city and cathedral (nice towpath walk out – or hire a canoe at the Quay), good big play area, camping, open all day *(Jackie Givens, the Didler, Mr and Mrs P D Titcomb, Richard Mason, LYM, Donna Delamain)*
Georges Meeting House EX1 1ED [South St]: Comfortable and vibrant Wetherspoons in grand former 18th-c chapel dominated by tall pulpit one end; stained-glass, original pews in three-sided gallery, some leather settees, their usual food and good west country cheese, fish and meat, six ales, good wine choice; children welcome when eating, quality furniture in attractive side garden, open all day *(Ryta Lyndley, Philip and Jude Simmons, Dr and Mrs M E Wilson)*
Great Western EX4 4NU [St Davids Hill]: Regulars enjoying up to a dozen or so changing real ales inc some choice rarities in large commercial hotel's straightforward plush-seated bar, friendly staff, wholesome good value fresh food all day from sandwiches and generous baked potatoes up (kitchen also supplies the hotel's restaurant), daily papers, no music; sports TV, pay parking; 35 bedrooms, open all day *(Andy and Jill Kassube, Joan and Michel Hooper-Immins, Phil and Sally Gorton, the Didler, BB)*
Honiton EX1 2JY [Paris St]: Small elegant pub with warmly lit rectangular bar, dark wood, counter with brass foot rail, patterned walls, divider with plants, tables, chairs and wall benches, simple food, Otter; soft piped music; conference room *(Dr and Mrs M E Wilson)*
Old Fire House EX4 4EP [New North Rd]: Cosy city centre pub in three-storey Georgian building (bar at top) approached through high arched wrought-iron gates, candlelit bistro feel, ten changing ales, good choice of wines, low-priced food, friendly staff, popular with young people evenings; piped music, live folk and jazz; big covered area outside *(the Didler, Mike Gorton, David Gray, Andy and Jill Kassube)*
Prospect EX2 4AN [The Quay (left bank, nr rowing club)]: Early 19th-c pub in good quayside position, enjoyable good value bar food from baguettes to good thai curry, Adnams, Fullers and Otter, friendly efficient young staff, plenty of comfortable tables inc raised river-view dining area; gentle piped music, live bands Mon/Tues; tables out by historic ship-canal basin, open all day *(Sue and Mike Todd, D W Stokes, Peter Salmon)*
Ship EX1 1EY [Martins Lane, nr cathedral]: Pretty 14th-c heavy-beamed building with olde-worlde city pub style, thriving friendly atmosphere, well kept Bass, Greene King Old Speckled Hen and Marstons Pedigree, farm cider; food can take a while (comfortable upstairs restaurant) *(Dr and Mrs M E Wilson, Andrew York, LYM)*
Welcome EX2 8DU [Haven Banks, off Haven Rd (which is first left off A377 heading S after Exe crossing)]: Two-room pub little changed since 60s (ditto the juke box), gas lighting and flagstones, very friendly old-school landlady, changing ales; a few tables out overlooking basin on Exeter Ship Canal, can be reached on foot via footbridges from The Quay *(the Didler)*
Well House EX1 1HB [Cathedral Yard, attached to Royal Clarence Hotel]: Big windows looking across to cathedral in open-plan bar divided by inner walls and partitions, good choice of local ales such as Otter, quick service, wide range of food, daily papers, sofa, lots of interesting Victorian prints, Roman well below (can be viewed when pub not busy); may be piped music; open all day *(Andy and Jill Kassube, Tony and*

Wendy Hobden, BB, Dr and Mrs M E Wilson, Meg and Colin Hamilton)

White Hart EX1 1EE [South St]: Attractively old-fashioned rambling bar, heavy beams, oak flooring, nice furnishings inc antiques, charming inner cobbled courtyard; now tied to Marstons, with their ales and reasonably priced standard food; bedrooms *(LYM, Joan and Michel Hooper-Immins, Dr and Mrs M E Wilson)*

EXMOUTH [SX9980]

Beach EX8 1DR [Victoria Rd]: Popular old quayside local with Bass, Greene King Old Speckled Hen and Otter, food, friendly landlord and staff, shipping and lifeboat memorabilia and photographs, beams, posts and panelling, cast-iron framed tables *(Dr and Mrs M E Wilson)*

Grove EX8 1BJ [Esplanade]: Roomy panelled Youngs outpost set back from beach, their beers kept well, decent house wines, good coffee, good value food inc plenty of local fish and children's menu, good friendly service, simple furnishings, caricatures and local prints, 1930s replicas, attractive fireplace at back, sea views from appealing upstairs dining room and balcony; live music Fri; picnic-sets in big garden (no view) with play area *(Dr and Mrs M E Wilson, Michael and Lynne Gittins)*

Imperial EX8 2SW [Esplanade]: Large Shearings hotel on seafront, comfortably shabby-chic lounge bar popular with older people, good value simple bar lunches though limited on the drinks side; garden and terrace tables, bedrooms *(MB, Mrs C Osgood)*

FOLLY GATE [SX5798]

Crossways EX20 3AH [A386 Hatherleigh—Okehampton]: Welcoming pub with homely comfortable atmosphere, consistently good food inc local seafood, well kept Sharps and Skinners, faultless service *(R J Walden)*

GEORGEHAM [SS4639]

☆ **Lower House** EX33 1JJ [B3231 Croyde—Woolacombe]: Doing well since its 2006 revamp; comfortable clean-cut contemporary style with sofas and fires, nice selection of good freshly cooked well presented food inc tapas, friendly service and owner, well kept St Austell and local guest ales, reasonably priced wines by the glass, daily papers, more elaborate food in upstairs restaurant; children welcome in downstairs eating area, tables out on small front terrace screened from road *(Paul and Ursula Randall, Wendda Johnson, John and Fiona McIlwain, Miss Lizzie Prescott)*

GOODLEIGH [SS5934]

New Inn EX32 7LX: Welcoming pubby atmosphere, chatty locals, two well kept changing ales, wide blackboard choice of good reasonably priced food cooked to order, log fire *(Gordon Tong, Ross Balaam)*

GRENOFEN [SX4971]

Halfway House PL19 9ER [A386 near Tavistock]: Recently redecorated dining pub with attractive plain décor, good choice of reasonably priced home-made food, Fullers London Pride, Sharps Doom Bar and a guest beer, farm cider, decent wines,; tables out overlooking Dartmoor, good value bedrooms *(Jacquie Jones)*

HARBERTON [SX7758]

☆ **Church House** TQ9 7SF [off A381 S of Totnes]: Ancient partly Norman village pub with welcoming efficient service, ales such as Butcombe, Courage Best, Marstons Pedigree and St Austell Tribute, good choice of wines by the glass, farm cider, decent bar food, woodburner in big inglenook, medieval latticed glass and oak panelling, attractive 17th- and 18th-c pews and settles, family room; bedrooms *(John Chambers, LYM, Dr Ian Mortimer)*

HARTLAND [SS2624]

Anchor EX39 6BD [Fore St]: Friendly pub dating from 16th c, food inc good Sun lunch, real ales, big log fire, restaurant and verandah at back; dogs and children welcome *(Dr D J and Mrs S C Walker)*

Hart EX39 6BL [The Square]: Village pub under new management, food from local suppliers, changing real ales: reports please *(Roger Chapple)*

HARTLAND QUAY [SS2224]

Hartland Quay Hotel EX39 6DU [off B3248 W of Bideford, down toll road (free Oct—Easter); OS Sheet 190 map ref 222248]: Unpretentious old hotel in formidable cliff scenery, fishing memorabilia and shipwreck pictures, down-to-earth friendly staff, may have well kept Sharps Doom Bar (often keg beer only), basic enjoyable food, good mix of customers; dogs welcome, lots of tables outside (very popular with holidaymakers in season), good value bedrooms, seawater swimming pool, rugged coast walks; cl midwinter *(S P Watkin, P A Taylor)*

HATHERLEIGH [SS5404]

☆ **Tally Ho** EX20 3JN [Market St (A386)]: Attractive heavy-beamed and timbered linked rooms, sturdy furnishings, big log fire and woodburner, ample enjoyable food from lunchtime sandwiches up, local Clearwater ales, quick friendly service, traditional games, restaurant; may be piped music; tables in nice sheltered garden, three pretty bedrooms, busy Tues market day *(LYM, Rona Murdoch, the Didler)*

HEXWORTHY [SX6572]

Forest Inn PL20 6SD [signed off B3357 Tavistock—Ashburton, E of B3212]: Lovely Dartmoor setting, roomy plush-seated open-plan bar and back walkers' bar, short daily-changing choice of generous bar and restaurant food using fresh local produce, prompt friendly service, well kept Teignworthy ales with a guest such as Otter, local cider, fire, daily papers; dogs and boots welcome, comfortable bedrooms (also bunkhouse), fishing permits, good walking and riding *(M G Hart, Robin M Corlett, LYM)*

HOLBETON [SX6150]

Dartmoor Union PL8 1NE [off A379 W of A3121 junction; Fore St]: Uncertain future for what was top-notch civilised pub, as small group running it went into administration earlier in 2008; has had own brews and guest beers, carefully chosen wines, chic spreading bar with nice mix of dining chairs, squashy leather sofas and fireside armchairs, smart restaurant, chatty relaxed atmosphere; children and dogs have been allowed, sheltered back terrace; news please *(LYM)*

HOLSWORTHY [SS3403]

Old Market EX22 6AY [Chapel St]: Town centre pub, four well kept ales, bar food from sandwiches up, restaurant, Sun carvery; function room, three bedrooms *(Pat Sycamore)*

HONITON [SY1198]

Greyhound EX14 3BJ [Fenny Bridges, B3177 4 miles W]: Big busy thatched family dining pub with wide food choice all day from good open sandwiches and baked potatoes up, friendly helpful service, good range of beers inc Otter, heavy beams, attractive restaurant; bedrooms *(John Roots, LYM)*

HOPE COVE [SX6740]

☆ *Hope & Anchor* TQ7 3HQ: Lively unpretentious inn, friendly and comfortably unfussy in lovely seaside spot (can get very busy in summer), good open fire, quick service, good value straightforward food inc lots of fish, well kept St Austell Dartmoor and a beer brewed for the pub, reasonably priced wines, flagstones and bare boards, dining room views to Burgh Island, big separate family room; piped music; children and dogs welcome, sea-view tables out on decking, great coast walks, bedrooms (can be noisy), open all day *(Mr and Mrs G Owens, LYM, Steve and Miriam Jones, David Barnes, Michael and Ann Cole, Theocsbrian, Simon J Barber)*

HORNS CROSS [SS3823]

☆ *Hoops* EX39 5DL [A39 Clovelly—Bideford, W of village]: Welcoming picturesque thatched inn with oak settles, beams and inglenook fires in pleasant bar, enjoyable food, good service even when busy, well kept Sharps and other ales tapped from the cask inc one brewed for the pub, local farm cider, good wine choice, daily papers, darts; background music, TV; well behaved children in eating area till 8, dogs allowed in bar, tables in small courtyard, bedrooms, open all day *(Nick Lawless, John and Jackie Chalcraft, LYM, Mr and Mrs A J Hudson)*

HORSEBRIDGE [SX4074]

☆ *Royal* PL19 8PJ [off A384 Tavistock—Launceston]: Cheerful old pub with dark

half-panelling, slate floors and interesting bric-a-brac, simple good value food from baguettes and baked potatoes to fresh scallops, friendly landlord and staff, well kept Bass, Blackawton and Sharps, Rich's farm cider, log fire, bar billiards, cribbage, dominoes, café-style side room, no music or machines; no children in evening, picnic-sets on back terrace and in big garden, quiet rustic spot by lovely old Tamar bridge *(LYM, Peter Craske)*

IDE [SX8990]

☆ *Poachers* EX2 9RW [3 miles from M5 junction 31, via A30; High St]: Friendly and individual, with nice non-standard mix of old chairs and sofas, good generous food, both traditional and inventive (worth booking evenings), Bass, Branscombe Vale Branoc, Otter and one brewed locally for the pub, good value house wines, big log fire; picnic-sets in pleasant garden, attractive and comfortable bedrooms, small quaint village, cl Mon lunchtime *(the Didler)*

IDEFORD [SX8977]

☆ *Royal Oak* TQ13 0AY [2 miles off A380]: Unpretentious 16th-c thatched and flagstoned village local with friendly helpful service, Greene King, Otter and Timothy Taylors, basic pub snacks, navy theme inc interesting Nelson and Churchill memorabilia, big log fireplace; children and dogs welcome, tables out at front and by car park over road *(the Didler)*

ILFRACOMBE [SS5247]

George & Dragon EX34 9ED [Fore St]: Oldest pub here, handy for harbour, with good local atmosphere, helpful friendly staff, mainstream real ales, decent wines, low-priced pubby food, attractive olde-worlde décor with stripped stone, open fireplaces, lots of ornaments, china etc; piped music, cash machine but no credit cards *(Philip and Jude Simmons, Miss J F Reay, Dave Braisted, B M Eldridge, Mrs C Osgood)*

INSTOW [SS4730]

Bar EX39 4HY [Marine Parade]: Minimalist contemporary café-bar style with plenty of chrome, reasonably priced enjoyable up-to-date food, good staff, well kept local ales, tables looking out over estuary; well behaved children and dogs welcome, disabled access, open all day *(Dr D J and Mrs S C Walker)*

Wayfarer EX39 4LB [Lane End]: Unpretentious locals' pub tucked away nr dunes and beach, welcoming staff, well kept ales tapped from the cask, good choice of enjoyable food using local fish and meats; children and dogs welcome, enclosed garden behind, six well presented bedrooms (some with sea view), open all day *(Wendda Johnson, Colin Canavan)*

KILMINGTON [SY2698]

New Inn EX13 7SF: Lively traditional thatched pub, originally three 14th-c cottages but carefully rebuilt after 2004 fire, pine-clad bar with stools, dark wood furniture, rich blue patterned carpet and banquettes, well kept Palmers ales, popular lunchtime food inc OAP specials (Mon-Thurs) and bargain Sun lunch (must book wknds), friendly service; lots of hanging baskets, picnic-sets in large garden with aviaries, good views *(David and Sue Smith)*

Old Inn EX13 7RB [A35]: Thatched 16th-c pub with enjoyable food using local supplies, Cotleigh and Otter, small character polished-floor front bar with traditional games, back lounge with leather armchairs by inglenook log fire, small restaurant; children welcome, skittle alley, two gardens *(Anthony Double, LYM)*

KING'S NYMPTON [SS6819]
Grove EX37 9ST [off B3226 SW of S Molton]: Attractive welcoming thatched village pub with popular landlord, flagstones, low beams and two log fires, Adnams and Exmoor ales, decent wine by the glass, food that can be most enjoyable, bookmark collection and interesting photographs of old-time villagers on red walls, skittle alley; small pretty enclosed terrace (defibrillator in porch), picturesque village *(LYM, MB, Mark Flynn)*

KINGSWEAR [SX8851]
Royal Dart TQ6 0AA [The Square]: Victorian building in fine setting by ferry and Dart Valley Railway terminal, great view of Dartmouth from balcony outside upstairs restaurant, enjoyable bargain food here and in unpretentious modernised bar, friendly staff, bargain South Hams and Teignworthy ales, interesting WWII history when used as naval base; riverside tables *(P Dawn, Chris Evans, N R White)*

LANDSCOVE [SX7766]
Live & Let Live TQ13 7LZ: Welcoming open-plan bar popular with locals, simple enjoyable food inc bargain lunches (Jan-Feb), well kept Ringwood, Teignworthy and occasional guest ale, ciders inc Winkleigh's, woodburner; decked terrace and more tables in small orchard across lane, cl Mon *(LYM, J D O Carter)*

LUPPITT [ST1606]
☆ *Luppitt Inn* EX14 4RT [back roads N of Honiton]: Unspoilt little basic farmhouse pub, amazing survivor of past times, friendly chatty landlady who keeps it open because she (and her cats) like the company; tiny room with corner bar and a table, another not much bigger with fireplace, cheap Otter tapped from the cask, intriguing metal puzzles made by neighbour, no food or music, lavatories across the yard; cl lunchtime and Sun evening *(the Didler)*

LUSTLEIGH [SX7881]
☆ *Cleave* TQ13 9TJ [off A382 Bovey Tracey—Moretonhampstead]: Friendly family left

this charming thatched pub as we went to press, and it will become a managed house; low-ceilinged bars, antique high-backed settles among other seats, log fire, Adnams Explorer, Otter and Wadworths 6X; children have been welcome, dogs in bar, sheltered garden, has been open all day in summer, cl Mon *(LYM)*

LUTON [SX9076]
☆ *Elizabethan* TQ13 0BL [Haldon Moor]: Charming low-beamed old-world pub once owned by Elizabeth I, welcoming owners and friendly efficient staff, good well presented food, real ales inc a local guest beer, several reasonably priced wines by the glass, thriving atmosphere; garden tables *(Paul and Dilys Wright)*

LYDFORD [SX5184]
☆ *Castle Inn* EX20 4BH [off A386 Okehampton—Tavistock]: Tudor inn with traditional twin bars, big slate flagstones, bowed low beams, log fire, brightly decorated plates, Hogarth prints, local Saxon pennies, notable stained-glass door, Bass, Fullers London Pride and Otter, darts, board games; provision for children and dogs, bedrooms, lovely nearby NT river gorge, open all day *(LYM, Dr Nigel Bowles, James and Ginette Read, Andrea Rampley, Michael and Ann Cole, Wendda Johnson, David Tindal, Dr and Mrs A K Clarke, Tom Evans)*

☆ *Dartmoor Inn* EX20 4AY [Downton, A386]: Attractive restaurant-with-rooms, several small civilised and relaxed stylishly decorated contemporary areas, interesting and imaginatively presented expensive food, separate bar menu (not Fri, Sat evenings), good wines by the glass; children welcome, dogs allowed in small front log-fire bar, terrace tables, three spacious comfortable bedrooms, good breakfast, cl Sun evening, Mon *(Andrea Rampley, R W Brooks, Terry and Linda Moseley, Guy Vowles, Mrs Elizabeth Powell, Dr Ian Mortimer, LYM)*

LYMPSTONE [SX9984]
Swan EX8 5ET [The Strand]: Pleasant olde-worlde décor; split-level dining area on left with leather sofas by large fire, good value generous food inc good fresh fish and italian specials, real ales inc Marstons, friendly staff, games room with pool; small front garden with smokers' area *(Dr and Mrs M E Wilson)*

LYNTON [SS6548]
Hunters EX31 4PY [pub well signed off A39 W of Lynton]: Superb Heddon Valley position by NT information centre down very steep hill, great walks inc one down to the sea; big spreading bar with plush banquettes and so forth, woodburner, 12 ales inc Exmoor, 16 whiskies, wide selection of generous food (may be a wait when crowded); piped music; picnic-sets on balconied terrace overlooking attractive pondside garden with peacocks,

open all day summer, hours may be restricted when season tails off (*B M Eldridge, Mick and Moira Brummell, BB*)

MANATON [SX7580]

☆ *Kestor* TQ13 9UF: Modern Dartmoor-edge inn in splendid spot nr Becky Falls, welcoming homely feel, good range of enjoyable home-made food from good lunchtime sandwiches up, well kept ales, farm cider, good wine choice, open fire, attractive dining room; piped music; nice bedrooms (*Barry and Anne, Mike Parkes*)

MARSH [ST2510]

Flintlock EX14 9AJ [pub signed just off A303 Ilminster—Honiton]: Long smartly kept and comfortable dining pub popular for wide choice of good food inc Sun lunches, well kept Fullers London Pride and Otter, good choice of wines, neat furnishings, woodburner in stone inglenook, beams and mainly stripped stone walls, copper and brass; piped music; cl Mon (*Mike Gorton, BB, Dr and Mrs M E Wilson*)

MODBURY [SX6551]

Modbury Inn PL21 0RQ [Brownston St]: Small traditional bar with well kept Otter, good value restaurant with enterprising country food, unfussy service; tables on attractive terrace, four nice bedrooms, open all day Sat (*Richard and Patricia Jefferson, MP*)

White Hart PL21 0QW [Church St]: Roomy flagstoned bar with soft leather chairs and sofas, open fire and old covered well, dining room with up-to-date minimalist décor, good imaginative well presented food inc bargain three-course bar lunch with glass of wine, Bass and Otter, wide choice of wines (inc local), pleasant welcoming staff; enclosed back terrace; five contemporary bedrooms (*Mr and Mrs W W Burke, Keith and Margaret Kettell, Bob and Ann Good*)

MORELEIGH [SX7652]

New Inn TQ9 7JH [B3207, off A381 Kingsbridge—Totnes in Stanborough]: Busy old-fashioned country local with attentive landlady (same family for several decades), limited choice of wholesome generous home cooking, reasonable prices, Palmers tapped from the cask, good inglenook log fire, character old furniture, nice pictures, candles in bottles; may be cl Sat lunchtime/race days (*Roger Wain-Heapy, LYM*)

MORETONHAMPSTEAD [SX7586]

White Horse TQ13 8PG [George St]: Newly refurbished and much improved pub, owner is chef; regular live music (*Dr Ian Mortimer*)

MORTEHOE [SS4545]

Chichester Arms EX34 7DU [off A361 Ilfracombe—Braunton]: Varied choice of enjoyable food from new chef, quick friendly service, real ales such as local Barum Original, reasonably priced wine,

plush and leatherette panelled lounge, comfortable dining room, pubby locals' bar with darts and pool, interesting old local photographs; skittle alley and games machines in summer children's room, tables out in front and in shaded pretty garden, good coast walk (*Mr and Mrs P Bland, B M Eldridge*)

Ship Aground EX34 7DT [signed off A361 Ilfracombe—Braunton]: Open-plan beamed village pub handy for coast walks, real ales such as Cotleigh Tawny and Greene King Abbot, decent wine, wide food choice, upstairs carvery some days, big log fires, massive rustic furnishings, interesting nautical brassware, big back family room with games area; sheltered sunny terrace with good views, by interesting church (*GSB, Chris Reading, LYM, B M Eldridge*)

NEWTON ABBOT [SX8571]

Dartmouth TQ12 2JP [East St]: Genuine old place with low ceilings, dark woodwork, roaring log fire, interesting changing local real ales, farm cider, decent wines; piped music; children welcome till 7, tables and barbecues in nice outside area, open all day (*the Didler, Dr and Mrs M E Wilson*)

Locomotive TQ12 2JP [East St]: Cheerful traditional town pub with friendly staff, well kept ales, linked rooms inc games room with pool; TV, juke box; open all day (*the Didler*)

☆ *Olde Cider Bar* TQ12 2LD [East St]: Basic old-fashioned cider house with casks of interesting low-priced farm ciders (helpful long-serving landlord may give you samples), a couple of perries, more in bottles, good country wines from the cask too, baguettes and pasties etc, great atmosphere, dark stools made from cask staves, barrel seats and wall benches, flagstones and bare boards; small back games room with machines; terrace tables (*the Didler, Dr Ian Mortimer*)

☆ *Two Mile Oak* TQ12 6DF [A381 2 miles S, at Denbury/Kingskerswell crossroads]: Another new licensee for appealing beamed coaching inn, log fires, traditional furnishings, black panelling and candlelit alcoves, well kept Bass and Otter tapped from the cask, straightforward bar food inc wkdy lunchtime bargains; piped music, TV, games machine; children in lounge, dogs in bar, terrace and lawn, open all day (*Peter Salmon, LYM, the Didler*)

NEWTON ST CYRES [SX8798]

☆ *Beer Engine* EX5 5AX [off A377 towards Thorverton]: Spacious former railway hotel brewing four good beers for last 25 years, wide choice of good food inc local fish, popular Sun lunch menu, good service; children welcome in eating areas, decked verandah, steps down to garden, open all day (*Philip and Jude Simmons, Mike Gorton, LYM, John and Bryony Coles, Roger and Carol Maden*)

NEWTON TRACEY [SS5226]
Hunters EX31 3PL [B3232 Barnstaple—Torrington]: Extended 15th-c pub doing well under new owners, massive low beams and log fire, good reasonably priced imaginative food, well kept St Austell and guest ale, decent wines, friendly service; disabled access, skittle alley popular with locals, tables on small terrace behind, open all day *(BB, Ken and Margaret Grinstead, Phil and Sally Gorton)*

PARKHAM [SS3821]
Bell EX39 5PL: Cheerful old thatched village pub with large comfortable family eating areas, enjoyable home-cooked food inc fresh fish, well kept Fullers London Pride, Greene King IPA and guest ale, decent choice of wine, lots of nooks and crannies, log fire, friendly staff *(Mrs J Hindley, K Skuse, LYM)*

PARRACOMBE [SS6644]
☆ *Fox & Goose* EX31 4PE [off A39 Blackmoor Gate—Lynton]: Relaxed rambling pub, hunting and farming memorabilia and interesting photographs, log fire, Cotleigh Barn Owl and Exmoor Fox, ten wines by the glass, farm cider, food sometimes using their own produce, separate dining room; children and dogs welcome, small front verandah, terraced garden leading to garden room, plans for bedrooms *(MB, LYM, Mark Sykes,B M Eldridge, David and Carole Sayliss, Tom Evans, Adrian and Dawn Collinge)*

PETROCKSTOWE [SS5109]
Laurels EX20 3HJ [signed off A386 N of Hatherleigh]: Recently refurbished former coaching inn, hospitable and well run, good generous freshly made food, well kept St Austell Tribute and other local beers *(R J Walden)*

PLYMOUTH [SX4854]
☆ *China House* PL4 0DW [Sutton Harbour, via Sutton Rd off Exeter St (A374)]: Attractive conversion of Plymouth's oldest warehouse, lovely boaty views, dimly lit and inviting interior with beams and flagstones, bare slate and stone walls, two good log fires, enjoyable food, good choice of real ales and wines by the glass, attentive staff; piped music, no dogs; good parking and disabled access/facilities, tables out on waterside balconies, open all day *(Mick and Moira Brummell, MB, Meg and Colin Hamilton, LYM)*
Dolphin PL1 2LS [Barbican]: Basic unchanging chatty local, good range of beers inc cask-tapped Bass, coal fire (not always lit), Beryl Cook paintings inc one of the friendly landlord; open all day *(the Didler, Ian Barker)*
Lounge PL1 4QT [Stopford Pl, Stoke]: Decent open-plan backstreet pub, good choice of drinks from oak-panelled counter *(Dr and Mrs A K Clarke, the Didler)*
Minerva PL4 0EA [Looe St (nr Barbican)]: Lively low-ceilinged backstreet pub dating from 16th c, good choice of mainstream

and less common ales, coal fire, good nostalgic juke box; quite small so can get packed; open all day *(the Didler)*
Thistle Park PL4 0LE [Commercial Rd]: Welcoming bare-boards pub nr National Maritime Aquarium, well kept South Hams ales (used to be brewed next door), friendly service, interesting décor, tasty food (pasties only wkdy lunchtime), live music wknds; children welcome, open all day till late *(the Didler, MP)*

POSTBRIDGE [SX6578]
East Dart PL20 6TJ [B3212]: Briskly run central Dartmoor hotel by pretty river, big comfortable open-plan bar, good value generous food from sandwiches with chips up, St Austell ales, good wines by the glass, good fire, hunting murals, pool room; can take coaches; dogs welcome, tables out in front and behind, decent bedrooms, some 30 miles of fishing *(Dennis Jenkin, Robin M Corlett, BB)*

RACKENFORD [SS8518]
☆ *Stag* EX16 8DT [pub signed off A361 NW of Tiverton]: 13th-c thatched pub reopened end 2007 after careful refurbishment, scrubbed pine tables and country furnishings, keeping huge inglenook fireplace, low beams, Jacobean panelling, flagstones and ancient cobbled entry passage between massive walls, friendly atmosphere, Cotleigh Tawny and Exmoor, food in bar and cottagey restaurant; disabled facilities, tables out behind *(Keith and Sue Ward, LYM)*

RINGMORE [SX6545]
Journeys End TQ7 4HL [signed off B3392 at Pickwick Inn, St Anns Chapel, nr Bigbury; best to park up opp church]: Ancient village inn with character panelled lounge, half a dozen changing local ales from casks behind bar, local farm cider, decent wines, food inc bargain lunches some wkdys, log fires, bar billiards (for over-16s), sunny back family dining conservatory with board games; pleasant big terraced garden with boules, attractive setting nr thatched cottages not far from sea, bedrooms antique but comfortable and well equipped, parking some distance away *(the Didler, LYM, David Barnes)*

ROBOROUGH [SS5717]
New Inn EX19 8SY [off B3217 N of Winkleigh]: 16th-c thatched country pub refurbished by friendly new owners, good value bistro-style food, good selection of local beers and ciders, locals' bar, lounge leading to snug dining area, inglenook log fire; small garden *(Nigel and Jenny Wallis, BB)*

SALCOMBE [SX7439]
☆ *Fortescue* TQ8 8BZ [Union St, end of Fore St]: Good proper pub with five linked nautical-theme rooms, friendly service, popular promptly served food from hot-filled rolls up, ales such as Bass, Courage Directors and Otter, decent wines, good

woodburner, old local black and white shipping pictures, big public bar with games, small dining room; children welcome, picnic-sets in courtyard *(Roger Wain-Heapy)*

Victoria TQ8 8BU [Fore St]: Neat and attractive 19th-c pub opp harbour car park, colourful window boxes, nautical décor and comfortable furnishings, enjoyable reasonably priced food, well kept St Austell ales, decent wines, friendly efficient service; piped music; large sheltered tiered garden behind with good play area, bedrooms *(Tom and Jill Jones, Roger Wain-Heapy, John and Julie Moon, Martin and Marion Vincent, Alan and Anne Driver)*

SAMPFORD COURTENAY [SS6300]

New Inn EX20 2TB [B3072 Crediton—Holsworthy]: Attractive 16th-c thatched pub with hospitable landlord, Otter, good food, pleasant décor in open-plan bar with locals' comments written on low beams, open fires; dogs welcome, nice garden with play area, picturesque village *(Conor McGaughey, Tom Evans)*

SAMPFORD PEVERELL [ST0314]

☆ *Globe* EX16 7BJ [a mile from M5 junction 27, village signed from Tiverton turn-off; Lower Town]: Spacious and comfortable village pub with thriving atmosphere, enjoyable good value home-made food from sandwiches to massive mixed grill and popular Sun carvery, well kept Otter ales, good wine choice, friendly efficient staff, lounge largely laid for eating, big-screen sports TV in bar, restaurant; piped music, children and dogs welcome, picnic-sets out in front, large garden, bedrooms, open all day *(John and Bryony Coles, Joan and Michel Hooper-Immins, LYM)*

SANDFORD [SS8202]

☆ *Lamb* EX17 4LW [The Square]: Relaxed homely local with small choice of interesting and very reasonably priced good food (bar snacks all day – from 9.30 wkdys), well kept O'Hanlons Royal Oak and Palmers Copper, village farm cider, good value wines by the glass, friendly efficient service, cheery young regulars, sofas by log fire, fresh flowers, daily papers, books and magazines; upstairs skittle alley/cinema; tables in attractive sheltered garden, open all day *(Miss Rachael Durbin, David J Cooke, Christopher Voaden, BB, Jane Wilkinson-Tancock)*

Rose & Crown EX17 4NH: Welcoming village pub with reasonably priced home-made food, good selection of beers; children welcome, garden *(Tom and Mandy Smith)*

SANDY GATE [SX9690]

☆ *Blue Ball* EX2 7JL [from M5 junction 30, take A376 and double back from A376/A3052 roundabout, turning off left towards Topsham just before getting back to M5 junction]: Extended thatched

dining pub under new management, popular and handy for M5, obliging young staff, enjoyable food, old wood and tile floors, beams, lovely settles, big inglenook, O'Hanlons Yellowhammer and Otter; gardens and play area *(Barry Steele-Perkins, BB, Dr and Mrs M E Wilson, Roger and Carol Maden)*

SEATON [SY4190]

Eyre Court EX12 2NY [Queen St]: Small welcoming hotel nr beach with several bar areas (inc conservatory bar) and a restaurant, popular with locals, well kept ales inc Greene King, enjoyable pubby food and fresh fish; large covered smoking area, garden, 10 bedrooms *(Laurence Milligan)*

SHALDON [SX9372]

Ferryboat TQ14 0DZ [Fore St]: Cosy and quaint little waterside local, basic but comfortable, long low-ceilinged bar overlooking estuary with Teignmouth ferry and lots of boats, welcoming helpful staff, Dartmoor and Greene King, interesting wines, enjoyable good value varied home-made food, open fires, seafaring artefacts; children and dogs on leads welcome, tables on small sunny terrace across narrow road by sandy beach *(John and Helen Rushton)*

London Inn TQ14 8AW [Bank St/The Green]: Lively and cheerfully bustling pub, good value generous food from good sandwiches to fresh fish, good friendly service even when busy, Greene King and Otter, decent wines; pool; juke box; children welcome, good value bedrooms, opp bowling green in pretty waterside village *(Roy and Lindsey Fentiman)*

☆ *Ness House* TQ14 0HP [Ness Dr]: Georgian hotel on Ness headland overlooking Teign estuary, comfortable nautical-theme bar, assorted furniture on bare boards, log fire, Badger ales, good range of food inc good fish in narrow beamed restaurant or brasserie; terrace superb on a summer evening, bedrooms *(John and Helen Rushton, Henry Tinny)*

SHEBBEAR [SS4309]

Devils Stone Inn EX21 5RU [off A3072 or A388 NE of Holsworthy]: Tucked-away 16th-c village pub with big oak-beamed bar, three other rooms, good value sensible food, cheerful staff and regulars, good range of well kept beers, may be winter mulled wine, small restaurant area with huge inglenook log fire, family room; handy for Tarka Trail; garden with play area, simple bedrooms *(Ryta Lyndley, LYM)*

SIDMOUTH [SY1287]

Dukes EX10 8AR [Esplanade]: Good central spot, long bar on left with linked areas, on right conservatory and flagstoned eating area (once a chapel), Branscombe Vale, Dartmoor and Otter ales, food all day from local produce inc good fish, young eager staff, daily papers; big-screen TV, may be summer queues; children welcome, disabled facilities, prom-view terrace tables, bedrooms in adjoining Elizabeth Hotel, open all day *(Dr and Mrs M E Wilson, Joan and Michel Hooper-Immins, Steve Whalley)*

☆ *Old Ship* EX10 8LP [Old Fore St]: Welcoming traditional pub in pedestrian zone near sea (local parking limited to 30 mins), partly 14th-c with low beams, mellow black woodwork inc early 17th-c carved panelling, nautical theme, good food (not Sun eve) from huge crab sandwiches to local fish and some adventurous dishes (may try to retain a credit card if running a tab), well kept Branscombe Vale Branoc, Fullers London Pride and Otter, decent wine choice, prompt friendly service even when busy, no piped music; close-set tables – raftered upstairs family area is more roomy; dogs allowed *(Phil and Sally Gorton, Mike Gorton, Steve Whalley, BB, Rona Murdoch)*

☆ *Swan* EX10 8BY [York St]: Cheerful old-fashioned town-centre local, well kept Wells & Youngs ales, good value food from doorstep sandwiches up, helpful long-serving licensees, lounge bar with interesting pictures and memorabilia, darts and warm coal fire in bigger light and airy public bar with boarded walls and ceilings, separate dining area; dogs welcome, nice small flower-filled garden *(David and Sue Smith, MB, Mike Gorton)*

SILVERTON [SS9503]
Lamb EX5 4HZ [Fore St]: Friendly flagstoned local with two or three changing ales tapped from the cask, food from sandwiches to good steaks, helpful family service, separate eating area; handy for Killerton (NT), open all day wknds *(the Didler)*

Three Tuns EX5 4HX [Exeter Rd]: 17th-c or older, with comfortable settees, period furniture and log fire in attractively old-fashioned beamed lounge, food here or in cosy restaurant welcoming children, Exe Valley and guest beers, fair-sized public bar; tables in pretty inner courtyard, handy for Killerton *(the Didler)*

SLAPTON [SX8245]
☆ *Queens Arms* TQ7 2PN: Neatly modernised village local with welcoming landlady, good inexpensive straightforward food using local suppliers, well kept Teignworthy and Otter, snug comfortable corners, World War II mementoes, dominoes and draughts; parking needs skill; children and dogs welcome, lots of tables in lovely suntrap stepped back garden *(Roger and Carol Maden, MP, Roger Wain-Heapy, Tom Evans)*

☆ *Tower* TQ7 2PN [off A379 Dartmouth—Kingsbridge]: Newish licensees and some refurbishment afoot as we went to press; has had real atmosphere in low-beamed flagstoned and bare-boards bar, log fires,

Badger Tanglefoot, Butcombe and St Austell Tribute; piped music, varied reports on food recently; pretty garden overlooked by ivy-covered 14th-c ruin, bedrooms, has been cl Sun evening, winter Mon *(the Didler, LYM, Jackie Givens, Adrian and Dawn Collinge, John and Doris Couper)*

SOURTON [SX5390]
☆ *Highwayman* EX20 4HN [A386, S of junction with A30]: Fantastical décor in warren of dimly lit stonework and flagstone-floored burrows and alcoves, all sorts of things to look at, even a make-believe sailing galleon; local farm cider (perhaps a real ale in summer), organic wines, good proper sandwiches or pasties, friendly chatty service, old penny fruit machine, 40s piped music; outside fairy-tale pumpkin house and an old-lady-who-lived-in-the-shoe house – children allowed to look around pub but can't stay inside; period bedrooms with four-posters and half-testers, bunk rooms for walkers and cyclists *(LYM, the Didler, Tom Evans)*

SOUTH BRENT [SX6960]
Royal Oak TQ10 9BE [Station Rd]: Popular food inc Sun carvery, four well kept ales such as Shepherd Neame and Teignworthy Reel, good choice of wines by the glass, helpful service, comfortable open-plan bar with some leather sofas, restaurant; children and dogs welcome, small courtyard, five new bedrooms *(anon)*

SOUTH ZEAL [SX6593]
☆ *Oxenham Arms* EX20 2JT [off A30/A382]: Stately interesting building with elegant mullioned windows and Stuart fireplaces in friendly beamed and partly panelled locals' front bar, small beamed family room with open fire, Sharps and guest ales tapped from the cask, quite a few wines by the glass, home-cooked food; dogs allowed in bar, imposing garden with lovely views, eight bedrooms *(Pete Baker, Michael and Ann Cole, the Didler, LYM, Dr Ian Mortimer, Peter Craske)*

STAVERTON [SX7964]
☆ *Sea Trout* TQ9 6PA [off A384 NW of Totnes]: Smartly kept and much extended beamed village inn/hotel, friendly efficient staff, enjoyable food, well kept Palmers ales, Thatcher's Gold cider, good choice of wines by the glass and single malts, neat and comfortable bars with fishing memorabilia, open fire; children welcome, seats under parasols in attractive paved back garden, 11 comfortable quiet bedrooms *(John Smart, LYM, Brian and Janet Ainscough)*

STOKE FLEMING [SX8648]
Green Dragon TQ6 0PX [Church St]: Local regulars in village pub with yachtsman landlord, beams and flagstones, boat pictures and burmese cats, snug with sofas and armchairs, adult board games, grandfather clock, open fire, Flowers IPA,

good choice of wines by the glass, food from lunchtime baguettes to restaurant meals; dogs welcome, tables out on partly covered heated terrace *(LYM, Dennis Jenkin)*
STOKENHAM [SX8042]

☆ *Tradesmans Arms* TQ7 2SZ [just off A379 Dartmouth—Kingsbridge]: Picturesque 15th-c thatched low-beamed pub overlooking village green, good pubby atmosphere, enjoyable reasonably priced home-cooked food from traditional favourites to fresh local fish, good Sun roasts and puddings, at least five good ales inc Brakspears and South Hams, Thatcher's and Weston's ciders, well chosen wines, woodburner, antique tables and interesting old pictures, lovely cat called Black, separate dining room; picnic-sets in attractive garden across lane *(Roger Wain-Heapy, LYM, Paul Boot)*
STRETE [SX8446]

☆ *Kings Arms* TQ6 0RW [A379 SW of Dartmouth]: Unusual cross between village local and seafood restaurant, very rewarding at its best, but service has had its ups and downs; same menu in terracotta-walled country-kitchen bar and more contemporary blue-green restaurant up steps, Adnams Best and Otter, good wines by the glass; piped music; children and dogs welcome, dogs in bar, back terrace and garden with views over Start Bay, open all day, cl Sun evening *(Cathryn and Richard Hicks, M G Hart, Michael B Griffith, Dr and Mrs M W A Haward, Roger Wain-Heapy, R D Howard, Jenny and Brian Seller, Paul Boot, LYM)*
SWIMBRIDGE [SS6229]

Jack Russell EX32 0PN [nr Barnstaple]: Well refurbished, with enjoyable food from generous doorstep sandwiches up, Winkleigh's farm cider, smart dining room; terrace, opp the eponymous 19th-c parson's church in pleasant village *(B M Eldridge, D P and M A Miles)*
TALATON [SY0699]

Talaton Inn EX5 2RQ [former B3176 N of Ottery St Mary]: Good choice of enjoyable interesting food inc bargain lunches in simply modernised country pub dating from 16th c, large carpeted public bar with pool in skittle alley beyond, roomy and comfortable timbered lounge bar/restaurant area on right with fresh flowers and candles, good service, well kept Otter ales; picnic-sets out in front *(Mrs Betty Williams, Revd R P Tickle)*
TEDBURN ST MARY [SX8194]

Kings Arms EX6 6EG [off A30 W of Exeter]: Picturesque thatched pub, open plan but comfortable and quietly welcoming, enjoyable pubby food, Otter and St Austell ales, local farm cider, efficient neatly dressed staff, heavy-beamed and panelled L-shaped bar, lantern lighting and snug stable-style alcoves, big log fire, lots of brass and hunting prints, modern restaurant, end

games bar with pool and big-screen TV; piped music; children in eating area, tables on back terrace, garden, bedrooms *(John Marsh, J J B Rowe, LYM, Dr and Mrs M E Wilson)*
THORVERTON [SS9202]

Thorverton Arms EX5 5NS: Nicely appointed 16th-c coaching inn with wide range of well prepared bar food from sandwiches up inc children's, charming welcoming service, three well kept ales, good coffee, lots of country magazines, small restaurant; tables in flower-filled garden, pleasant village, six comfortable bedrooms *(Frank and Gill Brown)*
TOPSHAM [SX9688]

Exeter EX3 0DY [High St]: Well run 17th-c roadside local with friendly chatty landlord, well kept Teignworthy Beachcomber and local Warrior ales, long bar and front area with pool table, reasonable prices; large TV for sport; open all day *(the Didler)*

☆ *Globe* EX3 0HR [Fore St; 2 miles from M5 junction 30]: Substantial traditional inn dating from 16th c, solid comfort in heavy-beamed bow-windowed bar (popular with locals), good interesting home-cooked food from tasty sandwiches up, reasonable prices, Bass, Sharps Doom Bar and guest beers, good value house wines, prompt service, log-effect gas fire, compact dining lounge, good value separate restaurant, back extension; children in eating area, well priced attractive bedrooms, open all day *(the Didler, Dr and Mrs M E Wilson, LYM, Barry Steele-Perkins)*

☆ *Lighter* EX3 0HZ [Fore St]: Big comfortable pub with tall windows and balcony looking out over tidal flats, quickly served food from good sandwiches and light dishes to fresh fish, some small helpings available, Badger ales, nautical décor, panelling and central log fire, friendly staff, good children's area; games machines, piped music; handy for antiques centre, a mass of tables out in lovely spot on old quay *(Gwyn and Anne Wake, Dr and Mrs M E Wilson, the Didler, BB)*

Passage House EX3 0JN [Ferry Rd, off main street]: Attractive 18th-c pub, good fresh fish choice and other pubby food from sandwiches up, thriving atmosphere even in winter, Adnams, Flowers and Otter, good wines, traditional black-beamed bar and slate-floored lower bistro area; peaceful terrace looking over moorings and river (lovely at sunset) to nature reserve beyond *(Philip and Jude Simmons, LYM, the Didler, Dr and Mrs M E Wilson)*
TORQUAY [SX9166]

Crown & Sceptre TQ1 4QA [Petitor Rd, St Marychurch]: Friendly two-bar local in 18th-c stone-built beamed coaching inn, eight mainstream and other changing ales, interesting naval memorabilia and chamber-pot collection, good-humoured long-serving landlord, basic good value lunchtime food (not Sun), snacks any time, frequent wknd jazz; dogs and children welcome *(the Didler)*

Hole in the Wall TQ1 2AU [Park Lane, opp clock tower]: Ancient unpretentious two-bar local nr harbour, consistently good value usual food, well kept Sharps Doom Bar and guest beers, Blackawton cider, proper old-fashioned landlord and friendly service, smooth cobbled floors, low beams and alcoves, lots of nautical brassware, ship models, old local photographs, chamber-pots, restaurant/function room (band nights); small terrace, open all day *(the Didler)*

TORRINGTON [SS4919]
Royal Exchange EX38 8BT [New St]: Good value home-made food, good drinks choice (early Jun beer festival), friendly efficient service, darts and pool; children welcome, good-sized garden *(anon)*

TOTNES [SX7960]
Bay Horse TQ9 5SP [Cistern St]: Welcoming traditional pub, good value home-made food, well kept ales; piped music, some live; nicely redone bedrooms *(John Goom, Matt Broadgate)*

Kingsbridge Inn TQ9 5SY [Leechwell St]: Attractive rambling bar with black beams, timbering and some stripped stone, eating areas inc small upper part (children allowed here), two log fires, plush seats, enjoyable food (not Mon lunchtime) from lunchtime baguettes up, real ales, pleasant staff; piped music *(LYM, John and Dinah Waters, Ronnie Jones)*

☆ *Royal Seven Stars* TQ9 5DD [Fore St, The Plains]: Civilised old hotel with roomy and cosy bay-windowed bars off flagstoned reception (former coach entry) with imposing staircase and sunny skylight, Courage Best and Greene King Old Speckled Hen, cheerful helpful service, reasonably priced bar food, pretty restaurant; tables out in front – ideal on a Tues market day when the tradespeople wear Elizabethan dress; bedrooms, river across busy main road *(Dr and Mrs M E Wilson, Roger Wain-Heapy)*

Rumour TQ9 5RY [High St]: Civilised almost trendy bar, well kept ales inc Greene King and Skinners, wide-ranging wines by the glass, local fruit juices, enjoyable up-to-date food from pizzas to some enterprising dishes using local produce, bare-boards bistro with bentwood chairs and informal contemporary décor; open all day, cl Sun lunchtime *(Giles and Annie Francis)*

TRUSHAM [SX8582]
☆ *Cridford Inn* TQ13 0NR [off B3193 NW of Chudleigh, just N of big ARC works]: New owners doing well in interesting 14th-c pub, Norman in parts, with Britain's oldest domestic window, lots of stripped stone, flagstones and stout timbers, pleasant bar

with enjoyable sensibly priced food, big woodburner, St Austell Dartmoor Best and Teignworthy Reel Ale, good chic restaurant; children in eating area, wide raised front terrace *(Mike Gorton, LYM)*

TURNCHAPEL [SX4953]
Clovelly Bay PL9 9TB [Boringdon Rd]: Friendly family-run waterside pub with great views across to Plymouth, good food, well kept Sharps Doom Bar and St Austell Tribute, Addlestone's cider, log fires; juke box; outside seating, five bedrooms *(Martin and Marion Vincent, Dino Riccobono)*

UGBOROUGH [SX6755]
Ship PL21 0NS [off A3121 SE of Ivybridge]: Quietly chatty dining pub extended from cosy 16th-c flagstoned core, nicely divided open-plan eating areas a step down from neat bar, wide choice of good home-made food, willing pleasant service, Butcombe and Skinners Heligan Honey; piped music; good tables out in front *(BB, PL, Simon Halsey)*

WESTON [ST1400]
☆ *Otter* EX14 3NZ [off A373, or A30 at W end of Honiton bypass]: Much enlarged busy family pub with heavy low beams, enjoyable food from light dishes to substantial meals and popular Sun carvery, OAP specials, quick cheerful helpful service, Cotleigh and Otter, good value wines, good log fire; piped music; children welcome, disabled access, picnic-sets on big lawn leading to River Otter, play area *(Anthony Double)*

WHIMPLE [SY0497]
Thirsty Farmer EX5 2QQ: Welcoming and helpful young licensees doing enjoyable food, inventive without being too clever, in tall brick-built pub with log fires and dark oak in large L-shaped bar, popular with locals, well kept Otter ale, side dining area; piped music (turned down on request), some band nights; garden tables *(Dr and Mrs M E Wilson)*

WIDECOMBE [SX7176]
Old Inn TQ13 7TA [B3387 W of Bovey Tracey]: Busy sleekly refurbished Badger dining pub with good-humoured landlord, large eating area and roomy side conservatory – get there before about 12.30 in summer to miss the coach-loads, well kept ales inc Greene King; nice garden with water features and pleasant terrace, great walks from this pretty moorland village *(LYM, Paul and Margaret Baker, JHW)*

WONSON [SX6789]
☆ *Northmore Arms* EX20 2JA [A30 at Merrymeet roundabout, take first left on old A30, through Whiddon Down; new roundabout and take left on to A382; then right down lane signposted Throwleigh/Gidleigh. Continue down lane over hump-back bridge; turn left to Wonson; OS Sheet 191 map reference 674903]: Far from smart and greatly

enjoyed by readers who take to its idiosyncratic style (not everyone does); two simple old-fashioned rooms, log fire and woodburner, low beams and stripped stone, well kept Adnams Broadside, Cotleigh Tawny and Exe Valley Dobs tapped from the cask, good house wines, cheap plain food (all day Mon-Sat), darts and board games; children and dogs welcome, picnic-sets outside, two modest bedrooms, beautiful remote walking country, normally open all day *(Michael and Ann Cole, the Didler, LYM, Dr and Mrs A K Clarke, Anthony Longden)*

WOODLAND [SX7869]

☆ *Rising Sun* TQ13 7JT [village signed off A38 just NE of Ashburton, then pub usually signed, nr Combe Cross]: Doing well under new hospitable licensees; good food from sandwiches to enterprising main dishes and local seafood, well kept Dartmoor Jail Ale and a local guest beer, good choice of wines by the glass, Luscombe farm cider; surprisingly plush and expansive with beams and soft lighting, snug corner by log fire, family area, restaurant; picnic-sets and play area in spacious garden, children and dogs welcome, four comfortable bedrooms *(Charlie and Chris Barker, Donna and Roger, David and Christine Francis, Neil Ingoe, LYM, Richard and Maria Gillespie)*

WOOLACOMBE [SS4543]

Red Barn EX34 7DF: Modern seaside bar and restaurant with good value food all day, well kept St Austell and guest ales (early Dec beer festival), pleasant service, surfing pictures and memorabilia; children and dogs welcome, open all day *(Bob and Margaret Holder)*

YARCOMBE [ST2408]

Yarcombe Inn EX14 9BD [A30 2 miles E of A303]: 14th-c thatched pub once owned by Sir Francis Drake, fresh attractive layout, flagstones and ancient stonework, has had well kept St Austell ales, good wines by the glass, friendly staff, pubby food inc OAP bargain lunch, but up for sale 2008; dogs welcome, small back terrace overlooking churchyard, bedrooms *(Dennis Jenkin)*

LUNDY

LUNDY [SS1344]

☆ *Marisco* EX39 2LY: One of England's most isolated pubs (yet full every night), great setting, steep trudge up from landing stage, galleried interior with lifebelts and shipwreck salvage, two St Austell ales labelled for the island, its spring water on tap, good value house wines, welcoming staff, good basic food (all day from breakfast on) using island produce and lots of fresh seafood, open fire, no music, TV or machines; children welcome, tables outside, souvenir shop, and doubles as general store for the island's few residents *(B M Eldridge, D Cheesbrough, Michael Roper)*

If a service charge is mentioned prominently on a menu or accommodation terms, you must pay it if service was satisfactory. If service is really bad, you are legally entitled to refuse to pay some or all of the service charge as compensation for not getting the service you might reasonably have expected.

Dorset

Pubs in Dorset this year have had mixed fortunes, with several falling from main entry status after some disappointing reports. However some have continued as very strong recommendations even though there have been changes at the top. The Hunters Moon at Middlemarsh, now under the mantle of Enterprise Inns, continues to do well, thanks to good service from helpful staff; and it doesn't seem to have lost any of its engagingly diverse paraphernalia. The Elm Tree at Langton Herring has changed hands since the last edition, and continues to provide a friendly welcome, now serving some interesting local produce. The Museum at Farnham makes a pleasant place to stay, with its bustling bar – now under the same landlord, David Sax, as the Cow at Poole. Both are lively dining pubs that have been stylishly and idiosyncratically decorated. As we go to press we hear that the much-liked George at Chideock is about to change hands, and we would very much welcome feedback when the new landlord takes over. For the time being the Ship at West Stour – a coaching inn with updated décor and imaginative food – is doing well, but the team responsible for it may move on, so again we would be grateful for your comments. We have three new main entries this year. The European at Piddletrenthide is an excellent newcomer, imaginatively refurbished and run with great enthusiasm and skill, with reasonably priced good food. We're happy to welcome back two coastal pubs – the West Bay in West Bay itself, where the seafood is deservedly popular, and the particularly family-friendly Smugglers at Osmington Mills, which copes really well with the appreciable summer crowds. Three pubs stand out for their appealingly unspoilt character. The Square & Compass at Worth Matravers is wonderfully individual: one of the best cider pubs around, it also has good beers, and is a perennial favourite with walkers – the rugged cliffs of the Purbeck coast are not far away. Also reassuringly unchanged is the Vine at Pamphill, on the National Trust's Kingston Lacy estate. In a side street in the centre of Sherborne, the Digby Tap is one to seek out for a drink; the well kept beers here are the one thing that does change, and very regularly. Our chosen pubs include several where the meals stand out. The Greyhound at Sydling St Nicholas has really special food, particularly fish and local meat; the beer is brewed for the pub by St Austell. Mudeford's Ship in Distress, aptly nautical in character, is a very useful place to know for its good seafood – and its quirkiness is much enjoyed. At Plush, the smart thatched Brace of Pheasants is another admirable dining pub, and now also offers accommodation. In beautiful countryside, the Three Horseshoes at Powerstock makes a point of using home-grown produce in its cooking. Not far away the Marquis of Lorne at Nettlecombe is a steady all-rounder, with its garden a lovely place to enjoy a pint of Palmers – in beautiful country near Eggardon Hill. Beneath Hambledon Hill the Cricketers at Shroton continues to be a welcoming and civilised place for a meal or a drink. The new European at Piddletrenthide is extremely promising on the food side, but we are staying with a trusted favourite, the Greyhound at Sydling St Nicholas, for our top title of Dorset Dining Pub of the Year. Some places to note particularly in the Lucky Dip section at the end of the chapter are the Beach & Barnicott in Bridport, Three Horseshoes in Burton Bradstock, Anchor on the coast near Chideock, Blue Raddle in Dorchester, Stocks at Furzehill, Pilot Boat and Royal Standard in Lyme Regis, Thimble at Piddlehinton, Crown at Puncknowle, Anchor at Shapwick, Red Lion in Sturminster Marshall, Bull in Sturminster Newton, Ilchester Arms at Symondsbury and Crown at Uploders. The county's main brewers are Ringwood and Palmers; Ringwood is now owned by Marstons, but Palmers remains family-owned (with a lot of appealing tenanted pubs). Badger is also based here – you'll now find its beers only in its own tied pubs, as it's sold its free trade business to Marstons. The only other local brewery we found supplying at least a few good pubs here was Dorset, of Weymouth.

CHIDEOCK   SY4292   MAP 1

George
A35 Bridport—Lyme Regis; DT6 6JD

Comfortable local with well liked food and some interesting photographs and drawings

Within range of some excellent walks towards the highest point of the cliffs at Golden Cap, this pleasantly traditional thatched village pub has been ticking over nicely for several years, but as we went to press we learned that the landlord was about to leave, so we hope it will continue its winning ways. Palmers Copper Ale, IPA and Palmers 200 are served on handpump from the horseshoe-shaped counter. The dark-beamed lounge bar has comfortable blue plush stools and wall and window seats, pewter tankards hanging from the mantelpiece above the big fireplace (with a good winter log fire), hundreds of banknotes pinned to the beams, boat drawings and attractively framed old local photographs on its cream walls and high shelves of bottles, plates, mugs and various items of brassware on the beams as well as an array of tools on the walls of the back bar. The snug is liked by locals; piped music and TV. In summer you can eat out on the terrace, although the busy main road is noisy. Reports on the new regime please.

🍴 Decent bar food has included lunchtime sandwiches, filled baguettes and baked potatoes, ploughman's, home-cooked ham or local sausages with free-range eggs and nice beer-battered haddock, with evening choices such as soup, local scallops, creamy garlic mushrooms, thai-style chicken, fish pie, vegetable lasagne, barnsley lamb chops, barbary duck breast, and puddings like hot chocolate pudding or lemon and lime cheesecake. *Starters/Snacks: £4.95 to £10.95. Main Courses: £10.95 to £18.95. Puddings: £4.00 to £4.50*

Palmers ~ Tenant Paul Crisp ~ Real ale ~ Bar food (12-2, 6-9.30; 12-3, 6-9 Sun) ~ Restaurant ~ (01297) 489419 ~ Children welcome ~ Dogs allowed in bar ~ Open 11-2.30(3 Sun), 6-11

Recommended by Roland and Wendy Chalu, John and Fiona McIlwain, Tim Venn, Terry and Linda Moseley, Peter Craske, Pat and Tony Martin, Mr and Mrs P D Titcomb, Penny and Peter Keevil, Dennis Jenkin, Gene and Kitty Rankin, Hazel Morgan, Bernard Patrick

---

Bedroom prices are for high summer. Even then you may get reductions for more than one night, or (outside tourist areas) weekends. Winter special rates are common, and many inns cut bedroom prices if you have a full evening meal.

CHURCH KNOWLE

SY9381 MAP 2

New Inn ♀

Village signposted off A351 just N of Corfe Castle; BH20 5NQ

An attractive 16th-c pub with pleasantly furnished rooms and an inviting garden; well positioned for walks

There's a lot of charm about this prettily placed pub, with views of the Purbecks from the good-sized garden. Inside it's full of bric-a-brac (including stuffed pheasants and a glass case with some interesting memorabilia, ration books and Horlicks tablets). The two main areas, linked by an arch, are attractively furnished with farmhouse chairs and tables, and a log fire at each end. You can choose wines (with help from the staff if you wish) from a tempting display in the walk-in wine cellar and there are several by the glass and a wine of the month; herefordshire apple juice. Flowers Original, Greene King Old Speckled Hen and Wadworths 6X are on handpump. There are disabled facilities, though there's a step down to the gents', and there is a function room with its own bar and dance floor. You can camp in two fields behind (you must book); fine surrounding walks.

🍴 Bar food includes lunchtime sandwiches and ploughman's as well as starters such as blue vinney soup or deep-fried goat's cheese, a choice of ten fish dishes daily such as grilled sardines, trout with almonds or whole-tail scampi, casseroles, roast of the day, and steak and stilton pie; best to book, especially at weekends. *Starters/Snacks: £4.25 to £7.50. Main Courses: £7.50 to £18.00. Puddings: £4.50 to £5.50*

Punch ~ Tenants Maurice and Rosemary Estop ~ Real ale ~ Bar food (12-2.15, 6-9.15) ~ Restaurant ~ (01929) 480357 ~ Children welcome ~ Open 10(12 Sun)-3, 6-11; closed Mon evening Jan-March

Recommended by Charles and Pauline Stride, Pat and Roger Davies, Mike and Sue Loseby, Joan and Michel Hooper-Immins, John Roots, JDM, KM, D R Robinson, Dr Phil Putwain, Colin Dorling, Michael Butler, Robert Watt

FARNHAM

ST9515 MAP 2

Museum ♀ 🛏

Village signposted off A354 Blandford Forum—Salisbury; DT11 8DE

Stylish and civilised inn with appealing rooms (and a bustling bar), and super bedrooms

David Sax who also runs the Cow at Poole took over this pleasantly extended pub with its interconnecting rooms early in 2008, and we hope it will continue with its winning ways. The little flagstoned bar remains a real focus for locals of all ages and has a lively atmosphere, light beams, a big inglenook fireplace, good comfortably cushioned furnishings and fresh flowers on all the tables. Cheery yellow walls and plentiful windows give the place a bright, fresh feel. To the right is a dining room with a fine antique dresser, while off to the left is a cosier room, with a very jolly hunting model and a seemingly sleeping stuffed fox curled in a corner. Another room feels rather like a contemporary baronial hall, soaring up to a high glass ceiling, with dozens of antlers and a stag's head looking down on a long refectory table and church-style pews. This leads to an outside terrace with more wooden tables. The bedrooms in the main building are very comfortable. An excellent choice of wines with a dozen by the glass and Ringwood Best Bitter and Timothy Taylors Landlord along with a guest such as Hidden Brewery Hidden Spring on handpump.

🍴 Bar food (not cheap) might include soup, lunchtime sandwiches, starters such as fishcake and caesar salad or warm red onion and goats cheese omelette, and main courses like aberdeen angus rump steak, calves liver with red onion marmalade and crispy bacon, wild rabbit loins wrapped in parma ham with smoked bacon and pearl barley risotto, and baked fillet of hake with steamed mussels. *Starters/Snacks: £5.00 to £8.50. Main Courses: £15.50 to £19.50. Puddings: £6.50 to £9.00*

Free house ~ Licensee David Sax ~ Real ale ~ Bar food (12-2(2.30 Sat), 7-9.30; 12-3, 7-9 Sun) ~ Restaurant (Fri and Sat evening and Sun lunch) ~ (01725) 516261 ~ Children over 5 only ~ Dogs allowed in bar and bedrooms ~ Open 12-3, 6-11; 12-3, 7-10.30 Sun ~ Bedrooms: £85B/£95B

Recommended by Colin and Janet Roe, Phil Bryant, Mrs L Saumarez Smith, JCW, Andrea Rampley, Steve Whalley, Andrew Hollingshead, John Robertson, R J Davies, Mrs J H S Lang, I H Curtis

LANGTON HERRING

SY6182   MAP 2

Elm Tree

Signed off B3157; DT3 4HU

Bustling pub with summer flowering tubs and baskets and lots of copper inside

This quietly situated village pub makes a handy starting point or objective for walks on the Dorset Coast Path alongside the Fleet, the eight-mile lagoon enclosed by Chesil Beach. There's a lot of character in the main beamed and carpeted rooms (where the Portland spy ring is said to have met) which have walls festooned with copper, brass and bellows, cushioned window seats, red leatherette stools, windsor chairs and lots of big old kitchen tables; one has some old-fashioned settles and an inglenook. The traditionally furnished extension gives more room for diners. Adnams Best Bitter and Courage Directors on handpump and several wines by the glass; piped music and darts. Outside, there are flower tubs, hanging baskets and a very pretty flower-filled sunken garden with outdoor heaters.

🍽 **Bar food includes sandwiches, soup, lasagne, steak and ale pie, spinach and feta roulade, interesting daily specials with an emphasis on local produce such as prawns, dabs or grey mullet from the Fleet or game in season from local shoots, and puddings such as bread and butter pudding or rhubarb crumble.** *Starters/Snacks: £3.95 to £5.95. Main Courses: £5.95 to £15.95. Puddings: £3.50 to £4.95*

Punch ~ Lease Andrew and Charlotte Dewell ~ Real ale ~ Bar food (12-2.15, 6.30-9.15; all day in summer) ~ Restaurant ~ (01305) 871257 ~ Children welcome ~ Dogs welcome ~ Folk music night first Tues in month, jazz every second Sun lunchtime ~ Open 11-11(10.30 Sun)

Recommended by Terry and Linda Moseley, Mr and Mrs W W Burke, Hugh Stafford, JDM, KM, Pat and Roger Davies, Fred and Lorraine Gill, Yana Pocklington, Patricia Owlett, Roland and Wendy Chalu

MARSHWOOD

SY3799   MAP 1

Bottle

B3165 Lyme Regis—Crewkerne; DT6 5QJ

Unchanging local, tasty food, summer beer festival and big back garden

In lovely, hilly country within strolling distance of Lambert's Castle Iron-Age hill fort, this unpretentious place has a generously sized garden with a play area, and a camping field beyond. Otter Bitter and Purbeck Fossil Fuel plus either Otter Ale or Palmers Dorset Gold, and perhaps a guest are on handpump. The simple cream-walled interior has down-to-earth furnishings including cushioned benches and there's an inglenook fireplace with (usually) a big log fire in winter. A more modern extension has pool, TV, a skittle alley and piped music; also table football, cards, darts, dominoes and backgammon. The annual world stinging-nettle eating championships are held at the same time as their beer festival, on the weekend before the summer solstice. Dogs are only allowed in the back bar, on a lead. More reports please.

🍽 **Bar food includes filled baguettes, soup, fillet steak rossini, beef, beer and mushroom pie, sausage and mash, baked cod in cheese and tarragon sauce, and puddings like dorset apple cake or bitter lemon tart with raspberry sorbet.** *Starters/Snacks: £3.75 to £6.00. Main Courses: £8.95 to £16.00. Puddings: £2.75 to £4.25*

Free house ~ Licensees Shane and Ellen Pym ~ Real ale ~ Bar food (12-2, 6.30-9; not Mon (except during summer hols)) ~ (01297) 678254 ~ Well-behaved children welcome if dining ~ Dogs allowed in bar ~ Rock disco last Sat of month ~ Open 12-3, 6.30-11(12 Fri, Sat); closed Mon except school hols

Recommended by R J and G M Townson, Terry and Linda Moseley, Roger Berry, Pat and Tony Martin

---

A few pubs try to make you leave a credit card at the bar, as a sort of deposit if you order food. This is a bad practice, and the banks and credit card firms warn you not to let your card go like this.

MIDDLEMARSH

ST6607   MAP 2

Hunters Moon

A352 Sherborne—Dorchester; DT9 5QN

Plenty of bric-a-brac in several linked areas, reasonably priced food, and a good choice of drinks

Readers continue to enjoy this cosy pub, which has remained largely unchanged since the present licensee took over in autumn 2007. The comfortably welcoming interior rambles around in several linked areas, with a great variety of tables and chairs, plenty of bric-a-brac from decorative teacups, china ornaments and glasses through horse tack and brassware, to quite a collection of spirits miniatures. Beams, some panelling, soft lighting from converted oil lamps, three log fires (one in a capacious inglenook), and the way that some attractively cushioned settles form booths all combine to give a cosy relaxed feel. Butcombe Bitter and a couple of guests such as Greene King Old Speckled Hen and Ringwood Fortyniner on handpump; faint piped music; children's books, colouring pads and puzzles; board games. A neat lawn has circular picnic-sets as well as the more usual ones, and the en-suite bedrooms are in what was formerly a skittle alley and stable block.

⏺ Bar food includes lunchtime filled baguettes and bloomers, soup, portland scallops, steak, goats cheese tart, lamb shank, battered cod, daily specials such as pheasant or venison, some 'smaller appetite meals', and puddings. *Starters/Snacks: £3.70 to £5.95. Main Courses: £6.75 to £14.75. Puddings: £3.75 to £4.25*

Enterprise ~ Lease Dean and Emma Mortimer ~ Real ale ~ Bar food (12-2, 6-9.30(9 Sun)) ~ (01963) 210966 ~ Children welcome ~ Dogs welcome ~ Open 11.30-3, 6-11; closed 25, 26 Dec ~ Bedrooms: £55S/£65S

Recommended by M G Hart, R J and G M Townson, Jill Bickerton, Dave Braisted, Joan and Michel Hooper-Immins

MUDEFORD

SZ1792   MAP 2

Ship in Distress ♀

Stanpit; off B3059 at roundabout; BH23 3NA

Wide choice of fish dishes, nautical décor, and friendly staff in cheerful cottage

A splendidly quirky and welcoming place, this former smugglers' haunt is well worth the effort of finding, whether to sample the real ales or for a meal. Adnams and Ringwood Best Bitter are served on handpump alongside a couple of guests that change about three times a week and might include such as Brains Bread of Heaven and Daleside Old Legover; 12 wines by the glass. It is crammed with nautical bric-a-brac from rope fancywork and brassware through lanterns, oars and ceiling nets and ensigns, to an aquarium, boat models (we particularly like the Mississippi steamboat), and the odd piratical figure; darts, games machine, board games, a couple of TV sets and piped music. Besides a good few boat pictures, the room on the right has masses of snapshots of locals caught up in various waterside japes, under its glass tabletops. A spreading two-room restaurant area, as cheerful in its way as the bar, has contemporary works by local artists for sale, and a light-hearted mural sketching out the impression of a window open on a sunny boating scene. There are tables out on the suntrap back terrace, and a covered area for smokers.

⏺ Enjoyable fresh local fish and seafood are the thing here: sandwiches, and reasonably priced bar food such as moules marinières or fish pie, as well as more expensive à la carte offerings (which you can eat in the bar or in the restaurant) like smoked salmon and halibut roulade, irish rock oysters, lamb cutlets with herb crust, confit duck leg with red onion marmalade and thyme jus, and whole roasted bream; puddings. *Starters/Snacks: £4.50 to £10.95. Main Courses: £5.95 to £10.95. Puddings: £4.95*

Punch ~ Tenants Colin Pond and Maggie Wheeler ~ Real ale ~ Bar food ~ Restaurant ~ (01202) 485123 ~ Children welcome ~ Dogs allowed in bar ~ Open 10am-midnight; 11-11 Sun

Recommended by David Randall, Chris Flynn, Wendy Jones, Katharine Cowherd, John and Annabel Hampshire, Martin and Karen Wake, Colin Wood

NETTLECOMBE   SY5195   MAP 2

Marquis of Lorne 🍺 🛏

Off A3066 Bridport—Beaminster, via W Milton; DT6 3SY

Tasty food and beer in welcoming country pub in beautiful countryside, with large, mature garden

The bars and dining rooms in this friendly 16th-c former farmhouse are named after local hills, one after Eggardon Hill, the site of one of Dorset's most spectacular Iron-Age hill forts, which is within walking distance. The comfortable bustling main bar has a log fire, mahogany panelling and old prints and photographs around its neatly matching chairs and tables; two dining areas lead off, the smaller of which has another log fire. The wooden-floored snug (liked by locals) has cribbage, dominoes, board games and table skittles. Three real ales from Palmers are well kept on handpump, with Copper, IPA and 200, and Tally Ho in winter, plus a decent wine list with several by the glass. The maturing big garden is full of pretty herbaceous borders, and has a rustic-style play area among the picnic-sets under its apple trees.

🍴 In addition to tasty sandwiches, filled baguettes and winter ploughman's, bar food includes soup, chicken and pork pâté with plum chutney, local scallops with herb risotto and pesto dressing, ham, egg and chips, beer-battered fresh cod, lasagne, pork tenderloin with apple and red onion in cider sauce and fillet steaks from a local farm. *Starters/Snacks: £4.50 to £7.50. Main Courses: £8.50 to £17.50. Puddings: £2.75 to £4.50*

Palmers ~ Tenants David and Julie Woodroffe ~ Real ale ~ Bar food (12-2.30, 7-9.30(9 winter)) ~ Restaurant ~ (01308) 485236 ~ No children under 10 in bedrooms ~ Dogs allowed in bar ~ Open 11-11 ~ Bedrooms: £50S/£95S

Recommended by Fred and Lorraine Gill, Michael Bayne, Dr Kevan Tucker, Roland and Wendy Chalu, R J and G M Townson, Brian and Jacky Wilson

OSMINGTON MILLS   SY7381   MAP 2

Smugglers

Off A353 NE of Weymouth; DT3 6HF

Centuries-old inn useful for the coastal path; copes well with the peak-time crowds

Open all day, this family-friendly inn is very efficiently run, even when crowded in summer, when the garden really comes into its own. There are picnic-sets out on crazy paving by a little stream, with a thatched summer bar (which offers Pimms and plates of smoked salmon) and a good play area (including a little assault course) beneath a steep lawn. Inside, woodwork divides the spacious bar into cosy, welcoming areas, with logs burning in two open stoves and old local pictures scattered about, and various quotes and words of wisdom painted on the wall ('a day without wine is a day without sunshine'). Some seats are tucked into alcoves and window embrasures. The games machines are kept sensibly out of the way; piped music. Three ales from Badger feature Tanglefoot and a seasonal brew like Fursty Ferret on handpump.

🍴 Handily served all day, bar food (they will do smaller helpings for children) includes soup, lunchtime sandwiches, eggs benedict, a larder board for two people, and main courses such as roast butternut squash, fish pie or steak, specials, and puddings like trifle or rhubarb crumble. *Starters/Snacks: £3.45 to £5.50. Main Courses: £7.95 to £12.95. Puddings: £4.50 to £4.95*

Badger ~ Manager Sonia Henderson ~ Real ale ~ Bar food (12-10(9 winter)) ~ (01305) 833125 ~ Children welcome ~ Dogs allowed in bar ~ Open 11-11; 12-10.30 Sun ~ Bedrooms: £62B/£72B

Recommended by Yana Pocklington, Patricia Owlett, Robert Watt, Chris and Jeanne Downing, Ann and Colin Hunt, the Didler, Pat and Tony Martin, Dr Kevan Tucker, Gerald and Gabrielle Culliford

---

Post Office address codings confusingly give the impression that some pubs are in Dorset, when they're really in Somerset (which is where we list them).

PAMPHILL   ST9900 MAP 2

Vine

Off B3082 on NW edge of Wimborne: turn on to Cowgrove Hill at Cowgrove signpost, then turn right up Vine Hill; BH21 4EE

Charming and unchanging, run by the same family for three generations

This well cared for little place will delight those who take pleasure in individual, simple country pubs. Frequented by locals but also welcoming to visitors, it's been run by the same family for three generations but is actually owned by the National Trust as part of the Kingston Lacy estate. Of its two tiny bars one, with a warm coal-effect gas fire, has only three tables, the other just half a dozen or so seats on its lino floor, some of them huddling under the stairs that lead up via narrow wooden steps to an upstairs games room; darts and board games. Local photographs (look out for the one of the regular with his giant pumpkin) and notices decorate the painted panelling; quiet piped music. Two real ales include one on handpump and one served from the cask, from brewers such as Fullers, Goddards or Ringwood; farm cider. There are picnic-sets and benches out on a sheltered gravel terrace and more share a fairy-lit, heated verandah with a grapevine. Round the back a patch of grass has a climbing frame; outside lavatories. The National Trust estate includes Kingston Lacy house and the huge Badbury Rings Iron-Age hill fort (itself good for wild flowers), and there are many paths. They don't accept credit cards or cheques.

🍴 **Lunchtime bar snacks such as good, fresh sandwiches and ploughman's.** *Starters/Snacks: £3.00 to £5.00*

Free house ~ Licensee Mrs Sweatland ~ Real ale ~ Bar food (11(12 Sun)-2; not evenings) ~ No credit cards ~ (01202) 882259 ~ Well behaved children in upper room (not evenings) ~ Dogs welcome ~ Open 11(12 Sun)-3, 7-10.30(11 Sat)

Recommended by the Didler, M R Phillips, Martin and Karen Wake, Mr and Mrs W W Burke, David Parker, Emma Smith, Pat and Roger Davies, Alan Wright, Mr and Mrs P D Titcomb

PIDDLETRENTHIDE   SY7198 MAP 2

European 🍴 🛏

B3143 N of Dorchester; DT2 7QT

Mellow, civilised and intimate dining pub with a fresh rustic look, caring staff and thoughtfully presented food

The former landlord of the Trout at Tadpole Bridge, Oxfordshire, has taken over this modest-looking inn and completely transformed it inside. The two opened-up linked beamed rooms are attractively furnished with quite a mix of dining chairs, lit church candles on all sorts of wooden tables, little country cushions on the comfortable, mushroom-coloured built-in wall seats, pretty window blinds, and nicely worn rugs on terracotta tiles. The yellow walls are hung with duck and hunting prints, fishy plates and a couple of fox masks, and there are interesting fresh flower arrangements, hand-made walking sticks for sale, newspapers to read and maybe one or more of the pub dogs on a cushion in front of the woodburning stove in the sandstone fireplace. Butcombe, Palmers Copper and a guest from a brewer such as Hidden Brewery on handpump, good wines by the glass, home-made elderflower cordial in season, and they have their own damson vodka and sloe gin too. The atmosphere is chatty and relaxed. There are a few picnic-sets in front and at the back, with an outdoor heater. The two new bedrooms have good views.

🍴 **Using some produce from their own farm and game from local estates, the sound cooking includes starters like portland scallops, home-smoked duck breast with apple and rosemary jelly, or blue vinney and port mushrooms, and main courses such as wild rabbit casserole, roasted red pepper and courgette, and fillet of bass with hollandaise sauce; super puddings might include lemon posset, hot chocolate fondant or english rhubarb fool with rhubarb sorbet and citrus shortbread.** *Starters/Snacks: £4.00 to £8.00. Main Courses: £8.00 to £14.00. Puddings: £4.00 to £5.00*

Free house ~ Licensees Mark and Emily Hammick ~ Bar food ~ (01300) 348308 ~ Children welcome ~ Dogs welcome ~ Open 11.30-3, 6-11; closed 2 weeks end of Jan-early Feb winter; closed Sun evening and all day Mon except bank hols ~ Bedrooms: £55B/£80B

Recommended by Paul and Annette Hallett, Dr R P Ashfield, Mr and Mrs Edward Mason, Joe Meier

PLUSH
ST7102   MAP 2

Brace of Pheasants
Off B3143 N of Dorchester; DT2 7RQ

Fairly smart but relaxed pub with friendly service, good beers, and decent garden; nearby walks

In a lovely position by Plush Brook and tucked into a fold of hills, this 16th-c thatched country pub continues to generate praise from readers, and now has en-suite bedrooms too; we would welcome reports from anyone who stays here. The airy beamed bar has good solid tables, windsor chairs, fresh flowers, a huge heavy-beamed inglenook at one end with cosy seating inside, and a good warming log fire at the other. Ringwood Best along with guests such as Cottage Whippet of Oz and Sharps Cornish Coaster are tapped from the cask and there's a good choice of wines with several by the glass; friendly service. A decent-sized garden and terrace include a lawn sloping up towards a rockery. From here an attractive bridleway behind goes to the left of the woods and over to Church Hill.

[] **Enjoyable bar food includes sandwiches, soup, warm garlic-marinated goats cheese, beer-battered pigeon strips with red onion marmalade, game terrine, lamb cutlets with fried piquant red wine sauce, poached skate wing and portland crab thermidor.** *Starters/Snacks: £4.00 to £8.00. Main Courses: £9.00 to £16.00. Puddings: £5.00*

Free house ~ Licensees Phil and Carol Bennett ~ Real ale ~ Bar food (12.30-2.30, 7.30-9.30) ~ (01300) 348357 ~ Children welcome ~ Dogs welcome ~ Open 12-3, 7-11; 12-4 Sun; closed Sun evening and all day Mon except bank hols ~ Bedrooms: £75B/£95B

Recommended by Dr and Mrs J Temporal, the Didier, Peter and Liz Holmes, Stewart Bingham, Edward Mirzoeff, Mr and Mrs W W Burke, Robert Watt, Mike and Sue Loseby, M G Hart, Phyl and Jack Street

POOLE
SZ0391   MAP 2

Cow ♀
Station Road, Ashley Cross, Parkstone; beside Parkstone Station; BH14 8UD

Interesting one-bar pub with contemporary décor, good modern food, and fine wines

The stylish open-plan interior is a real surprise here, as it's quite unassuming from the outside. It has a mix of wooden tables and dining chairs, a couple of low tables by some comfortable squashy sofas with huge colourful cushions and high leatherette bar chairs. A gas-effect coal fire in a brick fireplace, with another in the entrance hall and quite a discreet flat screen TV in one corner; piped music, board games and a good array of newspapers. Ochre ragged walls are hung with a vintage songsheet of Three Acres and a Cow, Twickenham Rugby Museum replicas of 1930s and 1940s rugby prints and big modern cow prints in bright pinks, yellows and blues. Fullers London Pride, Ringwood Best and a guest such as Gales HSB on handpump, and an extensive wine list with about ten wines by the glass and many remarkable bottles (the most expensive being a Château Pétrus at £650). In the evening you can eat in the sizeable bistro where there are more heavy stripped tables on bare boards and plenty of wine bottles lining the window sills. Seats outside on the enclosed and heated terrace area.

[] **From a sensibly short menu, the good modern lunchtime bar food includes filled baguettes, soup, sausages and mash with onion gravy, bacon, bubble-and-squeak and free-range eggs, fishcakes, warm leek and wild mushroom tart, cod and chips, steak, mushroom and ale pie, and puddings; more expensive evening options from a seasonally changing menu in the bistro.** *Starters/Snacks: £4.25 to £7.95. Main Courses: £9.50 to £14.50. Puddings: £6.00*

Free house ~ Licensee David Sax ~ Real ale ~ Bar food (not Sun evening) ~ Restaurant ~
(01202) 749569 ~ Children allowed in bistro, and in bar until 7pm ~ Dogs allowed in bar ~
Open 11-11(midnight Sat); 12-10.30 Sun

Recommended by JDM, KM, Terry and Linda Moseley, Alan Wright, Andy and Claire Barker, Mr and Mrs W W Burke

POWERSTOCK
SY5196   MAP 2

Three Horseshoes ♀

Off A3066 Beaminster—Bridport via W Milton; DT6 3TF

**Friendly inn in fine countryside with imaginative food and a fair choice of drinks; walks
nearby**

Part of the pleasure of visiting this secluded Victorian village inn is arriving there,
tucked away as it is among steep valleys and in tempting terrain for walkers. Inside, the
L-shaped bar has good log fires, magazines and newspapers to read, stripped panelling,
country furniture including settles, Palmers IPA and Copper on handpump, and several
wines by the glass served by friendly staff. There are local paintings for sale in the dining
room; piped music and board games. Smart teak seats and tables under large parasols on
the back terrace (steps down to it) have a lovely uninterrupted view towards the sea and
there's a big sloping garden. Two of the bedrooms have fine valley views.

🍴 Using home-grown vegetables, fruit and herbs, and cooked by the landlord/chef, the
enterprising food typically includes lunchtime filled rolls, interesting soup, deep-fried
tempura prawns with sweet chilli dipping sauce, rib-eye steak, wild mushroom and brie
risotto, apricot-braised partridge, loin of venison with a rich cherry jus, rabbit casserole
with chorizo dumplings, and organic lamb faggots, with puddings such as rum and raisin
chocolate torte or baked apple with maple syrup. *Starters/Snacks: £4.50 to £7.95. Main
Courses: £7.95 to £16.25. Puddings: £4.50*

Palmers ~ Tenant Andy Preece ~ Real ale ~ Bar food (12-3, 7-9.30; 12-4, 7-8.30 Sun) ~
Restaurant ~ (01308) 485328 ~ Children welcome ~ Dogs allowed in bar and bedrooms ~
Open 11-3, 6.30-11.30(midnight Sat); 11-4, 6.30-11 Sun ~ Bedrooms: /£80S

*Recommended by B D Nunn, Lewis Caplin, A J King, Roland and Wendy Chalu, Terry and Linda Moseley,
Noel Grundy*

SHAVE CROSS
SY4198   MAP 1

Shave Cross Inn

*On back lane Bridport—Marshwood, signposted locally; OS Sheet 193 map reference
415980; DT6 6HW*

Caribbean touches to food and drink in 14th-c pub; carefully tended garden

It's well worth a pilgrimage to this out-of-the-way flint and thatch inn, named because
travelling monks once lodged here, and got their heads shaved in preparation for the
final stage of their journey to the shrine of St Wita at Whitchurch. The original timbered
bar is a lovely flagstoned room, surprisingly roomy and full of character, with country
antiques, two armchairs either side of a warming fire in an enormous inglenook fireplace
and hops round the bar – a scene little altered from the last century. Branscombe Vale
Branoc, their own-label 4Ms and a guest on handpump, alongside half a dozen wines by
the glass, farm cider, several vintage rums and a caribbean beer; piped music (jazz or
caribbean). Pool, darts and a juke box (a real rarity now) are in the skittle alley. Lovingly
tended, the sheltered flower-filled garden with its thatched wishing-well, carp pool and
children's play area is very pretty. There are seven en-suite boutique hotel-style rooms.
🍴 With some caribbean influence, the bar food might include filled toasted panini and
ploughman's, caribbean chicken curry, boar or venison sausages and mash, spicy
aubergine, pimento, pepper and caribbean vegetable bake, and fish and seafood mornay,
along with a choice of specials; there's also a two- and three-course set restaurant menu.
Starters/Snacks: £6.95. Main Courses: £6.95 to £16.50. Puddings: £4.95 to £6.50

Free house ~ Licensee Mel Warburton ~ Real ale ~ Bar food (12-3, 7-9) ~ Restaurant (7-9.30) ~ (01308) 868358 ~ Children welcome ~ Dogs allowed in bar ~ Open 11-3, 6-11; 12-3, 7-11 Sun; 11-3, 6-1am Sat and 12-3, 7-1am Sun in winter; closed Mon except bank hols ~ Bedrooms: /£160B

Recommended by Fred and Lorraine Gill, Michael Doswell, the Didler, Roland and Wendy Chalu, Terry and Linda Moseley, Pat and Roger Davies, Pat and Tony Martin, Tim Venn, Gene and Kitty Rankin

SHERBORNE
ST6316 MAP 2

Digby Tap ▰ £

Cooks Lane; park in Digby Road and walk round corner; DT9 3NS

Regularly changing ales in simple tavern, usefully open all day; close to abbey

Refreshingly no-nonsense and no frills, this alehouse has a constantly changing array of interesting and reasonably priced beers, with one cornish ale among Sharps Cornish Coaster, St Austell Dartmoor or Tinners, and three others such as Moles Landlords Choice, Northumberland Legends of the Tyne and Scattor Rock Teign Valley Tipple. Its simple flagstoned bar is chatty and full of character. A little games room has pool and a quiz machine, and there's a TV room. There are some seats outside and the pub is only a couple of minutes' walk from the famous abbey.

▥ **Good value, straightforward bar lunchtime food includes sandwiches, filled baguettes and baked potatoes, chilli beef, and maybe liver and bacon, mixed grill or plaice stuffed with prawns; no puddings apart from ice-cream.** *Starters/Snacks: £1.65 to £3.00. Main Courses: £3.45 to £5.25*

Free house ~ Licensees Oliver Wilson and Nick Whigham ~ Real ale ~ Bar food (12-1.45, not Sun) ~ No credit cards ~ (01935) 813148 ~ Children welcome until 6pm ~ Dogs welcome ~ Open 11-11; 12-11 Sun

Recommended by JT, Mike and Mary Clark, Pat and Tony Martin, Michael B Griffith, Phil and Sally Gorton

SHROTON
ST8512 MAP 2

Cricketers ♀ ▰ ⇌

Off A350 N of Blandford (village also called Iwerne Courtney); follow signs; DT11 8QD

Well run pub with neatly uniformed and friendly staff, well liked food, and lots of wines by the glass; walks and nice views nearby

A cricket ball and stumps are attached to the front door of this elegantly charming red-brick dining pub, opposite the village green and within striding distance of Hambledon Hill, which is topped by one of the finest Iron-Age hill forts found anywhere; they welcome walkers if they leave their walking boots outside. The bright divided bar has a big stone fireplace, alcoves and cricketing memorabilia and Greene King IPA, Ringwood Best Bitter, St Austell Tribute and perhaps a guest from a brewery such as Butcombe are served from pumps with little cricket-bat handles. They've also several wines by the glass, and quite a few malt whiskies; good friendly service from the attentive landlord and his neatly uniformed staff. The comfortable back restaurant overlooks the garden and has a fresh neutral décor, and a sizeable games area has pool, darts, board games, games machine and piped music. The garden is secluded and pretty with big sturdy tables under cocktail parasols, well tended shrubs and a well stocked (and well used) herb garden by the kitchen door.

▥ **As well as filled baguettes, the well liked bar food might include soup, seared scallops with chive cream glaze, home-cured gravadlax, tagliatelle with mushroom, white wine and cream sauce, medallions of venison with port and wild mushroom jus, breast of chicken on dauphinoise potatoes with bacon and madeira cream, steak, mushroom and ale pie, and fillet of bass on mussel and saffron cream.** *Starters/Snacks: £5.95 to £6.95. Main Courses: £4.95 to £15.95. Puddings: £2.95 to £4.50*

Heartstone Inns ~ Managers Andrew and Natasha Edwards ~ Real ale ~ Bar food (12-2.30, 6.30-9.30; not Sun evening) ~ Restaurant ~ (01258) 860421 ~ Children welcome ~ Open 12-3, 6-11; 12-10.30 Sun

Recommended by Colin and Janet Roe, Edward Mirzoeff, Peter Salmon, R J Herd, Paul and Annette Hallett, Douglas and Ann Hare, Leslie and Barbara Owen, Terry and Linda Moseley, P and J Shapley

SYDLING ST NICHOLAS   SY6399 MAP 2

Greyhound 🍴 ♟ 🛏

Off A37 N of Dorchester; High Street; DT2 9PD

DORSET DINING PUB OF THE YEAR

Genuinely welcoming staff, attractively presented food, good range of drinks, and country décor in beamed rooms

In a peaceful streamside village, this supremely well run inn continues to hit top form consistently. Sydling Bitter brewed for the pub by St Austell is on handpump along with a couple of guests such as Fullers London Pride and Greene King Old Speckled Hen, and a dozen wines are sold by the glass; several malt whiskies; fairly unobtrusive piped music and board games. The beamed and flagstoned serving area is airy and alluring with a big bowl of lemons and limes, a backdrop of gleaming bottles and copper pans, and plenty of bar stools, with more opposite ranging against a drinking shelf. On one side a turkey-carpeted area with a warm coal fire in a handsome portland stone fireplace has a comfortable mix of straightforward tables and chairs and country decorations such as a stuffed fox eyeing a collection of china chickens and a few farm tools. At the other end, a cosy separate dining room with smart white table linen has some books and a glass-covered well set into its floor and a garden room with succulents and other plants on its sills has simple modern café furniture. The small front garden has a wooden climber and slide alongside its picnic-sets. The bedrooms are in a separate block.

🍴 **Extremely accomplished, if not cheap, bar food features meat reared in Dorset and a range of fish including shellfish from Lyme Bay; on a short lunchtime snack menu are sandwiches, filled baguettes, ploughman's and warm scallop and bacon salad; bar food includes mediterranean fish soup, goats cheese bruschetta with sun-dried tomato and olive tapenade, fresh cornish sardines, butternut squash and mascarpone risotto, rack of lamb on gratin potato, fillet of bass, steaks and daily specials such as chicken breast stuffed with fresh lobster or moroccan lamb tagine; vegetables are extra; puddings like vanilla and passion fruit brûlée and chocolate and coffee mousse pot with amaretto biscuit.** *Starters/Snacks: £3.95 to £9.50. Main Courses: £10.50 to £17.95. Puddings: £4.50*

Free house ~ Licensees John Ford, Karen Trimby, Ron Hobson, Cherry Ball ~ Real ale ~ Bar food (12-2(3 Sun), 6.30-9; not Sun evening) ~ Restaurant ~ (01300) 341303 ~ Children welcome ~ Dogs allowed in bar ~ Open 11-2.30, 6-11; 12-3.30 Sun; closed Sun evening ~ Bedrooms: /£70S(£80B)

Recommended by John Saville, Brian Thompson, Geoffrey Leather, Barbara Wright, Roland and Wendy Chalu, Peter Fish, Mr and Mrs W W Burke, Dennis Buckland, N M Penfold, Neil and Sue Cumming, Joan and Michel Hooper-Immins, Ian Malone, Russell New, Ann and Colin Hunt, M G Hart, Barrie and Anne King, P R Light, Terry and Linda Moseley, Donna Mason

WEST BAY   SY4690 MAP 1

West Bay 🍴 🛏

Station Road; DT6 4EW

Restauranty seaside inn with an emphasis on seafood

Looking out to sea and within strolling distance of the little harbour at West Bay, this dining pub is largely set out for eating, but you could just pop in for a drink; several local teams meet to play in the pub's skittles alley. An island servery separates the fairly simple bare-boards front part, with its coal-effect gas fire and mix of sea and nostalgic prints, from a cosier carpeted dining area with more of a country kitchen feel; piped music. Though its spaciousness means it never feels crowded, booking is virtually essential in season. Palmers 200, Copper Ale and IPA are served on handpump alongside good house wines (with eight by the glass); several malt whiskies. There are tables in the small side garden, with more in a large garden; plenty of parking. The bedrooms are quiet and comfortable.

🍽 Very enjoyable food (not cheap) focuses mostly on fish and shellfish; lunchtime ploughman's, sandwiches and a couple of simple items such as breaded scampi; soup, lyme scallops, cornish mussels, steak, chump chop of dorset lamb, rabbit and chicken pie, skate wing with nut brown butter, capers and chips, fish pie, and hot shellfish platter; puddings. *Starters/Snacks: £4.75 to £8.00. Main Courses: £7.50 to £32.00. Puddings: £4.50*

Palmers ~ Tenants Richard and Lorraine Barnard ~ Real ale ~ Bar food (12-2(3 Sun); 6.30-9.30) ~ Restaurant ~ (01308) 422157 ~ Children welcome ~ Dogs allowed in bar ~ Open 12-3, 6-11; closed Sun evening Oct-Jun ~ Bedrooms: £60B/£85B

Recommended by James A Waller, Nigel and Kath Thompson, David Parker, Emma Smith, Peter and Andrea Jacobs, B and F A Hannam, Roland and Wendy Chalu, George Atkinson, David and Julie Glover, Tony Baldwin, Terry and Linda Moseley, Dave Braisted, Robert Watt, Dr KevanTucker, Gaynor Gregory, George and Beverley Tucker, Pat and Tony Martin, R J Davies

WEST STOUR   ST7822   MAP 2

Ship 🍷 🛏
A30 W of Shaftesbury; SP8 5RP

Good imaginative fresh food in civilised and pleasantly updated roadside inn

This well cared for 18th-c coaching inn has been sympathetically modernised, and the neatly dressed staff give good service. On the right two carpeted dining rooms, with stripped pine dado and shutters, are furnished in a similar pleasantly informal style, and have some attractive contemporary nautical prints. The bar on the left, with a cool sage green décor and big sash windows, has a mix of seats around nice stripped tables on the dark boards or flagstones of its two smallish rooms; the gossipy inner one has a good log fire, and its bow window looks beyond the road and car park to a soothing view of rolling pastures; TV, darts, board games. As well as several malt whiskies, elderflower pressé and Frobishers bumbleberry, they have good wines by the glass, and Palmers Dorset Gold, IPA and a guest such as from a local brewery Otter on handpump. The bedlington terrier is called Douglas. As there's a sharp nearby bend, keep your fingers crossed that drivers are obeying the 30mph limit when you walk from or to the car park opposite.

🍽 The food continues to be the main draw, with a wide choice of lunchtime baguettes, ciabattas and panini, as well as soup, wild mushroom risotto, mussels, pot-roasted lamb shank with spring onion mash, duck breast marinated in balsamic vinegar and chilli on coriander noodles, rib-eye steak, cumberland sausage and mash, cottage pie, and a fresh fish board that could include a duo of cod and haddock in saffron mussel cream sauce, or grilled fillet of turbot. *Starters/Snacks: £3.95 to £6.95. Main Courses: £8.95 to £15.95. Puddings: £4.50*

Free house ~ Licensee Gavin Griggs ~ Real ale ~ Bar food (12-2.30, 6-9) ~ Restaurant ~ (01747) 838640 ~ Children welcome ~ Dogs allowed in bar ~ Open 12-3.30, 6-11.20; 12-11 Sun ~ Bedrooms: £55B/£80B

Recommended by Steve Jackson, Robert Watt, Colin and Janet Roe, Maria Furness

WIMBORNE MINSTER   SZ0199   MAP 2

Green Man £
Victoria Road at junction with West Street (B3082/B3073); BH21 1EN

Cosy and warm-hearted town pub with bargain simple food

The front of this lively, cheerful and efficiently run pub is lavished in summer with floral displays that have deservedly won awards. Inside, copper and brass ornaments brighten up the muted warm tones – soft lighting, dark red walls, maroon plush banquettes and polished dark pub tables in four small linked areas. One of these has a log fire in a biggish brick fireplace, another has a coal-effect gas fire, and they have two darts boards (the games machine is silenced, but they have piped music). Even early in the day quite a few regulars drop in for a chat. On handpump are Wadworths Henrys, IPA and Bishops Tipple, and Weston's farm cider; there's a nice little border terrier called Cooper. A back terrace has a couple of picnic-sets. More reports please.

⏮ As well as a very popular breakfast, they do light snacks such as baked beans on toast and burgers, as well as a wide choice of sandwiches, filled rolls and baked potatoes and simple pubby lunchtime dishes such as fish and chips or lasagne; good Sunday roasts. *Starters/Snacks: £1.50 to £4.75. Main Courses: £5.50 to £6.95. Puddings: £2.50*

Wadworths ~ Tenants Kate Kiff and Andrew Kiff ~ Real ale ~ Bar food (10-2) ~ Restaurant ~ (01202) 881021 ~ Children allowed until 8pm ~ Dogs welcome ~ Live music Fri, Sat and Sun evenings ~ Open 10am-12.30am(1am Sat)

Recommended by BOB

WORTH MATRAVERS

SY9777   MAP 2

Square & Compass ★ ⬛

At fork of both roads signposted to village from B3069; BH19 3LF

Unchanging country tavern, masses of character, in the same family for many years; lovely sea views and fine nearby walks

A firm favourite among readers, who treasure its marvellously individual character, this pub has been in the hands of the Newman family for 100 years now and to this day there's no bar counter. Ringwood Best and guests like Clearwater Olivers Nectar and Palmers Dorset Gold as well as up to 13 ciders, including one made on the premises, are tapped from a row of casks and passed to you in a drinking corridor through two serving hatches; several malt whiskies. A couple of basic unspoilt rooms have simple furniture on the flagstones, a woodburning stove and a loyal crowd of friendly locals; darts, cribbage, board games, shove-ha'penny and table skittles; a table tennis championship is held here twice a year. From benches out in front there's a fantastic view down over the village rooftops to the sea around St Aldhelm's Head; there may be free-roaming hens, chickens and other birds clucking around your feet. A little museum (free) exhibits local fossils and artefacts, mostly collected by the current friendly landlord and his father; mind your head on the way out. There are wonderful walks from here to some exciting switchback sections of the coast path above St Aldhelm's Head and Chapman's Pool; you will need to park in the public car park 100 yards along the Corfe Castle road (which has a £1 honesty box).

⏮ Bar food is limited to tasty home-made pasties, served till they run out. *Starters/Snacks: £2.60*

Free house ~ Licensee Charlie Newman ~ Real ale ~ Bar food (all day) ~ No credit cards ~ (01929) 439229 ~ Children welcome ~ Dogs welcome ~ Live music most Sats and some lunchtimes Fri and Sun ~ Open 12-11; closed weekdays 3-6 in winter

Recommended by Pete Baker, Rona Markland, Terry and Linda Moseley, JDM, KM, C J Fletcher, Mr and Mrs P D Titcomb, Mike and Sue Loseby, Michael Butler, Steve Derbyshire, Chris Flynn, Wendy Jones, Mrs Maricar Jagger, Mike and Eleanor Anderson, the Didler

LUCKY DIP

Besides the fully inspected pubs, you might like to try these Lucky Dips recommended to us and described by readers (if you do, please send us reports: feedback@thegoodpubguide.co.uk).

ANSTY [ST7603]
Fox DT2 7PN [NW of Milton Abbas]: Hotel with flourishing high-ceilinged bar side, comfortable if a bit sombre, with lots of toby jugs, Badger beers, good wines by the glass, very wide choice of good value food from baguettes up; piped music, separate locals' bar with pool and TV, skittle alley; children welcome in restaurant, garden tables, bedrooms, attractive countryside, open all day *(LYM, Pat and Roger Davies, Mr and Mrs W W Burke)*

ASKERSWELL [SY5393]
☆ *Spyway* DT2 9EP [off A35 Bridport—Dorchester]: Good value food from sandwiches up in prettily set beamed country pub, charming family service, real ales such as Otter tapped from the cask, old-fashioned high-backed settles, cushioned wall and window seats, old-world décor, local pictures for sale, dining area with steps down to overflow area; disabled access, children in eating areas, spectacular views from back terrace and large attractive garden, good walks,

comfortable bedrooms *(Roland and Wendy Chalu, the Didler, Mrs Hilarie Taylor, LYM)*

BLANDFORD FORUM [ST8806]
Crown DT11 7AJ [West St]: Best Western hotel's well furnished spacious bar areas used by locals as pub, full Badger range from nearby brewery, spacious adjacent informal eating area, good range of reasonably priced bar food inc good sandwiches and light meals, genteel restaurant; bedrooms *(Joan and Michel Hooper-Immins, Mr and Mrs W W Burke)*
Greyhound DT11 7EB [Market Pl]: Popular pub between Thurs/Sat market and main car park, Badger Best and Tanglefoot, good choice of generous sensibly priced food, friendly staff, long central bar, stripped brick, carved wood, comfortable seats, separate restaurant; tables out under giant parasols *(Stan Edwards)*

BLANDFORD ST MARY [ST8805]
Hall & Woodhouse DT11 9LS: Visitor centre for Badger brewery, their full beer range in top condition inc interesting bottled beers, lunchtime food from well filled baguettes up, friendly staff; spectacular chandelier made of Badger beer bottles, lots of memorabilia in centre and upper gallery; popular brewery tours *(Joan and Michel Hooper-Immins)*

BOURNEMOUTH [SZ0891]
Goat & Tricycle BH2 5PF [West Hill Rd]: More interesting than smart, two-level rambling Edwardian local (two former pubs knocked together) with Wadworths and guest beers kept well from pillared bar's impressive rank of ten or more handpumps, farm cider, bargain pubby food from sandwiches up inc Sun lunch, coal fire, lots of bric-a-brac inc hundreds of hats and helmets; can get rather noisily studenty; children welcome, good disabled access, heated yard with flower tubs, water feature and covered bower *(Joan and Michel Hooper-Immins)*
Sixty Million Postcards BH2 5AF [Exeter Rd]: Long ultra-modern bistro bar in 19th-c building, convivial at lunchtime with well kept Caledonian Deuchars IPA and Ringwood Best, good value contemporary food; more a lively young person's place evenings *(Val and Alan Green)*

BRADFORD ABBAS [ST5814]
Rose & Crown DT9 6RF [Church Rd]: Attractive and relaxed country local with four linked rooms, two with blond tables set for the enjoyable food inc good Sun lunch, well kept Wadworths from thatched counter, pleasant service, interesting collection of old village photographs and clippings; charming sheltered garden by fine medieval church, bedrooms *(Richard Burton, BB)*

BRIDPORT [SY4692]
☆ *Beach & Barnicott* DT6 3NQ [South St]: Three-floor café rather than pub, but has

well kept Branscombe Branoc tapped from the cask as well as decent wines by the glass, enjoyable bistro food all day (queue to order), convivial chatty atmosphere, nice informal mix of furnishings from huge sofas, ornate armchairs and big afghan cushions to pine tables and chairs, old pictures, timbering and panelling; children welcome, open all day *(Fred and Lorraine Gill, BB)*
George DT6 3NQ [South St]: Cheery well worn in two-bar town local, traditional dark décor, assorted furnishings and floor rugs, bargain home-made chip-free pub lunches (not Sun) cooked in sight, good crab sandwiches, well kept Palmers, good choice of wines by the glass, efficient service, hot coal fire, hatch-served family room; piped radio, upstairs lavatories; dogs welcome, open all day, from 9am for popular wkdy breakfast or coffee *(Roland and Wendy Chalu, Joan and Michel Hooper-Immins, L Hawkins, the Didler, LYM)*
Woodman DT6 3NZ [South St]: Lively local, well kept Branscombe Vale and guest beers, decent food even on Sun, skittle alley; attractive garden, open all day *(the Didler)*

BUCKHORN WESTON [ST7524]
☆ *Stapleton Arms* SP8 5HS [Church Hill]: Attractive upmarket bistro dining pub, enjoyable up-to-date daily-changing fresh food at a price from sandwiches up, bright quick young staff, Butcombe, Hidden, Otter and changing guest beers, Cheddar Valley cider, good range of wines and soft drinks; tables outside, pleasant countryside, four comfortable bedrooms, good breakfast, open all day wknds *(Richard Wyld, Joan and Michel Hooper-Immins)*

BUCKLAND NEWTON [ST6804]
☆ *Gaggle of Geese* DT2 7BS: Civilised country local with relaxed atmosphere and attractive décor, friendly helpful staff, Ringwood ales, good coffee, decent wines and spirits, good reasonably priced usual bar food, neat restaurant; goose auction May and Sept, games room and skittles, small garden but sizeable grounds (room for caravans) *(Ann and Colin Hunt, BB)*

BURTON BRADSTOCK [SY4889]
☆ *Three Horseshoes* DT6 4QZ [Mill St]: Attractive and comfortable thatched pub with warmly welcoming staff, Palmers' complete ale range particularly well kept (head brewer lives nearby), Thatcher's cider, enjoyable pubby food from sandwiches to fish, somewhat wider evening range, quick cheerful service, good wines by the glass, cottagey low-beamed L-shaped bar with log fire in big inglenook, rustic tables (mainly laid for eating) and lots of pictures, passage to pretty dining room; may be piped music;

dogs welcome, picnic-sets out on back terrace and lawn, charming village, pleasant shingle beach a few minutes' drive away (with NT car park) *(Bob and Margaret Holder, Norman and Sarah Keeping, LYM, George Atkinson, Rona Markland, Roland and Wendy Chalu, Fred and Lorraine Gill, L Hawkins)*

CATTISTOCK [SY5999]

☆ *Fox & Hounds* DT2 0JH [off A37 N of Dorchester]: Welcoming and attractive 17th-c or older pub, helpful service, enjoyable food inc generous OAP meals, Palmers ales from attractively carved counter, Taunton cider, good value wine choice, flagstones and nicely moulded Jacobean beams, stripped stone, log fire in huge inglenook, minimal décor, table skittles, pleasant side dining room, back public bar with well lit darts and TV, immaculate skittle alley; piped pop music, live some Sats; dogs welcome, comfortable bedrooms, cl Mon lunchtime, open all day wknds *(I A Herdman, Pat and Roger Davies, W F C Phillips, Hannah Elder, BB)*

CERNE ABBAS [ST6601]

☆ *New Inn* DT2 7JF [Long Street]: Handsome Tudor inn with mullioned window seats in neatly kept beamed bar, good service, enjoyable food inc interesting dishes, nice wine choice, Palmers IPA, comfortable restaurant; children welcome, lots of tables on coachyard terrace and attractive sheltered lawn beyond, eight bedrooms, open all day wknds and summer *(LYM, Alan Johnson, John Coatsworth, Joan and Michel Hooper-Immins, Ann and Colin Hunt)*

Royal Oak DT2 7JG [Long Street]: Unchanged pub in historic village centre, low beams, flagstones, all sorts of rustic memorabilia; has been a past favourite, but under temporary management as we go to press, with pubby food, Badger ales from long bar counter; children welcome, pleasant little back garden *(LYM)*

CHARMINSTER [SY6793]

Inn For All Seasons DT2 9QZ [North St]: Enjoyable food, attentive service, well kept real ales, bright airy back dining room; riverside garden, bedrooms *(Mr and Mrs Draper)*

CHARMOUTH [SY3693]

George DT6 6QE [off A35 W of Bridport; The Street]: Friendly and comfortably unpretentious open-plan family pub, reasonably priced tasty straightforward food, prompt cheerful service, well kept Otter and John Smiths, darts, pool and games machine in left-hand public bar; no credit cards; children and dogs welcome, big garden with play area and covered tables *(Rona Murdoch, BB, Derek and Sylvia Stephenson)*

Royal Oak DT6 6PE [off A3052/A35 E of Lyme Regis; The Street]: Chatty three-room village local with quite some

character, particularly welcoming staff and regulars, four Palmers ales, traditional games, usual lunchtime food, no TV or piped music; has been cl Tues *(Derek and Sylvia Stephenson)*

CHETNOLE [ST6008]

Chetnole Inn DT9 6NU [off A37 Dorchester—Yeovil]: Beams, flagstones and woodburner, enjoyable seasonal food using local supplies, four real ales; pleasant garden, three bedrooms *(Paul and Annette Hallett)*

CHIDEOCK [SY4191]

☆ *Anchor* DT6 6JU [Seatown signed off A35 from Chideock]: Simple seaside pub in outstanding spot, dramatic sea and cliff views and big front terrace, well kept Palmers ales, good choice of wines by the glass, local farm cider, good value straightforward food (all day in summer) from lunchtime sandwiches to lobster specials, quick friendly service despite crowds, woodburners, interesting local photographs; can get a bit untidy outside; children and dogs welcome, open all day in summer *(David and Sue Smith, Joan and Michel Hooper-Immins, LYM, the Didler, Mr and Mrs P D Titcomb, Mr and Mrs W W Burke, David and Julie Glover, R J and G M Townson, David Lamb, Roland and Wendy Chalu, Fred and Lorraine Gill, Rona Markland)*

CHILD OKEFORD [ST8213]

☆ *Saxon* DT11 8HD [signed off A350 Blandford—Shaftesbury and A357 Blandford—Sherborne; Gold Hill]: Welcoming village pub, quietly clubby snug bar with log fire and more spacious side room (where children allowed), four well kept changing ales inc Butcombe, good choice of wines and country wines, reasonably priced home-made food, traditional games; attractive back garden, good walks on neolithic Hambledon Hill, four comfortable new bedrooms *(LYM, Mrs Elaine Lee)*

CHRISTCHURCH [SZ1592]

Thomas Tripp BH23 1HX [Wick Lane]: Best known as a music pub, live acts most nights, but also has Ringwood, some interesting beers, lively staff, good atmosphere; attractive terrace *(Russell New)*

COLEHILL [SU0302]

☆ *Barley Mow* BH21 7AH [Colehill signed from A31/B3073 roundabout; Long Lane]: Enjoyable food (cooked to order so can take a while) inc great puddings in part-thatched and part-tiled pub with low-beamed main bar, open fire in brick inglenook, attractive oak panelling, some Hogarth prints, friendly service, well kept Badger ales, family area; piped music; pleasant enclosed lawn behind with terrace and boules *(LYM, Pat and Roger Davies, Robert Watt)*

CORFE CASTLE [SY9682]

Bankes Arms BH20 5ED [East St]: Big, busy and welcoming, on attractive village square, with flagstones and comfortable traditional décor, subtle lighting, enjoyable food, good choice of wines by the glass, well kept ales, restaurant; piped music; children and dogs welcome, tables on terrace and in long garden with end play area overlooking steam railway, ten bedrooms *(Peter Salmon)*

Castle Inn BH20 5EE [East St]: Neatly refurbished straightforward two-room pub mentioned in Hardy's *Hand of Ethelberta*, enjoyable home cooking using local supplies (get there early for a table), friendly licensees, Ringwood ales, good value wines, open fire, beams and flagstones; sizeable garden *(Nigel Thompson, John and Joan Calvert)*

☆ *Greyhound* BH20 5EZ [A351; The Square]: Bustling and picturesque old pub in centre of tourist village, three small low-ceilinged panelled rooms, steps and corridors, well kept changing ales and local farm cider, generous food from baguettes to seafood specialities, friendly well managed staff, traditional games inc Purbeck long board shove-ha'penny, family room; piped music, live Fri; garden with fine castle and countryside views, pretty courtyard opening on to castle bridge, open all day wknds and summer *(LYM, Mr and Mrs W W Burke, the Didler, John Roots, Fred and Lorraine Gill)*

CORFE MULLEN [SY9798]
Coventry Arms BH21 3RH [A31 W of Wimborne; Mill St]: Four-room dining pub with enjoyable bistro-style food (named suppliers, local fish, their own herbs, some unusual dishes and enterprising children's things), good sandwiches too, good choice of changing real ales and of wines, large central open fire, low ceilings, flagstones, bare boards, evening candles and fishing décor; they may try to hurry you on busy wknds; tables out by small river *(Robert Watt, Peter Salmon, Gerald and Gabrielle Culliford, M R Phillips, Mike and Shelley Woodroffe, Katharine Cowherd)*

CORSCOMBE [ST5205]
☆ *Fox* DT2 0NS [towards Halstock]: Beamed country dining pub with plenty of rustic charm, built-in settles, sporting prints, inglenook fire, Butcombe Bitter and Exmoor, several wines by the glass, quite ambitious if fairly pricy food; children in dining areas, streamside lawn across lane, bedrooms *(J S Burn, Alan M Pring, LYM, Gene and Kitty Rankin, Roland and Wendy Chalu, Paul and Annette Hallett)*

CRANBORNE [SU0513]
Fleur-de-Lys BH21 5PP [Wimborne St (B3078 N of Wimborne)]: 17th-c inn with long panelled lounge/dining room, flagstones and log fire, enjoyable pubby food from baguettes up, Badger ales, farm cider, decent wines, evening restaurant; games and TV in simple cheerful beamed public bar, piped music;

nice setting on edge of Cranborne Chase, comfortable pretty bedrooms *(LYM, Mr and Mrs P D Titcomb)*

DORCHESTER [SY6990]
☆ *Blue Raddle* DT1 1JN [Church St, nr central short stay car park]: Cheery unpretentious pub with welcoming service, relaxed atmosphere, well kept Otter, Sharps Doom Bar and guest beers such as Timothy Taylors Landlord, good wines and coffee, Weston's farm cider, modestly priced pubby food from generous sandwiches up, open fire; piped music; disabled access, but one step, cl Mon lunchtime *(Patrick and Daphne Darley, Gene and Kitty Rankin, Pat and Roger Davies, Joan and Michel Hooper-Immins, the Didler, Terry and Linda Moseley)*

☆ *Poet Laureate* DT1 3GW [Pummery Sq, Poundbury]: Substantial building in the Prince of Wales's Poundbury development, enjoyable food inc some interesting dishes, Fullers London Pride, Palmers Copper and Ringwood Fortyniner, decent wines by the glass, proper coffee, top-notch service, light and airy L-shaped bar with good décor, lots of chandeliers, good solid tables and chairs, daily papers, flame-effect stove, agreeable restaurant area; unobtrusive piped music; wheelchair access, a few picnic-sets on side terrace *(Terry and Linda Moseley)*

Tom Browns DT1 1HU [High East St]: Distinctive Goldfinch ales now brewed for them by Dorset Brewing of Weymouth (pending plans for reopening the pub's own microbrewery), unpretentious bare-boards L-shaped bar, friendly locals, traditional games; garden down to river, open all day Fri/Sat *(Joan and Michel Hooper-Immins, BB)*

EAST CHALDON [SY7983]
Sailors Return DT2 8DN [Village signposted from A352 Wareham—Dorchester; from village green, follow Dorchester, Weymouth signpost; note that the village is also known as Chaldon Herring; OS sheet 194 map reference 790834]: Thatched country pub useful for coast path, flagstoned bar with much of its original rural-tavern character, plain newer part with open beams showing the roof, Hampshire Strongs Best, Ringwood Best and guest beers, usual food; provision for children and dogs, plenty of seats outside, open all day in summer *(Peter and Anne Hollindale, Roland and Wendy Chalu, JT, Mike and Sue Loseby, LYM, Pat and Roger Davies)*

EAST LULWORTH [SY8581]
Weld Arms BH20 5QQ [B3070 SW of Wareham]: Civilised bar with log-fire sofas, well kept Palmers and Ringwood, pleasant service, two dining rooms; children and dogs welcome, picnic-sets out in big garden with play area *(LYM, Stewart Bingham)*

236 • DORSET

EAST MORDEN [SY9194]
☆ **Cock & Bottle** BH20 7DL [B3075 W of Poole]: Busy dining pub, interesting vintage car and motorcycle bric-a-brac, roaring log fire, bar food (not cheap, but can be very good), Badger ales, several wines by the glass, two dining areas with heavy rough beams; children in restaurant area only; garden and adjoining field, pleasant pastoral outlook *(Clive and Janice Sillitoe, Pat and Roger Davies, Yana Pocklington, Patricia Owlett, John and Joan Nash, Mr and Mrs P D Titcomb, Peter Veness, LYM, Mr and Mrs W W Burke, Andy Lickfold, Dr and Mrs J Temporal)*

EAST STOUR [ST8123]
Kings Arms SP8 5NB [B3095, 3 miles W towards Shaftesbury; The Common]: Current management doing good value pubby food inc all-day Sun roasts, Palmers and guest beers such as St Austell and Wadworths 6X, decent wines, friendly efficient staff, large bar with light and airy dining area; children welcome, big garden, bluebell walks nearby, bedrooms *(Richard Wyld, D M and B K Moores)*

EVERSHOT [ST5704]
Acorn DT2 0JW [off A37 S of Yeovil]: Upmarket inn with Branscombe Vale and Fullers London Pride, good choice of wines by the glass inc champagne, restauranty front part with up-to-date décor as well as log fires and oak panelling, bar snacks from interesting open sandwiches to salads and pubby hot dishes in beamed and flagstoned back bar with games and juke box, skittle alley; children allowed in eating areas, dogs in bar, terrace with dark oak furniture, bedrooms, pretty village, good surrounding walks, open all day *(Alan Johnson, LYM, Bob and Angela Brooks, Roland and Wendy Chalu)*

EYPE [SY4491]
Eypes Mouth DT6 6AL: Hotel not pub, good spot nr sea and coast paths, enjoyable food; children welcome, terrace tables, 18 bedrooms *(R J Herd)*
New Inn DT6 6AP: Welcoming simple two-bar village local, cheerful staff and african grey parrot, well kept Palmers, enjoyable popular food, coal fire, darts, two steps down to cottagey dining room; may be piped music; level access, magnificent views from back terrace, steps down to lawn *(Roland and Wendy Chalu, L Hawkins, John Coatsworth)*

FURZEHILL [SU0102]
☆ **Stocks** BH21 4HT [off B3078 N of Wimborne]: Partly thatched 17th-c country dining pub doing well under current management, good choice of enjoyable local food from lunchtime sandwiches up, well kept Ringwood and guest beers, attentive service, comfortable low-beamed rambling areas,

soft lighting and attractive décor, restaurant with huge mirror, darts; piped music; children welcome in eating areas, some outside tables, open all day *(Robert Watt, Jennifer Banks, Andy, LYM)*

GUSSAGE ALL SAINTS [SU0010]
☆ **Drovers** BH21 5ET [8 miles N of Wimborne]: Partly thatched pub with welcoming staff, good value generous home-made food from snacks to local fish, well kept Ringwood and a guest beer, good wines by the glass, log fire and pleasantly simple country furnishings, public bar with piano and darts; quiet village, tables on pretty front lawn with views across the Dorset hills *(LYM, John R Ringrose, Mr and Mrs W W Burke, Richard and Sue Fewkes, Pat and Roger Davies)*

HOLT [SU0304]
Old Inn BH21 7DJ: Busy and well run beamed Badger dining pub, their real ales kept well, helpful friendly service, good sensibly priced food inc fresh fish, small helpings available, plenty of comfortable tables, winter fires, good atmosphere; children welcome *(John R Ringrose, M R Phillips, June and Robin Savage)*

HORTON [SU0407]
Drusillas BH21 7JH [Wigbeth]: Picturesque 17th-c beamed pub restaurant, tablecloths even in the bar, wide choice of food inc lots of fish, good value wines, real ales, log fire, thatched extension; children welcome *(Robert Watt)*
Horton Inn BH21 5AD [B3078 Wimborne—Cranborne]: Good value food and several well kept ales, hard-working newish licensees, plenty of room in long bar and separate restaurant; garden with pleasant terrace, bedrooms *(Robert Watt)*

IBBERTON [ST7807]
Crown DT11 0EN: Nicely updated traditional village pub, ochre walls, flagstones, toby jugs and open fire, back dining area, Butcombe, Palmers and Ringwood, above-average pubby food inc interesting dishes, friendly helpful staff; lovely garden, beautiful spot under Bulbarrow Hill *(BB)*

IWERNE MINSTER [ST8614]
Talbot DT11 8QN [Blandford Rd]: Emphasis on enjoyable local food inc line-caught fish and popular Sun lunch, Badger ales, sensibly priced wines by the glass, friendly service and atmosphere, pleasant candlelit dining area, public bar with darts and pool; TV; tables on heated terrace, five comfortable bedrooms, good breakfast *(M R Eavis, Mary Bray, Colin and Janet Roe)*

KING'S STAG [ST7210]
Green Man DT10 2AY [B3143, S of A3030]: Bright and open local, with good-sized helpings of enjoyable food, well kept ales, interesting reasonably priced wine choice, farm cider, friendly

staff, restaurant area down on left, skittle alley (Robert Watt)

KINGSTON [SY9579]

Scott Arms BH20 5LH [West St (B3069)]: Extensively modernised holiday pub rambling through several levels, some sofas and easy chairs, beams, stripped stone, bare boards and log fires, well kept Ringwood and Wells & Youngs, lots of wines, low-priced food (can be slow to come), family dining area; darts, dominoes, pool and games machine, piped music; attractive garden with outstanding views of Corfe Castle and the Purbeck Hills, good walks (Michael Butler, John Roots, Peter Meister, LYM, the Didler)

LANGTON MATRAVERS [SY9978]

Kings Arms BH19 3HA [High St]: Lively old-fashioned village local with ancient flagstoned corridor to bar, simple rooms off, one with a fine local marble fireplace, nice pictures, well kept Fullers London Pride and Ringwood Best, friendly staff and regulars, well priced generous pubby food from tiny kitchen inc good Sun roasts, splendid antique Purbeck longboard for shove-ha'penny; sunny picnic-sets outside, good walks (LYM, Michael Butler)

LITTON CHENEY [SY5490]

☆ *White Horse* DT2 9AT: Relaxed and unpretentious, with good value food from sandwiches and traditional dishes to imaginative cooking with good fresh local ingredients, particularly well kept Palmers ales, decent reasonably priced wines by the glass, pleasant efficient service, big woodburner, lots of pictures, some pine panelling, stripped stone and flagstones, country kitchen chairs in dining area, table skittles; may be piped jazz; children and dogs welcome, disabled access, good spot on quiet lane into quaint village, picnic-sets on pleasant streamside front lawn (BB, L Hawkins, Dr Peter Andrews, Roland and Wendy Chalu)

LODERS [SY4994]

Loders Arms DT6 3SA [off A3066 just N of Bridport]: 17th-c stone-built pub, relaxed, friendly and unspoilt, with new licensees doing enjoyable food, well kept Palmers, good choice of wines by the glass, Thatcher's farm cider, log fire, daily papers, pretty dining room, skittle alley; children welcome, pleasant views from picnic-sets in small informal back garden, pretty thatched village, comfortable bedrooms, has been open all day Sun (LYM, L Hawkins, Dr Kevan Tucker)

LYME REGIS [SY3391]

Cobb Arms DT7 3JF [Marine Parade, Monmouth Beach]: Lively spaciously refurbished local with well kept Palmers ales, wide range of reasonably priced generous bar food inc local fish and Sun roasts, decent wines, quick service even when busy, good value cream teas, a couple of sofas, interesting ship pictures

and marine fish tank, pool, juke box – popular with local young people till late; next to harbour, beach and coastal walk, children and dogs welcome, open all day, tables on small back terrace, bedrooms, good breakfast (Mrs Jordan, Steve and Liz Tilley, David and Sue Smith)

☆ *Harbour Inn* DT7 3JF [Marine Parade]: More eating than pubby, with enjoyable range from lunchtime sandwiches to fresh local fish (great fish soup), friendly efficient service, good choice of wines by the glass, Otter and St Austell, farm cider, clean-cut modern décor keeping original flagstones and stone walls (lively acoustics), thriving family atmosphere, big paintings for sale, sea views from front windows; piped music; disabled access from street, verandah tables (Joan and Michel Hooper-Immins, Roland and Wendy Chalu, Terry and Linda Moseley, JT, Rosemary Richards)

☆ *Pilot Boat* DT7 3QA [Bridge St]: Popular good value modern all-day family food place nr waterfront, long-serving licensees, friendly service even when busy, well kept Palmers ales, good choice of wines by the glass, plenty of tables in cheery nautically themed areas, skittle alley; piped music; children and dogs welcome, tables out on terrace, open all day (Joan and Michel Hooper-Immins, Mrs Jordan, LYM, Steve Crick, Helen Preston, Pat and Tony Martin, Richard Pitcher)

☆ *Royal Standard* DT7 3JF [Marine Parade, The Cobb]: Right on broadest part of beach, properly pubby bar with fine built-in stripped high settles and even old-fashioned ring-up tills, quieter eating area with stripped brick and pine, friendly service, three Palmers ales, good choice of wines by the glass, popular food from massive crab sandwiches up inc local fish, good cream teas, log fire, darts, prominent pool table, some live music; may be piped pop, gets very busy in season – long waits then; children welcome, good-sized sheltered suntrap courtyard with own servery and wendy house (Mr and Mrs G Ives, Derek and Sylvia Stephenson, Pat and Tony Martin, Gene and Kitty Rankin, Sue and Mike Todd, Peter Salmon, BB, Steve and Liz Tilley)

Volunteer DT7 3QE [top of Broad St (A3052 towards Exeter)]: Easy-going local atmosphere in long cosy low-ceilinged bar, nice broad mix of customers, enjoyable food inc lots of modestly priced fresh local fish in dining lounge (children allowed here), changing real ales such as Sharps Doom Bar, farm cider, roaring fires; dogs welcome, open all day (LYM, Mrs Jordan)

LYTCHETT MINSTER [SY9693]

☆ *St Peters Finger* BH16 6JE [Dorchester Rd]: Well run two-part beamed Badger roadhouse with cheerful efficient staff, sensibly priced food from sandwiches and baguettes up, small helpings available, good wine choice, welcoming end log fire, cottagey mix of furnishings in different sections giving a cosy feel despite its size; good skittle alley, tables on big terrace, part covered and heated *(Leslie and Barbara Owen, B and K Hypher, Jennifer Banks)*

MANSTON [ST8116]

☆ *Plough* DT10 1HB [B3091 Shaftesbury—Sturminster Newton, just N]: Good-sized traditional country pub with well kept Palmers ales, plentiful appetising food from sandwiches up, prompt friendly considerate service, richly decorated plasterwork, ceilings and bar front; garden tables *(Steve Jackson)*

MARNHULL [ST7818]

☆ *Crown* DT10 1LN [about 3 miles N of Sturminster Newton; Crown Rd]: Part-thatched 17th-c dining pub with good value generous food, friendly attentive service, Badger Best and Tanglefoot, good wine choice, linked rooms with oak beams, huge flagstones or bare boards, old settles, stuffed animals and old prints and plates, log fire in big stone hearth in oldest part, more modern furnishings and carpet elsewhere; skittle alley, may be piped music; tables in peaceful enclosed garden, children welcome *(LYM, Robert Watt)*

MELPLASH [SY4897]

☆ *Half Moon* DT6 3UD [A3066 Bridport—Beaminster]: Friendly and cottagey 18th-c thatched pub, beams, brasses and pictures of local scenes and animals, well kept Palmers ales, landlord doing good range of good value standard food from sandwiches up, cheerful landlady, good choice of wines, log fire, carpeted bar, eating area and evening dining room (worth booking); may be unobtrusive piped music; tables and chairs in good-sized attractive garden with water feature, shares car park with cricket club next door *(L Hawkins, Roland and Wendy Chalu, George Atkinson)*

MOTCOMBE [ST8426]

Coppleridge SP7 9HW: Good value food from sandwiches to speciality steaks, real ales inc Butcombe, decent wines and welcoming service in former 18th-c farmhouse's bar/lounge and two smallish dining rooms; big airy bedrooms, good-sized grounds *(Colin and Janet Roe)*

☆ *Haven House* BH23 4AB [beyond huge seaside car park at Mudeford Pier]: Popular much-extended pub in great spot on beach with superb views and bird watching, good value pubby food and seafood, well kept Ringwood and other ales, cheerful efficient service, popular linked family cafeteria (all day in summer); nice in winter with old-fashioned feel in quaint little part-

flagstoned core and lovely seaside walks (dogs banned from beach May-Sept); tables on sheltered back terrace *(Kevin Flack, D W Stokes, LYM)*

Nelson BH23 3NJ [75 Mudeford]: Substantially renovated and well run, two real ales, pub food throughout, authentic thai dishes too in fresh and bright modern back dining area with big palms, white tablecloths and tan and cream chairs; brick terrace *(Mr and Mrs W W Burke)*

NORDEN HEATH [SY94834]

☆ *Halfway* BH20 5DU [A351 Wareham—Corfe Castle]: Cosily laid out partly thatched pub with friendly staff, Badger beers, good wines by the glass, enjoyable food all day, pitched-ceiling back serving bar where the locals congregate, front rooms with flagstones, log fires, stripped stonework, snug little side area; picnic-tables outside with play area, good nearby walks, open all day *(BB, Michael Butler)*

OSMINGTON [SY7282]

Sunray DT3 6EU [A353 Weymouth—Wareham]: Extended pub with hearty good value food (all day Sun) from open kitchen, good friendly service, well kept Ringwood and guest beers, relaxing atmosphere and light contemporary décor, card games; children welcome, large garden and terrace, play area *(Joan and Michel Hooper-Immins, Pat and Roger Davies)*

PIDDLEHINTON [SY7197]

☆ *Thimble* DT2 7TD [High St (B3143)]: Hospitable neatly kept partly thatched pub with two handsome fireplaces and deep glazed-over well in attractive low-beamed core, well kept Palmers and Ringwood, good wines by the glass, friendly staff, good value straightforward bar food from sandwiches up, interesting bottle collection, darts and cribbage; children and dogs welcome, floodlit garden with summer house, barbecues, stream and little bridge *(David Billington, Joan and Michel Hooper-Immins, Dennis Jenkin, LYM, P and J Shapley, M G Hart, Robert Watt, Michael Butler, John Coatsworth, Phil and Jane Hodson, P R Light, Mr and Mrs P D Titcomb, Gordon Tong)*

PIDDLETRENTHIDE [SY7099]

☆ *Piddle* DT2 7QF [B3143 N of Dorchester]: Most tables set for the good food (emphasis on fish) but comfortable leatherette sofas in refurbished bar, polite helpful staff, Ringwood Best, children's room, end pool room with sports TV; informal streamside garden with picnic-sets and play area, good bedrooms *(Ann and Colin Hunt, BB)*

Poachers DT2 7QX [B3143 N of Dorchester]: Bright up-to-date décor, comfortable lounge end, Butcombe, Palmers Tally Ho and Ringwood

Fortyniner, generous food, three linked beamed dining areas with local artwork for sale; piped music; dogs welcome, garden with tables on decking and stream at bottom, 21 comfortable good value motel-style bedrooms around residents' heated swimming pool, good breakfast (could perhaps be more flexible over special needs), open all day *(Richard Marjoram, Phyl and Jack Street)*
PIMPERNE [ST9009]
☆ *Anvil* DT11 8UQ [well back from A354]: Attractive 16th-c thatched family pub with wide choice of appetising food from enterprising and generous lunchtime baguettes to piping hot substantial main dishes, well kept Isle of Purbeck and Palmers ales, cheerful efficient young staff, bays of plush seating in bright and welcoming bar, neat black-beamed dining areas; fruit machine, piped music; good garden with fish pond and big weeping willow, 12 bedrooms with own bathrooms, nice surroundings *(Stan Edwards, Joan and Michel Hooper-Immins, BB, R J Davies)*
Farquharson Arms DT11 8TX [A354 NE of Blandford Forum]: Large neat and friendly Badger pub with enjoyable food inc some hefty dishes, four real ales, reasonably priced wines *(Stan Edwards)*
POOLE [SZ0090]
Antelope BH15 1BP [High St]: Former coaching inn just off quay, Greene King IPA and Abbot and Ringwood Best, enjoyable reasonably priced pubby food from sandwiches up in neatly kept character bar, refurbished back restaurant with more elaborate dishes, lots of RNLI photographs; lots of tables in partly decked back courtyard, bedrooms *(Michael Dandy, Michael Butler)*
Bermuda Triangle BH14 0JY [Parr St, Lower Parkstone (just off A35 at Ashley Cross)]: Old-fashioned bare-boards local with four interesting and particularly well kept changing real ales, two or three good continental lagers on tap and many other beers from around the world, good lunchtime food, friendly landlady, dark panelling, snug old corners and lots of nautical and other bric-a-brac, cloudscape ceiling, back room with sports TV; a bit too steppy for disabled access; pavement picnic-sets, open all day wknds *(Joan and Michel Hooper-Immins)*
Guildhall Tavern BH15 1NB [Market St]: Largely good french-run fish restaurant (not pub), friendly service, bright nautical décor, lots of yachting memorabilia, just a few bar stools by small front bar with Ringwood Best, decent house wine *(LYM, John Roots)*
Inn on the Quay BH15 1BW [High St]: Small bar/bistro in 18th-c former Kings Arms, some sofas and more formal seating, Ringwood ales, upstairs restaurant *(Michael Dandy)*

Lord Nelson BH15 1HJ [The Quay]: Handy quayside pub with wide choice of generous food, well kept varied ales, lots of nautical memorabilia, harbour views *(David and Julie Glover)*
Portsmouth Hoy BH15 1HJ [The Quay]: Proper chatty old bare-boards pub facing lively quay, well kept Badger ales, good food choice inc lots of fresh fish, cheerful service, bustling atmosphere, interesting brassware and ships' insignia, nice back dining area; quiet piped classical music *(Ian Barker)*
Sweet Home BH14 0RF [Ringwood Rd]: Neatly kept proper pub with simple good value food, down-to-earth friendly service, well kept Badger, darts; unobrtusive piped music; children welcome, big back garden and terrace *(Michael Bayne)*
PORTLAND [SY6872]
George DT5 2AP [Reforne]: Cheery 17th-c stone-built local mentioned by Thomas Hardy, low doorways and beams, flagstones, small rooms, reputed smugglers' tunnels, scrubbed tables carved with names of generations of sailors and quarrymen, interesting prints and mementoes, Courage Directors and Greene King Abbot and Addlestone's cider, basic bargain lunches, children's room, newer end bar, events most nights; pleasant back garden, open all day *(Joan and Michel Hooper-Immins, the Didler)*
Royal Portland Arms DT5 1LZ [Fortuneswell]: Busy local, large and comfortable, with fine range of ales tapped from the cask, farm cider, friendly licensees, wknd live bands; open all day *(the Didler)*
PORTLAND BILL [SY6768]
Pulpit DT5 2JT: Welcoming extended touristy pub in great spot nr Pulpit Rock, friendly long-serving landlord, landlady's steak and kidney pie popular, other quickly served food from good sandwiches to fried fish etc (they shout your name when it's ready), well kept Fullers London Pride or Ringwood Best, picture-window views, dark beams and stripped stone; may be piped music; dogs welcome, tiered sea-view terrace, short stroll to lighthouse and cliffs *(Philip Vernon, Kim Maidment, Joan and Michel Hooper-Immins, Dennis Jenkin)*
PRESTON [SY7083]
Spice Ship DT3 6BJ [A353 Weymouth—Osmington]: Big family pub, very nautical décor, one end like sailing ship's sterncastle, reasonably priced food all day, friendly staff, real ales; children and dogs welcome, garden with covered terrace and family amusements *(Phil and Jane Hodson)*
Spyglass DT3 6PN [Bowleaze Coveway]: Big busy family dining pub on Furzy Cliff, bright and airy, with picture-window

views over Weymouth Bay, wide choice of enjoyable generous food with plenty for children, real ales inc Ringwood Fortyniner; piped music; good outside area with big adventure playground *(Robert Watt)*

PUNCKNOWLE [SY5388]

☆ *Crown* DT2 9BN [off B3157 Bridport—Abbotsbury]: Comfortably unpretentious 16th-c thatched inn with welcoming staff, good value pubby food from lunchtime sandwiches and baked potatoes to several casseroles and steaks, full Palmers ale range kept well, a dozen wines by the glass, nice coffee, inglenook log fires each end of low-beamed stripped stone lounge, steps up to public bar with books, magazines and another log fire, children's books in family room, local paintings for sale; views from peaceful pretty back garden, good walks, bedrooms *(L Hawkins, LYM, Roland and Wendy Chalu, R J and G M Townson, Alan Johnson, Mr and Mrs P D Titcomb)*

SANDFORD ORCAS [ST6220]

☆ *Mitre* DT9 4RU [off B3148 and B3145 N of Sherborne]: Thriving tucked-away country local with welcoming landlord, well kept ales, wholesome home-made food from good soup and sandwiches up, flagstones, log fires and fresh flowers, small bar and larger pleasantly homely dining area; pretty terrace, has been cl Mon lunchtime *(LYM, D M and B K Moores)*

SHAFTESBURY [ST8722]

Half Moon SP7 8BS [Salisbury Rd, Ludwell (A30 E, by roundabout)]: Comfortable and pleasantly extended Badger family dining pub with their usual food inc popular Sun lunch, well kept if not cheap beers, quick helpful service, spotless housekeeping; garden with adventure playground *(Rodger and Yvonne MacDonald, Robert Watt)*

Mitre SP7 8JE [High St]: Imposing ancient building, unpretentious inside, with friendly efficient service, well kept Wells & Youngs ales, good range of wines, wide food choice, fine log fire, daily papers, varied mix of tables, Blackmore Vale views from back dining room and three-tier suntrap back decking; piped music; children and dogs welcome *(Stan Edwards, BB)*

Two Brewers SP7 8HE [St James St]: Nicely tucked away below steep famously photogenic Gold Hill, well divided open-plan plush-seated bar, log fire, lots of decorative plates, friendly staff, Fullers London Pride, Greene King Old Speckled Hen, Ringwood Best and Fortyniner and one from Sharps or St Austell, good value wines, Stowford Press cider, food from baguettes up (children's helpings of any dish), back dining room, skittle alley; children in eating areas, dogs in bar, picnic-sets in attractive good-sized garden with pretty views *(Pat and*

Roger Davies, Colin and Janet Roe, LYM, Mr and Mrs Draper)

SHAPWICK [ST9301]

☆ *Anchor* DT11 9LB [off A350 Blandford—Poole; West St]: Impressive and interesting generous food (not Mon, and freshly made so can take a while) in civilised pub with courteous helpful service, good wine choice, Greene King Abbot and Ringwood Best, varnished pine tables on quarry tiles, several small rooms with pleasant end dining room; piped music, occasional live; children welcome, brightly painted tables in front, more in attractive garden with terrace and play area behind, handy for Kingston Lacy *(Robert Watt, BB)*

SHERBORNE [ST6316]

George DT9 3JD [Higher Cheap St]: Proper local with generous food inc OAP bargains, several real ales, bustling service; sports TV *(Ken Russell)*

SHIPTON GORGE [SY4991]

New Inn DT6 4LT [off A35/B3157 E of Bridport]: Warmly welcoming licensees trying hard, well kept Palmers, good wines by the glass, enjoyable generous pubby food from lunchtime sandwiches up, neatly refurbished bar with a couple of sofas and dark blue carpet, extension dining area; piped music; small garden *(Roland and Wendy Chalu, L Hawkins, Terry and Linda Moseley)*

STOBOROUGH [SY9286]

Kings Arms BH20 5AB [B3075 S of Wareham; Corfe Rd]: Enjoyable food inc local fish in bar and restaurant, well kept Fullers London Pride and Ringwood, late May beer festival, Thatcher's farm cider, efficient service, live music Sat; children welcome, disabled access, views over marshes to River Frome from big terrace tables, open all day wknds *(Gerry and Rosemary Dobson, Dr Phil Putwain, Michael Butler, Ross Balaam, Adele Summers, Alan Black, JT, Alan M Pring)*

STOURPAINE [ST8609]

White Horse DT11 8TA [Shaston Rd; A350 NW of Blandford]: Traditional country pub carefully extended from original core, landlord/chef doing good choice of food from lunchtime sandwiches and bar meals to ambitious dishes (particularly evenings), friendly young staff, Badger ales, nice layout and décor, scrubbed tables; bedrooms *(Stan Edwards)*

STOURTON CAUNDLE [ST7115]

☆ *Trooper* DT10 2JW [village signed off A30 E of Milborne Port]: Pretty stone-built pub in lovely village setting, friendly staff and atmosphere, bargain good simple food, well kept ale, tiny low-ceilinged bar, stripped stone dining room, darts, cribbage, dominoes, shove-ha'penny, skittle alley; piped music, TV, outside gents'; children and dogs welcome, a few picnic-sets out in front, side garden with small play area, has been open all day summer wknds, cl Mon lunchtime *(Mr and Mrs W D Borthwick, LYM, Helen Boak)*

STRATTON [SY6593]

Saxon Arms DT2 9WG [off A37 NW of Dorchester; The Square]: Traditional but recently built thatched local, open-plan, bright and spacious, with open fire, part flagstones, part carpet, light oak tables and comfortable settles, helpful staff, well kept Ringwood Best, good value wines, generous food, large comfortable dining section on right, traditional games; piped music; children and dogs welcome, tables out overlooking village green *(John and Tania Wood, M G Hart, LYM)*

STURMINSTER MARSHALL [SY9500]

☆ *Red Lion* BH21 4BU [opp church; off A350 Blandford—Poole]: Attractive and civilised village pub opp handsome church, good friendly relaxed atmosphere, good value home-made food from sandwiches and substantial interesting starters up, cheerful landlady and neat staff, well kept Badger Best and Tanglefoot, good coffee, old-fashioned roomy U-shaped bar with good log fire, team photographs and caricatures, cabinet of sports trophies, good-sized dining room in former skittle alley *(BB, Mr and Mrs W W Burke, Pat and Roger Davies, JT, Peter Veness, Ann and Colin Hunt)*

STURMINSTER NEWTON [ST7813]

☆ *Bull* DT10 2BS [A357, S of centre]: Friendly thatched 16th-c country inn by River Stur, low beams and plenty of character, enjoyable food, Badger real ales, soft lighting; children welcome in compact eating area, roadside picnic-sets, more in pleasant secluded back garden *(Mr and Mrs W D Borthwick, LYM, Mr and Mrs W W Burke, Douglas Allen, Jill Bickerton)*

Swan DT10 1AR [off A357 Blandford—Sherborne, via B3092; Market Pl]: Civilised beamed market-town bar with fireside sofa, panelling and stripped brick, Badger ales, pleasant all-day dining area with usual food; piped music; terrace and garden, good value bedrooms, open all day *(Joan and Michel Hooper-Immins, LYM)*

SYMONDSBURY [SY4493]

☆ *Ilchester Arms* DT6 6HD [signed off A35 just W of Bridport]: Welcoming partly thatched old pub with short choice of traditional lunchtime food from sandwiches up, wider evening range inc local fish and more exotic things (can take a while), well kept Palmers ales, Taunton farm cider, snugly rustic open-plan low-beamed bar with high-backed settle built in by inglenook log fire, pretty restaurant with another fire, colourful flower displays, pub games, skittle alley doubling as family room (no children in bar); level entrance (steps

from car park), tables in brookside back garden with play area, peaceful village, good walks *(David and Julie Glover, Roland and Wendy Chalu, LYM, Joan and Michel Hooper-Immins, L Hawkins)*

TARRANT KEYNSTON [ST9204]

True Lovers Knot DT11 9JG [B3082 Blandford—Wimborne]: Good generous uncomplicated food using very local supplies such as red devon steaks, well kept Badger ales and welcoming landlord in neatly kept pub with uncluttered dining extension, modernised largely carpeted bar with some beams and flagstones, sensible prices, good value wines by the glass; children welcome, picnic-sets in good-sized garden with enclosed play area and camp site, four well equipped bedrooms (some road noise) *(Phil and Jane Hodson, B and K Hypher, Robert Watt, Paul Bunting)*

TARRANT MONKTON [ST9408]

☆ *Langton Arms* DT11 8RX [off A354]: Thatched dining pub with bar recently rebuilt after fire (modern feel despite the beams and flagstones), paintings for sale, Hidden, Ringwood and guest beers, bar food all day wknds, bistro restaurant in attractively reworked barn; juke box and TV in public bar (dogs allowed but no children there); comfortable modern bedroom block *(LYM, Colin and Janet Roe, Gene and Kitty Rankin, Noel Grundy, P and J Shapley, Robert Watt, Barry and Anne, Bruce and Sharon Eden, Mr and Mrs P D Titcomb, Hazel Morgan, Bernard Patrick, Julie Cox)*

UPLODERS [SY5093]

☆ *Crown* DT6 4NU [signed off A35 E of Bridport]: Appealing low-beamed flagstoned pub with warmly welcoming atmosphere and licensees, good country food from sandwiches, baguettes and bargain lunches to fresh local seafood, well kept Palmers ales, ten wines by the glass, prompt service, cheerful décor, candles, fresh flowers and log fires, daily papers, steps down to pretty evening restaurant; may be piped music; picnic-sets in small attractive two-tier garden *(L Hawkins, LYM, G F Couch, Roland and Wendy Chalu, John Saul)*

UPWEY [SY6785]

Old Ship DT3 5QQ [off A354; Ridgeway]: Quiet 16th-c beamed pub with traditional décor, lots of alcoves and log fires each end, new management doing enjoyable sensibly priced food, three real ales, friendly attentive staff; picnic-table sets in garden with terrace, interesting walks nearby *(Phil and Jane Hodson, Alan Johnson, LYM)*

WAREHAM [SY9287]

Duke of Wellington BH20 4NN [East St]: Small traditional 18th-c beamed pub with friendly service, several well kept ales, wide choice of reasonably priced food esp fish, some original features; piped music;

courtyard tables, open all day *(the Didler)*

WAREHAM FOREST [SY9089]

Silent Woman BH20 7PA [Wareham—Bere Regis]: Deceptively big all-day food pub, civilised traditional lounge bar extended into stripped-masonry dining area with country bygones, enjoyable food, welcoming service, well kept Badger ales, spotless housekeeping; no children; wheelchair access, walks nearby, has been cl Mon/Tues lunchtimes *(Mrs Suzy Miller)*

WAYTOWN [SY4797]

Hare & Hounds DT6 5LQ [between B3162 and A3066 N of Bridport]: Attractive 18th-c country local up and down steps, friendly caring staff, well kept Palmers ales tapped from the cask, good value food from sandwiches, baguettes up inc popular Sun lunch, coal fire, two small cottagey rooms and pretty dining room, no music; lovely Brit valley views from sizeable and unusual garden with good play area *(Roland and Wendy Chalu, John Norton, Fred and Lorraine Gill)*

WEST BAY [SY4690]

Bridport Arms DT6 4EN: Large light and airy two-level seaside bar, pleasantly stripped down areas around original inglenook flagstoned core, well kept Palmers, quick friendly service, quite a food operation majoring on fish, baguettes and pubby bar lunches too; piped music; children welcome, picnic-sets outside, paying public car park, bedrooms in adjoining hotel with own entrance *(BB, Pat and Tony Martin, Fred and Lorraine Gill, Roland and Wendy Chalu)*

WEST LULWORTH [SY8280]

Castle Inn BH20 5RN [B3070 SW of Wareham]: Pretty thatched inn in lovely spot nr Lulworth Cove, good walks and lots of summer visitors; flagstoned bar concentrating on food (not cheap, and may take a while) from sandwiches to local crab, friendly chatty staff, real ales such as Gales HSB and Ringwood Best, decent house wines, farm cider, maze of booth seating divided by ledges for board games and jigsaws, cosy more modern-feeling lounge bar, pleasant restaurant, splendid ladies'; they may try to keep your credit card while you eat, get cutlery yourself, piped music, video game; long attractive garden behind on several levels, front terrace too, giant chess boards, boules and barbecues, bedrooms *(Robert Gomme, Rona Markland, LYM, George Atkinson)*

WEYMOUTH [SY6778]

Boot DT4 8JH [High West St]: Friendly two-bar partly bare-boards local nr harbour dating from early 1600s, sloping beams, panelling and hooded stone-mullioned windows, well worn comfort, well kept Ringwood ales and a Marstons-related guest beer from fine brass handpumps; disabled access, pavement tables, open all day *(Roland and Wendy Chalu, the Didler, Joan and Michel Hooper-Immins, Dave Webster, Sue Holland)*

John Gregory DT4 9SS [Radipole Lane]: Modern suburban pub popular for wide choice of enjoyable food, Butcombe and Ringwood Best, picture windows *(Joan and Michel Hooper-Immins)*

Rock DT4 0AQ [Abbotsbury Rd]: Big pub recently reworked in fresh contemporary bare-boards style, enjoyable food, three well kept ales; tables out on back decking *(Tim Swift)*

Somerset DT4 7BH [King St]: Well kept Badger ales and good value straightforward bar lunches in neatly modernised pub with enthusiastic new tenants *(Joan and Michel Hooper-Immins)*

Spa DT3 5EQ [Dorchester Rd, Radipole; off A354 at Safeway roundabout]: Large open-plan family pub, good choice of generous food (all day Sun) inc pasta, curries, fish and grills, Marstons Bitter and Pedigree, peaceful picture-window back restaurant; good garden with terrace and play area, open all day *(Joan and Michel Hooper-Immins)*

Wellington Arms DT4 8PY [St Alban St]: Handsome green and gold 19th-c tiled façade, well restored panelled interior, carpets, banquettes, mirrors and lots of old local photographs, well kept Ringwood ales, bargain pubby food from sandwiches up inc daily roast, friendly landlord; children welcome in back dining room, disabled access, open all day from 10 *(Joan and Michel Hooper-Immins, the Didler, Roland and Wendy Chalu)*

WIMBORNE MINSTER [SU0000]

Kings Head BH21 1JG [The Square]: Appealing brasserie/bar in old-established hotel, Greene King ales, well trained staff, roomy bar areas; comfortable bedrooms *(J A Snell, Pat and Roger Davies, Mrs C Osgood)*

Olive Branch BH21 1PF [Hanham Rd/East Borough]: Opened-up 18th/19th-c town house, airy contemporary décor and coloured vases alongside handsome panelling and ceilings, welcoming service, up-to-date approach to enjoyable bistro food using local ingredients, Badger ales, nicely served coffee, big conservatory dining area; children welcome, picnic-sets on lawn running down to small river *(Joan and Michel Hooper-Immins)*

Willett Arms BH21 1RN [Oakley Hill (B3073, just off A31/A341)]: Comfortably refurbished chain pub popular for impressive choice of food from good snacks to some good value inventive main dishes *(F J Tucker)*

WIMBORNE ST GILES [SU0212]

Bull BH21 5NF [off B3078 N of Wimborne]: Comfortable and attractive former private house, friendly staff, enjoyable food using local fresh ingredients, Badger ales, farm cider; small

pleasant garden *(Robert Watt)*
WINFRITH NEWBURGH [SY8085]
Red Lion DT2 8LE [A352 Wareham—
Dorchester]: Comfortable Badger family
dining pub with wide choice of generous
enjoyable food inc fresh fish, young
attentive staff, real ales, reasonably
priced wines, beamy décor and candlelit
tables to give old-fashioned atmosphere;
TV room, piped music; children welcome,
tables in big sheltered garden (site for
caravans), good bedrooms *(John and
Tania Wood, Guy and Caroline Howard)*
WINKTON [SZ1696]
Fishermans Haunt BH23 7AS [B3347 N of
Christchurch]: Well divided big-windowed
bar comfortably refurbished by new
management, relaxed friendly atmosphere,
reasonably priced standard food,
Fullers/Gales and Ringwood, separate
dining room; disabled facilities, children
and dogs welcome, well kept gardens,
comfortable bedrooms, open all day
*(LYM, Sue and Mike Todd, Sara Fulton,
Roger Baker)*
Lamb BH23 7AN [Burley Rd/Bockhampton
Rd, Holfleet; off B3347 Christchurch—

Salisbury]: Two-bar country pub recently
refurbished under new licensees, helpful
cheerful staff, enjoyable pubby food from
baguettes to roasts, well kept Ringwood
Best and Timothy Taylors Landlord, Weds
jazz night; good-sized garden, nice
setting *(Mr and Mrs P D Titcomb)*
WINTERBORNE WHITECHURCH [ST8300]
Milton Arms DT11 0HW [A354
Blandford—Dorchester]: Good range of
well cooked generous inexpensive food in
refurbished village local, two busy bars,
pleasant atmosphere, helpful staff, good
beer range inc Ringwood *(Robert Watt)*
WINTERBOURNE ABBAS [SY6190]
Coach & Horses DT2 9LU: Big roadside
pub with long side dining area, wide
choice of pubby food (all day Sun) from
well filled rolls to carvery, Archers,
Palmers and Ringwood Best, sensibly
priced wines by the glass, pleasant
service, unusual pictures, games end with
darts and pool; piped music; children
welcome, a few picnic-sets outside with
play area and aviary, bedrooms
*(Phil and Jane Hodson, Roland and
Wendy Chalu, BB)*

Essex

The classic Essex pub is a low building with red tiles and white weatherboarding, often dating from Tudor times but simply modernised over the years, perhaps leaving little sign of their great age inside. You'll find plenty of examples in this chapter – but plenty of variety, too, with all sorts of other styles well represented. We've a happy batch of three good new main entries in Essex this year. Two of them – the friendly Axe & Compasses in Aythorpe Roding with its beers tapped straight from the cask, and cheery White Hart at Margaretting Tye with its unusual range and summer beer festival – go straight in with a Beer Award. The Kings Head at Gosfield is right up to date on the dining side but still keeps a proper public bar going. Among this county's old favourites, the Cricketers at Clavering is still nice and traditional following a sensitive refurbishment – it's run in the best possible way by an excellent landlord, with a very good chef, too. The friendly White Horse at Pleshey remains a jolly good all-rounder with tasty food, and the chatty Mole Trap at Stapleford Tawney, with its interesting local beers, is as full of real country character as ever. When it comes to choosing a place for a celebratory civilised meal out, we'd opt for the Sun at Dedham, with its emphasis on top-notch cooking using good seasonal ingredients – it's our Essex County Dining Pub this year. In the Lucky Dip section at the end of the chapter, we'd note particularly the Axe & Compasses at Arkesden and Crooked Billet in Leigh-on-Sea. It's also worth mentioning that the Chef & Brewer chain has quite a few good examples in the area. Three flourishing small independent brewers in the area produce good distinctive beers which are quite widely available: Crouch Vale, Nethergate and Mighty Oak. Another dozen or so are less commonly available, though we did find a couple – Brentwood and Farmers – in at least one or two of our pubs.

AYTHORPE RODING   TL5915   MAP 5
Axe & Compasses 🍴
B184 S of Dunmow; CM6 1PP

Friendly roadside stop, nice balance of eating and drinking

They look after their drinks carefully here, with Weston's farm cider on handpump as well as Nethergate IPA, and half a dozen temperature-stabilised casks of ale behind the bar, broached in rotation as they come to their prime (Highgate Quick Fix had just come on when we visited). The counter has comfortable bar chairs, with leatherette settles, stools and dark country chairs around a few pub tables on pale boards. On either side are more such tables, on turkey carpet; the original part on the left has dark old bent beams and wall timbers, with a two-way fireplace marking off a snug little raftered dining area, which has sentimental prints on dark masonry, and a big open-faced clock; piped music. The small garden behind has stylish modern tables and chairs.

🍴 As well as bar snacks such as olives, devilled chicken livers and mini fish and chips and sandwiches, bar food might include potted rabbit with tomato chutney, calves liver with sage butter and bacon, cod and chips with mushy peas, goats cheese and mushroom risotto with sage, rocket and parmesan crisp, rib-eye steak with horseradish butter and puddings such as coconut brûlée with Malibu and pineapple smoothie and hot chocolate fondu for two. *Starters/Snacks: £3.95 to £5.50. Main Courses: £7.95 to £15.95. Puddings: £4.95*

Free house ~ Licensee David Hunt ~ Real ale ~ Bar food (12-2.30, 6-9; 12-9(8 Sun) Sat) ~ Restaurant ~ (01279) 876648 ~ Children welcome ~ Dogs allowed in bar ~ Open 11-11(12 Fri, Sat); 12-11 Sun

Recommended by Paul and Ursula Randall, Mrs Margo Finlay, Jörg Kasprowski

BIRCHANGER   TL5122   MAP 5

Three Willows

Under a mile from M11 junction 8: A120 towards Bishops Stortford, then almost immediately right to Birchanger Village; don't be waylaid earlier by the Birchanger Services signpost! CM23 5QR

Full of cricketing memorabilia, a happy, civilised place serving good food

Reliable and deservedly popular, this cricket-themed pub is a great place for a good meal, and it's handily placed for Stansted Airport. The spacious carpeted main bar is full of cricketing prints, photographs, cartoons and other memorabilia and there's a small well furnished lounge bar; fruit machine. Friendly attentive staff serve well kept Greene King Abbot and IPA and a guest on handpump, and decent house wines. The generously served food draws quite a crowd, so it's best to arrive early if you want to eat, or book if you can. There are picnic-sets out on a terrace (with heaters) and on the lawn behind, which also has a sturdy climbing frame, swings and a basketball hoop (you can hear the motorway and airport out here).

🍴 Besides a wide range of pubby standards such as sandwiches, filled baked potatoes and ploughman's (all lunchtime only), and steak and ale pie, steaks and vegetable curry, they serve quite a lot of fresh fish – maybe cod, tuna steak, crab salad and lemon sole. Puddings might include raspberry and hazelnut meringue and jaffa puddle pudding. *Starters/Snacks: £4.95 to £8.95. Main Courses: £8.95 to £14.95. Puddings: £3.90*

Greene King ~ Tenants Paul and David Tucker ~ Real ale ~ Bar food (12-2, 6-9) ~ (01279) 815913 ~ Dogs welcome ~ Open 11.30-3, 6-11; 12-3 Sun; closed Sun evening

Recommended by Roy Hoing, David and Sue Smith, KC, Gordon Tong, John Saville, Justin and Emma King, Mrs M K Matthews, J Crosby, Marion and Bill Cross, Alvin and Yvonne Andrews, Charles Gysin, Grahame and Myra Williams, Martin Wilson, Mrs Hazel Rainer

BURNHAM-ON-CROUCH   TQ9495   MAP 5

White Harte

The Quay; CM0 8AS

Lovely waterside position, and with an aptly nautical twist to the décor

The relaxed partly carpeted bars at this comfortably old-fashioned hotel carry assorted nautical bric-a-brac and hardware, anything from models of Royal Navy ships to a compass set in the hearth. The other traditionally furnished high-ceilinged rooms have sea pictures on panelled or stripped brick walls, with cushioned seats set out around oak tables, and an enormous log fire making it cosy in winter. In summer they open the doors and windows, giving the place a nice airy feel. Charming staff serve Adnams and Crouch Vale Best from handpumps. They've a private jetty with a few tables and chairs just across the road – this is a lovely place to relax on a summer's evening idly taking in the yachts on the River Crouch.

🍴 Bar food includes lunchtime sandwiches, soup, steak and kidney pie, a choice of three local fish (cod, plaice and skate) and specials such as lasagne, curry and cottage pie. *Starters/Snacks: £3.50 to £6.20. Main Courses: £7.50 to £11.20. Puddings: £3.80*

Free house ~ Licensee G John Lewis ~ Real ale ~ Bar food ~ Restaurant ~ (01621) 782106 ~ Dogs welcome ~ Open 11-11; 12-10.30 Sun ~ Bedrooms: £28(£62B)/£50(£82B)

Recommended by John Wooll, George Atkinson, Sean A Smith, LM, Tina and David Woods-Taylor

CLAVERING

TL4832   MAP 5

Cricketers ⊕ 🛏

B1038 Newport—Buntingford, Newport end of village; CB11 4QT

Attractively updated traditional dining pub, very well run; a nice place to stay

When we heard that this old favourite of ours had been refurbished, we feared the worst. But knowing Mr Oliver, we shouldn't have worried. He's kept all its old-fashioned charm, with just a dash of extra sparkle from some new materials and furnishings. And there's a real feel throughout that they truly care about customers here. The main area has bays of deep purple button-back banquettes and neat padded leather dining chairs, dark floorboards, very low beams (the padding is a necessity, not a gimmick), and a big open fireplace. Back on the left is more obviously an eating part – two fairly compact carpeted areas, a step between them. The right side is similar but set more formally for dining, and has some big copper and brass pans on its dark beams and timbers. They have well kept Adnams Bitter and Broadside on handpump, a good choice of wines by the glass, freshly squeezed juices, and good coffee; piped music. Signed books by son Jamie are on sale. The attractive front terrace has wicker-look seats around teak tables among colourful flowering shrubs.

🍽 **As well as sandwiches and an interesting choice of salads, the seasonally changing menu might include starters such as king prawn and avocado tian with lime mascarpone cheese and dill, spicy venison patties with pea and mint yoghurt and cucumber salad, and antipasti and main courses such as roast duckling with orange and star anise jus and quince compote, organic salmon steak with lemon couscous and roasted tomato and sage sauce, spinach and mushroom lasagne with truffle crostini and roquette and parmesan salad, and well hung rump steak with rocket mustard pesto. They are strong on free-range and organic ingredients. Starters/Snacks: £4.50 to £8.50. Main Courses: £9.00 to £16.00. Puddings: £5.25 to £6.00.**

Free house ~ Licensee Trevor Oliver ~ Real ale ~ Bar food (12-2, 6.30-9.30) ~ Restaurant ~ (01799) 550442 ~ Children welcome ~ Open 10am-11pm ~ Bedrooms: £65B/£90B

Recommended by Philip Vernon, Kim Maidment, David and Ruth Hollands, Evelyn and Derek Walter, Mrs Margo Finlay, Jörg Kasprowski, Mr and Mrs B Watt, Paul Humphreys

DEDHAM

TM0533   MAP 5

Sun ⊕ 🍷 🍺 🛏

High Street (B2109); CO7 6DF
ESSEX DINING PUB OF THE YEAR

Popular stylish inn in Constable country, with elegant seasonal italian-biased food and an impressive wine selection

This fine old coaching inn is a lovely building and beautifully furnished. High carved beams, squared panelling, wall timbers and big log fires in splendid fireplaces provide a setting for high settles, sofas with sorbet coloured cushions and other good quality wooden tables and chairs. A charming little window seat in the bar looks across to the church, which is at least glimpsed in several of Constable's paintings. Relaxed and friendly but efficient young staff serve Adnams Broadside and Crouch Vale Brewers Gold and a couple of guests from brewers such as Earl Soham and Whitstable, a very good selection of more than 70 wines (20 by the glass) and some interesting soft drinks; piped music and board games. On the way out to picnic-sets on the quiet attractive back lawn, notice the unusual covered back staircase with what used to be a dovecote on top, and if you have time, beautiful walks into the heart of Constable country lead out of the village, over water meadows towards Flatford Mill. The panelled bedrooms are nicely done with abundant character, and an archway annexe houses their fruit and vegetable shop.

🍴 Food is not cheap but prices do reflect the quality of the ingredients used in a menu which places much emphasis on seasonal game, fish, fruit and vegetables. The daily changing choice might include antipasti, starters such as white peach, prosecco and basil risotto, ravioli stuffed with swiss chard, ricotta and sage butter, pork loin braised in milk, sage and lemon with celeriac, thyme, chestnuts and pancetta, shin of veal roasted with red wine vinegar, tomato and spring garlic and capers with gremolata, bass fillet baked with basil, vermouth and lentils, and puddings such as hazelnut and espresso cake or panna cotta with grappa and raspberries *Starters/Snacks: £9.00 to £10.50. Main Courses: £11.00 to £15.50. Puddings: £5.25*

Free house ~ Licensee Piers Baker ~ Real ale ~ Bar food (12-2.30(3 Sat, Sun), 6.30-9.30 (10 Fri, Sat)) ~ Restaurant ~ (01206) 323351 ~ Children welcome ~ Dogs allowed in bar ~ Open 12-11 ~ Bedrooms: £65B/£130B

Recommended by Bernard Phelvin, Marion and Bill Cross, N R White, Terry and Jackie Devine, John Saville, Sally Anne and Peter Goodale, A D Cross, Peter and Heather Elliott, John Wooll

FYFIELD
TL5706   MAP 5

Queens Head ♀ ◖

Corner of B184 and Queen Street; CM5 0RY

Very friendly 15th-c pub with good wine list and accent on food

The recently decorated low-beamed, compact L-shaped bar at this spotless 15th-c pub has some exposed timbers in cream and mocha walls, fresh flowers and pretty lamps on its nice sturdy elm tables and comfortable seating, from button-back wall banquettes to attractive and unusual high-backed chairs, some in a snug little side booth. In summer, two facing fireplaces have lighted church candles instead of a fire; piped music. The main focus is the very good food, but a pubby balance is maintained by their good range of half a dozen real ales: Adnams Bitter and Broadside and Crouch Vale Brewers Gold are well kept on handpump alongside guests from brewers such as Nethergate and Stonehenge. They've also Weston's Old Rosie farm cider, and about 17 wines by the glass (including champagne) and some very decent malts. A neat little prettily planted back garden by a weeping willow has a teak bench and half a dozen picnic-sets under canvas parasols, with the sleepy River Roding flowing past beyond.

🍴 Besides good lunchtime sandwiches, ploughman's and filled bagels, dishes from the daily changing menu might include pigeon and black pudding salad with mustard dressing, goats cheese baked with red grapes, pie of the day, roast mediterranean vegetables with goats cheese, scallops cooked in Pernod sauce with pasta, chicken breast stuffed with brie with sage sauce, smoked haddock on mash with creamy dill and horseradish sauce, sirloin steak with green peppercorn sauce. *Starters/Snacks: £3.50 to £9.50. Main Courses: £9.95 to £18.95. Puddings: £4.50*

Free house ~ Licensee Daniel Lemprecht ~ Real ale ~ Bar food (12-2.30, 7-9.30; 12-9.30 Sat, 12-7 Sun, not Sun evenings) ~ (01277) 899231 ~ Open 11-3.30, 6-11; 11-11 Sat; 12-10.30 Sun

Recommended by Marion and Bill Cross, Andy and Jill Kassube, Tina and David Woods-Taylor, Reg Fowle, Helen Rickwood

GOSFIELD
TL7829   MAP 5

Kings Head

The Street (A1017 Braintree—Halstead); CO9 1TP

Comfortably contemporary dining pub with separate proper public bar

The softly lit beamed main bar, with dark red panelled dado and ceiling, has neat modern black leather armchairs, bucket chairs and a settee as well as sturdy pale wood dining chairs and tables on its dark boards, and a log fire in a handsome old brick fireplace with big bellows. Black timbers mark off a red-carpeted and red-walled eating area with matching furnishings, opening into a carpeted conservatory; piped music. They have Adnams Broadside and Greene King IPA on handpump and a goodish choice of wines by the glass; neat black-clad young staff; daily papers. The good-sized quite separate public bar, with a purple pool table and TV, has its own partly covered terrace; the main terrace has round picnic-sets.

🍽 **Pubby meals include sandwiches, baguettes, baked potatoes, sausage and mash, chicken, leek and stilton pie, fish of the day, and changing specials such as confit of duck with orange jus, grilled haddock with king prawn and lemon sauce, pappardelle with mushroom sauce and rocket and parmesan salad and puddings such as crème brûlée, fruit crumble and meringue and strawberry compote.** *Starters/Snacks: £5.00 to £6.50. Main Courses: £8.50 to £17.50. Puddings: £5.00*

Enterprise ~ Lease Alastair and Katie Bols ~ Real ale ~ Bar food (12-2.30, 6-9.30; 12-6 Sun) ~ Restaurant ~ (01787) 474016 ~ Children welcome ~ Dogs allowed in bar ~ Open 12-3, 6-11; 12-10.30 Sun

Recommended by Patrick Reeve, Mrs Margo Finlay, Jörg Kasprowski

GREAT HENNY   TL8738   MAP 5

Henny Swan 🍽 ♟

Henny Street, signposted off A131 at traffic lights just SW of Sudbury, at the bottom of Ballingdon Hill; OS Sheet 155 map reference 879384; CO10 7LS

Stylish and restauranty place for a meal, with contemporary furnishings and a riverside garden

This dining pub occupies a converted barge-house by the River Stour. The smallish L-shaped contemporary bar has soft leather settees, armchairs and drum stools, carefully lit big bright modern prints contrasting with its stripped beams and dark walls and a woodburning stove in a big brick fireplace. The restaurant is bigger, and thanks to french windows along two walls, bright and airy. It has comfortable rather elegant modern dining furniture well spaced on polished oak boards, more modern artwork and another woodburning stove; disabled access and facilities. There are stylish metal tables and chairs (some under canvas parasols) out on the good-sized side terrace (with heaters), and picnic-sets across the quiet lane on a large informal lawn, beside which the river flows gently past willow trees and over a low weir (some people arrive here by boat). Drinks include Adnams Broadside and Greene King IPA on handpump, a dozen wines by the glass (including a champagne and a pudding wine) and summer jugs of Pimms. One or two readers have felt that service could be a bit kinder.

🍽 **Very good food includes grilled sardines, duck liver parfait with red onion marmalade, pork tenderloin with cider sauce, baked butternut squash, spinach and ricotta filo, rib-eye steak with black peppercorn sauce, and daily specials such as venison sausage and mash, moules marininères, salmon, cod and tiger prawn skewers with lime and tomato salsa and puddings such as pecan pie or fruit pavlova.** *Starters/Snacks: £4.25 to £7.95. Main Courses: £9.75 to £13.95. Puddings: £4.75*

Punch ~ Lease Harry and Sofia Charalambous ~ Real ale ~ Bar food (12-2.30, 6.30-9.30; 12-4 Sun) ~ Restaurant ~ (01787) 269238 ~ Children welcome ~ Open 11-3, 6-11; 11-11(11-3, 6-11 in winter) Sat; 12-10.30(5 in winter) Sun

Recommended by John and Enid Morris, Dave and Chris Watts, Adele Summers, Alan Black, Ryta Lyndley, Mrs Carolyn Dixon, Hunter and Christine Wright

HASTINGWOOD   TL4807   MAP 5

Rainbow & Dove £

0.25 miles from M11 junction 7; Hastingwood signposted after Ongar signs at exit roundabout; CM17 9JX

Useful for the motorway, a pleasantly traditional low-beamed pub with good value food

The very reasonably priced pubby meals at this unpretentious 16th-c cottage can draw quite a crowd and as it's not the biggest of pubs it's worth getting here early. Of its three little low-beamed rooms opening off the main bar area, the one on the left is particularly beamy, with the lower part of its wall stripped back to bare brick and decorated with brass pistols and plates. Adnams Broadside, Greene King IPA and a guest are on handpump; piped music, winter darts and occasional jazz nights. Hedged off from the car park, a stretch of grass has picnic-sets (one reader found sitting out here rather unappealing), and you can also eat out in front of the pub.

🍴 **The licensees tell us that all their food is home made. It includes lunchtime sandwiches and baked baguettes as well as ploughman's, chicken or vegetable curry, steak, kidney and ale pie, battered cod, and puddings such as apple pie or spotted dick.** *Starters/Snacks: £3.75 to £8.50. Main Courses: £8.15 to £14.75. Puddings: £3.60 to £5.25*

Punch ~ Lease Andrew Keep and Kathryn Chivrall ~ Real ale ~ Bar food (12-2(3 Sun), 7-9) ~ (01279) 415419 ~ Children welcome ~ Open 11.30-3, 6-11.30; 12-3.30, 6-12 midnight Sat; 12-4 Sun; closed Sun evening

Recommended by Tim and Claire Woodward, Donna and Roger, Sally Anne and Peter Goodale, Jeremy King

HORNDON-ON-THE-HILL   TQ6783   MAP 3

Bell ♀ 🍺 🛏

M25 junction 30 into A13, then left into B1007 after 7 miles, village signposted from here; SS17 8LD

Very popular ancient pub with mostly restauranty food and very good range of drinks

A curious collection of ossified hot cross buns hangs along a beam in the saloon bar at this lovely old Tudor inn. The first was put there some 90 years ago to mark the day that the licensee Jack Turnell took over the Bell – it was a Good Friday. Now the oldest person in the village (or at least the oldest available on the day) hangs the bun. During the war a concrete bun was hung, bearing witness to the shortage of food. Although emphasis is on the imaginative real food, the heavily beamed bar does maintain an unchanging pubby appearance with some antique high-backed settles and benches and rugs on the flagstones or highly polished oak floorboards. They keep an impressive range of drinks, including Bass (tapped straight from the cask), Greene King IPA, five guests from brewers such as Crouch Vale and over a hundred well chosen wines from all over the world (16 by the glass). You do need or get here early or book as tables are often all taken soon after opening time. More reports please.

🍴 **As well as a short bar menu (cheaper if served in the bar than in the restaurant) with lunchtime sandwiches and dishes such as poached haddock with poached egg and hollandaise, and lamb and chilli sausages with shallot mash, there are daily specials such as warm pigeon and rabbit terrine wrapped in parma ham with red onion marmalade, roast shoulder of lamb with sauté kidneys and tomato and tarragon jus, fried halibut with béarnaise sauce, fried scotch rib-eye beef with cèpe mushroom velouté and puddings such as baked banana and toffee crème brûlée with mild chocolate chip ice-cream and pistachio and hazelnut profiteroles with hot chocolate sauce and Baileys parfait.** *Starters/Snacks: £4.95 to £9.00. Main Courses: £8.50 to £9.95. Puddings: £5.10 to £6.95*

Free house ~ Licensee John Vereker ~ Real ale ~ Bar food (12-2, 6.30(7 Sun)-9.45; not bank hol Mon) ~ Restaurant ~ (01375) 642463 ~ Children in eating area of bar and restaurant ~ Dogs allowed in bar and bedrooms ~ Open 11-2.30, 5.30-11; 11-3, 6-11 Sat; 12-4, 7-10.30 Sun ~ Bedrooms: £44.50B/£49B

Recommended by Andy and Jill Kassube, Gordon and Margaret Ormondroyd, John and Enid Morris, John Silverman, Penny Turko

LITTLE BRAXTED   TL8413   MAP 5

Green Man £

Kelvedon Road; village signposted off B1389 by NE end of A12 Witham bypass – keep on patiently; OS Sheet 168 map reference 848133; CM8 3LB

Prettily traditional brick-built pub with a garden and reasonably priced food

Picnic-sets in the pleasant sheltered garden behind this tucked away house are a good place to while away an hour or two, and in winter the traditional little lounge is especially appealing with its warming open fire. Horsebrasses seem to be disappearing from pubs these days so the 200 or so here form quite an unusual collection. There's also some harness, mugs hanging from a beam, a lovely copper urn and other interesting bric-a-brac. The tiled public bar has books, darts, cribbage and dominoes; three Greene King beers and nine wines by the glass. More reports please.

🍴 **Reasonably priced bar food includes lunchtime sandwiches and warm baguettes, soup, ploughman's, baked potatoes, sausage and mash, and specials such as minted lamb shank in redcurrant gravy, thai chicken curry or steak and kidney pudding and good home-made puddings.** *Starters/Snacks: £3.95 to £4.50. Main Courses: £6.95 to £8.95. Puddings: £3.25*

Greene King ~ Tenant Matthew Ruffle ~ Real ale ~ Bar food (12-2.30, 6-9; 12-6 Sun) ~ Restaurant ~ (01621) 891659 ~ Children until 8pm ~ Dogs welcome ~ Open 11.30-3.30, 5-11.30(midnight Sat); 12-11 Sun

Recommended by Hazel Morgan, Bernard Patrick, Alvin and Yvonne Andrews, Gerald and Gabrielle Culliford

LITTLE WALDEN   TL5441   MAP 5

Crown 🍺

B1052 N of Saffron Walden; CB10 1XA

Bustling 18th-c cottage with a warming log fire and hearty food

This homely low-ceilinged pub has bookroom-red walls, flowery curtains and a mix of bare boards and navy carpeting. A higgledy-piggledy mix of chairs ranges from high-backed pews to little cushioned armchairs spaced around a good variety of closely arranged tables, mostly big, some stripped. The small red-tiled room on the right has two little tables. They light a fire in one of the three fireplaces, though not in the unusual walk-through one! Four or five beers are tapped straight from casks racked up behind the bar, normally Adnams, City of Cambridge Boathouse and Greene King Abbot with a guest or two such as Woodfordes Wherry; piped light music (one reader found it obtrusive); disabled access. Tables out on the terrace take in views of surrounding tranquil countryside; bedrooms are planned.

🍴 **The fairly traditional bar food is popular, so you may need to book at weekends: sandwiches (not Sun), whitebait, chicken liver pâté, lasagne, steak and mushroom pie, haddock, brazil nut loaf, thai curry, sirloin steak and puddings such as treacle sponge and cheesecake.** *Starters/Snacks: £3.95 to £6.25. Main Courses: £6.25 to £12.95. Puddings: £4.25 to £5.45*

Free house ~ Licensee Colin Hayling ~ Real ale ~ Bar food (not Sun and Mon evenings) ~ Restaurant ~ (01799) 522475 ~ Dogs welcome ~ Trad jazz Weds evening ~ Open 11.30-2.30, 6-11; 12-10 Sun ~ Bedrooms: £55B/£70B

Recommended by the Didler, Simon Watkins, Mrs Margo Finlay, Jörg Kasprowski

MARGARETTING TYE   TL6801   MAP 5

White Hart 🍺

From B1002 (just S of A12/A414 junction) follow Maldon Rd for 1.3 miles, then turn right immediately after river bridge, into Swan Lane, keeping on for 0.7 miles; The Tye; CM4 9JX

Fine choice of ales in cheery country pub with good family garden

Besides well kept Adnams Best and Broadside and a beer from Mighty Oak on handpump, they bring on a constant stream of unusual guest beers from all over the country – on our visit they had Archers Around The Maypole, Oxfordshire Marshmallow and Slaters Monkey Magic, with others due to take over later that same day. They do take-aways and have interesting bottled beers, too, and run a popular beer festival around midsummer. It's open-plan and unpretentious, with plenty of mixed seating, from comfortably worn wall banquettes to a group of housekeeper's chairs around a low table with country magazines. There are cosier areas on the left, and a neat dark-tiled back conservatory on the right, with John Ireland brewing cartoons; the front lobby has a charity paperback table; darts, quiz machine, skittles, board games and piped music. There are plenty of picnic-sets out on grass and terracing around the pub, with a sturdy play area, a safely fenced duck pond, an aviary with noisy cockatiels (they don't quite drown the larks), and pens of rabbits, guinea-pigs and a pygmy goat.

Ⓜ️ **Bar food includes sandwiches, pâté of the day, fried camembert with fruit coulis, king prawn cocktail, baked bass, steak and ale pie, liver and bacon, leek, red onion and feta quiche (the chef is vegetarian so the vegetarian dishes here should be good) and puddings such as mixed berry cheesecake and hot chocolate fudge cake.** *Starters/Snacks: £3.50 to £5.50. Main Courses: £5.50 to £15.00. Puddings: £3.00 to £5.50*

Free house ~ Licensee Elizabeth Haines ~ Real ale ~ Bar food (12-2, 6-9.30, 12-4.30, 6.30-8.30 Sun; not Mon evening) ~ (01277) 840478 ~ Children welcome away from main bar ~ Dogs allowed in bar ~ Open 11.30-3, 6-12; 12-12(11 Sun) Sat

Recommended by Mrs J Slowgrove, John and Enid Morris, Paul and Ursula Randall, Evelyn and Derek Walter, Mrs Roxanne Chamberlain

MILL GREEN   TL6401   MAP 5

Viper 🍺 £

The Common; from Fryerning (which is signposted off north-east bound A12 Ingatestone bypass) follow Writtle signposts; CM4 0PT

Timeless and charmingly unspoilt, with local ales, simple pub food and no modern intrusions

This delightfully unpretentious old local with its lovely cottagey garden is tucked quietly away in the woods. Its cosy lounge rooms have spindleback seats, armed country kitchen chairs and tapestried wall seats around neat little old tables, and there's a log fire. Booted walkers (and dogs) are directed towards the fairly basic parquet-floored tap room, which is more simply furnished with shiny wooden traditional wall seats and a coal fire, and beyond that another room has country kitchen chairs and sensibly placed darts, also dominoes and cribbage; the pub cat is Millie and the white west highland terrier is Jimmy. They stock an interesting range of five well kept beers on handpump: Viper (produced for the pub by Nethergate) and local brewery Mighty Oak Jake the Snake and Oscar Wilde and a couple of quickly changing guests from thoughtfully sourced brewers such as Maldon and Nethergate; also Wilkins' farm cider, straight from the barrel. Tables on the lawn overlook a beautifully tended cottage garden – a dazzling mass of colour in summer, further enhanced at the front by overflowing hanging baskets and window boxes. Morris men often dance here.

Ⓜ️ **Simple but tasty bar snacks might include sandwiches, soup, steak and ale pie, curry and lasagne; Sunday roasts. The tasty bread comes from a local baker a mile or so down the road.** *Starters/Snacks: £3.50 to £5.95. Main Courses: £3.50 to £7.95. Puddings: £3.25 to £3.75*

Free house ~ Licensees Peter White and Donna Torris ~ Real ale ~ Bar food (12-2(3 Sat, Sun); not evenings) ~ No credit cards ~ (01277) 352010 ~ Dogs allowed in bar ~ Open 12-3, 6-11(and Fri in winter) 12-11 Fri, Sat; 12-10.30 Sun

Recommended by Richard Pitcher, N R White, Philip Denton, Pete Baker, Donna and Roger, the Didler, Andy and Jill Kassube, Ian Phillips

PAGLESHAM   TQ9293   MAP 5

Punchbowl

Church End; from the Paglesham road out of Rochford, Church End is signposted on the left; SS4 2DP

Genuinely traditional pub with enjoyable food and east anglian beers

This partly white weatherboarded cottage began life in the 16th c as a sailmaker's loft. Its cosy beamed bar has exposed brick walls, low beams, pews, barrel chairs and other seats, lots of brass, mugs, pictures and other memorabilia. A lower room is laid out for dining. Besides Adnams, they usually have a beer from Cottage and Nethergate, and one from another brewery; cribbage, darts and piped music (mostly 1960s and 70s classic hits). There's a lovely rural view from tables in the little south facing front garden.

🍴 Straightforward but fairly priced tasty bar food includes sandwiches, ploughman's, Sunday roasts, rib-eye steak, lasagne, steak and stout pie, a fresh fish board (not Sunday), and puddings like crumble or plum pudding. *Starters/Snacks: £3.95 to £5.95. Main Courses: £6.50 to £12.50. Puddings: £3.75 to £4.25*

Free house ~ Licensees Bernie and Pat Cardy ~ Real ale ~ Bar food (12-1.30, 7-8.30; 12-8 Sun) ~ Restaurant ~ (01702) 258376 ~ Children usually welcome but ring first ~ Open 11.30-3, 6.30-11; 12-10.30 Sun

Recommended by Stuart and Doreen Ritchie, Louise English, George Atkinson, Sean A Smith

PELDON
TM0015   MAP 5

Rose 🍴 ♀ 🛏
B1025 Colchester—Mersea (do not turn left to Peldon village); CO5 7QJ

Friendly dining pub in an appealing building – good food, thoughtful staff and great wine choice

This very appealing pastel-coloured old inn has a delightfully traditional interior, with standing timbers supporting the heavy low ceilings with their dark bowed 17th-c oak beams, alcoves that conjure up smugglers discussing bygone contraband, little leaded-light windows and a gothick-arched brick fireplace. There are creaky close-set tables and some antique mahogany and padded wall banquettes. In contrast, the very spacious airy conservatory dining area (disabled access), with views over the garden, has a modern brightly lit feel. On handpump are Adnams Best and Broadside, Greene King IPA and a guest such as Wyre Piddle Piddle in the Wind; as the pub is run by the family-owned Essex wine merchant Lay & Wheeler, they have a very good wine list, with about 25 by the glass, listed with helpful descriptions on a blackboard. Staff are friendly and efficient, though as it does get very busy you may need to book. The spacious garden is very relaxing, with good teak seats and ducks on a pretty pond. More reports please.

🍴 Changing bar food might include a ploughman's, seared scallop and pancetta salad, and interesting sandwiches, starters such as fried crispy chilli beef with sweet chilli sauce and crispy seaweed, hot and sour marinated king prawns, main courses such as chicken curry, duck breast with cranberry jus, thai green vegetable curry, fried tuna on ratatouille with pesto dressing, sirloin steak with stilton rarebit and roast cherry tomatoes, with puddings such as white chocolate and lemon mousse, poached rhubarb cheesecake and hot cross bread and butter pudding with cinnamon anglaise. *Starters/Snacks: £4.25 to £8.25. Main Courses: £8.95 to £14.95. Puddings: £4.25*

Lay & Wheeler ~ Licensee Craig Formoy ~ Real ale ~ Bar food (12-2.15, 6.30-9(9.30 Fri, Sat); 12-9 Sun) ~ Restaurant ~ (01206) 735248 ~ Children welcome ~ Open 11-11; 12-10.30 Sun; 12-7 Sun in winter ~ Bedrooms: £40S/£60S

Recommended by John Wooll, Mrs P Lang, Mandy and Simon King, David Jackson

PLESHEY
TL6614   MAP 5

White Horse ♀
The Street; CM3 1HA

Packed to the gills with knick-knacks and crafts, an ancient inn nicely placed in a pretty village

This rather sweet little pub seems to be doing very well at the moment, with readers offering good general praise. It's crammed with cheerful clutter, sells crafts, locally made preserves, greetings cards and gifts, and even has its own little art gallery, with works for sale by local artists. Scattered all around are jugs, tankards, antlers, miscellaneous brass including an old ship's bell, prints, books and bottles. Furnishings take in wheelback and other chairs and tables with cloths, and a fireplace has an unusual curtain-like fireguard. Glass cabinets in the big sturdily furnished dining room are filled with lots of miniatures and silverware, and there are flowers on tables. A snug room by the tiny bar counter has brick and beamed walls, a comfortable sofa, some bar stools and a table with magazines to read. Maldon Gold is tapped straight from the cask and they've several wines by the glass; piped music. Doors from here open on to a terrace and a grass area with trees, shrubs and tables. The pub hosts monthly jazz buffets (not in summer) and a midsummer barbecue.

🍽 **Fairly priced and very enjoyable bar food includes lunchtime bar snacks such as toasted sandwiches, tasty herring roes fried in butter, ploughman's, thai chicken and vegetable dumplings, whitebait, steak and kidney pie, venison casserole, rabbit poached in cider with a creamy sauce and scampi.** *Starters/Snacks: £4.95 to £6.95. Main Courses: £8.75 to £13.75. Puddings: £3.95*

Free house ~ Licensees Mike and Jan Smail ~ Real ale ~ Bar food (12(11.30 Tues, Weds)-3, 7-9) ~ Restaurant ~ (01245) 237281 ~ Children welcome ~ Dogs allowed in bar ~ Open 11.30-3, 6.30-11; 12-4.30 Sun; closed Tues and Weds evenings, all day Mon

Recommended by David Twitchett, Roy and Lindsey Fentiman, Marion and Bill Cross, Philip Denton, Mrs Margo Finlay, Jörg Kasprowski, Paul and Ursula Randall, David Jackson

RICKLING GREEN
TL5129   MAP 5

Cricketers Arms 🛏
Just off B1383 N of Stansted Mountfichet; CB11 3YG

Attractive timbered pub with a relaxed atmosphere, handy for Stansted Airport

The atmosphere at this popular Elizabethan dining pub is pleasantly mellow, with leather sofas and stripped pine trunks as coffee tables on stone floors, an open fire, a handful of carefully selected prints on cream walls, thoughtful lighting and modern stools at the counter. Greene King IPA, Jennings Cumberland and a guest such as Greene King Abbot tapped straight from casks behind the bar. You can eat in the bar but they encourage you to eat in one of the two restaurants, which are gently contemporary with softly coloured walls, and solid uniform wood tables and chairs on wooden floors; piped music. Outside on a decked area, trellis screening and clusters of plants in pots partition off private little areas which are set out with wood and metal tables and chairs. More reports please.

🍽 **Under the new licensee, bar food includes a lunchtime menu with items such as steak baguette, burger or baked mackerel as well as thai fishcake, smoked chicken salad, crayfish risotto, baked mackerel with sweet potato mash, roast pork belly with cider sauce, red pepper and aubergine tart, roast salmon with polenta crust and creamed leeks, and rib-eye steak, with puddings such as apple and blueberry pie and white chocolate cheesecake with Baileys sauce.** *Starters/Snacks: £5.00 to £10.50. Main Courses: £10.50 to £19.00. Puddings: £5.00 to £6.00*

Punch ~ Lease Nicola Chamberlain ~ Real ale ~ Bar food (12-2.30, 6-9.30(9 Sun)) ~ Restaurant ~ (01799) 543210 ~ Children welcome away from the bar ~ Dogs allowed in bar ~ Open 11-11(10.30 Sun) ~ Bedrooms: £65B/£95B

Recommended by Alvin and Yvonne Andrews, Mrs Margo Finlay, Jörg Kasprowski

STAPLEFORD TAWNEY
TL5001   MAP 5

Mole Trap 🍺
Tawney Common, which is a couple of miles away from Stapleford Tawney and is signposted off A113 just N of M25 overpass – keep on; OS Sheet 167 map reference 500013; CM16 7PU

Tucked away but humming with customers; interesting selection of guest beers

Quirky as ever, this isolated little country pub is run with considerable individuality – it's the sort of place to fall into easy chat with the locals who prop themselves along the counter. The smallish carpeted bar (mind your head as you go in) has black dado, beams and joists, brocaded wall seats, library chairs and bentwood elbow chairs around plain pub tables, and steps down through a partly knocked-out timber stud wall to a similar area. There are a few small pictures, 3-D decorative plates, some dried-flower arrangements and (on the sloping ceiling formed by a staircase beyond) some regulars' snapshots, with a few dozen beermats stuck up around the serving bar, and warming fires; quiet piped radio. As well as Fullers London Pride on handpump, they have three constantly changing guests from smaller brewers such as Country Life, Crouch Vale and Sharps. The pub fills up quickly at lunchtimes, so it's worth getting here early if you want to eat. Outside are some plastic tables and chairs and a picnic-set, and across the road on the farm you might see a happy tribe of friendly cats, rabbits, a couple of dogs, hens, geese, a sheep, goats and horses. Note that food service stops very promptly, sometimes even before the allotted time.

🍴 **Besides sandwiches and popular Sunday roasts, bar food includes ploughman's, soup, lasagne, steak and kidney pie, ham, egg and chips and a vegetarian option like quiche, with puddings like cherry and apple pie.** *Starters/Snacks: £3.50 to £5.50. Main Courses: £8.95 to £10.50. Puddings: £3.95 to £4.50*

Free house ~ Licensees Mr and Mrs Kirtley ~ Real ale ~ Bar food (not Sun and Mon evenings) ~ No credit cards ~ (01992) 522394 ~ Dogs welcome ~ Open 11.30-2.30, 6-11; 12-3.30, 7-10.30 Sun

Recommended by the Didler, Evelyn and Derek Walter, Mrs Roxanne Chamberlain, N R White, David Jackson, H O Dickinson

STOCK   TQ6999 MAP 5
Hoop 🍺
B1007; from A12 Chelmsford bypass take Galleywood, Billericay turn-off; CM4 9BD

Weatherboarded pub with interesting range of beers and large garden

Standing timbers and beams in the open plan bustling bar at this weatherboarded pub hint at the building's great age, and its original layout as a row of three weavers' cottages. With all its wood fixtures and fittings, including a bare board floor, wooden tables and brocaded wooden settles, the fairly simple interior feels pubbily functional. In winter, a warm fire burns in a big brick walled fireplace. Hoop and Stock and Barrel (brewed for the pub by Brentwood) are on handpump with three guests from brewers such as Adnams, Crouch Vale and Mighty Oak. A restaurant up in the timbered eaves is light and airy with pale timbers set in white walls and more wood flooring. Prettily bordered with flowers, the large sheltered back garden has picnic-sets and a covered seating area.

🍴 **Very pubby bar food includes sandwiches, ploughman's battered cod, penne with tuna and olives, beef and mushroom, fish or chicken and leek pie, sausage and mash, rib-eye steak, with crumble of the day and jam roll and custard. They may ask to keep your credit card if you want to run a tab.** *Starters/Snacks: £3.95 to £6.95. Main Courses: £6.50 to £11.00. Puddings: £3.95 to £5.95*

Free house ~ Licensee Michelle Corrigan ~ Real ale ~ Bar food (12-2.30(3 Sun), 6-9(9.30 Fri, Sat); not Sun evening) ~ Restaurant ~ (01277) 841137 ~ Children welcome away from bar ~ Dogs allowed in bar ~ Open 11-11(12 Fri, 11.30 Sat); 12-10.30 Sun

Recommended by Evelyn and Derek Walter, John Saville, Ian Phillips, Paul A Moore, Louise English, MJVK, Mrs Margo Finlay, Jörg Kasprowski, Simon and Mandy King

STOW MARIES   TQ8399 MAP 5
Prince of Wales 🍺
B1012 between S Woodham Ferrers and Cold Norton Posters; CM3 6SA

Unfussy local with interesting beers

Few of the characterful little low-ceilinged rooms at this white weatherboard pub have space for more than one or two tables or wall benches on their tiled or bare-boards floors, though the room in the middle squeezes in quite a jumble of chairs and stools. The licensee worked for Crouch Vale Brewery before he came here so you can be sure of a good pint. As well as two real ales from Adnams, he stocks four widely sourced guests from brewers such as Dark Star, Everards, Hepworth and Hopback alongside bottled and draught belgian beers and several bottled fruit beers, all served from quite a little counter. There are seats and tables in the back garden, and between the picket fence and the pub's white weatherboarded frontage is a terrace, with herbs in Victorian chimneypots, sheltered by a huge umbrella. More reports please.

🍽 Besides sandwiches, the bar menu includes fish and chips, whitebait and burgers, with a choice of eight specials like steaks, fish pies, steak and kidney pie, and mediterranean vegetable hotpot. On Thursday evenings in winter they fire up the old bread oven to make pizzas in the room that used to be the village bakery, and on some summer Sundays, they barbecue steaks and all sorts of fish such as mahi-mahi and black barracuda. *Starters/Snacks: £5.25 to £6.25. Main Courses: £6.95 to £12.95. Puddings: £3.95*

Free house ~ Licensee Rob Walster ~ Real ale ~ Bar food (12-2.30, 6.30-9.30, 12-9.30 Sun) ~ (01621) 828971 ~ Children in family room ~ Open 11(12 Sun)-11(12 Fri, Sat)

Recommended by Reg Fowle, Helen Rickwood, N R White

YOUNGS END   TL7319   MAP 5

Green Dragon

Former A131 Braintree—Chelmsford (off new bypass), just N of Essex Showground; CM77 8QN

Nicely pubby dining pub with reasonably priced tasty food

A new licensee has freshened up the interior here. Its two bars have wood floors, traditional pub furnishings, stools at the counter and a log fire, and there's an extra low-ceilinged snug just beside the serving counter. Friendly staff serve Greene King Abbot and IPA and a Greene King guest by handpump; unobtrusive piped jazz. A lawn at the back has lots of picnic-sets under cocktail parasols and a terrace with outdoor heaters. More reports please.

🍽 Bar food includes lunchtime sandwiches and baguettes and possibly starters such as beetroot, watercress and goats cheese salad, asparagus and bacon bruschetta, main courses such as beef, ale and mushroom pie, tuna with lemon herb butter, mediterranean vegetable filo tart, chilli, venison with red wine sauce, steaks and puddings such as jam sponge pudding and caramel apple fudge cake. *Starters/Snacks: £3.50 to £5.95. Main Courses: £7.50 to £18.00. Puddings: £4.00*

Greene King ~ Lease Vanessa Scott ~ Real ale ~ Bar food (12-2.30, 6-9; 12-9 Sun) ~ Restaurant ~ (01245) 361030 ~ Children welcome till 8pm ~ Open 12-3, 6-11; 12-10.30 Sun

Recommended by Evelyn and Derek Walter, Justin and Emma King, Mrs Margo Finlay, Jörg Kasprowski, Roy and Lindsey Fentiman, Philip Denton, Peter and Jean Hoare

LUCKY DIP

Besides the fully inspected pubs, you might like to try these Lucky Dips recommended to us and described by readers (if you do, please send us reports: feedback@thegoodpubguide.co.uk).

ARDLEIGH [TM0429]
☆ *Wooden Fender* CO7 7PA [A137 towards Colchester]: Pleasantly extended and furnished old pub with friendly attentive service, beams and log fires, Greene King and a guest ale, decent wines; children welcome in large dining area, good-sized garden with water feature and play area (*N R White, LYM*)
ARKESDEN [TL4834]
☆ *Axe & Compasses* CB11 4EX [off B1038]: Enjoyable if not cheap food in thatched pub with welcoming staff, good choice of wines by the glass, Greene King ales, easy chairs, upholstered oak and elm seats, open fire and china trinkets in cosy lounge bar, built-in settles in smaller public bar with darts and board games, restaurant allowing children;

pretty hanging baskets, seats on side terrace, beautiful village (*Andrew Scarr, Simon Watkins, David Jackson, LYM, Gordon Neighbour*)
BELCHAMP ST PAUL [TL7942]
Half Moon CO10 7DP [Cole Green]: Thatched pub with well kept beers, generous good value honest food, friendly attentive service, snug beamed lounge, cheerful locals' bar, restaurant; children welcome, tables out in front and in back garden (*LYM*)
BOREHAM [TL7509]
Queens Head CM3 3EG [Church Rd, off B1137 Chelmsford—Hatfield Peverel]: Traditional friendly local tucked away by church, homely and spotless, with well kept Adnams, Crouch Vale Brewers Gold, Greene King IPA and Woodfordes Wherry, good service, tempting

food (not Sun evening) inc Sun roast, snug beams-and-brickwork saloon, more tables down one side of long public bar with darts at end; may be piped music; small garden, good walks *(Clare Phillips)*

Six Bells CM3 3JE [Main Rd (B1137)]: Well run dining pub with good value food cooked to order in comfortably opened-up bars and neat front restaurant, well kept Greene King and related ales, cheerful polite staff; play area in good-sized garden *(Paul and Ursula Randall, Justin and Emma King)*

BRENTWOOD [TQ5993]

Artichoke CM15 8DZ [Shenfield Common]: Large friendly Toby Carvery, interesting blow-ups of old postcards *(Robert Lester)*

BULMER TYE [TL8438]

Fox CO10 7EB [A131 S of Sudbury]: Well refurbished, with welcoming bustling staff, good range of food inc interesting dishes, Greene King IPA from small bar on left, pleasant conservatory; terrace tables *(Mrs P Lang, MDN, Oliver and Sue Rowell)*

CASTLE HEDINGHAM [TL7835]

☆ *Bell* CO9 3EJ [B1058]: Interesting beamed and timbered pub, unpretentious and well worn in, with galleried saloon, games in traditional bar, Adnams Best, Mighty Oak Maldon Gold and IPA and a guest beer, fairly priced pubby food; piped music, live Fri, trad jazz last Sun in month; children and dogs welcome (away from public bar), big informal garden with vine-covered terrace and children's toys, open all day Fri/Sat *(John Saville, G Dobson, LYM, Mrs Margo Finlay, Jörg Kasprowski)*

CHAPPEL [TL8928]

☆ *Swan* CO6 2DD [Wakes Colne; off A1124 Colchester—Halstead]: Spaciously rambling newly refurbished oak-beamed dining pub under new licensees (though keeping much of its former staff and popular menu), Greene King ales, good choice of other drinks; games machine, piped music; children away from bar, cobbled courtyard, view of Victorian viaduct from spreading garden by River Colne, open all day wknds *(LYM, Colin and Dot Savill)*

CHATHAM GREEN [TL7115]

Windmill CM3 3LE: Small hotel thriving under friendly new management, good value bar lunches in small beamed and flagstoned bar and dining room, Fullers London Pride and a Greene King beer labelled for them, reasonably priced wines by the glass, friendly service; a few picnic-sets, seven bedrooms *(Paul and Ursula Randall, Roy and Lindsey Fentiman)*

CHELMSFORD [TL7006]

☆ *Queens Head* CM2 0AS [Lower Anchor St]: Lively well run Victorian backstreet local with half a dozen or more interesting and well kept changing ales, summer farm cider, good value wines, friendly staff, winter log fires, bargain cheerful lunchtime food (not Sun) from separate counter; children welcome, colourful courtyard, open all day *(Joe Green, the Didler, PHB)*

Railway Tavern CM1 1LW [Duke St]: Small railway-theme pub with well kept ales inc Greene King Abbot, bargain freshly made simple lunchtime food, back seating area done like a railway carriage; pleasant garden behind *(Joe Green, PHB)*

CHIGNALL SMEALY [TL6711]

Pig & Whistle CM1 4SZ [NW of Chelmsford; Chignall Rd, just S of village]: Refurbished for new management, popular home-made food, traditional pub atmosphere with beams, soft lighting and pleasantly compact tables, well kept Shepherd Neame ales; no credit cards; children welcome, terrace tables with wide views *(Roy and Lindsey Fentiman, Paul and Ursula Randall)*

CHIGNALL ST JAMES [TL6709]

Three Elms CM1 4TZ: Friendly open-plan country dining pub with new chef/landlord doing good value straightforward food, changing ales such as Adnams, Fullers London Pride, St Austell Tribute and Woodfordes Wherry, monthly folk night last Mon *(Paul and Ursula Randall)*

CHIGWELL [TQ4493]

Olde Kings Head IG7 6QA [High Rd (A113)]: Large and handsome weatherboarded 17th-c pub, now a Chef & Brewer, with wide choice of sensibly priced food, quick friendly service, good choice of wines by the glass, real ales, some antique furnishings and interesting Dickens memorabilia (features in *Barnaby Rudge*), dark low-beamed décor, conservatory; piped music; children welcome, picnic-sets on attractive back terrace *(N R White, Robert Lester)*

COGGESHALL [TL8224]

☆ *Compasses* CM77 8BG [Pattiswick, signed off A120 W]: Attractively reworked as more country restaurant than pub, wide choice of good if not cheap food, keen attentive staff, neatly comfortable spacious beamed bars and barn restaurant; children welcome, plenty of lawn and orchard tables, rolling farmland beyond *(LYM, Mrs P Lang)*

Woolpack CO6 1UB [turn off main st opp Post Office and Barclays Bank]: Handsome timber-framed 15th-c inn opp church, nicely worn period lounge with big log fire, friendly chatty landlord, wide choice of interesting bar food, well kept Adnams; comfortable bedrooms *(PHB)*

COLCHESTER [TM9924]

Kings Arms CO3 3EY [Crouch St]: Simple bare-boards town pub with good changing ales, bargain food, daily papers; live music Thurs *(Ryta Lyndley)*

CRESSING [TL7920]

Willows CM77 8DQ: Pretty and popular, with good atmosphere in chatty locals' bar, good range of bar food, Adnams, Greene King and a guest beer, pleasant staff, lots of ornaments and knick-knacks, busy restaurant section, *(PHB)*

EAST HANNINGFIELD [TL7701]

Windmill CM3 8AA [The Tye]: Friendly L-shaped beamed bar, good standard food from baguettes to Sun roasts, well kept ales inc Crouch Vale, good prompt service, restaurant Thurs-Sat evenings and (must book) Sun lunch; plenty of tables out opp green (fairly busy road) *(George Atkinson)*

EPPING FOREST [TL4501]

Forest Gate CM16 4DZ [follow Ivy Chimneys signpost off]: Large open-plan pub dating from 17th c, good mix of customers, Adnams, Nethergate and guest beers, enjoyable home-made bar food; tables on front lawn *(the Didler)*

FEERING [TL8720]

☆ *Sun* CO5 9NH [Feering Hill, B1024]: Interesting old pub with 16th-c beams (watch out for the very low one over the inner entrance door), plenty of bric-a-brac, woodburners in huge inglenook fireplaces, nice carved bar counter with half a dozen well kept ales, efficient service, enjoyable food from sandwiches up, daily papers, board games; well behaved children allowed, partly covered paved terrace, attractive garden behind, some wknd barbecues *(LYM, the Didler, the Gray family, Matthew Shackle)*

FINCHINGFIELD [TL6832]

Red Lion CM7 4NN [Church Hill – B1053 just E of B1057 crossroads]: Beamed Tudor pub under new management, Adnams and Greene King ales, good value food inc enjoyable Sun roast, log fire in huge dividing chimney breast, recently refurbished dining room; attractive garden, bedrooms planned, nice spot opp churchyard and 15th-c guild hall, has been open all day *(anon)*

FINGRINGHOE [TM0220]

Whalebone CO5 7BG [off A134 just S of Colchester centre, or B1025]: Airy country-chic rooms with cream-painted tables on oak floors, Wells & Youngs Bombardier, Woodfordes Wherry and a guest beer, changing food choice with some interesting cooking (can be a long wait); TV, piped music, no children; charming back garden with peaceful valley view, front terrace, open all day wknds *(LYM, Dr and Mrs Michael Smith, Janelle Howell)*

FORDHAM HEATH [TL9426]

Cricketers CO3 9TG [Spring Ln]: Spruced up under new young manager, good choice of enjoyable rather upscale food, Greene King ales *(anon)*

FULLER STREET [TL7416]

Square & Compasses CM3 2BB [back rd Great Leighs—Hatfield Peverel]: Little country pub reopened after refurbishment, fresh local food from sandwiches up, choice of local ales and wines by the glass, big log fire in L-shaped beamed bar; unobtrusive piped music; gentle country views from tables outside *(Paul and Ursula Randall, LYM)*

FYFIELD [TL5707]

Black Bull CM5 0NN [Dunmow Rd (B184, N end)]: Traditional 15th-c pub with huge helpings of enjoyable food inc lots of fish and good steaks (ex-Smithfield chef), real ales such as Fullers London Pride and Greene King, friendly staff, heavy low beams and standing timbers in comfortably opened-up pubby bar and country-style dining area, open fire, traditional games; piped music, sports TV, games machine; tables out among flower tubs *(Jeremy King, LYM, Mrs Margo Finlay, Jörg Kasprowski, Marion and Bill Cross)*

GREAT BROMLEY [TM0923]

Snooty Fox CO7 7JW [Frating Rd (B1029)]: Welcoming beamed country pub with wide choice of good value fresh food inc interesting dishes (chef happy to talk things over), at least three real ales, good choice of wines by the glass, friendly service, leather sofas, separate dining area; good-sized garden *(Yana Pocklington, Patricia Owlett, Joan York)*

GREAT CHESTERFORD [TL5142]

Crown & Thistle CB10 1PL [just off M11 junction 9 (A11 exit roundabout); High St]: Gently upmarket pub/restaurant in affluent village, enjoyable if not cheap food inc home-baked bread and OAP bargains, friendly helpful landlord, range of wines by the glass, smartly served tea and coffee, well kept Greene King ales, log fire, well behaved children allowed, partly served tea and coffee, well kept Greene King ales, log fire, flowers, simple heavy furnishings on bare boards; Thurs quiz night; bedrooms *(Mrs Margo Finlay, Jörg Kasprowski, Roy Bromell)*

Plough CB10 1PL [off M11/A11 via B184; High St]: Busy beamed village pub, enjoyable food inc good value Sun lunch, Greene King ales, decent choice of wines by the glass, good coffee, pleasant staff, open fire; attractive garden, peaceful village *(Roy Bromell)*

GREAT SALING [TL7025]

☆ *White Hart* CM7 5DR [village signed from A120; The Street]: Friendly and distinctive Tudor pub with ancient beams, timbers and flooring tiles, lots of plates, brass and copperware, good reasonably priced food from speciality giant filled baps to fresh fish specialities, gallery restaurant, Greene King IPA and Abbot, decent wines, good service; well behaved children welcome, garden and terrace *(Roy and Lindsey Fentiman, LYM)*

GREAT TOTHAM [TL8613]

Compasses CM9 8BZ [Colchester Rd]: Appealing village pub with reasonably priced food from very long-serving cook, welcoming service *(Roy Hoing)*

GREAT WALTHAM [TL7013]

Rose & Crown CM3 1AG [about 0.75 mile from Ash Tree Corner, old A130/A131]: Friendly and comfortable little 16th-c local with well kept Fullers London Pride and changing ales from small breweries, cheerful and popular ex-farmer landlord, decent bar lunches; ghost said to use gents' *(Paul and Ursula Randall)*

GREAT WARLEY STREET [TQ5890]

Thatchers Arms CM13 3HU [Warley Rd]: Pretty beamed pub by village green, Greene King ales, varied decent food; may be piped music; tables on verandah and out behind *(Quentin and Carol Williamson)*

HARWICH [TM2632]

Alma CO12 3EE [Kings Head St]: Ancient seafarers' local now with upmarket dining area yet keeping its storm lamps, nauticalia, Greene King ales and friendly service; attractive back courtyard *(PHB)*

New Bell CO12 3EN [Outpart Eastward]: Small, bright and shiny traditional local, well kept ales inc Adnams, short menu inc choice of huffers and of enterprising soups, bargain crab salad, back dining lounge; tables on small terrace, open all day Sun in summer *(PHB)*

HATFIELD BROAD OAK [TL5416]

Dukes Head CM22 7HH [High St]: Comfortably reworked dining pub, wide food choice inc good fresh baguettes, good wines by the glass, well furnished conservatory; close to Hatfield Forest, and Stansted Airport *(Grahame Brooks)*

HATFIELD HEATH [TL5115]

Thatchers CM22 7DU [Stortford Rd (A1005)]: Olde-worlde beamed and thatched pub with good value fresh pubby food from sandwiches up, Greene King IPA and Wells & Youngs Bombardier from long counter, decent house wines, lovely log fire, copper kettles, jugs, brasses, plates and pictures in L-shaped bar, back dining area; no children in bar, may be piped music; at end of large green, tables out in front under cocktail parasols *(Mrs Margo Finlay, Jörg Kasprowski)*

HERONGATE [TQ6391]

Boars Head CM13 3PS [Billericay Rd, just off A128]: Picturesque low-beamed all-day dining pub with pleasant nooks and crannies, friendly staff, up to five changing real ales, reasonably priced wines; relaxing garden overlooking attractive reed-fringed pond with ducks, swans and moorhens *(Roy and Lindsey Fentiman, David Jackson)*

HEYBRIDGE BASIN [TL8706]

Old Ship CM9 4RX [Lockhill]: Now more restaurant than pub (friendly waitress service in the bar, drinkers may have to sit outside), with enjoyable home-made food inc breakfast all morning, pale wood chairs and tables, estuary views upstairs; dogs and children welcome, seats outside, some overlooking water by canal lock with lovely views of the saltings and across to Northey Island, open all day 8am-midnight *(David Jackson, John Wooll)*

KELVEDON [TL8518]

Angel CO5 9AN [St Marys Sq]: Doing well under newish chef/landlord, enjoyable food inc good value restaurant meals, good service, reasonably priced wines, well kept Courage Directors *(J B and M E Benson)*

LANGHAM [TM0232]

Shepherd & Dog CO4 5NR [Moor Rd/High St]: Chatty village pub decorated with entertaining miscellany of items, Greene King and Nethergate beers, wide choice of bar food inc curries; piped music; children and dogs welcome, enclosed side garden, open all day Sun *(Gill Brice, Gordon Prince, N R White, LYM)*

LEIGH-ON-SEA [TQ8385]

☆ *Crooked Billet* SS9 2EP [High St]: Homely old pub with waterfront views from big bay windows, well kept Adnams and two or three changing guest beers, good spring and autumn beer festivals, friendly attentive staff, basic pub food, log fires, beams, panelled dado and bare boards, local fishing pictures and bric-a-brac; piped music, jazz nights, no under-21s; open all day, side garden and terrace, seawall seating over road shared with Osbornes good shellfish stall (plastic glass if you drink outside); pay-and-display parking (free Sat/Sun) by fly-over *(LM, David Jackson, Andy and Jill Kassube, John and Enid Morris, LYM)*

LITTLE BADDOW [TL7807]

Generals Arms CM3 4SX [The Ridge; minor rd Hatfield Peverel—Danbury]: Roomily knocked through and airy, with friendly service, well kept Shepherd Neame, good range of pubby food from sandwiches up, reasonably priced wines; attractive terrace and good-sized back lawn with play area, good walks nearby *(LYM, John Saville)*

LITTLE DUNMOW [TL6521]

Flitch of Bacon CM6 3HT [off A120 E of Dunmow; The Street]: Informal country local, Fullers London Pride, Greene King IPA and a local Mild, enjoyable food from baguettes up (not Sun evening, and has been cl Mon lunchtime), simple and attractive small timbered bar kept spotless, flowery-cushioned pews and ochre walls, children welcome in back eating area; piped music; a few picnic-sets outside, peaceful views, bedrooms *(Paul Lucas, Joe Green, LYM)*

LITTLE TOTHAM [TL8811]

☆ *Swan* CM9 8LB [School Rd]: Country local with good changing range of real ales tapped from the cask such as Adnams, Crouch Vale, Mauldons and Mighty Oak, farm ciders and country wines, welcoming service, enjoyable straightforward food (not Sun evening), low 17th-c beams, coal fire, tiled games bar with darts and bar billiards, dining extension, Jun beer festival; children and dogs welcome, small terrace and picnic-sets under cocktail parasols on sizeable front lawn, open all day *(the Didler, Mrs Roxanne Chamberlain, Mrs M S Forbes)*

MALDON [TL8407]

☆ *Blue Boar* CM9 4QE [Silver St; car park round behind]: Quirky cross between coaching inn and antiques or auction showroom, most showy in the main building's lounge and dining room, interesting antique furnishings and pictures also in the separate smallish dark-timbered bar and its spectacular raftered upper room, good Farmers ales brewed at the back, Adnams and Crouch Vale too, enjoyable fresh food, friendly helpful staff; tables outside, open all day *(Pete Baker, Mrs Roxanne Chamberlain, LYM)*

Queens Head CM9 5HN [The Hythe]: Greene King IPA and Abbot, Mighty Oak Burntwood and Maldon Gold, good value standard food from good sandwiches up, friendly efficient staff, fresh and airy back lounge overlooking Thames barges on River Blackwater; good-sized quayside terrace *(Tony and Wendy Hobden, MDN)*

MARGARETTING [TL6701]
Black Bull CM4 9JA [Main Rd]: Friendly village local, neat and comfortable, with well kept Greene King IPA and Old Speckled Hen, popular usual food *(Mrs P J Pearce)*

MORETON [TL5307]
Nags Head CM5 0LF [signed off B184, at S end of Fyfield or opp Chipping Ongar school]: Cosy and friendly country pub with obliging new landlord, same chef doing good value food from tasty lunchtime sandwiches up, Greene King ales, three big log fires, comfortable mix of tables and medley of salvaged rustic beams and timbers, restaurant; children welcome, picnic-sets on side grass *(Roger and Pauline Pearce, Gordon Neighbour, Charles and Pauline Stride)*

MOUNT BURES [TL9031]
Thatchers Arms CO8 5AT: Bright country pub with good fresh food using local game and meats, midweek meal deals, well kept Adnams and local guest ales, good range of other drinks, friendly service, peaceful Stour valley views from dining room; dogs welcome, plenty of picnic-sets out on the grass, cl Mon, open all day wknds *(Sarah Mennell)*

NEWNEY GREEN [TL6506]
☆ **Duck** CM1 3SF [W of Chelmsford]: Attractive rambling dining bar, dark beams, timbering, panelling and interesting bric-a-brac, comfortable furnishings, enjoyable food inc good value lunches, well kept Shepherd Neame ales, decent wines by the glass, attentive service; pleasant terrace *(Paul and Ursula Randall, LYM)*

NORTH END [TL6617]
Butchers Arms CM6 3PJ [Dunmow Rd (A130 SE of Dunmow)]: Small attractively unpretentious 16th-c country pub with low beams, timbers, log fire and inglenook woodburner, Greene King ales, some emphasis on good value food (not Sun/Mon evenings), games room with pool; children welcome, sheltered garden and well equipped play area, open all day wknds *(Paul and Ursula Randall)*

NORTH FAMBRIDGE [TQ8596]
☆ **Ferry Boat** CM3 6LR [off B1012]: 15th-c flagstoned pub tucked prettily down by the marshes, friendly service, simple traditional furnishings, nautical memorabilia, log fire one end, woodburner the other, good value honest food from sandwiches to Sun lunches, well kept Greene King ales, traditional games, children in family room and low-beamed dining room; piped music, games machine, TV; garden with pond (ducks and carp), six comfortable bedrooms in separate block, good breakfast, good lonely walks *(LYM, LM)*

PAGLESHAM [TQ9492]
☆ **Plough & Sail** SS4 2EQ [East End]: Relaxed 17th-c dining pub in pretty spot, generally

good food from sandwiches through familiar favourites to interesting specials inc fresh fish, friendly attentive staff, well kept changing ales, decent house wines, low beams and big log fires, pine tables, lots of brasses and pictures, traditional games; unobtrusive piped music; attractive garden, open all day Sun *(Mrs Margo Finlay, Jörg Kasprowski, John Saville, Sean A Smith, LYM)*

RETTENDON [TQ7698]
Bell CM3 8DY [Main Rd]: Pleasantly smartened up, with good value food from sandwiches to good fish in beamed and carpeted lounge/dining area and popular separate restaurant, Fullers London Pride and Greene King ales *(George Atkinson)*

RIDGEWELL [TL7340]
White Horse CO9 4SG [Mill Rd (A1017 Haverhill—Halstead)]: Comfortable low-beamed village pub with good value range of well kept ales tapped from the cask and of generous food (changing bar and restaurant menus), friendly service, fireside sofa, no music; no dogs; terrace tables, bedroom block with good disabled access, open all day *(MLR)*

ROWHEDGE [TM0321]
Anchor CO5 7ES [off A134 just S of Colchester; High St]: Well kept Shepherd Neame ales, reasonably priced wines by the glass, good value substantial freshly made food, friendly attentive service, attractive flagstoned bar and pine furniture in nicely decorated tiled bistro, picture-window views over marshes and tidal River Colne with its swans, gulls and yachts; large waterside terrace, lovely lunchtime or summer evening setting *(George Atkinson, Mr and Mrs Brabants)*

ROXWELL [TL6508]
Hare CM1 4LU [Bishops Stortford Rd (A1060)]: Decent straightforward food cooked to order, Adnams, Courage Directors and Greene King IPA, cheerful staff, comfortably worn in beamed panelling-effect lounge, separate public bar, dining conservatory; piped music, small TV, games machine; children welcome, attractive garden with wendy house, swings and climber *(Paul and Ursula Randall, Reg Fowle, Helen Rickwood)*

SAFFRON WALDEN [TL5338]
Eight Bells CB10 1BU [Bridge St; B184 towards Cambridge]: Large pub with friendly young landlord, wide choice of enjoyable food, Adnams and Greene King IPA, linked rooms inc snug with leather chairs and flame-effect fire in big fireplace, carpeted back restaurant in handsomely raftered and timbered medieval hall, games room; children allowed, pleasant garden tables, handy for Audley End, good walks, open all day *(S Rowntree, LYM)*

STANSTED [TL5024]
Cock CM24 8HD [Silver St]: Refurbished in current dining pub style of unpretentious wooden furniture in bar and dining area, good choice of enjoyable bargain food nicely

served on modern china, friendly staff; garden with terrace tables *(Mrs Margo Finlay, Jörg Kasprowski)*

STISTED [TL7923]

☆ ***Dolphin*** CM77 8EU [A120 E of Braintree, by village turn]: Cheerful heavily beamed and timbered bar, good value straightforward food (not Tues or Sun evenings), chatty licensees, Greene King ales, log fire, bright eating area on left (children allowed); pretty garden, nice hanging baskets *(Ryta Lyndley, LYM, the Didler, Pete Baker)*

TENDRING [TM1523]

Cherry Tree CO16 9AP [Crow Lane, E of village centre]: Wide choice of enjoyable if not cheap home-made food, friendly efficient service, real ales such as Adnams and Black Sheep *(Sue Crees, Andrew Scarr)*

WALTHAM ABBEY [TQ4199]

Volunteer EN9 3QT [0.5 mile from M25 junction 26; A121 towards Loughton]: Roomy extensively refurbished family pub with reliable reasonably priced food, prompt friendly service, attractive conservatory, McMullens ales; piped music; some tables on side terrace, pretty hanging baskets, nice spot by Epping Forest *(BB, Nathaniel Catchpole)*

WENDENS AMBO [TL5136]

☆ ***Bell*** CB11 4JY [B1039 just W of village]: Small cottagey low-ceilinged pub with well kept Adnams, Woodfordes Wherry and changing ales, friendly service, bar food (not Sun/Mon evenings) from hearty baguettes up, good value coffee, open fire, ancient timbers, snug alcoves, quite a few pictures, cribbage and dominoes; piped music; children welcome in restaurant and family room, dogs in bar, lovely tree-sheltered garden with good play equipment, handy for Audley End, open all day Fri-Sun *(Mrs Margo Finlay, Jörg Kasprowski, LYM, Paul Humphreys, Andrew Scarr)*

WEST BERGHOLT [TL9528]

White Hart CO6 3DD [2 miles from Colchester on Sudbury rd]: Welcoming village pub, former old coaching inn, with good blackboard food choice inc plenty of fish and OAP lunches, Adnams ale, comfortable dining area; children welcome, big garden *(Tony and Shirley Albert)*

WIVENHOE [TM0321]

Black Buoy CO7 9BS [off A133]: Attractive open-plan partly timbered bar (16th-c behind the more recent façade), good cheerful service, wide choice of good generous food inc local fish, well kept ales inc Adnams and Greene King, good choice of wines by the glass, open fires, upper dining area glimpsing river over roofs; own parking (useful here), pleasant village *(Giles Barr, Eleanor Dandy, Charles Gysin, BB)*

Rose & Crown CO7 9BX [The Quay]: Unpretentious Georgian-faced pub on River Colne barge quay, low beams, lots of ship pictures, scrubbed floors and log fires, well kept Adnams Broadside with several guest beers, good house wines, wide choice of good value straightforward food all day from fresh baguettes up (next-door bakery), friendly young staff, local and nautical books and maps, no piped music; dogs welcome, lots of waterside picnic-sets, open all day Sun *(Mrs Jordan, BB)*

WRITTLE [TL6807]

Horse & Groom CM1 3RU [Roxwell Rd (A1060)]: Useful mock-Tudor Chef & Brewer family dining pub, well kept Adnams, decent wines, pleasant staff, spacious bar, big pine tables in good-sized all-day eating area, three log fires, evening candles; unobtrusive piped music; tables outside with country views *(Tina and David Woods-Taylor)*

Wheatsheaf CM1 3DU [The Green]: Friendly traditional two-room 19th-c local, well kept Greene King and Mighty Oak ales; terrace tables, open all day Fri-Sun *(the Didler)*

If a pub tries to make you leave a credit card behind the bar, be on your guard. The credit card firms and banks which issue them condemn this practice. After all, the publican who asks you to do this is in effect saying: 'I don't trust you'. Have you any more reason to trust his staff? If your card is used fraudulently while you have let it be kept out of your sight, the card company could say you've been negligent yourself – and refuse to make good your losses. So say that they can 'swipe' your card instead, but must hand it back to you. Please let us know if a pub does try to keep your card.

Gloucestershire

Although there's no doubt that this is a wealthy county which supports the high prices and good number of very smart dining pubs to be found here, there are some delightful, genuinely unspoilt places too. The new entries we have found this year might not exactly match this 'unspoilt' tag, but they do have a lot of character, and are run with great enthusiasm by hard-working licensees. These are the Bakers Arms in Broad Campden (a friendly village pub with traditional values and several real ales), the Tunnel House at Coates (fun and busy, and full of idiosyncratic knick-knacks), the Lamb at Great Rissington (rather civilised, with interesting things to look at and enjoyable food), the New Inn near North Nibley (doing well under its new owners, with a fine choice of real ales and ciders), and the Butchers Arms in a lovely spot at Sheepscombe (its friendly young licensees should do well, too). Other pubs doing especially well this year, generating particularly warm reports from readers, include the Bowl in Almondsbury (run by the same family for 25 years), the charming little Red Lion in Ampney St Peter (the very long-serving landlord and the wonderful atmosphere make it memorable), the Queens Arms in Ashleworth (consistently well run by the South African licensees), the Kings Head in Bledington (a good mix of villagers and visitors, and very popular as a place to stay), the Horse & Groom in Bourton-on-the-Hill (a super all-rounder), the Golden Heart near Brimpsfield (a lovely unchanging local), the Green Dragon near Cowley (a favourite with many readers), the Five Mile House at Duntisbourne Abbots (the licensees here are very special), the Old Spot in Dursley (up to ten real ales from all over the country), the Hollow Bottom at Guiting Power (lots of atmosphere and full of jockeys and trainers), the White Hart at Littleton-upon-Severn (new licensees this year, but still bustling and popular with enjoyable food), the Weighbridge in Nailsworth (their two-in-one pies are tremendous), the Ostrich in Newland (really friendly landlady, eight real ales and well liked food), the Anchor at Oldbury-on-Severn (the sort of place customers return to again and again), the Churchill Arms in Paxford (very well run by the helpful landlord), the Bell at Sapperton (another fantastic all-rounder), and the Ram in Woodchester (a lovely little country pub). In many of these, food is a major part of the appeal. Indeed, this area is exceptional for the number of pubs which offer outstanding meals. Those we'd particularly recommend for a special meal out are the Queens Arms in Ashleworth, the Village Pub in Barnsley, the Kings Head in Bledington, the Horse & Groom at Bourton-on-the-Hill, the Five Mile House at Duntisbourne Abbots, the Wild Duck at Ewen, the Inn for All Seasons at Little Barrington, the Fox at Lower Oddington (very much a dining pub, but with three ales as well), the Westcote Inn at Nether Westcote, the Churchill Arms at Paxford, the Bell at Sapperton, and the Horse & Groom at Upper Oddington. Our choice of Gloucestershire Dining Pub of the Year goes to the Horse & Groom at Bourton-on-the-Hill. Pubs and inns showing fine form recently in the Lucky Dip section at the end of the chapter include the Swan in Bibury, Twelve Bells in Cirencester, Yew Tree at Clifford's Mesne, Fossebridge Inn, Black Horse at Naunton, Fox at Old Down, Dog in Old Sodbury, Boat at Redbrook, Mount at Stanton, Eagle & Child and Queens Head in Stow-on-the-Wold, restauranty Gumstool near Tetbury and Plaisterers Arms in Winchcombe. Good news is that although a lot of pubs in the county were quite badly affected by the 2007 floods, almost all of these have been firmly back on track for quite some time now. Gloucestershire has a flourishing set of independent brewers, led by Donnington (probably Britain's prettiest brewery, still using its ancient watermill, as it has since the 19th century), Wickwar, Uley and Goffs. Other local brews we found in quite a few of the area's good pubs are Stroud, Cotswold Spring, Nailsworth, Festival, Stanway, Battledown and Freeminer.

ALMONDSBURY   ST6084   MAP 2

Bowl

1.25 miles from M5 junction 16 (and therefore quite handy for M4 junction 20); from A38 towards Thornbury, turn left signposted Lower Almondsbury, then first right down Sundays Hill, then at bottom right again into Church Road; BS32 4DT

Bustling pub handy for the M5; quite a few real ales and fairly priced food

In the same family for over 25 years, this friendly, cheerful pub always has a good mix of locals and visitors. The long beamed bar is neatly kept, with traditional settles, cushioned stools and mate's chairs around elm tables, horsebrasses on stripped bare stone walls and a big winter log fire at one end with a woodburning stove at the other. A fine choice of seven real ales on handpump might include Bass, Butcombe Bitter, Cotswold Spring Codrington Codger, Courage Best, an ale from Moles and a couple of guests; piped music. This is a pretty setting with the church next door and lovely flowering tubs, hanging baskets and window boxes. You will be asked to leave your credit card behind the bar.

🍴 **Quite a choice of bar food such as fresh baked filled baguettes and club sandwiches, chargrilled chicken with pancetta, avocado and parmesan caesar salad, macaroni cheese with garlic bread, beer-battered pollock and chips, beef and mushroom lasagne, chilli con carne, oriental duck noodles, dry-aged steaks and puddings like sticky date and walnut pudding with fudge sauce and lemon thyme cheesecake with lemon syrup.** *Starters/Snacks: £5.25 to £7.95. Main Courses: £7.95 to £19.95. Puddings: £4.95*

Free house ~ Licensee Mrs J Stephenson ~ Real ale ~ Bar food (12-2, 7-9; all day weekends) ~ Restaurant ~ (01454) 612757 ~ Children welcome ~ Open 11.30-3, 5-11; 12-11(10.30 Sun) Sat; closed 25 Dec ~ Bedrooms: £51.50S/£79S

Recommended by Donna and Roger, Gerry and Rosemary Dobson, Bob and Margaret Holder, Bruce and Sharon Eden, WAH, Dr and Mrs A K Clarke, Bob and Angela Brooks, Ellen Weld, David London

---

AMPNEY ST PETER   SP0801   MAP 4

Red Lion 🍺

A417, E of village; GL7 5SL

Friendly long-serving landlord in charmingly unspoilt little pub; note the limited opening hours

---

Held dear in the hearts of many of our readers, this smashing little place remains quite unchanged and unspoilt. It's run by a very friendly, long-serving landlord and there's always a chatty group of customers who will draw you into conversation. A central corridor, served by a hatch, gives on to the little right-hand tile-floor public bar. This has just one table, a wall seat, and one long bench facing a small open fire. Behind this bench is an open servery (no counter, just shelves of bottles and – by the corridor hatch – handpumps for the well kept Hook Norton Best plus weekend guest like Timothy Taylors Landlord; reasonably priced wine. There are old prints on the wall, and on the other side of the corridor is a small saloon with panelled wall seats around its single table, old local photographs, another open fire, and a print of Queen Victoria one could believe hasn't moved for a century – rather like the pub itself. The side garden has some seats. Please note the limited opening hours.

🍽 **No food at all.**

Free house ~ Licensee John Barnard ~ Real ale ~ No credit cards ~ (01285) 851596 ~ Children and dogs in the tiny games room ~ Open 6-10; 12-2, 7-10 Sun; closed lunchtimes except Sun

Recommended by the Didler, Ray J Carter, Giles and Annie Francis, Donna and Roger, E McCall, T McLean, D Irving, K Turner

ASHLEWORTH   SO8125   MAP 4

Queens Arms 🍽 ♈ 🍺
Village signposted off A417 at Hartpury; GL19 4HT

Neatly kept pub with civilised main bar, interesting food, thoughtful wines and ales, and sunny courtyard

You can be sure of a warm welcome from the friendly South African licensees in this spotless, low-beamed dining pub. It remains consistently well run and the comfortably laid out and civilised main bar has faintly patterned wallpaper and washed red ochre walls, big oak and mahogany tables and a nice mix of farmhouse and big brocaded dining chairs on a green carpet; at night it is softly lit by fringed wall lamps and candles. Brains Reverend James, Fullers London Pride and Timothy Taylors Landlord on handpump, 14 wines by the glass from a thoughtful wine list (including south african choices), and 22 malt whiskies; maybe summer home-made lemonade or winter mulled wine. Piped music, board games and (by arrangement) a skittle alley; the little black pub cat is called Bonnie and still entertains customers with her ping pong ball. Two perfectly clipped mushroom shaped yews dominate the front of the building. There are cast-iron tables and chairs in the sunny courtyard.

🍽 **Good and very popular bar food includes lunchtime filled baguettes, a pasta of the day, sausage, bacon, fried egg and mushrooms, greek or niçoise salads and grilled salmon with cherry tomatoes and thyme, plus interesting soups, deep-fried brie and stilton croquettes with cranberry sauce, sherried kidneys, steak and kidney pie, gammon with black cherries and crispy duck with orange sauce and daily specials like chicken satay kebab with peanut sauce, bobotie (a south african dish with spiced beef, savoury egg-custard, almonds and raisins), roast local partridge wrapped in bacon with a fresh sage and port sauce and black dory fillets on roasted butternut squash and sweet potato drizzled with a curry and raisin oil; puddings such as raspberry crème brûlée and cape brandy pudding.**
Starters/Snacks: £4.95 to £8.95. Main Courses: £7.75 to £21.95. Puddings: £4.95 to £5.50

Free house ~ Licensees Tony and Gill Burreddu ~ Real ale ~ Bar food (not Sun evening) ~ Restaurant ~ (01452) 700395 ~ Well-behaved children allowed ~ Open 12-3, 7-11; 12-3 Sun; closed Sun evening; 25 and 26 Dec

Recommended by Theocsbrian, Dave Kenward, J Crosby, Dr A J and Mrs Tompsett, Dr and Mrs C W Thomas, Mrs Jill Wyatt, Bernard Stradling, Paul Gavaghan, John and Helen Rushton, Michael Dallas, Kim Merrifield, Denys Gueroult, Tony and Tracy Constance

---

Please tell us if the décor, atmosphere, food or drink at a pub is different from our description. We rely on readers' reports to keep us up to date: feedback@thegoodpubguide.co.uk or (no stamp needed) The Good Pub Guide, FREEPOST TN1569, Wadhurst, E Sussex TN5 7BR.

ASHLEWORTH QUAY

SO8125   MAP 4

Boat ★ ◀

Ashleworth signposted off A417 N of Gloucester; quay signed from village; GL19 4HZ

Delightful and unchanging Severn-side pub with swiftly changing beers – and in the same family for hundreds of years

Renovated after the floods, this quaint and unpretentious pub still remains a special place – it's been in the same family since it was originally granted a licence by Charles II. The little front parlour has a built-in settle by a long scrubbed deal table that faces an old-fashioned open kitchen range with a side bread oven and a couple of elderly fireside chairs; there are rush mats on the scrubbed flagstones, houseplants in the window, fresh garden flowers, and old magazines to read; cribbage and dominoes in the front room. Two antique settles face each other in the back room where up to six swiftly changing beers such as Church End Gravediggers Fallen Angel and Mild, Hook Norton Hooky Gold, Slaters Top Totty, Stonehenge Pigswill and Wye Valley Butty Bach are tapped from the cask, along with a full range of Weston's farm ciders. The front suntrap crazy-paved courtyard is bright with plant tubs in summer, with a couple of picnic-sets under cocktail parasols; there are more seats and tables under cover at the sides.

🍽 **Lunchtime filled rolls as well as coffee, cakes and ice-cream.** *Starters/Snacks: £2.10*

Free house ~ Licensees Ron, Elisabeth and Louise Nicholls ~ Real ale ~ Bar food (lunchtime only; not Mon and Weds) ~ No credit cards ~ (01452) 700272 ~ Children welcome ~ Open 11.30-2.30(3 Sat), 6.30-11; 12-3, 7-11 Sun; evening opening 7 in winter; closed all day Mon, Weds lunchtime

Recommended by Pete Baker, Keith and Sue Ward, the Didler, Matthew Shackle, Dr W J M Gissane, Edna Jones, Theocsbrian, Phil and Sally Gorton

BARNSLEY

SP0705   MAP 4

Village Pub 🍴 ☖

B4425 Cirencester—Burford; GL7 5EF

Good mix of customers in civilised communicating rooms, candles and newspapers, and enjoyable food; comfortable bedrooms

Although most customers come to this smart, civilised country pub to enjoy the contemporary food, those popping in for a drink and chat (with or without their dogs) are made just as welcome. There's a good mix of customers, and the low-ceilinged communicating rooms have flagstones and oak floorboards, oil paintings, plush chairs, stools, and window settles around polished candlelit tables, three open fireplaces and country magazines and newspapers to read. Butcombe Bitter, Hook Norton Old Hooky, and St Austells Tribute on handpump, and an extensive wine list with over a dozen by the glass. The sheltered back courtyard has plenty of good solid wooden furniture under umbrellas, outdoor heaters and its own outside servery. More reports please.

🍽 **Good, modern food includes soup, salad of duck breast, chicory, lardons, mustard dressing and soft duck egg, chicken liver and foie gras parfait with pear chutney, mussels with chorizo and paprika cream sauce, linguine with sweet tomato, ricotta, olives and basil sauce, braised pork belly with spinach, lentils and red wine sauce, grilled brochette of lamb, crushed potatoes, field mushrooms, rocket and pesto, poached turbot with brown shrimps, chopped egg and garlic cream sauce, and puddings such as chocolate and caramel tart with mascarpone and honey bavarois with red wine poached pear.** *Starters/Snacks: £4.50 to £8.50. Main Courses: £10.50 to £16.50. Puddings: £6.50*

Free house ~ Licensees Tim Haigh and Rupert Pendered ~ Real ale ~ Bar food (12-2.30(3 Fri-Sun), 7-9.30(10 Fri and Sat)) ~ Restaurant ~ (01285) 740421 ~ Well-behaved children welcome ~ Dogs welcome ~ Open 11-3, 6-11.30; 11-11.30 Sat; 11-10.30 Sun ~ Bedrooms: £75S/£110B

Recommended by J Crosby, Mrs P Lang, Martin Lee, Graham Oddey, Derek Thomas, Charles Gysin, E McCall, T McLean, D Irving

BISLEY   SO9006   MAP 4

Bear ◀

Village signposted off A419 just E of Stroud; GL6 7BD

Friendly 16th-c inn with decent food and beer, and garden across quiet road

New licensees again for this elegantly gothic 16th-c inn. The meandering L-shaped bar
has a friendly, bustling atmosphere, a long shiny black built-in settle and a smaller but
even sturdier oak settle by the front entrance, and an enormously wide low stone
fireplace (not very high – the ochre ceiling's too low for that); the separate stripped-
stone area is used for families. Greene King Old Speckled Hen, Tetleys and Wells & Youngs
Bombardier on handpump; darts and board games. A small front colonnade supports the
upper floor of the pub, and the sheltered little flagstoned courtyard made by this has a
traditional bench. The garden is across the quiet road, and there's quite a collection of
stone mounting-blocks. The steep stone-built village is attractive. More reports please.

🍴 **Bar food includes filled baguettes, soup, creamy garlic mushrooms, mixed nut and lentil
loaf with fresh tomato sauce, home-baked ham with egg, lasagne, stilton chicken with a
port and cranberry sauce, steak and kidney pie, salmon fillet with a cream and chive sauce
and steaks.** *Starters/Snacks: £3.75 to £5.95. Main Courses: £7.95 to £13.95. Puddings: £3.75*

Punch ~ Lease Colin and Jane Pickford ~ Real ale ~ Bar food (12-2(3 weekends), 6-9) ~
(01452) 770265 ~ Children in own room ~ Dogs allowed in bar ~ Open 12-3, 6-11;
12-12 Sat and Sun ~ Bedrooms: £45S/£65S

*Recommended by Guy Vowles, Brian and Rosalie Laverick, Brian McBurnie, David Morgan, Evelyn and Derek Walter,
Paul and Shirley White, Nick and Meriel Cox*

BLAISDON   SO7016   MAP 4

Red Hart ◀

*Village signposted off A4136 just SW of junction with A40 W of Gloucester; OS Sheet 162
map reference 703169; GL17 0AH*

**Relaxed and friendly, some interesting bric-a-brac in attractive rooms, and several real
ales**

This is a bustling and friendly pub in a quiet, tucked away village with a fair choice of
real ales on handpump: Fullers London Pride, Harviestoun Bitter & Twisted, Hook Norton
Hooky Bitter, RCH Pitchfork, and Shepherd Neame Spitfire. The flagstoned main bar has
cushioned wall and window seats, traditional pub tables, a big sailing-ship painting
above the log fire and a thoroughly relaxing atmosphere – helped along by well
reproduced piped bluesy music and maybe Spotty the jack russell (who is now twelve).
On the right, there's an attractive, beamed restaurant with some interesting prints and
bric-a-brac, and on the left, you'll find additional dining space for families; board games
and table skittles. There are some picnic-sets in the garden and a children's play area,
and at the back of the building is a terrace for barbecues. The little church above the
village is worth a visit. More reports please.

🍴 **Bar food includes open ciabattas, soup, ham and egg with bubble and squeak, salmon
and coriander fishcakes, steak in ale pie and daily specials such as rump of lamb with red
wine and rosemary sauce, monkfish wrapped in parma ham with spinach, pork belly with
black pudding and pea and mint mash, and puddings.** *Starters/Snacks: £3.95 to £10.00. Main
Courses: £5.95 to £14.00. Puddings: £3.95*

Free house ~ Licensee Guy Wilkins ~ Real ale ~ Bar food ~ Restaurant ~ (01452) 830477 ~
Children allowed but must be well behaved ~ Dogs welcome ~ Open 12-3, 6(7 Sun)-11

*Recommended by Paul and Sue Merrick, Susan and Nigel Brookes, Neil and Anita Christopher, Mr and
Mrs A J Hudson, John and Tania Wood, Dave Braisted, MLR*

Pubs brewing their own beers are listed at the back of the book.

BLEDINGTON   SP2422   MAP 4

Kings Head 🍴 ⏷ 🍺 🛏

B4450; OX7 6XQ

Beams and atmospheric furnishings in rather smart old place, super wines by the glass, interesting food, and comfortable bedrooms

Although there is quite an emphasis on the interesting food and comfortable bedrooms in this rather smart 500-year-old inn, it's still popular with villagers popping in for a drink. The main bar is full of ancient beams and other atmospheric furnishings (high-backed wooden settles, gateleg or pedestal tables) and there's a warming log fire in the stone inglenook where there are bellows and a big black kettle; sporting memorabilia of rugby, racing, cricket and hunting. To the left of the bar a drinking space for locals has benches on the wooden floor and a woodburning stove. Hook Norton Best and guests such as Ballards Trotton Bitter, Hook Norton Best, Purity Pure Ubu and Wye Valley Bitter on handpump, an excellent wine list with ten by the glass, 20 malt whiskies and interesting bottled ciders; piped music and darts. There are seats at the front and in the back courtyard garden, and the pub is set back from the village green where there are usually ducks pottering about.

🍽 **Good, popular bar food includes lunchtime sandwiches and ploughman's, locally smoked trout and salmon pâté, devilled lambs kidneys with mushrooms and fried bread, free-range rosemary-baked chicken caesar salad, haddock and crayfish pie, spinach, gruyère and chive fritters with pepper marmalade, steak in ale pie, lamb cutlets with mustard and onion rösti and red wine jus and puddings such as toffee, chocolate and banana pie and rhubarb and custard cheesecake.** *Starters/Snacks: £4.50 to £7.95. Main Courses: £9.95 to £16.00. Puddings: £5.50*

Free house ~ Licensees Nicola and Archie Orr-Ewing ~ Real ale ~ Bar food ~ Restaurant ~ (01608) 658365 ~ Children allowed but away from bar area ~ Dogs allowed in bar ~ Open 11.30-3, 6-11; 11.30-11 Sat; 12-11 Sun; closed 25 and 26 Dec ~ Bedrooms: £55B/£70B

Recommended by Paul and Marion Watts, Fred and Kate Portnell, Myra Joyce, Richard Greaves, Mr and Mrs J Brown, John and Jackie Chalcraft, M and GR, Di and Mike Gillam, Derek Thomas, Lynda and Roy Mills, Simon Fox, Graham Oddey, Noel Grundy, Paul Humphreys, Mr and Mrs A J Hudson, Bernard Stradling

BOURTON-ON-THE-HILL   SP1732   MAP 4

Horse & Groom 🍴 ⏷ 🛏

A44 W of Moreton-in-Marsh; GL56 9AQ

GLOUCESTERSHIRE DINING PUB OF THE YEAR

Georgian inn with a relaxed, friendly atmosphere, super food, thoughtful choice of drinks, and fine views from seats outside; comfortable bedrooms

With a friendly welcome, delicious food and a fine choice of drinks, this honey-coloured stone inn is much enjoyed by our readers. There are plenty of original period features and the light and airy bar has a nice mix of wooden chairs and tables on bare boards, stripped stone walls, and a good log fire. Goffs Cheltenham Gold, Purity Pure Gold and a changing beer from Wye Valley on handpump, 14 wines including fizz by the glass, a local wheat beer and local lager and organic juices. Plenty of seats under smart umbrellas in the large back garden for eating and drinking, and lovely views over the surrounding countryside. The stylish bedrooms have been refurbished this year. It's best to get here early to be sure of a space in the smallish car park.

🍽 **Using their own free-range eggs and home-grown vegetables and local meat, the contemporary food might include interesting soups, warm terrine of braised shin with celeriac remoulade, sautéed mushrooms on toast with a poached egg and béarnaise sauce, beef pasty with onion gravy, gruyère stuffed chicken breast, prosciutto and braised leeks, roasted hake with lemon, anchovy and rosemary crust and shallot butter sauce, lamb and apricot tagine with lemon and spring onion couscous, and puddings such as chocolate nemesis and spiced pear and apple flapjack crumble.** *Starters/Snacks: £4.50 to £8.00. Main Courses: £10.00 to £16.50. Puddings: £4.50 to £6.00*

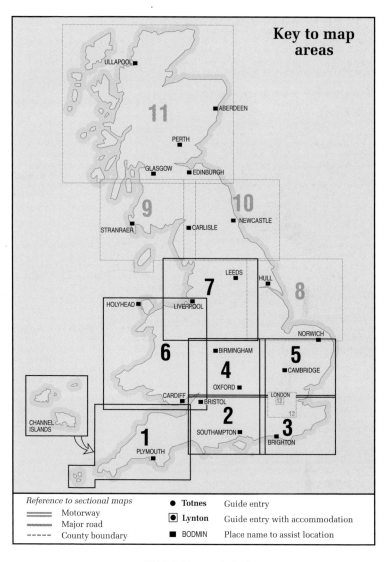

Key to map areas

ULLAPOOL

11

ABERDEEN

PERTH

GLASGOW EDINBURGH

9 **10**

NEWCASTLE

STRANRAER CARLISLE

LEEDS HULL

7 **8**

HOLYHEAD LIVERPOOL

6 BIRMINGHAM **5**

4 CAMBRIDGE

OXFORD

CARDIFF LONDON

BRISTOL **13**

2 **12**

CHANNEL ISLANDS

1 SOUTHAMPTON **3**

PLYMOUTH BRIGHTON

Reference to sectional maps

▬▬▬ Motorway
▬▬▬ Major road
----- County boundary

● **Totnes** Guide entry
◉ **Lynton** Guide entry with accommodation
■ BODMIN Place name to assist location

MAPS IN THIS SECTION

1

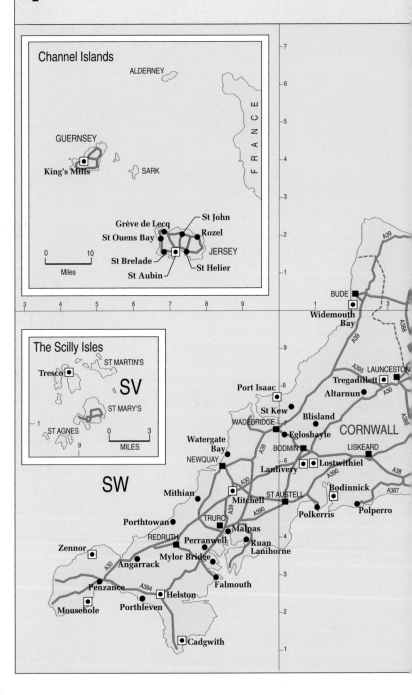

Channel Islands

ALDERNEY

GUERNSEY
King's Mills

SARK

FRANCE

Grève de Lecq
St John
St Ouens Bay
Rozel
St Brelade
JERSEY
St Helier
St Aubin

0   10
Miles

The Scilly Isles

ST MARTIN'S
Tresco
ST MARY'S
SV
ST AGNES

0   3
MILES

SW

BUDE
Widemouth Bay

LAUNCESTON
Tregadillett
Altarnun

Port Isaac
St Kew
Blisland
CORNWALL
WADEBRIDGE
Egloshayle
BODMIN
LISKEARD

Watergate Bay
NEWQUAY
Lanlivery
Lostwithiel
Bodinnick
Polperro

Mithian
Mitchell
ST AUSTELL
Polkerris

Porthtowan
TRURO
Malpas

Zennor
REDRUTH
Perranwell
Ruan Lanihorne
Mylor Bridge

Angarrack
Falmouth

Penzance
Helston

Mousehole
Porthleven

Cadgwith

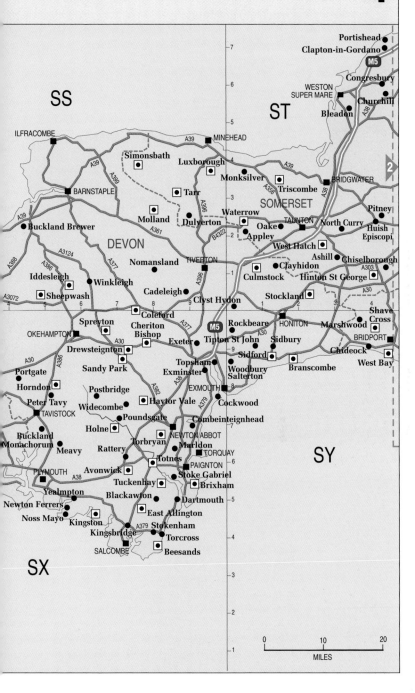

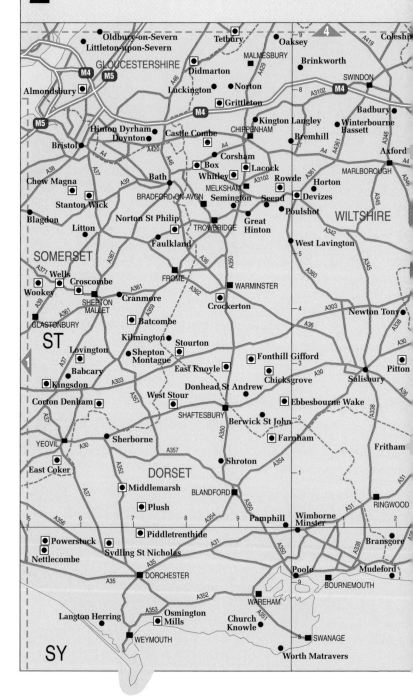

Oldbury-on-Severn
Littleton-upon-Severn
Tetbury
Oaksey
Coleshir
GLOUCESTERSHIRE
MALMESBURY
Brinkworth
Almondsbury
Didmarton
SWINDON
M4 M5
Luckington
Norton
Badbury
M5
Grittleton
Kington Langley
Winterbourne Bassett
Hinton Dyrham
Castle Combe
CHIPPENHAM
Bremhill
Axford
Doynton
Bristol
Corsham
Marlborough
Chew Magna
Box
Lacock
Rowde
Horton
Bath
Whitley
MELKSHAM
Devizes
Stanton Wick
BRADFORD-ON-AVON
Semington
Seend
WILTSHIRE
Blagdon
Norton St Philip
Great Hinton
Poulshot
Litton
TROWBRIDGE
SOMERSET
Faulkland
West Lavington
Wells
Croscombe
FROME
Wookey
Cranmore
WARMINSTER
SHEPTON MALLET
Crockerton
GLASTONBURY
Newton Tony
ST
Batcombe
Kilmington
Lovington
Stourton
Fonthill Gifford
Shepton Montague
Pitton
Babcary
East Knoyle
Chicksgrove
Salisbury
Kingsdon
Donhead St Andrew
Corton Denham
West Stour
Ebbesbourne Wake
SHAFTESBURY
YEOVIL
Berwick St John
Fritham
Sherborne
Farnham
East Coker
DORSET
Shroton
Middlemarsh
BLANDFORD
RINGWOOD
Plush
Pamphill
Wimborne Minster
Powerstock
Piddletrenthide
Bransgore
Nettlecombe
Sydling St Nicholas
Poole
Mudeford
DORCHESTER
BOURNEMOUTH
WAREHAM
Langton Herring
Osmington Mills
Church Knowle
SWANAGE
WEYMOUTH
SY
Worth Matravers

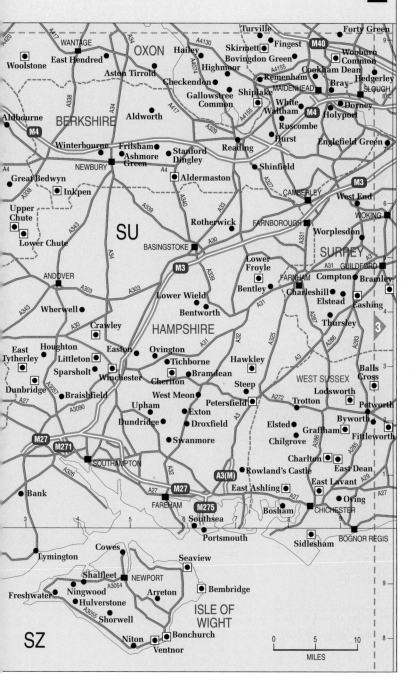

2

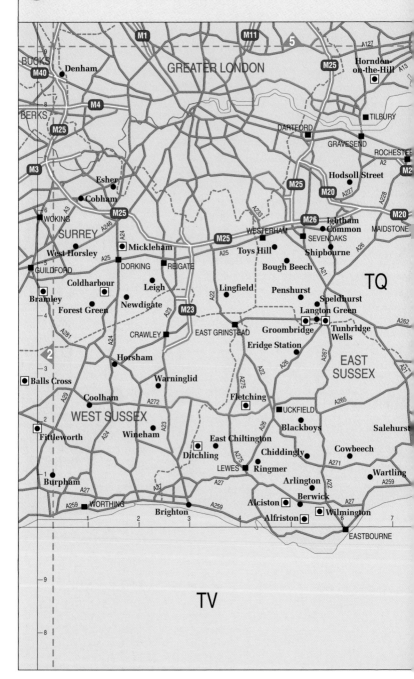

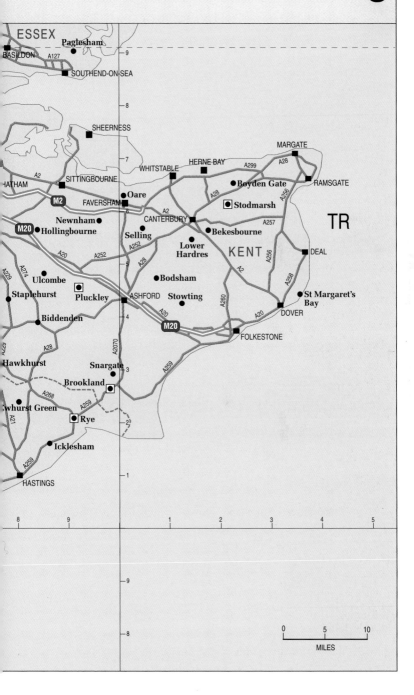

3

ESSEX
BASILDON Paglesham
A127
SOUTHEND-ON-SEA

SHEERNESS

MARGATE

HERNE BAY A299 A28
WHITSTABLE A28 RAMSGATE

CHATHAM SITTINGBOURNE Boyden Gate
A2 FAVERSHAM Oare A28 Stodmarsh
M2 6 A2 A256
Newnham CANTERBURY TR
M20 Hollingbourne Selling Bekesbourne A257
A20 A252 A252 Lower KENT DEAL
A274 A28 Hardres A256
Ulcombe 5 A2 A258
Staplehurst Bodsham St Margaret's
A229 Pluckley ASHFORD Stowting A260 Bay
Biddenden 4 A20 DOVER
A229 A28 M20 FOLKESTONE
Hawkhurst Snargate 3 A2070 A259
Brookland
A268
whurst Green A259
A21 Rye 2
Icklesham
A259
HASTINGS 1

8   9   1   2   3   4   5

                    9

                    8

0   5   10
MILES

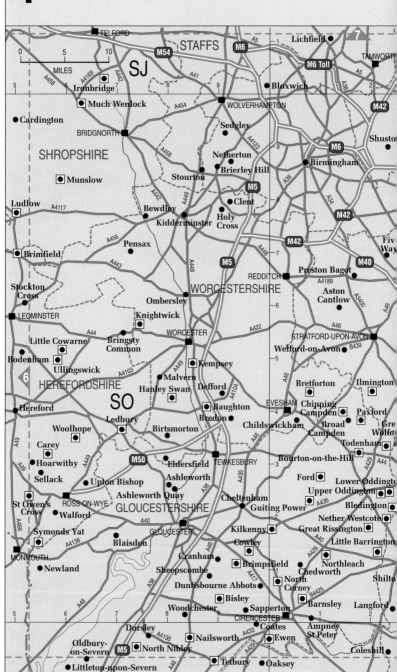

4

STAFFS

TELFORD ■

M54

M6

M6 Toll

Lichfield ●

TAMWORTI

SJ

A41

A5

A5

A458

A4169

A442

Ironbridge ●

Bloxwich ●

A38

M42

A454

Much Wenlock ●

WOLVERHAMPTON ■

● Cardington

BRIDGNORTH ■

Sedgley ●

A4123

M6

Shusto

SHROPSHIRE

A458

Netherton ●

Birmingham ●

Munslow ●

Stourton ●

Brierley Hill ●

M5

A38

M42

Bewdley ●

A442

A449

Clent ●

Holy
Cross

A34

Ludlow
●

A4117

Kidderminster ●

M42

Brimfield ●

A456

Pensax ●

A449

M5

Fiv
Way

A443

A4189

M40

Stockton
Cross

REDDITCH ■

Preston Bagot ●

WORCESTERSHIRE

A3400

LEOMINSTER ■

Ombersley ●

Aston
Cantlow ●

A46

Little Cowarne ●

A44

Knightwick ●

Bringsty
Common ●

WORCESTER ■

A422

A46

STRATFORD-UPON-AVON ■

Bodenham ●

Ullingswick ●

A4103

Kempsey ●

Welford-on-Avon ●

B439

HEREFORDSHIRE

SO

Malvern ●

Defford ●

A4104

Bretforton ●

Ilmington ●

Hanley Swan ●

EVESHAM ■

Hereford ●

Ledbury ●

Baughton ●

Chipping
Campden ●

Paxford ●

Woolhope ●

Birtsmorton ●

Bredon ●

Childswickham ●

Broad
Campden ●

Gre
Wolfo

Carey ●

A449

M50

Eldersfield ●

TEWKESBURY ■

Todenham ●

Hoarwithy ●

Ashleworth ●

A44

A429

Sellack ●

Upton Bishop ●

Ashleworth Quay ●

A435

Bourton-on-the-Hill ●

St Owen's
Cross ●

ROSS-ON-WYE ■

GLOUCESTERSHIRE

A38

Cheltenham ●

Ford ●

Lower Oddingto
Upper Oddington ●

Walford ●

A40

Guiting Power ●

A436

Bledington ●

A466

Symonds Yat ●

GLOUCESTER ■

Kilkenny ●

Nether Westcote ●

Great Rissington ●

MONMOUTH ■

A4136

Blaisdon ●

Cowley ●

A40

A429

Little Barrington ●

Newland ●

A38

Cranham ●

Brimpsfield ●

Chedworth ●

Northleach ●

Sheepscombe ●

North
Cerney ●

Shilto

Duntisbourne Abbots ●

A417

B4425

Bisley ●

Barnsley ●

Langford

Woodchester ●

Sapperton ●

CIRENCESTER ■

M5

Dorsley ●

A4135

Nailsworth ●

A433

Coates ●

Ampney
St Peter ●

Oldbury-
on-Severn ●

North Nibley ●

A429

Ewen ●

Coleshill ●

Littleton-upon-Severn ●

A46

Tetbury ●

Oaksey ●

0   5   10
MILES

A458

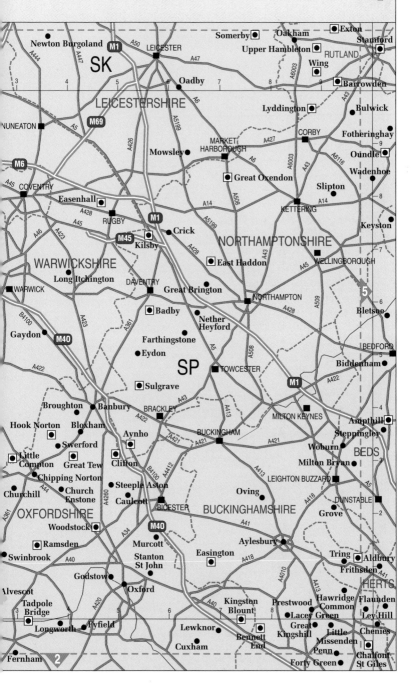

Newton Burgoland **M1** A50 LEICESTER A47

Somerby ● Oakham ● Exton ●
Stamford

Upper Hambleton ● RUTLAND

Wing ●

SK

M6 NUNEATON A5

M69

M6

A45 COVENTRY

Easenhall ●
A428
RUGBY
M45 Kilsby
Crick ●

M1

Oadby ● A6 7 8 9 Barrowden ●

LEICESTERSHIRE A6

Lyddington ● Bulwick ●

MARKET A427 CORBY Fotheringhay ●
Mowsley ● HARBOROUGH A6003 A43 Oundle ●
A426 A6 A43 Wadenhoe ●
● Great Oxendon A6116
A508 Slipton ●
A14 KETTERING A14 — 8

A5199 NORTHAMPTONSHIRE Keyston ●

● East Haddon A43 A45 WELLINGBOROUGH — 7

WARWICKSHIRE A428 A509 — 6
Long Itchington DAVENTRY Great Brington ● NORTHAMPTON Bletsoe ●

WARWICK ● Badby ● A428
A361 Nether A508 BEDFORD — 5
A423 Heyford
Gaydon ● **M40** Farthingstone ● A5 Biddenham ●
A422 ● Eydon SP ■ TOWCESTER
M1 A422 — 4
● Sulgrave A43
A413
Broughton ● Banbury ● BRACKLEY MILTON KEYNES Ampthill ●
Hook Norton ● Bloxham ● A422 BUCKINGHAM A421 Steppingley ●
● Aynho A421 A421 Woburn ● BEDS
● Swerford Clifton ● A413 Milton Bryan ●
● Little B4100 A4412 LEIGHTON BUZZARD ■
Compton Great Tew ● A5
Chipping Norton ● Steeple Aston ● Oving ● A418
Churchill ● Church A260 Caulcott ● BICESTER DUNSTABLE — 2
Enstone BUCKINGHAMSHIRE Grove ●
OXFORDSHIRE Woodstock ● **M40** A41
Ramsden ● A34 Aylesbury ● Tring ● Aldbury ●
Swinbrook ● A40 Murcott ● Frithsden ● A41
Stanton A418 HERTS
Godstow ● St John A413 Hawridge
Alvescot ● A420 A40 Kingston Prestwood ● Common Flaunden ●
Tadpole Oxford ● Blount ● ● Lacey Green Ley Hill ●
Bridge Lewknor ● Great
Longworth ● ● Fyfield Kingshill Little Chenies ●
Cuxham ● Bennett Missenden Chalfont
Fernham ● 2 End Penn ● St Giles ●
Forty Green ●

5

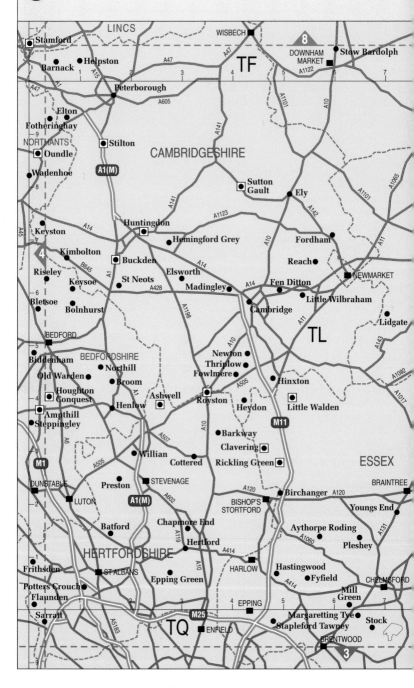

LINCS

WISBECH

☐ Stamford

TF

8

DOWNHAM
MARKET • Stow Bardolph

A47
A47

Barnack • Helpston

A15

A1122

A1101

A10

Peterborough

A605

A141

Elton

A101

NORTHANTS

Fotheringhay

• Stilton

CAMBRIDGESHIRE

☐ Oundle

A1(M)

• Wadenhoe

• Sutton
Gault

• Ely

A142

A1101

A1123

A14 • Keyston

Huntingdon

• Hemingford Grey

• Fordham

A10

4

• Kimbolton

☐ Buckden

Reach •

A11

NEWMARKET

Riseley •

B645

Elsworth

• Keysoe

• St Neots

A14

• Fen Ditton

• Madingley

• Little Wilbraham

• Bletsoe

A428

A1198

• Cambridge

A11

• Bolnhurst

TL

• Lidgate

A143

BEDFORD

A10

BEDFORDSHIRE

• Newton •

A1092

• Biddenham

• Northill

• Thriplow

A1017

• Old Warden

• Broom

Fowlmere •

• Houghton
Conquest

A1

Ashwell

Royston

• Hinxton

• Henlow

Heydon •

• Little Walden

• Ampthill

M11

• Steppingley

A6

A507

A10

• Barkway

M1

A505

• Willian

• Clavering ☐

DUNSTABLE

Cottered

Rickling Green ☐

ESSEX

• Preston

STEVENAGE

A120

• Birchanger

A120

BRAINTREE

LUTON

A1(M)

A602

BISHOP'S
STORTFORD

• Youngs End

A131

• Batford

Chapmore End

• Aythorpe Roding

A119

A1060

• Pleshey

Hertford

A414

HERTFORDSHIRE

A10

HARLOW

• Hastingwood

• Frithsden

ST ALBANS

Epping Green

A414

• Fyfield

CHELMSFORD

• Potters Crouch

• Mill
Green

• Flaunden

EPPING

• Margaretting Tye

• Stock

• Sarratt

A5183

M25

• Stapleford Tawney

TQ

ENFIELD

BRENTWOOD

3

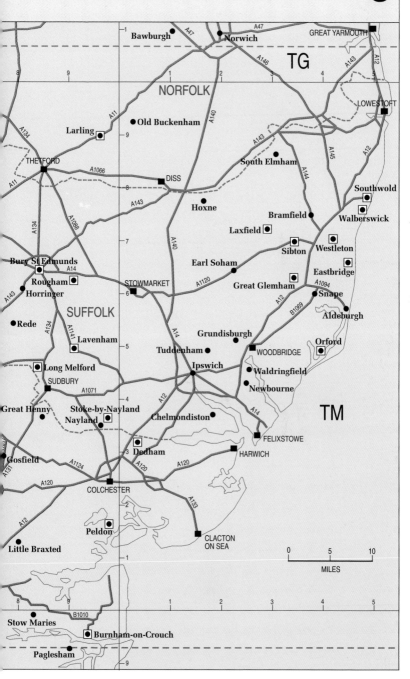

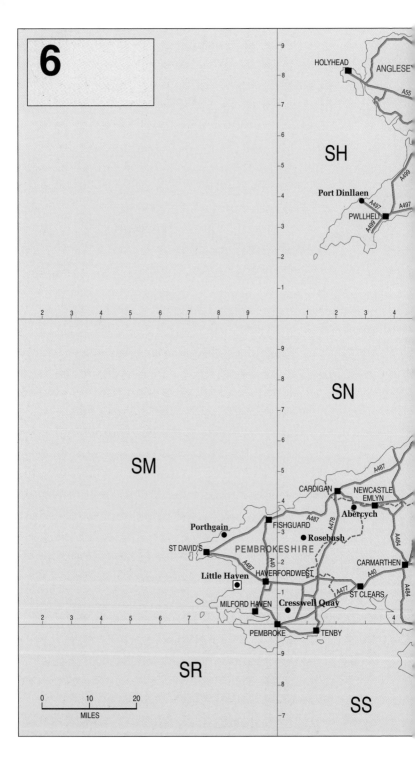

6

HOLYHEAD
ANGLESEY
A55

SH

Port Dinllaen
PWLLHELI
A497
A497
A499
A499

SN

SM

CARDIGAN
NEWCASTLE EMLYN
A487
Abercych
Porthgain
A487
FISHGUARD
A478
Rosebush
ST DAVID'S
PEMBROKESHIRE
A487
A40
CARMARTHEN
A484
Little Haven
HAVERFORDWEST
A40
A484
MILFORD HAVEN
Cresswell Quay
A477
ST CLEARS
PEMBROKE
TENBY

SR

SS

0   10   20
MILES

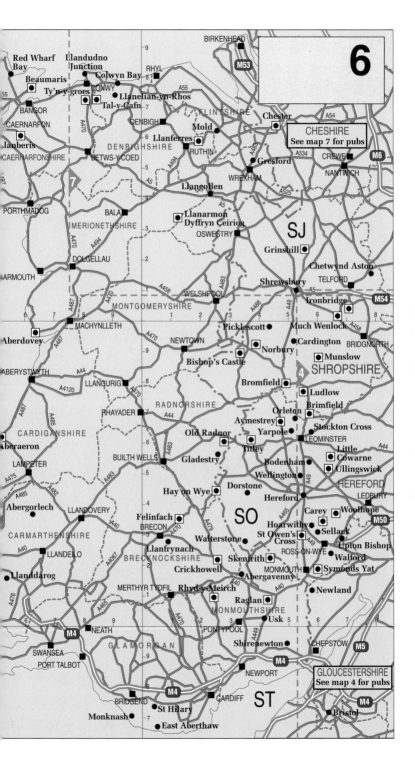

6

Red Wharf Bay
Beaumaris
Llandudno Junction
Ty'n-y-groes
Colwyn Bay
RHYL
BIRKENHEAD
M53
CONWY
Llanelian-yn-Rhos
Tal-y-Cafn
BANGOR
A55
CAERNARFON
Chester
A54
DENBIGH
FLINTSHIRE
CHESHIRE
See map 7 for pubs
Mold
lanberis
Llanferres
DENBIGHSHIRE
Gresford
M6
CAERNARFONSHIRE
BETWS-Y-COED
RUTHIN
CREWE
NANTWICH
WREXHAM
A534
PORTHMADOG
BALA
Llangollen
A525
MERIONETHSHIRE
Llanarmon Dyffryn Ceiriog
SJ
ARMOUTH
DOLGELLAU
OSWESTRY
Grinshill
Chetwynd Aston
WELSHPOOL
Shrewsbury
TELFORD
MONTGOMERYSHIRE
Ironbridge
M54
Aberdovey
MACHYNLLETH
Picklescott
Much Wenlock
BRIDGNORTH
NEWTOWN
Cardington
Munslow
ABERYSTWYTH
Norbury
SHROPSHIRE
Bishop's Castle
4
LLANGURIG
Bromfield
RADNORSHIRE
Ludlow
Brimfield
RHAYADER
Orleton
Aymestrey
Stockton Cross
CARDIGANSHIRE
Old Radnor
Yarpole
LEOMINSTER
aberaeron
Titley
Little Cowarne
LAMPETER
BUILTH WELLS
Gladestry
Bodenham
Ullingswick
Wellington
HEREFORD
Hay on Wye
Dorstone
LEDBURY
Abergorlech
Hereford
Carey
Woolhope
LLANDOVERY
Felinfach
SO
Hoarwithy
M50
BRECON
St Owen's Cross
Sellack
Walterstone
ROSS-ON-WYE
Upton Bishop
CARMARTHENSHIRE
Llanfrynach
BRECKNOCKSHIRE
Skenfrith
Walford
LLANDEILO
Crickhowell
MONMOUTH
Symonds Yat
Abergavenny
Llanddarog
MERTHYR TYDFIL
Rhyd-y-Meirch
Newland
Raglan
MONMOUTHSHIRE
M4
NEATH
Usk
GLAMORGAN
PONTYPOOL
Shirenewton
CHEPSTOW
M5
SWANSEA
M4
PORT TALBOT
NEWPORT
GLOUCESTERSHIRE
See map 4 for pubs
BRIDGEND
CARDIFF
ST
M4
Monknash
St Hilary
Bristol
East Aberthaw

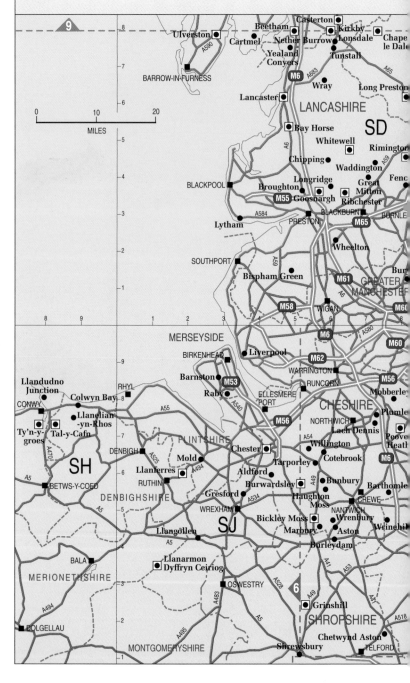

7

9

MILES
0   10   20

Ulverston A590

Beetham
Cartmel
Casterton
Kirkby
Lonsdale
Chapel le Dale
Nether Burrow
Yealand Conyers
Tunstall
BARROW-IN-FURNESS
M6 A683
Wray
Long Preston
Lancaster
LANCASHIRE
SD
A65
A6
Bay Horse
Whitewell
Rimington
Chipping
Waddington
A59
BLACKPOOL
Longridge
Great Mitton
Fence
M55
Broughton
Goosnargh
Ribchester
BLACKBURN
BURNLEY
PRESTON
M65
Lytham A584
Wheelton
SOUTHPORT A59
M61
Bur
Bispham Green
GREATER MANCHESTER
M58
A6
WIGAN
M60
M6
A580
M60
MERSEYSIDE
BIRKENHEAD
Liverpool
M62
WARRINGTON
M56
Barnston
M53
RUNCORN
Mobberley
Raby
ELLESMERE PORT
CHESHIRE
Plumley
A540
NORTHWICH
Peover Heath
Llandudno Junction
RHYL
Colwyn Bay
A55
Lach Dennis
M6
CONWY
Llanelian -yn-Rhos
Ty'n-y-groes
Tal-y-Cafn
SH
A470
DENBIGH
A525
Mold
Chester
A54
Willington
Tarporley
Cotebrook
FLINTSHIRE
A494
Bunbury
Barthomley
Llanferres
Aldford
Burwardsley
Haughton Moss
CREWE
BETWS-Y-COED
RUTHIN
Gresford
A534
NANTWICH
Wrenbury
Wrinehill
A5
DENBIGHSHIRE
WREXHAM
SJ
Bickley Moss
Aston
Llangollen
Marbury
Burleydam
A5
A41
A53
BALA
MERIONETHSHIRE
Llanarmon Dyffryn Ceiriog
A41
A494
OSWESTRY
6
A528
A49
DOLGELLAU
A483
Grinshill
A5
MONTGOMERYSHIRE
SHROPSHIRE
A518
A495
Chetwynd Aston
TELFORD
Shrewsbury

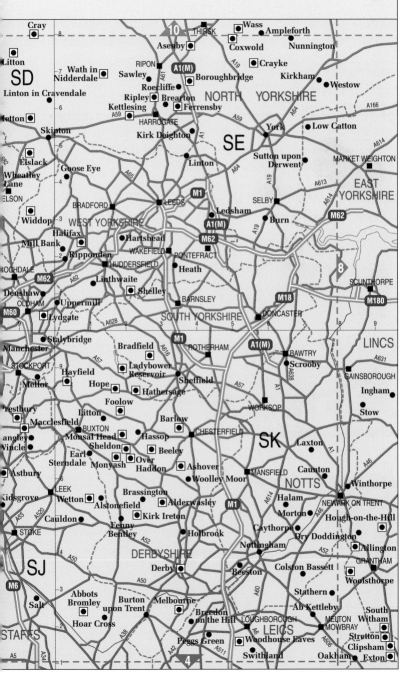

FIND THE NEAREST GOOD PUB ANYTIME, ANYWHERE!

Good Pub Guide Mobile – Text GOODPUB to 87080*

 Receive full details of your nearest good pub direct to your mobile. Our brand-new enhanced mobile phone system provides a complete description, contact details, map and directions, all displayed within our intuitive mobile phone application.

Visit **www.thegoodpubguide.co.uk/mobile** for full details.

* Texts cost 50p plus standard network charges

The Good Pub Guide Sat Nav Edition

 A digital version of The Good Pub Guide is now available for Garmin sat nav systems. Available on an SD card or as a download, the sat nav guide will find the nearest pubs in your area, shown in order of proximity together with their distance from your location, or you can track down a particular pub, and it will guide you there. With your phone connected by Bluetooth, you can even just tap the screen to phone ahead and reserve a table.

Visit **www.thegoodpubguide.co.uk/satnav** for full details.

You can purchase *The Good Pub Guide* and many other leading travel guides direct from the publisher at

www.rbooks.co.uk

Browse more than 10,000 titles from the UK's leading publishers

Pubs visited continued...

Your own name and address *(block capitals please)*

Postcode

Please return to
The Good Pub Guide,
FREEPOST TN1569,
WADHURST,
East Sussex
TN5 7BR

IF YOU PREFER, YOU CAN SEND US REPORTS
BY EMAIL:
feedback@thegoodpubguide.co.uk

I have been to the following pubs in *The Good Pub Guide 2009* in the last few months, found them as described, and confirm that they deserve continued inclusion:

Continued overleaf

PLEASE GIVE YOUR NAME AND ADDRESS ON THE BACK OF THIS FORM

When you write to The Good Pub Guide, FREEPOST TN1569, WADHURST, East Sussex TN5 7BR, you don't need a stamp in the UK. We'll gladly send you more forms (free) if you wish.

Though we try to answer all letters, please understand if there's a delay (particularly in summer, our busiest period). We now edit and inspect throughout the year, so reports are valuable at any time. Obviously it's most useful of all if you write soon after a pub visit, while everything's fresh in your mind, rather than storing things up for a later batch.

We'll assume we can print your name or initials as a recommender unless you tell us otherwise.

Please report to us: you can use the cut-out forms on the following pages, the card in the middle of the book, or just plain paper – whichever's easiest for you, or you can email us at **feedback@thegoodpubguide.co.uk**. We need to know what you think of the pubs in this edition. We need to know about other pubs worthy of inclusion. We need to know about ones that should not be included. And we need to know that vital factor – how good the landlord or landlady is.

The atmosphere and character of the pub are the most important features – why it would, or would not, appeal to strangers, so please try to describe what is special about it. In particular, we can't consider including a pub in the Lucky Dip section unless we know something about what it looks like inside, so that we can describe it to other readers. And obviously with existing entries, we need to know about any changes in décor and furnishings, too. But the bar food and the drink are also important – please tell us about them.

If the food is really quite outstanding, tick the FOOD AWARD box on the form, and tell us about the special quality that makes it stand out – the more detail, the better. And if you have stayed there, tell us about the standard of accommodation – whether it was comfortable, pleasant, good value for money. Again, if the pub or inn is worth special attention as a place to stay, tick the PLACE-TO-STAY AWARD box.

If you're in a position to gauge a pub's suitability or otherwise for **disabled people**, do please tell us about that.

Please try to gauge whether a pub should be a main entry, or is best as a Lucky Dip (and tick the relevant box). In general, main entries need qualities that would make it worth other readers' while to travel some distance to them; Lucky Dips are the pubs that are worth knowing about if you are nearby. But if a pub is an entirely new recommendation, the Lucky Dip may be the best place for it to start its career in the *Guide* – to encourage other readers to report on it.

The more detail you can put into your description of a Lucky Dip pub that's only scantily described in the current edition (or not in at all), the better. A description of its character and even furnishings is a tremendous boon.

It helps enormously if you can give the full address for any new pub – one not yet a main entry, or without a full address in the Lucky Dip sections. In a town, we need the street name; in the country, if it's hard to find, we need directions. Even better for us is the post code. If we can't find out a pub's post code, we no longer include it in the *Guide* – and the Post Office directories we use will not yet have caught up with new pubs, or ones which have changed their names. With any pub, it always helps to let us know about prices of food (and bedrooms, if there are any), and about any lunchtimes or evenings when food is not served. We'd also like to have your views on drinks quality – beer, wine, cider and so forth, even coffee and tea; and do let us know about bedrooms.

If you know that a Lucky Dip pub is open all day (or even late into the afternoon), please tell us – preferably saying which days.

When you go to a pub, don't tell them you're a reporter for the *Good Pub Guide*; we do make clear that all inspections are anonymous, and if you declare yourself as a reporter you risk getting special treatment – for better or for worse!

Sometimes pubs are dropped from the main entries simply because very few readers have written to us about them – and of course there's a risk that people may not write if they find the pub exactly as described in the entry. You can use the forms at the front of the batch of report forms just to list pubs you've been to, found as described, and can recommend.

Free house ~ Licensee Tom Greenstock ~ Real ale ~ Bar food (not Sun evening or Mon lunchtime) ~ Restaurant ~ (01386) 700413 ~ Children welcome ~ Open 11-2.30(3 Sat), 6-11; 12-3.30 Sun; closed Sun evening and Mon lunchtime, 25 Dec, 1 Jan ~ Bedrooms: £70B/£100B

Recommended by Jane and Alan Bush, Chris Glasson, Roger Braithwaite, Derek Thomas, Susan and Nigel Brookes, Martin and Pauline Jennings, Ian and Joan Blackwell, Keith and Sue Ward, Andrew and Ruth Triggs, Paul Humphreys

BRIMPSFIELD
SO9413   MAP 4

Golden Heart 🍺

Nettleton Bottom (not shown on road maps, so we list the pub instead under the name of the nearby village); on A417 N of the Brimpsfield turning northbound; GL4 8LA

Nice old-fashioned furnishings in several cosy areas, big log fire and fair choice of food and drink; suntrap terrace and nearby walks

'A timeless little gem' and 'probably my favourite local' are just a couple of the enthusiastic comments from regular visitors to this bustling roadside pub. It's a place of some genuine character and run by friendly, helpful licensees. The main low-ceilinged bar is divided into five cosily distinct areas; there's a roaring log fire in the huge stone inglenook fireplace in one, traditional built-in settles and other old-fashioned furnishings throughout, and quite a few brass items, typewriters, exposed stone and wood panelling. Newspapers to read. A comfortable parlour on the right has another decorative fireplace, and leads into a further room that opens on to the terrace. Archers Best Bitter, Festival Gold, Otter Bitter and Youngs Special on handpump, some rare ciders, and a few wines by the glass. From the tables and chairs under parasols on the suntrap terrace, there are pleasant views down over a valley; nearby walks. The bedrooms are at the back of the pub and so escape any road noise.

🍴 **Well liked bar food includes good sandwiches, filled baked potatoes, ploughman's, soup, avocado mousse with prawns, deep-fried brie, omelettes, vegetarian lasagne, calves liver and bacon with onion gravy, thai red chicken curry, hungarian goulash, salmon and pasta bake, venison, bacon and mushroom casserole, and puddings like banoffi pie and a duo of chocolate truffles.** *Starters/Snacks: £5.25 to £6.50. Main Courses: £9.95 to £14.95. Puddings: £4.25 to £4.95*

Free house ~ Licensee Catherine Stevens ~ Real ale ~ Bar food (12-3, 6-10; all day Fri, Sat and Sun) ~ Restaurant ~ (01242) 870261 ~ Children welcome ~ Dogs welcome ~ Open 11-3, 5.30-11; 11-11 Sat; 12-10.30 Sun ~ Bedrooms: £35S/£55S

Recommended by Colin Moore, Michael Doswell, Guy Vowles, Tracey and Stephen Groves, R T and J C Moggridge, R B Gardiner, Nigel and Sue Foster, Mike Vincent, E McCall, T McLean, D Irving, Adrian and Dawn Collinge, Di and Mike Gillam, Chris Flynn, Wendy Jones, Bob and Angela Brooks, Keith and Sue Ward, Eddie Edwards, R Huggins, M G Hart

BROAD CAMPDEN
SP1537   MAP 4

Bakers Arms 🍺

Off B4081; GL55 6UR

Friendly village pub with five real ales, traditional food and good mix of customers

Perhaps the part with the most character in this traditional and welcoming village pub is where the friendly locals tend to gather – the tiny beamed bar with its mix of tables and seats around the walls (which are stripped back to bare stone), and inglenook fireplace at one end. It's enjoyably chatty and relaxed and from the attractive oak bar counter you can get five real ales such as Donningtons BB, Goffs Tournament, Stanway Stanney Bitter, and Wells & Youngs Bombardier on handpump; darts and board games. The dining room is beamed, with exposed stone wall. There are seats on a terraced area with more by flower tubs on other terraces and in the back garden. Broad Campden is a peaceful village.

🍴 **As well as lunchtime sandwiches, filled baguettes, filled giant yorkshire puddings and ploughman's, the fairly priced bar food includes soup, breaded chicken goujons with garlic mayonnaise or chilli dip, lasagne, thai red vegetable curry, liver, bacon and onions, steak** and kidney suet pudding, chicken curry, smoked haddock bake, daily specials and puddings such as treacle tart or fruit crumble. *Starters/Snacks: £3.25 to £5.50. Main Courses: £7.50 to £9.75. Puddings: £3.95*

Free house ~ Licensees Ray and Sally Mayo ~ Real ale ~ Bar food (12-9 in summer; 12-2(2.30 Sat/Sun), 6-9(8.30 Sun) in winter;) ~ Restaurant ~ No credit cards ~ (01386) 840515 ~ Children welcome away from bar ~ Folk music third Tues evening of month ~ Open 11.30-11; 12-10.30 Sun; 11.30-2.30, 4.45-11 Mon-Thurs in winter; closed 25 Dec, evenings 26 and 31 Dec

Recommended by Noel Grundy, Michael Dandy, Brian and Anita Randall, B M Eldridge, Paul Humphreys, Keith and Sue Ward, R T and J C Moggridge

CHEDWORTH   SP0512   MAP 4

Seven Tuns ♀

Village signposted off A429 NE of Cirencester; then take second signposted right turn and bear left towards church; GL54 4AE

Handy for nearby Roman villa and with several open fires, lots of wines by the glass, good bar food, and plenty of seats outside

Delightful inside and out, this little 17th-c pub has exceptionally nice staff who offer a friendly welcome to all. The small snug lounge on the right has comfortable seats and decent tables, sizeable antique prints, tankards hanging from the beam over the serving bar, a partly boarded ceiling, and a good winter log fire in a big stone fireplace. Down a couple of steps, the public bar on the left has an open fire and leads into a dining room with another open fire. Wells & Youngs Bombardier and Youngs Special and a seasonal guest on handpump, ten wines by the glass and 15 malt whiskies; darts, skittle alley, dominoes and piped music. One sunny terrace has a boules pitch and across the road there's another little walled raised terrace with a waterwheel and a stream; plenty of tables and seats. There are nice walks through the valley.

🍽 **Well liked bar food at lunchtime includes sandwiches, ploughman's, soup, chicken caesar salad, home-made burger, sausages of the week with spring onion mash and redcurrant gravy, and herb and beer-battered fish with home-made tartare sauce, with evening dishes such as fried pigeon breast with white wine and mushroom sauce, home-made duck and chicken liver pâté with red onion marmalade, baked aubergine filled with chargrilled vegetables and topped with provençale sauce and mozzarella, slow-roasted pork belly on sautéed apple and potatoes with a red wine and bacon sauce, and puddings like apple and raspberry crumble and Baileys crème brûlée with home-made shortbread.** *Starters/Snacks: £4.95 to £6.95. Main Courses: £6.95 to £9.95. Puddings: £3.95 to £4.95*

Youngs ~ Tenant Mr Davenport-Jones ~ Real ale ~ Bar food (12-2.30(3 weekends), 6.30-9.30(10 weekends)) ~ Restaurant ~ (01285) 720242 ~ Children welcome ~ Dogs welcome ~ Open 12-midnight(2am Sat); 12-11 Sun; 12-3.30, 6-closing hours as above in winter

Recommended by E McCall, T McLean, D Irving, Neil and Anita Christopher, MBHJ, Edward Mirzoeff, KC

CHELTENHAM   SO9624   MAP 4

Royal Oak ♀ 🍺

Off B4348 just N of Cheltenham; The Burgage, Prestbury; GL52 3DL

Bustling and friendly with enjoyable food and drink (Sunday lunch all day), seats in sheltered garden and handy for Cheltenham racecourse

Run by an affable landlord, this attractive cotswold stone building is popular for its good choice of food and drink. The congenial low-beamed bar has fresh flowers and polished brasses, a comfortable mix of seating on the parquet flooring from country chairs and a cushioned pew to dark green wall banquettes built in on either side of its stone fireplace, and there are some interesting pictures on the ochre walls. Dark Star Hophead, Malvern Hills Black Pear and Timothy Taylors Landlord on handpump, nine wines by the glass and local soft drinks; they also hold an ale and sausage festival in May, a cider, perry and cheese one in August and a stout and oyster weekend in November. Service is efficient and friendly. Dining room tables are nicely spaced so that you don't feel crowded and the skittle alley can also be used as a function room; piped music. There are seats and tables under canopies on the heated terrace and a sheltered garden. This is the closest pub to Cheltenham racecourse so it does get busy on race days.

🍴 Bar food includes filled warm ciabattas and granary sandwiches, smoked mackerel pâté with horseradish and capers, potted shrimps and toast, beer-battered haddock with pea purée, ham, egg, tomato and chips, herb gnocchi with herb fondue, fried kidneys with oyster mushrooms and garlic croûton, fish pie with mussels, salmon, haddock and prawns, slow cooked pork belly stuffed with prunes with a sweet mustard sauce, rack of lamb with parsley mash and hazelnut dressing, and puddings; all-day roasts on Sunday. *Starters/Snacks: £5.75 to £7.95. Main Courses: £7.95 to £15.50. Puddings: £4.95*

Enterprise ~ Lease Simon and Kate Daws ~ Real ale ~ Bar food (12-2, 6.30-9; all day Sun) ~ Restaurant ~ (01242) 522344 ~ Children in bar before 7pm, in restaurant before 8pm ~ Open 11.30-3, 5.30(6 Sat)-11; 12-10.30 Sun; closed 25 Dec

Recommended by Michael Sargent, M Thomas, Keith and Sue Ward, B M Eldridge, Kerry Law, Stuart Doughty

CHIPPING CAMPDEN   SP1539   MAP 4
Eight Bells
Church Street (which is one way – entrance off B4035); GL55 6JG

Handsome inn with massive timbers and beams, log fires, well liked food, and seats in large terraced garden; handy for Cotswold Way

This handsome old inn has plenty of history. It was used, many hundreds of years ago, as a hostel for workmen building the nearby church and in the floor of the dining room is a glass inset showing part of the passage from the church by which Roman Catholic priests could escape from the Roundheads. The bars have heavy oak beams, massive timber supports and stripped stone walls with cushioned pews, sofas and solid dark wood furniture on the broad flagstones, and log fires in up to three restored stone fireplaces; daily papers to read. North Cotswold Pig Brook and three guest beers such as Brains Bread of Heaven, Everards Sunchaser and Goffs Jouster on handpump from the fine oak bar counter, quite a few wines by the glass, Old Rosie cider and country wines. Piped music and board games. There's a large terraced garden with plenty of seats, and striking views of the almshouses and church. The pub is handy for the Cotswold Way walk which takes you to Bath.

🍴 Enjoyable food at lunchtime includes sandwiches, soup, chicken liver parfait with apple and grape chutney, pasta dishes, omelettes, pork and leek sausages with red wine jus and home-battered onion rings, and beer-battered fish with pea and mint purée, with evening choices like spiced lamb kofta kebabs with minted couscous and lime and coriander dressing, sardines in garlic and parsley butter, slow-braised lamb shank with rissole potatoes and rosemary jus, fillet of scottish salmon wrapped in parma ham with a mild spiced chorizo bean cassoulet, and chicken supreme stuffed with brie and ham on tagliatelle with a mediterranean-style dressing; daily specials and puddings such as vanilla panna cotta with poached rhubarb and apricot and sultana bread and butter pudding with custard. *Starters/Snacks: £4.85 to £7.00. Main Courses: £10.00 to £16.50. Puddings: £5.50 to £6.75*

Free house ~ Licensee Neil Hargreaves ~ Real ale ~ Bar food (12-2(2.30 Fri-Sun), 6.30(7 Sun)-9(9.30 Fri and Sat)) ~ Restaurant ~ (01386) 840371 ~ Children must be well behaved and supervised by parents ~ Dogs allowed in bar ~ Open 12-11(10.30 Sun); closed 25 Dec ~ Bedrooms: £55S/£85B

Recommended by Jude Wright, Dru and Louisa Marshall, Stuart Doughty, Geoffrey Hughes, Michael Dandy, Ray J Carter, Graham Oddey, Martin and Pauline Jennings, Robert Ager, Dr and Mrs A K Clarke, Noel Grundy

We checked prices with the pubs as we went to press in summer 2008. They should hold until around spring 2009 – when our experience suggests that you can expect an increase of around 10p in the £.

COATES

SO9600   MAP 4

Tunnel House

Follow Tarlton signs (right then left) from village, pub up rough track on right after railway bridge; OS Sheet 163 map reference 965005; GL7 6PW

Warm welcome for all at friendly, interestingly decorated pub, lots of character, popular food and drink, and seats in sizeable garden; guards derelict canal tunnel

With plenty of character and an informal and relaxed atmosphere, this rather eccentric bow-fronted stone house has impressive views from tables on the pleasant terrace and a big garden sloping down to the derelict entrance tunnel of the old Thames and Severn Canal (which is under slow restoration). Inside, there are rambling rooms with beams, flagstones, a happy mix of furnishings including massive rustic benches and seats built into the sunny windows, lots of enamel advertising signs, race tickets and air travel labels, a stuffed wild boar's head and stuffed owl, plenty of copper and brass and an upside-down card table complete with cards and drinks fixed to the beams; there's a nice log fire with sofas in front of it. The more conventional dining extension and back conservatory fill up quickly at mealtimes. Three changing real ales from breweries such as Hook Norton, Stroud, Uley and Wickwar on handpump, several wines by the glass, and two draught ciders; quick, friendly service. Piped music and juke box. There may be an amiable black labrador and almost certainly lots of students from the Agricultural College (especially on term-time weekend evenings). Good walks nearby.

🍴 **Popular bar food at lunchtime includes sandwiches and filled baguettes, soup, chicken liver pâté with tomato chutney, beer-battered cod, a pie of the day, good burger with cheese and bacon, and ham and eggs, with evening meals such as smoked haddock kedgeree with a light curry dressing, seared pigeon breast with apple and celeriac remoulade, goats cheese parcels with herbed chickpeas and red pepper relish, calves liver with bacon and rich onion gravy, chicken breasts stuffed with sun-dried tomatoes and puddings like warm chocolate brownie with vanilla ice-cream and crème brûlée; take-away fish and chips on some evenings.** *Starters/Snacks: £4.00 to £6.95. Main Courses: £8.00 to £14.00. Puddings: £4.75*

Free house ~ Licensee Rupert Longsdon ~ Real ale ~ Bar food (12-2.15, 6.45-9.15) ~ (01285) 770280 ~ Children welcome ~ Dogs welcome ~ Open 11.30-3.30, 6-11.30; 11.30-11.30 Sat and Sun; closed 25 Dec

Recommended by Brian and Anita Randall, Neil and Anita Christopher, Pete Baker, Nick and Meriel Cox, Peter Meister, David Morgan, Alan Bulley, Giles and Annie Francis, Guy Vowles

COWLEY

SO9714   MAP 4

Green Dragon 🛏

Off A435 S of Cheltenham at Elkstone, Cockleford signpost; OS Sheet 163 map reference 970142; GL53 9NW

Cosy and old-fashioned bars with winter fires, good food, real ales, and terraces overlooking Cowley Lake; comfortable bedrooms

Extremely popular and exceptionally well run, this is a smashing country inn much loved by our readers. The two beamed bars have a cosy and genuinely old-fashioned feel with big flagstones and wooden boards, winter log fires in two stone fireplaces, candlelit tables, a woodburning stove and Butcombe Bitter, Courage Directors and Hook Norton on handpump. The furniture and the bar itself in the upper Mouse Bar were made by Robert Thompson, and little mice run over the hand-carved chairs, tables and mantelpiece; there's also a larger Lower Bar and upstairs restaurant; piped music. Terraces outside overlook Cowley Lake and the River Churn, and the pub is a good centre for the local walks. The bedrooms are very comfortable and well equipped and the breakfasts are good.

🍴 **Enjoyable bar food includes lunchtime sandwiches and light dishes such as home-made burger topped with beef tomato and mozzarella, vegetable curry, wild boar sausages with dark, rich gravy and chargrilled gammon with a free-range egg, as well as duck confit rillette with pink peppercorns and shallots and a prune and apple jam, savoury dill profiteroles filled with smoked mackerel and haddock with a lemon crème fraîche, pork** fillet with black pudding, apricots and chillies on colcannon potatoes with a smitaine sauce, steak and kidney suet pudding with minted mushy peas and fried ostrich steak with horseradish goulash; daily specials and puddings, too. *Starters/Snacks: £4.95 to £8.95. Main Courses: £9.95 to £15.95. Puddings: £4.00 to £4.95*

Buccaneer Holdings ~ Licensees Simon and Nicky Haly ~ Real ale ~ Bar food (12-2.30(3.30 Sun), 6-10(9 Sun)) ~ Restaurant ~ (01242) 870271 ~ Children welcome ~ Dogs allowed in bar and bedrooms ~ Open 11(12 Sun)-11; closed evenings 25 and 26 Dec and 1 Jan ~ Bedrooms: £65B/£85B

Recommended by Michael Doswell, E McCall, T McLean, D Irving, M S Lee, Guy Vowles, J Crosby, Keith and Sue Ward, Bruce and Sharon Eden, Mike Vincent, Michael and Joan Johnstone, H Paulinski, Pete Baker, Dave Braisted

CRANHAM   SO8912   MAP 4

Black Horse 🍺

Village signposted off A46 and B4070 N of Stroud; look out for small sign up village side turning; GL4 8HP

Friendly, old-fashioned country inn with obliging staff, homely food and real ales

Surrounded by woodland, this old-fashioned and unassuming 17th-c inn is popular with walkers – the Cotswold Way is only a mile away. A cosy little lounge has just three or four tables, the main bar has window seats and other traditional furniture and a good log fire, and the atmosphere is friendly and convivial; there are a couple of upstairs dining rooms, too (they take bookings up here but not in the bar or lounge). Butcombe Bitter, Hancocks HB, Sharps Doom Bar, and a guest beer on handpump. Outside, there are tables to the side of the pub and some in front; the labradoodle is called Percy and the jack russell, Baxter. They have a successful pub cricket team and regular morris dancers.

🍽 **Well priced, freshly cooked and popular bar food includes sandwiches, soup, ploughman's, various quiches, cumberland sausage and mash, chicken in stilton sauce, hungarian goulash, beef bourguignon, steak and kidney and fish pies, lamb kleftiko, and puddings like lemon shortcake or fruit crumbles.** *Starters/Snacks: £3.50 to £4.50. Main Courses: £6.75 to £11.95. Puddings: £3.25 to £3.95*

Free house ~ Licensees David and Julie Job ~ Real ale ~ Bar food (not Sun evening or Mon) ~ Restaurant ~ (01452) 812217 ~ Children welcome if well behaved; no small children evenings ~ Dogs allowed in bar ~ Open 12-2.30(3 Sat), 6.30-11; 12-3.30, 8-11 Sun; closed Mon

Recommended by Dr and Mrs Jackson, E McCall, T McLean, D Irving, Guy Vowles, Pete Baker, Andrew Shore, Maria Williams

DIDMARTON   ST8187   MAP 2

Kings Arms 🍷 🛏

A433 Tetbury road; GL9 1DT

Bustling pub with knocked-through rooms, pleasant back garden, and self-catering cottages

Westonbirt Arboretum is close by and so this carefully restored, 17th-c coaching inn can get pretty busy. The several knocked-through beamed bar rooms work their way around a big central counter with deep terracotta walls above a dark green dado, a pleasant mix of chairs on bare boards, quarry tiles and carpet, and a big stone fireplace. Cottage Champflower Ale, Otter Ale and Uley Bitter on handpump and ten wines by the glass; darts. There are seats out in the pleasant back garden, and as well as comfortable bedrooms, they have self-catering cottages in a converted barn and stable block. More reports please.

Prices of main dishes sometimes now don't include vegetables – if in doubt ask.

⏹ Enjoyable bar food at lunchtime includes nice sandwiches, ploughman's, a plate of antipasti, home-cooked ham and free-range eggs, macaroni cheese, beer-battered cod and gloucester old spot sausages and mash, with evening choices such as seared scallop and black pudding salad with parsley pesto, creamy garlic and peppercorn mushrooms, lime and ginger duck with buttered leeks, lamb chump with red wine and rosemary jus and 10oz rib-eye steak. *Starters/Snacks: £5.50 to £8.00. Main Courses: £9.95 to £16.00. Puddings: £5.50*

Free house ~ Licensees R A and S A Sadler ~ Real ale ~ Bar food (12-2, 6-9; 12-7.45 Sun) ~ Restaurant ~ (01454) 238245 ~ Children allowed away from bar ~ Dogs allowed in bar ~ Open 11am-11.30pm; 12-10.30 Sun ~ Bedrooms: £65S/£95S

Recommended by Matthew Shackle, Rod Stoneman, J Crosby, Derek and Sylvia Stephenson, Roger Price

DOYNTON

ST7174 MAP 2

Cross House ◖

Village signposted with Dyrham off A420 Bristol—Chippenham just E of Wick; High Street; BS30 5TF

Friendly staff and customers, honest food and beers and 15 wines by the glass; close to Dyrham Park and walking country

Always busy with both locals and visitors, this 18th-c village pub owes much of its charm to the convivial licensees and their staff. The softly lit carpeted bar has some beams and stripped stone, simple pub furniture brightened up with cheerful scatter cushions, a woodburning stove in a big stone fireplace and a chatty atmosphere. Two or three steps take you down to a cottagey candlelit dining room. Five real ales on handpump such as Bass, Bath Ales Gem Bitter, Courage Best, Sharps Doom Bar, and Timothy Taylors Landlord and 15 decent wines by the glass; darts, games machine and piped music. There are picnic-sets out by the road. This is fine walking country, and Dyrham Park is quite close.

⏹ Honest bar food at reasonable prices includes sandwiches, ham and egg with bubble and squeak, faggots, steak and kidney, rabbit and bacon and fish pies, salmon and broccoli fishcakes and roast rib of beef with yorkshire pudding. *Starters/Snacks: £3.95 to £5.25. Main Courses: £8.50 to £10.95. Puddings: £3.50 to £3.95*

Unique (Enterprise) ~ Lease André and Liz Large ~ Real ale ~ Bar food ~ Restaurant ~ (0117) 937 2261 ~ Children welcome ~ Dogs allowed in bar ~ Open 11.30-3, 6-11; 12-4, 7-10.30 Sun

Recommended by Ian and Joan Blackwell, Tony and Jill Radnor, Barry Gibbs, Michael Doswell, Dr and Mrs C W Thomas, John and Gloria Isaacs, Donna and Roger, Dr and Mrs A K Clarke, Dr and Mrs M E Wilson, Colin and Peggy Wilshire

DUNTISBOURNE ABBOTS

SO9709 MAP 4

Five Mile House ⏹ ◖

Off A417 at Duntisbourne Abbots exit sign; then, coming from Gloucester, pass filling station and keep on parallel to main road for 200 yards; coming from Cirencester, take Duntisbourne Abbots services sign, then immediate right and take underpass below main road, then turn right at T junction; avoid going into Duntisbourne Abbots village; pub is on the old main road; GL7 7JR

A lively landlord and a favourite with many for its good food, beer and atmosphere; plenty of original character, open fires and newspapers; nice views from garden

Thankfully, this extremely well run and genuinely friendly village pub doesn't change from year to year – and many of our readers go considerably out of their way to come back here on a regular basis. The atmosphere is always buoyant and bustling but no matter how busy it is, the cheerful Carriers make all their customers feel at home. There's plenty of original character and the front room has a companionable bare-boards drinking bar on the right (plenty of convivial banter from the locals), with wall seats around the big table in its bow window and just one other table. On the left is a flagstoned hallway tap room snug formed from two ancient high-backed settles by a stove in a tall carefully exposed old fireplace; newspapers to read. There's a small cellar bar, a back restaurant down steps and a family room on the far side; darts and board games. Donningtons BB, Timothy Taylors Landlord and Youngs Bitter on handpump (the cellar is temperature-controlled) and an interesting wine list (strong on new world ones); the friendly pub dog is called Sacha. The gardens have nice country views; the country lane was once Ermine Street, the main Roman road from Wales to London.

Ⅲ **Cooked by the landlord and his team, the very popular bar food includes sandwiches, soup, chicken liver pâté, hot brie with cranberry sauce, gammon with egg and pineapple, chicken breast stuffed with stilton, wrapped in bacon with a mushroom and brandy cream sauce, local trout with prawn and caper butter, lamb shoulder stuffed with redcurrant and mint, and daily specials such as spanish omelette, fish pie, chilli beef with noodles and prawn crackers, lambs liver with red onion and bacon in port jus, fillets of bass with crayfish tails in garlic butter, and roasted barbary duck breast on an orange and blackcurrant sauce; they offer several dishes in smaller helpings, too.** *Starters/Snacks: £3.95 to £6.50. Main Courses: £8.50 to £15.95. Puddings: £4.95 to £5.95*

Free house ~ Licensees Jo and Jon Carrier ~ Real ale ~ Bar food (12-2.30, 6(7 summer Sun)-9.30; not winter Sun evening) ~ Restaurant ~ (01285) 821432 ~ Children welcome if well behaved ~ Dogs allowed in bar ~ Open 12-3, 6-11; 12-3, 7-10.30 Sun

Recommended by Mr and Mrs J Brown, E McCall, T McLean, D Irving, Dr A J and Mrs Tompsett, Bren and Val Speed, Michael R B Taylor, Neil and Anita Christopher, George and Maureen Roby, David Morgan, the Didler, Graham and Helen Eastwood, Guy Vowles, Dennis Jenkin, Donna and Roger, Nick and Meriel Cox, Paul and Shirley White, J Crosby, Tom and Ruth Rees, Carol and Colin Broadbent, R Huggins, Mrs Roxanne Chamberlain, Mike and Jenny Beacon

DURSLEY   ST7598   MAP 4

Old Spot ◀ £
Hill Road; by bus station; GL11 4JQ

Unassuming and cheery town pub with up to ten real ales and regular beer festivals

With an excellent choice of changing real ales from all over the country, it's no wonder that beer lovers come here in droves. It's an unassuming and cheerful pub with plenty of good-humoured locals and as well as four annual beer festivals, the choices on handpump might include Butcombe Blonde and Uley Old Ric with changing guests such as Batemans Salem Porter, Bath Ales Wild Hare, Fullers London Pride, Hereford Pale Ale, St Austell HSD, Severn Vale Session, Strouds Tom Long, and Wye Valley Butty Bach; quite a few malt whiskies too. The front door opens into a deep pink little room with stools on shiny quarry tiles along its pine boarded bar counter and old enamel beer advertisements on the walls and ceiling; there's a profusion of porcine paraphernalia. A small room on the left leading off from here has shove-ha'penny, cribbage and dominoes, and the little dark wood floored room to the right has a stone fireplace. A step takes you down to a cosy Victorian tiled snug and (to the right) the meeting room.

Ⅲ **Bar food includes toasted ciabattas, ploughman's, a grazing board of meats, cheeses and fish (good for sharing), tagliatelle topped with roast vegetables and goats cheese, pork and apple burger with bacon and parmesan, home-cooked ham with parsley sauce, cottage pie, sausages with rich gravy, steak in ale or venison in stout pie, chicken fajitas, and puddings like white chocolate cheesecake and treacle tart.** *Starters/Snacks: £3.95 to £6.45. Main Courses: £6.45 to £9.45. Puddings: £3.75*

Free house ~ Licensee Steve Herbert ~ Real ale ~ Bar food (12-8 Mon-Thurs; 12-3 Fri-Sun; no food Fri-Sun evenings) ~ (01453) 542870 ~ Children in family room before 9pm; best to book ~ Dogs welcome ~ Open 11(12 Sun)-11

Recommended by Chris and Angela Buckell, Andy and Claire Barker, Mr and Mrs W W Burke, PL, Carol and Colin Broadbent, Neil and Anita Christopher, Michael and Joan Johnstone, Ben Guy, Andrew Birkinshaw, Stuart Paulley, Rob and Jane Woodward, the Didler

Please keep sending us reports. We rely on readers for news of new discoveries, and particularly for news of changes – however slight – at the fully described pubs: feedback@thegoodpubguide.co.uk or (no stamp needed) The Good Pub Guide, FREEPOST TN1569, Wadhurst, E Sussex TN5 7BR.

EWEN   SU0097   MAP 4

Wild Duck ⑪ ♀

Village signposted from A429 S of Cirencester; GL7 6BY

Bustling, civilised inn with open fires, a nice mix of furniture, and well liked food and drink; sheltered garden

Handy for Cirencester, this 16th-c inn is a fine old building on the edge of a peaceful village. The high-beamed main bar has a nice mix of comfortable armchairs and other seats, paintings on the red walls, crimson drapes, a winter open fire, and maybe candles on tables. The residents' lounge, which overlooks the garden, has a handsome Elizabethan fireplace and antique furnishings. Besides Duckpond Bitter (brewed especially for the pub), you'll find Butcombe Bitter, Theakstons Best and Old Peculier and Wells & Youngs Bombardier on handpump, 37 wines by the glass, several malts and local liqueurs; piped music and giant chess in the garden.There are wooden seats and tables under parasols and outdoor heaters in the neatly kept and enclosed courtyard garden; if you eat out here, you will be asked to leave your credit card behind the bar (but not if you eat inside).

⑪ **Good, interesting bar food includes soup, a plate of antipasti, duck liver pâté with red onion marmalade, roast chicken breast with wild mushrooms, pesto potatoes and red wine gravy finished with melted brie, moroccan lamb casserole with lemon couscous and toasted almonds, pork loin steak with garlic and rosemary potatoes and tomato and roast pepper sauce with olives, tandoori monkfish and tiger prawns with minty cucumber salad, daily specials such as moules marinières and pork sausage cassoulet with root vegetable mash, beans and smoked bacon, and puddings like pecan tart with chocolate sauce and coffee ice-cream and tiramisu with viennoise biscuits and white chocolate shavings.** *Starters/Snacks: £4.50 to £8.00. Main Courses: £6.95 to £23.00. Puddings: £5.95 to £6.95*

Free house ~ Licensees Tina and Dino Mussell ~ Real ale ~ Bar food (12-2, 6.45-10; 12-2, 2.30-10 Sat; 12-2.30, 3.30-6, 6.45-9.30 Sun) ~ Restaurant ~ (01285) 770310 ~ Children welcome ~ Dogs allowed in bar and bedrooms ~ Open 11-11(midnight Sat); 12-11 Sun ~ Bedrooms: £80B/£125B

Recommended by Evelyn and Derek Walter, E McCall, T McLean, D Irving, Ian and Joan Blackwell, Anne Morris, Mrs M B Gregg, Tom and Ruth Rees, Helen Hartley, Adrian and Dawn Collinge

FORD   SP0829   MAP 4

Plough

B4077 Stow—Alderton; GL54 5RU

A nice mix of customers in bustling, well run pub – gets packed on race days – and good food and beer

As this sociable pub is opposite a well known racehorse trainer's yard and many of the customers are stable hands and jockeys, it does get pretty packed on race meeting evenings. There's a chatty, friendly atmosphere and the beamed and stripped-stone bar has racing prints and photos on the walls, old settles and benches around the big tables on its uneven flagstones, oak tables in a snug alcove, open fires or woodburning stoves (a couple are the real thing), and darts, TV (for the races), board games and piped music. Donnington BB and SBA on handpump and efficient service, even when busy. There are benches in the garden, pretty hanging baskets and a play area at the back. The Cotswold Farm Park is nearby. The comfortable bedrooms away from the pub are the quietest.

⑪ **As well as lunchtime filled baguettes, ploughman's and pubby dishes like gloucester old spot sausages with rich onion gravy, baked ham with two free-range eggs and cottage pie, the enjoyable bar food includes soup, home-made thai crab fishcakes with sweet chilli sauce, a pâté of the day, smoked chicken salad with mango and sun-dried tomatoes, home-made steak and mushroom in ale pie, half a crisp roast duckling with a peach and thyme sauce, slow-roasted half shoulder of lamb with mint jelly, and venison with juniper sauce; also, vegetarian and fresh fish options, puddings, traditional asparagus feasts April-June, and good breakfasts.** *Starters/Snacks: £4.95 to £6.95. Main Courses: £9.95 to £17.95. Puddings: £4.95*

Donnington ~ Tenant Craig Brown ~ Real ale ~ Bar food (12-2, 6-9; all day weekends) ~ (01386) 584215 ~ Children welcome ~ Dogs allowed in bar ~ Open 10am-2am ~ Bedrooms: £40S/£70S

Recommended by Mr and Mrs Barrie, Guy Vowles, Clive and Fran Dutson, the Didler, Paul and Shirley White, Paul Humphreys, Andy and Claire Barker, Peter and Audrey Dowsett, Myra Joyce, Nick and Meriel Cox, Martin and Pauline Jennings

GREAT RISSINGTON   SP1917   MAP 4

Lamb ♀ 🛏

Off A40 W of Burford, via Gt Barrington; GL54 2LN

Well run, bustling inn, interesting, enjoyable bar food, fair choice of drinks and seats in sheltered garden; good surrounding walks

There's a really good balance between those popping in for a drink and a chat and customers hoping to enjoy the very good food in this warm and bright partly 17th-c inn – and the hard-working landlord and his friendly staff are sure to make everyone welcome. The rather civilised two-roomed bar has heritage red and stone coloured walls, fixed cushioned seating with fluted backs in a dark faux-aged suede, high-backed leather chairs grouped around polished tables, and a woodburning stove in the cotswold stone fireplace. Some interesting things to look out for are parts of a propeller, artefacts in display cases and pictures of the Canadian crew from the Wellington bomber that crashed in the garden in October 1943; also, photographs of the guide dogs that the staff, customers and owners have raised money to sponsor. The restaurant has another woodburning stove and various old agricultural tools on the walls. Hook Norton Old Hooky and Wye Valley Best Bitter on handpump, 11 wines by the glass from a comprehensive list and several malt whiskies; piped music, darts and TV for sports. You can sit outside on the front terrace or in the sheltered, well kept hillside garden. There's a local circular walk which takes in part of the idyllic village, church, River Windrush and stunning countryside surrounding the pub.

🍴 Attractively presented and using seasonal local produce, the popular bar food includes filled baguettes and baked potatoes, a soup and a sandwich deal, smoked haddock and spring onion fishcakes with red pepper relish, tartlet of poached chicken, chorizo and brie with a sweet red onion chutney, beer and poppy seed-battered fresh haddock, tagliatelle in a spinach, roasted pepper, blue cheese and pine nut cream sauce, steak, kidney and onion in ale pie, their speciality half roast shoulder of lamb with redcurrant and red wine gravy, and puddings. *Starters/Snacks: £4.50 to £6.95. Main Courses: £9.50 to £16.95. Puddings: £2.75 to £6.95*

Free house ~ Licensees Paul and Jacqueline Gabriel ~ Real ale ~ Bar food (12-2.30, 6.30-9.30; all day weekends) ~ Restaurant ~ (01451) 820388 ~ Children welcome ~ Dogs welcome ~ Open 12-11; closed evening 25 Dec ~ Bedrooms: £55B/£80B

Recommended by Guy Vowles, Mr and Mrs I and E Bell, David A Hammond, Lawrence Pearse, Betty Laker

GUITING POWER   SP0924   MAP 4

Hollow Bottom

Village signposted off B4068 SW of Stow-on-the-Wold (still called A436 on many maps); GL54 5UX

Popular old inn with lots of racing memorabilia and a good bustling atmosphere

This snug old stone cottage is liked by a wide mix of customers – in particular, jockeys, owners and trainers. The comfortable beamed bar has plenty of atmosphere, lots of racing memorabilia including racing silks, tunics and photographs and a winter log fire in an unusual pillar-supported stone fireplace. The public bar has flagstones and stripped stone masonry and racing on TV; newspapers to read, darts, board games and piped music. Fullers London Pride, North Cotswold Shagweaver and a beer named for the pub (from Badger) on handpump, 18 malt whiskies and several wines (including champagne) by the glass; obliging service. From the pleasant garden behind the pub are views towards the peaceful sloping fields; decent nearby walks.

🍴 Bar food includes good filled baguettes and baked potatoes, soup, ham and eggs, cottage pie, sausages with mash and gravy, gloucester old spot pork fillet in cider and cream, wild mushroom and spinach lasagne, slow-cooked lamb shoulder and daily specials. *Starters/Snacks: £3.50 to £7.50. Main Courses: £7.95 to £18.95. Puddings: £4.75 to £5.75*

Free house ~ Licensees Hugh Kelly and Charles Pettigrew ~ Real ale ~ Bar food (all day) ~ Restaurant ~ (01451) 850392 ~ Children welcome ~ Dogs allowed in bar and bedrooms ~ Live music during Cheltenham race meetings ~ Open 9am-12.30am ~ Bedrooms: £45B/£70B

Recommended by Michael and Jenny Back, Dennis and Gill Keen, Richard Marjoram, Keith and Sue Ward, Bernadette Fitzjohn, Mike and Mary Carter, Jeff and Sue Evans, Guy Vowles, Martin and Pauline Jennings, Ralph Kenber, Mr and Mrs Barrie, Jack and Sandra Clarfelt

HINTON DYRHAM

ST7376   MAP 2

Bull

2.4 miles from M4 junction 18; A46 towards Bath, then first right (opposite the Crown); SN14 8HG

17th-c stone pub in peaceful village with friendly atmosphere, enjoyable food, real ales and sizeable garden with children's play equipment

In its time, this pretty pub has been a farm and dairy as well as an inn. The main bar has a friendly, chatty atmosphere, two huge fireplaces, low beams, oak settles and pews on ancient flagstones and a nice window seat; there's also a stripped stone back area. Wadworths IPA and 6X and a couple of changing guests on handpump, several malt whiskies and 11 wines by the glass; piped music. Plenty of picnic-sets and play equipment in a sizeable sheltered upper garden with more seats on the sunny front balcony. The pub is handy for the M4.

🍴 As well as pork from their own herd of gloucester old spot pigs, the well liked bar food includes sandwiches and ploughman's (not Friday or Saturday evenings), soup, stilton, leek and mushroom crumble, ham and egg, steak in ale pie with horseradish pastry, home-made fishcakes with lemon butter sauce, breaded monkfish on a fennel and citrus fruit salad, roast leg and breast of guinea fowl with apple mash and thyme jus, and puddings like jaffa chocolate pudding with rich chocolate sauce and pineapple and banana fritters with maple syrup; there's a good value lunch for two people on Tuesday-Thursday lunchtimes. *Starters/Snacks: £5.50 to £8.50. Main Courses: £8.95 to £18.95. Puddings: £4.95 to £5.75*

Wadworths ~ Tenants David and Elizabeth White ~ Real ale ~ Bar food (12-2, 6-9(9.30 Fri and Sat); 12-3, 7-8.30 Sun) ~ Restaurant ~ (0117) 937 2332 ~ Children allowed in restaurant only until 7pm ~ Dogs allowed in bar ~ Open 12-3, 6-11; 12-11 Sat and Sun; closed Monday lunchtime

Recommended by Dr and Mrs A K Clarke, June and Robin Savage, Lise Chace, Meg and Colin Hamilton, Michael Doswell

KILKENNY

SP0118   MAP 4

Kilkeney Inn

On A436, 1 mile W of Andoversford, near Cheltenham – OS Sheet 163 map reference 007187; GL54 4LN

Popular food in contemporary dining pub with real ales and good, obliging service; seats outside with country views

Originally six stone cottages, this is now a modernised, spacious dining pub with quick, pleasant service. The extended, bright bar has neatly alternated stripped cotswold stone and white plasterwork, as well as gleaming dark wheelback chairs around the tables and an open fire. There's also a light and airy conservatory; piped music. St Austell Tribute and Wells & Youngs Bitter and Waggledance on handpump, and a good choice of wines by the glass. From the seats and tables out on the terrace and lawn there are attractive Cotswold views.

⊞ As well as light meals such as filled ciabattas, ham and egg, beef pie topped with stilton and puff pastry and cumberland sausage and mash with onion gravy, there's a more elaborate menu with chicken liver pâté made with orange and rosemary, thai salmon and crayfish fishcakes, warm goats cheese and sweet pepper tartlet with onion marmalade, chicken breast with thyme butter, wild mushrooms and red wine jus, pork steak with sage and grain mustard sauce, slow-roasted lamb shoulder with mint gravy, and puddings like **Baileys cheesecake and banoffi pie.** *Starters/Snacks: £4.95 to £9.95. Main Courses: £9.95 to £18.95. Puddings: £4.50 to £5.95*

Charles Wells ~ Lease Nigel and Jean White ~ Real ale ~ Bar food ~ Restaurant ~ (01242) 820341 ~ Well-behaved children allowed ~ Open 11-2.30, 5.30-11; 12-10.30 Sun ~ Bedrooms: /£95S

Recommended by JCW, Mr and Mrs C R Little, Russell Grimshaw, Kerry Purcell, Neil and Anita Christopher, Keith and Sue Ward, M Thomas

LITTLE BARRINGTON   SP2012   MAP 4

Inn For All Seasons

On the A40 3 miles W of Burford; OX18 4TN

Fish specials as well as other interesting food in creeper-covered old inn; fine wines, big log fire, and pleasant garden; very busy during Cheltenham Gold Cup Week

The Sharp family have now been running this handsome old coaching inn for over 20 years. The attractively decorated, mellow lounge bar has low beams, stripped stone and flagstones, old prints, leather-upholstered wing armchairs and other comfortable seats, country magazines to read, and a big log fire; the atmosphere is friendly and relaxed. 16 wines by the glass from a particularly good list, over 60 malt whiskies and a couple of real ales on handpump from breweries such as Bass, Sharps and Wadworths; friendly, kind service and newspapers to read. There's also a conservatory and restaurant. Cribbage, board games and piped music. The pleasant garden has tables, a play area, and aunt sally, and there are walks straight from the inn. It gets very busy during Cheltenham Gold Cup Week.

⊞ They specialise in fresh fish with dishes such as flash-fried squid with lime, irish rock oysters, seared scallops with crisp smoked bacon and coriander dressing, roast bass on a stir fry of ginger, spring onion, shredded chinese leaves and rice noodles with a spicy plum sauce, whole grilled dover sole with lemon and parsley butter, and whole cock crabs with garlic mayonnaise. Non-fishy choices include sandwiches, soup, italian cured meats and cheeses with pickles, game terrine with red onion chutney, home-made meatballs in tomato and basil sauce, smoked salmon omelette, ham and free-range eggs, moroccan-style lamb in mixed nut couscous, free-range chicken ballotine filled with black pudding and garlic with red wine jus, and puddings like lemon posset and warm banana sponge with coconut ice-cream. *Starters/Snacks: £4.50 to £9.50. Main Courses: £7.50 to £15.50. Puddings: £4.50 to £7.00*

Free house ~ Licensees Matthew and Heather Sharp ~ Real ale ~ Bar food (11.30-2.30, 6.30-9.30; 12-2, 7-9 Sun) ~ (01451) 844324 ~ Children welcome ~ Dogs allowed in bar and bedrooms ~ Open 10-2.30, 6-11; 10am-11pm Sat; 12-10.30 Sun ~ Bedrooms: £68B/£115B

Recommended by David Lamb, Edward Mirzoeff, Tom and Ruth Rees, John Holroyd, Richard Wyld, Graham Oddey, Richard Marjoram, Peter and Audrey Dowsett

LITTLETON-UPON-SEVERN   ST5989   MAP 2

White Hart

3.5 miles from M48 junction 1; B4461 towards Thornbury, then village signposted; BS35 1NR

A good mix of customers; log fires in three main rooms, nice country furnishings, and good beer and food; nearby walks

New licensees have taken over this cosy 17th-c farmhouse but have made no major changes and readers have been quick to voice their support. It's a popular place and the three main rooms have log fires and fine furnishings such as long cushioned wooden settles, high-backed settles, oak and elm tables and a loveseat in the big low inglenook fireplace. There are flagstones in the front, huge tiles at the back, and smaller tiles on the left, plus some old pots and pans, a lovely old White Hart Inn Simonds Ale sign and hops on beams; by the black wooden staircase are some nice little alcove seats. Similarly furnished, a family room has some sentimental engravings, plates on a delft shelf and a couple of high chairs; a back snug has pokerwork seats. Youngs Bitter and Special and guest beers like Bath Ales Gem and St Austells Tribute on handpump and several wines by the glass; even when stretched, the friendly staff cope admirably. Outside, there are picnic-sets on the neat front lawn with interesting cottagey flowerbeds, and by the good big back car park are some attractive shrubs and teak furniture on a small brick terrace. Several enjoyable walks from the pub.

🍴 **Decent bar food now includes lunchtime sandwiches and ploughman's as well as salads such as fresh seared tuna niçoise and warm ham hock with a poached egg, salmon and haddock fishcake with home-made tartare sauce, gloucester old spot sausages with caramelised onion and red wine gravy, butternut squash and green bean thai red curry, beer-battered haddock, confit shoulder of lamb with pommes anna, braised blade of beef with jerusalem artichoke purée, and puddings.** *Starters/Snacks: £4.95 to £8.95. Main Courses: £8.95 to £16.50. Puddings: £3.50 to £5.50*

Youngs ~ Managers Jamie and Diane Reed ~ Real ale ~ Bar food (12-2(3 Sun), 6.30(6 Sun)-9.30(9 Sun); all day Sat) ~ (01454) 412275 ~ Children in family areas ~ Dogs welcome ~ Open 12-midnight

Recommended by Michael Doswell, Chris and Angela Buckell, Will Stevens, Pete Devonish, Ian McIntyre, Dave Braisted, Mr and Mrs D J Nash, Tom Evans, Bob and Angela Brooks, Donna and Roger, Philip and Jude Simmons

LOWER ODDINGTON   SP2326 MAP 4

Fox 🍽️ 🍷 🛏️

Signposted off A436 between Stow and Chipping Norton; GL56 0UR

Popular dining inn with excellent food and wines, several real ales, and helpful staff

There's no doubt that this smart, busy inn places firm emphasis on the particularly good food but they do still offer Greene King Abbot, Hook Norton Bitter and a beer from Wickwar on handpump, and if you are lucky you might be able to sit on one of the bar stools in the small pubby bit by the bar counter; several wines by the glass. The simply furnished rooms have fresh flowers and flagstones, hunting scene figures above the mantelpiece, a display cabinet with pewter mugs and stone bottles, daily newspapers and an inglenook fireplace. The terrace has a custom-built awning and outdoor heaters, and the cottagey garden is pretty. A good eight-mile walk starts from here (though a stroll around the pretty village might be less taxing).

🍴 **Served by neat, uniformed staff, the interesting modern food might include soup, roasted red pepper and goats cheese tart, sautéed lambs kidneys, honey-roast duck salad with raspberry vinaigrette, salmon and leek cakes with hollandaise, mushroom, courgette and pesto lasagne, chicken breast baked with avocado and garlic, steak and kidney pie, fillet of pork with sage mash and dijon sauce, and puddings such as poached pears with chocolate sauce and orange and apricot brioche bread and butter pudding.** *Starters/Snacks: £5.00 to £6.75. Main Courses: £10.25 to £16.50. Puddings: £5.00*

Free house ~ Licensees James Cathcart and Ian MacKenzie ~ Real ale ~ Bar food (12-2(3.30 Sun), 6.30-9.30(7-9 Sun)) ~ Restaurant ~ (01451) 870555 ~ Children welcome ~ Dogs allowed in bar ~ Open 12-midnight(11 Sun); closed 25 Dec ~ Bedrooms: /£68S(£95B)

Recommended by Laurence and Kim Manning, Noel Grundy, Chris Glasson, Jay Bohmrich, MDN, Phil and Gill Wass, Evelyn and Derek Walter, Bruce and Sharon Eden, Richard Greaves, Graham Oddey, Jeff and Wendy Williams, Guy Vowles, Paul Boot, Fred and Kate Portnell, Keith and Sue Ward, Rod Stoneman

Post Office address codings confusingly give the impression that some pubs are in Gloucestershire, when they're really in Warwickshire (which is where we list them).

NAILSWORTH
ST8499   MAP 4

Egypt Mill 🛏️

Just off A46; heading N towards Stroud, first right after roundabout, then left; GL6 0AE

Stylishly converted mill with lovely summer terrace and interesting split-level bar

This is a stylish conversion of a three-floor stone-built mill still with working waterwheels and the millstream flowing through. The brick-and-stone-floored split-level bar gives good views of the wheels, and there are big pictures and lots of stripped beams in the comfortable carpeted lounge, along with some hefty yet elegant ironwork from the old mill machinery; maybe piped music. Nailsworth Mayor's Bitter and Stroud Tom Long on handpump, and several wines by the glass. Ideal for summer evenings, the floodlit terrace garden by the millpond is pretty, and there's a little bridge over from the car park. It can get quite crowded on fine weekends, but it's spacious enough to feel at its best when busy. More reports please.

🍽️ Well liked bar food at lunchtime includes sandwiches, soup, cauliflower cheese with mozzarella glaze and crispy bacon with garlic bread, home-cooked ham and egg, and home-made sausages with onion gravy; also, thai fishcakes with chilli jam, pressed ham hock terrine with home-made piccalilli, beer-battered haddock, vegetarian meatballs in tomato and basil sauce, slow roast pork belly with bean and chorizo casserole, steak and kidney suet pudding, and puddings such as rich chocolate fondant with chocolate sauce and strawberry and sherry trifle; they serve some kind of food all day on Sundays (main meals until 2.30). *Starters/Snacks: £4.95 to £6.95. Main Courses: £6.50 to £14.50. Puddings: £5.25*

Free house ~ Licensees Stephen Webb and Rob Aldridge ~ Real ale ~ Bar food (all day Sun) ~ Restaurant ~ (01453) 833449 ~ Children welcome ~ Open 11-11(midnight Sat); 12-11 Sun ~ Bedrooms: £80S/£90S

Recommended by Tom and Ruth Rees, J Crosby, Dr and Mrs C W Thomas, Karen Eliot, Andy and Claire Barker, Brian and Pat Wardrobe

Weighbridge

B4014 towards Tetbury; GL6 9AL

Super two-in-one pies served in cosy old-fashioned bar rooms, a fine choice of drinks, lots of black ironware hanging from beams, and sheltered landscaped garden

This is a really good pub with genuinely welcoming, helpful staff – it's the sort of place that customers happily return to again and again. The relaxed bar has three cosily old-fashioned rooms with stripped stone walls, antique settles and country chairs, window seats and open fires. The black beamed ceiling of the lounge bar is thickly festooned with black ironware – sheepshears, gin traps, lamps, and a large collection of keys, many from the old Longfords Mill opposite the pub. Upstairs is a raftered hayloft with an engaging mix of rustic tables. No noisy games machines or piped music. Well kept Uley Old Spot and Laurie Lee and Wadworths 6X on handpump, 15 wines (and champagne) by the glass, Weston's cider and several malt whiskies. Behind the building is a sheltered landscaped garden with picnic-sets under umbrellas. Good disabled access and facilities.

🍽️ The hugely popular two-in-one pies come in a large bowl, and half the bowl contains the filling of your choice whilst the other is full of home-made cauliflower cheese (or broccoli mornay or root vegetables), and topped with pastry: turkey and trimmings, salmon in a creamy sauce, steak and mushroom, roast root vegetables, pork, bacon and celery in stilton sauce or chicken, ham and leek in a cream and tarragon sauce; you can also have mini versions or straightforward pies, Other dishes include filled baguettes, filled baked potatoes, omelettes, lentil chilli, moussaka, duck breast in an orange and Grand Marnier sauce, and puddings such as lemon tart and banana crumble with butterscotch sauce. *Starters/Snacks: £3.95 to £7.85. Main Courses: £6.95 to £14.95. Puddings: £4.95 to £6.45*

Free house ~ Licensee Howard Parker ~ Real ale ~ Bar food (all day) ~ Restaurant ~ (01453) 832520 ~ Children allowed away from the bars until 9pm ~ Dogs welcome ~ Open 12-11(10.30 Sun); closed 25 Dec and ten days in Jan

Recommended by E McCall, T McLean, D Irving, Neil and Anita Christopher, Andy and Claire Barker, M G Hart, Norma and Noel Thomas, Ben Guy, Tom and Ruth Rees, Julian Saunders, Andrew Shore, Maria Williams, Jem Sweet, Dr and Mrs C W Thomas

NETHER WESTCOTE

SP2220 MAP 4

Westcote Inn 🍴 🍺 🛏️

Pub signposted off A424 Burford—Stow; OX7 6SD

Contemporary and stylish with fine food and drink and a friendly atmosphere

Although this very light and airy place is popular with the racing fraternity (some of the best racehorse trainers live in the area), there's a welcome for visitors, too. The main bar, the Tack Room, has stripped stone walls, beams, dark wooden tables and chairs and high bar stools on nice flagstones and lots of racing memorabilia such as Cheltenham Festival Tickets, passes, jockey colours and so forth. The pub even supports its own racehorse, Westcote, which is syndicated by enthusiasts from the village. There's a smart Champagne Bar with comfortable leather seats, wood-strip floor, an open fire and a high vaulted ceiling, a coffee lounge and a rather chic restaurant. Hook Norton Hooky Bitter and a couple of changing guest beers such as Flowers IPA and Timothy Taylors Landlord on handpump and over 20 wines (including champagne) by the glass from a carefully chosen list; piped music, TV, darts, and board games. There are seats on the terrace and in the garden and lovely views across the Evenlode Valley; spit-roasts and barbecues out here in summer.

🍴 **As well as lunchtime sandwiches, an upmarket ploughman's and a proper breakfast, the good bar food might include soup, scotch duck egg with caper mayonnaise, chicken liver pâté with onion marmalade, gloucestershire old spot sausages with onion gravy, burger with coleslaw and home-made chips, fish pie, tasty double baked stilton soufflé, rack of local lamb with tarragon sauce, loin of roe deer, smoked bacon mash and red wine sauce, and puddings such as marbled white and dark chocolate tart and blood orange cheesecake with grenadine syrup.** *Starters/Snacks: £5.00 to £7.95. Main Courses: £9.95 to £17.00. Puddings: £5.00 to £6.50*

Free house ~ Licensee Julia Reed ~ Real ale ~ Bar food (12-2.30, 7-9.30) ~ Restaurant ~ (01993) 830888 ~ Children welcome ~ Dogs allowed in bar and bedrooms ~ Open 8am-1am ~ Bedrooms: £85(£95B)/£110B

Recommended by Richard Greaves, Martin and Pauline Jennings, Guy Vowles, Noel Grundy, Paul Humphreys, Keith and Sue Ward, Bernard Stradling, David Glynne-Jones, David Howe, Dave Braisted, Myra Joyce, Michael Sargent, Julia Reed

NEWLAND

SO5509 MAP 4

Ostrich 🍺 🍷

Off B4228 in Coleford; or can be reached from the A466 in Redbrook, by the turning off at the England—Wales border – keep bearing right; GL16 8NP

Liked by walkers and their dogs with a friendly feel in spacious bar, super choice of beers, open fire, daily papers, and popular food

You can be sure of a genuinely friendly welcome from the cheerful landlady in this relaxed old pub, parts of which date back to the 13th c. The low-ceilinged bar is spacious but cosily traditional, refreshed by some light refurbishment in 2008. There are creaky floors, uneven walls with miners' lamps, window shutters, candles in bottles on the tables, and comfortable furnishings such as cushioned window seats, wall settles and rod-backed country-kitchen chairs. There's a fine big fireplace, newspapers to read, perhaps quiet piped jazz, and board games. The pub lurcher is called Alfie – and children who manage to tire him out with his rubber ball get an ice-cream for their efforts. A marvellous choice of up to eight well kept real ales on handpump might include Adnams Bitter, Fullers London Pride, Hook Norton Old Hooky, Greene King Abbot, Hop Back Summer Lightning, RCH Pitchfork, Timothy Taylors Landlord and Wye Valley Butty Bach. There are picnic-sets in a walled garden behind and out in front; the church, known as the Cathedral of the Forest, is well worth a visit, and this is a charmingly picturesque village.

🍴 Popular bar food includes good soup with home-made bread, ploughman's with home-made chutney, sausages with dauphinoise potatoes and onion gravy, salmon and spinach fishcakes with parsley sauce, pasta with fresh tomato and basil sauce, sizzling pork ribs, steak in ale pie and nice daily specials; you can also choose from the restaurant menu in the bar. *Starters/Snacks: £5.50 to £6.50. Main Courses: £5.50 to £9.50. Puddings: £4.50*

Free house ~ Licensee Kathryn Horton ~ Real ale ~ Bar food (12-2.30, 6.30(6 Sat)-9.30) ~ Restaurant ~ (01594) 833260 ~ Children welcome ~ Dogs allowed in bar ~ May have live jazz on summer evenings in garden ~ Open 12-3, 6.30-11; 12-3, 6-midnight Sat; 12-4, 6.30-10.30 Sun

Recommended by Richard and Sally Beardsley, LM, John and Gloria Isaacs, Chris and Angela Buckell, Rob and Penny Wakefield, Di and Mike Gillam, John and Tania Wood, Mr and Mrs D J Nash

NORTH CERNEY   SP0208   MAP 4

Bathurst Arms
A435 Cirencester—Cheltenham; GL7 7BZ

Plenty of character in beamed bar, real ales and a good wine list, and comfortable bedrooms

This handsome old inn has an original beamed and panelled bar with a fireplace at each end (one quite huge and housing an open woodburner), a good mix of old tables and nicely faded chairs, and old-fashioned window seats. There are country tables in an oak-floored room off the bar, as well as winged high-backed settles forming a few booths around other tables; board games and piped music. The restaurant has been refurbished this year and has leather sofas and a woodburning stove. Hook Norton Hooky Bitter, Wickwar Cotswold Way and a couple of guests such as Battledown Sunbeam and Festival Gold on handpump, decent wines, and locally produced soft drinks and juices. The pleasant riverside garden has picnic-sets sheltered by trees and shrubs, and there are plenty of surrounding walks. This has always been at its best when the landlord himself is around, and over the last few months he hasn't seemed so much in evidence – there have been some disappointments as a result. More reports on any changes, please.

🍴 Following a change of chef since its Gloucestershire Dining Pub of the Year glory days, bar food now includes sandwiches, soup, shredded ham hock and curried pea purée spring roll with apple dipping sauce, home-made faggots with wholegrain mustard mash and red onion gravy, wild mushroom risotto, beer-battered fish with home-made tartare sauce, chicken in garlic, dijon mustard and brandy sauce and chive mash, and puddings such as baked white chocolate vanilla cheesecake with mixed berry compote and rhubarb sponge with rhubarb sauce. *Starters/Snacks: £3.95 to £6.95. Main Courses: £9.95 to £16.95. Puddings: £4.95 to £6.95*

Free house ~ Licensee James Walker ~ Real ale ~ Bar food (12-2(2.30 Fri and Sat, 3 Sun), 6(7 Sun)-9(9.30 Fri and Sat) ~ Restaurant ~ (01285) 831281 ~ Children welcome ~ Dogs allowed in bar and bedrooms ~ Open 12-3, 6-11; 12-11(10.30 Sun) Sat; closed 25 Dec, evening 26 Dec ~ Bedrooms: £55B/£75B

Recommended by E McCall, T McLean, D Irving, Mr and Mrs J Brown, Cedric Robertshaw, Russell Grimshaw, Kerry Purcell, J Crosby, Alan Bulley, Guy Vowles, V Brogden, G Dunstan, Giles and Annie Francis, Melanie Harries, R Hebblethwaite, Christopher Pincher, John and Jackie Walsh, Peter Hadkins, Jude Wright, K Turner, Andrew Geraghty, Howard and Lorna Lambert, Fred and Lorraine Gill, Chris Flynn, Wendy Jones, Paul and Shirley White

NORTH NIBLEY   ST7596   MAP 4

New Inn 🍺
E of village itself; Waterley Bottom – OS Sheet 162 map reference 758963; GL11 6EF

Good choice of real ales and draught ciders in friendly country pub, tasty food and seats in garden

Peacefully tucked away in lovely south cotswold countryside, this bustling pub has a range of interesting real ales from antique beer pumps and holds two beer festivals a year (best to phone for dates): Cotleigh Tawny, Goffs Jouster, Matthews Brassknocker, and Wye Valley Butty Bach. Also, five draught ciders and an August cider festival. The lounge bar has cushioned windsor chairs and high-backed settles against the partly stripped stone walls and the simple, cosy public bar has darts. There are lots of tables on the lawn with more on a covered decked area (where there is an outdoor pool table).

🍴 **Enjoyable bar food includes filled baguettes, ploughman's, butternut squash tart with goats cheese, free-range chicken breast with a chestnut, bacon and parmesan sauce, pork tenderloin with black pudding, apple and cheese in a mustard sauce, wild alaskan salmon with watercress hollandaise, and puddings such as toffee and Malteser cheesecake and rhubarb and apple crumble.** *Starters/Snacks: £4.00 to £7.00. Main Courses: £8.00 to £14.00. Puddings: £3.50 to £4.50*

Free house ~ Licensee Les Smitherman ~ Real ale ~ Bar food (not Mon) ~ Restaurant ~ (01453) 543659 ~ Children welcome ~ Dogs welcome ~ Open 12-2.30, 6-11; 12-11 Sat; 12-10.30 Sun; closed Mon lunchtime and 2-15 Feb ~ Bedrooms: £40S/£60S

Recommended by Guy Vowles, Rob and Jane Woodward, Alain and Rose Foote

NORTHLEACH
SP1114   MAP 4

Wheatsheaf 🛏

West End; the inn is on your left as you come in following the sign off the A429, just SW of its junction with the A40; GL54 3EZ

Smart coaching inn run by three sisters with well liked food, real ales and a relaxed atmosphere; good bedrooms

Run by three sisters, this is a handsome 17th-c stone coaching inn. The big-windowed airy linked rooms have high ceilings, smart leather dining chairs around a mix of tables, flagstones in the central bar and wooden floors in the dining rooms, church candles and light modern paintwork and minimalist decor. Hook Norton Hooky Bitter on handpump and quite a few wines by the glass. There are seats in the pretty back garden. Cheltenham racecourse is nearby. More reports please.

🍴 **As well as lunchtime sandwiches, the good bar food includes soup, duck, smoked chicken and pork terrine wrapped in bacon with cumberland sauce, twice baked goats cheese soufflé, brie, walnut and rosemary lasagne, pure beefburger with toppings, a pie of the day, beer-battered cod with home-made tartare sauce, roast rack of lamb with dauphinoise potatoes and rosemary and red wine jus, daily specials, puddings like sticky toffee pudding and mango and passion fruit posset, and Sunday roasts.** *Starters/Snacks: £4.95 to £8.95. Main Courses: £9.95 to £17.95. Puddings: £4.95*

Punch ~ Lease Jo Champion ~ Real ale ~ Bar food (12-2.30, 6.30-10) ~ Restaurant ~ (01451) 860244 ~ Children welcome but must be with an adult ~ Open 11-11; 12-10.30 Sun ~ Bedrooms: £65S/£95S

Recommended by Dr and Mrs A K Clarke, Dennis Jenkin, Mike and Mary Carter, Guy Vowles, Ian and Joan Blackwell, Paul Goldman, George Atkinson, Jean and Douglas Troup

OLDBURY-ON-SEVERN
ST6092   MAP 2

Anchor ♀ 🍺

Village signposted from B4061; BS35 1QA

Bustling country pub with well liked food, a fine choice of drinks, and pretty garden and hanging baskets

Well priced for the area and kept on handpump in very good condition, the real ales in this popular and friendly pub continue to be quite a draw: Bass, Butcombe Bitter, Otter Bitter, Theakstons Old Peculier and Wickwar Spring Ale. They also have a fine range of 75 malt whiskies and 14 wines by the glass. The neatly kept lounge has an easy-going atmosphere, modern beams and stone, a mix of tables including an attractive oval oak gateleg, cushioned window seats, winged seats against the wall, oil paintings by a local artist and a big winter log fire. Diners can eat in the lounge or bar area or in the dining room at the back of the building (good for larger groups) and the menu is the same in all rooms. In summer, you can eat in the pretty garden and the hanging baskets and window boxes are lovely then; boules. They have wheelchair access and a disabled lavatory. Plenty of walks to the River Severn and along the many footpaths and bridleways, and St Arilda's church nearby is interesting, on its odd little knoll with wild flowers among the gravestones (the primroses and daffodils in spring are quite a show).

🍴 **Good, reasonably priced bar food includes ciabatta sandwiches, ploughman's, soup, warm goats cheese and chorizo salad with grilled red onions and peppers, lasagne, beef in ale pie, spinach and ricotta ravioli with wild mushroom sauce, lamb curry, steak and mushroom in ale pie, grilled salmon with an orange and chive sauce, half a gressingham duck with braised cabbage and dauphinoise potatoes, and puddings like crème brûlée with home-made shortbread and mixed berries with hot white chocolate sauce; there's also a good value two-course weekday lunch menu.** *Starters/Snacks: £3.95 to £8.95. Main Courses: £6.25 to £12.25. Puddings: £3.95*

Free house ~ Licensees Michael Dowdeswell and Mark Sorrell ~ Real ale ~ Bar food (12-2, 6(6.30 winter weekdays)-9) ~ Restaurant ~ (01454) 413331 ~ Children in dining room only ~ Dogs allowed in bar ~ Open 11.30-3, 6-midnight; 11.30-1am(midnight Sun) Sat; midday opening Sun and 6.30 evening opening all week in winter

Recommended by Mr and Mrs J P Blake, Dr and Mrs M E Wilson, James Morrell, Lawrence Pearse, J and F Gowers, Tom and Ruth Rees, Will Stevens, Andrew Shore, Maria Williams, Barry and Anne, Tom Evans, Pauline and Philip Darley, Bob and Angela Brooks, Colin and Peggy Wilshire, Bernard Stradling

PAXFORD   SP1837   MAP 4

Churchill Arms
B4479, SE of Chipping Campden; GL55 6XH

Very well run inn, super food and choice of drinks, first-class relaxed service and comfortable bedrooms

This is a thoroughly likeable and unpretentious pub with particularly good food and service and run by professional, hands-on licensees who genuinely care about their customers. The simply furnished flagstoned bar has low ceilings and some timbering, a happy assortment of old tables and chairs, laminated local maps showing walks of varying lengths, and a snug warmed by a good log fire in its big fireplace; there's also a dining extension – but to be sure of a table you must arrive early as they don't take bookings. Arkells Moonlight, Hook Norton Hooky Bitter, and a guest like Shepherd Neame Spitfire on handpump, some european and american bottled beers and several wines by the glass (including sweet ones) from a thoughtfully chosen list; excellent service from bright waitresses, board games. There are some seats outside and aunt sally. The four well equipped and comfortable little bedrooms have lovely views and the breakfasts are unusually creative.

🍴 **Delicious food might include nice soups, pork, venison and duck terrine with green tomato chutney, smoked haddock rarebit with a soft boiled egg, fishcake with spinach, dill and capers, breast of pheasant with port and green peppercorns, grilled pork chop, lentils with apple and mustard and a herb and parmesan crust, monkfish medallions with sweet and sour butternut squash, rump steak with balsamic onions and blue cheese glaze, and puddings such as maple and mascarpone baked cheesecake with pineapple and a shortbread biscuit and triple chocolate torte with raspberry parfait. The side dishes are interesting and they have a take-away menu as well.** *Starters/Snacks: £4.50 to £8.00. Main Courses: £9.00 to £18.00. Puddings: £4.00 to £6.50*

Enterprise ~ Licensees Sonya Kidney and Leo Brooke-Little ~ Real ale ~ Bar food ~ (01386) 594000 ~ Children welcome ~ Open 11-3, 6(6.30 Sun)-11 ~ Bedrooms: £40B/£70B

Recommended by Noel Grundy, Susan and Nigel Brookes, R J Herd, P Waterman, Stuart Doughty, Heather and Dick Martin, Laurence and Kim Manning, Derek Thomas

---

We mention bottled beers and spirits only if there is something unusual about them – imported belgian real ales, say, or dozens of malt whiskies; so do please let us know about them in your reports.

SAPPERTON
SO9403 MAP 4

Bell

Village signposted from A419 Stroud—Cirencester; OS Sheet 163 map reference 948033; GL7 6LE

Super pub with beamed cosy rooms, a really good mix of customers, delicious food, local ales, and very pretty courtyard

This is a delightful pub run with great care by the hard-working licensees and their staff. There is quite an emphasis on the excellent food but drinkers are most welcome too and they keep four real ales on handpump: Bath Ales Gem and Wild Hare, Otter Bitter and Uley Old Spot. Also, 16 wines by the glass or half litre carafe from a large and diverse wine list with very helpful notes, Ashton Press cider, 20 malt whiskies, several armagnacs and cognacs and local soft drinks. Harry's Bar (named after their sociable springer spaniel) has big cushion-strewn sofas, benches and armchairs where you can read the daily papers with a pint in front of the woodburning stove – or simply have a pre-dinner drink. The two other cosy rooms have stripped beams, a nice mix of wooden tables and chairs, country prints and modern art on stripped stone walls, one or two attractive rugs on the flagstones, fresh flowers and open fires. The gents' has schoolboy humour cartoons on the walls. There are tables out on a small front lawn and in a partly covered and very pretty courtyard, for eating outside. Horses have their own tethering rail (and bucket of water).

🍽 **As well as a lunchtime daily pub classic dish like beef and dumpling casserole, deep-fried fish and chips and pork sausages with onion gravy, the highly enjoyable food might include ploughman's, home-cured gravadlax of organic salmon with a soft poached egg on toasted brioche with a sweet mustard and dill dressing, breast of pigeon cooked rare with a home-made faggot, black pudding and apple sauce, home-made burger of local beef with spiced dill pickles, ravioli filled with spinach and mozzarella with sweet pepper dressing, crispy belly of gloucester old spot pork with a pork samosa and sage and parmesan polenta, slowly cooked local lamb shank in a thyme cream sauce, daily specials such as cornish mussels with white wine and cream and crisp skin whole roasted black bream with sea salt and herbs, and puddings like caramel bavarois with roasted pineapple and pineapple sorbet and rich bitter chocolate tart with poached pear and white chocolate sauce.** *Starters/Snacks: £4.95 to £9.00. Main Courses: £10.50 to £20.00. Puddings: £6.75*

Free house ~ Licensees Paul Davidson and Pat LeJeune ~ Real ale ~ Bar food ~ (01285) 760298 ~ Children allowed but must be over 10 in evenings ~ Dogs welcome ~ Open 11-2.30, 6.30-11; 12-3, 7-10.30 Sun; closed 25 Dec

Recommended by Michael Doswell, K Turner, Graham Oddey, Dr A J and Mrs Tompsett, John Holroyd, Brenda and Stuart Naylor, David Morgan, David Gunn, John Morgan, Pauline and Philip Darley, J Crosby, Carol Mills, Helene Grygar, John Balfour, James Morrell, Mr and Mrs A J Hudson, R S Jalbot, Bernard Stradling, Tom and Ruth Rees, Philip and Jude Simmons, Simon and Sally Small

SHEEPSCOMBE
SO8910 MAP 4

Butchers Arms

Off B4070 NE of Stroud; GL6 7RH

Fine views, real ales and pubby food and friendly young licensees

The views from this 17th-c cotswold stone pub over the lovely surrounding steep beech wood valley are terrific. It is thought that this area was once a royal hunting ground for King Henry VIII. Inside, the bustling lounge bar has a good mix of locals and visitors, beams, wheelback chairs and cushioned stools around simple wooden tables, built-in cushioned seats in the big bay windows, interesting oddments like assorted blow lamps, irons and plates, and a woodburning stove; friendly service. The restaurant has an open log fire. Butcombe Bitter, Wye Valley Butty Bach and a guest like St Austells Tribute on handpump, several wines by the glass and Weston's cider; darts, chess and cribbage. There are seats outside. The pub is part of a new pub group called Heartstone Inns. More reports please.

🍽 **As well as lunchtime sandwiches, bar food now includes crab, crayfish and orange salad, chicken liver pâté with red onion marmalade, local ham and free range eggs, wild** mushroom stroganoff, steak, stilton and ale pie, local cider, apple and pork sausages with cider gravy, home-made burger, beer-battered fish, apple and prune stuffed pork tenderloin with calvados sauce; puddings; Sunday roasts. *Starters/Snacks: £4.25 to £5.95. Main Courses: £7.95 to £16.50. Puddings: £3.75 to £4.25*

Free house ~ Licensee Mark Tallents ~ Real ale ~ Bar food (12-2.30, 6.30(7 winter)-9.30; all day weekends) ~ (01452) 812113 ~ Children welcome ~ Dogs allowed in bar ~ Open 11.30-3, 6-11; 11.30am-midnight Sat; 12-10.30 Sun; weekday evening opening 6.30 in winter

Recommended by Andrew Shore, Maria Williams, Paul and Shirley White, Alain and Rose Foote, Mr and Mrs I and E Bell, Neil and Anita Christopher, Giles and Annie Francis, Tom and Ruth Rees, John Holroyd

TETBURY ST8993 MAP 4

Snooty Fox ♀ 🛏

Market Place; small residents' car park, nearby pay & display; free car park some way down hill; GL8 8DD

Upmarket hotel with unstuffy bar, real ales, lots of wines by the glass, and popular food

Although this is a smart hotel, the bar here is unpretentious and friendly and has a good mix of chatty locals (often with their dogs) and visitors. It's a high-ceilinged, carpeted room with stripped stone, like much of the rest of the ground floor, comfortable sturdy leather-armed chairs around cast-iron tripod tables, a big log fireplace flanked by an imposing pair of brass flambeaux, brass ceiling fans, and Ronald Searle pony-club cartoons. Three real ales on handpump from breweries such as Otter, Nailsworth and Wickwar, lots of wines by the glass and a fine collection of armagnac, cognac, calvados and port; good service from neat young staff and unobtrusive piped music. Behind the main bar is a similar room with a colourful rug on bare boards and a leather sofa among other seats. On the right a smaller quieter room has church candles on the dining tables and subdued lighting. Outside, there's a sheltered entryway with teak tables and chairs facing the ancient central covered market. Comfortable, well equipped bedrooms and good breakfasts.

🍴 Interesting, well liked bar food at lunchtime includes sandwiches and filled baguettes, soup, ploughman's with proper cheddar, home-cooked ham and two free-range eggs, smoked bacon and smoked cheese sausages with onion gravy, and salmon and coriander fishcakes with chive beurre blanc; in the evening there might be gloucester old spot and duck liver terrine with port jelly, aubergine, potato and mussel tortilla with tapenade and marinated peppers, roast rabbit loin with sausage and a haricot bean and wild mushroom stew, chicken with roast garlic, thyme, bacon and field mushrooms, mutton braised in beer with horseradish and ham dumplings, and puddings like sticky toffee date pudding with date sauce and apple and hazelnut tarte tatin with a topping of caramel ice-cream. *Starters/Snacks: £3.95 to £5.95. Main Courses: £4.95 to £7.95. Puddings: £4.95*

Free house ~ Licensee Marc Gibbons ~ Real ale ~ Bar food ~ Restaurant ~ (01666) 502436 ~ Children welcome ~ Dogs allowed in bar and bedrooms ~ Open 11-11; 12-10.30 Sun ~ Bedrooms: £79B/£103B

Recommended by Pete Coxon, Nick and Meriel Cox, Ian Malone, George Atkinson

Trouble House ♀

A433 towards Cirencester, near Cherington turn; GL8 8SG

Smart and friendly bars with customers to match, an ambitious menu, good drinks, and attentive service

There's no doubt that most emphasis in this rather smart place is on the restaurant-style cooking although they do keep (in the small saggy-beamed middle room) Wadworths IPA and 6X on handpump and a dozen wines by the glass (including champagne). Furnishings are mainly close-set stripped pine or oak tables with chapel, wheelback and other chairs, and there are attractive mainly modern country prints on the cream or butter-coloured walls. On the left is a parquet-floored room with a big stone fireplace, a hop-girt mantelpiece and some big black beams; piped music, and attentive service. You can also sit out at picnic-sets on the gravel courtyard behind. More reports please.

🍴 Using carefully sourced local produce and making all their own ice-creams and bread, the interesting bar food includes sandwiches, soup, parfait of foie gras and chicken livers with pickled grapes, grilled scallops with caramelised cauliflower and cumin purée, raisins and capers, braised beef with smoked potato purée and bourguignon sauce, slow-cooked gloucestershire old spot pork belly with scottish langoustine scampi, langoustine sauce and shi-itake mushroom risotto, hereford rib-eye steak with béarnaise sauce, and puddings such as hot chocolate fondant with milk ice-cream and spiced pineapple tarte tatin with vanilla ice-cream. *Starters/Snacks: £5.80 to £9.50. Main Courses: £13.50 to £17.50. Puddings: £5.50*

Wadworths ~ Tenants Martin & Neringa Caws ~ Real ale ~ Bar food (not Sun evening or Mon) ~ (01666) 502206 ~ Children allowed away from bar area; must be over 10 in evening ~ Dogs welcome ~ Open 11.30-3, 6.30(7 winter)-11; 12-3 Sun; closed Sun evening, all day Mon; two weeks in Jan

Recommended by J Crosby, Joyce and Maurice Cottrell, Richard Wyld, David and Stella Martin, Mike and Sue Loseby, Graham Oddey, Geoff and Brigid Smithers

TODENHAM
SP2436   MAP 4

Farriers Arms ♀
Between A3400 and A429 N of Moreton-in-Marsh; GL56 9PF

Country pub with interesting décor and fine views

The bar in this unspoilt pub has nice wonky white plastered walls, hops on the beams, fine old polished flagstones by the stone bar counter and a woodburner in a huge inglenook fireplace. A tiny little room off to the side (full of old books and interesting old photographs) can seat parties of ten people. Hook Norton Hooky Bitter, Shepherd Neame Spitfire, and Wye Valley Butty Bach on handpump, and ten wines by the glass; piped music, darts and board games. The pub has fine views over the surrounding countryside from the back garden and there are a couple of tables with views of the church on a small terrace by the quiet little road; aunt sally. Good surrounding walks. More reports please.

🍴 Bar food includes sandwiches, soup, chicken liver parfait with cumberland sauce, king prawns in tempura batter with sweet chilli dip, ham and eggs, beef in ale pie, roast vegetables and goats cheese cannelloni with pesto and parmesan cream, pork tenderloin wrapped in parma ham with grain mustard mash and thyme gravy, puddings and Sunday roast beef. *Starters/Snacks: £4.00 to £9.00. Main Courses: £9.00 to £17.00. Puddings: £4.00 to £5.50*

Free house ~ Licensees Nigel and Louise Kirkwood ~ Real ale ~ Bar food (12-2.30(2 winter), 6.30(7 winter)-9) ~ Restaurant ~ (01608) 650901 ~ Children welcome ~ Dogs allowed in bar ~ Open 12-3, 6(6.30 Sun)-11 ~ Bedrooms: /£80S

Recommended by B R and M F Arnold, Keith and Sue Ward, John Holroyd, Peter and Jean Hoare, Clive and Fran Dutson, John Robertson, Alun and Jennifer Evans, Paul Butler, H O Dickinson, Phyl and Jack Street, Ken and Barbara Turner

UPPER ODDINGTON
SP2225   MAP 4

Horse & Groom 🍴 ♀
Village signposted from A436 E of Stow-on-the-Wold; GL56 0XH

Pretty 16th-c cotswold stone inn with imaginative food, lots of wines by the glass and local beers and other local drinks

Well run and friendly, this is a neat and attractive dining pub with a wide mix of customers. The bar has pale polished flagstones, a handsome antique oak box settle among other more modern seats, some nice armchairs at one end, oak beams in the ochre ceiling, stripped stone walls, and a log fire in the inglenook fireplace. Wickwar BOB and Wye Valley Bitter and Hereford Pale Ale on handpump, 25 wines by the glass (including champagne), local apple juice and a locally brewed premium lager. There are seats and tables under green parasols on the terrace and in the pretty garden. We've yet to hear from readers who have stayed here and would be grateful for any comments.

🍴 Taking great care to use local and regional suppliers (much of the vegetables and fruit used in their cooking is grown in the village), the very good food at lunchtime includes sandwiches, ploughman's, courgette and red onion tart, smoked haddock and spring onion fishcakes with horseradish cream, a trio of gloucester old spot pork sausages with wholegrain mustard mash and red onion gravy, home-cooked ham with free-range eggs, and seasonal fish pie; there's also rare thai beef salad with cashew nut and ginger dressing, venison terrine with red onion marmalade, crispy belly of gloucester old spot pork with a sauté of red peppers, pak choi and courgette, sesame noodles and sweet and sour sauce, and quality aged steaks from hereford breed herds and cut to any size you want. Puddings such as tiramisu iced parfait with chocolate triangle and kaluha cream and poached peaches with vanilla cheesecake ice-cream and shortbread biscuit. *Starters/Snacks: £5.75 to £7.75. Main Courses: £8.95 to £14.75. Puddings: £6.75*

Free house ~ Licensees Simon and Sally Jackson ~ Real ale ~ Bar food ~ Restaurant ~ (01451) 830584 ~ Children welcome ~ Open 12-3, 5.30-11; 12-3, 6-10.30 Sun ~ Bedrooms: £76S/£89S(£99B)

Recommended by Stuart Doughty, Keith and Sue Ward, Graham and Doreen Holden, B R and M F Arnold, Martin and Pauline Jennings, Alun and Jennifer Evans, Joan and Tony Walker, Julie and Bill Ryan, Graham Oddey, John and Elisabeth Cox, Julian Saunders

WOODCHESTER   SO8302   MAP 4

Ram 🍺

High Street, South Woodchester; off A46 S of Stroud; GL5 5EL

Half a dozen interesting ales, a friendly landlord and fair-priced food in attractive country pub

Most customers come to this friendly country pub to enjoy the six real ales on handpump kept particularly well by the welcoming and obliging landlord. They change constantly but might include Butcombe Bitter, Cotswold Spring Old English Rose, Goffs Jouster, Stroud Budding and Tom Long, and Uley Old Spot. The relaxed L-shaped beamed bar has a nice mix of traditional furnishings (including several cushioned antique panelled settles) on bare boards, stripped stonework, and an open fire. There are seats outside on the terrace and spectacular valley views; in summer they hold various events out here – open air theatre, live music and so forth.

🍴 Good value, enjoyable bar food includes sandwiches, soup, king prawns in filo pastry, spinach and ricotta cannelloni, gloucester old spot sausages with mash and onion gravy, steak in ale pie, cold poached salmon with lemon and dill dressing, chargrilled chicken breast with mango salsa, and puddings such as treacle sponge with custard or white chocolate and raspberry cheesecake; on Monday-Thursday they offer a £6 main course. *Starters/Snacks: £3.00 to £6.00. Main Courses: £6.00 to £11.50. Puddings: £3.95*

Free house ~ Licensee Tim Mullen ~ Real ale ~ Bar food ~ Restaurant ~ (01453) 873329 ~ Children welcome ~ Dogs welcome ~ Open 11-11

Recommended by Andrew Shore, Maria Williams, Tom and Ruth Rees, Dr A J and Mrs Tompsett, E McCall, T McLean, D Irving, Andy and Claire Barker, Chris and Angela Buckell

If a pub tries to make you leave a credit card behind the bar, be on your guard. The credit card firms and banks which issue them condemn this practice. After all, the publican who asks you to do this is in effect saying: 'I don't trust you'. Have you any more reason to trust his staff? If your card is used fraudulently while you have let it be kept out of your sight, the card company could say you've been negligent yourself – and refuse to make good your losses. So say that they can 'swipe' your card instead, but must hand it back to you. Please let us know if a pub does try to keep your card.

LUCKY DIP

Besides the fully inspected pubs, you might like to try these Lucky Dips recommended to us and described by readers (if you do, please send us reports: feedback@thegoodpubguide.co.uk).

AMBERLEY [SO8401]
Black Horse GL5 5AL [off A46 Stroud—Nailsworth; Littleworth]: Relaxed proper local with spectacular views from conservatory, Greene King IPA and Wells & Youngs Bombardier, open fire, flagstones and high-backed settles, lots of cheerful sporting pictures (and TV for big matches), large family area on left (huge food choice), games room; plenty of tables on pleasant back terrace with barbecue, more on secluded lawn *(LYM, E McCall, T McLean, D Irving, R B Gardiner, Karen Eliot, Ann and Colin Hunt, John Saville, Lawrence Pearse, N R White)*

APPERLEY [SO8528]
☆ *Coal House* GL19 4DN [village signed off B4213 S of Tewkesbury; Gabb Lane]: Light and airy pub in splendid riverside position, helpful cheerful staff, Hook Norton Best and a guest beer, Stowford Press cider, plenty of blackboards for inexpensive usual food, two dining areas, walkers welcome; no dogs; children welcome, wheelchair access possible, plenty of tables on front terrace and lawn with Severn views, play area, moorings *(Chris and Angela Buckell, BB, Neil and Anita Christopher)*
Farmers Arms GL19 4DR [Lower Apperley (B4213)]: Extended country local with mix of chairs and chesterfields, old prints, beams and huge open fire, popular dining area with good range of fish, Wadworths ales; children welcome, picnic-sets in garden with water feature and play area *(LYM, Andrew Shore, Maria Williams)*

AUST [ST5788]
Boars Head BS35 4AX [0.5 mile from M48, junction 1, off Avonmouth rd]: Marstons pub handy for the 'old' Severn bridge, their ales and Bath Gem, good house wines, wide food choice from baguettes to steak, dark furniture in linked rooms and alcoves, beams and some stripped stone, huge log fire; piped music; wheelchair access possible, children in eating area away from bar, dogs on lead in bar, pretty sheltered garden *(Mr and Mrs A J Hudson, Donna and Roger, LYM, Chris and Angela Buckell, Colin Moore)*

AWRE [SO7008]
☆ *Red Hart* GL14 1EW [off A48 S of Newnham]: Tall village inn with welcoming service, enjoyable home-made local food, real ale, farm cider, good wines by the glass, heavy-beamed and flagstoned bar, illuminated well and other interesting features, board games; piped music; children and dogs welcome, front picnic-sets, comfortable bedrooms, good breakfast, cl Sun evening and Mon/Tues lunchtimes in winter, open all day Sat *(Dr A J and Mrs Tompsett, Dr and Mrs C W Thomas, J Crosby, LYM, Rose Warwick, James Stephens, John and Alison Hamilton)*

BIBURY [SP1006]
Catherine Wheel GL7 5ND [Arlington; B4425 NE of Cirencester]: Now a Marstons pub, with open-plan main bar and smaller back rooms, low beams, stripped stone, good log fires, good range of bar food with unusual european flavour, raftered dining room; children welcome, picnic-sets out behind, famously beautiful village, handy for country and riverside walks, four bedrooms, open all day *(Keith and Sue Ward, LYM)*
☆ *Swan* GL7 5NW [B4425]: Hotel in lovely spot facing River Coln, friendly attentive staff, well kept Hook Norton, exemplary bar stools and blazing fire in comfortable and attractive side bar used by locals, nice modern adjoining brasserie with appealing up-to-date food, smart formal dining room; heated flagstoned terrace, pleasant waterside garden, luxurious bedrooms *(George Atkinson, Giles Barr, Eleanor Dandy, Keith and Sue Ward, V Brogden, BB)*

BIRDLIP [SO9214]
Royal George GL4 8JH: Welcoming two-level beamed bar beyond hotel reception, airy and open, wide food range from sandwiches up, good wine choice, three Greene King ales, prompt friendly service, soft lighting, part with armchairs and low tables, comfortable restaurant; piped music, busy Thurs quiz night; heated terrace, fine grounds, 34 bedrooms *(Guy Vowles, E McCall, T McLean, D Irving)*

BLAKENEY [SO6606]
Cock GL15 4DB [Nibley Hill/A48]: Enjoyable food, welcoming bar with real ales, local ciders and perry; children welcome, lovely view from big garden, six comfortable bedrooms *(Jessica Triggs)*

BLOCKLEY [SP1635]
Great Western Arms GL56 9DT [Station Rd (B4479)]: Smartly updated dining area, welcoming attentive licensees, well kept Hook Norton ales, enjoyable simple food, busy public bar; attractive village, lovely valley view *(Stuart Turner)*

BOURTON-ON-THE-WATER [SP1620]
Kingsbridge Inn GL54 2BS [Riverside]: Cheerful roomy open-plan pub, friendly efficient staff, emphasis on quickly served food inc two-for-one OAP bargains, well kept ales, log fire; pleasant village/river view from terrace tables *(Dr and Mrs Jackson)*
Old Manse GL54 2BX [Victoria St]: River Windrush view from front garden and end of long turkey-carpeted beamed bar (no under-21s), good choice of enjoyable food from all-day doorstep sandwiches up, Greene King ales, big log fire, attractive old prints, bookshelves, some stripped stone, pretty restaurant (children allowed here); TV, machines, piped music; 15 good bedrooms, open all day *(George Atkinson,*

BB, K H Frostick, M Greening, Keith and
Sue Ward)

BOX [SO8500]

☆ *Halfway House* GL6 9AE [by
Minchinhampton Common]: New licensees
again for smartly renovated light and airy
open-plan dining pub, good range of real
ales from central bar, friendly staff,
downstairs restaurant; piped music; children
and dogs welcome, garden tables, open all
day (E McCall, T McLean, D Irving, Tom and
Ruth Rees, LYM)

BROADOAK [SO6912]

White Hart GL14 1JB [A48 Gloucester—
Chepstow]: Overlooking tidal Severn, plenty
of tables out on high terrace by quay,
sensibly priced pubby food, Greene King
ales, carpeted bar and dining area, low
beams, nautical décor; piped music;
wheelchair access (Chris and Angela Buckell)

BROADWELL [SP2027]

☆ *Fox* GL56 0UF [off A429 2 miles N of Stow-
on-the-Wold]: Relaxing pub above broad
green in pleasant village, friendly staff, good
range of homely pub food (not Sun evening,
and stops early lunchtime) from sandwiches
to popular Sun lunch, low-priced Donnington
BB and SBA, decent wines, good summer
lemonade, nice coffee, stripped stone and
flagstones, beams hung with jugs, log fire,
darts, dominoes and chess, plain public bar
with pool room, pleasant restaurant; may be
piped music; tables out on gravel, good big
family-friendly garden with aunt sally,
meadow behind for Caravan Club members
(George Atkinson, Noel Grundy, BB, Keith and
Sue Ward)

BROCKHAMPTON [SP0322]

☆ *Craven Arms* GL54 5XQ [off A436
Andoversford—Naunton]: Attractive 17th-c
inn nicely tucked away in hillside hamlet with
lovely views and walks, sociable licensees,
good value food in sizeable linked eating
areas off smaller bar servery, well kept ales
such as Sharps and Tetleys, low beams, thick
stone walls, some tiled flooring, mainly pine
furniture with some wall settles, tub chairs,
shove-ha'penny; children welcome, sizeable
garden, comfortable bedrooms, cl Sun evening
(Helene Grygar, LYM, Brian McBurnie, Neil and
Anita Christopher, Stuart Doughty, Keith and
Sue Ward)

CAMBRIDGE [SO7403]

George GL2 7AL [3 miles from M5 junction
13 – A38 towards Bristol]: Two spacious
dining areas, good value generous food from
filled rolls inc bargain lunches, well kept
Adnams and Wickwar BOB, helpful well
organised service, log fire; garden with
barbecues, fowl pen and play area, also
pleasant small camp site, handy for
Slimbridge wildfowl centre, open all day Sun
(Meg and Colin Hamilton, Mike and
Mary Clark)

CAMP [SO9111]

☆ *Fostons Ash* GL6 7ES [B4070 Birdlip—
Stroud, junction with Calf Way]: Popular
open-plan dining pub with good food inc

interesting lunchtime sandwiches and
imaginative light dishes, Goffs Jouster and
Wickwar Cotswold Way and BOB, decent
wines by the glass, friendly efficient young
staff, log fire, one end with settees and easy
chairs; tables in garden with heated terrace
and play area, good walks (Guy Vowles,
Neil and Anita Christopher, David Morgan)

CERNEY WICK [SU0796]

Crown GL7 5QH: Roomy modern lounge bar,
comfortable conservatory dining extension,
enjoyable inexpensive popular food, well
kept real ales, friendly local landlord, coal-
effect gas fires, games in public bar;
children welcome, good-sized garden with
swings, small motel-style bedroom extension
(Giles and Annie Francis, BB, Tim and
Rosemary Wells)

CHARLTON KINGS [SO9619]

Clock Tower GL53 8DY [Cirencester Rd]:
Marstons all-day food pub with popular two-
for-one deals, good staff, well kept ales,
decent wines (A and B D Craig)

Langton GL52 6HT [189-191 London Rd]:
Comfortable contemporary bar/brasserie
rather than pub, but has a real ale among
good range of other beers, decent wines,
friendly attentive service, enjoyable food
from sharing tapas up, several linked rooms;
covered terrace tables, open all day at least
wknds (Guy Vowles)

Reservoir GL54 4HG [London Rd (A40)]:
Large roadside pub opp reservoir, wide
choice of reasonably priced food (Peter and
Audrey Dowsett, Mr and Mrs J Brown)

CHELTENHAM [SO9421]

Bath Tavern GL53 7JT [Bath Rd]: Compact
friendly bay-windowed local with well kept
Bath Spa and Gem, good choice of wines by
the glass, bargain generous pubby food
(Joe Green, Andy and Claire Barker)

Kemble GL52 2JF [Fairview St]: Friendly
civilised backstreet local with lunchtime
sandwiches and a bargain hot dish, well kept
real ales; small back garden (Joe Green)

Overton Lodge GL50 3EA [St Georges Rd]:
Pleasantly unassuming bar and dining room,
useful pub alternative, with one or two real
ales, good choice of wines by the glass,
enjoyable sensibly priced food; parking too
(Guy Vowles)

☆ *Plough* GL52 3BG [Mill St, Prestbury]:
Thatched village local opp church,
comfortable front lounge, service from corner
corridor hatch in flagstoned back tap room,
grandfather clock and big log fire, friendly
service, Adnams Best and Broadside and
Wells & Youngs Bombardier tapped from the
cask, Stowford Press farm cider, basic pub
food inc ready-filled rolls; outstanding good-
sized flower-filled back garden with
immaculate boules pitch (Guy Vowles,
B M Eldridge, P Dawn, M Thomas)

Retreat GL50 2AB [Suffolk Parade]:
Pub/wine bar with well kept beers, good
value wines, good choice of whiskies,
enjoyable generous pub food, deep red walls,
bare floors and dark wood furniture, friendly

staff and atmosphere; children welcome, small back terrace (Rod Stoneman)

Swan GL50 1DX [High St]: Friendly local with good value pub food (not Sat/Sun evenings), three well kept changing real ales, Thatcher's cider; courtyard tables, open all day (P Dawn, Alun Beach)

CHIPPING CAMPDEN [SP1539]

☆ **Kings Arms** GL55 6AW [High St]: Fresh eclectic contemporary décor in bar/brasserie and separate restaurant, cheery helpful service, food from lunchtime sandwiches and pubby dishes to more elaborate evening meals, Hook Norton beers, good choice of wines by the glass, good log fire, daily papers; secluded back garden with picnic-sets and terrace tables, 12 comfortable bedrooms, open all day Sat (Michael Dandy, LYM, Stuart Doughty)

☆ **Lygon Arms** GL55 6HB [High St]: Appealing low-beamed bar, good value food till late evening from good sandwiches to interesting more pricy dishes, good wine choice, real ales such as Hook Norton Old Hooky and Ringwood Fortyniner, open fires, stripped stone and lots of horse pictures, small back restaurant; children welcome, tables in shady courtyard, comfortable beamed bedrooms, good breakfast, open all day wknds and summer (Michael Dandy, Derek and Sylvia Stephenson, Barry and Anne, Donna and Roger, LYM, Ian and Judi Purches)

Noel Arms GL55 6AT [High St]: Handsome old inn with two popular bars, polished oak settles, attractive old tables, armour, antique prints, tools and traps on stripped stone walls, decent food from sandwiches to some interesting dishes, Hook Norton ales, coal fire, good restaurant; children welcome, courtyard tables, nice bedrooms, good breakfast (Michael Dandy, LYM, Derek and Sylvia Stephenson)

☆ **Red Lion** GL55 6AS [Lower High St]: Linked beamed rooms with flagstones, stripped stone and log fires, good value fresh food from sandwiches up, friendly efficient service, Greene King ales, decent wine choice, fine range of malt whiskies, roomy eating area and upstairs dining room; may be quiet piped classical music, big-screen sports TV and pool in games bar; sheltered back courtyard, five comfortable character bedrooms (Michael Dandy, Paul Goldman, Neil and Anita Christopher)

CIRENCESTER [SP0202]

☆ **Corinium** GL7 2DG [Dollar St/Gloucester St]: Civilised and comfortable, with big log fire, antique coaching prints, good mix of tables, sofas and small armchairs, three real ales, Thatcher's cider, decent wines, enjoyable bar food from sandwiches up, nicely decorated restaurant; piped music; entrance through charming courtyard with tables, attractive back garden, good bedrooms (E McCall, T McLean, D Irving, Guy Vowles, BB)

Drillmans Arms GL7 2JY [Gloucester Rd, Stratton]: Popular old two-room local, friendly and relaxing, with interesting

changing real ales, good log fires, usual food, low beams, skittle alley doubling as eating area; tables out by small car park (E McCall, T McLean, D Irving, R Huggins)

Fleece GL7 2NZ [Market Pl]: Well kept old hotel, good value enterprising food, friendly effective largely Hispanic staff, good choice of wines by the glass, Hook Norton and a guest beer, bay window looking up market place to parish church, roomy lounge and restaurant; terrace tables, bedrooms (June and Robin Savage, BB, George Atkinson, E McCall, T McLean, D Irving, Robert W Buckle)

☆ **Twelve Bells** GL7 1EA [Lewis Lane]: Cheery backstreet pub with dry-humoured landlord's son cooking bargain generous fresh local food inc some unusual dishes lunchtime and early evening (may be goose around Christmas), five or six quickly changing interesting ales all in fine condition, good coal fires in all three small old-fashioned low-ceilinged rooms, sturdy pine tables and rugs on quarry tiles in back dining area, pictures for sale, clay pipe collection; piped music; small sheltered unsmart back terrace (Giles and Annie Francis, Pete Baker, BB, E McCall, T McLean, D Irving, K Turner)

Wheatsheaf GL7 1JF [Cricklade St]: Busy unchanging local with five or so real ales, inexpensive pub food inc OAP bargains Weds and Fri, well used skittle alley; no children in bar, big-screen TV in back room, no credit cards; play area out behind, open all day (Peter and Audrey Dowsett)

CLEARWELL [SO5708]

Wyndham Arms GL16 8JT [The Cross]: Neat country bar with bare boards and big fire, friendly staff, local Freeminers ales, some interesting fresh food; attractive countryside nr Wye and Forest of Dean, comfortable spacious bedrooms in separate block (LYM, C D Watson)

CLIFFORD'S MESNE [SO6922]

☆ **Yew Tree** GL18 1JS [out of Newent, past Falconry Centre]: Large open-plan divided pub on slopes of May Hill (NT), good food (not Sun evening to Tues lunchtime) from home-baked rolls and home-cured gravadlax to rare-breed meats and clever vegetarian dishes, good wines, two or three real ales, relaxed atmosphere and genial staff; children welcome, sunny terrace, play area (Mike and Mary Carter, Neil and Anita Christopher, J E Shackleton, Alastair Stevenson, B M Eldridge)

COLD ASTON [SP1219]

☆ **Plough** GL54 3BN [aka Aston Blank; off A436 (B4068) or A429 SW of Stow-on-the-Wold]: Attractive little 17th-c pub with standing timbers, low black beams and flagstones, smart dining area; has had very good individual food inc upmarket dishes, well kept ales, good wines and a happy mix of customers, but the young managers who made it special moved in summer 2008 to the Mount at Stanton – news of the new regime, please; small side terraces, unspoilt village

with plenty of walks, has been cl Mon *(LYM)*
COLESBOURNE [SO9913]
Colesbourne Inn GL53 9NP [A435
Cirencester—Cheltenham]: Civilised 18th-c
grey stone gabled coaching inn, wide
changing choice of enjoyable if not cheap
food all home-made (can take a while),
friendly staff, Wadworths IPA and 6X, lots of
wines by the glass, linked rooms with partly
panelled dark red walls, log fires, soft
lighting, comfortable mix of settles and
softly padded seats, candlelit dining room;
dogs welcome, views from attractive back
garden and terrace, nine nice bedrooms in
converted stable block, good breakfast
*(Gary Roeder, LYM, Mike Sandford-West,
E McCall, T McLean, D Irving)*
COMPTON ABDALE [SP0717]
☆ *Puesdown Inn* GL54 4DN [A40 outside
village]: Spacious series of stylish bar areas,
wide choice of good enterprising food from
sandwiches up, neat friendly staff, Fullers
London Pride and Hook Norton ales, good
coffees and wines by the glass, log fire and
woodburner, leather or brightly upholstered
sofas and armchairs, big art posters and
other interesting pictures, bare boards,
bright rugs and rafter-effect ceilings, cream
and dark red walls, mainly stripped stone in
extensive eating areas, well reproduced
piped music, friendly chocolate labradors;
nice garden behind, bedrooms
(Rod Stoneman, BB, P and J Shapley)
DYMOCK [SO6931]
Beauchamp Arms GL18 2AQ: Friendly
recently extended parish-owned pub with
good licensees, well kept real ales, good
value pubby food (not Sun evening);
disabled facilities, small pleasant garden
with pond, cl Mon lunchtime *(KN-R)*
EASTLEACH TURVILLE [SP1905]
☆ *Victoria* GL7 3NQ [off A361 S of Burford]:
Low-ceilinged open-plan rooms around central
servery, attractive seats built in by log fire,
unusual Queen Victoria pictures, Arkells ales,
several wines by glass, good value
straightforward pub food (not winter Sun
evening) from good baguettes up, friendly
service; piped music; children and dogs
welcome, pleasant front garden overlooking
picturesque village *(Helene Grygar, Giles and
Annie Francis, Dennis and Doreen Haward,
C and R Bromage, P and J Shapley, LYM,
Meg and Colin Hamilton)*
EBRINGTON [SP1839]
☆ *Ebrington Arms* GL55 6NH [off B4035 E of
Chipping Campden or A429 N of Moreton-in-
Marsh]: Ancient stone-built pub newly
refurbished in unusual colours and fabrics,
good value food, cheerful service, well kept
ales inc local Purity, Thatcher's farm cider,
lively low-beamed bar with stripped stone,
flagstones and inglenooks, attractive dining
room; children welcome, picnic-sets on
pleasant sheltered terrace, good play area,
bedrooms *(Guy Vowles, LYM, Keith and
Sue Ward, Stuart Doughty, Michael Clatworthy,
P J F Cooper)*

ELKSTONE [SO9610]
☆ *Highwayman* GL53 9PL [Beechpike; A417
6 miles N of Cirencester]: Interesting
rambling 16th-c building, low beams,
stripped stone, log fires, cosy alcoves,
antique settles, armchairs and sofa among
more usual furnishings, good value home-
made food, full Arkells ale range, good house
wines, big back eating area; disabled access,
good family room, outside play area
*(Paul and Shirley White, G W Scarr, the Didler,
LYM)*
FAIRFORD [SP1501]
☆ *Bull* GL7 4AA [Market Place]: Sizeable
beamed and timbered bar, comfortably
old-fashioned pubby furnishings (nice bow
window seats overlooking little market
square), aircraft pictures and thespian
photographs, coal-effect gas fire, Arkells
ales, quite a choice of food, nice little
residents' lounge; dogs in bar, children
welcome, charming village and church,
22 bedrooms, open all day *(Dr Ron Cox,
Graham Oddey, Peter and Audrey Dowsett,
Paul Boot, LYM)*
Railway Inn GL7 4AR [London Rd]:
Comfortably refurbished under new licensees,
enjoyable reasonably priced food inc light
lunches, good range of beers and wines by
the glass, friendly service; terrace tables
(Gary Bloyce)
FOSSEBRIDGE [SP0711]
☆ *Fossebridge Inn* GL54 3JS [A429
Cirencester—Stow-on-the-Wold]: Handsome
Georgian inn doing well under father-and-
daughter management, attractive much older
two-room back bar with beams, arches,
stripped stone and good log fire, pleasant
more modern side area, tasty food from
sandwiches to good meals, friendly and
relaxed young staff, well kept real ales, good
value wines by the glass, two grand dining
rooms; children welcome, tables out in
attractive streamside garden with terrace,
comfortable bedrooms *(Giles and
Annie Francis, Guy Vowles, Keith and
Sue Ward, LYM, Tom and Ruth Rees)*
FRAMPTON COTTERELL [ST6681]
Globe BS36 2AB [Church Rd]: Friendly
efficient staff, well kept ales inc Butcombe
and local Cotswold Spring, hearty local food
(David and Jenny Gabriel)
Live & Let Live BS36 2EF [off A432; Clyde
Rd]: Attractive pub recently refurbished by
Bath brewery, their ales, helpful staff,
bargain food (not Sun evening) from
sandwiches to popular Sun lunch, decent
wines by the glass, daily papers, linked
rooms with carpeted bar and bare-boards
dining areas, pastel walls with panelled
dado, darts; piped music, no dogs; children
welcome, wheelchair access and facilities,
picnic-sets in big garden, open all day
(Chris and Angela Buckell)
FRAMPTON MANSELL [SO9202]
Crown GL6 8JG [brown sign to pub off A491
Cirencester—Stroud]: Welcoming new
licensees doing good range of fresh local pub

food, two log fires, heavy beams, stripped stone and rugs on bare boards, carpeted restaurant; picnic-sets in sunny front garden, pretty outlook, 12 decent bedrooms *(Ian and Melanie Henry, LYM)*

White Horse GL6 8HZ [A419 Cirencester—Stroud]: This good smart dining pub closed in 2008, and went into receivership *(LYM)*

FRAMPTON ON SEVERN [SO7408]

☆ *Bell* GL2 7EP [The Green (B4071, handy for M5 junction 13, via A38)]: Handsome creeper-covered Georgian inn, attractively opened-up, with extensive all-day family dining area, Bath Gem, Moles Tap and Sharps Doom Bar, some local liqueurs, several wines by glass, friendly staff, log fire, pool; piped music, games machine, TV; children and dogs welcome, plenty of seats outside, good play area and kids' farm, village cricket green opposite, open all day *(Roger Wain-Heapy, Mr and Mrs W W Burke, Dr and Mrs A K Clarke, Nigel and Sue Foster, Pauline and Philip Darley, Andy and Claire Barker, Mr and Mrs A J Hudson, LYM)*

Three Horseshoes GL2 7DY [The Green]: Cheerfully unpretentious 18th-c pub by splendid green, welcoming landlord, bargain lunchtime food inc good sandwiches and ploughman's (not Sun), well kept Hook Norton Old Hooky, Uley and a guest beer, farm cider, lounge/dining room for evening meals; dogs welcome, wheelchair access *(Chris and Angela Buckell, Comus and Sarah Elliott)*

GLASSHOUSE [SO7121]

☆ *Glasshouse Inn* GL17 0NN [off A40 just W of A4136]: Appealing old-fashioned and antique furnishings and décor, cavernous black hearth, flagstoned conservatory, well kept ales inc Butcombe tapped from the cask, Stowford Press cider, generous decent food inc thai; piped music, no children inside, no bookings, and they may try to keep your credit card while you eat; good disabled access, neat garden with interesting topiary and lovely hanging baskets, nearby paths up wooded May Hill, cl Sun evening *(LYM, Guy Vowles, the Didler, J E Shackleton, Phil and Sally Gorton, Dr A J and Mrs Tompsett, Ian and Nita Cooper)*

GLOUCESTER [SO8218]

☆ *Dick Whittingtons House* GL1 2PE [Westgate St]: Unusual in being listed Grade I, early Tudor behind its 18th-c façade, probably former guild hall and mansion house; welcoming staff, good straightforward food all day (not Mon or Sun evening), four changing ales, wide range of customers from shoppers to rugby supporters; attractive courtyard, open all day *(the Didler, P Dawn, Klaus and Elizabeth Leist, Theocsbrian)*

Fountain GL1 2NW [Westgate St/Berkeley St]: Popular and civilised, with good range of real ales, farm cider, reasonably priced usual food, attractive prints, handsome stone fireplace (pub dates from 17th c), plush seats and built-in wall benches, log-effect gas fire; good disabled access,

pleasant courtyard, handy for cathedral, open all day *(BB, B M Eldridge, Colin and Ruth Munro, the Didler)*

Longford Inn GL2 9BE [Tewkesbury Rd, Longford (A38)]: Beefeater well refurbished after flood damage, their usual food all day, good friendly service, well kept Greene King; wheelchair access, garden tables, bedrooms in attached Premier Inn *(Mike and Mary Carter)*

New Inn GL1 1SF [Northgate St]: Actually one of the city's oldest structures, lovely medieval building with galleried courtyard, three bars, half a dozen often local real ales, Black Rat farm cider, enjoyable inexpensive lunchtime food inc popular carvery, coffee shop, restaurant; good value bedrooms, open all day (till 1.30 Thurs-Sat) *(the Didler)*

Tall Ship GL1 2EX [Southgate St]: Extended Victorian pub by entry to docks, raised dining area with wide food choice inc seafood tapas and good fresh fish (can take a while at busy times), morning coffee and afternoon tea, Wadworths and a guest beer, cheerful young staff, landlady helpful on wine choice, pool in games area; pretty terrace, seafood barbecues, open all day *(B M Eldridge, P Dawn, Susan and Nigel Brookes)*

GOTHERINGTON [SO9629]

Shutter GL52 9EZ [off A435 N of Cheltenham; Shutter Lane]: Large bar with pine tables, pleasant new licensees, pubby food from lunchtime sandwiches up, changing real ales, decent house wines, restaurant; children welcome, disabled access, garden with play area, by GWR railway stn, good walks *(Neil and Anita Christopher)*

GREAT BARRINGTON [SP2013]

☆ *Fox* OX18 4TB [off A40 Burford—Northleach; pub towards Little Barrington]: 17th-c, with stripped stone, simple country furnishings and low ceiling, Donnington BB and SBA, farm cider and good apple juice, helpful staff, wide choice of quickly served food (all day Sun and summer Sat, not Mon night in winter) from sandwiches up, big river-view dining room, traditional games; can get very busy, games machine, TV; children welcome, heated terrace by River Windrush (swans and private fishing), informal orchard with pond, open all day *(LYM, the Didler, George Atkinson, M G Hart, Pete Baker, Richard Wyld, Brian and Rosalie Laverick, C and R·Bromage)*

GREET [SP0230]

Harvest Home GL54 5BH [Evesham Rd (B4078 by Winchcombe bridge)]: New licensees in neatly kept airy pub doing enjoyable sensibly priced food, good range of real ales inc Timothy Taylors Landlord, Stowford Press cider, decent house wines, beams, log fires and bay window seats, big raftered barn restaurant; sizeable garden, not far from medieval Sudeley Castle and Winchcombe GWR station *(LYM, Richard Hodges)*

GRETTON [SP0130]
Royal Oak GL54 5EP [off B4077 E of
Tewkesbury]: Civilised linked bare-boarded or
flagstoned rooms, enjoyable keenly priced
food, well kept Goffs and a guest ale, decent
wines, nice mix of furniture, beams hung
with tankards and chamber-pots, interesting
old motor-racing pictures, dining
conservatory; children and dogs welcome,
fine views from flower-filled terrace, big
pleasant garden with play area and tennis,
GWR private railway runs past, good nearby
walks, open all day summer wknds
(D J Lindsay, LYM, Giles and Annie Francis)
GUITING POWER [SP0924]
☆ *Farmers Arms* GL54 5TZ [Fosseway (A429)]:
Stripped stone, flagstones, cheap
Donnington BB and SBA, wide blackboard
range of unpretentious food from simple
sandwiches up, prompt friendly service, good
coal or log fire, carpeted back dining area,
skittle alley, games area with darts,
dominoes, cribbage, pool, skittle alley; piped
music, games machine; children welcome,
garden with quoits, lovely village, good
walks, bedrooms *(LYM, Dr A J and
Mrs Tompsett, the Didler)*
HAWKESBURY UPTON [ST7787]
Fox GL9 1AU [High St]: Comfortable village
pub with wide range of reasonably priced
food inc OAP menu, well kept local ales,
friendly staff, roomy dining area, huge
woodburner, lots of local photographs; five
good value bedrooms, pleasant village, open
all day Sun *(Peter and Audrey Dowsett, BB)*
HORSLEY [ST8497]
☆ *Tipputs* GL6 0QE [Tiltups End; A46 2 miles
S of Nailsworth]: Enjoyable food all day from
wide range of sandwiches and pubby things
to interesting evening meals, attentive
young staff, beams, stripped stone, big log
fire and abstract art, comfortable leather
seats in anteroom to galleried barn
restaurant; nice chairs and tables in pretty
garden with raised deck, lovely setting, open
all day *(Tom and Ruth Rees)*
IRON ACTON [ST6883]
Lamb BS37 9UZ [B4058/9 Bristol—Chipping
Sodbury]: Half a dozen well kept ales,
several farm ciders, pubby food all day from
sandwiches up, helpful cheerful staff, huge
fireplace in low-ceilinged carpeted bar,
panelling and stripped stone, old prints and
more modern art, pool upstairs; piped music,
games machine, no dogs; wheelchair access,
big garden with front terrace, bedrooms,
open all day *(Chris and Angela Buckell)*
White Hart BS37 9UG [High St]: Big open-
plan Greene King pub with their ales,
comfortably refurbished by welcoming new
South African landlord, enjoyable food esp
fresh fish, beams, carpet and open fire,
sensibly placed darts, pool room; garden
with play area, pasture beyond *(Dr and
Mrs C W Thomas, Donna and Roger)*
KEMBLE [ST9899]
Thames Head GL7 6NZ [A433 Cirencester—
Tetbury]: Stripped stone, timberwork, log

fire, intriguing little front alcove, pews in
cottagey back area with log-effect gas fire in
big fireplace, country-look dining room with
another big fire, good value wines, Arkells
2B and 3B, hearty food, friendly staff, skittle
alley; TV; children welcome, tables outside,
good value four-poster bedrooms, good
breakfast, nice walk to nearby Thames source
(LYM, Dan Farrall)
KILCOT [SO6925]
Kilcot Inn GL18 1NG [B4221, not far from
M50 junction 3]: Friendly and attractive
proper pub, enjoyable food from baguettes
and local cheeses to fresh fish and rare
breed meats, well kept Butcombe, Weston's
Old Rosie cider, good service, interesting
modern yew chairs among other wood
furniture on bare boards or flagstones,
woodburner, stripped beams, bare brick and
terracotta paintwork; dogs welcome, garden
picnic-sets *(Neil and Anita Christopher,
Clive, Dr A J and Mrs Tompsett, P Brown)*
KINETON [SP0926]
☆ *Halfway House* GL54 5UG [signed from
B4068 and B4077 W of Stow-on-the-Wold]:
Unpretentiously comfortable, with good
traditional food using local ingredients from
baguettes up, friendly unflappable staff,
cheap Donnington BB and SBA from nearby
brewery kept well, decent wines, farm cider,
pub games, restaurant; children welcome,
attractive sheltered back garden, simple
comfortable bedrooms, good walks
*(LYM, Alan Bulley, Keith and Sue Ward,
Helene Grygar)*
KINGSCOTE [ST8196]
☆ *Hunters Hall* GL8 8XZ [A4135 Dursley—
Tetbury]: Tudor beams, stripped stone, big
log fires and plenty of character in
individually furnished linked rooms, some
sofas and easy chairs, wide food choice from
lunchtime sandwiches up, Greene King and
Uley ales, friendly informal service,
flagstoned back bar with darts, pool and TV;
children and dogs welcome, garden with
good play area, bedrooms, open all day
*(Donna and Roger, Guy Vowles, LYM, Tom and
Ruth Rees, Mr and Mrs A J Hudson)*
LECHLADE [SU2199]
New Inn GL7 3AB [Market Sq (A361)]:
Prompt obliging service, wide choice of good
value generous food from good filled
baguettes up, huge log fire, several changing
real ales, roomy unpretentious front bar,
charming back restaurant; quiet piped music,
end games machine, big-screen sports TV;
play area in big garden leading to Thames,
good walks, 29 comfortable bedrooms
*(M Joyner, Peter and Audrey Dowsett,
E McCall, T McLean, D Irving)*
Trout GL7 3HA [A417, a mile E]: Refurbished
low-beamed pub (wood floor replacing the
nice old flagstones) three linked areas, three
real ales and a farm cider, good choice of
other drinks, good log fire, wide range of
enjoyable food at a price (can take a while if
busy), stuffed fish and fishing prints, local
paintings for sale, board games, dining

room, fishing rights, jazz nights Tues and Sun, early June steam rally; children welcome, nice big Thameside garden, boules, aunt sally, play area, camping, open all day summer Sat *(JJW, CMW, Kalman Kafetz, LYM)*

LEIGHTERTON [ST8290]

Royal Oak GL8 8UN [off A46 S of Nailsworth]: Neat stone-built pub, beams, log fires and mullioned windows, good value pubby food from soup and sandwiches to roasts, good OAP wkdy lunches, Butcombe, Wickwar Cotswold Way and a weekly guest beer, prompt helpful service; piped music; nice garden, quiet village, good walks, quite handy for Westonbirt Arboretum *(PL, Guy Vowles, J and F Gowers)*

LONGHOPE [SO6720]

Farmers Boy GL17 0LP [Boxbush, Ross Rd; A40 outside village]: Unpretentious and busy two-room country pub with friendly licensees, well kept real ales, food inc popular two in one pies, OAP bargains Thurs, heavy beams, log fire; piped music, separate bar with big-screen TV and electric organ; pleasant garden and terrace, may be cl Mon-Thurs lunchtime in winter *(Mrs Hazel Rainer, BB)*

Nags Head GL17 0LW [Ross Rd]: Friendly roadside pub with decent simple food inc bargain Sun lunch, Adnams, nice spot *(Reg Fowle, Helen Rickwood)*

LOWER LYDBROOK [SO5916]

Courtfield Arms GL17 9NU: Civilised refurbishment under new licensees, increasing emphasis on enjoyable upscale food; good spot overlooking River Wye *(Simon Fidler)*

MARSHFIELD [ST7773]

☆ *Catherine Wheel* SN14 8LR [High St; signed off A420 Bristol—Chippenham]: High-ceilinged stripped stone front part with medley of settles, chairs and stripped tables, cottagey back family bar, charming Georgian dining room with open fire in impressive fireplace, friendly staff, good range of real ales, farm cider, interesting wines by the glass, well priced food (can take a while), darts, dominoes, no music or machines; flower-decked back yard, unspoilt village, bedrooms, open all day Sat *(Lise Chace, Dr and Mrs A K Clarke, LYM, Graham Rooth, Donna and Roger, Julie and Bill Ryan, GSB, Geoff and Brigid Smithers)*

Lord Nelson SN14 8LP [A420 Bristol—Chippenham; High St]: Linked beamed rooms (inc former stables still with runnel down uneven flagstones), Bath and Courage ales, quickly served inexpensive generous food, plain tables and chairs, open fires, bistro restaurant, games bar with pool and machines; charming small courtyard, bedrooms in cottage annexe *(Donna and Roger, Dr and Mrs A K Clarke)*

MAYSHILL [ST6882]

☆ *New Inn* BS36 2NT [Badminton Rd (A432 Frampton Cotterell—Yate)]: Good food (all day Sun) in popular largely 17th-c coaching

inn with two comfortably carpeted bar rooms leading to restaurant, friendly staff, well kept changing ales inc Cotswold Spring, Stowford Press cider, log fire; children and dogs welcome, garden with play area *(Donna and Roger, E McCall, T McLean, D Irving)*

MEYSEY HAMPTON [SU1199]

☆ *Masons Arms* GL7 5JT [just off A417 Cirencester—Lechlade; High St]: 17th-c village pub with well kept changing ales, farm cider, friendly staff, enjoyable straightforward food, longish open-plan beamed bar with big inglenook log fire one end, restaurant; piped music; children and dogs welcome, tables out on green, pleasant compact bedrooms, good breakfast *(Sara Fulton, Roger Baker, Russell Grimshaw, Kerry Purcell, LYM, Matthew Shackle, E McCall, T McLean, D Irving)*

MICKLETON [SP1543]

☆ *Kings Arms* GL55 6RT [B4632 (ex A46)]: Civilised open-plan family lounge, good locally sourced food from well filled sandwiches to unusual specials and good value OAP lunches, welcoming service, Bass and Flowers, farm cider, nice mix of comfortable chairs, soft lighting, interesting homely décor, log fire, small locals' bar with darts, dominoes and cribbage; piped music; unusual tables in well remodelled garden, handy for Kiftsgate and Hidcote *(Ingrid Anson, Keith and Sue Ward, Martin and Pauline Jennings, BB)*

MORETON-IN-MARSH [SP2032]

Inn on the Marsh GL56 0DW [Stow Rd]: Interesting beamed bar with warm layout inc lovely curved sofa, quite a dutch flavour to the bric-a-brac, models, posters etc, Dutch chef doing national specialities alongside pubby favourites (cooked to order so allow for a wait), Marstons-related ales, inglenook woodburner, surprisingly pink modern conservatory restaurant; small back garden, bedrooms *(JCW, Catherine and Rob Dunster, Nigel and Sue Foster)*

☆ *Redesdale Arms* GL56 0AW [High St]: Relaxed old coaching inn with prettily lit alcoves, sofas and big stone fireplace in solidly furnished comfortable panelled bar on right, darts in flagstoned public bar, log fires, stripped stone, Hook Norton and Wye Valley, decent wines and coffee, enjoyable generous food, spacious back child-friendly brasserie and dining conservatory; piped music, TVs, games machine; heated floodlit courtyard decking, 24 comfortable bedrooms beyond, open all day from 8am *(Dr and Mrs A K Clarke, BB, Peter and Jean Hoare, Michael Dandy, Keith and Sue Ward, Catherine and Rob Dunster, George Atkinson)*

NAILSWORTH [ST8499]

☆ *Britannia* GL6 0DG [Cossack Sq]: Large open-plan food pub, quite elegant yet individual, very popular locally for wide range of good familiar bistro food (evening booking recommended), friendly efficient service even when busy, good choice of real ales and wines by the glass, thriving atmosphere, big log fire; good front garden (Tom and Ruth Rees, Miranda Spitteler, Colin Moore)

George GL6 0RF [Newmarket]: Good valley views, attractive central bar with lounge/eating area one side, dining room the other, beams and flagstones, above-average fresh food, four well kept ales inc Moles and Uley (the Didler)

Village Inn GL6 0HH [Bath Rd]: Brewing its own good value Nailsworth ales, bargain take-aways too, appealingly done series of rambling linked areas with steps down to back area for view of the process, woody décor with panelling, dividers and oak floors, log fire, pub food, brewery tours; open all day (E McCall, T McLean, D Irving, the Didler)

NAUNTON [SP1123]

☆ *Black Horse* GL54 3AD [off B4068 W of Stow]: Stripped-stone proper pub with friendly landlady, well priced Donnington BB and SBA, good simple fresh food from huge baguettes to Sun roasts (veg may come from local allotments), plain tables, flagstones, black beams and log fire, darts, cribbage, dominoes, dining room; piped music; children and dogs welcome, some nice seating outside, bedrooms, charming village, fine Cotswold walks (Pete Baker, Noel Grundy, Keith and Sue Ward, LYM, Malcolm Rand)

NORTHLEACH [SP1114]

Sherborne Arms GL54 3EE [Market Pl]: Comfortably traditional refurbishment, enjoyable food inc good Sun lunch, friendly attentive staff, real ales such as Sharps Doom Bar, good wines and coffee, bar on left stretching back from smallish front area, cosy lounge on right with wing armchairs and sofas around big stone fireplace, stripped stone restaurant area up a slope beyond; one or two picnic-sets out in front, three bedrooms (George Atkinson, BB)

NYMPSFIELD [SO7900]

Rose & Crown GL10 3TU [The Cross; signed off B4066 Stroud—Dursley]: Stone-built pub with plentiful food (through Sun afternoon) from sandwiches up, efficient friendly service, Bass Gem, Otter and Uley, decent wines, local farm cider, wide choice of coffees and teas, daily papers, log fire, pine tables and bare boards in beamed front bar, pews and other seats in large back dining area; piped music; children and dogs welcome, picnic-sets in side yard and sheltered lawn with good play area, bedrooms adjacent, handy for Cotswold walks and Woodchester (NT) (BB, Bruce and Sharon Eden, John and Gloria Isaacs, Neil and Anita Christopher)

OAKRIDGE LYNCH [SO9103]

Butchers Arms GL6 7NZ [off Eastcombe—Bisley rd E of Stroud]: Good sensibly priced food (not Sun evening or Mon) changing weekly in unpretentious pub with well kept Wadworths and a changing guest beer, rambling partly stripped stone bar, three open fires, dining room; children welcome, picnic-sets and play area on neat lawn overlooking valley, good walks, cl Mon lunchtime, open all day Fri-Sun in summer (LYM, David Morgan)

OLD DOWN [ST6187]

☆ *Fox* BS32 4PR [off A38 Bristol—Thornbury; Inner Down]: Fine range of real ales in low-beamed village local, hearty food with some interesting specials, friendly staff, farm cider and good choice of wines by the glass, log fire, carpeted eating area, high-backed settles in family room; children welcome, play area (Andrew Shore, Maria Williams, James Morrell, Chris and Angela Buckell, Donna and Roger)

OLD SODBURY [ST7581]

☆ *Dog* BS37 6LZ [3 miles from M4 junction 18, via A46 and A432; The Hill (a busy road)]: Two-level bar with low beams and stripped stone, extremely wide choice of good sensibly priced food from sandwiches up inc meal deals, quick friendly young staff, Wadworths 6X and other changing ales; games machine, juke box; children welcome, big garden with barbecues and good play area, bedrooms, open all day (Donna and Roger, Tom Evans, Dr and Mrs A K Clarke, Roy Hoing, J and F Gowers, Stephen Woad, LYM)

PAINSWICK [SO8609]

Falcon GL6 6UN [New St]: Sizeable old open-plan stone-built inn with new family doing enjoyable food inc enterprising dishes, real ale, good choice of wines by the glass, panelling, high ceilings, cheerfully rustic bare-boards front bar, mainly carpeted dining area with lots of prints, high bookshelves and shelves of ornaments by coal-effect fire; bedrooms, opp churchyard famous for its 99 yews (Guy Vowles, BB)

Royal Oak GL6 6QG [St Mary's St]: New mother-and-son tenants (he runs the kitchen) for partly 16th-c three-room local with appealing nooks and crannies, some attractive old or antique seats, plenty of prints, several real ales, decent wines, daily paper, open fire, small sun lounge; suntrap pretty courtyard (Brian McBurnie, Stuart Doughty, LYM)

PARKEND [SO6107]

Fountain GL15 4JD [just off B4234]: 18th-c village inn by terminus of restored Lydney—Parkend railway, three well kept ales inc local Freeminer, Stowford Press cider, decent wines, bargain food inc OAP lunches Tues/Thurs, welcoming helpful staff, real fire, assorted chairs and settles in two linked rooms, old local tools, bric-a-brac and photographs; children and dogs welcome, wheelchair access, eight bedrooms, bunkhouse (Pete Baker, B M Eldridge, Chris and Angela Buckell, Neil and Anita Christopher, Guy Vowles)

Woodman GL15 4JF [Folly Rd, Whitecroft]: Roomy and relaxed stripped-stone bar, two open fires, heavy beams, forest and forestry decorations, artwork for sale, smaller back bar and dining room, hearty fresh food from filled rolls up, Fullers, Greene King and Wadworths 6X, decent wines, pleasant service; picnic-sets on front terrace facing green, sheltered back courtyard and garden, bedrooms, good Forest of Dean walks *(Neil and Anita Christopher, BB)*

POULTON [SP1001]

Falcon GL7 5HN [London Rd]: This stylish and individual dining pub, a popular main entry in our last edition, was sold to a chain in 2007 then closed – news please *(LYM)*

PUCKLECHURCH [ST7076]

Star BS16 9RF [Castle Rd]: Attractive village pub with real ales tapped from the cask, farm ciders, enjoyable food, conservatory; open all day *(the Didler)*

QUENINGTON [SP1404]

Keepers Arms GL7 5BL [Church Rd]: Cosy and comfortable village pub, stripped stone, low beams and log fires, new licensees and chef giving a lift to the bar and restaurant food; picnic-sets outside, bedrooms *(E McCall, T McLean, D Irving)*

REDBROOK [SO5309]

☆ *Boat* NP25 4AJ [car park signed on A466 Chepstow—Monmouth, then 100-yard footbridge over Wye; or very narrow steep car access from Penallt in Wales]: Beautifully set Wyeside pub recently freshened up and warmly friendly, five changing well kept ales tapped from casks, good value simple food from baguettes up, country wines, stripped stone walls, flagstone floors and roaring woodburner; dogs and children welcome, rough home-built seats in informal tiered garden with stream spilling down waterfall cliffs into duck pond, open all day *(LYM, Bob and Margaret Holder, B M Eldridge, LM)*

SAPPERTON [SO9303]

Daneway Inn GL7 6LN [Daneway; off A419 Stroud—Cirencester]: Quiet local in charming wooded countryside, flagstones and bare boards, amazing floor-to-ceiling carved oak dutch fireplace, sporting prints, Wadworths ales, Weston's farm cider, reasonably priced generous simple food from filled baps up, friendly staff, small family room, traditional games in inglenook public bar; no dogs; camping possible, terrace tables and lovely sloping lawn, good walks by canal under restoration with tunnel to Coates *(E McCall, T McLean, D Irving, Martin and Marion Vincent, Guy Vowles, LYM)*

SHIPTON MOYNE [ST8989]

Cat & Custard Pot GL8 8PN [off B4040 Malmesbury—Bristol; The Street]: Popular robust food, often good, from sandwiches to restaurant dishes (booking recommended even wkdy lunch), well kept Flowers, Timothy Taylors Landlord and Wadworths IPA and 6X, Thatcher's cider, well priced wines, several dining areas, hunting prints (and back stables), cosy back snug; housekeeping slipped a bit in early 2008 – news please; dogs welcome, wheelchair access, picturesque village *(Chris and Angela Buckell, D M and B K Moores, Catherine Pitt, BB)*

SIDDINGTON [SU0399]

☆ *Greyhound* GL7 6HR [Ashton Rd; village signed from A419 roundabout at Tesco]:

Two linked rooms each with a big log fire, enjoyable pubby food from sandwiches up, some unusual specials, well kept Wadworths, welcoming service, slate-floored bar with darts and cribbage; piped music; garden tables, open all day *(LYM, Paul and Shirley White, E McCall, T McLean, D Irving, Neil and Anita Christopher)*

SLIMBRIDGE [SO7204]

Tudor Arms GL2 7BP [Shepherds Patch; off A38 towards Wildfowl & Wetlands Trust]: Welcoming and obliging, with plentiful generous food all day wknds, half a dozen interesting changing ales, good wines by the glass, farm cider, linked areas with parquet floor, flagstones or carpet, some leather chairs and settles, comfortable dining room, conservatory, darts, pool and skittle alley; children and dogs welcome, disabled facilities, picnic-sets outside, handy for Wildfowl Trust and canal boat trips, bedrooms in small annexe, open all day *(Neil and Anita Christopher, Betty Laker, Donna and Roger)*

SNOWSHILL [SP0933]

☆ *Snowshill Arms* WR12 7JU: Airy and unpretentious country pub in honeypot village, prompt helpful service even when busy, Donnington ales, reasonably priced simple food from sandwiches up, log fire, stripped stone, neat array of tables, local photographs; skittle alley, charming village views from bow windows and big back garden with little stream and play area, children welcome if eating, handy for Snowshill Manor and Cotswold Way walks *(LYM, Keith and Sue Ward, Robert Ager, Guy Vowles, Edna Jones)*

SOMERFORD KEYNES [SU0195]

☆ *Bakers Arms* GL7 6DN: Pretty stone-built pub popular for food from baguettes and ciabattas up, real ales, good house wine, two log fires, lots of pine tables in two linked stripped-stone areas with soft lighting and burgundy walls, young staff; children very welcome, big garden with play area and good barbecues, lovely Cotswold village *(E McCall, T McLean, D Irving, Julia Morris, Guy Vowles)*

SOUTH CERNEY [SU0497]

Eliot Arms GL7 5UA [signed off A419 SE of Cirencester; Clarks Hay]: Smart Marstons pub/hotel, interesting décor in relaxed and comfortable little rooms, friendly staff, affordable usual food; children welcome, pleasant garden, comfortable bedrooms *(LYM, Keith and Sue Ward)*

Royal Oak GL7 5UP [High St]: Thriving sympathetically extended ancient local, cosy bars and small back dining area, friendly staff, Fullers London Pride and guest beers, food from good value sandwiches up, woodburner; pleasant garden behind with big terrace and summer marquee *(Dr A Y Drummond, E McCall, T McLean, D Irving)*

SOUTHROP [SP2003]

Swan GL7 3NU [off A361 Lechlade—Burford]: Creeper-covered upscale dining pub in pretty village, a popular main entry in our last edition under its previous management, pleasant front dining rooms with flagstones and log fire, Hook Norton and two guest beers, lots of wines by the glass, public bar, skittle alley; children have been welcome, tables in sheltered back garden, pretty village esp at daffodil time *(Richard Wyld, LYM, J Crosby, Keith and Sue Ward)*

ST BRIAVELS [SO5504]

Crown GL15 6TE [Pystol Ln]: Obliging landlord, bargain pubby food, log fire, real ales *(Tom Evans)*

George GL15 6TA [High Street]: Now a Wadworths pub, with their real ales, wide food choice inc good value OAP meals, spotless rambling linked black-beamed rooms with attractive old-fashioned décor and big stone fireplace, restaurant; can get very busy wknds; children and dogs welcome, flagstoned terrace over former moat of neighbouring Norman fortress, four newly refurbished bedrooms *(LYM, Brian and Jacky Wilson, Tom Evans)*

STANTON [SP0634]

☆ *Mount* WR12 7NE [off B4632 SW of Broadway; no through road up hill, bear left]: Enthusiastic manager and chef who made great success of Plough at Cold Aston have now moved here, too late for us to try, but we'd expect them to make the most of huge potential here, with very good food; Donnington BB and SBA, heavy beams, flagstones and big log fire, horseracing memorabilia, roomy picture-window extensions, one with cricket memorabilia; attractive garden, great spot up steep lane from golden-stone village, views to welsh mountains, esp from large terrace (lovely on summer evenings) *(LYM)*

STOW-ON-THE-WOLD [SP1729]

Coach & Horses GL56 0QZ [Ganborough (A424 about 2.5 miles N)]: Beamed and flagstoned country pub, bright and clean, with friendly new tenants, well kept Donnington ales and farm cider, tasty proper cooking, good fires, steps up to carpeted dining area with high-backed settles; children welcome, popular skittle alley, garden *(K H Frostick, Clive and Fran Dutson, LYM)*

☆ *Eagle & Child* GL54 1BN [attached to Royalist Hotel, Digbeth Street]: Smart little bar attached to handsome old hotel, woodburner, flagstones, low beams and dark pink walls, back conservatory, nice mix of tables, enjoyable up-to-date food from sandwiches up, Goffs and Hook Norton, good if not cheap wine and malt whisky choice, friendly staff; may be piped music; children and dogs welcome, small back courtyard, good bedrooms, open all day *(Phil Bryant, Jude Wright, LYM, Michael Dandy, Myra Joyce, Mrs Brenda Calver)*

Grapevine GL54 1AU [Sheep St]: Substantial hotel with quiet comfortable bar, upscale bar food from sandwiches up, friendly staff, good coffee and choice of wines by the

glass, Hook Norton, attractive brasserie/restaurant with live vine; piped music; pavement tables, bedrooms, open all day *(Michael Dandy)*

Kings Arms GL54 1AF [The Square]: Enjoyable food from good sandwiches to lots of fish, real food for children, helpful staff, good choice of wines by the glass, Greene King IPA and Abbot, good coffee (opens early for this), daily papers, some Mackintosh-style chairs on polished boards, bowed black beams, some panelling and stripped stone, log fire, charming upstairs dining room; piped music; bedrooms, open all day *(BB, Michael Dandy)*

☆ *Queens Head* GL54 1AB [The Square]: Splendidly unpretentious for this upmarket town, well kept low-priced Donnington BB and SBA, good wines by the glass, good value sandwiches and basic pub meals (not Sun), cheerful helpful service, bustling and chatty stripped stone front lounge, heavily beamed and flagstoned back bar with high-backed settles, big log-effect fire, horse prints, usual games; quiet piped music; dogs and children positively welcome, tables in attractive sunny back courtyard, occasional jazz Sun lunchtime *(LYM, the Didler, Terry Miller, Noel Grundy, Lawrence Pearse, Neil and Anita Christopher, Tracey and Stephen Groves, Phil Bryant, Keith and Sue Ward, Michael Dandy)*

☆ *Talbot* GL54 1BQ [The Square]: Light and airy modern décor, relaxed café-bar feel, good up-to-date food, bright friendly service even when busy, Wadworths ales, lots of good value wines by the glass, good coffee, big log fire, plain tables and chairs on wood block floor, modern prints, daily papers; no children inside, may be piped radio, lavatories upstairs; bedrooms nearby, open all day *(Michael Dandy, BB)*

Unicorn GL54 1HQ [Sheep St (A429 edge of centre)]: Handsome hotel with log fire in comfortably traditional low-beamed and flagstoned upmarket bar, friendly young staff, Hook Norton and Wye Valley ale, good range of food from sandwiches up, restaurant; 20 bedrooms *(Mr and Mrs W W Burke, Neil and Anita Christopher)*

White Hart GL54 1AF [The Square]: Small former coaching inn, pubby food from baguettes up, Arkells ales; back courtyard, bedrooms *(Michael Dandy, BB)*

SWINEFORD [ST6969]

☆ *Swan* BS30 6LN [A431, right on the Somerset border]: Well kept Bath and guest ales, good value interesting food (not Sun evening), enterprising wine choice, friendly staff, big open fire, plain furniture on bare boards or tiles, pastel paintwork and panelled dado; wheelchair access, large lawn *(Donna and Roger, Chris and Angela Buckell, M G Hart)*

TETBURY [ST8494]

☆ *Gumstool* GL8 8YJ [Calcot Manor Hotel, A4135 W]: Civilised relaxed modern brasserie attached to good country hotel, too restauranty now for the main entries but well worth knowing for its imaginative food, stylish contented bustle, Butcombe and other good ales, fine choice of wines by the glass – and one corner has leather armchairs by a big log fire, with board games; piped music; children welcome, pleasant garden, nice bedrooms *(Bernard Stradling, Tom and Ruth Rees, Guy Vowles, Andy and Claire Barker, Donna and Roger, LYM, Dr and Mrs C W Thomas, Rod Stoneman)*

Ormond GL8 8AA [Long St]: Former Ormonds Head beheaded, enjoyable bar food from good lunchtime sandwiches up, decent wines, Sharps and Wickwar ales, open fire, stripped wood and leather furniture in comfortably reworked pastel and bare-boards bar, restaurant; children welcome, courtyard tables with play area, 15 comfortable bedrooms, open all day *(Michael and Veronica Collins)*

☆ *Priory* GL8 8JJ [London Rd]: More good civilised eating house than pub, with big central log fire in comfortable high-raftered stone-built former stables, and strong emphasis on local produce – not just the meat, veg and cheese, but beer and wine too, even a local slant to their wood-fired pizzas; good service, comfortable coffee lounge, live music Sun; children very welcome, terrace tables, 14 good bedrooms *(Mr and Mrs A Curry, Eleni Papandoniou)*

TEWKESBURY [SO8832]

Bell GL20 5SA [Church St]: Hotel bar interesting for its black oak beams and timbers, 17th-c oak panelling and medieval leaf-and-fruit frescoes; big log fire, tapestries and armchairs, decent bar food and house wines, good coffee; dogs welcome, garden above Severnside walk, bedrooms *(J and F Gowers, Chris Glasson, BB)*

Canterbury GL20 8BT [Ashchurch Rd (A438)]: 1960s pub flourishing under new landladies, Greene King ales, decent food, good atmosphere, fresh flowers *(Theocsbrian)*

☆ *Gupshill Manor* GL20 5SG [Gloucester Rd (off A38 S edge of town)]: Ancient black and white building with notably friendly service, good value food (all day Sun) from pubby dishes to interesting meals (some emphasis on the restaurant side), well kept Greene King IPA, sensible wine choice, accommodating low-ceilinged bars, log fires and flagstones; children welcome, disabled access, good-sized garden with heated terraces, open all day *(Jo Rees, Mrs J Carlill, Robert W Buckle, Andy and Claire Barker, Brian and Pat Wardrobe)*

☆ *Olde Black Bear* GL20 5BJ [High St]: County's oldest pub, well worth a look for its intricately rambling rooms with ancient tiles, heavy timbering and low beams; reasonably priced wines, up to five real ales, open fires, well worn furnishings, pubby food; piped music, and they may try to keep your credit card while you eat; children welcome, terrace and play area in riverside garden,

open all day *(the Didler, Dave Braisted, P Dawn, Jeremy King, S H Johnston, Maureen and Keith Gimson, Comus and Sarah Elliott, LYM, Ann and Colin Hunt)*

TOCKINGTON [ST6086]

Swan BS32 4NJ [Tockington Green]: Roomy Greene King pub with their ales and wide food choice, decent wines, log fire, beams and standing timbers, bric-a-brac on stripped stone walls; boules in tree-shaded garden, open all day wknds *(Chris and Angela Buckell, Dr and Mrs A K Clarke)*

TOLLDOWN [ST7577]

☆ *Crown* SN14 8HZ [a mile from M4 junction 18 – A46 towards Bath]: Heavy-beamed dining pub with generous interesting food from good ciabattas up, helpful service, Wadworths ales, good house wines, warm log fire, pine tables and light fresh décor; good disabled access, children in eating area and restaurant, good garden with play area, comfortable bedrooms, open all day *(Dr and Mrs A K Clarke, LYM, Tom and Ruth Rees)*

TYTHERINGTON [ST6788]

Swan GL12 8QB [Duck St]: Big well furnished family food pub with good choice (all day Sun) from sandwiches up, popular OAP lunches, well kept Wickwar, pleasant service; huge car park, busy wknds *(Tom Evans)*

ULEY [ST7998]

Old Crown GL11 5SN [The Green]: Rustic 17th-c pub prettily set by village green just off Cotswold Way, long narrow room with settles and pews on bare boards, step up to partitioned-off lounge area, good range of well kept changing ales and of wines by the glass, home-made pubby food from sandwiches up, quick friendly service, log fire, small games room up spiral stairs; attractive garden behind, four bedrooms *(Paul Booth, Martin and Pauline Jennings, Keith and Sue Ward)*

UPPER FRAMILODE [SO7510]

Ship GL2 7LH [Saul Rd; not far from M5 junction 13 via B4071]: Welcoming and relaxed, with sensibly priced pubby food from sandwiches up, well kept ales such as Cotswold Way and Wychwood, efficient friendly service, two bars and restaurant extension; children welcome, wheelchair access, big garden by Severn's Stroudwater Canal offshoot (being restored) *(James Skinner, Chris and Angela Buckell)*

WHITFIELD [ST6690]

White Horse GL12 8DX [Buckover; A38/B4461, N of Bristol]: Appealing L-shaped bar with spectacular Severn valley view, welcoming service, decent straightforward food from sandwiches up, real ale *(Meg and Colin Hamilton)*

WHITMINSTER [SO7607]

☆ *Frombridge Mill* GL2 7PD [Frombridge Lane (A38 nr M5 junction 13)]: Comfortable mill-based dining pub, some tables overlooking river, reliable reasonably priced food inc popular lunchtime carvery, attentive staff, well kept Greene King real ales; picnic-sets in good-sized garden with play area, pretty riverside setting *(Dr and Mrs C W Thomas, Dr A J and Mrs Tompsett)*

WICK [ST7072]

☆ *Rose & Crown* BS30 5QH [High St (A420)]: Nicely individual Chef & Brewer, plenty of character in linked 17th-c rooms, low beams, mixed furnishings and candlelight, coal fire in big stone fireplace, friendly helpful staff, Courage Best, Greene King Old Speckled Hen, Wells & Youngs Bombardier and an unusual guest beer, good wines by the glass, very wide food choice, daily papers; good disabled access, terrace picnic-sets, pleasant views, open all day *(Ian and Joan Blackwell, Dr and Mrs A K Clarke, BB)*

WILLERSEY [SP1039]

☆ *Bell* WR12 7PJ [B4632 Cheltenham— Stratford, nr Broadway]: Well run neatly modernised stone-built pub, comfortable front dining area with good home-made food (locally very popular – worth booking evenings), Aston Villa memorabilia and huge collection of model cars in back area past big L-shaped bar counter, reasonably priced Flowers Original, Hook Norton and Wadworths 6X, relaxed atmosphere, quick friendly helpful service; darts, Thurs evening chess ladder; overlooks village green and duck pond, lots of tables in big garden, bedrooms in outbuildings *(Noel Thomas, BB, Keith and Margaret Kettell, Keith and Sue Ward)*

WINCHCOMBE [SP0228]

☆ *Old Corner Cupboard* GL54 5LX [Gloucester St]: Attractive golden stone Tudor pub with good reasonably priced food well served in nice back dining room, Fullers, Hook Norton and seasonal local Stanway ales, good choice of wines by the glass, comfortable stripped-stone lounge bar with heavy-beamed Tudor core, traditional hatch-service lobby, small side room with woodburner in massive stone fireplace, traditional games; children welcome, tables in back garden, open all day *(D J Lindsay, LYM)*

☆ *Plaisterers Arms* GL54 5LL [Abbey Terr]: 18th-c, with stripped stonework, beams, Hogarth prints, bric-a-brac and flame-effect fires, friendly service, well kept Goffs Jouster and Timothy Taylors Landlord, good cider, wines and coffee, enterprising food, two chatty front bars both with steps down to dim-lit lower back dining area with stall tables, darts; dogs welcome, good play area in charming secluded back garden, long and narrow, comfortable simple bedrooms (tricky stairs) *(BB, Michael Dandy, Dr A J and Mrs Tompsett, M Greening, John Smart)*

White Hart GL54 5LJ [High St (B4632)]: Café-bar with big windows giving on to village street, decent food inc sausage specialities, interesting changing ales, integral wine shop (they add corkage charge if you buy to drink on the premises), cricket memorabilia, separate restaurant; children welcome, good bedrooms, open all day *(Guy Vowles, Michael Dandy, LYM, Ann and John Jordan)*

WITHINGTON [SP0315]

Kings Head GL54 4BD [Kings Head Lane]: Thriving old-fashioned back locals' bar, Hook Norton and a changing Wickwar beer tapped from the cask, friendly landlady and dog, pickled eggs, darts, shove-ha'penny, table skittles and pool, neat partly stripped stone lounge area; pleasant garden behind *(Giles and Annie Francis, Dr and Mrs M E Wilson, E McCall, T McLean, D Irving)*

Mill Inn GL54 4BE [off A436 or A40]: Idyllic streamside setting for mossy-roofed old stone inn, beams, flagstones, inglenook log fire, plenty of character with nice nooks and corners, darts and dominoes, standard food from baguettes and basket meals up, dining room; piped music, keg beer (but decent wine list); children very welcome, large pretty garden, splendid walks, four old-fashioned bedrooms, good breakfast *(LYM, Dr and Mrs M E Wilson)*

WOODCHESTER [SO8403]

☆ *Old Fleece* GL5 5NB [Rooksmoor; A46 a mile S of Stroud – not to be confused with Fleece at Lightpill a little closer in]: Wide choice of interesting fresh food from unusual lunchtime sandwiches up, children's helpings, friendly helpful staff, Bass and Greene King IPA, good wines by the glass, three unpretentious linked rooms, big windows and bare boards, big log fire, candles, daily papers, stripped stone or dark salmon pink walls; children welcome, two roadside terraces, one heated *(BB, E McCall, T McLean, D Irving, Alan Bulley, Andy and Claire Barker)*

YATE [ST7183]

Brimsham Park BS37 7PJ [Lark Rise]: Ember Inn with well kept real ales, food all day, open fires, some sofas and high-backed rounded settles *(Donna and Roger)*

Codrington Arms BS37 7LG [North Rd]: Welcoming and pleasantly refurbished, enjoyable lunchtime food and more elaborate evening menu, well kept Bass and a guest beer, light and airy dining area; unobtrusive piped music; attractive garden with play area *(Dr and Mrs C W Thomas)*

Please tell us if any Lucky Dips deserve to be upgraded to a main entry – and why: feedback@thegoodpubguide.co.uk or (no stamp needed) The Good Pub Guide, FREEPOST TN1569, Wadhurst, E Sussex TN5 7BR.

Hampshire

Quite a few pubs here gain a decided advantage from having long-serving landlords and landladies who have given them considerable individual appeal. There's quite an emphasis too on local beers, with the very high ratio of more than one in three main entries gaining a Beer Award; and we have tracked down some really inventive food in civilised surroundings. New to these pages as main entries are the friendly Fox & Hounds at Crawley (good value food and quite a choice of wines), the Bakers Arms in Droxford (the young chef/landlord's good country cooking brings it straight in with a Food Award), the Mill Arms at Dunbridge (with plenty of room for its good dining side, while keeping a pubby heart), the Star at East Tytherley (interesting food cooked by the landlord), the Anchor at Lower Froyle (engagingly reworked as a dining pub without losing its appeal for drinkers), and the Thomas Lord in West Meon (chatty friendly licensees, seven real ales and some unusual food). Other pubs doing particularly well here include the Sun at Bentworth (always busy thanks to lots of real ales and likeable meals), the Three Tuns at Bransgore (much enjoyed by readers, with a new licensee), the Flower Pots at Cheriton (40 years in the same family, and a favourite with many), the Chestnut Horse at Easton (a charming and popular dining pub), the Royal Oak at Fritham (a lovely simple New Forest pub), the Running Horse at Littleton (a well run dining pub), the Trooper near Petersfield (a genuine welcome from the charming landlord, and comfortable bedrooms), the Harrow at Steep (virtues that seem to have vanished from most pubs, preserved carefully here by the same family since 1929), the Rising Sun in Swanmore (the hands-on licensees give it a really enjoyable atmosphere), the Mayfly near Wherwell (an idyllic position and wide choice of good food), and the Wykeham Arms in Winchester (civilised and chatty, with super food and wines). Although prices for meals can be high, there's some fair value to be found too, and if you know where to spend your money you can find real rewards – one in eight pubs here has gained our Food Award. Shining above all others, it's the Wykeham Arms in Winchester which is Hampshire Dining Pub of the Year. The Lucky Dip section has a good many fine choices, too. In recent months pubs showing up particularly well – almost all inspected and vouched for by us – have been the Crown at Arford, Green Dragon at Brook, Five Bells at Buriton, White Buck near Burley, Red Lion at Chalton, Greyfriar at Chawton, New Forest at Emery Down, Jack Russell at Faccombe, Watership Down at Freefolk, Foresters Arms at Frogham, Peat Spade at Longstock, Fleur de Lys at Pilley, Selborne Arms in Selborne, Three Cups and White Hart in Stockbridge, Cricketers Arms at Tangley and Eclipse in Winchester. The county's main brewer is Ringwood, now owned by Marstons but still brewing locally (Gales, which used to be a Hampshire beer, is now part of Fullers and brewed by them up in London). Bowman, a small brewery started only a couple of years ago, is gaining very rapidly in popularity, and other good local beers to be found in quite a few pubs here are Hampshire, Flowerpots, Itchen Valley, fff and (perhaps less common) Oakleaf.

BANK   SU2806   MAP 2

Oak 🍺

Signposted just off A35 SW of Lyndhurst; SO43 7FD

Tucked-away New Forest pub with well liked food and interesting décor

Given its peaceful New Forest location, this tucked-away pub is surprisingly busy. On either side of the door in the bay windows of the L-shaped bar are built-in red-cushioned seats, and on the right there are two or three little pine-panelled booths with small built-in tables and bench seats. The rest of the bare-boarded bar has more space, with candles in individual brass holders on a line of stripped old and newer blond tables set against the wall, and more seats at the back; some low beams and joists, fishing rods, spears, a boomerang and old ski poles on the ceiling with brass platters, heavy knives, and guns on the walls. There's also a big fireplace, cushioned milk churns along the bar counter and little red lanterns among hop bines above the bar. Fullers London Pride, Gales HSB and Swing Low, and Ringwood Best on handpump; piped music. The pleasant side garden has picnic-sets and long tables and benches by the big yew trees.

🍴 Decent bar food includes lunchtime doorstep sandwiches, garlic mushrooms topped with melted cheese, baked brie with almonds and honey, home-cooked ham and eggs, vegetable and herb cakes with sweet chilli dip, a pie of the day, warm chicken and bacon salad, roasted lamb shank, daily specials such as soup, crayfish and avocado cocktail, pork medallions with creamy mustard sauce, and a trio of local venison sausages with onion jus, and puddings like chocolate crème brûlée and baked blueberry cheesecake. *Starters/Snacks: £4.25 to £6.95. Main Courses: £8.50 to £16.95. Puddings: £4.25*

Fullers ~ Manager Martin Sliva ~ Real ale ~ Bar food (12-2.30, 6-9.30; 12-2.30, 5-9 Sun) ~ (023) 8028 2350 ~ Children welcome until 6pm ~ Dogs welcome ~ Open 11.30-3.30, 6-11; 11.30-11 Sat; 12-10.30 Sun; 11.30-3, 6-11 weekdays in winter

Recommended by Pam and John Smith, Ian Wilson, Michael Dandy, George Atkinson, Philip and Susan Philcox, Simon Watkins, C J Cox, A Monro, Steve and Liz Tilley, Tom and Jill Jones, Kevin Flack, Leslie and Barbara Owen, Mike and Sue Loseby, Mr and Mrs A Garforth, P E Wareham, Dr D J R Martin, Bob and Margaret Holder, Mr and Mrs P D Titcomb

BENTLEY   SU8044   MAP 2

Bull

A31 Alton—Farnham dual carriageway, east of village itself; accessible from both carriageways, but tricky if westbound; GU10 5JH

Cosy old place with tasty food and four real ales – an unexpected trunk road respite

This is a welcoming and popular 15th-c inn with nice touches like flowers and candles on the tables. The main room on the right, restful despite some traffic noise, has soft lighting, witty sayings chalked on low black beams in its maroon ceiling, lots of local photographs on partly stripped brick walls and pub chairs around neat stripped pub tables. The back room on the left has a good log fire in a huge hearth, a cushioned pew by one long oak-planked table, and in a snug and narrow back alcove, another pew built around a nice mahogany table. Courage Best, Fullers London Pride, Ringwood Best, and Wells & Youngs Bitter on handpump and several wines by the glass; newspapers to read. There are plenty of pretty summer flowering tubs and hanging baskets outside and picnic-sets and a teak table and chairs on the side terrace.

🍴 Good changing blackboard food includes sandwiches, soup, ploughman's, chicken kidneys in mustard and honey on toast, sausages and mash, vegetarian tortilla stack with peppers, tomatoes and chilli, fresh fish from Brixham like moules marinières, sardines in orange and oregano and fresh tuna niçoise, lamb rump with redcurrant jus, chicken maryland with sweetcorn fritters, bananas and chilli, duck breast with blackberry jus and parsnip crisps, and puddings like apple and mixed berry crumble, and chocolate brownies with cream. *Starters/Snacks: £4.25 to £9.95. Main Courses: £8.95 to £19.95. Puddings: £5.00*

Enterprise ~ Lease Grant Edmead ~ Real ale ~ Bar food (12-2.30, 6.30-9.30; 12-8.30 Sun) ~ Restaurant ~ (01420) 22156 ~ Children allowed away from bar ~ Dogs allowed in bar ~ Open 10.30am-11pm; 12-10.30 Sun; closed evening 25 Dec

Recommended by Janet Whittaker, Ann and Colin Hunt, Ian Phillips, Steve Derbyshire

BENTWORTH
SU6640   MAP 2

Sun 🍺

Sun Hill; from the A339 coming from Alton the first turning takes you there direct; or in village follow Shalden 2¼, Alton 4¼ signpost; GU34 5JT

Marvellous choice of real ales and welcoming landlady in popular 17th-c country pub; nearby walks

To be sure of a table in this bustling and charming 17th-c country pub, you must book ahead as it's always busy. But despite plenty of customers, service remains efficient and friendly and the welcoming landlady is very hands-on. There's a fine choice of seven real ales on handpump such as Badger Hopping Hare, Fullers London Pride, Gales HSB, Ringwood Best and Old Thumper, Stonehenge Pigswill, and Timothy Taylors Landlord; several malt whiskies. The two little traditional communicating rooms have high-backed antique settles, pews and schoolroom chairs, olde-worlde prints and blacksmith's tools on the walls, and bare boards and scrubbed deal tables on the left; big fireplaces (one with an open fire) make it especially snug in winter; an arch leads to a brick-floored room with another open fire. There are seats out in front and in the back garden and pleasant nearby walks.

🍴 Well liked bar food includes sandwiches, soup (the creamy haddock chowder is popular), hummus with pitta bread, creamy garlic mushrooms, ham and egg, pork and leek sausages, liver and bacon, a thick, home-made burger, fresh tagliatelle with smoked salmon, lemon and dill cream sauce, steak and kidney pie, daily specials, and puddings such as banoffi pie and sticky toffee pudding. *Starters/Snacks: £4.25 to £4.75. Main Courses: £7.95 to £16.95. Puddings: £3.95 to £4.50*

Free house ~ Licensee Mary Holmes ~ Real ale ~ Bar food ~ (01420) 562338 ~ Children welcome ~ Dogs welcome ~ Open 12-3, 6-11; 12-10 Sun

Recommended by Tony and Jill Radnor, Simon Fox, Paul A Moore, Stephen Moss, Michael Sargent, R B Gardiner, S G N Bennett, Rob, the Didler, Phil and Sally Gorton, Mr and Mrs H J Langley, Martin and Karen Wake

BRAISHFIELD
SU3724   MAP 2

Wheatsheaf 🍷

Village signposted off A3090 on NW edge of Romsey, pub just S of village on Braishfield Road; SO51 0QE

Cheerful pub with interesting and unusual décor, good choice of wines, and food using some their own produce; nearby walks

All very friendly and laid-back, this rambling place has quite a mish-mash of idiosyncratic décor, but it does work well. There are all sorts of tables from elegant little oak ovals through handsome Regency-style drum tables to sturdy more rustic ones, with a similarly wide variety of chairs, and on the stripped brick or deep pink-painted walls a profusion of things to look at, from Spy caricatures and antique prints through staffordshire dogs and other decorative china to a leg in a fishnet stocking kicking out from the wall and a jokey 'Malteser grader' (a giant copper skimmer). Ringwood Best and a couple of guests like Bowmans Wallops Wood and Hampshire Pride of Romsey on handpump, and 18 wines by the glass; daily papers, several reference books, piped music and board games. Disabled access and facilities. Unusually, the chairs, tables and picnic-sets out on the terrace are painted in greek blue; boules. There are woodland walks nearby and the pub is handy for the Sir Harold Hillier Arboretum.

🍴 **Using their own rare breed pigs (they make their own sausages and black puddings) and local meat and game (the landlord can often be found plucking and preparing pheasants, rabbits and so forth), the bar food includes sandwiches, soup, pigeon and smoked bacon salad with orange and ginger dressing, goats cheese and caramelised onion tart, beer-battered pollack, chicken stuffed with cream cheese and wrapped in parma ham, cajun salmon, gloucester old spot pork chop with caramelised apple, and puddings such as chocolate sponge with chocolate sauce and lemon tart. Gourmet burgers on Wednesday evenings and Ladies' Night on Thursdays.** *Starters/Snacks: £4.25 to £7.95. Main Courses: £5.95 to £14.95. Puddings: £4.95 to £5.95*

Enterprise ~ Lease Peter and Jenny Jones ~ Real ale ~ Bar food (12-2.30, 6.30-9.30; all day Sun) ~ Restaurant ~ (01794) 368372 ~ Children welcome away from bar ~ Dogs welcome ~ Open 12-11.30

Recommended by Phyl and Jack Street, Tom and Jill Jones, Ann and Colin Hunt, Simon Watkins, John Chambers, Simon and Mandy King, Bettye Reynolds, Diana Brumfit

BRAMDEAN   SU6127   MAP 2

Fox 🍴

A272 Winchester—Petersfield; SO24 OLP

Civilised dining pub with popular food and friendly staff; no children inside

The licensees of this rather smart, weatherboarded dining pub have now been here for 23 years and continue to offer a warm welcome to all their customers. The carefully modernised black beamed open-plan bar is civilised and grown up (no children inside), with tall stools with proper backrests around the L-shaped counter and comfortably cushioned wall pews and wheelback chairs – the fox motif shows in a big painting over the fireplace and on much of the decorative china. Greene King Ruddles County on handpump, decent wine by the glass, and piped music. At the back of the building is a walled-in terraced area and a neatly kept spacious lawn spreading among the fruit trees. Good surrounding walks. Dogs are allowed in the bar if the pub is not too busy.

🍴 **Popular bar food includes lunchtime sandwiches, wild boar pâté, scallops fried with bacon, steak and kidney pie, chicken curry, fresh fillet of battered cod, confit of duck with an orange gravy, pork fillet with stilton and brandy sauce, skate wing with capers, and puddings such as apple, blackberry and almond crumble and chocolate st emilion.** *Starters/Snacks: £4.95 to £7.95. Main Courses: £8.95 to £15.95. Puddings: £4.25 to £5.25*

Greene King ~ Tenants Ian and Jane Inder ~ Real ale ~ Bar food ~ (01962) 771363 ~ Dogs allowed in bar ~ Open 11-3, 6.30-11; 12-3.30, 7-11 Sun; closed Sun evenings Jan-end May

Recommended by Phyl and Jack Street, Ann and Colin Hunt, Helen and Brian Edgeley, Janet Whittaker, J A Snell, Betty Laker

BRANSGORE   SZ1997   MAP 2

Three Tuns 🍺

Village signposted off A35 and off B3347 N of Christchurch; Ringwood Road, opposite church; BH23 8JH

Interesting food in pretty thatched pub with proper old-fashioned bar and good beers as well as civilised main dining area

A friendly, hard-working new licensee has taken over this thatched place and there's now a bar in the barn for special events and summer barbecues on the terrace. The roomy low-ceilinged and carpeted main area has a fireside 'codgers' corner' as well as its good mix of comfortably cushioned low chairs around a variety of dining tables, and opens on to an attractive and extensive shrub-sheltered terrace with picnic-sets on its brick pavers; beyond here are more tables out on the grass, looking out over pony paddocks. On the right is a separate traditional regulars' bar that seems almost taller than it is wide, with an impressive log-effect stove in a stripped brick hearth, some shiny black panelling, and individualistic pubby furnishings. Caledonian Deuchars IPA, Hop Back Summer Lightning, Ringwood Best and Fortyniner and Timothy Taylors Landlord on handpump, a good choice of wines by the glass, and hot drinks; service is well organised and polite.

🍴 As well as lunchtime sandwiches and ploughman's, the often interesting bar food now includes soup, a parcel of goats cheese and beetroot jelly, baby spinach and tomato pasta with cream and parmesan, caesar salad, fishcakes with sour cream and tomato sauce, aubergine and mushroom parcel, a curry of the day, liver and bacon with sherry cream sauce, daily specials like warm wild mushroom tart with garlic ice-cream, twice cooked rabbit with prunes, hazelnuts and mulled wine juices, and fried local bass with candied fennel and white balsamic juices, and puddings such as honey-roasted quince with crème fraîche and profiteroles with white chocolate sauce and blueberries; Sunday roasts.
Starters/Snacks: £3.95 to £7.95. Main Courses: £5.95 to £11.95. Puddings: £4.50 to £6.00

Enterprise ~ Lease Nigel Glenister ~ Real ale ~ Bar food (all day Sun) ~ Restaurant ~ (01425) 672232 ~ Children in restaurant and lounge but not main bar ~ Dogs allowed in bar ~ Open 11.30-11; 12-10.30 Sun

Recommended by Rodger and Yvonne MacDonald, Andy and Jill Kassube, Tony and Caroline Elwood, Mr and Mrs J Mandeville, Phyl and Jack Street, John and Penelope Massey Stewart

CHERITON   SU5828   MAP 2

Flower Pots ★ 🍺 £

Pub just off B3046 (main village road) towards Beauworth and Winchester; OS Sheet 185 map reference 581282; SO24 0QQ

Own-brew beers in rustic pub with simple rooms and simple food

'A little gem' is how several of our readers describe this homely village local, now family-owned for 40 years. The two straightforward little rooms are rustic and simple, though the one on the left is a favourite, almost like someone's front room with country pictures on its striped wallpaper, bunches of flowers and some ornaments on the mantelpiece over a small log fire. Behind the servery is disused copper filtering equipment, and lots of hanging gin traps, drag-hooks, scaleyards and other ironwork. The neat extended plain public bar (where there's a covered well) has board games. Their own-brewed beers (you can tour the brewery by arrangement) include Flower Pots Bitter, Goodens Gold and 2 Point 9 on handpump; several other pubs now carry their beers. The pretty front and back lawns have some old-fashioned seats and there's a summer marquee; maybe summer morris dancers. The pub is near the site of one of the final battles of the Civil War, and it got its name through once belonging to the retired head gardener of nearby Avington Park. No children inside.

🍴 Bar food from a fairly short straightforward menu includes sandwiches, toasties and baps, filled baked potatoes, ploughman's and various hotpots; on Wednesday evenings they serve only curries. The menu and serving times may be restricted if they're busy.
Starters/Snacks: £3.50 to £4.50. Main Courses: £6.50 to £10.00

Own brew ~ Licensees Jo and Patricia Bartlett ~ Real ale ~ Bar food (not Sun evening or bank hol evenings) ~ No credit cards ~ (01962) 771318 ~ Dogs welcome ~ Open 12-2.30(3 Sat), 6-11; 12-3, 7-10.30 Sun ~ Bedrooms: £45S/£70S

Recommended by Phyl and Jack Street, Ann and Colin Hunt, Paul and Shirley White, Peter and Liz Holmes, Val and Alan Green, A D Lealan, Janet Whittaker, the Didler, John R Ringrose, Peter Sampson, Colin and Janet Roe

CRAWLEY   SU4234   MAP 2

Fox & Hounds ♀

Off A272 or B3420 NW of Winchester; SO21 2PR

Attractive building, three roaring winter log fires, several real ales, and reasonably priced food; bedrooms

In a picturesque village, this is a striking, almost swiss-looking building with friendly licensees. The neat and attractive linked rooms have three log fires, a mix of attractive wooden tables and chairs on polished floors, and a civilised atmosphere. Ringwood Best and Fortyniner, Wadworths 6X, and Wells & Youngs Bombardier on handpump, and 14 wines by the glass; efficient young staff. There are tables in the garden. The bedrooms, in converted outbuildings, are named after the ducks on the village pond.

🍽 **An enjoyable mix of traditional and modern food at reasonable prices includes sandwiches, ploughman's, soup, pork and chicken liver pâté with plum and brandy sauce, thai ginger fish brochettes, a curry of the day, a trio of sausages with gravy, goats cheese tart, steak in ale pie and daily specials such as tempura-battered squid with sweet chilli chutney, moules marinières, wild mushroom stroganoff, slow-roasted minted lamb shoulder, chicken fillet stuffed with asparagus and wrapped in parma ham, and basil and parmesan crusted cod fillet.** *Starters/Snacks: £4.25 to £4.95. Main Courses: £7.95 to £15.95. Puddings: £4.25*

Enterprise ~ Lease Peter and Kathy Airey ~ Real ale ~ Bar food (12-2, 7-9; 12-4 Sun; not Sun evening) ~ Restaurant ~ (01962) 776006 ~ Children welcome ~ Dogs welcome ~ Open 11-3, 6-midnight; 11-4 Sun; closed Sun evening ~ Bedrooms: /£60B

Recommended by Phyl and Jack Street, Diana Brumfit

DROXFORD
SU6018   MAP 2

Bakers Arms

A32 5 miles N of Wickham; High Street; SO32 3PA

Good country cooking in attractively opened-up pub with well kept beers and cosy corners

The young couple who opened here in 2006 have already won a lot of support locally. Although the food is a big draw, the pub scores all round, with a warm atmosphere and attractive layout. It's been nicely cleaned up, keeping the central bar as the main focus: they have Bowman Swift One and Wallops Wood on handpump, Stowford Press cider, and a careful short choice of wines by the glass. Well spaced mixed tables on carpet or neat bare boards spread around the airy L-shaped open-plan bar, with low leather chesterfields and an assortment of comfortably cushioned chairs down at one end; a dark panelled dado, dark beams and joists and a modicum of country oddments emphasise the freshness of the crisp white paintwork. The hands-on landlady and her helpers are friendly and efficient. There's a good log fire, and board games. To one side, with a separate entrance, is the village post office. There are picnic-sets outside.

🍽 **Food here is top-notch country cooking with a deft light touch. Depending on what's available locally, the menu might include lunchtime ploughman's, a smoked haddock ramekin, boiled duck egg with parmesan soldiers or tongue and black pudding salad as starters, with main courses such as gloucester old spot sausages and mash, leek and blue cheese tart with a good salad, crispy duck leg with toasted couscous and thyme gravy, and bass with pasta, rocket pesto and samphire, and puddings like treacle tart with vanilla ice-cream and apple and rhubarb crumble with custard. Meats are melt-in-mouth, and fresh seasonal local vegetables, often unusual, are a highlight. The chef/landlord, who had previously worked in pub kitchens we have much admired, bakes some interesting breads, fresh for lunchtime and again for the evening. In puddings and pies, his pastry is admirably light and crisp.** *Starters/Snacks: £4.50 to £6.25. Main Courses: £10.95 to £16.95. Puddings: £4.95*

Free house ~ Licensees Adam and Anna Cordery ~ Real ale ~ Bar food ~ (01489) 877533 ~ Well behaved children welcome ~ Dogs welcome ~ Open 11.45-3, 6-11; 12-3 Sun; closed Sun evening and Mon

Recommended by Val and Alan Green, Diana Brumfit, Chris Sale

'Children welcome' means the pub says it lets children inside without any special restriction. If it allows them in, but to restricted areas such as an eating area or family room, we specify this. Some pubs may impose an evening time limit. We do not mention limits after 9pm as we assume children are home by then.

DUNBRIDGE   SU3225   MAP 2

Mill Arms ◀

Barley Hill, just by station on Portsmouth—Cardiff line; SO51 0LF

Extended coaching house with plenty of space, several real ales, bistro-style food and pretty garden; bedrooms

In fine Test Valley countryside where there are plenty of walks (and dogs on leads are welcome), this is an attractive 18th-c building, much extended since it was last in these pages. There's a relaxed, friendly atmosphere in the high-ceilinged rooms with scrubbed pine tables and farmhouse chairs on the oak or flagstone floors, a couple of log fires, several sofas, and Ringwood Best with guests such as Brains SA, Caledonian XPA, Gales (Fullers) HSB, and Wychwood Hobgoblin on handpump; several wines by the glass, and prompt service. There's also a dining conservatory (and by the time this book is published, a new dining area) and a skittle alley; piped music. The large, pretty garden has picnic-sets, and the bedrooms are bright and comfortable. Dunbridge railway station is opposite.

⊞ Good bistro-style bar food includes sandwiches, crab fritter with sweet chilli sauce, pumpkin and ricotta tortellini with hazelnut dressing, a trio of sausages with onion gravy, beer-battered fish and chips, home-baked ham with free-range eggs, lamb and rosemary pie, naturally smoked haddock with a soft poached egg, bubble and squeak and hollandaise sauce, crispy shoulder of lamb with smoked bacon and roast garlic, and puddings like treacle sponge with pumpkin jam and chocolate and chestnut cake with blood orange compote. *Starters/Snacks: £2.95 to £5.60. Main Courses: £6.95 to £9.95. Puddings: £4.95*

Enterprise ~ Lease Mr I Bentall ~ Real ale ~ Bar food (12-2.30, 6-9.30; 12-9.30 Sat(9 Sun)) ~
Restaurant ~ (01794) 340401 ~ Children welcome ~ Dogs allowed in bar ~
Open 12-11(10.30 Sun) ~ Bedrooms: £60B/£60B

Recommended by Phyl and Jack Street, P J Checksfield, Ann and Colin Hunt

DUNDRIDGE   SU5718   MAP 2

Hampshire Bowman ◀

Off B3035 towards Droxford, Swanmore, then right at Bishops W signpost; SO32 1GD

Friendly country pub with quickly changing real ales, homely food and peaceful garden with children's play equipment

Extremely popular with a good mix of customers, this extended country tavern has a friendly and relaxed atmosphere and a good range of real ales tapped from the cask: Archers Jackass, Bowman Swift One, Hop Back Summer Lightning, Ringwood Fortyniner, and Stonehenge Pigswill. There's a smart stable bar that sits comfortably alongside the cosy unassuming original bar, some colourful paintings, several wines by the glass, local apple juice, and cider (from April to October). Board games, puzzles and Daisy the pub dog. There are picnic-sets on the attractive lawn, a giant umbrella with lighting and heating on the terrace (where you can enjoy the lovely sunsets), and new children's play equipment; peaceful nearby downland walks.

⊞ Well liked homely bar food includes sandwiches, filled baguettes and baked potatoes, and soup, plus good daily specials such as creamy garlic mushrooms, half a pint of prawns, aubergine and tomato crumble, local sausages, various pies, lemon and mustard chicken breast with couscous, mixed game casserole, halibut fillet with prawns and mushrooms, duck leg with ginger, honey and spring onions, and puddings such as cherry and apricot lattice pie and chocolate waffle pudding. *Starters/Snacks: £3.95 to £5.50. Main Courses: £7.25 to £10.95. Puddings: £4.50*

Free house ~ Licensee Heather Seymour ~ Bar food (12-2, 6.30-9; all day Fri-Sun) ~
(01489) 892940 ~ Children welcome until 9pm ~ Dogs welcome ~ Open 12-11(10.30 Sun)

Recommended by Ann and Colin Hunt, Val and Alan Green, the Didler, Christine Bridgwater

EAST TYTHERLEY   SU2927   MAP 2

Star

Off B3084 N of Romsey; SO51 OLW

Warm welcome for drinkers and diners in pretty pub, inventive food, real ales, and comfortable bedrooms

The friendly, hard-working licensees in this pretty country pub have encouraged drinkers by creating more room for them in the main bar – they want to be, first and foremost, a village inn. The bar has comfortable sofas and tub armchairs, pub dining tables and chairs, bar stools and chairs, an overflowing bookcase to one side of the log fire, and rich red walls. The restaurant is attractive set with proper linen napkins and tablecloths. Ringwood Best Bitter and a guest plus Hidden Quest on handpump, several wines by the glass and malt whiskies and a range of apple juices; piped music and board games. There are picnic-set sets in front and tables and chairs on the back terrace by a giant chessboard. The bedrooms overlook the cricket pitch and the breakfasts are particularly good; nearby walks.

🍴 Cooked by the licensees' son, the inventive, attractively presented food might include lunchtime sandwiches and platters, soup, chicken liver and wild mushroom parfait with toasted soda bread and beetroot chutney, parsnip bread and butter pudding with red pepper coulis, cumberland sausages with wholegrain mustard mash and red onion confit, venison casserole, baked smoked haddock fillet with dijon mustard sauce, and puddings like warm chocolate brownie with orange curd and cardamom ice-cream and cappuccino crème brûlée; there's also a good value two-course set lunch menu. *Starters/Snacks: £4.25 to £5.75. Main Courses: £8.50 to £13.75. Puddings: £5.50*

Free house ~ Licensees Alan and Lesley Newitt ~ Real ale ~ Bar food ~ Restaurant ~ (01794) 340225 ~ Children welcome ~ Dogs allowed in bar and bedrooms ~ Open 11-3, 6-10.30; 11-4 Sun; closed Sun evening, Mon ~ Bedrooms: £55S/£80S

Recommended by Christopher and Elise Way, Peter Craske, Roger Price, Ann and Colin Hunt

EASTON   SU5132   MAP 2

Chestnut Horse 🍴 🍷

3.6 miles from M3 junction 9: A33 towards Kings Worthy, then B3047 towards Itchen Abbas; Easton then signposted on right – bear left in village; SO21 1EG

Cosy dining pub with log fires, fresh flowers and candles, deservedly popular food and friendly staff; Itchen Valley walks nearby

Cosy and well run, this is a busy dining pub with friendly, helpful staff. The open-plan interior manages to have a pleasantly rustic and intimate feel with a series of cosily separate areas and the snug décor takes in candles and fresh flowers on the tables, log fires in cottagey fireplaces and comfortable furnishings. The black beams and joists are hung with all sorts of jugs, mugs and chamber-pots, and there are lots of attractive pictures of wildlife and the local area. Badger K&B Sussex Bitter and Hopping Hare on handpump, several wines by the glass and 30 malt whiskies; piped music. There are good tables out on a smallish sheltered decked area with colourful flower tubs and baskets, and plenty of nearby walks in the Itchen Valley.

🍴 As well as lunchtime sandwiches, the good, carefully cooked (if not cheap) food might include soup, moules marinières, warm goats cheese crotin with pesto fettuccine and sun-blush peppers, confit duck and cherry terrine with parma ham and red chard and griottine dressing, wild mushroom and spinach pithiviers, confit plum tomatoes and tarragon sauce, steak and kidney pudding, roast chicken supreme stuffed with mozzarella, wrapped in bacon with a red wine jus, and puddings such as warm chocolate brownie with vanilla ice-cream and rhubarb and apple crumble; there's also a good value, seasonally changing two-course menu (not available weekend evenings or Sunday lunchtime). *Starters/Snacks: £5.50 to £7.95. Main Courses: £12.95 to £17.95. Puddings: £5.95 to £7.25*

Badger ~ Tenant Karen Wells ~ Real ale ~ Bar food ~ Restaurant ~ (01962) 779257 ~ Children welcome ~ Dogs allowed in bar ~ Open 11-3, 5.30-11.30; 11am-11.30pm Sat; 12-10.30 Sun; 12-6 Sun in winter; closed winter Sun evening

Recommended by Mrs S Barker-Ryder, John Robertson, Simon Fox, Phyl and Jack Street, Andy Reid, Dr D and Mrs B Woods, Mrs Ann Gray, Mike and Jayne Bastin, Michael Dandy, D and J Ashdown, Ann and Colin Hunt, Martin and Karen Wake, Stephen Moss

EXTON   SU6120   MAP 2

Shoe

Village signposted from A32 NE of Bishop's Waltham – brown sign to pub into Beacon Hill Lane; SO32 3NT

Hard-working licensees in country pub by River Meon with comfortable linked rooms and nice food

This is a pleasantly located country pub and the three linked rooms have a friendly relaxed atmosphere. Also, comfortable pub furnishings, cricket and country prints, and in the right-hand room (which is panelled), a log fire. Wadworths 6X, IPA and a seasonal guest on handpump and 14 wines by the glass; helpful, welcoming service. You can sit at picnic-sets and watch the ducks on the River Meon from beneath a floodlit sycamore across the road and there are seats under parasols at the front. They have baby-changing facilities, a disabled lavatory and ramp access.

🍽 **Cooked by the landlord using home-grown herbs, vegetables and fruit, the often imaginative food might include sandwiches and platters, soup, oriental crispy beef fillet salad, warm goats cheese, leek and red onion tart with tomato chutney, scallops with herb pancakes and sherry honey dressing, pork sausages with spring onion potato cake and vegetable casserole, chicken breast stuffed with mousseline, wrapped in parma ham on tomatoes and pasta, sea bream fillet on crab couscous with tomato and red pepper salsa, and puddings like hazelnut meringue with poached pear and rum and raisin ice-cream and sticky toffee pudding with cream. They make their own bread, pickles and chutneys.** *Starters/Snacks: £4.25 to £6.95. Main Courses: £9.95 to £14.95. Puddings: £5.50 to £5.95*

Wadworths ~ Tenants Mark and Carole Broadbent ~ Real ale ~ Bar food (12-2, 6-9(8.30 Sun, 9.30 Fri and Sat) ~ Restaurant ~ (01489) 877526 ~ Children welcome ~ Dogs allowed in bar ~ Open 11-3, 6-11(10 Sun); closed Mon evening; 25 Dec

Recommended by Stephen Moss, Brian Robinson, Ann and Colin Hunt, Simon Collett-Jones, Glenwys and Alan Lawrence, Tony Hewitt, Tony and Wendy Hobden, Michele Gunning, Tina and David Woods-Taylor, Matt and Cathy Fancett

FRITHAM   SU2314   MAP 2

Royal Oak 🍺

Village signed from exit roundabout, M27 junction 1; quickest via B3078, then left and straight through village; head for Eyeworth Pond; SO43 7HJ

Rural New Forest spot and part of a working farm; traditional rooms, log fires, seven real ales and simple lunchtime food

One nostalgic reader remembers this pub nearly fifty years ago when 'opening hours were whimsical and late night drinking guaranteed'. This is still a lovely, simple country tavern with plenty of chatty locals (almost invariably with a dog in tow), a genuinely warm welcome from the friendly staff and really enjoyable, good quality unfussy food. Three neatly kept black beamed rooms are straightforward but full of proper traditional character, with prints and pictures involving local characters on the white walls, restored panelling, antique wheelback, spindleback and other old chairs and stools with colourful seats around solid tables on new oak flooring, and two roaring log fires. The back bar has quite a few books. Half a dozen real ales are tapped from the cask: Hop Back Summer Lightning, Ringwood Best and Fortyniner and changing guests from brewers such as Bowman and Keysone. Also, a dozen wines by the glass (mulled wine in winter) and a September beer festival; darts. Summer barbecues are put on in the neatly kept big garden which has a marquee for poor weather and pétanque. The pub is part of a working farm so there are ponies and pigs out on the green and plenty of livestock nearby.

🍽 Using eggs from their free-range hens and pork from their own pigs, the much liked simple lunchtime food is limited to winter soups, ploughman's, pies and quiches, sausages and pork pie, and free-range smoked chicken breast wrapped in bacon. *Starters/Snacks: £4.50 to £6.50. Main Courses: £6.50 to £7.50*

Free house ~ Licensees Neil and Pauline McCulloch ~ Real ale ~ Bar food (lunchtime only (till 3pm weekends)) ~ No credit cards ~ (023) 8081 2606 ~ Children welcome if well behaved ~ Dogs welcome ~ Open 11-11; 11-11 Sat; 12-10.30 Sun; 11-3, 6-11 weekdays in winter

Recommended by N R White, Miss J F Reay, Kevin Flack, the Didler, Ann and Colin Hunt, Mr and Mrs W W Burke, Pete Baker, Mr and Mrs P D Titcomb, Janet Whittaker, Dick and Madeleine Brown, Mike and Linda Hudson, John Chambers, A D Lealan, Peter and Anne Hollindale, John Roots

HAWKLEY   SU7429   MAP 2

Hawkley Inn 🍺

Take first right turn off B3006, heading towards Liss 0.75 mile from its junction with A3; then after nearly 2 miles take first left turn into Hawkley village – Pococks Lane; OS Sheet 186 map reference 746292; GU33 6NE

Nine real ales in friendly country pub, home-cooked food and bedrooms

The new licensee here still keeps a fine range of nine real ales on handpump from breweries such as Bowmans, Dark Star, fff, Hogs Back, Hop Back, Ringwood, and Suthwyk. There are also a dozen malt whiskies and local cider. This is still a proper country pub with walking boots, wellies, horses, and bikes, and the unchanging front rooms have open fires, board games and piped music. The back rooms have been knocked through, effectively creating a central bar so you can now walk all round the pub. There are seats on the terrace and in the garden. The pub is on the Hangers Way Path, and at weekends there are plenty of walkers (and it does tend to be crowded then).

🍽 Bar food now includes filled rolls, filled baked potatoes and ploughman's, faggots with onion gravy, cottage pie, bacon, brie and mushroom tart, beef stew, and daily specials. *Starters/Snacks: £4.25 to £6.95. Main Courses: £8.50 to £14.50. Puddings: £3.50 to £5.50*

Free house ~ Licensee Jean Jamieson ~ Real ale ~ Bar food (12-2(2.30 Sat), 7-9.30) ~ (01730) 827205 ~ Children welcome until 8pm ~ Dogs allowed in bar ~ Open 12-3, 5.30-11; 12-11(10.30 Sun) Sat ~ Bedrooms: £69B/£75S(£85B)

Recommended by Susan and John Douglas, JMM, Tony and Jill Radnor, Simon Fox, P E Wareham, Martin and Karen Wake, R B Gardiner, Wendy Arnold, the Didler, Ann and Colin Hunt

HOUGHTON   SU3432   MAP 2

Boot

Village signposted off A30 in Stockbridge; SO20 6LH

Riverside pub with good generous food either in cheerful locals' bar or in roomy more decorous lounge/dining room

On a sunny day, this is an enchanting spot for lunch with the long sheltered back lawn runing down to a lovely tranquil stretch of the River Test (quick-flowing, and unfenced here); you may be able to arrange fishing with the pub – though one monster trout in the bar's generous assortment of stuffed creatures was actually taken on the Itchen. This nice country bar is bustling and pubby, with a good log fire, plenty of regulars both at the counter and around the various tables, and perhaps one or two dogs making themselves at home (visiting dogs may get a chew). Service is efficient and natural – treating people good-naturedly as individuals without being artificially over-friendly. Ringwood Best and Seventy Eight on handpump; faint piped music. On the left is a much more extensive part with cream and green décor and attractive high-backed, modern dining chairs around good solid tables. The Test Way cycle path is on the far side of the river.

🍽 Large helpings of good bar food include filled baguettes, croque monsieur, smoked halibut and smoked salmon with pickled cucumber, milano salami and parma ham salad with mustard dressing, duck confit on baby leaf salad, deep-fried chinese-style pigeon with plum rice, roasted field mushrooms filled with stilton and garlic on roasted peppers, a burger of the week, local sausages, chicken stuffed with apple and cheddar and wrapped in parma ham with a cream and garlic sauce, wild mushroom lasagne, smoked haddock in a sorrel and creamy butter sauce, and puddings such as white chocolate cheesecake and rhubarb fool. *Starters/Snacks: £4.50 to £5.50. Main Courses: £12.00 to £20.00. Puddings: £5.00*

Free house ~ Licensees Richard and Tessa Affleck ~ Real ale ~ Bar food ~ (01794) 388310 ~ Children welcome if well behaved ~ Dogs allowed in bar ~ Open 12-2.30, 6-11; 12-2.30, 7-10.30 Sun

Recommended by Phyl and Jack Street, Helen and Brian Edgeley, Edward Mirzoeff

LITTLETON
SU4532 MAP 2

Running Horse 🍴 🍷
Village signposted off B3049 just NW of Winchester; Main Road; S022 6QS

Inventive food in stylish, elegant rooms, a fine choice of drinks, and nice terraces

---

This is an enjoyable place with good food and helpful, friendly service. It's a smart, stylish dining pub and the bar has some deep leather chairs as well as ochre-cushioned metal and wicker ones around matching modern tables on its polished boards, up-to-date lighting, good colour photographs of hampshire landscapes and townscapes, a potted palm as well as a log fire, and venetian blinds in its bow windows. The neat modern marble and hardwood bar counter (with swish leather, wood and brass bar stools) has Flowerpots Bitter and Palmers IPA on handpump, 14 wines by the glass and good coffee. Linking openly from here, the back restaurant area has the same sort of elegant modern furniture on flagstones. Good disabled access and facilities and maybe piped pop music. There are green metal tables and chairs out on terraces front and back and picnic-sets on the back grass by a spreading sycamore.

🍴 Well presented, very popular food includes lunchtime sandwiches, soup, oriental crab and salmon fishcakes with wasabi mayonnaise, chicken caesar salad, grilled goats cheese with crispy bacon and a balsamic reduction, creamy wild mushroom tagliatelle, beer-battered haddock with mushy peas, steak in ale pie, chicken breast stuffed with apricot and chestnuts with a garlic bacon sauce, seared duck breast on lyonnaise potatoes with a honey, lime and ginger glaze, and puddings such as white and dark chocolate crème brulée with chocolate dipped shortbread biscuit and pecan pie with chantilly cream. *Starters/Snacks: £4.95 to £8.95. Main Courses: £10.95 to £17.95. Puddings: £3.95 to £6.95*

Free house ~ Licensee Kathryn Crawford ~ Real ale ~ Bar food (1) ~ Restaurant ~ (01962) 880218 ~ Children welcome if well behaved ~ Dogs allowed in bar ~ Open 11-3, 5.30-11; 12-9 Sun; closed 25 Dec ~ Bedrooms: £65B/£75B

Recommended by Ann and Colin Hunt, Phyl and Jack Street, Mr and Mrs M Stratton, John and Joan Calvert, David Jackson

LOWER FROYLE
SU7643 MAP 2

Anchor 🛏
Village signposted N of A31 W of Bentley; GU34 4NA

Interestingly refurbished, lots to look at, civilised but informal atmosphere, real ales and good wines, and enjoyable food; comfortable bedrooms

---

Rather civilised but with a relaxed and chatty atmosphere, this tile-hung 14th-c pub has been completely refurbished, the work complicated by a 2007 fire. There are low beams and standing timbers, flagstones in the bar and wood stripped floors elsewhere, sofas and armchairs dotted here and there, a mix of nice old tables and dining chairs, lit candles in candlesticks, an open fire, and high bar chairs at the counter. Throughout there are all sorts of interesting knick-knacks, books, lots of copper, horsebrasses, photographs (several of Charterhouse School), and all manner of pictures and prints; paint colours are fashionable, values are traditional, and they keep Hop Back Crop Circle and Ringwood Best and Fortyniner on handpump and good wines by the glass. There is quite an emphasis on the enjoyable food but those just wanting a drink are made genuinely welcome. The bedrooms are stylish.

🍴 **Good bar food includes welsh rarebit, soft herring roes with capers and parsley, seared scallops with celeriac and apple remoulade and blue cheese beignet, beer-battered haddock, toad-in-the-hole with shallot gravy, barnsley chop with crushed peas and mint sauce, rib-eye steak with béarnaise sauce, and puddings such as chocolate fondant with pistachio ice-cream and spotted dick with custard.** *Starters/Snacks: £5.00 to £9.50. Main Courses: £10.50 to £18.50. Puddings: £5.50 to £5.95*

Free house ~ Licensee Lucy Townsend ~ Real ale ~ Bar food ~ Restaurant ~ (01420) 23261 ~ Children welcome ~ Dogs allowed in bar ~ Open 11.30(12 Sun)-11 ~ Bedrooms: /£130S

Recommended by Barry Steele-Perkins, Martin and Karen Wake

LOWER WIELD
SU6339   MAP 2

Yew Tree ♀

Turn off A339 NW of Alton at Medstead, Bentworth 1 signpost, then follow village signposts; or off B3046 S of Basingstoke, signposted from Preston Candover; SO24 9RX

Relaxed atmosphere, super choice of wines and popular food in pleasant country pub; sizeable garden and nearby walks

This is the sort of place that once found, you'll want to come back to. It's a tile-hung country pub with an attractively informal atmosphere and a genuinely friendly and enthusiastic landlord. There's a small flagstoned bar area on the left with pictures above its stripped brick dado, a steadily ticking clock and log fire. Around to the right of the serving counter – which has a couple of stylish wrought-iron bar chairs – it's carpeted, with a few flower pictures; throughout there is a mix of tables, including some quite small ones for two, and miscellaneous chairs. 13 wines by the glass from a well chosen list which may include Louis Jadot burgundies from a shipper based just along the lane and summer rosé. Hammerpot Meteor and a beer from fff named after the pub on handpump. There are solid tables and chunky seats out on the front terrace, picnic-sets in a sizeable side garden, pleasant views, and a cricket field just across the quiet lane. Nearby walks.

🍴 **Carefully sourced, well liked bar food includes sandwiches, soup, chicken liver pâté with home-made spicy plum chutney, salmon and cornish crab cake with home-made tartare sauce, deep-fried camembert with redcurrant jelly, sausages of the week with mustard mash and onion gravy, spinach and ricotta cannelloni with cashew pesto, cream and cheese, chicken breast wrapped in parma ham with roasted vegetables and pepper sauce, half shoulder of lamb with parsnip and potato dauphinoise with red wine and rosemary jus, and puddings like prune and white chocolate bread and butter pudding and rhubarb, apple and ginger crumble.** *Starters/Snacks: £3.95 to £6.95. Main Courses: £8.95 to £17.95. Puddings: £4.50*

Free house ~ Licensee Tim Gray ~ Real ale ~ Bar food ~ (01256) 389224 ~ Children welcome ~ Dogs allowed in bar ~ Open 12-3, 6-11; 12-10.30 Sun; closed Mon; ten days in early Jan

Recommended by Roger Chacksfield, Stephen Moss, Tony and Jill Radnor, Matt and Cathy Fancett, R B Gardiner, Phyl and Jack Street, John Oates, Denise Walton, Shawn O'Rourke, P E Wareham, N B Vernon, Peter and Andrea Jacobs, Robert Davies, Simon Smith, Mr and Mrs W Mills

LYMINGTON
SZ3295   MAP 2

Kings Head ◀

Quay Hill; pedestrian alley at bottom of High Street, can park down on quay and walk up from Quay Street; SO41 3AR

Rambling beamed and timbered pub with nice mix of old-fashioned seating, several ales, and newspapers to read

A handsome sight at the top of a steep cobbled lane of smart small shops, this 17th-c pub is a popular place for a drink: Adnams Bitter, Gales HSB, Greene King Old Speckled

Hen and a beer from Fullers and Ringwood on handpump, and several wines by the glass. The mainly bare-boarded rooms ramble up and down steps and through timber dividers with tankards hanging from great rough beams. There's a nice old-fashioned variety of seating at a great mix of tables from an elegant gateleg to a huge chunk of elm, and the local pictures include good classic yacht photographs. A cosy upper corner past the serving counter has a log fire in a big fireplace, its mantelpiece a shrine to all sorts of drinking paraphernalia from beer tankards to port and champagne cases; an interesting clock, too. Daily papers in a rack and piped pop music.

Bar food includes sandwiches, brie wedges with orange and port sauce, lasagne, chicken curry, gammon with honey-glazed pineapple, duck breast with chinese-style stir-fried vegetables, and puddings. *Starters/Snacks: £3.95 to £6.95. Main Courses: £8.50 to £13.95. Puddings: £4.10 to £4.75*

Enterprise ~ Lease Paul Stratton ~ Real ale ~ Bar food (11-2.30(3 Fri, 3.30 weekends), 6-10) ~ (01590) 672709 ~ Children welcome ~ Dogs welcome ~ Open 11.30-3, 6-midnight; 11-midnight Sat; 12-midnight Sun; closed 25 and 26 Dec

Recommended by Mr and Mrs P D Titcomb, Mr and Mrs A Garforth, Fr Robert Marsh, Drs J and J Parker, Miss J F Reay, Mayur Shah, Stephen Moss, Richard and Sissel Harris, Michael Dandy

OVINGTON
SU5631   MAP 2

Bush

Village signposted from A31 on Winchester side of Alresford; SO24 ORE

Cottagey pub with seats in waterside back garden and several peaceful rooms

Especially busy at weekends, this tucked away pub is in a charming spot with picnic-sets by the River Itchen. It's attractively cottagey inside and the low-ceilinged bar is furnished with cushioned high-backed settles, elm tables with pews and kitchen chairs, masses of old pictures in heavy gilt frames on the walls, and a roaring fire on one side with an antique solid fuel stove opposite. Wadworths IPA, 6X, and Horizon on handpump, several wines by the glass and quite a few country wines. Look out for the sociable scottish springer spaniel, Paddy; board games. Please note that if you want to bring children it's best to book, as there are only a few tables set aside for families. Nice nearby walks.

As well as sandwiches and ploughman's (which are not cheap), bar food includes soup, organic smoked trout mousse, mushrooms with garlic and green peppercorns, french onion tart with goats cheese and olives, cumberland sausages with rich onion gravy, chargrilled chicken breast with chilli cheese, sour cream and tortilla crisps, steak, mushroom and thyme pie, tempura king prawns with chilli dip, and puddings such as plum in madeira crumble and Valrhona dark chocolate and raspberry crème brûlée; Sunday roasts. *Starters/Snacks: £5.95 to £11.50. Main Courses: £10.95 to £16.45. Puddings: £3.90 to £5.75*

Wadworths ~ Managers Nick and Cathy Young ~ Real ale ~ Bar food (12-4 Sun; not Sun evening) ~ (01962) 732764 ~ Children allowed but limited room for them ~ Dogs welcome ~ Open 11-3, 6-11(all day summer hols); 12-4, 7-10.30 Sun; closed 25 Dec

Recommended by Ann and Colin Hunt, Tracey and Stephen Groves, Peter Sampson, Martin and Karen Wake, Helen and Brian Edgeley, Matt and Cathy Fancett, Phyl and Jack Street, John and Tania Wood, Nick Lawless, R B Gardiner, Val and Alan Green

PETERSFIELD
SU7227   MAP 2

Trooper

From B2070 in Petersfield follow Steep signposts past station, but keep on up past Steep, on old coach road; OS Sheet 186 map reference 726273; GU32 1BD

Charming landlord, popular food, decent drinks, and little persian knick-knacks and local artists' work; comfortable bedrooms

Mr Matini continues to offer a genuinely friendly welcome to all his customers and this is the sort of well run all-rounder that people come back to again and again. There's an island bar, blond chairs and a mix of tripod tables on bare boards or red tiles, tall stools by a broad ledge facing big windows that look across to rolling downland fields, old film star photos and paintings by local artists for sale, little persian knick-knacks here and there, quite a few ogival mirrors, lit candles all over the place, fresh flowers, and a well tended log fire in the stone fireplace; carefully chosen piped music, and newspapers and magazines to read. Arundel Sussex Gold, Bowmans Swift One, and Ringwood Best on handpump and several wines by the glass. The attractive raftered restaurant has french windows to a paved terrace with views across the open countryside, and there are lots of picnic-sets on an upper lawn. The horse rail in the car park ('horses and camels only before 8pm') does get used, though probably not often by camels.

🍴 **Good, enjoyable bar food includes sandwiches, soup, baked brie and almonds with redcurrant jelly, carrot and chestnut cannelloni with watercress sauce, chilli con carne, sausage and mash, a pie of the day, free-range chicken with tarragon creamy sauce, roast duck breast with orange and Grand Marnier sauce, seared swordfish steak with pink peppercorn sauce, their speciality slow-roasted half shoulder of lamb, and puddings.** *Starters/Snacks: £5.00 to £12.50. Main Courses: £10.00 to £20.00. Puddings: £5.50 to £7.50*

Free house ~ Licensee Hassan Matini ~ Real ale ~ Bar food ~ Restaurant ~ (01730) 827293 ~ Children must be seated and supervised by an adult ~ Dogs allowed in bar ~ Open 12-3, 5-11; 12-11 Sat; 12-5 Sun; closed Sun evening and all day Mon (except for bank hols), 25 and 26 Dec, 1 Jan ~ Bedrooms: £69B/£89B

Recommended by Janet Whittaker, Bruce and Penny Wilkie, David and Sue Atkinson, Alex Harper, Roger and Lesley Everett, Tina and David Woods-Taylor, Ann and Colin Hunt, Sue Ruffhead

PORTSMOUTH
SZ6399 MAP 2

Old Customs House

Vernon Buildings, Gunwharf Quays; follow brown signs to Gunwharf Quays car park – usually quickest to park on lower level, come up escalator, turn left towards waterside then left again; PO1 3TY

Handsome historic building well converted in prime waterfront development

Although this fine brick building is now surrounded by the spacious walkways of a bright and extensive modern waterside shopping centre and is just around the corner from the graceful Spinnaker Tower (165 metres (540 ft) tall with staggering views from its viewing decks), it was indeed the former Georgian customs house, then an administration building for HMS *Vernon*, and the Royal Navy's mine clearance and diving school (it has some memorabilia of those days). It's a well laid out pub with several big-windowed high-ceilinged rooms off a long central spine which houses the serving bar and a separate food/coffee ordering counter – they have lots of good coffees and teas, as well as a decent range of wines by the glass, and Fullers ESB, HSB, London Pride, and Discovery and a guest such as Highgate Special on handpump. This floor, with good disabled access and facilities, has bare boards, nautical prints and photographs on pastel walls, coal-effect gas fires, nice unobtrusive lighting, and well padded chairs around sturdy tables in varying sizes; the sunny entrance area has leather sofas. Broad stairs take you up to a carpeted more restauranty floor, with similar décor. Staff are efficient, housekeeping is good, the piped music well reproduced, and the games machines silenced. Picnic-sets out in front are just yards from the water.

🍴 **Bar food includes a range of wraps and organic baps, moules marinières, farmhouse pâté, crayfish cocktail, vegetarian italian risotto, bangers and mash, chicken and pancetta melt, lamb shoulder in garlic and rosemary, steak pie, and puddings such as bakewell tart and four layer chocolate fudge cake.** *Starters/Snacks: £3.95 to £6.25. Main Courses: £6.95 to £12.95. Puddings: £3.95 to £5.65*

Fullers ~ Manager David Hughes ~ Real ale ~ Bar food ~ Restaurant ~ (023) 9283 2333 ~ Children allowed until 8pm but must go to upstairs restaurant after that ~ Open 9am-midnight(1am Fri, 2am Sat); 9am-11pm Sun

Recommended by Tony and Wendy Hobden, Ann and Colin Hunt, Alan and Eve Harding

Pubs with outstanding views are listed at the back of the book.

ROTHERWICK
SU7156   MAP 2

Falcon

4 miles from M3, junction 5; follow Newnham signpost from exit roundabout, then Rotherwick signpost, then turn right at Mattingley, Heckfield signpost; village also signposted from B3349 N of Hook, then brown signs to pub; RG27 9BL

Plenty of seating in various rooms, a relaxed country atmosphere, open fires, tasty food, and sizeable back garden

A friendly new Portuguese licensee has taken over this country pub but doesn't plan any major changes. The open-plan rooms have quite a mixture of dining chairs gathered around an informal variety of tables on varnished floorboards, big bay windows with sunny window seats, and minimal decoration on deep red walls. A rather more formal back dining area is round to the right, and on the left are an overstuffed sofa and a couple of ornate easy chairs by one log fire. Fullers London Pride and Sharps Doom Bar on handpump; piped music. You can sit out at tables and benches at the front and back of the building and the sizeable informal back garden looks into grazing pastures. Easy walks nearby. Reports on the new regime, please.

🍴 There's quite a choice of bar food including lunchtime sandwiches (their portuguese one is popular with chorizo, sausage, steak and an egg, topped with a special sauce), crab and avocado salad, ham or sausages with egg, steak in ale pie, lots of fish dishes, lamb steak with a lemon, cherry tomato and butter sauce, several vegetarian choices and puddings such as tiramisu and fruit crumble. *Starters/Snacks: £3.95 to £5.95. Main Courses: £7.95 to £17.50. Puddings: £5.50*

Enterprise ~ Lease Rui Gomes ~ Real ale ~ Bar food (12-2(2.30 Sun), 6-9.30(7-9 Sun) ~ Restaurant ~ (01256) 762586 ~ Children welcome ~ Dogs allowed in bar ~ Open 11-2.30, 6-11; 12-10.30 Sun

Recommended by Mr and Mrs W D Borthwick, Philip and June Caunt, John Cook, Stephen Moss, G Garvey, KC, Dr and Mrs Jackson, I A Herdman, Rob

ROWLAND'S CASTLE
SU7310   MAP 2

Castle Inn

Village signposted off B2148/B2149 N of Havant; Finchdean Road, by junction with Redhill Road and Woodberry Lane; PO9 6DA

A cheerful feel and generous food served by smart staff in bustling pub; largish garden

Well run and cheerful, this popular pub has friendly hands-on licensees. There are two appealing little eating rooms on the left. The front one has rather nice simple mahogany chairs around sturdy scrubbed pine tables, rugs on flagstones, a big fireplace, and quite a lot of old local photographs on its ochre walls. The back one is similar, but with bare boards and local watercolour landscapes by Bob Payne for sale. There is a small separate public bar on the right with a good fire and Fullers London Pride, Gales Butser and HSB and a guest like Fullers Festival Mild on handpump. The publicans' own ponies are in view from the largish garden, which is equipped with picnic-sets and a couple of swings; disabled access and facilities are good.

🍴 Served by smartly dressed staff, the pubby, fairly priced lunchtime menu includes filled baguettes, ploughman's, chilli con carne, sausage and mash, gammon and egg, and mixed grill, with evening choices such as smoked salmon and prawns on rocket leaves, smoked chicken and mango salad, duck confit with orange and Cointreau sauce and caramelised vegetables, fillet of sole stuffed with crab meat and scallops, and puddings like pear and amaretti crumble and treacle and pecan tart *Starters/Snacks: £3.75 to £5.25. Main Courses: £6.95 to £8.95. Puddings: £4.50*

Gales (Fullers) ~ Lease Jan and Roger Burrell ~ Real ale ~ Bar food (12-3, 6-9; not Sun evening) ~ Restaurant ~ (023) 9241 2494 ~ Children welcome ~ Dogs allowed in bar ~ Open 10.30am-midnight; 12-midnight Sun

Recommended by Tony and Wendy Hobden, Ann and Colin Hunt

SOUTHSEA   SZ6499   MAP 2

Wine Vaults ◀

Albert Road, opposite Kings Theatre; PO5 2SF

A fine range of real ales, reasonably priced food and a bustling atmosphere

Reliable and well run, this busy pub is popular for its fine range of eight real ales on
handpump. There are several rooms on different floors – all fairly straightforward and
chatty – and the main bar has wood-panelled walls, pubby tables and chairs on the
wooden floor, bar stools by the long plain bar counter, and Fullers Chiswick Bitter, ESB,
Discovery, HSB, London Pride, and four changing guests on handpump; there's a new
restaurant area away from the hustle and bustle of the bars. Maybe newspapers to read,
piped music and TV for sports events. It does get crowded at the weekend but is quieter
during the week.

🍴 **Some sort of food is offered all day and might include sandwiches (until 5pm), soup,
filled baked potatoes, gourmet burgers, various nachos, steak in ale pie, beer-battered
haddock, vegetable lasagne, bangers and mash, and honey-roast ham and wholegrain
mustard with two fried eggs; there may be a new tapas menu.** *Starters/Snacks: £2.95 to
£4.75. Main Courses: £6.95 to £15.00. Puddings: £3.95*

Fullers ~ Manager Sean Cochrane ~ Real ale ~ Bar food (all day) ~ Restaurant ~
(023) 9286 4712 ~ Children welcome until 9pm ~ Dogs allowed in bar ~
Open 12-11(12, Fri Sat; 10.30 Sun)
Recommended by Ann and Colin Hunt, the Didler

SPARSHOLT   SU4331   MAP 2

Plough 🍽 ♀

*Village signposted off B3049 (Winchester—Stockbridge), a little W of Winchester;
SO21 2NW*

**Neat, well run dining pub with interesting furnishings, an extensive wine list, and popular
bar food; garden with children's play fort**

As well as four real ales, this bustling pub is very popular for its extremely good food. It's
a neatly kept place and the main bar has an interesting mix of wooden tables and chairs
with farm tools, scythes and pitchforks attached to the ceiling. Wadworths IPA, 6X,
Horizon and a seasonal beer on handpump, and an extensive wine list with a fair
selection by the glass, including champagne and pudding wine; friendly, efficient service.
Disabled access and facilities; there's a children's play fort, and plenty of seats on the
terrace and lawn.

🍴 **Enjoyable bar food includes sandwiches, ciabattas and ploughman's, soup, a timbale of
salmon and prawns in a lemon dressing, grilled chorizo, feta cheese, olives and sun-dried
tomato salad, chicken liver parfait with fruit chutney, chicken breast stuffed with haggis
on a bacon and bean jus, venison steak with celeriac mash and roasted beetroots, lovely
steak, mushroom and ale pie, courgette, tomato and olive tart on pepper coulis, lamb
shank with parsley mash and rosemary jus, fillet of bass with wilted spinach and shrimp
butter, and puddings such as a trio of chocolate mousse, and orange and ginger panna
cotta.** *Starters/Snacks: £4.95 to £6.95. Main Courses: £8.95 to £17.95. Puddings: £3.95 to
£5.75*

Wadworths ~ Tenants Richard and Kathryn Crawford ~ Real ale ~ Bar food (12-2, 6-9(8.30 Sun))
~ (01962) 776353 ~ Children welcome in main bar area ~ Dogs welcome ~
Open 11-3, 6-11; 12-3, 6-10.30 Sun; closed 25 Dec
*Recommended by Michael Lewis, C and H Greenly, Mrs S Barker-Ryder, John and Joan Calvert, R Lake, Mr and
Mrs M Stratton, Keith and Sue Ward, Peter and Liz Holmes, Val and Alan Green, Glenwys and Alan Lawrence,
Ann and Colin Hunt, Mr and Mrs P D Titcomb, Karen Eliot, Fred and Kate Portnell*

We say if we know a pub allows dogs.

STEEP   SU7525   MAP 2

Harrow 🍺

Take Midhurst exit from Petersfield bypass, at exit roundabout first left towards Midhurst, then first turning on left opposite garage, and left again at Sheet church; follow over dual carriageway bridge to pub; GU32 2DA

Unchanging, simple place with long-serving landladies, beers tapped from cask, unfussy food, and big free-flowering garden; no children inside

In the same family since 1929, this genuinely unspoilt and unpretentious little pub is run by two sisters. Apart from some newish carpets and cushions, nothing changes and it all revolves around village chat and the friendly locals who will probably draw you into light-hearted conversation. There are adverts for logs next to calendars of local views being sold in support of local charities, news of various quirky competitions, and no pandering to modern methods – no credit cards, no waitress service, no restaurant, no music, and outside lavatories. The cosy public bar has hops and dried flowers hanging from the beams, built-in wall benches on the tiled floor, stripped pine wallboards, a good log fire in the big inglenook, and wild flowers on the scrubbed deal tables; board games. Bowmans Swift One and Ringwood Best are tapped straight from casks behind the counter, and they've local wine, and apple and pear juice; staff are polite and friendly, even when under pressure. The big garden is left free-flowering so that goldfinches can collect thistle seeds from the grass. The Petersfield bypass doesn't intrude on this idyll, though you will need to follow the directions above to find the pub. No children inside, and dogs must be on leads.

🍽 **Good helpings of unfussy bar food include sandwiches, home-made scotch eggs, hearty ham, split pea and vegetable soup, ploughman's, cottage pie, lasagne and quiches, and puddings such as super treacle tart or seasonal fruit pies.** *Starters/Snacks: £4.40. Main Courses: £8.00. Puddings: £4.00*

Free house ~ Licensees Claire and Denise McCutcheon ~ Real ale ~ Bar food (not Sun evening) ~ No credit cards ~ (01730) 262685 ~ Dogs welcome ~ Open 12-2.30, 6-11; 11-3, 6-11 Sat; 12-3, 7-10.30 Sun; closed winter Sun evenings

Recommended by Tracey and Stephen Groves, Phil and Sally Gorton, Jill Townsend, Tony and Jill Radnor, Mrs Rita Cox, Simon Fox, Keith and Sue Ward, Mike and Eleanor Anderson, Ann and Colin Hunt, the Didler, Sue Ruffhead

SWANMORE   SU5815   MAP 2

Rising Sun 🍷 🍺

Village signposted off A32 N of Wickham and B2177 S of Bishops Waltham; pub E of village centre, at Hillpound on the Droxford Road; SO32 2PS

Friendly licensees make this proper country pub a warmly welcoming all-rounder

The hard-working, hands-on licensees in this bustling 17th-c coaching inn make all their customers comfortable and welcome, and their young staff are attentive and helpful, too. The low-beamed carpeted bar has some easy chairs and a sofa by its good log fire, and a few tables with pubby seats. Beyond the fireplace on the right is a pleasant much roomier dining area, with similarly unpretentious furnishings, running back in an L past the bar; one part of this has stripped brick barrel vaulting. Marstons Pedigree and Ringwood Best and guests such as Adnams and Greene King Old Speckled Hen on handpump, and a good range of a dozen or so wines by the glass; faint piped music. There are picnic-sets out on the side grass with a play area, and the Kings Way long distance path is close by – some readers tell us it is best to head north where there is lovely downland country, fine views and interesting winding lanes.

🍽 **A fair choice of good value pubby food includes sandwiches and filled baguettes, filled baked potatoes, ploughman's, soup, omelettes, vegetable and stilton bake, a pie of the day, honey-baked ham and eggs, lasagne, smoked haddock and spring onion fishcakes, faggots with mushy peas, and lambs liver with bacon.** *Starters/Snacks: £4.75 to £7.95. Main Courses: £7.95 to £9.50. Puddings: £3.50 to £4.25*

Punch ~ Lease Mark and Sue Watts ~ Real ale ~ Bar food (12-2, 6-9) ~ Restaurant ~
(01489) 896663 ~ Children allowed but must be well behaved ~ Dogs allowed in bar ~
Open 11.30-3, 5.30-11; 12-3, 5.30-10.30 Sun

Recommended by Val and Alan Green, Stephen Moss, Ann and Colin Hunt, Phyl and Jack Street

TICHBORNE   SU5730   MAP 2
Tichborne Arms
Village signed off B3047; SO24 ONA

Traditional pub in rolling countryside and liked by walkers; big garden

Another new licensee for this attractive thatched pub but there's a good welcome and the
food, using seasonal produce, is good. The comfortable square-panelled room on the right
has wheelback chairs and settles (one very long), a stone fireplace and latticed windows.
On the left is a larger, livelier, partly panelled room used for eating. Pictures and
documents on the walls recall the bizarre Tichborne Case, in which a mystery man from
Australia claimed fraudulently to be the heir to this estate. Bowmans Swift One, Goddards
Ale of Wight, Ringwood Best, Sharps Doom Bar and a couple of guest beers are tapped
from the cask, alongside seven wines by the glass, and farm cider. There are picnic-sets
in the big, neat garden. The Wayfarers Walk and Itchen Way pass close by and the
countryside around is attractively rolling.

🍴 Totally home made (apart from the ice-creams), the good bar food now includes hearty
sandwiches, ploughman's with their own chutneys, soup, grilled scallops with garlic
butter, portobella mushrooms filled with stilton, asparagus and mushroom quiche, steak
and kidney pudding, whole lemon sole, bangers and mash, chicken stuffed with sun-dried
tomatoes and watercress, popular fish pie, lamb stew, winter game dishes, and puddings
such as lemon posset and chocolate mousse; Sunday roasts. *Starters/Snacks: £4.75 to £6.95.*
Main Courses: £7.50 to £12.95. Puddings: £3.95 to £4.50

Free house ~ Licensee Nicky Roper ~ Real ale ~ Bar food (12-2(3 Sat and Sun), 6.30-9.30) ~
(01962) 733760 ~ Children welcome ~ Dogs welcome ~ Open 11.30-3(4 Sat),
6.30-11(midnight Sat); 12-4, 7-11 Sun; closed evenings of 25 and 26 Dec and 1 Jan

Recommended by Matt and Cathy Fancett, Ann and Colin Hunt, Dr D and Mrs B Woods, the Didler,
Christine Bridgwater, Stephen and Jean Curtis, Gerald and Gabrielle Culliford, R B Gardiner, Sean A Smith

UPHAM   SU5320   MAP 2
Brushmakers Arms
Off Winchester—Bishops Waltham downs rd; Shoe Lane; SO32 1JJ

Friendly old place with extensive displays of brushes, local beers, and nice unfussy food

This is an enjoyable old local with a friendly landlord, helpful staff, and a good mix of
customers. Picking up on the pub's name, the walls in the L-shaped bar (divided in two
by a central brick chimney with a woodburning stove) are hung with quite a collection of
old and new brushes. A few beams in the low ceiling add to the cosiness, and there are
comfortably cushioned settles and chairs and a variety of tables including some in
country-style stripped wood; there's also a little back snug with fruit machine, dominoes
and board games. Hampshire Ironside and Uncle Bob, Ringwood Best and changing
guests on handpump; the pub cats are called Gilbert and Kera and the ghost is known as
Mr Chickett (apparently seen as a shadowy figure searching the pub for his lost money
and belongings). The big garden is well stocked with mature shrubs and trees and there
are picnic-sets on a sheltered back terrace amongst tubs of flowers, with more on the
tidy tree-sheltered lawn. It's best to park by the duck pond; good walks nearby.

🍴 Well liked, straightforward bar food includes lunchtime sandwiches, panini and
omelettes, soup, cheese and bacon potato skins, baked brie with redcurrant sauce,
vegetable lasagne, sausage and mash, cajun chicken, battered cod, liver and bacon with
onion gravy, cider-baked ham with grain mustard cream, and puddings. *Starters/Snacks:*
£4.95 to £5.55. Main Courses: £8.50 to £15.95. Puddings: £4.50

Free house ~ Licensee Keith Venton ~ Real ale ~ Bar food (12-2, 6(7 Sun)-9(9.30 Fri, Sat)) ~
(01489) 860231 ~ Children welcome ~ Dogs allowed in bar ~ Open 11-3, 5.45-11;
12-3, 7-10.30 Sun

Recommended by Jenny and Peter Lowater, Ann and Colin Hunt, Sean A Smith, Bruce and Penny Wilkie

WEST MEON   SU6424   MAP 2

Thomas Lord ◀

High Street; GU32 1LN

**Friendly pub, cheerful licensees, lots of wood in several rooms, interesting food and fine
choice of beers**

This is an individually decorated pub with a lively, warm-hearted atmosphere. There's an
interesting mix of wooden dining and pubby chairs around lots of different wooden
tables (each with a candle on it – lit on a dark day), bare boards, some cricketing prints
and memorabilia, various pictures and portraits above the wooden dados, and two blazing
fires. The back room is lined with books which you can buy for 50p. The welcoming,
chatty landlords keep a fine range of real ales tapped from the cask such as Ballards
Best, Bowmans Swift One and Wallops Wood, Goddards Ale of Wight, Itchen Valley
Winchester Ale, and Ringwood Best; also farm ciders, several wines by the glass and
decent coffee. The garden was being redesigned as we went to press and carpenters were
hard at work designing new seats and tables; there's an outside oven here, too. Good
walks to the west of the village.

🍽 **Enjoyable food using carefully sourced local produce includes sandwiches, soup,
steamed purple sprouting broccoli with a poached egg and hollandaise, salad of rump
steak with spinach, mashed parsnips and swede, home-cured duck with red cabbage
coleslaw, sausages with onion rings and ale sauce, vegetable and nut cottage pie with
local blue cheese sauce, goat burger with cheese, pasta with slow-braised leeks, bacon
and mushrooms, chicken and ox tongue pie, bass roasted in salt, rosemary and lemon
verbena butter, venison wellington with red cabbage, and puddings such as spiced apple
bread and butter pudding.** *Starters/Snacks: £5.00 to £7.00. Main Courses: £10.00 to £18.00.
Puddings: £4.00 to £5.50*

Enterprise ~ Lease David Thomas and Richard Taylor ~ Real ale ~ Bar food (not Sun evening) ~
Restaurant ~ (01730) 829244 ~ Children welcome ~ Dogs welcome ~ Open 11-3, 6-midnight;
11-midnight Sat; 12-11 Sun

*Recommended by Kevin Malam, Christine Bridgwater, Gerry Price, Val and Alan Green, Jennifer Hurst,
David M Smith, David and Ruth Hollands, Ann and Colin Hunt*

WHERWELL   SU3839   MAP 2

Mayfly

*Testcombe (over by Fullerton, and not in Wherwell itself); A3057 SE of Andover, between
B3420 turn-off and Leckford where road crosses River Test; OS Sheet 185 map reference
382390; SO20 6AX*

**Extremely (and deservedly) popular pub with decking and conservatory seats overlooking
the River Test, half a dozen ales, and wide range of enjoyable bar food, usefully served
throughout the day**

Mr and Mrs Lane have been running this idyllically placed pub for 21 years now. It's on
an island between the River Test and a smaller river to the back, and in good weather the
tables on the decking area overlooking the water are extremely popular – best to get
there early. Inside, the spacious, beamed and carpeted bar has fishing pictures and
fishing equipment on the cream walls, rustic pub furnishings, and a woodburning stove.
There's also a conservatory with riverside views; piped music. A fine choice of six real
ales on handpump served by friendly staff might include Hop Back Summer Lightning,
Palmers Gold, Ringwood Best, Wadworths 6X, Wychwood Hobgoblin, and a changing
guest; 20 wines by the glass.

🍴 Good, popular bar food is handily available all day and as well as a daily hot and cold buffet (at its largest in summer), there might be pork sausages in a rich onion gravy, lasagne, mushroom and red pepper stroganoff, smoked haddock and spring onion fishcakes, a curry such as caribbean chicken or vegetable balti, a dish of the day like chicken breast in white stilton and apricot cream sauce, five chef's specials such as lamb tagine or bass on a rocket and spring onion salad, and puddings like chocolate puddle pudding (chocolate sponge with a white chocolate centre and chocolate custard) and raspberry pavlova. They don't do sandwiches or chips. *Starters/Snacks: £4.95 to £6.95. Main Courses: £9.95 to £16.95. Puddings: £4.95*

Enterprise ~ Manager Barry Lane ~ Real ale ~ Bar food (11.30-9) ~ (01264) 860283 ~ Children welcome if well behaved ~ Dogs welcome ~ Open 10am-11pm; 10am-10pm winter

Recommended by Phyl and Jack Street, Ann and Colin Hunt, Stephen Allford, Sally and Tom Matson, Louise Gibbons

WINCHESTER
SU4828   MAP 2

Black Boy 🍺

A mile from M3 junction 10 northbound; B3403 towards city then left into Wharf Hill; rather further and less easy from junction 9, and anyway beware no nearby daytime parking – 220 metres from car park on B3403 N, or nice longer walk from town via College Street and College Walk, or via towpath; SO23 9NQ

Busy town pub with several different areas crammed full of interesting knick-knacks, straightforward lunchtime bar food and local ales

If you are seeking sophisticated surroundings, this old-fashioned place is not for you. It's full of fascinating things to look at and has plenty of eccentric character, and several different areas run from a bare-boards barn room with an open hayloft, down to an orange-painted room with big oriental rugs on red-painted floorboards. There are floor-to-ceiling books in some parts, lots of big clocks, mobiles made of wine bottles or strings of spectacles, some nice modern nature photographs in the lavatories and on the brightly stained walls on the way, and plenty of other things that you'll enjoy tracking down. Furnishings are similarly wide-ranging; two log fires. The five well kept beers on handpump are more or less local: Flower Pots Bitter, Hop Back Summer Lightning and Ringwood Best alongside a couple of guests from breweries such as Hampshire, Itchen Valley and Triple fff; decent wines, piped music, table football and board games. There are a couple of slate tables out in front with more seats on an attractive secluded terrace.

🍴 Lunchtime bar food includes sandwiches with chips or soup, a pasta dish, beer-battered cod and chips and caesar salad or shepherd's pie. *Starters/Snacks: £5.50 to £8.00. Main Courses: £8.00 to £10.00. Puddings: £3.50 to £5.00*

Free house ~ Licensee David Nicholson ~ Real ale ~ Bar food (not Sun evening, Mon, or Tues lunchtime) ~ Restaurant ~ (01962) 861754 ~ Children must be well behaved and supervised ~ Dogs welcome ~ Open 12-11(midnight Fri and Sat); 12-10.30 Sun

Recommended by John and Annabel Hampshire, Pete Baker, Ann and Colin Hunt, Val and Alan Green, Chris Sale, James Price, Michael and Alison Sandy, Simon Fox, Phil Bryant

Willow Tree

Durngate Terrace; no adjacent weekday daytime parking, but Durngate Car Park is around corner in North Walls; a mile from M3 junction 9, by Easton Lane into city; SO23 8QX

Snug Victorian pub with landlord/chef using much local produce for enjoyable food; nice riverside garden

Refurbished this year to include a new galleried kitchen and a smarter, more comfortable dining room, this is a popular local with a welcome for visitors, too. The carpeted lounge bar on the right has a relaxed atmosphere, wall banquettes, low ceilings and soft lighting; two bays of good sturdy dining tables at the back have quite a few books around them. There's a separate proper public bar, Greene King IPA and Old Speckled Hen and a summer guest from maybe Belhaven on handpump, a few wines by the glass, and several malt whiskies; piped music, TV, games machine, juke box (a rarity nowadays), chess, backgammon and pool. The young staff are cheerful and efficient. A narrow tree-shaded garden, partly paved and with plenty of heaters, stretches back between two branches of the River Itchen.

🍴 Done by the landlord, looking every inch a happy chef, the good, generous proper cooking here might include sandwiches, wraps and filled baguettes, ploughman's, omelettes, favourites like steak in ale pie, sizzling chicken fajitas, bangers and mash and half shoulder of lamb, and specials such as soup, terrine of foie gras with madeira jelly, grilled goats cheese salad with beetroot, salmon and haddock kedgeree, beef curry, and sweet and sour chicken, with puddings like warm chocolate fondant and prune and armagnac tart. *Starters/Snacks: £4.50 to £7.50. Main Courses: £8.50 to £16.50. Puddings: £4.50 to £5.50*

Greene King ~ Tenant James Yeoman ~ Real ale ~ Bar food (12-2.30, 6-10; 12-4 Sun; not Sun evening) ~ Restaurant ~ (01962) 877255 ~ Children welcome ~ Open 12-11.30(10.30 Sun)

Recommended by Diana Brumfit, Michael and Alison Sandy, Phil and Sally Gorton

Wykeham Arms ★ 🍴 🍷

Kingsgate Street (Kingsgate Arch and College Street are now closed to traffic; there is access via Canon Street); SO23 9PE

HAMPSHIRE DINING PUB OF THE YEAR

Lovely pub with excellent service, imaginative food, super wines, and lots to look at; no children inside

Civilised but genuinely friendly, this much loved town pub has an aura of calm but plenty of chatty customers – no piped music, mobile phones or children. A series of bustling rooms radiating from the central bar has 19th-c oak desks retired from nearby Winchester College, a redundant pew from the same source, kitchen chairs and candlelit deal tables, and big windows with swagged paisley curtains; all sorts of interesting collections are dotted around. A snug room at the back, known as the Jameson Room (after the late landlord Graeme Jameson), is decorated with a set of Ronald Searle 'Winespeak' prints, a second one is panelled, and all of them have log fires. Fullers London Pride, Chiswick, Gales Butser Bitter and a couple of guests on handpump, and a large number of wines by the glass (including champagne) from an extensive and interesting wine list. The neatly uniformed staff give first class service. There are tables on a covered back terrace (they will serve food at lunchtime only here), with more on a small courtyard.

🍴 Under the new managers, the extremely good, popular lunchtime bar food might include sandwiches, chicken liver parfait with home-made tomato and grain mustard chutney, salad of smoked salmon and smoked trout with an apple and celeriac remoulade and a grain mustard and dill dressing, tagliolini verde in a creamy wild mushroom and goats cheese sauce, cumberland sausages with onion gravy, and daily specials, evening choices such as fried sardine fillets in a sweet and sour escabeche sauce, seared pigeon breasts with black pudding and chorizo vierge, supreme of chicken, crushed minted peas and red wine cream sauce, and baked crab-crusted fillet of salmon on a warm salad of spinach, fine beans, mange tout and rocket with lemon oil; puddings like dark chocolate nemesis with pistachio anglaise and honeycomb and apple panna cotta, bramley apple jelly and raspberry coulis. *Starters/Snacks: £3.95 to £5.95. Main Courses: £6.95 to £22.95. Puddings: £4.50 to £4.95*

Gales (Fullers) ~ Managers Dennis and Ann Evans ~ Real ale ~ Bar food (12-2.30(sandwiches till 3 Sat), 7-9; 12.30-2 Sun; not Sun evenings) ~ Restaurant ~ (01962) 853834 ~ Dogs allowed in bar and bedrooms ~ Open 11-11; 12-10.30 Sun; closed 25 Dec ~ Bedrooms: £62B/£90B

Recommended by Chris and Libby Allen, Ellen Weld, David London, Simon Fox, John and Julie Moon, Martin and Karen Wake, R K Phillips, John Oates, Denise Walton, Peter and Liz Holmes, Fred and Kate Portnell, Janet Whittaker, Ann and Colin Hunt, Philip and June Caunt, John and Annabel Hampshire, David Dyson, Chris Flynn, Wendy Jones, J and F Gowers, Michael and Alison Sandy, David and Sheila Pearcey, Val and Alan Green, Barry and Anne, Phyl and Jack Street, Christopher and Elise Way, Pam and John Smith, the Didler, Cer, Chris Sale, James Price, I H Curtis

---

We say if we know a pub has piped music.

LUCKY DIP

Besides the fully inspected pubs, you might like to try these Lucky Dips recommended to us and described by readers (if you do, please send us reports: feedback@thegoodpubguide.co.uk).

ALRESFORD [SU5832]

☆ **Bell** SO24 9AT [West St]: Spotless Georgian coaching inn with welcoming licensees, interesting good value food from sandwiches and light dishes up, good real ales, fairly priced wines, log fire, daily papers, nice décor, smallish dining room; tables in attractive back courtyard, comfortable bedrooms, open all day (Ann and Colin Hunt, Val and Alan Green)

Swan SO24 9AD [West St]: Neatly kept long narrow panelled hotel bar with Fullers London Pride, large dining area inc Sun carvery; bedrooms in adjoining block (Ann and Colin Hunt)

ALTON [SU7138]

French Horn GU34 1RT [The Butts (A339 S of centre, by rly bridge)]: Bright and cheery local with six well kept ales from long counter such as Butcombe, Caledonian Deuchars IPA and Greene King IPA (beer festival late Nov), good coffee, bar food (all day Sun) from sandwiches to some more upmarket dishes, tankards and whisky-water jugs on beams, old photographs and inglenook log fires, partly stripped brick dining room, pleasant staff, sizeable restaurant, motorcyclists not spurned, separate skittle alley; piped pop music; picnic-sets and other tables outside, bedrooms, open all day (BB, Tony and Wendy Hobden)

Kings Head GU34 1HA [Market St]: Cheerfully bustling town pub, cheap home-made wkdy bar lunches, Courage Best and Ringwood Best, darts; play area in enclosed garden (Val and Alan Green)

AMPFIELD [SU4023]

White Horse SO51 9BQ [A3090 Winchester—Romsey]: Much extended open-plan pub, plenty of room for both eaters and drinkers, friendly staff, well kept Ringwood and Wadworths, good choice of wines by the glass, decent coffee, log fires, comfortable period-effect furniture, Victorian prints and advertisements in dining room; tables outside, pub backs on to village cricket green; handy for Hillier arboretum, good walks in Ampfield Woods (SJ, Ann and Colin Hunt, A and B D Craig, Phyl and Jack Street)

ARFORD [SU8236]

☆ **Crown** GU35 8BT [off B3002 W of Hindhead]: Low-beamed pub with coal and log fires in several areas from bustling local-feel bar to homely candlelit upper dining room, enjoyable if not cheap food from sandwiches to game and splendid puddings, friendly efficient staff, Adnams, Fullers London Pride, Greene King Abbot and a guest beer, decent wines by the glass; piped music; children welcome in eating areas, picnic-sets out in

peaceful dell by a tiny stream across the road (LYM, Tony and Jill Radnor, Keith and Margaret Jackson, R B Gardiner)

AXFORD [SU6043]

Crown RG25 2DZ [B3046 S of Basingstoke]: Efficient young staff, thriving atmosphere, real ales, several wines by the glass, home-made food, three newly refurnished linked rooms, small log fire; children welcome, suntrap terrace and sloping shrub-sheltered garden (Graham and Toni Sanders, John Cook, LYM)

BARTON STACEY [SU4341]

Swan SO21 3RL [village signed off A30]: Former coaching inn with enjoyable food, interesting mix of menus, pleasant staff, real ales inc Wadworths 6X, good choice of wines, chesterfields in nice little lounge area between beamed front bar and popular dining area, back restaurant (not always open); tables on front lawn and in informal back garden (Greta and Christopher Wells, B and F A Hannam, Colin Wood)

BASINGSTOKE [SU6352]

Queens Arms RG21 7JE [Bunnian Pl]: Friendly traditional old town pub with well kept ales such as Courage Best, Wadworths 6X and Wells & Youngs Bombardier, good value food (Tony and Wendy Hobden, Grahame Bann)

BATTRAMSLEY [SZ3098]

☆ **Hobler** SO41 8PT [Southampton Rd (A337 S of Brockenhurst)]: Stylish modern furnishings and décor contrasting with the ancient heavy-beamed structure, good reasonably priced food from sandwiches up using fresh local ingredients, friendly relaxed service, good choice of wines, Ringwood Best and Timothy Taylors Landlord, some sofas in bar; spacious lawn with play area, good Forest walks (Michael Dandy, Ann and Colin Hunt, LYM)

BAUGHURST [SU5860]

☆ **Wellington Arms** RG26 5LP [Baughurst Rd]: Neatly kept country pub with great emphasis on traceable largely organic fresh ingredients in enjoyable food (not Sun evening, Mon or lunch Tues) inc their own rare-breed eggs, herbs and honey, good wines and cheerful service, strong australian connections; picnic-sets in attractive garden (Colin and Bernardine Perry)

BEAULIEU [SU3902]

Montagu Arms SO42 7ZL [almost opp Palace House]: Civilised hotel's less formal Montys bar/brasserie, decent food from nice sandwiches up inc children's helpings, polite efficient service, Ringwood Best, good choice of wines by the glass, lots of malt whiskies, sofas and easy chairs, bare boards, books and panelling; may be piped music; children welcome, dogs allowed in bar, front courtyard picnic-sets, comfortable bedrooms,

attractive surroundings, open all day
(Ann and Colin Hunt, LYM)

BEAUWORTH [SU5624]
Milbury's SO24 0PB [off A272
Winchester/Petersfield]: Good atmosphere in
attractive ancient pub with four Greene King
and other ales, friendly landlord, simple
traditional bar food, reasonably priced wines
by the glass, log fires in huge fireplaces,
beams, panelling and stripped stone,
massive 17th-c treadmill for much older
incredibly deep well; piped music; children
in eating areas, garden with fine downland
views, good walks, has been open all day
wknds and summer *(Ann and Colin Hunt,
LYM, the Didler, Martin and Karen Wake,
Helen and Brian Edgeley)*

BINSTED [SU7741]
Cedars GU34 4PB [off A31 at Bentley, then
village signed; The Street]: New young
chef/landlord doing enjoyable food, friendly
family service, well kept ales, blazing fire in
chatty and airy bar with big windows and
high ceilings, pleasant dining room on right
with another fire, darts; dogs and muddy
boots welcome, big garden with huge further
family play garden *(BB, Tony and Jill Radnor)*

BISHOP'S WALTHAM [SU5517]
Barleycorn SO32 1AJ [Lower Basingwell St]:
Comfortable L-shaped main area with
cheerful staff, generous enjoyable food inc
popular Sun lunch, Greene King ales, log
fire, some low ceiling panelling; TV and
games in public bar; small back garden and
play area *(anon)*

☆ ***Bunch of Grapes*** SO32 1AD [St Peters St –
just along from entrance to central car park]:
Neat and civilised little pub in quiet
medieval street, smartly furnished keeping
individuality and unspoilt feel (run by same
family for a century), Courage Best and
Greene King IPA tapped from the cask, good
chatty landlord and regulars; charming back
terrace garden with own bar *(the Didler,
Stephen and Jean Curtis, BB, Val and
Alan Green)*

White Horse SO32 1FD [Beeches Hill, off
B3035 NE]: Open-plan pub with central log
fire, hop-hung beams and joists, fancy
knotwork, candles in bottles, friendly
licensees, Ringwood Best and Shepherd
Neame Spitfire, decent wines by the glass
and country wines, generous food inc
excellent vegetarian choice and bargain
lunches, all freshly made so may be a wait;
unobtrusive piped music; picnic-sets on
front terrace, small menagerie of rescued
domestic and farmyard animals, open all day
(Val and Alan Green, K Sloan, BB)

BLACKNEST [SU7941]
Jolly Farmer GU34 4QD [Binsted Rd]: Bright
and airy dining pub with reliable food inc
good puddings, friendly staff, real ales, open
fire one end, family room; tables on
sheltered terrace and in garden *(Betty Laker)*

BOLDRE [SZ3198]
☆ ***Red Lion*** SO41 8NE [off A337 N of
Lymington]: Attractive black-beamed rooms

with entertaining collection of bygones,
pews and other seats, log fires, friendly
young staff, Ringwood Best and Fortyniner
and a guest beer, great choice of wines by
the glass, generous food from sandwiches to
plenty of fish; children and dogs allowed,
tables out among flower tubs and baskets,
garden beyond, open all day *(Liz and
Brian Barnard, LYM, Dr D J R Martin,
Michael and Maggie Betton, Mr and
Mrs P D Titcomb, Nick Lawless, Mayur Shah,
Michael and Jenny Back, Ann and Colin Hunt,
Janet Whittaker)*

BRAMBRIDGE [SU4721]
☆ ***Dog & Crook*** SO50 6HZ [nr M3 junction 12,
via B3335]: New licensees for bustling pub,
emphasis on decent pubby food, cosy dining
room, beamed bar with lots of neat tables,
Fullers and Ringwood Best, lots of wines by
the glass; piped music, TV, regular events
and summer music nights; children and dogs
welcome, garden with decking and fairy-lit
arbour, Itchen Way walks nearby *(LYM)*

BRAMSHILL [SU7461]
Hatch Gate RG27 0JX [Heckfield rd]: Good
welcoming service, well kept Fullers London
Pride, some really exotic dishes, good wines
by the glass; big garden *(Peter Sampson)*

BRANSGORE [SZ1897]
Carpenters Arms BH23 8BA [Burley Rd]:
Wide choice of good value food inc popular
Sun roasts, polite cheerful staff, Fullers and
Ringwood ales, sensibly priced wines, long
bar, well spaced dining room tables; sports
TV at games end; pleasant garden *(Mr and
Mrs P D Titcomb)*

BREAMORE [SU1517]
Bat & Ball SP6 2EA [Salisbury Rd]:
Refurbished village pub with new chef doing
enjoyable food, well kept Ringwood, friendly
service, two linked bar areas, attractive
restaurant; pleasant side garden, bedrooms,
Avon fishing and walks, inc lovely ones up
by church and stately Breamore House
(Conrad Lanham, Jennifer Burnett)

BROCKENHURST [SU3002]
Foresters Arms SO42 7RR [Brookley Rd]:
Cheerful unspoilt village pub, low beams and
brickwork, carpeted lounge with good value
pubby food from sandwiches up, neat polite
staff, Fullers London Pride and Ringwood
Best and Fortyniner; TV in smaller bar with
pub games; roadside garden *(Ann and Colin
Hunt, Eithne Dandy, Peter Dandy)*

Rose & Crown SO42 7RH [Lyndhurst Rd
(A337)]: Large main-road pub with sizeable
dining area off small carpeted bar, good
choice of food from sandwiches up, Marstons
and related ales; covered terrace, good-sized
garden, bedrooms *(Michael Dandy)*

BROOK [SU2713]
☆ ***Green Dragon*** SO43 7HE [B3078 NW of
Cadnam, just off M27 junction 1]:
Immaculate big New Forest dining pub
dating from 15th c, good welcoming service
even when busy, enjoyable fresh food inc
plenty of seasonal game and fish as well as
sensibly priced pubby favourites, Fullers

London Pride and HSB and Ringwood, daily papers, bright linked areas with stripped pine and other pubby furnishings; attractive small terrace and larger garden, paddocks beyond, picturesque village (Bob and Angela Brooks, Philippe Victor, BB, George and Gill Rowley)

BUCKLERS HARD [SU4000]
Master Builders House SO42 7XB: Original small yachtsman's bar with beams, flagstones and big log fire, pricy Greene King ale and bar food; part of substantial Best Western hotel complex in charming carefully preserved waterside village (entrance fee), great views from terrace, good bedrooms (John Saville, LYM, Steve Whalley, Ann and Colin Hunt, A D Lealan)

BURGHCLERE [SU4660]
Carpenters Arms RG20 9JY [Harts Lane, off A34]: Pleasantly furnished small pub doing well under current cheerful helpful landlord, generous food from well presented sandwiches to some ambitious dishes, well kept Arkells, decent choice of wines by the glass, good country views from dining extension and terrace picnic-sets; unobtrusive piped music; children and dogs welcome (resident springers), handy for Sandham Memorial Chapel (NT), six comfortable annexe bedrooms, open all day (Mr and Mrs H J Langley)

BURITON [SU7320]
☆ *Five Bells* GU31 5RX [off A3 S of Petersfield]: Low-beamed 17th-c pub with pleasant staff, fresh pubby food from baguettes up, Badger beers, good wines by the glass, big log fire, daily papers, fresh flowers and church candles, some ancient stripped masonry and woodburner on public side; games machine, piped music; children and dogs welcome, nice garden and sheltered terraces, pretty village, good walks, self-catering in converted stables, open all day (LYM, Barry Steele-Perkins, Ann and Colin Hunt)

BURLEY [SU2202]
☆ *White Buck* BH24 4AZ [Bisterne Close; 0.7 miles E, OS Sheet 195 map ref 223028]: Long comfortable bar in 19th-c mock-Tudor hotel, vast choice of enjoyable generous food, Fullers/Gales and a guest beer, good wines by the glass and coffee, lots of worthwhile pictures, log fires each end, courteous attentive staff, pleasant end dining room with tables out on decking (should book – but no bookings Sun lunchtime); may be quiet piped music, Thurs jazz night; children and dogs welcome, pleasant front terrace and spacious lawn, lovely New Forest setting, superb walks towards Burley itself and over Mill Lawn, well equipped bedrooms, open all day (BB, Tom and Jill Jones, Mr and Mrs P D Titcomb, John and Joan Calvert, George Atkinson, Mrs Jordan, Conor McGaughey, N B Vernon, A and B D Craig)

BURSLEDON [SU4809]
☆ *Fox & Hounds* S031 8DE [Hungerford Bottom; 2 miles from M27 junction 8]:
Rambling 16th-c Chef & Brewer of unusual character, ancient beams, flagstones and big log fires, linked by pleasant family conservatory area to ancient back barn with buoyant rustic atmosphere, lantern-lit side stalls, lots of interesting farm equipment; Courage Best and Fullers London Pride, lots of wines, good coffee, enjoyable reasonably priced food from sandwiches up, cheerful obliging staff, daily papers; children allowed, tables outside (Ann and Colin Hunt, Philip Casey, LYM)

☆ *Jolly Sailor* S031 8DN [off A27 towards Bursledon Station, Lands End Rd; handy for M27 junction 8]: Busy efficiently laid out Badger dining pub in prime spot overlooking yachting inlet, good service, reliable food, their usual ales and good wine choice, log fires; open all day (Ann and Colin Hunt, Bettye Reynolds, LYM, Stuart and Doreen Ritchie, Mr and Mrs P D Titcomb)

CADNAM [SU2913]
☆ *Sir John Barleycorn* S040 2NP [Old Romsey Rd; by M27, junction 1]: Wide choice of enjoyable up-to-date food in picturesque low-slung thatched pub extended from low-beamed and timbered medieval core on left, charming prompt service, Ringwood and a guest such as Itchen Valley or Fullers, two good log fires, modern décor and stripped wood flooring; dogs and children welcome, suntrap benches in front and out in colourful garden, open all day (Michael Dandy, Mr and Mrs A Garforth, Chris and Meredith Owen, LYM, R J Davies, Colin Wood)

White Hart S040 2NP [0.5 mile from M27 junction 1; Old Romsey Rd]: Big rambling Blubeckers family restaurant pub, enjoyable food all day, Greene King ales, pleasant efficient service, spotless simple modern furnishings on parquet floors, stripped brickwork; well reproduced piped music, turned down on request; garden tables, play area (Michael Dandy, LYM)

CHALTON [SU7316]
☆ *Red Lion* P08 0BG [off A3 Petersfield—Horndean]: Largely extended thatched all-day dining pub with interesting 16th-c heart around ancient inglenook fireplace, wide range of food from good sandwiches up, Fullers ales and lots of country wines, helpful efficient service, well spaced tables; children and dogs allowed, good disabled access and facilities, nice views from neat rows of picnic-sets on rectangular lawn by large car park, handy for Queen Elizabeth Country Park, open all day (Ann and Colin Hunt, Ian Phillips, Phyl and Jack Street, Glen and Nola Armstrong, LYM, Janet Whittaker, Tony and Wendy Hobden, N B Vernon)

CHARTER ALLEY [SU5957]
White Hart RG26 5QA [White Hart Lane, off A340 N of Basingstoke]: Handsome beamed village pub with good changing ale choice, continental beers, summer farm cider, decent wines, impressive collection of whisky bottles, comfortable lounge bar with

woodburner in big fireplace, dining area, simple public bar with skittle alley; small garden with terrace *(J V Dadswell)*

CHAWTON [SU7037]

☆ *Greyfriar* GU34 1SB [off A31/A32 S of Alton; Winchester Rd]: Spick-and-span open-plan beamed dining pub opp Jane Austen's house, enjoyable food from good baguettes and sandwiches up, Fullers London Pride, ESB and guest beer, decent wines by the glass, good coffees, relaxed atmosphere and quite a few older midweek lunchers, comfortable seating and sturdy pine tables in neat linked areas, open fire in restaurant end; piped music; tables on terrace in small garden; dogs in bar, children until 9pm, good nearby walks, open all day *(Susan and Nigel Brookes, LYM, Meg and Colin Hamilton, Wendy Arnold, B M Eldridge, R B Gardiner, Tom and Jill Jones, David and Sue Smith, Roy and Lindsey Fentiman, I A Herdman, Ann and Colin Hunt, D and J Ashdown)*

CHILBOLTON [SU3939]

Abbots Mitre SO20 6BA [off A3051 S of Andover]: Good neat staff, enjoyable food, real ales such as Ringwood, side lounge and attractive restaurant with small log fire, separate front public bar; garden with pleasant covered terrace, baskets and tubs of flowers, play area, attractive village, River Test and other walks, open all day Sun *(Robert Watt)*

CHILWORTH [SU4118]

Chilworth Arms SO16 7JZ [Chilworth Rd (A27 S'ton—Romsey)]: Stylish modern dining pub, enjoyable food with adventurous contemporary touches, well kept Fullers London Pride and Greene King Old Speckled Hen, good choice of wines by the glass, friendly staff, chunky furniture, part divided off with leather sofas, armchairs and log fire; disabled facilities, large garden, open all day *(Phyl and Jack Street, Mrs C Osgood, Prof H G Allen, C J Pratt)*

CHURCH CROOKHAM [SU8252]

Foresters GU52 9EP [Aldershot Rd]: Wide choice of food from sandwiches up (can be a wait for interesting specials), Mon-Thurs fish supper deals, real ales, two beamed bar areas, high-ceilinged tiled-floor extension; french doors to garden, roadside verandah *(KC)*

COLDEN COMMON [SU4821]

☆ *Fishers Pond* SO50 7HG [Main Rd (B3354)]: Big busy well organised family pub in style of converted mill by pretty woodside lake, log fires and cosy old-world corners (get there early for window seats), Fullers London Pride and Ringwood Best, decent coffee, efficient service, food all day; tables on big part-covered terrace, handy for Marwell Zoo, open all day *(Phyl and Jack Street, Ann and Colin Hunt, Joan and Michel Hooper-Immins)*

Rising Sun SO21 1SB [Spring Lane]: Two welcoming bars, one with games area, bright dining room, cheerful cook doing sensibly priced straightforward food from sandwiches and baguettes up, OAP lunch, real ales such as Fullers/Gales and Ringwood Best; quiet

piped music; big garden with play area *(Diana Brumfit, Val and Alan Green)*

CRONDALL [SU7948]

Plume of Feathers GU10 5NT [The Borough]: Attractive smallish 15th-c village pub popular for good range of enjoyable hearty food from bar or more expensive restaurant menus, friendly helpful staff, Greene King and guest ales, good wines by the glass, beams and dark wood, prints on cream walls, log fire in big brick fireplace; children welcome, two red telephone boxes in garden, picturesque village *(Martin and Karen Wake, Roderick Braithwaite, Simon and Sally Small, KC, Tony and Jill Radnor)*

DAMERHAM [SU1016]

☆ *Compasses* SP6 3HQ [signed off B3078 in Fordingbridge, or off A354 via Martin; East End]: Appealing country inn continuing much as before under new licensees, well kept Fullers London Pride, Hop Back Summer Lightning, Palmers and guest beers, good choice of wines by the glass, lots of malt whiskies, good food from sandwiches up, small neat lounge bar divided by log fire from pleasant dining area with booth seating (children allowed here), pale wood tables and kitchen chairs, separate bar with pool, friendly locals and dogs; long pretty garden by attractive village's cricket ground, high downland walks, nice bedrooms *(Noel Grundy, Mr and Mrs P D Titcomb, John R Ringrose, Mr and Mrs D Renwick)*

DIBDEN PURLIEU [SU4106]

Heath SO45 4PU [Beaulieu Rd; B3054/A326 roundabout]: Enjoyable food pub with polished contemporary linked areas, good service, real ales such as Ringwood, Shepherd Neame Spitfire and Wadworths 6X; children welcome *(Phyl and Jack Street)*

DROXFORD [SU6118]

Hurdles SO32 3QT [Station Rd, Brockbridge]: Restaurant and bar with current licensees doing enjoyable food from simple baguettes up, three real ales, Victorian-style décor inc some booth seating and equestrian pictures *(Val and Alan Green)*

White Horse SO32 3PB [A32; South Hill]: Rambling pub with several small linked areas, low beams, bow windows, sofas, alcoves and log fires, two dining rooms, good wines by the glass, good indian food inc takeaways (some other dishes too inc good value ciabattas), character landlord and pleasant staff, roomy separate public bar with plenty of games, also TV and CD juke box; children and dogs welcome, tables out in sheltered flower-filled courtyard, open all day, rolling walking country *(LYM, Ann and Colin Hunt)*

DURLEY [SU5116]

Farmers Home SO32 2BT [B3354 and B2177; Heathen St/Curdridge rd]: Comfortable beamed bar with two-bay dining area and big restaurant, generous reasonably priced food inc fresh fish and lovely puddings, long-serving landlord, well kept Fullers/Gales ales and Ringwood Best, decent wine, log fire; children welcome, big garden with good play area, nice walks *(Diana Brumfit, Ann and Colin Hunt)*

EAST MEON [SU6822]

☆ *Olde George* GU32 1NH [Church St; signed off A272 W of Petersfield, and off A32 in West Meon]: Relaxing heavy-beamed rustic pub with enjoyable reasonably priced bar and restaurant food from sandwiches up, good service, inglenook log fires, cosy areas around central bar counter, Badger ales, good choice of wines, friendly pug cross; children welcome, nice back terrace, five comfortable bedrooms (book well ahead), good breakfast, pretty village with fine church, good walks *(V Brogden, Mr and Mrs A P Betts, Nigel Thompson, LYM, Ann and Colin Hunt, Phyl and Jack Street, Prof and Mrs S Barnett)*

Robin Hood SO32 2AA: Closed down as we went to press *(LYM)*

EAST WORLDHAM [SU7438]

Three Horseshoes GU34 3AE [Cakers Lane (B3004 Alton—Kingsley)]: Early 19th-c, comfortable and attractive, with good range of reasonably priced food, Fullers/Gales ales and a guest such as Adnams; secluded garden with pet rabbits, bedrooms *(Joan and Michel Hooper-Immins)*

ELLISFIELD [SU6345]

Fox RG25 2QW [Green Lane, Upper Common]: Village pub with new couple doing good country food using local meats, Wadworths 6X and interesting guest beers, nice range of wines by the glass, open fire, pleasant lounge area on left, main dining area opposite; attractive garden, good walks *(Stephen Allford)*

EMERY DOWN [SU2808]

☆ *New Forest* SO43 7DY [village signed off A35 just W of Lyndhurst]: In one of the best bits of the Forest for walking, with hard-working welcoming landlady, enjoyable food from filled baguettes and innovative snacks up, Ringwood and guest beers, good choice of wines by the glass, proper coffee, attractive softly lit separate areas on varying levels, each with its own character, hunting prints, two log fires; children allowed, small pleasant three-level garden; may change hands during the year *(Brian Collins, Mr and Mrs P D Titcomb, George Murdoch, LYM)*

EMSWORTH [SU7405]

Coal Exchange PO10 7EG [Ships Quay, South St]: Traditional L-shaped Victorian local, well kept Fullers ales inc HSB, good coffee and fresh pubby lunchtime food, Tues curry night, coal fire each end, low ceilings, lots of locals and yachtsmen; tables outside, handy for Wayfarers Walk and Solent Walk, open all day Fri-Sun *(Ann and Colin Hunt)*

EVERSLEY [SU7861]

☆ *Golden Pot* RG27 0NB [B3272]: Enjoyable food from baguettes up in neatly refurbished linked areas with nicely spaced tables, highly efficient cheerful service, Greene King ales, good wines by the glass; piped music; dogs allowed in bar, picnic-sets outside with

masses of colourful flowers, cl winter Sun evening *(D and J Ashdown, KC, LYM)*

FACCOMBE [SU3958]

☆ *Jack Russell* SP11 0DS [signed from A343 Newbury—Andover]: Light and airy creeper-covered pub in village-green setting opp pond by flint church, good bar food (not Sun evening) from snacks to Sun roasts, quick friendly service even on busy wknds, well kept Greene King IPA and Shepherd Neame Spitfire, good coffee, darts, decorous bar and carpeted conservatory restaurant; disabled facilities, lawn by beech trees, spotless cheerful bedrooms, good walks *(Angus and Rosemary Campbell, I A Herdman, Edward Leetham, Sue Demont, Tim Barrow, BB, Michael Dallas)*

FAREHAM [SU5705]

Castle in the Air PO16 0XH [Old Gosport Rd; was Coal Exchange]: Open-plan Greene King pub, friendly staff, their real ales, reasonably priced food, big fireplace, flagstones and bare boards, nice wooden chairs and settles, sailing photographs and gear, tidal Fareham Creek views from raised area and tables outside *(Stephen Moss)*

Cob & Pen PO16 8SL [Wallington Shore Rd, not far from M27 junction 11]: Well kept Bass, Ringwood Best and Wells & Youngs, fairly priced simple food, cheerful staff, pleasant pine furnishings, flagstones and carpets, nice separate games room; large garden, handy for waterside walks *(Val and Alan Green)*

Lord Arthur Lee PO16 0EP [West St]: Large open-plan Wetherspoons, eight well priced beers from small brewers, their usual good value food, family area; named for the local 1900s MP who presented Chequers to the nation *(Val and Alan Green)*

FARNBOROUGH [SU8756]

☆ *Prince of Wales* GU14 8AL [Rectory Rd, nr Farnborough North stn]: Half a dozen or more good changing ales in friendly Edwardian local, stripped brickwork, open fire and antiquey touches in its three small linked areas, popular lunchtime food (not Sun) from sandwiches to imaginative specials, good service, decent malt whiskies; open all day Sun *(Dr Martin Owton)*

FARRINGDON [SU7135]

Rose & Crown GU34 3ED [off A32 S of Alton; Crows Lane – follow Church, Selborne, Liss signpost]: Cheerful and attractive L-shaped bar mainly laid for the good choice of enjoyable food, friendly efficient service even when busy, real ales inc Adnams, decent wines and coffee, log fire, fresh flowers, candles and nice lighting, daily papers, spotless back dining room; wide views from big well kept back garden *(BB, Glen and Nola Armstrong, Ann and Colin Hunt, Tony and Jill Radnor)*

FINCHDEAN [SU7312]

George PO8 0AU: Good value food in roomy relaxing lounge, well kept Wells & Youngs ales, neat public bar; good nearby walks, open all day Sun *(Ann and Colin Hunt)*

FORDINGBRIDGE [SU1314]

Augustus John SP6 1DG [Station Rd]: Good unobtrusive service, enjoyable food, spotless housekeeping, reasonably priced wines; picnic-sets outside, four comfortable bedrooms *(Robert Watt)*

George SP6 1AH [Bridge St]: Lovely spot, refreshing contemporary décor keeping a pleasant degree of pubby cosiness, wide choice of enjoyable if not cheap food, Greene King ales; terrace and conservatory overlooking visibly trout-filled River Avon *(George Murdoch, Roy and Lindsey Fentiman)*

Ship SP6 1AX [High St]: Pleasantly old-fashioned, with enjoyable fresh food, attentive staff, well kept ales, well done nautical theme *(John Wheeler)*

FREEFOLK [SU4848]

☆ *Watership Down* RG28 7NJ [Freefolk Priors, N of B3400 Whitchurch—Overton; brown sign to pub]: Engaging unpretentious country pub, ancient brick flooring around bar counter with welcoming prompt service and chatty atmosphere, five well kept changing ales mainly from small brewers, good value food from sandwiches to Sun roasts, one neat carpeted area with rabbit pictures and well padded wall seating, another with darts, table football, veteran one-arm bandit and other games (TV too), comfortable dining conservatory; picnic-sets in big sloping informal garden with sturdy timber play area, more under heaters beside pub, pleasant walks *(BB, Tom Evans, Pete Baker, Ann and Colin Hunt)*

FROGHAM [SU1712]

☆ *Foresters Arms* SP6 2JA [Abbotswell Rd]: Busy New Forest pub comfortably refurbished in polished rustic style, chef/landlord doing good value blackboard food from sandwiches to very popular Sun lunch (get there early or book – compact dining room fills quickly), attentive young staff, Wadworths and guest ales, good wines by the glass; children welcome, pleasant garden with pretty front verandah and good play area, small camp site adjacent, nearby ponies, deer and good walks; cl Tues *(Phyl and Jack Street, Kevin Flack, John and Joan Calvert, LYM, Barrie Cornish)*

FROYLE [SU7542]

Hen & Chicken GU34 4JH [loop road just off A31 Alton—Farnham]: Comfortable and friendly 16th-c coaching inn with three attractive linked beamed rooms, inglenook log fire, well kept Badger ales; children warmly welcomed, big garden with play area, open all day *(David M Smith, David Poulter, LYM)*

GOSPORT [SZ5998]

Alverbank House PO12 2QT [Stokes Bay Rd, Alverstoke]: Pleasant partly divided hotel lounge, civilised bar with well kept Ringwood, guest beers and great choice of malt whiskies, good interesting food (not cheap) inc plenty for vegetarians, cheerful well trained staff; piped music; in woods at end of Stanley Park, nice big mature garden with Solent and Isle of Wight views and play area, good bedrooms *(Ann and Colin Hunt)*

☆ *Jolly Roger* PO12 4LQ [Priory Rd, Hardway]: Old beamed harbour-view pub with enjoyable fairly priced food, good friendly service, four real ales such as Adnams and Greene King Abbot, decent house wines, lots of bric-a-brac, attractive eating area *(Mr and Mrs J Underwood, Ann and Colin Hunt, Stephen Moss)*

Queens PO12 1LG [Queens Rd]: Classic bare-boards local whose long-serving landlady keeps five interesting changing ales in top condition, popular Oct beer festival, quick service, perhaps huge filled rolls and other simple food, three areas off bar with good log fire in interesting carved fireplace, sensibly placed darts; TV room – children welcome here daytime; cl lunchtimes Mon-Thurs, open all day Sat *(Ann and Colin Hunt)*

GREYWELL [SU7151]

Fox & Goose RG29 1BY [nr M3 junction 5; A287 towards Odiham then first right to village]: Two-bar village pub with nice atmosphere, country-kitchen furniture, friendly helpful service, food from good lunchtime sandwiches up, Courage Best; dogs welcome, good-sized garden behind, attractive village, handy for Basingstoke Canal walks *(D J and P M Taylor, Tony and Wendy Hobden, Ann and Colin Hunt)*

HAMBLE [SU4806]

Bugle SO31 4HA [3 miles from M27 junction 8]: Roomy waterside pub reopened after refurbishment, sturdy furniture, beams, flagstones and bare boards, enjoyable food (all day wknds) using local ingredients and fresh fish, good choice of wines by the glass, two or three real ales, log fires; river-view terrace, open all day *(Bob and Angela Brooks, LYM)*

HAMBLEDON [SU6414]

☆ *Vine* PO7 4RW [West St]: Appealing 400-year-old beamed village pub, very popular under previous licensees but awaiting new tenants as we go to press; lots of old sporting and country prints, plenty of bric-a-brac, nice mix of furnishings, Marstons guest beers, several wines by the glass, and has had enjoyable food; children and dogs have been welcome, garden with decking *(LYM)*

HARTLEY WINTNEY [SU7656]

Cricketers RG27 8QB [Cricket Green]: Friendly bar and good value linked french restaurant, real ales, good choice of wines by the glass, attentive french waitresses *(Graham and Toni Sanders)*

HECKFIELD [SU7260]

New Inn RG27 0LE [B3349 Hook—Reading (former A32)]: Well run rambling open-plan dining pub, good welcoming service, enjoyable food inc good light lunch selection, well kept Badger, good choice of wines by the glass, attractive layout with some traditional furniture in original core, two log fires; restaurant; good-sized heated terrace, bedrooms in comfortable and well equipped extension *(David and Sue Smith, LYM)*

HIGHCLERE [SU4358]
Yew Tree RG20 9SE [Hollington Cross]:
Smartly reworked country inn with good food
not too expensive in nicely furnished
comfortable low-beamed eating areas,
relaxed civilised atmosphere, serious wine
list, efficient service, stylish contemporary
bar, big inglenook log fire, attractive
lighting and pictures; picnic-sets under
cocktail parasols on pleasant terrace, six
good bedrooms *(LYM, Bernard Lawson)*

HILL HEAD [SU5402]
Osborne View PO14 3JR [Hill Head Rd]:
Modern extended clifftop Badger dining pub,
three stepped-back levels and picture
windows for stunning views to the Isle of
Wight, Badger beer, nautical prints and
memorabilia, lots of stripped wood and red
carpet, young staff; may be piped music,
busy wknds; garden and beach access, nr
Titchfield Haven bird reserve, open all day
(Val and Alan Green)

HOLYBOURNE [SU7341]
White Hart GU34 4EY [London Rd]:
Smartened up by good newish licensees,
enjoyable food, well kept ales *(Betty Laker)*

HOOK [SU7153]
Hogget RG27 9JJ [a mile W, A30/A287]:
Former Dorchester Arms, nicely refurbished
with emphasis on dining side, reopened
under helpful couple who previously ran the
good Vine in Hambledon, enjoyable food,
well kept ales, warmly friendly atmosphere;
reports please *(BOB)*

HORNDEAN [SU7013]
Ship & Bell PO8 0BZ [London Rd]: Pub/hotel
by former Gales brewery, Fullers ales, good
range of wines, enjoyable standard food,
pubby bar with deep well and log fire, broad
low steps up to comfortable lounge and
dining room, interesting photographs,
separate public bar/games room;
14 bedrooms, nice walk to Catherington
church *(Ann and Colin Hunt,
Conor McGaughey)*

HORSEBRIDGE [SU3430]
John o' Gaunt SO20 6PU [off A3057
Romsey—Andover, just SW of Kings
Somborne]: Nice spot in River Test village,
good value food inc some interesting dishes,
friendly service, well kept Ringwood ales, log
fire in simple L-shaped bar, nice prints in
small back dining area; picnic-sets out in
side arbour *(BB, Phyl and Jack Street, Ann
and Colin Hunt)*

HURSLEY [SU4225]
Kings Head SO21 2JW [A3090 Winchester—
Romsey]: Substantial food pub with
welcoming service, real ales such as Greene
King Abbot and Wells & Youngs Bombardier;
garden tables, six comfortable bedrooms,
open all day Fri and Sun *(Bruce M Drew)*

IBSLEY [SU1409]
Old Beams BH24 3PP [A338 Salisbury—
Ringwood]: Big busy black and white
thatched all-day family food pub, wide
choice and reasonable prices, helpful staff,
lots of modern pine furniture under aged oak

beams, also pleasant bar with Greene King
real ales and soft seating around log-effect
fire, conservatory; plenty of garden tables,
open all day *(Meg and Colin Hamilton, LYM)*

ITCHEN ABBAS [SU5332]
Trout SO21 1BQ [4 miles from M3 junction 9;
B3047]: Pleasant pub in good walking
country, enjoyable food using local
ingredients from baguettes and pubby
favourites to contemporary dishes, Greene
King ales, good value wines, simple décor in
quiet lounge and bare-boards dining room,
separate public bar; tables and play area in
sheltered pretty side garden, five bedrooms
(Alastair Maclean, LYM)

LANGSTONE [SU7104]
☆ *Ship* PO9 1RD [A3023]: Busy waterside
18th-c former grain store, lovely views to
Hayling Island from roomy softly lit nautical
bar with upper deck dining room, Fullers
ales, good choice of wines by the glass, log
fire, wide range of generous reasonably
priced food, quick friendly waitresses;
children welcome, plenty of tables on heated
terrace by quiet quay, good coast walks,
open all day *(Tony and Wendy Hobden)*

LINWOOD [SU1809]
Red Shoot BH24 3QT [signed from A338 via
Moyles Court, and from A31; go on up heath
to junction with Toms Lane]: Nice New
Forest setting, big picture-window bar with
attractive old tables, mixed chairs and rugs
on bare boards, country pictures on puce
walls, large back dining area, generous good
value food, friendly helpful staff, well kept
Wadworths and two or three ales brewed at
the pub; children, dogs and muddy boots
welcome, some disabled access, sheltered
side terrace, open all day wknds and summer
– very touristy then (by big campsite and
caravan park) *(BB, Peter Adcock, Len Clark)*

LITTLE LONDON [SU6259]
Plough RG26 5EP [Silchester Rd, off A340 N
of Basingstoke]: Cosy unspoilt tucked-away
local with well kept Ringwood, interesting
guest beers tapped from the cask, lots of
good value baguettes, log fires, draped hops,
very mixed furnishings on brick and tiled
floors (watch the step), low beams, darts,
bar billiards, no piped music; attractive
garden, handy for Pamber Forest and Calleva
Roman remains *(Prof Chris Bucke, Joan and
Michel Hooper-Immins)*

LOCKS HEATH [SU5006]
☆ *Jolly Farmer* SO31 9JH [2.5 miles from M27
junction 9; A27 towards Bursledon, left into
Locks Rd, at end T junction right into
Warsash Rd then left at hire shop into Fleet
End Rd]: Relaxing series of softly lit linked
rooms, nice old scrubbed tables and masses
of interesting bric-a-brac and prints, wide
choice of enjoyable food from filled baps to
fresh fish, local meats and good value
two-sitting Sun lunch, good quick friendly
service, interesting long-serving landlord,
Fullers/Gales ales, decent wines and country
wines, coal-effect gas fires; two sheltered
terraces (one with a play area and children's

lavatories), nice bedrooms *(Ann and Colin Hunt, LYM)*

LONG SUTTON [SU7447]

☆ *Four Horseshoes* RG29 1TA [signed off B3349 S of Hook]: Welcoming open-plan black-beamed country local with two log fires, long-serving landlord cooking good pubby food, friendly landlady, good range of changing ales such as Fullers/Gales, decent wines and country wine, daily papers, no piped music, small glazed-in verandah; disabled access, boules pitch and play area, picnic-sets on grass over road, good value bedrooms *(Tony and Jill Radnor, BB)*

LONGPARISH [SU4243]

☆ *Plough* SP11 6PB [B3048, off A303 just E of Andover]: Comfortably upmarket open-plan dining pub refurbished in country-house style, good if pricy food with larger evening menu and interesting lunchtime sandwiches, friendly helpful service, good choice of wines by the glass, real ales such as Hop Back Summer Lightning and Timothy Taylors Landlord, log fire; children in eating areas, disabled access and facilities, tables on terrace and in nice garden, bedrooms *(Edward Mirzoeff, LYM, Mr and Mrs J R Shrimpton, John Balfour)*

LONGSTOCK [SU3537]

☆ *Peat Spade* SO20 6DR [off A30 on W edge of Stockbridge]: Airy and attractive dining pub with enjoyable food (evenings are more restaurantly than pubby), friendly efficient service, Ringwood Best and a guest beer, quite a few wines by the glass, bistroish décor with quite a fishing and shooting theme, upstairs lounge with board games; no under-10s; dogs welcome in bar, pleasant courtyard tables, plenty of Test Way and water-meadow walks, good fishing by arrangement, nicely furnished if not over-large bedrooms, open all day *(Philip Vernon, Kim Maidment, Alun Jones, Max Dowse, Mrs S Barker-Ryder, Ann and Colin Hunt, LYM, I H Curtis)*

LYMINGTON [SZ3295]

Angel SO41 9AP [High St]: Roomy linked areas spreading comfortably around Georgian inn's central bar, panelling and black beams, food inc tapas, Marstons Burton and Pedigree; piped music; heated tables in attractive inner courtyard, bedrooms, open all day *(Michael Dandy, LYM)*

☆ *Chequers* SO41 8AH [Ridgeway Lane, Lower Woodside – dead end just S of A337 roundabout W of Lymington, by White Hart]: Welcoming local atmosphere, friendly landlord and pleasant young staff, generous enjoyable food, real ales such as Ringwood and Wadworths 6X, polished boards and quarry tiles, attractive pictures, plain chairs and wall pews, traditional games; may be piped music; well-behaved children allowed, tables and summer marquee in neat walled back family garden, attractive front terrace, handy for bird-watching on Pennington Marshes *(Mr and Mrs P D Titcomb, A and B D Craig, LYM)*

☆ *Fishermans* SO41 8FD [All Saints Rd, Woodside]: Under new management, with good choice of traditional and more interesting food inc popular Sun lunch, well kept Fullers/Gales ales, friendly helpful staff, pleasant atmosphere, decent wines *(Graham and Glenis Watkins, David Sizer)*

Ship SO41 3AY [Quay Rd]: One of Mitchells & Butlers' stylish new-look bistro pubs, interesting modern take on a nautical theme, enjoyable food from unusual sandwiches up, Fullers London Pride, Greene King Old Speckled Hen and Timothy Taylors Landlord, good choice of wines by the glass, plenty of tables, nice mix of new and old furnishings, log fires, tiles, flagstones, blue walls and brick arches; waterside terrace with big parasols *(Michael Dandy)*

LYNDHURST [SU2908]

Crown SO43 7NF [top end of High St opposite church]: Best Western hotel with cheerful log fire and comfortable leather seating in attractive traditional panelled bar, pleasant efficient young staff, Ringwood Best and Fortyniner, good coffee, several wines by the glass, bar food from sandwiches up as well as restaurant; piped music; comfortable bedrooms, good breakfast, open all day *(Michael Dandy, Steve and Liz Tilley)*

☆ *Crown Stirrup* SO43 7DE [Clay Hill (A337 just S)]: Two friendly old-fashioned low-beamed rooms, 17th-c or older, with well kept Fullers HSB, Ringwood Fortyniner and Timothy Taylors Landlord, reasonably priced pubby food, good service, pine furniture, log fires, stripped brick and plank panelling; children and dogs welcome, covered back terrace, picnic-sets in pleasant side garden with play area and gate to fine Forest walks *(Tony and Caroline Elwood, Ann and Colin Hunt, Michael Dandy)*

Fox & Hounds SO43 7BG [High St]: Big comfortable pub much modernised low-beamed dining pub with Fullers HSB, Ringwood Best and Fortyniner and Wychwood Hobgoblin, decent wines, welcoming staff, quick usual food, exposed brickwork and standing timbers, family room beyond former coach entry, games room *(Michael Dandy)*

Waterloo Arms SO43 7AS [Pikes Hill, just off A337 N]: Rambling thatched 17th-c New Forest pub with low beams and stripped brick, pleasant furnishings, log fire, Greene King Ruddles County, Ringwood Best and St Austell Tribute, pubby food, comfortable bar, roomy separate back dining area; heated terrace, attractive back garden with play area *(Michael Dandy, Alan M Pring)*

MAPLEDURWELL [SU6851]

Gamekeepers RG25 2LU [off A30, not far from M3 junction 6]: Dark-beamed dining pub with good if not cheap local food, friendly young staff, well kept Badger ales, a few sofas by flagstoned and panelled core, well spaced tables in large dining room; piped music, TV; children welcome, terrace and garden, lovely thatched village with duckpond, good walks, open all day *(LYM, LM)*

MARCHWOOD [SU3809]
Pilgrim SO40 4WU [Hythe Rd, off A326 at Twiggs Lane]: Picturesque thatched pub under newish management, reliable pubby food from sandwiches up, friendly service, Fullers ales, open fires, comfortable banquettes in long olde-worlde L-shaped bar, more expensive restaurant across road; neat garden *(LYM, Ann and Colin Hunt, Philip Vernon, Kim Maidment)*

MONXTON [SU3144]
☆ *Black Swan* SP11 8AW [High St]: Rambling 17th-c pub with decent food from baguettes up, courteous staff, real ales such as Ringwood Best and Timothy Taylors Landlord, good choice of wines by the glass, log fire, daily papers; piped music, car park down street; children welcome, lovely sheltered garden by stream with ducks, open all day *(Phyl and Jack Street, Mrs Joyce Robson, Edward Mirzoeff, B D Jones, Alec and Joan Laurence, LYM, Michael and Jenny Back)*

NEW CHERITON [SU5827]
☆ *Hinton Arms* SO24 0NH [A272 nr B3046 junction]: Neatly kept country pub with friendly atmosphere, enjoyable very generous food inc game specials, four real ales from Hampshire and Ringwood, nicely served wines by the glass, sporting pictures and memorabilia; TV lounge; terrace, big garden, very handy for Hinton Ampner House (NT) *(Val and Alan Green, BB, David and Sheila Pearcey, Christine Bridgwater)*

NORTH GORLEY [SU1611]
Royal Oak SP6 2PB [Ringwood Rd; village signed off A338 S of Fordingbridge]: 17th-c thatched pub by New Forest, neat lounge on left, busier main bar on right, well kept ales such as Ringwood Best and Timothy Taylors Landlord, decent wines, pleasant bare-boards L-shaped eating area with pine tables and old-fashioned chairs or booth seating; piped music, may be live, TV, games machine; children and dogs welcome, attractive sheltered back garden with play area for children, big duck pond over road, open all day *(LYM, Mr and Mrs W W Burke)*

NORTH WALTHAM [SU5645]
Fox RG25 2BE [signed off A30 SW of Basingstoke; handy for M3 junction 7]: Well kept Adnams Broadside, Ringwood Best and St Austell Tribute, enjoyable food from sandwiches to venison and popular Sun roasts (best to book), welcoming landlord and well trained staff, foxy décor, log fire in bright elongated dining area; children welcome, lovely outside with fine floral displays and farmland views, pleasant village in nice spot (walk to Jane Austen's church at Steventon) *(John R Ringrose)*

ODIHAM [SU7450]
Bell RG29 1LY [The Bury]: Simple unspoilt two-bar local in pretty square opp church, real ale *(Ann and Colin Hunt)*

OLD BASING [SU6653]
Bolton Arms RG24 7DA [The Street]: Welcoming village local with cheerful

atmosphere, willing staff, Itchen Valley ales, decent basic food *(Brian Robinson)*

OTTERBOURNE [SU4623]
Old Forge SO21 2EE [Main Rd]: Reliable and popular bistro-style chain pub, comfortable tables spread through linked rooms, plenty of friendly efficient young staff, generous food all day, real ales such as Everards Tiger and Timothy Taylors Landlord, log fires and rather individual décor *(Phyl and Jack Street, Diana Brumfit)*
Otter SO21 2HW [Boyatt Lane off Winchester Rd]: Unpretentious dining pub with enjoyable food, good staff, real ale; garden tables *(A and B D Craig)*

OVERTON [SU5149]
Red Lion RG25 3HQ: Village pub with good atmosphere and service, enjoyable food, sizeable eating area, well kept changing ales, open fires; children welcome, garden *(Jennifer Banks)*

OWSLEBURY [SU5123]
Ship SO21 1LT [off B2177 Fishers Pond—Lower Upham; Whites Hill]: Popular 17th-c pub with black oak beams and timbers, central log fire, well kept ales inc Greene King, good choice of wines by the glass, friendly service, pub games and skittle alley, comfortable dining area and restaurant; plenty of space outside with play area, toddler zone, pets corner and garden kitchen *(Paul and Shirley White, Ann and Colin Hunt, Mr and Mrs A H Young, LYM)*

PETERSFIELD [SU7129]
White Horse GU32 1DA [up on old downs rd about halfway between Steep and East Tisted, nr Priors Dean – OS Sheet 186 or 197, map ref 715290]: Charming building high and isolated on the downs, two well worn in idiosyncratically old-fashioned rustic parlours (candlelit at night), family dining room, open fires throughout, good range of real ales; children welcome, tables out by floodlit pond, open all day wknds *(Martin and Karen Wake, the Didler, Ann and Colin Hunt, LYM, N K Crace)*

PILLEY [SZ3298]
☆ *Fleur de Lys* SO41 5QG [off A337 Brockenhurst—Lymington; Pilley St]: Upscale dining pub with often good imaginative food, warmly welcoming service, real ales such as Ringwood and Timothy Taylors Landlord, decent wines, pretty contemporary décor keeping old boards, heavy beams, and dining room's huge inglenook log fire; may be piped music; fine forest and heathland walks *(LYM, Dr D J R Martin, Kevin Flack, William Ruxton, Graham and Glenis Watkins)*

PLAITFORD [SU2719]
Shoe SO51 6EE [Salisbury Rd]: Lively, roomy and attractively lit, with young welcoming staff, well kept ales inc Ringwood Best, good fresh food; children welcome, garden behind *(Stuart Turner)*

PORTSMOUTH [SZ6399]
American Bar PO1 2JA [White Hart Rd]: Spacious colonial-theme bar/restaurant

popular for reasonably priced food from all-day sandwiches, baguettes and bar meals to fresh local fish and seafood, Courage Directors and a guest beer, good friendly service; garden behind, handy for IOW ferry *(Colin Moore)*

Pembroke PO1 2NR [Pembroke Rd]: Buoyant atmosphere in well run traditional local, Bass and Fullers London Pride, fresh rolls; open all day *(Ann and Colin Hunt)*

☆ *Still & West* PO1 2JL [Bath Sq, Old Portsmouth]: Great location with super views of narrow harbour mouth and across to Isle of Wight, especially from glazed-in panoramic upper family dining area and waterfront terrace with lots of picnic-sets; nautical bar with fireside sofas and cosy colour scheme, food all day, efficient friendly service, Fullers ales, good choice of wines by the glass; piped music may be loud, nearby pay & display; children welcome, handy for Historic Dockyard, open all day *(LYM, Mike and Jennifer Marsh, Susan and John Douglas, Paul and Marion Watts, B M Eldridge, Ann and Colin Hunt, Joan York)*

PRESTON CANDOVER [SU6041]

Purefoy Arms RG25 2EJ [B3046]: Cheerful pub in attractive village, friendly staff, sensibly priced generous food, real ale, attractively laid-out restaurant; big peaceful garden with play area overlooking fields, nearby snowdrop walks, open all day Sun *(Ann and Colin Hunt)*

RINGWOOD [SU1405]

Fish BH24 2AA [off A31 W of town]: Large well divided pub with good value food, helpful staff, several real ales, log fire, eating area allowing children; piped music; riverside lawn (traffic noise) with play area, open all day *(Mrs C Osgood, LYM, Colin Wood)*

ROCKBOURNE [SU1118]

☆ *Rose & Thistle* SP6 3NL [signed off B3078 Fordingbridge—Cranborne]: Attractive 16th-c thatched pub with civilised flagstoned bar, antique settles, old engravings and cricket prints, good coal fire, traditional games, real ales such as Fullers/Gales and Hampshire, good range of wines, log fires in two-room restaurant; may be piped classical music; children and dogs welcome, tables by thatched dovecot in neat front garden, charming tranquil spot in lovely village, good walks *(Kevin Flack, Keith and Jean Symons, Mr and Mrs P D Titcomb, Mr and Mrs W W Burke, Robert Watt, LYM)*

ROCKFORD [SU1608]

Alice Lisle BH24 3NA: Big well laid-out open-plan family dining pub attractively placed on green by New Forest (can get very busy, popular with older folk wkdy lunchtimes), emphasis on big conservatory-style family eating area, generous helpings of usual food from sandwiches up, changing real ales, decent wines; baby-changing facilities, garden overlooking lake with peacock and other birds, ponies wander nearby, play area and summer children's entertainment, separate adults-only

garden, handy for Moyles Court *(Mr and Mrs P D Titcomb, BB)*

ROMSEY [SU3523]

☆ *Dukes Head* SO51 0HB [A3057 out towards Stockbridge]: Attractive 16th-c dining pub, picturesque series of small linked rooms each with own distinct, interesting décor (one has portraits of dukes on walls), big log fire, a few tables for drinkers, Hop Back Summer Lightning and Ringwood Best on handpump, several wines by glass, lots of fresh fish and seafood; cl Sun pm, live jazz Sun lunch, dogs in bar, children allowed, picnic-sets in front and nicer tables on sheltered back terrace, pleasant garden *(Phyl and Jack Street, BB, Val and Alan Green, David and Sheila Pearcey, Ann and Colin Hunt, J V Dadswell, Martin and Karen Wake, LYM)*

Old House At Home SO51 8DE [Love Lane]: Friendly and attractive 16th-c thatched pub surrounded by new development, appealingly individual and old-fashioned décor, good freshly made food from reasonably priced sandwiches up, good thoughtful service, well kept Fullers/Gales ales, good coffee *(Peter and Liz Holmes, Ann and Colin Hunt, A and B D Craig)*

☆ *Three Tuns* SO51 8HL [Middlebridge St (but car park signed straight off A27 bypass)]: Interesting bistro food inc reasonably priced up-to-date bar lunches from baguettes up in attractively furnished bow-windowed pub with flagstones, black beams and panelling, starched table linen, Ringwood ales, espresso machine, good amiable service; piped music; children allowed at lunchtime, nice back terrace *(Irene and Derek Flewin, LYM)*

SELBORNE [SU7433]

☆ *Selborne Arms* GU34 3JR [High St]: Character tables, pews and deep settles made from casks on antique boards in appealing bar, twinkly landlord and friendly staff, fine changing choice of largely local real ales, sensible range of promptly served good food from baguettes up, good choice of wines by the glass (three glass sizes), nice coffee, big log fire, daily papers, smart carpeted dining room with lots of local photographs; plenty of tables in garden with arbour, terrace, orchard and good play area, right by walks up Hanger, and handy for Gilbert White museum, open all day wknds *(Ann and Colin Hunt, David and Sue Atkinson, Gerald and Gabrielle Culliford, BB, Michael B Griffith, Martin and Karen Wake)*

SETLEY [SU3000]

Filly SO42 7UF [Lymington Rd (A337 Brockenhurst—Lymington)]: Wide choice of generous enjoyable home-made food inc Sun carvery, Ringwood ales, decent wines, helpful cheerful service, interesting if sometimes crowded beamed front bar with inglenook, other better spaced areas; sheltered tables outside, New Forest walks, open all day *(Mr and Mrs P D Titcomb,*

Ann and Colin Hunt, LYM, Guy and
Caroline Howard, Phyl and Jack Street)
SHAWFORD [SU4724]
Bridge Hotel SO21 2BP: Sprawling beamed
riverside Chef & Brewer useful for good
choice of promptly served food all day,
efficient friendly staff, Hogs Back TEA,
Palmers Copper and Ringwood Fortyniner,
decent wines, several interesting rooms,
smart décor, cosy nooks and corners;
pleasant terrace and large garden with play
area, downland and Itchen Way walks
*(Phyl and Jack Street, Tony Hobden,
Mrs Hilarie Taylor, Ann and Colin Hunt,
Val and Alan Green)*
SHERBORNE ST JOHN [SU6255]
Swan RG24 9HS [Kiln Rd]: Comfortably
divided 17th-c thatched pub, good choice of
good value fresh local food, good choice of
wines and beers, good friendly service; large
pleasant garden with play area, handy for
the Vyne (NT) *(Jennifer Banks, Mr and
Mrs J Alderton)*
SILCHESTER [SU6262]
☆ *Calleva Arms* RG7 2PH [The Common]: Good
varied food at sensible prices from
sandwiches and baguettes up, friendly
service, Fullers/Gales and a guest beer,
decent wines by the glass, interestingly
carved seats in roomy bar, smart dining
areas, family conservatory; handy for the
Roman site, sizeable attractive garden
*(Humphry and Angela Crum Ewing,
J V Dadswell, Mrs J H S Lang)*
SOUTHAMPTON [SU4112]
Cricketers Arms SO15 2DX [Carlton Pl]:
Generous pubby food, well kept beer
(Joe Green)
☆ *Duke of Wellington* SO14 2AH [Bugle St (or
walk along city wall from Bar Gate)]: Ancient
timber-framed building on 13th-c
foundations, recently freshened up,
Wadworths and a guest beer kept well, good
choice of wines by the glass, bargain food
(not Sun evening), friendly helpful service,
bare boards, great log fire; piped music in
cheery front bar, staider back area
welcoming children; very handy for Tudor
House Museum, open all day *(Val and
Alan Green, Joe Green)*
Guide Dog SO14 6SF [Earls Rd]: Great range
of half a dozen well kept changing ales and
Fullers ESB in friendly and comfortably
unpretentious local; quiet piped music,
sports TV *(Joe Green)*
South Western Arms SO17 2HW [Adelaide
Rd, by St Denys stn]: Ten or so well kept
changing ales, good friendly staff, easy-
going atmosphere, basic food and décor
(bare boards and brickwork, toby jugs and
stag's head on beams, lots of woodwork,
ceiling beer mats), darts, pool and table
football, eccentric cat, upper gallery
allowing children; terrace picnic-sets
(Joe Green, Warwick Payne)
Stile SO17 1TS [University Rd, Highfield]:
Friendly open-plan stone-floors-and-wood
pub with half a dozen real ales, wide variety

of low-priced college-canteen food *(Val and
Alan Green)*
Wellington Arms SO15 3DE [Park Rd,
Fremantle]: Cosy two-bar local which fought
the smoking ban ingeniously if
unsuccessfully, Adnams, Fullers London Pride,
Ringwood and guest ales, good choice of
whiskies, lots of Wellington memorabilia,
jazz nights; terrace tables *(Tony Hobden)*
SOUTHSEA [SZ6499]
Hole in the Wall PO5 3BY [Gt Southsea St]:
Small friendly unspoilt local in old part of
town, effectively tap for good Oakleaf ales
brewed nearby (head brewer was landlord),
also changing beers such as Bowman and
Dorset, three farm ciders, evening speciality
sausages and substantial home-made pies
(not Sun), old prints, dark panelling, daily
papers; side garden, cl till 5 exc Fri, open all
day wknds *(Mrs Maricar Jagger, Joan and
Michel Hooper-Immins)*
India Arms PO5 3BY [Gt Southsea St]:
Comfortable and interesting combination of
large pub (real ales such as Sharps Doom
Bar) and good indian tiffin room/restaurant;
nicely planted terrace with giant parasols
(Mrs Maricar Jagger, Joe Beardmore)
White Horse PO5 3AU [Southsea Terrace]:
Bright and airy modern décor, big windows
overlooking Solent-edge green, cheerful
young staff, well kept Fullers/Gales ales,
enjoyable pubby food; big well thought-out
garden *(Joan and Michel Hooper-Immins)*
SOUTHWICK [SU6208]
Red Lion PO17 6EF [High St]: Neatly kept
low-beamed village pub, prompt smiling
service even though busy, Fullers/Gales and
a guest ale, generous food, good value if not
cheap, from interesting baguettes up, good
choice of wines by the glass; good walks
(Val and Alan Green)
STOCKBRIDGE [SU3535]
Grosvenor SO20 6EU [High St]: Old-
fashioned coaching inn with relaxing high-
ceilinged main bar, log fire, Greene King
ales, oak-panelled restaurant, back
conservatory; piped music, TV; children and
dogs welcome, good-sized back garden,
26 bedrooms *(Ann and Colin Hunt, Phil and
Sally Gorton, LYM)*
☆ *Three Cups* SO20 6HB [High St]: Lovely low-
beamed building dating from 1500, more
restaurant than pub now, lots of smartly set
pine tables but still some high-backed
settles, country bric-a-brac and four well
kept ales inc Ringwood; good upscale food,
amiable service, good wines by the glass;
children and dogs welcome, vine-covered
verandah and charming cottage garden with
streamside terrace, bedrooms, open all day
*(LYM, Geoffrey Kemp, Dennis Jenkin,
Dr and Mrs A K Clarke, John and Julie Moon,
Brian Robinson, I H Curtis, Mr and
Mrs A Curry, Edward Mirzoeff)*
☆ *White Hart* SO20 6HF [High St; A272/A3057
roundabout]: Thriving welcoming divided
beamed bar, attractive décor with antique
prints, oak pews and other seats, quick

pleasant service, enjoyable generous fresh food from good sandwiches to game, Fullers ales, good coffee and wines by the glass, comfortable restaurant with blazing log fire (children allowed); disabled access and facilities, terrace tables, nice garden, good bedrooms, open all day *(Edward Mirzoeff, A and B D Craig, Diana Brumfit, Val and Alan Green, Mr and Mrs C Prentis, Helen and Brian Edgeley, LYM, D Hillaby)*

STRATFIELD TURGIS [SU6960]
Wellington Arms RG27 0AS: Handsome small country inn with relaxing armchairs and other individual furnishings in restful and surprisingly pubby tall-windowed two-room bar, part with polished flagstones, part carpeted, wide food choice inc enterprising lunchtime menu, good staff, Badger ales, open fire; garden, comfortable bedrooms *(Jennifer Banks)*

SUTTON SCOTNEY [SU4639]
Coach & Horses SO21 3JH [Oxford Rd, just off A30]: Welcoming new licensees doing reliable food, real ales such as Fullers HSB and Wadworths 6X, roomy carpeted beamed bar with big open fire; children welcome, pleasant garden, three bedrooms in adjacent former fire station *(Phyl and Jack Street)*

SWANMORE [SU5816]
Hunters SO32 2PZ [Hillgrove]: Popular and comfortably worn in dining pub, excellent for children, with big plain family room, winding garden with secluded tables (each with a buzzer for when your food's ready) and several substantial play areas for different age groups, plenty under cover and even one for babies; friendly and devoted long-serving landlord, two well kept ales tapped from the cask, good choice of wines, attentive service, lots of boxer pictures, bank notes, carpentry and farm tools; piped music; very busy wknds, nice walks N of village *(Val and Alan Green)*

SWAY [SZ2898]
Hare & Hounds SO41 6AL [Durns Town, just off B3055 SW of Brockenhurst]: Bright, airy and comfortable New Forest family dining pub, lots of children, good value enjoyable fresh food, Greene King and Ringwood ales, good coffee, neat friendly young staff, low beams, central log fire; piped music; dogs welcome, picnic-sets and play frame in neatly kept garden, open all day Sat *(Michael Dandy, Ann and Colin Hunt, LYM)*

TANGLEY [SU3252]
☆ *Cricketers Arms* SP11 0SH [towards the Chutes]: Relaxed old-fashioned tucked-away country pub with good food inc generous pizzas, well kept local ales tapped from the cask, friendly landlord and good staff, massive inglenook log fire in small tiled-floor front bar, bar billiards, friendly black labradors (Pots and Harvey), bistroish back flagstoned extension with a one-table alcove off, some good cricketing prints; dogs welcome, tables on neat terrace, good nordic-style back bedroom block, unspoilt countryside *(Phil and Sally Gorton, John and Julie Moon, I A Herdman, LYM)*

THRUXTON [SU2945]
George SP11 8LZ [just off A303]: Friendly service, Ringwood ales, bar with nooks and corners, roomy light and pleasant eating area overlooking garden with terrace and play area *(B and F A Hannam)*

☆ *White Horse* SP11 8EE [Mullens Pond, just off A303 eastbound]: Attractive and relaxed 16th-c thatched pub tucked below A303 embankment, good food (good value if not cheap), well kept Fullers London Pride and Greene King Abbot, good choice of wines by the glass, nice staff, log fire, a couple of sofas, very low beams, horse-racing décor, separate dining area; good-sized garden and terrace *(J D G Isherwood, Mark Flynn, Phyl and Jack Street)*

TIMSBURY [SU3325]
☆ *Bear & Ragged Staff* SO51 0LB [A3057 towards Stockbridge; pub marked on OS Sheet 185 map ref 334254]: Reliable roadside dining pub with wide blackboard choice of popular food all day, friendly efficient service, lots of wines by the glass, Greene King IPA, log fire, good-sized beamed interior; children in eating area, tables in extended garden with good play area, handy for Mottisfont, good walks *(Phyl and Jack Street, LYM, Ann and Colin Hunt)*

TITCHFIELD [SU5406]
Fishermans Rest PO15 5RA [Mill Lane, off A27 at Titchfield Abbey]: Spick and span pub/restaurant with wide choice of good value fresh food (can take a long while), well kept Greene King IPA and Ringwood Best, two log fires (not always lit), daily papers, fishing memorabilia; fine riverside position opp Titchfield Abbey, tables out behind overlooking water, open all day *(Ann and Colin Hunt, LYM)*

☆ *Titchfield Mill* PO15 5RF [A27, junction with Mill Lane]: Large popular Vintage Inn family dining pub in neatly kept converted watermill on River Meon, olde-worlde room off main bar, smarter dining room, upstairs gallery, stripped beams and interesting old machinery, efficient friendly service, good value wines by the glass, real ales, freshly squeezed orange juice; piped music; sunny terrace by mill stream with two waterwheels (food not served out here), open all day *(Phyl and Jack Street)*

TURGIS GREEN [SU6959]
Cricketers RG27 0AH [Bottle Lane]: Charming early 19th-c building reopened as welcoming dining pub, good set lunches, nice house wine *(George Williams, Colin and Bernardine Perry)*

TWYFORD [SU4824]
☆ *Bugle* SO21 1QT [Park Lane]: Reopened after appealing modern refurbishment keeping many period features, fireside leather chesterfield and armchairs one carpeted end, beech tables and flagstones, Bowmans, Flowerpots and Fullers, enterprising food, obliging young staff; attractive verandah *(Val and Alan Green, Phyl and Jack Street, Bruce and Penny Wilkie)*

Phoenix SO21 1RF [High St (B3335)]: Cheerful open-plan local with lots of prints, bric-a-brac and big end inglenook log fire, friendly long-serving landlord (here throughout the *Guide*'s life) and attentive staff, Greene King ales, good coffee, good value wines, raised dining area, pool, side skittle alley; unobtrusive piped music; children allowed at one end lunchtime, garden with smokers' area *(Geoffrey and Jo Pitt, Ann and Colin Hunt)*

UPTON [SU3555]

☆ *Crown* SP11 0JS [N of Hurstbourne Tarrant, off A343]: Linked cottagey rooms in bustling dining pub, Fullers ales, pine tables and chairs, pleasant modicum of sporting prints, horse tack and so forth, good log fires, back conservatory extension; piped music; small garden and terrace, nearby walks *(Michael Dallas, Ann and Colin Hunt, LYM)*

WALHAMPTON [SZ3396]

Walhampton Arms SO41 5RE [B3054 NE of Lymington; aka Walhampton Inn]: Large comfortable Georgian-style family roadhouse with emphasis on restauranty food inc reliable carvery (not Mon) in raftered former stables and two adjoining areas, pleasant lounge on right, Ringwood ales; attractive courtyard, good walks nearby inc Solent Way, open all day *(Phyl and Jack Street, David M Cundy, Rita and Keith Pollard)*

WALTHAM CHASE [SU5616]

Chase SO32 2LL [B2177]: Neat two-bar pub with changing ales inc a Hampshire seasonal beer, bargain generous food from baguettes to good Sun lunch, friendly helpful staff *(Val and Alan Green, Stephen and Jean Curtis)*

WELL [SU7646]

Chequers RG29 1TL [off A287 via Crondall, or A31 via Froyle and Lower Froyle]: Appealing low-beamed and panelled country pub with good service, well kept Badger Best, decent wines by the glass, roaring log fire, 18th-c country-life prints and old sepia photographs, pews, brocaded stools and a few GWR carriage lamps; picnic-sets on vine-covered terrace and in spacious back garden *(John R Ringrose, LYM, Martin and Karen Wake)*

WEST END [SU4714]

Southampton Arms SO30 2HG [Moorgreen Rd, off B3035]: Sizeable 1920s roadside pub with enjoyable reasonably priced food, Ringwood ales, comfortable and cosy bar, attractive conservatory restaurant; sports TV; good garden *(Val and Alan Green, B M Eldridge)*

White Swan SO18 3HW [Mansbridge Rd]: Pleasantly refurbished family food pub in nice spot, good beer range, carvery restaurant and conservatory; attractive terrace by River Itchen *(Phyl and Jack Street)*

WHERWELL [SU3840]

White Lion SP11 7JF [B3420]: Long-serving licensees who made this old-fashioned multi-

level beamed village pub rather special have now left; Bass and Ringwood Best, several wines by the glass, open fire, two dining rooms; piped music; dogs and well behaved children allowed, courtyard and terrace, Test Way walks, bedrooms *(LYM)*

WHITCHURCH [SU4648]

Bell RG28 7DD [Bell St]: Friendly local in attractive country town, small cosy lounge bar with inglenook and raised dining area, Fullers London Pride, good coffee; well equipped bedrooms; walled garden, open all day *(Ann and Colin Hunt)*

White Hart RG28 7DN [Newbury St]: Impressive former coaching inn now a busy and comfortably worn in pub with big public bar well away from dining areas, friendly staff, good value food (Sun carvery may be fully booked), well kept Arkells; bedrooms; open all day inc breakfast *(Val and Alan Green, Ann and Colin Hunt)*

WHITSBURY [SU1219]

Cartwheel SP6 3PZ [off A338 or A354 SW of Salisbury]: Welcoming and comfortable tucked-away pub with enjoyable straightforward food (not Mon evening), Ringwood ales, pitched high rafters in one part, lower beams elsewhere, snug little side areas; may be piped music; children welcome, garden with play area, open all day Sun *(Mr and Mrs P D Titcomb, LYM)*

WICKHAM [SU5711]

Greens PO17 5JQ [The Square]: Spotless and civilised, with friendly staff, enjoyable food from typical bar lunches to imaginative very local specials, changing real ales, steps down to restaurant; pleasant lawn overlooking watermeadows, cl Mon *(Val and Alan Green)*

Kings Head PO17 5JN [The Square]: Pretty small-town pub with good service, usual food, Fullers ales, good coffee, log fire, big-windowed and solidly furnished open-plan bar, restaurant nicely secluded up some steps; tables out on square and in back garden (former coach yard) with play area *(BB, Val and Alan Green, Peter and Anne Hollindale)*

WINCHESTER [SU4829]

Bakers Arms SO23 9JX [down passage off High St]: Busy central town pub with cheap quick bar food, Wells & Youngs and a guest such as Wychwood Hobgoblin; pretty wrought-iron and glass canopy over passageway tables *(Dave Braisted)*

☆ *Bell* SO23 9RE [St Cross Rd (B3335 off M3 junction 11)]: Good value fresh food inc good generous sandwiches, friendly helpful staff, well kept Greene King ales, decent wines by the glass, liner pictures and leather sofas in comfortable sunny lounge, plush modern chairs and pine tables; quiet piped music; nice walled garden with swing and slide, handy for St Cross Hospital (ancient monument, not a hospital), lovely water-meadows walk from centre, open all day *(Michael and Alison Sandy, R K Phillips, Phil and Sally Gorton)*

Bishop on the Bridge SO23 9JX [High St/Bridge St]: Neat smart Fullers pub with good beer range inc a guest, varied food not overpriced, efficient friendly staff, relaxing civilised atmosphere, leather sofas, old local prints; pleasant riverside back terrace (Michael and Alison Sandy, N B Vernon, John R Ringrose)

☆ **Eclipse** SO23 9EX [The Square, between High St and cathedral]: Chatty and welcoming licensees in picturesque 14th-c local with massive beams and timbers in its two small cheerful rooms, chilled ales inc Fullers London Pride and Ringwood, decent choice of wines by the glass, good value lunchtime food from ciabattas to popular Sun roasts, open fire, oak settles; children in back area, seats outside, very handy for cathedral (Simon Fox, Canon Michael Bourdeaux, Michael and Alison Sandy, Ann and Colin Hunt, June and Robin Savage, Mike and Mary Clark, Val and Alan Green, LYM)

Hyde Tavern SO23 7DY [Hyde St (B3047)]: New licensees in homely old 15th-c two-bar local, three changing real ales, two charming simply furnished bars with hardly a true right-angle; lovely secluded garden (Michael and Alison Sandy, Pete Baker, Phil and Sally Gorton, Val and Alan Green)

North Walls SO23 8DA [North Walls]: Restauranty make-over of former Foresters Arms, enjoyable food, good wines, well kept Flowerpots in welcoming bar area (John and Annabel Hampshire)

Old Gaol House SO23 8RZ [Jewry St]: Traditional Wetherspoons, good choice of real ales, knowledgeable barman, their usual food all day, decent coffee, walls of books; children welcome (Ann and Colin Hunt, Val and Alan Green)

☆ **Old Vine** SO23 9HA [Great Minster St]: Well kept Ringwood Best, Timothy Taylors Landlord and two guest ales, contemporary and more familiar bar lunches and restaurant meals, smart tables and chairs on oak boards, brisk friendly young staff, light and airy décor; opp cathedral, with sheltered terrace, partly covered and heated, charming bedrooms, open all day (Tony and Jill Radnor, Michael and Alison Sandy, James Price, Geoff Barden)

Queen SO23 9PG [Kingsgate Rd]: Roomy two-bar pub in attractive setting opp College cricket ground, wide choice of mainstream food from sandwiches up, well kept Greene King ales, decent wines, cheerful landlord and staff, low ceilings, cricketing and other prints on dark panelling, bric-a-brac on window-sills, central fireplace, darts, smart dining room; piped music; disabled facilities, front terrace, large attractive garden, open all day (Michael and Alison Sandy, Val and Alan Green)

Roebuck SO22 6RP [Stockbridge Rd (B3049)]: Smart Victorianised sitting-room style, Greene King ales, food from lunchtime sandwiches and light dishes up, young helpful staff, darts, attractive conservatory restaurant; piped music; terrace tables, disabled access, car park – rare in this city (Michael and Alison Sandy)

Royal SO23 8BS [St Peters St]: Traditional hotel bar and lounge, comfortable and relaxing, good range of bar food inc good value doorstep sandwiches; spacious secluded walled garden, 75 bedrooms (Mr and Mrs W W Burke)

St James SO22 5BE [Romsey Rd]: Unpretentious corner pub with scrubbed pine, flagstones, panelling, dark red and ochre décor, friendly landlord, relaxed atmosphere, Wadworths and guest beers kept well, good value pubby food from sandwiches up; small pleasant garden (Val and Alan Green)

Westgate Hotel SO22 5BE [Romsey Rd/Upper High St]: Big-windowed corner pub, good food inc organic produce and excellent meat in smallish white-panelled eating area with cheerful prints, friendly relaxed service, well kept changing ales, small choice of good wines, daily papers; bedrooms (Michael and Alison Sandy, BB)

WOLVERTON [SU5658]

George & Dragon RG26 5ST [Towns End; just N of A339 Newbury—Basingstoke]: Rambling open-plan beamed pub with wide choice of enjoyable unpretentious food, good beer range, decent wines, helpful service, log fires, pleasant dining area, no piped music, skittle alley; children welcome, large garden with small terrace, bedrooms (J V Dadswell, Mark and Ruth Brock)

Looking for a pub with a really special garden, or in lovely countryside, or with an outstanding view, or right by the water? They are listed separately, at the back of the book.

Herefordshire

There is plenty of relatively low-priced food to be found here, and some prime old-fashioned pubs. Also, the countryside provides some idyllic surroundings for some of our featured pubs – perhaps most notably with the county's star newcomer. This is the Live & Let Live, far from the road in the middle of Bringsty Common, a beautifully restored slice of the past, with enjoyable food and drink in quaint surroundings. The Three Horseshoes at Little Cowarne is another super rural place to come and enjoy sitting out on terrace or lawn at warmer times, and serves some own-grown or very local produce. On the fringes of the Black Mountains, the half-timbered, sensitively refurbished New Inn at St Owen's Cross has a spacious garden and an interesting range of drinks, while the remote Carpenters Arms at Walterstone is a thoroughly traditional and unpretentious country tavern run as a friendly family concern for many decades. The Saracens Head at Symonds Yat is a smashing place to linger by in the Wye gorge or stay the night (out of season is quieter); it serves imaginative modern food, and boasts the distinction of its very own ferry service. Also not far from the Wye are the Lough Pool at Sellack, in a black and white cottage with a very pretty garden, and the Cottage of Content at Carey, in a row of centuries-old former labourers' cottages. The county has a number of good all-rounders in character-laden old buildings, many half-timbered. Notable in this category, the Boot at Orleton is getting consistent reports for its welcome and pubby food, while Englands Gate at Bodenham and the Butchers Arms at Woolhope are both doing well and have pleasant gardens. The Feathers in Ledbury is a thoroughly civilised half-timbered hotel with enjoyable food, and makes a welcoming place to stay in a very attractive old town. Herefordshire's best dining pubs make up a distinguished group. The Stagg at Titley goes from strength to strength, creating really special food using their own produce, and is a good place to stay. Yet again the Stagg keeps its crown as Herefordshire Dining Pub of the Year. The Riverside Inn by the Lugg at Aymestrey is also hitting a winning formula, growing its own vegetables and using organic and local ingredients. There are also most enjoyable meals to be had at the Three Crowns at Ullingswick, the Bell at Yarpole, the Wellington at Wellington, and the Roebuck Inn at Brimfield. The county's most remarkable real ale pub is the extraordinary galleon-style Victory at Hereford, which brews its own good Spinning Dog beers and has an impressive range of local farm ciders and perries too. The New Harp at Hoarwithy has interesting real ales from local breweries as well as a huge array of interesting bottled beers; its menu recommends drinks for each dish. Wye Valley beers are by far the county's most popular local brews. There are several other smaller local breweries; apart from Spinning Dog, two we came across once or twice were Dunn Plowman and Shoes. Current stars in the Lucky Dip section at the end of the chapter include the Chequers in Leominster, Crown & Anchor at Lugwardine, Bell at Tillington and Crown at Woolhope.

AYMESTREY   SO4265   MAP 6

Riverside Inn ⊕ ♀ ⊨

A4110, at N end of village, W of Leominster; HR6 9ST

Lovely spot with seats making most of the view, and river fishing for residents; cosy, rambling rooms, open fires, enjoyable food, and warm welcome

In attractively folded wooded country, this half-timbered inn stands right by an ancient stone bridge over the River Lugg, and in warm weather the temptation to linger at picnic-sets in the tree-sheltered garden can be very strong. The rambling beamed bar has several cosy areas and the décor is drawn from a pleasant mix of periods and styles, with fine antique oak tables and chairs, stripped pine country kitchen tables, fresh flowers, hops strung from a ceiling wagon-wheel, horse tack and nice pictures. Warm log fires in winter, while in summer big overflowing flower pots frame the entrances; fairly quiet piped pop music. The service is both professional and friendly: the landlord really likes to talk to his customers. Wye Valley Hereford Pale Ale and a guest such as Wye Valley Butty Bach on handpump, Brook Farm cider (pressed in the next village), and more than 20 malt whiskies. Residents can try fly-fishing.

🍴 Using local specialist producers and growing much of their own vegetables and fruit, the enjoyable lunchtime bar food includes filled baguettes, soup, Wye Valley ale battered cod, beef lasagne and confit-cured organic belly pork with apple and rhubarb compote; they place emphasis on the more expensive restaurant menu, which might include fishcakes with tartare sauce, local trout, rack of welsh border lamb with wild garlic crust, supreme of organic free-range chicken wrapped in smoked bacon stuffed with sun-dried tomatoes and local goats cheese, moroccan spiced filo tart, and puddings, including home-made ice-creams and sorbets. *Starters/Snacks: £4.25 to £7.25. Main Courses: £7.95 to £12.95. Puddings: £5.25*

Free house ~ Licensees Richard and Liz Gresko ~ Real ale ~ Bar food (12-2.15, 7-9.15) ~ Restaurant ~ (01568) 708440 ~ Children welcome ~ Dogs allowed in bar and bedrooms ~ Open 11-3, 6-11; 12-3, 6.30-10.30 Sun; closed lunchtime Mon and 26 Dec-1 Jan ~ Bedrooms: £45B/£70B

Recommended by Doreen Maddock, Simon Fox, Mike and Lynn Robinson, Noel Grundy, Brian and Jacky Wilson, Denys Gueroult, Mike and Mary Carter, JHW, Alan and Eve Harding, David Morgan, Mr and Mrs D Moir, Stephen Bennett, Ian Stafford

BODENHAM   SO5454   MAP 4

Englands Gate

Just off A417 at Bodenham turn-off, about 6 miles S of Leominster; HR1 3HU

Some fine original features in comfortable 16th-c inn, several character rooms, and pleasant garden

This venerable 1540s building makes a relaxed place for a meal or a drink, and the service is efficient and polite. It has a vast central stone chimneypiece, heavy brown beams and joists in low ochre ceilings, well worn flagstones, sturdy timber props, one or two steps, and lantern-style lighting. One corner has a high-backed settle with scatter cushions, a cosy partly stripped-stone room has a long stripped table that would be just right for a party of eight and a lighter upper area with flowers on its tables has winged settles painted a soft eau de nil. Hobsons Best, Woods Shropshire Lad and Wye Valley Butty Bach are on handpump, and the pub holds a beer and sausage festival in July; piped pop music and TV. There are tables with sun umbrellas out in the garden and on the terrace.

🍴 Enjoyable bar food from the lunchtime and evening menus might include soup, a platter of cured meats, deep-fried goats cheese and fig filos, roasted breast of gressingham duck, salmon, tomato and fennel fishcakes, braised shank of lamb with parsnip and cardamom purée, steak and ale pie, and mixed grill. *Starters/Snacks: £3.95 to £5.75. Main Courses: £8.95 to £16.95. Puddings: £4.50*

Free house ~ Licensee Evelyn McNeil ~ Real ale ~ Bar food (12-2.30, 6-9.30; 12-3 Sun) ~ Restaurant ~ (01568) 797286 ~ Children welcome ~ Dogs allowed in bar ~ Open 12-11(midnight Sat, 10.30 Sun)

Recommended by Clive Watkin, Reg Fowle, Helen Rickwood, Dr A J and Mrs Tompsett, Carol and Colin Broadbent, Nigel Long, Ann and Colin Hunt

BRIMFIELD   SO5267   MAP 4

Roebuck Inn ⊕ 🍷 🛏

Village signposted just off A49 Shrewsbury—Leominster; SY8 4NE

Smartly refurbished dining pub with French owners, bistro-style food and updated bedrooms

Readers appreciate the efforts made by the owners to update this pub. Its front lounge bar has dark brown and orange club chairs, sofas and an open fire in the impressive inglenook fireplace. The middle bar area also has an open fire but has kept more of a pubby feel, and what was the dining room is now more of a bistro with chunky cord seating in brown and apricot around contemporary wooden tables and modern art on deep-coloured walls. The bedrooms have also been given a make-over. Banks's and Marstons Pedigree on handpump, farm cider and several wines by the glass; and piped jazz. There are some seats outside on the heated and sheltered terrace.

🍴 **Fine, contemporary food with a french influence includes a bar menu with lunchtime sandwiches and filled baguettes, soup, cheese tartlet, croque monsieur, carrot and pistachio strudel, sausage and mash, and fish of the day; the more expensive restaurant menu, available in the bar, could feature terrine of piglet and foie gras, caramelised fennel and goats cheese tartlet, raviolis of lobster with mussel and basil cream, millefeuilles of green asparagus with poached egg and hollandaise sauce, fish of the day, rump steak, coq au vin, slow-roast belly pork, and puddings like poached pear in sweet red wine and tiramisu. Starters/Snacks: £4.50 to £9.50. Main Courses: £10.95 to £22.50. Puddings: £4.50 to £5.50**

Union Pub Company ~ Tenant Oliver Bossut ~ Real ale ~ Bar food (12-2.30, 6.30-9.30) ~ Restaurant ~ (01584) 711230 ~ Children welcome ~ Dogs allowed in bar ~ Open 11.30-3, 6-11(1am Sat); 11.30-4 Sun; closed Sun evening ~ Bedrooms: £65B/£85S(£75B)

Recommended by Geoffrey Wordsworth, J E Shackleton, Ian Phillips, W H and E Thomas, Mike and Mary Carter, Michael and Joan Johnstone

BRINGSTY COMMON   SO6954   MAP 4

Live & Let Live ◧

Off A44 Knightwick—Bromyard 1.5 miles W of Whitbourne turn; take track southwards at black cat inn sign, bearing right at fork; WR6 5UW

Charmingly restored country tavern surrounded by rolling partly wooded common, enjoyable food and drink

This rustic 17th-c pub, beautifully restored and re-thatched, reopened in 2007 after more than ten years' closure. The restoration's been a long hard slog for its friendly local landlady, but her painstaking care has paid off well. The cosy bar has non-matching scrubbed or polished old tables on its flagstones, a very high-backed traditional winged settle by the log fire in the cavernous stone fireplace, and a variety of seats from comfortably cushioned little chairs to a long stripped pew. Earthenware jugs hang from the low stripped beams, with more bygones on the mantelshelf. The hop-hung bar counter, which has old casks built into its facing, has well kept Malvern Hills Black Pear on handpump, with a couple of guests, always local, such as Spinning Dog Herefordshire Owd Bull, and Oliver's cider and perry. A nicely joined new staircase takes you up to a pair of comfortable and attractively set cottagey little dining rooms tucked in under the steep rafters. Outside the timbered cottage with its massive stone chimney, a glass-topped well and big wooden hogshead have been pressed into service as tables for the flagstoned terrace, which has a splendid leather-cushioned bench, and the grassy former orchard blends into the partly scrubby and partly wooded slopes of this high ancient-feeling common, with picnic-sets giving long peaceful views. You really do feel miles from anywhere here.

🍴 **They do a short choice of bar lunches from soup and sandwiches (choice of breads) to three or four simple hot dishes such as fish pie or lamb chop – the lamb is usually from the black welsh mountain flock which grazes on the common, and other meats come from local farmers. The upstairs restaurant uses the same local supplies for its traditional**

country cooking – gammon, steaks, slow-cooked lamb or ham hock, for instance.
Starters/Snacks: £4.25 to £4.95. Main Courses: £6.75 to £9.95. Puddings: £4.95

Free house ~ Licensee Sue Dovey ~ Real ale ~ Bar food (12-2(3 Sun) 6-9, not Sun evening or Mon) ~ Restaurant ~ No credit cards ~ (01886) 821462 ~ Children welcome ~ Dogs allowed in bar ~ Open 12-2.30, 5-11, 12-11 Fri-Sun; closed Mon lunchtime except bank hols
Recommended by Chris Evans

CAREY   SO5631   MAP 4

Cottage of Content

Village signposted from good back road betweeen Ross-on-Wye and Hereford E of A49, through Hoarwithy; HR2 6NG

Country furnishings in rustic cottage, and seats on terraces

In a peaceful position close to the River Wye, this 15th-c building originated as three labourers' cottages that had its own integral cider and ale parlour. It has kept much of its old character, with a multitude of beams, prints on the walls and country furnishings such as stripped pine kitchen chairs, long pews by one big table and various old-fashioned tables on flagstones or bare boards. Hook Norton Best and Wye Valley Butty Bach are on handpump; piped music. There are picnic-sets on the flower-filled front terrace with a couple more on a back terrace. Since the last edition of the *Guide* the inn has had new owners; reports on the new regime please.

⊞ **Bar food includes starters such as smoked salmon and prawns in lime and paprika mayonnaise or smoked haddock chowder, and main courses like cinnamon-glazed slow-roasted duck leg on caramelised red cabbage with port wine jus, roasted pepper lasagne, grilled fillet of bream with chilli glaze on crab and tomato risotto, and grilled rib-eye of beef on mustard mash, with puddings such as lemon tart or raspberry spiked brownie.**
Starters/Snacks: £4.95 to £6.25. Main Courses: £6.25 to £15.50. Puddings: £5.00 to £6.75

Free house ~ Licensees Richard and Helen Moore ~ Real ale ~ Bar food ~ Restaurant ~ (01432) 840242 ~ Children welcome ~ Dogs allowed in bar ~ Acoustic guitar singer first Weds ~ Open 12-2, 6.30-10.30(11 Sat); 12-2.30 Sun; closed Sun evening and Mon ~ Bedrooms: £45(£55B)/£60(£70B)

Recommended by Dr and Mrs Michael Smith, Nick Lawless, Norman and Sarah Keeping, Noel Grundy, Dr W J M Gissane, Reg Fowle, Helen Rickwood, the Didler, Barry and Patricia Wooding, John Saville, Denys Gueroult

DORSTONE   SO3141   MAP 6

Pandy

Pub signed off B4348 E of Hay-on-Wye; HR3 6AN

Ancient and pretty inn by village green with flagstones, timbers and vast open fireplace, decent food, and seats and play area in side garden

In a bucolic setting in the Golden Valley, this is Herefordshire's oldest inn, with its origins as a building dating back to 1185. The neatly kept homely main room (on the right as you go in) has heavy beams in the ochre ceiling, stout timbers, upright chairs on its broad worn flagstones and in its various alcoves, and a vast open fireplace with logs; a side extension has been kept more or less in character. Wye Valley Butty Bach and a changing guest such as Bass on handpump, decent wines and several malt and irish whiskies; board games, TV, quoits and piped music. The handsome red setter is called Apache, and the neat side garden has picnic-sets and a play area. More reports please.

⊞ **Bar food includes filled baguettes, soup, scampi, fish pie, pizza, goats cheese salad, fried bass with chive, cream and Martini sauce, fillet of beef on red cabbage and mixed peppers, fish pie, lamb shank with redcurrant and red wine sauce, thai-style butternut squash curry, and puddings such as caribbean bread and butter pudding and chocolate pot; children's menu.** *Starters/Snacks: £4.50 to £7.50. Main Courses: £9.95 to £16.95. Puddings: £4.75*

Free house ~ Licensees Bill and Magdalena Gannon ~ Real ale ~ Bar food ~ Restaurant ~
(01981) 550273 ~ Children welcome ~ Dogs allowed in bar ~ Open 12-3, 6-11.30;
12-11.30 Sat; 12-3, 6.30-10.30 Sun; closed Mon lunchtime all year and all day Mon in winter

Recommended by Sue Demont, Tim Barrow, the Didler, Richard

HEREFORD   SO5139   MAP 6

Victory 🍺 £

St Owen Street, opposite fire station; HR1 2QD

**Extraordinary nautical décor in city pub with eight own-brewed beers plus guests, and
straightforward bar food**

Be prepared for a distinctly nautical surprise as you enter this externally unassuming-
looking city pub. The counter re-creates a miniature galleon complete with cannon
poking out of its top, and down a companionway the long back room is well decked out
as the inside of a man o' war: dark wood, rigging and netting everywhere, benches along
sides that curve towards a front fo'c'sle, stanchions and ropes forming an upper crow's
nest, and appropriate lamps. The remarkable choice of drinks is the reason for coming
here, with eight well kept own-brew beers: Hereford Best Bitter, Herefordshire Cathedral,
Organic Bitter, Owd Bull, Mutleys Dark, Mutleys Revenge, Mutts Nutts and Top Dog, as
well as seasonal brews such as Chase Your Tail and Light Ale; they also have several farm
ciders and a perry. Service is friendly and informal (they'll show you around the brewery if
they're not busy). Juke box (can be very loud), piped music, darts, games machine, TV,
skittle alley, table skittles, board games and a back pool table. The garden has a pagoda,
climbing plants and some seats. More reports please.

🍴 **Straightforward bar food (not available in winter) is limited to Sunday roasts only.** *Main
Courses: £5.95. Puddings: £1.50 to £2.50*

Own brew ~ Licensee James Kenyon ~ Real ale ~ Bar food (12-5 Sun (not winter)) ~ Restaurant
(Sun only) ~ No credit cards ~ (01432) 342125 ~ Children welcome until 9pm ~ Dogs welcome
~ Live band Fri, Sat, and Sun at bank holiday weekends ~ Open 3(11 Sat, 12 Sun)-midnight

Recommended by Reg Fowle, Helen Rickwood, Ann and Colin Hunt

HOARWITHY   SO5429   MAP 4

New Harp 🍷 🍺

Village signposted off A49 Hereford—Ross-on-Wye; HR2 6QH

**Contemporary décor in busy country pub where walkers and dogs are welcome; plenty of
outside seats, fair range of interesting drinks**

You can take your pick from a terrific range of drinks here: as well as Spinning Dog
Hereford Owd Bull and ales from breweries such as Cottage, Freeminer and Malvern Hills
on handpump, and herefordshire farm cider, there is a very extensive collection of
unusual bottled beers – among them wheat beers, trappist ales, lesser known lagers, fruit
beers and a fair range of wines by the glass. The bars are decorated in a contemporary
style with mainly crisp off-white paintwork, nicely lit modern artwork including cartoons
and caricatures, brown leather tub armchairs in front of a woodburning stove, a mix of
comfortable dining chairs around individual tables, stone floor tiling and some stripped
masonry. The bar angles round to a cosy dining room and the atmosphere is relaxed
throughout. Bow windows look up the hill to a remarkable italianate Victorian church
with a tall tower, and the little stream which runs through the pretty tree-sheltered
garden soon meets the nearby River Wye. The red labrador is called Foxy; piped music and
board games. There are plenty of picnic-sets, some on decking in a sort of arbour, and in
summer they have barbecues and erect a marquee. Service could be more welcoming at
times.

🍴 **Each item on the menu is paired with a drink or two that will complement it:**
sandwiches and platters, small plates such as indian-spiced mackerel fillet or crayfish and
crab vol-au-vent, and large plates such as fillet of bass on thai green king prawn and

coriander curry, roasted aubergine stuffed with ratatouille and mozzarella, and free-range chicken breast with apricot and mushroom stuffing; daily specials, often including game from local shoots, a fish night each Tuesday, and puddings. Booking is advisable. *Starters/Snacks: £4.00 to £6.00. Main Courses: £9.00 to £18.00. Puddings: £5.00 to £6.00*

Badger ~ Tenants Fleur and Andrew Cooper ~ Real ale ~ Bar food (12-2.30, 6-9.30) ~ (01432) 840900 ~ Children welcome ~ Dogs welcome ~ Open 12-11(10.30 Sun); 12-3, 6-11 Mon-Thurs in winter

Recommended by Mike and Mary Carter, Dr and Mrs A J Edwards, Nick Lawless, Guy Vowles, Reg Fowle, Helen Rickwood, Bernard Stradling, MLR, Dr W J M Gissane

LEDBURY   SO7137   MAP 4

Feathers 🍴 ♀ 🛏

High Street (A417); HR8 1DS

Chatty, relaxed bar in handsome timbered hotel, and more decorous lounges; good food, friendly staff and comfortable bedrooms

Within this comfortable and welcoming half-timbered hotel, you'll find a convivial mix of diners and chatty drinkers in the Top Bar. There are beams and restored brickwork, seats around oak tables on the oak flooring, as well as beams and timbers, hop bines, some country antiques, 19th-c caricatures and fancy fowl prints on the stripped brick chimneybreast (lovely winter fire), copper jam pots and fresh flowers on the tables – some very snug and cosy, in side bays. The lounge is a civilised place for afternoon teas, with high-sided armchairs and sofas in front of a big log fire and newspapers to read. Fullers London Pride and a guest such as Shepherd Neame Spitfire and Timothy Taylors Landlord on handpump, several wines by the glass, 30 malt whiskies and friendly, helpful staff. In summer, the sheltered back terrace has abundant pots and hanging baskets. 🍴 **Good food might include soup, smoked chicken caesar salad, confit duck terrine, salmon, prawn and leek fishcakes, mussels cooked with white wine, cream and shallot sauce, roast rump of lamb, fish and chips, chargrilled herefordshire sirloin, fresh penne pasta, and puddings such as dark chocolate torte or butterscotch pudding.** *Starters/Snacks: £5.25 to £9.50. Main Courses: £10.50 to £19.50. Puddings: £5.25*

Free house ~ Licensee David Elliston ~ Real ale ~ Bar food (12-2(2.30 Sat, Sun), 7-9.30(10 Fri, Sat; 9 Sun)) ~ Restaurant ~ (01531) 635266 ~ Children welcome ~ Dogs welcome ~ Open 11-11; 12-10.30 Sun ~ Bedrooms: £82.50B/£120B

Recommended by J E Shackleton, Rod Stoneman, Dr W J M Gissane, Mike and Mary Carter, Dr D J and Mrs S C Walker, Hansjoerg Landherr, Mr and Mrs A J Hudson, Jenny and Dave Hughes, Ann and Colin Hunt, George and Maureen Roby, J Crosby

LITTLE COWARNE   SO6050   MAP 4

Three Horseshoes ♀ 🛏

Pub signposted off A465 SW of Bromyard; towards Ullingswick; HR7 4RQ

Long-serving licensees and welcoming staff in bustling country pub with well liked food using their own chutneys and pickles and home-grown summer salad

The delightful rural position here makes the terrace or lawn in the garden a distinct lure at warmer times of year. The quarry tiled L-shaped middle bar has leather-seated bar stools, upholstered settles and dark brown kitchen chairs around sturdy old tables, old local photographs above the corner log fire, and hop-draped black beams in the dark peach ceiling. Opening off one side is a skylit sun room with wicker armchairs around more old tables; the other end has a games room with darts, pool, juke box and games machine; also cribbage. Greene King Old Speckled Hen and Ruddles Best, and Wye Valley Bitter on handpump, farm ciders and perry, and a dozen wines by the glass; obliging service, and disabled access. A roomy and attractive stripped-stone raftered restaurant extension has a Sunday lunchtime carvery. There are well sited tables on the terrace or on the neat prettily planted lawn. The refurbished bedrooms are comfortable.

🍴 Using their own-grown produce (and that of their neighbours and family, and other carefully sought out local producers), the enjoyable food might include sandwiches, soup, steak and ale pie, prawn and haddock smokies, fresh mussels with garlic and cream, cod fillet with scallop sauce, locally caught trout fillet with herb butter, lasagne, fillet of pork with crispy pork belly and damson sauce, and puddings such as steamed rhubarb and ginger sponge and home-made ice-cream; they do a good-value 'taste of Asia' menu on Wednesday evenings. *Starters/Snacks: £4.00 to £7.50. Main Courses: £6.95 to £9.95. Puddings: £3.75 to £3.95*

Free house ~ Licensees Norman and Janet Whittall ~ Real ale ~ Bar food ~ Restaurant ~ (01885) 400276 ~ Children welcome ~ Open 11-3(3.30 Sat), 6.30-11; 12-4, 7-10.30 Sun; closed Sun evening in winter ~ Bedrooms: £35S/£60S

Recommended by Mike and Mary Carter, Carol and Colin Broadbent, Theocsbrian, J E Shackleton, Denys Gueroult, Tim and Joan Wright, Reg Fowle, Helen Rickwood, Noel Grundy, Ann and Colin Hunt

ORLETON
S04967   MAP 6
Boot
Just off B4362 W of Woofferton; SY8 4HN

Small, welcoming pub with some original 16th-c features and much-enjoyed food

It doesn't take many people to fill up this likeable little place, in a pleasantly tucked-away village. The traditional-feeling bar has a mix of dining and cushioned carver chairs around a few old tables on the red tiles, one very high-backed settle, hops over the counter and a warming fire in the big fireplace with horsebrasses along its bressumer beam. Up a couple of steps, the lounge bar has green plush banquettes right the way around the walls, mullioned windows, an exposed section of wattle and daub, standing timbers and heavy wall beams. There's a restaurant on the left. Hobsons Best and Town Crier and a guest from a brewery like Ludlow or Wye Valley on handpump; cribbage and dominoes. There are seats in the garden under a huge ash tree, a barbecue area, and a fenced-in children's play area.

🍴 Consistently enjoyable bar food includes lunchtime sandwiches, filled hot baguettes, ploughman's, soup, whitebait, steak and ale pie, steaks, chicken breast stuffed with stilton wrapped in bacon, and daily specials such as vegetable bake, or pheasant casserole, and puddings. *Starters/Snacks: £2.95 to £5.50. Main Courses: £9.75 to £13.95. Puddings: £3.80*

Free house ~ Licensees Philip and Jane Dawson ~ Real ale ~ Bar food ~ Restaurant ~ (01568) 780228 ~ Children welcome ~ Dogs allowed in bar ~ Open 12-3, 6-11; 12-4, 7-11 Sun
Recommended by Mr and Mrs W W Burke, Doreen Maddock, Mr R Newbold, Ian Phillips, Carol and Colin Broadbent, Reg Fowle, Helen Rickwood, Mr and Mrs D Moir, George and Maureen Roby

SELLACK
S05526   MAP 4
Lough Pool ★ ♀
Back road Hoarwithy—Ross-on-Wye; HR9 6LX

Black and white cottage with individual furnishings in beamed bars, a good choice of food and drinks, lots of seats outside in pretty garden

Near the River Wye and Herefordshire Trail, this characterful, cottagey place is full of thoughtful touches, books and newspapers left out for customers, and crayons and paper for children, and dogs are made to feel welcome too. Outside are picnic-sets on an inviting front lawned area and a pretty array of hanging baskets. Its beamed central room has rustic chairs and cushioned window seats around wooden tables on the mainly flagstoned floor, sporting prints, bunches of dried flowers and fresh hop bines, and a log fire at one end with a woodburner at the other. Leading off are other rooms, gently brightened up with attractive individual furnishings and antique bottles, and nice touches such as a dresser of patterned plates. John Smiths and Wye Valley Bitter and Butty Bach and a guest such as Butcombe Bitter on handpump, several malt whiskies, local farm ciders, perries and apple juices, and several wines by the glass from a thoughtful wine list.

🍴 Using home-grown herbs and rare-breed meat from nearby farms, the food (not cheap) might include lunchtime open sandwiches, soup, seared fillet of salmon with mussels, confit of mackerel and potato terrine, fillets of red mullet, rump steak, saddle of lamb, fried breast of organic chicken, vegetarian options like sweet potato and coconut curry, and a children's menu, with puddings such as rhubarb posset or chocolate and walnut brownie. *Starters/Snacks: £4.95 to £13.50. Main Courses: £5.95 to £16.50. Puddings: £5.25 to £7.75*

Free house ~ Licensees David and Janice Birch ~ Real ale ~ Bar food ~ Restaurant ~ (01989) 730236 ~ Children welcome ~ Dogs allowed in bar ~ Open 11.30(12 Sun)-3, 6.30-11(10.30 Sun); 12-10.30 Sun; closed Sun evening and all day Mon in Nov, and mid Jan-Apr

Recommended by Nick Lawless, Jane McQuitty, Lucien Perring, J Crosby, Tom Evans, Bernard Stradling, Matt Anderson, Reg Fowle, Helen Rickwood, Noel Grundy, K S Whittaker

ST OWEN'S CROSS   SO5424   MAP 4

New Inn

Junction A4137 and B4521, W of Ross-on-Wye; HR2 8LQ

Huge inglenooks, beams and timbers, a friendly welcome, food served all day, and fine choice of drinks; big garden with views

From this half-timbered 16th-c inn, views extend to the Black Mountains, and in decent weather the spacious enclosed garden is particularly inviting. The friendly licensees have attractively refurbished the interior: lounge bar and restaurant have huge inglenook fireplaces, dark beams and timbers, various nooks and crannies, old pews and a mix of tables and chairs and lots of watercolours on warm red walls. Marstons Burton Bitter plus guests such as Hook Norton 303AD and Jennings Cocker Hoop on handpump, farm cider and perry, several malt whiskies and ten wines by the glass; piped music, table and outdoor games. The hanging baskets are quite a sight.

🍴 Served all day, bar food includes filled bloomers, soup, chicken liver pâté with home-made chutney, creamy garlic mushrooms, steak and ale pie, pork and leek sausages with onion sauce, tomato and red pepper tart, and puddings like apple crumble or dark chocolate mousse; children's menu. *Starters/Snacks: £3.50 to £6.25. Main Courses: £6.25 to £18.00. Puddings: £4.25 to £4.95*

Marstons ~ Lease Nigel Maud ~ Real ale ~ Bar food (12-9) ~ Restaurant ~ (01989) 730274 ~ Children welcome ~ Dogs allowed in bar ~ Open 11(9 Sat, Sun)-11 ~ Bedrooms: £45B/£70S(£80B)

Recommended by Dr and Mrs Michael Smith, Lucien Perring, Reg Fowle, Helen Rickwood, B M Eldridge, Tom Evans

STOCKTON CROSS   SO5161   MAP 4

Stockton Cross Inn

Kimbolton; A4112, off A49 just N of Leominster; HR6 0HD

Half-timbered pub with local ales and tasty food, huge log fire, seats in pretty garden

This pleasant old coaching inn is full of delightful nooks and crannies, with logs burning in a large stone fireplace in the character-laden, heavily beamed long bar, which has a handsome antique settle and old leather chairs and brocaded stools. At the far end is a woodburning stove with heavy cast-iron-framed tables and sturdy dining chairs, and up a step, a small area has more tables. Old-time prints, a couple of épées on one beam and lots of copper and brass complete the picture; piped music. Served by efficient staff are Hobsons Town Crier, Teme Valley This and Wye Valley Butty Bach on handpump, and several wines by the glass. There are tables out in the pretty garden. More reports please.

🍴 Reasonably priced bar food typically includes sandwiches, sirloin steak, roast black pudding with cider rarebit, poached haddock in smoked prawn sauce, fried lambs liver and bacon with onion gravy, goats cheese and pepper filo parcels, and puddings such as dark chocolate and orange tart. *Starters/Snacks: £3.95 to £5.95. Main Courses: £8.95 to £14.65. Puddings: £4.50 to £5.50*

Free house ~ Licensee Mike Betley ~ Real ale ~ Bar food ~ (01568) 612509 ~ Children welcome ~ Open mike night second Weds ~ Open 12-3, 7-11; 12-3 Sun; closed Sun and Mon evenings

Recommended by W H and E Thomas, Carol and Colin Broadbent, Reg Fowle, Helen Rickwood, Matthew Shackle, Mr and Mrs F E Boxell

SYMONDS YAT   SO5616   MAP 4

Saracens Head 🛏️

Symonds Yat E, by ferry, ie over on the Gloucs bank; HR9 6JL

Lovely riverside spot, contemporary food and a fine range of drinks in friendly inn; waterside terraces, comfortable bedrooms and plenty to do nearby

This idyllic inn far beneath the Symonds Yat viewpoint in the Wye gorge is a memorable place to arrive at on foot: a classic river walk crosses the Wye downstream by an entertainingly bouncy wire bridge at the Biblins and recrosses here by the long-extant hand-hauled chain ferry that one of the pub staff operates. There are lots of picnic-sets out on the waterside terrace. Inside, it's warm and relaxed with cheerful staff who make you feel at home. The busy, basic flagstoned public bar has Greene King Old Speckled Hen, Theakstons Old Peculier and Wye Valley Butty Bach and Hereford Pale Ale plus a guest such as Butcombe Bitter on handpump, and several wines by the glass; piped music, TV, games machine and pool. There's also a cosy lounge and a modernised bare-boards dining room. As well as bedrooms in the main building, there are two contemporary ones in the boathouse annexe. This is a nice place to stay out of season.

🍴 As well as lunchtime sandwiches, ciabatta bruschettas and ploughman's, the interesting modern food might include soup, mussels poached with honey and saffron, beetroot salmon gravadlax, rib-eye steak, steak in ale pie, confit leg of duck, courgette and sweet potato gateau, chargrilled tuna steak with tomato salsa, and some more expensive dinner menu items such as duet of local venison or fillet of beef; children's menu. *Starters/Snacks: £4.25 to £5.95. Main Courses: £8.95 to £14.95. Puddings: £5.50*

Free house ~ Licensees P K and C J Rollinson ~ Real ale ~ Bar food (12-2.30, 6.30-9) ~ Restaurant ~ (01600) 890435 ~ Children welcome ~ Dogs allowed in bar ~ Open 11-11(10.30 Sun) ~ Bedrooms: £50B/£74B

Recommended by Dr D J and Mrs S C Walker, Malcolm Pellatt, Keith and Chris O'Neill, John and Helen Rushton, David and Sue Atkinson, Mike and Lynn Robinson, B M Eldridge, Sue and Dave Harris

TITLEY   SO3359   MAP 6

Stagg 🍴 🍷 🛏️

B4355 N of Kington; HR5 3RL

HEREFORDSHIRE DINING PUB OF THE YEAR

Fantastic food using tip-top ingredients served in extensive dining rooms, a fine choice of drinks, two-acre garden, comfortable bedrooms

Consistently hitting the mark for many years as one of the top dining pubs in the country, this is a place for a special meal, and a lot of effort goes into creating an atmosphere that appeals to both visitors and locals. Readers also enjoy staying here, in bedrooms above the pub or in the additional rooms within a Georgian vicarage four minutes away, and the breakfasts are wonderful too. The bar, though comfortable and hospitable, is not large, and the atmosphere is civilised rather than lively. Hobsons Best and a couple of guests such as Brains Rev James and Timothy Taylors Landlord on handpump, several wines by the glass including champagne and pudding wines from a carefully chosen 100-bin wine list, home-made sloe gin, local ciders, perry, apple juice and pressés. The two-acre garden has seats on the terrace and a croquet lawn.

🍴 Outstanding food using their own-grown vegetables, pigs and free-range chickens includes a bar snack menu (not Saturday evenings or Sunday lunch) with filled baguettes, sausages and mash, three-cheese ploughman's with home-made pickle, smoked haddock risotto, faggots and mash, cod goujons with home-made chips, and devilled kidneys on rice; more elaborate choices such as foie gras with apple and pear jelly, bass with mussel broth, mushroom, leek and parmesan tart, belly pork with caramelised shallots and black pudding, fillet of beef with wild mushroom set cream and dauphinoise potato, and line-caught pollack with snail and white bean fricassee, with puddings such as white chocolate panna cotta with blackcurrant compote, lemon tart with raspberry sorbet, and three crème brûlées of vanilla, coffee and amaretto. The british cheeseboard is stupendous, with 23 different ones, mostly from Herefordshire and Wales. *Starters/Snacks: £3.90 to £7.90. Main Courses: £8.90 to £11.90. Puddings: £5.90*

Free house ~ Licensees Steve and Nicola Reynolds ~ Real ale ~ Bar food (12-2, 6.30-9; not Sun evening or Mon) ~ Restaurant ~ (01544) 230221 ~ Children welcome ~ Dogs allowed in bar and bedrooms ~ Open 12-3, 6.30-11; 12-3 Sun; closed Sun evening ~ Bedrooms: £70B/£85B

Recommended by J Crosby, Bruce and Sharon Eden, R Seifas, D and M T Ayres-Regan, Peter and Jean Hoare, P J and R D Greaves, J C Clark, Mr and Mrs W W Burke, Mr and Mrs R S Ashford, Dennis and Gill Keen

ULLINGSWICK   SO5949   MAP 4

Three Crowns

Village off A465 S of Bromyard (and just S of Stoke Lacy) and signposted off A417 N of A465 roundabout – keep straight on through village and past turn-off to church; pub at Bleak Acre, towards Little Cowarne; HR1 3JQ

Well presented food in busy dining pub with candlelight and proper napkins, and nice views from the terrace

Readers consistently praise the food and service at this very well run dining pub, where the emphasis leans distinctly towards the food rather than casual drinking, though some people do also pop in just for a drink. It has open fires, hops strung along the low beams of its smallish bar, traditional settles, old wooden tables, and more usual seats; there are one or two gently sophisticated touches such as candles on tables and proper napkins. Wye Valley Butty Bach and a guest such as Hobsons Best on handpump, several wines by the glass or sold in half bottles, and local apple juice. Tables out on the attractively planted lawn have pleasant views.

As well as a two- and three-course blackboard lunch menu (not Sunday), the interesting food includes starters like fish soup, home-smoked salmon with celeriac, apple and horseradish remoulade, and cheddar and spinach soufflé, with main courses such as grilled rump of herefordshire beef, grilled gurnard with bouillabaisse sauce, slow-cooked belly of pork and black pudding, and confit leg and seared breast of goosenargh duck; puddings include chocolate truffle torte and baked lemon and vanilla cheesecake. *Starters/Snacks: £4.50 to £6.50. Main Courses: £8.50 to £14.50. Puddings: £4.50 to £5.00*

Free house ~ Licensee Brent Castle ~ Real ale ~ Bar food ~ Restaurant ~ (01432) 820279 ~ Children welcome ~ Dogs allowed in bedrooms ~ Open 12-3, 7-11(10 Sun) ~ Bedrooms: /£95B

Recommended by Carol and Colin Broadbent, Mr and Mrs F E Boxell, Ann and Colin Hunt, Alan and Eve Harding, Bernard Stradling, J A Ellis, J E Shackleton, Denys Gueroult, M Sackett

UPTON BISHOP   SO6326   MAP 4

Moody Cow

2 miles from M50 junction 3 westbound (or junction 4 eastbound), via B4221; continue on B4221 to rejoin at next junction; HR9 7TT

Smart dining pub with interesting food, open fire and some cow-related ornaments

One reader brought a party of 36 here, and they were all very well looked after. It's laid out in snug areas that angle in an L around the bar counter, with rough sandstone walls, new slate flooring, an open fire, and a parade of cow-related ornaments and pictures. On the far right are a biggish rustic, candlelit restaurant with rafters, and a fireside area with armchairs and sofas. The far left has a second smaller dining area, just five or six tables with antique pine-style tables and chairs. Butcombe Bitter and Wye Valley Best on handpump.

🍴 **The enjoyable bar food might include sandwiches, soup, tempura-battered king prawns, caramelised red onion tart topped with melted goats cheese, sausages and mash, loin of lamb rolled with rosemary and roasted garlic, fish and chips, breast of duck with fondant potato and raspberry compote, pressed belly of pork with cider sauce, and puddings such as bread and butter pudding or chocolate rum truffle with lavender ice-cream.**
Starters/Snacks: £4.95 to £6.95. Main Courses: £11.95 to £17.95. Puddings: £4.50 to £5.95

Free house ~ Licensee James Lloyd ~ Real ale ~ Bar food (12-2, 6.30-9) ~ Restaurant ~ (01989) 780470 ~ Children welcome ~ Dogs allowed in bar ~ Open 12-2.30, 6.30-11; 12-3 Sun; closed Sun evening and Mon

Recommended by Mike and Mary Carter, Guy Vowles, Julian Cox, Carol and Colin Broadbent, Bob Broadhurst, Bernard Stradling, John and Helen Rushton, Nigel Clifton, Mr and Mrs F E Boxell, Dr W J M Gissane, JCW

WALFORD   SO5820   MAP 4

Mill Race ♀

B4234 Ross—Lydney; HR9 5QS

Contemporary furnishings in uncluttered rooms, a welcome for both diners and drinkers, and up-to-date daily specials served by attentive staff; terrace tables, nearby walks

The relaxed, crisply modern feel of this dining pub makes it a stylish place for a meal. The layout and décor are fresh and contemporary with a row of tall arched windows giving an airy feel in the main part, which has some comfortable leather armchairs and sofas on its flagstones, as well as smaller chairs around broad pedestal tables. The granite-topped modern bar counter stretching back from here has Wye Valley Bitter and a guest such as Wye Valley Dorothy Goodbody's Springtime on handpump, and a good choice of reasonably priced wines by the glass; opposite are a couple of tall nicely clean-cut tables with matching chairs. Service is friendly and attentive. The walls are mainly cream or dark pink, with just one or two carefully placed prints, and good unobtrusive lighting. One wall stripped back to the stonework has a woodburning stove, open also to the comfortable and compact dining area on the other side. There are tables out on the terrace; a leaflet available at the pub details a pleasant round walk of an hour or so. More reports please.

🍴 **They take pride in using named local suppliers for their careful mix of traditional and seasonal dishes with up-to-date specialities: the lunch menu includes sandwiches, baked potatoes, soup, goats cheese tart, burger and chips, sweet potato and spinach satay, and a fish dish; the more expensive evening menu features home-cured gravadlax, ham hock terrine with piccalilli, seared chicken livers with smoked bacon, roast farm chicken with braised lentils and air-dried ham, and chargrilled fillet of beef with smoked bacon, with puddings such as marmalade bread and butter pudding; Wednesday is fish night.**
Starters/Snacks: £4.50 to £6.95. Main Courses: £8.95 to £16.95. Puddings: £5.00

Free house ~ Licensee Jane Thompson ~ Real ale ~ Bar food (12-2, 6.30-9(9.30 Fri, Sat)) ~ (01989) 562891 ~ Children welcome ~ Open 11-3, 5-11; 11-11 Sat; 12-10.30 Sun

Recommended by R T and J C Moggridge, Paul Boot, Nick Lawless, Dr W J M Gissane

WALTERSTONE   SO3424   MAP 6

Carpenters Arms

Village signposted off A465 E of Abergavenny, beside Old Pandy Inn; follow village signs, and keep eyes skinned for sign to pub, off to right, by lane-side barn; HR2 0DX

Unchanging country tavern with traditional rooms, in same family for many years

Customers are instantly made to feel at home at this friendly, cottagey tavern near the Black Mountains. It has been in the same family for many years, and little has been altered. The traditional rooms have ancient settles against stripped stone walls, some pieces of carpet on broad polished flagstones, a roaring log fire in a gleaming black range (complete with pot-iron, hot-water tap, bread oven and salt cupboard), and pewter mugs hanging from beams. The snug main dining room has mahogany tables and oak corner cupboards and maybe a big vase of flowers on the dresser. Another little dining area has old oak tables and church pews on flagstones; piped music. Breconshire Golden Valley and Wadworths 6X, and a guest such as Breconshire Ramblers Ruin are tapped from the cask. The refurbished outside lavatories are cold but in character. More reports please.

🍴 **Straightforward food such as sandwiches and rolls, soup, chicken supreme, steaks, lamb cutlet with redcurrant and rosemary sauce, a vegetarian choice, daily specials, Sunday roasts, and puddings (made by the landlady's daughter) such as treacle tart and bread and butter pudding.** *Starters/Snacks: £4.00 to £4.75. Main Courses: £9.00 to £17.95. Puddings: £4.00*

Free house ~ Licensee Vera Watkins ~ Real ale ~ Bar food (12-2.30, 7-9.30) ~ Restaurant ~ No credit cards ~ (01873) 890353 ~ Children welcome ~ Open 12-11

Recommended by M J Winterton

WELLINGTON   SO4948   MAP 6

Wellington 🍺

Village signposted off A49 N of Hereford; pub at far end; HR4 8AT

Welcoming pub with good food and real ales, warm winter log fire, and summer barbecues in pleasant garden

This red-brick roadside pub has been imaginatively reworked inside to create a place where locals and diners alike feel comfortable and welcomed. The bar has big high-backed dark wooden settles, an open brick fireplace with a log fire in winter and fresh flowers in summer, historical photographs of the village, and antique farm and garden tools around the walls; the charming candlelit restaurant is in the former stables, and includes a conservatory. Hobsons Best, Wye Valley Hereford Pale Ale and a guest such as Shepherd Neame Spitfire on handpump, and a beer festival in July; several wines by the glass, a dozen malt whiskies and good, attentive service; board games and piped music. At the back is a pleasant garden with tables where they may hold summer barbecues.

🍴 **Good bar food includes sandwiches, soup, ham, egg and chips, sausage and mash, asparagus and cheese omelette, beer-battered fish and chips, and beefburger; the more expensive restaurant food, available in the bar at lunchtimes, might include starters like rabbit ravioli with cream and wholegrain mustard sauce, smoked haddock chowder or buffalo mozzarella with pomegranate and balsamic vinegar, and main courses such as fillet of venison, mushroom and roast garlic bourguignon, or sirloin steak, with puddings such as lemon tart or warm chocolate fondant pudding; roast Sunday lunches.** *Starters/Snacks: £4.95 to £8.50. Main Courses: £6.95 to £17.00. Puddings: £4.25 to £6.50*

Free house ~ Licensees Ross and Philippa Williams ~ Real ale ~ Bar food ~ Restaurant ~ (01432) 830367 ~ Children welcome ~ Dogs allowed in bar ~ Open 12-3, 6(7 Sun)-11; closed Sun evening in winter; closed Mon lunchtime

Recommended by Dr A J and Mrs Tompsett, Mrs J Gowan, Rosemary Richards, Reg Fowle, Helen Rickwood, H G Dyke, Alan and Eve Harding

WOOLHOPE   SO6135   MAP 4

Butchers Arms 🍺

Signposted from B4224 in Fownhope; carry straight on past Woolhope village; HR1 4RF

Pleasant country inn, peaceful setting and inviting garden, well kept beer and tasty food

Tucked away down a country lane through a gentle wood-rimmed valley, this friendly 14th-c inn takes a bit of finding. The welcoming staff serve four well kept real ales on handpump: Hook Norton Hooky Bitter, Shepherd Neame Spitfire, Wye Valley Butty Bach and a guest such as Wye Valley Golden Ale. One of the bars has very low beams decorated with hops, old-fashioned well worn built-in seats with brocaded cushions, high-backed chairs and stools around wooden tables, and a brick fireplace. Broadly similar though with fewer beams, the other bar has a large built-in settle and another log fire; piped music and darts. Breakfasts are good. The quiet garden has picnic-sets and flowering tubs and borders looking on to a willow-lined brook. To enjoy some of the best of the surroundings, turn left as you come out and take the tiny left-hand road at the end of the car park; this turns into a track and then into a path, and the view from the top of the hill is quite something.

🍴 **Enjoyable bar food includes sandwiches, ploughman's, steak, mushroom and ale casserole, vegetable lasagne, quiche of the day, sausages with spring onion mash and poached salmon fillet.** *Starters/Snacks: £3.95 to £5.75. Main Courses: £7.95 to £15.25. Puddings: £4.50*

Free house ~ Licensees Cheryl and Martin Baker ~ Real ale ~ Bar food (12-2, 6.30-9; 12-2 Sun) ~ Restaurant ~ (01432) 860281 ~ Children welcome ~ Dogs allowed in bedrooms ~ Open 12-2.30, 6.30-11(midnight Sat); 12-3, 7-10.30 Sun; closed Mon lunchtime and all day Mon in winter ~ Bedrooms: £35/£50

Recommended by Robert F Smith, Reg Fowle, Helen Rickwood, Nick Lawless, Noel Grundy, Ian and Denise Foster

YARPOLE   SO4664   MAP 6

Bell
Just off B4361 N of Leominster; HR6 0BD

Modern cooking using home-grown vegetables in black and white village pub, particularly good service, real ales and extensive gardens

Readers praise the service and food at this well run dining pub. In an ancient timbered building extended into a former cider mill, it has a basic tap room, a comfortable beamed lounge bar with a log fire and a large, high-raftered restaurant featuring a cider press and mill wheel; a mix of traditional furniture, some modern art on the walls and brass taps embedded into the stone bar counter. Hook Norton Hooky Bitter, Timothy Taylors Landlord and Wye Valley Hereford Pale Ale on handpump and a short but interesting wine list; efficient service even when busy. The golden labrador is called Marcus; piped music. There are picnic-sets under green parasols in the sunny flower-filled garden and the pub is very handy for Croft Castle.

🍴 **Using all home-grown vegetables and with a balance of innovative dishes and cheaper, pubbier dishes, the imaginative food includes items like sandwiches, soup, jerusalem artichoke and baby spinach risotto, fricassee of herefordshire snails with garlic and parsley, free-range chicken cordon bleu, fish pie, sausages and mash, and roast loin of pork with caramelised apple and black pudding.** *Starters/Snacks: £4.50 to £6.50. Main Courses: £7.50 to £16.00. Puddings: £4.95*

Enterprise ~ Lease Claude Bosi ~ Real ale ~ Bar food (12-2.30, 6.30-9.30) ~ Restaurant ~ (01568) 780359 ~ Children welcome ~ Dogs allowed in bar ~ Open 12-3, 6.30-11(10.30 Sun); closed Sun evening in winter; closed Mon

Recommended by Alan and Eve Harding, Reg Fowle, Helen Rickwood, Kevin Thorpe, Miss Jacquie Edwards, J E Shackleton, Don Beattie, Doreen Maddock, Dennis and Gill Keen

LUCKY DIP

Besides the fully inspected pubs, you might like to try these Lucky Dips recommended to us and described by readers (if you do, please send us reports: feedback@thegoodpubguide.co.uk).

ALLENSMORE [SO4533]
Three Horseshoes HR2 9AS: 17th-c timbered dining pub with attractive flowers and a good deal of character, well kept Black Sheep in cosy drinking area, enjoyable pub food, warmly friendly licensees, good walking country *(Reg Fowle, Helen Rickwood)*
ALMELEY [SO3351]
Bell HR3 6LF [off A480, A4111 or A4112 S of Kington]: Welcoming family-owned beamed country local with original jug-and-bottle entry lobby, well kept Wye Valley and a guest ale, small lounge with room for just a dozen or so people eating (inc good value

sandwiches and Sun roast), bar with traditional games, no piped music; boules pitch *(MLR)*
ASHPERTON [SO6441]
Hopton Arms HR8 2SE [A417]: Substantial Victorian inn with roomy bar and comfortable restaurant, friendly staff, food from usual bar snacks to reasonably priced Sun carvery, Flowers Original and Woods, Weston's farm cider, afternoon teas, fireside sofas and mix of contemporary style with carefully preserved original features; garden with good play area, camp site, 11 bedrooms *(Reg Fowle, Helen Rickwood)*

ASTON CREWS [SO6723]
☆ *Penny Farthing* HR9 7LW: Roomy and civilised partly 15th-c pub, Black Sheep, good value food and wines, good service, log fires, easy chairs, lots of beams, country bric-a-brac, feature well in bar, two restaurant areas, one with pretty valley and Forest of Dean views; tables in charming garden, bedrooms (*Lucien Perring, Julian Cox, BB*)

BISHOPS FROME [SO6648]
☆ *Green Dragon* WR6 5BP [just off B4214 Bromyard—Ledbury]: Up to half a dozen interesting well kept changing ales inc Timothy Taylors Landlord and Wye Valley, farm ciders, friendly licensees, good value lunchtime soup and sandwiches, evening hot dishes, four linked rooms with nice unspoilt rustic feel, flagstones and fine log fires; children welcome, newly reworked garden with smokers' shelter, on Herefordshire Trail, open all day Sat (*Reg Fowle, Helen Rickwood, LYM, Guy Vowles*)

BISHOPSTONE [SO4142]
Nelson HR4 7JN [A438 about 6 miles W of Hereford]: Comfortable roadside pub reopened after neat refurbishment, some medieval timbers, pitched rafters and wattle and daub preserved, log fire, friendly welcome, low-priced food from baguettes up, well kept Tetleys and Wye Valley, farm ciders, games end with pool; biggish side lawn (*LYM, Reg Fowle, Helen Rickwood*)

BROMYARD [SO6554]
Bay Horse HR7 4AA [High St]: Black and white 16th-c pub with good friendly service, enjoyable sensibly priced pubby food, well kept ales inc Ludlow, good choice of wines by the glass, attractive dining room; tables on back terrace (*Alan and Eve Harding*)

BROMYARD DOWNS [SO6755]
☆ *Royal Oak* HR7 4QP [just NE of Bromyard; pub signed off A44]: Beautifully placed open-plan low-beamed 18th-c pub with wide views, carpeted bar with interesting bric-a-brac, dining room with huge bay window, enjoyable reasonably priced food inc some interesting dishes, real ale, Weston's farm cider, friendly service; flagstoned bar with woodburner, pool, juke box and TV, piped music; walkers welcome (good area), picnic-sets on colourful front terrace, swings in orchard (*BB, Dave Braisted*)

BUSH BANK [SO4551]
Bush HR4 8EH: Enjoyable food, friendly inviting service (*A Wintour*)

CLODOCK [SO3227]
Cornewall Arms HR2 0PD [N of Walterstone]: Splendidly old-fashioned country local by historic church and facing Black Mountains, friendly landlady, good soft drinks choice, limited beers, no food to speak of, comfortable armchairs in stable-door bar, board games (*Reg Fowle, Helen Rickwood*)

COLWALL [SO7440]
☆ *Wellington* WR13 6HW [A449 Malvern—Ledbury]: Welcoming attentive newish landlord, wide choice of good reasonably priced food from home-baked bread up, well

kept ales such as Goffs, good wines by the glass, neat two-level bar and bright dining area; children welcome (*Chris Evans, M G Hughes, Dave Braisted, Karen Waller, Patricia Battelley*)

CRASWALL [SO2736]
Bulls Head HR2 0PN [Hay-on-Wye—Llanfihangel Crucorney Golden Valley rd]: Remote stone-built country pub reopened summer 2008 after light refurbishment keeping low beams and flagstones, log fire in old cast-iron stove, Hobsons and Wye Valley ales, several farm ciders tapped from the cask, plans to reopen smarter spacious dining area up steps; good-sized enclosed garden with play area, peaceful walking area (*LYM*)

EARDISLAND [SO4258]
Cross HR6 9BW [A44]: Friendly two-room local in lovely village, quick service, good value honest food (not Tues), a couple of real ales; open all day (*LYM, Ann and Colin Hunt*)

EARDISLEY [SO3149]
Tram HR3 6PG: Old beamed village local with chef/landlord doing good value home cooking, Wye Valley ales, one bar with woodburner, another served by hatch with log fire and pool, four cats; boules pitch (*H Paulinski, C E Clarke*)

EWYAS HAROLD [SO3828]
Temple Bar HR2 0EU: Friendly village pub, well kept Hook Norton Old Hooky, good service, enjoyable food from baguettes up inc Sun roasts and popular puddings, locals' bar with pool and juke box, pleasant lounge, small neat dining room (*Reg Fowle, Helen Rickwood*)

GARWAY [SO4622]
Moon HR2 8RF [Garway Common]: Friendly service, good choice of good value pubby food (*Ian and Denise Foster*)

GOODRICH [SO5618]
Cross Keys HR9 6JB [just off A40 outside village]: Four real ales, good farm cider, generous food, barn restaurant (*B M Eldridge, Dr A J and Mrs Tompsett*)

GORSLEY [SO6726]
Roadmaker HR9 7SW [B4221, just off M50 junction 3]: 19th-c village pub now run by group of retired Gurkha soldiers, good value pub food from baguettes up, also good nepalese curries, well kept Brains Rev James and Butcombe, large carpeted lounge bar with central log fire, evening restaurant (also Sun lunch); no dogs; terrace with water feature, open all day (*Neil and Anita Christopher, Mike and Mary Carter, Alastair Stevenson*)

GRAFTON [SO5038]
Grafton HR2 8ED [A49 2 miles S of Hereford]: Nicely decorated, with light warm dining area, friendly staff, well kept Rhymney Best and Wye Valley, rather pricy food, pool, conservatory; unobtrusive piped music; garden tables, new Travelodge to open Oct 2008 (*Reg Fowle, Helen Rickwood*)

HAMPTON BISHOP [SO5538]
Bunch of Carrots HR1 4JR: Spaciously
refurbished beamed country pub by River
Wye (fishing available), good helpful service,
consistently good carvery and wide choice of
other enjoyable food in bars and restaurant,
well kept real ales, local farm cider, lovely
log fires; children and dogs welcome, garden
with play area, open all day *(Steff Clegg,
Michael Lamm)*

HAREWOOD END [SO5227]
Harewood End Inn HR2 8JT [A49 Hereford—
Ross]: Attractive and comfortable panelled
dining lounge with wide choiceof reliable
food even Mon night, efficient staff, well
kept ales such as Brains Rev James and Wye
Valley, good value wines, magazines; nice
garden and walks, good bedrooms
*(Reg Fowle, Helen Rickwood, Dr and
Mrs Michael Smith)*

HEREFORD [SO4741]
Bay Horse HR4 0SD [Kings Acre Rd]: Large
freshly refurbished two-level main room and
smaller side room, conservatory extension,
friendly staff, decent food, real ales such as
Wye Valley, local farm cider *(Reg Fowle,
Helen Rickwood)*
Belmont Lodge & Golf Club HR2 9SA
[Ruckhall Lane; S of A465]: Non-members
welcome, good value Sun carvery with local
meats, Wye Valley ale, modern stripped-
stone bar, relaxed dining area; terrace views
(Reg Fowle, Helen Rickwood)
Litten Tree HR1 2BP [Commercial Rd]:
Comfortable chain pub in former repository,
good value food inc meal deals, competitive
drinks prices, darts; TVs; terrace tables
(Reg Fowle, Helen Rickwood)
Orange Tree HR4 9BX [King St]: Small 17th-c
beamed pub nr cathedral, enjoyable low-
priced food using local produce, Wye Valley
beers, civilised customers (popular with the
local constabulary), comfortable oak-
panelled dining area; disabled access,
children welcome, terrace tables, open all
day *(Reg Fowle, Helen Rickwood)*
Salmon HR1 1TQ [Hampton Park Rd]: Large
carpeted bar, cane chairs in pleasant
conservatory, Brains Rev James and Wye
Valley, bargain pub food inc OAP specials,
pleasant service; garden with terrace and
play area *(Neil and Anita Christopher)*
Spread Eagle HR4 9BW [King St]: Busy
beamed pub in side alley opp cathedral's
west front, several linked areas with
comfortable modern wood furniture,
generous bar food from pub staples to
imaginative dishes, well kept ales such as
Wychwood Hobgoblin, cheerful if not always
adept young staff, upstairs restaurant;
children welcome, tables in back courtyard
*(Reg Fowle, Helen Rickwood, Keith and
Chris O'Neill)*
Stagecoach HR4 0BX [West St]: 16th-c
black and white building, comfortable
lounge with dark oak panelling, John
Smiths, friendly service, two-for-one meal
deals, low-beamed upstairs restaurant; TV

in bar; open all day *(Reg Fowle,
Helen Rickwood)*

KINGSLAND [SO4461]
Angel HR6 9QS: Open-plan beamed and
timbered dining pub under new
management, bargain lunches, wider evening
choice, well kept Brains, decent wines,
comfortable bar with big hot stove, pool,
neat restaurant extension; picnic-sets on
front grass *(MLR, BB)*
Corner HR6 9RY [B4360 NW of Leominster]:
Friendly 16th-c black and white inn, good
service, good value food, well kept Hobsons
or Marstons, timbered bar and restaurant in
converted hay loft; good value bedrooms
(Alan and Eve Harding)

KINGTON [SO3056]
☆ *Olde Tavern* HR5 3BX [Victoria Rd, just off
A44 opp B4355 – follow sign to Town Centre,
Hospital, Cattle Mkt; pub on right opp
Elizabeth Rd, no inn sign but Estd 1767
notice]: Like stepping into an old sepia
photograph of a pub (except for the strip
lights – it's not at all twee), bargain local
Dunn Plowman ales, popular back bistro
using fresh local produce (Fri-Sat evening
and Sun lunch), hatch-served side room
opening off small plain parlour and public
bar, plenty of dark brown woodwork, big
windows, old settles and other antique
furniture on bare floors, gas fire, china,
pewter and curios, welcoming locals and
dog, no music or machines; children
welcome, though not a family pub; cl wkdy
lunchtimes, outside gents' *(Reg Fowle,
Helen Rickwood, the Didler, BB, Pete Baker,
MLR)*
Royal Oak HR5 3BE [Church Rd]: Cheerful
two-bar pub with good value generous pubby
food, well kept Hook Norton and Wye Valley,
friendly efficient service, restaurant; garden
with terrace, neat simple bedrooms, cl Mon
lunchtime *(Alan and Eve Harding)*

LEDBURY [SO7137]
☆ *Prince of Wales* HR8 1DL [Church Lane;
narrow passage from Town Hall]: Friendly
local, charmingly old-fashioned, tucked
nicely down narrow cobbled alley, well kept
ales such as Hobsons, Sharps Doom Bar and
Wye Valley, Weston's cider,foreign bottled
beers, bargain simple home-made food from
sandwiches up, attentive staff, low-beamed
front bars, long back room; a couple of
tables in flower-filled yard *(Simon Vernon,
Brian and Jacky Wilson, Simon Marley,
Reg Fowle, Helen Rickwood, Alan Bowker,
Malcolm Pellatt)*
Talbot HR8 2DX [New St]: Relaxed local
atmosphere in 16th-c inn's black-beamed bar
rambling around island servery, old hunting
prints, comfortably worn banquettes or more
traditional seats, log fire in big stone fireplace,
good value food from baguettes to full meals,
well kept Wye Valley ales, good house wines,
good service, black-panelled dining room, tales
of a friendly poltergeist; piped music; decent
bedrooms, open all day Sat *(Ian and
Denise Foster, Ann and Colin Hunt, BB)*

LEOMINSTER [SO4958]

☆ *Chequers* HR6 8AE [Etnam St]: Attractive 15th-c beamed and timbered two-bar pub with friendly and enthusiastic licensees doing good value food from sandwiches up, four or five well kept interesting real ales, cosy window seats and big log fires, newish back two-level dining room; children and dogs welcome, good heated and well lit courtyard, open all day *(MLR)*

LITTLE DEWCHURCH [SO5331]

Plough HR2 6PW: Friendly chatty country local with good value homely food, recently refurbished dining areas and games room; piped music *(Reg Fowle, Helen Rickwood)*

LONGTOWN [SO3228]

Crown HR2 0LT: Gently spruced up, with Wye Valley and another real ale, food lunchtime and evening from sandwiches up, woodburner in main bar, neat dining room, large back room with darts and pool; garden, good walks and scenery, cl Weds/Thurs lunchtimes *(MLR, Reg Fowle, Helen Rickwood)*

LUGWARDINE [SO5441]

☆ *Crown & Anchor* HR1 4AB [just off A438 E of Hereford; Cotts Lane]: Cheerful attractively cottagey timbered pub with good food inc plenty of lunchtime sandwiches and splendid ham and eggs, well kept Butcombe, Timothy Taylors Landlord and guest beers, several wines by the glass, several smallish rooms, some interesting furnishings, fresh flowers, big log fires, daily papers, no piped music or machines; children welcome, pretty garden, open all day *(Denys Gueroult, Paul Goldman, Noel Grundy, Martin and Jane Wright, Ken Millar, LYM)*

MADLEY [SO4138]

Red Lion HR2 9PH: Reasonably priced pub food, Banks's Best, friendly staff, log fire in comfortable dining area, flagstoned public bar, beams and interesting bric-a-brac, back pool table *(Reg Fowle, Helen Rickwood)*

MUCH BIRCH [SO4931]

Pilgrim HR2 8HJ: Substantially extended hotel, lounge bar with comfortable sofas and armchairs leading to dining room and conservatory, Wye Valley HPA, good value simple lunches and wider restaurant menu; beautiful grounds, terrace tables with sweeping Black Mountains view, 20 bedrooms *(MLR)*

MUCH DEWCHURCH [SO4831]

Black Swan HR2 8DJ [B4348 Ross—Hay]: Roomy and attractive beamed and timbered pub, partly 14th-c, with warm local atmosphere and log fires in cosy well worn bar and lounge with eating area, well kept ales such as Brains Rev James, Hook Norton, Rhymney and Timothy Taylors, decent wines, star barmaid; pool room with TV, juke box, no credit cards; dogs welcome *(Reg Fowle, Helen Rickwood, M J Winterton)*

MUCH MARCLE [SO6533]

☆ *Slip Tavern* HR8 2NG [off A449 SW of Ledbury]: Unpretentious country pub with splendidly colourful gardens overlooking cider orchards (Weston's Cider Centre is close

by), friendly informal service, good enterprising food, reasonable prices, Wye Valley ale and local farm cider, attractive conservatory restaurant *(Denys Gueroult, LYM)*

NORTON CANON [SO3748]

Three Horseshoes HR4 7BH [A480 Yazor—Eccles Green]: Basic two-bar rustic pub brewing its own good Shoes ales, inc fearsomely strong Farriers, log fire and old sofas in one room, vintage juke box in the other, even an indoor shooting gallery; may be home-pickled eggs; children welcome, tables in orchard – lovely countryside nr Davies Meadows wildflower reserve; cl lunchtimes exc Weds and wknds *(MLR)*

PEMBRIDGE [SO3958]

New Inn HR6 9DZ [Market Sq (A44)]: Timeless ancient inn overlooking small black-and-white town's church, unpretentious three-room bar with antique settles, beams, worn flagstones and substantial log fire, one room with sofas, pine furniture and books, Black Sheep and Fullers London Pride, farm cider, generous plain food (may stop serving lunch early), traditional games, quiet little family dining room; simple bedrooms *(Ann and Colin Hunt, LYM)*

PETERSTOW [SO5524]

Red Lion HR9 6LH [A49 W of Ross]: Country pub with wide range of food inc Sun lunch, small helpings available, good choice of real ales such as Otter and Wye Valley, farm cider, friendly staff, log fires, daily papers, open-plan bar with large dining area and modern conservatory; children welcome, back play area *(Rob and Penny Wakefield, Reg Fowle, Helen Rickwood)*

Yew Tree HR9 6JZ [A49 Ross—Hereford]: Unpretentious old-fashioned village pub with bargain home-made food, Flowers and Tetleys, friendly service, woodburner, games area with pool; adjacent caravan park *(Reg Fowle, Helen Rickwood)*

PRIORS FROME [SO5739]

☆ *Yew Tree* HR1 4EH [aka Len Gees; off A438 at Dormington, then second left and right at T; or off B4224 at Mordiford E of Hereford; OS Sheet 149 map ref 575390]: Friendly country pub with surprisingly good imaginative generous food at bargain prices inc carvery, rather more ambitious downstairs restaurant, changing real ales, summer farm cider; terrace, fine views to Black Mountains, cl Mon lunchtime and Tues *(BB, Reg Fowle, Helen Rickwood)*

ROSS-ON-WYE [SO6024]

Drop Inn HR9 7AG [Station St]: Long and narrow behind unpubby façade, Flowers IPA, pool, lots of Ross-on-Wye rugby memorabilia; sports TV; children welcome *(Reg Fowle, Helen Rickwood)*

Kings Head HR9 5HL [High St]: Comfortably old-fashioned beamed and panelled hotel bar, blazing log fire, lots of old pictures and some cosy armchairs, generous good value pubby food from good sandwiches and baked potatoes up, swift friendly service, two Wye Valley beers perhaps with a guest beer, airy dining extension; dogs welcome, bedrooms, open all day (Dr W J M Gissane, Mr and Mrs D J Nash, B M Eldridge)

Mail Rooms HR9 5BS [Gloucester Rd]: Open modern Wetherspoons, their usual food (using local ingredients) and attractively priced beers and wines, silenced TV; children in family area till 7, pleasant terrace, open all day (Mike and Mary Carter, B M Eldridge, Reg Fowle, Helen Rickwood)

Royal HR9 5HZ [Royal Parade]: Comfortably clean-cut river-view bar with Greene King IPA and Old Speckled Hen, enjoyable bar food and cream teas, sensible prices, pleasant service, restaurant; teak tables on heated decking, picnic-sets on steep lawn, 42 refurbished bedrooms, open all day (Paul Boot, Keith and Chris O'Neill, Ann and Colin Hunt)

SHOBDON [SO4061]

☆ *Bateman Arms* HR6 9LX: Striking 18th-c inn under welcoming new ex-Army licensees, good value food freshly made with local supplies (so can take a while; not Mon), well kept Wye Valley Buttie Bach and guest beers, good wines by the glass, cheerful service, log fire in comfortable beamed bar with relaxed local feel, a couple of shih tzus, well decorated restaurant; nine bedrooms, open all day (Alan and Eve Harding, Reg Fowle, Helen Rickwood)

STAUNTON ON WYE [SO3844]

Portway HR4 7NH [A438 Hereford—Hay, by Monnington turn]: Roomy 16th-c pub under new management, elegant oak-beamed lounge, bargain lunches, wider evening choice, well kept Brains, pool, restaurant (Reg Fowle, Helen Rickwood)

STIFFORDS BRIDGE [SO7348]

Red Lion WR13 5NN [A4103 3 miles W of Gt Malvern]: Cosy beamed roadside pub with good value food inc good baguettes and OAP bargains, prompt service, Greene King ales, farm ciders inc a local organic one; children welcome, tables in well kept garden (Dave Braisted)

STOKE PRIOR [SO5256]

Lamb HR6 0NB [off A49 or A44 1 mile SE of Leominster]: Good choice of reasonably priced food inc good value Sun lunch, Wye Valley ale; lovely garden with play area (Jonathan Neil-Smith)

STORRIDGE [SO7549]

New Inn WR13 5HB [A4103 SW of Worcester]: Pleasant pub with good value food in attractive new dining extension (Chris Evans)

SYMONDS YAT [SO5616]

Royal HR9 6JL: Enjoyable bar food in country hotel's roomy café/bar, Wye Valley ales; terrace tables, attractive riverside grounds, 20 bedrooms (John and Helen Rushton)

TARRINGTON [SO6140]

Tarrington Arms HR1 4HX [A438 E of Hereford]: Calm and welcoming, with

enjoyable reasonably priced food in bar and restaurant, efficient service, good choice of wines and ale; bellringers may be in at 9 after Fri practice (Reg Fowle, Helen Rickwood, Neasa Braham)

TILLINGTON [SO4645]

☆ *Bell* HR4 8LE: Family-run pub with warmly welcoming landlord, good proper home cooking (so can be a wait) in bar and compact restaurant from good baguettes and other lunchtime snacks up, good value Sun carvery (must book), Wye Valley and a guest beer, neat attentive service, daily papers, comfortable pine furniture with banquettes in lounge extension; children and dogs welcome, steps up to good big garden with play area (Reg Fowle, Helen Rickwood, Neasa Braham, A Wintour)

TRUMPET [SO6639]

☆ *Trumpet Inn* HR8 2RA: Beautiful black and white timbered pub dating from 15th c, good choice of good value home-made food largely from local farms and own garden, changing real ales, nice house wines, cheerful service, interesting horse-racing memorabilia, beams, log fires and stripped brickwork; tables in big garden behind, camp site with hard standings, open all day (Ann and Colin Hunt)

UPPER COLWALL [SO7643]

☆ *Chase* WR13 6DJ [Chase Rd, off B4218 Malvern—Colwall, 1st left after hilltop on bend going W]: Friendly staff in buoyant two-bar pub, plenty of tables for enjoyable good value generous food from sandwiches to good Sun lunch, good range of real ales and of wines by the glass; dogs and walkers welcome, attractive garden, wonderful views, open all day (Ian and Denise Foster, Dr and Mrs Jackson)

WEOBLEY [SO4051]

☆ *Red Lion* HR8 8SE [Bell Sq]: Recently reopened 14th-c black and white timbered and jettied inn, separated from graceful village church by bowling green; easy chairs, sofas, high-backed winged settles and huge stone fireplace in heavily beamed hotelish lounge, bar food, local real ales and ciders from small bar with pool, comfortable restaurant; lovely village, five comfortable bedrooms (Ann and Colin Hunt, LYM, MLR)

Salutation HR4 8SJ [off A4112 SW of Leominster]: Beamed and timbered old inn at top of delightful village green, chatty staff, local real ales, good range of wines by the glass, nice coffee, log fires, relaxed lounge, conservatory restaurant, public bar; children welcome, sheltered back terrace, bedrooms, open all day (the Didler, LYM, MLR, Ann and Colin Hunt)

Unicorn HR4 8SL [High St]: Unpretentious rustic local, plenty of character, games room with pool and juke box (Reg Fowle, Helen Rickwood)

WESTON-UNDER-PENYARD [SO6323]

Weston Cross Inn HR9 7NU [A40 E of Ross]: Substantial creeper-covered stone-built pub overlooking picturesque village, vast range of food cooked by friendly landlord's wife, special diets covered, Hancocks HB, Stowford Press cider, efficient service, comfortably worn in beamed dining lounge opening to garden, separate public bar; walkers welcome (they have a walks map), plenty of picnic-sets outside, play area (BB, Reg Fowle, Helen Rickwood)

WHITBOURNE [SO7156]
Live & Let Live WR6 5SP [off A44 Bromyard—Worcester at Wheatsheaf]: Two-bar pub under new owners, local ales such as Woods Shropshire Lad, enjoyable pubby food, good choice of wines by the glass, beams and big log fire, red plush seats and a couple of settees, darts, nice relaxed atmosphere in big-windowed restaurant; children welcome, garden with terrace and views (Chris Evans, Christopher Roberts, BB, M and GR)

WHITCHURCH [SO5417]
Crown HR9 6DB [just off A40 Ross—Monmouth]: Dating from 16th c, beams and stripped stone mixed with red and blue paintwork and modern art and furnishings in big wood-floored main bar, real ales inc Bass, good choice of food, log fire and settees, good-sized dining area and separate restaurant; dogs very welcome (they have five), tables outside, bedrooms (Neil and Anita Christopher)

WHITNEY-ON-WYE [SO2647]
Boat HR3 6EH: Spacious, quiet and neatly kept redbrick pub with big windows and picnic-sets in pleasant garden for lovely views (readers have watched riverside otter family playing); wide blackboard choice of good food, good friendly service, real ales inc a guest, farm cider, comfortable L-shaped lounge with dining area, games room with pool; children welcome, bedrooms, camp site (Neasa Braham, Dr and Mrs Michael Smith)

☆ *Rhydspence* HR3 6EU [A438 Hereford—Brecon]: Splendid half-timbered inn on the border with Wales, with comfortable bedrooms; views over Wye valley from

garden; smartly kept rooms with heavy beams and timbers, attractive old-fashioned furnishings, and there's a log fire in the fine big stone fireplace in the central bar; Bass and Robinson Best Bitter on handpump; tasty bar food and grills; children welcome, but no dogs inside (Rodney and Norma Stubington, Dr and Mrs Michael Smith, LYM, Guy Vowles, Mrs Ann Gray, John and Sylvia Harrop)

WIGMORE [SO4169]
Compasses HR6 9UN [Ford St]: Walker-friendly inn, olde-worlde behind its modern façade, with welcoming landlord (knowledgeable about local walks), good generous home cooking, well kept ales such as Timothy Taylors Landlord, daily papers, magazines and children's books, dining room, pool in plain public bar; good view from garden, four bedrooms, charming village with castle and lovely church (Alan and Eve Harding)

WOOLHOPE [SO6135]
☆ *Crown* HR1 4QP: Friendly hands-on licensees doing good range of food from sandwiches up, good Sun carvery, Black Sheep and Wye Valley ales, local farm cider, good hot drinks, open fire, neat comfortable lounge bar, dining area with old pews; piped music, sports TV; children welcome, big well kept garden with views, heaters and lighting, on Three Choirs Way, open all day Sat (Guy Vowles, Martin and Pauline Jennings, LYM, Reg Fowle, Helen Rickwood)

WOONTON [SO3552]
☆ *Lion* HR3 6QN [A480 SE of Kington]: Congenial country pub on busy road, warmly welcoming affable landlord and informal atmosphere, landlady using prime local produce for good plain cooking inc gluten-free and dishes suitable for vegans, sandwiches too, local and guest ales, inglenook bar, family restaurant, good views; monthly vintage sports car meeting second Tues; pleasant garden (W H and E Thomas, Reg Fowle, Helen Rickwood, Denys Gueroult)

Post Office address codings confusingly give the impression that a few pubs are in Herefordshire when they're really in Gloucestershire or even in Wales (which is where we list them).

Hertfordshire

Three new main entries here are the Beehive at Epping Green (good value food in cheerful surroundings, right out in the country), the hospitable Robin Hood in Tring (straight in with a Beer Award, enjoyable pubby food too), and the Tally Ho at Barkway (a winning combination of charming individuality with good food and Award-quality drinks). Hertfordshire is a particularly good county for real ale lovers. Its main brewer is McMullens, brewing here since the 18th century. Smaller and newer breweries we found represented in at least some pubs here are Tring, Buntingford, Alehouse and Red Squirrel. Nearly half the county's main entries have won our Beer Award – and what's more they are not pubs of a type, they range from simple down-to-earth places to up-to-the-minute dining pubs. Perhaps the most traditional are the lovely old unspoilt Valiant Trooper in Aldbury and the unpretentious White Horse in Hertford – with nine taps it has the widest range of beers. It's not just the beer they do well at the Holly Bush at Potters Crouch; this family-run place glows with loving care, and they have now started doing food in the evenings. The county's three food high flyers are the buoyant Aldford Arms at Frithsden (now with an exclusively european wine list as a response to concerns about wine miles), the civilised Fox in Willian (good wines and beers here too), and the restauranty Bricklayers Arms at Flaunden. It's the Bricklayers Arms, with its exceptionally good food carefully prepared by a team of French chefs, that is Hertfordshire Dining Pub of the Year. We'd also particularly note, from the Lucky Dip section at the end of the chapter, the Black Horse in Chorleywood, Boot at Sarratt and Six Bells in St Albans.

ALDBURY   SP9612   MAP 4

Greyhound

Stocks Road; village signposted from A4251 Tring—Berkhamsted, and from B4506; HP23 5RT

Spacious yet cosy old dining pub with traditional furnishings, popular food, and courtyard

The beamed interior of this handsome virginia creeper-covered inn shows some signs of considerable age (around the copper-hooded inglenook, for example), with plenty of tables in the two traditionally furnished rooms off either side of the drinks and food serving areas. In winter the lovely warm fire and subtle lighting make it feel really cosy. Three beers on handpump are usually Badger First Gold and Tanglefoot and King & Barnes Sussex. An airy oak floored restaurant at the back overlooks a suntrap gravel courtyard, and benches outside face a picturesque village green complete with stocks and a duck pond lively with wildfowl.

⑪ The tasty food here does draw a crowd, but the friendly staff cope well and meals are served promptly. The short but sensible menu includes something for most tastes: soup, panini, ploughman's, roast butternut squash, sage and pine nut risotto, gammon and eggs, cured meat platter with parmesan, smoked haddock on mash with poached egg and butter sauce, shepherds pie, thai king prawn curry, lamb tagine with lemon and honey couscous, parsley and cheese crusted cod loin and fillet of beef with pink peppercorn sauce. *Starters/Snacks: £4.75 to £7.50. Main Courses: £7.50 to £14.25. Puddings: £3.55 to £6.45*

Badger ~ Tenant Tim O'Gorman ~ Real ale ~ Bar food (12-2.30(4 Sun), 6.30-9.30; not Sun evenings) ~ Restaurant ~ (01442) 851228 ~ Children welcome away from bar ~ Dogs allowed in bar ~ Open 11-11; 12-10.30 Sun ~ Bedrooms: £65S/£75B

Recommended by Roy Hoing, Cathy Robinson, Ed Coombe, Mrs Deborah Chalmers, Dennis Jones

Valiant Trooper ◀
Trooper Road (towards Aldbury Common); off B4506 N of Berkhamsted; HP23 5RW

Cheery all-rounder with appealing interior, five interesting real ales, generous helpings of food, garden

This very pleasant old country pub consists of a lovely series of unspoilt rooms. The first is beamed and tiled in red and black, with built-in wall benches, a pew and small dining chairs around attractive country tables, and an inglenook fireplace. Futher in, the middle bar has spindleback chairs around tables on a wooden floor, some exposed brickwork, and signs warning you to 'mind the step'. The far room has nice country kitchen chairs around individually chosen tables, and a woodburning stove, and the back barn has been converted to house a restaurant. A jolly decent range of five very well kept beers on handpump might include Archers IPA, Fullers London Pride, Tring Jack o' Legs and Side Pocket for a Toad, with just under a dozen wines by the glass; dominoes, cribbage and bridge on Monday nights. The enclosed garden has a play house for children and the pub is nicely positioned for walks through the glorious beech woods of the National Trust's Ashridge Estate.

🍴 **Quickly served bar food includes well filled baked potatoes, open sandwiches or ciabattas and ploughman's, with daily specials such as soup, creamy mushroom carbonara, roast chicken and steak and kidney pie, and puddings such as chocolate and brandy torte.** *Starters/Snacks: £4.50 to £6.00. Main Courses: £7.50 to £16.00. Puddings: £4.50 to £5.00*

Free house ~ Licensee Tim O'Gorman ~ Real ale ~ Bar food (12-2(2.30 Sun), 6.30-9.15; not Mon and Sun evenings) ~ Restaurant ~ (01442) 851203 ~ Children in first bar and restaurant ~ Dogs allowed in bar ~ Open 11.30-11; 12-10.30 Sun

Recommended by Mrs Deborah Chalmers, Gordon Neighbour, Michael Butler, D J and P M Taylor, Paul Humphreys, N R White, Pam Adsley, Roy Hoing, Dave Braisted, Michael Dandy

ASHWELL   TL2739   MAP 5

Three Tuns ♀
Off A505 NE of Baldock; High Street; SG7 5NL

Comfortable gently old-fashioned hotel bars with generous helpings of tasty food, and substantial garden

As at all good pubs, there seems to be something for everyone at this well run hotel and pub – everything from boules in the shaded garden to breakfasts for non-residents. Wood panelling, relaxing chairs, big family tables, lots of pictures, stuffed pheasants and fish, piped light classical music and antiques lend an air of Victorian opulence to the cosy lounge. The recently refurbished public bar is more modern, with leather sofas on reclaimed oak flooring, and pool, cribbage, dominoes, a games machine and TV. They stock a good choice of wines (with 16 by the glass), as well as Greene King IPA, Abbot and a guest such as Bath Ales Gem on handpump. A big terrace has metal tables and chairs, while a large garden has picnic-sets under apple trees. The charming village is full of pleasant corners and is popular with walkers as the landscape around rolls enough to be rewarding.

🍴 **Nicely presented food might include filled baguettes, chicken liver pâté, herring fillets in madeira, ploughman's, chicken breast with stilton sauce, steak and kidney pie, seasonal game and 8oz fillet steak, with puddings such as bakewell tart and tiramisu; Sunday roast.** *Starters/Snacks: £4.95 to £7.45. Main Courses: £8.95 to £16.45. Puddings: £2.95 to £5.75*

Greene King ~ Tenants Claire and Darrell Stanley ~ Real ale ~ Bar food (12-2.30, 6.30-9.30;
12-9.30 Fri, Sat, Sun) ~ Restaurant ~ (01462) 742107 ~ Children welcome ~ Dogs allowed in
bar ~ Open 11-11; 12-10.30 Sun ~ Bedrooms: £39/£49(£59S)(£69B)

*Recommended by Colin McKerrow, Grahame Brooks, Gordon Neighbour, Mrs Margo Finlay, Jörg Kasprowski, R T and
J C Moggridge, Conor McGaughey, Eithne Dandy, Michael Dandy*

BARKWAY   TL3834   MAP 5

Tally Ho ♀ ◖

London Road (B1368, which parallels A10 S of Royston); SG8 8EX

**Appealing proper pub with all the traditional virtues including real country food – and a
decided dash of individuality**

In the cosy and cottagey little bar on the right, it looks as if the well kept changing ales
such as Brandon Best, Buntingford Highwayman and Greene King Ruddles Best are tapped
from big casks behind the bar, but in fact these are false and they are gently pumped.
Everything else couldn't be more genuine: the inviting old sofa and armchairs in the big
end bow window, the warm log fire, the good choice of wines by the glass, malt whiskies
and other spirits, the Aspall's farm cider, and the friendly professional service. There's
another fire through in the dining area angling back on the left – very old-world, with
fresh flowers and silver candelabra, old-fashioned prints on brown ply panelling, a dark
green ceiling. At the end here is a little terrace for smokers; beyond the car park is a
proper garden with well spaced picnic-sets, a weeping willow and fruit trees.

⑪ **Bar food might include smoked salmon with rocket and citrus dressing, chicken caesar
salad, cheese terrine with fruit chutney, home-made burger or haggis, duck breast with
thyme jus, red mullet wrapped in parma ham with sage leaves, beef casserole, sirloin
steak, and noteworthy puddings such as apple and cinnamon crumble, crème brûlée and
baked chocolate fondant.** *Starters/Snacks: £4.75 to £6.95. Main Courses: £7.95 to £17.95.
Puddings: £3.50 to £5.75*

Free house ~ Licensees Paul and Ros Danter ~ Real ale ~ Bar food (12-2, 6.30-9) ~ Restaurant ~
(01763) 848389 ~ Children welcome ~ Open 11.30-11; 12-4 Sun; closed Sun evening

Recommended by Conor McGaughey, Simon Watkins, M R D Foot

BATFORD   TL1415   MAP 5

Gibraltar Castle

Lower Luton Road; B653, S of B652 junction; AL5 5AH

**Pleasantly traditional pub with interesting militaria displays, some emphasis on food
(booking advised); terrace**

A most impressive collection of military paraphernalia, including rifles, swords, medals,
uniforms and bullets (with plenty of captions to read) is packed into this neatly kept
welcoming pub. The long carpeted bar has a pleasant old fireplace, comfortably
cushioned wall benches, and a couple of snugly intimate window alcoves, one with a fine
old clock. Pictures depict its namesake, and various moments in the Rock's history. In
one area the low beams give way to soaring rafters. Several board games are piled on top
of the piano, and they've piped music. They stock a thoughtful choice of wines by the
glass and a good range of malt whiskies, and serve three Fullers beers on handpump.
Hanging baskets and tubs dotted around lend colour to a decked back terrace, and there
are a few more tables and chairs in front by the road,

⑪ **Quickly served pubby food includes a good range of lunchtime sandwiches,
ploughman's, sausage and mash, cajun chicken, bacon and avocado salad, fish and chips,
chicken and mushroom pie and fillet steak; booking is recommended for Sunday roast.**
Starters/Snacks: £3.95 to £8.95. Main Courses: £8.95 to £17.95. Puddings: £3.95 to £6.95

Fullers ~ Lease Hamish Miller ~ Real ale ~ Bar food (12-2.30(4 Sun), 6-9; not Sun evening) ~
Restaurant ~ (01582) 460005 ~ Children welcome ~ Dogs allowed in bar ~ Live music
Tues evenings from 9pm ~ Open 11.30-11; 12-11 Sun

Recommended by Michael Dandy, David Jackson, Pat and Roger Davies, David and Ruth Shillitoe, Adrian Johnson, Grahame Brooks

CHAPMORE END   TL3216   MAP 5

Woodman 🍺

Off B158 Wadesmill—Bengeo; 300 yards W of A602 roundabout keep eyes skinned for discreet green sign to pub pointing up otherwise unmarked narrow lane; OS Sheet 166, map reference 328164; SG12 0HF

Peaceful country local with down-to-earth interior, beers straight from the cask, lunchtime snacks (occasionally more), cheery staff, and garden with play area

The two straightforward little linked rooms at this early Victorian local have plain seats around stripped pub tables, flooring tiles or broad bare boards, log fires in period fireplaces, cheerful pictures (for sale), lots of local notices, and darts over to one side. Three very well kept Greene King beers are tapped straight from the cask, and they've several malt whiskies; chess, backgammon, shove ha'penny and cribbage. There are picnic-sets out in front under a couple of walnut trees, and a bigger garden at the back has a good fenced play area where you can play boules.

🍴 **Under the new licensee, the minimal lunchtime menu includes sandwiches, soup and ploughman's. In winter they serve a Sunday lunchtime roast and in summer they have regular barbecues and tasty hog roasts.** *Starters/Snacks: £3.50 to £5.00. Main Courses: £4.50 to £8.00. Puddings: £2.50 to £3.50*

Greene King ~ Tenant Tony Dawes ~ Real ale ~ Bar food (12-2 Tues-Sat; 1-3 Sun; not Mon lunchtime) ~ (01920) 463143 ~ Children welcome till 8pm ~ Dogs welcome ~ Open 12-2, 5.30-11; 12-11 Sat; closed Mon lunchtime

Recommended by Andy and Jill Kassube, Ian Arthur

COTTERED   TL3229   MAP 5

Bull

A507 W of Buntingford; SG9 9QP

Neatly kept dining pub with polished antiques, good (though not cheap) food and big attractive garden

There's a rather pretty view of a row of charming old thatched cottages from the front window of this nice old pub – tables and benches set under majestic old trees make the best of this lovely setting. Inside, the airy low-beamed front lounge is well cared for, with good pieces of furniture on a stripped wood floor, a warming fire, Greene King IPA and Abbot and decent wines. A second bar has darts and a games machine; unobtrusive piped music.

🍴 **Thoughtfully presented bar food includes lunchtime sandwiches, toasties and ploughman's. Other dishes include fresh crab, steak and kidney pie, mushroom risotto, chicken fillet in cream, wine, garlic and mushroom sauce, salmon fillet with cheese and tomato sauce, rack of lamb with port sauce and fillet steak; 5% service charge except if dining in the Hunt Bar.** *Starters/Snacks: £4.80 to £7.25. Main Courses: £7.00 to £18.50. Puddings: £4.95 to £5.50*

Greene King ~ Tenant Darren Perkins ~ Real ale ~ Bar food (12-2, 6.30-9.30; 12-3.30, 6-9 Sun) ~ Restaurant ~ (01763) 281243 ~ No under sevens Mon-Sat, no prams ~ Open 12-3, 6.30-11; 12-10.30 Sun

Recommended by Simon Watkins, Charles Gysin, Brian and Rosalie Laverick, Pam and Wally Taylor, Jack and Sandra Clarfelt

---

Post Office address codings confusingly give the impression that some pubs are in Hertfordshire, when they're really in Bedfordshire, Buckinghamshire or Cambridgeshire (which is where we list them).

EPPING GREEN   TL2906   MAP 5

Beehive

Off B158 SW of Hertford, via Little Berkhamsted; back road towards Newgate Street and Cheshunt; SG13 8NB

Cheerful bustling country pub, very popular for its good value food

This well run pub has a pleasantly traditional feel, with its low shiny ceiling, wheelback chairs and brocaded benches around the dark tables on its patterned green carpet, and the stove in one brown-painted panelled corner. There's a warm chatty atmosphere, service is prompt and pleasant, and they have Adnams and Greene King IPA and Old Speckled Hen on handpump, and a good range of wines by the glass; piped music. There are picnic-sets out on the neat lawn betweeon the low tiled weatherboarded pub and the quiet country road; good woodland walks nearby.

Ⅲ **Bar food might include sandwiches, crab and mango salad, smoked haddock and spring onion fishcakes, grilled chicken breast wrapped in parma ham with brandy peppercorn sauce, steak, mushroom and ale pudding and baked cod with bacon and mushroom sauce and puddings such as vanilla and rosemary crème brûlée and white chocolate and blueberry sponge pudding.** *Starters/Snacks: £3.95 to £5.95. Main Courses: £5.95 to £16.00. Puddings: £4.25*

Punch ~ Lease Martin Squirrell ~ Real ale ~ Bar food (12-2.30, 6-9.30; 12-4 Sun) ~ Restaurant ~ (01707) 875959 ~ Children welcome ~ Open 11.30-3, 5.30-11; 12-5(8 Jun-Aug) Sun; closed Sun evening

Recommended by Kenneth and Mary Davies, J Marques, Professors Alan and Ann Clarke, Geoff and Sylvia Donald, Gordon Neighbour

FLAUNDEN   TL0101   MAP 5

Bricklayers Arms

Off A41; Hogpits Bottom; HP3 0PH
HERTFORDSHIRE DINING PUB OF THE YEAR

Cosy traditional country restaurant (drinkers welcome) with emphasis on beautifully prepared food (booking almost essential) and very good wine list

To experience exceptional food in a charming environment is likely to be your main reason for visiting this well refurbished, low brick and tiled 18th-c pub. Originally two cottages and now covered with virginia creeper, it's tucked away down a winding country lane. The low-beamed bar is snug and comfortable, with roaring winter log fires and dark brown wooden wall seats. Stubs of knocked-through oak-timbered walls keep some feeling of intimacy in the three areas that used to be separate rooms. They've a very good extensive wine list (with about 20 by the glass) as well as Fullers London Pride, Greene King IPA and Old Speckled Hen, Timothy Taylor and a guest such as Tring Jack o' Legs on handpump. This is a lovely peaceful spot in summer, when the beautifully kept old-fashioned garden with its foxgloves against sheltering hedges comes into its own. Just up the Belsize road there's a path on the left which goes through delightful woods to a forested area around Hollow Hedge.

Ⅲ **On the whole, food is fairly elaborate and not cheap, but the French chef does take tremendous care over preparation and ingredients. Some of the herbs and vegetables come from the pub's garden, and they smoke their own meats and fish. The menu (a fusion of anglo and gallic styles) might include starters such as french onion soup, smoked fish or smoked duck breast with grilled almonds, guinea fowl terrine with mustard and black pepper, main courses such as fried bass with creamy wine, red pepper and basil sauce, sausage and chive mash, battered cod with handcut chips, steak and kidney pie, kangaroo burger, boned quail stuffed with mushrooms with balsamic sauce, and puddings such as lemon tart with peach and redcurrant ice-cream, hot chocolate sponge pudding and bourbon vanilla crème brûlée.** *Starters/Snacks: £4.95 to £13.95. Main Courses: £9.95 to £18.95. Puddings: £4.60 to £6.95*

Free house ~ Licensee Alvin Michaels ~ Real ale ~ Bar food (12-2.30(4 Sun); 6.30-9.30(8.30 Sun)) ~ Restaurant ~ (01442) 833322 ~ Dogs allowed in bar ~ Open 12-11.30(10.30 Sun)

Recommended by Jarrod and Wendy Hopkinson, Sue Griffiths, Tracey and Stephen Groves, Martin Terry, James Paterson, Bruce and Penny Wilkie, Alex Gifford, Mike Turner, Peter and Jan Humphreys

FRITHSDEN   TL0109   MAP 5

Alford Arms ⑪ ♀

From Berkhamsted take unmarked road towards Potten End, pass Potten End turn on right, then take next left towards Ashridge College; HP1 3DD

Attractively located thriving dining pub with chic interior, good food from imaginative menu, and thoughtful wine list

Buzzing with cheerful diners and friendly staff, this stylish place is one of the county's most popular dining pubs (though locals still pop in to sit at the bar). You will probably need to book and it's worth getting here early as parking is limited. The fashionably elegant but understated interior has simple prints on pale cream walls, with blocks picked out in rich Victorian green or dark red, and an appealing mix of good antique furniture (from Georgian chairs to old commode stands) on bare boards and patterned quarry tiles. It's all pulled together by luxurious opulently patterned curtains; darts and piped jazz. In order to reduce 'wine miles' all the wines on their list are european, with most of them available by the glass, and they've Brakspears, Flowers Original, Marstons Pedigree and Rebellion IPA on handpump. The pub stands by a village green and is surrounded by lovely National Trust woodland. There are plenty of tables outside.

🍴 **The seasonally changing menu might include starters such as king prawn and spring onion bread and butter pudding with goats cheese and beetroot dressing, masala chicken salad with cumin spiced chicken heart kebab and green chutney yoghurt, main courses such as roast duck leg on white bean and duck faggot cassoulet, crispy pork belly and onion roly poly, parma ham wrapped monkfish with smoked garlic puy lentils and tomato butter sauce, and puddings such as treacle tart with lemon grass crème fraîche, vanilla and raisin rice pudding with nutmeg crust and sorbets with raspberry sauce. They've a british cheese plate and a liqueur list; Sunday roast.** *Starters/Snacks: £3.75 to £7.25. Main Courses: £11.00 to £15.75. Puddings: £4.00 to £6.75*

Salisbury Pubs ~ Lease Richard Coletta ~ Real ale ~ Bar food (12-2.30(4 Sun), 7-10) ~ (01442) 864480 ~ Children welcome ~ Dogs allowed in bar ~ Open 11-11; 12-10.30 Sun

Recommended by Gordon Davico, Michael Dandy, James Paterson, Susan and Nigel Brookes, Tim Maddison, John and Joyce Snell, Karen Eliot, Neil Ingoe, Howard Dell, Cathy Robinson, Ed Coombe, Giles Barr, Eleanor Dandy, Rosemary Smith

HERTFORD   TL3212   MAP 5

White Horse 🍺 £

Castle Street; SG14 1HH

Impressive range of real ales and very reasonably priced food at down-to-earth town-centre pub

Parts of this unpretentious tucked away little pub date from the 14th c – you can still see Tudor brickwork in the three quietly cosy upstairs family rooms. Its two downstairs rooms are small and homely, the one on the left being more basic, with bare boards, some brewery memorabilia, and a few rather well worn tables, stools and chairs. A warming open fire separates it from the more comfortable right-hand bar, which has a cosily tatty armchair, some old local photographs, beams and timbers, and a red-tiled floor. As well as four Fullers beers and Adnams Southwold, four guests, with the choice often changing from one day to the next, might be from brewers such as Brains, Butcombe and O'Hanlon. During their May and August bank holiday beer festivals they keep even more. They also have a dozen country wines. Service can be quite chatty and a good range of games includes bar billiards, darts, shove-ha'penny, shut-the-box, cribbage, dominoes, and a TV for some sports events. The pub faces the castle, and there are two simple benches on the pavement outside.

🍴 Very inexpensive home-made bar food includes sandwiches, soup, baguettes and ploughman's, and daily specials such as beef and vegetable pie, moroccan chicken, wild boar casserole, braised armenian lamb shanks and sausage and bubble and squeak with onion gravy. On Sunday they do a remarkably good value two-course and three-course lunch. The only evening they serve food is Monday, when they prepare one exotic dish such as a curry; they can do children's helpings. *Starters/Snacks: £2.40 to £4.50. Main Courses: £4.50 to £6.00*

Fullers ~ Lease Nigel Crofts ~ Real ale ~ Bar food (12-2(1-3 Sun); 6-until sold out (Mon only)) ~ (01992) 501950 ~ Children in family room ~ Dogs welcome ~ Open 12-2.30, 5.30-11; 12-11(10.30 Sun) Sat

Recommended by Pat and Tony Martin, Gordon Tong, N R White, Andy and Jill Kassube

POTTERS CROUCH   TL1105   MAP 5
Holly Bush 🍺 £

2.25 miles from M25 junction 21A: A405 towards St Albans, then first left, then after a mile turn left (ie away from Chiswell Green), then at T junction turn right into Blunts Lane; can also be reached fairly quickly, with a good map, from M1 exits 6 and 8 (and even M10); AL2 3NN

Lovingly kept cottage with gleaming furniture, fresh flowers, china, very well kept Fullers beers, good value food, and attractive garden

One gets a strong sense of this pretty wisteria-swamped white building being run with real loving care and sincerity. It's very much a family affair, with the licensees recently celebrating 30 years here. Everything is immaculate. Thoughtfully positioned fixtures create the illusion that there are lots of different rooms – some of which have the feel of a smart country house. In the evenings, neatly placed candles cast glimmering light over the mix of darkly varnished tables, all sporting fresh flowers. There are quite a few antique dressers (several filled with plates), a number of comfortably cushioned settles, the odd plant, a fox's mask, some antlers, a fine old clock, carefully lit prints and pictures, daily papers, and on the left as you go in, a big fireplace. The long, stepped bar has particularly well kept Fullers Chiswick, ESB, London Pride and a Fullers seasonal beer on handpump, and the sort of reassuringly old-fashioned till you hardly ever see these days. Led by the impeccably dressed landlord, service is calm, friendly and efficient, even when they're busy. Behind the pub, the fenced-off garden has a nice lawn, handsome trees, and sturdy picnic-sets – it's a very pleasant place to sit in summer. Though the pub seems to stand alone on a quiet little road, it's only a few minutes' drive from the centre of St Albans (or a pleasant 45-minute walk).

🍴 We've very good news on the food front here. Since the licensees' daughter and son-in-law became involved in the business they have been serving food most evenings. The good value (and very popular) lunchtime menu is still very pubby – sandwiches, baked potatoes, ploughman's, burgers and platters, but in the evening they now offer several heartier dishes such as chilli, casserole of the day, portabello mushrooms with stilton stuffing and cherry tomato stuffing and pork fillet with honey, mustard and thyme sauce. *Starters/Snacks: £3.00 to £4.20. Main Courses: £4.50 to £13.00. Puddings: £3.40 to £3.90*

Fullers ~ Tenants Ray and Karen Taylor ~ Real ale ~ Bar food (12-2, 6-9 (not Sun-Tues)) ~ (01727) 851792 ~ Open 12-2.30, 6-11(7-10.30 Sun)

Recommended by Michael Butler, Amy Farnham, John and Joyce Snell, Chris Edwards, Paul Goldman, Julie Oakes

PRESTON   TL1824   MAP 5
Red Lion 🍺

Village signposted off B656 S of Hitchin; The Green; SG4 7UD

Homely village local with changing beers and neatly kept colourful garden

Once you know the story behind this nice old village pub it becomes clear why there is such a feeling of local pride in the place. When Whitbread threatened its closure back in 1982 it became the first pub in the country to be acquired by a village. They keep very good beer, with Fullers London Pride and Youngs alongside three regularly changing guests from brewers such as Archers, Everards and Newby Wyke. They also tap farm cider from the cask, have several wines by the glass (including an english house wine), a perry and mulled wine in winter. The main room on the left has sturdy well varnished pub furnishings including padded country-kitchen chairs and cast-iron-framed tables on a patterned carpet, a log fire in a brick fireplace, and foxhunting prints. The somewhat smaller room on the right has steeplechasing prints, some varnished plank panelling, and brocaded bar stools on flagstones around the servery; dominoes. A few picnic-sets out on the front grass face across to lime trees on a peaceful village green. At the back, a pergola covered terrace gives way to many more picnic-sets (with some shade from a tall ash tree) in the good-sized sheltered garden beyond. It's all very neatly kept and there's a colourful herbaceous border.

🍽 **Under the new manager, very straightforward traditional bar food includes sandwiches and ploughman's, soup, pâté, quiche, sausage and mash, chilli, home-made pies and steaks.** *Starters/Snacks: £3.75 to £4.50. Main Courses: £5.95 to £13.95. Puddings: £3.75*

Free house ~ Licensee Rick Lewis ~ Real ale ~ Bar food (12-2(2.30 Sat, 3 Sun), 7-9; not Sun evenings and Mon) ~ No credit cards ~ (01462) 459585 ~ Children welcome away from bar ~ Open 12-2.30(3 Sat), 5.30-11(12 Fri); 12-4, 7-10.30 Sun

Recommended by Ben Williams, John Walker, John and Joyce Snell, R T and J C Moggridge

ROYSTON   TL3540   MAP 5

Old Bull £

High Street, off central A10 one-way system – has own car park, or use central car park; SG8 9AW

Bow-fronted town pub with pleasant spacious interior and good value food

The roomy high-beamed bar at this early Georgian coaching inn has handsome fireplaces, exposed timbers, big pictures and rather fine flooring, easy chairs, a leather sofa and a table of papers and magazines (and ready-to-pour coffee) at the entrance end with the bar counter. Further in, tables are set out for eating. They have Greene King Abbot and IPA and a Greene King guest on handpump and several decent wines by the glass. The atmosphere is chatty and relaxed with fairly unobtrusive piped music; cribbage and dominoes. In days of old, when up to 100 horses might have been stabled at this town hotel, the courtyard here would have been a bustling roar. Today it's a peaceful suntrap, equipped with outdoor heaters and modern tables and chairs.

🍽 **Under new licensee, good-value bar food includes sandwiches, soup, ploughman's, filled yorkshire pudding, lasagne, mushroom stroganoff, battered cod, crispy duck pancakes, rib-eye steak, and puddings such as pecan pie or lemon meringue roulade. There is a separate more formal restaurant; carvery.** *Starters/Snacks: £3.95 to £6.95. Main Courses: £7.95 to £15.95. Puddings: £4.50*

Greene King ~ Lease Peter Nightingale ~ Real ale ~ Bar food (12-2.30, 6-9; 12-9 Sat, Sun) ~ Restaurant ~ (01763) 242003 ~ Children welcome ~ Dogs allowed in bar ~ Open 11-11(midnight Thurs-Sat); 12-10.30 Sun ~ Bedrooms: £75S/£90S(£105B)

Recommended by Alistair and Kay Butler, Ross Balaam

SARRATT   TQ0498   MAP 5

Cock

Church End: a very pretty approach is via North Hill, a lane N off A404, just under a mile W of A405; WD3 6HH

Plush pub popular with older dining set at lunchtime and families at weekends; Badger beers, children's play area and summer bouncy castle

We very much hope that the new licensees at this nicely positioned 17th-c country local will bring it back on form as it seems to have floundered a little recently. It's a pretty cream-painted building, with a latched front door opening into a homely carpeted snug with a vaulted ceiling, original bread oven and a cluster of bar stools. Through an archway, the partly oak-panelled cream-walled lounge has a lovely log fire in an inglenook, pretty Liberty-style curtains, pink plush chairs at dark oak tables, and lots of interesting artefacts and several namesake pictures of cocks; Badger Best, Sussex, Tanglefoot and a Badger guest on handpump; piped music. The restaurant is in a nicely converted barn. Picnic-sets in front look out across a quiet lane towards the churchyard, while a pretty, sheltered lawn and terrace at the back give open country views (this is good walking country). There's also a children's play area and a bouncy castle during summer weekends.

🍽 **Bar food includes soup, sandwiches, whitebait, prawn and pineapple cocktail, vegetable lasagne, poached salmon salad, battered cod, steak and ale pie and specials such as chilli, bass, swordfish and vegetable lasagne.** *Starters/Snacks: £4.50 to £6.00. Main Courses: £8.95 to £15.00. Puddings: £4.75*

Badger ~ Tenants Brian and Marion Eccles ~ Real ale ~ Bar food (12-2.30(4 Sun), 6-8.30(9.30 Sat)) ~ Restaurant ~ (01923) 282908 ~ Children welcome ~ Dogs allowed in bar ~ Jazz Sun afternoon ~ Open 12-11(midnight Sat, 9 Sun)

Recommended by C Galloway, Howard Dell, D J and P M Taylor, Peter and Margaret Glenister, Roy Hoing, Jarrod and Wendy Hopkinson

TRING   SP9211   MAP 5

Robin Hood 🍺
Brook St (B486); HP23 5ED

Really welcoming pub with good beer and good pubby food

Doing very well under its fairly new licensees, this carefully run pub is a welcome new addition to the main entries. Its several immaculately kept smallish linked areas have quite a homely feel. Furnishings, on spotless bare boards or carpets, are quite traditional, taking in banquettes, standard pub chairs and the like. Early in the evening regulars pop in to occupy the stools lined along the counter, then later on, couples arrive for the tasty food. Beers include four very well kept Fullers brews, a seasonal Fullers guest, and a guest such as Adnams. The licensees' two little yorkshire terriers are called Toy and Teacup; piped music. There are tables out on small pleasant back terrace.

🍽 **Enjoyably pubby food includes filled baguettes, garlic breaded mushrooms, sausage and mash, ham, egg and chips, steak and kidney pudding, lamb shank in mint and rosemary sauce, chilli and lasagne.** *Starters/Snacks: £3.65 to £5.95. Main Courses: £7.65 to £14.95. Puddings: £3.75 to £3.95*

Fullers ~ Tenants Terry Johnson and Stewart Canham ~ Real ale ~ (01442) 824912 ~ Children welcome ~ Open 11.30-3, 5.30-11; 12-4, 6.30-11 Sat; 12-4, 7-11 Sun

Recommended by Roger E F Maxwell, Laura Rolfe, John Branston, Ross Balaam

WILLIAN   TL2230   MAP 5

Fox 🍽 🍷 🍺
A mile from A1(M) junction 9; A6141 W towards Letchworth then first left; SG6 2AE

Civilised dining pub with good food from pubby favourites to more imaginative dishes, nice range of drinks

Refurbished in a contemporary style a couple of years ago, this well run dining pub has a fresh clean-cut feel. There are comfortable light wood chairs and tables on stripped boards or big ceramic tiles, with modern pictures on white or pastel walls. Carefully lit, with boxy contemporary bar stools running along its pale blue frontage, the modern counter serves Adnams Best, Fullers London Pride, Woodfordes Wherry and a guest such as O'Hanlons Dry Stout from handpumps, a good wine list with just over a dozen by the glass and a nice range of spirits; well reproduced piped music, relatively unobtrusive TV. Young pleasantly attentive staff look as if they really enjoy their work. A side terrace has smart tables under cocktail parasols, and there are picnic-sets in the good-sized garden behind, below the handsome tower of the 14th-c All Saints church. Across the road is a large pond. More reports please.

🍴 The well executed changing menu might include sandwiches, starters such as watercress and stilton soup, native oysters, grilled sardines with citrus, caper and tomato salsa, main courses such as sausage and mash, battered cod, tiger prawns in linguine with tomato, lemon grass and lime sauce, garlic and thyme roast pork belly with apple purée, bean cassoulet in a filo basket, steaks, puddings such as pistachio crème brûlée and cherry and amaretto cheesecake, and a british cheese platter. *Starters/Snacks: £4.50 to £9.50. Main Courses: £8.95 to £16.50. Puddings: £5.25*

Free house ~ Licensee Cliff Nye ~ Real ale ~ Bar food (12-2(2.45 Sun), 6.30-9.15; not Sun evening) ~ Restaurant ~ (01462) 480233 ~ Children welcome ~ Dogs allowed in bar ~ Open 12-11(midnight Fri, Sat, 10.30 Sun)

Recommended by Ross Balaam, Gordon Neighbour, Peter and Margaret Glenister, Scott McGinlay

LUCKY DIP

Besides the fully inspected pubs, you might like to try these Lucky Dips recommended to us and described by readers (if you do, please send us reports: feedback@thegoodpubguide.co.uk).

ARDELEY [TL3027]
Rabbits Foot SG2 7AH [off B1037 NE of Stevenage]: Former Jolly Waggoner renamed by new licensees, enjoyable fresh home-made food inc game and rabbit in bar and restaurant, Greene King IPA and Abbot and a guest beer, decent wines, relaxed traditional pub with beams, timbering, lots of nooks and corners; children and dogs welcome, pleasant garden and terrace with play area, cl Sun evening, Tues lunchtime and Mon *(LYM)*

AYOT GREEN [TL2213]
Waggoners AL6 9AA [off B197 S of Welwyn]: Cosy low-beamed bar, comfortable good-sized restaurant extension, enjoyable well served food inc good lunchtime deals and wider more expensive evening choice, pleasant attentive staff, beers inc Adnams and Greene King; attractive and spacious suntrap back garden with sheltered terrace and play area (some A1(M) noise), wooded walks nearby, open all day *(Peter and Margaret Glenister, Ben Williams, BB, Alex Gifford)*

BARLEY [TL3938]
Chequers SG8 8JQ [London Rd]: Traditional unpretentious pub with generous food, friendly service, log fires, daily papers; dogs welcome, well kept flower garden *(Mrs Margo Finlay, Jörg Kasprowski)*

BERKHAMSTED [SP9907]
Crown HP4 3HH [High St]: Wetherspoons in former 17th-c coaching inn (so more pubby than some), low beams, quick service, good choice of beers and wines, usual cheap food inc bargain Sun lunch *(Mrs Margaret Peacock)*

BOURNE END [TL0206]
Anchor HP1 2RH [London Rd]: Friendly low-beamed 16th-c pub with good drinks range, wide choice of enjoyable food, bargain prices *(Mrs Margaret Peacock)*

☆ *Three Horseshoes* HP1 2RZ [Winkwell; just off A4251 Hemel—Berkhamsted]: Friendly 16th-c family pub in charming setting by

unusual swing bridge over Grand Union Canal, low-beamed three-room core with inglenooks, well kept Adnams Broadside, Black Sheep and Shepherd Neame Spitfire, reasonably priced food all day, efficient uniformed staff, bay-windowed extension overlooking canal; children welcome, tables out by water, open all day *(LYM, John Branston, John Faircloth, Ross Balaam)*

BRAUGHING [TL3925]
Axe & Compass SG11 2QR [just off B1368; The Street]: Pleasant country local in pretty village with ford, enjoyable straightforward food inc good steaks, real ales, friendly service, modern décor and mix of furnishings in two roomy bars (one an unusual corner-shape) and restaurant; well behaved dogs and children welcome *(Eleanor Dandy)*

BRICKET WOOD [TL1302]
Gate AL2 3PW [Station Rd/Smug Oak Lane]: Recently refurbished country pub with Wells & Youngs ales, well priced simple food, welcoming service, log fire; garden tables *(David M Smith)*

Old Fox AL2 3XU [School Lane; 2 miles from M1 junction 6 via Mount Pleasant Lane]: Surrounded by woodland and looking like converted 19th-c forester's cottage, with comfortable mix of furnishings, enthusiastic new landlady doing good value food, real ales such as Black Sheep, Greene King Old Speckled Hen and Shepherd Neame Spitfire; children welcome, large pleasant garden, good walks *(David M Smith)*

BUSHEY [TQ1394]
Horse & Chains WD23 1BL [High St]: Reopened under its original name after neat comfortable refurbishment, real ales, good choice of wines by the glass inc champagne, reasonably priced all-day bar food from sandwiches up, separate restaurant menu too (not Sun evening); no under-21s in bar; open all day *(anon)*

Swan WD23 3EE [Park Rd; turning off A411]: Homely atmosphere in rare surviving example of unspoilt single-room backstreet terraced pub, reminiscent of 1920s, changing ales such as Wells & Youngs, coal fires *(Conor McGaughey, LYM)*

CHISWELL GREEN [TL1304]

Three Hammers AL2 3EA [just S of St Albans; Watford Rd]: Neatly kept Ember Inn with four changing real ales, good value up-to-date food, prompt helpful service, several areas on different levels around central bar, a few rather low beams, abstracts and photographs of old St Albans; no children inside; garden tables *(KC, Val and Alan Green)*

CHORLEYWOOD [TQ0395]

☆ *Black Horse* WD3 5EG [Dog Kennel Lane, the Common]: Very welcoming to all, inc children, walkers and even dogs (biscuit basket on mantelpiece), good value food (not Mon) from good sandwiches up, OAP lunch some days, well kept Adnams, Shepherd Neame Spitfire, Wadworths 6X and Wells & Youngs Bitter and Bombardier, decent wines (and tea and coffee), quick helpful service, plenty of good-sized tables under low dark beams in attractively divided traditional room with thick carpet, daily papers, coal-effect fire, no music; family area, separate bar with SkyTV; pretty setting, picnic-sets overlooking common *(Tom Evans, Roy Hoing, Ian Phillips)*

☆ *Gate* WD3 5SQ [Rickmansworth Rd]: Open-plan family dining pub with clean-cut and attractive contemporary décor, wide range of enjoyable up-to-date food inc sharing plates, Bass and Timothy Taylors Landlord, good value wines by the glass, genial and helpful largely antipodean staff; plenty of garden tables *(Michael Dandy, Tom Evans, LYM, John Branston)*

Land of Liberty Peace & Plenty WD3 5BS [Long Lane, Heronsgate; just off M25, junction 17]: Relaxed old-fashioned open-plan pub with Red Squirrel and other interesting ales, Weston's cider and perry, good soft drinks choice, belgian bottled beers and brewery memorabilia, enjoyable bar lunches, cosy corner banquette, no music, skittles; no children inside; dogs welcome, garden behind, open all day *(LM, Tony Hobden)*

Stag WD3 5BT [Long Lane/Heronsgate Rd]: Spacious open-plan Edwardian pub with McMullens ales, good choice of reasonably priced wines by the glass, decent food, helpful staff, quiet relaxed atmosphere, large L-shaped bar with eating area extending into conservatory, no piped music; tables on back lawn, play area, open all day *(C Galloway, Tony Hobden)*

COLNEY HEATH [TL2007]

☆ *Plough* AL4 0SE [Sleapshyde; handy for A1(M) junction 3; A414 towards St Albans, doubling back at first roundabout then turning off left]: Cosily refurbished 18th-c low-beamed thatched local, chatty

atmosphere, good value generous home-made standard food from sandwiches up (lunchtime Mon-Sat, and Fri/Sat evening), well kept Greene King IPA and Abbot and Fullers London Pride, friendly efficient staff, big log fire, small brighter back dining area; white iron tables on pretty front terrace, picnic-sets on sheltered back terrace and lawn overlooking open fields *(Brian and Rosalie Laverick, BB, Robert Turnham)*

DATCHWORTH [TL2717]

☆ *Horns* SG3 6RZ [Bramfield Rd]: Pretty flower-decked Tudor pub facing small green, low beams and big inglenook one end, high rafters and rugs on patterned bricks the other, attractive décor, wide choice of good reasonably priced food from proper sandwiches to splendid paella (best to book Sun), quick friendly service, real ales inc one brewed for the pub; picnic-sets on front lawn *(LYM, Gordon Neighbour, Anthony and Marie Lewis)*

FLAMSTEAD [TL0714]

Three Blackbirds AL3 8BS [High St, just off A5]: Low-beamed partly Tudor pub, much modernised inside but still with roaring fire, old dark wood and brickwork, current chef doing enjoyable proper food, three well kept ales inc Shepherd Neame Spitfire from central bar, good coffee, pleasant service, high-backed settles in dining area; piped music; picnic-sets on terrace by car park behind, colourful hanging baskets *(David and Ruth Shillitoe, BB)*

FURNEUX PELHAM [TL4327]

Brewery Tap SG9 0LL [Bealey Croft End]: Generous and enjoyable home-made food, well kept Greene King IPA and Abbot, cheerful staff, pool, pleasant dining room; piped music; children welcome, back garden room and terrace overlooking neat attractive garden *(Philip Denton)*

GRAVESEND [TL4325]

Catherine Wheel SG11 2LW [off A120 at Little Hadham]: Recently reopened, rebuilt in sympathetic style after low-beamed partly early 15th-c original burnt down, luxurious interior, good choice of beers and wines by the glass inc champagne, wide food choice, welcoming staff; good outside seating *(Charles Gysin)*

GREAT OFFLEY [TL1427]

☆ *Green Man* SG5 3AR [signed off A505 Luton—Hitchin; High St]: Roomy and comfortably olde-worlde Chef & Brewer with very wide choice of enjoyable generous food, well organised friendly staff, Marstons Pedigree, Theakstons Bitter and Old Peculier and Wells & Youngs Bombardier, good choice of wines by the glass, good coffee, blazing log fires, large flagstoned conservatory; may be unobtrusive piped classical music; children welcome, peaceful country views from picnic-sets in back garden with pleasant terrace, striking inn-sign, open all day *(Ross Balaam, Michael Dandy, LYM, David and Ruth Shillitoe, Peter and Margaret Glenister)*

HARPENDEN [TL1415]

Amble AL5 4UL [Station Rd]: Newly reopened after comfortable reworking with mix of contemporary décor and familiar fittings, enjoyable food using local supplies, Black Sheep, Timothy Taylors Landlord, good coffees; open all day *(Nick Rowe)*

Cross Keys AL5 2SD [High St]: Compact low-beamed and flagstoned pub with well kept ales such as Fullers London Pride, Marlow Rebellion and Timothy Taylors Landlord from pewter-topped bar, log fire in public bar, simple lounge, basic lunchtime pub food (not Sun – hog roast last Sun of month) from sandwiches up, young staff; informal back garden *(M Thomas)*

Engineer AL5 1DJ [St Johns Rd]: Two-bar pub in residential area, Adnams, Greene King IPA, Shepherd Neame Spitfire and a guest beer, good choice of wines by the glass, reasonably priced pubby bar food from sandwiches up, welcoming helpful staff, conservatory restaurant with different menu inc Sun roasts; piped music, games, TV; pleasant garden with terrace and small fishpond *(Michael Dandy, Giles Barr, Eleanor Dandy)*

Fox AL5 3QE [Luton Rd, Kinsbourne Green; 2.2 miles from M1 junction 10; A1081 towards town]: Contemporary dining pub, tiled floor, usual leather armchairs and sofas, lots of modern dining tables in alcoved layout, enjoyably up-to-date pubby food, friendly helpful service, interesting wines by the glass, Timothy Taylors Landlord, open fire; piped music; terrace tables *(Michael Dandy, Giles Barr, Eleanor Dandy, Eithne Dandy)*

Old Bell AL5 3BN [Luton Rd (A1081)]: Compact Chef & Brewer with decent food, good choice of wines by the glass, Courage Best and Wells & Youngs Bombardier, daily papers, pub games; large back tree-shaded garden *(Michael Dandy)*

Rose & Crown AL5 1PS [Southdown Rd]: Enjoyable food from lunchtime sandwiches up, Adnams and Greene King Old Speckled Hen, good coffee, quick service, daily papers, contemporary décor and furnishings, small bar area with a couple of settees, airy back conservatory restaurant, games; piped music; side terrace and back garden *(Michael Dandy, M Thomas)*

Silver Cup AL5 2JF [St Albans Rd (A1081)]: Friendly neatly refurbished pub with four real ales such as Courage, St Austell Tribute and Wells & Youngs, good choice of wines by the glass, wide choice of food from sandwiches and pubby favourites to good upscale contemporary dishes, ample breakfast even for non-residents, attentive service, bare-boards bar and carpeted dining area, prints of old Harpenden; quiet piped music, TVs in bar; tables outside, four bedrooms, open all day from 7.30 *(Michael Dandy, Dr David Cockburn, Ian Arthur)*

☆ *White Horse* AL5 2JP [Hatching Green]: Timbered building well refurbished as smart dining pub, attractive modern furniture and décor though keeping log fire and original fabric, good food inc good value counter tapas and unusual dishes, front bar with Fullers London Pride and Tring Brock, good helpful service, daily papers; piped music; terrace tables *(Judi Lambeth, Michael Dandy)*

HEMEL HEMPSTEAD [TL0411]

☆ *Crown & Sceptre* HP2 6EY [Bridens Camp; leaving on A4146, right at Flamstead/ Markyate sign opp Red Lion]: New tenants in neatly refurbished rambling pub with well kept Greene King ales, enjoyable pubby food, friendly staff, log fires; children and dogs welcome, garden with play area, heated front picnic-sets, good walks, open all day summer wknds *(LYM, Ross Balaam)*

Olde Chequers HP2 6HH [Gaddesden Row; N, towards Markyate]: Well kept Adnams Bitter and Broadside and Greene King Abbot, good range of wines by the glass, generous sensibly priced usual food from sandwiches up, helpful service, small bar, large back dining areas with a mix of furnishings on carpet, flagstones or bare boards, log fires; garden picnic-sets and play area *(Michael Dandy, Giles Barr, Eleanor Dandy)*

HERTFORD [TL3212]

Old Barge SG14 1QD [The Folly]: Long low pub with main bar and tables outside (inc back ones covered for smokers) overlooking River Lee Navigation canal, Black Sheep, St Austell Tribute and Wells & Youngs, reasonably priced food from good freshly baked rolls up, lots of barge pictures etc; games machines; open all day *(LYM, Pat and Tony Martin)*

☆ *Old Cross Tavern* SG14 1JA [St Andrew St]: Chatty former antiques shop, very popular for its seven or eight particularly well kept real ales inc Dark Star, farm cider and perry, good home-made lunchtime food, cosy olde-worlde feel with settle, coal fire, brass, china etc, no music; dogs welcome, small heated back terrace, open all day *(Tony Hobden, N R White, Ian Arthur)*

HEXTON [TL1030]

Raven SG5 3JB [signed off B655]: Part of attractive mock-Tudor estate village, very popular for wide range of good value eclectic food from baguettes to swordfish and steaks, two children's menus, friendly efficient service, real ales such as Black Sheep, Fullers London Pride, Potton and Wadworths 6X, good choice of wines by the glass, open fire, plenty of dining tables in four linked areas, oil paintings (some for sale); piped music; big garden with heated terrace, barbecue, good play area *(Michael Dandy, Gordon Tong)*

HIGH WYCH [TL4614]

Rising Sun CM21 0HZ: Cosy old-fashioned local, serving hatch to carpeted lounge with log fire, central area with Courage Best, Mighty Oak and guest beers tapped from the cask, friendly landlord and locals, bar food (not Sun evening or Mon), bare-boards games room (children allowed) with darts and woodburner, no mobile phones; small garden *(the Didler, Pete Baker)*

HITCHIN [TL1828]
Sun SG5 1AF [Sun St]: Beamed and timbered bar with mix of furniture inc sofas, Greene King IPA and Abbot, good choice of wines by the glass, adjacent brasserie; piped music; courtyard tables *(Michael Dandy)*
KIMPTON [TL1718]
White Horse SG4 8RJ [High St]: Welcoming comfortably refurbished pub with good value food from pubby favourites to lots of fresh fish and seafood, friendly helpful service, nice old-fashioned traditional feel combined with fresh light décor, McMullens and a guest ale, good value small bottles of wine, log fire, airy and spotless dining area, darts in games area up a few steps, exemplary lavatories; some tables out by road or car park *(Mr and Mrs R A Buckler, David and Ruth Shillitoe, A Scowcroft)*
KINGS LANGLEY [TL0703]
Young Pretender WD4 8BR [Hempstead Rd]: Popular food inc good value carvery and OAP lunches, Greene King IPA *(anon)*
KNEBWORTH [TL2320]
☆ *Lytton Arms* SG3 6QB [Park Lane, Old Knebworth]: Spotless big-windowed rooms around large central servery, several changing real ales, two farm ciders, good choice of wines, good value food from interesting choice of sandwiches, baguettes and baked potatoes up, friendly staff, good log fire, daily papers, conservatory; children and dogs welcome, picnic-sets on front terrace, back garden with play area, nice surroundings, open all day wknds *(Pat and Tony Martin, LYM, David and Ruth Shillitoe)*
LEMSFORD [TL2212]
Sun AL8 7TN: Rather smart low-beamed and timbered pub nr River Lea, friendly enthusiastic licensees, half a dozen well kept changing ales, enjoyable generous food up to giant steaks, Victorian prints *(Jerry Brown, Anthony and Marie Lewis, LYM)*
LEY GREEN [TL1624]
Plough SG4 8LA [Plough Lane]: Simple country local with well kept Greene King ales, no music; lovely big informal garden with verandah and tall trees, peaceful views *(Conor McGaughey)*
LITTLE GADDESDEN [SP9913]
Bridgewater Arms HP4 1PD [Nettleden Rd, off B4506]: Pleasant dining pub with reasonably priced food from sandwiches up, Greene King IPA and Abbot, good wine choice, good coffee, friendly service, daily papers, carpeted bar with log fire, smart separate restaurant, games in small bare-boards public area; garden tables, good walks from the door *(LYM, John and Penelope Massey Stewart)*
LITTLE HADHAM [TL4322]
Nags Head SG11 2AX [Hadham Ford, towards Much Hadham]: Popular 16th-c country dining pub with small linked heavily black-beamed rooms, wide choice of reasonably priced food, small bar with three Greene King beers and decent wines, restaurant down a couple of steps; children in eating

areas, tables in pleasant garden *(Gordon Neighbour, LYM, Charles Gysin)*
LONDON COLNEY [TL1803]
Green Dragon AL2 1RB [Waterside; just off main st by bridge at S end]: Good value generous straightforward food (not Sun), real ales such as Adnams, Fullers London Pride and Shepherd Neame Spitfire, decent wine, cheerful efficient service, lots of ancient timbers, beams and brasses, soft lighting, woodburner, separate dining room; prettily set riverside picnic-sets – would be even nicer without the parked cars *(LYM, Pat and Tony Martin)*
MARKYATE [TL0616]
Swan AL3 8PB [High St]: Unusual combination of pub and good pasta parlour in buildings of some age and character, friendly service *(Stan Edwards)*
MUCH HADHAM [TL4219]
☆ *Bull* SG10 6BU [High St]: Neatly kept dining pub with good food changing daily, good choice of wines by the glass inc champagne, Greene King IPA, kind cheerful service even when busy, inglenook log fire in unspoilt bar, attractive pastel décor in roomy and civilised dining lounge and back dining room; children welcome, good-sized garden *(LYM, Sally Gagen)*
NORTHCHURCH [SP9708]
George & Dragon HP4 3QL [High St (A4251 Berkhamsted—Tring)]: Traditional low-beamed 18th-c coaching inn, welcoming licensees, log fire, good value food from good soups and sandwiches up (snacks only, evenings), well kept Greene King IPA and Shepherd Neame Spitfire, games bar with pool and darts; tables in yard and big garden, heated smokers' shelter, opp church where Peter the Wild Boy is buried, open all day wknds *(Mike Turner)*
NUTHAMPSTEAD [TL4134]
☆ *Woodman* SG8 8NB [off B1368 S of Barkway]: Tucked-away thatched and weatherboarded village pub, welcoming and well run, sofa and other furnishings in comfortable unspoilt core with worn tiled floor, nice inglenook log fire, another fire opposite and 17th-c low beams and timbers, plainer extension, enjoyable home-made food (not Sun evening) inc good home-baked bread, efficient friendly service, interesting USAF memorabilia (nearby World War II airfield), inc a memorial outside; benches out overlooking tranquil lane, comfortable bedrooms, open all day Sat *(BB, Ms Alexander, Mrs P J Pearce)*
PICCOTTS END [TL0508]
Boars Head HP1 3AT [just off A4146 N of Hemel]: Traditional two-bar local with welcoming service, popular straightforward food, real ales; pretty garden *(Conor McGaughey)*
REDBOURN [TL1111]
Chequers AL3 7AD [St Albans Rd (A5183), nr M1 junction 9]: Small rebuilt Chef & Brewer family dining pub with thatch, flagstones and dark wood, Adnams Broadside, Everards

Tiger and Wells & Youngs Bombardier, good choice of wines by the glass, friendly service; piped music, games; large back terrace and small pleasant garden *(Michael Dandy, Giles Barr, Eleanor Dandy)*
Hollybush AL3 7DU [Church End]: Picturesque old pub popular for its home-made pubby food, good friendly service, Brakspears and Wychwood, black-beamed lounge with big brick fireplace and heavy wooden doors, larger area with some built-in settles; sunny garden (some M1 noise), pretty spot nr medieval church *(Conor McGaughey, Ross Balaam)*
SARRATT [TQ0499]
☆ *Boot* WD3 6BL [The Green]: Attractive and civilised early 18th-c tiled pub with enjoyable pubby food inc some hearty sandwiches and OAP lunchtime specials, well kept Greene King ales, cosily cheerful rambling bar with unusual inglenook, more modern dining room; good-sized garden, pleasant spot facing green, handy for Chess Valley walks *(Jack and Sandra Clarfelt, LYM, John Branston, C Galloway, Julia Keeley, Brian and Rosalie Laverick, Tom Evans)*
SAWBRIDGEWORTH [TL4815]
Bull CM21 9BX [Cambridge Rd]: Attractive décor with lots of brass and beams, interesting bric-a-brac inc greyhound racing trophies, welcoming staff, decent generous food, changing ales such as Shepherd Neame Spitfire *(John Walker)*
Gate CM21 9JJ [London Rd (A1184)]: 18th-c local brewing its own low-priced beers, good range of guests (hundreds of ceiling pump clips show how quickly they change), bank hol beer festivals with live music, farm cider, bargain coffee, cheap fresh lunchtime food (not every Sun), roomy and relaxed front bar, back bar with pool and darts, little snug tucked behind bar; sports TVs; open all day wknds *(Ron Deighton)*
SOUTH MIMMS [TL2201]
Black Horse EN6 3PS [Blackhorse Ln; off B556]: Beamed village pub with friendly service, well kept Greene King, good value home-made food inc Sun roast and speciality sweet pancakes *(R T and J C Moggridge, Tony Liles)*
SPELLBROOK [TL4817]
Three Horseshoes CM22 7SE [Spellbrook Lane E]: Spacious Chef & Brewer dining pub largely extended from thatched and very low-beamed core, attentive young staff, usual food, Fullers ESB and Marstons Nightwatchman, good choice of wines by the glass; lots of tables on lawns and terrace, bridge from streamside car park *(George Atkinson)*
ST ALBANS [TL1307]
Black Lion AL3 4SB [Fishpool St]: Enterprising contemporary food, continental lagers and good coffee in spacious and relaxing bar, modern while keeping 18th-c inn's old beams and other original features, smart newly redesigned restaurant; 16 bedrooms, useful parking *(Michael Dandy)*

Blue Anchor AL3 4RY [Fishpool St]: Good value sandwiches and other more ambitious food (not Sun evening), McMullens ales, attractive prices, welcoming landlord, daily papers, real fire, recent refurbishment giving flagstoned bar and modern restaurant extension; sizeable garden, handy for Roman remains *(Andy and Jill Kassube, the Didler, Michael Dandy)*
Farmers Boy AL1 1PQ [London Rd]: Tastefully refurbished bay-windowed pub with its own Alehouse brews, continental bottled beers, log fire, back open kitchen doing bar lunches, helpful staff; SkyTV; suntrap back terrace, open all day *(the Didler)*
Farriers Arms AL3 4PT [Lower Dagnall St]: Plain friendly two-bar local in no-frills old part, McMullens Mild and guest beers, bar food wkdys, lots of old pictures of the pub (Campaign for Real Ale started here in the early 1970s) *(Andy and Jill Kassube, the Didler)*
Fighting Cocks AL3 4HE [Abbey Mill Lane; through abbey gateway – you can drive down]: Much modernised odd-shaped former abbey gatehouse with well kept Black Sheep, Fullers London Pride and Greene King ales, decent food, friendly helpful service, sunken Stuart cockpit, some low heavy beams and panelling, big inglenook fires; piped music; children welcome, attractive public park beyond garden, open all day *(Michael Dandy, Canon Michael Bourdeaux, LYM, John Roots)*
Garibaldi AL1 1RT [Albert St; left turn down Holywell Hill past White Hart – car park left at end]: Busy friendly Fullers local with their ales and guest beers, good wines by the glass, lunchtime food (not Sun/Mon) inc some unusual dishes; children welcome, open all day *(the Didler, Andy and Jill Kassube, LYM)*
Lower Red Lion AL3 4RX [Fishpool St]: Convivial beamed local dating from 17th c (right-hand bar has the most character), up to eight or so well kept changing ales inc local Alehouse, imported beers, friendly staff, inexpensive lunchtime food inc sandwiches, speciality sausages and popular Sun roast, red plush seats and carpet, board games; no nearby parking; tables in good-sized back garden, bedrooms (some sharing bath), open all day Fri-Sun *(Pete Baker, the Didler, Andy and Jill Kassube)*
Peahen AL1 1NQ [London Rd]: Much modernised, with woody contemporary furniture and décor, good range of wines by the glass and of lagers alongside McMullens real ale, reasonably priced up-to-date bar food from sandwiches up; heated courtyard tables *(Michael Dandy)*
☆ *Plough* AL4 0RW [Tyttenhanger Green, off A414 E]: Village pub with well kept Fullers and half-dozen changing guest beers, friendly efficient staff, bargain straightforward lunchtime food, good log fire, interesting old beer bottles and mats, longcase clock, back conservatory; big

garden with play area *(LYM, the Didler, John and Joyce Snell, Nick and Clare)*

Portland Arms AL3 4RA [Portland St/Verulam Rd]: Relaxed local with good value home-made food using local produce, Fullers full beer range kept well, friendly licensees, big open fire *(Andy and Jill Kassube)*

Rose & Crown AL3 4SG [St Michaels St]: 16th-c, with low beams, timbers and panelling, good speciality lunchtime sandwiches and a few hot dishes, Adnams, Fullers London Pride and Shepherd Neame Spitfire, welcoming service, big log fire, small snug; piped music; children and dogs welcome, lots of tables and benches outside, pretty floral and ivy-hung back yard *(LYM, Mike and Jennifer Marsh, Michael Dandy, Pat and Roger Davies)*

☆ **Six Bells** AL3 4SH [St Michaels St]: Well kept rambling food pub with good fresh generous food from lunchtime ciabattas to interesting specials, nice relaxed atmosphere, cheerful attentive service even when busy, several well kept ales such as Black Sheep, low beams and timbers, log fire, quieter panelled dining room; children welcome, occasional barbecues in small back garden, handy for Roman Verulam Museum, open all day *(P M Newsome, LYM, John Silverman, Gordon Prince, Ross Balaam)*

Verulam Arms AL3 4QE [Lower Dagnall St]: Comfortable and enjoyable bistro-style pub with some interesting dishes on quickly changing blackboard (not Mon evening), three real ales, modern décor, open all day *(Andy and Jill Kassube)*

White Lion AL1 1RN [Sopwell Lane]: Good atmosphere in small friendly front bar and roomy linked lounge areas, enjoyable proper cooking (not Sun evening or Mon) inc interesting dishes, well kept ales such as Adnams and Wells & Youngs, darts and other games; big back garden, play area *(Andy and Jill Kassube, Gordon Prince)*

ST PAULS WALDEN [TL1922]

Strathmore Arms SG4 8BT [Whitwell Rd]: Enjoyable limited bar lunches, well kept Fullers London Pride, Woodfordes Wherry and several guests such as Buntingford, friendly landlord, good service, occasional beer festivals, games area; open all day Fri-Sun, cl Mon lunchtime *(Ross Balaam)*

STEVENAGE [TL2324]

Chequers SG1 3LL [High St]: Open-plan high-ceilinged Greene King pub, comfortable U-shaped bar, quick friendly service, good value usual food (not Sun) from sandwiches up; well kept sunny courtyard *(Gordon Tong)*

THERFIELD [TL3337]

☆ **Fox & Duck** SG8 9PN [signed off A10 S of Royston; The Green]: Open-plan bow-windowed pub with country chairs and big stripped-top dark tables on stone flooring, enjoyable food inc enterprising sandwiches, Greene King IPA, decent wines and coffee, friendly helpful staff, good-sized carpeted back restaurant, darts in smaller boarded

area on left (TV and games machine); bedrooms, garden with good play equipment, more picnic-sets out on front green, quiet village, pleasant walks nearby *(BB, Ross Balaam)*

WATER END [TL2204]

Old Maypole AL9 7TT [Warrengate Rd, off Swanland Rd N of M25 junction 23 (back rd to North Mymms/Welham Green from South Mymms service area)]: Attractive 16th-c split-level pub, low ceilings, big inglenook log fire, lots of brasses, miniatures and bric-a-brac, well kept Greene King IPA and Abbot, bar meals, friendly service, family room; outside tables *(Colin Moore)*

WATFORD [TQ0997]

Essex Arms WD17 3EG [Langley Way, Cassiobury Park]: Well run Ember Inn with good cheerful staff, pleasant layout, usual food and beer *(David M Smith)*

WELWYN [TL2316]

Wellington AL6 9LZ [High St, old village – not the Garden City]: Restaurant rather than pub, though it has a small bar with Greene King Ruddles County; good interesting food (all day Sun) from lunchtime sandwiches up, small helpings and sharing plates available, interesting choice of wines by the glass, good tea and coffee range, cheerful attentive staff, smart up-to-date décor, open fires; heated terrace *(Chris and Angela Buckell)*

White Hart AL6 9EN [Prospect Pl]: Nicely refurbished beamed bar in Georgian-faced hotel doing well under current management, food from sandwiches up, smart but friendly restaurant; 13 comfortable bedrooms *(David and Ruth Shillitoe)*

WESTON [TL2529]

Cricketers SG4 7DA [Damask Green Rd]: Enjoyable pubby food with particularly good chips, well kept Church End and Fullers London Pride, good friendly service, recently redecorated restaurant *(Ross Balaam)*

WHEATHAMPSTEAD [TL1714]

Bull AL4 8BS [High St]: Miller & Carter chain dining pub, refurbished while keeping original features, decent food, good choice of wines by the glass, real ales *(Giles Barr, Eleanor Dandy)*

WHITWELL [TL1821]

Maidens Head SG4 8AH [High St (B651)]: Nice staff in immaculate old-fashioned local with McMullens and guest beers, generous usual food from simple sandwiches up, good coffee, interesting key-ring collection; tables in safe children's garden *(David and Ruth Shillitoe)*

WILDHILL [TL2606]

Woodman AL9 6EA [off B158 Brookmans Pk—Essendon]: Simple tucked-away country local with friendly licensees, well kept McMullens and interesting changing guest ales, good soft drinks choice, darts, open-plan bar and small back parlour, popular wkdy bar lunches; TV; picnic-sets on long grassy bank above car park, walks from pub *(Tim Maddison, JJW, CMW)*

Isle of Wight

It's well worth trying a pint of the island's local beers while you're here. Subject to a break or two, beers have been brewed on the site of the Ventnor Brewery, using spring water from the chalky downs above, for well over 150 years. Goddards, established much more recently, is now even more widely available on the island, and you may also come across Yates. The other thing to look out for is fresh fish and seafood: think particularly of the Crab & Lobster in Bembridge, doing well under its new switched-on licensees. Many of the island's pubs are well geared for families. Quite a number now serve food all through the day, at least in summer – particularly useful when you're on holiday. Our two new main entries here do this: the Horse & Groom at Ningwood, and the interesting old Buddle at Niton. Whatever you are looking for, whether it's a light pubby snack, a full-blown restaurant meal or somewhere lovely to stay, you can't go wrong with the Seaview Hotel in Seaview. With its top-notch service, this stands in a league of its own. Once again, the Seaview Hotel is the Isle of Wight Dining Pub of the Year. A handful of pubs we'd note particularly in the Lucky Dip section at the end of the chapter are the Yarbridge Inn near Brading, Blacksmiths Arms near Carisbrooke, Clarendon at Chale, Fishermans Cottage at Shanklin and Chequers at Rookley.

ARRETON   SZ5386   MAP 2
White Lion
A3056 Newport—Sandown; PO30 3AA

Pleasantly pubby local with basic food and three real ales

There's a good feeling of welcoming local character at this white-painted old village house, run by its long-serving licensees who really care about their pub. The beamed lounge is quite traditional, with dark pink walls or stripped brick above stained pine dado, gleaming brass and horse tack, and lots of cushioned wheelback chairs on the patterned red carpet. The piped music tends to be very quiet and the public bar has a games machine and darts; Badger Best, Fullers London Pride and Timothy Taylors Landlord on handpump. There's also a restaurant, family room and stable room. The pleasant garden has a small play area. More reports please.

🍴 Straightforward but very tasty food is served in generous helpings and includes sandwiches, baguettes, ploughman's, soup, creamy garlic mushrooms, moules marinineres, chilli, lasagne, vegetable or chicken curry, haddock and chips, pie of the day, steaks, and a handful of specials such as duck breast with orange and brandy sauce and lamb stew. *Starters/Snacks: £3.50 to £5.95. Main Courses: £5.95 to £14.95. Puddings: £4.25*

Enterprise ~ Lease Chris and Kate Cole ~ Real ale ~ Bar food (12-9) ~ (01983) 528479 ~ Children welcome in family area ~ Dogs allowed in bar ~ Open 11-11; 12-10.30 Sun

Recommended by Neil Ingoe, Neil and Anita Christopher, Penny and Peter Keevil

---

Our website is: www.thegoodpubguide.co.uk

BEMBRIDGE   SZ6587   MAP 2

Crab & Lobster £ 🛏

Foreland Fields Road, off Howgate Road (which is off B3395 via Hillway Road); PO35 5TR

Seafood speciality and prime location draw crowds; pleasant bedrooms

The island offers few better places on a summer's day than the terrace outside this well
positioned inn. It's perched on low cliffs within yards of the shore, with great views over
the Solent. The dining area and some of the bedrooms share the same view. Inside it's
roomier than you might expect (just as well as it does get busy) and it's done out in an
almost parlourish style, with lots of yachting memorabilia, old local photographs, and a
blazing fire in winter months; darts, dominoes and cribbage. Flowers Original, Goddards
Fuggle-Dee-Dum and Greene King IPA are on handpump, with decent house wines, about
20 malt whiskies, farm cider and good coffee; piped music (even in the lavatories).

🍽 **Under new licensees, seafood dishes take in crab cakes, seafood tagliatelle, a mixed
seafood grill, hot or cold crab and lobster platters for two, and a half or whole lobster.
Other generously served meals include sandwiches (including very good crab ones),
several light bites such as pasta with chicken and pesto, assorted pâtés, ploughman's,
lasagne, vegetarian curry, mixed grill and steaks, and ice-cream sundaes.** *Starters/Snacks:
£4.25 to £6.95. Main Courses: £8.50 to £16.95. Puddings: £4.25*

Enterprise ~ Lease Eric and Belinda Dewey and Caroline and Ian Quekett ~ Real ale ~ Bar food
(12-2.30, 6-9(9.30 Fri, Sat)) ~ (01983) 872244 ~ Children welcome ~ Dogs allowed in bar ~
Open 11-11; 12-10.30 Sun; 11-3, 6-11 in winter ~ Bedrooms: £50S(£55B)/£85S(£90B)

*Recommended by Philip Vernon, Kim Maidment, Alan and Paula McCully, Dr Alan and Mrs Sue Holder, Mr and
Mrs H J Langley, Mrs Brenda Calver, Pam and Alan Neale*

BONCHURCH   SZ5778   MAP 2

Bonchurch Inn

*Bonchurch Shute; from A3055 E of Ventnor turn down to Old Bonchurch opposite Leconfield
Hotel; PO38 1NU*

**Unusual italian-owned establishment rambling around central courtyard; italian influence
in menu and wines**

On warm summer days, the paved and cobbled courtyard here, with its tables, fountain
and pergola, has a slightly continental feel. The bar, restaurant, family room and kitchens
are spread around a sheltered courtyard, and the entire set-up is snuggled below a steep,
rocky slope. The unusual layout derives from its 1840s Victorian origins as the stables for
the nearby manor house. The furniture-packed bar has a good chatty local atmosphere,
and conjures up images of salvaged shipwrecks, with its floor of narrow-planked ship's
decking, and seats like the ones that old-fashioned steamers used to have. A separate
entrance leads to the fairly basic family room (it's a bit cut off from the congenial
atmosphere of the public bar). As well as Scottish Courage Directors and Best tapped
from the cask, there are a couple of italian wines by the glass and a few french ones;
piped music, darts, shove-ha'penny, dominoes and cribbage. The pub owns a holiday flat
for up to six people.

🍽 **Tasty bar food includes italian dishes such as lasagne, tagliatelle carbonara, seafood
risotto or spaghetti, as well as traditional dishes such as sandwiches, soup, a good crab
cocktail, grilled plaice, chicken cordon bleu and steak; there is a £1 charge for credit
cards.** *Starters/Snacks: £4.50 to £6.75. Main Courses: £7.50 to £14.50. Puddings: £3.00 to
£5.50*

Free house ~ Licensees Ulisse and Gillian Besozzi ~ Real ale ~ Bar food ~ Restaurant ~
(01983) 852611 ~ Children in family room ~ Open 12-3, 6.30(7 Sun)-11 ~ Bedrooms: /£70B

Recommended by David Jackson, Mr and Mrs W W Burke, Dr D and Mrs B Woods

COWES
SZ5092   MAP 2

Folly

Folly Lane – which is signposted off A3021 just S of Whippingham; PO32 6NB

Glorious water views from very popular place with cheery family holiday atmosphere, moorings, and good range of food served from breakfast on

You need to arrive early as this bustling family friendly place does get very busy in summer. Rumour has it that the splendidly positioned building originated from a french sea-going barge that beached here during a smuggling run in the early 1700s. The laid-back timbered interior certainly gives the sense of a ship's below decks. Straightforward but atmospheric furnishings include wooden tables (ready to be danced on come Saturday night) and chairs, and stools at the bar. All in all this is a cheery lighthearted place, with happy hands-on staff. Greene King IPA and Old Speckled Hen and Goddards on handpump; pool and piped music. Idling away the time watching all the nautical activity on the wide Medina estuary from seats on a waterside terrace is a lovely way to spend a summer afternoon – big windows in the bar share the same views, and if you're using the river, they have moorings, a water taxi and showers – they even keep an eye on weather forecasts and warnings, and they've long-term parking on a field. Watch out for the sleeping policemen along the lane if you come by car.

⑪ **Breakfast is served first thing, followed by the lunchtime and (more substantial) evening menus. Dishes are sensibly priced and include sandwiches, fish and chips, beef and ale pie, stuffed peppers, seafood, chicken and chorizo paella, chicken and bacon salad, 7oz sirloin steak, with daily specials such as roast duck in blueberry and port sauce, and puddings such as belgian chocolate cheesecake and tiramisu.** *Starters/Snacks: £4.30 to £6.95. Main Courses: £6.90 to £14.00. Puddings: £3.65*

Greene King ~ Managers Andy and Cheryl Greenwood ~ Real ale ~ Bar food (9am-9.30pm(9pm Sun, 10pm Sat in summer)) ~ Restaurant ~ (01983) 297171 ~ Children welcome ~ Dogs welcome ~ Live music Sat evening ~ Open 11-11(12 Sat in summer); 12-10.30 Sun

Recommended by Mrs Romey Heaton, Mr and Mrs H J Langley

FRESHWATER
SZ3487   MAP 2

Red Lion ♀

Church Place; from A3055 at E end of village by Freshwater Garage mini-roundabout follow Yarmouth signpost, then take first real right turn signed to Parish Church; PO40 9BP

Good mix of locals and visiting diners, reasonable range of drinks, decent food and no under-11s at understated tucked-away pub

Though food is quite a draw, chatting locals occupying stools along the counter keep a pubby feel at this firmly run place. The not over-done but comfortably furnished open-plan bar has fires, low grey sofas and sturdy country-kitchen style furnishings on mainly flagstoned floors, and bare board flooring too. The well executed paintings hung round the walls (between photographs and china platters) are by the licensee's brother and are worth a look. Flowers Original, Shepherd Neame Spitfire, Wadworths 6X and a guest such as Goddards are kept under light blanket pressure, and the good choice of wines includes 16 by the glass. Fines on mobile phone users go to charity (they collect a lot for the RNLI); there's a games machine but no music. There are tables on a carefully tended grass and gravel area at the back (some under cover), beside which is the kitchen's herb garden, and a couple of picnic-sets in a quiet square at the front have pleasant views of the church. The pub is virtually on the Freshwater Way footpath that connects Yarmouth with the southern coast at Freshwater Bay.

⑪ **Food is listed on blackboards behind the bar. As well as lunchtime filled baguettes and ploughman's it might include whitebait, mushroom stuffed with spinach and goats cheese, battered cod and mushy peas, steak and ale pie, sausage and mash, halibut steak with lemon sauce, roast pork belly with apple sauce, rib-eye steak with brandy cream, and puddings such as lime and chocolate cheesecake and bread and butter pudding.** *Starters/Snacks: £5.00 to £10.00. Main Courses: £9.50 to £16.00. Puddings: £4.50 to £5.00*

Enterprise ~ Lease Michael Mence ~ Real ale ~ Bar food (12-2, 6.30(7 Sun)-9) ~
(01983) 754925 ~ Children over 10 ~ Dogs welcome ~ Open 11.30-3, 5.30-11; 11.30-4,
6-11 Sat; 12-3, 7-10.30 Sun

Recommended by Rob Winstanley, Chris Sale, Derek and Sylvia Stephenson, Mr and Mrs A Garforth, Alan and Paula McCully, Dr D and Mrs B Woods

HULVERSTONE
SZ3984   MAP 2

Sun
B3399; PO30 4EH

Lovely thatched building with terrific coastal views, down-to-earth old-world appeal and four quickly changing real ales

The unpretentiously traditional and low-ceilinged bar at this thatched whitewashed country pub is full of friendly chatter, has a blazing fire at one end (with horsebrasses and ironwork hung around the fireplace), a nice mix of old furniture on flagstones and floorboards, and brick stone and walls; piped music, darts and board games. Leading off from one end is the traditionally decorated more modern dining area, with large windows making the most of the view. Four quickly changing real ales come from quite a range of brewers; maybe Charles Wells, Shepherd Neame, Timothy Taylor and Wychwood. Staff are helpful and friendly. The building is in a captivating setting, with views from its charmingly secluded cottagey garden (which has a terrace and several picnic-sets) down to a wild stretch of coast. It's very well positioned for some splendid walks along the cliffs, and up Mottistone Down to the prehistoric Long Stone.

Bar food includes sandwiches, whitebait, ploughman's, sausage and mash, lasagne, curry, pie of day and mixed grill. The specials board might include duck and hoi-sin spring rolls, soup, griddled black pudding with cranberry dip, swordfish steak, whole trout and 8oz fillet steak. They also do an 'all you can eat' curry night on Thursdays, and Sunday roasts. *Starters/Snacks: £3.95 to £5.25. Main Courses: £6.45 to £13.95. Puddings: £4.15*

Enterprise ~ Lease Chris and Kate Cole ~ Real ale ~ Bar food (12-9) ~ (01983) 741124 ~
Children welcome ~ Dogs allowed in bar ~ Open 11-11; 12-10.30 Sun

Recommended by Guy and Caroline Howard, Alan and Paula McCully, Louise Locock, J Hilary

NINGWOOD
SZ3989   MAP 2

Horse & Groom
A3054 Newport—Yarmouth, a mile W of Shalfleet; PO30 4NW

Spacious family dining pub with enjoyable all-day food and excellent play area

The roomy interior at this welcoming pub is thoughtfully arranged, with comfortable leather sofas grouped around low tables, leather wing chairs gathered by the fire, and a nice mix of sturdy tables and chairs that are given plenty of space for a relaxing meal. Walls are pale pink, which works nicely with the old flagstone flooring. Greene King IPA, Goddards Special and Ringwood Best are kept under light blanket pressure; staff are friendly and helpful; piped music, games machine. There are plenty of tables in the garden, which has a great fun children's play area.

Good value food includes sandwiches, burgers, ploughman's, whitebait, prawn and smoked salmon cocktail, pie, curry and grilled fish of the day, battered fish and steaks. They have a thoughtful children's menu, offer free baby food, and do a very good value Sunday carvery. *Starters/Snacks: £3.95 to £5.95. Main Courses: £7.95 to £16.95. Puddings: £2.95 to £4.95*

Enterprise ~ Lease Pete Tigwell ~ Real ale ~ Bar food (12-9) ~ (01983) 760672 ~ Children welcome ~ Dogs welcome ~ Open 11-11; 12-10.30 Sun

Recommended by E Brooks, Guy and Caroline Howard

NITON
SZ5075   MAP 2

Buddle ◀

St Catherines Road, Undercliff; off A3055 just S of village, towards St Catherines Point; PO38 2NE

Distinctive stone pub with good food and half a dozen real ales; nice clifftop garden

With a little imagination, the bar with its heavy black beams, big flagstones, broad stone fireplace and massive black oak mantelbeam does conjure up the time when this rambling old pub was the haunt of notorious local smugglers, though these days its most adventurous visitors are more likely to be cyclists and walkers with their dogs (it's handy for the coast path). Old-fashioned captain's chairs are arranged around solid wooden tables, and its walls are hung with pewter mugs and the like. Along one side of the lawn, and helping to shelter it, is what they call the Smugglers' Barn, which doubles as a family dining area. Six real ales will probably include Adnams Best, Hampshire Pride of Romsey, Ringwood Fortyniner, Shepherd Neame Spitfire and Yates. You can look out over the cliffs from the well cared for garden, with its tables spread over the sloping lawn and stone terraces, and there is a good walk to the nearby lighthouse – at night you may be able to see the beam of light sweeping the sea far below.

🍴 **Food service can slow down a little when it's busy, but the very helpful staff keep you well informed. Tasty dishes include soup, garlic mushrooms, crab salad, pork and leek sausages, beer-battered cod, a pie and curry of the day, and steaks.** *Starters/Snacks: £3.95 to £5.95. Main Courses: £7.95 to £13.95. Puddings: £2.20 to £4.25*

Enterprise ~ Lease Stephen Clayton ~ Real ale ~ Bar food (12-2.45, 6-9; 12-9 July, Aug) ~ (01983) 730243 ~ Children welcome ~ Dogs welcome ~ Open 11-11(12 Sat); 12-10.30 Sun

Recommended by Louise Locock, Rob Winstanley, K Almond, Glenn and Gillian Miller

SEAVIEW
SZ6291   MAP 2

Seaview Hotel 🍽 ♌ 🛏

High Street; off B3330 Ryde—Bembridge; PO34 5EX
ISLE OF WIGHT DINING PUB OF THE YEAR

Well run small relaxed hotel with pubby food in informal bar, top-notch attentive service, good wine list, and lovely bedrooms

The simple pubby bar here offers a genuinely laid-back alternative to the more sophisticated (and very attractive) reception rooms as this smashing 200-year-old hotel. The entire establishment is a hugely civilised yet enjoyably relaxed place, with a bustling atmosphere and proper old-fashioned service. The comfortable front bar, with good soft furnishings, is modelled on a naval wardroom and is home to one of the most extensive private collections of naval pictures, photographs and artefacts to be found on the island. You'll need to wander through the hotel to reach the bar at the back, which, with its traditional wooden furnishings on bare boards, lots of seafaring paraphernalia around its softly lit ochre walls, and a log fire has a relaxing down-to-earth atmosphere. Drinks include Ventnor Golden and a guest on handpump, a good selection of malt whiskies, a farm cider (in summer) and a good wine list (including a couple from local vineyards); piped music, TV, darts and board games. Tables on little terraces on either side of the path to the front door take in glimpses of the sea and coast, and some of the comfortable bedrooms also have a sea view. If you run a tab they may ask to keep your credit car behind the bar.

🍴 **Very good well presented and generously served bar food includes soup, hot crab ramekin, filled baguettes, fish pie, venison and wild boar sausages and mash, creamed leek, mushroom and stilton gratin, sirloin steak, battered haddock and mushy peas, and puddings such as sticky toffee pudding and vanilla rice pudding with chocolate soup; Sunday roast. There is a much more elaborate restaurant menu.** *Starters/Snacks: £4.75 to £7.25. Main Courses: £12.00 to £14.95. Puddings: £5.25 to £6.95*

Free house ~ Licensee Andrew Morgan ~ Real ale ~ Bar food (12-2.30(3 Sat, Sun), 6.30-9.30) ~ Restaurant ~ (01983) 612711 ~ No children under five in restaurant ~ Dogs allowed in bar and bedrooms ~ Open 10am-11pm; 12-10.30 Sun; 10-3, 6-11 in winter ~ Bedrooms: £155B/£155B

Recommended by Steve and Liz Tilley, Rob Winstanley, Derek and Sylvia Stephenson

SHALFLEET   SZ4089   MAP 2

New Inn ♀ ◀
A3054 Newport—Yarmouth; PO30 4NS

Cheerful old pub with great fresh seafood, good beers and wines too

The strengths of this 18th-c former fisherman's haunt lie equally in its cheery welcome, good seafood and well kept beer. It is popular so you will need to book – there may even be double sittings in summer. The partly panelled flagstoned public bar has yachting photographs and pictures, a boarded ceiling, scrubbed pine tables and a log fire in the big stone hearth. The carpeted beamed lounge bar has boating pictures and a coal fire, and the snug and gallery have slate floors, bric-a-brac and more scrubbed pine tables. Goddards Fuggle-Dee-Dum and Ventnor Golden and a couple of guests such as Bass and Flowers Original are kept under a light blanket pressure, and they stock around 60 wines; piped music. More reports please.

🍴 **Big draws here are their famous seafood platter and crab and lobster salads, which are served alongside a dozen or so other fish dishes – there might be crab and prawn cocktail, grilled grey mullet with mustard and horseradish sauce and grilled sole with lime, ginger and rocket. Other dishes are fairly pubby and include sandwiches, baguettes, ploughman's, sausage and mash, lasagne, leek and potato bake and lamb steak with moroccan bean salad.** *Starters/Snacks: £4.95 to £6.95. Main Courses: £7.95 to £19.95. Puddings: £4.25 to £5.50*

Enterprise ~ Lease Mr Bullock and Mr McDonald ~ Real ale ~ Bar food (12-2.30, 6-9.30) ~ (01983) 531314 ~ Children welcome ~ Dogs welcome ~ Open 12-11(10.30 Sun)

Recommended by Philip Vernon, Kim Maidment, Andrew Stephenson, Steve and Liz Tilley

SHORWELL   SZ4582   MAP 2

Crown
B3323 SW of Newport; PO30 3JZ

Popular rambling pub with good choice of decent food and pretty stream-side garden with play area

Now under new ownership, this peaceful country pub is in a lovely tranquil village a few miles from the sea. Four pleasant rooms, either carpeted, tiled or flagstoned, spread around a central bar, and chatty regulars who gather here lend some local character. The beamed knocked-through lounge has blue and white china in an attractive carved dresser, old country prints on stripped stone walls, other individual furnishings, and a winter log fire with a fancy tile-work surround. Black pews form bays around tables in a stripped-stone room off to the left with another log fire; piped music. Five real ales will probably be Adnams Broadside, Flowers Original, Goddards Special, Ringwood Best and Fortyniner, all on handpump. A pretty tree-sheltered garden has closely spaced picnic-sets and white garden chairs and tables set out by a sweet little stream, which broadens out into a small trout-filled pool, and a decent children's play area within easy view. Needless to say such a lovely spot can draw the summer crowds.

🍴 **The new licensees have taken the food up a little notch, now mainly cooking from fresh, with more fresh seafood on offer: sandwiches, ploughman's, soup, pâté of the day, crab cocktail, lasagne, vegetable curry and fisherman's pie, with daily specials such as venison sausages on smoked bacon mash, lemon crusted mackerel, steak and kidney pie, lamb tagine, haddock kedgeree, pheasant with calvados and sage gravy, and puddings such as treacle tart, fruit crumble and local ice-creams.** *Starters/Snacks: £4.25 to £6.25. Main Courses: £7.25 to £15.95. Puddings: £4.25*

Enterprise ~ Lease Nigel and Pam Wynn ~ Real ale ~ Bar food (12-9 (maybe not all day in winter)) ~ (01983) 740293 ~ Children welcome ~ Dogs allowed in bar ~ Open 10.30(11.30 Sun)-11; may close afternoons in winter

Recommended by Stephen Moss, Mr and Mrs H J Langley, Louise Locock

VENTNOR   SZ5677   MAP 2

Spyglass 🍺

Esplanade, SW end; road down very steep and twisty, and parking nearby can be difficult – best to use the pay-and-display (free in winter) about 100 yards up the road; PO38 1JX

Interesting waterside pub with appealing seafaring bric-a-brac, half a dozen very well kept beers and enjoyable food

No matter what the season, this cheery place always seems to be brimming with customers. It's in a super position, perched on the wall just above the beach, and tables outside on a terrace have lovely views over the sea. There are strolls westwards from here along the coast towards the Botanic Garden as well as heftier hikes up on to St Boniface Down and towards the eerie shell of Appuldurcombe House. Inside, a fascinating jumble of seafaring memorabilia fills the snug quarry-tiled interior – anything from wrecked rudders, ships' wheels, old local advertisements and rope-makers' tools to stuffed seagulls, an Admiral Benbow barometer and an old brass telescope; games machine and piped music. Ringwood Best and Fortyniner and Ventnor Gold are well kept alongside a couple of guests such as Marstons Pedigree and Goddards Special. They may ask to keep your credit card behind the bar.

🍴 **Generous helpings of very tasty bar food are promptly served and include sandwiches, soup, seafood chowder, ploughman's, crab tart, sausages and mash, steak and kidney or fisherman's pie, sirloin steak, and seafood stew, as well as several seasonal fish dishes and crab and lobster salad.** *Starters/Snacks: £4.75 to £5.75. Main Courses: £5.75 to £13.95. Puddings: £4.50*

Free house ~ Licensees Neil and Stephanie Gibbs ~ Real ale ~ Bar food (12-9.30) ~ (01983) 855338 ~ Children welcome away from main bar area, not in bedrooms ~ Dogs allowed in bar ~ Open 10.30am-11pm ~ Bedrooms: /£70B

Recommended by Penny and Peter Keevil, Neil and Anita Christopher, Daniel and Lynda Friel, Glenn and Gillian Miller, Andrew Stephenson, Mr and Mrs H J Langley, Steve and Liz Tilley, Stephen Moss

LUCKY DIP

Besides the fully inspected pubs, you might like to try these Lucky Dips recommended to us and described by readers (if you do, please send us reports: feedback@thegoodpubguide.co.uk).

BEMBRIDGE [SZ6488]
Pilot Boat PO35 5NN [Station Rd/Kings Rd]: Harbourside pub attractively reworked in style of a ship, enjoyable food, Greene King Old Speckled Hen; tables out overlooking water or in pleasant courtyard *(Quentin and Carol Williamson)*
BRADING [SZ6086]
☆ ***Yarbridge Inn*** PO36 0AA [Yarbridge, W]: Small pub full of local railway memorabilia, even an overhead model railway; fine well described range of quickly changing interesting real ales, happy staff, enjoyable food esp home-made pizzas, good changing choice of wines by the glass; children welcome, garden tables, open all day Sun and summer *(Joan and Michel Hooper-Immins)*
CALBOURNE [SZ4286]
Sun PO30 4JA [Sun Hill]: Family-friendly old roadside pub with enjoyable sensibly priced

food, quick friendly service, varying real ales, cosy no-frills bar, plain lower-level extension, extensive views across Brighstone Forest *(Guy and Caroline Howard)*
CARISBROOKE [SZ4687]
☆ ***Blacksmiths Arms*** PO30 5SS [B3401 1.5 miles W]: Quiet hillside pub with friendly staff, great choice of good fresh specials, decent wines and cider, scrubbed tables in neat flagstoned front bars, good Solent views from simple family dining extension; children, dogs and walkers welcome, smallish back garden with play area, open all day *(LYM, Penny and Peter Keevil)*
Eight Bells PO30 1NR [High St]: Big and busy with enjoyable quickly served straightforward food, Goddards ale, pleasant atmosphere, efficient helpful service; children welcome, charming garden behind running down to lovely lake with lots of

waterfowl, play area, handy for castle
(Quentin and Carol Williamson)

CHALE [SZ4877]

☆ *Clarendon (Wight Mouse)* PO38 2HA [off
A3055/B3399]: Big efficient family dining
pub rambling around with flagstones here,
carpet there, modern-look woody extension
around attractive traditional core with log
fire, Badger ales from long bar, good value
food using local produce, fast friendly service,
plenty to keep children occupied; extensive
outdoor seating with play area, great views
out over cliffs, good bedrooms in adjoining
hotel (LYM, Guy and Caroline Howard)

FRESHWATER [SZ3285]

Highdown PO39 0HY [Highdown Lane, SW off
Moons Hill]: Comfortable carpeted bar with
several real ales, log fire, popular food inc
local fish, restaurant; four bedrooms, some
sharing bathroom (Chris Sale)

GODSHILL [SZ5381]

Griffin PO38 3JD [High St]: Carefully
restored old pub in honeypot village, good
for families yet with plenty of places if you
want to be quiet, generous well presented
standard food from good hot rolls up (maybe
a toy for kids if they finish their meal),
friendly helpful staff, several well kept beers,
good wine choice; darts, pool and machines;
good-sized garden with play area and maze
(Glenn and Gillian Miller)

ROOKLEY [SZ5183]

☆ *Chequers* PO38 3NZ [S of village, Chequers
Inn Rd/Niton Rd]: Well equipped family pub
with usual food all day from sandwiches up,
puddings cabinet, real ales such as Goddards
and Wadworths 6X, close-set tables in
unpretentious dining lounge with log fire,
good children's games in plain and roomy
family area, flagstoned locals' bar with pool,
darts and TV, mother-and-baby room;
children and dogs welcome, large fenced
play area, downland views, handy for
Godshill, open all day (LYM, Alan and
Paula McCully, Penny and Peter Keevil)

SHANKLIN [SZ5881]

☆ *Fishermans Cottage* PO37 6BN [bottom of
Shanklin Chine]: Thatched shoreside cottage
in terrific setting surrounded by beached
boats, tucked into the cliffs, steep walk
down beautiful chine, lovely seaside walk to
Luccombe; flagstones and some stripped
stone, repro furniture, nets slung from low
beams, old local pictures and bric-a-brac,
simple bar lunches from sandwiches and
baked potatoes up, more enterprising
evening choice (till 8), convivial
atmosphere, helpful staff, well kept
Goddards, frequent entertainment; piped
music; wheelchair access, children welcome,
tables out on terrace, open all day in
summer when fine (David Jackson,
Michael Tack, BB)

Steamer PO37 6BS [Esplanade]: Nautical-
theme bar, fun for holiday families, with
good range of real ales, enjoyable fresh food
inc local seafood, live music most wknds;
fine sea views from covered floodlit terrace,
bedrooms, open all day (Kevin Flack)

TOTLAND [SZ3286]

Broadway PO39 0BL [Broadway]: Friendly
and homely, with several well kept beers,
farm cider, usual bar food; children and dogs
welcome (Chris Sale)

VENTNOR [SZ5677]

Crab & Lobster PO38 1TP [Grove Rd]:
Comfortable brightly lit old pub full of old-
world memorabilia, current tenants doing
good value food in bar and restaurant inc
local fish, fast service, two well kept ales,
decent house wines; dogs welcome, open
all day (Mr and Mrs B Watt)

WOOTTON BRIDGE [SZ5492]

Sloop PO33 4HS [Mill Sq (A3054 Ryde—
Newport)]: Now a Vintage Inn, comfortable
and well laid out, with improved food,
friendly quick service, good choice of wines
by the glass, proper cider and real ale; nice
setting, fine views over tidal yacht moorings
(Penny and Peter Keevil)

Kent

This county – on our doorstep – has a lot of well run and genuinely friendly pubs, and good local beers. Shepherd Neame, Kent's main independent brewer, is thought to be Britain's oldest that's been brewing continuously. You'll also find good beers from two younger competitors, Larkins and Goachers, quite widely available, and the even more recently established Westerham and Gadds gaining ground. A sprinkling of other small breweries includes Whitstable, Hopdaemon and Swan on the Green. We have five new main entries here this year: the Great House in Hawkhurst (good enterprising food in this stylish dining pub), the Green Man at Hodsoll Street (lots going on thanks to its hard-working licensees, the lovely little Rock near Penshurst (home base for those Larkins beers), the handsome old George & Dragon at Speldhurst (good food and wines) and the Fox & Hounds up at Toys Hill (lovely surroundings, well liked honest food). Other pubs currently on top form include the Unicorn at Bekesbourne (a smashing little pub with friendly owners and homely food), the Three Chimneys just outside Biddenden (civilised but informal, with delicious food), the Timber Batts at Bodsham (run by a charming French landlord, with lovely french food and wines), two Brookland pubs, the Royal Oak (very enjoyable, with interesting décor) and the Woolpack (award-winning hanging baskets and good value, honest food), the Chaser in Shipbourne (smart but relaxed, with a good choice of beers and food), the Red Lion at Snargate (in the same family for nearly a century), the Lord Raglan in Staplehurst (a bustling and friendly country pub), and the Red Lion at Stodmarsh (eccentric and interesting, with super food). Plenty of Kent pubs guarantee a good meal, whether homely and good value or imaginative and ahead of the trends. As well as the Three Chimneys, Timber Batts, Chaser and Red Lion, all mentioned above, other pubs to head for are the Harrow on Ightham Common and Sankeys in Tunbridge Wells. The charming old Three Chimneys near Biddenden is our Kent Dining Pub of the Year. The Lucky Dip section at the end of the chapter is a strong one: we'd particularly note the Dolphin in Canterbury, Bohemian in Deal, Kentish Rifleman at Dunks Green, Carpenters Arms at Eastling, Green Cross near Goudhurst, Duke William at Ickham, Cock at Luddesdown, Sportsman in Seasalter and Bell at Smarden.

Real ale may be served from handpumps, electric pumps (not just the on-off switches used for keg beer) or – common in Scotland – tall taps called founts (pronounced 'fonts') where a separate pump pushes the beer up under air pressure.

BEKESBOURNE

TR1856   MAP 3

Unicorn

Coming from Patrixbourne on A2, turn left up Bekesbourne Hill after passing railway line (and station); coming from Littlebourne on A257, pass Howletts Zoo – Bekesbourne Hill is then first turning on right; turning into pub car park is at bottom end of the little terrace of houses on the left (the pub is the far end of this terrace); CT4 5ED

Small, friendly pub, simply furnished bars and enjoyable food

Much enjoyed by our readers, this is a cosy little pub with friendly owners and really good homely food. There are just a few scrubbed old pine tables and bentwood café chairs on worn floorboards, a canary ceiling and walls above a dark green dado, minimal décor, and a handful of bar stools against the neat counter. Adnams Broadside and Shepherd Neame Master Brew on handpump, a carefully chosen wine list, local cider, apple and pear juice and a fair choice of coffees and teas; plenty of board games, piped music and a piano in one corner. A side terrace is prettily planted and there's a garden with benches and boules. Parking in front is tricky but there is a large car park at the back reached from the small track at the end of the adjacent terrace of cottages.

Ⅱ Popular bar meals include filled baguettes, soup, avocado and bacon salad, grilled mushrooms with stilton, gammon and egg, local sausages with onion gravy, cod in beer batter, liver and bacon, well liked steak in ale pie, daily specials such as lamb shank with rosemary, fish pie, thai chicken curry or fried bass in lemon butter sauce, and puddings such as lemon and almond torte with honeycomb ice-cream and fruit crumble.
Starters/Snacks: £3.95 to £4.95. Main Courses: £7.95 to £13.95. Puddings: £3.95 to £4.50

Free house ~ Licensees Mike and Monica Head ~ Real ale ~ Bar food (not Sun evening or Mon or Tues) ~ No credit cards ~ (01227) 830210 ~ Children welcome ~ Open 12-3, 6-11; 12-3 Sun; closed Sun evening, all day Mon and Tues

Recommended by Catherine and Rob Dunster, R J Anderson, Emma Ryan, Kevin Thorpe, Mr and Mrs G Wolstenhulme, Brian Munday, Laurence John, N R White, Basil Wynbergen

BIDDENDEN

TQ8238   MAP 3

Three Chimneys

A262, 1 mile W of village; TN27 8LW
KENT DINING PUB OF THE YEAR

Pubby beamed rooms of considerable individuality, log fires, imaginative food and pretty garden

This is a particularly well run pub and much enjoyed by our readers. It's a pretty, old-fashioned cottage with a series of low-beamed, very traditional little rooms with plain wooden furniture and old settles on flagstones and coir matting, some harness and sporting prints on the stripped brick walls and good log fires. The atmosphere is civilised and relaxed and service is friendly and efficient. Adnams Best, a seasonal beer from Harveys and a changing guest tapped straight from casks racked behind the counter, several wines by the glass, local cider and apple juice and ten malt whiskies. The simple public bar has darts, dominoes and cribbage. French windows in the candlelit bare-boards restaurant open on to the garden (ploughman's only out here) with picnic-sets in dappled shade, and the smart terrace area has tables and outdoor heaters. Sissinghurst Gardens are nearby.

Ⅱ Extremely good – if not cheap – bar food includes soup, ploughman's, baked field mushrooms with caramelised red onions and grilled goats cheese, deep-fried breadcrumbed brie with fruity cumberland sauce, sunblush tomato couscous topped with balsamic roast vegetables with grilled goats cheese, local port and sage sausages with red onion gravy, lambs liver and bacon, roast duck breast with bubble and squeak mash and a rich port sauce, roast cod fillet in brown butter with capers, lemon and prawns, rib-eye steak with béarnaise sauce, and puddings like apple and plum crumble and crème brûlée.
Starters/Snacks: £3.95 to £8.95. Main Courses: £11.95 to £17.95. Puddings: £4.50 to £6.50

Free house ~ Licensee Craig Smith ~ Real ale ~ Bar food ~ Restaurant ~ (01580) 291472 ~ Dogs welcome ~ Open 11.30-3, 6-11; 12-3.30, 6.30-10.30 Sun; closed 25 and 31 Dec

Recommended by Cathryn and Richard Hicks, Mr and Mrs Mike Pearson, B Forster, Oliver and Sue Rowell, M G Hart, the Didler, John Evans, Robin and Glenna Etheridge, Louise English, N R White, Jeff and Wendy Williams, Kevin Thorpe, Michael Doswell

BODSHAM
TR1045   MAP 3

Timber Batts 🍴 ♀

Following Bodsham, Wye sign off B2068 keep right at unsigned fork after about 1.5 miles; TN25 5JQ

Lovely french food (bar snacks too) and charming French owner in cottagey old country pub, good real ales, enjoyable wines and fine views

The charming French landlord in this 15th-c former farmhouse remains keen to keep a proper pubby feel and local drinkers in the public bar – despite a strong emphasis on the extremely good french food. The little heavy-beamed cottagey area to the right has a couple of comfortable armchairs and two wicker chairs each with a small table, an open fire in the brick fireplace with photographs of the pub above it, some hunting horns and a few high bar chairs; down a little step is more of a drinking part with a mix of cushioned dining chairs, a wall settle, two long tables and several bar stools. There are various froggy cushions and knick-knacks on the window sills (the pub is known locally as Froggies at the Timber Batts). To the left of the entrance is the large but informal beamed restaurant with a happy mix of attractive stripped pine tables and pews and all sorts of dark tables and dining chairs on the carpet, wine labels in a glass frame and wine box tops on the walls, a nice stripped pine cupboard in one corner, and a brick fireplace. Adnams Bitter, Fullers London Pride and Woodfordes Wherry on handpump and very good french wines by the glass (some from Mr Gross's cousin's vineyard). This hilltop pub is tucked away in lovely country with fine wide-spreading valley views from straightforward seats and tables in the back garden.

🍴 **As well as pubby choices such as filled baguettes, croque monsieur, omelettes, ham and egg, moules marinières and frites, and sausage and mash, the delicious french food using top local produce (cooked by the landlord's son) might include interesting soup, quail supreme wrapped in parma ham, duo of scallops and prawns, duck foie gras terrine, whitstable rock oysters, duck leg confit, beef bourguignonne, pheasant poached in cider, wild halibut in cider cream sauce, roasted rack of local lamb, and puddings such as crêpe suzette and tarte tatin (apricot in season or apple); lovely french cheeses. They list their suppliers on their menu; two- and three-course set Sunday lunch.** *Starters/Snacks: £6.00 to £8.50. Main Courses: £8.00 to £22.00. Puddings: £6.00 to £6.50*

Free house ~ Licensee Joel Gross ~ Real ale ~ Bar food (12-2.30, 7-9.30(9 Sun)) ~ Restaurant ~ (01233) 750237 ~ Children welcome ~ Dogs welcome ~ Open 12-3, 6.30-11; 12-3, 7-10.30 Sun; closed 24 Dec-3 Jan

Recommended by Derek Thomas, Virginia Williams

BOUGH BEECH
TQ4846   MAP 3

Wheatsheaf ♀ ◧

B2027, S of reservoir; TN8 7NU

Ex-hunting lodge with lots to look at, fine range of local drinks, popular food and plenty of seats in appealing garden

There's a lot of history and masses of interesting things to look at in this warmly welcoming, bustling pub. The neat central bar and the long front bar (with an attractive old settle carved with wheatsheaves) have unusually high ceilings with lofty oak timbers, a screen of standing timbers and a revealed king post; dominoes and board games. Divided from the central bar by two more rows of standing timbers – one formerly an outside wall to the building – are the snug and another bar. Other similarly aged features include a piece of 1607 graffiti, 'Foxy Holamby', thought to have been a whimsical local squire. On the walls and above the massive stone fireplaces there are quite a few horns and heads as well as a sword from Fiji, crocodiles, stuffed birds, swordfish spears and a matapee. Thoughtful touches include piles of smart magazines, tasty nibbles and winter chestnuts to roast. Harveys Best and from a village just three miles away, Westerham Brewery British Bulldog and Grasshopper Kentish Bitter on handpump, three farm ciders (one from nearby Biddenden), a decent wine list, several malt whiskies, summer Pimms and winter mulled wine. Outside is appealing too, with plenty of seats, flowerbeds and fruit trees in the sheltered side and back gardens. Shrubs help divide the garden into various areas, so it doesn't feel too crowded even when it's full.

🍴 **As well as light lunchtime dishes such as filled ciabattas, ploughman's, smoked haddock and spring onion fishcakes with lemon and parsley butter sauce and pie and mash, the popular food (using Kent or Sussex reared meat) includes falafels with chilli dip, hummus, mint yoghurt and pitta bread, moules marinières, honey-roast ham and egg, aberdeen angus beefburger, vegetable curry, poached smoked haddock on mash and spinach with a citrus cream sauce, lambs liver with bacon and black pudding, pork fillet with a cider, chestnut, bacon and cream sauce, and puddings such as chocolate tart and apple and blackberry crumble.** *Starters/Snacks: £5.95 to £9.95. Main Courses: £8.95 to £15.95. Puddings: £3.95 to £4.50*

Enterprise ~ Lease Liz and David Currie ~ Real ale ~ Bar food (12-10) ~ (01732) 700254 ~ Children welcome in one part of bar only ~ Dogs welcome ~ Open 11am-11.30pm(midnight Sat, 11pm Sun)

Recommended by Bob and Margaret Holder, Grahame Brooks, R and M Thomas, Mike and Sue Losebey, Oliver and Sue Rowell, Michael and Maggie Betton, Tina and David Woods-Taylor, Peter and Heather Elliott, B J Harding, Tom and Jill Jones

BOYDEN GATE   TR2265   MAP 3

Gate Inn ★ 🍺 £

Off A299 Herne Bay—Ramsgate – follow Chislet, Upstreet signpost opposite Roman Gallery; Chislet also signposted off A28 Canterbury—Margate at Upstreet – after turning right into Chislet main street keep right on to Boyden; the pub gives its address as Marshside, though Boyden Gate seems more usual on maps; CT3 4EB

Friendly, long-serving landlord in unchanging pub, well kept beers, simple food, and tame ducks and geese to feed

Right on the edge of the marshes, this unspoilt, traditional pub thankfully does not change at all from year to year. It's been run by the same landlord for 34 years now and you can be quite sure of a genuinely warm welcome – whether you are a regular or a visitor. The comfortably worn interior is properly pubby with an inglenook log fire serving both the well worn quarry-tiled rooms, flowery-cushioned pews around tables of considerable character, hop bines hanging from the beams and attractively etched windows. Shepherd Neame Master Brew, Spitfire and a seasonal ale are tapped from the cask and you can also get interesting bottled beers, and half a dozen wines by the glass; board games. The sheltered hollyhock flowered garden is bounded by two streams with tame ducks and geese (they sell bags of food, 10p), and on fine summer evenings you can hear the contented quacking of a multitude of ducks and geese, coots and moorhens out on the marshes. More reports please.

🍴 **Tasty bar food includes lots of different sandwiches and melts, soup, a big choice of baked potatoes and burgers, ploughman's, home-made vegetable flan, spicy hotpots and gammon and egg.** *Starters/Snacks: £0.75 to £4.80. Main Courses: £5.85 to £9.95. Puddings: £3.00*

Shepherd Neame ~ Tenant Chris Smith ~ Real ale ~ Bar food (12-2, 6(7 Sun)-9) ~ No credit cards ~ (01227) 860498 ~ Well behaved children in eating area of bar and family room ~ Dogs welcome ~ Open 11-2.30(3 Sat), 6-11; 12-4, 7-10.30 Sun

Recommended by Kevin Thorpe

Stars after the name of a pub show exceptional quality. One star means most people (after reading the report to see just why the star has been won) would think a special trip worth while. Two stars mean that the pub is really outstanding – for its particular qualities it could hardly be bettered.

BROOKLAND

TQ9825 MAP 3

Royal Oak

Just off A259 Rye—New Romney; High Street; TN29 9QR

Lovely old building with carefully modernised rooms, comfortable atmosphere, good bar food and garden

Doing extremely well and much enjoyed by our readers, this is a well proportioned cream-painted pub with ancient architectural features mixed with contemporary interior design. The bar is light and airy with creamy walls, pale solid timbering and lovely big windows hung with forest green velvet curtains. Leather upholstered chairs around oak tables and one nice old pew spread over a floor surface that runs from flagstones into oak boards then bricks; piped music and woodburner too. Locals pop in all evening to sit at the granite-topped counter (with Adnams and Harveys Sussex on handpump) on high cream leather backed bar stools and chat to the informative landlord – do ask him about the local area if you get a chance. His equestrian interests are manifest in a lovely set of racing watercolours and a couple of signed photographs on the lime white wall panelling in the bar, and in a rather special set of Cecil Aldin prints displayed in the restaurant (with its well spaced tables and big inglenook fireplace). French windows from here open on to a terrace with metal chairs and there are picnic-sets in the narrow garden which is laid out around a terrace; quaint views of the ancient church and graveyard next door.

🍴 Good, popular bar food includes bar snacks (not Saturday evening or Sunday lunchtime) such as filled baguettes, deep-fried squid rings with home-made tartare sauce, beer-battered cod fillet, home-cooked honey roasted ham with two local free-range eggs and free-range thai green chicken curry; there's also soup, fried prawns marinated in garlic and olive oil, pasta with buffalo mozzarella, cherry tomatoes, basil and olives, a trio of cumberland sausages with black pudding and onion gravy, braised shank of local lamb with rosemary mash and rich juniper berry sauce, grilled fresh fillet of cod with tomato, caper and lemon sauce and puddings like whisky and raisin bread and butter pudding and chocolate and Amaretto slice. *Starters/Snacks: £4.95 to £8.75. Main Courses: £7.95 to £10.50. Puddings: £5.25 to £5.95*

Enterprise ~ Lease David Rhys Jones ~ Real ale ~ Bar food (12-2.30, 6.30-9.30; not Sun evening) ~ Restaurant ~ (01797) 344215 ~ Well behaved children allowed; not in restaurant Fri or Sat evenings ~ Dogs allowed in bar ~ Open 12-3, 6-11; closed Sun evening ~ Bedrooms: /£60(£70B)

Recommended by Craig Turnbull, B and M Kendall, Peter Meister, Mr and Mrs Mike Pearson, V Brogden

Woolpack

On A259 from Rye, about 1 mile before Brookland, take the first right turn signposted Midley where the main road bends sharp left, just after the expanse of Walland Marsh; OS Sheet 189 map reference 977244; TN29 9TJ

15th-c pub with simple furnishings, massive inglenook fireplace, big helpings of tasty food and large garden

The award-winning hanging baskets in front of this pretty white pub are really quite a sight in summer and there are plenty of picnic-sets under parasols in the attractive garden with its barbecue area; it's all nicely lit up in the evenings. Inside, there's plenty of marshland character and a good, friendly bustling atmosphere. The ancient entrance lobby has an uneven brick floor and black-painted pine-panelled walls, and to the right, the simple quarry-tiled main bar has basic cushioned plank seats in the massive inglenook fireplace (with a lovely log fire on chilly days), a painted wood-effect bar counter hung with lots of water jugs and some very early ships' timbers (maybe 12th c) in the low-beamed ceiling; a long elm table has shove-ha'penny carved into one end and there are other old and newer wall benches, chairs at mixed tables with flowers and candles and photographs of locals on the walls. To the left of the lobby is a sparsely furnished little room and an open-plan family room; piped music. Shepherd Neame Master Brew, Spitfire and a seasonal brew on handpump; look out for the two pub cats, Liquorice and Charlie Girl.

🍴 Good value, honest bar food includes sandwiches, filled baguettes and baked potatoes, ploughman's, soup, garlic mushrooms, sausages, ham and egg, steak pie, vegetable curry, spaghetti bolognese, battered cod, moules marinières, lovely summer crab salad, and puddings such as honey and cinnamon pudding or bitter chocolate and orange sponge. *Starters/Snacks: £4.50 to £7.95. Main Courses: £7.45 to £16.95. Puddings: £4.50*

Shepherd Neame ~ Tenant Barry Morgan ~ Real ale ~ Bar food (12-2.30, 6-9; all day weekends) ~ (01797) 344321 ~ Children in family room ~ Dogs welcome ~ Open 11-3, 6-11; 11-11 Sat; 12-11 Sun

Recommended by Kevin Thorpe, Tim and Claire Woodward, V Brogden, Mike Gorton, Louise English, Arthur Pickering, Adrian Johnson, Conrad Freezer, Dave Braisted

GROOMBRIDGE   TQ5337   MAP 3

Crown

B2110; TN3 9QH

Charming village pub with quite a bit of bric-a-brac in snug, low-beamed rooms, and enjoyable food and drink

---

Part of a row of pretty tile-hung cottages, this friendly pub has picnic-sets out in front on a wonky but sunny brick terrace that overlooks the steep village green. Inside, the snug left-hand room has old tables on worn flagstones and a big brick inglenook with a cosy winter log fire – arrive early for a table in here. The other low-beamed rooms have roughly plastered walls, some squared panelling and timbering, and a quite a bit of bric-a-brac, from old teapots and pewter tankards to antique bottles. Walls are decorated with small topographical, game and sporting prints and there's a circular large-scale map with the pub at its centre. The end dining room has fairly close-spaced tables with a variety of good solid chairs, and a log-effect gas fire in a big fireplace. Three ales from Harveys, Larkins and Pilgrims on handpump and up to ten wines by the glass. There's a back car park and pub garden. A public footpath across the road beside the small chapel leads through a field to Groombridge Place Gardens.

🍴 Well liked bar food at lunchtime includes filled baguettes and baked potatoes, bruschetta and ploughman's, cumberland sausage with onion gravy, beer-battered haddock and home-cooked ham and eggs, as well as popular pasta dishes, good steak pie and more elaborate evening choices like smoked duck breast with apple and celeriac remoulade and walnuts and rump of lamb with rosemary potatoes and red wine jus. *Starters/Snacks: £5.25 to £6.90. Main Courses: £7.50 to £10.00. Puddings: £4.50*

Free house ~ Licensee Peter Kilshaw ~ Real ale ~ Bar food (12-2.30(3 Sat and Sun), 6.30-9(9.30 Sat); not Sun evening) ~ (01892) 864742 ~ Children welcome ~ Dogs allowed in bar ~ Open 11-3, 6-11; 11-11 Sat; 12-10.30 Sun; 12-5 Sun in winter; closed winter Sun evening ~ Bedrooms: £40/£45(£60S)

Recommended by B J Harding, N R White, Mrs Margo Finlay, Jörg Kasprowski

HAWKHURST   TQ7531   MAP 3

Great House ♀

Gills Green; pub signed just off A229 N; TN18 5EJ

Emphasis on good bistro-style food, drinkers' area too, several wines by the glass, attractive furnishings and plenty of space

---

Although there's much emphasis on the good food in this attractive white-weatherboarded pub, locals do pop in for a pint and a chat. Just inside the main door are a couple of heavy-beamed small drinking areas with sofas, armchairs, and bright scatter cushions, and there are high-backed bar chairs by the counter where they serve well kept Harveys Best on handpump; good wines by the glass. There are some dark wooden slatted dining tables and smart clothed dining chairs on the slate floor, gilt-framed pictures on the red or green walls, and a small brick fireplace. Stairs lead down to a light and airy dining room with big windows all round, carved, built-in seating with more colourful cushions and high-backed leather dining chairs around various wooden tables; Farrow & Ball paintwork and plenty of modern art. The atmosphere throughout is relaxed and chatty and the French staff are friendly. Outside on the terrace are some turquoise seats and tables.

🍴 **Good bistro-style food includes bar snacks (which might not be available if they are very busy on Friday or Saturday evenings) such as filled panini, ploughman's, cheese and ham omelette, sausage and mash with onion gravy and fish and chips, as well as several deli boards, soup, home-cured gravadlax, ballotine of foie gras with sultanas, chutney and brioche, seared scallops with tomato, bacon, orange and carrot sauce, interesting summer salads, chicken breast with parsley risotto and asparagus, pork belly with olive mash, roast apple and red wine sauce, sweet and sour duck magret with mango, coriander and noodles, and puddings like chocolate brownie with chocolate sauce and raspberry crème brûlée and a sable biscuit; popular Sunday roasts.** *Starters/Snacks: £4.45 to £8.75. Main Courses: £9.95 to £19.50. Puddings: £5.50 to £5.95*

Free house ~ Licensees Martial and Natasha Chaussy ~ Real ale ~ Bar food ~ Restaurant ~ (01580) 753119 ~ Children welcome ~ Dogs allowed in bar ~ Open 12-11

Recommended by BOB

HODSOLL STREET
TQ6263 MAP 3

Green Man

Hodsoll Street and pub signed off A227 S of Meopham; turn right in village; TN15 7LE

Bustling pub by village green, friendly atmosphere, lots of food specials, real ales and seats in garden

You can be sure of a friendly welcome from the hard-working licensees in this popular pub. There are big airy carpeted rooms that work their way around a hop-draped central bar, traditional neat tables and chairs spaced tidily around the walls, interesting old local photographs and antique plates on the walls, and a warm winter log fire; piped music. Greene King Old Speckled Hen, Harveys Best, Timothy Taylors Landlord and a changing guest on handpump and decent wines. The summer tubs and hanging baskets are pretty and there are seats on the well tended lawn; maybe summer morris dancers. The nearby North Downs have plenty of walks.

🍴 **As well as a popular two-course weekday lunch, they hold themed food evenings and lunchtime and evening Sunday roasts. Other generous dishes include lunchtime sandwiches, filled baguettes and wraps, soup, tempura prawns with sweet chilli sauce, chicken liver pâté, steak and kidney filo pie, spinach and ricotta tortellini in mushroom sauce, chicken breast stuffed with brie and topped with bacon, beer-battered cod, lamb shank in red wine jus, meat or fish mixed grill and daily specials.** *Starters/Snacks: £4.00 to £8.00. Main Courses: £9.00 to £14.00. Puddings: £4.50*

Enterprise ~ Lease John, Jean and David Haywood ~ Real ale ~ Bar food (12-2.30(3 weekends), 6.30-9.30) ~ (01732) 823575 ~ Children welcome ~ Dogs welcome ~ Live music second Thurs of month ~ Open 11-2.30, 6-11; 11-11 Sat; 12-10.30 Sun

Recommended by Martin Smith, Pat and Barbara Stancliffe, E D Bailey, M Greening, Annette Tress, Gary Smith, Jan and Rod Poulter, Jan and Alan Summers

HOLLINGBOURNE
TQ8354 MAP 3

Windmill

A mile from M20, junction 8: A20 towards Ashford (away from Maidstone), then left into B2163 – Eyhorne Street village; ME17 1TR

Small pubby core but mainly set for dining; sunny little garden

The pubbiest part of this attractive place can be found tucked away up steps towards the back with bar stools around the island serving bar. Flowers IPA, Fullers London Pride, Harveys Best and Shepherd Neame Masterbrew on handpump and several wines by the glass. Under heavy low black beams, several small or smallish mainly carpeted areas link together around this central core, sometimes partly separated by glazed or stained-glass panels; the solid pub tables have padded country or library chairs. Soft lighting, black timbers in ochre walls, shelves of books and the good log fire in the huge inglenook fireplace add up to a pleasantly old-world feel. Piped music. A neatly kept sunny little garden has picnic-sets under cocktail parasols and a play area.

⚕ **As well as lunchtime bar food such as sandwiches, filled baguettes and filled baked potatoes, ploughman's, ham and eggs, and lasagne, there might be soup, home-made gravadlax, breaded garlic mushrooms with sweet chilli sauce, a pie and a quiche of the day, oriental wok-tossed vegetables in honey and soy sauce, cajun chicken, burgers and steaks with various sauces, and daily specials like scallops in garlic butter, monkfish and tiger prawns in a chardonnay and tomato sauce and skate wing with lavender honey and capers.** *Starters/Snacks: £4.75 to £6.95. Main Courses: £8.75 to £24.95. Puddings: £3.50 to £5.95*

Enterprise ~ Lease Lee and Jan Atkinson ~ Real ale ~ Bar food (12-2.30, 6-10; 12-10 Sat(till 9.30 Sun) ~ Restaurant ~ (01622) 880280 ~ Children welcome ~ Open 11-3, 5-11; 11-11.30 Sat; 12-10.30 Sun; opens midday in winter

Recommended by E D Bailey, Stephen Moss, B and M Kendall, Tim and Claire Woodward

IGHTHAM COMMON   TQ5855   MAP 3

Harrow ⚕ ♀

Signposted off A25 just W of Ightham; pub sign may be hard to spot; TN15 9EB

Emphasis on good food in friendly, smart dining pub, fresh flowers and candles and pretty back garden

Most customers do come to this civilised country inn to enjoy the good food but there is a tiny bar inside the door and a larger bar area to the right. Both these two rooms are attractively decorated with fresh flowers and candles on tables, smart dining chairs on the herringbone-patterned wood floor and a winter fire. The bigger room is painted a cheerful sunny yellow above the wood-panelled dado, there's a charming little antiquated conservatory and a more formal dining room. Greene King IPA and Abbot on handpump, several wines by the glass and a friendly welcome from the amiable landlord. There are tables and chairs out on a pretty little pergola-enclosed back terrace and the pub is handy for Ightham Mote.

⚕ **Interesting, if not cheap, the food might include soup, smooth duck liver pâté with port wine jelly, salmon and chive fishcake with lemon butter sauce, goats cheese and caramelised red onion tart with grape salad, leek and parmesan tart with garlic and chive dressing, fillet of salmon and spinach in filo pastry with dill and lemon sauce, duck breast with plum and cinnamon tarte tatin and bubble and squeak, and daily specials like fillet of beef with foie gras, red wine jus and dauphinoise potatoes.** *Starters/Snacks: £5.50 to £7.50. Main Courses: £9.50 to £21.50. Puddings: £5.75*

Free house ~ Licensees John Elton and Claire Butler ~ Real ale ~ Bar food (not Sun evening or Mon) ~ Restaurant ~ (01732) 885912 ~ Children in family room and dining room only ~ Open 12-3, 6-11; 12-3 Sun; closed Sun evening and all day Mon; a few days over Christmas

Recommended by Andrea Rampley, Mr and Mrs Mike Pearson, Dave Braisted, Martin and Karen Wake, Gordon and Margaret Ormondroyd, Stuart and Doreen Ritchie, Derek Thomas, Alistair Forsyth, Mrs A Green, E D Bailey, Catherine and Richard Preston, Peter and Jan Humphreys, Dr L R Canning

LANGTON GREEN   TQ5439   MAP 3

Hare ♀

A264 W of Tunbridge Wells; TN3 0JA

Interestingly decorated Edwardian pub with a fine choice of drinks and popular food

Chatty and relaxed, this Edwardian roadside pub offers a good choice of food and drink. The front bar tends to be where drinkers gather and the knocked-through interior has big windows and high ceilings that give a spacious feel. Décor, more or less in period with the building, runs from dark-painted dados below light walls, 1930s oak furniture, and turkish-style carpets on stained wooden floors to old romantic pastels, and a huge collection of chamber-pots hanging from one beam. Interesting old books, pictures and two huge mahogany mirror-backed display cabinets crowd the walls of the big room at the back, which has lots of large tables (one big enough for at least a dozen) on a light brown carpet. Greene King IPA, Abbot and Old Speckled Hen and a couple of guests such as Bath Ales Gem Bitter and Hardys & Hansons Olde Tripe on handpump, over 100 whiskies, 20 vodkas, 18 wines by the glass and farm ciders; board games. French windows open on to a big terrace with picnic-sets and pleasant views of the tree-ringed village green. Parking is limited. More reports please.

🍴 Well liked bar food such as sandwiches, twice baked roquefort and tarragon soufflé, moules marinières, duck liver and basil pâté with plum and orange sauce, tagliatelle with chicken and bacon in a cream thyme sauce, goats cheese won ton and pear salad, rabbit and sausage casserole with steamed lemon and sage pudding, venison burger with pepper sauce, tempura battered plaice with prawn salad, and puddings such as chocolate brownie with vanilla ice-cream and apple and berry crumble. *Starters/Snacks: £4.50 to £6.75. Main Courses: £6.75 to £14.50. Puddings: £4.75 to £5.50*

Brunning & Price ~ Lease Christopher Little ~ Real ale ~ Bar food (12-9.30(10 Fri and Sat) ~ (01892) 862419 ~ Children allowed away from bar until 7pm ~ Dogs allowed in bar ~ Open 11-11; 11-midnight Sat; 12-10.30 Sun

Recommended by B and M Kendall, Colin and Janet Roe, Mrs Margo Finlay, Jörg Kasprowski, Revd R P Tickle, Dr and Mrs A K Clarke, Gerry and Rosemary Dobson

LOWER HARDRES   TR1453   MAP 3

Granville ♀

B2068 S of Canterbury; Faussett Hill, Street End; CT4 7AL

Surprisingly modern décor in several connected rooms, a fine choice of wines, good service and popular food; cosy little shady garden

Several linked areas inside this light and airy pub with its attractive contemporary furnishings have comfortable squashy sofas, a nice mix of pale and dark tables with cushioned dining chairs, and – through shelves of large coloured church candles – a glimpse of the chefs hard at work in the kitchen. The appealing décor includes interesting modern photographs and animal lino cuts on pale yellow walls above a dark red dado, a couple of large modern candelabra-type ceiling lights, one area with the floor attractively patterned in wood and tiles, and an unusual central fire with a large conical hood. There's a shelf with daily papers and board games, and a proper public bar with settles, farmhouse chairs and a woodburning stove. Shepherd Neame Master Brew and a seasonal beer on handpump and good wines from a long blackboard list; helpful, friendly bar ladies. French windows lead to the garden with rustic-style picnic-sets under a large spreading tree, and there are some more traditional picnic-sets on a small sunny terraced area.

🍴 Well liked bar food comes with slices of freshly made herby bread and a little dish of olives: soup, rock oysters with shallot vinegar, pear, walnut and roquefort salad, wild mushroom risotto, braised pork belly with crackling and apple sauce, crispy duck with smoked chilli salsa and sour cream, seared organic salmon with pea sauce and smoked pancetta, roast local leg of lamb and puddings such as rhubarb sorbet with burnt cream and flourless chocolate cake with blood orange ice-cream. *Starters/Snacks: £4.95 to £7.95. Main Courses: £11.95 to £18.95. Puddings: £5.50 to £7.50*

Shepherd Neame ~ Tenant Gabrielle Harris ~ Real ale ~ Bar food (not Sun evening or Mon) ~ Restaurant ~ (01227) 700402 ~ Children welcome ~ Dogs allowed in bar ~ Open 12-3, 5.30-11; 12-10.30 Sun; closed 25 and 26 Dec

Recommended by Catherine and Rob Dunster, Colin McKerrow

NEWNHAM   TQ9557   MAP 3

George

The Street; village signposted from A2 just W of Ospringe, outside Faversham; ME9 0LL

Old-world village pub with open-plan rooms, a fair choice of drinks and food, and seats in spacious garden; pleasant walks nearby

Blazing fires and hop-strung beams give this friendly local a kentish flavour. Happily, not much changes here and the series of spreading open-plan rooms still have stripped, polished floorboards, stripped brickwork, gas-type chandeliers, candles and lamps on handsome tables and attractively upholstered mahogany settles. Shepherd Neame Master Brew, Spitfire, and a seasonal beer on handpump, a dozen wines by the glass; piped music. The spacious sheltered garden has some picnic-sets and there are pleasant nearby walks. More reports please.

🍴 **Generous helpings of nice bar food include lunchtime sandwiches, filled baguettes and baked potatoes, ploughman's, ham and eggs, bangers and mash, vegetable curry, steak and kidney pudding, daily specials, and puddings such as gypsy tart and banoffi pie.** *Starters/Snacks: £4.95 to £6.50. Main Courses: £8.95 to £15.95. Puddings: £4.25 to £5.25*

Shepherd Neame ~ Tenants Chris and Marie Annand ~ Real ale ~ Bar food ~ Restaurant ~ (01795) 890237 ~ Children welcome ~ Open 11-3, 6.30-11; 12-4, 7-10.30 Sun

Recommended by Chris Bell, B and M Kendall, Norman Fox, N R White

OARE   TR0163   MAP 3

Shipwrights Arms

S shore of Oare Creek, E of village; coming from Faversham on the Oare road, turn right into Ham Road opposite Davington School; or off A2 on B2045, go into Oare village, then turn right towards Faversham, and then left into Ham Road opposite Davington School; OS Sheet 178 map reference 016635; ME13 7TU

Remote pub in marshland with lots of surrounding bird life and simple little bars

In the middle of marshland and almost alone by a boatyard, this unspoilt old tavern is actually three feet below sea level. The three simple little bars (redecorated this year) are dark, and separated by standing timbers and wood partitions or narrow door arches. A medley of seats runs from tapestry cushioned stools and chairs to black wood-panelled built-in settles forming little booths, there are pewter tankards over the bar counter, boating jumble and pictures, pottery boating figures, flags or boating pennants on the ceilings, several brick fireplaces and a good woodburning stove. Look out for the electronic wind gauge above the main door which takes its reading from the chimney. A beer from Goachers and Whitstable and maybe a couple of guests tapped from the cask and several wines by the glass; piped local radio. There are seats in the large garden and nearby walks. More reports please.

🍴 **Traditional bar food such as sandwiches, ploughman's, sausage and mash, liver and bacon and fish pie.** *Starters/Snacks: £2.95 to £6.95. Main Courses: £6.95 to £12.95. Puddings: £3.95 to £4.50*

Free house ~ Licensees Derek and Ruth Cole ~ Real ale ~ Bar food (12-2.30, 7-9; not Sun evening or Mon) ~ Restaurant ~ (01795) 590088 ~ Children welcome away from bar area ~ Dogs allowed in bar ~ Open 11-3(4 Sat), 6-11; 12-4, 6-10.30 Sun; closed Mon

Recommended by Gary Smith, R B Gardiner, Kevin Thorpe, Andrea Rampley, Louise English, the Didler

---

'Children welcome' means the pub says it lets children inside without any special restriction. If it allows them in, but to restricted areas such as an eating area or family room, we specify this. Places with separate restaurants often let children use them, hotels usually let them into public areas such as lounges. Some pubs impose an evening time limit – let us know if you find one earlier than 9pm.

PENSHURST

TQ4943 MAP 3

Rock 🍺

Hoath Corner, Chiddingstone Hoath, on back road Chiddingstone—Cowden; OS Sheet 188
map reference 497431; TN8 7BS

Tiny rural cottage, simple furnishings, local beer and tasty bar food

On a quiet lane in a little hamlet, this is a very small and unspoilt tile-hung cottage. It's
quite unpretentious inside, with beams, a lovely, uneven and very old brick floor, a
woodburning stove in a fine old brick inglenook, and pretty basic furniture – a few red
plush or brocaded stools, a couple of barrel tables, a well worn armchair, and a large
stuffed bull's head for ring-the-bull (well used by regulars). Up a step to the right is a
smaller room with a long wooden settle by an equally long and rather nice table, and a
couple of other tables with wheelback chairs. Larkins Best, Chiddingstone and Traditional
Ale on handpump, brewed on the Dockertys' nearby farm. There are usually several chatty
locals and their dogs, making visitors feel quite comfortable, too. In front of the building
are a couple of picnic-sets, with more on the back lawn.

🍴 **Tasty bar food includes sandwiches, home-made chicken liver pâté, garlic mushrooms,
proper ham and egg, chilli con carne, moussaka, lamb kofta kebab, salmon and dill
fishcakes, escalope of local veal, venison burgers, and puddings such as spotted dick and
custard and summer pavlovas.** *Starters/Snacks: £5.00 to £6.00. Main Courses: £7.95 to £12.95.
Puddings: £4.00*

Own brew ~ Licensee Robert Dockerty ~ Real ale ~ Bar food ~ (01892) 870296 ~ Children must
be well behaved ~ Dogs welcome ~ Open 11.30-3, 6-11; 12-3, 7-10.30 Sun; closed Sun evening
and Monday

Recommended by Andrea Rampley, Gwyn Jones, Heather and Dick Martin

PLUCKLEY

TQ9243 MAP 3

Dering Arms 🍷

*Pluckley Station, which is signposted from B2077; or follow Station Road (left turn off
Smarden Road in centre of Pluckley) for about 1.3 miles S, through Pluckley Thorne; TN27 0RR*

**Fine fish dishes plus other good food in handsome building, stylish main bar, carefully
chosen wines, and roaring log fire**

This striking old building was originally built as a hunting lodge on the Dering Estate.
The stylishly plain high-ceilinged main bar has a solid country feel with a variety of good
wooden furniture on stone floors, a roaring log fire in the great fireplace, country prints
and some fishing rods. The smaller half-panelled back bar has similar dark wood
furnishings, and an extension to this area has a woodburning stove, comfortable
armchairs and sofas and a grand piano; board games. Goachers Gold Star and a beer
named for the pub on handpump, a good wine list, local cider and quite a few malt
whiskies. Classic car meetings (the long-serving landlord has a couple of classics) are
held here on the second Sunday of the month.

🍴 **Fresh local fish is still the speciality here but they offer other good food too: soup,
oysters, soft herring roes with crispy smoked bacon, chicken liver, bacon and mushroom
pâté, a pie of the day, skate wing with capers and beurre noisette, confit duck with
bubble and squeak potato cake and wild mushroom sauce, venison steak with celeriac
purée and port sauce, monkfish with bacon, orange and cream sauce, lobster grilled with
garlic and cognac, and puddings like rich chocolate truffle with brandy cream and banana
and vanilla ice-cream pancake; the fruits de mer platter needs 24 hours' notice.**
Starters/Snacks: £4.65 to £6.95. Main Courses: £9.95 to £24.95. Puddings: £4.65 to £5.95

Free house ~ Licensee James Buss ~ Real ale ~ Bar food (not Sun evening, not Mon) ~
Restaurant ~ (01233) 840371 ~ Children in Club Room bar ~ Dogs allowed in bar ~
Open 11.30-4, 6-11; 12-4 Sun; closed Sun evening, all Mon, 25-27 Dec, 1 Jan ~
Bedrooms: £40(£60S)/£50(£75S)

Recommended by Michael Doswell, M G Hart, Peter Meister, Laurence Wynbergen, Philip and Cheryl Hill

Mundy Bois

*Mundy Bois – spelled Monday Boys on some maps – off Smarden Road SW of village centre;
TN27 0ST*

**Friendly country pub with relaxing bars, traditional bar food and more elaborate restaurant
menu, and play area in nice garden**

With a friendly welcome for families and dogs, this quietly set pub has a vibrant, cheerful
atmosphere. The informal main bar with its massive inglenook fireplace (favourite spot of
Ted the pub labrador) leads on to a little pool room; TV, darts, games machine, juke box
and piped music. The small snug bar has oak flooring and chesterfield sofas beside a
roaring log fire, and is also used as a pre and post drinking area for the restaurant.
Shepherd Neame Master Brew and Youngs Bitter with Wadworths 6X in summer and at
Christmas and maybe a guest beer on handpump and several wines by the glass. There are
seats in the pretty garden, which has a good children's play area, and you can eat on the
terrace which looks over to the hillside beyond.

Ⓜ **Using rare breed local meat and other local produce, the carefully cooked bar food
might include toasted sandwiches and filled baguettes, ploughman's, soup, steak and
kidney pie, popular vegetable or meaty lasagne, aberdeen angus burger, scampi and chips,
smoked haddock in a creamy white wine sauce with champ potatoes, crispy pork belly
with apple mash and apple gravy and puddings such as sticky toffee pudding and
chocolate torte; you can also eat from the pricier and more elaborate restaurant menu in
the bar.** *Starters/Snacks: £4.50 to £6.95. Main Courses: £7.50 to £9.95. Puddings: £4.25*

Free house ~ Licensees Peter and Helen Teare ~ Real ale ~ Bar food (12-2, 6.30-9(9.30 Sat);
12-4 Sun; not Sun or Mon evenings) ~ Restaurant ~ (01233) 840048 ~ Children welcome ~
Dogs allowed in bar ~ Open 11.30-3, 6-11; 11.30-11 Sat; 12-5 Sun; closed Sun and
Mon evenings; 25 Dec

*Recommended by M G Hart, Ian Barker, N R White, Philip and Cheryl Hill, Rod Stoneman, Kevin Thorpe, B and
M Kendall*

SELLING   TR0455   MAP 3

Rose & Crown

*Signposted from exit roundabout of M2 junction 7: keep right on through village and follow
Perry Wood signposts; or from A252 just W of junction with A28 at Chilham follow
Shottenden signpost, then right turn signposted Selling, then right signposted Perry Wood;
ME13 9RY*

Nice summer garden, winter log fires, hop-covered beams and several real ales

Tucked away up a very quiet lane through ancient woodland, this country pub has pretty
flowering tubs and hanging baskets in summer; the cottagey back garden is lovely then
too, with picnic-sets and a children's play area. Inside, there are comfortably cushioned
seats, winter log fires in two inglenook fireplaces, hop bines strung from the beams, and
fresh flowers; steps lead down to another timbered area. Adnams Southwold, Goachers
Mild, Harveys Sussex Best and a guest beer on handpump; piped music, cribbage,
dominoes, cards and shut-the-box. Good surrounding walks. More reports please.

Ⓜ **Standard bar food includes filled rolls and baked potatoes, ploughman's, soup, ham and
egg, steak and mushroom pudding, ricotta tortellini, fish pie, and puddings. They hold a
themed food evening on the last Thursday of the month.** *Starters/Snacks: £3.95 to £5.95.
Main Courses: £6.95 to £8.95. Puddings: £3.75 to £4.00*

Free house ~ Licensees Tim Robinson and Vanessa Grove ~ Real ale ~ Bar food (not Mon
evening) ~ Restaurant ~ (01227) 752214 ~ Children welcome ~ Dogs allowed in bar ~
Open 11.30-3(3.30 Sat), 6.30(6 Sat)-11; 12-3.30, 7-10.30 Sun; closed Mon evening and
evenings 25 and 26 Dec and 1 Jan

Recommended by Paul Jones, R and M Thomas, the Didler, Kevin Thorpe, Tom and Jill Jones

---

Pubs with attractive or unusually big gardens are listed at the back of the book.

SHIPBOURNE   TQ5952   MAP 3

Chaser ♀

Stumble Hill (A227 N of Tonbridge); TN11 9PE

Comfortable, civilised country pub, log fires, popular food, quite a few wines by the glass, and covered and heated outside terrace

'A really good all-rounder' is how one reader describes this bustling pub – and others tend to agree with him. It's civilised and rather smart with a friendly atmosphere and helpful, welcoming staff. There are several open-plan areas that meander into each other, all converging on a large central island bar counter: stripped wooden floors, frame-to-frame pictures on deepest red and cream walls, stripped pine wainscoting, an eclectic mix of solid old wood tables (with candles) and chairs, shelves of books, and open fires.
A striking school chapel-like restaurant, right at the back, has dark wood panelling and a high timber vaulted ceiling. Greene King IPA and Abbot and a couple of guest beers on handpump, quite a few wines by the glass and several malt whiskies; piped music and board games. French windows open on to a covered and heated central courtyard with teak furniture and big green parasols, and a side garden, with the pretty church rising behind, is nicely enclosed by hedges and shrubs. There is a small car park at the back or you can park in the lane opposite by a delightful green; farmer's market on Thursday morning.

〖¶〗 Enjoyable bar food includes sandwiches, ploughman's, soup, potted smoked mackerel with gooseberry chutney, seared scallops with chorizo butter sauce, honey-roast ham with two free-range eggs, salmon and smoked haddock fishcakes on tomato and spring onion salad with lemon mayonnaise, wild mushroom and tarragon risotto, roast chicken legs on bubble and squeak mash with thyme and roast garlic sauce, large beer-battered cod with mushy peas and salt and vinegar sauce, daily specials like moules marinières, baked camembert in a box with cranberry port sauce (ideal for sharing) and steak and Guinness pie, and puddings. *Starters/Snacks: £3.95 to £8.95. Main Courses: £6.95 to £24.95. Puddings: £4.25 to £5.45*

Whiting & Hammond ~ Lease Richard Barrett ~ Real ale ~ Bar food (all day) ~ (01732) 810360 ~ Children welcome ~ Dogs allowed in bar ~ Open 11-11(midnight Sat); 12-11 Sun

Recommended by B J Harding, Tina and David Woods-Taylor, Tom and Jill Jones, N R White, Gordon and Margaret Ormondroyd, Mrs G R Sharman, E D Bailey, Louise English, Derek Thomas

SNARGATE   TQ9928   MAP 3

Red Lion ★ 🍺

B2080 Appledore—Brenzett; TN29 9UQ

Unchanging, simple tavern, good chatty atmosphere and straightforward furnishings; no food

The timeless, old-fashioned charm of this quite unspoilt village local appeals very much to us – and to those who also love its simplicity. It's been run by the same family for 98 years, and the three little rooms still have their original cream tongue and groove wall panelling, heavy beams in a sagging ceiling, dark pine Victorian farmhouse chairs on bare boards, lots of old photographs and other memorabilia, and coal fire; outdoor lavatories, of course. Lighting is dim but they do light candles at night. One small room, with a frosted glass wall through to the bar and a sash window looking out to a cottage garden, has only two dark pine pews beside two long tables, a couple more farmhouse chairs and an old piano stacked with books. Toad in the hole, darts, shove-ha'penny, cribbage, dominoes, nine men's morris and table skittles. Goachers Light and Mild, and a guest beer or two are tapped straight from casks on a low rack behind an unusual shop-like marble-topped counter (little marks it out as a bar other than a few glasses on two small shelves, some crisps and half a dozen spirits bottles); you can also get Double Vision cider from nearby Staplehurst and country wines.

〖¶〗 No food served at all.

Free house ~ Licensee Mrs Jemison ~ Real ale ~ No credit cards ~ (01797) 344648 ~ Children in family room only ~ Dogs allowed in bar ~ Open 12-3, 7-11(10.30 Sun)
Recommended by Kevin Thorpe, N R White, Adrian Johnson, the Didler, Pete Baker, Phil and Sally Gorton, Louise English

SPELDHURST   TQ5541   MAP 3

George & Dragon ♀

Village signposted from A264 W of Tunbridge Wells; TN3 0NN

Fine old pub, beams, flagstones and huge fireplaces, local beers, good food, and attractive outside seating areas

Built around a 13th-c manorial hall, this is a fine half-timbered building with massive, ancient beams, some beautiful old flagstones, and in the main room, a huge sandstone fireplace with a fine winter log fire. The entrance hall (where there is a water bowl for thirsty dogs) is rather splendid – though we weren't sure about the chandelier. On the right, the half-panelled room is set for dining with a mix of old wheelback and other dining chairs and a cushioned wall pew around several tables, a few little pictures on the walls, horsebrasses on one huge beam, and a sizeable bar counter with Harveys and Larkins on handpump, and quite a few wines by the glass; friendly, efficient staff. A doorway leads through to another dining room with similar furnishings, and big copper pots and dried flowers in a big inglenook fireplace. To the left of the main door is a room more used for those wanting a drink and a chat (though people do eat in here, too) with a woodburning stove in a small fireplace, high-winged cushioned settles, and various wooden tables and dining chairs on the wooden-strip floor; piped music. There's also an upstairs restaurant. In front of the pub are teak tables, chairs and benches on a nicely planted gravel terrace, while at the back is a covered area with big church candles on wooden tables, and a lower terrace with good wooden seats and tables around a 300-year-old olive tree; more attractive planting here and some modern sculpturing.

🍽 Using local farm produce, the enjoyable – if not cheap – bar food includes sandwiches, ploughman's, soup, game terrine with pear and apple chutney, an attractively laid out platter of local cheeses, salamis, chutney and pickles, risotto verde with asparagus, broccoli and goats cheese, kentish hop sausages with onion marmalade, beer-battered cod with tartare sauce, steak in ale pie, slow roast belly of pork with apple compote, and hake fillet with samphire, lemon and brown shrimp. They add a 12.5% service charge to all bills – we've taken this into account in our prices. *Starters/Snacks: £6.20 to £10.70. Main Courses: £11.80 to £20.80. Puddings: £6.20*

Free house ~ Licensee Julian Leefe-Griffiths ~ Real ale ~ Bar food (12-2(3 Sun), 7-9) ~ Restaurant ~ (01892) 863125 ~ Children welcome ~ Dogs allowed in bar ~ Open 11-11(10.30 Sun); closed 25 Dec, 1 Jan

Recommended by Derek Thomas, N R White

ST MARGARET'S BAY   TR3744   MAP 3

Coastguard ♀ 🍺

Off A256 NE of Dover; keep on down through the village towards the bay, pub off on right; CT15 6DY

Bustling and friendly seaside place with terrific views, plenty of fish on menu, nautical décor, fine range of drinks, helpful uniformed staff

To make the best of the tremendous views in fine weather here, you must arrive early to bag one of the tables out on a prettily planted balcony that look across the Straits of Dover; there are more seats down by the beach below the National Trust cliffs. Inside, it's a cheerful and lively place and the warm, carpeted, wood-clad bar has some shipping memorabilia, three real ales from local Kentish breweries like Gadds or Goachers and from Scotland (they only use smaller breweries) on handpump, interesting continental beers, 40 malt whiskies, Weston's cider and a carefully chosen wine list including those from local vineyards; good service even when busy. The restaurant has wooden dining chairs and tables on a wood-strip floor and more fine views; piped music.

🍽 With quite an emphasis on local fish, the enjoyable food includes filled rolls, scallops with samphire, hot-devilled crab, a tart of the day like artichoke, tomato and pine nut, local sheep's milk cheese with apples, apple brandy and onion, beer-battered cod, smoked haddock omelette, john dory with anchovies, capers and sun-dried tomatoes, chicken with rosemary and cider, and puddings such as kentish pudding pie – a mixture between a

cheesecake and spongecake with dried fruit; their cheeseboard is particularly noteworthy.
Starters/Snacks: £4.00 to £7.00. Main Courses: £7.50 to £20.00. Puddings: £4.00 to £6.50

Free house ~ Licensee Nigel Wydymus ~ Real ale ~ Bar food (12.30-2.45, 6.30-8.45) ~
Restaurant ~ (01304) 853176 ~ Children allowed away from bar ~ Dogs allowed in bar ~
Open 11-11(10.30 Sun)

Recommended by Chris Parkins, Kevin Thorpe, Adrian Johnson, Arthur Pickering, Dr Kevan Tucker

STAPLEHURST   TQ7846   MAP 3

Lord Raglan

*About 1.5 miles from town centre towards Maidstone, turn right off A229 into Chart Hill
Road opposite Chart Cars; OS Sheet 188 map reference 785472; TN12 0DE*

**Simple and relaxed with chatty locals, beams and hops, good value bar snacks, and nice
little terrace**

Deservedly busy, this is a well run country pub with friendly licensees and swift, efficient
service. There's an enjoyably cheerful feel and the interior is cosy but compact, with a
narrow bar – you walk in almost on top of the counter and chatting locals – widening
slightly at one end to a small area with a big log fire in winter. In the other direction it
works its way round to an intimate area at the back, with lots of wine bottles lined up
on a low shelf. Low beams are covered with masses of hops, and the mixed collection of
comfortably worn dark wood furniture on quite well used dark brown carpet tiles and nice
old parquet flooring is mostly 1930s. Goachers Light, Harveys Best, and a guest like
Westerham Brewery British Bulldog on handpump, a good wine list, local Double Vision
farm cider and Weston's perry. Small french windows lead out to an enticing little
high-hedged terraced area with green plastic tables and chairs, and there are wooden
picnic-sets in the side orchard; reasonable wheelchair access.

🍴 **Good bar food includes sandwiches, filled baguettes, ploughman's, marinated anchovies
and apple and potato salad, smoked venison with pickled quince, ham and egg, macaroni
cheese, roast pork belly with puy lentils, apple and mash, stir-fried beef and peppers, cod
fillet with herb crust, duck breast with port and orange sauce, and home-made puddings.**
Starters/Snacks: £3.50 to £7.50. Main Courses: £7.95 to £19.50. Puddings: £4.50

Free house ~ Licensees Andrew and Annie Hutchison ~ Real ale ~ Bar food (12-2.30, 7-9.30;
not Sun) ~ (01622) 843747 ~ Children welcome ~ Dogs allowed in bar ~ Open 12-3,
6.30-11.30; closed Sun

Recommended by Mr and Mrs Mike Pearson, Richard Abnett, John and Joan Calvert

STODMARSH   TR2160   MAP 3

Red Lion 🛏

High Street; off A257 just E of Canterbury; CT3 4BA

**Super country pub with very cheerful landlord, lots to look at, super choice of food and
drink and pretty garden with roaming ducks and chickens**

This smashing country pub is hidden away down a network of lanes and run by an
exceptionally obliging if slightly eccentric and cheerful landlord. Full of character and
with lots to look at, the several idiosyncratic rooms wrap themselves around the big
island bar. You'll find lots of hops, wine bottles (some empty and some full) crammed
along mantelpieces and along one side of the bar, all manner of paintings and pictures,
copper kettles and old cooking implements, well used cookery books, big stone bottles
and milk churns, trugs and baskets, and old tennis racquets and straw hats; one part has
a collection of brass instruments, sheet music all over the walls, and some jazz records,
and a couple of little stall areas have hop sacks draped over the partitioning. There are
green-painted, cushioned mate's chairs around a mix of nice pine tables, lit candles in
unusual metal candleholders, a big log fire, and fresh flowers; piped jazz, and bat and
trap. The conservatory adds needed dining space. Greene King IPA and maybe a guest are
tapped straight from the cask, and they've a good wine list with several by the glass,

excellent summer Pimms and winter mulled wine, and cider. There are picnic-sets under umbrellas in the back garden, with pretty flowerbeds and roaming ducks and chickens. Please note that the bedrooms don't have their own bathrooms.

🍴 **Using allotment vegetables and home-reared meat, the good food might include filled baguettes (not Saturday evening or Sunday lunchtime), moules marinières, smoked haddock and salmon fishcakes with chilli sauce, lambs liver with onion gravy and horseradish mash, bass en papillote with lemon and tarragon, chicken, leek and cider pie, rack of local lamb stuffed with rosemary and garlic, duck breast with a summer fruit and vintage port sauce, and puddings.** *Starters/Snacks: £4.95 to £6.95. Main Courses: £11.25 to £17.50. Puddings: £4.50*

Free house ~ Licensee Robert Whigham ~ Real ale ~ Bar food (12.30-2.30, 7-9.30) ~ Restaurant ~ (01227) 721339 ~ Children welcome ~ Dogs allowed in bar ~ Open 11-11 ~ Bedrooms: £45/£70

Recommended by David Dyson, Norman Fox, N R White, M G Hart, Kevin Thorpe, Conor McGaughey, Dr Kevan Tucker, Tom and Ruth Rees, B and M Kendall

STOWTING   TR1241   MAP 3

Tiger

3.7 miles from M20 junction 11; B2068 N, then left at Stowting signpost, straight across crossroads, then fork left after 0.25 mile and pub is on right; coming from N, follow Brabourne, Wye, Ashford signpost to right at fork, then turn left towards Posting and Lyminge at T junction; TN25 6BA

Peaceful pub with friendly staff, interesting traditional furnishings and open fires; good walking country

This is a friendly country pub traditionally furnished with newly cushioned dark wooden pews on wooden floorboards and open fires at each end of the bar. There's an array of books meant to be read rather than left for decoration, candles in bottles, brewery memorabilia and paintings, lots of hops, and some faded rugs on the stone floor towards the back of the pub. Fullers London Pride and Shepherd Neame Master Brew and three guests like Harveys Best, Shepherd Neame Spitfire, and Theakstons Old Peculier on handpump, lots of malt whiskies, several wines by the glass and local cider. There are seats out on the front terrace and an outside smokers' shelter with an environmentally friendly heater and stools made from tractor seats. Plenty of nearby walks along the Wye Downs or North Downs Way. More reports please.

🍴 **Bar food at lunchtime includes filled baguettes and baked potatoes, soup, popular nachos, steak and mushroom in ale pie, roquefort, apple and toasted walnut risotto, cheeseburger, and lasagne, with evening choices such as spicy chilli and ginger chicken, pork loin with apple compote, fresh fish dishes, and puddings like banoffi pie and cranberry and Baileys bread and butter pudding.** *Starters/Snacks: £4.95 to £10.00. Main Courses: £8.95 to £20.00. Puddings: £4.25 to £5.25*

Free house ~ Licensees Emma Oliver and Benn Jarvis ~ Real ale ~ Bar food (all day; not Tues) ~ Restaurant ~ (01303) 862130 ~ Children welcome ~ Dogs allowed in bar ~ Jazz Mon evenings ~ Open 12-midnight; closed Tuesdays

Recommended by John Silverman, Dr Kevan Tucker, Eddie Edwards, Norman Fox

TOYS HILL   TQ4752   MAP 3

Fox & Hounds

Off A25 in Brasted, via Brasted Chart and The Chart; TN16 1QG

Country pub in fine surroundings with well liked food and nice garden

Surrounded by good walks, this bustling pub is in lovely countryside, and as you approach it from the pretty village you will glimpse one of the most magnificent views in Kent. The appealing tree-sheltered garden has picnic-sets, and a covered and heated area. Inside, the small first room has a few plain tables and chairs on dark boards and a small woodburning stove in a knocked-through fireplace which lets it also heat the main bar. Although modernised (including an unobtrusive wide-screen TV and blackboards promoting evening events), this is fondly reminiscent of the former landlady's slightly eccentric regime. Under the shiny pinkish ceiling which looks as old as the building itself are a low leather sofa and easy chair by the coffee table in front of the woodburner, a mix of tables and chairs, hunting prints, illustrated plates, old photographs, pewter mugs and copper jugs, and a small coal fire at the end. In a brick and stone extension is a carpeted dining room with big windows overlooking the garden. Greene King IPA, Abbot and Ruddles County on handpump and several wines by the glass; friendly helpful staff. Piped music and board games; no mobile phones. The pub is handy for Chartwell and Emmetts Garden.

🍴 Well liked bar food includes lunchtime sandwiches and filled baguettes that come with coleslaw, salad and crisps, soup, moules marinières, home-cooked ham with two free-range eggs, steak in ale pie, fresh cod in beer batter, pasta with tomatoes, spinach, olives and parmesan, lambs liver with bacon and red wine gravy, game casserole with herb dumplings, sirloin steak with madeira sauce, daily specials and puddings like raspberry crème brûlée and spotted dick and custard. *Starters/Snacks: £4.25 to £7.50. Main Courses: £7.95 to £19.90. Puddings: £4.95 to £6.25*

Greene King ~ Tenants Tony and Shirley Hickmott ~ Real ale ~ Bar food (12-2(2.30 Sat, 3 Sun), 7-9; not Sun or Mon evenings) ~ Restaurant ~ (01732) 750328 ~ Children welcome away from bar ~ Dogs allowed in bar ~ Live music last Fri of month ~ Open 11-3, 6-11; 11-10.30 Sat; 11-11(till 8 winter Sun) Sun; closed Mon evening

Recommended by Alan Cowell, Grahame Brooks, Glen and Nola Armstrong, Sheila Topham, Cathryn and Richard Hicks, N R White

TUNBRIDGE WELLS   TQ5638   MAP 3

Beacon ♀ 🛏

Tea Garden Lane; leaving Tunbridge Wells westwards on A264, this is the left turn-off on Rusthall Common after Nevill Park; TN3 9JH

Pleasant spreading bar, good bar food and local beers and fine views from seats on wooden decking

In fine weather, the seats under parasols on the raised wooden decked area at the back of this airy Victorian pub enjoy good sunsets and the grounds have footpaths between lakes and springs, as well as summer boules and (very rare for a pub these days) even rounders. Inside, there's a good bustling atmosphere and it's popular locally, especially at weekends. The dining area and spreading bar run freely into each other with stripped panelling, wooden floors and ornately built wall units giving a solidly comfortable feel; the brightly coloured sofas and upholstered cubes by the fireside are sought after in colder weather. Harveys Best, Larkins Traditional Ale and Timothy Taylors Landlord on handpump, and a dozen wines by the glass including champagne; board games. More reports please.

🍴 Interesting bar food includes lunchtime sandwiches, soup, terrine of confit duck with toasted pine nuts and beetroot pesto, teriyaki beef salad with pink ginger and crispy noodles, home-made fishcakes with chilli dipping sauce, lightly curried vegetable ragoût with crispy tofu and a tarragon and cucumber sour cream, boneless lamb shank with glazed dates and chestnut purée, beer-battered haddock, steak, kidney and wild mushroom pie, and garlic-roasted loin of local venison with sweet potato, onion purée and five spice jus. *Starters/Snacks: £4.25 to £6.95. Main Courses: £9.25 to £15.95. Puddings: £4.75*

Free house ~ Licensee John Cullen ~ Real ale ~ Bar food (12-2.30, 7-9.30; all day summer Sat; 12-4, 6.30-9 Sun) ~ Restaurant ~ (01892) 524252 ~ Children welcome ~ Dogs allowed in bar ~ Folk club second and fourth Mon of month ~ Open 11-11; 12-10.30 Sun; closed evenings 25 Dec and 1 Jan ~ Bedrooms: £68.50B/£97B

Recommended by Dr Ron Cox, Peter Meister, Chris and Sheila Smith, Kevin Thorpe, Colin and Janet Roe, V Brogden, Lorry Spooner, M Greening, Derek Thomas

---

If you know a pub's ever open all day, please tell us.

Sankeys 🍴 ♀ ◀

Mount Ephraim (A26 just N of junction with A267); TN4 8AA

Pubby street-level bar, informal downstairs brasserie, real ales and good wines, chatty atmosphere, and super fish dishes

There are two quite different choices in this interesting place – a pubby bar and a downstairs brasserie, both with Harveys Sussex Best and Larkins Traditional Ale on handpump, fruit beers and exotic brews, and a very good wine list with several by the glass. The street level bar is light and airy with big windows and high ceilings, a unique collection of rare enamel signs, antique brewery mirrors and old prints, framed cigarette cards, lots of old wine bottles, old soda syphons, comfortably laid-out leather sofas round low tables, pews round pubby tables on bare boards, and a big flat screen TV for sports (the landlord is a keen rugby fan, and runner); piped music. Downstairs, the central bar has gone and although the emphasis is on the excellent fresh fish (there's now a little oyster bar and a fresh fish display over ice) the atmosphere is cheerful, chatty and informal. Big mirrors spread the light and there are stripped brick walls, pews or chairs around sturdy tables, and french windows that open on to an inviting, suntrap decked garden with wicker and chrome chairs and wooden tables.

🍴 **Pubby choices at lunchtime in the upstairs bar include filled baguettes, ploughman's, baked camembert with french bread, fishcakes, chicken and bacon caesar salad, a changing pie, sharing plates of seafood, a weekend breakfast, and Sunday roast, whilst downstairs there's lots of fish dishes: potted shrimps, moules marinières, thai or masala-style, beer-battered fish, wild bream grilled with rosemary and garlic, roast perch with mango and mint salsa, wild bass stuffed with lemon and lime with sauce vierge, cornish cock and spider crabs, and lobster. From the oyster bar you can make up your own appetiser, starter, main course or shared platter, and there's a good value two- and three-course set lunch; a few non-fishy dishes, too.** *Starters/Snacks: £4.00 to £12.00. Main Courses: £8.50 to £17.50. Puddings: £4.50*

Free house ~ Licensee Guy Sankey ~ Real ale ~ Bar food (12-3, 6-10.30) ~ Restaurant ~ (01892) 511422 ~ Children welcome but not in bar after 7pm ~ Dogs allowed in bar ~ Live bands Sun evening ~ Open 12-11(1am Fri and Sat); restaurant closed Sun and Mon evenings

Recommended by BOB

ULCOMBE   TQ8550 MAP 3

Pepper Box ◀

Fairbourne Heath; signposted from A20 in Harrietsham, or follow Ulcombe signpost from A20, then turn left at crossroads with sign to pub, then right at next minor crossroads; ME17 1LP

Friendly country pub with homely bar, lovely log fire, consistently good food, fair choice of drinks and seats in pretty garden

Even when this extremely popular, traditional country pub is really packed, the friendly staff remain polite and efficient. The homely bar has standing timbers and low beams hung with hops, copper kettles and pans on window sills, some very low-seated windsor chairs, and two leather sofas by the splendid inglenook fireplace with its lovely log fire. A side area, more functionally furnished for eating, extends into the opened up dining room. Shepherd Neame Master Brew, Spitfire and a seasonal beer on handpump, local apple juice and a dozen wines by the glass; piped music. The two cats are called Murphy and Jim. There's a hop-covered terrace and a garden with shrubs, flowerbeds and a small pond. The name of the pub refers to the pepperbox pistol – an early type of revolver with numerous barrels; the village church is worth a look. The Greensand Way footpath is nearby. No children inside. More reports please.

🍴 **Consistently good bar food includes sandwiches and weekly changing specials as well as soup, home-made maryland crab cakes with tarragon butter, smoked duck breast with a fresh raspberry and balsamic dressing, garganelli pasta in a wild mushroom sauce, a sizzle platter of chicken in soy and sweet chilli sauce with sugar snap peas and peppers, lime,** lemon and rosemary chargrilled pork loin with crispy chorizo and a madeira glaze, calves liver in sage butter, fried sea bream fillet with brown butter, capers and parsley mashed potato, and puddings like crème brûlée and fruit platter with coulis. *Starters/Snacks: £6.00 to £9.50. Main Courses: £10.30 to £22.00. Puddings: £4.00*

Shepherd Neame ~ Tenants Geoff and Sarah Pemble ~ Real ale ~ Bar food (12-2, 7-9.45; 12-3 Sun; not Sun evening) ~ (01622) 842558 ~ Dogs allowed in bar ~ Open 11-3, 6.30-11.30; 12-4.30 Sun; closed Sun evening

Recommended by Philip and Cheryl Hill, N R White, John and Jackie Walsh, Michael Doswell, Mike Gorton, Jan and Alan Summers

---

LUCKY DIP

Besides the fully inspected pubs, you might like to try these Lucky Dips recommended to us and described by readers (if you do, please send us reports: feedback@thegoodpubguide.co.uk).

APPLEDORE [TQ9729]
Railway Hotel TN26 2DF [Station Rd (B2080 E)]: Friendly refurbished Victorian hotel with rail memorabilia and open fire in big front bar, Badger K&B and good value food, daily papers, pool, darts, big back children's room with toys and TV, restaurant; good disabled access and facilities, garden tables, 12 bedrooms in small motel wing *(Chris O'Donoghue)*

BARFRESTONE [TR2650]
Yew Tree CT15 7JH [off A256 N of Dover; or off A2 at Barham]: Country pub recently refreshed with stripped boards and pastel décor in airy up-to-date front dining area, great wine choice (new opera-singer landlord has a local vineyard), three real ales inc local Gadds from back bar, new chef doing enjoyable food, daily papers, woodburner; children welcome, back decking, wonderful Norman carvings in next-door church, open all day *(Kevin Thorpe, LYM)*

BARHAM [TR2050]
Duke of Cumberland CT4 6NY [The Street]: Open-plan country pub with welcoming licensees, good value enjoyable straightforward home cooking, three real ales, decent wines, attentive service, bare boards and flagstones, open fire; bedrooms *(Stuart Field)*

BISHOPSBOURNE [TR1952]
Mermaid CT4 5HX [signed off A2]: Traditional unspoilt two-room country local, local photographs, cricket memorabilia and old books, well kept Shepherd Neame, simple food inc good filled rolls, coal fire, darts, no machines; dogs and walkers welcome, lovely Kentish village nr Pilgrims Way and North Downs Way *(Richard Pitcher)*

BRAMLING [TR2256]
Haywain CT3 1NB: Friendly pub with two or three well kept ales inc Wells & Youngs Bombardier; garden *(Dr Michael Postlethwaite)*

BRIDGE [TR1854]
White Horse CT4 5LA [High St]: Relaxed chatty bar with big stone inglenook, homely mix of furnishings, good imaginative food from bar lunches to more elaborate restaurant dishes using local supplies, well kept Fullers London Pride and Shepherd

Neame ales, Biddenden farm cider, fine choice of wines by the glass, friendly efficient service; two-part restaurant with woodburner; unobtrusive piped music; dogs welcome, established back garden, attractive village *(Mr and Mrs Mike Pearson, N R White, BB)*

BROADSTAIRS [TR3967]
Neptunes Hall CT10 1ET [Harbour St]: Chatty early 19th-c two-bar Shepherd Neame local with attractive bow windows, original shelving and panelling, carpeted back lounge with open fire, lunchtime snacks, real ales, friendly landlord, pub dog, military photographs; occasional live folk (daily during Aug folk festival); children and dogs welcome, enclosed terrace, open all day *(the Didler, N R White, Kevin Thorpe)*

BROOMFIELD [TR1966]
Huntsman & Horn CT6 7AF [Margate Rd]: Small open-plan country pub with well kept changing ales such as Adnams, Black Sheep and Caledonian Deuchars IPA, welcoming young landlord, huge log fire, pubby food, daily papers; sports TV; dogs welcome, picnic-sets overlooking duck pond, open all day *(Kevin Thorpe)*

BURMARSH [TR1032]
Shepherd & Crook TN29 0JJ [Shear Way]: Friendly marshside pub, Adnams and a guest beer, Weston's cider, small dining room *(Kevin Thorpe)*

CANTERBURY [TR1458]
☆ *Dolphin* CT1 2AA [St Radigunds St]: Smartly redecorated dining pub, civilised and friendly, with books to read, board games, bric-a-brac on delft shelf, good choice of home-made blackboard food from baguettes to fish specials, several changing ales inc Sharps Doom Bar, country wines, flagstoned conservatory; popular Mon quiz night; disabled access, children and dogs welcome, good-sized back garden with heaters, open all day *(Kevin Thorpe, Dennis and Fiona Golchert)*
Millers Arms CT1 2AA [St Radigunds St/Mill Lane]: Shepherd Neame pub with young friendly staff, good value food inc good Sun lunch, changing guest beers, good wine choice, interesting pictures, basic

furnishings in bar and restaurant; unobtrusive piped music; bedrooms, quiet street nr river and handy for Marlow Theatre and cathedral *(N R White, Dr and Mrs Michael Smith, Keith and Chris O'Neill)*

Old Brewery Tavern CT1 2RX [Stour St, back of Abode Hotel]: Attractive and comfortable contemporary beamed bistro bar, good if not cheap food from sandwiches up, two well kept ales such as Hopdaemon and Shepherd Neame, pine flooring, modern prints on pastel walls, flame-effect fires, soft settees and more dining tables in adjoining high-ceilinged former warehouse, also good hotel restaurant; plasma TVs; children welcome, good bedrooms, open all day *(Kevin Thorpe, Keith and Chris O'Neill)*

Old Gate CT1 3EL [New Dover Rd (A2050 S)]: Big reliable Vintage Inn, stripped brick and beams, two large open fires, bookshelves, big prints, old wooden furniture, reasonably priced food all day, wide range of wines by the glass, real ale choice, well organised staff, daily papers; some piped music; easy disabled access, bedrooms in adjacent Innkeeper's Lodge, small back garden *(Kevin Thorpe, Michael Dandy)*

Parrot CT1 2AG [Church Lane – the one off St Radigund St, 100 yds E of St Radigunds car park]: Step down into basic pub in 14th-c building, pleasantly chatty front bar with heavy beams, broad boards, flagstones, some stripped masonry, two woodburners, dim-lit upstairs banqueting hall, friendly young staff, well kept Bass and lots of guest beers, good value simple lunchtime food inc sandwiches; good jazz nights; bought by Youngs as we went to press – news please; dogs welcome, tables in brick-paved courtyard, open all day *(Kath Hunt, N R White, Kevin Thorpe, Mr and Mrs John Taylor, Dr Kevan Tucker)*

Phoenix CT1 3DB [Old Dover Rd]: Two friendly linked rooms in olde-worlde beamed tavern with lots of prints and new central woodburner, several well kept changing ales, cheap all-day pub food, daily papers, pub games, books for sale; small TV; dogs welcome, open all day (Sun afternoon break) *(Kevin Thorpe, Tracey and Stephen Groves)*

CAPEL-LE-FERNE [TR2538]

Lighthouse CT18 7HT [Old Dover Rd]: Clifftop hotel built in 1802 overlooking Channel, large bar and restaurant, three real ales inc Camerons; eight bedrooms, open all day *(Arthur Pickering)*

Valiant Sailor CT18 7JJ [New Dover Rd (B2011)]: Pleasantly refurbished, with three or four ales inc well kept Fullers London Pride, good value food, good service; handy for cliff walks and Battle of Britain memorial, open all day *(Arthur Pickering)*

CHARTHAM HATCH [TR1056]

☆ **Chapter Arms** CT4 7LT [New Town St]: Sizeable 18th-c pub overlooking orchards, enjoyable generous meals, changing real ales, decent wine, friendly efficient staff, flowers and candles, heavily hop-hung

ceiling with brass instruments and fairy lights, attractive restaurant; quiet piped music; charming garden with good furniture and water features *(Keith and Chris O'Neill, Lady Dobson, Ron and Sheila Corbett, BB)*

CHIDDINGSTONE [TQ5045]

☆ **Castle Inn** TN8 7AH [off B2027 Tonbridge—Edenbridge]: Rambling old pub in pretty NT village, handsome, modernised beamed bar, settles forming booths around tables, cushioned sturdy wall benches, attractive mullioned window seat, woodburner, Harveys Best and local Larkins inc winter Porter (brewed in village), impressive wine list, quite a few whiskies, bar food and separate restaurant; dogs welcome and children away from bar, tables out in front and in secluded garden, circular walks from village, open all day *(Glenwys and Alan Lawrence, Kevin Thorpe, Tom and Jill Jones, LYM)*

CHIDDINGSTONE CAUSEWAY [TQ5146]

Little Brown Jug TN11 8JJ [B2027]: Whiting & Hammond pub with comfortable bar and big back dining extension, decent food from sandwiches to full meals, Greene King ales, friendly efficient service; attractive garden with play area, beer and music festivals, open all day wknds *(Oliver and Sue Rowell, Gerry and Rosemary Dobson, John Branston)*

CHILHAM [TR0753]

Woolpack CT4 8DL [off A28/A252; The Street]: Friendly old pub with traditional unfussy décor, pews, sofa, little armchairs, good inglenook, good value local food, well kept Shepherd Neame; quiet local radio; children allowed in restaurant, delightful village, bedrooms *(LYM, Phil and Jane Villiers)*

CHILLENDEN [TR2653]

☆ **Griffins Head** CT3 1PS: Attractive beamed, timbered and flagstoned 14th-c pub with two bar rooms and back flagstoned dining room, gently upscale local atmosphere, big log fire, Shepherd Neame real ales, popular food; pleasant garden surrounded by wild roses, super Sun barbecues, attractive countryside *(N R White, Philip and Cheryl Hill, Guy Vowles)*

CHIPSTEAD [TQ5056]

George & Dragon TN13 2RW [nr M25 junction 5]: Attractive country dining pub with heavy black beams and standing timbers, old tables and chapel chairs on bare boards, enjoyable fresh food, Fullers London Pride, Harveys Best and Timothy Taylors Landlord, good value wines, relaxed friendly service; children welcome, terrace and pleasant garden *(Derek Thomas, LYM)*

COBHAM [TQ6768]

Leather Bottle DA12 3BZ [handy for M2 junction 1]: Ancient beamed and timbered pub, much modernised, with interesting woodwork and lots of Dickens memorabilia, Courage Best and changing guest beer, young helpful staff, decent bar food, restaurant; disabled access, tables on big back lawn with play area, summer tuck shop and fishpond, pretty village, five bedrooms, open all day *(Alan Cowell, LYM)*

CRANBROOK [TQ7736]

George TN17 3HE [Stone St]: Stripped main bar with leather settees, armchairs and open fire, beamed dining room with huge inglenook, good evening meals, helpful staff, well kept Adnams and Harveys, smaller locals' bar; nicely old-fashioned bedrooms *(Tom and Jill Jones)*

CROCKHAM HILL [TQ4450]

Royal Oak TN8 6RD [Main Rd]: Friendly cosy village local popular lunchtime for good pubby food from sandwiches up, well kept Shepherd Neame, daily papers, comfortable high-backed seats, cartoons by local artist, no music or fruit machines; dogs welcome, small garden, handy for walks and Chartwell *(Godfrey Hurst, C and R Bromage)*

DARGATE [TR0761]

☆ *Dove* ME13 9HB [Village signposted from A299]: Tucked-away restauranty pub under new management, enjoyable and imaginative if not cheap food (not Mon), good service, well kept Shepherd Neame, unspoilt rambling rooms, plenty of stripped wood tables, log fire; quiet piped music; nice sheltered garden *(Sarah Martin, LYM, Mike and Brenda Day)*

DEAL [TR3752]

☆ *Bohemian* CT14 6HY [Beach St]: Relaxed chatty bar opp pier popular for its seven well kept changing ales and good range of continental beers, good choice of wines by the glass, friendly helpful staff, leather sofas, open fire, wooden floors and modern paintings, good seafront views from upstairs restaurant; easy wheelchair access, heated back decking, open all day Fri-Sun and summer, cl Mon in winter *(N R White, Kevin Thorpe, Dr Kevan Tucker, John and Annabel Hampshire)*

Green Berry CT14 7EQ [Canada Rd]: Small real ale pub opp old Royal Marine barracks, friendly couple, well kept real ales, farm cider and perry, no food; small vine-covered terrace, open all day wknds *(Dr Kevan Tucker)*

☆ *Kings Head* CT14 7AH [Beach St]: Handsome three-storey Georgian inn just across from promenade and sea, good landlord and atmosphere, interesting maritime décor and cricket memorabilia in comfortable areas around central servery with four real ales, flame-effect gas fires, usual food from cheap sandwiches up, darts; piped music, TV, popular with young locals wknd evenings; good front terrace area, good value bedrooms, open all day *(Kevin Thorpe, LYM, B J Harding, Rod Stoneman, John and Annabel Hampshire, David Gregory, Catherine and Rob Dunster)*

Prince Albert CT14 6LW [Middle St]: Small two-room immaculate pub in conservation area, ornate interior, three changing real ales, popular Sun carvery *(Dr Kevan Tucker)*

Ship CT14 6JZ [Middle St]: Neatly kept local, Caledonian Deuchars IPA, local Gadds ales and a guest beer, friendly landlord, lots of dark woodwork, stripped brick and local ship and wreck pictures, piano and woodburner in side bar; dogs welcome, small pretty walled garden, open all day *(N R White, Kevin Thorpe, Dr Kevan Tucker)*

DENTON [TR2147]

Jackdaw CT4 6QZ [A260 Canterbury—Folkestone]: Imposing old open-plan brick and flint pub, enjoyable family food all day, half a dozen real ales, friendly young staff, RAF memorabilia in front area, large back restaurant; quiet piped music; children welcome, pleasant garden, picturesque village, open all day *(Arthur Pickering)*

DOVER [TR3241]

Blakes CT16 1PJ [Castle St]: Four interesting changing ales in small flagstoned cellar bar, farm cider and perry, good choice of malt whiskies and of wines by the glass, good lunchtime bar food (not Sun) inc good value sandwiches and home-smoked food, upstairs restaurant, chatty licensees, daily papers, partly panelled brick and flint walls; well behaved children welcome, suntrap back terrace, bedrooms, open all day (till 4 Sun) *(Arthur Pickering, Kevin Thorpe)*

Three Cups CT17 0RX [Crabble Hill (A256)]: Bistro-style open-plan pub, comfortable settees, some high stools and bar tables, modern sunken fireplace, local panoramas, attentive staff, good value food from open kitchen, Marstons Pedigree, blackboard wines, daily papers, back pool table; piped music, TV; small terrace, open all day *(Kevin Thorpe)*

DUNKS GREEN [TQ6152]

☆ *Kentish Rifleman* TN11 9RU [Dunks Green Rd]: Timbered Tudor pub reopened Feb 2008 after careful restoration of serious 2007 fire damage, still plenty of character, particularly friendly helpful landlord and young staff, real ales such as Fullers London Pride, Greene King, Harveys and Westerham, reasonably priced pubby food, cosy log fire, rifles on low beams, enlarged dining room, small public bar; children welcome, tables in pretty garden behind, good walks *(Mr and Mrs C Prentis, Bob and Margaret Holder, BB, Simon and Sally Small)*

DUNTON GREEN [TQ5156]

Bullfinch TN13 2DR [London Rd, Riverhead]: Recently refurbished Geronimo pub, open-plan modern décor with mix of sofas, armchairs and banquettes, snacks and slightly upmarket traditional food, pleasant efficient staff, Adnams, Sharps and Westerham ales, good wine list, daily papers; nice garden, open all day wknds *(Mike Buckingham, Derek Thomas)*

EAST FARLEIGH [TQ7452]

Horseshoes ME15 0PR [Dean St]: Improved 15th-c pub next to riding stables, log fires and low beams, several cosy areas, Harveys Best, Timothy Taylors Landlord, enjoyable fresh food inc Sun roasts, pleasant efficient staff; disabled facilities, children welcome, terrace and large lawn *(Jo Hunt)*

EAST PECKHAM [TQ6548]

Man of Kent TN12 5LA [Tonbridge Rd]: Traditional friendly country pub dating from

15th c with later extension, low beams, well kept Adnams and Harveys, good choice of pubby food, log fire; front terrace and large back garden by River Bourne with greedy chub, orchard country, lots of walks *(Peter Meister)*

EASTLING [TQ9656]

☆ *Carpenters Arms* ME13 0AZ [off A251 S of M2 junction 6, via Painters Forstal; The Street]: Pretty, cosy and cottagey 14th-c oak-beamed pub with good imaginative food (not Sun evening), Shepherd Neame real ales, big log fireplaces front and back; children allowed in small candlelit restaurant, some tables outside, well equipped small bedrooms in separate building *(LYM, Mrs J A Stubblefield)*

EDENBRIDGE [TQ4445]

Old Eden TN8 5AX [High St]: Dim-lit 15th-c pub, old bricks and beams, low doors, open fires, blackboard food from sandwiches to fresh fish, home-baked bread and pies, three Westerham ales and Stowford Press cider; large games room with pool, machines and TV; back garden, open all day *(Kevin Thorpe)*

ELHAM [TR1743]

Kings Arms CT4 6TJ [St Marys Rd]: Attractive traditional pub with relaxing lounge bar, good open fire, good value standard food, well kept ales, good wine list, friendly attentive service, steps down to dining area, public bar with games; opp church in pretty village square, attractive sheltered garden *(David Barnes, B and E Palmer, D F Clarke)*

Rose & Crown CT4 6TD [High St]: Partly 16th-c inn in charming village in Kent's prettiest valley, low beams, uneven floors, inglenook and woodburner, comfortable pleasantly random furnishings, enjoyable pub food, Shepherd Neame ales, several wines by the glass, restaurant; children welcome, flagstoned back terrace, open all day wknds *(Richard Tingle, LYM, John and Annabel Hampshire)*

FAVERSHAM [TR0161]

Anchor ME13 7BP [Abbey St]: Friendly two-bar pub with good food from baguettes up, well kept Shepherd Neame ales, simple bare-boards bar with log fire, ancient beams, dark panelling, low lighting, frosted windows, boat pictures and models, small side room with pub games and books, restaurant; piped radio; dogs welcome, tables in pretty enclosed garden with bat and trap, attractive 17th-c street nr historic quay, open all day *(Peter Meister, Conor McGaughey, Kevin Flack, Kevin Thorpe, M and GR, Mrs M S Forbes)*

Bear ME13 7AG [Market Pl]: Late Victorian (back part from 16th c), locals' front bar, snug hung with chamber-pots and back dining lounge off side corridor, friendly service, relaxed atmosphere, Shepherd Neame ales, basic good value lunchtime home cooking; tables outside, lively musical following, open all day Sat *(Bob and Val Collman, the Didler, N R White)*

Elephant ME13 8JN [The Mall]: Picturesque flower-decked town pub under welcoming

young landlady, five changing real ales, belgian beers, local cider, central log fire, daily papers, modern prints on pastel walls, darts; juke box, games machine; children welcome, suntrap back terrace with fishpond, open from 3 wkdys, all day wknds *(the Didler, Kevin Thorpe, BB)*

Phoenix ME13 7BH [Abbey St]: Ancient two-bar pub with heavy beams and stripped stone, real ales such as Greene King K&B, Rother Valley and Shepherd Neame, bar food inc authentic thai dishes, central fireplace, smart candlelit oriental restaurant; games machine; open all day *(Kevin Thorpe)*

Railway Hotel ME13 8PE [Preston St]: Large handsomely refurbished Victorian hotel, good value restaurant, well kept Shepherd Neame from long highly polished bar with elaborate mirrored back, frosted glass and partitions, period lamps and warm red décor, leather settees and open fire in further room, daily papers, darts corner; seven bedrooms, open all day *(Kevin Thorpe)*

Sun ME13 7JE [West St]: Roomy rambling old-world 15th-c pub with good unpretentious atmosphere in small low-ceilinged partly panelled rooms, big inglenook, Shepherd Neame beers inc seasonal one from nearby brewery, OAP deals, smart restaurant; unobtrusive piped music; wheelchair access possible (small step), pleasant back courtyard, interesting street, eight bedrooms, open all day *(the Didler, Bob and Val Collman, Tony and Wendy Hobden)*

FINGLESHAM [TR3353]

☆ *Crown* CT14 0NA [just off A258 Sandwich—Deal; The Street]: Popular neatly kept low-beamed 16th-c country pub, good value generous food from usual pub dishes to interesting specials, warmly friendly helpful service, well kept ales inc Gadds, Biddenden cider, daily papers, softly lit carpeted split-level bar with stripped stone and inglenook log fire, two other attractive dining rooms; lovely big garden with play area, rabbits and bat and trap, field for caravans, open all day wknds *(N R White, Dr Kevan Tucker, Mrs S Etheridge, Kevin Thorpe, Sue Rowland)*

FRITTENDEN [TQ8141]

Bell & Jorrocks TN17 2EJ: Welcoming simple timber-framed village local with well kept ales inc Adnams Best, Black Sheep and Harveys Best, Stowford Press cider, good basic home-made food, end open fire, kentish darts, adjoining post office; sports TV; open all day *(Peter Meister, Kevin Thorpe)*

GOODNESTONE [TR2554]

Fitzwalter Arms CT3 1PJ [The Street; NB this is in East Kent NOT the other Goodnestone]: Old-fashioned early 18th-c beamed village local, Shepherd Neame ales, chatty atmosphere and friendly staff, three rooms off bar, log fire, dining area *(N R White)*

GOUDHURST [TQ7037]

☆ *Green Cross* TN17 1HA [Station Rd (A262 W)]: Particularly good interesting restauranty food, esp fish and seafood, well kept Harveys Best, good wines and own sloe gin, smart and roomy back restaurant, contrasting simple two-room bar with good fire and TV, friendly efficient service; no digs; terrace tables, light and airy good value bedrooms *(Kevin Thorpe, BB, Gillian Grist, Peter Hindley)*

☆ **Star & Eagle** TN17 1AL [High St]: Striking medieval building, now small hotel, with settles and Jacobean-style seats in heavily beamed open-plan areas, intriguing smuggling-days history, log fires, nice daily-changing food, well kept Adnams, Harveys and Westerham (bar itself fairly modern), lovely views from restaurant; children welcome, tables out behind with same views, attractive village, ten character bedrooms, open all day *(Tina and David Woods-Taylor, LYM, Grahame Brooks, D C O'Neill, Kevin Thorpe)*

HARBLEDOWN [TR1358]
Old Coach & Horses CT2 9AB [Church Hill]: Airy yet cosy modern two-room split-level bistro/bar with interesting enjoyable food, helpful friendly service, real ales inc Greene King, good wines by the glass; great views from garden, peaceful setting *(Hetty Dean, Kevin Thorpe, Jennifer Hurst)*

HEAVERHAM [TQ5758]
Chequers TN15 6NP [Watery Lane]: 16th-c pub with pleasantly unpretentious and friendly locals' bar, decent food (not Sun evening or Mon), Shepherd Neame ales, raftered barn restaurant; children welcome, big pretty garden *(N R White)*

HERNE [TR1865]
☆ **Butchers Arms** CT6 7HL [Herne St (A291)]: Tiny sawdust-floor pub with half a dozen well kept changing ales tapped from the cask inc Dark Star, Fullers and Harveys, interesting bottled beers and Biddenden farm cider, just a couple of benches and butcher's-block tables, some wines too but no food (you can bring your own) beyond fierce pickles and other nibbles, chess, no music or TV; dogs welcome, tables out under awning, cl Sun/Mon, short lunchtime opening *(Kevin Thorpe)*
First & Last CT6 7JU [Herne Common (A291)]: Large welcoming roadside pub with well kept real ales, nostalgic décor inc cigarette cards, motoring prints and team photographs, daily changing food from baguettes to Sun lunch *(Dr and Mrs A K Clarke)*
Smugglers CT6 7AN [School Ln]: Quaint traditional two-bar pub, one with dark beams, one with nautical décor and pool, well kept Shepherd Neame ales *(Dr and Mrs A K Clarke)*

HERNHILL [TR0660]
☆ **Red Lion** ME13 9JR [off A299 via Dargate, or A2 via Boughton Street and Staplestreet]: Pretty Tudor inn by church and attractive village green, densely beamed and flagstoned, log fires, pine tables, friendly helpful staff, enjoyable food, Fullers London

Pride, Shepherd Neame and a guest beer, decent house wines, upstairs restaurant; children welcome, big garden with good play area, bedrooms *(LYM, B and E Palmer, Mary McSweeney)*

HYTHE [TR1634]
Hope CT21 6DA [Stade St]: Proper pub with enjoyable low-priced lunches in friendly separately run simple restaurant *(Mr and Mrs Mike Pearson)*

ICKHAM [TR2258]
☆ **Duke William** CT3 1QP [off A257 E of Canterbury; The Street]: Cheerful open-plan beamed bar with log fire, polished boards and modern prints on pastel walls, good food from baguettes to daily fresh fish and Sun roasts, well kept Adnams, Harveys and Shepherd Neame, good wine list, daily papers, side dining room and back conservatory; piped music; disabled facilities, dogs welcome, large partly covered terrace, neat garden with play area, three bedrooms, open all day from 9.30 *(Kevin Thorpe, LYM, Catherine and Rob Dunster)*

IDE HILL [TQ4952]
Woodman TN14 6BU [Whitley Row, Goathurst Common; B2042 N]: Large well run popular pub, wide choice of all-day home-made food from hot baguettes to south african specialities (landlord's from there), helpful well trained young staff, well kept Larkins, decent wine, woodburner; manicured lawns, good walks *(Tina and David Woods-Taylor)*

IGHTHAM [TQ5956]
George & Dragon TN15 9HH [A227]: Picturesque roadside timbered dining pub, early 16th c but much modernised, good food from generous snacks (all day till 6.30, not Sun) up, friendly service, Shepherd Neame ales, decent wines, sofas among other furnishings in long sociable main bar, heavy-beamed end room, woodburner and open fires, restaurant; children in eating areas, back terrace, handy for Ightham Mote (NT), good walks, open all day *(Bob and Margaret Holder, LYM, Derek Thomas)*

IGHTHAM COMMON [TQ5955]
Old House TN15 9EE [Redwell, S of village; OS Sheet 188 map ref 591559]: Basic friendly two-room country local tucked down narrow lane, no inn sign, bare bricks and beams, huge inglenook, four interesting ales tapped from the cask, retired cash register and small TV in side room, darts; no food, cl wkdy lunchtimes, opens 7 (even later Tues) *(N R White, Pete Baker, BB, the Didler)*

IVY HATCH [TQ5854]
☆ **Plough** TN15 0NL [off A227 N of Tonbridge; High Cross Rd]: Tile-hung dining pub previously popular for pleasantly informal atmosphere and staff, cosy bar with inglenook, Harveys Best and perhaps a Kentish beer, decent wine list, unpretentiously cooked country food, conservatory-style dining room, nice location and gardens; closed for refurbishment under new licensees spring 2008; news please *(LYM)*

KILNDOWN [TQ7035]

☆ *Globe & Rainbow* TN17 2SG [signed off A21 S of Lamberhurst]: Welcoming well cared for pub with small cheerful bar, well kept Harveys and Fullers London Pride, decent wines, simple bare-boards dining room with good value fresh local food, efficient service; country views from decking out by cricket pitch *(V Brogden, Bob and Margaret Holder, H E Waters, BB)*

KINGSTON [TR2051]

☆ *Black Robin* CT4 6HS [Elham valley rd, off A2 S of Canterbury at Barham signpost]: Attractive dim-lit pub with enjoyable generous local food, good value Adnams and Shepherd Neame, decent wines by the glass, local apple juice, cheerful staff, daily papers, dark blue décor, mix of old furniture and pews on flagstones, candles and flowers, comfortable chairs by fire, woodburner in dining area, paintings for sale, darts and pool, back restaurant extension; piped music; disabled access, outside decking over stream, open all day *(Mr and Mrs Mike Pearson, Kevin Thorpe, BB)*

LAMBERHURST [TQ6535]

Elephants Head TN3 8LJ [Furnace Lane, Hook Green; B2169 towards T Wells]: Rambling 15th-c timber-framed pub, mullioned windows, heavy beams, brick or oak flooring, big inglenook, plush-cushioned pews etc, Harveys, good service, wide food choice inc popular Sun carvery; darts and games machine in small side area; children welcome, picnic-sets by front green and in big back garden with peaceful view, terrace and good play area, nr Bayham Abbey and Owl House *(N R White, LYM)*

Swan TN3 8EU [Lamberhurst Down]: Pretty dining pub by green (and vineyards), comfortable contemporary wine bar feel, some sofas, flagstones or bare boards, modern art on mushroom walls, good wines by the glass inc local ones, well kept Harveys and Westerham ales, log fires, cheery service, ambitious food from open sandwiches up; children welcome, back terrace *(BB, Daniel Winfield, Oliver and Sue Rowell)*

LOOSE [TQ7552]

Chequers ME15 0BL [Old Loose Hill]: Rambling 17th-c riverside dining pub, beamed, partly panelled and neatly kept, good fresh lunches inc enjoyable Sun roasts, four well kept ales inc Harveys Best and Timothy Taylors Landlord, nice atmosphere, friendly attentive service, flame-effect fire; small walled garden, good walks *(Peter Meister)*

LUDDESDOWN [TQ6667]

☆ *Cock* DA13 0XB [Henley St, N of village - OS Sheet 177 map reference 664672; off A227 in Meopham, or A228 in Cuxton]: Distinctive tucked-away early 18th-c country pub, friendly long-serving landlord, five well kept changing ales, farm ciders, all-day pubby food (not Sun evening) from wide choice of sandwiches up, rugs on polished boards in pleasant bay-windowed lounge bar, quarry-tiled locals' bar, two woodburners, pews and other miscellaneous furnishings, aircraft pictures, masses of beer mats and bric-a-brac inc stuffed animals, model cars and beer can collections, traditional games inc bar billiards and three types of darts board, back dining conservatory; no children in bar or heated back part-covered terrace; dogs welcome, big secure garden with boules, good walks, open all day *(LYM, N R White, Kevin Thorpe, LM)*

LYNSTED [TQ9460]

Black Lion ME9 0RJ: Sympathetically extended 16th-c local, well kept Goachers, good fresh home cooking inc popular Sun lunch (must book), Pawley's local farm cider, good-natured forthright landlord and two friendly dogs, settles and old tables on bare boards, log fires, old advertisements and something of a 1950s/60s feel; well behaved children welcome, garden with play area *(Richard Pitcher, Annette Tress, Gary Smith)*

MARSH GREEN [TQ4344]

Wheatsheaf TN8 5QL [Marsh Green Rd (B2028 SW of Edenbridge)]: At least half a dozen well kept changing ales, Biddenden cider, good value fresh food from lunchtime sandwiches up, friendly staff, simple linked areas with old photographs and wooden partitions, roomy conservatory; garden and small terrace, open all day *(Kevin Thorpe)*

MAYPOLE [TR2064]

Prince of Wales CT3 4LN [S of Herne Bay]: Popular for food all day in attractive extended back dining room with modern prints on warm red walls, good staff, good wine choice, Shepherd Neame and two guest beers, pine tables, two open fires, china and old photographs in front bar; very busy wknds, piped music, occasional live; children and dogs welcome, disabled facilities, garden with terrace tables, open all day *(Kevin Thorpe)*

NEW ROMNEY [TR0624]

Ship TN28 8BN [High St (A259)]: Tudor smugglers' pub with three airy up-to-date areas around L-shaped bar, Shepherd Neame ales, friendly staff, enjoyable reasonably priced food, attractive restaurant, darts, bar billiards; disabled facilities, covered terrace and lawn, seven bedrooms *(Mr and Mrs W W Burke)*

NEWENDEN [TQ8327]

White Hart TN18 5PN [Rye Rd (A268)]: Friendly 16th-c pub with long low-beamed bar, well kept ales such as Black Sheep, Harveys and Rother Valley, big stone fireplace, dining area with enjoyable food; popular with young people evenings, two sports TVs, pool in back games area, piped pop music; children welcome, large garden, nr river *(Tony Brace, V Brogden, Peter Meister, BB)*

OTFORD [TQ5259]

Bull TN14 5PG [High St]: Attractively laid out 15th-c Chef & Brewer, their usual huge food choice from sandwiches up all day, good Sun lunch, friendly attentive staff (can be stretched when busy), four well kept ales, decent wines, several quietly spacious rooms, two huge log fires, panelling, soft lighting and candles; nice garden, good walks nearby *(Robert Gomme, B J Harding, N R White)*

Crown TN14 5PQ [High St, pond end]: 16th-c two-bar local opp village pond, pleasantly chatty lounge with sofas, Black Sheep, cheerful friendly staff, reasonably priced lunchtime food inc good Sun roasts; walkers and dogs welcome *(N R White, Conor McGaughey)*

PENSHURST [TQ5142]

☆ **Bottle House** TN11 8ET [Coldharbour Lane, Smarts Hill; on B2188]: New licensee for tile-hung country pub, Harveys and Larkins Best (and very popular for food under its previous landlord), low-beamed front bar, well worn brick floor, big windows looking on to terrace, main bar with massive supporting beams, two large stone pillars with a small brick fireplace, low-ceilinged dining room, several cosy areas leading off main bar; piped music; children and dogs welcome, good surrounding walks, open all day *(Tina and David Woods-Taylor, LYM)*

Leicester Arms TN11 8BT [High St]: Cosily well worn old bars and country-view dining room up steps, Fullers London Pride and Greene King Old Speckled Hen, back extension eating area; lavatories down steps (disabled one in car park opp); children and dogs welcome, pretty back garden, seven bedrooms, open all day *(Tina and David Woods-Taylor)*

☆ **Spotted Dog** TN11 8EP [Smarts Hill, off B2188 S]: Quaint old clapboard pub with welcoming new landlady, heartening inglenook log fire, good choice of food from sandwiches up, local Larkins and a guest beer, local farm cider, heavy low beams and timbers, antique settles among other furnishings, rugs and tiles, attractive moulded panelling, restaurant, side shop selling local produce; unobtrusive piped music; children welcome till 7pm, attractive tiered back terrace, open all day *(Glenwys and Alan Lawrence, Oliver and Sue Rowell, Bob and Margaret Holder, N R White, B J Harding, Mrs G R Sharman, Nick Lawless, Mrs J Carlill, LYM)*

PLAXTOL [TQ6054]

☆ **Golding Hop** TN15 0PT [Sheet Hill (0.5 mile S of Ightham, between A25 and A227)]: Secluded country local, small and simple dim-lit two-level bar with hands-on landlord who can be very welcoming, Adnams, Wells & Youngs and guest beers, local farm ciders (sometimes even their own), basic good value fresh bar snacks (not Mon/Tues evenings), woodburner, bar billiards; portable TV for big sports events, games machine; suntrap streamside lawn and well fenced play area over lane, open all day Sat *(Bob and Margaret Holder, the Didler, LYM)*

PLUCKLEY [TQ9245]

Black Horse TN27 0QS [The Street]: Attractive medieval pub behind Georgian

façade, four log fires inc vast inglenook, bare boards, beams and flagstones, dark half-panelling, plenty to look at, wide food choice from baguettes up (just roasts on Sun), Adnams, Greene King Old Speckled Hen and Shepherd Neame, roomy carpeted dining areas; piped music, big-screen TV, games machines; children allowed if eating, spacious informal garden by tall sycamores, good walks, open all day Fri-Sun *(B and E Palmer, BB, Kevin Thorpe, Louise English)*

RAMSGATE [TR3764]

Artillery Arms CT11 9JS [West Cliff Rd]: Chatty open-plan local with Wells & Youngs Bombardier and unusual changing beers, farm ciders, cheap rolls all day, daily papers, fire at top end, artillery prints and interesting stained-glass windows dating from Napoleonic wars; juke box (free Sun) can be loud; good wheelchair access, children and dogs welcome, open all day *(Kevin Thorpe)*

Churchill Tavern CT11 9JX [Paragon (seafront)]: Big two-bar clifftop pub rebuilt 1980s with old beams, bare bricks, stained glass, pews and farm tools, Dark Star and up to half a dozen or so other changing ales, good value food, friendly young staff, open fire, dim lighting, pool in side room, popular back cottage restaurant, band nights; children and dogs welcome, harbour, marina and Channel views, open all day *(Kevin Thorpe, N R White)*

Montefiore Arms CT11 7HJ [Trinity Pl]: Chattily unpretentious traditional local, bargain Archers and guest beers, Biddenden cider, keen landlord, darts, pool in back room; TV, piped radio; children welcome away from bar, cl Weds lunchtime *(Kevin Thorpe)*

ROUGH COMMON [TR1259]

Dog CT2 9DE [Rough Common Rd]: Small friendly local, well kept Adnams Broadside and Fullers London Pride, food inc good value Sun roast *(Keith and Chris O'Neill)*

SANDWICH [TR3358]

George & Dragon CT13 9EJ [Fisher St]: Civilised open-plan 15th-c beamed pub keeping feel of small original rooms, welcoming landlady, enjoyable food inc wood-fired pizzas and unusual dishes from open-view kitchen, well kept ales such as Adnams, Harveys and Shepherd Neame, good choice of wines by the glass; children and dogs welcome, pretty back terrace *(N R White)*

SARRE [TR2564]

Crown CT7 0LF [Ramsgate Rd (A28)]: Bustling carefully restored pub with good interesting bar lunches and evening restaurant dishes, well kept Shepherd Neame, decent house wines, friendly attentive staff, two attractive beamed bars, log fires, celebrity pictures; garden tables, bedrooms, open all day *(Conor McGaughey)*

SEASALTER [TR0864]

☆ **Sportsman** CT5 4BP [Faversham Rd, off B2040]: Restaurany dining pub just inside sea wall, good imaginative contemporary cooking with plenty of seafood (not Sun evening or Mon, best to book and not cheap), two plain linked rooms and long conservatory, wooden floor, pine tables, big film star photographs, wheelback and basket-weave dining chairs, good wine choice, Shepherd Neame ales; children welcome, open all day Sun *(Dr Kevan Tucker, LYM, Gary Smith, Andrea Rampley, Colin and Stephanie McFie, Kevin Thorpe)*

SEVENOAKS [TQ5555]

☆ *Bucks Head* TN15 0JJ [Godden Green, just E]: Flower-decked pub with welcoming thoughtful service, good value blackboard food from sandwiches to lots of fish, well kept Shepherd Neame and a guest beer, log fires in splendid inglenooks, neatly kept bar and restaurant area, no piped music; no dogs or muddy boots; children welcome, front terrace overlooking informal green and duckpond, back lawn with mature trees, bird fountain, pergola and views over quiet country behind Knole *(Richard Pitcher, Neil Powell, Robert Gomme, Alison and Graham Hooper, Tina and David Woods-Taylor)*

Kings Head TN13 2QA [Bessels Green; A25 W, just off A21]: Popular village-green local, friendly young staff, fires, generous reasonably priced food, restaurant; dogs welcome, spacious garden (traffic noise) *(William Ruxton)*

White Hart TN13 1SG [Tonbridge Rd (A225 S, past Knole)]: 16th-c coaching inn now in Blubeckers chain, modern dining areas, good choice of food, real ales, good wine list, friendly service; pleasant lawns with well established shrubs, play area, open all day *(Martin and Pauline Jennings)*

SHATTERLING [TR2658]

· *Frog & Orange* CT3 1JR: Neat and welcoming 18th-c pub with lots of stripped pine, old maps and photographs on partly stripped walls, log fire, pubby food from baguettes up, popular Sun lunches, two changing ales, separate restaurant; children welcome, garden, four bedrooms, open all day *(Anne Clarke, Phil and Jane Hodson)*

SMARDEN [TQ8642]

☆ *Bell* TN27 8PW [from Smarden follow lane between church and Chequers, then left at T junction; or from A274 take unsignposted turn E a mile N of B2077 to Smarden]: Pretty 17th-c inn with welcoming landlady, enjoyable pub food from good ciabattas up, Shepherd Neame ales, local cider, country wines, winter mulled wine, inglenook fire, rambling low-beamed little rooms, dim-lit and snug, nicely creaky old furnishings on ancient brick and flagstones or quarry tiles, end games area; picnic-sets in attractive mature garden *(Peter Meister, John Currie, LYM, J H Bell, the Didler, Colin McKerrow)*

ST NICHOLAS AT WADE [TR2666]

Bell CT7 0NT [just off A299; The Street]: Olde-worlde 16th-c beamed two-bar pub busy wknds for good value generous unfussy food from baguettes to fresh fish and sell-out Sun roasts, ancient stripped brickwork,

big log fire in antique high grate, Black Sheep, Greene King IPA and a guest beer, friendly staff, restaurant, pool and games in big back room; children and dogs welcome, open all day wknds *(Kevin Thorpe, Conor McGaughey)*

STALISFIELD GREEN [TQ9552]

Plough ME13 0HY [off A252 in Charing]: 15th-c hall house on village green high on N Downs, beams and log fires, large old-fashioned tables and chairs in dining areas on either side of bar, enjoyable fresh food using local produce, changing local ales such as Whitstable; big pleasant garden, good view and walks *(Peter Meister, Annette Tress, Gary Smith)*

STONE IN OXNEY [TQ9428]

Ferry TN30 7JY: Attractive 17th-c smugglers' haunt, small bar with woodburner and separate inglenook, bare boards, steps to pleasant dining area, wide food choice from baguettes up, good friendly service, games room; front courtyard, big back garden *(Louise English, V Brogden)*

STONE STREET [TQ5755]

Padwell Arms TN15 0LQ [off A25 E of Sevenoaks, on Seal—Plaxtol by-road; OS Sheet 188 map ref 569551]: Orchard-view country pub with friendly and enthusiastic new young management, enjoyable fresh pub food (not Mon) using good local ingredients, changing real ales such as Larkins, nice wines and good coffee, comfortable banquettes and log fire, airy back dining area; front terrace and pleasant back garden, plenty of shade, good walks *(Malcolm Stapley, BB, the Didler, M J and C R Pope-Hattersley)*

☆ *Snail* TN15 0LT: Smart well run pub-styled restaurant, good food at big oak farmhouse tables, plenty of fish, good wines, Harveys and a guest beer, ad lib coffee, friendly relaxed brasserie layout with beams, oak panelling and some stripped stone; attractive rambling garden, handy for Ightham Mote *(Alan Cowell, BB, Derek Thomas, Gordon and Margaret Ormondroyd, Oliver and Sue Rowell)*

STOWTING [TR1140]

☆ *Black Horse* TN25 6AP [Fiddling Lane, Monks Horton]: Friendly pub with enjoyable fresh food inc home-made ice-cream, three well kept ales, Weston's farm cider, good choice of wines by the glass; garden overlooking fields, lovely surroundings *(Mr and Mrs Mike Pearson)*

SUNDRIDGE [TQ4855]

White Horse TN14 6EH [Main Rd]: Good interesting range of all-day fresh food from bar snacks to restaurant meals, well kept Fullers London Pride and guest beers, log fires and low beams; garden tables *(Mike Buckingham)*

SUTTON VALENCE [TQ8149]

Swan ME17 3AJ [Broad St]: Traditional heavy-beamed two-bar pub dating at least from 14th c, friendly service and chatty atmosphere, enjoyable blackboard food using local supplies, several real ales, moderately priced wines, pub games; pretty village nr Leeds Castle (N R White)

TENTERDEN [TQ8833]

Vine TN30 6AU [76 High St]: Refurbished 19th-c Shepherd Neame pub, airy entrance lobby with comfortable chairs and woodburner, steps down to small bar, large back restaurant and conservatory, Sun quiz night; piped music; children welcome, sunny terrace, open all day (Kevin Thorpe)

☆ *White Lion* TN30 6BD [High St]: 16th-c behind Georgian façade, beams and timbers, masses of pictures, china and books, cheerful helpful young staff, wide choice of generous popular food, Marstons and related beers, sensibly priced wines, big log fire, relaxed and friendly even when crowded with young people at night, cosy area off bar, softly lit back panelled restaurant; piped music, games machines; dogs welcome, heated terrace overlooking street, 15 comfortably creaky beamed bedrooms, good breakfast, open all day (Kevin Thorpe, Louise English)

☆ *William Caxton* TN30 6JR [West Cross; top of High St]: Timeless hospitable 15th-c local, heavy beams and bare boards, huge inglenook, woodburner in smaller back bar, wide choice of enjoyable reasonably priced food from moules frites to venison casserole, well kept Shepherd Neame, darts, daily papers, pleasant small dining room; piped music; children and dogs welcome, tables in attractive front area, back courtyard (Peter Meister, B J Harding, the Didler)

THURNHAM [TQ8057]

☆ *Black Horse* ME14 3LD [not far from M20 junction 7; off A249 at Detling]: Olde-worlde dining pub with enjoyable food all day, Fullers London Pride, Greene King IPA and Shepherd Neame Invicta, farm ciders and country wines, bare boards, hop bines and log fires; dogs welcome, pleasant garden with partly covered back terrace, water features and nice views, by Pilgrims Way, chic bedrooms, good breakfast (M Greening, Bob Pike, Phil Bryant)

TUNBRIDGE WELLS [TQ5839]

Black Pig TN1 1RZ [Grove Hill Rd]: Relaxed refurbished pub (former Orson Welles) under same ownership as George & Dragon at Speldhurst, good food using local and organic supplies, home-baked bread, Harveys Best, interesting wine list, long narrow front bar, big leather sofas by woodburner, balustraded raised area, elegant mix of dining chairs, decorative fireplace, fresh flowers, Hogarthesque prints, olive-painted panelling, back dining room (Derek Thomas, BB)

Bull TN2 5LH [Frant Rd]: Friendly refurbished pub with two linked areas, neatly set dining part with well spaced pine tables and chunky chairs on stripped wood, similar bar area, corner black sofa, Shepherd Neame Bitter and Spitfire, decent wine and food, daily papers; TV, piped pop music (BB)

UNDER RIVER [TQ5552]

☆ *White Rock* TN15 0SB [SE of Sevenoaks, off B245]: Well run village pub, attractive and relaxed, with enjoyable pubby food, coffee and cakes between times, Fullers London Pride, Harveys and one brewed by Westerham for them, friendly staff, beams, bare boards and stripped brickwork in cosy original part with adjacent dining area, public bar with pool in modern extension; quiet piped music; children welcome, pretty front garden, back terrace and large lawn, handy for Knole Park and Greensand Way (walkers asked to use side door) (Robert Gomme, R B Gardiner, E D Bailey)

UPNOR [TQ7570]

Kings Arms ME2 4XG [High St]: Old pub at top of cobbled street, four well kept ales inc Caledonian Deuchars IPA, enjoyable fresh food, friendly staff, three simple linked areas inc back restaurant, bar billiards; views to Chatham, attractive garden, delightful riverside village nr Upnor Castle, good walks (Pete Baker)

WEST FARLEIGH [TQ7152]

Tickled Trout ME15 0PE [B2010 SW of Maidstone]: Popular dining pub with good choice of decent food inc OAP specials (Tues-Thurs), Fullers London Pride, Greene King Old Speckled Hen and Shepherd Neame Spitfire, several wines by the glass, cheerful staff; Medway views (esp from big garden with play area), path down to river, good walks (LYM, Glenwys and Alan Lawrence)

WEST MALLING [TQ6857]

Lobster Pot ME19 6JU [Swan St]: Open fire in carpeted traditional bar with old posters, nets and lobster pots, step up to pleasant small panelled dining room, friendly service, Adnams and five other changing ales usually inc Larkins; darts and piped music in small dark-panelled public bar, upstairs skittle alley; open all day wknds (N R White)

WEST PECKHAM [TQ6452]

☆ *Swan on the Green* ME18 5JW [off A26/B2016 W of Maidstone]: Main draw here is the good range of beers brewed by the pub – and the charming village green is great for a summer drink (the church is partly Saxon); relaxed unpretentious open-plan beamed bar with modern artwork and some stripped brickwork, mixed furnishings, Biddenden farm cider, rather pricy food (not Sun/Mon evenings) from tapas to some ambitious dishes; piped classical music; children and dogs welcome, open all day summer wknds (Graham Burling, Philip and Cheryl Hill, N R White, Sue Demont, Tim Barrow, Annette Tress, Gary Smith, Dr Ron Cox, Kevin Thorpe, Martin and Pauline Jennings, Gordon and Margaret Ormondroyd, LYM)

WESTERHAM [TQ4454]

Grasshopper TN16 1AS [The Green]: Old village pub overlooking green with three linked bar areas, good log fire in back one, low ceilings, lots of bric-a-brac and Royal pictures, chatty atmosphere and friendly efficient staff, food from good value sandwiches up, Wells & Youngs ales, upstairs restaurant; children welcome, seating out at

front and in back garden, open all day
(N R White)
WESTWELL [TQ9847]
Wheel TN25 4LQ: Wide choice of good
imaginative food (not strong on vegetarian),
Shepherd Neame, efficient friendly service,
darts, pool; children and dogs welcome,
garden (Mr and Mrs Mike Pearson)
WHITSTABLE [TR1066]
Old Neptune CT5 1EJ [Marine Terr]: Seafront
pub, busy, friendly and relaxed, real ales
inc Greene King, enjoyable food; dogs and
children welcome, picnic-sets out on beach
(Keith and Chris O'Neill)
Pearsons CT5 1BT [Sea Wall]: Food pub
under welcoming new management, fresh
fish and seafood, Gadds beers, good service,
tiny upstairs restaurant (with oblique sea
view), nautical downstairs bar (no view)
with scrubbed wood tables and deep
armchairs; children welcome in eating areas,
open all day wknds, just above shingle
beach (LYM, Roger Thornington)
Ship Centurion CT5 1AY [High St]: Popular
and friendly unpretentious L-shaped bar,
bargain food inc german dishes (reflecting
landlord's roots), well kept Adnams and
changing guest beers from small breweries,
old local photographs, conservatory; TV
lounge, live music Thurs (Pete Baker)
Whitstable Brewery Bar CT5 2BP [East
Quay]: Beach bar with real ales and various
lagers and fruit beers from the associated
Whitstable brewery (over nr Maidstone),
light, airy and simple, with sea-view picture
windows, functional span ceiling, flagstone
floor with long tables and benches around
edge, corner leather settees, big log fire,
Fri music night; July beer festival; picnic-
sets out on the shingle, cl winter Mon-Weds,
open all day (Keith and Chris O'Neill)
WICKHAMBREAUX [TR2258]
Rose CT3 1RQ [The Green]: Attractive 16th-c
and partly older pub, good value home-made
food all day (not Sun evening), friendly
helpful staff, Adnams Broadside, Greene King
IPA and a guest beer, Addlestone's cider,
small bare-boards bar with log fire in big

fireplace, dining area beyond standing
timbers, beams, panelling and stripped brick;
no children or dogs (pub dog); garden, nice
spot across green from church and watermill,
open all day (Kevin Thorpe, Mrs M Grimwood)
WORTH [TR3356]
☆ *St Crispin* CT14 0DF [signed off A258 S of
Sandwich]: Dating from 16th c, with stripped
brickwork, bare boards and low beams in
comfortably refurbished bar, generous
popular home-made food here and in
restaurant and back conservatory from good
baguettes to some imaginative dishes,
welcoming attentive staff, changing real
ales, belgian beers, local farm cider, well
chosen wines, central log fire; good
bedrooms (inc motel-style extension),
charming big garden behind with terrace and
barbecue, lovely village position
(Rona Murdoch, Dr Kevan Tucker, N R White)
WYE [TR0546]
New Flying Horse TN25 5AN [Upper Bridge
St]: Civilised 17th-c Shepherd Neame inn
with beams and inglenook, comfortable
pleasantly light bar and restaurant,
straightforward good value food, good choice
of ales and wines; good-sized pretty garden,
bedrooms (Charles Gysin)
Tickled Trout TN25 5EB [signed off
A28 NE of Ashford]: Popular summer family
pub with lots of picnic-sets on lawn by
River Stour, spacious modern conservatory/
restaurant, rustic-style bar with beams and
stripped brickwork, stained glass and
partitions, food from baguettes up,
interesting changing real ales, good log fire;
children welcome (Arthur Pickering, LYM)
YALDING [TQ6950]
☆ *Walnut Tree* ME18 6JB [B2010 SW of
Maidstone]: Good country pub, warm and
friendly, pleasant brightly lit bar on several
levels with big fire, lots of old beams,
inglenook and interesting pictures, friendly
efficient staff, enjoyable generous from
tapas up, good-sized restaurant, well kept
Harveys Best, Timothy Taylors Landlord and a
guest beer; bedrooms, attractive village
(Steve Harvey)

Lancashire
(with Greater Manchester and Merseyside)

Lancashire's eminently good value pubs are joined by three new main entries here this year – and by over 70 new entrants to the Lucky Dip section at the end of the chapter. The Wheatsheaf at Raby, after a break of some years, rejoins the main entries on the strength of its welcoming chatty atmosphere, fine range of eight real ales, and enjoyable bar food. Also conspicuously friendly is the Lower Buck at Waddington, gaining its main entry for its much-praised food using meat and vegetables from farms nearby, as well as a choice of five local real ales. Our third find is the Inn at Wray, a most attractive dining pub which opened early in 2008. The choice of drinks particularly stands out in many of the pubs, notably the Sun in Lancaster, the Taps in Lytham, the Station Buffet in Stalybridge, the Britons Protection and Marble Arch in Manchester, the Lord Raglan, up above Bury, and the Church Inn at Uppermill. One of the most opulent Victorian pubs in the country is the Philharmonic Dining Rooms at Liverpool, now offering inexpensive food served throughout, as well as ten real ales. Top among Lancashire's food pubs, the Three Fishes at Great Mitton and (in only its second year under the present management) the Highwayman at Nether Burrow are run by the same team, and are doing exceptionally well in producing regional dishes; both have been sensitively revamped. Other pubs serving exceptional food are the Eagle & Child at Bispham Green, with its wild garden and adjacent bowling green, the Fence Gate at Fence (a sophisticated place with brasserie, notable wines and five real ales), the Lunesdale Arms at Tunstall (carefully prepared dishes made from local organic produce), and the White Bull at Ribchester (enjoyed particularly for food and accommodation). It's the Three Fishes at Great Mitton which takes the top title of Lancashire Dining Pub of the Year. The area has some fine all-rounders. The Bay Horse (at Bay Horse) has interesting drinks and thoughtful food served by helpful staff, while the Derby Arms at Longridge, looking across to the Forest of Bowland, is liked for its unchangingly traditional qualities, and has a decent wine list; similarly unchanged is the New Inn at Yealand Conyers, a friendly village pub with an attractive garden, and generous food all day. At Wheatley Lane, the Old Sparrow Hawk is engaging and convivial, with a good range of beers and wines, and its food is winning praise. The Black Bull at Rimington continues on fine form, readers enjoying its tasty food and fascinating transport-themed décor. In a very different style, Dukes 92 in Manchester is a vibrantly buzzy city pub in a rejuvenated area by the Rochdale Canal; food is good value here. Many readers appreciate the Devonshire Arms in Mellor for its cheery small-scale character, as well as its decent pubby food. Superb rural settings add to the appeal of the Rams Head at Denshaw (lots of old-world character inside, and tasty food), the Inn at Whitewell (a comfortable manor house hotel in the Hodder Valley), and the stylishly upmarket White Hart at Lydgate, overlooking Saddleworth Moor. A good few stars among the Lucky Dips include in Liverpool the Baltic Fleet, Cains Brewery Tap and the Dispensary, and in Manchester the Ape & Apple, Mr Thomas Chop House, Peveril of the Peak, Rain Bar and Sinclairs. Others are the Black Dog at Belmont, White House at Blackstone Edge, Craven Heifer near Clitheroe, Assheton Arms at Downham, Th'Owd Tithebarn in Garstang, Stags Head at Goosnargh, Red Lion in Hawkshaw, Hest Bank Inn, Millstone at Mellor (the one up near Blackburn), Hark to Bounty at Slaidburn, Arden Arms and Red Bull in Stockport, Waddington Arms in Waddington and Freemasons Arms at Wiswell. The area's two main brewers, both with several hundred tied pubs, are Thwaites and Robinsons. Three other good local brews which we found quite widely available in good pubs are Moorhouses, Phoenix and Bowland, with Cains (in administration as we went to press) very popular in and around Liverpool, and Hydes a major presence in Manchester. Holts, another Manchester brewer, deserves a special mention for its excellent keen pricing. Among some three dozen other independent brewers here, ones we found in at least some good pubs are Brimstage, Bank Top, Marble, Three Bs, Pennine, Boggart Hole Clough, Grindleton, Lancaster, Leyden, Pictish, Lees and Red Rose.

BARNSTON   SJ2783   MAP 7
Fox & Hounds 🍺 £
3 miles from M53 junction 3: A552 towards Woodchurch, then left on A551; CH61 1BW

Tidy pub with unusual collections, very reasonably priced lunchtime food and good range of drinks including interesting guest beers

They serve six real ales at this popular pub, with Brimstage Trappers Hat, Theakstons Best and Old Peculier and Scottish Courage Websters Yorkshire, along with two guests such as and Hanby Drawwell Bitter and Woodlands Oak Beauty on handpump; in addition are more than 60 whiskies and a dozen wines by the glass. The main part of the roomy carpeted bay-windowed lounge bar has blue plush pleated built-in banquettes and plush-cushioned captain's chairs around the solid tables, and plenty of old local prints on its cream walls below a delft shelf of china, with a collection of police and other headgear; darts and board games; TV and piped music. Tucked away opposite the serving counter is a charming old quarry-tiled corner with an antique kitchen range, copper kettles, built-in pine kitchen cupboards, and lots of earthenware or enamelled food bins. With its own entrance at the other end of the pub, a small locals' bar is worth a peek for its highly traditional layout – as well as a collection of hundreds of metal ashtrays on its delft shelf; beside it is a snug where children are allowed. There are some picnic-sets under cocktail parasols out in the yard behind, below a farm.

🍴 **Very traditional pubby food includes toasted ciabattas, open sandwiches, soup, filled baked potatoes, quiche, various platters such as coronation chicken, lamb shank, hot pie of the day, fish of the day, and Sunday roasts.** *Starters/Snacks: £24.50 to £4.50. Main Courses: £3.95 to £8.00. Puddings: £2.50 to £4.50*

Free house ~ Licensee Ralph Leech ~ Real ale ~ Bar food (12-2(2.30 Sun); not evenings) ~ (0151) 648 1323 ~ Children in snug until 9pm ~ Dogs allowed in bar ~ Open 11-11; 12-10.30 Sun

Recommended by Maurice and Gill McMahon, Ann and Tony Bennett-Hughes, Paul Boot, Derek and Sylvia Stephenson, Chris Glasson

BAY HORSE   SD4952   MAP 7

Bay Horse

1.25 miles from M6 junction 33: A6 southwards, then off on left; LA2 0HR

Comfortably stylish pub with emphasis on innovative food; good range of drinks, garden

With a cosily pubby atmosphere and efficient staff, this dining pub is a popular refuge for Lancaster University people. Its beamed red-walled bar is attractively decorated, with a good log fire, cushioned wall banquettes in bays, and gentle lighting, including table lamps on window sills – look out for the friendly cat. As well as a decent, fairly priced wine list (15 wines by the glass), 15 malt whiskies, freshly squeezed orange juice and pressed apple juices, very helpful staff serve Black Sheep, Moorhouses Pendle Witches Brew and a monthly guest such as Everards Pitch Black from handpumps. There are usually fresh flowers on the counter, and maybe quiet piped music. A series of small rambling dining areas has the feel of a civilised country restaurant, with red décor, another log fire, candle-flame-effect lights and nice tables, including one or two good-sized ones in intimate self-contained corners. The pub is in a peaceful location (though the railway is not far off), and there are tables out in the garden behind. Note they don't accept lunchtime bookings for parties of fewer than eight.

⌐ **A good deal of attention goes into the food here, with innovative use of carefully sourced ingredients, and though not cheap, helpings are generous. As well as imaginative lunchtime sandwiches, they have lunch and evening menus that might include starters such as black pudding with soused onions and english mustard, lancashire smoked salmon and home-cured salmon with beetroot and horseradish relish and warm potted morecambe bay shrimps. Main courses might be baked field mushrooms with garstang blue cheese, and roast fillet of aged lancashire beef; puddings such as chocolate pot, and treacle, walnut and fig tart; they also have a lancashire cheeseboard.** *Starters/Snacks: £4.45 to £7.75. Main Courses: £11.50 to £19.95. Puddings: £4.95 to £6.95*

Mitchells ~ Tenant Craig Wilkinson ~ Real ale ~ Bar food (12-2(3 Sun), 7-9.15) ~ Restaurant ~ (01524) 791204 ~ Children welcome ~ Open 12-3, 6.30-11(midnight Fri, Sat); 12-5 Sun; closed Mon except bank holidays, Tues after bank holidays ~ Bedrooms: /£110S(£89B)

Recommended by K S Whittaker, Sarah and Peter Gooderham, Mr and Mrs B Watt, Jo Lilley, Simon Calvert, Revd D Glover, Dr and Mrs A K Clarke, J S Burn, Dr Kevan Tucker, Margaret Dickinson, Mrs A Green

BISPHAM GREEN   SD4813   MAP 7

Eagle & Child

Maltkiln Lane (Parbold—Croston road, off B5246); L40 3SG

Well liked friendly pub with antiques in stylishly simple interior, interesting range of beers, very well prepared food, and nice garden

As well as an interesting range of changing real ales, there are some interesting diversions here, with crown green bowling to try, and a wild garden that is home to crested newts and moorhens; the pub's dogs are called Betty and Doris. In the largely open-plan bar, attractively understated old furnishings include a mix of small oak chairs around tables in corners, an oak coffer, several handsomely carved antique oak settles (the finest apparently made partly from a 16th-c wedding bed-head), and old hunting prints and engravings. There's coir matting in the snug, and oriental rugs on flagstones in front of the fine old stone fireplaces. An interesting range of five changing beers might typically include Three Bs Doff Cocker, Phoenix White Monk, Southport Golden Sands, Thwaites Original and Timothy Taylors Landlord, and they also keep a farm cider, decent wines and around 30 malt whiskies. They hold a popular beer festival over the first May bank holiday weekend. The handsome side barn was being converted into a deli as we went to press; smokers can retreat to the cart shed.

⌐ **There's quite an emphasis on the well cooked food (you should book) which includes soup, imaginative sandwiches, peppered carpaccio of beef fillet with truffle dressing, steak and ale pie, fish and chips, cajun beefburger, slow-cooked lamb shank, seared peppered medallions of tuna, thai-style vegetable curry, and specials.** *Starters/Snacks:*

£5.00 to £7.50. Main Courses: £9.00 to £12.50. Puddings: £4.50

Free house ~ Licensee David Anderson ~ Real ale ~ Bar food (12-2, 5.30-8.30(9 Fri, Sat); 12-8.30 Sun) ~ (01257) 462297 ~ Children welcome ~ Dogs welcome ~ Open 12-3, 5.30-11; 12-10.30 Sun

Recommended by Steve Whalley, Geoff and Teresa Salt, Andrea Rampley, Ian and Nita Cooper, Yvonne and Mike Meadley, K S Whittaker, Margaret Dickinson, Ann and Tony Bennett-Hughes, Dr Phil Putwain, Revd D Glover, Karen Eliot

BROUGHTON   SD4838   MAP 7

Plough at Eaves

A6 N through Broughton, first left into Station Lane just under a mile after traffic lights, then bear left after another 1.5 miles; PR4 0BJ

Cosy old place in very peaceful spot; good value traditional food

This pleasant old tavern is in a real backwater by a quiet country lane, with metal and wood-slat seats on the front terrace from which to watch the world go by. Inside, the two homely low-beamed lattice-windowed bars are traditionally furnished with a mixture of wooden chairs, tables and upholstered seats; there are three aged guns over a log-burning stove, and a row of Royal Doulton figurines above an open log fire in the restaurant bar, which extends into a conservatory; another area has a piano lounge doubling as a private function room. Thwaites Original and Lancaster Bomber on handpump, quiet piped music and games machine. There's a well equipped children's play area at the back. More reports please.

⑪ **Bar food includes sandwiches, potted shrimps, steak and kidney pie, fish, steaks, and home-made puddings including fresh fruit pavlova and chocolate fudge cake.** *Starters/Snacks: £3.95 to £7.00. Main Courses: £5.75 to £16.00. Puddings: £1.75 to £3.95*

Thwaites ~ Tenants Doreen and Mike Dawson ~ Real ale ~ Bar food (12-2.15(3.15 Sat), 6(5.30 Sat)-9.15; 12-8 Sun; 5.30-9 Mon) ~ Restaurant ~ (01772) 690233 ~ Children welcome away from bar ~ Open 12-3, 5.30-11.30; 12-12 Sat; 12-10.30 Sun; closed all day Mon in winter; closed Mon lunchtimes

Recommended by Robin and Janice Dewhurst, Margaret Dickinson

BURY   SD8015   MAP 7

Lord Raglan 🍺

2 miles off M66 northbound, junction 1; A56 S then left in Walmersley, up long cobbled lane to Mount Pleasant, Nangreaves; if coming from N, stay on A56 S instead of joining M66, and turn left in Walmersley as above; BL9 6SP

Individually run place with fabulous views and extensive range of own-brew beers

It's worth making the trek up to this moorland pub for the phenomenal views as well as for the eight well kept own-brew beers: Leyden Balaclava, Black Pudding, Crowning Glory, Forever Bury, Nanny Flyer, Raglan Sleeve and three seasonal brews including Sebastopol and Light Brigade. They've also 25 malt whiskies and interesting foreign bottled beers, and they hold a beer festival in June. All sorts of bric-a-brac is dotted around the snug beamed front bar, with lots of pewter, brass and interesting antique clocks, and there's a mix of spindleback chairs and old wooden settles. The back room has a huge open fire (not lit when one reader visited on a cold winter's day), china on a high delft shelf and welsh dresser, and windows giving a splendid view down the valley. A plainer but more spacious dining room on the left is panelled in light wood; piped music.

⑪ **Available in the bar or the restaurant, the menu includes open sandwiches, soup, smoked fish platter, ploughman's, steak and ale pie, prawn curry, red thai vegetable curry, chicken balti, poached salmon fillet, fried plaice, chicken chasseur, steaks, and specials. One or two readers have told us that food service stops very promptly, possibly even a bit early sometimes.** *Starters/Snacks: £2.95 to £4.95. Main Courses: £5.95 to £11.95. Puddings: £3.00 to £4.00*

Own brew ~ Licensee Brendan Leyden ~ Real ale ~ Bar food (12-2, 7(5 Fri)-9;12-9 Sat, Sun) ~
Restaurant ~ (0161) 764 6680 ~ Children welcome ~ Dogs allowed in bar ~ Open 12-2.30,
7(5 Fri)-11; 12-11(10.30 Sun) Sat

*Recommended by Mr and Mrs John Taylor, Dr Kevan Tucker, Brian Wainwright, Mark and Diane Grist,
Pauline Jepson*

CHIPPING   SD6141   MAP 7

Dog & Partridge

Hesketh Lane; crossroads Chipping—Longridge with Inglewhite—Clitheroe; PR3 2TH

Comfortable old-fashioned dining pub in grand countryside, with traditional food

Efficiently run by attentive staff, this old-fashioned pub near the Forest of Bowland dates
back nearly 500 years although it has been much modernised and extended over its
lifetime. The main lounge has small armchairs around fairly close-set low tables on a blue
patterned carpet, brown-painted beams, a good winter log fire, and multicoloured
lanterns; piped music. Tetleys Bitter and Mild with a weekly changing guest such as Black
Sheep Bitter are on handpump. Smart casual dress is preferred in the stable restaurant.
More reports please.

🍴 **Bar food includes soup, sandwiches, prawn cocktail, broccoli and stilton pancakes,
steak and kidney pie, roast beef with yorkshire pudding, roast duckling with apple sauce
and stuffing, and grilled sirloin steak with mushrooms, specials such as roast pheasant or
pork fillet in apricot sauce, with home-made puddings such as bakewell pie or mango
meringue with strawberry and lime coulis.** *Starters/Snacks: £3.30 to £5.50. Main Courses:
£9.00 to £14.75. Puddings: £4.00 to £4.30*

Free house ~ Licensee Peter Barr ~ Real ale ~ Bar food (12-1.45; 7(6.30 Sat)-9; 12-3,
3.30-8.30 Sun) ~ Restaurant (7(6.30 Sat)-9 Mon-Sat; 12-8.30 Sun) ~ (01995) 61201 ~
Children welcome ~ Open 11.45-3, 6.45-11; 11.45-10.30 Sun; closed Mon

Recommended by Mr and Mrs J L Blakey, Brian Wainwright, Jane Anne Ingleson

DENSHAW   SD9711   MAP 7

Rams Head

2 miles from M62 junction 2; A672 towards Oldham, pub N of village; OL3 5UN

Roaring fires and tasty food in inviting old-world moorland pub with farm shop

Placed 1,200 feet up in the moors, this snug retreat is a useful objective for walkers, and
the views are terrific too. Its cosily traditional interior has beam-and-plank ceilings and
good log fires, and is furnished with oak settles, and benches built into the panelling of
its four thick-walled little rooms; Daleside, Timothy Taylors and a guest on handpump;
piped music. You can buy locally sourced meat and other produce, and have a coffee, in
their adjacent shop.

🍴 **Tasty bar food features game in season and a wide range of seafood, and starters could
be soup, black pudding with roast apples, carpaccio of venison, or salmon and haddock
fishcake, with main courses like steaks, breast of pheasant wrapped in bacon, fish pie,
sausage and mash, pigeon risotto, and fried escalope of salmon on lemon roast fennel
with basil pesto terrine; good value three-course set menus.** *Starters/Snacks: £4.95 to
£9.95. Main Courses: £10.95 to £15.95. Puddings: £3.95 to £4.95*

Free house ~ Licensee Geoff Haigh ~ Real ale ~ Bar food ~ Restaurant ~ (01457) 874802 ~
Children welcome if well behaved and under supervision ~ Open 12-2.30, 6-10.30; 12-8.30 Sun;
closed Mon except bank holidays

*Recommended by John and Eleanor Holdsworth, K C and B Forman, Andy and Jill Kassube, Mrs P J Carroll,
Jak Radice*

Post Office address codings confusingly give the impression that some pubs are in
Lancashire when they're really in Cumbria or Yorkshire (which is where we list them).

FENCE

SD8237 MAP 7

Fence Gate ♀

2.6 miles from M65 junction 13; Wheatley Lane Road, just off A6068 W; BB12 9EE

Smartly refurbished pub and brasserie with great wine list, five real ales and popular tasty food

This imposing 17th-c building has been thoroughly refurbished into a smart and distinctly upmarket dining venue, while keeping some more traditional pubby features. There are often as many cosmopolitan groups sipping Pimms as there are locals downing pints, but somehow both seem completely at home. An almost bewildering array of blackboards above the bar counter shows off the good, comprehensive wine list (plenty by the glass), and they also have Caledonian Deuchars IPA, Courage Directors, Theakstons Best, two changing guests such as Copper Dragon Scotts 1816 and Moorhouses Pride of Pendle, and various teas and coffees. Plenty of polished panelling and timbers divide the carpeted bar into several distinct-feeling areas: there's an almost clubby corner with a small bookcase, a fish in a glass case, and a big fire, while just along from here is a part with sporting prints above the panelling, a number of stools, and a TV. Leading off the central section with its mix of wooden tables and chairs is a very comfortable area with red-patterned sofas and lots of cushions, and there's a more unusual bit with tables on a raised step beneath carved panelling; piped music.

🍴 **Bar food is popular, particularly their home-made sausages – organic meats are combined with all sorts of different ingredients, anything from local cheese or their own black pudding to blueberries and calvados or sun-dried tomato and chilli. Other dishes include lunchtime sandwiches, soup, vegetable lasagne, cod and chips, sirloin steak, steak, ale and mushroom pie, fish pie, a sausage menu, and puddings such as apple tart; separate, more expensive brasserie menu.** *Starters/Snacks: £4.50 to £8.75. Main Courses: £4.95 to £10.95. Puddings: £4.95 to £5.50*

Free house ~ Licensee Kevin Berkins ~ Real ale ~ Bar food (12-2.30, 6.30-9.30(8 Sat, 8.30 Sun)) ~ Restaurant ~ (01282) 618101 ~ Children welcome ~ Open 12-11.30(1am Fri, Sat, 10.30 Sun)

Recommended by GLD, Mike Horgan, Margaret Dickinson, Steve Whalley, Pat and Tony Martin, K C and B Forman

GOOSNARGH

SD5738 MAP 7

Horns ♀ 🛏

Pub signed from village, about 2 miles towards Chipping below Beacon Fell; PR3 2FJ

Traditional plush pub popular for dining; nice chintzy bedrooms

Not far from the M6, this mock-Tudor inn dates from 1782 and is a quietly relaxing place for a meal. The civilised, neatly kept rooms have patterned carpets, traditional red plush upholstered chairs around pub tables, colourful flower displays, and winter log fires. Beyond the lobby, the pleasant front bar opens into attractively decorated middle rooms; piped music. They stock an extensive wine list with a dozen by the glass, a fine choice of malt whiskies, and have two continually changing beers such as Grindleton Ribble Gold and Tirril Old Faithful on handpump.

🍴 **Bar food includes sandwiches, ploughman's, soup, duck liver pâté, spicy southport shrimps, prawns and salad, steak and kidney pie, beef hotpot, roast pheasant with cranberry sauce, and scampi, specials such as slow-cooked lamb, or you can eat a five-course meal from the elaborate restaurant menu; three-course Sunday lunch.** *Starters/Snacks: £4.95 to £5.25. Main Courses: £6.50 to £12.95. Puddings: £4.95*

Free house ~ Licensee Mark Woods ~ Real ale ~ Bar food ~ Restaurant ~ (01772) 865230 ~ Children welcome ~ Open 11.30-3, 6.30-11; 11.30-4, 6.30-10 Sun; closed Mon lunchtime ~ Bedrooms: £59B/£85B

Recommended by Susan and Nigel Brookes, GLD, Ken Richards, Mr and Mrs W W Burke, K C and B Forman, Piotr Chodzko-Zajko, Ray and Winifred Halliday

GREAT MITTON   SD7139   MAP 7

Three Fishes ⏶ ♀ ◀

Mitton Road (B6246, off A59 NW of Whalley); BB7 9PQ
LANCASHIRE DINING PUB OF THE YEAR

Stylish modern conversion, tremendous attention to detail, excellent regional food with a contemporary twist, interesting drinks

Although on a large scale, this stylishly revamped dining pub does things very well even at the busiest of times (which are often), with friendly staff serving very accomplished and thoughtful regional cuisine. The interior stretches back much further than you'd initially expect. The areas closest to the bar are elegantly traditional with a couple of big stone fireplaces, rugs on polished floors, newly upholstered stools, and a good chatty feel; then there's a series of individually furnished and painted rooms with exposed stone walls and floors, careful spotlighting, and wooden slatted blinds, ending with another impressive fireplace; facilities for the disabled. The long bar counter (with elaborate floral displays) serves Thwaites Lancaster Bomber and Wainwright, a guest from Bowland such as Golden Trough or Hen Harrier, cocktails, a good choice of wines by the glass and unusual soft drinks such as locally made sarsaparilla and dandelion and burdock. Overlooking the Ribble Valley, the garden has tables and perhaps its own menu in summer. They don't take bookings (except for groups of eight or more), but write your name on a blackboard when you arrive, and find you when a table becomes free – the system works surprisingly well. This pub is under the same ownership as the Highwayman at Nether Burrow.

⏶ You order your meal at various food points dotted around, and the emphasis is on traditional lancastrian dishes with a modern twist. Products are carefully sourced from small local suppliers, many of whom are immortalised in black and white photographs on the walls, and located on a map on the back of the menu. Most dish descriptions indicate the origins of the main ingredient – the beef particularly is exclusive to here. As well as imaginative lunchtime sandwiches, there might be starters such as treacle-baked cumbrian middle white ribs, crisp corn-fed goosnargh duck leg, or fondue of lancashire cheese with onions and poached egg, main courses such as mutton pudding, lamb hotpot, rib-eye steak, curd cheese and onion pie with shortcrust pastry, with puddings such as rice pudding with mead-soaked yellow raisins, rhubarb fool or bread and butter pudding with apricot glaze; children's menu. You may need to order side dishes with some main courses. *Starters/Snacks: £3.50 to £6.50. Main Courses: £8.50 to £17.00. Puddings: £4.50 to £5.00*

Free house ~ Lease Nigel Haworth, Andy Morris ~ Real ale ~ Bar food (12-2, 6(5.30 Sat)-9; 12-8.30 Sun) ~ (01254) 826888 ~ Children welcome ~ Dogs welcome ~ Open 12-11(10.30 Sun)

Recommended by Susan and Nigel Brookes, Gerry and Rosemary Dobson, GLD, Steve Whalley, Dr Kevan Tucker, Richard Pitcher, J F M and M West, Margaret Dickinson, Brian Wainwright, Paul Ribchester, Maurice and Gill McMahon, Paul Boot, John and Sylvia Harrop, Mark O'Sullivan, Ray and Winifred Halliday, Jo Lilley, Simon Calvert, Sally Anne and Peter Goodale

LANCASTER   SD4761   MAP 7

Sun ♀ ◀ ⇌

Church Street; LA1 1ET

Contemporary updates to lovely old building, fantastic range of drinks including eight real ales, food served from breakfast on, comfortably modern bedrooms

A successful blend of old and new, this town-centre pub has been thoughtfully restored, and is well worth seeking out for its outstanding selection of drinks. It's both warmly traditional and comfortably contemporary – and the food and drinks are impressive too. The beamed bar is atmospheric and characterful, with plenty of panelling, chunky modern tables on the part flagged and part wooden floors, a 300-year-old oak door (discovered during renovations), several fireplaces (the biggest filled with a huge oak cask), and subtly effective spotlighting. The size of the bar counter belies the range of drinks available: you'll generally find three real ales from the Lancaster Brewery (set up in

2005 by the company behind the pub's transformation), as well as five changing guests from brewers such as Jennings, Nethergate, Saltaire and Thwaites, 50 belgian and bottled beers, 15 or so well chosen wines by the glass, 50 whiskies and some unique teas and coffees from a local wholesaler. There's a discreet TV in a corner. A passageway leads to a long narrow room that's altogether cooler, still with exposed stone walls, but this time covered with changing art exhibitions; the furnishings in here are mostly soft and low, with lots of dark brown pouffes and stools. Some more substantial wooden tables and high-backed chairs lead into a conservatory; piped music.

🍴 **Bar food kicks off with an unusual breakfast menu (featuring devilled kidneys, smoked kippers and eggs benedict) where you pay for the number of components you pick. Lunchtime or evening food includes lunchtime ciabattas, soup, sausage and mash, omelette of the day, smoked haddock and leek fishcakes, meat or vegetarian hotpot, fish pie, venison casserole, and a cheeseboard with generous portions.** *Starters/Snacks: £3.50 to £6.00. Main Courses: £5.00 to £12.00. Puddings: £2.95 to £4.50*

Free house ~ Licensee Dominic Kiziuk ~ Real ale ~ Bar food (12-3(3.30 Sun), 4-9(7 Fri, Sat)) ~ (01524) 66006 ~ Children welcome away from bar ~ Quiz, theme or band nights on Weds ~ Open 10am-midnight(1am Fri, Sat) ~ Bedrooms: £60S/£60S(£70B)

Recommended by Les Baldwin, Ray and Winifred Halliday, Paul Boot, Jo Lilley, Simon Calvert, Jim and Maggie Cowell, Mike Horgan, John and Shirley North

LIVERPOOL
SJ3589   MAP 7

Philharmonic Dining Rooms ★ £
36 Hope Street; corner of Hardman Street; L1 9BX

Beautifully preserved Victorian pub with superb period interior, ten real ales

Originating as a gentlemen's club, this magnificent Victorian survival is full of astonishingly preserved period details, and draws in theatre-goers, students, locals and tourists. The centrepiece is a mosaic-faced serving counter, from which heavily carved and polished mahogany partitions radiate under the intricate plasterwork high ceiling. The echoing main hall is decorated with stained glass including contemporary portraits of Boer War heroes Baden-Powell and Lord Roberts, rich panelling, a huge mosaic floor, and copper panels of musicians in an alcove above the fireplace. More stained glass in one of the little lounges declares 'Music is the universal language of mankind', and backs this up with illustrations of musical instruments. Two side rooms are called Brahms and Liszt, and there are two plushly comfortable sitting rooms. Don't miss the original 1890s Adamant gents' lavatory (all pink marble and glinting mosaics); ladies are allowed a look if they ask first. They have up to ten changing guest ales on handpump, with usually an array of seasonal brews, as well as several malt whiskies; quiz machine, fruit machine and mellow piped jazz or blues.

🍴 **Reasonably priced food (available in the bar or in the table-service grand lounge dining room) could include soup, baked potatoes, sandwiches, ploughman's, steak pie, fish and chips and puddings; in the evenings they have starters including nachos or calamari, and main courses like roasted mushroom risotto, duck leg confit, sausage and mash, and pies.** *Starters/Snacks: £3.50. Main Courses: £6.95 to £9.95. Puddings: £2.65 to £3.65*

Mitchells & Butlers ~ Manager Marie-Louise Wong ~ Real ale ~ Bar food (10-10) ~ Restaurant ~ (0151) 707 2837 ~ Open 10am-midnight

Recommended by Tracey and Stephen Groves, David and Ros Hanley, Karen Eliot, Mark and Diane Grist, the Didler, Catherine and Rob Dunster, Darren Le Poidevin, Jeremy King, John and Helen Rushton

---

Stars after the name of a pub show exceptional character and appeal. They don't mean extra comfort. And they are nothing to do with food quality, for which there's a separate knife-and-fork symbol. Even quite a basic pub can win stars, if it's individual enough.

LONGRIDGE   SD6038   MAP 7
Derby Arms ♀

Chipping Road, Thornley; 1.5 miles N of Longridge on back road to Chipping; PR3 2NB

Convivial traditional country pub with hunting and fishing paraphernalia (and menu to match) and very decent wine list

The welcoming landlady here keeps things ticking over admirably well, and regulars report that it hits the mark consistently. Among the hunting and fishing items in its main bar, old photographs commemorate notable catches, and there's some nicely mounted bait above the comfortable red plush seats, together with a stuffed pheasant that seems to be flying in through the wall. To the right is a smaller room with sporting trophies and mementoes, and a regimental tie collection; piped music and darts. The gents' has dozens of riddles on the wall – you can buy a sheet of them in the bar and the money goes to charity. Along with a good range of wines, including several half-bottles and several by the glass (they're particularly strong on south african), you'll find Black Sheep and Marstons Pedigree on handpump. A few tables out in front, and another two behind the car park, have fine views across to the Forest of Bowland. Note that they sometimes close earlier than midnight during the week.

⚋ As well as several fresh fish dishes such as potted shrimps, mussels, fresh dressed crab, **oysters and monkfish, the enjoyable food might include sandwiches, soup, ploughman's, duck spring rolls, ham, egg and chips, vegetarian hotpot, steak and kidney pudding, venison platter and aberdeen angus fillet steak rossini; good chips and generous vegetables; the two- or three-course table d'hôte menu is good value. They also have pheasant, hare, rabbit, partridge, woodcock, rabbit and mallard in season; puddings such as home-baked fruit pies, sherry trifle and bread and butter pudding.** *Starters/Snacks: £3.50 to £6.50. Main Courses: £7.95 to £10.95. Puddings: £3.50 to £4.50*

Punch ~ Lease Mrs G M Walne ~ Real ale ~ Bar food (12-2.15, 6-9.30; 12-9.30 Sat, Sun) ~ Restaurant ~ (01772) 782623 ~ Children welcome away from main bar ~ Open 11-3, 6-12; 11-4, 5-12 Sat; 11am-midnight Sun

Recommended by Maurice and Gill McMahon, Roger Thornington, Peter Craske, Margaret Dickinson, Dr and Mrs T E Hothersall, Steve Whalley

LYDGATE   SD9704   MAP 7
White Hart ⬚ ♀ ⛬

Stockport Road; Lydgate not marked on some maps so not to be confused with the one near Todmorden; take A669 Oldham—Saddleworth, and after almost 2.5 miles turn right at brow of hill to A6050, Stockport Road; OL4 4JJ

Smart up-to-date dining pub (drinkers welcome too) with not cheap but excellent food, half a dozen beers, very good wine list, garden and comfortable bedrooms

A stylish place for an evening meal, this upmarket inn is just outside the eastern fringes of Oldham, on the moors of the Pennines and a few miles from the border of the Peak District National Park. Many come here to dine, but there are often a good few locals clustered round the bar, or in the two simpler rooms at the end. The building has kept a good number of its older features, but the overall style is fairly contemporary – beams and exposed stonework are blended skilfully with deep red or purple walls, punctuated with a mix of modern paintings, black and white photos, and stylised local scenes; most rooms have a fireplace and fresh flowers; piped music, and TV in front lounge. The warmly elegant brasserie is the biggest of the main rooms and service from the smartly dressed staff is good. The wine list includes around 20 by the glass and beers are Lees Bitter, Tetleys, Marble Manchester Bitter, Timothy Taylors Golden Best and Landlord and a changing guest from a brewer such as Pictish on handpump. There are picnic-sets on the lawn behind. They put on plenty of special events based around themed menus, including wine and beer tastings, and even a brass band contest. Bedrooms are comfortable, with free internet access. More reports please.

⚋ **The thoughtfully prepared meals are pricier than in most pubs around here, but the quality is consistently high. The bar food menu typically includes open and closed** sandwiches, deep fried king prawns in beer batter with soya and ginger dipping sauce, home-smoked salmon fishcake with tartare sauce, baked goats cheese with pickled beetroot salad, butternut squash risotto cake with wasabi mayonnaise, salads such as smoked goose with pickled mushrooms and watercress, honey-roasted goosenargh duck breast with roast figs and watercress risotto, steaks, baked fillet of smoked haddock, fish pies, spinach risotto with globe artichoke and nutmeg mascarpone, and puddings such as raspberry and whiskey oat crumble cheesecake, and chocolate and cherry parfait; there is also a separate restaurant menu. *Starters/Snacks: £5.20 to £6.75. Main Courses: £10.00 to £19.00. Puddings: £4.00 to £5.75*

Free house ~ Licensee Charles Brierley ~ Real ale ~ Bar food (12-2.30, 6-9.30; 1-7.30 Sun) ~ Restaurant ~ (01457) 872566 ~ Children welcome ~ Open 12-11(midnight Sat) ~ Bedrooms: £95B/£127.50B

Recommended by Revd D Glover, Paul Bailey, Marcus Mann

LYTHAM   SD3627   MAP 7

Taps 🍺 £

A584 S of Blackpool; Henry Street – in centre, one street in from West Beach; FY8 5LE

Thriving seaside pub with down-to-earth atmosphere, eight real ales and straightforward lunchtime snacks; open all day

The friendly staff run this town pub with real flair and keep on top of things even at busy times, and the choice of beers is particularly impressive. Greene King IPA and Taps Best (brewed for the pub by Titanic) are kept on handpump alongside six ever-changing real ales from brewers such as Batemans, Hopback, Okells and Nethergate – you can see them all in the view-in cellar; also country wines and a farm cider. With a good mix of customers, the Victorian-style bare-boarded bar has a sociable unassuming feel, plenty of stained-glass decoration in the windows, depictions of fish and gulls reflecting the pub's proximity to the beach (it's a couple of minutes' walk away), captain's chairs in bays around the sides, open fires, and a coal-effect gas fire between two built-in bookcases at one end. There's also an expanding collection of rugby memorabilia with old photographs and portraits of rugby stars on the walls; shove-ha'penny, dominoes, a quiz machine and a fruit machine. There are seat belts on the bar and headrests in the gents' to help keep you out of harm's way if you have one too many. There are a few seats and a heated canopied area outside. Parking is difficult near the pub so it's probably best to park at the West Beach car park on the seafront (free on Sunday), and walk.

🍴 A handful of cheap bar snacks includes sandwiches, soup and a hot roast sandwich, filled baked potatoes, burgers, chilli and curry. *Starters/Snacks: £1.95 to £3.95. Puddings: £1.50*

Greene King ~ Manager Ian Rigg ~ Real ale ~ Bar food (12-2, not Sun) ~ No credit cards ~ (01253) 736226 ~ Children welcome away from the bar till 7pm ~ Open 11-11(midnight Fri, Sat)

Recommended by Pam and John Smith, the Didler, Steve Whalley, J F M and M West, John Fiander, Ken Richards

MANCHESTER   SJ8397   MAP 7

Britons Protection 🍷 £

Great Bridgewater Street, corner of Lower Mosley Street; M1 5LE

Lively city pub with unspoilt small rooms, huge range of whiskies, five real ales, inexpensive lunchtime snacks, and garden

A tiled passage in this centrally located grade two listed pub is lined with battle murals depicting the Peterloo Massacre of 1819, which took place a few hundred yards away. The plush little front bar has a fine chequered tile floor, some glossy brown and russet wall tiles, solid woodwork and elaborate plastering. There are two cosy inner lounges, both served by hatch, with attractive brass and etched glass wall lamps, a mirror above the coal-effect gas fire in the simple art nouveau fireplace, and again good solidly comfortable furnishings. As something of a tribute to Manchester's notorious climate, the massive bar counter has a pair of heating pipes as its footrail. Although busy at lunchtime, it's usually quiet and relaxed in the evenings; piped music. As well as a terrific range of around 235 malt whiskies and bourbons, they have one changing guest real ale from a brewery such as Jennings on handpump, and good wines. There are tables out on the garden behind. They host various evening events, including poetry readings, storytelling, silent film shows and acoustic gigs. Football supporters are excluded on match days.

🍴 **Straightforward bar food includes soup, sandwiches, ploughman's, various pies, and home-made daily specials such as steak with mushroom sauce, hotpot, lasagne or minted lamb chop.** *Starters/Snacks: £3.75 to £4.95. Main Courses: £5.00 to £6.00. Puddings: £1.50*

Punch ~ Lease Peter Barnett ~ Real ale ~ Bar food (11-2) ~ Restaurant ~ (0161) 236 5895 ~ Children welcome ~ Open 11am-midnight; 12-11 Sun

Recommended by John Fiander, Mark and Diane Grist, Ian and Nita Cooper, Revd D Glover, Mrs Hazel Rainer, Pam and John Smith, GLD, the Didler, DC, Darren Le Poidevin, Dr and Mrs A K Clarke, Joe Green

Dukes 92 £
Castle Street, below the bottom end of Deansgate; M3 4LZ

Waterside pub with spacious interior, minimalist but comfortable modern and period furnishings and good value food till mid-afternoon

The waterside position is a real draw here, in a converted stable block by the basin and bottom lock of the Rochdale Canal among restored Victorian warehouses, and the tables (with heaters) outside make the most of it. Inside, black wrought-iron work contrasts boldly with whitewashed bare plaster walls, the handsome bar is granite-topped, and an elegant spiral staircase leads to an upper room and balcony. Down in the main room the fine mix of well spaced furnishings is mainly Edwardian in mood, with one particularly massive table, elegantly comfortable chaises-longues and deep armchairs. There are two real ales on handpump from a brewer such as Moorhouses, and they've decent wines, a wide choice of spirits, and the german wheat beer Erdinger on tap; piped jazz. A gallery has temporary exhibitions of local artwork.

🍴 **They do an excellent range of over three dozen cheeses, and several pâtés with generous helpings of granary bread. Other good value bar food includes soup, sandwiches, pizzas (served all day) and salads; puddings include chocolate fudge cake and sticky toffee pudding; the restaurant has a grill menu with burgers and steaks.** *Starters/Snacks: £2.95 to £5.95. Main Courses: £5.95 to £9.95. Puddings: £3.95 to £4.95*

Free house ~ Licensee James Ramsbottom ~ Real ale ~ Bar food (12-3(4.30 Fri-Sun); pizza available outside these times) ~ Restaurant ~ (0161) 839 8646 ~ Children welcome until 8.30pm ~ Dogs allowed in bar ~ Open 11.30-11(1 Sat); 12-10.30 Sun

Recommended by Howard and Sue Gascoyne, Ben Williams, Mrs Hazel Rainer, Darren Le Poidevin, Joe Green

Marble Arch ◖
Rochdale Road (A664), Ancoats; corner of Gould Street, just E of Victoria Station; M4 4HY

Cheery town pub with noteworthy Victorian interior, great range of real ales including own brews, very reasonably priced food, and small garden

With its range of ten real ales and decent, inexpensive bar food, this splendidly preserved Victorian alehouse is worth going out of your way to experience. The interior has a magnificently restored lightly barrel-vaulted high ceiling, and extensive marble and tiling – the frieze advertising various spirits and the chimney breast above the carved wooden mantelpiece particularly stand out, and the floor has a pronounced slope. Furniture is a cheerful mix of rustic tables and chairs, including a long communal table, and all the walls are stripped back to their original glazed brick; there's a collection of breweriana, and a display cabinet with pump clips; games machine and a juke box. From windows at the back, you can look out over the brewery (tours by arrangement) where they produce their distinctive Lagonda IPA, Manchester Bitter, Marble Best, Marble Ginger Ale and seasonal brews. They also have four guest ales from brewers such as Abbeydale, Ashover, Phoenix and Pictish, and a farm cider. The Laurel and Hardy Preservation Society meet here on the third Wednesday of the month and show old films; little garden.

🍴 Good-value food (some of it incorporating Marble beers in the recipe) includes soup, generously filled sandwiches, black pudding with new potatoes and poached egg, ploughman's, steak and ale or game pie, chunky vegetable hotpot, sausage and mash, lamb shank, and puddings such as bread and butter pudding. *Starters/Snacks: £5.50 to £6.75. Main Courses: £6.95 to £10.95. Puddings: £3.50 to £4.00*

Own brew ~ Licensee Jan Rogers ~ Real ale ~ Bar food (12-9) ~ (0161) 832 5914 ~ Children welcome if dining ~ Dogs welcome ~ Open 11.30-11(midnight Fri, Sat); 12-10.30 Sun

Recommended by Tony Hobden, Pat and Tony Martin, the Didler, Joe Green, Revd D Glover, Mark and Diane Grist, Darren Le Poidevin

MELLOR
SJ9888   MAP 7

Devonshire Arms

This is the Mellor nr Marple, S of Manchester; heading out of Marple on the A626 towards Glossop, Mellor is the next road after the B6102, signposted off on the right at Marple Bridge; Longhurst Lane; SK6 5PP

Charming little pub with wide choice of food, attractive gardens and play area

---

This cosily unpretentious little place has a delightful and extensive garden, with a waterfall tumbling into a well stocked fish pond, over which a japanese bridge leads to a covered terrace, and there's a children's play area tucked away in the small tree-sheltered lawn; it also has a boules piste and there are more picnic-sets out in front. The cheerful little front bar has a warming winter fire in a sizeable Victorian fireplace with a deep-chiming clock above it, an unusual curved bar (with Robinsons Best and Mild and a Robinsons guest and sangria in summer), and a couple of old leather-seated settles among other seats. Both of the two small back rooms have Victorian fireplaces – the one on the right has an unusual lion couchant in place of a mantelpiece, and one room has french windows opening on to the garden.

🍴 The wide choice of good generous pubby food includes pea and ham soup, mussel chowder, sandwiches, baked potatoes, ploughman's, spicy lamb and bean casserole, beef rogan josh, battered haddock, mixed grill, steaks and pies such as steak and kidney and chicken and ham; children's menu. *Starters/Snacks: £4.95 to £6.95. Main Courses: £8.50 to £17.95. Puddings: £3.95 to £4.25*

Robinsons ~ Tenants John and Liz Longworth ~ Real ale ~ Bar food (11.45-2, 6-9; 12-9 Sat, Sun) ~ Restaurant ~ (0161) 4272563 ~ Children welcome ~ Jazz second Tues ~ Open 11.45-3, 6-midnight; 11.45(12 Sun)-midnight summer holidays and Sat

Recommended by Hilary Forrest, David Hoult, Roger Yates

NETHER BURROW
SD6175   MAP 7

Highwayman 🍴 🍷

A683 S of Kirkby Lonsdale; LA6 2RJ

Substantial old stone house with country interior serving carefully sourced and prepared food; lovely gardens

---

Refurbished in 2007 by the owners of the Three Fishes at Great Mitton, this upmarket dining pub has struck a chord with readers for its cheerful service and food that uses locally sourced products. Although large, its flagstoned 17th-c interior is nicely divided into nooks and corners, with a big log fire at one end; this, another smaller fire and the informal wooden furnishings give it a relaxed comfortable feel. Black and white wall prints (and placemats) show local farmers and producers from whom the pub sources its ingredients – clearly real characters, some of these, and this seems to work nicely through into their produce. Thwaites Lancaster Bomber and Original and a guest such as Thwaites Wainwrights are served on handpump, alongside good wines by the glass and about 20 whiskies. French windows open to a big terrace and lovely gardens. They don't take bookings except for groups of eight or more.

🍴 Traditional lancastrian recipes are tweaked to bring them up-to-date, and prepared using very carefully sourced products from small local suppliers (marked on a map on the back of the menu). As well as bar nibbles and imaginative sandwiches, ploughman's and platters of local seafood and cured meats, starters include rope-grown mussels, slow-cooked goosnargh duck on toast, and day-old lancashire curd with crumpet and beetroot and mustard cress salad, with main courses such as fish pie, battered haddock, lamb hotpot with pickled red cabbage, rib-eye steak with chips cooked in dripping, and breast of chicken with avocado, organic curd and salad, and puddings such as apple crumble, and banana, rum and chocolate trifle with toasted hazelnuts. *Starters/Snacks: £3.50 to £6.50. Main Courses: £8.75 to £16.50. Puddings: £4.50 to £5.00*

Free house ~ Lease Andy Morris ~ Real ale ~ Bar food (12-2, 6(5.30 Sat)-9; 12-8.30 Sun) ~ (01254) 826888 ~ Children welcome ~ Dogs welcome ~ Open 12-11(10.30 Sun)

Recommended by Jane Taylor, David Dutton, Ray and Winifred Halliday, Jo Lilley, Simon Calvert, GLD, Michael Doswell, Karen Eliot, Margaret Dickinson, Maurice and Gill McMahon

RABY   SJ3179   MAP 7
Wheatsheaf
Off A540 S of Heswall; Raby Mere Rd; CH63 4JH

Small-windowed, cottagey village pub, decent bar food; eight real ales

The nicely chatty rambling rooms in this popular timbered and whitewashed country cottage (which is known simply as The Thatch) are simply furnished, with an old wall clock and homely black kitchen shelves in the cosy central bar, and a nice snug formed by antique settles built in around its fine old fireplace. A second, more spacious room has upholstered wall seats around the tables, small hunting prints on the cream walls, and a smaller coal fire. The spacious restaurant (Tuesdays to Saturday evening) is in a converted cowshed that leads into a larger conservatory; piped music is played in these areas only. Eight real ales are kept on handpump, with two guests like Elland Bargee and Hanby Golden Honey alongside half a dozen regular brews: Black Sheep, Brimstage Trappers Hat, Greene King Old Speckled Hen, Tetleys, Theakstons Best, Thwaites Original and Wells & Youngs Bombardier. There are picnic-sets on the terrace and in the pleasant garden behind, with more seats out front.

🍴 Good straightforward lunchtime bar food includes soup, a wide range of sandwiches and toasties, ploughman's, omelettes, steak and ale pie, mixed grill and braised knuckle of lamb; three-course Sunday lunch; more expensive à la carte restaurant food. *Starters/Snacks: £3.20 to £6.55. Main Courses: £6.95 to £13.45. Puddings: £3.95*

Free house ~ Licensee Wes Charlesworth ~ Real ale ~ Bar food (12-2(3 Sun), 6-9.30; not Mon or Sun evenings) ~ Restaurant (evenings 6-9.30, Tues-Sat; not Sun and Mon) ~ (0151) 336 3416 ~ Children welcome in restaurant if supervised ~ Dogs allowed in bar ~ Open 11.30-11; 12-10.30 Sun

Recommended by MLR, Paul Boot, Clive Watkin, Paul Humphreys

RIBCHESTER   SD6535   MAP 7
White Bull 🛏
Church Street; turn off B6245 at sharp corner by Black Bull; PR3 3XP

Friendly 18th-c inn with unusual views from pleasant garden, and interesting food

'Food is unquestionably the star of the show': one reader's comment was typical of many for this welcoming 18th-c inn, where the three ensuite double bedrooms are much enjoyed too. The floors are variously carpeted and bare floorboards, and in the traditional-looking spacious main bar is a stuffed fox in two halves that looks as if it's jumping through the wall; piped music, TV, games machine, pool and board games; service is usually very good. On handpump are real ales such as Bowland Chipping Steamer and Shepherd Neame Spitfire; several wines by the glass. In summer the big garden makes a pleasant spot to sit and contemplate the ruins of the adjacent Roman bathhouse; incidentally, look out for the tuscan pillars in the pub's porch – they came from a nearby building and are also thought to be of Roman origin.

🍴 Most areas are laid out for dining, and portions are generous. The menu and specials board might include starters such as soup, mussel and leek risotto, deep-fried roquefort fritters with beetroot and candied hazelnuts, main courses such as slow-cooked suckling pig with black pudding and apple and calvados stuffing, breast of goosnargh free-range chicken, a fish of the day, specials, and puddings such as apple and blackberry crumble or melting chocolate pudding. *Starters/Snacks: £3.75 to £6.00. Main Courses: £4.00 to £9.00. Puddings: £5.00 to £6.00*

Enterprise ~ Lease Chris Bell ~ Real ale ~ Bar food (12-2.30, 6-9.30; 12-8 Sun; not Mon) ~ Restaurant ~ (01254) 878303 ~ Children welcome ~ Open 12-12(11 Sun); closed Mon lunchtime Sept-Apr ~ Bedrooms: £55B/£70B

Recommended by David Morgan, A Benson, Steve Whalley, Howard Kissack, Trevor and Sylvia Millum, Carol Thompson, Mike Brock, Mark Blackburn, Brian and Janet Ainscough, DC, N R White

RIMINGTON
SD8045   MAP 7

Black Bull

Off A59 NW of Clitheroe, at Chatburn; or off A682 S of Gisburn; BB7 4DS

Comfortably civilised and rather unusual, with huge collection of transport models, and imaginative food

Quite a surprise awaits inside this comfortable stone-built pub, which houses an eye-popping collection of all things transport. The big traditional main bar has a model locomotive in a glass case beside an attractively tiled fireplace, a plane hanging from the ceiling, various platform signs on the walls, various model cars and ships, and comfortable banquettes and window seats; a central area with leatherette chairs leads through to a quietly refined dining room, with an exhibition of wildlife art on the walls; piped music, TV. Three real ales usually feature Copper Dragon, Thwaites and Timothy Taylors Landlord, all served on handpump. There is a special night for rail buffs on the last Thursday of each winter month, with pie and peas, film shows and soundtracks of vintage locos.

🍴 Very good bar food features soup, sausage and mash, beef and ale pie, black pudding and mash and steak pudding, plus a vegetarian option and a fish menu; more elaborate à la carte options (available in the restaurant or in the bar) typically include organic pork fillet roasted in port and apple sauce, steak rossini in parma ham topped with foie gras and truffle, and gressingham duck breast with honey glaze; puddings. *Starters/Snacks: £3.50 to £6.95. Main Courses: £9.95 to £19.95. Puddings: £4.75*

Free house ~ Licensee Neil Buckley ~ Real ale ~ Bar food (12-2.30, 6.30-9; 12-6.30 Sun; not Sun evening) ~ Restaurant ~ (01200) 445220 ~ Children welcome until 8pm ~ Open 12-3, 6.30-midnight; 12-midnight Sat; 12-11 Sun; closed Mon in winter ~ Bedrooms: £39.95S/£69.95S

Recommended by Steve Whalley, Gordon and Margaret Ormondroyd, Steve Kirby, Yvonne and Mike Meadley

STALYBRIDGE
SJ9598   MAP 7

Station Buffet 🍺 £

The Station, Rassbottom Street; SK15 1RF

Victorian station buffet bar with seven quickly changing beers and a few cheap basic meals

It's a positive pleasure to wait for a train at Stalybridge, on the Manchester to Huddersfield line, as you can linger on platform one in this atmospheric Victorian refreshment room. Friendly staff serve a marvellous range of seven real ales, with Bass, Boddingtons and Flowers alongside four guests that change rapidly from breweries such as Coach House, Elland and Boggart Hole Clough, alongside farm cider and belgian and other foreign bottled beers. The bar has a welcoming fire below an etched-glass mirror, old photographs of the station in its heyday, and other railway memorabilia; there's a little conservatory. An extension along the platform leads into what was the ladies' waiting room and part of the station-master's quarters. This has original ornate ceilings and a dining/function room with Victorian-style wallpaper; board games, cards, newspapers and magazines. On a sunny day you can sit out on the platform.

⏹ **They do cheap old-fashioned snacks such as tasty black peas and sandwiches, and three or four daily specials such as home-made pie with peas, bacon casserole and all day breakfast; freshly made coffee and tea by the pot.** *Starters/Snacks: £1.50 to £2.00. Main Courses: £2.40 to £3.50. Puddings: £0.75 to £1.20*

Free house ~ Licensees John Hesketh and Sylvia Wood ~ Real ale ~ Bar food (12-8) ~ No credit cards ~ (0161) 303 0007 ~ Children welcome ~ Dogs welcome ~ Open 11-11; 12-10.30 Sun

Recommended by John Fiander, the Didler, Len Beattie, Dennis Jones

TUNSTALL   SD6073   MAP 7

Lunesdale Arms ⓘⓘ ♀
A683 S of Kirkby Lonsdale; LA6 2QN

Light and airy civilised pub with emphasis on good imaginative food, separate area with traditional games

Readers are unanimous in their praise for this well run and cheerful country pub, where the main emphasis is on the excellent food. In the bright and airy bars, bare boards create a lively acoustic. On one side of the central bar part, a white-walled area has a good mix of stripped and sealed solid dining tables, and blue sofas facing each other across a low table (with daily papers) by a woodburning stove with a stone mantelpiece. Another area has pews and armchairs (some of the big unframed oil paintings are for sale), and at the other end, an airy games section has pool, table football, board games and TV. A snugger little flagstoned back part has another woodburning stove. Besides Black Sheep and a guest from a brewer such as Dent on handpump they have eight wines by the glass and 20 malts; piped music. The church in this village in the Lune Valley has Brontë associations.

⏹ **Food is prepared with admirable attention to detail – readers particularly praise the home-made bread and chips. The constantly changing menu might include lunchtime sandwiches, soup, lancashire cheese rarebit with smoked cumbrian ham, fish and chips, sausage and mash, slow-roast pork belly with haricot beans and smoked sausage, roasted fillet of salmon with lemon and chive mayonnaise, and puddings such as rhubarb and ginger panna cotta, and chocolate pot. They do Sunday lunch and smaller helpings of some main courses.** *Starters/Snacks: £4.95 to £7.95. Main Courses: £8.50 to £15.50. Puddings: £4.95*

Free house ~ Licensee Emma Gillibrand ~ Real ale ~ Bar food ~ (01524) 274203 ~ Children welcome ~ Dogs allowed in bar ~ Live piano music most Thurs nights ~ Open 11-3, 6-11; 11-3.30, 6-12.30 Sat; 12-3.30, 6-11 Sun; closed Mon except bank holidays

Recommended by Glenwys and Alan Lawrence, Mrs B Hemingway, John and Sylvia Harrop, W K Wood, Chris and Meredith Owen, Michael Doswell, Ken and Jenny Simmonds, Jo Lilley, Simon Calvert, Alun and Stephanie Llewellyn, Dr Kevan Tucker

UPPERMILL   SD0006   MAP 7

Church Inn ◼ £
From the main street (A607), look out for the sign for Saddleworth Church, and turn off up this steep narrow lane – keep on up!; OL3 6LW

Lively good value community pub with own brews from big range, lots of pets, and good food; children very welcome

Appealingly unconventional, this quirky place up in an elevated position on the moors has very inexpensive bar food and eight to 12 own-brew Saddleworth beers that start from just £1.50 a pint. Some of the seasonal ones (look out for Rubens, Ayrtons, Robins and Indya) are named after the licensee's children and appear around their birthdays.

When the spring water levels aren't high enough for brewing they bring in some guests such as Holts, Millstone and Robinsons; continental wheat beer and dark lager on tap too. On Wednesdays, local bellringers arrive to practise with a set of handbells that are kept here, while anyone is invited to join the morris dancers who meet here on Thursdays. Outside, there's a delightful assortment of pets roaming around in the garden or in view in the adjacent field – rabbits, chickens, dogs, ducks, geese, horses and a couple of peacocks, as well as an increasing army of rescued cats resident in an adjacent barn. Children and dogs are made to feel very welcome. The big unspoilt L-shaped main bar has high beams and some stripped stone; one window at the end of the bar counter looks down over the valley, and there's also a valley view from the quieter dining room; the conservatory opens on to a new terrace. Comfortable furnishings include settles and pews as well as a good individual mix of chairs, and there are lots of attractive prints, staffordshire and other china on a high delft shelf, jugs, brasses and so forth; TV (only when there's sport on) and unobtrusive piped music. The horse-collar on the wall is worn by the winner of their annual gurning (face-pulling) championship (part of the lively Rush Cart Festival, usually held over the August bank holiday).

🍴 **Reasonably priced bar food includes soup, sandwiches, steak and ale pudding, a range of pies, lasagne, jumbo cod, and puddings such as jam roly-poly or hot chocolate fudge cake.** *Starters/Snacks: £1.95 to £6.50. Main Courses: £5.75 to £11.75. Puddings: £2.50*

Own brew ~ Licensee Julian Taylor ~ Real ale ~ Bar food (12-2.30, 5.30-9; 12-9 Sat, Sun, bank hols) ~ (01457) 820902 ~ Children welcome ~ Dogs allowed in bar ~ Open 12-12(11 Sun)

Recommended by the Didler, John Fiander, Len Beattie, Bob Broadhurst

WADDINGTON   SD7243   MAP 7

Lower Buck
Edisford Road; BB7 3HU

Popular village pub with reasonably priced, tasty food; five real ales

In a lovely village, this chatty local is handily placed for walks in the Ribble Valley. The friendly landlord keeps a range of five local ales, with Moorhouses Black Cat Mild and guests such as Bowland Hen Harrier and Odd Shaped Balls, Moorhouses Premier and Timothy Taylors Landlord. The décor is nicely sympathetic with cream-painted walls hung with pictures, a built-in dresser in the front bar, and a welcoming coal fire; there are two dining rooms. There is seating outside in the garden.

🍴 **Using meat reared at a farm nearby in Longridge, and vegetables grown in Longridge too, the reasonably priced food includes lunchtime sandwiches and ploughman's, soup, morecambe bay shrimps, short-crust pastry pies, fish pie, hotpot, mixed grill, meat or vegetable lasagne, sirloin steak, and specials such as smoked haddock and poached egg pie, or steak and kidney pudding, with puddings such as apple pie.** *Starters/Snacks: £3.95 to £5.00. Main Courses: £7.75 to £16.25. Puddings: £3.50 to £4.50*

Free house ~ Licensee Andrew Warburton ~ Real ale ~ Bar food (12-2.30, 6-9; 12-9 Sat, Sun and bank hols) ~ Restaurant ~ (01200) 423342 ~ Children welcome ~ Dogs welcome ~ Open 11(12 Sun)-11(midnight Sat)

Recommended by Noel Grundy, Len Beattie

Several well known guide books make establishments pay for entry, either directly or as a fee for inspection. These fees can run to many hundreds of pounds. We do not. Unlike other guides, we never take payment for entries. We never accept a free meal, free drink, or any other freebie from a pub. We do not accept any sponsorship – let alone from commercial schemes linked to the pub trade. All our entries depend solely on merit. And we are the only guide in which virtually all the main entries have been gained by a unique two-stage sifting process: first, a build-up of favourable reports from our thousands of reader-reporters, then anonymous vetting by one of our senior editorial staff.

WHEATLEY LANE   SD8338   MAP 7

Old Sparrow Hawk

Wheatley Lane Road; towards E end of village road which runs N of and parallel to A6068; one way of reaching it is to follow Fence, Newchurch 1¼ signpost, then turn off at Barrowford ¾ signpost; BB12 9QG

Comfortably civilised dining pub, with very well prepared food and five real ales

This pleasantly chatty place has a good range of beers, with Bass, Black Sheep, Moorhouses Blonde Witch and Premier Bitter, and Thwaites on handpump, and draught Fransizkaner wheat beer, in addition to good wines by the glass. Locals pop in for an early evening drink and there's a buoyant relaxed atmosphere. Attractively laid out in several distinct areas, some with carpet and some with red tiles, it's nicely characterful, with interesting furnishings, dark oak panelling and timbers, stripped stonework, lots of snug corners including a nice area with a fire, and a sofa under a domed stained-glass skylight; daily papers, piped music and board games. Fresh flowers cheer up the cushioned leatherette bar counter. Heavy wood tables out on a spacious and attractive front terrace (pretty flower beds and a water feature) have good views to the moors beyond Nelson and Colne.

🍴 **Good fresh bar food includes interesting sandwiches, wraps and ciabattas, soup, pressed ham and black pudding terrine with beetroot salad, caesar salad, crispy duck salad, fish pie, sausage and mash, fish and chips, rib-eye steak, specials like goosnargh duck breast on bacon and lentil stew, and puddings such as rum and raisin cheesecake and eton mess.** *Starters/Snacks: £4.25 to £6.25. Main Courses: £9.25 to £14.95. Puddings: £4.50 to £6.95*

Mitchells & Butlers ~ Lease Stephen Turner ~ Real ale ~ Bar food (12-2.30, 5-9; 12-9.30 Sat; 12-8 Sun) ~ Restaurant ~ (01282) 603034 ~ Children welcome ~ Dogs welcome ~ Live music at bank hols ~ Open 12-11(12 Sat, 10.30 Sun)

Recommended by K C and B Forman, Steve Whalley, Dr Kevan Tucker, Margaret Dickinson

WHEELTON   SD6021   MAP 7

Dressers Arms 🍺

2.1 miles from M61 junction 8; Briers Brow, off A674 Blackburn road from Wheelton bypass (towards Brinscall); 3.6 miles from M65 junction 3, also via A674; PR6 8HD

Good choice of beer and big helpings of food at invitingly traditional pub run by warm friendly licensees

This converted cottage row usually keeps eight real ales, including their own Milk of Amnesia and Mild (now brewed off the site), Black Sheep and Tetleys, plus five guests from brewers such as Bank Top, Phoenix and Thwaites; also 16 malt whiskies, and some well chosen wines, with several by the glass. The snug low-beamed rooms are full of traditional features, including a handsome old woodburning stove in the flagstoned main bar; there are newspapers and magazines; piped music, juke box, pool table, games machine and TV. There are lots of picnic-sets, a large umbrella with lighting and heaters on a terrace in front of the pub. Their big car park is across the road. More reports please.

🍴 **Pubby bar food includes soup, breaded mushrooms, sandwiches, hot filled batons, cumberland ring, steak pudding, liver and onions, fish and chips and 14oz sirloin steak,** and there's a cantonese restaurant on the first floor; Sunday carvery; all-you-can-eat curry night on Thursdays; free supper for the quiz night on Tuesdays. *Starters/Snacks: £2.75 to £4.65. Main Courses: £7.95 to £14.95. Puddings: £3.50 to £4.95*

Own brew ~ Licensees Steve and Trudie Turner ~ Real ale ~ Bar food (12-2.30, 5-9; 12-9 weekends and bank hols) ~ Restaurant ~ (01254) 830041 ~ Children welcome ~ Dogs welcome ~ Open 11am-12.30am(1am Sat)

Recommended by Brian Wainwright, Norma and Noel Thomas, Ann and Tony Bennett-Hughes, Pam and John Smith, Mike and Linda Hudson, Keith and Chris O'Neill

WHITEWELL

SD6546 MAP 7

Inn at Whitewell ★★ ⑪ ♀ 🛏

Most easily reached by B6246 from Whalley; road through Dunsop Bridge from B6478 is also good; BB7 3AT

Very civilised hotel with smartly pubby atmosphere, enjoyable bar food and luxury bedrooms

Well positioned if you want to spend a day or two walking on the nearby moors of the Forest of Bowland, this relaxing and elegant manor house hotel owns several miles of trout, salmon and sea trout fishing on the Hodder, and with notice they'll arrange shooting and will make up a picnic hamper. It's beautifully decorated, with handsome furnishings standing out well against powder blue walls that are neatly hung with attractive prints. The old-fashioned pubby main bar has antique settles, oak gateleg tables, sonorous clocks, old cricketing and sporting prints, roaring log fires (the lounge has a very attractive stone fireplace), and heavy curtains on sturdy wooden rails; one area has a selection of newspapers and magazines, local maps and guide books, there's a piano for anyone who wants to play, and even an art gallery. In the early evening, there's a cheerful bustle but once the visitors have gone, the atmosphere is tranquil and relaxing. Their good wine list includes around 230 wines (there is a good wine shop in the reception area), and the three real ales on handpump might be from Bowland, Copper Dragon and Timothy Taylor. Staff are courteous and friendly. There are delightful views from the riverside bar and adjacent terrace.

⑪ Besides lunchtime sandwiches, well presented bar food includes soup, baked goats cheese wrapped in filo pastry, fish pie, grilled norfolk kipper, fish and chips, slow-cooked breast of lamb, chargrilled polenta with aubergine purée and slow-roast tomatoes, roast breast of goosnargh chicken, and delicious puddings like triple chocolate gateau with poached pears; also daily specials and a more expensive restaurant menu. *Starters/Snacks: £4.20 to £9.00. Main Courses: £7.60 to £17.00. Puddings: £5.00*

Free house ~ Licensee Charles Bowman ~ Real ale ~ Bar food ~ Restaurant ~ (01200) 448222 ~ Children welcome ~ Dogs allowed in bar and bedrooms ~ Open 10am-11pm(midnight Fri-Sun) ~ Bedrooms: £70B/£96B

Recommended by Jo Lilley, Simon Calvert, Derek and Sylvia Stephenson, Steve Whalley, Mr and Mrs W W Burke, N R White, J F M and M West, Anthony Longden, Mrs P J Carroll, Noel Grundy, Fiona Salvesen, Ross Murrell, Karen Eliot, John and Jackie Chalcraft, K S Whittaker, Revd R P Tickle, David and Sue Smith, GLD, Dr Kevan Tucker, Steve and Sarah Eardley, Steve Kirby, Revd D Glover, Michael Doswell

WRAY

SD6067 MAP 7

Inn at Wray

2 miles E of Hornby off A683 Kirkby Lonsdale—Lancaster; LA2 8QN

Comfortable and civilised new dining pub with good interesting local food

Formerly the New Inn, this was reopened under its new name early in 2008, after reworking as a dining pub. It's been well done, in a restrained way, keeping its original small-room layout. As you go in, a snug room opposite the serving bar has comfortable soft leather sofas and easy chairs by the coal fire, and magazines to read. A short corridor opens into further rooms, with oriental rugs on polished boards or flagstones, a log fire in one, a big woodburning stove in another, neat tables and chairs, and quite a few carefully placed pictures – one lot more a collection of grand frames, really. A larger end room has rather more imposing tables, and a cabinet of home-made preserves, cordials and country wines. Two carpeted dining rooms upstairs have comfortably upholstered chairs around a mix of tables, and a wall of books. Careful lighting and the soft pastel décor with a modicum of stripped stone make for a relaxed atmosphere, as does the welcoming and obliging service. They have Thwaites Original, a beer brewed for them by Tirril and a guest such as Lancaster Bomber on handpump, and do good coffee.

⑪ Good food here adds plenty of imaginative touches to proper country cooking. Besides sandwiches, they might have black pudding with mustard sauce and apple and chive compote or smoked haddock and pancetta fishcake as starters, perk up gressingham duck breast with their home-made marmalade, do good well hung local steaks, vegetarian dishes such as mixed vegetable and feta filo parcel and have puddings such as almond frangipane and caramel panna cotta. There's fresh fish on Fridays, and on weekdays they do bargain early suppers. *Starters/Snacks: £4.50 to £9.70. Main Courses: £8.95 to £17.50. Puddings: £4.50 to £6.50*

Free House ~ Licensee Greg Forbes ~ Real ale ~ Bar food (12-2, 6-9 (12-9 Sat, 8.30 Sun)) ~ Restaurant ~ (01524) 221722 ~ Children welcome ~ Dogs allowed in bar ~ Open 12-3, 6-11; 12-11 Sat; 12-10.30 Sun; closed Mon

Recommended by Michael Doswell, Karen Eliot

YEALAND CONYERS
SD5074 MAP 7

New Inn

3 miles from M6 junction 35; village signposted off A6; LA5 9SJ

Good generous food all day and warm welcome at village pub near M6

In a very attractive setting, this much-liked 17th-c village pub stays open all day and has a sheltered lawn at the side with picnic-sets among colourful roses and flowering shrubs. Inside, the simply furnished little beamed bar on the left has a cosy village atmosphere, with its log fire in the big stone fireplace. On the right, two communicating shiny beamed dining rooms are filled with closely set dark blue furniture and an attractive kitchen range. Robinsons Hartleys XB and another of their beers are served on handpump alongside around 30 malt whiskies; piped music and very friendly service. This makes a useful objective if you're walking in the area or visiting Leighton Moss RSPB reserve.

🕮 **Hearty helpings of bar food include sandwiches, baguettes and baked potatoes (all with interesting fillings), and soup, ploughman's, mussels with creamy garlic sauce, sausage with spinach mash, spicy mexican bean chilli tortilla, pie of the day, salmon fillet poached in white wine with prawn, cucumber and lemon reduction, and specials such as roast guinea fowl and pancake galette layered with cheese, fennel and tomato.** *Starters/Snacks: £3.95 to £6.50. Main Courses: £8.95 to £12.95. Puddings: £4.85*

Robinsons ~ Tenants Bill Tully and Charlotte Pinder ~ Real ale ~ Bar food (11.30(12 Sun)-9.30) ~ Restaurant ~ (01524) 732938 ~ Children welcome ~ Dogs allowed in bar ~ Open 11.30-11; 12-10.30 Sun

Recommended by Ray and Winifred Halliday, Jane and Martin Bailey, Don Bryan, Tony and Maggie Harwood, Bruce and Sharon Eden, Andrew York, Richard Greaves, Paul and Margaret Baker, Jo Lilley, Simon Calvert, Steve Whalley, John and Hilary Penny

LUCKY DIP

Besides the fully inspected pubs, you might like to try these Lucky Dips recommended to us and described by readers (if you do, please send us reports: feedback@thegoodpubguide.co.uk).

AFFETSIDE [SD7513]
Pack Horse BL8 3QW [Watling St]: Attractive neatly kept moorland pub on Roman road, particularly well kept Hydes, big helpings of good value lunchtime bar food, snug pool room, restaurant early evenings (not Sun); big car park, good walking country, open all day wknds *(Norma and Noel Thomas, Revd D Glover, Ian and Nita Cooper)*
ALTHAM [SD7732]
Walton Arms BB5 5UL [Burnley Rd (A678)]: Attractive and relaxed, with wide range of good reasonably priced food, well kept Jennings, very good value wines, friendly efficient service, oak furniture in flagstoned dining room *(Bob Broadhurst)*

ARKHOLME [SD5872]
Bay Horse LA6 1AS [B6254 Carnforth—Kirkby Lonsdale]: Neatly kept and homely old three-room country pub with one or two well kept changing ales such as Black Sheep and Moorhouses, friendly landlord and prompt service, good value basic food, lovely inglenook, pictures of long-lost London pubs; bowling green, handy for Lune valley walks, cl Mon *(Jane Taylor, David Dutton, MLR)*
AUGHTON [SD4106]
Dog & Gun L39 5BU [Long Lane]: Recently refurbished keeping old-fashioned charm, two rooms off bar, two fires, darts and dominoes, well kept Marstons-related ales, limited choice of enjoyable lunchtime food (not Mon/Tues); front and back gardens, bowling green *(Peter Black)*

BALDERSTONE [SD6131]
Myerscough Hotel BB2 7LE [Whalley Rd, Samlesbury; A59 Preston—Skipton, just over 2 miles from M6 junction 31]: Solid traditional furnishings in cosy and relaxed softly lit dark-beamed bar, four well kept Robinsons ales, good soft drinks choice, traditional games, good basic home-made food from sandwiches up, darts, quiz night; no dogs; children allowed in eating area, disabled access, garden picnic-sets, bedrooms (LYM, A Benson)

BARLEY [SD8240]
Pendle BB12 9JX: Friendly 1930s village pub in shadow of Pendle Hill, three cosy rooms, two open fires, well kept Moorhouses, enjoyable pub food (all day wknds), conservatory; garden, good walking country, bedrooms (J A Hooker, Dr Kevan Tucker)

BEBINGTON [SJ3385]
Travellers Rest CH62 1BQ [B5151, not far from M53 junction 4; New Ferry Rd, Higher Bebington]: Friendly semi-rural pub with several areas around central bar, good value popular bar lunches from good sandwiches to mixed grill (not Sun), up to eight real ales inc some from small breweries, efficient staff, alcoves, beams, brasses etc; no children; open all day (MLR)

BELMONT [SD6715]
☆ *Black Dog* BL7 8AB [Church St (A675)]: Nicely set Holts dining pub with their usual sensibly priced food (not Tues evening, all day Fri-Sun) and bargain beers, cheery small-roomed traditional core, coal fires, friendly attentive staff, picture-window extension; children welcome, seats outside with moorland views above village, good walks, decent bedrooms, open all day (the Didler, Steve Whalley, Norma and Noel Thomas, Tom and Jill Jones, Ben Williams, Pam and John Smith, LYM, Pat and Tony Martin, Peter Heaton)

BELTHORN [SD7324]
Grey Mare BB1 2PG [Elton Rd/Grane Rd (A6177), handy for M65 junction 5]: Bargain traditional food in popular welcoming Thwaites pub high on Oswaldtwistle Moor, their ales inc Dark Mild, attractive conservatory, fine views possibly to Blackpool (John and Helen Rushton, Brian Wainwright)

BILSBORROW [SD5039]
☆ *Owd Nells* PR3 0RS [off A6 N of Preston; at S end of village take Myerscough Coll of Agriculture turn into St Michaels Rd]: Nice pastiche of old rustic pub in busy thatched tourist complex by Lancaster Canal, huge range of real ales, good choice of generous bar food, good value wines, tea and coffee, flagstones and low beams by central bar counter, high pitched rafters each end, plenty of games, adjacent restaurant, hotel, craft and teashops; children welcome, good play area outside, two smoking shelters (one with TV) comfortable bedrooms, open all day (Stephen Hargreaves, Paul Ribchester)

BIRKENHEAD [SJ3288]
Crown CH41 6JE [Conway St]: Friendly three-room pub popular for interesting changing ales inc Cains, Weston's farm cider, good value generous food all day till 6, good tilework; terrace tables, open all day (the Didler)
Dispensary CH41 5DQ [Chester St]: Comfortable Cains pub with guest beers too, good value lunchtime food, handsome glass ceiling; handy for ferry, open all day (the Didler)
Stork CH41 6JN [Price St]: Early Victorian, four well restored civilised rooms around island bar, polished mosaic floor, old photographs, several changing ales, bargain basic food wkdy lunchtime and early evening, tiled façade; open all day (the Didler)

BLACKBURN [SD6921]
Black Horse BB3 2AF [Redearth Rd, Darwen]: Busy basic pub with local Three Bs Stokers Slake, popular monthly beer festivals, good value food, Thurs band night; open all day (the Didler)

BLACKSTONE EDGE [SD9617]
☆ *White House* OL15 0LG [A58 Ripponden—Littleborough, just W of B6138]: Beautifully placed moorland dining pub with remote views, emphasis on bargain hearty food from sandwiches up (all day Sun), prompt friendly service, Theakstons Best and changing guests, belgian bottled beers, cheerful atmosphere, carpeted main bar with hot coal fire, other areas off, most tables used for food; children welcome (Brian and Anna Marsden, K C and B Forman, LYM)

BOLTON [SD7109]
Howcroft BL1 2JU [Pool St]: Friendly local serving as tap for good Bank Top ales, also guest beers, bargain pubby lunches, lots of small screened-off rooms around central servery with fine glass and woodwork inc cosy snug with coal fire, bright and airy front room, conservatory, plenty of pub games, popular monthly poetry nights; crown bowling green, open all day (Joe Green, the Didler)
Spinning Mule BL1 1JT [Nelson Sq]: Typical Wetherspoons, good choice of real ales inc good value local ones, reasonably priced food all day, quick service; very busy with young people Sat night (Ben Williams)
Wilton Arms BL1 7BT [Belmont Rd, Horrocks Fold]: Friendly low-beamed roadside pub with enjoyable fresh food, well kept Timothy Taylors and Thwaites, open fires; garden overlooking valley, Pennine walks, open all day (Dave Davies)

BRINDLE [SD5924]
☆ *Cavendish Arms* PR6 8NG [3 miles from M6 junction 29, by A6 and B5256 (Sandy Lane)]: Refurbished village pub, sensibly priced pubby food inc good beef sandwiches, cosy snugs with stained-glass partitions, Marstons-related ales; children welcome, canopied terrace with water feature, open all day – may cl winter wkdy afternoons (John and Eleanor Holdsworth, Dr D J and Mrs S C Walker, LYM, David and Sue Smith)

BURY [SD8313]
Trackside BL9 0EY [East Lancs Railway Station, Bolton St]: Busy station bar by East Lancs steam railway, great range of ales and bottled imports, farm cider, bargain wkdy lunches (from breakfast time till 5 wknds); platform tables, open all day *(the Didler, Mrs Hazel Rainer)*

CARNFORTH [SD5173]
Longlands LA6 1JH [Tewitfield, about 2 miles N; A6070, off A6]: Bustling family-run village inn with good beer range, friendly helpful staff, good interesting food in bar and restaurant (worth booking); live music Mon, bedrooms, self-catering cottages *(Tony and Maggie Harwood)*

CATON [SD5364]
Ship LA2 9QJ [Lancaster Rd]: Roomy and reliable open-plan dining pub with good choice of reasonably priced enjoyable food from sandwiches to generous fresh fish and Sun lunch, well kept Thwaites and decent wines, efficient friendly staff, appealing nautical bric-a-brac, good fire in charming antique fireplace; subdued piped music; garden tables, handy for Lune valley and Forest of Bowland *(Chris and Meredith Owen, Margaret Dickinson)*

CHURCHTOWN [SD4842]
Punch Bowl PR3 0HT [Church St, off A586 Garstang—St Michaels-on-Wyre]: Attractive mock-Tudor pub/restaurant with wide choice of generous and reasonably priced good food, two small old-fashioned bar rooms, panelling, stained glass, lots of stuffed animals, billiards room, attractive back dining room, friendly staff, well kept Tetleys, good fires; disabled facilities, lovely village *(Pam and John Smith)*

CLITHEROE [SD6642]
☆ *Craven Heifer* BB7 3LX [Chipping Rd out of Chaigley through Walker Fold, off B6243 about 4 miles W]: Attractively refurbished civilised country dining pub with wide range of good food from bar favourites to smarter dishes, children's helpings, friendly attentive service, interesting wine choice, real ale such as Bowland, series of dining areas, bar with comfortable armchairs, sofas and big log fire, fine views; tables outside, cl Mon/Tues *(GLD, K C and B Forman, Phillip Marchant, Steve Whalley)*
Swan & Royal BB7 2BX [Castle St]: Large central former coaching inn, smaller rooms/alcoves off main bar, food from baguettes up, Jennings ales; bedrooms *(J A Snell)*

COLNE [SD8939]
Admiral Lord Rodney BB8 0TA [Mill Green]: Welcoming chatty three-room local, well kept Archers, Swales and guest ales from small breweries, bargain pubby food (not Mon), upside-down table and chairs on bar ceiling, football ties collection; children and dogs welcome *(Len Beattie)*
Black Lane Ends BB8 7EP [Skipton Old Rd, Foulridge]: Neatly kept country inn with good food inc some unusual dishes, welcoming relaxed atmosphere, Copper Dragon ales and guest, small restaurant; handy for canal and reservoir walks *(John and Helen Rushton, Richard and Karen Holt)*

COMPSTALL [SJ9690]
Andrew Arms SK6 5JD [George St (B6104)]: Enjoyable good value food, Robinsons ales, enterprising choice of wines by the glass, busy back dining room, bric-a-brac on walls; handy for Etherow Country Park *(Dennis Jones)*

COWAN BRIDGE [SD6277]
☆ *Whoop Hall* LA6 2HP [off A65 towards Kirkby Lonsdale]: Spacious and comfortable linked areas, wide choice of interesting quick food (all day from 8am) from popular buttery, pleasant neat staff, Black Sheep and Greene King, decent wines, log fire, pool; piped music; children welcome, garden well off road with back terrace views, play area, comfortable bedrooms *(Chris and Meredith Owen, Margaret Dickinson, LYM, Pat and Stewart Gordon)*

CROSBY [SJ3100]
Crows Nest L23 7XY [Victoria Rd, Gt Crosby]: Unspoilt and interesting roadside local with cosy bar, snug and Victorian-style lounge, chatty friendly landlady, well kept Cains, Theakstons and two guests; tables outside, open all day *(the Didler)*

CROSTON [SD4818]
Grapes PR26 9RA [Town Rd]: Popular village pub with wide choice of well kept beers inc Moorhouses, good lunchtime and evening food in bar or restaurant *(Yvonne and Mike Meadley)*

DENTON [SJ9395]
Lowes Arms M34 3FF [Hyde Rd (A57)]: Smart pub brewing its own cheap LAB ales, other guest beers, good well priced food, jovial landlord and efficient staff, separate large games room; tables outside, open all day wknds *(Dennis Jones)*

DIGGLE [SE0007]
Diggle Hotel OL3 5JZ [village signed off A670 just N of Dobcross]: Welcoming three-room hillside pub serving good value generous food (all day Sat, can be a wait), well kept ales inc Black Sheep and Timothy Taylors, daily papers; tables among the trees, quiet spot just below the moors, bedrooms *(BB, Brian and Anna Marsden)*

DOWNHAM [SD7844]
☆ *Assheton Arms* BB7 4BJ [off A59 NE of Clitheroe, via Chatburn]: Neatly kept pub in lovely village location, good value food using local produce from small open kitchen, quick service, lots of wines by the glass, Marstons ales, low-beamed L-shaped bar with pews, big oak tables and massive stone fireplace; piped music; children and dogs welcome, picnic-sets outside, open all day Sun *(Michael Lamm, K C and B Forman, Mr and Mrs John Taylor, Maurice and Gill McMahon, Norma and Noel Thomas, LYM)*

ECCLES [SJ7798]
Albert Edward M30 0LS [Church St]: Cheery roadside pub with three rooms, flagstones

and old tiles, fire, bargain Sam Smiths; small back terrace, open all day *(the Didler)*

Grapes M30 7HD [Liverpool Rd, Peel Green; A57 0.5 mile from M63 junction 2]: Handsome brawny Edwardian local with superb etched glass, wall tiling and mosaic floor, lots of mahogany, eye-catching staircase, bargain Holts and a good guest beer, fairly quiet roomy lounge areas (children welcome till 7), pool in classic billiards room, vault with Manchester darts, drinking corridor; tables outside, open all day *(Pam and John Smith, Pete Baker, the Didler)*

Lamb M30 0BP [Regent St (A57)]: Full-blooded Edwardian three-room local, splendid etched windows, fine woodwork and furnishings, extravagantly tiled stairway, trophies in display case, bargain Holts and lunchtime sandwiches, full-size snooker table in original billiards room; open all day *(the Didler, Pam and John Smith)*

Royal Oak M30 0EN [Barton Lane]: Large old-fashioned Edwardian pub on busy corner, several rooms off corridor, handsome tilework, mosaic floors and fittings, cheap Holts, good licensees, pool; children allowed daytime in back lounge (may be organ singalongs), open all day *(the Didler)*

Stanley Arms M30 0QN [Eliza Ann St/Liverpool Rd (A57), Patricroft]: Lively mid-Victorian corner local with bargain Holts, popular front bar, hatch serving lobby and corridor to small back rooms, one with cast-iron range, lunchtime filled rolls; open all day *(the Didler, Pam and John Smith)*

White Lion M30 0ND [Liverpool Rd, Patricroft, a mile from M63 junction 2]: Welcoming Edwardian traditional local, clean, tidy and popular with older people, great value Holts, games in lively public bar, other rooms off tiled side drinking corridor inc one with piano *(the Didler, Pete Baker)*

EGERTON [SD7014]

Thomas Egerton BL7 9SR [Blackburn Rd]: Former Globe under new management, interesting varied food much locally sourced, beers inc Bank Top *(Ann and Peter Tovell)*

ELSWICK [SD4138]

Ship PR4 3ZB [High St]: Contemporary dining pub with friendly service, good food all day, comfortable easy chairs in bar; children allowed if eating (till 8.30), good garden with terrace, open all day *(J F M and M West, Kate Lee)*

EUXTON [SD5518]

Euxton Mills PR7 6JD [A49 S, 3 miles from M6 junction 28]: Neatly kept roomy pub with wide choice of good value food from good sandwiches to daily roasts, popular wkdy lunchtime OAP deals, friendly service, well kept ales inc Burtonwood and Jennings *(Yvonne and Mike Meadley)*

Plough PR7 6HB [Runshaw Moor; a mile from A49/B5252 junction]: Spotless black-beamed country dining pub with olde-worlde décor and antiques, good atmosphere, enjoyable food inc good value imaginative dishes and popular Sun roasts), well kept Jennings and Theakstons, sympathetic extension; piped music, big-screen TV; big sheltered back garden with heated terrace under awning, lawn tables, small play area *(Margaret Dickinson)*

Railway PR7 6LA [The Ordnance, Wigan Rd]: Civilised pub with enjoyable food (all day Sun) from sandwiches and light dishes up, leather sofas in comfortable lounge, open-plan dining areas, Burtonwood ale; heated partly enclosed terrace *(Wendy Rogers)*

FORMBY [SD2908]

Freshfield L37 7BD [Massams Lane]: Good choice of well kept beers, usual lunchtime pub food (till 2.30, 4 wknds) inc special deals, evening events; open all day *(Pat and Tony Martin)*

FRECKLETON [SD4328]

Ship PR4 1HA [towards Naze Lane Ind Est, then right into Bunker St]: 17th-c, with roomy nautical-theme main bar, big windows overlooking watermeadows, generous bargain food, good Moorhouses and Theakstons, games area with big-screen TV; children allowed, tables outside *(LYM, Ben Williams)*

GARSTANG [SD4943]

Bradbeer Bar PR3 1YE [Garstang Country Hotel & Golf Club; B6430 S]: Best Western hotel with relaxed spacious bar overlooking golfing greens, good value imaginative food, good staff, big log fire; tables outside, bedrooms *(Margaret Dickinson)*

Crown PR3 1FA [High St]: Sympathetically modernised Thwaites pub, their full range kept well, bargain food, roaring coal fire, particularly friendly licensees *(Alan and Eve Harding)*

Royal Oak PR3 1ZA [Market Pl]: Comfortable roomy small-town inn dating from 16th c, attractive panelling, several eating areas inc charming snug, reliably enjoyable generous food (all day Sun) inc imaginative specials, small helpings for children or OAPs, Robinsons ales, good value coffee, restaurant, spotless housekeeping; disabled access, comfortable bedrooms, open all day Fri-Sun *(Pam and John Smith)*

☆ **Th'Owd Tithebarn** PR3 1PA [off Church St]: Large barn with flagstoned terrace overlooking Lancaster Canal marina, Victorian country life theme with very long refectory table, old kitchen range, masses of farm tools, stuffed animals and birds, flagstones and high rafters, simple food all day from filled baguettes up, Flowers IPA and Tetleys, good value wine by the glass, quieter parlour welcoming children; piped music; open all day summer *(Bruce and Sharon Eden, LYM, A Benson)*

GLASSON [SD4456]

Dalton Arms LA2 0BZ [Ten Row, Glasson Dock]: Friendly traditional three-room dining pub in port/marina area, good interesting food, well kept Thwaites; garden *(David and Rhian Peters)*

GOOSNARGH [SD5636]

☆ *Stags Head* PR3 2AU [Whittingham Lane (B5269)]: Lots of separate mainly old-world areas rambling around a central servery, plenty of nice features inc proper old-fashioned radiators, good value generous food from local produce (even make their own pork scratchings), children's helpings, good service, well kept ales, popular restaurant; piped music and live Fri nights; tables out in pleasant pergola with lawn (*Pam and John Smith, BB*)

GREAT HARWOOD [SD7332]

Royal BB6 7BA [Station Rd]: Substantial Victorian pub with good changing range of beers from small breweries, tap for nearby Red Rose brewery, good soft drinks choice (own sarsaparilla), great selection of bottled beers, simple traditional fittings, friendly atmosphere, pub games inc pool and darts; big-screen TV, live music Fri; partly covered terrace, bedrooms, cl lunchtime Mon-Thurs, open all day Fri-Sun (*the Didler*)

Victoria BB6 7EP [St Johns St]: Splendid beer range with Bowland Gold and half a dozen or more changing guests, friendly landlady and regulars, unspoilt traditional Edwardian layout with five rooms off central bar, one with darts, one with pool, two quiet snugs, some handsome tiling; tables out behind, opens 4.30 (3 Fri, all day wknds), cl wkdy lunchtimes (*Pam and John Smith, Richard Pitcher, the Didler, Pete Baker*)

GRIMSARGH [SD5934]

Plough PR2 5JR [Preston Rd (B6243 Preston—Longridge)]: Friendly and clean with wide range of good food from doorstep sandwiches to fish choices, well kept Moorhouses, Timothy Taylors and guest ales, helpful staff, appealing country décor (*David and Ruth Hollands, Dr and Mrs I J May*)

GRINDLETON [SD7646]

Buck BB7 4QS [Sawley Rd]: Recently reopened country pub in nice village, good value food (*Noel Grundy*)

HASKAYNE [SD3608]

Blue Bell L39 7JU [N on A5147]: Popular unpretentious local with L-shaped bar and separate back room, friendly staff and regulars, straightforward bargain food inc daily roast, two well kept ales (often Moorhouses); animal farm inc shetland pony (*Pete Baker*)

Kings Arms L39 7JJ [Delf Lane (A5147)]: Friendly traditional old-fashioned local with cosy L-shaped lounge and proper public bar, coal fires, interesting motoring memorabilia, four well kept ales, limited snacky lunchtime food, darts and table football (*Pete Baker*)

HASLINGDEN [SD7823]

Griffin BB4 5AF [Hud Rake, off A680 at N end]: Friendly basic local brewing its own cheap Pennine ales in the cellar, farm cider, L-shaped bar with views from comfortable lounge end, darts in public end; open all day (*Pete Baker*)

HAWKSHAW [SD7515]

☆ *Red Lion* BL8 4JS [Ramsbottom Rd]: Roomy, comfortable and attractive pub/hotel, friendly welcome and efficient cheerful service, good generous fresh local food in cosy bar and separate well run restaurant, good changing ales; comfortable if rather creaky bedrooms, quiet spot by River Irwell, open for food all day wknds (*K C and B Forman, John and Sylvia Harrop, W K Wood*)

HELMSHORE [SD7820]

White Horse BB4 4LU [Holcombe Rd]: Roomy stone-built inn reopened after spell as a restaurant, sympathetically modernised and low-ceilinged, up to four real ales, food; tables outside, Irwell valley views from front, walkers welcome (*Dave Endicott*)

HEST BANK [SD4766]

☆ *Hest Bank Inn* LA2 6DN [Hest Bank Lane; off A6 just N of Lancaster]: New management doing good fresh food in picturesque three-bar coaching inn, nice setting close to Morecambe Bay (so gets very wide range of customers in the easy-going bar areas), five well kept ales, decent wines, friendly helpful young staff, separate attractive refurbished restaurant area with pleasant conservatory; children welcome, plenty of tables out by Lancaster Canal, open all day (*MLR, Helen and Keith Bowers, Jane Taylor, David Dutton, BB*)

HESWALL [SJ2781]

Devon Doorway CH60 2SA [Telegraph Rd (A540)]: Large thatched low-beamed M&B dining pub with modern furniture on bare boards, inglenook fire, good value food, well kept Timothy Taylors Landlord, lots of continental beers, good service; back and front gardens (*Tom and Jill Jones*)

HEYSHAM [SD4161]

Royal LA3 2RN [Main St]: Four changing ales, well priced wines and decent food inc early evening bargains in charming early 16th-c low-beamed two-bar pub; no dogs at meal times; tables out in front and in good-sized sheltered garden, pretty fishing village with great views from interesting church (*A Benson, Tony and Maggie Harwood, Margaret Dickinson*)

HOGHTON [SD6225]

Boatyard PR5 0SP [A675 Preston—Bolton, NW of A674 junction]: Country dining pub above Leeds & Liverpool Canal, plenty of boats to watch, friendly staff, good value pubby food all day, Thwaites ales, Victorian-style décor; tables outside, beached barge in grounds (*Ben Williams*)

HOLDEN [SD7749]

☆ *Copy Nook* BB7 4NL [Bolton by Bowland Rd]: Roomy and attractive dining pub, friendly relaxing atmosphere, pleasant helpful staff, generous popular food from sandwiches up in bar's two dining areas and restaurant, reasonable prices, well kept ales such as Marstons Pedigree, good wine choice, log fire; piped music; children welcome, good walking area, six comfortable bedrooms *(BB, Brian and Janet Ainscough, Norma and Noel Thomas, Mrs P Beardsworth)*

HORNBY [SD5868]

Royal Oak LA2 8JY [Main St]: Long low-beamed bar with food inc good sandwiches, Thwaites, friendly service, pleasant décor inc HMS *Royal Oak* memorabilia *(Chris and Meredith Owen)*

HOYLAKE [SJ2188]

Green Lodge CH47 1HW [Stanley Rd, Kings Gap]: Pleasantly refurbished old hotel associated with nearby Royal Liverpool golf links, wide food choice inc two-for-one deals, spacious restaurant, real ales, friendly efficient service; outside seating, views, six bedrooms *(Colin Moore)*

HURST GREEN [SD6838]

Bayley Arms BB7 9QB [off B6243 Longridge—Clitheroe, towards Stoneyhurst Coll]: Comfortable bar with enjoyable good value food inc children's, friendly licensees, well kept Black Sheep Bitter, nice mix of old furniture, sporting and music memorabilia, brasses, log fire, inventive menu in more formal restaurant; comfortable bedrooms, attractive Ribble Valley village *(Len Beattie)*

HYDE [SJ9495]

Cheshire Ring SK14 2BJ [Manchester Rd (A57, between M67 junctions 2 and 3)]: Welcoming pub tied to Beartown brewery, their ales well priced, guest beers and imports on tap, beer festivals, farm cider, good house wines, good value sandwiches; piped music; opens 2 (1 Thurs-Sun) *(Dennis Jones, the Didler)*

Sportsman SK14 2NN [Mottram Rd]: Unpretentious basic Victorian local popular for its eight real ales, good prices, welcoming licensees, open fires and memorabilia, pub games, full-size snooker table upstairs; no food; children and dogs welcome *(the Didler)*

IRBY [SJ2586]

Irby Mill CH49 3NT [Irby Mill Hill, off Greasby rd]: Built on site of old mill in 1980, good choice of well kept beers, good value wines by the glass, decent food all day (can take a while) inc tapas, two low-beamed largely flagstoned rooms and carpeted lounge with comfortable pub furniture, coal-effect gas fire, interesting old photographs and history of mill; tables out on terraces and side grass, open all day *(MLR, Ann and Tony Bennett-Hughes, Pat and Tony Martin, BB)*

KNOWLE GREEN [SD6439]

Newdrop PR3 2YX [N off B6243, 2nd left at crossroads]: Good food, service, wine and beer inc Bowland; magnificent setting on Longridge Fell *(John and Helen Rushton)*

LANCASTER [SD4761]

Borough LA1 1PP [Dalton Sq]: Leather sofas and armchairs, high stools and elbow tables on wood floors, sizeable restaurant with some boothed areas, pillars and painted panelling, enjoyable food from good potted shrimps to steaks, eight ales inc Black Sheep, Bowland and Wainwrights, extensive wine list; dogs welcome, terrace with covered area *(Jo Lilley, Simon Calvert, Maria S)*

Ring o' Bells LA1 1RE [King St]: New management doing well, enjoyable food, well kept beer, good staff *(Tony and Maggie Harwood)*

LANESHAW BRIDGE [SD9141]

Alma BB8 7EG [Emmott Lane, off A6068 E of Colne]: Friendly country pub, enjoyable good value food, well kept beer *(Andy and Jill Kassube)*

LATHOM [SD4511]

Ship L40 4BX [off A5209 E of Burscough; Wheat Lane]: Big pub tucked below embankment at junction of Leeds & Liverpool and Rufford Branch canals, several beamed rooms, some interesting canal and naval memorabilia, Cains beers, decent bargain food inc three-course evening special, prompt service, games room with pool; TV, no dogs till after 9 – unusual local food rule; children welcome, lots of tables outside, open all day *(MLR, BB, J A Hooker, Nick Holding, Jeremy King)*

LEA TOWN [SD4730]

Smiths Arms PR4 0RP [Lea Lane; right off A583 at Clifton, right afer 2 miles at Windmill pub]: Recently refurbished under new licensees, Thwaites beers, wide food choice inc daily roast and OAP deals *(Jim and Maggie Cowell)*

LIMBRICK [SD6016]

Black Horse PR6 9EE [off A6 at Adlington; Long Lane]: Recently refurbished old-world low-ceilinged stone-built pub, the first recorded in Lancs (1577); well kept Greene King and Theakstons, coal fires, friendly service, good reasonably priced food (new Sicilian chef/landlord), small restaurant; garden behind, handy for West Pennine country park, open all day *(Peter Heaton)*

LITTLE LEVER [SD7407]

Jolly Carter BL3 1BW [Church St]: Bright and comfortable, with good value home-made food, Bank Top, Greene King Old Speckled Hen and Timothy Taylors Landlord, modern décor, friendly helpful long-serving licensees; handy for Bolton Branch of Manchester, Bolton & Bury Canal *(Ben Williams)*

LITTLEBOROUGH [SD9315]

Wine Press OL15 0AZ [Hollingworth Rd]: Renovated waterside pub with uncluttered split-level interior, well kept Black Sheep, hearty helpings of reasonably priced food *(Michael Butler)*

LIVERPOOL [SJ3489]

☆ *Baltic Fleet* L1 8DQ [Wapping, nr Albert Dock]: Triangular pub with own good Wapping brews and interesting guest ales, friendly service, lunch (not Sat) and evening food, nautical paraphernalia, bare boards, big arched windows, unpretentious mix of furnishings, newspapers, new upstairs lounge; piped music, TV; children welcome in eating areas, dogs in bar, back terrace, open all day *(LYM, Tracey and Stephen Groves,*

Mark and Diane Grist, the Didler, Paul Boot, Darren Le Poidevin)

Belvedere L7 7EB [Sugnall St]: Victorian pub with friendly chatty small bar, original fittings inc etched glass, open fire, well kept beers such as Copper Dragon and Spitting Feathers, good pizzas; open all day *(the Didler)*

☆ **Cains Brewery Tap** L8 5XJ [Stanhope St]: Victorian pub with full Cains range at reasonable prices, guest beers, friendly efficient staff, good value wkdy food till 6 (2 Sat), nicely understated décor, wooden floors, plush raised side snug, interesting old prints and breweriana, handsome bar, gas fire, daily papers; sports TV; brewery tours, open all day *(the Didler)*

Carnarvon Castle L1 1DS [Tarleton St]: Friendly pub in shopping area, long and narrow with compact bar and comfortable back lounge, Cains ales and two guests, breakfasts (from 10) and lunchtime bar snacks, Dinky toys and other eclectic collections; open all day, cl Sun evening, Mon/Tues lunchtime (opens 8pm then) *(the Didler)*

Crown L1 1JQ [Lime St]: Well preserved art nouveau showpiece with fine tiled fireplace and copper bar front, plush banquettes, splendid ceiling in airy corner bar, smaller back room with another good fireplace, impressive staircase sweeping up under splendid cupola to handsome area with ornate windows; generous bargain food till early evening, well priced Cains and guest beers *(Joe Green, the Didler, John and Helen Rushton)*

☆ **Dispensary** L1 2SP [Renshaw St]: Small chatty central pub with Cains ales and two guests, bottled imports, friendly staff, good value wkdy food 12-7, polished panelling, marvellous etched windows, bare boards, comfortable raised back bar, Victorian medical artefacts; open all day *(the Didler, Darren Le Poidevin, Jeremy King, Joe Green)*

☆ **Doctor Duncan** L1 1HF [St Johns Lane]: Friendly Victorian pub with several rooms inc impressive back area with pillared and vaulted tiled ceiling, particularly attentive staff, full Cains range and guest beers, belgians on tap, enjoyable good value food, pleasant helpful service, daily papers; may be piped music, can get lively evenings, busy wknds; family room, open all day *(the Didler)*

Everyman Bistro L1 9BH [Hope St, below Everyman Theatre]: Low-ceilinged tile-floor clattery basement with long wooden tables, four well kept ales such as Brimstage and Copper Dragon, side room with good value fresh food *(the Didler)*

Globe L1 1HW [Cases St, opp station]: Chatty comfortable old local in busy shopping area, pleasant staff, Cains and guest beers, lunchtime filled cobs, cosy snug, tiny quiet sloping-floor back lounge, prints of old Liverpool; 60s piped music; open all day *(the Didler, Joe Green)*

Grapes L2 6RE [Mathew St]: Friendly open-plan local with good Cains, Tetleys and guest ales, good value lunchtime bar food, cottagey décor with flagstones, old range, wall settles, mixed furnishings; open all day *(the Didler)*

Lion L2 2BP [Moorfields, off Tithebarn St]: Ornate Victorian tavern with great changing choice of real ales, friendly atmosphere and landlord interested in pub's history, lunchtime food inc splendid cheese and pie specialities, sparkling etched glass and serving hatches in central bar, unusual wallpaper, big mirrors, panelling and tilework, two small back lounges one with fine glass dome, coal fire; open all day *(the Didler, Mark and Diane Grist, Pete Baker)*

Ma Boyles L3 1LG [Tower Gardens, off Water St]: Backstreet pub with neat plain décor, good value bar food all day from pies to oysters, well kept Cains, Hydes and guest, quieter downstairs bar; open all day, cl Sat night and Sun *(the Didler, Tracey and Stephen Groves)*

Midland L1 1JP [Ranelagh St]: Well kept Victorian local with original décor, ornate lounge, long corner bar, nice etched glass, mirrors and chandeliers; keg beers *(the Didler)*

Peter Kavanaghs L8 7LY [Egerton St, off Catherine St]: Shuttered pub with interesting décor in several small rooms inc old-world murals, stained glass and lots of bric-a-brac (bicycle hanging from ceiling), wooden settles and real fires, Cains, Greene King, Wychwood and guests, friendly staff; open all day *(the Didler)*

Poste House L1 6BU [Cumberland St]: Small comfortably refurbished early 19th-c backstreet local surrounded by huge redevelopment, friendly licensees and chatty regulars, Cains beers and a guest, good wkdy lunches, daily papers, room upstairs; open all day *(the Didler, Jeremy King)*

Roscoe Head L1 2SX [Roscoe St]: Civilised old pub with three spotless little unspoilt rooms, friendly long-serving landlady, well kept Jennings, Tetleys and guest ale, good value home-made lunches, interesting memorabilia; Tues quiz, open all day *(Joe Green, David Martin, the Didler)*

Ship & Mitre L2 2JH [Dale St]: Friendly gaslit local popular with university people, up to 12 changing unusual ales, imported beers, two farm ciders, good-humoured staff, good value basic food lunchtime and (not Mon-Weds) early evening, pool, weekly themed beer nights; piped music; open all day, cl Sun lunchtime *(Mark and Diane Grist, the Didler)*

Swan L1 4DQ [Wood St]: Neon sign for this busy unsmart three-floor pub, bare boards, deep red lighting, Hydes, Phoenix and six guest beers, Weston's farm cider, good value cobs and wkdy lunches, friendly staff; rock juke box draws younger crowd *(the Didler, Jeremy King)*

☆ *Thomas Rigbys* L2 2EZ [Dale St]: Spacious beamed and panelled pub with great range of beers inc Okells and imports, impressively long bar, steps up to main area, table service, reasonably priced hearty home-made food (with accompanying beer recommendations) all day till 7; disabled access, outside seating, open all day *(the Didler, Jeremy King)*

Vines L1 1JQ [Lime St]: Comfortable and friendly with Victorian mahogany and mosaic tilework, handsome high-ceilinged room on right with stained glass; open all day *(the Didler)*

White Star L2 6PT [Rainford Gdns, off Matthew St]: Lively traditional local with lots of woodwork, boxing prints, White Star shipping line and Beatles memorabilia, Bowland and changing guest beers, friendly staff, quieter back room; big-screen sports TVs; open all day *(the Didler)*

LYDIATE [SD3604]

Scotch Piper L31 4HD [Southport Rd; A4157]: Medieval thatched pub, well worn in, with heavy low beams, flagstones, thick stone walls and dogs sprawled in front of roaring fires, well kept Banks's and guest ale from tiny counter in main room, corridor to middle room with darts and back snug, no food; bikers' night Weds, outside lavatories; big garden with aviary, chickens and donkey, open all day wknds *(the Didler, Pete Baker)*

MANCHESTER [SJ8398]

☆ *Ape & Apple* M2 6HQ [John Dalton St]: Big friendly open-plan pub with bargain Holts and hearty bar food, comfortable seats in bare-boards area with lots of old prints and posters, armchairs in upstairs lounge; piped music, TV area, games machines; unusual brick cube garden, bedrooms, open all day *(the Didler, Darren Le Poidevin)*

Bar Fringe M4 5JN [Swan St]: Long bare-boards café-bar specialising in continental beers, also four changing ales from small local breweries, farm cider, friendly staff, enjoyable food till 6 (4 Sat/Sun), daily papers, shelves of empty beer bottles, cartoons, posters and bank notes, polished motorcycle hung above door, games inc pinball; tables out behind, open all day *(the Didler)*

Castle M4 1LE [Oldham St, about 200 yards from Piccadilly, on right]: Simple traditional front bar, small snug, full Robinsons range from fine bank of handpumps, friendly locals, games in back room, nice tilework outside; no food, children allowed till 7, open all day (Sun 12-8) *(the Didler, Tony Hobden)*

Circus M1 4GX [Portland St]: Compact traditional pub with particularly well kept Tetleys from minute corridor bar (or may be table service), friendly landlord, celebrity photographs, leatherette banquettes in panelled back room; often looks closed but normally open all day (may have to knock) *(the Didler, Mark and Diane Grist)*

City Arms M2 4BQ [Kennedy St, off St Peters Sq]: Five or six quickly changing real ales, belgian bottled beers, occasional beer festivals, busy for bargain bar lunches, quick friendly service, coal fires, bare boards and banquettes, prints, panelling and masses of pump clips, handsome tiled façade and corridor; good piped music, TV, games machine; wheelchair access but steps down to back lounge, open all day *(the Didler)*

Coach & Horses M45 6TB [Old Bury Rd, Whitefield; A665 nr Besses o' the Barn Stn]: Early 19th-c, several separate rooms, popular and friendly, bargain Holts beers, table service, darts, cards; open all day *(the Didler)*

Crescent M5 4PF [Crescent (A6) – opp Salford Univ]: Three areas off central servery with up to 12 changing ales, friendly new licensees and young staff, buoyant local atmosphere (popular with uni), low-priced food inc good breakfast, bare boards and open fire, plenty of character, pool room; small enclosed terrace, open all day *(the Didler, Ben Williams, Jeremy King)*

Crown & Kettle M4 5EE [Oldham Rd/Gt Ancoats St]: Comfortably refurbished and partly panelled three-room Victorian pub, up to eight real ales, farm cider, popular bar food all day (till 6 wknds), coal fire, ornate high ceilings with remarkably intricate plasterwork (being restored), decorative windows *(the Didler, BB)*

Dutton Arms M3 1EU [Park St, Strangeways]: Welcoming old-fashioned backstreet local nr prison, three unusually shaped rooms, Hydes from central servery, lots of bric-a-brac; open all day *(the Didler)*

Egerton Arms M3 5FP [Gore St, Salford; A6 by stn]: Several rooms, chandeliers, art nouveau lamps, low-priced Holts and guest beers, friendly service; open all day *(the Didler, Ben Williams)*

Font M1 5NP [New Wakefield St]: Modern café-style bar by railway viaduct, good home-cooked food, two changing ales, lots of bottled beers, reasonable prices; loud music evenings when popular with students; open all day *(the Didler)*

Grey Horse M1 4QX [Portland St, nr Piccadilly]: Small traditional one-bar Hydes local, their Bitter and Mild, some unusual malt whiskies, panelled servery with colourful gantry, lots of prints, photographs and plates; piped 60s/70s music, small TV, net curtains; can bring good sandwiches from next door, open all day *(the Didler, Mark and Diane Grist)*

Hare & Hounds M4 4AA [Shudehill, behind Arndale]: Unpretentious 18th-c favourite of older locals, long narrow bar linking front snug and comfortable back lounge (with TV), notable tilework, panelling and stained glass, good Holts and Tetleys, friendly staff, games machine, karaoke nights; open all day *(Pete Baker, the Didler, Joe Green, Mark and Diane Grist)*

Jolly Angler M1 2JW [Ducie St]: Plain backstreet local, long a favourite, small and friendly, Hydes ales, coal or peat fire; darts, pool and sports TV, informal folk nights Thurs, Sat and Sun; open all day Sat *(Pete Baker, BB, the Didler)*

Kings Arms M3 6AN [Bloom St, Salford]: Plain tables, bare boards and flagstones contrasting with opulent maroon and purple décor and stained-glass, good changing real ale range, good value lunchtime food (till 6.30, not Sat); juke box, music, poetry or theatre nights upstairs; open all day (cl Sun evening) *(the Didler)*

Knott Fringe M3 4LY [Deansgate]: Friendly modern café-bar with Marble organic ales and guest beers, good range of continental imports, worthwhile inexpensive food all day; under railway arch, by Castlefield heritage site *(the Didler)*

Lass o' Gowrie M1 7DB [36 Charles St; off Oxford St at BBC]: Lively tiled Victorian sidestreet local with big-windowed long bar, stripped brickwork, hop pockets draped from the ceiling, good range of real ales inc Black Sheep, Greene King and house beer brewed by Titanic, good bargain food, open all day *(LYM, the Didler)*

Mark Addy M3 5EJ [Stanley St, off New Bailey St, Salford]: Unusual converted waiting rooms for boat passengers, barrel-vaulted red sandstone bays with wide glassed-in brick arches, cast-iron pillars and flagstones, views over river, limited bargain food inc good cheese and pâté choice, quite a few wines, fast friendly service; keg beers, piped music, sports TV facing bar; flower-filled waterside courtyard *(Jeremy King, LYM, Howard and Sue Gascoyne)*

☆ **Mr Thomas Chop House** M2 7AR [Cross St]: Good home-cooked traditional lunchtime food, friendly well informed staff who cope quickly however busy, good wines by the glass, well kept real ales, attractive Victorian décor, front bar with bare boards, panelling, original gas lamp fittings and stools at wall and window shelves, back tiled eating area, period features inc wrought-iron gates for wine racks; open all day *(Darren Le Poidevin, the Didler, GLD, Dennis Jones, Roger Yates)*

New Oxford M3 6DB [Bexley Sq, Salford]: Eight well kept changing beers and a house ale brewed by Northern, good range of imported beers, friendly staff, light and airy décor in small front bar and back lounge, coal fire, enjoyable basic food, good choice of wines; open all day *(the Didler, Ben Williams)*

Old Monkey M1 4GX [Portland St]: Holts showpiece recently built in traditional style, generous tasty food and their ales, bargain prices (beer even cheaper on Mon), bare boards, etched glass, mosaic tiling, interesting memorabilia, upstairs lounge *(Dr and Mrs A K Clarke, the Didler, Jeremy King)*

Old Wellington M3 1SW [Cathedral Gates, off Exchange Sq]: Tudor pub moved from Old Shambles Sq during Arndale rebuild, original flagstones, panelling and 16th-c gnarled

timbers, new bar fittings; open-plan with small bar and food area, restaurant and further bar on two floors above, real ales inc Jennings, courteous efficient staff; piped music; lots of tables out overlooking new Exchange Sq – plastic glasses here *(BB, Jeremy King)*

☆ **Peveril of the Peak** M1 5JQ [Gt Bridgewater St]: Vivid art nouveau green external tilework, interesting pictures, lots of mahogany, mirrors and stained or frosted glass, log fire, very welcoming family service, changing mainstream ales from central servery, cheap basic lunchtime food (not Sun), three sturdily furnished bare-boards rooms, busy lunchtime but friendly and homely evenings; TV; children welcome, pavement tables, cl wknd lunchtimes, open all day Fri *(the Didler, Joe Green, Mark and Diane Grist, GLD, LYM)*

Plough M18 7FB [Hyde Rd (A57), Gorton]: Classic tiling, windows and gantry in unspoilt Robinsons local, wooden benches in large public bar, two quieter back lounges, small pool room, lots of pub games; TV; open all day *(the Didler)*

☆ **Rain Bar** M1 5JG [Gt Bridgewater St]: Lots of woodwork and flagstones in former umbrella works, well kept Lees beers, masses of wines by the glass, good value pubby food all day inc 9am wknd breakfast, welcoming efficient staff, relaxed atmosphere, daily papers, coal fire in small snug, large upstairs café-bar too; piped music may be loud, can be busy with young people evenings; good back terrace overlooking spruced-up Rochdale Canal, handy for Bridgwater Hall, open all day *(Dr and Mrs A K Clarke, the Didler)*

Sams Chop House M2 1HN [Back Pool Fold, Chapel Walks]: Small pleasant dining pub, offshoot from Mr Thomas Chop House, with thriving atmosphere, good beers, huge helpings of good plain english food, good wine choice, formal waiters, original Victorian décor *(GLD)*

☆ **Sinclairs** M3 1SW [Cathedral Gates, off Exchange Sq]: Charming low-beamed and timbered 18th-c pub (rebuilt here in redevelopment), bargain Sam Smiths, good all-day menu inc fresh oysters, brisk friendly service, bustling atmosphere, quieter upstairs bar with snugs and Jacobean fireplace; tables out in Shambles Sq (plastic glasses), open all day *(Ben Williams, Pam and John Smith, LYM, Jeremy King, the Didler, Clive Flynn)*

Smithfield M4 5JZ [Swan St]: Unpretentious open-plan local with interesting well kept changing ales, some in jugs from the cellar, house beer brewed by Phoenix, beer festivals, bargain food from open kitchen, daily papers, friendly landlady, pool; games machine, juke box, sports TV; good value bedrooms in nearby building, open all day *(the Didler, Joe Green, BB)*

The Bar M21 0UE [Wilbraham Rd]: Tied to Marble with their organic beers and guests, good choice of bottled beers, good value food esp vegetarian, quick pleasant young staff, daily papers; smart pavement tables *(Pat and Tony Martin)*

Union M5 4LG [Liverpool St, Salford]: Down-to-earth local in industrial area, chatty bar with side room, bargain Holts and home-cooked food, pool room; open all day *(the Didler)*

Wetherspoons M1 2AP [Piccadilly]: Large three-roomed pub on two floors, can get busy without feeling overcrowded, good range of well kept beers, decent wines, friendly efficient service, sensibly priced food all day *(Bob)*

White Lion M3 4NQ [Liverpool Rd, Castlefield]: Lots of dark wood, tables for eating up one side of three-sided bar, good value home-made food all day, Phoenix, Timothy Taylors Landlord and changing guests, decent house wine, good tea, friendly service, real fire, lots of prints and Man Utd pictures, shelves of bottles and jugs; big-screen sports TVs, nostalgic discos Fri-Sun; disabled access, children welcome, tables out among Roman excavations overlooking fort gate, handy for Museum of Science and Industry and Royal Exchange Theatre, open all day *(the Didler, Dennis Jones)*

MARPLE [SJ9389]

Hare & Hounds SK6 7EJ [Dooley Lane (A627 W)]: Attractive old pub above River Goyt, modern layout and décor, new lunchtime and evening menus in restaurant, Hydes ales from stainless servery; sports TV, no dogs; well behaved children welcome, open all day *(Dennis Jones)*

MAWDESLEY [SD4914]

Red Lion L40 2QP [off B5246 N of Parbold]: Darkly traditional bars, enjoyable food in stylish and airy conservatory restaurant, friendly attentive service, well kept ales such as Caledonian Deuchars IPA and Timothy Taylors Landlord, decent wines by the glass; piped music; children in eating areas, tables in back courtyard and in front, walk to Harrock Hill for great views, open all day *(Norma and Noel Thomas, Don Bryan, LYM)*

Robin Hood L40 2RG [Blue Stone Lane (Croston—Eccleston road, N of village – keep going)]: Spotless open-plan dining pub with button-back wall banquettes, reproduction Victorian prints, decorative plates, stained-glass seat dividers, some stripped stone; generous home cooking (all day wknds) from sandwiches up, children's helpings, OAP bargain lunches, friendly staff coping well with the bustle, well kept Boddingtons, Timothy Taylors and four interesting guests, decent wines, children's room, small pretty upstairs evening restaurant; may be piped music, games machine; neat side terrace, good fenced play area, open all day *(Margaret Dickinson, Yvonne and Mike Meadley)*

MELLOR [SD6530]

☆ *Millstone* BB2 7JR [the one up nr Blackburn; Mellor Lane]: Stone-built village pub, smart and well run, panelled bar with comfortable lounge one side, enterprising dining extension the other, good food from all-day bar meals to enterprising cooking and popular substantial Sun lunch, obliging friendly staff, well kept Thwaites, good choice of wines by the glass, big log fire; good bedrooms, open all day *(Pam and John Smith, GLD, Ashley Dinsdale)*

Oddfellows Arms SK6 5PT [Moor End Rd, beyond Longhurst Lane]: Food pub on three floors, contemporary décor, several real ales, open fires, low-ceilinged flagstoned bar; has had several management changes; children welcome, cl Mon *(Dennis Jones, LYM)*

MERE BROW [SD4118]

Legh Arms PR4 6JX [The Gravel (B5246, off A565 W of Southport)]: Good choice of enjoyable food, friendly staff and atmosphere; children welcome, garden tables *(Pam and John Smith)*

MORECAMBE [SD4563]

Shrimp LA4 5TP [Lancaster Rd, Torrisholme]: Well run chain pub with good carvery, two real ales, good choice of wines by the glass, friendly efficient service, pleasant bar area *(Fred and Lorraine Gill)*

NEWTON [SD6950]

Parkers Arms BB7 3DY [B6478 7 miles N of Clitheroe]: New licensees refurbishing extensively as we go to press, with plans for highly local-based food in bar and restaurant (which has lovely views); real ales, good range of wines, log fires; children welcome, bedrooms, lovely spot; reports please *(LYM)*

ORMSKIRK [SD4109]

Hayfield L39 1NN [County Rd]: Relaxing pub attractively rebuilt some years ago using some old materials, good choice of real ales and inexpensive food *(Jean and Richard Phillips)*

OVER KELLET [SD5269]

Eagles Head LA6 1DL: Extended traditional village pub, good food, real ales, friendly staff; peaceful garden *(Gordon Tong)*

PARBOLD [SD4911]

Wayfarer WN8 7NL [A5209/Alder Lane]: Low-beamed civilised pub with enjoyable food and three real ales, sectionalised bar area, lots of stonework, good service, daily papers; piped music; children welcome *(Jeremy King)*

PAYTHORNE [SD8351]

Buck BB7 4JD: Welcoming country pub, busy in season (nr big caravan park), generous good value food largely local (not Tues, all day wknds), two local ales, reasonably priced wines, fire; outside seating *(Dudley and Moira Cockroft)*

PENDLETON [SD7539]

☆ *Swan With Two Necks* BB7 1PT: Welcoming olde-worlde pub in attractive streamside village below Pendle Hill, simply furnished, warm and tidy, good blackboard range of inexpensive generous home cooking (not Mon), friendly service, changing ales such as Moorhouses and Phoenix; large garden, open all day Sun, cl Tues *(LYM, Pete Baker)*

PRESTON [SD5329]

Black Horse PR1 2EJ [Friargate]: Friendly unspoilt pub in pedestrian street, good Robinsons ales, inexpensive lunchtime food, unusual ornate curved and mosaic-tiled Victorian main bar, panelling, stained-glass and old local photographs, two quiet cosy snugs, mirrored back area, upstairs 1920s-style bar, good juke box; no children, open all day from 10.30, cl Sun eve *(Pete Baker, the Didler, Pam and John Smith, Dr and Mrs A K Clarke)*

ROMILEY [SJ9390]

Duke of York SK6 3AN [Stockport Rd]: Old-fashioned real ale pub with good friendly atmosphere, lots of woodwork, bar opening into two smaller rooms, one up steps with creaky floorboards and hatch service, back vaults bar, limited bar snacks, popular upstairs restaurant (not Suns in Advent) *(Dennis Jones)*

SAWLEY [SD7746]

☆ *Spread Eagle* BB7 4NH [off A59 NE of Clitheroe]: This upmarket dining pub, by a pretty stretch of the River Ribble and nr 12th-c abbey ruins, and very popular for its food, service and atmosphere under its previous owners, changed hands and was closed for refurbishment as we went to press; reports on the new regime please *(LYM)*

SCOUTHEAD [SD9706]

Old Original OL4 3RX [Thurston Clough Rd, just off A62 Oldham—Huddersfield]: Homely and welcoming, open-plan but partitioned, spectacular Pennine and E Manchester views, reasonably priced food, beers such as Timothy Taylors Landlord and Thwaites, decent wines, soft lighting; piped music *(John Fiander, John R Tonge)*

Three Crowns OL4 4AT [Huddersfield Rd]: Enjoyable food from sandwiches to imaginative dishes, cheerful efficient service, real ales, good thriving atmosphere; children welcome, inoffensive piped music *(Ben Williams)*

SLAIDBURN [SD7152]

☆ *Hark to Bounty* BB7 3EP [B6478 N of Clitheroe]: Pretty old stone-built pub in charming Forest of Bowland village, neat rather modern décor in line of linked rooms, wide choice of fresh food (lots of tables) inc light dishes and old-fashioned puddings, good hospitable service, four real ales, decent wines and whiskies, comfortable chairs by open fire, games room one end, comfortable restaurant the other; pleasant garden behind, good walks, bedrooms, open all day *(Norma and Noel Thomas, LYM, Julian and Janet Dearden, Hilary Forrest, Mr and Mrs Barrie)*

SOUTHPORT [SD3317]

Scarisbrick PR8 1NZ [Lord St]: Relaxed hotel bar in medieval baronial style, comfortable armchairs, lots of real ales inc some rare for the area from central counter, adjoining café and bistro bar welcoming children, bargain food; open all day *(BB, Pat and Tony Martin)*

ST HELENS [SJ5095]

Turks Head WA10 2DQ [Morley St]: Friendly old-fashioned backstreet local with three rooms, wide choice of well kept ales inc Cains and Holts, farm cider and perry, may be mulled wine, good service, traditional pub games and pool, Tues quiz, Thurs curry night *(Julian and Janet Dearden)*

STOCKPORT [SJ8990]

☆ *Arden Arms* SK1 2LX [Millgate St, behind Asda]: Welcoming Victorian pub with good reasonably priced lunchtime food, well kept Robinsons, cheerful service (can slow when busy), well preserved traditional horseshoe bar, old-fashioned tiny snug through servery, two coal fires, longcase clocks, well restored tiling and panelling; tables in sheltered courtyard, open all day *(the Didler, Pete Baker, Dennis Jones)*

Armoury SK3 8BD [Shaw Heath]: Friendly refurbished old local, Robinsons Best and Hatters Mild, perhaps Old Tom tapped from cask, lunchtime family room upstairs; big-screen TV; open all day *(the Didler)*

Blossoms SK2 6NU [Buxton Rd (A6)]: Bustling main-road Victorian local, Robinsons ales inc Old Tom from bar-top cask, good home-made pies and other lunchtime food, three rooms off corridor inc attractive back lounge with handsome fireplace, pool room; open all day wknds *(the Didler)*

Crown SK4 1AR [Heaton Lane, Heaton Norris]: Partly open-plan Victorian pub popular for huge range of changing beers, three cosy lounge areas off gaslit bar, stylish décor, bargain lunches, farm cider, pool, darts; frequent live music; tables in cobbled courtyard, vast viaduct above *(the Didler, G D K Fraser, Ben Williams, Dennis Jones)*

Navigation SK4 1TY [Manchester Rd (B6167, former A626)]: Friendly pub with six Beartown ales and a guest beer, farm ciders tapped from cellar casks, continental bottled beers; open all day *(the Didler)*

Nursery SK4 2NA [Green Lane, Heaton Norris; off A6]: Very popular for enjoyable straightforward lunchtime food from kitchen servery on right, good Sun lunch, friendly efficient service, good value Hydes, big bays of banquettes in panelled front lounge, brocaded wall banquettes in back one; children welcome if eating, on narrow cobbled lane at E end of N part of Green Lane, immaculate bowling green behind, open all day wknds *(Pete Baker, the Didler, BB)*

Queens Head SK1 1JT [Little Underbank (can be reached by steps from St Petersgate)]: Splendid Victorian restoration, long and narrow, with charming separate snug and back dining area, rare brass cordials fountain, double bank of spirits taps and old spirit lamps, old posters and adverts, reasonably priced lunchtime snacks, bargain Sam Smiths, daily papers, good friendly bustle, bench seating and bare boards; famous tiny gents' upstairs, some live jazz; open all day *(the Didler, Ben Williams, Dennis Jones)*

Railway SK1 2BZ [Avenue St (just off M63 junction 13, via A560)]: Bright and airy L-shaped bar with Pennine and guest ales, lots of foreign beers, farm cider, home-made pub lunches (not Sun), bargain prices, friendly staff, old Stockport prints and memorabilia, bar billiards, tables out behind; open all day *(the Didler)*

☆ *Red Bull* SK1 3AY [Middle Hillgate]: Steps up to friendly well run local, impressive beamed and flagstoned bar with dark panelling, substantial settles and seats, open fires, lots of pictures, mirrors and brassware, traditional island servery with Robinsons ales, good value home-cooked bar lunches (not Sun); plans to expand into adjoining building, open all day (cl Sun afternoon) *(the Didler, LYM)*

Swan With Two Necks SK1 1RY [Princes St]: Traditional local under threat from redevelopment, comfortable panelled bar, back skylit lounge and drinking corridor, Robinsons ales, friendly efficient service, decent lunchtime food; open all day, cl Sun *(the Didler)*

Three Shires SK1 1NB [Great Underbank]: Former wine bar in Tudor building, four real ales inc Copper Dragon, interesting belgian beers and a helpful wine list, lunchtime food with drink offers; piped music; children welcome, open all day, cl 9pm Sun-Tues *(Dennis Jones, the Didler)*

TYLDESLEY [SD6902]
Mort Arms M29 8DG [Elliott St]: Bargain Holts ales in two-room 1930s pub, etched glass and polished panelling, comfortable lounge with old local photographs, friendly landlord and regulars, darts and dominoes, TV horseracing Sat; open all day *(the Didler)*

WADDINGTON [SD7243]
Higher Buck BB7 3HZ [The Square]: Pleasant pub in picturesque village, well kept Thwaites, very clean inside and out *(Noel Grundy)*

☆ *Waddington Arms* BB7 3HP [Clitheroe Rd]: Good reasonably priced food (all day wknds) using fresh local produce from sandwiches to well presented regional dishes, good cheerful staff, four or more well kept ales, flagstones and bare boards, woodburner in big 17th-c inglenook, room off with leather sofa and motor-racing pictures, neat quarry-tiled dining extension; children welcome, six good value bedrooms (church bells) *(Noel Grundy, Dr and Mrs T E Hothersall, Ashley Dinsdale, J A Snell)*

WEST BRADFORD [SD7444]
Three Millstones BB7 4SX [Waddington Rd]: Attractive old dining pub with good food in four comfortable linked areas, compact bar with Black Sheep and Moorhouses, good

coffee, friendly service, open fire *(John and Helen Rushton, John and Eleanor Holdsworth)*

WEST KIRBY [SJ2186]
White Lion CH48 4EE [Grange Rd (A540)]: Interesting 17th-c sandstone building, friendly proper pub with several small beamed areas on different levels, real ales such as John Smiths and Theakstons, good value simple bar lunches inc lots of sandwiches, coal stove; no children even in attractive secluded back garden up steep stone steps, open all day *(MLR, Clive Watkin)*

WHALLEY [SD7336]
Swan BB7 9SN [King St]: 17th-c coaching inn with long light-wood bar and high chairs, local Bowland and other beers, enjoyable food, good service; disabled access, bedrooms *(GLD)*

WHEELTON [SD5921]
Top Lock PR6 8LS [Copthurst Lane]: Jaunty barge-like pub in picturesque spot on Leeds & Liverpool Canal, friendly hard-working staff, canal-related décor, half a dozen well kept ales, beer festivals, upstairs dining room, good value food; picnic-sets outside *(Brian and Anna Marsden, Pam and John Smith)*

WIGAN [SD5805]
Anvil WN1 1ND [Dorning St]: Straightforward corner local with six real ales inc Hydes, fruit beers on tap; wrapped sandwiches behind bar, piped music *(anon)*

WISWELL [SD7437]
☆ *Freemasons Arms* BB7 9DF [Vicarage Fold; just NE of Whalley]: Good enterprising food freshly cooked to order in cosy, friendly and spotless tucked-away Victorian pub, well kept changing local ales such as Bowland and Moorhouses, remarkable choice of wines at very fair prices, lots of malt whiskies, friendly efficient service, small simple bar and upstairs restaurant (must book Fri/Sat evening); lovely village below Pendle Hill, limited parking, cl Mon/Tues, open all day Sun *(Dr Kevan Tucker, John and Eleanor Holdsworth, K C and B Forman)*

WOODLEY [SJ9391]
Lowes Arms SK6 1QG [Hyde Rd (A560)]: Well kept Robinsons on electric pump, carefully cooked food at sensible prices, friendly atmosphere; unobtrusive piped music *(Dennis Jones)*

WORSLEY [SD7500]
Barton Arms M28 2ED [Stablefold; just off Barton Rd (B5211, handy for M60 junction 13)]: Bright friendly modern pub with good value food, four real ales; children welcome *(Ben Williams)*

Boundary Stone M28 1AD [Bridgewater Rd, Mosley Common]: Bargain food and Brains and Marstons ales in bright modern estate pub *(Ben Williams)*

WORSTON [SD7642]
☆ *Calfs Head* BB7 1QA: Large old coaching inn, well run and busy, wide choice of moderately priced food inc popular Sun carvery in bar and spacious conservatory

looking towards Pendle Hill, well kept Jennings and Wychwood Hobgoblin; large attractive garden with summer house and stream, 11 comfortable bedrooms, open all day *(Steve Whalley, John and Helen Rushton, Alan and Eve Harding, Len Beattie, Brian Wainwright, Margaret Dickinson)*

WREA GREEN [SD3931]

Villa PR4 2PE [Moss Side Lane (B5259)]: Lots of small seating areas in smart hotel's welcoming panelled bar, well kept Copper Dragon and Jennings, enjoyable food, log fire, daily papers, Fri jazz; disabled facilities, good-sized garden, bedrooms, open all day *(the Didler)*

WRIGHTINGTON BAR [SD5313]

☆ *Mulberry Tree* WN6 9SE [B5250, N of M6 junction 27]: Light, airy and stylish restaurant pub with good generous if not cheap imaginatively served food (can take a while) from small sampler helpings to full meals, good wines, friendly attentive staff, plenty of tables *(Mr and Mrs John Taylor, Margaret and Jeff Graham)*

Ideas for a country day out? We list pubs in really attractive scenery at the back of the book – and there are separate lists for waterside pubs, ones with really good gardens, and ones with lovely views.

Leicestershire
and Rutland

The best pubs here are enjoyable places, often with a bustling, buoyant atmosphere and a friendly welcome from the licensees – our readers' reports are very positive this year. There's also some exceptionally good food to be found in this area, with almost half the main entries earning a Food Award – a far higher proportion than elsewhere. On the whole, it's fair to say that if you are after real quality, Rutland takes the palm, while if it's sheer value you are looking for, then you are more likely to find it in broader Leicestershire. Of course, there are notable exceptions to that general rule of thumb. The top places to head for are the Olive Branch at Clipsham (a thoroughly good all-rounder with a civilised atmosphere and delicious food), the Fox & Hounds at Exton (the Italian landlord offers mainly popular italian dishes), the Old White Hart at Lyddington (consistently enjoyable, and with a good value two-course set menu), the Staff of Life at Mowsley (a new Food Award this year for its imaginative choices), the Red Lion at Stathern (under the same ownership as the Olive Branch, and with the same very high standards), and the Kings Arms at Wing (they have their own smoke house and bake all their own bread). Our Leicestershire and Rutland Dining Pub of the Year – which has done so much to raise the game of other pubs here such as the Kings Arms at Wing – goes to the Olive Branch at Clipsham. Other pubs doing particularly well include the Finches Arms so nicely placed at Upper Hambleton (its good food brings it back into these pages after quite a break), the interesting old Belper Arms at Newton Burgoland, where the new licensees offer food all day and a fine range of drinks, the cheerful Cow & Plough at Oadby with its unusual breweriana and seven real ales, the own-brew Grainstore at Oakham, the bustling Griffin at Swithland with half a dozen good beers, and the friendly Wheatsheaf in Woodhouse Eaves – a fine all-rounder. Real ales feature strongly, with half the main entries qualifying for our Beer Award. Everards, the area's main brewer, has always set a high standard, and other newer local brewers such as Belvoir, Langton, Steamin' Billy, Parish, Wicked Hathern and, particularly, Grainstore make this a fine area for beer lovers. (The good Oakham beers, also widely available here, are despite their name brewed in Peterborough, Cambridgeshire.) In the Lucky Dip section at the end of the chapter, pubs gaining special praise recently include the Wheel at Branston, Dog & Hedgehog at Dadlington, Bell at Gumley, Fox & Goose at Illston on the Hill, Globe in Leicester, Swan in the Rushes in Loughborough, Three Swans in Market Harborough, Nevill Arms at Medbourne, Chandlers Arms at Shearsby and Bakers Arms at Thorpe Langton.

AB KETTLEBY

SK7519   MAP 7

Sugar Loaf

Nottingham Road (A606 NW of Melton); LE14 3JB

Well run friendly pub, reasonably priced tasty bar food and well kept beers

As we went to press, some refurbishment was about to take place here – nothing too drastic, just some freshening up of the décor. A new outside decked area was to be added, too. The open-plan bar remains comfortably modernised and warm, with big black and white photographs of Shipstones brewery dray horses and a variety of country prints on the ragged canary walls. A bare-boards end area with a coal-effect gas fire has darts, board games, a games machine and a quiet juke box. Good solid pale wood tables and chairs on the discreetly patterned carpet spread from here into a pleasant dining conservatory. Bass, a beer from Grainstore, Marstons Pedigree and a couple of guest beers on handpump served by friendly staff. There are a few picnic-sets out by the road and car park.

⊞ **Fair value bar food includes lunchtime filled baguettes and baked potatoes, ploughman's, soup, home-made pâté, burgers, a trio of sausages with red wine gravy, lasagne, chicken breast in stilton sauce, and steak in ale pie with evening choices like fried goats cheese topped with crispy parma ham and red onion marmalade, brie and cranberry wellington, a pasta of the day, peppered salmon fillet with braised courgettes, and honey-glazed duck breast with sweet chilli stir fry.** *Starters/Snacks: £4.95 to £6.95. Main Courses: £6.95 to £9.95. Puddings: £3.75*

Free house ~ Licensees Josephine and Dennis Donovan ~ Real ale ~ Bar food (12-9.30(9 Sun)) ~ Restaurant ~ (01664) 822473 ~ Children welcome if eating ~ Open 11am-11.30pm(12.30 Sat); 12-10.30 Sun

Recommended by Derek and Sylvia Stephenson, Robert F Smith, P Dawn, Jeff and Wendy Williams, Phil and Jane Hodson

BARROWDEN

SK9400   MAP 4

Exeter Arms ◀

Main Street, just off A47 Uppingham—Peterborough; LE15 8EQ

Own-brew beers and decent food in quietly set old pub; plenty of seats outside

The own-brew beers in this peaceful and neatly kept 17th-c coaching inn remain quite a draw. Brewed in an old free-standing barn behind they include Beach, Bevin, Hopgear and B,B,CEE and they also keep a couple of guests on handpump. The long cheery yellow open-plan bar stretches away either side of a long central counter, and is quite straightforwardly furnished with wheelback chairs at tables at either end of the bar, on bare boards or blue patterned carpet. There's quite a collection of pump clips, beer mats and brewery posters; cribbage, dominoes, piped music, and boules. On a narrow front terrace overlooking the pretty village green and ducks on the pond are some picnic-sets, with broader views stretching away beyond, and more well spaced picnic-sets in a big informal grassy garden at the back. There are red kites in the nearby Fineshades woods – nice walks here too.

⊞ **As well as lunchtime sandwiches and ploughman's, bar food includes soup, a changing pâté, mushrooms stuffed with stilton and walnuts, ham and egg, sausages with red wine gravy, steak in ale pie, chicken wrapped in bacon with a Boursin cheese sauce, baked salmon with cream and white wine sauce, and puddings such as chocolate sponge with hot chocolate sauce or treacle tart.** *Starters/Snacks: £4.75 to £6.50. Main Courses: £8.95 to £14.25. Puddings: £4.25*

Own brew ~ Licensee Martin Allsopp ~ Real ale ~ Bar food (not Sun evening, Mon) ~ Restaurant ~ (01572) 747247 ~ Children welcome away from the bar ~ Dogs allowed in bar ~ Live music Mon evening ~ Open 12-2.30(3.30 Sat), 6-11; 12-4, 7-10.30 Sun; 12-5 Sun in winter; closed Mon lunchtime, also Sun evening in winter ~ Bedrooms: £37.50S/£75S

Recommended by the Didler, Andy and Jill Kassube, Noel Grundy, Duncan Cloud, John Wooll, Jim Farmer, Michael Doswell, O K Smyth, Barry Collett, Barry and Sue Pladdys, Mike and Sue Loseby

BREEDON ON THE HILL   SK4022   MAP 7

Three Horse Shoes 🍴
Main Street (A453); DE73 1AN

Comfortable pub with imaginative food and friendly licensees

Most customers come to this pleasant pub to enjoy the particularly good – if not cheap –
food. It's been simply restored to reveal the attractive period heart of the building.
Heavy worn flagstones, a log fire, pubby tables, a dark wood counter and green walls and
ceilings give a timeless feel to the clean cut central bar: Marstons Pedigree on
handpump, 30 malt whiskies and decent house wines. Beyond here on the left is a step
up to a further eating room, with maroon walls, dark pews and cherry-stained tables. The
two-room dining area on the right has a comfortably civilised chatty feel with big quite
close-set antique tables on seagrass matting and colourful modern country prints and
antique engravings on canary walls. Even at lunchtime there are lighted candles in
elegant modern holders.

🍴 Although there are some pubby choices such as filled italian bread, baguettes and club
sandwiches, sausage with onion gravy and pasta with salmon and dill cream sauce, most
emphasis is on the restaurant-priced imaginative dishes: duck terrine with caramelised
oranges, grilled asparagus with parmesan, monkfish with stir-fried oriental vegetables,
leek and potato bake with cheese sauce, chicken breast with stilton cream sauce,
pheasant with whisky and savoy cabbage, lamb shank with mustard mash and puddings
like rhubarb crumble and treacle oat tart. *Starters/Snacks: £4.95 to £7.95. Main Courses:
£6.95 to £19.95. Puddings: £4.99 to £5.95*

Free house ~ Licensees Ian Davison, Jennie Ison, Stuart Marson ~ Real ale ~ Bar food ~
Restaurant ~ (01332) 695129 ~ Dogs allowed in bar ~ Open 11.30-2.30, 5.30-11; 12-3 Sun;
closed Sun evening, 25 Dec, evening 31 Dec and 1 Jan

*Recommended by Richard and Jean Green, H Paulinski, P Dawn, Phil and Jane Hodson, Alistair and Kay Butler,
Michael and Maggie Betton, Comus and Sarah Elliott, Gilly Middleburgh, Mrs Terry Dodd*

CLIPSHAM   SK9716   MAP 8

Olive Branch ★
*Take B668/Stretton exit off A1 N of Stamford; Clipsham signposted E from exit roundabout;
LE15 7SH*

LEICESTERSHIRE AND RUTLAND DINING PUB OF THE YEAR

**A very special place for an exceptional meal in comfortable surroundings, fine choice of
drinks and luxury bedrooms**

'You are made to feel like a special guest' and 'a wonderful place' are just two of the
enthusiastic comments from the many of our readers who love this civilised place. The
various smallish attractive rambling rooms have a relaxed and friendly atmosphere, dark
joists and beams, country furniture, an interesting mix of pictures (some by local artists),
candles on tables, and there's a cosy log fire in the stone inglenook fireplace. Many of
the books were bought at antiques fairs by one of the partners, so it's worth asking if
you see something you like, as much is for sale; piped music. A carefully chosen range of
drinks includes Grainstore Olive Oil and a guest beer on handpump, an enticing wine list
(with a dozen by the glass), a fine choice of malt whiskies, armagnacs and cognacs, and
quite a few different british and continental bottled beers; service is particularly good –
friendly and attentive. Outside, there are tables, chairs and big plant pots on a pretty
little terrace, with more on the neat lawn, sheltered in the L of its two low buildings. The
bedrooms (in their Beech House which is just opposite) are lovely and the breakfasts are
wonderful, too.

🍴 Excellent food includes sandwiches and salads, inventive soups, crab, brown shrimp and
avocado salad, lamb rillette terrine with tzatziki, shallot tatin with smoked duck breast,
wild mushroom risotto, fish and chips with minted peas and tomato sauce, lincolnshire
sausages with mustard mash and onion gravy, slow roast tamworth pork belly with sage
and onion mash, fried fillet of john dory with shellfish boulangère and baby fennel,
honey-roast gressingham duck breast with beetroot and turnip gratin, and puddings such

as banana brûlée with banana sorbet and chocolate tart with pistachio ice-cream; they also offer a two-course (£16.50) and three-course (£19.50) set lunch (Monday to Saturday). *Starters/Snacks: £5.00 to £11.50. Main Courses: £8.50 to £16.50. Puddings: £5.00 to £8.00*

Free house ~ Licensees Sean Hope and Ben Jones ~ Real ale ~ Bar food (12-2(3 Sun), 7-9.30(9 Sun)) ~ (01780) 410355 ~ Children welcome ~ Dogs allowed in bar and bedrooms ~ Open 12-3.30, 6-11; 12-11(10.30 Sun) Sat; closed 26 Dec, 1 Jan ~ Bedrooms: £85S(£95B)/£100S(£110B)

Recommended by Barry Collett, Noel Grundy, Bruce and Sharon Eden, Mrs Sheila Stothard, Dr and Mrs J Temporal, Michael Doswell, Di and Mike Gillam, Lin Ounsworth, Bettye Reynolds, Mrs Brenda Calver, Howard and Margaret Buchanan, W K Wood, Pat and Stewart Gordon, Paul Humphreys, Mike and Sue Loseby, Miss J F Reay, H Paulinski, Malcolm and Jane Levitt, Peter and Jean Hoare, M S Catling, Roy Bromell, Glenwys and Alan Lawrence, Gordon and Margaret Ormondroyd, Barry and Sue Pladdys

EXTON
SK9211 MAP 7

Fox & Hounds ⦿
Signposted off A606 Stamford—Oakham; LE15 8AP

Bustling and well run with italian emphasis on popular food, log fire in comfortable lounge and quiet garden

This splendid old coaching inn, facing the quiet village green, is handy for Rutland Water and the gardens at Barnsdale. The comfortable high-ceilinged lounge bar is traditionally civilised with some dark red plush easy chairs, as well as wheelback seats around lots of pine tables, maps and hunting prints on the walls, fresh flowers and a winter log fire in a large stone fireplace. Adnams Bitter, Grainstore Ten Fifty and Greene King IPA on handpump and a good range of wines by the glass; helpful, friendly service, piped music. The sheltered walled garden has seats among large rose beds on the pleasant well kept back lawn that looks out over paddocks.

⦿ As the landlord is from Italy, the menu includes quite a few italian dishes: lunchtime filled ciabattas and panini, a vast selection of handmade pizzas in almost every combination you could imagine (Monday-Saturday evenings only), italian sausages of the day, risotto with asparagus and sun-dried tomatoes, linguini with smoked salmon and king prawns in a garlic tomato sauce and spaghetti bolognese; also, gammon and egg, lambs liver and bacon, chicken stuffed with apricot and stilton in a light madeira and sage sauce, bass with niçoise-style salad, and home-made puddings. *Starters/Snacks: £3.75 to £6.95. Main Courses: £8.95 to £17.25. Puddings: £4.25 to £5.20*

Free house ~ Licensees Valter and Sandra Floris ~ Real ale ~ Bar food (not Sun evening or Mon) ~ Restaurant ~ (01572) 812403 ~ Children welcome ~ Dogs allowed in bar and bedrooms ~ Open 11-2.30, 6-11; 11-3, 8-11 Sun; closed Mon ~ Bedrooms: £45B/£60(£70B)

Recommended by Val and Alan Green, Michael Sargent, Jeff and Wendy Williams, Richard and Jean Green, Leslie and Barbara Owen, Paul Humphreys, MJB, Michael Dandy, S Holder, Jim Farmer, Barry Collett, Roy Bromell, Mrs Brenda Calver, P A Rowe, Ian Stafford, Mrs Hazel Rainer

LYDDINGTON
SP8796 MAP 4

Old White Hart ⦿
Village signposted off A6003 N of Corby; LE15 9LR

Well run, popular inn with welcoming staff, roaring fires, and very good food; pretty garden

The licensees in this fine old place are consistently friendly and attentive and nothing is too much trouble for them. The softly lit front bar has a glass-shielded roaring log fire, low ceilings and heavy bowed beams, a relaxed local atmosphere and just four close-set tables. This room opens into an attractive restaurant, and on the other side is another tiled-floor room with rugs, lots of fine hunting prints, cushioned wall seats and mate's chairs and a woodburning stove. Fullers London Pride and Timothy Taylors Golden Best on handpump and several wines by the glass; shove-ha'penny, cribbage and dominoes. The pretty walled garden (with eight floodlit boules pitches) is very pleasant and there are seats by outdoor heaters; if you sit out here on Thursday evening you may hear the church bell-ringers. The pub is handy for Bede House and there are good nearby walks.

🍽 From a sensibly short menu, the much enjoyed bar food includes filled panini, soup, breaded cambozola with orange, tomato and walnuts in a port dressing, duck liver parfait with tomato chutney, sausages with onion gravy, chicken breast filled with red leicester and pancetta with plum tomato and shallot sauce, rack of lamb with dauphinoise potatoes, calves liver with roast gravy, daily specials such as deep-fried grimsby haddock and butternut squash filled with red pepper risotto and parmesan, and puddings like chocolate marquise with crème de menthe choc chip ice-cream and sticky toffee pudding with butterscotch sauce. They have good value two- and three-course lunches and an early bird menu. *Starters/Snacks: £3.50 to £6.95. Main Courses: £9.95 to £15.00. Puddings: £5.95 to £6.95*

Free house ~ Licensees Stuart and Holly East ~ Real ale ~ Bar food (not winter Sun evening) ~ Restaurant ~ (01572) 821703 ~ Children welcome ~ Open 12-3, 6.15-11; 12-3.30, 7-10.30 Sun; closed 25 Dec ~ Bedrooms: £60B/£85B

Recommended by Ben and Helen Ingram, Jim Farmer, Dr Brian and Mrs Anne Hamilton, Noel Grundy, Jeff and Wendy Williams, Mike and Sue Loseby, Tracey and Stephen Groves, John Wooll, P A Rowe, John and Sylvia Harrop

MOWSLEY
SP6488 MAP 4
Staff of Life 🍽 ♓
Village signposted off A5199 S of Leicester; Main Street; LE17 6NT

Neat, high-gabled pub popular for a good meal out; seats in back garden

With friendly and helpful staff and very good food, it's not surprising that this high-gabled pub is so popular. It is spotlessly kept and the roomy bar is quite traditional with a panelled ceiling, comfortable seating, including some high-backed settles on flagstones, Banks's Bitter and Jennings Cumberland on handpump and up to 20 wines (and champagne) by the glass. The restaurant is rather like a country barn; piped music. The back garden has a large pergola and teak furniture.

🍽 As well as lunchtime sandwiches and dishes such as faggots on mash with rich gravy, home-cooked ham with two free-range eggs, grilled salmon on linguine with fish cream sauce and pork and leek sausages on wholegrain mustard mash, the very good food might include soup, chicken liver parfait with red onion marmalade, tian of fresh crab, avocado salsa and rocket with lemon vinaigrette, pork belly roasted with sage, onion and garlic on raisin mash with local black pudding and red wine jus, fillet of venison in pastry, baked whole bass with home-made spicy tomato and bramley apple chutney, and puddings such as crème brûlée of the day and Baileys cheesecake with forest fruit compote. *Starters/Snacks: £4.50 to £7.95. Main Courses: £8.50 to £17.95. Puddings: £5.00 to £6.50*

Free house ~ Licensee Spencer Farrell ~ Real ale ~ Bar food (12-2.30(3.30 Sun), 6.30-9.30(6-8.30 Mon); not Sun evening or Mon lunchtime) ~ Restaurant ~ (0116) 240 2359 ~ Children welcome but not in back garden ~ Open 12-3, 6-11; 12-10.30 Sun; closed Mon lunchtime except bank hols

Recommended by Duncan Cloud, Phil and Jane Hodson, Veronica Brown, P M Newsome, Leslie and Barbara Owen, Richard J Stanley

NEWTON BURGOLAND
SK3709 MAP 4
Belper Arms
Village signposted off B4116 S of Ashby or B586 W of Ibstock; LE67 2SE

Plenty of nooks and seating areas with original features in ancient pub, well liked food, changing ales and seats in rambling garden

Another new landlord for this bustling pub but readers have been quick to voice their warm enthusiasm. There's a warm welcome for all and although the original building is very opened up, there are lots of ancient interior features such as the heavy beams, changing floor levels and varying old floor and wall materials that break the place up into enjoyable little nooks and seating areas. Parts are said to date back to the 13th c and much of the exposed brickwork certainly looks at least three or four hundred years old. A big freestanding central chimney at the core of the building has a cottagey old black range on one side and open fire on the other, with chatty groups of nice old captain's chairs. And plenty to look at too, from a suit of old chain mail, to a collection of pewter teapots, some good antique furniture and, framed on the wall, the story of the pub ghost – Five to Four Fred. Black Sheep, Fullers London Pride, Greene King Abbot, Marstons Pedigree and Theakstons Old Peculier on handpump, 30 wines by the glass, quite a few malt whiskies and Stowford Press cider; piped music and dominoes. There are seats in the rambling garden and on the terrace.

⏍ Now usefully served all day, the popular food includes filled baguettes, soup, pressed terrine of slow-cooked barbary duck with roasted figs, pea and ham risotto topped with a poached egg, steak and mushroom in ale pie, venison sausages with caramelised onion gravy, garlic baked field mushrooms topped with goats cheese, chilli con carne with nachos, cheese, sour cream, salsa and guacamole, bass with spaghetti vegetables and chive lemon cream, rump of lamb with black olive and rosemary jus, and puddings; there's also a two- and three-course set menu. Starters/Snacks: £3.50 to £5.00. Main Courses: £4.50 to £12.50. Puddings: £3.50 to £4.50

Punch ~ Lease David Cordy ~ Real ale ~ Bar food (12-9) ~ Restaurant ~ (01530) 270530 ~ Children welcome ~ Dogs welcome ~ Open 12-12

Recommended by the Didler, R T and J C Moggridge, Mark Toussaint, Ian and Jane Irving, Dr and Mrs A K Clarke, R M Chard, Simon Fox, Lee Fraser, Robert F Smith

OADBY   SK6202   MAP 4

Cow & Plough ⏍
Gartree Road (B667 N of centre); LE2 2FB

Fantastic collection of brewery memorabilia, real ales and good, interesting food

The landlord in this interesting old place is a great collector of breweriana and the two dark back rooms known as the Vaults contain an extraordinary and ever-expanding collection – almost every piece has a story behind it: enamel signs and mirrors advertising long-forgotten brews, an aged brass cash register and furnishings and fittings salvaged from pubs and even churches (there's some splendid stained-glass behind the counter). The pub first opened about 20 years ago with just these cosily individual rooms, but it soon tripled in size when an extensive long, light, flagstoned conservatory was added to the front; it too has its share of brewery signs and the like, as well as plenty of plants and fresh flowers, a piano, beams liberally covered with hops, and a real mix of traditionally pubby tables and chairs, with lots of green leatherette sofas, and small round cast-iron tables. One section has descriptions of all Leicester's pubs. Beers from the very local Steamin' Billy brewery plus guests such as Abbeydale Absolution, Ossett Silver Fox and Roosters Cream on handpump, a dozen country wines, several wines by the glass and up to six ciders; TV, darts, board games and shove-ha'penny. There are picnic-sets outside.

⏍ Interesting bar food includes sandwiches, soup, duck confit with bean sprout salad and oriental dressing, crayfish and avocado timbale with lemon and lime oil, wild mushroom and fresh herb linguini, chicken, mozzarella, roast pepper and basil risotto, rump of lamb with spring onion mash and white onion sauce, fillet of sea trout with warm beetroot and shallot salad, 21-day hung sirloin steak with a thyme and horseradish rarebit and pan juices, and puddings like spiced plum crumble and rum chocolate truffles with raspberry dipping sauce. They also offer a fixed price early evening two-course menu. *Starters/Snacks: £3.95 to £8.95. Main Courses: £6.95 to £9.95. Puddings: £3.95 to £4.95*

Free house ~ Licensee Barry Lount ~ Real ale ~ Bar food (12-3(5 Sat and Sun), 6-9; not Sun evening) ~ Restaurant ~ (0116) 272 0852 ~ Children allowed but not in front of bars ~ Dogs welcome ~ Jazz Weds lunchtime ~ Open 11(midday Sun)-11; 11-3, 5-11 Mon-Thurs in winter

Recommended by Jim Farmer, the Didler, Rona Murdoch, Barry Collett, David Field, John Fiander, Duncan Cloud, Dr and Mrs A K Clarke

OAKHAM   SK8509   MAP 4

Grainstore ◀ £

Station Road, off A606; LE15 6RE

Super own-brewed beers in converted rail grain warehouse, friendly staff, cheerful customers and pubby food

Laid back or lively, depending on the time of day, and with noises of the brewery workings above, the interior of this converted three-storey Victorian grain warehouse is plain and functional. There are wide well worn bare floorboards, bare ceiling boards above massive joists which are supported by red metal pillars, a long brick-built bar counter with cast-iron bar stools, tall cask tables and simple elm chairs. Their own-brewed beers are served both traditionally at the left end of the bar counter and through swan necks with sparklers on the right: Grainstore Cooking Bitter, Rutland Panther, Rutland Rouses, Silly Billy, Ten Fifty and Triple B. The friendly staff are happy to give you samples. Games machine, darts, board games, shove-ha'penny, giant Jenga and bottle-walking. In summer they pull back the huge glass doors that open on to a terrace with picnic-sets, and often stacked with barrels; disabled access. You can tour the brewery by arrangement, they do take-aways, and hold a real ale festival with over 65 real ales and lots of live music during the August bank holiday weekend.

⫿ Decent unfussy pubby food includes sandwiches, soup, baguettes, baked potatoes, burgers, sausage and mash, chilli, and all day breakfast. *Starters/Snacks: £2.95 to £4.95. Main Courses: £4.95 to £8.95*

Own brew ~ Licensee Tony Davis ~ Real ale ~ Bar food (11-3; not Sun) ~ (01572) 770065 ~ Children welcome till 8pm ~ Dogs welcome ~ Live blues first Sun of month, jazz third and fourth Sun ~ Open 11-11(midnight Sat); 12-11 Sun

Recommended by Anthony Barnes, Mike and Sue Loseby, John Fiander, Jim Farmer, Barry Collett, the Didler, Richard and Karen Holt, Arthur Pickering, Alan and Eve Harding, Michael Dandy

PEGGS GREEN   SK4117   MAP 7

New Inn £

Signposted off A512 Ashby—Shepshed at roundabout, then turn immediately left down Zion Hill towards Newbold; pub is 100 yards down on the right with car park on opposite side of road; LE67 8JE

Intriguing bric-a-brac in unspoilt pub, a friendly welcome, good value food and drinks and cottagey garden

All are welcome at this warmly friendly and unspoilt little pub – though children and dogs must be well behaved. The two cosy tiled front rooms have plenty of chatty locals, an incredible collection of old bric-a-brac (it'll keep you busy looking for ages) which covers almost every inch of the walls and ceilings. The little room on the left, a bit like a kitchen parlour (they call it the Cabin), has china on the mantelpiece, lots of prints and photographs and little collections of this and that, three old cast-iron tables, wooden stools and a small stripped kitchen table. The room to the right has nice stripped panelling, and masses more appealing bric-a-brac. The small back Best room, with a stripped wooden floor, has a touching display of old local photographs including some colliery ones. Bass, Caledonian Deuchars IPA and Marstons Pedigree on handpump; cribbage and dominoes. Plenty of seats in front of the pub with more in the peaceful back garden.

⫿ As well as filled baps, the very good value, satisfying food includes ham and eggs, corned beef hash, steak in ale pie, faggots and peas, sausages in onion gravy and smoked haddock. *Main Courses: £3.95 to £5.50. Puddings: £1.95 to £2.50*

Enterprise ~ Lease Maria Christina Kell ~ Real ale ~ Bar food (12-2; 6-8 Mon; not Tues-Sat evenings; not Sun) ~ No credit cards ~ (01530) 222293 ~ Well-behaved children welcome ~ Dogs welcome ~ Open 12-2.30, 5.30-11; 12-3, 6.30-11 Sat; 12-3, 7-11 Sun

Recommended by Susan and John Douglas, JJW, CMW, Phil and Jane Hodson, B and M Kendall, David and Sue Atkinson, the Didler, Duncan Cloud, Clive and Fran Dutson

SOMERBY   SK7710   MAP 7

Stilton Cheese ◖

High Street; off A606 Oakham—Melton Mowbray, via Cold Overton, or Leesthorpe and Pickwell; can also be reached direct from Oakham via Knossington; LE14 2QB

Bustling and cheerful with chatty staff, local real ales, and seats on heated terrace

The cheerful traditional welcome and decent range of real ales continues to draw customers to this 17th-c village pub. Kept on handpump, there might be Grainstore Ten Fifty, Marstons Pedigree, Tetleys and guests like Hadrian & Borders Legion and Springhead Liberty; quite a few wines by the glass, over 30 malt whiskies and a proper cider. The comfortable hop-strung beamed bar/lounge has dark carpets, lots of country prints on its stripped stone walls, a collection of copper pots, a stuffed badger and plenty of seats; shove-ha'penny, cribbage and dominoes. There are seats and outdoor heaters on the terrace. More reports please.

🍴 **Bar food includes sandwiches, ploughman's, soup, deep-fried breaded mushrooms with garlic mayonnaise, macaroni cheese, lasagne, sausages and mash with onion gravy, battered cod and chilli con carne with daily specials such as duck liver and raisin pâté, wild mushroom risotto, liver and bacon with onion gravy and rutland water trout with prawn and tarragon butter.** *Starters/Snacks: £3.25 to £5.95. Main Courses: £7.25 to £12.95. Puddings: £3.75*

Free house ~ Licensees Carol and Jeff Evans ~ Real ale ~ Bar food (12-2, 6(7 Sun)-9) ~ Restaurant ~ (01664) 454394 ~ Children welcome ~ Dogs allowed in bedrooms ~ Open 12-3, 6-11; 12-3, 7-10.30 Sun ~ Bedrooms: £30/£40

Recommended by Jim Farmer, M and GR

STATHERN   SK7731   MAP 7

Red Lion 🍽 ♟ ◖

Off A52 W of Grantham via the brown-signed Belvoir road (keep on towards Harby – Stathern signposted on left); or off A606 Nottingham—Melton Mowbray via Long Clawson and Harby; LE14 4HS

Splendid range of drinks and imaginative food in civilised dining pub, open fires, good garden with play area; own shop too

Well run and rather civilised, this bustling place is under the same ownership as the Olive Branch in Clipsham and has the same high standards. There's a lot of emphasis on the imaginative food and a fine range of drinks but the atmosphere is relaxed and informal and the service very good indeed. The yellow room on the right has a country pub feel and the lounge bar has sofas, an open fire and a big table with books, newspapers and magazines; it leads off the smaller, more traditional flagstoned bar with terracotta walls, another fireplace with a pile of logs beside it, and lots of beams and hops. Dotted around are various oddities picked up by one of the licensees on visits to Newark Antiques Fair: some unusual lambing chairs for example and a collection of wooden spoons. A little room with tables set for eating leads to the long, narrow main dining room and out to a nicely arranged suntrap with good hardwood furnishings spread over its lawn and terrace. Brewsters Hophead, Fullers London Pride and Grainstore Olive Oil on handpump, alongside draught belgian beer and continental bottled beers, several ciders, a varied wine list with several by the glass, winter mulled wine and summer home-made lemonade. There's an unusually big play area behind the car park with swings, climbing frames and so on.

🍴 **Excellent bar food includes sandwiches, soup, brawn terrine with apple and apricot chutney, thai-style local pigeon with chilli and ginger dressing, spanish-style mussels, mediterranean vegetable tart with mozzarella, fish and chips with mushy peas and tartare sauce, lincolnshire sausages with mustard mash and onion gravy, braised lamb shoulder with rosemary fondant potato and ratatouille, local rabbit pithivier with carrot and cumin purée, wild bass with lobster gratin and dijon mustard sauce, and puddings such as hot chocolate fondant with irish liqueur ice-cream and lemon grass parfait with blackcurrant sorbet.** *Starters/Snacks: £4.50 to £8.50. Main Courses: £10.50 to £16.95. Puddings: £4.50 to £6.50*

Free house ~ Licensees Sean Hope and Ben Jones ~ Real ale ~ Bar food (12-2(3 Sun), 7-9.30; not Sun evening or Mon) ~ Restaurant ~ (01949) 860868 ~ Children welcome ~ Dogs allowed in bar ~ Open 12-3, 6-11; 12-11 Sat; 12-6.30 Sun; closed Sun evening, all day Mon, 1 Jan

Recommended by Philip and Susan Philcox, Jeff and Wendy Williams, Derek and Sylvia Stephenson, Dr and Mrs J Temporal, W K Wood, David Glynne-Jones, Richard, Phil and Jane Hodson, P Dawn, Leslie and Barbara Owen, Andy and Jill Kassube

STRETTON   SK9415   MAP 8

Jackson Stops

Rookery Lane; a mile or less off A1, at B668 (Oakham) exit; follow village sign, turning off Clipsham road into Manor Road, pub on left; LE15 7RA

Interesting former farmhouse with decent drinks and popular food

This thatched old place has new licensees again this year but remains on top form with particularly good food and a couple of real ales. The homely black-beamed country bar down on the left has some timbering in its ochre walls, a couple of bar stools, a cushioned stripped wall pew and an elderly settle on the worn tile and brick floor, with a coal fire in the corner. The smarter main room on the right is light and airy with linen napkins and lit candles in brass sticks on the nice mix of ancient and modern tables, dark blue carpeting, a couple of striking modern oils alongside a few tastefully disposed farm tools on the mainly canary coloured stone walls and another smokeless coal fire in a stone corner fireplace. Right along past the bar is a second dining room, older in style, with stripped stone walls, a tiled floor and an old open cooking range. The unobtrusive piped music in the main dining room doesn't disturb the chatty and relaxed atmosphere. Oakham JHB and a guest such as Bass or Greene King Ruddles Best on handpump and several good wines by the glass; board games and nurdles (they tell us it is a bit like pitch and toss). More reports please.

🍴 As well as sandwiches, the enjoyable food now includes soup, thai fishcakes with sweet chilli sauce, crayfish and avocado basket with aïoli capers, roasted pepper stuffed with couscous and italian herbs and topped with goats cheese, steak and mushroom pudding with stroganoff sauce, medallions of pork fillet with creamy spinach and crispy potato tart, chicken breast stuffed with brie, wrapped in bacon with a mushroom and tarragon cream and almond crusted bass fillet with saffron sauce. *Starters/Snacks: £3.95 to £5.25. Main Courses: £9.95 to £15.45. Puddings: £4.75 to £4.95*

Free house ~ Licensees Simon and Catherine Davy ~ Real ale ~ Bar food (12-2.15, 6.30-9.15; not Mon) ~ Restaurant ~ (01780) 410237 ~ Children welcome ~ Dogs allowed in bar ~ Open 12-3, 6-11; 12-11 Sat and Sun; closed Mon except bank hols

Recommended by Arthur Pickering, Phil and Jane Hodson, Maurice and Janet Thorpe

Ram Jam Inn ♀ 🛏

Just off A1: heading N, look out for warning signs some 8 miles N of Stamford, turning off at big inn sign through service station close to B668; heading S, look out for B668 Oakham turn-off, inn well signed on left 0.25 mile after roundabout; LE15 7QX

Popular A1 stop-off, even for breakfasts, with good drinks and modern food in appealing linked areas; comfortable bedrooms

So handy for the A1, this bustling dining place serves food from 7am to 7pm. As you go in, the first part of the big open-plan bar/dining area now has bucket chairs around a mix of tables on the new carpet, three cosy sofas and daily newspapers and a changing beer such as Wells & Youngs Bombardier on handpump; good house wines with several by the glass and excellent coffee. This area spreads on back to two more rooms, one with an open fire.

🍴 This year, all food is served buffet-style starting with breakfast (a full english breakfast plus croissants, danish pastries, fresh fruit and so forth) and then carrying on a lunch menu until 7pm: sandwiches, soup, pies like chicken, leek and mushroom, a daily pasta dish, sausage and mash, lamb shank with rosemary gravy, and plenty of salads and vegetables; Sunday roasts. *Main Courses: £6.95*

Oxford Hotels ~ Manager Sue Addnit ~ Real ale ~ Bar food (all day until 7pm; no food after that) ~ Restaurant ~ (01780) 410776 ~ Children welcome away from bar ~ Dogs welcome ~ Open 7am-11pm; closed 25 Dec ~ Bedrooms: £45B/£55B

Recommended by Eithne Dandy, DC, Paul and Ursula Randall, John Branston, Louise Gibbons, J F M and M West, B and M Kendall, Dr Kevan Tucker, Arthur Pickering

SWITHLAND
SK5512   MAP 7

Griffin 🍺

Main Street; between A6 and B5330, between Loughborough and Leicester; LE12 8TJ

A good mix of cheerful customers, well liked food and half a dozen real ales in bustling atmosphere

Bustling and friendly, this attractively converted and well run stone-built pub is liked by both locals and visitors. The beamed communicating rooms have some panelling, a nice mix of wooden tables and chairs and bar stools, Everards Beacon, Original and Tiger plus guests like Adnams Bitter and Marstons Pedigree on handpump, several malt whiskies and several wines by the glass from a good list. Piped music and skittle alley. The tidy streamside garden, overlooking open fields, has been reworked this year. The pub is handy for Bradgate Country Park and there are walks in Swithland Woods.

🍽 **Popular bar food includes sandwiches, soup, tempura battered prawns with lime and coriander mayonnaise dip, chicken liver pâté with chutney, roasted mediterranean vegetables with goats cheese, a trio of local sausages with rich onion gravy, lambs liver and bacon with red wine and sweet onion sauce, steak and mushroom in ale pie, salmon fillet with lemon pepper, and puddings.** *Starters/Snacks: £3.45 to £7.00. Main Courses: £4.95 to £17.95. Puddings: £3.95 to £4.95*

Everards ~ Tenant John Cooledge ~ Real ale ~ Bar food ~ Restaurant ~ (01509) 890535 ~ Well supervised children welcome ~ Open 10am-11pm; 11-10.30 Sun

Recommended by Duncan Cloud, Jim Farmer, John and Fiona Merritt, Pete Baker, Dr and Mrs A K Clarke, Derek and Sylvia Stephenson, JJW, CMW

UPPER HAMBLETON
SK8907   MAP 4

Finches Arms

Off A606; LE15 8TL

17th-c inn with lovely views, friendly staff, bustling bar and elegant restaurant, real ales and good, interesting food; bedrooms

From the suntrap hillside terrace behind this stone-built 17th-c inn there are lovely views over Rutland Water; good surroundings walks, too. Inside, you can expect a warm welcome from the friendly licensees and their staff, three roaring log fires, and a bustling bar with beams, fine old wooden chairs and settles around a mix of wooden tables on the flagstones, Greene King Abbot, Tetleys Bitter, Timothy Taylors Landlord and maybe a guest beer on handpump, and quite a few wines by the glass; piped music. The Garden Room restaurant is elegant with decorative bay trees amongst the wicker and chrome chairs around wooden tables on the stripped wooden floor and windows that look over the water. The comfortable bedrooms are popular.

🍽 **Using daily-delivered fresh fish, lots of seasonal game (venison, rabbit, pheasant, partridge and so forth), and very good local meat, the enjoyable food at lunchtime includes filled panini (which they also serve throughout the afternoon), soup, chicken caesar salad, bacon and broccoli flan, welsh rarebit, sausages with onion gravy, beer-battered haddock, aubergine lasagne, boneless pork chop with apple mash, and gressingham duck with braised leeks; evening choices such as pigeon with celery and bean salad, pork grilled with fennel and beetroot, fillet of bass, fresh plaice with peppers and pistachios, calves liver and bacon with béarnaise sauce, and puddings like mango and yoghurt mousse with mint sauce and chocolate pudding with hot chocolate sauce. They offer two- and three-course set menus at lunchtime and in the evening, cook early morning breakfasts for those dropping in from 8am, morning coffee, and proper cream teas.** *Starters/Snacks: £3.50 to £8.95. Main Courses: £9.95 to £14.95. Puddings: £4.95*

Free house ~ Licensees Celia and Colin Crawford ~ Real ale ~ Bar food (12-2.30, 6-9.30; 12-8 Sun) ~ Restaurant ~ (01572) 756575 ~ Children welcome ~ Open 11-11; 12-10.30 Sun ~ Bedrooms: £65B/£75B

Recommended by Bruce and Sharon Eden, Patrick Frew, Anthony Barnes, Roy Bromell, Gerry and Rosemary Dobson, Michael Dandy, Ian and Jane Irving

WING   SK8902   MAP 4

Kings Arms 🍽 ♈ ⌘

Village signposted off A6003 S of Oakham; Top Street; LE15 8SE

Nicely kept old pub, big log fires, super choice of wines by the glass and interesting modern cooking

On top form, this neatly kept 17th-c inn is a civilised place for an enjoyable drink or a meal. The attractive bar has various nooks and crannies, nice old beams and stripped stone, two large log fires (one in a copper-canopied central hearth), and flagstoned or wood-strip floors. Friendly, helpful staff serve 28 wines by the glass, as well as Grainstore Cooking, Shepherd Neame Spitfire and Timothy Taylors Landlord on handpump and several ciders. There are seats out in front, and more in the sunny yew-sheltered garden; the new car park has plenty of space. There's a medieval turf maze just up the road and we are told that the pub is just a couple of miles away from England's osprey hot-spot.

🍽 As well as naming their suppliers on their menu, having their own smoke house and baking their own bread and biscuits, the imaginative bar food includes sandwiches, interesting soups, hot smoked local pike with chive scrambled eggs on toast, shredded ham hock and pistachio terrine with home-made piccalilli, honey and mustard roast ham with free-range eggs and beef dripping chips, butternut squash and pumpkin risotto with mascarpone and parmesan, steak and mushroom pudding with ale gravy, saddle of fallow deer with pancetta, wild bass with warm herbed ratatouille-style relish, and puddings like kaffir lime and ginger scented crème brûlée and soft-centred chocolate fondant with white chocolate and cherry ice-cream; good cheeses, too. *Starters/Snacks: £4.75 to £7.50. Main Courses: £9.50 to £19.00. Puddings: £5.50*

Free house ~ Licensee David Goss ~ Real ale ~ Bar food (not Sun evening, Mon lunch and not winter Mon (except for residents)) ~ Restaurant ~ (01572) 737634 ~ Well supervised children welcome but not after 7.30pm ~ Open 12-3, 6.30-10.30(11.30 Sat); 12.3.30 Sun; closed Sun evening, Mon lunchtime and all day Mon Nov-April ~ Bedrooms: £65B/£75B

Recommended by Michael Doswell, Ben and Helen Ingram, O K Smyth, Mike and Sue Loseby, Phil and Jane Hodson, Jeff and Wendy Williams, Derek and Sylvia Stephenson, Michael Sargent, Roy Bromell

WOODHOUSE EAVES   SK5313   MAP 7

Wheatsheaf ⌘

Brand Hill; turn right into Main Street, off B591 S of Loughborough; LE12 8SS

Bustling and friendly country pub with charming licensees, interesting things to look at, good bistro-type food and fair choice of drinks; well equipped bedrooms

Even when really busy, the staff in this rather smart country pub remain welcoming and helpful. It's open plan with beams, has a log fire, newspapers to read, motor-racing memorabilia and pictures and artefacts to do with winter sports, a chatty bustling atmosphere, and Adnams Broadside, Greene King IPA, Shepherd Neame Spitfire, and Timothy Taylors Landlord on handpump with several wines including champagne by the glass from a thoughtful list. There's also a cosy area called The Mess for more intimate dining which has an RAF Hurricane propeller and (upstairs) a light and airy cottagey restaurant. The floodlit, heated terrace has plenty of seating.

🍽 As well as sandwiches, ciabattas, filled baguettes and ploughman's, the enjoyable bistro-style menu might include soup, chicken liver pâté, haddock smokies with wine, cream, tomatoes and cheese, chargrilled burger with bacon and cheese, mushroom stroganoff, a trio of sausages with red wine and redcurrant gravy, chicken strips on linguine with spinach, pine nuts and basil in a creamy cheese sauce, home-made fishcakes with parsley sauce, pork on apple mash with a calvados cream sauce, and puddings such as fruit crumble and meringues. *Starters/Snacks: £4.25 to £5.25. Main Courses: £9.55 to £15.00. Puddings: £4.95*

Free house ~ Licensees Richard and Bridget Dimblebee ~ Real ale ~ Bar food (12-2, 6.30-9.30; all day Sat; not Sun evening) ~ Restaurant ~ (01509) 890320 ~ Children welcome ~ Dogs allowed in bar ~ Open 11.30-3, 6-11; 11.30-11 Sat; 12-10.30 Sun; 11.30-3, 6-11 weekends in winter ~ Bedrooms: £60S/£80S

Recommended by C J Pratt, the Didler, Gordon and Margaret Ormondroyd, John and Helen Rushton, Michael Brunning, Peter and Joyce Hewitt, Gillian Grist, Adrian Johnson

LUCKY DIP

Besides the fully inspected pubs, you might like to try these Lucky Dips recommended to us and described by readers (if you do, please send us reports: feedback@thegoodpubguide.co.uk).

BARKBY [SK6309]
Malt Shovel LE7 3QG [Main St]: Old village pub with good value food inc bargain steak night Mon, half a dozen real ales, good choice of wines by the glass, charming service, U-shaped open-plan bar, small dining room; garden with partly covered heated terrace *(Phil and Jane Hodson)*
BELTON [SK4420]
Queens Head LE12 9TP [the one nr Loughborough, off A512/A453 between junctions 23 and 24, M1; Long St]: Relaxing former coaching inn with interesting up-to-date food in log-fire dining area and more formal restaurant, cool minimalist décor and leather seating, two bare-boards bar areas, good wines. proper coffee and a real ale, helpful and efficient young uniformed staff; tables out on decking and lawn, attractive village, six good bedrooms, cl Sun evening *(Michael Doswell)*
BOTCHESTON [SK4804]
Greyhound LE9 9FF [Main St, off B5380 E of Desford]: Beamed village pub with enjoyable fresh generous food from lunchtime special deals to unusual dishes, pine tables in two light and airy dining rooms, three well kept changing ales, friendly service; children welcome, garden with play area *(Duncan Cloud)*
BRANSTON [SK8129]
☆ *Wheel* NG32 1RU [Main St]: Beamed 18th-c village pub refurbished by new licensees, chef/landlord doing proper country food, some quite out of the ordinary, friendly attentive landlady, changing ales such as Adnams and Batemans from central servery, log fires, stylishly simple décor; attractive garden, next to church, splendid countryside nr Belvoir castle, has been cl Mon/Tues lunchtimes *(BB, Kate Davies, B R Wood)*
BRAUNSTON [SK8306]
Blue Ball LE15 8QS [off A606 in Oakham; Cedar St]: Pretty thatched and beamed dining pub refurbished by new licensees, enjoyable local food, good service, well kept ales, decent wines, log fire, candles, flowers and country pine in quiet linked rooms inc small conservatory; children welcome, tables outside, attractive village *(Keith and*

Sue Campbell, Colin McKerrow, Maurice and Janet Thorpe, LYM)
☆ *Old Plough* LE15 8QT [off A606 in Oakham; Church St]: Welcoming black-beamed pub, comfortably opened up, with log fire, well kept Grainstore and interesting guest ales, enjoyable food inc beer-based dishes, friendly staff, appealing back dining conservatory (children allowed); tables in sheltered garden, open all day *(Jim Farmer, LYM)*
BRUNTINGTHORPE [SP6089]
☆ *Joiners Arms* LE17 5QH [Church Walk/Cross St]: More bistro restaurant than pub, good imaginative up-to-date food and popular Sun lunches in three beamed areas of open-plan dining lounge, good friendly service, decent wines, Greene King IPA from small bar counter, lots of china and brasses; they don't serve tap water; cl Sun evening and Mon *(Gerry and Rosemary Dobson, Jeff and Wendy Williams)*
BURTON OVERY [SP6797]
☆ *Bell* LE8 9DL [Main St]: Interesting choice of consistently good if not cheap food using local produce in L-shaped open-plan bar and dining room, good log fire, comfortable settees, darts and games machine round corner; children welcome, nice garden, lovely village, open all day wknds *(R L Borthwick, Jim Farmer, David Field)*
CHURCH LANGTON [SP7293]
Langton Arms LE16 7SY [B6047 about 3 miles N of Mkt Harborough; just off A6]: Civilised extended village pub with good choice of pubby food, well kept Greene King, decent wines, friendly efficient service, small side eating area, restaurant; piped music; garden with play area *(David Field, Gerry and Rosemary Dobson)*
COLEORTON [SK4117]
George LE67 8HF [Loughborough Rd (A512 E)]: Attractive bar with lots of bric-a-brac, beams, stripped brick and timber, friendly landlord and staff, well kept changing ales such as Adnams, good value generous food inc light dishes; unobtrusive piped music; large garden behind with play area *(Phil and Jane Hodson)*
COPT OAK [SK4812]
Copt Oak LE67 9QB [Whitwick Rd, handy for M1 junction 22]: Comfortable family dining

pub with good views over Charnwood Forest, wide choice of food (all day Sun), quick friendly service, Marstons Pedigree, woodburner; piped music, can be very busy wknds (George Atkinson, Adrian Johnson)

COTTESMORE [SK9013]
☆ *Sun* LE15 7DH [B668 NE of Oakham]: 17th-c thatched stone-built village pub with good atmosphere and pleasant staff, good choice of wines by the glass, Adnams Best, Everards Tiger and guest, good coffee, wide choice of reasonably priced enjoyable bar food from lunchtime sandwiches up, stripped pine on flagstones, inglenook fire, lots of pictures and ornaments, carpeted back restaurant; piped music; dogs and children welcome, terrace tables, open all day wknds (Roy Bromell, Michael Dandy, Barry Collett, LYM)

CROPSTON [SK5411]
Badgers Sett LE7 7GQ [Reservoir Rd]: Rambling Vintage Inn family dining pub, wide choice all day, Everards ales and lots of wines by the glass, daily papers, log fires; nice garden (JJW, CMW)
Bradgate Arms LE7 7HG [Station Rd]: Much modernised extended village pub with traditional snug, wide range of pub food, well kept Marstons, lots of wines, attractive prices, lower family dining area, skittle alley; piped pop music, games machines; biggish garden with play area, handy for Bradgate Park (LYM, JJW, CMW, David Morgan)

CROXTON KERRIAL [SK8329]
☆ *Peacock* NG32 1QR [A607 SW of Grantham]: Much modernised 17th-c former coaching inn with good value straightforward food using good ingredients (can take a while), real ales such as Black Sheep, Greene King IPA and Wells & Youngs, decent wines, log fire in big open-plan bare boards beamed bar with chunky stripped tables, small simple dining room and garden room; said to be haunted by former landlord (never does anything that might upset customers); well-behaved children welcome, picnic-sets in inner courtyard and pleasant sloping garden with views, good bedroom block (Phil and Jane Hodson, Andy and Jill Kassube, BB, Derek and Sylvia Stephenson)

DADLINGTON [SP4097]
☆ *Dog & Hedgehog* CV13 6JB [The Green]: Comfortable extended dining pub with enjoyable interesting food inc early evening bargains and huge grills, friendly landlord, attentive staff, thriving atmosphere, well kept ales such as Chapel End and Hook Norton Old Hooky, great views over Ashby Canal and Bosworth Field, attractive village; may be piped music; children welcome (Mr and Mrs I Moules, Richard Atherton, Charles and Pauline Stride)

DESFORD [SK4902]
White Horse LE9 9JJ [B582 SE, nr A47 junction]: Recently pleasantly refurbished, enjoyable food inc good value lunches, Marstons and related guest beers, sensibly priced wines, pleasant staff,

comfortable bar with leather sofas, stylishly old-fashioned dining room; cl Sun/Mon evenings (C J Pratt)

EAST LANGTON [SP7292]
Bell LE16 7TW [off B6047; Main St]: Appealing country pub buzzing with locals and families, Brewsters, Greene King and local Langton ale, good if rather pricy food, popular Sun lunch (should book), good service, long low-ceilinged stripped-stone beamed bar, woodburner, plain wooden tables; tables on sloping front lawn (Joan and Tony Walker, LYM)

EMPINGHAM [SK9908]
☆ *White Horse* LE15 8PS [Main Street; A606 Stamford—Oakham]: Sizeable old stone pub handy for Rutland Water, bustling open-plan carpeted lounge bar, big log fire, Adnams, Oakham and Timothy Taylors Landlord, good choice of wines by the glass, pubby food with more elaborate specials; TV, piped music; children welcome, rustic tables out among flower tubs, bedrooms, open all day (Leslie and Barbara Owen, Glenwys and Alan Lawrence, LYM)

FOXTON [SP6989]
☆ *Foxton Locks* LE16 7RA [Foxton Locks, off A6 3m NW of Mkt Harboro (park by bridge 60/62 and walk)]: Large busy comfortably reworked L-shaped bar, good choice of usual food from baguettes up, quick friendly service, half a dozen real ales such as Caledonian Deuchars IPA, Fullers London Pride and Theakstons; large raised terrace and covered decking, steps down to fenced waterside lawn – nice setting at foot of long flight of canal locks (Jeff and Wendy Williams, John Wooll, Gerry and Rosemary Dobson, Jim Farmer, M J Winterton)

GLASTON [SK8900]
Old Pheasant LE15 9BP [A47 Leicester—Peterborough, E of Uppingham]: Attractively refurbished stone-built former Monckton Arms, friendly family service, good choice of wines by the glass, Greene King and a guest beer, spacious bar with central servery, alcoves, big woodburner in inglenook and some comfortable leather armchairs, restaurant; children welcome, picnic-sets on sheltered terrace, nine comfortable modern bedrooms (Colin McKerrow, LYM)

GREETHAM [SK9214]
Plough LE15 7NJ [B668 Stretton—Cottesmore]: Friendly popular village local tied to Grainstore, their beers kept well, enjoyable and interesting home-made food from baguettes up, coal-effect gas fire dividing cosy lounge from eating area, pub games; tables out behind (with quoits), handy for Rutland Water, open all day Fri-Sun (S Holder)
Wheatsheaf LE15 7NP [B668 Stretton—Cottesmore]: Linked L-shaped rooms, enjoyable food from short menu inc good open sandwiches using home-baked bread, friendly service through several management changes, Fullers London Pride and Greene King IPA, blazing open stove; soft piped

music, games room with darts, pool and big-screen sports TV; wheelchair access, front lawn and back terrace by pretty stream, annexe bedrooms, open all day Sat *(Michael and Jenny Back, BB)*

GRIMSTON [SK6821]

☆ *Black Horse* LE14 3BZ [off A6006 W of Melton Mowbray; Main St]: Popular pub with interesting interior, welcoming licensees, local ales, wide choice of good wholesome food, darts; attractive village with stocks and 13th-c church *(LYM, Duncan Cloud, S Holder)*

GUMLEY [SP6890]

☆ *Bell* LE16 7RU [NW of Market Harboro; Main St]: This cheerful neatly kept beamed village pub was for sale when we went to press; has had good value food (not Mon evening), friendly helpful staff and ales such as Adnams, Greene King and Timothy Taylors; traditional country décor, open fire, darts and cribbage, barn dining room; pretty terrace garden (not for children or dogs) with aviary, cl Sun evening *(Gerry and Rosemary Dobson, Barry Collett, LYM, P Tailyour, David Field, Jim Farmer, George Atkinson, Ken and Barbara Turner, Veronica Brown)*

HALLATON [SP7896]

Bewicke Arms LE16 8UB [off B6047 or B664]: New licensees for attractive thatched pub dating from 16th c, friendly staff, well kept Adnams, Fullers and Archers or Grainstore, two bar dining areas, restaurant of small linked areas, log fires, scrubbed pine tables, memorabilia of ancient local Easter Monday inter-village bottle-kicking match, darts, shove-ha'penny; piped music; children in eating areas, stables tearoom/gift shop across yard, big terrace overlooking paddock and lake, bedrooms, open all day Sun *(Jim Farmer, Mark Farrington, LYM)*

HATHERN [SK5021]

Dew Drop LE12 5HY [Loughborough Rd (A6)]: Traditional two-room beamed local with chatty landlord, Greene King ales, plenty of malt whiskies, coal fire, lunchtime cobs, darts and dominoes; tables outside *(the Didler)*

HEMINGTON [SK4527]

☆ *Jolly Sailor* DE74 2RB [Main St]: Cheerful and picturesque three-room village pub under new management, generous fresh food, six real ales, Weston's Old Rosie cider, decent wines by the glass, good range of soft drinks, warm log fire, big country pictures, bric-a-brac on heavy beams and shelves, prettily redone back restaurant, table skittles, daily papers; piped classical music; children welcome, picnic-sets out in front, open all day wknds *(JJW, CMW, Rona Murdoch, Richard and Jean Green, the Didler)*

HINCKLEY [SP4092]

Lime Kilns LE10 3ED [Watling St (A5)]: Pubby food, Bass, Marstons Pedigree and St Austell Tribute, small bar and compact upstairs lounge overlooking tranquil Ashby

Canal; waterside garden, some moorings *(Michael Dandy)*

HOSE [SK7329]

Black Horse LE14 4JE [Bolton Lane]: Down-to-earth beamed and quarry-tiled Tynemill pub with amiable landlord, interesting quickly served local food (not Sun/Mon evenings), well kept Castle Rock and changing ales, coal fire, darts, panelled restaurant; pretty village, nice countryside, cl Mon-Thurs lunchtimes *(the Didler, Eddie and Lynn Jarrett)*

HUNGARTON [SK6907]

Black Boy LE7 9JR [Main St]: Large partly divided open-plan bar, good food cooked to order (wknd booking advised), changing ales such as Batemans, Greene King Abbot and Wells & Youngs Bombardier, welcoming young couple, minimal decoration, open fire; cl Sun evening, Mon *(Jim Farmer, O K Smyth)*

ILLSTON ON THE HILL [SP7099]

☆ *Fox & Goose* LE7 9EG [Main St, off B6047 Mkt Harboro—Melton]: Individualistic two-bar local, plain, comfortable and convivial, with interesting pictures and assorted oddments, well kept Everards and guest ales, quick service, good coal fire, no food; cl Mon lunchtime *(Jim Farmer, LYM, the Didler, Rona Murdoch)*

KEGWORTH [SK4826]

☆ *Cap & Stocking* DE74 2FF [handy for M1 junction 24, via A6; Borough St]: Unchanging nicely old-fashioned three-room pub, brown paint, etched glass, coal fires, big cases of stuffed birds and locally caught fish, Bass (from the jug) and well kept guest beers such as Jennings and Wells & Youngs Bombardier, home-made food (not Weds evening) from fresh sandwiches to bargain Sun lunch, dominoes, back room opening to secluded garden with decking; piped music, no credit cards; children welcome *(LYM, Pete Baker, Bill Strang, Stuart Pearson)*

Red Lion DE74 2DA [a mile from M1 junction 24, via A6 towards Loughborough; High St]: Half a dozen or more good changing real ales and good range of whiskies and vodkas in four brightly lit traditional rooms around small servery, limited choice of good wholesome food (not Sun), assorted furnishings, coal and flame-effect fires, delft shelf of beer bottles, daily papers, darts and cards, family room; small back yard, garden with play area, well equipped bedrooms, open all day *(the Didler, Pete Baker, BB)*

KIBWORTH BEAUCHAMP [SP6894]

☆ *Coach & Horses* LE8 0NN [A6 S of Leicester]: Snug turkey-carpeted local with mugs on beams and relaxing candlelit restaurant, has had wide choice of good value home-made food (mainly roasts on Sun), with well kept Bass, Greene King IPA and a guest beer, and good staff, but friendly long-serving landlord may be giving up lease – news please *(P Tailyour, Jim Farmer, BB, Duncan Cloud)*

KILBY BRIDGE [SP6197]

Navigation LE18 3TE [Welford Rd (A5199 S of Leicester)]: Fine canalside position with waterside garden, nice old tiled-floor front bar, big dining area, generous food, real ales, good coffee; piped music; children welcome *(Veronica Brown)*

KIRBY MUXLOE [SK5104]

Royal Oak LE9 2AN [Main St]: Comfortable modernish pub with wide range of baguettes, good value bar dishes, fish specialities and Sun lunch, good friendly service, well kept Adnams and Everards, sizeable restaurant; nearby 15th-c castle ruins *(Gerry and Rosemary Dobson)*

KNIPTON [SK8231]

Manners Arms NG32 1RH [signed off A607 Grantham—Melton Mowbray; Croxton Rd]: Handsome Georgian hunting lodge beautifully renovated by Duke and Duchess of Rutland as upscale country inn, hunting prints and furniture from Belvoir Castle, log fire, well kept Belvoir and other ales, good choice of wines by the glass, sizeable restaurant with attractive conservatory, sumptuous lounge; terrace with ornamental pool, lovely views over pretty village, ten comfortable individually furnished bedrooms, open all day *(P Dawn, David Glynne-Jones, BB)*

LANGHAM [SK8411]

☆ *Noel Arms* LE15 7HU [Bridge St]: Pleasant country pub reopened 2007 after thorough refurbishment, low beams, flagstones, central log fire, new conservatory, food from bar or restaurant inc good value Sun lunch, Caledonian, Greene King and Marstons ales; children welcome *(LYM, Derek and Sylvia Stephenson)*

LEICESTER [SK5804]

Ale Wagon LE1 1RE [Rutland St/Charles St]: Basic 1930s two-room local with great beer choice inc Hoskins ales brewed for them, Weston's cider and perry, coal fire, events such as comedy nights; handy for station, open all day (Sun afternoon break) *(the Didler)*

Criterion LE1 5JN [Millstone Lane]: Great choice of changing real ales and continental beers in modern building with dark wood and burgundy décor in carpeted main room, decent wines by the glass, good value pizzas and more traditional pub food (not Sun evening/Mon), relaxed room on left with games, some live music; reasonable wheelchair access (small front step), picnic-sets outside, open all day *(the Didler, Jim Farmer, Tony Kelly)*

☆ *Globe* LE1 5EU [Silver St]: Lots of woodwork in cheerfully well worn partitioned areas off central bar, mirrors and wrought-iron gas lamps, charming more peaceful upstairs dining room, five Everards ales and four guest beers, pleasant staff, bargain food 12-7 from snacks up; piped pop music (not in snug), very popular with young people wknd evenings; children welcome, open all day *(the Didler, David and Sue Smith, Valerie Baker, LYM, Dave Braisted, Val and Alan Green)*

Marquis of Wellington LE2 1EF [London Rd]: Splendid Edwardian exterior, good open-plan refurbishment with intimate window seats and settles, panelling, well kept Everards and guest ales from long marble counter, good choice of continental beers, decent usual food, good friendly service, flame-effect gas fire; piped music may be loud, two TVs, games machine; disabled access and facilities, large glazed terrace, open all day *(Rona Murdoch)*

☆ *Out of the Vaults* LE1 6RL [King St/New Walk]: Remarkable changing range of real ales from a dozen handpumps in long high-ceilinged bar, friendly chatty landlady, enthusiast landlord, wkdy lunchtime cobs, baguettes and curries, decent reasonably priced wines by the glass, simple seating and stripped tables on bare boards; open all day *(Jim Farmer, the Didler)*

Pump & Tap LE3 5LX [Duns Gate (nr Polytechnic)]: Popular roadside pub with two long narrow rooms, panelling, old wicker chairs, large log fire and stove, old photographs, well kept ales; sports TV *(the Didler)*

Queen Victoria LE1 1SJ [Southampton St]: Reopened in 2008 by enthusiastic licensees, good local atmosphere, bar with stage, Sam Smiths OBB and eight changing guest ales, farm cider and wheat beers, enjoyable food; two gardens, beer festivals, open all day *(the Didler)*

Rutland & Derby Arms LE1 5JN [Millstone Lane]: Smartly renovated old pub with clean-cut modern bar/brasserie décor, friendly staff, interesting well priced food using local organic meat inc bargain two-course Sun lunch, home-baked sourdough bread, Everards and guest ales, very wide choice of lagers and impressive spirits range; well reproduced piped music; terrace tables *(Val and Alan Green, Kerry Law)*

☆ *Swan & Rushes* LE1 5WR [Oxford St/Infirmary Sq]: Well kept Oakham and fine range of guest and bottled beers, farm cider, thriving atmosphere in two rooms with big oak tables, enjoyable bar food lunchtime and Weds/Fri evening; live music Sat; open all day Fri-Sun *(the Didler, James Crouchman, Jim Farmer, Valerie Baker)*

LITTLE BOWDEN [SP7386]

Cherry Tree LE16 8AE [Church Walk; edge of Mkt Harboro, nr Sainsburys]: Attractive low-beamed thatched and timbered Everards pub, quick cheerful service, well kept ales, bargain food (not Sun evening) from baguettes up, two sitting rooms, lots of prints, dining room on left, Royal Naval Assoc room, back games bar (with TV); children welcome, front garden with picnic-sets and play area, heated child-free back one, open all day Fri-Sun, nr 12th-c church *(Michael Dandy)*

LONG CLAWSON [SK7227]

Crown & Plough LE14 4NG [off A606 NW of Melton Mowbray; East End]: 17th-c food pub with low bowed beams, stripped masonry, inglenooks, a mix of seats around scrubbed pine tables, some comfortable sofas, real ales such as Adnams, Everards Tiger and Marstons Pedigree; children and dogs welcome, tables in sheltered courtyard, five bedrooms, may cl Mon lunchtime *(Gwyn and Anne Wake, Phil and Jane Hodson, LYM)*

LOUGHBOROUGH [SK5320]

Albion LE11 1QA [canal bank, about 0.2 mile from Loughborough Wharf]: Cheerful chatty local by Grand Union Canal, emphasis on at least three changing real ales inc one from local Wicked Hathern, friendly owners, cheap straightforward home-made food, coal fire, darts room; children welcome, occasional barbecues, budgerigar aviary in nice big courtyard *(P Dawn, the Didler)*

☆ *Swan in the Rushes* LE11 5BE [The Rushes (A6)]: Bustling bare-boards town local with good value Castle Rock and lots of other interesting changing ales, plenty of foreign bottled beers, farm cider, good value straightforward chip-free food (not Sat/Sun evenings), good service, daily papers, traditional games, open fire, three smallish high-ceilinged rooms inc upgraded back dining room; good juke box, music nights; children in eating areas, tables outside, four bedrooms, open all day *(the Didler, P Dawn, Rona Murdoch, Pete Baker, Comus and Sarah Elliott, Sue Demont, Tim Barrow, Richard and Karen Holt, Mrs Hazel Rainer, Andrew Seymour, LYM, BB)*

Tap & Mallet LE11 1EU [Nottingham Rd]: Basic friendly pub noted for changing microbrews inc Church End, foreign beers, farm cider and perry, coal fire, pool, juke box; walled back garden with play area and pets corner, open all day wknds *(P Dawn, the Didler)*

MARKET BOSWORTH [SK4003]

☆ *Olde Red Lion* CV13 0LL [Park St; from centre follow Leicester and Hinckley signs]: Cheerful and civilised black-beamed split-level pub with good choice of well kept Marstons and other ales, sensibly priced food (not Sun/Mon evenings) from sandwiches and baked potatoes up inc proper steak and kidney pie, prompt efficient service, plushly tidy L-shaped bar; may be piped music; children welcome, picnic-sets and play area in sheltered courtyard, attractive village, five comfortable bedrooms, open all day Fri-Sun *(Pete Baker, LYM, C J Pratt, Derek and Sylvia Stephenson)*

MARKET HARBOROUGH [SP7387]

Angel LE16 7AF [High St]: Former coaching inn with good value food from sandwiches and other pubby lunchtime bar food to restaurant meals, friendly and efficient uniformed staff, Banks's and Everards Tiger, good coffee, daily papers; bedrooms *(Michael Dandy, Gerry and Rosemary Dobson)*

Oat Hill LE16 8AN [Kettering Rd]: Contemporary bar with mixed furnishings inc sofas, good choice of wines and lagers, Bass and Timothy Taylors Landlord, up-to-date food from sandwiches up, attentive staff, back restaurant; piped music; nice garden *(Michael Dandy)*

Sugar Loaf LE16 7NJ [High St]: Popular Wetherspoons, smaller than many, with half a dozen sensibly priced real ales, good value food all day; children allowed, frequent beer festivals, open all day *(Gerry and Rosemary Dobson, Michael Dandy, George Atkinson)*

☆ *Three Swans* LE16 7NJ [High St]: Handsome coaching inn now a Best Western conference hotel, comfortably refurbished beamed and panelled front bar, flagstoned back dining lounge and fine courtyard conservatory (used Weds-Fri evenings as good value bistro) in more modern part, friendly staff, wide range of good value bar lunches from sandwiches up, some bar food early evenings, Flowers and Wells & Youngs Bombardier, decent wines, good coffee, more formal upstairs restaurant; piped music; attractive suntrap courtyard, good bedroom extension *(Anthony Barnes, George Atkinson, Gerry and Rosemary Dobson, John Wooll, Michael Dandy)*

MARKET OVERTON [SK8816]

Black Bull LE15 7PW [off B668 in Cottesmore]: Attractive thatched and low-beamed stone-built pub in pretty village well placed for Rutland Water, friendly helpful landlord and energetic staff, good interesting home-made food in neat bar and dining room, well kept Fullers London Pride; children in eating areas, some tables out in front by small carp pool *(BB, Paul Bray, Dr C C S Wilson)*

MEDBOURNE [SP7992]

☆ *Nevill Arms* LE16 8EE [B664 Market Harborough—Uppingham]: Handsome streamside inn smartened up by welcoming new owners, helpful staff, decent bar food from sandwiches up, real ales such as Fullers London Pride. Greene King Abbot and St Austell Tribute, log fires, modern artwork, stylish new back restaurant; no dogs; seats out overlooking village green, nicely refurbished bedrooms, good breakfast *(R L Borthwick, Ian Stafford, John Saville, Mike and Sue Loseby, LYM, George Atkinson, Mark Farrington, John Wooll)*

MOUNTSORREL [SK5715]

Swan LE12 7AT [Loughborough Rd, off A6]: Log fires, old flagstones and stripped stone, friendly staff and locals, enjoyable food from baguettes and light dishes to full meals, Theakstons and a guest beer, good choice of wines, pine tables and gingham cloths in neat dining area and restaurant; pretty walled back garden down to canalised River Soar, self-contained accommodation, open all day Sat *(Rona Murdoch, Jim Farmer)*

MUSTON [SK8237]

Muston Gap NG13 0FD [Church Lane; just off A52 W of Grantham]: Big family-oriented M&B pub-restaurant with large bar and light and airy modern dining areas, bargain traditional food inc all-day carvery, neat staff, decent wines; good disabled access and facilities, garden with play area *(M J Winterton)*

OADBY [SP6399]

Grange LE2 4RH [Glen Rd (A6)]: Roomy Vintage Inn based on attractive early 19th-c farmhouse, friendly staff, good wine choice, Bass, log fires, old local photographs, daily papers, good mix of customers; children welcome, picnic-sets out in front, open all day (Leslie and Barbara Owen, Dr and Mrs A K Clarke)

OAKHAM [SK8508]

Admiral Hornblower LE15 6AS [High St]: Several differently decorated areas from panelling and tradition to fresher informality, warm and inviting with three log fires, interesting menu using own herbs, well organised service, well kept ales, conservatory; garden, comfortable bedrooms (P Dawn, H Paulinski)

Calico LE15 6EA [Mill St]: Modern bar/bistro with good value food from sandwiches up, good choice of wines by the glass, nice coffee, great staff, cosy corners; courtyard tables (Bruce and Sharon Eden)

Wheatsheaf LE15 6QS [Northgate]: Attractive 17th-c local nr church, friendly helpful service, Adnams, Everards and guest ales, enjoyable lunchtime pub food inc good puddings, open fire, plenty of bric-a-brac, cheerful bar, comfortable quieter lounge and conservatory (children welcome in it); pretty suntrap back courtyard with entertaining installation, nearby play park (Barry Collett, K H Frostick, John Fiander)

OLD DALBY [SK6723]

☆ *Crown* LE14 3LF [Debdale Hill]: Three or four intimate little farmhouse rooms up and down steps, black beams, one or two antique oak settles among other seats, rustic prints, open fires, several ales inc Belvoir from flagstoned servery, up-to-date fresh local food (not Sun evening or Mon), relaxed dining room; children and dogs welcome, nice terrace in attractive garden (the Didler, Dominic Markham, LYM)

PEATLING MAGNA [SP5992]

☆ *Cock* LE8 5UQ [off A5199 S of Leicester; Main St]: Friendly bustle in two-room village pub with good value generous food, may be help-yourself free brie and stilton Mon-Thurs evenings, Courage, John Smiths and a guest, decent house wines, horsey pictures and plates above fire and on beams, cushioned wall benches, plush stools, neat country dining area; lots of events (LYM, Mrs M B Gregg)

REDMILE [SK7935]

Windmill NG13 0GA [off A52 Grantham—Nottingham; Main St]: Dining pub with wide choice of enjoyable home-made food from baguettes to steaks, wkdy meal deals and Sun roasts, Greene King Ruddles, good wines by the glass, good friendly service, up-to-date décor keeping original features inc old fireplace; children welcome (P Dawn, David Glynne-Jones, N R White)

SADDINGTON [SP6591]

Queens Head LE8 0QH [S of Leicester between A5199 (ex A50) and A6; Main St]: Welcoming pub with well kept Everards and guest ales, decent wines, attentive staff, daily papers, lots of knick-knacks, steps from

area to area; children welcome, country and reservoir views from dining conservatory and tables in long sloping garden (Gerry and Rosemary Dobson, LYM, David Field)

SEATON [SP9098]

☆ *George & Dragon* LE15 9HU [Main St]: Good generous sensibly priced food from sandwiches up, Fri steak nights, Sun roasts, quick friendly service, real ales such as Adnams Broadside, Black Sheep, Grainstore Ten Fifty and Marstons Pedigree, good wine choice, daily papers, nice solid fuel stove, two cosy bars, one with lots of sports memorabilia; piped jazz; tables outside, unspoilt village, good views of famous viaduct (Jim Farmer, Barry Collett, BB, Noel Grundy)

SHEARSBY [SP6290]

☆ *Chandlers Arms* LE17 6PL [Fenny Lane, off A50 Leicester—Northampton]: Comfortable village pub doing well under current friendly owners, good value food inc some lunchtime bargains and more interesting evening menu, good choice of well kept changing ales inc Black Sheep and Grainstore, warm atmosphere, pub terrier, brocaded wall seats, wheelback chairs, flowers on tables, house plants, swagged curtains; tables in secluded raised garden, attractive village (Peter Cole, S Needham, Jeremy King, BB)

SHEPSHED [SK4719]

Pied Bull LE12 9AA [handy for M1 junction 23; Belton St]: Thatched two-bar local, neat and well organised, with enjoyable home-made food, cheerful accommodating staff, Marstons and guest ales from central bar, log fire in open-plan beamed lounge, back restaurant; children welcome, large colourful garden behind (Dr and Mrs A K Clarke)

SIBSON [SK3500]

Cock CV13 6LB [A444 N of Nuneaton; Twycross Rd]: Ancient picturesque black and white timbered and thatched building, Bass and Hook Norton, a dozen wines by the glass, low doorways, heavy black beams and genuine latticed windows, immense inglenook; piped music, games machine; children welcome, tables in courtyard and small garden, handy for Bosworth Field (Ian and Jane Irving, LYM, Helen Rowett)

SILEBY [SK6015]

☆ *White Swan* LE12 7NW [Swan St]: Bright and cheerful, with good choice of attractively priced home cooking (not Sun evening or Mon lunchtime, may be a wait if busy) from home-baked rolls to fine puddings, well kept Fullers London Pride, nice house wines, good friendly staff and chatty locals, comfortable dining lounge, small tasteful book-lined restaurant (booking needed) (Jim Farmer)

SOMERBY [SK7710]

☆ *Three Crowns* LE14 2PZ [off A606 Oakham—Melton Mowbray; High St]: Friendly low-beamed village pub with big log fire, good local Parish Bitter, Bass and Greene King IPA, bargain simple food, mix of old-fashioned chairs around dark oak tables, wknd live music; children and dogs welcome, tables in walled garden, nice bedrooms, open all day Sun; for sale 2008, plans for conversion to B&B and residential development – news please *(Ian Stafford, Barry Collett, Phil and Jane Hodson, LYM, O K Smyth, Gerry and Rosemary Dobson)*

SOUTH CROXTON [SK6810]

Golden Fleece LE7 3RL [Main St]: Large, clean and friendly, with enjoyable home-made food from good baguettes to popular Sun lunch, proper bar with some sofas, dark corners and attractive separate restaurant, good service, real ales such as Greene King, good house wine, log fire; lovely area *(Jim Farmer)*

SPROXTON [SK8524]

Crown LE14 4QB [Coston Rd]: Friendly enthusiastic landlord, enjoyable reasonably priced food running up to lobster, well kept Greene King, good coffee, light and airy bar with open fire, two dining rooms; back terrace, attractive village, nice walks *(Mike and Julia Porter)*

THORPE LANGTON [SP7492]

☆ *Bakers Arms* LE16 7TS [off B6047 N of Mkt Harboro']: Civilised restaurant rather than pub now, good imaginative meals in cottagey beamed linked areas (must book), stylishly simple country décor, well kept local Langton ale, good choice of wines by the glass, friendly attentive staff; no under-12s; garden picnic-sets, cl wkdy lunchtimes, Sun evening and Mon *(LYM, Gerry and Rosemary Dobson, Duncan Cloud, Mike and Sue Loseby)*

THORPE SATCHVILLE [SK7311]

Fox LE14 2DQ [Main St (B6047)]: 1930s pub/restaurant with French chef/landlord doing good food from interesting snacks to full french meals, carpeted front bars and back restaurant with open fire; tables in front and in back garden, cl Mon lunchtime and Sun *(Anna and Martyn Carey)*

THRINGSTONE [SK4217]

George & Dragon LE67 8UH [Ashby Rd]: Friendly new licensees doing enjoyable bar food using local farms, real ales such as Greene King, pleasant layout and décor, occasional beer festivals, Sun live music; garden with barbecues *(Gerry and Rosemary Dobson)*

THRUSSINGTON [SK6415]

Blue Lion LE7 4UD [off A46 N of Leicester; Rearsby Rd]: 18th-c two-bar village pub, good value standard food (not Sun evening), Marstons, good soft drinks range, friendly landlord, beams, woodburner, oak tables and comfortable settles, bric-a-brac inc lots of teapots; piped music, no credit cards; garden with play area *(JJW, CMW)*

TUGBY [SK7600]

Fox & Hounds LE7 9WB [A47 6 miles W of Uppingham]: Attractively refurbished village-green pub, enjoyable food inc midweek OAP bargains, fine range of well kept real ales, friendly service, Weston's farm cider, two-level layout with pleasant décor and relaxed atmosphere, central woodburner in dining

area on left; good-sized garden with terrace *(Jim Farmer, R L Borthwick, Michael and Jenny Back, O K Smyth, Andrew Cross)*

WALCOTE [SP5683]

Black Horse LE17 4JU [Lutterworth Rd (A4304 E of M1 junction 20)]: Attractive contemporary rebuild, half a dozen or more well kept real ales inc Timothy Taylors Landlord, enjoyable traditional food lunchtime inc OAP bargains, with the bonus of good thai food evenings and Fri lunchtime, friendly efficient service, comfortable games bar with pool, darts and sports TV; children welcome, disabled facilities, garden tables, open all day Fri-Sun *(LYM, Stuart and Bev Hutchesson)*

WALTHAM ON THE WOLDS [SK8024]

Marquis of Granby LE14 4AH [High St]: Friendly stone-built country local with good value generous pubby food inc lunchtime carvery, quick service, well kept ales, decent wines by the glass, upper games area with pool, skittle alley; children welcome, tables out on decking *(Phil and Jane Hodson)*

WESTON BY WELLAND [SP7791]

Wheel & Compass LE16 8HZ [Valley Rd]: Wide choice of enjoyable attractively priced food, Bass, Marstons Pedigree and three changing guest beers, friendly staff, comfortable bar, good-sized back dining area and restaurant; open all day wknds *(Jim Farmer, Guy and Caroline Howard)*

WHITWELL [SK9208]

Noel Arms LE15 8BW [Main Rd]: Smart spacious pub-restaurant handy for Rutland Water, enjoyable food inc good value two-course lunches, real ales, decent wines by the glass, good coffee; children welcome, suntrap tables outside, play area, bedrooms *(Roy Bromell, LYM)*

WHITWICK [SK4316]

Three Horseshoes LE67 5GN [Leicester Rd]: Utterly unpretentious local, friendly long bar and tiny snug, Bass and Marstons Pedigree, log fires, darts, dominoes and cards, no food; outdoor lavatories *(the Didler, Pete Baker)*

WIGSTON [SP6099]

William Wygston LE18 1DR [Leicester Rd]: Roomy Wetherspoons, bright and airy, with bargain food deals, well priced real ales, quick helpful service; accessible books – not exactly riveting except for specialists *(Veronica Brown, John Fiander)*

WOODHOUSE EAVES [SK5214]

Curzon Arms LE12 8QZ [Maplewell Rd]: Neatly kept proper pub with ample food choice (all day Sat) inc wkdy OAP lunches, changing ales such as Fullers London Pride, carpeted dining room; children and dogs welcome, good-sized front lawn and terrace *(Brian and Jean Hepworth)*

WYMESWOLD [SK6023]

☆ *Hammer & Pincers* LE12 6ST [East Rd (A6006)]: Restaurant rather than pub now, with good food (not Sun evening or Mon/Tues), good value Sat brunch, more expensive evening meals, small smart entrance bar with black leather settees and armchairs, shallow steps up to linked eating areas with chunky pine furniture, contemporary lighting and big cheery artworks, decent wines, neat helpful staff; piped music, no real ale; picnic-sets on sheltered well landscaped back terrace, sturdy play area behind; cl Mon (BB, R L Borthwick)

Three Crowns LE12 6TZ [Far St (A6006)]: Snug chatty 18th-c village local with good friendly staff, good value food inc lots of specials, four or five real ales such as Adnams, Belvoir and Marstons, good soft drinks choice, pleasant character furnishings in beamed bar and lounge, darts; picnic-sets out on decking (the Didler, Comus and Sarah Elliott, P Dawn)

Windmill LE12 6TT [Brook St]: Sidestreet village pub with good food using local ingredients, charming quick service, central servery separating bar and smallish dining area, minimalist décor – a few abstracts on pastel walls; children welcome (Phil and Jane Hodson, Francoise Vero, Comus and Sarah Elliott)

WYMONDHAM [SK8518]

Berkeley Arms LE14 2AG [Main St]: Attractive old stone building with friendly helpful staff, good generous fresh food inc imaginative dishes in main bar, dining lounge and elegant restaurant, changing ales such as Adnams, Greene King and Hydes, Addlestone's cider, good coffee, uncluttered décor with pine furniture; well spaced picnic-sets in pleasant garden, nice village, cl Mon lunchtime (Louise Etherington, George and Beverley Tucker)

Post Office address codings confusingly give the impression that some pubs are in Leicestershire, when they're really in Cambridgeshire (which is where we list them).

Lincolnshire

Once something of a desert for good food, Lincolnshire these days has its fair share of good pub dining. The benchmark is set by the well run George of Stamford. This grand old inn is in such a league of its own that it seems almost unfair to pit it against other pubs, but once again it romps away with the top title of Lincolnshire Dining Pub of the Year. When it comes to racking up our awards, it's something of a surprise to find that the pub which is closest on the George's heels is the Welby Arms at Allington. It's a much pubbier option – welcoming and relaxing, and a great place to stay. Another good all-rounder, with particularly good food, is the very thoughtfully run Chequers at Woolsthorpe. A new entry, the welcoming and comfortable Cross Keys in Stow, is a good food stop in a pleasantly traditional style. By contrast, the smart Blue Bell at Belchford is well worth knowing for its inventive modern cooking, and readers still love the civilised but chatty Wig & Mitre in Lincoln – so useful with its long food service hours. Another option in Lincoln, and a rather different one but not to be missed, is the much more down-to-earth and traditional Victoria, with its great range of nine real ales and straightforward but very good value tasty food. Current hot picks among the Lucky Dip entries at the end of the chapter are the Blue Pig in Grantham, Queens Head at Kirkby La Thorpe and Crown in Stamford. Batemans is the county's quintessential brewer – their brewery centre (see Wainfleet) is well worth a visit, and this family firm preserves a good many charmingly old-fashioned simple taverns. The good Tom Woods Highwood beers, going for little more than a decade, are increasingly widely available, and we also found Riverside, Brewsters and Poachers in one or two of our listed good pubs.

ALLINGTON

SK8540   MAP 7

Welby Arms ♀ ◼ ⇌

The Green; off A1 N of Grantham, or A52 W of Grantham; NG32 2EA

Friendly inn near A1 with agreeable food, six real ales and pleasant bedrooms

A jolly good all rounder is a fair description of this comfortably bustling pub which caters well for most needs. The large traditionally furnished bar is divided by a stone archway and has black beams and joists, log fires (one in an attractive arched brick fireplace), red velvet curtains and comfortable burgundy button-back wall banquettes and stools. Cheery staff serve the half a dozen very well kept real ales (through a sparkler) that include Charles Wells Bombardier, John Smiths, Timothy Taylors Landlord and three guests such as Adnams Broadside, Jennings Cumberland and St Austell Tribute; also ten wines by the glass, and 20 malt whiskies; dominoes, cribbage, and piped music. The civilised back dining lounge (where they prefer you to eat) looks out on to tables in a sheltered walled courtyard with pretty summer hanging baskets, and there are more picnic-sets out on the front lawn.

🍴 Popular bar food might include soup, filled baguettes (including hot sirloin steak and stilton), chicken liver pâté, chicken pasta, steak and mushroom in ale pie and chargrilled steaks, and specials such as pork and black pudding sausage, fresh grimsby haddock with mushy peas, lambs liver and onions, lamb shank and poached plaice with prawn sauce. Best to book to be sure of a table. *Starters/Snacks: £3.95 to £6.95. Main Courses: £6.95 to £7.95. Puddings: £3.50*

Enterprise ~ Lease Matt Rose ~ Real ale ~ Bar food ~ Restaurant ~ (01400) 281361 ~ Well behaved children in bar till 7pm, in restaurant till 9pm ~ Open 12-2(3 Sat), 6-11; 12-10.30 Sun ~ Bedrooms: £48S/£60S

Recommended by Michael and Jenny Back, Maurice and Janet Thorpe, JJW, CMW, Andy and Jill Kassube, Jill and Julian Tasker, Mrs Brenda Calver, Trevor Gaston, Bruce M Drew, W M Paton, Nigel and Sue Foster, Roger and Pauline Pearce, Maurice Ricketts, Sally Anne and Peter Goodale, Leslie and Barbara Owen, Mr and Mrs W D Borthwick

BARNOLDBY LE BECK   TA2303   MAP 8

Ship ♀

Village signposted off A18 Louth—Grimsby; DN37 0BG

Very good fish menu at tranquil plush dining pub

The sedately relaxed atmosphere at this neatly kept little cream painted pub is perfectly in keeping with the delightful collection of beautifully kept Edwardian and Victorian bric-a-brac that you'll find here. Charming items run from stand-up telephones and violins to a horn gramophone, as well as bowler and top hats, old racquets, crops, hockey sticks and a lace dress. Heavy dark-ringed drapes swathe the windows, with grandmotherly plants in ornate china bowls on the sills. Furnishings include comfortable dark green plush wall benches with lots of pretty propped-up cushions and heavily stuffed green plush Victorian-looking chairs on a green fleur de lys carpet. Tables may all be set for dining, but you can pop in for a drink as there are stools along the bar; well kept Black Sheep and Shepherd Neame Spitfire on handpump and a good wine list; piped music. A fenced-off sunny area behind has hanging baskets and a few picnic-sets under pink parasols. More reports please.

🍴 The licensees are passionate about the quality of the fish that they not only serve but some of which they also catch. There might be scallops with ginger and garlic butter, whitebait, skate wing with lemon and caper butter, red fish wrapped in parma ham with mushroom, bacon and shallot reduction, battered haddock, marinated catfish and halibut baked with orange segments. Other equally enjoyable food includes sandwiches, crispy duck with egg noodles, brie and cherry tomato tart, beef and ale pie, roast rack of lamb with mango, herb and parmesan crust and pork tenderloin with cranberry, port and rosemary jus. *Starters/Snacks: £4.25 to £7.00. Main Courses: £8.95 to £17.00. Puddings: £4.50*

Inn Business ~ Tenant Michele Hancock ~ Real ale ~ Bar food ~ Restaurant ~ (01472) 822308 ~ Children welcome ~ Open 12-3, 6-11(12 Sat)

Recommended by Maurice and Janet Thorpe, James Browne, Dr and Mrs J Temporal, Alistair and Kay Butler, Leslie and Barbara Owen

BELCHFORD   TF2975   MAP 8

Blue Bell 🍴

Village signposted off A153 Horncastle—Louth (and can be reached by the good Bluestone Heath Road off A16 just under 1.5 miles N of the A1104 roundabout); Main Road; LN9 6LQ

Emphasis on imaginative modern food at cottagey 18th-c dining pub

It's probably best to book a table if you are planning to visit this smart restauranty place at the weekend – drinkers are welcome but it does tend to fill up with diners. The cosy comfortable bar has a relaxing pastel décor, some armchairs and settees, as well as more upright chairs around good solid tables, with well kept Black Sheep and a guest such as Riverside Dixons Major on handpump. Service is pleasant and attentive. The neat terraced garden behind has picnic-sets, and this is a good base for Wolds walks and the Viking Way though hikers must take their boots off.

⑪ From an inventive changing (not cheap) menu, there might be sandwiches, starters such as goats cheese cheesecake, ham hock terrine with honey and grain mustard, confit of duck leg on puy lentil roast tomato, thyme and chorizo sauce, main courses such as beef and Guinness pie, sausage on truffle mash, cod baked with pumpkin crust and white wine cream sauce, twice-baked cheddar soufflé on spinach with red pepper coulis, saddle of venison wrapped in pancetta with lincoln blue cheese on parsnip purée with redcurrant sauce and fillet steak with green pepper and Guinness sauce, and puddings such as summer fruit pudding and warm chocolate brownie with pistachio ice-cream. *Starters/Snacks: £4.25 to £7.95. Main Courses: £7.95 to £18.95. Puddings: £4.95 to £5.50*

Free house ~ Licensees Darren and Shona Jackson ~ Real ale ~ Bar food (till 4 Sat) ~ Restaurant ~ (01507) 533602 ~ Children welcome ~ Open 11.30-2, 6.30-11; 12-4 Sun; closed Sun evening, Mon and second and third weeks in Jan

Recommended by Dr K A McLauchlan, D F Clarke, Mrs R McLauchlan, Derek and Sylvia Stephenson, Mrs P Bishop, David Barnes, Malcolm Brown, Mrs Brenda Calver, Chris Brooks

BILLINGBOROUGH   TF1134   MAP 8

Fortescue Arms

B1177, off A52 Grantham—Boston; NG34 0QB

Fresh flowers and good value food at welcoming low-beamed country pub; pretty gardens

The several turkey-carpeted characterful rooms at this fine old country inn have lots of ancient stonework, exposed brickwork, wood panelling and beams, bay window seats and a big see-through fireplace. Décor and bric-a-brac is that which you'd expect in a traditional rural pub – everything from Victorian prints to fresh flowers and pot plants, brass and copper, a stuffed badger and pheasant, and various quiz books. Attractive dining rooms at each end have flagstones and another open fire. Unusually, a long red and black tiled corridor runs right the way along behind the serving bar, making it an island. Here you'll find well kept Fullers London Pride, Greene King IPA, Timothy Taylors Landlord and a guest such as Greene King Abbot on handpump; piped music, games machine and TV. There are picnic-sets on a lawn under apple trees on one side, and on the other a sheltered courtyard with flowers planted in tubs and a manger.

⑪ Very generously served food includes sandwiches and baguettes, ploughman's, soup, crispy whitebait, smoked mackerel, several pies, thai curry, chicken breast in white wine and mushroom sauce, battered cod, goats cheese and red onion tart, roast duck in orange sauce and 16oz T-bone; Sunday roasts. *Starters/Snacks: £3.50 to £5.95. Main Courses: £7.95 to £18.95. Puddings: £3.95*

Churchill Taverns ~ Managers Terry and Nicola Williams ~ Real ale ~ Bar food (12-2(2.30 Sat), 6-9(9.30 Sat); 12-9 Sun) ~ Restaurant ~ (01529) 240228 ~ Children welcome ~ Open 12-3, 5.30-12; 12-midnight Sat; 12-11 Sun

Recommended by Brian and Jean Hepworth, W M Paton, Sally Anne and Peter Goodale

CONINGSBY   TF2458   MAP 8

Lea Gate Inn

Leagate Road (B1192 southwards, off A153 E); LN4 4RS

Cosy old-fashioned interior, attractive garden, play area

Full of evocative character, the unchanging ancient interior of this traditional 16th-c inn still conjures up the atmosphere of highwaymen lurking in snugs and visitors tucking themselves away from the bad weather. At the front of the inn is an enclosure known as Gibbet Nook Close, the site of the gibbet or gallows used for public executions (the bodies were left hanging). In the main lounge, above the fireplace, look out for the engraving titled the 'Last Supper'. It is believed that the last rites were given to the condemned criminals here. Three dimly lit areas have heavy low black beams supporting ochre ceiling boards, and two great antique oak high-backed settles with hunting-print cushions forming a snug around the biggest of the fireplaces. Fortunately, given all this darkly atmospheric character, the staff who serve the Batemans, Charles Wells Bombardier and a guest such as Adnams from handpumps are particularly cheerful – and there's piped music too. The appealing garden has tables and an enclosed play area.

🍴 Bar food includes soup, lunchtime sandwiches, grilled goats cheese on a croûton, mushroom stroganoff, steak and kidney pie, chicken breast filled with fresh spinach with tangy lemon and cream sauce, honey-glazed duck breast with plum and fresh ginger sauce, fried salmon with lime and coriander dressing and beef wellington, and puddings such as banoffi pie and Baileys and chocolate cheesecake. *Starters/Snacks: £4.95 to £7.95. Main Courses: £8.95 to £14.95. Puddings: £3.25*

Free house ~ Licensee Mark Dennison ~ Real ale ~ Bar food ~ Restaurant ~ (01526) 342370 ~ Children welcome ~ Open 11.30-3, 4-11; 12-10.30 Sun ~ Bedrooms: £60B/£80B

Recommended by Bill and Sheila McLardy, Janet and Peter Race, John Robertson, Mrs P Bishop, Ron and Sheila Corbett, the Didler

DRY DODDINGTON   SK8546   MAP 8
Wheatsheaf
1.5 miles off A1 N of Grantham; Main Street; NG23 5HU

Happy bustling pub with good food; handy for A1

Good news is that the new licensees here are maintaining the tremendously good spirits that have always been characteristic of this spotlessly kept mainly 16th-c colourwashed village pub. The front bar is basically two rooms, with a log fire, a variety of settles and chairs, and tables in the windows facing across to the green and the lovely 14th-c church with its crooked tower. The serving bar on the right has well kept Greene King Abbot, Timothy Taylors Landlord, Tom Woods Best and a guest such as Purity Pure Gold on handpump, and a nice choice of about ten wines by the glass. A slight slope takes you down to the comfortable thickly carpeted and recently extended dining room with its relaxing red and cream décor. Once a cow byre, this part is even more ancient than the rest of the building, perhaps dating from the 13th c. The front terrace has neat dark green tables under cocktail parasols, among tubs of flowers; disabled access at the side.

🍴 Good food might include hock and stilton terrine with apple and date chutney, fried scallops with black pudding and cauliflower purée, battered haddock, slow roast pork belly with honey jus, fillet of bream with warm salad of fennel and chorizo and braised blade of beef with celeriac purée. *Starters/Snacks: £4.25 to £6.25. Main Courses: £9.95 to £12.95. Puddings: £3.95 to £4.95*

Free house ~ Licensees Dan Bland and Kate Feetham ~ Real ale ~ Bar food (12-2.30(3 Sun)), 6-9(9.30 Fri, Sat, 5-8 Sun)) ~ Restaurant ~ (01400) 281458 ~ Children welcome ~ Dogs allowed in bar ~ Open 12-2.30, 5-11; 12-11 Sat; 12-10.30 Sun; closed Tues lunchtime and Mon

Recommended by Michael and Jenny Back, Alan Bowker, Andy and Jill Kassube, Mrs Roxanne Chamberlain, Frank Gorman

HOUGH-ON-THE-HILL   SK9246   MAP 8
Brownlow Arms
High Road; NG32 2AZ

Refined country house with beamed bar, imaginative food and graceful terrace

Our inspector reports that they didn't bat an eyelid when he arrived at this terribly smart upmarket old stone inn looking slightly scruffy, and ordered just one drink. In practice though, most people are here for the sophisticated dining experience (you will probably need to book). The beamed bar is comfortable with plenty of panelling, some exposed brickwork, local prints and scenes, a large mirror, and a pile of logs beside the big fireplace. Seating is on elegant stylishly mismatched upholstered armchairs, and the carefully arranged furnishings give the impression of several separate and surprisingly cosy areas; piped easy listening. Marstons Burton Bitter and Pedigree and Timothy

Taylors Landlord and a good choice of malt whiskies are served by friendly, impeccably polite staff. The well equipped bedrooms are attractive and breakfasts are hearty.

🍽 Very good (though not cheap) food might include starters such as butternut and parmesan soup, foie gras and chicken liver pâté with morello cherry chutney and toasted brioche, duck confit with honey and thyme glazed shallots, wild mushroom risotto with wilting spinach and parmesan, slow-cooked shoulder of lamb with crushed winter roots and red wine jus and fried rib-eye with cracked black peppercorns, shallots and armagnac cream, puddings such as panna cotta with orange and Grand Marnier fruit salad and double chocolate brownlow with white chocolate ice-cream, and a cheese plate. *Starters/Snacks: £4.95 to £8.25. Main Courses: £12.95 to £18.75. Puddings: £5.95*

Free house ~ Licensee Paul L Willoughby ~ Real ale ~ Bar food (12-2 Sun, 6.30-9.30) ~ Restaurant ~ (01400) 250234 ~ Open 6-11; 12-4 Sun; closed Mon, lunchtimes Tues-Sat, Sun evening, 1 week in September, 3 weeks in January ~ Bedrooms: £65B/£96B

Recommended by Ruby and Andrew Jones, Andy and Jill Kassube, Michael Holdsworth, Maurice and Janet Thorpe, D F Clarke

INGHAM   SK9483   MAP 8

Inn on the Green
The Green; LN1 2XT

Nicely modernised place popular for good thoughtfully prepared food; chatty atmosphere

Though there's some emphasis on the food at this welcoming place it does still feel like a proper pub, with a good chatty atmosphere throughout, particularly in the locals' bar, with its inglenook fireplace. It's quite likely that most tables elsewhere will be occupied by diners – no mean feat given that the beamed and timbered dining room is spread over two floors. There's lots of exposed brickwork, and a mix of brasses and copper, local prints and bric-a-brac. The brick bar counter has home-made jams, marmalade and chutney for sale alongside Black Sheep, a couple of guests such as Bass and Exmoor Gold and half a dozen or so wines by the glass. Opposite is a comfortably laid-back area with two red leather sofas; piped music; good service.

🍽 Good food is home-made, using seasonal produce – they even grow a proportion of the vegetables themselves. Dishes might include wild rabbit and sage strudel with cider jus, home-smoked salmon mousse with buckwheat pancakes, fried pigeon and black pudding, seared salmon with ratatouille and rocket pesto, beef bourguignon, chicken breast with mushroom stuffing baked in pastry and unashamedly indulgent puddings such as cranberry bakewell with custard, warm banana and syrup cake with rum raisin ice-cream and iced white chocolate and pistachio nut parfait. Readers have told us that they also do a very reasonably priced two-course lunchtime offer. *Starters/Snacks: £3.75 to £4.95. Main Courses: £5.95 to £13.95. Puddings: £3.60 to £4.95*

Free house ~ Licensees Andrew Cafferkey and Sarah Sharpe ~ Real ale ~ Bar food (12-2, 6.30-9.30; 12-6 Sun) ~ Restaurant ~ (01522) 730354 ~ Children welcome ~ Open 11.30-3, 6-11; 11-3, 6-midnight Sat; 12-10.30 Sun; closed Mon inc bank hols

Recommended by Mr and Mrs J L Blakey, Derek and Sylvia Stephenson, G Dobson

LINCOLN   SK9771   MAP 8

Victoria 🍺 £
Union Road; LN1 3BJ

Simple and popular real-ale pub with nine beers and very good value lunchtime food

Tucked away up a steep back street behind the castle, this down-to-earth early Victorian local is popular for its fine choice of up to nine real ales and good value straightforward food. Along with Batemans XB, Castle Rock Harvest Pale and Timothy Taylors Landlord, friendly staff serve five or six guests from brewers such as Belhaven, Phoenix and Riverside, as well as foreign draught and bottled beers, a farm cider on tap and cheap soft drinks. They hold beer festivals in the last week of October and the first week in

December. The simply furnished little tiled front lounge has a coal fire and pictures of Queen Victoria, and attracts a nicely mixed clientele. Being a proper town pub, it gets especially busy at lunchtime and later on in the evening. There's a small conservatory and a gravelled side garden, which has good views of the castle.

🍴 **Basic lunchtime food, from a short menu, includes filled cobs, toasties, baked potatoes, pies, sausage and mash; Sunday roast.** *Starters/Snacks: £1.50 to £3.75. Main Courses: £5.50 to £5.95*

Batemans ~ Tenant Neil Renshaw ~ Real ale ~ Bar food (12-2.30(2 Sun)) ~ (01522) 541000 ~ Children welcome ~ Dogs allowed in bar ~ Open 11(12 Sun)-midnight (1am Fri, Sat)

Recommended by the Didler, Andy and Jill Kassube, Joe Green, John Honnor, P Dawn, John Fiander, Fred and Lorraine Gill, John and Helen Rushton

Wig & Mitre ★ 🍴 ♀
Steep Hill; just below cathedral; LN2 1LU

Very popular multi-faceted town bar with imaginative (though not cheap) food all day and chatty bustling atmosphere

Year-on-year this civilised café-style dining pub remains as popular as ever. Dating from the 14th c and spreading over a couple of floors it has plenty of attractive period architectural features. The big-windowed beamed downstairs bar has exposed stone walls, pews and Gothic furniture on oak floorboards, and comfortable sofas in a carpeted back area. Upstairs, the somewhat calmer dining room is light and airy, with views of the castle walls and cathedral, shelves of old books and an open fire. Walls are hung with antique prints and caricatures of lawyers and clerics, and there are plenty of newspapers and periodicals lying about – even templates to tempt you to a game of noughts and crosses. They have nearly three dozen wines by the glass (from a good list), lots of liqueurs and spirits and well kept Batemans XB and Black Sheep on handpump. It can get busy at peak times so it's useful to know that you can pop in and get something to eat at almost any time of day.

🍴 **As well as a full breakfast and a sandwich menu, seasonal dishes might include starters such as pea and tarragon soup, iranian caviar, stilton mousse with apple and celery salad and walnut toast, main courses such as sausage and mash, roast salmon fillet with crab soufflé and thermidor sauce, roast rump of lamb with steamed kidney pudding and creamed spring greens, steamed leek and potato pudding with fricassee of mushrooms, leeks and peas and pudding such as apple and blackberry strudel with cinnamon custard and chocolate and orange pudding with tangerine ice-cream. Some readers have found the food a bit pricey, though most feel it's worth the money.** *Starters/Snacks: £4.95. Main Courses: £10.95 to £24.95. Puddings: £4.95 to £7.50*

Free house ~ Licensee Toby Hope ~ Real ale ~ Bar food (8am-midnight) ~ Restaurant ~ (01522) 535190 ~ Children welcome ~ Dogs allowed in bar ~ Open 8am-midnight

Recommended by Revd R P Tickle, Adrian Johnson, Christopher Turner, Bettye Reynolds, Richard, MDN, David and Ruth Hollands, Mike Vincent, Mr and Mrs Richard Osborne, Keith and Chris O'Neill, Michael Butler, Pete Coxon, Mrs R McLauchlan

ROTHWELL   TF1499   MAP 8

Blacksmiths Arms
Off B1225 S of Caistor; LN7 6AZ

Appealing beamed pub with decent food, five real ales and tables outside

Ideally situated for walks on the nearby Viking Way and Lincolnshire Wolds, this long white painted pub provides an agreeable drink and meal stop. The pleasant low beamed bar is divided by a couple of arches and has a warm central coal fire, attractive wildlife prints, comfortable chairs and tables and a relaxed atmosphere; piped music, games machine, pool, darts and dominoes. Black Sheep and Tom Woods Shepherds Delight are served on handpump alongside three guests from brewers such as Batemans and Steamin' Billy; 15 malt whiskies. There are plenty of tables outside.

🍽 Fairly pubby food includes sandwiches, soup, garlic mushrooms, burgers, salmon and prawn salad, lasagne, steak and ale pie, lamb shank in red wine sauce, battered haddock and steaks. They do a Sunday roast, an early evening special offer menu Monday to Friday and a curry night on Thursdays. *Starters/Snacks: £4.95 to £6.95. Main Courses: £7.95 to £16.95. Puddings: £3.50 to £4.95*

Free house ~ Licensee Rachel Flello ~ Real ale ~ Bar food (12-2(3 Sun), 5.30(6 Sun)-9(9.30 Fri, Sat)) ~ Restaurant ~ (01472) 371300 ~ Children welcome ~ Open 12-3, 5-11.30; 12-11.30 Sat; 12-11 Sun

Recommended by Tim and Claire Woodward, Alistair and Kay Butler

SOUTH WITHAM
SK9219 MAP 8

Blue Cow 🍺

Village signposted just off A1 Stamford—Grantham (with brown sign for pub); NG33 5QB

Tap for its own Blue Cow real ales; traditional interior, pubby food, garden

---

No one can accuse this country pub of racking up real-ale miles as all the beer sold here (Blue Cow Best and Witham Wobbler) is brewed on site. Its two appealing rooms (completely separated by a big central open-plan counter) have a relaxed pubby atmosphere, cottagey little windows, plush blue banquettes around a mix of tables (including some scrubbed pine ones), flowery carpets and floral upholstered stools along the counter. Dark low beams and standing timbers are set off against exposed stone walls – this is actually a much older building than a first glance at its exterior might suggest. Some areas have shiny flagstones, and there are cottagey pictures and a mantelpiece above the fireplace in one bar; piped music, darts and TV. The attractive garden has tables on a pleasant terrace.

🍽 Bar food might include sandwiches, soup, baked potatoes, fish and chips, pies, duck in port sauce, curries and steaks; popular Sunday roast. *Starters/Snacks: £3.50 to £4.50. Main Courses: £6.95 to £14.25. Puddings: £2.00 to £3.25*

Own brew ~ Licensee Simon Crathorn ~ Real ale ~ Bar food (10.30-9.30 (not 3-6 Sun)) ~ Restaurant ~ (01572) 768432 ~ Chidren welcome away from counter ~ Dogs welcome ~ Open 10.30(12 Sat, Sun)-11(10.30 Sun) ~ Bedrooms: £45S/£55S

Recommended by the Didler, Andy and Jill Kassube, Phil and Jane Hodson, Pete Coxon, B and M Kendall, Gordon and Margaret Ormondroyd

STAMFORD
TF0306 MAP 8

George of Stamford ★

High Street, St Martins (B1081 S of centre, not the quite different central pedestrianised High Street); PE9 2LB

LINCOLNSHIRE DINING PUB OF THE YEAR

Handsome coaching inn, beautifully relaxed and civilised, with very good food and wines, lovely courtyard, garden and bedrooms

---

It seems they can't put a foot wrong at this marvellously preserved grand old coaching inn with its various lovely reception areas and delightful courtyard and gardens. Though built in 1597 for Lord Burghley, there are visible parts of a much older Norman pilgrims' hospice, and a crypt under the cocktail bar that may be 1,000 years old. During the 18th and 19th centuries it was the hub of 20 coach trips a day between London and York (two of the front rooms take their names from these destinations). Seating in its beautifully furnished rooms ranges through leather, cane and antique wicker to soft settees and easy chairs. The central lounge has sturdy timbers, broad flagstones, heavy beams and massive stonework, and the York Bar (where you can get snacks) is surprisingly pubby with a local feel. More elaborate meals are served in the oak-panelled restaurant (jacket or tie required) and in the less formal Garden Lounge restaurant which has well spaced furniture on herringbone glazed bricks around a central tropical grove. The staff are professional and friendly, with waiter drinks service in the charming cobbled courtyard at the back: comfortable chairs and tables among attractive plant tubs and colourful hanging baskets on the ancient stone buildings. There's also an immaculately kept walled garden, with lovely plantings, and a sunken lawn where croquet is often played. The very good range of drinks includes Adnams Broadside, Fullers London Pride and Greene King Ruddles County on handpump, an excellent choice of wines (many of which are italian and good value, with about 17 by the glass), freshly squeezed orange juice and malt whiskies.

🍴 Snacks in the York Bar include soup, interesting sandwiches, chicken liver pâté with cumberland sauce and ploughman's. Besides a generous cold buffet, the menu in the Garden Lounge includes eight tempting pasta and risotto dishes (such as pea and pancetta risotto with a poached egg and half a lobster with spaghetti with tomato and mild chilli), shellfish, from oysters up to a seafood platter, with other delicious items such as vietnamese chicken rolls with hoi sin, grilled salmon with steamed pak choi, orange and ginger dressing, chickpea and vegetable tagine, fish and chips. They also serve full afternoon tea. *Starters/Snacks: £5.15 to £9.80. Main Courses: £8.95 to £32.50. Puddings: £6.00*

Free house ~ Licensees Chris Pitman and Ivo Vannocci ~ Real ale ~ Bar food (11-11) ~ Restaurant ~ (01780) 750750 ~ Children welcome ~ Dogs allowed in bar and bedrooms ~ Open 11(12 Sun)-11 ~ Bedrooms: £90B/£130B

Recommended by Louise English, Charles Gysin, Roy Bromell, Sally Anne and Peter Goodale, Ryta Lyndley, Paul Humphreys, Roy Hoing, Mike and Sue Loseby, J F M and M West, John Honnor, Michael Dandy, Rosemary K Germaine, John Wooll, Mrs Margo Finlay, Jörg Kasprowski, Mrs L Davies, Pete Coxon, the Didler, Di and Mike Gillam, P Dawn, Mike Ridgway, Sarah Miles, D F Clarke, David and Ruth Shillitoe

STOW   SK8881   MAP 8

Cross Keys
Stow Park Road; B1241 NW of Lincoln; LN1 2DD

Reliable dining pub with traditional décor

This extended dining pub, with its charmingly helpful staff, has recently been transformed by its long-serving licensees into an even more enjoyable place for a good meal. The carpeted bar is still fairly traditional, with a big woodburner, dark wheelback chairs and tables, dark wood panelling, country prints on cream walls and decorative china on a delft shelf; piped music. Further in, you'll find a couple of neatly laid dining areas. Fairly priced drinks include Everards and Theakstons on handpump, with a couple of guest beers such as Batemans XB and Springhead Charlies Angel. Well worth a visit, nearby Stow Minster is notable for its fantastic Saxon arches and among other things its Viking ship graffiti.

🍴 Bar food includes duck and port pâté, smoked salmon with lemon and dill mayonnaise, main courses such as lasagne, braised lamb shank with redcurrant and rosemary sauce, mushroom stroganoff, salmon fillet with lemon butter sauce, steak and mushroom pie and rib-eye with peppercorn sauce, and puddings such as banoffi pie and eton mess. *Starters/Snacks: £3.95 to £6.95. Main Courses: £8.00 to £19.50. Puddings: £4.75*

Free house ~ Licensees Richard and Helen Davies ~ Real ale ~ Bar food ~ Restaurant ~ (01427) 788314 ~ Children welcome ~ Open 12-2, 6-11; closed Mon lunchtime

Recommended by Dr and Mrs J Temporal, Mrs Jennifer Marris, David and Ruth Hollands

SURFLEET   TF2528   MAP 8

Mermaid
Just off A16 N of Spalding, on B1356 at bridge; PE11 4AB

Friendly old-fashioned pub with extensive waterside garden and good value food

This is a reliably traditional pub. Décor in the two long-established high-ceilinged rooms is largely Seventies in style, with green patterned carpets, horse tack on cream textured walls above red Anaglypta dado, huge netted sash windows, navigation lanterns, and a mixture of banquettes and stools; cribbage and dominoes. A small central glass-backed bar counter (complete with what is surely quite collectable Babycham décor) serves Adnams Broadside and Greene King IPA and Abbot on handpump, as well as quite a few malt whiskies. Down two steps the restaurant is decorated in a similar style; piped music. The pretty terraced garden has lots of seats with thatched parasols, and its own bar. The children's play area is safely walled from the River Glen which runs beside the pub.

🍽 **Bar food includes sandwiches filled ciabattas, crispy duck spring rolls, mushroom stroganoff, sausage and mash, lasagne, roast oxtail and mash, battered cod with chips and mushy peas, roast duck and 10oz sirloin steak and puddings such as fresh fruit pavlova and sticky toffee pudding.** *Starters/Snacks: £3.95 to £5.50. Main Courses: £8.50 to £19.95. Puddings: £4.50*

Free house ~ Licensee Chris Bustance ~ Real ale ~ Bar food (12-2, 6-9) ~ Restaurant ~ (01775) 680275 ~ Children welcome ~ Open 11.30-11; 12-10.30 Sun; closed 3-5.30 in winter

Recommended by Michael and Jenny Back, M J Winterton, Dr and Mrs R G J Telfer, Ryta Lyndley

WOOLSTHORPE   SK8334   MAP 8

Chequers 🍽 ♀

The one near Belvoir, signposted off A52 or A607 W of Grantham; NG32 1LU

Interesting food at comfortably relaxed inn with good drinks; appealing castle views from outside tables

'There was always a selection, even down to what gin to have with the tonic' is a reader's comment that gives a hint at the tremendous effort and attention to detail they put into making your visit at this excellent 17th-c coaching inn a satisfying one. Their fabulous range of drinks includes well kept Brewsters Marquis and a guest from a brewer such as Ridgeway on handpump, a selection of belgian beers, local fruit pressés, over 35 wines by the glass, over 20 champagnes and 50 malt whiskies. The heavy-beamed main bar has two big tables (one a massive oak construction), a comfortable mix of seating including some handsome leather chairs and leather banquettes, and a huge boar's head above a good log fire in the big brick fireplace. Among cartoons on the wall are some of the illustrated claret bottle labels from the series commissioned from famous artists, initiated by the late Baron Philippe de Rothschild. The lounge on the right has a deep red colour scheme, leather sofas and a big plasma TV, and on the left, there are more leather seats in a dining area in what was once the village bakery. A corridor leads off to the light and airy main restaurant which has contemporary pictures and another bar; piped music. There are good quality teak tables, chairs and benches outside and beyond these, some picnic-sets on the edge of the pub's cricket field, with views of Belvoir Castle.

🍽 **Food ranges from pub classics to more imaginative dishes, but it's all pretty good. There might be inventive sandwiches (such as red pepper, feta and rocket), starters such as cream of celeriac and celery soup with a stilton croûton, fried scallops with cauliflower purée, pancetta and red wine, warm salad of black pudding with chorizo, bacon, poached egg and hollandaise, main courses such as bass with steamed pak choi and red pepper and asian noodles, provençale vegetable pasta, sausage and mash, battered haddock and rib-eye steak with peppercorn sauce, puddings such as rhubarb and apple crumble, chocolate tart with coconut ice-cream and syrup sponges, and a local cheese platter; good value three-course weekday evening menu.** *Starters/Snacks: £4.50 to £6.50. Main Courses: £5.50 to £8.95. Puddings: £5.50*

Free house ~ Licensee Justin Chad ~ Real ale ~ Bar food (12-2.30, 6-9.30; 12-4, 6-8.30 Sun) ~ Restaurant ~ (01476) 870701 ~ Children welcome ~ Dogs allowed in bar and bedrooms ~ Open 12-3, 5.30-11; 12-11 Sat; 12-10.30 Sun ~ Bedrooms: £49B/£59B

Recommended by Alan and Jill Bull, J B Young, Ian Stafford, Bruce and Sharon Eden, M Mossman, Andy and Jill Kassube, MJB, Peter and Jo Smith, John Honnor, Trevor Gaston

Post Office address codings confusingly give the impression that a few pubs are in Lincolnshire, when they're really in Cambridgeshire (which is where we list them).

LUCKY DIP

Besides the fully inspected pubs, you might like to try these Lucky Dips recommended to us and described by readers (if you do, please send us reports: feedback@thegoodpubguide.co.uk).

ASWARBY [TF0639]
Tally Ho NG34 8SA [A15 S of Sleaford (but N of village turn-off)]: 17th-c beamed pub, nice spot, two fires, big-windowed comfortable front bar, enjoyable food using local ingredients, friendly helpful service, Bass and Batemans, good house wines, daily papers, airy restaurant; piped music; children welcome, tables among fruit trees *(Mrs Brenda Calver, LYM)*

BARHOLM [TF0810]
Five Horseshoes PE9 4RA: Old-fashioned relaxed village local, three rooms just right for a chat, clean, cosy and friendly, with well kept Adnams, Batemans and interesting guest beers, mini beer festivals, good range of wines, comfortable seats, rustic bric-a-brac; children welcome, charming small garden with shady arbour, paddocks behind *(Ian Stafford, LYM)*

BASSINGHAM [SK9160]
Five Bells LN5 9JZ [High St]: Cheerful beamed pub with good choice of real ales, usual food, two log fires, lots of brass and bric-a-brac, even a wishing well *(Maurice and Janet Thorpe)*

BOSTON [TF3344]
Coach & Horses PE21 6SY [Main Ridge]: Friendly traditional pub with well kept Batemans XB and XXB, good coal fire, darts, dominoes, pool; cl wkdy lunchtimes *(the Didler)*
Mill PE21 9QN [Spilsby Rd (A16)]: Roadside pub with enjoyable reasonably priced food from lunchtime sandwiches to steaks, plush dining rooms, helpful service, Batemans XB and guest beer, bar counter covered in old pennies; quiet piped music; seats out in front *(Terry Jones)*
White Hart PE21 8SH [High St/Lawrence Lane]: Substantial much-modernised building, comfortable carpeted hotel bar with well kept beer, enjoyable all-day bar food, friendly staff, separate restaurant; 23 bedrooms, open all day from 10 *(Michael Holdsworth, BB)*

BRANDY WHARF [TF0196]
☆ *Cider Centre* DN21 4RU [B1205 SE of Scunthorpe (off A15 about 16 miles N of Lincoln)]: Up to 15 draught ciders, many more in bottles etc, also country wines and meads; plain take-us-as-you-find-us bright main bar and dimmer lounge with lots of cider memorabilia and jokey bric-a-brac, reasonably priced straightforward food (all day Sun); piped music; children in eating area, simple glazed verandah, tables and play area in meadows or by river with moorings and slipway, open all day wknds, may be cl Mon *(the Didler, LYM, Rosemary K Germaine)*

BRIGG [TA0007]
White Horse DN20 8JR [Wrawby St]: Old inn with two real ales, good choice of traditional food (not Mon lunch), separate dining areas, Sun quiz night; quiet piped music; tables out at front *(JJW, CMW)*

BURGH LE MARSH [TO5065]
Fleece PE24 5JW [Market Pl]: Friendly and attractive pub in picturesque windmill village, real fire in lounge with Laurel and Hardy memorabilia, three real ales inc Greene King, bargain home cooking (not Sun evening) inc Sun carvery; children and dogs welcome, tables out among flower tubs, bedrooms *(Adrian Johnson)*

CASTLE BYTHAM [SK9818]
☆ *Castle Inn* NG33 4RZ [off A1 Stamford—Grantham, or B1176]: Comfortable black-beamed village pub with enjoyable home cooking from baguettes and ciabattas up, friendly staff, two or three changing ales, good hot drinks, sofas and huge fire, pub dogs called Skye, Benjie and Poppy, occasional beer festivals; disabled access, back terrace, open all day Sun, cl winter wkdy lunchtimes *(Michael and Jenny Back, LYM)*

CAYTHORPE [SK9348]
Red Lion NG32 3DN [signed just off A607 N of Grantham; High St]: Sensibly unpretentious food using local supplies, Adnams and Everards, several small and simply decorated linked areas, beams and big inglenook, immaculate lavatories; back terrace by car park *(Phil and Jane Hodson, David and Gilly Wilkins, BB, Maurice and Janet Thorpe)*

CLEETHORPES [TA3009]
No 2 Refreshment Room DN35 8AX [Station Approach]: Half a dozen well kept ales in comfortably refurbished carpeted platform bar, friendly staff, no food; tables out under heaters, open all day from 9 *(the Didler, P Dawn)*
☆ *Willys* DN35 8RQ [Highcliff Rd; south promenade]: Open-plan bistro-style seafront pub with panoramic Humber views, café tables, tiled floor and painted brick walls; visibly brews its own good beers, also Batemans and other changing ales, belgian beers, good value home-made lunches, friendly staff, nice mix of customers from young and trendy to weather-beaten fishermen; quiet juke box; a few tables out on the prom, open all day *(P Dawn, the Didler)*

FALDINGWORTH [TF0684]
Coach & Horses LN8 3SE [High St]: Beams, stripped bricks, banquettes, brass, copper and goldfish tank, three or four real ales, wide food choice inc Sun roast, woodburner; piped music; dogs and children allowed, garden with play area *(JJW, CMW)*

FULBECK [SK9450]
Hare & Hounds NG32 3JJ [The Green (A607 Leadenham—Grantham)]: Under helpful new management, converted 17th-c maltings

with tables, chairs and sofas in linked areas, enjoyable bar food from sandwiches up, attractive upstairs restaurant; nice village, ridge views *(Michael and Maggie Betton)*

GAINSBOROUGH [SK8189]

Eight Jolly Brewers DN21 2DW [Ship Court, Silver St]: Small comfortable real ale pub with up to eight from small breweries, farm cider, country wines, simple lunchtime food (not Sun), friendly staff and locals, beams, bare bricks and brewery posters, quieter bar upstairs; folk club, open all day *(the Didler)*

GEDNEY [TF4024]

Old Black Lion PE12 0BW [Main Rd]: Welcoming country pub with efficient service, Greene King IPA and John Smiths, decent house wines, straightforward good value menu, children's helpings; beer garden, bedrooms *(John Wooll)*

GRANTHAM [SK9135]

☆ *Angel & Royal* NG31 6PN [High St]: Comfortable hotel with elaborate carved 14th-c stone façade, well restored ancient upstairs bars with formidable inglenook fireplaces and a charming little medieval oriel window seat jutting over the road, stylish downstairs bistro/bar with elegant modern tables, comfortable chairs on pale oak boards, up-to-date pastels and some stripped stonework, two real ales, grand-manner wknd restaurant; piped music, TV; children in eating areas, well equipped bedrooms in modern bank extension alongside narrow flagstoned inner coachway, open all day *(LYM, Pete Coxon, David and Deirdre Renwick, Richard and Jean Green)*

☆ *Blue Pig* NG31 6RQ [Vine St]: Small three-bar Tudor pub with good value basic pub lunches, home-baked bread, OAP bargains, half a dozen interesting changing ales, quick cheerful service, low beams, panelling, stripped stone and flagstones, open fire, daily papers, lots of pig ornaments, prints and bric-a-brac; piped music, juke box, games machines, no children or dogs; tables out behind, open all day *(the Didler, Alan and Eve Harding, Trevor Gaston, BB, Nigel and Sue Foster)*

Nobody Inn NG31 6NU [North St]: Friendly bare-boards open-plan local with five or six good mainly local ales, back games room with pool, table footer; SkyTV; open all day *(the Didler)*

HARLAXTON [SK8833]

Gregory NG32 1AD [A607 Grantham—Melton]: Friendly roadside dining pub reopened under new licensees after losing its 'Arms' (and its deli), comfortably enlarged seating area and open airy restaurant, good imaginative food from local ingredients, good choice of wines by the glass, well kept ales inc Greene King and Marstons Pedigree; lovely walks, cl Sun evening and Mon *(Michael and Maggie Betton)*

INGHAM [SK9483]

Black Horse LN1 2YW [High St (off B1398)]: 200-year-old former cottages with good food inc some interesting dishes in two-level

back dining area, obliging staff, good beer; disabled access *(Alistair and Kay Butler)*

KIRKBY LA THORPE [TF0945]

☆ *Queens Head* NG34 9NW [Boston Rd, backing on to A17]: Attractive and comfortable dining pub with large bar, small cosy restaurant and airy conservatory, good choice of enjoyable food inc well filled sandwiches (home-baked bread), wkdy early evening deals, pleasant service, Batemans and Marstons Pedigree, decent house wine; easy disabled access, terrace tables *(Maurice and Janet Thorpe, Mr and Mrs J Brown)*

KIRMINGTON [TA1011]

Marrowbone & Cleaver DN39 6YZ [High St]: Friendly efficient staff, wide choice of good value food from baguettes up, well kept ales inc Timothy Taylors Landlord *(C A Hall)*

LINCOLN [SK9771]

Sippers LN5 7HW [Melville St, opp bus stn]: Two-bar pub with good value lunchtime food inc good Sun lunch (can book evening meals), Hop Back and guest ales; open all day (Sun afternoon break) *(the Didler, Joe Green)*

☆ *Strugglers* LN1 3BG [Westgate]: Smartly simple character local with thriving atmosphere, well kept Bass, Black Sheep, Fullers London Pride and Timothy Taylors Landlord, good value above-average lunchtime food inc fresh grimsby fish, coal-effect fire in back snug, interesting pictures; heaters and canopy for terrace tables, open all day *(David and Ruth Hollands, John and Helen Rushton, Michael Butler, Julian Saunders, Pete Coxon, the Didler)*

Tap & Spile LN1 1ES [Hungate]: Half a dozen well kept changing ales, farm cider and country wines, small choice of reasonably priced pubby food, friendly staff and atmosphere, central bar, linked areas with flagstones, bare boards and brickwork, breweriana; open all day *(the Didler, Joe Green)*

Treaty of Commerce LN5 7AF [High St]: Warmly welcoming, lively and simple pub in beamed Tudor building, fine stained-glass, panelling, etchings, good value bar lunches from generous baguettes up, well kept Batemans and guest beers, darts; open all day *(the Didler, Andy and Jill Kassube, John and Helen Rushton)*

LONG BENNINGTON [SK8344]

☆ *Reindeer* NG23 5DJ [just off A1 N of Grantham]: Thriving atmosphere in old inn with popular long-serving landlady, enjoyable home-made food from good sandwiches up in bar and more formal dining lounge, cut-price small helpings, well kept real ales, good wines *(D F Clarke, Maurice and Janet Thorpe, Grahame Brooks)*

LOUTH [TF3287]

Wheatsheaf LN11 9YD [Westgate]: Cheerful 17th-c low-beamed pub nr interesting church, coal fires in all three bars, changing ales under top pressure, old photographs; tables outside, open all day Sat *(Maurice and Janet Thorpe, Val and Alan Green, the Didler)*

NAVENBY [SK9857]

Kings Head LN5 0EE [A607 S of Lincoln]: Friendly roadside pub under popular new management, comfortable lounge bar, busy dining area, well kept Everards Tiger, Greene King IPA and John Smiths; small pretty garden *(Mark, Amanda, Luke and Jake Sheard, Maurice and Janet Thorpe, BB)*

NORTH KELSEY [TA0401]

Butchers Arms LN7 6EH [Middle St; off B1434 S of Brigg]: Busy village local with five well kept Tom Woods beers, enjoyable simple food, enthusiastic cheerful service, log fire, low ceilings, flagstones, bare boards, dim lighting, pub games; garden, opens 4 wkdys, open all day wknds *(the Didler, Stephen and Jean Curtis)*

NORTH THORESBY [TF2998]

New Inn DN36 5QS [Station Rd]: Attractive and friendly with enjoyable food (can slow when busy), several real ales, roomy restaurant, darts; TV; disabled facilities, pleasant terrace *(JJW, CMW)*

PETERBOROUGH []

Woodman PE3 6SQ [Thorpe Wood]: Sizeable open-plan pub overlooking golf course, well kept Greene King, pubby food, carpet throughout, leather sofas and suede bucket seats, conservatory, Sun quiz night; children welcome, disabled facilities, seats outside, smokers' shelter, open all day *(Michael Dandy)*

PINCHBECK [TF2325]

Bull PE11 3RA [Knight St]: Enjoyable good value food in bar and restaurant, good range of beers, friendly service *(Phillip Allen)*

SPALDING [TF2422]

White Horse PE11 2RA [Churchgate]: Attractive 17th-c thatched pub next to High Bridge over River Welland, three open-plan flagstoned rooms, lively and friendly, bargain Sam Smiths, pubby food inc good value Sun lunch; open all day *(John Honnor)*

STAMFORD [TF0306]

☆ *Bull & Swan* PE9 2LJ [High St, St Martins]: Nicely worn in traditional pub with three low-beamed connecting rooms, good log fires, friendly staff, enjoyable food from sandwiches up, real ales such as Caledonian Deuchars IPA and Greene King IPA; children welcome, tables out in former back coachyard, bedrooms *(LYM, Ray and Winifred Halliday, Mike Ridgway, Sarah Miles, P Dawn, Michael Dandy)*

☆ *Crown* PE9 2AG [All Saints Pl]: Substantial stone-built hotel with emphasis on good seasonal country cooking using local produce from good sandwiches up, very friendly staff, Adnams, Fullers and Ufford ales, decent wines, whiskies and coffee, spacious main bar, long leather-cushioned bar counter, substantial pillars, pinkish lighting, step up to more traditional flagstoned area with stripped stone and and lots of leather sofas

and armchairs, civilised dining room; heated outdoor area for smokers, comfortable quiet bedrooms, good breakfast, open all day *(BB, Paul Humphreys, Michael Dandy, Andy and Jill Kassube)*

Green Man PE9 2YQ [Scotgate]: Good range of changing ales inc Caledonian Deuchars IPA and Great Oakley, belgian beers, farm ciders, friendly staff, good value basic food, sturdy tables on flagstones, log fire, steps up to back room with bottle collection and TV; garden tables, comfortable bedrooms sharing bathroom, open all day *(P Dawn, Michael Dandy, the Didler)*

Jims Yard PE9 1PL [Ironmonger St]: Small ground floor bar with restaurant above, wide-ranging good food, no draught beer; outside seating *(Roy Bromell)*

Millstone PE9 2PA [All Saints St]: Recently refurbished stone-fronted 17th-c pub with one bar, wood floor, modern furniture, Black Sheep and Everards Tiger, limited basic food from sandwiches up; piped and live music, two TVs; children welcome, disabled facilities, sizeable back courtyard *(Michael Dandy)*

Periwig PE9 2AG [Red Lion Sq/All Saints Pl]: Contemporary bistro-style interior with upper gallery, basic good value food inc blackboard specials, Fullers London Pride and Ufford White Hart, smart efficient staff; piped music, sports TV, can get busy with lively young people evenings; open all day *(Tony and Wendy Hobden, Michael Dandy, Andy and Jill Kassube, Pete Coxon)*

SURFLEET SEAS END [TF2729]

☆ *Ship* PE11 4DH [Reservoir Rd; off A16 N of Spalding]: Handsomely rebuilt riverside pub with river view from smart big-windowed upstairs restaurant and balcony, broad steps up from flagstoned hall, woodburner and leather sofas in good-sized bar with well spaced old scrubbed tables in open bays, husband and wife chefs, good reasonably priced food esp pies, well kept ales; tables out on bank over road *(Sally Anne and Peter Goodale, Ken Marshall)*

SUSWORTH [SE8302]

☆ *Jenny Wren* DN17 3AS [East Ferry Rd]: Neatly kept, in nice setting overlooking River Trent, long partly divided bar/dining area, good enterprising reasonably priced food inc lots of fish and local produce, pleasant staff, real ales such as John Smiths and Tom Woods, good wines by the glass, two open fires, panelling, stripped brickwork, low beams and brasses, busy décor; terrace picnic-sets, more across quiet road by water *(BB)*

SUTTERTON [TF2835]

Thatched Cottage PE20 2EZ [B1397]: Welcoming 16th-c thatched pub opp village green, low beams and inglenook, L-shaped bar, small rooms set for fresh food inc Sun roasts, well kept beers, conservatory overlooking fields; small garden *(Sally Anne and Peter Goodale)*

TATTERSHALL THORPE [TF2159]
Blue Bell LN4 4PE [Thorpe Rd; B1192
Coningsby—Woodhall Spa]: Attractive very
low-beamed pub said to date from 13th c
and used by the Dambusters, RAF
memorabilia and appropriate real ales such
as Tom Woods Bomber County and Poachers
Pathfinders, well priced pubby bar food, log
fires, small dining room; garden tables,
impressive lavatera bushes, bedrooms
(Andy and Jill Kassube, the Didler)

WAINFLEET [TF5058]
☆ *Batemans Brewery* PE24 4JE [Mill Lane, off
A52 via B1195]: Circular bar in brewery's ivy-
covered windmill tower with Batemans ales
in top condition, czech and belgian beers on
tap, ground-floor dining area with
unpretentious lunchtime food such as local
sausages and pork pies, plenty of old pub
games (more .outside), lots of brewery
memorabilia and plenty for families to enjoy;
entertaining brewery tours at 2.30, brewery
shop (helpful service), tables out on terrace
and grass, opens 11.30-3.30 *(the Didler,
P Dawn, Andy and Jill Kassube, John Honnor)*

WESTON [TF2925]
☆ *Chequers* PE12 6RA [High Rd]: Reopened
2007 after extensive refurbishment, good
food (not Sun evening) using local produce
– best to book evenings and wknds, nice

wines, cool uncluttered contemporary décor,
bare boards, leather sofas and armchairs,
comfortable dining areas; disabled access,
garden with heated covered terrace and play
area, open all day Sun, cl Mon
(Sally Anne and Peter Goodale, Ken Marshall)

WOODHALL SPA [TF1962]
☆ *Abbey Lodge* LN10 6UH [B1192 towards
Coningsby]: Family-run roadside inn with
enjoyable reasonably priced food from
sandwiches up, affable staff, nice pubby
feel mixing eating and drinking sides
well, bustling discreetly decorated bar with
good choice of beers and wines, Victorian
and older furnishings, World War II RAF
pictures, Marstons Pedigree; children over
10 in restaurant, may be piped music;
cl Sun *(Mr and Mrs J Brown, LYM,
John Branston)*

Petwood LN10 6QG [Stixwould Rd]:.
Edwardian hotel in 30 acres, 1943 Dambusters
officers' mess, memorabilia making it
interesting for a drink or reasonably priced
meal; terrace tables, 53 bedrooms *(RS, ES)*

Village Limits LN10 6UJ [Stixwould Rd]:
Good choice of enjoyable local food inc
seafood, a well kept real ale, friendly service,
smallish bar with plush banquettes and
aeroplane prints; nine courtyard bedrooms
(Mr and Mrs J Brown, Mrs Brenda Calver)

If a service charge is mentioned prominently on a menu or accommodation terms, you
must pay it if service was satisfactory. If service is really bad, you are legally entitled to
refuse to pay some or all of the service charge as compensation for not getting the
service you might reasonably have expected.

Norfolk

What really stands out in Norfolk pubs is how friendly the licensees are. This filters through to the locals, which in turn creates a cheerful atmosphere for visitors, too. You can be sure of a particularly warm welcome at the Kings Arms in Blakeney, the Jolly Sailors in Brancaster Staithe (brewing its own beer), the Hoste Arms in Burnham Market (though perhaps this is more down to the well trained staff), the Saracens Head near Erpingham, the Adam & Eve in Norwich, the Gin Trap at Ringstead, the Rose & Crown at Snettisham, the Three Horseshoes at Warham, and the Fur & Feather at Woodbastwick. Our new entries here this year are also notably friendly, and include the attractively restored Black Boys in Aylsham (thriving atmosphere and good value food in this market-town inn), the Chequers at Binham (hands-on owners brewing their own beer, and with interesting food, too), the handsome Buckinghamshire Arms at Blickling (warmly welcoming, with a proper little bar as well as two attractive dining areas), the recently opened Pigs at Edgefield (breaking new ground on the food front, yet keeping a buoyant pubby atmosphere) and the Bell in Wiveton (stylish and carefully refurbished, with modern food and super bedrooms). Beer features strongly in this county, which now has some 30 independent brewers. By far the most popular local beer is Woodfordes. Yetmans, started in ancient farm buildings only three years ago, is already winning many friends in the north of the county, and others we've found recently in at least some good pubs are Fox, Winters, Wolf, Iceni, Chalk Hill, Blackfriars and Buffys. To find a good choice of interesting ales in pubs not mentioned already, head for the Lord Nelson at Burnham Thorpe (and try their speciality rum-based drink as well), the Walpole Arms at Itteringham, the Fat Cat in Norwich (with over two dozen real ales on at once, this is a beer lover's haven), Darbys at Swanton Morley, the Wheatsheaf at West Beckham and the Fisherman's Return in Winterton-on-Sea. There's a great deal of imaginative food from innovative chefs who make the most of the fantastic local fish and shellfish and local estate game. For a special meal, our pick would be the White Horse in Brancaster Staithe, the Hoste Arms in Burnham Market, the Saracens Head near Erpingham, the Gin Trap at Ringstead, the Rose & Crown at Snettisham, the Crown in Wells-next-the-Sea, and the Bell at Wiveton. We have particularly high hopes of several of these, which this year have promising new licensees (and one is new to the *Guide*); but the title of Norfolk Dining Pub of the Year is retained by a pub which has already more than earned its spurs – the Hoste Arms in Burnham Market. The Lucky Dip section at the end of the chapter has many more strong recommendations: we'd particularly pick out the Kings Head in Coltishall, Dabbling Duck at Great Massingham, Old Brewery House in Reepham, Dun Cow at Salthouse, Lobster in Sheringham and Wildebeest at Stoke Holy Cross.

AYLSHAM

TG1926   MAP 8

Black Boys ♀ 🍺 🛏

Market Place, just off B1145; NR11 6EH

Good value food with lots of fresh fish in nicely updated traditional market-place inn with a warm-hearted bar

The quite imposing Georgian façade fronts a building which dates back to 1650. It's been appealingly brought up to date inside, keeping the high dark beams in the ochre ceiling, stripping some walls back to the warm red brickwork, with a dark-panelled dado, neat new wood flooring, and comfortably old-fashioned chairs or built-in wall seats around good well spaced solid tables. Friendly helpful young staff jolly along the cheery thriving atmosphere in the bar and the adjoining dining area. Adnams Best and Woodfordes Wherry and couple of guests such as Adnams Broadside and Fullers London Pride are on handpump, and they've over a dozen decent wines by the glass. Neat modern tables and chairs out in front face the market place. The four bedrooms (there's a £5 charge for dogs if they stay) have been attractively refurbished.

🍽 Food from the wide-ranging menu is home-made, served generously, and well priced for its quality. They usually have a very good range of fresh fish. As well as snacky dishes such as filled baguettes and baked potatoes, club sandwich and salads (including crab), there might be wild mushroom risotto, steak and kidney pudding, bass on mediterranean vegetables, fried skate with parma ham and capers, and lobster. Puddings might be lemon meringue pie and raspberry and chocolate cheesecake; Sunday carvery. *Starters/Snacks: £4.50 to £6.95. Main Courses: £5.50 to £12.95. Puddings: £4.50*

Unique (Enterprise) ~ Lease Matthew Miller ~ Real ale ~ Bar food (12-2(6 Sun), 6.30-9(9.30 Fri Sat, 8.30 Sun)) ~ Restaurant ~ (01263) 732122 ~ Children welcome ~ Dogs allowed in bar and bedrooms ~ Open 11-12; 12-10.30 Sun ~ Bedrooms: £51.50B/£70.50B

Recommended by John Wooll, Mrs Hilarie Taylor, William Mack

BAWBURGH

TG1508   MAP 5

Kings Head ♀

Pub signposted down Harts Lane off B1108, which leads off A47 just W of Norwich; NR9 3LS

Bustling old pub, small rooms with plenty of atmosphere, cheerful service, wide choice of bar food and drinks

This popular old pub has been run by the same family for 24 years now. It's a 17th-c building and in an attractive spot opposite a small green. There are wooden floors, leather sofas and seats, a mix of nice old wooden tables and wooden or leather dining chairs, low beams and some standing timbers, a warming log fire in a large knocked-through canopied fireplace, and a couple of woodburning stoves in the restaurant areas. Adnams Bitter and Broadside and Woodfordes Wherry on handpump, 18 wines by the glass and several malt whiskies; piped music. There are seats outside in the garden.

🍽 At lunchtime, bar food might include filled rolls and ciabattas, chicken liver parfait with pickled courgettes and apple chutney, ham and free-range eggs, cumberland sausages with onion gravy, deep-fried cod with home-made tartare sauce, moroccan chicken with sweet potato chips, pea purée and crispy bacon, and roast pork belly with black pudding and red wine jus, with evening dishes such as home-made pork rillettes with orange marmalade, wood pigeon breast with bacon lardons, black pudding and pine nut salad, roast rump of lamb with caramelised shallots, potato tortilla and red wine jus, seared cod fillet with anya potatoes, cromer crab, spring onions, mascarpone, spinach, and bacon, and puddings such as baked white chocolate cheesecake and lime parfait with maple syrup; there's also a good value two- and three-course set lunch menu and themed evenings. *Starters/Snacks: £5.50 to £7.50. Main Courses: £9.00 to £17.50. Puddings: £5.50*

Free house ~ Licensee Anton Wimmer ~ Real ale ~ Bar food (12-2, 5.30(6 Sun)-9) ~ Restaurant ~ (01603) 744977 ~ Children welcome ~ Dogs allowed in bar ~ Open 11-11; 12-10.30 Sun

Recommended by Derek and Maggie Washington, Sally Anne and Peter Goodale, John Millwood, Ian and Nita Cooper, Alan Cowell

BINHAM   TF9839   MAP 8

Chequers 🍺

B1388 SW of Blakeney; NR21 0AL

Friendly, hard-working licensees, own-brewed beers and interesting food

Very hands-on and extremely friendly, the licensees in this 17th-c pub create a cheerful, happy atmosphere for all their customers – and their own-brewed Front Street ales are quite a draw too. Kept on handpump, there might be Binham Cheer, Callum's Ale, Ebony Stout, and Unity Strong; also, around 30 belgian bottled beers and decent house wines. The long low-beamed building has splendid coal fires at each end, sturdy plush seats, and some nice old local prints. There are picnic-sets out in front and on the grass behind the building. This is an interesting village with a huge priory church.

🍽 **Tasty, well liked bar food includes soup, deep-fried crumbed brie with home-made chutney, warm salad of smoked pigeon breast with pancetta, moussaka, steak in ale pie, asparagus and mushroom crumble, chicken supreme with a stilton and leek cream, seared tuna on crab risotto, braised venison forestière, and puddings such as white chocolate and brioche pudding and apple crumble.** *Starters/Snacks: £4.25 to £6.25. Main Courses: £8.95 to £12.75. Puddings: £4.25*

Free house ~ Licensees Mr and Mrs Chroscicki ~ Real ale ~ Bar food (12-2, 6(7 Sun)-9) ~ (01328) 830297 ~ Children welcome ~ Open 11.30-2.30, 6-11; 12-2.30, 7-11 Sun

Recommended by Martin Conybeare, Pete Baker, Judith Salter, Philip and Susan Philcox, David Rule, Derek and Sylvia Stephenson, Derek Field, Tracey and Stephen Groves, Julia Mann, R C Vincent

BLAKENEY   TG0243   MAP 8

Kings Arms 🍺

West Gate Street; NR25 7NQ

A stroll from the harbour, friendly and chatty, with popular home cooking and local ales; walled garden

Our readers enjoy their visits to this attractive white inn. It's a friendly place with a pleasant, welcoming atmosphere and courteous, helpful staff. The three simply furnished, knocked-through pubby rooms have a good mix of locals and visitors, low ceilings, some interesting photographs of the licensees' theatrical careers, other pictures including work by local artists, and what must be the smallest cartoon gallery in England – in a former telephone kiosk. Look out for the brass plaque on the wall that marks a flood level. There's an airy garden room, too; darts, games machine, and board games. Adnams Bitter and Woodfordes Nelsons Revenge and Wherry on handpump, and quite a few wines by the glass. The large garden has lots of tables and chairs; the harbour is a stroll away and the Norfolk Coast Path runs close by.

🍽 **Popular bar food includes sandwiches, soup, filled baked potatoes, chicken liver and madeira pâté, local mussels (winter only), cream cheese and broccoli bake, jumbo sausages with black pepper and brandy sauce, steak in ale pie, fish and chips, gammon and egg, seafood tagliatelle, and puddings such as apple and sultana crumble and chocolate brownie with Baileys cream.** *Starters/Snacks: £3.95 to £6.95. Main Courses: £7.00 to £13.00. Puddings: £3.50 to £5.50*

Free house ~ Licensees John Howard, Marjorie Davies and Nick Davies ~ Real ale ~ Bar food (all day) ~ (01263) 740341 ~ Children welcome ~ Dogs welcome ~ Open 11-11; 12-10.30 Sun ~ Bedrooms: £45S/£65S

Recommended by MDN, Pat and Tony Martin, Len Clark, Mrs B Barwick, David Carr, David Eberlin, Len Beattie, Christopher Turner, Joan York, Simon Cottrell, C and R Bromage, Jim Farmer, William Mack, Steve Whalley

---

> Post Office address codings confusingly give the impression that a few pubs are in Norfolk, when they're really in Cambridgeshire or Suffolk (which is where we list them).

White Horse

Off A149 W of Sheringham; High Street; NR25 7AL

Cheerful small hotel with popular dining conservatory, enjoyable food and drinks and helpful staff

Families like the bustling dining conservatory in this friendly little hotel, so to be sure of a table, it's best to book in advance. The informal long main bar is predominantly green with a venetian red ceiling and restrained but attractive décor, including watercolours by a local artist; the third dining area is a little more intimate and liked for evening meals. Adnams Bitter and Broadside, Woodfordes Wherry, and a guest from Yetmans on handpump, and 27 wines by the glass; board games. There are tables in a suntrap courtyard and a pleasant paved garden. The quayside is close by.

⑪ Using local estate produce and locally reared beef, the lunchtime menu includes sandwiches or ciabattas, ploughman's, smoked haddock kedgeree with a soft boiled egg, and fish pie, but you can also eat off the main menu then: seared scallops with anya potato and red onion salad with blood orange and pine nut dressing, moules marinières, chickpea, salsify and grilled courgette salad with harissa dressing, risotto of leeks, taleggio and sorrel with rocket and parmesan, beer-battered haddock, slow-roasted belly of pork with borlotti bean cassoulet, and puddings such as Baileys chocolate mousse with cookie dough ice-cream and prune and armagnac steamed pudding with toffee sauce and crème fraîche. *Starters/Snacks: £5.25 to £7.50. Main Courses: £9.95 to £15.95. Puddings: £4.25 to £6.25*

Free house ~ Licensees Dan Goff and Simon Scillitoe ~ Real ale ~ Bar food (12-2.15(2.30 Sun), 7-9) ~ Restaurant ~ (01263) 740574 ~ Children in conservatory ~ Open 11-11; 12-10.30 Sun ~ Bedrooms: /£110S(£70B)

Recommended by Michael Dandy, Mark Farrington, David Eberlin, John Wooll, Colin Goddard, Mrs Brenda Calver, MDN, David Field, Ken and Jenny Simmonds, A J Avery

BLICKLING   TG1728   MAP 8

Buckinghamshire Arms

B1354 NW of Aylsham; NR11 6NF

17th-c coaching inn, proper little bar and two dining areas, warmly friendly service, real ales, and good food; bedrooms

This handsome Jacobean inn is by the gates to the National Trust's Blickling Hall. It's run by a genuinely friendly landlady and her courteous staff and is liked by both drinkers and diners. There's a small and appealing proper unpretentious bar (the snug as they call it), a lounge bar with wheelbacks around circular tables on the stripped wooden floor, warm ochre-coloured walls, and a woodburning stove, and a smarter dining room with more formal wooden dining chairs and tables, another woodburning stove and a grandfather clock. Adnams Bitter, Fullers London Pride, and Woodfordes Wherry on handpump and ten wines by the glass. Outside on the lawn there are lots of tables.

⑪ Well presented bar food includes soup, caramelised red onion and spiced goats cheese tartlet with fresh pesto dressing, duck, chicken and pistachio terrine with home-made chutney, salmon and dill fishcakes with tomato sauce, old breed bangers and mash with rich red onion gravy, courgette, sweet pepper and cannellini bean gratin with a fresh herb and mozzarella crust, local venison and game casserole with parsley dumplings, and fillet of wild bass with saffron crushed potatoes and tomato and buttered spinach, and puddings. *Starters/Snacks: £4.95 to £6.75. Main Courses: £8.95 to £10.50. Puddings: £4.95 to £5.50*

Free house ~ Licensee Pip Wilkinson ~ Real ale ~ Bar food (not Sun or Mon evenings) ~ Restaurant ~ (01263) 732133 ~ Children welcome ~ Open 12-3, 6-11; 12-3, 7-10.30 Sun; closed 25 Dec ~ Bedrooms: £55S/£85S

Recommended by Mrs Mahni Pannett, Terry Mizen, Miss L Ward, Joan York, R C Vincent, Dr and Mrs R G J Telfer, Gaye Caulkett, Rob Winstanley

BRANCASTER STAITHE   TF7944   MAP 8

Jolly Sailors
Main Road (A149); PE31 8BJ

Own-brewed beers and good food in cosy rooms and plenty of seats in sizeable garden; great for bird-watching nearby

This is an enjoyable little pub with a friendly, unpretentious atmosphere. The three simply furnished and cosy rooms have a good mix of pubby seats and tables, and an open fire. The dining area has been smartened up and now feels less cluttered. From their on-site microbrewery they produce Brancaster Staithe Brewery Old Les and IPA and keep a guest like Woodfordes Norfolk Nog on handpump. There's a sizeable garden with a big new play area and a covered terrace with plenty of picnic-sets. This is prime bird-watching territory and the pub is set on the edge of thousands of acres of National Trust dunes and salt flats; walkers are welcome.

🍴 **Enjoyable freshly prepared food includes filled baguettes, soup, burgers, moules marinières, local oysters baked with sweet chilli sauce topped with stilton, sausages made with their own beer, roast vegetable and goats cheese tart, haddock in beer batter, fresh mackerel, chicken thai green curry, seasonal crab salad, T-bone steak, and puddings such as chocolate mousse and baked alaska.** *Starters/Snacks: £4.95 to £7.95. Main Courses: £8.95 to £18.95. Puddings: £2.95 to £5.50*

Free house ~ Licensee Mr Boughton ~ Real ale ~ Bar food (12-9) ~ Restaurant ~ (01485) 210314 ~ Children welcome ~ Dogs allowed in bar ~ Open 11-11; 12-10.30 Sun

Recommended by Tracey and Stephen Groves, David and Sue Smith, Eddie and Lynn Jarrett, Pete Baker, JJW, CMW, Len Clark, Philip and Susan Philcox, PHB, Mr and Mrs John Taylor, P Dawn

White Horse
A149 E of Hunstanton; PE31 8BY

Bustling, popular bar, big airy dining conservatory looking over tidal bird marshes, real ales and lovely food; comfortable bedrooms

They've cleverly managed to appeal to a very wide range of customers here and seem able to cater for most needs. It's a comfortable and enjoyable place to stay and the food in the bar and restaurant is particularly good, but what most appealed to one of our readers was the sign saying that they welcomed tired walkers and dogs, and he much appreciated sitting on the sun deck with a pint of beer looking out to Scolt Head across the salt marsh. The informal bar has plenty of locals dropping in, good photographs on the left, with bar billiards and maybe piped music, and on the right is a quieter group of cushioned wicker armchairs and sofas by a table with daily papers and local landscapes for sale; there are plenty of seats outside in front, some under cover and with heaters, for casual dining. The dining area and adjoining conservatory restaurant are at the back with well spaced furnishings in unvarnished country-style wood and some light-hearted seasidey decorations; the wide tidal marsh views seen through the big glass windows, are splendid. Adnams Bitter, Fullers London Pride, Woodfordes Wherry, and a guest like Timothy Taylors Landlord on handpump, several malt whiskies and about a dozen wines by the glass from an extensive and thoughtful wine list; friendly service. The coast path runs along the bottom of the garden.

🍴 **The food, using delicious local fish, is very good indeed. From the fair value little bar menu, there might be filled ciabattas, ploughman's, soup, caesar or cajun chicken salads, lamb kofta kebab with red onion and cucumber salsa, pitta bread and mint yoghurt, salmon and dill fishcakes with sorrel butter sauce, and beef chop steak with spiced tomato chutney; the restaurant has lunchtime dishes such as pork belly with caramelised apples and deep-fried cod fillet with pease pudding, evening choices like local mussels and oysters, fillet of halibut with bourguignon sauce and tartlet of lamb rump with confit sweet red onion, and daily specials, and there are puddings such as chocolate brownie with chocolate sauce and lemon tart.** *Starters/Snacks: £2.95 to £5.95. Main Courses: £4.95 to £9.50. Puddings: £3.95 to £4.95*

Free house ~ Licensees Cliff Nye and Kevin Nobes ~ Real ale ~ Bar food (all day in bar and on outside terrace; 12-2, 6.30-9 restaurant) ~ Restaurant ~ (01485) 210262 ~ Children welcome ~ Dogs allowed in bar and bedrooms ~ Open 11-11; 12-10.30 Sun ~ Bedrooms: £89B/£128B

Recommended by John Wooll, Michael Dandy, Len Beattie, John Honnor, Tracey and Stephen Groves, Mrs A J Robertson, Mike and Sue Loseby, M E and J R Hart, Peter Rozée, Steve Whalley, Simon Rodway, Leslie and Barbara Owen, PHB, Mrs Brenda Calver, K Christensen, Brian and Pamela Everett, Derek and Sylvia Stephenson, Glenwys and Alan Lawrence, R M Chard, Neil Ingoe, Mr and Mrs A H Young

BURNHAM MARKET
TF8342   MAP 8

Hoste Arms ⑪ � ⌂

The Green (B1155); PE31 8HD

NORFOLK DINING PUB OF THE YEAR

Civilised and stylish with delicious food and drinks, very good staff, plenty of different rooms and big eating area in lovely garden; super bedrooms

This smart and civilised 17th-c coaching inn is just as enjoyable whether you are dropping in for a pint and a chat, a first-rate lunch or evening meal, perhaps afternoon teas or staying overnight in their exceptional bedrooms – and the welcome from the friendly staff is as warm and genuine whatever your reason. The panelled proper bar on the right still retains the atmosphere of a village pub and there's a nice mix of chatty customers, a log fire and a series of watercolours showing scenes from local walks. A bow-windowed bar on the left has comfortable seats and there's a conservatory with leather armchairs and sofas and a lounge for afternoon tea; several restaurants, too. Adnams Bitter, Woodfordes Nelsons Revenge and Wherry, and a changing guest beer on handpump, over 20 wines by the glass from a fantastic list and 20 malt whiskies. The lovely walled garden has plenty of seats, and a big awning covers the sizeable eating area.

⑪ **Excellent food includes lunchtime sandwiches, interesting soups, salads like salmon, chinese leaf, pak choi and red pepper with chilli and ginger, and shredded duck with orange and pine nuts, oysters done several ways, mussels with white wine, parsley and cream, broccoli, red onion and walnut tart with goats cheese glaze, steak and kidney pudding with honey-glazed parsnips, pad thai chicken stir fry, loin of local venison with red wine and chocolate sauce, baked skate wing, confit cabbage and potato, thyme and brown shrimp and lime butter, and puddings such as vanilla and white chocolate mousse with dark chocolate and Baileys centre, and thyme panna cotta with an almond macaroon, red wine and kirsch sauce and pistachio nuts.** *Starters/Snacks: £4.75 to £7.95. Main Courses: £10.75 to £19.25. Puddings: £6.75*

Free house ~ Licensees Paul Whittome and Emma Tagg ~ Real ale ~ Bar food ~ Restaurant ~ (01328) 738777 ~ Children welcome ~ Dogs allowed in bar and bedrooms ~ Open 11-11(10.30 Sun) ~ Bedrooms: £90S/£122B

Recommended by Alan and Jill Bull, Philip Vernon, Kim Maidment, Walter and Susan Rinaldi-Butcher, John Winstanley, Dan and Holly Pitcher, Roy Hoing, D J Elliott, Sally Anne and Peter Goodale, Ken and Jenny Simmonds, Mike and Sue Loseby, Alistair and Kay Butler, Tracey and Stephen Groves, Michael and Maggie Betton, Sue Demont, Tim Barrow, Roger Wain-Heapy, Neil and Angela Huxter, Derek and Sylvia Stephenson, Mr and Mrs W W Burke, George Cowie, Frances Gosnell, Alan Cole, Kirstie Bruce

BURNHAM THORPE
TF8541   MAP 8

Lord Nelson ◀

Village signposted from B1155 and B1355, near Burnham Market; PE31 8HL

Interesting Nelson memorabilia, fine drinks including secret rum-based recipes, tasty food, and much character; play area in big garden

This spotlessly clean, 17th-c pub has plenty of memorabilia and pictures of Nelson (who was born in this sleepy village). The little bar has well waxed antique high-backed settles on the worn red flooring tiles and smoke ovens in the original fireplace, and there's a little snug leading off. The eating room has flagstones, an open fire and a history alongside more pictures of Nelson, and there's a separate dining room, too; board games. Greene King Abbot, Woodfordes Wherry and a guest like Fox Nelsons Blood tapped from the cask, a dozen wines by the glass and secret rum-based recipes called Nelson's Blood and Lady Hamilton's Nip; Nelson's Blood was first concocted in the 18th c and is passed down from landlord to landlord by word of mouth. There's a good-sized play area and pétanque in the very big garden (where there may be summer barbecues). They hold special Nelson events throughout the year.

📶 As well as lunchtime open sandwiches and ploughman's, the good bar food includes soup, toast with mushrooms and tarragon cream, salad of pigeon breast with shallots and red wine and cranberry sauce, steak and kidney pudding, venison sausages with red onion gravy, supreme of salmon with leeks and duchesse potatoes, lamb shank with rosemary sauce and roasted garlic, vegetarian options, and puddings such as orange and Cointreau panna cotta and chocolate brownie with mango coulis; there's also a surf and turf menu and a three-course set menu. *Starters/Snacks: £4.50 to £7.25. Main Courses: £8.25 to £22.50. Puddings: £5.50 to £6.50*

Greene King ~ Lease Simon Alper ~ Real ale ~ Bar food (12-2(2.30 Sat), 7-9(9.30 Sat); not Sun evening or Mon except summer school holidays) ~ Restaurant ~ (01328) 738241 ~ Children welcome ~ Dogs allowed in bar ~ Live bands Thurs evenings ~ Open 12-3(3.30 Sat), 6-11 (open all day during summer school holidays); 12-3.30, 6.30-11 Sun; closed Mon (except half term and school holidays)

Recommended by Jeremy and Jane Morrison, Pete Baker, John Wooll, Pat and Tony Martin, Sue Demont, Tim Barrow, John Honnor, Anthony Longden, Alan and Jill Bull, Kerry Law, Alan Cole, Kirstie Bruce, Barry Collett, Sheila Topham, the Didler

COLKIRK   TF9226   MAP 8

Crown ⚲

Village signposted off B1146 S of Fakenham, and off A1065; Crown Road; NR21 7AA

Neatly kept, bustling local with cheerful landlord, splendid wines, popular tasty food, and pleasant garden

This is still very much a proper village pub – even though you'll find a good few people enjoying the interesting food. The two bars are comfortable and cosy and kept spotless, with solid country furniture on the rugs and flooring tiles, interesting things to look at and open fires. Greene King IPA, Abbot and a guest such as Bath Ales Gem on handpump and a splendid range of wines, many by the glass; quick service even when busy. There's also a dining room. Outside, there's a suntrap terrace, a pleasant garden and plenty of picnic-sets.

📶 Popular bar food includes filled baguettes, soup, whitebait, deep-fried mushrooms with sweet chilli dip, asparagus and sun-dried tomato flan, steak in ale pie, baked chicken with melted cheese and bacon, braised lamb shank with onion gravy lasagne, and puddings such as cheesecake and bread and butter pudding. *Starters/Snacks: £4.25 to £5.75. Main Courses: £8.95 to £15.95. Puddings: £4.50*

Greene King ~ Tenant Roger Savell ~ Real ale ~ Bar food (12-1.45, 7-9) ~ Restaurant ~ (01328) 862172 ~ Children welcome ~ Dogs allowed in bar ~ Open 11-2.30, 6-11; 12-3, 7-10.30 Sun

Recommended by R C Vincent, Mr and Mrs T B Staples, Mark, Amanda, Luke and Jake Sheard, Jim Farmer, Dan and Holly Pitcher, Sally Anne and Peter Goodale

EDGEFIELD   TG0934   MAP 8

Pigs 🍽 ⚲ 🍺

Norwich Road; B1149 S of Holt; NR24 2RL

Good enterprising food and good range of drinks in enthusiastically run pub – still keeping a proper bar

In last year's Lucky Dip we gave this new venture a starred entry, on the strength of early visits by trusted reader-reporters. It's now thoroughly established itself as a splendid pub, good all round, and actually something of a front-runner on the food side. The carpeted central bar greets you with the reassuring sight of a good row of handpumps, with well kept Adnams Bitter and Broadside, Woodfordes Wherry, and a couple of changing guests. They have continental beers on tap, and a good range of wines by the glass, in two glass sizes; they do coffee in two sizes, too. No crisps – instead they do their own pork scratchings and interesting seed, bean and nut snacks. Service, under the very hands-on landlord, is uniformly cheerful and efficient. A games area has darts, dominoes, shove-ha'penny and bar billiards (Thursday is games night, and they have a Wednesday quiz night); there's a proper children's playroom, too. On the left, arches open through to a simply refurbished area with a mix of random dining chairs and built-in pews around the plain tables on broad stripped pine boards. On the right a light and airy dining extension is similar in style, with some tables in stalls formed by low brick stub walls and single standing timbers; the kitchen gives an open view. Outside, a big covered terrace has sturdy rustic tables and benches on flagstones, and there is an adventure play area. Wheelchair access is easy.

🍽 From a cheerfully set out menu, the good interesting food includes nibbly things like spiced almonds, salted broad beans and a sweet, spicy nut mix, sandwiches, beef dripping or herring roes on toast, a rarebit with local cheese, beer, grain mustard and apple chutney, soup, smoked haddock and shrimp kedgeree with a soft boiled free-range egg, pressed terrine of pork with dried fruits and pickled pear, a sharing charcuterie plate, beer-battered cod, leek, cheese and tomato tart with gherkin salad, lambs liver, crispy bacon, bubble and squeak and onion gravy, slow-cooked duck leg with orange salad and pickled red cabbage, beef casserole with dumplings, and puddings such as a proper trifle and warm double cream tapioca with prunes stewed in earl grey tea and orange. *Starters/Snacks: £2.50 to £5.95. Main Courses: £9.95 to £14.95. Puddings: £4.95*

Free house ~ Licensee Chloe Wasey ~ Real ale ~ Bar food (12-2.30(3 Sun), 6-9; not Sun evening or Mon (except bank hols)) ~ (01263) 587634 ~ Children welcome ~ Dogs allowed in bar ~ Open 11-3, 6-11; 12-4 Sun; closed Sun evening, Mon (except bank hols when they open 12-4)

Recommended by Tracey and Stephen Groves, William Mack, Derek Field, June and Ken Brooks, KN-R

ERPINGHAM

TG1732   MAP 8

Saracens Head 🍽 ♀ 🛏

At Wolterton – not shown on many maps; Erpingham signed off A140 N of Aylsham; keep on through Calthorpe, then where road bends right take the straight-ahead turn-off signposted Wolterton; NR11 7LZ

Charming long-serving landlord in simply furnished dining pub, gently civilised atmosphere, good food and well liked bedrooms

As we went to press, the convivial Mr Dawson-Smith told us that this rather civilised place was up for sale, so possibly some time during 2009, there could be quite a few changes here. The two-room bar is simple and stylish with high ceilings, terracotta walls, and red and white striped curtains at its tall windows – all lending a feeling of space, though it's not actually large. There's a mix of seats from built-in leather wall settles to wicker fireside chairs as well as log fires and flowers, and the windows look out on to a charming old-fashioned gravel stableyard with picnic-sets. A pretty six-table parlour on the right has another big log fire. Adnams Bitter and Woodfordes Wherry on handpump, an interesting wine list, local apple juice and decent malt whiskies; the atmosphere is enjoyably informal. The Shed next door (run by Mr Dawson-Smith's daughter Rachel) is a workshop and showcase for furniture and interior pieces. Lovely, comfortable bedrooms that our readers like very much.

🍽 Good, enjoyable food includes mussels with cider and cream, crispy fried aubergine with garlic mayonnaise, game and cranberry terrine, fried scallops with rosemary and cream, roast leg of lamb with red and white beans, baked cromer crab with apple and sherry, medallions of venison with red fruit jus, roast local pheasant with calvados, and puddings such as Baileys dark chocolate pot with orange jus and brown bread and butter pudding. *Starters/Snacks: £3.95 to £7.95. Main Courses: £11.95 to £15.95. Puddings: £4.95*

Free house ~ Licensee Robert Dawson-Smith ~ Real ale ~ Bar food (12-2-ish, 7.30-9-ish) ~ Restaurant ~ (01263) 768909 ~ Children welcome but must be well behaved ~ Dogs allowed in bedrooms ~ Open 11.30-3.30, 6-11.30; 12-3, 7-10.30 Sun; closed 25 Dec, Mon except bank holidays and maybe Tues lunchtime ~ Bedrooms: £45B/£85B

Recommended by Anthony Barnes, Bill Strang, Stuart Pearson, Dan and Holly Pitcher, Roddy and Kate Steen, Sally Anne and Peter Goodale, John Winstanley, Dr and Mrs P Truelove, Paul and Sue Dix, John Robertson, Brenda Crossley, Philip and Susan Philcox, Dennis and Gill Keen, Sue Demont, Tim Barrow, Pete Devonish, Ian McIntyre, John Wooll, Dr and Mrs M E Wilson

ITTERINGHAM   TG1430   MAP 8

Walpole Arms

Village signposted off B1354 NW of Aylsham; NR11 7AR

Ambitious food in popular dining pub, quietly chatty open-plan bar, decent drinks and good garden

New licensees have taken over this busy dining pub, but apart from the menu, little seems to have changed. The sizeable open-plan bar is rather civilised and has exposed beams, stripped brick walls, little windows, a mix of dining tables and quietly chatty atmosphere. Adnams Bitter, Wolf Golden Jackal, and Woodfordes Wherry on handpump, quite a few wines by the glass, and Aspall's cider; friendly young manager and his helpful staff. Behind the pub is a two-acre landscaped garden and there are seats on the vine-covered terrace. More reports on the new regime, please.

The interesting food now includes bruschetta with tomato, mozzarella and olive, ploughman's, borlotti bean soup, smoked haddock and herb potato cake, crayfish with vietnamese cabbage and mango purée, blue cheese salad with chicory, toasted walnuts and pickled pear, spinach and goats cheese parcel with tzimmes (sweet potato, carrot and dried fruit stew) and israeli couscous, home-made pork, basil and pepper sausages with a green bean, roast pepper and potato salad, corn-fed chicken piri piri with a portuguese salad, slow-roast pork belly with chickpea and chorizo stew and rouille, and fillet of black bream with potato salad, roast tomatoes and rocket. *Starters/Snacks: £6.00 to £7.00. Main Courses: £10.00 to £17.00. Puddings: £5.00 to £6.00*

Free house ~ Licensees Mr and Mrs Sayers ~ Real ale ~ Bar food (12-2(3 Sun), 7-9; not Sun evening) ~ Restaurant ~ (01263) 587258 ~ Children welcome ~ Dogs allowed in bar ~ Open 12-3, 6-11; 12-7 Sun; closed 25 Dec

Recommended by Barry and Patricia Wooding, John Winstanley, Pete Devonish, Ian McIntyre, Mike and Shelley Woodroffe, Mrs B Barwick, Philip and Susan Philcox, MDN, Charles and Pauline Stride, Joyce and Maurice Cottrell, Mrs Brenda Calver, Dennis and Gill Keen, Robert Tapsfield, Virginia Williams, Sheila Topham

LARLING   TL9889   MAP 5

Angel

From A11 Thetford—Attleborough, take B1111 turn-off and follow pub signs; NR16 2QU

In same family since 1913, with good-natured chatty atmosphere, real ales, and popular food; bedrooms

This very popular pub has been in the same family since 1913 and they still have the original visitors' books with guests from 1897 to 1909. There's a good mix of customers, the atmosphere is chatty and relaxed, and the comfortable 1930s-style lounge on the right has cushioned wheelback chairs, a nice long cushioned and panelled corner settle, some good solid tables for eating, and squared panelling; also, a collection of whisky-water jugs on the delft shelf over the big brick fireplace, a woodburning stove, a couple of copper kettles, and some hunting prints. Adnams Bitter and four guests from breweries like Crouch Vale, Iceni, Oakham, and Wolf on handpump, 100 malt whiskies, and ten wines by the glass. They hold an August beer festival with over 70 real ales and ciders, live music and barbecues. The quarry-tiled black-beamed public bar has a good local atmosphere, with darts, games machine, juke box (a rarity nowadays), board games and piped music. A neat grass area behind the car park has picnic-sets around a big fairy-lit apple tree, and there's a safely fenced play area. They also have a four-acre meadow and offer caravan and camping sites from March to October. Peter Beale's old-fashioned rose nursery is nearby.

Ⅲ Using local produce, the well liked, fair value bar food includes sandwiches, soup, filled baked potatoes, ploughman's, chicken liver pâté, burgers, ham and egg, stilton and mushroom bake, thai green chicken curry, smoked haddock mornay, peppered pork, and daily specials such as steak and kidney pie, smoked salmon and asparagus crêpes, and lamb chop in apple and cider sauce. *Starters/Snacks: £2.75 to £5.95. Main Courses: £5.25 to £18.95. Puddings: £4.75*

Free house ~ Licensee Andrew Stammers ~ Real ale ~ Bar food (all day) ~ Restaurant ~ (01953) 717963 ~ Children welcome ~ Open 10am-midnight ~ Bedrooms: £40B/£70S

Recommended by Julian and Janet Dearden, Edward Mirzoeff, George Atkinson, Roy Hoing, Alan Cowell, Mike and Shelley Woodroffe, Peter and Anne Hollindale, Kevin Thomas, Nina Randall, Stuart and Alison Ballantyne, Dr and Mrs A K Clarke, Mrs Jane Kingsbury

MORSTON   TG0043   MAP 8

Anchor

A149 Salthouse—Stiffkey; The Street; NR25 7AA

Quite a choice of rooms filled with bric-a-brac and prints, real ales, and well liked food

There's a good mix of rooms which offer something for everyone in this busy pub. The contemporary airy extension on the left has groups of deep leather sofas around low tables, grey-painted country dining furniture, fresh flowers and fish pictures. On the right are three more traditional rooms with pubby seating and tables on original wooden floors, coal fires, local 1950s beach photographs and lots of prints and bric-a-brac. Greene King IPA, Old Speckled Hen and local Winters Golden on handpump, several decent wines including vintage champagne by the glass, oyster shots (a local oyster in a short bloody mary), and daily papers. There are tables and benches out in front of the building. You can book seal-spotting trips from here and the surrounding area is wonderful for bird-watching and walking.

Ⅲ Good bar food includes sandwiches, soup, ham hock and parsley terrine with home-made piccalilli, six local oysters on ice with shallot vinegar, caesar salad with free-range chicken, liver and bacon, beer-battered haddock with mushy peas, portabello mushrooms stuffed with baby vine tomatoes and basil topped with goats cheese and pine nuts, beef in ale stew with horseradish dumplings, and puddings such as toffee cream tart and vanilla crème brûlée with almond shortbread. *Starters/Snacks: £4.50 to £8.50. Main Courses: £9.25 to £16.50. Puddings: £4.50 to £6.25*

Free house ~ Licensee Sam Handley ~ Real ale ~ Bar food (12-2.30, 6-9(9.30 Fri and Sat); 12-8 Sun) ~ Restaurant ~ (01263) 741392 ~ Children welcome ~ Dogs allowed in bar ~ Open 11-11(10.30 Sun)

Recommended by John Honnor, Fred and Lorraine Gill, Tracey and Stephen Groves, Derek Field, Colin McKerrow, Philip and Susan Philcox

NORWICH   TG2309   MAP 5

Adam & Eve £

Bishopgate; follow Palace Street from Tombland, N of cathedral; NR3 1RZ

Ancient, bustling pub, plenty of history, good mix of customers, real ales and fair value food, and seats by fantastic array of hanging baskets and tubs

There's always a really good mix of customers in this extremely popular and friendly pub: musicians and adult choir members from the nearby cathedral, lawyers, visitors and locals. The pub is thought to date back to at least 1249 (when it was used by workmen building the cathedral) and even has a Saxon well beneath the lower bar floor, though the striking dutch gables were added in the 14th and 15th centuries. The little old-fashioned bars have antique high-backed settles, cushioned benches built into partly panelled walls, and tiled or parquet floors. Adnams Bitter, Mauldons Moletrap Bitter, Theakstons Old Peculier, and Wells & Youngs Bombardier on handpump, over 50 malt whiskies, quite a few wines by the glass and Aspall's cider; piped music and board games.

The award-winning colourful tubs and hanging baskets here are quite a sight in summer and it's nice to admire them from one of the many picnic-sets. Comedy Horrid History of Norwich walks start and end here every evening from 1 April to 31 October, and there's also a Discover Norfolk tourist train that terminates here.

🍽 **Decent, good value pubby food includes sandwiches and filled baguettes, filled baked potatoes, ploughman's, soup, chilli con carne, steak and mushroom pie, cheese and vegetable bake, ham and eggs, king prawns in filo pastry with a sweet chilli dip, and daily specials.** *Starters/Snacks: £2.45 to £5.95. Main Courses: £5.95 to £9.95. Puddings: £3.95*

Unique (Enterprise) ~ Lease Rita McCluskey ~ Real ale ~ Bar food (12-7; 12-2.30 Sun; not Sun evening) ~ (01603) 667423 ~ Children in snug until 7pm ~ Open 11-11; 12-10.30 Sun

Recommended by John and Helen Rushton, Mr and Mrs W W Burke, Dennis Jones, John Wooll, Christopher Turner, Joan York, Revd R P Tickle, Ian Chisholm, the Didler, David and Sue Smith, David and Sue Atkinson, Dr and Mrs A K Clarke

Fat Cat 🍺
West End Street; NR2 4NA

A place of pilgrimage for beer lovers, and open all day

'The ulimate beer drinkers' heaven' is how one reader describes this extremely popular, well run little pub. As well as their own beers (brewed at their sister pub, The Shed) Fat Cat Bitter, Honey, Marmalade, Stout, and Top Cat, the fantastic choice (on handpump or tapped from the cask in a stillroom behind the bar – big windows reveal all) might include Acorn Old Moor Porter, Adnams Broadside and Southwold, Brains Dark Mild, Caledonian Deuchars IPA, Fullers ESB, Greene Jack Canary, Lurcher and Mahseer IPA, Greene King Abbot and Ale Fresco, Hopback Summer Lightning, Kelham Island Pale Rider, Oldershaw Bishops Farewell, Harrowby Pale Ale, Orkney Red McGregor, Pitfield Eco Warrier, Shepherd Neame Spitfire, Thornbridge Jaipur IPA, Timothy Taylors Landlord, Winters Storm Force, Wolf Prairie Gold, Woodfordes Wherry, and many more. You'll also find ten draught beers from Belgium and Germany, up to 80 bottled beers from around the world, and ciders and perries. There's a lively bustling atmosphere at busy times, with maybe tranquil lulls in the middle of the afternoon, and a good mix of cheerful customers. The no-nonsense furnishings include plain scrubbed pine tables and simple solid seats, lots of brewery memorabilia, bric-a-brac and stained glass. There are tables outside.

🍽 **Bar food consists of rolls and good pies at lunchtime (not Sunday).** *Starters/Snacks: £0.60*

Free house ~ Licensee Colin Keatley ~ Real ale ~ Bar food (filled rolls available until sold out; not Sun) ~ No credit cards ~ (01603) 624364 ~ Children allowed in conservatory until 7pm ~ Dogs allowed in bar ~ Open 12-11; 11(12 Fri)-midnight Sat; 12-10.30 Sun; closed evening 31 Dec

Recommended by the Didler, William Mack, David and Sue Atkinson, Dr and Mrs A K Clarke

OLD BUCKENHAM   TM0691   MAP 5

Gamekeeper
B1077 S of Attleborough; The Green; NR17 1RE

Carefully refurbished bar rooms liked by drinkers and diners, friendly service, interesting food, and seats on heated terrace

Refurbished throughout this year and no longer offering bedrooms, this pretty 16th-c pub is a civilised and friendly place with a new licensee. The beamed bar, with two main areas, has leather armchairs and a sofa in front of the big open woodburning stove in the capacious inglenook fireplace, a pleasant variety of nice old wooden seats and tables on the fine old flagstones or wooden flooring, and local watercolours on the walls; there are two unusual interior bow windows. Adnams Bitter, Timothy Taylors Landlord, and Woodfordes Wherry on handpump, and quite a few wines by the glass. Besides the comfortable main back dining area which includes some stripped high-backed settles and a grand piano, there's a small separate room used for private dining. The back heated terrace has seats and tables and there are picnic-sets on the grass beyond. More reports please.

🍴 At lunchtime, bar food includes sandwiches, ham hock and parsley terrine with bread sauce and toasted brioche, goats cheese and roasted pepper bruschetta with pesto, smoked prawns with basil mayonnaise, sausages with cheese mash and onion gravy, beetroot risotto with feta cheese, and sharing platters of charcuterie and antipasti; evening choices such as a duo of duck breast with a sausage and bean cassoulet, tempura-battered haddock with mint and broad bean risotto, popular slow-roasted moroccan lamb shoulder with chickpea and courgette rice and a yoghurt and lime dressing, and puddings like cherry and kirsch brûlée and sticky toffee pudding with muscovado sauce and vanilla ice-cream; Sunday roasts. *Starters/Snacks: £4.90 to £5.95. Main Courses: £6.95 to £16.95. Puddings: £4.95*

Enterprise ~ Lease David Francis ~ Real ale ~ Bar food (12-2.30(3.30 Sun), 6.30-9; not Sun evening) ~ Restaurant ~ (01953) 860397 ~ Children allowed away from bar ~ Dogs allowed in bar ~ Open 11.30-3, 5.30-11; 12-6 Sun; closed Sun evening

Recommended by Alan Cole, Kirstie Bruce, Ian Chisholm, John Wooll, Charles Gysin

RINGSTEAD
TF7040   MAP 8

Gin Trap 🍴 ♀

Village signposted off A149 near Hunstanton; OS Sheet 132 map reference 707403; PE36 5JU

Attractive coaching inn, caring, friendly licensees, good interesting food and wines; bedrooms

Customers are genuinely welcomed into this attractive white-painted 17th-c coaching inn by the hard-working, hands-on licensees. It's a friendly place with imaginative and enjoyable food and good, reasonably priced wines. The neat bar has beams, a woodburning stove, captain's chairs and cast-iron-framed tables, and Adnams Bitter, Greene King Abbot, and Woodfordes Wherry on handpump; piped music and board games. The dining conservatory overlooks the garden where there are seats and tables. In front of the building a handsome spreading chestnut tree shelters the car park. The Peddar's Way is close by.

🍴 Creative, well presented bar food includes sandwiches, interesting soups, pressed corn-fed chicken, apricot and sage terrine with home-made piccalilli, poached rillette of salmon with pickled cucumber papardelle and dill dressed fennel salad, organic burger with crispy onion rings, home-made relish and Monterey Jack cheese, home-cooked mustard-glazed ham with free-range eggs and bubble and squeak, hand-made saffron pasta with sauté wild mushrooms, madeira herb sauce and fresh parmesan shavings, warm mackerel escabeche with crushed coriander potatoes, toasted pine nuts and dressed pea shoot salad, and puddings such as bread and butter pudding with apricot coulis and crème caramel with poached fruits and mixed berries. *Starters/Snacks: £5.00 to £8.50. Main Courses: £8.50 to £13.00. Puddings: £5.50 to £7.00*

Free house ~ Licensees Cindy Cook and Steve Knowles ~ Real ale ~ Bar food (12-2(2.30 weekends), 6-9(9.30 Fri and Sat)) ~ Restaurant ~ (01485) 525264 ~ Children welcome ~ Dogs allowed in bar and bedrooms ~ Open 11.30-11(midnight Sat); 11.30-2.30, 6-11 in winter ~ Bedrooms: £60S(£70B)/£100S(£120B)

Recommended by John Wooll, Ian Woodroffe, Mrs Mary Jacobs, Tracey and Stephen Groves, KN-R, Roy Hoing, R C Vincent, JJW, CMW, Sue Demont, Tim Barrow, Mrs V Middlebrook

SNETTISHAM
TF6834   MAP 8

Rose & Crown 🍴 ♀ 🛏

Village signposted from A149 King's Lynn—Hunstanton just N of Sandringham; coming in on the B1440 from the roundabout just N of village, take first left turn into Old Church Road; PE31 7LX

Constantly improving old pub, log fires and interesting furnishings, thoughtful food, fine range of drinks, and stylish seating on heated terrace; well equipped, popular bedrooms

Many of our readers very much enjoy staying overnight at this pretty white cottage, and the upgrading of the bedrooms continues – they now have a lovely four-poster room, too.

It's a favourite with a lot of customers who enjoy the informal and relaxed feel of the place, helped no doubt by the presence of locals who are always popping in for a pint and a chat. The smallest of the three bars has had a facelift this year and is now a mocha coffee colour with coir flooring but still with the old prints of King's Lynn and Sandringham. The other two bars each has a separate character: an old-fashioned beamed front bar with black settles on its tiled floor and a big log fire, and a back bar with another large log fire and the landlord's sporting trophies and old sports equipment. There's also the Garden Room with inviting wicker-based wooden chairs, careful lighting and a quote by Dr Johnson in old-fashioned rolling script on a huge wall board. The residents' lounge is popular with non-residents too and has squashy armchairs and sofas, rugs on the floor, newspapers, magazines, jigsaws and board games – this can sometimes be dragooned into action as another dining room. Adnams Bitter, Bass, Fullers London Pride and Greene King IPA on handpump, quite a few wines by the glass, organic fruit juices and farm cider; friendly service. In the garden there are stylish café-style blue chairs and tables under cream parasols on the terrace, outdoor heaters, and colourful herbaceous borders. Two of the comfortable bedrooms are downstairs and there are disabled lavatories and wheelchair ramps.

🍽 **Usually very rewarding, the imaginative food includes lunchtime sandwiches (not Sunday), soup, potted crab, pigeon breast with broad bean and chorizo salad, antipasti and charcuterie platters, steak burger with bacon, cheese and real tomato ketchup (a vegetarian option too), barbecued spare ribs with buttered corn on the cob and coleslaw, seared sea trout with chilli and garlic and a lime dressing, roasted lamb rack with warm mint jam, and puddings such as vanilla fudge parfait, coffee millefeuilles and toffee wafer and crème caramel with soft fruit and mint kebabs.** *Starters/Snacks: £4.00 to £6.50. Main Courses: £7.75 to £14.50. Puddings: £4.50 to £4.75*

Free house ~ Licensee Anthony Goodrich ~ Real ale ~ Bar food (12-2(2.30 weekends and school holidays), 6.30-9(9.30 Fri and Sat) ~ Restaurant ~ (01485) 541382 ~ Children welcome ~ Dogs welcome ~ Open 11-11; 12-10.30 Sun ~ Bedrooms: £70B/£90B

Recommended by Alan Sutton, John Wooll, Philip Vernon, Kim Maidment, Conrad Freezer, Eithne Dandy, Sue Demont, Tim Barrow, Charlie and Chris Barker, Mark, Amanda, Luke and Jake Sheard, Peter Cole, Sally Anne and Peter Goodale, Ron and Sheila Corbett, Tracey and Stephen Groves, David Eberlin, Les and Sandra Brown, Michael Dandy, David Rule

SOUTH CREAKE   TF8635   MAP 8

Ostrich 🍺

B1355 Burnham Market—Fakenham; NR21 9PB

New owners for bustling village pub, some décor changes, real ales, well liked bar food, and seats in sheltered back terrace; bedrooms

In rolling countryside and within easy reach of bird reserves and lovely beaches, this bustling partly 17th-c village inn is under friendly new licensees this year. The bar and main seating area feel more pubby now, one room has shelves of books, and throughout there are modern paintings by local artists on the walls and a mix of wooden chairs and tables on polished bare boards. One of the dining room walls has been knocked through so that room is now open plan, and they have a spacious raftered second dining room as well. Adnams Broadside, Courage Directors, Greene King IPA, and Woodfordes Wherry on handpump, and several wines by the glass; piped music, magazines to read, and a woodburning stove. There are stylish tables and chairs on the sheltered back gravel terrace. More reports please.

🍽 **Bar food now includes sandwiches, soup, local moules marinières, monkfish tempura with thai sauce, chicken breast burger with garlic mayonnaise, sausages with onion gravy, mushroom or beef stroganoff, calves liver with creamy mash, duck breast with stir-fried vegetables in a black bean sauce, ostrich fillet, and puddings such as rhubarb possett and sticky toffee pudding with caramel sauce.** *Starters/Snacks: £3.25 to £5.95. Main Courses: £8.95 to £16.95. Puddings: £3.25 to £4.95*

Free house ~ Licensee Richard Millar ~ Real ale ~ Bar food (12-2, 6.30-9.30; all day weekends) ~ Restaurant ~ (01328) 823320 ~ Children welcome ~ Dogs welcome ~ Open 12-3, 5-11; 11am-midnight Sat; 12-10.30 Sun ~ Bedrooms: £50S/£75S

Recommended by Mrs M B Gregg, Tracey and Stephen Groves, M and GR, R C Vincent, Mike and Shelley Woodroffe

STIFFKEY

TF9643   MAP 8

Red Lion

A149 Wells—Blakeney; NR23 1AJ

New licensee, bustling atmosphere and attractive layout, good food, and new bedrooms

The new licensee of this bustling and traditional pub has opened up eco friendly bedrooms – the first floor rooms have views over the valley and ground floor ones have terraces. It's a friendly place with a wide mix of customers, and the oldest parts of the simple bars have a few beams, aged flooring tiles or bare floorboards, and big open fires. There's also a mix of pews, small settles and a couple of stripped high-backed settles, a nice old long deal table among quite a few others, Woodfordes Nelsons Revenge and Wherry and a guest like Yetmans Blue on handpump, and nine wines by the glass; good service, board games. A back gravel terrace has proper tables and seats, with more on grass further up beyond; there are some pleasant walks nearby.

Ⓜ **Good bar food now includes sandwiches, ploughman's, soup, chicken liver pâté with red onion marmalade, soft herring roes on garlic bruschetta, wild mushroom risotto, a trio of local sausages with creamy mash, honey and mustard ham with eggs, confit of duck with wilted spinach, jus and parsnip crisps, well liked beer-battered cod, fine mussels, daily specials, and puddings.** *Starters/Snacks: £4.25 to £6.50. Main Courses: £7.50 to £19.50. Puddings: £3.25 to £5.75*

Free house ~ Licensee Stephen Franklin ~ Real ale ~ Bar food (12-3, 6-9; all day weekends; breakfast from 8am) ~ (01328) 830552 ~ Children welcome ~ Dogs welcome ~ Live music monthly Fri evening ~ Open 8am-11pm ~ Bedrooms: £80B/£100B

Recommended by Robert Tapsfield, William Mack, the Didler, Sue Demont, Tim Barrow, Ken and Jenny Simmonds, Geoff and Pat Bell, Julia Mann, Tracey and Stephen Groves, John and Judith Jones, Trevor and Sheila Sharman, David Field, Dr D J and Mrs S C Walker

STOW BARDOLPH

TF6205   MAP 5

Hare Arms ♀

Just off A10 N of Downham Market; PE34 3HT

Long-serving licensees in bustling village pub, real ales, good mix of customers, and big back garden

The bustling bar in this neatly kept creeper-covered place has a proper village pub feel, and the licensees have now been here for 32 years. There's some interesting bric-a-brac, old advertising signs, fresh flowers, plenty of tables around its central servery and a good log fire; this bar opens into a well planted conservatory. Greene King IPA, Abbot, Old Speckled Hen, Ruddles County, and a guest beer on handpump, ten wines by the glass, and several malt whiskies. There are plenty of seats in the large garden behind with more in the pretty front garden, and chickens and peacocks roam freely. Church Farm Rare Breeds Centre is a five-minute walk away and is open April-October.

Ⓜ **As well as lunchtime sandwiches, filled baked potatoes and ploughman's, bar food includes lots of salads such as warm goats cheese with walnuts or chicken satay, a curry of the day, chilli con carne, gammon and pineapple, and daily specials such as nut cutlets with spicy chilli dip, locally smoked sprats with a horseradish dip, and chicken breast wrapped in streaky bacon with a stilton sauce.** *Starters/Snacks: £3.50 to £8.00. Main Courses: £8.25 to £16.00. Puddings: £3.75 to £4.25*

Greene King ~ Lease David and Trish McManus ~ Real ale ~ Bar food (12-2, 7-10; all day Sun) ~ Restaurant ~ (01366) 382229 ~ Children in small conservatory ~ Open 11-2.30, 6-11; 12-10.30 Sun; closed 25 and 26 Dec

Recommended by Tracey and Stephen Groves, John Wooll, John Saville, R C Vincent, Alan and Jill Bull

The ◖ symbol shows pubs which keep their beer unusually well, have a particularly good range or brew their own.

SWANTON MORLEY   TG0217 MAP 8

Darbys 🍺
B1147 NE of Dereham; NR20 4NY

Six or more real ales in unspoilt country local, plenty of farming knick-knacks, tasty bar food, and children's play area

The good choice of real ales in this busy local continues to draw plenty of customers. Kept on handpump, these might be Adnams Green and Bitter, Fullers Chiswick, Woodfordes Wherry and two regularly changing guests. The long bare-boarded country-style bar has a comfortable lived-in feel, with big stripped pine tables and chairs, lots of gin traps and farming memorabilia, a good log fire (with the original bread oven alongside) and tractor seats with folded sacks lining the long, attractive serving counter. A step up through a little doorway by the fireplace takes you through to the dining room. The children's room has a toy box and a glassed-over well, floodlit from inside; piped music. The garden has a children's play area. Plenty to do locally (B&B is available in carefully converted farm buildings a few minutes away) as the family also own the adjoining 720-acre estate.

🍽 **Bar food includes filled rolls, soup, garlic and stilton mushrooms, omelettes, various salad bowls, steak in ale pie, vegetable bake, chilli con carne, home-cooked ham and eggs, burgers, thai green chicken curry, and puddings.** *Starters/Snacks: £3.25 to £5.75. Main Courses: £6.00 to £13.25. Puddings: £4.50*

Free house ~ Licensees John Carrick and Louise Battle ~ Real ale ~ Bar food (12-2.15, 6.30-9.45) ~ Restaurant ~ (01362) 637647 ~ Children welcome ~ Dogs allowed in bar ~ Open 11.30-3, 6-11; 11.30-11 Sat; 12-10.30 Sun

Recommended by R C Vincent, Tony Middis, Bruce Bird

THORNHAM   TF7343 MAP 8

Lifeboat 🛏
Turn off A149 by Kings Head, then take first left turn; PE36 6LT

Good mix of customers and lots of character in traditional inn, five open fires, real ales and super surrounding walks

Extremely popular and with a lot of character, this bustling inn faces half a mile of coastal sea flats and there are lots of surrounding walks. The main Smugglers bar has low settles, window seats, pews, carved oak tables and rugs on the tiles, and masses of guns, swords, black metal mattocks, reed-slashers and other antique farm tools; lighting is by antique paraffin lamps suspended among an array of traps and yokes on its great oak-beamed ceiling. A couple of little rooms lead off here, and all in all there are five open fires. No games machines or piped music, though they still play the ancient game of 'pennies' which was outlawed in the late 1700s, and dominoes. Up some steps from the conservatory is a sunny terrace with picnic-sets, and further back is a children's playground with a fort and slide. Adnams Bitter, Greene King IPA and Abbot, Woodfordes Wherry, and a changing guest on handpump, several wines by the glass, farm cider and local apple juice; good service.

🍽 **Quite a choice of bar food might include sandwiches or filled ciabatta, ploughman's, soup, chicken and duck liver pâté with redcurrant sauce, a platter of smoked salmon and prawns with shellfish mayonnaise, malaysian-style vegetable curry, beer-battered fresh cod with home-made tartare sauce, home-made burger with bacon, emmenthal cheese and sticky onion marmalade, cajun chicken with a pineapple, cherry tomato and olive salad, hickory pork ribs, and gressingham duck breast with walnut and apricot stuffing and a mixed berry compote.** *Starters/Snacks: £3.65 to £6.90. Main Courses: £5.95 to £12.00. Puddings: £2.95 to £3.95*

Maypole Group ~ Manager Leon Mace ~ Real ale ~ Bar food ~ Restaurant ~ (01485) 512236 ~ Children welcome ~ Dogs allowed in bar and bedrooms ~ Open 12-11; 12-2.30, 6.30(6 Fri and Sat)-11 in winter ~ Bedrooms: £70B/£100B

WARHAM   TF9441   MAP 8

Three Horseshoes ★ ◖ ⇤

Warham All Saints; village signposted from A149 Wells-next-the-Sea—Blakeney, and from B1105 S of Wells; NR23 1NL

Old-fashioned pub with gas lighting in simple rooms, interesting furnishings and pubby food; gramophone museum

Happily, nothing changes here – it remains just the place for those who love genuinely friendly, unspoilt and old-fashioned pubs. The simple interior with its gas lighting looks little changed since the 1920s and parts of the building date back to the 1720s. There are stripped deal or mahogany tables (one marked for shove-ha'penny) on a stone floor, red leatherette settles built around the partly panelled walls of the public bar, royalist photographs and open fires in Victorian fireplaces. An antique American Mills one-arm bandit is still in working order (it takes 5p pieces), there's a big longcase clock with a clear piping strike and a twister on the ceiling to point out who gets the next round; darts and board games. Greene King IPA, Woodfordes Wherry and maybe a guest like Fox Fresh as a Daisy on handpump, local cider and home-made lemonade; friendly service. One of the outbuildings houses a wind-up gramophone museum – opened on request. There's a courtyard garden with flower tubs and a well, and a garden.

⊞ **Large helpings of proper pub food such as beans on toast, filled baked potatoes, home-cooked gammon, cheese and vegetable pie, rabbit, pigeon or pheasant casseroles, and puddings like spotted dick or syrup sponge.** *Starters/Snacks: £3.95 to £5.80. Main Courses: £8.50 to £10.50. Puddings: £3.50*

Free house ~ Licensee Iain Salmon ~ Real ale ~ Bar food (12-1.45, 6-8.30) ~ No credit cards ~ (01328) 710547 ~ Children welcome away from bar area; not in bedrooms ~ Dogs welcome ~ Open 11.30(12 Sun)-2.30, 6-11 ~ Bedrooms: £28/£56(£60S)

WELLS-NEXT-THE-SEA   TF9143   MAP 8

Crown ⊞ ♀ ⇤

The Buttlands; NR23 1EX

Smart coaching inn, friendly, informal bar, local ales, good, modern food, and stylish orangery; bedrooms

Although this is a rather smart 16th-c coaching inn, there's a bustling, cheerful atmosphere in the beamed bar and a good mix of both drinkers and diners. This bar has an informal mix of furnishings on the stripped wooden floor, local photographs on the red walls, a good selection of newspapers to read in front of the open fire, Adnams Bitter, Woodfordes Wherry and a guest like 3 Rivers IPA on handpump, quite a few wines by the glass and several whiskies and brandies; friendly, helpful staff. Piped music and board games. The conservatory is now a stylish orangery, and there's a pretty restaurant, too.

⊞ **Attractively presented and very good, the bar food includes lunchtime sandwiches, soup, scallops with green bean salad and chive butter sauce, cajun spiced lambs kidneys on toasted brioche, herring roe, rocket and apple salad with horseradish crème fraîche, herb roasted mediterranean vegetables with citrus couscous and balsamic glaze, thai watermelon curry with fish and coriander yoghurt, duck breast with swede purée and spiced lentils, daily specials, and puddings such as iced Baileys parfait with chocolate anglaise and crème brûlée.** *Starters/Snacks: £3.95 to £11.00. Main Courses: £10.45 to £19.95. Puddings: £5.00 to £5.95*

Free house ~ Licensees Chris and Jo Coubrough ~ Real ale ~ Bar food (12-2.30, 6.30-9.30) ~ Restaurant ~ (01328) 710209 ~ Children welcome ~ Dogs allowed in bar ~ Open 11-11 ~ Bedrooms: £110B/£120B

Recommended by John Wooll, Ian Chisholm, Simon Cottrell, Len Beattie, M and GR, Mrs J C Pank, Rod Stoneman, D J Elliott, Tracey and Stephen Groves, Walter and Susan Rinaldi-Butcher, Joyce and Maurice Cottrell, R C Vincent, David Carr, Mrs Romey Heaton, Robert Ager, Michael Dandy, David Field

Globe
The Buttlands; NR23 1EU

Attractive contemporary layout, good food and drink, and nice back courtyard; bedrooms

Just a short walk from the quay, this handsome Georgian inn is a popular place for a meal or a drink. The opened-up rooms have a relaxed contemporary feel and spread spaciously back from the front bar. Three big bow windows look over to a green lined by tall lime trees, there are well spaced tables on oak boards, walls in grey, cream or mulberry have moody local landscape photoprints, and the modern lighting is well judged; good service. Adnams Bitter and Broadside, and Woodfordes Wherry on handpump, a thoughtful choice of wines, and nice coffee; piped music and TV. An attractive heated back courtyard has dark green cast-iron furniture on pale flagstones among trellis tubs with lavender, roses and jasmine.

⊞ **Enjoyable bar food includes lunchtime sandwiches, a changing pâté with melba toast and red onion and tomato jam, baked field mushrooms with tapenade and garlic croûtons, dublin bay langoustines, a pie of the day, deep-fried haddock with tartare sauce, roast tomato confit with red onion pasta, ham with free-range eggs, steak with béarnaise sauce, daily specials, and puddings.** *Starters/Snacks: £4.50 to £10.00. Main Courses: £7.95 to £12.95. Puddings: £4.50 to £5.50*

Free house ~ Licensees Tom Coke and Ian Brereton ~ Real ale ~ Bar food ~ Restaurant ~ (01328) 710206 ~ Children welcome ~ Dogs allowed in bar ~ Open 11-11; 12-10.30 Sun ~ Bedrooms: £75B/£110B

Recommended by Tracey and Stephen Groves, Derek Field, Michael Dandy, Dan and Holly Pitcher, Amanda Goodrich, J D Taylor

WEST BECKHAM   TG1439   MAP 8
Wheatsheaf ◖
Off A148 Holt—Cromer; Church Road; NR25 6NX

Fine real ales and home-made food in nice, traditional pub, seats and children's play area in front garden

The charming, ramshackle garden here is a peaceful place for a drink or meal and there's an enclosed children's play area and some elusive rabbits and chickens; some seats on the covered terrace as well. Inside, it's pleasantly traditional and the bars have beams and cottagey doors, a roaring log fire in one part with a smaller coal one in another, comfortable chairs and banquettes and perhaps the enormous black pub cat. A fine choice of real ales tapped from the cask or on handpump might include Brakspears Bitter, Greene King IPA, Hook Norton Old Hooky, and Woodfordes Nelsons Revenge and Wherry; several wines by the glass, piped music. There is a purpose-built hut for smokers, with seats.

⊞ **As well as lunchtime sandwiches, filled baguettes and ciabattas, filled baked potatoes and ploughman's, the home-made bar food includes soup, creamy garlic mushrooms, pâté with a warm redcurrant sauce, venison and cranberry or steak and kidney pies, ham and eggs, sausages with creamy mash, roasted pepper and courgette risotto, chicken curry, daily specials such as mussels in white wine and garlic cream sauce, local rabbit casserole in beer and wine, and chicken in a coconut, chilli and asparagus sauce, and puddings like warm ginger sponge with toffee sauce or fruit crumble.** *Starters/Snacks: £4.00 to £5.95. Main Courses: £8.95 to £13.95. Puddings: £4.95*

Free house ~ Licensees Clare and Daniel Mercer ~ Real ale ~ Bar food (not Sun evening) ~ Restaurant ~ (01263) 822110 ~ Children welcome away from bar ~ Dogs allowed in bar ~ Open 12-3, 6.30-11; 12-3, 7-10.30 Sun; lunchtime closing 2.30 in winter

Recommended by Virginia Williams, Derek Field, Tracey and Stephen Groves, Sally Anne and Peter Goodale, Jim Farmer, D and M T Ayres-Regan, Ian Chisholm, Ryta Lyndley, Trevor and Sheila Sharman, Mr and Mrs John Taylor

WINTERTON-ON-SEA   TG4919   MAP 8

Fishermans Return 🍺

From B1159 turn into village at church on bend, then turn right into The Lane; NR29 4BN

Long-serving licensees in busy little local with half a dozen beers, warm log fire, and sheltered garden; nearby sandy beach

While locals tend to congregate in the public bar, visitors feel more comfortable in the white-painted lounge bar of this traditional brick and flint pub. This room has a roaring log fire, neat brass-studded red leatherette seats and maybe vases of fresh flowers. The panelled public bar has low ceilings and a glossily varnished nautical air (good fire in here too), and there's a family room and a dining room. The long-serving licensees have been here for over 30 years and keep up to six real ales on handpump: Adnams Bitter, Broadside and a seasonal beer, Woodfordes Nelsons Revenge and Wherry, and maybe a guest beer. Several malt whiskies and local cider; darts, pool, juke box and piped music. In fine weather you can sit on the attractive wrought-iron and wooden benches on a pretty front terrace with lovely views or in the sheltered garden. There's a sandy beach nearby. More reports please.

🍽 **Straightforward bar food includes toasties, filled baked potatoes, ploughman's, burgers, vegetarian omelette, fish pie, chilli con carne, daily specials such as beef in ale pie, smoked haddock and spinach mornay, and whole grilled plaice, and puddings.** *Starters/Snacks: £3.75 to £6.75. Main Courses: £5.25 to £12.25. Puddings: £3.75*

Free house ~ Licensees John and Kate Findlay ~ Real ale ~ Bar food ~ (01493) 393305 ~ Children welcome away from public bar ~ Dogs welcome ~ Open 11-2.30, 6-11; 11-11 Sat; 11.30-10.30 Sun ~ Bedrooms: £50B/£70B

Recommended by Mayur Shah, Steve Kirby, Mrs Romey Heaton, C Galloway

WIVETON   TG0442   MAP 8

Bell 🍽 🛏

Blakeney Rd; NR25 7TL

Refurbished open-plan dining pub, drinkers welcomed too, local beers, fine food, and seats outside; new bedrooms

Although the emphasis in this refurbished pub is on the good, modern food, they always keep some tables free for those popping in for a drink and a chat and the stools at the bar are well used too. It's all open-plan now, with fine old beams, an attractive mix of dining chairs around wooden tables on the stripped wooden floor, a log fire, and prints on the yellow walls. The sizeable conservatory has smart beige dining chairs around wooden tables on the coir flooring, and throughout, the atmosphere is chatty and relaxed. Friendly and helpful young staff serve Adnams Broadside, Woodfordes Wherry and a changing beer from Yetmans (the brewery is only a mile away) on handpump, and there are several good wines by the glass. Outside, there are picnic-sets on grass in front of the building looking across to the church, and at the back there are stylish wicker tables and chairs on several decked areas amongst decorative box hedging. Comfortable new bedrooms and they have a self-catering cottage as well.

🍽 **Using local game and fish, the enjoyable food includes sandwiches and various bruschetta, soup, crispy duck salad with sesame and soy dressing, duck, pigeon and foie gras terrine with quince chutney, field and wild mushrooms with thyme on toast with a fried duck egg, chicken caesar salad, slow-roasted pork belly on bubble and squeak with thyme jus, goats cheese tart, beer-battered fresh fish, roast lamb rump with pearl barley and asparagus risotto, and puddings such as lemon possett with shortbread and chocolate truffle torte with caramelised oranges.** *Starters/Snacks: £4.95 to £7.45. Main Courses: £6.95 to £14.95. Puddings: £4.95*

Free house ~ Licensee Berni Morritt ~ Real ale ~ Bar food (not winter Sun evening) ~ (01263) 740101 ~ Children welcome but not in bar in evening ~ Dogs allowed in bar ~ Open 12-3, 5-11; 12-10.30 Sun; 12-4.30 Sun in winter ~ Bedrooms: /£95S

Recommended by Mrs B Barwick

WOODBASTWICK   TG3214   MAP 8

Fur & Feather ◀

Off B1140 E of Norwich; NR13 6HQ

Full range of first-class beers from next-door Woodfordes brewery, tasty food, friendly service and suprisingly modern décor

Our readers love this pub. It's an attractively converted thatched cottage and very well run by friendly, efficient staff – and with the brewery next door, it's not surprising that the full range of Woodfordes beers are in tip-top condition. Tapped from the cask, they include Admirals Reserve, Headcracker, Mardlers, Nelsons Revenge, Norfolk Nip, Norfolk Nog, Sundew and Wherry; ten wines by the glass and quite a few malt whiskies. You can also visit the brewery shop. The style and atmosphere are not what you'd expect of a brewery tap as it's set out more like a dining pub and the décor is modern; piped music. The pub forms part of a very attractive estate village and has tables out in a pleasant garden.

🍴 Good bar food includes baps, filled baguettes and baked potatoes, soup, chicken livers with garlic, tarragon and madeira cream, salmon, pepper and watercress fishcake with a sweet chilli dip, home-baked ham with eggs, pure beef burgers, wild mushroom risotto, steak and kidney pudding, red snapper fillet with roasted sweet potato, red peppers and red onion and a rich butter sauce, and puddings such as rich chocolate pot and caramelised banana crème brûlée. *Starters/Snacks: £4.00 to £6.50. Main Courses: £8.50 to £16.95. Puddings: £5.25*

Woodfordes ~ Tenant Tim Ridley ~ Real ale ~ Bar food (12-2(3 Sun), 6-9) ~ Restaurant ~ (01603) 720003 ~ Children welcome but must be well behaved ~ Open 11.30-11; 12-10.30 Sun; 11.30-3, 6-11 Mon-Sat in winter

Recommended by R C Vincent, the Didler, Roy Hoing, Mayur Shah, Robert Ager, Anthony Barnes, Kerry Law, Mrs M B Gregg, Gerry and Rosemary Dobson, Mrs Romey Heaton, Revd R P Tickle

LUCKY DIP

Besides the fully inspected pubs, you might like to try these Lucky Dips recommended to us and described by readers (if you do, please send us reports: feedback@thegoodpubguide.co.uk).

BARFORD [TG1107]
☆ **Cock** NR9 4AS [B1108 7 miles W of Norwich]: Traditional main-road pub brewing its own good value Blue Moon ales, good food (fresh, so may take a time) from big lunchtime sandwiches to interesting main dishes and plenty of fish, friendly helpful service, pleasantly relaxed atmosphere, good mix of candlelit tables, shove-ha'penny, smarter back restaurant extension; well chosen piped music, occasional jazz *(BB, Bruce Bird, Ian and Nita Cooper)*
BLAKENEY [TG0244]
☆ **Manor** NR25 7ND [The Quay]: Friendly and attractive hotel opp wildfowl reserve and sea inlet, decorous bar, popular esp with older people for good fresh hearty bar food, not expensive, from well filled crab sandwiches up, good value wines by the glass, Adnams and Greene King Abbot, helpful attentive staff, conservatory; sunny tables in fountain

courtyard and walled garden with bowling green, good big bedrooms *(BB, Roy Bromell)*
BROOKE [TM2899]
Kings Head NR15 1AB [Norwich Rd (B1332)]: Good interesting food (home-baked bread too) in light and airy bar with log fire, stripped wood and scrubbed pine tables, smart eating area up a step, splendid choice of wines by the glass (and of glass sizes), Adnams, good value soft drinks, friendly efficient service, small back restaurant; picnic-sets in sheltered garden *(Roger and Lesley Everett)*
BROOME [TM3591]
Artichoke NR35 2NZ [Yarmouth Rd]: Eight well kept real ales, belgian fruit beers and good range of whiskies in properly unpretentious split-level pub with enjoyable food *(Neil Powell)*
BURSTON [TM1383]
☆ **Crown** IP22 5TW [Mill Rd]: Friendly and

relaxed two-bar country pub with lots of old woodwork, thoughtful home cooking using local supplies, well kept ales, small restaurant; nice front terrace *(Richard and Ruth Dean, Alan Cole, Kirstie Bruce)*

CASTLE ACRE [TF8115]

Albert Victor PE32 2AE [Stocks Green]: Dining pub with good interesting choice of tasty food from local meats to enterprising vegetarian dishes, well kept Greene King, pleasant staff, good range of wines by the glass; large attractive back garden and pergola *(Tim and Mark Allen, Chris and Susie Cammack)*

Ostrich PE32 2AE [Stocks Green]: Prettily placed pub overlooking attractive village's tree-lined green, reasonably priced food, real ales inc Woodfordes Wherry, ancient beams and masonry, huge inglenook fireplace; children welcome, large sheltered garden, open all day *(Charles Gysin, LYM, Len Beattie)*

CASTLE RISING [TF6624]

Black Horse PE31 6AG: All-day dining pub with plenty of tables in two front areas and back dining room, quick friendly service, real ales such as Adnams, Greene King and Woodfordes, decent choice of wines by the glass; piped music, no dogs; children particularly welcome, close-set tables out under parasols, by church and almshouses in pleasant unspoilt village *(John Wooll, R C Vincent, Ryta Lyndley, Tracey and Stephen Groves)*

CAWSTON [TG1422]

☆ *Ratcatchers* NR10 4HA [off B1145; Eastgate, S of village]: Beamed dining pub with old chairs and fine mix of walnut, beech, elm and oak tables, quieter candlelit dining room on right, Adnams Bitter and Broadside and a beer from Woodfordes, quite a few malt whiskies, conservatory; piped music, no dogs; children welcome, heated terrace, open all day Sun *(Philip and Susan Philcox, Dr and Mrs R G J Telfer, LYM, Jim Farmer, Roy Hoing, Barry Collett)*

CLEY NEXT THE SEA [TG0443]

☆ *Three Swallows* NR25 7TT [off A149; Newgate Green]: Straightforward food (all day wknds) from sandwiches up, unpretentious take-us-as-you-find-us style, banquettes around long high leathered tables, log fire, steps up to another small family eating area, second log fire in stripped pine dining room on left, Adnams and Greene King IPA and Abbot from unusual richly carved bar, decent wines, nice photographs, dominoes, cribbage; children and dogs welcome, big garden with budgerigars, surprisingly grandiose fountain, wooden climbing frame; handy for the salt marshes, simple bedrooms, open all day wknds and summer *(Geoff and Pat Bell, R C Vincent, Trevor and Sheila Sharman, C and R Bromage, Barry Collett, Roy Hoing, Derek Field, Jim Farmer, LYM, Mr and Mrs A H Young, Mrs M B Gregg, Pat and Tony Martin)*

COLTISHALL [TG2719]

☆ *Kings Head* NR12 7EA [Wroxham Rd (B1354)]: Welcoming dining pub close to river, good imaginative food esp fish, generous bar snacks and good value lunch deals, friendly helpful service, Adnams, good wines, open fire, fishing nets and stuffed fish inc monster pike (personable chef/landlord competes in international fishing contests); piped music; reasonably priced bedrooms, decent breakfast, moorings nearby *(BB, Andrew Gardner, Derek and Maggie Washington)*

CROMER [TG2242]

Red Lion NR27 9HD [off A149; Tucker St/Brook St]: Pubby carpeted bar in substantial Victorian hotel with elevated sea views, stripped flint and William Morris wallpaper, old bottles and chamber-pots, lots of lifeboat pictures, Adnams, Fullers London Pride and Woodfordes Wherry, friendly efficient staff, pleasant old-fashioned atmosphere, enjoyable standard food, restaurant, conservatory; tables in back courtyard, comfortable bedrooms *(MDN, B R and M F Arnold, Edward Mirzoeff)*

DERSINGHAM [TF6930]

Feathers PE31 6LN [B1440 towards Sandringham; Manor Rd]: Solid Jacobean sandstone inn with relaxed modernised dark-panelled bar, Adnams, Bass and a guest, friendly service, log fires, back eating room, more formal restaurant (not Sun evening), separate games room; children welcome, large family garden with elaborate play area, attractive secluded adults' garden with pond, comfortable well furnished bedrooms *(LYM, Tracey and Stephen Groves, Philip and Susan Philcox)*

EAST RUSTON [TG3428]

Butchers Arms NR12 9JG [back rd Horning—Happisburgh, N of Stalham]: Comfortable village local, friendly and well run, generous enjoyable food inc bargain lunchtime dish of the day, real ales, two dining rooms; attractive garden, handy for Old Vicarage garden *(Roy Hoing)*

GELDESTON [TM3990]

☆ *Locks* NR34 0HW [off A143/A146 NW of Beccles; off Station Rd S of village, obscurely signed down long rough track]: Remote candlelit pub at navigable head of River Waveney, ancient tiled-floor core with beams and big log fire, Green Jack and guest ales tapped from casks, enjoyable food, friendly informal service, large extension for summer crowds, wknd music nights; riverside garden, summer evening barbecues, open all day till late, cl Mon, Tues in winter *(LYM, P Dawn, the Didler, Alan Cole, Kirstie Bruce)*

GREAT BIRCHAM [TF7632]

☆ *Kings Head* PE31 6RJ [B1155, S end of village (called and signed Bircham locally)]: More hotel/restaurant than pub, yet with plenty of regulars and four real ales in small attractively contemporary bar with log fire and comfortable sofas; good innovative food inc lunch deals in light and airy modern restaurant, good sandwiches, house-proud staff; TV in bar; tables and chairs out front and back with rustic view, comfortable bedrooms, good breakfast (LYM, Tracey and Stephen Groves)

GREAT CRESSINGHAM [TF8401]

☆ *Windmill* IP25 6NN [village signed off A1065 S of Swaffham; Water End]: Interesting pictures and bric-a-brac in warren of rambling linked rooms, plenty of cosy corners, good value fresh bar food from baguettes to steak, three Sun roasts, log or coal fire, good changing beer range inc Windy Miller Quixote (brewed for the pub), good coffee, decent wines, plenty of malt whiskies, cheery staff, well lit pool room, pub games; piped music, big sports TV in side snug; children and dogs welcome, picnic-sets and good play area in big garden, bedroom extension (LYM, Mike and Shelley Woodroffe, Minda and Stanley Alexander, Simon and Mandy King, R C Vincent, Julian and Janet Dearden, Miss A G Drake, Gordon Neighbour, Mrs Shirley Hughes)

GREAT MASSINGHAM [TF7922]

☆ *Dabbling Duck* PE32 2HN [Abbey Rd]: Cheerful, attractive and civilised, reopened end 2006 by small group of villagers, with concise well thought out choice of good food (best to book), beers from small breweries, farm ciders, simple near-white décor, shelves of books, open fire, darts, board games, scrubbed kitchen tables in charming back dining room; children welcome, by village green with big duck ponds, three bedrooms (Tracey and Stephen Groves, Hansjoerg Landherr, Sally Anne and Peter Goodale, David Baines)

GREAT YARMOUTH [TG5206]

Red Herring NR30 3HQ [Havelock Rd]: Friendly open-plan alehouse with changing beers at attractive prices inc local Blackfriars, farm cider, rock collection, old local photographs, books to read, games area with pool; open all day wknds (the Didler)

Rumbold Arms NR31 0JX [Southtown Rd]: Neatly kept pub with good value food inc own smoked fish and Sun carvery, changing ales such as Adnams, Black Sheep and Camerons Strong Arm, huge fish tank in bar; good-sized garden with partly covered terrace, pets corner and play area (Rob Jenkins)

St Johns Head NR30 1JB [North Quay]: Traditional pub with friendly staff, four or five real ales, pool, juke box (P Dawn)

HAINFORD [TG2219]

Chequers NR10 3AY [Stratton Rd]: Comfortable and friendly rebuilt thatched cottage in charming setting, good food from baguettes up, several well kept ales, big airy bar and nicely furnished beamed dining areas; children welcome, well arranged gardens with play area (William Mack)

HARLESTON [TM2483]

J D Young IP20 9AD [Market Pl]: Refurbished hotel/pub, roomy dining lounge

area with pub atmosphere, wide range of beers, enjoyable reasonably priced food all day from 7, OAP deals, good coffee, efficient staff; bedrooms (Martin and Pauline Jennings)

Swan IP20 9AS [The Thoroughfare (narrow main st on one-way circuit, look out for narrow coach entry)]: Easy-going 16th-c coaching inn, friendly chatty locals, well kept Adnams, Greene King and guest, reasonably priced wine, decent good value food, two linked lounge rooms, ancient timbers, log fire in big inglenook, separate public bar; bedrooms (KC)

HARPLEY [TF7825]

☆ *Rose & Crown* PE31 6TW [off A148 Fakenham—Kings Lynn; Nethergate St]: Refreshing contemporary décor with local artwork and old wooden tables, good value food, interesting dishes as well as usual pubby things, friendly young staff, good choice of wines by the glass, well kept ales inc Greene King, big log fire, dining room on left; attractive garden, cl Mon, Tues lunchtime (Mrs Brenda Calver, Sally Anne and Peter Goodale, John Wooll, R C Vincent, BB)

HICKLING [TG4123]

Greyhound NR12 0YA [The Green]: Small busy pub with enjoyable food inc good Sun roasts in bar and neat restaurant, well kept ales, friendly long-serving landlord; well behaved children welcome, pretty garden with terrace tables, bedroom annexe (Robert Ager, Roy Hoing)

Pleasure Boat NR12 0YW: Spacious modern bar and fair-sized dining room in great spot – only building on short dyke at quiet end of Hickling Broad, friendly staff, Adnams Broadside and Greene King IPA, mix of sailors, bird-watchers and walkers, lots of birds, even a tiny beach; good moorings (Mrs Romey Heaton)

HOLKHAM [TF8943]

☆ *Victoria* NR23 1RG [A149 nr Holkham Hall]: Upmarket but informal small hotel, splendid place when on form (have been one or two let-downs this last year), most of ground floor opened up into quite individual linked areas, eclectic mix of furnishings inc deep low sofas, big log fire, fat lighted candles in heavy sticks, Adnams Bitter, Woodfordes Wherry and a guest beer, nice wines, good coffees, anglo-indian décor in linked dining rooms (best to book); piped music, TV; children welcome, dogs in bar, sheltered courtyard with retractable awning, walks to nature-reserve salt marshes and sea, some lovely bedrooms, open all day (Michael Dandy, Mike and Sue Loseby, Kevin Thomas, Nina Randall, LYM, Dan and Holly Pitcher, John Honnor)

HOLME NEXT THE SEA [TF7043]

White Horse PE36 6LH [Kirkgate St]: Attractive traditional pub with log fire, good value generous food inc notable fish and chips as well as more adventurous dishes, well kept real ales, small restaurant; big garden (Mr and Mrs P Bland)

HOLT [TG0738]
Feathers NR25 6BW [Market Pl]:
Unpretentious town hotel with bustling
locals' bar comfortably extended around
original panelled area with open fire,
attractive entrance/reception area with
antiques, quick friendly service, Greene King
ales, decent wines, good coffee, calm dining
room; piped music, busy on Sat market
day; dogs welcome, 15 bedrooms
*(Derek Field, Clive Flynn, John Wooll, Mr and
Mrs W W Burke, BB, Michael Tack)*
Kings Head NR25 6BN [High St/Bull St]:
Cheerful recently refurbished two-bar local,
reasonably priced fresh food all day, prompt
friendly service, four real ales inc Adnams
and Woodfordes, fair choice of wines,
pleasant dining conservatory; children
welcome, good-sized garden, may be
cl winter wkdy afternoons *(John Wooll,
Michael Tack)*
HORSEY [TG4622]
☆ *Nelson Head* NR29 4AD [off B1159; The
Street]: Friendly chatty licensees in nicely
placed simple country local with well kept
Woodfordes Wherry and Nelsons Revenge,
more-ish bar food from baguettes up, good
log fire and shiny bric-a-brac, small pleasant
side dining room, traditional games, local
pictures for sale, good-natured dog; piped
music; children welcome, garden picnic-sets,
good coast walks, open all day at least in
summer *(Tracey and Stephen Groves,
David Dickerson, LYM)*
HUNWORTH [TG0735]
Blue Bell NR24 2AA [aka Hunny Bell; signed
off B roads S of Holt]: Civilised country pub
nicely refurbished by new landlord, L-shaped
bar and flagstone dining room, wide food
choice, well kept ales, good staff; pleasant
garden with new terrace, charming village
(Charles Gysin, LYM, Derek Field)
KING'S LYNN [TF6120]
Crown & Mitre PE30 1LJ [Ferry St]:
Old-fashioned pub full of Naval and nautical
memorabilia, three or four well kept
changing ales, sandwiches and a freshly
made hot special, river views from back
conservatory *(John Wooll)*
Dukes Head PE30 1JS [Tuesday Market Pl]:
Imposing early 18th-c hotel with good value
food from baguettes to daily roast in
informal front café-bar (something of a well
run tea room in atmosphere), chatty jolly
staff, local pictures, sofas in inner lounge,
sedate back bar, more formal restaurant;
bedrooms *(Glenwys and Alan Lawrence,
John Wooll)*
Lloyds No 1 PE30 1EZ [King St/Tuesday
Market Pl]: Neatly kept Wetherspoons
popular in daytime for bargain food, good
beer and wine choice, efficient friendly
service; children welcome till 7, attractive
back garden down to river, pleasant
bedrooms, good value breakfast *(John Wooll,
David Carr)*
Wildfowler PE30 4EL [Gayton Rd, Gaywood]:
Neat, comfortable and relaxed even when

busy, enjoyable reasonably priced fresh food
in comfortable lounge bar and restaurant,
good beer range; garden tables *(Barry and
Sue Pladdys)*
LESSINGHAM [TG3928]
Star NR12 0DN [School Rd]: Small and
welcoming, with big inglenook and another
open fire, comfortable armchairs, low
ceilings, good beer and wine choice, good
side restaurant (not Mon/Tues lunchtime)
where chef/landlord uses only local produce;
dogs welcome, two bedrooms in back block
(Alison Bilyard)
LETHERINGSETT [TG0638]
Kings Head NR25 7AR [Holt Rd (A148)]:
A boon for young families, with plenty of
tables on extensive lawn, summer brass or
jazz bands, relaxed open-plan bar with sepia
prints of Norfolk life, prominent Union flags,
log fire, genial landlord, small lounge, games
room; piped music, live rock/blues winter
Sat night; dogs welcome, open all day
(R C Vincent, LYM, Clive Flynn, Simon Rodway)
MARLINGFORD [TG1309]
Bell NR9 5HX [Bawburgh Rd off Mill Rd]:
Friendly country local with enjoyable food
inc quickly served daily lunchtime carvery,
real ales such as Fullers London Pride and
Greene King, nicely furnished tiled-floor bar,
carpeted lounge and dining extension;
children and dogs welcome, terrace picnic-
sets *(Eugene Charlier)*
NORTH TUDDENHAM [TG0413]
Lodge NR20 3DJ [off A47]: Recently
refurbished as comfortable dining pub,
enjoyable home-made food from all-day bar
menu to more restauranty evening dishes,
local real ales, welcoming atmosphere; tables
outside, open all day, cl Sun evening *(anon)*
NORTH WOOTTON [TF6424]
House on the Green PE30 3RE [Ling Common
Rd]: Tidy and roomy, with enjoyable food
from baguettes up, basic garden menu, good
choice of well kept beers, friendly if not
always speedy service; children welcome,
lots of tables out on back terrace and lawn,
bowling green and some play equipment
(R C Vincent)
NORWICH [TG2108]
Alexandra NR2 3BB [Stafford St]:
Comfortable two-bar local with well kept
Chalk Hill and guest ales, friendly efficient
service, cheap home-made food, open fire,
pool, classic juke box; open all day
(the Didler)
Cidershed NR3 4LF [Lawson Rd]: Brewpub
under same ownership as Fat Cat, producing
its good ales, with many guests; interesting
layout, secondhand books, frequent live
music inc Sun jazz; open all day *(the Didler)*
Coach & Horses NR1 1BA [Thorpe Rd]: Light
and airy tap for Chalk Hill brewery, guest
beers too, friendly staff, good choice of
generous home cooking 12-9 (8 Sun), also
breakfast, bare-boards L-shaped bar with
open fire, dark wood, posters and prints,
pleasant back dining area; sports TV;
disabled access possible (not to lavatories),

front terrace, may be barbecues, open all day *(Dr and Mrs A K Clarke, the Didler)*

Duke of Wellington NR3 1EG [Waterloo Rd]: Great changing choice of well kept ales (some tapped from the cask) and foreign bottled beers in friendly rambling local, real fire, traditional games, Tues folk night; nice back terrace, Aug beer festival, open all day *(the Didler)*

☆ **Eagle** NR2 2HN [Eagle Walk/Newmarket Rd (A11)]: Attractive and comfortable, with sensible choice of good food, freshly made so takes a while, good ale range, friendly staff, second upstairs restaurant; pleasant lawn and play area, open all day *(Anthony Barnes)*

☆ **Kings Arms** NR1 3HQ [Hall Rd]: Woody Batemans local with lots of changing guest beers, good whisky and wine choice, brewery memorabilia, friendly landlord and atmosphere, may be lunchtime food (or bring your own or order out – plates, cutlery provided), airy garden room; unobtrusive sports TV; vines in courtyard, open all day *(the Didler)*

Kings Head NR3 1JE [Magdalen St]: Handsome Victorian-style renovation, up to 14 handpumps for well kept changing regional ales and a local farm cider, good choice of imported beers, enthusiastic landlord; open all day *(the Didler, Bruce Bird)*

Ribs of Beef NR3 1HY [Wensum St, S side of Fye Bridge]: Well used old pub, good range of real ales inc local brews, farm cider, good wine choice, deep leather settees and small tables upstairs, attractive smaller downstairs room with river view and some local river paintings, generous cheap food (till 5 Sat/Sun), quick friendly service; tables out on narrow riverside walkway *(John Wooll, John Cook)*

Trafford Arms NR1 3RL [Grove Rd, off A11/A140 Ipswich rd]: Large estate-type local with eight or more well kept ales, decent freshly made food (not Sun evening), pool; open all day *(the Didler)*

Wig & Pen NR3 1RN [St Martins Palace Plain]: Friendly beamed bar opp cathedral close, lawyer and judge prints, roaring stove, prompt generous food, Adnams, Buffys and guests, good value wines, staff who take an interest; piped music; terrace tables, open all day, cl Sun evening *(the Didler)*

OLD HUNSTANTON [TF6842]

Ancient Mariner PE36 6JJ [part of L'Estrange Arms Hotel, Golf Course Rd]: Cheerful rambling barn conversion, low beams, timbers, bare bricks, flagstones and maritime bric-a-brac, several little areas inc conservatory and upstairs family gallery, popular food from good sandwiches to fish, well kept Adnams and Woodfordes, good coffee and wines by the glass, courteous and efficient young staff, open fires, papers and magazines; racy piped music; hotel in prime spot, terrace and long sea-view garden down to dunes, children welcome, play area, nice

bedrooms, open all day Fri-Sun and summer *(Tracey and Stephen Groves, Bruce Bird)*

OVERSTRAND [TG2440]

White Horse NR27 0AB [High St]: Smart new art deco refurbishment, comfortable and stylish, with Greene King IPA, enjoyable up-to-date food in bar and restaurant, friendly staff; tables outside, newly done bedrooms *(anon)*

REEPHAM [TG0922]

☆ **Old Brewery House** NR10 4JJ [Market Sq]: Georgian hotel with big log fire in high-ceilinged panelled bar overlooking old-fashioned town square, farming and fishing bric-a-brac, changing ales inc Adnams, decent wines by the glass, attentive friendly staff, reasonably priced food from well filled sandwiches up, side lounge, dining area, public bar and restaurant; piped music; children and dogs welcome, tables in attractive courtyard with covered well and garden with pond and fountain, bedrooms, open all day *(John Wooll, the Didler, LYM)*

RUSHALL [TM1982]

☆ **Half Moon** IP21 4QD [The Street]: Hearty traditional food inc plenty of fish and big puddings (two sittings, 6 and 8.30, if you book), close-set tables on bare boards or brick flooring in chatty beamed bar, more space in picture-window carpeted dining room (children welcome here), Adnams, Boddingtons and Woodfordes Wherry, good friendly service, inglenook log fire; unobtrusive piped music; back brick terrace, neat grass beyond, simple good value separate motel block *(BB, Ian and Nita Cooper)*

SALTHOUSE [TG0743]

☆ **Dun Cow** NR25 7XA [A149 Blakeney—Sheringham; Purdy St]: Airy pub overlooking salt marshes, generous unpretentious food all day from good fresh crab sandwiches to local fish, fast friendly service, Adnams and Woodfordes, decent wines, open fires, high 18th-c rafters and cob walls in big main bar, family bar and games room with pool; piped radio, blues nights; coast views from attractive walled front garden, sheltered courtyard with figs and apples, separate family garden with play area, good walks and bird-watching, bedrooms and self-catering *(Derek Field, Tracey and Stephen Groves, Roy Hoing, John Millwood, Jim Farmer, David Rule, BB, David Eberlin, William Mack)*

SCULTHORPE [TF8930]

SEDGEFORD [TF7036]

☆ **King William IV** PE36 5LU [B1454, off A149 Kings Lynn—Hunstanton]: Friendly and roomy, with hard-working obliging staff, good value mainly traditional food, well chosen ales and wines, convivial panelled bar and expanded dining areas, warm woodburner; charming partly covered terrace, nice bedrooms (five more planned), good breakfast *(Tracey and Stephen Groves, Len Beattie, Mr and Mrs A Hetherington)*

SHERINGHAM [TG1543]

☆ **Lobster** NR26 8JP [High St]: Almost on seafront, seafaring décor in tidy panelled bar with old sewing-machine treadle tables and warm fire, well kept changing ales (ten in summer, dozens – and hog roasts – at bank hols), farm ciders, bottled belgians, good value quickly served generous bar meals (helpful with special diet needs), restaurant with good seafood, public bar with games inc pool; dogs on leads allowed, two courtyards, heated marquee, open all day *(Len Beattie, David Carr, Jerry Brown, Fred and Lorraine Gill, M J Winterton, Dr and Mrs P Truelove)*

Wyndham Arms NR26 8BA [Wyndham St]: Comfortable low-beamed lounge bar with real fire, good food with greek influences (chef/landlord is Greek), sensible prices, well kept ales inc Adnams and Woodfordes, cheap house wine, quick friendly service, restaurant; pool and piped music in busy public bar; courtyard picnic-sets, nr seafront, open all day *(Len Beattie)*

SKEYTON [TG2524]
Goat NR10 5DH [off A140 N of Aylsham; Long Rd]: Extended thatched and low-beamed food pub, good choice, well kept ales, good service, long dark-raftered dining area and small restaurant; pleasant terrace and tables under trees by pub's neat playing field – very quiet spot *(BB, Dr and Mrs R G J Telfer, Brian and Jean Hepworth)*

SMALLBURGH [TG3324]
☆ **Crown** NR12 9AD: 15th-c thatched and beamed village inn with friendly proper landlord, old-fashioned pub atmosphere, well kept Adnams and Black Sheep, good choice of wines by the glass, straightforward home-made food in bar and upstairs dining room, prompt service, daily papers, darts; no dogs or children inside; picnic-sets in sheltered and pretty back garden, bedrooms, cl Mon lunchtime, Sun evening *(Philip and Susan Philcox, Dr and Mrs P Truelove, BB)*

SOUTH LOPHAM [TM0481]
White Horse IP22 2LH [A1066 Diss—Thetford; The Street]: Cheerful beamed pub with enjoyable home-made food from good sandwiches up, good staff, well kept Adnams and Greene King; big garden, bedrooms, handy for Bressingham Gardens *(C Galloway)*

SOUTH WOOTTON [TF6622]
Farmers Arms PE30 3HQ [part of Knights Hill Hotel, Grimston Rd (off A148/A149)]: Hotel complex's olde-worlde barn and stables conversion, speedily served food all day, real ales inc Adnams and Fullers, good wines, abundant coffee, polite efficient service, stripped brick and timbers, quiet snugs and corners; piped music; children welcome, tables and play area outside, comfortable bedrooms, open all day *(R C Vincent, Tracey and Stephen Groves)*

Swan PE30 3NG [Nursery Lane]: Popular local overlooking village green, duckpond and bowling green, generous food in bar and conservatory restaurant, well kept ales inc Greene King; small enclosed garden with play area *(R C Vincent)*

STANHOE [TF8037]
☆ **Crown** PE31 8QD [B1155 towards Burnham Mkt]: Nice simple open-plan local with genial no-nonsense long-serving ex-RAF landlord, good value straightforward food (not Sun evening or Mon) cooked by his friendly wife, aircraft pictures, gas masks, guns, various military headgear, log fire, beams and joists (one beam densely studded with coins), Elgoods beers; well-behaved children and dogs allowed, side lawn and bigger one behind with room for caravans, may be free-running chickens *(R C Vincent, Sue Crees, J S Hurst, David Carr, LYM)*

STOKE HOLY CROSS [TG2302]
☆ **Wildebeest** NR14 8QJ [Norwich Rd]: Emphasis on good interesting bistro-style food but provision for drinkers in attractive old bar, good beer and wine by the glass, efficient friendly service, unusual decorations inc african wooden masks; shame about the piped music; delightful garden, well lit heated terrace with huge parasols *(J F M and M West, Roger and Lesley Everett, Sue Demont, Tim Barrow)*

TERRINGTON ST JOHN [TF5314]
☆ **Woolpack** PE14 7RR [off A47 W of King's Lynn]: Now run by son of former cheerful landlady, still with bright modern ceramics and contemporary prints, red plush banquettes, wheelbacks, dark pub tables, large back dining room, Greene King IPA and a couple of guest beers, pubby food, games machine, piped music; children allowed if eating, picnic-sets on neat grass, good disabled access *(LYM)*

THORNHAM [TF7343]
Orange Tree PE36 6NJ [Church St]: Pale wood furnishings in neatly updated beamed dining pub, bright and smart, with enjoyable contemporary food (all afternoon Sun) inc local seafood, very good choice of wines by the glass; good-sized garden with play area, six newish courtyard bedrooms *(Virginia Williams)*

TIVETSHALL ST MARY [TM1785]
☆ **Old Ram** NR15 2DE [A140, outside village]: New licensee for much extended popular dining pub, spacious country-style main room, lots of stripped beams and standing timbers, huge log fire, rosy brick floors, several smaller side areas, woodburner in dining room, second dining room and gallery, Adnams, Woodfordes Wherry and guest beers, quite a few wines by glass; piped music, games machine, TV; children welcome, sheltered heated terrace, comfortable bedrooms, open all day; more reports on new regime please *(LYM)*

UPWELL [TF5002]
Five Bells PE14 9AA [New Rd]: Under new management, wide choice of good value bar food (not Sun evening) inc enterprising dishes, Greene King and Woodfordes Wherry, decent short wine choice, restaurant (not Mon/Tues) *(Dr Malcolm Bridge)*

WEASENHAM ST PETER [TF8522]
Fox & Hounds PE32 2TD [A1065 Fakenham—

Swaffham; The Green]: 18th-c, with good range of beers inc Marstons Pedigree, bargain bar food, chatty landlord, restaurant; children welcome, nice garden *(Derek Field)*

WELLS-NEXT-THE-SEA [TF9143]

Bowling Green NR23 1JB [Church St]: Unpretentious 17th-c pub, L-shaped bar with flagstone and brick floor, good friendly staff, Greene King and Woodfordes ales, good value fresh traditional food, corner settles, two woodburners, raised dining end; tables on back terrace, quiet spot on outskirts *(David Carr, John Wooll, Eddie and Lynn Jarrett, Len Beattie, John Beeken)*

Edinburgh NR23 1AE [Station Rd/Church St]: Traditional pub with affordable pubby food from interesting filled rolls to good home-made puddings, Hancocks and Woodfordes, sizeable restaurant, local photographs for sale; piped music, no credit cards; children treated well, partly covered back courtyard, three bedrooms *(Mike Ridgway, Sarah Miles, Len Beattie, John Beeken, David Carr)*

WEST ACRE [TF7815]

Stag PE32 1TR [Low Rd]: Good choice of well kept changing ales in appealing local's unpretentious small bar, cheerful staff, good value limited food, neat dining room; attractive spot in quiet village, cl Mon *(BB, Tracey and Stephen Groves, Mark, Amanda, Luke and Jake Sheard)*

WEYBOURNE [TG1143]

Ship NR25 7SZ [The Street (A149 W of Sheringham)]: Wide choice of enterprising food (not Sun evening) inc OAP lunchtime specials and local game, friendly staff, Adnams and other ales, decent wines by the glass, big comfortably straightforward bar and two dining rooms; unobtrusive piped music; garden tables and tearoom, cl Mon *(Tony Middis, Derek Field)*

WIGHTON [TF9439]

☆ *Carpenters Arms* NR23 1PF [High St – off main rd, past church]: Cheerful chef doing enjoyable rather individual food inc lunchtime sandwiches, friendly service, Adnams, Woodfordes and a local beer bottled for them, leather sofas, brightly painted tables and chairs, mulberry dining room; picnic-sets in informal back garden *(BB, MDN)*

WRETHAM [TL9290]

Dog & Partridge IP24 1QS [Watton Rd; A1057]: Small country local reopened by friendly helpful landlady, enjoyable pubby food from baguettes up *(Paul J Robinshaw, Hugh and Anne Pinnock)*

WYMONDHAM [TG1001]

☆ *Green Dragon* NR18 0PH [Church Street]: Picturesque heavily timbered 14th-c inn, cosy unsmart beamed and timbered back bar, log fire under Tudor mantelpiece, interesting pictures, bigger dining area (children allowed), friendly helpful staff, Adnams and a guest beer, food inc fresh fish and good veg; children and dogs welcome, modest bedrooms, nr glorious 12th-c abbey church *(the Didler, LYM, P M Newsome, Mr and Mrs W W Burke)*

'Children welcome' means the pub says it lets children inside without any special restriction; some may impose an evening time limit earlier than 9pm – please tell us if you find this.

Northamptonshire

Northamptonshire has quite a number of fine pubs, run with real flair. Two of these this year gain our Food Award. The Falcon at Fotheringhay had a fine reputation as a civilised dining pub under former licensees. So we have been watching the progress of the present incumbents with particular interest, and are very pleased to confirm that the Falcon is indeed a good choice for a special meal out. The medieval Queens Head at Bulwick is a classic english pub, run with enthusiastic verve, and with plenty of local regulars and good drinks. Its robustly flavoured largely local food wins it not only a Food Award, but also the title of Northamptonshire Dining Pub of the Year. The county does even better when it comes to Beer Awards, with nearly half the main entries here sporting one. The ancient Fox & Hounds/Althorp Coaching Inn at Great Brington turns over a good selection of interesting guest beers as part of its impressive range of nine real ales, and the half-dozen beers at the Samuel Pepys at Slipton (a great all-rounder) are well sourced too. The cosy Great Western Arms at Aynho, the reliable and friendly Red Lion at Crick and the interesting Olde Sun at Nether Heyford all deserve a special mention as places which have that splendid knack of making people with widely different attitudes and tastes all feel well rewarded. A few pubs in the Lucky Dip section at the end of the chapter also stand out in that way: the New Inn at Buckby Wharf, White Swan at Harringworth, Saracens Head at Little Brington, Snooty Fox at Lowick and Malt Shovel in Northampton. The county has several worthwhile small breweries. Digfield, started quite recently, is coming to the fore with its distinctive beers. Others we have found locally this year, in rough order of frequency, are Frog Island, Great Oakley, Hoggleys, Potbelly, Rockingham and Nobbys.

AYNHO
SP4932 MAP 4

Great Western Arms
Just off B4031 W, towards Deddington; Aynho Wharf, Station Road; OX17 3BP

Civilised and attractive old pub, interesting railway memorabilia, well liked food, and moorings

The rather plain creeper-covered exterior of this much enjoyed pub gives little clue to its cosily inviting interior. Its series of linked rambling rooms is divided enough to give an intimate feel, and the golden stripped stone of some walling tones well with warm cream and deep red plasterwork. Fine furnishings include good solid country tables and regional chairs on broad flagstones and a homely log fire warms cosy seats in two of the areas. There are candles and fresh flowers throughout as well as daily papers and glossy magazines and readers enjoy the extensive GWR collection which includes lots of steam locomotive photographs; the dining area on the right is rather elegant. They have well kept Hook Norton and a guest on handpump, and good wines by the glass; service is welcoming and attentive; piped music. Opening out of the main bar, the former stable courtyard behind has white cast-iron tables and chairs and there are moorings and a marina nearby. The bedrooms here are comfortable but they don't serve breakfast.

🍽 **Lots of seafood and fish dishes feature amongst the freshly made food, which might include fried sardines, whitebait, sausage and mash, various pasta dishes, vegetable risotto, steak and kidney pie, kedgeree, grilled tuna with vegetable salsa, bass with red pepper sauce and rack of lamb with honey and rosemary.** *Starters/Snacks: £5.50 to £9.95. Main Courses: £7.95 to £16.95. Puddings: £3.95 to £6.75*

Hook Norton ~ Lease Frank Baldwin ~ Real ale ~ Bar food ~ Restaurant ~ (01869) 338288 ~ Dogs allowed in bar and bedrooms ~ Open 12-3, 6-11 ~ Bedrooms: £65B/£75B

Recommended by George Atkinson, Sir Nigel Foulkes, D A Bradford, Stuart Turner, Susan Crabbe, Charles and Pauline Stride, N R White, Trevor and Judith Pearson, Michael Sargent, Gerry and Rosemary Dobson

BADBY
SP5558   MAP 4

Windmill

Village signposted off A361 Daventry—Banbury; NN11 3AN

Homely thatched country dining pub with popular food and friendly service

The thatch hangs low over golden stone walls and snug little windows at this welcoming 300 year old pub. Inside, its two beamed and flagstoned bars have a nice country feel with an unusual woodburning stove in an enormous tiled inglenook fireplace, simple but good solid wood country furnishings, and cricketing and rugby pictures. There's also a comfortably cosy lounge. Cheery staff and licensees serve Bass, Flowers Original, Timothy Taylors Landlord and a guest such as Fullers London Pride from handpumps, and they've good fairly priced wines by the bottle. The brightly lit carpeted restaurant has a more modern feel; quiet piped music and TV. There's a pleasant terrace out by the green of this attractive ironstone village, and a nice path leads south through Badby Wood (carpeted with bluebells in spring) to a landscaped lake near Fawsley Hall.

🍽 **It can get full here so it is worth booking. Very decent bar food includes sandwiches, vegetable or beef lasagne, chilli, battered cod, pie of the day, steaks and daily specials.** *Starters/Snacks: £4.95 to £9.95. Main Courses: £5.95 to £13.95. Puddings: £4.25*

Free house ~ Licensees John Freestone and Carol Sutton ~ Real ale ~ Bar food (12-2(3 Sun), 6.30-9.30(9 Sun)) ~ Restaurant ~ (01327) 702363 ~ Children welcome ~ Dogs allowed in bar and bedrooms ~ Open 11.30-3, 5.30-11.30; 11.30am-12 midnight Sat; 12-11.30 Sun ~ Bedrooms: £59.50B/£72.50B

Recommended by George Atkinson, George Cowie, Frances Gosnell, Dennis and Gill Keen, John and Joyce Snell, Dave Braisted, Nigel and Sue Foster, Mr and Mrs W W Burke, Trevor and Judith Pearson

BULWICK
SP9694   MAP 4

Queens Head

Just off A43 Kettering—Duddington; NN17 3DY

NORTHAMPTONSHIRE DINING PUB OF THE YEAR

Ancient pub with cheery involved licensees; interesting beers, popular heartily flavoured food including game

A genuine happy love of all things country filters down from the enthusiastic licensees through all aspects of this lovely 600-year-old stone cottage row. Whilst its unaltered appearance and character remain those of a delightfully traditional village local (bellringers pop in after their Wednesday practice, and the darts and dominoes teams are very active), there's something extra here too. Thoughtfully sourced beers – well kept and served from a stone bar counter – include Shepherd Neame Spitfire, with three interesting guests from brewers such as Blythe, Elland and the very local Rockingham. The good wine list includes interesting bin-ends (nine by the glass), and they've over 25 malt whiskies. The timeless beamed bar has stone floors and a fire in a stone hearth at one end; darts, shove-ha'penny, dominoes and piped music. This is an attractive bypassed village in an area where you may be lucky enough to see red kites, and there can be few more pleasant experiences than a summer evening on the garden terrace (with its own well) listening to swallows and martins, sheep in the adjacent field and bells ringing in the nearby church.

⊞ The changing menu uses traditional european cooking methods and robustly flavoured ingredients, and much of the game served here is caught by the landlord. Dishes might include lunchtime sandwiches, pressed ox tongue with watercress salad, smoked eel with shaved fennel and lemon and horseradish crème fraîche, pork collar cooked in milk with cannellini beans and savoy cabbage, sausage and mash with onion and grainy mustard sauce, confit of duck leg with wilted greens and puy lentil and italian sausage cassoulet, steaks, and puddings such as chocolate terrine with caramel sauce or lemon polenta cake with lemon and vanilla syrup. *Starters/Snacks: £4.95 to £9.95. Main Courses: £9.95 to £20.95. Puddings: £4.95 to £5.95*

Free house ~ Licensee Geoff Smith ~ Real ale ~ Bar food (12-2.30, 6-9.30; not Sun evening) ~ Restaurant ~ (01780) 450272 ~ Children welcome away from bar ~ Dogs allowed in bar ~ Open 12-3, 6-11(7-10.30 Sun); closed Mon

Recommended by Ian Stafford, Michael and Jenny Back, Mike and Sue Losebey, Noel Grundy, Howard and Margaret Buchanan, Fred and Lorraine Gill, Val and Alan Green, Ian Judge, J C M Troughton, Tracey and Stephen Groves

CRICK   SP5872   MAP 4

Red Lion ◄ £

1 mile from M1 junction 18; in centre of village off A428; NN6 7TX

Nicely worn-in friendly coaching inn off M1 with good value straightforward lunchtime food and pricier more detailed evening menu

Not elaborate but very reliable, this old stone thatched pub is favoured by readers for its welcoming atmosphere and sensible prices. The cosy low-ceilinged bar is nice and traditional with lots of comfortable seating, some rare old horsebrasses, pictures of the pub in the days before it was surrounded by industrial estates, and a tiny log stove in a big inglenook. Four well kept beers on handpump include Wells & Youngs Bombardier, Greene King Old Speckled Hen, Theakstons Best and a guest from a brewer such as Sharpes. There are a few picnic-sets under parasols on grass by the car park, and in summer you can eat on the terrace in the old coachyard which is sheltered by a Perspex roof and decorated with lots of pretty hanging baskets.

⊞ Homely bar food includes sandwiches and ploughman's, chicken and mushroom pie, leek and smoky bacon bake, plaice and vegetable pancake rolls. Prices go up a little in the evening when they offer a wider range of dishes that might include stuffed salmon fillet, lamb shank, half a roast duck and sirloin steak; puddings such as lemon meringue pie; bargain-price Sunday roast. *Starters/Snacks: £2.20 to £3.60. Main Courses: £4.75 to £14.00. Puddings: £2.25 to £3.00*

Wellington ~ Tenants Tom and Paul Marks ~ Real ale ~ Bar food (12-2, 6.30-9; not Sun evening) ~ (01788) 822342 ~ Children under 14 welcome lunchtimes only ~ Dogs welcome ~ Open 11-2.30, 6.15-11; 12-3, 7-10.30 Sun

Recommended by George Atkinson, Dr and Mrs A K Clarke, Mrs Margaret Ball, Ian and Denise Foster, Edward Leetham, Ted George, Michael Dandy, JJW, CMW, Charles and Pauline Stride, Denis Newton, Mr and Mrs Staples, A R Mascall

EAST HADDON   SP6668   MAP 4

Red Lion

High Street; village signposted off A428 (turn right in village) and off A50 N of Northampton; NN6 8BU

Appealingly old hotel with very pleasant grounds and good food

The single spacious lounge bar at this rather smart substantially-built golden stone inn is split into drinking and dining areas. It's traditionally furnished with dark wood tables and chairs on green carpet, has attractive white-painted panelling with recessed china cabinets, a few old prints, and some beams. Well trained staff serve Courage Directors and Wells & Youngs Bombardier and Eagle from handpump and decent wines with about seven by the glass. The walled side garden is pretty with lilac, fruit trees, roses and neat flowerbeds. It leads back to the bigger lawn, which has well spaced picnic-sets. A small side terrace has more tables under parasols, and a big copper beech shades the gravel car park.

🍴 As well as filled baguettes, bar food might include crispy duck spring rolls, stilton mushrooms with basil pesto, braised lamb shank with red wine sauce, seafood mixed grill, baked choux pastry bun on mushrooms and spinach with hollandaise sauce and puddings such as bakewell tart. *Starters/Snacks: £3.95 to £6.95. Main Courses: £9.95 to £16.95. Puddings: £4.95*

Charles Wells ~ Lease Nick Bonner ~ Real ale ~ Bar food (12-2.30, 6-10; 12-7 Sun) ~ Restaurant ~ (01604) 770223 ~ Children in eating area of bar ~ Open 12-2.30, 5.30-11; 12-7.30 Sun; closed Sun evening ~ Bedrooms: £60S/£75S

Recommended by Gerry and Rosemary Dobson, R W Allen, George Atkinson, Ron and Sheila Corbett, Mrs B Barwick, Michael Dandy, Mrs E A Macdonald

EYDON   SP5450   MAP 7

Royal Oak

Lime Avenue; village signed off A361 Daventry—Banbury, and from B4525; NN11 3PG

Enjoyable low-beamed old place with good lunchtime snacks and imaginative evening menu

This attractive 300-year-old ironstone inn retains plenty of original features, including fine flagstone floors and leaded windows. The room on the right has cushioned wooden benches built into alcoves, seats in a bow window, some cottagey pictures, and an open fire in an inglenook fireplace. The bar counter (with bar stools) runs down a long central flagstoned corridor room and links several other small characterful rooms. An attractive covered terrace with hardwood furniture is a lovely place for a meal in fine weather. Friendy staff serve well kept Fullers London Pride, Greene King IPA, Timothy Taylors Landlord and a guest, usually from Archers, by handpump; piped music and table skittles. More reports please.

🍴 The lunchtime menu is fairy pubby, with maybe baguettes, smoked salmon plate, fishcakes and steak. More elaborate evening items might include starters such as curried parsnip soup with onion bhaji, seared pepper crusted venison fillet, main courses such as spicy vegetable tagine, fish and chips, roast shin of beef with root vegetables, red wine and thyme and beef fillet with stilton soufflé and cumberland sauce; Sunday roast. *Starters/Snacks: £4.95 to £6.50. Main Courses: £15.50. Puddings: £4.50*

Free house ~ Licensee Justin Lefevre ~ Real ale ~ Bar food ~ (01327) 263167 ~ Children welcome ~ Dogs welcome ~ Open 12-2.30, 6-11; 12-3, 7-10.30 Sun; closed Mon lunchtime

Recommended by Dave Braisted, Steve Piggott, RJH

FARTHINGSTONE   SP6155   MAP 4

Kings Arms 🍺

Off A5 SE of Daventry; village signposted from Litchborough on former B4525 (now declassified); NN12 8EZ

Individual place with carefully sourced regional foods, cosy traditional interior and lovely gardens; note limited opening times

Given that they serve food just a couple of sessions a week, the friendly licensee couple at this quirky gargoyle-embellished stone 18th-c country pub must be having some success at keeping it at the heart of the local community – they run regular quiz nights and even the occasional debating evening. The timelessly intimate flagstoned bar has a huge log fire, comfortable homely sofas and armchairs near the entrance, whisky-water jugs hanging from oak beams, and lots of pictures and decorative plates on the walls. A games room at the far end has darts, dominoes, cribbage, table skittles and board games. Thwaites Original and Wells & Youngs are well kept on handpump alongside a guest such as St Austell Tinners, the short wine list is quite decent, and they have a few country wines. Look out for the interesting newspaper-influenced décor in the outside gents'. The tranquil terrace is charmingly decorated with hanging baskets, flower and herb pots and plant-filled painted tractor tyres. They grow their own salad vegetables and there's a cosy little terrace by the herb garden. The list of retail food produce on sale – cheeses, cured and fresh meat and cured and fresh fish – are sourced for their originality of style, methods of rearing and smoking or organic farming methods. This is a picturesque village, and there are good walks including the Knightley Way. It's worth ringing ahead to check the opening and food serving times as the licensees are sometimes away unexpectedly. More reports please.

🍴 **Bar food might include soup, good filled baguettes, ploughman's, loch fyne fish platter and a british cheese platter, with a couple of main courses such as yorkshire pudding filled with steak and kidney or game casserole and cumbrian wild boar sausage and mash.** *Starters/Snacks: £4.25 to £6.75. Main Courses: £6.25 to £9.50. Puddings: £4.25 to £4.95*

Free house ~ Licensees Paul and Denise Egerton ~ Real ale ~ Bar food (12-2 Sat, Sun only) ~ No credit cards ~ (01327) 361604 ~ Children welcome ~ Dogs welcome ~ Open 7(6.30 Fri)-11; 12-3.30, 7-11.30 Sat; 12-4, 9-11 Sun; closed Mon, weekday lunchtimes and Weds evenings

Recommended by Pete Baker, George Atkinson

FOTHERINGHAY
TL0593   MAP 5

Falcon

Village signposted off A605 on Peterborough side of Oundle; PE8 5HZ

Upmarket dining pub, good food from snacks up, good range of drinks and attractive garden

The neatly kept little bar at this civilised pub is sedately furnished with cushioned slatback arm and bucket chairs, good winter log fires in a stone fireplace, and fresh flower arrangements. The conservatory restaurant is pretty, and if the weather's nice the attractively planted garden is particularly enjoyable. Though the main draw is dining, there is a thriving little locals' tap bar (and darts team) if you do just want a drink. The very good range of drinks includes three changing beers from brewers such as Digfield, Greene King IPA and Oakham on handpump, good wines (20 by the glass), organic cordials and fresh orange juice. The vast church behind is worth a visit, and the ruined Fotheringhay Castle, where Mary Queen of Scots was executed, is not far away.

🍴 **As well as imaginative sandwiches, thoughtful (if not cheap) bar food might include cauliflower and cheese soup, prawns cooked in garlic with mango, coconut and lime salad, grilled chicken breast with tarragon pasta and mushroom and sweetcorn broth, fried bream with cherry vine tomato and crab risotto, fillet steak with roast root vegetables and shallot and red wine jus and puddings such as treacle tart, spiced poached pear with caramel meringue and a cheese platter.** *Starters/Snacks: £5.25 to £5.95. Main Courses: £8.95 to £9.95. Puddings: £4.75 to £6.25*

Free house ~ Licensees Sally Facer and Jim Jeffries ~ Real ale ~ Bar food (12-2.15, 6.15-9.15; 12-3, 6.15-8.30 Sun) ~ Restaurant ~ (01832) 226254 ~ Children welcome ~ Dogs allowed in bar ~ Open 12-3, 6-11; 12-11 Sat; 12-10.30 Sun

Recommended by Mike and Sue Loseby, Jim Farmer, Keith and Sue Campbell, Noel Grundy, Howard and Margaret Buchanan, Oliver and Sue Rowell, O K Smyth, Bruce and Sharon Eden

---

Bedroom prices normally include full english breakfast, VAT and any inclusive service charge that we know of. Prices before the '/' are for single rooms, after for two people in double or twin (B includes a private bath, S a private shower). If there is no '/', the prices are only for twin or double rooms (as far as we know there are no singles). If there is no B or S, as far as we know no rooms have private facilities.

GREAT BRINGTON   SP6664   MAP 4

Fox & Hounds/Althorp Coaching Inn 🍺

Off A428 NW of Northampton, near Althorp Hall; NN7 4JA

Friendly golden stone thatched pub with great choice of real ales, tasty food, sheltered garden

'An olde worlde haven, often with a dog or two sprawled out' is the description one reader gives of the ancient bar at this cosy old coaching inn. It has all the features you'd expect of such a place, from old beams and saggy joists to an attractive mix of country chairs and tables (maybe with fresh flowers) on its broad flagstones and bare boards. Also plenty of snug alcoves, nooks and crannies, some stripped pine shutters and panelling, two fine log fires, and an eclectic medley of bric-a-brac from farming implements to an old typewriter and country pictures. A cellarish games room down some steps has a view of the casks in the cellar. Cheery staff serve the splendid range of nine real ales which include Greene King IPA, Abbot and Old Speckled Hen and Fullers London Pride, with up to five thoughtfully sourced guests from brewers such as Brewsters, Church End, Hoggleys (local to them), and they've about a dozen wines by the glass and a dozen malt whiskies; piped music. The coach entry from the road opens into a lovely little paved courtyard with sheltered tables and tubs of flowers, and there is more seating in the side garden.

🍴 Tasty bar food includes sandwiches and baguettes, pork and chicken liver pâté, grilled goats cheese croûton with roast onion coulis, leek and cheese macaroni, beef and Guinness casserole, lamb tagine, cajun chicken salad, grilled salmon with cream, white wine and chive sauce, sirloin steak, and puddings such as summer pudding and walnut and almond sponge. *Starters/Snacks: £4.25 to £5.95. Main Courses: £4.75 to £7.95. Puddings: £3.95 to £4.25*

Free house ~ Licensee Jacqui Ellard ~ Real ale ~ Bar food (12-2.30(3 Sat, Sun) 6.30-9.30) ~ Restaurant ~ (01604) 770164 ~ Dogs allowed in bar ~ Open 11am-12 midnight; 12-10.30 Sun

Recommended by Alain and Rose Foote, Trevor and Judith Pearson, George Atkinson, Michael Dandy, David and Sue Atkinson, Chris and Jeanne Downing

GREAT OXENDON   SP7383   MAP 4

George 🍷 🛏

A508 S of Market Harborough; LE16 8NA

Elegant 16th-c pub with emphasis on dining (you may need to book); garden and comfortable bedrooms

Dark walls, dark brown panelled dado, green leatherette bucket chairs around little tables, and a big log fire give the bar at this well run inn the intimate feel of a cosy gentleman's club – and the very helpful staff wouldn't be amiss in such an environment. The entrance lobby has easy chairs and a former inn-sign, and the turkey-carpeted conservatory overlooks a well tended shrub-sheltered garden; piped easy-listening music. The gents' lavatories are entertainingly decked out with rather stylish naughty pictures. Well kept Adnams and a guest such as Timothy Taylors Landlord on handpump, a dozen or so wines by the glass and around 15 malts.

🍴 Good bar food includes soup, gruyère fritters with cranberry sauce, fish and meat cold platters, filled baguettes, sausage and mash, thai vegetable curry in a filo tart, cod, chips and mushy peas, honey-roast lamb shank, duck breast with plum sauce, steaks and puddings such as chocolate fondant or bread and butter pudding; two or three-course Sunday lunch. *Starters/Snacks: £4.50 to £7.95. Main Courses: £10.95 to £17.95. Puddings: £4.75 to £5.75*

Free house ~ Licensee David Dudley ~ Real ale ~ Bar food (12-2, 6-9.30) ~ Restaurant ~ (01858) 465205 ~ Children welcome ~ Dogs allowed in bedrooms ~ Open 11.30-3, 6.30(7 Sat)-11.30; 12-3 Sun; closed Sun and bank holiday evenings ~ Bedrooms: £57.50B/£65.50B

Recommended by Julian Saunders, Gerry and Rosemary Dobson, Mrs M B Gregg, Jeff and Wendy Williams, Mr and Mrs W W Burke, David Kirkcaldy, Anthony Barnes, Michael Dandy, Alan Sutton, Adele Summers, Alan Black, O K Smyth, Sally Anne and Peter Goodale, Derek Stafford

KILSBY   SP5671   MAP 4

George

2.5 miles from M1 junction 18: A428 towards Daventry, left on to A5 – look out for pub off on right at roundabout; CV23 8YE

Handy for M1; warm welcome, good local atmosphere, proper public bar, old-fashioned décor and tasty wholesome food

Local myth suggests that this nice village inn was built with bricks pilfered during the construction of the nearby Kilsby tunnel in 1834 – white render (with woodwork prettily picked out in blue) makes it difficult to be sure either way. The very cheery landlady keeps a good balance between the popular dining aspect and the traditional public bar – this is just one of a handful of main entries that still has a pool table. The high-ceilinged wood panelled lounge on the right, with plush banquettes, a coal-effect gas stove and a big bay window, opens on the left into a smarter but relaxed attractive area with solidly comfortable furnishings. The long brightly decorated back public bar has a juke box, darts, that good pool table, a fruit machine and TV. Adnams, Fullers London Pride, Greene King Abbot and a guest such as Thwaites Lancaster Bomber are well kept on handpump, and they've a splendid range of malt whiskies, served in generous measures. There are wood picnic-sets out in the back garden, by the car park.

🍴 **The pubby lunch menu includes sandwiches, filled baguettes, soup, breaded brie with cranberry sauce, prawn cocktail, sausage, egg and chips, ploughman's, and beef or vegetable lasagne, while the evening menu typically features chicken liver pâté, steak, salmon fillet, penne with cream and mushroom sauce, beef and ale pie, and lamb shank; readers recommend the children's menu here. It's best to book if you go for Sunday lunch.** *Starters/Snacks: £4.50 to £5.90. Main Courses: £4.90 to £10.90. Puddings: £2.90 to £4.90*

Punch ~ Lease Maggie Chandler ~ Real ale ~ Bar food (12-2, 6-9; 12-4, 7.30-9) ~ Restaurant ~ (01788) 822229 ~ Children welcome ~ Dogs allowed in bar ~ Open 11.30-3, 5.30(6 Sat)-11(11.30 Sat); 12-5, 7.30-11 Sun ~ Bedrooms: £38/£56

Recommended by Keith and Chris O'Neill, George Atkinson, Keith and Sue Ward, Bruce and Sharon Eden, Denis Newton, Michael Dandy, Ted George

NETHER HEYFORD   SP6658   MAP 4

Olde Sun 🍴 £

1.75 miles from M1 junction 16: village signposted left off A45 westbound – Middle Street; NN7 3LL

Unpretentious place with diverting bric-a-brac, reasonably priced food, and garden with play area

All nature of curios and bric-a-brac is packed into nooks and crannies in the several small linked rooms at this 18th-c golden stone pub. There's gleaming brassware (one fireplace is a grotto of large brass animals), colourful relief plates, 1930s cigarette cards, railway memorabilia and advertising signs, World War II posters and rope fancywork. The nice old cash till on one of the two counters where they serve the well kept Banks's, Greene King Ruddles, Marstons Pedigree and a guest such as Everards Tiger, is wishfully stuck at one and a ha'penny. Furnishings are mostly properly pubby, with the odd easy chair. There are beams and low ceilings (one painted with a fine sunburst), partly glazed dividing panels, steps between some areas, rugs on parquet, red tiles or flagstones, a big inglenook log fire – and up on the left a room with full-sized hood skittles, a games machine, darts, TV, cribbage, dominoes and sports TV; piped music. The enjoyable collections continue into the garden, where there are blue-painted grain kibblers and other antiquated hand-operated farm machines, some with plants in their hoppers, beside a fairy-lit front terrace with picnic-sets.

⌂ **A short choice of snacky meals includes sandwiches, soup, scampi and chips, potato baked with bacon, onions and cream cheese, lasagne and coq au vin. There may be a few more dishes in the evening.** *Starters/Snacks: £5.00 to £7.00. Main Courses: £8.00 to £15.00. Puddings: £5.00 to £6.00*

Free house ~ Licensees P Yates and A Ford ~ Real ale ~ Bar food (till 4 Sun; not Sun evenings) ~ Restaurant ~ (01327) 340164 ~ Children welcome ~ Dogs allowed in bar ~ Open 12-2.30, 5-11; 12-11 Sat, Sun

Recommended by George Atkinson, Ian Stafford, Michael Dandy, Michael Butler, A R Mascall, Mr and Mrs W W Burke, Sam and Christine Kilburn, David and Karen Cuckney, Joan York, Margaret McPhee, Dennis and Doreen Haward, JJW, CMW, Gordon and Margaret Ormondroyd

OUNDLE
TL0388 MAP 5

Ship ◧
West Street; PE8 4EF

Bustling down-to-earth town pub with interesting beers and good value pubby food

---

This well worn enjoyable local is filled with the sound of hearty companionable chatter ('regulars in full cry' as one reader put it). None of it seems to disturb Midnight, the dozy black and white pub cat, though we suspect he might disappear when there's a live band or salsa class going on. The heavily beamed lounge bar (watch your head if you are tall) is made up of three cosy areas that lead off the central corridor. Up by the street there's a mix of leather and other seats, with sturdy tables and a warming log fire in a stone inglenook, and down one end a charming little panelled snug has button-back leather seats built in around it. The wood-floored public side has a TV, games machine, a juke box and board games; piped music. Friendly staff serve Brewsters Hophead and Digfield March Hare and an interesting guest or two such as Grainstore Rutland Panther and Oakham Bishops Farewell, and they've a good range of malt whiskies. The wooden tables and chairs out on the series of small sunny sheltered terraces are lit at night.

⌂ **Enjoyable bar food served in generous helpings might include soup, vegetarian or beef lasagne, haddock, chicken breast with mushroom sauce, pork curry and rib-eye steak; Sunday roast.** *Starters/Snacks: £2.00 to £5.50. Main Courses: £6.50 to £10.00. Puddings: £2.50 to £4.50*

Free house ~ Licensees Andrew and Robert Langridge ~ Real ale ~ Bar food (12-3, 6-9; 12-9 Sat, Sun) ~ Restaurant ~ (01832) 273918 ~ Children welcome ~ Dogs welcome ~ Disco Fri 8-11.45 and various other events inc salsa and live bands ~ Open 11-11(11.45 Fri, Sat); 12-11 Sun ~ Bedrooms: £30(£35S)/£60(£60S)(£70B)

Recommended by Keith and Margaret Kettell, the Didler, Ryta Lyndley, Howard and Margaret Buchanan, Barry Collett, Di and Mike Gillam, George Atkinson

SLIPTON
SP9579 MAP 4

Samuel Pepys ♀ ◧
Off A6116 at first roundabout N of A14 junction, towards Twywell and Slipton, bearing right to Slipton; the pub (in Slipton Lane) is well signed locally; NN14 3AR

Exemplary dining pub with prompt friendly service, good beers, nice surroundings and garden

---

Though popular for food, there's still a properly pubby feel and good range of beers in the long back bar of this smartly reworked old stone pub. It's gently modern and airy with good lighting, very heavy low beams, a log fire in the stone chimneybreast's big raised hearth (with plenty of logs stacked around), and chapel chairs on a simple mauve carpet. At one side, beyond a great central pillar that looks as if it was once part of a ship's mast, is an area with squashy leather seats around low tables. Beyond, the main dining room (with comfortably modern chairs around neatly set tables) extends into a fresh and roomy conservatory, with pleasant country views; piped music. The white painted bar counter stocks a good range of half a dozen real ales on handpump or tapped straight from the cask, including Greene King IPA, Hop Back Summer Lightning, John Smiths, Oakham JHB and Potbelly Aisling (from Kettering) and interesting changing guests from brewers such as Brewsters and Nethergate. They have an interesting choice of reasonably priced wines by the glass and bottle. Service is very friendly and helpful, and there is wheelchair access throughout. The sheltered garden is spacious and well laid out, with picnic-sets under cocktail parasols, and a terrace with heaters.

🍴 **Good value well presented and tasty bar food includes sandwiches, sausage with black pudding mash, cod and chips, steak and ale pie, thai green fish curry, mushroom risotto, duck breast with plum and caraway sauce, rib-eye steak, and puddings such as lemon and brandy syllabub and sticky toffee pudding.** *Starters/Snacks: £4.95 to £7.95. Main Courses: £10.95 to £19.95. Puddings: £4.95 to £7.60*

Mercury Inns ~ Manager Frazer Williams ~ Real ale ~ Bar food (12-3, 7-9.30) ~ Restaurant ~ (01832) 731739 ~ Children welcome ~ Dogs welcome ~ Open 12-3, 6-11.30; 12-11.30 Sat, Sun

Recommended by Michael and Jenny Back, Howard and Margaret Buchanan, Mike and Sue Losebey, Ryta Lyndley, Dave and Jen Harley, Oliver and Sue Rowell, Catherine and Rob Dunster, Mrs K Hooker, Michael Sargent

SULGRAVE   SP5545   MAP 4

Star

E of Banbury, signposted off B4525; Manor Road; OX17 2SA

Pleasant country pub with decent food and nice gardens

This lovely old creeper-covered farmhouse dates from the 17th c and is just a short walk from Sulgrave Manor, the ancestral home of George Washington (it's also handy for Silverstone). The peaceful little bar is unpretentiously furnished with small pews, cushioned window seats and wall benches, kitchen chairs and cast-iron-framed tables. Framed newspaper front pages record historic events such as Kennedy's assassination and the death of Churchill. There are polished flagstones in an area by the big inglenook fireplace, with red carpet elsewhere. Look out for the stuffed back end of a fox as it seems to leap into the wall. Hook Norton Hooky, Old Hooky and Hooky Gold are served from handpumps on the tiny counter. In summer you can eat outside under a vine-covered trellis, and there are benches at the front and in the back garden.

🍴 **Bar food includes sandwiches, soup, smoked trout pâté, sausage and mash, thai chicken curry, salmon steak with watercress sauce, and puddings such as lemon tart or chocolate brandy cream.** *Starters/Snacks: £4.95 to £8.95. Main Courses: £8.95 to £20.00. Puddings: £4.95 to £7.00*

Hook Norton ~ Tenant Andron Ingle ~ Real ale ~ Bar food ~ Restaurant ~ (01295) 760389 ~ Children welcome ~ Dogs allowed in bar ~ Open 11.30-3(4 Sun), 6-11; closed Sun evening, Mon ~ Bedrooms: £50S/£80S

Recommended by Alan Sutton, Mr and Mrs R A Buckler, Trevor and Judith Pearson, Tom Evans

WADENHOE   TL0183   MAP 5

Kings Head

Church Street; village signposted (in small print) off A605 S of Oundle; PE8 5ST

Country pub in idyllic riverside spot; decent range of beers, pubby food

Not to be missed in summer, this cheery stone-built 16th-c inn is in a wonderful spot with picnic-sets among willows and aspens on grass leading down to the River Nene – you can even arrive by boat and moor here. Inside, there's an uncluttered simplicity (maybe too much so for some) to the very welcoming partly stripped-stone main bar, which has pleasant old worn quarry-tiles, solid pale pine furniture with a couple of cushioned wall seats, and a leather-upholstered chair by the woodburning stove in the fine inglenook. The bare-boarded public bar has similar furnishings and another fire; steps lead up to a games room with dominoes and table skittles, and there's more of the pale pine furniture in an attractive little beamed dining room. As well as either Digfield

Barnwell or Digfield Kings Head they have a guest or two, maybe from Grainstore or Ruddles, and a dozen wines by the glass.

🍴 **Pubby bar food might include lunchtime sandwiches, ham, egg and chips, fish and chips, penne with goats cheese and olives, chicken wrapped in smoked bacon with white wine sauce, catch of the day, and 8oz rib-eye, with puddings such as bread and butter pudding and local ice-cream.** *Starters/Snacks: £4.95 to £6.95. Main Courses: £6.95 to £15.50. Puddings: £4.95*

Free house ~ Licensee Peter Hall ~ Real ale ~ Bar food (11.30-2.15(2.30 Sun), 6.30-9.15) ~ Restaurant ~ (01832) 720024 ~ Children welcome ~ Dogs allowed in bar ~ Open 11-11; 12-7.30 Sun

Recommended by Barry and Sue Pladdys, Michael Tack, Mike and Mary Carter, Barry Rolfe, Tom and Ruth Rees, Sally Anne and Peter Goodale, Ryta Lyndley

LUCKY DIP

Besides the fully inspected pubs, you might like to try these Lucky Dips recommended to us and described by readers (if you do, please send us reports: feedback@thegoodpubguide.co.uk).

APETHORPE [TL0295]
☆ *Kings Head* PE8 5DG [Kings Cliffe Rd]: Roomy and attractive stone-built pub in conservation village, comfortable and welcoming lounge with log fire, cosy bar, changing real ales, good coffee, friendly obliging service, arch to big dining area with wide choice of good fairly priced food inc fish, separate bar food menu (not Mon); children welcome, picnic-sets in charming sheltered courtyard *(Keith and Sue Campbell, R L Borthwick)*
ARTHINGWORTH [SP7581]
Bulls Head LE16 8JZ [Kelmarsh Rd, just above A14 by A508 junction; pub signed from A14]: Much extended local with open fires in big beamed L-shaped bar, enjoyable straightforward family food from good value sandwiches to steaks, Everards Tiger, Wells & Youngs Eagle and two guest beers, quick cheery service, dining room; disabled access, terrace tables, bedroom block, open all day Sun and perhaps summer *(Nick Roberts, Ian and Nita Cooper, Sally Anne and Peter Goodale)*
ASHBY ST LEDGERS [SP5768]
Olde Coach House CV23 8UN [off A361]: Now owned by Charles Wells and operated by same company as Samuel Pepys at Slipton, smartly refurbished and opened up, enjoyable up-to-date food, Wells & Youngs ales, light beige and white décor, leather sofas and armchairs in front room, leather dining chairs around stripped pine tables on carpet, service still settling down as we went to press; two new courtyards, lawn with fruit trees, interesting church nearby, open all day at least in summer, six comfortable new bedrooms *(LYM, Catherine and Rob Dunster)*
BRACKLEY [SP5836]
Crown NN13 7DP [Market Pl]: Smartly refurbished Georgian inn with open fire and some stripped masonry in comfortable carpeted bar, real ales such as St Austell, attentive staff, attractive dining room; 19 bedrooms *(George Atkinson)*

BRACKLEY HATCH [SP6441]
☆ *Green Man* NN13 5TX [A43 NE of Brackley (tricky exit)]: Big Chef & Brewer dining pub on busy dual carriageway nr Silverstone, comfortable old-look beamed lounge area, conservatory overlooking road, big family restaurant, wide range of all-day food, relaxed atmosphere, quick, friendly and helpful service, Greene King ales, good wines and coffee, daily papers, log fire; pervasive piped music, games; tables on lawn, bedrooms in Premier Lodge behind, open all day *(Michael Dandy, George Atkinson, Meg and Colin Hamilton, BB)*
BRAFIELD-ON-THE-GREEN [SP8258]
☆ *Red Lion* NN7 1BP [A428 5 miles from Northampton towards Bedford]: Smart comfortably modern bistro-style dining pub with generous upscale food from good glorified sandwiches up in two main rooms, small drinking area with a couple of settees, good choice of wines by the glass, Adnams and Great Oakley ales, friendly attentive staff; picnic-sets front and back, open all day *(Michael Dandy, Eithne Dandy)*
BRAUNSTON [SP5465]
Admiral Nelson NN11 7HJ [Dark Lane, Little Braunston, overlooking Lock 3 just N of Grand Union Canal tunnel]: 18th-c ex-farmhouse in peaceful setting by Grand Union Canal Lock 3 and hump bridge, good value food with interesting as well as basic dishes, well kept Black Sheep and Timothy Taylors Landlord, good choice of wines by the glass, cheery prompt service, canal pictures, cosy tiled-floor part by bar, longer dining end and back restaurant, lively games area with pool and table skittles; lots of picnic-sets in pleasant waterside garden over bridge, towpath walks *(Catherine and Rob Dunster, George Atkinson)*
Mill House NN11 7HB [London Rd (A45)]: Large modernised pub by Grand Union Canal, friendly quick service, enjoyable food inc Sun carvery, pool; six bedrooms *(E Clark)*

BRAYBROOKE [SP7684]

Swan LE16 8LH [Griffin Rd]: Nicely kept thatched pub with good drinks choice inc real ales, good value food (all day Sat), friendly service, fireside sofas; quiet piped music, games machine; garden with covered terrace (S Holder, JJW, CMW, Gerry and Rosemary Dobson)

BRIXWORTH [SP7470]

Coach & Horses NN6 9BX [Harborough Rd, just off A508 N of Northampton]: Welcoming unpretentious 17th-c stone-built beamed pub, helpful staff, good value food from sandwiches to fish, game and popular Sun lunch, log fire, Adnams and Marstons, decent house wines, pink walls with lots of horsebrasses and pictures, small restaurant; piped music; children welcome, tables on small back terrace, attractive village with famous Saxon church (J A Ellis)

☆ **New Inn** NN6 7PW [A5 N of Weedon]: Good range of tasty quickly served pubby food inc good baguettes, friendly staff, real ales such as Frog Island and Hook Norton, good short choice of wines, several rooms radiating from central servery inc small dining room with nice fire, games area with table skittles; TV; pleasant terrace by busy Grand Union Canal lock (Alison and Graham Hooper, Catherine and Rob Dunster, LYM, G Robinson, George Atkinson)

BUGBROOKE [SP6757]

Five Bells NN7 3PB [Church Lane]: Comfortable low-ceilinged dining areas off bar recently revamped and extended under enthusiastic new licensees, Caledonian Deuchars IPA, Fullers London Pride and Shepherd Neame Spitfire; children welcome, disabled access, garden with play area, attractive village, has been open all day wknds (George Atkinson)

Wharf Inn NN7 3QB [The Wharf; off A5 S of Weedon]: Super spot by Grand Union Canal, plenty of tables on big lawn with moorings and summer boat trips; emphasis on big water-view restaurant, also bar/lounge with small informal raised eating area either side, lots of stripped brickwork, wide choice of generous food from baguettes up, attentive staff, four or five real ales inc local Frog Island, farm cider, lots of wines by the glass, nice fire; piped music; children very welcome (George Atkinson, BB, JJW, CMW)

CASTLE ASHBY [SP8659]

Falcon NN7 1LF: Hotel in attractive preserved village, nice log fire in small lounge, 16th-c cellar bar (not always open, down tricky steps) with stone walls and hop-hung dark beams, Greene King ales; restaurant overlooking pretty gardens, bedrooms (some in nearby cottages) (George Atkinson)

CHACOMBE [SP4943]

☆ **George & Dragon** OX17 2JR [handy for M40 junction 11, via A361; Silver St]: Beams, flagstones, panelling, clock collection, log fire in massive fireplace and even an old

well, enjoyable food, good choice of wines by the glass, Everards ales, restaurant, darts and dominoes, attached Post Office; TV, piped music; children and dogs welcome, terrace tables and shelters, two bedrooms, pretty village with interesting church, open all day (George Atkinson, Mark and Diane Grist, BB, William Ruxton)

CHAPEL BRAMPTON [SP7366]

☆ **Brampton Halt** NN6 8BA [Pitsford Rd, off A5199 N of Northampton]: Well laid out pub on Northampton & Lamport Railway (which is open wknds), large restaurant, railway memorabilia and train theme throughout (some furnishings like railway carriages), popular generous food from sandwiches up, Everards Tiger and Original and Fullers London Pride, efficient attentive service, games and TV in bar; piped music; children welcome, lots of tables in garden with awnings and heaters, pretty views over small lake, Nene Valley Way walks (Gerry and Rosemary Dobson, LYM, George Atkinson)

Spencer Arms NN6 8AE [Northampton Rd]: Beamed Chef & Brewer family dining pub, plenty of stripped tables in long timber-divided L-shaped bar, decent sensibly priced food, good choice of wines by the glass, real ales, two log fires, daily papers; piped music; tables outside (Eithne Dandy, George Atkinson, Gerry and Rosemary Dobson)

CHARLTON [SP5235]

Rose & Crown OX17 3DP [Main St]: Thatched pub with friendly service, enjoyable food from bar snacks up, Greene King ales, beams, stripped stone and inglenook fireplaces, well spaced pale wood tables and chairs; picnic-sets outside, wisteria arbour, nice village (Sir Nigel Foulkes, E A and D C T Frewer, Tony Mason, LYM)

CHELVESTON [SP9969]

Star & Garter NN9 6AJ [The Green]: Small pub with friendly attentive new licensees, enjoyable food, Courage Directors and Wells & Youngs, decent wine by the glass, compact restaurant (Guy and Caroline Howard)

COLLINGTREE [SP7555]

☆ **Wooden Walls of Old England** NN4 0NE [1.2 miles from M1 junction 15; High St]: Low-beamed thatched stone-built village local doing well under current landlord, well kept Banks's and Black Sheep, good choice of wines by the glass, good value fresh pubby food (not Sun evening or Mon lunchtime), friendly staff, open fire; piped music, TV; children welcome, lots of picnic-sets and play area in nice big back garden with small terrace (BB, Keith and Sue Campbell, N A Hastings, R T and J C Moggridge, Michael Dandy)

COLLYWESTON [SK9902]

☆ **Collyweston Slater** PE9 3PU [A43; The Drove]: Stone-built stepped former cottage row recently refurbished as comfortable modern restaurant pub, sensibly short fresh menu, three ales inc Everards, friendly staff, good choice of wines by the glass, slate-mining memorabilia; children welcome, picnic-sets outside, five good bedrooms (double-glazed – traffic all night) *(Roy Bromell, Jan Murton)*

EVENLEY [SP5834]

☆ *Red Lion* NN13 5SH [The Green]: Small friendly well run local with particularly good value sandwiches and wide choice of other food, Marstons-related ales, decent coffee and choice of wines, inglenook, beams and some flagstones; piped music; neat garden, one or two seats out in front opp village cricket green *(George Atkinson, K H Frostick)*

GRAFTON REGIS [SP7546]

☆ *White Hart* NN12 7SR [A508 S of Northampton]: Good pubby food (not Sun evening) inc lots of splendid winter soups and fine range of baguettes in thatched dining pub with several linked rooms, Greene King ales, good wines by the glass, friendly hard-working helpful staff, african grey parrot (can be very vocal), small restaurant with open fire and separate menu; piped music; good-sized garden (food not served there) with terrace tables, cl Mon *(George Atkinson, BB)*

GREAT BILLING [SP8162]

Elwes Arms NN3 9DT [High St]: Thatched stone-built 16th-c village pub, two bars (steps between rooms), wide choice of good value food (all day Fri-Sun), three real ales, good choice of other drinks, pleasant dining room (children allowed), darts; piped music, TV, no dogs; garden tables, covered terrace, play area *(JJW, CMW)*

GREAT HOUGHTON [SP7959]

Old Cherry Tree NN4 7AT [Cherry Tree Lane; No Through Road off A428 just before White Hart]: Thatched village pub with low beams, open fires, stripped stone and panelling, decent fresh food from lunchtime baguettes up, wider evening choice, real ales such as Wells & Youngs, good wine choice, steps up to restaurant; quiet piped music; garden tables *(Gerry and Rosemary Dobson)*

White Hart NN4 7AF [off A428 Northampton—Bedford; High St]: Unpretentious thatched pub with steps between linked areas, good value food (not Mon evening) from sandwiches up, Adnams, Everards and Greene King, good choice of wines; piped music, TV, games machine, they may try to keep your credit card while you eat; attractive small garden with terrace *(Eithne Dandy, JJW, CMW)*

GREENS NORTON [SP6649]

Butchers Arms NN12 8BA [High St]: Large comfortably refurbished lounge, four well kept changing ales, wide food choice from sandwiches up, friendly staff, separate bar and games room with darts and pool; piped music, TV, games machines; children and dogs allowed, disabled access, picnic-sets and play area, pretty village nr Grafton Way walks *(JJW, CMW, Thomas Brigstocke)*

GRENDON [SP8760]

Half Moon NN7 1JW [Main Rd]: Thatched and stone-built 17th-c pub with new young licensees doing good value home cooking,

friendly attentive staff, Wells & Youngs real ale, long beamed bar with open fire and games end; small garden *(Martyn and Sue Smith)*

HARDINGSTONE [SP7657]

Sun NN4 7BT [High St]: Busy open-plan pub with three real ales, wide food choice (all day wknds), some 18th-c beams and stripped stone; piped music, games machine, TV, no dogs; children welcome, barn bar/function room, tables on attractive heated back terrace with play area *(JJW, CMW)*

HARLESTONE [SP7064]

Fox & Hounds NN7 4EW [A428, Lower Harlestone]: Contemporary M&B dining pub with pale wood furnishings and flooring, light and airy décor, prompt helpful waiter service throughout, Timothy Taylors Landlord, good choice of wines by the glass; tables in nice garden, handy for Althorp and Harlestone Firs walks, open all day *(Tim and Ann Newell, Michael Dandy)*

HARRINGTON [SP7780]

Tollemache Arms NN6 9NU [High St; off A508 S of Mkt Harboro]: Pretty thatched Tudor pub in lovely quiet ironstone village, very low ceilings in compact bar with log fire and in pleasant partly stripped stone dining room, good food choice from sandwiches up, well kept ales such as Clarkes and Wells & Youngs, neat, friendly and attentive young staff; children welcome, nice back garden with country views *(George Atkinson, BB)*

HARRINGWORTH [SP9197]

☆ *White Swan* NN17 3AF [SE of Uppingham; Seaton Rd]: Striking stone-built Tudor inn with imposing central gable, enjoyable food (not Sun evening) inc good value lunches, real ales such as Adnams and Fullers London Pride, good wines by the glass, solid tables and elaborate hand-crafted oak counter in friendly central bar, open fire dividing bar from roomy dining area with cottagey décor, interesting documentation on magnificent nearby viaduct, traditional games; may be piped music; terrace tables, six good bedrooms *(John Wooll, LYM, Barry Collett)*

HOLCOT [SP7969]

White Swan NN6 9SP [Main St; nr Pitsford Water, N of Northampton]: Good straightforward food inc wkdy lunch bargains and good value Sun lunch all afternoon, well kept Batemans and interesting guest beers, attractive partly thatched village pub with hospitable bar on right and dining rooms on left, pleasant service; open all day Sun and summer, children welcome *(George Atkinson, S Holder, Gerry and Rosemary Dobson)*

KETTERING [SP8778]

Alexandra Arms NN16 0BU [Victoria St]: Real ale pub, with ten changing quickly, hundreds each year, also their own Nobbys ale, may be sandwiches, back games bar with hood skittles; back terrace, open all day (from 2 wkdys) *(the Didler, P Dawn)*

KISLINGBURY [SP6959]

Old Red Lion NN7 4AQ [High St, off A45 W of Northampton]: Roomy old stone-fronted pub with new chef doing enjoyable bar and restaurant food, well kept Timothy Taylors Landlord and Wells & Youngs, good choice of other drinks, beams, bric-a-brac, brasses and horse tack; piped music; suntrap back terrace *(Robin M Corlett)*

LAMPORT [SP7574]

Lamport Swan NN6 9EZ: Modern pub/bistro in imposing stone building, good-sized front bar with Wells & Youngs and good choice of wines by the glass, emphasis on large side restaurant with big flame-effect fire one end, some pubby as well as more bistroish dishes, daily papers; piped music; outside tables with good views *(Michael Dandy)*

LITTLE BRINGTON [SP6663]

☆ *Saracens Head* NN7 4HS [4.5 miles from M1 junction 16, first right off A45 to Daventry; also signed off A428; Main St]: Friendly old pub with enjoyable food from interesting baguettes and wraps up, real ales such as Adnams Broadside, Greene King IPA, Shepherd Neame Spitfire and Timothy Taylors Landlord, roomy U-shaped lounge with good log fire, flagstones, chesterfields and lots of old prints, book-lined dining room; plenty of tables in neat back garden, handy for Althorp House and Holdenby House *(Gerry and Rosemary Dobson, Mrs S Hall, BB, George Atkinson, Tim and Ann Newell)*

LODDINGTON [SP8178]

Hare NN14 1LA [Main St]: Welcoming 17th-c stone-built dining pub, carpeted throughout, with wide choice of enjoyable good value food (not Sun evening or Mon) from good sandwiches to restaurant dishes, good-sized helpings, tablecloths and fresh flowers, Adnams Broadside and Timothy Taylors Landlord in small bar, good wine and soft drinks choice, good coffee, pleasant helpful service; piped music; picnic-sets on front lawn *(Alan Vann, Michael Dandy)*

LOWICK [SP9780]

☆ *Snooty Fox* NN14 3BH [off A6116 Corby—Raunds]: Attractively reworked and spacious 16th-c pub with leather sofas and chairs, beams and stripped stonework, log fire in huge stone fireplace, open kitchen doing bar food from sandwiches up inc steak counter, Greene King IPA and two guest beers, board games; piped music, games machine; dogs and children welcome, picnic-sets on front grass, open all day *(Mike and Sue Loseby, J C M Troughton, LYM, Ben and Helen Ingram)*

MAIDWELL [SP7477]

☆ *Stags Head* NN6 9JA [Harborough Rd (A508 N of Northampton)]: Comfortable carpeted areas off neatly kept beamed front bar with log fire, enjoyable pubby food very popular lunchtime with older people, friendly staff, Black Sheep, Greene King IPA and Tetleys, good choice of wines and soft drinks; quiet piped music; disabled facilities, terrace (dogs on leads allowed here) by neat back lawn with paddock beyond, bedrooms, not far from splendid Palladian Kelmarsh Hall in its parkland *(Gerry and Rosemary Dobson, Michael Dandy, JJW, CMW)*

MEARS ASHBY [SP8466]

Griffins Head NN6 0DX [Wilby Rd]: Good choice of changing ales and of food from sandwiches to much more ambitious dishes, substantial OAP bargain wkdy lunches, attentive staff, front lounge with pleasant outlook, hunting prints and log fire in huge fireplace, small dining room, basic back bar with juke box; children welcome, neat flower-filled garden, open all day *(Gerry and Rosemary Dobson)*

MIDDLETON CHENEY [SP5041]

New Inn OX17 2ND [Main Rd, off A422 E of M40 junction 11]: Good choice of well kept ales in hospitable 17th-c turnpike inn, reasonably priced food, bottle collection in bar and outer barn, back restaurant; dogs welcome, good-sized neatly kept garden with aunt sally, open all day Sat *(Alex Harper)*

MILTON MALSOR [SP7355]

Greyhound NN7 3AP [2.25 miles from M1 junction 15, via A508; Towcester Rd]: Big busy old-world beamed Chef & Brewer, cosy alcoves, old pictures and china, pewter-filled dresser, candlelit pine tables, good log fire, Greene King, Wells & Youngs Bombardier and a guest beer, good range of wines, usual food all day, cheerful service; piped music; well behaved children welcome, spreading front lawn with duck/fish pond, open all day *(Ryta Lyndley, LYM, George Atkinson)*

MOULTON [SP7866]

Artichoke NN3 7SP [Church St]: Large stone-built pub under new licensees, good friendly atmosphere, good value food, Everards ales *(S Holder)*

NASSINGTON [TL0696]

Queens Head PE8 6QB [Station Rd]: Very smartly refurbished, stylish bar/bistro and separate restaurant, wide choice of enjoyable food using local ingredients inc good value upscale lunches, pleasant staff, nice choice of wines by the glass, changing real ales, good coffee; pretty garden by River Nene, delightful village, nine chalet bedrooms *(Patrick Frew, Roy Bromell)*

NEWNHAM [SP5759]

Romer Arms NN11 3HB [The Green]: Pine panelling, mix of flagstones, quarry tiles and carpet, log fire, light and airy back dining conservatory, cheerful obliging licensees, reliably good generous home cooking (not Sun evening) inc good value Sun lunch, Greene King Old Speckled Hen, Wells & Youngs Eagle and a guest such as Jennings, good soft drinks choice, public bar with darts and pool; piped music; enclosed back garden looking over fields, small attractive village *(George Atkinson)*

NORTHAMPTON [SP7862]

Bold Dragoon NN3 3JW [High St, Weston Favell; off A4500 Wellingborough Rd]: Well run two-bar pub with wide choice of enjoyable up-to-date food inc imaginative dishes, interesting real ale choice, New World wines, friendly efficient staff, conservatory restaurant; disabled access, picnic-sets in garden with terrace *(Martin Kane)*

Fox & Hounds NN2 8DJ [Harborough Rd, Kingsthorpe (A508)]: Spacious pub with wide range of decent all-day food from sandwiches up, friendly service, Greene King IPA and Abbot and a guest beer; big-screen TV, games machine; open all day *(Gerry and Rosemary Dobson)*

Hopping Hare NN5 6DF [Harlestone Rd (A428), New Duston]: Stylish contemporary refurbishment, with sofas etc around big servery, real ales such as Greene King IPA, Marstons Pedigree and Wells & Youngs Bombardier, good choice of wines by the glass inc champagne, up-to-date food inc interesting salads, good friendly service, comfortable modern restaurant; nine modern bedrooms *(Michael Dandy)*

☆ *Malt Shovel* NN1 1QF [Bridge St (approach rd from M1 junction 15); best parking in Morrisons opp back entrance]: Full Great Oakley beer range and well kept guests inc local Frog Island, also Rich's farm cider, belgian bottled beers, good choice of other drinks, friendly landlord and staff, cheap pubby lunchtime food (not Sun), daily papers, breweriana inc some from Carlsberg Brewery opposite, open fire, darts; blues bands Weds; children and dogs welcome, disabled facilities, picnic-sets on small back terrace *(JJW, CMW, the Didler, George Atkinson, Bruce Bird, P Dawn)*

POTTERSPURY [SP7543]
Old Talbot NN12 7QD [A5; Watling St]: Family dining pub with chesterfields in small bar, pine furniture in large carpeted dining area behind, Greene King IPA and Abbot, reasonably priced food (not Sun evening) from sandwiches up; piped music; fenced garden behind, open all day wknds *(LYM, Michael Dandy)*

RAVENSTHORPE [SP6670]
☆ *Chequers* NN6 8ER [Chequers Lane]: Warmly welcoming extended local with reliable generous food from baguettes to popular Sun lunch, well kept ales such as Black Sheep, Greene King and Jennings, attentive staff, open fire, lots of bric-a-brac hung from beams and stripped stone walls, dining room, games room, home-made jam and free range eggs; TV, games machine; children welcome, small secluded back terrace and play area, open all day Sat *(George Atkinson, Gerry and Rosemary Dobson, Richard and Audrey Chase, JJW, CMW)*

RINGSTEAD [SP9875]
Axe & Compass NN14 4DW [Carlow Rd]: Extended stone-built village pub with flagstones and lots of bric-a-brac, enjoyable food, two-for-one bargains Tues-Thurs, Banks's and Marstons Pedigree, good wines and coffee; piped music, service can slow right down; garden and play area *(Ryta Lyndley)*

RUSHDEN [SP9566]
Station Bar NN10 0AW [Station Approach]: Not a pub, part of station HQ of Rushden Historical Transport Society (non-members can sign in), restored in 1940s/60s style, with Fullers London Pride and interesting guest beers, tea and coffee, friendly staff, filled rolls (perhaps some hot dishes), gas lighting, enamelled advertisements, old-fangled furnishings; authentic waiting room with piano, also museum and summer steam-ups; open all day Sat, cl wkdy lunchtimes *(the Didler)*

RUSHTON [SP8483]
Thornhill Arms NN14 1RL [Station Rd]: Pleasantly furnished rambling dining pub opp attractive village's cricket green, wide choice of good value food from speciality hot pork baguettes up in several neatly laid out dining areas inc smart high-beamed back restaurant, friendly helpful service, well kept Adnams, relaxed comfortable atmosphere, open fire; garden tables, bedrooms *(Alan Weedon, R T and J C Moggridge)*

SHUTLANGER [SP7249]
Plough NN12 7RU [Main Rd, off A43 N of Towcester]: Unpretentious bar with lots of hanging jugs, mugs and tankards, horse pictures and brasses, Wells & Youngs Eagle, darts and hood skittles prominent (just three tables), separate small restaurant with emphasis on fish; piped music; pleasant small garden with picnic-sets and play area, nearby walks *(Alan Sutton)*

SIBBERTOFT [SP6782]
☆ *Red Lion* LE16 9UD [off A4303 or A508 SW of Mkt Harboro; Welland Rise]: Good food, splendid wine list (they do tastings), quickly changing real ales such as Adnams, Greene King and Hydes, good friendly staff, small partly panelled bar with banquettes in linked dining area, light and airy contemporary back restaurant with clean-cut modern furnishings; covered terrace tables, large garden, two good self-catering bedrooms, cl Sun evening and Mon/Tues lunchtimes *(Jeff and Wendy Williams, George Atkinson, Gerry and Rosemary Dobson, E J Webster, Dr S Edwards, John Wooll)*

STOKE BRUERNE [SP7449]
Boat NN12 7SB [3.5 miles from M1 junction 15 – A508 towards Stony Stratford then signed on right; Bridge Rd]: Appealing old-world flagstoned bar in picturesque canalside spot by beautifully restored lock (plus more modern central-pillared back bar and bistro without the views – children allowed here), Marstons and guest ales, usual food from baguettes up, extension with all-day tearooms and comfortable upstairs restaurant; piped music; tables out by towpath opp British Waterways Museum and shop, canal boat trips, bar open all day summer Sats *(George Atkinson, LYM, Gerry and Rosemary Dobson)*

Navigation NN12 7SD: Large canalside Marstons pub, several levels and cosy corners, good choice of pubby food under current management, sturdy wood furniture, real ales and quite a few wines by the glass, friendly helpful young staff, separate family room, pub games; piped music; plenty of tables out overlooking water, big play area, open all day *(Simon Jones, Charles and Pauline Stride)*

TOWCESTER [SP6948]

Plough NN12 6BT [Watling St E (A5)]: Wells & Youngs Eagle and Bombardier and attractively priced food from sandwiches up in three traditionally furnished linked areas, cheerful efficient service; back terrace tables among flower tubs and baskets *(Michael Dandy)*

Saracens Head NN12 6BX [Watling St W]: Substantially modernised coaching inn with interesting *Pickwick Papers* connections (especially in the kitchen Dickens described, now a meeting room), open fire in long comfortable three-level lounge with dining area, Greene King ales, good value pub food, neat efficient staff, games bar; piped music, TV; children welcome, small back courtyard with smokers' shelter, well equipped bedrooms *(LYM, Michael Dandy, Pete Coxon)*

TURWESTON [SP6037]

Stratton Arms NN13 5JX [pub itself just inside Bucks]: Friendly chatty country pub, five well kept real ales, good choice of other drinks, reasonably priced food (not Sun evening or Mon), low ceilings, log fires; TV, games machine; children and dogs welcome, good-sized garden by Great Ouse, barbecues and play area *(JJW, CMW)*

UPPER BENEFIELD [SP9789]

Wheatsheaf PE8 5AN [Upper Main St]: Nicely placed and attractively smartened up country pub, enjoyable food from home-baked bread to beef and lamb raised for them by local farmers, well kept beers inc local Barnwell, fine house wines, friendly beamed bar with log fires, restaurant with stylish conservatory; garden tables, 19 good bedrooms *(Noel Grundy)*

WALGRAVE [SP8072]

Royal Oak NN6 9PN [Zion Hill, off A43 Northampton—Kettering]: Friendly old stone-built local with up to five changing real ales, good value food (not Sun evening) from sandwiches through fish and chips to wild boar, quick pleasant service, long three-part carpeted beamed bar with small lounge and restaurant extension behind; children welcome, small garden, play area, open all day Sun *(JJW, CMW, Barry Collett)*

WELLINGBOROUGH [SP9069]

Locomotive NN8 4AL [Finedon Rd (A5128)]: Traditional two-bar local with up to half a

dozen interesting changing real ales, big lunchtime baguettes, friendly landlord, lots of train memorabilia inc toy locomotive running above bar, log fire, daily papers, games room with pool, pin table and hood skittles; may be quiet piped music; dogs welcome, picnic-sets in small front garden, open all day (Sun afternoon break) *(the Didler)*

WELTON [SP5866]

☆ *White Horse* NN11 2JP [off A361/B4036 N of Daventry; behind church, High St]: Neatly simple beamed village pub on different levels, decent reasonably priced food, Adnams and interesting guest ales, nice house wines, cheerful attentive staff, big open fire, separate games bar, small dining room; attractively lit garden with play area, terrace and barbecue *(J V Dadswell, Robin M Corlett, George Atkinson)*

WILBY [SP8766]

George NN8 2UB [Main Rd (A4500 SW of Wellingboro)]: Friendly beamed pub with good value lunchtime food, five real ales, good soft drinks choice; big-screen TV, piped music, games machines; great views from nice garden with ancient mulberry, play area *(JJW, CMW)*

Horseshoe NN8 2UE [Main Rd]: Five real ales, good soft drinks choice, good value food (not Sun/Mon evenings) in friendly stone-built village pub with horseshoe bar, games area with darts and hood skittles; quiet piped music, no credit cards; children welcome, picnic-sets out in front, garden with play area *(JJW, CMW)*

WOODNEWTON [TL0394]

White Swan PE8 5EB [Main St]: This unpretentious traditional village pub was closed and boarded up as we went to press – news please *(LYM)*

YARDLEY HASTINGS [SP8656]

☆ *Red Lion* NN7 1ER [High St, just off A428 Bedford—Northampton]: Pretty thatched pub, friendly and relaxed, with good value pubby food from sandwiches up, wider evening choice (not Sun/Mon), Wells & Youngs Eagle and one or two guest beers, good range of soft drinks, linked rooms with beams and stripped stone, lots of pictures, plates and interesting brass and copper, small annexe with hood skittles; quiet piped music, TV, no dogs; children welcome, nicely planted sloping garden, open all day wknds *(Michael Dandy, BB, George Atkinson)*

Anyone claiming to arrange or prevent inclusion of a pub in the *Guide* is a fraud. Pubs are included only if recommended by genuine readers and if our own anonymous inspection confirms that they are suitable.

Please use this card to tell us which pubs *you* think should or should not be included in the next edition of *The Good Pub Guide*. Just fill it in and return it to us – no stamp or envelope needed. Don't forget you can also use the report forms at the end of the *Guide*

ALISDAIR AIRD

In returning this form I confirm my agreement that the information I provide may be used by The Random House Group Ltd, its assignees and/or licensees in any media or medium whatsoever.

YOUR NAME AND ADDRESS (BLOCK CAPITALS PLEASE)

☐ *Please tick this box if you would like extra report forms*

REPORT ON   *(pub's name)*

Pub's address

☐ **YES Main Entry**   ☐ **YES Lucky Dip**   ☐ **NO don't include**
Please tick one of these boxes to show your verdict, and give reasons and descriptive comments, prices etc

☐ Deserves FOOD award   ☐ Deserves PLACE-TO-STAY award

REPORT ON   *(pub's name)*

Pub's address

☐ **YES Main Entry**   ☐ **YES Lucky Dip**   ☐ **NO don't include**
Please tick one of these boxes to show your verdict, and give reasons and descriptive comments, prices etc

☐ Deserves FOOD award   ☐ Deserves PLACE-TO-STAY award

☐

THE GOOD PUB GUIDE

The Good Pub Guide
FREEPOST TN1569
WADHURST
E. SUSSEX
TN5 7BR

Northumbria
(County Durham, Northumberland and Tyneside)

This is a great part of the world in which to find real value. In general pubs here have done a fine job in holding their prices down, so that at one end of the scale there are plenty of food and drink bargains to be found, and at the other you can get really good pub meals without spending an arm and a leg. The area's three top pubs for food are the Feathers at Hedley on the Hill, overlooking the Cheviots (excellent carefully sourced food, good drinks selection), the thoughtfully run traditional Cook & Barker Arms at Newton-on-the-Moor, just off the A1 (good restaurant, and high food quality too at very fair prices in the bar), and the Rose & Crown at Romaldkirk (interesting food and super bedrooms – a good base for exploring the area). Building on their first year's success, the go-ahead newish owners of the Feathers at Hedley on the Hill retain its title of Northumbria Dining Pub of the Year. In the Rat at Anick, newish owners are winning praise for their food, as well as an interesting range of local real ales. The General Havelock at Haydon Bridge easily makes the main entry grade this year for its interesting locally sourced food, local beers and lovely river views. Another new main entry is the nicely placed Barrasford Arms at Barrasford, also using prime local ingredients for its good food, while keeping a thoroughly warm-hearted pub atmosphere. The Manor House Inn at Carterway Heads, the Pheasant near Kielder Water at Stannersburn, the Anglers Arms at Weldon Bridge (with the distinction of having its restaurant in a converted railway dining car; also fishing on the River Coquet) and the Morritt Arms at Greta Bridge are very civilised places to stay, eat or drink at. The Olde Ship in Seahouses is another favourite, for its splendid coastal views, loads of maritime memorabilia, and great atmosphere. The Carts Bog Inn in a pleasant rural spot up above Langley on Tyne, does well for its friendly service, local ales and food. With its monastic origins and extraordinarily atmospheric ancient vaulted bar, the Lord Crewe Arms at Blanchland is a memorable place to stay or have a drink. For visiting the key sites of Hadrian's Wall, the Milecastle Inn at Haltwhistle is very useful, its cosy beamed bar an appealing place for a drink. The Masons Arms at Rennington, in quiet countryside not far from Alnwick and the coast, has good accommodation and helpful staff. Three of our selected pubs are in city centres, with a notable choice of well kept beers: the Victoria in Durham (an evocatively untouched alehouse with heaps of character), the Crown Posada in Newcastle (a splendid old drinking haunt), and the Cluny there (an arty, upbeat place, with a good choice of drinks).

In a really special coastal position, the Ship Inn at Newton-by-the-Sea opened its own microbrewery in 2008, brewing four beers. Other notable brewpubs are the Dipton Mill Inn at Diptonmill (farm cider and malt whiskies, as well as its own Hexhamshire ales; pleasant garden) and the Keelman at Newburn, a popular destination for families and walkers (eight good own-brewed Big Lamp beers, not hard to find in other pubs, too). Several other small breweries flourish in the area, the most popular being Hadrian & Border, Wylam, Mordue, Durham and Jarrow. High House, a youngish farm brewery, is now making quite a name for itself. Other local beers to be found in the area's better pubs are Allendale, Consett Ale Works, Northumberland, Camerons, Hill Island and Darwin. In the Lucky Dip section at the end of the chapter, pubs to note particularly are the Ancient Unicorn at Bowes, Dun Cow in Durham, Black Bull at Frosterley, Horseshoes at Rennington, Boatside at Warden and Boathouse in Wylam.

ANICK   NY9565   MAP 10

Rat ◧

Village signposted NE of A69/A695 Hexham junction; NE46 4LN

Views over North Tyne Valley from terrace and garden, lots of interesting knick-knacks and six real ales

---

At cooler times you'll find fires blazing in this pleasantly relaxed country pub (under new owners since the last edition of the *Guide*), and there's a good selection of beers. It is full of interesting knick-knacks: antique floral chamber-pots hanging from the beams, china and glassware, maps and posters, and framed sets of cigarette cards. A coal fire blazes invitingly in the blackened kitchen range and lighting is soft and gentle. Furnishings keep up the cosily traditional mood with old-fashioned pub tables; piped music, daily papers and magazines. The conservatory has pleasant valley views. Half a dozen changing real ales on handpump always include Bass and Caledonian Deuchars together with guests usually from local breweries such as Allendale, Hadrian & Border, High House and Wylam. Parking is limited, but you can also park around the village green. From tables out on the terrace you look over the North Tyne Valley; the charming garden has a dovecote, statues and attractive flowers.

🍴 **Interesting and enjoyable bar food changes daily, and along with sandwiches and soup features starters such as local game terrine, and pea, celery and shropshire blue salad with walnuts, mains like roast rib of beef (for two people), fried bass with provençale prawns, fried duck breast with mushrooms and aubergine chutney, and rocket and herb risotto with goats cheese, with puddings like sticky toffee pudding or raspberry crème brûlée.** *Starters/Snacks: £3.50 to £4.95. Main Courses: £7.95 to £18.95. Puddings: £4.50*

Free house ~ Licensees Phil Mason and Karen Errington ~ Real ale ~ Bar food (12-2(3 Sun), 6-9; sandwiches only on Mon) ~ Restaurant ~ (01434) 602814 ~ Children welcome ~ Open 12-3, 6-11; 11.30-11 Sat; 11-10.30 Sun

Recommended by Shea Brookes Johnson, Comus and Sarah Elliott, K R Greenhalgh, Pat and Stewart Gordon, Dr Peter D Smart, Dr and Mrs R G J Telfer, Michael Doswell

---

The letters and figures after the name of each town are its Ordnance Survey map reference. 'Using the *Guide*' at the beginning of the book explains how it helps you find a pub, in road atlases or on large-scale maps as well as in our own maps.

Barrasford Arms

Village signposted off A6079 N of Hexham; NE48 4AA

Friendly proper pub with good country cooking, plenty of nearby walks; bedrooms

On the edge of a small North Tyne village quite close to Hadrian's Wall, this sandstone inn has lovely valley views and looks across to impressive medieval Haughton Castle (not open to the public); there may be sheep in the pasture just behind. The good-natured chef/landlord who took over a couple of years ago has made sure of keeping a genuinely local atmosphere – a quoits league, darts club, ladies' luncheon club and local vegetable shows have all evolved here. The compact traditional bar has a welcoming atmosphere, dark pink carpet and matching walls, old local photographs and a little country bric-a-brac such as horsebrasses, antlers and an oversized horseshoe. There's a good log fire, and they have a High House beer on handpump, with two guests from either Allendale, Hadrian & Border or Wylam, and good value wines by the glass. They make good coffee, and the young staff are friendly and attentive. One nice dining room, carefully decorated in greys and creams and dominated by a great stone chimneybreast hung with guns and copper pans, has wheelback chairs around half a dozen neat tables; a second, perhaps rather more restrained, has more comfortably upholstered dining chairs; piped music, TV. There are tables outside. We haven't yet heard from anyone staying here, but would expect it to be a nice place to stay; there is well equipped bunkhouse accommodation as well as the 11 proper bedrooms.

🍴 The cooking here is good, using carefully sourced local meats, game and fish to produce unpretentious and thoroughly rewarding dishes, full of flavour. The choice, changing daily, is usually kept sensibly short. Things which we or readers have enjoyed recently include the hearty soups such as lentil with bacon collar, warm black pudding and bacon salad with poached eggs, spiced beetroot and french bean salad, home-cured gammon, very tender braised beef, three-cheese risotto, and seared bass on saffron mash. The local cheeses are carefully chosen, the puddings are a high point worth saving space for and the roast potatoes on Sunday are said to be outstanding. *Starters/Snacks: £4.50 to £6.00. Main Courses: £8.00 to £15.00. Puddings: £5.00*

Free house ~ Licensee Tony Binks ~ Real ale ~ Bar food (12-2(3 Sun), 6.30-9; not Sun evening) ~ (01434) 681237 ~ Children welcome ~ Open 12-2, 6-11; 12-midnight Sat, Sun; closed Mon lunchtime ~ Bedrooms: £65B/£85B

Recommended by R L Borthwick, Margaret and Mike Iley, Michael Doswell

Lord Crewe Arms 🛏

B6306 S of Hexham; DH8 9SP

Ancient, historic building with some unusual features and straightforward bar food

Built by the Premonstratensians around 1235 as the abbot's lodging for their adjacent monastery – the lovely walled garden was formerly the cloisters – this comfortable hotel is a wonderful evocation of the past and is in a remote village beneath the moors. An ancient-feeling bar is housed in an unusual long and narrow stone barrel-vaulted crypt, its curving walls being up to eight feet thick in some places. Plush stools are lined along the bar counter on ancient flagstones and next to a narrow drinks shelf down the opposite wall; TV. Upstairs, the Derwent Room has low beams, old settles, and sepia photographs on its walls, and the Hilyard Room has a massive 13th-c fireplace once used as a hiding place by the Jacobite Tom Forster (part of the family who had owned the building before it was sold in 1704 to the formidable Lord Crewe, Bishop of Durham). Black Sheep Best Bitter and Ale on handpump, and a good selection of wines.

🍴 Straightforward bar food includes soup, filled rolls, generous ploughman's, cumberland sausage with black pudding and daily specials, as well as more elaborate restaurant food (available in the evening). *Starters/Snacks: £2.75 to £4.00. Main Courses: £7.00 to £10.00. Puddings: £3.60*

Free house ~ Licensees A Todd and Peter Gingell ~ Real ale ~ Bar food ~ Restaurant ~ (01434) 675251 ~ Children welcome ~ Dogs welcome ~ Open 11-11; 12-10.30 Sun ~ Bedrooms: £50B/£100B

Recommended by Tony and Maggie Harwood, Mike Vincent, Pat and Stewart Gordon, Ann and Tony Bennett-Hughes, Mr and Mrs P L Spencer

CARTERWAY HEADS   NZ0452 MAP 10

Manor House Inn ♀ ◀ ⌖

A68 just N of B6278, near Derwent Reservoir; DH8 9LX

Popular inn with a good choice of drinks, nice views and comfortable bedrooms

With good bar food available all day, and views towards the Derwent Valley and reservoir, this country inn is an enjoyable place to stay and eat. The locals' bar has an original boarded ceiling, pine tables, chairs and stools, old oak pews, and a mahogany counter. The comfortable lounge bar, warmed by a woodburning stove, and restaurant have picture windows that make the most of the setting. Courage Directors, Theakstons Best, Wells & Youngs Bombardier and a guest from a brewery such as Consett Ale Works or Mordue on handpump, 70 malt whiskies and a dozen wines by the glass; darts, dominoes, board games and piped music (only in the bar). There are rustic tables in the garden.

⑪ **Bar food includes sandwiches, soup, fried scallops with chilli jam, local trout, pheasant breast with black pudding, haggis and swede, chicken supreme with asparagus tips and cheese sauce, braised lamb shank, game casserole, baked salmon with braised fennel and puddings such as sticky toffee pudding. You can buy local produce, as well as chutneys, puddings and ice-cream made in the kitchens from their own little deli.** *Starters/Snacks: £3.75 to £8.50. Main Courses: £6.50 to £17.00. Puddings: £3.95 to £4.50*

Free house ~ Licensees Moira and Chris Brown ~ Real ale ~ Bar food (12-9.30(9 Sun)) ~ Restaurant ~ (01207) 255268 ~ Well behaved children welcome away from bar ~ Dogs welcome ~ Open 11-11; 12-10.30 Sun ~ Bedrooms: £43S/£65S

Recommended by Tony and Maggie Harwood, Adrian Johnson, Pat and Stewart Gordon, Brian Brooks, Andy and Jill Kassube, Fiona Salvesen, Ross Murrell, Arthur Pickering, D Hillaby, Mrs Carolyn Dixon, Sheena W Makin

CORBRIDGE   NY9868 MAP 10

Errington Arms

About 3 miles N of town; B6318, on A68 roundabout; NE45 5QB

18th-c stone-built inn restored after a fire, keeping its good father-and-son team; relaxed and friendly with enjoyable food

This 18th-c roadside inn is right beside Hadrians Wall and was stylishly revamped after a fire in 2006. Run by father and son, it has oak beams, a nice mix of candlelit tables on the light wooden floor, some pine planking and stripped stonework, burgundy paintwork, ornamental plaques, a large heavy mirror, and a log fire; there is still a modicum of bric-a-brac, on window sills and so forth. Jennings Cumberland and Wells & Youngs Special on handpump; piped music. Out on the front terrace are some sturdy metal and teak tables under canvas parasols. More reports please.

⑪ **As well as sandwiches, ploughman's and salads, the enjoyable food includes soup, duck and port mousse with redcurrant, orange and mint coulis, fried king prawns with bean sprout salad and a chilli soy broth, mushroom and spinach omelette, lamb and beef stew with orange and rosemary, breadcrumbed chicken topped with mozzarella, basil and tomato, wild boar and pheasant pie and seared duck breast with a chive and mushroom risotto and blueberry and red wine jus.** *Starters/Snacks: £3.50 to £4.95. Main Courses: £7.95 to £15.50. Puddings: £2.95 to £4.50*

Punch ~ Lease Nicholas Shotton ~ Real ale ~ Bar food (12-2.30(3 Sun), 6.30-9.30) ~ Restaurant ~ (01434) 672250 ~ Children welcome ~ Open 11-3, 6-11; 12-4 Sun; closed Sun evening, Mon (exc bank hols)

Recommended by Andy and Jill Kassube, Mrs Marion Matthewman, Mike Goddard, Michael Doswell

COTHERSTONE
NZ0119 MAP 10

Fox & Hounds 🛏

B6277 – incidentally a good quiet route to Scotland, through interesting scenery; DL12 9PF

Redecorated 18th-c inn with cheerful beamed bar, homely bar food and quite a few wines by the glass

This bustling and friendly Georgian country inn occupies an attractive spot by the village green. The simple but cheery beamed bar has a partly wooden floor (elsewhere it's carpeted), a good winter log fire, thickly cushioned wall seats and local photographs and country pictures on the walls in its various alcoves and recesses. Black Sheep Best and a guest such as Daleside Special on handpump, a dozen wines by the glass and several malt whiskies from smaller distilleries; efficient service from the friendly staff. Don't be surprised by the unusual lavatory attendant – an african grey parrot called Reva. Seats outside on the new terrace and quoits. More reports please.

🍽 **Bar food typically includes lunchtime sandwiches, soup, steak and ale pie, broccoli, leek and mushroom filled pancake, salmon, prawn and mackerel fishcake with home-made tartare sauce, fried pork tenderloin in marsala with mushroom cream sauce, beer-battered haddock, lambs liver and onions with red wine gravy, and puddings.** *Starters/Snacks: £3.90 to £5.95. Main Courses: £8.20 to £14.50. Puddings: £4.50*

Free house ~ Licensees Nichola and Ian Swinburn ~ Real ale ~ Bar food (12-2, 7-9(8.30 Sun)) ~ Restaurant ~ (01833) 650241 ~ Children allowed but not in bar unless eating ~ Dogs allowed in bedrooms ~ Open 12-2.30, 6.30-11 ~ Bedrooms: £47.50B/£75B

Recommended by David and Katharine Cooke, Maurice and Janet Thorpe, Brian and Rosalie Laverick, M J Winterton

DIPTONMILL
NY9261 MAP 10

Dipton Mill Inn 🍷 🍺 £

Just S of Hexham; off B6306 at Slaley, Blanchland and Dye House, Whitley Chapel signposts (and HGV route sign); not to be confused with the Dipton in Durham; NE46 1YA

Own-brew beers, good value bar food and garden with terrace and aviary

'All a pub should be,' enthused one reporter of this ivy-covered rural pub, which really deserves seeking out for its beers. In fine weather it's pleasant to sit out on the sunken crazy-paved terrace by the restored mill stream, or in the attractively planted garden with its aviary. The cheery landlord here is a brewer in the family-owned Hexhamshire Brewery and their Hexhamshire Devils Water, Devils Elbow, Old Humbug, Shire Bitter and Whapweasel are all well kept on handpump; 15 wines by the glass, over 20 malt whiskies, and Weston's Old Rosie cider. The neatly kept, snug bar has dark ply panelling, low ceilings, red furnishings, a dark red carpet and newspapers to read by two welcoming open fires. There's a nice walk through the woods along the little valley, and Hexham race course is not far away.

🍽 **As well as a fine range of northumbrian cheeses, the inexpensive food includes sandwiches, ploughman's, soup, mince and dumplings, duck breast with orange and cranberry, tagliatelle with creamy basil sauce and parmesan, lamb steak in wine and mustard sauce, and puddings such as rhubarb crumble and chocolate rum truffle torte.** *Starters/Snacks: £2.30 to £3.75. Main Courses: £7.00 to £8.00. Puddings: £2.25 to £3.00*

Own brew ~ Licensee Geoff Brooker ~ Real ale ~ Bar food (12-2, 6.30-8.30; not Sun evening) ~ No credit cards ~ (01434) 606577 ~ Children welcome ~ Open 12-2.30, 6-11; 12-3 Sun; closed Sun evening

Recommended by Alex and Claire Pearse, Andy and Jill Kassube, Michael Doswell, Neil Whitehead, Victoria Anderson, the Didler, Mr and Mrs T Stone

---

Cribbage is a card game using a block of wood with holes for matchsticks or special pins to score with; regulars in cribbage pubs are usually happy to teach strangers how to play.

DURHAM
NZ2742 MAP 10

Victoria 🍺 🛏
Hallgarth Street (A177, near Dunelm House); DH1 3AS

Unchanging and neatly kept Victorian pub with royal memorabilia, cheerful locals and well kept regional ales; good value bedrooms

There's a wonderful feeling of stepping back in time as you enter this admirably unaltered late Victorian tavern, and no piped music or modern contrivances sully the atmosphere. The very traditional layout means three little rooms lead off a central bar with typically Victorian décor: mahogany, etched and cut glass and mirrors, colourful William Morris wallpaper over a high panelled dado, some maroon plush seats in little booths, leatherette wall seats, long narrow drinkers' tables, handsome iron and tile fireplaces for the coal fires, a piano, and some photographs and articles showing a very proper pride in the pub; there are also lots of period prints and engravings of Queen Victoria and staffordshire figurines of her and the Prince Consort. Big Lamp Bitter, Durham Magus and three guests such as Hadrian & Border Gladiator, Mordue Five Bridge and Wylam Magic on handpump; also cheap house wines, around 40 malts and a great collection of 40 irish whiskeys. Dominoes. The good value bedrooms are simple but pleasant; a hearty breakfast (good vegetarian one too) is served in the upstairs dining room.

🍽 **They do only lunchtime toasties.** *Starters/Snacks: £1.50*

Free house ~ Licensee Michael Webster ~ Real ale ~ (0191) 386 5269 ~ Children welcome ~ Dogs welcome ~ Open 11.45-3, 6-11; 12-3, 7-10.30 Sun ~ Bedrooms: £48B/£62B

Recommended by Mark Walker, Tracey and Stephen Groves, the Didler, Pete Baker, Eric Larkham, Pam and John Smith, Dr and Mrs P Truelove, Sue and Derek Irvine, Chris Sale

GREAT WHITTINGTON
NZ0070 MAP 10

Queens Head 🍺
Village signposted off A68 and B6018 just N of Corbridge; NE19 2HP

Relaxed and civilised inn with log fires and outside seating

Rather elegant and mellow, this is a civilised place for a fireside drink, with three real ales from local brewers such as Hadrian & Border, High House and Matfen on handpump, and quite a few malt whiskies as well as several wines by the glass. Modern furnishings alongside contrast nicely with handsome carved oak settles and two roaring log fires. There are seats on the small front lawn and this attractive old building is in a smart stone-built village surrounded by partly wooded countryside. More reports please.

🍽 **As well as lunchtime sandwiches, bar food includes soup, fishcakes on bean sprout salad, confit duck leg pancakes with plum dipping sauce, seared scallops, battered cod and hand-cut chips, fish and prawn pie, wild mushroom and baby spinach crêpe with cheese, seared lambs liver, bacon and black pudding and braised pork belly with soy, ginger and garlic, with puddings such as rhubarb and strawberry crème brûlée and dark chocolate steamed pudding with chocolate and vanilla sauce.** *Starters/Snacks: £3.95 to £6.95. Main Courses: £8.25 to £14.95. Puddings: £3.25 to £5.25*

Free house ~ Licensee Claire Murray ~ Real ale ~ Bar food (12-2.30, 6-9; 12-9.30 Fri, Sat; 12-6 Sun) ~ Restaurant ~ (01434) 672267 ~ Children welcome ~ Open 12-3, 5.30-11; 12-midnight(10.30 Sun) Sat

Recommended by Michael Doswell

People named as recommenders after the main entries have told us that the pub should be included. But they have not written the report – we have, after anonymous on-the-spot inspection.

GRETA BRIDGE   NZ0813   MAP 10

Morritt Arms ♀ ⇌
Hotel signposted off A66 W of Scotch Corner; DL12 9SE

Country house hotel with nice pubby bar, extraordinary mural, interesting food, attractive garden and play area, nice bedrooms

The attractively laid out garden outside this imposing 17th-c former coaching inn has some seats with teak tables in a pretty side area looking along to the graceful old bridge by the stately gates to Rokeby Park; there's also a play area for children. Around the nicely pubby bar runs a remarkable mural painted in 1946 by J T Y Gilroy – better known for his old Guinness advertisements – of Dickensian characters; in 1839 Charles Dickens visited one of the three inns at Greta Bridge whilst researching *Nicholas Nickleby*. Big windsor armchairs and sturdy oak settles cluster around traditional cast-iron-framed tables, large windows look out on the extensive lawn, and there are nice open fires. A conservatory corridor leads from here through french windows to the function room. Black Sheep and Timothy Taylors Landlord on handpump, quite a few malt whiskies and an extensive wine list with a dozen wines by the glass. This pub stands on the site of a Roman settlement.

🍽 Good modern bar food includes sandwiches, soup, soufflé of northumberland cheese, steaks, sausage and mash, baked highland salmon with gravadlax risotto, roasted lamb rump, baked free-range chicken with grilled asparagus, line-caught bass, and puddings such as caramelised banana bavaroise or dark chocolate mousse; generous breakfasts. *Starters/Snacks: £5.00 to £9.00. Main Courses: £10.00 to £24.00. Puddings: £6.00 to £7.00*

Free house ~ Licensees Peter Phillips and Barbara Johnson ~ Real ale ~ Bar food (12-3(4 Sun, 6-9.30 (all day Mon-Sat summer)) ~ Restaurant ~ (01833) 627232 ~ Children welcome ~ Dogs allowed in bar and bedrooms ~ Open 11-11; 12-10.30 Sun ~ Bedrooms: £85B/£110B

Recommended by Pat and Stewart Gordon, David and Ruth Hollands, Barry Collett, Richard Cole, Dr and Mrs P Truelove, Tom and Jill Jones, Roger A Bellingham, Arthur Pickering, J Crosby

HALTWHISTLE   NY7166   MAP 10

Milecastle Inn
Military Road; B6318 NE – OS Sheet 86 map reference 715660; NE49 9NN

Close to Hadrian's Wall and some wild scenery, with cosy little rooms warmed by winter log fires; fine views and walled garden

This solitary 17th-c pub stands close to some of the most celebrated sites of Hadrian's Wall, and the straight moorland road it stands on was the military road that was contemporary with the Wall itself. The snug little rooms of the beamed bar are decorated with brasses, horsey and local landscape prints and attractive fresh flowers, and have two winter log fires; at lunchtime the small comfortable restaurant is used as an overflow. Friendly hard-working staff serve Big Lamp Bitter and Prince Bishop and a guest such as Camerons Castle Eden from handpump and they have a fair collection of malt whiskies and a good wine list. The tables and benches out in a pleasantly sheltered big walled garden with a dovecote and rather stunning views are popular in summer, and there are two self-catering cottages and a large car park.

🍽 Straightforward, sensible bar food includes sandwiches, soup, game pâté, filo duck rolls, scampi, stilton and vegetable crumble, various pies, and chicken tikka; daily specials, children's menu and puddings. *Starters/Snacks: £4.25 to £6.95. Main Courses: £7.25 to £14.95. Puddings: £4.25*

Free house ~ Licensees Clare and Kevin Hind ~ Real ale ~ Bar food (12-9; 12-3, 6-8.45 in winter) ~ Restaurant ~ (01434) 321372 ~ Children welcome ~ Open 12-11(10.30 Sun); 12-3, 6-10 in winter; closed 26 Dec

Recommended by Michael and Jean Hockings, Neil Whitehead, Victoria Anderson, Michael Dandy, Louise English, Edward Leetham, Tom and Jill Jones

HAYDON BRIDGE

NY8364 MAP 10

General Havelock

A69 Cobridge—Haltwhistle; NE47 6ER

Civilised, chatty riverside dining pub with local beers and interesting food

This old stone terrace house has been imaginatively decorated, and the stripped-stone back stone barn dining room and terrace make the most of the riverside views over the South Tyne. The attractively lit L-shaped bar is in shades of green, and is at its best in the back part – stripped pine chest-of-drawers topped with bric-a-brac, colourful cushions on long pine benches and a sturdy stripped settle, interestingly shaped mahogany-topped tables, good wildlife photographs and a stuffed mountain hare. They have a very local brew from Allendale or High House alongside a guest such as Durham Definitive on handpump, good wines and a choice of apple juices; they have no machines or background music but they do have board games and boules. Haydon Bridge itself is a short and very pretty stroll downstream.

🍴 **The food is well above average and helpings are generous, with home-made bread, local game and farm-assured meat; the menu might include lunchtime baguettes and panini, soup, breast of chicken stuffed with cheddar and leeks wrapped in bacon, sirloin steak and braised lamb shank, chicken and ham pie, a fish of the day, cumberland sausage with mash and game pie, with puddings like chocolate brownie or warm walnut tart; set evening meals and Sunday lunches.** *Starters/Snacks: £4.25 to £5.25. Main Courses: £6.50 to £11.50. Puddings: £4.85*

Free house ~ Licensees Gary and Joanna Thompson ~ Real ale ~ Bar food (12-2(4.30 Sun), 7-9; not Sun evening) ~ Restaurant ~ (01434) 684376 ~ Children welcome in lounge ~ Dogs allowed in bar ~ Open 12-3, 7-midnight; 12-3, 8-11 Sun; closed Mon and first week of Jan

Recommended by Bob Richardson, Michael Doswell, Mr and Mrs A Blofield, Marcus Byron

HEDLEY ON THE HILL

NZ0759 MAP 10

Feathers 🍴 🍺

Village signposted from New Ridley, which is signposted from B6309 N of Consett; OS Sheet 88 map reference 078592; NE43 7SW

NORTHUMBRIA DINING PUB OF THE YEAR

Interesting beers from small breweries, imaginative food and a friendly welcome in quaint tavern

Overlooking the Cheviots, this comfortably pubby hilltop tavern attracts a good mix of locals and visitors. Three neat bars have beams, open fires, stripped stonework, solid furniture, including settles, and old black and white photographs of local places and farm and country workers; a selection of traditional pub games, with dominoes, bar skittles and shove-ha'penny. Small-scale breweries are well represented and might feature Mordue Workie Ticket, Wylam Northern Kite, Hadrian & Border Gladiator and Orkney Red MacGregor on handpump; 31 wines by the glass, a fair range of bourbons and malt whiskies, and quite a choice of soft drinks. They hold a beer festival at Easter with over two dozen real ales (and a barrel race on Easter Monday). Picnic-sets in front are a nice place to sit and watch the world drift by.

🍴 **Details of their carefully chosen suppliers are listed on the menu, and the appealing choice of food features several regional dishes, using wild salmon from the South Tyne, game from local shoots and beef from rare breeds: the menu features items such as soup, ploughman's, purée of broccoli, asparagus and artichoke with poached free range egg, hot smoked eel with northumbrian bacon, leek, mushroom and cheese tart, cumberland sausage and mash, and fillet of mackerel with rhubarb and basil, with evening choices such as goosnargh chicken, sirloin steak, red mullet fillet with mussels, and chestnut and herb-stuffed field mushroom, with puddings like apple and blueberry crumble, and sticky toffee apricot pudding.** *Starters/Snacks: £3.00 to £7.00. Main Courses: £9.00 to £12.00. Puddings: £3.00 to £5.00*

Free house ~ Licensees Rhian Cradock and Helen Greer ~ Real ale ~ Bar food (12-2, 6-8.30; not Mon) ~ (01661) 843607 ~ Children welcome ~ Open 12(6 Mon)-11(10.30 Sun)

Recommended by M and GR, Jenny and Dave Hughes, M A Borthwick, Michael Doswell, Miss J Smith, Gail Squires, Bruce and Sharon Eden, Alex and Claire Pearse, Mike Goddard, Maddie Maughan, Andy and Jill Kassube, Rachel Greer, Christine and Phil Young

LANGLEY ON TYNE
NY8160   MAP 10

Carts Bog Inn
A686 S, junction B6305; NE47 5NW

Remote moorland pub with blazing log fire and well liked food in neat beamed rambling bar

In a fine rural setting between the Allen and Tyne valleys, this is an admirable well run and welcoming all-rounder. The neatly kept main black-beamed bar has a blazing log fire in the central stone fireplace, local photographs and horsebrasses, and windsor chairs and comfortably cushioned wall settles around the tables. It rambles about with flagstones here, carpet there, and mainly white walls with some stripped stone. A restaurant (once a cow byre) with more wall banquettes has pool, piped music, board games and quoits. Along with a brew from Big Lamp there are a couple of guests from brewers such as Consett Ale Works and Jarrow on handpump, several malt whiskies and a big choice of soft drinks and wines; quick, friendly service. Tables in the garden make the most of the view.

🍽 **Reasonably priced bar food includes filled baguettes, soup, haddock or haggis in beer batter, steak in ale casserole, vegetable moussaka, fillet steak, fried bass with spring garlic butter, pheasant with honey and prunes, and puddings such as baked orange and vanilla cheesecake and sticky toffee pudding with butterscotch sauce; they also do a 'little boggers' menu for children.** *Starters/Snacks: £4.25 to £6.75. Main Courses: £7.50 to £19.00. Puddings: £4.00 to £5.95*

Free house ~ Licensee Kelly Norman ~ Real ale ~ Bar food (12-2, 6-9; not Mon lunchtime) ~ Restaurant ~ (01434) 684338 ~ Children welcome ~ Dogs allowed in bar ~ Open 12-2.30, 5-11; 12-11(10.30 Sun) Sat; closed Mon lunchtime

Recommended by Comus and Sarah Elliott, Dr Kevan Tucker, Michael Dandy, Bob Richardson

NEW YORK
NZ3269   MAP 10

Shiremoor Farm
Middle Engine Lane/Norham Rd, off A191 bypass; NE29 8DZ

Large dining pub with interesting furnishings and décor, popular food all day, decent drinks, and covered and heated terrace

This is a clever and creative transformation of derelict agricultural buildings into a busy, large dining pub in somewhat unpromising suburban surroundings. The spacious interior is furnished with a mix of interesting and comfortable furniture and there's a big kelim on the broad flagstones, warmly colourful farmhouse paintwork on the bar counter and several tables, conical roof of the former gin-gan, a few farm tools and evocative country pictures. Gentle lighting in several well divided spacious areas cleverly picks up the surface modelling of the pale stone and beam ends. Black Sheep Ale, Timothy Taylors Landlord and a guest from a brewery like Wylam on handpump, together with decent wines by the glass. The granary extension is pleasant for families. There are seats outside on the covered, heated terrace.

🍽 **Popular food served all day might include sandwiches, starters like soup, honey roast pork fillet and cajun king prawns, main courses like vegetarian quiches and pasta dishes, spicy sausage, and szechuan and ginger marinated beef with king prawn kebab, and puddings like double chocolate and waffle cheesecake, and warm dutch apple pie.** *Starters/Snacks: £2.95 to £5.95. Main Courses: £6.95 to £12.95. Puddings: £3.95 to £4.95*

Free house ~ Licensee C W Kerridge ~ Real ale ~ Bar food (all day) ~ (0191) 2576302 ~ Children welcome away from one side of bar ~ Open 11-11

Recommended by Comus and Sarah Elliott, John R Ringrose

NEWBURN

NZ1665   MAP 10

Keelman 🍺 £ 🛏

Grange Road: follow Riverside Country Park brown signs off A6085 (the riverside road off A1 on Newcastle's W fringes); NE15 8ND

Impressive range of own-brewed beers in converted pumping station, easy-going atmosphere, excellent service, straightforward food, bedroom block

Popular with families because of the proximity of pub and public playgrounds as well as walks along the Tyne, the pub has a splendid array of beers from their own Big Lamp Brewery, on the same site. The bar counter's impressive array of eight handpumps usually dispenses the full range of their beers, obviously kept in tip-top condition and very reasonably priced. If you're confused about which one to go for, the neatly dressed staff will happily let you sample a couple first: Big Lamp Bitter, Blackout, Double M, Embers, Premium, Prince Bishop Ale, Summerhill Stout and Sunny Daze. Service is first-class, the hands-on landlord is quick to help out when needed and the whole place is kept spick and span; piped music. There's an easy-going atmosphere and a good mix of customers in the high-ceilinged bar, which has lofty arched windows, making it light and airy, and well spaced tables and chairs. There are more tables in an upper gallery and the modern all-glass conservatory dining area (pleasant at sunset) contrasts stylishly with the original old building. There are plenty of picnic-sets, tables and benches out on the terraces, among flower tubs and beds of shrubs. There are six up-to-date bedrooms in an adjoining block (prices are for room only, without breakfast).

🍴 **Reasonably priced and served in generous helpings, the straightforward food includes sandwiches, soup, filled baked potatoes, beef in ale pie, large fish and chips, grilled trout and chicken, bacon and leek dumpling in white wine sauce; they do an early evening special on weekdays from 5 till 7.** *Starters/Snacks: £2.95 to £5.50. Main Courses: £5.95 to £12.50. Puddings: £3.40*

Own brew ~ Licensee George Story ~ Real ale ~ Bar food (12-9(9.30 Sat)) ~ Restaurant ~ (0191) 267 0772 ~ Children welcome ~ Open 11-11; 12-10.30 Sun ~ Bedrooms: £41S/£55S

Recommended by Andy and Jill Kassube, GSB, M J Winterton, Graham Oddey, Celia Minoughan, Mr and Mrs Maurice Thompson, Arthur Pickering, Alan Thwaite, George Cowie, Frances Gosnell

NEWCASTLE UPON TYNE

NZ2664   MAP 10

Cluny 🍺 £

Lime Street (which runs between A193 and A186 E of centre); NE1 2PQ

Carefully converted whisky-bottling plant doubling as art gallery and studio; sparsely decorated bar, super ales from local breweries and simple bar food

By no means a conventional pub, this is a lively city venue with plenty going on and a splendid range of beers. It's an imaginatively converted early 19th-c whisky-bottling plant, and the back area has changing exhibitions of paintings, sculptures and pottery by local artists and craftspeople; each evening there is live music. The friendly L-shaped bar is trendy and gently bohemian-feeling despite its minimalist décor, with slightly scuffed bare boards, some chrome seating and overhead spotlights. There are seven changing real ales on handpump such as Jarrow River Cotcher, Hill Island Stout, Mordue Five Bridge Bitter and Wylom Magic; perry, Weston's farm cider, rotating continental and american beers on tap, lots of bottled world beers, a good range of soft drinks and a fine row of rums, malt whiskies and vodkas and banana smoothies. A raised area looking down on the river has comfortable seating including settees and there are daily papers and local arts magazines. A separate room has a stage for live bands; disabled access and facilities, fruit machine and well reproduced piped music. To get here – opposite the Ship on Lime Street look out for a cobbled bank leading down to the Ouseburn, by the Byker city farm, and stretching down here, the pub is below the clutch of bridges.

🍴 **Simple bar food, served by cheerful staff all day, includes soup, sandwiches, ciabattas, toasties, ploughman's, burgers, salads, spinach, chickpea and mushroom chilli, daily specials, Sunday roasts, and puddings such as fudge cake.** *Starters/Snacks: £2.50 to £4.50. Main Courses: £5.00 to £7.00. Puddings: £1.00 to £3.50*

Head of Steam ~ Licensee Julian Ive ~ Real ale ~ Bar food (12-9 daily) ~ (0191) 230 4474 ~
Children welcome until 7pm ~ Live bands every night ~ Open 11.30-11(midnight Sat);
12-10.30 Sun

Recommended by Mike and Lynn Robinson, Mrs Hazel Rainer, Eric Larkham, Graham Oddey

Crown Posada ◀

*The Side; off Dean Street, between and below the two high central bridges (A6125 and
A6127); NE1 3JE*

**Busy city-centre pub with grand architecture, lots of locals in long narrow bar, tip-top
beers and a warm welcome; almost no food**

This marvellously unchanged adults-only drinking pub, Newcastle's second oldest, is one
of the city's architectural glories but is easily missed. During the week regulars sit
reading papers in the front snug and it is an oasis of calm from the nearby quayside
area, but at weekends it is often packed. A golden crown and magnificent pre-Raphaelite
stained-glass windows add grandeur to an already imposing carved stone façade, while
inside highlights include the elaborate coffered ceiling, stained-glass in the counter
screens, a line of gilt mirrors each with a tulip lamp on a curly brass mount matching
the great ceiling candelabra. Fat low-level heating pipes make a popular footrest when
the east wind brings the rain off the North Sea. It's a very long and narrow room,
making quite a bottleneck by the serving counter; beyond that, a long soft green built-
in leather wall seat is flanked by narrow tables. An old record player in a wooden cabinet
provides mellow background music when the place is quiet. From half a dozen
handpumps and kept in fine condition, the real ales might include house beers like
Hadrian & Border Gladiator, Jarrow Bitter and Timothy Taylors Landlord with guests such
as Mordue IPA, Northumberland Bitter and Wylam Gold Tankard. It's only a few minutes'
stroll to the castle.

🍴 **Lunchtime sandwiches but nothing else.** *Starters/Snacks: £1.50*

Sir John Fitzgerald ~ Licensee Derek Raisbeck ~ Real ale ~ No credit cards ~ (0191) 232 1269 ~
Open 11(12 Sat)-11; 7-10.30 Sun; closed Sun lunchtime

*Recommended by Pete Baker, John and Gloria Isaacs, Andy and Jill Kassube, Dr and Mrs A K Clarke, Peter Smith,
Judith Brown, Mark and Diane Grist, Joe Green, Eric Larkham, the Didler, Arthur Pickering, Celia Minoughan,
Mrs Hazel Rainer*

NEWTON-BY-THE-SEA   NU2424   MAP 10

Ship

*Village signposted off B1339 N of Alnwick; Low Newton – paid parking 200 metres up road
on right, just before village (none in village); NE66 3EL*

**In charming square of fishermen's cottages by green sloping to sandy beach, good simple
food, fine spread of drinks; best to check winter opening times**

They started brewing their beers here at their own Ship Inn Brewery in 2008: Dolly
Daydream, Sandcastles at Dawn, Sea Wheat and Ship Hop are on handpump, with a guest
beer at busier times. The coastal setting is quite enchanting: a row of converted
fishermen's cottages and looking across a sloping village green to a sandy beach just
beyond. The plainly furnished bare-boards bar on the right has nautical charts on its
dark pink walls, beams and hop bines. Another simple room on the left has some bright
modern pictures on stripped-stone walls, and a woodburning stove in its stone fireplace;
darts, dominoes. It can get very busy indeed at lunchtimes (quieter at night and during
the winter) and service does slow down then (although we've generally had glowing
reports, a couple of readers have found service can leave a bit to be desired when the
staff are under pressure); booking at busier times is strongly recommended. Out in the
corner of the square are some tables among pots of flowers, with picnic-sets over on the
grass. There's no nearby parking, but there's a car park up the hill. There is a one-
bedroom flat on the premises (minimum stay two nights).

🍴 Using local free-range and organic produce, the well liked food at lunchtime includes toasties, stotties and ciabattas, ploughman's, fishcakes and kipper pâté, with evening choices such as grilled goats cheese with tomato and basil, lobster from Newton Bay, silver anchovies on wild rocket salad, hot mexican beans in a tortilla wrap with wild rice, cheese and sour cream, gammon with mustard mash, smoked haddock fillet on spring onion and parsley mash, and puddings like apple crumble and speciality ice-creams. *Starters/Snacks: £2.50 to £7.00. Main Courses: £6.50 to £15.00. Puddings: £3.50 to £5.00*

Free house ~ Licensee Christine Forsyth ~ Real ale ~ Bar food (12-2.30, 7-8 (not winter evenings except Thurs-Sat)) ~ No credit cards ~ (01665) 576262 ~ Children welcome ~ Dogs welcome ~ Live folk/blues/jazz; phone for details ~ Open 11(12 Sun)-11; 11-4 Sun-Weds; 11-4, 8-11 Thurs, Fri; 11-11 Sat winter; closed Sun-Weds evenings in winter

Recommended by Comus and Sarah Elliott, Lawrence Pearse, Graham Oddey, the Didler, Paul and Ursula Randall, P Dawn, Tony and Jill Radnor, Reg Fowle, Helen Rickwood, Michael Doswell, Mike and Sue Loseby, Michael Butler, Paul Newberry

NEWTON-ON-THE-MOOR
NU1705   MAP 10

Cook & Barker Arms 🍴 🛏

Village signposted from A1 Alnwick—Felton; NE65 9JY

Emphasis on generous food but with nicely traditional country-pub feel in the bar, and quite a range of drinks; comfortable bedrooms

The efficient staff cope really well here even when things get busy: it's a friendly stone-built inn with most customers here to enjoy the good food. The relaxed and unfussy long beamed bar feels distinctly pubby though, with stripped stone and partly panelled walls, brocade-seated settles around oak-topped tables, brasses, a highly polished oak servery, and a lovely fire at one end with a coal-effect gas fire at the other. An eating area has oak-topped tables with comfortable leather chairs and french windows leading on to the terrace; piped music. Black Sheep, Hadrian & Border Secret Kingdom and Timothy Taylors Landlord on handpump, a dozen wines by the glass from an extensive list and quite a few malt whiskies. Surprisingly quiet given its proximity to the A1, it has an inviting garden and the bedrooms are very comfortable.

🍴 The licensees have bought a farm and plan to grow organic vegetables and raise organic cattle, sheep and rare breed pigs for use in the pub. Popular, interesting and very fairly priced bar food includes sandwiches, interesting soups, crab and prawn risotto, goats cheese tart with beetroot, roast beef or pork, mixed grill, crispy vegetable spring rolls with chilli dipping sauce, seared tuna loin, and puddings; a more elaborate à la carte menu and a good value three-course evening menu, too. *Starters/Snacks: £4.00 to £8.00. Main Courses: £7.50 to £17.00. Puddings: £4.95*

Free house ~ Licensee Phil Farmer ~ Real ale ~ Bar food (12-2, 5-9) ~ Restaurant (12-2, 7-9) ~ (01665) 575234 ~ Children welcome ~ Open 11-11; 12-10.30 Sun ~ Bedrooms: £57B/£75B

Recommended by Philip and Susan Philcox, M A Borthwick, Arthur Pickering, Jennifer Hurst, Louise English, R N and M I Bailey, Alex and Claire Pearse, Michael Doswell, John and Sylvia Harrop, Comus and Sarah Elliott, Dr Peter D Smart, K S Whittaker, Brian Brooks, Charles and Pauline Stride, Tina and David Woods-Taylor, Mike and Sue Loseby

RENNINGTON
NU2118   MAP 10

Masons Arms 🛏

Stamford Cott; B1340 NE of Alnwick; NE66 3RX

Comfortable bedrooms make this a good base for nearby coast; very neatly kept pub, local beers and seats outside

In a quiet village a few miles from the coast, and handy for exploring Alnwick and Dunstanburgh castles, this spotless pub with accommodation is an attractive base, and the staff make every effort to get things right. The beamed lounge bar is pleasantly modernised and comfortable, with wheelback and mate's chairs around solid wood tables on a patterned carpet, plush bar stools, and plenty of pictures (some may be for sale), photographs and brass. The dining rooms have pine panelling and wrought-iron wall lights; piped classical music. Hadrian & Border Gladiator and Secret Kingdom and two guests like Hadrian & Border Farne Island Pale Ale and Northumberland Bedlington Terrier on handpump. There are sturdy rustic tables on the little front lavender-surrounded terrace, and picnic-sets at the back. The neat and well equipped bedrooms are in an adjacent stable block and annexe and the proper breakfasts are good.

🍴 **Straightforward bar food includes soup, craster kipper pâté, curry of the day, spinach and ricotta cannelloni, lemon sole stuffed with prawns, mixed grill, roast duck with orange sauce, and puddings like apple pie or lemon meringue pie.** *Starters/Snacks: £3.25 to £4.95. Main Courses: £5.95 to £16.95. Puddings: £3.95 to £4.25*

Free house ~ Licensees Bob and Alison Culverwell ~ Real ale ~ Bar food (12-2, 6.30-9) ~ Restaurant ~ (01665) 577275 ~ Children welcome ~ Dogs allowed in bedrooms ~ Open 12-11; 12-2, 4.30-10.30 Sun; closed 2-6.30 in winter ~ Bedrooms: £45B/£85S(£75B)

Recommended by Christine and Malcolm Ingram, Comus and Sarah Elliott, Stuart Paulley, Michael Butler, Robert Stephenson, Mr and Mrs P L Spencer

ROMALDKIRK   NY9922   MAP 10

Rose & Crown ★ 🍴 🍷 🛏

Just off B6277; DL12 9EB

Good base for the area, with accomplished cooking, civilised comfort and attentive service; lovely bedrooms

One couple returned to this comfortable country inn for a stay after more than 25 years after their last visit and found it as good as ever, with well kept beer, an excellent lunch and very helpful staff, and it has proved just as reliable with other readers. The cosy traditional beamed bar has old-fashioned seats facing a warming log fire, a Jacobean oak settle, lots of brass and copper, a grandfather clock, and gin traps, old farm tools, and black and white pictures of Romaldkirk on the walls. Black Sheep Best Bitter and Theakstons Best are on handpump alongside 14 wines by the glass, organic fruit juices and pressed vegetable juices. The smart brasserie-style Crown Room (bar food is served in here) has large cartoons of french waiters on dark red walls, a grey carpet and smart high-back chairs. The hall has farm tools, wine maps and other interesting prints, along with a photograph (taken by a customer) of the Hale Bopp comet over Romaldkirk church. There's also an oak-panelled restaurant. It's lovely outside in summer, with tables looking out over the village green, still with its original stocks and water pump. There are very well equipped bedrooms and bathrooms; the owners also provide their own in-house guide to tried and tested days out and about in the area and a *Walking in Teesdale* book. The village is close to the extraordinary Bowes Museum and High Force waterfall, and has an interesting old church.

🍴 **The imaginative food (only the frites and ice-cream are bought in and they make their own chutneys, jams, marmalades and bread) in the bar at lunchtime might include filled baguettes, stotties and ciabattas, ploughman's, soup, chicken liver pâté with port and orange sauce, baked goats cheese soufflé with a light chive cream, pork sausage with black pudding mustard mash and shallot gravy, welsh rarebit, steak, kidney and mushroom in ale pie, and smoked haddock kedgeree with prawns, quail eggs and parmesan; evening choices such as smoked salmon soufflé with tarragon gazpacho, fried pheasant with apple and prune compote and calvados cream, baked halibut with cotherstone cheese and red onion marmalade, confit of lamb shoulder, and chargrilled rump of venison with button mushrooms, oloroso sherry and cream; puddings like hot treacle tart and chocolate and brandy panna cotta. You do need to book to be sure of a table.** *Starters/Snacks: £4.25 to £6.25. Main Courses: £7.95 to £15.95. Puddings: £4.75*

Free house ~ Licensees Christopher and Alison Davy ~ Real ale ~ Bar food (12-1.30, 6.30-9.30) ~ Restaurant ~ (01833) 650213 ~ Children welcome but must be over 6 in restaurant ~ Dogs allowed in bar and bedrooms ~ Open 11(12 Sun)-11; closed 24-26 Dec ~ Bedrooms: £85B/£130S(£150B)

Recommended by Rodney and Norma Stubington, Pat and Tony Martin, Mike and Sue Loseby, J C Clark, Mrs Sheila Stothard, Pat and Stewart Gordon, Brian Brooks, J Crosby, Mrs Roxanne Chamberlain, Hunter and Christine Wright, Arthur Pickering

SEAHOUSES
NU2232   MAP 10

Olde Ship ★ ◖ 🛏
Just off B1340, towards harbour; NE68 7RD

Lots of atmosphere, fine choice of ales and maritime memorabilia in bustling little hotel; views across harbour to Farne Islands

You'll find a rich assemblage of nautical bits and pieces inside this busy hotel, which was first licensed in 1812 to serve visiting herring fishermen and has been in the same family for over a century. The bar, gently lit by stained-glass sea picture windows, lantern lights and a winter open fire, remains a tribute to the sea and seafarers. Even the floor is scrubbed ship's decking and, if it's working, an anemometer takes wind speed readings from the top of the chimney. Besides lots of other shiny brass fittings, ship's instruments and equipment, and a knotted anchor made by local fishermen, there are sea pictures and model ships, including fine ones of the North Sunderland lifeboat, and Seahouses' lifeboat the *Grace Darling*. There's also a model of the *Forfarshire*, the paddle steamer local heroine Grace Darling went to rescue in 1838 (you can read more of the story in the pub), and even the ship's nameboard. One clear glass window looks out across the harbour to the Farne Islands, and as dusk falls you can watch the Longstones lighthouse shine across the fading evening sky. A fine choice of beers features Black Sheep Best Bitter, Hadrian & Border Farne Island Pale Ale, Courage Directors and Greene King Old Speckled Hen and Ruddles County; also, a good wine list and quite a few malt whiskies. The pub has piped music and TV; it is not really suitable for children though there is a little family room, and along with walkers, they are welcome on the battlemented side terrace (you'll find fishing memorabilia even out here). This and a sun lounge look out on the harbour. You can book boat trips to the Farne Islands Bird Sanctuary at the harbour, and there are bracing coastal walks, particularly to Bamburgh, Grace Darling's birthplace.

🍴 **Standard bar food includes sandwiches, ploughman's, chicken liver pâté, soup, smoked fish chowder, fish or spicy lamb stew, chilli bean hotpot and puddings like plum crumble and apple and raspberry; breakfasts include kippers and local black pudding.** *Starters/Snacks: £4.50 to £5.00. Main Courses: £7.50 to £11.00. Puddings: £4.00 to £5.75*

Free house ~ Licensees Alan and Jean Glen ~ Real ale ~ Bar food (no evening food mid-Dec to mid-Jan) ~ Restaurant ~ (01665) 720200 ~ Children under 10 in small back lounge ~ Open 11(12 Sun)-11 ~ Bedrooms: £56S/£112B

Recommended by Andy and Jill Kassube, Tony and Maggie Harwood, Mr and Mrs Staples, Reg Fowle, Helen Rickwood, Mike and Sue Loseby, Mrs Marion Matthewman, M J Winterton, Mrs Brenda Calver, Mr and Mrs L Haines, Louise English, Sue and Dave Harris, Graham Findley, Comus and Sarah Elliott, the Didler, Paul and Ursula Randall

STANNERSBURN
NY7286   MAP 10

Pheasant
Kielder Water road signposted off B6320 in Bellingham; NE48 1DD

Warmly friendly village local close to Kielder Water with quite a mix of customers and nice homely bar food; streamside garden

In a restful valley amid quiet forests and not far from Kielder Water, this village inn is an inviting haven, with picnic-sets in the streamside garden and a pony paddock behind. The low-beamed comfortable traditional lounge has ranks of old local photographs on stripped stone and panelling, red patterned carpets, and upholstered stools ranged along the counter. A separate public bar is similar but simpler and opens into a further cosy seating area with beams and panelling. The evening sees a good mix of visitors and locals, when the small dining room can get quite crowded. Timothy Taylors Landlord and a couple of guests such as Wylam Bitter and Northern Kite on handpump (only one real ale during the winter), over 30 malt whiskies, and a decent reasonably priced wine list; courteous staff. The bedrooms were refurbished in 2008.

🍴 **Very good bar food typically includes lunchtime sandwiches, soup, caramelised onion and goats cheese tart, sweet marinated herring, poached bass, game and mushroom pie, roast lamb with redcurrant and rosemary jus, and puddings such as rhubarb and apple**

crumble and bread and butter marmalade pudding; northumbrian cheeseboard.
Starters/Snacks: £3.50 to £5.50. Main Courses: £7.95 to £10.95. Puddings: £3.95 to £4.25

Free house ~ Licensees Walter and Robin Kershaw ~ Real ale ~ Bar food ~ Restaurant ~
(01434) 240382 ~ Children welcome ~ Dogs allowed in bedrooms ~ Open 11-3, 6-11; 12-3,
7-11 Sun; closed Mon, Tues Nov-Mar ~ Bedrooms: £55S/£90S

Recommended by Pat and Stewart Gordon, Dr Peter D Smart, Dennis Jones, Mr and Mrs L Haines, Michael Dandy,
Pauline Shaw, David Cosham, Sara Fulton, Roger Baker, Arthur Pickering

STANNINGTON   NZ2179   MAP 10

Ridley Arms
Village signposted just off A1 S of Morpeth; NE61 6EL

Comfortably airy, with several differing linked rooms; good choice of real ales

They have seven real ales here, with Black Sheep alongside guests such as Caledonian
Deuchars IPA, Durham Magus, Theakstons XB and Wells & Youngs; also a good choice of
wines by the glass. It's arranged into several separate areas, each slightly different in
mood and style from its neighbours. The front is a proper bar area with darts and a fruit
machine and stools along the counter; piped music. The beamed dining areas lead back
from here, with a second bar counter, comfortable armchairs and upright chairs around
shiny dark wood tables on polished boards or carpet, portraits and cartoons on cream,
panelled or stripped stone walls, careful lighting and some horsey statuettes; brisk
service and good disabled access. There are tables outside on a terrace; the A1 is very
close by.

🍴 **Bar food includes sandwiches, soup, leek and wild mushroom tart, sticky spare ribs
with an orange and chilli glaze, fish and chips, harissa chicken with herby couscous,
aberdeen angus casserole with lentils, shallots and whisky, daily specials, and puddings.**
Starters/Snacks: £3.50 to £5.00. Main Courses: £7.50 to £16.00. Puddings: £3.95 to £4.75

Sir John Fitzgerald ~ Managers Lynn and Gary Reilly ~ Real ale ~ Bar food (12-9.30(9 Sun)) ~
(01670) 789216 ~ Children welcome ~ Open 11.30-11; 12-10.30 Sun

Recommended by Jan Moore, Comus and Sarah Elliott, Sheena W Makin, Dr Peter D Smart, Celia Minoughan

WARK   NY8676   MAP 10

Battlesteads 🍴 🛏

B6320 N of Hexham; NE48 3LS

Good local ales, fair value tasty food and relaxed atmosphere; comfortable bedrooms

In a village on a scenic road by the North Tyne River and close to Wark Forest, this
friendly inn originated as an 18th-c farmstead and served for a period as a temperance
hotel. The nicely restored carpeted bar has a wood-burning stove with traditional oak
surround, and on the low beams, comfortable seats including some low leather sofas, and
old *Punch* country life cartoons on the off-white walls above its dark dado; this leads
through to the restaurant and spacious conservatory. There's a relaxed unhurried
atmosphere and good changing local ales such as Black Sheep Ale and Best Bitter,
Durham Magus and a couple of guests such as Hadrian & Border Gladiator and Wylam
Gold Tankard from handpumps on the heavily carved dark oak bar counter; good coffee,
cheerful service. Some of the bedrooms are on the ground floor (with disabled access),
and in the roof space they plan to develop an observatory. There are tables on a terrace
in the walled garden. The hotel has won an award for green tourism initiatives: forest
wood chippings are used to fuel the heating and hot water system. More reports please.

🍴 **Good value food includes lunchtime sandwiches, soup, northumbrian smoked platter,
game terrine, chargrilled rib-eye steak, lamb cutlets, fresh coley fillet topped with
spinach and horseradish crumb, mussels with wild garlic leaves and cream, and globe
courgette with fresh beetroot and horseradish soufflé; daily specials, and puddings.**
Starters/Snacks: £3.25 to £7.95. Main Courses: £8.50 to £18.50. Puddings: £4.75 to £5.75

Free house ~ Licensees Richard and Dee Slade ~ Real ale ~ Bar food (12-3, 6.30-9.30) ~ Restaurant ~ (01434) 230209 ~ Children welcome ~ Dogs allowed in bar and bedrooms ~ Open 11-11; closed 3-6 Mon-Fri in winter ~ Bedrooms: £55S/£90B

Recommended by Dr A McCormick, Comus and Sarah Elliott, Andy and Jill Kassube, BOB, Michael Doswell

WELDON BRIDGE   NZ1398   MAP 10

Anglers Arms 🛏

B6344, just off A697; village signposted with Rothbury off A1 N of Morpeth; NE65 8AX

Large helpings of straightforward food in appealing and interesting bar or converted railway dining car, comfortable bedrooms, fishing on River Coquet

This sizeable hotel is beside a bridge over the River Coquet, and they have rights to fishing along a mile of the river bank. Nicely lit and comfortable, the traditional turkey-carpeted bar is divided into two parts: cream walls on the right, and oak panelling and some shiny black beams hung with copper pans on the left, with a grandfather clock and sofa by the coal fire, staffordshire cats and other antique ornaments on its mantelpiece, old fishing and other country prints, some in heavy gilt frames, a profusion of other fishing memorabilia, and some taxidermy. Some of the tables are lower than you'd expect for eating, but their chairs have short legs to match – different, and rather engaging. Timothy Taylors Landlord and three guests such as Black Sheep, Courage Directors and Greene King Old Speckled Hen on handpump, around 30 malt whiskies and decent wines; piped music. The restaurant is in a former railway dining car with crisp white linen and a pink carpet. There are tables in the attractive garden with a good play area that includes an assault course.

🍴 Generous helpings of bar food include sandwiches, home-made chicken liver pâté, prawn and smoked salmon salad, cod and chips, mince and dumplings, sausage casserole, steak in ale pie, sirloin steak, oriental platter, and puddings; the restaurant has more elaborate and more expensive dishes. *Starters/Snacks: £4.95 to £10.95. Main Courses: £7.95 to £18.95. Puddings: £4.95*

Enterprise ~ Lease John Young ~ Real ale ~ Bar food (12-9.30(9 Sun)) ~ Restaurant ~ (01665) 570271 ~ Children welcome ~ Dogs allowed in bedrooms ~ Open 11-11; 12-11 Sun ~ Bedrooms: £39.50S/£75S

Recommended by Richard C Morgan, Dr Peter D Smart, Sheena W Makin, Michael Doswell, Graham Oddey

LUCKY DIP

Besides the fully inspected pubs, you might like to try these Lucky Dips recommended to us and described by readers (if you do, please send us reports: feedback@thegoodpubguide.co.uk).

ALLENHEADS [NY8545]
☆ *Allenheads Inn* NE47 9HJ [just off B6295]: Country inn splendidly placed high in wild former lead-mining country (and on the C2C Sustrans cycle route), four well kept ales such as Black Sheep and Jarrow, decent wine, usual food from cheap toasties up, good-sized country dining room, room with forces memorabilia, games room with darts and pool; piped music, TV; children welcome, tables out beside some agricultural antiques, good value bedrooms, open all day *(Dennis Jones, LYM, Ann and Tony Bennett-Hughes)*

ALNWICK [NU1813]
☆ *Blackmores* NE66 1PN [Bondgate Without]: Black Sheep and Caledonian ales, good choice of wines by the glass and above-average food in former Plough, reworked as light and airy pub/boutique hotel by new landlord who previously made the Tankerville

Arms in Eglingham a popular main entry; bedrooms *(Comus and Sarah Elliott)*
John Bull NE66 1UY [Howick St]: Friendly real ale pub, essentially front room of early 19th-c terraced house, with great changing range, also bottled imports and dozens of malt whiskies; cl wkdy lunchtime *(the Didler, Eric Larkham, Ian Humphreys)*

AYCLIFFE [NZ2822]
☆ *County* DL5 6LX [off A1(M) junction 59, by A167]: Dining pub, very highly rated under previous regime, now under new owner, light minimalist décor in extended bar and bistro, good choice of wines by the glass, Wells & Youngs Bombardier and guest beers; piped music; children welcome, cl Sun evening *(LYM)*

BAMBURGH [NU1834]
Castle NE69 7BW [Front St]: Comfortably old-fashioned pub under new ownership, pleasant atmosphere, friendly staff, usual food *(John Woodman, Tony and Jill Radnor)*

Lord Crewe Arms NE69 7BL [Front St]: Small hotel prettily set in charming coastal village dominated by Norman castle, two-room bar with log fire, good choice of wines by the glass from penny-studded counter, Black Sheep and Wells & Youngs Bombardier, lunchtime bar food, separate modern restaurant; dogs and children welcome, suntrap terrace, short walk from splendid sandy beach, comfortable bedrooms *(LYM, Reg Fowle, Helen Rickwood)*

☆ *Victoria* NE69 7BP [Front St]: Substantial Victorian hotel with lots of mirrors and pictures in softly furnished two-part panelled bar, peaceful, light and airy, good quickly prepared food all day from sandwiches up, two rotating real ales from Black Sheep and/or Mordue, good wines by the glass, friendly young staff, smart more upmarket back brasserie, young children's playroom; comfortable bedrooms, lovely setting, open all day *(Comus and Sarah Elliott, Tina and David Woods-Taylor)*

BARDON MILL [NY7566]
Twice Brewed NE47 7AN [Military Rd (B6318 NE of Hexham)]: Large busy pub well placed for fell-walkers and major Wall sites, five local real ales, malt whiskies, reasonably priced wines, good value hearty pub food from baguettes up, quick friendly staff, nice photographs; quiet piped music; children allowed in restaurant, tables outside, warm bedrooms, open all day *(Michael Doswell)*

BEADNELL [NU2229]
Beadnell Towers NE67 5AU: Large welcoming off-season haven with above-average food, Black Sheep, Hadrian & Border and Mordue ales, reasonably priced wines by the glass, good service; can get more touristy in summer; good bedrooms *(Reg Fowle, Helen Rickwood, Comus and Sarah Elliott)*
Craster Arms NE67 5AX [The Wynding]: Enjoyable generous food inc wknd roasts, Black Sheep, friendly foreign staff, games area with pool, wknd entertainment; children welcome *(Reg Fowle, Helen Rickwood)*

BEAMISH [NZ2153]
☆ *Beamish Mary* DH9 0QH [off A693 signed No Place and Cooperative Villas, S of museum]: Friendly down-to-earth former pit village pub with up to ten well kept mainly local ales, two farm ciders, wide choice of good value generous food inc massive mixed grill and popular Sun lunch, efficient helpful staff, coal fires, two bars with 1960s-feel mix of furnishings, bric-a-brac, 1920s/30s memorabilia and Aga, Durham NUM banner in games room; piped music, live music most nights in converted stables concert room, annual beer festival; children allowed until evening, bedrooms *(Arthur Pickering, Mark Walker, Peter Smith, Judith Brown, Dr Roger Smith, Judy Nicholson)*

BELFORD [NU1033]
Salmon NE70 7NG [village signed off A1 S of Berwick]: Light and airy, with good value food inc curry specialities, efficient staff;

band nights, busy wknds *(LYM, Reg Fowle, Helen Rickwood)*

BELSAY [NZ1277]
Highlander NE20 0DN [A696 S of village]: Roomy country dining pub, bargain food from good lunchtime baguettes up, quick friendly service, Black Sheep and Timothy Taylors Landlord, good log fires, comfortable raised side area with nice plain wood tables and high-backed banquettes, plenty of nooks and corners for character, plainer locals' bar; unobtrusive piped music; open all day *(Michael Doswell, Guy and Caroline Howard, Dr Peter D Smart)*

BERWICK-UPON-TWEED [NT9952]
☆ *Foxtons* TD15 1AB [Hide Hill]: More chatty and comfortable two-level wine bar than pub, with wide choice of good imaginative food, prompt friendly service, good range of wines, whiskies and coffees, real ales such as Caledonian and Timothy Taylors, lively side bistro; busy, so worth booking evenings, open all day, cl Sun *(Mrs Marion Matthewman, John and Sylvia Harrop)*
Pilot TD15 1LZ [Low Greens]: Small beamed and panelled backstreet local, old nautical photographs and knick-knacks, comfortable back lounge, changing real ales from the region, darts and quoits; fiddle music Thurs; garden tables, bedrooms, open all day Fri-Sun and summer *(the Didler, Comus and Sarah Elliott)*
Queens Head TD15 1EP [Sandgate]: Welcoming pub with enjoyable pubby food, well kept Theakstons, comfortable seats at clean tables, daily papers *(Reg Fowle, Helen Rickwood)*

BIRTLEY [NZ2856]
Mill House DH3 1RE [Blackfell, via A1231 slip rd off southbound A1]: Extensively refurbished dining pub with enjoyable food all day inc bargain two-course lunches, compact bar area, changing real ale, decent house wines, dining room with olde-barn décor, alcoved eating areas and conservatory *(Gerry and Rosemary Dobson, Jenny and Dave Hughes)*
Moulders Arms DH3 2LW [Peareth Terr]: Friendly new licensees in pleasantly refurbished pub by church in old part of village, comfortable lounge with raised back area and wide views from front, three real ales, good value food from sandwiches up, small public bar; garden *(anon)*

BOULMER [NU2614]
Fishing Boat NE66 3BP: Well kept light airy pub, changing real ales, pubby food, interesting pictures; dogs welcome, decking overlooking sea, nice spot on Craster—Alnmouth coast walk *(Reg Fowle, Helen Rickwood, Peter and Eleanor Kenyon)*

BOURNMOOR [NZ3051]
Dun Cow DH4 6DY [Primrose Hill (A1052)]: Traditional country pub with comfortable bar and restaurant, friendly landlord, efficient staff, food all day, usually Jarrow and another ale; children welcome, garden with smokers' marquee *(Mark Walker)*

Floaters Mill DH4 6BQ [A1052]: Comfortable welcoming country pub with big lounge bar and conservatory, efficient young staff, three real ales, food inc popular Sun lunch; children welcome, outside seating, play area, open all day *(Mark Walker)*

BOWES [NY9913]

☆ *Ancient Unicorn* DL12 9HL: Substantial stone inn with some 17th-c parts and interesting *Nicholas Nickleby* connection, warmly welcoming licensees, two or three well kept ales (spring beer festival), good value generous fresh food from sandwiches and good hot-filled baguettes up, pleasant atmosphere in spacious and comfortable open-plan bar with small but hot open fire, coffee shop, pool; tables on split-level terrace, well refurbished bedrooms in converted stables block around big cobbled courtyard *(G Deacon, Nick Holding, Philip and Sally Tavener, LYM)*

BURNOPFIELD [NZ1857]

Pack Horse NE16 6NS [Crookgate (A692)]: Big friendly modern pub serving enjoyable food inc good well hung steaks, reasonable prices, open all day *(M and GR)*

CASTLE EDEN [NZ4237]

Castle Eden Inn TS27 4SD [B1281 S of Peterlee]: Revitalised by new landlord, Camerons and up to four changing ales, enjoyable interesting food, pool; juke box, sports TV; disabled access, open all day *(JHBS)*

CAUSEY PARK BRIDGE [NZ1894]

Oak NE61 3EL [off A1 5 miles N of Morpeth]: Open-plan country pub with friendly new management, enjoyable food inc bargain Sun lunch and cut-price small evening helpings, conservatory; children welcome, garden with play area *(Guy and Caroline Howard, Michael Doswell)*

CHATTON [NU0528]

Percy Arms NE66 5PS [B6348 E of Wooller]: Comfortable stone-built country inn with cheerful efficient staff, pubby food in bar and attractive panelled dining room from lunchtime sandwiches up, lounge bar extending through arch, public bar with games, plenty of malt whiskies, changing ales; piped music; children in good family area and dining room, small front lawn, bedrooms (12 miles of private fishing) *(Comus and Sarah Elliott, Paul and Ursula Randall, LYM)*

CORBRIDGE [NY9964]

Angel NE45 5LA [Main St]: Small 17th-c hotel with good fresh food (not cheap by northern standards) from sandwiches to stylish restaurant meals, up to half a dozen real ales such as Black Sheep, Marstons Pedigree, Mordue and Wylam Gold, good wines and coffees, large plain modern bar and adjoining plush panelled lounge; big-screen TV; children welcome, pleasant bedrooms, nr lovely bridge over River Tyne *(Blaise Vyner, Comus and Sarah Elliott, Carole Hall, Peter and Eleanor Kenyon, Michael Doswell, LYM, Dr Peter D Smart, Andy and Jill Kassube)*

☆ *Black Bull* NE45 5AT [Middle St]: Rambling linked rooms, reasonably priced food all day from sandwiches and light lunches up, good friendly service, four changing ales, good attractively priced wine choice, roaring fire, neat comfortable seating inc traditional settles in stone-floored low-ceilinged core; open all day *(Comus and Sarah Elliott, Pam and John Smith, Monica Shelley)*

CORNFORTH [NZ3035]

Old Mill DH6 5NX [Thinford Rd, off A177 just N]: Former mill now a country inn popular for its food, Durham Canny Lad and a guest beer *(Mr and Mrs Maurice Thompson)*

CORNSAY [NZ1443]

Black Horse DH7 9EL: Comfortable 18th-c former coaching inn in hilltop hamlet with great views, well kept Black Sheep and local ales (Easter beer festival), good range of malt whiskies, cheerful staff, well presented straightforward food Tues-Sat evenings; cl lunchtime exc Sun *(Alasdair Sutherland, Mrs L M Rutherford)*

CRAMLINGTON [NZ2373]

Snowy Owl NE23 8AU [just off A1/A19 junction via A1068; Blagdon Lane]: Large Vintage Inn, relaxed and comfortable, with reasonable prices, good choice of wines, reliable all-day food inc popular Sun lunch, friendly efficient service, Bass and Black Sheep, beams, flagstones, stripped stone and terracotta paintwork, soft lighting and an interesting mix of furnishings and decorations, daily papers; may be piped music; bedrooms in adjoining Innkeepers Lodge, open all day *(Dr Peter D Smart, Comus and Sarah Elliott)*

CRASTER [NU2519]

Jolly Fisherman NE66 3TR [off B1339, NE of Alnwick]: Simple local in great spot, a long-time favourite for its lovely sea and coast views from picture window and grass behind, and for its good value crab sandwiches, crab soup and locally smoked seafood; this makes up for the take-us-as-you-find-us style, which can verge on scruffiness; Black Sheep and Greene King, games area with pool; children and dogs welcome, open all day in summer *(the Didler, Paul Newberry, Arthur Pickering, Reg Fowle, Helen Rickwood, LYM, Phil Bryant)*

DUNSTAN [NU2419]

Cottage NE66 3SZ [off B1339 Alnmouth—Embleton]: Comfortable single-storey pub with low beams, dark wood and some stripped brickwork, banquettes and dimpled copper tables, enjoyable bar food, well kept Black Sheep, Mordue and Wylam, friendly efficient staff, restaurant, conservatory, games area; children welcome, terrace tables and attractive garden *(Phil Bryant, Dr Peter D Smart, LYM)*

DURHAM [NZ2742]

Court Inn DH1 3AW [Court Lane]: Unpretentious town pub with good hearty home-made food all day from sandwiches to steaks and late-evening bargains, real ales such as Bass, Marstons Pedigree and Mordue, extensive stripped brick eating area, no mobile phones; bustling in term-time with students and teachers, piped pop music; seats outside, open all day *(BB, David and Laraine Webster, Paul and Ursula Randall, Mark Walker, Pete Baker)*

☆ **Dun Cow** DH1 3HN [Old Elvet]: Unspoilt traditional town pub in pretty 16th-c black-and-white timbered cottage, cheerful licensees, tiny chatty front bar with wall benches, corridor to long narrow back lounge with banquettes, machines etc (can be packed with students), particularly well kept Camerons and other ales such as Black Sheep and Caledonian Deuchars IPA, good value basic lunchtime snacks, decent coffee; piped music; children welcome, open all day Mon-Sat, Sun too in summer *(Pete Baker, LYM, Chris Sale, Mark Walker, Paul and Ursula Randall, Pam and John Smith, the Didler)*

Swan & Three Cygnets DH1 3AG [Elvet Bridge]: Comfortably refurbished Victorian pub in good bridge-end spot high above river, city views from big windows and picnic-sets out on terrace, friendly service, bargain lunchtime food from hot filled baguettes up, cheap well kept Sam Smiths OB; open all day *(Mark Walker, BB, MDN)*

EBCHESTER [NZ1054]

☆ **Derwent Walk** DH8 0SX [Ebchester Hill (B6309 outside)]: Interesting pub by Gateshead—Consett walk of same name, wide range of consistently good value home-made food from unusual hot sandwiches through interesting dishes of the day to steaks, nice vegetarian menu, great choice of wines by the glass at reasonable prices, full Jennings range kept well and a guest beer, friendly staff, good log fire and appealing old photographs, conservatory with fine Derwent Valley views; walkers welcome, pleasant heated terrace *(Bruce and Sharon Eden, Arthur Pickering, Andy and Jill Kassube)*

EGLINGHAM [NU1019]

Tankerville Arms NE66 2TX [B6346 Alnwick—Wooler]: Pleasantly traditional, with helpful staff, real ales such as Black Sheep and Mordue, well chosen wines and malt whiskies, decent food inc evening restaurant and afternoon tea, coal fire each end of carpeted bar, plush banquettes, black joists, some stripped stone; quiet piped music; children welcome, nice views from garden, attractive village *(Michael Doswell, Peter and Eleanor Kenyon, LYM, Reg Fowle, Helen Rickwood)*

ELLINGHAM [NU1625]

Pack Horse NE67 5HA [signed off A1 N of Alnwick]: Compact stone-built country pub with light and airy dining room, feature fireplace in beamed bar, small comfortable lounge; enclosed garden, good value bedrooms, peaceful village *(David and Jane Hill, Comus and Sarah Elliott, Michael Doswell)*

ELWICK [NZ4532]

McOrville TS27 3EF [0.25 mile off A19 W of Hartlepool]: Open-plan dining pub with good blackboard food, Black Sheep and a changing ale, carved panelling, slippers provided for walkers *(Arthur Pickering, JHBS)*

EMBLETON [NU2322]

Greys NE66 3UY: Carpeted main front bar with pubby furniture, more lived-in area with old photographs and cuttings, large back dining area, good value home-made food inc excellent chips, Black Sheep ale, afternoon teas; small walled back garden, raised decking with village views *(Phil Bryant)*

Sportsman NE66 3XF: Large plain bar/bistro in pub/hotel with nearby beach and stunning views to Dunstanburgh Castle, impressive food using prime local produce inc fish and game, small interesting wine list, real ales such as Mordue Workie Ticket and Timothy Taylors Landlord, friendly cheerful service; frequent wknd live music; heated terrace, coast-view bedrooms, may cl in winter *(Reg Fowle, Helen Rickwood, Paul and Ursula Randall)*

FELTON [NU1800]

☆ **Northumberland Arms** NE65 9EE [West Thirston; B6345, off A1 N of Morpeth]: Attractive old inn with beams, stripped stone and good coal fires in roomy and comfortable open-plan bar, nice mix of furnishings inc big settees, elegant small restaurant; good well priced food, well kept Bass and Black Sheep, good coffee and wines, friendly service and atmosphere; well reproduced piped music, esp in conservatory pool room; dogs welcome, steps down to bench by River Coquet, five bedrooms, open all day *(Peter Jones, Comus and Sarah Elliott, BB)*

FOURSTONES [NY8867]

Railway Inn NE47 5DG: Doing well under new landlord, original fairly priced food, well kept Jennings *(Cedric Robertshaw)*

FROSTERLEY [NZ0236]

☆ **Black Bull** DL13 2SL [just off A689 W of centre]: Great atmosphere in three interesting traditional beamed and flagstoned rooms with two coal fires, landlord's own fine photographs, four well kept northern ales, farm cider and perry, carefully chosen wines and malt whiskies, good food using local and organic ingredients inc good choice of light lunchtime dishes and (not Sun/Mon) short and interesting evening menu, coffee and tempting pastries all day; live music Tues, occasional art shows; attractive no smoking terrace with wood-fired bread oven and old railway furnishings (opp steam station), open all day, cl Mon lunchtime *(Arthur Pickering, Joan Kureczka, Geoff and Angela Jacques, M J Winterton, JHBS, Mr and Mrs Maurice Thompson)*

GATESHEAD [NZ2559]

Aletaster NE9 6JA [Durham Rd (A167), Low Fell]: Wide range of real ales in friendly traditional pub, Newcastle United memorabilia; TV *(Dr and Mrs A K Clarke)*

Green NE10 8YB [White Mare Pool, Wardley; W of roundabout at end of A194(M)]: Large refurbished pub, light and airy, half a dozen or more reasonably priced ales inc local Mordue, good range of wines, good value freshly prepared bar/bistro food, friendly helpful staff, picture-window outlook on golf course; light piped music, very busy wknds *(Gerry and Rosemary Dobson)*

Lambton Arms NE9 7XR [Rockcliffe Way, Eighton Banks]: Comfortably updated pub with good range of straightforward food in bar and restaurant (should book wknds), Greene King ales, good wine choice, cafetière coffee, reasonable prices, pleasant friendly service; children welcome, open all day *(Gerry and Rosemary Dobson)*

HALTWHISTLE [NY7064]

☆ *Black Bull* NE49 OBL [just off Market Sq, behind indian restaurant]: Particularly well kept Big Lamp, Jennings and local guest ales, enterprising food all day (not till 7 Mon) inc seafood, game and bargain winter lunches, lively local atmosphere, friendly landlord, brasses on low beams, stripped stone with shelves of bric-a-brac, log fires, corridor to small dining room, darts and monthly quiz night; limited disabled access, dogs welcome in flagstoned part, attractive garden, open all day wknds and summer, cl Mon lunchtime *(Tony and Maggie Harwood, Helen Clarke)*

HART [NZ4634]

White Hart TS27 3AW [just off A179 W of Hartlepool; Front St]: Interesting nautical-theme pub with old ship's figurehead outside, fires in both bars, food cooked by new landlady-chef, two changing real ales; open all day (cl Mon afternoon) *(JHBS)*

HARTLEPOOL [NZ4832]

Golden Lion TS26 OEN [Dunston Rd]: Part of small local group, large pub with good value imaginatively presented food, wide choice of wines and four real ales inc Theakstons *(Jerry Brown)*

HAWTHORN [NZ4145]

Stapylton Arms SR7 8SD [off B1432 S of A19 Murton exit]: Chatty carpeted bar with old local photographs, a well kept ale such as Black Sheep, enjoyable food made by landlady from sandwiches to steaks and Sun roasts, friendly family service; dogs on leads allowed, may be open all day on busy wknds, nice wooded walk to sea (joins Durham Coastal Path) *(JHBS)*

HIGH HESLEDEN [NZ4538]

Ship TS27 4QD [off A19 via B1281]: Half a dozen good value changing ales from the region, log fire, sailing ship models inc big one hanging from ceiling, enjoyable bar food and some interesting restaurant dishes; yacht and shipping views from car park, six bedrooms in new block, cl Mon *(JHBS)*

HOLY ISLAND [NU1241]

Manor House TD15 2RX: Neat hotel bar with welcoming attentive staff, well kept local and national beers from corner servery, reasonably priced food inc OAP deals, afternoon teas, old-fashioned dining room; nice garden, bedrooms *(M J Winterton, Reg Fowle, Helen Rickwood)*

Ship TD15 2SJ [Marygate]: Nicely set pub (busy in season), renovated bar with stone walls, big stove, maritime/fishing memorabilia and pictures, bare-boards eating area, pubby food from sandwiches up, a Hadrian & Border ale brewed for the pub in summer, good choice of whiskies; children only in sheltered garden (no dogs), three bedrooms, may cl for three wks midwinter *(P Dawn, Comus and Sarah Elliott, Reg Fowle, Helen Rickwood)*

HORNCLIFFE [NT9249]

Fishers Arms TD15 2XW [off A698]: Nicely old-fashioned proper country pub in village high above River Tweed, obliging staff, well kept Caledonian Deuchars IPA and John Smiths, good value wines by the glass, simple home-made food inc well priced Sun lunch; monthly folk night first Sun, cl Tues *(Mrs Marion Matthewman)*

HORSLEY [NZ0965]

Lion & Lamb NE15 ONS [B6528, just off A69 Newcastle—Hexham]: Main bar with scrubbed tables, stripped stone, flagstones and panelling, lounge with big sofas, two local ales, small smart restaurant, good value unusual food; under-21s with parent/guardian only, Tyne views from attractive garden with roomy terrace, good adventure play area, open all day Fri-Sun *(Alex and Claire Pearse)*

HOUGHTON GATE [NZ2950]

Smiths Arms DH3 4HE [Castle Dene; off A183 Chester-le-Street—Sunderland via A1052 then Forge Lane]: Friendly traditional bar with open fire in old black range, up to four real ales, comfortable lounge with sloping floor and two more fires, games room, decorative upstairs restaurant with good interesting food inc set meal deals, lunchtime bar food; limited parking, has been cl Mon-Thurs lunchtime, open all day wknds *(Mark Walker)*

HURWORTH-ON-TEES [NZ3110]

Otter & Fish DL2 2AH [off A167 S of Darlington; Strait Lane]: Pleasantly up to date with armchairs and sofas by bar, nice mix of dining furniture, some wall banquettes, flagstones and stripped wood, good fresh local food (wise to book esp wknds), good wine selection, real ales, open fires and church candles *(Marcus Ware, Joan York)*

LAMESLEY [NZ2557]

Ravensworth Arms NE11 OER [just S of A1/Team Valley junction]: Popular stone-built Chef & Brewer, stripped brick and recycled timber dividers, fresh food from sandwiches to steak, fish and game, cheerful efficient staff, good wine choice, Wells & Youngs Bombardier, sofas in lounge; piped music; children welcome, play area outside, 13 bedrooms, open all day *(Christine and Phil Young, Michael Doswell, Mark Walker)*

LANGDON BECK [NY8531]

Langdon Beck Hotel DL12 OXP [B6277 Middleton—Alston]: Unpretentious isolated pub well placed for walks and Pennine Way, good choice of generous food, helpful friendly staff, real ales such as Black Sheep and Jarrow, wonderful views from dining room; bedrooms *(Mr and Mrs Maurice Thompson)*

LESBURY [NU2311]

☆ *Coach* NE66 3PP: Cosy stone-built pub with low-beamed bar, small lounge with sofas, pretty dining room, cheerful licensees, wide choice of enjoyable food from good crab sandwiches to full meals using local ingredients, well kept Black Sheep, good choice of wines, good coffee and tea (free refills); children welcome till 7.30, rustic tables outside with thatched umbrellas, lots of hanging baskets and tubs *(Gail and Simon Rowlands, Comus and Sarah Elliott, Michael Doswell)*

MELDON [NZ1185]

Dyke Neuk Inn NE61 3SL [B6343 W of Morpeth, 2 miles E of Hartburn]: Recently comfortably refurbished, with substantial food in beamed bar, quick service by friendly local staff, two local real ales, separate restaurant, lots of pictures; pleasant good-sized garden *(Guy and Caroline Howard, Mike and Lynn Robinson)*

MORPETH [NZ1985]

Sun NE61 2QT [High Church]: Large open-plan pub with emphasis on good value fresh local food from good generous baguettes through traditional pubby things to enterprising contemporary cooking (can take a while), well kept Caledonian Deuchars IPA and a guest beer, decent wines, good-sized partly stripped stone beamed dining area, more basic bar with pool beyond; piped music *(Bob Wright)*

NEWBIGGIN-BY-THE-SEA [NZ3188]

Queens Head NE64 6AT [High St]: Friendly talkative landlord, massed pump clips showing how many guest beers he gets besides bargain-price John Smiths, several high-ceilinged rooms, thriving atmosphere, dominoes; dogs welcome (not in sitting room), open all day from 10 *(the Didler, Tony and Maggie Harwood)*

NEWCASTLE UPON TYNE [NZ2464]

☆ *Bacchus* NE1 6BX [High Bridge East, between Pilgrim St and Grey St]: Smart and comfortable, with ocean liner look, good ship and shipbuilding photographs, good modern lunchtime food from interesting doorstep sandwiches and ciabattas through unusual light dishes to more substantial things all at keen prices, half a dozen changing real ales, plenty of bottled imports, perhaps farm cider, relaxed atmosphere; open all day (usually just evening Sun) *(Eric Larkham, Joe Green)*

Bodega NE1 4AG [Westgate Rd]: Majestic Edwardian drinking hall next to Tyne Theatre, particularly well kept Big Lamp Prince Bishop, Durham Magus, Mordue Geordie Pride (sold here as No 9) and three quickly changing interesting guest beers, farm cider, friendly service, lunchtime food, colourful walls and ceiling, snug front cubicles, spacious back area with two magnificent

stained-glass cupolas; piped music, machines, big-screen TV, very busy Newcastle United match days; open all day *(the Didler, Eric Larkham, Andy and Jill Kassube)*

☆ *Bridge Hotel* NE1 1RQ [Castle Sq, next to high level bridge]: Big cheery high-ceilinged room divided into several areas leaving plenty of space by the bar with replica slatted snob screens, particularly well kept Black Sheep, Caledonian Deuchars IPA, Durham, Mordue Workie Ticket and guest beers, farm cider, friendly staff, bargain lunchtime food (not Sat), Sun afternoon teas, magnificent fireplace, great views of river and bridges from raised back area; sports TV, piped music, games machines, live music upstairs inc long-standing Mon folk club; flagstoned back terrace overlooking part of old town wall, open all day *(Eric Larkham, the Didler, Brian and Rosalie Laverick, Dr and Mrs A K Clarke, LYM)*

Cooperage NE1 3RF [The Close, Quayside]: Ancient building in good waterfront setting, stripped stone bar and beamed lounge, small range of well kept ales; upstairs night club, pool, juke box; disabled facilities, cl Sun lunchtime *(LYM, Dr and Mrs A K Clarke, the Didler)*

Cumberland Arms NE6 1LD [Byker Buildings]: Friendly traditional local with four particularly well kept changing local ales (tapped straight from the cask if you wish), farm cider, organic beer festivals, good value toasties, obliging staff; live music or other events most nights (pub has its own ukelele band), tables out overlooking Ouseburn Valley, cl winter wkdy lunchtimes, open all day wknds *(Mike and Lynn Robinson, Eric Larkham)*

Falcons Nest NE3 5EH [Rotary Way, Gosforth – handy for racecourse]: Roomy Vintage Inn in their comfortably relaxing traditional style of olde-worlde linked rooms, good value food, pleasant staff, good choice of wines by the glass, well kept Black Sheep and Timothy Taylors Landlord; open all day, bedrooms in aadjacent Innkeepers Lodge *(Michael Doswell, J McKenna)*

Free Trade NE6 1AP [St Lawrence Rd, off Walker Rd (A186)]: Splendidly basic proper pub with outstanding views up river to bridges and the Gateshead arts centres from its big windows and from terrace tables and seats on grass, half a dozen changing largely local ales, warmly friendly atmosphere, good sandwiches, real fire, original Formica tables; steps down to back room and lavatories; open all day *(Eric Larkham)*

Newcastle Arms NE1 5SE [St Andrews St]: Open-plan pub on fringe of chinatown, several quickly changing real ales such as Black Sheep and Fullers, occasional farm cider (worth asking for if you don't see it) and mini beer festivals, friendly staff, decent food till 6 inc sandwiches, interesting old local photographs; piped music, big-screen sports TV, can get very busy esp on match days; open all day *(Eric Larkham)*

Slug & Lettuce NE1 3DW [Love Lane, Quayside]: Relaxed atmosphere, Tyne view, wide choice of enjoyable quickly served contemporary food, friendly staff, good wines by the glass (not cheap), daily papers *(Bruce and Sharon Eden)*

Tanners NE1 2NS [Byker Bridge]: By Byker Bridge, three real ales and half a dozen interesting bottled ciders, wkdy bar snacks and Sun lunch, pool; occasional live music *(Eric Larkham)*

Tilleys NE1 4AW [Corner Westgate Rd and Thornton St]: Large bar next to Tyne Theatre and nr performing arts college and live music centre, so interesting mix of customers, half a dozen well kept ales, farm cider, good choice of continental and bottled beers, generous home-made lunchtime food, artworks for sale; open all day *(Andy and Jill Kassube, Eric Larkham)*

Tyne NE6 1LP [Maling St]: Busy pub at end of quayside walk by confluence of Ouseburn and Tyne, four local real ales, exotic hot or cold sandwiches all day, lots of band posters and prints (live music upstairs Sun and Weds, monthly swing night first Tues); games machine, sports TV, stairs up to lavatories; all-weather fairy-lit garden (loudspeakers out here too) under arch of Glasshouse Bridge, also waterside picnic-sets, barbecues, open all day *(Eric Larkham)*

PONTELAND [NZ1771]

☆ *Badger* NE20 9BT [Street Houses; A696 SE, by garden centre]: Well done Vintage Inn, enjoyable food all day, real ales, good range of wines by the glass and good hot drinks, friendly attentive uniformed staff, good log fire, relaxing rooms and alcoves, old furnishings and olde-worlde décor; children welcome, open all day *(Peter and Eleanor Kenyon, Alan Cole, Kirstie Bruce, BB, Dr Peter D Smart)*

RENNINGTON [NU2118]

☆ *Horseshoes* NE66 3RS [B1340]: Comfortable flagstoned pub with friendly efficient service, well kept ales such as Hadrian & Border and John Smiths, good value generous food inc two-course lunch deals, good meat and smoked fish, decent wines by the glass, good local feel (may be horses in car park), simple neat bar with lots of horsebrasses, spotless compact restaurant with blue and white china; children welcome, tables outside, attractive quiet village nr coast *(Grahame Sherwin, Comus and Sarah Elliott, Michael Butler, Guy and Caroline Howard)*

RIDING MILL [NZ0161]

☆ *Wellington* NE44 6DQ [A695 just W of A68 roundabout]: Reliable and popular 17th-c Chef & Brewer, vast good value blackboard food choice from hot ciabatta sandwiches to nice puddings, good friendly staff, Courage Directors and Theakstons Bitter and Black Bull, good choice of wines by the glass, good coffee, beams and candlelight, two big log fires and mix of tables and chairs, some upholstered, some not; piped classical music,

can get busy; disabled access, children welcome, play area and picnic-sets outside, pretty village with nearby walks and river *(Dr Peter D Smart, Bruce and Sharon Eden, Louise Gibbons)*

ROKER [NZ4059]

Cliff SR6 9LG [Mere Knolls Rd]: Large open-plan pub in residential area, Batemans XXXB, Courage Directors and Theakstons Old Peculier, friendly helpful staff *(Mr and Mrs Maurice Thompson)*

SEDGEFIELD [NZ3528]

Dun Cow TS21 3AT [Front St]: Newly refurbished village inn with red-painted low-beamed bar, back tap room and comfortable dining room, wide choice of decent food from well filled sandwiches to game, fresh whitby fish and unusual puddings, cheerful staff, well kept ales such as Black Sheep and Camerons, whiskies in great variety; children welcome; good value bedrooms *(Andrew and Ruth Triggs, Louise English)*

SHINCLIFFE [NZ2940]

☆ *Seven Stars* DH1 2NU [High St N (A177 S of Durham)]: 18th-c village pub with enjoyable gently upmarket food at sensible prices, well kept ales inc Black Sheep, quick pleasant service, coal fire and plenty of atmosphere in lounge bar, candlelit dining room; children in eating areas, some picnic-sets outside, eight bedrooms, open all day *(LYM, Andy and Alice Jordan)*

SLAGGYFORD [NY6754]

Kirkstyle CA8 7PB [just N, signed off A689 at Knarsdale]: Attractive pleasantly refurbished old inn with relaxed atmosphere, friendly service and locals, wide range of good plain food inc children's helpings, well kept changing ales such as Geltsdale and Yates, decent wines, board games, darts and pool area, dining room, nice spot looking over South Tyne valley to hills beyond; active quoits, internet access, comfortable bedrooms, handy for Pennine Way and Cycle Way *(Marcus Byron)*

SOUTH SHIELDS [NZ3567]

Alum Ale House NE33 1JR [Ferry St (B1344)]: Relaxed 18th-c pub handy for ferry, big bars with good choice of guest beers, hot drinks, good value basic lunchtime bar food, coal fire in old inglenook range, polished boards, pictures and newspaper cuttings; piped music, machines, some live music, good beer festivals; children welcome, open all day *(Eric Larkham, the Didler)*

Beacon NE33 2AQ [Greens Pl]: Open-plan pub overlooking river mouth, well kept ales from central bar, good value lunchtime food, obliging service, stove in back room, two raised eating areas, sepia photographs and bric-a-brac, darts and dominoes; games machine, quiet piped music; open all day *(the Didler)*

STANHOPE [NY9939]

Grey Bull DL13 2PB [West Terr]: Jennings pub popular with walkers and cyclists, guest beers such as Banks's Original and Hop Back

Crop Circle, friendly staff and locals, toasted sandwiches *(Mr and Mrs Maurice Thompson)*

STANLEY [NZ2054]

South Causey DH9 0LS [South Causey Farm]: Recently refurbished stone inn by livery stables, beams, oak floors, open fires and nice mix of old furniture, food from thick-cut sandwiches to trout from own lakes, two-for-one and OAP deals, Wells & Youngs Bombardier and two local ales; picnic-sets outside, 15 bedrooms, open all day *(Jerry Brown)*

STOCKTON-ON-TEES [NZ4419]

Sun TS18 1SU [Knowles St]: Friendly town local noted for its Bass, good prices, quick service; folk night Mon, open all day *(the Didler)*

SUNDERLAND [NZ3956]

Fitzgeralds SR1 3PZ [Green Terr]: Bustling two-bar city pub popular for up to ten real ales inc several from local Darwin, helpful staff, friendly atmosphere, generous cheap bar lunches from toasties, baguettes and ciabattas to basic hot dishes; children welcome lunchtime *(Mr and Mrs Maurice Thompson, Mark Walker)*

Kings Arms SR4 6BU [Beach St, Deptford]: Chatty early 19th-c pub with several traditional panelled areas around central high-backed bar, well kept Timothy Taylors Landlord and half a dozen changing ales from small breweries, friendly staff and locals, two coal fires, easy chairs and lots of dark wood, food Weds-Sun evenings *(Mr and Mrs Maurice Thompson)*

SUNNISIDE [NZ2058]

Potters Wheel NE16 5EE [Sun St]: Light and airy pub with several areas off main bar, helpful staff, real ale such as Youngs Special *(Mr and Mrs Maurice Thompson)*

THORNLEY [NZ3340]

Three Horseshoes DH1 2SR [N on A181]: Country inn with welcoming landlord, a well kept real ale, good value food; six bedrooms *(Jerry Brown)*

THROPTON [NU0302]

Cross Keys NE65 7HX [B6341]: Attractive and friendly little village pub, enjoyable food with emphasis on fish, Black Sheep, open fires in small cosy beamed bar with rooms off inc snug with high-backed settles, games room with darts, pool, back dining area; sports TV; steeply terraced garden looking over village to hills beyond, open all day at least in summer *(Paul and Sue Merrick, LYM, Phil Bryant)*

☆ ***Three Wheat Heads*** NE65 7LR [B6341]: 300-year-old village inn favoured by older people for its sedate dining atmosphere, good coal fires (one in a fine tall stone fireplace), good bar food inc daily roasts (can take a while), well kept Black Sheep and Theakstons, pleasant hill-view dining area, darts and pool; piped music; children welcome, garden with play area and lovely views to Simonside Hills, good value comfortable bedrooms, good breakfast, handy for Cragside, open all day wknds *(Comus and Sarah Elliott, LYM,*

David Hassall, Christine and Malcolm Ingram, Richard C Morgan, Dr Peter D Smart)

WARDEN [NY9166]

☆ ***Boatside*** NE46 4SQ [0.5 mile N of A69]: Cheerful attractively modernised old stone-built pub with good service, enjoyable fresh pubby food inc good sandwiches, well kept Black Sheep, Tetleys and Wylam, pine dining room; children and muddy walkers welcome, small neat enclosed garden, active quoits, attractive spot by Tyne bridge, bedrooms in adjoining cottages *(Gerry Miller, Bruce and Sharon Eden, Comus and Sarah Elliott, R Macfarlane)*

WARENFORD [NU1330]

Purdy Lodge NE70 7JU [Adderstone Services, A1]: Enjoyable and unusual changing food relying on local produce in recently refurbished bar with interesting sporting memorabilia or in small comfortable country-view dining room, Belhaven ales, decent house wines *(Mrs Marion Matthewman)*

White Swan NE70 7HY [off A1 3 or 4 miles S of Belford]: Refurbished under newish owners, good friendly service, enjoyable food in bar and separate restaurant, Black Sheep, warm fires *(LYM, Mr and Mrs P L Spencer)*

WARKWORTH [NU2406]

Warkworth House NE65 0XB [Bridge St]: Hotel combining proper friendly pubby bar with bistro and restaurant, all with enjoyable generous reasonably priced food, friendly helpful staff, comfortable sofas, two changing real ales, good range of spirits and of good value wines by the glass, proper coffee, darts and bar billiards; dogs welcome, good bedrooms, open all day *(Sheena W Makin)*

WASHINGTON [NZ3054]

Courtyard NE38 8AB [Arts Centre, Biddick Lane]: Popular open-plan bar with up to six changing real ales, farm cider and perry, occasional beer festivals, good value food inc bargain Sun lunch; live music Mon; tables outside, open all day *(Mr and Mrs Maurice Thompson)*

WEST WOODBURN [NY8986]

Bay Horse NE48 2RX [A68]: Lively welcoming roadside pub, cosy neat bar with log fire, well kept ales, enjoyable food inc Sun lunch, dining room; riverside garden, refurbished bedrooms *(Joan York, LYM)*

WHITTONSTALL [NZ0757]

Anchor DH8 9JN [B6309 N of Consett]: Stone-built beamed pub with comfortable banquettes in L-shaped lounge, dining area with high-raftered pitched roof, attractive décor, interesting old north-east photographs and facsimile posters, interesting changing ales, huge choice of generous food from good sandwiches and baguettes to popular Sun lunch, friendly staff, separate locals' bar; piped music; nice countryside *(Alan Thwaite)*

WINSTON [NZ1416]

Bridgewater Arms DL2 3RN [B6274, just off A67 Darlington—Barnard Castle]: Attractively converted Victorian school house, light and airy high-ceilinged bar with book-lined corner, fine snugs, attractive dining room, pictures of old station and school plays, interesting food (not Sun/Mon) cooked fresh to order so may take time, early evening bargains Tues-Thurs, changing real ales such as Greene King Abbot and Timothy Taylors Landlord *(Alan Thwaite)*

WOLSINGHAM [NZ0737]

Mill Race DL13 3AP [West End]: Dining pub with good upscale food from all-day snacks up under enterprising new licensees, well kept Black Sheep ales, good wine choice, log-fire bar and dining area, back restaurant *(Roger Shipperley, Joan Kureczka)*

WOLVISTON [NZ4525]

Ship TS22 5JX [High St]: Gabled red-brick Victorian pub in centre of bypassed village, open-plan multi-level carpeted bar, bargain food, changing real ales from northern breweries, quiz nights; garden *(JHBS)*

WOOLER [NT9928]

Tankerville Arms NE71 6AD [A697 N]:

Pleasant hotel bar in tastefully modernised old building, reasonably priced food inc local meat and fish, small helpings on request, Black Sheep and Mordue ales, good wines by the glass, small smart restaurant and larger airy one overlooking nice garden; bedrooms *(Mrs Brenda Calver)*

WYLAM [NZ1164]

☆ *Boathouse* NE41 8HR [Station Rd, handy for Newcastle—Carlisle rail line; across Tyne from village (and Stephenson's birthplace)]: Thriving convivial riverside pub noted for splendid range of northern and other ales inc three local Wylam ones, keen prices, good choice of malt whiskies, bargain Sun lunch, polite helpful young staff, bright low-beamed bar with cheery open stove, separate dining room; loud band nights; children and dogs welcome, seats outside, open all day *(Comus and Sarah Elliott, Michael and Jean Hockings, the Didler, Lawrence Pearse, Andy and Jill Kassube, Arthur Pickering)*

Nottinghamshire

This county has plenty of good value simple pub food, and also – further up the price range – a handful of top-notch dining pubs. The smart Martins Arms at Colston Bassett is not cheap, but its imaginative food is worth the cost. The inventive cooking at the civilised Waggon & Horses in Halam ensures plenty of return visits. The warmly welcoming Caunton Beck at Caunton offers food for fully 15 hours a day, yet manages to keep its standards so uniformly high that it gratifies even the most critical judges. Of these top three food pubs, it's the Caunton Beck which is Nottinghamshire Dining Pub of the Year. Other pubs to note for food are two new main entries, the Lord Nelson at Winthorpe, a civilised and attractively reworked former watermill, and the Pilgrim Fathers at Scrooby; and also the enthusiastically run Victoria in Beeston, with award-quality cooking alongside a dozen real ales, and the Full Moon at Morton, recently de-cluttered by new licensees who have an interesting approach to pub food – one to watch in this next year. The county has quite a number of enthusiastic small breweries, mostly started within the last decade or so. The two most successful are Castle Rock, brewing for Tynemill (a small regional pub group specialising in unpretentious good value – even its soft drinks are cheap), and Nottingham. Others we found in good pubs are Mallard, Caythorpe (from the quaintly timeless Black Horse at Caythorpe, in the same family for about 40 years), Magpie, Milestone, Alcazar, Idle, Maypole and Springhead. The city of Nottingham itself, besides being home to several of these brews, has a splendid choice of real ale pubs, offering an astounding range of beers – the pumps at our six main entries alone tally over four dozen. Under the Tynemill wing here you can count a full dozen pumps at the down-to-earth Lincolnshire Poacher, eleven pumps under the caring hand of the landlady at the Vat & Fiddle (tap for Castle Rock), and half a dozen at the bustling Keans Head. You'll find another two dozen or so pubs in the city, in the Lucky Dip section at the end of the chapter: our pick of these would be the Canal House and Lion, and (out in West Bridgford) the Stratford Haven. Other notable Lucky Dip entries are the Horse & Plough in Bingham, Robin Hood at Elkesley, Marquis of Granby at Granby, Nelson & Railway in Kimberley, Beehive at Maplebeck and restauranty Mussel & Crab at West Markham.

BEESTON   SK5336   MAP 7

Victoria ♀ ◗

Dovecote Lane, backing on to railway station; NG9 1JG

Welcoming down-to-earth converted railway inn with impressive choice of drinks (including up to 12 real ales) and enjoyable fairly priced food

With a genuinely pubby feel, the three fairly simple rooms here have kept their original long narrow layout and are nicely unpretentious, with unfussy décor and simple solid traditional furnishings, stripped woodwork and floorboards (woodblock in some rooms), fires, stained-glass windows; newspapers, dominoes, cribbage and board games. The chatty lounge and bar back on to the railway station and a covered heated area outside has tables overlooking the platform, with trains passing just a few feet away. A nice varied crowd gathers here, but even at busy times service is helpful and efficient. Their extraordinary range of drinks takes in Batemans XB, Castle Rock Harvest Pale and Everards Tiger, which are well kept alongside up to nine guest ales. Running through as many as 500 widely sourced beers a year these could be from brewers such as Adnams, Copper Dragon, Elgoods, Harviestoun, Holt, Howard Town, Hydes, Isle of Skye and Oldershaw. They've also continental draught beers, two farm ciders, over 120 malt whiskies, 20 irish whiskeys, and about 30 wines by the glass. A lively time to visit is during their two week beer and music festival at the end of July; no mobile phones; limited parking.

🍽 **Tasty good value bar food is listed on a blackboard, and might include chicken liver pâté with tequila and cranberry, beef bourguignon, sausage and mash, chargrilled tuna loin on niçoise salad, goan vegetable curry (and quite a few more vegetarian dishes), and puddings such as apple and cinnamon crumble.** *Starters/Snacks: £2.50 to £5.95. Main Courses: £7.50 to £12.95. Puddings: £3.95 to £4.50*

Free house ~ Licensees Neil Kelso and Graham Smith ~ Real ale ~ Bar food (12-8.45(9.30 Weds-Sat)) ~ (0115) 925 4049 ~ Children welcome till 8pm ~ Dogs allowed in bar ~ Live folk Sun evening and jazz Mon evenings ~ Open 10.30am(12 Sun)-11pm

Recommended by Andy Lickfold, R T and J C Moggridge, David Eberlin, the Didler, Ian Stafford, C J Fletcher, B and M Kendall, Dr and Mrs A K Clarke, Tony and Wendy Hobden, P Dawn, Peter and Jean Hoare, Marianne Welsh, Andrew Stephenson, Chris Evans, G D K Fraser

---

CAUNTON   SK7459   MAP 7

Caunton Beck 🍴 ♀

Newark Road; NG23 6AE

NOTTINGHAMSHIRE DINING PUB OF THE YEAR

Civilised dining pub with very good (if not cheap) food all day from breakfasts first thing, good wine list, nice terrace

Warmly welcoming service contributes to making this lovely inn a memorable place. Surprisingly the building is almost new, but as it was reconstructed using original timbers and reclaimed oak, around the skeleton of the old Hole Arms, it seems old. Scrubbed pine tables, clever lighting, an open fire, country-kitchen chairs, low beams and rag-finished paintwork in a spacious interior create a comfortably relaxed atmosphere. Over two dozen of the wines on the very good wine list are available by the glass, and they've well kept Batemans Valiant, Marstons Pedigree and Tom Woods Farmers Blonde on handpump; also espresso coffee; daily papers and magazines, no music. With lots of flowers and plants in summer, the terrace is very pleasant when the weather is fine.

🍽 **You can get something to eat at most times of the day, from hearty english breakfasts (served until midday; 11.30 weekends and bank holidays), to delicious sandwiches and a fairly elaborate seasonally changing menu and specials list later on: twice-baked leek and local cheese soufflé, chilli and lime marinated anchovies with crostini and olive tapenade, caviar, roast pork belly on champ mash with sage and onion, garlic mushroom and gremolata bruschetta, grilled halibut with roast tomatoes and basil pesto, rib-eye steak with duck egg and brown sauce, and puddings such as lemon and lime tart and white chocolate mousse with home-made turkish delight.** *Starters/Snacks: £4.75 to £8.50. Main Courses: £10.95 to £18.50. Puddings: £4.95 to £7.50*

Free house ~ Licensee Julie Allwood ~ Real ale ~ Bar food (8am-11pm) ~ Restaurant ~
(01636) 636793 ~ Children welcome ~ Dogs allowed in bar ~ Open 8am-11pm

*Recommended by Ray and Winifred Halliday, Keith and Chris O'Neill, Susan and Nigel Brookes, Eithne Dandy,
Derek and Sylvia Stephenson, Maurice and Janet Thorpe, Catherine and Rob Dunster, Pete Coxon, Mrs Margo Finlay,
Jörg Kasprowski, K Bennett, Gerry and Rosemary Dobson, D A Bradford, Gordon and Margaret Ormondroyd,
Louise Gibbons, Mrs Brenda Calver, Richard Marjoram*

CAYTHORPE

SK6845   MAP 7

Black Horse 🍺

*Turn off A6097 0.25 mile SE of roundabout junction with A612, NE of Nottingham; into
Gunthorpe Road, then right into Caythorpe Road and keep on; NG14 7ED*

**Quaintly old-fashioned little pub brewing its own beer, simple interior and homely
enjoyable food; no children or credit cards**

Time seems to stand still at this 300-year-old country local – certainly little has changed
in the near-on 40 years that the current licensee family has been here. The uncluttered
carpeted bar has just five tables, brocaded wall banquettes and settles, a few bar stools
(for the cheerful evening regulars), a warm woodburning stove, decorative plates on a
delft shelf and a few horsebrasses on the ceiling joists. Off the front corridor is a partly
panelled inner room with a wall bench running right the way around three unusual long
copper-topped tables, and quite a few old local photographs; darts and dominoes. Down
on the left an end room has just one huge round table. The two tasty Caythorpe beers
are brewed in outbuildings here and are well kept alongside a couple of changing guests
such as Black Sheep and Greene King Abbot. There are some plastic tables outside, and
the River Trent is fairly close for waterside walks.

🍽 **Simple, but enjoyable freshly cooked and reasonably priced food from a shortish menu
includes soup, prawn cocktail, cod roe on toast and lambs kidneys in cream, seafood
salad, good fried cod, haddock or plaice, fillet steak, lemon brûlée and chocolate and
hazelnut meringue roulade. Booking is essential.** *Starters/Snacks: £3.00 to £6.00. Main
Courses: £6.00 to £14.00. Puddings: £3.50 to £5.00*

Own brew ~ Licensee Sharron Andrews ~ Real ale ~ Bar food (12-1.45 Tues-Sat,
6.30-8.30 Tues to Thurs; pre-booked sandwiches only Sun) ~ Restaurant ~ No credit cards ~
(0115) 966 3520 ~ Dogs welcome ~ Open 12-2.30, 5.30(6 Sat)-11; 12-5, 8-11 Sun;
closed Third Mon in month

Recommended by P Dawn, the Didler, Peter and Jean Hoare, Pam and Wally Taylor, Derek and Sylvia Stephenson

COLSTON BASSETT

SK6933   MAP 7

Martins Arms 🍷 🍺

*Village signposted off A46 E of Nottingham; School Lane, near market cross in village
centre; NG12 3FD*

**Smart dining pub with imaginative food (if pricy), good range of drinks including eight
real ales, and lovely grounds**

The restful bar at this lovely country pub is comfortably civilised with something of an
upmarket air. Neatly uniformed staff, antique furnishings, hunting prints and warm log
fires in the Jacobean fireplaces combine to convey this feel, and if you choose to eat in
the elegant restaurant (smartly decorated with period fabrics and colourings) you are
getting into serious dining. The little tap room has its own corner bar, where half a
dozen or so well kept real ales on handpump include Bass, Black Sheep, Jennings
Cumberland, Marstons Pedigree, Timothy Taylors Landlord and guest such as Woodfordes
Wherry, and they've a good range of malt whiskies and cognacs and an interesting wine
list; cribbage and dominoes. The sizeable attractive lawned garden (summer croquet
here) backs on to estate parkland – you might be asked to leave your credit card behind
the bar if you want to eat out here. They've converted the stables into an antiques shop
and readers recommend visiting the church opposite, and Colston Bassett Dairy just
outside the village, which sells its own stilton cheese.

🍴 The very good food is not cheap, but readers feel it's worth the price: lunchtime sandwiches and filled ciabattas, ploughman's, starters such as fried partridge breast with braised puy lentils, warm oriental beef salad and fried calamari with sweet chilli sauce, main courses such as battered fish and chips, roast butternut squash gnocchi with red onion marmalade, confit tomato and crème fraîche, seared bass fillet on crab and tomato mash with saffron and chive cream sauce, fillet steak with whisky and pâté sauce and puddings such as crumble of the day and lemon tart with blackcurrant compote. *Starters/Snacks: £4.95 to £7.50. Main Courses: £9.95 to £18.95. Puddings: £5.50*

Free house ~ Licensees Lynne Strafford Bryan and Salvatore Inguanta ~ Real ale ~ Bar food (12-2, 6-10; not Sun evenings) ~ Restaurant ~ (01949) 81361 ~ Children welcome ~ Open 12-3, 6-11

Recommended by the Didler, D F Clarke, Peter and Jo Smith, John Honnor, Richard, David Morgan, Brian and Jean Hepworth, Maurice and Janet Thorpe

HALAM   SK6754   MAP 7

Waggon & Horses 🍴
Off A612 in Southwell centre, via Halam Road; NG22 8AE

Civilised dining pub with inventive seasonally changing menu

Most people at this heavily oak-beamed pub are here for the good food, though drinkers are welcome. The recently tidied up open-plan interior has a congenial dining atmosphere, and is nicely divided into the cosy sections that are naturally formed by the layout of the original 17th-c building. Various floral pictures (some painted by the staff) hang on pale green walls, and good sturdy high-back rush-seat dining chairs are set around a mix of solid mainly stripped tables on wood floors. Two Thwaites beers are well kept on handpump; piped music. Out past a grandfather clock in the lobby are a few roadside picnic-sets by pretty window boxes.

🍴 Imaginative food might include starters such as partridge and rabbit terrine, lobster and king prawn risotto, warm scallop and pancetta salad, main courses such as monkfish with creamy mussels and parmesan crumb, pork, kale and apple hotpot, butternut, fennel and spinach risotto, fillet steak with melted stilton and port sauce and puddings such as rhubarb crème brûlée, chocolate bread and butter pudding and apple pancakes with gingerbread ice-cream. They also do a good value two-course menu (lunchtime (not Sun) and 6pm to 7pm Monday-Thursday). *Starters/Snacks: £4.00 to £10.00. Main Courses: £10.00 to £17.00. Puddings: £5.00 to £6.50*

Thwaites ~ Tenant Roy Wood ~ Real ale ~ Bar food (11.30-2.30, 5.30-9.30; not Sun evening) ~ (01636) 813109 ~ Children welcome ~ Open 11.30-3, 5.30-10.30(11 Fri, Sat); 11.30-4 Sun; closed Sun evening, Mon except bank hols

Recommended by R and M Tait, Derek and Sylvia Stephenson, Richard, JJW, CMW

LAXTON   SK7266   MAP 7

Dovecote
Signposted off A6075 E of Ollerton; NG22 0NU

Traditional village pub handy for A1; bar food and garden

The three dining areas at this red-brick free house are traditionally furnished with dark pubby tables and wheelback chairs on carpeted or wooden flooring. There's a coal-effect gas fire and a proper pool room with darts, fruit machine and dominoes; piped music. As well as a farm cider and around nine wines by the glass their three changing beers on handpump might be Fullers London Pride, Milestone Black Pearl and Wadworths 6X. Wooden tables and chairs on a small front terrace and sloping garden have views towards the village church. Campers can stay in the orchard and field. Laxton is famously home to three huge medieval open fields – it's one of the few places in the country still farmed using this system. Every year, in the third week of June, the grass is auctioned for haymaking, and anyone who lives in the parish is entitled to a bid and a drink. You can get more information about it all from the visitor centre behind the pub.

🍴 Served by friendly courteous staff, fairly priced tasty food might include whitebait, prawn cocktail, deep-fried brie with cumberland sauce, ploughman's, creamy mushroom hotpot, steak and ale pie, fish pie, lasagne, battered haddock and steaks, with puddings such as strawberry pavlova and chocolate fudge cake. *Starters/Snacks: £3.95 to £5.25. Main Courses: £6.95 to £16.75. Puddings: £1.95 to £3.95*

Free house ~ Licensees David and Linda Brown ~ Real ale ~ Bar food (12-2, 6.30-9; 12.30-6.30 Sun) ~ (01777) 871586 ~ Children welcome ~ Dogs allowed in bar ~ Open 11.30-3, 6.30(6 Sat)-11; 12-10.30 Sun

Recommended by Richard Cole, M Mossman, Gerry and Rosemary Dobson, Mrs Hazel Rainer, Noel Thomas, Derek and Sylvia Stephenson, Keith and Chris O'Neill, David and Ruth Hollands, Nick and Meriel Cox, DC, Mike and Linda Hudson, Ray and Winifred Halliday

MORTON
SK7251 MAP 7

Full Moon

Pub and village signposted off Bleasby—Fiskerton back road, SE of Southwell; NG25 OUT

Good food at friendly village pub with traditional plush décor; play area in nice garden

The enthusiastic new licensees at this cosy dining pub make every effort to ensure their customers are happy, whether they're here for a family celebration or for a quick drink after work. L-shaped and beamed, the main part is traditionally decorated with pink plush seats and cushioned black settles around a variety of pub tables, with wheelback chairs in the side dining area, and a couple of fireplaces. Batemans XB, Black Sheep, Charles Wells Bombardier, Greene King Ruddles and a changing guest such as Castle Rock Harvest Pale Ale are on handpump; TV, piped music, games machines and board games. Lots of effort has gone into the garden which comprises a peaceful shady back terrace with picnic-sets, a sizeable lawn, and some sturdy play equipment.

🍴 As well as lunchtime sandwiches, the thoughtfully pubby menu includes cream of celeriac and butternut squash soup, whitebait, half a pint of prawns, fish or chicken, leek and apricot pie, shepherd's pie with cauliflower cheese, battered haddock with mushy peas, sweet potato and chip pea chilli, with specials such as venison with beetroot and bubble and squeak. Puddings include sticky toffee pudding, rhubarb and vanilla trifle and grilled figs with honey, almond and mascarpone. *Starters/Snacks: £4.00 to £7.50. Main Courses: £9.00 to £16.50. Puddings: £4.50 to £5.50*

Free house ~ Licensees Will and Rebecca White ~ Real ale ~ Bar food (12-2.30, 6-9.30(9 Sun)) ~ Restaurant ~ (01636) 830251 ~ Children welcome ~ Open 11-3, 6-midnight(12.30 Sat); 11-11 Sun; 11-4, 6-11 Sun in winter

Recommended by M Mossman, the Didler, Maurice and Janet Thorpe, Derek and Sylvia Stephenson, Dean Rose, R and M Tait, Phil and Jane Hodson, P Dawn, David Glynne-Jones, Paul Humphreys, Simon Pyle, M Smith

NOTTINGHAM
SK5739 MAP 7

Bell 🍺 £

Angel Row, off Market Square; NG1 6HL

Great range of real ales from remarkable cellars in historic yet pubby place with regular live music and simple food

Masked by a late Georgian frontage, the two 500-year-old timber-framed buildings that form this pub were about to undergo a gradual restoration as we went to press – rooms will be done in sequence so that the pub can stay open. Reputed to have been part of a Carmelite friary, its venerable age is clearly evident throughout. Original timbers have been uncovered, and in the front Tudor bar glass protects patches of 300-year-old wallpaper. With quite a café feel in summer, this room is perhaps the brightest, with french windows opening to tables on the pavement, and bright blue walls. The room with the most aged feel is the very pubby low-beamed Elizabethan Bar, with its half-panelled walls, maple parquet floor and comfortable high-backed armchairs. Upstairs, at the back of the heavily panelled Belfry (usually open only at lunchtime), you can see the rafters of the 15th-c crown post roof, and look down on the busy street; TV, fruit machine and piped music. Down below, the labyrinthine cellars (tours 7.30pm Tues) are dug about ten metres into the sandstone rock – the efforts of the hardworking Norman monks who are said to have made them are still much appreciated as they now house the nine well kept beers that are served here – usually Greene King Abbot, IPA and Old Speckled Hen and guests from brewers such as Burton Bridge, Castle Rock, Nottingham, Oakham and Titanic. The friendly welcoming staff and landlord also serve ten wines by the glass, quite a few malt whiskies and a farm cider.

🍽 **Reasonably priced straightforward bar food includes soup, burgers, ploughman's, beef pie, battered cod, vegetable risotto, apple pie and rhubarb crumble.** *Starters/Snacks: £2.95 to £6.65. Main Courses: £4.50 to £8.95. Puddings: £3.50 to £4.50*

Greene King ~ Manager Brian Rigby ~ Real ale ~ Bar food (11-8.30) ~ Restaurant ~ (0115) 947 5241 ~ Children in restaurant ~ Dogs allowed in bar ~ Live jazz Sun lunchtime and Mon, Tues evenings ~ Open 10am-11pm(midnight Sat)

Recommended by the Didler, Dr and Mrs A K Clarke, C J Fletcher, David Carr, P Dawn, Bruce Bird

Fellows Morton & Clayton 🍺

Canal Street (part of inner ring road); NG1 7EH

Lively with canalside terrace, good value food and own brew beers

This former canal warehouse is popular with local workers at lunchtime and a younger set in the evening. The softly lit downstairs bar has a bustling town pub feel, with dark red plush seats built into alcoves on shiny blond wood floors, lots of exposed brickwork, a glossy dark green high ceiling, more tables on a raised balustraded carpeted area, and a rack of daily newspapers; piped pop music, games machines and several big TVs. Through a large window in a glassed-in area at the back you can see the little brewery where they make the tasty Samuel Fellows and Matthew Claytons Original served here. These are well kept alongside changing guests that might be Black Sheep, Fullers London Pride, Timothy Taylors Landlord and Mallard Duckling. A large decked terrace at the back overlooks the canal and is a great place for a summer evening drink; service is prompt and friendly and a reader tells us there is disabled access; parking at the back.

🍽 **Good value, quite pubby food, might include seasonal pâté, lunchtime sandwiches and wraps, haddock and chips, sausage and mash, spicy bean burger, chicken with chorizo, peppers, mozzarella and tomatoes, and steaks** *Starters/Snacks: £2.85 to £4.95. Main Courses: £4.95 to £10.75. Puddings: £3.25*

Enterprise ~ Licensees Les Howard and Keely Willans ~ Real ale ~ Bar food (11(10 Sat, Sun)-9; 10(6 Sun); not Sun evening) ~ Restaurant ~ (0115) 950 6795 ~ Children in restaurant ~ Live music Friday ~ Open 11-11(midnight Fri); 12 noon-1am Sat; 10am-10.30pm Sun

Recommended by Rona Murdoch, Mrs Hazel Rainer, Bruce Bird, David Carr, the Didler, Derek and Sylvia Stephenson, Michael Dandy, P Dawn, C J Fletcher

Keans Head 🍷 🍺 £

St Marys Gate; NG1 1QA

Bustling and friendly central pub, usefully serving good value food all day, wide choice of drinks, smiling service and informal chatty atmosphere

At first glance this unpretentious and cheery Tynemill pub looks a bit like a café. It's in the attractive Lace Market area and usefully offers enjoyable food all day. There's some exposed brickwork and red tiling, simple wooden furnishings on the wood-boarded floor, a low sofa by a big window overlooking the street, various pieces of artwork and beer advertisements on the walls, and a small fireplace. Friendly staff serve Batemans Valiant and Castle Rock Harvest Pale and Preservation with three well kept guests from brewers such as Oldershaw, Phoenix and Thornbridge from handpumps, draught belgian beers, interesting bottled beers and soft drinks, nearly two dozen wines by the glass and lots of coffees and teas; daily newspapers to read and piped music. Students often drop in for breakfast. St Mary's Church next door is worth a look.

🍴 An interesting mix of traditional english and italian food includes rosemary focaccia, antipasto, whitebait, made to order scotch egg, sandwiches, pizzas, carbonnara, pie of the day, sausage of the day and mash, ploughman's, spicy meatballs in pasatta, tuna burger and chicken, lemon and artichoke stew with white wine risotto. *Starters/Snacks: £3.25 to £5.95. Main Courses: £6.25 to £10.95. Puddings: £2.95 to £4.50*

Tynemill ~ Manager Charlotte Blomeley ~ Real ale ~ Bar food (12(10 Sat)-9; 12-5 only Sun, Mon) ~ (0115) 947 4052 ~ Children allowed until 5pm (6pm weekends) ~ Open 10.30am-11pm; 10am-12.30 midnight Sat; 12 noon-10.30pm Sun

Recommended by Simon J Barber, Gary Rollings, Debbie Porter, the Didler, David Carr, Richard, MP, P Dawn, Michael Dandy, Val and Alan Green, Andy and Jill Kassube

Lincolnshire Poacher 🍺 £

Mansfield Road; up hill from Victoria Centre; NG1 3FR

Chatty down-to-earth pub with great range of drinks (12 real ales), good value food, and outdoor seating

The impressive range of drinks at this relaxing place includes seven continental draught beers, around 20 continental bottled beers, good farm cider, around 70 malt whiskies and ten irish ones, and very good value soft drinks. Batemans Valiant, Everards Tiger and the local Castle Rock Harvest Pale are on as house beers alongside guests from a good variety of brewers such as Abbeydale, Archers, Oakham, Sarah Hughes and Thornbridge. The traditional big wood-floored front bar has a cheerful atmosphere, wall settles, plain wooden tables and breweriana. It opens on to a plain but lively room on the left with a corridor that takes you down to the chatty panelled back snug, with newspapers, cribbage, dominoes, cards and backgammon. A conservatory overlooks tables on a large heated area behind. It can get very busy in the evening when it's popular with a younger crowd.

🍴 Very good value tasty bar food from a changing blackboard menu might include haggis, neeps and tatties, cottage pie, leek and goats cheese pie, butternut squash thai curry, beef braised in beer with mash, and chicken breast with leeks and apples in a creamy cider sauce. *Starters/Snacks: £2.00 to £5.00. Main Courses: £4.50 to £8.00. Puddings: £2.00 to £3.00*

Tynemill ~ Manager Karen Williams ~ Real ale ~ Bar food (12-8(5 Sat, Sun)) ~ (0115) 941 1584 ~ Children welcome till 8pm ~ Dogs welcome ~ Live music Sun evening ~ Open 11-11(midnight Thurs, Fri); 10am-midnight Sat; 12 noon-11pm Sun

Recommended by Rona Murdoch, the Didler, MP, Derek and Sylvia Stephenson, David Carr, P Dawn

Olde Trip to Jerusalem ★ 🍺 £

Brewhouse Yard; from inner ring road follow The North, A6005 Long Eaton signpost until you are in Castle Boulevard, then almost at once turn right into Castle Road; pub is up on the left; NG1 6AD

Unusual pub partly built into sandstone caves, good range of real ales, reasonably priced pubby food

This famous place is unlike any other you'll visit, with some of its rambling rooms burrowed into the sandstone rock below the castle. The siting of the current building (largely 17th-c) is attributed to the days when a brewhouse was established here to supply the needs of the castle on the hill above. The panelled walls of the unusual upstairs bar soar narrowly into a dark cleft carved into the rock above. Also carved into the rock, the downstairs bar has leatherette-cushioned settles built into dark panelling, tables on flagstones, and snug banquettes built into low-ceilinged rocky alcoves. The pub's name refers to the 12th-c crusaders who used to meet nearby on their way to the Holy Land – pub collectors of today still make their own crusades to come here. If you prefer to experience it without the crowds, it's best to visit early evening or on a winter lunchtime, but staff do cope efficiently with the busy mix of tourists, conversational locals and students. Their nine ales (kept in top condition on handpump) include a Greene King stable and a couple of changing guests from brewers such as Nottingham and Saffron. They've ring the bull and a rather out of place games machine. There are seats in a snug courtyard, and the museum next door is interesting.

🍴 Straightforward bar food includes sandwiches, burgers, wraps, fish and chips, beef and ale pie, crab and prawn salad, red peppers in white wine with pasta and rump steak. *Starters/Snacks: £3.55 to £5.75. Main Courses: £5.95 to £8.55. Puddings: £3.55*

Greene King ~ Manager Allen Watson ~ Real ale ~ Bar food (12-8(6 Sun)) ~ (0115) 9473171 ~ Children allowed until 7pm ~ Storyteller last Thurs ~ Open 11(10.30 Sat)-midnight (11 Sun)

Recommended by Derek and Sylvia Stephenson, Colin Gooch, Barry Collett, David and Felicity Fox, Rona Murdoch, Michael Dandy, John Honnor, Bruce Bird, the Didler, Steve Kirby, Phil and Jane Hodson, P Dawn

Vat & Fiddle 🍺 £
Queens Bridge Road, alongside Sheriffs Way (near multi-storey car park); NG2 1NB

Ten real ales at very welcoming down-to-earth pub next to the Castle Rock brewery

It's the chatty relaxed character of this plain little brick pub that makes it stand out from other Nottingham entries (not to mention its fabulous range of beers). The fairly functional but well loved open-plan interior has a strong unspoilt 1930s feel, with cream and navy walls and ceiling, varnished pine tables and bentwood stools and chairs on parquet and terrazzo flooring, patterned blue curtains and some brewery memorabilia, and Kipper the landlady's cat. An interesting display of photographs depicts nearby demolished pubs and there are magazines and newspapers to read, piped music some of the time and a quiz machine. As well as four Castle Rock beers (the pub is right next door to the brewery – you'll probably see some comings and goings), they serve half a dozen interesting guests from brewers such as Burton Bridge, Crouch Vale, Hop Back, Magpie, Newby Wyke and Oakham. They also have around 70 malt whiskies, a changing farm cider, a good range of continental bottled beers, several polish vodkas and good value soft drinks, and have occasional beer festivals too. There are picnic-sets in front by the road.

🍴 Two or three specials such as chilli or curry are served at lunchtime and rolls are available until they run out of stock. *Starters/Snacks: £2.00. Main Courses: £4.95 to £6.75*

Tynemill ~ Manager Sarah Houghton ~ Real ale ~ Bar food (12-2.30 Mon-Fri; rolls all day) ~ (0115) 985 0611 ~ Children welcome away from bar till 8pm ~ Dogs allowed in bar ~ Open 11-11(midnight Fri, Sat); 12-11 Sun

Recommended by C J Fletcher, the Didler, Bruce Bird, Rona Murdoch

SCROOBY   SK6590   MAP 7
Pilgrim Fathers
Great North Rd (A638 S of Bawtry); DN10 6AT

Good enterprising food in spotless traditional pub

In the couple of years since the current licensees took over here they've brought this spotless beamed pub gently up to main entry standard. Its comfortably traditional interior remains unchanged (red patterned carpets, swirly white plastered walls, a leather wing armchair, panelled window seat and other traditional pub furniture) but the welcome and food are definitely up a notch (they prefer you to eat in the attractively set dining area and sizeable conservatory). The simpler public bar on the right is quite separate, with traditional games and a TV. Theakstons and a guest such as Adnams are well kept on handpump, they've decent wines and they do good coffee; unobtrusive piped music, daily papers and garden.

🍴 Cooked fresh to order, tasty bar food includes imaginative open sandwiches, pâté, sherry poached portabella mushrooms, main courses such as spiced salmon fishcakes with chilli crème fraîche dip, home-made pork, apple and mustard sausages on mustard mash, lambs liver on caramelised onion mash, roast vegetables in filo pastry and rib-eye steak with hand-cut chips, with puddings such as Amaretto and apricot sponge with Amaretto cream and white chocolate cheesecake with grenadine poached grapes, and a local cheeseboard. *Starters/Snacks: £2.95 to £6.95. Main Courses: £8.95 to £18.95. Puddings: £3.95*

Enterprise ~ Lease Geoff and Neece Francess-Allen ~ Real ale ~ Bar food (12-2.30, 6-9.30; 12-7 Sun) ~ Restaurant ~ (01302) 710446 ~ Children welcome ~ Dogs allowed in bar ~ Open 12(4 Tues)-11

Recommended by Stephen Woad

WINTHORPE   SK8156   MAP 7

Lord Nelson ◧

Handy for A1 Newark bypass, via A46 and A1133; Gainsborough Road; NG24 2NN

Smartly updated former watermill with reasonably priced imaginative food and good drinks choice

A civilised break from the A1, this recently reworked place greets you with relaxing leather sofas and easy chairs, and the seats around the chunky dining tables are very comfortable, too – dark leather, with well shaped high backs. There are beam and plank ceilings, flagstones and flooring bricks, a little stripped brickwork, prints on the cream or pastel walls, fresh flowers, a woodburning stove and an open fire. There are one or two slightly unusual Nelson mementoes; piped music and TV. Big windows in the dining area look out over a good-sized and attractive walled garden, sheltered by trees all around; children like the shallow former mill race which runs along the side of the building. They have well kept Black Sheep and up to three guests such as Gales HSB, Shepherd Neame Spitfire and Wadworths 6X on handpump, and eight wines by the glass. Service is good.

🍴 **Lunchtime bar food includes soup, fishcakes, chicken liver pâté, sandwiches, sausage and mash, quiche, scampi and steak. The evening dining here is a much more elaborate affair with complimentary canapés, home-made bread and pre-pudding sorbet; confit duck leg terrine, parmesan and tomato tart, spiced crab tian, chump of lamb with dauphinoise potatoes and lamb consommé, fried bass on saffron potato salad with roast aubergine and tomato, parsnip, salsify and sage risotto with asparagus and beetroot crisps and puddings such as crème brûlée of the day, bitter chocolate tart and whole poached baby pineapple.** *Starters/Snacks: £4.50 to £7.45. Main Courses: £8.45 to £17.25. Puddings: £4.95 to £5.25*

Enterprise ~ Lease Stuart Bagley ~ Real ale ~ Bar food (12-2(2.30 Fri, Sat), 6.30-9(9.30 Fri, 10 Sat); 12-3.30, 6.30-8.30 Sun) ~ (01636) 703578 ~ Children welcome ~ Dogs allowed in bar ~ Open 12-2.30(3 Fri), 6-11; 11.30-11 Sat, Sun; closed Mon, Tues

Recommended by Mrs Carolyn Dixon, Mr and Mrs W W Burke, David and Ruth Hollands, JJW, CMW

LUCKY DIP

Besides the fully inspected pubs, you might like to try these Lucky Dips recommended to us and described by readers (if you do, please send us reports: feedback@thegoodpubguide.co.uk).

AWSWORTH [SK4844]
Gate NG16 2RN [Main St, via A6096 off A610 Nuthall—Eastwood bypass]: Friendly old traditional local nr site of once-famous railway viaduct (photographs in passage), well kept Greene King ales, coal fire in quiet comfortable lounge, small pool room, skittle alley; tables out in front, open all day *(the Didler)*
BAGTHORPE [SK4751]
Dixies Arms NG16 5HF [2 miles from M1 junction 27; A608 towards Eastwood, then first right on to B600 via Sandhill Rd, then first left into School Rd; Lower Bagthorpe]: Reliably well kept ales such as Greene King Abbot and Theakstons Best in unspoilt 18th-c beamed and tiled-floor local, good fire in small part-panelled parlour's fine fireplace, entrance bar with tiny snug,

longer narrow room with toby jugs, darts and dominoes; good big garden with play area and football pitch, own pigeon, gun and morris dancing clubs, open all day, busy wknds *(the Didler, Derek and Sylvia Stephenson)*
Shepherds Rest NG16 5HF [2 miles from M1 junction 27, via A608 towards Eastwood, then off B600; Lower Bagthorpe]: Extensively refurbished old pub with pleasant staff, four changing ales, enjoyable food (not Sun evening) inc good fish and Thurs steak night; piped music; children and dogs welcome, garden with play area, pretty surroundings, open all day *(JJW, CMW, Derek and Sylvia Stephenson)*
BARKESTONE [SK7834]
☆ *Fig Tree* NG13 0HN [Rutland Sq]: Neatly refurbished country pub with comfortable

old tables in cosy pastel-walled linked areas around small servery, good enterprising food attractively served (cooked fresh so may take a while) inc good value lunches and home-baked bread, fine range of wines by the glass, well kept Greene King, pleasant attentive staff, interesting deli sales inc gluten/lactose-free; children welcome, open all day Sun *(Jennifer Hurst, Howard and Margaret Buchanan)*

BARNBY MOOR [SK6684]

White Horse DN22 8QS [Great North Rd]: Friendly village pub with good value home-made wkdy food all afternoon inc OAP bargains, four real ales, darts and pool room; piped music may obtrude, TV; disabled facilities, low-priced bedrooms, open all day *(JJW, CMW)*

BEESTON [SK5236]

Crown NG9 1FY [Church St]: Beamed traditional local with Greene King ales, small bar with high-backed settles, settles and darts in larger panelled room, comfortable lounge; terrace tables, open all day *(the Didler, Dr and Mrs A K Clarke)*

BINGHAM [SK7039]

☆ *Horse & Plough* NG13 8AF [off A52; Long Acre]: Low beams, flagstones and stripped brick, prints and old brewery memorabilia, comfortable open-plan seating inc pews, Bass, Caledonian Deuchars IPA, Wells & Youngs Bombardier and several guest beers (may offer tasters), good wine choice, generous wkdy lunchtime sandwiches and normally three or four hot bar dishes, popular upstairs evening grill room (Tues-Sat, and Sun lunch) with polished boards, hand-painted murals and open kitchen; piped music; open all day *(the Didler, P Dawn, Richard, BB)*

BLEASBY [SK7149]

Waggon & Horses NG14 7GG [Gypsy Lane]: Banquettes in carpeted lounge, coal fire in character bar with pub games, pleasant chatty landlord, wife makes good value fresh lunchtime food from snacks up, Marstons ales, comfortable back lobby with play area; piped music; tables outside, small camping area *(the Didler)*

BUNNY [SK5829]

☆ *Rancliffe Arms* NG11 6QT [Loughborough Rd (A60 S of Nottingham)]: Substantial early 18th-c former coaching inn reworked with emphasis on extensive bistro-style dining area, upscale food inc adventurous dishes, popular Sun carvery, friendly efficient service, sofas and armchairs in comfortable bar with interesting changing real ales and log fire; children welcome *(Gerry and Rosemary Dobson, P Dawn, Malcolm Pellatt, Gwyn and Anne Wake)*

CAR COLSTON [SK7242]

Royal Oak NG13 8JE [The Green, off Tenman Lane (off A46 not far from A6097 junction)]: Helpful young licensees doing reliably enjoyable food in biggish 18th-c pub opp one of England's largest village greens, Adnams, Jennings and other ales,

woodburner in main room, unusual vaulted brick ceiling in second room; picnic-sets on spacious back lawn, open all day wknds, cl Mon lunchtime *(Richard and Jean Green, David Glynne-Jones)*

CARLTON-ON-TRENT [SK7964]

Great Northern NG23 6NT [Ossington Rd; village signed just off A1 N of Newark]: Large busy local next to main railway line, very frequent trains and lots of railway memorabilia; usual food with good skillet dishes and fresh fish Fri, Greene King ales, big games room, family room; tables out overlooking trains *(Derek and Sylvia Stephenson)*

CHILWELL [SK5135]

Cadland NG9 5EG [High Rd]: Well divided open-plan Ember Inn with good choice of wines and beers, quick service, good value popular food all day, open fires; open all day *(Roy and Lindsey Fentiman)*

COTGRAVE [SK6435]

Rose & Crown NG12 3HQ [Main Rd, off A46 SE of Nottingham]: Friendly and comfortable village pub, good value generous food all day inc mid-week and early evening bargains, more elaborate evening/wknd dishes, young helpful staff, four changing ales such as Caledonian Deuchars IPA, good soft drinks choice, log fires, back eating area with fresh flowers and candles; children welcome, garden picnic-sets *(Piotr Chodzko-Zajko, P Dawn)*

EAST BRIDGFORD [SK6943]

Reindeer NG13 8PH [Kneeton Rd, a mile from A6075, can also be reached from A46]: Popular village pub with good value fresh home-made food, well kept ales such as Shepherd Neame Spitfire and Timothy Taylors Landlord, reasonably priced wine, nicely furnished beamed main bar and small dining room, back public bar, log-effect gas fires; children welcome *(BB)*

EASTWOOD [SK4846]

Foresters Arms NG16 2DN [Main St, Newthorpe]: Friendly local with Greene King ales, darts, dominoes and table skittles, open fire, old local photographs, lounge with wknd organ singalong; TV; nice garden *(the Didler)*

EDINGLEY [SK6655]

Old Reindeer NG22 8BE [off A617 Newark—Mansfield at Kirklington; Main St]: Early 18th-c, well kept Marstons-related and guest ales, good choice of other drinks, decent food (all day wknds), comfortably refurbished bar, pool in games area, upstairs restaurant; TV, games machines; children and dogs welcome, attractive garden, four bedrooms, open all day *(JJW, CMW)*

ELKESLEY [SK6875]

☆ *Robin Hood* DN22 8AJ [just off A1 Newark—Blyth; High St]: Neat dining pub with enjoyable food, friendly staff, Black Sheep and Marstons Pedigree, dark furnishings on patterned carpets, yellow walls, pool and board games; piped music, TV; children and dogs welcome, picnic-sets and play area, cl Sun evening, Mon lunchtime *(Alan Cole,*

Kirstie Bruce, Richard Cole, Christopher Turner, Gordon and Margaret Ormondroyd, Virginia Williams, Simon Collett-Jones, MJVK)

FISKERTON [SK7351]

Bromley Arms NG25 0UL [Main St]: Unpretentious Trentside pub with friendly helpful service, Greene King ales, reasonably priced wholesome food; can be busy in summer *(Alan Bulley)*

GOTHAM [SK5330]

Cuckoo Bush NG11 0JL [Leake Rd]: 19th-c local with comfortable L-shaped lounge bar, pictures, plates etc, three other rooms, good value usual food (not Sat-Weds nights), Bass and Wells & Youngs, sensibly segregated darts and TV (with sofa); quiet piped music; picnic-sets in small garden *(David and Sue Atkinson)*

GRANBY [SK7436]

☆ ***Marquis of Granby*** NG13 9PN [off A52 E of Nottingham; Dragon St]: Stylish yet friendly 18th-c pub in attractive Vale of Belvoir village, tap for Brewsters (just over near Plungar) with their ales and guest beers from chunky yew bar counter, decent local food (not Sun-Weds evenings), two small comfortable rooms with broad flagstones, some low beams and striking wallpaper, log fire; live music Sat; children and dogs welcome, open all day, cl Mon lunchtime *(the Didler, David Glynne-Jones, Richard, BB, Gary Rollings, Debbie Porter)*

HARBY [SK8870]

Bottle & Glass NG23 7EB [High St]: Smart civilised dining pub in same good family as Caunton Beck in Caunton and Wig & Mitre in Lincoln, good imaginative food – not cheap – in bar and restaurant, fine choice of wines by the glass inc good champagne, well kept ales inc Black Sheep; tables outside, open all day from 9.30 *(David and Ruth Hollands)*

HOVERINGHAM [SK6946]

☆ ***Reindeer*** NG14 7JR [Main St]: Unpretentious low-beamed pub with friendly staff, four or five good changing ales such as Castle Rock and Nottingham, good wines by the glass, good short choice of enjoyable food from pubby things to enterprising dishes, coal fires in bar and back dining lounge, daily papers; children welcome, picnic-sets outside, cl Sun evening, Tues lunchtime and Mon, open all day Sat, and Sun till 5 *(Richard, the Didler, Derek and Sylvia Stephenson)*

KIMBERLEY [SK4944]

☆ ***Nelson & Railway*** NG16 2NR [Station Rd; handy for M1 junction 26 via A610]: Cheery beamed Victorian pub with well kept Greene King ales, efficient service, mix of Edwardian-looking furniture, brewery prints and railway signs, good value dining extension, traditional games inc alley and table skittles; piped music, games machine; children and dogs allowed, tables and swings in good-sized cottagey garden, good value bedrooms, open all day *(LYM, the Didler, Barry Rolfe, Derek and Sylvia Stephenson, Pete Baker)*

Stag NG16 2NB [Nottingham Rd]: Friendly 16th-c traditional local kept spotless by devoted landlady, two cosy rooms, small central counter and corridor, low beams, dark panelling and settles, good range of real ales, vintage working penny slot machines and Shipstones brewery photographs; attractive back garden with play area, opens 5.30 (1.30 Sat, 12 Sun) *(the Didler)*

KINOULTON [SK6731]

Nevile Arms NG12 3EH [Owthorpe Lane]: Three well furnished beamed rooms, wide-ranging low-priced food (not Sun/Mon evenings) from sandwiches to Sun carvery, welcoming licensees, Greene King ales, good choice of wines; garden with play area *(M J Winterton)*

LAMBLEY [SK6245]

Robin Hood NG4 4PP [Main St]: Welcoming pub completely reworked after 2007 floods, two beamed bars off central servery, four Marstons ales, decent food choice (not Sun evening) inc wkdy bargain lunches, roaring log fires, dining room; piped music, Tues quiz night; garden, open all day *(JJW, CMW, David Glynne-Jones)*

LINBY [SK5351]

Horse & Groom NG15 8AE [Main St]: Picturesque three-room village pub, wide choice of decent straightforward food (not Sun-Thurs evenings), three or four changing ales inc Theakstons and Wells & Youngs, friendly staff, inglenook log fire, pleasant colour scheme, conservatory, no mobile phones; quiet piped music, big-screen TV, games machine in lobby; tables outside, big play area, attractive village nr Newstead Abbey, open all day *(the Didler, JJW, CMW, P Dawn)*

LOWDHAM [SK6646]

Worlds End NG14 7AT [Plough Lane]: Small village pub with reasonably priced food most of the day (not Sun evening) inc popular OAP wkdy lunches and other deals, three real ales, log fire in pubby beamed bar, restaurant; piped music; children welcome, garden picnic-sets, some covered, open all day *(Richard, JJW, CMW)*

MANSFIELD [SK5260]

Nell Gwynne NG18 5EX [Sutton Rd (A38 W of centre)]: Former gentlemen's club, much homelier now, with easy mix of age groups, Greene King Abbot and a guest beer, log-effect gas fire, old colliery plates and mementoes of old Mansfield pubs, games room; sports TV, piped music; has been cl Mon-Thurs lunchtimes *(Derek and Sylvia Stephenson, the Didler)*

Railway Inn NG18 1EF [Station St; best approached by viaduct from nr market pl]: Friendly local with long-serving landlady, attractively priced Batemans XB and two guest beers, bargain home-made lunches, bright front bar and cosier back room; handy for Robin Hood Line stn, normally open all day, cl Sun evening *(P Dawn, the Didler, Pete Baker)*

MANSFIELD WOODHOUSE [SK5463]
Greyhound NG19 8BD [High St]: Popular
village local with Greene King Abbot,
Theakstons Mild, Websters and one or two
guest beers, cosy lounge, darts, dominoes
and pool in busy bar; open all day
(the Didler)

MAPLEBECK [SK7160]
☆ *Beehive* NG22 0BS [signed down pretty
country lanes from A616 Newark—Ollerton
and from A617 Newark—Mansfield]: Relaxing
beamed country tavern in nice spot, chatty
landlady, tiny front bar, slightly bigger side
room, traditional furnishings, coal or log
fire, free antique juke box, changing ales
such as Maypole, no food; tables on small
terrace with flower tubs and grassy bank
running down to little stream, play area with
swings, may be cl winter wkdy lunchtimes,
very busy wknds and bank hols *(LYM,
Richard, the Didler)*

NEWARK [SK7953]
Castle & Falcon NG24 1TW [London Rd]:
John Smiths and two interesting guest
beers, friendly landlord, comfortable back
lounge and family conservatory, lively games
bar with darts, dominoes, pool and TV,
skittle alley; small terrace, evening opening
7, cl lunchtime Mon-Thurs *(the Didler)*
☆ *Fox & Crown* NG24 1JY [Appleton Gate]:
Convivial bare-boards open-plan Tynemill
pub with bargain simple food from filled
rolls, baguettes, panini and baked potatoes
up, Castle Rock ales and several interesting
guest beers from central servery, Stowford
Press cider, dozens of whiskies, vodkas and
other spirits, good tea, coffee and decent
wines by the glass, friendly obliging staff,
several side areas; piped pop music; children
welcome, good wheelchair access, open all
day *(P Dawn, the Didler, Stuart Paulley,
Mrs Hazel Rainer, Barbara Carver, David Carr, BB)*
Mail Coach NG24 1TN [London Rd, nr
Beaumont Cross]: Friendly open-plan
Georgian pub, three candlelit separate areas
with old-world décor, lots of chicken
pictures, hot coal fires and comfortable
chairs, Flowers IPA and Original and local
guest beers, pleasant staff, lunchtime food
(not Mon), pub games; upstairs ladies';
tables on back terrace *(the Didler, P Dawn)*
Navigation NG24 4TS [Mill Gate]: Lively
open-plan bar in converted warehouse, big
windows on to River Trent, flagstones, bare
boards and iron pillars, Everards Tiger and
Marstons Pedigree, bar food, nautical
decorations; weekly live music *(Keith and
Chris O'Neill)*

NEWSTEAD [SK5252]
Station Hotel NG15 0BZ [Station Rd]: Basic
red-brick village local opp Robin Hood line
station, low-priced Barnsley Bitter and
Oakwell Mild, chatty landlady, fine railway
photographs, pub games; juke box, TV
(the Didler)

NORTH MUSKHAM [SK7958]
Muskham Ferry NG23 6HB [Ferry Lane,
handy for A1 (which has small sign to pub)]:

Traditional well furnished panelled pub in
splendid location on River Trent, relaxing
views from bar/restaurant, usual food from
filled rolls up, Stones and Timothy Taylors
Landlord; children very welcome,
waterside terrace, moorings, open all day
(LYM, David and Ruth Hollands)

NOTTINGHAM [SK5739]
Approach NG1 6DQ [Friar Lane]: Big two-
floor bar, three local real ales, good wine
range, enjoyable food, comedy club Sun,
music Thurs; open all day *(P Dawn)*
Bread & Bitter NG3 5JL [Woodthorpe Dr]: New
Tynemill pub in former suburban bakery still
showing ovens, three bright airy rooms, Castle
Rock and great choice of other beers, farm
cider, decent wine choice, good value food all
day, defunct brewery memorabilia; open all
day from 9 *(Richard, the Didler)*
☆ *Canal House* NG1 7EH [Canal St]: Converted
wharf building, bridge over indoors canal
spur complete with narrowboat, lots of bare
brick and varnished wood, huge joists on
steel beams, long bar with good choice of
house wines, Castle Rock and changing guest
beers, lively efficient staff, sensibly priced
pubby food, lots of standing room; good
upstairs restaurant and second bar, masses
of tables out on attractive waterside terrace;
piped music (live Sun), busy with young
people at night; open all day *(Bruce Bird,
Michael Dandy, David Carr, P Dawn, Derek and
Sylvia Stephenson, BB, the Didler)*
Cast Bar NG1 5AL [Wellington Circus, nr
Playhouse Theatre]: Adjoining theatre, more
cool wine bar/restaurant than pub, lots of
chrome and glass, decent range of wines by
the glass, real ale such as Castle Rock or
Nottingham (handpumps hide below the
counter), good value light menu, more
adventurous restaurant meals, good integral
all-day deli; children welcome, plenty of
tables out on notable courtyard terrace by
huge Anish Kapoor *Sky Mirror*, open all day
(Richard)
Cock & Hoop NG1 1HF [High Pavement]: Tiny
front bar and flagstoned cellar bar attached
to decent hotel under new management,
imaginative food (all day, not cheap),
Caledonian Deuchars IPA, Fullers London
Pride, Nottingham Cock & Hoop, Timothy
Taylors Landlord and a guest; piped music,
TV, and they may add a service charge even
to bar snacks; children welcome with
restrictions, smart bedrooms (ones by the
street can be noisy wknds), open all day;
more reports on new regime please *(LYM)*
Fox & Crown NG6 0GA [Church St/Lincoln St,
Old Basford]: Good range of Alcazar beers
brewed behind refurbished open-plan pub
(window shows the brewery, tours Sat, next-
door beer shop), also guest beers, good
continental bottle choice, enjoyable fresh
food inc thai and wide choice of early
evening home-made pizzas; good piped
music, games machines, big-screen sports
TV; disabled access, tables out behind, open
all day *(the Didler)*

Gatehouse NG1 5FS [Maid Marion Way/Tollhouse Hill]: Below office block, interesting and surprisingly cosy, with easy chairs and sofas, four real ales, good choice of wines by the glass, good value food; pavement tables, open all day *(P Dawn)*

Gladstone NG5 2AW [Loscoe Rd, Carrington]: Welcoming local with well kept Fullers London Pride, Greene King Abbot and Timothy Taylors Landlord, good range of malt whiskies, comfortable lounge with reading matter, basic bar with old sports equipment and darts; piped music, big-screen sports TV; upstairs folk club Weds, quiz Thurs; tables in yard with lots of hanging baskets, cl wkdy lunchtimes, open all day wknds (from 3 Fri) *(the Didler, P Dawn, Jeremy King, MP, Richard, David and Sue Atkinson)*

Globe NG2 3BQ [London Rd]: Light and airy roadside pub with six well kept ales such as Mallard, Maple and Nottingham, coal fire; handy for cricket or football matches, open all day *(the Didler, P Dawn)*

Golden Fleece NG1 3FN [Mansfield Rd]: Frequent live music inc Mon open mike, contemporary refurbishment and young feel, up to date food all day, mainstream real ales and wide choice of other drinks; open all day *(Kathryn Pyer)*

Hemlockstone NG8 2QQ [Bramcote Lane, Wollaton]: Refurbished in modern traditional style, imaginatively reasonably priced food with separate restaurant menu, young enthusiastic staff, Batemans XB, Courage Directors and Shepherd Neame Spitfire *(Malcolm Pellatt)*

Horse & Groom NG7 7EA [Radford Rd, New Basford]: Eight good changing ales in well run unpretentious local by former Shipstones brewery, still with their name and other memorabilia, good value fresh straightforward food from sandwiches to Sun lunch, daily papers, nice snug, 60s/70s DJ Sun night; open all day *(the Didler, P Dawn)*

King William IV NG2 [Eyre St, Sneinton]: Newly refurbished real ale pub with Oakham and several other well kept changing ales, Weston's Old Rosie cider, bargain cobs, friendly staff, fresh flowers, pool upstairs, irish music Thurs; silenced sports TV; heated smokers' shelter, open all day *(the Didler)*

Larwood & Voce NG2 6AJ [Fox Rd, West Bridgford]: Revived by traditional/chic refurbishment, with good properly made pubby food, good value wines by the glass, great cocktails, Adnams; sports TV, on the edge of the cricket ground and handy for Notts Forest *(Kate Davies)*

☆ *Lion* NG7 7FQ [Lower Mosley St, New Basford]: Three or four Batemans ales and many changing guests such as Abbeydale and Mallard from one of city's deepest cellars (glass viewing panel – can be visited at quiet times), farm ciders, ten wines by the glass, good value home-made food all day inc doorstep sandwiches, children's helpings and summer barbecues; well fabricated feel of separate areas, bare bricks and polished

dark oak boards, coal or log fires, daily papers; wknd live music; children welcome, terrace and smokers' shelter, open all day *(David and Sue Atkinson, the Didler)*

Moot NG3 2DG [Carlton Rd, Sneinton – aka Old Moot Hall]: Bright refurbishment with comfortable banquettes, very wide choice of well kept ales, friendly staff; piped music *(the Didler, David and Sue Atkinson)*

News House NG1 7HB [Canal St]: Friendly two-room Tynemill pub with half a dozen or more well kept changing ales inc bargain Castle Rock, belgian and czech imports on tap, farm cider, good wine and hot drinks choice, decent fresh lunchtime food inc good value Sun lunch, mix of bare boards and carpet, one room filled with years of local newspaper front pages, bar billiards, attractive blue exterior tiling; big-screen sports TV; open all day *(the Didler, P Dawn, Andy and Jill Kassube, David Carr)*

Pit & Pendulum NG1 2EW [Victoria St]: Dark gothick theme bar with ghoulish carving and creeping ivy lit by heavy chandeliers and (electronically) flaring torches, all sorts of other more or less cinematic horror allusions in the décor, standard fairly priced all-day bar food, well reproduced piped music; keg beers; good wheelchair access, open all day *(David Carr, Jeremy King, Michael Dandy, LYM, Rona Murdoch)*

☆ *Plough* NG7 3EN [St Peters St, Radford]: Enthusiastic young new landlord for friendly 19th-c local brewing its own good value Nottingham ales, also a guest beer and farm cider, two coal fires, bar billiards and other traditional games, cheap food; prominent games machine and sports TV; open all day Fri-Sun *(the Didler)*

Salutation NG1 7AA [Hounds Gate/Maid Marion Way]: Proper pub, low beams, flagstones, ochre walls and cosy corners inc two small quiet rooms in ancient lower back part, plusher modern front lounge, half a dozen real ales, quickly served food till 7, helpful staff; piped music; open all day *(Val and Alan Green, Barry Collett, Michael Dandy, BB, P Dawn)*

Sir John Borlase Warren NG7 3GD [Ilkeston Rd/Canning Circus (A52 towards Derby)]: Good atmosphere in comfortable linked rooms with interesting Victorian decorations, enjoyable limited food, friendly staff, several real ales; children welcome (not Fri/Sat evenings), tables in nicely lit back garden *(BB, Peter and Jean Hoare, David Carr, P Dawn)*

Vale NG5 3GG [Mansfield Rd]: Half a dozen changing ales in 1930s local with original layout, panelling and woodwork, low-priced food; open all day *(the Didler)*

ORSTON [SK7741]

Durham Ox NG13 9NS [Church St]: Comfortable split-level open-plan village pub opp church, Fullers London Pride, Greene King IPA, Marstons Pedigree and local guest beers, hot coal fire, interesting RAF/USAF memorabilia; terrace tables, nice garden,

pleasant countryside, open all day Sat
(the Didler)

OXTON [SK6250]

Olde Bridge NG25 0SE [Nottingham Rd
(B6386, just off A6097)]: Immaculate partly
panelled 19th-c pub with profusely
cushioned sofas and armchairs, great choice
of wine by the glass, three Everards ales,
good soft drinks, hard-working staff, daily
papers, attractive traditional restaurant, lots
of potted plants; piped music, games
machines; children welcome, disabled
facilities, large garden, cl Mon, open all day
(N R White, Phil and Jane Hodson)

PAPPLEWICK [SK5450]

Griffins Head NG15 8EN [Moor Rd
(B683/B6011)]: Recently refurbished, food
from pubby favourites to local pigeon with
orange and rocket, well kept Black Sheep,
Brakspears and Timothy Taylors Landlord,
friendly efficient staff, log fire,
attractive raftered dining area; picnic-sets
outside, handy for Newstead Abbey
(David Glynne-Jones)

RADCLIFFE ON TRENT [SK6439]

Black Lion NG12 2FD [Main Rd (A52)]:
Courage Directors, Greene King IPA, Timothy
Taylors Landlord and quickly changing guest
beers, all-day food, big comfortable lounge
with coal fire; cheery bar with pool, big-
screen sports TV, may be discos or karaoke;
big enclosed garden behind, barbecues and
play area, open all day (the Didler,
Mrs Hazel Rainer)

Horse Chestnut NG12 2BE [Main Rd]: Smart
pub with eight well priced changing ales,
short tasty menu, friendly efficient staff,
two-level main bar, plenty of Victorian
features inc panelling, parquet, polished
brass and woodwork and impressive lamps,
handsome leather seating and fine
autobiography collection in lounge; disabled
access, attractive terrace, open all day
(M Mossman, the Didler, P Dawn,
David Glynne-Jones)

RANBY [SK6580]

Chequers DN22 8HT [off A620 Retford—
Worksop, just E of A1]: Several bays opening
off main area, some recent modern restyling
in black, gold and red, mix of furnishings inc
a sofa; Black Sheep, Timothy Taylors
Landlord and a guest beer, bar food and
carvery (they may try to keep your credit
card while you eat); piped music;
children welcome till 8, small terrace by
Chesterfield Canal (some mooring),
open all day wknds, cl Mon (M Mossman,
Derek and Sylvia Stephenson, LYM, Mr and
Mrs P Eastwood)

RUDDINGTON [SK5733]

Three Crowns NG11 6LB [Easthorpe St]:
Open-plan village local with well kept ales
such as Adnams and Nottingham, popular
back thai restaurant (evenings, not
Sun/Mon); open all day wknds (the Didler,
P Dawn)

White Horse NG11 6HD [Church St]: Cheerful
two-room 1930s village local with half a

dozen real ales, old photographs, games inc
pool; TV, heated terrace, nice garden, open
all day wknds (P Dawn, the Didler)

SELSTON [SK4553]

Horse & Jockey NG16 6FB [handy for M1
junctions 27/28; Church Lane]: Dating from
17th c, intelligently renovated with
interesting 18th/19th-c survivals and good
carving, different levels, low beams and
flagstones, friendly staff, half a dozen real
ales, bargain cobs wkdys, good log fire in
cast-iron range, games area with darts
and pool; dogs welcome, top-end smokers'
shelter (Roger Noyes, Derek and
Sylvia Stephenson, the Didler)

SOUTH LEVERTON [SK7881]

Plough DN22 0BT [Town St]: Tiny local
doubling as morning post office, basic
trestle tables, benches and pews, log fire,
helpful staff, Greene King and a guest beer,
traditional games; nice garden, open all day
(from early afternoon wkdys) (the Didler,
Paul J Robinshaw)

STAUNTON IN THE VALE [SK8043]

Staunton Arms NG13 9PE: Welcoming and
spotless country pub with helpful attentive
licensees, real ales, good choice of other
drinks, bar food, lots of varnished pine in
L-shaped bar with dining area up a step or
two, RAF pictures; front terrace, back
garden, rolling Vale of Belvoir views
(Phil and Jane Hodson)

THURGARTON [SK6949]

☆ *Red Lion* NG14 7GP [Southwell Rd (A612)]:
Cheery 16th-c pub with good sensibly priced
food (all day wknds and bank hols) inc fresh
fish and some adventurous dishes in brightly
decorated split-level beamed bars and
restaurant, well kept Black Sheep, Marstons
and Springhead, comfortable banquettes and
other seating, flame-effect fire, lots of nooks
and crannies, big windows to attractive
good-sized two-level back garden with well
spaced picnic-sets (dogs on leads allowed
here); unobtrusive games machine, steepish
walk back up to car park; children welcome
(Maurice and Janet Thorpe, Derek and
Sylvia Stephenson, David Glynne-Jones, BB,
Dean Rose)

WALKERINGHAM [SK7692]

Brickmakers Arms DN10 4LT [Fountain Hill
Rd, off B1403]: Busy pub expanded into
hotel and restaurant too, huge helpings of
good value pubby food, well kept beers inc
Idle, helpful staff; 16 bedrooms (Anne and
Paul Horscraft)

WATNALL CHAWORTH [SK5046]

☆ *Queens Head* NG16 1HT [3 miles from M1
junction 26: A610 towards Nottingham, left
on B600, then keep right; Main Rd]: Good
value pubby food (all day summer) in
tastefully extended low-beamed pub with
well kept ales such as Adnams, Everards,
Greene King and Marstons Pedigree,
efficient staff, beams and stripped pine, coal
fire, intimate snug, dining area; piped
music; picnic-sets on attractive back lawn
with big play area, open all day (Derek and

Sylvia Stephenson, the Didler, Glen and Nola Armstrong)

Royal Oak NG16 1HS [Main Rd; B600
N of Kimberley]: Friendly beamed village local with interesting plates and pictures, Greene King ales, fresh cobs, woodburner, back games room and pool room, upstairs lounge open Fri-Sun; sports TV, some live music; tables outside, open all day (the Didler)

WEST BRIDGFORD [SK5837]

Monkey Tree NG2 6AP [Bridgford Rd]: Bright stylish bar, three local real ales, decent wines, good service, good value upstairs restaurant – busy wknds and summer; tables out under front tree, open all day (P Dawn)

☆ **Stratford Haven** NG2 6BA [Stratford Rd, Trent Bridge]: One of Tynemill's best pubs, bare-boards front bar leading to linked areas inc airy skylit back part with relaxed local atmosphere, Batemans, Castle Rock and interesting changing guest beers, exotic bottled beers, farm ciders, ample whiskies and wines, good value simple home-made food all day, daily papers, some live music (nothing too noisy), dogs welcome, handy for cricket ground and Nottingham Forest FC, tables outside, open all day (the Didler, Derek and Sylvia Stephenson, Rona Murdoch, Richard, BB)

WEST MARKHAM [SK7273]

☆ **Mussel & Crab** NG22 0PJ [Sibthorpe Hill; B1164 nr A1/A57/A638 roundabout N of Tuxford]: More roomy restaurant than pub (you can have just a drink in the interesting open-plan bar), good fish and seafood fresh from Brancaster and Brixham, vast array of

other blackboard food, beams, stripped stone, some big pastel fishy murals, nice conservatory, prompt friendly service, good wines by the glass (wine racks around the room), Tetleys, good coffee; good disabled access, terrace picnic-sets, play area, farmland views (Mrs Brenda Calver, Derek and Sylvia Stephenson)

WEST STOCKWITH [SK7994]

White Hart DN10 4EY [Main St]: Small friendly country pub at junction of Chesterfield Canal with River Trent, five of its own good Idle ales, enjoyable food, friendly atmosphere, games room with pool; TV; children and dogs welcome, waterside tables, bedrooms (JJW, CMW)

WIDMERPOOL [SK6429]

☆ **Pullman** NG12 5PR [1st left off A606 coming towards Nottingham from A46 junction; Kinoulton Lane]: Thriving family dining pub in well converted station building, well kept Greene King, good value generous food inc fish and carvery nights, friendly helpful service, good wine choice, abundant locomotive and train paintings; piped music; tables and picnic-sets outside (Nigel and Sue Foster, John and Sylvia Harrop)

WYSALL [SK6027]

Plough NG12 5QQ [Keyworth Rd; off A60 at Costock, or A6006 at Wymeswold]: Attractive 17th-c beamed village pub popular for sensibly short choice of good value generous food, cheerful staff, changing real ales, rooms either side of bar with nice mix of furnishings, soft lighting, big log fire; french doors to pretty terrace with flower tubs and baskets (M Mossman, P Dawn)

Post Office address codings confusingly give the impression that a few pubs are in Nottinghamshire, when they're really in Derbyshire (which is where we list them).

Oxfordshire

This county has a great line in really enjoyable well run pubs. These range from unchanging and unspoilt little places through bustling inns in the heart of some lovely towns and cities to top-notch dining pubs, several with chef/patrons. There's also a healthy clutch of new entries, including some making a welcome return to the *Guide*, in quite a new guise, after a break of several years. The newcomers are the Joiners Arms in Bloxham (appealing rooms on several levels, plenty of outside seating), the Crown at Church Enstone (most enjoyable under its friendly landlady, while the landlord cooks the good food), the King William IV at Hailey (a pleasant country pub with fantastic views), the Nut Tree at Murcott (enthusiastic young licensees using their own-grown produce and home-reared pigs to great advantage), the Eagle & Child in Oxford (lots of atmosphere and a palpable sense of history), and the White Horse at Woolstone (the hard-working landlord has turned it into a great local favourite). Other pubs doing especially well this year are the Plough at Alvescot (the genial landlord has lots of interesting collections), the Reindeer in Banbury (unpretentious and chatty, with plenty to look at), the Saye & Sele Arms at Broughton (the landlord cooks well), the Black Horse at Checkendon (over a century in the same family – and it shows), the Chequers in Chipping Norton (bustling and friendly all day), the Chequers at Churchill (Mrs Golding's amazing memory for faces makes for a splendidly warm atmosphere), the lovely old White Hart at Fyfield (delicious food), the Bell at Langford (the landlord's smashing cooking earns it a new Food Award), the Olde Leathern Bottel at Lewknor (friendly timelessness, with a nice mix of customers), the welcoming Blue Boar at Longworth (splendid long-serving landlord), the traditional Rose & Crown and classic old Turf Tavern in Oxford, the Royal Oak at Ramsden (super wines, enjoyable food and genuinely warm welcome for all), the Rose & Crown at Shilton (simple but upmarket, with nice food), the Baskerville Arms at Shiplake (emphasis on interesting food), the Masons Arms at Swerford (good modern cooking by the landlord, and a warm relaxed atmosphere), the Swan at Swinbrook (civilised and smart, with lovely contemporary food), the Trout at Tadpole Bridge (especially smart since it had to be refurbished twice in a year after flooding), and the Kings Arms in Woodstock (stylish Georgian hotel, handy for something to eat at any time). From this long list, it's clear that there is some delicious food to be had – at a price, it has to be noted. This is not a cheap county, but at least for your money you are getting some pretty special pub meals here. With so many strong contenders, it's been a close-run contest, but the top title of Oxfordshire Dining Pub of the Year goes to the Swan at Swinbrook. The Lucky Dip section at the end of the chapter again shows how rich the county's range of good pubs is, with plenty of strong picks – most notably the Red Lion in Adderbury, Angel in Burford, Clanfield Tavern, Lamb at Crawley, Unicorn in Deddington, Plough at Finstock, Carpenters Arms at Fulbrook, Anchor in Henley, Dog & Duck at Highmoor, Sun in Hook

Norton, Plough at Kingham, Crown at Nuffield, Crown at Pishill, Bell at Shenington, Duck on the Pond at South Newington, and two fine restaurarty pubs in or near Stoke Row, the Cherry Tree and Crooked Billet. Hook Norton is the county's leading independent brewer. Brakspears, brewed by Wychwood, is also very widely available here; Wychwood has now been bought by the Marstons combine, but is likely to keep brewing. Other local beers we found in at least some good pubs here are Loddon, White Horse, Lovibonds, Butlers, Cotswold, Ridgeway and Old Bog; instead of the usual real ales, Cotswold brews distinctive lagers – well worth trying.

ALVESCOT   SP2704   MAP 4

Plough
B4020 Carterton—Clanfield, SW of Witney; OX18 2PU

Useful for wide choice of popular food all day, bric-a-brac and aircraft prints in neat pubby bar, colourful hanging baskets

Quite a few changes to this bustling pub include a new skittle alley, new pubby furniture, refurbished lavatories, a new pet, and new chickens in the children's play area. It remains extremely popular under the genial landlord and to be sure of a table, it's now best to book ahead at peak times. As well as a collection of keys in the entrance hall, the neatly kept bar with its good pubby atmosphere has aircraft prints and a large poster of Concorde's last flight, as well as plenty of cottagey pictures, china ornaments and house plants, a big antique case of stuffed birds of prey, sundry bric-a-brac, and a log fire. Comfortable seating includes cream, red and green cushioned dark wooden chairs around dark wooden tables, some cushioned settles, and of course the bar stools bagged by cheerful regulars in the early evening. Wadworths IPA, 6X and Horizon on handpump. There's a proper public bar with TV, games machine, darts and piped music. There are picnic-sets on the back terrace and a couple out in front below particularly colourful hanging baskets by the quiet village road; aunt sally. The pub cats Dino and Bo have been joined by a very friendly stray called Patch.

🍴 From a sizeable menu, bar food might include cheese and garlic mushrooms, brussels pâté with redcurrant jelly, egg mayonnaise, macaroni cheese, fish pie, ham and free-range eggs, lasagne, half a chicken in smoked hickory sauce, beef and mushroom in ale pie, lamb cobbler, daily specials such as game pie or cajun tuna steak, and puddings like sticky ginger pudding and tiramisu. *Starters/Snacks: £4.50 to £8.95. Main Courses: £8.50 to £14.75. Puddings: £3.95 to £4.50*

Wadworths ~ Tenant Kevin Robert Keeling ~ Real ale ~ Bar food (all day) ~ (01993) 842281 ~ Children allowed until 8.30pm ~ Open 11.30(11 Fri)-11(midnight Fri); 12-10.30 Sun

Recommended by Keith and Sue Ward, KN-R, Peter and Audrey Dowsett, Paul Humphreys, Pat and Roger Davies

---

ASTON TIRROLD   SU5586   MAP 2

Chequers 🍴 ☼
Village signposted off A417 Streatley—Wantage; Fullers Road; OX11 9EN

Atmosphere and food of a rustic french restaurant in pubby surroundings, nice french wines, restrained décor and stylish service; charming cottagey garden

There's no doubt that this charming place – formally calling itself the Sweet Olive at the Chequers – is almost more of a rustic french restaurant than a village pub, but readers have much enjoyed their visits and it does have a relaxed pubby feel, and Brakspears Bitter and Fullers London Pride on handpump. The chatty main room has a proper bar counter, complete with sturdy bar stools (and people using them), grass matting over its quarry tiles, six or seven sturdy stripped tables with mate's chairs and cushioned high-backed settles against the walls, a small fireplace, and plain white walls. There are two or three wine cartoons, and wine box-ends, mainly claret and sauternes, panelling the back of the servery, a nice range of french wines by the glass, including a pudding wine, and good coffees; attentive service. A second rather smaller room, set more formally as a restaurant, has a similarly restrained décor of pale grey dado, white-panelled ceiling and red and black flooring tile; piped music. A charming small cottagey garden, well sheltered by flowering shrubs, angles around the pub, with picnic-sets under cocktail parasols and a play tree; aunt sally.

🍴 **Changing daily, the very good food comes with a slate of olives and good breads as well as a handsomely ringed linen napkin: filled baguettes, mediterranean fish soup with garlic mayonnaise, croutons and cheese, sautéed lambs sweetbreads with grainy mustard, spinach and wild mushrooms, slow cooked moroccan-style lamb, scottish scallops with lime butter sauce, mushroom risotto and rocket salad, escalope of venison with port wine sauce, oxtail in puff pastry with red burgundy sauce, and puddings such as dark chocolate mousse with espresso ice-cream and vanilla sauce and lemon cheesecake with raspberry coulis and passion fruit sorbet.** *Starters/Snacks: £4.50 to £9.95. Main Courses: £11.95 to £16.95. Puddings: £5.96*

Enterprise ~ Lease Olivier Bouet and Stephane Brun ~ Real ale ~ Bar food (not Sun evening, all day Weds, all Feb, 1 week July) ~ Restaurant ~ (01235) 851272 ~ Children welcome ~ Dogs allowed in bar ~ Open 12-3, 6-midnight; 12-4 Sun; closed Weds, Sun evening, all Feb and 1 week July

Recommended by I H G Busby, Rob Winstanley, J V Dadswell, Susan and John Douglas, Gordon Davico, Malcolm Rand

BANBURY   SP4540   MAP 4

Reindeer 🍴 £

Parsons Street, off Market Place; OX16 5NA

Plenty of shoppers and regulars in interesting town pub, fine real ales, simple food and roaring log fires; no under-21s

'The best type of town pub' is how one reader describes this very well run and unpretentious place. The warmly welcoming front bar has a relaxed and friendly atmosphere, a good mix of chatty customers, heavy 16th-c beams, very broad polished oak floorboards, magnificent carved overmantel for one of the two roaring log fires, and traditional solid furnishings. It's worth looking at the handsomely proportioned Globe Room used by Cromwell as his base during the Civil War. Quite a sight, it still has some wonderfully carved 17th-c dark oak panelling. Hook Norton Best Bitter, Old Hooky, Hooky Mild and a guest such as Marstons Pedigree on handpump, country wines, several whiskies and winter mulled wines; piped music. The little back courtyard has tables and benches under parasols, aunt sally and pretty flowering baskets. No under-21s (but see below).

🍴 **Served only at lunchtime, straightforward bar food in generous helpings might include sandwiches, soup, omelettes, good filled baked potatoes, all day breakfast and daily specials.** *Starters/Snacks: £2.50 to £3.15. Main Courses: £4.90 to £7.50. Puddings: £2.95 to £3.50*

Hook Norton ~ Tenants Tony and Dot Puddifoot ~ Real ale ~ Bar food (11-2.30) ~ Restaurant ~ (01295) 264031 ~ Children allowed away from main bar area ~ Dogs allowed in bar ~ Open 11-11; 12-3 Sun; closed Sun evening

Recommended by the Didler, Mark and Diane Grist, Nick and Meriel Cox, David and Felicity Fox, Stuart Doughty, Ted George, Derek and Sylvia Stephenson, Sally and Tom Matson, Keith and Sue Ward

---

A few pubs try to make you leave a credit card at the bar, as a sort of deposit if you order food. This is a bad practice, and the banks and credit card firms warn you not to let your card go like this.

BLOXHAM   SP4235 MAP 4

Joiners Arms
Off A361; Old Bridge Road; OX15 4LY

Interestingly furnished rooms on several levels, a good mix of customers, and well liked food; attractive seating areas outside

Although this bustling place has been attractively modernised, there's a good, relaxed pubby atmosphere, quite a mix of customers, and welcoming service. Several rambling, appealing rooms have careful spotlighting and some light furnishings that give them a nice airy feel. The main bar has a big stone fireplace, traditional wooden chairs and tables, half-panelled walls, and Greene King Abbot and Theakstons Best on handpump. A big room just off the bar has rafters in the high ceiling and an exposed well in the floor. Outside, there are plenty of seats on the various levels – the most popular is down some steps by a stream, with picnic-sets and heater.

⑪ **Tasty bar food includes lunchtime sandwiches, soup, deep-fried brie with a port and cranberry sauce, smokies in cheese sauce, chicken liver pâté with red onion marmalade, home-cooked ham and egg, pork and leek sausages with onion rings and gravy, steak and mushroom in ale pie, goats cheese and spinach filo tart, chicken in honey and mustard, medallions of pork in orange and sage, and puddings like Malteser cheesecake and raspberry and white chocolate crème brûlée.** *Starters/Snacks: £3.25 to £4.95. Main Courses: £6.95 to £10.95. Puddings: £4.00*

Free house ~ Licensee Matthew Hanson ~ Real ale ~ Bar food ~ Restaurant ~ (01295) 720223 ~ Children welcome ~ Dogs allowed in bar ~ Open 11-11
Recommended by Keith and Sue Ward

BROUGHTON   SP4238 MAP 4

Saye & Sele Arms
B4035 SW of Banbury; OX15 5ED

Smartly refurbished 16th-c house with generously served food, several real ales and particularly attentive service

This attractive old stone house is on the Broughton Castle Estate and was first licensed in 1782. The landlord is also the chef and is passionate about food – which is very much at the heart of things here, though locals do pop in for a drink and they keep Adnams Best and guests such as Brains Rev James, Brakspears Bitter, and Wadworths 6X on handpump; friendly service. Though essentially one long room, the refurbished bar has three distinct areas – a dining room at one end, with dozens of tankards and cups hanging from the beams, and neatly folded napkins on the tables, then a tiled area beside the bar counter, with cushioned window seats, a few brasses, and dark wooden furnishings, and finally a carpeted room with red walls and a mirror above the big fireplace. A pleasant terrace with picnic-sets leads to a nice lawn with plastic tables, and aunt sally. Broughton Castle is open on Sunday and Wednesday afternoons in season (and Thursday afternoons in summer).

⑪ **Cooked by the landlord, the popular bar food includes lunchtime sandwiches, filled baked potatoes and ploughman's, jumbo sausages with onion gravy, ham and eggs, an upside-down tart with caramelised red onion, mushrooms and courgettes topped with a cheese, tomato and basil fondue, a well liked pie of the day such as gammon, leek, mustard and cheese, seared tuna, salmon fillet and aubergine tower with a white wine, cream, tarragon and mushroom sauce, daily specials like grilled loin of lamb fillet with redcurrant, garlic and rosemary sauce, and puddings such as soufflé bread and butter pudding and chocolate cheesecake with dark chocolate ice-cream.** *Starters/Snacks: £3.95 to £7.95. Main Courses: £8.75 to £16.95. Puddings: £4.95*

Free house ~ Licensees Danny and Liz McGeehan ~ Real ale ~ Bar food (not Sun evening) ~ Restaurant ~ (01295) 263348 ~ Children allowed if dining with an adult ~ Open 11.30-2.30(3 Sat), 7-11; 12-5 Sun; closed Sun evenings, 25 and evening 26 Dec
Recommended by Paul Humphreys, George Atkinson, John and Sharon Hancock

CAULCOTT

SP5024 MAP 4

Horse & Groom 🍽 ◖

Lower Heyford Road (B4030); OX25 4ND

Bustling and friendly cottage with obliging licensees (he is also the chef), french-influenced food, and changing beers

This is a lovely, traditional cottage where you can be sure of a warm welcome from the friendly licensee and from the chatty locals, too. It's not a huge place: an L-shaped red-carpeted room angles around the servery, with plush-cushioned settles, chairs and stools around a few dark tables at the low-ceilinged bar end and a blazing fire in the big inglenook, with brassware under its long bressumer beam; shove-ha'penny and board games. The far end, up a shallow step, is set for dining with lots of decorative jugs hanging on black joists, and some decorative plates; also, some attractive watercolours and original drawings dotted around. The friendly staffordshire bull terrier is called Minnie. Hook Norton Bitter and three changing guests on handpump, and decent house wines. There is a small side sun lounge (which has been refurbished this year) and picnic-sets under cocktail parasols on a neat lawn.

🍽 Delicious bar food cooked by the French landlord using home-grown herbs and local produce includes lunchtime sandwiches, croque monsieur, guinea fowl and pistachio pâté with baby onion chutney, king prawns in garlic butter, a first-class burger, speciality sausages (12 different types), roasted poussin with a lemon and thyme sauce, sea trout with saffron beurre blanc and spring onion mash, fillet of beef with oyster mushrooms in madeira sauce, and puddings like crêpes suzette and sticky toffee pudding with butterscotch sauce. *Starters/Snacks: £4.50 to £7.50. Main Courses: £9.95 to £15.95. Puddings: £4.50 to £5.50*

Free house ~ Licensees Anne Gallacher and Jerome Prigent ~ Real ale ~ Bar food (not Sun or Mon evenings) ~ Restaurant ~ (01869) 343257 ~ Children over 10 and only in dining room ~ Dogs welcome ~ Open 12-3, 6-11; 12-3, 7-10.30 Sun

Recommended by D P and M A Miles, Stephen Moss, Dick and Madeleine Brown, Dennis and Doreen Haward, Ken and Barbara Turner

CHECKENDON

SU6684 MAP 2

Black Horse

Village signposted off A4074 Reading—Wallingford; coming from that direction, go straight through village towards Stoke Row, then turn left (the second turn left after the village church); OS Sheet 175 map reference 666841; RG8 OTE

Simple place liked by walkers and cyclists for a pint and snack

Luckily, nothing changes here and this unpretentious, simple country local has now been run by the same family for 103 years. The back still room where three changing West Berkshire beers are tapped from the cask has a relaxed, unchanging feel and the room with the bar counter has some tent pegs ranged above the fireplace, a reminder that they used to be made here. A homely side room has some splendidly unfashionable 1950s-look armchairs and there's another room beyond that. There are seats out on a verandah and in the garden. The surrounding countryside is very attractive and enjoyed by walkers and cyclists.

🍽 They offer only filled rolls and pickled eggs.

Free house ~ Licensees Margaret and Martin Morgan ~ Real ale ~ No credit cards ~ (01491) 680418 ~ Children allowed but must be very well behaved ~ Open 12-2(2.30 Sat), 7-11; 12-3, 7-10.30 Sun; closed evening 25 Dec

Recommended by Pete Baker, the Didler, Phil and Sally Gorton, Susan and John Douglas, Torrens Lyster

CHIPPING NORTON   SP3127   MAP 4

Chequers ★ ♀ ◖
Goddards Lane; OX7 5NP

Busy, friendly town pub open all day, with cheerful mix of customers and simple bars

Readers much enjoy this bustling town pub – there's a good, cheerful atmosphere and plenty of loyal customers. The three softly lit beamed rooms have no frills, but are clean and comfortable with low ochre ceilings, lots of character, and blazing log fires. Efficient staff serve very well kept Fullers Chiswick, London Pride, ESB and Discovery on handpump and they have good house wines, all available by the glass. The conservatory restaurant is light and airy and used for more formal dining. The town's theatre is next door.

⌘ **Seasonally changing bar food includes lunchtime sandwiches, ploughman's with home-made chutneys, soup, potted duck with pickles, chicken pot pie, local braised rabbit with rosemary, bacon and white wine sauce, wild mushroom risotto, pork and black pudding sausages with parsley mash and apple gravy and shin of beef with chive and thyme dumplings and braised vegetables.** *Starters/Snacks: £4.00 to £7.00. Main Courses: £6.00 to £15.00. Puddings: £4.00 to £5.00*

Fullers ~ Lease John Cooper ~ Real ale ~ Bar food (12-2.30, 6-9.30; 12-5 Sun; not Sun evening) ~ Restaurant ~ (01608) 644717 ~ Children allowed until 8.30 but no facilities for them ~ Dogs allowed in bar ~ Open 11-11(11.30 Fri and Sat); 12-10.30 Sun; closed 25 Dec

Recommended by Robert Gomme, the Didler, Barry Collett, Brian and Rosalie Laverick, Michael Dandy, Chris Glasson, Nick and Meriel Cox, Richard Greaves, Keith and Sue Ward, George Atkinson, M Joyner, R C Vincent, Bruce M Drew, Peter and Anne Hollindale, Simon D H Robarts Briggs, Mike and Mary Carter, Michael Butler, P and J Shapley

CHURCH ENSTONE   SP3725   MAP 4

Crown
Mill Lane; from A44 take B4030 turn off at Enstone; OX7 4NN

Friendly country pub with helpful licensees, enjoyable food cooked by the landlord, and well kept real ales

This popular and attractive old pub is run by friendly, helpful licensees and Mr Warburton himself does the cooking. It's smart and uncluttered with a congenial beamed bar, wheelback chairs and built-in cushioned wall seats around heavy wooden tables, country pictures on the stone walls, and a good log fire in the large stone fireplace with horsebrasses along its bressumer beam. Butcombe Bitter, Hook Norton Bitter, and Shepherd Neame Spitfire on handpump and several decent wines by the glass. There's also a beamed, pink-walled, carpeted dining room and an airy slate-floored conservatory, both with farmhouse chairs and tables. On the front terrace are some white metal tables and chairs overlooking the quiet lane, with picnic-sets in the sheltered back garden.

⌘ **Good enjoyable bar food at lunchtime includes filled baguettes, goats cheese salad, scallops and bacon, sausage and mash and steak in ale pie, with evening choices such as smoked salmon and spinach roulade, roast pigeon breast with caramelised endive and oranges, crisp roast duck leg with honey-roast vegetables and sirloin steak with cracked peppercorns, dolcelatte and garlic butter, and puddings like warm chocolate pudding with fudge sauce and vanilla crème brûlée.** *Starters/Snacks: £4.50 to £8.50. Main Courses: £7.95 to £14.95. Puddings: £4.50*

Free house ~ Licensees Tony and Caroline Warburton ~ Real ale ~ Bar food (not Sun evening) ~ Restaurant ~ (01608) 677262 ~ Children welcome ~ Dogs allowed in bar ~ Open 12-3, 6-11; 12-4 Sun; closed Sun evening, 26 Dec, 1 Jan

Recommended by Stuart Turner, Richard Marjoram, Keith and Sue Ward, M E and J R Hart, Mrs M B Gregg

---

There are report forms at the back of the book.

CHURCHILL   SP2824   MAP 4

Chequers

B4450 Chipping Norton—Stow (and village signposted off A361 Chipping Norton—Burford); Church Road; OX7 6NJ

Exceptionally welcoming licensees in busy village pub with plenty of space and popular food

Mrs Golding's remarkable memory means that you will be remembered and warmly welcomed into this 18th-c village pub even after just one visit. It's been refurbished in a country house style but the relaxed and friendly atmosphere remains. The front bar has a light stone flagstoned floor, a couple of old timbers, modern oak furnishings, some exposed stone walls around a big inglenook (with a good winter log fire) and country prints on the walls; newspapers are laid out on a table. At the back is a big extension that's a bit like a church with soaring rafters and there's a cosy but easily missed area upstairs, now mainly laid out for eating. Hook Norton Hooky Bitter and a couple of changing guest beers like Fullers London Pride and Greene King Old Speckled Hen on handpump and a good wine list. The pub's outside is cotswold stone at its most golden, and the village church opposite is impressive.

⑪ As well as regular themed evenings, the popular bar food includes a lunchtime sandwich and soup choice, poached egg florentine, chicken and black pudding ballottine with fruit chutney, wild mushroom risotto, tenderloin of pork with port wine sauce, fish pie, braised leg of lamb with thyme roasted shallots, bacon mash and cucumber and mint relish, daily specials such as duck liver and whisky parfait with walnut bread, crab and ginger fishcakes with lemon grass and white wine sauce and venison loin with juniper berry and orange segments, and puddings like rhubarb and apple crumble and warm chocolate sponge pudding with vanilla ice-cream. *Starters/Snacks: £5.00 to £6.50. Main Courses: £11.00 to £13.50. Puddings: £5.00*

Free house ~ Licensees Peter and Assumpta Golding ~ Real ale ~ Bar food (12-2(3 Sun), 6.30-9) ~ Restaurant ~ (01608) 659393 ~ Children welcome ~ Dogs allowed in bar ~ Irish music several times a year ~ Open 11-11(10.30 Sun); 25 Dec winter

Recommended by J Crosby, Caroline and Michael Abbey, Sir Nigel Foulkes, Stuart Turner, Richard Greaves, Mr and Mrs Hignell, Colin McKerrow, Dennis and Doreen Haward, Tracey and Stephen Groves, Graham Oddey, Tom Evans, Richard Atherton

CLIFTON   SP4931   MAP 4

Duke of Cumberlands Head ♀

B4031 Deddington—Aynho; OX15 0PE

Homely touches and big log fire in low-beamed bar, tasty food, and short walk to canal

The son of the previous landlord is now running this thatched and golden stone pub and he hasn't made any major changes. The low-beamed turkey-carpeted lounge has a good log fire in a vast stone fireplace, attractive paintings by the landlord's grandmother of lilies and rhododendrons grown by her on the west coast of Scotland, and mainly sturdy kitchen tables, with a few more through in the little dining room, which has some stripped stone; none of the walls or ceilings are straight. Black Sheep, Hook Norton Hooky Bitter Best and guests such as Archers Village and Wyre Piddle Piddle in the Cellar on handpump, plenty of wines to choose from, and 30 malt whiskies. Picnic-sets out on the grass behind. The canal is a short walk away.

⑪ Bar food now includes lunchtime filled baguettes and panini, soup, deep-fried mushrooms with garlic dip, chicken liver pâté, scallops in leek and saffron sauce, fish and chips, sausages with onion gravy, salmon in butter sauce, minted lamb shank, chicken dijonnaise, pork normandy, and puddings such as banoffi pie and vanilla cheesecake; **Sunday roasts.** *Starters/Snacks: £3.50 to £5.50. Main Courses: £6.50 to £15.00. Puddings: £4.50*

Free house ~ Licensee Robert Huntington ~ Real ale ~ Bar food ~ (01869) 338534 ~ Children welcome ~ Dogs allowed in bar and bedrooms ~ Open 12-3, 6.30-11; 12-3, 6.30-10.30 Sun ~ Bedrooms: £60B/£75B

Recommended by John and Heather Phipps, Mr and Mrs John Taylor, Sir Nigel Foulkes, George Atkinson, Richard Marjoram, K H Frostick, Stephen Moss, Andy and Jill Kassube, JJW, CMW, J and F Gowers

COLESHILL

SU2393 MAP 4

Radnor Arms 🍽 🍷 ◀

B4019 Faringdon—Highworth; village signposted off A417 in Faringdon and A361 in Highworth; SN6 7PR

Bustling pub with imaginative food, good choice of drinks and friendly service; small back garden and good nearby walks

The National Trust owns this pub – and the attractive village, too. It's a popular place for an imaginative meal though there's often a couple of locals chatting over a pint of Ramsbury Bitter or Youngs Bitter tapped from casks behind the counter and the atmosphere is relaxed and informal. A good range of wines by the glass, a few malt whiskies and summer Pimms and home-made lemonade. This room has a couple of cushioned settles as well as comfortable plush carver chairs, and a woodburning stove; a back alcove has a few more tables. Steps take you down into the main dining area, once a blacksmith's forge: with a lofty beamed ceiling, this has kept its brick chimney stack angling up (with a log fire now) and its canary walls are decorated with dozens of forged tools and smith's gear. A small garden up behind, with a big yew tree, has picnic-sets under cocktail parasols; plenty of good walking nearby.

🍴 **Using organic local produce where possible, the interesting bar food includes lunchtime sandwiches, soup, home-smoked duck with honeyed pear and watercress salad, scallops with orange and pink grapefruit and beurre blanc, rabbit cooked two ways with mushrooms, creamy dauphinoise and madeira sauce, pork belly twice cooked on a sage and apple potato cake with calvados jus, and daily specials such as local sausages with onion jus, fillets of mackerel with chilli and ginger butter and stir-fried pak choi and whole plaice fried with prawns, capers and lemon butter; Sunday roasts.** *Starters/Snacks: £4.25 to £8.50. Main Courses: £9.50 to £15.75. Puddings: £4.95 to £6.75*

Free house ~ Licensees Chris Green and Shelley Crowhurst ~ Real ale ~ Bar food (no food Sun evening or Mon) ~ Restaurant ~ (01793) 861575 ~ Children welcome ~ Dogs allowed in bar ~ Open 11.30-3, 6-11; 12-3, 7-10.30 Sun; closed Mon

Recommended by Tony and Tracy Constance, Evelyn and Derek Walter, Helene Grygar, D R Ellis, Edward Mirzoeff, William Goodhart, Derek Allpass

CUXHAM

SU6695 MAP 4

Half Moon 🍽

4 miles from M40, junction 6; S on B4009, then right on to B480 at Watlington; OX49 5NF

Lovely 16th-c country pub with relaxed atmosphere and delicious food cooked by friendly landlord

Well worth the detour from the motorway, this attractive 16th-c thatched pub is run by obliging young licensees. Both diners and drinkers are welcomed equally and there's a relaxed pubby atmosphere and cheerful service. The small red and black tiled bar has a brick fireplace and two main eating areas have old beams, Edwardian tables and chairs and Brakspears Bitter on handpump and several wines by the glass. There are wooden-slatted chairs and tables in the good-sized garden and pretty window boxes. This is a sleepy hamlet surrounded by fine countryside.

🍴 **Using home-grown vegetables and produce from their own cold smokehouse, the excellent food might include sandwiches, interesting soup, chicken liver pâté with pear chutney, beetroot marinated salmon with sorrel salad, potted crab, home-made sausages with onion gravy, steak and Guinness pie with cheddar and suet crust, confit pork belly with scallops, lentils and green sauce, roast hake, white bean and chorizo stew, orkney island mutton with capers and mash, and puddings like orange and elderflower trifle and chocolate and raspberry torte; good Sunday roasts.** *Starters/Snacks: £4.75 to £6.50. Main Courses: £9.50 to £12.50. Puddings: £5.00 to £6.50*

Brakspears ~ Tenants Andrew Hill and Eilidh Ferguson ~ Real ale ~ Bar food (12-2(3 Sun), 6-9; not Sun evening ~ (01491) 614151 ~ Children welcome ~ Dogs welcome ~ Open 12-3, 5.30-11; 12-11(10.30) Sat; closed Sun evening

Recommended by David Lamb, Jeremy Hebblethwaite, Karen Eliot, Mrs E A Macdonald, Tim and Gill Bullivant, I H G Busby, Malcolm and Barbara Lewis, R K Phillips, Dennis and Doreen Haward, Richard Endacott

EAST HENDRED   SU4588   MAP 2

Eyston Arms

Village signposted off A417 E of Wantage; High Street; OX12 8JY

Attractive bar areas with low beams, flagstones, log fires and candles, imaginative food and helpful service

---

There are a couple of tables for drinkers and some seats at the bar but most customers are here to eat the good, interesting food. There's a friendly welcome from the cheerful staff, and the several separate-seeming areas are furnished in modern country style: nice tables and chairs on the flagstones and carpet, some cushioned wall-seats, stripped timbers, particularly low ceilings and beams, a piano, and a pleasant atmosphere. An attractive inglenook has a winter log fire. The bar counter has olives to pick at and even on a sunny day the candles may be lit. Hook Norton Old Hooky and Wadworths 6X on handpump, good wines, piped easy-listening music, cribbage, chess and dominoes. Picnic-sets outside overlook the pretty village lane.

🍴 **Inventive bar food includes lunchtime sandwiches, roast beetroot risotto with crumbled goats cheese and tempura courgettes, a plate of cold rare rib of beef with string chips, a fish and shellfish stew, canon of lamb with a rich red wine, redcurrant and rosemary reduction with bubble and squeak cake, crab, salmon and undyed smoked haddock fishcakes with creamy chive sauce, chargrilled rib-eye steak with green peppercorn sauce, daily specials, and puddings such as dark chilli chocolate pot with shortbread biscuit and orange and rhubarb panna cotta with gingerbread ice-cream.** *Starters/Snacks: £5.00 to £8.00. Main Courses: £10.00 to £17.95. Puddings: £5.50*

Free house ~ Licensees George Dailey and Daisy Barton ~ Real ale ~ Bar food ~ Restaurant ~ (01235) 833320 ~ Children must be well behaved; no babies ~ Dogs allowed in bar ~ Open 11-11

Recommended by Alan and Audrey Moulds, Bob and Margaret Holder, Trevor and Sylvia Millum, Susan and John Douglas, Tony Winckworth, Roger Thornington, Dr D Scott, Ken and Margaret Grinstead, Guy Vowles, C R Crofton, Terry Miller

---

FERNHAM   SU2991   MAP 4

Woodman

A420 SW of Oxford, then left into B4508 after about 11 miles; village a further 6 miles on; SN7 7NX

Half a dozen real ales and generous food in charming old-world country pub

---

The heavily beamed rooms in this bustling country pub are full of an amazing assortment of old objects like clay pipes, milkmaids' yokes, leather tack, coach horns, an old screw press, some original oil paintings and good black and white photographs of horses. Comfortable seating includes cushioned benches, pews and windsor chairs, and the candlelit tables are simply made from old casks; big wood fire. At least six real ales are tapped from the cask: Butts Traditional, Brakspears Bitter, Greene King Abbot, Hop Back Crop Circle and Summer Lightning and Timothy Taylors Landlord. Several wines by the glass and winter mulled wine; piped music, TV and pool. There are seats outside on the terrace. Disabled lavatories. More reports please.

🍴 **Quite a choice of bar food includes lunchtime filled baguettes and panini, ploughman's, deep-fried camembert with cranberry sauce, chicken liver pâté with red onion marmalade, ham and free-range eggs, steak mushroom in ale pie, a curry of the day, and pasta with red pepper sauce and pesto, with evening choices such as slow-roasted lamb shank, fillet of pork souvlaki with greek salad, and breast of barbary duck with plum and apple sauce.** *Starters/Snacks: £4.50 to £7.95. Main Courses: £9.95 to £16.95. Puddings: £4.95*

Free house ~ Licensee Steven Whiting ~ Real ale ~ Bar food ~ Restaurant ~ (01367) 820643 ~ Children welcome ~ Dogs welcome ~ Open 11-11; 12-10.30 Sun

Recommended by Tony and Tracy Constance, Peter and Audrey Dowsett, Mark and Ruth Brock, Mary Rayner

FYFIELD   SU4298   MAP 4

White Hart ⑪ ♀ ◖

In village, off A420 8 miles SW of Oxford; OX13 5LW

Impressive place with grand main hall, minstrel's gallery and interesting side rooms, imaginative modern food, fine choice of drinks, and seats outside

A civilised and impressive place, this former medieval chantry house has been refurbished this year by the friendly young licensees – it still has many original features though, and is well worth wandering around. The bustling main restaurant is a grand hall with soaring rafters; inside, its huge stone-flanked window embrasures and flagstoned floors are overlooked by a minstrel's gallery on one side and several other charming and characterful side rooms on the other. In contrast, the side bar is cosy with a large inglenook fireplace at its centre and a low beamed ceiling; there are flowers all around and evening candles. Bath Ales Gem, Hook Norton Old Hooky, Loddon Hullabaloo, Nethergate Azzaparrot, and White Horse Village Idiot on handpump, around 16 wines by the glass including champagne and pudding wines, Thatcher's cider, and several malt whiskies; they hold beer festivals on May and August bank holiday weekends. Piped music and board games. There are elegant metal seats around tables under smart umbrellas on the spacious heated terrace, and the garden was about to be re-landscaped as we went to press. Plenty to see nearby and the Thames-side walks are well worth taking. More reports please.

🍽 **Carefully sourced excellent food, cooked by the licensee (who makes his own bread and pasta and grows some of his own herbs, fruit and vegetables), includes soup, chicken and duck liver parfait with spiced apricot chutney, grilled mackerel fillet with slow-roasted vine tomatoes and horseradish cream, sharing boards of mezze, antipasti or fish, herb pancakes with ricotta, parmesan and spinach with a herb salad and walnut sauce, roast chicken breast, brie and mushroom tartlet and creamed leeks, slow-roasted kelmscott pork with celeriac purée and cider jus, wild line-caught fillet of bass with tomato and fennel salsa, chorizo and piquillo peppers, and puddings such as hot chocolate fondant with pistachio ice-cream and vanilla panna cotta with poached rhubarb; there are two- and three-course set lunches, too.** *Starters/Snacks: £5.50 to £8.00. Main Courses: £12.50 to £17.50. Puddings: £5.50 to £6.95*

Free house ~ Licensee Mark Chandler ~ Real ale ~ Bar food (12-2.30, 7(though they have nibbles from 6pm)-9.30; 12-4 Sun; not Sun evening and Mon) ~ Restaurant ~ (01865) 390585 ~ Children welcome but must be well behaved ~ Open 12-3, 5.30-11; 12-11(10.30 Sun) Sat; closed Mon

Recommended by Dr and Mrs A K Clarke, J Crosby, E A and D C T Frewer, Dick and Madeleine Brown, Andrea and Guy Bradley, William Goodhart, Keith and Margaret Kettell, Shirley Sandilands, David and Elaine Shaw, Yvonne and Mike Meadley

GALLOWSTREE COMMON   SU7081   MAP 2

Greyhound ⑪ ♀

Gallowstree Road, Shiplake Bottom (though heading E from Gallowstree Common it's past the sign for Rotherfield Peppard); off B481 at N end of Sonning Common; RG9 5HT

Attractive restauranty country pub (Antony Worrall Thompson's), very good food, local beers and a pretty garden

Of course most customers come to this extraordinarily popular and civilised place to enjoy the consistently good food and there's no escape who the owner is since Antony Worrall Thompson's name is on the water and some of the condiments – and indeed some of the meat is from his own farms. This celebrity link is part of the big appeal for many of the people who flock here every night, but don't expect the man himself to be cooking your meal, or even be around – though he does occasionally pop in. Most of the tables throughout are set for eating, with wine glasses. The nicest and certainly the cosiest part is what they call the bottom restaurant, to the left of the door; it has more of the feel of an upmarket country pub, with beams and timbers, comfortable and plentiful cushions on wall benches beside chunky wooden tables, and smart curtains around the small windows. The main restaurant is at the other end and is much busier, with rafters from the high ceiling, lots of packed-together tables, plenty more cushions, and some stuffed animal heads; both rooms are candlelit at night. In between is the bar, which has Fullers London Pride, Loddon Hoppit, Lovibonds Henley Gold, and Rebellion IPA on handpump, and several wines by the glass from a good wine list. Though not at all individual, service is polite and generally efficient. There are tables on a back terrace, and plenty more in the attractive front garden, with a pond. Booking is recommended (and essential at weekends). The ubiquitous chef's other pub, the Lamb, is a few minutes away at Satwell.

⚏ There's a strong emphasis on the steaks and burgers, all using 35-day-hung prime aberdeen angus beef, but the main menu also has pork, ham and pickle terrine with a herb and egg dressing, home-made potted shrimps, hand picked crab on toast, baked field mushrooms, olive toast and melting taleggio, free-range prosciutto-wrapped chicken breast with white bean stew and chorizo, scottish salmon and smoked haddock fishcake with sorrel hollandaise, duck breast à l'orange, and roast middle white porchetta with sage and onion stuffing and apple chilli jelly (evenings only); there's a set dish and rare breed pork dish of the day, and a good value two-course set menu Monday-Thursday lunchtimes and early evenings on those days until 8pm. *Starters/Snacks: £5.45 to £9.25. Main Courses: £11.50 to £28.95. Puddings: £5.50 to £7.50*

Free house ~ Licensee David Wilby ~ Real ale ~ Bar food (12-2.30, 6-9.30(10 Fri, 10.30 Sat); 12-9.30 Sun) ~ Restaurant ~ (0118) 9722 227 ~ Children welcome ~ Dogs allowed in bar ~ Open 12-3.30, 5.30-11; 12-11(10.30 Sun) Sat; closed evenings 25 and 26 Dec and 1 Jan

Recommended by BOB

GODSTOW   SP4809   MAP 4

Trout ⚏ ♀

Off A34 Oxford bypass northbound, via Wytham, or A40/A44 roundabout via Wolvercote; OX2 8PN

Busy pub blending original features with modern touches, good contemporary food and plenty of wines by the glass, real ales, and relaxed atmosphere; charming waterside terrace

---

Extremely popular and well run, this pretty medieval pub is in a lovely riverside spot with plenty of seats and tables under large parasols on the terrace, and a bridge across to an island; the peacocks wander freely. Inside, it's been opened up and there are four different areas combining many original old features with contemporary furnishings. What was the old bar is the Wine Room, there's an Alice in Wonderland room, a Morse Room (still with the framed book covers) and a restaurant. It's all very attractively done with beams, flagstones, bare floorboards and log fires alongside a mix of high-backed plush or leather dining chairs (and some extraordinarily high-backed chairs in the Alice in Wonderland room), church chairs, a mix of wooden tables and plenty of prints; piped music. Adnams Best and Timothy Taylors Landlord on handpump and quite a few wines by the glass; good service.

⚏ As well as sharing plates (such as barbecue ribs and sticky oriental chicken wings) and pizzas from a wood-fired oven, the enjoyable food might include soup, potted salmon and prawns with grebiche sauce, asparagus with cumbrian air-dried ham, a poached free-range egg and hollandaise, smoked chicken caesar salad, tagliatelle with beef ragú, beer-battered haddock with minted pea purée, from the spit roast a half duck with bitter orange sauce and chicken with lemon aïoli, thyme and frites, organic salmon with wasabi mash, sesame pink ginger and soy dressing, and steaks with a choice of salsa, relish and butters; Sunday roasts. *Starters/Snacks: £5.00 to £9.00. Main Courses: £8.50 to £12.50. Puddings: £5.00 to £6.00*

Mitchells & Butlers ~ Manager Stuart Challand ~ Real ale ~ Bar food (all day) ~ Restaurant ~ (01865) 302071 ~ Children allowed but must leave bar area by 7pm ~ Open 11-11

Recommended by Peter Sampson, Martin and Pauline Jennings, P and J Shapley, John Silverman, Mrs P Lang, Geoff and Teresa Salt, Phil and Jane Hodson, Dr and Mrs Michael Smith

GREAT TEW   SP3929   MAP 4

Falkland Arms 🍺

Off B4022 about 5 miles E of Chipping Norton; The Green; OX7 4DB

Idyllic golden-stone cottage in lovely village with plenty of character in unspoilt bar and fine choice of ales

New licensees have taken over this busy thatched pub – just one of the untouched golden-stone buildings in this idyllic village. The unspoilt and partly panelled bar has high-backed settles and a diversity of stools around plain stripped tables on flagstones and bare boards, one, two and three-handled mugs hanging from the beam-and-board ceiling, dim converted oil lamps, shutters for the stone-mullioned latticed windows, and an open fire in the fine inglenook fireplace. Wadworths IPA, 6X and a seasonal ale plus guests such as Beartown Kodiak Gold, Timothy Taylors Landlord, and Wychwood Hobgoblin on handpump. The counter is decorated with tobacco jars and different varieties of snuff which you can buy, and you'll also find 30 malt whiskies, country wines, and farm cider; darts and board games. You have to go out into the lane and then back in again to use the lavatories; and they may try to keep your credit card while you eat. There are tables out in front of the pub and picnic-sets under cocktail parasols in the garden behind. Dogs must be on a lead. Small good value bedrooms (no under-16s). No mobile phones.

🍴 **Lunchtime bar food includes filled baguettes, ploughman's, soup, smoked fish plate and a charcuterie plate (both for sharing), sausages of the day, tomato and herb pasta, gammon and egg, and daily specials; more elaborate evening meals are on offer in the restaurant (best to book in advance).** *Starters/Snacks: £4.50 to £7.25. Main Courses: £7.95 to £9.95. Puddings: £4.95*

Wadworths ~ Managers Paula and James Meredith ~ Real ale ~ Bar food (12-2, 7-8; not Sun evening) ~ Restaurant ~ (01608) 683653 ~ Children in restaurant lunchtimes only ~ Dogs allowed in bar ~ Live folk Sun evening ~ Open 11.30-2.30(3 Sat), 6-11(midnight Sat); 12-3, 7-10.30 Sun ~ Bedrooms: £50S/£80S(£110B)

Recommended by Graham and Doreen Holden, Guy Vowles, Paul Boot, Trevor and Judith Pearson, Stuart Turner, Rona Murdoch, the Didler, Dr and Mrs Michael Smith, Barry Collett, R L Borthwick, Stephen Moss

HAILEY   SU6485   MAP 2

King William IV

The Hailey near Ipsden, off A4074 or A4130 SE of Wallingford; OX10 6AD

Attractive old pub, wonderful views from seats in garden, friendly staff, well liked food and several real ales

There are outstanding, wide-ranging views from this 400-year-old pub looking across peaceful, rolling pastures. Inside, the thriving, beamed bar has some good, sturdy furniture on the tiles in front of the big winter log fire; three other cosy seating areas open off here. Brakspears Bitter and guest ales are tapped from the cask, there's an interesting wine list, and farm cider; food, friendly service. The terrace and large garden have plenty of seats and tables. The pub is popular with walkers.

🍴 **Enjoyable bar food includes lunchtime filled baguettes (not Sunday), soup, chicken liver pâté, goats cheese salad, sausages and chips, popular spaghetti carbonara, steak in ale pie, liver and bacon, baked haddock with new potatoes, pork medallions in a mushroom, white wine and cream sauce, and puddings such as sticky toffee pudding with butterscotch sauce and various cheesecakes. Sunday roasts and summer barbecues.** *Starters/Snacks: £4.95 to £6.50. Main Courses: £8.95 to £11.95. Puddings: £4.50 to £4.95*

Brakspears ~ Tenant Neal Frankel ~ Real ale ~ Bar food ~ (01491) 681845 ~ Childen allowed in two rooms off bar area ~ Dogs allowed in bar ~ Open 11.30-2.30, 6-11; 12-3, 6.30-10.30 Sun

Recommended by Mr and Mrs C Prentis, the Didler, Colin and Bernardine Perry, Malcolm and Barbara Lewis, Jane and Martin Bailey

HIGHMOOR

SU6984 MAP 2

Rising Sun

Witheridge Hill, signposted off B481; OS Sheet 175 map reference 697841; RG9 5PF

Thoughtfully run and pretty pub with a mix of diners and drinkers; interesting daily specials

The two front rooms in this pretty black and cream pub are for those just wanting a drink – the rest of the place is laid out for dining. On the right by the bar, there are wooden tables and chairs and a sofa on the stripped wooden floors, cream and terracotta walls and an open fire in the big brick inglenook fireplace. The main area spreading back from here has shiny bare boards and a swathe of carpeting with well spaced tables and attractive pictures on the walls. Brakspears Bitter and a seasonal beer on handpump; piped music and board games. Seats and tables in the back garden; boules. More reports please.

Popular bar food includes sandwiches, soup, chicken liver, Cointreau and orange pâté with home-made chutney, roasted giant field mushroom stuffed with almond and basil pesto, a sharing plate of parma ham, salami, hummus, olives and garlic bread, smoked haddock pie, pearl barley risotto with roasted pumpkin, shallots and chestnuts, wild boar, apple and cider sausages with cider mustard sauce, lambs liver with cranberry and orange gravy, pheasant and venison cassoulet with toulouse sausages and beans, and puddings. *Starters/Snacks: £1.50 to £6.50. Main Courses: £8.95 to £13.50. Puddings: £4.00 to £6.50*

Brakspears ~ Tenant Judith Bishop ~ Real ale ~ Bar food (12-2(2.30 Sat), 7-9(9.30 Fri and Sat); 12-3 Sun (all day summer; not winter Sun evening)) ~ Restaurant ~ (01491) 640856 ~ Children allowed if eating and must be strictly supervised by parents ~ Dogs allowed in bar ~ Open 12-3, 6-11; 12-11 Sat; 12-10(8 in winter) Sun; closed two days after New Year

Recommended by Susan and John Douglas, Anthony and Marie Lewis, Bob and Margaret Holder

HOOK NORTON

SP3534 MAP 4

Gate Hangs High ◀

Banbury Road; a mile N of village towards Sibford, at Banbury—Rollright crossroads; OX15 5DF

Friendly country pub with traditional bar, real ales, and pretty courtyard garden; bedrooms

The bar in this tucked-away country pub has joists in the long, low ceiling, assorted chairs and stools around traditional tables, a gleaming copper hood over the hearth in the inglenook fireplace and Hook Norton Best and Old Hooky and a guest such as Wadworths 6X on handpump, bottled beers and decent wines. You'll need to book for Saturday evening and Sunday lunch in the slightly chintzy side dining extension; piped music and dominoes. There's a pretty courtyard garden and seats on a broad lawn behind the building with holly and apple trees and fine views; the flower tubs and wall baskets are very colourful. More reports please.

Bar food includes lunchtime sandwiches, soup, goats cheese and bacon salad, steak in ale pie, rack of lamb with garlic butter, duck with marmalade and orange sauce, steaks, and puddings. *Starters/Snacks: £3.75 to £6.95. Main Courses: £7.25 to £14.95. Puddings: £4.50 to £6.00*

Hook Norton ~ Tenant Stephen Coots-Williams ~ Real ale ~ Bar food (12-2.30, 6-9.30; all day Sat and Sun) ~ Restaurant ~ (01608) 737387 ~ Children welcome ~ Dogs allowed in bar and bedrooms ~ Open 12-2.30, 6-11; 12-11(10.30 Sun) Sat ~ Bedrooms: £45B/£60B

Recommended by J Crosby, Stuart Turner, Keith and Sue Ward, Mrs Pam Mattinson, Chester Armstrong, Sir Nigel Foulkes, Mary McSweeney, R C Vincent, Paul Humphreys

---

We accept no free drinks, meals or payment for inclusion. We take no advertising, and are not sponsored by the brewing industry – or by anyone else. So all reports are independent.

KINGSTON BLOUNT

SU7399 MAP 4

Cherry Tree

1.9 miles from M40 junction 6: B4009 towards Chinnor; Park Lane; OX39 4SL

Interesting up-to-date décor, ambitious food and decent choice of wines in bustling pub

This is a friendly place and the staff take their cue well from the young licensees. It's smart and uncluttered with a surprisingly contemporary interior and the long single-room bar has light school chairs around chunky tables on its stripped wood floor, with soft leather sofas facing each other beside a small brick fireplace at one end. The cool décor of cream and olive-beige, set off by fresh flowers, big modern abstracts and modern lighting, makes for a light and airy feel. This relaxed chatty atmosphere continues into the good-sized popular back dining room. Brakspears Bitter and a seasonal beer and a guest such as Wychwood Hobgoblin on handpump and a fair choice of wines by the glass; piped music.

🍴 Interesting bar food includes sandwiches, soup, duck and pistachio nut pâté with red onion marmalade, mussels in white wine, garlic and cream, courgette en croûte with brie and vegetable stuffing and tomato sauce, oxtail and beef tongue stew with horseradish cream, butterflied chicken grilled with tomatoes and mozzarella in a provençale sauce, crab and lobster cannelloni with shellfish sauce, honey-roast shoulder of lamb with rosemary jus, and Sunday roasts; good breakfasts. *Starters/Snacks: £3.75 to £6.50. Main Courses: £9.00 to £16.00. Puddings: £4.95 to £5.95*

Brakspears ~ Tenant Sharon Dallacosta ~ Real ale ~ Bar food (12-2.30, 7-9.30; 12-5 Sun; not Sun evening) ~ Restaurant ~ (01844) 352273 ~ Children welcome ~ Dogs allowed in bar ~ Open 12-midnight; 12-6 Sun; closed Sun evening, 25 and 26 Dec, 1 Jan ~ Bedrooms: £70B/£80B

Recommended by Gerry and Rosemary Dobson, Nina Randall, Kevin Thomas, Tom and Jill Jones

LANGFORD

SP2402 MAP 4

Bell 🍴 ♈ 🍺

Village signposted off A361 N of Lechlade, then pub signed; GL7 3LF

Beams, flagstones, a good log fire, well chosen wines and beer and enjoyable bar food in civilised pub

This is a popular little dining pub and whilst Mr Wynne produces the consistently enjoyable food, Mrs Wynne offers a friendly welcome to all – even dogs may be offered a doggy treat. The simple low-key furnishings and décor add to the appeal here: the main bar has just six sanded and sealed mixed tables on grass matting, a variety of chairs, three nice cushioned window seats, an attractive carved oak settle, polished broad flagstones by a big stone inglenook fireplace with a good log fire, low beams and butter-coloured walls with two or three antique engravings. A second even smaller room on the right is similar in character; daily papers on a little corner table. Hook Norton Hooky Bitter, Timothy Taylors Landlord and Wells & Youngs Bombardier on handpump, farm cider and ten wines by the glass. The bearded collie is called Madison; piped music, board games and summer aunt sally. There are two or three picnic-sets out in a small garden with a play house. This is a quiet and charming village.

🍴 As well as lunchtime sandwiches and filled rolls, the restaurant quality food includes soup, warm salad of black pudding, pancetta and quail eggs with a sun-dried tomato, fennel and tarragon dressing, fried tiger prawns in garlic butter, pork and herb sausages with wholegrain mustard mash and onion gravy, steak and mushroom pie, gammon and eggs, slow-roasted pork belly with red wine jus and creamed leeks, braised lamb shank with swede mash and red wine jus, seared king scallops with bacon and basil and balsamic dressing, and puddings such as chocolate panna cotta with berry coulis and treacle tart with crème anglaise. *Starters/Snacks: £3.95 to £8.95. Main Courses: £7.95 to £15.95. Puddings: £4.95*

Free house ~ Licensees Paul and Jackie Wynne ~ Real ale ~ Bar food (not Sun evening or Mon) ~ Restaurant ~ (01367) 860249 ~ Children welcome but babies must leave before 7pm ~ Dogs welcome ~ Open 12-3, 7-11(midnight Fri, 11.30 Sat); 12-4 Sun; closed Sun evening, all day Mon

Recommended by Grahame and Myra Williams, Tony and Jill Radnor, Guy Charrison, Thomas Holman, KN-R, Graham Oddey

LEWKNOR   SU7197   MAP 4

Olde Leathern Bottel

Under a mile from M40 junction 6; just off B4009 towards Watlington; OX49 5TH

Unchanging bustling country local with decent food and beer and seats in sizeable garden

Happily unchanging, this friendly place has a good mix of customers; it does get busy at lunchtimes (being so close to the M40) so it's best to arrive early to be sure of a table. There are heavy beams and low ceilings in the two bar rooms as well as rustic furnishings, open fires, and an understated décor of old beer taps and the like; the family room is separated only by standing timbers, so you won't feel segregated from the rest of the pub. Brakspears Bitter and Wychwood Hobgoblin and Dirty Tackle on handpump, and all their wines are available by the glass. The attractive sizeable garden has plenty of picnic-sets under parasols and a children's play area.

🍴 Bar food includes lunchtime filled baguettes or ploughman's, soup, thai crab cakes, duck liver pâté, prawns in filo pastry with chilli dip, ham and eggs, chicken korma, vegetable lasagne, fresh beer-battered cod with mushy peas, steaks, and puddings such as apple pie and sticky toffee pudding. *Starters/Snacks: £4.95 to £6.95. Main Courses: £7.95 to £15.95. Puddings: £3.40 to £4.95*

Brakspears ~ Tenant L S Gordon ~ Real ale ~ Bar food (12-2, 7-9.30) ~ (01844) 351482 ~ Children in restaurant and family room ~ Dogs welcome ~ Open 11-2.30(3 Sat), 6-11; 12-3, 7-10.30 Sun

Recommended by P Tailyour, Dr D J and Mrs S C Walker, Mark and Ruth Brock, N R White, D Hillaby, William Goodhart, Torrens Lyster

LONGWORTH   SU3899   MAP 4

Blue Boar

Off A420/A415; Tucks Lane off Cow Lane; OX13 5ET

Smashing old pub with a friendly welcome for all, good wines and beer and fairly priced good food; Thames-side walks nearby

With a good choice of food and drink, open fires, and a welcome to both locals and visitors, it's not surprising that this 17th-c thatched stone pub is so bustling and popular. The three low-beamed, characterful little rooms are warmly traditional with well worn fixtures and furnishings, and two blazing log fires, one beside a fine old settle. Brasses, hops and assorted knick-knacks like skis and an old clocking-in machine line the ceilings and walls, there are fresh flowers on the bar and scrubbed wooden tables, and faded rugs on the tiled floor; benches are firmly wooden rather than upholstered. The main eating area is the red-painted room at the end and there's a newer restaurant extension, too; quiet piped music. Brakspears, Fullers London Pride, and Timothy Taylors Landlord on handpump, 30 malt whiskies, 15 wines by the glass, summer Pimms and quite a few brandies and ports. The licensee has been here for 30 years, though his friendly young team are generally more in evidence. There are tables in front and on the back terrace, and the Thames is a short walk away.

🍴 Good, reasonably priced bar food includes sandwiches and ploughman's, soup, chicken liver parfait with poached pears, an antipasti plate, roasted vegetable and goats cheese terrine with pumpkin seed vinaigrette, popular burger with brie, stilton or cheddar, pork and leek sausages, beer-battered cod with home-made tartare sauce, steak in Guinness pie, a curry of the day, half a rack of barbecued pork ribs, and puddings such as chocolate mocha brownies with fudge sauce and vanilla ice-ream and apple crumble; there's a pig roast on the bank holiday at the end of May. *Starters/Snacks: £4.50 to £6.95. Main Courses: £7.50 to £16.95. Puddings: £4.50 to £5.95*

Free house ~ Licensee Paul Dailey ~ Real ale ~ Bar food (12-2(2.30 Sat, 3 Sun), 7-10(9 Sun)) ~
Restaurant ~ (01865) 820494 ~ Children welcome ~ Dogs allowed in bar ~
Open 12-11(midnight Fri and Sat); closed 25 Dec, 1 Jan

Recommended by Peter and Audrey Dowsett, BOB, Barry and Anne, George Atkinson, William Goodhart, Dick and Madeleine Brown

MURCOTT   SP5815   MAP 4

Nut Tree 🍴 ♀
Off B4027 NE of Oxford; OX5 2RE

Very much a village pub with a friendly welcome and real ales but much emphasis on the imaginative food

Back in these pages with enthusiastic newish licensees, this neatly thatched pub has
seen some changes, though Mr and Mrs North are determined the place should remain
very much at the centre of the village community. The bar counter is now at one end of
the main room and has a comfortable seating area for those just popping in for a chat
and a pint. The dining area is split into three areas – the main room, the conservatory,
and a room behind the bar which is popular for private parties; there are a couple of
woodburning stoves. Hook Norton and a couple of guests such as Slaters Top Totty and
Vale Black Beauty Porter on handpump and 11 wines (including champagne) by the glass
from a carefully chosen list. There are seats outside in the garden and pretty hanging
baskets and tubs; aunt sally. On a wall in front of the pub is an unusual collection of
gargoyles, each loosely modelled on one of the local characters. There are ducks on the
village pond.

🍴 **Using their own gloucester old spot pigs and growing their own salads and vegetables,
the interesting – if not cheap – bar food includes filled baguettes, soup, ploughman's,
wild mushrooms on toast, home-smoked orkney salmon and scrambled eggs, baked crottin
de chavignol with apple purée, pickled girolles and roasted shallot, grilled diver-caught
scallops with bacon and parsnip purée, risotto of wild mushrooms with parmesan and
white truffle oil, roast breast of gressingham duck with savoy cabbage à la crème, chicory
tart and beetroot jus, olive oil poached fillet of wild scottish halibut with a risotto of
herbs, and puddings such as sticky toffee pudding, caramelised apple tart and praline ice-
cream and glazed lemon cream with champagne yorkshire rhubarb and rhubarb sherbet.
There's a good value set menu, and from May to October they offer Sunday evening dinner
and a pint for £10.** *Starters/Snacks: £4.50 to £9.00. Main Courses: £14.00 to £22.00. Puddings:
£5.50 to £7.50.*

Free house ~ Licensees Mike and Imogen North ~ Real ale ~ Bar food ~ Restaurant ~
(01865) 331253 ~ Children welcome ~ Dogs welcome ~ Open 12-11(10.30 Sun); 12-7 Sun in
winter; closed winter Sun evenings

Recommended by Mr and Mrs J C Cetti, Jenny and Peter Lowater, E A and D C T Frewer

OXFORD   SP5106   MAP 4

Eagle & Child
St Giles; OX1 3LU

**Lots of genuine atmosphere in bustling town pub, well kept real ales, wide choice of well
liked pubby food, and friendly welcome**

J R R Tolkien and C S Lewis used to meet at this proper pub for discussions and a pint
and there's a memorial plaque, a couple of portraits and a framed paper with their
signatures (along with others of their group, the Inklings) saying they had drunk to the
landlord's health. The two charmingly old-fashioned panelled front rooms have plenty of
atmosphere, a friendly welcome from the staff, and Brakspears and guests such as Fullers
London Pride, Hop Back Spring Zing, and Stonehenge Sign of Spring on handpump; also,
17 wines by the glass and Weston's cider; newspapers to read, piped music, games
machine and board games. There's a stripped-brick back dining extension with a
conservatory.

🍴 Good value bar food includes sandwiches, breakfast waffles with maple syrup and banana, nachos with cheddar, sour cream and guacamole, bacon and free-range eggs, beer-battered cod, mushroom risotto, aberdeen angus burger, steak in ale pie, tuna niçoise, platters with meat or fish and vegetable, duck leg confit with redcurrant jus, lemon and dill corn-fed chicken, and puddings such as apple and rhubarb crumble and chocolate fudge cake. *Starters/Snacks: £3.50 to £7.45. Main Courses: £5.75 to £9.45. Puddings: £2.65 to £3.65*

Mitchells & Butlers ~ Manager Darren Amena ~ Real ale ~ Bar food (all day) ~ (01865) 302925 ~ Children in back room only until 6pm ~ Open 10am-11pm(11.30 Fri and Sat); 12-10.30 Sun; closed 25 Dec, 1 Jan

Recommended by Phil and Sally Gorton, Chris Glasson, Roger Shipperley, Dennis Jones, the Didler, Sapna Thottathil, Michael Dandy, Dick and Madeleine Brown

Rose & Crown

North Parade Avenue; very narrow, so best to park in a nearby street; OX2 6LX

Long-serving licensees in lively friendly local, a good mix of customers, fine choice of drinks and proper home cooking

Sharp-witted Mr Hall and his wife have now been running this rather straightforward but friendly pub for 25 years now. All well behaved customers are made welcome (not children or dogs) and the front door opens into little more than a passage by the bar counter. The panelled back room, with traditional pub furnishings, is slightly bigger, and you'll find reference books for crossword buffs; no mobile phones, piped music or noisy games machines but they do have board games. Adnams Bitter and Broadside and Hook Norton Old Hooky on handpump, around 30 malt whiskies and a large choice of wines. The pleasant walled and heated back yard can be completely covered with a huge awning; at the far end is a 12-seater dining/meeting room. The lavatories are pretty basic.

🍴 Traditional but enjoyable food at honest prices includes a good choice of interesting sandwiches and baguettes, various dips with pitta bread, filled baked potatoes, ploughman's, omelettes, sausage or ham with egg, chips and beans, and a hot dish of the day such as moroccan lamb with dates and apricots, mussels in a creamy white wine sauce and beef stew with mustard dumplings; popular Sunday roast. *Starters/Snacks: £3.95 to £5.95. Main Courses: £7.00 to £10.95. Puddings: £2.95 to £4.95*

Punch ~ Tenants Andrew and Debbie Hall ~ Real ale ~ Bar food (12-2.15(3.15 Sun), 7-9) ~ No credit cards ~ (01865) 510551 ~ Open 10am-midnight(1am Sat); best to check for opening hours over public holiday times

Recommended by Jane Taylor, David Dutton, the Didler, Torrens Lyster

Turf Tavern 🍺

Tavern Bath Place; via St Helen's Passage, between Holywell Street and New College Lane; OX1 3SU

Interesting pub hidden away behind high walls with a dozen ales, regular beer festivals, nice food, and knowledgeable staff

There's always a really good mix of customers of all ages in this busy pub, hidden away down little passages and alleyways in the shadows of the city walls. The two dark-beamed and low ceilinged small bars fill up quickly, though many prefer (whatever the time of year) to sit outside in the three attractive walled-in flagstoned or gravelled courtyards (one has its own bar); in winter, they have coal braziers so you can roast chestnuts or toast marshmallows and there are canopies with lights and heaters. Up to a dozen real ales on handpump: Butts Barbus Barbus, Crouch Vale Brewers Gold, Green King Ruddles Best, Nethergate Augustinian Ale, Rebellion Mutiny, Titanic Golden Age, Vale Wychert Ale, West Berkshire Good Old Boy, and three from the White Horse Brewery including one named for the pub and Black Beauty Mild. Regular beer festivals, Weston's Old Rosie cider and winter mulled wine; bright, knowledgeable service.

🍴 Reasonably priced bar food includes sandwiches, filled baked potatoes, soup, chicken liver and mushroom pâté, lasagne, tomato and mediterranean vegetable risotto, chicken caesar salad, beer-battered fish and chips, lamb shoulder in rich minted gravy, a curry of the week, and puddings such as rhubarb crumble and apple pie. *Starters/Snacks: £3.55 to £4.25. Main Courses: £6.45 to £9.40. Puddings: £3.45*

Greene King ~ Manager Darren Kent ~ Real ale ~ Bar food (12-7.30(7 Sun)) ~ (01865) 243235 ~ Dogs welcome ~ Live music Thurs evening ~ Open 11-11; 12-10.30 Sun

Recommended by Gordon Davico, Michael Dandy, Tim and Ann Newell, B J Harding, Lawrence Pearse, Peter Dandy, Roger Shipperley, the Didler, Phil and Sally Gorton, David Heath, Michael Butler, Mrs Margo Finlay, Jörg Kasprowski, Veronica Brown

RAMSDEN   SP3515   MAP 4

Royal Oak 🍴 ♀ 🍺

Village signposted off B4022 Witney—Charlbury; OX7 3AU

Chatty, unpretentious pub with friendly licensees, 30 wines by the glass, very good food and heated back terrace

You can be sure of a splendid welcome from the friendly staff in this well run and unpretentious village inn. The basic furnishings are comfortable, with fresh flowers, bookcases with old and new copies of *Country Life* and, when the weather gets cold, a cheerful log fire; no piped music or games machines – just a relaxed and chatty atmosphere. Hook Norton Best Bitter, White Horse Village Idiot, and Wye Valley Springtime Ale on handpump, a fine choice of 30 wines by the glass from a carefully chosen list, farm cider and several armagnacs. There are tables and chairs out in front and on the heated terrace behind the restaurant (folding back doors give easy access). The bedrooms are in separate cottages.

🍴 Generous helpings of highly enjoyable bar food using local seasonal produce include lunchtime sandwiches, soup, chicken liver parfait with raisins and cognac, moules marinières, devilled lambs kidneys with dijon mustard sauce, fresh crab and smoked salmon fishcakes, a pie of the week, half shoulder of lamb with rosemary and garlic jus, aberdeen angus steak and kidney suet pudding with rich onion gravy, fresh pasta with a wild mushroom truffle sauce, a sri lankan curry, daily specials and puddings. *Starters/Snacks: £3.95 to £7.95. Main Courses: £6.95 to £18.00. Puddings: £5.50*

Free house ~ Licensee Jon Oldham ~ Real ale ~ Bar food (12-2, 7-10.30(9.30 Sun) ~ Restaurant ~ (01993) 868213 ~ Children in dining room with parents ~ Dogs allowed in bar ~ Open 11.30-3, 6.30-11; 12-3, 7-10.30 Sun; closed 25 and 26 Dec ~ Bedrooms: £45S/£65S

Recommended by Simon Cottrell, Sue Demont, Tim Barrow, Matthew Shackle, Graham Oddey, Michael and Wendy Howl, Mr and Mrs John Taylor, P and J Shapley, Howard and Margaret Buchanan, J Crosby, Richard Marjoram, Mrs D Rawlings

SHILTON   SP2608   MAP 4

Rose & Crown

Just off B4020 SE of Burford; OX18 4AB

Simple and appealing little village pub, with relaxed civilised atmosphere and good locally sourced food

Some changes to this 17th-c stone-built village pub this year include original beams and stone walls being uncovered in the back room and a fire opened up in the original fireplace. It remains a simple and unfussy place with a lovely, unspoilt feel in a subtly upmarket way. It's all very understated: the small front bar has proper wooden beams and timbers, exposed stone walls, and a stove in a big fireplace, with half a dozen or so wonky tables on the red tiled floor, and a few locals at the planked counter. This opens into a similar, bigger room used mainly for eating, with flowers on the tables, and another fireplace. Hook Norton Old Hooky, Youngs Bitter, and Ramsbury Kennet Valley on handpump and several wines by the glass. At the side, an attractive garden has picnic-sets.

🍴 Using meat reared just over a mile away and plenty of local game, the enjoyable food might include lunchtime ciabattas, interesting soups, fresh and smoked salmon rillettes with cucumber pickle, venison terrine with plum chutney, ham and egg, sausages with onion gravy, aubergine parmigiana baked with mozzarella, steak and mushroom in ale pie, harissa chicken with couscous, sultanas and pine nuts, salmon fillet with spinach and dill sauce, and puddings such as chocolate and armagnac mousse and tuscan plum tart with vanilla ice-cream. *Starters/Snacks: £4.50 to £5.50. Main Courses: £8.00 to £14.50. Puddings: £4.00 to £4.50*

Free house ~ Licensee Martin Coldicott ~ Bar food (12-2(2.45 weekends and bank hols), 7-9; not winter Sun evening) ~ (01993) 842280 ~ Well behaved children allowed ~ Dogs allowed in bar ~ Open 12-3, 6-11; 12-12 Fri, Sat; 12-10.30 Sun; closed 25 Dec

Recommended by Helene Grygar, David Lamb, Pete Baker

SHIPLAKE
SU7779 MAP 2

Baskerville Arms 🍴 ♀
Station Road, Lower Shiplake (off A4155 just S of Henley); RG9 3NY

Emphasis on imaginative food though proper public bar too, real ales, several wines by the glass, interesting sporting memorabilia and pretty garden

Locals do gather around the high bar chairs in the public bar of this neat brick pub for a pint and a chat and there are also blue armchairs, darts and piles of magazines – but mostly, it's laid out for eating. Apart from the wooden flooring around the light, modern bar counter, it's all carpeted and there are a few beams, pale wooden furnishings (lit candles on all the tables), plush red banquettes around the windows, and a brick fireplace with plenty of logs next to it. A fair amount of sporting memorabilia and pictures, especially old rowing photos (the pub is very close to Henley) and signed rugby shirts and photographs (the pub runs its own rugby club), plus some maps of the Thames are hung on the red walls, and there are flowers and large houseplants dotted about. It all feels quite homely, but in a smart way, with some chintzy touches such as a shelf of china dogs. Loddon Hoppit and a couple of changing guests on handpump, 30 malt whiskies and ten wines by the glass. The pretty garden has a proper covered barbecue area and smart teak furniture under huge parasols. There is a new manager – though the owners remain the same – and there may be some changes to the furnishings.

🍴 Good, interesting food at lunchtime includes open sandwiches using home-made bread, soup, spanish tortilla, spaghetti in a rich tomato sauce with red onion, capers, basil and chilli, steak and kidney pie, beer-battered haddock, tuna burger, and chicken, chorizo and seafood paella, with evening choices such as fried chicken livers finished with jus, mustard and cream served with celeriac purée, terrine of pork and black pudding with mustard and pear mayonnaise, roast pepper and feta risotto with herb salsa, fillets of bass on lemon and chive crushed potato with mussel and tomato sauce, braised shoulder of lamb with bubble and squeak and rosemary jus, and confit of duck leg with madeira jus, potato rösti and parsnip crisps; there's also a good value, two-course menu of the day. *Starters/Snacks: £6.50 to £14.00. Main Courses: £7.95 to £15.00. Puddings: £5.25*

Free house ~ Licensee Allan Hannah ~ Real ale ~ Bar food (12-2, 7-9.30(10 Fri and Sat); not Sun evening) ~ Restaurant ~ (0118) 940 3332 ~ Children welcome but no babies in evening restaurant ~ Dogs allowed in bar ~ Open 11.30-2.30, 6-11; 12-5 Sun; closed Sun evening ~ Bedrooms: £50S/£85S

Recommended by Rob Winstanley, Paul Humphreys, Mark and Diane Grist, Graham and Toni Sanders, G Fry, Michael Dandy, David Heath, Joe Green

---

Please keep sending us reports. We rely on readers for news of new discoveries, and particularly for news of changes – however slight – at the fully described pubs: feedback@thegoodpubguide.co.uk or (no stamp needed) The Good Pub Guide, FREEPOST TN1569, Wadhurst, E Sussex TN5 7BR.

STANTON ST JOHN   SP5709   MAP 4

Star

Pub signposted off B4027, in Middle Lane; village is signposted off A40 heading E of Oxford (heading W, you have to go to the Oxford ring-road roundabout and take unclassified road signposted to Stanton St John, Forest Hill etc); OX33 1EX

Nice old village pub with interesting rooms, friendly landlord, fair value food and Wadworths beers

This is a friendly old place – chatty and relaxed and popular for its good value food. It is appealingly arranged over two levels and the oldest parts are two characterful little low-beamed rooms, one with ancient brick flooring tiles and the other with quite close-set tables. Up some stairs is an attractive extension on a level with the car park with old-fashioned dining chairs, an interesting mix of dark oak and elm tables, rugs on flagstones, bookshelves on each side of an attractive inglenook fireplace (good blazing fires in winter), shelves of good pewter, terracotta-coloured walls with a portrait in oils, and a stuffed ermine. Wadworths IPA and 6X on handpump and ten wines by the glass. There's a family room and conservatory, too; piped music, darts and board games. The walled garden has seats among the flower beds; children's play equipment.

🍴 A good choice of bar food includes sandwiches, ploughman's, filled baked potatoes, soup, cheddar and broccoli quiche, lasagne, beef in ale pie, seafood pasta, red thai chicken curry, lamb shank in redcurrant and rosemary sauce, whole bass in ginger, coriander and lime, and slow-roast pork belly in barbecue sauce. *Starters/Snacks: £4.25 to £8.95. Main Courses: £8.95 to £13.50. Puddings: £4.50*

Wadworths ~ Tenant Michael Urwin ~ Real ale ~ Bar food ~ (01865) 351277 ~ Children welcome ~ Dogs welcome ~ Open 12-3, 6.30-11; 12-3, 7-10.30 Sun

Recommended by Brian and Rosalie Laverick, Tracey and Stephen Groves, Roy Hoing, W N Murphy, Peter Sampson, M Greening, Robert Gomme

STEEPLE ASTON   SP4725   MAP 4

Red Lion

Off A4260 12 miles N of Oxford; OX25 4RY

Friendly village pub with beamed bar, nice straightforward food, local beers, and suntrap terrace

The comfortable partly panelled bar in this little stone village pub is welcoming and relaxed with beams, an antique settle and other good furnishings – and you can be sure of a friendly welcome from the hard-working licensees. Hook Norton Hooky and Hooky Gold on handpump and several wines by the glass; good service. There's a back conservatory-style dining extension, too. The suntrap front terrace has lovely flowers and shrubs. More reports please.

🍴 As well as lunchtime filled baguettes, the well liked bar food includes soup, coarse country pâté with red onion chutney, king prawns with sweet chilli sauce, proper ham with free-range eggs, feta cheese, red onion and tomato tart, steak and kidney suet pudding, cornish crab risotto, popular fish and chips, daily specials like lamb korma or shepherd's pie, and puddings such as crème brûlée and chocolate mousse. They list suppliers on their menu and try to use as much organic local produce as possible. *Starters/Snacks: £4.00 to £6.50. Main Courses: £7.00 to £14.00. Puddings: £3.00 to £5.50*

Hook Norton ~ Tenants Melvin and Sarah Phipps ~ Real ale ~ Bar food (12-2.30, 6-9; 12-4 Sun (not Sun evening)) ~ Restaurant ~ (01869) 340225 ~ Children allowed only when dining with adults ~ Dogs allowed in bar ~ Open 12-3, 5.30-11; 12-11(10.30 Sun) Sat; 12-4, 7-10.30 Sun in winter; closed evenings 25 and 26 Dec and 1 Jan

Recommended by John and Heather Phipps, J and M Taylor, Craig Turnbull, Nigel and Jean Eames, BOB, Paul Humphreys

SWERFORD

SP3830   MAP 4

Masons Arms ⑪ ♀

A361 Banbury—Chipping Norton; OX7 4AP

Attractive dining pub with modern cooking by chef/landlord, airy dining extension, civilised and relaxed atmosphere, country views from outside tables

Not surprisingly, this attractive dining pub is always extremely busy and our readers enjoy their visits here very much. Mr Leadbeater, the chef/patron, cooks interesting food at reasonable prices and although most customers are here to eat, the atmosphere is friendly, relaxed and bustling which prevents it becoming an out-and-out restaurant. The dining extension is light and airy and the bar has pale wooden floors with rugs, a carefully illuminated stone fireplace, thoughtful spotlighting, and beige and red armchairs around big round tables in light wood. Doors open on to a small terrace with a couple of stylish tables, while steps lead down into a cream-painted room with chunky tables and contemporary pictures. Round the other side of the bar is another roomy dining room with great views by day, candles at night, and a civilised feel. Hook Norton Best and a guest beer on handpump and several wines by the glass. Behind is a neat square lawn with picnic-sets and views over the Oxfordshire countryside.

⑪ Enjoyable food at lunchtime includes ploughman's, nachos with tomato salsa, guacamole, sour cream and melted cheese, home-baked ham with free-range eggs, a vegetarian pasta of the day, chicken korma and supreme of salmon with mustard beets and new potato salad; in the evening there's a two- and three-course menu with choices such as coarse chicken liver terrine with apple and ale chutney, home-cured ox tongue, egg mayonnaise, gherkins and ox jelly, five spice marinated barramundi fillet with noodle salad, chilli and coriander, confit of lamb shoulder with mixed bean stew and rosemary jus, and slow cooked shorthorn beef with potato gnocchi and roast carrots with honey and cumin; puddings like chocolate truffle cake with poached morello cherries and raspberry and Drambuie crème brûlée with raspberry sorbet. *Starters/Snacks: £4.50 to £6.50. Main Courses: £6.95 to £9.95. Puddings: £5.50*

Free house ~ Licensee Bill Leadbeater ~ Real ale ~ Bar food (12-2, 7-9; 12-4 Sun; not Sun evening) ~ Restaurant ~ (01608) 683212 ~ Children welcome ~ Open 10-3, 6-11; 12-4 Sun; closed Sun evening; 25 and 26 Dec

Recommended by Paul Butler, K H Frostick, P Brown, Phil and Jane Hodson, E A and D C T Frewer, Richard Marjoram, Martin and Pauline Jennings, Dr Nigel Bowles, Sir Nigel Foulkes, Michael Dandy, P and J Shapley, Carole Hall

SWINBROOK

SP2812   MAP 4

Swan ⑪ ♀

Back road a mile N of A40, 2 miles E of Burford; OX18 4DY
OXFORDSHIRE DINING PUB OF THE YEAR

Civilised 17th-c pub with handsome oak garden room, nice, smart bars, local beers and contemporary food

Extremely well run, this is a smart, civilised and very popular 17th-c pub. Even on a Monday lunchtime there are lots of customers so it is advisable to book a table in advance. There's a little bar with simple antique furnishings, settles and benches, an open fire, and (in an alcove) a stuffed swan; locals do still drop in here for a pint and a chat. The small dining room to the right of the entrance opens into this room, and there's a green oak garden room with high-backed beige and green dining chairs around pale wood tables and views over the garden and orchard. As the pub is owned by the Duchess of Devonshire – the last of the Mitford sisters who grew up in the village – there are lots of old Mitford family photographs blown up on the walls. Hook Norton Hooky Bitter, and a couple of guests from maybe Cottage Brewery or Sharps on handpump, 13 wines by the glass, Weston's organic cider, a proper bloody mary and local apple juice; piped music. This is a lovely spot by a bridge over the River Windrush and seats by the fuchsia hedge make the best of the view. The bedrooms should be up and running just after this edition is published. The licensees also run the Kings Head at Bledington in Gloucestershire.

⑪ Imaginative modern bar food includes lunchtime sandwiches, soup, home-made taramasalata, terrine of locally smoked guinea fowl with chutney, crab linguine with chilli, garlic and herbs, a good burger, roasted butternut squash and gorgonzola pasta, beer-battered fish with mushy peas and home-made tartare sauce, slowly braised feather blade of beef on truffle mash with wild mushrooms, daily specials such as locally smoked venison carpaccio with rocket and parmesan and whole lemon sole with lemon and parsley butter, and puddings like coconut and lemon grass crème brûlée with passion fruit sorbet and chocolate mousse with champagne rhubarb jelly and whipped cream. *Starters/Snacks: £5.00 to £7.00. Main Courses: £12.00 to £16.00. Puddings: £6.00*

Free house ~ Licensees Archie and Nicola Orr-Ewing ~ Real ale ~ Bar food (12-2(3 Sun), 7-9(9.30 weekends)) ~ Restaurant ~ (01993) 823339 ~ Children welcome ~ Dogs allowed in bar ~ Live music monthly Sun ~ Open 11-3, 6-11; 12-11 Sat and Sun; closed Mon evenings; 25 Dec

Recommended by Klaus and Elizabeth Leist, Malcolm and Jo Hart, David Handforth, Guy Vowles, Gill and Keith Croxton, J L Wedel, E A and D C T Frewer, Mr and Mrs C Prentis, Dennis and Doreen Haward, Richard Greaves, Keith and Sue Ward, David Glynne-Jones, A G Marx, Richard Marjoram

TADPOLE BRIDGE   SP3200   MAP 4

Trout ⑪ ♌ ⇐

Back road Bampton—Buckland, 4 miles NE of Faringdon; SN7 8RF

Busy country inn with River Thames moorings, fine choice of drinks, particularly good restaurant-style food, lovely summer garden; super bedrooms

Having just refurbished this civilised and comfortable place, extensive flood damage meant they had to refurbish yet again, so the whole place is extremely smart now. It's in a peaceful spot by the Thames and the L-shaped bar has attractive pink and cream checked chairs around a mix of nice wooden tables, some rugs on the flagstones, a modern wooden bar counter with terracotta paintwork behind, fresh flowers, a woodburning stove and a large stuffed trout. The airy restaurant is appealingly candlelit in the evenings. Ramsbury Bitter, Wells & Youngs Bitter and guests like Arkells Moonlight and Butts Barbus Barbus on handpump, a dozen wines by the glass from a wide-ranging and carefully chosen list, some fine sherries and several malt whiskies; the hard-working licensees positively welcome locals who pop in for a pint and a chat. There are good quality teak chairs and tables under blue parasols in the lovely garden and six moorings for visiting boats; you can also hire punts with champagne hampers. The bedrooms are exceptionally well equipped and extremely attractive.

⑪ As well as lunchtime filled baguettes (not Sunday), the attractively presented food includes terrine of chicken and foie gras wrapped in prosciutto with fig chutney and melba toast, tian of brixham crab with citrus infused, warm vichyssoise, beetroot and pear risotto, rump of lamb with roasted root vegetables and cider fondant, herb-crusted chicken breast with mushroom and thyme gravy, daily specials like cornish mussels thai-style, roast pigeon breast with celeriac potato cake and fine bean salad, turbot poached in merlot with braised onions and salsify and steamed beef and smoked oyster pudding, and puddings such as crème brûlée with rosemary and a pineapple compote and steamed chocolate pudding with double chocolate chip ice-cream and chocolate sauce. *Starters/Snacks: £4.95 to £8.95. Main Courses: £10.95 to £18.95. Puddings: £5.95 to £6.95*

Free house ~ Licensees Gareth and Helen Pugh ~ Real ale ~ Bar food (not winter Sun evening) ~ Restaurant ~ (01367) 870382 ~ Children welcome ~ Dogs welcome ~ Open 11.30-3, 6-11; 12-3.30, 6.30-10.30 Sun; closed winter Sun evening ~ Bedrooms: £75B/£110B

Recommended by Derek Thomas, Sally Anne and Peter Goodale, Simon Collett-Jones, Jim and Nancy Forbes, J Crosby, Mary Rayner, Mr and Mrs J C Cetti, Julia and Richard Tredgett, M S Pizer, Fred Beckett, Jeff and Wendy Williams, Bob and Margaret Holder, Terry Miller, Paul Humphreys

---

Post Office address codings confusingly give the impression that some pubs are in Oxfordshire, when they're really in Berkshire, Buckinghamshire, Gloucestershire or Warwickshire (which is where we list them).

WOODSTOCK   SP4416   MAP 4

Kings Arms 🛏

Market Street/Park Lane (A44); OX20 1SU

Stylish hotel in centre of attractive town, good creative food, enjoyable atmosphere, comfortable bedrooms

Although this is a smart, Georgian, town centre hotel, both locals and visitors enjoy its stylish décor and friendly, relaxed atmosphere. It has been gradually improved by the friendly owners over some years now and they feel they've got things as they want them – traditional but with a modern twist. The bar is simple and unfussy, yet still comfortable and characterful, with brown leather furnishings, smart blinds and black and white photos throughout, and at the front an old wooden settle and interesting little woodburner. There's a marble bar counter, and, in the room leading to the brasserie-style dining room, an unusual stained-glass structure used for newspapers and magazines; the restaurant is attractive, with its hanging baskets and fine old fireplace. Marstons Pedigree and Theakstons Best on handpump, good coffees and afternoon tea, freshly squeezed orange juice, and a dozen or so malt whiskies; efficient service from smartly uniformed staff, piped music. Comfortable bedrooms and good breakfasts (available from 7.30-noon for non-residents too). There are a couple of tables on the street outside.

🍴 As well as filled rolls, the lunchtime menu includes soup, potted crab pâté with onion chutney, honey roast ham with free-range eggs, warm shredded chicken and bacon salad with elderflower and cracked pepper dressing, home-made burger using organic beef with tomato and lime chutney, cider-battered cod with hand-cut chips, and roast butternut squash, red onion and spinach tart with somerset brie; evening choices such as beetroot-cured salmon with dill and potato cake, grilled chicken with lemon and fennel salad, braised pig cheeks with sage gravy, slow honey-roast rump of lamb with shallot sauce and tomato and thyme dauphinoise potatoes, free-range chicken breast stuffed with mushrooms, roast asparagus and tarragon and mustard sauce, and puddings like apple and cinnamon bread and butter pudding with butterscotch sauce and white chocolate and orange mousse with milk chocolate brownie. *Starters/Snacks: £4.75 to £6.75. Main Courses: £7.75 to £19.50. Puddings: £5.75 to £7.50*

Free house ~ Licensees David and Sara Sykes ~ Bar food (12-2.30, 6.30-9.30; 12-3, 6.30-10 Sat; all day Sun) ~ Restaurant ~ (01993) 813636 ~ Children welcome in bar and restaurant but no under 12s in bedrooms ~ Dogs allowed in bar ~ Open 11-11(10.30 Sun) ~ Bedrooms: £75S/£140S

Recommended by Michael Dandy, Guy Vowles, J and M Taylor, Michael and Maggie Betton

WOOLSTONE   SU2987   MAP 2

White Horse

Village signed off B4507; SN7 7QL

Gabled old pub with hard-working, friendly landlord, enjoyable food and drink, seats in front and back garden and bedrooms

Handy for White Horse and Ridgeway walkers, this partly thatched, 16th-c pub with steep Victorian gables, is just the place for a drink or meal. It's plushly refurbished, with two big open fires in the spacious and eclectically decorated beamed and part-panelled bar and has Arkells 2B, 3B and Moonlight Ale on handpump, decent wines and lots of whiskies; good coffee, too. There's an evening restaurant and the staff are friendly and helpful. The well organised back garden has plenty of seats with more in the small front garden. The bedrooms are charming and they offer big breakfasts. This is a secluded and interesting village.

🍴 Generous helpings of good bar food using local suppliers and cornish fish includes sandwiches, good ploughman's, soup, grilled mackerel fillets with potato and chive salad, a bowl of mussels with white wine and cream, coq au vin with roasted garlic mash, tomato and black olive risotto, steak and mushroom in ale pie, fillet of bass with noodles and stir-fried vegetables, slow-braised rump of lamb with puy lentils and root vegetables, and puddings like rich chocolate tart and lemon posset with fresh raspberries.

Starters/Snacks: £4.50 to £6.50. Main Courses: £8.00 to £15.00. Puddings: £5.00

Arkells ~ Tenant Angus Tucker ~ Bar food (not Sunday evening) ~ Restaurant ~ (01367) 820726 ~ Children welcome ~ Dogs welcome ~ Open 11am-midnight ~ Bedrooms: £70B/£75B

Recommended by Paul Humphreys, J and F Gowers

LUCKY DIP

Besides the fully inspected pubs, you might like to try these Lucky Dips recommended to us and described by readers (if you do, please send us reports: feedback@thegoodpubguide.co.uk).

ADDERBURY [SP4735]
Bell OX17 3LS [High St; just off A4260, turn opp Red Lion]: Unpretentious ancient beamed village local with chiming grandfather clock, some panelling, relaxed atmosphere, generous good fresh food, well kept Hook Norton, homely front room with sofas by huge log fire, sewing machines and standard lamp, candlelit restaurant, smaller back music room with two pianos, old settles, and folk nights 1st and 3rd Mon of month *(BB, Andy and Jill Kassube, Giles and Annie Francis)*
Plough OX17 3NL [Aynho Rd]: Welcoming and attractively furnished medieval thatched pub under newish licensees, enjoyable nicely presented food, real ales, good choice of wines by the glass, log fire in small L-shaped bar, larger separate restaurant; piped music, TV, games; tables outside *(Carole Hall, E A and D C T Frewer, Helen Rowett)*
☆ *Red Lion* OX17 3NG [The Green; off A4260 S of Banbury]: Attractive and congenial, with enjoyable pubby food (all day wknds), helpful friendly staff, Greene King ales, good wine range and coffee, three linked bar rooms, big inglenook log fire, panelling, high stripped beams and stonework, old books and Victorian and Edwardian pictures, daily papers, games area on left; piped music; children in eating area, picnic-sets out on roadside terrace, 12 comfortable bedrooms, open all day summer *(Conor McGaughey, E A and D C T Frewer, I A Herdman, LYM)*
ASCOTT UNDER WYCHWOOD [SP2918]
Swan OX7 6AY [Shipton Rd]: Fresh contemporary refurbishment after flood damage, enjoyable food from ciabattas to upscaled main dishes in bar and restaurant, Brakspears, Hook Norton and Wadworths 6X, helpful staff, beams and some stripped stone, woodburner; terrace tables, good bedrooms *(Caroline and Michael Abbey)*
ASTHALL [SP2811]
Maytime OX18 4HW [off A40 at W end of Witney bypass, then 1st left]: Good reasonably priced food from sandwiches and snacks up (just set lunch Sun) in genteel dining pub comfortably refurbished after flooding, welcoming helpful service, nice wine range, small proper bar with two changing real ales, flagstones and log fire, Beryl Cook prints, slightly raised neat dining lounge, airy conservatory restaurant with

family area; piped music; nice views of Asthall Manor and watermeadows from garden, attractive walks, quiet comfortable bedrooms around pretty courtyard garden *(David Handforth, BB, Martin and Pauline Jennings, Theocsbrian)*
BANBURY [SP4540]
Woolpack OX16 0AE [Horse Fair]: Two bars and back restaurant, half a dozen ales mostly from smaller brewers, good value food inc OAP deals, some Sat live music; small back terrace, open all day (cl Mon 2.30-5) *(Tony and Wendy Hobden)*
BECKLEY [SP5611]
☆ *Abingdon Arms* OX3 9UU [signed off B4027; High St]: Well worn in old pub in unspoilt village with good generous food from sandwiches to nicely presented main dishes inc some imaginative things, quick willing service, Brakspears, good value wines, bare boards, lots of beams and stripped stone, two real fires, mixed seating inc pews, board games, separate dining room; extensive informal garden dropping away from floodlit terrace to orchard with superb views over RSPB Otmoor reserve – good walks *(Martin and Pauline Jennings, Peter and Audrey Dowsett, Peter and Anne Hollindale, LYM, Colin McKerrow)*
BLETCHINGDON [SP5017]
Blacks Head OX5 3DA [Station Rd; B4027 N of Oxford]: Early 18th-c Cotswold stone pub with two neat bars, wide choice of enjoyable food, Black Sheep, Fullers, Marstons and Wells & Youngs, conservatory; pleasant garden *(Dave Braisted)*
BLEWBURY [SU5385]
Red Lion OX11 9PQ [Nottingham Fee – narrow turning N from A417]: Attractive downland village pub with good service, enjoyable honest food, well kept Brakspears and a guest beer, beams, tiled floor and big log fire, cribbage, dominoes, no piped music or machines, restaurant (children allowed); terrace tables in quiet back garden, pretty surroundings *(Ray J Carter, William Goodhart, LYM, D and M T Ayres-Regan)*
BOARS HILL [SP4901]
Fox OX1 5DR [between A34 and B4017; Fox Lane]: Attractive Chef & Brewer in pretty wooded countryside, comfortable and spacious, with interesting rambling rooms on different levels, huge log fireplaces, prompt service, decent food and wines by the glass, well kept ales, day's paper framed in gents';

may be soft piped classical music or jazz; children welcome, pleasant raised verandah, charming big sloping garden with play area, open all day *(William Goodhart)*

BODICOTE [SP4637]

Plough OX15 4BZ [Goose Lane/High St; off A4260 S of Banbury]: Pleasantly refurbished 14th-c pub with low heavy beams, stripped stone and small open fire, well kept Wadworths, good value simple lunches, good service and friendly locals; darts, TV and games machine in public bar
(John R Ringrose, BB, the Didler)

BRIGHTWELL BALDWIN [SU6594]

☆ *Lord Nelson* OX49 5NP [off B480 Chalgrove—Watlington, or B4009 Benson—Watlington]: Civilised dining pub with wide range of enjoyable if not cheap food esp game (two-course set lunch is good value), stylish décor, dining chairs around big candlelit tables, pleasant staff, well kept ales inc Black Sheep, good house wines, good log fires, snug armchair area, plenty of Nelson memorabilia; service may slow on busy Sundays; children and dogs welcome, front verandah, charming back garden
(Di and Mike Gillam, LYM, Hunter and Christine Wright, Torrens Lyster)

BRIZE NORTON [SP3007]

Chequers OX18 3PR [Station Rd]: Big smart open-plan dining pub with wide choice inc OAP lunches, friendly staff, real ales, RAF theme; big garden with play area *(Peter and Audrey Dowsett)*

BUCKLAND [SU3497]

Lamb SN7 8QN [off A420 NE of Faringdon]: Smart 18th-c stone-built dining pub with popular food (not Mon) from lunchtime special deals to grander and more expensive evening menus, Hook Norton Best, good choice of wines by the glass, lamb motif everywhere, formal restaurant; piped music; children welcome, pleasant tree-shaded garden, good walks nearby, comfortable bedrooms, cl Sun evening and over Christmas/New Year *(the Didler, Pat and Roger Davies, Alan and Carolin Tidbury, Mr and Mrs John Taylor, Hon Richard Godber, Tony Winckworth, LYM)*

BUCKNELL [SP5525]

☆ *Trigger Pond* OX27 7NE [handy for M40 junction 10; Bicester Rd]: Neatly kept and welcoming stone-built pub opp the pond, good range of enjoyable sensibly priced food from sandwiches up (must book Sun lunch), helpful staff and friendly obliging young licensee, full Wadworths beer range, good value wines, restaurant; colourful terrace and garden *(David Lamb, John and Joyce Snell, Trevor and Judith Pearson)*

BURCOT [SU5695]

Chequers OX14 3DP [A415 Dorchester—Abingdon]: Friendly thatched dining pub with newish chef-landlord doing enjoyable food using good local supplies from lunchtime sandwiches and other pubby dishes up, real ales such as Adnams, Hook Norton and Ridgeway, good wine range,

leather sofas around big log fire, neat contemporary black and white décor; children welcome, wheelchair access, floodlit terrace and lawn with flowers and fruit trees *(Roy Hoing, LYM)*

BURFORD [SP2512]

☆ *Angel* OX18 4SN [Witney St]: Long heavy-beamed dining pub in attractive ancient building, warmly welcoming and more pubby under current licensees, good reasonably priced brasserie food, good range of drinks; big secluded garden, three comfortable bedrooms *(KN-R, Mr and Mrs M Pattinson, David Glynne-Jones, LYM)*

Cotswold Arms OX18 4QF [High St]: Cosy bar and larger back dining area, wide choice of enjoyable good value pubby food from sandwiches to steak, good selection of real ales, welcoming staff, beautiful stonework, two flame-effect stoves; children welcome, tables out in front and in back garden *(Michael Dandy, Jason Reynolds)*

Golden Pheasant OX18 4QA [High St]: Small early 18th-c hotel's flagstoned split-level bar, civilised yet relaxed and pubby, settees, armchairs, well spaced tables and woodburner, enjoyable bar food from sandwiches through pub standbys to more unusual things, well kept Greene King ales, good house wines, back dining room down steps; children welcome, pleasant back terrace, open all day *(Michael Dandy, Rona Murdoch, C and R Bromage, Peter Dandy, Michael Butler, Maureen and Keith Gimson, David Spurgeon, BB, Peter and Jan Humphreys)*

Highway OX18 4RG [High St (A361)]: 15th-c coaching inn reopened 2006, log fires, stripped stone and some modern touches, popular restaurant, local real ales; dogs welcome, 11 bedrooms *(anon)*

☆ *Lamb* OX18 4LR [Sheep St (B4425)]: 16th-c stone-built inn well worth a visit for its broad flagstones, polished oak boards and fine log fireplace – one of the nicest pub buildings around, with a lovely suntrap garden as well as its timeless bar; bar food value has been good in recent months (some interesting dishes from sandwiches up), Hook Norton and Wadworths 6X; children and dogs welcome, comfortable bedrooms, open all day *(LYM, Malcolm Ward, Michael Dandy, the Didler, Mr and Mrs M Pattinson, Carol Mills, Richard Marjoram, Peter Dandy, Julie and Bill Ryan, P R Waights, Nick and Meriel Cox)*

Mermaid OX18 4QF [High St]: Handsome jettied Tudor dining pub with beams, flagstones, panelling and stripped stone, good log fire, well kept real ales, lots of wines by the glass, nice winter mulled wine, enjoyable sensibly priced food from lunchtime baguettes up, good fresh veg, prompt service, bay seating around row of close-set tables on the left, further airy back dining room and upstairs restaurant; piped music, games machine; children in eating areas, picnic-sets under cocktail parasols outside, open all day

(Mike and Mary Carter, Dr Phil Putwain, Peter Dandy, LYM, Guy Vowles)

Old Bull OX18 4RG [High St]: Handsomely rebuilt in the 1980s with beams, panelling and big fireplaces, then smartly refurbished in wine bar/bistro style, comfortable seating and open fire, steps down to further eating area, restaurant behind, good friendly service, Greene King ales, decent wines, wide choice of usual food from baguettes up; piped music; children welcome, tables out in front or back through old coach entry, comfortable bedrooms, open all day *(C and R Bromage, LYM, Michael Dandy, Peter Dandy)*

☆ **Royal Oak** OX18 4SN [Witney St]: Relaxed homely 17th-c stripped-stone local, an oasis in this smart village, with long-serving friendly landlord, Courage Best from central servery, sensible choice of generous good value food using local produce from filled rolls up, good service, over a thousand beer mugs and steins hanging from beams, antlers over big log fire (underfloor heating too), some comfortable sofas as well as pine tables, chairs and benches on flagstones, more in carpeted back room with bar billiards; terrace tables, sensibly priced bedrooms by garden behind *(Stuart Turner, Pete Baker, Michael Dandy, Mr and Mrs C Prentis)*

CHADLINGTON [SP3222]

☆ **Tite** OX7 3NY [off A361 S of Chipping Norton; Mill End]: 17th-c country pub reopened under new hard-working owners early 2008, inviting choice of reasonably priced good food, big log fire in huge fireplace, settles, wooden chairs, prints, rack of guide books, daily papers, small vine-covered back restaurant; big terrace and attractive garden full of shrubs, some quite unusual, with stream running under pub, good walks nearby *(Helene Grygar, BB, Martin and Pauline Jennings)*

CHARLBURY [SP3519]

☆ **Bell** OX7 3PP [Church St]: Attractive civilised two-room bar in small olde-worlde 17th-c hotel, welcoming and relaxed, flagstones, stripped stonework and huge inglenook log fire, good bar lunches (not Sun) from sandwiches to short choice of imaginative dishes, friendly attentive service, Greene King and a guest ale, good value wines, wide choice of malt whiskies, restaurant; children welcome in eating area, dogs in bar, pleasant garden tables, comfortable quiet bedrooms, good breakfast *(M E and J R Hart, E A and D C T Frewer, LYM)*

CHAZEY HEATH [SU6977]

Pack Saddle RG4 7UD [A4074 Reading—Wallingford]: Eclectic bric-a-brac, pine panelling, wood floors, dark red walls and log fire, well kept Wadworths, good wine choice, sensibly priced pubby food, bar billiards; children welcome, garden *(BB, Susan and John Douglas)*

CHESTERTON [SP5521]

Red Cow OX26 1UU [The Green]: Comfortably updated softly lit traditional local with

beams, brasses, old photographs, two log fires, enjoyable lunchtime food from baguettes to good value hot dishes, Greene King ales, good coffee, small dining area; dogs welcome, picnic-sets out under parasols *(E A and D C T Frewer, Chris Glasson)*

CHIPPING NORTON [SP3127]

Fox OX7 5DD [Market Pl]: Well placed unpretentious pub with lots of pictures and open fire in quiet lounge, well kept Hook Norton, good coffee, simple inexpensive bar food, welcoming landlord, upstairs dining room; children and dogs welcome, good value bedrooms *(Chris Glasson, LYM)*

Kings Arms OX7 5AA [West St]: Former early 18th-c coaching inn, usual pub food, relaxed service, two pool tables; lots of TVs; outside decking, 13 bedrooms, hearty breakfast, useful small car park *(Michael Butler)*

CHISLEHAMPTON [SU5998]

☆ **Coach & Horses** OX44 7UX [B480 Oxford—Watlington, opp B4015 to Abingdon]: Extended former 16th-c coaching inn with two beamed bars, homely and civilised, and sizeable restaurant (polished oak tables and wall banquettes); good value well prepared food from baguettes and good ploughman's to game specials, friendly obliging service, well kept Fullers London Pride and Hook Norton, big log fire; piped music; neat terraced gardens overlooking fields by River Thame, some tables out in front, good bedrooms in back courtyard block *(Anne and Jeff Peel, Roy Hoing, BB)*

CHRISTMAS COMMON [SU7193]

Fox & Hounds OX49 5HL [off B480/B481]: Upmarket Chilterns pub in lovely countryside, emphasis on airy and spacious front barn restaurant and conservatory with interesting food from open kitchen, Brakspears and Wychwood, proper coffee, two compact beamed rooms simply but comfortably furnished, bow windows, red and black tiles and big inglenook, snug little back room; children and dogs welcome, rustic benches and tables outside, open all day wknds *(Fred and Kate Portnell, the Didler, Dr and Mrs R E S Tanner, LYM)*

CHURCH HANBOROUGH [SP4212]

Hand & Shears OX29 8AB [opp church; signed off A4095 at Long Hanborough, or off A40 at Eynsham roundabout]: Open-feeling bistro-style pub with enjoyable fresh food from light dishes and generous if pricy sandwiches up, Hook Norton and Wells & Youngs, long gleaming bar, sofa one end, open fires, steps down into roomy back dining extension *(E A and D C T Frewer, BB)*

CLANFIELD [SP2802]

☆ **Clanfield Tavern** OX18 2RG [Bampton Rd (A4095 S of Witney)]: New licensees in pretty 17th-c pub, friendly service, enjoyable bar food and enterprising main menu using seasonal local ingredients inc own veg and herbs, home-smoked salmon, popular Sun roasts, Adnams, Banks's and Marstons Sunburst (sampling trays available), interesting wines, daily papers, linked beamed, flagstoned and stripped-stone rooms, log fires, modern conservatory restaurant; picnic-sets in pleasant front garden (LYM, Ian Phillips)

Plough OX18 2RB [Bourton Rd]: Substantial old stone inn with lovely Elizabethan façade, civilised atmosphere, log fire in comfortable lounge bar, enjoyable food, particularly fish and game, good wine list, attentive service; dogs welcome, attractive gardens with teak tables under giant parasols in nice front courtyard, bedrooms (LYM, Terry Miller)

CRAWLEY [SP3412]

☆ **Lamb** OX29 9TW [Steep Hill; just NW of Witney]: Comfortably extended 17th-c stone-built pub with simple beamed bar, lovely fireplace and cricket bats above counter, steps to candlelit dining room, wide choice of well liked food from baguettes and usual dishes to interesting specials, good choice of wines by the glass, well kept ales such as Brakspears and Wychwood Hobgoblin, quick, helpful and friendly service; views from tables on terraced lawn behind, pretty village, good walks – on Palladian Way (Guy Vowles, Brenda and Stuart Naylor, BB, Richard Atherton, Richard Marjoram)

CRAYS POND [SU6380]

☆ **White Lion** RG8 7SH [Goring Rd [B471 nr junction with B4526, about 3 miles E of Goring]]: Low-ceilinged pub with friendly newish licensees doing good food from bar lunches to full meals, attentive efficient service, well kept beer, good wine choice, relaxed casual atmosphere with proper front bar, open fire, attractive conservatory; big garden with play area, lovely countryside (I H G Busby, Rob Winstanley)

CROPREDY [SP4646]

Red Lion OX17 1PB [off A423 N of Banbury]: Rambling old thatched stone-built pub charmingly placed opp pretty village's churchyard, welcoming helpful landlady, good value food from sandwiches up inc Sun lunch, several changing ales, low beams, inglenook log fire, high-backed settles, brass, plates and pictures, unusual dining room mural, games room; piped music, limited parking; children allowed in dining part, picnic-sets under cocktail parasols on back terrace (Dennis and Doreen Haward, LYM, Charles and Pauline Stride)

CROWELL [SU7499]

Shepherds Crook OX39 4RR [B4009, 2 miles from M40 junction 6]: Traditional local, for sale as we went to press, so things may change; unpretentious beamed bar with stripped brick and flagstones, open fire, high-raftered dining are, has had interesting real ales, board games; children and dogs welcome, tables out on green, decent walks (LYM, Torrens Lyster)

CUDDESDON [SP5902]

Bat & Ball OX44 9HJ [S of Wheatley; High St]: Civilised pub full of cricket memorabilia, low beams, some flagstones, Banks's LBW, Marstons Pedigree and a guest beer, decent wines, food inc good focaccia sandwiches,

cheery service, big dining extension; piped music; children welcome, pleasant back terrace with good views, aunt sally, comfortable annexe bedrooms (some small), open all day (Peter and Anne Hollindale, LYM)

CUMNOR [SP4503]

☆ **Bear & Ragged Staff** OX2 9QH [signed from A420; Appleton Rd]: Busy comfortably rambling dining pub with interesting furnishings and kitsch bric-a-brac, five dim-lit partly flagstoned small rooms and separate restaurant, good reasonably priced food inc popular Sun roasts and enterprising vegetarian dishes, efficient friendly staff, well kept changing ales (there's a proper drinking area), two big log fires; children in eating areas, open all day Sun in summer (LYM)

CURBRIDGE [SP3208]

Lord Kitchener OX29 7PD [Lew Rd (A4095 towards Bampton)]: Bustling local atmosphere, quick welcoming service, good value extensive menu inc two-for-one lunch deals (not Sun) in neat, light and roomy dining extension, old local photographs, big log fire, real ales; piped music may obtrude; garden with play area, open all day (Peter and Audrey Dowsett, David Lamb)

DEDDINGTON [SP4631]

Crown & Tuns OX15 0SP [New St]: Bistro-style pub with interesting range of pies, good range of Hook Norton ales, log fires (Andy and Jill Kassube)

☆ **Deddington Arms** OX15 0SH [off A4260 (B4031) Banbury—Oxford; Horse Fair]: Beamed and timbered hotel with emphasis on sizeable contemporary back dining room with tiled floor, comfortable bar with mullioned windows and log fire, enjoyable bar food, real ales such as Black Sheep, Greene King, Jennings and Tetleys, good choice of wines by the glass; unobtrusive piped music; open all day, comfortable chalet bedrooms around courtyard, good breakfast, attractive village with lots of antiques shops and good farmers' market 4th Sat (R C Vincent, Trevor and Judith Pearson, LYM, Michael Dandy, George Atkinson, Les and Sandra Brown, Paul Humphreys)

Red Lion OX15 0SE [Market Pl]: Smartly up-to-date bar and bistro with reasonably priced food from lunchtime sandwiches and baked potatoes up, Greene King IPA and Oxfordshire ale, good choice of wines by the glass, good inexpensive coffee, friendly staff, daily papers; piped music, games; back courtyard tables (Michael Dandy)

☆ **Unicorn** OX15 0SE [Market Pl]: Cheerful 17th-c inn run by helpful mother and daughter, good reasonably priced generous food (not Sun evening) inc plenty of fish in L-shaped bar and beamed dining areas off, Hook Norton and Wells & Youngs, good choice of wines by the glass, proper coffee, daily papers, inglenook fireplace, pub games; dogs welcome in bar, cobbled courtyard leading to long walled back garden, open all day (from 9 for good 4th Sat farmers' market), good bedrooms and breakfast *(Paul Wilson, BB, Trevor and Judith Pearson, George Atkinson, Andy and Jill Kassube, Michael Dandy)*

DENCHWORTH [SU3891]

Fox OX12 0DX [off A338 or A417 N of Wantage; Hyde Rd]: Picturesque thatched village pub doing well under newish landlord, reasonably priced food inc good Sun carvery, friendly young staff, Greene King ales, good house wines, two good log fires and plush seats in low-ceilinged connecting areas, old prints and paintings, airy dining extension; children welcome, pleasant sheltered garden, peaceful village *(Dick and Madeleine Brown, BB)*

DUCKLINGTON [SP3507]

☆ *Bell* OX29 7UP [off A415, a mile SE of Witney; Standlake Rd]: Pretty thatched local with generous good value home-made food (not Sun eve) inc particularly good sandwiches, Greene King ales, good house wines, friendly service; big stripped stone and flagstoned bar with scrubbed tables, log fires, glass-covered walls, old local photographs, farm tools, hatch-served public bar, roomy and attractive well laid out back restaurant, its beams festooned with bells; cards and dominoes, no piped music; small garden behind with play area, colourful hanging baskets, nine bedrooms *(Helene Grygar, Pete Baker, BB)*

EAST HENDRED [SU4588]

Plough OX12 8JW [off A417 E of Wantage; Orchard Lane]: Big beamed village pub with friendly staff, wide blackboard range of enjoyable food, well kept Greene King ale, usual public bar and airy and lofty-raftered main room, interesting farming and wartime memorabilia; piped music, big-screen TV; pleasant garden with good play area, attractive village *(Harvey Smith, BB)*

FEWCOTT [SP5327]

White Lion OX27 7NZ [a mile from M40 junction 10, via B430 then 1st right; Fritwell Rd]: Cosy village local with four changing real ales from small breweries; children welcome, open all day wknds, cl wkdy lunchtimes and Sun evening *(Roger Shipperley)*

FIFIELD [SP2318]

☆ *Merrymouth* OX7 6HR [A424 Burford—Stow]: New licensees for this 13th-c inn, simple but comfortable L-shaped bar, nice bay-window seats, flagstones, brasses and antique bottles hanging from low beams, some walls stripped back to old masonry, warm stove; Hook Norton Old Hooky and West Berkshire Good Old Boy; piped music; children and dogs welcome, tables on terrace and in back garden *(Chris and Jeanne Downing, LYM, Neil and Anita Christopher, Gavin, Canon Michael Bourdeaux)*

FILKINS [SP2304]

Five Alls GL7 3JQ [signed off A361 Lechlade—Burford]: Big 18th-c Cotswold stone pub with relaxed local atmosphere,

good value traditional home cooking, well kept Brakspears and a guest beer, decent house wines, beams, flagstones, stripped stone and good log fire, settees, armchairs and rugs on polished boards, good-sized eating areas; quiz and theme nights; plenty of tables on terrace and neat lawns, five good bedrooms, nice village *(Tadeus Pfeifer, BB, Graham Oddey)*

FINSTOCK [SP3616]

Crown OX7 3DJ [School Rd]: Welcoming old-fashioned family pub with bar and dining area, three real ales, reasonably priced enjoyable food *(Keith Puddefoot)*

☆ *Plough* OX7 3BY [just off B4022 N of Witney; High St]: Rambling thatched and low-beamed village pub, chef brings out good food from lunchtime sandwiches to local venison, well kept ales such as Adnams, Brakspears and Hook Norton, small sensibly priced choice of decent wines, Weston's farm cider and perry, pleasant service, long carpeted bar and flagstoned locals' bar, leather sofas around welcoming log fire in tiled snug's massive stone inglenook, stripped-stone dining room; children and dogs welcome, courtyard tables, sizeable garden with old-fashioned roses and aunt sally, good walks *(Mr and Mrs J C Cetti, LYM, Stuart Turner)*

FOREST HILL [SP5807]

White Horse OX33 1EH [B4027 just off A40 E of Oxford; turn off Eastbound only]: Welcoming beamed village pub with good thai food (must book evenings), central log fire in restaurant; handy for Oxfordshire Way *(BB, Tim Venn)*

FRINGFORD [SP6028]

Butchers Arms OX27 8EB [off A421 N of Bicester; Main St]: Picturesque partly thatched Victorian local in Flora Thompson's 'Candleford' village, good welcoming service, wide choice of low-priced generous pubby food from sandwiches and ciabattas up, Adnams Broadside, Caledonian Deuchars IPA and Marstons Pedigree, darts in L-shaped bar, separate smaller dining room; piped music, TV; dogs welcome, tables out under parasols facing cricket green *(JJW, CMW, E A and D C T Frewer, Conor McGaughey, Guy Vowles)*

FRITWELL [SP5229]

Kings Head OX27 7QF [quite handy for M40 junction 10; East St]: Well run pub in small village, welcoming young licensees, good beer range, generous food in bar and dining room, darts and pool; children welcome *(Dr and Mrs M E Wilson, David Campbell, Vicki McLean)*

FULBROOK [SP2512]

☆ *Carpenters Arms* OX18 4BH [Fulbrook Hill]: Old Cotswold stone pub with new licensees doing good interesting food inc fish specialities, cheerful service, well kept Greene King Abbot and good wines by the glass from long bar serving smartly redecorated beamed rooms with neat country furnishings, good-sized dining room and conservatory; children and dogs welcome, disabled access and facilities, attractive terrace tables in garden behind, good play area, cl Sun evening and Mon *(Chris Glasson)*

GORING [SU5980]

☆ *Catherine Wheel* RG8 9HB [Station Rd]: Smart and well run, with friendly landlord and good informal atmosphere in two neat and cosily traditional bar areas, especially the more individual lower room with its low beams and big inglenook log fireplace; very wide choice of well priced generous home-made food, Brakspears, Hook Norton and Wychwood ales, Stowford Press cider, good value house wine, good coffee; back restaurant (children welcome here), notable door to gents'; nice courtyard and garden behind, handy for Thames Path, attractive village, open all day *(the Didler, Paul Humphreys, Rob Winstanley, Iwan and Sion Roberts, BB)*

☆ *Miller of Mansfield* RG8 9AW [High St]: Contemporary very dark green décor, lots of easy chairs and log fires in three linked areas of large bow-windowed bar, good if not cheap bar food all day, Butts Jester, Marlow Rebellion and West Berkshire Good Old Boy, friendly young staff, up-to-date meals in large smart and airy back restaurant; well reproduced piped pop music; children welcome, good tables under big canopy on heated terrace, open all day *(Rob Winstanley, BB)*

GOZZARD'S FORD [SU4698]

Black Horse OX13 6JH [off B4017 NW of Abingdon; N of A415 by Marcham—Cothill rd]: Ancient traditional pub in tiny hamlet, well kept beer, sensibly short choice of good generous food esp fish and seafood, decent wines, cheerful family service; nice garden *(William Goodhart)*

HARWELL [SU4988]

Kingswell OX11 0LZ [A417; Reading Rd]: Substantial hotel with good imaginative bar food as well as restaurant meals, helpful staff; comfortable bedrooms *(Henry Midwinter)*

HEADINGTON [SP5406]

Butchers Arms OX3 7AN [Wilberforce St]: Welcoming bare-boards backstreet local with long narrow seating area, good value wkdy lunchtime food, well kept Fullers beers, roaring fire, lots of sports trophies and memorabilia, games corner with darts, bar billiards and sports TV; big heated terrace with barbecues *(Dr and Mrs A K Clarke)*

Masons Arms OX3 8LH [Quarry School Pl]: Open-plan local with Caledonian Deuchars IPA, St Austell Tribute, two guest beers and its own Old Bog brews, darts, Sat quiz night; children welcome, heated outside seating, aunt sally, cl wkdy lunchtimes, open all day Sat *(Roger Shipperley)*

White Hart OX3 9DL [St Andrews Rd, Old Town]: Attractive multi-level stone-built pub with wooden benches and tables, intimate nooks and corners, well kept Everards and changing ales, bar food; piped music; delightful garden *(Dr and Mrs A K Clarke)*

HENLEY [SU7682]

☆ *Anchor* RG9 1AH [Friday St]: Old-fashioned, homely and individualistic (not a place for people who insist on order and neatness), two slightly cluttered and nicely lived-in front rooms, hearty food (not Sun/Mon evenings) from lunchtime open sandwiches up, lovely traditional puddings, well kept Brakspears ales, good range of malt whiskies and New World wines by the glass, friendly chocolate lab called Ruger, straight-talking landlady, simple back dining room; well behaved children welcome, charming back terrace, open all day *(Tracey and Stephen Groves, Anthony Longden, Ian Phillips, Mrs M S Forbes, the Didler, Peter Smith, Judith Brown, Clive Watkin, Geoff Simms, David Heath, LYM)*

HETHE [SP5929]

Whitmore Arms OX27 8ES [Main St]: A couple of steps up to large quiet low-ceilinged bar, small blackboard choice of sensibly priced freshly home-made food, Brakspears, Fullers London Pride and Hook Norton from oak counter, pleasantly relaxed service, inglenook log fire, rustic bygones, games area on right; lovely village, cl wkdy lunchtimes *(David Lamb)*

HIGHMOOR [SU7084]

☆ *Dog & Duck* RG9 5DL [B481]: Appealing country pub with careful choice of good traditional food, well kept Brakspears ales, good choice of wines by the glass, helpful friendly staff, cheery log fires in small beamed bar and not much larger flagstoned dining room with old prints and pictures, family room leading off; children and dogs welcome, attractive long garden with some play equipment and small sheep paddock, plenty of surrounding walks *(the Didler, Howard Dell, Robert Watt, Mrs M Phythian, LYM, Roy Hoing)*

HOOK NORTON [SP3533]

Pear Tree OX15 5NU [Scotland End]: Take-us-as-you-find-us village pub with full Hook Norton beer range kept well from nearby brewery, country wines, bar food (not Sun evening) from doorstep sandwiches up, knocked-together bar area with country-kitchen furniture, good log fire, daily papers; TV; children and dogs welcome, sizeable attractive garden with play area, bedrooms, open all day *(P Rose, LYM, Barry Collett, Tom Evans, Tracey and Stephen Groves)*

☆ *Sun* OX15 5NH [High Street]: Beamed bar with good atmosphere, friendly staff, huge log fire and flagstones, cosy carpeted back room leading into attractive dining room, enjoyable entirely local food from bar snacks to restaurant meals, well kept Hook Norton ales, several wines by the glass, darts and dominoes; children and dogs welcome, disabled facilities, tables out in front and on back terrace, well equipped bedrooms, good breakfast *(Robert Gomme, Michael Clatworthy, Pete Baker, Chris Brooks, Sir Nigel Foulkes, K H Frostick, LYM, Richard Greaves)*

KELMSCOTT [SU2499]
☆ *Plough* GL7 3HG [NW of Faringdon, off B4449 between A417 and A4095]: Reopened after flood refurbishment, beams, ancient flagstones, stripped stone and log fire, friendly relaxed atmosphere, wide choice of food (all day wknds), Archers Best, Hook Norton Best, Timothy Taylors Landlord, and Wychwood Hobgoblin, farm cider; children, dogs and booted walkers welcome, garden with aunt sally, lovely spot nr upper Thames (good moorings a few mins' walk away), eight good bedrooms, open all day *(LYM, Canon Michael Bourdeaux, David Handforth, Dr and Mrs M E Wilson, Mary McSweeney, Peter and Audrey Dowsett, Colin Piper, Paul Boot, Charles and Pauline Stride)*

KINGHAM [SP2624]
☆ *Plough* OX7 6YD [The Green]: Young chef/landlady doing short imaginative daily-changing choice of good food from enterprising bar snacks to restaurant meals in two small attractive dining rooms, reasonable prices, well kept Greene King and a guest beer, good value wines by the glass and fine wines by the bottle (or try their bloody mary), tastefully refurbished pubby flagstoned bar with rustic furniture and open fires; children welcome, terrace tables, seven comfortable bedrooms *(Myra Joyce, A G Marx, Richard Greaves, Bernard Stradling)*

☆ *Tollgate* OX7 6YA [Church St]: Civilised beamed and flagstoned former Georgian farmhouse with contemporary styling, good choice of well cooked food (not Sun evening or Mon) from lunchtime baguettes and light dishes to restaurant meals inc good if not cheap Sun lunch, Hook Norton and unusual local Cotswold Lager, good wines by the glass, friendly landlord, prompt service; dogs welcome (theirs is called Guinness), outside seating, nine comfortable bedrooms *(Guy Vowles)*

KINGSTON LISLE [SU3287]
Blowing Stone OX12 9QL [signed off B4507 W of Wantage]: Friendly pub/restaurant with good food choice from sandwiches to steaks, West Berkshire real ale, daily papers, log fire, comfortable lounge, cheerful modernised bar and attractive dining conservatory; children welcome, tables out in lovely garden with goldfish pond, pretty bedrooms, handy for Uffington Castle hill fort and the downs *(Tony Winckworth, LYM)*

KIRTLINGTON [SP4919]
☆ *Oxford Arms* OX5 3HA [Troy Lane]: Oak-beamed pub popular for generous food from proper sandwiches and imaginative starters up using good local produce, genial hands-on landlord and charming young staff, good reasonably priced wines by the large glass, Hook Norton Best and two other ales from congenial central bar with small standing area, leather settees and log fire one end, separate dining room; small sunny back garden, heated awning *(Briege Gormley, Colin and Ruth Munro, Phillip and Margaret-Ann Minty, Guy Vowles)*

LAUNTON [SP6022]
Bull OX26 5DQ [just E of Bicester]: Convivial village local with enjoyable food inc OAP lunches, good steaks and Sun roasts, welcoming efficient service *(Meg and Colin Hamilton)*

LONG WITTENHAM [SU5493]
Plough OX14 4QH [High St]: Friendly pub with well kept Greene King ales, good value wines by the glass and coffee, wide choice of good value food (all day wknds), good service, low beams and lots of brass, inglenook fires, dining room, games in public bar; dogs welcome, Thames moorings at bottom of long spacious garden with aunt sally, bedrooms *(Chris Glasson, David Lamb)*

LOWER HEYFORD [SP4824]
☆ *Bell* OX25 5NY [Market Sq]: Charming creeper-clad building in small thatched village square, good range of generous enjoyable fresh food inc popular specials and several elaborate ice-cream concoctions, well kept ales such as Adnams and Youngs, good coffees inc flavoured lattes, cheerful helpful staff, uncluttered pleasantly refurbished rooms around central beamed bar; children welcome, disabled facilities, nice long lawned garden with aunt sally, nearby Oxford Canal walks *(Trevor and Judith Pearson, K H Frostick, BB, William Goodhart)*

MAIDENSGROVE [SU7288]
☆ *Five Horseshoes* RG9 6EX [off B480 and B481, W of village]: 17th-c dining pub with lovely views from common high in the Chilterns, rambling bar with low ceiling and log fire, friendly efficient staff, enjoyable bar food from sandwiches and pork pie platter up, Brakspears, good choice of wines by the glass, airy conservatory restaurant with its own good menu; children and dogs welcome, plenty of tables outside (wknd barbecues or hog roasts), good walks, open all day summer wknds, cl winter Sun evening *(Julia and Richard Tredgett, Edward Mirzoeff, LYM, Malcolm and Barbara Lewis, Mrs L M Beard)*

MILTON [SU4891]
Apple Cart OX14 4TX: Reasonably priced food inc good value steaks; bedrooms in adjoining Travel Inn *(Chris Evans)*

MINSTER LOVELL [SP3111]
New Inn OX29 0RZ [Burford Rd]: Handsomely reworked and extended restauranty pub with enjoyable food from antipasti, lunchtime sandwiches and light dishes to major meals, good choice of wines by the glass, Hook Norton and Wadworths 6X, tremendous views over pretty Windrush valley; children welcome, tables on big heated terrace, lovely setting *(Paul and Sue Merrick, Sarah and Peter Gooderham, Mrs Ann Gray)*

NORTHMOOR [SP4202]
Red Lion OX29 5SX [B4449 SE of Stanton Harcourt]: Comfortable 15th-c stone-built village pub with friendly staff, good value generous traditional food cooked to order, Greene King and a guest ale, good log fires each end, heavy beams, stripped stone,

small dining room, Thurs morning post office; no dogs, no credit cards; walkers welcome, garden *(Tony Winckworth, Mr and Mrs H J Stephens)*

NUFFIELD [SU6787]

☆ *Crown* RG9 5SJ [A4130/B481]: Attractive small country pub continuing well under new management, decent food from sandwiches to grills, good service, well kept Brakspears, good house wines, simple country furniture and inglenook log fire in beamed lounge bar; children in small family room, walkers welcome (good walks nearby), pleasant garden with tables front and back *(Howard Dell, Roy Hoing, LYM, David Lamb, Bruce Horne)*

OXFORD [SP5106]

☆ *Bear* OX1 4EH [Alfred St/Wheatsheaf Alley]: Two charming little low-ceilinged and partly panelled ancient rooms, not over-smart and often packed with students, thousands of vintage ties on walls and beams, simple reasonably priced lunchtime food most days inc sandwiches, four well kept changing ales from centenarian handpumps on pewter bar counter; upstairs ladies'; tables outside, open all day summer *(the Didler, LYM, Sapna Thottathil, Tracey and Stephen Groves, Michael Dandy)*

Chequers OX1 4DH [off High St]: Narrow 16th-c courtyard pub with several areas on three floors, interesting architectural features, panelling and stained-glass, up to three real ales, sausage specialities, quick friendly service, games room with balcony; walled garden *(Dave Braisted)*

☆ *Kings Arms* OX1 3SP [Holywell St]: Dating from early 17th c, convivial and relaxed, with quick helpful service, Wells & Youngs and guests, fine choice of wines by the glass, cosy comfortably worn in partly panelled side and back rooms, daily papers, eating area with counter servery doing usual food (all day wknds, children allowed) from sandwiches up; a few tables outside, open all day from 10.30 *(the Didler, LYM, Michael Dandy, Roger Shipperley, J C Burgis, Lawrence Pearse)*

Lamb & Flag OX1 3JS [St Giles/Banbury Rd]: Old pub owned by nearby college, modern airy front room with big windows over street, more atmosphere in back rooms with stripped stonework and low boarded ceilings, a beer brewed by Palmers for the pub (L&F Gold), Shepherd Neame Spitfire and Theakstons Old Peculier, good value lunchtime food from baguettes to suet puddings, cheerful service *(Roger Shipperley, Sapna Thottathil, David Campbell, Vicki McLean, Michael Dandy)*

Old Bookbinders OX2 6BT [Victor St]: Dark and mellow local tucked away in Jericho area, friendly and unpretentious, with masses of interesting bric-a-brac, good range of well kept ales, reasonably priced simple food, free peanuts, darts, cards and shove ha'penny; open all day wknds *(Len Beattie, Phil and Sally Gorton)*

☆ *White Horse* OX1 3BB [Broad St]: Bustling and studenty, squeezed between bits of Blackwells bookshop, small narrow bar with snug one-table raised back alcove, low beams and timbers, ochre ceiling, beautiful view of the Clarendon building and Sheldonian, Brakspears, St Austell and Timothy Taylors Landlord, friendly staff, good value simple lunchtime food (the few tables reserved for this) *(Roger Shipperley, the Didler, Mike Vincent, Michael Dandy, Phil and Sally Gorton, BB)*

PISHILL [SU7190]

☆ *Crown* RG9 6HH [B480 Nettlebed—Watlington]: Popular well kept dining pub in wisteria-covered ancient building, black beams and timbers, good log fires and candlelight, wholesome home-made food from carefully chosen ingredients, good friendly service, Brakspears; children welcome in restaurant, picnic-sets on attractive side lawn, pleasant cottage bedroom, pretty country setting, walks *(Susan and John Douglas, Peter Dandy, the Didler, LYM, E Seymour)*

ROKE [SU6293]

Home Sweet Home OX10 6JD [off B4009 Benson—Watlington]: This Wadworths pub, previously a popular main entry, changed hands in 2007 *(LYM)*

ROTHERFIELD GREYS [SU7282]

Maltsters Arms RG9 4QD: Welcoming recently refurbished country local with friendly staff, Brakspears ales, reasonably priced enjoyable food from panini to piping hot specials and good Sun lunch (best to book wknds), good wines by the glass, lots of cricket memorabilia; small garden, not far from Greys Court (NT), lovely country views *(Roy Hoing, Fred and Kate Portnell, Paul Humphreys, Malcolm and Barbara Lewis)*

ROTHERFIELD PEPPARD [SU7081]

Unicorn RG9 5LX [Colmore Ln]: Well kept Brakspears and Hook Norton, good food from open sandwiches in the bar to full meals, roaring log fire, friendly welcome *(Ken and Janet Bracey)*

SATWELL [SU7083]

Lamb RG9 4QZ [2 miles S of Nettlebed; follow Shepherds Green signpost]: 16th-c low-beamed dining pub in same ownership as Greyhound on Gallowstree Common (see main entries), big log fireplace, informal rustic décor with simple wood furniture and tiled floors, good wholesome country food not too expensive, good mix of ages inc plenty of young people, pleasant foreign staff, Butlers and Fullers London Pride; tables out in good-sized garden with terrace and barbecues *(P M Newsome, LYM, Fred and Kate Portnell)*

SHENINGTON [SP3742]

☆ *Bell* OX15 6NQ [off A422 NW of Banbury]: Good hearty wholesome home cooking in hospitable 17th-c two-room pub, good sandwiches too, well kept Hook Norton Best, good wine choice, fair prices, friendly informal service and long-serving licensees, relaxed atmosphere, heavy beams, some flagstones, stripped stone and pine panelling, coal fire, amiable dogs, cribbage, dominoes; children in eating areas, nice tables out in front, small attractive back garden, charming quiet village, good walks, bedrooms, cl Mon (and perhaps other wkdy) lunchtimes *(Graham and Nicky Westwood, Paul Humphreys, LYM, Sir Nigel Foulkes, K H Frostick)*

SHIPLAKE [SU7678]

Plowden Arms RG9 4BX [Reading Rd (A4155)]: Neat and cheerful with hard-working landlord, three linked rooms and side dining room, log fire, good range of home-made food from well filled baguettes up, Brakspears, good coffee; handy for Thames walk *(Roy Hoing, Roy and Jean Russell)*

SHIPLAKE ROW [SU7478]

White Hart RG9 4DP [off A4155 W of Shiplake]: Pretty pub with three simple friendly linked rooms mainly set for good choice of food (just roasts Sun lunchtime), cheerful attentive service, Brakspears, decent house wines, log fires; lovely garden, nice spot, fine views, good walks *(Paul Humphreys)*

SHIPTON-UNDER-WYCHWOOD [SP2717]

☆ *Lamb* OX7 6DQ [off A361 to Burford; High St]: A welcome for all (not just diners) under new family management, revamped racing-theme bar with some stripped stone and log fire, good food, Greene King and a guest ale, good value wines, restaurant area in fascinating Elizabethan core; children and dogs welcome, front suntrap garden with tables, five attractive bedrooms (some over bar) *(LYM)*

☆ *Shaven Crown* OX7 6BA [High St (A361)]: Ancient building, in line for major update, with magnificent lofty medieval rafters and imposing double stairway in hotel part's hall, separate more down-to-earth back bar with booth seating, quick friendly service, lovely log fires, good value food from sandwiches up, Archers, Hook Norton and Wychwood Hobgoblin, several wines by the glass, restaurant; piped music; children and dogs welcome, peaceful courtyard with outside heaters, bowling green *(Keith and Sue Ward, LYM)*

SHUTFORD [SP3840]

☆ *George & Dragon* OX15 6PG [Church Lane]: Ancient stone-built pub with good friendly service, enjoyable food inc good ploughman's and Sun lunches, Hook Norton Best and changing ales such as Everards Original, fine choice of wines by the glass, cosy flagstoned L-shaped bar with impressive fireplace, oak-panelled beamed dining room; children and dogs welcome, small garden, pretty village, cl Mon, open all day Sun *(BB, Guy Vowles)*

SOUTH NEWINGTON [SP4033]

☆ *Duck on the Pond* OX15 4JE: Thriving dining pub with tidy modern-rustic décor in small flagstoned bar and linked carpeted eating areas up a step with fresh flowers and lit

candles, interesting choice of generous enjoyable food from wraps, melts and other light dishes to steak and family Sun lunch, changing ales such as Archers Golden and Exmoor Fox, attentive landlord and neat and friendly young staff, woodburner; piped music; lots of tables out on deck and lawn, pretty pond with waterfowl, open all day *(BB, George Atkinson, Jay Bohmrich)*

STEVENTON [SU4691]

North Star OX13 6SG [Stocks Lane, The Causeway, central westward turn off B4017]: Carefully restored old-fangled village pub with tiled entrance corridor, main area with ancient high-backed settles around central table, Greene King ales from pump set tucked away in side tap room, hatch service to another room with plain seating, a couple of tables and good coal fire, simple lunchtime food, young friendly staff; piped music, sports TV, games machine; tables on side grass, front gateway through living yew tree *(Pete Baker, Alan and Carolin Tidbury, the Didler, Phil and Sally Gorton, LYM)*

STOKE LYNE [SP5628]

Peyton Arms OX27 8SD [from minor road off B4110 N of Bicester fork left into village]: Largely unspoilt stone-built pub, Hook Norton from casks behind small corner bar in sparsely decorated front snug, filled rolls, tiled floor, inglenook fire, games room with darts and pool; no children or dogs; pleasant garden with aunt sally, open all day Sat, cl Sun evening and Mon *(Roger Shipperley, the Didler, Pete Baker, Torrens Lyster)*

STOKE ROW [SU6884]

☆ *Cherry Tree* RG9 5QA [off B481 at Highmoor]: Contemporary upscale pub restaurant with particularly good if not cheap food (freshly made so can take a while at busy times), Brakspears ales, good choice of wines by the glass, enthusiastic young staff, minimalist décor and solid country furniture in four linked rooms with stripped wood, heavy low beams and some flagstones; TV in bar; good seating in attractive garden, nice nearby walks, five good bedrooms in new block *(Richard Endacott, I H G Busby, Mrs Pam Mattinson, Bob and Margaret Holder, Roy Hoing, BB, Penny and Peter Keevil)*

☆ *Crooked Billet* RG9 5PU [Nottwood Lane, off B491 N of Reading – OS Sheet 175 map ref 684844]: Very nice place, but restaurant not pub (you can't have just a drink); charming rustic pub layout though, with heavy beams, flagstones, antique pubby furnishings and great inglenook log fire as well as crimsonly Victorian dining room; wide choice of well cooked interesting meals using local produce inc good value lunch (you can have just a starter), helpful friendly staff, Brakspears tapped from the cask (no bar counter), good wines, relaxed homely atmosphere – like a french country restaurant; children truly welcome, occasional live music, big garden by Chilterns beechwoods *(Bob and Margaret Holder, LYM, Tim Venn, the Didler)*

SUNNINGWELL [SP4900]
Flowing Well OX13 6RB [just N of Abingdon]: Attractive timbered pub redecorated under friendly new landlord, relaxed and unpretentious bar/lounge, neatly set tablecloth dining room, enjoyable food (not Tues night, and can take quite a while), good choice of wines and other drinks, Tues quiz night; TV; children welcome, garden with small well and picnic-sets under cocktail parasols *(BB, Henry Bennet-Clark)*

SUTTON COURTENAY [SU5094]
Fish OX14 4NQ [Appleford Rd]: Civilised well run restaurant rather than pub, small front bar opening into attractive three-part dining room, nice prints toning in with the dark green décor, good fresh-cooked food with some emphasis on fish, starters that can double as interesting bar snacks, good fairly priced house wines, top-notch service, stylish back conservatory; children welcome, tables out in terrace arbour and on neat lawn *(Alan and Audrey Moulds, BB)*

George & Dragon OX14 4NJ [Church St]: Chatty and friendly 16th-c local, attractive mix of furnishings, dark beams and nice log fire in traditional bar, smoother dining area on right, good choice of substantial bar food, well kept Greene King Morlands and Ruddles, good wine choice; big back terrace overlooking graveyard where Orwell is buried – church worth a visit but may be locked *(Dick and Madeleine Brown, BB)*

SWINFORD [SP4308]
Talbot OX29 4BT [B4044 just S of Eynsham]: Roomy and confortable beamed pub with good friendly staff, very wide changing choice of good value generous fresh food, four well kept ales inc Arkells 3B, friendly landlord and staff, long attractive bar with some stripped stone, cheerful log-effect gas fire, games room; tables in garden (some traffic noise), pleasant walk along lovely stretch of the Thames towpath *(Anthony Double)*

THAME [SP7005]
Black Horse OX9 2BL [High St]: Traditional old local with attractive panelled and chintzy back lounge, simple dining area and conservatory, reasonably priced standard food (not Fri/Sat nights or Sun), well kept Greene King IPA, good coffee, friendly atmosphere, games room with two pool tables; bedrooms sharing bathroom *(Tim and Ann Newell, LYM)*

Falcon OX9 3JA [Thame Park Rd]: Open-plan local with well kept Hook Norton ales, friendly service, decent food (not Sat lunchtime); open all day *(Roger Shipperley, Tim and Ann Newell)*

Swan OX9 3ER [Upper High St]: Heavily beamed 16th-c former coaching inn with well kept changing real ales such as Brakspears, Hydes and Skinners, baguettes and light lunches, upstairs evening restaurant with medieval ceiling, friendly informal service, big log fire; big-screen sports TV in main bar, two more in back

bars, some live music; children and dogs welcome, open all day, bedrooms *(Tim and Ann Newell, LYM)*

☆ *Thatch* OX9 2AA [High St]: Attractive timbered and thatched building, more upmarket restaurant than pub but does have small bar with ancient floor tiles and big inglenook log fire, nice collection of small higgledy-piggledy heavily beamed dining rooms, good food from the traditional to more enterprising inc good value set lunches, Vale real ale; six bedrooms *(BB, Jane Taylor, David Dutton, Jestyn Phillips)*

THRUPP [SP4815]
☆ *Boat* OX5 1JY [off A4260 just N of Kidlington]: Stone-built pub in good spot near Oxford Canal, good upscale meals, friendly landlord, Greene King ales, decent wine, coal fire, old canal pictures and artefacts, bare boards and stripped pine, restaurant; gets busy in summer; fenced garden behind with plenty of tables *(Pete Baker, Sue Demont, Tim Barrow, D A Bradford, Bob and Laura Brock)*

TOOT BALDON [SP5600]
☆ *Mole* OX44 9NG [between A4074 and B480 SE of Oxford]: Light bright open-plan dining pub with sensibly shortish choice of good food, good wines by the glass inc champagne, real ale, leather sofas by bar, neat country furniture or more formal leather dining chairs in nice choice of linked eating areas inc conservatory, woodburners and stripped beams; garden tables *(Mrs D Rawlings)*

TOWERSEY [SP7304]
Three Horseshoes OX9 3QY [Chinnor Rd]: Unpretentious flagstoned country local with well kept ales such as Black Sheep and Wadworths 6X, enjoyable pubby food from baguettes up, old-fashioned furnishings in two low-beamed bars, good log fire, darts, small restaurant; children allowed lunchtime, biggish garden with fruit trees and play area *(LYM, David Lamb, Jestyn Phillips)*

UPTON [SU5186]
George & Dragon OX11 9JJ [A417 Harwell—Blewbury]: Welcoming little pub with enjoyable reasonably priced food, Greene King Morlands, small end dining area *(Chris Evans)*

WARBOROUGH [SU5993]
Cricketers Arms OX10 7DD [Thame Rd (off A329)]: Good choice of sensibly priced food in neat pleasantly decorated pub, Greene King ales and a guest, proper bar and dining area, friendly welcome esp from ginger cat Ben; tables outside, cl Mon lunchtime *(David Lamb)*

Six Bells OX10 7DN [The Green S; just E of A329, 4 miles N of Wallingford]: Attentive and welcoming new licensees doing good food in thatched 16th-c pub facing cricket green, Brakspears ales, attractive country furnishings in linked small areas off bar, low beams, stripped stone, big log fire; tables in pleasant orchard garden *(LYM, Barry Collett)*

WENDLEBURY [SP5619]
Red Lion OX25 2PW [a mile from M40

junction 9; signposted from A41 Bicester—Oxford]: Spacious low-beamed stone-built pub with traditional furnishings, atmosphere and food (steak and kidney pudding recommended), friendly attentive staff, well kept ales such as Fullers London Pride, several wines by the glass, big log fire, two comfortable dining areas; large garden *(M Coultish)*

WEST HANNEY [SU4092]

☆ *Plough* OX12 0LN [Church St]: Unspoilt and pretty 16th-c thatched family local with attractive timbered upper storey, original timbers and uneven low ceilings, homely lounge with good log fire in stone fireplace, genial landlord, pubby atmosphere, popular sensibly priced food from sandwiches and baguettes up, well kept ales such as Brakspears, Butts, Greene King Abbot and Timothy Taylors Landlord, interesting whiskies, good coffee, small dining room, friendly cat; children and dogs welcome, tables on back terrace, play area, good walks *(D R Williams, Dick and Madeleine Brown, Alan and Carolin Tidbury, BB)*

WESTON-ON-THE-GREEN [SP5318]

Ben Jonson OX25 3RA [B430 nr M40 junction 9]: Ancient thatched and stone-built country pub, smart beamed bar with oak furniture, pastel décor and interesting sculpture, enjoyable if not cheap food from baguettes up, well kept Hook Norton, decent wines, newish dining room *(Tom McLean, Val and Alan Green, E A and D C T Frewer)*

Chequers OX25 3QH [handy for M40 junction 9, via A34; Northampton Rd (B430)]: Extended thatched pub with three smart areas off large semicircular raftered bar, Fullers ales, good value wines by the glass, welcoming service, enjoyable food all day from thick beef sandwiches up; tables under parasols in attractive garden *(Miss E Ackrill, Val and Alan Green, Paul Goldman, Conor McGaughey)*

WITNEY [SP3509]

Fleece OX28 4AZ [Church Green]: Wide choice of enjoyable food in smart and civilised town pub on green, Greene King ales, daily papers and leather armchairs; piped music; children welcome, tables outside *(Richard Atherton)*

Hollybush OX28 6BT [Corn St]: 18th-c building nicely smartened up without entirely losing its pub character, though emphasis now on enjoyable food inc good burgers as well as more elaborate dishes, a real ale *(Joe McCorry)*

Royal Oak OX28 6HW [High St]: Small cosy lounge and larger bar, good choice of generous lunchtime food, Brakspears and Wychwood ales, cheery staff *(Richard Marjoram, Pete Baker)*

WOLVERCOTE [SP4909]

Plough OX2 8AH [First Turn/Wolvercote Green]: Comfortably well worn in pubby linked areas, friendly helpful service, bustling atmosphere, armchairs and Victorian-style carpeted bays in main lounge, well kept Greene King ales, farm cider, decent wines, good value usual food in flagstoned ex-stables dining room and library (children allowed here), traditional snug, woodburner; picnic-sets on front terrace looking over rough meadow to canal and woods *(Mike and Mary Clark, BB)*

WOODSTOCK [SP4416]

☆ *Bear* OX20 1SZ [Park St]: Small heavy-beamed bar at front of smart and attractive ancient hotel, cosy alcoves, immaculate and tastefully casual mix of antique oak, mahogany and leather furniture, paintings and sporting trophies, blazing inglenook log fire, good fresh sandwiches and hot bar lunches (not cheap), quick friendly service, good choice of wines by the glass, may be a real ale, restaurant; no dogs; tables in back courtyard, good bedrooms, open all day *(Chris Glasson, Conor McGaughey, BB, C Galloway, Michael Dandy, David Glynne-Jones)*

WOOTTON [SP4320]

Killingworth Castle OX20 1EJ [Glympton Rd; B4027 N of Woodstock]: Striking three-storey 17th-c coaching inn with new licensees doing enjoyable food, Greene King ales, long narrow main bar with pine furnishings, parquet floor, brasses and log fire, bar billiards, darts and shove ha'penny in smaller games end; garden, bedrooms *(Pete Baker, BB)*

WROXTON [SP4141]

North Arms OX15 6PY [Mills Lane; off A422 at hotel, pub at back of village]: Prettily thatched stone pub with good fresh well prepared food from generous snacks up, well kept Greene King, friendly atmosphere, log fire in huge inglenook, nice wooden furnishings, character restaurant; attractive quiet garden in peaceful part of lovely village, walks in abbey gardens opposite (now the grounds of a US college) during term time *(Ian Phillips, LYM)*

YARNTON [SP4812]

Turnpike OX5 1PJ [A44 N of Oxford]: Large Vintage Inn pub/restaurant with good atmosphere in spacious low-ceilinged bar areas, prompt pleasant service, reliable food all day, log fire *(A and B D Craig, David Green)*

Real ale to us means beer which has matured naturally in its cask – not pressurised or filtered. We name all real ales stocked. We usually name ales preserved under a light blanket of carbon dioxide too, though purists – pointing out that this stops the natural yeasts developing – would disagree (most people, including us, can't tell the difference!).

Shropshire

Shropshire is a great county for a good pint: more than half our main entries have our Beer Award. It's also home to some great little brewers. Over a dozen small independent brewers are based here – in rough order of popularity, the main ones are Hobsons, Woods, Three Tuns, Six Bells, Ludlow, Hanby and Salopian, and this year we've also come across Bridgnorth and Corvedale. Pubs here are loyal to their local brewers, so you will certainly find at least some of these, normally at attractive prices. For beer lovers, three rather special pubs are the Three Tuns in Bishop's Castle (for the original Victorian tower brewery across the yard – and have a look at their new dining room), the popular Six Bells in the same town, for the beers brewed by its jovial landlord, and the Church Inn in Ludlow, for its good range of regional beers. For a county with rather fewer main entries than some in the *Guide*, there's been good competition for Shropshire Dining Pub of the Year. Two strong contenders are both in the Brunning & Price group: the cosmopolitan-feeling Armoury in Shrewsbury, and the substantial Fox at Chetwynd Aston. A third, the elegant Inn at Grinshill, is independently owned. All three are on top form these days. The title goes to the Inn at Grinshill – it's very restauranty, and with its carefully prepared food and stylish atmosphere is a fine destination for a special meal out. Though it's far from cheap, its prices are fair for the quality, and it does have good value early bird and lunch deals. Two other pubs deserve special mention this year for their good food: the lively Three Tuns in Bishop's Castle is popular for its tasty generous meals, and the very special Sun at Norbury puts a lot of care into sourcing its sensibly short choice of dishes (but note its limited opening times). In the Lucky Dip section at the end of the chapter, we've noted strong recent support among readers for the Riverside at Cressage, Black Lion in Ellesmere, Bear at Hodnet, Sun at Marton and Stiperstones Inn.

BISHOP'S CASTLE   SO3288   MAP 6
Castle Hotel ⇐
Market Square, just off B4385; SY9 5BN

Substantial coaching inn with bags of old-fashioned charm; bedrooms

One feels part of the long line of travellers to have received hospitality at this pleasantly old-fashioned inn – it has been taking guests since 1719. Neatly kept and attractively furnished, the clubby little beamed and panelled bar, glazed off from the entrance, has a good coal fire, old hunting prints and sturdy leather chairs on its muted carpet. It opens into a much bigger room, with maroon plush wall seats and stools, big Victorian engravings, and another coal fire in an attractive cast-iron fireplace. The lighting in both rooms is gentle and relaxing, and the pub tables have unusually elaborate cast-iron frames; bar billiards and board games. Hobsons Best and local Six Bells Goldings and Big Nevs are well kept on handpump, they've decent wines, and over 30 malt whiskies. The handsome panelled dining room is open in the evening and on Sunday lunchtime. The bedrooms are spacious and full of period character, and the breakfasts are good. In summer the pub is festooned with pretty hanging baskets, and the back garden has terraces with blue chairs on either side of a large formal raised fish pond, pergolas and climbing plants, and stone walls; it looks out over the town rooftops to the surrounding gentle countryside; disabled access.

🍴 **Served in the bar or dining area, enjoyable bar food is made with good quality ingredients. The very short lunchtime menu includes filled baguettes and vegetarian flan, and perhaps steak and kidney pie or chicken curry. The evening menu is a bit more extensive, with lamb samosas with sweet chilli dip, duck breast with orange and redcurrant gravy, rump or fillet steak, and a few specials such as chicken breast wrapped in pancetta and stuffed with garlic cheese, and white wine poached salmon fillet with creamy tarragon and lemon sauce.** *Starters/Snacks: £3.95 to £5.95. Main Courses: £9.50 to £15.95. Puddings: £4.50*

Free house ~ Licensees David and Nicky Simpson ~ Real ale ~ Bar food ~ (01588) 638403 ~ Dogs welcome ~ Open 12-2.30, 6-11(7-10.30 Sun); closed bank hol Mon ~ Bedrooms: £50B/£90S

Recommended by the Didler, Bruce Purvis, Kevin Thorpe, J C Clark, Steven and Victoria James, Richard C Morgan

Six Bells

Church Street; SY9 5AA

Deservedly popular own-brew pub

If the licensee isn't brewing and is behind the bar when you visit this unpretentious inn his is a really cheerful chatty presence – the staff are particularly friendly too. The excellent beers he brews include Big Nevs (most people's favourite), Cloud Nine, Goldings Best and a seasonal brew; they also keep a wide range of country wines. You can arrange a tour of the brewery, and they have a beer festival on the second full weekend in July. The no-frills bar is really quite small, with an assortment of well worn furniture and old local photographs and prints. The second, bigger room has bare boards, some stripped stone, a roaring woodburner in the inglenook, plenty of sociable locals on the benches around plain tables, and lots of board games (you may find people absorbed in Scrabble or darts). The service is very friendly. It can be packed here at the weekend.

🍴 **Good value tasty bar food includes lunchtime soup, sandwiches, ploughman's and quiche, and in the evening there could be sausages and mash, salmon fillet or pork tenderloin with mustard and cider sauce.** *Starters/Snacks: £3.50 to £6.00. Main Courses: £8.00 to £10.00. Puddings: £4.00*

Own brew ~ Licensee Neville Richards ~ Real ale ~ Bar food (12-1.45, 6.30-8.45; not Sun evening or Mon except bank hols) ~ Restaurant ~ No credit cards ~ (01588) 630144 ~ Children welcome ~ Dogs allowed in bar ~ Open 12-2.30, 5-11; 12-11 Sat; 12-3.30, 7-10.30 Sun; closed Mon lunchtime

Recommended by Alan and Eve Harding, Kevin Thorpe, David Field, the Didler, Andrew Stephenson, Steven and Victoria James, Tracey and Stephen Groves, D Hillaby

Three Tuns 🍺

Salop Street; SY9 5BW

Unpretentious own-brew pub scoring well for food as well as beer from its unique four-storey Victorian brewhouse

They've recently modernised the dining room and added a smart new oak and glass dining room here, but left the front bar at this markedly individual pub as characterfully ungimmicky as it's always been. It's genuinely part of the local community – you might chance upon the film club, live jazz, morris dancers, a brass band playing in the garden or the local rugby club enjoying a drink, and in July they hold a popular annual beer festival. They serve four of the excellent beers that are brewed in the Victorian John Roberts brewhouse across the yard from old-fashioned handpumps, always have a farm cider or perry and about eight wines by the glass, and do carry-out kegs. The brewery (which is a separate business) sells beer by the barrel. There are newspapers to read, and a good range of board games.

🍽 **Tasty, and in generous portions, bar food might include starters such as organic smoked salmon with sour cream and salmon roe, baked camembert, chicken satay, main courses such as beef and wild mushroom in beer with root vegetable mash, rump steak burger with tomato and coriander salsa and stir-fried tofu with basil, fennel, ginger and mushrooms.** *Starters/Snacks: £3.75 to £4.95. Main Courses: £5.95 to £11.95. Puddings: £3.95*

Free house ~ Licensee Tim Curtis-Evans ~ Real ale ~ Bar food (12-3, 7-9; not Sun evening) ~ (01588) 638797 ~ Children welcome ~ Dogs allowed in bar ~ Open 12-11

Recommended by Mike and Lynn Robinson, Robert Turnham, Pat and Tony Martin, Andrew Stephenson, David Field, Kevin Thorpe, the Didler, Kerry Law

BROMFIELD   SO4877   MAP 6
Clive ♀ 🛏
A49 2 miles NW of Ludlow; SY8 2JR

Elegant minimalist dining pub with similarly stylish bedrooms

The interior of this sophisticated dining pub has a crisp minimalist look that contrasts pleasingly with its a Georgian brick structure. The focus is on the dining room, with its modern light wood tables. A door leads through into the bar, sparse but neat and welcoming, with round glass tables and metal chairs running down to a sleek bar counter with fresh flowers, newspapers and spotlights. Then it's down a step to the Clive Arms Bar, where traditional features like the huge brick fireplace (with woodburning stove), exposed stonework, and soaring beams and rafters are appealingly juxtaposed with well worn sofas and new glass tables; piped jazz. The good wine list includes several by the glass, and Hobsons Best and a guest such as Ludlow Gold are on handpump; they also have a range of coffees and teas. An attractive secluded terrace has tables under cocktail parasols and a fish pond. They have 15 stylishly modern, good-sized bedrooms, and breakfast is excellent.

🍽 **Besides interestingly filled baguettes and sandwiches, good bar food includes battered cod, ham, egg and chips, sirloin with hand-cut chips, puddings such as white chocolate and orange cheesecake with fig and vanilla jam. There is a longer more elaborate restaurant menu that might include roast duck breast with black treacle and sherry vinegar.** *Starters/Snacks: £3.95 to £7.95. Main Courses: £8.95 to £16.95. Puddings: £4.95 to £5.95*

Free house ~ Licensee Paul Brooks ~ Real ale ~ Bar food (12-3, 6.30-9.30; 12-9.30 Sat, Sun) ~ Restaurant ~ (01584) 856565 ~ Children welcome ~ Open 11-11; 12-10.30 Sun ~ Bedrooms: £60B/£85B

Recommended by P J and R D Greaves, Alan and Eve Harding, L and D Webster, Mike and Mary Carter, Guy Vowles, Ian Phillips, Mr and Mrs W W Burke, Michael Sargent

CARDINGTON   SO5095   MAP 4
Royal Oak
Village signposted off B4371 Church Stretton—Much Wenlock, pub behind church; also reached via narrow lanes from A49; SY6 7JZ

Wonderful rural position, heaps of character inside too

Not much has changed over the centuries at this enjoyable place which is said to be the oldest continually licensed pub in the county. The rambling low-beamed bar has a roaring winter log fire, cauldron, black kettle and pewter jugs in its vast inglenook fireplace, the old standing timbers of a knocked-through wall, and red and green tapestry seats solidly capped in elm; darts and dominoes. A comfortable dining area has exposed old beams and studwork. Hobsons, Wye Valley Butty Bach and a couple of guests such as Flowers Original and Six Bells 1859 are on handpump. This is glorious country for walks, like the one to the summit of Caer Caradoc a couple of miles to the west (ask for directions at the pub), and the front courtyard makes the most of the setting. Dogs are only allowed in the bar when food isn't being served.

🍴 Using seasonal produce such as game and local specialities, bar food from the menu and specials board might include celery and stilton soup, tuna carpaccio with garlic butter, baguettes, ploughman's, moroccan lamb stew, fidget pie, battered cod, salmon fillet with creamy watercress sauce and lentil curry. *Starters/Snacks: £3.50 to £8.50. Main Courses: £7.95 to £15.95. Puddings: £2.50 to £3.95*

Free house ~ Licensees Steve Oldham and Eira Williams ~ Real ale ~ Bar food (not Sun evening) ~ Restaurant ~ (01694) 771266 ~ Children welcome ~ Open 12-2.30(3.30 Sun), 7-midnight(1 Fri, Sat); closed Mon except bank hol lunchtimes

Recommended by MLR, TOH, Tracey and Stephen Groves, Carol and Colin Broadbent, D Hillaby, David Edwards

CHETWYND ASTON   SJ7517   MAP 7

Fox

Village signposted off A41 and A518 just S of Newport; TF10 9LQ

Civilised dining pub with generous food and interesting ales served by ever-attentive staff

This substantial dining pub goes from strength to strength, with readers enthusing about its delicious food and good range of ales, and friendly staff who keep up a high level of service even at busy times. The 1920s building was handsomely done up by Brunning & Price a few of years ago – its style will be familiar to anyone who has tried their other pubs. A series of linked semi-separate areas, one with a broad arched ceiling, has plenty of tables in all shapes and sizes, some quite elegant, and a vaguely matching diversity of comfortable chairs, all laid out in a way that's fine for eating but serves equally well for just drinking and chatting. There are masses of attractive prints, three open fires, a few oriental rugs on polished parquet or boards, some attractive floor tiling; big windows and careful lighting help towards the relaxed and effortless atmosphere. The handsome bar counter, with a decent complement of bar stools, serves an excellent changing range of about a dozen wines by the glass, and Thwaites Original, Woods Shropshire Lad and three or four guests from brewers such as Batemans, Hanby and Woodlands are well kept on handpump. The staff, mainly young, are well trained, cheerful and attentive. Disabled access and facilities are good (no push chairs or baby buggies, though); there is a selection of board games. The spreading garden is quite lovely, with a sunny terrace, picnic-sets tucked into the shade of mature trees and extensive views across quiet country fields.

🍴 Served in generous helpings, well liked food from a changing menu could include sandwiches, ploughman's with local cheeses, sweet potato and coriander soup, waldforf salad, fried scallops with bacon salad, thai noodles and king prawns in a lemon grass and ginger broth, beef and ale pie, vegetable and chickpea tagine with mint couscous, grilled mackerel fillets on chorizo, butterbean and potato cassoulet and sirloin steak, and puddings such as white chocolate, marshmallow and Malteser parfait and baked apple and cinnamon cheesecake. *Starters/Snacks: £4.50 to £8.95. Main Courses: £8.95 to £15.95. Puddings: £4.50 to £5.25*

Brunning & Price ~ Manager Samantha Malloy ~ Real ale ~ Bar food (12-10(9.30 Sun)) ~ (01952) 815940 ~ Children welcome till 7pm ~ Dogs allowed in bar ~ Open 12-11(10.30 Sun)

Recommended by Gary Rollings, Debbie Porter, J S Burn, Alan and Eve Harding, R T and J C Moggridge, Steve Whalley, Leslie and Barbara Owen, Dr Phil Putwain, Mark Blackburn, D Weston, Bruce and Sharon Eden, Dennis Jenkin, Mrs Philippa Wilson, Paul and Margaret Baker, Kevin Thomas, Nina Randall

GRINSHILL   SJ5223   MAP 7

Inn at Grinshill 🍴 ♀ ⛵

Off A49 N of Shrewsbury; SY4 3BL

SHROPSHIRE DINING PUB OF THE YEAR

Looks after its customers admirably: a civilised place to stay or dine

This elegantly refurbished early Georgian country inn enjoys a good reputation for its excellent food (it gains a Food Award this year) and welcoming staff. Hanby Drawwell and three guests from a brewer such as Greene King, John Smiths and Theakstons are on handpump, and they have over a dozen wines by the glass. The smartly comfortable 19th-c bar has an open log fire, while the spacious contemporary main restaurant has a view straight into the kitchen, and doors into the back garden, which is laid out with tables and chairs; TV, piped music, dominoes, and an evening pianist on Friday. Beautifully decorated bedrooms have wide-screen TV and broadband access. Though not at all high, the nearby hill of Grinshill has an astonishingly far-ranging view.

🍴 Prepared with care, the very good (though not cheap) food might include mussels, warm avocado tartlet with balsamic fig and air-dried cumbrian ham, smoked salmon and herb cheese crêpe gateau with tomato, cucumber and horseradish salsa, seared king scallops with black pudding croûte and spiced apple sauce, pea and mushroom fritters with coriander cream sauce, sirloin steak, fish and chips or sausage and mash, puddings such as crème brûlée with shortbread and chocolate truffle torte with chocolate sauce, and a local cheeseboard. They do lunchtime sandwiches, and a good value lunchtime and early bird menu. *Starters/Snacks: £5.25 to £8.00. Main Courses: £10.95 to £17.00. Puddings: £4.95 to £7.50*

Free house ~ Licensees Kevin and Victoria Brazier ~ Real ale ~ Bar food (12-2.30(3 Sun), 6.30-9.30) ~ Restaurant ~ (01939) 220410 ~ Children welcome ~ Dogs welcome ~ Open 11-3, 6-11; 11-11 Sat; 12-4 Sun; closed Sun and bank hol evenings ~ Bedrooms: £60S/£120B

Recommended by Alan and Eve Harding, Ken Marshall, J S Burn, M Thomas, Brian and Diane Mugford, Tom and Jill Jones, Noel Grundy, David Field, Martin Stafford

IRONBRIDGE   SJ6603   MAP 6

Malthouse ♀

The Wharfage (bottom road alongside Severn); TF8 7NH

Right in the heart of the historic Gorge, with pleasantly airy décor and tasty bar food

What with its position right down in the Gorge and hulking great structure, it's still fairly apparent that this imaginatively converted 18th-c building was originally constructed as a malthouse. Tucked down below, the spacious bar is broken up by white-painted iron pillars supporting heavy pine beams. A mix of scrubbed light wooden tables with candles, cream-painted banquettes and bright pictures keeps it feeling light; piped music and TV. Greene King IPA and Scottish Courage Directors are on handpump, and they've a wide choice of wines including several by the glass. The atmosphere is quite different in the restaurant, which has a much more elaborate menu. There are a few tables outside in front by the car park. Note that they may retain your credit card if you eat in the bar. More reports please.

🍴 Appropriately informal, the bar menu includes dishes such as soup, chicken and sausage terrine with beetroot jam, filled baguettes, burgers, chilli, fish and chips, wild mushroom and goats cheese tagliatelle, pork loin stuffed with sun-dried tomato and basil with saffron cream sauce and steaks. *Starters/Snacks: £3.00 to £8.95. Main Courses: £6.95 to £14.95. Puddings: £4.50*

Free house ~ Licensees Alex and Andrea Nicoll ~ Real ale ~ Bar food (12-2.30, 6.30-9.30; 12-8 Sun) ~ Restaurant ~ (01952) 433712 ~ Children welcome ~ Dogs allowed in bar ~ Live music Weds, Sat evenings ~ Open 11-11.30(midnight Sat); 12-11 Sun ~ Bedrooms: £59B/£65B

Recommended by Chris Glasson, Linda Dickins, R T and J C Moggridge

---

Waterside pubs are listed at the back of the book.

LUDLOW

Church Inn 🍺
Church Street, behind Butter Cross; SY8 1AW

Characterful town-centre inn with impressive range of real ales

One reader's report sums this place up so well it's worth quoting: 'yet more fantastic beers, great character, interesting people popping in and out, dog asleep by door, interesting chats about local beers with the staff'. Right in the centre of this handsome country town and behind the ancient Butter Cross, this bustling inn generates a welcoming atmosphere. They serve a great choice of eight well kept real beers including Hobsons Mild and Town Crier, Ludlow Boiling Well and Gold, Weetwood Eastgate and Wye Valley, as well as a couple of guests from brewers such as Blue Bear and Three Tuns; also several malt whiskies and country wines. Appealingly decorated, with comfortable banquettes in cosy alcoves off the island bar, and pews and stripped stonework from the church (part of the bar is a pulpit), the interior is divided into three areas; hops hang from the heavy beams; daily papers and piped music. There are displays of old photographic equipment, plants on windowsills, and church prints in the side room; a long central area with a fine stone fireplace (good winter fires) leads to lavatories. The more basic side bar has old black and white photos of the town. The civilised upstairs lounge has vaulted ceilings and long windows overlooking the church, display cases of glass, china and old bottles, and musical instruments on the walls, along with a mix of new and old pictures. In summer you can get three different types of Pimms, while in winter there's mulled wine and hot toddy, and they do a roaring trade in tea and coffee too. The bedrooms are simple but comfortable; good breakfasts. Car parking is some way off. The landlord (a former mayor of Ludlow) is also the owner of the Charlton Arms, down the hill on Ludford Bridge.

🍴 **Straightforward pubby food includes sandwiches, ludlow sausage baguette, soup, sausage and mash, cod in beer batter, sirloin steak, shropshire pork pies and a changing choice of vegetarian dishes such as quiche.** *Starters/Snacks: £3.70 to £4.50. Main Courses: £7.45 to £10.45. Puddings: £3.95*

Free house ~ Licensee Graham Willson-Lloyd ~ Real ale ~ Bar food (12-2.30(3.30 Sat), 6.30-9; 12-3, 6.30-8.30 Sun) ~ Restaurant ~ (01584) 872174 ~ Children welcome ~ Dogs welcome ~ Open 11-11(midnight Fri, Sat); 12-11 Sun ~ Bedrooms: £40B/£70B

Recommended by Ian Stafford, Kevin Thorpe, Malcolm Pellatt, Pam and John Smith, Paul J Robinshaw, Mr and Mrs W W Burke, Joe Green, Theo, Anne and Jane Gaskin, Dave Braisted, Mike and Lynn Robinson

MUCH WENLOCK

George & Dragon 🍺
High Street (A458); TF13 6AA

Bustling, cosily atmospheric, plenty to look at, good food and usefully open all day

This friendly town-centre local has a fascinating stash of memorabilia. There are old brewery and cigarette advertisements, bottle labels and beer trays, and George-and-the-Dragon pictures, as well as around 500 jugs hanging from the beams. Furnishings such as antique settles are among more conventional seats, and there are a couple of attractive Victorian fireplaces (with coal-effect gas fires). At the back is the restaurant. Black Sheep, Greene King Abbot, Hobsons Town Crier, Shepherd Neame Spitfire and a guest such as Titanic Stout are on handpump, and they also have country wines; piped music and occasional TV for major events.

🍴 **Available in the restaurant or bar, tasty food includes lunchtime sandwiches, soup, fish and chips, faggots and peas and evening dishes such as black pudding with caramelised red cabbage, rack of lamb, thai chicken curry and vegetable lasagne.** *Starters/Snacks: £4.95 to £5.95. Main Courses: £7.95 to £12.95. Puddings: £4.50*

Punch ~ Lease Angela Gray ~ Real ale ~ Bar food (12-2.30, 6-9 (not Weds or Sun evenings)) ~ Restaurant ~ (01952) 727312 ~ Children welcome ~ Dogs allowed in bar ~ Open 11-11(12 Fri); 12-10.30 Sun

Recommended by Jenny and Peter Lowater, Steve Whalley, Pat and Tony Martin, Pete Baker, Alan and Eve Harding, Maurice and Gill McMahon, Paul and Margaret Baker

Talbot 🛏

High Street (A458); TF13 6AA

Ancient building with friendly welcome, tasty food, pretty courtyard, and bedrooms

Doing equally well as the George & Dragon but with the advantage of accommodation, this 14th-c building was once part of Wenlock Abbey, the ruins of which still stand nearby. Its several neatly kept traditional areas (good for both drinkers or diners) have low ceilings, and comfortable red tapestry button-back wall banquettes around their tables. The walls are decorated with local pictures and cottagey plates, and there are art deco-style lamps and gleaming brasses. Bass and a guest such as Woods Beauty are served on handpump, and they've several malt whiskies, and nine wines by the glass; quiet piped music. It also has a little courtyard with green metal and wood garden furniture and pretty flower tubs. There's a cheap car park close by.

🍴 **The lunchtime menu is fairly pubby with soup, stilton and walnut pâté, coquilles st jacques, liver and onions, lamb and leek pie, lasagne, seared halibut with dill seed and lemon zest with prawn and spinach stuffing, smoked haddock and pasta bake and pheasant wrapped in bacon with a creamy whisky sauce.** Starters/Snacks: £4.50 to £6.50. Main Courses: £8.50 to £9.95. Puddings: £4.25

Free house ~ Licensees Mark and Maggie Tennant ~ Real ale ~ Bar food (12-2.30, 6-9 (8.30 Sun)) ~ Restaurant ~ (01952) 727077 ~ Children welcome ~ Open 10(12 Sat)-midnight ~ Bedrooms: £40B/£80B

Recommended by Adrian Johnson, Brian Goodson, John Oates, Denise Walton, R J Herd, Jennifer Banks, Mr and Mrs W W Burke, John Wooll, Alan and Eve Harding, Steve Whalley

MUNSLOW   SO5287   MAP 2

Crown ♀ ◖

B4368 Much Wenlock—Craven Arms; SY7 9ET

Cosy, ancient village inn with local ales, cider, good wines and imaginative food

It's evident that plenty of loving care goes into the running of this fairly traditional former court house. Although it looks Georgian from outside, it feels much more ancient as soon as you step inside. It's full of comfortable corners, and the welcome is particularly warm. The split-level lounge bar has a pleasantly old-fashioned mix of furnishings on its broad flagstones, a collection of old bottles, country pictures, and a bread oven by its good log fire. There are more seats in a traditional snug with its own fire, and the eating area has tables around a central oven chimney, stripped stone walls, and more beams and flagstones; piped music. Three beers on handpump are Holdens Black Country and Golden Glow and Three Tuns XXX, alongside a local farm cider, several malt whiskies and a good wine list. Look out for Jenna, the boxer who usually makes her rounds at the end of the evening. More reports please.

🍴 **The imaginative food is produced with thought – they display a list of their locals suppliers up on the bar wall. As well as lunchtime sandwiches, the changing menu might include butternut risotto with goats cheese and toasted pine nuts, faggots cooked in red wine, madeira and rosemary sauce, lamb tagine, pork and leek sausages in a yorkshire pudding with onion gravy, slow-cooked pork belly with rösti potato, onion marmalade, chorizo and chive cream sauce, and puddings such as warm mincemeat and almond frangipane with vanilla custard, and crème brûlée with caramel glazed pineapple and brandy snap biscuit, and an english and welsh cheese board.** Starters/Snacks: £4.75 to £7.50. Main Courses: £8.95 to £17.95. Puddings: £4.95

Free house ~ Licensees Richard and Jane Arnold ~ Real ale ~ Bar food (12-1.45, 6.45-8.45) ~ Restaurant ~ (01584) 841205 ~ Children welcome ~ Open 12-2.30(3 Sun), 6.45-11; closed Sun evening, Mon ~ Bedrooms: £50S/£70S(£75B)

Recommended by James and Lucinda Woodcock, Alan and Eve Harding, Colin Wood, Julia and Richard Tredgett, Sue Demont, Tim Barrow

NORBURY   SO3692   MAP 6

Sun 🛏

Off A488 or A489 NE of Bishop's Castle; OS Sheet 137 map reference 363928; SY9 5DX

Civilised dining pub with lovely bar and bedrooms, in prime hill-walking country not far from the Stiperstones

Do note the unusual opening times of this delightful little dining pub. Its proper tiled-floor bar has settees and Victorian tables and chairs, cushioned stone seats along the wall by the woodburning stove, and a few mysterious farming implements (the kind that it's fun to guess about) on its neat white walls. The restaurant side has a charming lounge with button-back leather wing chairs, easy chairs and a chesterfield on its deep-pile green carpet, as well as a welcoming log fire, nice lighting, willow-pattern china on a good dark oak dresser, fresh flowers, candles and magazines; service is friendly. Wye Valley Bitter is on handpump under a light blanket pressure, and they have several malts and decent house wines; piped music. It's in a charmingly sleepy village beneath the southern flank of Norbury and has a particularly pretty little rustic garden and pond.

🍽 The bar menu is fairly short but food is carefully sourced and dishes are cooked to order: with baguettes, ploughman's, cumberland sausage and chips, shropshire rump steak, smoked trout and scampi. The elegantly furnished dining room has a very short menu for evening meals and Sunday lunch (booking required) that might include leek and watercress soup, fillet steak with cognac and green pepper sauce and lemon syllabub. *Starters/Snacks: £4.95. Main Courses: £9.75 to £11.75. Puddings: £4.25 to £4.95*

Free house ~ Licensee Carol Cahan ~ Real ale ~ Bar food (7-9 Weds-Sat; 12-2.30 Sun) ~ Restaurant ~ (01588) 650680 ~ Children welcome Sunday lunchtime only; no children in bedrooms ~ Open 7-11; 12-3 Sun; closed lunchtimes (except Sun), Sun evening and all day Mon, Tues ~ Bedrooms: /£90S

Recommended by S J and C C Davidson, M J Daly, Jan and Alan Summers, Susan Batten

PICKLESCOTT   SO4399   MAP 6

Bottle & Glass

Village signposted off A49 N of Church Stretton; SY6 6NR

Remote village pub with a charismatic and hospitable landlord who gets all the details right

This 16th-c pub has a lovely position 1,000 feet above sea level and near the Long Mynd. Remote but surprisingly busy, it's well worth the pilgrimage along tortuous country lanes. It's run by a charismatic, bow-tied landlord who makes things tick along with great aplomb. He works hard to make sure everyone is happy, easily running the bar and striking up conversations with customers – ask him to tell you about the antics of the resident ghost of the former landlord, Victor. Much to the delight surely of the two resident cats, Hello and Cookie, the fire rarely goes out in the small low-beamed and quarry-tiled cosy candlelit bar. The lounge, dining area and library area (for dining or sitting in) have open fires. Beers brewed by Hobsons, Three Tuns and Woods are on handpump; unobtrusive piped classical music. There are picnic-sets in front.

🍽 Very good home-made bar food (promptly served, in hearty helpings) includes sandwiches, soup, ploughman's, roquefort stuffed pear with green mayonnaise, steak, kidney and Guinness pie, fish pie, sausages in red wine and onion gravy, feta and spinach filo pie, and rosemary and garlic-crusted rack of lamb with red wine, honey and redcurrant sauce; very tasty puddings such as sticky toffee pudding or chocolate mint roulade. *Starters/Snacks: £5.50 to £6.50. Main Courses: £8.50 to £17.50. Puddings: £3.50 to £4.50*

Free house ~ Licensees Paul and Jo Stretton-Downes ~ Real ale ~ Bar food (not over the Christmas period) ~ Restaurant ~ (01694) 751345 ~ Children welcome ~ Dogs allowed in bar ~ Open 12-3, 6-midnight; closed Sun evening, Mon

Recommended by Carol and Colin Broadbent, Phil and Jane Hodson, George and Maureen Roby, David Field, Angus and Carol Johnson, Dave Braisted

SHREWSBURY   SJ4812   MAP 6

Armoury
Victoria Quay, Victoria Avenue; SY1 1HH

Smart pub in interestingly converted riverside warehouse, run by friendly and enthusiastic young staff, good food all day

The food, beer and buzzy atmosphere all come in for high praise at this large, airy 18th-c former warehouse. With an initial wow factor, and lit by long runs of big arched windows with views across the broad river, the spacious open-plan interior is light and fresh, but the eclectic décor, furniture layout and lively bustle give a personal feel. Mixed wood tables and chairs are grouped on expanses of stripped wood floors, a display of floor-to-ceiling books dominates two huge walls, there's a grand stone fireplace at one end, and masses of old prints mounted edge to edge on the stripped brick walls. Colonial-style fans whirr away on the ceilings, which are supported by occasional green-painted standing timbers, and small glass cabinets display collections of smoking pipes. The long bar counter has a terrific choice of drinks with up to seven real ales from brewers such as Hanby, Salopian, Three Tuns and Woods well kept on handpump, a great wine list (with 20 by the glass), around 50 malt whiskies, a dozen different gins, lots of rums and vodkas, a variety of brandies, and some unusual liqueurs. Tables at one end are laid out for eating. The massive uniform red brick exteriors are interspersed with hanging baskets and smart coach lights at the front, and there may be queues at the weekend. The pub doesn't have its own parking, but there are plenty of places nearby.

🍴 Superbly cooked bar food, from an interesting daily changing (and fairly priced) menu, could include sandwiches, ploughman's, spiced parsnip and apple soup, smoked haddock and salmon fishcake with tomato and onion salad, vegetarian moussaka, braised lamb shoulder with champ and cabbage, steamed salmon with olives, fennel and pesto, pork chop with sweet potato wedges and pear chutney; puddings might feature sticky toffee pudding with toffee sauce, banana split and blueberry pancakes with maple syrup. *Starters/Snacks: £4.25 to £7.95. Main Courses: £7.95 to £16.95. Puddings: £3.95 to £5.50*

Brunning & Price ~ Manager Angharad Williams ~ Real ale ~ Bar food (12-9.30) ~ (01743) 340525 ~ Children welcome till 7pm ~ Dogs allowed in bar ~ Open 12-11(10.30 Sun)

Recommended by Richard C Morgan, Steve Whalley, P Dawn, Kerry Law, Mrs Hazel Rainer, Gerry and Rosemary Dobson, Steve and Liz Tilley

LUCKY DIP

Besides the fully inspected pubs, you might like to try these Lucky Dips recommended to us and described by readers (if you do, please send us reports: feedback@thegoodpubguide.co.uk).

ADMASTON [SJ6313]
Pheasant TF5 0AD [Shawbirch Rd]: Newish owners producing enjoyable food at reasonable prices, pleasant staff, real ales such as Greene King, Sadlers and Salopian *(Anne Wileman)*
ASH [SJ5739]
White Lion SY13 4DR: Two-room village pub with cheerful character landlord and good service, enjoyable evening food (and Sun lunch) inc landlady's german specialities, Sat lunchtime snacks, well kept Bass, Timothy Taylors Landlord, Worthington and a summer guest beer, blazing log fires *(Alan and Eve Harding)*
ASTON MUNSLOW [SO5187]
Swan SY7 9ER: Ancient pub with several rambling linked areas in varying styles, good friendly service, good choice of food inc good value dining-room lunches, well kept

Hobsons, fairly priced wines, log fires; garden with shady areas *(Alan and Eve Harding)*
ASTON ON CLUN [SO3981]
Kangaroo SY7 8EW [Clun Rd]: Open-plan country pub with limited good value bar lunches inc notable ploughman's, wider evening choice, four well kept ales inc one brewed for them by Six Bells, friendly service, central log fire, front public bar with railway memorabilia inc large model train, little side dining room; games machine; large back garden, interesting village below Hopesay Hill, open all day Fri-Sun *(Alan and Eve Harding, Robert W Buckle)*
BIRDSGREEN [SO7785]
Royal Oak WV15 6LL [A442 Kidderminster—Bridgnorth]: Pleasant main-road pub with good value food in bar and restaurant extension, Banks's and Sadlers Windsor Castle ales; garden behind *(Dave Braisted)*

BISHOP'S CASTLE [SO3288]
Boars Head SY9 5AE [Church St]:
Comfortable beamed and stripped-stone bar
with well made wall benches around pleasant
tables, big log fire, welcoming young staff,
well kept Weetwood, good value pubby food
(all day in summer); four good roomy high-
raftered bedrooms in converted barn
(Alan and Eve Harding)

BRIDGES [SO3996]
☆ *Horseshoe* SY5 0ST [nr Ratlinghope]: Down
to earth yet comfortable, with light oak
beams, woodburners and lots of rustic
bygones, three local real ales, small dining
room, bar food (not Sun evening) inc Weds
bargain supper, frequent live music; piped
music, no credit cards; children and dogs
welcome, tables out by the little River Onny,
bedrooms, open all day (may cl Sun evening)
(Chris Flynn, Wendy Jones, J S Burn)

BRIDGNORTH [SO6890]
☆ *Down* WV16 6UA [The Down, Ludlow Rd,
3 miles S]: Attractive old stone-built pub
overlooking rolling countryside, good value
food inc good carvery and vegetarian choice,
good cheerful service even when busy, local
real ales inc one brewed for the pub by
Three Tuns *(Alan and Eve Harding,
Jennifer Banks, Mr and Mrs F E Boxell)*
Friars WV16 4DW [St Marys St, Central Ct
(down passage from High St)]: Homely town
pub in quaint location in sheltered courtyard
of half-timbered buildings, well kept ales inc
local Bridgnorth, cheerful service, good
value simple bar lunches, good coffee; piped
music; bedrooms, open all day wknds and
summer *(George Atkinson)*
Old Castle WV16 4AB [West Castle St]:
Dating from 14th c, newish landlord putting
more emphasis on food, real ales such as
Caledonian Deuchars IPA, friendly efficient
service; good-sized garden overlooking town,
may be bouncy castle in summer
(Karl Becker)
☆ *Railwaymans Arms* WV16 5DT [Severn Valley
Stn, Hollybush Rd (off A458 towards
Stourbridge)]: Bathams, Hobsons and other
good value local ales kept well in chatty old-
fashioned converted waiting-room at Severn
Valley steam railway terminus, bustling on
summer days, with coal fire, station
nameplates, superb mirror over fireplace,
may be simple summer snacks; children
welcome, wheelchair access, tables out on
platform – the train to Kidderminster
(another bar there) has an all-day bar and
bookable Sun lunches *(the Didler, Joe Green,
Kerry Law, LYM, Ian Stafford)*

BROOME [SO4081]
Engine & Tender SY7 0NT: One or two well
kept local ales from simple bar's art deco
servery, larger lounge with cosy eating areas
and sizeable dining room with interesting
teapots and shelves of jugs, good pubby
food (not Mon) inc Thurs OAP lunch,
generous Sun roast and good puddings,
good value wines, cheerful helpful
unhurried service, railway memorabilia

and other bric-a-brac, lushly planted
conservatory, games room with pool and
glassed-over well; tables out under cover,
well equipped caravan site, nice countryside
(MLR)

BUCKNELL [SO3574]
Baron of Beef SY7 0AH [Chapel Lawn Rd;
just off B4367 Knighton Rd]: Rather smart
dining pub, friendly efficient staff, well kept
ales inc Hobsons and Wye Valley, farm cider,
decent house wines, big log fire in front bar,
back dining lounge/garden room, interesting
prints, rustic memorabilia inc grindstone and
cider press, largish upstairs restaurant with
own bar and popular wknd carvery; wknd live
music; well behaved children and dogs
welcome, lovely views, big garden with
skittles and play area, camping field *(MLR,
Alan and Eve Harding)*

BURLTON [SJ4526]
☆ *Burlton Inn* SY4 5TB [A528 Shrewsbury—
Ellesmere, nr B4397 junction]: Attractively
refurbished old pub with friendly new
landlord, wide food choice at well spaced
tables, Robinsons ales, sporting prints, log
fires, comfortable snug, restaurant with
garden dining room; children welcome,
disabled facilities, garden with pleasant
terrace, bedrooms, good breakfast *(LYM,
Noel Grundy, Mrs Jane Kingsbury, Alan and
Eve Harding, Bruce and Sharon Eden)*

CLUN [SO3080]
☆ *White Horse* SY7 8JA [The Square]: Recently
refurbished pub dating from 18th c, helpful
cheerful staff, generous good value food inc
old-fashioned casseroles and lunchtime
cheese-cookery specialities, half a dozen
well priced changing ales such as Hobsons,
Salopian, Six Bells and Wye Valley, Weston's
farm cider, good coffee, daily papers, low
beams, inglenook and open woodburner,
country bric-a-brac, pool and juke box in
panelled games end; children welcome, front
pavement tables, small back garden, freshly
renovated bedrooms, open all day *(Alan and
Eve Harding, Peter and Sheila Longland, MLR)*

CLUNTON [SO3381]
Crown SY7 0HU: Cosy old country local with
welcoming landlady and good-humoured
service (even just after the 2007 floods),
good changing ales such as Hobsons and Six
Bells, good value wines by the glass, log fire
in small flagstoned bar, dining room with
good choice of popular food inc Sun lunch,
small games room *(A N Bance, Alan and
Eve Harding)*

COALBROOKDALE [SJ6604]
☆ *Coalbrookdale Inn* TF8 7DX [Wellington Rd,
opp Museum of Iron]: Handsome dark brick
18th-c pub with half a dozen quickly
changing ales from square counter in simple
convivial tiled-floor bar, good sensibly priced
food cooked to order using local produce
here or in quieter dining room, farm ciders,
country wines, good log fire, local pictures,
piano, naughty beach murals in lavatories;
long flight of steps to entrance; dogs
welcome, a few tables outside, comfortable

well equipped bedrooms *(Warren Marsh, the Didler, BB, DC)*

CORFTON [SO4985]

☆ *Sun* SY7 9DF [B4368 Much Wenlock—Craven Arms]: Very welcoming chatty landlord (if he's not busy in the back brewery) in unsmart two-bar country local with its own good unfined Corvedale ales and a guest beer, lots of breweriana, public bar with internet access as well as darts and pool, good value pubby food from generous baguettes to bargain Sun lunch (service can slow if busy), dining room with covered well, tourist information; piped music; particularly good disabled access throughout, tables on terrace and in good-sized garden with good play area *(MLR, BB, Carol and Colin Broadbent)*

CRESSAGE [SJ5704]

☆ *Riverside* SY5 6AF [A458 NW, nr Cound]: Spacious pub/hotel, neat, light and airy, with limited choice of enjoyable food inc lunchtime baguettes (and their own free range eggs), reasonable prices, unrushed service, good value wines by the glass, well kept changing ales inc Salopian, lovely Severn views from roomy conservatory; dogs welcome in public bar, big terraced garden with wandering rare-breed chickens, comfortable bedrooms, good breakfast, open all day wknds *(John Oates, Denise Walton, Neil and Brenda Skidmore, Bob and Val Collman, D Hillaby, Dennis Jenkin, LYM, Mr and Mrs M Sykes)*

DORRINGTON [SJ4703]

Bridge Inn SY5 7ED [A49 N]: Attractively refurbished streamside pub with bargain lunches Mon-Sat inc choice of roasts, Sun carvery lunch too, settees and armchairs as well as plenty of tables and chairs in roomy lounge bar, well spaced tables in conservatory restaurant; tables outside, caravan spaces in paddock behind *(TOH)*

ELLESMERE [SJ3934]

☆ *Black Lion* SY12 0EG [Scotland St; back car park on A495]: Good simple substantial food at bargain prices, helpful enthusiastic staff, relaxed beamed bar with interesting décor and some nice unusual features such as the traditional wood-and-glass screen along its tiled entrance corridor, quiet and comfortable roomy dining room; piped music; bedrooms, handy car park, not far from canal wharf *(A Darroch Harkness, Adrian Johnson, Meg and Colin Hamilton, BB, Rita and Keith Pollard, D Hillaby)*

GRINDLEY BROOK [SJ5242]

Horse & Jockey SY13 4QJ [A41]: Enjoyable food (all day wknds) inc good value Sun lunch, good friendly service, well kept Black Sheep; handy for Sandstone Trail and Llangollen Canal *(Alan and Eve Harding)*

HADNALL [SJ5219]

New Inn SY4 4AE [A49 6 miles N of Shrewsbury]: Enjoyable pubby food, well kept Marstons Pedigree and friendly service in newly refurbished pub *(Alan and Eve Harding)*

Saracens Head SY4 4AG [A49 6 miles N of Shrewsbury]: Snug and friendly, with interesting old photographs, enjoyable changing food inc midweek lunch deals, good service and wine choice, Marstons ales, restaurant with feature well *(Alan and Eve Harding)*

HINDFORD [SJ3333]

Jack Mytton SY11 4NL: Enjoyable food from bar snacks up, good atmosphere, good choice of changing real ales, pleasant rustic bar with log fire, airy raftered dining room; picnic-sets in attractive garden by Llangollen Canal, good-sized courtyard with carved bear and summer bar, moorings *(Meg and Colin Hamilton)*

HINSTOCK [SJ6927]

Falcon TF9 2TA [just off A41 9 miles N of Newport; Wood Lane]: Friendly traditional beamed local with Salopian and interesting guest beers, Stowford Press cider, decent wines and malt whiskies, enjoyable food from generous open sandwiches up in open-plan bar and separate dining room, settles and other dark wood furniture, log fire, board games; TV *(Richard and Jean Phillips)*

HODNET [SJ6128]

☆ *Bear* TF9 3NH [Drayton Rd (A53)]: Under new management, with friendly efficient service, good fairly priced food, four well kept ales inc Woods Shropshire Lad, good wines by the glass, rambling open-plan carpeted main area with blond seats and tables, snug end alcoves with heavy 16th-c beams and timbers, small beamed quarry-tiled bar with log fire; children welcome, six good value bedrooms, opp Hodnet Hall gardens and handy for Hawkstone Park, open all day *(Bob and Margaret Holder, BB, Alan and Eve Harding)*

HOPTON WAFERS [SO6376]

☆ *Crown* DY14 0NB [A4117]: Attractive 16th-c beamed and creeper-covered inn with relaxed atmosphere and cheerful staff, enjoyable food (all day Sun) from home-baked bread up, big inglenook, light and comfortable décor and furnishings, well kept ales inc Hobsons and Ludlow, good choice of wines; children and dogs welcome, pretty bedrooms, inviting garden with duck pond, stream and terraces, open all day *(Lynda and Trevor Smith, K S Whittaker, Mrs A J Evans, Alan and Eve Harding, LYM, Julian Saunders, Mike and Lynn Robinson)*

IRONBRIDGE [SJ6703]

Horse & Jockey TF8 7PD [Jockey Bank, off Madeley rd]: Good value home cooking inc real steak and kidney pie and good steaks, cheerful staff, thriving atmosphere, well kept ales such as Salopian; open during meal times only, best to book evenings *(Alan and Eve Harding)*

Robin Hood TF8 7HQ [Waterloo St]: Severnside pub with five comfortable linked rooms, various alcoves inc barrel-vaulted dining room, well kept Holdens, lots of brass and old clocks; attractive seating area out in front, nice setting handy for museums, bedrooms, good breakfast *(Adrian Johnson)*

KNOCKIN [SJ3322]

Bradford Arms SY10 8HJ [B4396 NW of Shrewsbury]: Neatly kept unpretentious modernised pub, bargain generous bar food from baguettes up, well kept Banks's, good sensibly priced wine range, interesting RAF prints *(Dave Braisted)*

LEEBOTWOOD [SO4798]

☆ *Pound* SY6 6ND [A49 Church Stretton—Shrewsbury]: Smartly modernised dining pub in thatched 16th-c building, good food inc interesting dishes as well as ham and eggs and so forth, pleasant staff, Fullers London Pride and Greene King IPA or Abbot, decent wines by the glass; garden tables *(Carol and Colin Broadbent, Pat Crabb, BB)*

LITTLE STRETTON [SO4492]

☆ *Ragleth* SY6 6RB [off A49; Ludlow Rd]: New licensee in nicely opened up and refurbished 17th-c pub with light wood old tables and chairs in airy bay-windowed front bar, heavily beamed brick-and-tile-floored public bar with huge inglenook, home-made food from bar snacks to full meals, real ales, darts, board games; piped music; tulip-tree by lawn looking across to thatched and timbered church, good play area, open all day summer wknds *(LYM)*

LONGVILLE [SO5393]

☆ *Longville Arms* TF13 6DT [B4371 Church Stretton—Much Wenlock]: Two neat and spacious bars with beams, stripped stone and some oak panelling, good service, real ales inc Woods, decent food in bar and large comfortable restaurant, games room with darts and pool; piped music; disabled facilities, children and dogs welcome, terraced side garden with good play area, lovely countryside, bedrooms, open all day wknds *(TOH, LYM)*

LOPPINGTON [SJ4729]

Dickin Arms SY4 5SR [B4397]: Cheerful two-bar country local, comfortably plush banquettes, shallow steps to neat back dining room with good value food inc lunchtime deals, well kept Bass and an interesting guest beer, open fire; play area, pretty village *(Alan and Eve Harding, BB)*

LUDLOW [SO5174]

Blue Boar SY8 1BB [Mill St]: Big rambling pub, lots of linked areas, old-world décor with woodwork, old prints and notices, country bygones and boar memorabilia, cheerful efficient service, bargain food from lunchtime sandwiches up, well kept Black Sheep; piped music, TVs, popular with younger people; lovely back suntrap courtyard with tables under parasols, big bedrooms, open all day *(Alan and Eve Braisted, Dave Braisted)*

Charlton Arms SY8 1PJ [Ludford Bridge]: Former coaching inn in great spot overlooking River Teme and the town, cheerful efficient service, good choice of real ales inc local Ludlow Gold, limited range of enjoyable food, two comfortable and attractively refurbished bars; waterside

garden and terrace, bedrooms (may be traffic noise), open all day *(Joe Green, Alan and Eve Harding)*

Feathers SY8 1AA [Bull Ring]: Superb timbered building with Jacobean panelling and carving, and fine period furnishings inc charming ancient sitting room for coffee, though for a bar snack (inc good sandwiches) you'll probably be diverted to a less distinguished side café-bar, which has Woods real ale; good parking, lift to comfortable bedrooms, not cheap *(Hugh Tattersall, David and Ros Hanley, the Didler, LYM)*

Globe SY8 1BP [Market St]: Friendly town pub with good service, pleasant bar dining area, good value thai restaurant; terrace *(Alan and Eve Harding)*

Old Bull Ring Tavern SY8 1AB [Bull Ring]: Striking timbered building run well by friendly family, home-made food inc great pies and roasts, good sandwiches too, real ales, upstairs restaurant; children welcome, terrace tables *(Joe Green)*

Unicorn SY8 1DU [Corve St, bottom end]: Small 17th-c coaching inn, its low-beamed and partly panelled bar restored after flooding, good food using local produce, real ales such as Bass, Black Sheep and Wye Valley; children and dogs welcome, terrace among willows by river, open all day wknds *(Joe Green, LYM)*

Wheatsheaf SY8 1PQ [Lower Broad St]: Traditional 17th-c beamed pub spectacularly built into medieval town gate, good value generous pubby food, Sun carvery, efficient cheerful staff, well kept Marstons and related ales; attractive comfortable bedrooms *(Alan and Eve Harding, Dr and Mrs Jackson)*

MARTON [SJ2802]

☆ *Sun* SY21 8JP [B4386 NE of Chirbury]: Proper village pub with welcoming efficient service, enjoyable pubby food, well kept Banks's and Hobsons at good prices, decent wines by the glass, locals playing dominoes; also separate more contemporary restaurant with good serious cooking and good choice of reasonably priced wines – best to book evenings *(Alan and Eve Harding, William Ruxton)*

NEWPORT [SJ7516]

Fox TF10 9LQ: Large 1920s pub now owned by Brunning & Price, different areas around central bar inc room with unusual barrel-vaulted ceiling, wood floors and rugs, panelled dado, open fires, mix of old tables and chairs, masses of pictures, interesting food from sandwiches up, changing ales from small brewers; terrace, garden and paddock – good for families in summer *(Dr Phil Putwain)*

NORTON [SJ7200]

☆ *Hundred House* TF11 9EE [A442 Telford—Bridgnorth]: Neatly kept bar with appealing gothic décor, Highgate and a Bitter and Mild brewed to the pub's recipes, good wine choice, enjoyable food in bar and two tucked-away dining areas inc two-course deals, log fires in handsome old fireplaces or working coalbrookdale ranges, good service; piped music; lovely garden (sell seeds for charity), comfortable and individual bedrooms *(Maurice and Gill McMahon, Mr and Mrs M Stratton, Tracey and Stephen Groves, Alan and Eve Harding, LYM, John Silverman)*

SHIFNAL [SJ7407]

Odfellows TF11 9AU [Market Pl]: Friendly bistro-style pub with wide range of interesting sensibly priced food in four linked rooms, well kept ales such as Holdens, Salopian and Wye Valley, good wine choice, foreign lagers, large unusual conservatory; tables outside, seven bedrooms, open all day *(Trevor and Sheila Sharman)*

Wheatsheaf TF11 8BB [Broadway]: Friendly pub with oak beams and original wooden partitioning, open fires, good value pubby food, well kept Banks's, traditional games; sports TV; open all day *(Alan and Eve Harding)*

SHREWSBURY [SO4912]

Coach & Horses SY1 1NF [Swan Hill/Cross Hill]: Friendly old-fashioned Victorian local, panelled throughout, with main bar, cosy little side room and back dining room, good value fresh food inc daily roast and some unusual dishes, Bass, Goodalls Gold (brewed for pub by Salopian) and a guest beer, relaxed atmosphere, prompt helpful service even when busy, interesting prints; pretty flower boxes outside, open all day *(Alan and Eve Harding, Joe Green, P Dawn, Pete Baker, the Didler)*

Cromwells SY1 1EN [Dogpole]: Warm, cosy and friendly, with good value fresh food from baguettes to inventive puddings in smallish dim-lit bar and attractive panelled restaurant, well kept ales inc Hobsons and Woods, good house wines, cheerful efficient service; well chosen piped music; raised garden and attractive heated terrace behind, six nice bedrooms, good breakfast, open all day Sat *(Alan and Eve Harding)*

Golden Cross SY1 1LP [Princess St]: Attractive partly Tudor hotel with restaurant and quiet bar, welcoming attentive service, short choice of good interesting food inc home-baked bread and midweek lunch deals, good range of wines by the glass, well kept ales such as Banks's and Salopian, pleasant helpful staff; four good value bedrooms *(Alan and Eve Harding)*

☆ *Loggerheads* SY1 1UG [Church St]: Chatty old-fashioned local, panelled back room with flagstones, scrubbed-top tables, high-backed settles and coal fire, three other rooms with lots of prints, flagstones and bare boards, quaint linking corridor and hatch service of Banks's Bitter and Mild and other Marstons-related ales, exemplary bar staff, bargain lunchtime food (not Sun); darts, dominoes, poetry society, occasional live music; open all day *(Pete Baker, Joe Green, P Dawn, the Didler)*

Old Bucks Head SY3 8JR [Frankwell]: Quietly placed old pub with traditional bar and

restaurant, cheerful staff, broad choice of enjoyable pubby food inc bargain Sun lunch, well kept Salopian; garden with sun deck, ten bedrooms, open all day Sat *(Alan and Eve Harding)*

Prince of Wales SY3 7NZ [Bynner St]: Popular for its half-dozen well kept changing ales inc Ansells Mild, Greene King IPA and St Austell Tribute, Weston's farm cider and cheap cheerful bar lunches; terrace tables, bowling green, open all day Fri-Sun, cl Mon/Tues lunchtimes in winter *(Jim Elliott)*

STIPERSTONES [SJ3600]

☆ *Stiperstones Inn* SY5 0LZ [signed off A488 S of Minsterley; OS Sheet 126 map ref 364005]: Great value simple fresh food all day in warm-hearted walkers' pub (they sell maps) with Six Bells or Woods Parish, small modernised lounge bar, comfortable leatherette wall banquettes, lots of brassware on ply-panelled walls, good value wine, real fire, darts in plainer public bar, restaurant; tables outside, cheap bedrooms (small dogs welcome), good breakfast *(Bruce and Sharon Eden, Jeff Davies, BB)*

STREET DINAS [SJ3338]

Greyhound SY11 3HD [B5069 St Martin's—Oswestry]: Unpretentious comfort, with profuse décor of pictures, interesting Ifton colliery memorabilia, hundreds of beer bottles and whisky miniatures, chamber-pots hanging from beams, welcoming landlady, Banks's Best and Greene King Old Speckled Hen, good value food (not Mon) from good baguettes up, dining room, back pool table; big-screen TV; disabled access, tables in individualistic garden with water features, Reliant Robin as a sort of sculpture *(Michael and Jenny Back, Jeremy King)*

UPPER AFFCOT [SO4486]

Travellers Rest SY6 6RL [A49 S of Church Stretton]: Spacious and comfortable, with enjoyable standard food inc good value carvery, four well kept ales inc Ludlow, decent wines, friendly service, carpeted conservatory extension; children and dogs welcome, four ground-floor bedrooms *(Alan and Eve Harding)*

WELLINGTON [SJ6410]

Wickets TF1 2EB [Holyhead Rd]: Light modern refurbishment but keeping some interesting memorabilia dating from World War I, generous good value food from snacks up, Greene King Old Speckled Hen and Wells & Youngs Bombardier, good seating in tiled bar, dining area *(David Field, Gill and Keith Croxton)*

WENTNOR [SO3892]

☆ *Crown* SY9 5EE [off A489]: Popular dining pub dating from 16th c, quick friendly service, good value pubby food, real ales such as Greene King Old Speckled Hen, Hobsons Best, John Roberts XXX and Woods Shropshire Lad, decent wines, good choice of malt whiskies, warm log fires, daily papers, dominoes and cribbage, big restaurant; terrace tables, bedrooms, open all day wknds *(LYM, Phil and Jane Hodson, Julia and Richard Tredgett, Jan and Alan Summers)*

WHITCHURCH [SJ5441]
Horse & Jockey SY13 1LB [Church St]: Three or four cosy and comfortable dining areas with good value food, friendly attentive service, well kept Black Sheep *(Alan and Eve Harding)*

WHITTINGTON [SJ3231]
White Lion SY11 4DF [Castle St]: Sizeable nicely refurbished pub just below castle, good value food, lots of cheerful young staff, Bass and Wells & Youngs Bombardier, good wines by the glass, light wood tables in front bar, smaller area with leather sofas, dining room and conservatory beyond; plenty of tables in good outdoor area *(Alan and Eve Harding, Jeremy King, Jill Sparrow)*

WOORE [SJ7342]
Falcon CW3 9SE [The Square (A51)]: Refurbished as comfortable dining pub with sensible tables, enjoyable food inc good starters, well kept Marstons-related ales, lots of flowers inside and out; nr Bridgemere Garden World *(Paul and Gail Betteley)*

Post Office address codings confusingly give the impression that some pubs are in Shropshire, when they're really in Cheshire (which is where we list them).

Somerset

This chapter includes Bristol, as well as Bath. More than one-third of our main entries here hold one of our Food Awards, and all of these are keen to support local producers – especially fishermen and gamekeepers (rabbit, pheasant and venison feature strongly on many menus). Local beers, ciders and fruit juices abound too, one main entry even makes its own cider. And, as we mentioned last year, the pubs in this large county have plenty of genuine individuality and character, with a loyal regular following – though all are welcoming to visitors as well. We are pleased with the new entries, all quite different to each other, that we've found this year. These are the New Inn at Blagdon (popular with older lunchers for its good value food), the Albion in Bristol (in Clifton – chatty and relaxed, with good modern cooking), the White Hart in Congresbury (they have three dozen different gins – though that's certainly not their only claim for inclusion), the Rock at Waterrow (its mother and son team produce a civilised but informal atmosphere and bistro-style food), and the Farmers at West Hatch (attractively decorated spreading rooms, with a good choice of drinks and interesting food). Other pubs which have been bringing particular pleasure to readers recently are the Square & Compass at Ashill (a traditional little pub with hard-working licensees), the Red Lion at Babcary (a smashing all-rounder), the Old Green Tree in Bath (even when crowded, it stays a favourite), the Cat Head at Chiselborough (a degree of sophistication nicely balanced against a village pub atmosphere), the Crown at Churchill (up to ten real ales, with a really friendly landlord), the George in Croscombe (the Canadian landlord is refreshingly welcoming, and there are lots of homely knick-knacks), the tiny Tuckers Grave at Faulkland (quite unspoilt), the Lord Poulett Arms at Hinton St George (fine antiques, and a relaxed but civilised feel), the Royal Oak at Luxborough (a lively mix of locals and visitors, comfortable bedrooms), the Halfway House at Pitney (doing very well, and with ten real ales), and the Carpenters Arms at Stanton Wick (very well run and neatly kept, with quickly served imaginative food). Many of these are Food Award holders, but one shines out and is our Somerset Dining Pub of the Year – it is the Lord Poulett Arms at Hinton St George. The Lucky Dip section at the end of the chapter is a particularly strong one – this is yet another county where we really wish we had space in the *Guide* for extra main entries. Pubs we'd shortlist for that are the Ring o' Bells at Ashcott, Coeur de Lion and George in Bath, White Horse at Bradford-on-Tone, Commercial Rooms and Kings Head in Bristol, Crown at Catcott, Carew Arms at Crowcombe, Luttrell Arms in Dunster, Inn at Freshford, Holcombe Inn, Hope & Anchor at Midford, Globe at Newton St Loe, Priory at Portbury, Pack Horse at South Stoke, Lowtrow Cross Inn at Upton, Vobster Inn, Pub at Wanstrow, Slab House at West Horrington, Royal Oak at Winsford and Seymour Arms at Witham Friary. This is also a remarkable area for interesting local beers. Much the most widely available is Butcombe. Other very popular local ales are Exmoor, Cotleigh,

Bath, RCH, Cheddar, Cottage, Blindmans, Bristol and Abbey; other names to look out for are Glastonbury, Matthews, Moor, Masters, Newmans, Dunkery, Milk Street, Taunton Vale and Yeovil.

APPLEY   ST0721   MAP 1

Globe 🍴

Hamlet signposted from the network of back roads between A361 and A38, W of B3187 and W of Milverton and Wellington; OS Sheet 181 map reference 072215; TA21 OHJ

Friendly new licensee for bustling country pub, tasty food, real ales, and seats in garden

A friendly new licensee has taken over this 15th-c pub and there's a happy mix of both locals and visitors. The simple beamed front room has a built-in settle and bare wood tables on the brick floor, and another room has a GWR bench and 1930s railway posters; there's a further room with easy chairs and other more traditional ones, open fires, a growing collection of musical posters and instruments, and art deco items and *Titanic* pictures; skittle alley. A brick entry corridor leads to a serving hatch with Masters Appley Ale and Sharps Doom Bar on handpump. There are seats outside in the garden; the path opposite leads eventually to the River Tone.

🍴 **Bar food now includes lunchtime filled baguettes, spicy vegetable chilli, pasta of the day, beef in Guinness stew, and goats cheese and red onion marmalade salad, as well as soup, king prawns in garlic butter, smoked mackerel pâté, chicken, leek and mushroom pie, grilled lamb steak with an aubergine, courgette and red pepper ratatouille, pork chops with garlic oil, rosemary and cannellini beans, and puddings such as chocolate and walnut brownie with vanilla ice-cream and lemon tart.** *Starters/Snacks: £2.95 to £6.95. Main Courses: £7.50 to £15.95. Puddings: £4.95 to £5.25*

Free house ~ Licensee LeBurn Maddox ~ Real ale ~ Bar food (11-2, 7-9.30) ~ Restaurant ~ (01823) 672327 ~ Children welcome ~ Open 11-3, 6.30-11.30; 12-3, 7-10.30 Sun; closed Mon except bank hols, and 25 and 26 Dec

Recommended by Bob and Margaret Holder, MB, the Didler, Dr and Mrs C W Thomas, Peter John West, Sara Fulton, Roger Baker

ASHILL   ST3116   MAP 1

Square & Compass

Windmill Hill; off A358 between Ilminster and Taunton; up Wood Road for 1 mile behind Stewley Cross service station; OS Sheet 193 map reference 310166; TA19 9NX

Friendly simple pub with local ales, tasty food and good regular live music in sound-proofed barn

Much enjoyed by our readers, this is a traditional pub with genuinely welcoming licensees and a nice mix of friendly customers. The sweeping views over the rolling pastures around Neroche Forest can be enjoyed from the upholstered window seats in the little bar, and there are other seats, an open winter fire – and perhaps the pub cat, Lilly. Exmoor Ale and Otter Bitter on handpump and good house wines by the glass. The piped music is often classical. There's a garden with picnic-sets, a large glass-covered walled terrace, and good regular live music in their sound-proofed Barn.

🍴 **Generously served bar food includes sandwiches, filled baguettes and baked potatoes, ploughman's, soup, hot garlic king prawns, fried brie, local sausages with onion gravy, ham and egg, mushroom stroganoff, sweet and sour pork, chicken curry, lambs kidneys braised with sherry and dijon mustard, mixed grill, and puddings such as banoffi pie or chocolate fudge cake; Sunday roasts.** *Starters/Snacks: £3.95 to £5.50. Main Courses: £6.50 to £14.00. Puddings: £4.00*

Free house ~ Licensees Chris, Janet and Beth Slow ~ Real ale ~ Bar food (not Tues, Weds or Thurs lunchtimes) ~ Restaurant ~ (01823) 480467 ~ Children welcome ~ Dogs welcome ~ Monthly live music in separate barn ~ Open 12-2.30, 6.30(7 Sun)-11; closed Tues, Weds and Thurs lunchtimes

Recommended by Kieran Charles-Neale, M Jav, Nick Hawksley

BABCARY   ST5628   MAP 2

Red Lion 🍽 �ီ

Off A37 south of Shepton Mallett; 2 miles or so north of roundabout where A37 meets A303 and A372; TA11 7ED

Relaxed, friendly thatched pub with interesting food, local beers and comfortable rambling rooms

Convenient for A303 travellers, this is a well run golden stone thatched pub with welcoming staff and very good food. Several distinct areas work their way around the carefully refurbished bar. To the left of the entrance is a longish room with dark pink walls, a squashy leather sofa and two housekeeper's chairs around a low table by the woodburning stove and a few well spaced tables and captain's chairs including a big one in a bay window with built-in seats. There are elegant rustic wall lights, some clay pipes in a cabinet, and local papers to read; board games and gardening magazines too. Leading off here, with lovely dark flagstones, is a more dimly lit public bar area with a panelled dado, a high-backed old settle other more straightforward chairs; darts, board games and bar billiards. The good-sized smart dining room has a large stone lion's head on a plinth above the open fire (with a huge stack of logs to one side), a big rug on polished boards, and properly set tables. Otter Bright, Teignworthy Reel Ale, and a changing ale from Glastonbury on handpump, around ten wines by the glass, and a few malt whiskies. There's a long informal garden with picnic-sets and a play area with slide for children.

🍽 **Good bar food includes sandwiches, soup, salmon fishcake with citrus butter, crispy beef with angel hair noodles and chilli jam, honey-glazed ham with poached egg, fried egg and chips, mussels steamed with shallots, white wine and cream, herbed ricotta rigatoni, kalamata olives, black grapes and parmesan, chicken breast, roast mediterranean vegetables, sherry and wild mushroom cream sauce, steak and Guinness pie, grilled pork chop with courgette relish and caramelised apple sauce, and puddings such as Tia Maria tiramisu with chantilly cream and fresh fruit brûlée with an almond biscuit.** *Starters/Snacks: £3.95 to £8.50. Main Courses: £5.95 to £12.50. Puddings: £4.95*

Free house ~ Licensee Charles Garrard ~ Real ale ~ Bar food (12-3(2.30 in winter), 7-9(10 Fri and Sat)) ~ Restaurant ~ (01458) 223230 ~ Children welcome ~ Dogs welcome ~ Open 12-3, 6-midnight; 12-10 Sun

Recommended by Bob and Margaret Holder, Paul and Annette Hallett, Guy Vowles, M G Hart, Dr and Mrs C W Thomas, Di and Mike Gillam, Tom Evans, Brian and Bett Cox, Chris and Angela Buckell, Roger and Carol Maden, Tony Winckworth, Edward Mirzoeff

BATCOMBE   ST6839   MAP 2

Three Horseshoes 🍽 ♍ ᕦ

Village signposted off A359 Bruton—Frome; BA4 6HE

Well run, attractive dining pub with smart rooms, friendly staff, elaborate food and quite a choice of drinks; comfortable bedrooms

This 17th-c coaching inn is a neatly kept honey-coloured stone building with quite an emphasis on the brasserie-style food. There's a warm welcome from the friendly staff, and the long, rather narrow main room is smartly traditional: beams, local pictures on the lightly ragged dark pink walls, built-in cushioned window seats and solid chairs around a nice mix of old tables, and a woodburning stove at one end with a big open fire at the other. At the back on the left, the Gallery Bar has dark light panelled walls, tiled floors and modern pictures for sale and there's also a pretty stripped stone dining room (no mobile phones); best to book to be sure of a table, especially at weekends. Butcombe Bitter, Palmers IPA, and Bats in the Belfry (brewed for the pub) on handpump, eight wines by the glass, and farm cider. There are picnic-sets on the heated back terrace with more on the grass and a pond with koi carp. The pub is on a quiet village lane by the church which has a very striking tower. The bedrooms are comfortable and the breakfasts are good.

▥ **Seasonally changing bar food at lunchtime includes filled ciabattas, chicken liver pâté, home-made fillet of beef burger, goujons of fresh beer-battered fish served in paper with tartare sauce, bangers and mash with onion gravy, and pasta with sunblush tomatoes and pesto; there's also oriental five-spice lamb with little gem lettuce and hoi sin sauce, slow braised quarter shoulder of lamb with confit garlic and red wine gravy, cassoulet of shellfish and white fish with rouille, local free-range chicken farci with creamed potato, savoy cabbage and crispy bacon, and puddings such as a duo of white and dark chocolate bavarois and sticky toffee pudding with butterscotch sauce.** *Starters/Snacks: £4.75 to £7.25. Main Courses: £8.75 to £21.50. Puddings: £5.50*

Free house ~ Licensees Bob Wood and Shirley Greaves ~ Real ale ~ Bar food (not Sun evening or Mon) ~ Restaurant ~ (01749) 850359 ~ Children in eating areas but must be 13 in evening ~ Dogs allowed in bar and bedrooms ~ Live music some Thurs ~ Open 12-3, 6-11; 12-3, 8-11 Sun; closed Mon ~ Bedrooms: /£75B

Recommended by Dennis and Gill Keen, Michael Doswell, Mark Flynn

BATH
ST7565 MAP 2

King William ♀
Thomas Street, corner with A4 London Road – may be no nearby parking; BA1 5NN

Simple bars in small corner pub with informally friendly service, interesting food and drink; upstairs dining room

It's quite a surprise to find such individual food in this little corner pub. Many customers are here for a drink and a chat, and the two plain, un-smart rooms have straightfoward seating and just three chunky old tables each on dark bare boards; big windows look out on the busy street. Bristol Beer Factory Sunrise, Newmans Red Stag Bitter, and Palmers Dorset Gold on handpump and a fine choice of good wines by the glass. Daily papers, a few lighted church candles, and perhaps a big bunch of flowers on the counter. Steep stairs go up to a simple and attractive dining room, used mainly on Wednesday to Saturday evenings, decorated with Jane Grigson British Cooking prints. More reports please.

▥ **Using free-range or organic meat, the interesting bar food might include sandwiches, linguine with seasonal vegetables, wild garlic and pine nut dressing, popular beefburger with bacon, apple and cheese, grey mullet with pickled rhubarb and syrup, lambs liver with bacon and green sauce, chicken with duck fat potatoes, braised brisket with bacon, sweet onions and horseradish cream, beer-battered hake, and puddings such as steamed lemon sponge with custard and iced elderflower cream with strawberries and mint syrup; the restaurant has a two- and three-course set menu.** *Starters/Snacks: £4.00 to £9.00. Main Courses: £9.00 to £14.00. Puddings: £5.50 to £7.00*

Free house ~ Licensees Charlie and Amanda Digney ~ Real ale ~ Bar food (12-3, 6-10; not Sun evening) ~ Restaurant ~ (01225) 428096 ~ Well-behaved children welcome until 9pm ~ Dogs allowed in bar ~ Open 12-3, 5-11.30(midnight Fri); 12-midnight(11pm Sun) Sat

Recommended by Trevor and Sylvia Millum, Dr and Mrs A K Clarke

Old Green Tree ◀
Green Street; BA1 2JZ

Super little pub with fine choice of real ales, enjoyable traditional food, lots of cheerful customers and friendly service

Full of atmosphere and with a good mix of customers of all ages, this very well run pub remains much loved by our readers; it can get packed, so to get a table you must arrive before midday. Green Tree Bitter (brewed for them by Blindmans Brewery), plus

Butcombe Gold, RCH Pitchfork, Wickwar Brand Oak and two changing guest beers on handpump, a dozen wines by the glass from a nice little list with helpful notes, 35 malt whiskies, winter hot toddies and a proper Pimms. It's laid-back and cosy rather than particularly smart, and the three small oak-panelled and low wood-and-plaster ceilinged rooms include a comfortable lounge on the left as you go in, its walls decorated with wartime aircraft pictures in winter and local artists' work during spring and summer, and a back bar; the big skylight lightens things up attractively. No music or machines; chess, cribbage, dominoes, backgammon, shut the box, Jenga. The gents' is down steep steps. No children.

🍴 **Generous helpings of popular lunchtime bar food include soup and sandwiches, ploughman's, a changing pâté, bangers and mash with beer and onion sauce, mussels with white wine, cream and saffron, tagliatelle with mediterranean vegetables, beef in ale pie, lamb tagine, and daily specials; no puddings.** *Main Courses: £6.50 to £10.00*

Free house ~ Licensees Nick Luke and Tim Bethune ~ Real ale ~ Bar food (12-3; not evenings, not Sun) ~ No credit cards ~ Open 11-11; 12-10.30 Sun; closed 25 and 26 Dec

Recommended by Dr and Mrs M E Wilson, Tony and Jill Radnor, Pete Coxon, the Didler, Ian Phillips, Malcolm Ward, Dr and Mrs A K Clarke, Colin and Peggy Wilshire, Martin and Marion Vincent, Roger Wain-Heapy, Susan and Nigel Wilson, John Saville, Comus and Sarah Elliott, Donna and Roger, Pete Baker, Derek and Sylvia Stephenson, Michael Dandy, Tom and Ruth Rees

Star 🍺

Vineyards; The Paragon (A4), junction with Guinea Lane; BA1 5NA

Quietly chatty and unchanging old town local, brewery tap for Abbey Ales; filled rolls only

As the brewery tap for Abbey Ales, this honest old town pub keeps Bellringer plus Bass, St Austell Tribute, Thwaites Lancaster Bomber, and a couple of guests on handpump; they hold a July weekend beer festival. The interior is quite unchanging and there's a quiet, chatty atmosphere not spoilt by noisy fruit machines or music. The four (well, more like three and a half) small linked rooms are served from a single bar, separated by panelling with glass inserts. They are furnished with traditional leatherette wall benches and the like – even one hard bench that the regulars call Death Row – and the lighting's dim, and not rudely interrupted by too much daylight. Friendly staff and customers; it does get busy at weekends.

🍴 **Filled rolls only, though they may have bar nibbles on Thursday evening.** *Starters/Snacks: £1.90*

Punch ~ Lease Paul Waters and Alan Morgan ~ Real ale ~ Bar food (see text) ~ (01225) 425072 ~ Children welcome ~ Dogs welcome ~ Open 12-2.30, 5.30-midnight(1am Fri); 12 noon-1am Sat; 12-midnight Sun

Recommended by the Didler, Dr and Mrs A K Clarke, Catherine Pitt, Pete Baker, Donna and Roger, Roger Wain-Heapy, Pete Coxon, Ian Phillips

BLAGDON   ST5058 MAP 2

New Inn

Off A368; Park Lane; BS40 7SB

Lovely view over Blagdon Lake from nicely set pub, comfortable old furnishings in bustling bar, real ales, and decent food

Tables outside this nicely set pub look down over fields to the wood-fringed Blagdon Lake and to the low hills beyond. Inside, there are two log fires in inglenook fireplaces, heavy beams hung with horsebrasses and a few tankards, some comfortable antique settles and mate's chairs among more modern furnishings, old prints and photographs, and Wadworths IPA, 6X and JCB on handpump; several wines by the glass. There's a plainer side bar, too; cheerful, helpful service. Wheelchair access but no disabled facilities.

🍴 Tasty bar food includes filled rolls, soup, ploughman's, ham and egg, vegetarian lasagne, beer-battered haddock, local trout, cajun chicken, pork steak in a cider, cream and mustard sauce, pies such as game or beef in ale, and puddings like bakewell tart or strawberry pavlova. *Starters/Snacks: £4.50 to £5.95. Main Courses: £5.25 to £15.00. Puddings: £3.50*

Wadworths ~ Tenant Roger Owen ~ Real ale ~ Bar food ~ (01761) 462475 ~ Dogs welcome ~ Open 11-3, 6-11; 12-3, 7-10.30 Sun

Recommended by Paul Booth, John and Gloria Isaacs, Steve and Liz Tilley, Stuart Paulley, Bob and Angela Brooks, Steve Pocock, Chris and Angela Buckell, Hugh Roberts

BLEADON   ST3457   MAP 1

Queens Arms 🍺
Village signed just off A370 S of Weston; Celtic Way; BS24 0NF

Busy, cheerful pub with some interesting décor in linked rooms, real ales tapped from the cask, well liked bar food, and seats on pretty terrace

Enjoyed by quite a mix of customers, this 16th-c village pub has a cosy, informal and chatty atmosphere. The carefully divided areas have plenty of distinctive touches that include the dark flagstones of the terracotta-walled restaurant and back bar area, candles on sturdy tables flanked by winged settles, old hunting prints, a frieze of quaint sayings in Old English print, and above all, the focal servery where the real ales are tapped from the cask: Butcombe Bitter and Gold, and guests from Bath Ales or Cottage. Several wines by the glass. There is a big solid fuel stove in the main bar and a woodburning stove in the stripped-stone back tap bar; games machine and darts. The pretty, heated terrace has picnic-sets on flagstones and there's a pergola, shrubs and flowers.

🍴 **Reasonably priced bar food includes lunchtime filled baguettes, ploughman's, soup, moules marinières, mushroom stroganoff, faggots and mash, beer-battered haddock, stilton and bacon chicken, braised shoulder of lamb, gammon with home-made onion rings, pork casserole, and rump steak; Sunday roasts.** *Starters/Snacks: £4.25 to £7.50. Main Courses: £7.95 to £17.95. Puddings: £3.95 to £4.50*

Butcombe ~ Manager Andrew Pearson ~ Real ale ~ Bar food (12-6 Sun; not Sun evening) ~ Restaurant ~ (01934) 812080 ~ Children welcome away from bar ~ Dogs allowed in bar ~ Open 11.30-11; 12-10.30 Sun

Recommended by Bob and Margaret Holder, Chris and Angela Buckell, Tom Evans, Donna and Roger, R T and J C Moggridge, JCW, Comus and Sarah Elliott, P and J Shapley

BRISTOL   ST5773   MAP 2

Albion
Boyce's Avenue, Clifton; BS8 4AA

Chatty and cheerful local close to boutiquey shops, with interesting food and a good choice of drinks

Just ten minutes from the famous suspension bridge, this is a bustling and friendly little 18th-c pub down a cobbled alley in the heart of Clifton village. On the covered and heated terrace in front of the building are picnic-sets and other seats, fairy lights and church candles in hurricane lanterns. Inside by the main door, is a flagstoned area with a big old pine table and a couple of candlesticks, a dresser filled with jars of pickles, and an open kitchen. Further in, the L-shaped bar has high chairs by the counter with its extravagant flower arrangement, chapel chairs around good oak tables on the stripped wooden floor, brown leather sofas and armchairs in front of the coal-effect gas fire with its neat log stacks on either side of the brick fireplace, and some cushioned wall seats; up a step is an end room with a rather fine and very long high-backed new settle right the way across one wall, similar tables and chairs and unusual silvery peony-type wallpaper (elswhere, the sage green half-panelled walls are hung with modern photographs of the village). On our early evening visit, there was quite a mix of chatty customers and a couple of well behaved dogs. Butcombe Bitter, St Austell Tribute, Sharps

Doom Bar, and Wye Valley Bitter on handpump, good wines by the glass, farm cider, 20 malt whiskies, and winter hot cider; piped music and board games.

🔟 **Interesting modern cooking (not cheap) might include sandwiches, soup, home-cured charcuterie (rabbit terrine, jellied ham, foie gras, rilletes of pork belly and pickles), deep-fried pollock with tartare sauce, pot-roast chicken with garlic, bacon and anna potatoes, slow-cooked shoulder of lamb with potato gnocchi and confit shallots, bouillabaisse, 35-day aged roast rib of Aberdeen Angus, and puddings such as rhubarb and frangipane tart and hot Valrhona chocolate fondant with milk sorbet and salt butter caramel.** *Starters/Snacks: £5.00 to £8.50. Main Courses: £10.50 to £19.00. Puddings: £6.00 to £7.50*

Enterprise ~ Lease James Phillips ~ Real ale ~ Bar food (12-3, 7-9.30; not Sun evening or Mon) ~ Restaurant ~ (0117) 973 3522 ~ Children welcome until 9pm ~ Dogs allowed in bar ~ Open 12-midnight(11 Sun); 5-11 Mon; closed Mon lunchtime; 25 and 26 Dec

Recommended by Philip and Jude Simmons

CHEW MAGNA

ST5763   MAP 2

Bear & Swan 🔟 ♀

B3130 (South Parade), off A37 S of Bristol; BS40 8SL

Successfully ambitious food in relaxed and civilised linked rooms, good range of drinks, and friendly welcome; bedrooms

Run by friendly people, this carefully laid out, open-plan pub is popular for its particularly good food. It splendidly mixes the traditional with the modern, and the left hand end, beyond a piano, is an L-shaped dining room with stripped stone walls, dark dining tables, a woodburning stove, bare boards and an oriental rug. The other half, also bare boards with the odd oriental rug, has various sizes of pine tables, pews and raffia-seat dining chairs. In this part, a relaxed and civilised mix of customers runs from young men chatting on the bar stools through smart lunching mothers sipping champagne to older people reading the racing form; there may also be a friendly golden labrador. Décor is minimal, really just plants in the windows with their heavy dark blue curtains and some china above the huge bressumer beam over a splendid log fire; a wide-screen TV may be on with its sound turned down; cribbage.The long bar counter has Butcombe Bitter, Otter Bitter, and Sharps Doom Bar on handpump, and around 20 wines by the glass. The car park is small, and street parking needs care (and patience). The bedrooms are old-fashioned but nice and you prepare your own breakfasts.

🔟 **As well as bar staples such as filled baguettes, ploughman's, fishcakes with sweet chilli, gammon and eggs and sausages with mash and gravy, the enjoyable food includes moules marinières, pork and duck rillette with cumberland sauce, warm chicken liver salad with pine nuts, figs and cherry tomatoes, grilled bass on a tarragon mustard cream sauce, roast lamb rump on horseradish creamed potato, veal escalope with a sherry mushroom sauce and parmesan, duck breast on hoi sin poached pear with passion fruit sauce, and puddings such as chocolate brownie with white and dark chocolate sauce and vanilla crème brûlée.** *Starters/Snacks: £4.50 to £7.50. Main Courses: £6.50 to £10.00. Puddings: £5.00*

Free house ~ Licensees Nigel and Caroline Pushman ~ Real ale ~ Bar food (12-2(2.30 Sun), 7-9; not Sun evening) ~ Restaurant ~ (01275) 331100 ~ Well-behaved children welcome ~ Dogs allowed in bar ~ Open 9am-midnight; 10-6 Sun; closed Sun evening ~ Bedrooms: £50S/£80S

Recommended by Michael Doswell, Dr and Mrs A K Clarke, M G Hart, Gaynor Gregory, Mrs Jane Kingsbury, John Urquhart, Dr and Mrs C W Thomas

---

Bedroom prices normally include full english breakfast, VAT and any inclusive service charge that we know of. Prices before the '/' are for single rooms, after for two people in a double or twin (B includes a private bath, S a private shower). If there is no '/', the prices are only for twin or double rooms (as far as we know there are no singles).

CHISELBOROUGH

ST4614   MAP 1

Cat Head

Leave A303 on A356 towards Crewkerne; take the third left turn (at 1.4 miles), signposted Chiselborough, then after another 0.2 miles turn left; Cat Street; TA14 6TT

Handy for the A303, with consistently warm welcome, neat attractive bars, enjoyable food and thoughtful choice of drinks; pretty garden

Extremely well run and genuinely friendly, this bustling old sandstone pub has a degree of sophistication with the atmosphere of a village local, and so is much enjoyed by our readers. The spotless, traditional flagstoned rooms have light wooden tables and chairs, some high-backed cushioned settles, flowers and plants, a woodburning stove and curtains around the small mullioned windows. Butcombe Bitter, Otter Bitter and Sharps Doom Bar on handpump, a good wine list and Thatcher's cider; piped music, darts, skittle alley, shove-ha'penny, and board games. There are seats on the terrace and in the attractive garden where there are plenty of colourful plants; nice views over the peaceful village, too.

⑪ **As well as lunchtime filled rolls, ploughman's, soup, duck liver and herb pâté and grilled rib-eye steak, the popular, well presented food includes king prawns in lime and ginger, lambs kidneys in madeira sauce, three cheese and wild mushroom pasta, pork tenderloin with dijon mustard and calvados sauce, chicken breast stuffed with dorset blue cheese, daily specials like braised oxtail in Guinness, wild rabbit with mustard and thyme, and haddock and prawn fishcake with dill mayonnaise, and puddings such as chocolate and pecan pie and bakewell tart with almond ice-cream.** *Starters/Snacks: £4.80 to £6.90. Main Courses: £6.10 to £10.20. Puddings: £4.20*

Enterprise ~ Lease Duncan and Avril Gordon ~ Real ale ~ Bar food ~ Restaurant ~ (01935) 881231 ~ Children welcome ~ Open 12-3, 6-11(10.30 Sun); closed evening 25 Dec

Recommended by Peter Craske, Patricia Jones, Ray Edwards, Frank Willy, Mike Gorton, Sheila Topham, Mr and Mrs P D Titcomb, R T and J C Moggridge, Douglas Allen, I D Barnett, Kate and Ian Hodge, Jill Healing

CHURCHILL

ST4459   MAP 1

Crown 🍺 £

The Batch; in village, turn off A368 into Skinners Lane at Nelson Arms, then bear right; BS25 5PP

Unspoilt and unchanging small cottage with friendly customers and staff, super range of real ales and homely lunchtime food

'As good as ever' has been the comment used by several of our readers to describe this much enjoyed and unpretentious little cottage. Not much has changed over many years and the small and rather local-feeling stone-floored and cross-beamed room on the right has a wooden window seat, an unusually sturdy settle, built-in wall benches, and chatty, friendly customers; the left-hand room has a slate floor, and some steps past the big log fire in a big stone fireplace lead to more sitting space. No noise from music or games (except perhaps dominoes) and a fine range of real ales tapped from the cask: Bass, Butcombe Bitter, Cheddar Best Bitter, Cotleigh Batch, Palmers IPA and Tally Ho, RCH Hewish IPA and PG Steam, St Austells Tribute and Black Prince. Several wines by the glass and local ciders. Outside lavatories. There are garden tables at the front, a smallish back lawn and hill views; the Mendip Morris Men come in summer. Good walks nearby.

⑪ **Straightforward lunchtime bar food includes sandwiches (the rare roast beef is popular), good soup, filled baked potatoes, ploughman's, chilli con carne, beef casserole, broccoli and stilton bake and puddings like fruit crumbles and treacle tart.** *Starters/Snacks: £4.25 to £5.25. Main Courses: £5.25 to £7.95. Puddings: £3.90*

Free house ~ Licensee Tim Rogers ~ Real ale ~ Bar food (12-2.30; not evenings) ~ No credit cards ~ (01934) 852995 ~ Children welcome away from bar ~ Dogs welcome ~ Open 11-11(midnight Fri); 11-10.30 Sun

Recommended by Tom Evans, Roger Wain-Heapy, the Didler, Bob and Margaret Holder, Barry and Anne, John and Gloria Isaacs, Andrea Rampley

CLAPTON-IN-GORDANO   ST4773 MAP 1

Black Horse 🍺

4 miles from M5 junction 19; A369 towards Portishead, then B3124 towards Clevedon; in N Weston opp school turn left signposted Clapton, then in village take second right, maybe signed Clevedon, Clapton Wick; BS20 7RH

Ancient pub with lots of cheerful customers, friendly service, real ales and cider and straightforward bar food; pretty garden

This is a proper, old-fashioned pub run by friendly people and always with a good mix of cheerful, chatty customers. The partly flagstoned and partly red-tiled main room has winged settles and built-in wall benches around narrow, dark wooden tables, window seats, a big log fire with stirrups and bits on the mantelbeam, and amusing cartoons and photographs of the pub. A window in an inner snug is still barred from the days when this room was the petty-sessions gaol; high-backed settles – one a marvellous carved and canopied creature, another with an art nouveau copper insert reading East, West, Hame's Best – lots of mugs hanging from its black beams, and plenty of little prints and photographs. There's also a simply furnished room which is the only place families are allowed; piped music, darts, and TV. Butcombe Bitter, Courage Best, St Austell Tribute, Shepherd Neame Spitfire, and Wadworths 6X on handpump or tapped from the cask, several wines by the glass, farm ciders and efficient service. There are some old rustic tables and benches in the garden, with more to one side of the car park, and the summer flowers are really quite a sight. Paths from the pub lead up Naish Hill or along to Cadbury Camp.

🍴 **Straightforward lunchtime bar food includes filled baguettes, ploughman's and a few hot dishes like soup, lamb hotpot, cottage pie, moussaka and chilli.** *Starters/Snacks: £3.40 to £4.75. Main Courses: £4.60 to £6.95*

Enterprise ~ Licensee Nicholas Evans ~ Real ale ~ Bar food (not evenings, not Sun) ~ No credit cards ~ (01275) 842105 ~ Children in very plain family room only ~ Dogs welcome ~ Live music Mon evening ~ Open 11-11; 12-10.30 Sun

Recommended by J and F Gowers, Rona Murdoch, Dr and Mrs A K Clarke, Will Stevens, the Didler, Dave Braisted, Dr D J and Mrs S C Walker, Gaynor Gregory, R T and J C Moggridge, Philip and Jude Simmons, Chris and Angela Buckell, Tom Evans, Roy Hoing

CONGRESBURY   ST4563 MAP 1

White Hart

Wrington Rd, off A370 Bristol—Weston; BS49 5AR

Friendly new licensee, specialist gin menu, real ales, decent food and seats in sizeable garden

You can be sure of a friendly welcome from the new licensee here. It's a companionable country pub with a few heavy black beams in the bowed ceiling of the L-shaped main bar, big stone ingelnook fireplaces at each end, country kitchen furniture and Badger K&B Sussex Bitter, Tanglefoot and a seasonal beer on handpump; they specialise in gin, with 36 different types, and have several wines by the glass. Two areas lead off, and there's a big bright conservatory; piped music, table skittles and board games. Outside, there are picnic-sets under a back terrace arbour with more in the big garden. The hills you can see are the Mendips.

🍴 **Using fresh local produce, bar food now includes lunchtime filled baguettes, a quiche of the day, and ham and egg, as well as soup, fishcakes with onion marmalade and sweet chilli dressing, a terrine of the week, home-made burger, steak in ale pie, wild mushroom risotto, liver and bacon, roast rump of lamb with rosemary and red wine sauce, and puddings such as fruit crumbles.** *Starters/Snacks: £4.35 to £7.95. Main Courses: £9.95 to £11.50. Puddings: £3.50 to £4.50*

Badger ~ Tenant Murat Gumus ~ Real ale ~ Bar food (11.30-3, 6-9.30) ~ Restaurant ~ (01934) 833303 ~ Children welcome away from bar area ~ Dogs allowed in bar ~ live turkish music and belly dancers monthly ~ Open 11-midnight

Recommended by Bob and Margaret Holder, Stuart Paulley, John and Bryony Coles, Bob and Angela Brooks

CORTON DENHAM

ST6322   MAP 2

Queens Arms

Village signposted off B3145 N of Sherborne; DT9 4LR

Informally smart, honey-coloured stone inn, super choice of drinks, interesting food, and seats in sunny garden

As this Georgian honey-coloured stone inn is very popular, it's probably best to book a table in advance. The plain high-beamed bar has a woodburning stove in the inglenook at one end with rugs on flagstones in front of the raised fireplace at the other end, some old pews, barrel seats and a sofa, church candles and maybe a big bowl of flowers; a little room off here has just one big table – nice for a party of eight or so. On the left, the comfortable dining room (dark pink with crisp white paintwork), has good oak tables and a log fire. Butcombe Bitter, Otter Bitter, Timothy Taylors Landlord and guests like Bath Ales Wild Hare, Cheddar Potholer, and Highgate Dark Mild on handpump, local ciders and apple juice, 40 malt whiskies, several wines by the glass, and lots of bottled beers from around the world. A south-facing back terrace has teak tables and chairs under cocktail parasols (or heaters if it's cool), with colourful flower tubs. The village lane has some parking nearby, though not a great deal.

🍽 Using their own pigs and chickens, the food can be very good and at lunchtime might include sandwiches, ploughman's, soup, terrine of chicken liver, black pudding, and parma ham with tomato chutney, goose egg omelette with port salut and fresh herbs, shepherd's pie with minty mash, and wild mushroom and honey-roast chestnut tagliatelle with 24-month-old parmesan; evening choices such as seared cornish scallops with confit of old spot pork belly and cress, bourbon marinated salmon with honey mustard mayonnaise, loin of lamb on celeriac purée with thyme jus, and duo of rabbit with crispy haggis, fondant potato and root vegetable purée. Puddings like rich triple chocolate stack with chocolate brittle and apple and rhubarb crumble with custard. *Starters/Snacks: £4.75 to £6.10. Main Courses: £9.70 to £13.90. Puddings: £5.50 to £5.90*

Free house ~ Licensees Rupert and Victoria Reeves ~ Real ale ~ Bar food (12-3, 6-10; 12-4, 6-9.30 Sun) ~ Restaurant ~ (01963) 220317 ~ Children welcome ~ Dogs allowed in bar ~ Open 11-3, 6-11; 11-11 Sat; 12-10.30 Sun ~ Bedrooms: £60S(£70B)/£75S(£90B)

Recommended by Christine Cox, Colin and Janet Roe, Mrs Angela Graham, Mike and Heather Watson, Robert and Christina Jones, Graham and Toni Sanders

CRANMORE

ST6643   MAP 2

Strode Arms 🍽 ♀

West Cranmore; signposted with pub off A361 Frome—Shepton Mallet; BA4 4QJ

Interesting food and wide choice of drinks in pretty country pub with attractive, comfortable bars; pretty outside

An enjoyable place for a meal, this is a pretty and popular former farmhouse. The rooms have charming country furnishings, fresh flowers and pot plants, a grandfather clock on the flagstones, remarkable old locomotive engineering drawings and big black and white steam train murals in a central lobby; there are newspapers to read and lovely log fires in handsome fireplaces. Wadworths 6X, IPA and seasonal brews on handpump, eight wines by the glass from an interesting list, several malt whiskies and quite a few liqueurs and ports. In summer, the building is an attractive sight with its neat stonework, cartwheels on the walls, pretty tubs and hanging baskets, and seats under umbrellas on the front terrace, looking across to the village pond; there are more seats in the back garden. The East Somerset Light Railway is nearby and there may be a vintage sports car meeting on the first Tuesday of each month.

🍽 Well presented and very good, the bar food includes filled baguettes, ploughman's, soup, pork and leek sausages with onion gravy, ham and eggs, chicken, bacon and cider pie, bubble and squeak with asparagus, mushrooms, cheese and onion marmalade, pasta with mussels, prawns and pesto, and duck breast with morello cherry compote and red wine sauce; daily specials such as home-made faggots in rich gravy with colcannon potato, beef in ale casserole with a stilton cobbler topping and bass fillet with seared

scallops and an oriental dressing, and puddings like spotted dick with vanilla custard and warm treacle tart with honeycomb cream. *Starters/Snacks: £3.00 to £5.95. Main Courses: £7.10 to £15.00. Puddings: £4.50*

Wadworths ~ Tenants Tim and Ann-Marie Gould ~ Real ale ~ Bar food (not Sun evening) ~ Restaurant ~ (01749) 880450 ~ Children in one bar area and in restaurant until 7pm ~ Dogs allowed in bar ~ Open 11.30-3, 6-11; 12-3, 7-10.30 Sun

Recommended by Frank Willy, Meg and Colin Hamilton, Gaynor Gregory, Tony and Rosemary Warren, Col and Mrs Patrick Kaye, Bob and Margaret Holder, Richard Wyld, Cathryn and Richard Hicks, John Urquhart, Sylvia and Tony Birbeck, M G Hart

CROSCOMBE
ST5844   MAP 2

George

Long Street (A371 Wells—Shepton Mallet); BA5 3QH

Carefully renovated old coaching inn, cheerful Canadian landlord, bar food cooked by landlady, good local beers, attractive garden

Family-run and genuinely friendly, this is a 17th-c coaching inn with a warm, homely atmosphere and plenty of interesting mementoes and pictures. The main bar has some stripped stone, a winter log fire in the inglenook fireplace, dark wooden tables and chairs and more comfortable seats, and the family grandfather clock. The attractive dining room has more stripped stone, local artwork and photographs on the dark orange walls, and high-backed cushioned dining chairs around a mix of tables. King George the Thirst is brewed exclusively for them by Blindmans, and they also keep Butcombe Bitter, Cottage Gold Cup, and Sharps Doom Bar on handpump; local farm ciders and a short choice of sensibly priced wines. Darts, board games, a skittle alley, shut-the-box, and a canadian wooden table game called crokinole; occasional piped music. The friendly pub dog is called Tessa. The attractive, sizeable garden has seats on the heated and covered terrace; children's area and boules.

🍴 Cooked by the landlady, the bar food includes sandwiches, filled baked potatoes, ploughman's, soup, smoked fish pâté, vegetable lasagne, bangers and mash with onion gravy, crab au gratin, ham with mustard and pineapple sauce, steak in ale pie, daily specials, and puddings like crème brûlée and sticky toffee pudding. Curry night is on the last Thursday of the month. *Starters/Snacks: £3.95 to £6.85. Main Courses: £7.35 to £15.95. Puddings: £4.35 to £4.85*

Free house ~ Licensees Peter and Veryan Graham ~ Real ale ~ Bar food ~ Restaurant ~ (01749) 342306 ~ Children welcome ~ Dogs allowed in bar ~ Live jazz monthly ~ Open 12-2.30(3 Sat), 6-11; 12-3, 6-10.30 Sun ~ Bedrooms: £35S/£70S

Recommended by Peter Dearing, M G Hart, Terry Buckland, Barbara Close

DULVERTON
SS9127   MAP 1

Woods ★

Bank Square; TA22 9BU

Smartly informal place with exceptional wines and enjoyable food

You can order any of the 400 or so wines from an amazing wine list by the glass in this mildly upmarket place, and the landlord also keeps an unlisted collection of about 500 well aged new world wines which he will happily chat about. It's all comfortably relaxed and very Exmoor – plenty of good sporting prints on the salmon pink walls, some antlers, other hunting trophies and stuffed birds and a couple of salmon rods. There are bare boards on the left by the bar counter, which has well kept Exmoor Ale, Otter Head and St Austells Tribute tapped from the cask, a farm cider, many sherries, and some unusual spirits; daily papers to read. Its tables partly separated by stable-style timbering and masonry dividers, the bit on the right is carpeted and has a woodburning stove in the big fireplace set into its end wall, which has varnished plank panelling; maybe unobjectionable piped music. Big windows keep you in touch with what's going on out in the quiet town centre (or you can sit out on the pavement at a couple of metal tables). A small suntrap back courtyard has a few picnic-sets.

🍽 **Extremely good bar food** includes filled baguettes, ploughman's, soup, chicken liver parfait with celeriac remoulade, pickled beetroot, and red wine syrup, seared steak salad with crispy bacon, red onions and balsamic vinegar dressing, local wild boar sausages with spicy oriental sauce, risotto of wild mushrooms scented with truffle, calves liver and bacon, ballotine of organic corn-fed chicken wrapped in parma ham with chinese cabbage and pancetta poultry juices, gilthead bream with anchovy, samphire and fennel salad and caper nut brown butter, local lamb three ways with thyme sauce, and puddings such as lemon grass poached peach, bellini jelly and ginger ice-cream and rich chocolate tart with banana sorbet and mocha sauce. *Starters/Snacks: £6.50 to £8.50. Main Courses: £8.50 to £10.00. Puddings: £5.00 to £7.00*

Free house ~ Licensee Patrick Groves ~ Real ale ~ Bar food (12-2(3 Sun), 6-9.30) ~ Restaurant ~ (01398) 324007 ~ Well behaved children welcome ~ Dogs welcome ~ Open 11-3, 6-midnight(1am Sat); 12-3, 7-11 Sun; closed evenings 25 and 26 Dec

Recommended by James Crouchman, Sheila Topham, Richard and Anne Ansell, Roger and Carol Maden, Peter Craske, Mr and Mrs P D Titcomb, Len Clark

EAST COKER   ST5412 MAP 2

Helyar Arms ♀ 🛏

Village signposted off A37 or A30 SW of Yeovil; Moor Lane; BA22 9JR

Neat pub, comfortable big bar, well liked bar food, and lots of wines by the glass; bedrooms

A new licensee has taken over this neatly kept, heavy-beamed pub – but as Mr Eke was the head chef under the last people, things shouldn't change too much. There's a spacious and comfortable turkey-carpeted bar carefully laid out to give a degree of intimacy to its various candlelit tables, helped by soft lighting, a couple of high-backed settles, and squashy leather sofas at each end. There are lots of hunting and other country pictures, brass and copper ware and a log fire. Steps lead up to a good-sized back high-raftered dining room with well spaced tables. Butcombe Bitter and a couple of changing guest beers on handpump, local farm cider, 17 wines by the glass, and daily papers; piped music, board games, TV, and skittle alley. There are a few picnic-sets out on a neat lawn. This is an enjoyable place to stay and the breakfasts are good.

🍽 **Bar food can be very good:** sandwiches, ploughman's, soup, a platter of antipasti, thai vegetarian curry, seafood tagliatelle with lemon and dill cream, home-baked honey-glazed ham and free-range eggs, beer-battered haddock with home-made tartare sauce, liver and bacon with sage butter, steak and kidney pudding, slow-braised pork belly with black pudding, cider and sage jus, and puddings such as steamed treacle and orange sponge with prune and armagnac ice-cream and hot chocolate fondant with plum and rosemary compote and clotted cream; there's a £5 weekday lunch meal. *Starters/Snacks: £5.00 to £8.00. Main Courses: £7.00 to £17.00. Puddings: £4.00 to £7.00*

Punch ~ Lease Mathieu Eke ~ Real ale ~ Bar food (12-2.30, 6.30-9.30(9 Sun)) ~ Restaurant ~ (01935) 862332 ~ Children welcome ~ Dogs welcome ~ Open 11-3, 6-11; 11am-midnight Sat; 11-10.30 Sun; 11-3, 6-midnight Sat in winter ~ Bedrooms: £65S/£89S

Recommended by Charles Gysin, Paul and Gail Betteley, Roland and Wendy Chalu, Mrs Angela Graham, Mike and Heather Watson, Ian Malone

FAULKLAND   ST7555 MAP 2

Tuckers Grave ★ £

A366 E of village; BA3 5XF

Quite unspoilt and unchanging little cider house with friendly locals and charming licensees

As one reader told us, 'This timeless pub should remain a main entry until hell freezes over.' It's an unchanging little gem, at its best when you can chat to the friendly locals and charming licensees. Little is certainly the operative word – it's one of the two tiniest pubs in the *Guide*. The flagstoned entry opens into a teeny unspoilt room with casks of Bass and Butcombe Bitter on tap and Thatcher's Cheddar Valley cider in an alcove on the left. Two old cream-painted high-backed settles face each other across a single table on the right and a side room has shove-ha'penny. There are winter fires and maybe newspapers to read; also a skittle alley and lots of tables and chairs on an attractive back lawn with good views.

🍴 **There may be lunchtime sandwiches.**

Free house ~ Licensees Ivan and Glenda Swift ~ Real ale ~ No credit cards ~ (01373) 834230 ~ Children allowed but with restrictions ~ Open 12-3, 6-11; 12-3, 7-10.30 Sun; closed 25 Dec

Recommended by the Didler, Dr and Mrs A K Clarke, Pete Baker, Ian Phillips, Ann and Colin Hunt, E McCall, T McLean, D Irving, R Huggins

HINTON ST GEORGE
ST4212   MAP 1

Lord Poulett Arms 🍴 ♀ 🛏

Off A30 W of Crewkerne, and off Merriott road (declassified – former A356, off B3165) N of Crewkerne; TA17 8SE

SOMERSET DINING PUB OF THE YEAR

Attractive old stone inn with friendly licensees, charming antiques-filled rooms, imaginative food, good choice of drinks, pretty garden; nice bedrooms

This substantial 17th-c thatched pub is in a charming and peaceful golden hamstone village. It's been carefully restored and is extremely attractive inside with several cosy linked areas: rugs on bare boards or flagstones, open fires – one in an inglenook and one in a raised fireplace that separates two rooms – walls of honey-coloured stone or painted in bold Farrow & Ball colours, hops on beams, antique brass candelabra, fresh flowers and candles, and some lovely old farmhouse, windsor and ladderback chairs around fine oak or elm tables. The atmosphere is civilised and relaxed with plenty of locals dropping in for a drink. Branscombe Branoc and Otter Ale on handpump, several wines by the glass, mulled wine, and summer Pimms and cider by the jug. The cat is called Honey. Outside, under a wisteria-clad pergola, there are white metalwork tables and chairs in a mediterranean-style lavender-edged gravelled area, a couple of boules pistes (two keen pub teams) and picnic-sets in a wild flower meadow. The bedrooms (some are being refurbished this year) are pretty with some proper character and the breakfasts are good; nearby walks.

🍴 **Well presented, extremely good bar food (using home-made bread and home-grown herbs) includes lunchtime dishes such as sandwiches, soup, mussels in a thai red curry broth, herb gnocchi with smoked bacon, sage, brown butter, spinach and parmesan, home-made beef burger with smoked streaky bacon and mature cheddar, pork and chive sausage with apple and onion gravy, and fried gurnard fillet with candied lemon, roasted red pepper and tomato confit; evening choices like citrus-cured organic salmon with pomegranate, blood orange and ginger, cauliflower cheese, cumin and apple glazed pork belly with roasted beetroot and spinach and roasted polenta, roasted venison loin with parsnip purée, and puddings such as molten chocolate tart and raspberry trifle.**
Starters/Snacks: £4.50 to £10.00. Main Courses: £9.00 to £16.00. Puddings: £4.50 to £6.00

Free house ~ Licensees Steve Hill and Michelle Paynton ~ Real ale ~ Bar food ~ (01460) 73149 ~ Children welcome ~ Dogs allowed in bar ~ Open 12-3, 6.30-11; closed 26 Dec, 1 Jan ~ Bedrooms: /£88B

Recommended by Glen and Nola Armstrong, Cathryn and Richard Hicks, Bob and Margaret Holder, Pamela and Alan Neale, Fred Beckett, Ian Malone, Theo, Anne and Jane Gaskin, Steven and Nic, Heidi Montgomery

---

'Children welcome' means the pub says it lets children inside without any special restriction. If it allows them in, but to restricted areas such as an eating area or family room, we specify this. Some pubs may impose an evening time limit. We do not mention limits after 9pm as we assume children are home by then.

HUISH EPISCOPI

ST4326 MAP 1

Rose & Crown £

Off A372 E of Langport; TA10 9QT

In the same family for over 140 years and a real throwback; local ciders and beers, simple food and friendly welcome

Very sadly as we went to press, we heard that the long-serving landlady, Eileen Pittard, had passed away. Her son and daughters (who were also born in the pub as Mrs Pittard was) will continue to run this determinedly unpretentious, unspoilt thatched tavern. There's no bar as such – to get a drink, you just walk into the central flagstoned still room and choose from the casks of Teignworthy Reel Ale and guests such as Branscombe Vale Summa That, Glastonbury Mystery Tor, and Hopback Crop Circle; farm cider, too. This servery is the only thoroughfare between the casual little front parlours with their unusual pointed-arch windows – and genuinely friendly locals; good helpful service. Shove-ha'penny, dominoes and cribbage, and a much more orthodox big back extension family room has pool, darts, games machine and juke box; skittle alley and popular quiz nights. There are tables in a garden and a second enclosed garden has a children's play area. Summer morris men, fine nearby walks and the site of the Battle of Langport (1645) is close by.

🍴 **Using some home-grown fruit and vegetables, the simple, cheap food includes generously filled sandwiches, filled baked potatoes, ploughman's, pork, apple and cider cobbler, steak in ale pie, stilton and broccoli tart, chicken breast in tarragon sauce and puddings such as chocolate torte with chocolate sauce and lemon sponge pudding with lemon cream.** *Starters/Snacks: £3.20. Main Courses: £6.50 to £6.95. Puddings: £3.50*

Free house ~ Licensee Stephen Pittard ~ Real ale ~ Bar food (12-2, 5.30-7.30; not Sun or Mon evenings) ~ No credit cards ~ (01458) 250494 ~ Children welcome ~ Dogs welcome ~ Singalongs every third Sat (Sept-May) and irish night last Thurs in month ~ Open 11.30-2.30, 5.30-11; 11.30-11 Fri and Sat; 12-10.30 Sun

Recommended by Meg and Colin Hamilton, Rona Murdoch, Neil and Anita Christopher, the Didler, Dr and Mrs M E Wilson, Pete Baker, Phil and Sally Gorton

KINGSDON

ST5126 MAP 2

Kingsdon Inn ♀

At Podimore roundabout junction of A303, A372 and A37 take A372, then turn right on to B3151, right into village, and right again opposite post office; TA11 7LG

Charming old cottage with low-ceilinged rooms, local cider, west country beers and nice food

This is an enjoyable and pretty thatched cottage with friendly, efficient staff and several low-ceilinged, attractively decorated rooms with farmhouse and wheelback chairs and a mix of stripped pine tables. The main part has built-in wooden and cushioned wall seats, high bar chairs by the curved counter, quarry tiles, and a warm coal fire in the rather nice raised stone fireplace. Up some steps to a blue carpeted area with half-panelled walls, a few low sagging beams, the same tables and chairs, and some seats in what was a small inglenook fireplace. There are two other rooms as well. The atmosphere throughout is relaxed and chatty. Butcombe Bitter, Otter Bitter and Cheddar Ales Potholer on handpump, local cider, and good wines by the glass. There are some picnic-sets on the grass in front and the pub is handy for Lytes Cary (National Trust) and the Fleet Air Arm Museum.

🍴 **Rewarding bar food at lunchtime includes ploughman's, soup, duck liver pâté, poached salmon with parsley sauce, steak and kidney or walnut, leek and stilton pies, and chicken in cider, mushrooms and cream; evening choices such as mussels in white wine sauce, braised oxtail, grilled haddock fillet with a herb crust, calves liver with onion and garlic, pork fillet with toasted almonds and apricots, roast rack of lamb in a port and redcurrant sauce, and venison casserole; Sunday roast set menu.** *Starters/Snacks: £3.80 to £5.90. Main Courses: £8.20 to £10.95. Puddings: £4.50*

Game Bird Inns ~ Managers Linda Woods and Martin Brelsford ~ Real ale ~ Bar food ~
(01935) 840543 ~ Children welcome ~ Dogs welcome ~ Open 12-3, 5.30-11; 12-3, 6-10.30 Sun;
closed evening 25 Dec ~ Bedrooms: £60S/£80S

*Recommended by Jenny and Brian Seller, Dr and Mrs M E Wilson, Piotr Chodzko-Zajko, John and Enid Morris,
Brian and Bett Cox, Tony and Rosemary Warren, KC, Bob and Ann Good, Clare West, David Morgan, Mike and
Heather Watson, John Chambers, Col and Mrs Patrick Kaye, Mr and Mrs Gordon Turner, Robert Watt, Pamela and
Alan Neale, Andrew Shore, Maria Williams, J D O Carter*

LITTON   ST5954   MAP 2

Kings Arms

B3114, NW of Chewton Mendip on A39 Bath—Wells; BA3 4PW

Bustling pub, good choice of drinks, modern cooking, and seats on riverside terrace

The new licensees in this partly 15th-c dining pub have carried out some refurbishment,
though most of the original features remain untouched. There's a big entrance hall with
polished flagstones, and bars lead off to the left with low heavy beams and more
flagstones; a nice bit on the right beyond the huge fireplace has a big old-fashioned
settle and a mix of other settles and wheelback chairs. Throughout there are paintings,
four open fires, and the rooms are divided up into areas by standing timbers. Greene
King IPA, Old Speckled Hen, and Ruddles County on handpump, ciders, several malt
whiskies, summer Pimms and an extensive wine list. The terrace overlooking the River
Chew has plenty of wooden tables and chairs and there are good quality picnic-sets on
the lawn; good walks nearby. They hope to open bedrooms. More reports please.

🍴 As well as some pubby lunchtime food such as sandwiches, ploughman's, welsh rarebit,
ham and egg, sausage and mash, and burgers, there are more elaborate choices like free-
range pork loin with apple and sage butter, chicken caesar salad, crayfish tails with
poached wild salmon, dressed crab with avocado and bitter leaf salad, and puddings such
as chocolate brownie with trinity cream and summer pudding. *Starters/Snacks: £3.50 to
£7.00. Main Courses: £6.50 to £12.50. Puddings: £5.00*

Greene King ~ Lease Jason Woodger ~ Real ale ~ Bar food (12-3(4 Sat), 6-10; 12-5 Sun) ~
Restaurant ~ (01761) 241301 ~ Children welcome ~ Dogs welcome ~ Jazz Sun evening,
folk Weds evening ~ Open 11-11; 10am-11pm Sat; 12-10.30 Sun

*Recommended by Clare West, Dr and Mrs A K Clarke, Richard Fendick, Terry Buckland, Liz and Tony Colman,
M G Hart*

LOVINGTON   ST5831   MAP 2

Pilgrims 🍴 🍷

B3153 Castle Cary—Keinton Mandeville; BA7 7PT

**Rather smart but relaxed dining pub with particularly good food cooked by landlord, local
beer and cider, and decked terrace; bedrooms**

The emphasis in this civilised and rather upmarket dining pub is very much on the
enjoyable food cooked by the landlord. But the bar is chatty and relaxed with a few
stools by a corner counter, a rack of daily papers, 16 wines by the glass, local cider and
cider brandy, and Cottage Champflower on handpump from the nearby brewery. A cosy
little dark green inner area has sunny modern country and city prints, a couple of
shelves of books and china, a cushioned pew, and some settees by the big fireplace.
With flagstones throughout, this runs into the compact eating area, with candles on
tables and some stripped stone. There's also a separate, more formal carpeted dining
room. The landlady's service is efficient and friendly. The enclosed garden has tables,
chairs and umbrellas on a decked terrace. The car park exit has its own traffic lights –
on your way out line your car up carefully or you may wait for ever for them to change.
More reports please.

🍴 Using the best local produce and cooked by the landlord, the rewarding lunchtime food
includes various soups, hot potted haddock in cheese sauce on piquant tomato salsa, pork
and veal terrine with home-made bread, smoked eel and bacon, bangers and mash with

onion gravy, fishcakes with tartare sauce, and free-range chicken stuffed with goats cheese with cider brandy and cream; evening dishes such as smoked salmon mousse, tiger prawns in tempura batter with soy and lime dipping sauce, veal escalopes with sage and parma ham, tuna on chickpeas with chorizo, and sirloin steak, with puddings like rhubarb crumble and chocolate mousse with mango and passion fruit sorbet. *Starters/Snacks: £4.00 to £8.00. Main Courses: £8.00 to £23.00. Puddings: £5.00 to £7.00*

Free house ~ Licensees Sally and Jools Mitchison ~ Real ale ~ Bar food (not Sun evening, Mon, Tues lunchtime) ~ Restaurant ~ (01963) 240597 ~ Children welcome ~ Dogs allowed in bar ~ Open 12-3, 7-11; 12-3 Sun; closed Sun evening, Mon, Tues lunchtime ~ Bedrooms: /£95B

Recommended by Paul and Annette Hallett, Michael Doswell

LUXBOROUGH   SS9837   MAP 1

Royal Oak

Kingsbridge; S of Dunster on minor roads into Brendon Hills – OS Sheet 181 map reference 983378; TA23 0SH

Smashing place to stay in wonderful countryside, often inventive food, local beers and ciders; especially attentive staff

This is a proper Exmoor inn with a good mix of chatty locals (often with their dogs) and visitors here for a meal; the recently refurbished bedrooms are a popular place to stay, too – though the breakfasts are rather early for some. The compact bar, which has the most character, has lovely old flagstones, several rather fine settles (one with a very high back and one still with its book rest), scrubbed kitchen tables, lots of beer mats on beams, a cart horse saddle, and a huge brick fireplace with a warm log fire; a simpler back room has an ancient cobbled floor, some quarry tiles, and a stone fireplace. One room just off the bar is set for dining, with attractive old pine furniture and horse and hunting prints, and there are two dining rooms – one green-painted, and a larger end one with stuffed fish in glass cabinets, fish paintings and fishing rods on the dark red walls, leather and brass-tack dining chairs and more formal ones around quite a mix of old tables, and turkey rugs on the black slate floor. The atmosphere throughout is cheerful and relaxed, and the staff are all friendly and helpful. Cotleigh Tawny, Exmoor Gold and Stag, and Palmers IPA on handpump; board games. There are some seats out in the charming back courtyard, and memorable nearby walks in the wonderful surrounding countryside; they hope to have a tethering area for horses soon.

Using local produce – organic where possible – the well liked bar food includes lunchtime filled baguettes, mussels with white wine, garlic and shallot butter, terrine of duck and foie gras with toasted brioche and sauternes dressing butternut squash, roasted garlic and spring onion ravioli with a sage and pine nut butter, roast rump of lamb with rich jus and gremolata, loin of pork with calvados-soaked sultanas and crème fraîche, fresh crab and coriander strudel with seared scallops and sweet mirin dressing, daily specials, and puddings. Best to book a table as there are often walking and shooting parties in. *Starters/Snacks: £4.50 to £7.25. Main Courses: £9.95 to £15.75. Puddings: £3.75 to £4.75*

Free house ~ Licensees James and Sian Waller ~ Real ale ~ Bar food (they plan to serve snacks and cream teas on summer afternoons) ~ Restaurant ~ (01984) 640319 ~ Children must be over 10 in evening and in bedrooms ~ Dogs allowed in bar and bedrooms ~ Open 12-11; 12-2.30, 6-11 (Oct-end May) winter ~ Bedrooms: £55B/£65B

Recommended by Mike and Eleanor Anderson, J Roy Smylie, Andrew Shore, Maria Williams, Roy and Jean Russell, Sue Demont, Tim Barrow, Paul and Karen Cornock, R G Stollery, Mr and Mrs Peter Larkman, John and Alison Hamilton, Lynda and Trevor Smith, Martin Hatcher, Gaynor Gregory, the Didler, Dave Braisted, Bob and Margaret Holder, Dr and Mrs Michael Smith, Chris and Meredith Owen, John Urquhart, Andrew and Debbie Ettle, J L Wedel

---

Bedroom prices are for high summer. Even then you may get reductions for more than one night, or (outside tourist areas) weekends. Winter special rates are common, and many inns cut bedroom prices if you have a full evening meal.

MONKSILVER ST0737 MAP 1

Notley Arms

B3188; TA4 4JB

Friendly, busy pub in lovely village with beamed rooms, a fair choice of drinks and well liked food; neat streamside garden

In fine weather, the immaculate garden of this bustling pub has plenty of tables, and there's a swift clear stream at the bottom. The beamed and L-shaped bar has small settles and kitchen chairs around the plain country wooden and candlelit tables, original paintings on the ochre-coloured walls, fresh flowers and a couple of woodburning stoves. The Tack Room is decorated with horse tack (saddles, bridles and so forth) and has some toys. Bath Ales Gem, Exmoor Ale and Wadworths 6X on handpump, farm ciders and several wines by the glass; piped classical music, and good service from the friendly staff. This is a lovely village. More reports please.

🍽 **Well liked bar food includes soup, whitebait with home-made tartare sauce, chicken and almond tikka masala, pheasant pie, beer-battered cod, butternut and cherry tomato laksa with egg noodles, lambs liver with crispy bacon, black pudding and redcurrant gravy, and slow-braised shin of beef with valencia oranges in red wine.** *Starters/Snacks: £4.95 to £5.95. Main Courses: £8.95 to £10.95. Puddings: £4.50 to £5.50*

Unique (Enterprise) ~ Lease Russell and Jane Deary ~ Real ale ~ Bar food (not Mon lunchtime or winter Mon) ~ (01984) 656217 ~ Children are encouraged to be in family room with books and toys ~ Dogs welcome ~ Open 12-2.30, 6.30-10.30(11 Sat); 12-2.45, 7-10.30 Sun; closed Mon lunchtime (all day Mon in winter)

Recommended by the Didler, Terry Miller, Nick Lawless, R G Stollery

NORTH CURRY ST3125 MAP 1

Bird in Hand

Queens Square; off A378 (or A358) E of Taunton; TA3 6LT

Village pub with beams and timbers, cricketing memorabilia, friendly staff and decent food and drink

Though there may be some changes due to rebuilding after a fire, this remains a bustling village pub with a friendly atmosphere. The cosy main bar has nice old pews, settles, benches, and old yew tables on the flagstones, some original beams and timbers, locally woven willow work, cricketing memorabilia, and a log fire in the inglenook fireplace. Otter Bitter and a couple of guests like Butcombe Gold and Exmoor Fox on handpump, Rich's farm cider, and ten wines by the glass; piped music.

🍽 **Well cooked and tasty, the bar food includes sandwiches, baked garlic mushrooms topped with goats cheese, tiger prawns in garlic butter, scallops and bacon on mixed leaf salad, breast of chicken with leek, bacon and stilton sauce, mahi mahi with lime and chilli butter, duck breast with port, orange and redcurrant sauce, gilt bream with prawns and wine sauce, rack of lamb, and puddings such as apricot and brandy brûlée and chocolate brownie with chocolate sauce.** *Starters/Snacks: £3.75 to £7.50. Main Courses: £8.75 to £15.95. Puddings: £4.50*

Free house ~ Licensee James Mogg ~ Real ale ~ Bar food ~ Restaurant ~ (01823) 490248 ~ Children welcome ~ Dogs allowed in bar ~ Open 12-3, 6-11.30; 12-3, 6(7 Sun)-midnight Sat

Recommended by Alan and Pam Atkinson, PLC, Brian and Bett Cox, Steve and Liz Tilley, Bob and Margaret Holder, R T and J C Moggridge, Gary Rollings, Debbie Porter, K Turner, John Day

---

The letters and figures after the name of each town are its Ordnance Survey map reference. 'Using the *Guide*' at the beginning of the book explains how it helps you find a pub, in road atlases or on large-scale maps as well as in our own maps.

NORTON ST PHILIP

ST7755   MAP 2

George 🛏

A366; BA2 7LH

Wonderful ancient building full of history and interest, with well liked food, pleasant service and fine spacious bedrooms

Apart from a new licensee, nothing much changes in this exceptional place. It was built around 700 years ago to house merchants buying wool and cloth from the rich sheep-farming Hinton Priory at the great August cloth market. The central Norton Room, which was the original bar, has really heavy beams, an oak panelled settle and solid dining chairs on the narrow strip wooden floor, a variety of 18th-c pictures, an open fire in the handsome stone fireplace, and a low wooden bar counter. Wadworths IPA, 6X, Bishops Tipple and Horizon, and a changing guest beer on handpump and pleasant service. As you enter the building, there's a room on the right with high dark beams, squared dark half-panelling, a broad carved stone fireplace with an old iron fireback and pewter plates on the mantelpiece, a big mullioned window with leaded lights, and a round oak 17th-c table reputed to have been used by the Duke of Monmouth who stayed here before the Battle of Sedgemoor – after their defeat, his men were imprisoned in what is now the Monmouth Bar. The Charterhouse Bar is mostly used by those enjoying a drink before a meal: a wonderful pitched ceiling with trusses and timbering, heraldic shields and standards, jousting lances, and swords on the walls, a fine old stone fireplace, high backed cushioned heraldic-fabric dining chairs on the big rug over the wood plank floor, and an oak dresser with some pewter. The dining room (a restored barn with original oak ceiling beams, a pleasant if haphazard mix of early 19th-c portraits and hunting prints, and the same mix of vaguely old-looking furnishings) has a good relaxing, chatty atmosphere. The bedrooms are very atmospheric and comfortable – some reached by an external Norman stone stair-turret, and some across the cobbled and flagstoned courtyard and up into a fine half-timbered upper gallery (where there's a lovely 18th-c carved oak settle). A stroll over the meadow behind the pub (past the picnic-sets on the narrow grass pub garden) leads to an attractive churchyard around the medieval church whose bells struck Pepys (here on 12 June 1668) as 'mighty tuneable'.

🍴 **Well liked bar food includes sandwiches and filled baguettes, gloucester old spot sausages with onion gravy, gammon with pineapple and cheese, beef in ale pie, chicken curry, home-made burgers, and vegetable, cheese, cider and sage casserole with olive bread; the more elaborate restaurant menu might have salmon and asparagus with lemon, parsley butter, half a roast duck with rhubarb, venison with redcurrant sauce, and puddings such as bread and butter pudding with Baileys and sultanas and chocolate brownie with chocolate sauce.** *Starters/Snacks: £4.95 to £6.95. Main Courses: £7.95 to £12.95. Puddings: £4.95*

Wadworths ~ Manager Mark Jenkinson ~ Real ale ~ Bar food (12-2, 6-9; all day weekends) ~ Restaurant ~ (01373) 834224 ~ Well-behaved children welcome ~ Dogs allowed in bar and bedrooms ~ Open 11.30-11; 12-10.30 Sun ~ Bedrooms: £70B/£90B

Recommended by Ian Phillips, David Field, the Didler, Simon Collett-Jones, Dr and Mrs A K Clarke, Pete Coxon, Ann and Colin Hunt

OAKE

ST1526   MAP 1

Royal Oak 🍺

Hillcommon, N; B3227 W of Taunton; if coming from Taunton, ignore signpost on left for Oake and go 200 yards, pub is on left directly off B3227; TA4 1DS

Decent real ales and Easter beer festival, fresh meat and fish counter in neat pub

They've now set up a fresh meat and fish counter in this neat country pub so you can choose your evening specials; the produce is all from the west country. The spacious bar has several separate-seeming areas around the central servery; on the left is a little tiled fireplace, with a big woodburning stove on the other side. The windows have smart curtains, with plenty of fresh flowers and lots of brasses on the beams and walls. As well as holding a real ale festival with live jazz at Easter, there might be Cotleigh Barn

Owl, Exe Valley Devon Glory, Exmoor Gold, and Sharps Eden Pure Ale on handpump or tapped from the cask; quite a few malt whiskies. At the back is a long dining area which leads out to a pleasant sheltered garden. Skittle alley in winter and piped music. More reports please.

🍽 **As well as lunchtime sandwiches, the bar food might include soup, home-made fishcake, breaded somerset brie with cranberry and orange jam, mussels done several different ways, burgers, bangers and mash with onion gravy, steak and kidney pudding, outdoor reared pork with warm cider apple compote, roasted fillet of salmon on tagliatelle with cherry tomato, dill and cream sauce, chicken korma, and puddings.** *Starters/Snacks: £4.25 to £6.95. Main Courses: £5.95 to £19.95. Puddings: £2.95 to £4.50*

Free house ~ Licensee Richard Bolwell ~ Real ale ~ Bar food (12-2.30, 6.30-9.30; all day weekends) ~ Restaurant ~ (01823) 400295 ~ Children welcome ~ Open 12-3, 5.30-11; 12-midnight(10.30 Sun) Sat

Recommended by J L Wedel, Theo, Anne and Jane Gaskin

PITNEY   ST4527   MAP 1

Halfway House 🍺

Just off B3153 W of Somerton; TA10 9AB

Up to ten real ales, local ciders and continental bottled beers in bustling friendly local; good simple food

Warm and friendly with helpful, welcoming staff, this traditional village local keeps a fine range of ten real ales tapped from the cask. Changing regularly, these might include Bath Ales SPA, Branscombe Vale Branoc, Butcombe Bitter, Exmoor Fox, Hop Back Crop Circle and Summer Lightning, Moor Peat Porter, Otter Ale, RCH Pitchfork, and Teignworthy Reel Ale. They also have 20 or so continental bottled beers, three farm ciders, several wines by the glass, and 15 malt whiskies; cribbage, dominoes and board games. There's a good mix of people chatting at communal tables in the three old-fashioned rooms, all with roaring log fires and a homely feel underlined by a profusion of books, maps and newspapers. There are tables outside.

🍽 **Good simple filling food includes hot smoked foods from their own garden smokery as well as sandwiches, soup, filled baked potatoes, ploughman's with home-made pickle, lamb stew with dumplings and fish pie; in the evening they do about half a dozen home-made curries.** *Starters/Snacks: £4.25 to £5.95. Main Courses: £6.95 to £10.50. Puddings: £2.00 to £3.50*

Free house ~ Licensee Julian Lichfield ~ Real ale ~ Bar food (12-2.30, 7.30-9; not Sun) ~ (01458) 252513 ~ Children welcome ~ Dogs welcome ~ Open 11.30-3, 5.30-11(midnight Fri and Sat); 12-3, 7-11 Sun; closed evening 25 Dec

Recommended by the Didler, R T and J C Moggridge, Theo, Anne and Jane Gaskin, Evelyn and Derek Walter, Andrea Rampley, Mrs M B Gregg

PORTISHEAD   ST4576   MAP 1

Windmill 🍺

3.7 miles from M5 junction 19; A369 into town, then follow Sea Front sign off left and into Nore Road; BS20 6JZ

Large and efficient family dining pub in lovely spot with quite a few real ales and decent food

Don't come to this popular, bustling place expecting a traditional village pub – it's very far from that. But it is a well run and reliable, three-level family dining pub and an efficient mealtime stop from the motorway. And the views in fine weather from the wall of picture windows on the top and bottom floors, are marvellous, looking out over the Bristol Channel to Newport and Cardiff (with the bridges on the right). The bottom floor is a simple easy-going family area, the top one a shade more elegant with its turkey carpet, muted green and cream wallpaper and dark panelled dado. The middle floor, set back from here, is quieter and (with its black-painted ceiling boards) more softly lit. Unexpectedly, they have up to six quickly changing real ales on handpump such as Bass, Butcombe Gold, Courage Best, RCH PG Steam, and two guest beers such as Bristol Beer Factory Exhibition and Matthews Brassknocker. Out on the seaward side are picnic-sets on three tiers of lantern-lit terrace; disabled access.

🍴 To eat, you find a numbered table, present yourself at the order desk (by a slimline pudding show-cabinet), pay for your order, and return to the table with a tin (well, stainless steel) tray of cutlery, condiments and sauce packets. It works well: sandwiches, filled baked potatoes, ploughman's, soup, thai green vegetable curry, steak in ale pie, barbecue chicken, daily specials such as liver and bacon casserole, mild chicken curry, and cajun pork escalope, and puddings like fruit crumble of the day and dark chocolate truffle. *Starters/Snacks: £2.25 to £6.25. Main Courses: £6.95 to £12.95. Puddings: £1.75 to £4.95*

Free house ~ Licensee J S Churchill ~ Real ale ~ Bar food (all day) ~ (01275) 843677 ~ Children in family area ~ Dogs allowed in bar ~ Open 11-11; 12-10.30 Sun

Recommended by Tom Evans, Ian Legge, J and F Gowers, Dave Braisted, Andrea and Guy Bradley, Chris and Angela Buckell, P and J Shapley, R T and J C Moggridge

SHEPTON MONTAGUE   ST6731   MAP 2

Montague Inn ♀
Village signposted just off A359 Bruton—Castle Cary; BA9 8JW

Friendly licensees in busy country pub with real ales, good bar food, and pretty, heated terrace

The pretty terrace behind this popular little country pub has smart new teak seats and tables this year and the views from here are very pleasant; more seats in the garden, too. Inside, there's a good welcome from the friendly landlord and the rooms are simply but tastefully furnished with stripped wooden tables and kitchen chairs, and there's a log fire in the attractive inglenook fireplace. French windows in the restaurant lead to the terrace. Wadworths IPA and 6X and maybe Bath Ales Gem tapped from the cask, local cider, several wines by the glass, and smiling, helpful service.

🍴 Good food includes lunchtime open sandwiches, soup, duck, chicken and pork terrine with home-made cumberland sauce, bacon, avocado and blue cheese salad topped with a soft poached egg, thai fishcake with a sweet chilli and mango sauce, beer-battered fish, chicken, bacon and mushroom pancakes, grilled whole plaice, crusted, slow-baked pork, duckling with bacon, pine nuts and savoy cabbage with a shallot and lentil sauce, and puddings such as white chocolate and passion fruit mousse and apple and calvados tarte tatin. *Starters/Snacks: £4.95 to £6.50. Main Courses: £12.95 to £18.00. Puddings: £5.50*

Free house ~ Licensee Sean O'Callaghan ~ Real ale ~ Bar food (12-2(3 Sun and bank hols), 7-9; not Sun evening or Mon) ~ Restaurant ~ (01749) 813213 ~ Well behaved children welcome ~ Dogs allowed in bar ~ Open 12-3, 6-11; closed Sun evening and all day Mon (except bank hols)

Recommended by Derek and Heather Manning, G Vyse, J L and C J Hamilton

SIMONSBATH   SS7739   MAP 1

Exmoor Forest Inn 🛏
B3223/B3358; TA24 7SH

In lovely surroundings with plenty of fine walks, comfortable inn with enjoyable food, good range of drinks and friendly licensees

As we went to press we heard that this popular inn was up for sale. It's a friendly place and even on a wet, miserable day there are usually plenty of customers. The bar has a few red plush stools around little circular tables by the bar counter and steps up to a larger area with joists in the ceiling, cushioned settles, upholstered stools and mate's chairs around a mix of dark tables, a woodburning stove with two shelves of stone flagons to one side and hunting prints, trophies and antlers on the walls. The walls of the Tack Room are covered in all sorts of horse tack – saddles, bridles, stirrups, horseshoes and so forth with similar tables and chairs as well as one nice long table for a bigger party. Otter Bright, Quantock Bitter and a couple of summer guests such as Cotleigh Honey Buzzard and St Austell Black Prince on handpump, local cider and local juices, 30 malt whiskies and several wines by the glass. There's a cosy little residents' lounge and an airy dining room. Piped music, board games, bar skittles, and skittle alley. Picnic-sets and wooden and metal benches around tables under parasols in the front garden. The dogs are Billy the lurcher, Noddy the collie and Pip the jack russell. The inn is in lovely surroundings and perfectly positioned for a first or last night's stay on the Two Moors Walk linking Exmoor to Dartmoor; they provide dog beds, bowls and towels.

🍴 **Using some home-grown vegetables and local suppliers, the reliable bar food includes lunchtime filled rolls and filled baked potatoes, soup, terrine of duck and confit duck with home-made crab apple and chilli jelly, garlic field mushrooms in pesto toast, sausages with mash and onion gravy, ham and free-range eggs, saffron and roast vegetable organic risotto, free-range chicken supreme with wild garlic cream sauce, gurnard with a prawn and star anise sauce, and wild local venison casserole with red wine and bacon; daily specials and puddings as well.** *Starters/Snacks: £3.95 to £8.95. Main Courses: £8.50 to £16.95. Puddings: £4.75 to £5.50*

Free house ~ Licensees Chris and Barry Kift ~ Real ale ~ Bar food ~ Restaurant ~ (01643) 831341 ~ Children welcome ~ Dogs allowed in bar and bedrooms ~ Open 12-3, 6.30-11(10.30 Sun); closed Mon lunchtime except bank hols; Sun evening and all day Mon Nov-March ~ Bedrooms: £45S/£85S

Recommended by Laurence Smith, John Urquhart, Michael David Doyle, Lynda and Trevor Smith, Mark Okunie Wski, John and Jackie Walsh

STANTON WICK
ST6162 MAP 2

Carpenters Arms 🍴 🍷 🛏️
Village signposted off A368, just W of junction with A37 S of Bristol; BS39 4BX

Bustling warm-hearted dining pub in nice country setting with imaginative food, friendly staff and good drinks

Well run by a friendly licensee and his attentive staff, this is a civilised and neatly kept dining pub with quick service, blazing fires, and plenty of chatty customers. The Coopers Parlour on the right (which will have been refurbished by the time this *Guide* is published) has one or two beams, seats around heavy tables and attractive curtains and plants in the windows; on the angle between here and the bar area there's a fat woodburning stove in an opened-through corner fireplace. The bar (also refurbished) has wood-backed built-in wall seats and some leather fabric-cushioned stools, stripped stone walls and a big log fire. There's also a snug inner room (lightened by mirrors in arched 'windows') and a restaurant with leather sofas and easy chairs in a comfortable lounge area. Butcombe Bitter, Wadworths 6X, and a beer named after the pub on handpump, ten wines by the glass, and several malt whiskies; games machine and TV. They may ask you to leave your credit card behind the bar. This is a lovely rural setting and there are picnic-sets on the front terrace; pretty flowerbeds and attractive hanging baskets and tubs. This is only ten minutes' drive to the Chew Valley – the perfect place to walk off lunch.

🍴 **Quickly served and rather good, the bar food includes lunchtime sandwiches, mussels in cider and thyme, honey-roast ham with eggs, beefburger with bacon and mozzarella, and roasted red pepper and sunblush tomato and parmesan risotto, and there's also soup, warm duck salad with orange and maple glazed walnuts, a trio of smoked salmon, halibut and trout with horseradish dressing, stir-fried sweet chilli pork with spring onion, ginger, pineapple and egg noodles, steak and kidney in ale pie, pork and apple sausages on bubble and squeak with caramelised shallot gravy, steamed fillets of bass with tomato, chive and prawn butter, and puddings like warm chocolate and nut brownie with orange and Cointreau ice-cream and vanilla panna cotta with apricot, fig and prune compote.** *Starters/Snacks: £4.50 to £8.95. Main Courses: £10.95 to £16.95. Puddings: £4.95 to £6.50*

Buccaneer Holdings ~ Manager Simon Pledge ~ Real ale ~ Bar food (12-2, 7-10; they offer afternoon sandwiches on Sat; all day Sun) ~ Restaurant ~ (01761) 490202 ~ Children welcome ~ Dogs allowed in bar ~ Open 11-11; 12-10.30 Sun; closed evenings 25 and 26 Dec ~ Bedrooms: £72.50B/£105B

Recommended by M G Hart, Terry Buckland, Bettye Reynolds, Mrs Suzy Miller, Bob and Angela Brooks, Carl and Sheila Randall, Andrew Shore, Maria Williams, Mrs Angela Graham, Chris Brooks, John Urquhart, Steve and Liz Tilley, Donna and Roger, Dr and Mrs A K Clarke, MRSM

TARR   SS8632   MAP 1

Tarr Farm ⓦⓨ 🛏

Tarr Steps – rather narrow road off B3223 N of Dulverton, very little nearby parking (paying car park quarter-mile up road); OS Sheet 181 map reference 868322 – as the inn is on the E bank, don't be tempted to approach by car from the W unless you can cope with a deep ford; TA22 9PY

Lovely Exmoor setting looking over Tarr Steps and lots to do nearby; popular food, a fine range of drinks, and friendly staff; bedrooms

Despite being in a remote – if glorious – setting, there are plenty of locals (and visitors) popping in and out of this busy inn throughout the day. It's set on an Exmoor hillside looking down on Tarr Steps just below – that much-photographed clapper bridge of massive granite slabs for medieval packhorses crossing the River Barle as it winds through this lightly wooded combe. The pub part consists of a line of compact and unpretentious rooms, with plenty of good views, slabby rustic tables, stall seating, wall seats and pub chairs, a woodburning stove at one end, salmon pink walls, nice game bird pictures and a pair of stuffed pheasants. The serving bar up a step or two has Exmoor Ale and Gold on handpump, eight wines by the glass and a good choice of other drinks. The residents' end has a smart little evening restaurant (you can eat from this menu in the bar), and a pleasant log-fire lounge with dark leather armchairs and sofas. Outside, lots of chaffinches hop around between slate-topped stone tables above the steep lawn.

🍴 **Bar food can be very rewarding: lunchtime sandwiches and ciabattas and omelettes, as well as soup, chicken, leek and red pepper terrine with piccalilli, home-cured gravadlax with capers and horseradish mustard sauce, honey-roast ham with free-range eggs, beefburger, thai chicken curry, plaice goujons with garlic mayonnaise, calves liver with spring onion mash, crispy bacon and madeira jus, and puddings like apple and plum crumble and sticky toffee pudding with toffee sauce and vanilla bean ice-cream; more elaborate dishes might be a plate of antipasti, roast rack of local lamb with fine ratatouille, and duck breast, chicory tart, creamed leeks and orange scented jus. Cream teas are served all day until 5pm.** *Starters/Snacks: £3.50 to £5.95. Main Courses: £7.00 to £13.00. Puddings: £4.00 to £5.00*

Free house ~ Licensees Richard Benn and Judy Carless ~ Real ale ~ Bar food (11.30-2.30, 6.30-9.30) ~ Restaurant ~ (01643) 851507 ~ Children allowed if over 10 ~ Dogs allowed in bar and bedrooms ~ Open 11-11; closed 1-10 Feb ~ Bedrooms: £90B/£150B

Recommended by Tony and Tracy Constance, George and Gill Rowley, John and Jackie Walsh, John and Jackie Chalcraft, Martin and Pauline Jennings, Glenwys and Alan Lawrence, Mr and Mrs P D Titcomb

TRISCOMBE   ST1535   MAP 1

Blue Ball ⓦⓨ ⓨ

Village signposted off A358 Crowcombe—Bagborough; turn off opposite sign to youth hostel; OS Sheet 181 map reference 155355; TA4 3HE

Fine old building with enjoyable food and drink, and seats on decking making the most of the views; bedrooms

Although there is quite an emphasis on the very good food in this 15th-c thatched stone-built inn – most tables are given over to eating – the licensees are still happy for customers to drop in for a drink and a chat. On the first floor of the original stables, it's a smart place, sloping down gently on three levels, each with its own fire, and cleverly divided into seating by hand-cut beech partitions. Cotleigh Tawny, and a couple of guest beers from Cottage, Exmoor and St Austell on handpump and eight wines by the glass; piped music. The decking at the top of the woodside, terraced garden makes the most of the views. There is a chair lift to the bar/restaurant area for the disabled.

🍴 Good, interesting food includes lunchtime filled rolls and ploughman's, soup, goats cheese, roasted pepper and leek tart with pesto leaves, terrine of rabbit and duck with avocado dressing and caramelised shallots, ham and eggs, burger with bacon and cheese, lasagne, white bean, mushroom and goats cheese cassoulet, ginger and lemon-scented free-range chicken breast with poppy seed rice and sesame vegetables, grilled loin of pork on bubble and squeak with roasted vegetables and stilton infusion, rib-eye steak on rösti with wild funghi, shallots, creamy leeks and jus, and white chocolate and raspberry brûlée with shortbread finger and warm apple flan with caramel ice-cream. *Starters/Snacks: £3.95 to £6.95. Main Courses: £7.95 to £14.95. Puddings: £4.95*

Punch ~ Lease Sue and Gerald Rogers ~ Real ale ~ Bar food (12-2.30, 7-9.30) ~ Restaurant ~ (01984) 618242 ~ Well behaved children welcome ~ Dogs allowed in bar ~ Open 12-4, 6-11(10.30) Sun); closed evenings 25 and 26 Dec and 1 Jan ~ Bedrooms: £40B/£60B

Recommended by Mr and Mrs C R Little, P Dawn, Mr and Mrs P D Titcomb, Mike and Sue Loseby, A J Bowen, Peter Meister, John A Barker, Mrs P Bishop, Terry Miller

WATERROW   ST0525   MAP 1

Rock ♀ 🛏

A361 Wiveliscombe—Bampton; TA4 2AX

Friendly, family-run half-timbered inn, local ales and good food, and nice mix of customers; bedrooms

Civilised and friendly, this striking timbered inn – run by a mother and son partnership – is on the edge of Exmoor National Park. There's quite an emphasis on the imaginative food and attractive bedrooms, but locals do drop in for a pint and a chat. The bar area has a dark brown leather sofa and low table with newspapers and books in front of the stone fireplace with its log fire and big blackboard menus. There's a mix of dining chairs and wooden tables on the partly wood and partly red carpeted floor, a few high-backed bar chairs, hunting paintings and photographs, a couple of built-in cushioned window seats, Cotleigh Tawny, Exmoor Ale, and Otter Ale on handpump, Sheppy's cider, and 15 wines by the glass. A back room has a popular pool table; darts and piped music. Up some steps from the bar is the heavily beamed restaurant (set up on our visit for a cheerful shooting party). The welsh collie is called Meg. There are a few seats under umbrellas by the road.

🍴 Using local produce and beef from their own farm, the good bar food at lunchtime includes filled baguettes, ploughman's, soup, chicken liver parfait with toasted brioche and red onion confit, moules marinière, home-cooked ham and free-range eggs, lasagne, pork sausages with port and onion jus, and a risotto of the day such as pea and mint with parmesan crisps; evening choices like doubled-baked cheese soufflé, fried pigeon breasts with black pudding and a quail egg, beef in red wine pie, fresh beer-battered haddock, roasted barbary duck with Grand Marnier and orange sauce, and fillet of venison with cumberland sauce. *Starters/Snacks: £4.50 to £7.95. Main Courses: £10.95 to £16.95. Puddings: £4.50 to £6.95*

Free house ~ Licensees Matt Harvey and Joanna Oldman ~ Real ale ~ Bar food (12-2.30, 6-9.30) ~ Restaurant ~ (01984) 623293 ~ Children welcome ~ Dogs allowed in bar and bedrooms ~ Open 12-3, 6-11(10.30); closed 25 and 26 Dec ~ Bedrooms: £45S/£75S

Recommended by Bob and Margaret Holder, John and Fiona McIlwain, Heather Coulson, Neil Cross, Nigel Cant

WELLS   ST5445   MAP 2

City Arms 🍺

High Street; BA5 2AG

Busy town centre pub with seven real ales, fine choice of whiskies and wines, and food served all day from 9am

Usefully serving food all day (and their breakfasts are good), this is a busy old pub with plenty of customers popping in and out. The main bar has been refurbished and has leather sofas around low tables, dark wooden pubby chairs around large, heavy tables with carved legs, a gas-effect log fire, and plenty of prints and paintings on the cream walls. There's also a first floor terrace in the cobbled courtyard. Board games and piped music. Up to seven real ales are kept on handpump: Butcombe Bitter and Gold, Cheddar Ales Potholer, Greene King Abbot, IPA and Old Speckled Hen, and Sharps Doom Bar; 35 malt whiskies and 16 wines by the glass. The building was originally a jail, and you can still see a couple of small, barred windows in the courtyard.

🍴 As well as the breakfasts, the popular bar food includes sandwiches, soup, duck and orange pâté with onion marmalade, warm mushroom tartlet with stilton and rocket, beer-battered cod, home-cooked honey and mustard glazed ham with free-range eggs, prime beefburger, steak and kidney suet pudding, salmon pasta, cajun chicken, and daily specials like cottage pie, macaroni cheese and baked haddock with bubble and squeak and a wholegrain mustard sauce. *Starters/Snacks: £3.25 to £4.95. Main Courses: £5.95 to £9.95. Puddings: £3.25 to £3.50*

Free house ~ Licensee Penelope Lee ~ Real ale ~ Bar food (all day till 9.30) ~ Restaurant ~ (01749) 673916 ~ Children welcome ~ Dogs allowed in bar ~ Open 9am(10am Sun)-11.30pm (midnight Sat)

Recommended by Terry Buckland, Mr and Mrs Sandhurst, Joe Green, Ann and Colin Hunt, John and Alison Hamilton, J Roy Smylie, Dr and Mrs A K Clarke

Crown 🛏️

Market Place; BA5 2RF

Handy for the centre, bustling bars open all day for coffee, real ales, and several wines by the glass; bedrooms

As this brightly modernised former coaching inn is in a fine spot in the Market Place overlooked by the cathedral, it's a useful place to pop into for a pint: Butcombe Bitter, Moles Rucking Mole, and Sharps Doom Bar on handpump.The walls in the various bustling bar areas are painted white or blue, there's light wooden flooring, and plenty of matching chairs and cushioned wall benches; up a step is a comfortable area with a sofa and newspapers. A sunny back room (where children tend to go) has an exposed stone fireplace, GWR prints, and a couple of games machines, piped music, and TV; it opens on to a small courtyard with a few tables. More reports please.

🍴 Straightforward bar food such as sandwiches, ploughman's, soup, battered cod, ham and eggs, vegetable pasta, and steak. *Starters/Snacks: £4.50 to £6.50. Main Courses: £6.95 to £13.50. Puddings: £4.95*

Free house ~ Licensees Adrian Lawrence and Matthew Hailingbiggs ~ Real ale ~ Bar food (12-2, 6-9.30) ~ Restaurant ~ (01749) 673457 ~ Children welcome until 8pm ~ Dogs allowed in bedrooms ~ Open 10am-11.30pm(midnight Sat); closed 25 Dec ~ Bedrooms: £60S/£90S

Recommended by John Coatsworth, Dr and Mrs A K Clarke, Steve and Liz Tilley

WEST HATCH   ST2719 MAP 1

Farmers 🛏️

W of village, at Slough Green; from A358 head for RSPCA centre and keep past; TA3 5RS

Attractively decorated rooms, civilised but relaxed atmosphere, bright young staff, a good choice of drinks, and interesting food

The four attractively decorated rooms in this spreading pub are linked by open doorways and decorated in pastels of magnolia, mushroom and green, with bits of stone wall here and there. There are nice stripped floorboards throughout, low ceilings with pale beams, good farmhouse and wheelback chairs around a mix of tables, wooden wall lamps, various large plants, and black and white photographs of teasels and old and modern prints; piped jazz. One fireplace is filled with hundreds of logs and another has a woodburning stove, with some brown leather sofas, little armchairs and a couple of low copper tables in front of it. The atmosphere is civilised and relaxing, and the neat young staff are helpful. Exmoor Ale and Otter Ale on handpump, several wines by the glass, home-made cider, and on our visit winter Pimms, hot toddy and whisky mac. The labrador is called Pickle. Smart picnic-sets on the terrace, covered floodlit area and small neat lawn.

🍴 **Using home-grown vegetables, the often inventive bistro-style bar food includes focaccia sandwiches and filled baguettes, soup, wild mushroom open ravioli with horseradish cream sauce and basil oil, sautéed chicken livers with smoked bacon and madeira sauce, home-baked ham with free-range eggs, beef and watercress burger with peppered sour cream or mushroom, feta and oregano burger with tomato salsa, home-made fishcakes with roasted mediterranean vegetables, crispy leeks and parsley sauce, roasted pork belly filled with apricots with a pancetta cassoulet, and puddings such as baked white chocolate and Kahlua cheesecake with a cappuccino anglaise and passion fruit charlotte with a honey crème fraîche.** *Starters/Snacks: £4.95 to £7.50. Main Courses: £7.50 to £10.95. Puddings: £5.00 to £6.00*

Free house ~ Licensees Debbie Cunliffe and Tom Warren ~ Real ale ~ Bar food (12-2(3 weekends), 7-9(9.30 weekends)) ~ Restaurant ~ (01823) 480480 ~ Well behaved children welcome away from bar area ~ Dogs allowed in bar ~ Open 12-2.30(3 weekends), 6(7 weekends)-11 ~ Bedrooms: £70(£80B)/£120B

Recommended by A H Latham, Bob and Margaret Holder, Tony Winckworth, Simon and Amanda Holder

WOOKEY

ST5245   MAP 2

Burcott 🍺

B3139 W of Wells; BA5 1NJ

Unspoilt, friendly roadside pub with neat bars, west country beers, and reliable food; bedrooms

---

Many of our readers enjoy this neat roadside pub for its warm welcome and reliably good food. The two simply furnished and old-fashioned small front bar rooms have exposed flagstoned floors, lantern-style lights on the walls and a woodburning stove. The lounge has a square corner bar counter, fresh flowers at either end of the mantelpiece above the tiny stone fireplace, Parker-Knollish brocaded chairs around a couple of tables, and high bar stools; the other bar has beams (some willow pattern plates on one), a solid settle by the window and a high backed old pine settle by one wall, cushioned mate's chairs and fresh flowers on the mix of nice old pine tables, and a hunting horn on the bressumer above the fireplace. Darts, shove-ha'penny, cribbage, dominoes, and board games, and built-in wall seats and little framed advertisements in a small right-hand room; piped music. Hop Back Summer Lightning, RCH Pitchfork and Teignworthy Old Moggie on handpump, and several wines by the glass. The window boxes and tubs in front of the building are pretty in summer and a sizeable garden has picnic-sets, plenty of small trees and shrubs and Mendip Hill views. The bedrooms are in converted stables.

🍴 **As well as sandwiches, the well liked food includes chicken liver and wild mushroom pâté with a spicy tomato and caramelised onion chutney, garlic mushrooms, honey roast ham and eggs, steak in ale pie, chicken breast goujons in an apricot and stilton cream sauce, vegetable and cashew nut bake, salmon steak in a white wine and prawn mornay sauce, roasted lamb rump with a fresh mint and honey glaze, daily specials and puddings; three-course Sunday roast.** *Starters/Snacks: £3.95 to £6.95. Main Courses: £7.50 to £9.50. Puddings: £4.25*

Free house ~ Licensees Ian and Anne Stead ~ Real ale ~ Bar food (not Sun or Mon evenings) ~ Restaurant ~ (01749) 673874 ~ Children in restaurant but must be well behaved ~ Open 11.30-2.30, 6-11; 12-3, 6-11 Sat; 12-3, 7-10.30 Sun; closed 25 and 26 Dec, 1 Jan ~ Bedrooms: /£60S

Recommended by Phil and Sally Gorton, Tom Evans, Mr and Mrs R Duys

---

Bedroom prices normally include full english breakfast, VAT and any inclusive service charge that we know of. Prices before the '/' are for single rooms, after for two people in a double or twin (B includes a private bath, S a private shower).

LUCKY DIP

Besides the fully inspected pubs, you might like to try these Lucky Dips recommended to us and described by readers (if you do, please send us reports: feedback@thegoodpubguide.co.uk).

ACTON TURVILLE [ST8080]
Fox & Hounds GL9 1HW: Wide range of pubby food, Greene King Abbot and Shepherd Neame Spitfire, three pleasant rooms off panelled main bar, settee and TV in one *(Donna and Roger)*

ASHCOTT [ST4436]
Pipers TA7 9QL [A39/A361, SE of village]: Reasonably priced food still above average despite staff changes (chef won lottery £5m in summer 2007) in nicely restored beamed dining pub, large lounge, neat bright dining area, cheerful efficient service, Butcombe, Courage Best and Wadworths 6X, Addlestone's cider, good choice of wines by the glass, woodburner, leather armchairs, pictures for sale and potted plants; unobtrusive piped music; pleasant roadside garden *(Jenny and Brian Seller, Comus and Sarah Elliott, Dr and Mrs C W Thomas)*
☆ *Ring o' Bells* TA7 9PZ [High St; pub well signed off A39 W of Street]: Wide choice of good value fresh home-made food from sandwiches to good fish in friendly neatly kept local, quickly changing ales such as Marlow, Moor and RCH, Wilkins's farm cider, steps up and down making snug comfortably modernised areas, decent wines, helpful service, inglenook woodburner; piped music, games machines, skittle alley; attractive back garden with play area and shaded terrace, camping *(Liz and Tony Colman, Joe Green, Meg and Colin Hamilton, Frank Willy, BB)*

AXBRIDGE [ST4354]
Crown BS26 2BN [St Marys St]: Good value unpretentious food from good baguettes up, real ales such as Butcombe or Skinners, friendly staff, dogs allowed in locals' bar (popular table skittles) *(Dennis Jenkin)*
☆ *Lamb* BS26 2AP [The Square; off A371 Cheddar—Winscombe]: Big rambling bar, heavy beams and timbers, open fire in one great stone fireplace, Bath Ales Gem, Butcombe Bitter and Gold and perhaps Fullers London Pride, board games, table skittles, skittle alley; they may try to keep your credit card while you eat; children and dogs allowed, pretty and sheltered small back garden, medieval King John's Hunting Lodge opp (NT), open all day wknds *(Peter Craske, LYM)*
Oak House BS26 2AP [The Square]: Civilised contemporary bar/restaurant, local real ale, good coffee, daily papers *(anon)*

BARRINGTON [ST3918]
☆ *Royal Oak* TA19 0JB: Roomy updated stone-built dining pub with good if not cheap food with a fresh modern twist from enterprising sandwiches to steaks and speciality fish (veg may come from nearby Barrington Court), friendly efficient service, real ales inc Bass

and Butcombe, solid modern furnishings in light and airy lounge bar (children welcome here), no piped music; large outdoor area, opp church in beautiful village *(Dr and Mrs R G J Telfer, Anneliese Cooke, Mrs M K Matthews)*

BATH [ST7565]
Bell BA1 5BW [Walcot St]: Eight regular real ales, interesting guest beers and farm cider in long narrow split-level dark-ceilinged pub with lots of pump clips and gig notices, good value baguettes, bar billiards; packed and lively evenings with loud music; canopied garden, open all day *(Pete Baker, Dr and Mrs A K Clarke, the Didler, Donna and Roger)*
☆ *Coeur de Lion* BA1 5AR [Northumberland Pl; off High St by W H Smith]: Tiny single-room pub, perhaps Bath's prettiest, simple, cosy and friendly, with well kept Abbey ales and guest beers, candles and log-effect gas fire, good mulled wine at Christmas, lunchtime filled rolls in summer; may be piped music, stairs to lavatories; tables out in charming flower-filled flagstoned pedestrian alley, open all day *(Dr and Mrs A K Clarke, LYM, Michael Dandy, Pete Coxon, the Didler, Roger Wain-Heapy)*
Cross Keys BA2 5RZ [Midford Rd (B3110)]: Another change of licensee, minimalist décor with plain walls and arty black-and-white pictures, enjoyable standard food, good choice of real ales; live music and quiz nights planned; big garden *(Meg and Colin Hamilton, Pete Coxon, Dr and Mrs A K Clarke)*
Crystal Palace BA1 1NW [Abbey Green]: Cheerfully busy two-room pub with something of a winebar feel, dark panelling and tiled floors, freshly prepared straightforward food (not Sun evening) inc lunchtime snacks, speedy friendly service, well kept ales such as Abbey Bellringer, Jennings and Marstons Pedigree, log fire, family room and conservatory; piped music; sheltered heated courtyard with lovely hanging baskets *(Dr and Mrs A K Clarke, Tom and Jill Jones, Dr and Mrs M E Wilson, LYM, Ian Phillips, Donna and Roger)*
Forester & Flower BA2 5BZ [Bradford Rd, Combe Down]: Friendly good value dining pub with good Sun roasts and a couple of well kept ales *(Mark O'Sullivan, Dr and Mrs A K Clarke)*
☆ *Garricks Head* BA1 1ET [Theatre Royal, St Johns Pl]: Relaxed and attractive food pub, armchairs, sofa and big wooden tables on bare boards, two open fires, good food (that bit different without being affected) served quickly if not cheaply, notably friendly helpful staff, interesting wines by the glass, Milk Street and guest

ales such as Palmers, daily papers; pavement tables, handy for Theatre Royal *(Dr and Mrs M E Wilson, Dr and Mrs A K Clarke, Steve and Liz Tilley, Mr and Mrs W W Burke, Edward Mirzoeff)*

Gascoyne Place BA1 1EY [Sawclose]: Stylish comfortable new pub in 18th-c building, good choice of drinks, bar food all day, front bar with gallery, boarded ceiling and stripped masonry in long back bar, upstairs restaurant; Sun jazz night; open all day *(Dr and Mrs A K Clarke)*

☆ *George* BA2 6TR [Bathampton, E of Bath centre, off A36 or (via toll bridge) off A4; Mill Lane]: Beautifully placed canalside Chef & Brewer dining pub, wide blackboard food choice all day at good spread of prices, five real ales and good choice of wines by the glass, plenty of well organised young uniformed staff, good-sized bar opening through arches into rambling beamed rooms with soft lighting, three log fires, candles on nice mix of tables, rugs on polished boards, dark panelling, period portraits and plates; may be quiet piped music; children welcome, enclosed suntrap terrace and waterside tables (may be drinks only, out here) *(Dr and Mrs M E Wilson, Richard Fendick, Meg and Colin Hamilton, Norman and Sarah Keeping, Dr and Mrs A K Clarke, Pete Coxon, Donna and Roger)*

Hare & Hounds BA1 5TJ [Lansdown Rd, Lansdown Hill]: Elegant stone building with superb views from big garden and terrace, attractive and comfortably furnished long well divided bar, Abbey Bellringer and Courage, enjoyable food, friendly staff, leaded lights in mullioned windows, lots of woodwork, hanging bird cages and shelves of bric-a-brac, roomy eating area and conservatory, open all day *(Dr and Mrs A K Clarke, Mr and Mrs A H Young)*

☆ *Hop Pole* BA1 3AR [Albion Buildings, Upper Bristol Rd]: Bustling friendly Bath Ales pub with guest beers, farm cider, decent wines by the glass, enjoyable food (not Sun evening) from sandwiches to full meals in bar and former skittle alley restaurant, traditional settles and other pub furniture on bare boards in four tastefully reworked linked areas, lots of black woodwork and ochre walls; Mon quiz night; children welcome, wheelchair accessible, attractive two-level back courtyard with boules, terrace tables, fairy-lit vine arbour and summer houses with heaters, opp Victoria Park with its great play area, open all day *(Colin and Peggy Wilshire, Roger Wain-Heapy, Dr and Mrs M E Wilson, Chris and Angela Buckell, the Didler, BB, Dr and Mrs A K Clarke)*

Marlborough BA1 2LY [Marlborough Buildings]: Nicely updated over the years, sensibly priced fresh bar food inc interesting dishes, welcoming mix of ages; courtyard garden *(Dr and Mrs A K Clarke, Mary Docherty, Mr and Mrs A H Young)*

Pig & Fiddle BA1 5BR [Saracen St]: Lively pub, not smart, with good sensibly priced

ales such as Abbey, Bath and Butcombe, pleasant staff, two big open fires, clocks set to different time zones, bare boards and bright paintwork, steps up to darker bustling servery and little dining area, games area and several TVs; lots of students at night, good piped trendy pop music then; picnic-sets on big heated front terrace, open all day *(Derek and Sylvia Stephenson, Dr and Mrs M E Wilson, Dr and Mrs A K Clarke, BB, the Didler, Donna and Roger)*

Raven BA1 1HE [Queen St]: Small friendly pub with Blindmans and guest ales, a changing farm cider, particularly good lunchtime pies, sausages and savoury mash, cheerful helpful staff, open fire, charity bookshelves, some stripped stone, upstairs dining room, live music; open all day *(Pete Coxon, John Robertson, Dr and Mrs M E Wilson, Dr and Mrs A K Clarke, the Didler, Meg and Colin Hamilton, Catherine Pitt, Andrew and Debbie Ettle)*

Richmond Arms BA1 5PZ [Richmond Pl, off Lansdown Rd]: Small 18th-c house with friendly licensees, good imaginative food, good wine choice, Bass and Butcombe, bare boards, pine tables and chairs, unusual quiet setting off the tourist track; children welcome, enclosed pretty front garden *(Dr and Mrs A K Clarke, Trevor and Sylvia Millum)*

Salamander BA1 2JL [John St]: Busy city local tied to Bath Ales, their full range and guest beers, bare boards, black woodwork and dark ochre walls, bargain basic bar lunches (get there early for a table), two rooms downstairs, open-kitchen upstairs restaurant, decent wines, daily papers, live irish music Tues; open all day *(Dr and Mrs A K Clarke, Dr and Mrs M E Wilson, BB, the Didler, Derek and Sylvia Stephenson, Pete Coxon, LM, Steve and Liz Tilley, Ian Phillips)*

Volunteer Riflemans Arms BA1 1BH [New Bond St Place]: Compact pub with four well kept quickly changing ales, friendly landlord, cheery locals, old light wood furnishings, upstairs eating area; pavement tables *(Dr and Mrs M E Wilson)*

BECKINGTON [ST8051]

☆ *Woolpack* BA11 6SP [Warminster Rd, off A36 bypass]: Well refurbished and civilised old inn with charming helpful staff, unusual and well prepared if not cheap food from well filled ciabattas up, well kept Greene King, decent wines, farm cider, big log fire and chunky candlelit tables in flagstoned bar, attractive smarter oak-panelled dining room and conservatory; children welcome, appealing period bedrooms, open all day *(Simon and Sally Small, LYM, Dr and Mrs M E Wilson)*

BLAGDON HILL [ST2118]

Blagdon Inn TA3 7SG [4 miles S of Taunton]: Stylish contemporary country pub with good choice of enjoyable good value food, well kept beers, good choice of wines, lively friendly service, plenty of room for eating

or relaxing, log fire; terrace tables
(I H G Busby, Heather Coulson, Neil Cross, MB)

BRADFORD-ON-TONE [ST1722]

☆ *White Horse* TA4 1HF [fairly nr M5 junction 26, off A38 towards Taunton]: Neat and comfortable 17th-c stone-built local in quiet village, wide choice of good reasonably priced fresh food in straightforward bar eating area and cheerfully decorated dining room, welcoming licensees and staff, Badger Tanglefoot and Cotleigh Tawny, decent wines, malt whiskies, armchairs by ornate woodburner, hunting cartoons, bar billiards, skittle alley; piped music; pretty back garden with fairy-lit arbour and boules (Bob and Margaret Holder, BB, Charles, Richard Fendick)

BRENDON HILLS [ST0334]

☆ *Raleghs Cross* TA23 0LN [junction B3190/B3224]: Busy family-friendly upland inn with helpful friendly staff, wide choice of well priced generous food, good puddings, Cotleigh, Exmoor and a guest beer, rows of plush banquettes in big bar, back restaurant/carvery; children in restaurant and family room, no dogs; plenty of tables outside with play area, views to Wales on clear days, good walking country, 17 comfortable bedrooms, open all day summer (B M Eldridge, John and Bryony Coles, Paul Thompson, Bob and Angela Brooks, Roy and Jean Russell, LYM)

BRENT KNOLL [ST3251]

Red Cow TA9 4BE [2 miles from M5 junction 22; right on to A38, then first left into Brent St]: Well run pub with well prepared standard food in dining lounge (children allowed), well kept Butcombe, family room, skittle alley; no dogs inside; pretty gardens front and back (MP, BB)

BRIDGWATER [ST3140]

Admirals Table TA6 4TN [A38 N, just off M5 junction 23]: Big Marstons pub useful as motorway break, wide food choice inc wknd carvery, attentive young staff, lots of beamery, old-fashioned prints, some bric-a-brac; quiet piped music; small back decked area, open all day (Richard Fendick)

BRISTOL [ST5773]

Alma BS8 2HY [Alma Vale Rd, Clifton]: Two-bar pub under newish ownership, decent food from sandwiches to some quite imaginative dishes, good value wines, real ales such as Black Sheep, Sharps Doom Bar and Shepherd Neame Spitfire, good choice of malt whiskies, cheerful helpful staff, sofas and armchairs as well as plain tables and chairs; piped music, games machines, students can get noisy evenings; popular upstairs theatre Tues-Sat – best to book; wheelchair access, small back terrace (not late evening) (Chris and Angela Buckell)

Apple BS1 4SB [Welsh Back]: Barge specialising in ciders, cheap comfort food – popular with students; quayside seating under huge umbrella (Kerry Law)

☆ *Bag o' Nails* BS1 5UW [St Georges Rd, by B4466/A4 Hotwells roundabout]: Proudly old-fashioned and popular for its half a dozen or more changing ales and bottled beers, good cobs; piped music; beer festivals, open all day Fri-Sun (the Didler, Simon and Amanda Southwell)

Bell BS2 8JT [Hillgrove St off Jamaica St]: Two-room local with well kept Butcombe ales, choice of farm ciders, pubby food; no disabled access; back terrace (Chris and Angela Buckell)

Berkeley BS8 1QE [Queens Rd, Clifton]: Weatherspoons conversion of old shopping arcade, double doors to main bar, long narrower bar to right and interconnecting rooms, one with surprising stained-glass dome, their usual value pricing; popular with students; disabled access and facilities (Chris and Angela Buckell)

Bridge Inn BS2 0JF [Passage St]: Neat little one-bar city pub nr floating harbour, good friendly service, lots of film stills and posters, Bath and guest ales, lunchtime sandwiches and quick hot food, padded wall seats; well reproduced music; tables outside, open all day (the Didler)

Colston Yard BS1 5BD [Upper Maudlin St/Colston St]: Former Smiles Brewery Tap reopened as a Butcombe pub, their full range, interesting bottled beers, good value wines, wide food choice from lunchtime sandwiches to grills and evening restaurant menu, two floors in current minimalist pastel style; wheelchair access (Chris and Angela Buckell)

☆ *Commercial Rooms* BS1 1HT [Corn St]: Spacious Wetherspoons with lofty domed ceiling and snug cubicles along one side, gas lighting, comfortable quieter room with ornate balcony; wide changing choice of good real ales, sensibly priced food all day, friendly chatty bustle, wind indicator, and surprising ladies' with chesterfields and open fire; good location, very busy wknd evenings, side wheelchair access (Gordon Tong, Dr and Mrs A K Clarke, Donna and Roger, the Didler, Simon and Amanda Southwell)

☆ *Cornubia* BS1 6EN [Temple St]: Well run 18th-c backstreet real ale pub with good Hidden ales and several recherché guest beers, interesting bottled beers, farm cider and perry, wkdy food till 7.30, small woody seating areas; can be crowded evenings, not for wheelchairs; picnic-sets on cobbles outside, open all day (from 7pm Sat, cl Sun) (the Didler, Alan Pratt-Walters)

Eldon House BS8 1BT [Lower Clifton Hill]: Friendly and individual, with three unassuming slightly bohemian rooms, candles, flowers and plain wood, sympathetic staff, decent food inc some interesting evening dishes, Bath ales, good value wines, some live jazz or blues; wheelchair access, metal tables and chairs out by pavement (Chris and Angela Buckell)

Grain Barge BS8 4RU [Hotwell Rd]: Floating barge tied to Bristol Beer Factory, their good beers and freshly made food inc ale sausages/pies and beer-battered fish, picnic-sets on top deck, sofas downstairs; live music Fri night, open all day (the Didler, Kerry Law)

Hare on the Hill BS2 8LX [Thomas St N]: Traditional friendly corner local, well kept Bath ales and guest, lots of malt whiskies, good value pubby food, pictures by local artists, live music Sun; not for wheelchairs, sports TV; open all day Fri-Sun (Chris and Angela Buckell, the Didler)

Hatchet BS1 5NA [Frogmore St]: Lively lunchtime atmosphere with well priced simple food from sandwiches up, well kept Butcombe (Steve and Liz Tilley, Dr and Mrs A K Clarke)

Highbury Vaults BS2 8DE [St Michaels Hill, Cotham]: Well kept Bath, St Austell and Wells & Youngs ales in studenty pub with small partly dark-panelled rooms, cheap food (not Sat/Sun evenings), old-fashioned furniture and prints, bar billiards, dominoes, cribbage; wheelchair access (staff help you to the main bar, but steep steps to lavatories); children welcome, attractive back terrace with heated arbour, open all day (LM, Chris and Angela Buckell, the Didler, LYM)

Hillgrove Porter Stores BS2 8LT [Hillgrove St N]: Friendly unfussy local with basic interior inc comfortable lounge, four mainly local well kept changing ales (prices reduced on Mon), good choice of wines by the glass, welcoming landlady, Sun quiz night; not for wheelchairs; back terrace, open 4-12 (Chris and Angela Buckell, the Didler)

Hope & Anchor BS8 1DR [Jacobs Wells Rd, Clifton]: Bare-boards 18th-c pub with half a dozen changing ales from central bar, large shared pine tables, good service, good value substantial food all day inc lots of sandwiches, interesting dishes and sumptuous ploughman's – very popular lunchtime; piped music, occasional live, can get crowded late evening; disabled access, summer evening barbecues in good-sized tiered back garden with interesting niches (Jeremy King, the Didler, Simon and Amanda Southwell)

Hophouse BS8 4AB [16 Kings Rd, Clifton]: Refurbished Wadworths pub with sofas and wooden chairs in big-windowed bar, upstairs dining room; TV, live music Mon; open all day (Donna and Roger)

Horts City Tavern BS1 2EJ [Broad St]: Well refurbished 18th-c pub with well kept Bath Gem, Wells & Youngs and guest beers, food inc huge choice of sandwiches served quickly in two main bars and eating area, friendly helpful service, some panelling, ornate ironwork dividers, chesterfields and old prints, pool in games area; piped music; open all day, terrace tables (Donna and Roger)

☆ **Kensington Arms** BS6 6NP [Stanley Rd]: Smart newish dining pub in discreet shades of grey and cream, cheerful helpful staff, enjoyable food from light pub lunches to bigger pricier evening dishes, well kept Greene King ales, good if not cheap wine choice, interesting rums etc, flowers and lit candles; may be piped music; wheelchair facilities and access (not to dining room/upstairs dining room), well behaved children and dogs welcome, heated terrace (Gaynor Gregory, Chris and Angela Buckell, John and Gloria Isaacs)

☆ **Kings Head** BS1 6DE [Victoria St]: Friendly relaxed 17th-c pub with big front window and splendid mirrored bar back, corridor to cosy panelled back snug with serving hatch, Courage, Wadworths and other ales, toby jugs on joists, old-fashioned local prints and photographs, interesting gas pressure gauge, generous reasonably priced food wkdy lunchtimes (get there early if you want a seat); no credit cards; pavement tables, cl Sat lunchtime, open all day Weds-Fri (Pete Baker, the Didler, Gordon Tong, Dr and Mrs A K Clarke, BB, Di and Mike Gillam)

Lamplighters BS11 9XA [Station Rd, Shirehampton]: Riverside pub with decent sensibly priced straightforward food, good range of beers, efficient friendly service, upstairs balcony, daily papers; piped music may obtrude, games machines; good-sized garden with play area (Chris and Angela Buckell, John and Gloria Isaacs)

Llandoger Trow BS1 4ER [off King St/Welsh Back]: By docks, interesting as the last timber-framed building built here, impressive flower-decked façade, reasonably priced bar food inc daytime bargains (not Sun), upstairs restaurant, Greene King IPA and Old Speckled Hen, friendly staff, some small alcoves and rooms with original fireplaces and carvings around central servery, wide mix from students to tourists; piped music; picnic-sets out by cobbled pedestrianised street, bedrooms in adjacent Premier Lodge (Jeremy King, Sue and Mike Todd)

Merchants Arms BS8 4PZ [Merchants Rd, Hotwells]: Tiny two-room pub close to historic dockside, well kept Bath ales, Ashton Press cider, interesting ports (monthly port and local cheese night), limited food inc local pies, impromptu folk and sea shanty sessions; wheelchair access with determined help (Chris and Angela Buckell)

Nova Scotia BS1 6XJ [Baltic Wharf, Cumberland Basin]: Unreconstructed old local on S side of Floating Harbour, views to Clifton and Avon Gorge, Bass, Courage Best and guest beers, Thatcher's farm cider, bargain hearty food inc Sun roasts, pubby seats in four linked areas, snob screen, mahogany and mirrors, nautical charts as wallpaper; wheelchair access (two steps), plenty of tables out by water, bedrooms sharing bathroom (Dr and Mrs A K Clarke, Chris and Angela Buckell, LM)

Old Fish Market BS1 1QZ [Baldwin St]: Imposing red and cream brick building converted to roomy pub, good mural showing it in 1790s, green décor, lots of dark wood inc handsome counter, parquet floor, relaxed friendly atmosphere, good value mainly thai food all day, four well kept Fullers ales and guest such as Butcombe, good coffee, daily papers; quiet piped music, unobtrusive sports TV, games machines; open all day *(Jeremy King, Dr and Mrs A K Clarke, Dr and Mrs M E Wilson, Simon and Amanda Southwell)*

Orchard BS1 6XT [Hanover Pl]: Friendly one-room local with fine range of well kept real ales and ciders, may be food such as hot pies; tables out in front, handy for SS Great Britain *(Pete Baker)*

Penny Farthing BS8 2PB [Whiteladies Rd, Clifton]: Bright panelled ex-bank with Bath Gem and full Wadworths range racked behind bar, late Victorian bric-a-brac inc penny-farthing (and photographs of them), armchairs opp bar, lots of table seating, very good value home-made food lunchtime and evening, friendly helpful staff; big-screen TV, can get very busy evenings; pavement tables *(Donna and Roger, the Didler)*

Robin Hoods Retreat BS7 8BG [Gloucester Rd, Bishopston]: Smartly refurbished horseshoe bar with eight well kept ales, good wines by the glass, good food with freshly podded veg, cheerful young staff, daily papers, small dining area just off bar (which can be noisy Fri night) *(Dr and Mrs A K Clarke, Gaynor Gregory, D C Leggatt)*

Staple Hill Oak BS16 5HN [High St]: Welcoming modern Wetherspoons with well kept range of interesting real ales at bargain prices *(Dr and Mrs A K Clarke)*

White Lion BS8 4LD [Avon Gorge Hotel, Princes Buildings, Clifton]: Worth knowing for terrace bar overlooking Clifton Bridge; simple inside, with high tables and stools, leather sofas and chairs, Butcombe and blackboard bar food from baguettes up; sports TV; bedrooms *(Donna and Roger)*

Whitehall BS5 9AD [Devon Rd]: Lively friendly local with jolly landlord, well kept Courage Best, wood floors and stripped stone; horseracing on two TVs *(Dr and Mrs A K Clarke)*

Windmill BS3 4LU [Windmill Hill, Bedminster]: Sofas and bare boards, pleasant décor, buoyant casual relaxed atmosphere, Bath, Bristol Beer Factory and guest ales, two farm ciders, wholesome and interesting soups, pies and tapas, good home-made puddings, pub games; 1970s juke box, TV; tables out on small deck *(Gaynor Gregory, Mrs Jane Kingsbury, Dr M E Williams)*

BROMPTON REGIS [SS9531]

☆ *George* TA22 9NL: 17th-c country local in quiet remote village, warmly welcoming and accommodating chef/landlord, wide choice of reasonably priced home-made food inc local trout, imaginative dishes and good Sun roast, well kept ales such as Exmoor, organic wines, woodburners, pub games (no juke box or machines), active skittle alley, pleasant dining lounge; may be quiet piped music; children and dogs welcome (Huckleberry is the character pub dog), Exmoor views from

pleasant garden by churchyard, good walks, cl Mon *(John and Christine Cross, BB)*

CASTLE CARY [ST6432]

George BA7 7AH [just off A371 Shepton Mallet—Wincanton; Market Pl]: Thatched country-town hotel, quiet and civilised, with big inglenook in small front bar, inner no smoking lounge off main central reception area, enjoyable straightforward food from sandwiches up, Greene King ales, decent house wines; children welcome, 16 bedrooms, open all day *(LYM, Derek and Sylvia Stephenson)*

CATCOTT [ST3939]

☆ *Crown* TA7 9HQ [off A39 W of Street; Nidon Lane, via Brook Lane]: Roomy country pub under new ownership, wide choice of generous pub food inc good Sun carvery, real ales such as Butcombe and Fullers London Pride, farm cider, decent wines by the glass, cosy area by log fire, skittle alley; children welcome, picnic-sets and play area out behind, bedrooms *(LYM, Frank Willy, KC, Mr and Mrs H J Stephens)*

King William TA7 9HU [signed off A39 Street—Bridgwater]: Spacious and spotless, with central bar, rugs on flagstones, big stone fireplaces, traditional furnishings, old prints, food inc good value Sun lunch, well kept Palmers ales, good range of malt whiskies, darts, cribbage, dominoes, big back extension with skittle alley and glass-topped well; piped music; children welcome *(LYM, Joe Green)*

CHARLTON ADAM [ST5328]

Fox & Hounds TA11 7AU [Broadway Rd, just off A37 about 3 m N of Ilchester]: Big friendly and neatly refurbished pub with prompt pleasant service, enjoyable home-made food *(Richard Marjoram, J Stickland)*

CHEDDAR [ST4553]

☆ *Gardeners Arms* BS27 3LE [Silver St]: Relaxed and cheerful, tucked away in the old part, with enjoyable food (service can suffer when busy) from familiar pub lunches to beautifully presented exotic dishes, well kept Adnams, Butcombe and Courage Best, cheery log fires, attractive two-room beamed dining area, interesting old local photographs; children and dogs welcome, playthings and wendy house in quiet back garden, open all day *(JCW, LYM, Richard Fendick, John and Gloria Isaacs)*

CHEW MAGNA [ST5861]

☆ *Pony & Trap* BS40 8TQ [Knowle Hill, New Town; back rd to Bishop Sutton]: Enjoyable food, good relaxing atmosphere and welcoming helpful staff in small gently refurbished tucked-away pub with comfortable layout, flagstones, antiques and lit candles, Butcombe, Courage Best and Exmoor Stag, good wines by the glass and coffee, downstairs conservatory restaurant – great views from here and garden picnic-sets; wheelchair access to bar, good walks, delightfully rural hillside setting nr Chew Valley Lake *(Chris and Angela Buckell, Nigel Long, Gaynor Gregory)*

CLEVEDON [ST4071]

☆ *Old Inn* BS21 6AE [Walton Rd (B3124 on outskirts)]: Friendly mix of regulars and visitors in neatly extended beamed pub, good solid furniture on carpets, good value generous food (all day Sat), well kept Otter Head and Theakstons Old Peculier; bedrooms, open all day (*Tom Evans, Will Stevens, Tim and Rosemary Wells*)

CLUTTON HILL [ST6360]

Hunters Rest BS39 5QL [off A39 Bristol—Wells]: Extended pub with tasteful mix of stone and plaster walls, black beams and joists, Butcombe, Matthews, Otter and a guest beer, Thatcher's farm cider, wide choice of enjoyable bar food from interestingly filled home-baked rolls and pastries to hearty home cooking, family room, log fires, restaurant, no piped music; disabled facilities, big garden with play area and view to Mendips, five bedrooms (*Stuart Paulley*)

COLEFORD [ST6848]

Kings Head BA3 5LU [Underhill]: Popular extended village pub with friendly landlord, local Blindmans Buff, Box Steam Dark & Handsome and Cheddar Valley farm cider in big bar with woodburner, bar food, separate pool room; large lawn, plenty of walks (*Ian Phillips*)

COMBE FLOREY [ST1531]

☆ *Farmers Arms* TA4 3HZ [off A358 Taunton—Williton, just N of main village turn-off]: Neatly kept thatched and beamed dining pub, enjoyable food using prime local produce, real ales such as Exmoor and Otter, local farm cider, comfortable drinking area with log fire; children welcome, plenty of tables in attractive garden, by summer steam line (*Bob and Margaret Holder, David Barnes, BB, Dr and Mrs P Humphrey*)

COMBE HAY [ST7359]

☆ *Wheatsheaf* BA2 7EG [off A367 or B3110 S of Bath]: Upscale food from sandwiches and tasty home-baked breads through short changing choice of up-to-date starters and main dishes to tempting puddings, Butcombe beers, local farm cider, good wine choice, quick friendly service, plush fireside sofas, big fresh and airy dining area with trendy light modern furnishings (a radical change for this 1576 pub); tables in attractive terraced garden overlooking church and steep valley, dovecotes built into the walls, plenty of good nearby walks, comfortable bedrooms in outbuildings, cl Mon (*J and J Palmer, Adele Barton, Donna and Roger, LYM, Dr and Mrs A K Clarke*)

COMPTON DUNDON [ST4832]

Castlebrook Inn TA11 6PR [Castlebrook]: Cheerful two-bar village local, warm and friendly, with super flagstone floors, blazing log fire, Greene King IPA, Sharps Doom Bar and Wadworths 6X, quick service, good value enjoyable straightforward food from open-view kitchen, big back simple family restaurant, Sun carvery, daily papers; big lawn behind with play area (*R J and G M Townson, Ian Phillips*)

COMPTON MARTIN [ST5457]

☆ *Ring o' Bells* BS40 6JE [A368 Bath—Weston]: Country pub in attractive spot, another new licensee, traditional front part with rugs on flagstones, inglenook seats by log fire, up step to spacious carpeted back part, stripped stone, Butcombe Bitter and Gold and Bath Gem, ciders, Thurs jazz night; piped music; well behaved children and dogs welcome, big garden with play area, open all day wknds (*LYM*)

COSSINGTON [ST3640]

Red Tile TA7 8LN [Middle Rd]: Attractive pub with enjoyable generous food, changing ales such as Butcombe, Cheddar and Sharps, cosy fire; children and dogs welcome, garden tables under walnut tree, adventure play area (*Richard Fendick*)

CROSS [ST4254]

New Inn BS26 2EE [A38 Bristol—Bridgwater, junction A371]: Friendly roadside pub with good atmosphere, limited but interesting choice of enjoyable food from filling sandwiches up, pleasant dining area, well kept weekly-changing ales, reasonable prices, fine views, upstairs games room (*Hugh Roberts*)

CROWCOMBE [ST1336]

☆ *Carew Arms* TA4 4AD [just off A358 Taunton—Minehead]: Interesting 17th-c beamed inn with hunting trophies and inglenook woodburner in appealingly old-fashioned front public bar, well kept Exe Valley, Exmoor and Otter ales, Lane's strong farm cider and good choice of wines by the glass, enjoyable food from pubby things to more expensive specials, friendly service, traditional games and skittle alley, neat dining room allowing children; dogs welcome (wandering jack russells), informal garden with good play things, open all day summer wknds (*the Didler, LYM, Mike and Sue Loseby, Tony Winckworth, Mr and Mrs Sandhurst, Terry Miller, Bob and Margaret Holder, Peter Meister*)

CURRY RIVEL [ST3925]

Olde Forge TA10 0HE [Church St]: Small welcoming bar, attractive décor, mugs on beams, light beamed dining room, good food and service, real ales; cellar bar with fine 14th-c vaulted ceiling for small parties, art shows (*Elizabeth Mawson*)

DONYATT [ST3314]

George TA19 0RW [A358, a mile S of A303]: Friendly and civilised, with relaxing traditional décor, well kept Butcombe and Fullers London Pride, decent wines by the glass, good service, interesting choice of reasonably priced enjoyable food from well filled rolls to plenty of fish; games machine in smaller side room (*Roger Weldhen*)

DOWLISH WAKE [ST3712]

New Inn TA19 0NZ [off A3037 S of Ilminster, via Kingstone]: Dark-beamed village pub reopened under hard-working family, popular food using fresh local produce, well kept Butcombe and Otter, local farm cider, woodburners in stone inglenooks, pleasant dining room; attractive garden and village, four comfortable bedrooms *(LYM, Douglas Allen)*

DULVERTON [SS9127]

Bridge Inn TA22 9HJ [Bridge St]: Unpretentious local with *Lorna Doone* connections, home-made food from local suppliers, good choice of beers, ciders and wines, welcoming young licensees, log fire; dogs welcome, riverside garden *(David and Carol Foster)*

DUNSTER [SS9943]

☆ *Luttrell Arms* TA24 6SG [High St; A396]: Small hotel in 15th-c timber-framed abbey building, well used high-beamed back bar hung with bottles, clogs and horseshoes, stag's head and rifles on walls above old settles and more modern furniture, big log fires, enjoyable if not cheap bar food inc substantial sandwiches with home-baked bread, small helpings available, friendly attentive staff, well kept ales inc Exmoor Fox, good wines in three glass sizes; dogs welcome in bar, ancient glazed partition dividing off small galleried and flagstoned courtyard, upstairs access to quiet attractive garden with Civil War cannon emplacements and great views, comfortable if pricy bedrooms (have to stay two nights wknds) *(Mr and Mrs P D Titcomb, Sue Demont, Tim Barrow, Glenwys and Alan Lawrence, BB, Tom and Ruth Rees, Peter and Margaret Glenister, Paul Humphreys)*

☆ *Stags Head* TA24 6SN [West St]: Good sensibly priced food from traditional pub dishes to eastern exotics in 15th-c inn on flintstone pavement below castle, lively friendly atmosphere, brisk service by attentive entertaining staff, Archers, Cotleigh and Exmoor ales, candles, beams, timbers and inglenooks; dogs welcome, comfortable bedrooms *(Peter and Jean Hoare, Andrew and Debbie Ettle, Paul and Karen Cornock, Allan Worth)*

EAST HARPTREE [ST5655]

Waldegrave Arms BS40 6BD [Church Lane]: Very welcoming stone-floored 17th-c pub largely set out for newish chef/landlord's enjoyable food, cheerful young staff, Bath ales, traditional décor, log fires in beamed bar and dining room; children and dogs welcome, picnic-sets in attractive sheltered garden *(Stuart Paulley, Tom Evans)*

EAST LAMBROOK [ST4218]

☆ *Rose & Crown* TA13 5HF: Neatly kept stone-built dining pub spreading extensively from compact 17th-c core with inglenook log fire, efficient friendly staff and relaxed atmosphere, good generous inexpensive food freshly made using local supplies inc very popular wkdy OAP lunches, full Palmers real ale range, farm cider, decent wines by the glass, restaurant extension showing old well through central glass floor panel; picnic-sets on neat lawn, opp East Lambrook Manor Garden *(Evelyn and Derek Walter, Nick Hawksley, BB, Meg and Colin Hamilton)*

EASTON-IN-GORDANO [ST5175]

Rudgleigh Inn BS20 0QD [A369 a mile from M5 junction 19]: Two-bar refurbished roadside pub popular for enjoyable promptly served food at sensible prices from baguettes up, Bath and Courage ales, extension restaurant suiting families, welcoming service; piped music; big well tended enclosed garden with willows, tamarisks, play area and cricket-field view, open all day wkdys *(Tom Evans, LYM)*

ENMORE [ST2635]

Enmore Inn TA5 2AH [Enmore Rd]: Enjoyable good value home-made food inc Sun carvery using good local meat, real ales, nice atmosphere, popular wknds *(Brian and Genie Smart, Bob and Margaret Holder)*

Tynte Arms TA5 2DP: Open-plan low-beamed pub with wide choice of good generous food cooked by landlady inc lots of fish, good puddings and good value set menus, relaxed atmosphere and pleasant staff, west country ales from long bar, plenty of dining tables, chesterfields and settles, end inglenook, china collection; car park over road, good walking country *(Bob and Margaret Holder, T K Baker, B M Eldridge)*

EVERCREECH [ST6336]

Natterjack BA4 6NA [A371 Shepton Mallet—Castle Cary]: Wide choice of generous good value food, Butcombe and another real ale, pleasant helpful staff, long bar with eating areas off *(Michael and Jenny Back)*

EXFORD [SS8538]

☆ *White Horse* TA24 7PY [B3224]: Three-storey creeper-covered inn, more or less open-plan bar, high-backed antique settle among more conventional seats, scrubbed deal tables, hunting prints and local photographs, good log fire, Exmoor Ale, Dunkery Ale and Gold and Sharps Doom Bar, over 100 malt whiskies, Thatcher's cider, hearty food from sandwiches up, daily Land Rover Exmoor safaris; children and dogs welcome, play area and outside tables, comfortable bedrooms, pretty village, open all day from 8 *(LYM, Martin and Pauline Jennings, Lynda and Trevor Smith, Paul Humphreys, Nick Lawless, J L Wedel)*

FAILAND [ST5171]

Failand Inn BS8 3TU [B3128 Bristol—Clevedon]: Simply furnished old coaching inn with wide choice of popular family food, Butcombe and Courage, good wines by the glass, comfortable dining extension; may be piped music; dogs and children welcome, garden with play area *(Comus and Sarah Elliott, Mr and Mrs A Curry, John and Gloria Isaacs)*

FARMBOROUGH [ST6661]

New Inn BA2 0BY [Bath Rd (A39)]: Roomy roadside Greene King pub, friendly staff, generous traditional food *(Dr and Mrs A K Clarke)*

FRESHFORD [ST7960]

☆ *Inn at Freshford* BA2 7WG [off A36 or B3108]: Roomy beamed stone-built dining pub now tied to Box Steam with their ales and a guest, good choice of wines by the glass, comfortable traditional layout inc area with leather sofas and chairs by fire, enjoyable food inc cream teas, good staff, live jazz and quiz nights; piped music; children and dogs welcome, pretty hillside garden, attractive spot nr river *(Ann and Colin Hunt, MRSM, LYM, Roger Wain-Heapy, Andrew Shore, Maria Williams, Dr and Mrs M E Wilson, Dr and Mrs A K Clarke, Chris and Angela Buckell, Ian Phillips)*

FROME [ST7748]
Sun BA11 1DA [Catherine St]: Friendly local with well kept real ales, good choice of other drinks (popular with young people for its cocktails and shooters); sports TV; dogs welcome (the great dane's called Taylor), attractive courtyard, bedrooms *(Kate Turnbull)*
Wheatsheaf BA11 1DJ [Bath St]: Large comfortable open-plan bar in former coaching inn, modern décor, Bath, Brakspears, Sharps and St Austell, food from sandwiches up, daily papers *(Ian Phillips)*

GLASTONBURY [ST4938]
George & Pilgrims BA6 9DP [High St]: Comfortable 15th-c inn with magnificent carved stone façade and some interesting features – handsome stone fireplace (flame-effect gas fire), oak panelling and traceried stained-glass bay window (rest of pub more ordinary); well kept Butcombe Gold, St Austell Tribute and a house beer, local country wine, decent food; children in buffet and upstairs restaurant, bedrooms *(LYM, Joe Green, Joan and Michel Hooper-Immins)*
Hawthorns BA6 9JJ [Northload St]: Neatly kept and welcoming, well kept Wadworths, decent wines, daily good value curry buffet, local art for sale *(Joe Green)*
King Arthur BA6 9NB [Benedict St]: Great atmosphere in friendly refurbished pub with fine range of real ales at good prices, farm ciders, good live music Fri – can get packed; nice outside area *(Joe Green)*
☆ *Who'd A Thought It* BA6 9JJ [Northload St]: High-backed curved settle, coal fire, pine panelling, stripped brick, beams and flagstones, nicely quirky oddments, well kept Palmers ales, good choice of wines by the glass, good value food from toasties to good steaks, daily papers; children and dogs welcome, pleasant garden, comfortable bedrooms, open all day *(Terry Buckland, LYM, Joe Green, Bob and Angela Brooks, Fred and Lorraine Gill)*

HALLATROW [ST6357]
☆ *Old Station* BS39 6EN [A39 S of Bristol]: Reliable bar food and well kept ales such as Bass and Butcombe in idiosyncratic bar packed with cluttered railway, musical and other bric-a-brac, also italian evening dishes in Flying Scotsman railcar restaurant (can look in, daytime); piped music; children in eating areas, garden with well equipped play area, bedrooms *(Richard Fendick, LYM, John and Fiona McIlwain)*

HALSE [ST1428]
New Inn TA4 3AF [off B3227 Taunton—Bampton]: Traditional 17th-c stone-built inn, roomy and neatly kept, with its own Taunton Vale ales and guest beers, local farm ciders, generous food, woodburner in big inglenook, oak beams, dining room, separate games area and skittle alley; tables in garden, lovely village *(I H G Busby)*

HILLFARRANCE [ST1624]
Anchor TA4 1AW: Comfortable pub with dining area off attractive two-part bar, good choice of enjoyable food, pleasant atmosphere, Butcombe and Exmoor, family room; garden with play area, bedrooms, caravan site, holiday apartments *(Bob and Margaret Holder)*

HINTON CHARTERHOUSE [ST7758]
Rose & Crown BA2 7SN [B3110 about 4 miles S of Bath]: New licensees for popular country pub with roomy linked partly panelled areas, big log fire in ornate fireplace, Bass, Butcombe and two or three other ales tapped from casks, reasonably priced wines, decent food, restaurant, skittle alley; children welcome, small terrace, bedrooms, open all day Sat *(BB, Dr and Mrs M E Wilson, Meg and Colin Hamilton)*

HOLCOMBE [ST6649]
☆ *Holcombe Inn* BA3 5EB [off A367; Stratton Rd]: Extensively modernised quietly placed country pub, Otter ales and a guest, local cider, several wines by the glass, pleasant layout with several linked areas inc pubby tables on flagstones, sofas, easy chairs, panelling and carpet elsewhere, woodburners, good-sized dining area – the food, not cheap, can be very good indeed; piped music; children, dogs and walkers welcome, picnic-sets outside, peaceful farmland views, bedrooms, open all day wkdys *(LYM, Brian England, Ian Phillips, Stephen Bennett, Terry Buckland)*

HOLTON [ST6826]
Old Inn BA9 8AR [off A303 W of Wincanton]: Charming rustic 16th-c pub, unaffectedly comfortable, with beams, ancient flagstones, log fire, hundreds of key fobs, nice bric-a-brac, big open woodburner, long-serving landlord, well kept Butcombe and Wadworths 6X, good interesting attractively priced food in bar and restaurant (must book Sun lunch); tables outside, sheltered garden up steps *(BB, Mark Flynn)*

HOLYWELL LAKE [ST1020]
Holywell Inn TA21 0EJ [off A38]: Comfortable and relaxed, with good value food inc remarkable vegetarian range with their Sunday carvery, Cotleigh and Wadworths 6X *(Peter Barnes)*

HOWLEY [ST2609]
Howley Tavern TA20 3DX: New licensees in comfortable pub, enjoyable food, attentive service, well kept ales, decent wines; attractive spot, good views *(D M and B K Moores)*

HUNTWORTH [ST3134]
Boat & Anchor TA7 0AQ [just off M5

junction 24, signed off exit roundabout, then turn right towards narrow swing bridge]: Good choice of enjoyable pub food from baguettes to good steaks, Sun carvery, roomy eating areas inc new conservatory, young friendly staff, well kept Butcombe and Otter, nice house wines, inscrutable parrot called Barney; lovely garden by Bridgwater & Taunton Canal, eight bedrooms *(Richard Fendick, Bob and Margaret Holder)*

KELSTON [ST7067]

Old Crown BA1 9AQ [Bitton Rd; A431 W of Bath]: Four small convivial traditional rooms with beams and polished flagstones, carved settles and cask tables, logs burning in ancient open range, two more coal-effect fires, well kept ales such as Bath Gem, Butcombe Gold and Blonde and Wadworths 6X tapped from the cask, Thatcher's cider, well priced wines, friendly staff, cheap wholesome bar food (not Sun or Mon evenings) inc good salads, small restaurant (not Sun), no machines or music; dogs welcome, children in eating areas, picnic-sets under apple trees in sunny sheltered back garden, open all day wknds *(Andrew and Debbie Ettle, LYM, Donna and Roger)*

KENN [ST4169]

Drum & Monkey BS21 6TJ [B3133 Yatton—Clevedon]: Neatly kept village pub, well priced food, good friendly service, well kept ales, thriving local atmosphere, open fires, brasses and copper-topped tables *(Frank Willy)*

KEYNSHAM [ST6669]

☆ *Lock-Keeper* BS31 2DD [Keynsham Rd (A4175)]: Bustling and popular, in lovely spot on Avon island with lots of picnic-sets out under glazed canopy, big heated deck and steps down to shady garden by lock, marina and weir; well kept Wells & Youngs ales, good choice of wines by the glass, good value food served promptly from sandwiches to good old-fashioned puddings, friendly helpful young staff, small room by bar, arches to unpretentious main divided room with rust and dark blue décor, black beams and bare boards, barrel-vaulted lower area; wheelchair access; piped music may obtrude; boules *(Dr and Mrs A K Clarke, Matthew Shackle, Andrew and Debbie Ettle, Chris and Angela Buckell)*

KILMERSDON [ST6952]

Jolliffe Arms BA3 5TD: Large attractive stone-built Georgian local overlooking pretty churchyard, Butcombe and Fullers London Pride, good wines by the glass, reasonably priced home-made pub food, friendly service, linked areas reminiscent of unpretentious farmhouse parlour, some huge black flagstones; piped music; front picnic-sets *(Terry Buckland, Ian Phillips)*

KILVE [ST1442]

Hood Arms TA5 1EA [A39 E of Williton]: Neatly kept country pub with decent bar food cooked to order, well kept ales such as Yeovil, pleasant service, cosy plush lounge,

warm woodburner in bar, restaurant; skittle alley, nice back garden with tables on sheltered terrace, 12 bedrooms – back are quietest *(Bob and Margaret Holder, LYM, Peter Meister)*

KINGSTON ST MARY [ST2229]

Swan TA2 8HW: New owners putting emphasis on good value food, real ales, good choice of wines, big log fires, daily papers; dogs welcome *(W N Murphy, Bob and Margaret Holder)*

LANGFORD BUDVILLE [ST1122]

☆ *Martlet* TA21 0QZ [off B3187 NW of Wellington]: Cosy and comfortably refurbished, with nice mix of locals and diners, good value food, friendly staff, good range of real ales, open fires, inglenook, beams and flagstones, central woodburner, steps up to carpeted lounge with another woodburner; skittle alley *(Heather Coulson, Neil Cross, John Hopkins)*

LANSDOWN [ST7268]

Blathwayt Arms BA1 9BT: Interesting old building with helpful service, enjoyable food inc some unusual dishes and good Sun roast, well kept ales, decent wines; children welcome, racecourse view from garden, open all day *(Tom and Ruth Rees)*

LEIGH UPON MENDIP [ST6947]

Bell BA3 5QQ [Leigh St]: Friendly L-shaped village pub with good value food from baguettes to interesting specials, efficient service, Butcombe and other ales; garden *(M G Hart)*

LONG ASHTON [ST5570]

Dovecote BS41 9LX: Roomy Vintage Inn with their usual food and reasonably priced drinks inc good choice of wines by the glass, attentive young staff, upstairs gents'; open all day *(MB)*

Miners Rest BS41 9DJ [Providence Lane]: Friendly pub, comfortable and unpretentious, with good farm ciders, well kept Bass and Fullers London Pride, reasonably priced wines, bargain pub lunches, cheerful staff (help with wheelchair access), local mining memorabilia; children welcome, vine-covered verandah and terrace picnic-sets *(Chris and Angela Buckell)*

LONG SUTTON [ST4625]

☆ *Devonshire Arms* TA10 9LP [B3165 Somerton—Martock, just off A372 E of Langport]: Tall gabled stone inn with squashy leather settees by log fire, roomy restaurant area on left, sporting and country prints, courteous young staff, interesting blackboard food from enterprising sandwiches up, real ale, good local farm cider, quite a few wines by the glass, homely flagstoned back bar with darts and TV; may be piped music; children in eating areas, open all day, bedrooms *(LYM, Clare West)*

MELLS [ST7249]

☆ *Talbot* BA11 3PN [W of Frome, off A362 or A361]: New licensee for this interesting old inn, austere public bar in carefully restored tithe barn, farm tools on stone walls, big mural behind counter, attractive dining room in main building, sporting and riding pictures, solid dining tables and chairs, Butcombe tapped from cask, darts; piped music, TV; children and dogs welcome, pleasant cobbled courtyard, comfortable bedrooms (Colin Watt, LYM, Pete Coxon)

MIDDLEZOY [ST3732]

George TA7 0NN [off A372 E of Bridgwater]: Friendly 16th-c country local with low-ceilinged flagstoned bar, wooden tables, chairs and settles, Butcombe and other well kept ales, decent food inc local steaks; good outside tables (Liz and Jeremy Baker)

MIDFORD [ST7660]

☆ *Hope & Anchor* BA2 7DD [Bath Rd (B3110)]: Good well presented interesting food from light dishes to mouth-watering more elaborate things and imaginative puddings in civilised bar, heavy-beamed and flagstoned restaurant end, and new back conservatory, six changing ales such as Bath Gem, Butcombe Gold and Sharps Doom Bar, good house wines, proper coffee, relaxed atmosphere, log fire; tables on sheltered back terrace with upper tier beyond, pleasant walks on disused Somerset & Dorset railway track, open all day (Chris and Ann Coy, Gaynor Gregory, M G Hart, BB, Roger Wain-Heapy, Bryan Pearson)

MIDSOMER NORTON [ST6654]

White Hart BA3 2HQ [The Island]: Well worn chatty Victorian local with several rooms, Bass, Butcombe and a guest tapped from the cask, two farm ciders, local coal-mining memorabilia, bargain simple lunchtime food, cheerful helpful staff; no credit cards; dogs welcome, open all day (the Didler)

MILVERTON [ST1225]

Globe TA4 1JX [Fore St]: Smartly reworked as dining pub, enjoyable if not cheap food, well kept Exmoor ale (Giles and Annie Francis)

MONTACUTE [ST4916]

Phelips Arms TA15 6XB [The Borough; off A3088 W of Yeovil]: Newish young licensees, welcoming and obliging, in roomy and airy open-plan bar, well kept Palmers ales, good choice of wines by the glass, farm cider, nice fireplace and old-fashioned décor, restaurant; children welcome, skittle alley, attractive walled garden behind, pretty square next to Montacute House, nicely refurbished bedrooms (Ian Malone, Peter Holmes, BB, Paul and Annette Hallett, Bob and Margaret Holder)

MOORLINCH [ST3936]

Ring o' Bells TA7 9BT [signed off A39]: Fine old building, log fire in attractive lounge, keen chef/landlord doing good value hearty food inc good Sun roasts, well kept changing ales such as Bath and Cotleigh; sports TV in public bar (Joe Green)

NAILSEA [ST4469]

Blue Flame BS48 4DE [West End]: Small well worn 19th-c farmers' local, two rooms with mixed furnishings, Butcombe and RCH ales from casks behind bar, Thatcher's farm cider, filled rolls, coal fire, pub games; plain-speaking landlord, outside lavatories

inc roofless gents', limited parking (may be filled with Land Rovers and tractors); children's room, sizeable informal garden, open all day summer wknds (Philip and Jude Simmons, the Didler, Catherine Pitt)

Moorend Spout BS48 4BB [Union St]: Low-priced straightforward food (not Sun evening) inc midwk two-course bargains in neatly kept early 18th-c beamed local, friendly helpful family service, Bass, Butcombe and Greene King; may be piped music; terrace and sheltered lawn (Geoff and Brigid Smithers, Richard Fendick)

Old Farmhouse BS48 2PF [Trendlewood Way, off B3130]: Roomy pub with olde-worlde bric-a-brac in stone-built farmhouse-kitchen dining annexe, good value inventive food, carvery Fri-Sun, Badger ales, good friendly staff; may be piped music; disabled facilities, tables outside, good play area (Richard Fendick)

NEWTON ST LOE [ST7065]

☆ *Globe* BA2 9BB [A4/A36 roundabout]: Large rambling Vintage Inn with pleasant décor and dark wood partitions, pillars and timbers giving secluded feel, enjoyable food all day, well kept beer, prompt helpful service from friendly young staff, good atmosphere; pleasant back terrace (Guy Vowles, J and F Gowers, Dr and Mrs A K Clarke, Meg and Colin Hamilton, Lady Heath)

NORTH PERROTT [ST4709]

Manor Arms TA18 7SG [A3066 W of Crewkerne; Middle St]: Attractive 16th-c inn on pretty village green, concentrating on restaurant and bedroom side, with imaginative freshly made meals rather than snacks, small but good wine choice, well kept ales inc Butcombe, good coffee, friendly staff, long tidily restored bar, beams and mellow stripped stone, log fire and plenty of character; simple comfortable bedrooms, good breakfast, pleasant garden with adventure play area, open all day (John Wymer)

NORTON FITZWARREN [ST2026]

Cross Keys TA2 6NR [A358 roundabout NW of Taunton]: Comfortably extended and newly refurbished 19th-c pub, stone-tiled bar and carpeted dining area with some plank panelling, friendly cheerful staff, sensibly priced food all day, well kept ales such as Brains, Exmoor Fox, Otter and St Austell, decent wines by the glass, generous coffee, log fire in big hearth; riverside garden, open all day (Ian Phillips, Richard Foskett, Stephanie Lang)

NORTON ST PHILIP [ST7755]

☆ *Fleur de Lys* BA2 7LG [High St]: Chatty local in 13th-c stone cottages, friendly landlord, Wadworths beers, good value home-made food from baguettes up, log fire in huge fireplace, steps and pillars giving cosy feel of separate rooms in beamed and flagstoned areas around central servery; children welcome, skittle alley (Dr and Mrs M E Wilson, the Didler, Donna and Roger, BB, Ann and Colin Hunt, Dr and Mrs A K Clarke)

PANBOROUGH [ST4745]
Panborough Inn BA5 1PN [B3139
Wedmore—Wells]: Large well run 17th-c
dining pub, good welcoming service, wide
range of enjoyable generous food, several
attractive rooms, inglenook, beams,
gleaming brass and copper, fresh and dried
flowers, well kept ales such as Butcombe,
Fri music night; skittle alley, quiet views
from tables on front terrace *(BB, Jenny and
Brian Seller)*

PITMINSTER [ST2219]
Queens Arms TA3 7AZ [off B3170 S of
Taunton (or reached direct); nr church]:
Village pub with enjoyable local food inc
good fish choice and some interesting dishes
(can take a while at busy times), real ales
inc Cotleigh and Otter, good choice of wines
by the glass, log fires, simple wooden bar
furniture, pleasant dining room *(John and
Fiona Merritt)*

PORLOCK WEIR [SS8846]
☆ *Ship* TA24 8QD [separate from but run in
tandem with neighbouring Anchor Hotel]:
Unpretentious old-world thatched bar in
wonderful spot by peaceful harbour (so can
get packed), dark low beams signed by
customers, flagstones and stripped stone,
big log fire, simple pub furniture, four ales
inc Cotleigh Barn Owl and Exmoor, Inch's
cider, good whisky and soft drinks choice,
friendly young staff, usual generous food
from thick sandwiches up, plainer overflow
rooms across small back yard; piped music,
big-screen TV, little free parking but pay &
display opposite; children and dogs
welcome, sturdy picnic-sets on side terraces,
good coast walks, decent bedrooms
(Paul Humphreys, BB)

PORTBURY [ST4975]
☆ *Priory* BS20 7TN [Station Rd, 0.5 mile from
A369 (just S of M5 junction 19)]:
Consistently good well extended Vintage Inn
dining pub/hotel, several beamed rooms
with appealing mix of comfortable
furnishings in alcoves, log fire, plenty of
friendly prompt staff, well kept ales, good
range of wines by the glass, interesting fresh
fruit juices, wide choice of reasonably
priced food all day till 10 inc good fish
specials; piped music; front and back garden
tables, bedrooms, open all day *(JCW,
George and Gill Rowley, Richard Fendick,
Dr and Mrs C W Thomas, Bob and
Margaret Holder, MB)*

PORTISHEAD [ST4676]
Poacher BS20 6AJ [High St]: Large pub
popular with older lunchers for wide range of
freshly made low-priced food, well kept
Courage Best and three other ales (a proper
part for village beer-drinkers, with a big
fireplace), friendly staff, quiz nights, cl Sun
pm *(Tom Evans)*
Royal BS20 7HG [Pier Rd (NE end of town,
nr sea)]: 1830s former hotel popular in
summer for superb location overlooking
Severn estuary and bridges, light and
spacious with linked Victorian parlours, well

kept Butcombe and Sharps Doom Bar, good
food inc children's helpings and wider
evening choice, friendly staff; piped music;
large terrace, open all day, cl Sun evening
(Richard Fendick, George and Gill Rowley)

PRIDDY [ST5450]
Hunters Lodge BA5 3AR [from Wells on A39
pass hill with TV mast on left, then next
left]: Welcoming and unchanging walkers'
and potholers' pub above ice-age cavern, in
same family for generations, well kept
Butcombe and Exmoor tapped from casks
behind the bar, Weston's farm cider,
wholesome cheap snacks such as fresh rolls
and local cheeses, log fires, flagstones and
panelling; garden picnic-sets, bedrooms
*(Phil and Sally Gorton, the Didler,
Gaynor Gregory, LYM)*
New Inn BA5 3BB [off B3135; The Green]:
Low-beamed stripped-stone 15th-c pub
under welcoming new owners, well kept
Bath, Cheddar and Exmoor ales, Thatcher's
ciders, big helpings of appealing good value
food inc Sun carvery in bar, refurbished
lounge with warm coal fire, and spacious
conservatory, beer and folk festivals;
children welcome, tables out facing quiet
village green, bedrooms *(Stuart Paulley,
Terry Buckland)*
☆ *Queen Victoria* BA5 3BA [village signed off
B3135; Pelting Drove]: Relaxed character
country local with chatty staff and regulars,
three good log fires (one open on two
sides), well kept Butcombe ales tapped from
the cask, organic beers, three local ciders,
good coffee, wholesome food inc good
steaks and fish, stripped stone and
flagstones, interesting bric-a-brac, collected
furnishings inc miscellaneous tables and old
pews; good garden for children over road,
great walks, cl lunchtime Oct-Apr exc hols,
open all day wknds and high season
(Terry Buckland, M Mossman, J and F Gowers)

PURITON [ST3141]
Puriton Inn TA7 8AF [just off M5 junction
23; Puriton Hill]: Character pub well
screened from motorway, dark, clean and
tidy, with ample straightforward food, well
kept Butcombe, Flowers and Wadworths,
warmly welcoming service even when busy,
pool; good disabled access, front terrace and
back garden with play area *(Richard Fendick)*

QUEEN CAMEL [ST5924]
Mildmay Arms BA22 7NJ [A359 S of A303
roundabout]: Chef/landlord doing good food
all day inc interesting specials and notable
puddings *(David Morgan)*

RICKFORD [ST4859]
Plume of Feathers BS40 7AH [very sharp
turn off A368]: Unspoilt cottagey and partly
flagstoned local with limited choice of
simple reasonably priced home-made food,
relaxed atmosphere, four well kept ales such
as Butcombe and St Austell Tribute, country
ciders, friendly family service, ochre walls
and pale green panelling, mix of furniture
inc cast-iron tables and settles, log fires,
table skittles, pool; well-behaved children

and dogs welcome, rustic tables on narrow front terrace, pretty streamside hamlet *(Chris and Angela Buckell, BB)*

☆ *Bell* BA11 6PW [Frome Rd (A361)]: Neatly kept and roomy sparely decorated bar with a couple of armchairs as well as pleasantly practical furnishings, step up to good-sized pool room, smaller lounge bar on right leading to busy attractively set restaurant with popular carvery, friendly attentive staff, well kept ales; dogs welcome, plenty of tables on spreading lawn *(Dr and Mrs A K Clarke, Ted George)*

ROWBERROW [ST4458]

☆ *Swan* BS25 1QL [off A38 S of A368 junction]: Neat and spacious dining pub opp pond, olde-worlde beamery and so forth, friendly atmosphere esp in nicely unsophisticated old bar part, popular food from substantial lunchtime sandwiches up, well kept Butcombe ales, good choice of wines by the glass, Thatcher's cider, good log fires; good-sized garden over road *(LYM, Tom Evans, Bob and Angela Brooks, Philip Kingsbury, Ian Legge, M G Hart, Steve and Liz Tilley, Mrs Sheila Clarke)*

RUISHTON [ST2524]

Blackbrook TA3 5LU [just off M5 junction 25]: Busy recently refurbished chain dining pub, a useful stop, various kinds of generous decent food in several different roomy areas, quick friendly service, real ales, beams, conservatory; good-sized garden with play area *(Richard Fendick)*

SALTFORD [ST6867]

Bird in Hand BS31 3EJ [High St]: Comfortable and friendly, with lively front bar, good range of beers such as Abbey and Butcombe, farm cider, attractive back conservatory dining area popular locally for good value fresh food from mini-ploughman's to daily roast, huge omelettes and whitby fish, quick service even when quite a queue for food, lots of bird pictures, small family area; live entertainment; picnic-sets down towards river, handy for Bristol—Bath railway path *(Andrew and Debbie Ettle, Dr and Mrs M E Wilson)*

☆ *Jolly Sailor* BS31 3ER [off A4 Bath—Keynsham; Mead Lane]: Great spot by lock and weir on River Avon, with dozens of picnic-sets, garden heaters and own island between lock and pub; enjoyable standard food from lunchtime sandwiches to several fish dishes, cheerful efficient service, well kept Butcombe, Courage Best and Hop Back Crop Circle, good value wines by the glass, flagstones, low beams, log fires, daily papers, conservatory restaurant; children allowed if eating, disabled facilities, open all day *(Roger Edward-Jones, Chris and Angela Buckell, John and Gloria Isaacs)*

SIDCOT [ST4256]

Sidcot Hotel BS25 1NN [Bridgwater Rd (A38)]: Clean, bright and friendly Brewers Fayre, lovely views, Wadworths 6X, decent choice of wines, good staff, promptly served

food all day; disabled access, Premier Lodge bedrooms *(Comus and Sarah Elliott)*

SOUTH STOKE [ST7461]

☆ *Pack Horse* BA2 7DU [off B3110, S edge of Bath]: Former medieval priory (central passageway still a public right of way to the church), with heavy beams, handsome inglenook log fire, antique settles and scrubbed tables on flagstones, friendly helpful staff, good choice of robust good value food, real ales such as Butcombe and Wadworths 6X, plenty of farm cider; children welcome, lots of tables in spacious back garden, open all day wknds *(Roger Wain-Heapy, Donna and Roger, David Hoult, Guy Vowles, Dr and Mrs A K Clarke, LYM)*

SPARKFORD [ST6026]

Sparkford Inn BA22 7JH [just W of Wincanton; High St]: Big softly lit low-beamed rambling pub now tied to Marstons, cheerful helpful staff, popular pubby food from sandwiches up, their real ales, reasonably priced wines, real ale and decent wines by the glass; wheelchair access, children welcome to eat, dogs allowed in bar (not Sun lunchtime), outside tables and play area, well equipped bedrooms, open all day *(Chris and Angela Buckell, LYM, J Stickland, B J Harding)*

STAPLE FITZPAINE [ST2618]

☆ *Greyhound* TA3 5SP [off A358 or B3170 S of Taunton]: Light rambling country pub with good choice of enjoyable food and of changing ales, good wines by the glass, welcoming atmosphere and attentive staff, flagstones, inglenooks, pleasant mix of settles and chairs, log fires throughout, olde-worlde pictures, farm tools and so forth; children welcome, comfortable bedrooms, good breakfast *(Roy and Jean Russell, Bob and Margaret Holder, LYM)*

STAR [ST4358]

Star BS25 1QE [A38 NE of Winscombe]: Reopened after extensive reworking as rambling dining pub, busy at peak times, good value carvery, Butcombe and Marstons Pedigree, inglenook log fire in old bar area; heated terrace, picnic-sets behind, open all day *(Tom Evans, George and Gill Rowley)*

STOGUMBER [ST0937]

White Horse TA4 3TA [off A358 at Crowcombe]: Friendly village pub with well kept Cotleigh, Greene King and Marstons, enjoyable food from sandwiches to Sun roasts, long neat bar, old village photographs with more recent ones for comparison, good log fires, games room and skittle alley; children welcome, nice quiet back terrace, bedrooms, open all day wknds and summer *(LYM, Terry Miller, John Marsh)*

STOGURSEY [ST2042]

Greyhound TA5 1QR [Lime St]: Friendly family-run village local with home-made pub food, Sun carvery, armchairs by log fire in low-ceilinged bar, cosy dining room; large back garden *(Christopher Johnson)*

STOKE ST GREGORY [ST3527]
☆ *Rose & Crown* TA3 6EW [off A378/A358; Woodhill]: This very popular main entry, good value with a happy atmosphere and helpful family service, was gutted by fire in March 2008 – we hope for its reopening some time in 2009 *(LYM)*

STOKE ST MARY [ST2622]
Half Moon TA3 5BY [from M5 junction 25 take A358 towards Ilminster, 1st right, right in Henlade]: Much-modernised village pub very popular lunchtime for wide choice of hearty good value food inc daily carvery, pleasant staff but service can be slow, Butcombe, Boddingtons, Fullers London Pride and Greene King Abbot, nice coffee, quite a few malt whiskies, thriving local atmosphere in several comfortable open-plan areas inc restaurant; children welcome, well tended garden *(Comus and Sarah Elliott, LYM, Bob and Margaret Holder, Richard Fendick)*

STOKE SUB HAMDON [ST4717]
Prince of Wales TA14 6RW [Ham Hill]: On top of Ham Hill with superb views, changing real ales tapped from the cask, good value food, friendly staff; children, dogs and muddy boots welcome, open all day *(Jenny and Brian Seller)*

STREET [ST4836]
Bear BA16 0EF [associated with Clarks Shopping Village]: Large newly refurbished open-plan Marstons inn, carpeted and screened into different areas, wide selection of good value food inc OAP and other deals served at well spaced tables, lots of old prints, posters and other paraphernalia; good wheelchair access, 25 bedrooms *(Phil and Jane Hodson)*

TAUNTON [ST2525]
☆ *Hankridge Arms* TA1 2LR [Hankridge Way, Deane Gate (nr Sainsbury); just off M5 junction 25 – A358 towards city, then right at roundabout, right at next roundabout]: Well appointed Badger dining pub based on 16th-c former farm, splendid contrast to the modern shopping complex around it, different-sized linked areas, well kept ales, generous enjoyable food from interesting soups and sandwiches through sensibly priced pubby things to restaurant dishes, quick friendly young staff, decent wines, big log fire; piped music; dogs welcome, plenty of tables in pleasant outside area *(Gill and Keith Croxton, Dr and Mrs A K Clarke, Chris Glasson)*
Vivary Arms TA1 3JR [Wilton St; across Vivary Park from centre]: Quiet and pretty low-beamed 18th-c local (Taunton's oldest), good value distinctive fresh food in snug plush lounge and small dining room, prompt helpful young staff, relaxed atmosphere, well kept ales inc Cotleigh, decent wines, interesting collection of drink-related items; bedrooms in Georgian house next door *(Richard Fendick, John Marsh, Bob and Margaret Holder)*

TIMSBURY [ST6758]
Seven Stars BA2 0JJ [North Rd]: Bright and cheerful stone-built village pub with some

emphasis on good value unusual if not exactly cheap food, Butcombe and other well kept local ales, several small eating areas off locals' bar; good wheelchair facilities, garden with adventure playground and pet goats *(LYM, Stuart Paulley)*

TINTINHULL [ST5019]
Crown & Victoria BA22 8PZ [Farm St, village signed off A303]: Roomy, light and airy main bar, good fire, attractive choice of generous fairly priced food cooked to order, Butcombe and Wadworths, wine in big glasses, good service, pleasant conservatory; disabled facilities, well kept big garden with play area, bedrooms, handy for Tintinhull House (NT) *(LYM, Dr and Mrs M E Wilson, Neil and Anita Christopher)*

TYTHERINGTON [ST7645]
Fox & Hounds BA11 5BN: 17th-c, with roomy and tidy L-shaped stripped-stone bar, generous food (not Mon) inc unusual curries and Sun roasts, Bass, Butcombe and a guest beer tapped from the cask, farm ciders, welcoming landlord and atmosphere, sleepy chocolate labrador (likes the side lounge's best sofa), small dining area; tables outside, comfortable bedrooms, good breakfast *(Edward Mirzoeff, MRSM)*

UPTON [ST0129]
☆ *Lowtrow Cross Inn* TA4 2DB: Well run by cheery landlord and staff, good fresh home-made food, nice relaxed mix of locals and diners, character low-beamed bar with log fire, bare boards and flagstones, two carpeted country-kitchen dining areas, one with enormous inglenook, plenty of atmosphere, well kept ales such as Cotleigh Tawny and Exmoor Fox; no dogs; children welcome, attractive surroundings, bedrooms *(BB, John Hopkins, Richard and Anne Ansell)*

UPTON NOBLE [ST7139]
Lamb BA4 6AS [Church St; off A359 SW of Frome]: Friendly 17th-c village local with wide blackboard choice of good unfussy home-made food, efficient staff, well kept ales inc Butcombe, reasonable prices, comfortable lounge bar, beams, stripped stone, brasses and ornaments, lovely view from restaurant, darts and pool in public bar; big garden, nice location, cl Mon lunchtime *(Henry Tinny)*

VOBSTER [ST7049]
☆ *Vobster Inn* BA3 5RJ [Lower Vobster]: Roomy old stone-built dining pub, good reasonably priced food from Spanish chef/landlord inc good local cheese plate, some spanish dishes and fish fresh daily from Cornwall, friendly staff, Butcombe and a Blindmans seasonal ale, good wines by the glass, three comfortable open-plan areas with antique furniture inc plenty of room for just a drink; side lawn with colourful bantams, peaceful views, boules, adventure playground behind *(Gaynor Gregory, Donna and Roger, Sylvia and Tony Birbeck, Ian Phillips, M G Hart, BB)*

WAMBROOK [ST2907]
☆ *Cotley Inn* TA20 3EN [off A30 W of Chard; don't follow the small signs to Cotley itself]:

Smartly unpretentious stone-built pub with good fairly priced food, welcoming efficient staff, Otter ales, simple flagstoned entrance bar opening on one side into small plush bar, several open fires, popular two-room dining area (best to book, children allowed here); piped music, skittle alley; lovely view from terrace tables, play area in nice garden below, good bedrooms, quiet spot with plenty of surrounding walks *(Mike Gorton, Phil and Sally Gorton, LYM, Bob and Margaret Holder, Douglas Allen, Stephen and Jean Curtis)*

WANSTROW [ST7141]

☆ *Pub* BA4 4SZ [Station Rd (A359 Nunney—Bruton)]: Proper old-fashioned local, attractive, individual and civilised, with friendly owners, bargain genuine home cooking by landlady, five or six well kept changing ales inc local Blindmans, interesting wines by the glass, comfortable traditional furniture on flagstones, settles snugged around log fire, case of interesting books in dining room, bar billiards, games room, skittle alley; tables in charming little floral courtyard, cl Mon lunchtime *(Mark O'Sullivan, Philip and Jude Simmons, BB, Susan and Nigel Wilson)*

WATCHFIELD [ST3447]

Watchfield TA9 4RD: Nicely placed country pub much extended from original cottage core with some unusual features, reasonably priced enjoyable food, Butcombe, Cheddar and Marstons, morning teas and coffees, friendly relaxed service, various rooms off central servery, pool; piped music; sunny terrace, garden, small campsite *(Richard Fendick)*

WELLOW [ST7358]

☆ *Fox & Badger* BA2 8QG [signed off A367 SW of Bath]: Recently opened up, flagstones one end, bare boards the other, some snug corners, woodburner in massive hearth, real ales such as Butcombe and Theakstons, Thatcher's farm cider, warmly welcoming service, wide range of good value bar food; children and dogs welcome, picnic-sets in covered courtyard, open all day Fri-Sun *(Donna and Roger, LYM)*

WELLS [ST5546]

☆ *Fountain* BA5 2UU [St Thomas St]: Comfortable and friendly big-windowed dining pub, largely laid out for eating in the downstairs bar (good log fire), steep stairs up to original dining room, enthusiastic staff, popular sensibly priced food from filled baguettes to good value meals inc fresh fish, interesting dishes and good Sun lunch, Butcombe and good choice of wines, good coffee, daily papers; can be fully booked even wkdys, may be piped music; children welcome, by cathedral and moated Bishop's Palace *(R K Phillips, Terry Buckland, John Coatsworth, BB)*

WEST HORRINGTON [ST5948]

☆ *Slab House* BA5 3EQ [B3139 Wells-Emborough, NE of village]: Enthusiastic new management and some gentle redecoration in pretty open-plan country dining pub, smallish partly flagstoned bar area with

cottagey corners, old engravings and interesting clocks, roaring log fires, wide choice of good generous food from sandwiches to imaginative dishes, attentive service (can slow when busy), relaxed atmosphere, Cheddar Best, good-sized comfortable restaurant; discreet piped music, no dogs; spotless lavatories, tables out on floodlit nicely planted sunken terrace and on big neat lawns, play area *(Terry Buckland, Dr and Mrs C W Thomas, BB, M G Hart)*

WEST HUNTSPILL [ST3145]

☆ *Crossways* TA9 3RA [A38 (between M5 exits 22 and 23)]: Friendly elderly pub with several rambling areas inc a family room, interesting decorations, beams and log fires, bargain food, five good real ales, local farm cider, decent wines, quick attentive service, skittle alley and pub games; fruit trees in sizeable informal garden *(LYM, Tom Evans)*

WEST MONKTON [ST2628]

Monkton TA2 8NP: Comfortable firmly run dining pub popular for its fresh food (not Sun evening) inc lunch deals, linked areas inc smallish bar; lots of tables in streamside meadow, peaceful spot, open all day Fri-Sun, cl Mon *(Brian Monaghan, Bob and Margaret Holder)*

WESTHAY [ST4342]

Bird in Hand BA6 9TN: Small friendly country local, Butcombe ales, food inc good value Sun lunch; handy for Shapwick Heath peatland nature reserve *(Richard Burton)*

WESTON-SUPER-MARE [ST3762]

Woolpack BS22 7XE [St Georges, just off M5, junction 21]: Opened-up 17th-c coaching inn with full Butcombe range, low-priced pubby food, friendly atmosphere, pleasant window seats and library-theme area, small attractive restaurant, conservatory, skittle alley *(Comus and Sarah Elliott)*

WINSCOMBE [ST4257]

Woodborough BS25 1HD [Sandford Rd]: Big beamed dining pub, smart, comfortable and busy, with good range of above-average local food, helpful friendly staff, good wine choice, separate drinking areas *(Hugh Roberts, George and Gill Rowley)*

WINSFORD [SS9034]

☆ *Royal Oak* TA24 7JE [off A396 about 10 miles S of Dunster]: New owners settling in well at prettily placed thatched and beamed Exmoor inn, buoyant chatty atmosphere in attractively furnished lounge bar with big stone fireplace and big bay-window seat looking across towards village green and foot and packhorse bridges over River Winn, more eating space in second bar, several pretty and comfortable lounges, enjoyable food strong on local meats and game, Brakspears and Butcombe tapped from the cask, good wines by the glass; children and dogs welcome, good bedrooms *(LYM, GSB, Philip and Jude Simmons, B M Eldridge, Mrs P Bishop)*

WITHAM FRIARY [ST7440]

☆ *Seymour Arms* BA11 5HF [signed from B3092 S of Frome]: Well worn in flagstoned

SOMERSET • 633

country tavern, two simple rooms off 19th-c
hatch-service lobby, one with darts, the
other with central table skittles; well kept
Butcombe and Rich's local cider tapped from
backroom casks, veteran landlord, open fires,
panelled benches, cards and dominoes, no
food; good-sized attractive garden by main
rail line, open all day wknds *(Pete Baker,
the Didler, Phil and Sally Gorton, Edward
Mirzoeff)*

WITHYPOOL [SS8435]

☆ *Royal Oak* TA24 7QP [off B3233]: Easy-going
pub with steps between two beamed bars,
Exmoor Ale and a guest beer, several wines
by the glass, reasonably priced food, lovely
log fire and some nice old oak tables;
children and dogs welcome, terrace seating,
pretty riverside village tucked below
some of Exmoor's finest parts, nicely
redecorated bedrooms, good breakfast, open
all day *(Mike and Nicky Pleass, John and
Jackie Walsh, Bob and Margaret Holder,
LYM, Ian and Angela Redley, Mr and
Mrs P D Titcomb)*

WRANTAGE [ST3022]

Canal Inn TA3 6DF [A378 E of M5 junction
25]: Welcoming three-room country pub with
lively young licensees, enjoyable fresh food
(not Sun evening) in bar and dining room,
all local sourcing plus daily brixham fish,
changing ales inc one brewed for them by
Blackwater, Burrow Hill farm cider, log fires,
interesting old furniture, parrot; dogs
welcome, good garden with play area and
chickens, has been cl Mon lunchtime
(Bruce Bird)

WRAXALL [ST4971]

☆ *Old Barn* BS48 1LQ [just off Bristol Rd
(B3130)]: Idiosyncratic gabled barn
conversion with scrubbed tables, school
benches and soft sofas under oak rafters,
stripped boards, flagstones and festoons of
dried flowers; welcoming atmosphere and
friendly service, Butcombe, Fullers London
Pride, St Austell Tribute and Timothy Taylors
Landlord tapped from the cask (plans for
their own brews too), farm ciders, good
wines by the glass; sports TV; nice garden
with good play area, smokers' shelter,
barbecues (can bring your own meat) on
cobbled terrace *(Steve and Liz Tilley,
the Didler)*

WRINGTON [ST4762]

Plough BS40 5QA [2.5 miles off A370
Bristol—Weston, from bottom of Rhodiate
Hill]: Large popular pub rambling around
central servery with Wells & Youngs and a
guest ale, decent choice of wines and
whiskies, good value food inc sandwiches and
bargain light lunches, beams and stripped
stone, step up to long dining area, two coal
or log fires; children and dogs welcome,
wheelchair access, lots of picnic-sets out on
sloping grass, more under cover on heated
terrace, open all day *(Bob and
Margaret Holder, BB, Chris and Angela Buckell)*

Please tell us if any Lucky Dips deserve to be upgraded to a main entry
– and why: feedback@thegoodpubguide.co.uk or (no stamp needed)
The Good Pub Guide, FREEPOST TN1569, Wadhurst, E Sussex TN5 7BR.

Staffordshire

Staffordshire is one of Britain's best counties for pub value, with plenty of sensibly priced food to be found, and drinks tending to be relatively very cheap. What's more, pubs here, whatever their speciality, have lots of individuality. Outstanding in this respect is the marvellously eccentric Yew Tree at Cauldon – it's one of only three pubs in the *Guide* to carry two of our Stars. The charming licensee here has amassed a distinguished collection of all sorts of interesting things to look at. Conjuring up childhood memories of old-fashioned museums, it's all in a lovely tumble, complete with a decent coating of dust. An added pleasure here is rock-bottom pricing. The timeless Olde Royal Oak at Wetton ticks all the right pubby boxes with its beams and cosy fire, but it's the personal hands-on welcome from the friendly couple running it that really pulls it all together. The happy Burton Bridge Inn in Burton upon Trent does well this year to gain a Wine Award for its fine range of wines by the glass – surprising broad-mindedness, considering its successful Burton Bridge brewing operation, across the yard. The George at Alstonefield, also charmingly simple, has proved particularly popular with readers this year – thanks above all to the hands-on landlady, so cheerful and helpful. As we've said, on the food side the Staffordshire trade mark is good value (especially at the Burton Bridge Inn, the Queens Head in Lichfield and the Olde Royal Oak at Wetton). However, there's real quality to be found, too, notably at the Hand & Trumpet at Wrinehill, which wins the title of Staffordshire Dining Pub of the Year. Another pub to pick out for food is the Boat near Lichfield, back in the *Guide* after a break: well placed as a good refreshment stop. Pubs to note in the Lucky Dip section at the end of the chapter are the Plum Pudding in Armitage, Coopers Tavern in Burton upon Trent, Boat at Cheddleton, White Swan at Fradley and Horseshoe at Tatenhill, and this is an area where chain pubs such as Vintage Inns and Chef & Brewers are more than usually worth patronising. The area's dominant brewer is Marstons, but there is also a flourishing small brewery scene, with nearly 20 active here. Besides Burton Bridge, ones we found supplying at least some good pubs here this year were Enville, Beowulf, Blythe, Townhouse, Tower, Black Hole, Old Cottage and Titanic.

Post Office address codings confusingly give the impression that some pubs are in Staffordshire, when they're really in Cheshire or Derbyshire (which is where we list them).

ABBOTS BROMLEY

SK0824 MAP 7

Goats Head

Market Place; WS15 3BP

Well run old-world pub with good food, attractive location

Readers make particular mention of the fairly priced tasty food and welcoming atmosphere at this charming old black and white timbered pub. It's at the centre of an unspoilt village, which is famous for a still thriving ancient tradition, its annual horn dance. The opened-up cream painted interior has attractive oak floors, a warm fire in a big inglenook, and furniture running from the odd traditional oak settle. Served by attentive staff, the Black Sheep, Greene King Abbot, Marstons Pedigree and a guest such as Wells & Youngs Bombardier are well kept on handpump, and you can have any of the wines on their good wine list by the glass; piped music, TV. Picnic-sets and teak tables out on a neat sheltered lawn look up to the church tower behind.

🍴 Generously served enjoyable bar food is all home-made, and the chips here are good: sandwiches, soup, thai fishcakes, salmon fillet with hollandaise, daily specials such as bacon wrapped chicken breast with pesto, grilled sardines and halibut steak with prawns, and puddings such as lemon pie or plum crumble. Steaks are discounted Monday to Wednesday evenings. *Starters/Snacks: £4.95 to £5.95. Main Courses: £7.95 to £16.95. Puddings: £3.95*

Punch ~ Lease Dawn Skelton ~ Real ale ~ Bar food (12-2.30, 6-9(9.30 Fri); 12-9.30 Sat; 12-8(6 in winter) Sun) ~ Restaurant ~ (01283) 840254 ~ Children welcome ~ Open 12-midnight (1 Sat, 11 Sun) ~ Bedrooms: /£40

Recommended by Gwyn and Anne Wake, R T and J C Moggridge, S J and C C Davidson, Richard and Jean Green, Neil and Brenda Skidmore, C J Fletcher, David J Austin, Susan and Nigel Brookes, Lawrence Bacon, Jean Scott, Roger and Anne Newbury

ALSTONEFIELD

SK1355 MAP 7

George ♀

Village signposted from A515 Ashbourne—Buxton; DE6 2FX

Nice old pub with good range of fairly priced food, a Peak District classic

We're happy to report that under the caring hand of its very friendly landlady this stone-built peak district pub has gently gone from strength to strength since she took over a couple of years ago. It's by the green in a peaceful farming hamlet (sitting out beneath the inn-sign and watching the world go by, or in the big sheltered stableyard behind the pub is a real pleasure) and is popular with a good variety of customers (including plenty of walkers) soaking up the charming atmosphere. The unchanging straightforward low-beamed bar has a collection of old Peak District photographs and pictures, a warming coal fire, and a copper-topped counter with well kept Marstons Pedigree, Burtonwood and a guest such as Adnams Broadside on handpump and a dozen wines by the glass; dominoes. The neatened up dining room has a woodburning stove.

🍴 The menu is fairly short but it's well balanced, fairly priced, and pubby feeling with an imaginative twist. As well as lunchtime sandwiches there might be duck and ham hock terrine, home-made pork pie, sausage and spring onion mash, lemon and dill battered cod fillet, roast cherry tomato risotto with mozzarella and rocket, game and ale pie, grilled rib-eye steak with chilli and garlic chips and rosemary stuffed tomato, with puddings such as sticky toffee pudding. *Starters/Snacks: £4.00 to £6.00. Main Courses: £7.00 to £16.00. Puddings: £4.00 to £5.00*

Marstons ~ Lease Emily Hammond ~ Real ale ~ Bar food (12-2.30, 7-9(6.30-8 Sun)) ~ Restaurant ~ (01335) 310205 ~ Children welcome ~ Dogs allowed in bar ~ Open 11-3, 6-11; 11.30-11 Sat; 12-10.30 Sun

Recommended by R T and J C Moggridge, Susan and Nigel Brookes, Andy and Claire Barker, the Didler, Roderick Braithwaite, J and E Dakin, Paul J Robinshaw, Verity Kemp, Richard Mills, Mr and Mrs John Taylor, Richard, B and M Kendall, Maurice and Gill McMahon, Eileen Tierney, Annette Tress, Gary Smith, Peter F Marshall

BURTON UPON TRENT   SK2523   MAP 7

Burton Bridge Inn ♀ ◖ £
Bridge Street (A50); DE14 1SY

Straightforward cheery tap for the Burton Bridge Brewery; lunchtime snacks only

'What a gem,' says one reader of this genuinely friendly down-to-earth old brick local. It's the showcase for the superbly kept beers (Bitter, Festival, Golden Delicious, Porter and XL) that are brewed by Burton Bridge Brewery who are housed across the long old-fashioned yard at the back (there's a blue-brick terrace out here too). These are served on handpump alongside a guest such as Timothy Taylors Landlord, around 20 whiskies, an impressive 17 wines by the glass and over a dozen country wines. The simple little front area leads into an adjacent bar with wooden pews, and plain walls hung with notices, awards and brewery memorabilia. Separated from the bar by the serving counter, the little oak beamed lounge is snugly oak panelled and has a flame-effect fire and a mix of furnishings; skittle alley. The panelled upstairs dining room is open only at lunchtime.

🍽 Simple but hearty bar snacks take in filled cobs (including roast beef and pork), cheese filled oatcakes, baked potatoes, filled giant yorkshire puddings and ploughman's. *Starters/Snacks: £1.90 to £4.30*

Own brew ~ Licensees Kevin and Jan McDonald ~ Real ale ~ Bar food (lunchtime only, not Sun) ~ No credit cards ~ (01283) 536596 ~ Dogs welcome ~ Open 11.30-2.15, 5-11; 12-2, 7-10.30 Sun; closed bank hol Mon lunchtime

Recommended by P Dawn, Paul J Robinshaw, the Didler, C J Fletcher, Theo, Anne and Jane Gaskin, Pete Baker, R T and J C Moggridge

CAULDON   SK0749   MAP 7

Yew Tree ★★ £
Village signposted from A523 and A52 about 8 miles W of Ashbourne; ST10 3EJ

Treasure-trove of fascinating antiques and dusty bric-a-brac, very idiosyncratic

One reader told us it was worth the 180-mile detour that her husband persuaded her to make just to visit this unique pub. It's an idiosyncratic place (you will either love or hate it) that another reader has affectionately described as a junk shop with a bar. Over the years, the charming landlord has amassed a museum's-worth of curiosities. The most impressive pieces are perhaps the working polyphons and symphonions – 19th-c developments of the musical box, often taller than a person, each with quite a repertoire of tunes and elaborate sound-effects. But there are also two pairs of Queen Victoria's stockings, ancient guns and pistols, several penny-farthings, an old sit-and-stride boneshaker, a rocking horse, swordfish blades, a little 800 BC greek vase, and even a fine marquetry cabinet crammed with notable early staffordshire pottery. Soggily sprung sofas mingle with 18th-c settles, plenty of little wooden tables and a four-person oak church choir seat with carved heads which came from St Mary's church in Stafford; above the bar is an odd iron dog-carrier. As well as all this there's an expanding choir of fine tuneful longcase clocks in the gallery just above the entrance, a collection of six pianolas (one of which is played most nights) with an excellent repertoire of piano rolls, a working vintage valve radio set, a crank-handle telephone, a sinuous medieval wind instrument made of leather, and a Jacobean four-poster which was once owned by Josiah Wedgwood and still has his original wig hook on the headboard. Clearly it would be almost an overwhelming task to keep all that sprucely clean. The drinks here are very reasonably priced (so no wonder it's popular with locals), and you'll find well kept Bass, Burton Bridge and Grays Dark Mild on handpump or tapped from the cask, along with about a dozen interesting malt whiskies; piped music (probably Radio 2), darts, shove-ha'penny, table skittles, dominoes and cribbage. When you arrive don't be put off by the plain exterior, or the fact that the pub is tucked unpromisingly between enormous cement works and quarries and almost hidden by a towering yew tree.

🍽 Simple good value tasty snacks include pork, meat and potato, chicken and mushroom and steak pies, hot big filled baps and sandwiches, quiche, smoked mackerel or ham salad, and home-made puddings. *Starters/Snacks: £0.80 to £1.90. Puddings: £1.60 to £1.80*

Free house ~ Licensee Alan East ~ Real ale ~ Bar food ~ No credit cards ~ (01538) 308348 ~
Children in polyphon room ~ Dogs welcome ~ Folk music first Tues in month ~
Open 10-2.30(3 Sat), 6-midnight; 12-3, 7-midnight Sun

*Recommended by N R White, Simon Fox, the Didler, John and Enid Morris, D and J Ashdown, Mike Horgan,
Andy and Claire Barker, Susan and John Douglas, Susan and Nigel Brookes, R W Allen, Richard*

HOAR CROSS
SK1323 MAP 7
Meynell Ingram Arms
Abbots Bromley Road, off A515 Yoxall—Sudbury; DE13 8RB

**Interesting choice of food in cheery traditional bar and smarter dining areas; courtyard
and garden**

Several neat little rooms ramble round the central counter at this attractive, bustling
place. The smartest area is the brightly painted room leading to the dining room, with its
elegant red curtains and coal effect fire. Elsewhere there's a traditional red-tiled bar with
stools along the counter, a log fire in a brick fireplace, hunting pictures and a
bespectacled fox's head among other stuffed creatures, comfortably upholstered seats, a
few beams and brasses, and local notices on yellow walls. Marstons Pedigree is kept on
handpump alongside a couple of guests such as Wells & Youngs Bombardier, Timothy
Taylors Landlord, and nine wines by the glass; helpful young staff. There are tables in a
courtyard behind, and some on the grass in front; it's a pretty spot in summer. More
reports please.

🍴 **Under the new licensee, it's essential to book a table at the weekend. Bar food
includes mixed olives and toasted provençale herb bread, potted chicken liver pâté with
toasted onion bread, warm potato and bacon salad, chicken caesar salad, roasted scallops
with creamed champ potatoes, parma ham and shallot dressing and apple purée, moules
marinières, lamb sausages with pea and spring onion mash and caramelised pear and lamb
jus, braised shin of beef with horseradish potatoes, caramelised onions and beer sauce,
grilled swordfish with crab and leek risotto, cucumber and fennel salad, confit parsnip
tart with baby onions, coriander salad and vegetable curry purée and puddings such as
crème brûlée with almond shortbread biscuit and apple and calvados sorbet.**
Starters/Snacks: £3.90 to £6.95. Main Courses: £8.95 to £15.50. Puddings: £3.75 to £5.50

Free house ~ Licensee Guy Wallis ~ Real ale ~ Bar food (12-2.30, 6-9; 12-6 only Sun) ~
Restaurant ~ (01283) 575202 ~ Children welcome ~ Dogs allowed in bar ~ Open 12-11(12 Sat);
12-10.30 Sun

Recommended by Pete Baker, Susan and Nigel Brookes

KIDSGROVE
SJ8354 MAP 7
Blue Bell 🍺
25 Hardings Wood; off A50 NW edge of town; ST7 1EG

**Astonishing tally of thoughtfully sourced real ales on six constantly changing pumps at
simple little beer pub**

In the last ten years over 2500 brews have passed through the beer pumps at this quirky
double cottage at the junction of the Trent & Mersey and Macclesfield canals. The
constantly changing range is carefully selected from smaller, often unusual brewers, such
as Acorn, Castle Rock, Crouch Vale, Oakham, Townhouse and Whim. Lagers are restricted
to german or belgian brews, they've usually a draught continental beer, at least one farm
cider, around 30 bottled beers, and various coffees and soft drinks. Service is friendly and
knowledgeable. The four small, carpeted rooms are unfussy and straightforward, with blue
upholstered benches running around ivory-painted walls, a gas effect coal fire, just a few
tables, and maybe soft piped music. There are tables in front, and more on a little back
lawn. Note the limited opening hours.

🍴 **Food is limited to filled rolls at the weekend.**

Free house ~ Licensees Dave and Kay Washbrook ~ Real ale ~ No credit cards ~ (01782) 774052 ~ Children welcome ~ Dogs welcome ~ Impromptu acoustic Sun evenings ~ Open 7.30-11; 1-4, 7-11 Sat; 12-10.30 Sun; closed lunchtimes and Mon except bank hols

Recommended by Dave Webster, Sue Holland, the Didler, John R Ringrose

LICHFIELD   SK0705   MAP 4

Boat

3.8 miles from M6 Toll junction T6 (pay again when you rejoin it); head E on A5, turning right at first roundabout into B4155, keeping straight ahead into Barrack Lane at first crossroads, then left on to A461 Walsall Rd; leaving pub, keep straight on to rejoin A5 at Muckley Corner roundabout; WS14 0BU

Efficiently run dining pub makes handy break for imaginative meal off M6

The first area you enter at this neatly kept place is well lit from above by a big skylight, and dominated by huge floor-to-ceiling food blackboards, reflecting the emphasis on the carefully prepared food here. Bright plastic flooring, views straight into the kitchen, striking photoprints, leather club chairs and sofas around coffee tables and potted palms all lend a cheery café atmosphere to this part. The solid light wood bar counter has three thoughtfully sourced changing real ales from brewers such as Beowulf, Blythe and Robinsons on handpump, and around ten wines by the glass. The comfortable dining areas are more conventional with sturdy modern pale pine furniture on russet pink carpets and prints on white walls. Windows to the left have views on to the canal (currently undergoing restoration); faint piped music. A landscaped area outside is paved with a central raised decking area; good wheelchair access throughout.

🍴 **Attractively presented good bar food from a fairly extensive menu includes soup, seafood terrine wrapped in smoked salmon, lemon risotto with balsamic dressing and parmesan, scallops with black pudding and rocket salad, honey and chestnut roast duck breast with juniper sauce, pear and blue cheese tart, bass with shallot and lemon sauce, chicken with serrano ham and basil mousse with smoked garlic and lemon thyme dressing, and puddings such as pear and almond flan or panettone bread and butter pudding.** *Starters/Snacks: £3.50 to £7.75. Main Courses: £7.25 to £16.95. Puddings: £3.25 to £5.25*

Free house ~ Licensee Ann Holden ~ Real ale ~ Bar food (12-2.15, 6-9.30; 12-8.30 Sun) ~ (01543) 361692 ~ Children welcome ~ Dogs welcome ~ Open 12-4, 6-midnight; 12-11 Sun

Recommended by Trevor and Sheila Sharman, Karen Eliot, David Green, Oliver Richardson, Ian and Jane Irving, Louise Gibbons, Glenwys and Alan Lawrence, Clifford Blakemore, David Wright, N R White, R T and J C Moggridge, John Balfour, Peter and Heather Elliott, Philand Jane Hodson, Julia and Richard Tredgett, Brian and Jacky Wilson, Mrs Ann Gray

Queens Head 🍺 £

Queen Street; public car park just round corner in Swan Road, off A51 roundabout; WS13 6QD

Friendly with great cheese counter, bargain lunchtime hot dishes, good range of real ales

It's well worth making the short walk from the city centre to find this handsome Georgian brick building, which is done up inside as an old-fashioned alehouse. Its single long room has a mix of comfortable aged furniture on bare boards, some stripped brick, Lichfield and other pictures on ochre walls above a panelled dado, and big sash windows. The atmosphere is comfortably relaxed and grown-up and staff are friendly and helpful. The pub is a keen supporter of local sports teams and they've a terrestrial TV for sports events. As well as a couple of interesting guests, usually from smaller brewers, beers include Adnams, Marstons Pedigree and Timothy Taylors Landlord; small garden.

🍴 **The highlight is the cold cabinet of cheeses on the left of the bar, including some interesting local ones such as Dovedale Blue. Throughout the day (unless it gets too busy) you can make up your own very generous ploughman's, perhaps with some pâté too, with a basket of their good crusty granary bread, home-made pickles, onions and gherkins. At lunchtime (not Sunday) they also have a good range of over two dozen enjoyable pubby hot dishes at amazingly low prices, such as their pedi pie (steak pie made with Marstons Pedigree).** *Starters/Snacks: £3.50 to £5.50*

Marstons ~ Lease Denise Harvey ~ Real ale ~ Bar food (12-2.15 (cheese all day and only cheese Sun)) ~ No credit cards ~ (01543) 410932 ~ Dogs welcome ~ Open 12-11(11.30 Fri, Sat); 12-3, 7-11 Sun

Recommended by Alan and Eve Harding, Nicola Ridding, Richard Green

SALT   SJ9527   MAP 7

Holly Bush
Off A51 S of Stone; ST18 OBX

Delightful medieval pub popular for generous mainly traditional all-day food

The interior of this very lovely white-painted 14th-c house is as charming as the deep-thatched, flower bedecked exterior suggests. The oldest part has a heavy beamed and planked ceiling (some of the beams are attractively carved), a woodburning stove and salt cupboard built into the big inglenook, with other nice old-fashioned touches such as an ancient pair of riding boots on the mantelpiece. Several cosy areas spread off from the standing-room serving section, with high backed cushioned pews, old tables and more orthodox seats. A modern back extension, with beams, stripped brickwork and a small coal fire, blends in well. Adnams, Marstons Pedigree and a guest such as Black Sheep are on handpump, alongside a fairly priced house wine and a dozen wines by the glass. The back of the pub is beautifully tended, with rustic picnic-sets on a big lawn. They operate a type of locker system for credit cards, which they will ask to keep if you are running a tab.

⏪ **The pub has its own commercial smoking oven, which allows them to make their own smoked meats and fish, and an 18th-c-styled wood fired oven (in the beer garden) for pizzas, hearth breads and other interesting dishes. Based on traditional british recipes and using carefully sourced ingredients, food might include handmade pork, leek and stilton sausage, egg and chips, battered cod with mushy peas, steak and kidney pudding, a lunchtime roast, braised venison with beer and spiced dumplings, grilled red snapper with jamaican spiced tomato chutney, traditional puddings such as apple crumble and bread and butter pudding and an english cheeseboard.** *Starters/Snacks: £1.95 to £3.95. Main Courses: £7.25 to £13.95. Puddings: £3.95 to £7.95*

Pyramid ~ Licensees Geoffrey and Joseph Holland ~ Real ale ~ Bar food (12-9.30(9 Sun)) ~ (01889) 508234 ~ Children welcome till 8.30pm ~ Open 12-11

Recommended by Trevor and Sheila Sharman, Glen and Nola Armstrong, Simon and Sally Small, Pat and Tony Martin, Roger and Anne Newbury, Susan and Nigel Brookes, Maurice and Gill McMahon, R M Chard, Mayur Shah, M and GR, Michael and Jenny Back, Richard Endacott, S J and C C Davidson, John and Yvonne Davies, Ian and Nita Cooper, R T and J C Moggridge

STOURTON   SO8485   MAP 4

Fox
A458 W of junction with A449, towards Enville; DY7 5BL

Cosy series of rooms at welcoming country pub, nice bar food and garden

The warm atmosphere at this neatly kept roadside pub is largely down to the welcoming family who've been running it with loving care for over 30 years. Don't get the impression though that it's at all old-fashioned. Where appropriate, they've kept things perky and neatly up to date. Several cosily small areas ramble back from the small serving bar by the entrance, with its well kept Bathams Best and guest such as Enville Ale on handpump (and a noticeboard of hand-written travel offers). Tables are mostly sturdy and varnished, with pews, settles and comfortable library or dining chairs on the green or dark blue carpet and bare boards. A good positive colour scheme is picked up nicely by the curtains, some framed exotic menus and well chosen prints (jazz and golf both feature). The woodburning stoves may be opened to give a cheery blaze on cold days, they put out big bunches of flowers, and the lighting (mainly low voltage spots) has been done very carefully, giving an intimate bistro feel in the areas round on the right. Dining areas include a smart conservatory which has neat bentwood furniture and proper tablecloths; piped music. There are well spaced picnic-sets on a terrace and big stretch of sloping grass and the pub is well placed for Kinver Country Park walks and the Staffordshire Way.

🍴 Bar food includes **lunchtime sandwiches, as well as soup, garlic mushrooms, tomato and basil pasta, mediterranean risotto, battered cod, curry, fish or steak and stout pie and 8oz sirloin steak; it's a good idea to book if you want to go to one of their fortnightly fish evenings.** *Starters/Snacks: £4.95 to £8.95. Main Courses: £10.95 to £18.50. Puddings: £3.95*

Free house ~ Licensee Stefan Caron ~ Real ale ~ Bar food (12-2.30, 7-9.30; 12-5.30 Sun; not Mon evening) ~ Restaurant ~ (01384) 872614 ~ Children welcome in conservatory til 8pm ~ Open 10.30-3, 5-11; 10.30-11 Sat; 12-10.30 Sun

Recommended by Theo, Anne and Jane Gaskin, Chris Glasson, George and Maureen Roby, R T and J C Moggridge

WETTON
SK1055 MAP 7

Olde Royal Oak

Village signposted off Hulme End—Alstonefield road, between B5054 and A515; DE6 2AF

Friendly traditional pub in lovely location; good value straightforward food

---

In the words of one happy reader, 'Here is a real old village pub with open fires and beams.' As he suggests, this aged white-painted and shuttered stone-built village house is just the sort of traditionally welcoming place you'd hope to find tucked in at the heart of this lovely National Trust countryside, with Wetton Mill and the Manifold Valley nearby. There's a good convivial atmosphere in the bar, with white ceiling boards above its black beams, small dining chairs around rustic tables, an oak corner cupboard, and a coal fire in the stone fireplace. The bar extends into a more modern-feeling area, which in turn leads to a carpeted sun lounge that looks over the small garden; piped music, darts, TV, shove-ha'penny, cribbage and dominoes. You can choose from more than 30 whiskies, and they've well kept Greene King Morlands Original and a guest from a small brewer such as Cottage on handpump. There's a croft behind the pub for caravans and tents, and boot covers for muddy walkers at both doors.

🍴 Reasonably priced pubby food includes **filled baps, leek and potato soup, breaded mushrooms, spicy chicken dippers, battered cod, parsnip, sweet potato and chestnut bake, gammon with pineapple and egg, chicken tikka and steaks, and puddings such as treacle sponge or home-made bread and butter pudding.** *Starters/Snacks: £3.45 to £4.95. Main Courses: £5.95 to £12.95. Puddings: £3.75*

Free house ~ Licensees Brian and Janet Morley ~ Real ale ~ Bar food ~ (01335) 310287 ~ Dogs welcome ~ Open 12-2.30(3 Sat in winter, Sun), 7-11; 12-11 Sat high summer; closed Mon, Tues ~ Bedrooms: /£40S

Recommended by Malcolm Pellatt, Peter F Marshall, B M Eldridge, Paul J Robinshaw, the Didler, Andy and Claire Barker

WRINEHILL
SJ7547 MAP 7

Hand & Trumpet 🍴 ♀ ◀

A531 Newcastle—Nantwich; CW3 9BJ

STAFFORDSHIRE DINING PUB OF THE YEAR

Big attractive dining pub with good food all day, professional service, nice range of real ales and wines; pleasant garden

---

Cleverly open plan and stylish yet still intimate feeling this sturdy building has been handsomely converted with top quality fixtures and fittings. At its heart, the solidly built counter has half a dozen handpumps dispensing well kept Caledonian Deuchars IPA, Thwaites Original, Timothy Taylors Landlord and three guests from brewers such as Derby, Salopian and Woodlands. They also keep a fine range of about 22 wines by the glass and about 85 whiskies. Linked open-plan areas working around the counter have a good mix of dining chairs and varying-sized tables on polished tiles or stripped oak boards, and several big oriental rugs that soften the acoustics as well as the appearance. There are lots of nicely lit prints on cream walls above mainly dark dado and below deep red ceilings. It's all brightened up with good natural light from bow windows and in one area a big skylight. Service is relaxed and friendly; good disabled access and facilities; board games. French windows open on to a stylish balustraded deck with teak tables and chairs looking down to ducks swimming on a big pond in the sizeable garden, which has plenty of trees.

🍴 Imaginative bar food includes interesting sandwiches, starters such as white onion and wild garlic soup, creamed leek risotto with parmesan crisp, crab cakes with tarragon mayonnaise, main courses such as battered haddock with mushy peas and hand cut chips, roast squash and thyme bread pudding, fried salmon fillet with bacon potato cake and horseradish sauce, chicken breast with chorizo risotto and chargrilled vegetables and rump steak with peppercorn sauce. Puddings might be custard tart with poached pear and chocolate sauce and knickerbocker glory; british cheeseboard. *Starters/Snacks: £4.50 to £7.95. Main Courses: £8.95 to £15.50. Puddings: £4.25 to £5.95*

Brunning & Price ~ Manager John Unsworth ~ Real ale ~ Bar food (12-10(9.30 Sun)) ~ (01270) 820048 ~ Children welcome till 7pm ~ Dogs allowed in bar ~ Open 12-11(10.30 Sun)

Recommended by R T and J C Moggridge, Sue Leighton, Dr Peter Crawshaw, Liese Collier-Jones, John R Ringrose, Dave Webster, Sue Holland, Paul and Gail Betteley, Karen Eliot, Alistair and Kay Butler, J Metcalfe, Gary Rollings, Debbie Porter

LUCKY DIP

Besides the fully inspected pubs, you might like to try these Lucky Dips recommended to us and described by readers (if you do, please send us reports: feedback@thegoodpubguide.co.uk).

ALSTONEFIELD [SK1255]
☆ *Watts Russell Arms* DE6 2GD [Hopedale]: Cheerful nicely placed light and airy beamed pub, sandwiches, hearty dishes and more enterprising food, well kept Black Sheep, Timothy Taylors Landlord and an occasional guest beer, decent range of soft drinks, traditional games; can get busy wknds; children welcome, picnic-sets on sheltered tiered terrace and in garden, cl Mon and winter Sun evening *(LYM, the Didler, John Tav)*
ALTON [SK0742]
Bulls Head ST10 4AQ [High St]: Good value bar lunches and pleasant restaurant, Greene King Abbot, friendly helpful staff; piped music; children welcome *(D and J Ashdown)*
AMINGTON [SK2204]
Gate B77 3BY [Tamworth Rd, by Coventry Canal bridge 69]: Pleasantly decorated local with good value food in bar and restaurant, well kept Marstons Pedigree, good value wines, good service; nice waterside terrace, moorings *(Chris Reading)*
ANSLOW [SK2125]
Bell DE13 9QD [Main Rd]: Friendly flagstoned bar with settles and log fire, enjoyable enterprising food, good service, choice of real ales, good wines by the glass; restaurant cl Mon, Sun evening *(Paul Humphreys, B M Eldridge)*
☆ *Burnt Gate* DE13 9PY [Hopley Rd]: Comfortable country dining pub with good fresh food inc some imaginative dishes and speciality kebabs (full lunches not bar snacks Sun), friendly efficient staff, good choice of wines by the glass, Bass and Marstons

Pedigree, proper bar with coal fire as well as restaurant *(Paul Humphreys, John and Helen Rushton, C J Fletcher)*
ARMITAGE [SK0716]
☆ *Plum Pudding* WS15 4AZ [Rugeley Rd (A513)]: Canalside pub and brasserie with modern warm colour scheme, good contemporary food inc good value set menu, sandwiches and light dishes, Greene King Old Speckled Hen, Marstons Pedigree and Bass or Tetleys, decent wines (choice of large or giant glasses), friendly service; no dogs, live music Fri; tables on waterside terrace and narrow canal bank (moorings available), bedrooms in neighbouring cottage *(John and Helen Rushton, Bren and Val Speed, BB, S J and C C Davidson)*
BIDDULPH [SJ8959]
Talbot ST8 7RY [Grange Rd (N, right off A527)]: Well laid out Vintage Inn family dining pub, decent fresh food, well kept ales; handy for Biddulph Grange gardens *(Paul J Robinshaw, Oliver Richardson)*
BLITHBURY [SK0819]
Bull & Spectacles WS15 3HY [Uttoxeter Rd (B5014 S of Abbots Bromley)]: Obliging friendly service, wide choice of homely food inc bargain lunchtime Hot Table – half a dozen or so generous main dishes with help-yourself veg, and some puddings; no credit cards *(David Green, Helen Rowett)*
BLYTHE BRIDGE [SJ9640]
Black Cock ST11 9NT [Uttoxeter Rd (A521)]: Roadside local with good staff, some tables set for the enjoyable fresh food, several real ales, good wine choice, great 50s and Beatles memorabilia *(the Didler)*

BOBBINGTON [SO8190]

Red Lion DY7 5DU [Six Ashes Rd, off A458 Stourbridge—Bridgnorth]: Enjoyable food from sandwiches and bargain lunches up, good range of wines by the glass, Theakstons Old Peculier and Wye Valley, roomy bar areas with pool and table footer; children welcome, good-sized garden with robust play area, 17 comfortable bedrooms in modern block, open all day wknds *(John and Helen Rushton)*

BRANSTON [SK2221]

Bridge Inn DE14 3EZ [off A5121 just SW of Burton; Tatenhill Lane, by Trent & Mersey Canal bridge 34]: Cosy low-beamed canalside pub very popular at wknds for Italian landlord's good reasonably priced pizzas and pastas (so may be a wait for a table – hang in there for his rather special tiramisu), particularly well kept Marstons Pedigree, friendly helpful staff, warm log fire; tables in waterside garden, good moorings, basic supplies for boaters and caravanners *(C J Fletcher, Paul J Robinshaw)*

Riverside DE14 3EP [Riverside Dr]: Good-sized pub in lovely spot by River Trent, good value pubby food, good choice of wines by the glass, Greene King ales, friendly efficient service; lots of tables in big waterside garden, 20 bedrooms *(Mr and Mrs P L Spencer, Roy and Lindsey Fentiman)*

BURTON UPON TRENT [SK2523]

Brewery Tap DE14 1YQ [part of Museum of Brewing, Horninglow St]: Comfortably refurbished modern bar with unusual local real ales and interesting lagers, prompt service, adjoining brewing museum (interesting outing) and restaurant *(C J Fletcher)*

☆ *Coopers Tavern* DE14 1EG [Cross St]: Appealing traditional pub well run by friendly family, Hop Back Summer Lightning, Tower and other well kept changing ales from casks in back room with cask tables, lunchtime food, coal fire in homely front parlour *(C J Fletcher, the Didler, LYM, Pete Baker)*

Derby Inn DE14 1RU [Derby Rd]: Well worn in idiosyncratic local with particularly good Marstons Pedigree, friendly long-serving landlord (talking of retirement – go while you can), local produce for sale wknd, brewery glasses collection in cosy panelled lounge, lots of steam railway memorabilia in long narrow bar; sports TV; dogs welcome, open all day Fri/Sat *(the Didler, C J Fletcher)*

Devonshire Arms DE14 1BT [Station St]: Obliging new licensees doing good value food inc good Sun lunch in two-bar pub with lots of snug corners and back restaurant, well kept Burton Bridge ales, continental bottled beers; pleasant back terrace with water feature, open all day Fri/Sat *(Chris Evans, the Didler, C J Fletcher)*

Elms DE15 9AE [Stapenhill Rd (A444)]: Bass, Tower and changing guest beers in compact bar with wall benches, larger lounge; open all day Fri-Sun *(the Didler)*

Old Cottage Tavern DE14 2EG [Rangemoor St/Byrkley St]: Tied to local small brewery Old Cottage, their tasty beers and guest ales, bargain specials and good Sun lunch, solid fuel stove, four rooms inc games room and compact back restaurant; open all day *(the Didler, C J Fletcher)*

Wetmore Whistle DE14 1SH [Wetmore Rd]: Well renovated Tynemill pub under welcoming new licensees, two unpretentiously comfortable linked areas and back café, good value simple nourishing food all day inc bargain Sun roast, Castle Rock, Marstons Pedigree and guest beers tapped from the cask, continental beers and farm ciders, good choice of wines by the glass; open all day *(C J Fletcher, the Didler, Rona Murdoch)*

BUTTERTON [SK0756]

Black Lion ST13 7SP [off B5053]: Traditional 18th-c low-beamed stone-built inn in Peak District conservation village, logs blazing in inner room's kitchen range, some banquettes, good-humoured efficient service even when busy, enjoyable bar food from filled rolls up, half a dozen well kept ales, reasonable prices, traditional games and pool room; piped music; children in eating areas, terrace tables, tidy bedrooms, cl Mon and Tues lunchtimes *(DC, LYM, the Didler)*

CANNOCK [SJ9710]

Linford Arms WS11 1BN [High Green]: Wetherspoons in attractive 18th-c building, eight well kept ales and their usual keenly priced food, good house wine, friendly fast service and hands-on manager, quiet family area upstairs; tables outside, open all day *(R T and J C Moggridge, John Tav)*

Shoal Hill WS11 1RF [Sandy Lane]: Smart pub popular with walkers for low-priced bar food from baguettes and baked potatoes up, friendly helpful staff, Thwaites ales, large light restaurant *(Neil and Brenda Skidmore, Robert Garner)*

CHASETOWN [SK0407]

Uxbridge Arms WS7 3QL [Church St]: Large local with some interesting real ales such as Black Hole, food in bar and upstairs restaurant; open all day Fri-Sun *(Tony and Wendy Hobden)*

CHEADLE [SK0342]

☆ *Queens at Freehay* ST10 1RF [Counslow Rd, SE]: Friendly family dining pub with wide range of good mainly familiar food inc attractively priced light lunchtime dishes, real ales, polite attentive staff, arch to neat and airy dining area from comfortable lounge; tables and chairs in attractive back garden *(Mr and Mrs J Morris, Mrs R A Collard, LYM)*

CHEDDLETON [SJ9751]

☆ *Boat* ST13 7EQ [Basford Bridge Lane, off A520]: Cheerful local handy for Churnet Valley steam railway, flint mill and country park, neat long bar, low plank ceilings, well kept Marstons-related and other ales, friendly staff and locals, good value generous simple food from sandwiches and filled oatcakes up, interesting pictures, attractive dining room with polished floor, black-leaded range and brass fittings; children and dogs welcome, marquee and fairy-lit heated terrace out overlooking Cauldon Canal *(Dr D J and Mrs S C Walker, Susan and Nigel Brookes, John and Helen Rushton, LYM)*

CLIFTON CAMPVILLE [SK2511]

☆ *Green Man* B79 0AX [Main St]: Low-beamed 15th-c village pub with inglenook and chubby armchair in public bar, airy modernised dining lounge, good service, Bass, Marstons Pedigree and a guest beer, good range of generous food from hot baguettes to good value Sun roast, games area with pool; children in back family room, garden with play area *(Geoff Ziola, LYM, John and Helen Rushton)*

CODSALL [SJ8603]

Codsall Station WV8 1BY [Chapel Lane/Station Rd]: Pub in simply restored vintage waiting room and ticket office (station still used by trains) with added conservatory, Holdens beers inc one brewed for the pub, helpful staff, good value plentiful basic food (not Sun/Mon) from sandwiches up, lots of railway memorabilia; terrace, open all day wknds *(the Didler, Neil and Brenda Skidmore)*

CONSALL [SK0049]

☆ *Black Lion* ST9 0AJ [Consall Forge, OS Sheet 118 map ref 000491; best approach from Nature Park, off A522, using car park 0.5 miles past Nature Centre]: Traditional take-us-as-you-find-us tavern tucked away in rustic old-fashioned canalside settlement by restored steam railway station, enjoyable generous unpretentious food made by landlord (may be only sandwiches midweek), well kept Black Sheep and Moorhouses, good coal fire; piped music, no muddy boots, busy wknd lunchtimes; good walking area *(Gwyn and Anne Wake, the Didler, Clive and Fran Dutson, S J and C C Davidson, LYM)*

DERRINGTON [SJ8922]

Red Lion ST18 9LR [Billington Lane]: Welcoming country pub popular for its good value lunches (not Mon), real ales such as Wells & Youngs Bombardier *(B M Eldridge)*

DRAYCOTT IN THE CLAY [SK1529]

Roebuck DE6 5BT [Toby's Hill]: Attractive Marstons pub with jovial licensees, well kept beer, fresh food from lunchtime sandwiches and hot dishes to evening meals, big inglenook *(BB, B M Eldridge)*

ENVILLE [SO8286]

☆ *Cat* DY7 5HA [A458 W of Stourbridge (Bridgnorth Rd)]: Ancient beamed pub on Staffordshire Way, log fire in two appealingly old-fashioned rooms on one side of servery, plush banquettes on the other, four local Enville ales and three or four interesting guests, bar food inc sandwiches and mix-and-match range of sausage, mash and gravies, restaurant; children in family room and main lounge, dogs in bar, pretty courtyard sheltered by massive estate wall,

cl Sun evening, Mon *(the Didler, Lynda and Trevor Smith, LYM)*

FRADLEY [SK1414]

☆ *White Swan* DE13 7DN [Fradley Junction]: Perfect canalside location at Trent & Mersey and Coventry junction, bargain food from sandwiches to Sun carvery, well kept ales inc Marstons Pedigree, cheery traditional public bar, quieter plusher lounge and lower vaulted back bar (where children allowed), real fire, cribbage, dominoes; waterside tables *(LYM, Paul J Robinshaw, John Hopkins)*

GNOSALL [SJ8221]

Royal Oak ST20 0BL [Newport Rd]: Small, civilised and friendly two-bar pub with enjoyable home-made food (all day till 8 Sun, not Tues) inc notable vegetarian choice, Greene King IPA and Abbot, Highgate Mild and a weekly guest beer, dogs welcome, good-sized garden *(Mike and Julia Porter)*

HANLEY [SJ8847]

Coachmakers Arms ST1 3EA [Lichfield St]: Chatty traditional town local, three small rooms and drinking corridor, half a dozen or more changing ales, farm cider, darts, cards and dominoes, original seating and local tilework; children welcome, open all day, cl lunchtime Sun *(the Didler)*

HARLASTON [SK2110]

White Lion B79 9HT [off A513 N of Tamworth; Main St]: Friendly relaxed two-bar village pub with enjoyable fresh food, good value Sun lunch worth booking, good range of real ales such as Adnams and Wells & Youngs Bombardier; children welcome *(Steve Jennings)*

HIMLEY [SO8990]

☆ *Crooked House* DY3 4DA [signed down rather grim lane from B4176 Gornalwood—Himley, OS Sheet 139 map ref 896908]: Extraordinary sight, building thrown wildly out of kilter (mining subsidence), slopes so weird that things look as if they roll up not down them; otherwise a basic well worn low-priced pub with Banks's Bitter and Mild and guest beers, Weston's Old Rosie cider, cheery staff, straightforward food (all day in summer), some local antiques in level more modern extension, conservatory; children in eating areas, big outside terrace, open all day wknds and summer *(the Didler, Dave Braisted, R T and J C Moggridge, LYM)*

HOLLINGTON [SK0539]

Raddle ST10 4HQ [the one between Alton and Uttoxeter]: Extended country pub with neatly modernised rambling bar, low beams and brasses, generous pubby food, good choice of well kept ales inc Black Sheep, helpful young staff, conservatory; sweeping views from garden *(BB, R T and J C Moggridge)*

HOPWAS [SK1704]

Tame Otter B78 3AT [Hints Rd (A51 Tamworth—Lichfield)]: Vintage Inn by Birmingham & Fazeley Canal, beams and cosy corners, three log fires, nice mixed furnishings, old photographs and canalia, good value food all day, well kept ales inc Timothy Taylors Landlord, good choice of wines; large garden *(Colin Gooch, Derek and Heather Manning, Paul J Robinshaw)*

HUDDLESFORD [SK1509]

Plough WS13 8PY [off A38 2 miles E of Lichfield, by Coventry Canal]: Waterside dining pub extended from 17th-c cottage, good food from good value lunchtime dishes to more expensive evening choice, children's helpings, four neat areas, cheerful attentive staff, well kept ales such as Greene King and Marstons Pedigree, good range of wines; attractive hanging baskets, canalside tables, hitching posts *(Deb and John Arthur, Leslie and Barbara Owen)*

HULME END [SK1059]

☆ *Manifold Inn* SK17 0EX [B5054 Warslow— Hartington]: Light and airy 18th-c country dining pub nr river, enjoyable food inc some interesting and greek dishes using local produce, pleasant staff, well kept Whim ales, good choice of whiskies, log-effect gas fires and some stripped stone, conservatory, silver band practice night Sun; children welcome, disabled facilities, tables outside, camp site, simple bedrooms off secluded back courtyard *(Greta and Christopher Wells, Derek Stapley, BB, Annette Tress, Gary Smith)*

LEEK [SJ9856]

Den Engel ST13 5HG [Stanley St]: Belgian-style bar in high-ceilinged former bank, many dozens of belgian beers inc lots on tap, three dozen genevers, three or four changing real ales; piped classical music; tables on back terrace, open all day Weds-Sun, cl Mon/Tues lunchtimes *(the Didler)*

☆ *Swan* ST13 5DS [St Edward St]: Well worn in old pub popular for cheap lunchtime food from sandwiches up, quick helpful service, changing real ales, lots of malt whiskies, choice of coffees, pleasant front lounge, two bars behind central servery, downstairs wine bar, folk club; courtyard seats *(John Wooll)*

☆ *Wilkes Head* ST13 5DS [St Edward St]: Convivial three-room local dating from 18th c (still has back coaching stables), tied to Whim with their ales and interesting guest beers, good choice of whiskies, farm cider, friendly chatty landlord, welcoming regulars and dogs, filled rolls, pub games, gas fire, lots of pump clips; juke box in back room, Mon music night; children allowed in one room (but not really a family pub), fair disabled access, tables outside, open all day exc Mon lunchtime *(the Didler, Pete Baker)*

LICHFIELD [SK1010]

Hedgehog WS13 8JB [Stafford Rd (A51)]: Large Vintage Inn with lots of well spaced tables and plenty of nooks and corners, friendly staff, well kept Marstons Pedigree; children welcome, picnic-sets outside, bedrooms *(S J and C C Davidson, John and Yvonne Davies)*

Horse & Jockey WS14 9JE [Tamworth Rd (A51 Lichfield—Tamworth)]: Dining pub with friendly helpful service, enjoyable

generous food, four linked softly lit rooms with some panelling, settles, sepia photographs, books, plates and so forth, Black Sheep, Marstons, Timothy Taylors Landlord and guest beers *(S P Watkin, P A Taylor, David Green)*

Kings Head WS13 6PW [Bird St]: Beams, stripped wood and old prints, bargain home-made food from sandwiches up, well kept Marstons and guest beers, friendly service, coachyard conservatory, some live music; children welcome *(Colin Gooch)*

LITTLE HAY [SK1203]

Holly Bush WS14 0QA [E of A5127 N of Birmingham]: Cottagey Chef & Brewer with wide choice of reasonably priced food inc game and venison, friendly staff, pleasant layout with log fires and different levels *(Rita Gibbs)*

LONGNOR [SK0864]

☆ *Crewe & Harpur Arms* SK17 0NS: Well run pub, Marstons and several guest beers, good choice of wines by the glass, good food from sandwiches to restaurant meals, friendly efficient service, landlord plays piano Fri; bedrooms *(John Branston, Emma and Steve Ryland, John Lowe, Malcolm Pellatt, John Wooll)*

Olde Cheshire Cheese SK17 0NS: 14th-c, a pub for 250 years, well kept Robinsons, friendly service, tasty food inc Sun carvery, plenty of bric-a-brac and pictures in traditional main bar and two attractive dining rooms with their own bar; hikers welcome, bedrooms *(John Dwane, David Abbot)*

MARCHINGTON [SK1330]

Dog & Partridge ST14 8LJ [Church Lane]: Traditional village pub with warm fires, good range of well kept guest beers, helpful staff, good value evening restaurant Mon-Sat, and Sun lunch; live music Sun *(B M Eldridge)*

MEERBROOK [SJ9960]

Lazy Trout ST13 8SN: Good value food from traditional bar dishes to restaurant meals, good quick friendly service, three well kept changing ales, decent wines, cosily old-fashioned bar, comfortable lounge with log fire and dining area; no dogs, games machines; plenty of tables in pleasant garden behind, attractive setting, good walks *(John and Helen Rushton, DC, Dr D J and Mrs S C Walker)*

MILWICH [SJ9533]

Red Lion ST15 8RU [Dayhills; B5027 towards Stone]: Unpretentious bar at end of working farmhouse, old settles, tiled floor, inglenook log or coal fire, Bass and one or two guest beers tapped from the cask, friendly welcome, darts, dominoes and cribbage; cl lunchtimes exc Sun, cl Sun evening *(the Didler)*

NEWCASTLE-UNDER-LYME [SJ8547]

New Smithy ST5 0EH [Church Lane, Wolstanton]: Friendly bustling local with good mix of ages and low-priced well kept Hop Back ales *(John R Ringrose)*

NORTON CANES [SK0107]
Railway Tavern WS11 9PR [Norton Green Lane]: Large refurbished pub with Banks's and guest ales, food only Weds/Thurs lunchtime and some evenings, old local photographs; play area in big back garden *(Tony and Wendy Hobden)*

OAKEN [SJ8402]
Foaming Jug WV8 2HX [Holyhead Rd; A41 just E of A464 junction]: Interesting olde-worlde Vintage Inn, fair-priced food, helpful staff, good choice of wines by the glass, well kept ale, plenty of jugs on show; children welcome, neat garden *(Neil and Brenda Skidmore)*

PENKRIDGE [SJ9214]
Littleton Arms ST19 5AL [St Michaels Sq/A449 – M6 detour between junctions 12 and 13]: Busy M&B dining pub with contemporary layout, low leather stools and sofa, up-to-date brasserie food inc pizzas, good choice of wines by the glass, real ales, quick helpful service from friendly young staff; children welcome, bedrooms, open all day *(John and Helen Rushton, Colin Gooch, John and Alison Hamilton)*

☆ *Star* ST19 5DJ [Market Pl]: Charming open-plan local with good value food, Marstons-related ales, efficient friendly service, lots of low black beams and button-back red plush, open fires; piped music, sports TV; open all day, terrace tables *(Dr and Mrs A K Clarke, Robert Garner, Colin Gooch, R T and J C Moggridge, BB)*

RANTON [SJ8422]
☆ *Hand & Cleaver* ST18 9JZ [Butt Lane, Ranton Green]: New landlord doing good enterprising food from tapas and sharing plates up in tastefully extended country pub, good wines by the glass, four changing well kept ales, log fires, lots of exposed beams and timber; children and dogs welcome, cl Mon *(Jonathon Bell)*

ROLLESTON ON DOVE [SK2427]
Jinnie DE13 9AB [Station Rd]: Comfortable and friendly two-room pub with generous inexpensive food, four Marstons-related ales, coal-effect gas fires, pale blue décor; picnic-sets on small lawn by pony paddock *(Dennis Jones)*

Spread Eagle DE13 9BE [Church Rd]: Vintage Inn family dining pub with sensibly priced standard food all day, great choice of wines by the glass, Bass and Marstons Pedigree, three linked areas and separate dining room; disabled access and facilities, attractive shrubby streamside garden, bedrooms *(Dennis Jones, B M Eldridge)*

RUSHTON SPENCER [SJ9362]
Royal Oak SK11 0SE [A523 Leek—Macclesfield]: Good proper home cooking, warmly friendly service, well kept ales inc Banks's, pleasant lounge bar and restaurant, log fires *(Dr D J and Mrs S C Walker)*

SEIGHFORD [SJ8725]
Holly Bush ST18 9PQ [3 miles from M6 junction 14 via A5013/B5405]: Neatly kept extended dining pub with generous food inc very popular bargain lunches, two real ales;

neat back rose garden, cl Sun evening and Mon *(LYM, John and Helen Rushton)*

SHENSTONE [SK1004]
Fox & Hounds WS14 0NB [Main St]: Adnams, Greene King IPA, Marstons Pedigree and Timothy Taylors Landlord, good service even though busy, extended restaurant (not Mon); open all day wknds *(John and Helen Rushton)*

Railway Inn WS14 0LZ [Main St]: Pleasantly refurbished (once a butcher's shop and chapel), enjoyable food in airy dining area, three Marstons-related ales, good choice of wines by the glass, comfortable lounge; garden *(John and Helen Rushton)*

SLITTING MILL [SK0217]
Horns WS15 2UW [Slitting Mill Rd]: Light and airy, nicely set out, with good choice of food inc good value lunches, pleasant staff, five or six real ales inc Bass, Caledonian, Marstons and Timothy Taylors Landlord *(David Green, Robert Garner)*

STAFFORD [SJ9223]
Greyhound ST16 2PU [County Rd]: Unpretentious two-bar town pub with many well kept ales from all over, landlord may offer a taster; sports TVs and usual games in lively public bar *(Pete Baker)*

Picture House ST16 2HL [Bridge St/Lichfield St]: Art deco cinema converted by Wetherspoons keeping ornate ceiling plasterwork and stained-glass name sign, bar on stage with up to five real ales at competitive prices, farm cider, seating in stalls, circle and upper circle, popular food all day, lively atmosphere, film posters, Peter Cushing mannequin in preserved ticket box; good disabled facilities, spacious terrace overlooking river, open all day *(Alan and Eve Harding)*

Star & Garter ST17 4AW [Wolverhampton Rd (A449)]: Busy town local with four reasonably priced real ales, friendly licensees; some live music; garden facing road *(Mark Hannan, John Tav)*

Telegraph ST17 4AW [Wolverhampton Rd (A449)]: Neatly kept two-bar with real ales such as Banks's, Black Sheep and Wells & Youngs Bombardier, quick friendly service, daily papers *(John Tav)*

Vine ST16 2JU [Salter St]: Large traditional hotel with comfortable well divided bar, wide food choice inc restaurant bargains for two, well kept low-priced Banks's; children welcome, 27 bedrooms *(John Tav)*

STOKE-ON-TRENT [SJ8649]
Bulls Head ST6 3AJ [St Johns Sq, Burslem]: Lots of belgian beers as well as good Titanic and guest beers in two-room town pub with good service even when busy, coal fire, bar billiards; good juke box; cl till 3 wkdys, open all day Fri-Sun *(the Didler, P Dawn, R T and J C Moggridge)*

Potter ST4 3DB [King St, Fenton]: Unpretentious three-room local with several changing ales such as Coach House and Greene King; sports TV; open all day *(the Didler)*

STONE [SJ9033]

Swan ST15 8QW [Stafford St (A520)]: Immaculate converted warehouse by Trent & Mersey Canal, up to ten well kept ales inc interesting local brews, log fires, buoyant atmosphere, good friendly service, bar lunches (not Sun/Mon); frequent live music nights; terrace tables, open all day *(John Tav)*

STOWE [SK0027]

Cock ST18 0LF [off A518 Stafford—Uttoxeter]: Nicely laid out bistro-style conversion of village pub, good value light lunches, pleasant efficient service *(Leslie and Barbara Owen)*

SWYNNERTON [SJ8535]

Fitzherbert Arms ST15 0RA [village signposted off A51 Stone—Nantwich]: Olde-worlde beamed pub with well kept Caledonian Deuchars IPA, friendly helpful staff, usual food *(R T and J C Moggridge)*

TAMWORTH [SK2004]

Market Vaults B79 7LU [Market St]: Splendidly unpretentious little two-bar pub, lots of brass, dark oak, original fireplaces and even tales of lost secret tunnel, hard-working welcoming landlord, well kept Banks's Original and Bitter and a guest beer, bargain lunchtime food – pounce quickly for a table in the small back dining area; piped music/juke box *(Pete Baker, Colin Gooch)*

Tweeddale Arms B79 7JS [Albert Rd/Victoria Rd]: Substantial building with modern airy atmosphere, spacious restaurant with reasonably priced food inc good steaks, attentive service, Marstons Pedigree, daily papers; games machines; bedrooms *(Colin Gooch)*

TATENHILL [SK2021]

☆ *Horseshoe* DE13 9SD [off A38 W of Burton; Main St]: Friendly and pubby, with bargain food all day (can take a while) inc good children's food and puddings, Marstons ales, good wine range, friendly service, tiled-floor bar, cosy side snug with woodburner, two-level restaurant and back family area; pleasant garden, good play area with pets corner *(C J Fletcher, Brian and Jacky Wilson, David and Felicity Fox, LYM, Paul J Robinshaw, John and Helen Rushton)*

TEAN [SK0138]

Dog & Partridge ST10 4LN [Uttoxeter Rd]: Good imaginative food, reasonably priced and well served, in pleasant conservatory restaurant, good range of ales and wines, nice countryside *(B M Eldridge)*

THORNCLIFFE [SK0158]

Red Lion ST13 7LP: Comfortable and attractive traditional 17th-c pub with prompt friendly service, enjoyable fresh food (all day Sun) from sandwiches up, warm atmosphere, log fires, wide range of wines and beers, dining room, games area with pool; children welcome, pretty garden with fish pond *(P and M Rudlin)*

TRYSULL [SO8594]

Bell WV5 7JB [Bell Rd]: Extended village local, softly lit lounge with lots of table lamps, big grandfather clock, inglenook fire and good chatty atmosphere, cosy bar with brasses and locomotive number-plates, Holdens, Bathams Best and a guest beer, interesting bar food from sandwiches up at fair prices, evening restaurant Weds-Sat; open all day wknds *(the Didler)*

TUTBURY [SK2128]

☆ *Olde Dog & Partridge* DE13 9LS [High St; off A50 N of Burton]: Chef & Brewer in handsome Tudor inn, rambling extensively back with heavy beams, timbers, various small rooms, nooks and corners, half a dozen real ales, their usual food all day, prompt friendly service, good log fire; comfortable bedrooms, open all day *(Derek and Sylvia Stephenson, Paul and Margaret Baker, LYM, Susan and Nigel Brookes)*

WARSLOW [SK0858]

Hare & Greyhound SK17 0JN [B5053 S of Buxton]: Former Greyhound reopened under friendly new owners, comfortably refurbished keeping beams, open fires and some stripped stone, good choice of good value food, well priced wine; garden picnic-sets under ash trees, pretty countryside *(LYM, David Jones)*

WHITMORE [SJ8040]

Mainwaring Arms ST5 5HR [3 miles from M6 junction 15 – A53 towards Mkt Drayton]: Popular old place of quiet character, with good value simple local food, real ales such as Bass and Marstons Pedigree, wide range of foreign bottled beers and ciders, quick friendly service, rambling linked rooms with beams, stripped stone, four open fires, antique settles among more modern seats; children in eating area, seats outside, open all day Fri/Sat *(Brian and Christina Dowsett)*

WHITTINGTON [SK1608]

Bell WS14 9JR [Main St]: Two smallish rooms, good value food from lunchtime sandwiches up (Thurs fish and chips night), three well kept real ales, friendly staff; terrace picnic-sets, big well planted garden with play area, pleasant village, open all day wknds *(David M Smith)*

Dog WS14 9JU [the one nr Lichfield; Main St]: Recently refurbished family-run village local with wide choice of generous home-made food from sandwiches up, Adnams Bitter and Broadside and Marstons Pedigree, lots of beams, brassware, old prints and team photographs, restaurant; big-screen TV; small terrace, bedrooms *(Sarah Shelton, Deb and John Arthur)*

YOXALL [SK1418]

Crown DE13 8NQ [Main St]: Friendly informal pub with enjoyable food using fresh local supplies in recently redecorated lounge bar, Marstons and related ales, decent wines by the glass, lively public bar; sports TV *(B M Eldridge)*

You can send reports to us at feedback@thegoodpubguide.co.uk.

Suffolk

This county has a healthy clutch of new entries this year, all very different from each other: the Cross Keys in Aldeburgh (chatty and friendly, near the beach), the Eels Foot at Eastbridge (handy for Minsmere and liked by cyclists and walkers, too), the Swan at Hoxne (a striking building with interesting food and wine), the properly pubby Kings Head in Orford (owned by a well known cookery writer), the Brewers Arms at Rattlesden (the return of former licensees has given it a new lease of life), the White Horse in Sibton (a nicely old-fashioned local), and two pubs in Snape, the Golden Key (an extremely friendly young landlord who keeps his own bees, animals and chickens for use in the imaginative food) and the Plough & Sail (near the Maltings and its interesting shopping complex). Real ales play a strong part in pubs here, with nearly half the main entries holding one of our Beer Awards. The county is home to one of Britain's biggest brewers, Greene King, though it is the smaller Adnams which is most often the beer of choice for Suffolk's good pubs. Other local brews we've found here this year are Earl Soham, Green Jack, Brandon, St Peters, Fat Cat, Old Cannon, Mauldons and Old Chimneys. When it comes to food, with the bountiful produce around – local game, fish and shellfish and salt marsh lamb for starters – it's not surprising that enthusiastic pub chefs here are creating some delicious dishes. There are plenty of good choices for a special meal out: the Dog at Grundisburgh, the Beehive at Horringer, the Angel in Lavenham, the Black Lion in Long Melford, the Anchor at Nayland, the Brewers Arms at Rattlesden, the Plough at Rede, the Ravenwood Hall at Rougham, the Golden Key in Snape, the Crown in Southwold, the Crown at Stoke-by-Nayland, the Anchor in Walberswick, and the Crown at Westleton. From this distinguished company the Crown in Southwold stands out, for its consistency and its all-round appeal, with splendid wines by the glass and beers as well as enterprising food. The Crown in Southwold is Suffolk Dining Pub of the Year. Finally, a note about the Lucky Dip section at the end of the chapter: it does have a good many starred entries, often already inspected and approved by us. We'd particularly note the Cock at Brent Eleigh, restaurany Froize at Chillesford, Kings Head in East Bergholt, Crown at Hartest and Ship at Levington.

ALDEBURGH   TM4656   MAP 5
Cross Keys ◀
Crabbe Street; IP15 5BN

Seats outside near beach, chatty atmosphere, friendly licensee, and local beer

It's fun to sit with a pint of beer on the terrace outside this 16th-c pub and watch people walking down Crag Path, especially during the Aldeburgh Festival when you may hear outside events (or at least, rehearsals for those events); there are seats in the garden, too, and the hanging baskets are pretty. This is one of the few places in Suffolk where you can eat outside by the beach. Inside, there's a happy, jolly atmosphere helped along by the obliging licensee and his staff. The interconnecting bars have two inglenook fireplaces, antique and other pubby furniture, the landlord's collection of oils and Victorian watercolours, and paintings by local artists on the walls. Adnams Bitter, Broadside and Explorer on handpump, and decent wines by the glass; games machine. The bedrooms are elegant.

🍴 **Simple bar food includes sandwiches, ploughman's, fish and chips, moules frites, steak and kidney pie, summer cromer crab, daily specials such as braised oxtail and coq au vin, and puddings like treacle sponge and summer pudding.** *Starters/Snacks: £3.95 to £7.75. Main Courses: £6.50 to £10.95. Puddings: £3.25*

Adnams ~ Tenants Mike and Janet Clement ~ Real ale ~ Bar food (not winter Sun evening) ~ No credit cards ~ (01728) 452637 ~ Children welcome ~ Dogs welcome ~ Open 11am(12am Sun)-midnight

Recommended by Tracey and Stephen Groves, MDN, Hilary Edwards, Michael Dandy, P Dawn, Simon Cottrell

BRAMFIELD
TM3973 MAP 5

Queens Head

The Street; A144 S of Halesworth; IP19 9HT

Popular pub with pretty garden, organic produce for bar food, and decent choice of drinks

The high-raftered lounge here has been redecorated this year with a new carpet, curtains and lighting; they still have the scrubbed pine tables, good log fire in the impressive fireplace, and sprinkling of farm tools on the walls. The separate side bar is now a lounge with comfortable leather furniture around the brick fireplace. Adnams Bitter and Broadside on handpump, several wines by the glass, Aspall's cider and seasonal home-made elderflower cordial; friendly service. Cheerful blue-painted picnic-sets under blue and white umbrellas in the pretty garden and there's a dome-shaped bower made of willow. The church next door is rather lovely.

🍴 **With an emphasis on local organic produce and making their own bread, the bar food includes lunchtime sandwiches, soup, crab claw meat, king prawns and apple cocktail, chicken liver pâté with cumberland sauce, grilled dates wrapped in bacon on a mild mustard sauce, mushroom omelette, fresh tagliatelle with cream, stilton and walnuts, pork sausages braised in onion gravy, lamb and vegetable pie, seafood crumble, steaks, and puddings such as steamed stem ginger and orange pudding with ginger sauce and lemon and lime mascarpone cheesecake; home-made preserves and cakes for sale.** *Starters/Snacks: £3.95 to £6.95. Main Courses: £6.95 to £15.95. Puddings: £3.25 to £4.35*

Adnams ~ Tenants Mark and Amanda Corcoran ~ Real ale ~ Bar food (12-2, 6.30-9.15) ~ (01986) 784214 ~ Children welcome away from main bar area ~ Dogs welcome ~ Live music monthly Fri evenings ~ Open 11.45-2.30, 6.30-11; 12-3, 7-10.30 Sun; closed 26 Dec

Recommended by Robert F Smith, Neil Powell, Charles and Pauline Stride, Anne Morris, Roger and Lesley Everett, Philip and Susan Philcox, Gerry and Rosemary Dobson, Derek and Sylvia Stephenson, Richard and Margaret McPhee, Tina and David Woods-Taylor, Rosemary Smith, V Brogden, Mike and Shelley Woodroffe, Mrs L Pratt, Jim and Sheila Prideaux

BURY ST EDMUNDS
TL8564 MAP 5

Nutshell

The Traverse, central pedestrian link off Abbeygate Street; IP33 1BJ

Teeny, simple local with lots of interest on the walls and a couple of real ales

Really tiny and quaint, this 17th-c bare-boards local is friendly and interesting. The timeless interior contains a short wooden bench along its shop-front corner windows, one cut-down sewing-machine table, an elbow rest running along its rather battered counter, and Greene King IPA and Abbot on handpump. A mummified cat, which was found walled up here (something our ancestors did quite commonly to ward off evil spirits) hangs from the dark brown ceiling (and also seems to have a companion rat), along with stacks of other bric-a-brac, from bits of a skeleton through vintage bank notes, cigarette packets and military and other badges to spears and a great metal halberd; piped music, chess and dominoes. The stairs up to the lavatories are very steep and narrow. The modern curved inn sign is appealing. No children. More reports please.

🍴 **No food at all.**

Greene King ~ Lease Jack Burton ~ Real ale ~ No credit cards ~ (01284) 764867 ~ Dogs welcome ~ Open 11-11; 12-10.30 Sun; closed 1 Jan

Recommended by David and Sue Smith, R T and J C Moggridge, the Didler, Joe Green

Old Cannon 🍺

Cannon Street, just off A134/A1101 roundabout N end of town; IP33 1JR

Busy own-brew town pub with guest beers, farm cider and tasty bar food

This bustling place looks more like a stylish private town house than a pub, and the bar has miscellaneous chairs around a few tables on dark bare boards, dark red or ochre walls (one with a big mirror), and plenty of standing space. The main feature of the bar is the two huge, gleaming stainless steel brewing vessels (in use each Monday) which produce the pub's own Old Cannon Best, Gunner's Daughter, and Blonde Bombshell, and they also have a couple of guest beers like Adnams Bitter and Crouch Vale Brewers Gold on handpump; farm cider, continental beers and a dozen wines by the glass. Piped music. Behind, through the old side coach arch, is a good-sized cobbled courtyard neatly set with planters and hanging baskets, with rather stylish metal tables and chairs. The recently refurbished bedrooms are in what was the old brewhouse across the courtyard. Dogs allowed on Sunday and Monday evenings. No children. More reports please.

🍴 **Bar food at lunchtime includes filled baguettes, soup, spinach, mushroom and ricotta pasta on fresh tomato coulis, sugar-baked ham and egg, beer-battered cod, and steak and mushroom in ale pie, with evening choices such as leek, blue cheese and toasted pine nut risotto with crispy bacon lardons, corn-fed chicken breast with wild mushroom stuffing, caramelised red onions, and a creamy madeira and watercress sauce, and roast cod fillet with a parsley crust, mustard mash and a cockle and sorrel cream sauce.** *Starters/Snacks: £4.25 to £5.25. Main Courses: £7.95 to £9.95. Puddings: £4.25 to £4.95*

Free house ~ Licensees Mike and Judith Shallow ~ Real ale ~ Bar food (12-2, 6.15-9.15; not Sun evening or all day Mon) ~ (01284) 768769 ~ Folk club every third Mon of month ~ Open 12-3, 5-11; 12-3, 7-10.30 Sun; closed Mon lunchtime, 25 and 26 Dec, 1 Jan ~ Bedrooms: £65S/£79S

Recommended by Ryta Lyndley, Joe Green, Julia Mann, M and GR, John and Patricia White

CHELMONDISTON   TM2037   MAP 5

Butt & Oyster

Pin Mill – signposted from B1456 SE of Ipswich; IP9 1JW

Chatty old pub above River Orwell with nice views, decent food and drink, and seats on the terrace

Named for the flounders and oysters which used to be caught here, this simple old bargeman's pub has fine riverside views from the window seats inside; you can watch the ships coming down from Ipswich and look across to the long lines of moored black sailing barges – the suntrap terrace shares the same view. The half-panelled timeless little smoke room is pleasantly worn and unfussy and has model sailing ships around the walls and high-backed and other old-fashioned settles on the tiled floor. Adnams Bitter and Broadside, and Greene King IPA and Explorer on handpump or tapped from the cask, and several wines by the glass; board games and dominoes. The annual Thames Barge Race (end June/beginning July) is fun.

> If we know a pub does summer barbecues, we say so.

🍴 Well liked bar food includes sandwiches, good soup, mussels done several different ways, chicken liver parfait with real ale chutney, beer-battered cod, home-cooked ham and free-range eggs, honey-glazed goats cheese with toasted pine nut and olive salad, burgers with various toppings, italian sausage pasta with mediterranean vegetables in pesto sauce, smoked paprika chicken breast with a tomato and herb dressing, and steaks. *Starters/Snacks: £3.95 to £5.95. Main Courses: £7.45 to £16.95. Puddings: £3.95 to £4.95*

Deben Inns ~ Lease Steve Lomas ~ Real ale ~ Bar food (all day) ~ (01473) 780764 ~ Children welcome ~ Dogs allowed in bar ~ Regular folk evenings ~ Open 11-11

Recommended by Pamela Goodwyn, the Didler, Pat and Tony Martin, Sue Demont, Tim Barrow, Bob and Margaret Holder, Mrs Romey Heaton, JDM, KM

EARL SOHAM
TM2263 MAP 5

Victoria 🍺 £
A1120 Yoxford—Stowmarket; IP13 7RL

Nice beers from brewery across the road in friendly, informal local

With the Earl Soham brewery just across the road (it used be brewed at the pub), the beers on handpump in this unpretentious, friendly pub are, not surprisingly, very well kept: Albert Ale, Gold, Sir Roger's Porter, and Victoria Bitter. Farm cider too. The well worn bar has an easy-going local atmosphere and is fairly basic. It's sparsely furnished with kitchen chairs and pews, plank-topped trestle sewing-machine tables and other simple scrubbed pine country tables, and there's stripped panelling, tiled or board floors, an interesting range of pictures of Queen Victoria and her reign, and open fires. On a raised back lawn are some seats, with more out in front. The pub is quite close to a wild fritillary meadow at Framlingham, and a working windmill at Saxtead.

🍴 Straightforward bar food includes sandwiches, ploughman's, soup, corned beef hash, vegetarian pasta dishes, an enjoyable changing curry, and puddings. *Starters/Snacks: £3.95 to £4.95. Main Courses: £5.50 to £9.95. Puddings: £3.95*

Own brew ~ Licensee Paul Hooper ~ Real ale ~ Bar food (12-2, 7-10) ~ (01728) 685758 ~ Children welcome ~ Dogs welcome ~ Open 11.30-3, 6-11; 12-3, 7-10.30 Sun

Recommended by Pete Baker, Mike and Sue Loseby, Stephen P Edwards, Julia Mann

EASTBRIDGE
TM4566 MAP 5

Eels Foot
Off B1122 N of Leiston; IP16 4SN

Handy for Minsmere bird reserve, friendly welcome, real ales, fair value food, and long-standing live Thursday evening folk music; bedrooms

This cheerful beamed country local is a popular spot with bird watchers, cyclists and walkers and the fresh water marshes bordering the inn offer plenty of opportunity for watching the abundance of birds and butterflies; a footpath leads you directly to the sea. Inside, the upper and lower parts of the bar have light modern furnishings, a friendly welcome from the helpful staff, a log fire, and Adnams Bitter, Broadside, Old Ale and seasonal beers on handpump, several wines by the glass, and Aspall's cider. Darts in a side area, board games, and a neat back dining room. There are seats on the terrace and in the extensive garden. The bedrooms (one with wheelchair access) in the newish building are comfortable and attractive.

🍴 Popular bar food includes sandwiches, whitebait, wild boar terrine, warm goats cheese salad with caramelised onion chutney, beer-battered cod, steak in ale pie, smoked haddock and spring onion fishcakes, three-cheese cannelloni, and puddings like treacle tart and white chocolate and berry pudding. *Starters/Snacks: £4.50 to £6.25. Main Courses: £7.25 to £12.95. Puddings: £2.95 to £4.25*

Adnams ~ Tenants Simon and Corinne Webber ~ Real ale ~ Bar food (12-2.30, 7-9 (6.30-8 Thurs evening)) ~ Restaurant ~ (01728) 830154 ~ Children welcome ~ Dogs allowed in bar ~ Live acoustic music Thurs evening and last Sun of month ~ Open 12-3, 6-11; 11am-midnight Sat; 12-10.30 Sun ~ Bedrooms: £55B/£80B

Recommended by Julia Mann, Mrs M S Forbes, A G Marx, S P Watkin, P A Taylor, RS, ES, Charles and Pauline Stride, Joan York

GREAT GLEMHAM
TM3461   MAP 5

Crown

Between A12 Wickham Market—Saxmundham and B1119 Saxmundham—Framlingham; IP17 2DA

Friendly, pleasant pub in pretty village, log fires and fresh flowers, real ales and enjoyable food

This is a neat, friendly pub in a particularly pretty village. There's a big entrance hall with sofas on rush matting, and an open-plan beamed lounge with wooden pews and captain's chairs around stripped and waxed kitchen tables, and local photographs and interesting paintings on cream walls; fresh flowers, some brass ornaments and log fires in two big fireplaces. Adnams Bitter, Earl Soham Victoria, and St Austell Tribute are served from old brass handpumps and they've eight wines (including sparkling) by the glass, Aspall's cider and several malt whiskies. A tidy flower-ringed lawn, raised above the corner of the quiet village lane by a retaining wall, has some seats and tables under cocktail parasols; there's a smokers' shelter and disabled access.

Enjoyable bar food – available in smaller helpings too – includes sandwiches, soup, smoked duck with roast figs and home-made plum sauce, tempura of king prawns with sweet chilli and ginger sauce, roast pepper, rocket, halloumi and tomato quiche, shepherd's pie, wild boar sausages with onion gravy, chicken breast with wild mushrooms, tarragon and tagliatelle with a white wine and cream sauce, shredded shoulder of lamb with roast pepper, coriander and couscous and wild garlic crème fraîche, and puddings such as chocolate and orange sponge with chocolate sauce and passion fruit cheesecake. *Starters/Snacks: £3.95 to £5.25. Main Courses: £5.75 to £12.95. Puddings: £4.50*

Free house ~ Licensee Dave Cottle ~ Real ale ~ Bar food (12-2.30, 6.30-9; not Mon) ~ (01728) 663693 ~ Well-behaved children welcome ~ Dogs welcome ~ Occasional live music ~ Open 11.30-3, 6.30-11.30; 12-3, 7-10.30 Sun; closed Mon except bank hols ~ Bedrooms: /£80B

Recommended by Simon Cottrell, George Atkinson, Roger White, Pamela Goodwyn, Charles and Pauline Stride, Chris and Vannessa O'Neill, Neil Powell, Simon Rodway, Brenda Crossley, Peter and Pat Frogley, Derek and Maggie Washington

GRUNDISBURGH
TM2250   MAP 5

Dog

Off A12 via B1079 from Woodbridge bypass; The Green – village signposted; IP13 6TA

Civilised, friendly pub run by two brothers with enjoyable food, nice choice of drinks and log fire; garden with play area

Run with care and commitment by two brothers, this pink-washed pub is much enjoyed by our readers. The public bar on the left has oak settles and dark wooden carvers around a mix of tables on the tiles, and an open log fire. The softly lit and relaxing carpeted lounge bar has comfortable seating around dark oak tables, antique engravings on the crushed raspberry walls, and unusual flowers in the windows; it links with a similar bare-boards dining room, with some attractive antique oak settles. Adnams Bitter, Timothy Taylors Landlord, and a couple of guests like Black Sheep Best Bitter and Fullers London Pride on handpump, half a dozen wines by the glass, ciders, and good espresso coffee; the atmosphere is civilised and relaxed. The jack russell is called Poppy. There are quite a few picnic-sets out in front by flowering tubs and the fenced back garden has a play area.

🔟 Cooked by one of the landlords using seasonal produce, game from local estates, and meat from local farms (they list all their suppliers), the particularly good bar food includes lunchtime sandwiches, soup, free-range ham hock terrine with apple chutney, poached scottish salmon with horseradish and lemon crème dressing, lambs liver with bacon and caramelised onion gravy, roast rump of lamb with ratatouille and redcurrant jus, confit of gressingham duck with bitter sweet port sauce, daily specials such as fried pigeon with damson plums, roast loin of venison with rich beer and redcurrant gravy, and thick cut cod on pea and mint purée, and puddings such as white chocolate and raspberry crème brûlée and a changing baked cheesecake with chantilly cream; there's also a two- and three-course set lunch. *Starters/Snacks: £3.50 to £5.50. Main Courses: £4.50 to £8.50. Puddings: £3.25 to £4.50*

Punch ~ Lease Charles and James Rogers ~ Real ale ~ Bar food (12-2, 5.30-9; 12-2.30, 5-9 Sun; not Mon) ~ Restaurant ~ (01473) 735267 ~ Children welcome away from bar area ~ Dogs allowed in bar ~ Open 12-2.30, 5.30-11; 12-11 Fri and Sat; 12-10.30 Sun; closed Mon

Recommended by Richard and Margaret McPhee, J F M and M West, John Saul, Pamela Goodwyn, Charles and Pauline Stride, Wendy and Fred Cole, Tom Gondris

HORRINGER   TL8261   MAP 5

Beehive 🍴 ♀
A143; IP29 5SN

Imaginative food in civilised pub with long-serving licensees and nice little rambling rooms; attractive back terrace

Always warm and friendly, this is a civilised pub with long-serving licensees who have now been here 23 years. The rambling series of little rooms is furnished with good quality old country furniture on the sage green carpet or flagstones and there's a cottagey feel, largely because they've refrained from pulling walls down to create an open-plan layout favoured by many places nowadays. Despite some very low beams, stripped panelling and brickwork, good chalky heritage wall colours keep it fairly light and airy. Greene King IPA and Abbot on handpump, and several wines by the glass. An attractively planted back terrace has picnic-sets and more seats on a raised lawn. Their friendly, elderly dog Muffin might make a lunchtime appearance and they also have Skye the westie.

🔟 Well presented and interesting, the bar food might include soup, flash fried chicken breast, bacon and egg salad, country pâté with apricots and pistachio nuts, home-made potted brown shrimps, warm blue cheese and rocket tart, local venison sausages with port wine and orange zest gravy, low cooked wild boar with dates and juniper berries, fried skate wing with lime and hot ginger, and puddings such as floating island of berries and vanilla custard and iced banana parfait with rich chocolate sauce. *Starters/Snacks: £1.95 to £6.95. Main Courses: £7.95 to £15.95. Puddings: £4.95*

Greene King ~ Tenants Gary and Dianne Kingshott ~ Real ale ~ Bar food (not Sun evening) ~ (01284) 735260 ~ Well behaved children welcome ~ Open 12-3, 7-11; closed Sun evening, 25 and 26 Dec

Recommended by Mrs Carolyn Dixon, John Saville, Simon Cottrell, Bettye Reynolds, Edward Mirzoeff

HOXNE   TM1877   MAP 5

Swan ♀
Off B1118, signed off A140 S of Diss; Low St; IP21 5AS

15th-c pub, friendly and relaxed, interesting bar food, good choice of drinks and seats in large garden; lots going on

Built in 1480 for the Bishop of Norwich, this striking pub is run by friendly people. The relaxed bar has two solid oak counters, broad oak floorboards, and a deep-set inglenook fireplace; you can still see the ancient timber and mortar of the walls. A fire in the back bar divides the bar area and snug, and there's an original wooden fireplace in the restaurant. Adnams Bitter and Broadside, Wells & Youngs Bombardier, and Woodfordes Wherry on handpump or tapped from the cask, ten wines by the glass, and Aspall's cider;

they hold an annual beer festival. There are seats under parasols on two sheltered terraces, and an extensive garden by a small stream. They hold a Pudding Club evening, outdoor theatre performances and a monthly quiz night, and have regular live music. Nearby, the tree to which King Edmund was tied at his execution is said to form part of a screen in the neighbouring church.

🍴 **Good bar food includes filled baguettes, ploughman's, soup, chicken, apricot and pork terrine with red onion chutney, colcannon cakes with crispy pancetta and stilton, smoked haddock poached and served on wholegrain mustard mash with wilted spinach and topped with a poached egg, slow-roast honey-glazed pork belly with sausagemeat and apricot stuffing, leek, cauliflower and cheese puff pastry parcels with a mustard cream sauce, and daily specials such as creamy garlic king prawns, wild mushroom lasagne and tilapia on roasted red peppers with a feta and rocket salad.** *Starters/Snacks: £4.00 to £6.50. Main Courses: £9.00 to £15.95. Puddings: £4.50 to £5.00*

Enterprise ~ Lease Jo-Anne and David Rye ~ Real ale ~ Bar food (12-2(3.30 Sun), 6.30-9) ~ Restaurant ~ (01379) 668275 ~ Children welcome ~ Dogs allowed in bar ~ Open 12-3, 6-11; 12-10.30 Sun

Recommended by Conrad Freezer, Alan Cole, Kirstie Bruce, John Saville

IPSWICH   TM1844   MAP 5

Fat Cat

Spring Road, opposite junction with Nelson Road (best bet for parking up there); IP4 5NL

Fantastic range of changing real ales in well run town pub; garden

Although the real ales in this very busy and friendly town pub come from all over the country, they always make sure that some of the 20 on handpump or tapped from the cask in the tap room, are local: Adnams Bitter, Arundel Sussex Gold, Coach House Gunpowder Mild, Crouch Vale Brewers Gold, Dark Star Original and Hophead, Elgoods Black Dog, Everards Tiger Best Bitter, Fat Cat Top Cat and Honey Cat, Fullers London Pride, Grainstore 1050, Green Jack Orange Wheat, Moles Barley Mole, Oakham JHB, St Peters Golden and Mild, RCH Hewish IPA, Traditional Scottish Ales Bannockburn Ale, Woodfordes Wherry and many more. Also, quite a few belgian bottled beers, farm cider and fruit wines. The bare-boarded bars have a mix of café and bar stools, unpadded wall benches and cushioned seats around cast-iron and wooden pub tables, and lots of enamel brewery signs of varying ages on the canary yellow walls; no noisy machines or music to spoil the cheerful and chatty atmosphere. The pub cat is called Dave and the sausage dog, Stanley. There's also a spacious and useful back conservatory, and several picnic-sets on the terrace and lawn. Very little nearby parking. No children or dogs.

🍴 **They do only scotch eggs, pasties and filled baguettes.** *Starters/Snacks: £2.30 to £2.50*

Free house ~ Licensees John and Ann Keatley ~ Real ale ~ Bar food ~ (01473) 726524 ~ Open 12-11; 11am-midnight Sat

Recommended by G Coates, Kerry Law, Ian and Nita Cooper, Mrs Hazel Rainer, the Didler

LAVENHAM   TL9149   MAP 5

Angel

Market Place; CO10 9QZ

Handsome and civilised Tudor inn, good range of drinks, popular food, and sizeable back garden; comfortable bedrooms

Owned by the Maypole Group and with new managers, this is an attractive Tudor inn in a pretty village and it's a popular place to spend a weekend – though they won't take bookings for one night, then; lots of walks in fine surrounding countryside. The light and airy long bar area has plenty of polished dark tables, a big inglenook log fire under a heavy mantelbeam, and some attractive 16th-c ceiling plasterwork – even more elaborate pargeting in the residents' sitting room upstairs. Round towards the back on the right of the central servery, is a further dining area with heavy stripped pine country furnishings. They have shelves of books, dominoes and lots of board games. Adnams Bitter, Greene King IPA and Nethergate Suffolk County, and Woodfordes Wherry on handpump, Aspall's cider, and nine wines by the glass. Picnic-sets out in front overlook the former market square and there are tables under parasols in a sizeable sheltered back garden; it's worth asking if they've time to show you the interesting Tudor cellar.

🍽 **Rewarding food includes sandwiches, soup, good pigeon, pork and rabbit terrine with damson apple jelly, tiger prawns with chinese spices, seared, herbed carpaccio of beef with fresh horseradish cream, pork tenderloin with apple, prune and sage stuffing, roast rump of lamb with sweet potato and rosemary couscous, grilled lemon sole fillets with potted brown shrimps and lemon and dill carrots, gressingham duck with roast beetroot and layered potatoes, daily specials such as thai crab cakes with sweet chilli sauce, wild boar sausages with onion gravy, chickpea, chilli and coriander cakes, and steak in ale pie.** *Starters/Snacks: £4.50 to £8.95. Main Courses: £9.95 to £16.95. Puddings: £4.50 to £5.75*

Maypole Group ~ Managers Katherine Thompson and James Haggar ~ Real ale ~ Bar food (12-2.15, 6.45-9.15) ~ Restaurant ~ (01787) 247388 ~ Children welcome ~ Dogs allowed in bar and bedrooms ~ Open 11-11; 12-10.30 Sun ~ Bedrooms: £70B/£85B

Recommended by John Saville, the Didler, Mrs M B Gregg, P A Rowe, Michael and Maggie Betton, Pamela Goodwyn, Mrs Carolyn Dixon, N R White, Jim and Sheila Prideaux, C Galloway, Tom and Jill Jones, Peter Meister, Tina and David Woods-Taylor, Stuart Orton, Anne Walton, Tina Humphrey, John and Patricia White, Stephen and Jean Curtis

LAXFIELD   TM2972   MAP 5

Kings Head ★ 🍺

Behind church, off road toward Banyards Green; IP13 8DW

Unspoilt old pub of real character, helpful staff, well liked bar food and several real ales; bedrooms and self-contained flat

Although this unspoilt 15th-c pub does change hands fairly regularly, the charming rooms always keep their tremendously informal atmosphere and old-fashioned character. Lots of people like the front room best, with a high-backed built-in settle on the tiled floor and an open fire. Two other equally unspoilt rooms – the card and tap rooms – have pews, old seats, scrubbed deal tables and some interesting wall prints. There's no bar – instead, the helpful staff potter in and out of a cellar tap room to pour pints of Adnams Bitter, Broadside, and East Green with guests such as Woodfordes Wherry straight from the cask; several wines by the glass, piped music, cards and board games. Outside, the garden has plenty of benches and tables, there's an arbour covered by grape and hop vines, and a small pavilion for cooler evenings. They now have letting bedrooms and still rent out their self-contained flat.

🍽 **Bar food now includes sandwiches, soup, smoked mackerel pâté, dublin bay prawns, bananas in stilton, vegetable lasagne, a fine choice of local sausages such as chilli or apricot and ginger, roast pork belly, chump of lamb, chicken curry, beef stir fry, good sirloin steaks, and puddings like boozy sherry trifle and sticky toffee pudding.** *Starters/Snacks: £3.50 to £4.95. Main Courses: £6.95 to £13.95. Puddings: £3.95*

Adnams ~ Tenant Bob Wilson ~ Real ale ~ Bar food ~ Restaurant ~ (01986) 798395 ~ Children welcome ~ Dogs welcome ~ Open 12-3, 6-11; 12-11 Sat and Sun ~ Bedrooms: /£50S

Recommended by Pete Baker, Ian and Nita Cooper, Tracey and Stephen Groves, the Didler, Richard Armstrong, Jeremy and Jane Morrison, Alan Cole, Kirstie Bruce, Philip and Susan Philcox, Michael Clatworthy, Charles and Pauline Stride

---

If a pub tries to make you leave a credit card behind the bar, be on your guard. The credit card firms and banks which issue them condemn this practice. After all, the publican who asks you to do this is in effect saying: 'I don't trust you.' Have you any more reason to trust his staff? If your card is used fraudulently while you have let it be kept out of your sight, the card company could say you've been negligent yourself – and refuse to make good your losses. So say that they can 'swipe' your card instead, but must hand it back to you. Please let us know if a pub does try to keep your card.

LIDGATE

TL7257   MAP 5

Star ♀

B1063 SE of Newmarket; CB8 9PP

Attentive service, spanish and english food, a warm welcome and seats out in front and in back garden

Most customers come to this friendly village pub to enjoy the wide choice of interesting food.The main room has handsomely moulded heavy beams, a good big log fire, candles in iron candelabra on polished oak or stripped pine tables, and some antique catalan plates over the bar; darts, ring the bull and piped music. Besides a second similar room on the right, there's a cosy little dining room on the left. Greene King IPA, Abbot and Ruddles County on handpump and decent house wines. There are some tables out on the raised lawn in front and in a pretty little rustic back garden. Dogs may be allowed with permission from the landlady.

🍴 **The Spanish landlady features both spanish and english dishes on her menu, and whilst the food is good and interesting, the main course prices are pretty high for a pub: soup including gazpacho, boquerones (fresh anchovies floured and fried), catalan salad, carpaccio of salmon, grilled squid, spanish meatballs, lasagne, lamb steaks in blackcurrant, pig cheeks, daube of beef, venison steaks in port, paella valenciana, seafood casserole, and magret of duck.** *Starters/Snacks: £5.50 to £6.90. Main Courses: £15.95 to £18.95*

Greene King ~ Lease Maria Teresa Axon ~ Real ale ~ Bar food (12-2, 7-10; not Sun evening) ~ Restaurant ~ (01638) 500275 ~ Well-behaved children welcome ~ Open 12-3, 6-11; 12-3, 7-11 Sun; closed 26 Dec, 1 Jan

Recommended by M and GR, John Saville, Michael Sargent, P and D Carpenter, Jim and Sheila Prideaux

LONG MELFORD

TL8646   MAP 5

Black Lion 🍴 ♀ 🛏

Church Walk; CO10 9DN

Civilised hotel with relaxed and comfortable bar, a couple of real ales, modern bar food, attentive uniformed staff; lovely bedrooms

Of course this is not a straightforward pub, it's a civilised and comfortable hotel, but customers do continue to drop in for just a drink, and they do keep Adnams Bitter and Broadside on handpump; several wines by the glass and malt whiskies, too. One side of the oak serving counter is decorated in ochre and has bar stools, deeply cushioned sofas, leather wing armchairs and antique fireside settles, while the other side, decorated in shades of terracotta, has leather dining chairs around handsome tables set for the good modern food; open fires in both rooms. Big windows with swagged-back curtains have a pleasant outlook over the village green and there are large portraits of racehorses and of people. Service by neatly uniformed staff is friendly and efficient. There are seats and tables under terracotta parasols on the terrace and more in the appealing Victorian walled garden. More reports please.

🍴 **Under the new licensee, the inventive and attractively presented – if not cheap – food includes filled huffers (a type of roll), soup, indian wood-smoked duck samosas with tamarind salsa, cockle, brown shrimp and wild garlic linguine, warm tart of caramelised red onion, feta and slow-roast plum tomatoes with pesto dressing, local sausages, beer-battered haddock with tartare sauce, whole spring chicken roasted with rock salt and lemons with thyme gravy, ewes milk risotto with peas and mint, local rabbit with caramelised apples and cider sauce, bass baked in a paper parcel with roasted fennel butter, and puddings such as chocolate and rum crushed pineapple mousse with orange cream and seasonal knickerbocker glory.** *Starters/Snacks: £4.95 to £8.50. Main Courses: £10.95 to £24.95. Puddings: £5.50 to £6.50*

Ravenwood Group ~ Manager Craig Jarvis ~ Real ale ~ Bar food ~ Restaurant ~ (01787) 312356 ~ Children welcome ~ Dogs allowed in bar and bedrooms ~ Open 9am-11pm ~ Bedrooms: £97.50B/£150B

Recommended by Jim and Sheila Prideaux, John Saville

NAYLAND TL9734 MAP 5

Anchor 🍽 🍷

Court Street; just off A134 – turn off S of signposted B1087 main village turn; CO6 4JL

Friendly well run pub with interesting food using own farm and smokehouse produce, real ales, wines from own vineyard; riverside terrace

Although the food in this popular, well run pub is one of the main reasons for coming here, the bare-boards front bar is liked by regulars who gather for a pint and a chat. The whole pub is light and sunny with interesting old photographs of pipe-smoking customers and village characters on its pale yellow walls, farmhouse chairs around a mix of tables, and coal and log fires at each end. Another room behind has similar furniture and an open fire and leads into a small carpeted sun room. Up some quite steep stairs is the stylish restaurant; to be sure of a table, you must book in advance. Adnams Bitter, Greene King IPA, Pitfield East Kent Goldings and maybe a seasonal guest from Greene King on handpump and several wines by the glass (some from their own vineyard); piped music. In warm weather you can sit at picnic-sets on the back terrace and look across to the peaceful River Stour and its quacking ducks. Their farmland next door is being worked by suffolk punch horses using traditional farming methods. The suffolk punch is a seriously endangered species and visitors are welcome to watch these magnificent animals or maybe try their hands at the reins – which our readers have enjoyed very much.

🍽 From their Heritage Farm next door they produce free-range eggs, vegetables and home-reared lambs, pigs, beef, game, trout and venison; they also have their own smokehouse. As well as lunchtime sandwiches and nibbles, the imaginative food might include interesting soups, asparagus lasagne, dodine of wild goose and foie gras with apple chutney, salmon paupiette with crème fraîche and cucumber salad, a smoked platter of fish, meat and cheeses, home-made sage and onion pork sausages with thyme gravy, fried wild bass with ratatouille and tapenade jus, ox liver and bacon, kebabs with sweet chilli sauce and yoghurt and cucumber dressing, and puddings such as orange cheesecake with marmalade sauce and summer pudding. *Starters/Snacks: £3.80 to £6.00. Main Courses: £8.50 to £14.50. Puddings: £4.00*

Free house ~ Licensee Daniel Bunting ~ Real ale ~ Bar food (12-2(2.30 Sat), 6.30-9(9.30 Sat); 10-3, 5-8.30 Sun) ~ Restaurant ~ (01206) 262313 ~ Children welcome ~ Open 11-11; 10am-10.30pm Sun; 11-3, 5-11 weekdays in winter

Recommended by Mrs P Lang, Robert Turnham, Rosemary Smith, Ray J Carter, Bernard Phelvin, Adele Summers, Alan Black, Mrs Carolyn Dixon

NEWBOURNE TM2743 MAP 5

Fox

Off A12 at roundabout 1.7 miles N of A14 junction; The Street; IP12 4NY

Friendly, relaxed pub with good generous food in attractive rooms; seats by lovely hanging baskets and in nice garden

This is a peaceful spot and there are picnic-sets out in front of this pink-washed 16th-c pub by the lovely flowering baskets, with more seats in the attractive grounds with its secluded rose garden and well stocked pond. Inside, the atmosphere is relaxed and pubby, even though food has pride of place. As you come in, there's an eye-catching array of some two or three dozen little black hanging panels showing, in white writing, one dish to each, what's on offer. Also, a few shiny black beams in the low rather bowed ceiling, slabby elm and other dark tables on the bar's tiled floor, a stuffed fox sitting among other decorations in an inglenook, and a warm décor in crushed raspberry. A comfortable carpeted dining room with a large modern artwork and several antique mirrors on its warm yellow walls opens off on the left and overlooks the courtyard. Adnams Bitter and Greene King IPA with a couple of guests like Adnams Broadside and Shepherd Neame Spitfire on handpump, decent wines by the glass, and prompt, friendly service; piped music. More reports please.

🍽 As well as daily specials and lunchtime sandwiches, the quickly served food might include soup, chicken liver and port pâté with real ale chutney, goats cheese and mediterranean vegetable tartlets, crispy chicken strips with a sweet plum sauce, beer-battered cod with home-made tartare sauce, steak in ale pie, stilton and vegetable crumble, tuscan-style chicken, minted rack of lamb, and seafood gratin. *Starters/Snacks: £3.95 to £5.95. Main Courses: £7.95 to £13.95. Puddings: £1.50 to £4.95*

Deben Inns ~ Lease Steve and Louise Lomas ~ Real ale ~ Bar food (all day weekends) ~ Restaurant ~ (01473) 736307 ~ Children welcome ~ Dogs allowed in bar ~ Open 11-11

Recommended by Mrs Hilarie Taylor, Pamela Goodwyn, P Clark

ORFORD
TM4249   MAP 5

Kings Head
Front Street; IP12 2LW

Under same ownership as Crown & Castle but a proper pub, straightforward rooms, real ales, friendly service and good, pubby food; refurbished bedrooms

---

Although under the same ownership as the nearby Crown & Castle (Ruth Watson is a food writer and TV presenter), this is a quite different operation. Of course the food is very good but it's a proper pub with a straightforward, comfortable bar serving Adnams Bitter, Broadside and Explorer on handpump, half a dozen wines by the glass, and Aspall's cider; good humoured young staff who cope cheerfully even on sunny weekends. There's also a stripped brick dining room with ancient bare boards but as they don't take bookings, you must get here early to be sure of a table; Sunday evening quiz night. They tell us there is a garden to the left and back of the pub but 'you have to scramble through the neighbouring basket shop's wares to get to it'. The bedrooms have been newly refurbished.

🍽 Using top-notch local produce, the enjoyable pubby food at lunchtime includes doorstop sandwiches, soup, a large slab of gloucester old spot pork pie with home-made courgette pickle, goats cheese, spinach and roast garlic quiche, free-range three-egg parmesan omelette, beer-battered fresh plaice fillets, and steak in ale pie; evening choices such as potted (fresh and smoked) salmon, greek feta, roast beetroot and orange salad, tagliatelle with peas, ham and cream sauce, pork sausages with onion gravy, smoked haddock fishcakes with parsley sauce, and griddled, butterflied chicken breast with chunky tomato salsa, and puddings like warm chocolate and walnut brownie with vanilla ice-cream and a sundae with banana, crushed meringue, cinnamon and honey ice-cream. The Sunday roast pork is popular. *Starters/Snacks: £3.95 to £6.95. Main Courses: £6.50 to £10.95. Puddings: £1.50 to £4.95*

Adnams ~ Tenants Ruth and David Watson ~ Real ale ~ Bar food (12-2.30(3 Sun), 6.30(7 Sun)-9; no food winter Sun evenings) ~ (01394) 450271 ~ Children welcome ~ Dogs welcome ~ Open 11-3, 6-11(11.30 Fri and Sat); 12-4, 7-10.30 Sun(10 in winter) ~ Bedrooms: £50S/£60S

Recommended by RS, ES, Edward Mirzoeff, Neil Powell, Conrad Freezer, Michael Dandy, Malcolm Pellatt, A J Murray

RATTLESDEN
TL9758   MAP 5

Brewers Arms 🍽
Off B1115 or A45 W of Stowmarket; Lower Road; IP30 0RJ

Former licensees now back in 16th-c village pub, refurbished bars, friendly welcome, real ales, and interesting food

---

Now that Mr and Mrs Chamberlain are back running this solidly built 16th-c village local, all is well again. They have refurbished the whole building, refitted the kitchen and refurnished the bars – and the locals are delighted. There's a mix of pubby seating and more comfortable chairs and a beamed lounge bar on the left that winds back through standing timbers to the main eating area – a partly flint-walled room with a magnificent old bread oven. French windows open on to the garden. Greene King IPA and Old Speckled Hen and a changing guest beer on handpump; very helpful staff. They hold regular themed evenings like jazz and thai or quizzes. More reports on the changes, please.

🍴 Good, interesting bar food includes some inventive sandwiches and filled baguettes (like fish fingers and minted pea mayonnaise or cheese with coleslaw and crispy bacon), soup, stilton and port rarebit, and lunchtime dishes such as fried chorizo with mixed peppers, red onions and sautéed potatoes topped with a fried egg, chilli con carne, mixed nut loaf layered with ricotta and spinach with a white wine and mushroom cream sauce, and crab linguine; evening choices like fresh salmon fishcakes with roasted red pepper sauce, slow-roasted belly of pork with a smooth apple and calvados sauce, steamed steak pudding, minted lamb shank with port and mint gravy, and fillets of bass with brown shrimps. Puddings include crunchy chocolate honeycomb slice and syrup sponge pudding. *Starters/Snacks: £3.95 to £6.95. Main Courses: £11.95 to £16.95. Puddings: £4.95*

Greene King ~ Tenants Jeff and Nina Chamberlain ~ Real ale ~ Bar food (12-2, 6.45-9.15; not Sun evening or Mon) ~ Restaurant ~ (01449) 736377 ~ Well behaved children in eating area of bar and restaurant ~ Dogs allowed in bar ~ Open 12-3, 6.30-11.30(midnight Sat); 12-3.30, 9-11.30 Sun; closed Mon

Recommended by Charles and Pauline Stride, J F M and M West

REDE   TL8055   MAP 5

Plough 🍴 ⅁

Village signposted off A143 Bury St Edmunds—Haverhill; IP29 4BE

Promptly served, well liked food in 16th-c pub, several wines by the glass and friendly service

Run by a friendly, helpful landlord, this cream-painted thatched old pub is a popular place for a meal, especially at weekends; best to book ahead to be sure of a table. It's a very neat and pretty place, and the traditional bar has low beams, comfortable seating and a solid-fuel stove in its brick fireplace. Adnams Bitter, Greene King IPA and a guest like Fullers London Pride on handpump and quite a few wines by the glass; piped music. There are picnic-sets in front and a sheltered cottage garden at the back.

🍴 Generous helpings of quickly changing bar food include grilled scallops, shrimps with aïoli, wild boar sausages with mash, braised local rabbit with tarragon and spring onion sauce, mediterranean beef with salami and pepperoni, crispy belly of pork with bacon and sage butter, hock of local venison in red wine and port, and puddings such as bread and butter pudding and amaretti chocolate crunch. *Starters/Snacks: £3.95 to £6.95. Main Courses: £9.95 to £19.95. Puddings: £4.50*

Admiral Taverns ~ Tenant Brian Desborough ~ Real ale ~ Bar food (not Sun evening) ~ Restaurant ~ (01284) 789208 ~ Children welcome until 8pm ~ Open 11-3, 6.30-midnight; 12-3, 7-11 Sun

Recommended by Bettye Reynolds, John Saville, Philip and Susan Philcox

ROUGHAM   TL9063   MAP 5

Ravenwood Hall 🍴 ⅁ 🛏

Just off A14 E of Bury St Edmunds; IP30 9JA

Welcoming and civilised all-day bar in comfortable country house hotel – a peaceful A14 break; real ales, fine wines, imaginative food and good service; lovely grounds

Although this is a civilised and very well run country house hotel, it's the thoroughly welcoming all-day bar that earns it a place in this particular guidebook. Basically two fairly compact rooms, this has tall ceilings, gently patterned wallpaper, and heavily draped curtains for big windows overlooking a sweeping lawn with a stately cedar. The part by the back serving counter is set for food, its nice furnishings including well upholstered settles and dining chairs, sporting prints and a log fire. Adnams Bitter and Broadside on handpump, good wines by the glass, mulled wine around Christmas, and freshly squeezed orange juice; neat unobtrusive staff give good service. The other end of the bar has horse pictures, several sofas and armchairs with lots of plump cushions, one or two attractively moulded beams, and a good-sized fragment of early Tudor wall decoration above its big inglenook log fire; piped music. They have a more formal quite separate restaurant. The Garden Room has a high ceiling, a large fireplace and views over the swimming pool and grounds. Outside, teak tables and chairs (some under a summer house) stand around a swimming pool; big enclosures by the car park hold geese and pygmy goats. Croquet. The bedrooms are very comfortable.

🍴 Unfailingly good and often imaginative, the attractively presented bar food uses their own smoked meats and fish and home-made preserves: sandwiches, soup, roasted pigeon with honey-glazed beetroot and sorrel, crispy fried calamari in a light curry dust with mango and coriander mayonnaise, carpaccio of seared, line-caught tuna with a peppered lime foam, sausages with caramelised onion gravy, beer-battered cod, local rabbit with elderflower cream and sautéed morels, slow-braised belly pork in cider with caramelised apples, star anise and chilli, sauté of shitake mushrooms with pineapple and avocado in a crispy buckwheat pancake, and puddings such as a little pot of pure chocolate filled with mango mousse and bakewell tart with damson jam and real custard. *Starters/Snacks: £4.25 to £8.50. Main Courses: £9.75 to £22.50. Puddings: £5.25 to £6.50*

Free house ~ Licensee Craig Jarvis ~ Real ale ~ Bar food (12-2.30, 7-9.30(10 Fri and Sat)) ~ Restaurant ~ (01359) 270345 ~ Children welcome ~ Dogs welcome ~ Open 9am-midnight ~ Bedrooms: £97.50B/£135B

Recommended by J F M and M West, Derek Field, Alan Cole, Kirstie Bruce

SIBTON   TM3570   MAP 5

White Horse
Halesworth Road; IP17 2JJ

Friendly, nicely old-fashioned bar, good mix of customers, real ales, and enjoyable food; bedrooms

A pleasant place to unwind, this is a comfortable and nicely laid out 16th-c inn decorated in a genuine old-fashioned style. The bar has horsebrasses and tack on the walls, old settles and pews, a large inglenook fireplace with a roaring log fire, and plenty of amiable locals; there's a viewing panel showing the working cellar and its Roman floor. Steps take you up past an ancient partly knocked-through timbered wall into a carpeted gallery; there's a smart dining room, too. Adnams Bitter, Greene King Abbot, and a guest such as Brandon Rusty Bucket on handpump from the old oak servery, and nine wines by the glass. The big garden has plenty of seats, and the comfortable bedrooms are in a converted outbuilding.

🍴 Enjoyable bar food at lunchtime includes warm filled rolls and sandwiches, ploughman's, ham and free-range eggs, cumberland sausages with onion gravy, 100% beefburger topped with bacon, brie and red onion marmalade, smoked chicken caesar salad, and beer-battered cod; in the evening, there might be warm pigeon breast with watercress salad and walnuts drizzled in honey and herbs, honey-roasted free-range pork belly with apple sauce and cider jus, steak and kidney suet pudding with sage mash, vegetable pie, grilled salmon supreme with a herb crust and lemon butter, daily specials, and puddings like rhubarb tart with lemon and ginger ice-cream and apple strudel with nutmeg anglaise. *Starters/Snacks: £3.75 to £5.50. Main Courses: £6.95 to £13.95. Puddings: £3.95 to £4.75*

Free house ~ Licensees Neil and Jill Mason ~ Real ale ~ Bar food ~ Restaurant ~ (01728) 660337 ~ Well behaved children welcome ~ Dogs allowed in bar ~ Open 12-3, 6.30-11(10.30 Sun); closed Mon lunchtime ~ Bedrooms: £60S/£90S

Recommended by R Chessells, Neil Powell, Brent and Gillian Payne, Stuart and Joan Bloomer, S Norton, Lorraine Brennan, Robin Jackson, K G Moore

SNAPE   TM4058   MAP 5

Golden Key 🍴 ☟
Priory Lane; IP17 1SA

Handy for Maltings Concert Hall – they arrange pre- and post-theatre meals – with friendly landlord, cottagey rooms, and enjoyable food and drink

Under the friendly and enthusiastic young landlord, this 17th-c pub is extremely popular and things have changed quite a bit. The low-beamed lounge bar has an old-fashioned settle curving around a couple of venerable stripped tables on the tiled floor, a winter open fire, a mix of pubby tables and chairs, and local art and horsebrasses on the walls. This leads through to a cottagey little dining room with older style stripped pine tables and chairs on the carpet, and more local art including some embroidery and sheepskins from Mr Attfield's own sheep on the light yellow walls. The low-ceilinged larger dining room is similarly furnished and has small oil paintings of the landlord's animals and so forth on its walls; fresh flowers throughout. Adnams Bitter, Broadside and Explorer on handpump, a dozen wines by the glass, Aspall's cider, and good coffee; attentive, efficient service. Outside, there are two terraces (one for the morning and a suntrap evening one) both with contemporary wood and steel tables and chairs under large green parasols, and plenty of hanging baskets. The garden has a herb bed, beehives and a greenhouse and in a field beyond are the landlord's sheep and pigs. A big back lobby sells sheep rugs, cook books and so forth.

⊞ Using their own chickens, rare breed sheep and pigs, their own honey and herbs and other local produce, the rewarding bar food includes sandwiches, soup, venison terrine with beetroot chutney, crayfish tails in dill and lime mayonnaise, baked camembert studded with garlic, rosemary and rock salt and served with an apricot coulis, sweet potato and spinach curry, organic chicken supreme stuffed with prosciutto and blue cheese with a light jus, lamb burger topped with Monterey Jack cheese and bacon with cucumber relish, steak and mushroom in ale pie, wild rabbit casserole in cider and mustard sauce, skate wing with caper and almond butter, and puddings such as vanilla pod panna cotta with cherries macerated in kirsch and sticky toffee pudding with butterscotch sauce and stem ginger ice-cream. *Starters/Snacks: £4.50 to £7.50. Main Courses: £8.50 to £15.00. Puddings: £4.00 to £5.50*

Adnams ~ Tenant Nick Attfield ~ Real ale ~ Bar food (12-2(2.30 Sun), 6.30(7 Sun)-9; pre and post theatre bookings taken outside these hours) ~ Restaurant ~ (01728) 688510 ~ Children welcome ~ Dogs allowed in bar ~ Open 12-11; 12-3(4 weekends), 6-11 in winter

Recommended by Tom Gondris, Peter and Pat Frogley, Charles and Pauline Stride, Terry and Jackie Devine, Ron and Betty Broom, Michael Dandy, Neil Powell

Plough & Sail

The Maltings, Snape Bridge (B1069 S); IP17 1SR

Nicely placed dining pub extended airily around older bar, real ales, several wines by the glass, seats outside

There's more space in the pink-washed roadside cottage than you'd think. The older part has a woodburning stove, some high bar chairs by the serving counter, and rustic pine dining chairs and tables on terracotta tiling, and a cosy little room has comfortable sofas and low coffee tables. Most diners head for the simply furnished bar hall and large main dining room with blue-cushioned dining chairs around straightforward tables on the light, woodstrip flooring, and high ceilings with A-frame beams; motifs illustrating the history of the Maltings decorate the walls. Upstairs is another restaurant area with similar furnishings. Adnams Best and Broadside and Timothy Taylors Landlord on handpump, and several wines by the glass. The flower-filled terrace has plenty of teak chairs and tables, and there are some picnic-sets in front of the building. The shops and other buildings in the attractive complex are interesting to wander through.

⊞ Usefully served all day at the weekends, the bar food includes sandwiches, filled baguettes and baked potatoes, ploughman's, soup, filo-wrapped field mushroom stuffed with berries and brie, steamed mussels cooked in a basil and parmesan cream sauce, roasted squash, pepper and ricotta lasagne, beer-battered cod, steak in ale suet pudding, slow braised lamb shank with rosemary gravy, and puddings such as espresso brûlée and profiteroles with hot chocolate sauce. *Starters/Snacks: £3.75 to £6.95. Main Courses: £5.95 to £13.95. Puddings: £4.45*

Deben Inns ~ Licensees Steve and Louise Lomas ~ Real ale ~ Bar food (all day weekends) ~ Restaurant ~ (01728) 688413 ~ Children welcome ~ Dogs allowed in bar ~ Open 11-11

Recommended by C and R Bromage, Oliver and Sue Rowell, Tony Middis, Simon Cottrell, Terry and Jackie Devine, Dr and Mrs M E Wilson, Michael Dandy

---

We say if we know a pub allows dogs.

SOUTH ELMHAM
TM3385 MAP 5

St Peters Brewery
St Peter S Elmham; off B1062 SW of Bungay; NR35 1NQ

Lovely manor dating back to 13th c with some fine original features, own brew beers, and inventive food

Rather like a small stately home, this is a medieval manor under new management this year. St Peter's Hall, to which the brewery is attached, itself dates back to the late 13th c but was much extended in 1539 using materials from the recently dissoved Flixton Priory. Genuinely old tapestries and furnishings make having a drink in the small main bar feel rather special, and the atmosphere is relaxed and welcoming. It does feel more restauranty these days with candles and fresh flowers on crisp white-clothed dining tables and smart dining chairs – though they tell us there are still some of the cushioned pews and settles. Their beers are made using water from a 100-metre (300-ft) bore hole, in brewery buildings laid out around a courtyard; gift shop, too. On handpump and served by warmly friendly staff, the three real ales might include St Peters Best Bitter, Organic Ale and Golden Ale and the others are available by bottle. There's a particularly dramatic high-ceilinged dining hall with elaborate woodwork, a big flagstoned floor and an imposing chandelier, as well as a couple of other appealing old rooms reached up some steepish stairs. Outside, tables overlook the original moat where there are friendly black swans. More reports please.

🍴 Enjoyable food at lunchtime now includes soup, quinelles of smooth chicken liver pâté with cumberland port sauce, beer-battered black pudding with onion marmalade, a platter of cured meats with olives, sunblush tomatoes and capers, pasta with wild mushrooms, pesto and a rich red wine and tomato sauce, beef in ale pie, home-baked ham and free-range eggs, and chicken breast marinated in a garlic, rosemary and thyme cream sauce; evening choices such as fried scallops in a lemon and chive butter with chorizo, mushroom stroganoff finished with brandy and sour cream, pheasant breast on a honey cassis sauce, pork fillet topped with stilton and grilled with a marsala and sage jus, seared tuna steak with ginger, lemon and coriander, and puddings like apple and apricot crumble and sticky toffee and date pudding with hot toffee sauce. *Starters/Snacks: £5.00 to £8.00. Main Courses: £10.00 to £19.00. Puddings: £5.00*

Own brew ~ Licensee Sam Goodbourne ~ Real ale ~ Bar food (12-2(4 Sun), 7-9) ~ Restaurant ~ (01986) 782288 ~ Well-behaved children welcome ~ Open 12-3, 6-11; 12-4 Sun; closed Sun evening

Recommended by Mike and Shelley Woodroffe, Adele Summers, Alan Black, Mrs M B Gregg, Peter and Pat Frogley, Richard Pitcher, P Dawn, Mayur Shah, John Saville, the Didler, Adrian Johnson, Charles and Pauline Stride, Tony Middis, Simon and Mandy King, Philip and Susan Philcox, Sue Demont, Tim Barrow

SOUTHWOLD
TM5076 MAP 5

Crown
High Street; IP18 6DP
SUFFOLK DINING PUB OF THE YEAR

Civilised and smart old hotel with relaxed bars, a fine choice of drinks, papers to read, interesting food and seats outside; bedrooms

Although most customers do come to this smart old hotel to enjoy the extremely good, imaginative food, the cosy and smaller back oak-panelled locals' bar, with its pubby atmosphere and red leatherette wall benches on the red carpet, remains a favourite with many readers – and the other customers are chatty and friendly. The extended elegant beamed main bar has a relaxed, informal atmosphere, a stripped curved high-backed settle and other dark varnished settles, kitchen chairs and some bar stools, pretty flowers on the tables and a carefully restored and rather fine carved wooden fireplace; maybe newspapers to read. Adnams Bitter, Broadside, Explorer and maybe Spindrift on handpump, a splendid wine list with a monthly changing choice of 20 interesting varieties by the glass or bottle, quite a few malt whiskies and local cider. The tables out in a sunny sheltered corner are very pleasant, and the bedrooms are comfortable, light and airy.

Ⓜ Using local, organic produce, the interesting bar food includes soup, crab and saffron tart with lemon dressing, pistachio and orange roasted quail with chicory, orange and chilli salad, sri lankan-style chicken thigh, pineapple rice and satay dressing, sharing platters of meats and seafood, white onion, wild garlic, plum tomato, artichoke and pine nut pizza, salt fish tagine with chickpeas and couscous, pork cooked two ways with cider apple balsamic and red chard, fried sea trout with crème fraîche potatoes and tomato beurre blanc, daily specials such as confit duck hash, free-range poached egg and beurre blanc, whole plaice with razor clam, bacon and onion sauce, and oysters cooked three ways, and puddings such as raspberry assiette including muffin, raspberry jelly, parfait and smoothie and lavender panna cotta with passion fruit and mint salsa. Please note – as it's first come, first served, you must arrive early to bag a table. *Starters/Snacks: £4.95 to £7.00. Main Courses: £12.95 to £17.50. Puddings: £5.75 to £7.00*

Adnams ~ Manager Francis Guildea ~ Real ale ~ Bar food ~ (01502) 722275 ~ Children welcome ~ Open 11-3, 6-11(10.30 Sun) ~ Bedrooms: £90B/£140B

Recommended by Catherine and Rob Dunster, Richard Pitcher, Mike and Sue Loseby, Andrea Rampley, Sheila Topham, Michael Dandy, Ray J Carter, Gerald and Gabrielle Culliford, MJVK, P Dawn, Tina and David Woods-Taylor, Julia Mann, Guy Vowles, Stephanie Sanders, Sue Demont, Tim Barrow

Harbour Inn ⬛

Blackshore, by the boats; from A1095, turn right at the Kings Head, and keep on past the golf course and water tower; IP18 6TA

Bustling waterside pub with lots of outside seats, interesting nautical décor, plenty of fish, and real ales

The position by the Blyth Estuary and the good fish and chips continue to draw visitors to this busy pub. The nautical character inside is pretty genuine as the friendly licensee is a lifeboatman. The back bar has a wind speed indicator, model ships, a lot of local ship and boat photographs, smoked fish hanging from a line on a beam, a lifeboat line launcher and brass shellcases on the mantelpiece over a stove; also, rustic stools and cushioned wooden benches built into its stripped panelling. The tiny, low-beamed, tiled and panelled front bar has antique settles and there's a dining extension with a raised deck in front of it. Adnams Bitter, Broadside, Explorer and maybe a seasonal guest on handpump, and several wines by the glass. There are seats in front of the building so you can watch the waterside activity and more seats and tables on a little terrace with fine views across the marshy fields towards the town and lighthouse. Look out for the 1953 flood level marked on the outside of the pub.

Ⓜ Popular bar food includes lunchtime filled baguettes, soup, grilled local smoked sprats, stuffed moroccan-style peppers, smoked haddock and prawn gratin, liver and bacon, beer-battered cod, haddock or plaice (served wrapped in paper on Friday evenings), daily specials, and puddings such as chocolate sponge with chocolate sauce and rhubarb and ginger crumble. *Starters/Snacks: £4.50 to £5.95. Main Courses: £8.95 to £13.95. Puddings: £4.95*

Adnams ~ Tenant Colin Fraser ~ Real ale ~ Bar food (12-2.30, 6-9) ~ Restaurant ~ (01502) 722381 ~ Children in bottom bar and dining room ~ Dogs allowed in bar ~ Open 11-11; 11-10.30 Sun

Recommended by Michael Dandy, Mike and Sue Loseby, Hilary Edwards, John and Jackie Walsh, Pete Baker, Richard Pitcher, the Didler, Steve Whalley, Eddie and Lynn Jarrett, Andrea Rampley

Lord Nelson ⬛

East Street, off High Street (A1095); IP18 6EJ

Smashing town pub with lots of locals and visitors, cheerful and chatty, excellent service, home-made pubby food and good choice of drinks; seats outside

Just moments away from the seafront, this smashing town pub remains as popular as ever. It's lively and friendly (and carefully redecorated this year) with lots of locals and visitors coming and going – but even when really busy, the good-natured service remains quick and attentive. The partly panelled bar and its two small side rooms are kept spotless, with good lighting, a small but extremely hot coal fire, light wood furniture on the tiled floor, lamps in nice nooks and corners and some interesting Nelson memorabilia, including attractive nautical prints and a fine model of HMS *Victory*. Adnams Bitter, Broadside, Explorer and a seasonal guest on handpump, Aspall's cider, and several good wines by the glass. Daily papers and board games but no piped music or games machines. There are nice seats out in front with a sidelong view down to the sea and more in a sheltered (and heated) back garden, with the brewery in sight (and often the appetising fragrance of brewing in progress). Disabled access is not perfect but is possible, and they will help.

🍴 **Under the new licensee and using local and organic produce, the well liked bar food includes sandwiches, ploughman's, soup, ham with pineapple, half a roast chicken with chips, vegetable or chicken curry, chilli con carne, popular beer-battered cod, and daily specials.** *Starters/Snacks: £3.95 to £5.95. Main Courses: £7.25 to £13.95. Puddings: £4.25*

Adnams ~ Tenant David Sanchez ~ Real ale ~ Bar food ~ (01502) 722079 ~ Children in areas to side of bar ~ Dogs welcome ~ Open 10.30am-11pm; 12-10.30 Sun

Recommended by Mrs M B Gregg, Malcolm Pellatt, N R White, Derek and Sylvia Stephenson, P Dawn, Michael Dandy, Derek Field, Pete Baker, Andrea Rampley, Richard Armstrong, Mike and Sue Loseby, Bob and Margaret Holder, Mr and Mrs B Watt, the Didler, Alan and Eve Harding, Sheila Topham, Blaise Vyner, Jeff Davies, Sue Demont, Tim Barrow, Richard Pitcher

STOKE-BY-NAYLAND

TL9836 MAP 5

Crown ★
Park Street (B1068); CO6 4SE

Smart dining pub with attractive modern furnishings, bistro-style food, and fantastic wine choice; comfortable bedrooms

Although most emphasis in this busy, smart and friendly dining pub is on the interesting, bistro-style food, those popping in for a drink and a chat, are just as welcome. Most of the place is open to the three-sided bar servery, yet it's well divided, and with two or three more tucked-away areas too. The main part, with a big woodburning stove, has quite a lot of fairly closely spaced tables in a variety of shapes, styles and sizes; elsewhere, several smaller areas have just three or four tables each. Seating varies from deep armchairs and sofas to elegant dining chairs and comfortable high-backed woven rush seats – and there are plenty of bar stools. This all gives a good choice between conviviality and varying degrees of cosiness and privacy. There are cheerful wildlife and landscape paintings on the pale walls, quite a lot of attractive table lamps, low ceilings (some with a good deal of stripped old beams), and floors varying from old tiles through broad boards or dark new flagstones to beige carpet; daily papers. Adnams Bitter, Crouch Vale Brewery Gold, and Woodfordes on handpump and a fantastic choice of 37 wines by the glass from a list of around 200 kept in an unusual glass-walled wine 'cellar' in one corner. A sheltered back terrace, with cushioned teak chairs and tables under big canvas parasols, looks out over a neat lawn to a landscaped shrubbery. There are many more picnic-sets out on the front terrace. Disabled access is good and the car park is big.

🍴 **Imaginative modern food using carefully sourced local produce includes soup, smoked eel, beetroot, grilled prosciutto and horseradish mousse, fried haggis, bacon and egg salad, soft shell crab tempura with wasabi, orecchiette with roasted baby aubergines, ricotta, chilli, rocket and lemon, pork fillet with caramelised apple, black pudding and sage and caper gravy, deep-fried local rabbit, watercress and aïoli, smoked gloucester old spot bacon with parsley sauce and cabbage parcel, steak and kidney pie with horseradish mash, salt marsh rump of lamb with roasted garlic and lemon thyme and creamed vegetables, and puddings such as hot jam doughnut with home-made condensed milk ice-cream and lemon mousse with raspberry tuiles.** *Starters/Snacks: £4.25 to £7.95. Main Courses: £10.50 to £17.50. Puddings: £4.75 to £5.95*

Free house ~ Licensee Richard Sunderland ~ Real ale ~ Bar food (12-2.30, 6-9.30 (10 Fri, Sat); 12-9 Sun) ~ (01206) 262001 ~ Children allowed but no facilities for them ~ Dogs allowed in bar ~ Open 11-11; 12-10.30 Sun; closed 25 and 26 Dec ~ Bedrooms: £90S(£100B)/£110S(£135B)

Recommended by Mrs P Lang, Mark Farrington, Mrs M B Gregg, Ken Millar, MDN, Marion and Bill Cross, N R White

TUDDENHAM

TM1948   MAP 5

Fountain ♀

Village signposted off B1077 N of Ipswich; The Street; IP6 9BT

17th-c village dining pub with well thought-of contemporary cooking; plenty of outside seating

This 17th-c dining pub was once a stopping point for drovers on their way to Ipswich Market. It's still popular with visitors but most customers now come to enjoy the good modern cooking – though there is a nod to drinkers who do still pop in, with space in the bar and Adnams Bitter on handpump. The several linked almost café-style rooms have original heavy beams and timbering, stripped wooden floors, a mix of wooden dining chairs around a medley of light wood tables, an open fire and a few prints (including some Giles ones; he spent some time here after World War II) on the white walls – décor is minimal. Several wines by the glass and piped music. Outside on the covered and heated terrace are wicker and metal chairs and wooden tables, and there are lots of picnic-sets on a sizeable lawn.

⌽ As well as a two- and three-course set menu, the contemporary food might include filled baguettes or focaccia, smoked chicken caesar salad, duck and spring onion samosas with chilli sesame soy sauce, smoked salmon, prawn and crème fraîche tian with red pepper dressing, grilled smoked haddock kedgeree with poached egg and butter sauce, organic salmon fillet with potato bean salad and mustard tarragon dressing, roasted lamb rump with a mint crust and red wine gravy, gressingham duck breast on curried parsnips with dauphinoise potatoes, and puddings such as rhubarb and ginger streusel with mascarpone sweet ginger cream and bread and butter pudding with whisky sauce. *Starters/Snacks: £4.60 to £9.95. Main Courses: £7.90 to £14.50. Puddings: £4.75*

Punch ~ Lease Charles Lewis and Scott Davidson ~ Real ale ~ Bar food (12-2(3 Sun), 6-9(9.30 Sat); not Sun evening) ~ Restaurant ~ (01473) 785377 ~ Children welcome ~ Open 12-3, 6-11; 12-4 Sun; closed Sun evening

Recommended by Tom Gondris, J F M and M West, Pamela Goodwyn, Mrs Carolyn Dixon, Mrs Hilarie Taylor

WALBERSWICK

TM4974   MAP 5

Anchor ⦅⑪⦆ ♀ ◖

Village signposted off A12; The Street (B1387); IP18 6UA

Good mix of locals and visitors in well run, attractively furnished inn, fine range of drinks, appetising modern cooking, and friendly, helpful service; bedrooms

The newly renovated flint barn here is used for private dining and other meetings, they hope to renovate the bedrooms soon, and there's now a garden bar serving the flagstoned terrace that overlooks the beach and village allotments. Inside, there's a genuine mix of both locals and visitors and the big-windowed comfortable front bar has heavy stripped tables on its dark blue carpet, sturdy built-in wall seats cushioned in green leather and nicely framed black and white photographs of local fishermen and their boats on the varnished plank panelling. Log fires in the chimneybreast divide this room into two snug halves. They have loads of bottled beers from all over the world, 23 interesting wines by the glass including champagne and a pudding one, Adnams Bitter, Broadside and a seasonal beer on handpump (they are holding an Old Ale festival in December 2008), and good coffee; particularly good service, daily papers, darts and board games. Quite an extensive dining area stretching back from a more modern-feeling small lounge on the left is furnished much like the bar – though perhaps a bit more minimalist – and looks out on a good-sized sheltered and nicely planted garden. The pub is right by the coast path, and there's a pleasant walk across to Southwold; in summer there may be a pedestrian ferry – though you won't know if it is running until you get there.

⌽ Using local producers (and vegetables from their allotment), the extremely good food (with a suggested beer to go with each dish) includes proper fish soup with rouille and croûtons, duck liver parfait with pear chutney, double-baked cheddar soufflé with caramelised onions, salmon and cod fishcake with creamy leeks, lamb curry with spiced rice, dhal and chutney, ham, bubble and squeak and a free-range poached egg with mustard cream (or a field mushroom with blue stilton and bubble and squeak), ox cheek in spices and red wine with parsnip and horseradish mash, and puddings such as date and walnut pudding with crème fraîche and toffee sauce and bakewell tart with clotted cream ice-cream. *Starters/Snacks: £4.50 to £7.75. Main Courses: £11.25 to £17.75. Puddings: £3.50 to £5.50*

Adnams ~ Lease Mark and Sophie Dorber ~ Real ale ~ Bar food (12-3, 6-9) ~ Restaurant ~ (01502) 722112 ~ Children welcome ~ Dogs allowed in bar and bedrooms ~ Open 11-4, 6-11; 11-11 Sat and Sun ~ Bedrooms: £75B/£90B

Recommended by Ryta Lyndley, Pete and Sue Robbins, Mr and Mrs B Watt, W K Wood, Jim and Sheila Prideaux, P Dawn, Bob and Margaret Holder, Evelyn and Derek Walter, Mrs M S Forbes, Adrian Johnson, Roger and Lesley Everett, Richard Pitcher, Mrs Brenda Calver, Mike and Sue Loseby, P A Rowe, Catherine and Rob Dunster, J F M and M West, Tracey and Stephen Groves, Michael and Ann Cole, Maurice Ricketts

Bell ♀ 🛏
Just off B1387; IP18 6TN

Busy well run inn close to beach, nice original features, fine choice of drinks and well liked food; bedrooms

Lively and usually extremely busy, this efficiently run pub is in a fine setting close to the beach, and most of the well appointed bedrooms look over the sea or river; the tables on the sizeable lawn are sheltered from the worst of the winds by a well placed hedge.The bars have brick floors, well worn uneven flagstones and wonky steps and oak beams that were here 400 years ago when the sleepy little village was a flourishing port. The rambling traditional main bar has curved high-backed settles, tankards hanging from oars above the counter and a woodburning stove in the big fireplace; a second bar has a very large open fire. Adnams Bitter, Broadside, Explorer and a seasonal ale on handpump, up to 20 wines by the glass, local cider, mulled wine and hot spiced ginger in winter and several malt whiskies; darts and board games. The landlady's daughter runs a ceramics business from a shed in the garden.

🍴 **Well liked bar food includes lunchtime sandwiches, soup, potted shrimps, smokies in creamy cheese sauce, locally smoked sprats, local sausages, macaroni cheese, fish and chips, sweet potato, spinach and cumin curry, spicy chilli with sour cream, shepherd's pie topped with cheese and leeks, and puddings such as sticky toffee pudding with vanilla pod ice-cream and lemon posset.** *Starters/Snacks: £5.95 to £6.95. Main Courses: £8.50 to £12.00. Puddings: £4.50*

Adnams ~ Tenant Sue Ireland Cutting ~ Real ale ~ Bar food ~ (01502) 723109 ~ Children welcome except in one bar ~ Dogs allowed in bar and bedrooms ~ Open 11-11(midnight Sat; 10.30 Sun); 11-3, 6-11 in winter ~ Bedrooms: £70S/£90S(£100B)

Recommended by Conrad Freezer, the Didler, Guy Vowles, Giles and Annie Francis, Michael Dandy, Nick Lawless, Mr and Mrs B Watt, Stephanie Sanders, Blaise Vyner, P Dawn, Mike and Sue Loseby, Catherine and Rob Dunster, Ryta Lyndley, Evelyn and Derek Walter, E Rankin,Bob and Margaret Holder, Sue Demont, Tim Barrow

WALDRINGFIELD   TM2844   MAP 5
Maybush
Off A12 S of Martlesham; The Quay, Cliff Road; IP12 4QL

Busy pub in lovely riverside position with plenty of tables making the most of the view, lots of room inside, nautical décor and fair choice of drinks and bar food

As the sizeable terrace in front of this busy, extended pub overlooks the River Deben and boating activity, the seats and tables under the umbrellas and big parasols are much prized – get here early if you want to bag one. Inside, the spacious bar has quite a nautical theme with lots of old lanterns, pistols and so forth, as well as aerial photographs, an original Twister board and fresh flowers. Alhough it's all been knocked through, it's divided into separate areas by fireplaces or steps; piped music, cards and dominoes. A glass case has an elaborate ship's model and there are a few more in a lighter, high-ceilinged extension. Adnams Bitter and Broadside and Greene King IPA on handpump and a fair choice of wines by the glass. There are river cruises available nearby but you have to pre-book them.

🍴 Popular bar food includes sandwiches, soup, pâté of the day, deep-fried garlic mushrooms with mayonnaise, breaded brie and camembert with a plum sauce, burgers with various toppings, much enjoyed fresh large fillets of cod and haddock, spinach and ricotta cannelloni, chicken curry, steak and kidney pudding, lamb shank with redcurrant and rosemary jus, and mixed grill. *Starters/Snacks: £3.95 to £5.95. Main Courses: £7.95 to £16.95. Puddings: £4.75*

Deben Inns ~ Lease Steve and Louise Lomas ~ Real ale ~ Bar food (all day) ~ Restaurant ~ (01473) 736215 ~ Children welcome ~ Dogs allowed in bar ~ Open 11-11

Recommended by Michael Clatworthy, Peter Meister, Bob and Margaret Holder, Mrs A J Robertson, Pamela Goodwyn, Mrs Romey Heaton, Howard and Sue Gascoyne

WESTLETON
TM4469   MAP 5

Crown

B1125 Blythburgh—Leiston; IP17 3AD

Lovely old coaching inn with cosy chatty bar, plenty of dining areas, carefully chosen drinks and particularly good food; comfortable, stylish bedrooms

Although this fine old coaching inn is a comfortable and stylish place to stay and the carefully cooked food is very good, its heart is still in the genuinely local bar. This area is really cosy and attractive with a lovely log fire, plenty of original features, and Adnams Bitter and guests like Brandon Rusty Bucket and Green Jack Gone Fishing on handpump, local cider, and a thoughtfully chosen wine list; piped music. There's also a parlour, a dining room and a conservatory. The charming terraced gardens have plenty of seats. Lots to do nearby.

🍴 Only using fresh local produce and making their own bread, chutneys and ice-creams, the imaginative food includes sandwiches, soup, home-cured gravadlax with a watercress and pine nut salad, wild duck and pheasant terrine with a beer and mixed fruit chutney, spinach, onion, wild mushroom and brie tart, cod and chips with home-made tartare sauce, steamed steak and kidney suet pudding, daily specials such as scallops with chilli, lime and ginger dipping sauce, grilled fillet of black bream with provençale tomato stew, and 21-day hung beef with wild mushroom jus, and puddings like warm chocolate brownie with caramel sauce and crème chantilly and caramelised vanilla crème brûlée topped with bananas with raisin shortbread. *Starters/Snacks: £4.50 to £6.50. Main Courses: £9.50 to £19.95. Puddings: £5.00 to £6.00*

Free house ~ Licensee Matthew Goodwin ~ Real ale ~ Bar food (12-2.30, 7-9.30) ~ Restaurant ~ (01728) 648777 ~ Children welcome ~ Dogs allowed in bar and bedrooms ~ Occasional live piano ~ Open 11-11; closed 25 Dec ~ Bedrooms: £90B/£120B

Recommended by Michael and Ann Cole, Tracey and Stephen Groves, Giles and Annie Francis, Michael Dandy, Lorraine Brennan, Richard and Margaret McPhee

LUCKY DIP

Besides the fully inspected pubs, you might like to try these Lucky Dips recommended to us and described by readers (if you do, please send us reports: feedback@thegoodpubguide.co.uk).

ALDEBURGH [TM4656]
☆ *Mill* IP15 5BJ [Market Cross Pl, opp Moot Hall]: Bustling 1920s seaside pub, cheerful and chatty, with good value fresh food (not Sun evening) from sandwiches and baguettes to very local fish and crabs, hard-working staff, well kept Adnams, decent coffee, three smallish rooms inc back dining room, RNLI and military memorabilia, cushioned wall seats and padded stools, cosy beamed dining room, cream teas July/Aug; games machine; dogs welcome, bedrooms, open all day (*RS, ES, Peter and Pat Frogley, the Didler,*

Edward Mirzoeff, Michael Dandy, Steve Whalley, Terry Buckland, P Dawn)

Wentworth IP15 5BB [Wentworth Rd]: Old-fashioned hotel not pub, popular with older people for good value bar food (not Sun evening), well kept Adnams and a good choice of wines by the glass, pleasant long-serving staff; conservatory, colourful seafront flagstoned terrace and suntrap sunken garden, bedrooms (*Steve Whalley, Terry Mizen, Pamela Goodwyn, Mr and Mrs T B Staples, Michael Dandy*)

White Hart IP15 5AJ [High St]: Friendly beamed and panelled Victorian local with four real ales inc Adnams, pubby food from bargain lunchtime sandwiches up, log fire, heavy stripped tables, folk nights; open all day *(P Dawn)*

ALDRINGHAM [TM4461]
Parrot & Punchbowl IP16 4PY [B1122/B1353 S of Leiston]: Attractive and welcoming beamed pub with good fairly priced food inc local fish, good wine choice, well kept Adnams and Greene King IPA, decent coffee, two-level restaurant; children welcome; nice sheltered garden, also family garden with adventure play area *(BB, Charles and Pauline Stride, Simon Rodway)*

BILDESTON [TL9949]
☆ *Crown* IP7 7EB [B1115 SW of Stowmarket]: Good upmarket food in picturesque and impressively refurbished 15th-c timbered country inn, smart beamed main bar with inglenook log fire, Adnams ales, good choice of wines by the glass, farm cider, kind service, dining room; children welcome, nice tables out in courtyard, more in large attractive garden, quiet comfortable bedrooms *(Pamela Goodwyn, J F M and M West, LYM)*

BLYTHBURGH [TM4575]
☆ *White Hart* IP19 9LQ [A12]: Open-plan family dining pub with fine ancient beams, woodwork and staircase, full Adnams ale range and good range of wines, good coffee, friendly efficient service; children in eating areas, spacious lawns looking down on tidal bird marshes (barbecues), magnificent church over road, four bedrooms, open all day *(B J Harding, Edward Mirzoeff, RS, ES, LYM, Derek and Sylvia Stephenson)*

BOXFORD [TL9640]
☆ *Fleece* CO10 5DX [Broad St]: Unpretentious partly 15th-c pub with friendly landlord, good home-made food, Adnams, cosy panelled bar, airy lounge bar with wonderful medieval fireplace, armchairs and some distinctive old seats among more conventional furnishings *(Mrs Carolyn Dixon, LYM)*

White Hart CO10 5DX [Broad St]: Contemporary dining pub with light modern furniture and décor in old building, enjoyable food (can take a while), friendly helpful service, Greene King ales *(MDN, Mrs P Lang)*

BRANTHAM [TM1234]
Bull CO11 1PN [E, junction A137/B1080]: Modern refurbishment emphasising food side, friendly service, cheerful big-windowed restaurant extension, views to Stour estuary; children welcome, good-sized garden with play area *(N R White, Pamela Goodwyn)*

BRENT ELEIGH [TL9348]
☆ *Cock* CO10 9PB [A1141 SE of Lavenham]: Classic thatched country local now serving limited food such as casseroles, Adnams and Greene King IPA and Abbot, organic farm cider, piano in clean and cosy snug, darts in second small room, antique flooring tiles,

lovely coal fire, ochre walls with old photographs of local villages (village church well worth a look); picnic-sets up on side grass with summer hatch service, attractive inn-sign, bedrooms *(Giles and Annie Francis, the Didler, Mrs M B Gregg, BB)*

BROCKLEY GREEN [TL7247]
☆ *Plough* CO10 8DT: Friendly neatly kept knocked-through bar, beams, timbers and stripped brick, scrubbed tables and open fire, enjoyable food from lunchtime sandwiches to some enterprising dishes, cheerful staff, Greene King IPA, Woodfordes Wherry and a guest beer, good choice of wines by the glass and malt whiskies, restaurant; children and dogs welcome, extensive attractive grounds with good tables and terrace, newly refurbished bedrooms *(Dave Braisted, LYM)*

BURY ST EDMUNDS [TL8563]
☆ *Rose & Crown* IP33 1NP [Whiting St]: Unassuming black-beamed town local with affable helpful landlord, bargain simple lunchtime home cooking (not Sun), particularly well kept Greene King ales inc Mild, pleasant lounge with lots of piggy pictures and bric-a-brac, good games-oriented public bar with darts, cards and dominoes, rare separate off-sales counter; pretty back courtyard, open all day wkdys *(Julia Mann, Tony and Jill Radnor, Pete Baker, Ryta Lyndley, Tom and Jill Jones)*

BUTLEY [TM3650]
Oyster IP12 3NZ [B1084 E of Woodbridge]: Friendly country local, well kept Adnams, good value fresh food (not Sun evening), good wine by the glass, helpful staff, stripped pine tables and pews, high-backed settles and more orthodox seats on bare boards, good coal fire, darts, dominoes; children and dogs welcome *(LYM, Jeremy and Jane Morrison)*

BUXHALL [TM9957]
Crown IP14 3DW [off B1115 W of Stowmarket; Mill Rd]: Cosy low-beamed inglenook bar, leather chairs, pews, airy dining room off, Greene King ales; children and dogs welcome, plenty of tables on heated terrace, pretty enclosed garden, nice country views, cl Sun pm, Mon; the Goltons who made this tucked-away country pub a favourite for their good food and friendly service have now moved to the Hand & Cleaver at Ranton *(LYM)*

CHILLESFORD [TM3852]
☆ *Froize* IP12 3PU [B1084 E of Woodbridge]: Restaurant rather than pub (open only when they serve food, ie not Mon, nor Sun-Weds evenings), reliably good cooking in pleasant bar and restaurant, warmly welcoming service, good value two-course buffet-style or carvery lunch, wide choice of more elaborate evening meals, local fish, pork, game and venison, original puddings, good wines by the glass, Adnams; may be cl Feb for hols *(Simon Cottrell, Tony and Shirley Albert, LYM, C and R Bromage, Mr and Mrs A Curry)*

CLARE [TL7645]
Bell CO10 8NN [Market Hill]: Large timbered inn with comfortably rambling lounge, log fires, splendidly carved black beams, old panelling and woodwork, friendly service, Greene King ales and decent wines, food from sandwiches up inc afternoon teas, dining room, conservatory opening on to terrace, darts and pool in public bar; games machine, TV; nice bedrooms off back courtyard (special village, lovely church), open all day Sun (*Mrs Margo Finlay, Jörg Kasprowski, Tom and Jill Jones, LYM, Dave Braisted*)

COCKFIELD [TL9152]
Three Horseshoes IP30 0JB [Stows Hill (A1141 towards Lavenham)]: Partly thatched village local dating from 14th c, well kept changing ales, reasonably priced generous food (not Tues), friendly attentive staff, cosy bar, dining lounge, conservatory restaurant; children welcome (*Clive Flynn*)

COTTON [TM0667]
☆ *Trowel & Hammer* IP14 4QL [off B1113 N of Stowmarket; Mill Rd]: Spreading linked areas, lots of beamery and timber baulks, plenty of wheelbacks and one or two older chairs and settles around a mix of tables, big log fire, Adnams and Greene King, some food available all day, pool, may be live music Sat; piped music, games machine, juke box; well behaved children welcome, colourful back garden great for them, swimming pool, open all day (*Stephen P Edwards, LYM, Ian and Nita Cooper, Andrew Gardner*)

CREETING ST MARY [TM1155]
Highwayman IP6 8PD [A140, just N of junction with A14]: Attractively modernised two-bar pub with pleasant barn extension, relaxed atmosphere, welcoming landlord, good interesting food, Adnams, Fullers London Pride and Woodfordes Wherry, decent wines, gallery overflow; unobtrusive piped music; tables on back lawn with pretty pond, cl Sun evening and Mon (*Ian and Nita Cooper*)

CRETINGHAM [TM2260]
☆ *Bell* IP13 7BJ [The Street]: Attractive pub taken in hand by two brothers and their partners, good value pubby food with spanish specials, several real ales, neat new leather armchairs in bare-boards bar, sofa and dining tables in quarry-tiled second room, fine old fireplace, beams and timbers; attractive garden, two tidy bedrooms (*J F M and M West, John and Patricia White, LYM*)

DENNINGTON [TM2867]
Queens Head IP13 8AB [A1120; The Square]: New landlord for beamed and timbered Tudor pub prettily placed by church, neat, L-shaped main bar, Adnams and maybe a guest, local cider, straightforward food (can take a while); piped music; children in family room, side lawn by noble lime trees, pond at back with ducks and carp, backs on to Dennington Park with swings and so forth for children (*LYM*)

DUNWICH [TM4770]
Ship IP17 3DT [St James St]: Handy halt in charming seaside village, woodburner and lots of sea prints and nauticalia in well worn tiled bar, Adnams and Mauldons from antique handpumps, popular fish and chips, simple conservatory; children and dogs welcome, large sheltered garden, bedrooms, open all day (*Julia Mann, Michael and Ann Cole, Edward Mirzoeff, LYM, Tracey and Stephen Groves, Giles and Annie Francis, Dave Braisted, Evelyn and Derek Walter, Mike and Sue Loseby, Tina and David Woods-Taylor, Roy Hoing, Tony Middis, Simon Rodway, P Dawn, SimonCottrell, Michael Dandy*)

EAST BERGHOLT [TM0734]
☆ *Kings Head* CO7 6TL [Burnt Oak, towards Flatford Mill]: Enjoyable food inc unusual dishes in popular well laid out dining pub, friendly obliging staff, well kept ales inc Adnams Broadside, decent wines and coffee, beamed lounge with comfortable sofas in softly lit part by servery, interesting decorations; piped classical music; lots of room in garden (*Mrs Carolyn Dixon, Mike and Mary Carter, MDN, N R White*)

EASTON [TM2858]
White Horse IP13 0ED [N of Wickham Market on back rd to Earl Soham and Framlingham]: Neatly kept pink-washed two-bar country pub, bigger than it looks, doing well under new licensees, good choice of enjoyable food in bar and dining room, Adnams, good wines by the glass (they are starting a wine business); welcoming staff, open fires; children in eating area, nice garden (*Pamela Goodwyn, Simon Cottrell, LYM*)

EDWARDSTONE [TL9542]
White Horse CO10 5PX [Mill Green]: Something of an eco-pub (wind turbine out behind), up to half a dozen well kept changing ales inc a Mild (dark beer festivals every few months), hoping to brew their own soon, also strong local farm cider, hearty food (not Mon), rustic décor; nice big garden, camp site, has been cl lunchtimes on Mon, Tues and Thurs (*Giles and Annie Francis*)

ERWARTON [TM2134]
☆ *Queens Head* IP9 1LN [off B1456 Ipswich—Shotley Gate]: 16th-c pub newly refurbished for more emphasis on dining side, bowed oak beams, wooden flooring, sea paintings and photographs, coal fire, Adnams, Greene King and Shepherd Neame, pleasant conservatory; piped music; children allowed lunchtimes, front picnic-sets under summer hanging baskets may have view to Stour Estuary (if foliage trimmed enough), cl Sun pm (*LYM*)

FELIXSTOWE FERRY [TM3237]
Ferry Boat IP11 9RZ: Much modernised 17th-c pub tucked between golf links and dunes nr harbour, Martello tower and summer rowing-boat ferry, good value food from snacks to fresh fish (lunch stops 2 on the dot), Adnams and Greene King, good log fire; piped music, busy summer wknds, and

they may try to keep your credit card while you eat; dogs welcome, tables out in front, on green opposite, and in fenced garden, good coast walks *(Peter Meister, Mrs Hazel Rainer, LYM)*

FELSHAM [TL9457]

Six Bells IP30 0PJ [Church Rd]: Open-plan beamed country local with darts and cribbage in good lively bar, cosy quiet restaurant, nice décor and fresh flowers, Greene King ales, friendly relaxed licensees, pubby food inc home-baked bread; children and dogs welcome *(Ben and Chris Francis, J F M and M West, Clive Flynn)*

FORWARD GREEN [TM0959]

☆ *Shepherd & Dog* IP14 5HN: Good modern dining-pub refurbishment with attractive pastel décor, comfortable dining tables and some sofas, good interesting food in contemporary bar and restaurant, well kept Greene King IPA, good wines by the glass and coffee; disabled access, terrace tables, cl Sun evening and Mon *(Alan Cole, Kirstie Bruce, Richard Siebert, Tom Gondris, J F M and M West, Charles and Pauline Stride)*

FRAMLINGHAM [TM2863]

Crown IP13 9AP [Market Hill]: Traditional heavy-beamed front bar, log-fire lounge and eating area, Greene King ales, several wines by the glass, contemporary bar extension restaurant (evenings, Sun carvery); courtyard tables, 14 comfortable period bedrooms *(LYM, Michael Dandy)*

FRISTON [TM4160]

☆ *Old Chequers* IP17 1NP [just off A1094 Aldeburgh—Snape]: Reopened under new licensees, enjoyable daily-changing food, Adnams and Timothy Taylors Landlord, Aspall's local cider, smartly reworked L-shaped bar with nicely spaced varying-sized tables, log fires; children welcome, good walk from Aldeburgh *(LYM, Charles and Pauline Stride)*

HALESWORTH [TM3979]

Triple Plea IP19 8QW [Broadway (A144 N)]: Popular two-bar dining pub with sensibly short choice of enjoyable home-made food, good service, leather sofas and open fire in relaxed lounge, pleasant raftered restaurant with conservatory; two bedrooms, open all day Fri-Sun, cl Mon lunchtime *(N Murphy, Julie Gilbert, Michael R B Taylor)*

White Hart IP19 8AH [Thoroughfare]: Roomy well restored open-plan pub, well arranged and nicely furnished, with short choice of good value food, well kept Adnams and guest beers *(RS, ES)*

HARTEST [TL8352]

☆ *Crown* IP29 4DH [B1066 S of Bury St Edmunds]: Pink-washed pub by church behind pretty village green, friendly staff, good food choice inc good value midweek lunches, well kept Greene King, smart minimalist décor with quality tables and chairs on tiled floor, good log fire in impressive fireplace, two dining rooms and conservatory; piped music; children and dogs welcome, tables on big back lawn and in

sheltered side courtyard, good play area *(John Saville, LYM, Clive Flynn)*

HAUGHLEY [TM0262]

Kings Arms IP14 3NT [off A45/B1113 N of Stowmarket; Old St]: Enjoyable pub food and well kept Adnams Broadside and Greene King Abbot in 16th-c timbered pub with airy 1950s back part refurbished to match, decent wines, busy public bar with games, log fire; piped music; tables in colourful back garden *(BB, Conrad Freezer)*

HENLEY [TM1552]

Cross Keys IP6 0QP [Main Rd]: Busy refurbished local, good value unpretentious food all day, well kept beer, enthusiastic young licencees; children welcome *(J F M and M West)*

HESSETT [TL9361]

☆ *Five Bells* IP30 9AX [off A14 E of Bury; The Street]: New licensee (too late for us to gauge) for this nice low-ceilinged open-plan pub nr spectacular Norman church, good mix of tables, country prints, big rugs on flooring tiles, good log fire; has had well kept Greene King ales and a guest beer and attractively varied home cooking; piped music; children and dogs welcome, sheltered garden with boules, has been cl Mon; reports on new regime please *(LYM)*

HONINGTON [TL9174]

Fox IP31 1RD [Troston Rd]: Simple pubby food, Courage and Theakstons, darts and pool; garden tables, doubles as post office, open all day *(Dave Braisted)*

HUNTINGFIELD [TM3473]

Huntingfield Arms IP19 0PU [The Street]: Handsome building by green, friendly landlord (and dog Archie), enjoyable home cooking inc fresh and smoked fish, well kept Adnams and a guest beer, light wood tables and chairs, beams and stripped brickwork, blazing woodburner in front room, pleasant back games area with pool, restaurant; tables outside, cl Sun evening *(Charman family)*

ICKLINGHAM [TL7872]

☆ *Red Lion* IP28 6PS [A1101 Mildenhall—Bury St Edmunds]: Civilised 16th-c thatched dining pub with newish young chef/landlord doing good fresh food, attractive beamed open-plan bar with cavernous inglenook fireplace, friendly staff, Greene King ales, interesting short choice of wines by the glass; picnic-sets out on front lawn and back terrace overlooking fields *(LYM, Dan Graham, Stephen Read, George Cowie, Frances Gosnell, Sheila Topham)*

IPSWICH [TM1644]

Dove Street IP4 2LA [76 St Helens St]: Great choice of well kept quickly changing ales, farm ciders, bottled beers and whiskies, cheap hot drinks, friendly staff, bargain basic food; dogs welcome *(David Carr)*

Greyhound IP1 3SE [Henley Rd/Anglesea Rd]: Comfortable Victorian décor, well kept Adnams and guest ales, good substantial home cooking inc plenty for vegetarians, quick service by well trained young staff;

children welcome, quiet back terrace (the Didler)

Lord Nelson IP4 1JZ [Fore St]: Ancient local with friendly prompt service, well kept Adnams ales tapped from the cask, tasty food (not Sun evening) inc wider evening choice, bare boards, timbering, huge fireplace and barrels; sunny garden, handy for waterfront, bedrooms *(Tony Hobden, G Coates, Allison and Graham Thackery)*

Milestone IP4 2EA [Woodbridge Rd]: Open-plan mock-Tudor pub with up to a dozen or so changing ales, farm ciders, several dozen whiskies, home-made food lunchtime and Mon-Weds evening, real fire; big-screen sports TV, live bands; disabled access, large front terrace, open all day wknds *(Mrs Hazel Rainer, G Coates, the Didler)*

KERSEY [TM0044]

Bell IP7 6DY [signed off A1141 N of Hadleigh; The Street]: Tudor pub in notably picturesque village, quick friendly service, good value pubby food from sandwiches up, Adnams and Greene King IPA, decent house wines, modernised low-beamed bar with log fire, two dining rooms; children allowed, sheltered back terrace with fairy-lit side canopy, open all day *(Adele Summers, Alan Black, LYM)*

LAVENHAM [TL9148]

Cock CO10 9SA [Church St]: Comfortable thatched village pub with friendly attentive service, Adnams and Greene King ales, good wine choice, generous food inc popular Sun roasts, separate family dining room, plush lounge, basic bar; no dogs; seats out in front, back garden, nice view of church *(the Didler, Mrs Carolyn Dixon, Clive Flynn)*

LAXFIELD [TM2972]

Royal Oak IP13 8DH [High St]: Newly refurbished Tudor pub, well kept Adnams and Woodfordes, good value lunchtime bar food (roasts on Sun) and evening restaurant (not Mon); open all day, cl Mon lunchtime *(Andrew Selwyn)*

LEVINGTON [TM2339]

☆ ***Ship*** IP10 0LQ [Gun Hill/Church Lane]: Charming old pub with good informal dining inc fair-priced fresh fish and seafood (no bookings), good choice of wines by the glass, Adnams Best and Broadside, friendly efficient staff, old-fashioned wooden furnishings on flagstone floor, nautical décor and pictures; no children inside, front picnic-sets with a bit of an estuary view, more out behind, attractive surroundings, good walks, cl Sun evening *(J F M and M West, Peter Meister, Mrs Carolyn Dixon, Andrew Shore, Maria Williams, Rosemary Smith, Allison and Graham Thackery, Charles and Pauline Stride, LYM, George Cowie, Frances Gosnell, Ian and Nita Cooper, Pamela Goodwyn)*

LINDSEY TYE [TL9846]

Red Rose IP7 6PP: Ancient beamed pub thriving under new management, simple good value food, good friendly staff, good value wines, continuing improvements inside

and out; tables outside front and back, open all day Sun *(Mrs Carolyn Dixon, MDN)*

LONG MELFORD [TL8645]

☆ ***Bull*** CO10 9JG [Hall St (B1064)]: Lovely medieval great hall, now a hotel, with beautifully carved beams in old-fashioned timbered front lounge, antique furnishings, log fire in huge fireplace, more spacious back bar with sporting prints, well kept Greene King ales, bar food from good filled huffers to one-price hot dishes inc imaginative salads and fresh fish, friendly helpful staff, daily papers, restaurant; children welcome, courtyard tables, comfortable bedrooms, open all day Sat/Sun *(C and R Bromage, LYM, I A Herdman)*

LOWESTOFT [TM5593]

Triangle NR32 1QA [St Peters St]: Jovial pub brewing its own good Green Jack ales, several guest beers and two farm ciders, open fire you can cook on, frequent live music and all-day jam sessions, pool and juke box in back bar; open all day *(P Dawn)*

MARKET WESTON [TL9777]

☆ ***Mill*** IP22 2PD [Bury Rd (B1111)]: Opened-up pub with attractively priced lunches using local produce, OAP discounts, thoughtful evening menu, Adnams, Greene King IPA, Woodfordes Wherry and an Old Chimneys beer from the village brewery, local farm cider, enthusiastic effective service, two log fires, dominoes; children welcome, small well kept garden *(Derek Field)*

MELTON [TM2850]

Wilford Bridge IP12 2PA [Wilford Bridge Rd]: Light, roomy and well organised, with reliable good value food from good sandwiches to local fish in two spacious bars and restaurant, Adnams and Greene King Old Speckled Hen, good wines by the glass, prompt friendly service; nearby river walks *(P Clark, Pamela Goodwyn)*

METTINGHAM [TM3690]

Tally Ho NR35 1TL [B1062 E of Bungay]: Roomy food-oriented pub, unpretentiously comfortable, with wide choice from sandwiches up, friendly service, Fullers and Woodfordes Wherry *(John Robertson)*

MONKS ELEIGH [TL9647]

Swan IP7 7AU [B1115 Sudbury—Stowmarket]: Proper pub with chef/landlord doing good freshly made rather restaurant food (and recipe books), real ales inc Adnams and Greene King, good value wines, welcoming efficient service, comfortably modernised lounge bar, open fire, two dining areas; bedrooms *(Mrs Carolyn Dixon, Clive Flynn)*

OCCOLD [TM1570]

Beaconsfield Arms IP23 7PN [Mill Rd]: Village local with enthusiastic newish licensees, well kept Adnams and Greene King, home-made food *(Mrs B R Walker, Chris Mawson)*

ORFORD [TM4249]

Crown & Castle IP12 2LJ: Restaurant with rooms rather than pub, small smartly minimalist bar (used largely for pre-meal drinks – well kept Greene King and good wines by the glass), good individual food from light lunches up, good service; tables outside, residents' garden, 18 good chalet bedrooms *(Conrad Freezer, Michael Dandy, A J Murray, C and R Bromage)*

PETTISTREE [TM2954]

Greyhound IP13 0HP [off A12 just S of Wickham Mkt]: 15th-c beamed village pub reopened under new owners, enjoyable home-made food (not Mon), Earl Soham, Greene King and Woodfordes Wherry, good soft drinks, plenty of neat tables in carpeted bar and pleasant dining room, open fires; garden picnic-sets *(Justin and Emma King)*

POLSTEAD [TL9938]

Cock CO6 5AL [signed off B1068 and A1071 E of Sudbury, then pub signed; Polstead Green]: Beamed and timbered local with unassuming pink-walled bar, woodburner and open fire, Adnams Broadside and Greene King IPA, good choice of wines and malt whiskies, good coffee, friendly young staff, bar food from big lunchtime rolls up, smarter light and airy barn restaurant; piped music; good disabled access and facilities, children and dogs welcome, picnic-sets out overlooking quiet green, side play area, cl Mon *(BB, N R White)*

RAMSHOLT [TM3041]

☆ *Ramsholt Arms* IP12 3AB [signed off B1083; Dock Rd]: Lovely isolated spot overlooking River Deben, easy-going open-plan nautical bar busy on summer wknds and handy for bird walks and Sutton Hoo; quickly served food inc good value seafood and game, two sittings for Sun lunch, Adnams and a guest beer, decent wines by the glass, winter mulled wine, good log fire; children welcome and very happy here, plenty of tables outside with summer afternoon terrace bar (not Sun), roomy bedrooms with stunning view, open all day *(LYM, J F M and M West, John Coatsworth, Pamela Goodwyn, Peter Meister)*

REYDON [TM4977]

☆ *Randolph* IP18 6PZ [Wangford Rd]: Light and airy contemporary décor, light wood furniture on parquet and blinds for the big windows, friendly obliging staff, good food choice from sandwiches to plenty of fish and interesting puddings, Adnams beers and wines, reasonable prices; children welcome in attractive dining area, garden, ten good value bedrooms *(Derek and Sylvia Stephenson, Guy Vowles, Tracey and Stephen Groves)*

RUMBURGH [TM3481]

Buck IP19 0NT: Pretty and hospitable rambling country local, enjoyable food inc generous Sun roasts, lots of character with flagstones and old settles, well kept Adnams and guest beers, decent wines; quiet back lawn, lovely church nearby, nice walks *(Simon Cottrell)*

SHADINGFIELD [TM4385]

Fox NR34 8DD [London Rd]: Character 16th-c pub refurbished under friendly new

management, enjoyable fresh food from home-baked lunchtime sandwiches to some interesting cooking, Adnams and Greene King, well chosen wines, nicely set tables *(Jemma Mills, Anne Morris)*

SHIMPLING STREET [TL8753]

Bush IP29 4HU [off A134 Sudbury—Bury; The Street]: Friendly pub with good value food inc bargain lunches Tues-Thurs, neat dining room; good-sized garden *(Mrs Carolyn Dixon)*

SHOTTISHAM [TM3244]

Sorrel Horse IP12 3HD [Hollesley Rd]: Charming two-bar thatched Tudor local, attentive helpful landlord, Greene King ales tapped from the cask, limited tasty home-made food from granary baguettes up, good log fire in tiled-floor bar with games area, attractive dining room, game prints; tables out on green, open all day wknds *(J F M and M West, the Didler, C and R Bromage)*

SNAPE [TM3958]

Crown IP17 1SL [Bridge Rd (B1069)]: New tenants have streamlined the décor (not as quaint as it was, but at least they've kept the beams and inglenook log fire), Adnams ales, good choice of wines by the glass, food from light dishes up; children and dogs welcome, newly landscaped garden, bedrooms up steep stairs *(LYM)*

SOUTHWOLD [TM5076]

☆ *Red Lion* IP18 6ET [South Green]: Good atmosphere, warm friendly service, reasonably priced pubby food from sandwiches up, well kept Adnams, big windows looking over green to sea, pale panelling, ship pictures, lots of brassware and copper, pub games, separate dining room; children and dogs welcome, lots of tables outside, right by the Adnams retail shop *(BB, Roger and Lesley Everett, Trevor and Sylvia Millum, Sue Demont, Tim Barrow, Ian and Nita Cooper, Michael Dandy, P Dawn, Janet Whittaker)*

Sole Bay IP18 6JN [East Green]: Bright café-bar with full Adnams ale range and good wine choice, cheerful and efficient smartly dressed staff, good simple food from impressive doorstep sandwiches up, mix of furnishings from pale wood to settles, conservatory; side terrace, moments from sea and lighthouse *(Pat and Tony Martin, Michael Dandy, Adrian Johnson, Richard and Margaret McPhee, LYM, P Dawn)*

☆ *Swan* IP18 6EG [Market Pl]: Relaxed and comfortable back bar in smart hotel, full range of Adnams ales and bottled beers, fine wines and malt whiskies, good bar lunches (not cheap, but worth it), pleasant staff, pricy coffee and teas in luxurious chintzy front lounge, restaurant; bedrooms inc separate block where (by arrangement) dogs can stay too *(Michael Dandy, LYM, P Dawn)*

STOKE-BY-NAYLAND [TL9836]

☆ *Angel* CO6 4SA [B1068 Sudbury—East Bergholt]: This handsomely beamed dining pub, a former favourite for its civilised individual style and good food, has been sold to a new small pub investment company (run by an ex Greene King operations director); with a new manageress, it's been refurbished throughout, with some stripped brickwork and timbers, a mix of pubby furnishings, big log fire, straightforward bar food (all day Sun), elegantly furnished high-ceilinged restaurant, Adnams and guest beers, good choice of wines by glass; children welcome, sheltered terrace, comfortable bedrooms, open all day; more reports on new regime please *(LYM)*

STRATFORD ST MARY [TM0434]

Anchor CO7 6LW [Upper St]: Thriving local atmosphere, wide food choice from bargain pub lunches up, Adnams; tables among flower tubs in front, back garden with play area *(PHB)*

STUTTON [TM1434]

Gardeners Arms IP9 2TG [Manningtree Rd, Upper Street (B1080)]: Well kept Adnams and Mighty Oak, friendly landlord, enjoyable fresh straightforward food inc OAP meals and good value Sun lunch, lots of bric-a-brac, dining room; garden, open all day *(Tony and Shirley Albert, N R White)*

☆ **SWILLAND** [TM1852]

Moon & Mushroom IP6 9LR [off B1078]: Cheerfully old-fashioned, with area ales like Adnams, Buffys, Crouch Vale, Wolf and Woodfordes tapped from casks racked up behind long counter, old tables and chairs on quarry tiles, log fires, game and fish dishes plus pubby choices; children and dogs welcome, terrace tables with grapevines and roses, cl Sun pm and Mon *(Neil Powell, Ian and Nita Cooper, Peter Comeau, N R White, Mrs Carolyn Dixon, LYM, the Didler)*

TATTINGSTONE [TM1338]

White Horse IP9 2NU [White Horse Hill]: Tastefully renovated, with wide choice of food, friendly landlord, reasonably priced ales such as Adnams and Woodfordes (talk of brewing their own), restaurant *(Tony and Shirley Albert)*

THORNHAM MAGNA [TM1070]

☆ **Four Horseshoes** IP23 8HD [off A140 S of Diss; Wickham Rd]: Extensive thatched pub with dim-lit rambling well divided bar, helpful friendly young staff, wide food choice, Greene King ales, good choice of wines and whiskies, very low heavy black beams, plush banquettes, country pictures, big log fireplaces, inside well; piped music; handy for Thornham Walks and interesting thatched church, picnic-sets on big sheltered lawn, ten comfortable bedrooms, good breakfast, open all day *(Ian and Nita Cooper, Guy and Caroline Howard, LYM)*

THORPENESS [TM4759]

☆ **Dolphin** IP16 4NB: Smart almost scandinavian décor, light and bright, very busy lunchtime for enjoyable food from sandwiches up, Adnams, good wine range, welcoming landlord and relaxed helpful service, interesting photographs of this quaint purpose-built seaside holiday village with its boating lake; children and dogs welcome, large attractive garden with

summer bar and barbecue, three comfortable and attractive bedrooms *(Adrian Johnson, Mrs Romey Heaton, Pamela Goodwyn)*

TOSTOCK [TL9563]

Gardeners Arms IP30 9PA [off A14 or A1088]: Low-beamed village pub, Greene King and a guest ale, enjoyable pubby food, quick friendly service, log fire, games in tiled separate bar; nicely planted sheltered garden *(LYM, J F M and M West, Pat and Tony Martin)*

WANGFORD [TM4679]

☆ **Angel** NR34 8RL [signed just off A12 by B1126 junction; High St]: Handsome 17th-c village inn with well spaced tables in light and airy bar, Adnams, Fullers London Pride, Greene King Abbot and Shepherd Neame Spitfire, decent wines, friendly new licensees doing good value plentiful food, family dining room; comfortable bedrooms (the church clock sounds on the quarter), good breakfast *(Brett Massey, Marcus Mann, LYM)*

WENHASTON [TM4274]

Star IP19 9HF [Hall Rd]: Village pub with Adnams and good wine choice, wide range of home-made food in pleasant dining areas with some bric-a-brac for sale, sun lounge, pleasant views, games in tiled-floor locals' bar; dogs welcome, sizeable lawn with boules *(Adrian Johnson, LYM)*

WESTLETON [TM4469]

☆ **White Horse** IP17 3AH [Darsham Rd, off B1125 Blythburgh—Leiston]: Homely comfort and friendly staff in traditional pub with generous straightforward food inc good sandwiches, OAP bargain lunch, Adnams, unassuming high-ceilinged bar with bric-a-brac and central fire, steps down to attractive Victorian back dining room; children in eating area, picnic-sets in cottagey back garden with climbing frame, more out by village duckpond, bedrooms, good breakfast *(Michael Dandy, Robert F Smith)*

WINGFIELD [TM2276]

☆ **De La Pole Arms** IP21 5RA [off B1118 N of Stradbroke; Church Rd]: Timbered 16th-c pub with friendly staff, short choice of enjoyable country cooking using prime local ingredients, well kept Adnams, Aspall's farm cider, good choice of wines by the glass, bare boards and quarry tiles, leather easy chairs and solid country dining tables and chairs, log fires in big inglenooks; unobtrusive piped music; children and dogs welcome, good disabled access, cl Sun evening *(Jane Greenwood, Mr and Mrs A Campbell, LYM, David Barnes)*

WOODBRIDGE [TM2749]

Olde Bell & Steelyard IP12 1DZ [New St, off Market Sq]: Ancient and unpretentious, with friendly landlord, Greene King IPA and Abbot, short good value choice of usual food from bargain soup and sandwich to local fish, darts, steelyard still overhanging street; back terrace *(Mr and Mrs W W Burke, Jeremy and Jane Morrison, Alan and Eve Harding)*

Seckford Hall IP13 6NU [signed off A12 bypass, N of town; Seckford Hall Rd, Great Bealings]: Civilised Tudor country-house hotel not pub, but its dark and friendly comfortable bar makes a good coffee break, and has good bar snacks, helpful staff, Adnams, good wines inc lots of half bottles, also good value if not cheap restaurant meals, sunny conservatory; terrace tables, extensive grounds with lake, leisure centre and swimming pool, good bedrooms

(George Atkinson, Mrs Ann Faulkner, J F M and M West, Pamela Goodwyn)
YAXLEY [TM1173]
Auberge IP23 8BZ [Ipswich Rd (A140 Ipswich—Norwich)]: Former Bull, with good food using local supplies, big fireplace in pretty dining area, beams and timbers; bedrooms *(Sarah Flynn)*

Post Office address codings confusingly give the impression that some pubs are in Suffolk, when they're really in Cambridgeshire, Essex or Norfolk (which is where we list them).

Surrey

Pubs here are among the country's most expensive, both for drinks and for food. So in our choices, both for the main section and among the small-print entries at the end of the chapter, we have done our best to point you towards the pubs which – even if they are more expensive than elsewhere – give good value in comparison with the local competition. Despite its proximity to large towns and London, Surrey has some delightful rural enclaves, and fortunately it's in these that a good many of our main entries are to be found. Our three new main entries are each in or close to pleasant countryside. The Jolly Farmer in Bramley has a terrific range of real ales, with scope for walks nearby; the Cricketers near Cobham has a lovely setting and garden, and its food, though somewhat pricy, is above average; and the Fox & Hounds at Englefield Green is a very friendly all-rounder, handy for walks in Windsor Park. Other pubs here have been winning recent warm praise for quite a variety of different qualities. The charmingly unspoilt Seven Stars at Leigh stands out particularly for its delightfully welcoming licensees, who provide consistently interesting food and wines, and now have their own smokery for meat and fish. Carefully sourced food and outstandingly well chosen wines are keynotes at the Inn at West End, though it keeps a bar area where you can feel comfortable just enjoying a drink. The Running Horses at Mickleham is another smartly upmarket all-rounder, with very good food and drinks. The Surrey Oaks at Newdigate has much more modestly priced bar food, and its choice of particularly interesting real ales from uncommon breweries is really special. Other pubs doing well, and all in fine country settings, are the Donkey at Charleshill (very welcoming, and with generous food), the Plough in Cobham (a fine all-rounder on the edge of parkland, useful for the Watts Gallery), the Withies at Compton (an upscale dining pub with abundant character, and some enjoyably pubby aspects too, as well as an attractive garden), the Parrot at Forest Green (with meat from their own farm, fine gardens, very interesting drinks, and a choice view of the village cricket pitch), and the Three Horseshoes at Thursley (saved from redevelopment by local villagers who have turned it into a very civilised all-rounder, with interesting very locally sourced food). The Mill at Elstead, a well converted watermill, enjoys a particularly appealing waterside garden. As you can see above, there is plenty of good food to be found here. For a special meal out, its consistently rewarding and interesting food in civilised surroundings make the Inn at West End our choice as Surrey Dining Pub of the Year. In the Lucky Dip section at the end of the chapter you'll find quite a few Chef & Brewers and Vintage Inns; this is an area where these chains have obviously found it rewarding to invest in often substantial improvements. Perhaps for much the same reason, it's also an area which has quite a lot of good modern refurbishments, bright and clean, of old or ancient buildings. Whatever their nature, pubs in this section which currently stand out include the Abinger Hatch on Abinger Common, Jolly Farmers at Buckland, Prince of Wales in Esher, Good Intent at Puttenham, Anchor at Pyrford Lock, Skimmington Castle on Reigate Heath, White Horse in Shere, and Old Crown and Prince of Wales, both in Weybridge. The most popular local brewer is Hogs Back, and Surrey Hills, started only very recently, is gaining ground rapidly; you may also find Pilgrim, Waylands and Leith Hill.

BRAMLEY
TQ0044 MAP 3

Jolly Farmer 🍺
High Street; GU5 0HB

Relaxed village inn near the Surrey hills, with very wide selection of beers, pleasant staff and daily specials

'Everything a pub should be,' enthused one reader of this welcoming village inn within a few miles of Winkworth Arboretum and walks up St Martha's Hill. Its attractive interior is a mixture of brick and timbering, with an open fireplace and timbered semi-partitions, and furnished with a homely miscellany of wooden tables and chairs; various assemblages of plates, enamel advertising signs, antique bottles, prints and old tools hang from the walls; the back restaurant area is inviting, piped music, dominoes and board games. Friendly staff serve up to 20 different national and local real ales each week, typically with eight on at a time, with Badger First Gold and Hogsback HBB alongside guests from brewers such as B&T, Brentwood, Harwich, Kings, Rebellion and Rudgate; also three changing belgian draught beers and 18 wines by the glass. There are six cottagey bedrooms and a serviced flat; we would welcome reports from readers who stay here.

🍽 The bar menu specials change daily, and could include starters such as soup, tiger prawns in garlic butter, caesar salad or mediterranean vegetable tart, and main courses such as beef, bacon and mushroom pie, double lamb chop with mediterranean vegetable stack and grilled halloumi cheese, king scallops, vegetarian olive tapenade risotto, and sausages and mash. *Starters/Snacks: £4.50 to £6.50. Main Courses: £7.50 to £17.50. Puddings: £4.50 to £4.95*

Free house ~ Licensees Steve and Chris Hardstone ~ Real ale ~ Bar food (12-2.30, 6(7 Sun)-9.30) ~ Restaurant ~ (01483) 893355 ~ Children welcome until 9.30pm ~ Dogs allowed in bar ~ Live music first or second Tues ~ Open 11am-11.30pm(midnight Sat); 12-11.30 Sun ~ Bedrooms: £60S(£65B)/£70S(£75B)

Recommended by Phil Bryant, Guy Wightman

CHARLESHILL
SU8844 MAP 2

Donkey
B3001 Milford—Farnham near Tilford; coming from Elstead, turn left as soon as you see pub sign; GU10 2AU

Beamed, cottagey dining pub with attractive garden and good local walks

Readers enjoy the warm welcome and generous portions of food here, and you might meet its two friendly donkeys, Pip and Dusty, a reminder that the pub takes its name from much earlier donkeys that were once kept to transport loads up the hill opposite. Its saloon has lots of tables for dining, polished stirrups, lamps and watering cans on the walls, and prettily cushioned built-in wall benches, while the lounge has a fine high-backed settle, highly polished horsebrasses, and swords on the walls and beams. All their wines (including champagne) are available by the glass, and you'll also find two real ales on handpump, with Greene Abbot and Old Speckled Hen, or a guest such as Fullers London Pride or Harveys Sussex on handpump; piped music. The attractive garden also has a terrace and plenty of seats and there's a wendy house. On the edge of woodlands, it has been a pub since 1850. Attractive local walking areas through heathlands include Crooksbury Common, and there are paths into the woods around the pub.

⑪ Friendly staff serve lunchtime sandwiches, soup, chicken liver and brandy pâté, grilled field mushroom with melted goats cheese, moules marinières, scampi, medallions of fillet steak with madeira and stilton sauce, and daily specials that take in quite a few fish dishes such as dover sole, cod mornay, crab or lobster; Sunday roast. *Starters/Snacks: £4.50 to £9.95. Main Courses: £4.50 to £19.95. Puddings: £4.95*

Greene King ~ Lease Lee and Helen Francis ~ Real ale ~ Bar food (12-2.30(4 Sun), 6-9.30(8.30 Sun)) ~ Restaurant ~ (01252) 702124 ~ Children welcome ~ Dogs welcome ~ Open 11.30-3, 6-11; 12-10.30 Sun

Recommended by Michael Sargent, John and Joyce Snell, J and E Dakin, Mr and Mrs A Curry, Richard and Sissel Harris, PHB, Peter Sampson

COBHAM
TQ1058   MAP 3

Cricketers

Downside Common, S of town past Cobham Park; KT11 3NX

Lots of character, with idyllic village green location, pretty garden, low beams; good bar food, served all day on Sunday

You get classic views over the village green from metal tables on a terrace outside this characterful pub or from its delightful neatly kept garden – itself stocked with standard roses, magnolias, dahlias, bedding plants, urns and hanging baskets. Inside, watch your head on the low, heavy oak beams (some have crash-pads on them), where crooked standing timbers create a comfortable open-plan layout, warmed by a blazing log fire. In places you can see the wide oak ceiling boards and ancient plastering laths. Furnishings are quite simple, and there are horsebrasses and big brass platters on the walls. Fullers London Pride and Greene King IPA and Old Speckled Hen are on handpump alongside a guest such as Hogs Back TEA, and there's a good choice of wines including several by the glass; piped music. It's worth arriving early (particularly on Sunday) to be sure of a table; one reader reported there were no high chairs available; they may retain your credit card as you dine.

⑪ Bar food (not cheap but well above average) includes sandwiches (weekdays only), soup, duck pâté with mango chutney and toast, smoked haddock and spring onion fishcakes with crème fraîche, haddock in beer batter with chips, various pies such as steak and Guinness or chicken, mushroom and leek, and pork and leek sausages with mash, plus daily specials; there's also a separate, more elaborate restaurant menu. *Starters/Snacks: £4.25 to £10.50. Main Courses: £8.95 to £16.95. Puddings: £4.95*

Enterprise ~ Tenant Mustafa Ozcan ~ Real ale ~ Bar food (12-3, 6.30-10; 12-8 Sun) ~ Restaurant ~ (01932) 862105 ~ Children welcome ~ Dogs welcome ~ Open 11-11; 12-10.30 Sun

Recommended by K F Winknorth, Phil Bryant, Ian Phillips, Mr and Mrs Mike Pearson, Geoffrey Kemp, Stephen Funnell, Dr Ron Cox, Susan and John Douglas

Plough ♀

3.2 miles from M25 junction 10; A3, then right on A245 at roundabout; in Cobham, right at Downside signpost into Downside Bridge Road; Plough Lane; KT11 3LT

Civilised and welcoming country local with reasonably priced lunchtime snacks, more elaborate pricier evening menu, and garden

Very popular, this thriving pub has a buoyant and cheerful local atmosphere in its attractive low-beamed bar. Round to the right, a cosy parquet-floored snug has cushioned seats built into nice stripped pine panelling, and horseracing prints. The main part is carpeted, with a mix of pubby furnishings, and past some standing timbers a few softly padded banquettes around good-sized tables by a log fire in the ancient stone fireplace. Adnams Bitter, Badger K&B Sussex Bitter and Hogs Back TEA are on handpump, a fine choice of wines by the glass including champagne, and good coffee – served with hot milk. The restaurant part (with pews, bare boards and white table linen) rambles around behind this. A terrace has picnic-sets sheltering beside a very high garden wall. Service is swift and good-natured and there are disabled access and facilities.

⌘ You order your meal from a separate servery. The lunchtime snack menu includes sandwiches, filled baguettes, soup, ploughman's, omelettes, pasta of the day, cheeseburger, rib-eye steak, and daily specials; the evening à la carte menu features whitebait, trout, steaks, rack of lamb with rosemary, steak, kidney and mushroom pie, and seasonal dishes such as pheasant, asparagus or lobster; puddings. *Starters/Snacks: £4.95 to £8.95. Main Courses: £6.95 to £12.95. Puddings: £4.95*

Massive ~ Manager Joe Worley ~ Real ale ~ Bar food (12-2.30(3 Sat, 6 Sun), 7-9.30; not Fri, Sat evening) ~ Restaurant ~ (01932) 862514 ~ Children welcome ~ Dogs allowed in bar ~ Occasional live music ~ Open 11-11; 12-10.30 Sun

Recommended by Rita and Keith Pollard, C and R Bromage, David M Smith, Ian Phillips, Phil Bryant, Geoffrey Kemp, Piotr Chodzko-Zajko, David Twitchett, Tom and Ruth Rees

COLDHARBOUR   TQ1544   MAP 3

Plough ⌘

Village signposted in the network of small roads around Leith Hill; RH5 6HD

Good walkers' drinks stop with own-brew beers

A useful place to know about if you're walking or cycling in some of the best scenery in the Surrey hills – around Leith Hill or Friday Street for instance – this pub has its own brewery (Leith Hill) which produces the excellent Crooked Furrow, Hoppily Ever After and Tallywhacker which are served here on handpump, alongside a couple of guests such as Ringwood Best and Timothy Taylors Landlord; also Biddenden farm cider and several wines by the glass; note that they may charge for tap water, a policy on which we're not at all keen. As we went to press, the brewery was temporarily closed due to illness, but we understand it will reopen by the time the *Guide* is published. Two bars (each with a lovely open fire) have stripped light beams and timbering in warm-coloured dark ochre walls, with quite unusual little chairs around the tables in the snug red-carpeted games room on the left (with darts, board games and cards), and little decorative plates on the walls; the one on the right leads through to the candlelit restaurant; at busy times it may be hard to find somewhere to sit if you're not dining; piped music, TV. If you stay here, it may be advisable to ask for a quieter room not over the bar. The front and the terraced back gardens have picnic-sets and tubs. More reports please.

⌘ Straightforward bar food includes soup and pies; children's portions available. *Starters/Snacks: £5.95 to £7.95. Main Courses: £7.95 to £15.95. Puddings: £5.95*

Own brew ~ Licensees Richard and Anna Abrehart ~ Real ale ~ Bar food (12-2.30(3 Sat, Sun), 6-9.30(9 Sun)) ~ Restaurant ~ (01306) 711793 ~ Children welcome if dining; not in accommodation ~ Dogs welcome ~ Open 11.30-11.30; 12-10.30 Sun ~ Bedrooms: £69.50S/£79.50S(£95B)

Recommended by Pete Baker, John Branston, Tony and Jill Radnor, Kevin Thorpe, Sara Fulton, Roger Baker, Tony Hobden, Norma and Noel Thomas, T S Meakin, Susan and John Douglas, Phil and Sally Gorton, A J Longshaw, Derek and Heather Manning

COMPTON   SU9646   MAP 2

Withies

Withies Lane; pub signposted from B3000; GU3 1JA

Great atmosphere in 16th-c pub of considerable character, with a slight french slant to its food side

On the edge of Loseley Park and close to the extraordinary Watts Gallery of works by the Victorian artist GF Watts, this 16th-c tavern has been sympathetically altered over the years, and keeps a cosy low-beamed bar. It's a very civilised place, with logs burning even on cool summer days in its massive inglenook, some fine 17th-c carved panels between the windows, and a splendid art nouveau settle among the old sewing-machine tables. Even when it's busy, the pleasant uniformed staff are helpful and efficient; they have Adnams, Badger K&B and Hogs Back TEA on handpump. A mass of flowers borders the neat lawn in front, and weeping willows overhang the immaculate garden, where there are plenty of dining tables under an arbour of creeper-hung trellises, with more on a crazy-paved terrace and others under old apple trees.

▥ Good bar food includes sandwiches, filled baked potatoes, ploughman's, seafood platter, cumberland sausage with onion gravy, and more elaborate choices such as seafood crêpe mornay, pawpaw with fresh crab, half a roast duckling with orange sauce, veal escalope marsala and roasted rack of lamb with rosemary. *Starters/Snacks: £4.00 to £9.50. Main Courses: £12.50 to £22.75. Puddings: £5.75*

Free house ~ Licensees Brian and Hugh Thomas ~ Real ale ~ Bar food (12-2.30, 7-9.30) ~ Restaurant ~ (01483) 421158 ~ Children welcome ~ Open 11-4, 6-11; 12-4 Sun; closed Sun evening

Recommended by Marianne and Peter Stevens, Helen and Brian Edgeley, Ian Phillips, Derek and Heather Manning, R and M Thomas, R Lake, Andrea Rampley, Michael Sargent, Mrs Margo Finlay, Jörg Kasprowski, Norma and Noel Thomas, P and J Shapley, John Evans

EASHING   SU9543   MAP 2

Stag ♀

Lower Eashing; Eashing signposted off A3 southbound, S of Hurtmore turn-off; or pub signposted off A283 just SE of exit roundabout at N end of A3 Milford bypass; GU7 2QG

Gentle improvements by to lovely old riverside pub with attractive garden

The Georgian brick façade masks a much older, attractively opened-up interior including a charming old-fashioned locals' bar on the right with red and black quarry tiles by the counter. A cosy gently lit snug beyond has a low white plank ceiling, a big stag print and stag's head on dark green walls, books on shelves by the log fire, and sturdy cushioned housekeeper's chairs grouped around dark tables on the brick floor. An extensive blue-carpeted area rambles around on the left, with similar comfortable dark furniture, some smaller country prints and decorative plates on red, brown or cream walls, and towards the back a big woodburning stove in a capacious fireplace under a long mantelbeam; piped music and daily papers. Hogs Back TEA and a couple of guests such as Fullers London Pride and Shepherd Neame Spitfire on handpump, and several wines by the glass. The river room looks out on to mature trees by a millstream, and there are picnic-sets and tables under cocktail parasols set out on a terrace and in a lantern-lit arbour. A couple of readers have found the service lacked warmth. More reports please.

▥ As well as ploughman's, hot ciabattas and steaks, the seasonally changing blackboard menu might include starters like leek and ham hock terrine, halloumi and roast pepper tartlets, and fish or meat platters, with main courses like ham, egg and chips, baked salmon and smoked haddock fishcake, free-range chicken breast stuffed with feta cheese and sunblush tomato, home-smoked duck breast salad, tempura prawns, and burgers, with puddings like chocolate summer fruit cheesecake. *Starters/Snacks: £5.00 to £10.00. Main Courses: £9.00 to £19.00. Puddings: £4.00 to £8.00*

Punch ~ Lease Mark Robson ~ Real ale ~ Restaurant ~ (01483) 421568 ~ Dogs allowed in bar ~ Open 12-3, 5-11; 12-11 Sat; 12-10.30 Sun ~ Bedrooms: /£65S

Recommended by Ian Phillips, Conor McGaughey, Liz and Brian Barnard

ELSTEAD   SU9044   MAP 2

Mill at Elstead ♀ ◧

Farnham Road (B3001 just W of village, which is itself between Farnham and Milford); GU8 6LE

Fascinating and beautifully located watermill conversion, great service, big attractive waterside garden, Fullers beers, bar food

This is a really special location for a pub, in a sensitively converted largely 18th-c watermill that rises through four storeys, with the River Wey beneath. Inside, you are greeted by a great internal waterwheel, and the gentle rush of the stream turning below your feet. Throughout, big windows make the most of the charming surroundings – the broad millpond, swans and weeping willows. The spacious building (which can feel a bit cavernously empty at quieter times) has a good rambling series of linked bar areas on the ground floor, and further seating including a restaurant area upstairs. It changes in mood from one part to the next: brown leather armchairs and antique engravings by a longcase clock; neat modern tables and dining chairs on pale woodstrip flooring; big country tables and rustic prints on broad ceramic tiles; dark boards and beams, iron pillars and stripped masonry; a log fire in a huge inglenook, or a trendy finned stove with a fat black stovepipe. Service is commendably helpful, friendly and personal. They have Fullers Discovery, London Pride, ESB and perhaps a seasonal beer on handpump and a good range of wines by the glass; piped music; dogs allowed in certain areas only. There are plenty of picnic-sets in a variety of appealing waterside seating areas outside, with flares and good floodlighting at night.

🍴 **Freshly prepared bar food includes soup, tortilla and dips, sharing platters, greek salad, sweet potato risotto, organic salmon, battered hake and chips, steakburger, and tuna steak salad, with a carvery on winter Sundays.** *Starters/Snacks: £3.95. Main Courses: £8.95. Puddings: £4.25*

Fullers ~ Managers Carol and Brian Jewell ~ Real ale ~ Bar food (12-9.30(10 Fri, Sat; 8 Sun)) ~ Restaurant ~ (01252) 703333 ~ Children welcome ~ Open 10(11 Sat)-11; 11.30-10.30 Sun

Recommended by Ian Phillips, Phil Bryant, Susan and Nigel Brookes, Martin and Karen Wake, Simon and Sally Small, R Lake

ENGLEFIELD GREEN   SU9872   MAP 2
Fox & Hounds
Bishopsgate Rd, off A328 N of Egham; TW20 0XU

Spotless and friendly tavern, useful for Windsor Park; log fires, and tasty bar food

Very usefully placed for strolls in Windsor Park, this friendly 17th-c pub is close to the main gate to the Savile Garden. It's a civilised place with good sturdy wooden tables and chairs, three log fires, bare floorboards and leather sofas around the bar area, and brick walls, hung with modern prints, in the J-shaped dining area (which extends out into the conservatory). Courage Best, Hogs Back Brewery TEA and a guest from a brewery such as Brakspears on handpump, and an extensive wine list with ten wines by the glass as well as several malt whiskies. There are picnic-sets on the terrace, on the decking and on the front lawn.

🍴 **Enjoyable bar food includes an interesting choice of sandwiches, soup, fishcakes, chicken liver parfait, mussel and clam linguini, chicken breast wrapped in bacon, sausages and mash, wild mushroom and mascarpone risotto, roast shoulder of lamb, rib-eye steak, and puddings; good value two-course menu.** *Starters/Snacks: £4.95 to £7.25. Main Courses: £9.95 to £15.95. Puddings: £4.75 to £7.25*

Old Monk ~ Lease Andy Eaton-Carr ~ Real ale ~ Bar food (12-2.30 Mon-Thurs; 12-4 Fri-Sun; filled baguettes only Sun) ~ Restaurant ~ (01784) 433098 ~ Children welcome ~ Dogs allowed in bar ~ Live jazz Mon evening ~ Open 11-11; 12-10.30 Sun

Recommended by Martin and Karen Wake, Ian Phillips, Jack and Sandra Clarfelt

ESHER   TQ1566   MAP 3
Marneys ♀
Alma Road (one way only), Weston Green; heading N on A309 from A307 roundabout, after Lamb & Star pub turn left into Lime Tree Avenue (signposted to All Saints Parish Church), then left at T junction into Chestnut Avenue; KT10 8JN

Cottagey little pub with nordic influence (particularly in the menu), and attractive garden

With a pleasant location by a rural-feeling wooded common, this cottagey pub is an unexpected scandinavian enclave, whose norwegian owners put some interesting national dishes on the menu, and the norwegian national anthem and flags feature in the décor. The chatty low-beamed and black and white plank-panelled bar (it's worth arriving early as it does get full) has shelves of hens and ducks and other ornaments, small blue-curtained windows, and perhaps horseracing on the unobtrusive corner TV. On the left, past a little cast-iron woodburning stove, a dining area (somewhat roomier but still small) has big pine tables, pews and pale country kitchen chairs, with attractive goose pictures. Drinks include Courage Best, Fullers London Pride and Wells & Youngs Bombardier on handpump, about 16 wines by the glass, norwegian schnapps and good coffee. Service by friendly staff is quick and efficient; and they have daily papers on sticks. The pleasantly planted sheltered garden has a decked area, bar, black picnic-sets and tables under green and blue canvas parasols, and occasionally a spanish guitarist playing under the willow tree on summer afternoons to accompany a barbecue, weather allowing; the front terrace has dark blue cast-iron tables and chairs under matching parasols, with some more black tables too, with table lighting and views over the common and duck pond. More reports please.

🍴 The sensibly small choice of well liked food includes some scandinavian dishes: baguettes, warm smoked salmon blinis, frikadellen (danish pork meat cake), dill-marinated herring fillets topped with onion and apple cream, specials and pudding. *Starters/Snacks: £6.50 to £7.50. Main Courses: £7.00 to £11.00. Puddings: £4.95*

Free house ~ Licensee Henrik Platou ~ Real ale ~ Bar food (12-2.15(12.30-3 Sun); not evenings) ~ (020) 8398 4444 ~ Children welcome until 6pm ~ Dogs welcome ~ Open 11-11; 12-10.30 Sun

Recommended by Ian Phillips, LM

FOREST GREEN
TQ1241 MAP 3

Parrot ★

B2127 just W of junction with B2126, SW of Dorking; RH5 5RZ

Beamed pub with produce from the owners' farm on the menu and in attached shop, good range of drinks, and lovely garden

With truly local food and a range of five real ales, this is a well known venue yet retains its character of a village pub too. As well as a huge inglenook fireplace, it has a fine profusion of heavy beams, timbers and flagstones, with a couple of cosy rambling areas hidden away behind the fireplace. There are some more tables opposite the long brick bar counter, which has a few unusual wooden chairs in front. Ringwood Best and Wells & Youngs Pale Ale are served alongside three guests such as Timothy Taylors Landlord, Wells & Youngs Bombardier and Wychwood Hobgoblin on handpump, freshly squeezed orange juice, local farm apple juice and 15 wines by the glass; newspapers. Tables outside in front face the village cricket field and there are more among several attractive gardens, one with apple trees and rose beds. The owners have their own farm not far away at Coldharbour and you can buy their meats, as well as cheese, cured and smoked hams, pies, bread and preserves in their farm shop at the pub.

🍴 With the pork, beef and lamb on the frequently changing menu coming from their own farm, the accent is particularly on meat; dishes might include soup, pork, venison and cognac terrine, roasted mediterranean vegetables and haloumi bruschetta, slow-braised beef in Guinness, grilled pollack fillet with wilted spinach and chive cream sauce, pork rib-eye with cider sauce, lamb and coriander burger with hand-cut chips, roasted butternut squash stuffed with vegetables and goats cheese, with puddings like rhubarb fool or treacle and pistachio tart, and an english cheese platter. *Starters/Snacks: £4.50 to £5.75. Main Courses: £9.50 to £14.50. Puddings: £3.50 to £5.75*

Free house ~ Licensee Charles Gotto ~ Real ale ~ Bar food (12-3(5 Sun), 6-10; not Sun evening) ~ Restaurant ~ (01306) 621339 ~ No children in restaurant after 7pm ~ Dogs allowed in bar ~ Open 11(12 Sun)-11(midnight Sat)

Recommended by Gordon Stevenson, Sheila Topham, Derek Thomas, Tony and Jill Radnor, Mike Gorton, Susan and John Douglas, Ian and Barbara Rankin, Tim and Alice Wright, R Lake, Tom and Ruth Rees, Mike and Lynn Robinson, C and R Bromage, Guy Vowles, Bernard Stradling, Derek and Maggie Washington, Pam and Alan Neale, Mr and Mrs A H Young, Conor McGaughey, Tim Crook, Hunter and Christine Wright

LEIGH   TQ2147   MAP 3

Seven Stars ♀

Dawes Green, S of A25 Dorking—Reigate; RH2 8NP

Popular welcoming dining pub with really enjoyable food and good wines

With no piped music or other modern sound intrusions, this extremely welcoming tile-hung 17th-c tavern has just the murmur of contented chatter to greet you as you enter, and the flair of the licensees has attracted much praise from readers. The comfortable saloon bar has a 1633 inglenook fireback with the royal coat of arms, and there's a plainer public bar. The sympathetically done restaurant extension at the side incorporates 17th-c floor timbers imported from a granary. Greene King Old Speckled Hen, Fullers London Pride and Wells & Youngs Bitter are served from handpump, alongside decent wines with ten by the glass. Outside, there's plenty of room in the beer garden at the front, on the terrace and in the side garden.

🍽 **Available in both the bar or restaurant very good food includes lunchtime ciabattas and baked potatoes, soup, risotto of the day as a starter or main course, whitebait, warm goats cheese salad with roasted beetroot and walnuts, rib-eye steak, spiced lamb shank with dauphinoise potatoes, roasted chicken with truffle-scented mash and morel mushroom sauce, breast of duck, and puddings like chocolate marquise or bread and butter pudding. Using their own smoker, they smoke meats and fish during the summer months for dishes such as smoked chicken and avocado salad and hickory-smoked ribs. They do two sittings for Sunday lunch. It's advisable to book at all times.** *Starters/Snacks: £4.50 to £6.95. Main Courses: £8.50 to £14.95. Puddings: £3.95 to £4.95*

Punch ~ Lease David and Rebecca Pellen ~ Real ale ~ Bar food (12-2.30(4 Sun), 6-9(9.30 Fri, Sat); not Sun evening) ~ Restaurant ~ (01306) 611254 ~ Dogs allowed in bar ~ Open 12-11(9 Sun)

Recommended by Colin McKerrow, Ian Macro, C and R Bromage, Terry Buckland, Grahame Brooks

LINGFIELD   TQ3844   MAP 3

Hare & Hounds 🍴

Turn off B2029 N at the Crowhurst/Edenbridge signpost, into Lingfield Common Road (coming from the A22 towards Lingfield on B2029, this is the second road on your left); RH7 6BZ

Interesting bar food at easy-going pub, interestingly decorated and more sophisticated than it looks; garden

By no means smartened up, this dining pub is comfortably individual and informal in style. The smallish open-plan bar is light and airy by day, with soft lighting and nightlights burning on a good mix of different-sized tables at night – when it's full of the chatter of happy customers, some drinking, some eating. Partly bare boards and partly flagstones, it has a variety of well worn scatter-cushioned dining chairs and other seats from pews to a button-back leather chesterfield, and black and white pictures of jazz musicians on brown tongue-and-groove panelling. The bar opens into a quieter dining area with big abstract-expressionist paintings. Adnams, Fullers London Pride and a guest such as Shepherd Neame Spitfire are on handpump, and eight of their decent wines are available by the glass. Tables are set out in a pleasant split-level garden, with some on decking. This is good walking country near Haxted Mill – walkers can leave their boots in the porch.

🍽 **Daily changing bar food (booking advised) might include starters such as soup, smoked leg of free-range lamb with baby beetroot and goats cheese, seared pigeon breast with red onion tart, or poached asparagus, main courses like braised duck, cumberland sausage and mash, slow-roast pork belly with steamed clams, and fried black bream with fish chowder, and puddings like passion fruit crème caramel or plum and walnut samosas.** *Starters/Snacks: £6.50 to £9.95. Main Courses: £7.95 to £17.50. Puddings: £5.50*

Punch ~ Lease Fergus Greer ~ Real ale ~ Bar food (12-2.30(3 Sun), 7-9.30) ~ Restaurant ~ (01342) 832351 ~ Children welcome ~ Dogs allowed in bar ~ Open 12-11 (midnight Sat); 12-4 Sun; closed Sun evening

Recommended by R J Anderson, Kevin Thorpe, Evelyn and Derek Walter, Ian Wilson, Annette Tress, Gary Smith, Neil Hardwick, Grahame Brooks

MICKLEHAM   TQ1753   MAP 3

Running Horses 🍴 ☐ 🛏

Old London Road (B2209); RH5 6DU

Upmarket pub with elegant restaurant and comfortable bar, sandwiches through to very imaginative dishes

Run with care by attentive staff, this is an accomplished all-rounder, much liked both as a drinking haunt and as a place to eat. It has two calmly relaxing bar rooms, neatly kept and spaciously open-plan, with fresh flowers or a fire in an inglenook at one end, lots of race tickets hanging from a beam, some really good racing cartoons, hunting pictures and Hogarth prints, dark carpets, cushioned wall settles and other dining chairs around straightforward pubby tables and bar stools. Adnams, Fullers London Pride, Shepherd Neame Spitfire and Wells & Youngs Bitter are on handpump alongside good wines by the glass, from a serious list; piped music. The extensive restaurant leads straight out of the bar and, although it is set out quite formally with crisp white cloths and candles on each table, it shares the thriving atmosphere of the bar. There are picnic-sets on a terrace in front by lovely flowering tubs and hanging baskets, with a peaceful view of the old church with its strange stubby steeple.

🍴 **There is a tempting choice of food, with a bar menu including soup, well filled lunchtime chunky sandwiches, fish pie, croque monsieur, pea and spinach risotto, salmon and crab fishcakes, steak and Guinness pudding, and bubble and squeak topped with ham and poached egg with mornay sauce, as well as a more expensive restaurant menu (which you can eat from in the bar) featuring items like smoked bacon and duck liver parfait, tunisian aubergine, basil and mozzarella roulade, shellfish chowder, seared monkfish wrapped in parma ham, roast rump of lamb with garlic confit and beetroot chips, grilled fillet or sirloin, and honey-glazed duck breast with blackberry and port sauce, with puddings such as dark chocolate mousse or pear, apple and cinnamon cheesecake.**
Starters/Snacks: £5.25 to £9.50. Main Courses: £9.50 to £14.75. Puddings: £5.75

Punch ~ Lease Steve and Josie Slayford ~ Real ale ~ Bar food (12-2.30(3 Sat, Sun), 7(6.30 Sun)-9.30) ~ Restaurant ~ (01372) 372279 ~ Children in function room only ~ Dogs allowed in bar ~ Open 11.30-11; 12-10.30 Sun ~ Bedrooms: £90(£90S)(£105B)/£105(£105S)(£130B)

Recommended by Sheila Topham, Ian Phillips, Conor McGaughey, Pam and Alan Neale, N R White, Paul Humphreys

NEWDIGATE   TQ2043   MAP 3

Surrey Oaks 🍺

Off A24 S of Dorking, via Beare Green; Parkgate Road; RH5 5DZ

Interesting real ales at traditional pub with straightforward bar food and enjoyable garden for children

The friendly landlord at this former wheelwright's cottage serves an excellent range of beers from small breweries along with a choice of sensibly priced home-made bar food. The pubby interior is interestingly divided into four areas; in the older part locals gather by an open fire in a snug little beamed room, and a standing area with unusually large flagstones has a woodburning stove in an inglenook fireplace. Rustic tables are dotted around the light and airy main lounge to the left, and there's a pool table in the separate games room; fruit machine and piped classical music. You can try five well kept real ales on handpump, with Harveys Best and Surrey Hills Ranmore alongside three constantly rotating guests such as Millstones Vale mill, Titanic Stout and Tower Spring Equinox; there are also belgian bottled beers, several wines by the glass and a farm cider like Mole's Black Rat and a farm perry such as Weston's Country, and there are beer festivals over the May Whitsun and August bank holiday weekends. The garden is nicely complicated, with a terrace, and a rockery with pools and a waterfall, with a play area and two goats to keep children amused.

🍴 Reasonably priced bar food includes filled baguettes, ploughman's, ham, eggs and chips, battered fish, with specials such as sausage and mash, fish pie, steak and ale pie and lambs liver, bacon and onion gravy; Sunday lunch features a choice of three roasts. They may retain your credit card while you eat. *Starters/Snacks: £4.00 to £5.00. Main Courses: £7.00 to £8.00. Puddings: £3.50*

Admiral Taverns ~ Lease Ken Proctor ~ Real ale ~ Bar food (12-2(2.15 Sat, Sun), 6.30(7 Sat)-9; not Sun or Mon evenings) ~ Restaurant ~ (01306) 631200 ~ Children welcome ~ Dogs allowed in bar ~ Open 11.30-2.30, 5.30-11; 11.30-3, 6-11 Sat; 12-10.30 Sun

Recommended by Ian Phillips, Conor McGaughey, Norma and Noel Thomas, Sara Fulton, Roger Baker, C and R Bromage, Bruce Bird

THURSLEY   SU9039   MAP 2

Three Horseshoes

Dye House Road, just off A3 SW of Godalming; GU8 6QD

Appealing and civilised cottagey village pub with good restaurant food as well as bar snacks

An appealing combination of mildly upmarket country local and attractive restaurant, and run by a group of locals who rescued it from closure, this congenial tile-hung village pub is well placed for bracing heathland walks over Thursley Common. The beamed front bar has Fullers London Pride, Hogs Back TEA and a guest such as Surrey Hills Shere Drop on handpump, farm ciders, a winter log fire, and warmly welcoming service; piped music. There's some emphasis on the attractive restaurant area behind, with beamery and paintings of local scenes. The attractive two-acre garden has picnic-sets and a big play fort, and there are smarter comfortable chairs around terrace tables; pleasant views over the green. During summer they hold various events such as jazz evenings, barbecues and folk-dancing festivals.

🍴 Using vegetables grown in gardens in the village and trout caught in local streams and game shot in woods nearby, bar food includes chicken liver parfait, beetroot-cured salmon with crab salad, terrine of duck, rabbit and pigeon, cottage pie, smoked haddock and salmon fishcakes, black pudding with poached duck egg and bacon, fried skate, and puddings like cappuccino crème brûlée or warm chocolate brownie; Sunday roast; they make their own bread, ice-cream and pasta. *Starters/Snacks: £5.00 to £12.00. Main Courses: £9.00 to £20.00. Puddings: £4.50 to £5.50*

Free house ~ Licensees David Alders and Sandra Proni ~ Real ale ~ Bar food (12.30-2.15, 7-9.15; 12-3 Sun; not Sun evening) ~ Restaurant ~ (01252) 703268 ~ Children welcome ~ Dogs allowed in bar ~ Open 12-3, 5.30-11; 12-11 Sat; 12-10 Sun

Recommended by Richard Freeman, Michael Sargent, Ian Phillips, Phil and Sally Gorton, Christopher and Elise Way, Michael B Griffith, Dan and Holly Pitcher, Mr and Mrs Gordon Turner, Bernard Stradling

WEST END   SU9461   MAP 2

Inn at West End 🍴 🍷

Just under 2.5 miles from M3 junction 3; A322 S, on right; GU24 9PW
SURREY DINING PUB OF THE YEAR

Enjoyable fresh-feeling dining pub, with prompt and friendly service; excellent food, good wines, and terrace

The thoughtfully created food here is well complemented by the knowledgeably chosen house wines (16 by the glass) that lean particularly towards Spain and Portugal (they also hold wine tastings here), several sherries and dessert wines, and as the very enthusiastic landlord is a wine merchant they can supply by the case. The interior is open-plan, with bare boards, attractive modern prints on canary yellow walls above a red dado, and a line of dining tables with crisp white linen over pale yellow tablecloths on the left. The bar counter (Fullers London Pride and a guest such as Wells & Youngs Bitter on handpump), straight ahead as you come in, is quite a focus, with chatting regulars on the comfortable bar stools. The area on the right has a pleasant relaxed atmosphere, with blue-cushioned wall benches and dining chairs around solid pale wood tables, broadsheet daily papers, magazines and a row of reference books on the brick chimneybreast above a woodburning stove. This opens into a garden room, which in turn leads to a pergola-covered (with grapevine and clematis) terrace.

🍴 **Skilfully prepared using carefully sourced ingredients (some of the herbs and vegetables are grown here, they pluck their own game and use organic meat), not cheap but very good bar food might include soup, roasted field mushroom filled with welsh rarebit, lightly curried smoked haddock kedgeree, cumberland sausages with mash, selection of fresh fish with warm roasted red pepper and fennel salad, slow-roasted lamb and caramelised onion filo parcel, spinach, mushroom and mozzarella bake in garlic cream, and sirloin steak, with puddings such as banana bavarois or crème brûlée.** *Starters/Snacks: £5.25 to £7.95. Main Courses: £11.95 to £17.75. Puddings: £5.25 to £7.25*

Enterprise ~ Lease Gerry and Ann Price ~ Real ale ~ Bar food (12-2.30, 6.30-9.30; 12-3, 6-9 Sun) ~ Restaurant ~ (01276) 858652 ~ Well-behaved children over 7 welcome in restaurant if dining ~ Dogs allowed in bar ~ Open 12-3, 5-11; 12-11 Sat; 12-10.30 Sun

Recommended by Guy Vowles, Guy Consterdine, Bernard Stradling, Philip and Jude Simmons, Ian Phillips, Guy Charrison, Edward Mirzoeff, John and Rosemary Haynes, P Waterman, Miss A E Dare

WEST HORSLEY   TQ0853   MAP 3
Barley Mow
Off A246 Leatherhead—Guildford at Bell & Colvill garage roundabout; The Street; KT24 6HR

Nice country pub with lunchtime snacks and more in the evening; garden

Just as we went to press this much-liked pub gained a new licensee, Mustafa Ozcan – who also runs the Cricketers at Cobham (another main entry), so we trust it will continue to hit good form. The low-beamed bar has Fullers London Pride, Greene King IPA, Shepherd Neame Spitfire and Wells & Youngs Special on handpump, several wines by the glass and decent spirits; daily papers, unobtrusive piped music and a wide-screen TV. The flagstoned part on the right probably dates from the 16th c, and with its big log fire under an unusual domed smoke canopy is quite a magnet for dogs and their owners at weekends. The left-hand side is carpeted, with comfortable library chairs, pubby tables (two of them copper-topped and framed with cast iron), cottagey lantern lighting, and another fireplace; there's also a less ancient front extension. On the left, the comfortable and softly lit restaurant includes what looks like a former barn, with pitched rafters. The good-sized garden, sheltered, well planted and neatly kept, has picnic-sets. Reports on the new regime please.

🍴 **You can eat from the same menu in the restaurant or the bar; food includes lunchtime baguettes, duck pâté, asparagus and poached egg with hollandaise sauce, chicken pie, steak and ale pie, tuna steak, rib-eye steak and filleted bass, with puddings like summer pudding or apple pie.** *Starters/Snacks: £5.50 to £7.50. Main Courses: £7.95 to £13.50. Puddings: £4.50*

Punch ~ Lease Mustafa Ozcan ~ Real ale ~ Bar food (12-2.30, 6-9(9.30 Fri, Sat); 12-4.30 Sun, not Sun evening) ~ Restaurant ~ (01483) 282693 ~ Children welcome away from bar ~ Dogs allowed in bar ~ Open 11-11; 12-10.30 Sun

Recommended by BOB

WORPLESDON   SU9854   MAP 3
Jolly Farmer
Burdenshott Road, off A320 Guildford—Woking, not in village – heading N from Guildford on the A320, turn left after Jacobs Well roundabout towards Worplesdon Station; OS Sheet 186 map reference 987542; GU3 3RN

Traditional place with pubby food, good service and attractive sheltered garden

With a very pleasant woodland setting, this village pub has a garden with grape vines and fruit trees, and picnic-sets under cocktail parasols. Inside, the bar retains a pubby feel, with dark beams and pub furniture; Fullers Discovery, London Pride and HSB are on handpump, with a guest such as Fullers IPA, and there's a large wine list with about 15 by the glass, as well as several malt whiskies. You can eat here, or in a dining extension with stripped brickwork, rugs on bare boards and well spaced tables; piped music. The car park is shared with Whitmore Common.

⚟ **Bar food (not cheap) includes sandwiches, soup, king crab and avocado salad, dill-cured salmon trout, chargrilled cape malay lamb rump, spinach and ricotta tortellini, steaks, monkfish, trio of gourmet sausages, tempura-battered cod and chips, stilton soufflé, picnic baskets for eating in or taking out, and puddings such as apple crumble and bread and butter pudding.** *Starters/Snacks: £4.95 to £8.95. Main Courses: £10.50 to £18.50. Puddings: £5.50*

Fullers ~ Managers Tara and Owen Bossert ~ Real ale ~ Bar food (12-3, 6-9.30; 12-8 Sun) ~ Restaurant ~ (01483) 234658 ~ No children in bar area after 9pm ~ Open 12-11(10.30 Sun)

Recommended by Ian Phillips, Gerry and Rosemary Dobson, Phil Bryant, John and Rosemary Haynes

LUCKY DIP

Besides the fully inspected pubs, you might like to try these Lucky Dips recommended to us and described by readers (if you do, please send us reports: feedback@thegoodpubguide.co.uk).

ABINGER COMMON [TQ1146]
☆ *Abinger Hatch* RH5 6HZ [off A25 W of Dorking, towards Abinger Hammer]: Nicely modernised dining pub in beautiful woodland spot, popular food (not Sun evening) from interesting light dishes up, Fullers London Pride and Ringwood Best and Fortyniner, sociable landlord and good service, heavy beams and flagstones, log fires, pews forming booths around oak tables in carpeted side area, plenty of space (very busy wknds); piped music, plain family extension; dogs welcome, tables and friendly ducks in nice garden, nr pretty church and pond, summer barbecues, open all day *(Conor McGaughey, C and R Bromage, Sue and Mike Todd, Richard and Sissel Harris, LYM, P Waterman, Ian Phillips)*

ADDLESTONE [TQ0563]
White Hart KT15 2DS [New Haw Rd (corner A318/B385)]: Smartly reworked in grey and white, bare boards and dark leather, rattan chairs in light dining area, food from baguettes to steaks inc full thai menu, Courage Best, Harveys and Wells & Youngs; play area in attractive garden by fast stream around Wey Navigation canal lock *(Ian Phillips, LYM)*

ASH VALE [SU8952]
Swan GU12 5HA [Hutton Rd, off Ash Vale Rd (B3411) via Heathvale Bridge Rd]: Big friendly three-room Chef & Brewer on the workaday Basingstoke Canal, huge choice of decent food all day (can take a while when very busy), good sandwiches, Courage Directors, Wells & Youngs and a guest beer, good value wines by the glass, good cheerful staff inc chefs in tall white hats, large log fire; piped classical music; children welcome, attractive garden, neat heated terraces and window boxes, open all day *(KC)*

BATTS CORNER [SU8140]
Blue Bell GU10 4EX: Light décor in country pub with enjoyable fresh food from

good choice of lunchtime sandwiches and salads up, pleasant chatty atmosphere, well kept fff Moondance, a beer brewed by them for the pub and Hogs Back TEA, half a dozen wines by the glass, log fire, restaurant; dogs and muddy boots welcome (numerous good walks nearby), big garden with rolling views and play area, handy for Alice Holt Forest *(N R White, BB, Phil and Sally Gorton)*

BETCHWORTH [TQ1950]
Arkle Manor RH3 7HB [Reigate Rd]: Smart M&B dining pub with enjoyable gently upscale food, attractive rambling layout with easy chairs and so forth, real ales, good choice of wines by the glass *(Mike and Heather Watson, John Branston)*
☆ *Dolphin* RH3 7DW [off A25 W of Reigate; The Street]: 16th-c village pub on Greensand Way, plain tables on ancient flagstones in neat front bar, smaller bar, panelled restaurant bar with blazing fire and chiming grandfather clock, nice old local photographs, Wells & Youngs ales perhaps inc a seasonal guest; children and dogs welcome, small front courtyard, back garden, open all day *(LM, the Didler, LYM, B and M Kendall)*
Red Lion RH3 7DS [Old Rd, Buckland]: Light and airy dining pub with stylish long flagstoned room and rather Tuscan-seeming candlelit dining room, modern furnishings, Adnams Broadside and guest beers, some enjoyable cooking by Cypriot chef; children welcome, picnic-sets on lawn with play area and cricket ground beyond, dining terrace, bedroom block, open all day *(Jenny and Brian Seller, LYM)*

BLACKBROOK [TQ1846]
☆ *Plough* RH5 4DS [just S of Dorking]: White-fronted pub nicely placed by oak woods, new licensees doing decent pubby food from good ploughman's to fish specials, well kept Badger ales, good choice of wines by the glass and of hot drinks, neat red saloon bar,

steps down to public bar with brass-topped treadle tables; children and dogs welcome, terrace tables, sheltered garden, has been open all day Sun *(Norma and Noel Thomas, John and Joyce Snell, LYM, Michael and Barbara Calverley)*

BLETCHINGLEY [TQ3251]

William IV RH1 4QF [3 miles from M25 junction 6; Little Common Lane, off A25 on Redhill side of village]: Tile-hung and weatherboarded country local down pretty lane, real ales such as Adnams, Fullers London Pride and Greene King IPA, good wines, limited choice of food, two separate bar rooms and back pool room; two-level garden *(C and R Bromage, Grahame Brooks, LYM)*

BLINDLEY HEATH [TQ3645]

☆ *Red Barn* RH7 6LL [Tandridge Lane]: Former Brewers Fayre charmingly reworked and newly reopened as attractive upscale dining pub, relaxed country décor with stripped timbers and high rafters, books, sofas, wing armchairs and central feature fire, carefully thought through food from sandwiches (not cheap but worth the price) up, good wines by the glass and coffee, well trained staff, adjoining farm shop *(Grahame Brooks)*

BROOK [SU9238]

Dog & Pheasant GU8 5UJ [Haslemere Rd (A286)]: Big take-us-as-you-find-us low-beamed traditional pub in attractive spot opp cricket green nr Witley Common, Fullers London Pride, Greene King Abbot, Ringwood Best and Wells & Youngs Bombardier, good choice of wines, food inc antipodean specialities, log fire, shove-ha'penny, small restaurant, family eating area; picnic-sets in garden and on small front terrace *(R B Gardiner, Phil Hanson)*

BUCKLAND [TQ2250]

☆ *Jolly Farmers* RH3 7BG [Reigate Rd (A25)]: Convivial and interesting dining pub with good if not cheap food from a few lunchtime sandwiches and familiar favourites using good ingredients to wider evening choice, thriving atmosphere, cheerful expert staff, real ale such as Hop Back Summer Lightning or Timothy Taylors Landlord, enterprising choice of soft drinks, integral farm shop *(Conor McGaughey, Dan and Holly Pitcher, John Branston, Cathryn and Richard Hicks)*

BURROWHILL [SU9763]

Four Horseshoes GU24 8QP [B383 N of Chobham]: Unpretentious old-fashioned local, log fires in both bars, three well kept changing ales, sensibly priced pubby food from sandwiches up, dining room; lots of picnic-sets out overlooking green (some under ancient yew) *(Ian Phillips)*

BYFLEET [TQ0661]

Plough KT14 7QT [High Rd]: Outstanding range of eight or so interesting changing real ales, comfortably relaxed atmosphere, limited food from sandwiches to three or four bargain hot dishes lunchtime and Weds evening, two log fires, rustic medley of

furnishings, lots of farm tools, brass and copper, dominoes; picnic-sets in pleasant back garden *(Ian Phillips, Phil Bryant)*

CHERTSEY [TQ0566]

Kingfisher KT16 8LF [Chertsey Bridge Rd (Shepperton side of river)]: Big Vintage Inn particularly liked by older people for its delightful spot nr Thames lock, repro period décor and furnishings in spreading series of small intimate areas, efficient friendly staff, Adnams and Fullers London Pride, good wine choice, reasonably priced food, friendly attentive staff, good log fires, daily papers, large-scale map for walkers, interesting old photographs and prints; soft piped music; families welcome if eating (no other under-21s), roadside garden, open all day *(Ron and Sheila Corbett, Ian Phillips, Mike Longman)*

Olde Swan KT16 8AY [Windsor St]: Old-fashioned exterior, but up-to-date main bar with back eating area, good value bar lunches from baguettes or soup up, good service, cosy lower seating area with sofas, quiet lunchtimes, can be busy evenings; bedrooms, open all day *(Shirley Mackenzie)*

CHIDDINGFOLD [SU9635]

☆ *Swan* GU8 4TY [Petworth Rd (A283 S)]: Attractive dining pub, comfortably up to date, with good choice of food inc tempting if not cheap sandwich range in light and airy dining bar and restaurant, several well kept ales, thoughtful wine choice, friendly relaxed service; pleasant back terrace with big sunshades, good bedrooms *(Christopher and Elise Way, Hunter and Christine Wright, LYM, Gerry and Rosemary Dobson, Martin and Karen Wake)*

CHIPSTEAD [TQ2757]

Ramblers Rest CR5 3NP [Outwood Lane (B2032)]: Picturesque aggregation of partly 14th-c former farm buildings, modern furnishings keeping panelling, flagstones, low beams and log fires, Fullers London Pride and Pilgrim, good value wines by the glass, up-to-date food inc popular Sun lunch, chummy efficient service, daily papers; children and dogs welcome, big pleasant garden with terrace, attractive views, good walks nearby, open all day *(BB, Sheila Topham, Grahame Brooks)*

Well House CR5 3SQ [Chipstead signed with Mugswell off A217, N of M25 junction 8]: Partly 14th-c, cottagey, comfortable and friendly, with log fires in all three rooms, Adnams, Fullers London Pride, Surrey Hills Shere Drop and a seasonal ale, huge helpings of plainly served food (not Sun evening) from hefty sandwiches up, conservatory; dogs allowed (they have cats); large attractive hillside garden with well reputed to be mentioned in Domesday Book, delightful setting *(LYM, John Coatsworth, Conor McGaughey, LM)*

CHOBHAM [SU9761]

Sun GU24 8AF [High St, off A319]: Congenial low-beamed timbered pub with Courage Directors, Fullers London Pride and Hogs Back TEA, pubby food, friendly staff, lots of

daily papers, woodburner, shining brasses
(LYM, Ian Phillips)

CHURT [SU8538]

Crossways GU10 2JE: Two distinct down-to-earth bar areas busy evenings for great changing beer range at reasonable prices, good value home-made pub lunches (not Sun) from good sandwiches up, simple suppers Weds, cheerful young staff; garden, open all day Fri/Sat (Mr and Mrs A Curry, R B Gardiner, Tony and Jill Radnor)

Frensham Pond GU10 2QD [L off A287 into Pond Ln to Bacon Ln]: Hotel not pub, but bar has Hogs Back TEA, bar food, and lovely views of Frensham Great Pond, as do dining room and picnic-sets outside; bedrooms (Ian Phillips)

CLAYGATE [TQ1563]

Foley Arms KT10 0LZ [Hare Lane]: Unpretentious Victorian two-bar local with chatty landlord, real fires, food from filling baguettes up, well kept Wells & Youngs ales; good folk club Fri; open all day, long garden with heated shelter and play area (Conor McGaughey, Stephen Funnell)

DORKING [TQ1649]

☆ *Kings Arms* RH4 1BU [West St]: Rambling 16th-c pub in antiques area, masses of timbers and low beams, nice lived-in furniture in olde-worlde part-panelled lounge, warm relaxed atmosphere, mainstream and interesting guest ales, friendly efficient service, bargain home-made food from sandwiches to roasts and a good pie of the day, prompt polite service, attractive old-fashioned back dining area; piped music; open all day (Conor McGaughey)

DORMANSLAND [TQ4042]

Old House At Home RH7 6QP [West St]: Warmly friendly comfortable country local with well kept Shepherd Neame ales, wide choice of good generous food using fresh produce (booking recommended for Sun lunch), good-natured proper landlord (Tony Carter)

Plough RH7 6PS [Plough Rd, off B2028 NE]: Hard-working licensees and friendly staff in traditional old pub in quiet village, well kept Fullers and Harveys, log fires, original features, enjoyable bar lunches and sizeable thai restaurant; children welcome, disabled facilities, good-sized garden with splendid barbecues (Lorry Spooner)

EAST CLANDON [TQ0551]

☆ *Queens Head* GU4 7RY [just off A246 Guildford—Leatherhead; The Street]: Rambling dining pub, part of same small group as Stag at Eashing, with enjoyable reasonably priced food from baguettes and light dishes to popular Sun roasts, good friendly service, real ales such as Shepherd Neame from fine old elm bar counter, comfortable linked rooms, big inglenook log-effect fire; children welcome, picnic-sets on pretty front terrace and in quiet side garden, handy for two NT properties, cl Sun evening (LYM, John Evans, KC)

EFFINGHAM [TQ1153]

Sir Douglas Haig KT24 5LU [off A246 Leatherhead—Guildford]: Large open-plan beamed pub with good value standard food from sandwiches up, good-sized helpings, real ales inc Fullers London Pride, good choice of coffees; piped music; children in eating area, attractive terrace and back lawn, decent bedrooms, open all day (DWAJ, LYM)

EGHAM [TQ0071]

Beehive TW20 0JQ [Middle Hill]: Small friendly local with good value home-made pubby food, Fullers ales with a guest such as Brains Rev James, polite service, neat tables on polished boards, small dining area; nice small garden with picnic-sets (Ian Phillips)

ENGLEFIELD GREEN [SU9971]

Barley Mow TW20 0NX [Northcroft Rd]: Pretty pub with good value food from good reasonably priced snacks up, good choice of mainstream ales, usual refurbished interior, back dining area, darts; quiet piped music; pleasant back garden with play area, café tables out in front overlooking cricket green (summer steam fairs) (Martin Wilson)

Happy Man TW20 0QS [Harvest Rd]: Friendly and unpretentious two-bar late Victorian backstreet local with inexpensive pubby food, four well kept changing ales mainly from smaller breweries, darts area; open all day (Pete Baker)

Sun TW20 0UF [Wick Lane, Bishopsgate]: Well used beamed local, well kept Courage Best, Greene King Abbot, Hogs Back TEA and Timothy Taylors Landlord, good blackboard wine choice, bargain food from good sandwiches to Sun lunch, daily papers, good log fire in back conservatory, biscuit and water for dogs, interesting beer bottle and bank note collections; soft piped music; quiet garden with aviary, handy for Savill Garden and Windsor Park (LM, Ian Phillips, Simon Collett-Jones)

EPSOM [TQ2158]

Rubbing House KT18 5LJ [Epsom Downs]: Restaurant dining pub with attractive modern décor, good value food promptly served even when busy, Fullers London Pride and Greene King IPA, serious wine list, racecourse views, upper balcony; tables outside (Sue and Mike Todd, Mrs G R Sharman, DWAJ, Mike and Sue Richardson, Conor McGaughey)

ESHER [TQ1264]

☆ *Prince of Wales* KT10 8LA [West End Lane; off A244 towards Hersham, by Princess Alice Hospice]: Warm and homely Chef & Brewer dining pub, particularly welcoming and well run, with wide choice of reasonably priced food from doorstep sandwiches up (can take a while on busy wknds), calm corners, turkey carpets, old furniture, prints and photographs, real ales such as Fullers London Pride, Greene King Old Speckled Hen and Wells & Youngs Bombardier, good wine choice, daily papers; children welcome, big shady garden with good decking, lovely

village setting nr green and pond
*(Ian Phillips, LM, Tom and Ruth Rees,
Ron and Sheila Corbett, Phil Bryant)*

EWHURST [TQ0940]

Bulls Head GU6 7QD [The Street]: Rambling
Victorian village pub busy wkdy lunchtimes
with good value OAP specials; attractive
garden, opp village green *(Conor McGaughey)*

FARNHAM [SU8457]

Shepherd & Flock GU9 9JB [Moor Park Lane,
on A31/A324/A325 roundabout]: Flower-
decked pub with helpful friendly licensees,
interesting changing well kept ales,
enjoyable pub lunches from sandwiches up,
good atmosphere, simple up-to-date décor;
they may try to keep your credit card while
you eat; picnic-sets out in front and in
pleasant enclosed back garden with
barbecue, open all day wknds
(David M Smith, E Ling, Ian Phillips)

Spotted Cow GU10 3QT [Bourne Grove,
Lower Bourne (towards Tilford)]: Pleasantly
reworked as contemporary dining pub with
pastel décor, enjoyable straightforward food
inc proper pies and good home-made
puddings, smart friendly helpful young staff,
well kept changing ales, jazz and curry
nights; little room for wheelchairs; play area
in big attractive garden, nice surroundings,
open all day Fri-Sun *(Tony and Jill Radnor,
Liz and Brian Barnard)*

FRENSHAM [SU8442]

Holly Bush GU10 3BJ: Bright and friendly
pub nr Frensham Ponds, new landlady doing
enjoyable food from sandwiches up, Greene
King and other ales, decent house wines;
attractive garden, pleasant covered area off
public bar *(Gordon Stevenson)*

FRIDAY STREET [TQ1245]

Stephan Langton RH5 6JR [off B2126]:
Prettily placed pub with good nearby walks
inc Leith Hill, Fullers London Pride, Hogs
Back TEA and Surrey Hills Ranmore, farm
cider, good choice of other drinks inc dozens
of whiskies, sensible home-made food (not
Sun evening or Mon), welcoming log fire in
bar, woodburner in dining area; children and
dogs welcome, tables outside, open
all day *(LYM, Ian Phillips, Gordon and
Margaret Ormondroyd, Gerald and
Gabrielle Culliford, Stephen Funnell)*

GODALMING [SU9743]

☆ *Bel & the Dragon* GU7 1HY [Old Church,
Bridge St]: Well converted church keeping
gothic-style features, impressive vaulted
ceiling and upper gallery, emphasis on good
fairly priced food, well kept Hogs Back TEA,
good choice of wines by the glass,
enthusiastic helpful young staff, solid tables
and chairs on bare boards, sofas and low
tables in good-sized bar area; tables out in
herb garden *(Phil Bryant)*

GODSTONE [TQ3551]

Bell RH9 8DX [under a mile from M25
junction 6, via B2236]: Good choice of up-
to-date and more traditional food in open-
plan M&B dining pub, comfortably modern
furnishings and lighting in handsome old

building, good-sized restaurant, separate bar
with one draught beer; attractive garden
(LYM, Grahame Brooks, A Flynn)

GOMSHALL [TQ0847]

Compasses GU5 9LA [A25]: Plain bar
(open all day) and much bigger neat and
comfortable dining area, very popular for
good value generous food from sandwiches
up, small helpings available, good service,
real ales and decent wines by the glass; may
be piped music, very busy in summer;
children welcome, pretty garden sloping
down to roadside mill stream, open all day
(DWAJ, Gordon Prince, LYM)

GRAYSWOOD [SU9134]

Wheatsheaf GU27 2DE [Grayswood Rd (A286
NE of Haslemere)]: Civilised dining pub, light
and airy décor, enjoyable food in bar and
restaurant (they bake their own bread), well
kept ales inc Ringwood, friendly helpful
service; front verandah, side terrace,
conference/bedroom extension *(N R White)*

GUILDFORD [SU9948]

Olde Ship GU2 4EB [Portsmouth Rd (St
Catherine's, A3100 S)]: Three cosy areas
around central bar, ancient beams, bare
boards and flagstones, good log fire in big
fireplace, woodburner the other end,
comfortable mix of furniture, good wood-
fired pizzas and interesting but
unpretentious and fairly priced bistro-style
food, well kept Greene King and guests such
as Black Country and Hook Norton, decent
wines, quick, friendly and helpful service; no
music (unless you count the occasional
morris men) *(Ian Phillips, Phil and
Sally Gorton)*

HAMBLEDON [SU9639]

☆ *Merry Harriers* GU8 4DR [off A283; just N of
village]: New licensees in homely country
local popular with walkers, huge inglenook
log fire, dark wood with cream and
terracotta paintwork, pine tables, impressive
collection of chamber-pots hanging from
beams, Greene King IPA and Abbot, Hogs
Back TEA and Hop Back Crop Circle, farm
cider, decent wines and coffee, attentive
staff, reasonably priced fresh simple food
from sandwiches up, daily papers, pool room;
big back garden in attractive walking
countryside near Greensand Way, picnic-sets
in front and over road – caravan parking
(Phil and Sally Gorton)

HEADLEY [TQ2054]

Cock KT18 6LE [Church Lane]: Good value
up-to-date food from lunchtime doorstep
sandwiches up, well kept Adnams and
Harveys, choice of coffees, pleasant young
staff, contemporary décor (pub actually
dates back to the 15th c) with several light
and airy dining areas; tables outside –
attractive setting, good woodland walks
(LM)

HERSHAM [TQ1164]

Bricklayers Arms KT12 5LS [Queens Rd]:
Friendly and well run, back servery doing
good value home-made food from lots of
sandwiches and snacks up, Badger

Tanglefoot, Flowers IPA, Hogs Back TEA and Wells & Youngs, decent wines, log-effect gas fire, separate public bar with pool; parking down by green in Faulkners Rd; small secluded garden, comfortable bedrooms *(Ian Phillips)*

HOLMBURY ST MARY [TQ1144]

☆ *Kings Head* RH5 6NP: Popular bare-boards pub in walking country (leave muddy boots in porch), sensibly short choice of good fresh food using local supplies, friendly atmosphere and helpful young licensees, well kept ales such as Kings and Surrey Hills, good wines by the glass, two-way log fire, small traditional back restaurant (fish recommended), public bar with darts, TV and games machine; pretty spot with seats out facing village green, more in big sloping back garden, open all day at least wknds and summer *(Tom and Ruth Rees, Barry Steele-Perkins, Kevin Flack)*

Royal Oak RH5 6PF: Low-beamed 17th-c coaching inn with enjoyable food from baguettes to some interesting dishes (can take a while), helpful staff, well kept ales such as Everards, decent wine by the glass, fresh flowers, log fire; tables on front lawn, pleasant spot by green and church, good walks, bedrooms *(Mike and Heather Watson, Tom and Ruth Rees, C and R Bromage, Conor McGaughey, Kevin Flack, Tom and Rosemary Hall)*

HORSELL [SU9859]

Cricketers GU21 4XB [Horsell Birch]: Warm and friendly country local, long neatly kept bar, quietly comfortable end sections, extended back eating area, carpet and shiny boards, good sensibly priced straightforward food (all day Sun and bank hols), Greene King and Fullers London Pride, cheerful service, children well catered for; picnic-sets out in front and in big well kept garden, wide views over Horsell Common *(Phil Bryant, Ian Phillips)*

Plough GU21 4JL [off South Rd; Cheapside]: Small friendly local overlooking wooded heath, relaxed atmosphere, well kept changing ales such as Fullers London Pride, Shepherd Neame Spitfire, St Austell Dartmoor Best and Thwaites Lancaster Bomber, good choice of wines by the glass and of malt whiskies, good value fresh pubby food (all day Sat, not Sun evening) from sandwiches up, quiet dining area one side of L, games machines and TV the other; children and dogs welcome (and hay for visiting horses), garden tables, play area, open all day *(Ian Phillips)*

Red Lion GU21 4SS [High St]: Large pub doing very well under new management, smart contemporary décor with bare boards and brickwork, back picture-filled barn restaurant where children allowed, good pubby and more sophisticated food from sandwiches up, Adnams, Courage and Fullers London Pride, decent wines, friendly attentive service, daily papers; ivy-clad passage to garden and comfortable terrace, good walks nearby *(Ian Phillips, Phil Bryant)*

HORSELL COMMON [TQ0160]

☆ *Bleak House* GU21 5NL [Chertsey Rd, The Anthonys; A320 Woking—Ottershaw]: Smart restauranty pub aka Sands at Bleak House, grey split sandstone for floor and face of bar counter, cool décor with black tables, sofas and stools, new back section, good if not cheap food from fresh baguettes up, Hogs Back TEA, Surrey Hills Shere Drop and Wells & Youngs Bombardier, fresh juices, friendly attentive uniformed staff; lively acoustics; smokers' marquee in pleasant back garden merging into woods with good shortish walks to sandpits which inspired H G Wells's *War of the Worlds*, bedrooms *(Ian Phillips, Phil Bryant)*

HURTMORE [SU9445]

Squirrel GU7 2RN [just off A3 nr Godalming, via Priorsfield Rd]: Fresh and airy bar with well kept changing ales inc Hogs Back, decent wines, good choice of enjoyable bar food from panini up, friendly young staff, cosy corners with sofas, good log fire, bar billiards, informal back restaurant and conservatory; piped music, sports TV; disabled facilities, sizeable pleasant garden with heated terrace and play area, comfortable bedrooms, good breakfast, open all day *(BB, Phil Bryant, Catherine and Rob Dunster)*

IRONS BOTTOM [TQ2546]

Three Horseshoes RH2 8PT [Sidlow Bridge, off A217]: Down-to-earth country local with short choice of good value carefully made food from hot baguettes up, good friendly service, Fullers London Pride and Harveys, darts; tables outside, summer barbecues *(John Branston, C and R Bromage)*

KINGSWOOD [TQ2456]

☆ *Kingswood Arms* KT20 6EB [Waterhouse Lane]: Attractive old roadhouse, good bustling atmosphere in rambling bar, enjoyable generous food from good sandwiches up, real ales such as Adnams, Fullers London Pride and Wells & Youngs, hanging plants in light and airy conservatory dining extension; piped music; spacious rolling garden with play area *(Gordon Neighbour)*

LALEHAM [TQ0470]

☆ *Anglers Retreat* TW18 2RT [Staines Rd (B376)]: Roomy and comfortable 1930s pub, reasonably priced pubby food (all day wknds) from sandwiches up, pale panelling, big tropical aquarium set into wall, even larger one in smart restaurant area extended into conservatory, two bright coal fires, Brakspears and Wychwood ales, decent wines, daily papers; no dogs; children welcome, seats out in front, play area in back garden, open all day *(Ian Phillips, Mayur Shah, LYM)*

Three Horseshoes TW18 1SE [Shepperton Rd (B376)]: Light and airy beamed and flagstoned bar with contemporary décor, comfortable sofas, daily papers, log fire, two restaurant areas and conservatory, bar food (all day wknds), Brakspears, Courage Best,

Fullers London Pride and Wells & Youngs Bombardier, lots of wines by the glass; piped music, big-screen TV; children welcome, concrete tables in garden, nicer ones out in front, nr pleasant stretch of the Thames, open all day *(JMM, LYM, Ian Phillips)*

LIMPSFIELD [TQ4053]

Bull RH8 0DR [High St]: Friendly village local dating from 16th c, limited choice of well cooked food all day inc breakfast, good choice of modestly priced wines, Adnams and Marstons Pedigree, good service, darts; sports TVs, juke box; children welcome, terrace tables, *(Colin and Stephanie McFie)*

LYNE [TQ0166]

Royal Marine KT16 0AN [Lyne Lane]: Cosy little pub, neat as a new pin, real ales such as Courage Best, Hogs Back TEA and Kings Harvest, good value simple pub food, welcoming landlord, lots of nautical bric-a-brac and fine collection of pewter mugs; some picnic-sets out in front, attractive small back garden, cl Sat/Sun evenings *(Ian Phillips, Hunter and Christine Wright)*

MICKLEHAM [TQ1753]

☆ *King William IV* RH5 6EL [just off A24 Leatherhead—Dorking; Byttom Hill]: Nicely placed country pub smartened up under newish licensees, Adnams Best, Badger Best, Hogs Back TEA and a guest beer, well presented pubby and more elaborate food with good veg, generally very friendly if not always speedy service, pleasant outlook from snug plank-panelled front bar; may be piped music, no under-12s; plenty of tables (some in extended open-sided heated shelter) in lovely terraced garden with great valley views, cl Mon and Sun evening *(Cathryn and Richard Hicks, N R White, Paul Humphreys, Susan and John Douglas, LYM, C and R Bromage, Tom and Rosemary Hall)*

NEWDIGATE [TQ1942]

Six Bells RH5 5DH [Village St]: Good atmosphere in refurbished pub with four blackboards of good value food in the popular and pleasant eating section, good range of real ales, good service and cheery hands-on landlord; children really welcome, plenty of tables in pleasant garden, lovely outlook over wooden-towered church *(Jenny and Brian Seller)*

NUTFIELD [TQ3050]

☆ *Queens Head* RH1 4HH [A25 E of Redhill]: Congenial atmosphere, good fresh unpretentious food from good value rare beef sandwiches up, cheerful helpful staff, three or four well kept ales inc Shepherd Neame Spitfire, simple bare wood décor in tiled bar with eating area one side, compact carpeted restaurant the other *(John Branston, Hamish and Gillian Turner)*

OCKHAM [TQ0756]

Hautboy GU23 6NP: This remarkable red stone Gothick folly, with its high-vaulted upstairs brasserie bar, nice outside area and bedrooms, closed at the end of 2008, amid objectionable plans to turn it into offices or

have housing built around it; fingers crossed for its future *(LYM)*

OCKLEY [TQ1440]

Inn on the Green RH5 5TD [Billingshurst Rd (A29)]: Friendly former 17th-c coaching inn on green of attractive village, enjoyable fresh food, well kept ales inc Adnams and Greene King, attentive staff, quiet eating area away from bar and leading to conservatory; tables in secluded garden, six comfortable bedrooms, good breakfast *(BB, Derek and Heather Manning)*

☆ *Kings Arms* RH5 5TS [Stane St (A29)]: Attractive 17th-c country inn comfortably reworked as upscale dining pubs while keeping proper bar, several well kept mainstream ales, good choice of wines by the glass, attentive friendly staff, starched napkins and pretty tablecloths, comfortable olde-worlde décor inc lots of antique prints, good inglenook log fire, heavy beams and timbers, low lighting; children welcome, immaculate big back garden, good bedrooms *(LYM, David Dyson, Gordon and Margaret Ormondroyd, Mike and Heather Watson, Ian and Barbara Rankin, Gerald and Gabrielle Culliford)*

☆ *Punchbowl* RH5 5PU [Oakwood Hill, signed off A29 S]: Cosily old-fashioned country pub, smart and clean, with friendly landlord, cheerful relaxed atmosphere, wide choice of imaginative inexpensive food (all day wknds), Badger ales, daily papers, huge inglenook, polished flagstones, lots of low beams and hunting décor, restaurant off on one side, public bar with darts and pool the other; children allowed in dining area, picnic-sets in pretty garden, smokers' awning, quiet spot with good walks inc Sussex Border Path *(Conor McGaughey, LYM, C and R Bromage)*

OTTERSHAW [TQ0263]

☆ *Castle* KT16 0LW [Brox Rd, off A320 not far from M25 junction 11]: Friendly early Victorian local with log fires, paraphernalia on black ceiling joists and walls hung with horse tack and an armoury of guns, six real ales inc Adnams, Greene King and Harveys, Addlestone's cider, lunchtime and evening bar food (not Sun eve); TV, piped music; children welcome in conservatory till 7, dogs in bar, tables on terrace and grass, open all day wknds *(Simon Collett-Jones, Dr and Mrs A K Clarke, Ian Phillips, Phil Bryant, JMM, LYM, S J and C C Davidson)*

OUTWOOD [TQ3246]

Bell RH1 5PN [Outwood Common, just E of village; off A23 S of Redhill]: Attractive extended 17th-c country pub/restaurant, friendly prompt service, mildly upscale food in softly lit smartly rustic beamed bar and restaurant area, Fullers ales and a guest such as Harveys, good wines by the glass, log fires; children and dogs welcome, piped music; summer barbecues and cream teas, pretty garden with play area and country views, handy for windmill *(N R White, LYM, C and R Bromage)*

PEASLAKE [TQ0844]
☆ **Hurtwood** GU5 9RR [off A25 S of Gomshall;
Walking Bottom]: Homely and warmly
welcoming 1920 country hotel (was the first
Trust House), comfortable bar and lounge
largely set for the reasonably priced bar food
from sandwiches up, Hogs Back TEA, Kings
Broadsword and two Surrey Hills ales, good
range of wines by the glass, coffee and malt
whiskies, helpful staff, daily papers and
magazines, two coal-effect fires, sizeable
interesting restaurant; dogs welcome, good
walks from the door, bedrooms, good
breakfast (BB, Ian Phillips)

PIRBRIGHT [SU9455]
Cricketers GU24 0JT [The Green]: Chatty
local overlooking green and duck pond, well
kept Fullers London Pride, Surrey Hills Shere
Drop and St Austell Proper Job, plain
extension with pool and games
machines (Shirley Mackenzie, Phil Bryant,
Paul A Moore)
White Hart GU24 0LP [The Green]: Reliable
dining pub with modern décor, sturdy pale
wood furniture on black and white tartan
carpet, some original flagstones, sofas by
log fires in restored fireplaces, well kept
Hogs Back TEA and Timothy Taylors Landlord,
good service, daily papers, area up steps
popular with ladies who lunch; soft piped
music; good tables and chairs in pleasant
fenced front garden, play area behind
(KC, Michael Dandy, Ian Phillips)

PUTTENHAM [SU9347]
☆ **Good Intent** GU3 1AR [signed off B3000 just
S of A31 junction; The Street/Seale Lane]:
Well worn in beamed village local with up to
half a dozen well kept changing ales,
friendly enthusiastic licensees, good value
generous pubby food (not Sun/Mon
evenings) from sandwiches up, popular Weds
fish night, pre-ordering for muddy walkers
available, farm cider, decent wine choice, log
fire in cosy front bar with alcove seating,
old photographs of the pub, simple dining
area; children and dogs welcome, small
sunny garden, good walks, open all day
wknds (Phil Bryant, N R White, E Ling,
Phil and Sally Gorton, BB)

PYRFORD LOCK [TQ0559]
☆ **Anchor** GU23 6QW [3 miles from M25
junction 10 – S on A3, then take Wisley slip
rd and go on past RHS Garden]: Bustling
light and airy Badger family dining pub with
pubby food all day (small helpings available),
lunchtime sandwiches and baguettes too,
good value wines, quick cheerful service,
daily papers, simple tables on bare boards,
quieter more comfortable panelled back area,
narrow-boat memorabilia, rebuilt
conservatory; children welcome, dogs allowed
in part of bar, splendid terrace with brazier
and dozens of tables in lovely spot by bridge
and locks on River Wey Navigation (very
handy for RHS Wisley), fenced-off
play area, open all day (Ian Phillips, Mr and
Mrs W W Burke, Phil Bryant, Mrs G R Sharman,
Susan and Erik Falck-Therkelsen, LYM,

David and Sue Smith, Sue and Mike Todd,
Susan and John Douglas, Shirley Mackenzie)

REDHILL [TQ2750]
Garland RH1 6PP [Brighton Rd]: Well run
19th-c Harveys local, their full range kept
well, friendly chatty atmosphere, dim
lighting, darts (N R White)

REIGATE [TQ2349]
Black Horse RH2 9JZ [West St (A25)]:
Friendly pub with sofas in relaxing bar area,
emphasis on enjoyable food, attractive
good-sized modern dining extension; nice
spot by heathland (Dan and Holly Pitcher)
Nutley Hall RH2 9HS [Nutley Lane]:
Individual and cheerful high-ceilinged one-
room Victorian local with well kept keenly
priced Badger ales, darts; piped music; dogs
welcome, picnic-sets outside, handy for
Colley Hill (Neil Powell)

REIGATE HEATH [TQ2349]
☆ **Skimmington Castle** RH2 8RL [off A25
Reigate—Dorking via Flanchford Rd and
Bonny's Rd]: Charming small country pub
popular with walkers and riders, cosy dark-
panelled beamed rooms with miscellany of
furniture, big log fireplace, good value food,
Adnams, Greene King K&B and a guest such
as Wells & Youngs Waggle Dance, lots of
wines by the glass, Addlestone's farm cider,
ring-the-bull; piped music; children in back
room, open all day Sun (George Davidson,
Conor McGaughey, Nick Lawless, Dr Ron Cox,
LM, Ian Phillips, N R White, Dan and
Holly Pitcher, P and J Shapley, Martin and
Karen Wake, LYM)

RIPLEY [TQ0455]
Jovial Sailor GU23 6EZ [Portsmouth Rd]:
Large well divided Chef & Brewer, cheerful
helpful staff, well kept changing ales such as
Black Sheep and Hogs Back TEA, good wine
choice, their usual food all day, log fires,
daily papers, standing timbers, beams,
stripped brickwork and country bric-a-brac;
piped music; good-sized garden (Ian Phillips,
Phil Bryant)
Seven Stars GU23 6DL [Newark Lane
(B367)]: Neat well run traditional 1930s pub
popular lunchtimes for good value generous
food from sandwiches to plenty of seafood,
lots of blackboards, good Sun lunches, well
kept Fullers London Pride, Greene King
Abbot, Shepherd Neame Spitfire and Wells &
Youngs Special, good wines and coffee, open
fire; quiet piped music; picnic-sets in large
tidy garden (Ian Phillips, N R White,
Shirley Mackenzie)

ROWLEDGE [SU8243]
Hare & Hounds GU10 4AA [The Square]: New
landlord doing enjoyable generous food, esp
fish and steaks, welcoming atmosphere,
Greene King ales; attractive garden
(Janet Whittaker)

SEND [TQ0156]
New Inn GU23 7EN [Send Rd, Cartbridge]:
Well placed by Wey Navigation canal, long
bar decorated to suit, Fullers London Pride,
Greene King Abbot and Ringwood Best,
reasonably priced food from toasted

sandwiches up, two log-effect gas fires; large waterside garden with moorings and smokers' shelter *(Ian Phillips)*

SENDMARSH [TQ0455]

☆ **Saddlers Arms** GU23 6JQ [Send Marsh Rd]: Genial and attentive licensees in unpretentious low-beamed local, homely and warm, with Courage Best, Fullers London Pride and Shepherd Neame Spitfire, good value generous home-made food (all day Sun) from sandwiches to pizzas and pubby favourites, open fire, toby jugs, brassware etc, no music or TV; picnic-sets out front and back *(Ian Phillips, Phil Bryant, DWAJ, Shirley Mackenzie)*

SHALFORD [SU9946]

Parrot GU4 8DW [Broadford]: Big pub with rows of neat pine tables for the good value food from good sandwiches up, some easy chairs around low tables, Fullers London Pride, Hogs Back TEA and Surrey Hills Shere Drop, quick friendly staff, pleasant conservatory grill restaurant; attractive garden *(Mrs P J Pearce)*

SHAMLEY GREEN [TQ0343]

☆ **Red Lion** GU5 0UB [The Green]: Welcoming dining pub with smart décor, dark polished furniture, rows of books, open fires, local cricketing photographs, enjoyable food all day from good well filled sandwiches with chips to steaks, children's helpings and unusual puddings, good service, well kept Adnams Broadside and Wells & Youngs, farm cider, good choice of wines, cafetière coffee, restaurant; open all day, children welcome, sturdy tables in nice garden by village green, another behind with heated covered terrace *(S and N McLean, LYM, Shirley Mackenzie, Rodney and Mary Milne-Day)*

SHEPPERTON [TQ0766]

Anchor TW17 9JY [Church Sq]: Roomy panelled front bar with friendly helpful staff, decent pubby food at sensible prices, real ale; seats out in front, short walk to river *(Tom Evans)*

Thames Court TW17 9LJ [Shepperton Lock, Ferry Lane; turn left off B375 towards Chertsey, 100yds from Square]: Huge Vintage Inn dining pub well placed by Thames, heaters on extensive and attractive tree-shaded terrace, good choice of wines by the glass, Fullers London Pride, Greene King Old Speckled Hen, Marstons Pedigree and John Smiths, reasonably priced usual food from sandwiches up all day, galleried central atrium with separate attractive panelled areas up and down stairs, two good log fires, daily papers; children welcome, open all day *(Mayur Shah, Ian Phillips)*

SHERE [TQ0747]

☆ **White Horse** GU5 9HF [signed off A25 3 miles E of Guildford; Middle St]: Well run Chef & Brewer, popular with families and a lovely place to take foreign visitors – uneven floors, massive beams and timbers, Tudor stonework, olde-worlde décor with oak wall seats and two log fires, one in a huge inglenook, several rooms off small busy bar,

good value food all day from sandwiches up, friendly efficient staff and warm atmosphere, real ales such as Courage, Hogs Back TEA and Greene King, lots of sensibly priced wines by the glass; dogs welcome, big back garden, beautiful film-set village, open all day *(R B Gardiner, Ian Phillips, LYM, John Branston, Kevin Flack)*

SOUTH GODSTONE [TQ3549]

Fox & Hounds RH9 8LY [Tilburstow Hill Rd/Harts Lane, off A22]: Pleasant country pub with racing prints and woodburner in low-beamed bar, welcoming staff, enjoyable food from pubby staples to good seafood, nice puddings, well kept Greene King ales from tiny bar counter, evening restaurant (not Sun/Mon evenings); *(LYM, Geoffrey Kemp)*

STAINES [TQ0371]

Swan TW18 3JB [The Hythe; south bank, over Staines Bridge]: Splendid Thameside setting, with moorings, good tables on riverside verandah and terrace, big conservatory, several distinctly different areas inc river-view upstairs restaurant, enjoyable food from sandwiches up, prompt friendly service, well kept Fullers ales and a guest such as St Austell HSD; can be very busy Sun lunchtime and packed with under-30s on summer evenings; comfortable bedrooms, open all day *(LYM, Ian Phillips)*

Wheatsheaf & Pigeon TW18 2JX [Penton Rd]: Welcoming 1920s suburban local with indelicate nick-name, noted for its choice of fish and chips; well kept Courage Best, Fullers London Pride, Grand Union Special and Marstons Pedigree, largish bar/lounge and small dining area – fills quickly, even midweek *(Ian Phillips)*

SUNBURY [TQ1068]

Admiral Hawke TW16 6RD [Green St]: Cheerful, warm and comfortable, with reasonably priced pubby food, hospitable staff, real ales inc Adnams and Courage, back dining conservatory; TV *(Gerry and Rosemary Dobson)*

Flower Pot TW16 6AA [Thames St, handy for M3 junction 1, via Green St off exit roundabout]: Trendy décor and nice artwork in friendly and brightly updated 18th-c inn, good home-made food from nice sandwiches to restaurant dishes with emphasis on fish, Brakspears, Fullers London Pride and Greene King, good choice of wines by the glass, helpful cheerful young staff; five bedrooms *(Gerry and Rosemary Dobson, Ian Phillips, Neil and Anita Christopher, Edward Mirzoeff)*

Magpie TW16 6AF [Thames St]: Lovely Thames views from upper bar and small heated terrace by boat club, steps up from moorings; bare boards and panelling, several levels, reliable standard food from sandwiches up, Greene King ales, decent wines; smokers' shelter planned *(Ian Phillips)*

Three Fishes TW16 6RE [Green St, Lower Sunbury]: 16th-c timber-framed building with two welcoming low-ceilinged bars,

Adnams and Courage Best, reasonably priced pizzas, hooded Tudor fireplace *(Ian Phillips)*

SUTTON GREEN [TQ0054]

Olive Tree GU4 7QD [Sutton Green Rd]: Modern dining pub with good honest food (not Sun/Mon evenings) inc fish and seafood, cheaper bar menu inc sandwiches, well kept Fullers London Pride, Harveys and Timothy Taylors Landlord, good choice of wines by the glass, attentive staff, relaxing back dining room with minimalist décor *(Phil Bryant, C and R Bromage, Ian Phillips)*

TADWORTH [TQ2356]

Inn on the Green KT20 5RX [Dorking Rd (B2032)]: Small welcoming bar, Adnams and Harveys, wide choice of enjoyable food, restaurant *(C and R Bromage)*

TANDRIDGE [TQ3748]

Brickmakers Arms RH8 9NS [Tandridge Lane, off A25 W of Oxted]: Civilised and relaxed country dining pub, dating from 15th c but much extended and modernised, beams and stripped brick in two-level carpeted bar, real ales such as Fullers London Pride, Harveys and Larkins, pubby bar food from sandwiches up, help-yourself Sun buffet, log fires, cosy back restaurant; piped music may obtrude; dogs and walkers welcome, picnic-sets out under cover *(Phil Bryant)*

THAMES DITTON [TQ1567]

Albany KT7 0QY [Queens Rd, signed off Summer Rd]: Smartly refurbished M&B bar-with-restaurant in lovely Thames-side position, upscale food, good choice of wines by the glass, log fire, daily papers, river pictures; nice balconies and lots of tables on terrace and lawn with great views across river, moorings, open all day *(Gordon Stevenson, Dr Ron Cox)*

☆ *Olde Swan* KT7 0QQ [Summer Rd]: Large reliable riverside pub (one of very few listed Grade I) with helpful service, good reasonably priced food (all day wknds, inc Sun carvery), well kept Greene King and a guest beer, good choice of wines by the glass, cosy Victorian-style décor, log fires, one long bar with three good-sized areas inc civilised black-panelled upper bar overlooking quiet Thames backwater, restaurant; provision for children and dogs, moorings and plenty of waterside tables, open all day *(BB, Tom and Ruth Rees)*

THE SANDS [SU8846]

Barley Mow GU10 1NE [Littleworth Rd, Seale; E of Farnham]: Quiet village pub with shiny pine tables and simple chairs on polished boards, a step or two down to small dining area, well kept Hogs Back TEA, Fullers London Pride and Hook Norton Old Hooky, good if pricy home-made food, pleasant service, log fire; picnic-sets in secluded attractive garden with terrace, well placed for woodland walks *(Liz and Brian Barnard, N R White, Tony and Jill Radnor)*

TILFORD [SU8742]

Duke of Cambridge GU10 2DD [Tilford Rd]: Civilised pub in same small local group as Stag at Eashing and Queens Head at East

Clandon, enjoyable food inc good fish, efficient service; piped music; garden tables, good play area *(R B Gardiner)*

WALTON-ON-THAMES [TQ0966]

Swan KT12 2PF [Manor Rd, off A3050]: Three-bar riverside Youngs pub due for refurbishment, several linked rooms, decent food from sandwiches up in bar and attractive restaurant, well kept ales, good wine choice, prompt friendly service; dogs welcome, lots of tables in huge garden leading down to Thames, moorings, riverside walks *(Ian Phillips)*

WARLINGHAM [TQ3955]

☆ *Botley Hill Farmhouse* CR6 9QH [S on Limpsfield Rd (B269)]: Busy dining pub with good choice from interesting lunchtime snacks to plenty of fish and popular Sun lunch, well kept Greene King ales and Kings Horsham, good house wines, hard-working friendly staff, low-ceilinged linked rooms up and down steps, soft lighting, spreading carpet, quite close-set tables, big log fireplace in one attractive flagstoned room, restaurant with overhead fishing net and seashells; loud live music some nights; children welcome, cream teas, wknd entertainments, courtyard tables, neat garden with play area and toddlers' park, ducks and aviary *(N R White, LM, BB, Ian Phillips, Conor McGaughey)*

WEST CLANDON [TQ0451]

☆ *Bulls Head* GU4 7ST [A247 SE of Woking]: Friendly and comfortable, based on 1540s timbered hall house, very popular esp with older people lunchtime for good value hearty food from sandwiches up inc home-made proper pies, small lantern-lit beamed front bar with open fire and some stripped brick, contemporary artwork for sale, older local prints and bric-a-brac, simple raised back inglenook dining area, helpful staff, Courage Best, Greene King and Wadworths 6X, good coffee, no piped music, games room with darts and pool; no credit cards; children and dogs on leads welcome, good play area in pleasant garden, handy for Clandon Park, good walking country *(DWAJ, R Lake, Mike and Heather Watson)*

☆ *Onslow Arms* GU4 7TE [A247 SE of Woking]: Popular partly 17th-c country pub with beams, flagstones, dark nooks and corners, warm seats by inglenook log fires, welcoming staff, good value food (not Sun evening) from baguettes up, good value lunches in stylish restaurant, Courage Best and Directors, Greene King Old Speckled Hen and Ringwood Fortyniner, decent wines; piped music; children welcome (and dogs in bar), great well lit garden, open all day *(Phil Bryant, Geoffrey Kemp, Tom and Ruth Rees, LYM, Michael Sargent)*

WEST HORSLEY [TQ0752]

King William IV KT24 6BG [The Street]: Comfortable early 19th-c pub with very low-beamed open-plan rambling bar, reasonably priced proper food from sandwiches up here and in conservatory restaurant, good choice of wines by the glass, well kept Courage Best and Directors and Surrey Hills Shere Drop, good coffee, log fire, board games; children and dogs very welcome, good disabled access, small garden with decking and gorgeous hanging baskets *(Ian Phillips, Michael Dandy, Shirley Mackenzie)*

WESTHUMBLE [TQ1751]

Stepping Stones RH5 6BS [just off A24 below Box Hill]: Comfortable dining pub with reliable good sensibly priced lunchtime food and more elaborate evening menu, good friendly service even when busy, circular bar with Fullers London Pride, Greene King Abbot and a guest beer (drinks brought to table), clean uncluttered décor, open fire, no music; children and walkers welcome, terrace and garden with summer barbecue and play area *(DWAJ)*

WEYBRIDGE [TQ0763]

Hand & Spear KT13 8TX [Old Heath Rd/Station Rd]: Big Youngs pub well refurbished as more of a dining pub, plenty of atmosphere, friendly staff, enjoyable generous food, several different areas, large informal tables and more formal dining room, *(Minda and Stanley Alexander)*

Jolly Farmer KT13 9BN [Princes Rd]: Attractive and civilised small low-beamed local opp picturesque cricket ground, friendly efficient service, enjoyable plentiful pubby food from sandwiches up, reasonable prices, several Marstons-related ales, good choice of wines by the glass, daily papers, toby jugs and interesting old photographs, no music or TV; smart tables out on front terrace, nice back garden *(Ian Phillips, Phil Bryant)*

Oatlands Chaser KT13 9RW [Oatlands Chase]: Attractive building in quiet residential road, large rambling bar with stylish modern décor, pastels and glazed panels, carefully mismatched furnishings mainly laid out for the wide range of food (popular with older lunchers), Fullers London Pride and Timothy Taylors Landlord, good wine choice; lots of tables on alluringly lit front terrace and lawn, immaculate bedrooms *(Phil Bryant)*

☆ *Old Crown* KT13 8LP [Thames St]: Comfortably old-fashioned three-bar pub dating from 16th c and run by same friendly family for many decades, very popular for good value traditional food (not Sun-Tues evenings) from sandwiches up, fresh Grimsby fish, Courage Directors, Fullers London Pride, local Waylands and Wells & Youngs, good choice of wines by the glass, service good even when busy, family lounge and conservatory, coal-effect gas fire; may be sports TV in back bar with Lions RFC photographs; children welcome, suntrap streamside garden *(DWAJ, Ian Phillips, Phil Bryant)*

☆ *Prince of Wales* KT13 9NX [Cross Rd/Anderson Rd off Oatlands Drive]: Civilised and attractively restored, good value generous pubby food inc Sun roasts, real ales such as Adnams, Fullers ESB and

London Pride, Wells & Youngs and one brewed for the pub, ten wines by the glass, relaxed lunchtime atmosphere, friendly service, daily papers, log-effect fire, tribal mask collection, stripped pine dining room down a couple of steps; big-screen TVs for major sports events; well-behaved children welcome *(Ian Phillips, Phil Bryant, Minda and Stanley Alexander)*

Queens Head KT13 8XS [Bridge Rd]: Real ales such as Courage Best, Sharps Doom Bar and St Austell Tribute, comfortable bar with reasonably priced food from baguettes up, good value bistro restaurant, friendly helpful staff; picnic-sets out by pavement and in back yard *(Ian Phillips, Hunter and Christine Wright)*

WINDLESHAM [SU9363]

☆ *Half Moon* GU20 6BN [Church Rd]: Enjoyable if not cheap much extended pub mainly laid for pubby food from sandwiches up, well kept ales such as Fullers London Pride, Hogs Back TEA, Ringwood Fortyniner, Timothy Taylors Landlord and Theakstons Old Peculier, Weston's farm cider, decent wines, plenty of children's drinks, cheerful young staff, log fires, World War II pictures, modern furnishings, attractive barn restaurant out along covered flagstoned walkway; piped music, silenced games machine; children welcome, huge tidy garden with two terraces and play area *(Ian Phillips, Martin Wilson, Phil Bryant)*

Windmill GU20 6PJ [London Rd (A30/B3020 junction)]: Recently refurbished M&B dining pub, light and airy, good range of food with both standard and more adventurous dishes, well kept Fullers London Pride, good choice of wines by the glass, polite helpful staff, log fire, daily papers; handy for Ascot racecourse, some tables outside *(Nigel and Sue Foster)*

WITLEY [SU9439]

White Hart GU8 5PH [Petworth Rd]: Picture-book beamed Tudor local with friendly helpful staff, well kept Shepherd Neame ales, enjoyable home-made pubby food (not Sun evening) from sandwiches up, daily papers, good oak furniture and log fire in cosy panelled inglenook snug where George Eliot drank, games in public bar, restaurant; tables on flower-filled cobbled terrace, lower meadow with picnic-sets and play area, open all day Sat *(Phil Bryant, LYM)*

WOKING [TQ0058]

Sovereigns GU22 7QQ [Guildford Rd/Victoria Rd]: Large Ember Inn with their usual food all day, well kept changing ales such as Butcombe, Caledonian Deuchars IPA, Elgoods and Harveys Best, daily papers, nice layout of comfortable linked rooms; open all day *(Tony and Wendy Hobden)*

Wetherspoons GU21 5AJ [Chertsey Rd]: Large and busy with shoppers yet with lots of cosy areas and side snugs, good range of food all day, half a dozen or more interesting well kept real ales, good choice of coffees, fair prices, friendly helpful staff, daily

papers, interesting old local pictures, no
music; open all day *(Tony Hobden)*
Wheatsheaf GU21 4AL [Chobham Rd]: Ember
Inn with enthusiastic and capable young staff,
good choice of real ales, quickly served tasty
food, nice atmosphere, lots of alcoves and
smaller areas; open all day *(David M Smith)*
WOTTON [TQ1247]
☆ *Wotton Hatch* RH5 6QQ [A25 Dorking—
Guildford]: Stylish modern M&B dining pub,
angular tub chairs, pony skin rugs, imposing
zinc bar with belgian beers as well as
Adnams and Hogs Back TEA, good choice of
decent wines, generous soft drinks, still a
log fire in the 17th-c core, good generous
reasonably priced food inc some adventurous
dishes, hospitable landlord and staff, daily
papers, conservatory; no dogs; children
welcome, smartly furnished neat garden with
impressive views, open all day *(Mr and
Mrs Mike Pearson, LYM, Ian Phillips)*
WRECCLESHAM [SU8344]
☆ *Bat & Ball* GU10 4SA [Bat & Ball Lane,
South Farnham; approach from Sandrock Hill
and Upper Bourne Lane then narrow steep
lane to pub]: Neatly refurbished pub tucked

away in hidden valley, wide range of above-
average pubby and more upmarket food
(small helpings available) inc good puddings
display, up to half a dozen or more changing
ales such as one brewed for them by Itchen
Valley, good choice of wines by the glass,
friendly staff; they may try to keep your
credit card while you eat, sports TV; disabled
facilities, dogs welcome, provision for
children, tables out on attractive heated
terrace with vine arbour and in garden with
substantial play fort, open all day *(BB,
R Lake)*
Sandrock GU10 4NS [Sandrock Hill Road]:
Popular and unpretentious real ale tavern
with Bathams Best, Enville White, Holdens
Special, Surrey Hills and several interesting
changing guest beers, friendly helpful staff,
reasonably priced food from huge lunchtime
sandwiches through pubby standards to
steaks and a good fish stew, good choice of
sensibly priced wines by the glass, real fire,
bar billiards in games room, annual beer
festival; children and dogs welcome,
pleasant heated terrace, open all day
(Janet Whittaker, Simon Fletcher)

Post Office address codings confusingly give the impression that some pubs are in Surrey
when they're really in Hampshire or London (which is where we list them). And there's
further confusion from the way the Post Office still talks about Middlesex – which
disappeared in local government reorganisation over 40 years ago.

Sussex

With some fine walking country here, many of the pubs – whether nice little locals or smart dining pubs – are happy to welcome walkers, and often their dogs too. This is a friendly county with quite a few long-serving licensees who work really hard at keeping their pubs on top form. Some unspoilt pubs doing well this year, and often giving real value in what tends to be an expensive county, include the Rose Cottage at Alciston (in the same family for over 40 years), the cottagey Cricketers Arms at Berwick (the bearded Victorian cricketer on its inn sign giving a nice idea of its old-fashioned appeal), the Black Horse at Byworth (a new licensee but still with a quietly chatty feel, newspapers to read and open fires), the Six Bells at Chiddingly (lively and unpretentious, with very good value food and popular live music), the Royal Oak at Chilgrove (a friendly and relaxed country local), and the Giants Rest at Wilmington (friendly licensees, well liked country cooking and fine surrounding walks). Food plays a strong part in many of the pubs here (excellent fresh fish and seafood, game and beef and lamb). For a particularly good meal head for Greys in Brighton (interesting food in an unusual pub with very good live music on Monday evenings), the Jolly Sportsman at East Chiltington (professionally run restauranty place with delicious modern cooking, but with a proper little bar, too), the Star & Garter at East Dean (again, restauranty with smart food, but some provision for drinkers), the Royal Oak at East Lavant (new licensees determined to keep its appeal to chatting drinkers, despite much emphasis on the imaginative food), the Three Horseshoes at Elsted (a smashing, relaxed but civilised feel and proper home cooking), the Griffin in Fletching (interesting dishes at a price, popular with a wide mix of customers), the Crab & Lobster at Sidlesham (a new entry this year, almost a restaurant-with-rooms), the Keepers Arms at Trotton (a hard-working landlord and good contemporary cooking), and the newly extended Half Moon at Warninglid (deservedly very popular for both food and drink). Our Sussex Dining Pub of the Year is the Jolly Sportsman at East Chiltington. Other pubs doing well include the Anchor Bleu in Bosham (a new entry and with a lovely waterside position), the Basketmakers in Brighton (a really well run local, friendly and bustling, with surprisingly good food), the Fox Goes Free at Charlton (exceptionally nice, just the place to while away a lazy lunch), the Bull in Ditchling (much enjoyed by cyclists and walkers, especially at weekends), the White Dog at Ewhurst Green (new licensees committed to making the most of this well placed pub's potential have quickly cracked the main entry barrier), the Foresters Arms in Graffham (another new entry, with hard-working young licensees, an informal atmosphere, a roaring log fire and tasty food from a sensibly short menu), the Queens Head at Icklesham (much loved by customers of all ages, who return again and again), and the Ypres Castle in Rye (another pub where a fresh hand at the helm has deftly raised standards and gained a new main entry). This is a big county, and the Lucky Dip section at the end of the chapter also includes quite a few strong contenders. A shortlist might include the Black Horse at Amberley, Black Rabbit just outside Arundel, Cricketers in Brighton, White Horse at Chilgrove (too restauranty now for the main entries, but top-notch), Coach & Horses at Danehill, Crown & Anchor at Dell Quay, Bulls Head at Fishbourne, Anglesey Arms at Halnaker, Royal Oak at Handcross, Haywaggon in Hartfield, Sussex Brewery at Hermitage, Arun View in Littlehampton and Dorset Arms in Withyham. The dominant local brewer is Harveys, and you will quite often come across Dark Star, Arundel, Ballards and Kings. Other independent local brews we've found in at least some good pubs this year are Gribble, Hammerpot, Hepworths, Whites, Langham, Rother Valley and Weltons, and there are another nine or ten which we didn't come across ourselves but which you may be lucky enough to find. Another Sussex-sounding beer, which turns up in Badger pubs, is K&B Sussex – actually brewed by them down in Dorset, the name if not the taste recalling beers brewed in Horsham by King & Barnes until Badger bought them and closed the brewery in 2000.

ALCISTON   TQ5005   MAP 3
Rose Cottage
Village signposted off A27 Polegate—Lewes; BN26 6UW

Old-fashioned cottage with fresh local food, cosy fires and country bric-a-brac, a good little wine list and local beers; bedrooms

This old-fashioned little pub, run by the same family for more than 40 years, has a lovely country cottage feel and a good mix of locals and visitors. There are cosy winter log fires, half a dozen tables with cushioned pews under quite a forest of harness, traps, a thatcher's blade and lots of other black ironware, and more bric-a-brac on the shelves above the stripped pine dado or in the etched-glass windows; in the mornings you may also find Jasper the parrot (he gets too noisy in the evenings and is moved upstairs). There's a lunchtime overflow into the restaurant area as they don't take bookings in the bar then. Harveys Best and a guest like Dark Star Hophead on handpump, a good little wine list with fair value house wines and a few nice bin ends, and two local farm ciders; the landlord is quite a plain-speaking character. Piped music, darts and board games. There are heaters outside for cooler evenings and the small paddock in the garden has ducks and chickens; boules. Nearby fishing and shooting. The charming small village (and local church) are certainly worth a look. They take bedroom bookings for a minimum of two nights.

ⓘ Using fresh local and often organic produce, the well liked food includes ploughman's, soup, potted brown shrimps, pâté, grilled flat mushrooms with garlic and mixed fresh herbs, breast of free-range chicken with a cream cheese, sun-dried tomato and herb stuffing and wrapped in pancetta, escalope of free-range pork with button onions, bacon and pears in a cream and white port sauce, and daily specials such as local sausages with onion gravy, popular cheesy-topped garlic mussels, coq au vin and wild rabbit pie. They do add a 10% service charge to all meals. *Starters/Snacks: £3.95 to £5.95. Main Courses: £9.75 to £13.95. Puddings: £4.50*

Free house ~ Licensee Ian Lewis ~ Real ale ~ Bar food ~ Restaurant ~ (01323) 870377 ~ Children allowed if over 10 ~ Dogs allowed in bar ~ Open 11.30-3, 6.30-11; 12-3, 6.30-10.30 Sun; closed evenings 25 Dec and 1 Jan, 26 Dec ~ Bedrooms: /£60S

Recommended by Paul Boot, Alan Cowell, Andrea Rampley, Paul Lucas, the Didler, N R White, P and J Shapley, Jenny and Peter Lowater, Mrs L M Beard

ALFRISTON
TQ5203 MAP 3

George
High Street; BN26 5SY

Venerable inn in lovely village with comfortable, heavily beamed bars, good wines, several real ales, and bedrooms; fine nearby walks

This 14th-c timbered inn is a popular place to drop into after a wander around this lovely village. The long bar has massive low beams hung with hops, appropriately soft lighting and a log fire (or summer flower arrangement) in a huge stone inglenook fireplace that dominates the room, with lots of copper and brass around it. There are settles and chairs around sturdy stripped tables, Greene King IPA and Abbot, and a guest like Bath Ales Gem on handpump, decent wines including champagne by the glass, board games, and piped music; the lounge has comfortable sofas, standing timbers and rugs on the wooden floor. The restaurant is cosy and candlelit – or you can sit out in the charming flint-walled garden behind. Two long-distance paths, the South Downs Way and Vanguard Way, cross here and Cuckmere Haven is close by.

Bar food at lunchtime includes sandwiches, a rustic sharing board, mussels in garlic and cream with chips and mayonnaise, flat mushrooms sautéed in garlic and topped with smoked bacon and goats cheese, pork and leek sausages, and steak, mushroom and Guinness suet pudding; evening choices such as confit of pork belly with red cabbage, fried tofu with cabbage, bean sprouts and crispy noodles, and monkfish wrapped in parma ham on a mixed bean cassoulet. *Starters/Snacks: £4.00 to £6.50. Main Courses: £7.50 to £16.95. Puddings: £4.50 to £4.95*

Greene King ~ Lease Roland and Cate Couch ~ Real ale ~ Bar food (12-2.30, 7-9(10 Fri and Sat)) ~ Restaurant ~ (01323) 870319 ~ Children welcome ~ Dogs allowed in bar and bedrooms ~ Open 11-11(midnight Fri and Sat); closed 25 and 26 Dec ~ Bedrooms: £60S/£110B

Recommended by Trevor and Sylvia Millum, Catherine and Richard Preston, C and R Bromage, Mrs L M Beard, Ann and Colin Hunt, J A Snell, Mrs Hazel Rainer, Guy Vowles

ARLINGTON
TQ5507 MAP 3

Old Oak
Caneheath, off A22 or A27 NW of Polegate; BN26 6SJ

Beamed comfortable rooms in pleasant country pub, tasty pubby food, real ales and quiet garden

Although this old place was built in 1733 as an almshouse, it didn't become a pub until the early 1900s. The L-shaped bar is open-plan with heavy beams, well spaced tables and comfortable seating, log fires, and Badger K&B, Harveys Best, and a changing guest such as Dark Star Hophead tapped from the cask; several malt whiskies, piped music, and toad in the hole (a Sussex coin game). There are seats in the peaceful garden, and walks in the nearby Abbot's Wood nature reserve.

Decent bar food includes filled baguettes and baked potatoes, soup, ploughman's, duck and orange pâté, tiger prawns in garlic oil with a sweet chilli dip, home-baked honey and mustard ham with eggs, spinach and mascarpone lasagne, steak in ale pie, curry with mango chutney, a roast of the day, bass with mediterranean vegetables, and puddings. *Starters/Snacks: £3.95 to £5.95. Main Courses: £6.95 to £8.95. Puddings: £2.95 to £3.95*

Free house ~ Licensees Mr J Boots and Mr B Slattery ~ Real ale ~ Bar food (12-2.30, 6.30-9.30; all day weekends) ~ Restaurant ~ (01323) 482072 ~ Children welcome ~ Dogs allowed in bar ~ Open 11-11

Recommended by Jenny and Peter Lowater, Fr Robert Marsh, Stuart and Diana Hughes

---

Planning a day in the country? We list pubs in really attractive scenery at the back of the book.

BALLS CROSS

SU9826   MAP 2

Stag ◖

Village signposted off A283 at N edge of Petworth, brown sign to pub there too; GU28 9JP

Popular little local with a friendly landlord, well kept beer, nice traditional food and seats in sizeable garden

Unchanging and unspoilt, this 17th-c place is an enjoyable little country pub. The tiny flagstoned bar has a winter log fire in a huge inglenook fireplace, just a couple of tables, a window seat, and a few chairs and leather-seated bar stools. On the right, a second room with a rug on its bare boards has space for just a single table. Beyond is an appealing old-fashioned dining room with quite a few horsey pictures. There are yellowing cream walls and low shiny ochre ceilings throughout, with soft lighting from little fringed wall lamps, and fishing rods and country knick-knacks hanging from the ceilings. On the left a separate carpeted room with a couple of big Victorian prints has table skittles, darts and board games. Badger K&B Sussex Bitter, First Gold and Hopping Hare on handpump, decent wines by the glass, summer cider and some nice malt whiskies. The good-sized garden behind, divided by a shrubbery, has teak or cast-iron tables and chairs, picnic-sets, and in summer a couple of canvas awnings; there are more picnic-sets out under green canvas parasols in front, and the hitching rail does get used. The veteran gents' (and ladies') are outside.

🍽 **Traditional bar food (using game bagged by the landlord) includes lunchtime filled baguettes and baked potatoes, soup, fried garlic mushrooms, cumberland sausage and chips, home-baked ham and eggs, chilli con carne, battered cod with mushy peas, macaroni cheese, steak and kidney pudding and slow-cooked venison casserole.** *Starters/Snacks: £3.50 to £7.00. Main Courses: £8.00 to £13.50. Puddings: £4.00 to £4.50*

Badger ~ Tenant Hamish Barrie Hiddleston ~ Real ale ~ Bar food (not Sun evening) ~ Restaurant ~ (01403) 820241 ~ Well-behaved children welcome ~ Dogs welcome ~ Open 11-3, 6-11; 12-3.30, 7-10.30 Sun ~ Bedrooms: £35/£60

Recommended by R B Gardiner, Phil and Sally Gorton

BERWICK

TQ5105   MAP 3

Cricketers Arms

Lower Road, S of A27; BN26 6SP

Cottagey and unchanging in a quiet setting with welcoming little bars, nice staff, traditional food (all day weekends and summer weekdays); charming garden

In fine weather, the garden in front of this charming cottage is delightful, with seats amidst small brick paths and mature flowering shrubs and plants; there are more seats behind the building. Inside, the three small cottagey rooms are all similarly furnished with simple benches against the half-panelled walls, a pleasant mix of old country tables and chairs, a few bar stools and some country prints; quarry tiles on the floors (nice worn ones in the middle room), two log fires in little brick fireplaces, a huge black supporting beam in each of the low ochre ceilings, and (in the end room) some attractive cricketing pastels; some of the beams are hung with cricket bats. Harveys Best and two seasonal ales tapped from the cask and decent wine; cribbage, dominoes and an old Sussex coin game called toad in the hole. The wall paintings in the nearby church done by the Bloomsbury Group during World War II are worth a look.

🍽 **Popular bar food includes chicken liver and mushroom terrine with real ale chutney, crayfish cocktail, various platters (the spanish one is much liked), warm halloumi and pine nut salad, local pork sausages with egg, warm chicken caesar salad, summer dressed crab salad, daily specials, and puddings.** *Starters/Snacks: £4.50 to £6.95. Main Courses: £7.50 to £15.95. Puddings: £4.50*

Harveys ~ Lease Peter Brown ~ Real ale ~ Bar food (12-2.15, 6.15-9; all day weekends and summer weekdays); not 25 Dec or evening 26 Dec) ~ (01323) 870469 ~ Children in family room only ~ Dogs welcome ~ Open 11-11; 12-10.30 Sun; 11-3, 6-11 weekdays in winter; closed 25 Dec

Recommended by Simon and Mandy King, Kevin Thorpe, the Didler, Jenny and Peter Lowater, Richard Endacott, C and R Bromage, Mrs Mahni Pannett, Andrea Rampley

BLACKBOYS

TQ5220 MAP 3

Blackboys Inn

B2192, S edge of village; TN22 5LG

Pretty 14th-c pub, bustling locals' bar, nice old dining rooms, good choice of drinks, often interesting food, and plenty of seats in attractive garden

In warm weather, the garden to the side of this pretty 14th-c pub has plenty of rustic tables overlooking the pond, and there are more under the chestnut trees. Inside, the bustling locals' bar to the left has a good, chatty atmosphere, there's a bar area to the right with bar stools and a couple of tables, and the other rooms – used for dining – have dark oak beams, bare boards or parquet, antique prints, and usually, a good log fire in the inglenook fireplace. Harveys Best, Hadlow and a couple of seasonal guests on handpump and ten wines by the glass; piped music. The Vanguard Way passes the pub, the Wealdway goes close by, and there's the Woodland Trust opposite. More reports please.

🍽 **Often interesting – though there may be quite a wait – the food includes soup, chorizo and bacon salad, chicken with red pepper sauce, pork medallions with creamed leeks, seared salmon with watercress and beetroot salad, calves liver, pancetta, pine nuts and balsamic, daily specials such as grilled fresh sardines, home-made venison sausages with onion gravy, and local beef fillet on watercress, stilton and rocket, and puddings like chocolate torte and apple crumble.** *Starters/Snacks: £4.50 to £8.50. Main Courses: £6.50 to £14.95. Puddings: £5.50*

Harveys ~ Tenant Paul James ~ Real ale ~ Bar food (12-3, 6-10; all day weekends) ~ Restaurant ~ (01825) 890283 ~ Children welcome ~ Dogs allowed in bar ~ Open 12-11(midnight Sat)

Recommended by Alec and Joan Laurence, the Didler, Steve Godfrey

BOSHAM

SU8003 MAP 2

Anchor Bleu

High Street; PO18 8LS

Waterside inn overlooking Chichester harbour and usefully open all day in summer, several real ales in snug old bars, and decent food (lots of summer fish dishes)

At high tide, the water comes right up to the windows of this 16th-c pub, and there's an attractive view over the ducks and boats on this sheltered inlet of Chichester harbour, which dries to mud flats at low tide. There are seats on the terrace making the most of the view, and a massive wheel-operated bulkhead door to ward off high tides (cars parked on the seaward side are often submerged). Inside, two nicely simple bars have low shiny ochre ceilings, some beams, worn flagstones and exposed timbered brickwork, lots of nautical bric-a-brac, and robust, simple furniture. Gribble Best Bitter, Hogs Back TEA, Hop Back Summer Lightning, and Ringwood Fortyniner on handpump, and winter mulled wine; friendly, helpful staff. As King Canute had a palace here, this may be the spot where he showed his courtiers that however much they flattered him as all-powerful, he couldn't turn the tide back. The church a few yards up the lane figures in the Bayeux tapestry. This is a charming village.

🍽 **Lunchtime bar food includes filled baguettes, ploughman's, soup, crayfish with lime mayonnaise, poached salmon, battered haddock, moussaka, and shepherd's pie, with evening dishes such as whole plaice with caper butter, sea bream with herbs and lemon, leg of lamb steak with bacon and onion gravy, vegetable and sweet chilli stir fry with pumpkin seeds, chicken with parma ham, brie and leek sauce, and puddings such as pear and Amaretto crumble and pecan pie.** *Starters/Snacks: £4.25 to £6.75. Main Courses: £7.50 to £12.00. Puddings: £2.95 to £4.25*

Enterprise ~ Lease Kate Walford ~ Real ale ~ Bar food (12-3(2.30 winter), 6.30(7 winter)-9.30(9 winter); 12-4, 6.30-9.30 Fri-Sun but all day Sun in summer) ~ Restaurant ~ (01243) 573956 ~ Children welcome ~ Dogs allowed in bar ~ Open 11.30(10.30)-11; 12-10.30 Sun; 12-3, 5.30-11 weekdays in winter

Recommended by Michael B Griffith, Bruce Bird, Francis Vernon, Mr and Mrs P D Titcomb, David H T Dimock

BRIGHTON   TQ3104   MAP 3

Basketmakers Arms £

Gloucester Road – the E end, near Cheltenham Place; off Marlborough Place (A23) via
Gloucester Street; BN1 4AD

Bustling backstreet pub with friendly landlord, plenty of chatty customers, great drinks range, and enjoyable food

There's always a really good mix of customers and a chatty, bustling atmosphere in this thriving local. The two small low-ceilinged rooms have brocaded wall benches and stools on the stripped wood floor, lots of interesting old tins all over the walls, cigarette cards on one beam with whisky labels on another, beermats, and some old advertisements, photographs and posters; piped music. A fine choice of up to eight real ales such as Fullers London Pride, Butser, Discover, ESB, and HSB and guests like Adnams Bitter, and Fullers IPA and Festival Mild on handpump, good wines by the glass, at least 90 malt whiskies, and quite a range of vodkas, gins and rums; staff are helpful and cheerful. There are three metal tables out on the pavement.

🍽 **Good value enjoyable bar food using local, organic produce includes lots of sandwiches, filled baguettes and baked potatoes, ploughman's, soup, particularly good home-made meaty and vegetarian burgers, mexican meaty and vegetarian chillis, steak in ale pie, vegetable lasagne, lambs liver and bacon, and fresh crab salad; popular Sunday roasts.** *Starters/Snacks: £4.25 to £5.95. Main Courses: £5.75 to £7.95. Puddings: £3.75*

Gales (Fullers) ~ Lease P Dowd and A Mawer ~ Real ale ~ Bar food (12-8.30(7 Fri, 6 Sat, 5 Sun)) ~ (01273) 689006 ~ Children welcome until 8pm ~ Dogs allowed in bar ~ Open 11-11(midnight Fri and Sat); 12-11 Sun

Recommended by Michael Dandy, the Didler, N R White, Ian Phillips, Richard and Sissel Harris

Greys 🍽 🍷

Southover Street, off A270 Lewes Road opposite The Level (public park); BN2 9UA

A good mix of drinkers and diners in friendly, bustling and interesting local, thoughtful choice of drinks, popular food; live music Monday evenings

On Monday evenings when they have interesting live music (tickets only), this friendly place is absolutely packed. At other times – do check the opening hours carefully – it can be quiet and relaxed. There's a cheerful atmosphere, smiling and efficient staff, and basic furnishings like simple wall seats and stools around mixed pub tables on bare boards and flagstones, ochre walls, and some wood panelling around a flame-effect stove below a big metal canopy; piped music is at a reasonable level. The serving bar is on the right, with Harveys Best and Timothy Taylors Landlord on handpump, a carefully chosen wine list, 16 bottled belgian beers, Weston's organic cider and a breton cider, and a local crowd on the bar stools and at the nearby tables. The five or six tables on the left, each with a little vase of flowers and lighted tea lamp, are the food bit – one corner table is snugged in by a high-backed settle, and another at the back is tucked into a quiet corner. The stair wall is papered with posters and flyers from bands, singers and poets who have performed here. The house wines, from Burgundy, are excellent value. There is not much daytime parking on this steep lane or the nearby streets. No children inside.

🍽 **From a shortish menu, the good food might include a light prawn curry with pineapple, duck liver pâté, garlic mushrooms in truffle oil, moules marinière, a small roast chicken with dijonnaise mustard sauce, grilled lamb cutlets with a crispy crust of garlic, breadcrumbs, fresh thyme and parsley, fresh tortellini stuffed with mozzarella in a rich tomato sauce, and puddings such as edwardian-style trifle and vanilla and butterscotch ice-cream with crunchy biscuits; they may offer good value two- and three-course set meals, too.** *Starters/Snacks: £4.25 to £4.50. Main Courses: £9.00 to £12.50. Puddings: £4.50*

Free house ~ Licensees Chris Taylor and Gill Perkins ~ Real ale ~ Bar food (6-9; not Sun evening, not Mon, not Tues-Fri lunch) ~ Restaurant ~ (01273) 680734 ~ Dogs welcome ~ Live music Mon evening (tickets only) ~ Open 4-11; 12-midnight Fri and Sat; 12am-11pm Sun; closed lunchtimes Mon-Thurs

Recommended by Sue Demont, Tim Barrow, Guy Vowles, N R White, Francis Vernon, Ann and Colin Hunt

BURPHAM

TQ0308   MAP 3

George & Dragon 🍺

Warningcamp turn off A27 outside Arundel: follow road up and up; BN18 9RR

Interesting food and real ales in bustling dining pub

Under the new licensees, this remains a popular dining pub in a hilltop village; just a short walk away are splendid views down to Arundel Castle and the river. The front part is a restaurant with tables set for dining on the wooden floor, and there's a small area where drinkers can enjoy Arundel Gold, Harveys Best, and Skinners Betty Stogs on handpump. The lane up to this remote hill village is long and winding and the pub is at the end of the village between the partly Norman church (which has some unusual decoration) and cricket ground. More reports please.

🍴 **Interesting bar food includes soup, caramelised red onion, fig and pear tartlet with stilton dressing, game terrine with ale chutney, tian of smoked salmon, guacamole, and crab with dill crème fraîche, chicken breast stuffed with haggis with a whisky cream sauce, wild mushroom, leek and thyme crumble topped with cheese, rump of lamb on red onion confit with red wine and cranberry sauce, honey roast scotch salmon fillet on citrus couscous with a soy dressing, and slow cooked beef in ale with chive mash and horseradish dumplings; Sunday roasts.** *Starters/Snacks: £5.25 to £6.50. Main Courses: £8.95 to £16.95. Puddings: £5.25*

Free house ~ Licensees Sarah and Michael Cheney ~ Real ale ~ Bar food ~ Restaurant ~ (01903) 883131 ~ Children welcome ~ Dogs allowed in bar ~ Open 11.30am-midnight; 12-11.30 Sun

Recommended by Cathryn and Richard Hicks, Bruce Bird, Sue Demont, Tim Barrow, Martin and Karen Wake

BYWORTH

SU9821   MAP 2

Black Horse 🍺

Off A283; GU28 0HL

Enjoyable country pub with open fires, newspapers to read, several real ales, tasty food, and nice garden

This is an understated and very enjoyable country pub with a new landlord. There's a good mix of customers, a quietly chatty atmosphere, and large open fires, and the simply furnished though smart bar has pews and scrubbed wooden tables on its bare floorboards, pictures and old photographs on the walls and newspapers to read. The back dining room has lots of nooks and crannies, there's a spiral staircase to a heavily beamed function room, and stairs up to a games room with pool, bar billiards, darts, two games machines and board games; lovely views of the downs. Dark Star Hophead, Flowerpots Bitter, Fullers London Pride, and Sharps Doom Bar on handpump. The particularly attractive garden has tables on a steep series of grassy terraces sheltered by banks of flowering shrubs that look across a drowsy valley to swelling woodland.

🍴 **As well as filled baguettes, filled baked potatoes and ploughman's, the bar food includes soup, thai fishcakes with sweet chilli sauce, a pie of the day, home-cooked ham and free range eggs, cheesy-topped cottage pie, beer-battered cod, scallops and bacon, and slow-roasted lamb shoulder in mint gravy.** *Starters/Snacks: £3.95 to £6.95. Main Courses: £8.95 to £18.95. Puddings: £3.95*

Free house ~ Licensee Jeff Paddock ~ Real ale ~ Bar food (12-3, 6-9(9.30 Fri and Sat, 8.30 Sun)) ~ Restaurant ~ (01798) 342424 ~ Children welcome ~ Dogs allowed in bar ~ Open 11.30-11; 12-11 Sun

Recommended by R B Gardiner, Nick Lawless, Tracey and Stephen Groves, Bruce Bird, Jonathan Neil-Smith, John and Annabel Hampshire

---

The 🍺 symbol shows pubs which keep their beer unusually well, have a particularly good range or brew their own.

CHARLTON   SU8812   MAP 2

Fox Goes Free

Village signposted off A286 Chichester—Midhurst in Singleton, also from Chichester—
Petworth via East Dean; PO18 0HU

Comfortable old pub with well organised staff, popular food and drink; nice surrounding walks; bedrooms

This is a lovely place to while away a lunchtime – especially in good weather when you can sit at one of the picnic-sets under the apple trees in the attractive back garden with the downs as a backdrop; there are rustic benches and tables on the gravelled front terrace, too. Inside, the bustling bar has an informal and relaxed atmosphere and is the first of the dark and cosy series of separate rooms: old irish settles, tables and chapel chairs, and an open fire. Standing timbers divide a larger beamed bar which has a huge brick fireplace with a woodburning stove and old local photographs on the walls. A dining area with hunting prints looks over the garden. The family extension is a clever conversion from horse boxes and the stables where the 1926 Goodwood winner was housed; darts, games machine, board games, and piped music. Ballards Best and a beer named for the pub on handpump, and eight wines by the glass; friendly, helpful staff. It's handy for Goodwood (and does get crowded on race days) and for the Weald and Downland Open Air Museum and West Dean gardens; good surrounding walks.

🍴 Well presented bar food includes filled baguettes, ploughman's, soup, caramelised onion tart with grilled goats cheese and spicy olives, pork terrine with tomato chutney, honey-roast ham and egg, sausages with onion gravy, wild mushroom risotto, steak and mushroom pie, chicken breast with creamed leeks and red wine jus, belly of pork with apple chutney, fillet of sole with a crab and herb cream, and puddings such as raspberry crème brûlée and vanilla cheesecake, both with home-made ice-cream. *Starters/Snacks: £2.50 to £7.50. Main Courses: £8.50 to £16.95. Puddings: £5.50*

Free house ~ Licensee David Coxon ~ Real ale ~ Bar food (12-2.30, 6.30-10; all day weekends) ~ Restaurant ~ (01243) 811461 ~ Children welcome ~ Dogs allowed in bar ~ Live music Weds evenings ~ Open 11-11(11.30 Sat); 12-11 Sun ~ Bedrooms: £60S/£85S

Recommended by Tony and Wendy Hobden, Peter Meister, Alec and Joan Laurence, LM, Francis Vernon, Paul and Shirley White, Bruce Bird, Roger and Lesley Everett, Tony Brace, John Evans, Tom and Jill Jones, Ann and Colin Hunt

CHIDDINGLY   TQ5414   MAP 3

Six Bells ★ £

Village signed off A22 Uckfield—Hailsham; BN8 6HE

Lively, unpretentious village local with good weekend live music, extremely good value bar food and friendly long-serving landlord

There's a cheerful atmosphere and a good mix of customers in this unspoilt old local. The bars have a shabby charm, lots of fusty artefacts and interesting bric-a-brac collected over the years by the long-serving landlord, solid old wood pews and antique seats, plenty of local pictures and posters, and log fires. The live weekend music is very popular. A sensitive extension provides some much needed family space; board games. Courage Directors, Harveys Best and a guest beer on handpump. Outside at the back, there are some tables beyond a big raised goldfish pond and a boules pitch; the church opposite has an interesting Jefferay monument. Vintage and Kit car meetings outside the pub every month. This is a pleasant area for walks.

🍴 The tasty but traditional bar food is exceptionally good value: sandwiches, french onion soup, filled baked potatoes, ploughman's, stilton and walnut pie, lasagne, shepherd's or steak and kidney pies, chicken curry, barbecue spare ribs, ham hock, and puddings such as banana split and steamed puddings. *Starters/Snacks: £3.50 to £6.00. Main Courses: £4.75 to £9.50. Puddings: £3.60*

Free house ~ Licensees Paul Newman and Emma Bannister ~ Real ale ~ Bar food (11.30-2.30, 6-9; all day Fri-Sun) ~ (01825) 872227 ~ Children in family room ~ Dogs allowed in bedrooms ~ Live music Fri and Sat evenings and Sun lunchtime ~ Open 10-3, 6-11; 10am-midnight Fri and Sat; 10am-11pm Sun

Recommended by Ann and Colin Hunt, Jenny and Peter Lowater, John Roots, Mayur Shah, N R White, Kevin Thorpe, John Beeken, C Shaw

CHILGROVE   SU8116   MAP 2

Royal Oak
Off B2141 Petersfield—Chichester, signed Hooksway down steep single track; PO18 9JZ

Unchanging and peaceful country pub with welcoming landlord, decent traditional bar food and big pretty garden

In fine walking and riding country and close to the South Downs Way, this is an unchanging and bustling pub with friendly, long-serving licensees. It's simply furnished with plain country-kitchen tables and chairs and there are huge log fires in the two cosy rooms of the partly brick-floored beamed bar. There's also a cottagey dining room with a woodburning stove, and plainer family room. Gribble Best, Hammerpot Madgwick Gold, and Hogs Back HBB and OTT on handpump; piped music, cribbage and shut-the-box. There are plenty of picnic-sets under parasols on the grass of the big, pretty garden.

🍴 **Sensibly priced traditional bar food includes ploughman's, filled baked potatoes, creamy garlic mushrooms, pâté with cranberry sauce, chicken curry, slow-cooked pork hock with apple and cider sauce, salmon fillet with red thai sauce, mixed grill, and venison steak with mulled wine and redcurrant jelly.** *Starters/Snacks: £4.95. Main Courses: £6.50 to £13.95. Puddings: £3.50 to £4.50*

Free house ~ Licensee Dave Jeffery ~ Real ale ~ Bar food (not Sun evening or Mon) ~ Restaurant ~ (01243) 535257 ~ Children in family room until 8pm ~ Dogs allowed in bar ~ Live music second Fri evening of the month ~ Open 11.30-2.30, 6-11; 12-3 Sun; closed Sun evening and all day Mon

Recommended by R C Vincent, Marianne and Peter Stevens, John Beeken, Prof and Mrs S Barnett, Ann and Colin Hunt, R B Gardiner

COOLHAM   TQ1423   MAP 3

George & Dragon
Dragons Green, Dragons Lane; pub signed just off A272, about 1.5 miles E of village; RH13 8GE

Pleasant little country cottage with beamed bars, and decent food and drink

New licensees for this tile-hung cottage – but happily, little has changed. The cosy bar has heavily timbered walls, a partly woodblock and partly polished-tile-floor, unusually low and massive black beams (see if you can decide whether the date cut into one is 1677 or 1577), simple chairs and rustic stools, some brass, and a big inglenook fireplace with an early 17th-c grate. There's also a smaller back bar and restaurant. Badger K&B, Tanglefoot, and a seasonal ale on handpump, and a chatty, relaxed atmosphere. The sizeable orchard garden which is neatly kept with pretty flowers and shrubs has quite a few picnic-sets; the little front garden has a sad 19th-c memorial to the son of a previous innkeeper. More reports please.

🍴 **Bar food now includes lunchtime filled baguettes, ploughman's, soup, garlic mushrooms, baked brie with cranberry sauce, whitebait, popular bacon and onion suet pudding, spicy burger, vegetable risotto, giant yorkshire pudding filled with sausage and mash, steak in Guinness or lamb pie, and puddings such as spotted dick and a fruit pie.** *Starters/Snacks: £3.50 to £4.95. Main Courses: £7.00 to £12.00. Puddings: £3.95*

Badger ~ Tenants Peter and Anne Snelling ~ Real ale ~ Bar food ~ Restaurant ~ (01403) 741320 ~ Children welcome ~ Dogs allowed in bar ~ Open 12-3, 6-11; 12-midnight(11 Sun) Sat

Recommended by John Beeken, Francis Vernon, David Coleman, Terry Buckland, Katharine Cowherd, Philip and Cheryl Hill

COWBEECH
Merrie Harriers
Village signposted from A271; BN27 4JQ

Pleasant village pub with log fire and chatty locals, real ales and popular food, and seats in terraced garden

The smallish beamed and panelled bar in this white clapboarded village local is popular with friendly regulars, but there's a welcome for visitors, too. There's a log fire in the brick inglenook, a high-backed settle and mixed tables and chairs, and an L-shaped counter with bar stools; the quieter lounge is off to the left. Harveys Best and Timothy Taylors Landlord on handpump, and several wines by the glass. There's also a brick-walled and oak-ceilinged back restaurant. The terraced garden – with country views – has rustic seats amongst colourful shrubs and pots.

⚟ Bar food includes sandwiches, pork and chicken liver terrine, steamed mussels with white wine and garlic, beer-battered cod with home-made tartare sauce, sausages with apple mash and red onion gravy, fried noodles with seared tofu, vegetables and cashew nuts, rack of lamb with redcurrant jus, slow-roast pork belly with red onion marmalade and mustard mash, and fillet of beef with a wild mushroom sauce. *Starters/Snacks: £4.50 to £6.25. Main Courses: £7.95 to £16.95. Puddings: £5.00*

Free house ~ Licensee Duncan Smart ~ Real ale ~ Bar food ~ Restaurant ~ (01323) 833108 ~ Children welcome ~ Dogs allowed in bar ~ Open 11.30-3, 6-11; 12-4, 6-11 Sun

Recommended by Mike Gorton, Paul Boot, Conor McGaughey

DITCHLING
Bull ♀
High Street (B2112); BN6 8TA

Handsome old building with cosy atmosphere in rambling traditional bars, good choice of drinks, and quite an emphasis on food; nearby walks

At weekends particularly, this 16th-c inn is popular with walkers and cyclists (the South Downs Way is close by) but there are plenty of staff to keep things running smoothly. The invitingly cosy main bar on the right is quite large, rambling and pleasantly traditional with well worn old wooden furniture, beams and floorboards, and a blazing winter fire. To the left, the nicely furnished rooms have a calm, restrained mellow décor and candles, and beyond that there's a snug area with chesterfields around a low table; piped music. Harveys Best and Timothy Taylors Landlord with a couple of changing guests on handpump and a dozen wines by the glass. Picnic-sets in the good-sized pretty downland garden which is gently lit at night look up towards Ditchling Beacon and there are more tables on a suntrap back terrace; good wheelchair access.

⚟ Well liked bar food includes sandwiches, soup, thai-style fishcakes with soy and honey dip, chicken and beetroot salad with tomato and mozzarella relish, smoked salmon and herring terrine, local sausages with herb mash and gravy, roast pepper, celeriac and feta cheese risotto, smoked haddock and king prawn linguini, lamb rump steak with fondant potato, roast guinea fowl breast with bacon and mushrooms, and puddings; Sunday roasts. *Starters/Snacks: £5.00 to £6.50. Main Courses: £9.50 to £16.00. Puddings: £5.50*

Free house ~ Licensee Dominic Worrall ~ Real ale ~ Bar food (12-2.30, 7-9.30; 12-6 Sun) ~ Restaurant ~ (01273) 843147 ~ Children welcome ~ Dogs allowed in bar ~ Live music monthly Fri ~ Open 11-11; 12-10.30 Sun ~ Bedrooms: /£80S(£100B)

Recommended by Alec and Joan Laurence, Tracey and Stephen Groves, John Silverman, Martin and Karen Wake, Tina and David Woods-Taylor, Andy and Claire Barker

---

By law pubs must show a price list of their drinks. Let us know if you are inconvenienced by any breach of this law.

EAST ASHLING
SU8207   MAP 2
Horse & Groom ♀ ◀
B2178 NW of Chichester; PO18 9AX

Busy country pub with real ales in unchanging front drinkers' bar, plenty of dining space and decent food

If it's just a drink you're after in this bustling country pub, you'd be best to head for the front part with its old pale flagstones and woodburning stove in the big inglenook on the right; the carpeted area is nice too, with its old wireless set, scrubbed trestle tables, and bar stools lining the counter. Dark Star Hophead, Harveys Hadlow, Hop Back Summer Lightning, and Wells & Youngs Bitter on handpump, and several wines by the glass; board games. There's also a small light flagstoned middle area with a couple of tables. The back part of the pub, angling right round behind the bar servery, with a further extension beyond one set of internal windows, has solid pale country-kitchen furniture on neat bare boards, and a fresh and airy décor, with a little bleached pine panelling and long white curtains. French windows lead out to a garden with picnic-sets under umbrellas. It does get extremely busy on Goodwood race days, and is handy for Kingly Vale Nature Reserve.

🍴 **As well as sandwiches and filled baguettes, the bar food might include filled baked potatoes, ploughman's, home-cooked ham and eggs, steak in ale pie, lasagne, lamb cutlets with rosemary jus, whole baked plaice with lemon butter, and puddings.** *Starters/Snacks: £4.50 to £5.50. Main Courses: £9.50 to £12.95. Puddings: £5.00*

Free house ~ Licensee Michael Martell ~ Real ale ~ Bar food ~ Restaurant ~ (01243) 575339 ~ Children welcome before 9pm ~ Dogs allowed in bar and bedrooms ~ Open 11-3, 6-11; 12-2.30 Sun; closed Sun evening ~ Bedrooms: £45B/£70B

Recommended by Paul and Shirley White, J A Snell, Bruce Bird, David Coleman, Ann and Colin Hunt, R and M Thomas, Gordon Neighbour, Ian and Joan Blackwell, Malcolm Pellatt

EAST CHILTINGTON
TQ3715   MAP 3
Jolly Sportsman 🍽 ♀
2 miles N of B2116; Chapel Lane – follow sign to 13th-c church; BN7 3BA
SUSSEX DINING PUB OF THE YEAR

Excellent modern food in civilised, rather smart place, small bar for drinkers, contemporary furnishings, fine wine list and huge range of malt whiskies; nice garden

Professionally run and rather civilised, this is an enjoyable dining pub with a cosy and friendly little bar which is set aside for drinkers. There's a roaring winter fire, a mix of furniture on the stripped wood floors, Dark Star Hophead and Whitstable Native tapped from the cask, a remarkably good wine list with nine by the glass, over 100 malt whiskies, and an extensive list of cognacs, armagnacs and grappa. The larger restaurant is smart but informal with contemporary light wood furniture and modern landscapes on coffee coloured walls. There are rustic tables and benches under gnarled trees in a pretty cottagey front garden with more on the terrace and the front bricked area, and the large back lawn with a children's play area looks out towards the South Downs; good walks nearby.

🍴 **As well as a two- and three-course set lunch menu, the carefully sourced, imaginative – if not cheap – food might include ploughman's, roast quail, pomegranate and red onion salad, grilled squid with fennel, chilli and rocket, confit pig's cheek with bacon and parsnip salad, wild mushroom risotto, herb-roasted rump of lamb with dauphinoise potatoes, belly of organic saddleback pork with spring vegetables, hake fillet with vermouth sauce, daily specials such as a plate of charcuterie and crispy duck, haggis, mashed neeps and tatties, and merguez sausages with tzatziki, and puddings like chocolate griottine cherry and espresso mascarpone cake and Kahlua sauce and apricot, walnut and ginger toffee pudding.** *Starters/Snacks: £4.85 to £8.50. Main Courses: £9.75 to £16.95. Puddings: £4.85 to £6.50*

Free house ~ Licensee Bruce Wass ~ Real ale ~ Bar food (12.30-2.30, 7-9.30(10 Fri and Sat);
12-3 Sun; not Sun evening) ~ Restaurant ~ (01273) 890400 ~ Children welcome ~ Dogs
welcome ~ Open 12-11; 12-11 Sat; 12-4 Sun; 12-3, 6-11 Tues-Sat in winter; closed Sun
evening, all day Mon, two days Christmas

*Recommended by Susan and John Douglas, David Cumberland, Jane and Alan Bush, Barry and Victoria Lister,
June Pullen, Sue Demont, Tim Barrow*

EAST DEAN   SU9012   MAP 2

Star & Garter 🍴 ♀

*Village signposted with Charlton off A286 in Singleton; also signposted off A285; note that
there are two East Deans in Sussex (this one is N of Chichester) – OS Sheet 197 map
reference 904129; PO18 OJG*

**Attractively furnished bar and restaurant in light and airy well run pub, relaxed
atmosphere, friendly, attentive staff, and enjoyable food and drink; bedrooms**

Popular with racegoers at Goodwood, downland walkers, and locals, this traditional brick
and flint pub does make some provision for drinkers, but most customers are here to eat.
There's some stripped wooden panelling, exposed brickwork and solid oak floors and the
more or less roomy square area has sturdy, individual, mainly stripped and scrubbed
tables in various sizes and an interesting mix of seats from country kitchen chairs
through chunky modern dining chairs to cushioned pews and some 17th-c and 18th-c
carved oak settles. The high ceilings, big sash windows and uncluttered walls give a light
and airy feel. The bar counter, with a few bar stools, is on the left, with Arundel Best
and Ballards Best tapped from the cask, ten wines by the glass, a couple of farm ciders,
and a few malt whiskies; tables in this area are usually left unlaid whilst those to the
right of the front door and further on are set for diners. Newspapers to read and piped
music. The sheltered terrace behind has teak tables and chairs with big canvas parasols
and heaters, and a gazebo for smokers; steps go up to a walled lawn with picnic-sets. A
gate provides level access from the road to the terrace and into the pub for those who
might not manage the front steps. The South Downs Way is close by.

🍴 **The popular fresh seafood is listed on a board over the fireplace and might include
selsey crab and lobster, line caught bass, local mackerel, cod, mussels, scallops, and fine
platters; there are non-fishy choices too such as lunchtime filled baguettes, ploughman's,
home-cooked ham and free-range eggs, liver and bacon, and steak in ale pie, as well as a
sauté of wild mushrooms with crispy saffron risotto cake, couscous-crusted goats cheese
with red onion salad, salad of pigeon breast with beetroot and walnuts, supreme of
chicken wrapped in pancetta with a white wine and tarragon sauce, breast of barbary duck
with a rhubarb and port sauce, half a roast guinea fowl, scotch fillet steak with madeira
sauce, and puddings.** *Starters/Snacks: £5.00 to £10.50. Main Courses: £9.00 to £18.50.
Puddings: £5.50*

Free house ~ Licensee Oliver Ligertwood ~ Real ale ~ Bar food (12-2.30, 6.30-10;
all day weekends) ~ Restaurant ~ (01243) 811318 ~ Children welcome ~ Dogs allowed in bar ~
Open 11-3, 6-11; 11am-11pm Sat; 12-10.30 Sun; closed evenings 25 and 26 Dec ~ Bedrooms:
£60S(£80B)/£80S(£100B)

*Recommended by Jennifer Hurst, Sue Ruffhead, Ann and Colin Hunt, Tony and Wendy Hobden, William Goodhart,
Bruce and Penny Wilkie, Mrs Romey Heaton, R B Gardiner, Cathy Robinson, Ed Coombe*

EAST LAVANT   SU8608   MAP 2

Royal Oak 🍴 ♀ 🛏

Village signposted off A286 N of Chichester; Pook Lane; PO18 OAX

**Bustling and friendly dining pub with proper drinking area, excellent food, extensive wine
list and real ales; super bedrooms**

A new licensee has taken over this pretty little white house and is keen that this should
remain a proper village pub where you can drop in for a drink after a walk, whilst also
offering fine food in relaxed surroundings. It's all open plan with low beams and exposed

brickwork, crooked timbers, winter log fires, and church candles. The well used drinking area at the front has wall seats and sofas, Arundel Gold, Badger K&B, Palmers IPA, and Skinners Betty Stogs tapped from the cask, 17 wines by the glass from an extensive list, and a friendly welcome from the attentive staff. The attached seating area is focused on dining and sensitively furnished with brown suede and leather dining chairs around scrubbed pine tables, and pictures of local scenes and of motor sport on the walls. Outside, there are cushioned seats and tables under green parasols on the flagstoned front terrace and far-reaching views to the downs; rambling around the side and back are terraced, brick and grass areas with more seats and attractive tubs and baskets. The bedrooms are stylish and well equipped and they also have self-catering cottages. The car park is across the road; good walks. More reports please.

🍴 Enjoyable food now includes salt and pepper squid with greek salad and crab mayonnaise, sliced smoked duck breast with cassis and blueberry jus, seared local black pudding and fried duck egg with pancetta dressing, beer-battered fish with minted pea purée, mushroom burger with sweet potato chips and home-made sweetcorn relish, pork loin steak with puy lentil sauce, seared king fish and chervil-poached scallops on citrus-crushed new potatoes, brochette of chicken on herby bulgar wheat with tzatziki and tamarind chutney, and puddings such as baked cheesecake with chargrilled pineapple and pistachio praline and bay-leaf-scented crème brûlée. *Starters/Snacks: £5.25 to £9.95. Main Courses: £12.50 to £21.00. Puddings: £4.95 to £6.95*

Free house ~ Licensee Charles Ullmann ~ Real ale ~ Bar food (12-2.30, 6-9.30) ~ (01243) 527434 ~ Children welcome ~ Dogs allowed in bar ~ Open 11-11; closed 1 Jan ~ Bedrooms: £75B/£95B

Recommended by David M Godfrey, Tony Brace, MDN, Ian and Joan Blackwell, Tracey and Stephen Groves

ELSTED   SU8119   MAP 2

Three Horseshoes 🍷 🍺

Village signposted from B2141 Chichester—Petersfield; also reached easily from A272 about 2 miles W of Midhurst, turning left heading W; GU29 0JY

Bustling, friendly and well run country pub, congenial little beamed rooms, enjoyable food, and good drinks; wonderful views from flower-filled garden

The snug little rooms in this much enjoyed 16th-c pub have a cosy, chatty atmosphere and the staff are helpful and friendly. There are ancient beams and flooring, antique furnishings, log fires and candlelight, fresh flowers on the tables, and attractive prints and photographs; it's best to book to be sure of a table. Racked on a stillage behind the bar counter, the real ales include a changing beer from Bowman, Ballards Best, Timothy Taylors Landlord, Youngs Bitter and a guest such as Hop Back Spring Zing or Sharps Doom Bar; summer cider; dominoes. The flower-filled garden in summer is lovely with plenty of tables and stunning views of the South Downs. Good nearby walks.

🍴 Generous helpings of good, popular food include ploughman's with a good choice of cheeses, potted shrimps on toast, prawn mayonnaise wrapped in smoked salmon, smoked duck, roasted pepper and bacon salad, pork and herb sausages, venison either as a fillet with a port and redcurrant sauce or in a winter stew, steak and kidney in Guinness pie, lamb with apples and apricots, seasonal crab and lobster, and puddings such as lemon posset and panna cotta with blueberries. *Starters/Snacks: £4.50 to £8.95. Main Courses: £8.95 to £15.95. Puddings: £4.95*

Free house ~ Licensee Sue Beavis ~ Real ale ~ Bar food ~ Restaurant ~ (01730) 825746 ~ Well-behaved children allowed ~ Dogs allowed in bar ~ Open 11-2.30, 6-11; 12-3, 7-10.30 Sun

Recommended by Tony and Jill Radnor, Michael B Griffith, Miss J F Reay, Jeff Davies, Ian and Joan Blackwell, Mrs K Hooker, R B Gardiner, Nick Lawless, Jennifer Hurst, John Evans, John Beeken, J A Snell, N B Vernon, Mrs Romey Heaton, Miss A E Dare

---

We mention bottled beers and spirits only if there is something unusual about them – imported belgian real ales, say, or dozens of malt whiskies; so do please let us know about them in your reports.

ERIDGE STATION

TQ5434   MAP 3

Huntsman ♀ ◖

Signposted off A26 S of Eridge Green; Eridge Road; TN3 9LE

Little country local with friendly landlord, interesting bar food (lots of seasonal game), excellent wines and seats in sizeable garden

There's a good range of drinks in this small and unpretentious country local – the quietly friendly landlord has considerable wine expertise (they offer a fantastic choice of over two dozen wines by the glass) and they keep Badger K&B and First Gold and a seasonal guest on handpump, and farm cider. The two opened-up rooms have dark wooden dining chairs and a nice mix of matching tables on the wooden floorboards, and plenty of amusing pictures of hunting scenes on the walls. There are picnic-sets and outdoor heaters on the decking, an outside bar, and more seating on the lawn among weeping willows and other trees. The pub is virtually alone here apart from the station itself – which on weekdays is responsible for filling the hamlet's roadside verges with commuters' cars. Plenty of space at weekends, though. More reports please.

🍽 **As well as sandwiches, the interesting bar food might include soup, fried duck livers with puy lentils, courgette blinis with smoked salmon and sour cream, game terrine with home-made chutney, smoked haddock florentine, goats cheese, red onion and cranberry tart, chicken leg stuffed with pistachios, bacon and tarragon with a brandy cream sauce, thai-style bass with lime dressing, wild boar casserole, and puddings such as fig panna cotta and banana and chocolate roulade.** *Starters/Snacks: £4.50 to £7.25. Main Courses: £8.50 to £16.95. Puddings: £4.50 to £5.50*

Badger ~ Tenants Simon Wood and Nicola Tester ~ Real ale ~ Bar food (not Sun evening or Mon (except bank hol lunchtime)) ~ (01892) 864258 ~ Children welcome ~ Dogs allowed in bar ~ Open 11.30-3, 5.30-11; 11.30-11 Sat; 12-11 Sun; closed Mon (except bank hols when open 12-4) and first two weeks in Jan

Recommended by BOB

EWHURST GREEN

TQ7924   MAP 3

White Dog

Turn off A21 to Bodiam at S end of Hurst Green, cross B2244, pass Bodiam Castle, cross river then bear left uphill at Ewhurst Green sign; TN32 5TD

Bustling local handy for Bodiam Castle, nice little bar, popular food, and real ales

In a fine spot above Bodiam Castle (and quite handy for Great Dixter), this is an attractive, partly 17th-c pub/restaurant with new owners. The bar on the left has a proper pubby feel with a fine inglenook fireplace, hop-draped beams, wood-panelled walls, farm implements and horsebrasses, just a few tables with high-backed, rush-seated dining chairs and quite a few red plush-topped bar stools by the curved wooden counter on the old brick or flagstoned floor; there's also a high-backed cushioned settle by the counter, and Harveys Best plus guests like Fullers London Pride and Shepherd Neame Whitstable Bay on handpump. To the right of the door is the busy but fairly plain dining room with more big flagstones, the same tables and chairs as the bar, fresh flowers, black joists and hops, paintings by local artists for sale, and again, one high-backed settle by the bar. There's also a games room with darts, pool and a games machine. They are hoping to build a new terrace with smart seats and tables under big umbrellas to make the most of the fine view over the castle.

🍽 **Well liked bar food includes sandwiches, monkfish and smoked salmon terrine, crab and prawn fishcakes, roasted beetroot and peppered duck risotto, a home-made pudding of the day (the steak and onion is good), corn-fed chicken topped with parma ham and mozzarella with tomato sauce, perch fillet wrapped in bacon with a red wine sauce, rib-eye steak, and puddings like strawberry crème brûlée and sticky toffee pudding.** *Starters/Snacks: £4.95 to £6.75. Main Courses: £11.50 to £16.50. Puddings: £5.25*

Free house ~ Licensees Bill and Jacqui Tipples ~ Real ale ~ Bar food ~ Restaurant ~ (01580) 830264 ~ Children welcome ~ Dogs allowed in bar ~ Open 12-3, 6-11; 12-10.30 Sun

Recommended by V Brogden

FITTLEWORTH

TQ0118 MAP 2

Swan 🛏

Lower Street (B2138, off A283 W of Pulborough); RH20 1EL

Pretty tile-hung inn with comfortable beamed bar and plenty of seats in big back garden; bedrooms

This pretty tile-hung inn is a nice place to stay and the bedrooms are newly refurbished. The beamed main bar is comfortable and relaxed with windsor armchairs and bar stools on the part-stripped wood and part-carpeted floor, there are wooden truncheons over the big inglenook fireplace (which has good winter log fires), and Fullers London Pride and Youngs on handpump; piped music. There's a big back lawn with plenty of well spaced tables and flowering shrubs and benches in front by the village lane; good nearby walks in beech woods. They do take your credit card if you are eating in the garden.

🍽 **Well liked food might include sandwiches, ploughman's, soup, goats cheese tart with roasted peppers, devilled kidneys, bacon and walnut salad with stilton croûtons, a pie of the day, stuffed aubergine rolls with tomato salsa, ham and egg, cajun chicken with yoghurt and cucumber dressing, pork medallions in cider sauce, haddock mornay, and puddings such as orange panna cotta with Cointreau syrup and double chocolate torte with kumquat compote.** *Starters/Snacks: £4.50 to £8.95. Main Courses: £9.95 to £16.95. Puddings: £4.50 to £5.50*

Enterprise ~ Lease Paul and Gillian Warriner ~ Real ale ~ Bar food (12-2.30, 6-9.30) ~ Restaurant ~ (01798) 865429 ~ Children allowed until 9pm ~ Dogs allowed in bar ~ Open 11-3, 5-11; 11-4, 7-10.30 Sun ~ Bedrooms: £60B/£90B

Recommended by Glen and Nola Armstrong, R B Gardiner, Ian Phillips, BOB, Karen Eliot, MDN, Barry Collett, Jude Wright

FLETCHING

TQ4223 MAP 3

Griffin 🍴 🍷

Village signposted off A272 W of Uckfield; TN22 3SS

Busy, gently upmarket inn with a fine wine list, bistro-style bar food, real ales and big garden with far-reaching views; bedrooms

Usually extremely busy, this rather civilised old inn is an integral part of village life but has a good mix of visitors and locals. There are beamed and quaintly panelled bar rooms with blazing log fires, old photographs and hunting prints, straightforward close-set furniture including some captain's chairs, and china on a delft shelf. There's a small bare-boarded serving area off to one side and a snug separate bar with sofas and TV. Harveys Best, Hepworths Iron Horse, and Kings Horsham Best on handpump and a fine wine list with 16 (including champagne and sweet wine) by the glass. The two acres of garden behind the pub look across fine rolling countryside towards Sheffield Park and there are plenty of seats here and on the sandstone terrace with its woodburning oven. They may try to keep your credit card while you eat.

🍽 **As well as a more elaborate restaurant menu, the often interesting – if not cheap – food in the bar might include confit rabbit terrine with parma ham and figs on toasted sourdough bread, steamed razor-clams with chilli and parsley, sautéed chicken livers with pancetta, balsamic and rocket salad, risotto of wild garlic with courgettes, tomato and pine nuts, pasta with tuscan sausage, tomato, rosemary and garlic, calves liver with smoked bacon and onion gravy, lamb pie, local plaice with caper and herb butter, and puddings such as orange and almond tart and apple and cinnamon crumble.** *Starters/Snacks: £5.50 to £9.00. Main Courses: £10.00 to £17.00. Puddings: £6.00*

Free house ~ Licensees J Pullan, T Erlam, M W Wright ~ Real ale ~ Bar food (12-2.30(3 weekends), 7-9.30(9 Sun)) ~ Restaurant ~ (01825) 722890 ~ Children welcome if supervised ~ Dogs allowed in bar ~ Live jazz Fri evening and Sun lunchtime ~ Open 12-11(midnight Sat); closed 25 Dec and evening 1 Jan ~ Bedrooms: £80B/£85S(£95B)

Recommended by Peter Meister, Phil Bryant, Richard and Sissel Harris, P Waterman, Mr and Mrs M Stratton, J A Snell, Alan Clark, John Ralph, Gerry and Rosemary Dobson, R B Gardiner, Alan Cowell, John and Jackie Chalcraft, Ann and Colin Hunt, Andrea Rampley, Martin and Karen Wake, Susan and John Douglas, Ian and Sue Hiscock

GRAFFHAM

SU9218 MAP 2

Foresters Arms

Left off A285 to Graffham, left after 1 mile signed Graffham, pub on left after 1 mile; GU28 0QA

Neat 16th-c inn run by enthusiastic young couple with local beers, a fine choice of wines by the glass and good quality food from a short, seasonal menu

In good walking country, this neat and friendly 16th-c pub is run by hard-working young owners. There are three connected rooms with heavy beams and joists, a few big contemporary hunting photographs and sizeable mirrors on the cream walls, quiet piped jazz and church candles and fresh flowers. The main bar area has a big log fire in the huge brick fireplace, pews with cushions and pale windsor chairs around light modern tables on the dark wooden floor, a fine old butcher's block, Horsham beers and lots of good quality wines by the glass. A brick pillar with an open fireplace separates this room with an end brick-walled one furnished with chapel chairs and a nice mix of tables. To the left of the bar is a room with more wheelbacks and one long pew beside a similarly long table on the sisal flooring, what was a fireplace now filled with neatly stacked logs and a couple of large flagons on the broad windowsill. There are some picnic-sets out at the back. Breakfasts can be delivered to your bedroom in a hamper or taken in the bar.

🍴 **Naming their suppliers and using much local produce, the very good food from a short, seasonal menu might include sandwiches, soup, ham hock terrine and red onion marmalade, chicken wings in tomato sauce, parsnip and red lentil roast with pesto cauliflower, lamb shoulder slow cooked in red wines and tomatoes, griddled sardines, duck sausages with warm chive and wholegrain mustard potato salad, and puddings such as rhubarb syllabub and caramelised apples with toffee sauce.** *Starters/Snacks: £4.00 to £7.00. Main Courses: £9.00 to £15.00. Puddings: £4.00 to £6.00*

Free house ~ Licensees Robert and Clare Pearce ~ Real ale ~ Bar food (12-3, 6-9; 12-5 Sun) ~ Restaurant ~ (01798) 867202 ~ Children lunchtimes only ~ Dogs allowed in bar ~ Open 12-11; closed from 5pm Sun and all day Mon ~ Bedrooms: /£98S

Recommended by Bruce Bird

HORSHAM

TQ1730 MAP 3

Black Jug ♀

North Street; RH12 1RJ

Bustling town pub with wide choice of drinks, efficient staff, well liked food

Inside this bustling town pub, it's basically one large open-plan, turn-of-the-century bar room. There's a large central bar, a nice collection of sizeable dark wood tables and comfortable chairs on a stripped wood floor, and interesting old prints and photographs above a dark wood panelled dado on the cream walls. A spacious conservatory has similar furniture and lots of hanging baskets. Caledonian 80/-, Greene King IPA and Old Speckled Hen, Harveys Best, Harviestoun Bitter & Twisted, and Ringwood Fortyniner on handpump, around 100 malt whiskies, lots of gins, vodkas and rums, 30 wines by the glass, and draught cider. The pretty flower-filled back terrace has plenty of garden furniture. The small car park is for staff and deliveries only but you can park next door in the council car park.

🍴 **Interesting bar food includes sandwiches, ploughman's, soup, pork and green peppercorn terrine, roasted artichoke, shallot and baby spinach salad with poached egg, smoked salmon and scrambled egg on toast, antipasti platter, pork and leek sausages with bubble and squeak and onion gravy, sweet potato, lentil and coconut curry, 8oz burger with mozzarella and bacon, beef in ale pie, grilled salmon fillet with pea and crayfish risotto, braised lamb shank with roasted garlic mash, and puddings like chocolate, rum and raisin cheesecake and honey and pecan tart.** *Starters/Snacks: £3.50 to £8.50. Main Courses: £8.75 to £15.50. Puddings: £4.95 to £5.25*

Brunning & Price ~ Manager Neil Gander ~ Real ale ~ Bar food (all day) ~ (01403) 253526 ~ Children over 5 lunchtime only ~ Dogs allowed in bar ~ Open 12-11(10.30 Sun)

Recommended by Tony and Wendy Hobden, Jude Wright, Francis Vernon, Ian Phillips

ICKLESHAM

TQ8716   MAP 3

Queens Head ♀ ◖
Just off A259 Rye—Hastings; TN36 4BL

Friendly, well run country pub, extremely popular with locals and visitors, with a good range of beers, proper home cooking and seats in garden with fine views

Much enjoyed by our readers, this is a particularly well run pub where the long-serving landlord and his friendly staff are certain to make you welcome. The open-plan areas work round a very big serving counter which stands under a vaulted beamed roof, the high beamed walls and ceiling of the easy-going bar are lined with shelves of bottles and covered with farming implements and animal traps, and there are well used pub tables and old pews on the brown patterned carpet. Other areas have big inglenook fireplaces, and the back room has some old bikes hanging from the ceiling and is decorated with old bicycle and motorbike prints. Greene King IPA and Abbot, Harveys Best, Kings Red River, Ringwood Fortyniner, and Whitstable India Pale Ale on handpump, ciders and perries, and a dozen wines by the glass. Piped jazz or blues, board games, and darts. Picnic-sets look out over the vast, gently sloping plain of the Brede Valley from the little garden, there's a children's play area, and boules. Good local walks.

Ⅱ **Popular, reasonably priced bar food using local produce includes sandwiches, filled baked potatoes, ploughman's, soup, chicken liver pâté, soft herring roes, tiger prawns in ginger, chilli and garlic, large steak and kidney pie, all day breakfasts, leek, brie and bacon pasta, ham and eggs, a curry of the day, minted lamb chops, mixed grill, fresh local grilled fish (cod, haddock, halibut, plaice and skate), and puddings like profiteroles with chocolate sauce and apple pie.** *Starters/Snacks: £4.95 to £6.50. Main Courses: £8.25 to £14.95. Puddings: £3.50 to £3.95*

Free house ~ Licensee Ian Mitchell ~ Real ale ~ Bar food (12-2.30, 6-9.30; all day weekends) ~ (01424) 814552 ~ Well behaved children in eating area of bar until 8.30pm ~ Dogs allowed in bar ~ Live music Sun 4-6pm ~ Open 11-11; 12-10.30 Sun; closed evenings 25 and 26 Dec

Recommended by Tony Brace, Kevin Thorpe, Peter Meister, Tom and Jill Jones, V Brogden, Chris Maynard, Gene and Tony Freemantle, Lucien Perring, Conrad Freezer, Tina and David Woods-Taylor, Lorry Spooner, Dr A J and Mrs Tompsett, Mike Gorton, Danielle Glann

LODSWORTH

SU9321   MAP 2

Halfway Bridge Inn ♀ 🛏
Just before village, on A272 Midhurst—Petworth; GU28 9BP

Smart, contemporary décor in several dining areas, log fires, real ales, quite a few wines by the glass, modern food; lovely bedrooms

Perhaps with more emphasis nowadays on the dining side, this smart and civilised 17th-c inn does still welcome those dropping in for a drink and a chat. The three or four bar rooms are carefully furnished with good oak chairs and an individual mix of tables, and one of the log fires is contained in a well polished kitchen range. The inter-connecting restaurant rooms have beams, wooden floors and a cosy atmosphere. Ballards Best, Ringwood Best, and Skinners Betty Stogs on handpump and 14 wines by the glass; piped music. At the back there are seats on a small terrace. The bedrooms in the former stable yard are extremely stylish and comfortable.

Ⅱ **Served by friendly staff, the imaginative food includes lunchtime sandwiches, soup, rabbit and pancetta terrine with cranberry chutney, twice-cooked belly of pork with sage and bacon lardons, seared scallops with rosemary and celeriac purée, chestnut and wild mushroom risotto with apple compote and parmesan crisp, beer-battered fresh cod with tartare sauce, roasted lamb shank with rich rosemary jus, trio of partridge, pheasant and pigeon breasts with parsnip, sweet potato and swede purées and red wine jus, and puddings such as dark and white chocolate mousse and orange and cardamom brûlée with a brandy snap.** *Starters/Snacks: £4.95 to £9.50. Main Courses: £10.95 to £18.95. Puddings: £4.75 to £7.50*

Free house ~ Licensee Paul Carter ~ Real ale ~ Bar food (12-2.30, 6.30-9.15) ~ Restaurant ~ (01798) 861281 ~ Children welcome ~ Dogs allowed in bar ~ Open 11-11; 12-10.30 Sun; closed 25 Dec ~ Bedrooms: £85B/£120B

Recommended by Hunter and Christine Wright, Ralph and Jean Whitehouse, Derek Thomas, Colin and Janet Roe

OVING   SU9005   MAP 2

Gribble Inn ⬛

Between A27 and A259 just E of Chichester, then should be signposted just off village road; OS Sheet 197 map reference 900050; PO20 2BP

Own-brewed beers in bustling thatched pub with beamed and timbered linked rooms, traditional bar food, and pretty garden

The own-brewed real ales and changing guests in this 16th-c thatched pub remain quite a draw, and include Gribble Ale, Plucking Pheasant, and Reg's Tipple, plus Badger Best, First Gold, and Hopping Hare on handpump. The chatty bar has lots of heavy beams and timbering, old country-kitchen furnishings and pews and the several linked rooms have a cottagey feel and huge winter log fires; the basset hound is called Puzzle. Decent wine and farm cider. Board games and skittle alley with its own bar. There are seats outside under a covered area and more chairs in the pretty garden with apple and pear trees; at the end of the garden are some rabbits.

🍽 **Bar food at lunchtime includes doorstop sandwiches, filled baked potatoes, ploughman's, soup, mushrooms in garlic, steak and kidney pudding, beery sausages with gravy, a daily vegetarian pasta dish, lambs liver and bacon, and home-cooked ham and egg; in the evening, there are quite a few daily specials and fresh fish dishes.** *Starters/Snacks: £4.95 to £6.95. Main Courses: £7.95 to £14.95. Puddings: £4.50*

Badger ~ Licensees Dave and Linda Stone ~ Real ale ~ Bar food (12-2.30, 6.30-9.30(8.30 Sun)) ~ Restaurant ~ (01243) 786893 ~ Children welcome ~ Dogs allowed in bar ~ Jazz first Tues of month, live bands last Fri of month ~ Open 11-3, 5.30-11; 11-11 Sat; 12-10.30 Sun

Recommended by R B Gardiner, David H T Dimock, Paul and Shirley White, Stephen Moss, Mike and Lynn Robinson, Mr and Mrs P D Titcomb, Tony and Wendy Hobden, Ann and Colin Hunt

PETWORTH   SU9921   MAP 2

Welldiggers Arms

Low Heath; A283 towards Pulborough; GU28 0HG

Country pub with long-serving landlord, unassuming bar rooms and home-cooked bar food

Run by a long-serving, friendly landlord, this is a popular country pub liked by both locals and visitors. The smallish L-shaped bar has an unassuming style and appearance, low beams, a few pictures (Churchill and gun dogs are prominent) on shiny ochre walls above a panelled dado, a couple of very long rustic settles with tables to match, and some other stripped tables (many are laid for eating); a second rather lower side room has a somewhat lighter décor. No music or machines. Wells & Youngs bitter on handpump, and decent wines by the glass. Outside, screened from the road by a thick high hedge, are plenty of tables and chairs on pleasant lawns and a terrace, with nice country views.

🍽 **As well as two-course set menus, the well liked bar food includes sandwiches, ploughman's, soup, grilled king prawns in garlic, smooth duck pâté, half-a-dozen oysters, steak, Guinness and stilton pie, home-cooked ham and eggs, braised oxtail with dumplings, smoked haddock with parsley sauce, half a roast duck with apple sauce, and daily specials.** *Starters/Snacks: £5.50 to £10.50. Main Courses: £7.50 to £24.00. Puddings: £4.95 to £5.95*

Free house ~ Licensee Ted Whitcomb ~ Real ale ~ Bar food (12-2(3 Sun), 6.30-9 but also see opening hours) ~ Restaurant ~ (01798) 342287 ~ Children in saloon bar only ~ Dogs welcome ~ Open 11-3.30, 6-11.30; 12-4 Sun; closed Mon; closed Tues, Weds and Sun evenings

Recommended by Christopher and Elise Way, Peter Sampson, R B Gardiner

RINGMER

Cock

Uckfield Road – blocked-off section of road off A26 N of village turn-off; BN8 5RX

Popular food in 16th-c pub, log fire in heavily beamed bar, a fine choice of drinks, garden with wide views – nice sunsets

This is a 16th-c former coaching inn where the landlords personally welcome all customers. The unspoilt, heavily beamed bar has traditional pubby furniture on flagstones, a log fire in the inglenook fireplace (lit from October to May), and Harveys Best and winter Old, and a guest like Fullers London Pride on handpump; Weston's cider, nine wines by the glass, and a dozen malt whiskies; piped music. There are dining areas. Outside on the terrace and in the garden, there are lots of picnic-sets with views across open fields to the South Downs; visiting dogs are offered a bowl of water and a chew, and their own dogs are called Fred and Tally.

🍴 An extensive choice of popular bar food includes soup, chicken liver pâté, egg and prawn mayonnaise, spicy cajun chicken strips, pork and herb sausages, mixed nut roast with red wine sauce, home-cooked ham and free-range eggs, steak and kidney pudding, lamb chops in garlic and rosemary, liver and bacon with onion gravy, bass fillets with a white wine, cream and mushroom sauce, daily specials such as thai-style mussels, various quiches and moussaka, and puddings like treacle tart or rhubarb crumble. *Starters/Snacks: £4.25 to £5.50. Main Courses: £6.50 to £16.95. Puddings: £3.95 to £5.25*

Free house ~ Licensees Ian and Matt Ridley ~ Real ale ~ Bar food (12-2.15(2.30 Sat), 6-9.30; all day Sun) ~ Restaurant ~ (01273) 812040 ~ Children welcome ~ Dogs allowed in bar ~ Open 11-3, 6-11.30; 11am-11.30pm Sun

Recommended by John Branston, Ann and Colin Hunt, Tony and Wendy Hobden, Conor McGaughey

RYE

Mermaid 🍷 🛏

Mermaid Street; TN31 7EY

Lovely old timbered inn on famous cobbled street with civilised, antiques-filled bar and other rooms, good wine list, and short choice of decent bar food; smart restaurant and bedrooms

A special place to stay overnight and full of history and interest, this fine old inn – on a steeply cobbled street – was built in the 15th and 16th centuries, and its black and white timbered façade is beautiful. It's extremely civilised with prices to match, and the little bar is where those in search of a light lunch and a drink tend to head: quite a mix of quaint, closely set furnishings such as Victorian gothic carved oak chairs, older but plainer oak seats, and a massive deeply polished bressumer beam across one wall for the huge inglenook fireplace. Three antique but not ancient wall paintings show old english scenes. Courage Best, Fullers London Pride, and Greene King Old Speckled Hen on handpump, and a good wine list; piped music in the bar only. Seats on a small back terrace overlook the car park where – on bank holiday weekends – there are morris dancers.

🍴 A short choice of lunchtime bar food includes sandwiches, soup, goats cheese and spinach omelette, moules marinières, smoked haddock and salmon fishcakes, steak and kidney pudding, minute steak with a blue cheese salad, and puddings such as crème brûlée with fresh berries and strawberry pavlova with chantilly cream. The smart restaurant offers two- and three-course set lunches. *Starters/Snacks: £6.75 to £7.50. Main Courses: £8.50 to £16.00. Puddings: £5.50*

Free house ~ Licensees Robert Pinwill and Mrs J Blincow ~ Real ale ~ Bar food (12-2.30, 7-9.30; all day in summer) ~ Restaurant ~ (01797) 223065 ~ Children welcome away from main bar ~ Open 12-11 ~ Bedrooms: £90B/£180B

Recommended by Lorry Spooner, Mrs Hazel Rainer, B and M Kendall, Mr and Mrs W W Burke, Adrian Johnson, the Didler

Ypres Castle ◖

Gun Garden; steps up from A259, or down past Ypres Tower; TN31 7HH

Traditional pub with views of Ypres Castle, enjoyable bar food, lots of fish, several real ales, and friendly service; seats in sheltered garden

---

Doing well under its newish management, this is a traditional and nicely placed pub with views of Ypres Castle and the River Rother. The bars have not changed much, still with a mix of old tables and chairs, and somehow, the informal almost scruffy feel adds to its character; there are comfortable seats by the winter log fire, local artwork, and a restaurant area. Adnams Broadside, Harveys Best, local Pevensey Bay White Gold, and Timothy Taylors Landlord on handpump, and friendly, helpful service. Outside in the sheltered garden, there is some new garden furniture; boules.

🍴 Good bar food includes lots of fish such as plaice, beer-battered fresh cod, and bass with basil mash and a white wine sauce – they also have a Scallop Festival – plus filled baguettes, ploughman's, soup, chicken liver parfait with red onion marmalade, ham and fig salad, butternut squash and mediterranean vegetables with red pesto, cider-simmered honey-roast ham, romney marsh marinated lamb on a skewer with fruit couscous salad, chicken with mozzarella wrapped in pancetta with a green pesto sauce, and puddings such as triple chocolate cake and passion fruit crème brûlée. *Starters/Snacks: £5.00 to £6.50. Main Courses: £8.00 to £18.00. Puddings: £4.50 to £5.50*

Free house ~ Licensee Ian Fenn ~ Real ale ~ Bar food (11-3, 6-9(8 Fri); 11-9 Sat; 12-4 Sun) ~ Restaurant ~ (01797) 223248 ~ Children welcome in back bar ~ Dogs allowed in bar ~ Live music Fri evening ~ Open 11-midnight; 11-9 Sun; closed Sun evening

Recommended by Richard Endacott, Peter Meister, Tom and Jill Jones

---

SALEHURST   TQ7424   MAP 3

Salehurst Halt

Village signposted from Robertsbridge bypass on A21 Tunbridge Wells—Battle; Church Lane; TN32 5PH

Pleasant little local in quiet hamlet, chatty atmosphere, and real ales; nice little back garden

---

To find this chatty and relaxed little local, just head for the church. It's at its busiest in the evening when there's quite a mix of customers of all ages. To the right of the door there's a small area with a big squishy black sofa, a sizeable cushioned wooden settle and just one small table on the stone floor, a TV and an open fire. To the left there's a nice long scrubbed pine table with a sofa and cushions, a mix of more ordinary pubby tables and wheelback and mates' chairs on the wood-strip floor, and maybe piped folk music; board games. Harveys Best and Dark Star Hophead on handpump and decent wines by the glass. There's a back terrace with metal chairs and tiled tables with more seats in the landscaped garden. More reports please.

🍴 Bar food – which can be limited at times – usually includes filled baguettes, soup, greek salad, a large, popular fishcake with tartare sauce, proper burgers, local cod in beer batter, ham and eggs, and puddings. *Starters/Snacks: £4.00 to £5.00. Main Courses: £7.00 to £15.00. Puddings: £3.80*

Free house ~ Licensee Andrew Augarde ~ Real ale ~ Bar food (12-3, 7-9; not Mon, not Tues evening) ~ (01580) 880620 ~ Children welcome ~ Dogs welcome ~ Live music 2nd Sun of month 4-7pm ~ Open 12-3, 6-11; 12-11(10 Sun) Sat; closed Mon

Recommended by Mrs Hazel Rainer, Nigel and Jean Eames

> If a service charge is mentioned prominently on a menu or accommodation terms, you must pay it if service was satisfactory. If service is really bad, you are legally entitled to refuse to pay some or all of the service charge as compensation for not getting the service you might reasonably have expected.

SIDLESHAM

SZ8697 MAP 2

Crab & Lobster 🍴 ♀ 🛏

Mill Lane; off B2145 S of Chichester; PO20 7NB

Welcoming to walkers and drinkers but more of a restaurant-with-rooms, plenty of fresh fish dishes, real ales and a dozen wines by the glass, stylish furnishings, and seats on terrace overlooking bird reserve; new bedrooms

Just minutes from Chichester, this rather handsome inn has seats and tables on the back terrace that look over to the bird reserve of silted Pagham Harbour. Inside, there's a flagstoned bar for walkers and drinkers with comfortable bucket seats around a mix of wooden tables, some bar stools by the light wooden-topped bar counter, a log fire, Harveys Best and Timothy Taylors Landlord on handpump, and a dozen wines by the glass. But the main emphasis here is on the stylish, upmarket restaurant side with fabric dining chairs around tables set for eating, and walls painted in pale pastel colours. Good lighting, piped music, and friendly, helpful staff. The newly opened bedrooms are stylish, and there's also a self-catering cottage. This is under the same ownership as the Royal Oak at East Lavant and the Halfway Bridge Inn at Lodsworth, both Sussex main entries.

🍴 Specialising in fresh fish, the imaginative food includes lunchtime open sandwiches, soup, home-smoked breast of barbary duck with mango and pumpkin seed salad and a pomegranate molasses dressing, flaked smoked haddock and smoked cheddar omelette, crab and crayfish in crème fraîche cocktail sauce wrapped in smoked salmon and served on pickled cucumber topped with caviar, spinach, ricotta, pepperonata and garlic mushroom filo pie with goats cheese sauce, fresh fish in light beer batter, monkfish and tiger prawn thai green curry, seafood risotto with wild rocket, and roast rump of local lamb with black olive and tomato jus. *Starters/Snacks: £5.50 to £10.50. Main Courses: £12.50 to £18.00. Puddings: £5.75*

Free house ~ Licensee Sam Bakose ~ Real ale ~ Bar food (12-2.30, 6-10(9 Sun) ~ Restaurant ~ (01243) 641233 ~ Children welcome ~ Open 11-11 ~ Bedrooms: /£120B
Recommended by J A Snell

TROTTON

SU8322 MAP 2

Keepers Arms 🍴 ♀

A272 Midhurst—Petersfield; pub tucked up above road, on S side; GU31 5ER

Low ceilings, comfortable furnishings on polished wooden boards, open fires, real ales, contemporary food, and seats on sunny terrace

Originally a smithy, this is now an interestingly furnished pub with good modern bar food and pleasant sitting areas for those who just want a drink. The beamed L-shaped bar has timbered walls and some standing timbers, comfortable sofas and winged-back old leather armchairs around the big log fire, and simple rustic tables on the oak flooring. Elsewhere, there are a couple of unusual adult high chairs at an oak refectory table, two huge Georgian leather high-backed chairs around another table and, in the dining room, elegant oak tables, comfortable dining chairs and a woodburning stove; there's another cosy little dining room with bench seating around all four walls and a large central table. Ballards Best, Dark Star Hophead, and Ringwood Best on handpump, and several wines from a comprehensive list. There are tables and seats on the south-facing terrace.

🍴 Good, locally sourced, contemporary bar food includes soup, wild mushroom tartlet with a poached egg and hollandaise sauce, ballotine of rabbit and foie gras, risotto of sun-dried tomatoes, goats cheese and pesto, trio of pork with apple and parsnip purée, honey-roasted gressingham duck breast with creamed savoy cabbage, shi-itake mushrooms and puy lentils, daily specials such as cod fillet in light beer batter, seared tuna with niçoise salad and roast rump of lamb with chargrilled vegetables and olive sauce, and puddings like salted peanut parfait with caramelised bananas and mango mousse with tropical fruit salad; popular Sunday roasts. *Starters/Snacks: £4.50 to £6.75. Main Courses: £8.50 to £15.00. Puddings: £5.00 to £6.50*

Free house ~ Licensee Nick Troth ~ Real ale ~ Bar food ~ Restaurant ~ (01730) 813724 ~
Children welcome ~ Dogs allowed in bar ~ Open 12-3.30, 6-11; 12-3.30, 7-10.30 Sun

Recommended by Martin and Karen Wake, BOB, Jennifer Hurst, Janet Whittaker, Bruce Young

WARNINGLID   TQ2425   MAP 3

Half Moon 🍴

*B2115 off A23 S of Handcross, or off B2110 Handcross—Lower Beeding – village is
signposted; The Street; RH17 5TR*

**Good modern cooking in simply furnished, newly extended village local, informal chatty
atmosphere, friendly service, real ales and decent wines, and seats in sizeable garden**

As we went to press, a new, larger dining area was being added to this traditional village
local and new kitchens were being fitted. But the hard-working licensees are very keen
that at least half the place will be kept for those just wanting a drink and a chat. There's
a lively little locals' bar with straightforward pubby furniture on the bare boards and a
small victorian fireplace. A couple of steps leads from here down to the main bar which
again, is pretty unpretentious, with an informal chatty feel, plank panelling and bare
brick, old photographs of the village, built-in cushioned wall settles, and a mix of tables
(all with candles and fresh flowers) on bare boards; another step down to a smaller
carpeted area with big paintings. It's all spotless. Harveys Best and changing guests like
Greene King Old Speckled Hen, and Ringwood Best and Fortyniner on handpump, several
decent wines by the glass, and some malt whiskies; friendly service. There are quite a few
picnic-sets outside on the lawn in the sheltered, sizeable garden. No children inside.

🍴 Very popular and extremely good, the totally home-made bar food includes lunchtime
filled ciabattas and ploughman's as well as pumpkin seed risotto cakes with beetroot coulis
and grilled goats cheese salad, beer-battered fish with home-made ketchup, home-made
beefburger with horseradish mayonnaise, chicken breast with ginger and satay coleslaw,
mango salsa and parmentier potatoes, beef, field mushroom and ale pie, roast salmon fillet
with tartare velouté and pea purée, specials like a trio of local estate venison and lamb
tagine with mint crème fraîche and couscous, and puddings such as chocolate and rum
mousse cake with orange crème fraîche and muscovado cheesecake with kumquat compote.
Starters/Snacks: £5.25 to £6.25. Main Courses: £9.00 to £18.50. Puddings: £5.00 to £7.00

Free house ~ Licensees John Lea and James Amico ~ Real ale ~ Bar food (12-2, 6-9.30; 12-3;
not Sun evening) ~ Restaurant ~ (01444) 461227 ~ Dogs allowed in bar ~ Open 11.30-2.30,
5.30-11; 12-10.30 Sun; closed 25 Dec

*Recommended by Mr and Mrs R Green, Terry Buckland, C and R Bromage, N R White, David Cosham, Chris Wall,
Karen Eliot, Martin and Karen Wake, Derek and Maggie Washington*

WARTLING   TQ6509   MAP 3

Lamb 🍷

Village signposted with Herstmonceux Castle off A271 Herstmonceux—Battle; BN27 1RY

**Newly refurbished, friendly pub, comfortable seating areas, cosy little bar, changing real
ales, popular bar food, and seats on pretty back terrace**

Closed for a few months and newly refurbished, this remains a relaxed and cheerful pub with
friendly staff. There's a little entrance bar with a couple of tables and this leads through to
the beamed and timbered snug (mind your head on the low entrance beam) with comfortable
leather sofas and some wooden chairs and tables; the separate restaurant is off here. Log
fires, Harveys Best and a couple of guest beers on handpump, and ten wines by the glass. Up
some steps at the back of the building there are seats on a pretty, flower-filled terrace.

Bedroom prices normally include full english breakfast, VAT and any inclusive service
charge that we know of. Prices before the '/' are for single rooms, after for two people in
a double or twin (B includes a private bath, S a private shower).

🍴 Well liked bar food includes filled ciabattas, ploughman's, soup, caesar salads with chicken, cajun or large prawns, chicken and mushroom pâté, spaghetti with crab, prawns, chilli and crayfish, wellington of mushrooms, leeks, asparagus and goats cheese with a mushroom and thyme sauce, braised chicken with fennel, shank of lamb with mushrooms, marsala, peppercorns, nutmeg and cinammon on garlic mash, escalopes of gloucester old spot pork with blue cheese, prosciutto, sage and white wine and caramelised onion mash, and puddings such as lemon and sultana bread and butter pudding with clotted cream and iced chocolate and Tia Maria parfait. *Starters/Snacks: £4.25 to £6.50. Main Courses: £8.50 to £13.95. Puddings: £4.95*

Free house ~ Licensees Robert and Alison Farncombe ~ Real ale ~ Bar food (11.45-2.15, 6.45-9; 12-2.30 Sun; not Sun evening) ~ Restaurant ~ (01323) 832116 ~ Children in eating areas ~ Dogs allowed in bar ~ Open 11-3, 6-11; 12-3 Sun; closed Sun evening

Recommended by Conrad Freezer, Christopher Turner, V Brogden, Barry and Victoria Lister, P and J Shapley

WILMINGTON
TQ5404 MAP 3

Giants Rest

Just off A27; BN26 5SQ

Busy country pub with friendly welcome from cheerful landlord, informal atmosphere, popular bar food, and real ales; bedrooms

In a peaceful village, this inviting pub has now been run by the same friendly family for ten years. It's a popular place and the long wood-floored bar and adjacent open areas have simple chairs and tables, wooden table games, Beryl Cook paintings, candles on tables, an open fire and a nice informal atmosphere; you must book to be sure of a table, especially on Sunday lunchtimes. Harveys Best, Hop Back Summer Lightning and Timothy Taylors Landlord on handpump; piped music, and puzzles and games on the tables. Plenty of seats in the front garden. Elizabeth David the famous cookery writer is buried in the churchyard at nearby Folkington; her headstone is beautifully carved and features mediterranean vegetables and a casserole. Plenty of walks nearby on the South Downs, and the majestic chalk-carved figure of the Long Man of Wilmington is nearby.

🍴 Reasonably priced and well liked, the bar food includes sandwiches, filled baked potatoes, ploughman's, soup, smoked duck and bacon warm salad, king prawns cooked in wild garlic, local sausages or home-cooked ham with bubble and squeak and home-made chutney, roast vegetable, watercress and goats cheese lasagne, hake, coriander, spring onion and chilli fishcakes, rabbit and bacon pie, daily specials, and puddings such as sticky date and walnut pudding and warm chocolate fudge brownie. *Starters/Snacks: £4.00 to £6.00. Main Courses: £7.00 to £13.50. Puddings: £3.50 to £5.00*

Free house ~ Licensees Adrian and Rebecca Hillman ~ Real ale ~ Bar food (all day Sun and bank hol Mon) ~ (01323) 870207 ~ Children welcome if well behaved ~ Dogs allowed in bar ~ Open 11-3, 6-11; 11-11 Sat; 12-10.30 Sun ~ Bedrooms: /£60

Recommended by Bettye Reynolds, Barry and Victoria Lister, Jenny and Peter Lowater, Paul Boot, N R White, Bob and Val Collman, Kevin Thorpe

WINEHAM
TQ2320 MAP 3

Royal Oak

Village signposted from A272 and B2116; BN5 9AY

Splendidly old-fashioned local with interesting bric-a-brac in simple rooms, real ales and well liked food

A new licensee has taken over this old-fashioned local but has no plans to make major changes to the décor. Logs burn in an enormous inglenook fireplace with a cast-iron Royal Oak fireback, and there's a collection of cigarette boxes, a stuffed stoat and crocodile, some jugs and ancient corkscrews on the very low beams above the serving counter, and other bits of bric-a-brac; views of quiet countryside from the back parlour, and the bearded collie is called Bella. Harveys Best and maybe a guest beer tapped from the cask in a still room, and 14 wines by the glass. There are some picnic-sets outside – picturesque if you are facing the pub. More reports on the new regime, please.

🍴 Using local, seasonal produce, the bar food now includes sandwiches, soup, ploughman's (attractively set out on big boards), fishcakes, venison sausages, various pies, and puddings such as baked cheesecake with stem ginger and walnut tart; on Mondays they do home-cooked ham with bubble and squeak and parsley sauce and their Sunday roasts are popular. *Starters/Snacks: £4.25 to £6.00. Main Courses: £6.75 to £11.50. Puddings: £4.75*

Punch ~ Tenants Sharon and Michael Bailey ~ Real ale ~ Bar food (12-2.30(3 Sun), 7-9.30; no food Sun evening) ~ (01444) 881252 ~ Children welcome ~ Dogs welcome ~ Open 11-2.30(3.30 Sat), 5.30(6 Sat)-11; 12-5, 7-10.30 Sun

Recommended by B and M Kendall, N R White, Mrs Mahni Pannett, Barry and Sue Pladdys, Phil and Sally Gorton

LUCKY DIP

Besides the fully inspected pubs, you might like to try these Lucky Dips recommended to us and described by readers (if you do, please send us reports: feedback@thegoodpubguide.co.uk).

☆ *Olde Smugglers* BN26 5UE [Waterloo Sq]: Charming ancient pub, low beams and panelling, huge inglenook in white-panelled bar, masses of bric-a-brac and smuggling mementoes, good friendly service, good value bar food from sandwiches to steaks, Harveys Best and Timothy Taylors Landlord, good choice of wines by the glass; can get crowded as this lovely village draws many visitors; children allowed in eating area and conservatory, nice well planted back suntrap terrace *(LYM, Pam Adsley, Bruce Bird)*
Star BN26 5TA [High St]: Fascinating fine painted medieval carvings outside, heavy-beamed old-fashioned bar (busy lunchtime, quiet evenings) with some interesting features inc medieval sanctuary post, antique furnishings and big log fire in Tudor fireplace, easy chairs in comfortable lounge, more space behind for eating; some 35 good modern bedrooms in up-to-date part behind, open all day summer *(the Didler, LYM)*
AMBERLEY [S00313]
☆ *Black Horse* BN18 9NL [off B2139]: Pretty pub with character main bar (dogs allowed), plenty of pictures, high-backed settles on flagstones, beams over serving counter festooned with sheep bells and shepherds' tools, lounge with many antiques and artefacts, log fires in both bars and restaurant, straightforward bar food (all day Sun), sandwiches served with potato wedges and salad (and no sharing of main courses), well kept Greene King IPA and Wells & Youngs Bombardier; piped music, children must be well behaved; nice sheltered raised garden, open all day *(LM, Tina and David Woods-Taylor, LYM)*
Bridge BN18 9LR [B2139]: Popular open-plan dining pub, comfortable and relaxed even when busy, with welcoming staff, pleasant bar and separate two-room dining area, decent range of reasonably priced food from good sandwiches up, well kept Harveys and other ales; children and dogs welcome, seats out in front, more tables in side garden, open all day *(Lawrence Pearse, LYM, Sian Morris, Mrs M K Matthews)*

☆ *Sportsmans* BN18 9NR [Crossgates; Rackham Rd, off B2139]: Warmly welcoming new licensees, well kept Fullers, Harveys and guests such as Dark Star, enjoyable food, three bars inc brick-floored games room, great views over Amberley Wild Brooks from pretty back conservatory restaurant and tables outside, good walks; neat up-to-date bedrooms *(LYM, Bruce Bird)*
ANGMERING [TQ0704]
☆ *Spotted Cow* BN16 4AW [High St]: Good interesting generous food (very popular wkdy lunchtimes with older people) from sandwiches up, friendly and enthusiastic chef/landlord, real ales such as Arundel, Fullers, Greene King and Harveys, good choice of wines by the glass, smallish bar on left, long dining extension with large conservatory on right, two log fires, smuggling history, sporting caricatures, no piped music; children welcome, big garden with boules and play area; open all day Sun, afternoon jazz sometimes then, lovely walk to Highdown hill fort *(Bruce Bird, Tony and Wendy Hobden, N R White)*
ARDINGLY [TQ3430]
☆ *Gardeners Arms* RH17 6TJ [B2028 2 miles N]: Reliable reasonably priced pub food in olde-worlde linked rooms, Badger beers, pleasant efficient service, daily papers, standing timbers and inglenooks, scrubbed pine on flagstones and broad boards, old local photographs, mural in back part; attractive wooden furniture on pretty terrace, lots of picnic-sets in side garden, opp S of England show ground and handy for Borde Hill and Wakehurst Place, open all day at least wknds *(Susan and John Douglas, BB, Harvey Smith, Tony and Wendy Hobden)*
Oak RH17 6UA [Street Lane]: Low-beamed 14th-c dining pub with Harveys Best and guest beers such as Hop Back Summer Lightning and Sharps Doom Bar, good range of wines by the glass, good value food servery, efficient staff, olde-worlde décor with lots of brass, bric-a-brac and lace curtains, magnificent inglenook, simple bright restaurant extension, games in public bar; good-sized garden with slide, handy for

show ground and reservoir walks *(Bruce Bird, Gary and Karen Turner)*

ARLINGTON [TQ5407]

Yew Tree BN26 6RX [off A22 nr Hailsham, or A27 W of Polegate]: Neatly modernised Victorian village pub popular for generous food (can ask for smaller helpings) from hot filled rolls up, Harveys Best and decent wines, log fires, prompt service even when busy, darts in thriving bare-boards bar, plush lounge, comfortable conservatory; children welcome, good big garden with play area by paddock with farm animals, good walks *(BB, John Beeken, Stuart and Diana Hughes)*

ARUNDEL [TQ0208]

☆ *Black Rabbit* BN18 9PB [Mill Rd; Offham; keep on and don't give up!]: Long nicely refurbished riverside pub well organised for families, lovely spot nr wildfowl reserve, lots of tables outside, timeless views of water-meadows and castle; enjoyable range of all-day food, Badger ales, good choice of decent wines by the glass, friendly service, log fires; piped music; doubles as summer tea shop, with boat trips, good walks, open all day *(M Greening, Val and Alan Green, Mr and Mrs P D Titcomb, Gene and Kitty Rankin, LYM)*

ASHURST [TQ1816]

☆ *Fountain* BN44 3AP [B2135 S of Partridge Green]: Attractive and well run 16th-c country local with fine old flagstones, friendly rustic tap room on right with some antique polished trestle tables and housekeeper's chairs by inglenook log fire, second inglenook in opened-up heavy-beamed snug, attentive young staff, interesting blackboard food as well as pub staples, Fullers London Pride, Harveys and Kings; no under-10s; dogs welcome, pretty garden with duck pond (pay ahead if you eat out here) *(Karen Eliot, LYM, Terry Buckland)*

ASHURSTWOOD [TQ4136]

Three Crowns RH19 3TJ [Hammerwood Rd]: Roomy, well decorated and good value, local meats and fish, good service *(Glenn and Gillian Miller)*

BECKLEY [TQ8423]

Rose & Crown TN31 6SE [Northiam Rd (B2088)]: Comfortably refurbished village pub with good friendly service, good value generous standard food from sandwiches to good fish, well kept changing ales such as Harveys Best, Rother Valley and Timothy Taylors Landlord from hop-draped bar, cosy lower eating area with log fire and model boat; children welcome, views from pleasant garden *(Bruce Bird, Conrad Freezer)*

BINSTED [SU9806]

Black Horse BN18 0LP [Binsted Lane; about 2 miles W of Arundel, turn S off A27 towards Binsted]: Pretty 17th-c pub opened up by current welcoming licensees as roomy dining pub, sensible choice of reasonably priced food with some more expensive specials, Courage Best and Fullers London Pride, good coffee, back conservatory restaurant; piped music may obtrude; terrace tables,

attractive garden, valley views *(Tony and Wendy Hobden, BB)*

BODIAM [TQ7626]

☆ *Curlew* TN32 5UY [B2244 S of Hawkhurst]: In administration as we went to press, this has been a good smart dining pub (but with drinkers popping in too – Fullers London Pride, Wells & Youngs Bombardier and good wines by the glass), with beams, timbering and some red walls, neatly set tables, more formal back restaurant with woodburner; children and dogs welcome, small pretty garden; has been open all day in summer, cl Sun evening; news please *(LYM)*

BOGNOR REGIS [SZ9298]

Navigator PO21 2QA [Marine Drive West]: Good value pubby food in picture-window seafront dining area, Greene King, good staff, lively local atmosphere in carpeted bar; comfortable bedrooms, some with sea view *(David H T Dimock, Diana King)*

BRIGHTON [TQ3104]

Black Lion BN1 1ND [Black Lion St]: Big open-plan pub with stripped pine tables and some leather sofas on wooden floor, prints and soft lighting, Adnams and Wychwood Hobgoblin, pubby food, good choice of wines by the glass; piped music, games machine; tables outside *(Michael Dandy)*

☆ *Cricketers* BN1 1ND [Black Lion St]: Cheerful and genuine town pub, friendly bustle at busy times, good relaxed atmosphere when quieter, cosy and darkly Victorian with loads of interesting bric-a-brac – even a stuffed bear; attentive quick service, Adnams, Fullers, Greene King and Harveys tapped from the cask, good coffee, well priced pubby lunchtime food from sandwiches up in covered ex-stables courtyard and upstairs bar, restaurant (where children allowed); piped music; tall tables out in front, open all day *(LYM, Sue Demont, Tim Barrow, Bruce Bird, Michael Dandy, Keith and Chris O'Neill)*

☆ *Evening Star* BN1 3PB [Surrey St]: Chatty pub with several good Dark Star beers (originally brewed here), lots of changing guest beers and belgian cherry beers, friendly staff (may let you sample before you buy), farm ciders and perries, country wines, good lunchtime baguettes (rolls Sun), simple pale wood furniture on bare boards, good mix of customers; unobtrusive piped music, some live; pavement tables, open all day *(N R White, Michael Dandy, BB, Sue Demont, Tim Barrow)*

King & Queen BN1 1UB [Marlborough Pl]: Surprising medieval-style lofty main hall with mullioned windows and original décor, real ales such as Greene King Abbot from long bar, bargain food inc good Sun roasts, friendly service; portcullised entry to flagstoned courtyard, open all day Sun *(LYM, Ian Phillips)*

Mitre BN1 4JN [Baker St]: Welcoming traditional town pub, well kept Harveys, small snug *(Ann and Colin Hunt)*

Preston Park BN1 6GF [Havelock Rd]: Opened 2006, with short changing choice of enjoyable food, Adnams and Harveys, good service, contemporary décor, modern art on white walls, big windows *(William Goodhart)*

Romans BN42 4NG [Manor Hall Rd, Southwick]: 1930s estate pub, changing ales such as Arundel, Caledonian, Fullers and Wells & Youngs, sensibly priced food all day (not Sun evening), games bar; big garden, summer barbecues *(Tony and Wendy Hobden)*

Setting Sun BN2 0GN [Windmill St]: Two linked bars, several real ales, evening food (may do you something at lunchtime), reasonably priced house wines, high views from conservatory *(Guy Vowles)*

Waggon & Horses BN1 1UD [Church St]: Well run mid 19th-c town pub, bare boards and basic wall seating, Adnams Broadside, Fullers London Pride and Harveys Best, cheap pub lunches; seats outside *(Ian Phillips)*

BROWNBREAD STREET [TQ6714]

☆ *Ash Tree* TN33 9NX [off A271 (was B2204) W of Battle; 1st northward rd W of Ashburnham Pl, then 1st fork left, then bear right into Brownbread Street]: Tranquil country local tucked away in isolated hamlet, tasty food, wide choice of wines, well kept ales inc Harveys, cheerful service, good inglenook log fires, cosy beamed bars with nice old settles and chairs, stripped brickwork, interesting dining areas with timbered dividers; children in eating area, pretty garden, open all day *(Vivienne Bell, Jeremy Billingham, LYM, Ronald Donovan)*

BURGESS HILL [TQ3019]

Woolpack RH15 8TS [Howard Ave]: Useful reasonably priced family dining pub in big 1930s-look roadhouse, Courage Best, Wadworths 6X and guest beers; piped music; plenty of tables outside *(Tony and Wendy Hobden)*

BURY [TQ0013]

Squire & Horse RH20 1NS [Bury Common; A29 Fontwell—Pulborough]: Smartly kept beamed roadside pub with wide range of good generous home-made food inc good fish (worth booking as can get very busy), well kept Fullers and Harveys, good choice of wines, several attractive partly divided areas, pink plush wall seats, hunting prints and ornaments, log fire, fresh flowers; pleasant garden with pretty terrace (some road noise) *(Ann and Colin Hunt, Tony and Wendy Hobden, David Coleman, Lawrence Pearse, BB, Terry and Nice Williams, J Bryant)*

CATSFIELD [TQ7213]

White Hart TN33 9DJ [B2204, off A269; The Green]: Welcoming staff, enjoyable honest food from good value lunchtime snacks up, well kept Harveys, warm log fire; good walks *(Christopher Turner)*

CHAILEY [TQ3919]

☆ *Five Bells* BN8 4DA [A275 9 miles N of Lewes]: New licensees in attractive rambling roadside pub, spacious and interesting, with enjoyable food putting unusual touches to

good local and organic ingredients, friendly staff, several real ales, decent wine choice, lots of different rooms and alcoves leading from low-beamed bar area with fine old brick floor, brick walls and inglenook, leather sofas and log fire; picnic-sets in pretty garden *(Anne Clarke, BB)*

CHICHESTER [SU8605]

Bell PO19 6AT [Broyle Rd]: Friendly and comfortable country-pub feel, good interesting changing real ales and wines, generous reasonably priced food from separate counter inc good puddings, good service even when busy, daily papers, bric-a-brac on high beams; children welcome, pleasant partly covered back terrace, opp Festival Theatre *(Craig Turnbull, Val and Alan Green, Bruce Bird, David Carr)*

Dolphin & Anchor PO19 1QD [West St]: Wetherspoons opp cathedral well run as straightforward town pub, low prices, half a dozen ales, food from 9am breakfast on; TVs, small family area till 7 (not wknds); very busy with young people Sat night, doorman and queues to get in; disabled access, pleasant back terrace, open all day *(John Beeken, David Carr)*

Eastgate PO19 7JG [The Hornet]: Town pub with reasonably priced straightforward food inc a daily meat pudding, three Fullers ales and a guest beer, back dining area; children and dogs welcome, small back terrace *(Tony and Wendy Hobden)*

Four Chestnuts PO19 7EJ [Oving Rd]: Roomy open-plan pub, well kept interesting changing ales (annual beer festival), good generous basic lunchtime food (not Mon/Tues) inc good pie of the day, friendly helpful family service, daily papers, games room, skittle alley, some live music; open all day *(Bruce Bird)*

George & Dragon PO19 1NQ [North St]: Bustling simply refurbished bare-boards bar with sensibly priced food from sandwiches up, Adnams, Caledonian Deuchars IPA, Fullers London Pride and Wells & Youngs, pleasant service, log fires, conservatory extension; quiet back terrace, good value bedrooms *(David Carr, J A Snell, David H T Dimock, Michael Dandy, Ann and Colin Hunt)*

Old Cross PO19 1LP [North St]: Reopened open-plan pub in partly 16th-c building, sensibly priced pubby food, Ringwood Best and Wells & Youngs Bombardier *(Michael Dandy)*

☆ *Park Tavern* PO19 1NS [Priory Rd, opp Jubilee Park]: Comfortably reworked pub in attractive spot opp Jubilee Park, cheerful friendly service, enjoyable lunchtime food using fresh local produce and the day's fish, also good value sandwiches and some thai dishes, Fullers ales, relaxing smallish front bar, huge mirrors on right, extensive back eating area *(Michael Dandy, BB)*

Ship PO19 1NH [North St]: Bar/brasserie in modernised Georgian hotel, Gribble Best, bar lunches from sandwiches up; 36 bedrooms *(Michael Dandy)*

Waterside PO19 8DT [Stockbridge Rd]: Smart split-level pub with enjoyable interesting home-made food, friendly unhurried atmosphere, no swearing; downstairs lavatories can be reached instead from sloping side road, tables out by canal basin *(Valerie Baker)*

CHIDHAM [SU7804]

☆ *Old House At Home* PO18 8SU [off A259 at Barleycorn pub in Nutbourne; Cot Lane]: Cottagey old pub gently updated under newish management, enjoyable if not cheap food esp good local fish, several real ales, log fire, low beams and timbering, restaurant area, no piped music or machines; children in eating areas, tables outside, remote unspoilt farm-hamlet location, nearby walks by Chichester Harbour, open all day wknds *(Ann and Colin Hunt, LYM, J A Snell, William Ruxton)*

CHILGROVE [SU8214]

☆ *White Horse* PO18 9HX [B2141 Petersfield—Chichester]: As we went to press, this was closed with major changes intended

CLAPHAM [TQ1105]

Coach & Horses BN13 3UA [Arundel Rd (A27 Worthing—Arundel)]: Brightly modern uncluttered restauranty dining pub, informally smart, with hard-working chatty landlord, well cooked food, good wines by the glass, Greene King Abbot; tables outside *(Tony and Wendy Hobden, Val and Alan Green)*

CLAYTON [TQ2914]

Jack & Jill BN6 9PD [Brighton Rd (A273)]: Friendly unsmart country pub with proper cooking inc local lamb, well kept changing ales such as Shepherd Neame and Whites, open fires, corner settles, small restaurant area; children and dogs welcome, big back garden with play area, bedrooms *(Tony and Wendy Hobden, John Beeken)*

CLIMPING [TQ0001]

Black Horse BN17 5RL [Climping St]: Attractive olde-worlde pub popular lunchtime for good value food (best to book Sun lunch), friendly newish management, Courage Best and Directors, good choice of wines by the glass, log fire, pleasant dining rooms, back room with leather sofas; tables out behind, walk to beach *(Colin McKerrow, Mrs M K Matthews)*

Oystercatcher BN17 5RU [A259/B2233]: Roomy thatched Vintage Inn dining pub, olde-worlde décor, friendly young well trained staff, reasonably priced traditional food all day from sandwiches and starters doubling as light dishes up, Bass and Harveys Best, good choice of wines by the glass, nicely served coffee, log fires; disabled lavatories, picnic-sets in pleasant front garden (some traffic noise) *(David H T Dimock)*

COCKING CAUSEWAY [SU8819]

Greyhound GU29 9QH [A286 Cocking—Midhurst]: Pretty tile-hung 18th-c pub under new licensees, enjoyable reasonably priced food (booking advised wknds), real ales such

as Fullers London Pride, Greene King and St Austell, cosy olde-worlde beamed bar with open fires, pine furniture in big new conservatory, nice and light; garden with play area *(Miss A E Dare)*

COLDWALTHAM [TQ0216]

Labouring Man RH20 1LF [pub signed down lane off A29 about 2 miles S of Pulborough]: Recently refurbished, friendly and comfortable, with great atmosphere, enjoyable food, real ales, log fires; children welcome, five comfortable new downs-view bedrooms *(Sian Morris)*

COLGATE [TQ2232]

Dragon RH12 4SY [Forest Rd]: Small two-bar pub with friendly staff, good value home-made food from tasty baguettes to local game, lovely log fire, well kept Badger ales, dining area; big garden, pleasant and secluded – good for children *(Francis Vernon, Terry Buckland)*

COMPTON [SU7714]

Coach & Horses PO18 9HA [B2146 S of Petersfield]: 17th-c two-bar local in pleasant village not far from Uppark (NT), open fire, pine shutters and panelling, three or four interesting changing ales, friendly landlady, bar food from baguettes up (can take a while), bar billiards; games machine; children and dogs welcome, tables out by village square *(LYM, Tony and Wendy Hobden, Ann and Colin Hunt)*

COOLHAM [TQ1223]

Selsey Arms RH13 8QJ [A272/B2139]: Welcoming landlord, Fullers London Pride and several Harveys ales, good value blackboard food from sandwiches up, three linked areas with flagstones, bare boards or carpet, two blazing log fires; pretty gardens, lots of trees in back one *(Tony and Wendy Hobden, M Greening, Bruce Bird)*

CRAWLEY [TQ2836]

LB1 RH10 1QA [Gales Dr, Three Bridges]: Stylish modern bar/café, enjoyable food from snacks and cream teas to pies and steaks (all day Sat), good Sun roast, speciality coffees and teas; open all day from 9 *(Eamonn and Natasha Skyrme)*

DANEHILL [TQ4128]

☆ *Coach & Horses* RH17 7JF [off A275, via School Lane towards Chelwood Common]: Well run dining pub in attractive countryside, good if not cheap restauranty food (not Sun evening) served with style, Harveys Best and Wychwood Shires, good wines by the glass, little hatch-served public bar with small woodburner and simple furniture on polished boards, main bar with big Victorian prints, attractive old tables and fine brick floor, dining extension, darts, home-made chutneys and jams for sale; may try to keep your credit card while you eat outside; children and dogs welcome (nice pub dog), lovely views from big attractive garden with terrace under huge maple *(Oliver and Sue Rowell, Susan and John Douglas, John and Patricia Deller, Michael Hasslacher, LYM)*

DELL QUAY [SU8302]

☆ *Crown & Anchor* PO20 7EE [off A286 S of Chichester – look out for small sign]: Modernised 15th-c beamed pub in splendid spot overlooking Chichester Harbour – best at high tide and quiet times, can be packed on sunny days; comfortable bow-windowed lounge bar, panelled public bar (dogs welcome), two log fires, lots of wines by the glass, four Wells & Youngs ales, polite cheerful staff, all-day servery doing popular food inc plenty of seafood (good crab sandwiches); terrace, nice walks *(Dick and Madeleine Brown, Derek and Heather Manning, Mr and Mrs W W Burke, Mrs Romey Heaton, John Beeken, Nigel and Kath Thompson, R and M Thomas, BB, David Carr, Mr and Mrs P D Titcomb)*

DENTON [TQ4502]

☆ *Flying Fish* BN9 0QB [Denton Rd]: French chef/landlord doing good well priced food from interesting baguettes up inc seasonal food esp game and fresh fish from nearby Newhaven, in attractive 17th-c flint village pub by South Downs Way, heavy beams, lots of settles and rustic bric-a-brac, two log fires, tiled floors throughout, comfortable high-ceilinged dining room and two smaller rooms off bar, well kept Shepherd Neame, friendly prompt service; attractive sloping garden behind, more tables on long deck and out in front, bedrooms *(John Beeken, the Didler)*

DIAL POST [TQ1519]

Crown RH13 8NH [Worthing Rd (off A24 S of Horsham)]: Friendly hard-working licensees, enjoyable food using local sources inc tapas and lunchtime sandwiches, well kept Harveys, Kings and a seasonal ale, good wines, two log fires, lots of beams, country bric-a-brac, front sun lounge, back dining room with extension down steps; garden *(Bruce Bird, Jennifer Hurst, A D Lealan, Tony and Wendy Hobden)*

DONNINGTON [SU8501]

☆ *Blacksmiths Arms* PO20 7PR [B2201 S of Chichester]: Small white roadside cottage, low ceilings, Victorian prints, solid comfortable furnishings, relaxed atmosphere, back restaurant, Fullers London Pride, Greene King Abbot and a guest beer, enjoyable but pricy food; children and dogs welcome, big garden with good play area, three miniature schnauzers, a cat and four tortoises, open all day Sun *(Lawrence Pearse, Nigel and Kath Thompson, Val and Alan Green, Joan York, Bob and Margaret Holder, LYM)*

DUNCTON [SU9517]

☆ *Cricketers* GU28 0LB [set back from A285]: Friendly family service, well kept Kings, Skinners Betty Stogs and a local guest such as Arundel or Langham, enjoyable food from sandwiches up, decent wines by the glass, inglenook fireplace, cricketing memorabilia, traditional games; piped music; children and dogs welcome, charming garden behind with creeper-covered bower and proper barbecue, open all day (till 8 Sun) *(LYM, Bruce Bird)*

EAST DEAN [TV5597]

Tiger BN20 0DA [off A259 Eastbourne—Seaford]: Pretty pub overlooking delightful cottage-lined sloping green, just a very few tables in two smallish rooms, low beams hung with pewter and china, polished rustic tables and distinctive antique settles, old prints and so forth, Harveys, Hepworths and Whites, Stowford Press farm cider, good wines by the glass; good spot for walkers, open all day wknds *(Guy Vowles, Andrea Rampley, Kevin Thorpe, LYM)*

EAST GRINSTEAD [TQ3936]

☆ *Old Mill* RH19 4AT [Dunnings Rd, S towards Saint Hill]: Low-ceilinged 16th-c former mill cottage built right over stream, attractively reworked as good informal Whiting & Hammond dining pub, with hearty fresh food, four Harveys ales, wide choice of wines by the glass, friendly service; children welcome, pretty garden, handy for Standen (NT) *(LYM, Mrs Stella Knight)*

EAST PRESTON [TQ0701]

Sea View BN16 1PD [Sea Rd]: Comfortable seaside pub with neat, friendly and efficient staff, well kept ales inc Arundel Castle, good value home-made food (not Sun/Mon evenings), OAP lunches Mon/Tues; nice garden *(Bruce Bird)*

EASTBOURNE [TV6198]

Buccaneer BN21 4BW [Compton St, by Winter Gardens]: Shaped like a galleon, with friendly helpful young staff, well kept Adnams Broadside and Wells & Youngs, enjoyable food inc two-for-one deals, theatre memorabilia; open all day *(Bruce Bird, the Didler)*

Dolphin BN21 4XF [South St]: Sensitively refurbished keeping its panelling and open fires, with leather settees alongside traditional pub furnishings, consistently enjoyable food using good local ingredients, changing ales such as Timothy Taylors Landlord *(Marcus and Lienna Gomm)*

Farm at Friday Street BN23 8AP [Friday St (B2104, Langney)]: Careful modern take on the rustic theme in newish Whiting & Hammond pub, beams, flagstones and leather sofas, good log fire, wide-ranging food (all day wknds) from lunchtime sandwiches to good puddings, good choice of wines by the glass, Harveys, friendly staff; children welcome, disabled facilities, tables outside, open all day *(anon)*

Pilot BN20 7RW [Holywell Rd, Meads; just off front below approach from Beachy Head]: Well worn friendly local, engaging Irish landlord, ample enjoyable food inc fresh fish, prompt service, well kept Harveys Best and Wells & Youngs Bombardier, good ship and aeroplane photographs, log fire in side bar; piped music, occasional live, TV, games machine, Tues quiz night; steeply terraced garden behind, open all day *(Kevin Thorpe, Christopher Turner)*

Ship BN20 7RH [Meads St]: Roomy pub, friendly and relaxed, with big leather sofas, comfortable chairs, pot plants and mirrors, enjoyable food inc fresh local fish, relaxed atmosphere, Bass, Fullers London Pride and Harveys Best, daily papers; TV, no dogs; disabled access, nicely planted garden with huge decked area and all-day summer barbecues, open all day *(David Burston, Guy Vowles, Michael and Ann Cole)*

Terminus BN21 3NS [Terminus Rd]: Enjoyable generous home-made lunches inc OAP deals and choice of daily roasts, full Harveys ale range kept well, welcoming licensees, interesting railway photographs (even section of ancient track, found in renovations), exotic plants in small sun lounge; tables outside *(Bruce Bird)*

EASTERGATE [SU9405]

Wilkes Head PO20 3UT [just off A29 Fontwell—Bognor; Church Lane]: Small friendly local with flagstones and big log fires, reasonably priced food, Adnams, pleasant service; garden tables *(D and J Guyoncourt)*

ELSTED [SU8320]

Elsted Inn GU29 0JT [Elsted Marsh]: Quietly civilised two-bar country pub with enjoyable food, good choice of wines by the glass, real ales such as Ballards, welcoming staff, log fires, nice country furniture and neat pastel décor; lovely enclosed downs-view garden with big terrace, four comfortable bedrooms, cl Sun evening *(LYM)*

FERNHURST [SU9028]

Red Lion GU27 3HY [The Green, off A286 via Church Lane]: Wisteria-covered 16th-c pub tucked quietly away by green and cricket pitch nr church, heavy beams and timbers, attractive furnishings, pricy food from interesting sandwiches and snacks to fresh fish, well kept Fullers, good wines, friendly efficient staff, restaurant; children welcome, pretty gardens front and back *(John Beeken, BB, Tony and Wendy Hobden)*

FERRING [TQ0903]

Henty Arms BN12 6QY [Ferring Lane]: Well kept Caledonian Deuchars IPA, Fullers London Pride, Wells & Youngs and other changing ales, beer festival late July, generous attractively priced food even Sun evening, neat friendly staff, log fire, opened-up lounge/dining area, separate bar with games and TV; garden tables *(Bruce Bird, Tony and Wendy Hobden)*

FINDON [TQ1208]

Snooty Fox BN14 0TA [bar of Findon Manor Hotel]: Quiet and comfortable, with well kept Harveys Best and Skinners Betty Stogs, good coffee, enjoyable food from sandwiches up, 16th-c beams, wall settles, hunting caricatures and other foxy decorations, old advertisements and local photographs; pleasant tree-sheltered lawn, open all day Sun *(Tony and Wendy Hobden, Bruce Bird)*

FIRLE [TQ4607]

☆ *Ram* BN8 6NS [village signed off A27 Lewes—Polegate]: 17th-c village pub with chatty local atmosphere, individual décor with good mix of unassuming furnishings inc some big comfortable armchairs, contrasting coloured walls, log fires, friendly staff, well kept low-priced Harveys, food from sandwiches and some interesting light dishes up; children and dogs welcome, big walled garden behind, open all day *(Kevin Thorpe, Huw and Sarah, BB, J H Bell)*

FISHBOURNE [SU8304]

☆ *Bulls Head* PO19 3JP [Fishbourne Rd (A259 Chichester—Emsworth)]: Comfortable beamed village pub with popular quickly served food (not Sun evening), Fullers ales, neat attentive staff, good log fire, daily papers, fair-sized main bar, children's area, restaurant area, outstanding lavatories; skittle alley, terrace picnic-sets and pretty window-boxes, bedrooms *(Klaus and Elizabeth Leist, Ann and Colin Hunt, J A Snell, Mrs K Hooker)*

Woolpack PO19 3JJ [Fishbourne Rd W; just off A27 Chichester—Emsworth]: Big open-plan 1950s-ish roadside pub, nice variety of seats inc settees, Greene King Abbot, Wells & Youngs Special and two guest beers, friendly dog; dogs welcome, big garden, ten bedrooms *(J A Snell)*

FORD [SU0003]

Ship & Anchor BN18 0BJ [Station Rd]: Changing ales such as Goddards, Ringwood Fortyniner and Wells & Youngs Bombardier, sensibly priced pubby food all day from generous baguettes up, games room and family area, pub dog and cats; tables out by small marina, open all day *(Tony and Wendy Hobden)*

FRANT [TQ5935]

George TN3 9DU [High St, off A267]: Tucked down charming quiet lane by ancient church and cottages, new owners doing enjoyable traditional bar food and wider wknd evening choice, convivial low-ceilinged bar with several rooms rambling round servery, coal-effect gas fire in big inglenook, real ales, lots of wines by the glass, pleasant dining room; children and dogs welcome, play area, smokers' shelter and picnic-sets in pretty walled garden *(BB)*

GATWICK [TQ2539]

Flight Tavern RH11 0QA [Charlwood Rd]: Roomy former Aero Club, lots of Spitfire and other memorabilia, decent generous pubby food, good drinks choice, conservatory dining area; children welcome, good for plane-spotting – runway 300 metres away beyond trees *(Terry Buckland)*

GLYNDE [TQ4508]

☆ *Trevor Arms* BN8 6SS: Bargain food from ploughman's and baked potatoes to good Sun roasts, well kept Harveys, congenial landlord and staff, good range of spirits, small bar with corridor to impressive dining room, Glyndebourne posters and photographs; large garden with downland backdrop, Glyndebourne musicians may play out here on summer Suns *(John Beeken, Oliver Wright, John Tav, G H Wagstaff)*

GORING-BY-SEA [TQ1002]

Bulls Head BN12 5AR [Goring St]: Recently refurbished and renamed former Bull, several linked beamed areas inc barn-style dining room, friendly efficient young staff, real ales such as Black Sheep, Harveys and Wells & Youngs Bombardier, usual food all day inc afternoon discounts Mon-Thurs, pictures and old photographs; large walled garden *(Tony and Wendy Hobden)*

GUN HILL [TQ5614]

☆ *Gun* TN21 0JU [off A22 NW of Hailsham, or off A267]: Big welcoming country dining pub thriving under current licensees, several interesting rambling areas either side of large central bar, beams and log fires, generous fresh food using local supplies, two real ales (not always on), good wines, efficient pleasant service, locals' shop in former coach house; children welcome, hay for visiting horses, lovely garden with play area, right on Wealden Way *(LYM, Mike and Eleanor Anderson)*

HADLOW DOWN [TQ5324]

New Inn TN22 4HJ [Main Rd (A272 E of Uckfield)]: Unspoilt Edwardian pub with traditional brown décor, well kept Harveys; outside lavatories *(Phil and Sally Gorton)*

HALNAKER [SU9008]

☆ *Anglesey Arms* PO18 0NQ [A285 Chichester—Petworth]: Bare boards, settles and log fire, Adnams Best, Wells & Youngs and local guest beers, decent wines, good generous if not cheap food inc local organic produce and Selsey fish, friendly accommodating licensees, simple but smart L-shaped dining room with woodburners, stripped pine and some flagstones (children allowed), traditional games, amiable dog; tables in large tree-lined garden *(Leslie and Barbara Owen, R B Gardiner, Bruce Bird, John Beeken, Val and Alan Green, LYM, David H T Dimock)*

HAMMERPOT [TQ0605]

☆ *Woodmans Arms* BN16 4EU: Pretty thatched pub comfortably rebuilt after 2004 fire, beams and timbers, enjoyable pubby food from sandwiches and baked potatoes up, Fullers and a guest beer, Sun bar nibbles, quick service by neat polite staff, log fire in big fireplace; piped music; tables outside with summer marquee, open all day Fri/Sat and summer Sun, may be cl Sun evening *(Tony and Wendy Hobden, Ann and Colin Hunt, LYM)*

HANDCROSS [TQ2529]

☆ *Royal Oak* RH17 6DJ [Horsham Rd (A279, off A23)]: Handy for Nymans, very popular for generous food from light dishes to seasonal game and Sun lunch, friendly atmosphere and prompt obliging service, well kept Fullers, Harveys and guest beers, old photographs and curios; comfortable terrace with pleasant arbour overlooking fields and woods, interesting vintage motorcycle shop nearby *(C and R Bromage, Terry Buckland, Jack and Sandra Clarfelt, Glen and Nola Armstrong)*

HARTFIELD [TQ4735]

Anchor TN7 4AG [Church St]: Popular 15th-c local with good-natured atmosphere, quick

friendly service, Adnams, Bass, Flowers IPA, Fullers ESB and Harveys Best, generous usual bar food, heavy beams and flagstones, little country pictures and houseplants, inglenook log fire and woodburner, comfortable dining area, darts in lower room; piped music; children welcome, front verandah, garden with play area, open all day *(Adele Summers, Alan Black, LYM, N R White)*

☆ *Haywaggon* TN7 4AB [High St (A264)]: Two big log fires, pews and lots of large tables in spacious low-beamed bar, enjoyable blackboard bar food and good value former bakehouse restaurant, cheerful helpful staff, well kept Harveys, good choice of wines by the glass; dogs welcome, picnic-sets outside, comfortable bedrooms in recently converted stable block, good breakfast *(Cathy Robinson, Ed Coombe, William Ruxton, John Saville, Mike Gorton)*

HASTINGS [TQ8311]

Old King John TN35 5DL [Middle Rd]: Friendly local with well kept Greene King and Harveys, darts, shove-ha'penny, no machines *(anon)*

HEATHFIELD [TQ5920]

☆ *Star* TN21 9AH [Old Heathfield, off A265/B2096 E; Church St]: Lovely ancient pub with great potential and gentle country views from pretty garden, L-shaped beamed bar with inglenook log fire, built-in wall settles and window seats, a few old wooden tables, further room off, Harveys and Shepherd Neame ales; piped music, and has had a series of recent management changes; children and dogs have been allowed *(LYM)*

HENFIELD [TQ2115]

George BN5 9DB [High St]: Roomy and neatly kept beamed former coaching inn, good value food (particularly popular with older lunchers), well kept Harveys and Shepherd Neame, special wine offers, open fires, panelled restaurant; nostalgic piped music; children welcome *(Terry Buckland)*

White Hart BN5 9HP [High St (A281)]: Relaxing chatty 16th-c village pub with interesting tiled roof, cheery landlord, good service, Badger beers, farm cider, large civilised dining area with enjoyable food inc tempting puddings, decent wines with choice of glass sizes, comfortable L-shaped lounge, log fire, lots of panelling, tools hanging from low beams, horsebrasses, lots of pictures and fresh flowers; children welcome, small pleasant courtyard garden with play things *(Terry Buckland, William Ruxton)*

HENLEY [SU8925]

☆ *Duke of Cumberland Arms* GU27 3HQ [off A286 S of Fernhurst]: Rather special wisteria-covered 15th-c stone-built pub with big scrubbed pine or oak tables in two small rooms each with a bright log fire, low ceilings, white-painted wall boards and rustic decorations; reopened under new licensees summer 2007, initially limited food, several real ales tapped from the cask, farm cider, good wine choice; children welcome, beautiful hill views from gnarled seats in charming big sloping garden criss-crossed by stream and trout ponds, open all day *(Miss A E Dare, LYM, Phil and Sally Gorton, A J Longshaw)*

HERMITAGE [SU7505]

☆ *Sussex Brewery* PO10 8AU [A259 just W of Emsworth]: Bustling, welcoming and interesting, with small boards-and-sawdust bar, good winter fire in huge brick fireplace, simple furniture, little flagstoned snug, Wells & Youngs ales and a guest beer, several wines by the glass, good value hearty straightforward food inc wide choice of speciality sausages, two dining rooms, one overlooking garden; children and dogs welcome, picnic-sets in small back courtyard, open all day *(LYM, Ann and Colin Hunt, Ian Phillips, R and M Thomas, Harriette Scowen, Mr and Mrs P D Titcomb)*

HILL BROW [SU7826]

Jolly Drover GU33 7QL [B2070]: Smartened up as dining pub, leather sofas and big log fire, wide choice of enjoyable blackboard food, real ales such as fff Alton Pride, Fullers London Pride, Ringwood Best, Sharps Doom Bar and Timothy Taylors Landlord, friendly staff and atmosphere; bedrooms *(Tony Hobden)*

HOOE [TQ6708]

Lamb TN33 9HH [A259 E of Pevensey]: Quick friendly young staff in prettily placed olde-worlde Vintage Inn with lots of stripped brick and flintwork, one snug area around huge log fire and lots of other seats, big tables, good choice of wines by the glass and a couple of real ales, streamlined but enjoyable food range; children welcome *(Simon and Philippa Hughes)*

HORAM [TQ5717]

Horam Inn TN21 0EL: Tidied up under current welcoming management, enjoyable food, subdued lighting *(Phil and Sally Gorton)*

HORSHAM [TQ1730]

Crown RH12 1DW [Carfax]: Comfortably modernised, with polite efficient young staff, good range of food from light meals up, real ales such as Elgoods Black Dog and Greene King Old Speckled Hen, decent wines by the glass, some settees *(Neil Hardwick)*

HORSTED KEYNES [TQ3828]

Green Man RH17 7AS [The Green]: Open-plan pub in attractive spot handy for Bluebell Line, good value food from sandwiches up, well kept Greene King ales, decent wines by the glass, efficient friendly service, massive open fireplace, popular beamed dining area; lots of tables out in front and on green *(Tony and Wendy Hobden)*

HOUGHTON [TQ0111]

George & Dragon BN18 9LW [B2139 W of Storrington]: Elizabethan beams and timbers, attractive old-world bar rambling up and down steps, Arun valley views from back extension, reasonably priced generous food (all day wknds), attentive service, Marstons-

related ales such as Jennings and Ringwood, decent wines; they may try to keep your credit card while you eat, piped music; children welcome, charming well organised sloping garden, good walks *(LYM, Tony and Wendy Hobden, David Coleman, Ann and Colin Hunt)*

HUNSTON [SU8601]

Spotted Cow PO20 1PD [B2145 S of Chichester]: Flagstoned pub with friendly staff, locals and dog, wide choice of enjoyable if not cheap food, chilled Fullers/Gales ales, big fires, up-to-date décor, small front bar, roomier side lounge with armchairs, sofas and low tables as anteroom for airy high-ceilinged restaurant; may be piped music; good disabled access, children welcome to eat, big pretty garden, handy for towpath walkers *(Nigel and Kath Thompson, David H T Dimock)*

HURSTPIERPOINT [TQ2816]

☆ *New Inn* BN6 9RQ [High St]: Nicely refurbished 16th-c pub now under same management as Bull in Ditchling, well kept Harveys, good wines by the glass, enjoyable food, good friendly service, several softly lit linked beamed areas, comfortable leather seating; garden tables, open all day *(LYM, James and Ginette Read)*

ICKLESHAM [TQ8716]

☆ *Robin Hood* TN36 4BD [Main Rd]: Friendly no-frills pub with cheerful attentive staff, great local atmosphere, bargain unpretentious food, well kept Greene King ales, log fire, games area with pool, back dining extension; fortnightly summer Sun car boot sale, big garden with Brede valley views *(Peter Meister, Tom and Jill Jones, Arthur Pickering)*

ISFIELD [TQ4417]

Laughing Fish TN22 5XB: Opened-up Victorian local with good value pubby food, several Greene King ales, friendly staff, open fire, traditional games, entertaining beer race Easter bank hol Mon; children welcome, small pleasantly shaded walled garden with enclosed play area, right by Lavender Line *(Mrs Hazel Rainer, John Beeken, BB)*

JEVINGTON [TQ5601]

☆ *Eight Bells* BN26 5QB: Friendly and relaxed, with good value hearty home-made food (all day Sun) from good lunchtime filled rolls up, nice puddings, Adnams Broadside, Flowers Original and Harveys Best and winter Old, simple furnishings, beams, parquet floor, flame-effect fire in inglenook; piped music; dogs welcome, South Downs Way, Weald Way and 1066 Trail all nearby, quiet village with interesting church; dogs welcome, front terrace, secluded downs-view garden with some sturdy tables under cover, adjacent cricket field, open all day *(BB, Mike and Carol Williams)*

KINGSFOLD [TQ1635]

Wise Old Owl RH12 3SA [Dorking Rd (A24 Dorking—Horsham, nr A29 junction)]: Nicely rambling olde-worlde reworking of 1930s pub, good sharing platters from their integral deli/farm shop and other enjoyable food from sandwiches up, Badger K&B and Hogs Back TEA, good choice of wines by the glass, log fires, restaurant very welcoming to children (worth booking Sun); open all day from 9.30am *(Anna and Martyn Carey, Ian Phillips)*

KINGSTON NEAR LEWES [TQ3908]

☆ *Juggs* BN7 3NT [village signed off A27 by roundabout W of Lewes]: Ancient rose-covered pub with heavy 15th-c beams and very low front door, lots of neatly stripped masonry, sturdy wooden furniture on bare boards and stone slabs, smaller eating areas inc family room, good welcoming service, enjoyable straightforward food, well kept Shepherd Neame ales, good coffee and wine list, log fires, dominoes and shove-ha'penny; piped music; nice seating areas outside, compact well equipped play area *(Tom and Rosemary Hall, Fr Robert Marsh, LYM, R and M Thomas)*

LANCING [TQ1704]

Crabtree BN15 9NQ [Crabtree Lane]: Friendly pub with good staff, Fullers London Pride and changing ales from small brewers, bargain lunches, games area in large public bar, comfortable Spitfire lounge with unusual 30s ceiling, art deco lights, model planes and old photographs; garden with downs views and play area *(Bruce Bird, Tony and Wendy Hobden)*

LAVANT [SU8508]

Earl of March PO18 0BQ [A286, Mid Lavant]: Charming new landlord in smart pub with lots of Goodwood car and aircraft photographs, fireside leather sofas and flagstones, enjoyable traditional food, changing guest beers tapped from the cask, good wines by the glass, attractive restaurant; piped music; good views from garden, local walks, handy for Centurion Way cycle path *(J A Snell, Tony Brace, Kathryn Gill)*

LEWES [TQ4210]

Dorset BN7 2RD [Malling St]: Reopened after extensive refurbishment, light and airy, with large mellow area around central bar, smaller snug, lots of bare wood, neat welcoming staff, decent value food from panini to lots of fish, well kept Harveys, smart restaurant; large terrace, six comfortable bedrooms *(Tony Hobden, Ann and Colin Hunt, Tony and Wendy Hobden, BB)*

John Harvey BN7 2AN [Bear Yard, just off Cliffe High St]: No-nonsense tap for nearby Harveys brewery, all their beers inc seasonal kept perfectly, some tapped from the cask, decent value food from huge lunchtime sandwiches, baked potatoes and ciabattas up, friendly efficient young staff, basic dark flagstoned bar with one great vat halved to make two towering 'snugs' for several people, lighter room on left; piped music and machines; a few tables outside, open all day, breakfast from 10am *(Mrs Hazel Rainer, Phil Bryant, BB, David Swift, Tony and Wendy Hobden, Ann and Colin Hunt)*

☆ *Lewes Arms* BN7 1YH [Castle Ditch Lane/Mount Pl – tucked behind castle ruins]: Well worn corner local built into castle ramparts, chatty and friendly, small front bar and hatchway, larger lounge with eating area off, well kept Harveys Best as well as Greene King ales, Old Rat farm cider, good wines by the glass, bargain simple food from good baguettes and tapas up 12-6, daily papers, local pictures, good fire in traditional games room, no music or mobiles; small heated terrace, open all day *(Kevin Thorpe, Geoff and Carol Thorp, Sue Demont, Tim Barrow, BB, Conor McGaughey, John Beeken)*

Snowdrop BN7 2BU [South St]: Tucked under the cliffs, unpretentious pub reopened under new management, exclusively vegetarian food, well kept Adnams and Harveys, distinctive atmosphere and maritime décor with figureheads, ship lamps etc; piped music, no nearby parking if pub's small space full; children and dogs welcome, open all day *(Sue Demont, Tim Barrow, Kevin Thorpe, LYM)*

LINDFIELD [TQ3425]

Stand Up RH16 2HN [High St]: Traditional local tied to Dark Star with their ales and guests from Crouch Vale, Moles, and Red Squirrel, beams and joists, a mix of dining chairs and various tables on the well worn carpet, cushioned window seats, and loud piped pop music; end dining room with new laminate wood floor, blonde chunky furnishings, dried flowers and various nature prints and photographs; farm ciders and maybe bargain pasties; darts; tables in yard, open all day *(Andrew and Susan Kerry-Bedell, Mike and Eleanor Anderson)*

LITTLE COMMON [TQ7107]

Wheatsheaf TN39 4LR: Very popular bargain lunch inc four roasts Mon-Sat, friendly helpful staff, well kept Harveys in recently refurbished pub with tables in front bar and two comfortable dining areas *(C and R Bromage)*

LITTLEHAMPTON [TQ0202]

☆ *Arun View* BN17 5DD [Wharf Rd; W towards Chichester]: Airy and attractive 18th-c pub in lovely spot right on harbour with busy waterway directly below windows, very popular lunchtime with older people, a younger crowd evenings, for its interesting food (all day Sun) from sandwiches to good fresh fish, Ringwood Best and Old Thumper and Youngs Special, good wine list, good cheerful service even when busy, lots of drawings, caricatures and nautical collectables, flagstoned and panelled back public bar, large waterside conservatory and flower-filled terrace, interesting newish waterside walkway to coast; disabled facilities, summer barbecues evenings and wknds, winter live music, bright and modest good value bedrooms *(Craig Turnbull, Terry Buckland, Tony and Wendy Hobden, Valerie Baker, Allison and Graham Thackery)*

George BN17 5BG [Surrey St]: Bright Wetherspoons with their usual food, impressive drinks choice, local pictures; heated back terrace (Valerie Baker)

LODSWORTH [SU9223]

☆ **Hollist Arms** GU28 9BZ [off A272 Midhurst—Petworth]: Civilised village pub overlooking small green, Kings Horsham Best, Timothy Taylors Landlord and Wells & Youngs, good wines by the glass and coffee, good range of generous enjoyable bar food inc fresh fish and shellfish, popular Sun lunch, relaxed atmosphere, cheerful landlord and helpful service, interesting books and magazines, country prints, sofas by log fire, high-ceilinged dining room; must book Sat night, outside lavatories; children welcome, nice tree-lined back garden, good walks (R B Gardiner, Mike and Eleanor Anderson, Martin and Karen Wake)

MARESFIELD [TQ4623]

Chequers TN22 2EH [High St]: Imposing three-storey Georgian coaching inn with rather smart bar, enjoyable food here and in restaurant, Harveys and guest beers, good coffee, decent house wine, friendly staff, daily papers; picnic-sets under cocktail parasols in neat garden, bedrooms (Anne Clarke)

MARK CROSS [TQ5831]

☆ **Mark Cross Inn** TN6 3NP [A267 N of Mayfield]: Big Whiting & Hammond pub, linked areas on varying levels, good informal service, real ales inc Harveys Best and Timothy Taylors Landlord, good wines by the glass, nice coffee, huge helpings of hearty food, real mix of dark wood tables and cushioned dining chairs, walls crowded with prints, old photographs and postcards, church candles, houseplants; decking with nice teak furniture, picnic-sets out on grass, broad Weald views (Peter Meister, Colin McKerrow, Conor McGaughey, Mrs M Merritt, BB)

MAYFIELD [TQ5927]

Rose & Crown TN20 6TE [Fletching St]: Pretty weather-boarded old local under new sister licensees, well kept Greene King Abbot and Harveys Best, decent wines, popular bar food, two-room front bar with low beams, big inglenook and attractive bow-window seat, nicely laid dining room (down a step or two) and tiny room behind servery; nostalgic piped music, rustic tables out by village lane, five bedrooms (LYM)

MIDDLETON-ON-SEA [SU9800]

Elmer PO22 6HD [Elmer Rd]: Comfortable central bar with front games room and back restaurant, attractively priced food from baguettes up, friendly efficient service, Fullers ales; bedrooms (Tony and Wendy Hobden)

MIDHURST [SU8821]

Bricklayers Arms GU29 9BX [Wool Lane/West St]: Two cosy olde-worlde bars, welcoming local atmosphere, enjoyable generous home-made food inc good sandwiches and Sun roast, Greene King ales, good coffee, friendly efficient service, oak furniture, 17th-c

beams, old photographs and bric-a-brac; courtyard tables out under cocktail parasols (Craig Turnbull, Colin McKerrow)

MILLAND [SU8328]

Rising Sun GU30 7NA [Iping Rd junction with main rd through village]: Light and cheery main bar with Fullers ales at a price, pubby food from sandwiches up, bar billiards; children welcome (very popular with large families wknds), good-sized neat garden with heated terrace, good walking area (BB)

MILTON STREET [TQ5304]

☆ **Sussex Ox** BN26 5RL [off A27 just E of Alfriston – brown sign to pub]: Attractive and friendly country pub with magnificent downs views, smallish beamed and brick-floored bar with roaring woodburner, enjoyable food, well kept Dark Star, Harveys and an interesting guest beer, enthusiastic young licensees and quick service even when busy, good family dining area (book well ahead in summer) with nice prints; piped music; big lawn and terrace, lots of good walks (Julian Thomas, LYM, Michael B Griffith, Bruce Bird)

NEWHAVEN [TQ4500]

Hope BN9 9DN [follow West Beach signs from A259 westbound]: Big-windowed nautical-theme pub overlooking busy harbour entrance, settles forming booths in long bar, upstairs dining conservatory and breezy balcony tables with even better view towards Seaford Head, Fullers London Pride and Harveys, bargain food, good choice of wines, friendly staff; piped music may obtrude; waterside terrace (John Beeken, LYM)

NORTH CHAILEY [TQ3921]

Kings Head BN8 4DH [A275/A272]: Bargain pub food under new landlord, well kept Greene King ales, long light bar and eating area with log fire, darts and pool in games end; piped music may obtrude; garden behind (John Beeken)

NUTBOURNE [SU7805]

Barleycorn PO18 8RS [A259 W of Chichester]: Unpretentious open-plan local with welcoming staff, reasonably priced usual food; tables outside (Tony and Jill Radnor)

Rising Sun RH20 2HE [off A283 E of Pulborough; The Street]: Unspoilt creeper-covered village pub dating partly from 16th c, beams, bare boards and scrubbed tables, friendly helpful young landlord, well kept ales such as Adnams, Fullers and Hammerpot, good value food from pubby favourites to exotics, big log fire, daily papers, enamel advertising signs and 1920s fashion and dance posters, chess and cosy games room, attractive back family room; children and dogs allowed, two garden areas with small back terrace under apple tree (Bruce Bird, John Beeken, Sarah Hutchinson)

OFFHAM [TQ4011]

Chalk Pit BN7 3QF [Offham Rd (A275 N of Lewes)]: Bright and pleasant, on four levels, with well kept Harveys, decent wines by the glass, generous standard food all day, attentive staff, neat restaurant extension, skittle alley; bedrooms, open all day *(Tony and Wendy Hobden, John Beeken)*

PAGHAM [SZ8998]

Bear PO21 3QB [Pagham Rd]: Generous good value food from bar snacks to hearty main dishes, Fullers London Pride and Greene King Ruddles County and Old Speckled Hen, friendly staff; bedrooms *(Nigel and Kath Thompson)*

Lamb PO21 4NJ [Pagham Rd]: Rambling flower-decked pub with generous enjoyable food, Fullers, Greene King and Wells & Youngs, prompt service even when busy, lots of beams, timbers and paintings; unobtrusive piped music; garden tables *(David H T Dimock, Bruce Bird)*

PATCHING [TQ0705]

Fox BN13 3UJ [Arundel Rd; signed off A27 eastbound just W of Worthing]: Generous good value fresh food from imaginative sandwiches up, popular Sun roasts (book ahead for these), well trained young staff, well kept Harveys Best and a guest beer, good wine choice, daily papers, large dining area off roomy panelled bar, hunting pictures; quiet piped music, nice tree-shaded garden with play area, small caravan site, open all day wknds *(Bruce Bird, Tony and Wendy Hobden, Jude Wright)*

PETT [TQ8713]

Royal Oak TN35 4HG [Pett Rd]: Well run friendly local, roomy main bar with big log fireplace, attractive dining areas each end, Harveys Best, Timothy Taylors Landlord and a guest beer, quick service, popular Sun lunch; well cared for small garden behind *(Lucien Perring, Peter Meister)*

PETWORTH [SU9722]

☆ *Stonemasons* GU28 9NL [North St]: Attractive old low-beamed pub, enjoyable food from sandwiches to enterprising dishes, Badger K&B, Fullers London Pride, Langham Halfway to Heaven and Skinners Betty Stogs, comfortable eating areas in former adjoining cottages (opp Petworth House so best to book in summer); picnic-sets in pleasant sheltered garden with arbour, nine comfortable bedrooms, good breakfast *(Ian Phillips)*

PLUMPTON GREEN [TQ3617]

☆ *Plough* BN7 3DF: Whiting & Hammond pub with enjoyable food from filled bagels up (they list many of their suppliers), notably friendly attentive service, Harveys ales inc seasonal, good value wines, log fires in both bars, striking Spitfire and Hurricane pictures as well as books and bric-a-brac; covered terrace and large attractive downs-view garden with play area, open all day *(Bruce Bird, Terry Buckland, John Beeken)*

POYNINGS [TQ2611]

☆ *Royal Oak* BN45 7AQ [The Street]: Large darkly beamed chatty bar with wide choice of good food (best to book Sun lunch), fair prices, good service even when very busy, Courage Directors, Greene King Old Speckled

Hen and Harveys from three-sided servery, woodburner, no piped music; dogs welcome, big attractive garden with barbecue, climbing frame and country/downs views *(J Graveling, Mrs Mahni Pannett, William Goodhart, Adele Summers, Alan Black)*

ROBERTSBRIDGE [TQ7323]

☆ *George* TN32 5AW [High St]: Attractive contemporary dining pub, armchairs and sofa by inglenook log fire on right, friendly helpful licensees, Adnams, Harveys, Hop Back Crop Circle and Timothy Taylors Landlord, good wines by the glass, enterprising and enjoyable reasonably priced food, bustling, chatty atmosphere; piped music, live lunchtime last Sun of month; children and dogs welcome, back courtyard *(Nigel and Jean Eames, BB, Alan Covall)*

Ostrich TN32 5DG [Station Rd]: Cheerful open-plan former station hotel, enjoyable food from filled rolls up, Adnams, Harveys and a guest beer, coal fire, eye-catching artworks, games room; attractive garden, bedrooms, open all day *(the Didler)*

RODMELL [TQ4105]

Abergavenny Arms BN7 3EZ [back rd Lewes—Newhaven]: Open-plan beamed and raftered ex-barn pub with some interesting bric-a-brac and furnishings, generous pubby food, Harveys Best and Hogs Back RIP, Thatcher's cider, log fire, further upper dining area; piped music may obtrude; dogs on leads welcome, large two-level back terrace, good walks and handy for Virginia Woolf's Monks Cottage *(John Beeken)*

ROGATE [SU8023]

☆ *White Horse* GU31 5EA [East St; A272 Midhurst—Petersfield]: Rambling heavy-beamed local in front of village cricket field, civilised and friendly, with Harveys full range kept particularly well, relaxed atmosphere, flagstones, stripped stone, timbers and big log fire, attractive candlelit sunken dining area, good generous reasonably priced food (not Sun eve), friendly staff, traditional games (and quite a collection of trophy cups), no music or machines; quiz and folk nights; some tables on back terrace, open all day Sun *(Michael B Griffith, Bruce Bird, LYM)*

RUDGWICK [TQ0934]

Kings Head RH12 3EB [off A281; Church St (B2128)]: Well kept Harveys and good italian cooking inc lots of seafood, reasonable prices; by fine old church in pretty village *(Ian Scott-Thompson)*

RUSHLAKE GREEN [TQ6218]

☆ *Horse & Groom* TN21 9QE [off B2096 Heathfield—Battle]: Cheerful village-green local, little L-shaped low-beamed bar with small brick fireplace and local pictures, small room down a step with horsey décor, simple beamed restaurant, friendly landlady and sister, food inc local fish and game, Shepherd Neame ales, decent wines by the glass; children and dogs welcome, cottagey garden with pretty country views, nice walks *(David Barnes, R L Borthwick,*

Conor McGaughey, J H Bell, E D Bailey, LYM)
RUSPER [TQ1836]
Royal Oak RH12 4QA [Friday St, towards
Warnham; back rd N of Horsham, E of A24]:
Cosy linked areas with interesting bric-a-brac
big and small, prints and panelling, up to
nine changing well kept ales such as Dark
Star, Goddards and Surrey Hills, farm cider,
enjoyable food, big log fire; very rural spot
on Sussex Border Path *(Bruce Bird)*
RYE [TQ9220]
Globe TN31 7NX [Military Rd]: Reworked
under newish ownership as 1940s-theme
dining pub, enjoyable local food from bar
dishes to upscale lunchtime specials,
Harveys Best and Fullers ESB, friendly staff
and good atmosphere, barmaids in high
heels and bright red lipstick, period piped
music, sofas and easy chairs, light wood
dining furniture, light airy décor; picnic-sets
out under cocktail parasols *(Peter Meister)*
Hope Anchor TN31 7HA [Watchbell St]: Fine
views from family-run 18th-c hotel, well kept
Harveys and other ales, pleasant staff, good
value food inc sandwiches and fresh fish in
attractive day, log-fire lounge and roomy and
tasteful dining room; 14 bedrooms
(V Brogden)
Ship TN31 7DB [The Strand]: Lots of space,
wooden tables on bare boards, good value
pubby food, Harveys and Youngs; bedrooms
(Conrad Freezer)
Union TN31 7JY [East St]: Attractive beamed
pub with friendly helpful service, enjoyable
home-made food from sandwiches to fresh
local fish, Harveys and Hop Back Summer
Lightning, good atmosphere; children
welcome *(Ian Phillips)*
RYE HARBOUR [TQ9419]
☆ *Inkerman Arms* TN31 7TQ [Rye Harbour Rd]:
Friendly plain pub nr nature reserve, stools
around the bar but otherwise mainly tables
for the wide choice of good food inc local
scallops Nov-Apr and lots of low-priced fresh
fish, fine home-made pies and old-fashioned
puddings, Greene King IPA, Harveys Best
and perhaps a guest beer; tables out in
small sheltered back area, cl Mon evening
and winter Mon lunchtime *(V Brogden,
Conrad Freezer)*
SCAYNES HILL [TQ3824]
Sloop RH17 7NP [Freshfield Lock]: Promptly
served blackboard food (all day Sun), Greene
King and guest ales, decent wines, bar
billiards and traditional games, interesting
photographs in pleasantly furnished linked
areas; children in eating areas, lots of tables
in sheltered garden *(LYM, Mrs Hazel Rainer,
C and R Bromage)*
SELHAM [SU9320]
☆ *Three Moles* GU28 0PN [village signed off
A272 Petworth—Midhurst]: Small simple old-
fashioned pub tucked away in woodland
village with tiny late Saxon church, quiet
and relaxing, friendly enthusiastic landlady,
unusual ales collected direct from small
breweries (one always a Mild, others often
west country), farm cider, blazing coal fires,

daily papers, darts, bar billiards, plenty of
board games, very mixed furniture, a few oil
lamps and pictures, no mobile phones – but
has internet link; steep steps up to bar, no
food or children, monthly singsongs, June
beer festival; garden tables, nice walks, open
all day wknds *(Phil and Sally Gorton,
J A Snell)*
SELSEY [SZ8692]
Lifeboat PO20 0DJ [Albion Rd, nr seafront]:
Congenial unpretentious bar (dogs allowed)
with dining extension, enjoyable food inc
fish from new landlord's own boat, well kept
Arundel ASB and Fullers London Pride;
flower-decked verandah *(Tony and
Wendy Hobden, Nigel and Kath Thompson,
J A Snell)*
Seal PO20 0JX [Hillfield Rd]: Lively
refurbished local with helpful staff, real ales
such as Dark Star, Hop Back and Wells &
Youngs, good value food inc local fish, good
choice of wines by the glass, old local
lifeboat and other photographs; tables out
on decking *(Bruce Bird)*
SHIPLEY [TQ1321]
☆ *Countryman* RH13 8PZ [SW of village, off
A272 E of Coolham]: Particularly friendly and
neatly kept country pub, public bar with
cushioned pews either side of woodburning
stove in inglenook fireplace, red bucket
leather armchairs and high-backed black
leather dining chairs around small tables,
blue plush bar stools and Fullers London
Pride, Harveys Best and Horsham Best on
handpump; spreading dining areas with warm
coal fire in brick fireplace, heavy beams and
joists (water jugs, small flagons and copper
pieces), proper napkins and clothes on all
tables, musical instruments, piped jazz,
Dixieland prints, fresh flowers and house
plants and charming staff; picnic-sets,
garden seats, pergolas, and small marquees
in country garden *(Terry Buckland)*
SHOREHAM-BY-SEA [TQ2105]
Red Lion BN43 5TE [Upper Shoreham Rd]:
Modest dim-lit low-beamed and timbered
16th-c pub with settles in snug alcoves,
good value generous pubby food inc good
Sun lunch, half a dozen well kept changing
ales such as Harveys and Kings, decent
wines, farm cider, friendly efficient staff, log
fire in unusual fireplace, another open fire in
dining room, further bar with covered
terrace; pretty sheltered garden behind,
lovely Norman church opp, good downs
views and walks *(Tony and Wendy Hobden,
Ian Phillips, Jestyn Phillips, Val and
Alan Green)*
SHORTBRIDGE [TQ4521]
☆ *Peacock* TN22 3XA [Piltdown; OS Sheet 198
map ref 450215]: Civilised and comfortable
traditional dining pub with beams, timbers
and big inglenook, enjoyable generous food
inc good fish, well kept Fullers London
Pride, Harveys Best and Wadworths 6X,
friendly staff, restaurant; piped music;
children welcome, good-sized garden *(BB,
Phil Bryant, Mrs Stella Knight)*

SINGLETON [SU8713]

☆ *Partridge* PO18 0EY [just off A286 Midhurst—Chichester]: Pretty black and cream pub handy for Weald & Downland Open Air Museum, polished boards, flagstones and daily papers, some small rooms with red settles, log fires, roomy back bar extension, Fullers London Pride, Goddards Fuggle-Dee-Dum and Kings Horsham Best, attentive staff, standard bar food; piped music; children and dogs allowed, terrace and big walled garden, bedrooms planned, open all day wknds *(Mr and Mrs P D Titcomb, Prof and Mrs S Barnett, James Edwards, Ann and Colin Hunt, LYM)*

SLAUGHAM [TQ2528]

Chequers RH17 6AQ [off A23 S of Handcross]: Leather sofas, polished boards and soft lighting, rustic wooden furniture around chatty bar, wide choice of home-made food from simple bar lunches to smart evening meals, real ales such as Kings, good wines by the glass, young staff, open fire, modern back extension; dogs welcome, sloping garden with country views, lakeside walks *(Terry Buckland, N R White)*

SOUTH HARTING [SU7819]

Ship GU31 5PZ [North Lane (B2146)]: Welcoming 17th-c pub, unpretentious and informal, with fine log fires, good value food (not Sun evening) from sandwiches up, well kept ales from small breweries, decent wines, friendly helpful service, old photographs in dimly lit main bar, plain wooden settles in locals' bar, dominoes; may be piped music; nice setting in village, good walks *(Chris and Sarah Dowdeswell, J A Snell)*

STAPLEFIELD [TQ2728]

Jolly Tanners RH17 6EF [Handcross Rd, just off A23]: Neatly kept two-level local by cricket green, two good log fires, lots of china, brasses and old photographs, well kept Elgoods Black Dog Mild, Fullers London Pride, Harveys and guest beers, Addlestone's and Weston's cider, good early May bank hol beer festival, pubby food, friendly landlord and chatty atmosphere; piped music, jazz Sun evening, fortnightly quiz Thurs; children and dogs welcome, attractive garden with lots of space for children, quite handy for Nymans (NT) *(Mike and Eleanor Anderson, N R White)*

STEDHAM [SU8522]

Hamilton Arms GU29 0NZ [School Lane (off A272)]: Proper english local but decorated with thai artefacts and run by friendly thai family, basic pub food but also good interesting thai bar snacks and restaurant dishes (cl Mon); pretty hanging baskets, tables out by village green and quiet lane, village shop in car park, good walks nearby *(J A Snell)*

STEYNING [TQ1711]

Chequer BN44 3RE [High St]: Rambling low-beamed timber-framed Tudor pub under friendly new local landlord, well kept Dark Star, Kings Horsham Best, Timothy Taylors Landlord, and a guest such as Arundel, good choice of wines, generous usual food from sandwiches and snacks up, friendly service, log fire, antique snooker table; smokers' shelter, bedrooms, open all day *(Bruce Bird, Tony and Wendy Hobden)*

STOPHAM [TQ0318]

☆ *White Hart* RH20 1DS [off A283 E of village, W of Pulborough]: Fine old pub by medieval River Arun bridge, gently smartened up under friendly new management, heavy beams, timbers and panelling, log fire and sofas in one of its three snug rooms, well kept Arundel Gold, Hogs Back TEA and Weltons, enjoyable generous home-made food (unusual pictorial puddings menu), some interesting bric-a-brac; children welcome, waterside tables, some under cover *(Bruce Bird, John Beeken, R B Gardiner, LYM, Colin McKerrow)*

THAKEHAM [TQ1017]

☆ *White Lion* RH20 3EP [off B2139 N of Storrington; The Street]: Two-bar 16th-c pub still smoking hams in the chimney (big log fire), robust home-made food (not Sun-Weds evenings) from open kitchen, friendly informal service, real ales such as Caledonian, Harveys and Hogs Back, good choice of wines by the glass, heavy beams, panelling, bare boards and traditional furnishings inc corner settles, pleasant separate eating area; dogs welcome, terrace tables, more on small lawn, small pretty village, open all day *(Bruce Bird)*

TICEHURST [TQ6930]

Cherry Tree TN5 7DG [B2087 towards Flimwell, by Dale Hill golf club]: Neatly opened-up beamed bar with sofas as well as dark wood pub furniture, decent generous home-made food, cheerful service; pleasant terrace and small roadside garden *(BB)*

TILLINGTON [SU9621]

Horse Guards GU28 9AF [off A272 Midhurst—Petworth]: Prettily set dining pub with friendly new young licensees, some sensibly priced traditional dishes as well as fancier pricier things, changing ales such as Harveys, good choice of wines by the glass, log fire and country furniture in neat low-beamed front bar, lovely views from bow window, simple pine tables in dining room; terrace tables and sheltered garden behind, attractive ancient church opposite, three neat bedrooms, good breakfast *(LYM, Sally and Tom Matson)*

TURNERS HILL [TQ3435]

Crown RH10 4PT [East St]: Low-beamed bar, steps down to attractive dining area with pitched rafters, wide choice of reliable reasonably priced pubby food, real ales such as Greene King Ruddles and Harveys Best, good coffee and wine choice, log fire; soft piped music; children welcome, sheltered back garden with pleasant valley views, tables out in front, two bedrooms *(Michael Dandy, BB, Andy and Jill Kassube)*

☆ **Red Lion** RH10 4NU [Lion Lane, just off B2028]: Warmly welcoming traditional local with great range of customers, proper landlord, Harveys ales, good choice of wines by the glass, good value home-made bar lunches from sandwiches up, narrow high-beamed bar with small fire, three steps up to smallish low-ceilinged dining area with inglenook log fire, cushioned pews and built-in settles, fresh flowers, lots of memorabilia; children and well behaved dogs welcome, quiet side garden *(BB, Louise English, William Ruxton)*

UCKFIELD [TQ4720]

Highlands TN22 5SP [Eastbourne Rd/Lewes Rd]: Roomy 1930s pub with sensibly priced food inc Sun roasts, Adnams Broadside, Fullers London Pride and Harveys Best, sofas in lounge with dining areas, bar with games and TV *(Tony and Wendy Hobden)*

UDIMORE [TQ8519]

Kings Head TN31 6BG: Proper traditional chatty village pub with consistently well kept Harveys, Youngs and Timothy Taylors Landlord or Best from long bar, good-sized helpings of low-priced pubby food inc popular Sun lunch in dining area, pains-taking long-serving licensees, open fires, low beams, plain tables and chairs on bare boards *(Peter Meister, Conrad Freezer, PL)*

☆ **Plough** TN31 6AL [Cock Marling (B2089 W of Rye)]: Civilised and popular, with good fresh home-made food from soup and nice lamb sandwiches up, Greene King IPA, Ringwood Fortyniner and a guest beer, reasonably priced wines, relaxed friendly service, basic front bar with brass bric-a-brac and woodburner, open fire and farming prints in small pleasant carpeted dining area, books for sale; dogs welcome, tables on good-sized suntrap back terrace, open all day *(Kevin Thorpe, Mrs Hazel Rainer, Conrad Freezer)*

UPPER DICKER [TQ5409]

Plough BN27 3QJ [Coldharbour Rd]: Good food at fair prices (all day wknds) in much-extended ancient pub, well kept Shepherd Neame ales, friendly service, armchairs and sofas, woodburners, restaurant; public bar with darts and big-screen TV; garden tables *(Fr Robert Marsh)*

WALBERTON [SU9705]

Holly Tree BN18 0PH [The Street]: Traditional two-room pub with Fullers London Pride, Harveys Best and Wells & Youngs Bombardier from central bar, wide choice of generous food from baguettes and baked potatoes up; attractive hanging baskets and flower tubs, drive due for resurfacing *(Tony and Wendy Hobden)*

WALDERTON [SU7910]

☆ **Barley Mow** PO18 9ED [Stoughton rd, just off B2146 Chichester—Petersfield]: Recently refurbished flagstoned country pub with good value generous food from baguettes up, real ales such as Fullers, Ringwood and Youngs, good wine choice, friendly efficient service even on busy wknds, two log fires and rustic

bric-a-brac in U-shaped bar with roomy dining areas, no music; children welcome, skittle alley, nice furniture in big pleasant streamside back garden with fish pond, aviary and swings, good walks, handy for Stansted House *(R and M Thomas, J A Snell)*

WALDRON [TQ5419]

Star TN21 0RA [Blackboys—Horam side road]: Big inglenook log fire in beamed and panelled bar, Bass, Harveys and a guest beer, reliable food from good lunchtime sandwiches up, friendly helpful service, separate back dining room; pleasant garden, seats out in front overlooking pretty village *(Phil and Sally Gorton, PL, BB)*

WARNHAM [TQ1533]

☆ **Sussex Oak** RH12 3QW [just off A24 Horsham—Dorking; Church St]: Cheerful country pub with big inglenook log fireplace, mix of flagstones, tiles, wood and carpeting, heavy beams and timbers, comfortable sofas, Adnams, Fullers London Pride, Timothy Taylors Landlord, Wells & Youngs and a guest beer from carved servery, Weston's farm cider, plenty of wines by the glass, enjoyable food (all day wknds, not Mon evenings) from sandwiches and baked potatoes to steaks, high-raftered restaurant, bar billiards; piped music; children and dogs welcome, disabled facilities, picnic-sets in large pleasant garden, open all day *(Kevin Thorpe, Phil Bryant, LYM)*

WASHINGTON [TQ1213]

Frankland Arms RH20 4AL [just off A24 Horsham—Worthing]: Village pub below Chanctonbury Ring, wide choice of unpretentious food all day, good service, two or three real ales, good value wines by the glass, log fires, sizeable restaurant, public bar with pool and TV in games area; disabled facilities, walkers welcome, neat garden *(Tony and Wendy Hobden, Alec and Joan Laurence, N R White)*

WEST CHILTINGTON [TQ0917]

Five Bells RH20 2QX [Smock Alley, off B2139 SE]: Large open-plan beamed and panelled bar with old photographs, unusual brass bric-a-brac, changing ales inc a Mild kept carefully by friendly landlord, farm cider, pubby food (not Sun evening or Mon) inc good pies, log fire, daily papers, big pleasant conservatory dining room; peaceful garden with terrace, bedrooms *(Bruce Bird, Tony and Wendy Hobden)*

WEST HOATHLY [TQ3632]

☆ **Cat** RH19 4PP [signed from A22 and B2028 S of E Grinstead; North Lane]: Attractive country dining pub with enjoyable food from sandwiches to interesting main dishes, attentive landlord and cheerful efficient staff, well kept Harveys and guest beers, decent wines, several pleasant seating areas, beams, panelling, fresh flowers and inglenook log fires; pleasant terrace, quiet view of church *(Bruce Bird, LYM)*

Intrepid Fox RH19 4QG [Hammingden Lane/North Lane, towards Sharpthorne]: Good generous food inc restaurant dishes, good wines by the glass, Harveys and guest beers, genial landlord, comfortably updated furnishings and décor, cosy log fire; walkers welcome *(C and R Bromage)*

WEST MARDEN [SU7713]

Victoria PO18 9EN [B2146 2 miles S of Uppark]: Light fresh décor, short choice of good food esp fish in bar and small back candlelit restaurant, well kept Harveys, good choice of reasonably priced wines, decent coffee, friendly attentive staff, old Royal wedding photographs, pleasant end alcove with old-fashioned sofa by log fire; attractive garden, good walks nearby *(Ann and Colin Hunt)*

WEST WITTERING [SZ8099]

Lamb PO20 8QA [Chichester Rd; B2179/A286 towards Birdham]: Warmly friendly staff in spotless 18th-c country pub, reasonably priced food from separate servery inc OAP bargains, Badger ales, decent wines, rugs on tiles, blazing fire; dogs on leads allowed, lots of tables in front and in small sheltered back garden – good for children; busy in summer – handy for beach *(R and M Thomas, Ian and Joan Blackwell, BB, E J Seddon)*

WESTFIELD [TQ8115]

Old Courthouse TN35 4QE [Main Rd]: Friendly neatly updated panelled pub with well kept Harveys and two quickly changing guests from small brewers, generous food all day, simple décor; seats out at side and back *(Bruce Bird)*

WINCHELSEA [TQ9017]

☆ *New Inn* TN36 4EN [German St; just off A259]: Well run attractive pub with Georgian décor in front part, log fire, turkey carpet and some slate flagstones, new chef doing good value food (all day Sat) from sandwiches up, four well kept Greene King ales, separate back bar with darts, pool and machines; piped music; children in eating area, pleasant walled garden, six pretty

bedrooms (some sharing bathrooms), delightful setting opp church – Spike Milligan buried in graveyard *(Lucien Perring, Peter Meister, Adrian Johnson, LYM)*

WITHYHAM [TQ4935]

☆ *Dorset Arms* TN7 4BD [B2110]: Pleasantly unpretentious 16th-c pub handy for Forest Way walks (not to mention nearby Ferrari garage), good friendly service, Harveys ales kept well, decent wines inc local ones, young landlord cooks good traditional food from filled rolls to seasonal game, reasonable prices, good log fire in Tudor fireplace, sturdy tables and simple country seats on wide oak boards (sometimes a bit uneven – beware of wobbles), darts, dominoes, shove-ha'penny, cribbage, pretty restaurant; piped music; dogs welcome, white tables on brick terrace by small green, cl Mon *(Geoffrey Kemp, LYM, Michael and Ann Cole, N R White, Angus and Carol Johnson)*

WIVELSFIELD [TQ3319]

Royal Oak RH15 0SJ [Ditchling Common, S on B2112]: Food a cut above the norm, good ale range changing weekly; big child-friendly garden *(Karen Reid)*

WORTHING [TQ1502]

Selden Arms BN11 2DB [Lyndhurst Rd, between Waitrose and hospital]: Friendly local with half a dozen good real ales inc Dark Star Hophead and Ringwood Fortyniner, farm cider, welcoming Lancashire landlady and locals, bargain lunchtime food inc popular doorstep sandwiches, log fire, lots of old pub photographs; dogs welcome, open all day *(Tony and Wendy Hobden, Bruce Bird)*

WYCH CROSS [TQ4121]

Roebuck RH18 5JL: Hotel rather than pub, but worth knowing for its Sun carvery, pleasant bar with Greene King ales, friendly efficient staff; nice garden, 30 bedrooms *(Klaus and Elizabeth Leist)*

Warwickshire
(with Birmingham and West Midlands)

Pub prices in the urban West Midlands are among Britain's lowest; value is king here. What's more, you can easily escape the dreaded sameness often produced by the trend for contemporary refurbished pub interiors. The area has a good many unspoilt pubs, places well worth a visit for their individuality, often with a strong sense of history that's very much alive and kicking. The Beacon in Sedgley's front door opens straight on to locals propped against the stair wall, chatting to the waistcoated barman behind the hatch of his island servery. This is the tap for the distinctive Sarah Hughes beers, brewed in the traditional Victorian tower at the back. Going into the timelessly eccentric Turf in Bloxwich, you might doubt that you are in a pub at all – in the 130 years that it's been in the same family it can't have changed much. The decorations in the friendly Old Swan in Netherton are well worth a look, though the beers brewed on the premises will quickly divert your attention. The happily old-fashioned Case is Altered at Five Ways, filled only with the sound of chatting customers, has been licensed and seemingly unchanged for over 300 years; we keep a picture of its interior on our office wall, to remind us of what pubs are all about. The cheery Vine in Brierley Hill, a classic no-nonsense town pub, has very good value food, while the Griffin out at Shustoke is an equally unpretentious country local, much enjoyed for its good beer, friendly welcome and good value simple tasty food. Out in the countryside, memorable dining pubs include the cosy old Fox & Hounds at Great Wolford, again a lovely unspoilt building, but here you'll find the rewarding results of a creative chef working with top-notch ingredients, as you will at the calmly civilised Howard Arms in Ilmington – a lovely place for a weekend break or a special meal out. Showing genuine care in their business, the licensees at the very appealing Bell at Welford-on-Avon have made it a bastion of good service; their thoughtful menu lists their local suppliers, and food here is delicious – it is the Warwickshire Dining Pub of the Year. In the Lucky Dip section at the end of the chapter, some particularly promising entries include the Bell at Alderminster, Golden Cross at Ardens Grafton, Barnt Green Inn, Wellington in Birmingham (the real ale pub here), Red Lion at Long Compton, Bell at Monks Kirby, Zetland Arms in Warwick and Saxon Mill just outside at Guy's Cliffe. The area has nearly 20 different breweries at work. Apart from Banks's, part of the Marstons empire, the most popular are Holdens, Bathams and now Purity, started only in 2005; highly environment-conscious, it is doing very well. Other worthwhile local beers to be found in at least some of our listed pubs are Warwickshire, Slaughterhouse, Toll End, Black Country, Church End and Tunnel.

ASTON CANTLOW   SP1360   MAP 4

Kings Head ♀

Village signposted just off A3400 NW of Stratford; B95 6HY

Gently civilised Tudor pub with nice old interior, imaginative (if not cheap) food, and pleasant garden

The beautifully kept bar on the right of this creeper swathed pub is charmingly old, with flagstones, low beams, and old-fashioned settles around its massive inglenook log fireplace. The chatty quarry-tiled main room has attractive window seats and big country oak tables – it's all the perfect setting for a civilised meal out. A good range of drinks includes Greene King Abbot, M&B Brew XI and a guest such as Purity Pure Gold on handpump, with ten wines by the glass from a very decent list; piped jazz. A big chestnut tree graces the lovely garden, and the pub looks really pretty in summer with its colourful hanging baskets and wisteria. It's in the middle of a very pretty village, and Shakespeare's parents are said to have married in the church next door.

🍽 They offer several menus that variously include chicken with chilli and lime mayonnaise sandwich, battered fish and crushed peas, sausage and mash, seared scallops with orange, rocket and potato salad, duck breast with confit leg, ginger and soy jus, fried bass fillet with grilled fennel, tomatoes and garlic, grilled veal cutlet with parsley and caper potato croquettes, pumpkin ravioli with wild mushroom, sage, walnuts and blue cheese, roast pork belly with potato, onion and sage fritters, puddings such as chocolate mousse with orange crisps and fresh berries, lemon and vanilla cheesecake with raspberry coulis and a british cheeseboard. *Starters/Snacks: £3.95 to £7.20. Main Courses: £12.50 to £19.90. Puddings: £5.50*

Enterprise ~ Lease Peter and Louise Sadler ~ Real ale ~ Bar food (12-2.30, 6.30-9.30; 12.30-3 Sun, not Sun evening) ~ Restaurant ~ (01789) 488242 ~ Children welcome ~ Dogs allowed in bar ~ Open 12-3, 5.30-11; 12-11 Sat; 12-8.30 Sun

Recommended by Mrs Philippa Wilson, Gordon Davico, Dr D Scott, Martin and Pauline Jennings, Di and Mike Gillam, Michael and Maggie Betton, John and Jackie Walsh, Trevor and Sylvia Millum, Ian and Jane Irving, Dennis and Gill Keen, Simon Fox, Graham Findlay, Pete Coxon, Keith and Sue Ward, David Spurgeon, Joyce and Maurice Cottrell, Cedric Robertshaw

BIRMINGHAM   SP0686   MAP 4

Old Joint Stock ◀

Temple Row West; B2 5NY

Big bustling city Fullers pie-and-ale pub with impressive Victorian façade and interior and small back terrace

Housed in what used to be the Stock Exchange, this well run cheery city centre pub (opposite the cathedral) has a rather impressive interior. Chandeliers hang from the soaring pink and gilt ceiling, gently illuminated busts line the top of the ornately plastered walls, and there's a splendid, if well worn, cupola above the centre of the room. Big portraits and smart long curtains create an air of unexpected elegance. Around the walls are plenty of tables and chairs, some in cosy corners, with more on a big balcony overlooking the bar, reached by a very grand wide staircase. A separate room with panelling and a fireplace has a more intimate, clubby feel. Well kept Fullers Chiswick, Discovery, ESB and London Pride, a guest from local Beowulf and a decent range of about a dozen wines by the glass are served from a handsome dark wood island bar counter. It does get busy, particularly with local office workers, but effortlessly absorbs what seems like huge numbers of people; helpful friendly service, teas, coffees, daily papers, TV, games machine, board games and piped music (can be loud in the evening). The building is owned by London-based brewer Fullers (their only premises N of Bristol as far as we know) who've recently spent a considerable sum on a smart purpose built little theatre above the pub. A small back terrace has some cast-iron tables and chairs and wall mounted heaters.

🍽 Very reasonably priced pubby food includes soup, sandwiches, lots of pies such as steak in ale or chicken and ham, fish and chips and a vegetarian dish. *Starters/Snacks: £2.25 to £5.95. Main Courses: £6.75 to £9.25. Puddings: £3.75*

Fullers ~ Manager Alison Robins ~ Real ale ~ Bar food (12-8) ~ (0121) 200 1892 ~ Children welcome if attending theatre ~ Open 11-11; closed Sun and bank hols
Recommended by the Didler, Barry Collett, Simon Fox, Ian and Jane Irving, Michael Dandy, Dr and Mrs A K Clarke, R T and J C Moggridge

BLOXWICH

SJ9902   MAP 4

Turf 🍺

Wolverhampton Road, off A34 just S of A4124, N fringes of Walsall; aka Tinky's; WS3 2EZ

Simple eccentric family-run pub, utterly uncontrived, with five good beers

This basic but very special place has been in the same family for over 130 years, remaining virtually unchanged in all that time. From the outside it appears to be a rather run-down terraced Victorian house. Once through the front door it still doesn't immediately look like a pub, but more like the hall of a 1930s home. The public bar is through a door on the right, and reminiscent of a waiting room, it has wooden slatted benches running around the walls, with a big heating pipe clearly visible underneath; there's a tiled floor, three small tables, William Morris curtains and wallpaper and a simple fireplace. What's particularly nice is that even though the unspoilt rooms are Grade II listed, it's far more than just a museum piece but is alive and chatty with friendly locals happy to tell you the history of the place. The friendly landlady serves a particularly impressive changing range of five beers, always very well kept, usually from Bathams, Beowulf, Holdens, RCH and Titanic. There's hatch service out to the hall, on the other side of the old smoking room, which is slightly more comfortable, with unusual padded wall settles with armrests. There's also a tiny back parlour with chairs around a tiled fireplace. The pub's basic charms won't appeal to those who like their creature comforts; the no-frills lavatories are outside, at the end of a simple but pleasant garden, and they don't do food – it almost goes without saying that there's no music or machines. Do please check opening times before you visit.

🍴 **No food at all.**

Free house ~ Licensees Doris and Zena Hiscott-Wilkes ~ Real ale ~ No credit cards ~ (01922) 407745 ~ Open 12-2.30, 7-11(10.30 Sun)
Recommended by Pete Baker, the Didler, John Dwane, Mike Begley, Simon and Mandy King, R T and J C Moggridge

BRIERLEY HILL

SO9286   MAP 4

Vine 🍺 £

B4172 between A461 and (nearer) A4100; straight after the turn into Delph Road; DY5 2TN

Incredibly good value, very friendly classic down-to-earth Bathams tap; tables in back yard and lunchtime snacks

The good stained-glass bull's heads and very approximate bunches of grapes in the front bow windows of this no-nonsense Black Country pub are a reference to its nickname, the Bull & Bladder – this name harks back to its previous life as a butcher's shop. It's often bustling with chatty locals, and the cheery down-to-earth landlord and staff are friendly and welcoming. The interior meanders through a series of rooms, each different in character. The traditional little front bar has wall benches and simple leatherette-topped oak stools, the comfortable extended snug on the left has solidly built red plush seats, and the tartan decorated larger back bar has brass chandeliers, darts, dominoes and a big-screen TV. A couple of tables and games machines stand in a corridor. Some of the memorabilia you'll see, including one huge pair of horns over a mantelpiece, relates to the Royal Ancient Order of Buffalos, who meet in a room here. The very cheap Bitter and Mild (with perhaps Delph Strong in winter) are kept in top condition and come from the next-door Bathams brewery. There are tables in a back yard, and the car park is opposite.

Pubs brewing their own beers are listed at the back of the book.

🍽 A couple of simple but wholesome fresh lunchtime snacks (sandwiches, baguettes, steak and mushroom pie and faggots, chips and peas) are sold at prices that prove a landlord can make money (yes, we asked) and offer his customers fantastic value for money at the same time. *Starters/Snacks: £1.00 to £3.00. Main Courses: £2.50 to £4.50*

Bathams ~ Manager Melvyn Wood ~ Real ale ~ Bar food (12-1.30 Mon-Fri) ~ No credit cards ~ (01384) 78293 ~ Dogs allowed in bar ~ Open 12-11(10.30 Sun)

Recommended by the Didler, Theo, Anne and Jane Gaskin, R T and J C Moggridge

EASENHALL

SP4679 MAP 4

Golden Lion £ 🛏

Village signposted from B4112 Newbold—Pailton, and from B4455 at Brinklow; Main Street; CV23 0JA

Comfortable hotel with traditional bar, good food and large garden

---

Tucked away at the heart of this busy extended hotel you'll find this spotlessly kept and welcoming little 17th-c bar. It still has many of its original features, including tiles, flagstones, low beams, timbers and a fine carved settle. Yellow walls have occasional stencilled lion motifs or latin phrases, while a slightly raised area has a comfortable little alcove with padding overhead; the lower level has a brick fireplace. Friendly attentive staff serve Greene King Ruddles and Black Sheep; piped music. There are tables at the side, and a good few picnic-sets on a spacious lawn.

🍽 Bar food includes soup of the day, thai fishcake and sweet chilli sauce, £5 weekday lunchtime specials such as chicken balti and mushroom and pepper stroganoff, steak burger, steak and ale pie, roast vegetable tart stopped with melted brie, battered cod and mushy peas and sirloin steak; Sunday carvery. *Starters/Snacks: £3.80 to £7.40. Main Courses: £5.00 to £14.95. Puddings: £2.50 to £5.10*

Free house ~ Licensee James Austin ~ Real ale ~ Bar food (12-2, 4.30-9.30(12-2.30, 4-8.45 Sun)) ~ Restaurant ~ (01788) 832265 ~ Children welcome ~ Open 11-11 ~ Bedrooms: £50S(£50B)/£60B

Recommended by Martin and Pauline Jennings, Catherine and Rob Dunster, George Atkinson, Gerry and Rosemary Dobson, Alan Johnson, Trevor and Sheila Sharman, Dr and Mrs A K Clarke, R T and J C Moggridge, Michael and Maggie Betton, Ian Phillips

FIVE WAYS

SP2270 MAP 4

Case is Altered 🍺

Follow Rowington signposts at junction roundabout off A4177/A4141 N of Warwick, then right into Case Lane; CV35 7JD

Unspoilt convivial local serving well kept beers, including a couple of interesting guests

---

It's the sound of happy conversation, undisturbed by noisy games machines, music or children, that fills the old-fashioned rooms at this tiled white-painted brick cottage. The servery here has been licensed to sell beer for over three centuries – these days the friendly landlady serves Greene King IPA, Sharps Doom Bar, Slaughterhouse Saddleback and a couple of guests such as Hook Norton Old Hooky and Vale Black Swan and, all served by a rare type of handpump mounted on the casks that are stilled behind the counter. A door at the back of the building leads into a modest little room with a tiled floor, and an antique bar billiards table protected by an ancient leather cover (it takes pre-decimal sixpences). From here, the simple little main bar has a fine old poster showing the old Lucas Blackwell & Arkwright brewery (now flats) and a clock with its hours spelling out Thornleys Ale – another defunct brewery; there are just a few sturdy old-fashioned tables, with a couple of stout leather-covered settles facing each other over the spotless tiles. Behind a wrought-iron gate is a little brick-paved courtyard with a stone table. Full disabled access.

🍽 No food at all.

Free house ~ Licensee Jackie Willacy ~ Real ale ~ No credit cards ~ (01926) 484206 ~
Open 12-2.30, 6-11; 12-2, 7-10.30 Sun

Recommended by Pete Baker, Kerry Law, the Didler, Steve and Liz Tilley, Dr and Mrs A K Clarke

GAYDON

SP3654   MAP 4

Malt Shovel 🍺

M40 junction 12; Church Rd; CV35 0ET

**In quiet village just off M40; nice mix of pubby bar and smarter restaurant, tasty food and
five real ales**

The slightly unusual layout of this bustling pub sees a sort of pathway in mahogany-
varnished boards running through bright carpeting to link the entrance, the bar counter
on the right and the blazing log fire on the left. The central area has a high pitched
ceiling, milk churns and earthenware containers in a loft above the bar. A few stools are
lined up along the counter where they serve five changing real ales which might include
Adnams Best, Bass, Fullers London Pride, Everards Tiger and Wadworths 6X, and most of
their dozen or so wines are available by the glass. Three steps take you up to a snug
little space with some comfortable sofas overlooked by a big stained-glass window and
reproductions of classic posters. At the other end is a busy dining area with flowers on
the mix of kitchen, pub and dining tables. Service is friendly and efficient (though they
may try to keep your credit card while you eat); piped music, darts, and games machine.
The springer spaniel is called Rosie, and the jack russell is Mollie.

🍴 **Enjoyable food, cooked by the chef-landlord, includes good lunchtime sandwiches and
panini, soup, ploughman's, tempura prawns, salads, moroccan lamb shank, duck with
orange, lemon and honey, gammon egg and chips, battered fish, sticky toffee pudding and
lemon cheesecake.** *Starters/Snacks: £3.95 to £6.95. Main Courses: £5.95 to £15.95. Puddings:
£3.50 to £4.95*

Enterprise ~ Lease Richard and Debi Morisot ~ Real ale ~ Bar food (12-2, 6.30-9) ~ Restaurant
~ (01926) 641221 ~ Children welcome ~ Dogs welcome ~ Open 11-3, 5-11; 11-11 Fri, Sat;
12-10.30 Sun

*Recommended by Michael and Judy Buckley, Dennis Jones, I A Herdman, N R White, George Atkinson, Tina and
David Woods-Taylor, Tom and Jill Jones, Craig Turnbull, Dennis Jenkin, Catherine and Rob Dunster, Phil and
Jane Hodson, Karen Eliot, Dr and Mrs A K Clarke, Piotr Chodzko-Zajko, Clive Watkin, Mary McSweeney, Val and
Alan Green*

GREAT WOLFORD

SP2434   MAP 4

Fox & Hounds

Village signposted on right on A3400 3 miles S of Shipston-on-Stour; CV36 5NQ

Thoughtfully prepared food at cosy old country inn

It's nice to find such good food in an atmosphere as unspoilt and pubby as this. The
unpretentious aged bar at this very handsome 16th-c stone inn has hops strung from its
low beams, an appealing collection of chairs and old candlelit tables on spotless
flagstones, antique hunting prints, and a roaring log fire in the inglenook fireplace with
its fine old bread oven. An old-fashioned little tap room serves Hook Norton Hooky,
Purity Pure UBU and a guest such as Bass on handpump and around 60 malt whiskies;
piped music. A terrace has solid wood furniture and a well.

🍴 **The chef here is careful about sourcing ingredients, and cooks from fresh virtually
everything (including the breads) that appear on the fairly elaborate bar and restaurant
menus: roast garlic and potato soup, crab and spring onion salad with crab and coriander
fritter, lamb loin with home-made black pudding, celeriac purée and braised puy lentils,**

Real ale to us means beer which has matured naturally in its cask –
not pressurised or filtered.

broad bean and pea risotto with soft cheese and cherry tomato salad, hare, chianti and home-cured bacon casserole with celeriac mash, home-made sausages and mash with cider onion gravy and honey and lavender crème brûlée or warm chocolate brownie with bitter chocolate sauce and hazelnut ice-cream. *Starters/Snacks: £4.50 to £7.00. Main Courses: £12.00 to £16.00. Puddings: £5.95 to £7.50*

Free house ~ Licensee Gillian Tarbox ~ Real ale ~ Bar food (not Sun evening) ~ (01608) 674220 ~ Children welcome ~ Dogs welcome ~ Open 12-2.30(3 Sat), 6-11.30; 12-3, 7-11 Sun; closed Mon ~ Bedrooms: £50B/£80B

Recommended by H O Dickinson, Ted George, J C Burgis, Clive and Fran Dutson, Keith and Sue Ward, Mrs Philippa Wilson

ILMINGTON
SP2143 MAP 4

Howard Arms 🍴 🍷 🛏️

Village signposted with Wimpstone off A3400 S of Stratford; CV36 4LT

Emphasis on imaginative food and good wine list in lovely mellow-toned interior; attractive bedrooms

This top-notch golden-stone inn is a lovely place for a deliciously civilised meal out or weekend away. The stylishly simple interior is light, airy and gently traditional, with a few good prints on warm golden walls, rugs on broad polished flagstones, and a nice mix of furniture from hardwood pews to old church seats. The cosy log fire in a huge stone inglenook seems to be alight most of the year. Drinks include Hook Norton Old Hooky, Purity Pure Gold and a guest from a local brewer such as Wyre Piddle on handpump, organic soft drinks and 18 wines by the glass. The garden is charming with fruit trees sheltering the lawn, a colourful herbaceous border, and a handful of tables on a neat york stone terrace. Readers very much enjoy staying in the comfortable bedrooms – the breakfasts are particularly good. The pub is nicely set beside the village green, and there are lovely walks on the nearby hills and pleasant strolls around the village outskirts.

🍴 Ingredients are thoughtfully sourced, often from local suppliers and the imaginative (though not cheap) menu which changes every week or so and might include smoked organic salmon, pigeon, pork and peppercorn terrine with red onion marmalade, crab beignets with sweet chilli and coriander dip, beef, ale and mustard pie, roast duck breast with braised puy lentils and red wine jus, roast cod with potato, garlic and saffron broth, calves liver and rib-eye steak, with puddings such as apple and pear flapjack crumble or vanilla cheesecake with berry compote and organic ice-creams; british cheeseboard. *Starters/Snacks: £5.50 to £7.50. Main Courses: £11.50 to £15.50. Puddings: £5.00 to £6.50*

Free house ~ Licensee Martin Devereux ~ Real ale ~ Bar food (12-2.30(3 Fri-Sun), 6.30-9.30(10 Fri, Sat, 9 Sun)) ~ Restaurant ~ (01608) 682226 ~ Children welcome ~ Open 11-11; 12-10.30 Sun ~ Bedrooms: £87.50B/£120B

Recommended by Noel Grundy, Mary McSweeney, Bernard Stradling, Keith and Sue Ward, Robin and Glenna Etheridge, Ian and Jane Haslock, Robert and Elaine Smyth, Theo, Anne and Jane Gaskin, Hugh Bower, Donna and Roger, Mr and Mrs A H Young, K H Frostick, David Handforth, David Gunn, Rob, Stuart Doughty, Graham Findlay, Julian Saunders, Chris Glasson, Andrea Rampley, Martin and Pauline Jennings, K Turner, Mrs Philippa Wilson, Nina Sohal

LITTLE COMPTON
SP2530 MAP 4

Red Lion

Off A44 Moreton-in-Marsh—Chipping Norton; GL56 0RT

Comfortably unpretentious country pub serving generous tasty food; nice garden

The simple traditionally decorated lounge at this friendly 16th-c cotswold stone local is low-beamed, with pews and settles in snug alcoves and a couple of little tables by the log fire; service is friendly. The plainer public bar has another log fire, Donnington BB and SBA on handpump, several wines by the glass and a farm cider; darts, pool, games machine, TV and juke box, board games, aunt sally and croquet. The garden is well enclosed and rather pretty. More reports please.

🍴 **Bar food is served in generous helpings and includes lunchtime sandwiches, filled baguettes and ciabattas, ploughman's, soup, crispy whitebait, battered cod, chicken caesar salad, pie of the day, rump of lamb with rosemary mash, sticky toffee pudding.** *Starters/Snacks: £4.00 to £6.50. Main Courses: £7.75 to £9.75. Puddings: £1.40 to £4.50*

Donnington ~ Tenants Ian and Jacqui Sergeant ~ Real ale ~ Bar food ~ Restaurant ~ (01608) 674397 ~ Children welcome ~ Dogs allowed in bar ~ Open 12-3(3.30 Sat, Sun), 6(7 Sun)-11; 12-3, 6-11 in winter ~ Bedrooms: £59S/£69S

Recommended by Clive and Fran Dutson, Alec and Joan Laurence, Paul Goldman, P and J Shapley, Keith and Sue Ward, Tracey and Stephen Groves

LONG ITCHINGTON
SP4165   MAP 4

Duck on the Pond
Just off A423 Coventry—Southam; The Green; CV47 9QJ

Well laid out friendly dining pub with attentive staff serving decent food

A steady main entry, this welcoming pub is a pleasant place for a relaxed meal out. Its surprisingly eclectic and somewhat individual interior is vaguely reminiscent of a 1970s french bistro. The central bar, with a few scattered rugs on dark wooden floorboards, has dark pine ceiling planks, royal blue banquettes, some barrel tables, bacchanalian carvings around its coal fire and some big brass wading birds. Wicker panels provide an unusual frontage to the counter, which has Wells & Youngs Bombardier and a couple of guests such as Courage Directors and Wells & Youngs Waggledance on handpump, and about ten wines by the glass from a fairly extensive list. Service is friendly and attentive. On each end of the bar, inviting dining rooms have pine furniture (some tables painted in light red chequers), a wall of wine bottles, big Edwardian prints on sienna red walls, a crystal chandelier and a grandfather clock. Well produced piped pop or jazzy soul music. Tables and chairs in front look down on a pond, which does indeed have ducks; the main road is quite busy.

🍴 **Good bar food from a useful menu might include soup, smoked haddock and spring onion fishcake with hollandaise sauce, game terrine with pear and ginger chutney, roast mediterranean pasta with tomato, basil and cream sauce, grilled bass fillets on leek and potato rösti with lemon herb butter, sausage of the week and mash, confit duck on oriental noodles with garlic, spring onion and chilli and rib-eye and fillet steak.** *Starters/Snacks: £4.50 to £6.50. Main Courses: £10.95 to £15.95. Puddings: £4.95 to £5.50*

Charles Wells ~ Lease Andrew and Wendy Parry ~ Real ale (12-2.30, 6.30-9.30; 12-10 Sat, 12-8.30 Sun) ~ Restaurant ~ (01926) 815876 ~ No children after 7pm Fri, Sat ~ Open 12-2.30, 5-11; 12-11(10.30 Sun) Sat; closed Mon except bank hols

Recommended by Nigel and Sue Foster, Dr and Mrs A K Clarke, George Atkinson, Dennis and Gill Keen, Dr and Mrs C W Thomas, Leslie and Barbara Owen, Dr Kevan Tucker, John Cook, Peter Sampson

NETHERTON
SO9488   MAP 4

Old Swan 🍺 £
Halesowen Road (A459 just S of centre); DY2 9PY

Traditional unspoilt friendly local serving own-brew beers and bar food

The unchanged multi-roomed layout at this characterful local should appeal to readers who are keen on original interiors. The front public bar is a delightful piece of unspoilt pub history, with a lovely patterned enamel ceiling with a big swan centrepiece, mirrors behind the bar engraved with a swan design, an old-fashioned cylinder stove with its chimney angling away to the wall, and traditional furnishings. The cosy back snug is fitted out very much in keeping with the rest of the building, using recycled bricks and woodwork, and even matching etched window panels. The beers they brew here are Old Swan Original, Dark Swan, Entire, Bumble Hole, and usually one more seasonal one. Parking in front is difficult but there's a good car park at the back.

🍽 The recently expanded lunchtime menu now takes in cobs, baked potatoes, ploughman's, fish and chips, warm roast pepper with melted brie and steaks. The longer evening menu includes smoked fish pâté, minted shoulder of lamb, mediterranean quiche, chicken curry. Traditional home-made puddings include cheesecake, steamed sponge and bakewell tart. *Starters/Snacks: £2.80 to £4.25. Main Courses: £7.10 to £13.50. Puddings: £2.25 to £3.75*

Punch ~ Tenant Tim Newey ~ Real ale ~ Bar food (12-2, 6.30-9; 12-2 Sun) ~ Restaurant ~ (01384) 253075 ~ Dogs allowed in bar ~ Open 11-11; 12-4, 7-11 Sun

Recommended by the Didler, P Dawn, Dr and Mrs A K Clarke, R T and J C Moggridge, Pete Baker, Mark and Diane Grist, Helen Maynard

PRESTON BAGOT   SP1765   MAP 4

Crabmill ♀

A4189 Henley-in-Arden—Warwick; B95 5EE

Contemporary mill conversion with comfortable modern décor, relaxed atmosphere, and smart bar food

They've used strikingly unusual but pleasing colours in the stylish transformation of this rambling old cider mill. The smart two-level lounge area has soft leather settees and easy chairs, low tables, big table lamps and one or two rugs on bare boards, the elegant and roomy low-beamed dining area has candles and fresh flowers, and a beamed and flagstoned bar area has some stripped pine country tables and chairs, snug corners and a gleaming metal bar serving Greene King Abbot, Purity Pure Ubu and a guest such as Tetleys from handpump, with eight wines by the glass from a mostly new world list. Piped music is well chosen and well reproduced. There are lots of tables (some of them under cover) out in a large attractive decked garden. Booking is advised, especially Sunday lunchtime when it's popular with families.

🍽 Imaginative bar food includes soup, tuna carpaccio with pickled ginger, wasabi, soy and prawn crackers, caramelised onion, parmesan and thyme tart, fish and chips with pea purée, braised pork belly stuffed with chorizo and oregano with dauphinoise potatoes, bass fillets with sun-dried tomato pappardelle and basil mascarpone, beef bourguignon, sweet potato, spinach and goats cheese lasagne; vegetables are extra. *Starters/Snacks: £3.95 to £7.95. Main Courses: £13.20 to £19.45. Puddings: £5.25 to £5.95*

Enterprise ~ Lease Sally Coll ~ Real ale ~ Bar food (12-2.30(3.30 Sun), 6.30-9.30) ~ Restaurant ~ (01926) 843342 ~ Children welcome ~ Dogs allowed in bar ~ Open 11-11; 12-6 Sun; closed Sun evening

Recommended by Karen Eliot, Paul Boot, Rod Stoneman, Dr Ron Cox, Andrew Stephenson, Andy and Claire Barker, Peter and Heather Elliott, Hansjoerg Landherr, R L Borthwick, Keith and Sue Ward, Gordon Davico, Tim and Sue Jolley

SEDGLEY   SO9293   MAP 4

Beacon ★ ◧

Bilston Street (no pub sign on our visit, but by Beacon Lane); A463, off A4123 Wolverhampton—Dudley; DY3 1JE

Good unusual own-brew beers and interesting guests at beautifully preserved down-to-earth Victorian pub

Once parked, it's worth walking round to the front door of this plain-looking old brick pub. It opens into a simple quarry-tiled drinking corridor where you may find a couple of cheery locals leaning up the stair wall, chatting to the waistcoated barman propped in the doorway of his little central serving booth. Go through the door into the little snug on your left and you can easily imagine a 19th-c traveller tucked up on one of the wall settles, next to the imposing green-tiled marble fireplace with its big misty mirror, the door closed for privacy and warmth and a drink handed through the glazed hatch. The dark woodwork, turkey carpet, velvet and net curtains, heavy mahogany tables, old piano and little landscape prints all seem unchanged since those times. A timelessly sparse snug on the right has a black kettle and embroidered mantel over a blackened range, and a nice old stripped wooden wall bench. The corridor then runs round the serving booth, past the stairs and into a big well proportioned dark-panelled old smoking room with impressively sturdy red leather wall settles down the length of each side, gilt-based cast-iron tables, a big blue carpet on the lino, and dramatic old sea prints. Round a corner (where you would have come in from the car park) the conservatory is densely filled with plants, and has no seats. Named after a former landlady, the well kept Sarah Hughes beers brewed and served here include Dark Ruby, Pale Amber and Surprise Bitter – you can arrange to look around the traditional Victorian brewery at the back. They also keep a couple of guests such as Fernandes Ale to the Tsar and Toll End Tipton Pride. A children's play area in the garden has a slide, climbing frame and roundabout.

🍴 **The only food served is cheese and onion and maybe ham cobs.** *Starters/Snacks: £1.40 to £1.50*

Own brew ~ Licensee John Hughes ~ Real ale ~ No credit cards ~ (01902) 883380 ~ Chidren allowed in the verandah ~ Dogs welcome ~ Open 12-2.30, 5.30-11; 12-3, 6-11 Sat; 12-3, 7-10.30 Sun

Recommended by Mark and Diane Grist, Pete Baker, the Didler, R T and J C Moggridge

SHUSTOKE
SP2290   MAP 4

Griffin 🍺 £

5 miles from M6 junction 4; A446 towards Tamworth, then right on to B4114 and go straight through Coleshill; pub is at Church End, a mile E of village; B46 2LB

Ten real ales and simple good value lunchtime snacks at unpretentious country local; garden and play area

Usually busy with a cheery crowd, the low-beamed L-shaped bar at this friendly place has log fires in two stone fireplaces (one's a big inglenook), fairly simple décor from cushioned café seats (some quite closely spaced) and sturdily elm-topped sewing trestles to one nice old-fashioned settle, lots of old jugs on the beams, beer mats on the ceiling and a games machine. The smashing choice of real ales here is well kept on handpump and dispensed (by the chatty landlord) from a servery under a very low heavy beam. Beers come from an enterprising range of brewers such as Holdens, Hook Norton, Jennings, Marstons, Moorhouses, RCH and Thornbridge; also lots of english wines, farm cider, and mulled wine in winter. Outside, there are old-fashioned seats and tables outside on the back grass, a play area and a large terrace with plants in raised beds.

🍴 **Straightforward but tasty bar food includes sandwiches, ploughman's, cheese and broccoli bake, scampi, steak and ale pie, mixed grill and 10oz sirloin steak.** *Starters/Snacks: £2.50 to £5.50. Main Courses: £5.75 to £8.50*

Free house ~ Licensee Michael Pugh ~ Real ale ~ Bar food (12-2; not Sun or evenings) ~ No credit cards ~ (01675) 481205 ~ Children in conservatory ~ Dogs welcome ~ Open 12-2.30, 7-11; 12-3, 7-10.30 Sun

Recommended by R T and J C Moggridge, Catherine and Rob Dunster, Carol and Colin Broadbent, John Dwane

WELFORD-ON-AVON
SP1452   MAP 4

Bell 🍴 🍷 🍺

Off B439 W of Stratford; High Street; CV37 8EB
WARWICKSHIRE DINING PUB OF THE YEAR

Enjoyably civilised pub with appealing ancient interior, good food and great range of drinks including five real ales; terrace

The charming service at this delightful 17th-c place is the sort where the customer really does come first – staff are knowledgeable, organised and kind. As most people are here to dine booking is advised. The attractive interior (full of signs of the building's great age) is divided into five comfortable areas, each with its own character, from the cosy terracotta-painted bar to a light and airy gallery room with its antique wood panelling, solid oak floor and contemporary Lloyd Loom chairs. Flagstone floors, stripped or well polished antique or period-style furniture, and three good fires (one in an inglenook) add warmth and cosiness. Flowers Original, Hobsons, Hook Norton Old Hooky, Purity Pure Gold and Pure UBU are well kept on handpump, and they've 16 wines including champagne and local wines by the glass; piped music. In summer the creeper-covered exterior is hung with lots of colourful baskets, and there are tables and chairs on a vine-covered dining terrace. This riverside village has an appealing church and pretty thatched black and white cottages.

⑪ Using local suppliers – which they list on the menu – food ranges from the traditional pubby dishes up to more imaginative specials: soup, sandwiches, fried brie with a ginger and apricot compote, ploughman's, lasagne, beer-battered cod and minty lamb curry, spinach and potato bhaji with coconut, coriander and green chilli chutney, tuna loin on red thai roast butternut, roast duck breast with raspberry coulis, with puddings such as mint crème brûlée with lemon poppy shortbread and blueberry steamed pudding with mixed berry compote. *Starters/Snacks: £4.95 to £6.95. Main Courses: £9.95 to £16.95. Puddings: £5.50*

Laurel (Enterprise) ~ Lease Colin and Teresa Ombler ~ Real ale ~ Bar food (11.30-2.30(3 Sat), 6-9.30(10 Fri, Sat); 12-9.30 Sun) ~ (01789) 750353 ~ Children welcome ~ Open 11.30-3, 6-11.30; 11.30-11.30 Sat; 12-10.30 Sun

Recommended by Glenwys and Alan Lawrence, Muriel and John Hobbs, Malcolm Brown, Keith and Sue Ward, Jean and Richard Phillips, Rod Stoneman, Leslie and Barbara Owen, Denys Gueroult, K S Whittaker, R T and J C Moggridge, Martin and Pauline Jennings, John Wooll, David Heath, Graham Findlay, John Saville, Lyn Ellwood

LUCKY DIP

Besides the fully inspected pubs, you might like to try these Lucky Dips recommended to us and described by readers (if you do, please send us reports: feedback@thegoodpubguide.co.uk).

ALCESTER [SP0957]
☆ *Holly Bush* B49 5QX [Henley St]: Unpretentious 17th-c panelled rooms off darkish central bar, enjoyable fair-priced food (not Mon) from good sandwiches and simple dishes to some interesting blackboard items, enterprising changing range of real ales, farm cider, dozens of whiskies, hard-working landlady and friendly staff, good easy-going atmosphere, nice dining room; disabled access, attractive sheltered back garden, open all day *(Pete Baker, Derek and Sylvia Stephenson, Martin and Pauline Jennings, Andrew McKeand)*
Three Tuns B49 5AB [High St]: Unspoilt bar with flagstones, heavy Jacobean beams, whited wattle and daub walls, plain furniture, half a dozen changing well kept ales, interesting antique beer bottles, friendly service, cheery customers, no food, music or machines; open all day *(Pete Baker)*
ALDERMINSTER [SP2348]
☆ *Bell* CV37 8NY [A3400 Oxford—Stratford]: Neatly kept open-plan Georgian dining pub, good imaginative food, flagstones or polished wood floors, inglenook stove, modern prints on green walls, small proper bar with well kept Greene King ales, great range of wines by the glass, conservatory with Stour Valley views; children and dogs welcome, terrace and garden, bedrooms *(Graham Findlay, Denys Gueroult, Robert Ager, LYM, Gordon Davico, Keith and Sue Ward)*
ANSLEY [SP2991]
Boot CV10 9PL [Birmingham Rd]: Welcoming

and neatly kept family-run pub with good value food from bargain sandwiches to generous Sun carvery (three sizes), some spooky stories *(Jacqui Methley)*
Lord Nelson CV10 9PQ [Birmingham Rd]: Enjoyable reasonably priced food in ample space (two restaurants), good beers from neighbouring Tunnel microbrewery (tours available), great staff; terrace tables, open all day wknds *(Chris Evans)*
ARDENS GRAFTON [SP1153]
☆ *Golden Cross* B50 4LG [off A46 or B439 W of Stratford, OS Sheet 150 map ref 114538; Wixford Rd]: Attractive open-plan stone-built dining pub with good affordable generous food from lunchtime sandwiches up, alert attentive staff, Wells & Youngs and a guest such as local Purity, decent wines, comfortable light wood furniture on flagstones, log fire, nice décor and good lighting; piped music; wheelchair access, charming garden, nice views *(Neil and Brenda Skidmore, Mr and Mrs F E Boxell, George Atkinson, Keith and Sue Ward, Carol and Colin Broadbent)*
ARMSCOTE [SP2444]
☆ *Fox & Goose* CV37 8DD [off A3400 Stratford—Shipston]: Former blacksmith's forge with locals' bar and woodburner in dining area, Black Sheep, Butcombe, Hook Norton Old Hooky and a guest such as Warwickshire, pies and country-style food (all day Fri-Sun); piped music, TV; children and dogs welcome, vine-covered deck overlooking lawn, brightly painted

bedrooms named after characters in *Cluedo*, open from 9am, all day Fri-Sun *(Dr and Mrs A K Clarke, J Crosby, Susan and John Douglas, Carol and Colin Broadbent, George Atkinson, Noel Grundy, LYM)*

AVON DASSETT [SP4049]

Avon CV47 2AS [off B4100 Banbury—Warwick]: Pleasant décor, relaxing atmosphere, chatty friendly staff, good value hearty fresh food inc great variety of sausages and mash, Greene King IPA, Hook Norton Bitter and Dark and Timothy Taylors Landlord, several wines by the glass, interesting Civil War memorabilia, nice restaurant; dogs and muddy walkers welcome – bar's flagstones cope well; tables out in front and small side garden, attractive village by country park *(George Atkinson, Gill and Keith Croxton)*

BAGINTON [SP3474]

Oak CV8 3AU [Coventry Rd]: Large friendly pub by Coventry Airport, nicely modernised keeping beams and open fire; dogs welcome, tables outside, 13 bedrooms *(Alex Henderson)*

☆ *Old Mill* CV8 3AH [Mill Hill]: Olde-worlde Chef & Brewer conversion of watermill nr airport (and Lunt Roman fort), heavy beams, timbers and candlelight, warm rustic-theme bar, linked dining areas, good wine choice, Courage, Greene King and Theakstons, friendly uniformed staff; lovely terraced gardens down to River Sower, 28 bedrooms *(LYM, Richard Tosswill, Susan and John Douglas, Nigel and Sue Foster, Duncan Cloud)*

BARFORD [SP2660]

☆ *Granville* CV35 8DS [off A429 S of Warwick; Wellesbourne Rd]: New owner doing good enterprising food all day from doorstep sandwiches up in attractively refurbished beamed dining pub, charming service, well kept Hook Norton and Purity Pure Gold, bar with leather sofas by open fire, candles and flowers in raftered restaurant with stripped brickwork; children welcome, tables under red canopies in good-sized garden with terrace, open all day *(Dr and Mrs A K Clarke, Keith and Sue Ward, Clive and Fran Dutson, Trevor and Sheila Sharman)*

BARNT GREEN [SP0074]

☆ *Barnt Green Inn* B45 8PZ [Kendal End Rd]: Large civilised Elizabethan dining pub with friendly young staff, good innovative food from breads with dipping oils through shared tapas and wood-fired pizzas to rotisserie, real ales such as Black Sheep and Greene King Old Speckled Hen, log fire, relaxed atmosphere, comfortable contemporary décor, clubby seating in panelled front bar, large brasserie area; tables outside, handy for Lickey Hills walks *(Paul J Robinshaw, Mike and Mary Carter, Nigel and Sue Foster)*

BARSTON [SP2078]

☆ *Bulls Head* B92 0JU [from M42 junction 5, A4141 towards Warwick, first left, then signed down Barston Lane]: Unassuming partly Tudor village pub, friendly landlord and efficient service, well kept ales such as Adnams, Hook Norton, Hydes and Timothy Taylors Landlord, enjoyable traditional food from sandwiches to good fresh fish and Sun lunch, log fires, comfortable lounge with pictures and plates, oak-beamed bar with a little Buddy Holly memorabilia, separate dining room; good-sized secluded garden alongside, hay barn behind, open all day wknds *(Pete Baker, Geoffrey Hughes, Chris Evans)*

BARTON [SP1051]

Cottage of Content B50 4NP [pub signed off B4085, just S of Bidford-on-Avon]: Traditional flagstoned low-beamed bar with new licensees doing good helpings of affordable pubby food, solid fuel stove in inglenook, easy-going local atmosphere, Hook Norton and Shepherd Neame Spitfire, restaurant; picnic-sets in front of the pretty house, touring caravan site with good play area behind, day fishing on River Avon but no nearby moorings *(Keith and Sue Ward, BB)*

BILSTON [SO9496]

Trumpet WV14 0EP [High St]: Well kept Holdens and perhaps a guest ale, good free nightly jazz bands (quiet early evening before they start), trumpets and other instruments hang from ceiling, lots of musical memorabilia and photographs, back conservatory *(the Didler)*

BINLEY WOODS [SP3977]

Cocked Hat CV3 2AX [A428 Coventry—Warwicks]: Two-bar pub dating from 17th c, enjoyable bar food, real ale, some live music inc Sun lunchtime jazz, quiz nights, restaurant; no children or dogs; garden, terrace and smokers' shelter, bedrooms, open all day wknds *(Alan Johnson)*

BIRMINGHAM [SP0786]

Anchor B5 6ET [Bradford St, Digbeth]: Well preserved Edwardian pub with ten or so changing ales and lots of bottled beers, friendly staff, two-part front public bar with carefully restored art nouveau windows, bench seating, tall counter and much polished brasswork and mirrors, back lounge set for eating (well priced simple food till 6), games area with pool and sports TV; tables out behind, open all day *(Roger Shipperley)*

☆ *Bartons Arms* B6 4UP [High St, Aston (A34)]: Magnificent Edwardian landmark, a trouble-free oasis in rather a daunting area, impressive linked richly decorated rooms from the palatial to the snug, original tilework murals, stained glass and mahogany, decorative fireplaces, sweeping stairs to handsome rooms upstairs, well kept Oakham and guests from ornate island bar with snob screens in one section, interesting imported bottled beers and frequent mini beer festivals, good choice of well priced thai food (not Mon), good young staff; open all day *(BB, the Didler, R T and J C Moggridge)*

Bennetts B2 5RS [Bennetts Hill]: Bank conversion with egyptian/french theme, big mural, high carved domed ceiling, snugger side areas with lots of old pictures, ironwork and wood, relaxed atmosphere, comfortably worn seating, well kept Marstons-related ales, good choice of wines by the glass, good coffee, friendly staff, low-priced food; piped music; good wheelchair access, but parking restrictions *(Dr and Mrs A K Clarke, Mrs Hazel Rainer, Michael Dandy)*

Black Eagle B18 5JU [Factory Rd, Hockley]: Welcoming late 19th-c pub with half a dozen well kept ales, generous popular home-made food inc bargain specials, friendly traditional landlord and efficient service, small bare-boards bar, three-part lounge inc one area with banquettes, bay window and old pictures, some original Minton tilework, compact back dining room, summer beer festival with live music; shaded tables in nice small garden, open all day Fri, cl Sun evening *(Roger Shipperley, John Dwane)*

Brasshouse B1 2HP [Broad St]: Handsome bank conversion with lots of dark oak and brass, enjoyable reasonably priced food from sandwiches up, Fullers London Pride, Marstons Pedigree and Timothy Taylors Landlord, attractive dining area; canalside seats, handy for National Sea Life Centre and convention centre *(Michael Dandy, Colin Gooch, Dr and Mrs A K Clarke)*

Briar Rose B2 5RE [Bennetts Hill]: Civilised open-plan Wetherspoons with deep pink décor, well kept changing guest beers, their usual food offers from breakfast on, friendly staff, separate back family dining room; lavatories down stairs, can get busy; reasonably priced bedrooms, open all day *(Michael Dandy, Joe Green, the Didler, Roger Shipperley)*

British Oak B30 2XS [Pershore Rd, Stirchley]: Large 1920s roadhouse with many original fittings in lively front bar and other quieter rooms, Black Sheep, M&B and Wickwar ales, bargain pubby food; big garden behind, open all day *(Tony and Wendy Hobden)*

Bulls Head B4 6JU [Price St, Aston; off A34]: Corner local with two main areas served from central bar, china collection, easy chairs in more private back room, good value generous food, Ansells Mild, Marstons Pedigree and Robinsons Original; open all day, cl Sun *(Tony Hobden)*

Country Girl B29 6HJ [Raddlebarn Rd]: Well run Ember Inn, roomy and comfortable, with two fires, several separate areas, bargain piping hot generous food, friendly landlady and prompt service; no under-12s; garden tables *(Miss L Ward)*

Jewellers Arms B18 6BW [Hockley St]: Traditional Victorian corner pub still catering for local jewellery trade (and handy for good Museum of Jewellery Quarter), several small rooms, attentive friendly staff, bargain basic lunchtime food; keg beer *(M J Winterton, Julian Saunders)*

Shakespeare B2 4JD [Lower Temple St]: Victorian pub with good value food, well

kept ales inc Timothy Taylors Landlord, friendly staff *(Richard Tingle)*

Tap & Spile B1 2JT [Gas St]: Well used basic pub with picnic-sets out by Gas Street canal basin, three tasting levels, low-priced lunchtime bar food from baguettes up, several real ales, darts and dominoes; piped music, games machine, no children; open all day *(LYM, Dr and Mrs A K Clarke, Colin Gooch)*

☆ **Wellington** B2 5SN [Bennetts Hill]: Superb range of changing real ales all from small breweries, also farm ciders, in roomy old-fashioned high-ceilinged pub, experienced landlord and friendly staff, can get very busy; no food, but plates and cutlery if you bring your own – on cheese nights people bring different ones that are pooled; tables out behind, open all day *(John Dwane, Dr and Mrs A K Clarke, Roger Shipperley, Richard Tingle, Michael Dandy, the Didler, John Rushton)*

BRETFORD [SP4277]

Queens Head CV23 0JY [A428 Coventry—Rugby]: Roomy dining pub popular for its lunchtime food (all day Sun), real ales; garden with big play area *(R W Allen)*

BRINKLOW [SP4379]

Bulls Head CV23 0NE [A427, fairly handy for M6 junction 2]: Enjoyable family pub with play areas indoors and outdoors, generous popular food from fresh sandwiches up inc plenty for children, friendly staff, several real ales, collection of old pub signs, shove-ha'penny and table skittles; heated terrace, good bedrooms *(Alan Johnson)*

BROWNHILLS [SK0504]

Royal Oak WS8 6DU [Chester Rd]: Good village-local atmosphere, well kept ales such as Caledonian Deuchars IPA and Greene King, pleasant staff, back eating area with bargain food from sandwiches up from open kitchen, comfortable art deco lounge with Clarice Cliff pottery etc, 1930s-feel public bar; reasonable disabled access, pleasant garden *(R T and J C Moggridge)*

BUBBENHALL [SP3672]

Malt Shovel CV8 3BW [off A445 S of Coventry; Lower End]: Friendly and attractive, with affordable sensible pub food, Black Sheep, Greene King IPA and Wells & Youngs Bombardier, small bar and larger L-shaped lounge, beams, brass and copper, comfortable banquettes; delightful village *(Keith and Sue Ward)*

CHURCHOVER [SP5180]

Haywaggon CV23 0EP [handy for M6 junction 1, off A426; The Green]: Neapolitan landlord does some italian dishes as well as pubbier staples (must book Sun lunch), changing ales such as Fullers London Pride and Shepherd Neame Spitfire, good coffee and wines by the glass, pleasant young staff, two snug eating areas, lots of beams, standing timbers, brasses, nooks and crannies; may be piped music; tables outside with play area, on edge of quiet village, beautiful views over Swift valley *(BB, John Wooll, Catherine and Rob Dunster)*

CORLEY MOOR [SP2885]
Bull & Butcher CV7 8AQ [Common Lane]: Traditional low-beamed country pub, small tidy front lounge and bar with hot log fires and tiled floor, Hook Norton ale, back dining room; garden with play area, walks nearby *(Geoffrey Hughes)*

COVENTRY [SP3279]
Old Windmill CV1 3BA [Spon St]: Well worn timber-framed 15th-c pub with lots of tiny old rooms, exposed beams in uneven ceilings, carved oak seats on flagstones, inglenook woodburner, half a dozen real ales, farm cider, basic lunchtime bar food (not Mon) served from the kitchen door, restaurant; popular with students and busy at wknds, games machine and juke box, no credit cards; open all day *(the Didler, LYM)*
Town Wall CV1 4AH [Bond St, among car parks behind Belgrade Theatre]: Busy Victorian town local with real ales inc Adnams, farm cider, nice hot drinks choice, good generous lunchtime doorstep sandwiches, filled rolls and cheap hot dishes, unspoilt basic front bar and tiny snug, engraved windows and open fires, bigger back lounge with actor and playwright photographs; big-screen sports TV; open all day *(Alan Johnson, BB)*
☆ *Whitefriars* CV1 5DL [Gosford St]: Pair of well preserved medieval town houses, three old-fashioned rooms on both floors, lots of ancient beams, timbers and furniture, flagstones, cobbles and coal fire, up to nine well kept changing ales (more during beer festivals), daily papers, bar lunches; some live music, no children; smokers' shelter on good-sized terrace behind, open all day *(Alan Johnson, BB)*

DEPPERS BRIDGE [SP3959]
Great Western CV47 2ST [4 miles N of M40 junction 12; B4451]: Welcoming roomy and airy pub with model train often clattering round overhead, Adnams and Wells & Youngs Bombardier, short lunchtime menu, more elaborate evening choice, friendly attentive staff; terrace tables *(George Atkinson)*

DUDLEY [SO9591]
☆ *Bottle & Glass* DY1 4SQ [Black Country Museum, Tipton Rd]: Reconstruction of local alehouse in extensive open-air working Black Country Museum (well worth a visit for its re-created period village complete with shops, fairground, school, barge wharf and tram system); friendly staff in costume, well kept Banks's, good chunky filled rolls and smokies, wall benches, sawdust on old boards, woodburner, family rooms *(Chris Evans)*
Park DY2 9PN [George St/Chapel St]: Tap for adjacent Holdens brewery, their beers kept well, basic lunchtime food inc good hot roast meat sandwiches, low prices, friendly service, conservatory, small games room; sports TV; open all day *(the Didler)*

DUNCHURCH [SP4871]
Dun Cow CV22 6NJ [a mile from M45 junction 1: A45/A426]: Handsomely beamed Vintage Inn with massive log fires and other traditional features, friendly staff, food all day, good range of wines by the glass, real ales from small bar counter; piped music; children welcome, tables out in attractive former coachyard and on sheltered side lawn, bedrooms in adjacent Innkeepers Lodge, open all day *(David Green, George Atkinson, LYM, Donna and Roger, John Cook, Martin and Pauline Jennings)*

EARLSWOOD [SP1274]
Blue Bell B94 6BP [Warings Green Rd, not far from M42 junction 2]: By Stratford Canal, roomy lounge, generous bargain Sun carvery (doggie bags provided), Robinsons and guest beers; children welcome, plenty of outside seating *(Tony and Wendy Hobden)*

EATHORPE [SP3968]
☆ *Plough* CV33 9DQ [car park off B4455 NW of Leamington Spa]: Good value generous pub food cooked by landlord, exuberant landlady and speedy jolly service, good wine choice and coffee, Caledonian Deuchars IPA and Greene King Abbot, small bar with open fire, beams and flagstones, step up to long neat dining room, games room; garden picnic-sets *(David Green, Keith and Sue Ward, Joan and Tony Walker, Michael and Jenny Back)*

EDGE HILL [SP3747]
☆ *Castle* OX15 6DJ [off A422]: Curious crenellated octagonal tower perched on steep hill, built 1749 as Gothic folly, arched doorways, Civil War memorabilia and armoury, Hook Norton beers, Stowford Press cider, splendid log fire, darts, pool, board games; fairly basic bar food, piped music, games machine, TV, juke box; children and dogs welcome, big attractive garden with aunt sally and winter views, bedrooms, open all day *(I A Herdman, N R White, Roger and Anne Newbury, Susan and John Douglas, LYM, Tracey and Stephen Groves, John Branston, G Coates, Barry and Susanne Hurst, William Ruxton)*

FARNBOROUGH [SP4349]
☆ *Inn at Farnborough* OX17 1DZ [off A423 N of Banbury]: Upmarket dining pub with wide choice of enjoyable food from pubby things like sausages and mash to pricier more restauranty dishes, Greene King ales, good choice of wines by the glass, modern minimalist décor blending attractively with flagstones and mullioned windows; garden picnic-sets, cl Mon lunchtime *(J Crosby, LYM, Mary McSweeney, Mrs Philippa Wilson, David Wright, George Atkinson)*

FILLONGLEY [SP2787]
Cottage CV7 8EG [Black Hall Lane]: Comfortable and civilised dining pub with wide choice of enjoyable reasonably priced food, unpretentious yet with plenty of interest, Church End, Marstons and Tetleys ales *(David Green)*

HALESOWEN [SO9683]
Waggon & Horses B63 3TU [Stourbridge Rd]: Regular beers inc Bathams and up to seven or so changing ales from small brewers in chatty bare-boards bar and more spacious

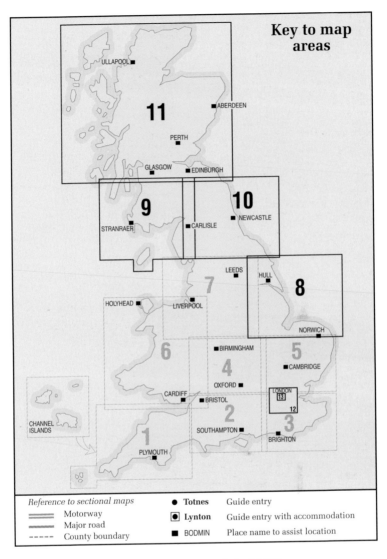

Key to map areas

ULLAPOOL ■

11

■ ABERDEEN

PERTH ■

GLASGOW ■ ■ EDINBURGH

9

10

STRANRAER ■

■ CARLISLE

■ NEWCASTLE

LEEDS ■

HULL ■

8

HOLYHEAD ■

7

LIVERPOOL ■

■ NORWICH

6

■ BIRMINGHAM

5

4

■ CAMBRIDGE

OXFORD ■

LONDON [13]

12

CHANNEL ISLANDS

CARDIFF ■ ■ BRISTOL

2

3

1

SOUTHAMPTON ■

■ BRIGHTON

PLYMOUTH ■

Reference to sectional maps

━━━ Motorway
━━━ Major road
╌╌╌ County boundary

● **Totnes** Guide entry
◉ **Lynton** Guide entry with accommodation
■ BODMIN Place name to assist location

MAPS IN THIS SECTION

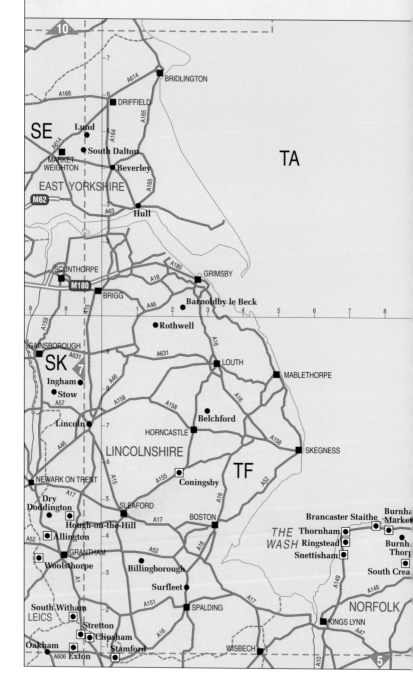

10

7

A614

BRIDLINGTON

A166

6 ■ DRIFFIELD

A165

SE

A164

Lund ●

TA

A814

● **South Dalton**

MARKET
WEIGHTON ■

● **Beverley**

A165

EAST YORKSHIRE

M62

3

A63

■ **Hull**

2

A180

SCUNTHORPE ■

M180

GRIMSBY

A18

■ **BRIGG**

A46

Barnoldby le Beck ●

8   9   1   2   3   4   5   6   7   8

A159

A15

● **Rothwell**

A631

GAINSBOROUGH ■

A631

A16

SK   **7**

9

■ **LOUTH**

Ingham ●

A46

■ **MABLETHORPE**

● Stow

8

A57

A158

A158

Belchford ●

■ **Lincoln**

HORNCASTLE

A16

A16

7

A158

A46

LINCOLNSHIRE

SKEGNESS ■

6

A15

A155

□ **Coningsby**

TF

A52

NEWARK ON TRENT ■

5

A17

Dry
Doddington ●

□ **SLEAFORD**

A16

A17

A15

□ **Hough-on-the-Hill**

BOSTON ■

Brancaster Staithe   Burnha

4

A52

□ **Allington**

A17

□
Market

THE   **Thornham** □

□ **GRANTHAM**

A52

WASH   **Ringstead** □

Burnh
Thorp

A1

□ **Woolsthorpe**

● **Billingborough**

3

Snettisham □

A149

South Crea

A148

● **Surfleet**

NORFOLK

South Witham   2

A151

□

LEICS   □

Stretton

A16

□ **Clipsham**

SPALDING ■

KINGS LYNN ■

A47

Oakham ●   1

□ **Stamford**

WISBECH ■

A606   **Exton** □

A10

5

8

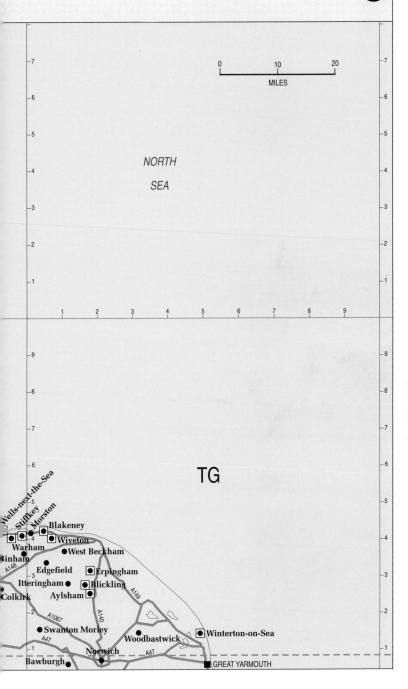

NORTH

SEA

0   10   20
MILES

TG

Wells-next-the-Sea
Stiffkey
Morston
Blakeney
Wiveton
Warham
West Beckham
inham
Edgefield
Erpingham
Itteringham
Blickling
Colkirk
Aylsham
Swanton Morley
Woodbastwick
Winterton-on-Sea
Bawburgh
Norwich
GREAT YARMOUTH

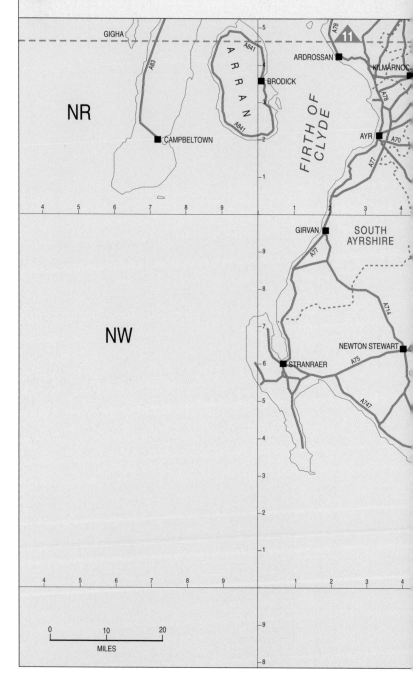

GIGHA

A83

A841

A R R A N

BRODICK

ARDROSSAN

A78

11

KILMARNOC

NR

CAMPBELTOWN

FIRTH OF CLYDE

AYR

A70

A77

4   5   6   7   8   9

1   2   3   4

GIRVAN

SOUTH AYRSHIRE

A77

NW

A714

NEWTON STEWART

STRANRAER

A75

A747

4   5   6   7   8   9

1   2   3   4

0   10   20

MILES

-5

-4

-3

-2

-1

-9

-8

-7

-6

-5

-4

-3

-2

-1

-9

-8

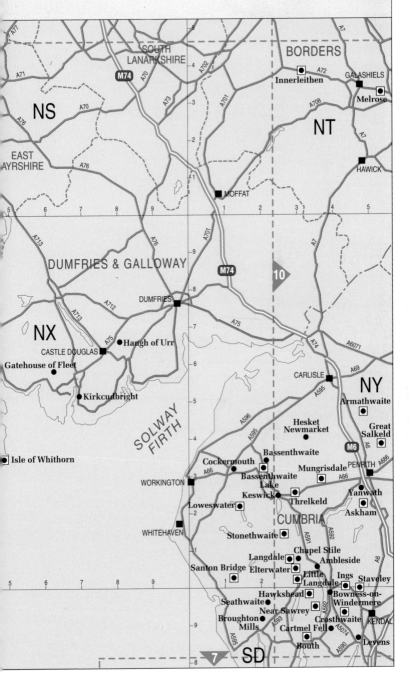

9

NS

SOUTH
LANARKSHIRE

BORDERS

M74

A77

A71

A70

A70

A73

A76

A702

A701

Innerleithen

A72

GALASHIELS

A708

Melrose

NT

A7

EAST
AYRSHIRE

A76

A701

HAWICK

MOFFAT

5   6   7   8   9   1   2   3   4   5

A713

A76

A701

DUMFRIES & GALLOWAY

M74

10

NX

A713

A712

A713

DUMFRIES

A75

A74

A6071

A69

Haugh of Urr

A75

CASTLE DOUGLAS

Gatehouse of Fleet

Kirkcudbright

CARLISLE

NY

Armathwaite

SOLWAY
FIRTH

A596

A595

A595

Hesket
Newmarket

Great
Salkeld

M6

A6

Isle of Whithorn

Cockermouth

Bassenthwaite

Mungrisdale

PENRITH

A686

A66

WORKINGTON

A66

Bassenthwaite
Lake

Keswick

Threlkeld

Yanwath

Askham

Loweswater

CUMBRIA

WHITEHAVEN

Stonethwaite

A591

A592

Chapel Stile

Langdale

Ambleside

Ings   Staveley

A6

Santon Bridge

Elterwater

Little
Langdale

Hawkshead

Bowness-on-
Windermere

Seathwaite

Near Sawrey

A592

Broughton
Mills

A593

Crosthwaite

KENDAL

Cartmel Fell

A5074

Bouth

Levens

A595

A590

SD

7

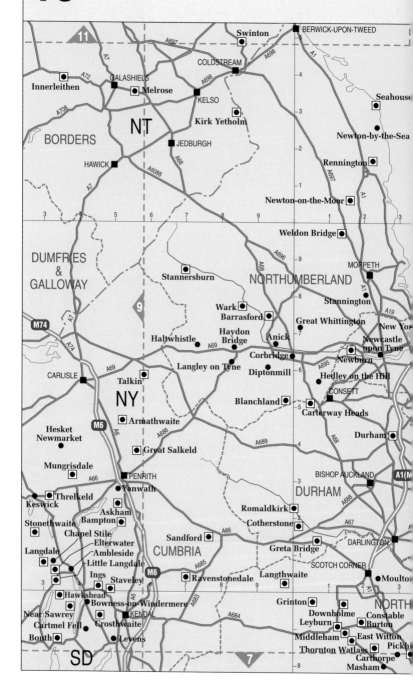

11

Swinton

BERWICK-UPON-TWEED

A697

A698

COLDSTREAM

A72

GALASHIELS

A698

Innerleithen

A7

Melrose

KELSO

Seahouse

A708

Kirk Yetholm

Newton-by-the-Sea

NT

BORDERS

JEDBURGH

Rennington

HAWICK

A6088

A68

Newton-on-the-Moor

A697

A1

Weldon Bridge

DUMFRIES & GALLOWAY

MORPETH

Stannersburn

NORTHUMBERLAND

9

Stannington

A19

Wark

Barrasford

Great Whittington

New Yor

M74

A7

A74

Haltwhistle

Haydon Bridge

A69

Anick

Newcastle upon Tyne

Langley on Tyne

Corbridge

A695

Newburn

CARLISLE

A69

Diptonmill

Hedley on the Hill

Talkin

CONSETT

NY

Blanchland

Carterway Heads

Armathwaite

A686

Durham

Hesket Newmarket

M6

A6

Great Salkeld

A689

A68

Mungrisdale

PENRITH

BISHOP AUCKLAND

A1(M

A66

Threlkeld

Yanwath

DURHAM

Keswick

Askham

Romaldkirk

A688

Stonethwaite

Bampton

Cotherstone

A67

Chapel Stile

Sandford

DARLINGTON

Elterwater

CUMBRIA

Greta Bridge

Langdale

Ambleside

Little Langdale

M6

A685

SCOTCH CORNER

Ings

Staveley

A683

Ravenstonedale

Langthwaite

A1

Moulto

Hawkshead

Bowness-on-Windermere

A6

A684

Grinton

NORTH

Near Sawrey

KENDAL

Downholme

Constable Burton

Cartmel Fell

Crosthwaite

Leyburn

Bouth

Levens

Middleham

East Witton

Thornton Watlass

Pickhi

SD

7

Carthorpe

Masham

NU

NORTH

SEA

0   10   20
MILES

SOUTH SHIELDS

SUNDERLAND   NZ

A19

HARTLEPOOL

MIDDLESBROUGH A174

A171

A172   Whitby

Egton Bridge   Robin Hood's Bay
Beck Hole

A169   A171

Osmotherley

YORKSHIRE   Blakey Ridge
SE   Lastingham
Fadmoor   Cropton
Appleton-le-Moors   SCARBOROUGH
Felixkirk   Sinnington   TA
Kirkbymoorside

A170   A170   A165

Harome   Marton   Pickering

8

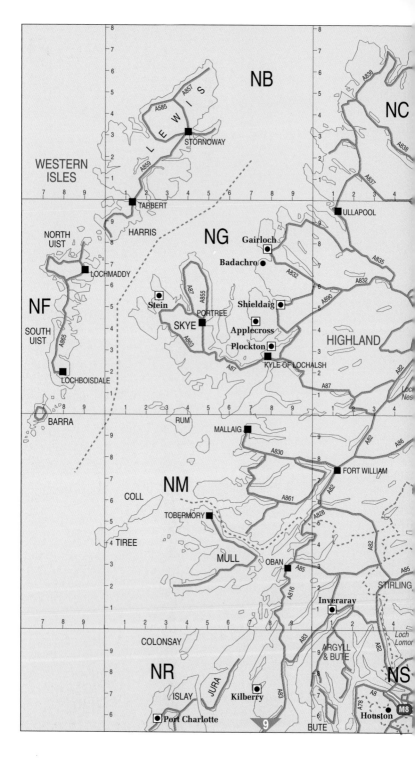

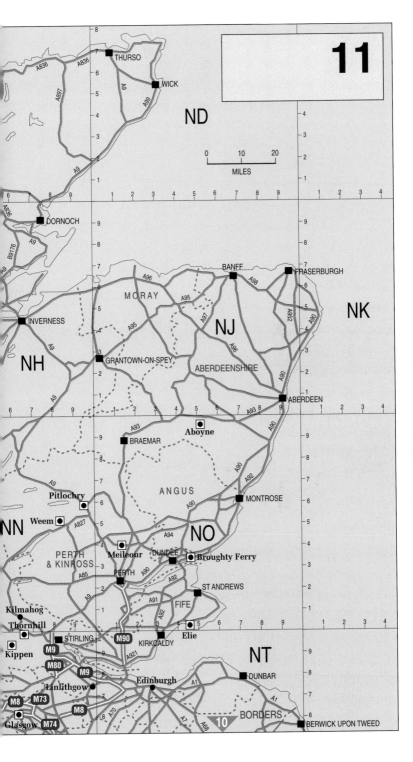

11

THURSO

WICK

ND

A836
A836
A887
A9
A99

0   10   20
MILES

DORNOCH

A836
B9176
A9

BANFF
FRASERBURGH

MORAY

A96
A95
A97
A95

NJ

A952
A90

NK

INVERNESS

A95

GRANTOWN-ON-SPEY

A96

ABERDEENSHIRE

NH

A9

ABERDEEN

A90
A93

Aboyne

A93

BRAEMAR

A90

ANGUS

A90
A92

MONTROSE

A9

Pitlochry

Weem
A827

A94

NO

Meileour

DUNDEE
Broughty Ferry

NN

PERTH
& KINROSS

A85

PERTH

A90
A92

ST ANDREWS

A9

A91
A92

FIFE

Kilmahog
Thornhill

STIRLING

Kippen

M9

M90

Elie

KIRKCALDY

NT

M80
M9

A921

DUNBAR

Linlithgow

Edinburgh

A1

A1

M8
M73

Glasgow

M8

M74

A70

BORDERS

10

BERWICK UPON TWEED

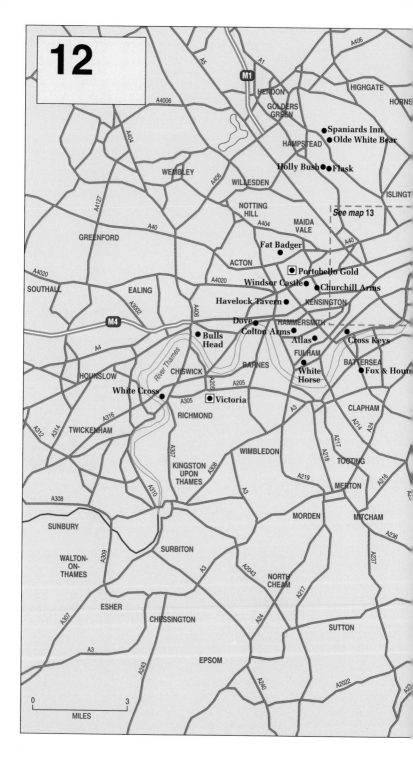

12

TOTTENHAM
WALTHAMSTOW
A406
A112
A12
STOKE
NEWINGTON
A503
A10
A11
A12
A118
A12
A406
●Compton Arms
●Crown
WEST HAM
A13
Marquess
Tavern
BARKING
A11
A124
A13
CITY
A13
A12
Prospect of Whitby●
●Grapes
●Narrow
A102
River Thames
WOOLWICH
A206
A2
●Cutty Sark
PLUMSTEAD
A205
CAMBERWELL
Greenwich Union●
GREENWICH
A202
A2
A207
BEXLEYHEATH
PECKHAM
LEWISHAM
A20
A2
A2
●Crown & Greyhound
ELTHAM
A211
BEXLEY
DULWICH
A205
A20
A222
STREATHAM
SYDENHAM
A21
A212
SIDCUP
A223
A208
SOUTH
NORWOOD
A222
A222
CHISLEHURST
A20
A224
SWANLEY
A208
BROMLEY
PETTS
WOOD
A21
CROYDON
A232
A232
ORPINGTON
A2022
FARNBOROUGH
●Bo-Peep
A23
NEW
ADDINGTON
A233
A21
PURLEY
A2
BIGGIN
HILL
●Old Jail

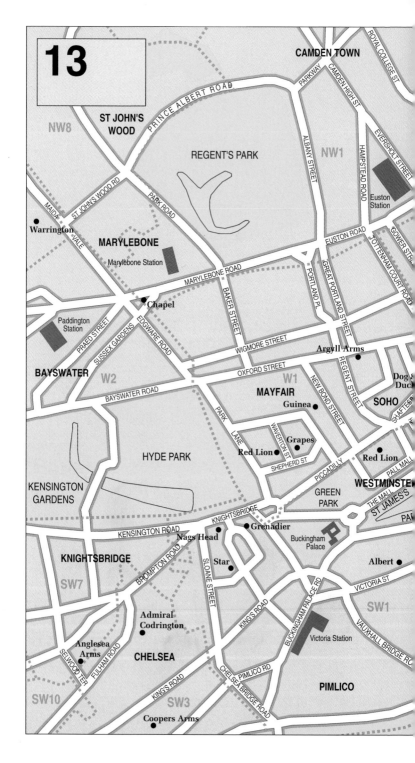

13

CAMDEN TOWN

ROYAL COLLEGE ST

PARKWAY

CAMDEN HIGH ST

EVERSHOLT STREET

PRINCE ALBERT ROAD

ST JOHN'S WOOD

NW8

REGENT'S PARK

ALBANY STREET

NW1

HAMPSTEAD ROAD

ST JOHN'S WOOD RD

PARK ROAD

GOWER STH

Euston Station

MAIDA VALE

Warrington

MARYLEBONE

EUSTON ROAD

Marylebone Station

PORTLAND PL

GREAT PORTLAND STREET

TOTTENHAM COURT ROAD

PRAED STREET

EDGWARE ROAD

MARYLEBONE ROAD

Chapel

BAKER STREET

Paddington Station

SUSSEX GARDENS

WIGMORE STREET

Argyll Arms

BAYSWATER

W2

OXFORD STREET

W1

REGENT STREET

BAYSWATER ROAD

MAYFAIR

NEW BOND STREET

Dog & Duck

SOHO

SHAFTESB

Guinea

PARK LANE

KENSINGTON GARDENS

HYDE PARK

WAVERTON ST

Grapes

Red Lion

SHEPHERD ST

Red Lion

PICCADILLY

PALL MALL

WESTMINSTE

GREEN PARK

THE MALL

ST JAMES'S

PA

KNIGHTSBRIDGE

KENSINGTON ROAD

Nags Head

Grenadier

Buckingham Palace

Albert

KNIGHTSBRIDGE

SW7

Star

BROMPTON ROAD

SLOANE STREET

VICTORIA ST

SW1

VAUXHALL BRIDGE RO

Admiral Codrington

KING'S ROAD

BUCKINGHAM PALACE RD

Anglesea Arms

SELWOOD TER

FULHAM ROAD

CHELSEA

Victoria Station

SW10

KING'S ROAD

SW3

CHELSEA BRIDGE ROAD

PIMLICO RD

PIMLICO

Coopers Arms

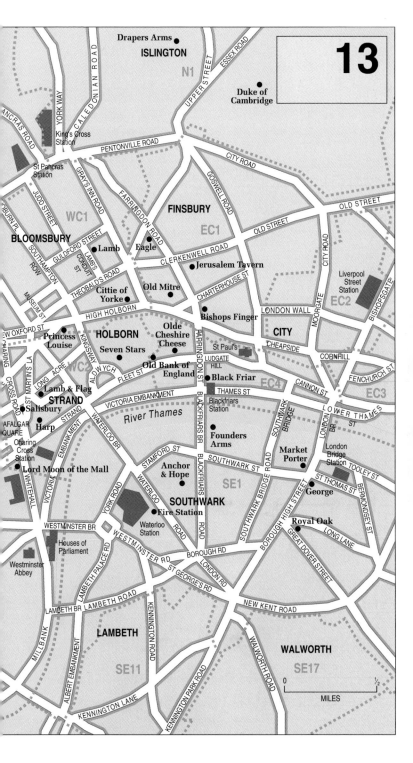

13

Drapers Arms ●
ISLINGTON
N1

UPPER STREET
ESSEX ROAD

YORK WAY
CALEDONIAN ROAD

Duke of
Cambridge ●

King's Cross
Station
PANCRAS ROAD

PENTONVILLE ROAD
CITY ROAD

St Pancras
Station

GRAY'S INN ROAD
FARRINGDON ROAD
GOSWELL ROAD
OLD STREET

JUDD STREET
HOLBURN PL
WC1
FINSBURY
EC1
OLD STREET

BLOOMSBURY
SOUTHAMPTON ROW
GUILDFORD STREET
LAMB'S
CONDUIT ST
THEOBALD'S ROAD

● Lamb
Eagle ●
CLERKENWELL ROAD
● Jerusalem Tavern

CITY ROAD

MUSEUM ST
Cittie of
Yorke ●
● Old Mitre
CHARTERHOUSE ST

Liverpool
Street
Station
BISHOPSGATE

EW OXFORD ST
HIGH HOLBORN
● Bishops Finger
LONDON WALL
EC2

CHARING
Princess
Louise ●
HOLBORN
Olde
Cheshire
Cheese
FARRINGDON ST
CITY
MOORGATE

KINGSWAY
Seven Stars ●
St Paul's
CHEAPSIDE
CORNHILL

ST MARTIN'S LA
LONG ACRE
WC2
ALDWYCH
● Old Bank of
England
LUDGATE
HILL
Black Friar ●
EC4
FENCHURCH ST

CROSS ROAD
● Lamb & Flag
FLEET ST
THAMES ST
CANNON ST
EC3

STRAND
● Salisbury
VICTORIA EMBANKMENT
BLACKFRIARS RD
Blackfriars
Station
LOWER THAMES

AFALGAR
QUARE
● Harp
STRAND
River Thames
SOUTHWARK
BRIDGE
LONDON BR
ST

Charing
Cross
Station
EMBANKMENT
WATERLOO BR
STAMFORD ST
● Founders
Arms
SOUTHWARK BRIDGE ROAD
Market
Porter ●
London
Bridge
Station
TOOLEY ST

● Lord Moon of the Mall
VICTORIA
WHITEHALL
YORK ROAD
WATERLOO ROAD
● Anchor
& Hope
BLACKFRIARS RD
SOUTHWARK ST
SE1
ST THOMAS ST
● George
BERMONDSEY ST

WESTMINSTER BR
SOUTHWARK
● Fire Station
Waterloo
Station
BOROUGH HIGH STREET
● Royal Oak
LONG LANE

Houses of
Parliament
WESTMINSTER RD
BOROUGH RD
LONDON RD
GREAT DOVER STREET

Westminster
Abbey
LAMBETH PALACE RD
ST GEORGE'S RD
NEW KENT ROAD

LAMBETH BR
LAMBETH ROAD
KENNINGTON ROAD

MILLBANK
ALBERT EMBANKMENT
LAMBETH
SE11
KENNINGTON PARK ROAD
WALWORTH ROAD
WALWORTH
SE17

KENNINGTON LANE
0   ½
MILES

'Since I've discovered *The Good Pub Guide* I haven't
had to suffer a bad pub again'
Simon Heptinstall, Mail on Sunday

'Easily the best'
Time Out

'The definitive guide to boozing'
The Times

* Since it was first published 27 years ago, *The Good Pub
Guide* has received many fabulous recommendations
because, unlike other guide books, it is totally
independent. We never take payment for entries.

* Pubs are inspected anonymously by the editorial team,
and we rely on reports from readers to tell us whether
pubs deserve to be in the next edition.

* Don't forget to report to us on any pubs you visit over the
coming year. You can use the card in the middle of the
book, the forms at the back, or you can send reports to us
at **feedback@thegoodpubguide.co.uk**

Write and tell us about your favourite pub!

We'll send you more forms (free) if you wish.
You don't need a stamp in the UK.
Simply write to us at:

**The Good Pub Guide,
FREEPOST TN1569, WADHURST,
East Sussex TN5 7BR**

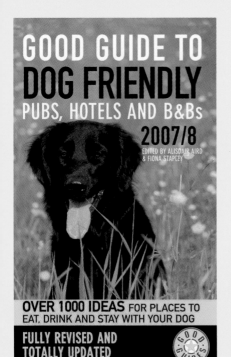

THE GOOD PUB GUIDE ONLINE
BIGGER AND BETTER

Everyone at *The Good Pub Guide* has been hard at work to bring you not only the latest edition – but also a brand new website. **www.thegoodpubguide.co.uk** provides all of the information on the 5,000 *Good Pub Guide*-recommended pubs as well as listing over 50,000 pubs across the country.

We also need your help and feedback. Come to the new website and tell the world about your favourite pubs, the best food, the best service – whatever it was that particularly impressed you. With over 50,000 pubs out there, there is no shortage of places to choose from.

So please come and try out **www.thegoodpubguide.co.uk**

- * Search for *Good Pub Guide* recommended pubs
- * Over 50,000 licensed premises across the UK listed
- * Use the site to search for pubs with specific amenities
- * Add your own opinion on your favourite pubs
- * Integrated maps help you find new pubs

lounge, country wines and belgian brews, good snacks, low prices, brewery memorabilia; TV, Tues music night; open all day *(the Didler)*

HALFORD [SP2645]

☆ *Halford Bridge* CV36 5BN [Fosse Way (A429)]: Solid Cotswold stone inn with unusual contemporary furniture in roomy civilised bar, armchair lounge, tasty food from lunchtime baguettes and pubby favourites to more interesting dishes, good choice of wines by the glass, well kept Hook Norton and perhaps a guest beer, friendly helpful staff, good solid tables in restaurant with open fire; attractive inner courtyard, 12 bedrooms, open all day *(Clive and Fran Dutson, Ian and Jackie Robertson, Keith and Sue Ward)*

HAMPTON IN ARDEN [SP2080]

White Lion B92 0AA [High St; handy for M42 junction 6]: Civilised traditional beamed pub with good straightforward food inc interesting sandwiches, friendly service, well kept Adnams, open fires, brasses and local memorabilia in carpeted bar, back restaurant; seven bedrooms, attractive village, handy for NEC *(LYM, Trevor and Sylvia Millum, R T and J C Moggridge)*

HAMPTON LUCY [SP2557]

Boars Head CV35 8BE [Church St, E of Stratford]: Recently refurbished roomy low-beamed two-bar local next to lovely church, five quickly changing real ales, good value pubby food inc lunchtime baguettes, good choice of wines by the glass, log fire; discreet piped music; neat and attractive secluded back garden, pretty village nr Charlcote House *(Joan and Tony Walker, Keith and Sue Ward)*

HARBOROUGH MAGNA [SP4779]

Old Lion CV23 0HL [3 miles from M6 junction 1; B4122]: Welcoming village pub with Greene King ales, decent wines by the glass, good helpings of food from sandwiches up inc popular OAP lunches and some interesting dishes, friendly side restaurant, pool room; children welcome, family events, open all day wknds *(Alan Johnson, John Wooll)*

HATTON [SP2467]

Waterman CV35 7JJ [A4177, by Grand Union Canal]: Above Hatton flight of 21 locks, far views from sunny balcony and huge garden, nice variety of furnishings in linked rooms, good range of food from modern sandwiches up all day, local ales, great choice of wines by the glass, friendly efficient staff; good walks nearby, moorings *(anon)*

HOCKLEY HEATH [SP1572]

Wharf B94 6QT [Stratford Rd (A3400)]: Friendly modernised local by Stratford Canal, open-plan but cosily divided, lounge extension, quick generous food inc bargain daily carvery, Courage and Theakstons, good canal photographs; children welcome, attractive garden with play area, interesting towpath walks *(Tony Hobden)*

HUNNINGHAM [SP3768]

☆ *Red Lion* CV33 9DY [off B4453 Leamington—Rugby]: New chef/landlord doing good generous food, individual but not pretentious, from sandwiches up, cheery staff, Greene King Abbot and Hook Norton Old Hooky, log fires, airy spacious layout, décor strong on comics; no children after 7.30, attractive riverside spot *(Geoffrey Hughes, Myles Abell, Martin Stafford)*

ILMINGTON [SP2143]

Red Lion CV36 4LX [Front St]: Stone-built village local, flagstoned bar with fire, smarter lounge, traditional furnishings, well kept Hook Norton, farm cider, enjoyable simple good value food, good wine list, friendly helpful licensees, evening dining room; secluded garden with aunt sally *(Stephen Wright, K H Frostick)*

KENILWORTH [SP2872]

Clarendon Arms CV8 1NB [Castle Hill]: Busy pub opp castle, huge helpings of good value food in several rooms off long partly flagstoned bustling bar, largish peaceful upstairs dining room, good friendly staff, several real ales; daytime car park fee deducted from bill *(Martin Kane, Alan Johnson, John and Yvonne Davies, I A Herdman)*

☆ *Clarendon House* CV8 1LZ [High St]: Interesting enjoyable snacks (all day) and meals in ancient timber building with leather armchairs and sofas in large front lounge with contemporary prints and china, Greene King ales and decent wines from long serving counter, back dining room; piped music; comfortable bedrooms, good breakfast, open all day *(Andy and Jill Kassube, LYM, Donna and Roger)*

KNOWLE [SP1875]

☆ *Herons Nest* B93 0EE [A4110 (Warwick Rd) about a mile S]: Beamed Vintage Inn dining pub, updated keeping character, sensibly priced traditional food all day, well organised friendly staff, plenty of good value wines by the glass, real ales, open fires, interesting décor, some flagstones and high-backed settles, big dining room overlooking Grand Union Canal; lots of tables out by water, moorings, Innkeepers Lodge bedrooms, open all day *(Susan and Nigel Brookes, Martin Kane, David Green, Hugh Bower)*

LAPWORTH [SP1970]

Navigation B94 6NA [Old Warwick Rd (B4439 S)]: New management for busy two-bar beamed and flagstoned local by Grand Union Canal, warm coal fire and some bright canal ware, modern back dining room, wide range of generous food from sandwiches up, real ales such as Holdens, Timothy Taylors Landlord and Warwickshire; children welcome, hatch service to waterside terrace, open all day *(Michael and Alison Sandy, LYM)*

LEAMINGTON SPA [SP3266]

Somerville Arms CV32 4SX [Campion Terr]: Neat local with cosy unspoilt Victorian back lounge, well kept Adnams Broadside, Fullers London Pride and Greene King, friendly staff, darts; quiz and music nights; tables out on wide pavement and in small courtyard, cl lunchtime *(Steve and Liz Tilley, Antony Townsend, Katie Carter)*

LEEK WOOTTON [SP2868]

Anchor CV35 7QX [Warwick Rd]: Neat and well run dining lounge popular for enjoyable fresh food inc cheaper lunchtime specials, well kept Bass, Hook Norton Old Hooky and M&B Brew XI, decent wine, good soft drinks choice, attentive service, lots of close-set tables, overflow into smaller bar with darts, TV and machines; may be piped pop music; long garden behind *(George Atkinson)*

LONG COMPTON [SP2832]

☆ *Red Lion* CV36 5JS [A3400 S of Shipston-on-Stour]: Old-fashioned built-in settles among other pleasantly assorted seats and tables, beams, panelling, flagstones, stripped stone, old prints, good value substantial food from good sandwiches up in bar and restaurant areas, children's helpings, real ales such as Adnams Broadside and Hook Norton, good wines by the glass, welcoming landlady (second landlady in charge of the kitchen), log fires and woodburners, simple public bar with pool; dogs and children welcome, big back garden with terrace, picnic-sets and climber, comfortable bedrooms *(John Wooll, LYM, S M Livingstone, Chris Glasson, K H Frostick)*

LONG ITCHINGTON [SP4165]

Blue Lias CV47 8LD [Stockton Rd, off A423]: Pretty pub by Grand Union Canal, good choice of ales inc Adnams Broadside, Greene King Old Speckled Hen and Wychwood Hobgoblin, quick pleasant service, snug booth seating in eating area; plenty of tables in waterside grounds, also a separate outbuilding bar with tables under a dome *(Adrian Johnson, Nigel and Sue Foster, Catherine and Rob Dunster, Charles and Pauline Stride)*

LOWER GORNAL [SO9291]

Black Bear DY3 2AE [Deepdale Lane]: Simple split-level local based on 18th-c former farmhouse, up to seven changing ales, good choice of whiskies, coal fire; open all day wknds, cl wkdy lunchtimes *(the Didler)*

Fountain DY3 2PE [Temple St]: Lively two-room local with helpful landlord and staff, eight real ales such as Enville and RCH, two farm ciders, country wines and imported beers, enjoyable inexpensive food all day (not Sun evening), back dining area, pigs-and-pen skittles; piped music; beer festivals, open all day *(the Didler)*

Old Bulls Head DY3 2NU [Redhall Rd]: Busy Victorian local with own Black Country ales from back microbrewery and two guest beers, may be good filled cobs, open fire, back games room, some live music; open all day wknds (from 4 wkdys) *(the Didler)*

LYE [SO9284]

Windsor Castle DY9 7DG [Stourbridge Rd]: Contemporary minimalist décor and

furnishings, good value Sadlers ales brewed here (tours available), guest beers too, friendly helpful staff, good range of enjoyable cheap food inc some imaginative dishes often using ale in the recipe (snacks all day, no evening meals Sun), bright lighting and lively acoustics, some brewing memorabilia; open all day *(J Rowlands-Roberts, Nigel Espley, Liane Purnell)*

MONKS KIRBY [SP4682]

☆ *Bell* CV23 0QY [just off B4027 W of Pailton]: Hospitable long-serving Spanish landlord and his sweet dogs enlivening this dimly lit pub, dark beams, timber dividers, flagstones and cobbles, very wide choice of largely good spanish food inc starters doubling as tapas, fine range of spanish wines and of brandies and malt whiskies, relaxed informal service, Greene King ales, plenty of brandies and malt whiskies, appropriate piped music; children and dogs welcome, streamside back terrace with country view, may be cl Mon *(Susan and John Douglas, Trevor and Sheila Sharman, Catherine and Rob Dunster, LYM, Jill and Julian Tasker, Michael Doswell)*

NAPTON [SP4661]

Napton Bridge Inn CV47 8NQ [Southam Rd (A425), Oxford Canal Napton Bottom Lock]: Big family-run canalside pub with pine panelling, open fires and comfortable mixed furnishings in three smallish rooms, good food and service, changing real ales, lots of canal pictures, dining area overlooking water; piped music, no dogs; children welcome, garden behind *(E Clark)*

OFFCHURCH [SP3565]

Stags Head CV33 9AQ [Welsh Rd, off A425 at Radford Semele]: Low-beamed olde-worlde thatched village pub with good value usual food, spacious dining area with conservatory, friendly efficient service, log fire, John Smiths and a guest beer; quiet piped music; good-sized garden with play area *(Joan and Tony Walker, Keith and Sue Ward)*

OLD HILL [SO9686]

Waterfall B64 6RG [Waterfall Lane]: Good value unpretentious two-room local, friendly staff, well kept Holdens, Bathams and guests, good value plain home-made food from hot filled baguettes with chips to Sun lunch, tankards and jugs hanging from boarded ceiling; piped music; children welcome, back garden with play area, open all day Fri-Sun *(the Didler)*

OLDBURY [SO9989]

Waggon & Horses B69 3AD [Church St, nr Savacentre]: Copper ceiling, original etched windows, open fire and Black Country memorabilia in busy town pub with Enville and two or three guest beers, wide choice of generous lunchtime food (not wknds) from sandwiches up inc lots of puddings, decent wines, friendly efficient service even when busy, ornate Victorian tiles in corridor to lively comfortable back lounge with tie collection, side room with high-backed settles and big old tables, bookable upstairs

bistro Weds-Fri nights; open all day
(the Didler, Pete Baker)

OXHILL [SP3149]

☆ *Peacock* CV35 0QU [off A422 Stratford—
Banbury]: Pleasantly upgraded stone-built
pub with good traditional food, Timothy
Taylors Landlord and more local ales, cosy
bar and dining room; pretty village, open all
day wknds, cl Mon *(Roger M Hancock,
Prof H G Allen)*

PRINCETHORPE [SP4070]

Three Horseshoes CV23 9PR [High Town;
junction A423/B4453]: Friendly old beamed
village pub, Marstons Pedigree and Wells &
Youngs Bombardier, enjoyable food, open
fire, decorative plates, pictures, comfortable
settles and chairs; end TV; pleasant big
garden with terrace and play area, bedrooms
(Catherine and Rob Dunster, Alan Johnson)

PRIORS HARDWICK [SP4756]

☆ *Butchers Arms* CV47 7SN [off A423 via
Wormleighton or A361 via Boddington,
N of Banbury; Church End]: Upmarket
old-fashioned restaurant in pleasantly
reworked 14th-c building, oak beams,
flagstones, panelling, antiques and soft
lighting, huge choice of good if pricy food
inc good value lunches, friendly Portuguese
landlord, punctilious formal service,
distinguished wine list (the beer is keg),
small bar with inglenook used mainly by
people waiting for tables, also simple
public bar; country garden, lovely setting
(BB, K H Frostick)

PRIORS MARSTON [SP4857]

Holly Bush CV47 7RW [off A361 S of
Daventry; Holly Bush Lane]: Beams,
flagstones and lots of stripped stone in
rambling linked rooms, hefty tables, some
squashy leather sofas, Adnams, Brakspears
and Hook Norton, cheery landlord, usual
food, big log fire and woodburners (not
always lit), games area with bar billiards,
pool and board games; piped music, TV, juke
box, games machine; children and dogs
welcome, sheltered garden with covered
pergola, open all day wknds *(Joan and
Tony Walker, LYM, George Atkinson)*

RADFORD SEMELE [SP3464]

White Lion CV31 1TE [A425 2 miles E of
Leamington Spa]: Relaxed beamed Chef &
Brewer, friendly staff, their usual food all
day from baguettes up, real ales such as
Adnams and Caledonian Deuchars IPA, good
coffee and choice of wines by the glass,
candles and open fires; children welcome,
disabled access and facilities, terrace tables
and heaters *(Patrick Andrews)*

REDHILL [SP1356]

Stag B49 6NQ [Alcester Rd (A46 Alcester—
Stratford)]: Airy linked beamed and timbered
rooms around central bar, some with pine
tables, others with leather sofas, open fires,
Greene King ales, good choice of wines by
the glass, wide food choice from sandwiches
up; children welcome, large terrace (traffic
noise out here), 10 bedrooms *(Keith and
Sue Ward)*

RYTON-ON-DUNSMORE [SP3872]

Old Bull & Butcher CV8 3EP [Oxford Rd]:
Roomy refurbished pub with usual food inc
bargain lunches, two real ales, restaurant
and conservatory; no dogs; children
welcome, good-sized garden with play area,
open all day *(Alan Johnson)*

SEDGLEY [SO9194]

Mount Pleasant DY3 1RH [High St]: Mock-
Tudor pub nr town centre, comfortable homely
front bar with fire, cosy split-level back
lounge, RCH and six changing guest beers
such as Enville, cl Sun till 7 *(the Didler)*

SHIPSTON-ON-STOUR [SP2540]

Black Horse CV36 4BT [Station Rd (off
A3400)]: 16th-c thatched pub reopened
after wine-bar-style refurbishment, keeping
good inglenook log fire and low-beamed bars
off central entrance passage, good choice of
wines by the glass, Adnams Broadside and
Greene King IPA, enjoyable home-made food
(not Sun evening), darts, dominoes and
cribbage, small dining room; back garden
with terrace and aunt sally, open all day Sun
(K H Frostick)

George CV36 4AJ [High St]: Splendid early
Georgian façade, bistro-style inside with
several linked areas inc one with deep
leather armchairs and log fire, enjoyable
mildly upmarket blackboard food, good
friendly service, real ales such as Fullers
London Pride from central marble-topped
counter; 16 well modernised bedrooms, open
all day *(JHBS)*

☆ *Horseshoe* CV36 4AP [Church St]: Good food
(not Sun evening) from new chef inc OAP
bargains in pretty timbered inn, recently
refurbished open-plan bar with big fireplace,
separate restaurant, friendly staff, three
changing ales such as Greene King and local
Wizard, decent wines and coffee, darts, live
music Weds; children very welcome, small
flower-decked back terrace, nice bedrooms,
open all day Sat *(BB, K H Frostick)*

SHIRLEY [SP1376]

Plough B90 4EP [Stratford Rd]: Comfortable
and reliable Beefeater; disabled facilities,
garden tables, Premier Inn bedrooms
(Chris Evans)

STOURBRIDGE [SO9083]

Shrubbery Cottage DY8 1RQ [Heath Lane,
Old Swinford (B4186 S)]: Welcoming
L-shaped local with full Holdens ale range
kept well, basic cobs, darts one end, cards
and dominoes the other; central
wide-screen sports TV; open all day *(R T and
J C Moggridge, Pete Baker)*

STRATFORD-UPON-AVON [SP2054]

Dirty Duck CV37 6BA [Waterside]: Bustling
16th-c Greene King Wayside Inn nr Memorial
Theatre, their real ales, open fire, food all
day, lots of signed RSC photographs, modern
conservatory restaurant (best to book
wknds); children allowed in dining area,
attractive small terrace looking over riverside
public gardens which tend to act as
summer overflow, open all day *(Roger and
Anne Newbury, LYM, Mrs Hazel Rainer,*

Adrian Johnson, Roger Thornington, Martin Kane, Peter Dandy)

☆ **Garrick** CV37 6AU [High St]: Bustling ancient pub with heavy beams and timbers, odd-shaped rooms and simple furnishings on bare boards, good-natured efficient staff, Greene King ales, decent wines by the glass, food from sandwiches and light dishes up all day, small air-conditioned back restaurant; piped music, TV, games machine; children welcome, open all day (Peter Dandy, Val and Alan Green, LYM, Ted George, John Millwood, Roger Thornington, Giles Barr, Eleanor Dandy, Derek and Sylvia Stephenson)

Lamplighter CV37 6LP [Rother St, opp United Reform Church; handy for Friday Market]: Civilised proper local with several areas off central servery, bargain food, well kept Marstons-related ales, friendly staff, nice mix of wooden chairs and settles, alcoves, pillars, stripped brick and some flagstones (watch the steps), lots of show business pictures, guns on walls and beams; TV, games machines (Dave Braisted)

Pen & Parchment CV37 6YY [Bridgefoot, by canal basin]: Wayside Inn comfortably restored after 2007 floods, well divided, with bare boards, flagstones and carpet, big open fire in old fireplace, prompt helpful service, good wine choice, Greene King IPA and Abbot and Timothy Taylors Landlord, wide choice of good value usual food all day; children welcome, disabled facilities, good-sized terrace, good canal basin views (busy road), open all day (Mrs Hazel Rainer, Tim and Ann Newell, Adrian Johnson, Meg and Colin Hamilton)

Windmill CV37 6HB [Church St]: Ancient pub beyond the attractive Guild Chapel, with town's oldest licence, very low black beams and big log fire; typical old-fashioned town local, complete with piped music, sports TV, games machines, given visitor appeal by its friendly efficient staff, wide choice of attractively priced food (till 7 wkdys) from sandwiches to substantial Sun lunch and some unusual main dishes, Flowers Original, Greene King IPA; tables outside, open all day from noon (David Coleman, Roger Thornington, Ted George, Edward Mirzoeff)

STRETTON-ON-FOSSE [SP2238]

☆ **Plough** GL56 9QX [just off A429]: Unpretentious olde-worlde 17th-c village pub, enjoyable food from baguettes to spit roasts, inglenook log fire, happy local atmosphere, Hook Norton and interesting guest beers, small bar and larger lounge, stripped stone and some flagstones, jugs and mugs on oak beams, small attractive candlelit dining room on right, darts, dominoes and cribbage; dogs welcome, a few tables outside, has been cl Mon lunchtime (Keith and Sue Ward, BB)

SUTTON COLDFIELD [SP1195]

Duke B72 1RJ [Duke St]: Great atmosphere in smallish chatty local, friendly and comfortable, good choice of real ales, lunchtime rolls (Stephen Corfield)

Queslett B74 2EY [Queslett Rd E]: Ember Inn worth knowing for its wide range of well kept changing ales; their usual food (Stephen Corfield)

Station B73 6AT [Station St]: Enjoyable simple food, friendly staff, good range of real ales, model train circling overhead; unobtrusive piped music; large outdoor area (Stephen Corfield)

TANWORTH-IN-ARDEN [SP1170]

☆ **Bell** B94 5AL [The Green]: Smartly comfortable contemporary bar-style décor, enjoyable food from light lunchtime dishes to full meals, good choice of wines by the glass, well kept ales such as Black Sheep and Timothy Taylors Landlord, friendly staff; also houses deli and back post office; children in eating areas, outlook on pretty village's green and lovely 14th-c church, back terrace with alloy planters, stylish modern bedrooms – good base for walks (Rosanna Luke, Matt Curzon, LYM, Hansjoerg Landherr)

TEMPLE GRAFTON [SP1355]

☆ **Blue Boar** B49 6NR [a mile E, towards Binton; off A422 W of Stratford]: Refurbished stone-built dining pub with enjoyable food from imaginative sandwiches up, well kept Marstons ales and a guest such as local Shakespeares Taming of the Brew, good coffee and wine choice, friendly efficient young staff, beams, stripped stonework and log fires, dining room with attractive farmhouse-kitchen mural; big-screen TVs; children and dogs welcome, picnic-sets outside, pretty flower plantings, comfortable well equipped bedrooms, open all day summer wknds (Reg Fowle, Helen Rickwood, Mike and Mary Carter, LYM, Joan and Tony Walker)

TIPTON [SO9792]

Rising Sun DY4 7NH [Horseley Rd (B4517, off A461)]: Friendly Victorian pub with well kept Banks's, Oakham and six guests, farm ciders, back lounge with coal fires, alcoves and original bare boards and tiles, lunchtime food; tables outside, open all day wknds (the Didler)

UPPER BRAILES [SP3039]

Gate OX15 5AX: Attractively old-fashioned low-beamed village pub, welcoming landlord, wife cooks good generous well priced country food (not lunchtime Tues) inc good fresh fish Tues/Weds, well kept Hook Norton and guest beers, big log fire, sizeable part-panelled bar, smaller stripped stone lounge, alsatian called Shade; piped music in stripped stone restaurant; dogs and well behaved children welcome, tables in extensive back garden with wendy house, pretty hillside spot, lovely walks, cl Sun evening/Mon lunchtime (JHBS, Martin and Pauline Jennings)

UPPER GORNAL [SO9292]

☆ **Britannia** DY3 1UX [Kent St (A459)]: 19th-c chatty old-fashioned local with particularly well kept Bathams Best and Mild (bargain prices), tiled floors, coal fires in front bar and time-trapped back room down corridor; sports TV; nice flower-filled back yard, cl lunchtimes Mon-Thurs, open all day Fri/Sat *(the Didler)*

Jolly Crispin DY3 1UL [Clarence St (A459)]: Friendly well run 18th-c local with eight interesting quickly changing ales, two farm ciders or perry, compact front bar, wall seats and mixed tables and chairs on tiled floor, aircraft pictures in larger back room, beer festivals; open all day Fri-Sun, cl lunchtime Mon-Thurs *(the Didler)*

WALSALL [SP0198]

Arbor Lights WS1 1SY [Lichfield St]: Relaxed modern open-plan brasserie-style bar and restaurant, wide choice of wines, Fullers London Pride and Wadworths 6X, enjoyable fresh food all day from sandwiches and unusual starter/light dishes to good fish choice, smart friendly staff *(Tony and Wendy Hobden)*

Tap & Spile WS2 8AF [John St]: Victorian backstreet local (aka Pretty Bricks), friendly new management, good value bar lunches, three or four well kept ales, coal fire *(John Dwane)*

WARWICK [SP2766]

Cape of Good Hope CV34 5DP [Lower Cape]: Traditional unsmart two-room pub on Grand Union Canal by Warwick Top Lock, half a dozen changing real ales, darts, hatch service for waterside seats *(Pete Baker)*

☆ *Rose & Crown* CV34 4SH [Market Pl]: Up-to-date uncluttered refurbishment with big leather sofas and low tables by open fire in front, red-walled dining area behind on left with large modern photographs, interesting food all day at sensible prices from sandwiches and self-choice deli platters up, relaxed atmosphere, two well kept ales such as Wells & Youngs Bombardier and plenty of fancy keg dispensers, good wines by the glass, good strong coffee, friendly efficient service; tables out under parasols, comfortable good-sized bedrooms *(Martin and Karen Wake, LYM)*

☆ *Saxon Mill* CV34 5YN [Guy's Cliffe, A429 just N]: Well run M&B dining pub in charmingly set converted mill, mill race and turning wheel behind glass, smart contemporary chairs and tables on polished boards and flagstones below the beams, cosy corners with leather armchairs and big rugs, smiling service, enjoyable good value food in bar and (best to book) upstairs family restaurant, good choice of wines by the glass; shame about the piped music; teak tables out on terraces by broad willow-flanked river, bridge to more tables on far side, delightful views across to Grade I ruins of Guy's Cliffe House, open all day *(Terry Buckland, Paul Goldman, Stuart Doughty, Roy Bromell, Andy and Alice Jordan, LYM)*

☆ *Zetland Arms* CV34 4AB [Church St]: Cosy town pub with good sensibly priced traditional food (not wknd evenings) inc good sandwich choice, friendly quick

service even when busy, Marstons Pedigree and Tetleys, decent wines in generous glasses, neat but relaxing small panelled front bar with toby jug collection, comfortable larger L-shaped back eating area with small conservatory; sports TV; children welcome, interestingly planted sheltered back garden, bedrooms sharing bathroom *(Graham Findlay, LYM, Martin Kane)*

WELFORD-ON-AVON [SP1452]

Four Alls CV37 8PW [Binton Rd]: Reopened with new staff after restoration of 2008 flood damage, keen welcoming service, wide choice of good value food inc unusual dishes, real ales, good wines by the glass, attractive light modern décor and furnishings in large L-shaped dining area; pleasant terrace with heaters, fine spot by River Avon *(Martin and Pauline Jennings, Keith and Sue Ward, Chris Glasson)*

Shakespeare CV37 8PX [Chapel St]: Modernised and recently refurbished family-run 18th-c dining pub, freshly prepared food inc home-baked bread and lots of fish, bargain fixed-price lunches and Sun roasts, children's menu, well kept real ales, farm ciders, good choice of wines inc local; front and back gardens *(anon)*

WELLESBOURNE [SP2755]

Kings Head CV35 9LT: Recently refurbished Vintage Inn dining pub, wide choice of wines by the glass, well kept beers, pleasant staff, contemporary high-ceilinged lounge bar, log fire and smaller areas leading off; piped music, no dogs; good tables on small front terrace, more in prettily placed back garden facing church, Innkeepers Lodge bedrooms (handy for Stratford but cheaper), open all day *(Prof H G Allen, LYM, Tom and Jill Jones, Barry Rolfe)*

WHATCOTE [SP2944]

☆ *Royal Oak* CV36 5EF: Dating from 12th c, quaint and unpretentious low-beamed small room with Civil War connections and lots of knick-knacks and curios, good log fire in huge inglenook, cheery helpful landlord, well kept Hook Norton ales, reasonably priced food from baguettes up, decent wines, quiet dining room; children welcome, picnic-sets in informal garden *(LYM, Michael and Jenny Back, Prof H G Allen)*

WHICHFORD [SP3134]

Norman Knight CV36 5PE: Unpretentious two-room pub with good interesting changing beers, reasonably priced food from appealing sandwiches to good Sun roasts, decent wines, darts and dominoes, flagstones and stone walls; some live music; dogs welcome, tables out by attractive village green, aunt sally, small back campsite, cl Mon lunchtime *(David Campbell, Vicki McLean, JHBS, Guy Vowles, Helene Grygar, Pete Baker)*

WILLENHALL [SO9701]

Duke of Cambridge WV12 5QD [Coltham Rd]: Family-run pub in former farm cottages, two small front rooms with displays of model commercial vehicles, real ales such as Timothy Taylors Landlord and Wye Valley Butty Bach, big back games room with pool and table football; cl Mon/Tues lunchtime *(Tony and Wendy Hobden)*

Falcon WV13 2NR [Gomer St W]: Traditional two-bar 1930s backstreet local, up to nine real ales, basic lunchtime snacks, darts and dominoes; wheelchair access possible, open all day *(the Didler)*

WITHYBROOK [SP4384]

Pheasant CV7 9LT [B4112 NE of Coventry, not far from M6, junction 2]: Comfortable dining pub with very wide choice of usual food from sandwiches up, mainstream real ales, good coffee, big log fires, lots of dark tables with plush-cushioned chairs; piped music; children welcome, tables under lanterns on brookside terrace, open all day Sun *(Alan Johnson, LYM)*

WOLLASTON [SO8884]

Unicorn DY8 3NX [Bridgnorth Rd (A458)]: Friendly traditional local with well kept low-priced Bathams Bitter and Mild, unpretentious L-shaped bar and unspoilt back parlour, lots of brasses and knick-knacks, good lunchtime sandwiches; tables outside, open all day, Sun afternoon break *(the Didler)*

WOLVERHAMPTON [SO9298]

☆ *Great Western* WV10 0DG [Corn Hill/Sun St, behind BR station]: Cheerful and down to earth, hidden away by cobbled lane down from main line station to GWR low-level one, with friendly very prompt service, particularly well kept Bathams and several Holdens ales at bargain prices, guest beers too, winter mulled wine, cheap hearty home-made lunchtime food (not Sun) from good filled cobs up, interesting railway and motorcycle photographs, traditional front bar, other rooms inc neat dining conservatory; Sky TV; yard with good barbecues, open all day (Sun afternoon break) *(Pete Baker, Tony and Wendy Hobden, BB, the Didler, P Dawn, R T and J C Moggridge, Andrew Bosi, John Tav)*

WOOTTON WAWEN [SP1563]

☆ *Bulls Head* B95 6BD [Stratford Rd, just off A3400]: Good well priced food in attractive black and white dining pub, quick friendly service, well kept Marstons-related ales, log fire, low Elizabethan beams and timbers, leather sofas and armchairs, comfortable low-beamed dining room with rich colours, brocaded seats and tapestries; children welcome, garden tables, handy for one of England's finest churches and Stratford Canal walks *(Carol and Colin Broadbent, LYM, Mr and Mrs F E Boxell, Mark Sykes, Len Clark)*

'Children welcome' means the pub says it lets children inside without any special restriction. If it allows them in, but to restricted areas such as an eating area or family room, we specify this. Places with separate restaurants often let children use them, hotels usually let them into public areas such as lounges. Some pubs impose an evening time limit – let us know if you find one earlier than 9pm.

Wiltshire

Although this county has some exceptional dining pubs, it's nice to find quite a few properly pubby places, too, with plenty of unpretentious character and a genuinely warm welcome from the licensees. Those doing well here this year include the Two Pigs in Corsham (Monday nights especially popular for their live music), the Horseshoe at Ebbesbourne Wake (five real ales and a kindly landlord in this classic country pub), the Neeld Arms at Grittleton (chatty cheery locals and staff, and a happy atmosphere), the Red Lion at Kilmington (an exemplary host in this no-nonsense pub), the Hatchet at Lower Chute (off the beaten track and all very traditional), the Silver Plough at Pitton (relaxing and with lots to look at), and the Cross Keys at Upper Chute (unstuffy and warm-hearted, with good honest food). If it's a special meal in civilised surroundings that you want, then you could head for the Three Crowns in Brinkworth (elaborate cooking but with five real ales as well), the Compasses at Chicksgrove (enjoyable food, local ales and a nice play to stay, too), the Forester at Donhead St Andrew (a new Food Award this year, and plenty of fresh fish from Cornwall and Devon), the Linnet at Great Hinton (elaborate meals including a two- or three-course set lunch), the Malet Arms at Newton Tony (bustling and cheerful, with nice food and well chosen beers), the Vine Tree at Norton (civilised and busy, with super food and wines), the Wheatsheaf at Oaksey (stylish contemporary furnishings and uncomplicated but much liked food), the George & Dragon at Rowde (very much a dining pub, yet with genuine character), the Lamb at Semington (proper pubby meals of real quality), and the Bridge at West Lavington (the French chef uses organic free-range produce wherever possible). With its classy cooking, great wines and charming environment, it's the Vine Tree at Norton which takes the title of Wiltshire Dining Pub of the Year. After quite a crop of newcomers in recent years, we have no new main entries here this year, but have our eye on several bright prospects in the Lucky Dip section at the end of the chapter: the Boot at Berwick St James (promising new tenants, just too recently arrived for us to check them out for this edition), Fox at Broughton Giffard, Horse & Groom at Charlton, Lamb at Edington, Hit or Miss at Kington Langley, Wheatsheaf at Lower Woodford, Rattlebone at Sherston and Royal Oak at Swallowcliffe. If you try any of these, do let us know what you think. The county has a dozen or so thriving independent brewers. By far the most popular is Wadworths (they supply good wines, too). Others we have found quite widely available this year are Hop Back, Arkells, Hidden, Keystone, Moles, Archers, Ramsbury, Wessex and Stonehenge, with Box Steam and Three Castles cropping up more rarely.

ALDBOURNE

SU2675   MAP 2

Blue Boar

The Green (off B4192 in centre); SN8 2EN

Bags of character in low-beamed traditional pub

Cheerful serving staff and plenty of locals create a relaxed, chatty atmosphere here. The left-hand bar is homely, with partly bare boards, partly faded carpet, pubby seats around heavily rustic tables, lots of low black beams in the ochre ceiling, a boar's head above the bigger of the two fireplaces, a stuffed pine marten over one table, darts, and a corner cupboard of village trophies. Lots of unusual bottled beers line the rail above the dark pine dado. Wadworths IPA and 6X and a guest from Jennings on handpump and beer festivals twice a year during April and October. A separate bare-boards dining bar on the right, stretching back further, has more table space, and is rather more modern in style, with its country pictures on cream or dark pink walls, but has a similar nicely pubby atmosphere. Picnic-sets and a couple of tall hogshead tables under big green canvas parasols out in front face the village green (and its parked cars).

▥ **Very generous helpings of food from a shortish menu include well filled baguettes, and things like minted shoulder of lamb, wild boar with apple cream and horseradish, popular steak and kidney pie, venison cooked with blackberries, and puddings like apple pie.** *Starters/Snacks: £4.00 to £7.00. Main Courses: £8.25 to £16.00. Puddings: £3.75*

Wadworths ~ Tenants Jez and Mandy Hill ~ Real ale ~ Bar food ~ Restaurant ~ (01672) 540237 ~ Children welcome ~ Dogs welcome ~ Open 11.30-3, 5.30-11; 11.30-11.30 Sat; 12-11 Sun

Recommended by Mary Rayner, Dr and Mrs Ellison, Sheila and Robert Robinson, Guy Vowles, Paul A Moore

AXFORD

SU2470   MAP 2

Red Lion ♀

Off A4 E of Marlborough; on back road Mildenhall—Ramsbury; SN8 2HA

Pretty pub with careful service from friendly staff, locally brewed beers and wide choice of food

Most customers are here to enjoy the popular food in this flint-and-brick pub, though they do keep Cottage Durassic Bark, Ramsbury Axford Ale from the little brewery on the edge of the village, and West Berkshire Good Old Boy on handpump, 15 wines by the glass and 20 malt whiskies. The beamed and pine-panelled bar has a big inglenook fireplace, and a pleasant mix of comfortable sofas, cask seats and other solid chairs on the parquet floor; the pictures by local artists are for sale. There are lovely views over a valley from good hardwood tables and chairs on the terrace outside the restaurant, and you get the same views from picture windows in the restaurant and lounge. The sheltered garden has picnic-sets under parasols overlooking the river.

▥ **As well as lunchtime filled rolls (not Sunday), the well liked bar food includes home-baked ham and eggs, sausages with onion gravy, spinach and ricotta crêpe, crab, prawn and dill fishcakes, and steak and kidney and chicken and mushroom pies; there's a more elaborate menu, too, with quite an emphasis on (more pricy) fish dishes such as grilled fillet of halibut with green pesto broth and whole bass baked with fennel and orange.** *Starters/Snacks: £5.25 to £7.25. Main Courses: £9.00 to £16.95. Puddings: £3.75 to £5.00*

Free house ~ Licensee Seamus Lecky ~ Real ale ~ Bar food (not Sun evening or 25 Dec) ~ Restaurant ~ (01672) 520271 ~ Children welcome ~ Dogs allowed in bar ~ Open 12-2.30, 6.30-11; 12-2.30 Sun; closed Sun evening and 25 Dec

Recommended by Graham Cooper, Robert Watt, Mr and Mrs A Curry, Mike Vincent, Guy Vowles, I A Herdman, Alvin and Yvonne Andrews, Mr and Mrs Mike Pearson, Mrs Jill Wyatt, Bernard Stradling, Mrs L M Beard, Mary Rayner, Mr and Mrs P D Titcomb

BADBURY   SU1980   MAP 2

Bakers Arms

A mile from M4 junction 15; first left off A346 S, then bear left; SN4 0EU

Comfortably old-fashioned atmosphere in true village pub, a nice motorway escape

Very handy for the M4, this is a traditional village pub with proper old-fashioned values.
There are three smallish red-carpeted areas – house plants and red velvet curtains in the
bow window, scatter cushions on grey leatherette seating, old clippings and photographs
of the pub on cream-painted plank panelling, and a hot coal or log fire; a proper pool
and darts area, TV, a silenced games machine, friendly licensees, and perhaps even piped
Frank Sinatra. Arkells 2B and 3B on handpump, and picnic-sets in a prettily tended
garden (with a heated area for smokers).

🍴 **Good value food runs from speciality sandwiches through a fair choice of pubby
favourites like ploughman's, vegetable lasagne, steak and kidney pie and fish and chips,
to specials such as lamb shank and liver, bacon and onions.** *Starters/Snacks: £4.00 to £9.00.
Main Courses: £7.00 to £9.00. Puddings: £4.50 to £6.00*

Arkells ~ Tenants Dennis and Sandra Fairall ~ Real ale ~ Bar food (12.30-2.30,
6.30-9 Mon-Thurs, 7-9.30 Fri/Sat; no food Sun evening) ~ Restaurant ~ (01793) 740313 ~
Children over 10 only ~ Open 12-3, 5.30-11; 12-4, 7-midnight Sat; 12-4, 7-11 Sun

Recommended by JJW, CMW, Dr and Mrs A K Clarke, Bill and Sally Leckey, Paul Humphreys

BERWICK ST JOHN   ST9422   MAP 2

Talbot

Village signposted from A30 E of Shaftesbury; SP7 0HA

**Unspoilt and friendly pub in attractive village, with simple furnishings and tasty,
reasonably priced food**

In a pretty village full of thatched old houses, this is an enjoyable pub with friendly
locals. The heavily beamed bar has plenty of character and is simply furnished with
cushioned solid wall and window seats, spindleback chairs, a high-backed built-in settle
at one end, and a huge inglenook fireplace with a good iron fireback and bread ovens.
Bass, Ringwood Best, Wadworths 6X and a guest such as Ringwood Fortyniner on
handpump; darts and cribbage. There are seats outside.

🍴 **Good, reasonably priced bar food at lunchtime includes sandwiches, filled baguettes,
ploughman's, garlic mushrooms, tasty ham and egg, sausage and mash with onion gravy,
cheese and mushroom omelette and battered fish with chips, with evening choices such
as pasta vegetable stir fry, cajun-style chicken and mixed grill, and daily specials like cod
loin wrapped in parma ham with a saffron sauce, braised lamb shank, and venison steak
with juniper berry marinade; Sunday roasts.** *Starters/Snacks: £4.00 to £8.00. Main Courses:
£7.50 to £15.50. Puddings: £3.50 to £5.50*

Free house ~ Licensees Pete and Marilyn Hawkins ~ Real ale ~ Bar food (not Sun evening) ~
Restaurant ~ (01747) 828222 ~ Children welcome ~ Dogs welcome ~ Open 12-2.30, 6.30-11;
12-4 Sun; closed Sun evening, all day Mon

Recommended by D and J Ashdown, Colin and Janet Roe, Mr and Mrs P D Titcomb

---

Please keep sending us reports. We rely on readers for news of new discoveries, and
particularly for news of changes – however slight – at the fully described pubs:
feedback@thegoodpubguide.co.uk or (no stamp needed) The Good Pub Guide,
FREEPOST TN1569, Wadhurst, E Sussex TN5 7BR.

BOX

ST8369 MAP 2

Quarrymans Arms

Box Hill; coming from Bath on A4 turn right into Bargates 50 yards before railway bridge, then at T junction turn left up Quarry Hill, turning left again near the top at grassy triangle; from Corsham, turn left after Rudloe Park Hotel into Beech Road, then third left on to Barnetts Hill, and finally right at the top of the hill; OS Sheet 173 map reference 834694; SN13 8HN

Cheerful and unpretentious, with great views, real ales and good value food

There's plenty of mining-related photographs and memorabilia dotted around the interior of this easy-going and friendly place – it was once the local of the Bath stone miners and the welcoming licensees run interesting guided trips down the mine itself. It's atmospheric and comfortable rather than overly smart (some parts have an air of mild untidiness) and one modernised room with an open fire is entirely set aside for drinking, with Butcombe Best, Moles Best, Wadworths 6X and a couple of changing guests on handpump, as well as Black Rat cider and up to 60 malt whiskies. There are lovely sweeping views from the big windows of the dining room; games machine and board game. An attractive outside terrace has picnic-sets; boules. The pub is ideally placed for cavers, potholers and walkers.

🍴 **Good value traditional bar food includes sandwiches, soup, macaroni cheese, ham, egg and chips, spaghetti carbonara, steak in ale pie, daily specials such as liver and bacon, and a pudding such as bread and butter pudding.** *Starters/Snacks: £2.50 to £8.00. Main Courses: £6.50 to £16.00. Puddings: £2.50 to £5.00*

Free house ~ Licensees John and Ginny Arundel ~ Real ale ~ Bar food (11-3, 6-9) ~ Restaurant ~ (01225) 743569 ~ Children welcome ~ Dogs allowed in bar ~ Open 11-3, 6-midnight Mon-Thurs; 11am-midnight Fri, Sat and Sun ~ Bedrooms: £35B/£65B

Recommended by Guy Vowles, Jeff Davies, Dr and Mrs A K Clarke, Colin and Peggy Wilshire, Gene and Kitty Rankin, Richard and Judy Winn, Mr Reader

BREMHILL

ST9772 MAP 2

Dumb Post

Off A4/A3102 just NW of Calne; Hazeland, just SW of village itself, OS Sheet 173 map reference 976727; SN11 9LJ

Quirky and unspoilt; a proper country local with no frills, but some real character

Not huge, this pub has something of the air of a once-grand but now rather faded hunting lodge. It isn't for those with fussier tastes, but is run by and for people who like their pubs unpretentious and with some genuine character. The main lounge is a glorious mix of mismatched, faded furnishings, vivid patterned wallpaper, and stuffed animal heads, its two big windows boasting an unexpectedly fine view down over the surrounding countryside. There are half a dozen or so tables, a big woodburner in a brick fireplace (not always lit), a log fire on the opposite side of the room, comfortably-worn armchairs and plush banquettes, a standard lamp, mugs, bread and a sombrero hanging from the beams, and a scaled-down model house between the windows; in a cage is an occasionally vocal parrot, Oscar. The narrow bar leading to the lounge is more dimly lit, but has a few more tables, exposed stonework, and quite a collection of toby jugs around the counter; there's a plainer third room with pool, darts, and piped music. Archers Best and Wadworths 6X on handpump; an amiable landlord. There are a couple of picnic-sets outside, and some wooden play equipment. Note the limited lunchtime opening times.

🍴 **Bar food (served lunchtimes only) is simple, hearty and well liked by locals: toasted sandwiches, ploughman's, sausage, egg and chips, steak and kidney pudding, and fish and chips; Sunday roasts.** *Starters/Snacks: £2.00 to £2.90. Main Courses: £5.25 to £6.50*

Free house ~ Licensee Mr Pitt ~ Real ale ~ Bar food (lunchtimes only Fri-Sun) ~ No credit cards ~ (01249) 813192 ~ Children in eating area of bar ~ Dogs allowed in bar ~ Open 12-2.30, 7-11(midnight Sat); closed Mon-Thurs lunchtimes

Recommended by Phil and Sally Gorton, Guy Vowles, JJW, CMW

BRINKWORTH   SU0184   MAP 2

Three Crowns ⑪ ⚲
The Street; B4042 Wootton Bassett—Malmesbury; SN15 5AF

Excellent food deservedly takes centre stage here, but this is still a pub, with five good beers and a carefully chosen wine list

They do keep five real ales on handpump in this bustling place, so although many customers are here to enjoy the impressive food (particularly in the evenings), you'll still be made welcome if all you want is a drink: Abbey Ales Bellringer, Bath Ales Gem, Greene King IPA, Marstons Pedigree, and Wadworths 6X, a carefully chosen, extensive wine list with 25 by the glass, and around 20 malt whiskies. The bar part of the building is the most traditional, with big landscape prints and other pictures, some horsebrasses on dark beams, a log fire, a dresser with a collection of old bottles, big tapestry-upholstered pews, a stripped deal table, and a couple more made from gigantic forge bellows. Sensibly placed darts, shove-ha'penny, dominoes, cribbage, board games, games machine, and piped music. Most people choose to eat in the conservatory or the light and airy garden room. There's a terrace with outdoor heating to the side of the conservatory. The garden stretches around the side and back, with well spaced tables and a climbing frame, and looks over a side lane to the church, and out over rolling prosperous farmland. They do have a smoking shelter.

⑪ Changing every day, the extensive menu covers an entire wall; at lunchtimes, as well as filled double decker rolls, baked potatoes and ploughman's, they might have chicken curry, home-made crab cakes with home-made mayonnaise and sweet chilli sauce, liver and bacon with tomato mash and onion gravy, and crispy belly pork with fresh sage mash and onion gravy. From a more elaborate (and more expensive) menu, there might also be half a smoked chicken with a sherry, dijon mustard and cream sauce, steak and kidney or seafood pies, fresh tuna in puff pastry with french brie and prawns in a madeira and cream sauce, slices of kangaroo, venison and ostrich marinated in a secret recipe and cooked with sun-dried tomatoes, wild mushrooms and button onions flamed with brandy and finished with cream, half a crispy duck with cherry wine, redcurrant jelly and cream sauce, and puddings such as popular banoffi pie and swiss chocolate fondue with dipping fruit and biscuits. *Starters/Snacks: £8.00 to £13.00. Main Courses: £10.00 to £18.00. Puddings: £5.25 to £6.25*

Enterprise ~ Lease Anthony Windle ~ Real ale ~ Bar food (12-2(3 Sun), 6-9.30 (9 Sun)) ~ Restaurant ~ (01666) 510366 ~ Well-behaved children allowed until 7.30pm ~ Dogs allowed in bar ~ Open 10-3, 6-11.30; 11-4, 6-midnight Sat; 12-5, 6-11 Sun; closed 25 and 26 Dec
Recommended by Andrew Shore, Maria Williams, Nigel and Sue Foster, Tom and Ruth Rees, Robyn Selley

CASTLE COMBE   ST8477   MAP 2

Castle Inn ⚲ 🛏
Off A420; SN14 7HN

Some sort of food all day in friendly pubby bar of well run small hotel, in perhaps the most lovely English village

Although this is a stylish little hotel, the beamed bar is bustling and friendly and quite happy to accommodate all the different hordes who descend on this timless village. There's some stripped stone, a big inglenook log fire, comfortably padded bar stools as well as a handsome old oak settle and other good seats around the sturdy tables, and hunting and vintage motor racing pictures on the walls. Butcombe Bitter and Shepherd Neame Spitfire on handpump, good wines by the glass, a fine choice of spirits, and well liked morning coffee and afternoon cream teas; efficient, obliging service. On either side of the bar are two snug old-world sitting rooms with comfortable settees and easy chairs, and besides the smart and attractive high-ceilinged formal dining room there is a big light-hearted upstairs eating room with a very effective sunblind system for its conservatory-style roof. This opens on to a charming small roof terrace with good cast-iron furniture, and there are more tables out in front, looking down this idyllic village street. The medieval church clock is fascinating. Very limited parking (if you're staying and have mobility problems they do try to help).

🍴 Enjoyable bar food includes filled baguettes, ploughman's, soup, smoked haddock fishcake on baby spinach with a herb and cream sauce, interesting summer salads like thai noodles with cashew nuts and prawns or toulouse sausage, new potatoes, wild garlic leaf and baby sweetcorn, a pie of the day, tagliatelle with roast vegetables and feta cheese, chicken curry, fillet of salmon with stir-fried vegetables and coriander pesto, and puddings such as strawberry and Grand Marnier crème brûlée and treacle tart with clotted cream; there's also a more elaborate menu as well. *Starters/Snacks: £4.50 to £7.50. Main Courses: £8.00 to £17.50. Puddings: £5.25*

Free house ~ Licensees Ann and Bill Cross ~ Real ale ~ Bar food (12-3, 6-9) ~ Restaurant ~ (01249) 783030 ~ Children welcome ~ Dogs allowed in bar ~ Open 9.30am-11pm; closed 25 Dec ~ Bedrooms: £69S(£85B)/£110B

Recommended by Guy Vowles, Peter and Audrey Dowsett, Ian Phillips

CHICKSGROVE   ST9729   MAP 2

Compasses ★ 🍴 ⌷ 🛏

From A30 5.5 miles W of B3089 junction, take lane on N side signposted Sutton Mandeville, Sutton Row, then first left fork (small signs point the way to the pub, in Lower Chicksgrove; look out for the car park); SP3 6NB

Ancient thatched house with enjoyable food, a genuine welcome, and splendid bedrooms – an excellent all-rounder

You can be sure of a warm welcome from the friendly landlord and his family in this reassuringly unchanging old place – and the food is particularly good, too. The bar has old bottles and jugs hanging from beams above the roughly timbered counter, farm tools and traps on the partly stripped stone walls, and high-backed wooden settles forming snug booths around tables on the mainly flagstoned floor. Bass, Keytone Bed Rock and Large One and a guest such as Hidden Quest on handpump, 20 wines by the glass and several malt whiskies. The quiet garden, terraces and flagstoned farm courtyard are very pleasant places to sit, and this really is a smashing place to stay, with lovely surrounding walks and plenty to do in the area.

🍴 Carefully sourced food includes lunchtime filled loaves and ploughman's plus toulouse sausages with mustard mash, smoked salmon and scrambled eggs, steak and kidney pie and ham and eggs, as well as duck liver and Grand Marnier parfait with spiced compote, mussels in a bacon, white wine and onion cream sauce, roasted vegetable cassoulet, chicken breast filled with goats cheese, wrapped in bacon with a red onion confit, rump of lamb with shitake mushrooms and caramelised onion jus, bass and monkfish risotto flavoured with lemons and fresh herbs, buttered asparagus and parmesan, and puddings such as bitter chocolate torte with lemon sorbet and brioche and butter pudding with rum-soaked banana and sultanas. *Starters/Snacks: £5.00 to £9.00. Main Courses: £9.00 to £20.00. Puddings: £5.00*

Free house ~ Licensee Alan Stoneham ~ Real ale ~ Bar food ~ (01722) 714318 ~ Children welcome ~ Dogs welcome ~ Open 12-3, 6-11; 12-3, 7-10.30 Sun; closed 25 and 26 Dec ~ Bedrooms: £65B/£85S(£90B)

Recommended by Edward Mirzoeff, Andrew Hollingshead, Colin and Janet Roe, Mrs J H S Lang, Helen and Brian Edgeley, Mr and Mrs Draper, Nick Lawless, Dr and Mrs Michael Smith, Mr and Mrs A J Hudson, Mark Coppin, John and Jane Hayter, Andy and Claire Barker, Mike and Linda Hudson

CORSHAM   ST8770   MAP 2

Flemish Weaver

High Street; SN13 0EZ

Smart town centre pub with a relaxed atmosphere and well liked bar food

In the heart of town, this is a civilised and attractive mellow-stone building which was built in the early 17th c to house drovers in the wool trade. It's been sensitively modernised, but the three main areas – mostly set for eating – still have many original features, as well as patterned blue banquettes and matching chairs on slate floors, flowers on the tables, and tealights in the fireplaces; old black and white photographs on the walls. Bath Ales Gem, Hook Norton Hooky Bitter, and Sharps Doom Bar on handpump and several wines by the glass; friendly staff, even when busy. Piped classical music or jazz, board games and table skittles. There are tables in the back courtyard and the pub is opposite Corsham Court.

🍴 **Under the new licensees, bar food now includes lunchtime sandwiches, filled baguettes, filled baked potatoes, sausage and mash, cottage pie, and fish and chips, with evening choices such as mediterranean vegetable pasta with a tomato sauce, monkfish wrapped in bacon with a roasted pepper sauce, and guinea fowl breast in an apple, cider and mushroom sauce, daily specials like fish pie and pork tenderloin with a vegetable stir fry and puddings such as fruit crumble and chocolate fudge cake with clotted cream.** *Starters/Snacks: £3.95 to £6.50. Main Courses: £8.25 to £15.50. Puddings: £3.95*

Enterprise ~ Lease Adam and David Klewin ~ Real ale ~ Bar food (not Sun evening) ~ Restaurant ~ (01249) 701929 ~ Children welcome away from bar ~ Dogs allowed in bar ~ Open 11-2.30, 5.30-11; 12-3 Sun; closed Sun evening
Recommended by Jean and Douglas Troup, Dr and Mrs A K Clarke, Michael Doswell, John Robertson, Paul A Moore

Two Pigs 🍺
A4, Pickwick; SN13 0HY

Wonderfully eccentric pub for fans of beer and music, open evenings only (except Sun), and at its best on Monday nights

Monday evening in this delightfully unusual place is great fun and lively and the most popular night of the week – there's always a big crowd enjoying the live music with a handpumped pint of Butcombe Bitter, Goffs Jouster, or Hop Back Summer Lightning. The cheerfully eccentric feel owes much to the individualistic landlord, and there's a zany collection of bric-a-brac in the narrow and dimly lit flagstoned bar including enamel advertising signs on the wood-clad walls, pig-theme ornaments, and old radios. There's usually a good mix of customers around the long dark wood tables and benches, and friendly staff; piped blues. A covered yard outside is called the Sty. Do note their opening times – the pub is closed every lunchtime, except on Sunday. No under 21s.

🍴 **No food at all.**

Free house ~ Licensees Dickie and Ann Doyle ~ Real ale ~ No credit cards ~ (01249) 712515 ~ Live blues/rock Mon evening ~ Open 7-11; 12-2.30, 7-10.30 Sun
Recommended by Catherine Pitt, Dr and Mrs A K Clarke

CROCKERTON   ST8642   MAP 2

Bath Arms
Just off A350 Warminster—Blandford; BA12 8AJ

Excellent food cooked by chef/landlord at attractively modernised dining pub, with pretty gardens, relaxed atmosphere, and two very stylish bedrooms

The imaginative food remains quite a draw to this attractive old dining pub and even on a Monday, there are lots of customers. The building is very appealing from outside with plenty of picnic-sets in various garden areas. Inside, it's warmly welcoming with a thriving informal atmosphere, lots of well spaced tables on the parquet floor in the long, stylishly modernised two-roomed bar, beams in the whitewashed ceiling, and brasses. There's a restaurant at one end and a log fire in a stone fireplace at the other. Courage Best and Wessex Crockerton Classic and Naughty Ferrets on handpump and quite a few wines by the glass; piped music. We've yet to hear from readers who've stayed in the two splendidly stylish bedrooms, but imagine they would merit one of our stay awards – they're what you might expect to find in a chic boutique hotel rather than a country pub. Longleat is very close by.

🍴 Cooked by the landlord using local produce, the good, attractively presented food might include filled baguettes, nice soups, pressed tomato terrine with cornish crab mayonnaise, smoked duck breast and lambs sweetbreads with apple and watercress, sausages and champ, roast fennel with artichokes and parmesan, belly of pork with spiced aubergine and merguez sausage, sticky beef with braised cabbage, poached duck in a scallop and vegetable broth and puddings such as rhubarb trifle with vanilla cream and hot chocolate fondant with caramel ice-cream. *Starters/Snacks: £4.50 to £5.50. Main Courses: £9.95 to £14.00. Puddings: £4.75*

Wellington ~ Lease Dean Carr ~ Real ale ~ Bar food ~ Restaurant ~ (01985) 212262 ~ Children welcome ~ Dogs allowed in bar ~ Open 11-3, 6-11(10.30 Sun); closed evenings 25 and 26 Dec ~ Bedrooms: /£75S

Recommended by J Stickland, Colin and Janet Roe, Edward Mirzoeff, Dr and Mrs J Temporal, R J Herd, Ian Phillips, Richard Fendick, I H Curtis, Mr and Mrs P R Thomas, Jill Bickerton

DEVIZES
SU0061   MAP 2

Bear ♀ 🍺
Market Place; SN10 1HS

Comfortable coaching inn with plenty of history, beers fresh from the local brewery, pleasant terrace, and unpretentious food

This individual and pleasant old coaching inn has a great deal of character and although it has been carefully upgraded over the years, it dates from 1559 so there are plenty of reminders of the past. The big main carpeted bar has log fires, black winged wall settles and muted cloth-upholstered bucket armchairs around oak tripod tables; the classic bar counter has shiny black woodwork and small panes of glass. Separated from here by some steps, a room named after the portrait painter Thomas Lawrence (his father ran the establishment in the 1770s) has dark oak-panelled walls, a parquet floor, a big open fireplace, shining copper pans, and plates around the walls. Wadworths IPA, 6X and a seasonal guest on handpump, a good choice of wines (including 16 by the glass), and quite a few malt whiskies. A mediterranean-style courtyard with olive trees, hibiscus and bougainvillea has some outside tables. The brewery is just 150 yards away – you can buy beer in splendid old-fashioned half-gallon earthenware jars. They will keep your credit card behind the bar if you wish to run a food tab.

🍴 Served by friendly staff, the well liked bar food at lunchtime includes a sizeable choice of sandwiches and filled ciabattas and baguettes, filled baked potatoes, ploughman's, omelettes, all-day breakfast, gammon and egg, chicken breast with mexican salad and beer-battered fish, with evening dishes such as sautéed chicken livers, fettucine with mushroom cream sauce, grilled lamb loin chop, and puddings. *Starters/Snacks: £3.50 to £6.25. Main Courses: £5.15 to £7.50. Puddings: £2.95 to £3.50*

Wadworths ~ Tenants Andrew and Angela Maclachlan ~ Real ale ~ Bar food (11.30-2.30, 7.30-9.45 Mon-Sat; 11.30-2, 7-8.45 Sun) ~ Restaurant ~ (01380) 722444 ~ Children welcome ~ Dogs allowed in bar ~ Live jazz Sat evening in cellar bar ~ Open 9.30am-11pm(10pm Sun) ~ Bedrooms: £80S/£105B

Recommended by Dr and Mrs A K Clarke, Steven and Victoria James, Mary Rayner, the Didler, Mr and Mrs P D Titcomb, Ann and Colin Hunt

DONHEAD ST ANDREW
ST9124   MAP 2

Forester 🍴 ♀
Village signposted off A30 E of Shaftesbury, just E of Ludwell; Lower Street; SP7 9EE

Attractive old thatched pub in charming village, good food – especially fish – and fine views from very pleasant big terrace

'Everything is just right here' is how one of our readers describes this 14th-c thatched pub – and others agree with him. The appealing bar has a welcoming atmosphere, stripped tables on wooden floors, a log fire in its big inglenook fireplace, and usually a few locals chatting around the servery: Butcombe Bitter, Butts Traditional and Ringwood

Best on handpump, and 12 wines (including champagne) by the glass. Off here is an alcove with a sofa and table and magazines to read. The comfortable main dining room has country-kitchen tables in varying sizes and there's also a second smaller and cosier dining room. Outside, seats on a good-sized terrace have fine country views. Good walks nearby, for example to the old and 'new' Wardour castles. The neighbouring cottage used to be the pub's coach house.

🍴 As well as lunchtime sandwiches, the interesting food includes good soups, a charcuterie plate, tiger prawn and sorrel ravioli with garlic wilted spinach and bouillabaisse sauce, their own cured gravadlax of scottish smoked salmon, seared calves liver with leek and sage mash, crisp bacon and sauce diable, local lamb chops with green olive and herb crust, garlic potato purée and thyme jus, and roast breast of gressingham duck with bubble and squeak. Fresh fish from cornwall and devon also features strongly and can be had as two- and three-course menu option: moules marinières, fish soup with rouille and pecorino, mackerel with horseradish mash, crisp pancetta and beetroot and whole plaice with fresh herb butter. Puddings such as dark chocolate risotto with caramelised pear and pistachios and elderberry and basil jelly with almond beignet and raspberry sorbet and a good cheeseboard. *Starters/Snacks: £4.50 to £8.95. Main Courses: £8.95 to £18.50. Puddings: £4.95 to £6.95*

Free house ~ Licensee Chris Matthew ~ Real ale ~ Bar food ~ Restaurant ~ (01747) 828038 ~ Children welcome ~ Dogs allowed in bar ~ Open 12-3, 6.30-11; closed winter Sun evenings

Recommended by Keith and Jean Symons, Mrs J H S Lang, Mr and Mrs W W Burke, Robert Watt, John Robertson, Paul Goldman, Michael Doswell, Colin and Janet Roe

EAST KNOYLE
ST8731 MAP 2

Fox & Hounds ♀

Village signposted off A350 S of A303; The Green (named on some road atlases), a mile NW at OS Sheet 183 map reference 872313; or follow signpost off B3089, about 0.5 mile E of A303 junction near Little Chef; SP3 6BN

Beautiful thatched village pub with splendid views, welcoming service, good beers, and popular food

It's well worth the effort negotiating the little lanes to reach this ancient pretty pub, especially on a clear day when you can enjoy the remarkable views right over into Somerset and Dorset from picnic-sets facing the green. Inside, there's the warmly welcoming feel of a proper long-established pub (rather than a more formal pub/restaurant), and service is prompt and cheerful. Around the central horseshoe-shaped servery are three linked areas on different levels, with big log fires, plentiful oak woodwork and flagstones, comfortably padded dining chairs around big scrubbed tables with vases of flowers, and a couple of leather settees; the furnishings are all very individual and uncluttered. There's a small light-painted conservatory restaurant. Butcombe Bitter, Hidden Potential, Keystone Large One, Palmers 200, and Youngs Bitter on handpump, 15 wines by the glass and Thatcher's Cheddar Valley cider. Piped music and skittle alley. The nearby woods are good for a stroll.

🍴 At lunchtime, the well liked food includes ploughman's, stone baked pizzas, crab pâté, lasagne, aubergine stuffed with pine nuts, spinach and pecorino cheese and beef, mushroom and shallot casserole; evening extras such as bacon wrapped chicken breast with a wild mushroom sauce, pork tenderloin with a calvados and prune sauce and venison haunch steak with a port and cranberry sauce and puddings like blackberry and apple crumble and sticky toffee pudding. *Starters/Snacks: £4.00 to £8.50. Main Courses: £8.75 to £16.00. Puddings: £4.50 to £4.75*

Free house ~ Licensee Murray Seator ~ Real ale ~ Bar food (12-2.30, 6-9) ~ (01747) 830573 ~ Well-behaved children welcome ~ Dogs welcome ~ Open 11.30-3, 5.30-11(10.30 Sun); closed 25 Dec

Recommended by Hugh Stafford, Paul Goldman, Mr and Mrs W W Burke, Dr and Mrs J Temporal, Chris and Meredith Owen, Roy Hoing, Edward Mirzoeff

You can send reports to us at feedback@thegoodpubguide.co.uk.

Seymour Arms

The Street; just off A350 S of Warminster; SP3 6AJ

Neatly kept and friendly, quite handy for A303, with decent food, rambling seating areas, real ales, and garden; bedrooms

Even when really pushed, the hard-working staff in this creeper-covered stone-built pub remain efficient and friendly. The rambling L-shaped bar is attractively divided into separate snug seating areas though perhaps the cosiest beamed part is where there's a high-backed settle by the log fire, and a built-in window settle and farmhouse chairs by a nice little table; some brass bits and bobs dotted about, Wadworths IPA and 6X and a guest beer on handpump, and several wines by the glass. There are tables in the garden. Sir Christopher Wren was born in the village in 1632 – his father was rector of the church.

🍽 **Reasonably priced, well cooked bar food includes lunchtime sandwiches, soup, garlic mushrooms in a puff pastry case, ham and eggs, vegetable bake, cumberland sausage with onion gravy, beer-battered cod and steak and mushroom pie, plus daily specials, more elaborate evening meals, and puddings.** *Starters/Snacks: £3.50 to £5.50. Main Courses: £7.50 to £14.95. Puddings: £3.95 to £4.20*

Wadworths ~ Tenants Bruno and Terena Burgess ~ Real ale ~ Bar food (not Mon) ~ (01747) 830374 ~ Children welcome ~ Dogs allowed in bar ~ Open 12-3, 7-11; closed Mon except bank hols ~ Bedrooms: £30S/£50S

Recommended by Roger and Pauline Pearce, Colin and Janet Roe, Chris and Ann Coy, David Sizer, B and E Palmer

EBBESBOURNE WAKE   ST9924 MAP 2

Horseshoe ★ 🍺 🛏

On A354 S of Salisbury, right at signpost at Coombe Bissett; village is around 8 miles further on; SP5 5JF

Restful, unspoilt country pub with a good welcome, beers tapped from the cask, and views from pretty garden

There's always a kind welcome from the attentive landlord in this charmingly unspoilt old country pub. The neatly kept, comfortably furnished bar has fresh home-grown flowers on the tables, lanterns, a large collection of farm tools and other bric-a-brac crowded along its beams, and an open fire; a conservatory extension seats ten people. Bowmans Swift One, Otter Best, Ramsbury Bitter, and Ringwood Best and Old Thumper tapped from the cask, farm cider, and several malt whiskies. Booking is advisable for the small restaurant, especially at weekends when it can fill quite quickly. There are pleasant views over the steep sleepy valley of the River Ebble from seats in the pretty little garden, a jack russell, and two goats in a paddock; good nearby walks. Morris dancers may call some evenings in summer.

🍽 **Traditional bar food includes lunchtime sausages, ploughman's, ham and eggs, vegetarian lasagne, venison and mushroom pie, half a roast duck with a choice of sauces, and puddings like treacle tart.** *Starters/Snacks: £6.95 to £10.25. Main Courses: £7.95 to £15.00. Puddings: £4.50*

Free house ~ Licensees Tony and Pat Bath ~ Real ale ~ Bar food (not Sun evening or Mon) ~ Restaurant ~ (01722) 780474 ~ Children welcome but not in main bar ~ Open 12-3, 6.30-11; 12-4 Sun; closed Sun evening and Mon lunchtime; 26 Dec ~ Bedrooms: /£75B

Recommended by John Robertson, Mr and Mrs P D Titcomb, the Didler, Mr and Mrs Draper

---

Stars after the name of a pub show exceptional character and appeal. They don't mean extra comfort. And they are nothing to do with food quality, for which there's a separate knife-and-fork symbol. Even quite a basic pub can win stars, if it's individual enough.

FONTHILL GIFFORD   ST9231   MAP 2

Beckford Arms

Off B3089 W of Wilton at Fonthill Bishop; SP3 6PX

Civilised 18th-c country inn with smartly informal feel, and good food, especially in the evening

A new licensee has taken over this civilised country house set on the edge of a fine parkland estate with a lake and sweeping vistas. The big, light and airy rooms are smartly informal with stripped bare wood, a parquet floor and a pleasant mix of chunky tables with church candles. In winter, a big log fire burns in the lounge bar, which leads into a light back garden room with a high pitched plank ceiling and picture windows looking on to a terrace. Locals tend to gather in the straightforward games room: darts, pool, board games, and piped music. Hop Back GFB, Keystone Large One and Wadworths IPA and 6X on handpump and several wines by the glass. More reports please.

🍽 **Bar food at lunchtime now includes sandwiches, filled baked potatoes, burger with home-made coleslaw, ham and eggs, and a trio of local sausages with onion gravy, with more elaborate evening dishes such as duck liver, toasted pine nut and bacon salad, gravadlax, home-cured with dill, wholegrain mustard and vodka with a mango and chilli salsa, honey and cinnamon glazed duck breast with slow-braised red cabbage and bacon bubble and squeak, fillets of bass on a coriander noodle omelette, rocket, grapefruit and stir-fry vegetable salad, and rack of lamb with roast garlic and shallot mash, poached spiced fig and red wine jus.** *Starters/Snacks: £4.95 to £7.95. Main Courses: £9.99 to £18.95. Puddings: £3.95 to £7.95*

Free house ~ Licensee Feargal Powell ~ Real ale ~ Bar food (12-2, 7-9; 12-6 Sun; not Sun evening) ~ Restaurant ~ (01747) 870385 ~ Well-behaved children welcome ~ Dogs welcome ~ Open 12-11(10.30 Sun) ~ Bedrooms: £60S/£90B

Recommended by Dr and Mrs M E Wilson, Shirley Mackenzie, MDN, Andy and Claire Barker, Peter Preston, Colin and Janet Roe

GREAT BEDWYN   SU2764   MAP 2

Three Tuns

Village signposted off A338 S of Hungerford, or off A4 W of Hungerford via Little Bedwyn; High Street; SN8 3NU

Thriving village pub with good food, several real ales, helpful staff, and eclectic décor

Although new licensees have taken over this cheerful place, the manageress is one of the former licensees so things are running as smoothly as before. There's a genuinely pubby atmosphere despite the emphasis on good food, and you won't feel out of place if you just want a pint. The traditional décor in the beamed, bare-boards front bar is lifted out of the ordinary by some quirky touches and almost every inch of the walls and ceiling is covered by either the usual brasses, jugs, hops and agricultural implements, or more unusual collections such as ribbons from ships' hats, showbiz photos, and yellowing cuttings about the royal family. There's an inglenook fireplace, lighted candles in the evenings, and Black Sheep, Flowers IPA, Fullers London Pride and Wadworths 6X on handpump (the cellar was once the village morgue), several wines by the glass and quite a few malt whiskies; helpful service and board games. The whitewashed building has quite a few plants in front, and a raised garden behind (with a heated smoking area). It does get pretty packed at weekends.

🍽 **Enjoyable bar food now includes lunchtime warm salads such as chicken and bacon or niçoise, fresh sardines marinated in garlic and herbs, warm goats cheese with onion marmalade, fish stew, lamb and apricot pie, chicken breast stuffed with garlic mushrooms and mozzarella, slow-roasted belly of pork with cider sauce and bubble and squeak, fillet of bass with celeriac mash, roast cherries, lemon and white wine, and puddings such as chocolate brownie and rhubarb and ginger fool with home-made ginger cookies.** *Starters/Snacks: £3.95 to £7.95. Main Courses: £8.95 to £15.95. Puddings: £3.95 to £4.95*

Punch ~ Lease Amanda and Jason Gard ~ Real ale ~ Bar food (not winter Sun evening) ~
Restaurant ~ (01672) 870280 ~ Well-behaved children welcome away fom bar ~ Dogs allowed in
bar ~ Open 12-3, 6-11; 12-6 Sun; closed winter Sun evening

Recommended by Mary Rayner, Mark Farrington, Geoff and Sylvia Donald, Evelyn and Derek Walter

GREAT HINTON   ST9059   MAP 2

Linnet ⊗

*3.5 miles E of Trowbridge, village signposted off A361 opposite Lamb at Semington;
BA14 6BU*

Attractive dining pub, very much a place to come for a good meal rather than just a drink

Such is the reputation for the interesting food in this pretty brick dining pub that you
have to book some time ahead to be sure of a table. The comfortable bar to the right of
the door has Wadworths 6X on electric pump, several wines by the glass and around two
dozen malt whiskies; there are bookshelves in a snug end part of the room. The
restaurant is candlelit at night; piped music. In summer, the window boxes and flowering
tubs with seats dotted among them are quite a sight. More reports please.

⊞ **Served by efficient staff, the popular food at lunchtime includes sandwiches, garlic
mushroom risotto on plum tomato and watercress salad, mackerel and dill fishcake with
cucumber sour cream, steak in ale pie with mustard mash and onion gravy, sautéed
chicken, bacon and poached egg salad with stilton dressing, and venison steak; there's
also dish of the day and a two- and three-course set menu. In the evening, there might be
baked pork and thyme tart on mushy peas with mint pesto, honey-roast duck breast on
watercress and orange couscous, deep-fried salmon fillet in lemon batter on caper and
parsley mash with roasted tomato sauce, and baked tenderloin of pork filled with prunes
and spinach and wrapped in smoked bacon on a wild mushroom sauce, and puddings like
rhubarb and vanilla mascarpone cheesecake and stem ginger pudding with toffee sauce.**
Starters/Snacks: £4.95 to £6.95. Main Courses: £14.50 to £20.95. Puddings: £4.95 to £6.95

Wadworths ~ Tenant Jonathan Furby ~ Real ale ~ Bar food (not Mon) ~ Restaurant ~
(01380) 870354 ~ Children welcome ~ Dogs allowed in bar ~ Open 12-3.30, 6-11;
12-4, 7-10 Sun; closed Mon, 25-27 Dec, 1 Jan

Recommended by Lise Chace, Mr and Mrs A Curry, Dennis and Gill Keen

GRITTLETON   ST8680   MAP 2

Neeld Arms ♀ 🍺 🛏

Off A350 NW of Chippenham; The Street; SN14 6AP

**Good, chatty atmosphere in bustling village pub with popular food and comfortable
bedrooms**

With friendly, cheerful staff and chatty locals, it's not surprising that our readers enjoy
this 17th-c village pub so much. It's largely open plan, with stripped stone and some
black beams, a log fire in the big inglenook on the right and a smaller coal-effect fire on
the left, flowers on tables, and a pleasant mix of seating from windsor chairs through
scatter-cushioned window seats to some nice arts and crafts chairs and a traditional
settle. The back dining area has yet another inglenook, with a big woodburning stove –
even back here, you still feel thoroughly part of the action. Wadworths IPA and 6X and
guests like Butcombe Bitter and Sharps Cornish Coaster on handpump from the substantial
central bar counter, and a good choice of reasonably priced wines by the glass; board
games. There's an outdoor terrace, with pergola. The golden retriever is called Soaky.

⊞ **Good, reasonably priced bar food at lunchtime includes filled ciabattas, soup,
ploughman's, ham and egg, and scampi, as well as moules marinière, chicken liver pâté,
stuffed peppers with couscous and mediterranean vegetables, beef and chorizo meatballs
on tagliatelle with fresh tomato sauce, beef, Guinness and mushroom pie, lamb noisettes
with fresh rosemary and port gravy, bass stuffed with fresh herbs and lemon, and
puddings such as chocolate brownies and sticky toffee pudding; Sunday roasts.**
Starters/Snacks: £3.95 to £7.95. Main Courses: £7.95 to £13.50. Puddings: £3.95

Free house ~ Licensees Charlie and Boo West ~ Real ale ~ Bar food ~ (01249) 782470 ~
Children welcome ~ Dogs welcome ~ Open 12-3(3.30 Sat), 5.30-midnight; 12-4, 7-11 Sun ~
Bedrooms: £60B/£80B

*Recommended by Ian Phillips, Peter and Audrey Dowsett, Sara Fulton, Roger Baker, Bettye Reynolds,
David Collison, Paul A Moore, K Turner, Carol and Phil Byng, Henry Snell, Alistair Forsyth*

HORTON   SU0363   MAP 2

Bridge Inn

*Signposted off A361 Beckhampton road just inside the Devizes limit; Horton Road;
SN10 2JS*

**Well run and distinctive canalside pub, with good traditional pub food, and pleasant
garden with aviary**

A new licensee has taken over this neatly kept canalside pub and has retained the aviary
and fantail doves in the safely-fenced garden area where there are also picnic-sets;
moorings for boats as well. Inside, on the red walls above a high panelled dado are black
and white photos of bargee families and their barges among other old photographs and
country pictures. In the carpeted area on the left all the sturdy pale pine tables may be
set for food, and there's a log fire at the front; to the right of the bar is a pubbier part
with similar country-kitchen furniture on reconstituted flagstones and some stripped
brickwork. Wadworths IPA and 6X tapped from the cask and several decent wines by the
glass. Disabled lavatories, piped music, TV, board games, table skittles and shove-
ha'penny. In 1810, the building was extended to include a flour mill and bakery using
grain transported along the Kennet & Avon Canal. It's handy for walks on the downs and
along the canal tow path. More reports on the new regime, please.

🍴 **As well as filled baguettes, crusty rolls and ploughman's, bar food now includes soup,
pâté with toast, ham or sausage and eggs, steak in ale pie, aubergine bake, local trout
stuffed with prawns with lemon and butter, chicken in a garlic, mushroom and cream
sauce and duck breast with an orange and redcurrant sauce.** *Starters/Snacks: £3.00 to £7.95.
Main Courses: £9.95 to £15.95. Puddings: £4.00 to £5.50*

Wadworths ~ Tenant Adrian Softley ~ Real ale ~ Bar food (11.30-2.30, 6.30-9) ~ Restaurant ~
(01380) 860273 ~ Well behaved children welcome ~ Dogs allowed in bar ~ Open 11-2.30, 6-11;
11-11 Sat; 12-10.30 Sun; 11(12 Sun)-3, 6-11 Sat in winter

*Recommended by David Barnes, Michael Doswell, Dr and Mrs M E Wilson, Mr and Mrs A H Young, Sheila and
Robert Robinson, Andrew Gardner*

KILMINGTON   ST7835   MAP 2

Red Lion £

*B3092 Mere—Frome, 2.5 miles S of Maiden Bradley; 3 miles from A303 Mere turn-off;
BA12 6RP*

**Atmospheric, no nonsense country inn owned by the National Trust, with good value
traditional lunches, and attractive garden**

Run by an exemplary host, this ivy-covered country inn thankfully remains quite
unchanging and down-to-earth. The snug, low-ceilinged bar has a good convivial
atmosphere, pleasant furnishings such as a curved high-backed settle and red leatherette
wall and window seats on the flagstones, photographs of locals pinned up on the black
beams, and a couple of big fireplaces (one with a fine old iron fireback) with log fires in
winter. A newer big-windowed eating area is decorated with brasses, a large leather horse
collar, and hanging plates. Darts, shove-ha'penny, dominoes and board games. Butcombe
Bitter, Butts Jester, and Hidden Spring on handpump, Thatcher's Cheddar Valley cider and
several wines by the glass; helpful service. There are picnic-sets in the big attractive
garden (look out for Kim the labrador). A gate gives on to the lane which leads to White
Sheet Hill, where there are riding, hang gliding and radio-controlled gliders, and
Stourhead Gardens are only a mile away. Though dogs are generally welcome, they're not
allowed at lunchtime. There's a smokers' shelter in a corner of the car park.

🍴 **Served only at lunchtime, the straightforward bar food includes soup, sandwiches, toasties, filled baked potatoes, ploughman's, pasties, steak and kidney, fish or game pies, meat or vegetable lasagne, and daily specials.** *Starters/Snacks: £1.95 to £3.00. Main Courses: £3.65 to £8.50. Puddings: £4.50*

Free house ~ Licensee Chris Gibbs ~ Real ale ~ Bar food (12-1.50; not evenings or 25 and 26 Dec, 1 Jan) ~ No credit cards ~ (01985) 844263 ~ Children welcome in eating area of bar till 8.30pm ~ Dogs allowed in bar ~ Open 11.30-2.30, 6.30-11; 12-3, 7-11 Sun

Recommended by Andrea Rampley, Mr and Mrs P D Titcomb, Edward Mirzoeff, Jenny and Peter Lowater, Geoff and Carol Thorp, Steve Jackson

KINGTON LANGLEY   ST9277   MAP 2

Hit or Miss

Handy for M4 junction 17, off A350 S; Days Lane; SN15 5NS

Friendly village pub with good food and beer

In a quiet village handy for the motorway, this long, cottagey pub is run by warmly welcoming licensees. There's some emphasis on the left-hand restaurant with its good log fire, but the cosiest room is the small, rather plush middle bar with low beams, just a few tables, cricket memorabilia and Hydes 1863, Robinsons Dizzy Blonde and Timothy Taylors Landlord on handpump or tapped from the cask; several wines by the glass and malt whiskies; darts. There are some tables out in front.

🍴 **Good bar food includes filled baguettes, soup, duck and orange pâté, ham and eggs, goats cheese and broccoli pancakes, steak and mushrooms in ale pie, a curry of the day, cajun chicken breast, calves liver and bacon in red wine, braised lamb shank with a redcurrant and mint gravy, fresh fish dishes, and crispy duck leg with dauphinoise potatoes and ginger marmalade.** *Starters/Snacks: £3.00 to £6.00. Main Courses: £6.50 to £10.50. Puddings: £5.00*

Free house ~ Licensees Susan Heasman and J Crowle ~ Real ale ~ Bar food (12-2, 7-9(8 Sun)) ~ Restaurant ~ (01249) 758830 ~ Well behaved children welcome ~ Dogs allowed in bar ~ Open 11.30-2.30, 6.30-11

Recommended by Dr and Mrs A K Clarke, John and Gloria Isaacs

LACOCK   ST9168   MAP 2

George

West Street; village signposted off A350 S of Chippenham; SN15 2LH

Unspoilt and homely, with plenty of character and attractive back garden in summer

Long-serving Mr Glass has now handed over the reigns of this cosy pub – one of the oldest buildings in this particularly lovely village and dating back to 1361 – to his son. It's just the place for a drink and the low-beamed bar has upright timbers in the place of knocked-through walls making cosy rambling corners, armchairs and windsor chairs around close-set tables, seats in the stone-mullioned windows, and flagstones just by the counter; piped music. The treadwheel set into the outer breast of the original great central fireplace is a talking point – worked by a dog, it was used to turn a spit for roasting. Wadworths IPA and 6X on handpump. Outside, there are picnic-sets with umbrellas in the attractive back garden. As we went to press we heard that an exhibition had been set up on William Henry Fox Talbot in a corner of the pub. More reports on the food, please.

🍴 **Bar food now includes sandwiches and snacks, quite a few different pies and puddings such as bread and butter pudding.** *Starters/Snacks: £3.95 to £5.55. Main Courses: £7.95 to £12.50. Puddings: £4.75*

Wadworths ~ Manager John Glass ~ Real ale ~ Bar food (12-2.15, 6-9) ~ Restaurant ~ (01249) 730263 ~ Children in eating area of bar ~ Dogs allowed in bar ~ Open 9am(10 Sun)-11pm; 9am-3, 5-11 Mon-Thurs in winter

Recommended by Tom and Ruth Rees, David Field, Andrew Shore, Maria Williams, I A Herdman, Michael Doswell, Dr and Mrs M E Wilson, J Stickland, Dr and Mrs A K Clarke

Red Lion
High Street; SN15 2LQ

Nicely pubby Georgian inn, with interesting bar, cosy snug, and popular home-made casseroles and pies

Busy but with enough space to cope, this is an imposing National-Trust-owned Georgian inn. The long, airy pink-painted bar has a nice pubby atmosphere, heavy dark wood tables with candles and tapestried chairs, turkey rugs on the partly flagstoned floor, a fine old log fire at one end, aged-looking paintings, and branding irons hanging from the ceiling. The cosy snug has comfortable leather armchairs. Wadworths IPA, 6X and a seasonal beer on handpump and several malt whiskies; piped music. In fine weather, the seats outside are a pleasant place for a drink. The pub is handy for Lacock Abbey and the Fox Talbot Museum.

🍴 **Well liked food includes lunchtime sandwiches, filled baguettes and ploughman's, soup, duck liver pâté with grape chutney, beer-battered fish and chips, home-cooked ham and free-range eggs, asparagus and potato filo tart, sausages with onion gravy, a pie and a casserole of the day, rib-eye steak with garlic butter and puddings such as walnut and treacle tart and a fruit crumble.** *Starters/Snacks: £4.50 to £6.95. Main Courses: £6.95 to £10.95. Puddings: £4.75 to £5.25*

Wadworths ~ Managers Jack Warmington and John Whitfield ~ Real ale ~ Bar food (12-2.30, 6-9.30; all day weekends (though restricted menu)) ~ (01249) 730456 ~ Children welcome ~ Dogs allowed in bar ~ Open 11-11(10.30 Sun); closed evenings 25 and 26 Dec ~ Bedrooms: £80B/£120B

Recommended by Ian Phillips, Keith and Sue Ward, Donna and Roger, Gwyn Pickering, JCW

Rising Sun 🍺
Bewley Common, Bowden Hill – out towards Sandy Lane, up hill past Abbey; OS Sheet 173 map reference 935679; SN15 2PP

Unassuming stone pub with welcoming atmosphere and great views from garden

The untouched interior here is charming. It's an unpretentious stone-built pub with three welcoming little rooms knocked together to form one simply furnished area, with a mix of old chairs and basic kitchen tables on stone floors, country pictures, and open fires. Welcoming staff serve Moles Best Bitter, Tap, Rucking Mole, Capture and a seasonal guest on handpump, several wines by the glass and summer farm cider; darts, board games and piped music; their live music on Wednesdays is popular. The conservatory shares the same fantastic views as the big two-level terrace (where there are plenty of seats) – on a clear day you can see up to 25 miles over the Avon Valley; the sunsets can be stunning.

🍴 **Bar food includes filled baguettes, potato boats filled with mushrooms, bacon and stilton, smoked chicken salad with honey and mustard dressing, home-made broccoli and cheese lasagne or beef in ale pie, daily specials, and puddings such as apple and blackberry flapjack.** *Starters/Snacks: £4.50 to £6.25. Main Courses: £7.95 to £13.25. Puddings: £2.50 to £4.50*

Moles ~ Managers Patricia and Tom Russell ~ Real ale ~ Bar food (12-2(3 Sun), 6-9(8.30 Weds and Sun) ~ Restaurant ~ (01249) 730363 ~ Children welcome ~ Dogs allowed in bar ~ Live entertainment every Weds evening ~ Open 12-3, 6-11; 12-11 Sun

Recommended by Dr and Mrs M E Wilson, Michael Doswell, Jeff Davies, Paul and Shirley White, Simon Rodway, Dr and Mrs A K Clarke, Mrs Sheila Pearley, I A Herdman

LOWER CHUTE   SU3153   MAP 2
Hatchet
The Chutes well signposted via Appleshaw off A342, 2.5 miles W of Andover; SP11 9DX

One of the county's most attractive pubs with restful atmosphere

'A remote rural paradise' is how one reader describes this neat and friendly 16th-c thatched pub. The very low-beamed bar has a splendid 17th-c fireback in the huge fireplace (and a roaring winter log fire), a mix of captain's chairs and cushioned wheelbacks around oak tables, and a peaceful local feel. Timothy Taylors Landlord and Golden Best and Wickwar Penny Black on handpump; piped music. There are seats out on a terrace by the front car park, or on the side grass, as well as a smokers' hut, and a children's sandpit.

Thursday night is curry night and other bar food includes lunchtime filled baguettes, ploughman's, liver and bacon, steak in ale pie, mushroom tortellini with sun-dried tomatoes and pesto, and daily specials such as fishcakes and calves liver with dijon mash. *Starters/Snacks: £5.25 to £6.50. Main Courses: £8.25 to £9.95. Puddings: £3.95*

Free house ~ Licensee Jeremy McKay ~ Real ale ~ Bar food (12-2.15, 6.30-9.45) ~ Restaurant ~ (01264) 730229 ~ Children in restaurant and side bar only ~ Dogs allowed in bar and bedrooms ~ Open 11.30-3, 6-11; 12-3, 7-10.30 Sun ~ Bedrooms: £60S/£70S

Recommended by N B Vernon, J Stickland, Steven and Victoria James, Phyl and Jack Street, I A Herdman, Mrs J H S Lang, Mr and Mrs H J Langley

LUCKINGTON   ST8384   MAP 2
Old Royal Ship
Off B4040 SW of Malmesbury; SN14 6PA

Friendly pub by village green, with fair choice of drinks and decent bar food

This is a likeable, bustling partly 17th-c pub with friendly staff. It's been pleasantly opened up, making in effect one long bar divided into three areas, and the central servery has Archers Village, Bass, Wadworths 6X and a changing guest such as Wickwar Long John Silver on handpump, and ten decent wines by the glass. On the right are neat tables, spindleback chairs and small cushioned settles on dark bare boards, with a small open fireplace and some stripped masonry. Skittle alley, games machine and piped music. The garden beyond the car park has boules, a play area with a big wooden climbing frame, and plenty of seats on the terrace or grass. More reports please.

Bar food includes sandwiches, deep-fried chicken goujons with chilli dip, steak and mushroom pie, ham and eggs, chicken caesar salad, and specials like spinach and brie tart or braised lamb shank in a red wine, rosemary and garlic sauce. *Starters/Snacks: £3.25 to £9.00. Main Courses: £5.75 to £17.00. Puddings: £2.50 to £4.50*

Free house ~ Licensee Helen Johnson-Greening ~ Real ale ~ Bar food (12-2.15, 6(7 Sun)-9.30) ~ Restaurant ~ (01666) 840222 ~ Children allowed away from bar area ~ Jazz monthly ~ Open 11.30-3, 6-11; 11.30-11 Sat; 12-4, 7-10.30 Sun

Recommended by Conor McGaughey, Paul A Moore, Michael Doswell, Neil and Anita Christopher

NEWTON TONY   SU2140   MAP 2
Malet Arms 🍴 🍺
Village signposted off A338 Swindon—Salisbury; SP4 0HF

Smashing village pub with no pretensions, a good choice of local beers and tasty home-made food

There's a lot of genuine character in this cheerful, bustling pub. The two low-beamed interconnecting rooms have nice furnishings including a mix of different-sized tables with high winged wall settles, carved pews, chapel and carver chairs, and lots of pictures, mainly from imperial days. The main front windows are said to have come from the stern of a ship, and there's a log and coal fire in a huge fireplace. At the back is a homely dining room. As well as beers from breweries such as Hogs Back, Hop Back, Palmers, and Stonehenge, there might be Fullers London Pride and Wadworths St George's on handpump, farm cider and several malt whiskies. The small front terrace has old-fashioned garden seats and some picnic-sets on the grass, and there are more tables in the back garden, along with a wendy house. There's also a little aviary, and a horse paddock behind. Getting to the pub takes you through a ford and it may be best to use an alternative route in winter, as it can be quite deep.

⊞ Chalked up on a blackboard, the very good, changing range of home-made food might include soup, olives and antipasti with hot ciabatta, pasta with gorgonzola and walnuts in pesto sauce, thai salmon fishcakes with sweet chilli, popular burgers with blue cheese and bacon, gammon with free-range eggs, chicken curry, venison dishes (the landlord runs the deer management on a local estate) and puddings such as bakewell tart and chocolate brownies. *Starters/Snacks: £4.50 to £6.25. Main Courses: £8.75 to £16.00. Puddings: £4.50*

Free house ~ Licensee Noel Cardew ~ Real ale ~ Bar food (12-2.30, 6.30-10 (7-9.30 Sun)) ~ (01980) 629279 ~ Children allowed but not in bar area ~ Dogs allowed in bar ~ Open 11-3, 6-11; 12-3, 7-10.30 Sun; closed 25 and 26 Dec, 1 Jan

Recommended by Keith and Jean Symons, Howard and Margaret Buchanan, J Stickland, Michael Rigby, John Robertson, Bren and Val Speed, Mr and Mrs P D Titcomb, John Driver

NORTON   ST8884   MAP 2

Vine Tree ⊞ ♀

4 miles from M4 junction 17; A429 towards Malmesbury, then left at Hullavington, Sherston signpost, then follow Norton signposts; in village turn right at Foxley signpost, which takes you into Honey Lane; SN16 0JP

WILTSHIRE DINING PUB OF THE YEAR

Civilised, friendly dining pub, beams and candlelight, super food using local, seasonal produce, fine choice of drinks, and big garden

---

Although the first-rate, imaginative food remains one of the main draws to this well run and civilised place, there's always a good mix of customers and locals do still pop in for a drink and a chat. Three neatly kept little rooms open together, with old beams, some aged settles and unvarnished wooden tables on the flagstone floors, big cream church altar candles, a woodburning stove at one end of the restaurant and a large open fireplace in the central bar, and limited edition and sporting prints; look out for Clementine, the friendly and docile black labrador. Butcombe Bitter and a couple of guest beers like Bath Ales Gem and St Austell Tinners on handpump, around 28 wines by the glass from an impressive list (they do monthly tutored tastings), and quite a choice of malt whiskies and armagnacs; helpful, attentive staff. It's best to book if you want to eat here, especially at weekends. There are picnic-sets and a children's play area in a two-acre garden plus a pretty suntrap terrace with teak furniture under big cream umbrellas, a lion fountain, lots of lavender, and box hedging; there's an attractive smoking shelter, too. They have a busy calendar of events, with outdoor music in summer, vintage car rallies and lots going on during the Badminton horse trials. It's not the easiest place to find, and feels pleasantly remote despite its proximity to the motorway.

⊞ Using local seasonal produce (and listing suppliers), the excellent food includes sandwiches, interesting soups, parfait of foie gras and chicken livers with grape and sauternes jelly, a mediterranean charcuterie board, warm salad of pigeon breast and black pudding with orange ginger chutney, good caesar salad topped with free-range organic chicken, roasted artichoke hearts or asparagus spears, moules marinières, squash and spinach cannelloni with baby roast leeks and a vine tomato and herb sauce, roast rack of lamb with pea and mint purée and rosemary stock jus, venison and juniper pie, gloucestershire old spot pork tenderloin coated in honey wholegrain mustard with black pudding and caramelised apples, fresh lobster open ravioli with a crayfish velouté, and puddings like pink champagne and wild strawberry jelly with a sabayon of white peach and almond shortbread and white and dark chocolate torte with caramel toffee sauce. *Starters/Snacks: £3.95 to £8.95. Main Courses: £10.95 to £17.95. Puddings: £4.95 to £6.95*

Free house ~ Licensees Charles Walker and Tiggi Wood ~ Real ale ~ Bar food (12-2(2.30 Sat, 3.30 Sun), 7-9.30(9.45 Fri, 10 Sat)) ~ Restaurant ~ (01666) 837654 ~ Children welcome ~ Dogs allowed in bar ~ Live jazz and blues once a month but maybe every Sun in summer ~ Open 11.45-3-ish, 6-midnight; 11.45am-midnight Sun; they try to close winter Sun afternoons winter

Recommended by Chris and Libby Allen, Evelyn and Derek Walter, J Crosby, John and Gloria Isaacs, Mrs Ann Gray, David Parker, Emma Smith, Susan and Nigel Wilson, Andy and Claire Barker, Nina Randall, Kevin Thomas, Mr and Mrs J Brown, Rod Stoneman, M Fitzpatrick, Philip and Jude Simmons, Rob Holt, Guy Vowles

OAKSEY
ST9993   MAP 4

Wheatsheaf 🍴 🍺

Village signposted off A429 SW of Cirencester; turn left after church into Wheatsheaf Lane; SN16 9TB

Notable food showing flair in even simple things, in unpretentious tucked-away village pub – good beer, too

This is a neat little village pub with imaginative food and a relaxed pubby atmosphere. The smallish parquet-floored bar has stylishly modern padded chairs and matching bar stools, a soft leather armchair by the log fire in its big stone hearth (with a 17th-c coffin lid above), latticed windows in stripped-stone walls, and a few black beams in its low ochre ceiling; darts are over on the right. The part on the left, with a second log fire in a raised contemporary hearth, is set for eating, and a slope takes you up to a carpeted back area, also fairly compact, with more comfortably modern dining furniture around bookable tables. Bath Ales Gem, Hook Norton Old Hooky, and a guest beer on handpump, and a good choice of wines by the glass; there may be local artwork for sale, piped music. There are picnic-sets out on the quiet front terrace and a garden.

🍴 Good, well prepared bar food includes sandwiches, a choice of breads and marinated olives, ham hock terrine with piccalilli and brioche, salmon fishcake with sweet and sour sauce, proper ham with free-range egg and fresh tomato sauce, award-winning rump steak burger with dijon mayonnaise, roast tomato and basil risotto, chicken with thyme mash and bacon, old spot pork sausages with bubble and squeak and onion gravy, and puddings like baked rice pudding with cinnamon and raspberry jam and baked hot chocolate fondant with rum and raisin ice-cream; popular Sunday lunch. *Starters/Snacks: £4.50 to £6.95. Main Courses: £6.95 to £14.95. Puddings: £4.50 to £5.50*

Enterprise ~ Licensee Tony Robson-Burrell ~ Real ale ~ Bar food (12-2(3 Sun), 6.30-9; not Sun evening or Mon) ~ Restaurant ~ (01666) 577348 ~ Children welcome ~ Dogs allowed in bar ~ Open 11.30-2.30, 6-11; 11.30-3, 6-12 Sat; 12-10 Sun; closed Mon

Recommended by E McCall, T McLean, D Irving, M G Hart, Michael Doswell, J Crosby, Holly Brand, KC, Dr and Mrs J Temporal

PITTON
SU2131   MAP 2

Silver Plough 🍷

Village signposted from A30 E of Salisbury (follow brown tourist signs); SP5 1DU

Bustling country dining pub that feels instantly welcoming, good food and beer and nearby walks

You can be sure of a genuinely warm welcome in this bustling village pub and readers have, again, much enjoyed their visits. The comfortable front bar has plenty to look at, as the black beams are strung with hundreds of antique boot-warmers and stretchers, pewter and china tankards, copper kettles, toby jugs, earthenware and glass rolling pins, painted clogs, glass net-floats, and coach horns and so forth. Seats include half a dozen cushioned antique oak settles (one elaborately carved, beside a very fine reproduction of an Elizabethan oak table), and the timbered white walls are hung with Thorburn and other game bird prints, and a big naval battle glass-painting. The back bar is simpler, but still has a big winged high-backed settle, cased antique guns, substantial pictures, and – like the front room – flowers on its tables. There's a skittle alley next to the snug bar; piped music. Badger Gold, Sussex Bitter, and a seasonal guest on handpump and quite a few country wines. A quiet lawn has picnic-sets and other tables under cocktail parasols, and on the terrace is a heated area for smokers. The pub is well placed for good downland and woodland walks.

🍴 Good bar food (quite a few dishes come in two sizes) includes lunchtime filled baguettes, ploughman's and various salads like caesar with locally smoked chicken, goats cheese and caramelised pepper tart, lasagne, steak and kidney pie, pork and leek sausages with onion gravy, chicken with asparagus in a creamy tarragon sauce, pork loin stuffed with apricot and thyme on red wine gravy, and half a honey-roast duck with orange sauce; **Sunday roasts.** *Starters/Snacks: £3.95 to £7.95. Main Courses: £5.95 to £12.95. Puddings: £4.95*

Badger ~ Tenants Hughen and Joyce Riley ~ Real ale ~ Bar food (12-2, 6-9; 11-3, 6-9 Fri and Sat; 12-2, 6.30-8.30 Sun) ~ Restaurant ~ (01722) 712266 ~ Children allowed but not in main bar or restaurant ~ Dogs allowed in bar ~ Open 11-3, 6-11.30(12.30 Sat); 12-3, 6.30-11 Sun; closed 25 and evening 26 Dec ~ Bedrooms: /£50S

Recommended by Virginia Williams, Phyl and Jack Street, Chris Glasson, John Robertson, Howard and Margaret Buchanan, Helen and Brian Edgeley, Richard Fendick

POULSHOT   ST9760   MAP 2

Raven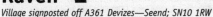
Village signposted off A361 Devizes—Seend; SN10 1RW

Reliable food and service in pretty setting

In the centre of the village and just across from the green, this is a friendly pub with well kept beer and dependable food. The two cosy black-beamed rooms are traditionally furnished with sturdy tables and chairs and comfortable banquettes, and Wadworths IPA, 6X and maybe a seasonal ale are tapped straight from the cask. Obliging service. The gents' is outside. More reports please.

🍽 **Bar food includes filled ciabattas, smoked salmon pâté, devilled whitebait, fresh battered cod, ham and eggs, steak and kidney pie, pork stroganoff, mixed grill, specials such as salmon fishcakes with sweet chilli sauce, mexican bean casserole, chicken in a creamy mushroom and stilton sauce, and pork in a leek, apple and cider sauce, and puddings such as apple and blackberry pie and lemon and ginger cheesecake.** *Starters/Snacks: £3.85 to £5.95. Main Courses: £9.70 to £15.70. Puddings: £3.25 to £4.90*

Wadworths ~ Tenants Philip and Susan Henshaw ~ Real ale ~ Bar food (not Mon) ~ Restaurant ~ (01380) 828271 ~ Well-behaved children allowed ~ Dogs allowed in bar ~ Open 11-2.30, 6.30-11; 12-3, 7-10.30 Sun; closed Mon
Recommended by Dr and Mrs A K Clarke, Mr and Mrs J Brown

ROWDE   ST9762   MAP 2

George & Dragon 🍽 ⬭
A342 Devizes—Chippenham; SN10 2PN

Gently upmarket coaching inn with good, varied food and nice atmosphere

Charming inside, this is an attractive 17th-c coaching inn with quite an emphasis on the interesting food – though they do keep Butcombe Bitter and Cottage Golden Arrow on handpump; several wines by the glass. The two low-ceilinged rooms have plenty of wood, beams, and open fireplaces and there are large wooden tables, antique rugs, and walls covered with old pictures and portraits; the atmosphere is pleasantly chatty. Board games and piped music. A pretty garden at the back has tables and chairs; maybe summer barbecues. The Kennet & Avon Canal is nearby. Smart contemporary bedrooms.

🍽 **Good, if not cheap, bar food includes baked fresh fig with goats cheese and prosciutto, grilled baked field mushroom with pesto, crab and tomato risotto, spicy meatballs with aïoli, local sausages with mash, chicken breast with roast tomatoes, goats cheese and balsamic dressing, roast cod fillet with chorizo and garlic new potato compote, devilled lambs kidneys on toast with onion gravy, wild bass with soy and ginger, and puddings such as banana sponge with custard sauce and chocolate and orange brioche bread and butter pudding.** *Starters/Snacks: £5.00 to £9.50. Main Courses: £13.50 to £32.50. Puddings: £6.75*

Free house ~ Licensees Philip and Michelle Hale, Christopher Day ~ Real ale ~ Bar food (12-3, 7-10; 12-4, 6.30-10 Sat; not Sun evening) ~ Restaurant ~ (01380) 723053 ~ Children in restaurant ~ Dogs allowed in bar ~ Open 12-3, 7-11; 12-4, 6.30-11 Sat; 12-4 Sun; closed Sun evening ~ Bedrooms: /£105S(£95B)

Recommended by Mrs Joanna Jensen, Mr and Mrs A H Young, Dr and Mrs A K Clarke, Chris and Meredith Owen, Mary Rayner, Andrew Shore, Maria Williams

SALISBURY

SU1429   MAP 2

Haunch of Venison

Minster Street, opposite Market Cross; SP1 1TB

Ancient pub oozing history, with tiny beamed rooms, unique fittings, and famous mummified hand; lovely atmosphere and well kept beers

The two tiny downstairs rooms in this splendidly characterful place (that dates back to 1320) are a delight for lovers of the unspoilt. They are quite spit-and-sawdust in spirit, with massive beams in the white ceiling, stout oak benches built into the timbered walls, black and white floor tiles, and an open fire. A tiny snug (popular with locals, but historically said to be where the ladies drank) opens off the entrance lobby. Courage Best, Greene King IPA, and a guest such as Hop Back Summer Lightning on handpump from a unique pewter bar counter, and there's a rare set of antique taps for gravity-fed spirits and liqueurs. They've also 80 malt whiskies, decent wines (ten by the glass), herbal teas, and a range of brandies. Halfway up the stairs is a panelled room they call the House of Lords, which has a small-paned window looking down on to the main bar, and a splendid fireplace that dates back to the building's early years; behind glass in a small wall slit is the smoke-preserved mummified hand of an 18th-c card sharp still clutching his cards.

❚❶ As well as filled baguettes, cottage pie, steak and mushroom in ale pudding, toad in the hole and ham with bubble and squeak, there are more elaborate dishes such as duck mousse with red onion and orange salsa, cornish brown crabcakes with sweet chilli and lime dressing, lamb noisettes with paprika and rosemary potatoes and redcurrant sauce, and local estate venison goulash, with puddings such as chocolate brownie with hot chocolate sauce and fresh fruit salad. *Starters/Snacks: £3.95 to £4.95. Main Courses: £8.50 to £13.50. Puddings: £3.90 to £5.50*

Scottish Courage ~ Lease Anthony Leroy and Justyna Miller ~ Real ale ~ Bar food (12-2.30, 6-9.30(10 Sat)) ~ Restaurant ~ (01722) 411313 ~ Children welcome ~ Dogs allowed in bar ~ Open 11am-11.30pm; 12-10.30 Sun; closed evening 25 Dec

Recommended by Andrea Rampley, Stuart Doughty, Ann and Colin Hunt, Mike Parkes, John Saville, Colin and Peggy Wilshire, Philip and June Caunt, Phil and Sally Gorton, the Didler, Donna and Roger, Andy and Claire Barker

SEEND

ST9361   MAP 2

Barge

Seend Cleeve; signposted off A361 Devizes—Trowbridge, between Seend village and signpost to Seend Head; SN12 6QB

Popular canalside pub, nice garden to watch the boats, and decent beer and food

In good weather, the neatly kept garden of this busy waterside pub is an excellent place to watch the bustle of boats on the Kennet & Avon Canal – and moorings by the humpy bridge are very useful for thirsty bargees. The bar has a medley of eye-catching seats which includes milk churns, unusual high-backed chairs (made from old boat-parts), a seat made from an upturned canoe, and the occasional small oak settle among the rugs on the parquet floor; there's a well stocked aquarium, and a pretty Victorian fireplace. Wadworths IPA, 6X and a seasonal beer on handpump, 40 wines by the glass and Weston's cider; friendly, helpful staff.

❚❶ Bar food includes filled baguettes, duck liver and pistachio pâté with cumberland sauce, thai-style crab cakes with sweet chilli sauce, fish, cheese and meat boards with crusty bread for sharing, lamb and rosemary sausages with caramelised onion gravy, free-range chicken on roasted pepper and rocket linguine, beer-battered hake, daily specials such as deep-fried breaded brie, fish pie and confit of duck with spiced grape sauce, and puddings such as sticky chocolate and almond sponge pudding and mixed berry pavlova; Sunday roasts. *Starters/Snacks: £4.75 to £9.50. Main Courses: £8.25 to £13.50. Puddings: £4.75 to £5.50*

Wadworths ~ Managers Paul and Sarah Haynes ~ Real ale ~ Bar food (all day (more limited between 3 and 5)) ~ Restaurant ~ (01380) 828230 ~ Children welcome ~ Dogs allowed in bar ~ Open 11-11

Recommended by Dr and Mrs M E Wilson, Tom and Jill Jones, Dr and Mrs A K Clarke, John Saville, Richard and Jean Green, Helen and Brian Edgeley, Meg and Colin Hamilton, Mr and Mrs P D Titcomb, Paul and Shirley White, Michael Doswell

SEMINGTON   ST9259   MAP 2

Lamb 🍴 ♈

The Strand; A361 Devizes—Trowbridge; BA14 6LL

Very good food in busy, ivy-covered dining pub, with wide range of wines and spirits, reliable service, and attractive garden

Although the large majority of customers come to this civilised creeper-covered dining pub to enjoy the popular food, they won't discourage you if you just want a pint. A series of corridors and attractively decorated separate rooms radiates from the serving counter, with antique settles, a woodburning stove, and a log fire. Tables in the bar are kept on a first-come, first-serve basis and tend to be snapped up rather quickly (particularly on Saturday evening or Sunday lunchtime) but you can reserve a table in advance in the dining areas. Butcombe, Ringwood Best and a guest like Keystone Large One on handpump, a good wine list with 16 by the glass, and an interesting range of armagnacs, cognacs and rums. There is a pleasant colourfully planted walled garden with seats and tables, and views towards the Bowood Estate. More reports please.

🍽 **Good bar food includes sandwiches, soup, smoked mackerel pâté with red onion marmalade, smoked duck breast with apple chutney, warm salad of scallops and cripsy bacon, sausages of the day with mash and onion gravy, ham, egg and sauté potatoes, chicken and flageolet beans in white wine and thyme, fillet of salmon with chive hollandaise, steak and mushroom pie, and puddings; the fresh fish is delivered daily.** *Starters/Snacks: £5.25 to £7.50. Main Courses: £8.50 to £15.00. Puddings: £4.95*

Free house ~ Licensees Philip Roose-Francis and Sue and Tim Smith ~ Real ale ~ Bar food (not Sun evening) ~ (01380) 870263 ~ Children welcome ~ Dogs allowed in bar ~ Open 11.30-3, 6.30-11; 12-3 Sun; closed Sun evening, 25 Dec, 1 Jan

Recommended by Dr and Mrs M E Wilson, Dr and Mrs A K Clarke, Andrew Shore, Maria Williams, Mr and Mrs A Curry, Alan and Audrey Moulds

STOURTON   ST7733   MAP 2

Spread Eagle 🛏

Church Lawn; follow Stourhead brown signs off B3092, N of junction with A303 just W of Mere; BA12 6QE

Comfortably civilised country inn next to famous gardens; some food all day in summer; busy at lunchtimes, quieter later on

A new licensee has taken over this handsome brick house – it's right next to the National Trust gardens and so does get busy at peak times. The interior has an old-fashioned, rather civilised feel with antique panel-back settles, a mix of new and old solid tables and chairs, handsome fireplaces with good winter log fires, smoky old sporting prints, prints of Stourhead, and standard lamps or brass swan's-neck wall lamps. One room by the entrance has armchairs, a longcase clock and a corner china cupboard. Butcombe Bitter, Cheddar Potholer, and Wessex Kilmington Best on handpump and several wines by the glass. There are benches in the courtyard behind. If you stay overnight, you can wander freely around the gardens outside their normal opening times – a nice way of enjoying them away from the crowds.

🍽 **Bar food at lunchtime includes sandwiches, ploughman's, soup, chicken liver and wild mushroom pâté with chutney, ham and free-range eggs, and pies such as goats cheese and sweet potato, fish, and steak and kidney; evening dishes such as baked camembert with cranberry coulis, scottish smoked salmon and home-cured gravadlax with sour cream and chives, three local cheeses and spring onion risotto, and confit of barbary duck leg with rissole potatoes and haricot bean dressing, with puddings like sticky toffee pudding with caramel sauce and Baileys chocolate and banana bread and butter pudding.** *Starters/Snacks: £4.95 to £6.95. Main Courses: £9.95 to £16.50. Puddings: £3.50 to £4.95*

Prices of main dishes sometimes now don't include vegetables – if in doubt ask.

Free house ~ Licensee Andrew Wilson ~ Real ale ~ Bar food (all day during summer (light snacks in afternoons)) ~ Restaurant (evening) ~ (01747) 840587 ~ Children welcome ~ Open 11-11; 12-10.30 Sun ~ Bedrooms: £80B/£110B

Recommended by Jenny and Brian Seller, Andrea Rampley, Sue Demont, Tim Barrow, Mayur Shah, J L and C J Hamilton, Laurence Milligan, Martin and Karen Wake, Sheila Topham, Ian Phillips, Colin and Janet Roe

UPPER CHUTE   SU2953   MAP 2

Cross Keys ♀ ◖

Tucked-away village N of Andover, best reached off A343 via Tangley, or off A342 in Weyhill via Clanville; SP11 9ER

Peacefully set, proper country pub, welcoming and relaxed, with enjoyable food and good beer and wines

As they have two stables at the back of this country pub, customers staying overnight can now bring their horses with them; there's around 80 square miles of open countryside to explore. (We have not yet heard from readers who have stayed here, but would expect it to be good value.) The back garden has been tidied up and has a children's play area, and picnic-sets out under flowering cherries on the front south-facing terrace give far views over rolling wooded uplands. Inside, it's open plan and well run with a relaxed, unstuffy atmosphere, early 18th-c beams, some sofas, a cushioned pew built around the window, and a good log fire in the big hearth on the left; pubby tables and a couple of leather armchairs by the woodburning stove on the right, darts sensibly placed in an alcove, and shut-the-box, chess, TV and piped music. Fullers London Pride, Discovery and Butser and a changing guest beer such as Everards Beacon on handpump, and good wines by the glass; service is welcoming and helpful, and the charming bulldogs are called Pepper, Pudding and Mouse.

🍴 Deliberately unpretentious and very good food using seasonal ingredients includes sandwiches, tasty soup, salmon and haddock fishcakes, cottage or steak in ale pies, liver and bacon casserole, beer-battered haddock, chicken breast with bacon and mushrooms in a creamy sauce, tuna steak on sweet chilli noodles, and puddings such as banoffi pie and crème brûlée; steak night is on Wednesdays and fish night on Fridays. *Starters/Snacks: £3.95 to £4.00. Main Courses: £7.95 to £15.95. Puddings: £4.25*

Free house ~ Licensees George and Sonia Humphrey ~ Bar food (12-2(2.30 Sat and Sun), 6-9; not Sun evening) ~ Restaurant ~ (01264) 730295 ~ Children allowed until 9pm ~ Dogs allowed in bar and bedrooms ~ Open 11-2.30, 5-11; 11-midnight Sat; 12-11 Sun ~ Bedrooms: £55S/£65S

Recommended by Paul A Moore, Ian Thomasson

WEST LAVINGTON   SU0052   MAP 2

Bridge Inn 🍴

A360 S of Devizes; Church Street; SN10 4LD

Welcoming village pub with good, french-influenced food and a light, comfortable bar

This is a thoroughly nice pub, much enjoyed by both locals and visitors. It's comfortable and quietly civilised, and the light, spacious bar mixes contemporary features such as spotlights in the ceiling with firmly traditional fixtures like the enormous brick inglenook that may be filled with big logs and candles; at the opposite end is a smaller modern fireplace, in an area set mostly for eating. Pictures on the cream-painted or exposed brick walls are for sale, as are local jams, and there are plenty of fresh flowers on the tables and bar; timbers and the occasional step divide the various areas. Brakspears Bitter, Wadworths IPA, and Wychwood Hobgoblin on handpump, a dozen wines by the glass and several malt whiskies; piped music in the evenings. At the back is a nice raised lawn area with several tables under a big tree; boules. No children inside.

🍴 Extremely good food with a french leaning includes lunchtime filled baguettes, fish soup, warm smoked duck with croûtons, chestnut mushroom and emmenthal cheese salad with a strawberry vinegar and olive oil dressing, a plate of salami and cured ham with pickled onions, gherkins and sunblush tomatoes, baked snails in their shells with garlic and herb butter, a choice of soufflés, coq au vin, local venison fillet with a port and shallot sauce, daily specials such as salmon, haddock and dill fishcakes, ham with organic, free-range eggs and pommes frites and haddock in organic beer batter, and puddings like organic dark chocolate and cherry torte with white chocolate sauce and a trio of crème brûlée. *Starters/Snacks: £4.50 to £6.25. Main Courses: £8.25 to £22.00. Puddings: £5.10 to £6.50*

Enterprise ~ Lease Cyrille and Paula Portier ~ Real ale ~ Bar food (12-2, 6.30-9; not Sun evening or Mon) ~ Restaurant ~ (01380) 813213 ~ Open 12-3, 7-11; 12-3 Sun; closed Sun evening and all day Mon; last two weeks Feb

Recommended by L and D Webster, Michael Doswell, B and F A Hannam, Mr and Mrs A Curry, Ken and Margaret Grinstead

WHITLEY   ST8866   MAP 2

Pear Tree � 🛏

Off B3353 S of Corsham, at Atworth 1.5, Purlpit 1 signpost; or from A350 Chippenham—Melksham in Beanacre turn off on Westlands Lane at Whitley 1 signpost, then left and right at B3353; SN12 8QX

Attractive, upmarket old farmhouse, a good choice of drinks and comfortable bedrooms; plenty of seats in neat gardens

A new licensee has taken over this honey-coloured stone farmhouse and is to open up a new area for diners and drinkers in the garden; the major improvements to the car park have been a great success. The charming front bar has quite a pubby feel, with cushioned window seats, some stripped shutters, a mix of dining chairs around good solid tables, a variety of country pictures and a Wiltshire Regiment sampler on the walls, a little fireplace on the left, and a lovely old stripped stone one on the right. Candlelit at night, the popular big back restaurant (best to book) has dark wood cushioned dining chairs, quite a mix of tables, and a pitched ceiling at one end with a quirky farmyard theme – wrought-iron cockerels and white scythe sculpture. Black Sheep, Wadworths 6X and Wells & Youngs Bitter on handpump, and quite a few wines by the glass. A bright spacious garden room opens on to a terrace with good teak furniture and views over the carefully maintained gardens, which are prettily lit at night to show features like the ruined pigsty; more seats on the terrace, and boules. More reports on the new regime, please.

🍴 Using local produce, the bar food now includes lunchtime sandwiches, middlewhite pork, prune and brandy pâté with home-made piccalilli and sourdough toast, bruschetta of warm marinated squid and mussels with chorizo, rocket, chilli, garlic and parsley, home-made sausages with bubble and squeak and onion gravy, steak pie, free-range chicken breast with bacon and tarragon stuffing, pan haggerty, parsnip purée and mushroom sauce, monkfish tail wrapped in parma ham with risotto of hand-picked crab, chive butter and mascarpone and salsa verde, specials (one reader found they were not available on a Sunday evening), and puddings such as chilled rhubarb and custard crumble and vanilla crème brûlée with ginger snap biscuit. *Starters/Snacks: £5.50 to £6.50. Main Courses: £10.30 to £19.50. Puddings: £5.95*

Punch ~ Lease Alex McEwen ~ Real ale ~ Bar food (12-2.30(3 Sun), 6.30-9.30(10 Fri and Sat) ~ Restaurant ~ (01225) 709131 ~ Children welcome ~ Dogs welcome ~ Open 11(12 Sun)-11 ~ Bedrooms: £75B/£110B

Recommended by Pete Devonish, Ian McIntyre, Dr and Mrs M E Wilson, P and J Shapley, Joyce and Maurice Cottrell, Ian Malone, David Parker, Emma Smith, Ian and Jane Irving, Mr and Mrs A J Hudson, Ray and Winifred Halliday, John Robertson, Alun Jones, Mr and Mrs A H Young, Roger Wain-Heapy, Dr and Mrs A K Clarke, M G Hart, Alistair and Kay Butler

---

Bedroom prices normally include full english breakfast, VAT and any inclusive service charge that we know of. Prices before the '/' are for single rooms, after for two people in a double or twin (B includes a private bath, S a private shower). If there is no '/', the prices are only for twin or double rooms (as far as we know there are no singles).

WINTERBOURNE BASSETT

SU1075 MAP 2

White Horse

Off A4361 S of Swindon; SN4 9QB

Neat dining pub, wide choice of enjoyable food, thoughtful choice of drinks, and sizeable garden

'Bright and cheerful as always' is how a regular customer describes this civilised dining pub. It's well run by helpful, friendly licensees and the neat big-windowed bar is attractively extended with traditional tables and chairs on the waxed wooden floors, old prints and paintings on the walls, plants dotted about, and a little brick fireplace. There's a comfortable dining room and warm conservatory, too. Wadworths IPA and 6X and a seasonal guest on handpump, a dozen wines by the glass, and maybe winter mulled wine and summer Pimms by the jug; piped music, darts and board games. There are tables outside on a good-sized lawn and lovely hanging baskets.

🍴 As well as using local produce and making their own bread and ice-creams, they offer a wide choice of well liked bar food including filled baguettes, ploughman's, soup, duck liver pâté, almond and nut roast, yorkshire pudding filled with four different sausages, mash and gravy, fillet of cod mornay, chicken curry, liver and onions, braised beef casserole, specials such as pork dijonnaise and fillet steak stuffed with stilton, wrapped in bacon with a red wine sauce, and puddings such as fresh fruit crumble and thick cut marmalade sponge pudding with custard; also, a good value two-course lunch, an early evening menu, and Sunday roasts. *Starters/Snacks: £3.95 to £5.50. Main Courses: £5.95 to £17.95. Puddings: £4.65 to £5.50*

Wadworths ~ Tenants Chris and Kathy Stone ~ Real ale ~ Bar food (12-2(3 Sun), 6(7 Sun)-9; they will offer snacks outside these hours if possible) ~ Restaurant ~ (01793) 731257 ~ Children welcome ~ Open 11.30-3, 6-11; 12-4, 7-11 Sun

Recommended by Tony Baldwin, Sheila and Robert Robinson, Eric and Mary Barrett, Mrs B S Clarke

LUCKY DIP

Besides the fully inspected pubs, you might like to try these Lucky Dips recommended to us and described by readers (if you do, please send us reports: feedback@thegoodpubguide.co.uk).

ALL CANNINGS [SU0761]
Kings Arms SN10 3PA [The Street]: Warmly welcoming Victorian pub in charming village, well kept Wadworths IPA, 6X and a guest beer, good wine range, good choice of reasonably priced pubby food from sandwiches up inc some unusual touches; children welcome, large garden, not far from Kennet & Avon Canal moorings, cl Mon lunchtime *(Bob and Laura Brock, Anne and Alan Fleming)*
AMESBURY [SU1541]
☆ *Antrobus Arms* SP4 7EU [Church St]: Handsome hotel, quiet, comfortable and relaxed, with good food, friendly helpful staff, changing real ales, log fires in warmly welcoming smart yet pubby bar and communicating lounge overlooking beautiful walled garden, two dining rooms; children and dogs welcome, 17 attractive bedrooms, open all day *(Gwyneth and Salvo Spadaro-Dutturi, Stephen Corfield)*
BADBURY [SU1980]
☆ *Plough* SN4 0EP [A346 (Marlborough Rd) just S of M4 junction 15]: Good simple food at attractive prices inc afternoon snacks and all-day Sun roasts in light and airy dining room (children allowed) looking over road to

Vale of the White Horse, friendly atmosphere, cheerful efficient staff, well kept Arkells ales, decent wines, large rambling bar area, pianola, daily papers, darts; piped music; play area in sunny garden above, open all day *(Richard and Judy Winn, Alistair Forsyth, Nigel and Sue Foster, Mary Rayner, Keith and Sue Ward)*
BARFORD ST MARTIN [SU0531]
☆ *Barford Inn* SP3 4AB [B3098 W of Salisbury (Grovely Rd), just off A30]: Panelled front bar with big log fire, other chatty interlinking rooms and bars, restaurant, wide choice of enjoyable food inc good fresh fish, quick unfussy friendly service, Badger ales; disabled facilities, children and dogs welcome, terrace tables, more in back garden, charming affordable bedrooms, good walks, open all day (has been cl Sun afternoon) *(LYM, Alec and Sheelagh Knight)*
BECKHAMPTON [SU0868]
☆ *Waggon & Horses* SN8 1QJ [A4 Marlborough—Calne]: Handsome old stone-and-thatch pub handy for Avebury, old-fashioned settles and comfortably cushioned wall benches in open-plan beamed bar with what some might call the patina of ages, friendly staff, dining area, sensible food (not

Sun evening), well kept Wadworths ales and a guest, pool and pub games; piped music turned down on request; children in restaurant, pleasant raised garden with good play area, open all day, bedrooms *(LYM, Susan and John Douglas, Martin and Sarah, Sheila and Robert Robinson, Conor McGaughey, David Barnes, T R and B C Jenkins)*

BERWICK ST JAMES [SU0739]
☆ *Boot* SP3 4TN [High St (B3083)]: Flint and stone pub not far from Stonehenge, new tenants spring 2008; former landlady a very hard act to follow, but early reports most promising – enjoyable local-sourced food, Wadworths and possible guest ale, huge log fire in inglenook one end, sporting prints over small brick fireplace at other, small back dining room with collection of celebrity boots; dogs and children have been welcome, sheltered side lawn *(Bryan Reed, LYM, Howard and Margaret Buchanan)*

BISHOPS CANNINGS [SU0364]
Crown SN10 2JZ [Chandlers Lane; off A361 NE of Devizes]: Friendly two-bar local with wide choice of good value generous food inc good Sun lunch, Wadworths ales, decent wines, good mix of customers, popular quiz Thurs; dogs welcome, tables in garden behind, next to handsome old church in pretty village, walk to Kennet & Avon Canal *(Roger Wain-Heapy, Andrew Campbell)*

BISHOPSTONE [SU2483]
Royal Oak SN6 8PP [the one nr Swindon; Cue's Lane]: Two-bar pub taken over by local organic farmers and opened up in light and airy refurbishment, emphasis on organic supplies such as bath chaps, properly hung home-reared steaks, veg from the school allotment, even home-made elderflower cordial and pork scratchings alongside well kept Arkells, some beams, oak panelling and wood floors, good landlord; sizeable garden, bedrooms in outbuildings, beautiful village below Ridgeway and White Horse *(Tony and Tracy Constance, Guy Taylor)*

White Hart SP5 4AA [Butts Lane; the one nr Salisbury]: Good atmosphere, pleasant helpful staff, reasonably priced food inc good Sun lunch, log fire, attractive layout and décor, roomy restaurant; garden picnic-sets *(N Bullock)*

BOX [ST8168]
Northey Arms SN13 8AE [A4, Bath side]: Stone-built dining pub with simple contemporary décor, chunky modern furniture on pale hardwood floor, food from tapas and satisfying bar lunches to more ambitious evening menu, Wadworths ales, decent wines by the glass; children welcome, garden tables *(Dr and Mrs A K Clarke, Michael Doswell)*

BRADFORD LEIGH [ST8362]
Plough BA15 2RW [B2109 N of Bradford]: Emphasis on meals in extended and smartened up dining area (no baps or sandwiches), friendly efficient service, Moles and Wadworths 6X, cheery public bar with fire, darts and pool; children welcome, big garden with play area *(Dr and Mrs A K Clarke, MRSM, Dr and Mrs M E Wilson)*

BRADFORD-ON-AVON [ST8359]
Beehive BA15 1UA [A363 out towards Trowbridge]: Friendly old-fashioned L-shaped pub nr canal on outskirts, good choice of changing ales, reasonably priced pubby food, good range of wines, helpful staff, cosy log fires, candlelit tables, 19th-c playbills, cricketing prints and cigarette cards, darts; children and dogs welcome; attractive back garden, play area, barbecues *(Mike Gorton, BB, Pete Baker, Dr and Mrs A K Clarke)*

Castle BA15 1SJ [Mount Pleasant/Masons Lane]: Major refurbishment of imposing 18th-c stone building blending old materials with relaxed contemporary feel, largish low-ceilinged flagstoned bar with long farmhouse tables and fireside armchairs, sofas in cosy snug, ligher bare-boards dining room, enjoyable up-to-date food (all day), well kept Three Castles Barbury Castle, friendly staff; children welcome, nice garden, good spot above town, new boutique bedrooms, open all day *(Dr and Mrs M E Wilson, Keith Burnell)*

Cross Guns BA15 2HB [Avoncliff, 2 miles W; OS Sheet 173 map ref 805600]: Almost a fairground atmosphere on busy summer days, hard-working friendly staff generally coping pretty well with swarms of people in floodlit partly concreted areas steeply terraced above the bridges, aqueducts and river (dogs allowed out here); appealingly quaint at quieter times, with friendly stripped-stone low-beamed bar, well kept ales such as Butcombe, Box Steam and Theakstons Old Peculier, lots of malt whiskies and country wines, 16th-c inglenook, upstairs river-view restaurant; children welcome, open all day *(John and Gloria Isaacs, Dr and Mrs M E Wilson, LYM, Ian Phillips)*

Dandy Lion BA15 1LL [Market St]: More continental café bar than typical local, old-fashioned chairs, stripped wood floor and panelling, steps to snug bare-boarded back room, restaurant upstairs, Butcombe and Wadworths IPA, several wines by glass, good coffee, friendly atmosphere; children away from bar area, may be open all day *(Simon Collett-Jones, Douglas and Ann Hare, Guy Vowles, LYM)*

Three Horseshoes BA15 1LA [Frome Rd, by station car park entrance]: Popular old local with well kept sensibly priced Butcombe and Wadworths 6X, quickly served enjoyable food, friendly service, some tall tables and chairs in simple bar with plenty of nooks and corners, small restaurant; big-screen TV; tables out on decking *(Dr and Mrs M E Wilson, Bob and Laura Brock)*

BROAD CHALKE [SU0325]
Queens Head SP5 5EN [Ebble Valley SW of Salisbury; North St]: Roomy, with heavy beams, inglenook with woodburner, padded settles and chairs, some stripped brickwork, good value home-made food, well kept

Badger ales, decent wines, farm ciders and country wines, good coffee, helpful staff; may be piped music; wheelchair access from back car park, pretty courtyard overlooked by comfortable well equipped bedroom block (Mike and Linda Hudson)

BROAD HINTON [SU1176]

Bell SN4 9PF [A4361 Swindon—Devizes]: Contemporary open-plan L-shaped refurbishment, popular locally for enjoyable reasonably priced pubby food, well kept Greene King and Wadworths, decent wines by the glass, friendly informal service; children welcome, pleasant garden (Tony Baldwin, Keith and Jean Symons, Mary Rayner)

BROKENBOROUGH [ST9189]

Rose & Crown SN16 0HZ: Open-plan bar, lower back part mainly a restaurant area, enjoyable hearty food from baguettes to good steaks (best to book Fri/Sat night), welcoming owners, two well kept Uley ales, good value wines (Guy Vowles)

BROMHAM [ST9665]

Greyhound SN15 2HA [off A342; High St]: Old beamed pub under newish management, light modern décor, comfortable leather sofas and log fires, old walk-across well in back bar, wide choice of good value food inc home-made pizzas and Sun roasts (booking advised wknds), friendly efficient staff, well kept Wadworths, good wine choice, upstairs skittle alley for extra dining space when busy; quiz nights, live musicians; big enclosed garden (dogs allowed here) with decking and boules (Andy Fawthrop, Karen Rogers)

BROUGHTON GIFFORD [ST8764]

Bell on the Common SN12 8LX [The Common]: Imposing rose-draped stone-built local on huge village green, traditional furnishings, long-serving landlord and friendly staff, Wadworths from handpumps on back wall, big coal fire, enjoyable homely food, dining lounge full of copper and old country prints, rustic bar with local photographs, small pool room with darts; juke box; children welcome, charming flower-filled crazy-paved garden (occasional pig roasts and live music), bowls club next door (Dr and Mrs M E Wilson)

☆ *Fox* SN12 8PN [The Street]: Former Fox & Hounds, friendly chef/landlord doing good fresh food from lunchtime standbys to more inventive evening dishes, well kept Greene King and other ales, helpful service, fresh décor alongside traditional timbers, armchairs and sofa by entrance; big well kept garden behind (Dr and Mrs M E Wilson, Catherine Pitt)

BURCOMBE [SU0631]

☆ *Ship* SP2 0EJ [Burcombe Lane]: Cosy two-level dining pub with young chef/landlord doing good choice of good value fresh food inc enterprising dishes, friendly efficient staff, Wadworths 6X, decent wines, two log fires, unpretentious bistro atmosphere, low beams, panelling and window seats, pleasant décor, candles and soft lighting; unobtrusive

piped music; children welcome, tables on front terrace and in peaceful riverside garden, pretty village (Colin and Janet Roe, Mr and Mrs P D Titcomb, Ken Marshall)

CASTLE EATON [SU1495]

Red Lion SN6 6JZ [The Street]: Thames-side dining pub with cosy linked rooms inc sizeable pleasant conservatory, usual pubby food even Mon lunchtime, well kept ales inc one named for the pub, log fire, settees and hunting prints, darts in pool room; children welcome, shrubby riverside garden, popular with Thames Path walkers, open all day Fri-Sun (LYM, Evelyn and Derek Walter)

CHARLTON [ST9688]

☆ *Horse & Groom* SN16 9DL [B4040 towards Cricklade]: Recently smartly refurbished stone-built pub, appealing and relaxing, keeping flagstones and log fire in proper bar (dogs welcome), stylish dining rooms, interesting choice of good fresh modern food, polished obliging service, Archers and a guest beer, good choice of wines by the glass; tables out under trees, five good bedrooms (Eric and Mary Barrett, John Monks, LYM)

CHILMARK [ST9732]

Black Dog SP3 5AH [B3089 Salisbury—Hindon]: Smartly updated 15th-c beamed village pub with enjoyable if not cheap food from lunchtime baguettes to good local steaks, warm welcome and attentive polite service, Wadworths ales, wide range of good value wines, civilised local atmosphere, several cosy linked areas, inglenook woodburner; good-sized attractive roadside garden (Mr and Mrs W W Burke, Mrs J H S Lang, Edward Mirzoeff, Basil and Sylvia Walden, Colin and Janet Roe, LYM)

CHIPPENHAM [ST9073]

Kingfisher SN14 0JL [Hungerdown Lane]: Welcoming local with Wadworths 6X, interesting spirits, good lunchtime sandwiches and salads, antique prints, board games; soft piped music, frequent live music and quiz nights; tables outside (Dr and Mrs A K Clarke)

CHIRTON [SU0757]

Wiltshire Yeoman SN10 3QN [Andover Rd (A342)]: Current chef/landlord doing some imaginative cooking inc good fish and bargain two-course lunches without losing the local atmosphere, enthusiastic cheerful service, well kept Wadworths, Stowford Press cider, pool in back bar area; cl Mon (I H G Busby, Alan and Audrey Moulds, Eric and Mary Barrett, Anthony Bowes, Roger Edward-Jones)

CHITTERNE [ST9843]

☆ *Kings Head* BA12 0LJ [B390 Heytesbury—Shrewton]: Welcoming local, relaxed and understated, well liked for food from short choice of good bar lunches to inventive evening meals inc good fish, local Keystone and Wadworths 6X, friendly tenants, good log fire one end (the best end if it's cold), simple traditional décor with wooden floors, panelled dado and chunky old pine tables;

lovely hanging baskets, tables on back terrace, pretty village, good Salisbury Plain walks (Terry Buckland, Edward Mirzoeff, Ian Phillips, BB)

CHOLDERTON [SU2242]

Crown SP4 0DW [A338 Tidworth—Salisbury roundabout, just off A303]: Thatched low-beamed cottage with nicely informal eating area in L-shaped bar, friendly staff, Ringwood and Timothy Taylors Landlord, good unexpectedly sophisticated food, open fire, restaurant; terrace tables (Alec and Susan Hamilton)

COLLINGBOURNE KINGSTON [SU2355]

Barleycorn SN8 3SD [A338]: Neat comfortable village pub with several well kept ales inc Hook Norton and Wadworths, decent wines, good coffee, wide blackboard choice of enjoyable bar food (can take quite a while – attractive restaurant may take priority), roaring fire, friendly owners, pool room; piped music; small garden (Stuart Doughty, Robin and Tricia Walker)

CORSHAM [ST8670]

Hare & Hounds SN13 0HY [Pickwick (A4 E)]: Traditional local with well kept changing ales such as Bass, Caledonian Deuchars IPA, Fullers London Pride and Marstons Pedigree, annual beer festival, usual food, panelled log-fire lounge, busy main bar with unobtrusive piped music and sports TV, another room with alcove seating, darts and pool; open all day Fri-Sun (and lunchtimes when the Two Pigs is not) (Dr and Mrs A K Clarke, David Parker, Emma Smith)

CORSLEY HEATH [ST8145]

Royal Oak BA12 7PR [A362 Frome—Warminster]: Large comfortable 19th-c pub very popular lunchtime for generous reasonably priced home-made pub food from sandwiches and baked potatoes to duck and steaks, friendly landlady and attentive staff, Wadworths IPA and a guest such as Batemans XXXB, roomy beamed and panelled bar (no dogs here, but welcome in small side bar), good fire, pleasant big back family extension with pool, restaurant; disabled facilities, attractive terrace and big garden, valley views, handy for Longleat (Richard Fendick, Terry Buckland)

CORTON [ST9340]

☆ *Dove* BA12 0SZ [off A36 at Upton Lovell, SE of Warminster]: Cheerful helpful landlord and good service, enterprising range of good food from baguettes to fresh fish and steaks, three well kept ales, good wines by the glass, daily papers, pleasant partly flagstoned main bar with central log fire and good pictures, conservatory; children welcome, tables on neat back lawn (lovely valley), comfortable wheelchair-friendly bedrooms, good fishing available (Edward Mirzoeff, LYM, Dr and Mrs M E Wilson, C and R Bromage, Mr and Mrs Draper, David Morgan)

CRICKLADE [SU1093]

Red Lion SN6 6DD [off A419 Swindon—Cirencester; High St]: 16th-c former

coaching inn with great ale range – Moles Best, Wadworths 6X and half a dozen or more guests, two farm ciders, good choice of malt whiskies, friendly landlord and helpful staff, pubby food (not Mon/Tues), log fire, interesting signs and bric-a-brac in large bar, less cluttered front lounge, no music or mobile phones; neat garden, bedrooms, open all day (E McCall, T McLean, D Irving, Pete Baker)

Vale SN6 6AY [High St]: Recently smartened up beamed and timbered pub, dining rooms off pleasant bar with woodburner in each room, wide food choice from lunchtime sandwiches and other snacks to hearty evening dishes and popular Sun roasts, helpful friendly staff, good choice of well kept ales; piped music; bedrooms (E McCall, T McLean, D Irving)

White Lion SN6 6DA [High St]: Two-bar pub with good service, good value generous food (limited lunchtime menu), real ales such as Black Sheep and Wychwood, good choice of soft drinks, pleasantly relaxed restaurant, games room; tables out under parasols behind (Alan and Eve Harding, R T and J C Moggridge)

DERRY HILL [ST9570]

Lansdowne Arms SN11 9NS [Church Rd]: Stately stone-built pub opposite one of Bowood's grand gatehouses, roomy, airy and civilised, with relaxed period flavour, hearty log fire and candles in bottles, Wadworths ales, good value wines by the glass, prompt attentive cheerful service, wide food choice from good range of huge sandwiches with chips up in bar and restaurant; faint piped music; fine views, neat side garden, good play area (Dr and Mrs A K Clarke, BB, Matthew Shackle)

EASTON ROYAL [SU1961]

Bruce Arms SN9 5LR [Easton Rd]: Chatty 19th-c local with benches by two long scrubbed antique pine tables on bar's brick floor, homely carpeted and curtained parlour with easy chairs, old pictures, flowers and piano, well kept Wadworths and guest ale, Pewsey organic cider, good filled rolls only, darts, extension with pool and TV; camping field, open all day Sun (the Didler)

EDINGTON [ST9353]

☆ *Lamb* BA13 4PG [Westbury Rd (B3098)]: Open-plan traditional beamed village pub with assorted pine furniture on bare boards, friendly atmosphere and cheerful staff, log fire, real ales such as Butcombe, Otter and Wadworths 6X, enjoyable food (not Sun evening or Mon lunchtime) in bar and dining room; children welcome, pleasant garden tables (access to pretty village's play area beyond), great views, good walks (Dr and Mrs M E Wilson, Mike Gorton)

ENFORD [SU14351]

Swan SN9 6DD [Long St, off A345]: Friendly thatched village-owned dining pub, thriving relaxed atmosphere, wide choice of good enterprising food at sensible prices, well kept local ales such as Stonehenge, helpful staff; dogs welcome, garden with small play area (Chris and Meredith Owen)

FARLEIGH WICK [ST8063]

Fox & Hounds BA15 2PU [A363 Bathford—Bradford, 2.5 miles NW of Bradford]: Well extended low-beamed rambling 18th-c pub with friendly efficient landlord, changing choice of enjoyable food inc some interesting dishes, real ales such as Bath Gem and Bass, log fire in big oak-floored dining area; attractive garden (Dr and Mrs M E Wilson, MRSM)

FORD [ST8474]

White Hart SN14 8RP [off A420 Chippenham—Bristol]: Comfortably updated 16th-c stone-built Marstons country inn, their ales and a guest such as Abbey Bellringer kept well, food all day, quietly friendly landlord, heavy black beams and good log fire in ancient fireplace; attractive stream-side grounds, comfortable bedrooms (some in annexe), open all day (Dr and Mrs A K Clarke, Julie and Bill Ryan, Phil and Jane Hodson, Michael Doswell, LYM)

FROXFIELD [SU2968]

Pelican SN8 3JY [A4]: Former coaching inn thoroughly refurbished in uncluttered almost hotel-like style, attractively priced food (all day Fri-Sun), good choice of wines by the glass and of real ales inc local Ramsbury, relaxed atmosphere; pleasant streamside garden with terrace, dovecot and duck pond, Kennet & Avon Canal walks, open all day (Geoff and Sylvia Donald, Mark Farrington, Mr and Mrs A Curry)

GREAT DURNFORD [SU1337]

☆ *Black Horse* SP4 6AY [follow Woodfords sign from A345 High Post traffic lights]: Cheery and homely, with some nice alcoves, one room with ship pictures, models and huge ensigns, another with a large inglenook woodburner, masses of bric-a-brac, Fullers London Pride, Ringwood and other ales, genial staff, food from baguettes up, traditional pub games; piped blues and jazz, jokey notices, even talking lavatories; children and dogs welcome, big informal garden with play area and barbecues, decent bedrooms, cl Sun evening and Mon in winter (Dr and Mrs M E Wilson, LYM)

GREAT WISHFORD [SU0735]

☆ *Royal Oak* SP2 0PD [off A36 NW of Salisbury]: Emphasis on enjoyable food in appealing two-bar pub with big family dining area and restaurant, prompt service by friendly helpful young staff, three well kept changing ales (useful tasting notes), decent wines, pleasant décor with beams, panelling, rugs on bare boards and log fires; pretty village (Ian Phillips, Mr and Mrs P D Titcomb, Mr and Mrs Draper, LYM)

HEDDINGTON [ST9966]

☆ *Ivy* SN11 0PL [off A3102 S of Calne]: Picturesque thatched 15th-c village pub with good inglenook log fire in take-us-as-you-find-us old-fashioned L-shaped bar, heavy low beams, timbered walls, assorted furnishings on parquet floor, brass and

copper, Wadworths IPA, 6X and a seasonal beer tapped from the cask, good plain fresh home-made food (not Sun-Weds evenings, and may take a time if many locals in) from great lunchtime club sandwiches up, back family eating room, sensibly placed darts, piano, dog and cat; may be piped music; disabled access, front garden, open all day wknds (Pete Baker, LYM, the Didler)

HEYTESBURY [ST9242]

Angel BA12 0ED [just off A36 E of Warminster; High St]: Upscale dining pub in quiet village just below Salisbury Plain, good value lunches and other pricier food inc notable steaks, good if not cheap wines by the glass, relaxed atmosphere (service can be slow), two linked dining areas, one very softly lit, comfortable if compact pre-dinner lounge, log fire (not always lit), daily papers, straightforward furnishings and some attractive prints and old photographs, Greene King ales; piped music; children welcome, open all day (I A Herdman, Ian Malone, Ian Phillips, LYM, Edward Mirzoeff, Stephen P Edwards)

HIGHWORTH [SU1891]

Freke Arms SN6 7RN [Swanborough; B4019, a mile W on Honnington turning]: Airy, smart and relaxed, four comfortable rooms on different levels, real ales inc Arkells, blackboard food inc good popular Sun roast, efficient service; quiet piped music; small garden with play area, nice views (Peter and Audrey Dowsett)

☆ *Saracens Head* SN6 7AG [High St]: Civilised and relaxed rambling bar, several real ales inc Arkells 2B and 3B tapped from casks in bar area, reasonably priced blackboard food, good soft drinks choice, comfortably cushioned pews in several interesting areas around great four-way central log fireplace, timbers and panelling, no mobile phones; quiet piped music; children in eating area, tables in smart partly covered courtyard with heaters, comfortable bedrooms, open all day wkdys (LYM, Dr and Mrs M E Wilson, Peter and Audrey Dowsett)

HILMARTON [SU0175]

Duke SN11 8SD: Friendly helpful staff, enjoyable straightforward food with local ingredients, quirky pleasing interior, good selection of beers; children welcome, bedrooms (Nick and Lorelei Freeman)

HINDON [ST9032]

☆ *Angel* SP3 6DJ [B3089 Wilton—Mere]: Dining pub with welcoming new landlord, huge window showing kitchen, good food inc set-price choices, hard-working staff, well kept ales such as Archers from chrome bar counter, decent wines, big log fire, flagstones and other coaching-inn survivals; children in eating areas, tables outside, seven refurbished bedrooms, good breakfast, open all day in summer (Robert Watt, Steve Jackson, John Evans, Colin and Janet Roe, Helen and Brian Edgeley, MDN, LYM, Mrs M S Turner-Jones)

☆ *Lamb* SP3 6DP [B3089 Wilton—Mere]: New management for this attractive old hotel, long roomy bar with log fire, two flagstoned lower sections with very long polished table, high-backed pews and settles, up steps a third, bigger area, Wells & Youngs Bitter, Special and guest beer, good choice of wines by the glass and whiskies; children and dogs welcome, picnic-sets over the road, bedrooms, open all day *(LYM)*

HODSON [SU1780]

Calley Arms SN4 0QG [not far from M4 junction 15, via Chiseldon; off B4005 S of Swindon]: Open-plan pub with new licensees doing generous enjoyable fresh food, pleasant service, well kept Wadworths, open fire in main area, woodburner in bare-boards part; picnic-sets on sheltered back grass (hear the larks singing), pleasant walk from pub *(Sheila and Robert Robinson, Nigel and Sue Foster, BB)*

HOLT [ST8561]

☆ *Toll Gate* BA14 6PX [Ham Green; B3107 W of Melksham]: Appealing individual décor and furnishings and thriving atmosphere in comfortable bar, friendly helpful service, five good interesting changing ales, good choice of wines by the glass, farm cider, daily papers, log fire, another in more sedate high-raftered ex-chapel restaurant up steps; piped music may obtrude; dogs welcome, no under-12s, back terrace, compact bedrooms, cl Sun evening, Mon *(Mr and Mrs A H Young, Dr and Mrs M E Wilson, Bryan Pearson, Dr and Mrs A K Clarke, LYM, Ian Phillips)*

HOOK [SU0785]

Bolingbroke Arms SN4 8DZ [B4041, off A420 just W of M4 junction 16]: Well spaced tables in informal airy bare-boards bar with lots of light pine, armchair lounge, discreet lighting, pleasantly decorated restaurant popular with older lunchers, Arkells ales, good soft drinks choice, generous well prepared food from sandwiches up; quiet piped music; children welcome, garden with pond and fountain, bedrooms, cl Sun evening *(JJW, CMW, Nigel and Sue Foster)*

HORNINGSHAM [ST8041]

Bath Arms BA12 7LY [by entrance to Longleat House]: Handsome old stone-built inn stylishly opened up as welcoming dining pub with several linked areas inc a proper bar, enjoyable fresh food inc delicious puddings, Wessex ales and local cider, good wine choice, charming staff, log fire, daily papers, side restaurant and conservatory; attractive garden with neat terraces, 15 good bedrooms, on sloping green of pretty village *(BB, Clare West)*

KINGTON ST MICHAEL [ST9077]

Jolly Huntsman SN14 6JB [handy for M4 junction 17]: Roomy stone-built pub with charming service, well kept Greene King ales and Wadworths 6X, popular dining end, scrubbed tables, comfortable settees, good log fire, pleasant décor; six well equipped bedrooms in separate block *(Deb Thomas)*

LACOCK [ST9168]

Carpenters Arms SN15 2LB [Church St]: Enjoyable quickly served home-made food,

well kept Wadworths 6X and a guest beer, decent wines by the glass, long-serving landlord, cottagey-style rambling bar with log fire, country prints and panelled dado, back restaurant; children in eating area, bedrooms *(Mr and Mrs A Curry, LYM)*

LANDFORD [SU2419]

☆ *Cuckoo* SP5 2DU [village signed down B3079 off A36, then right towards Redlynch]: Unpretentious proper old thatched pub with friendly chatty local atmosphere, four simple rooms (three with fires), well kept Hop Back Summer Lightning and Ringwood Best tapped from the cask, farm cider, pasties and baguettes, traditional games; dogs and muddy walkers welcome, nice gardens front and back, play area, on edge of New Forest, open all day wknds *(the Didler, Christopher Owen, LYM)*

LIDDINGTON [SU2081]

Village Inn SN4 0HE [handy for M4 junction 15, via A419 and B4192; Bell Lane]: Comfortable, warm and welcoming, some emphasis on huge choice of good value food inc popular Sun roasts, linked bar areas and stripped stone and raftered back dining extension, Arkells ales, log fire, conservatory; no under-8s, service may slow if busy; disabled facilities, terrace tables *(KC)*

LOCKERIDGE [SU1467]

☆ *Who'd A Thought It* SN8 4EL [signed just off A4 Marlborough—Calne just W of Fyfield]: Friendly pub with two linked rooms set for good plentiful food from good value baguettes up (kitchen may close early if not busy), evening meals with fish emphasis, reasonable prices, small side drinking area, well kept Wadworths and a guest beer, good choice of wines by the glass, coal or log fire, interesting collection of cooperage tools, family room; piped music turned down on request; pleasant back garden with play area, delightful scenery, lovely walks *(J Stickland, Robert W Buckle, BB)*

LOWER WOODFORD [SU1235]

☆ *Wheatsheaf* SP4 6NQ [signed off A360 just N of Salisbury]: Well run 18th-c Badger dining pub, large, warm and friendly, with generous traditional food using local ingredients (some small helpings available), efficient service, well kept ales, good wines, log fire, comfortable furnishings on oak floor with miniature footbridge over indoor goldfish pool; piped music; children welcome, baby-changing, good disabled access, good big tree-lined garden with play area, pretty setting *(J Stickland, Keith and Sue Ward, B and F A Hannam, LYM, David Barnes, Mr and Mrs A Curry)*

LYDIARD MILLICENT [SU0985]

Sun SN5 3LU [The Street]: Pleasantly refurbished 18th-c pub bought in 2007 by its good manageress, well kept changing ales such as Hidden and West Berkshire, interesting enjoyable food, daily papers, restaurant; good-sized pretty garden with terrace *(anon)*

MAIDEN BRADLEY [ST8038]
Somerset Arms BA12 7HW [Church St]: Two-bar Georgian pub under new friendly family management, simple but accomplished food, Wadworths ales kept well, pleasant Victorian décor, daily papers; nice garden, bedrooms *(Edward Mirzoeff)*

MARDEN [SU0857]
☆ *Millstream* SN10 3RH [off A342]: Comfortably upmarket and well appointed open-plan bar/restaurant with good food from home-baked bread to imaginative dishes using fresh local organic ingredients, well kept Wadworths and great wine choice inc champagne by the glass, beams, flagstones, log fires and woodburners, charming service, maps and guides as well as daily papers; children and well behaved dogs welcome, pleasant garden with neat terrace, cl Mon *(Mr and Mrs A H Young)*

MARKET LAVINGTON [SU0154]
Green Dragon SN10 4AG [High St]: Rambling early 17th-c pub with enjoyable food, well kept Wadworths and guest beers, good value wines; wheelchair access, garden with play area and aunt sally *(John and Lesley Bennett, LYM)*

MARLBOROUGH [SU1869]
Castle & Ball SN8 1LZ [High St]: Georgian coaching inn with plenty of atmosphere in comfortably worn lounge bar, unusually wide choice of decent food inc good speciality pie, quieter and slightly simpler eating area, Greene King ales, good range of well listed wines by the glass, young enthusiastic staff; seats out under projecting colonnade, good value bedrooms *(Jennifer Banks)*
Green Dragon SN8 1AA [High St]: Bustling unspoilt town pub with friendly service, full Wadworths range kept well, good value bar food inc popular OAP lunch, big coal-effect gas fire, stripped brickwork, lots of blue and white plates, leatherette wall banquettes, pine furniture, steps down to back games room, skittle alley; back terrace, bedrooms, pretty little breakfast room *(Paul Butler)*
Lamb SN8 1NE [The Parade]: Family-run 17th-c coaching inn with further stable-block eating area, good value up-to-date food, Wadworths, farm cider, good choice of wines; pretty courtyard with assorted tables under parasols, six attractive bedrooms *(anon)*

MARSTON MEYSEY [SU1297]
Old Spotted Cow SN6 6LQ [off A419 Swindon—Cirencester]: Smartly refurbished as dining pub with enjoyable upscale food, choice of real ales from proper bar, good value wines, welcoming staff, two open fires, light wood furniture and cosy sofas, rugs on bare boards and parquet, plants and cow pictures on stripped stone walls, no piped music; spacious garden with picnic-sets and play area, open all day wknds, cl Mon *(Catherine Turnbull)*

MONKTON FARLEIGH [ST8065]
Kings Arms BA15 2QH [signed off A363 Bradford—Bath]: Imposing 17th-c building

with pleasantly up-to-date feel inside, sofas, open fire and dining tables in one bar, huge inglenook and more dining tables in L-shaped beamed lounge, Bass, Butcombe and Wadworths 6X, good wine and whisky choice, good if not cheap food (all day wknds) using local supplies; piped music, unobtrusive big-screen TV; front partly flagstoned courtyard, well tended two-level back garden, lovely village, has been open all day wknds *(Dr and Mrs M E Wilson, John and Gloria Isaacs, Frank and Bridget Crowe)*

NETHERHAMPTON [SU1129]
☆ *Victoria & Albert* SP2 8PU [just off A3094 W of Salisbury]: Cosy black-beamed bar in simple thatched cottage with good generous food from nicely presented sandwiches up, sensible prices and local supplies, four well kept changing ales, farm cider, decent house wine, nicely cushioned old-fashioned wall settles on ancient floor tiles, restaurant; children welcome, hatch service for sizeable terrace and garden behind, handy for Wilton House and Nadder Valley walks *(Joan and Michel Hooper-Immins, Colin and Janet Roe, LYM)*

NOMANSLAND [SU2517]
Lamb SP5 2BP [signed off B3078 and B3079]: Lovely New Forest village-green setting for unpretentious bustling pub with wide range of bargain fresh food inc lots of pasta and fish, children's menu and popular Sun roasts, Ringwood ales, short sensible wine list, friendly informal service, log fire in lounge bar, small dining room; pool and TV in public bar; tables out on terrace, green and garden behind, good walks, open all day *(Ann and Colin Hunt, Sally and Tom Matson, BB)*

NUNTON [SU1526]
☆ *Radnor Arms* SP5 4HS [off A338 S of Salisbury]: Pretty ivy-clad village pub very popular for its food inc fish and local game, friendly staff (very helpful with wheelchairs), Badger real ales, three pleasantly decorated and furnished linked rooms inc cheerfully busy yet relaxing bar and staider restaurant, log fires; wknd booking essential; attractive garden good for children *(Mr and Mrs W W Burke)*

PEWSEY [SU1561]
French Horn SN9 5NT [A345 towards Marlborough; Pewsey Wharf]: Two-part back bar with steps down to pleasant rather smarter front dining area (children allowed here), flagstones and log fire, enjoyable food if a bit pricy, well kept Wadworths, good choice of wines by the glass, cheery staff; piped music; one or two picnic-sets out behind, walks by Kennet & Avon Canal below, cl Tues *(Meg and Colin Hamilton, BB, Bob and Laura Brock, David Barnes, M G Hart)*

RAMSBURY [SU2771]
☆ *Bell* SN8 2PE [off B4192 NW of Hungerford, or A4 W]: Neat dining pub with log fires in small airy beamed bar, sunny bay windows, Ramsbury Gold (brewed for the pub) and a guest, Black Rat cider, several malt whiskies,

good choice of wines by the glass, enjoyable if not cheap mildly upmarket food using local produce in bar or restaurant; children and dogs welcome, picnic-sets on raised lawn, cl Sun evening *(Mary Rayner, LYM, Nina Randall, Kevin Thomas, Dr and Mrs J Temporal)*

SALISBURY [SU1430]

☆ *Avon Brewery* SP1 3SP [Castle St]: Long narrow city bar, busy and friendly, with dark mahogany, frosted and engraved bow windows, friezes and attractive pictures, two open fires, sensibly priced food (not Sun evening) from sandwiches up, mainstream real ales, decent wines; piped music; long sheltered courtyard garden overlooking river, open all day *(Craig Turnbull, LYM, John Robertson)*

☆ *New Inn* SP1 2PH [New St]: Good value food from sandwiches to grills, Badger ales, decent house wines and good cheerful service, inglenook log fire, massive beams and timbers, quiet cosy alcoves, children's area; walled garden with striking view of nearby cathedral spire, open all day summer wknds *(Ann and Colin Hunt, John and Julie Moon, Colin and Peggy Wilshire, LYM, Alan and Eve Harding)*

☆ *Old Mill* SP2 8EU [Town Path, W Harnham]: Charming 17th-c pub/hotel in glorious tranquil out-of-centre setting, unpretentious beamed bars with prized window tables, good value food from sandwiches up, helpful staff, real ales, good wines and malt whiskies, attractive restaurant showing mill race; children welcome, small floodlit garden by duck-filled millpond, delightful stroll across water-meadows from cathedral (classic view of it from bridge beyond garden), bedrooms *(Tony and Wendy Hobden, LYM, Charles Gysin)*

Rai d'Or SP1 2AS [Brown St]: 16th-c former Star, back to an earlier name after reworking with emphasis on enjoyable thai food, but keeping relaxed and friendly pub atmosphere, with local ales inc Stonehenge Great Bustard and reasonably priced wines; cl lunchtimes and Sun *(Gavin Robinson)*

☆ *Wig & Quill* SP1 2PH [New St]: Low-beamed 15th-c former shop with good value fresh standard food (not winter evenings) from sandwiches up, prompt friendly service and relaxed atmosphere, well kept Wadworths and guest beers tapped from the cask, decent wines and interesting summer drinks, open fires, daily papers, soft lighting, rugs, sofa, worn leather armchairs, stuffed birds and low arches to linked rooms, tiled back eating room; dogs welcome, sunny sheltered courtyard behind with cathedral spire views, open all day *(Edward Mirzoeff, Tom and Jill Jones, Chris Glasson, Stephen Corfield)*

Wyndham Arms SP1 3AS [Estcourt Rd]: Friendly modern corner local with Hop Back beers (originally brewed here, now from Downton), country wines, simple bar food, small front room, longer main bar; children welcome in front room, open all day wknds, cl lunchtime other days *(the Didler)*

SEEND [ST9361]

Brewery SN12 6PX [Seend Cleeve]: Genuine village local, friendly helpful licensees, great choice of farm ciders, well kept Sharps Doom Bar and perhaps a guest beer, pubby food (all day Fri/Sat, not Sun evening or Mon); pleasant garden with play area, open all day Fri-Sun *(Bob and Laura Brock)*

SEMLEY [ST8926]

☆ *Benett Arms* SP7 9AS [off A350 N of Shaftesbury]: The long-serving Duthies left this character village inn in 2007, but their welcoming replacements and staff give good service, with good value food (the cook's stayed on), Butcombe and Ringwood Best, decent wines, log fire, bright cheery dining rooms; children and well behaved dogs allowed, pleasant tables outside *(Steve Jackson, LYM, Graham Jones, Colin and Janet Roe)*

SHAW [ST8765]

Golden Fleece SN12 8HB [Folly Lane (A365 towards Atworth)]: Attractive former coaching inn with good atmosphere in bright and clean low-ceilinged L-shaped bar and long sympathetic front dining extension, good range of food inc good bargain lunches – very popular with older people, good welcoming service, well kept ales such as Bass, Fullers London Pride and Moles, farm cider, flame-effect fires; garden tables *(D S and J M Jackson, Dr and Mrs A K Clarke)*

SHERSTON [ST8585]

☆ *Rattlebone* SN16 0LR [Church St (B4040 Malmesbury—Chipping Sodbury)]: Rambling beamed and stone-walled 17th-c village pub with welcoming licensees and good atmosphere, popular food with some unusual choices, Wells & Youngs ales, farm cider, decent wines inc interesting bin-ends, log fire, cosy corners with pews, settles and country-kitchen chairs; children in restaurant, skittle alley, picnic-sets in back garden, has been open all day *(Donna and Roger, D Nightingale, Kate Hosier, Bob and Angela Brooks, LYM)*

SOUTH WRAXALL [ST8364]

☆ *Long Arms* BA15 2SB [Upper S Wraxall, off B3109 N of Bradford on Avon]: Partly 17th-c country pub very popular locally for good value food inc bargain daily roast and homely puddings, friendly efficient staff and cheerful atmosphere, Wadworths, good range of wines by the glass, character dark décor with flagstones and some stripped stone, log fire; pretty garden *(Mark Flynn, Mr and Mrs P R Thomas)*

STAVERTON [ST8560]

☆ *Old Bear* BA14 6PB [B3105 Trowbridge—Bradford-on-Avon]: Warm, friendly and increasingly popular for wide choice of reasonably priced good food inc fish and upmarket dishes from huge ciabattas up in neatly kept long bar divided into four sections, obliging landlord, real ales such as Bass, Sharps Doom Bar and Wadworths 6X, nice mix of seats inc some high-backed settles, stone fireplaces (biggest in end dining area); booking recommended Sun lunchtime *(Dr and Mrs M E Wilson, Mrs P Bishop, BB)*

STIBB GREEN [SU2262]

☆ *Three Horseshoes* SN8 3AE [just N of Burbage]: Friendly old-world local with landlady's good honest home cooking (not Sun evening or Mon), speciality pies, competitive prices, quick service, Wadworths IPA and 6X, farm cider, inglenook log fire in comfortable beamed front bar, railway memorabilia and pictures (enthusiast landlord), small dining room; beautifully kept garden, cl Mon *(Pete Baker, Alan and Audrey Moulds)*

SWALLOWCLIFFE [ST9627]

☆ *Royal Oak* SP3 5PA [signed just off A30 Wilton—Shaftesbury; Common Lane]: Pretty little partly 16th-c partly thatched pub with good interesting frequently changing food, friendly staff (and cat and dog), fine range of wines, modest choice of good real ales, good mix of chairs around varying-sized solid tables in pink-walled carpeted bar with sofa by nice log fire, cosy bistro beyond; picnic-sets under cocktail parasols in big sheltered back garden, good walks *(BB, Louise Gibbons)*

SWINDON [SU1484]

Glue Pot SN1 5BP [Emlyn Sq]: No-frills alehouse in Brunel's Railway Village, eight or so well kept beers, honest but sometimes very limited pub food, prompt service, pub games and high-backed settles around pine tables; sports TV, can get very busy; terrace tables, open all day *(M Joyner, Howard and Margaret Buchanan)*

TISBURY [ST9429]

Boot SP3 6PS [High St]: Ancient unpretentious village local with jovial landlord, well kept Marstons Bitter and Pedigree tapped from the cask, good value pubby food, smashing fireplace *(Tony and Wendy Hobden)*

TROWBRIDGE [ST8557]

Sir Isaac Pitman BA14 8AL [Castle Pl]: Useful Wetherspoons well done out in elm-coloured wood, comfortable alcoves and different levels below cupola, the shorthand Sir Isaac invented along the beams, good value beer and food, pleasant staff *(Mike Gorton)*

WANBOROUGH [SU2183]

Brewers Arms SN4 0AE [High St]: Friendly country pub with pleasant modern décor, good range of enjoyable food, well kept Arkells; garden *(Nigel and Sue Foster)*

WEST OVERTON [SU1368]

Bell SN8 1QD [A4 Marlboro—Calne]: Pleasant and homely, with cosy well used furnishings, Wadworths and guest ales such as Shepherd Neame kept well, bargain generous straightforward food, affable attentive landlord; open all day *(Sheila and Robert Robinson)*

WESTWOOD [ST8159]

New Inn BA15 2AE [off B3109 S of Bradford-on-Avon]: Traditional country pub, busy

wknds but quiet midweek, with several linked rooms, beams and stripped stone, scrubbed tables on slate floor, generous popular food in bar and restaurant, well kept Wadworths; a few tables out behind, lovely hanging baskets, walks nearby, pretty village *(Meg and Colin Hamilton, BB)*

WILCOT [SU1461]

Golden Swan SN9 5NN [signed off A345 N of Pewsey, and in Pewsey itself]: Pretty steeply thatched country local nr Kennet & Avon Canal, unpretentiously welcoming, lots of china hanging from beams of two small rooms, well kept Wadworths, basic good value home-made bar food (not Sun evening or Mon), dining room, games room with bar billiards; children welcome, rustic tables on front lawn, field with camping, occasional folk and barbecue wknds, good value simple bedrooms *(LYM, Andrew Gardner)*

WILTON [SU0931]

☆ *Pembroke Arms* SP2 0BH [Minster St (A30)]: Elegant and friendly Georgian hotel handy for Wilton House, bar not cheap but roomy and comfortable, good food from new chef, Badger ale, good coffee and wines by the glass, open fire, fresh flowers and candles, daily papers and magazines, restaurant; some outside tables, attractive bedrooms with marble bathrooms *(BB, John Robertson, A D Lealan)*

WOOTTON BASSETT [SU0682]

Five Bells SN4 7BD [Wood St]: Friendly town local with great atmosphere, well kept Fullers London Pride and four changing guests, farm cider, imaginative food a cut above usual pub style inc good value substantial sandwiches and special menus/theme nights, board games, darts; TV; shaded courtyard, open all day Fri-Sun *(Pete Baker, BB)*

WOOTTON RIVERS [SU1963]

Royal Oak SN8 4NQ [off A346, A345 or B3087]: 16th-c beamed and thatched pub, wide range of enjoyable food from lunchtime sandwiches up, Fullers London Pride, Wadworths 6X and perhaps a guest beer, good choice of wines by the glass, cheerful service, comfortable L-shaped dining lounge with woodburner, timbered bar with small games area; children and dogs welcome, tables out in yard, pleasant village, bedrooms in adjoining house *(Mr and Mrs P D Titcomb, LYM, Gwyneth and Salvo Spadaro-Dutturi)*

WROUGHTON [SU1480]

White Hart SN4 9JX [High St]: Thatched former blacksmith's with nicely smartened up L-shaped beamed lounge, big old stone fireplace with woodburner, moderately priced food inc blackboard specials, well kept Wadworths and a guest, welcoming service *(Nigel and Sue Foster, LYM)*

WYLYE [SU0037]

☆ *Bell* BA12 0QP [just off A303/A36; High St]: Partly 14th-c, prettily set in peaceful village, neat black-beamed front bar, big log fire, sturdy rustic furnishings, stripped stone and herringbone brickwork, well kept local

Hidden ales, restaurant; children and dogs welcome, pleasant walled terrace and back garden attractively flanked by church's clipped yews, fine downland walks nearby, good value bedrooms *(LYM, Mary Rayner, Richard J Mullarkey, David Morgan, John Coatsworth, C and R Bromage, Roy Hoing)*

YATTON KEYNELL [ST8676]
Bell SN14 7BG [B4039 NW of Chippenham]: Cosy village pub popular for good value hearty food, friendly staff, real ales and decent wines, nicely decorated bar and country-feel dining area; well spaced picnic-sets in good-sized fenced garden *(Mr and Mrs P R Thomas)*

Worcestershire

We've often pondered the conundrum as to how there can be a single wild mushroom left growing in the entire country, given the number of 'wild mushrooms' we see on menus. We suspect that many are not as wild as they profess to be. But when one new main entry here, the Butchers Arms at Eldersfield, has them on the menu, you can be quite sure that they have indeed been freshly gathered from round about. The enthusiastic young couple who run this tiny place serve really good food, yet have managed to preserve the pub's essential simplicity. Worcestershire has a handful of other rather special slightly unusual pubs. The cheery King & Castle in Kidderminster is a very rewarding re-creation of an Edwardian station waiting room, bustling with happy customers here for the good value food and very reasonably priced beers. Owned by the National Trust, the Fleece at Bretforton is virtually a museum piece, while the Monkey House at Defford, in the same family for a century and a half, is an old-fashioned rustic cider house, virtually unique. Among the best pubs in this county, the Farmers Arms at Birtsmorton, is a relaxing country village pub with good value pubby food, and the Nags Head in Malvern is a great place with a tremendous range of beers. The handsome Kings Arms in Ombersley (our other new entry) returns to the *Guide* after a longish break, doing very well under its newish landlady, and we have high hopes for the Walter de Cantelupe at Kempsey, now that it has a full-time chef on board – this nice pub did struggle a bit when the landlord was doubling as both chef and front man. The welcoming Bell & Cross at Holy Cross is a charming place where you can pop in for a drink or eat from a varied menu that seems geared to cater for most occasions – it's this pub that we choose as Worcestershire Dining Pub of the Year. Some pubs to note in the Lucky Dip section at the end of the chapter are the Three Kings at Hanley Castle, Royal Oaks at Kinnersley and at Leigh Sinton, Malvern Hills Hotel just outside Malvern and Brewers Arms at West Malvern. And this county has some bargains to look out for in the food line, especially if you are eligible for OAP deals. Worcestershire also has several small independent brewers, also well worth looking out for: this year we have found Malvern Hills, Cannon Royall, St Georges, Teme Valley, Wyre Piddle, Blue Bear and Weatheroak.

Real ale to us means beer which has matured naturally in its cask – not pressurised or filtered. We name all real ales stocked. We usually name ales preserved under a light blanket of carbon dioxide too, though purists – pointing out that this stops the natural yeasts developing – would disagree (most people, including us, can't tell the difference!).

BAUGHTON   SO8742   MAP 4

Jockey ♀

4 miles from M50 junction 1; A38 northwards, then right on to A4104 Upton—Pershore;
WR8 9DQ

Thoughtfully run dining pub with an appealing layout

This steady dining pub tends to be popular with an older lunchtime set here to enjoy the
warm welcome extended by the friendly licensees. The open plan layout is nicely divided
by stripped brick half walls, some with open timbering to the ceiling, and there's a mix
of good-sized tables, a few horse-racing pictures on butter-coloured walls, and a cream
Rayburn in one brick inglenook; piped music. Drinks include Courage Directors,
Theakstons and a changing guest such as Goffs Tournament, and they've farm cider and a
rewarding choice of wines, with ten by the glass. There are picnic-sets out in front, with
an array of flowers. Out here, you may hear the motorway in the distance if there's an
east wind.

🍴 **As well as lunchtime sandwiches, baguettes and baked potatoes (not Sundays), bar
food includes starters like whitebait or smoked duck breast, and main courses like
poached salmon fillet with oyster mushroom white wine sauce, steak and kidney pie,
sirloin or fillet steak, and specials that could include loin of lamb or poached scallops in
creamy light curry sauce.** *Starters/Snacks: £4.25 to £6.95. Main Courses: £8.95 to £18.95.
Puddings: £3.95 to £4.75*

Free house ~ Licensee Colin Clarke ~ Real ale ~ Bar food (12-2(2.30 Sun), 6(7 Sun)-9) ~
Restaurant ~ (01684) 592153 ~ Children welcome ~ Open 11.30-3, 6-11; 11.30-11 Sat;
12-10.30 Sun; 11.30-3, 6-11 winter Sat, 12-4 Sun in winter ~ Bedrooms: £40B/£60B

Recommended by Joyce and Maurice Cottrell, Carol and Colin Broadbent, J E Shackleton, Mike and Mary Carter

BEWDLEY   SO7875   MAP 4

Little Pack Horse

High Street; no nearby parking – best to park in main car park, cross A4117 Cleobury road,
and keep walking on down narrowing High Street; DY12 2DH

Friendly town pub full of interesting paraphernalia, decent food

This chatty welcoming place is tucked away in a quiet back street in a very attractive
riverside town. There's no parking so it's best to leave your car in the public car park
near the river in the town, and walk down. Warmed by a woodburning stove, the interior
has reclaimed oak panelling and floorboards, as well as an eye-catching array of old
advertisements, photos and other memorabilia. Alongside Black Sheep they have a couple
of guests such as Sharps Doom Bar and Wood Quaff, a selection of bottled ciders, a
couple of draught belgian beers and just under two dozen wines; piped music. An area
outside has heaters.

🍴 **Some of the sensibly priced pubby dishes are very usefully offered in two sizes:
sandwiches, filled baguettes, pork, liver and brandy pâté, fishcake and salad, beef and ale
or five bean and vegetable pie, sausage and mash, chicken balti, battered haddock and
steaks.** *Starters/Snacks: £3.00 to £6.00. Main Courses: £5.35 to £14.75. Puddings: £3.65 to
£4.75*

Punch ~ Lease Mark Payne ~ Real ale ~ Bar food (12-2.15, 6-9.15; 12-3, 6-9.30 Fri; 12-4,
5.30-9.30(8.30 Sun) Sat, Sun) ~ Restaurant ~ (01299) 403762 ~ Children welcome until 8pm ~
Dogs allowed in bar ~ Open 12-3, 6-11(midnight Fri and Sat); 12-10.30 Sun

Recommended by Alan and Eve Harding, N R White

BIRTSMORTON

SO7936 MAP 4

Farmers Arms ◀ £

Birts Street, off B4208 W; WR13 6AP

Unrushed half-timbered village local with plenty of character

Calm and relaxing, this unchanging half-timbered pubby place is quietly free of piped music or games machines, but is home to the local cribbage and darts teams – you can also play shove-ha'penny or dominoes. Chatty locals gather at the bar for Hook Norton Hooky and Old Hooky, which are on handpump alongside a changing guest from a brewer such as Wye Valley. The big flagstoned room on the right rambles away under very low dark beams, with some standing timbers, a big inglenook, and flowery-panelled cushioned settles as well as spindleback chairs. A lower-beamed room on the left seems even cosier, and in both the white walls are broken up by black timbering. You'll find seats and swings out on the lovely big lawn with view over the Malvern Hills – the pub is surrounded by plenty of walks. More reports please.

🍴 **Very inexpensive simple bar food typically includes sandwiches, soup, ploughman's, cauliflower cheese, steak and kidney pie and burgers.** *Starters/Snacks: £2.65 to £4.50. Main Courses: £3.35 to £7.20. Puddings: £1.75 to £2.95*

Free house ~ Licensees Jill and Julie Moore ~ Real ale ~ Bar food (11-2, 6.30-9.30; 12-2, 7-9 Sun) ~ (01684) 833308 ~ Children welcome ~ Dogs welcome ~ Open 11-4.30, 6-midnight; 12-4.30, 7-midnight Sun

Recommended by Dave Braisted, the Didler, Steve Bailey, Dr A J and Mrs Tompsett, Sue and Dave Harris

BREDON

SO9236 MAP 4

Fox & Hounds

4.5 miles from M5 junction 9; A438 to Northway, left at B4079, then in Bredon follow signpost to church and river on right; GL20 7LA

An appealingly old-fashioned 15th-c pub not far off the motorway

A useful all-rounder, this friendly timber and stone thatched building stands by the church in a village beside the River Avon, and close to a magnificent barn owned by the National Trust. The exterior is especially pretty in summer when it's decked with brightly coloured hanging baskets; some of the picnic-sets out here are sheltered under Perspex. The open-plan carpeted bar has low beams, stone pillars and stripped timbers, a central woodburning stove, upholstered settles, a variety of wheelback, tub and kitchen chairs around handsome mahogany and cast-iron-framed tables, dried grasses and flowers and elegant wall lamps. There's a smaller side bar. Friendly efficient staff serve Banks's Bitter and Greene King Old Speckled Hen along with a guest such as Charles Wells Bombardier on handpump, and eight wines by the glass; piped music.

🍴 **Decent bar food includes lunchtime sandwiches, salads, ploughman's, as well as chicken liver pâté, roast mediterranean vegetable terrine, pork and leek sausages, smoked haddock on spring onion mash, scampi, mushroom risotto, beef bourguignon, battered cod, onion mash and mushroom risotto; half a crispy duck with orange and Grand Marnier sauce and steaks, with daily specials such as scallops in pernod sauce and cod loin wrapped in parma ham.** *Starters/Snacks: £3.95 to £5.95. Main Courses: £8.25 to £15.95. Puddings: £4.50*

Enterprise ~ Lease Cilla and Christopher Lamb ~ Real ale ~ Bar food (not Sun evening) ~ Restaurant ~ (01684) 772377 ~ Children welcome ~ Dogs allowed in bar ~ Open 12-3, 6.30-11(midnight Sat)

Recommended by Dr A J and Mrs Tompsett, Richard and Maria Gillespie, J S Burn, Gerry and Rosemary Dobson, Tom and Jill Jones, M Mossman

> Food details, prices, timing etc refer to bar food (if that's separate and different from any restaurant there).

BRETFORTON   SP0943   MAP 4

Fleece ★ £

B4035 E of Evesham: turn S off this road into village; pub is in centre square by church;
there's a sizeable car park at one side of the church; WR11 7JE

Marvellously unspoilt and deservedly popular medieval pub owned by the National Trust

Bequeathed to the National Trust in 1977, this museum-like old farmhouse and its
contents are pretty famous these days and as such it can draw the crowds. Before
becoming a pub in 1848 the building was owned by the same family for nearly 500 years
and many of the furnishings, such as the great oak dresser that holds a priceless 48-
piece set of Stuart pewter, are heirlooms passed down generations of that family, now
back in place. The rooms have massive beams and exposed timbers, and marks scored on
the worn and crazed flagstones to keep out demons. There are two fine grandfather
clocks, ancient kitchen chairs, curved high-backed settles, a rocking chair, and a rack of
heavy pointed iron shafts, probably for spit roasting, in one of the huge inglenook
fireplaces, and two more log fires. Plenty of oddities include a great cheese-press and set
of cheese moulds, and a rare dough-proving table; a leaflet details the more bizarre
items, and photographs report the terrible fire that struck this place several years ago.
Four or five real ales include Hook Norton Best and Uley Pigs Ear, with a couple of
guests from brewers such as Cannon Royall and Holdens on handpump, along with a farm
cider, local apple juices, german wheat bear and fruit wines, and ten wines by the glass;
darts and various board games. As part of the Vale of Evesham Asparagus Festival they
hold an asparagus auction at the end of May and host the village fête on August bank
holiday Monday; there's sometimes morris dancing, and the village silver band plays here
regularly too. The lawn (with its fruit trees) around the beautifully restored thatched and
timbered barn is a lovely place to sit, and there are more picnic-sets, and a stone pump-
trough in the front courtyard.

🍴 A shortish choice of bar food includes sandwiches, soup, baked camembert with
cranberry sauce, sausages or faggots and mash, steak and mushroom casserole with suet
dumplings, fish dish of the day and beefburger. *Starters/Snacks: £3.75 to £5.50. Main
Courses: £6.95 to £12.95. Puddings: £3.75 to £5.50*

Free house ~ Licensee Nigel Smith ~ Real ale ~ Bar food (12-2.30(4 Sun), 6.30-9(8.30 Sun)) ~
(01386) 831173 ~ Children welcome ~ Folk session Thurs evening ~ Open 11(12 Sun)-11;
11-3, 6-11 Mon-Thurs in winter ~ Bedrooms: /£85S

Recommended by Bob Broadhurst, Susan and John Douglas, Noel Grundy, Di and Mike Gillam, Ted George,
Carol and Colin Broadbent, MLR, Andrea Rampley, Pat and Tony Martin, John Wooll, Steve Whalley,
David A Hammond, Ann and Colin Hunt

CHILDSWICKHAM   SP0738   MAP 4

Childswickham Inn ♀

Village signposted off A44 just NW of Broadway; WR12 7HP

Dining pub with plenty of pleasant corners, contemporary furnishings and good food

The main area at this modernised place focuses on dining. It's attractively decorated
with big rugs on boards or broad terracotta tiles, more or less abstract contemporary
prints on part timbered walls painted cream and pale violet or mauve, candlesticks in
great variety, a woodburning stove and a piano. A carefully lit modern-style lounge-like
bar off to the right (snacks only, such as baguettes, in here) is light and airy, with a
similarly modern colour-scheme, paintings by local artists, leather armchairs and sofas,
and bamboo furniture; piped music. Hook Norton Hooky and Greene King Old Speckled
Hen on handpump, a good choice of over 50 french, italian and other wines (with ten by
the glass), and good coffee in elegant cups is served by friendly attentive staff from a
counter that seems made from old doors; good disabled access and facilities. A large
sunny deck outside has tables, and the garden, with its lawns and borders, is nicely
cottagey. More reports please.

⚑ Typical items on the lunchtime menu are baguettes, soup, curry and pie of the day, mushroom macaroni cheese. In the evening well presented food might be venison and juniper terrine, breaded brie with cranberry sauce, roast duck with honey, ginger and kumquat sauce, rack of lamb in red wine, garlic and thyme jus and puddings such as apple and berry crumble and sticky toffee pudding. *Starters/Snacks: £4.95 to £6.95. Main Courses: £6.95 to £10.95. Puddings: £4.50*

Punch ~ Tenant Carol Marshall ~ Real ale ~ Bar food (12-5 Sun) ~ Restaurant (not Sun evening or Mon lunch) ~ (01386) 852461 ~ Children welcome ~ Dogs allowed in bar ~ Open 12-3, 5.30-11; 12-5 Sun; closed Sun evening, Mon

Recommended by Michael Dandy, Edna Jones

CLENT
SO9279   MAP 4

Fountain ♀

Off A491 at Holy Cross/Clent exit roundabout, via Violet Lane, then turn right at T junction; Adams Hill/Odnall Lane; DY9 9PU

Often packed to overflowing, a restauranty pub popular with the well-heeled set

Although drinkers are welcome to stand at the bar (or sit if there is a table free) they may feel in the minority at this hugely popular, upmarket dining pub (booking is advised). With a buoyant atmosphere, the long carpeted dining bar (three knocked-together areas) is filled mainly by teak chairs and pedestal tables, with some comfortably cushioned brocaded wall seats. There are nicely framed local photographs on the ragged pinkish walls above a dark panelled dado, pretty wall lights, and candles on the tables (flowers in summer). Keen to please uniformed staff are friendly and efficient. Three changing real ales might be from brewers such as Jennings, Marstons and Wadworths, and 34 of their 40 wines are served by the glass; also a choice of speciality teas and good coffees, and freshly squeezed orange juice; alley skittles. There are tables out on a deck.

⚑ As well as a good selection of sandwiches at lunchtime, the daily changing menu might include apple and celery soup, chicken and partridge terrine, tiger prawns, battered haddock and chips, spinach, tomato, mozzarella and suet pudding, lamb pot roast, duck with red wine and cherry sauce, confit of pork with seared bass and cider cream sauce, and rather tasty-sounding puddings such as crème brûlée, chocolate Drambuie slice and bread and butter pudding; they may barbecue in summer. *Starters/Snacks: £4.95 to £7.50. Main Courses: £8.95 to £16.95. Puddings: £4.95 to £6.25*

Union Pub Company ~ Lease Richard and Jacque Macey ~ Real ale ~ Bar food (12-2.15(4.30 Sun), 6-9(9.30 Fri, Sat); sandwiches only, Sun evening) ~ (01562) 883286 ~ Children welcome till 8pm ~ Open 11am-12 midnight; 12-10.30(cl Sun evening in winter) Sun

Recommended by Theo, Anne and Jane Gaskin, Dr and Mrs A K Clarke, Susan and John Douglas, Dave Braisted, Neil and Brenda Skidmore, Lynda and Trevor Smith

DEFFORD
SO9042   MAP 4

Monkey House

A4104 towards Upton – immediately after passing Oak public house on right, there's a small group of cottages, of which this is the last; WR8 9BW

Astonishingly unspoilt time-warp survival with farm cider and a menagerie of animals

A lovely relic of a bygone age, this simple black and white thatched cider house has been in the same family for some 150 years. With no inn sign outside, it at first sight hardly resembles a pub at all. Drinks are limited to very inexpensive Bulmer's Medium or Special Dry cider tapped from barrels, poured by jug into pottery mugs (some locals have their own) and then served from a hatch beside the door. In the summer you could find yourself sharing the garden with the hens and cockerels that wander in from an adjacent collection of caravans and sheds; there's also a pony called Mandy, Tapper the jack russell, and Marie the rottweiler. Alternatively you can retreat to a small and spartan side outbuilding with a couple of plain tables, a settle and an open fire. The pub's name is said to come from a story about a drunken customer who, some years ago, fell into bramble bushes and swore that he was attacked by monkeys. Please note the limited opening times below.

🍴 **Apart from crisps and nuts they don't do food, but you can bring your own.**

Free house ~ Licensee Graham Collins ~ No credit cards ~ (01386) 750234 ~ Open 11-2, 6-10;
12-3 Sun; closed Tues, evenings Sun-Mon, lunchtimes Weds-Thurs

Recommended by Pete Baker, the Didler, R T and J C Moggridge

ELDERSFIELD   SO8131   MAP 4

Butchers Arms

Village signposted from B4211; Lime Street (coming from A417, go past the Eldersfield turn and take the next one), OS Sheet 150 map ref 815314; also signposted from B4208 N of Staunton; GL19 4NX

Good interesting cooking of prime ingredients in unspoilt country local's compact dining room

The food here is really rather special – so top marks to the new young chef/landlord and his wife for their determination in keeping the unpretentious local feel of the simple bar. With farm cider and well kept changing ales such as Malvern Hills Black Pear and Wye Valley Butty Bach tapped from the cask, this has one or two high bar chairs, plain but individual wooden chairs and tables on bare oak boards, a big woodburner in quite a cavernous fireplace, black beams and clean cut cream paintwork, and a traditional quoits board. Service is warmly friendly, as are the local regulars, and they have a short but well chosen choice of wines. The lavatories are strikingly modern, with an unusual mosaic in the gents'. Newish picnic-sets in the good-sized sheltered tree-shaded garden look out on pasture grazed by their own steers.

🍴 The little candlelit dining room, also simple, has just three tables, and at lunchtime James Winter cooks only for those who have booked – so you must ring (it's virtually essential to book evenings, too). Using first-class ingredients from named local farms, including rare-breed meats, line-caught fresh fish and all sorts of freshly gathered wild mushrooms (something of a speciality here), he keeps the choice short and seasonal, and changes it day by day. The results are full of flavour and interest. Starters might include tangy crab and avocado, fried pigeon breast with varying accompaniments, seared scallops with pork belly, and leek and stilton tartlet. For main course, perhaps sea trout with samphire, well hung hereford beef rib, rack of lamb with lentils, bacon and mint from the garden, and goats cheese gnocchi with local mushrooms. There's usually a substantial nursery pudding such as marmalade pudding with Drambuie custard, alongside interesting combinations of lighter tarts or cheesecake with fresh or cooked fruits. *Starters/Snacks: £5.50 to £9.00. Main Courses: £14.50 to £19.00. Puddings: £4.95 to £6.00*

Free house ~ Licensees James and Liz Winter ~ Real ale ~ Bar food (12-2, 7-8.30;
not Tues lunchtime or Sun evening) ~ (01452) 840381 ~ Children welcome ~ Open 12-2.30,
7-12(12.30 Fri, Sat); 12-3, 7-11.30 Sun; closed Mon

Recommended by Dr A J and Mrs Tompsett

HANLEY SWAN   SO8142   MAP 4

Swan 🛏

B4209 Malvern—Upton; WR8 0EA

Cheerful staff, stylish décor, and appealing rural setting

Clever contemporary elements contrast very successfully with original features at this well maintained country pub. Fresh cream paintwork, attractive new oak panelling, well chosen prints, and bright upholstery work well with older rough timbering and low beams, some stripped masonry, bare boards and logs heaped up by the fire. The layout comprises two main areas: the extended back part set for dining, with french windows looking out over the picnic-sets on the good-sized side lawn and its play area, and the front part, which is more conventional; each area has its own servery. Good sturdy dining tables have comfortably high-backed chairs, and one part of the bar has dark leather bucket armchairs; piped music, TV. On handpump, are Adnams, Charles Wells Bombardier and Shepherd Neame Spitfire; disabled access and facilities. The building is set well back from the road in lovely countryside, facing a classic village green, complete with duck pond and massive oak tree. They allow dogs in the bar only if the pub is quiet.

🍽 **Under new licensees bar food includes a good choice of wraps, baguettes and baked potatoes, and might include prawn cocktail, mussels in coconut milk with coriander, tasty home-made beefburger, steak and ale pie, red snapper fillet with apple and ginger chutney and chive mash, battered cod and mushy peas, greek salad, mushroom and parmesan tagliatelle with rocket salad and steaks; Sunday carvery.** *Starters/Snacks: £3.95 to £5.95. Main Courses: £8.95 to £12.95. Puddings: £3.95 to £6.00*

Punch ~ Lease Malcolm Heale and Julia Northover ~ Real ale ~ Bar food (12-2.30, 6.30-9) ~ Restaurant ~ (01684) 311870 ~ Children welcome ~ Dogs allowed in bar and bedrooms ~ Open 12-3, 6-11 ~ Bedrooms: /£65B

Recommended by P Dawn

HOLY CROSS
SO9278   MAP 4

Bell & Cross 🍽 ♀

4 miles from M5 junction 4: A491 towards Stourbridge, then follow Clent signpost off on left; DY9 9QL

WORCESTERSHIRE DINING PUB OF THE YEAR

Super food, staff with a can-do attitude, delightful old interior and pretty garden

This charming pub is the sort of rewarding place that works well as a dining pub and yet remains extremely welcoming if you're just popping in for a drink. Arranged in a classic unspoilt early 19th-c layout, five quaint little rooms and a kitchen open off a central corridor with a black and white tiled floor: they give a choice of carpet, bare boards, lino or nice old quarry tiles, a variety of moods from snug and chatty to bright and airy, and an individual décor in each – theatrical engravings on red walls here, nice sporting prints on pale green walls there, racing and gundog pictures above the black panelled dado in another room. Two of the rooms have small serving bars, with Timothy Taylors Landlord, Enville and Wye Valley HPA on handpump. You'll find over 50 wines (with 14 sold by the glass), a variety of coffees, daily papers, coal fires in most rooms, perhaps regulars playing cards in one of the two front ones, and piped music. You get pleasant views from the garden terrace. More reports please.

🍽 **As well as lunchtime sandwiches and panini, delicious dishes from a changing seasonal menu might include peking duck salad, cheeseburger, fishcakes with white wine and chive sauce, gnocchi with smoked salmon, leeks and chive cream sauce, steak pie, roast cod with prawn and parsley butter, sirloin steak, with puddings such as treacle sponge and Baileys crème brûlée with coffee ice-cream and biscotti biscuit.** *Starters/Snacks: £4.50 to £7.00. Main Courses: £7.95 to £14.50. Puddings: £5.00 to £5.50*

Enterprise ~ Managers Roger and Jo Narbett ~ Real ale ~ Bar food (12-2, 6.30-9.15(12-7 Sun)) ~ Restaurant ~ (01562) 730319 ~ Children welcome ~ Dogs allowed in bar ~ Open 12-3, 6-11; 12-10.30 Sun

Recommended by Pete Baker, Dr and Mrs A K Clarke, Paul and Bryony Walker, W H and E Thomas, David and Pauline, Dr D J and Mrs S C Walker, Dr Kevan Tucker, Susan and John Douglas

---

A very few pubs try to make you leave a credit card at the bar, as a sort of deposit if you order food. They are not entitled to do this. The credit card firms and banks which issue them warn you not to let them out of your sight. If someone behind the counter used your card fraudulently, the card company or bank could in theory hold you liable, because of your negligence in letting a stranger hang on to your card. Suggest instead that if they feel the need for security, they 'swipe' your card and give it back to you. And do name and shame the pub to us.

KEMPSEY   SO8548   MAP 4

Walter de Cantelupe ♀
A38, handy for M5 junction 7 via A44 and A4440; WR5 3NA

A warmly welcoming and unpretentious roadside inn, with enjoyable food and interesting drinks

We've always been keen on this friendly informal pub so we're very pleased to relay that since a new chef was employed (thus freeing up the charming landlord) reader reports have been full of praise, with no hint of service being overwhelmed by too many customers. It's a comfortably relaxed place, with a pleasant mix of well worn furniture, an old wind-up HMV gramophone and a good big fireplace. Drinks include Cannon Royall Kings Shilling, and three guests such as Jennings Cumberland, Timothy Taylors Landlord and Wye Valley Golden Ale on handpump, locally grown and pressed apple juices and a farm cider in summer, and wines from a local vineyard. Decorated in neutral colours, the dining area has various plush or yellow leather dining chairs, an old settle, a sonorous clock, and candles and flowers on the tables, piped music in the evenings, board games, cribbage, dominoes and table skittles. There's a pretty suntrap walled garden at the back and readers have enjoyed staying here. They sell jars of home-made chutney and marmalade.

🍴 **Food is good value and increasingly popular. The lunchtime bar menu includes sandwiches, soup, very good ploughman's, sausages and mash, pasta of the day, chicken curry and grilled gammon steak and egg. In the evening there might be ham hock terrine with pear and cider chutney, chickpea and coriander pâté, fish of the day, duck and sweet pepper stir fry on egg noodles, braised lamb shank with redcurrant and fresh rosemary sauce and sirloin steak, with puddings such as Baileys cheesecake with chocolate truffle and whisky crème brûlée.** *Starters/Snacks: £3.75 to £6.50. Main Courses: £7.50 to £10.50. Puddings: £3.75 to £4.50*

Free house ~ Licensee Martin Lloyd Morris ~ Real ale ~ Bar food (12-2, 7-9; 12-7 Sun and bank hols) ~ Restaurant ~ (01905) 820572 ~ Children in dining area until 8.15 ~ Dogs welcome ~ Folk music second Sun evening of month ~ Open 12-2.30(3 Sat), 6-11; 12-10.30 Sun; closed Mon except bank hols ~ Bedrooms: £50B/£65S(£80B)

Recommended by Dr and Mrs A K Clarke, David Morgan, Richard and Judy Winn, Peter and Jean Hoare, Ken Marshall, Comus and Sarah Elliott, Dr W J M Gissane, Mr and Mrs W D Borthwick, Hywel and Marilyn Roberts, Brian and Janet Ainscough

---

KIDDERMINSTER   SO8376   MAP 4

King & Castle ◀ £
Railway Station, Comberton Hill; DY10 1QX

Railway refreshment room within earshot of steam locos, and with one of the cheapest pints around

Owned and run by the Severn Valley Railway, this splendidly evocative place is a loving re-creation of an Edwardian refreshment room. It's right by the platform, so you can take your drink outside and happily while away time watching steam trains shunt in and out and passionate enthusiasts as they go about their work. Inside, the atmosphere is lively and sometimes noisily good-humoured, with a good mix of customers. Furnishings are solid and in character, and there's the railway memorabilia that you'd expect. Bathams and remarkably low-priced Wyre Piddle Royal Piddle (just £1.65 a pint) are superbly kept alongside a couple of changing guests from brewers such as Enville, Hobsons and Holdens on handpump, and they've several malt whiskies. The cheerful landlady and friendly staff cope well with the bank holiday and railway gala day crowds, though you'll be lucky to find a seat then. You can use a Rover ticket to shuttle between here and the Railwaymans Arms in Bridgnorth (see Shropshire chapter).

🍴 **The very reasonably priced straightforward menu includes toasted sandwiches, soup, ploughman's, hamburger in bap with chips, vegetable or chicken kiev, cottage pie, chicken tikka masala, battered cod and all-day breakfast; they also do children's meals, and sometimes Sunday lunch.** *Starters/Snacks: £2.75 to £5.00. Main Courses: £5.25 to £6.25. Puddings: £3.25*

Free house ~ Licensee Rosemary Hyde ~ Real ale ~ Bar food (12-3.30, 10-3 wknds) ~ No credit cards ~ (01562) 747505 ~ Children welcome if seated ~ Dogs allowed in bar ~ Monthly quiz night ~ Open 11-11; 12-10.30 Sun

Recommended by Joe Green, Andrew Bosi, Dennis Jones, R T and J C Moggridge

KNIGHTWICK

S07355   MAP 4

Talbot ♀ ◼ 🛏

Knightsford Bridge; B4197 just off A44 Worcester—Bromyard; WR6 5PH

Interesting old coaching inn with good beer from its own brewery, and riverside garden

Well kept on handpump and reasonably priced, the beers This, That, T'other and the seasonal ale at this friendly 15th-c coaching inn are brewed in their own Teme Valley microbrewery using locally grown hops. Efficient and welcoming uniformed staff also serve a guest such as Hobsons Bitter, as well as several different wines by the glass and a number of malt whiskies. With a good log fire in winter, the heavily beamed and extended carpeted lounge bar opens on to a terrace and arbour with summer roses and clematis. A variety of traditional seats runs from small carved or leatherette armchairs to the winged settles by the windows, and a vast stove squats in the big central stone hearth. The well furnished back public bar has pool on a raised side area, a games machine and juke box; cribbage. The pub has a lovely lawn across the lane by the River Teme (they serve out here too), or you can sit out in front on old-fashioned seats. A farmers' market takes place here on the second Sunday in the month.

🍽 **Bar food includes rolls, ploughman's, burgers, pork and game pie, moussaka, vegetarian quiche, battered fish and sirloin steak. There is a more expensive restaurant menu.**
Starters/Snacks: £6.50 to £8.50. Main Courses: £10.00 to £15.00. Puddings: £6.00

Own brew ~ Licensee Annie Clift ~ Real ale ~ Bar food (12-2, 6.30(7 Sun)-9) ~ Restaurant ~ (01886) 821235 ~ Children welcome ~ Dogs allowed in bar and bedrooms ~ Open 11-11; 12-10.30 Sun ~ Bedrooms: £50S/£84B

Recommended by John Holroyd, Ann and Colin Hunt, David Dyson, MP, Noel Grundy, Kevin Thorpe

MALVERN

S07845   MAP 4

Nags Head ◼

Bottom end of Bank Street, steep turn down off A449; WR14 2JG

Remarkable range of real ales, appealing layout and décor, and warmly welcoming atmosphere

This is a terrifically enjoyable little pub, with readers loving its splendid individuality. Its superb range of well kept beer and tasty bar food attract a good mix of customers, including plenty of locals, and the mood is chatty and easy-going. A series of snug individually decorated rooms, with one or two steps between, gives plenty of options on where to sit. Each is charactefully filled with all sorts of chairs including leather armchairs, pews sometimes arranged as booths, a mix of tables with sturdy ones stained different colours, bare boards here, flagstones there, carpet elsewhere, and plenty of interesting pictures and homely touches such as house plants and shelves of well thumbed books, a coal fire opposite the central servery, broadsheet newspapers, shove-ha'penny, cribbage and dominoes, and a good juke box; piped music. If you feel confused by the astonishing range of 16 beers here they will happily help you with a taster. House beers are Banks's, Bathams, Marstons Pedigree, St Georges Charger, Dragon Blood, Maidens Saviour, and Woods Shropshire Lad and their nine changing guests (last year they got through over 1,000) come from a tremendous spread of brewers far and wide. They also keep a fine range of malt whiskies, belgian beers, Barbourne farm cider and decent wines by the glass. Outside are picnic-sets and rustic tables and benches on the front terrace (with heaters and umbrellas) and in a garden.

🍽 Tasty lunchtime bar food includes good sandwiches, ploughman's, soup, an antipasti board, ham, egg and chips and fish and chips. In the evenings they do meals (more expensive) only in the extension barn dining room. It's worth arriving early as they don't take bookings. *Starters/Snacks: £3.50 to £10.50. Main Courses: £8.50 to £10.80. Puddings: £4.00 to £5.00.*

Free house ~ Licensee Clare Willets ~ Real ale ~ Bar food (12-2, 6.30-8.30) ~ Restaurant ~ (01684) 574373 ~ Children welcome ~ Dogs welcome ~ Open 11am-11.15pm(11.30 Fri, Sat); 12-11 Sun

Recommended by Alistair Forsyth, C Galloway, Dr and Mrs Jackson, P Dawn, Chris Evans, Mike and Mary Carter, R T and J C Moggridge, Steve Whalley, Richard, Arthur S Maxted, Paul J Robinshaw, Barry Collett, Ray and Winifred Halliday

OMBERSLEY   SO8463   MAP 4
Kings Arms
Main Road (A4133); WR9 0EW

Cosy Tudor building with tasty food and attractive courtyard

King Charles is reputed to have stopped at this striking black and white timbered inn after fleeing the Battle of Worcester in 1651 – one room has his coat of arms moulded into its decorated plaster ceiling as a trophy of the visit. The building is said to date from about the 1400s, and the various wood-floored cosy nooks and crannies, and three splendid fireplaces with good log fires, certainly show signs of great age. The charming rambling interior has fresh flowers throughout, and lots of rustic bric-a-brac. Service is warmly friendly, Marstons Best and Pedigree and a couple of guests such as Black Sheep and Jennings Cocker Hoop on handpump are well kept, and they've darts and board games. A tree-sheltered courtyard has tables under cocktail parasols, and colourful hanging baskets and tubs in summer, and there's another terrace.

🍽 As well as lunchtime sandwiches, enjoyable sensibly priced bar food might include steamed thai mussels, antipasti, smoked haddock risotto, lamb kebab with mint yoghurt and couscous, seared tuna with caper and dill butter, fish pie, mustard and beer-battered fish with pea and mint purée, 28-day-aged ribeye steak, with puddings such as treacle pudding and jam roly-poly. *Starters/Snacks: £4.50 to £10.95. Main Courses: £7.95 to £19.95. Puddings: £4.50 to £5.00.*

Banks's (Marstons) ~ Lease Caroline Cassell ~ Real ale ~ Bar food (12-2.30, 6-8.30) ~ (01905) 620142 ~ Children welcome ~ Dogs allowed in bar ~ Open 12-11(midnight Sat); 12-10.30 Sun

Recommended by Paul and Sue Merrick, Robert W Buckle, Nigel and Sue Foster, Arthur S Maxted

PENSAX   SO7368   MAP 4
Bell 🍺 £
B4202 Abberley—Clows Top, SE of the Snead Common part of the village; WR6 6AE

Admirably welcoming all-rounder, good fire and tasty, reasonably priced tasty food

Very much a proper pub, this mock-Tudor place extends a genuinely friendly welcome – a great backdrop for its tasty food and good range of drinks. As well as Hobsons Best, four or five changing beers on handpump might be from brewers such as Cannon Royall, Timothy Taylors, Woods and Wye Valley, they've three local ciders and a local perry and organic fruit juices; they host a beer festival during the last weekend of June. The L-shaped main bar has a restrained traditional décor, with long cushioned pews on its bare boards, good solid pub tables and a woodburning stove. Beyond a small area on the left, with a couple more tables, is a more airy dining room, with french windows opening on to a wooden deck. Picnic-sets in the back garden look out over rolling fields and copses to the Wyre Forest.

🍴 Besides sandwiches a short choice of good value tasty lunchtime weekday specials such as steak and ale pie, vegetable stir fry, sausage and mash and pasta bake, hearty enjoyable evening specials could include steaks, faggots and pork chop with black pudding; Sunday roast and children's menu. *Starters/Snacks: £3.50 to £4.95. Main Courses: £7.50 to £13.95. Puddings: £3.75*

Free house ~ Licensees John and Trudy Greaves ~ Real ale ~ Bar food (12-2(3 Sun), 6-9; not Sun evening) ~ (01299) 896677 ~ Children welcome away from the bar ~ Dogs allowed in bar ~ Open 12-2.30, 5-11; 12-10.30 Sun; closed Mon lunchtime except bank hols

Recommended by Lynda and Trevor Smith, Ian Stafford, Dr A J and Mrs Tompsett, Jean Stidwell, Chris and Maggie Kent, Dennis and Gill Keen

LUCKY DIP

Besides the fully inspected pubs, you might like to try these Lucky Dips recommended to us and described by readers (if you do, please send us reports: feedback@thegoodpubguide.co.uk).

ABBERLEY [SO7567]
Manor Arms WR6 6BN: Good value comfortable country inn nicely tucked away in quiet village backwater, façade emblazoned with coats of arms, warm welcome, quick friendly service, Timothy Taylors Landlord and Wye Valley HPA, generous food from tasty baguettes up, two bars and restaurant, interesting toby jug collection; ten bedrooms *(Carol and Colin Broadbent, W H and E Thomas, Alan and Eve Harding)*
ALVECHURCH [SP0172]
Weighbridge B48 7SQ [Scarfield Wharf]: Recently converted house by Worcester & Birmingham Canal marina, several neat linked rooms, well kept ales such as Blue Bear, Sadlers and Weatheroak, bargain unpretentious food with home-grown veg; tables outside *(Dave Braisted)*
ASHTON UNDER HILL [SO9938]
Star WR11 7SN [Elmley Rd]: Small comfortably carpeted pub in quiet village below Bredon Hill, decent quickly served pubby food from fresh baguettes up, real ales inc Shepherd Neame Spitfire, friendly staff; good garden, has been cl Mon/Tues lunchtimes *(Pat Crabb, Martin and Pauline Jennings)*
BADSEY [SP0743]
☆*Round of Gras* WR11 7XQ [B4035 (Bretforton Rd) 2 miles E of Evesham]: Popular for substantial well priced food inc Weds and Sun carvery, seasonal asparagus feasts, comfortable carpeted open-plan bar with log fire, lots of polished wood and panelling, welcoming staff, good ale range, Weston's farm cider, raised restaurant section, games area with darts, pool and TV; children welcome, fair-sized tree-shaded garden with pets corner, open all day *(BB, Martin and Pauline Jennings)*
Wheatsheaf WR11 7EJ [E of Evesham; High St]: Friendly country-style pub with enjoyable home-made food inc local asparagus in season, well kept ales such as Fullers London Pride, good wines by the glass, efficient service even when busy, beams, flagstones, darts and log fire, comfortable carpeted

stripped-stone dining room; garden tables, four bedrooms *(K H Frostick)*
BASTONFORD [SO8150]
Halfway House WR2 4SL [A449 Worcester—Malvern]: Spacious and bright restauranty pub with good traditional food (separate meat and fish menus), well kept local ales and farm cider, no machines or juke box; tables and play area in garden, has been open all day Sat in summer *(Chris Evans, BB)*
BECKFORD [SO9835]
☆*Beckford Hotel* GL20 7AN [A435]: Attractive up-to-date furnishings along with bar's beams, log fires and some stripped stone, real ales such as Fullers London Pride, Purity and Theakstons XB, good range of wines by the glass, good service, some emphasis on wide choice of good value food from sandwiches up, smart dining room; large well kept garden, eight comfortable bedrooms, good breakfast *(Joyce and Maurice Cottrell)*
BELBROUGHTON [SO9277]
Olde Horse Shoe DY9 9ST [High St]: Extensively reworked by new owners, enjoyable fresh food inc good value lunches in separate restaurant area, good service, real ales, good value wines, properly pubby bar *(Ian Jones)*
BERROW GREEN [SO7458]
☆*Admiral Rodney* WR6 6PL [B4197, off A44 W of Worcester]: Light and roomy high-beamed dining pub, big stripped kitchen tables and woodburner, Wye Valley and a couple of guest ales, good coffee and choice of wines by the glass, enjoyable generous food inc interesting vegetarian dishes, charming end restaurant in rebuilt barn; children and dogs welcome, tables outside with pretty view and heated covered terrace, good walks, three good bedrooms, cl Mon lunchtime, open all day wknds *(Chris Evans, Antony Townsend, Katie Carter, Denys Gueroult, LYM)*
BIRLINGHAM [SO9343]
Swan WR10 3AQ [off A4104 and B4080 S of Pershore; Church St]: Friendly thatched and timbered country pub in quiet village backwater, good reasonably priced straightforward food (great faggots), well kept and interesting quickly changing real

ales; nice garden (and snowdrops in village churchyard well worth seeing in season) *(Caroline and Michael Abbey, Chris Evans)*

BRANSFORD [SO8052]

☆ *Bear & Ragged Staff* WR6 5JH [off A4103 SW of Worcester; Station Rd]: Popular upscale dining pub (use some of their own veg), friendly licensees and staff, good range of wines by the glass, lots of malt whiskies, St Georges Best and a guest such as Fullers London Pride, open fire, country views from relaxed linked rooms; piped music; children welcome, good disabled access and facilities, pleasant secluded garden *(Michael and Maggie Betton, John Saville, Ken Millar, Jeff and Wendy Williams, LYM, Ann and Colin Hunt)*

Fox WR6 5JL [Bransford Court Lane (A4103 Worcester—Hereford)]: Attractive Chef & Brewer well divided to give cosy areas, decent food all day, local suppliers, friendly staff, real ales *(Chris Evans, A J N Johnston)*

BROADWAY [SP0937]

☆ *Crown & Trumpet* WR12 7AE [Church St]: Cheerful 17th-c golden stone beamed local just behind green, friendly staff, changing ales such as Flowers, Greene King and local Stanway, pub food, log fires, traditional games; they may try to keep your credit card while you eat, piped music, live Sat, games machines; children welcome, front terrace, bedrooms, open all day wknds and summer *(Robert Ager, Ted George, LYM, Malcolm Pellatt, Michael Dandy)*

☆ *Lygon Arms* WR12 7DU [High St]: Handsome Cotswold hotel with interesting old rooms rambling away from attractive oak-panelled bar, splendid restaurant; adjoining bar/brasserie has good imaginative food, quick attentive service, good wines; children welcome, prettily planted courtyard (dogs allowed here), well kept gardens, smart comfortable bedrooms, open all day in summer *(LYM, Michael Dandy)*

BROMSGROVE [SO9570]

Red Lion B61 8AQ [High St]: Cheap cheerful bar lunches and good beer in congenial Banks's pub - typical of how high-street pubs used to be; covered terrace, open all day, cl Sun evening *(Dave Braisted)*

BROUGHTON HACKETT [SO9254]

March Hare WR7 4BE [A422 Worcester—Alcester]: Marstons food pub with good specials and tempting puddings, well kept Banks's, good coffee, country décor, glass-covered floodlit well; garden with play area *(BB, Chris Evans)*

CALLOW END [SO8349]

Old Bush WR2 4TE [Upton Rd]: Good range of Marstons-related ales, good value standard bar meals inc great range of lunchtime baguettes, pleasant staff, cosy small areas around central bar, restaurant *(Dr and Mrs Jackson)*

CALLOW HILL [SO7473]

Royal Forester DY14 9XW [nr Wyre Forest visitors' centre]: Dining pub dating in part

from 15th c, good if not cheap food from lunchtime sandwiches to full meals, modern leather settees and bucket armchairs in lounge bar with two well kept ales such as Caledonian Deuchars IPA and Timothy Taylors Landlord, pleasant service; children welcome, seven stylish contemporary bedrooms *(Chris and Maggie Kent, W H and E Thomas)*

CASTLEMORTON [SO7838]

Plume of Feathers WR13 6JB [B4208]: Friendly country local with well kept changing ales such as Hobsons and St Georges, heavy black beams (one studded with regulars' holiday PCs), big log fire snugged in by built-in settles, side room with darts and games machine, attractively priced home cooking (not Sun evening), small neat dining room; children welcome, swings on side lawn, good views, open all day *(Dr and Mrs Jackson, BB)*

Robin Hood WR13 6BS [Gloucester Rd (B4208, 1.2 miles S of Welland crossroads)]: Charming old timbered and beamed country pub below Malvern Hills, good value food, well kept Wadworths 6X, Weston's cider, welcoming service, relaxed atmosphere, medley of cushioned pews etc, big brick fireplace, lots of jugs and horsebrasses, dining room; big lawns and space for caravans behind *(Chris Evans)*

CHADDESLEY CORBETT [SO8973]

Fox DY10 4QN [A448 Bromsgrove—Kidderminster]: Several eating and drinking areas, very popular for bargain OAP lunches (need to book) and carvery, four real ales inc Enville, Hobsons and Theakstons, pleasant attentive service; open all day wknds *(W H and E Thomas)*

CLAINES [SO8558]

Mug House WR3 7RN [Claines Lane, off A449 3 miles W of M5 junction 3]: Fine views from ancient country tavern in unique churchyard setting by fields below the Malvern Hills, sympathetically refurbished keeping low doorways and heavy oak beams, well kept Banks's Bitter and Mild, bargain simple generous snacks (not Sun); children allowed in snug away from servery *(Andy and Jill Kassube, LYM, Dave Braisted)*

CLENT [SO9279]

☆ *Hill Tavern* DY9 9PS [Adams Hill]: At foot of Clent Hills (right by the car park), with new licensees doing good home-made food all day from baguettes to restaurant dishes, Sun carvery, well kept real ales, farm cider, good choice of wines by the glass, skittle alley; children welcome, pork scratchings etc for dogs, disabled facilities, pleasant terrace *(L Davies, L Coghlan)*

CROPTHORNE [SO9944]

New Inn WR10 3NE [Main Rd (B4084 former A44 Evesham—Pershore)]: Popular food pub, good choice (all day wknds) using local produce from ciabattas up, well kept changing ales such as Black Sheep and Hook Norton, paintings for sale; piped music may be loud, food service may stop if busy; children welcome, large garden, open all day wknds *(Steve and Liz Tilley, K H Frostick, Phyllis McCombie, Matt)*

CUTNALL GREEN [SO8868]
Chequers WR9 OPJ [Kidderminster Rd]: Comfortable and stylish beamed country dining pub with enjoyable food from pubby lunchtime snacks and sandwiches to some good imaginative dishes and pretty little puddings, pleasant atmosphere, good wine choice, real ales *(W H and E Thomas)*

DRAKES BROUGHTON [SO9248]
☆ *Plough & Harrow* WR10 2AG [A44 NW of Pershore]: Well run dining pub with sensible prices and bargain OAP helpings, friendly courteous staff, two or three well kept ales changing weekly, good-sized restaurant area, comfortable and attractive rambling lounge, log fire; may be two sittings on busy days; good disabled access, pleasant terrace, big orchard-side garden with play area, open all day *(Mr and Mrs F E Boxell, W H and E Thomas, Theo, Anne and Jane Gaskin)*

DROITWICH [SO9063]
Hop Pole WR9 8ED [Friar St]: Heavy-beamed 16th-c local with friendly staff, well kept ales such as Malvern Hills and Wye Valley, bargain basic home-made lunchtime food from sandwiches to popular Sun roasts, dominoes, darts, pool; loud music Thurs-Sat evenings, otherwise quiet; partly canopied back garden, open all day *(Andy and Jill Kassube, Dr B and Mrs P B Baker, Pete Baker, R T and J C Moggridge)*
Old Cock WR9 8EQ [Friar St]: Several distinctive rooms, beams and stained-glass, friendly staff, well kept real ales, sensibly short choice of good fresh local food, reasonable prices; garden courtyard with pool and fountain *(Michael and Lynne Gittins)*

ECKINGTON [SO9241]
Bell WR10 3AN [Church St (B4080)]: Smart and attractive village pub with enjoyable food from sandwiches to more sophisticated main dishes, good range of beers and wines, nice staff, central servery for pleasant bar and big dining area, cool dining conservatory, pool *(Mr and Mrs F E Boxell, Dr A J and Mrs Tompsett)*

EVESHAM [SP0344]
Evesham Hotel WR11 6DA [Coopers Lane]: Large hotel worth knowing for its bar's amazing range of malt whiskies and spirits, good if quirky wine list, interesting menu inc good value lunchtime buffet, remarkable lavatories; children welcome, indoor swimming pool, 40 bedrooms *(Denys Gueroult)*

FAR FOREST [SO7274]
Plough DY14 9TE [A4117 Bewdley—Ludlow, just W of junction with A456]: Bright and cosy beamed dining area popular lunchtime with older people for wide-ranging good value food inc carvery, Greene King Abbot, quick friendly service, small bar, woodburner, lots of brass and china; plenty of picnic-sets on neat lawn, good walks *(J Roy Smylie)*

FECKENHAM [SP0061]
☆ *Lygon Arms* B96 6JE [B4090 Droitwich—Alcester]: Welcoming timber-framed pub with good interesting specials using fresh ingredients, small helpings available, real ales inc two local ones brewed for them, reasonably priced wines, traditional bar, attractive dining conservatory *(Dave Braisted)*

FINSTALL [SO9870]
Cross B60 1EW [Alcester Rd]: New licensees doing short range of hearty old-fashioned specials alongside good value usual pub food, well kept Enville ale, pine-panelled lounge and small timbered snug; perched high above road, tables on sheltered lawn *(LYM, Dave Braisted)*

FORHILL [SP0575]
☆ *Peacock* B38 0EH [handy for M42, junctions 2 and 3; pub at junction Lea End Lane and Icknield St]: Attractive, quietly placed and well run Chef & Brewer with wide range of generous enjoyable food, plenty of tables in comfortably fitted knocked-through beamed rooms, woodburner in big inglenook, Enville, Hobsons Best, Theakstons Old Peculier and two changing ales, friendly prompt helpful service; piped classical music; children welcome, picnic-sets on back terrace and front grass, open all day *(John Beeken, Dennis and Gill Keen, LYM)*

GREAT WITLEY [SO7566]
☆ *Hundred House* WR6 6HS [Worcester Rd]: Handsome much-modernised hotel (former Georgian coaching inn and magistrates' court), friendly quick service, well kept Banks's ales, good house wines, good choice of good value food from sandwiches up inc good Sun lunch, pleasant restaurant; no dogs; 27 bedrooms, handy for ruined Witley Court and remarkable church *(Chris Evans, Alan and Eve Harding)*

GRIMLEY [SO8359]
Camp House WR2 6LX [A443 5 miles N from Worcester, right to Grimley, right at village T]: Unspoilt old character pub in pleasant Severnside setting with own landing stage, generous bargain food from huge cobs to good seafood, Bathams, local farm cider as well as Thatcher's, friendly staff; children and well behaved dogs welcome, attractive lawns *(Chris Evans, Kerry Law)*

GUARLFORD [SO8245]
Plough & Harrow WR13 6NY [B4211 W of Malvern]: Charmingly updated timbered country pub, friendly helpful young licensees, good if not cheap food inc their own produce, well kept Wadworths, good choice of wines by the glass, comfortable cottagey bar and beamed dining room; attractive good-sized garden, nice spot on open common, cl Sun evening and Mon *(Peter Wickens, P Dawn, W H and E Thomas)*

HANLEY CASTLE [SO8342]
☆ *Three Kings* WR8 0BL [Church End, off B4211 N of Upton upon Severn]: By no means smart, even a little unkempt, a favourite for those who put unspoilt character and individuality first; friendly and homely, with huge inglenook and hatch service in little tiled-floor tap room, consistently well kept

Butcombe, Hobsons Best and two or three changing beers from small breweries usually inc a Mild, Nov beer festival, farm cider, dozens of malt whiskies, two other larger rooms, one with fire in open range, low-priced food (not Sun evening - singer then; be prepared for a possibly longish wait other times), seats of a sort outside *(Carol and Colin Broadbent, Mrs M B Gregg, Pete Baker, the Didler, LYM)*

INKBERROW [SP0157]

☆ *Old Bull* WR7 4DZ [off A422 - note that this is quite different from the nearby Bulls Head]: Photogenic Tudor pub with lots of *Archers* memorabilia (it's the model for the Ambridge Bull), friendly service, bargain pub lunches and Fri night fish and chips, real ales, big log fire in huge inglenook, bulging walls, flagstones, oak beams and trusses, some old-fashioned high-backed settles among more modern furnishings; children allowed in eating area, plenty of tables outside *(Dave Braisted, LYM)*

KEMERTON [SO9437]

Crown GL20 7HP [back rd Bredon—Beckford]: 18th-c pub with modern light furnishings in smallish L-shaped lounge bar and dining area, bargain pubby food from sandwiches up, three real ales, farm cider, friendly service; peaceful garden, upmarket village worth a look around, good walks over Bredon Hill *(Warren Marsh)*

KIDDERMINSTER [SO8376]

Olde Seven Stars DY10 2BG [Coventry St]: Cosy and friendly recently reopened town pub, bare boards, panelling and coal fire, good range of well kept changing ales such as Adnams, Hobsons Mild and Ludlow, may be filled cobs, plates and cutlery provided if you bring a takeaway; terrace with smokers' shelter, open all day (Sun afternoon break) *(Kevin Bridgewater)*

KINNERSLEY [SO8743]

☆ *Royal Oak* WR8 9JR [off A38 S of Worcester]: Welcoming well run 18th-c pub with chef/landlord doing interesting reasonably priced food from lunchtime sandwiches up, friendly staff, good atmosphere and log fire in comfortable carpeted bar, well kept ales such as Fullers London Pride, Hook Norton and Timothy Taylors Landlord, good choice of wines by the glass, conservatory restaurant; three bedrooms in newly refurbished back block *(Chris Evans, Moira Terrett, Dr A J and Mrs Tompsett, J Graveling, C D Watson)*

LEIGH SINTON [SO7850]

☆ *Royal Oak* WR13 5DZ [Malvern Rd, junction with A4103 SW of Worcester]: Well run dining pub with enjoyable cheap pubby food very popular with older lunchers for its value, notable Sun lunch and bargain Mon buffet, charming efficient staff, Marstons-related ales, short choice of reasonably priced wines, coal fire, cheerful cartoons and polished bric-a-brac in carpeted beamed bar, attractive smallish restaurant quickly fills; flower-filled garden behind with cushioned seats in sheltered alcoves *(Denys Gueroult, Chris Evans, JCW)*

LONGDON [SO8434]

☆ *Hunters Inn* GL20 6AR [B4211 S, towards Tewkesbury]: Attractive décor with beams, flagstones, timbers, some stripped brick and log fires, welcoming young licensees, imaginative food (all day wknds) inc fresh fish, exotic dishes and good value Sun lunch, real ales such as Malvern Hills and Wells & Youngs Bombardier, good choice of wines by the glass, raftered dining area, good views; new bedrooms, extensive well tended garden *(Dr A J and Mrs Tompsett, Carol and Colin Broadbent, Mr and Mrs F E Boxell, LYM)*

LOWER BROADHEATH [SO8055]

Plough WR2 6RH [off A44 into Crown East Lane W of Worcester (first right, after A4103/A4440 roundabout)]: Village pub next to Elgar's birthplace museum, good value food inc popular OAP bargain lunches, friendly staff, real ales; garden with play area *(Chris Evans)*

MALVERN [SO7640]

☆ *Malvern Hills Hotel* WR13 6DW [opp British Camp car park, Wynds Point; junction A449/B4232 S]: Big comfortable dark-panelled lounge bar, very popular wknds (plenty of friendly staff), decent bar food, well kept changing ales such as Wye Valley and local Malvern Hills, quite a few malt whiskies, good coffee, open fire, downstairs pool room, smart more expensive restaurant, well reproduced piped music; they may try to keep your credit card while you eat; dogs welcome, great views from terrace, bedrooms small but comfortable, open all day - fine position high in the hills *(Mark Farrington, Dr and Mrs Jackson, Lawrence Pearse, BB, P Dawn)*

MALVERN WELLS [SO7742]

Railway Inn WR14 4PA [Wells Rd (A449 towards Ledbury)]: Nicely placed pub with wide choice of enjoyable food, friendly staff, Marstons-related ales, restaurant, skittle alley and pool table; terrace tables, fine views *(P Dawn, Maureen and Keith Gimson)*

MAMBLE [SO6971]

Sun & Slipper DY14 9JL [just off A456 Bewdley—Tenbury Wells]: Chatty and attractive two-room 16th-c village pub, well kept Banks's, Hobsons and a guest beer, good value food, log fires, friendly dog, darts, dominoes and pool; picnic-sets outside, cl Mon *(Pete Baker, BB, Dave Braisted)*

MARTLEY [SO7560]

Crown WR6 6PA: Pleasant light décor, friendly staff, enjoyable fresh food using local supplies, several real ales, good wines by the glass and nice coffee, comfortable contemporary furniture on bare wood floors, separate dining area, charity book sales; children and dogs welcome (hitching rail for horses too), good big garden with play area, lovely walks nearby *(anon)*

Masons Arms WR6 6YA [B4204 E]: Unusually good thai food as well as standard dishes, charming attentive service, four real ales, good coffee, decent wines, comfortable bar and dining lounge, separate raftered restaurant (acoustics rather lively); garden with country views and play area *(Denys Gueroult)*

OFFENHAM [SP0545]
Bridge WR11 8QZ [Boat Lane]: Smart light refurbishment after 2007 Avon floods - perhaps easier to find by boat than by road (the bridge went years ago, as did the ferry that replaced it); friendly landlord, mulled and country wines, enjoyable food (can take a while) from baguettes up; pleasant riverside garden *(Caroline and Michael Abbey)*

OMBERSLEY [SO8463]
☆ *Cross Keys* WR9 0DS [just off A449; Main Rd (A4133, Kidderminster end)]: Nicely decorated beamed front bar with cosy areas inc armchairs and sofa, Banks's and Timothy Taylors, good value wines by the glass, good-humoured helpful and efficient service, good food inc enterprising dishes, smart conservatory restaurant *(Dr and Mrs Jackson, Dave Braisted)*

PEOPLETON [SO9350]
Crown WR10 2EE: Peaceful village pub, pretty and cosy, beamed bar with big inglenook fireplace, enterprising if not cheap food, good wines by the glass and coffee, friendly efficient service; flower-filled back garden *(Chris Evans, Caroline and Michael Abbey)*

PERSHORE [SO9545]
☆ *Brandy Cask* WR10 1AJ [Bridge St]: Plain high-ceilinged bow-windowed bar, back courtyard brewery producing their own good ales, guest beers too, Aug beer festival, quick friendly helpful service, coal fire, food from sandwiches to steaks, quaintly decorated dining room; well behaved children allowed, long attractive garden down to river (keep a careful eye on the kids), with terrace, vine arbour and koi pond *(the Didler, BB, Kerry Law)*

RASHWOOD [SO9165]
Robin Hood WR9 0BS [A38, 0.5 mile SW of M5 junction 5]: Bustling dining pub with good reasonably priced homely food, friendly staff, well kept Bass, log fire; picnic-sets on small side terrace *(Nigel and Sue Foster)*

REDDITCH [SP0367]
Golden Cross B97 4RA [Unicorn Hill]: Banks's and guest beers such as Black Sheep and Freeminer, attractive arthurian-theme carvery *(Roger Fletcher)*

SEDGEBERROW [SP0238]
Queens Head WR11 7UE [Main St (B4078, just off A46 S of Evesham)]: Friendly village local with good value simple food, cheerful service, Hook Norton and one or two guest beers, farm cider, attractive plain redecoration (see the 2007 flood marker), comfortable settees one end, darts, dining end allowing children; open all day wknds *(Pete Baker, Stuart Doughty)*

SHATTERFORD [SO7981]
☆ *Bellmans Cross* DY12 1RN [Bridgnorth Rd (A442)]: French-mood dining pub with good interesting food from sandwiches up inc good Sun lunch, smart tasteful restaurant with kitchen view, french chefs and bar staff, pleasant deft service, neat timber-effect bar with Bass, Greene King Old Speckled Hen and a guest beer, good choice of wines by the glass inc champagne, teas and coffees; picnic-sets outside, handy for Severn Woods walks, open all day wknds *(BB, Lynda and Trevor Smith, Theo, Anne and Jane Gaskin, Richard Tosswill)*

SHENSTONE [SO8573]
Granary DY10 4BS [Heath Lane]: Contemporary bar, lounge and dining room very popular for good value OAP carvery, good friendly service; 18 comfortable bedrooms *(W H and E Thomas)*

SINTON GREEN [SO8160]
Hunters Lodge WR2 6NT: Quiet and attractive country pub with owner cooking enjoyable generous fresh food *(Chris Evans)*

STOKE POUND [SO9667]
☆ *Queens* B60 3AU [Sugarbrook Lane, by Bridge 48, Worcester & Birmingham Canal]: Waterside dining pub with enjoyable promptly served food in bar and restaurant, generous if not cheap, inc popular Sun lunch, friendly staff, attractive minimalist contemporary décor, exemplary lavatories; nice garden with play area, large covered waterside terrace, moorings, good walk up the 36 locks of the Tardebigge Steps, quite handy for Avoncroft buildings museum *(Mike and Mary Carter, Bob Dudley, Mrs B H Adams)*

STOKE PRIOR [SO9467]
Ewe & Lamb B60 4DN [Hanbury Rd (B4091)]: Beamed dining pub with some interesting dishes, pleasant décor; attractive garden *(Dave Braisted)*
Gate Hangs Well B60 4HG [Woodgate Rd, off B4091 Hanbury Rd via Moorgate Rd]: Well divided open-plan dining pub keeping balance between its popular carvery (and other good value generous food from sandwiches up, not Mon lunchtime) and its bar side, with good local atmosphere, Banks's special brews and three or four well kept guest beers, friendly service, conservatory and country views; garden picnic-sets, some on decking, open all day wknds *(Dave Braisted)*

STOKE WHARF [SO9468]
Navigation B60 4LB [Hanbury Rd (B4091), by Worcester & Birmingham Canal]: Friendly and comfortabe, popular for good value food and well kept changing ales *(Paul J Robinshaw, Dave Braisted)*

STOKE WORKS [SO9365]
Boat & Railway B60 4EQ [Shaw Lane, by Bridge 42 of Worcester & Birmingham Canal]: Popular and unpretentious, with happy old-fashioned atmosphere, efficient service with a smile, Banks's and related ales, bargain

generous lunchtime food, good carvery in former skittle alley; pretty hanging baskets, pleasant covered waterside terrace *(Dave Braisted)*

Bowling Green B60 4BH [a mile from M5 Junction 5, via Stoke Lane; handy for Worcester & Birmingham Canal]: Attractive and comfortable, with bargain traditional food, Banks's Bitter and Mild, good atmosphere, polished fireplace; big garden with neat bowling green *(Dave Braisted)*

TENBURY WELLS [SO5968]

☆ *Pembroke House* WR15 8EQ [Cross St]: Striking timbered building, oldest in town, combining bustling pub side (lots to look at in well divided open-plan beamed bars) with upmarket dining side, popular with older people lunchtime (not Mon) for fair-priced above-average food from sandwiches up, more elaborate evening meals (not Sun/Mon), friendly helpful staff, Hobsons and a guest beer such as Bathams, woodburner; open all day wknds *(MLR, Ann and Colin Hunt, Denys Gueroult)*

UPTON UPON SEVERN [SO8540]

White Lion WR8 0HJ [High St]: Family-run hotel's pleasant relaxed bar, well kept Greene King and other ales, helpful staff, comfortable bucket chairs, sofas and old prints, food in bar and brasserie; covered courtyard, 13 bedrooms *(P Dawn, Chris Evans, BB)*

WEST MALVERN [SO7645]

☆ *Brewers Arms* WR14 4BQ [The Dingle]: Friendly and energetic landlord keeping Marstons Bitter and Pedigree and three guest beers in top condition (Oct beer festival) in spotless and attractive little two-room beamed country local down steep path from the road, good atmosphere, good value food (all day wknds, breakfast from 9 then) from good fresh sandwiches up, OAP wkdy lunches, neat and airy separate dining room, amiable pub cat; glorious view from small

garden, well placed for walks *(Alan Bowker, Ian and Denise Foster)*

Lamb WR14 4NG [West Malvern Rd]: Intriguing mix of customers and quirky décor, not a place for shrinking violets, with well kept ales such as Black Sheep and Timothy Taylors Landlord, farm cider, frequent live music *(Dr and Mrs Jackson)*

WILLERSEY [SP1039]

New Inn WR12 7PJ [Main St]: Friendly and attractive old stone-built local, good value straightforward food all day from good range of sandwiches up, Donnington ales, ancient flagstones, darts and raised end area in simple main bar, pool in separate public bar; tables outside *(Neil and Anita Christopher)*

WORCESTER [SO8455]

Dragon WR1 1JT [The Tything]: Lively simply furnished open-plan alehouse with half a dozen well described and well kept unusual changing microbrews inc a Mild and Porter, local farm cider, friendly staff, bargain wkdy lunchtime food; piped pop music, folksy live bands; partly covered back terrace, open all day Sat *(Alan and Eve Harding, Joe Green)*

Five Ways WR1 3QN [Angel Pl]: Good value traditional town pub, bargain food, sensibly priced Websters *(Angela Davies)*

Ketch WR5 3HW [Bath Rd]: Big Toby family pub useful for bargain carvery; children welcome *(Chris Evans)*

Maple Leaf WR2 4XA [Canada Way, Lower Wick]: Low-priced generous food, well kept Banks's *(Chris Evans)*

Oak Apple WR5 2NL [Spetchley Rd]: Low prices, well kept beer, food inc huge baguettes *(Chris Evans)*

Plough WR1 2HN [Fish St]: Two simple rooms off entrance lobby, plain wkdy food 12-5.30 (not Sun/Mon) inc bargain OAP lunches, four changing real ales, farm cider; pleasant back courtyard, open all day *(Barry Collett, Pete Baker, Chris Evans, Dr B and Mrs P B Baker)*

Post Office address codings confusingly give the impression that some pubs are in Worcestershire, when they're really in Gloucestershire, Herefordshire, Shropshire or Warwickshire (which is where we list them).

Yorkshire

This is the biggest chapter in the *Guide*, as this huge county has such a splendid diversity of pubs from simple moorland locals in wonderful walking country, through city pubs with a fine choice of ales and a buzzy atmosphere, to civilised dining pubs with stylish modern food, and smart hotels with comfortable bedrooms and informal little bars. The common theme that runs through them – and really defines Yorkshire pubs – is the genuine friendliness of the licensees and their staff, with a warm and interested welcome for all, whether regulars or just visitors passing through. Places combining a really good pub side with an appealing accommodation side include the Crab & Lobster at Asenby (much emphasis on the hotel and dining side but with a lively, interesting bar, too), the Blue Lion in East Witton (despite the much enjoyed food and bedrooms, the bar is lively and informal), the Charles Bathurst near Langthwaite (despite the imaginative food, there's a proper pubby feel), the Star at Harome (the young chef creates fantastic food – but at a price), the Maypole at Long Preston (a happy and cheerful atmosphere in this traditional pub where many stay to enjoy the walking), the White Swan in Pickering (a civilised old coaching inn with fabulous restauranty food), the Boars Head in Ripley (smart hotel but with an informal bar liked by locals), the Three Acres in Shelley (a smashing place to stay with excellent food and a bustling bar), the Fox & Hounds in Sinnington (doing very well all round and much liked by our readers), the Wombwell Arms in Wass (a super landlord who looks after his customers and with reliable, good food), and the Sportsmans Arms in Wath in Nidderdale (comfortable hotel run by a charming landlord for 30 years, and with a nice little bar). Other pubs doing especially well this year are the Black Bull in Boroughbridge (an amiable landlord creates a cheerful atmosphere for this town pub), the Malt Shovel in Brearton (run by two opera singers with impromptu music and excellent food), the Fox & Hounds in Carthorpe (a good break from the A1 for tasty food), the Wyvill Arms in Constable Burton (efficiently run and hugely popular dining pub with tip-top food), the Durham Ox in Crayke (a winning all-rounder), the Plough at Fadmoor (a well run and welcoming dining pub), the Gray Ox in Hartshead (good attentive service, fine views and impressive meals), the Angel at Hetton (on top form with delicious food and a pubby bar), the Stone Trough at Kirkham (popular for both its appealing bar food and real ales), the Gold Cup at Low Catton (relaxing atmosphere, good food and first-class service), and the Maltings in York (quirky décor and interesting ales in this lively city tavern). Half a dozen new main entries this year, or pubs back in the *Guide* after a few years' absence, usually under enthusiastic new management, are the White Swan at Ampleforth (civilised individuality, a good all-rounder), the Fauconberg Arms at Coxwold (good food and comfortable bedrooms in this nicely updated village inn), the Bolton Arms at Downholme (interestingly placed Swaledale dining pub), the Tempest Arms at Elslack (good food and bedrooms), the Black Bull in Moulton (very strong on seafood), and the Crown at Roecliffe (doing very well all round since its reopening under first-class new management who have proved themselves well to the Guide in their previous pub). Food plays a strong part in Yorkshire pubs' appeal, with some really innovative young chef/landlords making the best of the marvellous local produce – there's much emphasis on game and fish, and several grow their own herbs and vegetables. Helpings tend to be generous, and you do get value for your money here. As well as quite a few pubs picked out above for good food, further contenders for our dining pub award include the Carpenters Arms at Felixkirk (run by a mother and daughter team), the General Tarleton at Ferrensby (smart, well run dining pub, if a bit pricy – vegetables are extra), the Wellington in Lund (first-class food in this smart pub), the Appletree at Marton (last year's winner, and still a fantastic place), the Millbank at Mill Bank (the new licensees' mix of contemporary and popular dishes is going down well), the Nags Head in Pickhill (a popular dining pub and handy for the A1), the Pipe & Glass at South Dalton (the young chef/landlord creates some very different dishes), the St Vincent Arms in Sutton upon Derwent (elaborate evening cooking but with nine real ales as well), and the Blacksmiths at Westow (a bustling pub with imaginative food but plenty of space for drinkers). It's an extremely difficult choice to make with so many marvellous chefs creating genuinely special food, but our Yorkshire Dining Pub of the Year is the Durham Ox at Crayke – on tip-top form, it's been giving great pleasure over the last few months. From the Lucky Dip section at the end of the chapter, we have picked out some very strong current performers, by area. North Yorkshire has the most: the Falcon at Arncliffe, Hare & Hounds at Burton Leonard, Foresters Arms at Carlton, Olde Sun at Colton, Coverbridge Inn near East Witton, Hales and Old Bell in Harrogate, Blue Bell in Kettlewell, Red Lion at Langthwaite, Fox & Rabbit at Lockton, Freemasons Arms at Nosterfield, Hare at Scawton, Golden Lion in Settle, and Ackhorne and Blue Bell in York. Others to note are, just inside East Yorkshire, the Three Cups at Stamford Bridge; in South Yorkshire, the Devonshire Cat in Sheffield and Boat at Sprotbrough; and in West Yorkshire, the Fleece at Addingham, Black Horse at Clifton, White Lion in Hebden Bridge and Grouse at Oakworth. The county has a great brewing tradition. Besides John Smiths and Tetleys (both now owned by a foreign brewing conglomerate), Yorkshire has five or six dozen independent breweries, and this wealth of choice has helped to keep beer prices down here. Much the most popular are Black Sheep, Timothy Taylors, Theakstons (its Best beer brewed for it by John Smiths) and Copper Dragon. Others we found in quite a few good pubs are York, Daleside, Abbeydale, Cropton, Hambleton, Roosters, Wold Top, Sam Smiths, Ossett, Bradfield, Eastwood/Elland, Kelham Island, Rudgate, Brown Cow, Acorn, Salamander and Wharfedale.

Real ale to us means beer which has matured naturally in its cask –
not pressurised or filtered.

AMPLEFORTH   SE5878   MAP 10

White Swan

Off A170 W of Helmsley; East End; YO62 4DA

Quite a choice of seating areas in friendly pub, attentive service, enjoyable food, and real ales; seats on back terrace

Just a couple of miles from Ampleforth Abbey, this is a friendly pub with an extensive series of seating areas, and a civilised atmosphere. The back part is the nicest and you can choose from the large lounge area with beams, handsome and polished oak floor boards, cream-coloured décor, sporting prints, and all sorts of tables and seats or the more formal, recently extended restaurant area with plush furnishings and crisp, white linen-covered tables. There's also a more conventional beamed and quarry-tiled front bar liked by locals, with a blazing log fire, plenty of standing room as well as seating, and Black Sheep Best and John Smiths Bitter on handpump, and good wines by the glass; genuinely friendly, helpful service. Piped music, TV, darts and dominoes. There are seats and tables on the large, attractive back terrace.

⚏ Enjoyable bar food at lunchtime includes sandwiches and toasties, ploughman's, soup, smoked chicken caesar salad, chicken liver pâté with chutney, tasty black pudding with apple and redcurrant potato cake, deep-fried haddock with mushy peas, lasagne, chicken in a light curry sauce, and steak in ale pie, with evening dishes such as duck terrine with mango and honey dressing, smoked, fresh and marinated seafood on mixed leaves, lamb steaks in rosemary and red wine, tiger prawns and avocado with tagliatelle and a sweet chilli and red pepper sauce, and half a gressingham duckling with orange sauce; Sunday roasts. *Starters/Snacks: £4.50 to £6.95. Main Courses: £7.95 to £16.95. Puddings: £4.25 to £5.95*

Free house ~ Licensees Mr and Mrs R Thompson ~ Real ale ~ Bar food (12-2, 6-9) ~ Restaurant ~ (01439) 788239 ~ Children welcome ~ Open 12-3, 6-11.15; 12 noon-12.30am(11.15 Sun) Sat; closed 25 Dec

Recommended by Walter and Susan Rinaldi-Butcher, R L Borthwick, Janet and Peter Race, R Pearce, WW

APPLETON-LE-MOORS   SE7388   MAP 10

Moors ⇐

Village N of A170 just under 1.5 miles E of Kirkby Mooride; YO62 6TF

Neat and unfussy pub with a good choice of drinks, proper country cooking using own-grown produce, and plenty of nearby walks; comfortable bedrooms

The landlady of this little stone-built pub is thinking of retiring, so to be sure of her cooking this is perhaps a place to head for sooner rather than later. It's all strikingly neat and surprisingly bare of the usual bric-a-brac; sparse decorations include just a few copper pans and earthenware mugs in a little alcove, a couple of plates, one or two pieces of country ironwork, and a delft shelf with miniature whiskies. The whiteness of walls and ceiling is underlined by the black beams and joists, and the bristly grey carpet. Perfect for a cold winter evening, there's a nice built-in high-backed stripped settle next to an old kitchen fireplace, and other seating includes an unusual rustic seat for two cleverly made out of stripped cartwheels; plenty of standing space. To the left of the bar you'll probably find a few regulars chatting on the backed padded stools: Black Sheep Best on handpump, over 50 malt whiskies and a reasonably priced wine list. Darts and board games. There are tables in the lovely walled garden with quiet country views and walks straight from here to Rosedale Abbey or Hartoft End, as well as paths to Hutton-le-Hole, Cropton and Sinnington. More reports on any changes, please.

⚏ Using own-grown vegetables and salads and local organic produce, the enjoyable food might include soup, chicken liver pâté, crispy breaded mushrooms with garlic dip, fruit and vegetable curry, fish pie, lasagne, lemon and saffron chicken, pheasant casserole, pork medallions with ginger sauce, smoked haddock flan, half a duck in a tangy orange sauce, peppered steak with a creamy green peppercorn sauce, daily specials, and puddings. *Starters/Snacks: £3.95 to £4.95. Main Courses: £8.50 to £12.00. Puddings: £4.25*

Free house ~ Licensee Janet Frank ~ Real ale ~ Bar food (see opening hours; not Mon (except for residents)) ~ Restaurant ~ No credit cards ~ (01751) 417435 ~ Children welcome ~ Dogs allowed in bar and bedrooms ~ Open 7-11; 12-3, 7-11 Sun; closed Mon; closed Tues-Sat lunchtimes ~ Bedrooms: £45B/£70B

Recommended by BOB

ASENBY   SE3975   MAP 7

Crab & Lobster 🍴 🍷 🛏
Village signposted off A168 – handy for A1; YO7 3QL

Interesting furnishings and décor in rambling bar, ambitious and enjoyable restauranty food, good drinks choice, attractive terrace; smart bedrooms

Of course this civilised place is more of a hotel and restaurant than a pub, but there is a friendly bar and they do keep Copper Dragon Golden Pippin, John Smiths Bitter, and Theakstons Best on handpump. This rambling, L-shaped bar has an interesting jumble of seats from antique high-backed and other settles through settees and wing armchairs heaped with cushions, to tall and rather theatrical corner seats; the tables are almost as much of a mix, and the walls and available surfaces are quite a jungle of bric-a-brac, with standard and table lamps and candles keeping even the lighting pleasantly informal. There's also a cosy main restaurant and a dining pavilion with big tropical plants, nautical bits and pieces, and Edwardian sofas. Quite a few wines by the glass and maybe piped music. The gardens have bamboo and palm trees lining the paths, there's a gazebo at the end of the walkways, and seats on a mediterranean-style terrace. The opulent bedrooms (based on famous hotels around the world) are in the surrounding house which has seven acres of mature gardens, and a 180-metre golf hole with full practice facilities.

🍴 **Imaginative – if not cheap – food includes a lunchtime fish club sandwich (not Sunday), terrine of spiced lamb with mango, peach and lime pickle and an onion fritter, barbecue spare ribs with sticky plum, orange and ginger sauce, mussels with shallots, thyme, garlic, white wine and cream, pasta with roast tomatoes, italian vegetables, pesto and garlic and parmesan toasts, fresh local haddock in beer batter, breast of chicken with ricotta, oven-dried tomatoes in pancetta with saffron and garlic mash and chicken cream, moroccan-spiced confit of lamb with dried fruit couscous and minted cucumber yoghurt, roast scarborough woof with sweet potato purée, shallot confit and brown shrimp roast gravy, and honey-roast gressingham duck breast with onion confit, duck mash and crisp parcel of duck à l'orange.** *Starters/Snacks: £8.50 to £10.00. Main Courses: £14.50 to £21.00. Puddings: £6.30 to £11.50*

Vimac Leisure ~ Licensee Mark Spenceley ~ Real ale ~ Bar food ~ Restaurant ~ (01845) 577286 ~ Well-behaved children allowed ~ Open 11.30-11 ~ Bedrooms: £120B/£150B

Recommended by Peter and Lesley Yeoward, Gordon and Margaret Ormondroyd, W K Wood, Ian and Jane Haslock, Sally Anne and Peter Goodale, Jennifer Hurst, Dr and Mrs R G J Telfer, Gerry and Rosemary Dobson, Tim and Liz Sherbourne

BECK HOLE   NZ8202   MAP 10

Birch Hall
Signed off A169 SW of Whitby, from top of Sleights Moor; YO22 5LE

Extraordinary pub-cum-village-shop in lovely valley with friendly landlady, real ales and simple snacks, seats outside and wonderful surrounding walks

If it wasn't for the chatty atmosphere and the many thirsty customers, you could almost believe this unique pub-cum-village-shop was a heritage museum. It's quite unchanging and there are two rooms, with the shop selling postcards, sweeties and ice-creams in between, and hatch service to both sides. Furnishings are simple – built-in cushioned wall seats and wooden tables (spot the one with 136 pennies, all heads up, embedded in the top) and chairs on the flagstones in one room, composition in the other and there are some strange items about, such as french breakfast cereal boxes and a tube of Macleans toothpaste priced 1/3d. Black Sheep Best, Daleside Stout, and York Birds &

Bees on handpump; several malt whiskies. Friendly, welcoming staff, dominoes and quoits. Outside, an ancient oil painting of the view up the steeply wooded river valley hangs on the pub wall, there are benches out in front, and steps up to a little steeply terraced side garden. They have a self-catering cottage attached to the pub. It's in a beautiful steep valley and surrounded by marvellous walks; you can walk along the disused railway line from Goathland – part of the path from Beck Hole to Grosmont is surfaced with mussel shells.

🍴 **Bar snacks such as locally made pies, butties and home-made scones and cakes that include their lovely beer cake.**

Free house ~ Licensee Glenys Crampton ~ Real ale ~ Bar food (available during all opening hours) ~ No credit cards ~ (01947) 896245 ~ Children in small family room ~ Dogs welcome ~ Open 11-11; 12-10.30 Sun; 11-3, 7.30-11 Weds-Sun in winter; closed winter Mon evening, all day Tues Nov-March

Recommended by Pete Baker, Pat and Tony Martin, Paul Newberry, the Didler, Peter and Jo Smith, Phil Bryant, Rona Murdoch, Maurice and Gill McMahon, Malcolm and Jane Levitt, Alison and Pete, Arthur Pickering, Amanda Russell

BEVERLEY   TA0339   MAP 8

White Horse £

Hengate, close to the imposing Church of St Mary's; runs off North Bar; HU17 8BN

Unspoilt Victorian pub with basic little rooms, simple furnishings, open fires, and traditional bar food

'A national treasure,' is how one reader describes this quite-without-frills pub. It has a carefully preserved Victorian feel and the basic but very atmospheric little rooms are huddled around the central bar: brown leatherette seats (high-backed settles in one little snug) and basic wooden chairs and benches on bare floorboards, antique cartoons and sentimental engravings on the nicotine-stained walls, a gaslit pulley-controlled chandelier, a deeply reverberating chiming clock, and open fires – one with an attractively tiled old fireplace. A framed history of the pub now hangs on the wall. Very cheap Sam Smiths OB on handpump; a separate games room has pool and a games machine. Upstairs is a large area with a sideboard full of children's toys and an open fire. John Wesley preached in the back yard in the mid-18th c.

🍴 **Simple food includes sandwiches, bangers and mash, steak in ale pie, lasagne, somerset pork, and puddings like spotted dick and custard.** *Starters/Snacks: £1.95 to £3.95. Main Courses: £3.95 to £5.95. Puddings: £2.00 to £2.95*

Sam Smiths ~ Manager Anna ~ Real ale ~ Bar food (11-2.45 Mon-Sat; no food Sun) ~ No credit cards ~ (01482) 861973 ~ Children welcome away from bar areas ~ Open 11-11; 12-10.30 Sun
Recommended by David Carr, Alison and Pete, Pam and John Smith, Pete Baker, the Didler, Mark Walker

BLAKEY RIDGE   SE6799   MAP 10

Lion 🍴 🛏

From A171 Guisborough—Whitby follow Castleton, Hutton le Hole signposts; from A170 Kirkby Moorside—Pickering follow Keldholm, Hutton le Hole, Castleton signposts; OS Sheet 100 map reference 679996; YO62 7LQ

Extended pub in fine scenery and open all day; bedrooms

As this extended pub is usefully open all day and serves food until 10pm, it's popular with walkers on the nearby Coast to Coast Footpath; there are plenty of other surrounding hikes – this is the highest point of the North York Moors National Park. The views are stunning. The beamed and rambling bars have warm open fires, a few big high-backed rustic settles around cast-iron-framed tables, lots of small dining chairs, a nice leather settee, and stone walls hung with some old engravings and photographs of the pub under snow (it can easily get cut off in winter). Greene King Old Speckled Hen, John

Smiths, and Theakstons Best, Old Peculier, Black Bull and XB on handpump; piped music and games machine. If you are thinking of staying, you must book well in advance. This is a regular stop-off for coach parties.

🍴 Generous helpings of basic bar food include lunchtime sandwiches and filled baked potatoes as well as soup, deep-fried brie with cranberry sauce, chicken goujons with barbecue dip, home-cooked ham and egg, chicken curry, battered cod, vegetable lasagne, daily specials like steak in ale pie and sausage casserole, and puddings like treacle roly-poly and strawberry cheesecake. *Starters/Snacks: £2.95 to £3.95. Main Courses: £8.95 to £14.25. Puddings: £1.95 to £3.95*

Free house ~ Licensee Barry Crossland ~ Real ale ~ Bar food (12-10) ~ Restaurant ~ (01751) 417320 ~ Children welcome ~ Dogs allowed in bar ~ Open 10am-11pm ~ Bedrooms: £20(£41.50B)/£54(£68B)

Recommended by R M Jones, DC, Sean A Smith, WW, John and Helen Rushton, Dr and Mrs Jackson, Joan York, Pete Coxon, Maurice and Gill McMahon

BOROUGHBRIDGE
SE3966 MAP 7

Black Bull ♀
St James Square; B6265, just off A1(M); YO51 9AR

Bustling and friendly old town pub with reliable food, real ales and several wines by the glass

Handy for the A1, this is an attractive old town pub with a friendly landlord and lots of separate drinking and eating areas. The main bar area has a big stone fireplace and comfortable seats and is served through an old-fashioned hatch; there's also a cosy snug with traditional wall settles, a tap room, lounge bar and restaurant. The two rooms at the front are liked by local drinkers. John Smiths, Theakstons Best, and Timothy Taylors Landlord on handpump, ten wines by the glass and 19 malt whiskies; dominoes. The two borzoi dogs are called Charlie and Sadie, and the cat Mimi; the local mummers perform here on the first Sunday of every month. The hanging baskets are lovely.

🍴 As well as lots of hot and cold sandwiches, the enjoyable bar food includes soup, pork and chive sausages with onion gravy, a pie of the day, smoked salmon and scrambled eggs, chinese pork with mushrooms, water chestnuts and baby corn, battered haddock goujons, daily specials such as lamb shank with port and honey gravy, tuna steak on wild mushrooms topped with smoked cheese, and venison steak with smoked bacon, blue cheese and a wild berry glaze, and puddings such as jam sponge and banana and toffee roulade. *Starters/Snacks: £5.95 to £9.25. Main Courses: £6.95 to £9.25. Puddings: £3.95*

Free house ~ Licensees Anthony and Jillian Burgess ~ Real ale ~ Bar food (12-2(2.30 Sun), 6-9(9.30 Fri and Sat)) ~ Restaurant ~ (01423) 322413 ~ Children welcome ~ Dogs allowed in bar and bedrooms ~ Folk music first Sun of month, 12-5 ~ Open 11-11(midnight Fri and Sat); 12-11 Sun ~ Bedrooms: £40S/£60S

Recommended by the Didler, Janet and Peter Race, Pete Baker, John R Ringrose, Comus and Sarah Elliott

BRADFIELD
SK2290 MAP 7

Strines Inn 🛏
From A57 heading E of junction with A6013 (Ladybower Reservoir) take first left turn (signposted with Bradfield) then bear left; with a map can also be reached more circuitously from Strines signpost on A616 at head of Underbank Reservoir, W of Stocksbridge; S6 6JE

Friendly, bustling inn with fine surrounding scenery, good mix of customers, well liked food, and changing real ales; four-poster bedrooms

Although there's a 16th-c coat of arms over the door into this moorland inn, the place probably dates back 300 years before that. It's surrounded by superb scenery on the edge of the High Peak National Park and there are fine views, plenty of picnic-sets, a children's play area, and peacocks, geese and chickens. Inside, it's well run and enjoyable, and the main bar has a welcoming atmosphere, a good mix of customers, black beams liberally decked with copper kettles and so forth, quite a menagerie of stuffed animals, homely red-plush-cushioned traditional wooden wall benches and small chairs, and a coal fire in the rather grand stone fireplace. A room off on the right has another coal fire, hunting photographs and prints, and lots of brass and china, and on the left is another similarly furnished room. Bradfield Farmers Pale Ale, Jennings Cocker Hoop, and Marstons Pedigree on handpump and several malt whiskies; piped music. The bedrooms have four-poster beds and a dining table as the good breakfasts are served in your room – and the front room overlooks the reservoir. More reports please.

🍴 **Enjoyable bar food includes sandwiches and panini, filled baked potatoes, ploughman's, soup, garlic mushrooms, giant yorkshire pudding filled with sausages, a pie of the day, meaty or vegetable lasagne, liver and onions, fresh fish dishes, and puddings such as treacle sponge and Bailey's and toffee cheesecake.** *Starters/Snacks: £3.10 to £4.40. Main Courses: £4.30 to £14.95. Puddings: £3.40 to £3.60*

Free house ~ Licensee Bruce Howarth ~ Real ale ~ Bar food (12-2.30, 6-9 winter weekdays; all day weekends and summer weekdays) ~ (0114) 285 1247 ~ Children welcome ~ Dogs welcome ~ Open 10.30am-11pm; 10.30-3, 6-11 in winter; closed 25 Dec ~ Bedrooms: £60B/£80B

Recommended by JJW, CMW, the Didler, Susan and John Douglas, Mrs Jane Kingsbury, Dr and Mrs R G J Telfer, David and Ruth Hollands

BREARTON

SE3260 MAP 7

Malt Shovel 🍴 🍷 🍺

Village signposted off A61 N of Harrogate; HG3 3BX

Friendly, family-run dining pub with imaginative food and good choice of drinks in heavily beamed rooms; airy new conservatory

Now a dining pub and calling itself 'Bleikers at The Malt Shovel, Brearton', this is a family run, 16th-c place with a warm and friendly atmosphere. Two of the young licensees are professional opera singers and there are regular live opera evenings and impromptu piano playing. Heavily beamed rooms radiate from the attractive linenfold oak bar counter, with painted walls and light blue skirting, an attractive mix of wooden dining chairs around pristine white-clothed tables on wood or slate floors, and some partitioning that separates several candlelit dining areas. The conservatory is light and airy with lemon trees and a piano. Black Sheep Best and guests like Daleside Blonde and Timothy Taylors Landlord on handpump, and a very good wine list with 13 by the glass; competent, attentive staff. There are seats in the parasoled garden. The family are also associated with Bleiker's Smokehouse near Harrogate.

🍴 **Using top quality produce, the excellent, if not cheap, food includes sandwiches, soup, lamb sweetbreads with mustard sauce, warm slow-cooked rabbit salad with black truffle shavings, a trio of peat-smoked salmon, romanov smoked salmon (marinated in beetroot and lightly smoked with apple wood) and home-cured gravadlax, scallops with black pudding, tagliatelle with creamy wild mushroom sauce, fish pie, home-made pork sausages with caramelised onion mash, good sautéed pheasant breast with pheasant dumpling wrapped in pancetta with chestnut mash and a cider and calvados sauce, slow-cooked moroccan lamb with potato pancake, wienerschnitzel, daily specials such as moules marinières and ocean perch with green ginger wine and almonds, and puddings like knickerbocker glory and dark chocolate truffle cake.** *Starters/Snacks: £4.50 to £9.95. Main Courses: £9.95 to £19.95. Puddings: £5.95 to £6.95*

Free house ~ Licensee Jurg Bleiker ~ Real ale ~ Bar food (12-2, 6-9 Weds-Sat; 12-7 Sun; not Sun evening or Mon or Tues) ~ Restaurant ~ (01423) 862929 ~ Children welcome ~ Mrs Bleiker regularly plays the piano, and live opera evenings ~ Open 12-3, 6-11; 12-9 Sun; closed Mon and Tues

Recommended by Peter and Anne-Marie O'Malley, Rona Murdoch, Les and Sandra Brown, Tim and Claire Woodward, Dr Ian S Morley, Jeremy King, Michael Doswell, David Coleman, Brian and Janet Ainscough

---

The knife-and-fork award distinguishes pubs where the food is of exceptional quality.

BURN   SE5928   MAP 7

Wheatsheaf 🍺 £
A19 Selby—Doncaster; Main Road; YO8 8LJ

Plenty to look at and a friendly welcome, half a dozen real ales and good value straightforward food

Most customers come to this friendly roadside pub to look at the amazing collections of memorabilia while enjoying one of the half a dozen real ales. There really are masses to see: gleaming copper kettles, black dagging shears, polished buffalo horns and the like around its good log and coal fire (and a drying rack with bunches of herbs above it), decorative mugs above one bow-window seat, and cases of model wines and lorries on the cream walls. The highly polished pub tables in the partly divided, open-plan bar have comfortable seats around them and John Smiths and Timothy Taylors Best and guests such as Brown Cow Montana Pale, Fernandes Triple O, Milestone Black Pearl, and Ossett Pale Gold on handpump at attractive prices and over 30 malt whiskies. A pool table is out of the way on the left, cribbage, dominoes, games machine, TV, and maybe unobtrusive piped music. A small garden behind has picnic-sets on a heated terrace.

🍴 **Straightforward bar food at very fair prices includes sandwiches, filled baked potatoes, ploughman's, burgers, chicken curry, breaded plaice, steak in ale pie, daily specials such as moussaka and lamb shank, and Sunday roasts.** *Starters/Snacks: £2.95 to £3.75. Main Courses: £5.50 to £9.20. Puddings: £2.50*

Free house ~ Licensee Andrew Howdall ~ Real ale ~ Bar food (12-2 daily, 6.30-8.30 Thurs, Fri and Sat; no food Sun-Weds evenings) ~ (01757) 270614 ~ Children welcome ~ Dogs welcome ~ Open 12 noon-midnight

Recommended by DC, Tim and Claire Woodward, Matt Waite, Roger and Anne Newbury, Mrs Margaret Ball, R T and J C Moggridge

CARTHORPE   SE3083   MAP 10

Fox & Hounds 🍴 🍷
Village signposted from A1 N of Ripon, via B6285; DL8 2LG

Emphasis on ambitious food in friendly dining pub but drinkers welcome too; real ales and extensive wine list

For several of our readers, this neatly kept and friendly dining pub is a regular lunchtime break from the A1. It's been run by the same family for 24 years and you can be sure of a warm welcome. The cosy L-shaped bar has quite a few mistily evocative Victorian photographs of Whitby, a couple of nice seats by the larger of its two log fires, plush button-back built-in wall banquettes and chairs, plates on stripped beams, and some limed panelling; piped light classical music. There is some theatrical memorabilia in the corridors and an attractive high-raftered restaurant with lots of neatly black-painted farm and smithy tools. Black Sheep Best and Worthingtons on handpump and an extensive wine list; helpful service.

🍴 **Their local producers are listed on the menu and the popular restaurant-style food includes sandwiches, soup, grilled black pudding with roasted apple and red onion marmalade, duck-filled filo parcels with plum sauce, fillet of bass with roasted tomato salad and citrus butter, caramelised onion and goats cheese tart, chicken breast filled with blue cheese and leeks in a creamy sauce, poached salmon fillet with a white wine and parsley sauce, roast rack of lamb on a blackcurrant croûton with redcurrant gravy, and puddings such as orange panna cotta with cinnamon shortbread and chocolate fudge pudding with chocolate sauce; they also offer a Tuesday-Thursday two- and three-course set menu.** *Starters/Snacks: £3.55 to £6.95. Main Courses: £9.95 to £15.95. Puddings: £4.85 to £10.95*

Free house ~ Licensees Vince and Helen Taylor ~ Real ale ~ Bar food (not Mon) ~ Restaurant ~ (01845) 567433 ~ Children welcome ~ Open 12-3, 7-11(10.30 Sun); closed Mon and first week Jan

Recommended by David Carr, Jill and Julian Tasker, Dennis and Amanda Parkyn, Janet and Peter Race, Jill Angold-Stevens, Dr Ian S Morley, Brian Brooks, Mr and Mrs Ian King, R N and M I Bailey, Alan Thwaite

CHAPEL LE DALE

SD7477 MAP 7

Hill Inn ◧

B5655 Ingleton—Hawes, 3 miles N of Ingleton; LA6 3AR

Friendly inn with fine surrounding walks, appealing food cooked by the licensees, and a fair choice of real ales; comfortable bedrooms

You can be sure of a warm and friendly welcome in this bustling ex-farmhouse, run by a family of chefs. There are wonderful remote walks all round and fantastic views to Ingleborough and Whernside from the bedrooms; many of the customers are walkers who create a relaxed and chatty atmosphere. There are beams and log fires, straightforward seats and tables on the stripped wooden floors, nice pictures on the walls, stripped-stone recesses, and Black Sheep Best, Dent Aviator, Theakstons Best, and Timothy Taylors Landlord on handpump; several wines by the glass. There's a dining room and a well worn-in sun lounge.

🍽 Cooked by the licensees, the enjoyable food might include sandwiches, soup, butternut squash risotto with pine nuts, fishcakes with sweet chilli sauce, beef in ale casserole, chicken breast flavoured with lemon and herbs and wrapped in bacon, lamb shank with rich gravy and redcurrant jelly, duck breast with parsley mash and orange sauce, and puddings like sticky toffee pudding with home-made vanilla ice-cream and lemon tart with raspberry coulis and home-made lemon and mascarpone ice-cream. *Starters/Snacks: £3.95 to £5.95. Main Courses: £9.95 to £15.50. Puddings: £5.50*

Free house ~ Licensee Sabena Martin ~ Real ale ~ Bar food (12-2.30, 6.30-8.45; not Mon except bank hols) ~ Restaurant ~ (015242) 41256 ~ Children in dining areas if eating ~ Dogs allowed in bar ~ Open 12-3.30, 6.30-11; 12-11 Sat; 12-4, 6.30-11 Sun; closed Mon (except bank hols), 24 and 25 Dec ~ Bedrooms: /£70S

Recommended by S Gainsley, Karen Eliot

CONSTABLE BURTON

SE1690 MAP 10

Wyvill Arms 🍴 � 🛇

A684 E of Leyburn; DL8 5LH

Well run and friendly dining pub with excellent food, a dozen wines by the glass, real ales and efficient helpful service; bedrooms

Very efficiently run, this is a spotless and friendly dining pub with particularly good, popular food, and as we went to press they were starting work on creating a kitchen that will be partly on view to diners. But drinkers are catered for too – there's a small bar area with a mix of seating, a finely worked plaster ceiling with the Wyvill family's coat of arms, and an elaborate stone fireplace. The second bar, where food is served (though they also have a sizeable restaurant), has upholstered alcoves, hunting prints, and old oak tables; the reception area of this room includes a huge chesterfield which can seat up to eight people, another carved stone fireplace, and an old leaded church stained-glass window partition. Both rooms are hung with pictures of local scenes. Copper Dragon Golden Pippin, Theakstons Best, and a couple of changing guests on handpump, a dozen wines by the glass, and some rare malt whiskies; board games and darts. There are several large wooden benches under large white parasols for outdoor dining. Constable Burton Gardens are opposite and worth a visit.

🍽 Using seasonal produce, herbs from their own big garden and game from the estate across the road, the first class food includes sandwiches, soup, crispy duck leg on wilted greens with a chinese plum sauce, terrine of smoked ham, wensleydale cheese and duck mousse with pear and apple chutney, salmon fishcakes on tomato carpaccio with spring onion and chilli jam, mediterranean risotto, pork fillet wrapped in smoked pancetta with a prune and armagnac sauce, steak and onion pie, lamb shank on sweet potato mash with a thyme and lamb jus, and daily specials such as seared scallops on chorizo with a minted hollandaise sauce, fried fillet of sea bream with brown shrimps, prawns, anchovies and capers and a lemon butter sauce, and rib-eye steak with a mustard, mushroom and caper sauce. *Starters/Snacks: £4.50 to £7.50. Main Courses: £9.75 to £18.50. Puddings: £5.00 to £5.95*

Free house ~ Licensee Nigel Stevens ~ Real ale ~ Bar food ~ Restaurant ~ (01677) 450581 ~ Children welcome but must be well supervised ~ Dogs allowed in bar and bedrooms ~ Open 11-3, 5.30-11; closed Mon ~ Bedrooms: £60B/£80B

Recommended by Mrs Brenda Calver, Ben and Helen Ingram, Mr and Mrs Ian King, Michael Tack, Dr and Mrs R G J Telfer, Janet and Peter Race, Anna Cooper, M and GR, Jane and Alan Bush, Stephen Woad

COXWOLD
SE5377 MAP 7

Fauconberg Arms ♀ 🛏

off A170 Thirsk—Helmsley, via Kilburn or Wass; easily found off A19, too; YO61 4AD

Friendly family running nicely updated 17th-c inn, enjoyable generous food, comfortable bedrooms

Reopened under new owners a couple of years ago, this now fits perfectly in mood with the relaxed style of the charming unchanging village, and quaint nearby Shandy Hall, the home of Laurence Stern the eccentric 18th-c novelist. In summer, picnic-sets and teak benches out on the cobbles look along the village's broad tree-lined verges, bright with flower tubs. In winter, the heavily beamed and flagstoned bar welcomes you with log fires in both linked areas, one in an unusual arched fireplace in a broad low inglenook. Both generations of the family are helpful and cheerful. They have well kept Theakstons Best and Thwaites Best with a couple of guests like John Smiths and Thwaites Dark Mild on handpump, and a thoughtful choice of wines by the glass. Muted Farrow & Ball colours, some attractive oak chairs by local craftsmen alongside more usual pub furnishings, and nicely chosen old local photographs and other pictures and china give a stylish feel without being at all pretentious. The candlelit dining room is quietly elegant, gently upmarket yet relaxed.

🍴 As well as lunchtime sandwiches, ploughman's, and burgers like prime beef or pork and apple, the generous helpings of well liked bar food include soup with their own bread, garlic mushrooms, salmon fishcake with a sweet chilli dip, ham and egg, goats cheese tart, warm, spicy chicken salad, lamb rump with a rosemary and red wine reduction, slow-roast belly pork with fresh ginger, apple and cider gravy, duck with an orange, honey and Cointreau sauce, and Sunday roasts; they have a super cheeseboard. *Starters/Snacks: £4.95 to £7.50. Main Courses: £7.50 to £14.50. Puddings: £4.95*

Free house ~ Licensee Simon Rheinberg ~ Real ale ~ Bar food (12.30-2.30(3 Sat), 6.30-9.30; 12.30-6 Sun; not Sun evening or Tues) ~ Restaurant ~ (01347) 868214 ~ Children welcome ~ Dogs allowed in bar ~ Live impromptu music Sun evenings ~ Open 11-3, 6-11(midnight Fri); 11-midnight(11 Sun) Sat; closed Tues ~ Bedrooms: £75S/£85S

Recommended by Nigel Long, R Pearce, Earl and Chris Pick, Karen Powell, E M Mason

CRAY
SD9479 MAP 7

White Lion 🍺 🛏

B6160, Upper Wharfedale N of Kettlewell; BD23 5JB

Useful for walkers, with simply furnished rooms and real ales

The countryside surrounding this former drovers' hostelry is superb and it's the highest pub in Wharfedale – walkers and their well behaved dogs are welcome. The simply furnished bar has an open fire, seats around tables on the flagstone floor, shelves of china, iron tools, old painted metal adverts for animal feed and so forth, and a high dark beam-and-plank ceiling; there's also a back room. Copper Dragon 1816 and Golden Pippin, John Smiths, and Timothy Taylors Golden Best and Landlord on handpump, several wines by the glass, and around 20 malt whiskies; board games, ring the bull, and giant Jenga. In fine weather, you can sit at picnic benches above the very quiet steep lane or on the great flat limestone slabs in the shallow stream which tumbles down opposite. More reports please.

🍴 Basic bar food includes filled baguettes and ploughman's, soup, steak and mushroom pie, a vegetarian dish, and liver and bacon. *Starters/Snacks: £4.50 to £4.95. Main Courses: £9.50 to £14.95. Puddings: £2.75 to £3.75*

Enterprise ~ Lease Kevin and Debbie Roe ~ Real ale ~ Bar food ~ Restaurant ~ (01756) 760262 ~ Children welcome ~ Dogs allowed in bar ~ Open 11-11 ~ Bedrooms: £55S/£70S

Recommended by Dr A McCormick, Bruce and Sharon Eden, Lawrence Pearse, Mr and Mrs Maurice Thompson, Richard, the Didler, Peter Smith, Judith Brown, Dr D and Mrs B Woods, Lynda and Trevor Smith, Peter F Marshall, Len Beattie, Terry Mizen, Greta and Christopher Wells, Richard Tosswill

CRAYKE

SE5670 MAP 7

Durham Ox ⊕ 🍷 🛏

Off B1363 at Brandsby, towards Easingwold; West Way; YO61 4TE

YORKSHIRE DINING PUB OF THE YEAR

Friendly, particularly well run inn, interesting décor in old-fashioned, relaxing rooms, fine drinks and excellent food; lovely views and comfortable bedrooms

In an attractive village, this bustling inn is very well run and genuinely friendly, and our readers really enjoy staying in the newly refurbished bedrooms – which are in converted farm buildings; the breakfasts are good, too. The old-fashioned lounge bar has an enormous inglenook fireplace, pictures and photographs on the dark red walls, interesting satirical carvings in its panelling (Victorian copies of medieval pew ends), polished copper and brass, and venerable tables and antique seats and settles on the flagstones. In the bottom bar is a framed illustrated account of the local history (some of it gruesome) dating back to the 12th c, and a large framed print of the original famous Durham Ox which weighed 171 stone. Black Sheep Best, Theakstons Best, Timothy Taylors Landlord and a guest like Everards Sly Fox on handpump, several wines by the glass, a dozen malt whiskies and organic juices, all served by knowledgeable, welcoming staff; piped music. There are seats outside on a terrace and in the covered courtyard and fantastic views over the Vale of York on three sides; on the fourth side there's a charming view up the hill to the medieval church. The tale is that this is the hill up which the Grand Old Duke of York marched his men.

🍴 **Excellent food using home-made bread and ice-creams includes open sandwiches, soup, scottish salmon and haddock fishcake with tomato chutney, eggs benedict, baked queen scallops with garlic and parsley butter and a gruyère and cheddar crust, beer-battered haddock, chargrilled free-range corn-fed chicken breast with grilled vine tomato and field mushrooms, baked puy lentils and chargrilled vegetables with roasted garlic and herb potatoes, roast lamb rump with minted crushed new potatoes and lamb reduction, popular steak frites, daily specials such as ham hock terrine with home-made piccalilli, smoked cheddar soufflé with red onion marmalade, and steamed black bream with wilted pak choi, coriander, ginger and lemon grass, and puddings like apricot and Amaretto tart with clotted cream ice-cream and chocolate brownie sundae with hot chocolate sauce.** *Starters/Snacks: £3.95 to £6.95. Main Courses: £8.95 to £15.95. Puddings: £3.95 to £5.95*

Free house ~ Licensee Michael Ibbotson ~ Real ale ~ Bar food (12-2.30(3 Sun), 6-9.30(10 Sat; 8.30 Sun); not 25 Dec) ~ Restaurant ~ (01347) 821506 ~ Children welcome but must be well behaved ~ Dogs allowed in bedrooms ~ Open 12-2.30, 6-11.30; 12-midnight Sat; 12-10.30 Sun; closed 25 Dec ~ Bedrooms: £60B/£80B

Recommended by David S Allen, Dr Peter Crawshaw, John and Sylvia Harrop, S and N McLean, Ian Malone, Pat and Graham Williamson, Gordon and Margaret Ormondroyd, Joan York, Keith and Margaret Kettell

CROPTON

SE7588 MAP 10

New Inn 🍺 🛏

Village signposted off A170 W of Pickering; YO18 8HH

Own-brew beers in friendly modernised village inn, traditional rooms, and home cooking; brewery tours, bedrooms

The own-brewed beers on handpump in this comfortably modernised, bustling village inn remain quite a draw: Cropton Endeavour Ale, Honey Gold, King Billy, Monkmans Slaughter, Two Pints and Yorkshire Moors Bitter. They also have a guest such as Greene King IPA, several malt whiskies, and half a dozen wines by the glass. The traditional village bar has wooden panelling, terracotta and plush seats, lots of brass, and a small fire. A local artist has designed historical posters all around the downstairs conservatory that doubles as a visitor centre during busy times. The elegant restaurant has locally made furniture and paintings by local artists. Games machine, juke box, and TV. There's a neat terrace, a garden with a pond, and a brewery shop. Brewery Tours (not Sunday or Monday), 11.30-2.30, £4.95 per person.

Bar food includes lunchtime sandwiches, ploughman's, soup, wensleydale parcels, vegetable stroganoff, steak in ale pie, pork fillet stuffed with mozzarella and smoked bacon with a creamy red pepper sauce, and puddings such as rhubarb and apple crumble and chocolate brownie. *Starters/Snacks: £3.95 to £5.95. Main Courses: £8.95 to £13.95. Puddings: £3.95*

Own brew ~ Licensee Philip Lee ~ Real ale ~ Bar food (12-2, 6-9) ~ Restaurant ~ (01751) 417330 ~ Children welcome ~ Open 11am-midnight; 11-11 Sun ~ Bedrooms: £45B/£80B

Recommended by Maurice and Gill McMahon, Rona Murdoch, Pat and Graham Williamson, Rosemary K Germaine, Anne and Paul Horscraft, Christopher Turner, Ann and Tony Bennett-Hughes, Pete Coxon, P Dawn, Mrs Roxanne Chamberlain, J F M and M West

DOWNHOLME   SE1197   MAP 10

Bolton Arms

Village signposted just off A6108 Leyburn—Richmond; DL11 6AE

Enjoyable food in unusual village's cosy country pub, lovely views

The little stone-built pub, like the village itself, is owned by the Ministry of Defence, and surrounded by MoD land – a largely unspoilt swathe of Swaledale, with great views over it from the red-walled back conservatory dining room. This is simple, quiet and attractive, up a few steps from the bar. If you eat, they take your order down there, then call you through when it's ready. The black-beamed and carpeted bar, warm, friendly and softly lit, has two smallish linked areas off the servery, with Black Sheep Best and Theakstons Best on handpump from a small stone counter, and good wines by the glass at fair prices. There are comfortable plush wall banquettes, a log fire in one neat fireplace, and quite a lot of gleaming brass, a few small country pictures and drinks advertisements on pinkish rough-plastered walls. Service is friendly and efficient; there may be piped music. The neat garden, on the same level as the dining room (and up steps from the front), shares its view; there are also some lower picnic-sets and benches. The two bedrooms, sharing a bathroom, are good value.

Good bar food cooked by the landlord includes sandwiches, soup, ploughman's, garlic mushrooms, seafood pancake, caesar salad with chicken and bacon, mushroom tagliatelle, thai chicken stir fry, gammon and egg, liver and bacon, fillet of salmon with prawn sauce, lamb with redcurrant gravy, and puddings such as banoffi cheesecake with toffee sauce and stem ginger and syrup sponge with custard. *Starters/Snacks: £3.75 to £5.95. Main Courses: £7.95 to £19.50. Puddings: £4.50*

Free house ~ Licensees Steve and Nicola Ross ~ Real ale ~ Bar food (11.30-2, 6.30-9; not Tues) ~ Restaurant ~ (01748) 823716 ~ Children welcome ~ Open 11-3, 6.30-11; closed Tues lunchtime ~ Bedrooms: /£60S

Recommended by John and Sylvia Harrop, Anna Cooper

EAST WITTON   SE1486   MAP 10

Blue Lion 🍴 ☆ 🛏

A6108 Leyburn—Ripon; DL8 4SN

Civilised dining pub with interesting rooms, daily papers and real ales, inventive food, and courteous service; comfortable bedrooms

With first class food and very comfortable bedrooms, this smart and civilised dining pub also cleverly manages to have a proper bar that welcomes drinkers, too. This big squarish bar has high-backed antique settles and old windsor chairs on the turkey rugs and flagstones, ham-hooks in the high ceiling decorated with dried wheat, teazles and so forth, a delft shelf filled with appropriate bric-a-brac, several prints, sporting caricatures and other pictures on the walls, a log fire, and daily papers; the friendly labrador is called Archie. Black Sheep Best and Riggwelter, and Theakstons Best on handpump and an impressive wine list with quite a few (plus champagne) by the glass; courteous, attentive service. Picnic-sets on the gravel outside look beyond the stone houses on the far side of the village green to Witton Fell and there's a big, pretty back garden.

🍴 **Whilst not cheap, the food is excellent and might include sandwiches, soft shell crab deep fried with chilli and ginger with a fennel salad, terrine of ham hock, parsley and foie gras with yellow split pea purée, smoked salmon with creamed horseradish and walnut bread, home-made tagliatelle with wild mushrooms, cured bacon and parmesan, sautéed fillet of pork, crispy belly pork and fried black pudding with a honey and apple sauce, poached fillet of smoked haddock topped with a poached egg, leek and mushroom sauce and toasted with gruyère, flash-roasted venison with red wine, chestnut and vegetable risotto, sautéed breast of duck and confit duck leg with slow-braised cumbrian dried ham, and puddings such as dark chocolate terrine with tiramisu ice-cream and raspberry crème brûlée.** *Starters/Snacks: £5.85 to £9.75. Main Courses: £10.50 to £25.50. Puddings: £4.95 to £6.50*

Free house ~ Licensee Paul Klein ~ Real ale ~ Bar food ~ Restaurant ~ (01969) 624273 ~ Children welcome ~ Dogs allowed in bar and bedrooms ~ Open 11-11 ~ Bedrooms: £67.50S/£89S(£99B)

Recommended by Dr Kevan Tucker, Jane Taylor, David Dutton, Terry Mizen, Michael and Maggie Betton, Mrs Sheila Stothard, J and S Grabiner, Dr Ian S Morley, Neil and Angela Huxter, Simon Rodway, Peter Hacker, Lynda and Trevor Smith, Dr Peter Crawshaw, Comus and Sarah Elliott, the Didler, Anthony Longden

EGTON BRIDGE

NZ8005   MAP 10

Horseshoe

Village signposted from A171 W of Whitby; via Grosmont from A169 S of Whitby; YO21 1XE

Charmingly placed inn, refurbished rooms, several real ales, and seats in attractive gardens; bedrooms

Considerable refurbishment is taking place throughout this bustling inn, so by the time this *Guide* is published, the bedrooms, main bar and dining areas should all have been completely redecorated. The bar has had old oak tables, high-backed built-in winged settles, wall seats and spindleback chairs, a big stuffed trout (caught near here in 1913), and a warm log fire. Black Sheep Best, John Smiths, and three guests like Durham Definitive, Theakstons Paradise, and Wells & Youngs Bombardier on handpump; piped music and board games. This is a peaceful spot and the attractive gardens have pretty roses and mature redwoods, and seats on a quiet terrace and lawn. A different way to reach the pub is to park by the Roman Catholic church, walk through the village and cross the River Esk by stepping stones. Not to be confused with a similarly named pub up at Egton. More reports please.

🍴 **Bar food includes lunchtime sandwiches, filled baguettes and baked potatoes, and ploughman's, as well as soup, chicken liver pâté, home-baked ham and egg, lasagne, fish pie, a casserole of the day, scampi, and steaks; they plan to serve cream teas throughout the afternoon in summer.** *Starters/Snacks: £3.70 to £6.00. Main Courses: £7.95 to £15.00. Puddings: £2.75 to £4.00*

Free house ~ Licensee Alison Underwood ~ Real ale ~ Bar food ~ Restaurant ~ (01947) 895245 ~ Children in restaurant and small back room ~ Dogs allowed in bar ~ Open 11.30-4(3 winter weekdays), 6.30-11(10.30 winter weekdays); 11.30-11 Sat; 12-10.30 Sun ~ Bedrooms: /£50(£60S)

Recommended by Pete Baker, Peter and Jo Smith, Paul Vates, Dr and Mrs R G J Telfer, Chris and Jeanne Downing, Dave Braisted, Phil and Jane Hodson, Rona Murdoch, Brian Brooks, Alex and Claire Pearse, Sean A Smith, Neil Ingoe

ELSLACK
SD9249 MAP 7

Tempest Arms 🍴 ♀ 🍺 🛏
just off A56 Earby—Skipton; BD23 3AY

Friendly inn with three log fires in stylish rooms, several real ales, good food, and tables outside; bedrooms

Now back on top form, this is a bustling and friendly inn with a genuine welcome from the helpful staff. It's stylish but understated with cushioned armchairs, built-in wall seats with lots of comfortable cushions, stools and lots of tables, and three log fires – one greets you at the entrance and divides the bar and restaurant. There's quite a bit of exposed stonework, amusing prints on the cream walls, and maybe Molly the friendly back labrador. Moorhouses Premier Bitter, Theakstons Best, Timothy Taylors Landlord, and a changing guest beer on handpump, ten wines by the glass, and several malt whiskies. There are tables outside largely screened from the road by a raised bank, and a smokers' shelter. The bedrooms, in the newish purpose built extension, are comfortable.

🍴 **Good food – using the same menu in bar and restaurant – includes lunchtime sandwiches, soup, fried bread topped with devilled lambs kidneys and crispy smoked bacon, deep-fried brie in a light crumb with a stawberry and citrus coulis, wensleydale cheese and onion pie with asparagus sauce, beer-battered haddock with mushy peas and tartare sauce, chicken breast with tiger prawns and fresh coriander with a creamy mild curry sauce and egg-fried rice, popular marinated lamb on the bone with mint and redcurrant gravy, confit duck leg on bubble and squeak with madeira sauce, and steak frites.** *Starters/Snacks: £2.95 to £6.95. Main Courses: £8.25 to £15.50. Puddings: £4.70 to £5.75*

Free house ~ Licensees Martin and Veronica Clarkson ~ Real ale ~ Bar food (12-2, 6-9(9.30 Fri and Sat); 12-7.30 Sun) ~ Restaurant ~ (01282) 842450 ~ Children welcome ~ Dogs allowed in bedrooms ~ Open 11-11; 12-10.30 Sun ~ Bedrooms: £59.95B/£74.95B

Recommended by Pat and Graham Williamson, Dr Kevan Tucker, Geoffrey and Brenda Wilson, Fred and Lorraine Gill, Dudley and Moira Cockroft, Mr and Mrs P Eastwood, Neil Kellett, Richard, Pat and Stewart Gordon, Ian Stafford, Karen Eliot, Brian Wainwright, Mrs R A Cartwright, John and Alison Hamilton, Brian and Janet Ainscough, Andrew and Christine Gagg, Steve Whalley

FADMOOR
SE6789 MAP 10

Plough 🍴 ♀
Village signposted off A170 in or just W of Kirkbymoorside; YO62 7HY

Particularly well run and enjoyable dining pub with a friendly welcome, civilised little rooms, particularly good food, and fine wines

Overlooking the quiet village green, this very well run pub remains as popular as ever for its smashing food and welcoming staff. The elegantly simple little rooms have cushioned settles and a range of armed wheelbacks and other wooden dining chairs on seagrass floors (some fine rugs too), horse tack attached to beams, all sorts of prints and pictures on the yellow walls, and lots of wine bottles on display. Black Sheep Best and Tetleys on handpump, and an extensive wine list; piped music. There are seats on the terrace. They also have a quiet little caravan site for Caravan Club registered members.

🍴 **First rate bar food includes sandwiches, soup, chicken liver pâté with home-made fruit chutney, black pudding and blue stilton salad with a warm poached duck egg, crayfish cocktail, steak in ale pie, slow-roast lamb shank with red wine and rosemary gravy, chicken breast with a mushroom and creamy white wine sauce, fillet of cod wrapped in pancetta with a rustic tomato, white wine and herb sauce, slow-roasted boneless half gressingham duckling with an orange, mandarin and brandy sauce, and puddings such as steamed ginger and syrup sponge and and rhubarb and honey crème brûlée with rhubarb ice-cream; they also offer a good value two-course set menu (not Saturday evening or Sunday lunchtime).** *Starters/Snacks: £4.95 to £7.95. Main Courses: £8.95 to £17.95. Puddings: £5.00*

Holf Leisure Ltd ~ Licensee Neil Nicholson ~ Real ale ~ Bar food (12-1.45, 6.30(7 Sun)-8.45) ~ Restaurant ~ (01751) 431515 ~ Children welcome ~ Open 12-3, 6.30-11; 12-4, 7-10.30 Sun; closed 25 and 26 Dec, 1 Jan

Recommended by Joyce and Maurice Cottrell, WW, Sylvia and Tony Birbeck, Maurice and Gill McMahon, Margaret Dickinson, John and Verna Aspinall, Christopher Turner, Dennis and Gill Keen, Ann and Tony Bennett-Hughes, Greta and Christopher Wells, Jean and Douglas Troup, Pauline and Derek Hodgkiss

FELIXKIRK

SE4684   MAP 10

Carpenters Arms 🍴 🍷

Village signposted off A170 E of Thirsk; YO7 2DP

Busy family-run dining pub with pubby choices and more interesting dishes, good wine list, and several real ales

The quiet setting of this busy dining pub in a little yorkshire village is most appealing. It's run by a mother and daughter team, and there are three or four cosy areas that ramble around the bar counter (made partly from three huge casks), with dark beams and joists hung with carpentry tools and other bric-a-brac, and comfortable seats around tables with check tablecloths; also, little lighted oil burners, a stone fireplace, Batemans Hooker, Black Sheep Best, John Smiths, and Timothy Taylors Mild on handpump, a good wine list and lots of coffees. Piped music and board games. The two dalmatians are called Lola and Lloyd. The church is prettily floodlit at night.

🍴 Well liked bar dishes (not available on Saturday evenings or Sunday lunchtimes) include sandwiches, bangers and mash with onion gravy, smoked haddock and spring onion risotto with a soft poached egg, chicken curry, fish pie, and field mushroom and bacon pasta with fresh herbs; there's also terrine of duck confit, foie gras and belly pork with english mustard butter, queen scallops with lemon, garlic and gruyère, baked avocado with stilton, celery and walnuts and avocado oil dressing, calves liver with crispy bacon, caramelised onions and port sauce, whole bass with fresh ginger, orange and spring onions, and puddings such as a trio of crème brûlée with home-made shortbreads and banana and golden syrup cake with caramel ice-cream, toffee bananas and caramel sauce. *Starters/Snacks: £4.95 to £6.95. Main Courses: £9.50 to £16.50. Puddings: £4.95*

Free house ~ Licensee Karen Bumby ~ Real ale ~ Bar food (not Sun evening or Mon) ~ Restaurant ~ (01845) 537369 ~ Children welcome ~ Open 11.30-3, 6.30-11; 12-3 Sun; closed Sun evening, Mon, 25 Dec, 1 week Feb

Recommended by WW, H Bramwell, M and GR, R Pearce, Peter Burton, Derek and Sylvia Stephenson, Sally Anne and Peter Goodale, J Crosby

FERRENSBY

SE3660   MAP 7

General Tarleton 🍴 🍷 🛏

A655 N of Knaresborough; HG5 0PZ

Civilised coaching inn with interesting food, lots of wines by the glass, friendly service, and relaxed atmosphere; comfortable bedrooms

Most customers are here to enjoy the interesting food in this civilised and rather smart old coaching inn. The beamed bar/brasserie has brick pillars dividing up the several different areas to create the occasional cosy alcove, some exposed stonework, and neatly framed pictures of staff on the cream walls. Dark brown leather chairs are grouped around wooden tables, there's a big open fire, a friendly, relaxed atmosphere and a door leading out to a pleasant tree-lined garden – seats here as well as in a covered courtyard. If you reserve a table, they put your name on it rather than just the word 'reserved' which readers feel adds a nice personal touch. Black Sheep Best and Timothy Taylors Landlord on handpump, 17 good wines by the glass, and quite a few coffees. The bedrooms are comfortable.

🍴 Good – if not cheap – food includes lunchtime open sandwiches, asian-spiced crispy belly pork with pak choi, sweet potato and sweet ginger dressing, queenie scallops in garlic and lemon butter with gruyère and cheddar, aubergine and potato terrine with goats cheese fondue, beetroot jelly and basil oil, beer-battered fresh fish, crisped slow-braised shoulder of lamb with puy lentils, bacon lardons, roast shallots and thyme, steak in ale pudding, breast of goosnargh corn-fed duckling with rhubarb and gingerbread spiced sauce, and puddings like baked custard tart with armagnac-soaked d'agen prunes and sticky toffee pudding with butterscotch sauce and vanilla pod ice-cream; side dishes (potatoes, vegetables and salad) are extra. *Starters/Snacks: £4.95 to £9.95. Main Courses: £9.95 to £17.95. Puddings: £4.95 to £6.75*

Free house ~ Licensee John Topham ~ Real ale ~ Bar food (12-2, 6-9.15) ~ Restaurant ~ (01423) 340284 ~ Children welcome ~ Open 12-3, 6(5.30 Sat)-11 ~ Bedrooms: £85B/£129B

Recommended by Keith and Margaret Kettell, Janet and Peter Race, Brian and Janet Ainscough, Graham and Doreen Holden, Dr Ian S Morley, Alison and Pete, Comus and Sarah Elliott, WW

GOOSE EYE   SE0240   MAP 7

Turkey 🍺

Just S of Laycock on road to Oakworth and Haworth, W of Keighley; OS Sheet 104 map reference 028406; BD22 0PD

Friendly local, several real ales including their own-brewed ones, roaring log fires, and tasty, straightforward bar food

A new licensee has taken over this pleasant old pub and as we went to press had shut the brewery for refurbishment; it will certainly be up and running by the time this *Guide* is published. As well as their own Turkey Bitter, guest beers include Adnams Bitter, Brakspears Oxford Gold, Fullers London Pride, Greene King Abbot, Springhead Leveller, Tetleys, and Timothy Taylors Golden Best and Landlord on handpump; their beer festival is on the first May Bank Holiday. Also, around 40 malt whiskies, and a separate games area with pool, darts and a games machine. There are various cosy and snug alcoves, straightforward pubby furniture, beams, walls covered with pictures of surrounding areas, and two roaring log fires; both walkers and their dogs are welcome.

🍽 **Generous helpings of decent, straightforward bar food include sandwiches, soup, a pie of the day, daily specials and puddings.** *Starters/Snacks: £3.25 to £4.95. Main Courses: £7.95 to £16.00. Puddings: £3.95*

Own brew ~ Licensee Neil Armitage ~ Real ale ~ Bar food (12-2.30, 6-9; 12-8.30 Sun) ~ Restaurant ~ (01535) 681339 ~ Children welcome until 9pm ~ Dogs allowed in bar ~ Open 12-11(midnight Fri and Sat)

Recommended by Greta and Christopher Wells, Priscilla Sandford, Matt Waite, Noel Thomas

GRINTON   SE0498   MAP 10

Bridge Inn 🍺 🛏

B6270 W of Richmond; DL11 6HH

Bustling pub with welcoming landlord, comfortable bars, log fires, a fine choice of drinks, and good food; neat bedrooms

After enjoying one of the good walks surrounding this well run and friendly country pub, both wet walkers and their dogs are welcome in the bar. This is cheerful, gently lit and red-carpeted, with bow window seats and a pair of stripped traditional settles among more usual pub seats, all well cushioned, a good log fire, Jennings Cumberland and Cocker Hoop, and guests such as Marstons Sun Bright and York Yorkshire Terrier on handpump, nice wines by the glass, and 20 malt whiskies. On the right a few steps take you down into a dark red room with darts, board games, a well lit pool table, ring-the-bull, and piped music. Friendly, helpful service. On the left, past leather armchairs and a sofa by a second log fire (and a glass chess set), is an extensive two-part dining room. The décor is in mint green and shades of brown, with a modicum of fishing memorabilia. There are picnic-sets outside, and the inn is right opposite a lovely church known as the Cathedral of the Dales. The bedrooms are neat and simple, and breakfasts are good. This is a pretty Swaledale village.

🍽 **Using their own herbs, making their own jams, marmalade and chutneys, and sourcing seasonal produce from local suppliers, the often interesting bar food includes filled baguettes and baked potatoes, soup, smoked mackerel pâté, chicken goujons wrapped in** bacon and stacked on garlic spinach with a tomato and olive dressing, **butternut squash risotto with basil, oregano and white wine, cumberland sausage with onion gravy, honey-glazed duck breast on roast celeriac and red onion, lamb shank braised in red wine, rosemary and onions on sweet potato mash, and puddings such as three-chocolate brownie and changing fruit crumbles.** *Starters/Snacks: £4.95 to £5.45. Main Courses: £7.95 to £16.95. Puddings: £4.25 to £4.95*

Jennings (Marstons) ~ Lease Andrew Atkin ~ Real ale ~ Bar food (all day) ~ Restaurant ~ (01748) 884224 ~ Children welcome ~ Dogs allowed in bar and bedrooms ~ Open 12-midnight(1am Sat) ~ Bedrooms: £46B/£72B

Recommended by Lucien Perring, Lynda and Trevor Smith, Jill and Julian Tasker, Jo Lilley, Simon Calvert, M and GR, Chris and Jeanne Downing, Mr and Mrs Ian King, Stephen Woad, Ken and Barbara Turner, Dr and Mrs P Truelove, Dr A McCormick, David and Jean Hall, Arthur Pickering, David and Karen Cuckney

HALIFAX
SE1027   MAP 7

Shibden Mill ♀ 🍺

Off A58 into Kell Lane at Stump Cross Inn, near A6036 junction; keep on, pub signposted from Kell Lane on left; HX3 7UL

Tucked-away restored mill with cosy rambling bar, five real ales, and well liked bar food

This restored mill is hidden away in a wooded valley; there are plenty of seats and tables on an attractive heated terrace, and the building is prettily floodlit at night. Inside, the rambling bar has cosy side areas with banquettes heaped with cushions and rugs, there are well spaced nice old tables and chairs on the flagstones, and the candles in elegant iron holders give a feeling of real intimacy; also, old hunting prints, country landscapes and so forth, and a couple of big log fireplaces. John Smiths, Theakstons XB, a beer brewed for them by Moorhouses, and a couple of guest beers like Copper Dragon Golden Pippin and Stonehenge Pigswill on handpump, and several wines by the glass. There's an upstairs restaurant; piped music.

🍴 Well liked **bar food includes sandwiches, good ploughman's with home-made bread and pickles and scotch egg, warm terrine of smoked haddock with wholegrain mustard sauce, leek and morel risotto with herby butter sauce, burger with extra toppings, fish and chips with tartare sauce, cold ham hock with two fried eggs and spicy tomato chutney, sausages of the day with onion gravy, steak and kidney pudding, and puddings such as white chocolate cheesecake and glazed lemon tart with chantilly cream and raspberry coulis.** *Starters/Snacks: £4.25 to £7.25. Main Courses: £8.95 to £17.95. Puddings: £5.75 to £6.25*

Free house ~ Licensee Glen Pearson ~ Real ale ~ Bar food (12-2, 6-9.30; 12-7.30 Sun) ~ Restaurant ~ (01422) 365840 ~ Children welcome ~ Dogs allowed in bar ~ Open 12-2.30, 5.30-11 Sat; 12-10.30 Sun; closed evenings of 25 and 26 Dec and 1 Jan ~ Bedrooms: £75B/£90B

Recommended by MDN, Gordon and Margaret Ormondroyd, Jane and Alan Bush, Jo Lilley, Simon Calvert, Brian and Ruth Young, Richard Marjoram, John Honnor, Clive Flynn, Pat and Tony Martin, Hunter and Christine Wright, Simon Marley, Greta and Christopher Wells

HAROME
SE6482   MAP 10

Star ★ ⑪ ♀ 🍺 🛏

Village signposted S of A170, E of Helmsley; YO62 5JE

Ambitious modern cooking by young landlord in pretty thatched pub, proper bar with real ales and first-class wines, and seats on terrace and in garden; stylish bedrooms

Most customers come to this pretty, thatched 14th-c inn to enjoy the imaginative modern food cooked by the young chef/patron. But the bar still has a proper pubby atmosphere, a dark bowed beam-and-plank ceiling, plenty of bric-a-brac, interesting furniture (this was the first pub that 'Mousey Thompson' ever populated with his famous dark wood furniture), a fine log fire, a well polished tiled kitchen range, and daily papers and magazines; as they don't take bar reservations, it's best to arrive early to get a seat. There's also a private dining room, a popular coffee loft in the eaves, and a separate restaurant. Black Sheep Best, Copper Dragon Golden Pippin, Hambleton Stallion and a seasonal ale, and Timothy Taylors Landlord on handpump, 17 wines by the glass, and home-made fruit liqueurs, with coffees, teas and hot chocolate with marshmallows, all with home-made chocolates; piped music. There are some seats and tables on a sheltered front terrace with more in the garden with fruit trees. You may have to book the stylish bedrooms and suites a long way ahead. They own a traditional butcher and delicatessen in the Market Place in Helmsley, and also have a village cricket team.

{¶} Using their own herbs and vegetables and other local produce, the inventive, if expensive, food includes sandwiches and filled buns, a posh ploughman's, scrambled duck eggs with wild garlic, mushrooms and sherried juices, chicken liver and foie gras parfait with a little fig salad and relish, calves liver with bubble and squeak mash, peppered saddleback pancetta and real ale juices, saddle of roe deer with a small venison cottage pie, black trumpet mushrooms, ham lardons, and juniper juices, casserole of saddleback pig with sage and onion mash, apples, black pudding and dry cider juices, and puddings like steamed blood orange and golden syrup sponge with marmalade ice-cream and dark chocolate and rosemary mousse with clotted cream, boozy cherries and berry sauce; there's a fine cheeseboard and a bakery/delicatessen that sells take-away meals and snacks as well as all manner of other goodies. *Starters/Snacks: £4.50 to £13.95. Main Courses: £12.50 to £24.00. Puddings: £5.00 to £9.00*

Free house ~ Licensees Andrew and Jacquie Pern ~ Real ale ~ Bar food (11.30-2, 6.15-9.30; 12-6 Sun; not Mon lunchtime) ~ Restaurant ~ (01439) 770397 ~ Children welcome ~ Open 11.30-3, 6.15-11; 12-11 Sun; closed Mon lunchtime, bank hols, 25 Dec ~ Bedrooms: /£140B

Recommended by Ian and Jane Haslock, David Thornton, Sally Anne and Peter Goodale, J Crosby, Phil and Jane Hodson, John Lane, Mr and Mrs P L Spencer, Maurice and Gill McMahon, Richard Cole, Derek Thomas, Andy and Jill Kassube, P R Stevens

HARTSHEAD
SE1822 MAP 7

Gray Ox {¶} ♀

3.5 miles from M62 junction 25; A644 towards Dewsbury, left on to A62, next left on to B6119, then second left on to Hartshead Lane (past Hartshead Hall Lane); pub on right; WF15 8AL

Appealing modern cooking in attractive dining pub, cosy beamed bars, real ales, several wines by the glass, and fine views

With reliably good food and drink and attentive, friendly service, it's not surprising that this attractive stone-built dining pub is so popular. The bars have beams and flagstones, a cosy décor, bentwood chairs and stripped pine tables, roaring log fires and a buoyant atmosphere; comfortable carpeted dining areas with bold paintwork and leather dining chairs around polished tables lead off. Jennings Cumberland and Cocker Hoop with guests like Hook Norton 303 AD and Jennings Mountain Man on handpump, and several wines by the glass; piped music. There are picnic-sets outside, and fine views through the latticed pub windows across the Calder Valley to the distant outskirts of Huddersfield – the lights are pretty at night.

{¶} Impressive modern food at lunchtime might include sandwiches, fresh crab and spring onion risotto, smoked salmon and scrambled egg on toasted brioche, beer-battered haddock with mushy peas, pork and leek sausages, slow-braised lamb shank with red wine and redcurrant jus and steak in ale pie; evening choices such as queenie scallops with garlic butter and gruyère, a vegetarian tapas plate, pigeon breast, chorizo and black pudding salad, seafood risotto with mascarpone cheese, chicken breast stuffed with a wild mushroom and tarragon mousse with blue cheese sauce, and roast rack of venison with a game suet pudding and barley broth, and puddings like Baileys crème brûlée with a chocolate brownie and lemon posset with home-made loganberry ice-cream. *Starters/Snacks: £3.95 to £8.50. Main Courses: £7.95 to £15.95. Puddings: £4.95 to £5.25*

Banks's (Marstons) ~ Lease Bernadette McCarron ~ Real ale ~ Bar food (12-2, 6-9; 12-7 Sun, not Sun evening) ~ Restaurant ~ (01274) 872845 ~ Children welcome ~ Open 12-3, 6-midnight; 12 noon-midnight Sat; 12-11 Sun

Recommended by Gordon and Margaret Ormondroyd, Andy and Jill Kassube, Bernie, Marcus Mann, Dr Kevan Tucker, AP, Michael Jones, Roger Newton

HEATH

SE3520 MAP 7

Kings Arms

Village signposted from A655 Wakefield—Normanton – or, more directly, turn off to the left opposite Horse & Groom; WF1 5SL

Old-fashioned gaslit pub in interesting location with dark-panelled original bar, real ales, and standard bar food; seats outside

This is an old-fashioned pub that makes the most of the village green setting opposite, surrounded by 19th-c stone merchants' houses; there are benches in front, picnic-sets on a side lawn, and a nice walled garden. Inside, the gas lighting adds a lot to the atmosphere, and the original bar has a fire burning in the old black range (with a long row of smoothing irons on the mantelpiece), plain elm stools and oak settles built into the walls, and dark panelling. A more comfortable extension has carefully preserved the original style, down to good wood-pegged oak panelling (two embossed with royal arms), and a high shelf of plates; there are also two other small flagstoned rooms and the conservatory opens on to the garden. Clarks Classic Blonde and Rams Revenge, and a couple of guest beers on handpump.

🍴 Straightforward bar food includes sandwiches, soup, yorkshire pudding and onion gravy, steak in ale pie, beer-battered haddock, daily specials, and puddings like lemon cheesecake and chocolate fudge cake. *Starters/Snacks: £3.50 to £4.95. Main Courses: £5.25 to £9.95. Puddings: £3.95*

Clarks ~ Manager Andrew Shepherd ~ Real ale ~ Bar food (12-2(2.30 Sun), 6-9.30; 12-5 Sun) ~ Restaurant ~ (01924) 377527 ~ Children allowed away from main lounge ~ Dogs allowed in bar ~ Open 12-11(midnight Sat); 12-3, 5-11 weekdays in winter

Recommended by the Didler, Greta and Christopher Wells, Rosemary K Germaine, R T and J C Moggridge, John Saville, Dr and Mrs A K Clarke

HETTON

SD9658 MAP 7

Angel 🍴 ♆ 🛏

Just off B6265 Skipton—Grassington; BD23 6LT

Dining pub with rambling timbered rooms, lots of wines by the glass, real ales and imaginative food; seats on the heated terrace

You can expect a warm welcome from the courteous staff and first class food in this particularly well run and very popular dining pub. There are three timbered and panelled rambling rooms, though perhaps the one with the most pubby atmosphere (and where you can feel comfortable just popping in for a drink) is the main bar with a Victorian farmhouse range in the big stone fireplace. There are lots of cosy alcoves, comfortable country-kitchen chairs or button-back green plush seats, Ronald Searle wine-snob cartoons and older engravings and photographs, and log fires. Black Sheep Best, Timothy Taylors Landlord, and a guest beer on handpump, around 20 wines by the glass including champagne, and quite a few malt whiskies. Outside on a decked area with canopies and outdoor heaters, there are lots of seats.

🍴 Excellent bar food using top quality, local produce includes sandwiches, local rare breed pork, pistachio and prune terrine with port and madeira jelly, a little moneybag (seafood baked in crisp pastry with lobster sauce), potato gnocchi with cherry tomatoes, spinach and buffalo mozzarella, goosnargh chicken breast with rocket and red onion salad, goats cheese and rosemary sauce, pheasant wrapped in bacon with a herb and chestnut butter, wild halibut fillet with pomme purée, asparagus, queenie scallops, lobster reduction and lemon and chilli oil, duck breast with honey-roasted apple, red wine shallots, and thyme jus, and puddings such as orange and lemon tart with a light citrus crème pâtissière and sticky toffee pudding with butterscotch sauce and crème chantilly; there's also a good value two- and three-course early bird menu (until 6.45pm), and good Sunday roasts. *Starters/Snacks: £3.95 to £6.95. Main Courses: £10.95 to £16.95. Puddings: £4.50 to £6.95*

Free house ~ Licensee Bruce Elsworth ~ Real ale ~ Bar food (12-2.15(2.30 Sun), 6-9(10 Sat)) ~ Restaurant ~ (01756) 730263 ~ Children welcome ~ Dogs allowed in bedrooms ~ Open 12-3, 6-11(10 Sun); 12-2.30, 6-10.30(11 Sat) in winter; closed 25 Dec, one week Jan ~ Bedrooms: £115B/£130B

Recommended by Michael Doswell, Richard and Mary Bailey, Dr Kevan Tucker, Richard, Margaret and Jeff Graham, Karen Eliot, Revd D Glover, Ray and Winifred Halliday, Jeremy King, Hunter and Christine Wright

HULL   TA1028   MAP 8

Olde White Harte ★ £

Off 25 Silver Street, a continuation of Whitefriargate; pub is up narrow passage, and should not be confused with the much more modern White Hart nearby; HU1 1JG

Some fine original features in busy old pub, lots of malt whiskies, several real ales, good value bar food, and seats in heated courtyard

Despite its heritage, this is very much a bustling and friendly working pub. The three bar rooms have some fine features. The downstairs one has attractive stained-glass windows that look out above the bow window seat, carved heavy beams support black ceiling boards, and there are two big brick inglenooks with a frieze of delft tiles. There's an upstairs restaurant. The curved copper-topped counter serves Caledonian Deuchars IPA, McEwans 80/-, Theakstons Old Peculier and a guest like Theakstons Best on handpump, and 80 malt whiskies. It was in the heavily panelled room up the oak staircase that in 1642 the town's governor Sir John Hotham made the fateful decision to lock the nearby gate against Charles I, depriving him of Hull's arsenal; it didn't do him much good, as in the Civil War that followed, Hotham, like the king, was executed by the parliamentarians. There are seats in the heated courtyard.

🍴 **Good value bar food includes lunchtime sandwiches and filled baguettes, soup, chicken liver pâté with sweet red onion chutney, fishcake with home-made tartare sauce, spinach and ricotta cannelloni, steak in ale pie, stuffed chicken breast with a creamy pesto sauce, and steaks.** *Starters/Snacks: £3.25 to £5.95. Main Courses: £5.25 to £9.95. Puddings: £2.95 to £3.50*

Scottish Courage ~ Lease Bernard Copley ~ Real ale ~ Bar food (11.30-3, 6-9.30; 12-4 Sun; evening food restaurant only (Weds-Sat); no food Mon or Tues evenings) ~ Restaurant ~ (01482) 326363 ~ Children in restaurant only ~ Dogs allowed in bar ~ Open 11am-midnight(1am Sat); 12 noon-midnight Sun

Recommended by the Didler, Alison and Pete, Pam and John Smith, Pat and Graham Williamson

KETTLESING   SE2257   MAP 7

Queens Head 🍺

Village signposted off A59 W of Harrogate; HG3 2LB

Lots to look at in friendly stone pub with open fires, chatty atmosphere, real ales and decent food; bedrooms

There's a warm, convivial atmosphere in this solid, quietly placed pub – it's very popular with older people at lunchtime. The L-shaped, carpeted main bar is decorated with Victorian song sheet covers, lithographs of Queen Victoria, little heraldic shields, and a delft shelf of blue and white china. There are also lots of quite close-set elm and other tables around its walls, with cushioned country seats, coal or log fires at each end and maybe unobtrusive piped radio. A smaller bar on the left, with built-in red banquettes, has cricketing prints and cigarette cards, coins and banknotes, and in the lobby there's a life-size portrait of Elizabeth I. Goose Eye Barm Pot Bitter, Roosters Hooligan, and Theakstons Old Peculier on handpump; good service. Seats in the neatly kept suntrap back garden, and benches in front by the lane.

Tipping is not normal for bar meals, and not usually expected.

🍴 Well liked bar food includes sandwiches, soup, filled yorkshire puddings, home-made burger, salads, omelettes, battered haddock, gammon and egg, and daily specials such as seafood bake, goats cheese and cherry tomato en croûte, medallions of pork fillet with apple and cider sauce, and homely puddings; they also do a good value three-course meal. *Starters/Snacks: £3.95 to £10.95. Main Courses: £5.95 to £19.95. Puddings: £3.95 to £4.95*

Free house ~ Licensees Louise and Glen Garbutt ~ Real ale ~ Bar food ~ (01423) 770263 ~ Children welcome ~ Open 11-2.30, 6-11; 12-10.30 Sun ~ Bedrooms: £76.37S/£88.12S

Recommended by B and M Kendall, Walter and Susan Rinaldi-Butcher, Tim and Claire Woodward, Mr and Mrs Staples, L and D Webster, M E Hutchinson, Brian Wainwright, Peter Hacker

KIRK DEIGHTON

Bay Horse ♀
B6164 N of Wetherby; Main Street; LS22 4DZ

Attractive dining pub with flagstoned entrance bar, candlelit tables in dining area, friendly service, decent wines and well liked bar food

For those who come to this attractive dining pub for just a drink, there's a small flagstoned bar by the entrance with Black Sheep Best, Copper Dragon Best Bitter, John Smiths and Timothy Taylors Landlord on handpump. Also, 12 wines by the glass and good coffees from a solid mahogany bar counter with proper brass foot and elbow rails. The main dark terracotta dining area is not large, with perhaps a dozen or so candlelit tables, comfortable banquettes and other seats, rugs on flagstones, beams and pictures, and a relaxed atmosphere. It's worth booking quite well ahead, especially for evenings or weekends. Service is friendly and efficient; piped music and games machine. More reports please.

🍴 As well as lunchtime sandwiches, the popular food includes good crab soup, duck terrine with plum and apple chutney, seared king scallops with celeriac purée, bacon and truffle oil, free-range organic chicken breast stuffed with smoked cheese, local estate venison roasted over cauliflower and sage purée with juniper sauce, saddle of lamb stuffed with oranges and apricots, whole lemon with prawn and lemon butter sauce, and puddings such as chocolate and hazelnut brownie with crème anglaise and vanilla ice-cream and lemon zest crème brûlée with blackberry compote and shortbread biscuits; good two-course set Sunday lunch menu. *Starters/Snacks: £4.25 to £6.75. Main Courses: £8.50 to £16.50. Puddings: £5.50*

Enterprise ~ Lease Karl and Amanda Maney ~ Real ale ~ Bar food (not Sun evening, not Mon lunchtime) ~ Restaurant ~ (01937) 580058 ~ Children welcome away from bar ~ Dogs allowed in bar ~ Open 12-3(5 Mon), 5-midnight; 12-11 Sun; closed Mon lunchtime

Recommended by Alyson and Andrew Jackson, Michael and Maggie Betton, Dr and Mrs A K Clarke, Michael Doswell, Brian and Janet Ainscough

KIRKBYMOORSIDE

George & Dragon 🛏
Market Place; YO62 6AA

17th-c coaching inn with convivial front bar, snug and bistro, good wines, real ales, and decent bar food; comfortable bedrooms

In a pretty little town, this handsome 17th-c coaching inn is a bustling place, especially on Wednesdays (which is market day). The convivial front bar has beams and panelling, smart orange-patterned tub seats around a mix of wooden tables on the part-carpet and part-solid-oak flooring, a roaring log fire in a rather fine fireplace, Black Sheep Best, Copper Dragon Challenger IPA and Scotts 1816, and Fullers London Pride on handpump from the hand-made ash counter, and ten wines by the glass; piped music. There's also a snug and a bistro. Outside on both the front and back terraces, there are plenty of seats under giant parasols and outdoor heater. More reports please.

🍴 Bar food includes sandwiches and panini, soup, pâté with chutney, salmon and crab fishcakes with a duo of sauces, sharing platters, beer-battered fresh haddock, steak in ale pie, vegetarian choices, slow-braised lamb shank, spicy mexican beef, a pasta of the day, steaks, and puddings. *Starters/Snacks: £4.00 to £5.50. Main Courses: £7.50 to £13.50. Puddings: £4.50*

Free house ~ Licensees David and Alison Nicholas ~ Real ale ~ Bar food ~ Restaurant ~ (01751) 433334 ~ Children welcome ~ Dogs allowed in bedrooms ~ Open 10.30am-11pm; 12-11 Sun ~ Bedrooms: £60B/£90B

Recommended by Pat and Tony Martin, Ann and Tony Bennett-Hughes

KIRKHAM
SE7365   MAP 7

Stone Trough 🍴 ♟ ◀
Kirkham Abbey; YO60 7JS

Beamed, cosy rooms in well run country pub, interesting bar food, five real ales, quite a few wines by the glass, and lovely valley views

Although the good, popular bar food in this bustling country inn remains quite a draw, the atmosphere is cosy and relaxed with a proper pubby feel. The several beamed and cosy rooms have warm log fires, Black Sheep Best, Tetleys, Timothy Taylors Landlord, and a couple of guests such as Copper Dragon Golden Pippin and Theakstons Old Peculier on handpump, and 11 wines by the glass; friendly service. There's also a snug, a lounge area for drinkers and diners, and a restaurant; piped music, TV and board games. From seats outside there are lovely views down the valley, and Kirkham Abbey and Castle Howard are nearby.

🍴 First rate bar food includes lunchtime sandwiches, soup, potted brown shrimps and whitby crab with tartare sauce, deep-fried herb breadcrumbed goats cheese with beetroot and walnut salad, pork and herb sausages on chive mash with real ale gravy and apple chutney, mature cheddar and caramelised shallot pasty with grain mustard and lentil sauce, parmesan-crumbed chicken escalope with roast garlic and tarragon butter, salmon, cod and prawn pie topped with cheddar mash and parsley crumb, and puddings such as dark chocolate cheesecake with caramelised oranges and Bailey's whipped cream and apricot bread and butter pudding with orange custard. *Starters/Snacks: £4.75 to £7.50. Main Courses: £8.95 to £16.95. Puddings: £5.25 to £5.95*

Free house ~ Licensees Sarah and Adam Richardson ~ Real ale (12-2, 6.30-8.30; not Mon) ~ Restaurant ~ (01653) 618713 ~ Well-behaved children welcome ~ Open 12-2.30, 6-11; 11.45-10.30 Sun; closed Mon (exc bank hols), 2-5 Jan

Recommended by Eileen McCall, Tim and Liz Sherbourne, DC, Michael Butler, WW, Michael Dandy, J Crosby, R L Graham, Christopher Turner, Pat and Graham Williamson, Jeff and Wendy Williams, S P Watkin, P A Taylor

LANGTHWAITE
NY9902   MAP 10

Charles Bathurst 🍴 ◀
Arkengarthdale, a mile N towards Tan Hill; generally known as the CB Inn; DL11 6EN

Friendly country pub with bustling atmosphere, good mix of customers, thoughtful wine list, decent real ales, and interesting bar food; comfortable bedrooms, lots of walks

You can be sure of a genuinely friendly welcome in this well run country pub, whether you are a local or a visitor. And whilst the place does major on the good food, it still feels like a pub with a bustling, relaxed atmosphere. The long bar has light pine scrubbed tables, country chairs and benches on stripped floors, plenty of snug alcoves, and a roaring fire. There's also a wooden floored dining room with views of Scar House (a shooting lodge owned by the Duke of Norfolk), Robert 'the Mouseman' Thompson tables and chairs, and an open truss ceiling; there are other dining areas as well. The island bar counter has bar stools, Black Sheep Best and Riggwelter, John Smiths and Theakstons Best on handpump, and ten wines by the glass from a sensibly laid-out list with helpful notes. Piped music, darts, pool, TV, dominoes, board games and quoits. The bedrooms are pretty and comfortable. This is a lovely spot with fine views over Langthwaite village and Arkengarthdale, and super surrounding walks.

🍴 **Imaginative food includes filled baguettes, soup, hare sausage with yorkshire pudding and apple and sultana compote, deep-fried fillet of smoked haddock on baby leaf spinach with quail egg and sweet mustard dressing, aubergine, tomato and feta cheese gratin, supreme of corn-fed chicken with crisp pancetta, savoy cabbage and dijon cream, shank of lamb with mixed bean du puy and juniper jus, monkfish wrapped in parma ham, lime rösti and spiced aubergine and mint yoghurt, and chocolate and walnut brownie with white chocolate ice-cream and chocolate sauce and glazed lemon tart with raspberry sorbet.** *Starters/Snacks: £4.75 to £6.00. Main Courses: £10.25 to £19.95. Puddings: £4.95 to £5.25*

Free house ~ Licensees Charles and Stacy Cody ~ Real ale ~ Bar food ~ Restaurant ~ (01748) 884567 ~ Children welcome ~ Dogs allowed in bedrooms ~ Open 11am-midnight; closed 25 Dec ~ Bedrooms: /£92.50B

Recommended by K S Whittaker, Bruce and Sharon Eden, John Coatsworth, Ben and Helen Ingram, Jane and Alan Bush, J Crosby, Richard and Sissel Harris, Professors Alan and Ann Clarke, Jill and Julian Tasker, David Thornton, Lynda and Trevor Smith, David and Jean Hall, Arthur Pickering

LASTINGHAM   SE7290   MAP 10

Blacksmiths Arms 🍺

Off A170 W of Pickering at Wrelton, forking off Rosedale road N of Cropton; or via Appleton or Hutton-le-Hole; YO62 6TL

Friendly village pub liked by walkers, with lively atmosphere, good service, traditional bars, quite a choice of drinks, and decent food; bedrooms

Bustling and friendly, with a wide range of customers – there are always plenty of walkers and cyclists – this is a comfortable and neatly kept stone inn at the foot of the moors in the National Park. The cosily old-fashioned beamed bar has a cheerful atmosphere, a log fire in an open range, traditional furnishings, Theakstons Best and guests like Copper Dragon Golden Pippin and Greene King Abbot on handpump, eight wines by the glass, Cropton cider (brewed a couple of miles away), and several malt whiskies. Piped music, darts, and board games. There are seats in the back garden and the village is very pretty. It's worth a visit to the church as it has a unique Saxon crypt built as a shrine to St Cedd.

🍴 **Fairly priced and popular, the bar food at lunchtime includes filled rolls and hot toasted panini (not Sunday lunchtime), soup, steak in ale pie, vegetable balti, beer-battered cod, and whitby scampi, with evening choices like stuffed mushrooms, brie wedges with red onion marmalade, beef hotpot in a giant yorkshire pudding, stuffed chicken fillet with stilton and asparagus sauce, chargrilled sirloin steak, and puddings. They do a frozen home-made take-away service, too.** *Starters/Snacks: £2.75 to £5.25. Main Courses: £8.50 to £17.95. Puddings: £3.65*

Free house ~ Licensee Peter Trafford ~ Real ale ~ Bar food (12-2(5 Sun), 7-9; not winter Tues lunchtime) ~ Restaurant ~ (01751) 417247 ~ Children welcome ~ Jamming session second Sun of month ~ Open 12-11.30; 12-2.30, 6-11 Mon-Thurs in winter; closed winter Tues lunchtime ~ Bedrooms: £50B/£70B

Recommended by Janet and Peter Race, Ann and Tony Bennett-Hughes, David Barnes, WW, P Dawn

LEDSHAM   SE4529   MAP 7

Chequers 🍺

1.5 miles from A1(M) junction 42: follow Leeds signs, then Ledsham signposted; also some 4 miles N of junction M62; Claypit Lane; LS25 5LP

Ambitious restauranty food – some bar snacks too – in friendly village pub, log fires in several beamed rooms, and real ales; pretty back terrace

This 16th-c stone-built inn is a very popular and restful place to take a break from the busy A1. There are several small, individually decorated rooms with low beams, lots of cosy alcoves, toby jugs and all sorts of knick-knacks on the walls and ceilings, and log fires. From the old-fashioned little central panelled-in servery they dispense Brown Cow Bitter, John Smiths, Theakstons Best, Timothy Taylors Landlord and a guest beer on handpump; good, attentive service. A sheltered two-level terrace behind the house has tables among roses and the hanging baskets and flowers are very pretty.

🍴 As well as bar food like sandwiches, smoked salmon and scrambled eggs, sausage and mash, and steak and mushroom pie, there's an elaborately described, restauranty menu (with prices to match). To give you the full flavour, we've kept their wording: 'dishes such as warm spinach and woodland mushroom tart sheeted with brie and caressed by a white onion glaze, warm baby goats cheese and caramelised apples brought together with an orange glaze, slow-cooked shoulder of lamb relaxing beside buttered chilli mash and coated with a provençale sauce and a duvet of smoked mozzarella, halibut baked with a crust of herbs and garlic and set in a pool of mussel and dill cream, rosemary-dusted venison noisettes with red cabbage brought together by a cranberry marmalade.' They do puddings like raspberry and almond tart and treacle sponge and custard. *Starters/Snacks: £4.65 to £9.45. Main Courses: £10.85 to £17.95. Puddings: £4.95 to £5.25*

Free house ~ Licensee Chris Wraith ~ Real ale ~ Bar food (12-9 Mon-Sat; not Sun) ~ Restaurant ~ (01977) 683135 ~ Well-behaved children allowed ~ Dogs allowed in bar ~ Open 11-11; closed Sun

Recommended by Andy and Jill Kassube, the Didler, David and Pam Wilcox, Louise Gibbons, Pat and Stewart Gordon, Peter and Jean Hoare, Dr and Mrs J Temporal

LEYBURN
SE1190   MAP 10

Sandpiper 🍴 ♟
Just off Market Place; DL8 5AT

Emphasis on appealing food though cosy bar for drinkers in 17th-c cottage, real ales, amazing choice of whiskies; bedrooms

In good weather, you can enjoy a drink on the front terrace of this little 17th-c stone cottage amongst the lovely hanging baskets and flowering climbers. Inside, the small cosy bar – liked by locals – has a couple of black beams in the low ceiling and a few tables and chairs, and the back room up three steps has attractive Dales photographs; get here early to be sure of a seat. Down by the nice linenfold panelled bar counter there are stuffed sandpipers, more photographs, and a woodburning stove in the stone fireplace; to the left is the restaurant. Black Sheep Best and Special and Copper Dragon Best on handpump, over 100 malt whiskies, and a decent wine list with several by the glass; piped music.

🍴 Cooked by the landlord, the interesting food includes lunchtime sandwiches, soup, coq au vin terrine, blood orange and blue cheese salad, fish in beer batter, gammon and eggs, asparagus and wild mushroom risotto, pollack wrapped in parma ham with tomato and basil sauce, crispy duck leg with fried potatoes and a plum and orange sauce, breast of chicken topped with bacon on bubble and squeak, a duo of fish on a crab, lime and coriander pasta, daily specials, puddings, and Sunday roasts. *Starters/Snacks: £6.55 to £7.50. Main Courses: £8.25 to £16.95. Puddings: £5.00 to £6.75*

Free house ~ Licensee Jonathan Harrison ~ Real ale ~ Bar food (12-2.30(2 Sun), 6.30(7 Sun)-9; not Mon or winter Tues) ~ Restaurant ~ (01969) 622206 ~ Well-behaved children allowed in restaurant only, until 8pm ~ Dogs allowed in bar ~ Open 11.30-3, 6.30-11; 12-3, 6.30-10.30 Sun; closed Mon, winter Tues ~ Bedrooms: £65S(£70B)/£75S(£80B)

Recommended by Stuart Paulley, John and Sharon Hancock, John Robertson, J Crosby, Jane and Alan Bush, C and H Greenly, Mr and Mrs W W Burke, Ian and Celia Abbott, Dr Ian S Morley, David S Allen, B and M Kendall, Stephen Wood, Richard and Sissel Harris

---

'Children welcome' means the pub says it lets children inside without any special restriction. If it allows them in, but to restricted areas such as an eating area or family room, we specify this. Some pubs may impose an evening time limit. We do not mention limits after 9pm as we assume children are home by then.

LINTHWAITE

SE1014   MAP 7

Sair 🍺

Hoyle Ing, off A62; 3.5 miles after Huddersfield look out for two water storage tanks (painted with a shepherd scene) on your right – the street is on your left, burrowing very steeply up between works buildings; OS Sheet 110 map reference 101143; HD7 5SG

A fine choice of own-brew beers in old-fashioned pub; open fires, simple furnishings, fine view from outside seats; no food

It's the nine own-brewed beers that draw customers into this old-fashioned pub. On handpump, they include Linfit Bitter, Dark Mild, Special, Swift, Gold Medal, Autumn Gold, Old Eli, English Guineas Stout and Leadboiler. Also, Weston's farm cider and a few malt whiskies. The four rooms are furnished with pews or smaller chairs on the rough flagstones or wooden floors and there are log-burning ranges in three rooms; the one to the left of the entrance has dominoes, a juke box, shove-ha'penny and cribbage. In summer, there are plenty of seats and tables in front of the pub that have a striking view across the Colne Valley. The Huddersfield Narrow Canal is restored through to Ashton; in the 3.5 miles from Linthwaite to the highest, deepest and longest tunnel in Britain, there are 25 working locks and some lovely countryside. More reports please.

🍽 **No food at all.**

Own brew ~ Licensee Ron Crabtree ~ Real ale ~ No credit cards ~ (01484) 842370 ~ Children welcome until 8pm ~ Dogs welcome ~ Open 5-11; 12-11 Sat; 12-10.30 Sun; closed weekday lunchtimes

Recommended by the Didler

LINTON

SE3846   MAP 7

Windmill

Leaving Wetherby W on A661, fork left just before hospital and bear left; also signposted from A659, leaving Collingham towards Harewood; LS22 4HT

Small beamed rooms, chatty civilised atmosphere, real ales, lunchtime snacks and more elaborate evening food; sunny terrace and sheltered garden

This is an enjoyable pub for either a drink or a meal and service is cheerful and efficient. The small beamed rooms have a good relaxed atmosphere, walls stripped back to bare stone, polished antique oak settles around copper-topped cast-iron tables, pots hanging from the oak beams, a high shelf of plates, and log fires. There's also a sizeable restaurant. John Smiths, Theakstons Best, and a guest like Harviestoun Bitter & Twisted or Robinsons Top Tipple on handpump and several wines by the glass; piped music. The pear tree outside was raised from seed brought back from the Napoleonic Wars, and there are seats in the sheltered garden and on the sunny terrace at the back of the building.

🍽 **Well liked bar food includes lunchtime sandwiches and snacks, soup, chicken liver parfait with plum and apple chutney, carpaccio of fennel and melon with a pink grapefruit dressing, crayfish tail salad with spiced mango aïoli, grilled chicken breast with roasted butternut squash and creamy tarragon and rocket sauce, caramelised red onion and goats cheese filo tart, salmon fillet with a light sweet and sour sauce, rack of lamb with a port and redcurrant reduction and creamed leek potatoes, and puddings.** *Starters/Snacks: £4.95 to £8.95. Main Courses: £5.95 to £11.95. Puddings: £3.95 to £4.95*

Scottish Courage ~ Lease Janet Rowley and John Littler ~ Real ale ~ Bar food (12-2(2.30 Sat), 5.30-9; 12-5.45 Sun; not Sun evening) ~ Restaurant ~ (01937) 582209 ~ Children welcome until 7.30pm ~ Dogs allowed in bar ~ Open 11.30-3, 5.30-11; 11-11 Sat; 12-10.30 Sun

Recommended by Maurice and Janet Thorpe, Ray and Winifred Halliday, Mrs F Brooker, David Crook, Dr and Mrs A K Clarke, Di and Mike Gillam

---

Smoking is not allowed inside any pub. Some pubs now have outdoor shelters, open on two sides and sometimes heated, where smoking is allowed.

LINTON IN CRAVEN   SD9962 MAP 7

Fountaine

Just off B6265 Skipton—Grassington; BD23 5HJ

Neatly kept pub in charming village, attractive furnishings, open fires, five real ales, decent wines and well liked bar food; seats on terrace

Bustling and neatly kept, this pub looks down over the village green to the narrow stream that runs through this delightful hamlet; there are fine surrounding walks in the lovely Dales countryside. There's a welcoming atmosphere, beams and white-painted joists in the low ceilings, log fires (one in a beautifully carved heavy wooden fireplace), attractive built-in cushioned wall benches and stools around a mix of copper-topped tables, little wall lamps and quite a few prints on the pale walls. John Smiths, Tetleys, and guests like Copper Dragon 1816, Moorhouses Premier Bitter, and Theakstons Best on handpump and several wines by the glass; piped music, darts, and dominoes. Outside on the terrace there are teak benches and tables under green parasols and pretty hanging baskets.

🍴 As well as hearty sandwiches in different breads, the attractively presented food might include chicken liver pâté with onion marmalade, mediterranean prawn pot, garlic mushrooms, beer-battered haddock, steak in ale pie, cumberland sausage, mixed bean chilli, gammon and eggs, chicken stir fry, slow-cooked lamb shoulder with redcurrant and mint gravy, and puddings like white chocolate cheesecake with berry compote and jam roly-poly and custard. *Starters/Snacks: £3.95 to £5.95. Main Courses: £7.95 to £15.00. Puddings: £4.50*

Individual Inns ~ Manager Christopher Gregson ~ Real ale ~ Bar food (12-9) ~ Restaurant ~ (01756) 752210 ~ Children must be well behaved ~ Dogs allowed in bar ~ Open 11-11; 12-10.30 Sun

Recommended by WW, Lynda and Trevor Smith, Richard, Hunter and Christine Wright, Alyson and Andrew Jackson, Pat and Graham Williamson, Gordon and Margaret Ormondroyd, Fred and Lorraine Gill, B and M Kendall, Simon and Mandy King

LITTON   SD9074 MAP 7

Queens Arms 🍺

From B6160 N of Grassington, after Kilnsey take second left fork; can also be reached off B6479 at Stainforth N of Settle, via Halton Gill; BD23 5QJ

Friendly pub in fantastic walking area, own-brew beers, good homely food and simply furnished bars; bedrooms including a walkers' room

Hard-working, thoughtful new licensees have taken over this friendly pub. The main bar on the right has a good coal fire, stripped rough stone walls, a brown beam-and-plank ceiling, stools around cast-iron-framed tables on the stone and concrete floor, a seat built into the stone-mullioned window, and signed cricket bats. The left-hand room is an eating area with old photographs of the Dales around the walls. From their own microbrewery, they offer Litton Ale and Potts Beck Ale, and there's usually a guest such as Tetleys on handpump. Darts and board games. There's a safe area for children in the two-level garden and plenty of surrounding walks – a track behind the inn leads over Ackerley Moor to Buckden, and the quiet lane through the valley leads on to Pen-y-ghent. Walkers enjoy staying here and there is a walkers' room (price on request).

🍴 Hearty helpings of bar food include sandwiches, soup, yorkshire pudding with gravy, vegetable samosas with home-made mint dip, smoked bacon chops with apple, sage and onion, pies like rabbit or lamb and kidney in red wine, beer-battered haddock (using their own ale), local cumberland sausage ring, mushroom stroganoff, stilton chicken, and daily specials such as fresh tuna steak with sweet peppers and teriyaki sauce, and lamb and mint and pork and leek sausages on garlic mash with red wine gravy. *Starters/Snacks: £4.50 to £6.50. Main Courses: £8.10 to £16.50. Puddings: £2.50 to £4.20*

Own brew ~ Licensees Jayne and Doug Goldie ~ Real ale ~ Bar food (12-2.30, 6.30(7 Sun)-9) ~ Restaurant ~ (01756) 770208 ~ Children welcome away from bar ~ Dogs welcome ~ Open 12-3(3.30 Sat), 6.30-11; 12-3, 7-10.30 Sun ~ Bedrooms: /£75S

Recommended by Greta and Christopher Wells, Alyson and Andrew Jackson, Richard, Comus and Sarah Elliott, Dr D and Mrs B Woods, MDN

LONG PRESTON

SD8358   MAP 7

Maypole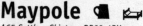

A65 Settle—Skipton; BD23 4PH

A good base for walkers with friendly staff, bustling atmosphere, well liked pubby food and fair choice of real ales

With friendly, hard-working licensees, this is a well run and enjoyable pub – our readers like it very much. The carpeted two-room bar has a good mix of locals and visitors, sporting prints and local photographs and a list of landlords dating back to 1695 on its butter-coloured walls, a delft shelf with whisky-water jugs and decorative plates, a couple of stags' heads, and good solid pub furnishings – heavy carved wall settles and the like, and heavy cast-iron-framed pub tables with unusual inset leather tops. There is a separate country dining room. Moorhouses Premier Bitter, Timothy Taylors Landlord and two changing ales from breweries such as Bowland and Copper Dragon on handpump, ten wines by the glass, Weston's cider (in summer), and several malt whiskies. There's a room on the left with darts, board games, dominoes and TV for important sporting events. Out behind is a terrace with a couple of picnic-sets under an ornamental cherry tree and another terrace with large tables under umbrellas and outdoor heaters, making it ideal for dining. This makes a good base for walking in the Dales and the bedrooms do get booked up quite a way ahead; good breakfasts.

🍴 Tasty, reasonably priced bar food includes sandwiches, soup, garlic mushrooms, smoked trout pâté, hot black pudding and chorizo with wholegrain mustard sauce, wensleydale and spinach lasagne, ham and eggs, breadcrumbed fillet of plaice, steak in ale pie, trout with fresh tarragon and lemon butter, and daily specials like slow-cooked oxtail in brown sugar and stout, wild rabbit and mushroom pie, and salmon fillet with a herb crust and a leek and cheese sauce. *Starters/Snacks: £3.50 to £5.25. Main Courses: £6.00 to £11.75. Puddings: £3.75 to £4.50*

Enterprise ~ Lease Robert Palmer ~ Real ale ~ Bar food (12-2, 6.30-9(9.30 Fri); all day weekends) ~ Restaurant ~ (01729) 840219 ~ Children welcome ~ Dogs allowed in bar and bedrooms ~ Occasional jazz Fri evenings; quiz first Weds of month ~ Open 11.30-3, 6-11; 11.30-midnight Sat; 11.30-11 Sun ~ Bedrooms: £35S/£60B

Recommended by Michael Butler, Mr and Mrs Ian King, Len Beattie, Steve Whalley, Mike and Linda Hudson, Adam F Padel, Andy and Jill Kassube

LOW CATTON

SE7053   MAP 7

Gold Cup

Village signposted with High Catton off A166 in Stamford Bridge or A1079 at Kexby Bridge; YO41 1EA

Enjoyable food and a friendly welcome in pleasant, bustling pub; real ales, seats in garden and ponies in paddock

At weekends, this white-rendered house usefully serves good food all day. It's a bustling and spacious pub with first-class service from the helpful and friendly staff, and several comfortable, communicating rooms. There's a fire at one end, plush wall seats and stools around good solid tables, some decorative plates and brasswork on the walls, and a relaxed atmosphere. The back bar has a woodburning stove in a brick fireplace and the restaurant has solid wooden pews and tables (said to be made from a single oak tree), and pleasant views of the surrounding fields. John Smiths and Theakstons Best on handpump; piped music, pool, and TV. The garden has a grassed area for children and the back paddock houses Candy the horse and Polly the shetland pony. They also own Boris the retired greyhound and have fishing rights on the adjoining River Derwent.

🍴 Using local farm meat and summer produce from local allotments, the good bar food includes sandwiches, soup, warm bacon and brie salad, battered mushrooms with a garlic mayonnaise dip, melon fan with parma ham and peach coulis, roasted vegetable stroganoff, prawns and poached salmon in a filo basket with lemon and dill mayonnaise, cajun chicken, beef in ale pie, venison steak braised in red wine, roast rack of lamb with redcurrant gravy, and puddings such as orange and Cointreau cheesecake and bakewell tart; they also offer two- and three-course set evening meals. *Starters/Snacks: £3.50 to £6.50. Main Courses: £6.96 to £15.50. Puddings: £3.95*

Free house ~ Licensees Pat and Ray Hales ~ Real ale ~ Bar food (12-2, 6-9; all day weekends; not Mon lunchtime) ~ Restaurant ~ (01759) 371354 ~ Children welcome ~ Dogs allowed in bar ~ Open 12-2.30, 6-11; 12-11(10.30 Sun) Sat; closed Mon lunchtime, evenings 25 and 26 Dec

Recommended by Gordon and Margaret Ormondroyd, Pat and Graham Williamson, Alistair and Kay Butler, Roger A Bellingham, Pat and Tony Martin, David Carr, R T and J C Moggridge, Peter and Anne Hollindale

LUND   SE9748   MAP 8

Wellington 🍴 🍷
Off B1248 SW of Driffield; YO25 9TE

Busy, smart pub with plenty of space in several rooms, real ales and helpfully noted wine list, and interesting changing food

There's always a good mix of drinkers and diners in this smart pub, and a friendly welcome for all. Perhaps the most atmospheric part is the cosy Farmers Bar – a small heavily beamed room with an interesting fireplace and some old agricultural equipment. The neatly kept main bar is much brighter with a brick fireplace and bar counter, well polished wooden banquettes and square tables, dried flowers, and local prints on the textured cream-painted walls. Off to one side is a plainer flagstoned room, while at the other a york-stoned walkway leads to a room with a display case showing off the village's Britain in Bloom awards. The restaurant is supported by a back dining area where you cannot reserve a table – this seems to work well and the main bar in the evening remains a haven for drinkers only. Black Sheep Best, John Smiths, Timothy Taylors Landlord and a guest such as Copper Dragon Golden Pippin on handpump, a good wine list with a helpfully labelled choice by the glass, and 30 malt whiskies. Piped music, pool, and TV. A small courtyard beside the car park has a couple of benches. More reports please.

🍴 Good bar food includes sandwiches, soup, chicken liver parfait with peach, apple and apricot chutney, warm mild goats cheese and chilli cheesecake with red pepper coulis and balsamic syrup, calves liver with a bacon and herb croquette and fresh raspberry dressing, confit shoulder of lamb with lentil jus, fresh wild sea trout with samphire and fresh crab velouté, roast gressingham duck with wild mushrooms and pan jus, and puddings like chocolate brownie with chocolate sauce and vanilla ice-cream and marmalade sponge with suzette sauce and crème fraîche. *Starters/Snacks: £5.45 to £8.95. Main Courses: £6.95 to £10.95. Puddings: £5.95*

Free house ~ Licensees Russell Jeffery and Sarah Jeffery ~ Real ale ~ Bar food (not Sun evening or Mon lunchtime) ~ Restaurant (Tues-Sat evenings) ~ (01377) 217294 ~ Children welcome ~ Open 12-3, 6.30-11; 12-11 Sun; closed Mon lunch

Recommended by Colin McKerrow, Pat and Graham Williamson, J Crosby, Fred and Lorraine Gill, Pat and Tony Martin, Marcus Mann

MARTON   SE7383   MAP 10

Appletree 🍴 🍷 🍺
Village signposted off A170 W of Pickering; YO62 6RD

Carefully run and civilised pub with relaxed rooms, friendly welcome, super range of drinks and excellent food using the best (usually local) produce available

Although many customers are here to enjoy the particularly good, imaginative food cooked by the landlord in this civilised and neatly kept pub, drinkers do pop in for a pint, and there's a warm, genuine welcome to all from the landlady and her staff. The relaxed beamed lounge has comfortable settees in red or cream around polished low tables, an open fire in the stone fireplace and a modicum of carefully placed decorations on the red walls. There's also a small bar with Moorhouses TJs Tipple (named for the pub), Suddabys Windfall (brewed specially for them) and a guest such as Great Newsome

Holderness Dark on handpump, 19 wines by the glass (including champagne) from an extensive list with helpful notes, home-made gins such as sloe, bramble, and raspberry, sloe vodka, and quite a collection of teas and coffees. The busy red-walled dining room has well spaced farmhouse tables, fresh flowers, and masses of evening candles; a small bay off here has more dining tables and is decorated in a musical theme with brass instruments on the walls. Piped music. There are cast-iron tables and chairs out on a sheltered flagstoned courtyard behind. This year, they've opened a shop attached to the pub selling delicatessen-type goodies.

🍴 **They are using more home-grown produce than ever and working closely with local farmers and other producers, and the food is first rate. This might include various nibbles, steamed mussels with dill butter, crispy duck and bacon salad with honey and mustard dressing, whitby crab cheesecake with parmesan crisp and a chilli mango salsa, caramelised jerusalem artichoke and onion tarte tatin with roasted red peppers and watercress, posh fish and chips, confit belly pork with black pudding, crisp prosciutto and grainy mustard cream, roast salmon steak with a herb crust, saffron and a wine velouté, gressingham duck breast with roast beetroot, beetroot mash and orange sauce, and puddings like chocolate mousse with boozy cherries and dark treacle tart with lemon curd ice-cream and lime syrup; the cheeseboard is particularly good.** *Starters/Snacks: £3.00 to £7.00. Main Courses: £8.50 to £17.00. Puddings: £3.00 to £7.50*

Free house ~ Licensees Melanie and T J Drew ~ Bar food (12-2, 6(6.30 Sun)-9.30(9 Sun); not Mon or Tues) ~ Restaurant ~ (01751) 431457 ~ Children welcome away from bar ~ Dogs allowed in bar ~ Open 12-2.30, 6-11; 12-3, 6.30-10.30 Sun; closed Mon and Tues, two weeks Jan

Recommended by Brian and Pat Wardrobe, Dennis and Gill Keen, Gordon and Margaret Ormondroyd, Janet and Peter Race, Richard and Mary Bailey, Michael and Anne McDonald, David Varley

MASHAM

SE2281   MAP 10

Black Sheep Brewery 🍺

Crosshills; HG4 4EN

Lively place with friendly staff, quite a mix of customers, unusual décor in big warehouse room, well kept beers (brewery tours and shop) and interesting food

There's a thriving mix of customers of all ages in this lively and well run place. A huge upper warehouse room has a bar serving well kept Black Sheep Best, Ale, and Riggwelter on handpump, several wines by the glass, and a fair choice of soft drinks. Most of the good-sized tables have cheery american-cloth patterned tablecloths and brightly cushioned green café chairs but there are some modern pubbier tables near the bar. There's a good deal of bare woodwork, with some rough stonework painted cream, and green-painted steel girders and pillars. This big area is partly divided up by free-standing partitions and some big plants; piped music and friendly service. Interesting brewery tours and a shop selling beers and more or less beer-related items from pub games and T-shirts to pottery and fudge. A glass wall lets you see into the brewing exhibition centre. Picnic-sets out on the grass.

🍴 **Using locally sourced food, the well liked food includes sandwiches, filled baguettes and baked potatoes, ploughman's, soup, salads such as hot crispy duck, black pudding and bacon with a raspberry dressing or bacon, mushrooms, onions and croûtons, fishcakes with a spicy dip, omelettes, steak in ale pie, ricotta and spinach cannelloni topped with tomato concasse, chicken chasseur, gammon and egg, grilled lambs liver, bacon and black pudding with onion sauce, and puddings such as crème brûlée and a changing cheesecake. They also offer cream teas plus cakes and tray bakes, milk shakes, lots of coffees and hot chocolates, and an ice-cream menu.** *Starters/Snacks: £4.25 to £6.95. Main Courses: £7.95 to £9.95. Puddings: £4.25*

Free house ~ Licensee Paul Theakston ~ Real ale ~ Bar food (food served during opening hours) ~ Restaurant ~ (01765) 680100 ~ Children welcome ~ Open 10.30-5.30 Mon-Weds; 10.30am-11pm Thurs, Fri and Sat; 10.30-5 Sun; closed two weeks Jan for refurbishment

Recommended by Adrian Johnson, WW, M and GR, Mark Walker, Janet and Peter Race, Mr and Mrs Maurice Thompson, Mr and Mrs John Taylor

MIDDLEHAM   SE1287   MAP 10

White Swan ♀ ⇌

Market Place; DL8 4PE

Still has proper pubby bar in smartly extended inn, well liked food and real ales; individually decorated bedrooms

If you are lucky, you can bag one of the seats in the window of the bar in this pleasant, extended coaching inn that look across the cobbled market square. There's a beamed and flagstoned entrance bar with a proper pubby atmosphere, a long dark pew built into a big window, a mix of chairs around a handful of biggish tables, and an open woodburning stove. Black Sheep Best and Ale, John Smiths and Theakstons Best on handpump from the curved counter, 12 wines by the glass, 20 malt whiskies and quite a few teas and coffees. The dining room is light, spacious and modern with some popular window tables, a large fireplace, and in an area opposite the bar, some contemporary leather chairs and a sofa. The back room offers more dining space; piped music. The bedrooms are comfortable and well appointed.

🍴 Popular bar food includes sandwiches, soup, moules marinière, king prawns with sesame and ginger, steak in ale pie, spicy pork pot with chilli, tomatoes and butter beans, tagliatelle carbonara, various pizzas, vegetable curry, chicken breast stuffed with blue wensleydale and served with a smoked bacon and parmesan risotto, braised lamb shank with spring onion mash, and puddings such as iced liquorice terrine with caramel sauce and white chocolate and raspberry trifle; they offer a dish of the day and a two- and three-course early bird menu (6.30-7.30 Sunday-Friday). *Starters/Snacks: £4.75 to £7.25. Main Courses: £7.50 to £15.50. Puddings: £5.25*

Free house ~ Licensee Kim Woodcock ~ Real ale ~ Bar food (12-2.15, 6.30-9.30) ~ Restaurant ~ (01969) 622093 ~ Children welcome ~ Dogs allowed in bar ~ Open 11-11(midnight Sat); 12-10.30 Sun ~ Bedrooms: £55B/£89S(£79B)

Recommended by John Robertson, WW, Richard, Anthony Barnes, Bruce and Sharon Eden, Janet and Peter Race, Michael Tack

MILL BANK   SE0321   MAP 7

Millbank 🍴 ♀

Mill Bank Road, off A58 SW of Sowerby Bridge; HX6 3DY

Imaginative food in cottagey-looking dining pub, real ales, fine wines and specialist gin list; friendly staff and interesting garden sculptures; walks nearby and good views

Although this impressive dining pub looks cottagey and traditional from the outside, once you get inside, the rooms have a clean-cut minimalist modern décor, and there are local photographs for sale. It's divided into the tap room, bar and restaurant, with Tetleys and Timothy Taylors Landlord on handpump, 20 wines by the glass including champagne, port and pudding wines, and a specialised gin list; friendly staff. Outside, the terrace has a glass roof and fold-away windows that make the most of the glorious setting overlooking an old textile mill. The Calderdale Way is easily accessible from the pub.

🍴 Under the new licensee, the food remains good and contemporary: sandwiches (available until 7pm), soup, roast scallops with crisp belly pork, carrot and ginger purée and sesame seeds, crab fritters with chilli oil, roast tomato and raita, pancetta and quail egg salad with tarragon mayonnaise, lasagne of butternut squash with pickled mushrooms, toasted almonds and parmesan, bass fillet with savoy cabbage and lobster pie with saffron, haddock kiev with salami, sweet and sour onions and sweet potato purée, loin of lamb with shepherd's pie of the shoulder, roast pimento, pea purée and mint oil, and puddings such as chocolate fondant cake with yoghurt ice-cream and peanut praline and prune and brandy crème brûlée with caramel ice-cream; there's also a two-course set menu (not Saturday evening or Sunday). *Starters/Snacks: £4.95 to £9.50. Main Courses: £8.95 to £12.50. Puddings: £4.95 to £5.95*

Free house ~ Licensee Glenn Futter ~ Real ale ~ Bar food (12-2.30, 6-9.30(10 Fri and Sat);
12.30-4.30, 6-8 Sun; not Mon) ~ Restaurant ~ (01422) 825588 ~ Children welcome ~
Dogs allowed in bar ~ Open 12-3, 5.30-11; 12-10.30 Sun; closed Mon, first week Jan,
first two weeks Oct

Recommended by Stuart Doughty, David and Cathrine Whiting, Dr Kevan Tucker, Gordon and Margaret Ormondroyd

MOULTON

NZ2303   MAP 10

Black Bull ⊛ ♀

Just off A1 nr Scotch Corner; DL10 6QJ

**Civilised, enjoyable dining pub, characterful bar with interesting furnishings, very good
bar food and more elaborate restaurant menu, seafood bar, and smart dining areas (one is
a Pullman dining car)**

There's always a good mix of both locals and visitors in this civilised and enjoyable
dining pub. The bar has a lot of character, as well as an antique panelled oak settle and
an old elm housekeeper's chair, built-in red cushioned black settles and pews around
cast-iron tables, silver-plated turkish coffee pots and copper cooking utensils hanging
from black beams, fresh flowers, and a huge winter log fire; there's a seafood bar with
high seats at the marble-topped counter. In the evening you can also eat in the polished
brick-tiled conservatory with bentwood cane chairs or in the Bright Belle dining car.
Eight wines, including champagne by the glass, and 50 malt whiskies. There are some
seats outside in the central court.

⊞ **The food is extremely good, and at lunchtime the bar food includes lovely smoked
salmon in baguettes, on a plate, and in pâté, as well as soup served in little tureens, six,
nine or a dozen oysters, welsh rarebit and bacon, feuilleté of smoked haddock, prawns,
parsley and mash, queenie scallops in garlic butter with mature cheddar and thyme
crumb, pork sausages with mash and onion gravy, fried pigeon breast, wild mushroom,
beetroot and bacon salad, and beer-battered cod with pea purée and balsamic syrup.
There are puddings like hot orange liqueur pancakes with vanilla ice-cream and baked egg
custard tart with blackcurrant compote, a far more elaborate (and expensive) restaurant
menu, and a two- and three-course set menu for Sunday lunch.** *Starters/Snacks: £4.25 to
£9.95. Main Courses: £5.95 to £13.75. Puddings: £4.95*

Free house ~ Licensee Mr Barker ~ Bar food (12-2.30, 6.30-9.45; 12-4 Sun) ~ Restaurant
(evening) ~ (01325) 377289 ~ Children welcome ~ Open 12-3, 6-midnight; 12-6 Sun;
closed Sun evening

*Recommended by Jill and Julian Tasker, John and Eleanor Holdsworth, Patrick and Barbara Knights,
Rebecca Sutton, Greta and Christopher Wells*

NUNNINGTON

SE6679   MAP 7

Royal Oak

Church Street; at back of village, which is signposted from A170 and B1257; YO62 5US

**Friendly staff and good food in reliable, neat pub, lots to look at in beamed bar, open
fires, and real ales**

After a visit to nearby Nunnington Hall (National Trust), this attractive little pub is just
the place for a drink or a meal. The neatly kept bar has high black beams strung with
earthenware flagons, copper jugs and lots of antique keys, one of the walls is stripped
back to the bare stone to display a fine collection of antique farm tools, and there are
open fires; carefully chosen furniture such as kitchen and country dining chairs or a long
pew around the sturdy tables on the turkey carpet, and a lectern in one corner. Black
Sheep Best, Theakstons XB, and Wold Top Wolds Way on handpump and several wines by
the glass; friendly, efficient staff, and piped music. More reports please.

⊞ **Enjoyable bar food includes chicken liver pâté with red onion marmalade, egg
mayonnaise with prawns, toasted goats cheese with crispy bacon and apple and tomato
chutney, lasagne, fisherman's pot, sweet and sour vegetables, steak and kidney casserole
with herb dumplings, chicken breast in cheese and mustard sauce, crispy roast duckling**

with orange sauce, and puddings such as seasonal fruit crumble and sticky toffee pudding with toffee sauce. *Starters/Snacks: £4.50 to £6.95. Main Courses: £10.95 to £18.50. Puddings: £5.50*

Free house ~ Licensee Anita Hilton ~ Real ale ~ Bar food (not Mon) ~ Restaurant ~ (01439) 748271 ~ Children welcome ~ Open 11.45-2.30, 6.30(7 Sun)-11; closed Mon

Recommended by Peter Burton, Pat and Graham Williamson, Roger A Bellingham

OSMOTHERLEY   SE4597   MAP 10

Golden Lion
The Green, West End; off A19 N of Thirsk; DL6 3AA

Welcoming, busy pub with simply furnished rooms, lots of malt whiskies, real ales, interesting bar food, and fine surrounding walks

Run by a friendly landlord, this attractive old stone pub has an enjoyably bustling atmosphere. The roomy beamed bar on the left is simply furnished with old pews and just a few decorations on its white walls, candles on tables, John Smiths, Timothy Taylors Landlord and a guest from Salamander on handpump, several wines by the glass, and 50 malt whiskies. On the right, there's a similarly unpretentious and well worn-in eating area; best to book to be sure of a table as it does get pretty packed. There's also a separate dining room, mainly open at weekends, and a covered courtyard; piped music. Benches out in front look across the village green to the market cross, and there's a new terrace. As the inn is the start of the 44-mile Lyke Wakes Walk on the Cleveland Way and quite handy for the Coast to Coast Walk, it is naturally popular with walkers. More reports please.

Ⅱ **Popular, interesting bar food includes soup, mussels in wine, cream and shallots, spicy pork ribs, goats cheese and red pepper terrine with onion and apricot relish, deep-fried soft shell crab with lime mayonnaise, home-made beef burger with mexican salsa, lasagne, steak and kidney pie, pork with parma ham, sage and marsala wine sauce, charcoal-grilled poussin with rosemary and garlic, fresh salmon with cream basil sauce, calves liver with fried onions, and puddings such as raspberry ripple cheesecake with raspberry coulis and warm apple, prune and walnut cake with whipped cream.** *Starters/Snacks: £4.95 to £8.00. Main Courses: £7.95 to £19.00. Puddings: £4.95*

Free house ~ Licensee Christie Connelly ~ Real ale ~ Bar food (12-2.30, 6-9) ~ Restaurant ~ (01609) 883526 ~ Children welcome ~ Dogs allowed in bar ~ Open 12-3, 6-11; 12-11(10.30 Sun) Sat; closed Mon and Tues lunchtime ~ Bedrooms: £60S/£90S

Recommended by Christopher Turner, Sylvia and Tony Birbeck, Dr and Mrs R G J Telfer, Neil and Anita Christopher, Arthur Pickering, Roger Noyes, Stuart Paulley, Pat Bradbury, Dr and Mrs P Truelove, Blaise Vyner

PICKERING   SE7984   MAP 10

White Swan
Market Place, just off A170; YO18 7AA

Relaxed little bar in civilised coaching inn, several smart lounges, attractive restaurant, real ales and an excellent wine list, and first-class food; luxurious bedrooms

This smart old coaching inn is first and foremost a hotel with a terrific restaurant, but there is a small bar with real ales and a friendly welcome. This room has a relaxed atmosphere, wood panelling, sofas and just four tables, a log fire, and Black Sheep Best and Timothy Taylors Landlord on handpump, 17 wines by the glass from an extensive list that includes super old St Emilions and pudding wines, and 20 malt whiskies. Opposite, a bare-boards room with a few more tables has another fire in a handsome art nouveau iron fireplace, a big bow window, and pear prints on its plum-coloured walls. The restaurant has flagstones, a fine open fire, rich tweed soft furnishings, comfortable settles and gothic screens, and the residents' lounge is in a converted beamed barn. The old coach entry to the car park is very narrow. The bedrooms are lovely and staying here is a real treat.

🕮 At lunchtime, you can enjoy the excellent food in both the bar and restaurant but in the evening you may eat only in the restaurant. Some lunchtime snacks like good sandwiches, interesting soups, caesar salad with chicken, smoked salmon or roast smoked haddock, and ploughman's, as well as whitby fishcakes with herb shrimp salad and tartare sauce, venison carpaccio, hand-dived king scallops with jerusalem artichoke purée and smoked bacon, slow-roasted belly pork with mustard mash and bramley apple sauce, posh fish and chips, free-range chicken with toulouse sausage and smoked bacon casserole, fried halibut with sage butter and red wine mushroom risotto, and puddings such as crème caramel with rum-soaked raisins and fruit and nut biscotti and poached rhubarb layered with tuile biscuits and a lemon and ginger syllabub; fine cheeses, too. *Starters/Snacks: £4.95 to £8.25. Main Courses: £10.95 to £19.50. Puddings: £6.50*

Free house ~ Licensees Marion and Victor Buchanan ~ Real ale ~ Bar food ~ Restaurant ~ (01751) 472288 ~ Children welcome ~ Dogs allowed in bar and bedrooms ~ Open 10am-11.30pm; 11am-10.30pm Sun ~ Bedrooms: £110B/£145B

Recommended by Derek Thomas, Dr Ian S Morley, Arthur Pickering, J Crosby, Phil Bryant, P Dawn, Sylvia and Tony Birbeck, Michael Dandy, Pat and Graham Williamson, John and Barbara Hirst, David Carr, Margaret Walker

PICKHILL   SE3483   MAP 10

Nags Head 🍴 ☐ 🛏

Take the Masham turn-off from A1 both N and S, and village signposted off B6267 in Ainderby Quernhow; YO7 4JG

Busy dining pub with excellent food, a fine choice of carefully chosen drinks, a tap room and smarter lounge, and friendly service

Just the place to take a break from the A1, this is a popular dining pub with particularly good food and a friendly welcome. Most of the tables are laid for eating so if it is just a drink you're after, head for the bustling tap room on the left: beams hung with jugs, coach horns, ale-yards and so forth, and masses of ties hanging as a frieze from a rail around the red ceiling. The smarter lounge bar has deep green plush banquettes on the matching carpet, pictures for sale on its neat cream walls, and an open fire. There's also a library-themed restaurant; piped music. Black Sheep Best, Hambleton Bitter, and Theakstons Black Bull on handpump, a good choice of malt whiskies, vintage armagnacs, and a carefully chosen wine list with several by the glass. One table is inset with a chessboard and they also have board games. There's a front verandah, a boules and quoits pitch, and nine-hole putting green.

🕮 Good, interesting food includes sandwiches, soup, twice-baked cheddar and blue stilton soufflé with a rocket, chard and pine nut salad, potted brown shrimps with five spice and lime herb croûton, scottish moules marinière, pigeon breast with toasted walnut vinaigrette and roast beetroot and apple salad, rare breed old spot pork sausages with onion gravy, roasted pepper, wild mushroom and fennel risotto, fried halibut fillet with sautéed wild mushrooms and a white wine and dill reduction, seared gressingham duck breast with apple and rosemary compote and orange jus, and puddings such as warm treacle tart with red berry compote and dark chocolate fondant with liquorice ice-cream. *Starters/Snacks: £3.95 to £8.95. Main Courses: £8.50 to £17.95. Puddings: £3.95 to £5.95*

Free house ~ Licensee Edward Boynton ~ Real ale ~ Bar food (12-2, 6-9.30; 12-2.30, 6-9 Sun) ~ Restaurant ~ (01845) 567391 ~ Well-behaved children welcome ~ Dogs allowed in bedrooms ~ Open 11-11 ~ Bedrooms: £55B/£80B

Recommended by Peter and Anne Hollindale, Ginny Barbour, J A West, Janet and Peter Race, Mr and Mrs Maurice Thompson, Gordon and Margaret Ormondroyd, Robert Stephenson, Jill and Julian Tasker, Mrs Brenda Calver, Michael Doswell

---

Bedroom prices normally include full english breakfast, VAT and any inclusive service charge that we know of. Prices before the '/' are for single rooms, after for two people in double or twin (B includes a private bath, S a private shower). If there is no '/', the prices are only for twin or double rooms (as far as we know there are no singles). If there is no B or S, as far as we know no rooms have private facilities.

RIPLEY   SE2860   MAP 7

Boars Head 🍴 ⏥ 🍺 🛏

Off A61 Harrogate—Ripon; HG3 3AY

Friendly bar liked by locals in smart hotel, real ales, excellent wine list and malt whiskies, good food and helpful service; comfortable bedrooms

The relaxed and informal bar in this smart, comfortable hotel is always bustling and friendly, with plenty of chatty locals, Black Sheep Best, Daleside Bitter, Hambleton White Boar, and Theakstons Old Peculier on handpump, an excellent wine list (with ten or so by the glass), around 20 malt whiskies, and lots of teas and coffees. It's a long flagstoned room with green checked tablecloths and olive oil on all the tables, most of which are arranged to form individual booths. The warm yellow walls have jolly little drawings of cricketers or huntsmen running along the bottom, as well as a boar's head (part of the family coat of arms), an interesting religious carving, and a couple of cricket bats; efficient staff even when very busy. Some of the furnishings in the hotel came from the attic of next door Ripley Castle, where the Ingilbys have lived for over 650 years. A pleasant little garden has plenty of tables.

🍽 **Enjoyable food includes good sandwiches, soup, terrine of salmon and smoked salmon, wensleydale cheese tartlet, wild boar sausages with rosemary and onion crushed potatoes, sweet potato and chestnut risotto, corn-fed chicken breast with bacon, mushrooms and button onions, seared fillet of bass with spiced couscous, slow-cooked lamb with braised lettuce and tomato, daily specials, and puddings like banana and toffee crème brûlée with chocolate ice-cream and crumble-topped apple tart with crème anglaise.** *Starters/Snacks: £3.95 to £5.95. Main Courses: £9.95 to £18.50. Puddings: £4.75*

Free house ~ Licensee Sir Thomas Ingilby ~ Real ale ~ Bar food ~ Restaurant ~ (01423) 771888 ~ Children welcome ~ Dogs allowed in bedrooms ~ Open 11(12 Sun)-11 ~ Bedrooms: £105B/£125B

Recommended by Janet and Peter Race, Dr and Mrs Jackson, Christopher Turner, Tim and Ann Newell, David Coleman, J F M and M West, the Didler, Jack Morley, Stephen R Holman, Mr and Mrs Maurice Thompson

RIPPONDEN   SE0419   MAP 7

Old Bridge ⏥ 🍺

From A58, best approach is Elland Road (opposite Golden Lion), park opposite the church in pub's car park and walk back over ancient hump-back bridge; HX6 4DF

Pleasant old pub by medieval bridge with relaxed communicating rooms, half a dozen real ales, quite a few wines by the glass, lots of whiskies, and well liked food

If this 15th-c pub is proving hard to find, just head for the church, which is opposite it. There are three communicating rooms, each on a slightly different level, and all with a relaxed, friendly atmosphere. Oak settles are built into the window recesses of the thick stone walls, and there are antique oak tables, rush-seated chairs, a few well chosen pictures and prints, and a big woodburning stove. Timothy Taylors Best, Golden Best and Landlord and three changing guests on handpump, a dozen wines by the glass, 30 malt whiskies, and a good choice of foreign bottled beers. This is a pleasant spot by the medieval pack-horse bridge over the little River Ryburn, and there's a garden overlooking the water. More reports please.

🍽 **On weekday lunchtimes, bar food includes only sandwiches and soup or the popular help-yourself carvery and salad buffet; at weekends and in the evening, there might be dolcelatte cheesecake with pickled pear, country-style terrine with apricot chutney, meat and potato pie, smoked haddock and spinach pancakes, gressingham duck on oriental noodles, slow-roast shoulder of lamb with rosemary, red wine and garlic, and puddings.** *Starters/Snacks: £3.50 to £5.50. Main Courses: £7.50 to £12.00. Puddings: £3.50*

Free house ~ Licensees Tim and Lindsay Eaton Walker ~ Real ale ~ Bar food (12-2, 6.30-9.30; not Sat or Sun evening) ~ (01422) 822595 ~ Children in eating area of bar until 8pm but must be well behaved ~ Open 12-3, 5.30-11; 12-11(10.30 Sun) Sat

Recommended by Greta and Christopher Wells

ROBIN HOOD'S BAY

NZ9505 MAP 10

Laurel

Village signposted off A171 S of Whitby; YO22 4SE

Charming little pub in unspoilt fishing village, neat friendly bar, and three real ales

At the heart of one of the prettiest and most unspoilt fishing villages on the north-east coast sits this charming little local. The beamed and welcoming main bar is neatly kept and is decorated with old local photographs, Victorian prints and brasses, and lager bottles from all over the world. There's an open fire and Caledonian Deuchars IPA and maybe Theakstons Best and Old Peculier on handpump; darts, board games, TV and piped music. In summer, the hanging baskets and window boxes are lovely. They have a self-contained apartment for two people.

🍴 **You can buy sandwiches from the Old Bakery Tearooms and eat them in the pub.**

Free house ~ Licensee Brian Catling ~ Real ale ~ Bar food ~ No credit cards ~ (01947) 880400 ~ Children in snug bar only ~ Dogs welcome ~ Open 12-11(10.30 Sun); opening time 2pm Mon-Fri in winter

Recommended by P Dawn, Peter and Jo Smith, Amanda Russell, Alison and Pete

ROECLIFFE

SE3765 MAP 7

Crown 🍴 🍷

Off A168 just W of Boroughbridge; handy for A1(M) junction 48; YO51 9LY

Smartly updated by new owners, with civilised bar and good enterprising food

This large attractively placed pub, facing an appealing tree-shaded village green, has been reopened by the Maneys who previously made such a success of the Bay Horse over at Kirk Deighton. The bar has a contemporary colour scheme of dark reds and near-whites, with attractive prints carefully grouped and lit; one area has chunky pine tables on flagstones, another part, with a log fire, has dark tables on plaid carpet. John Smiths, Theakstons Best and changing guests like Caledonian Deuchars IPA and Fullers Summer Ale on handpump, and as well as a decent range of wines by the glass, their list includes some useful half bottles. The neatly dressed staff are warmly welcoming. For meals, you have a choice between a small candlelit olive-green bistro, with nice tables, a longcase clock and one or two paintings, and a more formal restaurant; at weekends, it's already wise to book ahead. As we went to press they were still refurbishing the bedrooms; we'd expect this to be a nice place to stay in, and look forward to reports on this aspect.

🍴 **Good, modern bar food includes lunchtime sandwiches on a choice of their own interesting breads and ploughman's, as well as soup (the crab is well liked), sweet soy belly pork, crisp fried and tossed in ginger and lime soy dipping sauce, queenie scallop gratin glazed with parmesan with white wine and parsley, cod and chips with home-made tartare sauce and organic tomato sauce, rare breed minced beef in ale pie, organic chicken coq au vin, fresh wild mushroom risotto laced with smoked wensleydale and crisp leeks, fishcakes with creamed leeks, suckling pig with home-made black pudding, an impressive seafood platter, and particularly good puddings such as a trio of crème brûlée and pear and almond tartlet with lemon mascarpone and sweet calvados sauce; they do charge extra for vegetables.** *Starters/Snacks: £4.00 to £6.00. Main Courses: £9.95 to £17.00. Puddings: £6.00*

Free house ~ Licensee Karl Mainy ~ Real ale ~ Bar food (12-2.30, 6-9.30; 12-7 Sun; not Sun evening) ~ Restaurant ~ (01423) 322300 ~ Children welcome ~ Dogs allowed in bar ~ Open 12-3.30, 5-11.30; 12-11.30 Sun

Recommended by Michael Williamson, Les and Sandra Brown, Michael Doswell, DC

The details at the end of each main entry start by saying whether the pub is a free house, or if it belongs to a brewery or pub group (which we name).

SAWLEY   SE2467   MAP 7

Sawley Arms ♀
Village signposted off B6265 W of Ripon; HG4 3EQ

Old-fashioned dining pub with good restaurnty food, decent house wines, and comfortable furnishings in small carpeted rooms; pretty garden

Mrs Hawes – now with help from her son and daughter-in-law – has been running this spotlessly kept dining pub for nearly 40 years. It's ultra-civilised in an old-fashioned, decorous sort of way and particularly popular with older customers. The small turkey-carpeted rooms have log fires and comfortable furniture ranging from small softly cushioned armed dining chairs and settees, to the wing armchairs down a couple of steps in a side snug; maybe daily papers and magazines to read, piped music. There's also a conservatory; good house wines. In fine weather you can sit in the pretty garden where the flowering tubs and baskets are lovely; two stone cottages in the grounds for rent. Fountains Abbey (the most extensive of the great monastic remains – floodlit on late summer Friday and Saturday evenings, with a live choir on the Saturday) – is not far away.

⊞ Restaurnty food includes lunchtime sandwiches, soup with croutons, duck liver and orange pâté with cumberland sauce, deep-fried brie with pineapple and apple chutney, steak pie with rich gravy, chicken breast in a mild curry sauce, goats cheese and cherry tomato tarte tatin with sweet pepper sauce, plaice mornay, braised lamb shank with madeira gravy, and puddings like bread and butter pudding and rich apricot trifle. *Starters/Snacks: £4.10 to £6.75. Main Courses: £10.45 to £16.50. Puddings: £4.00 to £4.75*

Free house ~ Licensee Mrs June Hawes ~ Bar food (not Mon evening or winter Sun evening) ~ Restaurant ~ (01765) 620642 ~ Well behaved children over 9 ~ Open 11.30-3, 6.30-10.30; 12-3, 6-10.30 Sun; Sun and Mon evenings in winter

Recommended by WW, P and J Shapley, David Coleman, Brian Wainwright

SHEFFIELD   SK3687   MAP 7

Fat Cat ⬛ £
23 Alma Street; S3 8SA

Super own-brewed beers and guests in friendly, bustling town local, plenty of bottled beers too, remarkably cheap tasty food; brewery visits

With up to 11 real ales on handpump, it's not surprising that this busy and friendly town local is so popular. As well as their own-brewed Kelham Island Bitter, Pale Rider, and Easy Rider, there's Timothy Taylors Landlord, and guests such as Derby Splendiforous, Foxfield Stout, Rudgate Shield, and Townes IPA, all well kept on handpump. Also, draught and bottled belgian beers, farm cider and country wines. The two small downstairs rooms have brewery-related prints on the walls, coal fires, simple wooden tables and cushioned seats around the walls, and jugs, bottles and some advertising mirrors; cards and dominoes and maybe the pub cat wandering around. The upstairs room has a TV for sport. The Brewery Visitor Centre (you can book brewery trips (0114) 249 4804) has framed beer mats, pump clips and prints on the walls. There are picnic-sets in a fairylit back courtyard.

⊞ Under the new licensee, the popular and incredibly cheap bar food includes sandwiches, soup, ploughman's, leek and cheese pie, pork casserole, chickpea and pepper stew, mushroom and tomato pasta with melted mozzarella, steak pie, and puddings like apple crumble and spotted dick; Sunday roast. *Starters/Snacks: £1.50 to £3.00. Main Courses: £4.20 to £4.50. Puddings: £1.75 to £2.50*

Own brew ~ Licensee Duncan Shaw ~ Real ale ~ Bar food (12-2.30, 6-8; all day Sat; not Sun evening) ~ No credit cards ~ (0114) 249 4801 ~ Children welcome away from main bar ~ Dogs welcome ~ Open 12-11(midnight Fri and Sat); closed 25 Dec, evening 26 Dec

Recommended by Pete Baker, the Didler, P Dawn, Brian and Anna Marsden, Mark and Diane Grist, B and M Kendall, David Carr, John Honnor, Giles and Annie Francis

New Barrack 🍺 £

601 Penistone Road, Hillsborough; S6 2GA

Lively and friendly, with 11 real ales and fine range of other drinks, good value food and lots going on

---

There's always something going on in the evenings at this really friendly and popular pub. On Tuesdays there's a music quiz, on Wednesdays a general knowledge quiz, Thursday is games night, and there's live music at weekends; it's even busier on match days. The comfortable front lounge has upholstered seats, old pine floors, and a log fire, the tap room has another log fire and darts, and the back room can be used for small functions. TV, dominoes, cards, cribbage, piped music, and daily papers to read. As well as regular beers such as Abbeydale Moonshine, Acorn Barnsley Bitter, Castle Rock Elsie Mo, Harvest Pale, and Sherrif's Tipple, there are six constantly changing guests; also, real cider, a range of bottled belgian beers, and 28 malt whiskies. The small walled back garden has won awards. Local parking is not easy.

🍴 **Tasty bar food includes sandwiches and filled baguettes, all day breakfast, pie and peas, pizzas, sausage and mash, mixed grill, and their very popular beer-battered cod.** *Starters/Snacks: £2.00 to £4.95. Main Courses: £4.50 to £9.95. Puddings: £1.50 to £3.50.*

Tynemill ~ Managers Kevin and Stephanie Woods ~ Real ale ~ Bar food (11-3, 5-9; 12-4, 7-9 Sun) ~ (0114) 234 9148 ~ Children welcome until 9pm ~ Dogs welcome ~ Live music Sat, alternate Fri evenings and monthly Sun ~ Open 11-11; 11am-midnight Fri and Sat; 12-11 Sun

Recommended by the Didler, Don and Shirley Parrish, Andy and Jill Kassube, David Carr

SHELLEY   SE2112   MAP 7

Three Acres 🍴 🍷 🍺 🛏️

Roydhouse (not signposted); from B6116 heading for Skelmanthorpe, turn left in Shelley (signposted Flockton, Elmley, Elmley Moor) and go up lane for 2 miles towards radio mast; HD8 8LR

Delicious food and friendly service in busy, smart dining pub, several real ales and fine choice of other drinks, and relaxed atmosphere; fine views, good bedrooms

---

Only ten minutes from the M1 and with plenty to do nearby, this civilised former coaching inn is a comfortable and friendly place to stay. Most customers are here to enjoy the stylish food but they do keep Black Sheep Best, Tetleys, and Timothy Taylors Landlord on handpump, over 40 whiskies and a fantastic (if not cheap) choice of wines with at least 17 by the glass; attentive staff. The roomy lounge bar has a relaxed, informal atmosphere, tankards hanging from the main beam, high bar chairs and stools, button-back leather sofas, and old prints and so forth. To be sure of a table you must book quite a way ahead – try to get a place with a view across to Elmley Moor; piped music. There are also more formal dining rooms.

🍴 **Food is excellent (though pricy) from a sizeable menu: super open sandwiches on home-made bread, interesting soups, pressed ham hock, parsley and sauternes terrine with cornichons, dijon mustard, and toasted onion bread, devilled lambs kidneys and chicken livers with spiced onion rings and mango chutney, potted shrimps with smoked salmon and a sweet mustard and dill dressing, potato and cheese kofta with spiced tomato and chickpea stew, a lunchtime roast of the day, beer-battered haddock with proper beef dripping chips, rabbit and vegetable pasty, free-range chicken with field mushrooms and a creamy pea, pancetta and tarragon sauce, slow-roast crispy belly pork with star anise and hoi sin jus and a cucumber, chilli and mint salad, and puddings such as dark chocolate mousse torte with griottine cherries, white chocolate sauce, and basil syrup and caramelised clotted cream rice pudding with fresh raspberry purée.** *Starters/Snacks: £4.50 to £9.95. Main Courses: £14.95 to £24.95. Puddings: £6.25*

Free house ~ Licensees Neil Truelove and Brian Orme ~ Real ale ~ Bar food (12-2, 6.30-9.30) ~ Restaurant ~ (01484) 602606 ~ Children welcome ~ Pianist Weds and Thurs evenings ~ Open 12-3, 6-11(10.30 Sun); closed 25 and 26 Dec, 1 and 2 Jan ~ Bedrooms: £70B/£100B

If we know a pub does summer barbecues, we say so.

Recommended by Simon Fox, Michael and Maggie Betton, Colin McKerrow, Pat and Stewart Gordon, Gordon and Margaret Ormondroyd, Revd D Glover, Derek and Sylvia Stephenson, Richard Cole, John and Barbara Hirst, Cedric Robertshaw, Geoff and Teresa Salt, Michael Jones, Richard Marjoram, Dr and Mrs M W A Haward, K S Whittaker, Hunter and Christine Wright

SINNINGTON   SE7485   MAP 10

Fox & Hounds 🍽 ♟ 🛏

Just off A170 W of Pickering; YO62 6SQ

Proficiently run coaching inn with welcoming staff, fine choice of drinks, imaginative food, and comfortable beamed bar; comfortable bedrooms

Our readers continue to very much enjoy coming to this genuinely friendly and well run coaching inn for either a drink, a meal or to stay overnight in the comfortable, quiet bedrooms. The beamed bar has various pictures and old artefacts, a woodburning stove and comfortable wall seats and carver chairs around the tables on its carpet. The curved corner bar counter has Black Sheep Special and John Smiths on handpump, several wines by the glass and some rare malt whiskies. There's a lounge and separate restaurant, too. The cartoons in the gents' are worth a peek, piped music, and dominoes. In front of the building are some picnic-sets, with more in the garden. The charming village is well worth strolling around.

🍽 **Exceptionally good food includes lunchtime sandwiches, soup, seared king scallops with pea purée, smoked bacon and sherry vinaigrette, warm tart of smoked haddock and gruyère with a poached egg, spinach and hollandaise, asparagus and goats cheese pudding with watercress sauce, lambs liver with spring onion mashed potato, pancetta and red wine jus, daube of beef with horseradish croquettes, roast breast of guinea fowl with apricot and sage stuffing, cider fondants, spring onions and scrumpy jus, slow-braised rare breed belly pork with a casserole of broad beans, thyme and onions with little herb dumplings, daily specials, and puddings like lemon tart and bread and butter pudding.** *Starters/Snacks: £4.50 to £7.45. Main Courses: £9.50 to £19.95. Puddings: £4.50 to £5.25*

Free house ~ Licensees Andrew and Catherine Stephens ~ Real ale ~ Bar food ~ Restaurant (evening) ~ (01751) 431577 ~ Children welcome away from bar ~ Dogs allowed in bar and bedrooms ~ Open 12-2, 6(6.30 Sun)-11; closed 25 and 26 Dec ~ Bedrooms: £59S(£69B)/£90S(£100B)

Recommended by Derek and Sylvia Stephenson, Catherine Hyde, Ann and Tony Bennett-Hughes, Alison and Pete, Julie Preddy, Jill and Julian Tasker, Maurice and Gill McMahon, I H M Milne, Christopher Turner, Pat and Stewart Gordon, Janet and Peter Race, M S Catling, I D Barnett

SKIPTON   SD9851   MAP 7

Narrow Boat 🍺

Victoria Street; pub signed down alley off Coach Street; BD23 1JE

Extended pub near canal with eight real ales, proper home cooking, and good mix of customers

The fine choice of eight real ales on handpump remains quite a draw to this extended pub: Black Sheep Best, Copper Dragon Best Bitter and Golden Pippin, Timothy Taylors Landlord, and four guests like Abbeydale Last Rites, Daleside Stout, Elland Dragon Hunter, and Phoenix Navvy. Several continental beers and decent wines, too. The bar has a good mix of both locals and visitors, old brewery posters and nice mirrors decorated with framed beer advertisements on the walls, church pews, dining chairs and stools around wooden tables, and an upstairs gallery area with an interesting canal mural. The pub is down a cobbled alley, with picnic-sets under a front colonnade, and the Leeds & Liverpool Canal is nearby.

🍽 **Bar food includes filled baguettes, soup, home-made pies, and daily specials like tuscan bean stew, spanish-style meatballs, sausage and mash, and slow-roast lamb. Popular bar food at lunchtime includes sandwiches, soup, shepherd's pie, sausage and slow-roasted lamb.** *Starters/Snacks: £3.50 to £4.95. Main Courses: £7.95 to £10.95. Puddings: £3.75*

Market Town Taverns ~ Manager Tim Hughes ~ Real ale ~ Bar food (12-2.30, 5.30-8.30;
12-4 Sun; not Sun evening) ~ (01756) 797922 ~ Children welcome if dining ~ Dogs welcome ~
Open 12-11

*Recommended by Alan and Eve Harding, Jo Lilley, Simon Calvert, Michael and Lynne Gittins, Richard, Bruce Bird,
Richard and Karen Holt, the Didler, Alyson and Andrew Jackson, Phil and Carol Jones, Mr and Mrs Maurice Thompson*

SOUTH DALTON   SE9645   MAP 8

Pipe & Glass 🍴 🍷

West End; brown sign to pub off B1248 NW of Beverley; HU17 7PN

**Attractive dining pub with proper bar area, real ales, interesting modern cooking by young
chef/landlord, good service, and garden and front terrace**

The excellent, imaginative food cooked by the young chef/landlord in this attractive
white-washed dining pub is as good as ever. But despite the emphasis on the eating
side, there is a proper bar area where they don't take bookings. This is beamed and bow-
windowed, with a log fire, some old prints, plush stools and traditional pubby chairs
around a mix of tables, and even high-backed settles. Beyond that, all is airy and
comfortably contemporary, angling around past some soft modern dark leather
chesterfields into a light restaurant area overlooking Dalton Park, with high-backed
stylish dining chairs around well spaced country tables on bare boards. The decorations –
a row of serious cookery books, and framed big-name restaurant menus – show how high
the licensee aims. Black Sheep Best, guest beers from breweries like Copper Dragon,
Cropton, and Wold Top on handpump, ten wines by the glass, and Old Rosie cider. Service
is friendly and prompt by bright and attentive young staff; disabled access, piped music.
There are tables out on the garden's peaceful lawn beside the park and picnic-sets on
the front terrace; people say the yew tree is some 500 years old. The village is charming,
and its elegant Victorian church spire, 62 metres (204 ft) tall, is visible for miles around.
More reports please.

🍴 Contemporary and interesting, the food includes sandwiches, deep-fried wild rabbit
rissoles with sorrel salad and cockle and caper vinaigrette, a little jar of potted spiced
gloucester old spot pork with sticky apples and crackling salad, hay-baked chicken breast
with leeks, wild garlic, creamed smoked bacon broth and crispy black pudding, baked
truffled field mushroom and spinach tart with rarebit, poached egg, and hazelnut pesto,
barnsley lamb chop with devilled kidneys, boulangère potato, pickled red cabbage and
nettle and mint sauce, daily specials like deep-fried pollack croquettes with potted
shrimp and flat parsley salad and wild garlic velouté, line-caught bass with cauliflower
champ and cockle and langoustine stew, and beer-braised oxtails with roast beetroot,
mash, and oyster fritter, and puddings such as hot dark chocolate and cherry pudding with
cherry blossom ice-cream and lemon burnt cream with blood orange and thyme compote.
Starters/Snacks: £3.85 to £9.95. Main Courses: £8.95 to £19.95. Puddings: £5.45 to £6.95

Free house ~ Licensees Kate and James Mackenzie ~ Real ale ~ Bar food (12-2, 6.30-9.30;
12-4 Sun; not Sun evening or Mon) ~ Restaurant ~ (01430) 810246 ~ Children welcome ~
Open 12-3, 6.30-11; 12-11 Sat; 12-10.30 Sun; closed Mon, two weeks Jan

*Recommended by J Crosby, Pat and Graham Williamson, Walter and Susan Rinaldi-Butcher, David and
Cathrine Whiting*

SUTTON UPON DERWENT   SE7047   MAP 7

St Vincent Arms 🍴 🍷

B1228 SE of York; YO41 4BN

**Consistently cheerful, with nine real ales plus other drinks, well liked bar food and more
elaborate menu, and friendly service**

To be sure of a seat in the bustling bar here, you must arrive early – or book a table in
advance. There's a cheerful atmosphere, and this parlour-style, panelled front room has
traditional high-backed settles, a cushioned bow-window seat, windsor chairs and a gas-

effect coal fire; another lounge and separate dining room open off. On handpump, the beers might include Fullers London Pride and ESB, Gales HSB, Old Mill Bitter, Theakstons XB, Timothy Taylors Landlord and Golden Best, York Yorkshire Terrier, and Wells & Youngs Bombardier; 14 wines and two champagnes by the glass, and several malt whiskies. There are seats in the garden. The pub is named after the admiral who was granted the village and lands by the nation as thanks for his successful commands – and for coping with Nelson's infatuation with Lady Hamilton. Handy for the Yorkshire Air Museum. More reports please.

🍴 At lunchtime, the tasty bar food might include sandwiches and hot ciabatta, soup, salads like griddled chicken caesar and prawn and egg, steak and mushroom in ale pie, lasagne, and haddock and chips with mushy peas, with more elaborate evening dishes such as seared scallops on celeriac purée with balsamic reduction, confit of duck with cucumber salad and hoi sin sauce, thai green chicken curry, vegetable stir fry, beef stroganoff, rack of lamb with herb crust and a garlic and rosemary jus, steak au poivre, and puddings like red berry trifle and sticky toffee pudding with toffee sauce. *Starters/Snacks: £3.50 to £7.50. Main Courses: £9.00 to £17.95. Puddings: £4.90*

Free house ~ Licensee Simon Hopwood ~ Real ale ~ Bar food ~ Restaurant ~ (01904) 608349 ~ Children welcome ~ Open 11.30-3, 6-11; 12-3, 7-10.30 Sun

Recommended by Dr and Mrs J Temporal, J Crosby, Tim and Liz Sherbourne, Susan and Nigel Brookes

THORNTON WATLASS   SE2385   MAP 10

Buck 🍺 🛏

Village signposted off B6268 Bedale—Masham; HG4 4AH

Friendly village pub with five real ales, traditional bars, well liked food, and popular Sunday jazz

The pleasantly traditional bar on the right is where our readers like to head for in this honest village pub (in the same hands for 22 years now). This bar has upholstered old-fashioned wall settles on the carpet, a fine mahogany bar counter, a high shelf packed with ancient bottles, several mounted fox masks and brushes, and a brick fireplace. The Long Room (which overlooks the cricket green) has large prints of old Thornton Watlass cricket teams, signed bats, and cricket balls and so forth. Black Sheep Best, John Smiths and Theakstons Bitter with guests like Black Dog Rhatas and Copper Dragon Scotts 1816 on handpump, over 40 interesting malt whiskies, and seven wines by the glass; darts, cribbage and dominoes. The sheltered garden has an equipped children's play area and summer barbecues, and they have their own cricket team; quoits.

🍴 Traditional bar food includes sandwiches, soup, ploughman's, pâté with cumberland sauce, omelettes, mediterranean spaghetti, steak and kidney pie, lasagne, beer-battered fish, and daily specials such as moules marinières, lambs liver and smoked bacon, and marinated duck breast. *Starters/Snacks: £4.25 to £6.95. Main Courses: £7.95 to £13.95. Puddings: £3.50 to £4.50*

Free house ~ Licensees Michael and Margaret Fox ~ Real ale ~ Bar food (12-2(3 Sun), 6.30-9.30) ~ Restaurant ~ (01677) 422461 ~ Children welcome ~ Dogs allowed in bedrooms ~ Jazz Sun lunchtimes ~ Open 11am-midnight; closed evening 25 Dec ~ Bedrooms: £55S/£70(£80B)

Recommended by David Hoult, Bill and Sheila McLardy, Michael Doswell, Michael Butler, John R Ringrose, Jill and Julian Tasker

Real ale to us means beer which has matured naturally in its cask – not pressurised or filtered. We name all real ales stocked. We usually name ales preserved under a light blanket of carbon dioxide too, though purists – pointing out that this stops the natural yeasts developing – would disagree (most people, including us, can't tell the difference!).

WASS SE5579 MAP 7

Wombwell Arms

Back road W of Ampleforth; or follow brown tourist-attraction sign for Byland Abbey off A170 Thirsk—Helmsley; YO61 4BE

Consistently enjoyable village pub, friendly, bustling atmosphere, good mix of locals and visitors, appealing bar food, and real ales

'A thoroughly nice pub,' says one of our readers – and many others agree with him. The licensees and their staff are warmly friendly and the place is often packed with a good mix of both locals and visitors. The two cosy and neatly kept bars have plenty of simple character, log fires, Black Sheep Best, Copper Dragon Golden Pippin, and Timothy Taylors Landlord on handpump, seven wines by the glass, and several malt whiskies; darts and board games. The two restaurants are incorporated into a 17th-c former granary.

🍴 Enjoyable bar food includes sandwiches, soup, a trio of smoked fish, seared pigeon breasts with mushrooms on a croûton, mussels in a lightly spiced creamy sauce, aubergine and goats cheese stack with a light basil oil dressing, casserole of rabbit, venison, pheasant and shallots in a beer and port sauce, good mushroom risotto with chicken, red mullet fillets with a beurre blanc sauce on fennel and sweet potato, slow-roasted lamb shank in red wine and rosemary sauce, popular steak, mushroom and Guinness pie, crispy gressingham duck with a piquant cherry sauce, and puddings. *Starters/Snacks: £3.95 to £7.75. Main Courses: £9.25 to £16.95. Puddings: £4.25 to £5.00*

Free house ~ Licensees Steve and Mary Wykes ~ Real ale ~ Bar food (12-2(2.30 weekends), 6.30-8.45(9 Sat); not Sun evening or Mon) ~ Restaurant ~ (01347) 868280 ~ Children welcome ~ Open 12-2.30(4 Sat and Sun), 6.15-11; closed Sun evening and all day Mon (open summer bank hol Mon) ~ Bedrooms: £50S/£70S

Recommended by Michael Doswell, I H G Busby, WW, D Mills, Hansjoerg Landherr, Alyson and Andrew Jackson, Jill Angold-Stevens, Dr Peter Crawshaw, R Pearce, Pat and Tony Martin, Jeff and Wendy Williams

WATH IN NIDDERDALE

SE1467 MAP 7

Sportsmans Arms

Nidderdale road off B6265 in Pateley Bridge; village and pub signposted over hump-back bridge on right after a couple of miles; HG3 5PP

Beautifully placed restaurant-with-rooms plus welcoming bar, real ales and super choice of other drinks, imaginative food; comfortable bedrooms

Extremely well run by the charming Mr Carter for over 30 years, this civilised and friendly 17th-c restaurant-with-rooms is consistently enjoyed by our readers. Of course, it's not a traditional inn but it does have a welcoming bar with an open fire, Black Sheep Best and Ale on handpump, and locals who do still pop in – though most customers are here to enjoy the particularly good food. There's a very sensible and extensive wine list with 15 by the glass (including champagne), over 30 malt whiskies and several russian vodkas; quiet piped music. Benches and tables outside and seats in the pretty garden; croquet. As well as their own fishing on the River Nidd, this is an ideal spot for walkers, hikers and ornithologists, and there are plenty of country houses, gardens and cities to explore.

🍴 Using the best local produce for the imaginative menu, the food in the bar includes lunchtime filled rolls and sandwiches, terrine of local game with pistachios and home-made chutney, home-cured gravadlax with warm asparagus and mustard mayonnaise, seared scallops with garlic butter and an emmenthal glaze, sausages with red wine and haricot bean gravy, pheasant with bacon and wild mushrooms, bass on spinach mash with a red pepper sauce, and rib-eye steak with fries and aïoli; more elaborate choices also, such as warm camembert goats cheese on roasted peppers with caramelised red onions, pear, roquefort and walnut salad, a trio of seafood (local smoked salmon, trout mousse and portland crab), fillet of hake with olive oil mash and tapenade and roast cherry tomatos with home-made rocket pesto, best end of lamb with provençale tomatoes and natural jus, roast loin of venison with home-made aubergine chutney and a prune and brandy sauce, and puddings like orange and Grand Marnier crème brûlée and sticky toffee pudding with toffee sauce. *Starters/Snacks: £4.00 to £9.50. Main Courses: £9.50 to £18.00. Puddings: £3.95 to £6.50*

Free house ~ Licensee Ray Carter ~ Real ale ~ Bar food (during opening hours though only until 7pm Sun evening) ~ Restaurant ~ (01423) 711306 ~ Children allowed until 9pm ~ Dogs allowed in bar ~ Open 12-2.30, 6.30-11(10.30 Sun); closed 25 Dec, evening 1 Jan ~ Bedrooms: £70B/£120B

Recommended by Stephen Woad, Richard Cole, Mr and Mrs D J Nash, Janet and Peter Race, Hunter and Christine Wright, Lynda and Trevor Smith, Peter and Lesley Yeoward

WESTOW   SE7565   MAP 7

Blacksmiths 🍴

Off A64 York—Malton; Main Street; YO60 7NE

Bustling dining pub with plenty of space for drinkers, imaginative food, and real ales

Although this is a busy dining pub, there's plenty of space for drinkers in the bar, and tables can only be booked before 7pm. This beamed area has traditional high-backed settles around sturdy stripped tables, each with a fat candle, a big open woodburning stove in the capacious brick inglenook, and a few small engravings (farm animals, scenes from *Mr Sponge's Sporting Tour* and the like) on the cream walls. Jennings Bitter and Cumberland and a guest such as Thwaites Double Century on handpump, and several wines by the glass; piped music and TV. The main dining area is basically two linked smallish rooms with a medley of comfortable dining chairs including some distinctive antiques around candlelit stripped dining tables on the wooden floor. There are picnic-sets on a side terrace. More reports please.

🍴 Very good, interesting food includes sandwiches, soup, garlic and white wine steamed mussels with soft herbs, goats cheese and caramelised onion puff pastry tartlet, seared scallops with minted cucumber and mango chutney, pork with roasted apple and ginger, herb-crusted rack of lamb with garlic and rosemary roast potatoes, red mullet with cauliflower purée and ratatouille sauce, fried venison and venison skewer with caramelised parsnips, and puddings like baby banana tatin with mini chocolate fondant and coconut panna cotta with pineapple carpaccio and pina colada. *Starters/Snacks: £3.95 to £5.95. Main Courses: £7.95 to £12.95. Puddings: £4.95 to £6.95*

Free house ~ Licensee Jonathan Cliff ~ Bar food (12-2, 5.30-9; 12-4 Sun; not Sun evening, not Mon, not Tues lunchtime) ~ Restaurant ~ (01653) 618365 ~ Children welcome ~ Open 12-2, 5.30(6.30 Tues)-11; 12-11(10.30 Sun) Sat; closed Mon all day, Tues lunchtime

Recommended by R L Graham, Christopher Turner, David and Cathrine Whiting, John H Smith, Julie Preddy, Dr Ian S Morley

WHITBY   NZ9011   MAP 10

Duke of York

124 Church Street, Harbour East Side; YO22 4DE

Fine harbourside position, window seats and bedrooms enjoy the view, several real ales, and standard bar food

From the windows in this busy pub there's a fine view over the harbour entrance and the western cliff. The comfortable beamed lounge bar – some refurbishment this year – has fishing memorabilia (including the pennant numbers of local trawlers chalked on the beams) and Caledonian Deuchars IPA, Courage Directors, John Smiths and Shepherd Neame Spitfire on handpump; decent wines by the glass and quite a few malt whiskies, piped music, TV, and games machine. All the bedrooms (apart from one) overlook the water. The pub is close to the famous 199 Steps that lead up to the abbey. There is no nearby parking.

🍴 Straightforward bar food includes sandwiches, chilli con carne, steak in ale or fish pie, and large local cod or haddock in batter. *Starters/Snacks: £3.95 to £4.50. Main Courses: £6.95 to £11.95. Puddings: £3.50*

Enterprise ~ Lease Lawrence Bradley ~ Real ale ~ Bar food (all day) ~ (01947) 600324 ~ Children welcome ~ Live music Mon evening ~ Open 11-11(midnight Sat); 12-11 Sun ~ Bedrooms: /£60B

Recommended by Ann and Tony Bennett-Hughes, Ben Williams, the Didler, Chris and Jeanne Downing, Amanda Russell, David Carr, P Dawn, Pat and Graham Williamson, Patrick Wiegand, Michael Dandy, Tim and Claire Woodward

WIDDOP   SD9531   MAP 7

Pack Horse 🐴

The Ridge; from A646 on W side of Hebden Bridge, turn off at Heptonstall signpost (as it's a sharp turn, coming out of Hebden Bridge road signs direct you around a turning circle), then follow Slack and Widdop signposts; can also be reached from Nelson and Colne, on high, pretty road; OS Sheet 103 map reference 952317; HX7 7AT

Friendly pub high up on the moors and liked by walkers for generous, tasty food, five real ales, and lots of malt whiskies; bedrooms

A real oasis for walkers on the Pennine Way and Pennine Bridleway, this isolated pub has a good, bustling atmosphere. There's a welcome from the friendly staff, and the bar has warm winter fires, window seats cut into the partly panelled stripped stone walls that take in the moorland view, sturdy furnishings, horsey mementos, and Black Sheep Best and Special, Greene King Old Speckled Hen, and Thwaites Bitter and Lancaster Bomber on handpump, around 130 single malt whiskies and some irish ones as well, and eight wines by the glass. The friendly golden retrievers are called Padge and Purdey, and there's another dog called Holly. Seats outside and pretty summer hanging baskets. Leave your boots and backpacks in the porch.

🍽 **Decent bar food at fair prices includes sandwiches, ploughman's, soup, pâté, garlic mushrooms, large burgers, steak and kidney pie, lasagne, vegetable bake, gammon and eggs, seafood thermidor, and daily specials. They do stop food service promptly.**
Starters/Snacks: £3.95 to £5.95. Main Courses: £5.95 to £12.95. Puddings: £3.50 to £4.50

Free house ~ Licensee Andrew Hollinrake ~ Real ale ~ Bar food (not Mon or Tues-Thurs winter lunchtimes) ~ (01422) 842803 ~ Children in eating area of bar until 8pm ~ Dogs allowed in bar ~ Open 12-3, 7-11; 12-11 Sun; closed lunchtimes Mon-Thurs in winter; closed Mon ~ Bedrooms: £43S/£48B

Recommended by Brian Wainwright, Greta and Christopher Wells, Len Beattie, Dr Kevan Tucker, Ian and Nita Cooper

YORK   SE5951   MAP 7

Maltings 🍺 £

Tanners Moat/Wellington Row, below Lendal Bridge; YO1 6HU

Bustling, friendly city pub with cheerful landlord, interesting real ales and other drinks, and good value food

Tucked away by the riverside, this lively city pub is very popular with a wide range of customers for its half a dozen interesting beers, good value food, and friendly welcome. The tricksy décor is entirely contrived and strong on salvaged somewhat quirky junk: old doors for the bar front and much of the ceiling, a marvellous collection of railway signs and amusing notices, an old chocolate dispensing machine, cigarette and tobacco advertisements alongside cough and chest remedies, what looks like a suburban front door for the entrance to the ladies', partly stripped orange brick walls, and even a lavatory pan in one corner. As well as Black Sheep Bitter, the jovial landlord keeps six guest ales on handpump including one each from Roosters and York, and four that change daily. He also has four or five continental beers on tap, lots of bottled beers, up to four farm ciders, a dozen or so country wines, and more irish whiskeys than you normally see. Get there early to be sure of a seat; games machine. The day's papers are framed in the gents'. Nearby parking is difficult; the pub is very handy for the Rail Museum and the Yorkshire Eye.

Pubs with outstanding views are listed at the back of the book.

⑪ **Generous helpings of tasty bar food include sandwiches, extremely good, truly home-made chips with chilli or curry, filled baked potatoes, haddock, beef in ale pie and stilton and leek bake.** *Main Courses: £2.85 to £5.50*

Free house ~ Licensee Shaun Collinge ~ Real ale ~ Bar food (12-2 weekdays, 12-4 weekends; not evenings) ~ No credit cards ~ (01904) 655387 ~ Children allowed only during meal times ~ Dogs welcome ~ Live folk music Tues evening ~ Open 11-11; 12-10.30 Sun

Recommended by Mark and Diane Grist, Michael Butler, the Didler, Bruce Bird, Neil Whitehead, Victoria Anderson, Brian Wainwright, Alison and Pete, David Carr, Pete Coxon, Andy and Jill Kassube, Mark Walker

LUCKY DIP

Besides the fully inspected pubs, you might like to try these Lucky Dips recommended to us and described by readers (if you do, please send us reports: feedback@thegoodpubguide.co.uk).

ABERFORD [SE4337]
Swan LS25 3AA [best to use A642 junction to leave A1; Main St N]: Useful dining pub, vast choice of generous food from sandwiches to bargain carvery, lots of black timber, prints, pistols, cutlasses, stuffed animals and hunting trophies, well kept Black Sheep and Tetleys, generous glasses of wine, quick service by uniformed staff, upstairs evening restaurant; children welcome, tables outside *(Michael Butler)*
ADDINGHAM [SE0749]
☆ **Fleece** LS29 0LY [Main St]: Nice farmhouse-style eating area on right with good value home-made food from hearty sandwiches using their own baked bread to sophisticated blackboard meals using good local ingredients, popular Sun roasts (all day then), quick friendly service, well kept Yorkshire ales and good choice of wines by the glass, low ceilings, flagstones, candles and log fire, plain tap room with darts and dominoes; very busy wknds; children welcome, lots of picnic-sets on terrace, open all day *(Michael and Lynne Gittins, Michael Doswell, Gerry Miller, Stuart Doughty, Lucie Ware)*
Swan LS29 0NS [Main St]: Haunted time-warp pub with open fires in comfortably worn linked rooms around central servery, flagstones and ancient iron range, well kept changing ales inc Copper Dragon, good value food inc tapas, sausage specialities and game, friendly dog *(Stuart Doughty)*
AINDERBY QUERNHOW [SE3480]
Black Horse YO7 4HX [B6267, just off A1]: Relaxed, friendly and well refurbished, enjoyable fresh food, Black Sheep and John Smiths, coal fire *(John Robertson)*
ALDBOROUGH [SE4166]
Ship YO51 9ER [off B6265 just S of Boroughbridge, close to A1]: Attractive creeper-clad 14th-c village pub with heavy beams, some old-fashioned seats around cast-iron-framed tables, lots of copper and brass, inglenook fire, enjoyable food, friendly staff, John Smiths, Theakstons and Timothy Taylors Landlord; piped music; children welcome, front terrace, handy for Roman remains and museum, comfortable

bedrooms, open all day wknds *(Graham and Doreen Holden, Malcolm and Jane Levitt, LYM, Brian and Janet Ainscough, Pat and Graham Williamson)*
ALNE [SE4965]
Blue Bell YO61 1RR [off A19 NW of York; Main St]: Restauranty place open evenings only (though all day Sun), two linked front areas, coal fire and stove, old engravings, stripped joists in dark red ceiling, mix of furnishings, fine bow-window seat around good-sized round table, sun lounge, further L-shaped room, John Smiths, Timothy Taylors Landlord and a guest beer; children welcome, neat garden behind, new bedrooms *(Pat and Graham Williamson, Mr and Mrs P M Jennings, John R Ringrose, LYM)*
APPLETREEWICK [SE0560]
☆ **Craven Arms** BD23 6DA [off B6160 Burnsall—Bolton Abbey]: Creeper-covered 17th-c beamed pub with comfortably down-to-earth settles and rugs on flagstones, brown-painted ply panelling, coal fire in old range, good friendly service, three well kept ales such as Black Sheep and Wharfedale, good choice of wines by the glass, enjoyable reasonably priced home-made food from good sandwiches up, small dining room and splendid thatched and raftered barn extension with gallery; dogs and walking boots welcome (plenty of surrounding walks), nice views from front picnic-sets, more seats in back garden *(Greta and Christopher Wells, LYM, Colin McIlwain, Lucien Perring, WW, Pat and Graham Williamson)*
New Inn BD23 6DA: Unpretentious warmly welcoming country local with lovely views, well kept ales such as Daleside, several belgian beers, generous tasty home cooking, distinctive décor, interesting photographs (HQ of local soi-disant dangerous sports club); garden, good walking, bedrooms *(LYM, David and Sue Smith)*
ARNCLIFFE [SD9371]
☆ **Falcon** BD23 5QE [off B6160 N of Grassington]: Basic country tavern in same family for generations, lovely setting on moorland village green, no frills, coal fire in small bar with elderly furnishings, well kept Timothy Taylors Landlord tapped from cask to stoneware jugs in central hatch-style

servery, good plain lunchtime and early evening filled rolls and snacks from old family kitchen, attractive watercolours, sepia photographs and humorous sporting prints, simple back sunroom (children allowed lunchtime) overlooking pleasant garden; no credit cards, cl winter Thurs evenings; two plain bedrooms (not all year), miles of trout fishing, good breakfast and evening meal *(WW, Sarah Watkinson, Ann and Tony Bennett-Hughes, Comus and Sarah Elliott, Michael B Griffith, the Didler, Gerry Miller, LYM, B and M Kendall, Neil and Angela Huxter)*

ARTHINGTON [SE2644]

Wharfedale LS21 1NL [A659 E of Otley (Arthington Lane)]: Good value food from sandwiches and pub staples to popular Sun lunch, well kept Black Sheep and Tetleys, several wines by the glass, efficient friendly service, roomy and comfortably old-fashioned open-plan bar, intimate alcoves, soft lighting, half-panelling and Yorkshire landscapes, separate more modern restaurant; disabled access and facilities, three bedrooms *(Jeremy King, Ray and Winifred Halliday)*

ASKRIGG [SD9491]

☆ *Crown* DL8 3HQ [Main St]: Friendly open-plan local in James Herriot village, three areas off main bar, blazing fires inc old-fashioned range, relaxed atmosphere, simple home-made food inc cut-price small helpings, cheerful staff, Black Sheep, Theakstons XB and guest beers; children, dogs and walkers welcome, tables outside *(Dr D Scott, Lawrence Pearse, Derek Allpass, Robin and Ann Taylor, David and Karen Cuckney, Mrs Margo Finlay, Jörg Kasprowski)*

☆ *Kings Arms* DL8 3HQ [signed from A684 Leyburn—Sedbergh in Bainbridge]: Great log fire in former coaching inn's flagstoned and high-ceilinged main bar, traditional furnishings and décor, real ales such as Black Sheep, John Smiths and Theakstons, decent wines by the glass, good choice of malt whiskies, upscale bar food, another log fire in restaurant, pool in barrel-vaulted former beer cellar; piped music; dogs welcome, pleasant courtyard, bedrooms run separately as part of Holiday Property Bond complex behind *(Robin and Ann Taylor, Ian and Celia Abbott, Greta and Christopher Wells, Lawrence Pearse, LYM, John and Enid Morris, Mrs Margo Finlay, Jörg Kasprowski)*

White Rose DL8 3HG [Main St]: Good value food from lunchtime sandwiches up in neat and friendly carpeted bar or dining room with conservatory, local real ales, pool; 12 comfortable bedrooms *(Mrs Margo Finlay, Jörg Kasprowski, Derek Allpass)*

AUSTWICK [SD7668]

☆ *Game Cock* LA2 8BB [just off A65 Settle—Kirkby Lonsdale]: Pretty spot below Three Peaks, friendly barman and good log fire in homely old-fashioned beamed bare-boards

back bar, Thwaites ales, nice coffee, most space devoted to the food side, with good fairly priced choice from sandwiches up inc good game pie, two dining rooms and modern front conservatory-type extension; dogs welcome, tables out in front with good play area, five neat bedrooms, good walks, open all day Sun *(BB, MDN, Lucien Perring, Margaret Dickinson)*

AYSGARTH [SE0088]

George & Dragon DL8 3AD [just off A684]: 17th-c posting inn with emphasis on good varied food from sandwiches up (service has been slow), two big dining areas, small beamed and panelled bar with log fire, good choice of wines by the glass, Black Sheep Bitter and Theakstons Best; may be piped music; children welcome, nice paved garden, lovely scenery, compact bedrooms, open all day *(Mr and Mrs W W Burke, Michael and Maggie Betton, LYM, Janet and Peter Race, P R Stevens)*

BAILDON [SE1538]

Junction BD17 6AB [Baildon Rd]: Traditional welcoming alehouse with linked rooms, good range of ales inc Fullers and locals such as Saltaire, brewery memorabilia, basic food served till 7pm, popular Tues curry night, pool *(Jeremy King, Andy and Jill Kassube)*

BARKISLAND [SE0419]

Fleece HX4 0DJ [B6113 towards Ripponden]: 18th-c two-bar moorland pub, food counter with good choice inc local meat, Black Sheep and Timothy Taylors, feature fireplace, comfortable settles, beams, stripped stone and mezzanine; good-sized garden with play frame and Pennine views, four bedrooms *(BB, Tony Carter)*

BECKWITHSHAW [SE2853]

Pine Marten HG3 1UE [Otley Rd, Beckwith Knowle; B6162 towards Harrogate]: Rambling Victorian M&B dining pub, big comfortable rooms and cosy nooks, mullioned windows, panelling, settles and open fires, sensibly priced food all day from sandwiches up, efficient polite service, real ale, decent wines; handy for Harlow Carr gardens, Innkeepers Lodge bedrooms *(Ian and Nita Cooper)*

BEDALE [SE2688]

Old Black Swan DL8 1ED [Market Pl]: Attractive façade, welcoming efficient staff, bargain bar lunches, Theakstons ales, log fire, darts, pool; sports TV; children welcome, disabled facilities, small back terrace, open all day *(Margaret Dickinson)*

BEVERLEY [TA0339]

Oddfellows Arms HU17 0DR [Eastgate]: Friendly corner local, small comfortable front snug, large bar, lunchtime food, real ale; silenced TV *(Mark Walker)*

Rose & Crown HU17 7AB [North Bar Without]: Prompt cheerful service even when busy, good value food inc Mon and Thurs night bargains, three real ales *(Clive Gibson)*

BILBROUGH [SE5346]

Three Hares YO23 3PH [off A64 York—Tadcaster]: Smart neatly kept village dining pub with decent food, well kept real ale, good choice of wines by the glass, leather sofas and log fire (BB, Gordon and Margaret Ormondroyd)

BILTON [SE4750]

☆ *Chequers* YO26 7NN [B1224]: Good sensibly priced fresh food, well kept Caledonian Deuchars IPA and Jennings Cockerhoop, good house wines and coffee, young helpful staff, comfortably refurbished linked bar areas and part-panelled dining room; piped music; three bedrooms (Les and Sandra Brown, Malcolm Pellatt, John and Eleanor Holdsworth, Rita and Keith Pollard)

BINGLEY [SE1242]

Dick Hudsons BD16 3BA [Otley Rd, High Eldwick]: Comfortable Vintage Inn family dining pub, a couple of real ales, good choice of wines by the glass, quick service; tables out by cricket field, great views, open all day (David Coupe, Pat and Graham Williamson, R M Chard)

BISHOP WILTON [SE7955]

Fleece YO42 1RU [just off A166 York—Bridlington; Main St]: Partly panelled open-plan village inn with good changing beer range, enterprising food, pleasant landlord, moderately priced wines, several areas off flagstoned entrance hall, lots of pictures and bric-a-brac; four compact comfortable bedrooms across courtyard, nice spot nr interesting church and Wolds (Pat and Graham Williamson)

BISHOPDALE [SD9985]

Street Head DL8 3TE [B6160 W Burton—Cray]: 17th-c coaching inn, three comfortably modernised linked rooms, enjoyable food, Black Sheep, John Smiths and Theakstons; five good bedrooms (Mr and Mrs Ian King)

BOLSTERSTONE [SK2796]

Castle Inn S36 3ZB [off A616]: Open-plan stone-built local in small hilltop conservation-area village, spectacular surroundings by Ewden Valley at edge of Peak Park, great views from picnic-sets outside; Black Sheep, Bradfield Blonde and Stones, enjoyable basic food, unofficial HQ of award-winning male voice choir (Giles and Annie Francis)

BRADFORD [SE1633]

Cock & Bottle BD3 9AA [Barkerend Rd, up Church Bank from centre]: Carefully restored Victorian décor, deep-cut and etched windows and mirrors, stained-glass, enamel intaglios, heavily carved woodwork and traditional furniture,Copper Dragon and guest ales, coal fire, Thurs folk night; open all day (BB, the Didler)

Fighting Cock BD7 1JE [Preston St (off B6145)]: Busy bare-boards alehouse by industrial estate, a dozen well kept changing real ales inc Theakstons and Timothy Taylors, foreign bottled beers, farm ciders, lively atmosphere, all-day doorstep sandwiches and good simple lunchtime hot dishes (not Sun), low prices, coal fires; open all day (Gordon and Margaret Ormondroyd, the Didler)

Haigys BD8 7QU [Lumb Lane]: Friendly, lively and distinctive local with cosy lounge area, Ossett, Phoenix and four guests, revolving pool table, music area; cl lunchtimes (the Didler)

New Beehive BD1 3AA [Westgate]: Robustly old-fashioned Edwardian inn with several rooms inc good pool room, wide range of changing ales, gas lighting, candles and coal fires; basement music nights; nice back courtyard, bedrooms, open all day (till 2am Fri/Sat) (the Didler)

Stansfield Arms BD10 0NP [Apperley Lane, Apperley Bridge; off A658 NE]: Attractive creeper-covered pub smartly refurbished as roomy dining pub, enjoyable food, well kept Black Sheep, Timothy Taylors Landlord and Tetleys, cheerful attentive staff, beams, stripped stone and dark panelling, pleasant setting (Gordon and Margaret Ormondroyd)

BRADWAY [SK3280]

Old Mother Redcap S17 4JA [Prospect Rd]: Recently refurbished L-shaped open-plan lounge, comfortable banquettes, friendly staff, cheap Sam Smiths OB, fair-priced food; no cards; picnic-sets on back terrace (JJW, CMW)

BRAMHAM [SE4242]

Swan LS23 6QA [just off A1 2 miles N of A64]: Civilised three-room country local with engaging long-serving landlady, Black Sheep, Caledonian Deuchers IPA and John Smiths, no food, machines or music (Les and Sandra Brown)

BRIDGE HEWICK [SE3370]

Black-a-moor HG4 5AA [Boroughbridge Rd (B6265 E of Ripon)]: Roomy dining pub locally very popular for its food using prime local produce, well kept Black Sheep, well chosen wines by the glass, friendly and willing young staff, good coffee, sofas in bar area; bedrooms (Michael Doswell, I D Barnett, Janet and Peter Race)

BRIGHOUSE [SE1320]

Roundhill HD6 3QL [Clough Lane]: Friendly cosy two-room local with energetic landlady, well kept Black Sheep, Timothy Taylors and a guest beer, open fire and bric-a-brac; cl wkdy lunchtimes, open all day wknds (Gordon and Margaret Ormondroyd)

Sun HX3 8TH [N, on A649; Wakefield Rd, Lightcliffe]: Comfortably updated and extended 18th-c stone building, real ales inc Timothy Taylors, wide choice of food, carvery (Thurs/Fri/Sat evenings, all day Sun) (Gordon and Margaret Ormondroyd)

Tipp HD6 1ES [Atlas Mill Rd]: Tap for good Atlas Mill brewery above, converted mill premises with stone walls, brick barrel-vaulted ceiling, extraordinary salvaged Victorian bar back, usual pubby furnishings, friendly staff; big-screen TV; smokers' shelter (David, Pat and Tony Martin)

BURNISTON [TA0192]

Oak Wheel YO13 0HR [A171 N of Scarborough]: Thriving under current licensees, quick friendly service, lively atmosphere, enjoyable pubby food inc fresh local fish, well kept ales; five bedrooms, cl lunchtime, opens 4 *(Joan York)*

BURNT YATES [SE2561]

New Inn HG3 3EG [Pateley Bridge Rd]: Prompt cheerful service, well kept ales inc Theakstons, Viking and York, good wines by the glass, short blackboard choice of good value country cooking, lots of interesting bric-a-brac, nicely panelled back restaurant; terrace tables, eight comfortable bedrooms *(Michael Swallow, Tim and Ann Newell, Comus and Sarah Elliott, John Robertson)*

BURTON LEONARD [SE3263]

☆ *Hare & Hounds* HG3 3SG [off A61 Ripon—Harrogate, handy for A1(M) exit 48]: Civilised country dining pub, enjoyable reasonably priced food inc special deals, well kept Black Sheep from long counter, several wines by the glass and good choice of other drinks, welcoming service, large carpeted main area divided by log fire, traditional furnishings, bright little side room with sofa and easy chairs; children in eating areas, pretty back garden *(Justin and Emma King, B and M Kendall, Mrs Mahni Pannett, John and Jill Milton, LYM)*

BURYTHORPE [SE7964]

☆ *Bay Horse* YO17 9LJ [5 miles S of Malton]: Charming dining pub, bar well used by locals too, careful décor keeping linked rooms cosy yet up-to-date, pictures, books and armchairs; welcoming service, good value generous food (not Sun/Mon evenings), Black Sheep and Timothy Taylors, decent wines by the glass; nice Wolds-edge village *(Christopher Turner, Dr Ian S Morley)*

BYLAND ABBEY [SE5478]

☆ *Abbey Inn* YO61 4BD [off A170 Thirsk—Helmsley]: By the beautiful abbey ruins and now too owned by English Heritage, prettily refurbished to include Thompsons of Kilburn sturdy oak furniture, polished boards and flagstones, big fireplaces, some discreet stripping back of plaster to show signs of venerable past, Black Sheep Best and a guest beer, several wines by the glass, nice jugs from local potter; newish management and chef, restaurant meals and lunchtime snacks; may close for private functions; children allowed if eating, terrace tables and pretty garden, three comfortable bedrooms, cl Sun pm, Mon lunchtime *(LYM, Peter Burton, H Bramwell)*

CARLTON [SE0684]

☆ *Foresters Arms* DL8 4BB [off A684 W of Leyburn]: Friendly landlord, good food inc local game and venison, their own-brewed Wensleydale and guest ales, decent wines by the glass, log fire, low beams and flagstones; children welcome, picnic-sets out among tubs of flowers, pretty village in heart of Yorkshire Dales National Park, comfortable bedrooms, lovely views *(LYM, Gerry Miller, Mr and Mrs Maurice Thompson, the Didler, Ken and Barbara Turner, Terry Mizen, Dr and Mrs R G J Telfer)*

Smiths Arms TS21 1EA: Gabled end-of-terrace brick-built pub with bare-boards bar

and carpeted restaurant, Caledonian Deuchars IPA and changing guest, bargain lunchtime food such as lamb skewers on couscous, higher evening prices *(JHBS)*

CAWOOD [SE5737]

Ferry YO8 3TL [King St (B1222 NW of Selby), by Ouse swing bridge]: Unspoilt neatly kept 16th-c inn, several comfortable areas, well kept ales such as Black Sheep, Mansfield, Timothy Taylors Landlord and a couple of local beers tapped from the cask in corner bar, friendly helpful staff, limited food inc bargain steak baguette and lots for children, Sun roast, log fire in massive inglenook, low beams, stripped brickwork, bare boards; well behaved children and dogs welcome, flagstone terrace and lawn by interesting River Ouse swing bridge, three good value bedrooms, open all day Fri-Sun, cl Mon/Tues lunchtime *(Matt Waite)*

CAWTHORNE [SE2808]

Spencer Arms S75 4HL [off A635 W of Barnsley]: Low-beamed stone-built pub in attractive village by Cannon Hall, lots of cosy alcoves, contemporary restaurant, good standard food, friendly helpful staff *(Marcus Mann)*

CLAPHAM [SD7469]

New Inn LA2 8HH [off A65 N of Settle]: Welcoming riverside inn in famously pretty village, log fires, cartoons and landlady's tapestries in small comfortable lounge, changing well kept Yorkshire ales, obliging staff, good honest food, public bar with pool in games area, restaurant; dogs welcome, tables outside, handy for walk to Ingleborough Cavern and more adventurous hikes, 20 comfortable bedrooms *(Roy and Lindsey Fentiman, Adam F Padel, Mr and Mrs Maurice Thompson, MDN)*

CLAYTON WEST [SE2510]

Green Man HD8 9PD [High St]: Hospitable village pub with enjoyable food (all day Fri/Sat; not Sun evening, Mon or lunchtime Tues-Thurs); handy for Sculpture Park and National Mining Museum *(W G O'Brien)*

CLIFTON [SE1622]

☆ *Black Horse* HD6 4HJ [Westgate/Coalpit Lane; signed off Brighouse rd from M62 junction 25]: 17th-c pub/hotel with pleasant décor featuring sports and variety artistes, front dining rooms with good generous food from lunchtime snacks up, can be pricy but good value set meals, cosy back bar area, beam and plank ceiling, open fire, well kept Black Sheep and Timothy Taylors Landlord, decent wines, english setter called Arthur; 23 comfortable bedrooms, pleasant village *(Michael Butler, BB, Marcus Mann)*

Old Mill HD6 4HA [A644 (Wakefield Rd) off M62 J25]: Vast Chef & Brewer in former corn mill, old-world rooms around central bar, wide food choice all day, well kept Old Mill and Theakstons; lots of tables in riverside grounds *(Gordon and Margaret Ormondroyd)*

COLTON [SE5444]

☆ *Olde Sun* LS24 8EP [off A64 York—Tadcaster]: Immaculate 17th-c beamed dining pub with wide choice of good upscale food using prime local produce (must book Sun lunch), good welcoming service, well kept ales such as Black Sheep and Greene King, good choice of wines by the glass, several linked low-ceilinged rooms with nice collection of old chairs inc an antique settle around good solid tables, log fires, back delicatessen; quiet front terrace and decking, cl Mon (BB, Tom and Jill Jones, Pete Coxon, Paul Dickinson, Matt Waite, Tim and Sue Halstead)

CONEYTHORPE [SE3958]

☆ **Tiger** HG5 0RY [E of Knaresborough]: Pretty dining pub on green of charming village, friendly efficient staff, wholesome food from lunchtime sandwiches and pub favourites to some tempting originals, Black Sheep and Tetleys, fresh open-plan décor in linked areas around bar and adjoining dining room (WW, Michael Doswell)

CRACOE [SD9760]

Devonshire Arms BD23 6LA [B6265 Skipton—Grassington]: Reopened after sympathetic updating while keeping the low beams, good value standard food, Marstons and related ales, log fire; garden with terrace, comfortable bedrooms (Dudley and Moira Cockroft, LYM)

CRIGGLESTONE [SE3217]

Red Kite WF4 3BB [Denby Dale Rd, Durkar (A636, by M1 junction 39)]: Vintage Inn dining pub done like a Georgian house adjoining a cottage row, good service, their usual good value food and wide range of wines by the glass, Black Sheep, Fullers and Tetleys, log fire, pleasant décor, daily papers; lots of tables outside, bedrooms in adjacent Holiday Inn Express (Michael Butler, Derek and Sylvia Stephenson)

CROFTON [SE3817]

Cock & Crown WF4 1PP [A638 SE of Wakefield]: Roomy and busy modern M&B bargain carvery pub; children welcome, open all day (Marcus Mann)

CROSS HILLS [SE0045]

Old White Bear BD20 7RN [Keighley Rd]: Cheery bustling local brewing its own Naylors ales, quick friendly service, wide choice of popular home cooking, two rooms off central bar, beams and open fires, pub games; piped music, games machine, TV (Stuart Doughty, Len Beattie)

DACRE BANKS [SE1961]

☆ **Royal Oak** HG3 4EN [B6451 S of Pateley Bridge]: Solidly comfortable 18th-c pub with Nidderdale views, good value often enterprising food from sandwiches up, helpful staff, Boddingtons, Rudgate and Theakstons, good wine choice, beams and panelling, log-fire dining room, games room with darts, dominoes and pool; TV, piped music; children in eating areas, terrace tables, informal back garden, three good value character bedrooms (bar below can stay lively till late), good breakfast (LYM, Michael Butler, Mrs M Tippett, Pat and Tony Martin)

DARLEY [SE1959]

Wellington HG3 2QQ [B6451 S of Pateley Bridge]: Comfortable stone-built country inn, wide choice of imaginative food from hearty sandwiches up, friendly staff, heavily panelled bar and large dining area, real ales, log fires; lovely Nidderdale views, 12 good reasonably priced bedrooms, good breakfast (H Bramwell)

DEWSBURY [SE2622]

Huntsman WF12 7SW [Walker Cottages, Chidswell Lane, Shaw Cross - pub signed]: Cosy low-beamed converted cottages alongside urban-fringe farm, lots of agricultural bric-a-brac, friendly locals, Black Sheep, Timothy Taylors Landlord and Chidswell (brewed for them by Tom Woods), hot log fire, small front extension, decent food (not evening or Sun/Mon lunchtime) (Michael Butler, the Didler)

Leggers WF12 9BD [Robinsons Boat Yard, Savile Town Wharf, Mill St E (SE of B6409)]: Good value basic hayloft conversion by Calder & Hebble Navigation marina, low-beamed upstairs bar, good value ales such as Everards and Three Rivers, bottled belgian beers, farm cider, pies and rolls all day, real fire, friendly staff, daily papers, brewery and pub memorabilia, pool; picnic-sets outside, boat trips, open all day (the Didler, Andy and Jill Kassube)

Shepherds Boy WF13 2RP [Huddersfield Rd, Ravensthorpe]: Bargain generous basic lunchtime food, four Ossett ales and interesting guest beers, good range of foreign lagers, bottled beers and wines; open all day (Andy and Jill Kassube, the Didler)

☆ **West Riding Licensed Refreshment Rooms** WF13 1HF [Station, Wellington Rd]: Convivial three-room early Victorian station bar, particularly well kept Timothy Taylors and interesting changing ales, farm ciders, bargain wkdy lunchtime food on scrubbed tables, popular pie night Tues and curry night Weds, friendly staff, daily papers, coal fire, lots of steam memorabilia inc paintings by local artists, impressive juke box, jazz nights; disabled access, open all day (Andrew York, the Didler, Pat and Tony Martin)

DONCASTER [SK6299]

Hare & Tortoise DN4 7PB [Parrots Corner, Bawtry Rd, Bessacarr (A638)]: Civilised Vintage Inn all-day dining pub, varying-sized antique tables in several small rooms off bar, pleasant young staff, well priced food, good choice of wines by the glass and other drinks, log fire (Stephen Woad, Mr and Mrs W W Burke)

EASINGWOLD [SE5270]

☆ **George** YO61 3AD [Market Pl]: Neat, bright and airy market town hotel popular with older people, pleasant bustle though quiet corners even when busy, good cheerful service, Black Sheep, Daleside and Moorhouses, decent food inc generous sandwiches, warm log fires, interesting bric-a-brac; good value bedrooms, good breakfast

(Derek and Sylvia Stephenson, Pete Coxon, Margaret Dickinson)

EAST MARTON [SD9050]

Cross Keys BD23 3LP [A59 Gisburn—Skipton]: Behind small green nr Leeds & Liverpool Canal (and Pennine Way), abstract prints on pastel walls contrasting with heavy beams, antique oak furniture and big log or coal fire, reasonably priced food from good fresh sandwiches up, well kept Copper Dragon ales with a guest such as Black Sheep, decent wines, quick friendly helpful service, more restauranty dining room; quiet piped music; tables outside *(LYM, Len Beattie, Steve Whalley, D W Stokes)*

EAST WITTON [SE1487]

☆ *Coverbridge Inn* DL8 4SQ [A6108 out towards Middleham]: Homely 16th-c flagstoned country local with eight well kept yorkshire ales, good generous home-made food inc prime local steak and their renowned ham and eggs, sensible prices, helpful knowledgeable landlord and welcoming staff, small character bar and larger eating areas off, roaring fires; children and dogs welcome, riverside garden and play area, three bedrooms, open all day *(Mr and Mrs Ian King, the Didler, Dr Ian S Morley, Comus and Sarah Elliott, Mr and Mrs Maurice Thompson, David and Karen Cuckney, LYM, WW)*

EGTON BRIDGE [NZ8005]

Postgate YO21 1UX [signed off A171 W of Whitby]: Moorland village pub, wide choice of enjoyable food, friendly staff, real ales, traditional quarry-tiled panelled bar with beams, panelled dado and coal fire in antique range, elegant restaurant; children and dogs welcome, garden picnic-sets, three nice bedrooms *(LYM, Jane and Alan Bush)*

ELLAND [SE1021]

☆ *Barge & Barrel* HX5 9HP [quite handy for M62 junction 24; Park Rd (A6025, via A629 and B6114)]: Large welcoming pub with several changing ales inc local Eastwood/Elland, farm cider, pleasant staff, limited but generous low-priced tasty lunchtime food (not Mon), real fire, family room (with air hockey), some live music; piped radio, seats by Calder & Hebble Canal, limited parking, open all day *(the Didler, Stuart Paulley)*

EMBSAY [SE0053]

Elm Tree BD23 6RB [Elm Tree Sq]: Good value open-plan beamed village pub, hearty popular food from tasty sandwiches up, good range of well kept ales inc Goose Eye, Moorhouses and Wells & Youngs, friendly young staff, settles and old-fashioned prints, log-effect gas fire, dining room, games area; busy wknds esp evenings; comfortable bedrooms, handy for steam railway *(Michael Butler, Mr and Mrs D J Nash, Dudley and Moira Cockroft)*

FIXBY [SE1119]

Nags Head HD2 2EA [New Hey Rd, by M62 junction 24 south side, past Hilton]: Newly refurbished chain food pub, attractive outside and comfortable in, four well kept ales, decent food inc sandwiches and buffet restaurant, four well kept ales, linked areas with wood and slate floors; garden tables, bedrooms in adjoining Premier Inn *(Gordon and Margaret Ormondroyd)*

FLAMBOROUGH [TA2270]

☆ *Seabirds* YO15 1PD [Tower St (B1255/B1229)]: Friendly pub with shipping-theme bar, woodburner and local pictures in comfortable lounge, smart light and airy dining extension; has had enjoyable food from sandwiches to fresh fish, good cheerful service, well kept Wold Top ale, decent wine list, but for sale early 2008; children welcome, tables in sizeable garden *(DC, John and Sylvia Harrop, Pat and Graham Williamson, Susan and Nigel Brookes, LYM)*

GARGRAVE [SD9253]

Masons Arms BD23 3NL [Church St/Marton Rd (off A65 NW of Skipton)]: Attractive and well run, friendly and homely, good value straightforward food from good sandwiches up, well kept northern ales, copper-canopied log-effect gas fire dividing two linked areas; well behaved children welcome, garden tables, bowling green behind - charming village on Pennine Way, between river and church and not far from Leeds & Liverpool Canal *(Derek and Sylvia Stephenson)*

GARSDALE HEAD [SD7992]

☆ *Moorcock* LA10 5PU [junction A684/B6259; marked on many maps, nr Garsdale stn on Settle—Carlisle line]: Isolated stone-built inn with Black Sheep and own Moorcock ale brewed in Hawes, good value food all day from overstuffed sandwiches up, good choice of wines by the glass, good coffee, welcoming landlord and helpful staff, pleasantly informal eclectic décor, log fire in small flagstone bar, cosy corners in lounge bar, occasional live music such as classical guitar; muddy walkers welcome, tables outside with views of viaduct and Settle—Carlisle railway, bedrooms, open all day *(Bruce and Sharon Eden, Mr and Mrs Maurice Thompson, David and Karen Cuckney)*

GIGGLESWICK [SD8164]

☆ *Black Horse* BD24 0BE [Church St]: Very hospitable father-and-son landlords in prettily set 17th-c village pub, spotless cosy bar with horsey bric-a-brac and gleaming brasses, good value hearty food inc sandwiches and nice home-made puddings, John Smiths, Timothy Taylors and Tetleys, coal fire, intimate dining room; three comfortable bedrooms, good breakfast *(Michael Butler)*

Harts Head BD24 0BA [Belle Hill]: Cheerful family-run inn, real ales such as Black Sheep, a bargain malt whisky, good choice of wines by the glass, public bar with dominoes (dogs welcome), Fri folk night, good value restaurant; bedrooms *(Mr and Mrs Maurice Thompson, Adam F Padel, Michael Butler)*

GILLING EAST [SE6176]

☆ *Fairfax Arms* YO62 4JH [Main St (B1363)]: Attractive stone-built country inn with cheerfully informal service, good appealingly presented food in bar and restaurant, big helpings, real ales such as Black Sheep and Jennings, good wine choice, beams and log fires; streamside front lawn, pleasant village with castle and miniature steam railway, ten good bedrooms (WW, John and Verna Aspinall, Michael and Anne McDonald)

GILLING WEST [NZ1805]

White Swan DL10 5JG [High St (B6274 just N of Richmond)]: 18th-c inn with well kept Black Sheep, log fire, enjoyable home-made food inc good curries in bar and dining room (bargain suppers Mon/Tues), pleasant accommodating staff, good local atmosphere, darts; tables in quirkily decorated yard, attractive village, four bedrooms (John R Ringrose, Jill and Julian Tasker)

GLAISDALE [NZ7805]

Arncliffe Arms YO21 2QL: Stone-built pub nr Esk Valley stn, traditional beamed bar, steps up to attractive contemporary bistro with good value food, three Yorkshire ales, darts and pool; children and dogs welcome, five bedrooms, open all day wknds and summer (Phil and Jane Hodson, JHBS)

GLUSBURN [SD9944]

Dog & Gun BD20 8DS [Colne Rd (A6068 W)]: Comfortably refurbished traditional pub very popular for wide choice of enjoyable bargain food, good friendly service, Timothy Taylors ales (Rob Bowran)

GOATHLAND [NZ8200]

Mallyan Spout Hotel YO22 5AN [opp church]: More hotel than pub, popular from its use for TV's Heartbeat cast, three spacious lounges, friendly traditional bar, good open fires, fine views, enjoyable bar lunches, well kept Theakstons, good malt whiskies and wines; children in eating area, usually open all day, handy for namesake waterfall; comfortable bedrooms (LYM, Roger A Bellingham)

GOMERSAL [SE2025]

Old Saw BD19 4PJ [Spen Lane]: Small pub popular for good value food, friendly service (John and Eleanor Holdsworth)

GRANGE MOOR [SE2215]

Kaye Arms WF4 4BG [A642 Huddersfield—Wakefield]: Civilised dining pub under new management, pleasant surroundings and log fire, menu strong on fish; handy for Mining Museum (Dr Rob Watson, LYM)

GRASSINGTON [SE0064]

Black Horse BD23 5AT [Garrs Lane]: Comfortably modern open-plan pub, very popular in summer, with good food from sandwiches up, welcoming service, well kept Black Sheep, Cains and Tetleys, open fire, darts in back room, small attractive restaurant; piped music, TV; children welcome, sheltered terrace, good value comfortable bedrooms, open all day (BB, David and Sally Cullen, Jeremy King, B and M Kendall)

Foresters Arms BD23 5AA [Main St]: Cheerful opened-up old coaching inn with friendly

efficient staff, bargain food, real ales inc Black Sheep, Tetleys and Wharfedale Folly, log fire, dining room off on right; pool and sports TV on left; children welcome, 14 reasonably priced bedrooms, open all day (B and M Kendall, Dave Braisted, the Didler, Edna Jones, Michael Butler, Rita and Keith Pollard)

GREAT HABTON [SE7576]

☆ *Grapes* YO17 6TU: Homely and cosy traditionally refurbished dining pub in small village, good cooking inc fresh local fish and game, hard-working young couple; nice walks (David S Allen)

GREAT OUSEBURN [SE4461]

Crown YO26 9RF [off B6265 SE of Boroughbridge]: Recently reopened, with good choice of well kept ales, decent honest food from pubby to more restaurany dishes, back dining extension; garden with terrace tables (James Martin, LYM)

GUISELEY [SE1941]

Coopers LS20 8AH [Otley Rd]: Impressive Market Town Taverns café-bar with good food from lunchtime sandwiches through pastas and pies to evening paella and steaks, eight real ales such as Copper Dragon, jazz and blues nights in upstairs function/dining room (Andy and Jill Kassube)

HALIFAX [SE1026]

Stump Cross HX3 7AY: Newly reopened as smart dining pub, airy and modern, with enjoyable reasonably priced food, efficient friendly staff, new bar, good coffee; attractive terrace (Gordon and Margaret Ormondroyd)

HAMPSTHWAITE [SE2558]

Joiners Arms HG3 2EU [about 5 miles W of Harrogate; High St]: Friendly staff and locals, Rudgate Viking and Tetleys, decent wines, popular food, big fireplace, decorative plates on lounge beams, public bar and barrel-vaulted snug, spacious and airy back dining extension with dozens of sauceboats on beams and corner chest of joiner's tools; unobtrusive piped music; tables out in front and pleasant back garden, attractive village (Mr and Mrs Maurice Thompson)

HARDROW [SD8691]

Green Dragon DL8 3LZ: Traditional Dales pub full of character, stripped stone, antique settles on flagstones, lots of bric-a-brac, low-beamed snug with log fire in old iron range, another in big main bar, real ales such as Black Sheep and Timothy Taylors Landlord, small neat restaurant; access (for a small fee) to Britain's highest single-drop waterfall; children welcome, bedrooms (LYM, Tom and Ruth Rees, David and Karen Cuckney, Jane and Alan Bush)

HAREWOOD [SE3245]

Harewood Arms LS17 9LH [A61 opp Harewood House]: Two comfortable rooms off busy hotel's spacious L-shaped lounge bar, attractive dark green décor with Harewood family memorabilia, friendly courteous staff, cheap Sam Smiths OB, decent house wines, good coffee, popular food from sandwiches up (breakfast and afternoon teas too), leisurely old-fashioned restaurant; back disabled access, bedrooms *(Stuart Paulley, P and J Shapley)*

HARROGATE [SE3055]

Blues Bar HG1 2TJ [Montpellier Parade]: The atmosphere and music you'd expect from the name, Beartown and Fullers ales, food inc egyptian specialities, little window tables overlooking The Stray, live bands nightly *(Ian Phillips)*

Coach & Horses HG1 1BJ [West Park]: Friendly bustling pub (can be almost too busy) with speciality pies and other reasonably priced food, several good Yorkshire ales; open all day *(the Didler, Ian Phillips)*

Gardeners Arms HG1 4DH [Bilton Lane (off A59 either in Bilton itself or on outskirts towards Harrogate - via Bilton Hall Dr)]: Stone-built house converted into friendly down-to-earth local, tiny bar and three small rooms, flagstone floors, panelling, old prints and little else; very cheap Sam Smiths OB, decent bar lunches (not Weds), big fire in stone fireplace, dominoes; children welcome, surrounding streamside garden with play area, lovely peaceful setting nr Nidd Gorge *(the Didler, Hunter and Christine Wright)*

☆ *Hales* HG1 2RS [Crescent Rd]: Classic Victorian décor in gas-lit18th-c local close to Pump Rooms, stuffed birds, comfortable saloon and tiny snug, Bass, Daleside and guest beers, simple good value lunchtime bar food inc Sun roast *(Eric Larkham, Ian Phillips)*

☆ *Old Bell* HG1 2SZ [Royal Parade]: Thriving Market Town Taverns pub with eight mainly Yorkshire ales from handsome bar counter, lots of continental bottled beers, impressive choice of wines by the glass, friendly helpful staff, good sandwiches with interesting choice of breads, good value hot dishes, daily papers, panelling, old sweet shop ads and breweriana, upstairs brasserie, no music or machines; no children; open all day *(Canon Michael Bourdeaux, Martin and Pamela Clark, the Didler, Dr Andy Wilkinson, Arthur S Maxted, Mrs J King, Jo Lilley, Simon Calvert, Bruce Bird, Ian Phillips)*

Tap & Spile HG1 1HS [Tower St]: Up to ten changing ales, friendly staff, good value basic lunchtime food, daily papers, old photographs, stripped stone and panelling; open all day *(Ian Phillips, the Didler, Joe Green)*

HARTHILL [SK4980]

Beehive S26 7YH [Union St]: Smart two-bar village pub opp attractive church, welcoming service, chef/landlord doing wide choice of enjoyable well priced food (not Mon lunchtime) inc proper pies and Sun lunch, good choice of real ales, wines and soft drinks, games room with pool; piped music; children welcome, picnic-sets in attractive garden, walks nearby *(Mrs Hazel Rainer)*

HARTOFT END [SE7493]

☆ *Blacksmiths* YO18 8EN [Pickering—Rosedale Abbey rd]: Good enterprising food inc fresh

fish and veg and wider evening choice in civilised and relaxing 16th-c moorland inn, well kept Jennings, good wines, friendly staff, three linked rooms with open fires, lots of original stonework, brasses, cosy nooks and corners, attractive restaurant; sports TV; children welcome, 19 comfortable bedrooms *(WW, Maurice and Gill McMahon, S P Watkin, P A Taylor, Anne and Paul Horscraft)*

HAWNBY [SE5489]

Inn at Hawnby YO62 5QS [aka Hawnby Hotel; off B1257 NW of Helmsley]: Attractive and spotless, with enjoyable generous food inc imaginative up-to-date dishes, helpful welcoming service, real ales inc Black Sheep and John Smiths, owl theme in lounge, darts in tap room; views from pleasant garden tables, lovely village in walking country, nine bedrooms, open all day Fri-Sun *(Dr and Mrs R G J Telfer, Arthur Pickering)*

HAWORTH [SE0337]

Fleece BD22 8DA [Main St]: Open bar and small lounge, some panelling and flagstones, coal fires, full Timothy Taylors range kept well, good bottled beers, popular food inc wknd breakfasts, *Railway Children* film stills, restaurant *(Andy and Jill Kassube)*

Haworth Old Hall BD22 8BP [Sun St]: Bustling open-plan 17th-c beamed and panelled pub with valley views, long bar, log fire, stripped stonework, appropriately plain furnishings, well kept Jennings ales, quick cheerful young staff, unpretentious food; piped music; plenty of tables out in front, bedrooms, good breakfast, open all day *(Greta and Christopher Wells, C A Hall, the Didler, Richard Tosswill)*

Old White Lion BD22 8DU [West Lane]: Wide choice of good value bar food, more upscale beamed restaurant, Tetleys and Theakstons, friendly attentive staff, warm comfortable lounge with plush banquettes, soft lighting; TV; children welcome, very handy for museum, comfortable bedrooms (but not much parking), open all day *(Geoffrey and Brenda Wilson, DC, Andy and Jill Kassube)*

HEBDEN BRIDGE [SD9827]

Fox & Goose HX7 6AZ [Heptonstall Rd (A646)]: Proper basic pub with quickly changing real ales inc one brewed for them, several small rooms, bar billiards, occasional live music; open all day *(Tony Hobden, Fred and Lorraine Gill)*

Moyles HX7 8AD [New Rd]: Stylish contemporary bar and restaurant, enjoyable food, real ales such as Abbeydale, Salamander and Woodfordes; 12 comfortable bedrooms *(Andy and Jill Kassube)*

☆ *White Lion* HX7 8EX [Bridge Gate]: Solid stone-built inn with welcoming comfortable bar and country-furnished bare-boards back area with coal fire, sound reasonably priced home cooking all day (just lunchtime Sun), fish specialities, well kept Timothy Taylors Landlord and a guest beer, good service; disabled access and facilities, attractive secluded riverside garden, ten comfortable bedrooms *(John Fiander,*

Derek and Sylvia Stephenson, Mrs Hazel Rainer, V Brogden, Ian and Nita Cooper)

HELMSLEY [SE6183]

☆ **Crown** YO62 5BJ [Market Pl]: Pleasant beamed pub opening into bigger unpretentious central dining bar, enjoyable food (all day Sun) from sandwiches up, real ales, good wines by the glass, efficient staff, roaring fires, separate restaurant with conservatory; piped music; dogs welcome, sheltered garden behind, nice bedrooms *(Margaret Dickinson, JJW, CMW, BB, Elizabeth Whelan)*

HIGH HOYLAND [SE2710]

Cherry Tree S75 4BE [Bank End Lane; 3 miles W of M1 junction 38]: Attractive split-level stone-built village pub, friendly prompt service, interesting local Eastwood & Sanders ales, good range of enjoyable simple food cooked to order (so may be a wait if busy) inc good Sun lunch, low beams, brasses, cigarette card collections, open fire, dining areas each end of bar and separate small restaurant; piped music; children welcome, front picnic-sets under cocktail parasols with lovely views over Cannon Hall Country Park *(Bob Richardson)*

HIPPERHOLME [SE1224]

☆ **Cock o' the North** HX3 8EF [Southedge Works, Brighouse Rd (A644)]: Industrial estate portacabin transformed into comfortable and thoroughly pubby tap for adjacent Halifax Steam brewery, half a dozen or more of their own interesting ales, a guest beer, fruit cordials, Burts crisps, discreet corner TV; seats outside, open all day wknds, cl wkdy lunchtimes *(Pat and Tony Martin)*

Travellers HX3 8HN [Tanhouse Hill, off A58]: Stone-built roadside pub now owned by Ossett, eight reasonably priced ales, good range of bottled beers; no food exc Weds curry night *(Andy and Jill Kassube)*

HOLMFIRTH [SD1605]

Fox House HD9 2TR [Penistone Rd (B6106 S)]: Wide choice of enjoyable well priced food, several big old rooms, friendly staff *(Trevor and Sylvia Millum)*

Sycamore HD9 7SH [New Mill Rd]: Friendly local with good value simple home-made food and local real ales, folk and blues nights *(Andy and Jill Kassube)*

HORBURY [SE2918]

Boons WF4 6LP [Queen St]: Lively, chatty and comfortably unpretentious flagstoned local, Clarks, John Smiths, Timothy Taylors Landlord and three or four quickly changing guest beers, bare walls, Rugby League memorabilia, back tap room with pool; TV, no children; courtyard tables *(Michael Butler)*

Bulls Head WF4 5AR [Southfield Lane]: Large well divided pub deservedly popular for food, smart attentive staff, Cains and Greene King, lots of wines by the glass, panelling and wood floors, relaxing linked rooms inc library, snug and restaurant; front picnic-sets *(Mr and Mrs Ian King, Michael Butler)*

HORNBY [NZ3605]

Grange Arms DL6 2JQ: Neat country local run by friendly family, son cooks enjoyable food, well kept real ale, dining area one side *(Tim and Ann Newell)*

HORSFORTH [SE2438]

Town Street Tavern LS18 4RJ [Town St]: A Market Town Taverns pub with eight well kept ales inc Black Sheep, Copper Dragon, Leeds Pale and Timothy Taylors Best, lots of continental bottled beers, good bar food and (Tues-Sat) upstairs evening bistro; small terrace, open all day *(Andy and Jill Kassube)*

HORTON IN RIBBLESDALE [SD8072]

Crown BD24 0HF [B6479 N of Settle]: Pretty pub by river, well placed for walkers (Pennine Way goes through car park, short walk from Settle—Carlisle line station), dark woodwork and lots of brass in low-ceilinged locals' bar and larger lounge, good fire in both, cheap and cheerful home cooking, well kept Black Sheep, nice wines by the glass, friendly helpful staff, restaurant, no music or machines; big attractive garden behind, good value bedrooms *(MDN, David and Karen Cuckney)*

HOTHAM [SE8934]

Hotham Arms YO43 4UD [Main St; 2.9 miles from M62 junction 38]: Friendly and busy, with proper landlord, good-natured attentive service, enjoyable food, real ales such as Black Sheep, comfortable banquettes, back dining area *(Matthew James)*

HUBBERHOLME [SD9278]

☆ **George** BD23 5JE: Beautifully placed ancient Dales inn with River Wharfe fishing rights, heavy beams, flagstones and stripped stone, quick simple food, well kept Black Sheep and Copper Dragon, good log fire, perpetual candle on bar; may charge for water, no dogs, outside lavatories; children allowed in dining area, terrace, seven bedrooms, cl Mon *(LYM, Dr and Mrs Jackson, Michael and Maggie Betton, Michael Tack, Robin M Corlett, Richard, Matt Waite, Richard Tosswill, Ben and Helen Ingram, Ann and Tony Bennett-Hughes, Terry Mizen)*

HUDDERSFIELD [SE1416]

Albert HD1 2QF [Victoria Lane]: Well preserved high Victorian pub with new licensees, good choice of changing ales, handsome mahogany, marble, mirrors, etched glass and chandeliers, traditional red leather wall seats, steps up to compact lounge and dining room; bedrooms *(the Didler, Greta and Christopher Wells)*

Cherry Tree HD1 1BA [John William St]: Open-plan split-level Wetherspoons with good choice of mainly yorkshire beers, farm cider, decent food in back dining room, good views, more seating downstairs *(the Didler)*

Grove HD1 4BP [Spring Grove St]: Lots of exotic bottled beers, Timothy Taylors Landlord and fine range of changing guest ales, huge vodka choice, snacks from latvian crisps to dried anchovies; back terrace, open all day (own microbrewery planned) *(John R Ringrose, the Didler)*

☆ **Head of Steam** HD1 1JF [Station, St Georges Sq]: Railway memorabilia, model trains, cars, buses and planes for sale, friendly staff, long bar with up to eight changing ales, lots of bottled beers, farm ciders and perry, fruit wines, black leather easy chairs and sofas, hot coal fire, good value enjoyable back buffet, some live jazz and blues nights; unobtrusive piped music, can be very busy; open all day (Mrs Jane Kingsbury, C J Fletcher, Andrew York, David Hoult, the Didler, Peter Smith, Judith Brown, Pat and Tony Martin)

Rat & Ratchet HD1 3EB [Chapel Hill]: Flagstoned pub with several well kept Ossett ales and lots of guest beers, cheap lunchtime food (not Sun-Tues), friendly staff, more comfortable seating up steps, brewery memorabilia and music posters; open all day (the Didler)

Royal & Ancient HD5 0RE [Colne Bridge; B6118 just off A62 NE]: Long roadside pub, well kept Marstons and related ales with a guest such as Titanic, log fires, wide food choice inc popular Sun lunch, reasonable prices, attractive golfing theme bar with extended dining area, backwards clock; tables out at front, nr Huddersfield Broad Canal (Gordon and Margaret Ormondroyd, Jeremy King)

Shoulder of Mutton HD1 3TN [Neale Rd, Lockwood (off A616/B6108)]: Walnut-panelled four-room pub with well kept Timothy Taylors Landlord and guest ales, soft lighting; good juke box, big-screen TV (the Didler)

Star HD1 3PJ [Albert St, Lockwood]: Unpretentious local with seven changing ales particularly well kept by enthusiastic landlady, continental beers, farm cider, well organised beer festivals, bric-a-brac and customers' paintings; cl Mon, and lunchtime Tues-Thurs, open all day wknds (Andy and Jill Kassube, the Didler, Gordon and Margaret Ormondroyd)

Station Tavern HD1 1JF [St Georges Sq]: Handsome station building housing friendly and well run basic pub, eight regularly changing ales, bargain cobs, live folk and blues, monthly piano singalongs; open all day (the Didler)

White Cross HD2 1XD [Bradley Rd, Colne Bridge (A62/A6107)]: Six particularly well kept changing ales and nicely cooked bargain food in small simple two-room pub, popular Feb beer festival; open all day (the Didler)

HULL [TA0928]

☆ **Minerva** HU1 1XE [Pier St/Nelson St]: Shut until Easter 2009 for major refurbishment, has been good pub at heart of restored waterfront and marina, with seats in front to watch passing boats, several rambling rooms, tiny snug and back room, coal fires, has had good range of real ales, darts; piped music, TV, games machine; children in restaurant, open all day; news please (LYM)

Pave HU5 3QA [Princes Avenue, nr Thoresby St]: Comfortable minimalist café-bar, good

value interesting food from all-day breakfast to tapas, Caledonian Deuchars IPA, belgian beers, decent wines, friendly staff, sofas and dining tables, open stove, pleasant décor; live music, poetry (Fred and Lorraine Gill)

HUTTON-LE-HOLE [SE7089]

Crown YO62 6UA [The Green]: Spotless pub overlooking pretty village green with wandering sheep in classic coach-trip country, good sandwiches and huge helpings of no-fuss food (all day Sun), well kept Black Sheep, efficient service, opened-up bar with varnished woodwork and whisky-water jugs, dining area; children and dogs welcome, nr Folk Museum and handy for Farndale walks (Phil and Jane Hodson, Simon Collett-Jones)

ILKLEY [SE1147]

Bar t'at LS29 9DZ [Cunliffe Rd]: Market Towns Tavern pub with eight mainly Yorkshire ales, good wine choice, lively lunchtime bistro atmosphere with good sandwiches and bargain hot dishes, more elaborate evening food (candlelit cellar dining area may open then), quick polite service, daily papers, front conservatory; dogs welcome, heated back terrace, open all day (Pat and Tony Martin, WW)

INGBIRCHWORTH [SE2106]

Fountain S36 7GJ [off A629 Shepley—Penistone; Wellthorne Lane]: Relaxed and enjoyable beamed dining pub, well kept ales such as Black Sheep, good value coffee, log fires, roomy red plush lounge, cosy front bar and family room; well reproduced piped music; garden tables overlooking reservoir with pretty walks, good bedrooms, hearty breakfast (Michael Butler, BB, Roger A Bellingham)

INGLETON [SD6973]

Three Horseshoes LA6 3EH [Main St]: Nicely refurbished by new landlord, home-made local food inc good sandwiches, well kept Thwaites, friendly staff; children and dogs welcome, terrace tables (Alison Bembridge)

KEIGHLEY [SE0641]

Boltmakers Arms BD21 5HX [East Parade]: Friendly split-level open-plan local with well kept Timothy Taylors ales and guests, good value basic food all day, coal fire, nice brewing pictures; sports TV; short walk from Worth Valley Railway, open all day (the Didler)

Brown Cow BD21 2LQ [Cross Leeds St]: Popular and friendly extensively refurbished local with particularly well kept Timothy Taylors ales and guest beers; open all day wknds (the Didler)

Globe BD21 4QR [Parkwood St]: Comfortable friendly local by Worth Valley steam railway track, wkdy lunches, Timothy Taylors and a guest, farm cider, coal fire; tables out behind, open all day (the Didler)

KETTLEWELL [SD9672]

☆ **Blue Bell** BD23 5QX [Middle Lane]: Roomy knocked-through 17th-c pub thriving since takeover by Copper Dragon, their ales kept well, good food from sandwiches to lots of fresh fish, friendly obliging service, good wine choice, snug simple furnishings, log fire, low beams and flagstones, old country photographs, attractive restaurant, daily papers; pool room; children welcome, picnic-sets out on cobbles facing Wharfe bridge, more on good-sized back terrace, decent bedrooms mainly in annexe, good breakfast *(Comus and Sarah Elliott, Stephen Corfield, DA, Bruce Bird, LYM, B and M Kendall, Dr A McCormick)*

Kings Head BD23 5RD: Hearty flavourful food in old pub tucked away near church, flagstoned main bar with log fire in big inglenook, tartan-carpeted snug around corner, discreet dining room, interesting ales inc local Litton; four comfortable bedrooms *(David and Sue Smith, Brian and Janet Ainscough, BB, David and Sally Cullen)*

☆ *Racehorses* BD23 5QZ [B6160 N of Skipton]: Comfortable, civilised and friendly, with generous good value food from substantial lunchtime rolls and baguettes to local game, popular early evening bargains Sun-Thurs, well kept Tetleys and Timothy Taylors, good choice of wines by the glass, good log fire; children welcome (dogs too in front bar), attractive terrace, well placed for Wharfedale walks, good bedrooms, open all day *(BB, Brian and Janet Ainscough, Dr D and Mrs B Woods, B and M Kendall, Stephen Corfield)*

KILNSEY [SD9767]

☆ *Tennants Arms* BD23 5PS: Good Wharfedale walking area, views of spectacular overhanging crag from restaurant, prompt friendly service, good range of good food, well kept ales inc Black Sheep, log fire, several comfortable rooms, interesting decorations; piped music; children welcome, good value bedrooms *(B and M Kendall)*

KIRKBY MALHAM [SD8960]

Victoria BD23 4BS: Understated Victorian décor in small simple rooms, enjoyable pub food, well kept ales inc Timothy Taylors and Tetleys, good wine choice, nice fire, separate restaurant (not always in use); children welcome, lovely village with interesting church, attractive good value bedrooms *(Dr Kevan Tucker)*

KIRKBY OVERBLOW [SE3249]

Shoulder of Mutton HG3 1HD [Main St]: Three linked areas with rugs on bare boards, two fires, well kept Black Sheep, Tetleys, Timothy Taylors and a guest, several wines by the glass, good fresh well priced pub food, friendly attentive service, upstairs restaurant; garden behind *(Les and Sandra Brown)*

Star & Garter HG3 1HD [off A61 S of Harrogate]: Relaxing old-fashioned pub with cheerful helpful licensees, very popular lunchtime with older people for generous good value food inc substantial light dishes, decent wines, well kept Black Sheep and Fullers, huge log fires, separate dining room; open all day, nice village setting *(H Bramwell)*

KNARESBOROUGH [SE3556]

☆ *Blind Jacks* HG5 8AL [Market Pl]: Friendly individualistic multi-floor tavern in 18th-c building, simple attractive furnishings, brewery posters etc, particularly well kept Black Sheep, Timothy Taylors (inc their great Dark Mild) and other changing ales, farm cider and foreign bottled beers, staff helpful over choice, bubbly atmosphere downstairs, quieter up; well behaved children allowed away from bar, open all day wknds, cl Mon till 5.30; Beer Ritz two doors away sells all sorts of rare bottled beers *(Rona Murdoch, the Didler, John R Ringrose, Paul Smurthwaite, LYM, Joe Green)*

Old Royal Oak HG5 8AL [Market Pl]: Traditional town tavern with bargain hearty bar lunches, prompt friendly service; six recently done bedrooms *(D W Stokes)*

LANGTHWAITE [NZ0002]

☆ *Red Lion* DL11 6RE [just off Reeth—Brough Arkengarthdale rd]: A favourite proper pub dating from 17th c, homely and relaxing, in beguiling Dales village with ancient bridge; cheap nourishing lunchtime sandwiches, pasties and sausage rolls, well kept Black Sheep ales, Thatcher's farm cider, country wines, tea and coffee, character landlady; well behaved children allowed lunchtime in low-ceilinged side snug; the ladies' is a genuine bathroom; seats outside, good walks, inc organised circular ones from the pub - maps and guides for sale *(David and Jean Hall, Ann and Tony Bennett-Hughes, LYM, Arthur Pickering, Joan York, David Thornton, David and Karen Cuckney)*

LAUGHTON EN LE MORTHEN [SK5189]

Travellers Rest S25 1YA [Brookhouse, towards Thurcroft]: Pleasant 1970s-style stone-built pub with lounge/dining room and public bar, three Greene King ales, enjoyable fresh food (Fri/Sat evening and Sun lunch), flowers on tables; piped music; children welcome, streamside picnic-sets outside, pleasant village, open all day Sun *(JJW, CMW)*

LEAVENING [SE7863]

Jolly Farmers YO17 9SA [Main St]: Bustling welcoming village local, good choice of changing ales, good value pubby food with lots of fresh veg, friendly licensees, front bar with eating area behind, separate dining room *(Tim and Liz Sherbourne, Christopher Turner)*

LEEDS [SE3033]

Duck & Drake LS2 7DR [Kirkgate, between indoor market and Parish Church]: Basic two-room proper pub with a dozen or more interesting reasonably priced real ales from central servery, farm cider, pleasant hard-working staff, good coal fires, bare boards, beer posters and mirrors, low-priced wkdy lunchtime bar snacks, games room with Yorkshire doubles dartboard as well as pool etc; juke box, big-screen TV, games machines; open all day *(Joe Green, Pete Baker, the Didler)*

Fox & Grapes LS15 4NJ [York Rd]: Pleasant Vintage Inn with sensibly priced enjoyable food, ales such as Black Sheep and Timothy Taylors *(Andy and Jill Kassube)*

Palace LS2 7DJ [Kirkgate]: Pleasantly uncityfied, with stripped boards and polished panelling, unusual lighting from electric candelabra to mock street lamps, lots of old prints, friendly helpful staff, good value lunchtime food till 7 from sandwiches up inc popular Sun roasts in dining area, fine changing choice of ales, may be bargain wine offers; games end with pool, TV, good piped music; tables out in front and in small heated back courtyard, open all day *(Joe Green, David Hoult, the Didler)*

Scarbrough LS1 5DY [Bishopgate St, opp stn]: Ornate art nouveau tiled curved façade, bare boards, barrel tables, lots of wood and stone, shelves of Victoriana, showy fireplace, many well kept changing ales, farm cider, wide range of lunchtime sandwiches and bargain basic hot dishes, friendly young staff, music-hall posters; busy lunchtime and early evening, machines, big-screen sports TV; open all day *(Bruce Bird, the Didler, Andy and Jill Kassube)*

☆ *Victoria* LS1 3DL [Gt George St]: Opulent early Victorian pub with grand cut and etched mirrors, impressive globe lamps extending from majestic bar, carved beams, leather-seat booths with working snob-screens, smaller rooms off, changing ales such as Cottage, Leeds, Timothy Taylors and Tetleys, friendly efficient service by smart bar staff, reasonably priced food 12-6 from sandwiches and light dishes up in luncheon room with end serving hatch; open all day *(Joe Green, the Didler, Jeremy King)*

☆ *Whitelocks* LS1 6HB [Turks Head Yard, off Briggate]: Classic Victorian pub nicely restored 2007 by new owners, long narrow old-fashioned bar, tiled counter, grand mirrors, mahogany and glass screens, heavy copper-topped tables and green leather, with Caledonian Deuchars IPA, John Smiths, Theakstons Best and Old Peculier and fine range of guest beers, all-day bar food (not Sun evening), hard-working young staff; children in restaurant and top bar, tables out in narrow courtyard, open all day *(David Carr, Joe Green, the Didler, LYM, Janet and Peter Race, Neil Whitehead, Victoria Anderson)*

LEVISHAM [SE8390]

☆ *Horseshoe* YO18 7NL [off A169 N of Pickering]: Attractive inn recently taken over by good team from Fox & Rabbit at Lockton, old beams, simple attractive furnishings on broad boards, handsome log fire, enjoyable country food, real ale such as Black Sheep; picnic-sets on pretty green, delightful unspoilt village a steep walk up from station, good walks, eight nicely refurbished bedrooms, cl Sun evening, Tues *(Helen Royds, LYM)*

LEYBURN [SE1190]

Black Swan DL8 5AS [Market Pl]: Attractive creeper-covered old hotel with chatty locals in cheerful open-plan bar, entertaining landlord, fast efficient service, decent range of food inc popular Sun carvery, well kept ales such as Black Sheep, good wines by the glass; no credit cards; children and dogs welcome, good disabled access, tables on cobbled terrace, nine bedrooms, open all day *(David and Karen Cuckney, B and M Kendall, Michael Tack, A and B D Craig, the Didler)*

LOCKTON [SE8488]

☆ *Fox & Rabbit* YO18 7NQ [A169 N of Pickering]: Smart and neatly kept by young brothers, one cooks good generous food (sandwiches too), quick cheerful service, well kept ales inc Black Sheep, plush banquettes, fresh flowers, brasses, big log fire, busy locals' bar with pool, good views from comfortable restaurant; tables outside and in sun lounge, nice spot on moors edge *(Michael Dandy, Sara Fulton, Roger Baker, Dave Braisted, Helen Royds, LYM)*

LONG PRESTON [SD8358]

Boars Head BD23 4ND [Main St]: Welcoming local atmosphere, good value home-made food inc OAP wkdy lunches, Sun carvery, well kept Caledonian and Copper Dragon, beams and log fire in unpretentious recently refurbished bar, live music Sat; four comfortable bedrooms *(Karen Eliot)*

LOW BRADFIELD [SK2691]

☆ *Plough* S6 6HW [New Rd]: Recently attractively refurbished under new management, good value home-made food (not Mon/Tues evenings), well kept local Bradfield and guest beers, cheery efficient service, inglenook log fire, restaurant; children welcome, picnic-sets in attractive garden, lovely scenery *(JJW, CMW, Peter F Marshall)*

LOW ROW [SD9898]

☆ *Punch Bowl* DL11 6PF [B6270 Reeth—Muker]: Under same ownership as Charles Bathurst at Langthwaite (see main entries), fresh, light and almost scandinavian in style, with friendly staff, good interesting food inc superb steak, a dozen good wines by the glass, well kept Black Sheep, log fire, leather armchairs, sturdy tables and chairs, minimal décor; great Swaledale views from terrace, 11 comfortable bedrooms, great breakfast, open all day in summer *(Bruce and Sharon Eden, Richard, Professors Alan and Ann Clarke)*

MALHAM [SD9062]

Lister Arms BD23 4DB [off A65 NW of Skipton]: Creeper-covered stone-built inn now tied to Thwaites, their ales kept well, lots of bottled imports, good value food inc lunchtime sandwiches, roaring fire, lively bustle (pool and games machines popular with young locals); children and dogs welcome, seats out overlooking small green, more in back garden, nice spot by river, good walking country, comfortable modern bedrooms, good breakfast *(David Field, Lynda and Trevor Smith, Arthur Pickering)*

MARKET WEIGHTON [SE8741]

Griffin YO43 3AW [Market Pl]: Well kept Thwaites and range of wines, good value pubby food, friendly efficient staff, attractive décor; tables outside inc covered decking (David Simmonds)

MARSDEN [SE0411]

☆ *Riverhead* HD7 6BR [Peel St, next to Co-op; just off A62 Huddersfield—Oldham]: Spruced up pub with Ossett ales, perhaps also beers from pub's own microbrewery, good value food from sandwiches to interesting dishes in airy upstairs beamed dining room with stripped tables and open kitchen; unobtrusive piped music; dogs welcome, wheelchair access, streamside tables, open all day (the Didler, Pat and Tony Martin, John Fiander)

MASHAM [SE2280]

Kings Head HG4 4EF [Market Pl]: Handsome stone inn, two much-modernised linked rooms with imposing fireplace and clock, well kept Theakstons ales and up to 20 wines by the glass, enjoyable bar food (all day wknds), restaurant; piped music, games machine, TV; children in eating areas, good bedrooms in back courtyard area (some for disabled), open all day (Dr and Mrs Jackson, Janet and Peter Race, LYM, Angus Lyon, Pat and Tony Martin)

☆ *White Bear* HG4 4EN [Wellgarth, Crosshills; signed off A6108 opp turn into town]: Cheerful comfortably refurbished stone-built beamed pub, small public bar with well kept local ales and darts, comfortable larger lounge with coal fire, good fairly priced food choice (not Sun evening) from sandwiches up, decent wines by the glass, neat efficient staff; piped radio; children and dogs welcome, terrace tables, 14 bedrooms, open all day (BB, the Didler, Stuart Paulley, WW, Janet and Peter Race)

MENSTON [SE1744]

Fox LS29 6EB [A65/A6038]: Contemporary M&B dining pub in former coaching inn, enjoyable fairly priced food, efficient friendly staff, Black Sheep, Timothy Taylors Landlord and a guest such as Adnams, big fireplace, flagstones and polished boards in one part; two terraces looking beyond car park to cricket field (Gordon and Margaret Ormondroyd)

MIDDLEHAM [SE1287]

Black Swan DL8 4NP [Market Pl]: Sold to Enterprise who have put in a manager; heavy-beamed bar with high-backed settles built-in by big stone fireplace, John Smiths, Theakstons Best, guest such as Yorkshire Dales; piped music, TV; children welcome, dogs have been allowed in bar, tables on cobbles outside and in back garden, good walking country, bedrooms, open all day (LYM)

MILLINGTON [SE8351]

Gait YO42 1TX [aka Gate]: Friendly 16th-c beamed pub respelled but still unspoilt, good straightforward food, happy staff, well kept ales, nice mix of old and newer furnishings, big inglenook fire; children welcome, garden picnic-sets, appealing village in good Wolds walking country,

cl Mon-Thurs lunchtimes, open all day Sun (LYM, Pat and Graham Williamson)

MIRFIELD [SE2017]

Hare & Hounds WF14 8EE [Liley Lane (B6118 2m S)]: Popular smartly refurbished Vintage Inn dining pub, Greene King Old Speckled Hen and John Smiths, decent wines by the glass, cheerful helpful staff; tables outside with good Pennine views (Michael Butler, Gordon and Margaret Ormondroyd)

Navigation WF14 8NL [Station Rd]: By Calder & Hebble Navigation canal, interesting food using local ingredients in back restaurant, good Sun lunch and early evening bargains, well kept Theakstons (Andy and Jill Kassube)

MUKER [SD9097]

☆ *Farmers Arms* DL11 6QG [B6270 W of Reeth]: Plain walkers' pub in beautiful valley village, warm fire, friendly staff and locals, Black Sheep and Theakstons, wines, teas and coffees, enjoyable straightforward good value food from sandwiches to generous pies, casseroles and so forth, simple modern pine furniture, flagstones and panelling, darts and dominoes; children welcome, hill views from terrace tables, self-catering flat (the Didler, Arthur Pickering, LYM, Dr D Scott, David and Karen Cuckney, Bruce and Sharon Eden, David and Jean Hall)

MYTHOLMROYD [SE0126]

☆ *Dusty Miller* HX7 5LH [Burnley Rd]: Stylishly refurbished, with good enterprising generous food from open kitchen inc well priced lunchtime bar snacks and lunch/early evening deals, friendly helpful staff, contemporary comfort and décor; five comfortable bedrooms (John and Eleanor Holdsworth, Andy and Jill Kassube, Ian and Nita Cooper)

Shoulder of Mutton HX7 5DZ [New Rd, just across river bridge (B6138)]: Comfortable friendly local, emphasis on generous good value home cooking (not Tues) inc carvery, fish, good range of puddings, OAP lunches and children's helpings, family dining areas and cosy child- and food-free areas, well kept Black Sheep Best, Timothy Taylors and guests, toby jugs and other china; streamside terrace (Pete Baker, Bruce Bird)

NEWLAY [SE2346]

Abbey LS13 1EQ [Bridge 221, Leeds & Liverpool Canal]: Up to eight well kept ales inc locals such as Naylors, good value enjoyable food from sandwiches to steaks (Andy and Jill Kassube)

NEWTON-ON-RAWCLIFFE [SE8190]

Mucky Duck YO18 8QA: Friendly country local overlooking village green and duckpond, enjoyable inexpensive traditional food, well kept beer with a monthly guest, attentive service, cosy bar with railway memorabilia, TV and music in another room; tables outside, bedrooms, back field for caravans (Patricia Walker)

NORTH GRIMSTON [SE8467]

Middleton Arms YO17 8AX: Comfortable, with good value simple food from sandwiches up, well kept ales, homely dining area; garden tables, nice Wolds-edge spot *(WW)*

NORTHALLERTON [SE3693]

Golden Lion DL7 8PP [High St]: Large Georgian ex-coaching inn, generous food in two big bars and attractive dining room, well kept Yorkshire ales, good coffee; 25 bedrooms *(Margaret Dickinson)*

Tithe Bar DL6 1DP [Friarage St]: Market Town Tavern with half a dozen quickly changing ales such as Durham and Timothy Taylors, plenty of continental beers, friendly staff, tasty food lunchtime and early evening, two traditional rooms with tables and chairs, settle and armchairs, upstairs evening brasserie; open all day *(Mr and Mrs Maurice Thompson)*

NORWOOD GREEN [SE1326]

☆ *Old White Beare* HX3 8QG [signed off A641 in Wyke, or off A58 Halifax—Leeds just W of Wyke; Village St]: Large 17th-c building well renovated and extended, beams and panelling, friendly attentive staff, well kept Timothy Taylors, good value enjoyable food esp seafood, friendly helpful staff, small character snug, imposing flagstoned barn restaurant with gallery; front terrace, back garden with barbecue, Calderdale Way and Brontë Way pass the door *(Gordon and Margaret Ormondroyd, Clive Flynn)*

NOSTERFIELD [SE2780]

☆ *Freemasons Arms* DL8 2QP [B6267]: Warm-hearted pub with lots to look at, flagstones, booths, pews and settles, low black beams hung with bric-a-brac, big Queen Victoria prints, many old enamel advertisements, hot coal fires, popular generous food, well kept Black Sheep and Theakstons, several wines by the glass, dominoes; piped music; well behaved children and dogs welcome, picnic-sets out in front with pretty flower tubs and baskets, self-catering flat, open all day Sun, cl Mon *(Pete Baker, LYM, Michael Butler)*

OAKWORTH [SE0138]

☆ *Grouse* BD22 0RX [Harehills, Oldfield; 2 miles towards Colne]: Comfortable old Timothy Taylors pub well altered and extended, their ales kept well, good value wines, wide range of enjoyable hearty and interesting food all day, good friendly staff, lots of bric-a-brac, gleaming copper and china, prints, cartoons and caricatures, charming evening restaurant; undisturbed hamlet in fine moorland surroundings, Pennine views, open all day *(Brian and Ruth Young, Andy and Jill Kassube)*

OLDSTEAD [SE5380]

☆ *Black Swan* YO61 4BL [Main St]: Doing well under current friendly owners (local farmers), very good traditional food from home-baked bread up in comfortable and attractive back dining areas (good disabled access here) with antique furnishings, simpler beamed and flagstoned bar with pretty valley views from two big bay windows, log fire, Black Sheep and Copper Dragon; children welcome, picnic-sets outside, newly refurbished

bedroom extension, beautiful surroundings *(WW, John and Eleanor Holdsworth, Hansjoerg Landherr, Walter and Susan Rinaldi-Butcher, BB)*

OSMOTHERLEY [SE4597]

☆ *Three Tuns* DL6 3BN [South End, off A19 N of Thirsk]: Small stylish restaurant-with-rooms rather than pub, good individual upmarket food (they warn you it will take a while) in a bistro atmosphere and setting, light and open, mixing local sandstone with pale oak panelling and furniture, good service; children welcome, charming mediterranean-style terrace, good nearby walks, comfortable bedrooms, open all day *(LYM, Hunter and Christine Wright, Kevin Jeavons, Alison Turner)*

OSSETT [SE2719]

☆ *Brewers Pride* WF5 8ND [Low Mill Rd/Healey Lane (long cul-de-sac by railway sidings, off B6128)]: Friendly basic local with Rooster, Timothy Taylors and its own Ossett beers (now brewed nearby - the pub may still brew occasional ales), enjoyable lunchtime food (not Sun), cosy front room and bar both with open fires, flagstones, brewery memorabilia, small games room; big back garden with local entertainment summer wknds, nr Calder & Hebble Canal, open all day wknds *(the Didler)*

Tap WF5 8JS [The Green]: Former Masons Arms, renamed with retro refurbishment by Ossett, their ales and guest beers, friendly service, several wines by the glass *(Michael Butler)*

OULTON [SE3628]

New Masons Arms LS26 8JR [Aberford Rd]: Popular welcoming pub with decent good value pubby food; bedrooms *(Marcus Mann)*

Three Horseshoes LS26 8JU [Leeds Rd]: Spacious old open-plan dining pub with reasonably priced decent food, warm friendly atmosphere, real ales, brass plates and memorabilia; children welcome *(Marcus Mann)*

OUTLANE [SE0717]

Dog & Partridge HX4 9LB [Forest Hill Rd]: Small comfortable two-room country local with well kept Black Sheep and Timothy Taylors, may do simple food with notice; cl wkdy lunchtimes *(Gordon and Margaret Ormondroyd)*

OVERTON [SE2516]

Black Swan WF4 4RF [off A642 Wakefield—Huddersfield; Green Lane]: Traditional local, two knocked-together low-beamed rooms full of brasses and bric-a-brac, well kept John Smiths, popular Thurs quiz night *(Michael Butler)*

OXENHOPE [SE0434]

☆ *Dog & Gun* BD22 9SN [Long Causeway; off B6141 towards Denholme]: Beautifully placed roomy moorland pub, smartly extended and comfortable, with good varied generous food from sandwiches to lots of fish and Sun roasts (worth booking then), thriving atmosphere, cheerful landlord and staff, full Timothy Taylors beer range kept well, beamery, copper, brasses, plates and jugs, big log fire each end, padded settles and stools, wonderful views; five bedrooms in adjoining hotel *(Gordon and Margaret Ormondroyd)*

POOL [SE2445]

White Hart LS21 1LH [just off A658 S of Harrogate, A659 E of Otley]: M&B dining pub with enjoyable italian-leaning food all day, friendly quick service, good choice of wines by the glass, well kept Greene King and Timothy Taylors, stylishly simple bistro eating areas, armchairs and sofas on bar's flagstones and bare boards; tables outside *(Michael Butler, Pat and Graham Williamson, LYM)*

RAMSGILL [SE1171]

☆ *Yorke Arms* HG3 5RL [Nidderdale]: Upmarket small hotel (not a pub), small smart bar with some heavy Jacobean furniture and log fires, Black Sheep Special, a fine wine list, good choice of spirits and fresh juices, good restaurant; piped music, no under-12s even in restaurant; comfortable bedrooms, good quiet moorland and reservoir walks *(Hunter and Christine Wright, LYM)*

RAVENSWORTH [NZ1407]

Bay Horse DL11 7ET [off A66]: Small attractive stone-built split-level beamed local, three or four real ales, simple good value food; children welcome, picnic-table sets facing village green, castle ruin below *(Guy Vowles)*

REDMIRE [SE0491]

Bolton Arms DL8 4EA: Nicely refurbished village inn with good food cooked by landlady, well kept Black Sheep, Lees and John Smiths, convivial landlord, comfortable carpeted bar, attractive dining room, darts, exemplary lavatories; garden with quoits, handy for Wensleydale Railway and Bolton Castle, three new courtyard bedrooms *(Lynda and Trevor Smith, Mr and Mrs Ian King, Michael Tack, Mr and Mrs Maurice Thompson)*

RIBBLEHEAD [SD7678]

Station Inn LA6 3AS [B6255 Ingleton—Hawes]: Great spot up on the moors by Ribblehead Viaduct (Settle—Carlisle trains), friendly newish licensees doing varied food from good ciabattas up, log fire, real ales, low-priced coffee and wine, simple public bar with darts and pool, dining room with viaduct mural (the bar has relevant photographs, some you can buy); piped music, TV; children welcome, picnic-sets outside, five bedrooms (some sharing bath), bunkhouse, open all day *(Ann and Tony Bennett-Hughes, BB)*

RICHMOND [NZ1700]

Castle Tavern DL10 4HU [Market Pl]: Small refurbished pub with divided seating in part-panelled bar, lots of pictures and bric-a-brac, Flowers and Tetleys, cheap food (not Sun), dining room with panelling and stripped stone; piped music; bedrooms *(Michael and Alison Sandy, Nick Holding)*

Kings Head DL10 4HS [Market Pl]: Friendly Best Western hotel, good value food and wine in comfortable bar and bistro, log fire;

30 bedrooms *(Bruce and Sharon Eden)*

RIPON [SE3171]

☆ *One-Eyed Rat* HG4 1LQ [Allhallowgate]: Friendly bare-boards pub with numerous real ales inc Black Sheep and Everards, farm cider, lots of bottled beers and country wines, long narrow bar with fire, fresh flowers, cigarette cards, framed beer mats, bank notes and old pictures, no food but may be free black pudding, pool; pleasant outside area, open all day Sat, cl wkdy lunchtimes *(Joe Green, Michael Butler)*

RISHWORTH [SE0318]

Malthouse HX6 4QB [Oldham Rd (A672 S of Ripponden)]: Former Royal, reworked as smart modern dining pub, enjoyable food, well kept Shepherd Neame Spitfire and a guest beer, log fires; five new bedrooms, open all day *(Gordon and Margaret Ormondroyd)*

ROBIN HOOD'S BAY [NZ9504]

Bay Hotel YO22 4SJ [The Dock, Bay Town]: Friendly old village inn, fine sea views from cosy picture-window upstairs bar (downstairs open too if busy), three real ales, log fires, good value home-made food in bar and separate dining area; tables outside, cosy bedrooms, open all day *(Ian and Sue Wells, Amanda Russell, P Dawn, Arthur Pickering)*

ROTHERHAM [SK4292]

Blue Coat S60 2DJ [The Crofts]: Civilised Wetherspoons with friendly staff, good well kept ales, upstairs seating; open all day *(Mrs Hazel Rainer)*

SANCTON [SE9039]

Star YO43 4QP [King St (A1034 S of Mkt Weighton)]: Neatly modernised dining pub, young chef/landlord doing good blackboard food listing sources, evening booking advised, good wines by the glass, Black Sheep and Fullers, good friendly service, small restaurant *(Pat and Graham Williamson, E M Mason)*

SANDHUTTON [SE3882]

☆ *Kings Arms* YO7 4RW [A167]: Charmingly refurbished village-edge pub, good food at reasonable prices from current chef-landlord, local real ales, friendly attentive service, small convivial dining room; open all day *(Mr and Mrs J Culf, Dr J Garside, Dennis and Amanda Parkyn)*

SCARBOROUGH [TA0388]

Lord Rosebery YO11 1JW [Westborough]: Wetherspoons in former local Liberal HQ (and Co-op), galleried upper bar, good beer range, enjoyable quickly served food inc Sun roast, obliging staff, local prints; busy and lively evenings; disabled facilities, open all day *(MDN, Mrs Hazel Rainer, David Carr)*

Scarborough Arms YO11 1HU [North Terr]: Comfortably unpretentious mock-Tudor pub, good value filling meals (not Sun evening), several real ales, helpful landlady, friendly staff, warm open range, weaponry displays, darts, pool; children welcome, good outside seating, open all day *(Gordon and Margaret Ormondroyd, David Carr)*

Valley YO11 2LX [Valley Rd]: L-shaped bar with banquettes, friendly efficient service, good value simple food using local produce inc popular speciality nights (authentic sri lankan curries Weds), seven farm ciders, up to eight real ales such as Copper Dragon and Roosters, beer festivals *(Dave and Shirley Shaw)*

SCAWTON [SE5483]

☆ *Hare* YO7 2HG [off A170 Thirsk—Helmsley]: Attractive dining pub with carefully cooked well presented food, hospitable landlord, good wines by the glass, well kept Black Sheep, stripped pine tables, heavy beams and some flagstones, old-fashioned range and woodburner, William Morris wallpaper, appealing prints and old books; children welcome, wrought-iron garden furniture, open all day summer, cl Mon *(LYM, Peter and Anne-Marie O'Malley, Michael and Anne McDonald, John Lane, Michael Doswell, Mrs Margo Finlay, Jörg Kasprowski, John and Verna Aspinall)*

SEAMER [TA0183]

Copper Horse YO12 4RF [just S of Scarboro; Main St]: Good choice of generous tasty usual food in dining areas off main bar, bright and clean with beams, brasses, stripped stone, part wood-floored and part carpeted, welcoming staff, John Smiths and Theakstons; pretty village *(Keith and Margaret Kettell, Barry Collett)*

SETTLE [SD8163]

☆ *Golden Lion* BD24 9DU [B6480 (main rd through town), off A65 bypass]: Warm friendly old-fashioned atmosphere in market-town inn with grand staircase sweeping down into old-fashioned baronial-style high-beamed hall bar, lovely log fire, comfortably worn settles, plush seats, brass, prints and plates on dark panelling; good value food (all day wknds) inc interesting specials, well kept Thwaites, decent wines by the glass, splendid dining room; public bar with darts, pool, games machines and TV; children in eating area, 12 good-sized comfortable bedrooms, hearty breakfast, open all day *(C and G Mangham, Michael and Maggie Betton, Michael Butler, John and Helen Rushton, LYM, Phil Bryant, Gerry Miller, Arthur Pickering)*

SHEFFIELD [SK3586]

Bungalows & Bears S1 4GF [Division St]: Relaxed daytime bar with good simple food, decent wines by the glass, lots of settees, daily papers, board games, big windows, room for pushchairs; trendy and lively young people's place at night, with loud live music *(Paul Newberry)*

Castle Inn S17 4PT [Twentywell Rd, Bradway]: Two-bar stone-built pub in attractive spot, sensibly priced food (not Sun evening or Weds), three real ales, good choice of other drinks, friendly service, beamed dining room, pub games; piped music, games machine; children welcome, front picnic-sets *(JJW, CMW)*

Corner Pin S4 7QN [Carlisle St East]: Restored 19th-c pub with changing ales such as Abbeydale, Acorn, Bradfield and Ossett,

bar food changing daily, basic locals' bar, quiet lounge; cl 8.30 Mon-Thurs, open all day Fri/Sat, cl Sun *(the Didler)*

☆ *Devonshire Cat* S1 4HG [Wellington St (some local parking)]: Plain contemporary bar with friendly staff knowledgeable about the dozen mainly Yorkshire real ales inc Abbeydale and Kelham Island, some tapped from the cask, eight foreign beers on tap, masses of bottled beers in glass-walled cool room, two farm ciders, tea and coffee, cheap food more interesting than usual from end servery, plenty of room, polished light wood, big modern prints, board games; well reproduced piped music, wide-screen TV, silenced games machine, ATM, Weds folk night; good disabled access and facilities, open all day *(Don and Shirley Parrish, Brian and Anna Marsden, BB, Valerie Baker, the Didler, Mrs Hazel Rainer, James Tringham)*

Fagans S1 4BS [Broad Lane]: Simple two-room local with friendly popular landlord, well kept Abbeydale and Tetleys, lots of malt whiskies, bargain food (not Sun evening or Sat), good staff, frequent folk nights; dogs welcome, open all day *(Bob, Valerie Baker)*

Gardeners Rest S3 8AT [Neepsend Lane]: Still shut after 2007 floods as we went to press, but should reopen soon, with welcoming beer-enthusiast landlord selling his own good Sheffield ales as well as several changing guest beers tapped from the cask, farm cider and continental beers; has had old brewery memorabilia, lunchtime food, daily papers, games inc bar billiards, changing local artwork, various events; disabled access and facilities, back conservatory and tables out overlooking River Don; was open all day Fri-Sun, perhaps not till mid-afternoon other days *(the Didler, Pete Baker)*

Harlequin S3 8GG [Nursery St]: Comfortable open-plan pub with eight well kept ales such as Bradfield and John Smiths, imports and farm cider too, bargain food, good staff, some live music; open all day *(the Didler, Valerie Baker)*

☆ *Hillsborough* S6 2UB [Langsett Rd/Wood St; by Primrose View tram stop]: Chatty and friendly pub-in-hotel, eight beers inc own microbrews and quickly changing guests, good soft drinks choice, bargain food inc Sun roasts, daily papers, open fire, bare-boards bar, lounge, views to ski slope from attractive back conservatory and terrace tables; piped music, TV; children and dogs welcome, good value simple bedrooms, covered parking, open all day *(the Didler, JJW, CMW, Don and Shirley Parrish)*

☆ *Kelham Island Tavern* S3 8RY [Kelham Island]: Very popular backstreet local, friendly and comfortable, with Acorn, Pictish and lots of interesting guest beers, continental imports, farm cider, nice artwork, filled cobs and other bar lunches (not Sun/Mon), Sun folk night; disabled facilities, sheltered flower-filled back terrace, open all day *(Sun afternoon break)*

(Mrs Hazel Rainer, the Didler, Mark and Diane Grist, David Carr, P Dawn)

Milestone S3 8SE [Green Ln]: Compact pub with enjoyable fresh food in bar and impressive upstairs restaurant, Kelham Island, Sheffield and Thornbridge ales, good range of foreign bottled beers, friendly staff *(the Didler)*

Old Queens Head S1 2BG [Pond Hill]: Oldest commercial building here, carvings, dark panelling, red plush, brass elephant head bar rail supports, well kept Thwaites, good value generous food inc bargain Sun lunch, upstairs family room; good disabled access, terrace tables *(Valerie Baker)*

Rawson Spring S6 2LN [Langsett Rd]: Newish Wetherspoons, their usual value, impressive décor with unusual skylights, inviting atmosphere; TV *(the Didler)*

Red Deer S1 4DD [Pitt St]: Thriving backstreet local among Univ buildings, changing ales from central bar, good value simple wkdy lunchtime food, pleasant raised back area; dogs welcome, tables outside, open all day, cl Sun lunchtime *(the Didler, Don and Shirley Parrish, Bob)*

Sheaf View S2 3AA [Gleadless Rd, Heeley Bottom]: Attractively refurbished in unpretentious 1960s/70s style, wide range of local and other changing ales, farm cider, spotless unusually shaped bar, pleasant staff; disabled facilities, tables outside, open all day wknds, cl Mon lunchtime *(Don and Shirley Parrish)*

Sportsman S10 4LJ [Redmires Rd]: Pleasant old pub with jovial landlord, friendly atmosphere, sports jersey décor, three real ales, good soft drinks range, good value food; children and dogs welcome, views *(JJW, CMW)*

Three Merry Lads S10 4LJ [W on Redmires Rd]: Refurbished under new management, enjoyable freshly made food bargains for two, good choice of wines by the glass, four real ales inc Kelham Island, pleasant well trained staff, chatty bar and dining extension with uninterrupted views; children welcome, terrace picnic-sets, open all day wknds *(Derek Stapley)*

Walkley Cottage S6 5DD [Bole Hill Rd]: Warm-hearted 1930s pub with half a dozen or more real ales, decent well priced food (not Sun evening or Mon) inc bargain OAP lunch and good Sun roasts, some take-aways, farm cider, good coffee and other drinks choice, daily papers, games room with darts, pool etc; children and dogs welcome, views from picnic-sets in small back garden with play area, lovely hanging baskets, open all day *(JJW, CMW, Valerie Baker)*

☆ **Wellington** S3 7EQ [Henry St; Shalesmoor tram stop right outside]: Back to former name after spell as Cask & Cutler, unpretentious relaxed pub with up to ten changing real ales, bottled imports, farm cider, coal fire in lounge, daily papers, pub games, good Nov beer festival, friendly staff;

wheelchair access, tables in nice back garden, open all day Fri/Sat, has been cl Mon lunchtime *(David Carr, the Didler, Pete Baker)*

White Swan S8 7RB [Greenhill Main Rd (not the B6054 bit)]: Friendly four-room local with enjoyable food (not Sun evening), freshly cooked so may be a wait, real ales such as Black Sheep; piped music, TV; open all day *(JJW, CMW)*

SHELF [SE1127]

Duke of York HX3 7LN [West St; A644 Brighouse—Queensbury]: 17th-c beamed dining pub, eating areas off light open bar, reasonably priced generous food inc proper pies, friendly quick service, well kept ales such as Ossett, open fires; bedrooms *(Pat and Tony Martin)*

SHEPLEY [SE1809]

Farmers Boy HD8 8AP [links A629 and A635, from village centre by Black Bull]: Cleanly refurbished beamed cottage conversion favoured by diners for current chef/landlord's good if pricy food, well kept Black Sheep, Flowers and Greene King *(Gordon and Margaret Ormondroyd)*

SHERBURN IN ELMET [SE4933]

Oddfellows Arms LS25 6BA [Low Street]: Friendly local with bargain blackboard food and wine by the glass, John Smiths *(Ian and Anne Read)*

SHIPLEY [SE1437]

Fannys Ale & Cider House BD18 3JN [Saltaire Rd]: Interesting gaslit two-room roadside local with up to nine changing ales inc Timothy Taylors, foreign beers, farm cider; open all day Fri/Sat, cl Mon lunchtime *(the Didler)*

SKIPTON [SD9851]

☆ **Royal Shepherd** BD23 1LB [Canal St; from Water St (A65) turn into Coach St, then left after bridge over Leeds & Liverpool Canal]: Convivial old-fashioned local with big bustling bar, snug and dining room, open fires, local Copper Dragon ales, decent wine, interesting whiskies, cheery landlord and brisk service, low-priced standard food from sandwiches up, photographs of Yorks CCC in its golden days; games and piped music; children welcome in side room, tables out in pretty spot by canal *(Chris and Jeanne Downing, John and Alison Hamilton, the Didler)*

Woolly Sheep BD23 1HY [Sheep St]: Big bustling pub with full range of Timothy Taylors ales, prompt friendly enthusiastic service, daily papers, two beamed bars off flagstoned passage, exposed brickwork, stone fireplace, lots of sheep prints and bric-a-brac, attractive and comfortable raised lunchtime dining area, good value food (plenty for children); unobtrusive piped music; spacious pretty garden, six good value bedrooms, good breakfast *(David and Ruth Hollands, Clive Flynn)*

SKIPWITH [SE6638]

Drovers Arms YO8 5SF [follow Escrick sign off A163 NE of Selby]: Comfortable country pub in smart village by Skipwith Common nature reserve, Black Sheep and a guest beer, enjoyable home-made food, good log fires, two linked bars and dining room; wheelchair access, open all day wknds *(Bob Deacon)*

SLAITHWAITE [SE0513]

Rose & Crown HD7 5XA [Cop Hill, up Nabbs Lane then Holme Lane]: New management doing good value pubby food in isolated pub with great Colne Valley and Pennine views, real ales such as Daleside and Timothy Taylors, three rooms off friendly bar, log fire, end restaurant; good walks *(Andy and Jill Kassube)*

SLEDMERE [SE9364]

Triton YO25 3XQ [junction B1252/B1253 NW of Gt Driffield]: Good food (all day Sun) inc delicious puddings and children's helpings in refurbished 18th-c inn, welcoming attentive staff, well kept ales inc Wold Top, good log fire, games room with darts, dominoes and pool; children welcome, five neat bedrooms, cl Mon lunchtime *(C A Hall, Roger A Bellingham, LYM, Mrs R Mehlman)*

SLEIGHTS [NZ8606]

Plough YO22 5EN [Coach Rd]: Two-bar stone-built pub with friendly landlord, well kept Black Sheep, John Smiths and Wells & Youngs Bombardier, bargain locally sourced food, back restaurant; tables outside, good views, three bedrooms *(Michael Butler)*

SNAPE [SE2684]

☆ *Castle Arms* DL8 2TB [off B6268 Masham—Bedale]: Immaculately updated low-ceilinged pub with good fresh enterprising food from interesting sandwiches up, well kept Marstons-related ales, helpful landlord, decent wines, good coffee, relaxed happy atmosphere, flagstoned bar with big inglenook coal fire, second flagstoned room and attractive rather smart small carpeted dining room, sporting prints; children and dogs welcome, charming courtyard, pretty village very handy for Thorp Perrow, comfortable bedrooms *(Comus and Sarah Elliott, Michael Swallow, BB)*

SOWERBY BRIDGE [SE0623]

Moorings HX6 2AG [canal basin]: Spacious multi-level canal warehouse conversion, enjoyable interesting food (all day Sat, not Sun evening), real ales inc Black Sheep, good wine choice, big windows overlooking boat basin, high beams, flagstones and stripped stone, solid booth seating; unobtrusive piped music; canopied terrace tables *(John Honnor, LYM)*

Works HX6 2QG [Hollins Mill Lane, off A58]: Big airy two-room bareboards pub in converted joinery workshop, seating from pews to comfortable sofas, at least eight real ales, bargain lunchtime food, poetry readings, live music in back yard (covered in inclement weather); open all day *(Andy and Jill Kassube, Tony Hobden, Pat and Tony Martin)*

SPROTBROUGH [SE5301]

☆ *Boat* DN5 7NB [3.5 miles from M18 junction 2, less from A1(M) junction 36 via A630 and

Mill Lane; Nursery Lane]: Reopened after restoration of 2007 flood damage, several snug flagstoned areas, log fires in big stone fireplaces, latticed windows, dark beams, decent food, well kept Black Sheep and Timothy Taylors Landlord, friendly service; tables in big sheltered prettily lit courtyard, River Don walks, open all day *(Comus and Sarah Elliott, Derek and Sylvia Stephenson, LYM)*

Ivanhoe DN5 7NS [quite handy for A1(M)]: Large friendly mock-Tudor pub, bargain Sam Smiths and pubby food (not Sun evening) from hot servery inc popular Sun carvery, three linked rooms with conservatory extension overlooking cricket ground, uniformed waitresses, games bar with pool; games machines; children in eating areas, flagstoned terrace with play area, open all day *(JJW, CMW, JHBS)*

STAITHES [NZ7818]

Captain Cook TS13 5AD [Staithes Ln/Top of Bank]: Ruggedly old-fashioned unpretentious local with changing real ales such as bargain Rudgate Viking, dining room (food Fri-Sun evenings and Sun lunchtime), back family games room with pool, live music most wknds; open all day *(Pete Baker)*

STAMFORD BRIDGE [SE7055]

☆ *Three Cups* YO41 1AX [A166 W of town]: Spacious Vintage Inn family dining pub in cosy timbered country style, reliable food all day, good range of wines by the glass, real ales, good staff, two blazing fires, glass-topped well; children welcome, good play area behind, good disabled access, bedrooms *(Joan York, LYM, David Carr, Pat and Graham Williamson)*

STAPLETON [NZ2612]

Bridge DL2 2QQ [nr spur from A1(M); The Green]: Remarkably wide food choice inc generous Sun carvery (three plate sizes) in two warmly decorated comfortable bars and raftered restaurant, genial landlord; picnic-sets in neatly kept garden *(John C and Anne Morley)*

STARBOTTON [SD9574]

Fox & Hounds BD23 5HY [B6160]: Unspoilt small Dales local in pretty village, big log fire in attractively traditional beamed and flagstoned bar, compact dining room; has had Black Sheep and Timothy Taylors Landlord and decent usual food, welcoming children, but for sale summer 2008 - news please *(LYM)*

STAVELEY [SE3662]

Royal Oak HG5 9LD [signed off A6055 Knaresborough—Boroughbridge]: Popular and welcoming beamed pub with well kept Black Sheep, enjoyable food from standard to thai dishes in bar and restaurant, broad bow window overlooking front lawn *(Mike and Terry Wass, LYM)*

STAXTON [TA0179]

Hare & Hounds YO12 4TA [Main St]: Friendly family-run pub, five real ales inc Black Sheep, Stones and Theakstons, good wines by the glass, enjoyable food running to lobster salad (C A Hall)

STOKESLEY [NZ5208]

Spread Eagle TS9 5AD [High St]: Smallish former coaching inn, four real ales, good choice of drinks and of enjoyable food all day (fresh, so may take a while), no mobile phones; piped music, live Tues, big TV; children and dogs welcome, garden down to river, open all day (Elizabeth Whelan, JJW, CMW)

☆ **White Swan** TS9 5BL [West End]: Good Captain Cook ales brewed in neat and attractive pub, friendly young staff, three relaxing seating areas in L-shaped bar, log fire, lots of brass on elegant dark panelling, lovely bar counter carving, hat display, unusual clock, no food, music or machines; cl Tues lunchtime, open all day Fri/Sat (Blaise Vyner, Michael Butler, Pete Baker, Don and Shirley Parrish, the Didler)

STUTTON [SE4841]

☆ **Hare & Hounds** LS24 9BR [Manor Rd]: Attractive stone-built pub with cosy low-ceilinged rooms, enjoyable food (not Sun evening) from sandwiches up, quick friendly service even though busy (helpful with wheelchairs), well kept cheap Sam Smiths OB, decent wine, well behaved children in restaurant; tables, some under cover, in long pretty sloping garden, has been cl Mon (Mrs P J Pearce, LYM, Rosemary K Germaine, Gordon and Margaret Ormondroyd)

SUTTON-ON-THE-FOREST [SE5864]

Rose & Crown YO61 1DP [B1363 N of York]: Neat beamed pub, small bar on right with parquet floor, old engravings, traditional pub furnishings, Black Sheep Best and Timothy Taylors Landlord from intricately carved counter, several wines and malt whiskies, L-shaped dining room with former inglenook, decent food, conservatory; children welcome, big decked terrace and garden with sizeable heated thatched gazebo, cl Sun pm and Mon (LYM)

SUTTON-UNDER-WHITESTONECLIFFE [SE4983]

Whitestonecliffe Inn YO7 2PR [A170 E of Thirsk]: Beamed roadside pub with wide choice of good value food from sandwiches up in bar and restaurant, OAP lunches, friendly staff, well kept ales, log fire, games room with darts and pool; children welcome, s/c cottages (Don and Shirley Parrish)

SWAINBY [NZ4702]

Black Horse DL6 3ED [High St]: Pleasant streamside spot in nice village, appealing beamed bar with local photographs, wide range of generous appetising home-made food from substantial doorstep sandwiches to good value Sun roasts, well kept Camerons and John Smiths, friendly efficient service even when busy; well spaced picnic-sets in attractive garden with play area (Michael Butler)

TAN HILL [NY8906]

Tan Hill Inn DL11 6ED [Arkengarthdale rd Reeth—Brough, at junction Keld/W Stonesdale rd]: Basic old pub in wonderful bleak setting on Pennine Way - Britain's highest, full of bric-a-brac and interesting photographs, simple sturdy furniture, flagstones, ever-burning big log fire (with prized stone side seats, even a pub duck toasting itself last winter); chatty atmosphere, four real ales, good cheap pubby food, pool in family room; often snowbound, can get overcrowded; swaledale sheep show here last Thurs in May; children and dogs welcome (even a pub duck last winter), bedrooms, open all day (Tim and Ann Newell, Nick Holding, LYM)

TERRINGTON [SE6770]

☆ **Bay Horse** YO60 6PP [W of Malton]: Cosy log-fire lounge bar, good thai food in handsome dining area and back family conservatory with old farm tools, decent real ales and wines, over 100 whiskies, traditional public bar with darts, shove-ha'penny, cribbage and dominoes; children welcome in eating areas, garden tables, unspoilt village (LYM, J F M and M West)

THOLTHORPE [SE4766]

New Inn YO61 1SL: Beamed bar and candlelit dining room, friendly staff, good food from local sources (not Sun evening/Mon), early evening deals and Sun roasts, real ales; children welcome, bedrooms (Rosemary Platt)

THORNTON IN LONSDALE [SD6873]

Marton Arms LA6 3PB [off A65 just NW of Ingleton]: Change of management, quite a few real ales (perhaps too many to keep fresh), has had 361 malt whiskies, beamed bar with stripped pine tables and chairs, pews and built-in seats in airy main part, curtained-off flagstoned public bar with darts and piped music, log fires; children have been allowed, picnic-sets on front terrace and at back, great walking country, 13th-c church opp, bedrooms (Jo Lilley, Simon Calvert, Karen Eliot, LYM)

THRESHFIELD [SD9863]

Old Hall Inn BD23 5HB [B6160/B6265 just outside Grassington]: Three old-world linked rooms inc smart candlelit dining room, enjoyable food, well kept Timothy Taylors, helpful friendly staff, log fires, high beam-and-plank ceiling, cushioned wall pews, tall well blacked kitchen range; children in eating area, neat garden (Mr and Mrs D Moir, V Brogden, LYM)

THRUSCROSS [SE1558]

Stone House HG3 4AH [Blubberhouses—Greenhow Hill rd, between A59 and B6265]: Good generous sensibly priced food in warm and cosy moorland pub's bar or dining room, beams, flagstones, stripped stone, dark panelling, attentive friendly staff, good log fires, well kept ales; children welcome, sheltered tables outside (LYM, Helen Burns)

THURSTONLAND [SE1610]

Rose & Crown HD4 6XU [off A629 Huddersfield—Sheffield, via Thunder Bridge and Stocksmoor]: Spacious open-plan village pub, banquettes and some stripped stone, new owners doing good value food inc Weds curry and Fri fish and chips nights, five real ales inc Bradfield; some tables out in front, exhilarating countryside *(Andy and Jill Kassube)*

TOCKWITH [SE4652]

Spotted Ox YO26 7PY [Westfield Rd, off B1224]: Welcoming traditional beamed village local, three areas open off central bar with well kept Black Sheep, Tetleys and Timothy Taylors Landlord carefully served the old-fashioned way, good choice of sensibly priced home-made food inc OAP bargains, attentive staff, relaxed atmosphere, interesting local history; open all day Fri-Sun *(Les and Sandra Brown)*

TODMORDEN [SD9223]

Masons Arms OL14 7PN [A681/A6033, S of centre]: Welcoming traditional local, well kept Copper Dragon ales and local guest beers, enthusiastic landlord, decent food till 6, pump clips on beams and interesting photographs and cuttings in two knocked-together rooms, darts, cards and pool in popular games end *(Bruce Bird)*

TONG [SE2230]

Greyhound BD4 0RR [Tong Lane]: Traditional low-beamed and flagstoned local by village cricket field, distinctive areas inc small dining room, good value food, Black Sheep, Greene King Abbot and Tetleys, friendly staff; tables outside *(Dudley and Moira Cockroft)*

TOPCLIFFE [SE4076]

Angel YO7 3RW [off A1, take A168 to Thirsk, after 3 miles follow signs for Topcliffe; Long St]: Big bustling place with friendly helpful service, several well kept ales, wide choice of good value food from good sandwiches up, decent wines, separately themed areas inc attractive and softly lit stripped-stone faux-irish bar, also billiards room and two dining rooms; unobtrusive piped music; tables outside, bedrooms, good breakfast *(Gerry and Rosemary Dobson)*

TOTLEY [SK3080]

Cricket S17 3AZ [signed from A621; Penny Lane]: Reopened 2007 in dining pub style, pews, mixed chairs and pine tables on bare boards and flagstones, hearty blackboard food (all day wknds) from sandwiches and pubby staples to some interesting dishes, Thornbridge ales, log fires, bay-window views of rustic cricket field; children and dogs welcome, terrace tables, open all day *(anon)*

Crown S17 3AX [Hillfoot Rd]: Old-fashioned country pub with two rooms off central bar, friendly landlord and good staff, four or five real ales, good choice of other drinks, good plain home-cooked food (not Sun/Mon evenings); TV; dogs welcome, picnic-sets outside *(James A Waller, DC)*

WAKEFIELD [SE3320]

Fernandes Brewery Tap WF1 1UA [Avison Yard, Kirkgate]: Now owned by Ossett but still brewing own ales, interesting guest beers, bottled imports, farm cider, new ground-floor bar with flagstones, bare brick

and panelling, original raftered top-floor bar with unusual breweriana, plans for middle café-bar; cl Mon-Thurs lunchtime, open all day Fri-Sun with lunchtime soup and sandwiches *(the Didler)*

WALES [SK4782]

Duke of Leeds S26 5LQ [Church St]: Comfortable 18th-c village pub with good value food (all day Fri-Sun, at least in summer), early evening and wkdy OAP bargains, Sun carvery, John Smiths, Theakstons and guest beers, good wine and soft drinks choice, quick friendly service, long dining lounge, lots of photographs, brass and copper, flame-effect gas fire, Thurs quiz nights; piped music, TV, may be cl Sat afternoon for functions; children welcome, tables outside, nearby walks *(JJW, CMW, Mrs Hazel Rainer)*

WEAVERTHORPE [SE9670]

☆ *Blue Bell* YO17 8EX: Upscale country dining pub with beautifully presented good food, fine choice of wines, well kept Black Sheep, pre-meal home-made crisps and dips, cosy and cheerful bar with a mass of wine bottles and other drinks packaging, intimate back restaurant also with wine décor, charming efficient waitresses; 12 bedrooms, good breakfast *(Colin McKerrow)*

WELL [SE2682]

Milbank Arms DL8 2PX [Bedale Rd]: Well restored beamed bar, cheery landlord, enjoyable food inc light lunchtime dishes, well kept Black Sheep and Viking, good coffee, log fire; picnic-sets out in front *(Michael Doswell, Peter Hacker)*

WENSLEY [SE0989]

Three Horseshoes DL8 4HJ: Three smartly simple flagstoned rooms, friendly helpful staff, warm fire, well kept Wensleydale and guest ales (they may offer tasters), straightforward food (not Sun evening); immaculate outside lavatories; tables outside, open all day *(Ben and Helen Ingram, Mr and Mrs Maurice Thompson, John and Sharon Hancock)*

WENTWORTH [SK3898]

☆ *George & Dragon* S62 7TN [3 miles from M1 junction 36; Main St]: Friendly rambling split-level bar, good range of real ales and of generous good value food cooked to order (worth the wait), flagstones and assorted old-fashioned furnishings, ornate stove in lounge, small back games room; tables out on big back lawn, crafts and antiques shop - pleasant village *(Jo Lilley, Simon Calvert, LYM)*

WEST TANFIELD [SE2678]

Bruce Arms HG4 5JJ [Main St (A6108 N of Ripon)]: Current landlord doing good food inc interesting dishes, friendly landlady, log fire in one dining room; two bedrooms, cl Sun evening and Mon *(Janet and Peter Race, Steve Clarke, LYM)*

WEST WITTON [SE0588]

☆ *Wensleydale Heifer* DL8 4LS [A684 W of Leyburn]: Stylish restaurant-with-rooms rather than pub, good local meat and fresh fish and seafood, cosy informal upmarket food bar as well as extensive main formal restaurant, daily papers; nice comfortable bedrooms (back ones quietest), good big breakfast *(M S Catling, Mr and Mrs P L Spencer, Brian Young, BB)*

WETHERBY [SE4048]

Muse café LS22 6NQ [Bank St]: Very popular bistro-bar with good brasserie food inc early-bird two-course deals, four real ales such as Black Sheep, continental lagers, good coffee, young friendly helpful staff; open all day *(Stuart Paulley, Andy and Jill Kassube, WW)*

Swan & Talbot LS22 6NN [handy for A1; North St]: Traditional town pub, linked rooms each side of main bar, modestly priced tasty food esp fish and grills, Caledonian Deuchars IPA, Fullers London Pride and John Smiths, busy attentive staff; courtyard tables, four bedrooms, open all day *(Tim and Ann Newell, Comus and Sarah Elliott)*

WHITBY [NZ9011]

Dolphin YO22 4BG [Bridge St, just over bridge to E/Old Whitby]: Harbourside pub with straightforward generous food from good crab brasserie to local fish, quick service, real ale; terrace with nice marina and sea view, bedrooms *(David Carr)*

Endeavour YO22 4AS [Church St]: One-room local with real ales such as Caledonian Deuchars IPA and Timothy Taylors, settles and coal fire, nautical memorabilia and Frank Sutcliffe Whitby photographs *(P Dawn)*

Granby YO21 3AJ [Skinner St, off West Cliff]: Friendly traditional local with good value generous food inc Sun roasts, three real ales, Victorian photographs, hexagonal ceiling design with mirror centrepiece; children and dogs welcome *(Elizabeth Whelan, JJW, CMW)*

Middle Earth Tavern YO22 4AE [Church St]: Well used pub in quiet spot facing river and harbour, bar food, may be Black Sheep and Tetleys in summer; tables outside *(P Dawn, David Carr)*

Station Inn YO21 1DH [New Quay Rd]: Three-room bare-boards pub with eight well kept changing ales, farm cider, friendly licensees, proper lunchtime home cooking inc local fish, good choice of wines by the glass, thriving atmosphere, traditional games; piped music, live Weds; open all day *(P Dawn)*

WIGGLESWORTH [SD8056]

☆ *Plough* BD23 4RJ [B6478, off A65 S of Settle]: Friendly dining pub with good reasonably priced bar food (not Sun evening or Mon in winter) from baguettes up, takeaways too, efficient service, Black Sheep and Tetleys, attractive bar with log fire, little rooms off, panelled dining room, snug and attractive conservatory restaurant with panoramic Dales views; pleasant garden, nine comfortable bedrooms also with views *(Norma and Noel Thomas)*

WORMALD GREEN [SE3065]

George HG3 3PR [A61 Ripon—Harrogate]: Reopened 2006 after comfortable reworking, stylish contemporary linked areas (smaller one for bar food, larger for main meals), good choice of wines by the glass, good coffee, friendly helpful staff; garden picnic-sets, five well equipped bedrooms *(LYM, Roy Bromell)*

WRELTON [SE7685]

Buck YO18 8PJ [Wrelton Cliff Rd]: Chef/landlord doing good value food esp Thurs steak night, good young polish staff *(Peter and Anne-Marie O'Malley)*

YORK [SE5951]

☆ *Ackhorne* YO1 6LN [St Martins Lane, Micklegate]: Good real ales such as Daleside, Rooster and Village, beams, panelling, stained-glass, leather wall seats, open fire, Civil War prints, bottles and jugs, carpeted snug one end, friendly helpful family service, up to four farm ciders, perry, country wines, foreign bottled beers, bargain basic food, not Sun, from good choice of sandwiches up, daily papers, traditional games; silenced games machine; smokers' shelter and suntrap back terrace, open all day *(David Carr, Pat and Tony Martin, Bruce Bird, Mark Walker, the Didler, Roger A Bellingham, Mark and Diane Grist)*

☆ *Black Swan* YO1 7PR [Peaseholme Green (inner ring road)]: Striking timbered and jettied Tudor building, compact panelled front bar, crooked-floored central hall with fine period staircase, black-beamed back bar with vast inglenook, great atmosphere, good choice of real ales, cheerful service, basic low-priced food, decent wines, jazz and folk nights; piped music, useful car park *(Pete Baker, Pete Coxon, the Didler, Peter Dandy, LYM)*

☆ *Blue Bell* YO1 9TF [Fossgate]: Delightfully old-fashioned Edwardian pub with super friendly atmosphere, chatty locals and landlady, well kept Timothy Taylors Landlord, Tetleys Mild and guest beers, good value sandwiches and tapas all day till 5 (not Sun), daily papers, tiny tiled-floor front bar with roaring fire, panelled ceiling, stained-glass, bar pots and decanters, corridor to back room not much bigger, hatch service, lamps and flickering candles, pub games; may be piped music; open all day *(Eric Larkham, Pete Baker, Mark Walker, David Carr, Mark and Diane Grist, Pete Coxon, the Didler, WW, Bruce Bird)*

☆ *Brigantes* YO1 6JX [Micklegate]: Comfortably traditional Market Town Taverns bar/bistro, eight real ales and good range of bottled beers, good wines and coffee, enjoyable unpretentious brasserie food all day, friendly helpful staff, simple pleasant décor, upstairs dining room; open all day *(WW, Bruce Bird, the Didler, Mark and Diane Grist, Pete Coxon, Sue Demont, Tim Barrow)*

Crystal Palace YO24 4AB [Holgate Rd]: Well kept Sam Smiths at bargain price, good range of basic food, pleasant lounge bar; children welcome *(Andrew Bosi)*

Golden Fleece YO1 9UP [Pavement]: Black Sheep, Greene King and Timothy Taylors, good value usual food from sandwiches up all afternoon, long corridor from bar to comfortable back lounge (beware the sloping floors - it dates from 1503), interesting décor with quite a library, lots of pictures and ghost stories, pub games; piped music; children welcome, bedrooms *(David Carr, Michael and Alison Sandy, Pete Coxon)*

Golden Lion YO1 8BG [Church St]: Big comfortable open-plan pub done up in bare-boards Edwardian style (in fact first licensed 1771), beams, plenty of lamps, old photographs and brewery signs, good changing real ale choice, sensible food all day from good sandwiches up, good range of wines by the glass, pleasant young staff; piped music; open all day *(Pat and Tony Martin, Mark Walker, Pete Coxon)*

Golden Slipper YO1 7LG [Goodramgate]: Dating from 15th c, unpretentious bar and three comfortably old-fashioned small rooms, one lined with books, cheerful staff, good cheap plain lunchtime food from sandwiches up, well kept ales inc Caledonian Deuchars IPA and Fullers London Pride; TV; tables in back courtyard *(Mark Walker, Pat and Graham Williamson, Pete Coxon, Alan Thwaite)*

Hansom Cab YO1 8SL [Market St]: Dark panelling and leather seating, low-priced Sam Smiths, enjoyable cheap quick food counter, plenty of tables, side alcoves, interesting ceiling (like a glass pyramid surrounded by plants); children allowed lunchtime *(Mark Walker)*

Harkers YO1 8QN [St Helens Sq]: Handsome late Georgian building (basement has part of Roman gateway) converted to good value high-ceilinged bar, Black Sheep, Greene King IPA and good new world wines from the long serving counter, pubby food and more contemporary dishes from sandwiches up, panelling and marble fireplace in one room; TV; open all day *(Michael Dandy)*

Hole in the Wall YO1 7EH [High Petergate]: Handy for Minster, rambling comfortably modernised linked areas, low beams, panelling and stripped masonry, lots of prints, good friendly service, real ales, decent wine choice and coffee, very busy lunchtime for good value food; children welcome, open all day *(LYM, Mark Walker)*

Kings Arms YO1 9SN [King's Staithe, by Clifford St]: Fine riverside position (so can get flooded), bowed black beams, flagstones, lunchtime food from sandwiches up; keg beers; picnic-sets out on cobbled waterside terrace, open all day *(Mark Walker, LYM, David Carr)*

☆ **Last Drop** YO1 8BN [Colliergate]: Basic traditional York Brewery pub, their own beers and one or two well kept guests, decent wines and country wines, friendly helpful young staff, big windows, bare boards, barrel tables and comfortable seats (some up a few steps), no music, machines or children, nice simple fresh food 12-4 inc sandwiches and good salads; piped music, no children, can get very busy lunchtime, attic lavatories;

tables out behind, open all day *(WW, Mark and Diane Grist, Susan and Nigel Brookes, David Carr, Mark Walker, Bruce Bird, the Didler)*

Lendal Cellars YO1 8AA [Lendal]: Bustling rather studenty split-level ale house in broad-vaulted 17th-c cellars, stripped brickwork, stone floor, linked rooms and alcoves, good choice of fairly priced changing ales and wines by the glass, farm cider, decent coffee, foreign bottled beers, daily papers, good plain food 11.30-7(5 Fri/Sat), well reproduced piped music; service can slow, can get packed; children allowed if eating, open all day *(Dave Webster, Sue Holland, the Didler, Peter Dandy, Dr D J and Mrs S C Walker, LYM)*

Masons Arms YO10 4AB [Fishergate]: Friendly 1930s local, well priced food inc unusual dishes, changing real ales, two fires in panelled front bar with blow lamps and pig ornaments, attractive fireplaces; comfortable bedroom block (no breakfast), tables out in front and on back riverside terrace *(Robin and Ann Taylor, Mrs Hazel Rainer)*

Minster Inn YO30 7BH [Marygate]: Modest Edwardian local, bric-a-brac and dark old settles, fires and woodburners, corridor to distinctive back room, friendly staff, well kept changing Marstons-related ales, sandwiches, table games; tables out behind *(David Carr, Bruce Bird, the Didler)*

Old White Swan YO1 7LF [Goodramgate]: Victorian, Georgian and Tudor themed bars, enjoyable lunchtime food, several real ales, pleasant busy staff, big L-shaped dining area, central covered courtyard good for families; piped music, frequent live (busy then), big-screen sports TV, games machines *(David Carr)*

Olde Starre YO1 8AS [Stonegate]: City's oldest licensed pub, a big tourist draw, with 'gallows' sign across town's prettiest street, original panelling and prints, green plush wall seats, several other little carpeted rooms off porch-like lobby, four changing ales from long counter, cheerful young staff, low-priced food, daily papers; piped music, TV, games machines; children welcome away from bar, flower-filled back garden and front courtyard, open all day *(Pete Coxon, David Carr, Michael Dandy, Peter Dandy, LYM)*

Red Lion YO1 9TU [Merchantgate, between Fossgate and Piccadilly]: Low-beamed rambling rooms with plenty of atmosphere, some stripped Tudor brickwork, relaxed old-fashioned furnishings, well kept Black Sheep and John Smiths, reasonably priced bar lunches, good staff; piped music; children welcome for lunch, picnic-sets outside *(Pete Coxon, Mark Walker, David Carr, LYM)*

Rook & Gaskill YO10 3WP [Lawrence St]: Traditional Tynemill pub, up to a dozen ales inc local York, enjoyable food (not Sun), dark wood tables, banquettes, chairs and high stools, back conservatory; open all day *(the Didler, David Carr, Pete Coxon, Eric Larkham)*

Snickleway YO1 7LS [Goodramgate]: Interesting little open-plan pub behind big shop-front window, lots of antiques, copper and brass, cosy fire, Black Sheep, Greene King Old Speckled Hen and John Smiths, good value fresh well filled doorstep sandwiches, baked potatoes and a coupe of hot dishes lunchtimes, cheerful landlord, prompt service, splendid cartoons in gents', exemplary ladies'; unobtrusive piped music *(Pete Coxon, David Carr, Alan Thwaite, Mark Walker)*

Swan YO23 1JH [Bishopgate St, Clementhorpe]: Unspoilt 1930s interior, friendly and chatty, hatch service to lobby for two small rooms off main bar, great staff, several changing ales inc Caledonian Deuchars IPA and Timothy Taylors Landlord, rotating farm ciders; busy with young people wknds; small pleasant walled garden, nr city walls, open all day wknds *(the Didler, Fred and Lorraine Gill, Pete Baker, Alison and Pete)*

☆ *Tap & Spile* YO31 7PB [Monkgate]: Friendly open-plan late Victorian pub with Roosters and other mainly northern ales, farm cider and country wines, decent wines by the glass, bookshelves, games in raised back area, cheap straightforward lunchtime bar food (not Mon); children in eating area, garden and heated terrace, open all day *(Pete Coxon, the Didler, LYM)*

☆ *Three Legged Mare* YO1 7EN [High Petergate]: Bustling light and airy modern café-bar with York Brewery's full beer range kept well, good range of belgian beers, quick cheerful young staff, interesting sandwiches and one or two basic lunchtime hot dishes, some comfortable sofas, back conservatory; no children; disabled facilities (other lavatories down spiral stairs), back garden with replica of the local gallows of the pub's name, open all day *(Pete Coxon, Bruce Bird, WW, Pat and Tony Martin, David Carr)*

☆ *York Arms* YO1 7EH [High Petergate]: Cheerful Sam Smiths pub by Minster, quick helpful service, good value sandwiches and simple hot dishes lunchtime to early evening (not Sun-Tues), snug little basic panelled bar, big modern back lounge, cosier partly panelled parlour full of old bric-a-brac, prints, brown-cushioned wall settles and open fire, pub games, no piped music; open all day *(David Carr, BB, Peter Dandy)*

☆ *York Brewery Tap* YO1 6JT [Toft Green, Micklegate]: Members only for York Brewery's upstairs lounge (annual fee £3 unless you live in York or go on brewery tour), their own full cask range in top condition at bargain price, also bottled beers, nice clubby atmosphere with friendly staff happy to talk about the beers, lots of breweriana and view of brewing plant, comfortable settees and armchairs, magazines and daily papers, brewery shop; no food; children allowed, open 11.30-7, cl Sun *(Sue Demont, Tim Barrow, Peter F Marshall, the Didler, David Carr)*

Yorkshire Terrier YO1 8AS [Stonegate]: York Brewery shop, behind this a smallish well worn in bar with their full beer range, tasting trays of four one-third pints, interesting bottled beers too, winter mulled wine, lunchtime dining room upstairs (where the lavatories are – there's a stair lift) allowing children; soup, sandwiches and limited range of other good value food noon, small light and airy conservatory; open all day *(Pete Coxon, David Carr, WW, Pat and Tony Martin, Mrs Roxanne Chamberlain, Mark and Diane Grist, Dave Webster, Sue Holland, Matt Waite)*

If a pub tries to make you leave a credit card behind the bar, be on your guard. The credit card firms and banks which issue them condemn this practice. After all, the publican who asks you to do this is in effect saying: 'I don't trust you.' Have you any more reason to trust his staff? If your card is used fraudulently while you have let it be kept out of your sight, the card company could say you've been negligent yourself – and refuse to make good your losses. So say that they can 'swipe' your card instead, but must hand it back to you. Please let us know if a pub does try to keep your card.

London

London
Scotland
Wales
Channel Islands

London

Pub prices in London are highly contradictory. On one hand, the beer is very expensive, with many pubs now pricing their pints at well over £3 (though both Sam Smiths beers and pubs in the Wetherspoons chain are much cheaper than that). On the other hand, food prices are much lower than in most parts of the country. Given that the food is often proper home cooking, that makes for real value. A great many of the main entries here have fascinating interiors and histories; the architecture in some is amazing. The Black Friar in central London and the Warrington in west London are remarkably ornate art nouveau buildings. For pubs in central London with handsome original Victorian fittings, head for the Albert, the Argyll Arms, the Lamb, the Princess Louise, and the Red Lion in Duke of York Street (not to be confused with various other Red Lions nearby). There are restored coffee houses, a couple of converted former banks, what was once a vinegar factory, a toll house, stable blocks, an outstanding example of a historic coaching inn, where the Great Train Robbery was planned, even a former fire station. And despite this being a vast metropolis, some London pubs have an engaging country feel: the Nags Head and the Waverton Street Red Lion in central London, the Compton Arms and the Flask in north London, the Old Jail in south London, and the Colton Arms in west London. Certainly in central London, all our main entries do get extremely crowded at peak times, when customers spill out on to the streets and pack out the bars; it's probably best to avoid lunchtime and just after work finishes if you want to enjoy these places at their best. Pubs doing particularly well this year in central London include the Argyll Arms (a lot of character and with a new landlord), the Bishops Finger (a swish little place with ten varieties of sausage), the Black Friar (marvellous décor and super beers), the Cittie of York (a unique old pub with a really interesting back bar), the Dog & Duck (a cosy little gem), the chatty little Harp (new to the *Guide*, a good central refuge), the Jerusalem Tavern (a firm favourite with readers), the Lamb & Flag (extremely popular – well worth avoiding peak times), the Olde Cheshire Cheese (a real mix of customers keen to enjoy its history and character), and the Olde Mitre (a proper refuge from the modern city nearby). In east London, there's the Narrow (Gordon Ramsay's pub and with super food) and the Prospect of Whitby (it is a tourist haven but much liked by our readers); in the north, the Holly Bush (a lovely timeless interior); and in the south, the Anchor & Hope (usually packed for its distinctive food), the Cutty Sark (splendid Thames views), the Founders Arms (again, fine Thames views and a good mix of customers), the Market Porter (fantastic beers), and the Royal Oak (tied to Harveys, with all of their beers). If you want a meal, you can be sure of finding plenty of places offering pies, fish and chips, sausage and mash and so forth (as we say above, prices are extremely fair), but there are also plenty of good gastropubs with imaginative, restaurant-style cooking at comparatively reasonable prices: the

Crown in East London, another new main entry, is a fine example. Run on sound eco values, using only seasonal produce from small producers and producing super food, our London Dining Pub of the Year is the Duke of Cambridge in north London. The Lucky Dip section at the end of the chapter is divided into Central, East, North, South and West (with the pubs grouped by postal district). Outer London suburbs come last, by name, after the numbered postal districts. In this section, Central London pubs currently showing particularly well include the Hamilton Hall (EC2), Lamb (EC3), Banker (EC4), Buckingham Arms (SW1), Audley (W1), Victoria (W2), Chandos and Cross Keys (WC2); in East London, the Pride of Spitalfields (E1); in North London, the Queens Head & Artichoke (NW1); in South London, the Brown Dog (SW13), Telegraph (SW15) and Cats Back (SW18); in West London, the Duke of Sussex (W4) and Anglesea Arms (W6); and in the suburbs, the Kings Arms at Hampton Court and Star at Malden Rushett. London's dominant local brewer is Fullers, now very widely available (Fullers pubs tend to have good wines by the glass, too). The Wells & Youngs beers in Youngs pubs are now brewed out in Bedford; also widely available. The city has about ten much smaller breweries. Meantime is well worth trying, and we also found Twickenham and Grand Union in one or two pubs.

CENTRAL LONDON · MAP 13

Admiral Codrington ♀

Mossop Street; ☻ South Kensington; SW3 2LY

Bustling Chelsea pub with real ales, fine wines, enjoyable lunchtime food and more elaborate evening menu

The bar here has a pleasing café feel with comfortable sofas and cushioned wall seats, neatly polished floorboards and panelling, spotlights in the ceiling and lamps on elegant wooden tables, a handsome central counter, sporting prints on the yellow walls, and house plants around the big bow windows. There's a model ship in a case just above the entrance to the dining room. Black Sheep Best and Shepherd Neame Spitfire on handpump (not cheap, even for round here), and an excellent wine list, with nearly all available by the glass; various coffees, a range of havana cigars, and friendly service from smartly uniformed young staff. There may be piped pop or jazz – though in the evenings it will be drowned out by the sound of animated conversation; the dining room is quieter and especially nice in fine weather when the retractable glass roof slides open. At the side is a little terrace with tables, benches and heaters.

🍴 The lunchtime bar food might include soup, scrambled eggs with smoked salmon, cumberland sausages, grain mustard mash and red onion gravy, home-made rib-eye burger with fontina cheese and dry-cured bacon, tarte tatin of red onion and grilled goats cheese with balsamic dressing, popular fish and chips with tartare sauce, and puddings such as sticky toffee pudding with caramel sauce and rhubarb crème brûlée; evening restaurant dishes like salt and pepper crispy squid with lemon aïoli, seared scallops and rosemary risotto, and veal with caper and anchovy beurre noisette and a fried duck egg; Sunday roast beef. *Starters/Snacks: £4.50 to £6.50. Main Courses: £6.95 to £13.95. Puddings: £5.50*

Punch ~ Lease Alexander Langlands Pearse ~ Real ale ~ Bar food (12-2.30(3.30 Sat), 6.30-11; 12-4, 7-10 Sun) ~ Restaurant ~ (020) 7581 0005 ~ Children welcome ~ Dogs allowed in bar ~ Open 11.30am-midnight; 12-10.30 Sun; closed 24-26 Dec

Recommended by N R White, Tracey and Stephen Groves

Albert

Victoria Street; ✆ St James's Park; SW1H 0NP

Imposing old building with some interesting original features, good value food all day, popular upstairs carvery

There's always a fine mix of customers in this well run, bustling pub – tourists, civil servants and even the occasional MP: the Division Bell is rung to remind them when it's time to get back to Westminster. It's especially busy on weekday lunchtimes and after work but service from the big island counter is efficient and friendly. The original heavily cut and etched windows, running along three sides of the open-plan bar, give the place a surprisingly airy feel, and there's some gleaming mahogany, an ornate ceiling, and good solid comfortable furnishings. Fullers London Pride and Wells & Youngs Bomardier, with guests like Adnams Broadside, Caledonian Deuchars IPA, and Courage Directors on handpump, 24 wines by the glass and a few malt whiskies. The handsome staircase leading up to the dining room is lined with portraits of prime ministers; piped music, fruit machine. Handily placed between Victoria and Westminster, the pub was one of the few buildings in this part of Victoria to escape the Blitz, and is one of the area's most striking sights (though it's now rather dwarfed by the surrounding faceless cliffs of dark modern glass).

🍴 **Usefully and promptly served all day, the good bar food includes sandwiches and filled baguettes, filled baked potatoes, soup, chicken liver and honey pâté with bramley apple chutney, caesar salad, bacon steaks and free-range eggs, fish and chips, various sausages with red onion gravy, beef in ale pie, mushroom risotto, daily specials like cottage pie or lamb hotpot, and puddings such as treacle sponge and custard and profiteroles with chocolate sauce; the upstairs carvery is good, and they also serve afternoon teas.** *Starters/Snacks: £3.49 to £4.75. Main Courses: £6.99 to £11.99. Puddings: £2.99 to £3.19*

Spirit ~ Manager Declan Clancy ~ Real ale ~ Bar food (8am-10pm) ~ Restaurant ~ (020) 7222 5577 ~ Children in eating area of bar if eating, until 9pm ~ Open 8am-11pm(10.30 Sun)

Recommended by Donna and Roger, Darren Le Poidevin, Michael Dandy, Mike and Sue Loseby

Argyll Arms 🍺

Argyll Street; ✆ Oxford Circus, opposite tube side exit; W1F 7TP

Unexpectedly individual pub just off Oxford Street, with interesting little front rooms, appealing range of beers, and good value straightforward food all day

This Victorian pub is always busy, though there's space for drinking outside, and has a surprising amount of genuine character. Particularly unusual are the three atmospheric and secluded little cubicle rooms at the front, essentially unchanged since they were built in the 1860s. All oddly angular, they're made by wooden partitions with remarkable frosted and engraved glass, with hops trailing above. A long mirrored corridor leads to the spacious back room; newspapers to read, two fruit machines, piped music. Black Sheep Best, Caledonian Deuchars IPA, Fullers London Pride, Harviestoun Bitter & Twisted, Shepherd Neame Spitfire, and Timothy Taylors Landlord on handpump, and quite a few malt whiskies. The quieter upstairs bar (with theatrical photographs) overlooks the pedestrianised street – and the Palladium theatre if you can see through the impressive foliage outside the window.

🍴 **Under the new licensee, the decent bar food includes sandwiches, all-day breakfast, fish and chips, steak in ale pie, sunblush tomato ravioli, and puddings like rhubarb and apple crumble and eton mess.** *Starters/Snacks: £3.50 to £5.25. Main Courses: £6.45 to £9.95. Puddings: £3.75*

Mitchells & Butlers ~ Manager Gillian Newman ~ Real ale ~ Bar food (10am-10pm) ~ Restaurant ~ (020) 7734 6117 ~ Children in upstairs bar till 9pm ~ Open 10am-11pm(10.30 Sun); closed 24 Dec

Recommended by the Didler, Joe Green, Mike and Sue Loseby, Mrs Hazel Rainer, Mike Gorton, Michael Dandy, Barry Collett, Derek Thomas, Peter Dandy, Dr and Mrs A K Clarke, Tracey and Stephen Groves, DC, Andrea Rampley

Bishops Finger ♀

West Smithfield – opposite Bart's Hospital; ⊖ ⇄ *Farringdon; EC1A 9JR*

Nicely civilised little pub with particularly welcoming atmosphere, and good beers

Well known for its sausages, this swish little pub has a sparkle to it. Comfortable and smartly civilised, the well laid out bar room has cream walls, big windows, elegant tables with fresh flowers on the polished bare boards, a few pillars, and cushioned chairs under one wall lined with framed prints of the market. It can be busy after work, but rather relaxed and peaceful during the day; the atmosphere is friendly and welcoming. Shepherd Neame Bitter, Spitfire, Bishops Finger and seasonal brews on handpump, with a wide choice of wines (eight by the glass), ten malt whiskies, and several ports and champagnes; friendly, efficient service. There are a couple of tables outside.

🍴 **Most people go for one of the ten or so varieties of sausage from a speciality shop nearby, all served with mash, but they also do sandwiches, burgers, steaks, and specials like gammon, or beer-battered cod.** *Main Courses: £6.50 to £9.95*

Shepherd Neame ~ Manager Paul Potts ~ Real ale ~ Bar food (12-3, 6-9 (not Fri, or weekends)) ~ Restaurant ~ (020) 7248 2341 ~ Children welcome ~ Open 11-11; closed weekends and bank hols

Recommended by N R White, Peter Dandy, Dr and Mrs M E Wilson, John and Gloria Isaacs, Steve Kirby, Michael Dandy, David Hall

Black Friar

Queen Victoria Street; ⊖ ⇄ *Blackfriars; EC4V 4EG*

Remarkable art nouveau décor, a good choice of beers, friendly atmosphere, and decent food all day

Always busy – though it's big enough to swallow the crowds – this old favourite has some unique and quite extraordinary décor, which includes some of the best Edwardian bronze and marble art nouveau work to be found anywhere. The inner back room (known as the Grotto) has big bas-relief friezes of jolly monks set into richly coloured florentine marble walls, an opulent marble-pillared inglenook fireplace, a low vaulted mosaic ceiling, gleaming mirrors, seats built into rich golden marble recesses, and tongue-in-cheek verbal embellishments such as Silence is Golden and Finery is Foolish. See if you can spot the opium-smoking hints modelled into the fireplace of the front room. The other large room has a fireplace and plenty of seats and tables. Fullers London Pride and Timothy Taylors Landlord on handpump are joined by guests such as Harveys Best, St Austell Tribute, and Stonehenge Sign of Spring, and there's a decent range of wines by the glass; piped music, and prompt, friendly service. In the evenings, lots of people spill out on to the wide forecourt, near the approach to Blackfriars Bridge; there's some smart furniture out here (and in spring some rather impressive tulips). If you're coming by Tube, choose your exit carefully – it's all too easy to emerge from the network of passageways and find yourself on the wrong side of the street, or marooned on a traffic island.

🍴 **They specialise in pies such as chicken and asparagus, steak and stilton, or spinach, brie and redcurrant; other traditional meals, served all day, include sausages and mash, steak in ale pie, a vegetarian dish of the day, and fish and chips, some in a choice of sizes.** *Starters/Snacks: £3.50 to £4.95. Main Courses: £6.95 to £9.95. Puddings: £3.65 to £4.65*

Mitchells & Butlers ~ Manager Cecilia Soderholm ~ Real ale ~ Bar food (10-10; 12-10 Sun) ~ (020) 7236 5474 ~ Children welcome until 9pm ~ Open 10am-11pm(11.30 Thurs and Fri); 10-11 Sat; 12-10.30 Sun; closed 25 and 26 Dec

Recommended by Barry Collett, the Didler, N R White, Peter Dandy, Ian Phillips, Eithne Dandy, Tom McLean, Lawrence Pearse, Ewan McCall, Dr and Mrs A K Clarke, C J Fletcher, B and M Kendall, Anthony Longden

---

Pubs with particularly interesting histories, or in unusually interesting buildings, are listed at the back of the book.

Cittie of Yorke 🍺

High Holborn – find it by looking out for its big black and gold clock; ⊖ *Chancery Lane; WC1V 6BN*

Bustling old pub where the splendid back bar with its old-fashioned cubicles rarely fails to impress – and the beer is refreshingly low priced

As popular as ever with a fine mix of customers from students to lawyers, and City types, this is another pub where the building itself is the main attraction. The impressive back bar is rather like a baronial hall, with its extraordinarily extended bar counter stretching off into the distance. There are thousand-gallon wine vats resting above the gantry, big, bulbous lights hanging from the soaring high-raftered roof, and a nice glow from the fire. It can get busy in the evenings, but there's plenty of space to absorb the crowds – and indeed it's at the busiest times that the pub is at its most magnificent (it never feels quite right when it's quiet). Most people tend to congregate in the middle, so you should still be able to bag one of the intimate, old-fashioned and ornately carved booths that run along both sides. As it's a Sam Smiths pub, a bonus is the refreshingly cheap real ale, with the OB on handpump around a pound less than a typical London pint. The triangular Waterloo fireplace, with grates on all three sides and a figure of Peace among laurels, used to stand in the Hall of Grays Inn Common Room until less obtrusive heating was introduced. A smaller, comfortable panelled room has lots of little prints of York and attractive brass lights, while the ceiling of the entrance hall has medieval-style painted panels and plaster York roses. Fruit machine. A pub has stood on this site since 1430, though the current building owes more to the 1695 coffee house erected here behind a garden; it was reconstructed in Victorian times, using 17th-c materials and parts.

🍴 **Served from buffet counters in the main hall and cellar bar, bar food (not perhaps the pub's finest feature) includes sandwiches, soup, and half a dozen daily-changing hot dishes.** *Main Courses: £5.50 to £6.50. Puddings: £2.95*

Sam Smiths ~ Manager Stuart Browning ~ Real ale ~ Bar food (12-3, 5-9; all day Sat) ~ (020) 7242 7670 ~ Children welcome until 5pm ~ Open 11.30(12 Sat)-11; closed Sun, bank hols, 24 and 25 Dec

Recommended by Dr and Mrs A K Clarke, C J Fletcher, P Dawn, Pete Coxon, N R White, Ian Phillips, Ewan McCall, the Didler, Bruce Bird, Barry Collett, Anthony Longden, Dr and Mrs Jackson, Simon Collett-Jones, Phil and Sally Gorton, Tom McLean, Keith and Chris O'Neill

Coopers Arms

Flood Street; ⊖ *Sloane Square, but quite a walk; SW3 5TB*

Well positioned with real ales and decent food, and a useful bolthole for Kings Road shoppers

Relaxed and properly pubby (especially in the evenings), this spacious pub is a useful retreat from the hustle of the Kings Road.The open-plan bar has interesting furnishings such as kitchen chairs and some dark brown plush chairs on the floorboards, a mix of nice old good-sized tables, and a pre-war sideboard and dresser; also, LNER posters and maps of Chelsea and the Thames on the walls, an enormous railway clock, a fireplace with dried flowers, and tea-shop chandeliers – all watched over by the heads of a moose and a tusky boar. Wells & Youngs Bitter, Special, and Waggledance on handpump, and 11 wines by the glass. There are seats in the courtyard garden.

🍴 **Bar food might include club sandwiches, soup, salads like smoked salmon and tiger prawn with aïoli and chicken caesar, spinach and courgette risotto, fish and chips, cumberland sausage with red wine and shallot gravy, home-made steak burger topped with mature cheddar and home-made tomato chutney, and sharing plates of antipasti or baked camembert with rosemary, garlic and crusty bread.** *Starters/Snacks: £6.95 to £9.75. Main Courses: £9.50 to £16.95. Puddings: £5.00*

Youngs ~ Manager Colin Ryan ~ Real ale ~ Bar food (11-10; 12-9 Sun) ~ (020) 7376 3120 ~ Well behaved children allowed until 7pm ~ Dogs allowed in bar ~ Open 11-11; 12-10.30 Sun

Recommended by BOB, Ian Phillips

Cross Keys

Lawrence Street; ↔ Sloane Square, but some distance away; SW3 5NB

Civilised and warmly convivial, with an unusual style and décor, very short choice of bar food, and decent choice of drinks

The designer obviously had some fun while decorating this bustling pub. There's an unusual array of brassware hanging from the rafters, including trumpets and a diver's helmet, as well as animal-skin prints on the furnishings, and quite a mix of sculptures, paintings and objects. The roomy high-ceilinged flagstoned bar also has an island servery, a roaring fire, lots of atmosphere, and a good range of customers; there's a light and airy conservatory-style back restaurant, with an ironic twist to its appealing gardening décor. Courage Directors and Theakstons Best on handpump (not cheap, even for this area), and a good choice of wines by the glass. Attentive young staff; piped music. Like most pubs in the area, this can be busy and lively on Saturday evenings. More reports please.

🍽 The very short bar menu includes club sandwiches, spinach and ricotta ravioli, crispy organic chicken, baked aubergine, steak grilled with rosemary jus, and puddings such as crème brûlée and pavlovas. *Starters/Snacks: £4.50 to £7.40. Main Courses: £11.90 to £16.90. Puddings: £5.90*

Free house ~ Licensee Michael Bertorelli ~ Bar food (12-2.30(4 Sat and Sun), 6-11(10 Sun) ~ Restaurant ~ (020) 7349 9111 ~ Children welcome ~ Dogs allowed in bar ~ Open 11am-midnight; 11-11 Sun; closed bank holidays

Recommended by BOB

Dog & Duck 🐕

Bateman Street, on corner with Frith Street; ↔ Tottenham Court Road, Leicester Square; W1D 3AJ

Tiny Soho pub squeezing in bags of character, with unusual old tiles and mosaics, good beers, and warmly welcoming atmosphere

'A cosy little gem' is how several of our readers describe this pint-sized corner house. A Soho landmark, it hasn't really changed in the last 40 years and has a consistently enjoyable atmosphere. In the evenings it can be very busy indeed, packing a lot of atmosphere into a small space, so afternoons are probably the best time to fully appreciate the décor, which has some interesting detail and individual touches. On the floor near the door is an engaging mosaic showing a dog with its tongue out in hot pursuit of a duck; the same theme is embossed on some of the shiny tiles that frame the heavy old advertising mirrors. There are some high stools by the ledge along the back wall, further seats in a slightly roomier area at one end, and a fire in winter; the piped music is usually drowned out by the good-natured chatter. Fullers London Pride, Timothy Taylors Landlord and two changing guest beers on handpump from the unusual little bar counter; also Addlestone's cider, and 15 wines by the glass. In good weather especially, most people tend to spill on to the bustling street, though even when the pub is at its busiest you may find plenty of space in the rather cosy upstairs bar. The pub is said to be where George Orwell celebrated when the American Book of the Month Club chose *Animal Farm* as its monthly selection. Ronnie Scott's jazz club is near by.

🍽 Served all day, good value bar snacks include quite a range of sausages, from cumberland to venison, juniper berry and gin, as well as sandwiches, a breakfast, burgers, fish and chips, summer salads, rump steak, and puddings. *Starters/Snacks: £3.50. Main Courses: £5.95 to £7.95. Puddings: £3.65*

Mitchells & Butlers ~ Manager Natalie Hubbard ~ Real ale ~ Bar food (10-10; 12-9 Sun) ~ (020) 7494 0697 ~ Children allowed in dining room ~ Dogs allowed in bar ~ Open 10am-11pm(11.30 Fri and Sat); 12-10.30 Sun

Recommended by Dr and Mrs M E Wilson, P Dawn, Ewan McCall, LM, the Didler, Mike Gorton, Mel Smith, Tom McLean

---

We say if we know a pub allows dogs.

Eagle 🍽 ♀

Farringdon Road; opposite Bowling Green Lane car park; ⊖ ⇄ Farringdon, Old Street; EC1R 3AL

Still exceptional for food, London's original gastropub is busy and noisy, with a couple of real ales and quite a few wines by the glass

This was London's first gastropub and to enjoy the mediterranean-style, almost rustic cooking, you must get there before serving time starts, to be sure of a table. On weekday lunchtimes especially (when staff from the *Guardian* offices next door can be a major part of the mix), dishes from the blackboard menu can run out or change fairly quickly. The open-plan room is dominated by the open kitchen, and it's all pretty busy, noisy, and slightly scruffy for some tastes. Furnishings are basic and well worn – school chairs, a random assortment of tables, a couple of sofas on bare boards, and modern paintings on the walls (there's an art gallery upstairs, with direct access from the bar). Wells & Youngs Eagle and Bombardier on handpump, good wines including around 14 by the glass, and decent coffee; piped music (sometimes loud). Not the ideal choice for a quiet dinner, or a smart night out, the pub is generally quieter at weekends.

🍽 **The short choice of very good food might include a proper minestrone soup, sandwiches, linguine with clams, skate with spinach, pine nuts, sultanas and garlic, skirt of beef with rocket and balsamic, leg of lamb with barley, mint and yoghurt salad, and a handful of tapas like smoked salmon in crème fraîche and hot spicy prawns; well chosen cheeses and portuguese custard tarts.** *Starters/Snacks: £4.00 to £6.00. Main Courses: £8.00 to £15.00. Puddings: £1.20*

Free house ~ Licensee Michael Belben ~ Real ale ~ Bar food (12.30-3(3.30 weekends), 6.30-10.30; not Sun evening) ~ (020) 7837 1353 ~ Children welcome ~ Dogs welcome ~ Open 12-11(5 Sun); closed Sun evening, bank hols and a week at Christmas

Recommended by Barry Collett, John and Gloria Isaacs, Andy and Claire Barker, Simon and Mandy King, Conor McGaughey

Grapes 🍺

Shepherd Market; ⊖ Green Park; W1J 7QQ

Genuinely old-fashioned and individual, and always packed in the evenings for the six real ales and thai food

The half a dozen real ales in this engagingly old-fashioned pub continue to draw in the crowds: Fullers London Pride, Sharps Doom Bar, Wells & Youngs Bombardier, and three changing guests on handpump. Genuinely atmospheric, the bar is enjoyable at lunchtime when you can more easily take in its traditional charms, but is perhaps at its best when it's so very busy in the evenings, and the cheery bustle rather adds to the allure. The dimly lit bar has plenty of well worn plush red furnishings, stuffed birds and fish in glass display cases, wooden floors and panelling, a welcoming coal fire, and a snug little alcove at the back. You'll generally see smart-suited drinkers spilling on to the square outside. The pub is in the heart of Shepherd Market, one of Central London's best-kept secrets.

🍽 **As well as thai dishes cooked by a Thai chef, there are also other traditional english dishes like a pie or fish and chips.** *Starters/Snacks: £2.00 to £6.95. Main Courses: £5.95 to £10.95*

Free house ~ Licensees John Shannon, Leigh Kelly ~ Real ale ~ Bar food (12-3.30(2.30 Sat), 5-9.30; 12-5 Sun; not Sun evening) ~ Restaurant ~ (020) 7493 4216 ~ Children allowed until 5pm ~ Open 11.30-11; 12-10.30 Sun

Recommended by the Didler, Conor McGaughey, N R White, Peter Dandy, Michael Dandy, Dr and Mrs A K Clarke, Ian Phillips

---

Children – if the details at the end of a main entry don't mention them, you should assume that the pub does not allow them inside.

Grenadier

Wilton Row; the turning off Wilton Crescent looks prohibitive, but the barrier and watchman are there to keep out cars; walk straight past – the pub is just around the corner; ✪ Knightsbridge; SW1X 7NR

Atmospheric old pub with lots of character and military history – though not much space; famous for its ghost, and its bloody marys

Built in 1720 as the officers' mess for the First Royal Regiment of Foot Guards, this is a cosy and characterful little pub. A portrait of the Duke of Wellington hangs above the fireplace, alongside neat prints of guardsmen through the ages, and there's a sentry box out in front. Even at the busiest of times the atmosphere is good-natured and smartly civilised, and you should generally be able to plonk yourself on one of the stools or wooden benches in the simple, unfussy bar. Fullers London Pride, Shepherd Neame Spitfire, Timothy Taylors Landlord, and Wells & Youngs Bombardier on handpump at the rare pewter-topped bar counter, though on Sundays especially you'll find several of the customers here to sample their famous bloody marys, made to a unique recipe. At the back is an intimate restaurant. There's a single table outside in the attractive mews – surprisingly peaceful given the proximity to Knightsbridge and Hyde Park Corner. They may be closed to all but ticket holders on events such as the anniversary of the Battle of Waterloo, or Wellington's birthday. No children. More reports please.

🍴 Well liked bar food includes sandwiches, soup, garlic pesto mushrooms, chicken liver pâté with damson and elderflower chutney, angels on horseback, a pie of the day, vegetable tart, fish and chips, steak and oyster in ale pie, venison medallions with smoked bacon and onions in a red wine sauce, moroccan-style lamb, beef wellington, and puddings like chocolate pudding and apple pie; Sunday roasts. *Starters/Snacks: £5.25 to £7.95. Main Courses: £9.95 to £17.95. Puddings: £5.95*

Spirit ~ Manager Cynthia Weston ~ Real ale ~ Bar food (12-2.30(4 Sat), 6-9.30; 12-4, 6-8.30 Sun) ~ Restaurant ~ (020) 7235 3074 ~ Dogs allowed in bar ~ Occasional live solo artists ~ Open 12-11(10.30 Sun)

Recommended by Ian Phillips, Simon and Sally Small, N R White, Andrea Rampley, Franki McCabe, Darren Le Poidevin

Guinea

Bruton Place; ✪ Bond Street, Green Park, Piccadilly Circus, Oxford Circus; W1J 6NL

Prize-winning steak and kidney pie in tiny old-fashioned pub with friendly staff, and bustling atmosphere after work – when customers spill on to the street

The main draw to this old-fashioned little place is their steak and kidney pie, served on weekday lunchtimes, though there's a friendly after-work atmosphere, when a mix of suited workers, tourists, and diners for the upmarket restaurant spill out on to the little mews in front, even in winter. Inside, it's almost standing room only, and the look of the place is appealingly simple: bare boards, yellow walls, old-fashioned prints, and a red-planked ceiling with raj fans. Three cushioned wooden seats and tables are tucked to the left of the entrance to the bar, with a couple more in a snug area at the back, underneath a big old clock; most people tend to prop themselves against a little shelf running along the side of the small room. Pleasant, cheery staff serve Wells & Youngs Bitter, Special, and seasonal brews from the striking bar counter, which has some nice wrought-iron work above it. Take care to pick the right entrance – it's all too easy to walk into the upscale Guinea Grill which takes up much of the same building; uniformed doormen will politely redirect you if you've picked the door to that by mistake. No children.

🍴 Served lunchtimes only, the steak and kidney pies (the prize winners) are still the thing here – beyond these, the bar menu is limited to a few elaborate grilled ciabattas (these have won awards too), such as chicken siciliano, or a good one with steak and anchovy; there's also a vegetarian one. The adjacent restaurant serves the pies, albeit more expensively. *Main Courses: £5.50 to £8.50*

Youngs ~ Manager Carl Smith ~ Real ale ~ Bar food (12.30-3, 6-10.30; not Sat lunchtime or Sun) ~ Restaurant ~ (020) 7409 1728 ~ Open 11.30-11; 6-11 Sat; closed Sat lunchtime, all day Sun, bank hols, Christmas and Easter

Recommended by Peter Dandy, Sue Demont, Tim Barrow, the Didler, Derek Thomas, Barry and Anne, N R White

Harp £

47 Chandos Place; ⊖ ⇌ Leicester Square, Charing Cross; WC2N 4HS

Quietly civilised little pub with half a dozen real ales, friendly service, and nice sausages

With six real ales kept well by the warmly friendly landlady, it's not surprising that this rather civilised little pub is so popular. There's an unpretentious, relaxed atmosphere in the long, narrow bar, a mix of quietly chatty customers, lots of high bar stools along the wall counter and around elbow tables, big mirrors on the red walls, some lovely front stained-glass, and lots of interesting if not always well executed star portraits. If it's not too busy you may be able to get one of the prized seats looking out through the front windows. Black Sheep Best, Harveys Best, Timothy Taylors Landlord and three quickly changing guest beers on handpump, decent wines by the glass, farm cider, and a good collection of whiskies. Upstairs, there's a little room with comfortable furniture and a window looking over the road below; you can get out into the back alley, too.

🍴 **Good sausages such as kangaroo, venison, wild boar, pork in ale and so forth served in baps.** *Starters/Snacks: £2.50*

Punch ~ Lease Bridget Walsh ~ Real ale ~ Bar food (11.30-7) ~ (020) 7836 0291 ~ Open 10.30-11; 12-10.30 Sun

Recommended by Jarrod and Wendy Hopkinson, Joe Green, Tracey and Stephen Groves, John Branston, Dr and Mrs M E Wilson, N R White, Michael Dandy

Jerusalem Tavern ★

Britton Street; ⊖ ⇌ Farringdon; EC1M 5UQ

A London favourite, delightfully atmospheric, even at its busiest, with full range of splendid St Peters beers, good lunchtime food, and helpful staff

Still a first class pub and much enjoyed by our readers, this carefully restored old coffee house can get horribly packed just after work towards the end of the week – but you can get a seat a little later in the evening and the staff are always friendly and attentive. It's the only place to stock the whole range of brews from the Suffolk-based St Peter's other than the brewery itself, with half a dozen tapped from casks behind the little bar counter, and the rest available in their elegant, distinctively shaped bottles. Depending on the season you'll find St Peters Best, Golden Ale, Grapefruit, Organic Best, and two other changing guests from their range, and you can buy them to take away too. Particularly inviting when it's candlelit on a cold winter's evening, the pub is a vivid re-creation of a dark 18th-c tavern, seeming so genuinely old that you'd hardly guess the work was done only a few years ago. The current building was developed around 1720, originally as a merchant's house, then becoming a clock and watchmaker's. It still has the shopfront added in 1810, immediately behind which is a light little room with a couple of wooden tables and benches, a stack of *Country Life* magazines, and some remarkable old tiles on the walls at either side. This leads to the tiny dimly lit bar, which has a couple of unpretentious tables on the bare boards, and another up some stairs on a discreetly precarious-feeling though perfectly secure balcony – a prized vantage point. A plainer back room has a few more tables, a fireplace, and a stuffed fox in a case. There may be a couple of tables outside. Note the pub is closed at weekends. The brewery's headquarters in South Elmham is a main entry in our Suffolk chapter. No children.

🍴 **Blackboards list the simple but well liked weekly-changing lunchtime food: sourdough sandwiches with potato wedges, home-made minted lamb burger with chilli aïoli, chickpea, feta and roasted red pepper salad with green pesto, a choice of sausages with gravy, haddock, salmon and prawn pie, ham and organic eggs, beef in ale stew with cream cheese dumplings, and pork cheeks with mushroom sauce.** *Starters/Snacks: £5.00 to £7.50. Main Courses: £8.00 to £9.50*

St Peters ~ Manager Cheryl Jacob ~ Real ale ~ Bar food (12-3, plus 5-9.30 Tues-Thurs evenings only) ~ (020) 7490 4281 ~ Dogs welcome ~ Open 11-11; closed weekends, bank holidays, 25 Dec-1 Jan

Recommended by Anthony Longden, Susan and John Douglas, Ewan McCall, the Didler, Stephen and Jean Curtis, Revd R P Tickle, Michael Dandy, Donna and Roger, Mike Gorton, N R White, Tracey and Stephen Groves, Giles and Annie Francis, Sue Demont, Tim Barrow, P Dawn, Bruce Bird, Peter Dandy

Lamb ★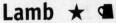

Lamb's Conduit Street; ⊖ Holborn; WC1N 3LZ

Famously unspoilt Victorian pub, full of character, with unique fittings and atmosphere

Quite unchanging, this characterful pub offers a genuine welcome to its many customers. It stands out for its unique Victorian fittings and atmosphere, with the highlight the bank of cut-glass swivelling snob-screens all the way around the U-shaped bar counter. Sepia photographs of 1890s actresses on the ochre panelled walls, and traditional cast-iron-framed tables with neat brass rails around the rim add to the overall effect. It can get busy in the evenings, but there's a very peaceful, relaxed atmosphere at quieter times (particularly the afternoons), when this can be a lovely place to unwind. Wells & Youngs Bitter, Bombardier, and Special on handpump, and a good choice of malt whiskies. No machines or music. There's a snug little room at the back, slatted wooden seats out in front, and more in a little courtyard beyond. Like the street, the pub is named for the kentish clothmaker William Lamb who brought fresh water to Holborn in 1577. No children.

⊞ Standard bar food includes sandwiches, soup, ploughman's, vegetable curry, chicken or lamb burgers, and steak pie. *Starters/Snacks: £4.50 to £5.95. Main Courses: £7.50 to £10.50. Puddings: £3.95 to £4.50*

Youngs ~ Manager Suzanne Simpson ~ Real ale ~ Bar food (12-9) ~ (020) 7405 0713 ~ Open 11am-midnight; 12-10.30 Sun

Recommended by Bruce Bird, Tracey and Stephen Groves, Derek and Sylvia Stephenson, Donna and Roger, Sue Demont, Tim Barrow, the Didler, Derek Thomas, P Dawn, Dr and Mrs A K Clarke, Brian and Anna Marsden, Roy Hoing, James A Waller

Lamb & Flag ▮ £

Rose Street, off Garrick Street; ⊖ Leicester Square; WC2E 9EB

Historic yet unpretentious, full of character and atmosphere; busy in the evenings, it's this area's most interesting pub

In the evenings, this characterful pub is enormously popular with after-work drinkers and visitors. It can be empty at 5pm and cheerfully heaving by 6, and always has an overflow of people chatting in the little alleyways outside, even in winter. It's an unspoilt and in places rather basic old tavern, and the more spartan front room leads into a snugly atmospheric low-ceilinged back bar, with high-backed black settles and an open fire; in Regency times this was known as the Bucket of Blood thanks to the bare-knuckle prize-fights held here. Half a dozen well kept real ales typically include Caledonian Deuchars IPA, Courage Best and Directors, Greene King Abbot, and Wells & Youngs Bitter and Special on handpump; also, a good few malt whiskies. The upstairs Dryden Room is often less crowded, and has more seats (though fewer beers). The pub has a lively and well documented history: Dryden was nearly beaten to death by hired thugs outside, and Dickens made fun of the Middle Temple lawyers who frequented it when he was working in nearby Catherine Street.

⊞ A short choice of simple food is served upstairs, lunchtimes only: soup, baked potatoes, a few daily changing specials like cottage pie, cauliflower cheese or fish and chips, and a choice of roasts. *Starters/Snacks: £4.00 to £5.75. Main Courses: £6.25 to £8.50*

Free house ~ Licensees Terry Archer and Adrian and Sandra Zimmerman ~ Real ale ~ Bar food (11-3 Mon-Fri; 11-5.30 weekends) ~ (020) 7497 9504 ~ Children in upstairs dining room lunchtime only ~ Open 11-11(11.40 Fri and Sat); 12-10.30 Sun; closed 25 and 26 Dec, 1 Jan

Recommended by Derek Thomas, Dr Kevan Tucker, Ewan McCall, Michael Dandy, Mike and Sue Loseby, Dr and Mrs Jackson, Tom McLean, the Didler, Ian Phillips, Rosemary K Germaine, N R White

---

Please tell us if the décor, atmosphere, food or drink at a pub is different from our description. We rely on readers' reports to keep us up to date: feedback@thegoodpubguide.co.uk or (no stamp needed) The Good Pub Guide, FREEPOST TN1569, Wadhurst, E Sussex TN5 7BR.

Lord Moon of the Mall ◖ £

Whitehall; ⊖ ⇌ Charing Cross; SW1A 2DY

Superior Wetherspoons pub with excellent value food and drink in perfect location close to all the sights; up to nine real ales, often unusual

Incredible value for both food and drink, this Wetherspoons pub is in a nicely converted former bank, and is handy for families and visitors touring the nearby sights. The impressive main room has a splendid high ceiling and quite an elegant feel, with old prints, big arched windows looking out over Whitehall, and a huge painting that seems to show a well-to-do 18th-c gentleman; in fact it's Tim Martin, founder of the Wetherspoons chain. Once through an arch the style is more recognisably Wetherspoons, with a couple of neatly tiled areas and bookshelves opposite the long bar; silenced fruit machines, trivia, and a cash machine. There's a fine range of real ales, including rapidly changing guests: Batemans Hooker, Bath Ales Festivity, Cotleigh Tawny, Evans Evans FBA, Fullers London Pride, Grand Union Liberty Blonde, Greene King Abbot, and Oakham Inferno on handpump, and Weston's cider. The back doors (now only an emergency exit) were apparently built as a secret entrance for the bank's account holders living in Buckingham Palace (Edward VII had an account here from the age of three). As you come out, Nelson's Column is immediately to the left, and Big Ben a walk of ten minutes or so to the right.

🍴 **Good value bar food from the standard Wetherspoons menu includes sandwiches, bangers and mash, barbecue chicken melt, beef in ale pie (extra gravy in a little boat), liver and bacon, and puddings like rhubarb, apple and ginger crumble with ice-cream.** *Main Courses: £6.50 to £8.00. Puddings: £2.50 to £4.00*

Wetherspoons ~ Manager Jay Blower ~ Real ale ~ Bar food (9am-11pm) ~ (020) 7839 7701 ~ Children welcome till 7pm if eating ~ Open 9am-11.30pm(midnight Fri and Sat; 11pm Sun)

Recommended by Ian Phillips, Richard, E McCall, T McLean, D Irving, Meg and Colin Hamilton, Phil Bryant, Peter Dandy, Keith and Chris O'Neill, Dr and Mrs A K Clarke, Alan Thwaite, Michael Dandy

Nags Head ◖

Kinnerton Street; ⊖ Knightsbridge; SW1X 8ED

Genuinely unspoilt pub, its distinctive bar filled with theatrical mementoes, and friendly locals

Very un-london, this is one of the city's most unspoilt pubs hidden away in an attractive and peaceful mews, and rarely getting too busy or crowded. There's a snugly relaxed, cosy feel in the small, panelled and low-ceilinged front room, where friendly regulars sit chatting around the unusual sunken bar counter. The seats by the log-effect gas fire in an old cooking range are snapped up pretty quickly and a narrow passage leads down steps to an even smaller back bar with stools and a mix of comfortable seats. Adnams Best, Broadside and Regatta are pulled on attractive 19th-c china, pewter and brass handpumps, while other interesting old features include a 1930s what-the-butler-saw machine and a one-armed bandit that takes old pennies. The piped music is rather individual: often jazz, folk or 1920s-40s show tunes, and around the walls are drawings of actors and fading programmes from variety performances. There are a few seats and sometimes a couple of tables outside. The landlord's individual style of management gives the pub its particular personality, which appeals a lot to many readers though not perhaps to all.

🍴 **Bar food (which often sells out) includes sandwiches, ploughman's, salads, sausage, mash and beans, chilli con carne, daily specials, and a choice of roasts; there's usually a £1.50 surcharge added to all dishes in the evenings, and at weekends.** *Starters/Snacks: £4.50 to £5.50. Main Courses: £6.50 to £8.50. Puddings: £3.50 to £4.50*

Free house ~ Licensee Kevin Moran ~ Real ale ~ Bar food (11-9.30; 12-9.30 Sun) ~ (020) 7235 1135 ~ Children welcome ~ Dogs allowed in bar ~ Open 11-11; 12-10.30 Sun

Recommended by Pete Baker, the Didler, John and Gloria Isaacs, Sue Demont, Tim Barrow, LM, Barry and Anne

---

There are report forms at the back of the book.

Old Bank of England ♀

Fleet Street; ⊖ *Temple; EC4A 2LT*

Dramatically converted former bank building, with gleaming chandeliers in impressive, soaring bar, well kept Fullers beers, and good pies

The opulent décor here can take your breath away and visitors from abroad are quite amazed by its sheer scale. It's a splendid conversion of a former branch of the Bank of England which you can best appreciate at quieter times (perhaps not straight after work). The soaring, spacious bar has three gleaming chandeliers hanging from the exquisitely plastered ceiling, high above an unusually tall island bar counter, crowned with a clock. The end wall has big paintings and murals that look like 18th-c depictions of Justice, but in fact feature members of the Fuller, Smith and Turner families, who run the brewery the pub belongs to. There are well polished dark wooden furnishings, plenty of framed prints, and, despite the grandeur, some surprisingly cosy corners, with screens between some of the tables creating an unexpectedly intimate feel which readers really enjoy. Tables in a quieter galleried section upstairs offer a bird's-eye view of the action, and some smaller rooms (used mainly for functions) open off. Fullers Chiswick, Discovery, ESB, London Pride and seasonal brews on handpump, a good choice of malt whiskies, and a dozen wines by the glass. At lunchtimes the piped music is generally classical or easy listening; it's louder and livelier in the evenings. There's also a garden with seats (one of the few pubs in the area to have one). Pies have a long if rather dubious pedigree in this area; it was in the vaults and tunnels below the Old Bank and the surrounding buildings that Sweeney Todd butchered the clients destined to provide the fillings in his mistress Mrs Lovett's nearby pie shop. No children.

🍴 **Available all day, the good bar food has an emphasis on well liked homemade pies such as sweet potato and goats cheese, chicken, broccoli or gammon, leek and whole grain mustard, but also includes sandwiches, soup, welsh rarebit, ploughman's, sausages and mash, lemon chicken and courgette salad, and fish and chips. Also, puddings like banoffi pie and spotted dick, and afternoon teas.** *Main Courses: £8.50 to £10.00. Puddings: £3.95 to £4.50*

Fullers ~ Manager Jo Farquhar ~ Real ale ~ Bar food (12-9) ~ (020) 7430 2255 ~ Open 11-11; closed weekends, bank hols

Recommended by Bruce Bird, Peter Dandy, P Dawn, the Didler, Barry Collett, Anthony Longden, Dr and Mrs A K Clarke, Ian Phillips, David and Sue Smith, Tracey and Stephen Groves, N R White, Michael Dandy

Olde Cheshire Cheese

Wine Office Court, off 145 Fleet Street; ⊖ ⇌ *Blackfriars; EC4A 2BU*

Much bigger than it looks, soaked in history, with lots of warmly old-fashioned rooms, cheap Sam Smiths beer, and a convivial atmosphere

Over the years Congreve, Pope, Voltaire, Thackeray, Dickens, Conan Doyle, Yeats and perhaps Dr Johnson have all called in to this 17th-c former chop house. Many of the warren of dark, historic rooms have hardly changed since, and although it can get busy with tourists, there are plenty of hidden corners to absorb the crowds. The unpretentious rooms have bare wooden benches built in to the walls, bare boards, and, on the ground floor, high beams, crackly old black varnish, Victorian paintings on the dark brown walls, and big open fires in winter. A particularly snug room is the tiny one on the right as you enter, but the most rewarding bit is the Cellar Bar, down steep narrow stone steps that look as if they're only going to lead to the loo, but in fact take you to an unexpected series of cosy areas with stone walls and ceilings, and some secluded alcoves. Sam Smiths OB on handpump, as usual for this brewery, extraordinarily well priced (over £1 less than the beer in some of our other London main entries). Service from smartly dressed staff is helpful, though sometimes less quick for food than it is for drinks. In the early 20th c the pub was well known for its famous parrot that for over 40 years entertained princes, ambassadors, and other distinguished guests; she's still around today, stuffed and silent, in the restaurant on the ground floor.

🍴 **Bar food includes macaroni cheese, fish and chips, lamb shank, pheasant, and puddings such as sticky toffee pudding; the cellar serves a lunchtime pie and mash buffet.** *Main Courses: £5.95 to £7.75. Puddings: £2.95*

Sam Smiths ~ Manager Gordon Garrity ~ Real ale ~ Bar food (12-10; not Sun) ~ Restaurant ~ (020) 7353 6170 ~ Children allowed in eating area ~ Open 11-11; 12-4 Sun; closed Sun evening

Recommended by LM, Anthony Longden, Eithne Dandy, Richard Marjoram, the Didler, Barry Collett, Roy and Lindsey Fentiman, Dr and Mrs M E Wilson, N R White, Bruce Bird, B and M Kendall, Phil and Sally Gorton, C J Fletcher, P Dawn, Peter Dandy, Sue Demont, Tim Barrow

Olde Mitre 🍺 £

Ely Place; the easiest way to find it is from the narrow passageway beside 8 Hatton Garden; ⊖ *Chancery Lane; EC1N 6SJ*

Hard to find but well worth it – an unspoilt old pub with lovely atmosphere, unusual guest beers, and bargain toasted sandwiches

'This really is a gem,' say several of our readers. It's a lovely little pub and a refuge from the modern city nearby, with unspoilt and cosy small rooms, lots of dark panelling, as well as antique settles and – particularly in the popular back room, where there are more seats – old local pictures and so forth. It gets good-naturedly packed between 12.30 and 2.15, filling up again in the early evening, but in the early afternoons and by around 9pm becomes a good deal more tranquil. An upstairs room, mainly used for functions, may double as an overflow at peak periods. Adnams Bitter and Broadside, Caledonian Deuchars IPA, and a guest like Bearton Kodiak Gold on handpump; friendly service from the convivial landlord and obliging staff. No music, TV or machines – the only games here are cribbage and dominoes. There's some space for outside drinking by the pot plants and jasmine in the narrow yard between the pub and St Ethelreda's church (which is worth a look). Note the pub doesn't open weekends. The iron gates that guard one entrance to Ely Place are a reminder of the days when the law in this district was administered by the Bishops of Ely. The best approach is from Hatton Garden, walking up the right-hand side away from Chancery Lane; an easily missed sign on a lamppost points the way down a narrow alley. No children.

🍴 **Served all day, bar snacks are limited to scotch eggs, pork pies and sausage rolls, and really good value toasted sandwiches with cheese, ham, pickle or tomato.** *Starters/Snacks: £0.60 to £1.95*

Punch ~ Managers Eamon and Kathy Scott ~ Real ale ~ Bar food (11.30-9.30) ~ No credit cards ~ (020) 7405 4751 ~ Open 11-11; closed weekends, bank holidays, 25 Dec, and 1 Jan

Recommended by the Didler, Tracey and Stephen Groves, N R White, Dr and Mrs Jackson, Phil and Sally Gorton, Steve Kirby, Tom McLean, Ewan McCall, Joe Green, Sue Demont, Tim Barrow, Anthony Longden, P Dawn

Princess Louise

High Holborn; ⊖ *Holborn; WC1V 7EP*

Beautifully refurbished Victorian gin-palace with fabulously extravagant décor

After a major refurbishment, this splendid Victorian gin-palace has been restored to its former glory. It had been created by the finest craftsmen of the day and the gloriously opulent main bar once again has wood and glass partitions in lots of different areas, splendid etched and gilt mirrors, brightly coloured and fruity-shaped tiles, and slender portland stone columns soaring towards the lofty and deeply moulded plaster ceiling. Its architectural appeal is unique (even the gents' has its own preservation order) but the pub has also won praise for its friendly, bustling atmosphere, and of course its very nicely priced Sam Smiths OB on handpump from the long main bar counter. It's generally quite crowded on early weekday evenings (for some, adding to the appeal), but is usually quieter later on. No children.

🍴 **From a menu limited to pies, there might be steak in ale, cottage, chicken and mushroom, and fish.** *Main Courses: £5.95. Puddings: £2.90*

Sam Smiths ~ Manager Campbell Mackay ~ Real ale ~ Bar food ~ (020) 7405 8816 ~
Open 11-11; 12-11(10.30 Sun) Sat; closed 25 and 26 Dec, 1 Jan
Recommended by the Didler, Mike Gorton, Bruce Bird, Joe Green, Barry Collett, Tom McLean, Ewan McCall

Red Lion

Duke of York Street; **⊖** *Piccadilly Circus; SW1Y 6JP*

Remarkably preserved Victorian pub, all gleaming mirrors and polished mahogany, though right in the heart of town, so does get busy

It's probably best to come to this remarkably well preserved Victorian pub at opening time to appreciate its period charms in peace and quiet. When it was built its profusion of mirrors was said to enable the landlord to keep a watchful eye on local prostitutes, but the gleaming glasswork isn't the only feature of note: the series of small rooms also has a good deal of polished mahogany, as well as crystal chandeliers and cut and etched windows, and a striking ornamental plaster ceiling. Fullers London Pride, Jennings Cumberland, Timothy Taylors Landlord, and changing guests like Elgoods Golden Newt, Moorhouses Black Cat, O'Hanlons Yellowhammer, and Skinners Betty Stogs on handpump. Diners have priority on a few of the front tables. It can be very crowded at lunchtime and early evening (try inching through to the back room where there's sometimes more space); many customers spill out on to the pavement, in front of a mass of foliage and flowers cascading down the wall. No children.

🍽 **Now served all day, simple dishes include sandwiches, filled baked potatoes, salads, pies like steak and stilton and cottage, and fish and chips.** *Starters/Snacks: £3.50 to £4.50. Main Courses: £5.95 to £8.95. Puddings: £2.65 to £3.65*

Mitchells & Butlers ~ Manager Paul McCallion ~ Real ale ~ Bar food (11-9.45) ~
(020) 7321 0782 ~ Open 11-11; closed Sun, bank hols
Recommended by Dr and Mrs A K Clarke, the Didler, Michael Dandy, Dr and Mrs M E Wilson, N R White, Sue Demont, Tim Barrow, Tracey and Stephen Groves, LM, Barry and Anne

Red Lion

Waverton Street; **⊖** *Green Park; W1J 5QN*

Civilised Mayfair pub with the feel of a village local, particularly welcoming service, and enjoyably cosy atmosphere; good beers and food, too

Built in the 1820s for the servants and tradesmen of the mansions, this comfortably civilised pub is in one of Mayfair's quietest and prettiest corners. It feels like a rather smart village local, and on warm evenings you'll generally find plenty of drinkers chatting outside. It can get very busy indeed after work, but always keeps its warmly cosy feel. The main L-shaped bar has small winged settles on the partly carpeted scrubbed floorboards, and carefully framed London prints below the high shelf of china on the well polished, dark-panelled walls. Greene King IPA, Hydes 1863, Woodfordes Wherry, and a guest beer on handpump, and they do rather good bloody marys (with a Very Spicy option); also a dozen malt whiskies, and around 14 wines by the glass; friendly, smiling service. The gents' usually has a copy of *The Times* at eye level.

🍽 **Good, honest bar food (served from a corner at the front) includes sandwiches, good toasties, soup, ploughman's, cumberland sausage and mash, battered haddock, scampi, steak and stilton pie, and daily specials.** *Starters/Snacks: £2.95 to £4.00. Main Courses: £7.50 to £8.50. Puddings: £4.00*

Punch ~ Manager Greg Peck ~ Real ale ~ Bar food (12-3 (not weekends), 6-9.30; not Sun) ~
Restaurant ~ (020) 7499 1307 ~ Children in restaurant ~ Dogs allowed in bar ~ Open 12-11;
6-11 Sat; 6-10.30 Sun; closed Sat lunchtime, all day Sun, bank hols, 25 Dec, and 1 Jan
Recommended by Barry and Anne, Jeremy King, Sue Demont, Tim Barrow, N R White, Ian Phillips, Giles and Annie Francis

It's very helpful if you let us know up-to-date food prices when you report on pubs.

Salisbury ♀ ◀

St Martins Lane; ➔ Leicester Square; WC2N 4AP

Gleaming Victorian pub surviving unchanged in the heart of the West End, good atmosphere, wide choice of drinks; it does get crowded

Not much has changed in this Victorian pub since it was opened in 1892. There's a wealth of cut glass and mahogany, and the busily pubby main bar is perhaps best enjoyed mid-afternoon on a weekday – it can be rather packed in the evenings. A curved upholstered wall seat creates the impression of several distinct areas, framed by wonderfully ornate bronze light fittings shaped like ethereal nymphs each holding stems of flowers; there are only four of these, but mirrors all around make it seem as though there are more, and that the room extends much further than it does. A back room, popular for eating, has plenty more glasswork, and there's a separate little side room with its own entrance. On the walls are old photographs and prints, and, tucked behind the main door, a well known picture of Marianne Faithfull taken here in 1964. Every inch of the walls and ceiling around the stairs down to the lavatories is coated with theatre posters (the pub is right in the heart of the West End). Cheerful staff serve six real ales such as Caledonian Deuchars IPA, Wadworths 6X, Wells & Youngs Bitter and Bombardier, and guests like Hook Norton Old Hooky, Fox Branthill Best, and Timothy Taylors Landlord on handpump, as well as almost 20 wines by the glass, coffees, and summer Pimms. There are some fine details on the exterior of the building too, and tables in a pedestrianised side alley.

🍴 **Bar food includes sandwiches, filled baked potatoes, soup, speciality pies and sausages, popular fish and chips, chicken kiev, and plenty of pasta dishes and salads.** *Starters/Snacks: £3.25 to £3.99. Main Courses: £5.50 to £8.75. Puddings: £2.99 to £3.75*

Spirit ~ Manager Jas Teensa ~ Bar food (12-9.30) ~ (020) 7836 5863 ~ Children allowed in inside bar only till 5pm ~ Open 11-11(11.30 Thurs, midnight Fri); 12-12(10.30 Sun) Sat; closed 25 Dec

Recommended by Joe Green, the Didler, N R White, Alan Thwaite, David M Smith, Mike Gorton, Michael Dandy, Pete Coxon

Seven Stars ◀

Carey Street; ➔ Holborn (just as handy from Temple or Chancery Lane, but the walk through Lincoln's Inn Fields can be rather pleasant); WC2A 2JB

Quirky pub with cheerful landlady, an interesting mix of customers, and good choice of drinks

At its best when the cheerful landlady is here, this popular little pub faces the back of the Law Courts and is therefore a favourite with lawyers and reporters covering notable trials – it has plenty of caricatures of barristers and judges on the red-painted walls of the two main rooms. There are also posters of legal-themed british films, big ceiling fans, and a relaxed, intimate atmosphere; checked table cloths add a quirky, almost continental touch. A third area is in what was formerly a legal wig shop next door – it still retains the original frontage, with a neat display of wigs in the window. Despite the extra space, the pub can fill up very quickly, with lots of the tables snapped up by people here for the often individual food. Adnams Best and Broadside, Black Sheep Best, and Harveys Best on handpump, and they might mix a proper martini. On busy evenings there's an overflow of customers on to the quiet road in front; things generally quieten down after 8pm, and there can be a nice, sleepy atmosphere some afternoons. The Elizabethan stairs up to the lavatories are rather steep, but there's a good strong handrail. Tom Paine, the large and somewhat po-faced pub cat, remains very much a centre of attention. The licensees have a second pub, the Bountiful Cow, on Eagle Street near Holborn, which specialises in beef. No children.

🍴 **Changing daily, the blackboard menu might include dill-cured herring with potato salad, mussels, a plate of charcuterie, tabbouleh with merguez sausage, beef and potato pie, half a corn-fed chicken, and vegetarian chinese stir fry.** *Starters/Snacks: £5.00 to £9.00. Main Courses: £9.00 to £16.50. Puddings: £4.00 to £7.00*

Enterprise ~ Lease Roxy Beaujolais ~ Real ale ~ Bar food (12-3, 5-9 weekdays, 1-4, 6-9 weekends) ~ Restaurant ~ (020) 7242 8521 ~ Open 11-11; 12-11 Sat; 12-10.30 Sun; closed some bank hols (usually including Christmas)

Recommended by Pete Coxon, David and Sue Smith, Ewan McCall, Joe Green, Ian Phillips, the Didler, Tracey and Stephen Groves, N R White, Bruce Bird, Dr and Mrs A K Clarke, Humphry and Angela Crum Ewing, Sue Demont, Tim Barrow, Tom McLean, Anthony Longden, P Dawn, Phil and Sally Gorton, Edward Mirzoeff

Star ◖

Belgrave Mews West, behind the German Embassy, off Belgrave Square; ⊖ Knightsbridge; SW1X 8HT

Refurbished, bustling local with restful bar, new upstairs dining room, Fullers ales, and colourful hanging baskets

Just refurbished, this pleasant pub now has sash windows, wooden floors, and an upstairs dining room. The small bar has a restful local feel outside peak times (when it is busy), stools by the counter and tall windows, an arch leading to the main seating area with well polished tables and chairs, and improved lighting. Fullers Chiswick, Discovery, ESB, and London Pride with a changing guest beer on handpump. The pub is said to be where the Great Train Robbery was planned. The astonishing array of hanging baskets and flowering tubs makes a lovely sight in summer. No children.

🍴 **Bar food includes rib-eye steak baguette, seared scallops, chicken burger, slow braised lamb shank, calves liver and bacon, steak and kidney in ale pie, Saturday all-day breakfasts, and Sunday roasts.** *Starters/Snacks: £3.70 to £6.20. Main Courses: £7.80 to £13.50. Puddings: £3.50 to £4.50*

Fullers ~ Managers Jason and Karen Tinklin ~ Real ale ~ Bar food (12-2, 5-9; 12-7 weekends) ~ (020) 7235 3019 ~ Dogs allowed in bar ~ Open 11.30(11 Sat)-11; 12-10.30 Sun; closed 25 and 26 Dec, 1 Jan

Recommended by N R White, the Didler, Sue Demont, Tim Barrow

EAST LONDON   MAP 12

Crown ♀

Grove Road/Old Ford Road, E3; ⊖ Mile End; E3 5SN

Stylish new dining pub with civilised bar, interesting food and choice of moods in upstairs dining rooms

Light and airy and full of lively chat, this sizeable pub has had a complete makeover. The bar is relaxed and informal, with contemporary furnishings, Greene King East Green and Endeavour and Sharps Doom Bar on handpump, and a good choice of wines by the glass. There are high bar stools covered with faux animal hides by the simple bar counter, two-person stools in the same material around chunky pine tables on the polished boards, candles in coloured glass holders, a big bay window with a comfortable built-in seated area with cushions in browns, pinks and greens, a brown leather sofa beside a couple of cream easy chairs, and a scattering of books and objects on open shelves. Upstairs, the three individually decorated dining areas – again, with simple contemporary but stylish furniture on carpeted or wooden floors – overlook Victoria Park.

🍴 **From a sensibly short menu, the lunchtime food might include granary bread topped with honey-baked ham and mustard mayonnaise or smoked salmon with horseradish cream, soup, ham hock terrine with marinated beetroot, burgers, cumberland sausage, and apple, sage and prune meatballs with chicken liquor, with evening dishes such as devilled kidneys, potted shrimps, fried gnocchi with tomato fondue and parmesan, jellied eels with parsley sauce, and peppered rib-eye steak; puddings like lemon tart with chantilly cream and pistachio and olive oil cake with strawberries.** *Starters/Snacks: £4.50 to £7.00. Main Courses: £8.50 to £17.00. Puddings: £3.50 to £5.00*

Geronimo Inns ~ Lease Tanya Stafford ~ Real ale ~ Bar food (12-3, 7-10; 12-5 Sun; not Sun evening) ~ Restaurant ~ (020) 8880 7261 ~ Children allowed until 3pm ~ Dogs allowed in bar ~ Open 12-11

Recommended by BOB

Grapes

Narrow Street; ⊖ Shadwell (some distance away) or Westferry on the Docklands Light Railway; the Limehouse link has made it hard to find by car – turn off Commercial Road at signs for Rotherhithe tunnel, then from the Tunnel Approach slip road, fork left leading into Branch Road, turn left and then left again into Narrow Street; E14 8BP

Relaxed waterside pub, unchanged since Dickens knew it, with particularly appealing cosy back room, helpful friendly staff, well liked Sunday roasts, and good upstairs fish restaurant

This 16th-c place is a pub for all seasons. In winter, there's an open fire in the cosy back part, and in summer, the small back balcony is a fine place for a sheltered waterside drink, and steps lead down to the foreshore. The chatty, partly panelled bar has lots of prints, mainly of actors, and old local maps, as well as some elaborately etched windows, plates along a shelf, and newspapers to read. The pub remains almost exactly as Charles Dickens knew it – all the more remarkable considering the ultra-modern buildings that now surround it. Piped classical or jazz, and board games. Adnams Best, Marstons Pedigree, Timothy Taylors Landlord, and a guest like Shepherd Neame Bishops Finger on handpump, a choice of malt whiskies, and a good wine list; efficient, friendly service. The upstairs fish restaurant is very good, with fine views of the river. The pub was a favourite with Rex Whistler, who used it as the viewpoint for his rather special river paintings. No children.

🍴 Decent bar food includes soup, sandwiches, ploughman's, bangers and mash, home-made fishcakes with caper sauce, popular fish and chips, a Saturday brunch, and a highly regarded, generous Sunday roast (no other meals then, when it can be busy, particularly in season). *Starters/Snacks: £3.60 to £5.95. Main Courses: £7.50 to £7.95. Puddings: £3.60*

Free house ~ Licensee Barbara Haigh ~ Real ale ~ Bar food (12-2.30, 7-9.30; 12-4; not Sun evening) ~ Restaurant ~ (020) 7987 4396 ~ Dogs allowed in bar ~ Open 12-3.30, 5.30-11; 12-11 Sat; 12-10.30 Sun; closed 25 Dec, 1 Jan

Recommended by N R White, Andy and Jill Kassube, Mike Gorton, David Hall, LM, Edward Leetham, Derek Thomas, Steve Kirby

Narrow

Narrow Street; ⊖ ⇌ Limehouse; E14 8DJ

Stylish and popular with interesting contemporary food, real ales, good wines by the glass, and seats outside on waterside terrace; will need to book well ahead

Of course, most customers come here to eat, given that the owner of this stylish place is Gordon Ramsay. It's modern, brasserie-style fare rather than fine restaurant dining, and although there are a few bar snacks, the main menu is served only in the small, sunny dining room (with limited tables), and you may need to book up some time in advance. The bar itself – nicely lightened up but with a pubby feel – is simple and smart, with white-painted walls and ceilings, and dark blue doors and woodwork. There are two mosaic-tiled fireplaces, each with a mirror above, a couple of hat stands, and some colourfully striped armchairs; piped music. Caledonian Deuchars IPA, Fullers London Pride and perhaps a guest on handpump at the long bar counter, which also has a good range of bottled beers, and a varied wine list. The dining room is white too, with a glass skylight and big window, the floors are polished wood, and the furnishings simple, matching, and dark; on the walls are maps and prints of the area, and a couple of oars. This room now opens on to the sizeable terrace where there are plenty of riverside tables with views around a breezy bend of the Thames.

🍴 Excellent quality bar snacks include a mug of soup, potted salt beef with pickles, welsh rarebit, devilled lambs kidneys, ploughman's, fishcake with tartare sauce, cocktail sausages with grain mustard mayonnaise, and dressed crab or half lobster; from the main menu there might be soup, smoked ham hock terrine with home-made piccalilli, hake and chips with marrowfat peas, chicken, mushroom and tarragon pie, old spot bangers with champ and onion gravy, braised lamb neck, confit duck leg with port sauce, and puddings like chocolate tart with hokey pokey ice-cream and earl grey tea cream with goosnargh cakes. *Starters/Snacks: £5.50 to £6.50. Main Courses: £8.00 to £15.50. Puddings: £4.50 to £5.50*

Free house ~ Licensee Marina Anderson ~ Real ale ~ Bar food (12-3, 6-11; 12-4, 5-11 Sat) ~
Restaurant ~ (020) 7592 7950 ~ Children in restaurant only ~ Open 12-11(10.30 Sun)

Recommended by Tina and David Woods-Taylor, Mike Gorton

Prospect of Whitby

Wapping Wall; ⊖ Wapping; E1W 3SH

**Waterside pub with colourful history and good river views – welcoming to visitors and
families**

Although this cheerful place rather plays upon its colourful history (which tourists love
and it's a favourite with evening coach tours), this is all part of the fun. It claims to be
the oldest pub on the Thames (dating back to 1543), and for a long while was better
known as the Devil's Tavern, thanks to its popularity with smugglers and other ne'er-do-
wells. Pepys and Dickens both regularly popped in, Turner came for weeks at a time to
study the scene, and in the 17th c the notorious Hanging Judge Jeffreys was able to
combine two of his interests by enjoying a drink at the back while looking down over
the grisly goings-on in Execution Dock. Plenty of bare beams, bare boards, panelling and
flagstones in the L-shaped bar (where the long pewter counter is over 400 years old),
and an unbeatable river view towards Docklands from tables in the waterfront courtyard.
Adnams Best, Courage Directors, Fullers London Pride, Greene King IPA and Old Speckled
Hen, and Timothy Taylors Landlord on handpump, 22 wines by the glass, and a dozen
malt whiskies; very friendly, efficient staff.

🍴 Bar food includes sandwiches, fish and chips, burgers, steak and mushroom pie, and
puddings like chocolate fondant and treacle sponge pudding. *Starters/Snacks: £3.50 to
£4.99. Main Courses: £7.99 to £9.95. Puddings: £3.99*

Spirit ~ Manager Terry Standing ~ Real ale ~ Bar food (12-9.45) ~ (020) 7481 1095 ~
Children welcome ~ Dogs welcome ~ Occasional live music ~ Open 12-11(midnight Fri and Sat);
12-10.30 Sun

Recommended by the Didler, Stuart and Alison Ballantyne, Ross Balaam

NORTH LONDON   MAP 13

Chapel 🍴 🍷

Chapel Street; ⊖ Edgware Road; NW1 5DP

**Very good food in bustling modern gastropub; it does get busy and sometimes noisy – all
part of the atmosphere**

This is very much a gastropub with good, contemporary food. There's a rather
cosmopolitan atmosphere – perhaps more relaxed and civilised at lunchtime, when it's a
favourite with chic local office workers, and then altogether busier and louder in the
evenings. The cream-painted rooms are light and spacious and dominated by the open
kitchen, and the furnishings are smart but simple, with plenty of plain wooden tables
around the bar, a couple of comfortable sofas at the lounge end, and a big fireplace. You
may have to wait for a table during busier periods. A real bonus is the spacious and
rather calming outside terrace with canopies and heaters. Adnams Best and Greene King
IPA on handpump, a decent choice of wines by the glass, cappuccino and espresso, fresh
orange juice, and a choice of tisanes such as peppermint or strawberry and vanilla. In
the evening trade is more evenly split between diners and drinkers, and the music is
more noticeable then, especially at weekends. More reports please.

🍴 As well as a choice of antipasti, the interesting food might include unusual soups,
lunchtime open sandwiches, rosemary and sultana calves liver pâté, deep-fried brie with
cranberry sauce, goats cheese wrapped in parma ham with tomato marmalade, feta, cherry
tomato, peppers, red onion and cucumber greek salad with pitta bread and tzatziki, wok-
fried goose breast with ginger sauce and berries, fillet of sea bream with potato, tomato,
aubergine and onion gratin, chargrilled rib-eye steak with red wine sauce, and puddings
such as banoffi pie and Baileys crème brûlée. *Starters/Snacks: £4.00 to £6.00. Main Courses:
£8.50 to £15.50. Puddings: £4.50*

Punch ~ Lease Lakis Hondrogiannis ~ Real ale ~ Bar food (12-2.30, 7-10) ~ (020) 7402 9220 ~
Children welcome ~ Dogs welcome ~ Open 12-11(10.30 Sun); closed 25-26 Dec, Easter
Recommended by Sue Demont, Tim Barrow

Compton Arms £

Compton Avenue, off Canonbury Road; ⊖ ⇌ Highbury & Islington; N1 2XD

Tiny, well run pub with particularly good value food, and very pleasant garden

Just a mile from the city and tucked away in a quiet mews, this tiny, well run place has a real pubby atmosphere and feels like an appealing village local. The unpretentious low-ceilinged rooms are simply furnished with wooden settles and assorted stools and chairs, with local pictures on the walls; TV (one reader feels it might be used a bit too much). Greene King Abbot and IPA and a couple of changing guests like Bath Ales Gem and Greene King Tanners Jack on handpump, and a choice of malt whiskies. An unexpected bonus is the very pleasant back terrace, with tables among flowers under a big sycamore tree, and a new glass-covered, heated area. The pub is deep in Arsenal country, so can get busy on match days. More reports please.

🍴 **Decent, very good value bar food includes baguettes, filled baked potatoes, various burgers, fish and chips, steak in ale pie, eight different types of sausage with mashed potato and home-made red onion gravy, and particularly well liked daily specials; popular Sunday roasts.** *Starters/Snacks: £2.25 to £4.95. Main Courses: £5.95 to £8.95. Puddings: £3.00*

Greene King ~ Tenants Scott Plomer and Eileen Shelock ~ Real ale ~ Bar food (12-2.30, 6-8.30; 12-4 weekends; not Mon) ~ (020) 7359 6883 ~ Children welcome away from main bar until 7pm ~ Dogs welcome ~ Open 12-11(10.30 Sun)
Recommended by Joe Green, Tracey and Stephen Groves, Steve Kirby

Drapers Arms 🍴 ☐

Far west end of Barnsbury Street; ⊖ ⇌ Highbury & Islington; N1 1ER

Hard to find but well worth it – a top-notch gastropub with especially memorable meals, and excellent range of wines

Most customers come to this striking Georgian townhouse to enjoy the first-rate food – not cheap, but rewarding for a special night out. It's in a quiet residential street away from Islington's main drag, and the overall effect is not unlike a bright, elegant wine bar. There are seating areas – in subdued colours – that horseshoe around the bar, with sofas and armchairs grouped together at the front, a nice area to the right with inset shelves of paperbacks and board games and high-backed dining furniture on dark bare boards, and a more sparsely furnished area on the left; a pair of large fireplaces and mirrors precisely facing each other across the front area. Adnams Best and Greene King IPA on handpump, a fine choice of wines and champagne by the glass, and several malt whiskies; piped jazz or swing. Service is helpful and unobtrusive. More reports please.

🍴 **At lunchtime, the brasserie-style modern cooking might include sandwiches, chicken liver and foie gras pâté with pineapple and caraway chutney, soup, spaghetti with queen scallops, garlic butter and fresh tomato fondue, fish and chips with pea purée and crème fraîche tartare sauce, and corn-fed chicken with sweet potato fondant and niçoise vegetables, with evening choices like chorizo and baby squid with frisée salad, artichoke and thyme tart with a soft poached egg and hollandaise, rock oysters with shallot vinegar, double pork chop with lentil and black pudding jus, aged rib-eye steak with béarnaise sauce, and puddings like raspberry and white chocolate crème brûlée and spiced apple and berry crumble with clotted cream.** *Starters/Snacks: £6.00 to £11.00. Main Courses: £12.50 to £15.50. Puddings: £6.00*

Free house ~ Licensees Mark Emberton and Paul McElhinney ~ Real ale ~ Bar food (12-3, 7-10 (6.30-9.30 Sun)) ~ Restaurant ~ (020) 7619 0348 ~ No children after 7pm unless eating ~ Dogs allowed in bar ~ Open 12-11(10.30 Sun); closed 24-27 Dec
Recommended by Jeremy King

Pubs with attractive or unusually big gardens are listed at the back of the book.

Duke of Cambridge 🍴 ♀ 🍺

St Peter's Street; ✚ Angel, though some distance away; N1 8JT
LONDON DINING PUB OF THE YEAR

Trail-blazing organic pub with very good, carefully sourced food, and excellent range of unusual drinks; nice, chatty atmosphere too, with the feel of a comfortably upmarket local

For ten years, this award-winning pub has continued to follow its eco-friendly policies. It was London's first organic pub (and is the UK's first and only Soil Association-certified gastropub) and its founder uses only high quality produce at its seasonal peak from small producers. As much as possible is re-used and re-cycled, and the electricity here is wind and solar generated. Even the real ales on handpump are organic: Pitfield East Kent Goldings, Eco Warrior, and SB, and St Peters Best. They also have organic draught lagers and cider, organic spirits, and a very wide range of good, organic wines, many of which are available by the glass. The full range of drinks is chalked on a blackboard, and also coffees and teas, and a spicy ginger ale. The atmosphere is warmly inviting, and it's the kind of place that somehow encourages conversation, with a steady stream of civilised chat from the varied customers. The big, busy main room is simply decorated and furnished, with lots of chunky wooden tables, pews and benches on bare boards, a couple of big metal vases with colourful flowers, daily papers, and carefully positioned soft lighting around the otherwise bare walls. A corridor leads off past a few tables and an open kitchen to a couple of smaller candlelit rooms, more formally set for eating, and a conservatory. It's worth arriving early to eat, as they can get very busy. More reports please.

🍽 **Enjoyable, interesting food might include soup, pigs cheek and cornichon pâté with onion relish, twice baked roquefort soufflé with chicory and walnuts, diver-caught scallops with buttered leeks and white wine in puff pastry, pressed lamb breast with creamed flageolet and broad beans with mint jus, crispy pork belly with apple, watercress and mangetout, tapenade-crusted pollock with a lemon and black pepper dressing, venison and chocolate stew with celeriac dauphinoise, and puddings such as sherry trifle and pot au chocolate.** *Starters/Snacks: £4.50 to £9.00. Main Courses: £11.00 to £21.00. Puddings: £6.50 to £8.50*

Free house ~ Licensee Geetie Singh ~ Real ale ~ Bar food (12.30-3(3.30 weekends), 6.30-10.30(10 Sun)) ~ Restaurant ~ (020) 7359 3066 ~ Children welcome ~ Dogs welcome ~ Open 12-11(10.30 Sun); closed 24-26 Dec, 31 Dec, 1 Jan
Recommended by P Dawn, Tracey and Stephen Groves

Flask ♀

Flask Walk; ✚ Hampstead; NW3 1HE

Properly old-fashioned and villagey local, five real ales, a fine choice of wines by the glass, and pubby food; well liked by Hampstead characters

There has been some refurbishment to this peaceful old local, and because much of the interior is listed, the changes are to do with the furnishings rather than the fabric of the building. The bar – a popular haunt of Hampstead artists, actors, and local characters – is unassuming, properly old-fashioned and rather villagey, with a nice old wooden counter and pubby tables and chairs; a unique Victorian screen divides this from the cosy lounge at the front with smart red plush banquettes curving round the panelled walls, and an attractive fireplace. There are some nice old wooden tables and dining chairs on rugs or on the dark wooden floorboards, lots of little prints on the walls, and quite a few wine and champagne bottles dotted about. Courage Directors, Greene King Old Speckled Hen, and Wells & Youngs Bitter, Special and Bombardier on handpump, around 30 wines by the glass, and lots of malt whiskies; friendly service, and piped music and darts. There are quite a few tables out in the alley. The pub's name is a reminder of the days when it distributed mineral water from Hampstead's springs.

🍽 **Decent bar food includes sandwiches, wild mixed mushrooms on toast, various sharing boards, chicken caesar salad, steak in ale pie, macaroni cheese, corn-fed, free-range chicken breast with a wine sauce, sausage and mash with caramelised shallot and onion gravy, smoked haddock kedgeree topped with a soft poached egg, pork chop with bubble**

and squeak, black pudding, and an english mustard cream sauce, and puddings such as treacle tart and rice pudding with fruit compote. *Starters/Snacks: £4.50 to £6.50. Main Courses: £7.95 to £13.95. Puddings: £4.95*

Youngs ~ Manager Natalie Chapman ~ Real ale ~ Bar food (12-3, 6-10; all day weekends) ~ Restaurant ~ (020) 7435 4580 ~ Children welcome till 8pm in dining room ~ Dogs allowed in bar ~ Live acoustic guitar Weds evening ~ Open 11-11(midnight Fri and Sat); 12-10.30 Sun

Recommended by P Dawn, Barry Collett, the Didler, Sue Demont, Tim Barrow

Holly Bush

Holly Mount; ⊖ Hampstead; NW3 6SG

Unique village local, with good food and drinks, and lovely unspoilt feel

Tucked charmingly away among some of Hampstead's most villagey streets is this rather special, nostalgically individual place, where even in the height of summer the light is timelessly dim. Under the dark sagging ceiling of its attractively old-fashioned front bar are brown and cream panelled walls (decorated with old advertisements and a few hanging plates), open fires, bare boards, and cosy bays formed by partly glazed partitions. Slightly more intimate, the back room, named after the painter George Romney, has an embossed red ceiling, panelled and etched glass alcoves, and ochre-painted brick walls covered with small prints; lots of board and card games. Interesting local characters pop in here for a pint of well kept beer – they've Adnams Broadside, Fullers London Pride, Harveys Sussex and a couple of quickly changing guests on handpump, as well as plenty of whiskies, and a good, seasonally changing wine list. The upstairs dining room has table service from Tuesday to Sunday – as does the rest of the pub on Sunday. There are benches on the pavement outside. The pub was originally the stable block of a nearby house.

Now served all day, generally the food includes a half pint of prawns, smoked duck, fig and mint salad, various sausages with cheddar mash and gravy, salmon fillet with tarragon and white wine sauce, pies such as chicken, mushroom and ale or beef and ale, roast lamb shank cooked with beer, puddings like marmalade and vanilla bread and butter pudding and apple and pear crumble, and some good cheeses. Some of their meat is organic and they do Sunday roasts. *Starters/Snacks: £2.00 to £8.00. Main Courses: £8.00 to £18.00. Puddings: £4.00 to £7.00*

Punch ~ Lease Nicolai Outzen ~ Real ale ~ Bar food (12-10(9 Sun)) ~ Restaurant ~ (020) 7435 2892 ~ Children welcome away from bar ~ Dogs allowed in bar ~ Open 12-11(10.30 Sun)

Recommended by Pat and Tony Martin, Sue Demont, Tim Barrow, Barry Collett, the Didler, Mike and Mary Clark, Tracey and Stephen Groves, David M Smith, Steve Kirby, Russell and Alison Hunt

Marquess Tavern

Canonbury Street/Marquess Road; ⊖ ⇌ Highbury & Islington, Angel; N1 2TB

Gastropub with honest seasonal british food, a very good range of drinks, and the feel of a proper local at the front

Though this imposing Victorian place (in a nice villagey corner of Islington) is now fairly well known as a dining pub, it still maintains the relaxed, chatty feel of a local, with quite a few regulars coming for just a drink. The bar is reassuringly traditional and fairly plain, with bare boards and a mix of candlelit wooden tables arranged around a big, horseshoe servery; there's a fireplace either side, one topped by a very tall mirror, as well as an old leather sofa and faded old pictures; piped music. You can eat either in the bar or in the slightly more formal back dining room, feeling much brighter with its white paint and skylight; it has an impressive brass chandelier. Two real ales are usually from Wells & Youngs, with a guest such as Charles Wells Bombardier, and they have a cask-conditioned cider or perry, a very good range of unusual bottled beers, well chosen wines (including several british) and 50 malt whiskies. There are some peaceful picnic-sets in front. Note they don't open weekday lunchtimes.

🍽 Although the pub was changing hands just as we went to press, it's not anticipated that there will be a change in the style of cooking, which focuses on seasonal british food. There might be starters such as globe artichokes and vinaigrette, smoked sprats, rabbit, black pudding and quail eggs, brown trout with trout mousse and watercress sauce, venison with roast prunes and shallots, braised fennel, mushrooms and cheese, and puddings such as raspberry fool, pear tart and summer pudding. *Starters/Snacks: £5.00 to £7.00. Main Courses: £10.50 to £17.50. Puddings: £5.60 to £6.00*

Youngs ~ Lease Bridie Hall ~ Real ale ~ Bar food (6-10; 12-6, 8-10 Sun) ~ Restaurant ~ (020) 7354 2975 ~ Children welcome ~ Dogs allowed in bar ~ Open 5-11(12 Fri); 12-12 Sat; 12-10.30 Sun; closed weekday lunchtimes

Recommended by BOB

Olde White Bear 🍷 🍺

Well Road; ⊖ Hampstead; NW3 1LJ

Particularly friendly and atmospheric, with a wonderfully varied mix of customers; good range of beers, and sensibly priced food all day

The dimly lit knocked-through bar at this neo-Victorian pub is smart but relaxed, with elegant panelling, wooden venetian blinds, and three separate-seeming areas: the biggest has lots of Victorian prints and cartoons on the walls, as well as wooden stools, cushioned chairs, a couple of big tasselled armchairs, a sofa, a handsome fireplace and an ornate Edwardian sideboard. A brighter section at the end has elaborate brocaded pews, while a central area has signed photographs of actors and playwrights. Half a dozen constantly changing beers on handpump might be from brewers such as Badger, Batemans, Daleside and Otter; also a decent range of whiskies and over a dozen wines by the glass. There are a few tables in front, and more in a courtyard behind. Still attracting a wonderfully diverse mix of customers, it is reckoned by many to be Hampstead's friendliest place. Piped music may be louder in the evenings – perhaps reflecting its popularity then with a younger crowd (though the cheery, helpful staff are very proud of the eclectic range); cards, chess, TV, and fun Thursday quiz nights. Parking nearby is mostly by permits only (there are no restrictions on Sundays), but the pub sells visitors permits for up to two hours. The Heath is close by.

🍽 Bar food is served all day, from a range including soup, sandwiches and ciabattas, various salads, home-made beef and lamb burgers, haddock in beer batter, sausages and mash, beef in Guinness pie, and puddings like apple crumble and spotted dick; their choice of roasts on Sundays is very popular. *Starters/Snacks: £4.00 to £7.00. Main Courses: £7.00 to £11.00. Puddings: £4.00*

Punch ~ Lease Christopher Ely ~ Real ale ~ Bar food (12-9) ~ (020) 7435 3758 ~ Children welcome ~ Dogs welcome ~ quiz Thurs ~ Open 11.30-11(11.30 Thurs, Fri); 11-11.30 Sat; 12-11 Sun

Recommended by the Didler, N R White

Spaniards Inn 🍷 🍺

Spaniards Lane; ⊖ Hampstead, but some distance away, or from Golders Green station take 220 bus; NW3 7JJ

Very popular old pub with lots of character and history, delightful big garden, and wide range of drinks and good food

Definitely a real plus, this busy and historic former toll house has a very large and quite charming garden. It's nicely arranged in a series of areas separated by judicious planting of shrubs. A crazy paved terrace with slatted wooden tables and chairs opens on to a flagstoned walk around a small raised area with roses and a side arbour of wisteria, clematis and hops. There are even some chickens down at the end. It's popular with families (including those with dogs) and you may need to move fast to bag a table. There's an outside bar, regular summer barbecues, and a new area for smokers. Dating back to 1585, the pub is well known for its tales of hauntings and highwaymen (some of which are best taken with a very large pinch of salt), and the low-ceilinged oak-panelled rooms are attractive and full of character, with open fires, genuinely antique winged settles, candle-shaped lamps in shades, and snug little alcoves. The atmosphere is friendly and chatty, and there's an impressive range of drinks, with half a dozen ales including Adnams, Fullers London Pride, Harveys and Marstons Old Empire with a couple of guests such as Fullers London Porter and Timothy Taylors Golden Best; they have occasional themed beer festivals – the most recent showcased beers with dog-related names. They also have a couple of ciders on handpump, an incredible range of continental draught lagers, and 20 wines by the glass – though in summer you might find the most popular drink is their big jug of Pimms. The pub is believed to have been named after the spanish ambassador to the court of James I, who had a private residence here. It's fairly handy for Kenwood. The car park fills up fast, and other parking nearby is difficult.

🍴 Served all day, the well liked pubby food might include soup, lunchtime sandwiches, ploughmans, mushrooms on toast, whitebait, pork chop with cider gravy, fish and chips, pie of the day, warm goats cheese, apple, pistachio and rocket salad, rib-eye steak and puddings such as apple crumble and custard and baked vanilla cheesecake. *Starters/Snacks: £3.80 to £5.95. Main Courses: £6.90 to £12.00. Puddings: £3.50 to £4.20*

Mitchells & Butlers ~ Manager David Nichol ~ Real ale ~ Bar food (11.30(12 Sun)-10) ~ (020) 8731 6571 ~ Children welcome ~ Dogs welcome ~ Open 11(10 Sat, Sun)-11

Recommended by N R White, Jo Lilley, Simon Calvert

SOUTH LONDON

MAP 13

Anchor & Hope 🍴 ♀

The Cut (B300, turning E off A301 Waterloo Road, S of Waterloo Station); ⊖ ⇌ Waterloo, Waterloo East; SE1 8LP

Fashionable destination with excellent, distinctive food in bustling informal atmosphere

Tucked surprisingly behind a slightly scruffy exterior is this vibrant bare-boards gastropub, currently one of London's most fashionable places to eat. Its sometimes quite unusual dishes are thoughtfully prepared using excellent seasonal ingredients, and the atmosphere is determinedly informal. It's very much of the Eagle school: open kitchen and absolutely no booking (except on Sunday when you must book for their three-course set menu) – even well known faces have been made to wait. It perhaps appeals to the same sort of people, but here there's a separate dining room, and on arrival you can add your name to the list to be seated there. Alternatively you can join the throng in the bar, which shares the same menu, but the dining room tables are better for an unhurried meal; those in the bar are rather low and small. The bar is fairly plain, with a big mirror behind the counter, dark red-painted walls and big windows that open up in summer. On the other side of a big curtain, the dining room is similar, but with contemporary paintings on the walls. Well kept Wells & Youngs Bombardier, Youngs and a guest such as Jennings Cumberland on handpump; there's a good wine list – wines are served in carafes and tumblers rather than smart glasses, but a popular choice before dinner is one of their sherries. It's all rather relaxed and unstuffy, and the kind of place where strangers cheerfully ask what you're eating; service is welcoming. There are a few metal tables in front on the street. The owners also have a restaurant with rooms in the heart of the Livradois-Forez in France.

🍴 Meals here are listed on a blackboard that changes twice a day: it might include soups such as pea and ham, potted shrimps and pickled cucumber, hereford steak tartare, whole crab, salt cod brandade with green beans and olives, duck confit with lentils, radishes and wild garlic, roast squab with liver toast and bread sauce, fish stew, with puddings such as pear and almond tart, chocolate pot and lemon meringues. *Starters/Snacks: £4.80 to £8.00. Main Courses: £10.80 to £16.00. Puddings: £3.80 to £5.00*

Charles Wells ~ Lease Robert Shaw ~ Real ale ~ Bar food (12-2.30, 6-10.30) ~ Restaurant ~ No credit cards ~ (020) 7928 9898 ~ Children welcome ~ Dogs welcome ~ Open 11(5 Mon)-11; 11-11 Sat; 12.30-5 Sun; closed Mon lunchtime, Sun evening; Easter weekend, and between Christmas and New Year

Recommended by Canon Michael Bourdeaux, John Watson, Mike and Sue Loseby, Ian Phillips, M Fitzpatrick

Bo-Peep

Chelsfield; 1.7 miles from M25 junction 4; Hewitts Road, which is last road off exit roundabout; BR6 7QL

Useful motorway meal-stop with good fish and other meals popular with older diners at lunchtime

Very handy from the M25, this is a surprisingly proper little country pub. The food is particularly popular with older people at lunchtimes, and indeed there's a nice, genuinely old-fashioned air throughout. The attractive tile-hung house is said to date from the 16th c, and the main bar – about to have a new stone floor as we went to press – still has very low old beams, and an enormous inglenook, as well as flowers on the tables, and a board with local notices. Two cosy little rooms for eating open off, one with smart cushions and a wooden floor, and there's a light side room looking over the country lane. The pub is candlelit at night. Courage Best, Greene King Old Speckled Hen and Harveys Sussex on handpump; efficient service from cheery, helpful staff, and look out for Milo, the licensees' miniature english bull terrier; piped easy listening. A terrace behind has lots of picnic-sets.

🍴 **The landlord is a fishmonger, so the fresh fish (typically salmon, bass, and sometimes monkfish and skate wing) are particularly well liked. As well as ploughman's and sandwiches, other reliable home-made dishes might include soup of the day, toasted brioche with garlic and stilton mushrooms, steak and ale pie, sausage and mash in giant yorkshire pudding and sirloin steak.** *Starters/Snacks: £4.25 to £6.95. Main Courses: £7.95 to £16.95. Puddings: £4.25*

Enterprise ~ Lease Kate Mansfield, Graham Buckley ~ Real ale ~ Bar food (12-2 (5.30 Sun), 7-9.30) ~ Restaurant ~ (01959) 534457 ~ Children welcome ~ Open 11.30-11

Recommended by B and M Kendall, Derek Thomas

Crown & Greyhound ♀

Dulwich Village; ⇌ North Dulwich; SE21 7BJ

Comfortable Victorian pub with big back garden, good beers, and popular Sunday carvery

Handy for walks through the park, and Dulwich Picture Gallery, this big, relaxed Victorian pub boasts a very pleasant back garden, with tables shaded by a chestnut tree, and barbecues on summer weekends. The fence has murals painted by local schoolchildren, and they've french boules, and over-sized versions of games like Connect 4 and dominoes. A big back dining room and conservatory open on to here, leading from the pleasantly furnished roomy main bar at the front. Retaining many of its original features, this has some quite ornate plasterwork and lamps over on the right, and a variety of nicely distinct seating areas, some with traditional upholstered and panelled settles, others with stripped kitchen tables on stripped boards; there's a coal-effect gas fire and some old prints; piped music. Drinks include a dozen wines by the glass, Fullers London Pride, Harveys and Wells & Youngs and a guest such as Everards Sunchaser Blonde on handpump; they hold an Easter beer festival and perhaps some other bank holidays. Known locally as the Dog, it was built at the turn of the century to replace two inns that had stood here previously, hence the unusual name. Busy in the evenings, but quieter during the day. More reports please.

🍴 **Under the new licensee, bar food might include sandwiches, devilled whitebait, three choices of sausages and mash, baked trout stuffed with lemon, spinach and lentil burger, well hung steaks, and puddings such as chocolate brownie with vanilla pod ice-cream. It's best to arrive early for the popular Sunday carvery as they don't take bookings.** *Starters/Snacks: £3.50 to £6.00. Main Courses: £6.90 to £12.00. Puddings: £3.50*

Mitchells & Butlers ~ Manager Mike Earp ~ Real ale ~ Bar food (12-10(9.30 Sun)) ~ (020) 8299 4976 ~ Children in restaurant ~ Dogs welcome ~ Open 11-11(12 Thurs-Sat)

Recommended by Giles and Annie Francis, Dave W Holliday

If we know a pub has an outdoor play area for children, we mention it.

Cutty Sark

Ballast Quay, off Lassell Street; ⇌ Maze Hill, from London Bridge; or from the river front walk past the Yacht in Crane Street and Trinity Hospital; SE10 9PD

Interesting old tavern with genuinely unspoilt bar, great Thames views, organic wines, and wide range of fairly straightforward but popular food

Alive with young people on Friday and Saturday evenings and at the weekends, but surprisingly quiet some weekday lunchtimes, the unspoilt, dark flagstoned bar at this white-painted house has a genuinely old-fashioned feel, with rough brick walls, wooden settles, barrel tables, open fires, low lighting and narrow openings to tiny side snugs; you can just imagine smugglers and blackguards lurking here. An elaborate central staircase leads to an upstairs room that feels just like a ship's deck, and a big bow window jutting out over the pavement – and splendid views of the Thames and Millennium Dome. Adnams Broadside, Fullers London Pride, St Austell Tribute and a guest on handpump, with a good choice of malt whiskies, and a range of organic wines; juke box. There's a busy riverside terrace across the narrow cobbled lane; morris dancers occasionally drop by. Parking is limited nearby – though, unusually for London, if you can bag a space it's free.

🍽 **A wide range of well cooked, promptly served meals includes sandwiches, scampi, mussels, caesar salad, sweet and sour chicken, lasagne, steak and ale pie, rib-eye steak and puddings such as knickerbocker glory. Tuesday fish and chips night, with two helpings of battered haddock for £10.** *Starters/Snacks: £4.50 to £4.95. Main Courses: £9.95 to £12.95. Puddings: £4.95.*

Free house ~ Licensee Denny Davies ~ Real ale ~ Bar food (12-9(10 Sat)) ~ (020) 8858 3146 ~ Children welcome ~ Dogs allowed in bar ~ Open 11-11(10.30 Sun)

Recommended by John Saville, Mrs Margo Finlay, Jörg Kasprowski, N R White, Ian Phillips, Mike Gorton, the Didler, Susan and John Douglas

Fire Station ♀

Waterloo Road; ⊖ ⇌ Waterloo, Waterloo East; SE1 8SB

Unusual conversion of former fire station, with lively after-work atmosphere (it does get crowded then), and good food all day

Without fail, there seems to be a crowd at this busy conversion of the former LCC central fire station: even by 5pm it can be standing room only, though it's calmer at lunchtimes, and at weekends. The loud chat and music combine in a cheery cacophony that most readers thoroughly enjoy, but some find a little overpowering. The bar is two huge knocked-through tiled rooms (one reader described it as feeling like an old-fashioned public bath), with lots of wooden tables and a mix of chairs, a couple of pews and worn leather armchairs, some sizeable plants, and distinctive box-shaped floral lampshades hanging from the high ceilings; the back wall has three back-lit mirrored panels, and some red fire buckets on a shelf. Some of the walls – and the bar counter – have nice black, brick-shaped tiles. The back dining room has smarter chairs and tables. Fullers London Pride, Marstons Pedigree and a guest are on handpump, and they've an excellent choice of wines, and a good range of spirits and cocktails. There are tables in front, and picnic-sets in a scruffy side alley. It's very handy for the Old Vic and Waterloo Station.

🍽 **They do breakfasts from 9am, then have an all-day bar menu with baguettes, interesting burgers (lamb and rosemary, or olive and sun-dried tomato), sausage and mash with savoy cabbage, and daily specials such as roast belly of pork, new forest lamb, and moroccan seafood stew, while the dining room menu has things like gilt-head bream and lemon butter with red chard and sweet potato mash, roast fillet of beef with watercress purée and wholegrain mustard mash, pan-fried haddock fillet with lightly spiced chickpea and pepper salad, and 28-day hung rib-eye steak.** *Starters/Snacks: £3.00 to £7.00. Main Courses: £7.00 to £9.00*

Marstons ~ Manager Tom Alabaster ~ Real ale ~ Bar food (9-11) ~ Restaurant ~ (020) 7620 2226 ~ Children welcome till 6pm ~ Open 9-midnight

Recommended by Ian Phillips, Simon Collett-Jones, Susan and John Douglas, Peter Dandy, Jane Taylor, David Dutton

Founders Arms ♀

Hopton Street (Bankside); ⊖ ⇌ Blackfriars, and cross Blackfriars Bridge; SE1 9JH

Superb location, with outstanding terrace views along the Thames, and handy for Tate Modern and Shakespeare's Globe; decent efficiently served food

Great for a pre-theatre dinner (Shakespeare's Globe, as well as Tate Modern are just a short stroll away) this big modern pub, feeling rather like a huge conservatory, is cleverly lit at night so that you can still see out across the Thames. The menu provides a useful cross reference to the terrific views: along the bottom it very handily identifies all the main buildings you can see with information on when they were built. Taking in St Paul's, the Millennium Bridge, and even the Tower of London way off in the distance, it's probably the best view you'll find at any pub along the river, particularly in the City – you get the best views from seats out on the waterside terrace. It's a bustling place, popular with a good mix of city types, tourists, theatre and gallery goers. Wells & Youngs Bitter, Special and seasonal brews and maybe a guest such as Courage Directors are served from the modern bar counter angling along one side; there's a good range of other drinks too, including well over a dozen wines by the glass, and various coffees, tea and hot chocolate. Efficient, cheerful service; piped music.

⑪ Available all day (starting at 9am for breakfast at the weekend), and served without fuss or too much waiting around the very useful menu might include sandwiches, ciabattas, moules and frites, fish and cheeseboards for one or to share, duck breast niçoise, warm goats cheese salad, battered fish, beef, mushroom and ale pie, butternut squash tagine, tomato, basil and olive fettuccine, *Starters/Snacks: £4.45 to £5.95. Main Courses: £7.95 to £13.70. Puddings: £3.95*

Youngs ~ Manager Paul Raynor ~ Real ale ~ Bar food (10(Sat, Sun)-10) ~ (020) 7928 1899 ~ Children welcome away from bar ~ Open 10(9 Sun)-11(midnight Fri); 9-midnight Sat

Recommended by the Didler, N R White, Meg and Colin Hamilton, Dr and Mrs M E Wilson, Dr Ron Cox, Mike and Sue Loseby, Eithne Dandy, John Saville, Ian Phillips, Howard and Margaret Buchanan, Val and Alan Green, Dr and Mrs A K Clarke

Fox & Hounds ⑪ ♀

Latchmere Road; ⇌ Clapham Junction; SW11 2JU

Victorian local standing out for its excellent mediterranean cooking; mostly evenings only, but some lunchtimes too

We'd love to hear more from readers about the excellent mediterranean cooking (evenings only) at this otherwise unremarkable big Victorian local. It's run by the two brothers who transformed the Atlas (see West London, below), and has a very similar style and menu. The pub can fill quickly, so you may have to move fast to grab a table. It's still very much the kind of place where locals happily come to drink – and they're a more varied bunch than you might find filling the Atlas. The spacious, straightforward bar has bare boards, mismatched tables and chairs, two narrow pillars supporting the dark red ceiling, photographs on the walls, and big windows overlooking the street (the view partially obscured by colourful window boxes). There are fresh flowers and daily papers on the bar, and a view of the kitchen behind. Two rooms lead off, one more cosy with its two red leatherette sofas. Fullers London Pride, Harveys and a guest such as Black Sheep are on handpump; the carefully chosen wine list (which includes over a dozen by the glass) is written out on a blackboard; the varied piped music fits in rather well; TV. The garden has big parasols and heaters for winter.

⑪ Changing every day, a typical choice might include roast aubergine soup with cumin and ricotta, antipasti to share, squid and chorizo salad with grilled sweet potato, asparagus, porcini and field mushroom risotto, rigatoni with italian sausage ragú, roast tomato and herb aïoli, tuscan sausage and mash, poached haddock with shaved fennel and mixed pepper salad, roast venison steak with celeriac and parsnip mash and red onion marmalade, rib-eye steak and kidney beans with tomato, red wine and rosemary, and puddings such as apple and date crumble and lime cheesecake with honey. *Starters/Snacks: £4.50 to £8.50. Main Courses: £9.00 to £14.50. Puddings: £4.50 to £6.50*

Free house ~ Licensees Richard and George Manners ~ Real ale ~ Bar food (12.30-3(4 Sun) Fri-Sat; 7-10.30(10 Sun); not Mon-Thurs lunchtimes) ~ (020) 7924 5483 ~ Children welcome till 7pm ~ Dogs welcome ~ Open 12-3, 5-11; 12-11 Fri, Sat; 12-10.30 Sun; closed Mon lunchtime; 24 Dec-1 Jan

Recommended by BOB

George ★

Off 77 Borough High Street; ⊖ ⇌ *Borough, London Bridge; SE1 1NH*

Beautifully preserved 16th-c coaching inn, with lots of tables in bustling courtyard to take in the galleried exterior.

Whatever the season, readers head for tables in the bustling cobbled courtyard so they can sit and soak up the unusual exterior of this splendidly preserved building. It's perhaps the country's best example of a historic coaching inn, and is well known for its tiers of outside open galleries. Owned by the National Trust, the building dates from the 16th c, but was rebuilt to the original plan after the great Southwark fire of 1676. What survives today is only a third of the original building; it was 'mercilessly reduced' as E V Lucas put it, during the period when it was owned by the Great Northern Railway Company. Unless you know where you're going (or you're in one of the many tourist groups that flock here in summer) you may well miss it, as apart from the great gates and sign there's little to indicate that such a gem still exists behind the less auspicious-looking buildings on the busy high street. Less appealing than its façade, the row of no-frills ground-floor rooms and bars has square-latticed windows, black beams, bare floorboards, some panelling, plain oak or elm tables and old-fashioned built-in settles, along with a 1797 'Act of Parliament' clock, dimpled glass lantern-lamps and so forth. The best seats indoors are in a snug room nearest the street, where there's an ancient beer engine that looks like a cash register. In summer they open a bar with direct service into the courtyard (when it's busy it may be quicker to order your drinks inside) and though staff cope well with the crowds, for some readers it can have the same impersonal feel as other National Trust pubs. Greene King Abbot, IPA, Old Speckled Hen and a beer brewed by them for the pub on handpump; mulled wine in winter, tea and coffee. An impressive central staircase goes up to a series of dining rooms and to a gaslit balcony; darts, trivia games machine. Please be careful here as one reporter told us about handbag thefts.

🍴 Good value lunchtime bar food includes baguettes and wraps, soup, filled baked potatoes, ham, egg and chips, primavera risotto, scampi, sausage and mash, fish and chips, and puddings like black forest gateau or apple crumble; they do a Sunday carvery. In the evenings they do meals only in the balcony restaurant. *Starters/Snacks: £4.95 to £6.25. Main Courses: £7.25 to £9.95. Puddings: £4.25*

Greene King ~ Manager Scott Masterson ~ Real ale ~ Bar food (12-5, 6-9; Sun evening) ~ Restaurant (5-10 (not Sun)) ~ (020) 7407 2056 ~ Children welcome at lunchtimes ~ Open 11-11; 12-10.30 Sun

Recommended by Tom McLean, David and Sue Smith, the Didler, N R White, Derek and Sylvia Stephenson, Ian and Nita Cooper, Mike and Sue Loseby, Ewan McCall, Ian Phillips, Tracey and Stephen Groves, Susan and John Douglas, Roy and Lindsey Fentiman, Dr and Mrs A K Clarke, Howard and Margaret Buchanan

Greenwich Union 🍺

Royal Hill; ⊖ ⇌ *Greenwich; SE10 8RT*

Enterprising refurbished pub with distinctive beers from small local Meantime Brewery, plus other unusual drinks and good, popular food

Established by Alastair Hook, who also founded the Freedom Brewery and the microbrew restaurant Mash, this enterprising and nicely renovated pub is the tap for the small Meantime Brewery in nearby Charlton, and is the only place with all their distinctive unpasteurised beers on draught. The range includes a traditional pale ale (served cool, under pressure) a mix of proper pilsners, lagers and wheat beers, one a deliciously refreshing raspberry flavour, and a stout. The helpful, knowledgeable staff will generally offer small tasters to help you choose. They also have Adnams on handpump, and a draught cider, as well as a helpfully annotated list of unusual bottled beers including some of their own. The rest of the drinks can be unfamiliar too, as they try to avoid the more common brands. Perhaps feeling a little more like a bar than a pub, the long, narrow stoneflagged room has several different parts: a simple area at the front with a few wooden chairs and tables, a stove and newspapers, then, past the counter with its headings recalling the branding of the brewery's first beers, several brown leather cushioned pews and armchairs under framed editions of *Picture Post* on the yellow walls; piped music. Beyond here a much lighter, more moden-feeling conservatory has comfortable brown leather wallbenches, a few original pictures and paintings, and white fairy lights under the glass roof; it leads out to an appealing back patio with green picnic-sets and a couple of old-fashioned lampposts. The fence at the end is painted to resemble a poppy field, and the one at the side to represent wheat growing. Though there are plenty of tables out here, it can get busy in summer (as can the whole pub on weekday evenings). In front are a couple of tables overlooking the street. The pub is slightly removed from Greenwich's many attractions and there's a particularly good traditional cheese shop as you walk towards the pub.

🍴 **Good and popular, from a seasonally changing menu that might include lunchtime sandwiches, a risotto, crumbed cod fillet with minted pea purée, smoked eel with salsa verde and soft boiled eggs, poached haddock, low cooked pork belly with carrot purée and braised lentils, rib-eye steak, and puddings such as vanilla panna cotta with champagne poached rhubarb and apple sorbet and chocolate and walnut brownies with white chocolate ice-cream. They do brunch on Saturdays, and a choice of roasts on Sunday.**
Starters/Snacks: £3.95 to £8.90. Main Courses: £7.90 to £13.90. Puddings: £3.95 to £4.50

Free house ~ Licensee Andrew Ward ~ Real ale ~ Bar food (12-4, 5.30-10; 12-9(10 Sun) Sat) ~ (020) 8692 6258 ~ Children welcome ~ Dogs welcome ~ Open 12-11; 11-11 Sat; 11.30-10.30 Sun
Recommended by the Didler, N R White

Market Porter 🍺
Stoney Street; ⊖ ⇄ London Bridge; SE1 9AA

Up to ten unusual real ales in very popular, properly pubby place opening at 6am for workers at neighbouring market

Ashamedly, we haven't yet made it here at the crack of dawn for their 6 to 8.30 weekday morning opening when they do breakfasts for the workers and porters from Borough Market. We have however popped in many a time to inspect their impressive selection of around ten carefully chosen and perfectly kept beers, often from unusual brewers that you might not have come across before. The range changes every day (they get through around 60 different ones a week), but as we went to press they had beers from Alcazar, Atlas, Copper Dragon, Goachers, Old Bear, Purple Moose, Saltaire, Springhead and Stonehenge, alongside the regular Harveys – you may find you can't read the names on all the beer pumps at lunchtimes and after work, when it can get crowded and noisy with good-natured chatter; most readers feel that's all part of the atmosphere. Service is particularly helpful and friendly, and it's usually quieter in the afternoons (or in the upstairs restaurant, looking over the market). The main part of the bar is pretty straightforward (making one reader nostalgic for the sort of pubs he used to know in London) with rough wooden ceiling beams with beer barrels balanced on them, a heavy wooden counter with a beamed gantry, cushioned bar stools, an open fire, and 1920s-style wall lamps – it gets more old-fashioned the further you venture in; piped music. The company that owns the pub has various others around London; ones with similarly unusual beers (if not quite so many) can be found in Stamford Street and Seymour Place.

🍴 **Usually served in the upstairs restaurant (but everywhere on Sun), well liked sensibly priced lunchtime bar food includes sandwiches, sausage and mash, various pies such as steak and mushroom, mushroom and spinach tagliatelle and fish and chips; good Sunday roasts.** *Starters/Snacks: £4.25 to £5.45. Main Courses: £7.25 to £12.95*

Free house ~ Licensee Sarah Nixon ~ Real ale ~ Bar food (12-3) ~ Restaurant ~ (020) 7407 2495 ~ Children in restaurant ~ Open 6-8.30am weekdays, then 11-11; 12-11 Sat; 12-10.30 Sun

Recommended by John Saville, Tracey and Stephen Groves, Tom McLean, Ewan McCall, E McCall, T McLean, D Irving, the Didler, Ian and Julia Beard, Joe Green, P Dawn, Phil Bryant, Bruce Bird, Mike Gorton, Mike and Sue Loseby, Ian Phillips, Steve Kirby, Sue Demont, Tim Barrow, B and M Kendall

Old Jail

Jail Lane, Biggin Hill (first turn E off A233 S of airport and industrial estate, towards Berry's Hill and Cudham); no station near; TN16 3AX

Country pub close to the city, with big garden, interesting traditional bars with RAF memorabilia, and good daily specials

With its lovely big garden – well spaced picnic-sets on the grass, several substantial trees, and a nicely maintained play area – it's easy to forget that this good all-rounder is only ten minutes or so from the bustle of Croydon and Bromley. Situated on a narrow leafy lane and feeling very much in the countryside it's popular with families at the weekend. Inside, several traditional beamed and low-ceilinged rooms ramble around a central servery, the nicest parts being the two cosy little areas to the right of the front entrance; divided by dark timbers, one has a very big inglenook fireplace with lots of logs and brasses, and the other has a cabinet of Battle of Britain plates – a reference perhaps to the pub's popularity with RAF pilots based at nearby Biggin Hill. Other parts have wartime prints and plates too, especially around the edge of the dining room, up a step beyond a second, smaller fireplace. There's also a plainer, flagstoned room; discreet, low piped music. Fullers London Pride, Harveys and Shepherd Neame Spitfire on handpump; friendly, efficient service. With nice hanging baskets in front, the attractive building wasn't itself part of any jail, but was a beef shop until becoming a pub in 1869. More reports please.

🍴 There's a standard menu with things like good value sandwiches, soup, baked potatoes, and ploughman's, but the food to go for is the wide choice of good, blackboard specials, which might include local sausages with mash and red onion gravy, chicken tarragon with bacon and onion potato cake, slow cooked beef with new potatoes and swede mash, roast spiced duck with parmentier potatoes and lemon grass jus, and rib-eye steak; they do a choice of roasts on Sundays. *Starters/Snacks: £2.95 to £4.95. Main Courses: £7.95 to £16.95. Puddings: £2.95 to £4.50*

Punch ~ Lease Richard Hards ~ Real ale ~ Bar food (12-2.30(2 Sat, 3 Sun), 7-9.15(9.30 Sat); not Sun evening or bank hols) ~ (01959) 572979 ~ Children welcome ~ Dogs welcome ~ Open 11.30-3, 6-11.30; 11.30-11 Fri, Sat; 12-10.30 Sun

Recommended by Rob Liddiard, Debbie and Neil Hayter, LM

Royal Oak 🍺

Tabard Street; ⊖ ⇌ Borough; SE1 4JU

Old-fashioned corner house owned by Sussex brewer Harveys, with all their beers excellently kept; good, honest food too

This very enjoyable old-fashioned corner house is the only London pub belonging to Sussex brewer Harveys. It's slightly off the beaten track (in rather unprepossessing surroundings), but well worth the detour, both for its cheery atmosphere, and for the full range of Harveys beers, all impeccably kept. Best-loved among these is perhaps their Sussex Best, but you'll also find their stronger Armada, as well as Mild, Pale Ale, and changing seasonal brews. The brewery transformed the pub when they took over, and painstakingly re-created the look and feel of a traditional London alehouse – you'd never imagine it wasn't like this all along. Filled with the noisy sounds of happy chat, two busy little L-shaped rooms meander around the central wooden servery, which has a fine old clock in the middle. They're done out in a cosy, traditional style: patterned rugs on the wooden floors, plates running along a delft shelf, black and white scenes or period sheet music on the red-painted walls, and an assortment of wooden tables and chairs. It almost goes without saying, but there's no music or machines.

🍴 Well liked by readers, honest good value bar food includes impressive doorstep sandwiches, and generously served daily specials like fillets of bass, or pies such as vegetable and stilton, lamb and apricot, or game and steak and kidney pudding; Sunday roasts. *Starters/Snacks: £4.50 to £6.75. Main Courses: £10.50 to £3.95*

Harveys ~ Tenants John Porteous, Frank Taylor ~ Real ale ~ Bar food (12-2.30, 5-9; 12-4 Sun) ~ (020) 7357 7173 ~ Dogs allowed in bar ~ Open 11-11; 12-11 Sat; 12-6 Sun

Recommended by Sue Demont, Tim Barrow, Andrew Bosi, the Didler, Derek and Sylvia Stephenson, Mike and Sue Loseby, Brian and Rosalie Laverick, N R White, Mike Gorton, Darren Le Poidevin

Victoria ♀ 🛏

West Temple Sheen; ⇌ Mortlake; SW14 7RT

Sophisticated reworked local with excellent food and wines, and smart contemporary style; good for families, comfortable bedrooms

As we went to press, this stylish gastropub with rooms (simple and smart) was about to re-open with a new licensee. One big thoughtfully designed room, with wooden floors and armchairs, and separate-seeming areas with a fireplace, and plenty of contemporary touches leads into a huge glass room at the back which is especially stunning in the evening. Plenty of thought seems to have gone into the wine list, and they will have Fullers London Pride and Timothy Taylors Landlord on handpump. The garden is a rather smartly renovated affair, with paving and a sheltered play area and the pub is just a short stroll from Richmond Park's Sheen Gate.

🍴 **Pubby snacks from a changing menu will be on offer in the bar, and are likely to include things like home-made scotch eggs with green tomato chutney, steak sandwich and mussel chowder. The dining room will feature modern british cooking.** *Starters/Snacks: £4.50 to £9.00. Puddings: £4.50 to £6.50*

Enterprise ~ Lease Greg Bellamy ~ Real ale ~ Bar food (coffee and cakes 9-12, then bar food till 11) ~ Restaurant ~ (020) 8876 4238 ~ Children welcome ~ Dogs allowed in bar ~ Open 9-11; 12-11 Sun ~ Bedrooms: £110S/£125S

Recommended by Maggie Atherton

White Cross ♀

Water Lane; ⊖ ⇌ Richmond; TW9 1TH

Splendidly set Thames-side pub with paved waterside area; busy in fine weather, but comfortable in winter too – though watch out for the tides

The very pleasant paved garden in front of this perfectly set Thames-side pub enjoys terrific river views. It gets quite busy out here in summer, when it can even feel rather like a cosmopolitan seaside resort, and there's an outside bar to make the most of the sunshine (they may use plastic glasses for outside drinking). Boats leave from immediately outside for Kingston and Hampton Court and it's not unknown for the water to reach right up the steps into the bar and cut off the towpath at the front – if you're leaving your car by the river check tide times so as not to return to find it marooned in a rapidly swelling pool of water. Inside, the two chatty main rooms have something of the air of the hotel this once was, with local prints and photographs, an old-fashioned wooden island servery, and a good mix of variously aged customers. Two of the three log fires have mirrors above them – unusually, the third is below a window. A bright and airy upstairs room has lots more tables, and a pretty cast-iron balcony opening off, with a splendid view down to the water; piped music, TV. Wells & Youngs Bitter and Special and a couple of guests such as Caledonian Deuchars IPA and Wells & Youngs Bombardier on handpump, and a dozen or so carefully chosen wines by the glass; welcoming service.

🍴 **Served all day from a food counter (thus eliminating a wait even when it's busy) bar food includes sandwiches, salads, sausage and mash, fish and chips, home-made pies, daily roasts, and (in summer) scones and clotted cream.** *Starters/Snacks: £3.95 to £6.95. Main Courses: £7.95 to £9.95. Puddings: £4.25*

Youngs ~ Manager Alex Gibson ~ Real ale ~ Bar food (12-9.30(8 Sun)) ~ (020) 8940 6844 ~ Children welcome in upstairs room till 6pm ~ Dogs welcome ~ Occasional live music Thurs ~ Open 11-11; 12-10.30 Sun

Recommended by Bruce Bird, the Didler, Tracey and Stephen Groves, N R White, Peter Dandy, Alan and Carolin Tidbury

---

We checked prices with the pubs as we went to press in summer 2008. They should hold until around spring 2009 – when our experience suggests that you can expect an increase of around 10p in the £.

WEST LONDON

MAP 13

Anglesea Arms ♀ ◀

Selwood Terrace; ● South Kensington; SW7 3QG

Busy old local with good range of beers, enjoyably chatty atmosphere in the evenings (when it can get packed)

With an enjoyably chatty, traditional atmosphere, the characterful bar at this bustling pub has something of the feel of a late Victorian local. It has a mix of cast-iron tables on the bare wood-strip floor, panelling, and big windows with attractive swagged curtains; at one end several booths with partly glazed screens have worn cushioned pews and spindleback chairs. If there weren't so many people, there might be an air of rather faded grandeur, heightened by some heavy portraits, prints of London, and large brass chandeliers; perhaps incongruously, there's a TV too. On particularly busy days – when well heeled young locals are very much part of the mix – you'll need to move fast to grab a seat, but most people seem happy leaning on the central elbow tables. A good choice of half a dozen real ales takes in Adnams Bitter and Broadside, Brakspears, Fullers London Pride, Hogs Back TEA and a guest such as Sharps Doom Bar; also a few bottled belgian beers, around 15 whiskies, and a varied wine list of about 20 wines with everything available by the glass. Down some steps is a dining room with a fireplace and table service – and generally a bit more space if you're eating; service is friendly and helpful. In summer the place to be is the leafy front terrace, with outside heaters for chillier evenings (and smokers).

🍴 Changing every day, the menu might include a couple of lunchtime sandwiches (such as crayfish and rocket), pea and mint soup, linguini with crab, chilli, parsley and garlic, half a pint of prawns, cavalo nero, taleggio and pecorino risotto, battered whiting and chips, sausage and mash with onion gravy and crisp sage, duck ragoût with pappardelle, sirloin steak, and puddings such as apple and rhubarb crumble. *Starters/Snacks: £5.00 to £8.00. Main Courses: £9.00 to £16.00. Puddings: £3.75 to £4.50*

Free house ~ Licensee Jenny Podmore ~ Real ale ~ Bar food (12-3, 6.30-10; 12-5, 6-10(9.30 Sun) Sat, Sun) ~ Restaurant ~ (020) 7373 7960 ~ Children welcome ~ Dogs welcome ~ Open 11-11; 12-10.30 Sun

Recommended by P Dawn, Brian and Janet Ainscough, Revd R P Tickle, Sue Demont, Tim Barrow, the Didler, Susan and John Douglas, John and Jill Perkins

Atlas 🍽 ♀

Seagrave Road; ● West Brompton; SW6 1RX

Spruced-up local with consistently excellent southern mediterranean cooking, very popular, especially in the evenings, when tables are highly prized

Providing something of an oasis in this part of London, this souped-up local offers a constantly changing choice of innovative, varied food in a very good, bustling atmosphere. The creative combination of flavours results in a very satisfying, enjoyable meal, and if there's a downside it's simply the place's popularity; tables are highly prized, so if you're planning a meal, arrive early, or swoop quickly. The long, simple knocked-together bar has been well renovated without removing the original features; there's plenty of panelling and dark wooden wall benches, a couple of brick fireplaces, a mix of school chairs, and well spaced tables. Smart young people figure prominently in the mix, but there are plenty of locals too, as well as visitors to the Exhibition Centre at Earls Court (one of the biggest car parks is next door). Well kept Caledonian Deuchars IPA, Fullers London Pride and a guest are on handpump, and they've a very good, carefully chosen wine list, with plenty by the glass; big mugs of coffee; friendly service. The piped music covers a real cross section – on various visits we've come across everything from salsa and jazz to vintage TV themes; it can be loud at times, and with all the chat too, this isn't the place to come for a quiet dinner. Down at the end, by a hatch to the kitchen, is a TV (though big sports events are shown in a room upstairs). Outside is an attractively planted narrow side terrace, with an overhead awning; heaters make it comfortable even in winter.

Ⅲ Influenced by recipes from North Africa, Turkey and Italy, the menu changes twice a day but might include things like tomato bruschetta, antipasti, grilled vegetable skewer with cracked wheat, harissa and yoghurt, rabbit, porcini and sage risotto, roast sea trout with puy lentils with balsamic and dill, grilled italian sausages with red onion marmalade, pork and bean stew with chorizo, morcilla and pancetta and crackling and rib-eye steak with salsa verde. *Starters/Snacks: £5.00 to £7.50. Main Courses: £8.00 to £14.50. Puddings: £4.50 to £6.50*

Enterprise ~ Lease Toby Ellis, Richard and George Manners ~ Real ale ~ Bar food (12.30-3, 7-10.30 Mon-Sat; 12.30-4, 7-10 Sun) ~ (020) 7385 9129 ~ Children welcome till 7pm ~ Dogs welcome ~ Open 12-11(10.30 Sun); closed 24 Dec-1 Jan

Recommended by Robert Lester, Alistair Forsyth, Derek Thomas, Evelyn and Derek Walter

Bulls Head 🍺
Strand-on-the-Green; ⇌ Kew Bridge; W4 3PQ

Cosy old Thames-side pub with tables by river with atmospheric little rooms, half a dozen real ales and pubby food all day

One of the best examples from the chain, this cosy Chef & Brewer pub enjoys a delightful Thames-side setting, with a few tables in front by the river. On cooler days, if you get here early enough (the pub can fill up fast) you should be able to bag one of the highly prized tables by the little windows, with nice views of the river past the attractively planted hanging flower baskets (a very pleasant place to sit and read one of the newspapers they lay out for customers). Inside, the series of beamed rooms rambles up and down steps, with plenty of polished dark wood and beams, and old-fashioned benches built into the simple panelling. The black-panelled alcoves make useful cubby-holes (especially snug on chilly autumn days), and there are lots of empty wine bottles dotted around. All in all the refurbishments give (and in truth, the building itself is actually very old – it served as Cromwell's HQ several times during the Civil War) a good mock historic pubby setting for a decent meal. Coming from all sorts of brewers, far and wide, six changing real ales on handpump might be from Adnams, Black Sheep, Highgate, Old Bear and Wells & Youngs. They do pitchers of Pimms in summer, and have around 20 wines by the glass; good service from friendly uniformed staff.

Ⅲ Served all day, food is fairly pubby, running from good sandwiches and filled baguettes, through fish and chips and beef and ale pie, to thai king prawn curry and tagliatelle with asparagus; popular Sunday roasts. *Starters/Snacks: £3.50 to £5.95. Main Courses: £6.50 to £13.95. Puddings: £3.95 to £4.95*

Spirit ~ Manager Julie Whittingham ~ Real ale ~ Bar food (12-10(9.30 Sun)) ~ (020) 8994 1204 ~ Children welcome ~ Open 12-11.30(10.30 Sun)

Recommended by Susan and John Douglas, N R White, John Saville, Sue Demont, Tim Barrow

Churchill Arms 🍷 🍺 £
Kensington Church Street; ⊖ Notting Hill Gate, Kensington High Street; W8 7LN

Cheery Irish landlord at bustling old favourite that's like a friendly local, with very well kept beers and excellent thai food; even at its most crowded, it stays relaxed and welcoming

The wonderfully cheery atmosphere at this flower swamped pub owes a lot to the enthusiasm and commitment of the amiable Irish landlord. He's very much in evidence, delightedly mixing with customers as he threads his way through the evening crowds, making everyone feel at home, even when it's really busy. A few years ago his buoyant enthusiasm led him to start planting up flower pots and baskets. It quickly became something of an obsession (indeed the façade has pretty much disappeared behind the glorious display) and a year or two ago his efforts were rewarded when the pub's 85 window boxes and 42 hanging baskets won the Chelsea Flower Show's first-ever Boozers in Bloom competition. Another of his hobbies is collecting butterflies – you'll see a variety of prints and books on the subject dotted around the bar. He wasn't ready to stop there though – the pub is also filled with countless lamps, miners' lights, horse tack, bedpans and brasses hanging from the ceiling, a couple of interesting carved figures and statuettes behind the central bar counter, prints of american presidents, and lots of Churchill memorabilia. On handpump, the Fullers Chiswick, ESB, London Pride, and seasonal beers are particularly well kept, and he offers two dozen wines by the glass. The spacious and rather smart plant-filled dining conservatory may be used for hatching butterflies, but is better known for its big choice of excellent thai food. Look out for special events and decorations around Christmas, Hallowe'en, St Patrick's Day, St George's Day, and Churchill's birthday (30 November) – along with more people than you'd ever imagine could feasibly fit inside this place; they have their own cricket and football teams; fruit machine and TV. There can be quite an overspill on to the street, where there are some chrome tables and chairs.

🍴 **Good quality and splendid value, the conservatory has authentic thai food with everything from a proper thai curry to various rice, noodle and stir-fried dishes. At lunchtimes they usually also have a very few traditional dishes such as fish and chips or sausage and chips, and they do a good value Sunday roast.** *Starters/Snacks: £2.50. Main Courses: £6.00. Puddings: £2.00*

Fullers ~ Manager Jerry O'Brien ~ Real ale ~ Bar food (12-10) ~ Restaurant ~ (020) 7727 4242 ~ Children welcome ~ Dogs welcome ~ Open 11-11(12 Thurs-Sat); 12-10.30 Sun

Recommended by LM, P Dawn, David M Smith, Derek Thomas, the Didler, Brian and Anna Marsden, Tracey and Stephen Groves

Colton Arms

Greyhound Road; ⊖ Barons Court; W14 9SD

Unspoilt little pub kept unchanged thanks to its dedicated landlord; it's peaceful and genuinely old-fashioned, with well kept beer

Do go out of your way for a pint at this unspoilt little gem, and when you get there, don't be deterred by its inconspicuous exterior. Thanks to the friendly, dedicated landlord (and his son) this peaceful, unassuming place has survived intact down the years – it's been exactly the same for the last 40 years. As he says, 'A pub like this is a little strange in London nowadays, but most people seem to like it.' Like an old-fashioned country pub in town, the main U-shaped front bar has a log fire blazing in winter, highly polished brasses, a fox's mask, hunting crops and plates decorated with hunting scenes on the walls, and a remarkable collection of handsomely carved antique oak furniture. That room is small enough, but the two back rooms, each with their own little serving counter with a bell to ring for service, are tiny. Well kept Adnams, Fullers London Pride and Harveys on handpump, with, in summer, Caledonian Deuchars IPA, and in winter, Greene King Old Speckled Hen. When you pay, note the old-fashioned brass-bound till. Pull the curtain aside for the door out to a charming back terrace with a neat rose arbour. The pub is next to the Queens Club tennis courts and gardens. More reports please.

🍴 **Just sandwiches, weekday lunchtimes only.** *Starters/Snacks: £3.75*

Enterprise ~ Lease N J and J A Nunn ~ Real ale ~ Bar food (weekday lunchtimes only) ~ No credit cards ~ (020) 7385 6956 ~ Children over three welcome till 7pm ~ Dogs allowed in bar ~ Open 12-3, 5.30-11.30; 12-4, 7-11.30(11 Sun) weekends

Recommended by Susan and John Douglas, Sue Demont, Tim Barrow

Dove

Upper Mall; ⊖ Ravenscourt Park; W6 9TA

One of London's best-known pubs with lovely back terrace overlooking river, and cosily traditional front bar; interesting history, and sometimes unusual specials

So many writers, actors and artists have been drawn through the doors of this famous riverside pub over the years that there's a rather fascinating framed list of them all on a wall. It's said to be where 'Rule Britannia' was composed, and it was a favourite with Turner, who painted the view of the Thames from the delightful back terrace, and Graham Greene. The street itself is associated with the foundation of the Arts and Crafts movement – William Morris's old residence (open certain afternoons) is nearby. By the entrance from the quiet alley, the front snug (said to be Britain's smallest and apparently listed in *The Guinness Book of Records*) is cosy and traditional, with black panelling, and red leatherette cushioned built-in wall settles and stools around dimpled copper tables; it leads to a bigger, similarly furnished room, with old framed advertisements and photographs of the pub. That opens on to the terrace, where the main flagstoned area, down some steps, has a verandah and some highly prized tables looking over the low river wall to the Thames reach just above Hammersmith Bridge. There's a tiny exclusive area up a spiral staircase, a prime spot for watching the rowing crews out on the water. They stock the full range of Fullers beers, with Chiswick, Discovery, ESB, London Pride and seasonal beers on handpump. The pub isn't quite so crowded at lunchtimes as it is in the evenings. A plaque marks the level of the highest-ever tide in 1928. More reports please.

🍴 **They make a real effort in sourcing their ingredients for the well liked bar food which typically includes lunchtime sandwiches, vegetable moussaka, sausage and mash, salads, fish and chips, popular platters for sharing, and perhaps some more unexpected specials such as tuscan vegetable fritatta, grilled fig salad and venison on truffled sweet potato purée.** *Starters/Snacks: £5.50 to £6.50. Main Courses: £9.75 to £13.75. Puddings: £3.25 to £5.50*

Fullers ~ Manager Nick Kiley ~ Real ale ~ Bar food (12-3, 6-9; 12-4, 5-9 Sat; 12-5 Sun) ~ (020) 8748 9474 ~ Dogs welcome ~ Open 11-11; 12-10.30 Sun

Recommended by Pat and Tony Martin, N R White, the Didler

Fat Badger 🍴 🍷

Portobello Road; ⊖ Ladbroke Grove, Westbourne Park (though perhaps the nicest walk is the long one from Notting Hill Gate); W10 5TA

Stylish but easy-going gastropub with enjoyable, individual food – not overly fancy, but good quality and properly cooked; a laid-back pubby feel too

Relaxed and comfortably trendy yet welcoming and pubby at the same time, this reworked old local is run by a team with a pedigree at some of London's best-known eating places. Not surprisingly then the food is exceptional. The chef is influenced by the slow-food movement, so he sources well reared animals and birds and cooks them in honest, traditional ways. It's not fancy, and some will think it expensive, but the meats in particular are full of flavour, and it's all a refreshing and unusual change to most London gastropubs. At the end of the Portobello Road fewer people seem to get to, it can be pleasantly uncrowded some evenings, though tending to be busier Fridays and weekends. The downstairs bar – quite spacious – has the expected polished bare boards and worn furnishings (some of the comfortable armchairs and leather sofas very much so), with scrubbed wooden tables, a mix of benches and pews, and a big mirror propped against one wall; a ledge beneath one of the big windows has plenty of board games, and above a door there's a stuffed badger in a glass case. More unusual is the pink toile de jouy wallpaper, at first glance the sort you might find in a country house, but look more closely and these aren't tranquil rural scenes – they're fiercely contemporary vignettes of urban life, replete with hoodies and even muggings. The good wine list is on a clipboard on the bar, where you'll also find two changing beers such as Greene King IPA and Timothy Taylors Landlord. Upstairs, the dining room has simple wooden furnishings and standard lamps; a small scruffy roof terrace opens off. They may have an oyster counter in summer. More reports please.

🍴 **Bar snacks might include welsh rarebit, skillets of chicken and duck livers with bacon and thyme and baked sardines, while the main menu could have oysters, pickled beetroot with boiled egg and mustard cream, runner bean and goats cheese salad with walnut dressing, smoked eel with beetroot apple and watercresss, steamed mussels, pork and prune pie, confit of duck with orange and red onion salad, roast bream with anchovy and dill oil, roast partridge with lentils, black cabbage and green sauce, and puddings such as apple, prune and almond tart, walnut tiramisu and steamed orange pudding.** *Starters/Snacks: £5.50 to £8.00. Main Courses: £9.00 to £16.00. Puddings: £5.00 to £7.50*

Enterprise ~ Lease Rupert Walsh and Joad Hall ~ Real ale ~ Bar food (12-3, 6.30-10; 11-5, 6.30-10.30(9 Sun) weekends) ~ Restaurant ~ (020) 8969 4500 ~ Children in restaurant ~ Dogs allowed in bar ~ Open 12-11; 11-midnight Sat; 12-10.30 Sun

Recommended by BOB

Havelock Tavern 🍽 ♀

Masbro Road; ⊖ ⇄ Kensington(Olympia); W14 0LS

Popular gastropub with friendly, often vibrant, atmosphere, very good food, and well chosen wines

Until 1932 this blue-tiled building was two separate shops (one was a wine merchant, but no one can remember much about the other), and it still has huge shop-front windows. Step inside and the atmosphere is buoyant with smart chatting customers – at busy times it can seem really quite noisy. You may have to wait for a table in the evenings (when some dishes can run out quite quickly), but it can be quieter at lunchtimes, and in the afternoons can have something of the feel of a civilised private club. As all was going very well here when they took over, new licensees have kept things just as they were. Light and airy, the L-shaped bar is welcoming but plain and unfussy: bare boards, long wooden tables (you may end up sharing at busy times), a mix of chairs and stools, a few soft spotlights, and a fireplace. A second little room with pews leads to a small paved terrace, with benches, a tree, and wall climbers. Friendly staff serve Adnams, Fullers London Pride and Sharps Doom Bar from handpumps at the elegant modern bar counter, as well as a good range of well chosen wines, with around a dozen by the glass; mulled wine in winter, and in May and June perhaps home-made elderflower soda; backgammon, chess, Scrabble and other board games. On weekdays, nearby parking is metered, though restrictions stop at 5pm.

🍽 The well conceived and executed cooking is full of flavour – as with the fabric of the place it remains just the same under the new licensees. The choice changes every day but might include things like courgette, fennel and chilli soup, warm leek, spinach and goats cheese tart, fillets of red mullet wrapped in parma ham with baby spinach, green beans and salsa verde, thai red beef curry, chargrilled whole poussin with parsley and garlic butter, pan-fried bass with chickpeas, tomato, fennel and white wine, grilled leg of lamb with spinach, roast potatoes, peppers, aubergine, fennel and tzatziki, puddings like chocolate brownie or summer berry trifle, and some unusual cheeses served with apple chutney; you can't book tables. *Starters/Snacks: £4.50 to £8.50. Main Courses: £9.00 to £14.00. Puddings: £4.50 to £6.50*

Free house ~ Licensees Helen Watson and Andrew Cooper ~ Real ale ~ Bar food (12.30-2.30(3 Sun), 7-10(9.30 Sun)) ~ (020) 7603 5374 ~ Children welcome ~ Dogs welcome ~ Open 11-11; 12-10.30 Sun

Recommended by Martin and Karen Wake, Derek Thomas

Portobello Gold ♀

Portobello Road; ⊖ Notting Hill Gate; W11 2QB

Engaging combination of pub, hotel, restaurant and even Internet café, with relaxed atmosphere, wide choice of enjoyable food (especially in attractive dining room), excellent range of drinks, and good value bedrooms

Going some way back now, this enterprising Notting Hill stalwart (known as the Gold) was the first place in the UK to serve oyster shooters (a shot glass with an oyster, parmesan, horseradish, crushed chillies, Tabasco and lime). We remember it too when the garden (now the rather exotic-seeming back dining room) was a favourite Hells Angels hangout. Though a bit tamer these days the lively almost bohemian air has filtered down the years to the current enterprising licensees who open up from 9am (so you can pop in and read the daily papers over a coffee and fresh pastry) and always seem to be on the go organising live music sessions, growing herbs on the roof, or changing the art and photographs on the walls. Our favourite part is that dining room mentioned above, with big tropical plants, an impressive wall-to-wall mirror, comfortable wicker chairs, stained wooden tables, and a cage of vocal canaries adding to the outdoor effect – in summer they open up the sliding roof. The smaller front bar has a nice old fireplace, cushioned banquettes, and, more unusually, several Internet terminals (which disappear in the evening). It's all very relaxed, cheerful and informal, though can get a bit rushed when they're busy in the evening. The very well stocked bar has Fullers London Pride and Harveys, as well as several draught belgian beers, Thatcher's farm cider, a good selection of bottled beers from around the world, a wide range of interesting tequilas and other well sourced spirits and a particularly good wine list (with just under two dozen by the glass) which can be attributed to the landlady who has written books on matching wine with food. They also have a cigar menu; piped music, TV, chess, backgammon. There are one or two tables and chairs on the pretty street outside, which, like the pub, is named in recognition of the 1769 battle of Portobello, fought over control of the lucrative gold route to Panama. Parking nearby is metered but you can usually find a space, though Saturday can be a problem. Some of the bedrooms are small, but they're all particularly good value for the area (you get the best price by booking on line), and there's a spacious apartment with rooftop terrace and putting green.

🍴 With meats carefully sourced from a known farm in Oxfordshire, bar food includes dips and nibbles, soup, toasted sandwiches, caesar salad, cajun jumbo shrimp, irish rock oysters (with a choice of dressings), moules marinières, fish and chips, wild boar and apple sausages with red onion gravy, chicken fajitas, linguini with puttanesca sauce, rib-eye steak, a seafood platter, and puddings such as pecan nut pie, chocolate and amaretti torte. There's a choice of Sunday roasts, and at lunchtime they usually do a good value set menu; also children's helpings, and cream teas; a reader told us that they add a 10% service charge to the bill. *Starters/Snacks: £6.00 to £8.00. Main Courses: £10.00 to £15.00. Puddings: £4.50*

Enterprise ~ Lease Michael Bell and Linda Johnson-Bell ~ Real ale ~ Bar food (12-9) ~ Restaurant ~ (020) 7460 4910 ~ Children welcome away from the bar ~ Dogs allowed in bar ~ Live music Sun evening ~ Open 9-midnight(12.30 Fri, Sat); 10-10.30 Sun; closed 25-31 Dec ~ Bedrooms: £85S/£105S(£130B)

Recommended by Brian and Anna Marsden, Brian and Janet Ainscough

Warrington

Warrington Crescent; ⊖ Maida Vale; W9 1EH

Gordon Ramsay's second London pub, a Victorian gin palace with extaordinary décor; pie and mash bar menu and upstairs restaurant

This dazzling building, restored at huge expense by Gordon Ramsay, reopened about a year ago. Nor can any expense have been spared when the opulent art nouveau interior was originally constructed. A splendid marble and mahogany bar counter is topped by an extraordinary structure that's rather like a cross between a carousel and a ship's hull, with cherubs thrown in for good measure. Throughout are elaborately patterned tiles, ceilings and stained-glass, and a remarkable number of big lamps and original light fittings; there's a small coal fire, and two exquisitely tiled pillars. The drawings of nubile young women here and above a row of mirrors on the opposite wall are later additions, very much in keeping with the overall style, and hinting at the days when the building's trade was rather less respectable than it is today. Three real ales include Adnams Broadside, Fullers London Pride and Greene King IPA, they've several unusual bottled beers and a beer from London brewer Meantime, as well as a fine choice of wines.

🍴 The short bar menu is very traditional, with soup, pork pie with piccalilli, scotch egg with HP sauce, ploughman's and pies. *Starters/Snacks: £3.50 to £6.50. Main Courses: £9.50*

Free house ~ Licensee Oliver Williams ~ Real ale ~ Bar food (12-2.30(4 Sat, Sun), 6-10(10.30 Fri, Sat)) ~ (020) 7592 7960 ~ Children welcome ~ Open 11-11; 12-12 Fri; 12-11 Sat; 12-11.30 Sun

Recommended by BOB

White Horse ♀ 🍺

Parsons Green; ⊖ Parsons Green; SW6 4UL

Cheerfully relaxed local with emphasis on the excellent range of carefully sourced drinks, and superior food

On summer evenings and at weekends the front terrace overlooking the green at this easy-going place has something of a continental feel, with a cheery crowd drinking al fresco, and they have barbecues out here most sunny evenings. The stylishly modernised

U-shaped bar has plenty of sofas, wooden tables, and huge windows with slatted wooden blinds, and winter coal and log fires, one in an elegant marble fireplace. The pub is usually busy (and can feel crowded at times), but there are enough smiling, helpful staff behind the solid panelled central servery to ensure you'll rarely have to wait too long to be served. They stock an impressive range of drinks, with Adnams and Harveys and half a dozen nicely varied guests on handpump from brewers such as Abbeydale, Dark Star, Jennings, O'Hanlons, Otter and Whitstable, 14 well chosen draught beers from overseas (usually belgian and german but occasionally from further afield), 15 trappist beers, around 120 other foreign bottled beers, ten or so malt whiskies, and a constantly expanding range of about 100 good, interesting and reasonably priced wines. They have quarterly beer festivals, often spotlighting regional breweries.

🍴 Changing bar food might include butternut squash and watercress risotto, ricotta and aubergine ravioli, slow braised pork belly, beer-battered haddock, sausage and mash, and specials like lemon sole with pea mash, or seafood linguini. They still have a weekend brunch menu, and a popular Sunday lunch. *Starters/Snacks: £3.50 to £8.00. Main Courses: £9.00 to £16.00. Puddings: £4.50 to £6.50*

Mitchells & Butlers ~ Manager Dan Fox ~ Real ale ~ Bar food (9.30am-10.30pm) ~ Restaurant ~ (020) 7736 2115 ~ Children welcome ~ Dogs welcome ~ Open 9.30am-11.30pm(12 Sat, Sun)
Recommended by Sue Demont, Tim Barrow, the Didler, LM, Jonathan Evans, Steve Kirby

Windsor Castle

Campden Hill Road; ✆ *Holland Park, Notting Hill Gate; W8 7AR*

Genuinely unspoilt, with lots of atmosphere in the tiny, dark rooms, and a bustling summer garden; good beers, and reliable food

Each of the tiny unspoilt rooms at this warmly characterful Victorian pub has its own entrance from the street, but it's much more fun trying to navigate through the minuscule doors between them inside (one leads to a cosy pre-war-style dining room), and finding people you've arranged to meet can be quite a challenge; more often than not they'll be hidden behind the high backs of the sturdy built-in elm benches. With its wealth of dark oak furnishings, time-smoked ceilings, soft lighting and a coal-effect fire it oozes with genuine old-fashioned charm. Usually fairly quiet at lunchtime, the pub is packed most evenings, and you'll need to move fast to bag a table. It's especially cosy in winter, but the pub's appeal is just as strong in summer, thanks to the little, tree-shaped garden behind, easily one of the best pub gardens in London. It's always busy out here when the sun's shining, but there's quite a secluded feel thanks to the high ivy-covered sheltering walls. They have a bar out here in summer, as well as heaters for cooler days, and lots of tables and chairs on the flagstones. Adnams Broadside, Fullers London Pride and Timothy Taylors Landlord are well kept on handpump, with decent house wines, various malt whiskies, jugs of Pimms in summer, and perhaps mulled wine in winter, and they have occasional beer festivals. No fruit machines or piped music. The bones of Thomas Paine are said to be buried in the cellar, after his son sold them to the landlord to settle a beer debt.

🍴 Under the new licensee, bar food includes sandwiches, good ploughman's, fish and chips, pies, salmon salad and puddings such as apple crumble. *Starters/Snacks: £3.80 to £6.95. Main Courses: £6.70 to £10.90. Puddings: £3.80*

Mitchells & Butlers ~ Manager James Platford ~ Real ale ~ Bar food (12-3, 5-10, 12-10 Sat, 12-9 Sun) ~ (020) 7243 8797 ~ Children welcome till 7pm ~ Dogs allowed in bar ~ Open 12-11(10.30 Sun)
Recommended by Tracey and Stephen Groves, N R White, Brian and Anna Marsden, the Didler, J V Dadswell, Giles and Annie Francis

---

If a service charge is mentioned prominently on a menu or accommodation terms, you must pay it if service was satisfactory. If service is really bad, you are legally entitled to refuse to pay some or all of the service charge as compensation for not getting the service you might reasonably have expected.

LUCKY DIP

Besides the fully inspected pubs, you might like to try these Lucky Dips recommended to us and described by readers (if you do, please send us reports: feedback@thegoodpubguide.co.uk).

CENTRAL LONDON

EC1

☆ *Bleeding Heart* EC1N 8SJ [Bleeding Heart Yard, off Greville St]: Airy contemporary bar with café tables on scrubbed boards, neat staff, well kept Adnams ales from ornate mahogany-and-mirrors counter, good choice of wines by the glass; emphasis on good if not cheap french food in smart downstairs open-kitchen candlelit restaurant – an extraordinary maze of cellars (beware service charge); breakfast from 7, cl wknds *(N R White, BB)*

Butchers Hook & Cleaver EC1A 9DY [W Smithfield]: Fullers bank conversion with their full ale range and pubby food all day esp pies, breakfast from 7.30am, friendly staff, daily papers, relaxed atmosphere, nice mix of chairs inc some button-back leather armchairs, wrought-iron spiral stairs to pleasant mezzanine with waitress service; piped music, big-screen sports TV; open all day, cl wknds *(Peter Dandy, Steve Kirby, Michael Dandy, Derek Thomas, BB, DC)*

Fence EC1M 6BP [Cowcross St]: Contemporary furniture on bare boards, up-to-date food, good choice of wines and lagers, daily papers; piped music, TV; tables out on sizeable back deck and terrace *(Michael Dandy)*

☆ *Hand & Shears* EC1A 7JA [Middle St]: Traditional panelled Smithfield pub dating from 16th c, three basic bright rooms and small snug off central servery, bustling at lunchtime, quiet evenings, Adnams and Courage Directors, quick friendly service, interesting bric-a-brac and old photographs, short choice of low-priced pub food; open all day but cl wknds *(Dr Ron Cox, Michael Dandy, LYM, N R White)*

Hope & Sirloin EC1M 6BH [Cowcross St]: One-bar Victorian pub, Wells & Youngs ales from small bar, some decent wines by the glass, popular carvery at bar with Smithfield meats for sandwiches, dark panelling, crimson walls, frosted glass, some original tiling, simple varied dark wood furniture, upstairs restaurant with good steaks and roasts; good wheelchair access, some tables outside, open all day from 6am (wkdy breakfast from 7) *(Valerie Baker)*

St Pauls EC1Y 4SA [Chiswell St]: Extended corner pub with mixed décor and furnishings, low-priced pubby food from baguettes up, Greene King ales *(Michael Dandy)*

EC2

☆ *Dirty Dicks* EC2M 4NR [Bishopsgate]: Busy re-creation of traditional City tavern, fun for foreign visitors, booths and barrel tables in rather laddish low-beamed bar, interesting old prints inc one of Nathaniel Bentley the weird original Dirty Dick, Wells & Youngs ales, enjoyable food inc interesting sandwiches and sharing platters, pleasant service, calmer cellar wine bar with wine racks overhead in brick barrel-vaulted ceiling, further upstairs area too; piped music, games machines and TV; cl wknds *(LYM, Michael Dandy, the Didler, Ian Phillips)*

Globe EC2M 6SA [Moorgate]: Adnams Broadside, Elgoods Cambridge, Fullers London Pride and Sharps Doom Bar in modest-sized bar with mixed furniture, pubby bar food from sandwiches up (breakfast from 8am), daily papers, restaurant and pool room upstairs; TV *(Michael Dandy, Peter Dandy)*

☆ *Hamilton Hall* EC2M 7PY [Bishopsgate; also entrance from L'pool St Stn]: Showpiece Wetherspoons with flamboyant Victorian baroque décor, plaster nudes and fruit mouldings, chandeliers, mirrors, good-sized comfortable mezzanine, reliable food all day, lots of real ales inc interesting guest beers, decent wines and coffee, good prices; silenced machines, can get crowded; good disabled access, tables outside, open all day *(Valerie Baker, Tracey and Stephen Groves, LYM, Ian Phillips)*

Kings Arms EC2M 1RP [Wormwood St]: Low-ceilinged bar with reasonably priced pubby food from sandwiches up, Courage Directors, Fullers London Pride and Greene King IPA, pool downstairs; piped music; back terrace *(Michael Dandy)*

Lord Aberconway EC2M 1QT [Old Broad St]: Victorian feel with dark panelling and furniture, Caledonian Deuchars IPA, Fullers London Pride, St Austell Tribute and Timothy Taylors Landlord, reasonably priced food from sandwiches up, wrought-iron railed upper dining gallery *(Michael Dandy)*

Railway Tavern EC2M 7NX [Liverpool St]: Light and airy, with high ceilings and vast front windows, Greene King ales and several wines by the glass from long bar, pubby food from sandwiches up inc sharing platters, second room upstairs; pavement tables *(Michael Dandy)*

White Hart EC2M 3TH [Bishopsgate]: Typical City pub with plenty of tables and standing shelves, appealing candlelit vaulted dining basement, Caledonian Deuchars IPA, Fullers London Pride, Timothy Taylors Landlord and Wells & Youngs Bombardier, lots of wines by the glass, pubby food from sandwiches up *(Michael Dandy)*

EC3

Bunch of Grapes EC3M 7AN [Lime St]: Long narrow City pub, Adnams, Greene King IPA and Wells & Youngs Bombardier, pubby food, turkey carpet and anaglypta ceiling *(Michael Dandy, Ian Phillips)*

Chamberlain EC3N 1NU [Minories]: Neat high-ceilinged bar in substantial hotel, Fullers ales, sensibly priced bar food from sandwiches up, smart back restaurant; handy for Tower, 64 bedrooms *(Michael Dandy)*

East India Arms EC3M 4BR [Fenchurch St]: Neat Victorian pub refurbished by Shepherd Neame, good service even with the lunchtime crowds; unobtrusive TV; cl wknds and perhaps later evenings *(Ian Phillips, N R White)*

Elephant EC3M 5BA [Fenchurch St]: Small ground-floor bar, larger basement lounge, Wells & Youngs ales, good sandwiches and other lunchtime food, friendly helpful staff *(Ian Phillips)*

☆ **Lamb** EC3V 1LR [Leadenhall Mkt]: Well run traditional stand-up bar, staff always polite and efficient even when very busy with sharp City lads, Wells & Youngs ales, good choice of wines by the glass, engraved glass, plenty of ledges and shelves, spiral stairs up to tables and seating in small light and airy carpeted gallery overlooking market's central crossing, corner servery doing good lunchtime carvery baguettes, separate stairs to bright and airy dining room (not cheap), also basement bar with shiny wall tiling and own entrance; discreet TV, silenced games machine; cl wknds *(Ian Phillips, N R White, Dr and Mrs M E Wilson, Michael Dandy, Derek Thomas, Valerie Baker)*

New Moon EC3V 0DN [Gracechurch St, Leadenhall Mkt]: Long busy bare-boards market-view bar, fancy plasterwork in high red ceiling, Greene King ales; big-screen TV *(Dr and Mrs M E Wilson, Michael Dandy)*

Ship EC3V 0BP [Talbot Ct, off Eastcheap]: Interesting bare-boards pub, quieter upstairs with old prints and dark décor, friendly staff, several well kept ales, simple low-priced lunchtime food; alley overflow, open all day, cl wknds *(N R White)*

Swan EC3V 1LY [Ship Tavern Passage, off Gracechurch St]: Bustling narrow flagstoned bar, particularly well kept Fullers ales, proper hands-on landlord and friendly chatty service, generous lunchtime sandwiches and snacks, neatly kept Victorian panelled décor, larger carpeted upstairs bar; silent corner TV, can get packed early wkdy evenings; usually cl 9, cl wknds *(N R White, Dr and Mrs M E Wilson, Ian Phillips, Michael Dandy)*

EC4

☆ **Banker** EC4R 3TE [Cousin Lane, by Cannon St Stn]: Attractive multi-level pub just below Cannon St railway bridge, stripped brick, mirrors and big chandelier in high-ceilinged bar, steps up to two small rooms (one very cosy, with leather sofas – you can hear the trains rumbling overhead), linking to long narrow glass-fronted room with thrilling Thames view shared by small outdoor deck; good range of Fullers ales and of wines by the glass, enjoyable food inc sharing plates

(some nice cheeses), may be spit-roasts, smart attentive staff, relaxed chatty atmosphere, framed banknotes and railway posters; open all day *(BB, Derek Thomas, Dr and Mrs M E Wilson)*

Centre Page EC4V 5BH [aka the Horn; Knightrider St]: Modernised old pub with window booths or 'traps' in narrow entrance room, more space beyond, traditional style with panelling and subdued lighting, chatty atmosphere, mix of after-work drinkers and tourists having cappuccino; friendly efficient staff, simple appetising bar menu (from breakfast at 9), downstairs dining room, well kept Fullers beers, good tea, various coffees; piped music may be a bit loud; tables outside have good view of St Pauls *(BB, N R White, Tim and Ann Newell)*

Old Bell EC4Y 1DH [Fleet St, nr Ludgate Circus]: 17th-c tavern backing on to St Brides the wedding-cake church, heavy black beams, brass-topped tables, dim lighting, stained-glass bow window, good changing choice of real ales from island servery, friendly efficient young foreign staff, good value standard food, coal fire, cheerful atmosphere; piped music *(N R White, BB, Michael Dandy, the Didler, Tracey and Stephen Groves)*

Punch EC4Y 1DE [Fleet St]: New chef doing enjoyable food all day inc good home-made pies and sausages and lunchtime buffet, Timothy Taylors or Theakstons, good choice of wines by the glass, friendly young staff, pleasant informal atmosphere, light and airy, with colourful cushions and modern tables alongside Victorian features such as superb tiled entrance with mirrored lobby; children welcome, open all day *(Michael Dandy)*

Tipperary EC4Y 1HT [Fleet St]: Tiny irish-theme downstairs bar with counter seating, Fullers London Pride and Greene King IPA, more room upstairs *(Tracey and Stephen Groves, Michael Dandy)*

SE1

Rake SE1 9AG [Winchester Walk]: Tiny discreetly modern bar with amazing bottled beer range in wall-wide cooler as well as half a dozen continental lagers on tap and perhaps a couple of rare real ales; fair-sized terrace with decking and heated marquee *(E McCall, T McLean, D Irving)*

SW1

Adam & Eve SW1H 9EX [Petty France]: Nicely redecorated with dark ceilings and furniture but big light windows, Adnams, Caledonian 80/-, Wadworths 6X and Wells & Youngs, low-priced pubby food from sandwiches and baked potatoes up, friendly service; piped music, TV and games machine *(Michael Dandy)*

☆ **Buckingham Arms** SW1H 9EU [Petty France]: Relaxed chatty 18th-c local with welcoming landlord and friendly regulars, good value pubby food (evenings too) from back open kitchen, Wells & Youngs ales from long bar, good wines by the glass, elegant mirrors and woodwork, unusual side corridor fitted out with elbow ledge for drinkers, friendly pub dog; two TVs; dogs welcome, handy for Buckingham Palace, Westminster Abbey and St James's Park, open all day *(LYM, the Didler, Robert F Smith, N R White, Dr and Mrs A K Clarke, Michael Dandy)*

Chequers SW1Y 6DB [Duke St]: Long beamed and carpeted bar with well kept Fullers, interesting Prime Minister prints *(Tracey and Stephen Groves)*

Clarence SW1A 2HP [Whitehall]: Civilised olde-worlde beamed pub with well spaced tables, varied seating inc tub chairs and banquettes, real ales such as Old Mill, Timothy Taylors Landlord and Wells & Youngs Bombardier, decent wines by the glass, friendly chatty landlord, popular reasonably priced food all day from sandwiches up, upstairs dining area; pavement tables *(Phil Bryant)*

Feathers SW1H 0BH [Broadway]: Large comfortable pub, a Scotland Yard local, pubby food from sandwiches up, restaurant upstairs, well kept Fullers London Pride, Marstons Pedigree, Wadworths 6X and Wells & Youngs Bombardier, several wines by the glass; open all day (from 8 for breakfast) *(Michael Dandy, BB)*

☆ *Fox & Hounds* SW1W 8HR [Passmore St/Graham Terr]: Small convivial local, Wells & Youngs ales, friendly staff and civilised customers, wall benches, warm red décor with big hunting prints, old sepia photographs of pubs and customers, some sofas and toby jugs, book-lined back room, hanging plants under attractive skylight, coal-effect gas fire and organ; can be very busy Fri night, quieter wkdy lunchtimes *(the Didler, Jeremy King, N R White, Sue Demont, Tim Barrow)*

Golden Lion SW1Y 6QY [King St]: Imposing bow-fronted Victorian pub opp Christies auction rooms, well kept Fullers, Greene King and Wells & Youngs from decorative servery, decent wines by the glass, good value food, friendly service, ornate 1900 Jacobean décor and dark panelling; piped dance music can be obtrusive; seats usually available in passageway alongside or upstairs bar *(PHB, N R White)*

Grouse & Claret SW1X 7AP [Little Chester St]: This attractively old-fashioned and civilised mews pub has now closed, redevelopment likely *(BB)*

Jugged Hare SW1V 1DX [Vauxhall Bridge Rd/Rochester Row]: Popular Fullers Ale & Pie pub in impressive former colonnaded bank with balustraded balcony, chandelier, prints and busts; their real ales, friendly efficient service, reasonably priced traditional food from sandwiches up, cream teas; games machine, piped music; open all day *(Jeremy King, the Didler, BB)*

☆ *Morpeth Arms* SW1P 4RW [Millbank]: Sparkling clean Victorian pub facing Thames, roomy and comfortable, some etched and cut glass, old books and prints, photographs, earthenware jars and bottles, well kept Wells & Youngs, good choice of wines and of good value food all day from sandwiches up, good welcoming service even at busy lunchtimes, upstairs dining room; games machine, may be unobtrusive sports TV; seats outside (a lot of traffic), handy for Tate Britain *(Dr Ron Cox, BB, the Didler, JJW, CMW, PHB, Robert W Buckle, Mrs Margaret Ball)*

Old Monk Exchange SW1H 0HW [Victoria St]: Welcoming basement pub/wine bar, reasonably priced changing food choice, well kept real ales, good choice of wines; cl wknds *(Peter Handley)*

Old Star SW1H 0DB [Broadway]: Small partly carpeted ground-floor bar, Greene King ales, usual food, some tables and sofas in partly vaulted basement, upstairs area (not always open); piped music, sports TV *(Michael Dandy)*

Orange Brewery SW1W 8NE [Pimlico Rd]: Friendly panelled bar, all-day cheap food inc various pies and good sausages, well kept ales inc Adnams Broadside; pavement tables *(LYM, N R White)*

Plumbers Arms SW1W 0LN [Lower Belgrave St]: Small, friendly and carefully refurbished to keep homely feel, well kept Fullers London Pride, Greene King and Wells & Youngs, enjoyable bar food from sandwiches up; cl wknds *(Conor McGaughey)*

Red Lion SW1A 2NH [Parliament St]: Congenial pub by Houses of Parliament, used by Foreign Office staff and MPs – has Division Bell; parliamentary cartoons and prints, decent wines by the glass, Caledonian Deuchars IPA, Fullers London Pride and Greene King Old Speckled Hen, good range of food from good panini to steaks, efficient staff who welcome visitors, also cellar bar and small narrow upstairs dining room *(Peter Dandy, Michael Dandy)*

☆ *Red Lion* SW1Y 6PP [Crown Passage, behind St James's St]: Cheerful brightly lit early Victorian local tucked down narrow passage nr St James's Palace, red décor, dark panelling, nice prints, settles and leaded lights, well kept ales inc Adnams, friendly service, busy lunchtime (good bargain sandwiches), room upstairs; unobtrusive corner TV *(N R White, John and Gloria Isaacs, Tracey and Stephen Groves, Sue Demont, Tim Barrow, BB)*

Royal Oak SW1P 4BZ [Regency St/Rutherford St]: Compact one-bar Youngs pub with good choice of wines by the glass as well as their real ales, good value home-made wkdy lunchtime bar food, friendly mainly antipodean staff *(anon)*

Sanctuary House SW1H 9LA [Tothill St]: Pub/hotel's roomy high-ceilinged bar with Fullers ales, pubby food from sandwiches to steaks, cheerful helpful staff, plenty of tables, nice stools and armchairs, raised and balustraded back area with monkish mural, ornate outside scrollwork; piped music;

children welcome, 30 or more bedrooms, open all day *(Eithne Dandy)*

Speaker SW1P 2HA [Great Peter St]: Pleasant chatty atmosphere in unpretentious corner pub, well kept Shepherd Neame Spitfire, Wells & Youngs and two guest beers, lots of whiskies, limited popular food, friendly helpful staff, political cartoons and prints *(PHB, N R White, Mike Begley)*

☆ **St Stephens Tavern** SW1A 2JR [Parliament St]: Elegantly refurbished Victorian pub opp Houses of Parliament and Big Ben, lofty ceilings with brass chandeliers, tall windows with etched glass and swagged gold curtains, gleaming mahogany, charming upper gallery bar, four Badger ales from handsome counter with pedestal lamps, pleasant staff, usual food, Division Bell for MPs; can get packed; open all day *(Phil Bryant, BB)*

Westminster Arms SW1P 3AT [Storey's Gate; Westminster]: Unpretentious local near Westminster Abbey and Houses of Parliament, quite a mix of customers, lots of real ales like Adnams Best, Brakspears Bitter, Greene King IPA and Abbot, Thwaites Lancaster Bomber, and a beer named for the pub brewed by Hogs Back on handpump, several malt whiskies, straightforward food, old-fashioned furnishings, a good deal of panelling, piped music, not much room; children in eating areas lunchtime, tables outside, pen all day, cl Sun pm, food all day in week, not wknd pm *(P Dawn, N R White, Dr and Mrs A K Clarke, Ian Phillips, Peter Dandy, Michael Dandy, LYM, Dr Ron Cox, Andrew Hollingshead)*

White Swan SW1V 2SA [Vauxhall Bridge Rd]: Roomy pub handy for the Tate, lots of dark dining tables on three levels in long room, good value pubby food from sandwiches up, Fullers London Pride, Greene King and Wells & Youngs Bitter, lots of wines by the glass, quick helpful uniformed staff; quiet piped music; open all day *(John Wooll, JJW, CMW, BB)*

SW3

Hour Glass SW3 2DY [Brompton Rd]: Small well run pub handy for V&A and other nearby museums, well kept Black Sheep and Fullers London Pride, freshly squeezed fruit juice, good value pubby food (not Sun), friendly landlady and quick young staff; sports TV; pavement picnic-sets *(LM)*

Phoenix SW3 4EE [Smith St]: Light and airy comfortably modern two-room bar mixing sofas and low tables with leatherette chairs and dining tables, good range of wines by the glass, up-to-date food from good lunchtime light dishes to interesting specials *(Ian Phillips)*

☆ **Pigs Ear** SW3 5BS [Old Church St]: Civilised but carefully unsmart L-shaped pub with short interesting bar food choice, lots of wines by the glass inc champagne, Caledonian Deuchars IPA and Uley Pigs Ear, good coffee and service, solid wooden

furnishings, butterflies and 60s artwork on white-painted panelling, huge windows, upstairs restaurant; piped music *(LYM, Jeremy King)*

W1

Albany W1W 5QU [Great Portland St]: Eclectic mix of furnishings inc some big sofas and large tables, bare boards, unusual lamps (quite low lighting), dramatic patterned ceiling, Caledonian Deuchars IPA and Wells & Youngs Bombardier from long bar, Weston's farm cider, fruit beers, good choice of juices and smoothies, sensibly priced generous comfort food *(Jeremy King)*

☆ **Audley** W1K 2RX [Mount St]: Classic Mayfair pub, classy and relaxed, with opulent red plush, mahogany panelling and engraved glass, chandelier and clock hanging in lovely carved wood bracket from ornately corniced ceiling, Courage Best, Fullers London Pride, Greene King IPA and Wells & Youngs Bombardier from long polished bar, friendly efficient service, good standard food (reasonably priced for the area) and service, good coffee, upstairs panelled dining room; pavement tables, open all day *(LYM, Ian Phillips)*

Blue Posts W1B 5PX [Kingly St]: Compact pub with Greene King ales, good choice of food, upstairs dining area; attractive hanging baskets, a few pavement tables *(Peter Dandy, Michael Dandy)*

Carpenters Arms W1H 7NE [Seymour Pl]: Chatty local with up to half a dozen good changing ales, bare boards, helpful friendly staff, decently priced usual food; can get busy early evening, sports TVs, piped music *(Michael Mellers, BB)*

Champion W1T 3PA [Wells St]: Popular Sam Smiths pub with lots of stained-glass, brighter L-shaped upstairs area *(Tracey and Stephen Groves)*

Clachan W1B 5QH [Kingly St]: Ornate plaster ceiling supported by two large fluted and decorated pillars, comfortable screened leather banquettes, smaller drinking alcove up three or four steps, changing ales such as Batemans, Fullers and Timothy Taylors from handsome counter, food from sandwiches up; can get busy, but very relaxed in afternoons *(Sue Demont, Tim Barrow, Michael Dandy, Peter Dandy, BB)*

Coach & Horses W1J 6PT [Bruton St]: Cosy little timbered local among modern buildings, small welcoming bar with upstairs dining room (not always open), five well kept ales such as Sharps Doom Bar *(David M Smith, E McCall, T McLean, D Irving)*

Cock W1W 8QE [Great Portland St]: Big corner local with enormous lamps over picnic-sets outside, florid Victorian/ Edwardian décor with gleaming mahogany and plasterwork, some cut and etched glass, high tiled ceiling and mosaic floor, velvet curtains, coal-effect gas fire, cheap Sam Smiths OB from all four handpumps, popular food (not Fri-Sun evenings) in upstairs lounge with two more coal-effect gas fires, ploughman's downstairs too 12-6, friendly efficient service; open all day *(Michael Dandy, Peter Dandy, the Didler, Tracey and Stephen Groves, BB)*

Fitzroy W1T 2LY [Charlotte St]: Thriving traditional pub with grand mahogany servery, maroon leather and handsome frosted glass and mirrors, photographs of customers Augustus John, Dylan Thomas and the young Richard Attenborough, George Orwell's NUJ card and so forth, quieter carpeted downstairs bar, low-priced Sam Smiths OB, good value food inc filled baguettes, expert friendly staff; plenty of tables outside *(Darren Le Poidevin)*

French House W1D 5BG [Dean St]: Theatre memorabilia, good wines by the glass, plenty of bottled beers and lively chatty atmosphere – mainly standing room, windows keeping good eye on passers-by; can get very busy, open all day *(Peter Dandy, Mike Gorton)*

George W1W 7LQ [Gt Portland St]: Solid old-fashioned pub with lots of mahogany, chandeliers and engraved mirrors, standard pubby food from sandwiches up, well kept Greene King ales *(Michael Dandy)*

☆ **Golden Eagle** W1U 2NY [Marylebone Lane]: Well updated Victorian local with well kept Fullers and St Austell ales from elegant curving bar with plenty of bar stools, relaxing perimeter seating, friendly barman, blue and yellow décor, fresh flowers, popular informal piano singalong Thurs and Fri; piped music *(Terry Buckland)*

Jack Horner W1T 7QN [Tottenham Ct Rd]: Fullers bank conversion with full range of their ales from island bar counter, good service, pie-based food, neat tables in quiet areas *(Peter Dandy)*

Kings Arms W1J 7QA [Shepherd Market]: Minimalist décor in old low-ceilinged pub with good value standard bar food, Fullers London Pride, Greene King IPA and Wells & Youngs Bombardier, upper dining gallery *(Michael Dandy, LYM)*

Masons Arms W1S 1PY [Maddox St]: Nicely old-fashioned and traditional behind its florid Victorian façade, english staff and food, Fullers London Pride, Greene King Old Speckled Hen *(Quentin and Carol Williamson)*

Pontefract Castle W1U 1QA [Wigmore St/ St Christopher Pl]: Pleasantly traditional décor and civilised atmosphere, helpful staff, Fullers London Pride, Greene King Old Speckled Hen and St Austell Tribute, bargain wines, enjoyable food esp home-made sausages in variety and bargain fishcakes *(Robert Gomme, John Branston)*

Punch Bowl W1J 5RP [Farm St]: Attractive 18th-c Mayfair local, quiet and civilised, relaxing bar and dining room off panelled entrance corridor, decent bar lunches and wines by the glass; open all day *(Tracey and Stephen Groves)*

Red Lion W1B 5PR [Kingly St]: Dark panelling, narrow front bar with deep leather banquettes, back bar with darts, bargain simple lunches in comfortable upstairs lounge, cheap Sam Smiths keg beers *(Peter Dandy, DC, Michael Dandy, BB)*

Windmill W1S 2AZ [Mill St]: Plush and civilised, with gilt plaster cherubs, nice wall banquette, lots of small tables, Wells & Youngs Bombardier, some emphasis on wines, popular pies, pleasant dining areas on two floors *(Tracey and Stephen Groves)*

W2

Mad Bishop & Bear W2 1HB [Paddington Stn]: Up escalators from concourse, full Fullers ale range and a guest beer, good wine choice, good value standard food inc breakfast (7.30 on), ornate plasterwork, etched mirrors and fancy lamps inc big brass chandeliers, parquet, tiles and carpet, booths with leather banquettes, lots of wood and prints, train departures screen; TV, piped music, games machine; open all day, tables out overlooking concourse *(E McCall, T McLean, D Irving, Dr and Mrs M E Wilson, Dr and Mrs A K Clarke, BB, Michael Dandy)*

☆ **Victoria** W2 2NH [Strathearn Pl]: Lots of Victorian pictures and memorabilia, cast-iron fireplaces, wonderful gilded mirrors and mahogany panelling, brass mock-gas lamps above attractive horseshoe bar, bare boards and banquettes, relaxed atmosphere, friendly attentive service, full Fullers ale range, good choice of wines by the glass, well priced food counter; upstairs has leather club chairs in small library/snug (and, mostly used for private functions now, replica of Gaiety Theatre bar, all gilt and red plush); quiet piped music, TV (off unless people ask); pavement picnic-sets, open all day *(Tracey and Stephen Groves, LYM, Sue Demont, Tim Barrow)*

WC1

Bountiful Cow WC1R 4AP [Eagle St]: Distinctive pub with large cellar restaurant strong on burgers and steaks, Adnams ales with a guest such as Crouch Vale Brewers Gold *(Dr Martin Owton)*

Calthorpe Arms WC1X 8JR [Grays Inn Rd]: Civilised corner pub with plush wall seats, Wells & Youngs ales, big helpings of popular food upstairs lunchtime and evening, good staff; nice pavement tables, open all day *(the Didler)*

Penderels Oak WC1V 7HJ [High Holborn]: Vast Wetherspoons with attractive décor and woodwork, lots of books, pew seating around central tables, their usual well priced food and huge choice of good value real ales, charming staff; open all day *(Tracey and Stephen Groves, Dr and Mrs A K Clarke)*

Queens Head WC1X 8SF [Theobalds Rd]: Plushly comfortable and well decorated, with well kept Adnams, good service; lots of sports TVs *(Giles and Annie Francis)*

Rugby WC1N 3ES [Great James St]: Sizeable corner pub with Shepherd Neame ales from central servery, decent usual food, good service, darts, appropriate photographs; pleasant terrace *(the Didler)*

Swintons WC1X 9NT [Swinton St]: Modern dining pub, comfortable and spacious, with efficient friendly service, real ale such as Black Sheep, extensive wine list, impressive choice of reasonably priced food from contemporary snacks up; no TVs or machines *(Joe Green)*

WC2

Brewmaster WC2H 7AD [Cranbourn St]: Busy pub with standard pubby food from sandwiches and sharing platters up, Greene King ales, quick friendly service, room upstairs *(Michael Dandy)*

☆ **Chandos** WC2N 4ER [St Martins Lane]: Busy bare-boards bar with snug cubicles, lots of theatre memorabilia on stairs up to more comfortable lounge with opera photographs, low wooden tables, panelling, leather sofas, coloured windows; cheap Sam Smiths OB, prompt cheerful service, generous reasonably priced food from sandwiches to Sun roasts, air conditioning, darts; can get packed early evening, piped music and games machines; note the automaton on the roof (working 10-2 and 4-9); children upstairs till 6, open all day from 9 (for breakfast) *(Conor McGaughey, Michael Dandy, Dr and Mrs M E Wilson, Ian Phillips, LYM, Bruce Bird, Susan and Nigel Wilson)*

Coach & Horses WC2E 7BD [Wellington St]: Small irish pub with old-fashioned copper-topped bar, Fullers London Pride and Marstons Pedigree, lots of whiskeys, good lunchtime hot roast beef baps, irish sports mementoes and cartoons; can get crowded, handy for Royal Opera House *(John and Gloria Isaacs)*

Coal Hole WC2R 0DW [Strand]: Chatty and comfortable front bar, softly lit relaxed downstairs dining bar with wall reliefs, mock-baronial high ceiling and raised back gallery, cosy basement snug, good range of beers, decent wines by the glass, standard pubby food from sandwiches up *(N R White, Valerie Baker, BB, Michael Dandy, Pete Coxon)*

Cove WC2E 8HB [Piazza, Covent Garden]: Cornish-style nautical-theme bar up steep stairs, good pasties from shop below, Skinners Cornish Knocker and Betty Stogs, friendly staff, low beams and flagstones; piped music, may be crowded (door staff can put off at peak times); balcony overlooking cobbled piazza and its entertainers *(N R White)*

☆ **Cross Keys** WC2H 9EB [Endell St/Betterton St]: Relaxed retreat, masses of photographs and posters inc Beatles memorabilia, brassware and tasteful bric-a-brac on dark walls, impressive range of lunchtime sandwiches and a few bargain hot dishes, Courage Best and Wells & Youngs ales, decent wines by the glass, quick friendly service even at busy times; games machine, gents' down stairs; sheltered picnic-sets out on cobbles, pretty flower tubs and hanging baskets, open all day *(John and Gloria Isaacs, the Didler)*

Edgar Wallace WC2R 3JE [Essex St]: Simple spacious open-plan pub dating from 18th c despite its modern name, well kept Adnams, a beer brewed for them by Nethergate and several unusual guest beers (tasters offered), friendly relaxed staff, decent all-day food inc good sandwiches, interesting maps and prints of old London, stairs to room of Edgar Wallace memorabilia; open all day, cl wknds *(Bruce Bird, N R White, LM, Tracey and Stephen Groves)*

Freemasons Arms WC2E 9NG [Long Acre]: Roomy and relaxed two-level pub with ornate woodwork and cupola ceiling, big windows, pleasing semicircular bar, nice raised back area, interesting prints (and FA inaugurated here), small tables and lots of wood, Shepherd Neame ales, attentive staff, sensibly priced food; big-screen TV; open all day *(BB, Tracey and Stephen Groves, Bruce Bird)*

Hercules Pillars WC2B 5DG [Great Queen St]: Useful traditional mirrored pub with pubby food inc sausage specialities, good range of real ales, efficient staff; seats outside *(Martin and Pauline Jennings)*

Marquess of Anglesey WC2E 7AU [Bow St/Russell St]: Well refurbished, quiet, light and airy, with Wells & Youngs and a guest beer, decent food, friendly staff, a couple of big sofas, more room upstairs *(Michael Dandy)*

Nell Gwynne WC2R 0NP [Bull Inn Court]: Narrow dimly lit open-plan pub, lively atmosphere, real ales such as Greene King Old Speckled Hen and Wells & Youngs Bombardier, good juke box; TV, games machines; under threat of redevelopment – news please *(Tracey and Stephen Groves)*

Opera Tavern WC2B 5JS [Catherine St, opp Theatre Royal]: Cheerful bare-boards Victorian pub, not too touristy, five quickly changing real ales (over 20 a week), enjoyable bar food, some interesting fittings, lamps and windows *(Bruce Bird)*

☆ **Porterhouse** WC2E 7NA [Maiden Lane]: Good daytime pub (can be crammed evenings), London outpost of Dublin's Porterhouse microbrewery, their interesting if pricy draught beers inc Porter and two Stouts (comprehensive tasting tray), also their TSB real ale and a guest, lots of bottled imports, good choice of wines by the glass, reasonably priced food from soup and open sandwiches up with some emphasis on rock oysters, shiny three-level labyrinth of stairs (lifts for disabled), galleries and copper ducting and piping, some nice design touches, sonorous openwork clock, neatly cased bottled beer displays; piped music, irish live music, big-screen sports TV (repeated in gents'); tables on front terrace, open all day *(G Coates, Tracey and Stephen Groves, BB, Peter Dandy)*

☆ **Sherlock Holmes** WC2N 5DB [Northumberland St; aka Northumberland Arms]: Fine collection of Holmes memorabilia, also silent videos of black and white Holmes films; well kept Greene King ales, usual furnishings, quick service at good value lunchtime food counter, friendly young staff, quieter upstairs restaurant by replica of his study; tables out in front *(John Saville, BB)*

Ship WC2A 3HP [Gate St]: Tucked-away bare-boards pub with pews and high-backed settles, leaded lights, painted plaster relief ceiling and upstairs overflow, changing real ales, decent pubby food inc good ploughman's, friendly service; piped music *(Joe Green, Tracey and Stephen Groves)*

☆ *Ship & Shovell* WC2N 5PH [Craven Passage, off Craven St]: Four well kept Badger ales, good friendly staff, decent reasonably priced food inc wide range of baguettes etc, bright lighting, interesting prints, mainly naval (to support a fanciful connection between this former coal-heavers' pub properly called Ship & Shovel with Sir Cloudesley Shovell the early 18th-c admiral), open fire, compact back section, separate partitioned bar across *Underneath the Arches* alley; TV; open all day *(John A Barker, N R White, the Didler, Sue Demont, Tim Barrow)*

Wellington WC2R 0HS [Strand/Wellington St]: Long narrow corner pub with room upstairs, Fullers London Pride, Greene King Abbot and Timothy Taylors Landlord, low-priced standard simple food from sandwiches up, friendly staff; tables outside *(Michael Dandy, Conor McGaughey)*

White Hart WC2B 5QD [Drury Lane]: Linked room areas with some appealing Regency touches to comfortable recent refurbishment (nicest near the front), good value food all day, Fullers; cl Sun *(Dave Braisted)*

EAST LONDON

E1

☆ *Dickens Inn* E1W 1UH [Marble Quay, St Katharines Way]: Outstanding position looking over smart docklands marina to Tower Bridge, bare boards, baulks and timbers, wide choice of enjoyable food from separate servery (or pizza/pasta upstairs, and smarter restaurant above that), friendly helpful staff, real ales such as Adnams, Greene King Old Speckled Hen and Wells & Youngs Bombardier, decent wines by the glass; piped music, machines; tables outside *(the Didler, N R White, John Saville, LYM)*

☆ *Pride of Spitalfields* E1 5LJ [Heneage St]: Nicely worn in little East End local with cheery regulars and friendly cat called Lenny, well kept Crouch Vale, Sharps and interesting guest beers from central servery, bargain simple food, prompt efficient service, atmospheric lighting, interesting prints, comfortable banquettes, coal fire; two pavement tables *(Tracey and Stephen Groves, Derek and Sylvia Stephenson, Jerry Brown, Mike and Eleanor Anderson, David Hoult)*

Princess of Prussia E1 8AZ [Prescot St]: Recently refurbished, with well kept

Shepherd Neame ales, chatty atmosphere, lively and friendly hands-on landlady, enjoyable seasonal cooking by her mother; large secluded back terrace *(Gary Hodson, N R White)*

Town of Ramsgate E1W 2PN [Wapping High St]: Interesting old-London Thames-side setting, with restricted but evocative river view from small back floodlit terrace and wooden deck; long narrow bar with squared oak panelling, real ales inc Adnams, friendly service, good choice of food inc daily specials; piped music; open all day *(Mrs M S Forbes, BB)*

E3

Palm Tree E3 5BH [Haverfield Rd]: Lone survivor of blitzed East End terrace, by Regents Canal and beside windmill and ecology centre in futuristic-looking Mile End Park; two Edwardian bars around oval servery, changing ales such as Mauldons, thriving local atmosphere, live music Fri-Sun *(Pete Baker)*

E4

Royal Forest E4 7QH [Rangers Rd (A1069)]: Large timbered Brewers Fayre backing on to Epping Forest and dating partly from 17th c, friendly service, Fullers London Pride, reasonably priced food; play area *(Robert Lester)*

E8

Prince Arthur E8 3BH [Forest Rd]: 19th-c, with some emphasis on enjoyable proper food inc some impressive puddings, Caledonian Deuchars IPA, Fullers London Pride and a beer from Meantime, period décor inc deep colours, leather chesterfields, stag's head, fox masks, big portraits and local photographs; open all day wknds, cl till 4 wkdys *(anon)*

E11

Birkbeck Tavern E11 4HL [Langthorne Rd]: Interesting local with good value snacks and well kept unusual ales *(Andrew Bosi)*

Eagle E11 1PE [Hollybush (A11/Eagle Lane)]: Some interesting show business pictures, low-priced carvery, picnic-sets outside, bedrooms in adjoining Innkeepers Lodge *(Robert Lester)*

George E11 2RL [High St Wanstead]: Large popular Wetherspoons in former 18th-c coaching inn, their usual good value food and real ales; plenty of books to read, pictures of famous Georges down the ages *(Robert Lester)*

Nightingale E11 2EY [Nightingale Ln]: Popular all-rounder with wide choice of food from sandwiches up, half a dozen mainly mainstream ales from island bar serving several linked areas *(Pete Baker)*

E14

Cat & Canary E14 4DH [Fishermans Walk]: Very good choice of wines by the glass,

Fullers and guest ales, decent bar food inc speciality burgers, traditional décor; tables out by dockside with heating and lights, nice spot (Colin Moore)

☆ *Gun* E14 9NS [Cold Harbour, Canary Wharf]: Well restored early 19th-c building, smart front dining bar, dark wood, white walls and naval battle painting, two back Thames-view bar rooms with good log fires, comfortable leather armchairs and chesterfields, settles, Adnams Broadside and Wells & Youngs, interesting food, good choice of wines by the glass inc champagne, good coffees; attractive riverside terrace with good tables and views, adjacent new portuguese barbecue restaurant, open all day (Susan and John Douglas, Jamie May)

E17

Celsius E17 4QH [Hoe St]: Neat pub/wine bar/tapas bar/club combination, contemporary décor inc settees and leather cubes, reasonably priced food, speciality wheat beers; music Fri evenings, monthly disco first Sun, big-screen TV; open all day Sat (Ron Deighton)

NORTH LONDON

N1

Angel N1 9LQ [High St, opp Angel tube stn]: Large, light and airy open-plan Wetherspoons with feel of a comfortable modern continental bar, busy with lively acoustics, cheerful staff, good choice of well kept beers (some bargains), their usual food all day; silenced games machine, no music, open all day (Alan Thwaite)
Barnsbury N1 1LX [Liverpool Rd]: Enjoyable food (all day Sun), wines inc organic ones, real ales and belgian beers, original woodwork and fireplaces, interesting chandeliers, pubby front part, back restaurant, contemporary art for sale; attractive back terrace (Mrs Margo Finlay, Jörg Kasprowski)
Camden Head N1 8DY [Camden Walk]: Well preserved Victorian pub very handy for the antiques market, spacious and comfortably elegant, plenty of etched glass, well kept Fullers London Pride, Greene King and St Austell Tribute from oval island servery, enjoyable food inc good specials, comedy nights upstairs; front terrace (Jeremy King)
Lord Clyde N1 3PB [Essex Rd]: Civilised dining pub with mix of furnishings inc some comfortable sofas, Timothy Taylors Landlord, reasonable prices (Andrew Bosi)
Steam Passage N1 0PN [Upper St]: Typical London pub with nice atmosphere, enjoyable hearty food, Adnams, Fullers London Pride and Greene King Abbot; pavement tables (Ian Phillips)
Wenlock Arms N1 7TA [Wenlock Rd]: Popular open-plan carpeted local in a bleak bit of London, friendly service, half a dozen or more well kept changing ales from central servery, always inc a Mild, farm cider and

perry, foreign bottled beers, doorstep sandwiches inc good salt beef, alcove seating, piano in pride of place, coal fires, darts, back pool table, Fri/Sat jazz nights, piano Sun afternoon; piped music; open all day (the Didler)

N4

White Lion of Mortimer N4 3PX [Stroud Green Rd]: One of the earliest Wetherspoons pubs, brightly lit, convivial and comfortable, good choice of changing regional ales, country wines and farm cider, good value food, restful back conservatory; TVs (LYM, Giles and Annie Francis)

N6

Angel N6 5JT [Highgate High St]: Long neat L-shaped bar with well kept ales such as Caledonian Deuchars IPA, decent wines by the glass, up-to-date food from sandwiches up for most of the day, friendly management and efficient staff, tables round the sides, dim lighting; open all day (John Wooll, Tracey and Stephen Groves)
Gatehouse N6 4BD [North Rd]: Above-average Wetherspoons with some unusual angles and private corners, effective service; upstairs theatre, tables in back yard (Tracey and Stephen Groves)
Wrestlers N6 4AA [North Rd]: L-shaped bar with 1920s panelling, cosy corners, comfortable sofa, well kept Fullers and Greene King Abbot, friendly efficient service, games (Tracey and Stephen Groves, Brian and Rosalie Laverick)

N16

Three Crowns N16 0LH [High St]: Nicely modernised bustling pub, very woody, with well kept Harveys and a guest such as Sharps, enjoyable food, compact dining area one side of bar standing area (Tracey and Stephen Groves)

N17

Bell & Hare N17 0AG [High St]: Friendly new couple in panelled pub nr Tottenham Hotspur FC – busy on match days, with big-screen TVs and free sandwiches after (P Davies)

NW1

☆ *Doric Arch* NW1 2DN [Eversholt St]: Virtually part of Euston Station, up stairs from bus terminus with raised back part overlooking it, Fullers and interesting guest beers inc seasonal, Weston's farm cider, friendly helpful staff, good value basic food lunchtime and from 4.30 wkdys, extended lunchtime wknds, pleasantly nostalgic atmosphere, intriguing train and other transport memorabilia, downstairs restaurant; discreet sports TV, lavatories on combination lock; open all day (Simon Marley, BB, Ian Phillips, N R White, Dr and Mrs A K Clarke, C J Fletcher, the Didler, Sue Demont, Tim Barrow)

Euston Flyer NW1 2RA [Euston Rd, opp British Library]: Open-plan pub opp British Library, genuine welcome, full Fullers beer range, good value food all day from big well filled fresh sandwiches up, relaxed lunchtime atmosphere, plenty of light wood, tile and wood floors, smaller more private raised areas, big doors open to street in warm weather; piped music, big-screen TVs, games machines, can get packed early evening, then again later; open all day, cl 8.30 Sun (*Dr and Mrs A K Clarke, Simon Marley*)
Metropolitan NW1 5LA [Baker St Stn, Marylebone Rd]: Wetherspoons in impressively ornate Victorian hall, large and rarely crowded, lots of tables on one side, very long bar the other, good beer choice and prices, friendly efficient staff, good coffee, inexpensive food; family area, open all day (*John Branston, Tony and Wendy Hobden, Robert Lester, Stephen and Jean Curtis*)
☆ *Queens Head & Artichoke* NW1 4EA [Albany St]: Unusual choice of good sensibly priced serious food (all day Sun) inc tapas, good choice of wines by the glass, Adnams and Greene King ales, lots of pub tables on big-windowed bar's bare boards, leather settees, some panelling, conservatory, smart upstairs dining room; service charge, may be piped music; pavement picnic-sets (*David Morgan, Sue Demont, Tim Barrow*)

NW3
Duke of Hamilton NW3 1JD [New End]: Well worn unsmart Fullers local with tall Edwardian central servery, interesting prints, bric-a-brac and signed cricket bats, farm cider and malt whiskies; raised back suntrap terrace, next to New End Theatre, open all day (*the Didler*)

NW6
North London Tavern NW6 7QB [Kilburn High Rd]: Decent food, beer and wine, good restaurant service even when busy; no bar food Sun (*John and Helen Rushton*)

NW7
☆ *Rising Sun* NW7 4EY [Marsh Lane/Highwood Hill, Mill Hill]: Beautiful wisteria-covered local dating from 17th c, nicely worn in cottagey bar and tiny low-ceilinged candlelit snug on right, lots of dark panelling, timber and coal fires, antique tables, prints and old local photographs, big plainer lounge on left, friendly helpful staff, Adnams, Greene King Abbot and Wells & Youngs, good wines by the glass and malt whiskies, enjoyable quickly served food from fresh lunchtime sandwiches up; children welcome, picnic-sets on suntrap back terrace, good walks nearby (inc London Loop), open all day (*Jestyn Phillips, Barry and Anne*)

NW8
Lords Tavern NW8 8QP [St Johns Wood Rd]: Next to Lords Cricket Ground, light and airy

with lots of glass and modern bare-boards décor, Fullers London Pride, good wine choice, decent food (breakfast available some match days), friendly service; tables out on decking (*BB, Michael Dandy, Eleanor Dandy*)

SOUTH LONDON

SE1
☆ *Anchor* SE1 9EF [Bankside]: In great spot nr Thames, reopened summer 2007 after extensive redevelopment, river views from upper floors and new roof terrace with barbecue, beams, stripped brickwork and old-world corners, good choice of wines by the glass, real ales, popular new fish and chip bar inc take-aways, other all-day food inc breakfast and tearoom, good atmosphere; piped music; provision for children, bedrooms in friendly quiet Premier Travel Inn behind, open all day (*LYM*)
Barrow Boy & Banker SE1 9QQ [Borough High St, by London Bridge station]: Comfortable civilised bank conversion with roomy upper gallery, full Fullers beer range kept well, decent wines, efficient young staff, no-nonsense food inc good pies, music-free; right by Southwark cathedral (*Charles Gysin, Sue and Mike Todd, Bruce Bird*)
Bridge House SE1 2UP [Tower Bridge Rd]: Relaxed Adnams bar with upmarket modern décor and sofas, their full ale range and good wine choice, good value generous food, friendly efficient service, downstairs dining area (*Richard Siebert, N R White*)
Charles Dickens SE1 0LH [Union St]: Bustling pub with well kept Adnams and other changing ales, sensibly priced pubby food, Dickens memorabilia, neat simple furnishings; pavement tables (*Bruce Bird*)
Doggetts Coat & Badge SE1 9UD [by Blackfriars Bridge]: Well run modern pub on several floors, good Thames views, pleasant outside drinking area, well kept range of real ales, pleasant service, usual food (*Dr and Mrs M E Wilson, BB*)
Duke of York SE1 1DR [Borough Rd]: Airy burgundy and cream décor, sofas and light wood furniture, polished boards, panelling and chandeliers, popular home-made sausages and mash, well kept Shepherd Neame real ales and shelves of belgian beers, good service; piped music; picnic-sets and colourful planters outside (*Valerie Baker*)
☆ *Hole in the Wall* SE1 8SQ [Mepham St]: Quirky and decidely unsmart no-frills hideaway in railway arch virtually underneath Waterloo, rumbles and shakes with the trains, well kept Adnams Bitter and Broadside, Greene King IPA and Abbot, Hogs Back TEA, Sharps Doom Bar and Twickenham Original, bargain basic food all day, small front bar, well worn mix of tables set well back from long bar in bigger back room; open all day, cl wknd afternoons

(Ian Phillips, LM, Stephen and Jean Curtis, Sue Demont, Tim Barrow, Tracey and Stephen Groves, LYM)

☆ *Horniman* SE1 2HD [Hays Galleria, off Battlebridge Lane]: Spacious, bright and airy Thames-side drinking hall with lots of polished wood, comfortable seating inc a few sofas, upstairs seating, several real ales with unusual guests (may offer tasters), teas and coffees at good prices, lunchtime bar food from soup and big sandwiches up, snacks other times, efficient service coping with large numbers after work; unobtrusive piped music; fine river views from picnic-sets outside, open all day *(Tracey and Stephen Groves, Dr and Mrs Jackson, LYM)*

☆ *Kings Arms* SE1 8TB [Roupell St]: Proper corner local, bustling and friendly, curved servery dividing traditional bar and lounge, Adnams, Fullers London Pride, Greene King IPA and Wells & Youngs Bombardier, good friendly service, flame-effect fires, food from thai dishes to good Sun roast, big back extension with conservatory/courtyard dining area, long central table and high side tables, attractive local prints and eccentric bric-a-brac; piped music gets a bit keen Fri night; open all day *(Ian Phillips, Sue Demont, Tim Barrow, Tracey and Stephen Groves, Phil Bryant, Giles and Annie Francis)*

Leather Exchange SE1 3HN [Leathermarket St]: Smart Fullers pub well refurbished in red, gold and cream, very popular lunchtime for good value generous food, their real ales, decent wines, helpful friendly staff, deep leather settees, nice prints; disabled facilities *(Valerie Baker)*

☆ *Lord Clyde* SE1 1ER [Clennam St]: Neat panelled L-shaped local in same friendly efficient family for 50 years, well kept Adnams Best, Fullers London Pride, Greene King IPA, Shepherd Neame Spitfire and Wells & Youngs, good value simple home-made food from good salt beef sandwiches up wkdy lunchtimes and early evenings, darts in small hatch-service back public bar; striking tiled façade, open all day (Sat early evening break, cl 7 Sun) *(Pete Baker, Mike and Sue Loseby)*

Mudlark SE1 9DA [Montague Cl (office estate off arch under London Bridge to Tooley St)]: Comfortable multi-level pub handy for Southwark Cathedral, Fullers London Pride and Wells & Youngs, fair choice of wines, popular bar lunches; small terrace *(Valerie Baker)*

Old Thameside SE1 9DG [Pickfords Wharf, Clink St]: Good 1980s pastiche of ancient tavern beside dock with replica *Golden Hind*, two floors, hefty beams and timbers, pews, flagstones, candles; splendid river view upstairs and from charming waterside terrace, several changing ales, fresh baguettes from salad bar, lunchtime hot buffet; pool down spiral stairs, piped music, service can slow when busy after work; open all day but cl 3 at wknds *(LYM, Valerie Baker, Dave Braisted)*

Rose & Crown SE1 8DP [Colombo St]: Straightforward L-shaped local with full Shepherd Neame range, simple good value bar lunches from sandwiches up, upstairs room; back terrace *(Tony Hobden)*

Ship SE1 1DX [Borough Rd]: Attractive Fullers pub, long, narrow and comfortable, with lots of wood, candles and flowers, well kept ales, good choice of wines by the glass, good value food from sandwiches and light dishes through omelettes and platters up, friendly young uniformed staff, popular comedy club Fri; wrought iron furniture on back terrace with heated gazebo *(Valerie Baker)*

Wheatsheaf SE1 9AA [Stoney St]: Bare-boards Borough Market local, well kept Wells & Youngs ales from central servery, decent wine choice, lunchtime food, friendly staff, some brown panelling; piped music, sports TV, games machine; small back terrace, open all day, cl Sun *(the Didler)*

White Hart SE1 8TJ [Cornwall Rd/Whittlesey St]: Vibrant local in upcoming area, friendly bustle, comfortable sofas, stripped boards and so forth, Fullers London Pride, Greene King IPA, Wells & Youngs Bitter, several belgian beers, good range of ciders, sensibly priced up-to-date food; piped music *(Ian Phillips, Giles and Annie Francis)*

SE3

Railway SE3 9LE [Lee Rd/Blackheath Village]: Comfortably trendy, with deep easy chairs and chesterfields, Adnams Broadside, Shepherd Neame Spitfire and Youngs, good choice of lagers and bottled beers inc belgian fruit beers, lots of wines by the glass inc champagne, generous coffee, enjoyable if not cheap up-to-date food all day; lively young crowd for wknd live music; wheelchair access, small garden behind *(Valerie Baker)*

SE8

Dog & Bell SE8 3JD [Prince St]: Friendly tucked-away local on Thames Path, well kept changing ales inc Fullers, prompt friendly service, reasonably priced pub food inc good sandwiches; corner TV; tables outside *(N R White)*

SE10

Ashburnham Arms SE10 8UH [Ashburnham Grove]: Friendly chatty Shepherd Neame local with good pasta and other food (not Mon), mixed décor and customers young and old; pleasant garden with barbecues *(N R White, the Didler)*

Kings Arms SE10 9JH [King William Walk]: New management in well placed pub with lots of dark wood panelling and furniture, chintzy country-inn décor, enjoyable food, Greene King Old Speckled Hen, Timothy Taylors Landlord and Wells & Youngs; back terrace *(Valerie Baker)*

Plume of Feathers SE10 9LZ [Park Vista]: Low-ceilinged Georgian local with good value food from sandwiches up, Adnams, Fullers London Pride and Greene King from central bar, good coffee, cheerful service, flame-effect fire in large attractive fireplace, lots of pictures and plates on ochre walls, back dining area; sports TV; children welcome, play room across back yard with trees (Greenwich Park playground nearby too), handy for Maritime Museum *(Pete Baker, N R White, LM, Tom and Rosemary Hall)*

☆ *Richard I* SE10 8RT [Royal Hill]: Well run traditional two-bar Youngs local, friendly and chatty, with real ales, decent bar food, bare boards and panelling; children welcome, picnic-sets out in front, lots more in pleasant paved back garden with wknd barbecues – busy summer wknds and evenings *(N R White, the Didler)*

Spanish Galleon SE10 9BL [Greenwich Church St]: Large old-fashioned local handy for Cutty Sark restoration exhibition and Greenwich markets, good value food all day, well kept Shepherd Neame beers and nice range of wines, attentive friendly staff *(Mike and Mary Clark, Neil Hardwick)*

☆ *Trafalgar* SE10 9NW [Park Row]: Substantial 18th-c building with splendid river views from big windows directly above water in four still quite elegant if slightly worn rooms inc end dining room, all with oak panelling and good maritime and local prints, Adnams and Fullers London Pride, popular food all day from standard menu (more interesting in dining room), good house wines, brisk friendly service, atmosphere, though spacious bars can get packed Fri/Sat evenings, piped music can be unusual; tables out by Nelson statue, handy for Maritime Museum *(BB, Ian Phillips)*

Yacht SE10 9NP [Crane St]: Neatly modernised, with great river views from spacious room up a few steps from bar, good value food inc particularly good fish and chips, well kept Fullers London Pride, Greene King IPA and two guest beers, cosy banquettes, light wood panelling, portholes, yacht pictures *(Ian Phillips)*

SE16

☆ *Angel* SE16 4NB [Bermondsey Wall E]: Handsomely renovated Thames-side pub, appealing and civilised, with superb views to Tower Bridge and the City upstream, and the Pool of London downstream, from back lounge, upstairs area, back jetty and side garden, softly lit front bars with two public areas on either side of snug, low-backed settles, old local photographs and memorabilia, etched glass and glossy varnish, enjoyable pubby food from baguettes to popular Sun roast, cheap Sam Smiths, kind friendly service; children and dogs welcome, interesting walks round Surrey Quays *(Valerie Baker, LYM, N R White)*

Blacksmiths Arms SE16 5EJ [Rotherhithe St (Nelson Dock)]: Neatly restored Fullers local

in up-and-coming area, friendly staff, well kept London Pride and Porter, enjoyable fresh thai food; quiet lunchtime, busy evenings *(David M Smith)*

☆ *Mayflower* SE16 4NF [Rotherhithe St]: Cosy old riverside pub with surprisingly wide choice of enjoyable generous food all day from sandwiches up inc good chips, black beams, panelling, nautical bric-a-brac, high-backed settles and coal fires, good Thames views from upstairs restaurant (cl Sat lunchtime), Greene King ales, good coffee and good value wines; piped music; children welcome, nice jetty/terrace over water, open all day, in unusual street with lovely Wren church *(Jeremy King, LYM, N R White, the Didler)*

Ship & Whale SE16 7LT [Gulliver St]: Opened-up Victorian pub with pleasant bar-style décor and distinct areas, full Shepherd Neame range kept well, friendly young staff, enjoyable well presented fresh food from sandwiches to round-the-world dishes, choice of teas and coffees, Sun comedy club; garden behind with barbecues Thurs-Sun *(Valerie Baker)*

SE24

Florence SE24 0NG [Dulwich Rd]: Handsome Victorian pub visibly brewing its own Weasel ale, also guests such as Adnams, farm cider, enjoyable food, friendly atmosphere, glossy bar and appealing contemporary décor, comfortable booth seating, dining conservatory; children welcome, good terrace tables *(Dave W Holliday, Giles and Annie Francis)*

SE26

☆ *Dulwich Wood House* SE26 6RS [Sydenham Hill]: Extended Youngs pub in Victorian lodge gatehouse complete with turret, nice local atmosphere, friendly service, decent food cooked to order; steps up to entrance (and stiff walk up from station); big pleasant back garden with old-fashioned street lamps and barbecues, handy for Dulwich Wood *(Ian and Nita Cooper, David M Smith)*

SW11

Eagle SW11 6HG [Chatham Rd]: Attractive and warmly welcoming old backstreet local, real ales such as Fullers London Pride, Timothy Taylors Landlord and Westerham British Bulldog, friendly helpful service, leather sofas in fireside corner of L-shaped bar; big-screen sports TV; back terrace with marquee, small front terrace too *(Sue Demont, Tim Barrow, Stephen Funnell)*

Falcon SW11 1RU [St Johns Hill]: Edwardian pub with well kept Fullers London Pride from remarkably long light oak bar, bargain pub food such as pie and mash, friendly service, lively front bar, period partitions, cut glass and mirrors, quieter back dining area, daily papers; big-screen TV *(Dr Ron Cox, Sue Demont, Tim Barrow)*

SW13

☆ **Brown Dog** SW13 0AP [Cross St]: Impressively renovated former Rose of Denmark, thriving atmosphere, enjoyable food, good choice of wines, friendly helpful staff, subtle lighting and open fires; children and dogs welcome (Sandy Taylor, BB)

Castelnau SW13 9ER [Castelnau]: Big pub with great garden, had been doing well as part of the former Auberge group, combining pubby bars with decent french-style eating areas, but no news since the group's sale in April; reports please (Charles and Christina McComb)

Red Lion SW13 9RU [Castelnau]: Spaciously refurbished Fullers pub with impressive Victorian woodwork, reliable food inc sandwiches, children's helpings and popular Sun lunch, good staff, good choice of reasonably priced wines by the glass, good atmosphere, three separate areas; big garden with good play area and barbecue (Peter Rozée, Edward Mirzoeff, BB)

Sun SW13 9HE [Church Rd]: Open-plan pub with Greene King ales and wines by the glass from central servery, sofas as well as lots of tables and chairs, appealing food inc winter soup and sandwich deals; piped music; tables over road overlooking green and duckpond (Edward Mirzoeff)

SW14

Ship SW14 7QR [Thames Bank]: Comfortable pub with good Thames views, prompt friendly service, good range of reasonably priced generous pubby food from sandwiches up, Fullers London Pride, Greene King IPA and Wells & Youngs Bombardier, conservatory; terrace tables, not on river side (John Wooll, Peter Dandy)

SW15

☆ **Boathouse** SW15 2JX [Brewhouse Lane, Putney Wharf; Putney Bridge, then cross the Thames – from the bridge you can see the pub on your left]: Busy Thames-side pub in new development, Wells & Youngs ales from long bar in tall glazed extension from former Victorian vinegar factory, low modern seating, young chatty atmosphere, quieter panelled room on another level behind, cosy upstairs panelled restaurant with another pubby bar; piped pop music; children in eating areas, glass-sided balcony and attractive riverside terrace, open all day (Tracey and Stephen Groves, Michael Tack, Peter Rozée, LYM)

Bricklayers Arms SW15 1DD [down cul-de-sac off Lower Richmond Rd nr Putney Bridge]: Traditional local with well kept Timothy Taylors ale range and guest beers, friendly young staff, scrubbed tables, woodburner, dim lighting; side terrace (Steve Derbyshire, N R White, Peter Dandy)

Green Man SW15 3NG [Wildcroft Rd, Putney Heath]: Small friendly old local by Putney Heath, cosy main bar, quiet sitting room, enjoyable bar lunches, well kept Wells & Youngs; attractive garden, open all day (LYM, Colin McKerrow)

Prince of Wales SW15 2SP [Upper Richmond Rd]: Neatly refurbished by new young landlord, country-pub feel, good reasonably priced unusual food inc game and tasty rotisserie chicken, well kept Fullers London Pride, efficient friendly staff, bar lined with pewter mugs, good countryside photographs and interesting skylight in back restaurant (Richard Greaves)

☆ **Telegraph** SW15 3TU [Telegraph Rd]: Big attractively modernised pub with buoyant atmosphere, top-notch cheerful service, St Austell Tribute, Timothy Taylors Landlord and several guests such as Adnams, Twickenham and Weltons, French chef doing short choice of enjoyable fresh food (all day Fri-Sun) from pubby favourites to some minor french classics, Fri jazz or blues; sports TV, can get packed wknds; children and dogs welcome, attractive garden, nice spot opp cricket pitch (Peter Dandy, Shannone Parsons, Charles and Christina McComb, Colin McKerrow)

SW18

Brewers SW18 2QB [East Hill]: Large Youngs pub recently refurbished as an enjoyable food pub, sharing platters as well as other dishes, several wines by the glass, Wells & Youngs ales (Peter Dandy)

☆ **Cats Back** SW18 1NN [Point Pleasant]: Distinctive backstreet haven with half a dozen interesting ales, good choice of wines by the glass, popular new upstairs restaurant, good sandwiches too, good service, motley furnishings from pews and scrubbed pine tables to pensioned-off chairs and sofas, loads of bric-a-brac, pictures on red walls, dimmed chandeliers and lit candelabra, customers in keeping with the eccentric décor, blazing fire in small fireplace; well chosen piped music; pavement tables and diverse chairs, open all day (LM, BB)

Pig & Whistle SW18 5LD [Merton Rd (A218)]: Neatly kept, with pleasant décor, Wells & Youngs ales, decent food inc good roasts, smart bar staff; TV; open all day (Peter Dandy)

SW19

Alexandra SW19 7NE [Wimbledon Hill Rd]: Large busy Youngs pub with Wells & Youngs ales and good choice of wines by the glass from central bar, enjoyable food from sandwiches to good Sun roasts, helpful service, comfortably up-to-date décor in three linked areas inc bare-boards back dining areas; TV; attractive roof terrace, tables also out in mews (Peter Dandy, Michael Dandy)

Colliers Tup SW19 2BH [High St Colliers Wood]: Lively atmosphere, enthusiastic landlord, four well kept ales, plenty of activities; good garden (Charles and Christina McComb)

Dog & Fox SW19 5EA [Wimbledon High St]: Striking large pub, smartly modernised, with contemporary furniture, Wells & Youngs ales, good coffee, enjoyable food from sandwiches up, friendly staff, sizeable dining area *(Michael Dandy, Peter Dandy)*

Fox & Grapes SW19 4UN [Camp Rd]: By common, with enjoyable contemporary food, well kept ales, attractive mural behind food servery, big-screen sports TV in larger high-beamed bar; piped music; children welcome till 7, pleasant on summer evenings when you can sit out on the grass, open all day *(Peter Dandy, BB)*

Hand in Hand SW19 4RQ [Crooked Billet]: Good new landlord in friendly recently refurbished Youngs local, several areas off central bar inc family room with games, good choice of wines by the glass and Wells & Youngs ales, popular traditional food, log fire; front courtyard with vine and hanging baskets, benches out by common (plastic glasses there) *(Jonty and Karen Bloom, N R White, BB)*

☆ **Rose & Crown** SW19 5BA [Wimbledon High St]: Quiet comfortably refurbished 17th-c Youngs pub with alcove seating in roomy bar, friendly attentive staff, pubby feel, old prints inc interesting religious texts and drawings, back dining conservatory; neat partly covered former coachyard, bedrooms *(LYM, Peter Dandy, Colin McKerrow, MRSM, Michael Dandy)*

Trafalgar SW19 2JY [High Path]: Proper little traditional local with half a dozen real ales, friendly staff, jazz Sun afternoon *(David North)*

TW10 [TQ1771]

Legless Frog TW10 5LA [Upper Ham Rd]: Smart and attractive french-run common-side pub with light and airy cricket-theme bar, lower snugs and eating area, friendly landlady, enjoyable food, Greene King and Wells & Youngs, smart tiled verandah opening into big sheltered garden, banks of greenery with grotto, waterfall and pond, unobtrusive play area *(Richard and Sissel Harris)*

WEST LONDON

SW6

Duke on the Green SW6 4XG [New Kings Rd, Parsons Green]: Bar/brasserie in Edwardian former Duke of Cumberland, sensibly limited choice of enjoyable food, Wells & Youngs ale, well laid out high tables and chairs, a few settles in front part, back restaurant (and come evening they pretty much expect you to eat); chrome tables out by pavement *(Peter Rozée, BB, the Didler)*

George & Dragon SW6 1UD [Ibis Hotel, Lillie Rd]: Good value food in mirrored upstairs bar with woody décor, popular with staff from nearby police admin building *(Robert Lester)*

SW7

Queens Arms SW7 5QL [Queens Gate Mews]: Victorian pub with enjoyable home cooking, good wines by the glass, real ales inc Fullers London Pride, period furniture, heavy plush seating, massive mahogany bookcases, lithographs inc two of nearby Albert Hall *(Pat and Roger Davies)*

SW10

Lots Road Pub & Dining Rooms SW10 0RJ [Lots Rd, opp entrance to Chelsea Harbour]: Unusually curved corner house with big windows and plenty of space, wide choice of beers and wines, enjoyable food, caring staff *(Peter Rozée, Giles and Annie Francis, LYM)*

W4

Bell & Crown W4 3PF [Strand on the Green]: Well run panelled Fullers local, big and busy, with their ales, friendly attentive service, sensibly priced food, cosy log fire, great Thames views from back bar and conservatory; may be piped music; terrace out by towpath, good walks, open all day *(Susan and John Douglas, N R White)*

City Barge W4 3PH [Strand on the Green]: Small panelled riverside bars with some nice original features in picturesque front part (kept for diners lunchtime), airy newer back part done out with maritime signs and bird prints, bar food (not Sun) from sandwiches up, real ales, open fire, back conservatory; waterside picnic-sets – nice spot to watch sun set over Kew Bridge *(N R White, LYM)*

☆ **Duke of Sussex** W4 5LF [South Parade]: Imposing and impressively restored 1898 building, light and airy, with booth seating by large windows, interesting if not cheap changing ales, good proper food all day inc some spanish dishes, slow-roast rare breed pork and winter game and stews, good choice of wines in half-bottle carafes, handsome back dining room with cherub-framed skylight; shaded outside seating, open all day *(G Coates)*

Swan W4 5HH [Evershed Walk, Acton Lane]: Enjoyable food with some interesting dishes, informal style, friendly overseas staff, good range of wines by the glass, three real ales; they may try to keep your credit card while you eat *(Simon Rodway)*

W6

☆ **Anglesea Arms** W6 0UR [Wingate Rd; Ravenscourt Park]: Good interesting food inc wkdy set lunches in lively and bustling gastropub, most enjoyable, with good choice of wines by the glass and of real ales, close-set tables in dining room facing kitchen, roaring fire in simply decorated panelled bar; children welcome, tables out by quiet street, open all day *(John and Annabel Hampshire, Martin and Karen Wake, the Didler, LYM)*

W7

Fox W7 2PJ [Green Lane]: Friendly open-plan 19th-c local in quiet cul de sac nr Grand

Union Canal, Black Sheep, Fullers London Pride, Timothy Taylors Landlord and Twickenham ale, decent wines, entertaining scroll menu of good value pub lunches, evening food now too, panelling and stained-glass one end, wildlife pictures and big fish tank, farm tools hung from ceiling, darts end; dogs welcome, small side garden, towpath walks (Tony Hobden)

W8

☆ Uxbridge Arms W8 7TQ [Uxbridge St]: Friendly and cottagey backstreet local with three brightly furnished linked areas, well kept Fullers and a guest such as St Austell Tribute, good choice of bottled beers, china, prints and photographs; sports TV; open all day (the Didler, Tracey and Stephen Groves)

W9

Prince Alfred W9 1EE [Formosa St]: Well preserved austerely ornate Victorian pub with five separate bars, snob-screens and duck-through doors, beautiful etched glass bow window, enjoyable proper food in airy new dining room; piped music can be loud evenings (Tracey and Stephen Groves)

W11

Ladbroke Arms W11 3NW [Ladbroke Rd]: Smart and busy dining pub with good food, good choice of real ales, pleasant staff, daily papers; tables on front terrace (LYM, Dr Martin Owton)

W14

Crown & Sceptre W14 8BA [Holland Rd]: Mellow and relaxed mix of wine bar and pub, bare boards, some Edwardian features, well kept changing ales such as Butcombe and Hogs Back TEA, good value interesting pub food esp mexican dishes, friendly staff; unobtrusive piped music (David M Smith, Stephen Corfield)

Radnor Arms W14 8PX [Warwick Rd]: Classic pub architecture, convivial and pubby inside, interesting regional ales, friendly staff who are real ale enthusiasts, good choice of whiskies, plenty of small tables in both rooms, pub games; open all day (the Didler, Tracey and Stephen Groves)

OUTER LONDON

BECKENHAM [TQ3769]

Jolly Woodman BR3 6NR [Chancery Lane]: Small friendly old-fashioned local popular for good changing real ales inc Caledonian Deuchars IPA, Harveys and Timothy Taylors Landlord, welcoming service, good value fresh lunchtime food from sandwiches up; flower-filled back yard and pavement tables, open all day, cl Mon lunchtime (N R White, Gwyn Berry)

BOTANY BAY [TQ2999]

Robin Hood EN2 8AP [2 miles from M25 junction 24; Ridgeway (A1005 Enfield rd)]: Neatly kept open-plan 1930s roadhouse,

wide choice of enjoyable food all day inc exceptional puddings range, well kept McMullens ales, decent wines, friendly uniformed staff; good-sized garden with roses and weeping willow, open all day (Colin Moore)

BROMLEY [TQ4069]

Red Lion BR1 3LG [North Rd]: Chatty backstreet local, soft lighting, shelves of books, green velvet drapes, well kept Greene King, Harveys and guest beers, good service; front terrace (N R White)

Two Doves BR2 8HD [Oakley Rd (A233)]: Popular unpretentious pub notable for its lovely garden with terrace tables; friendly staff and locals, well kept Courage Directors, St Austell Tribute and Wells & Youngs Premium, nice range of snacks, modern back conservatory (N R White, Mr and Mrs Rob W Miles)

CHEAM [TQ2463]

Olde Red Lion SM3 8QB [Park Rd]: Friendly 16th-c family pub, quite roomy, with low ceilings and panelling, reasonably priced food, several real ales from island bar; attractive terrace (Conor McGaughey)

CHELSFIELD [TQ4864]

Five Bells BR6 7RE [Church Rd; just off A224 Orpington by-pass]: Ancient chatty village local with two separate bars and dining area, friendly staff, well kept Adnams, Courage Best and Harveys, well priced food from good fresh sandwiches up; picnic-sets among flowers out in front (LM)

CHISLEHURST [TQ4369]

Ramblers Rest BR7 5ND [Mill Place; just off Bickley Park Rd and Old Hill, by Summer Hill (A222)]: White weatherboarded local in picturesque hillside setting on edge of Chislehurst Common, particularly well kept Adnams Broadside, Brakspears, Courage Best, Fullers London Pride and Wells & Youngs Bombardier, good value basic food, friendly staff, pleasant unpretentious grown-up atmosphere, upper and lower bars; garden behind, grassy slope out in front (plastic glasses for there), handy for Chislehurst Caves (Tony and Glenys Dyer, John Saville)

CROYDON [TQ3466]

Claret CR0 7AA [5 Bingham Corner, Lower Addiscombe Road]: Half a dozen changing ales such as Dark Star, Palmers and Sharps, wknd snacks; sports TV; dogs welcome, garden overlooking Tramlink stn, open all day (Tony and Wendy Hobden)

Spread Eagle CR0 1NX [Katharine St]: Large well staffed Edwardian Fullers Ale & Pie pub with sensible prices, high ceilings and panelling; sports TVs (Tony and Wendy Hobden, Sue and Mike Todd)

DOWNE [TQ4361]

Queens Head BR6 7US [High St]: Civilised and comfortable, with green and cream décor, latticed windows, lanterns and hops, Darwin texts and splendid log fire in lounge, Adnams Bitter and Broadside, friendly staff, plush dining room; big-screen sports TV in locals' bar, well equipped children's room;

picnic-sets on pavement, more in small tree-shaded back courtyard, handy for Darwin's Down House, good walks, open all day *(N R White)*

ENFIELD [TQ3198]

Fallow Buck EN2 9JD [Clay Hill]: Beamed green belt pub with wide choice of reliable food inc popular Sun lunch, a couple of real ales such as Adnams Broadside, good-sized eating area; tables outside, nice walks *(Colin Moore)*

Navigation EN3 4XX [Wharf Rd, Ponders End]: Big Harvester recently nicely restored, good friendly service, good value food; canalside terrace *(Robert Lester)*

HAMPTON COURT [TQ1668]

☆ *Kings Arms* KT8 9DD [Hampton Court Rd, by Lion Gate]: Civilised pub by Hampton Court itself, with comfortable furnishings inc sofas in back area, attractive Farrow & Ball colours, good open fires, lots of oak panelling, beams and some stained-glass, well kept Badger beers, good choice of wines by the glass, friendly service, sensibly priced pubby food from sandwiches up, restaurant too; piped music; children and dogs welcome, picnic-sets on roadside front terrace, charming new bedrooms, open all day *(Susan and John Douglas, Michael Butler, LYM, N R White)*

HARROW [TQ1588]

Moon on the Hill HA1 2AW [Station Rd, nr tube]: Wetherspoons, with their sensibly priced food and six guest beers, efficient staff, old local photographs *(Mike and Mary Clark)*

ILFORD [TQ4589]

Dick Turpin IG2 7TD [Aldborough Rd N, off A12 Newbury Park]: Well refurbished and reopened as M&B Miller & Carter steakhouse, their standard good value menu, friendly efficient service, real ale *(Robert Lester, John Saville)*

Beehive IG4 5DR [Beehive Lane (B192), Gants Hill]: Friendly Harvester restaurant with their usual food and separate bar, Fullers; bedrooms in adjoining Travelodge *(Robert Lester)*

Red House IG4 5BG [Redbridge Lane E; just off A12, handy for M11 via A406]: Popular multi-level Beefeater with friendly service, good value food; disabled facilities, bedrooms in adjoining Premier Inn *(Robert Lester)*

KEW [TQ1977]

Coach & Horses TW9 3BH [Kew Green]: Modernised open-plan pub with Wells & Youngs ales and good coffees, standard bar food from sandwiches up, young friendly staff, armchairs and sofas, restaurant; sports TV; teak tables on front terrace, nice setting handy for Kew Gardens and National Archive *(Pat and Tony Martin, Alan and Carolin Tidbury)*

Inn at Kew Gardens TW9 3NG [Sandycombe Rd, close to tube stn]: Roomy pub/hotel with comfortably refurbished Victorian bar, friendly and relaxed, well kept ales such as

Hogs Back TEA and Twickenham Crane, helpful friendly staff, enjoyable fresh food inc good sandwich choice, nice dining room; tables outside, 19 good bedrooms *(Chris Smith)*

Railway TW9 3PZ [Station Parade]: Appealing former station buffet, Adnams Broadside, Shepherd Neame Spitfire and Wells & Youngs Bombardier, decent choice of wines by the glass, reasonably priced food, mix of comfortable sofas, tall and more regular tables; TVs; large covered and heated area outside *(Ian Phillips)*

KINGSTON [TQ1970]

Albert Arms KT2 7PX [Kingston Hill]: Sprucely modernised multi-level Youngs pub with contemporary décor, decent food all day; children and dogs welcome, tables outside *(Meg and Colin Hamilton)*

Canbury Arms KT2 6LQ [Canbury Pk Rd]: Big-windowed open-plan local with good value enterprising up-to-date food inc breakfast from 9 (not Sun), well kept ales such as Harveys, Sharps, Timothy Taylors and Twickenham Spring, very good choice of wines by the glass, young staff, simple fresh contemporary décor, cosy easy chairs as well as neat tables and chairs, large side conservatory, frequent events; children and dogs welcome, heated terrace with retractable awning *(Myles Woodley, LM)*

LONGFORD [TQ0576]

White Horse UB7 0EE [Bath Rd, off A3044 (and A4)]: Brasses on low 16th-c black beams, fireplace between the two spotless areas, comfortable seats, cosy and friendly with pot plants in windows and rustic decorations such as antique rifles and equestrian bronzes, good value fresh lunchtime bar food, good service, well kept Courage Best, Fullers London Pride, Marstons Pedigree and Wells & Youngs Bombardier; shame about the piped music, games machine; flower tubs and picnic-sets outside, one in a little barn, surprisingly villagey surroundings despite the parking meters, open all day *(Les and Sandra Brown)*

MALDEN RUSHETT [TQ1763]

☆ *Star* KT22 0DP [Kingston Rd (A243 just N of M25 junction 9)]: Reliable and well run family dining pub on Surrey border, well kept Courage and Greene King, good value food (separate order point), friendly service and atmosphere, nice log fire; quiet piped music, Harley-Davidson monthly meet 2nd Thurs; terrace and covered tables outside *(the Didler, DWAJ, LM)*

OSTERLEY [TQ1578]

☆ *Hare & Hounds* TW7 5PR [Windmill Lane (B454, off A4 – called Syon Lane at that point)]: Roomy suburban Fullers dining pub, wide choice of enjoyable food from sandwiches to hearty reasonably priced main dishes, prompt friendly service, pleasant dining extension; spacious terrace and big floodlit mature garden, nice setting opp beautiful Osterley Park *(Tom and Ruth Rees, Mrs M S Forbes, Roy and Lindsey Fentiman)*

RICHMOND [TQ1774]
Cricketers TW9 1LX [The Green]: Several linked rooms, Greene King ales, bargain food from sandwiches up, pubby furnishings, cricket and rugby prints, big windows looking out over green, more room upstairs; piped music, TV; pavement picnic-sets *(Michael Dandy)*
Duke TW9 1HP [Duke St]: Former Racing Page, reopened as open-plan dining pub by small London pubs and bars group, Fullers London Pride and Sharps Doom Bar, good choice of wines by the glass, mixed furnishings on bare boards; nice spot nr theatre and green *(Michael Dandy)*
Old Ship TW9 1ND [King St]: Two bustling linked bars, fine panelling upstairs, stained-glass, old photographs, model ships and nauticalia, hands-on landlord and helpful staff, well kept Wells & Youngs ales, enjoyable pubby food inc good Sun roast; TV; open all day *(Bruce Bird, Michael Dandy)*
Pitcher & Piano TW9 1TQ [Bridge St, by Richmond Bridge]: Modern bar chain, this one in converted riverside villa with lower conservatory and big terrace overlooking Thames, Marstons Pedigree and good choice of wines by the glass, up-to-date food from sandwiches up *(Michael Dandy)*
Princes Head TW9 1LX [The Green]: Large open-plan pub overlooking cricket green nr theatre, low-ceilinged panelled areas off big island bar, full Fullers range, fresh bar food from sandwiches to steak, relaxed mature atmosphere, open fire; seats outside – fine spot *(Michael Dandy)*
Rose & Crown TW9 3AH [Kew Green]: Popular 18th-c Chef & Brewer handy for Kew Gardens, dark interior with panelling, old prints and cosy corners, their usual food, Wells & Youngs Bombardier, friendly service; raised front terrace overlooking cricket green, tree-shaded back terrace *(Michael Butler)*
White Swan TW9 1PG [Old Palace Lane]: Civilised and relaxed, with dark-beamed open-plan plush bar, friendly service, real ales such as Fullers London Pride and Wells & Youngs Bombardier, fresh wholesome bar lunches, coal-effect fires, popular upstairs restaurant; piped music, children allowed in conservatory, pretty little walled back terrace below railway *(LYM, N R White)*
New Inn TW10 7DB [Petersham Rd (A307, Ham Common)]: Attractive Georgian pub in good spot on Ham Common, comfortable banquettes and stools, brown décor, Adnams Broadside, Fullers London Pride and Wells & Youngs Bitter, food inc ciabattas, steaks, good fish and chips and interesting specials, pleasant dining area, quick service, big log fire one side, coal the other; disabled facilities, picnic-sets out among flowers front and back *(Chris Evans)*
Roebuck TW10 6RN [Richmond Hill]: Comfortable and attractive 18th-c bay-windowed pub with neat staff, well kept changing ales such as McMullens, reasonably

priced food, some substantial bygones, old Thames photographs and prints, fine views of meadows and Thames itself; open all day *(Bruce Bird)*
ROMFORD [TQ4889]
Moby Dick RM6 6QU [A1112/A12 (Whalebone Lane N)]: Large recently refurbished main-road pub/restaurant, all-day food inc good value carvery, open for breakfast from 7 (8 wknds), Fullers London Pride and Greene King IPA, games in public bar; bedrooms in adjoining Premier Travel Inn, open all day *(Robert Lester)*
TEDDINGTON [TQ1671]
Adelaide TW11 0AU [Park Rd]: Good friendly pub with hospitable Irish licensees, well kept Shepherd Neame ales, wines on show, coffee machine, good value slightly upmarket food inc good filled baguettes and sandwiches, pews around tables, red paintwork; attractive tables and seats in pretty honeysuckle-clad back yard with barbecue counter *(Eunice Gilks)*
Kings Head TW11 8HG [High St]: Five changing ales such as Fullers London Pride, Harveys and Twickenham, amusing landlord and friendly atmosphere, sensibly priced bar food, comfortable restaurant; sports TV; terrace tables *(Charles and Christina McComb)*
Oak TW11 8HU [High St]: Former Royal Oak reworked in discreet contemporary style with smart minimalist modern furnishings, bare boards and spotlights, Twickenham ale, good choice of wines by the glass, up-to-date pubby bar food (all day wknds, not Sun evening) and lift to basement restaurant *(anon)*
Tide End Cottage TW11 9NN [Broom Rd/Ferry Rd, nr bridge at Teddington Lock]: Friendly low-ceilinged pub in Victorian cottage terrace, two rooms united by big log-effect gas fire, well kept Greene King IPA, decent reasonably priced bar food to numbered tables from sandwiches up, lots of river, fishing and rowing memorabilia and photographs, interesting Dunkirk evacuation link, back dining extension; sports TV in front bar, minimal parking; children welcome till 7.30, circular picnic-sets on front terrace *(Chris Evans, LM)*
TWICKENHAM [TQ1673]
Barmy Arms TW1 3DU [The Embankment]: Biggish riverside pub with enjoyable generous food, good beer choice; plenty of terrace tables with gazebo, outside bar on match days *(Pat and Tony Martin)*
Eel Pie TW1 3NJ [Church St]: Unpretentious and good-natured, Badger ales, foreign beers in their individual branded glasses, usual bar food (lunchtime not Sun), good friendly service even when busy, lots of rugby caricatures, bar billiards and other pub games; piped music, TV for rugby; tables outside, children allowed till 6, open all day *(N R White, LYM)*
Ranch TW1 3JZ [York St]: Nicely refurbished, with comfortable alcoves, cheery service, good deals early evening *(Mayur Shah)*

White Swan TW1 3DN [Riverside]: Unpretentious 17th-c Thames-side house up steep anti-flood steps (the gents' can get flooded by spring tides), little waterside terrace across quiet lane, traditional bare-boards bar with big rustic tables and blazing fires, back room full of rugby memorabilia, changing ales such as Adnams, Caledonian, Fullers and Greene King, good choice of wines by the glass, pub food from filled rolls up, backgammon, cribbage; piped blues or jazz; children welcome, open all day summer *(Pat and Tony Martin, LYM)*

Old Goat TW2 5NG [Hampton Rd]: Freshened up with cream décor and bare boards, well kept Twickenham and dozens of belgian beers, prompt pleasant service, separate belgian bistro area, jazz nights *(Simon Collett-Jones)*

Prince of Wales TW2 5QR [Hampton Rd]: Transformed by new owners, with well kept changing ales such as Adnams, Black Sheep and Twickenham, enjoyable bargain food from tapas snacks to imaginative daily specials *(Steve Derbyshire)*

UXBRIDGE [TQ0582]

Malt Shovel UB8 2JE [Iver Lane, Cowley (B470)]: Good beer range, interesting sensibly priced food all day (not Sun) inc sustaining fresh sandwiches from 5pm, quick service; by Grand Union Canal *(Geoff and Sylvia Donald, David Lamb)*

Scotland

Scotland's pubs and inns have improved enormously in the last few years. Prompt service with a smile is now the order of the day – something which we could not, with honesty, have asserted in the past. Moreover, standards all round have improved significantly. Not so long ago quite a few places seemed to rely on their magnificent settings to keep their customers happy, and managed to get by with indifferent furnishings, and without putting much effort into the food and drink side. Our hearts used to sink at the way so many of Scotland's pubs even right on the coast relied on freezer packs for their fish, when the country is surrounded by such rich seas. Very few publicans here took the trouble even to stock real ales (and to keep them properly does take trouble). All that has now changed. It's become clear that customers, much better informed than they used to be, now demand real value for their money – in terms of food, drink, surroundings, service and atmosphere. Scotland's pub keepers have responded to this by aiming at much more of a top-notch experience all round. Pubs that deserve particular note are the Applecross Inn, reached by such a memorable drive, the Badachro Inn with its decking down by the water's edge, the happily pubby Four Marys in Linlithgow, the lovingly run Moulin in Pitlochry, the unique Plockton Hotel, the remotely set Stein Inn, and the cheery Lion & Unicorn in Thornhill. Several new main entries also exemplify the impact of committed customer-friendly management: the cheery Laurie Arms at Haugh of Urr (the newish team here gaining it both a Beer Award and a Bargain Award), the attractive Selkirk Arms in Kirkcudbright (flourishing under its enthusiastic new management) and the immaculately well run Meikleour Hotel. Mouth-wateringly fresh seafood now features heavily on many menus here (the Tigh an Eilean Hotel at Shieldaig, Applecross Inn, Badachro Inn and Plockton Hotel all stand out), with delicious scallops, oysters, mussels, langoustines and lobsters, often caught in the waters that you are relaxing by. With all this great seafood, not to mention excellent local beef, lamb and game, there's now a splendid choice of pubs and inns here for a special meal out. Once again, the Applecross Inn (run in an intimate but down-to-earth way by its landlady Judith Fish) stands out for its fairly priced, not over-elaborate and sensibly balanced choice, particularly strong on good locally sourced meat and seafood, and is our Scotland Dining Pub of the Year. Old hands as we are, the incredible range of whiskies at some pubs in Scotland still astounds even us. Take for instance another of our new main entries this year, the Port Charlotte Hotel on Islay. The landlord there stocks an exceptional collection of about 140 malts – all from his island alone. The highest number though is probably at the pubby Bon Accord in Glasgow (with a great range of real ales too) – they keep around 170 malts; plenty of pubs have around 50, and a good number have 100 or so. Pubs in Edinburgh deserve a special mention – you could spend days exploring them, anything from the sumptuous architectural grandeur of places like the Café Royal to snugly traditional taverns like the Bow Bar. To help you pick out places in particular areas, we have split the Lucky Dip section at the end of the chapter into counties: stars here include, in Argyll, the Clachaig in Glencoe; in Berwickshire, the Allanton Inn; in Dumfries-shire, the Black Bull in Moffat; in Inverness-shire, the Cluanie Inn in Glen Shiel and Old Forge at Inverie; in Lanarkshire, the Horseshoe in Glasgow; in Midlothian, the Canny Man's in Edinburgh; in Perthsire, the Killiecrankie Hotel near Pitlochry; in Ross-shire, the Plockton Inn; and out on Mull, the Bellachroy at Dervaig, and on Skye the Old Inn at Carbost. Scotland now has three or four dozen breweries. Much the most widely available is Caledonian and its subsidiary Harviestoun (Caledonian has ties to the Scottish & Newcastle combine, which is now foreign-owned). Other beers which we have found in at least some of our good pubs this year are, in rough order of popularity, Isle of Skye, Kelburn (started quite recently, making great progress), Inveralmond, Cairngorm, Broughton, Stewart, Belhaven (now part of the Greene King empire), Atlas, An Teallach, Houston, Orkney, Islay and Sulwath and Fyne. Others cropping up more rarely were Bridge of Allan, Moulin, Traquair, Arran, Black Isle, Cuillin, Hebridean, Williams and Windie Goat.

ABOYNE

NO5298 MAP 11

Boat

Charlestown Road (B968, just off A93); AB34 5EL

Welcoming pub by the River Dee with good food; open all day, bedrooms

The first thing you will see as you go into this pleasantly pubby inn is a model train, often chugging around just below the ceiling, making appropriate noises. The partly carpeted bar – with a counter running along through the narrower linking section – also has scottish pictures and brasses, a woodburning stove in a stone fireplace, and games in the public-bar end; piped music and games machine. Spiral stairs take you up to a roomy additional dining area. They have Timothy Taylors Landlord and a couple of scottish guest beers such as Caledonian Deuchars IPA and Inveralmond Thrapplesouser on handpump; also 40 malt whiskies. The pub – right by the River Dee – used to serve the ferry that it's named for; outside there are tables and they've recently opened six bedrooms so do let us know how you find them if you stay here.

🍴 Using plenty of fresh local produce, lunchtime bar food includes soup, sandwiches, traditional meals like very good fresh battered haddock, tasty liver and bacon and lasagne (all served in a choice of sizes), several vegetarian dishes, grilled fillet of bass with sweet cucumber salsa, pan-fried lemon and chilli chicken breast, daily specials (maybe including turbot, venison and salmon), and puddings like rhubarb and gingerbread fool or sticky toffee. *Starters/Snacks: £2.75 to £5.25. Main Courses: £4.75 to £13.50. Puddings: £3.75 to £4.75*

Free house ~ Licensees Wilson and Jacqui Clark ~ Real ale ~ Bar food (12-2, 5.30-9) ~ Restaurant ~ (01339) 886137 ~ Dogs welcome ~ Open 11-11(12 Sat) ~ Bedrooms: £57.50B/£57.50B

Recommended by J A West, David and Betty Gittins, Jean and Douglas Troup

---

If we know a pub does sandwiches we always say so – if they're not mentioned, you'll have to assume you can't get one.

APPLECROSS

NG7144   MAP 11

Applecross Inn ★ ⑪ 🛏

Off A896 S of Shieldaig; IV54 8LR

SCOTLAND DINING PUB OF THE YEAR

Wonderfully remote pub reached by extraordinarily scenic drive; particularly friendly welcome, and excellent sensibly priced fresh seafood

The long drive to get to this splendidly remote waterside pub is rewarding in itself – providing there is no low cloud. It's reached by what's undoubtedly one of Britain's greatest scenic drives, over the hair-raising Pass of the Cattle (Beallach na Ba). The alternative route, along the single-track lane winding round the coast from just south of Shieldaig, has equally glorious sea loch and then sea views nearly all the way; some readers like to go one way, then back the other. Tables in the nice shoreside garden enjoy magnificent views across to the Cuillin Hills on Skye. With a friendly mix of locals and visitors, the no-nonsense bar has a woodburning stove, exposed stone walls, and upholstered pine furnishings on the stone floor; Isle of Skye Blaven and Red Cuillin, and over 50 malt whiskies; pool (winter only), board games and juke box (musicians may take over instead); some disabled facilities.

⑪ Most ingredients are local, with the keenly priced fresh seafood a real draw; chalked up on boards, the menu might include starters such as white bean, rosemary and celery minestrone, rollmop herring, lobster cocktail, half a dozen oysters, haggis flambéed in Drambuie and topped with cream, main courses such as ploughman's, battered haddock, dressed crab, green thai curry, local venison sausages and sirloin steak, with puddings such as hot chocolate fudge cake, creamy rice pudding with berry compote and raspberry cranachan; they also do very good sandwiches. *Starters/Snacks: £3.00 to £7.00. Main Courses: £8.00 to £16.00. Puddings: £4.00 to £6.00*

Free house ~ Licensee Judith Fish ~ Real ale ~ Bar food (12-9) ~ Restaurant ~ (01520) 744242 ~ Children welcome ~ Dogs welcome ~ Open 11am-11.30pm; 12.30-11 Sun ~ Bedrooms: /£90B

Recommended by Richard and Emily Whitworth, Barry Collett, Revd D Glover, Peter Black, Peter Meister, the Dutchman, Chris Evans, Comus and Sarah Elliott, Mrs A J Robertson, Mr and Mrs G D Brooks

BADACHRO

NG7873   MAP 11

Badachro Inn ⑪

2.5 miles S of Gairloch village turn off A832 on to B8056, then after another 3.25 miles turn right in Badachro to the quay and inn; IV21 2AA

Convivial waterside pub with chatty local atmosphere, great views, and excellent fresh fish

Decking, done in a nautical style with sails and rigging, runs right down to the water, making the most of the lovely views over Loch Gairloch at this very friendly white-painted house. There are three pub moorings (free for visitors), and showers are available at a small charge. Sailing visitors and chatty locals mix happily in the welcoming bar, which can get quite busy in summer. In the bar you'll find some interesting photographs and collages on the walls, and they put out the Sunday newspapers. The quieter dining area on the left has big tables by a huge log fire, and there's a dining conservatory overlooking the bay. Friendly staff serve a couple of beers from the An Teallach or Caledonian breweries and a farm cider on handpump, and they've over 50 malt whiskies, and a good changing wine list, with several by the glass; piped music. Look out for the sociable pub spaniel Kenzie. The pub is in a tiny village, and its quiet road comes to a dead end a few miles further on at the lovely Redpoint beach. The bay is very sheltered, virtually landlocked by Eilean Horrisdale just opposite; you may see seals in the water, and occasionally even otters.

⑪ Enjoyable food – with the good fresh fish earning the place its food award – might include snacks such as sandwiches, soups, smoked salmon, locally smoked mussels and local venison terrine, creel-caught prawns, haggis, neeps and tatties, ploughman's, beef and spring onion burger, chicken breast on crushed haggis, neeps and tatties, locally smoked haddock topped with welsh rarebit and locally caught langoustines and bass en

papillote, with home-made puddings such as chocolate marquise and sticky toffee
pudding. *Starters/Snacks: £3.25 to £6.95. Main Courses: £9.95 to £14.95. Puddings: £1.75 to
£5.25*

Free house ~ Licensee Martyn Pearson ~ Real ale ~ Bar food (12(12.30 Sun)-3(2.30 Sat in winter),
6-9(8 in winter)) ~ (01445) 741255 ~ Children welcome ~ Dogs allowed in bar ~ Open 12-12;
12.30-11 Sun; 4.30-11 Mon-Fri, 12.30-6 Sun in winter

*Recommended by R M Jones, Walter and Susan Rinaldi-Butcher, Comus and Sarah Elliott, Peter Meister,
Mrs A J Robertson, Revd D Glover, Mr and Mrs G D Brooks*

BROUGHTY FERRY   NO4630   MAP 11

Fishermans Tavern ♀ ◁

Fort Street; turning off shore road; DD5 2AD

Welcoming pub with good choice of beers and enjoyable food

This friendly place carries a good range of beers. As well as Caledonian Deuchars IPA,
five guests on handpump might typically be from Bass, Bridge of Allan, Greene King and
Hanby. They also have draught wheat beer, a dozen wines by the glass, and a good range
of malt whiskies. It's been a pub since 1827, when it was converted from a row of
fishermen's cottages. On the right, a secluded lounge area with an open coal fire runs
into a little carpeted snug with nautical tables, light pink soft fabric seating, basket-
weave wall panels and beige lamps. The carpeted back bar (popular with diners) has a
Victorian fireplace, dominoes, TV and fruit machine, and a coal fire. On summer evenings
there are tables on the front pavement or you can sit out in the secluded walled garden
(where they hold an annual beer festival on the last weekend in May). They have
disabled lavatories, and baby changing facilities. More reports please.

▥ Bar food includes soup, sandwiches, fisherman's crêpe, smoked fish pie, chicken
stuffed with haggis, lambs liver on black pudding mash, burgers and salads.
Starters/Snacks: £2.75 to £3.95. Main Courses: £5.95 to £8.95. Puddings: £3.25

Free house ~ Licensee Rhys Martinson ~ Real ale ~ Bar food (12(12.30 Sun)-2.30 (3 Sat, Sun),
5-7) ~ Restaurant ~ (01382) 775941 ~ Children welcome till 6pm (8pm if dining) ~
Dogs allowed in bar ~ Scots fiddle music Thurs night from 10 ~ Open 11am-midnight(1 Thurs-
Sat); 12.30-midnight Sun ~ Bedrooms: £39B/£64B

Recommended by Derek Thomas, BOB

EDINBURGH   NT2574   MAP 11

Abbotsford ◁

Rose Street; E end, beside South St David Street; EH2 2PR

Bustling well preserved Victorian pub with constantly changing beers and good value food

This traditional city-centre pub was purpose built in 1902 and continues to this day
virtually unaltered since its construction. Perched at its centre is a hefty and very
impressive highly polished Victorian island bar ornately carved from dark spanish
mahogany. Long wooden tables and leatherette benches run the lengths of its dark
wooden high-panelled walls and a rather handsome plaster-moulded high ceiling has
recently been restored to its original green and gold. Five changing real ales, usually
Scottish, might be from Arran, Cairngorm, Hadrian & Border, Inveralmond and Stewart,
and are served from a set of air pressure tall founts; around 50 malt whiskies. Low level
or silent large screen sports TV.

🍴 Bar food includes soup, sandwiches, haggis, neeps and tatties, battered haddock, coq au vin, burger, leek and parmesan risotto cakes with baked portobella mushrooms, rump steak, and good home-made puddings. There's a smarter restaurant upstairs. *Starters/Snacks: £3.50 to £5.95. Main Courses: £7.95 to £12.95. Puddings: £3.95 to £6.50*

Free house ~ Licensee Daniel Jackson ~ Real ale ~ Bar food (12(12.30 Sun)-3, 3.30-5.30(10 Fri, Sat)) ~ Restaurant (12-2.15, 5.30-9.30) ~ (0131) 225 5276 ~ Children in restaurant ~ Open 11-11(12 Fri, Sat); 12.30-11 Sun

Recommended by the Didler, Janet and Peter Race, Dr and Mrs A K Clarke, Michael Dandy, Jeremy King, Dave Webster, Sue Holland, Doug Christian, Joe Green

Bow Bar ★ 🍺
West Bow; EH1 2HH

Eight splendidly kept beers – and lots of malts – in well run and friendly alehouse of considerable character

For many readers, this very traditional character-laden one room alehouse is their favourite pub in the city. The simple, neatly kept rectangular bar – busy and friendly with a jolly good welcome – stars an impressive carved mahogany gantry, home to over 160 malts, including cask strength whiskies; a good choice of rums and gins too. A fine collection of enamel advertising signs and handsome antique brewery mirrors festoons the walls, with sturdy leatherette wall seats and heavy narrow tables on its wooden floor, and café-style bar seats. The tall founts on the bar counter date from the 1920s, and dispense eight superbly kept beers from Belhaven 80/-, Caledonian Deuchars IPA, Timothy Taylors Landlord, plus various changing guests from brewers such as Cairngorm, Inveralmond, Kelham Island, Stewart and York.

🍴 Lunchtime snacks are limited to tasty pies and toasties. *Starters/Snacks: £1.75*

Free house ~ Licensee Helen McLoughlin ~ Real ale ~ Bar food (12-2; not Sun) ~ (0131) 226 7667 ~ Dogs welcome ~ Open 12-11.30; 12.30-11 Sun

Recommended by the Didler, Dave Webster, Sue Holland, Pam and John Smith, Tracey and Stephen Groves, Doug Christian, Joe Green, Dr and Mrs A K Clarke, Colin and Ruth Munro

Café Royal
West Register Street; EH2 2AA

Stunning listed interior, bustling atmosphere and rewarding food

Do call in here, even if only in passing, as the wonderfully preserved listed interior is well worth a look. The building was constructed with late Victorian grandeur and no expense spared, in 1863, with state-of-the art plumbing and gas fittings that were probably the pride and joy of its owner Robert Hume who was a local plumber. Its floors and stairway are laid with marble, chandeliers hang from the magnificent plasterwork ceilings, and the substantial island bar is graced by a carefully re-created gantry. The high-ceilinged vienna café style rooms have a particularly impressive series of highly detailed Doulton tilework portraits of historical innovators Watt, Faraday, Stephenson, Caxton, Benjamin Franklin and Robert Peel (forget police – his importance here is as the introducer of calico printing), and the stained-glass well in the restaurant is well worth a look. Alongside a decent choice of wines, with a dozen by the glass, they've 15 malt whiskies, and Caledonian Deuchars IPA and 80/- on handpump. They may also have a couple of scottish guests like Isle of Skye Young Pretender and Kelburn Red Smiddy, but reader reports suggest not often; games machine and piped music. It can get very busy at lunchtimes (when the acoustics lend themselves to a lively lunch rather than intimate chat), so if you're keen to fully take in the look of the place, try and visit on a quieter afternoon.

If you have to cancel a reservation for a bedroom or restaurant, please telephone or write to warn them. You may lose your deposit if you've paid one.

🍴 Bar food includes some seafood: mussels (half a kilo, or a kilo – that's a lot of mussels), fine oysters with lovely bread, cullen skink and fish stew, as well as sandwiches, beef and ale pie, haggis pie with neeps, tatties and whisky cream and steak, with puddings such as plum cranachan with heather honey and oats or white chocolate and raspberry tart and a local cheese plate. *Starters/Snacks: £3.95 to £5.50. Main Courses: £7.95 to £11.95. Puddings: £2.95 to £5.95*

Spirit ~ Manager Valerie Graham ~ Real ale ~ Bar food (11(12.30 Sun)-10) ~ Restaurant ~ (0131) 556 1884 ~ Open 11-12(1 Sat); 12.30-11 Sun

Recommended by the Didler, Tracey and Stephen Groves, Joe Green, Janet and Peter Race, Dr and Mrs A K Clarke, Michael Dandy, Pam and John Smith, Comus and Sarah Elliott, Geoff and Pat Bell, Dr Kevan Tucker, Dave Webster, Sue Holland, Doug Christian, David M Smith

Guildford Arms 🍺

West Register Street; EH2 2AA

Busy and friendly, with sumptuous Victorian décor, and an extraordinary range of real ales

The resplendent interior of this elaborately façaded Victorian pub is opulently excessive with ornate painted plasterwork, dark mahogany fittings, heavy swagged velvet curtains at the huge arched windows and a busy patterned carpet. The snug little upstairs gallery restaurant, with strongly contrasting modern décor, gives a fine dress-circle view of the main bar (notice the lovely old mirror decorated with two tigers on the way up). Another key part of the appeal is the extraordinary range of ten very well kept beers – typically Caledonian Deuchars IPA and XPA, Harviestoun Bitter & Twisted, Orkney Dark Island, Stewart 80/-, with quickly changing guests from brewers such as Buffys, Kelburn and Vale; the helpful, friendly staff may offer a taste before you buy. Also, 18 wines by the glass, and two dozen or so malt whiskies; board games, TV, fruit machine, piped music. They may have occasional mini beer festivals.

🍴 The menu includes sandwiches, soup, haggis with whisky and warm oatcakes, thai green chicken curry, lamb chops with port gravy and mint, steak and ale pie, breaded haddock, various steaks, and specials such as a fish of the day; in the evenings food from the same menu is served only in the gallery restaurant. *Starters/Snacks: £3.25 to £5.20. Main Courses: £8.95 to £15.00. Puddings: £4.00*

Free house ~ Licensee Scott Wilkinson ~ Real ale ~ Bar food (12(12.30 Sun)-2.30(3 Fri-Sun), 6-9.30(10 Fri, Sat)) ~ Restaurant (12(12.30 Sun)-2.30, 6-9.30(10 Fri/Sat)) ~ (0131) 556 4312 ~ Live jazz, folk and blues during Festival ~ Open 11-11(12 Fri, Sat); 12.30-11 Sun

Recommended by Dr Kevan Tucker, Dr and Mrs A K Clarke, Pam and John Smith, Joe Green, Geoff and Pat Bell, Nick Holding, Comus and Sarah Elliott, the Didler, Michael Dandy

Kays Bar 🍺 £

Jamaica Street W; off India Street; EH3 6HF

Unpretentious and cosy back-street pub with excellent choice of well kept beers, and the feel of a friendly local

Attracting an eclectic and sometimes lively mix of customers, this busy little back-street pub has a very enjoyable local feel, and is not at all touristy. They stock a great range of beers and whiskies, including more than 50 malts between eight and 50 years old and ten blended whiskies and, superbly well kept on handpump, Caledonian Deuchars IPA and Theakstons Best alongside five guests from brewers such as Fyne and Harviestoun. The no frills interior is decked out with various casks and vats, old wine and spirits merchant notices, gas-type lamps, well worn red plush wall banquettes and stools around cast-iron tables, and red pillars supporting a red ceiling. A quiet panelled back room (a bit like a library) leads off, with a narrow plank-panelled pitched ceiling and a collection of books ranging from dictionaries to ancient steam-train books for boys; lovely warming coal fire in winter. In days past, the pub was owned by John Kay, a whisky and wine merchant; wine barrels were hoisted up to the first floor and dispensed through pipes attached to nipples which can still be seen around the light rose. Service is friendly, obliging, and occasionally idiosyncratic; TV, dominoes and cribbage, Scrabble and backgammon.

⑪ Straightforward but good value lunchtime bar food includes soup, sandwiches, haggis and neeps, mince and tatties, steak pie, beefburger and chips, and chicken balti. *Starters/Snacks: £1.50 to £2.50. Main Courses: £3.50 to £5.00. Puddings: £2.50*

Free house ~ Licensee David Mackenzie ~ Real ale ~ Bar food (12(12.30 Sun)-2.30; not on rugby international days) ~ (0131) 225 1858 ~ Children allowed in back room until 6 ~ Dogs welcome ~ Open 11am-midnight (1 Fri, 1.30 Sat); 12.30-11 Sun

Recommended by Nick Holding, the Didler, Dr and Mrs A K Clarke, Peter F Marshall, John and Annabel Hampshire, Doug Christian, Pam and John Smith, R T and J C Moggridge

Starbank ♀ ▣ £

Laverockbank Road, off Starbank Road, just off A901 Granton—Leith; EH5 3BZ

Half a dozen real ales, good value food and great views over Firth of Forth at cheery well run pub

It's the impressive waterside views that really make this pub stand out, but it's a friendly, comfortably elegant place too. The long, light and airy bare-boarded bar looks out over the Firth of Forth, and has around six real ales, with Belhaven 80/, Caledonian Deuchars IPA, and Timothy Taylors Landlord alongside guests from breweries all over Britain such as Broughton, Everards, Greene King and Harviestoun. They serve about a dozen wines by the glass and have a good selection of malt whiskies. You can eat in the conservatory restaurant, and there's a sheltered back terrace; TV. Dogs must be on a lead. Parking is on the adjacent hilly street.

⑪ Good-value bar food includes soup, herring rollmop salad, a daily vegetarian dish, ploughman's, steak and ale pie, smoked haddock with poached egg, poached salmon, and minute steak. *Starters/Snacks: £3.75 to £3.95. Main Courses: £6.50 to £7.50. Puddings: £3.25*

Free house ~ Licensee Valerie West ~ Real ale ~ Bar food (12-2.30, 6-9; 12-9 Sat, Sun) ~ Restaurant ~ (0131) 552 4141 ~ Children welcome ~ Dogs welcome ~ Open 11-11(midnight Thurs-Sat); 12.30-11 Sun

Recommended by Dr and Mrs A K Clarke, Ken Richards, John and Annabel Hampshire

ELIE   NO4999   MAP 11

Ship 🛏

The Toft, off A917 (High Street) towards harbour; KY9 1DT

Friendly seaside inn with views over broad sandy bay, unspoilt bar, and good seafood

On alternate summer Sundays you can sit on the terrace outside this popular harbourside pub and watch the progress of the pub's cricket team going through the overs out on the wide sandy bay, itself neatly enclosed by headlands. It has to be said though that a walk here on a fresh, windy day in December is just as rewarding. The very positive licensees here are hands-on and interested, and the pub is very much a cheery part of the local community. The unspoilt, villagey beamed bar has a buoyantly nautical feel, with friendly locals and staff, warming winter coal fires, partly panelled walls studded with old prints and maps, Caledonian Deuchars IPA, several wines by the glass, and half a dozen malt whiskies. There's also a simple carpeted back room; cards, dominoes and shut-the-box. The comfortable bedrooms are in a guesthouse next door. More reports please.

⑪ Well presented very fairly priced bar food includes lunchtime sandwiches, good soup, lentil dhal, hot salmon tart with a dill dressing, battered haddock and chips, mussels in season, smoked haddock crêpe, steak and Guinness pie, lamb curry, steaks and plenty of fresh fish. *Starters/Snacks: £3.00 to £6.00. Main Courses: £9.00 to £15.00. Puddings: £4.00*

Free house ~ Licensees Richard and Jill Philip ~ Real ale ~ Bar food (12-2.30(2 in winter, 12.30-3 Sun), 6-9(9.30 Fri, Sat); not Sun evening) ~ Restaurant ~ (01333) 330246 ~ Children welcome ~ Dogs allowed in bar ~ Open 11am-midnight (1 Fri, Sat); 12.30-midnight Sun ~ Bedrooms: £55B/£80B

Recommended by Comus and Sarah Elliott, Joyce and Maurice Cottrell

GAIRLOCH   NG8075   MAP 11

Old Inn ♀ 🍺

Just off A832/B8021; IV21 2BD

Delightful old pub with fish and seafood from neighbouring harbour; good beers too, especially in summer

The chef at this delightfully set 18th-c inn sometimes walks down to the adjacent pier to see what's being landed in the little fishing harbour – needless to say fresh seafood is a speciality here. Manned by welcoming staff, the cheerfully relaxed public bar is popular with chatty locals, no doubt here for the decent range of drinks, which include Greene King Abbot and Isle of Skye Blind Piper (a blend of Isle of Skye ales made for the pub and named after a famed 17th-c local piper), three guests such as Adnams, An Teallach Crofters Pale Ale and Isle of Skye Blaven, quite a few fairly priced wines by the glass, a decent collection of 30 malt whiskies, and speciality coffees. It's quite traditional, with paintings and murals on exposed stone walls and stools lined up along the counter; darts, TV, fruit machine, pool and juke box. The pub is nicely tucked away from the main shoreside road, with picnic-sets prettily placed by the trees alongside a stream that flows past under the old stone bridge and is well placed for strolls up Flowerdale valley to a waterfall – you might spot eagles over the crags above. Credit (but not debit) cards incur a surcharge of £1.75.

🍽 Bouillabaisse, seared scallops and langoustines are commonly on the board, and mussels, crabs, lobster, skate, haddock and hake often crop up too. Otherwise, the menu usually includes a good mix of dishes including soup, cullen skink, game pâté, venison steak with garlic confit and blue cheese, whisky and basil mash, fish and chips, vegetable stuffed cannelloni, steak and ale pie, and puddings such as clootie dumpling and sticky date pudding. *Starters/Snacks: £3.50 to £5.25. Main Courses: £7.50 to £16.50. Puddings: £3.75 to £4.95*

Free house ~ Licensees Alastair and Ute Pearson ~ Real ale ~ Bar food (12-9.30 in summer) ~ Restaurant ~ (01445) 712006 ~ Children welcome ~ Dogs welcome ~ Open 11am-1am (midnight Sun); open only 4pm-midnight weekdays in winter ~ Bedrooms: £40B/£75B

Recommended by Barry Collett, Mr and Mrs G D Brooks, WAH, Carol and Phil Byng, Di and Mike Gillam, Peter Meister

GATEHOUSE OF FLEET   NX6056   MAP 9

Masonic Arms 🍽 ♀

Ann Street, off B727; DG7 2HU

Nicely transformed pub with really excellent, very popular food, and relaxed traditional bar

Though food is quite a draw here (it's well worth booking) the comfortable two-room beamed bar is still pubby, with Caledonian Deuchars IPA and a guest such as Houston Auld Copperhead on handpump, and a good choice of whiskies and wines by the glass, traditional seating, pictures on its lightly timbered walls, and blue and white plates on a delft shelf; piped music, TV and pool. Service is friendly and efficient, and there is a relaxed warm-hearted atmosphere. The bar opens into an airily attractive conservatory, with comfortable cane bucket chairs around good tables on its terracotta tiles, pot plants, and colourful pictures on one wall. The conservatory then opens through into a contemporary restaurant, with high-backed dark leather chairs around modern tables on bare boards. There are picnic-sets under cocktail parasols out in the neatly kept sheltered garden, and seats out in front of the flower-decked black and white building; this is an appealing small town, between the Solway Firth and the Galloway Forest Park.

🍽 Good food includes lunchtime baguettes, soup, venison and chicken terrine with roast hazelnuts and home-made beetroot chutney, locally smoked salmon, seared scallops with celeriac purée, fish and chips, goan beef curry, local scampi, bass fillet with tomato crust on parmesan mash, mediterranean vegetable and pesto ricotta tart, steaks, and puddings such as milk chocolate brûlée with baked polenta biscuits, chocolate gingerbread pudding with honeycomb ice-cream and cherry and frangipane tart. *Starters/Snacks: £3.95 to £7.25. Main Courses: £9.75 to £18.50. Puddings: £4.50 to £5.50*

Challenger Inns ~ Lease Paul Shepherd ~ Real ale ~ Bar food (12-2, 6-9) ~ Restaurant ~ (01557) 814335 ~ Children welcome ~ Dogs allowed in bar ~ Open 11.30-2.30, 5.30-11.30; 11.30-11.30 Sat, Sun

Recommended by Pat Crabb, Ken and Jenny Simmonds, Nick Holding

GLASGOW

NS5965 MAP 11

Babbity Bowster ⊕☺ ♀

Blackfriars Street; G1 1PE

Glasgow institution: friendly, comfortable and sometimes lively mix of traditional and modern, with almost continental feel, and good food

Genuinely welcoming and often lively, this fine city-centre pub is a sprightly blend of both scottish and continental, traditional and modern. A big ceramic of a kilted dancer and piper in the bar illustrates the mildly cheeky 18th-c lowland wedding pipe tune (Bab at the Bowster) from which the pub takes its name – the friendly landlord or his staff will be happy to explain further. The simply decorated light interior has fine tall windows, well lit photographs and big pen-and-wash drawings of the city, its people and musicians, dark grey stools and wall seats around dark grey tables on the stripped wooden boards, and a peat fire. The bar opens on to a pleasant terrace with tables under cocktail parasols, trellised vines and shrubs; they may have barbecues out here in summer. You'll find Caledonian Deuchars IPA, Kelburn Misty Law and a guest such as Hook Norton on air pressure tall fount, and a remarkably sound collection of wines, malt whiskies, and farm cider; good tea and coffee too. On Saturday evenings they have live traditional scottish music, while at other times you may find games of boules in progress outside. Note the bedroom price is for the room only.

⊞ A short but interesting bar menu includes scottish and french items such as hearty home-made soup, cullen skink, potted rabbit, croques monsieur, haggis, neeps and tatties (they also do a vegetarian version), stovies, mussels, cauliflower and mung bean moussaka, platter of scottish smoked salmon, roast leg of duck on a bed of haricot beans and sautéed potatoes, and a daily special. The airy upstairs restaurant has more elaborate meals. *Starters/Snacks: £3.50 to £4.95. Main Courses: £5.95 to £8.50. Puddings: £3.25 to £4.50*

Free house ~ Licensee Fraser Laurie ~ Real ale ~ Bar food (12-10.30) ~ Restaurant ~ (0141) 552 5055 ~ children welcome till 8pm ~ Live traditional music on Sat ~ Open 11(12.30 Sun)-midnight ~ Bedrooms: £45S/£60S

Recommended by Barry Collett, Andy and Claire Barker

Bon Accord ◀ £

North Street; G3 7DA

Fabulous choice of drinks, with a choice of ten often uncommon real ales and lots of whiskies; a good welcome too, and bargain food

With Caledonian Deuchars IPA and Marstons Pedigree as house beers, an astonishing eight hundred or so daily changing guest beers pass through the pumps each year at this very welcoming pubby place. These are sourced from smaller breweries around Britain – maybe Brakspears, Broughton, Durham, Hop Back, Fullers, Harviestoun, Houston and Kelham Island. Spirit drinkers have lots to keep them happy too, with over 170 malts (this number seems to grow each year), lots of gins, vodkas and brandies. All 13 of their wines are available by the glass and they keep a farm cider. With a good mix of customers (women find it comfortable here), the interior is neatly kept; partly polished bare-boards and partly carpeted, with a mix of tables and chairs, terracotta walls, and pot plants throughout; TV, fruit machine, cribbage, chess and piped music. More reports please.

Places with gardens or terraces usually let children sit there – we note in the text the very few exceptions that don't.

---

⑪ **Very reasonably priced bar food includes baguettes, baked potatoes, lasagne, scampi and steak; they do a bargain two-course lunch.** *Starters/Snacks: £1.90 to £2.70. Main Courses: £4.25 to £7.95. Puddings: £1.50*

Scottish Courage ~ Tenant Paul McDonagh ~ Real ale ~ Bar food (12(12.30 Sun)-8) ~ (0141) 248 4427 ~ Children allowed till 8pm ~ Live band Sat, open mike Tues ~ Open 11am-midnight; 12.30-11 Sun

Recommended by Nick Holding

Counting House ◖ £

St Vincent Place/George Square; G1 2DH

Impressive conversion of former bank with great range of mostly scottish beers, and food all day

This former bank is one of Wetherspoons' more striking conversions. The imposing interior rises into a lofty, richly decorated coffered ceiling which culminates in a great central dome, with well lit nubile caryatids doing a fine supporting job in the corners. You'll also find the sort of decorative glasswork that nowadays seems more appropriate to a landmark pub than to a bank, as well as wall-safes, plenty of prints and local history, and big windows overlooking George Square. Away from the bar, several areas have solidly comfortable seating, while a series of smaller rooms – once the managers' offices – lead around the perimeter of the building. Some of these are surprisingly cosy, one is like a well stocked library, and a few are themed with pictures and prints of historical characters such as Walter Scott or Mary, Queen of Scots. The very reasonable prices surely contribute to drawing in the crowd here, but even when really busy the atmosphere remains civilised, and staff are friendly and efficient. The central island servery has a splendid choice of up to eight real ales on handpump, with Greene King IPA and Abbot and half a dozen guests from brewers such as Exmoor, Harviestoun, Kelburn, Oakham and Shepherd Neame. They also do a good choice of bottled beers, 22 malt whiskies, a farmhouse cider and seven wines by the glass; games machines.

⑪ **Served all day, by friendly staff, the usual wide choice of straightforward Wetherspoons food: baguettes and wraps, haggis, neeps and tatties, chilli con carne, liver and bacon casserole, breaded scampi, pasta, sausages and mash, Sunday roasts, and children's meals. Steak night is now Tuesday, with curry club on Thursday.** *Starters/Snacks: £1.49 to £7.79. Main Courses: £3.49 to £9.49. Puddings: £1.69 to £3.69*

Wetherspoons ~ Manager Rhoda Thompson ~ Real ale ~ Bar food (9am-10pm) ~ (0141) 225 0160 ~ Children welcome till 7pm ~ Open 9am-midnight

Recommended by Andrew York, Nick Holding, Barry Collett, Dave Braisted

HAUGH OF URR   NX8066   MAP 11

Laurie Arms ◖ £

B794 N of Dalbeattie; Main Street; DG7 3YA

Comfortable village pub with enjoyable attractively priced food and local beers

This has a few of those notices dotted around – at a glance, the 'Please park considerately...' sort that you tend not to look at because you think you've seen them so often before. But these are rather different: sharp little bundles of spiky humour. And the gents' well repays a visit, with its splendid old Bamforth comic postcards. Neatly kept and attractively decorated, with some bric-a-brac and small pictures, the bar has a log fire in its stone fireplace, and just a few pub tables, with a couple of steps up to a further similar area. They have decent wines by the glass, and two or three well kept real ales on handpump. These change quite quickly and usually include one or two scottish beers such as Harviestoun and Inveralmond and perhaps an english one such as Timothy Taylors Landlord. Service is welcoming and attentive without being pushy. On the right is a pleasant restaurant; you can eat anywhere except in the games room, which has darts, pool and a juke box. There are picnic-sets and one or two teak benches out on the pavement in front of the white-painted 19th-c building, with more on a sheltered terrace behind.

⚷ The people who took this over a couple of years ago have extended the menu while keeping their eye firmly on quality and value. They usually have two or three fish dishes as well as a game dish or two. The familiar pub favourites such as lunchtime sandwiches (not Sunday), pâté with oatcakes, haggis, neeps and tatties, steak pie or haddock and chips use good fresh ingredients including tender local beef and lamb. Puddings might include sticky toffee pudding and a brûlée. It's worth booking at weekends. *Starters/Snacks: £2.70 to £6.00. Main Courses: £6.50 to £13.45. Puddings: £3.95*

Free house ~ Licensee Sandra Yates ~ Real ale ~ Bar food (12-2, 5.30-9) ~ Restaurant ~ (01556) 660246 ~ Children welcome ~ Open 12-3, 5.30-midnight; 12-midnight Sat, Sun
Recommended by Nick Holding, J M Renshaw, Mark O'Sullivan, C A Hall

HOUSTON
NS4066 MAP 11

Fox & Hounds ♀ ⚷

South Street at junction with Main Street (B789, off B790 at Langbank signpost E of Bridge of Weir); PA6 7EN

Welcoming village pub best known for the award-winning beers from their own Houston Brewery

Over the last few years the tasty beers produced at this welcoming village pub (run by the same family for over 30 years) have won several national awards – they are now sold throughout the UK, by cask and bottle. In the meanwhile, as you enjoy your pint of Killellan, St Peters Well, Texas, or Warlock Stout you can look through a window in the bar to the little brewery where they are produced. They also stock a guest such as Caledonian Deuchars IPA, 12 wines by the glass, around 100 malt whiskies, and freshly squeezed orange juice. The clean plush hunting-theme lounge has comfortable seats by a fire and polished brass and copper; piped music. Popular with a younger crowd, the lively downstairs bar has a large-screen TV, pool, juke box and fruit machines; board games, piped music. At the back is a covered and heated area with decking. More reports please.

⚷ Served upstairs (downstairs they do only substantial sandwiches), a good choice of enjoyable bar food might include soup, crayfish and scallop skewer with coriander and tomato salsa, courgette fritters with shaved parmesan and garlic mayonnaise, steak burger, steak, mushroom and ale pie, apple, celery and mushroom stroganoff, battered haddock, pork ribs in spicy sauce, and puddings such as banana split and warm chocolate fudge cake. *Starters/Snacks: £3.00 to £8.00. Main Courses: £7.00 to £14.00. Puddings: £3.00 to £5.00*

Own brew ~ Licensee Jonathan Wengel ~ Real ale ~ Bar food (12-10(9 Sun)) ~ Restaurant ~ (01505) 612448 ~ Children in lounge and restaurant till 8pm ~ Dogs allowed in bar ~ Quiz Tues ~ Open 11(12 Sun)-midnight(1am Sat)
Recommended by BOB

INNERLEITHEN
NT3336 MAP 9

Traquair Arms ⚷

B709, just off A72 Peebles—Galashiels; follow signs for Traquair House; EH44 6PD

Comfortably refurbished village inn, popular with families, with friendly welcome and nice food (great puddings); a good bet if exploring the Borders

This is an attractively modernised inn in a pretty village, cheerily hospitable, with an easy mix of locals and visitors around the warm open fire in the main bar. It's one of only three places where you can taste draught Traquair ale, which is produced using original oak vessels in the 18th-c brewhouse at nearby Traquair House. They also stock a couple of guests such as Caledonian Deuchars IPA and Timothy Taylors Landlord, several malt whiskies and draught cider; piped music, TV. Both the relaxed light and airy bistro style restaurant and the italian restaurant have high chairs. The garden at the back has picnic-sets and a big tree on a neatly kept lawn. Bedrooms are comfortable, clean and fresh.

🍽 Well liked bar food includes sandwiches, ciabattas, steak and ale pie, local venison, chilli, rack of lamb, pizza and pasta dishes, and traditional puddings. *Starters/Snacks: £3.95 to £5.95. Main Courses: £7.95 to £11.75. Puddings: £3.95 to £4.25*

Free house ~ Licensee Dave Rogers ~ Real ale ~ Bar food (12-2, 7-9; 12-9 Sat, Sun) ~ Restaurant ~ (01896) 830229 ~ Children welcome ~ Dogs welcome ~ Open 11(12 Sun)-midnight ~ Bedrooms: £50S/£80B

Recommended by Angus Lyon, Nick Holding, Tom and Jill Jones, R T and J C Moggridge

INVERARAY
NN0908   MAP 11

George £ 🛏
Main Street E; PA32 8TT

Well placed and attractive, with atmospheric old bar, enjoyable food and pleasant garden; comfortable bedrooms

Run by the same family since 1860, this handsome Georgian inn has plenty to offer. Its dark bustling pubby bar oozes Scottish history from its bare stone walls, and shows plenty of age in its exposed joists, old tiles and big flagstones. It has antique settles, cushioned stone slabs along the walls, carved wooden benches, nicely grained wooden-topped cast-iron tables and four cosy log fires. The bar carries over 100 malt whiskies and a couple of beers from Fyne on handpump; darts. A smarter flagstoned restaurant has french windows that open to tables tucked into nice private corners on a series of well laid-out terraces. This is a civilised place to stay, the individually decorated bedrooms (reached by a grand wooden staircase) with jacuzzis or four-poster beds. It's near Inveraray Castle, and the shore of Loch Fyne (where you may glimpse seals or even a basking shark or whale), and well placed for the great Argyll woodland gardens, best for their rhododendrons in May and early June.

🍽 Generously served enjoyable bar food (you order at the table) includes soup, ploughman's, haggis, neeps and tatties, steak pie, venison sausages, spaghetti bolognaise, and evening dishes like crispy duck pancakes, a vegetarian dish of the day, haddock and chips, venison collops with red wine and morello cherry sauce, with home-made puddings such as crumble or warm chocolate cake; proper children's meals. *Starters/Snacks: £2.95 to £6.25. Main Courses: £5.25 to £14.95. Puddings: £3.95 to £4.95*

Free house ~ Licensee Donald Clark ~ Real ale ~ Bar food (12-9) ~ Restaurant ~ (01499) 302111 ~ Children welcome ~ Dogs welcome ~ Live entertainment Fri/Sat ~ Open 11-midnight ~ Bedrooms: £35B/£70B

Recommended by David Heath, Les and Sandra Brown, Peter Black, Dave Braisted, Alistair and Kay Butler, Peter Craske, David and Sue Atkinson, Dr A McCormick

ISLE OF WHITHORN
NX4736   MAP 9

Steam Packet ♀ 🛏
Harbour Row; DG8 8LL

Unfussy family-run inn with splendid views of working harbour from bar and some bedrooms, and good food – especially the inventive specials

Big picture windows at this modernised inn have fine views out over a busy crowd of yachts and fishing boats in the harbour, and then beyond to calmer waters. Run by the same family for over 26 years, this is an unfussy but welcoming place. The comfortable low-ceilinged bar is split into two: on the right, plush button-back banquettes and boat pictures, and on the left, green leatherette stools around cast-iron-framed tables on big stone tiles, and a woodburning stove in the bare stone wall. Bar food can be served in the lower-beamed dining room, which has excellent colour wildlife photographs, rugs on its wooden floor, and a solid fuel stove, and there's also a small eating area off the lounge bar, as well as a conservatory. Three guests from brewers such as Batemans and Kelburn are kept alongside the Theakstons XB on handpump, and they've quite a few malt whiskies, and a good wine list; TV, pool and board games. There are white tables and chairs in the garden. You can walk from here up to the remains of St Ninian's Kirk, on a headland behind the village.

🍴 **Bar food might include lunchtime open sandwiches and ciabatta, haggis, neeps and tatties, chicken pie and scampi, with interesting changing specials such as chorizo salad, devilled whitebait, warm fig and goats cheese salad, smoked haddock with prawn, cream and white wine sauce, scallops with pea purée and black pudding salad, cumberland sausage and mash and rump steak with red wine jus, with puddings such as oat flapjack with whisky ice-cream, lemon posset and local ice-creams, and a scottish cheese platter.** *Starters/Snacks: £2.75 to £7.95. Main Courses: £7.95 to £17.95. Puddings: £1.25 to £3.50*

Free house ~ Licensee Alastair Scoular ~ Real ale ~ Bar food (12-2, 6.30-9) ~ Restaurant ~ (01988) 500334 ~ Children welcome except in bar ~ Dogs allowed in bar and bedrooms ~ Open 11(12 Sun)-11(midnight Sat); closed 2.30-6 Tues-Thurs in winter ~ Bedrooms: £30B/£60B

Recommended by Pat Crabb, Mark O'Sullivan, Karen Eliot, Nick Holding

KILBERRY

Kilberry Inn 🛏

NR7164   MAP 11

B8024; PA29 6YD

A stylish place to stay in wonderfully remote setting; no real ale but pubby feel to bar, and excellent, locally sourced food

It really is worth the long splendid single-track drive (with stunning views of the coast) to reach this rather special gently upmarket place with its excellent, locally sourced food (as they say, the cattle you saw on the way here may later make it on to the menu) and very comfortable bedrooms. Topped by its trademark pinky red corrugated iron roof, it's a simple low slung whitewashed building, ready to batten down the hatches in winter but lovely when they put tables outside in summer. The small beamed dining room, tastefully and simply furnished, is relaxed and warmly sociable, with a good log fire; piped music. There's no real ale, but they do Fyne bottled beers, have a selection of malt whiskies (with quite a few local ones) and a good wine list. Do tell us about your visit if you go as we get barely any reports on this place and we'd love to know what you think.

🍴 **Thoughtfully prepared food from the delicious lunchtime or evening menus might include gazpacho soup, local potted crab, scallops with minted pea purée, braised pork belly with garlic and celeriac purée, grilled halibut with creamy leeks and grainy mustard mash, rump of roast lamb with puy lentils and rib-eye steak with roast red peppers and café de paris butter, with puddings like sticky toffee pudding, chocolate amaretti cake with orange syrup and mascarpone sorbet, and a local cheese platter.** *Starters/Snacks: £4.50 to £7.95. Main Courses: £10.25 to £15.95. Puddings: £5.00 to £6.50*

Free house ~ Licensees Clare Johnson and David Wilson ~ Bar food (12.15-2.15, 6.30-9) ~ Restaurant ~ (01880) 770223 ~ Children welcome away from restaurant ~ Dogs allowed in bedrooms ~ Open 12.15-2.15, 6.30-11; closed Mon, plus Mon-Thurs in Nov and Dec, and also closed all Jan to mid-Mar ~ Bedrooms: /£155S

Recommended by BOB

KILMAHOG

Lade 🍷 ☕

NN6008   MAP 11

A84 just NW of Callander, by A821 junction; FK17 8HD

Lively and pubby, with own brew beers, and shop specialising in scottish brews; traditional scottish music at weekends, and good home-made food

It's all family hands on deck to offer a cheery welcome at this lively inn. One of the licensees is passionate about real ale, which explains not just their own excellent beers, but also the scottish real ale shop with over 120 bottled brews from 26 microbreweries around Scotland. In the bar they always have their own WayLade, LadeBack and LadeOut on handpump, along with a guest such as Broughton Clipper, nine wines by the glass and about 30 malts. There's plenty of character in the several small beamed areas – cosy with red walls, panelling and stripped stone, and decorated with highland prints and works by local artists; piped music. A big windowed restaurant (with a more ambitious menu) opens on to a terrace and a pleasant garden with three fish ponds.

🍴 Using local ingredients, food includes soup, sandwiches, baked potatoes, battered haggis balls, fresh battered haddock, steak and ale pie, vegetables lasagne, whole fried local trout, deer burgers, and puddings like raspberry cranachan and chocolate fudge cake. *Starters/Snacks: £3.95 to £7.00. Main Courses: £7.75 to £17.50. Puddings: £3.60 to £5.50*

Own brew ~ Licensees Frank and Rita Park ~ Real ale ~ Bar food (12(12.30 Sun)-9; 12-3, 5-9 Mon-Fri in winter) ~ Restaurant ~ (01877) 330152 ~ Children welcome ~ Dogs allowed in bar ~ Ceilidhs Fri and Sat evenings ~ Open 12(12.30 Sun)-11(1 Fri, Sat)

Recommended by Paul and Margaret Baker, Alan Sutton

KIPPEN
NS6594   MAP 11

Cross Keys 🛏

Main Street; village signposted off A811 W of Stirling; FK8 3DN

Cosy village inn, popular with locals and visitors

The recent addition (by new licensees) of a few extra comforts has not detracted from the timeless local atmosphere which has always been a large part of the appeal here. The cosy bar is stylish with lovely dark panelling and subdued lighting. A straightforward lounge has a good log fire, and there's a coal fire in the attractive family dining room. They have Harviestoun Bitter & Twisted on handpump, and over 30 malt whiskies; cards, dominoes, TV in the separate public bar; piped music. Tables in the garden have good views towards the Trossachs.

🍴 Bar food might include cream of sweet corn soup, smoked haddock and spinach tart, mussels, chicken and chorizo terrine, braised lamb shank with garlic thyme mash, chicken breast stuffed with haggis, battered haddock with crushed peas, five cheese ravioli with tomato and basil sauce, and puddings such as dark chocolate rum mousse, and a cheeseboard. *Starters/Snacks: £4.00 to £6.00. Main Courses: £7.00 to £16.00. Puddings: £4.00 to £6.00*

Free house ~ Licensees Debby McGregor and Brian Horsburgh ~ Real ale ~ Bar food (12-9(8 Sat)) ~ Restaurant ~ (01786) 870293 ~ Children welcome ~ Dogs allowed in bar and bedrooms ~ Open 12-11(1 Fri, Sat); closed Mon ~ Bedrooms: £70S/£90S

Recommended by Mr and Mrs M Stratton, Lucien Perring

KIRK YETHOLM
NT8328   MAP 10

Border 🛏

Village signposted off B6352/B6401 crossroads, SE of Kelso; The Green; TD5 8PQ

Welcoming and comfortable hotel with good inventive food and a famous beer story
Run by a warmly hospitable couple, this well tended hotel has good, interesting food, comfortable bedrooms, and owing to an old tradition, a particularly good welcome for walkers (and a water bowl for dogs). Alfred Wainwright determined that anyone who walked the entire 256 miles of the Pennine Way National Trail would get a free drink. He left some money here to cover the bill, but it has long since run out, and the pub has generously footed the bill. In recent times the Broughton Brewery has helped out by producing an exclusive beer, Pennine Way. They usually have another Scottish beer on handpump too, such as Atlas Three Sisters, decent wines by the glass and a good range of malt whiskies. The cheerfully unpretentious bar has beams and flagstones, a log fire, a signed photograph of Wainwright and other souvenirs of the Pennine Way, and appropriate borders scenery etchings and murals; snug side rooms lead off. There's a roomy pink-walled dining room, a comfortable lounge with a second log fire, and a neat conservatory; piped music, TV, darts, board games, and children's games and books. A sheltered back terrace has picnic-sets and a play area, and the colourful window boxes and floral tubs make a very attractive display outside.

🍴 Using carefully sourced ingredients (including local fish, game and organic pork), food from the seasonal menu is inventive without being at all pretentious: seafood ravioli on rocket, mushroom soup, suet pastry venison pie, steamed cod fillet with straw vegetables and crispy bacon dressing, pork fillet stuffed with black pudding wrapped in bacon with port and cranberry jus, venison steak and roast of the day. *Starters/Snacks: £3.25 to £5.95. Main Courses: £7.95 to £12.95. Puddings: £3.95 to £4.95*

Free house ~ Licensees Philip and Margaret Blackburn ~ Real ale ~ Bar food (12-2, 6-9(8.30 winter), unless booked for weddings) ~ Restaurant ~ (01573) 420237 ~ Children welcome away from public bar ~ Dogs allowed in bar and bedrooms ~ Open 11(12 Sun)-11 ~ Bedrooms: £45B/£90B

Recommended by Tina and David Woods-Taylor, Joe Green, Brian McCaucs, John Evans, Mairi Reynolds

KIRKCUDBRIGHT
NX6850   MAP 11

Selkirk Arms
High Street; DG6 4JG

Comfortable well run hotel with good service, enjoyable imaginative food and local sports bar

There's a tradition that Burns composed the Selkirk Grace while staying in this well kept and much modernised 18th-c hotel (though a rival school of thought is that he did so while staying at St Mary's Isle with Lord Daer, Selkirk's son). Either way, this place stocks a beer called The Grace, which is brewed especially for them by Sulwath, alongside a guest beer such as Timothy Taylors Landlord. The bars here range from the very simple locals' front bar which has its own street entrance, a TV for live sport, darts and dominoes, to a welcoming partitioned high-ceilinged lounge bar at the heart of the hotel, with comfortable upholstered armchairs and wall banquettes and original paintings which are for sale. There's also a bistro and restaurant. Service is thoughtful and efficient and there's a nice friendly atmosphere. A neatly set out garden has smart wooden furniture with contrasting blue umbrellas and a 15th-c font. The hotel is in the older part of this attractive historic town at the mouth of the Dee where a handful of fishing boats land their catch on the quay.

🍴 Food in the locals' bar is limited to sandwiches, burgers and fish and chips, but the enjoyable food served in the bistro might include prawn cocktail, haggis and tattie scone tower with Drambuie cream sauce, chicken and pistachio terrine, fish and meat antipasti, sausage and mash, organic beefburger, roast duck breast with cranberry and lime jus, spinach and cream cheese roulade, king scallops fried with chorizo, steaks, and puddings such as chocolate and pecan nut brownie, berry cranachan, and a local cheeseboard. *Starters/Snacks: £3.95 to £6.95. Main Courses: £8.95 to £16.95. Puddings: £4.10*

Free house ~ Licensees Douglas McDavid and Chris Walker ~ Real ale ~ Bar food (12-2, 6-9) ~ Restaurant ~ (01557) 330402 ~ Children welcome away from public bar ~ Dogs welcome ~ Open 11-11(12 Sat)

Recommended by Nick Holding, Pat Crabb

LINLITHGOW
NS0077   MAP 11

Four Marys 🍺 £
High Street; 2 miles from M9 junction 3 (and little further from junction 4) – town signposted; EH49 7ED

Very popular old pub with Mary, Queen of Scots memorabilia, excellent range of beers, and good food and service

This terrific pub is one of those happy places that ticks every box – as one reader said, it's 'all that a pub should be'. In the same hands for quite a few years now, it has a good steady well cared for feel, and service is very friendly. The building dates from the 16th c and takes its name from the four ladies-in-waiting of Mary, Queen of Scots, born at nearby Linlithgow Palace in 1542. Accordingly the pub is stashed with mementoes of the ill-fated queen, such as pictures and written records, a piece of bed curtain said to be hers, part of a 16th-c cloth and swansdown vest of the type she's likely to have worn, and a facsimile of her death-mask. Spotlessly kept, the L-shaped bar has mahogany dining chairs around stripped period and antique tables, a couple of attractive antique corner cupboards, and an elaborate Victorian dresser serving as a bar gantry. The walls are mainly stripped stone, including some remarkable masonry in the inner area; piped music. Eight real ales are kept on handpump, with changing guests such as Atlas Three Sisters, Cairngorm Tradewinds, Caledonian Deuchars IPA, Fullers London Pride joining the regular Belhaven 80/- and St Andrews and Greene King IPA and Abbot; they also have a good range of malt whiskies (including a bargain malt of the month) and several wines by the glass. During their May and October beer festivals they have 20 real ale pumps and live entertainment. There's an outdoor smoking area with heaters, and tables and chairs. Parking can be difficult, but the pub is handy for the station.

🍴 Generously served good value bar food (with around half a dozen qualifying for our Bargain Award) includes sandwiches, baked potatoes, ploughman's, good cullen skink, haddock and chips, steak and ale pie, curry, tasty haggis, neeps and tatties, scampi, roast cod and cherry tomatoes wrapped in parma ham, roast duck breast with citrus fruit jus and mustard mash, steaks, and puddings such as banoffi pie and baked apple pie. *Starters/Snacks: £2.45 to £4.95. Main Courses: £5.95 to £12.95. Puddings: £3.95*

Belhaven (Greene King) ~ Managers Eve and Ian Forrest ~ Real ale ~ Bar food (12-3, 5-9; 12-9 Sat; 12.30-8.30 Sun) ~ Restaurant ~ (01506) 842171 ~ Children in dining area till 8pm ~ Open 12(12.30 Sun)-11(midnight Sat)

Recommended by Christine and Malcolm Ingram, Peter F Marshall, A Darroch Harkness, Tony and Wendy Hobden, PL

MEIKLEOUR   NO1539   MAP 11

Meikleour Hotel 🛏

A984 W of Coupar Angus; PH2 6EB

Friendly, civilised and well run, with good bar food and real ales, comfortable bedrooms

This early 19th-c inn is an attractive building, low and creeper-covered, with broad eaves and a long back wing. The main lounge bar is a friendly place, basically two rooms, both with log fires. One is carpeted and decorated in gentle toning colours, with comfortable seating, chintz curtains and a log fire in its elegant white-painted fireplace, the other is broadly similar, again with well padded seats, but on flagstones, with some stripped stone around its fireplace. There is a modicum of fishing equipment (the River Tay is nearby), and a few small pictures. Service is welcoming and efficient, and they have local bottled water as well as two or three beers from Inveralmond, one of which, Lure of Meikleour, is brewed especially for them. The elegant fully panelled restaurant specialises in local game and fish; piped music. There are a few Victorian-style seats out in a small colonnaded verandah, and tables and picnic-sets under tall conifers on the gently sloping lawn of a garden sheltered by clipped box. You can see the distant hills over the hedges – talking of which, don't miss the spectacular nearby beech hedge, planted over 250 years ago and the grandest in the world. If you stay, the breakfast is good.

🍴 The good pubby bar menu includes especially tasty sandwiches, panini, burgers, beef and ale pie, and their very popular beer-battered scampi and haddock. This is balanced against much more elaborate daily specials that might include tomato and roasted red pepper soup, ballotine of rabbit wrapped in bacon with orange and pine nut salad, fried breast of guinea fowl with a black pudding and potato rösti and madeira jus, roast beef fillet topped with chicken and tarragon mousse with marsala sauce, braised halibut with fried courgettes and citrus fruit butter sauce and ratatouille stuffed beef tomatoes, with puddings such as brûléed lemon tart with red berry coulis, dark chocolate marquise with minted cream biscuits, and a scottish cheese platter. *Starters/Snacks: £4.25 to £5.80. Main Courses: £8.50 to £16.95. Puddings: £4.50*

Free house ~ Licensee Kia Mathieson ~ Real ale ~ Bar food (12.15(12.30 Sun)-2.30, 6.30-9) ~ Restaurant ~ (01250) 883206 ~ Children welcome ~ Dogs allowed in bedrooms ~ Open 11-3, 6-11; 11-11.45 Fri, Sat; 12-11 Sun ~ Bedrooms: £75B/£120B

Recommended by Dr A McCormick, G Dobson, David and Katharine Cooke

MELROSE   NT5433   MAP 9

Burts Hotel 🍴 🛏

B6374, Market Square; TD6 9PL

Comfortably civilised hotel with tasty food and lots of malt whiskies

Emphasis at this quite smart 200-year-old hotel is on the food and accommodation but you can pop in for just a drink if you prefer – service by smartly uniformed staff is polite and good and it's well run. Pleasantly informal and inviting, the lounge bar has lots of cushioned wall seats and windsor armchairs, and scottish prints on the walls; piped music. There are 90 malt whiskies to choose from, and Caledonian Deuchars IPA and 80/- and a guest such as Timothy Taylors Landlord are kept on handpump; there's a good wine list too, with eight by the glass. In summer you can sit out in the well tended garden. It's situated at the heart of this attractive border town, in the market square, a few steps away from the abbey ruins.

🍴 Gently imaginative bar food might include soup, chicken liver parfait, crab and sweet chilli cakes with lime and chive mayonnaise, seared king scallops and black pudding with cauliflower purée, chicken caesar salad, battered haddock, burger, organic salmon, pea and ham risotto, sausage and mash with red onion jus and steaks, with puddings such as chocolate tart with crème fraîche sorbet and marmalade syrup and apple, rhubarb and raspberry crumble with berry ice-cream. *Starters/Snacks: £3.50 to £8.95. Main Courses: £9.25 to £17.50. Puddings: £5.00 to £5.50*

Free house ~ Licensees Graham and Anne Henderson ~ Real ale ~ Bar food ~ Restaurant ~ (01896) 822285 ~ Dogs allowed in bar and bedrooms ~ Open 11-2.30, 5-11; 12-2.30, 6-11 Sun ~ Bedrooms: £60B/£112B

Recommended by John Evans, Mrs J H S Lang, Nick Holding

PITLOCHRY   NN9459   MAP 11

Moulin 🍺 🛏

Kirkmichael Road, Moulin; A924 NE of Pitlochry centre; PH16 5EH

Attractive old inn with excellent own-brewed beers, nicely pubby bar, well presented tasty food all day; comfortable bedrooms

Everything seems to be going very well at this most enjoyable 17th-c family run inn. With an all round comfortably traditional atmosphere and great friendly service, it has a lively bar (serving their great own-brew beers), very good food in a calmer dining room, and is a comfortably relaxing place to stay. Although much extended over the years, the bar, in the oldest part of the building, still seems an entity in itself, nicely pubby, with plenty of character. Above the fireplace in the smaller room is an interesting painting of the village before the road was built (Moulin used to be a bustling market town, far busier than upstart Pitlochry), while the bigger carpeted area has a good few tables and cushioned banquettes in little booths divided by stained-glass country scenes, another big fireplace, some exposed stonework, fresh flowers, and golf clubs and local and sporting prints around the walls; bar billiards and board games. The superbly kept Ale of Atholl, Braveheart, Light and the stronger Old Remedial served here on handpump are brewed in the little stables across the street; they also have around 40 malt whiskies, and a good choice of wines by the glass and carafe. On a gravelled area and surrounded by tubs of flowers, picnic-sets look across to the village kirk in front, and there are excellent walks nearby.

🍴 The extensive bar menu includes baked potatoes and sandwiches served right through the afternoon, as well as soup, deep-fried haggis with piquant sauce, a platter of local smoked meats with oatcakes and rowan sauce, fish, chips and peas, grilled salmon steak with lemon and herb butter sauce, haggis, neeps and tatties, stuffed peppers, steak and ale pie, game casserole, fried strips of venison with mushrooms and their own beer, 6oz minute steak stuffed with haggis, and puddings like bread and butter pudding or apple pie. *Starters/Snacks: £3.95 to £7.95. Main Courses: £6.95 to £13.95. Puddings: £3.05 to £4.50*

Own brew ~ Licensee Heather Reeves ~ Real ale ~ Bar food (12-9.30) ~ Restaurant ~
(01796) 472196 ~ Children welcome ~ Open 11(12 Sun)-11(11.45 Sat) ~ Bedrooms: £55B/£70B

*Recommended by Comus and Sarah Elliott, Joan York, Derek Thomas, Paul and Ursula Randall, Charles and
Pauline Stride, the Dutchman, Barry Collett, Ian Wilson*

PLOCKTON   NG8033   MAP 11

Plockton Hotel ★ 🍴 🛏

Village signposted from A87 near Kyle of Lochalsh; IV52 8TN

**Welcoming loch-side hotel with wonderful views, excellent food, and particularly friendly
staff – a real favourite with many readers**

Thanks to the welcome, the seafood, and the delightful location this place draws several
readers back year after year – it's much loved and receives plenty of praise. Forming part
of a long, low terrace of stone-built houses, it's set in a delightful waterfront National
Trust for Scotland village. Tables in the front garden look out past the village's trademark
palm trees and colourfully flowering shrub-lined shore, and across the sheltered
anchorage to the rugged mountainous surrounds of Loch Carron; a stream runs down the
hill into a pond in the landscaped back garden. With a buoyant, bustling atmosphere,
the welcoming comfortably furnished lounge bar has window seats looking out to the
boats on the water, as well as antiqued dark red leather seating around neat Regency-
style tables on a tartan carpet, three model ships set into the woodwork, and partly
panelled stone walls. The separate public bar has darts, pool, board games, TV and piped
music, and on Wednesday evenings they have live traditional folk music. Drinks include
Isle of Skye Hebridean Gold and Crags from a fairly new little village brewery on
handpump, bottled beers from the Isle of Skye brewery, a good collection of malt
whiskies, and a short wine list. Most of the comfortable bedrooms (it's worth booking
well ahead) are in the adjacent building – one has a balcony and woodburning stove and
half of them have extraordinary views over the loch ('ridiculously pretty', says one
reader), and you can expect good breakfasts. A hotel nearby changed its name a few
years ago to the Plockton Inn, so don't get the two confused. The family who have run
the hotel so well for 20 years have put it on the market; fingers crossed any buyer
doesn't change a thing.

🍴 **Especially good for fresh, local seafood, bar dishes include cream of smoked fish soup,
salad of pickled herrings and prawns, haggis and whisky, venison casserole, wild boar
burgers, trout grilled with almonds, fish and chips, chargrilled prawns, and a seafood
platter.** *Starters/Snacks: £3.50 to £9.75. Main Courses: £7.50 to £20.25. Puddings: £3.95 to
£4.75*

Free house ~ Licensee Tom Pearson ~ Real ale ~ Bar food (12(12.30 Sun)-2.15, 6-9.15) ~
Restaurant ~ (01599) 544274 ~ Children welcome ~ Dogs allowed in bar ~ Traditional folk
music Weds evenings ~ Open 11-midnight; 12.30-11 Sun ~ Bedrooms: £60B/£100B

*Recommended by Joan York, Richard and Emily Whitworth, Joan and Tony Walker, Mr and Mrs G D Brooks,
Mike and Sue Loseby, Brian McBurnie, Peter Black, Les and Sandra Brown, R M Jones, Barry Collett, Comus and
Sarah Elliott, Di and Mike Gillam, Richard Tosswill, Christine and Phil Young, Revd D Glover, J D Taylor*

PORT CHARLOTTE   NR2558   MAP 11

Port Charlotte Hotel 🛏

Main St, Isle of Islay; PA48 7TU

**Welcoming inn with exceptional collection of local malts, cheery bar, lots of seafood,
lovely views and comfortable bedrooms**

With lovely views over Loch Indaal (a sea inlet) and across to the mountains of Jura,
this occupies a prime spot in the most beautiful of Islay's carefully planned Georgian
villages. We have been getting warm reports from readers ever since the present owners
took it on some five years ago, but all our attempts to integrate it sensibly into one of
our usual anonymous inspection tours have failed. So we have departed from our normal

procedure and have in effect used a posse of deputies to do our job – a number of trusted reader/reporters who have been able to check the inn out for us during a holiday on the island (or in one case a yachting visit). Pride of place in the rounded central bar goes to an exceptional collection of about 140 Islay and rare Islay malts (Port Charlotte was built originally as a distillery village – its own Lochindaal distillery closed in 1929, though the island still has another eight). It also has real ales such as Black Sheep and local Islay Angus Og and Saligo, and good wines by the glass; service is welcoming and helpful. There is a good log and peat fire, with well padded wall seats and pubby chairs on bare boards, attractive charcoal prints (the inn has nice pictures throughout), and big windows giving a light and airy feel. The comfortable and relaxed back lounge has a case of books about the area, and there is a good restaurant. The roomy conservatory, with well upholstered seats around its tables, opens on to a garden with more seats. Just a short stroll from a sandy beach, this is a good spot for families with children.

🍴 The island has good local lamb and beef, so even the straightforward dishes are full of flavour. There is often local seafood, too – maybe scallops, oysters, langoustines, bass on minted pea mash with caper sauce and a seafood platter – and game in season. Other dishes might include lunchtime sandwiches and salads, as well as red thai curry, couscous and stir-fried vegetables, chilli and mushroom stroganoff. *Starters/Snacks: £3.50 to £7.75. Main Courses: £8.50 to £14.75. Puddings: £4.95*

Free house ~ Licensee Graham Allison ~ Real ale ~ Bar food (12-2, 5.30-8.30) ~ Restaurant ~ (01496) 850360 ~ Children welcome ~ Dogs allowed in bedrooms ~ Traditional live music weekly ~ Open 12 noon-1am ~ Bedrooms: £85B/£130B

Recommended by Alan Cole, Kirstie Bruce, D S and J M Jackson

SHIELDAIG

NG8153   MAP 11

Tigh an Eilean Hotel 🛏

Village signposted just off A896 Lochcarron—Gairloch; IV54 8XN

Particularly fine views, good beers, and well liked food, especially seafood, in newly built bar

The new bar here was not quite finished as we went to press (it will be open by the time this *Guide* is in the shops) so please forgive our slightly vague description. Separate from the civilised little hotel itself, it will be on two storeys with an open staircase, dining on the first floor, and a decked balcony with what should be magnificent 270-degree views of the sea. The interior will be gently contemporary and nicely relaxed with timbered floors, timber boarded walls, and shiny bolts through the timber roof beams. Please do tell us about it if you go as we may not be able to get up here for a year or two. Isle of Skye Black Cuillin and Red Cuillin and maybe a summer guest will be on handpump, as well as up to ten wines by the glass, and several malt whiskies; winter darts and pool. Tables outside in a sheltered little courtyard are well placed to enjoy the gorgeous position at the head of Loch Shieldaig (which merges into Loch Torridon), beneath some of the most dramatic of all the highland peaks, and looking out to Shieldaig Island – a sanctuary for a stand of ancient caledonian pines. Next door, the main building's bedrooms are comfortable and peaceful.

🍴 Fresh fish and seafood, all hand-dived or creel-caught by local fishermen, feature heavily on the menu, and particularly among the daily specials, which might take in battered haddock, smoked haddock omelette, grilled bream in lemon and garlic butter, catalan seafood stew, moules marinières and shieldaig spiny lobsters. Other dishes include sandwiches, butties, venison sausages and mash and rib-eye steak, with puddings such as sticky toffee pudding and rum, orange and almond cake. *Starters/Snacks: £3.75 to £8.00. Main Courses: £7.25 to £14.75. Puddings: £3.25 to £4.00*

Free house ~ Licensee Cathryn Field ~ Real ale ~ Bar food (12-8.30 (winter 12-2.30, 6-8.30)) ~ Restaurant ~ (01520) 755251 ~ Children welcome ~ Dogs welcome ~ Traditional live folk music some weekends and holidays ~ Open 11-11; 12-10 Sun ~ Bedrooms: £75B/£160B

Recommended by Comus and Sarah Elliott

You can send reports to us at feedback@thegoodpubguide.co.uk.

STEIN   NG2656   MAP 11

Stein Inn 🛏

End of B886 N of Dunvegan in Waternish, off A850 Dunvegan—Portree; OS Sheet 23 map reference 263564; IV55 8GA

Lovely setting on northern corner of Skye, especially welcoming inn with good, simple food, and lots of whiskies; rewarding place to stay

This welcoming 18th-c inn has an extremely restful location by the water's edge on a far-flung northern corner of Skye. The tables outside are an ideal place to sit with a malt whisky (they've over 125 to choose from), and watch the sunset. Inside, the unpretentious original public bar has great character, with its sturdy country furnishings, flagstone floor, beam and plank ceiling, partly panelled stripped-stone walls and peat fire in a grate between the two rooms. The atmosphere can be surprisingly lively, and there's a good welcome from the owners and the evening crowd of local regulars (where do they all appear from?). Good service from the smartly uniformed staff. There's a games area with pool table, darts, board games, dominoes and cribbage, and maybe piped music. Caledonian Deuchars IPA and a couple of guests such as Cairngorm Trade Winds and Isle of Skye Red Cuillin are kept on handpump, and in summer they have several wines by the glass. There's a lively children's inside play area, and showers for yachtsmen. All the bedrooms have sea views, and breakfasts are good – it's well worth pre-ordering the tasty smoked kippers if you stay here.

🍽 **Using local fish and highland meat, the short choice of good, simple and very sensibly priced food includes good value sandwiches, various salads, battered haddock, and 8oz sirloin steak, with specials such as home-made soup, mussels, venison casserole, lamb chops with cranberry sauce, chicken supreme stuffed with haggis, and fresh langoustines, and local cheeses.** *Starters/Snacks: £4.50 to £7.50. Main Courses: £5.65 to £13.50. Puddings: £3.10 to £6.50*

Free house ~ Licensees Angus and Teresa Mcghie ~ Real ale ~ Bar food (12-4, 6-9.30) ~ Restaurant ~ (01470) 592362 ~ Children welcome ~ Open 11-midnight(12.30 Sat); 12.30-11 Sun; 12-11 Mon-Sat in winter ~ Bedrooms: £35S/£60S(£90B)

Recommended by Ann O'Sullivan-Hollingnorth, Mike and Sue Loseby, Joan and Tony Walker, Ian and Barbara Rankin, Comus and Sarah Elliott

SWINTON   NT8347   MAP 10

Wheatsheaf 🍽 🍷 🛏

A6112 N of Coldstream; TD11 3JJ

Civilised, upmarket restaurant with imaginative, elaborate food – not cheap, but rewarding; well chosen wines, comfortable bedrooms

If they're not busy here they will serve just a drink, but this is really very much a restaurant-with-rooms so be aware that priority is given to residents (and surprisingly, the handful of locals who still turn up here) – it's probably best to ring first. The carefully thought-out main lounge area has an attractive long oak settle and comfortable armchairs, with sporting prints and plates on the bottle-green wall covering; a small lower-ceilinged part by the counter has pubbier furnishings, and small agricultural prints on the walls, especially sheep. A further lounge area has a fishing-theme décor (with a detailed fishing map of the River Tweed). The front conservatory has a vaulted pine ceiling and walls of local stone. Caledonian Deuchars IPA on handpump, around 40 malt whiskies, and a fine choice of 150 wines (with a dozen by the glass). Breakfasts are good, with freshly squeezed orange juice.

🍽 **Skilfully prepared with fresh local ingredients, bar food might include starters such as soup, paris brown mushrooms with bacon in filo pastry topped with local cheddar, woodpigeon breast on black pudding with cumberland sauce, fried feta wrapped in filo with local honey, garlic and lemon prawn skewer, main courses such as linguine with rocket, prosciutto and chilli, goats cheese and spinach omelette, pork, leek and sage meatballs with cider gravy, braised oxtail in red wine, sirloin steak with pink peppercorn and brandy sauce, and puddings such as warm chocolate and pistachio brownie with**

Malteser ice-cream and ginger and pear pudding with warm fudge sauce. *Starters/Snacks: £5.20 to £9.95. Main Courses: £11.90 to £21.00. Puddings: £5.45 to £7.95*

Free house ~ Licensees Chris and Jan Winson ~ Real ale ~ Bar food (12-2, 6-9(9.30 Fri, Sat; 8.30 Sun)) ~ Restaurant ~ (01890) 860257 ~ Children welcome ~ Open 11(12 Sun)-3, 6-11 ~ Bedrooms: £71B/£108B

Recommended by Les and Sheila Gee, Christine and Malcolm Ingram, Dr Peter D Smart, Alan Cole, Kirstie Bruce, John Evans, Mrs Marion Matthewman, John and Annabel Hampshire

THORNHILL

NS6699 MAP 11

Lion & Unicorn

A873; FK8 3PJ

Busy and interesting pub with some emphasis on its good home-made food (all day), well liked locally

Readers who pop in at this welcoming family owned pub are immediately cheered by the happy atmosphere, blazing log fires and especially good natured service, and if you're here for a tasty meal you can be pretty sure that it will be a positive experience too (around meal times most tables may be set for eating). Parts of the building date back in part to 1635 – one dining room (with its own entrance) still has its original massive fireplace, almost big enough to drive a car into. The carpeted front room has old walls, a beamed ceiling, and comfortable seating. One or two real ales such as Caledonian Deuchars IPA and Harviestoun Bitter and Twisted, are on handpump (it's cheaper in the public bar than it is in the lounge), and they have a good choice of malt whiskies. A games room has a juke box, pool, fruit machine, TV, darts, and board games; quiz nights and piped music. There's a play area in the garden.

🍽 Served all day, enjoyable bar food includes soup, baked potatoes, steak pie, battered haddock, scampi, stir-fried vegetables, lamb shank with red wine and rosemary, chicken and haggis wrapped in bacon with a whisky sauce, duck with teriyaki sauce, baked bass with tomato salsa, and puddings such as cherry anglaise pancake stack, lemon tart and chocolate ice-cream sundae. *Starters/Snacks: £3.50 to £4.95. Main Courses: £4.50 to £9.50. Puddings: £3.00 to £4.95*

Free house ~ Licensees Fiona and Bobby Stevenson ~ Real ale ~ Bar food (12-9) ~ Restaurant ~ (01786) 850204 ~ Children welcome ~ Open 11am-midnight(1 Sat); 12.30-midnight Sun ~ Bedrooms: £55B/£75B

Recommended by the Dutchman, Tom and Rosemary Hall, Karen Eliot, John and Joan Nash

WEEM

NN8449 MAP 11

Ailean Chraggan 🍽 ♟ 🛏

B846; PH15 2LD

Changing range of well sourced creative food in friendly family-run hotel – a particularly nice place to stay

Beautifully kept, small and friendly, this family-run hotel is a lovely place to stay – as one reader put it, 'every request was promptly met and with a smile'. You're likely to find chatty locals in the bar which carries around 100 malt whiskies, a couple of beers from the local Inveralmond Brewery on handpump, and a very good wine list with several by the glass; winter darts and board games. The lovely views from its two flower filled terraces look to the mountains beyond the Tay, and up to Ben Lawers – the highest peak in this part of Scotland – and the owners can arrange fishing nearby. More reports please.

🍽 As well as sandwiches, the changing menu, served in either the comfortably carpeted modern lounge or the dining room, might include starters such as broccoli and toasted almond soup, pigeon breast with black pudding and roast plums, warm courgette, goats cheese and mustard tart, moules marinières, main courses such as bacon wrapped scallops, halibut with tomato beurre blanc, roast pork fillet stuffed with chorizo, smoked mozzarella and pesto, braised lamb shank with rosemary jus, and puddings such as sticky toffee pudding, sherry trifle and pistachio crème brûlée. It's worth booking at busy times. *Starters/Snacks: £2.95 to £4.95. Main Courses: £9.85 to £17.95. Puddings: £4.95*

Free house ~ Licensee Alastair Gillespie ~ Real ale ~ Bar food ~ Restaurant ~ (01887) 820346 ~ Children welcome ~ Dogs allowed in bar and bedrooms ~ Open 11-11 ~ Bedrooms: £57.50B/£95B

Recommended by Comus and Sarah Elliott, Ian Stafford

LUCKY DIP

Besides the fully inspected pubs, you might like to try these Lucky Dips recommended to us and described by readers (if you do, please send us reports: feedback@thegoodpubguide.co.uk).

ABERDEENSHIRE

ABERDEEN [NJ9305]
Grill AB11 6BA [Union St]: Old-fashioned traditional local with enormous range of whiskies, well kept Caledonian 80/- and guest beers, polished dark panelling, basic snacks; open all day *(the Didler)*
☆ *Prince of Wales* AB10 1HF [St Nicholas Lane]: Eight changing ales from individual and convivial old tavern's very long bar counter, bargain hearty food, flagstones, pews and screened booths, smarter lounge; children welcome in eating area at lunchtime, open all day *(LYM, Gwyn and Anne Wake, the Didler, Joe Green)*
CRATHIE [NO2293]
Inver AB35 5XN [A93 Balmoral—Braemar]: Friendly family-run 18th-c inn by River Dee, sensitively and comfortably refurbished bar areas with log fires, some stripped stone and good solid furnishings inc leather settees, sensible choice of enjoyable fresh home-made food esp in restaurant, decent wine by the glass, lots of whiskies, may possibly stock a real ale in summer; comfortable bedrooms *(Peter Cobb, J F M and M West, Ken and Jenny Simmonds)*
GLENKINDIE [NJ4413]
Glenkindie Arms AB33 8SX [A97]: Hard-working licensees now brewing their own good ale, food from good toasties to wide choice of fresh fish; bedrooms, cl winter wkdy lunchtimes *(David and Betty Gittins)*
MONYMUSK [NJ6815]
Grant Arms AB51 7HJ [signed from B993 SW of Kemnay]: Recently refurbished small stone-built inn with enjoyable pub food and full evening meals, pleasant helpful table service, real ales, lots of malt whiskies, modern take on traditional décor, cane chairs in panelled dining lounge divided by log fire, separate dining room and simpler public bar; children welcome, 12 bedrooms, attractive countryside nr River Don (good fishing) *(LYM)*
OLDMELDRUM [NJ8127]
☆ *Redgarth* AB51 0DJ [Kirk Brae]: Good-sized comfortable lounge, traditional décor and subdued lighting, Caledonian Deuchars IPA, Timothy Taylors Landlord and a guest beer, good range of malt whiskies, enjoyable

bargain food, cheerful attentive service, restaurant; gorgeous views to Bennachie, immaculate bedrooms *(David and Betty Gittins)*

ANGUS

BROUGHTY FERRY [NO4630]
Royal Arch DD5 2DS [Brook St]: 19th-c pub with restored traditional bar and simple comfort in art deco lounge, well kept real ales such as Belhaven Best and McEwans 80/-, enjoyable food *(anon)*

ARGYLL

BRIDGE OF ORCHY [NN2939]
☆ *Bridge of Orchy Hotel* PA36 4AB [A82 Tyndrum—Glencoe]: Comfortable and lively bar with nice views, good choice of well kept ales, house wines and malt whiskies, friendly young staff, fairly priced food in bar and restaurant, interesting mountain photographs; lovely bedrooms, good value bunkhouse, spectacular spot on West Highland Way *(Sarah and Peter Gooderham, Michael and Maggie Betton)*
DUNBEG [NM8833]
Wide Mouthed Frog PA37 1PX [Dunstaffnage Marina]: Enjoyable food inc lots of good enterprisingly cooked fish in long bar and small attractive restaurant, good staff, Fyne Highlander, interesting wines; verandah and huge covered terrace overlooking marina, bay and Dunstaffnage Castle, good bedrooms in same complex *(Pat and Sam Roberts)*
GLENCOE [NN1058]
☆ *Clachaig* PH49 4HX [old Glencoe rd, behind NTS Visitor Centre]: Lively extended inn doubling as mountain rescue post and cheerfully crowded with outdoors people in season, mountain photographs in basic flagstoned walkers' bar (two woodburners and pool), quieter pine-panelled snug and big modern-feeling dining lounge, hearty all-day bar food, wider evening choice, great real ale choice inc An Teallach, Glenfinnan and Williams, unusual bottled beers, over 120 malt whiskies, children in restaurant; live music Sat – great atmosphere; good warm simple bedrooms, spectacular setting

surrounded by soaring mountains
(Andy and Jill Kassube, LYM, Mr and
Mrs Maurice Thompson, Peter Black,
Jarrod and Wendy Hopkinson, R M Jones)

KINLOCHLEVEN [NN1862]

Tailrace PH50 4QH [Riverside Rd]: Friendly,
quiet and very neatly kept, with well kept
Atlas seasonal ales from nearby brewery,
good value simple food all day from
sandwiches up, pleasantly decorated partly
carpeted bar, separate restaurant; picnic-sets
outside, six bedrooms, open all day
(Andy and Jill Kassube)

OBAN [NM8530]

Cuan Mor PA34 5SD [George St]: Reworked
as dining pub using reclaimed scottish
materials, good value food (Jack Burnett)

TAYVALLICH [NR7487]

Tayvallich Inn PA31 8PL [B8025]: Simple
conversion specialising in local seafood, pale
pine furnishings on quarry tiles, local
nautical charts, full range of Islay malts,
Loch Fyne ales; piped music; children
welcome, decking with lovely views over
yacht anchorage, open all day, cl Mon/Tues
in winter (LYM)

AYRSHIRE

AYR [NS3321]

West Kirk KA7 1BX [Sandgate]: Outstanding
Wetherspoons conversion of a former church,
keeping its original stained-glass, pulpit,
balconies, doors and so forth; good real ales
and their usual food (Nick Holding)

FAILFORD [NS4526]

Failford Inn KA5 5TF [B743 Mauchline—
Ayr]: Wide choice of freshly made pubby
food (all day Fri-Sun) and particularly well
kept ales inc their own good Windie Goat
brews, bar and lounge with back dining area
overlooking River Ayr (anon)

SYMINGTON [NS3831]

Wheatsheaf KA1 5QB [just off A77 Ayr—
Kilmarnock; Main St]: Rambling 17th-c pub
in quiet pretty village, charming and cosy,
two dining rooms with wide blackboard
choice of consistently good original food
served all day esp fish and local produce,
quick friendly service, racehorse décor; keg
beers, must book wknd, can be seething
with customers lunchtime; attractively set
tables outside, open all day (Christine and
Malcolm Ingram)

BERWICKSHIRE

ALLANTON [NT8654]

☆ *Allanton Inn* TD11 3JZ [B6347 S of
Chirnside]: Pretty stone-built village inn,
light and airy, with friendly chef/landlord
doing short choice of good modestly priced
food inc fresh fish (not Mon/Tues lunch),
helpful kind service, changing ales such as
Harviestoun, farm cider, good choice of
wines by the glass, log fire in attractive side
dining room; sheltered garden behind, five

comfortable bedrooms, open all day wknds
(BB, Comus and Sarah Elliott)

CAITHNESS

LYBSTER [ND2436]

☆ *Portland Arms* KW3 6BS [A9 S of Wick]:
Civilised 19th-c hotel, part attractively laid
out as cosy country kitchen with Aga, pine
furnishings and farmhouse crockery, smart
bar-bistro with easy chairs on tartan carpet
and cosy fire, good straightforward bar food
(all day Sun and summer), friendly efficient
service, good selection of malt whiskies (keg
beers), board games, restaurant; piped
music; children welcome away from bar area,
bedrooms, good spot nr spectacular cliffs
and stacks, open all day wknds and summer
(David Poulter, Mr and Mrs G D Brooks,
Bill Strang, Stuart Pearson, LYM, David Heath)

MEY [ND2872]

Castle Arms KW14 8XH: 19th-c former
coaching inn, quiet décor in understated
stripped pine and so forth, good usual bar
food, wider choice in dining room (notable
steak pie), friendly helpful service, decent
wines by the glass, photographs of the late
Queen Mother during her Caithness holidays;
eight bedrooms in back extension, well
placed for N coast of Caithness and for
Castle of Mey (which has no refreshments)
(David Poulter)

DUMFRIESSHIRE

DUMFRIES [NX9776]

☆ *Cavens Arms* DG1 2AH [Buccleuch St]: Good
food (all day Sat, not Mon) from pubby
standards to enterprising dishes using prime
ingredients, well kept interesting ales with
up to half a dozen changing guest beers,
Stowford Press farm cider and perhaps a
perry, fine choice of malt whiskies, friendly
landlord and staff, civilised front part with
lots of wood, bar stools and a few
comfortable drinkers at the back; can
can get very busy (efficient table-queuing
system), unobtrusive TV, no children or dogs;
open all day (Joe Green, Nick Holding)

KINGHOLM QUAY [NX9773]

☆ *Swan* DG1 4SU [B726 just S of Dumfries]:
Small dining pub in quiet spot overlooking
old fishing jetty on River Nith, handy for
Caerlaverock nature reserve, coal fire in well
ordered dining lounge, neat and nicely
furnished public bar, Timothy Taylors
Landlord, standard pub food; quiet piped
music, TV; children welcome, pleasant
garden, open all day Thurs-Sun (Joe Green,
Richard J Holloway, Mark O'Sullivan, LYM)

MOFFAT [NT0805]

☆ *Black Bull* DG10 9EG [Churchgate]:
Attractive small hotel, plush dimly lit bar
with Burns memorabilia, willing helpful staff,
good value pubby food all day, real ales such
as Caledonian Deuchars IPA and Theakstons
XB, several dozen malt whiskies, good value

wine by the glass, friendly public bar across courtyard with railway memorabilia and good open fire, simply furnished tiled-floor dining room; piped music, side games bar, big-screen TV for golf; children welcome, tables in courtyard, comfortable bedroom annexe (come back quietly from late night revels), open all day (*Pat and Stewart Gordon, Julian Knights, Ray and Winifred Halliday, LYM, John Urquhart, Joe Green, Patricia Walker*)

DUNBARTONSHIRE

INVERARNAN [NN3118]
Drovers Inn G83 7DX [A82 N of Loch Lomond; signed also as Stagger Inn]: Highly idiosyncratic in its extreme scottishness, with tartan, loch and mountain pictures, decrepit stuffed animals and other elderly scottish bric-a-brac, great range of whiskies, Caledonian Deuchars IPA (at a price), good log fires, all-day bar food; appropriate piped music, live wknds – lots of atmosphere then; children welcome till 8, tables outside, modern bedrooms and restaurant across rd, open all day (*Peter Black, LYM*)

EAST LOTHIAN

EAST LINTON [NT5977]
Crown EH40 3AG [Bridge St]: Appealing choice of good food, friendly staff, real ales such as Adnams, Caledonian and Wells & Youngs, reasonably priced wines (*Tom Riddell, Meg Robbins, Keith and Ann Arnold*)

GARVALD [NT5870]
Garvald Inn EH41 4LN: Enjoyable food inc good fish chowder and other dishes using local ingredients (*Fiona Salvesen, Ross Murrell*)

GIFFORD [NT5368]
Goblin Ha' EH41 4QH [Main St]: Contemporary décor and colour scheme in roomy and comfortable front dining lounge, sensibly priced pubby food (all day at least wknds), quick friendly foreign service, four real ales, airy back conservatory, lively stripped-stone public bar with games area; children welcome in lounge and conservatory, tables and chairs in good big garden with small play area, bedrooms, open all day at least Fri-Sun (*C and H Greenly, Comus and Sarah Elliott*)
Tweeddale Arms EH41 4QU [S of Haddington; High St (B6355)]: Old-fashioned hotel in peaceful setting overlooking attractive village green, simple lounge bar with several malt whiskies and interesting modestly priced wines (keg beers), decent bar food from sandwiches up, public bar with games machine and darts, comfortably chintzy hotel lounge with antique tables and paintings, good restaurant meals; children welcome, bedrooms, open all day (*LYM, Dr A McCormick, Angus Lyon, Christine and Phil Young*)

FIFE

CULROSS [NS9885]
Red Lion KY12 8HN [Low Causeway]: Well kept Inveralmond Independence, good value food and efficient attentive staff (*David M Smith*)

LATHONES [NO4708]
Inn at Lathones KY9 1JE [A915 Leven—St Andrews, just S of B940]: Relaxed and friendly small hotel, elegant bar with courteous helpful staff, beams, stripped masonry, armchairs and sofas, soft lighting, two woodburners, imaginative nicely presented fresh food, not cheap but good, from serious lunchtime sandwiches up, children's helpings, light and airy cheerfully decorated restaurant area, occasional top-line live music; two well equipped playrooms, outdoor play area, pretty terrace, good bedrooms (*anon*)

LIMEKILNS [NT0783]
Ship KY11 3HJ [Halketts Hall, towards Charlestown; off A985]: Good lunchtime pub food (best to book) in comfortable pub/bistro, unusual well kept ales (such as one from the Isle of Man), good views over the Forth, mainly nautical décor; children welcome, pavement seats, interesting waterside conservation area, open all day (*David M Smith*)

INVERNESS-SHIRE

AVIEMORE [NH8612]
Cairngorm PH22 1PE [Grampian Rd (A9)]: Large flagstoned bar, lively and friendly, with prompt service, good value bar food using local produce, a real ale and good choice of other drinks, informal restaurant; sports TV; children welcome, comfortable bedrooms (*Gwyn and Anne Wake, Michael and Maggie Betton*)
Old Bridge PH22 1PU [Dalfaber Rd, southern outskirts off B970]: Stripped stone and wood, local books and memorabilia, log fire, short choice of good value lunchtime bar food, friendly staff, changing ales such as Caledonian Deuchars IPA and 80/- and Isle of Skye Red Cuillin, good choice of wines by the glass, large restaurant extension; may be piped music; children welcome (*Christine and Phil Young*)

CAOL [NN1176]
Lochy PH33 7HL [Kilmallie Rd (B8006, off A830 N of Fort William)]: Good value generous usual food from 11am, quite a favourite with walkers (*Sarah and Peter Gooderham*)

CARRBRIDGE [NH9022]
Cairn PH23 3AS [Main Rd]: Friendly tartan-carpeted bar with attentive staff, bargain all-day snacks, lunches and suppers, well kept ales such as Cairngorm and Isle of Skye Red Cuillin, log fire, old local pictures; children and dogs welcome, seven comfortable bedrooms, open all day (*anon*)

FORT WILLIAM [NN1073]
Ben Nevis Bar PH33 6DG [High St]: Stylish pub with several real ales, good value food, harbour views from upstairs restaurant *(Andy and Jill Kassube)*
Ben Nevis Inn PH33 6TE [N off A82: Achintee]: Roomy well converted raftered barn by path up to Ben Nevis, good value mainly straightforward food, Isle of Skye Hebridean Gold, prompt cheery service, some wknd bands; bunk house below *(Michael and Maggie Betton, Sarah and Peter Gooderham)*
Grog & Gruel PH33 6AD [High St]: Busy alehouse-style pub in pedestrian part, barrel tables, dark woodwork and bygones, friendly helpful staff, half a dozen well kept changing ales such as An Teallach, Atlas, Glenfinnan and Orkney, good value food all day from baguettes, pasta and pizzas to upstairs tex-mex restaurant; piped music, machines; dogs and children welcome, live music nights, open all day *(Andy and Jill Kassube)*
GLEN SHIEL [NH0711]
☆ *Cluanie Inn* IV63 7YW [A87 Invergarry—Kyle of Lochalsh, on Loch Cluanie]: Welcoming inn in lovely isolated setting by Loch Cluanie, stunning views, friendly table service for drinks inc well kept local ale, fine range of malt whiskies, big helpings of enjoyable bar food in three knocked-together rooms with dining chairs around polished tables, overspill into restaurant, warm log fire; children welcome, big comfortable modern bedrooms nicely furnished in pine, new bunk house too, great breakfasts inc non-residents *(R M Jones, Peter Black, Revd D Glover)*
INVERIE [NG7500]
☆ *Old Forge* PH41 4PL: Utterly remote waterside pub with fabulous views, comfortable mix of antique furnishings, lots of charts and sailing prints, buoyant atmosphere, open fire, good reasonably priced bar food inc fresh local seafood, even two well kept ales in season, also lots of whiskies and good wine choice; restaurant extension, open all day, late wknds, occasional live music and ceilidhs; the snag's getting there – boat (jetty moorings, even new pier for small cruise ships), Mallaig foot ferry three days a week, or 15-mile walk through Knoydart from nearest road *(Dave Braisted, David Hoult)*
INVERNESS [NH6644]
Castle Tavern IV2 4SA [1-2 View Pl, top of Castle St]: Now under same management as Clachnaharry, relaxed and chatty bare-boards bar with four well kept ales inc one brewed for them by Isle of Skye, fine whisky choice, good value pubby food using local produce, informal upstairs restaurant; castle-view terrace *(Gwyn and Anne Wake)*
☆ *Clachnaharry Inn* IV3 8RB [High St, Clachnaharry (A862 NW of city)]: Congenial and pleasantly updated beamed real ale bar with Greene King and lots of well kept

interesting guest beers, warm chatty atmosphere, bargain freshly made food all day, good staff, great log fire as well as gas stove, bottom lounge with picture windows looking over Beauly Firth; children welcome, heated terrace overlooking railway, lovely walks by big flight of Caledonian Canal locks, open all day *(Joe Green)*
Columba IV3 5NF [Ness Walk]: Smart arty bar, attentive table service, good atmosphere *(Sarah and Peter Gooderham)*
KEPPANACH [NN0263]
Corran PH33 6SE [N on A82]: Decent simple snacks, Isle of Skye ale, good spot next to ferry quay; bedrooms *(Andy and Jill Kassube)*

KINCARDINESHIRE

POTARCH [NO6097]
Potarch Hotel AB31 4BD [B993, just off A93 5 miles W of Banchory]: Good log fire in tartan-carpeted bar, smiling service, well kept real ale, enjoyable bar food and restaurant meals; six comfortably reworked bedrooms, beautiful spot by River Dee, open all day *(David and Betty Gittins)*
STONEHAVEN [NO8785]
Marine Hotel AB39 2JY [Shore Head]: Busy harbourside pub under new management, up to five well kept ales, good choice of whiskies, good value food esp local fish, large lively stripped stone bar with log fire in cosy side room, upstairs lounge bar and seaview restaurant; children welcome, pavement seats, open all day *(Mark Walker)*
Ship AB39 2JY [Shore Head]: Bustling local atmosphere, one or two well kept ales, good choice of whiskies, enjoyable generous food, good prices, friendly staff, simple bar, small lounge off, smarter back restaurant area; children welcome in lounge and restaurant, tables out overlooking pretty harbour with plenty going on, bedrooms, open all day *(Robert Watt, Mark Walker)*

KIRKCUDBRIGHTSHIRE

GATEHOUSE OF FLEET [NX5956]
Ship DG7 2JT [Fleet St]: Decent bar food, Belhaven beers, good choice of malt whiskies, log fires, good service even for big groups, comfortable restaurant; riverside garden, well refurbished bedrooms *(John and Helen Rushton)*
KIPPFORD [NX8355]
☆ *Anchor* DG5 4LN [off A710 S of Dalbeattie]: Popular waterfront inn in lovely spot overlooking yachting estuary and peaceful hills, nautical theme décor with panelling and slight 1960s feel, good fire in small traditional back bar (dogs welcome here only, free treats), more tables in area off, simple bright and roomy dining room, usual pubby fare from sandwiches up, two or three ales inc local Sulwath, lots of malt whiskies, lounge bar (cl out of season); piped music, TV and machines; children welcome, tables

on front terrace, good walks and birdwatching, open all day in summer *(John Foord, LYM, Nick Holding)*

LANARKSHIRE

GLASGOW [NS5865]

Drum & Monkey G2 5TF [St Vincent St]: Former bank, with ornate ceiling, granite pillars, lots of carved mahogany, good range of real ales and wines from island bar, good value basic food using local produce, quieter back area *(Gwyn and Anne Wake)*

☆ *Horseshoe* G2 5AE [Drury St, nr Central Stn]: Classic high-ceilinged standing-room pub with enormous island bar, gleaming mahogany and mirrors, snob screens, other high Victorian features and interesting music-hall era memorabilia and musical instruments; friendly jovial staff and atmosphere, well kept and priced ales inc Caledonian Deuchars IPA and 80/-, lots of malt whiskies, bargain simple food served speedily in plainer upstairs bar and restaurant (where children allowed), inc long-served McGhees hot pies; sports TVs, games machine, piped music; open all day inc breakfast from 9 *(Gwyn and Anne Wake, Nick Holding, LYM, Joe Green, Pat and Bill Chalmers)*

Ingram G1 3BX [Queen St]: Civilised and well run Greene King (Belhaven) pub with Orkney Dark Island as a guest beer, several dozen malt whiskies ranked along island bar, enterprising sandwiches and bargain generous home-made hot dishes, dark panelling, interesting *Daily Herald* papers from 1953 (pub's opening) lining narrow stairs down to lavatories *(Nick Holding, Joe Green)*

MIDLOTHIAN

BALERNO [NT1566]

Johnsburn House EH14 7BB [Johnsburn Rd]: Handsome old-fashioned beamed bar in 18th-c former mansion with masterpiece 1911 ceiling by Robert Lorimer; Caledonian Deuchars IPA and interesting changing ales, coal fire, panelled dining lounge with good food inc shellfish and game, more formal evening dining rooms; children and dogs welcome, open all day wknds, cl Mon *(the Didler)*

EDINBURGH [NT2574]

Barony EH1 3RJ [Broughton St]: L-shaped Victorian pub with ornate tiles, mahogany, mirrors and brass, coal fire, well kept ales such as Caledonian 80/- and Jennings Cocker Hoop, cheap pubby food all day inc good pies; live music Sat; open all day *(Tony and Wendy Hobden)*

☆ *Bennets* EH3 9LG [Leven St]: Ornate Victorian bar with original glass, mirrors, arcades, fine panelling and tiles, friendly service, real ales inc Caledonian Deuchars IPA from tall founts, masses of malt

whiskies, bar snacks and bargain homely lunchtime hot dishes (not Sun; children allowed in eating area), second bar with counter salvaged from old ship; open all day, cl Sun *(the Didler, Nick Holding, LYM, Pam and John Smith)*

☆ *Canny Man's* EH10 4QU [Morningside Rd; aka Volunteer Arms]: Utterly individual and distinctive, saloon, lounge and snug with all sorts of fascinating bric-a-brac, ceiling papered with sheet music, huge range of appetising smorgasbord served with great efficiency and friendliness, lots of whiskies, real ales such as Caledonian Deuchars IPA, cheap children's drinks; courtyard tables *(Dr and Mrs R G J Telfer)*

Canons Gait EH8 8DQ [Canongate]: Smart Royal Mile bar with plush booth seating and old-city map mural, pleasant atmosphere, sensibly priced lunchtime food, several real ales, bare-boards basement bar; piped music; open all day *(Michael Dandy)*

Cloisters EH3 9JH [Brougham St]: Friendly and interesting ex-parsonage alehouse with Caledonian Deuchars and 80/- and half a dozen or so interesting guest beers, dozens of malt whiskies, several wines by the glass, decent food till 4 (6 Tues-Thurs) from toasties to Sun roasts, pews and bar gantry recycled from redundant church, bare boards and lots of brewery mirrors; lavatories down spiral stairs, folk music Fri/Sat; dogs welcome, open all day *(the Didler, Pam and John Smith)*

Ensign Ewart EH1 2PE [Lawnmarket, Royal Mile; last pub on right before castle]: Charming old-world pub handy for castle (so can get very full), huge painting of Ewart at Waterloo capturing the french banner (on show in the castle), friendly efficient staff, well kept ales, wide range of whiskies, usual food lunchtime and some summer evenings; games machine, traditional music most nights; open all day *(Peter F Marshall)*

Milnes EH2 2PJ [Rose St/Hanover St]: Much reworked traditional city pub rambling down to several areas below street level, old-fashioned bare-boards feel, dark décor and panelling, cask tables, lots of old photographs and mementoes of poets who used the 'Little Kremlin' room here, four real ales, good choice of wines by the glass, good value coffees, open fire, reasonably priced bar food all day, breakfast from 10; piped music, games; pavement seats, open all day *(Nick Holding, Tony and Wendy Hobden, the Didler, Michael Dandy, BB, Doug Christian)*

Mitre EH1 1SG [High St, nr Festival Theatre]: Busy interesting Victorian pub with enjoyable pubby food inc haggis and bashed neeps, Caledonian Deuchars IPA and 80/- from high curved counter; piped music, TV, games machine; pavement tables *(Michael Dandy)*

☆ *Old Peacock* EH6 4TZ [Lindsay Rd, Newhaven]: Good value food all day inc fresh fish in massive helpings in neat plushly comfortable beamed pub with several linked areas inc conservatory-style back room leading to garden, friendly efficient staff, McEwans 80/- and a guest such as Orkney Dark Island, bright family room; very popular, best to book evenings and Sun lunchtime; children welcome, open all day *(Mike and Sue Shirley, LYM)*

Oxford EH2 4JB [Young St]: Friendly no-frills pub with two built-in wall settles and unchanging welcoming regulars in tiny bustling front bar, steps up to quieter back room with dominoes, lino floor, well kept Caledonian Deuchars IPA and Belhaven 80/-, good range of whiskies, cheap filled cobs *(Joe Green, Peter F Marshall, Dave Webster, Sue Holland, Pam and John Smith)*

Royal McGregor EH1 1QS [High St]: Family-run long modern traditional-style bar with enjoyable real food in raised back area from sandwiches up (with good bread or oatcakes), well kept ales such as Broughton Merlin and Caledonian Deuchars IPA, good coffee, friendly staff, Georgian Edinburgh prints; piped music, TV; pavement tables, open all day *(Michael Dandy)*

☆ *Standing Order* EH2 2JP [George St]: Grand Wetherspoons bank conversion in three elegant Georgian houses, imposing columns, enormous main room with elaborate colourful high ceiling, lots of tables, smaller side booths, other rooms inc two with floor-to-ceiling bookshelves, comfortable clubby seats, Adam fireplace and portraits; civilised atmosphere, efficient young international staff, good value food (inc Sun evening), coffee and pastries, real ales inc interesting guest beers from very long counter; wknd live music, extremely popular Sat night; disabled facilities, open all day *(Doug Christian, Ian and Jane Haslock, David M Smith, Joe Green, BB)*

MUSSELBURGH [NT3372]

Volunteer Arms EH21 6JE [N High St; aka Staggs]: Same family since 1858, unspoilt busy bar, dark panelling, old brewery mirrors, great gantry with ancient casks, Caledonian Deuchars IPA and guest beers, overflow lounge wknds; dogs welcome, open all day *(the Didler, Joe Green)*

MORAYSHIRE

FINDHORN [NJ0464]

☆ *Kimberley* IV36 3YG: Unpretentious wood-floored seaside pub with good generous food inc particularly good fresh seafood collected by landlord from Buckie dawn fish market, quick friendly service, two ales such as Black Isle and Timothy Taylors, loads of whiskies, jovial company, big log fire; children and dogs welcome, heated sea-view terrace *(Ken and Jenny Simmonds, Lee Fraser)*

NAIRNSHIRE

CAWDOR [NH8449]

☆ *Cawdor Tavern* IV12 5XP [just off B9090]: Now owned by owner of Atlas and Orkney breweries, ales from those, lots of bottled beers, proper seasonal food cooked fresh (worth the wait), great choice of malt whiskies, pleasant attentive staff, elegant panelled lounge, nice features in public bar, restaurant; children in eating areas, attractive front terrace, lovely conservation village, has been open all day wknds and summer *(LYM, the Dutchman)*

PERTHSHIRE

COMRIE [NN7722]

Royal PH6 2DN [Melville Sq]: Pleasant country hotel with good value bar food using local produce, friendly laid-back service, limited choice of well kept beer, lounge and separate public bar, good dining room menu; bedrooms *(A J Longshaw)*

GUILDTOWN [NO1331]

Anglers PH2 6BS [Main Rd]: Opened 2007 after refurbishment by owners of popular Perth restaurant, fresh local food and local real ale *(anon)*

KENMORE [NN7745]

Mains of Taymouth Courtyard PH15 2HN [A827 just W]: Holiday village's welcoming contemporary bistro bar and restaurant, enjoyable if not cheap food inc indoor barbecue, well kept Caledonian Deuchars IPA, lots of malt whiskies, good friendly service; neat modern tables out on decking *(Les and Sandra Brown, Andy Cole)*

KILLIN [NN5732]

Falls of Dochart FK21 8SL [Gray St]: Former coaching inn near the falls, big log fire in attractive flagstoned bar (dogs welcome), two real ales, interesting home-made food; bedrooms *(Paul Steeples)*

KIRKMICHAEL [NS0760]

Kirkmichael Hotel PH10 7NT [Main St]: Attractive whitewashed village inn with friendly helpful owners, enjoyable food, pleasantly rambling rooms inc simple comfortable bar with log fire and some stripped stone; five bedrooms *(Leanne Price)*

LOCH TUMMEL [NN8160]

Loch Tummel Inn PH16 5RP [B8019 4 miles E of Tummel Bridge]: This attractive loch-side inn was closed and for sale in the first half of 2008; news please *(LYM)*

PITLOCHRY [NN9163]

☆ *Killiecrankie Hotel* PH16 5LG [Killiecrankie, off A9 N]: Friendly new owner in comfortable and splendidly placed country hotel with extensive peaceful grounds and dramatic views, attractive panelled bar, airy and relaxed conservatory dining area, nicely varied reasonably priced enjoyable food here and in restaurant, well kept if not cheap real ales, good choice of wines; children in eating area, bedrooms, open all day in summer (LYM, David Hunt, Joan and Tony Walker)

SCONE [NO1325]

Scone Arms PH2 6LR [A94; Cross St]: Neatly kept, with good value pubby food (not Mon), efficient prompt service and good drinks choice (Ian and Sandra Thornton)

STRATHYRE [NN5617]

Inn at Strathyre FK18 8NA [Main St]: Well kept real ales, enjoyable food, good staff, neatly kept bar and colourful dining room; children welcome, garden and terrace, bedrooms (Mr and Mrs D T Hill)

RENFREWSHIRE

GREENOCK [NS2876]

James Watt PA15 1DD [Cathcart St]: Smart Wetherspoons in busy ferry town, some scottish dishes, perhaos local real ales such as Houston, good service (Andy and Jill Kassube)

ROSS-SHIRE

ACHILTIBUIE [NC0208]

☆ *Summer Isles* IV26 2YQ: Locally popular small bar attached to hotel, good fresh food from sandwiches up inc notable seafood and organic supplies from nearby Hydroponicum, real ales such as Isle of Skye or Orkney, good wines by the glass, friendly service, lovely views of the Summer Isles from small terrace; hotel side warm, friendly and well furnished, bedrooms comfortable and good value, though the cheapest are not lavish (J F M and M West)

ALTANDHU [NB9812]

Fuaran IV26 2YR [15 miles off A835 N of Ullapool]: Splendidly remote, in gorgeous coastal scenery, enjoyable food inc good value toasties and take-aways, good whiskies and wine by the glass, old local photographs and farm tools; beautiful views across to Summer Isles from new decking (J F M and M West)

CROMARTY [NH7867]

Royal IV11 8YN [Marine Terrace]: Pleasant old-fashioned harbourside hotel with cheerful helpful management, lots of malt whiskies (keg beers), sleepy sea views across Cromarty Firth to Ben Wyvis from covered front verandah, games etc in separate locals' bar; children and dogs welcome, comfortable bedrooms (not all have the view), open all day (Charles and Pauline Stride, LYM, Ken and Jenny Simmonds)

FORTROSE [NH7256]

☆ *Anderson* IV10 8TD [Union St, off A832]: Good small 19th-c hotel with appealing pub side, over 200 malt whiskies, well kept changing ales from interesting small breweries, dozens of bottled belgian beers, fine choice of wine, settees by log fire,

friendly helpful landlord, enterprising food with a scottish touch in bar and restaurant; children welcome (games for them), nine comfortable bedrooms, open all day (anon)

GLENELG [NG8119]

☆ *Glenelg Inn* IV40 8JR [unmarked rd from Shiel Bridge (A87) towards Skye]: Unpretentious mountain cabin-like bar in smart hotel reached by dramatic drive with spectacular views of Loch Duich to Skye, big fireplace, black and white photographs, just a few tables, some refurbishment as we went to press, may have two real ales, fresh local food (inc Sun roasts), winter pool; may be piped music (usually scottish) and TV (possibly loud); children and dogs welcome, lovely garden, views from some bedrooms, open all day (Mr and Mrs G D Brooks, Mike and Sue Loseby, LYM)

KYLE OF LOCHALSH [NG7627]

Cuchulainns IV40 8AE [Station Rd]: Locals' and walkers' bar with pool, bar lunches; good value hostel alongside, open all day (Dave Braisted)

LOCHCARRON [NG9039]

☆ *Rockvilla* IV54 8YB: Small hotel with friendly helpful staff, good reasonably priced fresh food from sandwiches to local seafood and venison, up to three rotating local real ales, dozens of malt whiskies, light and comfortable homely bar with loch view, separate restaurant; good bedrooms (Mr and Mrs G D Brooks, David and Jane Hill)

PLOCKTON [NG8033]

☆ *Plockton Inn* IV52 8TW [Innes St; unconnected to Plockton Hotel]: Fresh substantial well cooked food at appealing prices inc good fish and smoked seafood from back smokery, congenial bustling atmosphere even in winter, friendly efficient service, well kept usually english ales such as Adnams and Fullers London Pride, good range of malt whiskies; lively separate bar for the younger element, some live traditional music; comfortable bedrooms (good value deals) (Peter Black, Revd D Glover, Joan York)

ULLAPOOL [NH1293]

Arch IV26 2UR [West Shore St]: Neatly kept and welcoming, popular with locals and visitors for food from good soup and hearty sandwiches up, reasonably priced beer, magnificent sea loch views, local paintings for sale; seats out by quay wall (J F M and M West)

Ferry Boat IV26 2UJ [Shore St; from S, go straight when A835 turns right into Mill St]: Unpretentious pub with big windows for harbour and Loch Broom views, may be coal fire in smaller room, has had real ales and hearty evening food, cribbage, dominoes, board games; games machine, piped music; dogs allowed until food serving times, children in eating areas till 8, may be ceilidh band Thurs, open all day; more reports please (LYM, Joan York, David and Sue Smith)

ROXBURGHSHIRE

KELSO [NT7234]
Cobbles TD5 7JH [Bowmont St]: Small ornate dining pub with new owners doing good value home-made food emphasising Borders produce, two real ales now too, along with decent wines and malt whiskies from end bar, wall banquettes, some panelling, cheerful log-effect fire; children welcome, disabled facilities *(Comus and Sarah Elliott)*
MELROSE [NT5434]
George & Abbotsford TD6 9PD [High St]: Comfortable linked areas in civilised bar/lounge with friendly staff, enjoyable freshly made all-day food, decent wines and beers, quite a few malt whiskies, restaurant; 30 bedrooms, open all day *(Trevor and Sylvia Millum)*

STIRLINGSHIRE

DRYMEN [NS4788]
Winnock G63 0BL [just off A811; The Square]: Well kept Caledonian 80/- in big Best Western hotel's modern split-level stripped-stone and beamed lounge bar, with blazing log fire, leather sofas and easy chairs, neat helpful young staff, good choice of malt whiskies, steps down to popular restaurant area; piped music; big garden, 48 bedrooms *(J M Renshaw)*

STRATHCLYDE

BEARSDEN [NS5573]
Burnbrae G61 3DQ [Milngavie Rd; A81]: Well run Chef & Brewer with attentive service, enjoyable specials, well kept ales inc Courage Directors and Theakstons, good choice of wines by the glass; children welcome, disabled facilities, heated terrace, Premier Inn bedrooms, open all day *(Andy and Jill Kassube)*

SUTHERLAND

ROGART [NC7201]
Pittentrail Inn IV28 3XA: Friendly local in beautiful Highland crofting valley of River Fleet, deer, eagles and otters nearby, good specials such as venison, aberdeen angus beef and cranachan pudding (with oatmeal, whisky and raspberries), dozens of malt whiskies inc bargain malt of the month; cl winter lunchtimes early part of week, and 9.30 most nights *(Dave Braisted)*
ROSEHALL [NC4701]
Achness IV27 4BD: Hotel with typical bar used by locals, traditional restaurant meals and back to the lounge for coffee; good area for fishing, walking or mountain biking, bedrooms *(Julia and Richard Tredgett)*

WEST LOTHIAN

LINLITHGOW [NS0077]
Platform 3 EH49 7AB [High St/Railway Approach]: Smart bar with some red leather armchairs, model train running along one wall, Caledonian Deuchars IPA and a guest beer; large TV *(Tony and Wendy Hobden)*

WIGTOWNSHIRE

BLADNOCH [NX4254]
Bladnoch Inn DG8 9AB: Cheerful bar, neat and bright, with eating area, enjoyable pubby food from sandwiches up using quality ingredients, friendly obliging service, well proportioned restaurant; keg beer, piped radio; children and dogs welcome, picturesque riverside setting across from Bladnoch distillery (tours available), good value modernised bedrooms *(Richard J Holloway)*
DRUMMORE [NX1336]
Ship DG9 9PU [Shore St]: Friendly staff, good value carefully cooked pubby food, landlady aiming to stock real ale *(Don and Shirley Parrish)*
PORTPATRICK [NW9954]
Crown DG9 8SX [North Crescent]: Seafront hotel in delightful harbourside village, good choice of food from good crab sandwiches up, good staff, several dozen malt whiskies, decent wine by the glass, warm fire in rambling old-fashioned bar with cosy nooks and crannies, attractively decorated early 20th-c dining room opening through quiet conservatory into sheltered back garden; TV, games machine, piped music; children and dogs welcome, tables out in front, open all day *(LYM, Pat Crabb, A and B D Craig)*

SCOTTISH ISLANDS

ARRAN

LOCHRANZA [NR9350]
Lochranza Hotel KA27 8HL: Nice mix of hotel and pub, waterside setting, deer grazing outside, good landlord; bedrooms *(Stuart Turner)*
WHITING BAY [NS0425]
Eden Lodge KA27 8QH: Hotel's public bar with impressive range of enjoyable fresh food inc good local steaks, cheerful service, good drinks choice (esp whiskies), partly stone-floored bar, airy modern décor and big contemporary pictures; next to bowling green, great sea and mainland views from beachside terrace picnic-sets and attractive modern bedrooms, open all year *(P and D Carpenter)*

BARRA

BAYHERIVAGH [NF7002]
Heathbank HS9 5YQ: Enjoyable usual bar food using local produce, young friendly staff; open all day at least in summer *(Alistair and Kay Butler)*

CASTLEBAY [NL6698]
Castlebay Hotel HS9 5XD: Big but cosy and lively bar with pool etc annexed to hotel with great harbour view, enjoyable food, pleasant young staff; decent bedrooms (dogs allowed) *(Alistair and Kay Butler)*

TANGASDALE [NL6599]
Isle of Barra Hotel HS9 5XW: Great spot on sweep of sandy beach by dolphin bay, spectacular sea and sunset views from dining room and terrace tables, friendly public bar; 30 bedrooms (newish owners planning refurbishment), has been cl winter exc New Year *(Alistair and Kay Butler, Dave Braisted)*

COLL

ARINAGOUR [NM2257]
☆ *Coll Hotel* PA78 6SZ: Wonderful fresh seafood cooked by landlady, Pipers Gold and 70/-, good not over-costly wine range, friendly public bar (post box for yachtsmen and others) and panelled lounge with old photographs; simple comfortable bedrooms, great views *(Dave Braisted, Pat and Stewart Gordon)*

COLONSAY

SCALASAIG [NR3893]
☆ *Colonsay* PA61 7YP: Haven for ramblers and birders, cool and trendy décor with log fires, interesting old islander pictures, pastel walls and polished painted boards, bar with sofas and board games, enjoyable food from soup and toasties to fresh seafood, game and venison, good local Colonsay ale, lots of malt whiskies, informal restaurant; children and dogs welcome, pleasant views from gardens, comfortable bedrooms *(Dave Braisted, David Hoult)*

HARRIS

RODEL [NG0483]
☆ *Rodel Hotel* HS5 3TW [A859 at southern tip of South Harris (hotel itself may be unsigned)]: Comfortably rebuilt, light and contemporary, with enjoyable food esp seafood, bottled Hebridean ales, local art in modernist bar and linked dining room, separate locals' and residents' bar; four bedrooms and self-catering, idyllic setting in small harbour (nearby St Clement's church well worth a visit) *(Dave Braisted, David Heath)*

TARBERT [NB1500]
☆ *Harris Hotel* HS3 3DL [Scott Rd]: Large hotel with nice small panelled bar, local Skye and Hebridean real ales, rare malt whiskies, enjoyable bar lunches from good range of sandwiches through some interesting light dishes to steak, good choice of evening restaurant meals; comfortable bedrooms *(Bob and Angela Brooks, Dr A McCormick, BB)*

ISLAY

BOWMORE [NR3159]
☆ *Harbour Inn* PA43 7JR [The Square]: Fine inn with traditional local bar, lovely harbour and sea views from comfortable dining lounge, good food inc local seafood and delicious puddings, good choice of wines and local malts inc attractively priced rare ones, warmly welcoming service; good value bedrooms *(Alan Cole, Kirstie Bruce)*

Lochside Hotel PA43 7LB [Shore St]: Spacious and neatly modernised family-run hotel, great collection of Islay malts, Islay ales (draught and bottled, bottled Colonsay beer too), enjoyable straightforward food inc local fish and lamb, two bars and new conservatory-style back restaurant with lovely views over Loch Indaal; ten recently refurbished bedrooms *(David Hoult)*

PORTNAHAVEN [NN1652]
An Tighe Seinnse PA47 7SJ [Queen St]: Good food inc fresh local seafood in small end-of-terrace harbourside pub tucked away in remote and attractive fishing village, cosy bar and room off, good choice of malt whiskies, bottled local Islay ales, open fire *(David Hoult)*

MULL

DERVAIG [NM4251]
☆ *Bellachroy* PA75 6QW: Island's oldest inn, really well run, with traditional basic bar, informal dining area and lounge used more by residents, landlady cooks good pub and restaurant food inc local seafood and plenty of other fresh produce, reasonable prices, children's helpings, well kept Caledonian Deuchars IPA, local whiskies and wide wine choice, fine atmosphere, nice spot in sleepy village; well behaved dogs welcome, six comfortable bedrooms, open all year *(T Walker, Miss E Thorne)*

NORTH UIST

LOCHMADDY [NF9168]
Lochmaddy Hotel HS6 5AA: Clean and smart, in great spot, with good home-made bar lunches and evening meals, helpful pleasant staff, popular public bar; good bedrooms *(Dr A McCormick)*

SKYE

CARBOST [NG3731]

☆ *Old Inn* IV47 8SR [B8009]: Unpretentious simply furnished bare-boards bar in idyllic peaceful spot close to Talisker distillery, friendly staff, limited but good home-made bar food, perhaps a real ale such as Isle of Skye, peat fire, darts, pool, cribbage and dominoes; TV, piped traditional music; children welcome, terrace with fine Loch Harport and Cuillin views (bar's at the back though), sea-view bedrooms in annexe (breakfast for non-residents too if you book the night before), bunkhouse, moorings and showers for yachtsmen, open all day, cl midwinter afternoons (Peter Black, LYM)

SLIGACHAN [NG4930]

☆ *Sligachan Hotel* IV47 8SW [A87 Broadford—Portree, junction with A863]: Remote hotel with almost a monopoly on the Cuillins, huge modern pine-clad bar (play area, games room) between original basic climbers' and walkers' bar and plusher more sedate hotel side; quickly served popular food all day from home-made cakes with tea or coffee through decent bar food to fresh local seafood, fine log or coal fire, efficient pleasant staff, their own Cuillin Pinnacle and Skye ales, scottish guest beers, 200 malt whiskies, good meals in hotel restaurant; piped highland and islands music, very lively some nights, with summer live music and big campsite opp; children welcome, tables outside, 22 good value bedrooms, open all day (BB, Michael Garner, Walter and Susan Rinaldi-Butcher)

SOUTH UIST

LOCH CARNAN [NF8144]

Orasay Inn HS8 5PD [signed off A865 S of Creagorry]: Lovely remote spot overlooking sea, friendly service and tempting local seafood in comfortable modern lounge and conservatory, pleasant public bar; open all day at least in summer, compact comfortable bedrooms (Dr A McCormick)

LOCHBOISDALE [NF7819]

Lochboisdale Hotel HS8 5TH [nr ferry dock]: Fine location with sea views, decent food, separate public bar – very friendly; modern building, nice bedrooms (Dr A McCormick)

'Children welcome' means the pub says it lets children inside without any special restriction. If it allows them in, but to restricted areas such as an eating area or family room, we specify this. Places with separate restaurants often let children use them, hotels usually let them into public areas such as lounges. Some pubs impose an evening time limit – let us know if you find one earlier than 9pm.

Wales

Our four newcomers here this year are the Hardwick near Abergavenny, a friendly dining pub with top-notch food; the Blue Boar in Hay-on-Wye, combining a cosy little traditional bar with a bright and cheerful eating area; the St Brides Inn in Little Haven, returning to the *Guide* under friendly newish owners; and the Tal-y-Cafn Hotel, a welcoming place with enjoyable food usefully placed in northern Snowdonia. In the same area, the Groes at Ty'n-y-Groes is doing really well these days, with very friendly staff, smashing bedrooms, and Great Orme beers brewed by the family. Also doing well in north Wales are the Queens Head near Llandudno Junction, a most reliable dining pub, and the Olde Bulls Head in Beaumaris on Anglesey, a strong all-rounder near the castle, with good food. Four splendid Brunning & Price pubs continue to brighten the northern Wales pub scene, all efficiently run by friendly staff: the Pen-y-Bryn above Colwyn Bay (great views), the Pant-yr-Ochain in Gresford (a very good drinks selection and tasty food all day, lakeside garden), the Corn Mill in Llangollen (interesting drinks and food, and a fine riverside position) and the open-plan Glasfryn in Mold (imaginative food, very good drinks selection). On the southern welsh borders, the Keys family have now been welcoming customers to their Nags Head in Usk for 40 years, and continue to get everything right about running a pub; also doing well in that part of Wales are the Bell at Skenfrith (fine wine and food, and a good place to stay, right opposite the castle), and the elegant Clytha Arms on the edge of Clytha Park near Raglan. In mid Wales, a firm recommendation is the Harp near the border with Herefordshire at Old Radnor (liked for its character-laden rustic bar, accommodation, food, and splendid views over Radnor Forest), and the Griffin at Felinfach just outside the Brecon Beacons National Park, with its carefully sourced food and wines. In western Wales, highlights include the Harbourmaster in Aberaeron on Cardigan Bay (revamped this year with new bar, not very pubby but stylish with attractive food and bedrooms, and good wines), and the interesting Sloop tucked into its sheltered cove at Porthgain on the Pembrokeshire Coast Path. The Old Black Lion in Hay-on-Wye and the Bear in Crickhowell are also doing well. A good many of our selected pubs are in very special locations. The Ship at Red Wharf Bay (with a good drinks selection) is splendidly placed on the Anglesey coast, while the Ty Coch at Porth Dinllaen on the Lleyn Peninsula has perhaps the best beachside location of all. The delightfully unchanging Cresselly Arms at Cresswell Quay is a simple place on a river creek in Pembrokeshire; the Nags Head at Abercych is another fine riverside pub (near Cardigan) with own-brew beer and hefty helpings of bar food. In the Brecon Beacons National Park are the unassuming Goose & Cuckoo at Rhyd-y-Meirch, liked especially for its beer and remote rural position, and the upmarket, food-oriented White Swan at Llanfrynach. In north Wales, the Druid at Llanferres is a good all-rounder, with lovely views of the Clwydian Hills, while the Pen-y-Gwryd near Llanberis is a splendidly placed mountaineers' haunt amid the wilds of Snowdonia, and has very inexpensive bar food. For sheer curiosity value, the corrugated iron Tafarn Sinc at Rosebush in Pembrokeshire must be one of the strangest buildings in this book, while other buildings of special character are the cheery 600-year-old White Hart at Llanddarog in Carmarthenshire (generous food and own-brew beers) and the Plough & Harrow at Monknash (in a superb old building near the Glamorgan coast, with a fine range of beers). Other good all-rounders include the Carpenters Arms at Shirenewton (a nicely unspoilt village pub near the M4 bridges in south Wales), the thatched Bush at St Hilary near Cardiff, and the White Lion at Llanelian-yn-Rhos, positioned above Colwyn Bay. Good food is a particular draw at many of the pubs we have picked out above. For a special meal out, our final shortlist would include the Olde Bulls Head in Beaumaris, the Glasfryn in Mold, the Bell at Skenfrith, the Groes, the Nags Head in Usk and that new entry, the Hardwick near Abergavenny. We'd add another place not far from there, but in the Lucky Dip section at the end of the chapter, the Walnut Tree at Llandewi Skirrid; we thought it rather too restaurany for the main entries – we'd be interested to know whether you agree. Our final choice for Wales Dining Pub of the Year is the Groes at Ty'n-y-Groes. Other pubs to note in that Lucky Dip section are, in Dyfed, the Old Point House at Angle, Druidstone Hotel near Broad Haven, Carew Inn, Dyffryn Arms at Cwm Gwaun, Georges in Haverfordwest, Butchers Arms at Llanddarog, Angel in Llandeilo, Royal Oak in Saundersfoot and Stackpole Inn; in Glamorgan, the Prince of Wales at Kenfig; in Gwent, the Raglan Arms at Llandenny; in Gwynedd, the Ty Gwyn in Betws-y-Coed, Castle Hotel in Conwy and Goat at Glandwyfach; and in Powys, the Red Lion at Llanfihangel-nant-Melan, Green at Llangedwyn and Dragon in Montgomery. Wales has some three dozen independent brewers. Much the most widely available is Brains (who also brew Hancocks). We also found Rhymney, Felinfoel, Tomos Watkins and Conwy fairly readily available, and Evan Evans, Breconshire, Great Orme, Otley, Facers, Coles, Plassey, Bullmastiff, Purple Moose and Swansea in at least some good pubs.

ABERAERON
SN4562 MAP 6

Harbourmaster 🍴 🍷 🛏
Harbour Lane; SA46 0BA

Stylish, thriving waterside dining pub/hotel, interesting food (at a price), up-to-date bedrooms

There's been a comprehensive revamp of this waterside pub since the last edition of the *Guide*, and although it's far removed from a traditional pub in character you can still just come in to enjoy a drink. The building has been extended into a former grain warehouse, which now contains the zinc-clad and blue-walled new bar, with french windows overlooking the yacht-filled harbour with its array of colourwashed buildings; there's an array of leather sofas, as well as a stuffed albatross reputed to have collided with a ship belonging to the owner's great-grandfather. The former panelled bar and restaurant have been knocked through into one large dining area, where new light wood furniture looks stylishly modern on light wood floors against light and aqua blue walls, while there's also a four-seater cwtch, or snug, within the former porch; piped music. Evan Evans Best Bitter and Tomos Watkins on handpump, and a good wine list, with a dozen sold by the glass. The owners are chatty and welcoming, and if you stay the breakfasts are good; disabled access.

🍽 Tasty bar meals served in here include soup, carpaccio of beef, welsh rarebit, risotto, fish and chips, yswyth valley sirloin, gnocchi with roasted tomatoes and pine nuts, sweet-cured gammon with organic egg, and puddings like lemon tart or chocolate brownie; children's menu. In the restaurant there's a choice of good, fashionable food (not cheap). *Starters/Snacks: £4.50 to £8.50. Main Courses: £9.00 to £14.00. Puddings: £5.50*

Free house ~ Licensees Glyn and Menna Heulyn ~ Real ale ~ Bar food (12-2.30, 6-9; not Mon lunchtime) ~ Restaurant ~ (01545) 570755 ~ Children welcome ~ Open 11-11 ~ Bedrooms: £60S/£120B

Recommended by Patrick and Daphne Darley, M J Daly, Mr and Mrs P R Thomas, Blaise Vyner, B and M Kendall, Mike and Mary Carter, M Fitzpatrick

ABERCYCH   SN2539   MAP 6

Nags Head 🍺

Off B4332 Cenarth—Boncath; SA37 0HJ

Enticing riverside position, good value own-brew beer and gargantuan quantities of bar food

---

Benches in the garden at this nicely tucked-away village pub look over the river, where you might see a coracle being rowed – and there's one hanging from the wall inside. One thing to try here is the much-enjoyed Old Emrys beer, made in a microbrewery and named after one of the regulars; others might include Brains Rev James, Marstons Pedigree and Otley OG. The dimly lit beamed and flagstoned bar has a big fireplace, clocks showing the time around the world, stripped wood tables, a piano, photographs and postcards of locals, and hundreds of beer bottles displayed around the brick and stone walls – look out for the big stuffed rat. A plainer small room leads down to a couple of big dining areas, and there's another little room behind the bar; piped music and TV. Service is pleasant and efficient. They sometimes have barbecues out here in summer, and outside it's lit by fairy lights in the evening; there's a children's play area.

🍽 Served in huge helpings (so you might struggle to get through a three-course meal), the bar food might include sandwiches, cawl (stew), steak and Old Emrys ale pie, mixed grill, cardigan island crab salad, faggots with chips and mushy peas, lamb steak marinated with rosemary and redcurrant, and cottage pie with swede mash, plus specials such as salmon with sweet chilli jam, honey-roasted duck, or pork chops with wholegrain mustard sauce. *Starters/Snacks: £3.50 to £5.50. Main Courses: £6.50 to £15.95. Puddings: £3.95*

Own brew ~ Licensee Samantha Jamieson ~ Real ale ~ Bar food (12-2, 6-9) ~ Restaurant ~ (01239) 841200 ~ Children welcome ~ Dogs allowed in bar ~ Open 11.30-3, 6-11.30; 12-10.30 Sun; closed Mon

Recommended by Colin Moore, Dr and Mrs A K Clarke, B and M Kendall, John and Enid Morris

ABERDOVEY   SN6196   MAP 6

Penhelig Arms

Opposite Penhelig railway station; LL35 0LT

Fine harbourside location, and a nice place to stay

The water views over the Dyfi Estuary from this pleasant old hotel are really special. Good log fires in the small original beamed bar make it especially cosy in winter, and there's nothing in the way of fruit machines or piped music. On handpump are Brains Bitter, Rev James and SA, with a guest such as Brains Milkwood; two dozen malt whiskies and a good wine selection with 20 by the glass. The bedrooms are comfortable (some have balconies overlooking the estuary) but the ones nearest the road can be noisy. Since the last edition of the *Guide* the hotel has been taken over by Brains, who have installed a manager; more reports on the new regime please.

🍴 **In addition to lunchtime sandwiches, the daily lunch and dinner menus could include soup, fish or meat platters, grilled sardines, seared fillet of bass, fried lambs liver and bacon, rib-eye steak, honey-roasted duck, and vegetarian brie and basil filo tart.** *Starters/Snacks: £3.95 to £8.95. Main Courses: £8.95 to £16.95. Puddings: £3.95 to £5.95*

Brains ~ Manager Frederick Oxlade ~ Real ale ~ Bar food ~ Restaurant ~ (01654) 767215 ~ Children welcome (until 9pm in bar) ~ Dogs allowed in bar and bedrooms ~ Open 11-11; 12-10.30 Sun; closed 24-26 Dec ~ Bedrooms: £49S/£78S

Recommended by Mike and Mary Carter, David Glynne-Jones, Gerry and Rosemary Dobson, Jacquie Jones, C J Fletcher, Colin Moore, Clive Watkin, Philip Hesketh, Di and Mike Gillam, Brian and Anna Marsden

ABERGAVENNY

SO3111   MAP 6

Hardwick 🍴 🍷

Hardwick; B4598 SE, off A40 at A465/A4042 exit – coming from E on A40, go right round the exit system, as B4598 is final road out; NP7 9AA

Very good interesting food in smartly simple dining pub, good beers and wines too

---

This plain white-painted building gives no hint externally of the top-quality cooking you can expect here; it's decidedly somewhere to come for a meal, rather than just a drink, though they do have two well kept changing ales on handpump, one of them normally from Rhymney, and farm cider, as well as a splendid choice of good interesting wines by the glass, in a choice of glass sizes. Their coffee is good, too. The bar, with a small functional corner servery, is a simple room with spindleback chairs around pub tables, and some stripped brickwork around a disused fireplace. The better of the two dining rooms actually has rather more of a pub feel, given its dark beams, a winged high-backed settle by the end serving counter, another facing a small pew across one table tucked in by a huge fireplace, and a nice mix of other tables and chairs on bare boards with a big rug (the lack of soft furnishings here can make the acoustics rather lively). The second dining room in a carpeted extension is lighter and simpler, more modern in style, with big windows; there is some interesting artwork. Service is welcoming and helpful; there may be piped music. They have teak tables and chairs out under umbrellas by the car park, and the garden is neatly kept. They plan to open bedrooms.

🍴 **We have greatly enjoyed Stephen Terry's work in at least two of his previous haunts, and here, in his very own place for the first time, he is giving free rein to his talented use of extremely carefully selected largely local ingredients, for a mixture of supercharged variations on familiar dishes with more inventive or esoteric recipes. Nothing's cheap here, but given the quality it's all good value. To take the familiar, his crisp thrice-cooked chips add something special to the tender home-baked ham and eggs, and the grilled lunchtime sandwiches might include delicate goats cheese with tapenade and mixed vegetables as an eye-opening variant on the humble cheese toastie. Some more elaborate choices might include provençal-style fish soup, confit duck hash with fried local duck egg, mustard mayonnaise and watercress, white crab meat with coriander, mint and chilli on toast with pea shoots, samphire, amalfi lemon and brown crab meat mayonnaise, home-made goucester old spot pork, onion and sage sausages with spring greens, fried polenta, celeriac mash, lentil gravy, rocket and parmesan, roast cod with spanish butter beans, black pudding and chorizo sausage with flat parsley and sherry vinegar, slow-cooked, boned and rolled shoulder of lamb with braising juices, and puddings such as triple chocolate, nut and raisin brownie with peanut butter and jelly ice-cream and panna cotta with consit san marzano tomatoes and basil syrup; the two- and three-course set lunches are very fair value.** *Starters/Snacks: £4.95 to £10.95. Main Courses: £11.95 to £17.95. Puddings: £5.00 to £6.50*

Free house ~ Licensees Stephen and Joanna Terry ~ Real ale ~ Bar food (12-3, 6.30-10; not Sun evening or Mon) ~ Restaurant ~ (01873) 854220 ~ Children welcome ~ Open 12-3, 6.30-11.30; 12-3 Sun; closed Sun evening, Mon

Recommended by Michael and Maggie Betton, Joyce and Maurice Cottrell, Jane McQuitty, John Bromley, June Whitworth, John Smart, Alastair Stevenson, Duncan Cloud

ABERGORLECH
SN5833 MAP 6

Black Lion £

B4310 (a pretty road roughly NE of Carmarthen); SA32 7SN

Delightful old pub in a super rural position, with caring staff

At the start of the Gorlech Trail mountain-bike route in the Brechfa Forest and in a blissfully tranquil spot in the wooded Cothi Valley not far from the Dolaucothi Gold Mines at Pumsaint, this old coaching inn is a popular stop for cyclists. The plain but comfortably cosy stripped-stone bar is traditionally furnished with oak tables and chairs, and high-backed black settles facing each other across the flagstones by the coal stove. There are horsebrasses and copper pans on the black beams, old jugs on shelves, fresh flowers, and paintings by a local artist. The dining extension has french windows opening on to a landscaped enclosed garden. The one or two real ales are likely to come from Merthyr Tydfil's Rhymney Brewery, and are kept under a light blanket pressure on handpump; also welsh whisky, mulled wine in winter and lots of fruit juices. Board games, darts and piped music. The picnic-sets, wooden seats and benches have lovely views, and the garden slopes down towards the River Cothi where there's a Roman triple-arched bridge. The present licensees took over since our last edition; more reports on the new regime please.

Ⅱ **Very reasonably priced bar food (there may be a wait at busy times) includes soup, sandwiches, ploughman's, curry, steaks, and vegetable and stilton crumble; on Sunday evenings they prepare their own pizzas, and there are one- to three-course Sunday lunches and changing specials like steak and ale pie, lamb and mint pie, with puddings like chocolate truffle torte and fruit crumble (with some fruit from their own garden); children's meals.** *Starters/Snacks: £3.75 to £4.50. Main Courses: £6.00 to £17.95. Puddings: £3.75 to £4.50*

Free house ~ Licensees George and Louis Rashbrook ~ Real ale ~ Bar food ~ Restaurant ~ (01558) 685271 ~ Children welcome ~ Dogs allowed in bar ~ Open 12-3, 7-11; 12-11 Sat, Sun; closed Mon in winter

Recommended by Mrs Margo Finlay, Jörg Kasprowski

BEAUMARIS
SH6076 MAP 6

Olde Bulls Head 🍴 ♀ 🛏

Castle Street; LL58 8AP

Interesting and much-liked historic pub; spot on for food, accommodation and wines

Enjoyed by visitors and locals, and with friendly and efficient service, this 15th-c inn near the castle is an excellent place to stay, eat or drink. Its low-beamed bar is a genuinely pubby, rambling place, with plenty of interesting reminders of the town's past: a rare 17th-c brass water clock, a bloodthirsty crew of cutlasses and even an oak ducking stool tucked among the snug alcoves. There are also lots of copper and china jugs, comfortable low-seated settles, leather-cushioned window seats, a good log fire, and Bass, Hancocks and a guest such as Everards Sly Fox on handpump. Quite a contrast, the busy brasserie behind is lively and stylishly modern, with a wine list including a dozen available by the glass; the restaurant list runs to 120 bottles. The entrance to the pretty courtyard is closed by what is listed in *The Guinness Book of Records* as the biggest simple-hinged door in Britain (11 feet wide and 13 feet high). Named after characters in Dickens's novels, the bedrooms are very well equipped; some are traditional, and others more up to date, and they plan to open further bedrooms in an adjacent property by the time this edition is published; very good breakfast.

Half pints: by law, a pub should not charge more for half a pint than half the price of a full pint, unless it shows that half-pint price on its price list.

[!] The brasserie menu includes sandwiches, soup, clam chowder, burger with cheese and bacon, corn-fed chicken supreme, indian spiced salmon, rib-eye steak, and several puddings such as rhubarb and raspberry crumble sundae; small but decent children's menu. There is also a smart restaurant upstairs. *Starters/Snacks: £3.50 to £5.50. Main Courses: £8.50 to £10.95. Puddings: £3.70 to £5.65*

Free house ~ Licensee David Robertson ~ Real ale ~ Bar food (12-2(3 Sun), 6-9; not 25, 26 Dec or evening 1 Jan) ~ Restaurant ~ (01248) 810329 ~ Children welcome in brasserie but no under 7s in loft restaurant ~ Open 11-11; 12-10.30 Sun ~ Bedrooms: £80B/£105B

Recommended by Simon Cottrell, Neil Whitehead, Victoria Anderson, Gordon and Margaret Ormondroyd, Chris Brooks, Ken and Margaret Grinstead, Dave Webster, Sue Holland, Michael Dandy, John McDonald, Ann Bond, Di and Mike Gillam, Phil and Jane Hodson, Bob and Val Collman, Revd D Glover, Mrs Jane Kingsbury, Mike and Mary Carter, Mrs Angela Graham

COLWYN BAY   SH8478   MAP 6

Pen-y-Bryn 🍴 🍷 ☕

B5113 Llanwrst Road, on S outskirts; when you see the pub turn off into Wentworth Avenue for its car park; LL29 6DD

Modern pub in great position overlooking the bay, reliable food all day, good range of drinks, obliging staff

'Far and away the best pub for miles around, loads of ambience, superb affordable food,' enthused one couple about this wonderfully placed Brunning & Price pub – who found the landlord remembered them from their visit two years earlier. Although it looks like a suburban bungalow from outside, it is actually a former school, with a light and airy open-plan interior giving terrific views over the bay and the Great Orme (it's worth booking a window table). Extending around the three long sides of the bar counter, the mix of seating and well spaced tables, oriental rugs on pale stripped boards, shelves of books, welcoming coal fires, profusion of pictures, big pot plants, careful lighting and dark green school radiators are all typical of the pubs in this small chain. Besides Great Orme Best, Thwaites Original and Wadworths 6X, you'll find three changing guests such as Black Sheep Best Bitter, Conwy Welsh Pride and Timothy Taylors Landlord on handpump. They also have well chosen good value wines including 20 by the glass, 70 malts and several irish whiskeys, and proper coffee; board games. Outside there are sturdy tables and chairs on a side terrace and a lower one, by a lawn with picnic-sets.

[!] Served all day, the reliable and much liked food from a changing menu could typically include sandwiches, ploughman's with welsh cheeses, soup, welsh rarebit, mussels cooked in white wine with garlic and cream, braised half shoulder of lamb, chicken and leek with mushroom pie, fish stew, roast butternut squash risotto, rump steak with garlic butter, and puddings such as chocolate brownie or cinnamon choux pastry fritters with apricot sauce; efficient service from friendly staff. *Starters/Snacks: £4.50 to £8.95. Main Courses: £7.95 to £15.95. Puddings: £4.25 to £4.95*

Brunning & Price ~ Licensees Graham Arathoon and Graham Price ~ Real ale ~ Bar food (12-9.30(9 Sun)) ~ (01492) 533360 ~ Children under 14 welcome till 7pm ~ Open 11.30-11; 12-10.30 Sun

Recommended by Paul and Margaret Baker, Dr Dale Archer, R T and J C Moggridge, William Ruxton, Keith and Sue Ward, G Robinson

CRESSWELL QUAY   SN0506   MAP 6

Cresselly Arms

Village signposted from A4075; SA68 0TE

Marvellously simple alehouse, with benches outside overlooking a tidal creek

Totally unsophisticated and unfussy, this unchanging tavern has a lovely position looking out to a creek of the Cresswell River, and if you time the tides right, you can arrive by boat, and seats outside make the most of the view. Often full of locals, the two simple and comfortably old-fashioned communicating rooms have a relaxed and jaunty air, as well as red and black floor tiles, built-in wall benches, kitchen chairs and plain tables, an open fire in one room, a working Aga in the other, and a high beam-and-plank ceiling hung with lots of pictorial china. A third red-carpeted room is more conventionally furnished, with red-cushioned mate's chairs around neat tables. Worthington BB and a winter guest beer are tapped straight from the cask into glass jugs by the landlord, whose presence is a key ingredient of the atmosphere. No children.

🏵 **No food, except filled rolls on Saturday mornings.** *Starters/Snacks: £0.70*

Free house ~ Licensees Maurice and Janet Cole ~ Real ale ~ No credit cards ~ (01646) 651210 ~ Open 12-3, 5-11; 11-11 Sat; 12-3, 5(7 winter)-10.30 Sun

Recommended by Mark Farrington, Pete Baker, Richard Pitcher, the Didler

CRICKHOWELL
SO2118   MAP 6

Bear ★ ♀ 🛏
Brecon Road; A40; NP8 1BW

Civilised and interesting inn with splendid old-fashioned bar area warmed by a log fire, good food and bedrooms

This comfortably traditional coaching inn, in the heart of this delightful little town, has been run by the same owners for over 30 years now, and although some things have been carefully refreshed (the dining area has been given an overhaul for instance) they remark that they don't want to change things just for change's sake, and are constantly being told to keep it just as it is. The comfortably decorated, heavily beamed lounge has fresh flowers on tables, lots of little plush-seated bentwood armchairs and handsome cushioned antique settles, and a window seat looking down on the market square. Up by the great roaring log fire, a big sofa and leather easy chairs are spread among rugs on the oak parquet floor. Other good antiques include a fine oak dresser filled with pewter mugs and brass, a longcase clock, and interesting prints. Brains Rev James, Greene King Ruddles Best and a guest such as Skirrid on handpump, as well as 24 malt whiskies, vintage and late-bottled ports, unusual wines (with several by the glass) and liqueurs; disabled lavatories. Successfully blending its charms with efficient service, it is a welcoming place to stay – some refurbished bedrooms are in a country style, though the older rooms have antiques; more expensive rooms have jacuzzis and four-poster beds.

🏵 **Usually very rewarding bar food could include items such as sandwiches, shank of lamb, faggots and peas, bubble and squeak with poached egg and black pudding, butternut squash ravioli on braised leeks and courgettes, welsh black beef sirloin and fillet steaks, and venison pie; they do a popular three-course Sunday lunch. You can eat in the small garden in summer.** *Starters/Snacks: £3.75 to £5.95. Main Courses: £6.95 to £17.95. Puddings: £4.25 to £5.50*

Free house ~ Licensee Judy Hindmarsh ~ Real ale ~ Bar food (12-2, 6-10; 12-2, 7-9.30 Sun) ~ Restaurant ~ (01873) 810408 ~ Children welcome with restrictions ~ Dogs allowed in bar and bedrooms ~ Open 11-3, 6-11; 12-3, 7-10.30 Sun ~ Bedrooms: £70S/£86S(£133B)

Recommended by Tom and Ruth Rees, Mr and Mrs A J Hudson, Steven and Victoria James, Patrick and Daphne Darley, Denys Gueroult, Roy Hoing, LM, Colin Moore, Malcolm and Sue Scott, Mrs Margo Finlay, Jörg Kasprowski, Mike and Mary Carter, Herbert and Susan Verity, Bob and Angela Brooks, Blaise Vyner, Guy Vowles

EAST ABERTHAW
ST0366   MAP 6

Blue Anchor 🍺
B4265; CF62 3DD

Ancient waterside pub, loaded with character and a popular place for a beer

Flower baskets and ivy adorn the ancient stone walls of this atmospheric thatched pub, which dates back to 1380 and has been run by the same family since 1941. The building has massive walls, low-beamed rooms and tiny doorways, with open fires everywhere,

including one in an inglenook with antique oak seats built into its stripped stonework.
Other seats and tables are worked into a series of chatty little alcoves, and the more
open front bar still has an ancient lime-ash floor. Friendly staff serve Brains Bitter,
Theakstons Old Peculier, Wadworths 6X and Wye Valley Hereford Pale Ale on handpump,
alongside a changing guest such as Moles Rucking Mole. Rustic seats shelter peacefully
among tubs and troughs of flowers outside, with more stone tables on a newer terrace.
From here a path leads to the shingly flats of the estuary. The pub can get very full in
the evenings and on summer weekends, and it's used as a base by a couple of local
motorbike clubs. More reports please.

🍴 As well as lunchtime baguettes and filled baked potatoes, bar food might include soup,
chicken liver parfait, pork and apple faggots with mash, jamaican jerk chicken with
potato wedges, lamb stew, rib-eye steak and roasted aubergine linguine pasta, and
specials such as beetroot risotto or turnkey escalope with couscous and tagine sauce.
Starters/Snacks: £3.95 to £4.50. Main Courses: £8.25 to £10.95. Puddings: £3.95

Free house ~ Licensee Jeremy Coleman ~ Real ale ~ Bar food (12-2, 6-9; not Sun evening) ~
Restaurant ~ (01446) 750329 ~ Children welcome ~ Dogs allowed in bar ~ Open 11-11;
12-10.30 Sun

Recommended by BOB

FELINFACH

SO0933   MAP 6

Griffin 🍴 ☐ 🛏
A470 NE of Brecon; LD3 0UB

**A classy dining pub for enjoying good, unpretentious cooking featuring lots of home-
grown vegetables; upbeat rustic décor, nice bedrooms**

With a nice mixture of locals coming in for a drink and diners enjoying the interesting
food, this friendly and stylish inn is tucked away in a hamlet on the Dulas valley just
west of the Black Mountains. The back bar is quite pubby in an up-to-date way, with
three leather sofas around a low table on pitted quarry tiles, by a high slate hearth with
a log fire, and behind them mixed stripped seats around scrubbed kitchen tables on bare
boards, and a bright blue-and-ochre colour scheme, with some modern prints. The
acoustics are pretty lively, with so much bare flooring and uncurtained windows; maybe
piped radio. The two smallish front dining rooms, linking through to the back bar, are
attractive: on the left, mixed dining chairs around mainly stripped tables on flagstones,
and white-painted rough stone walls, with a cream-coloured Aga in a big stripped-stone
embrasure; on the right, similar furniture on bare boards, with big modern prints on
terracotta walls, and good dark curtains. They have a thoughtful choice of wines
including 12 by the glass, welsh spirits, cocktails and Breconshire Cribyn, Tomos Watkins
OSB and a guest like Tomos Watkins Cwrw Braf on handpump; local bottled ciders and
apple juice, and a fine range of spirits, cocktails and sherries. Wheelchair access is good,
and there are tables outside. Bedrooms are comfortable and tastefully decorated, and the
hearty breakfasts nicely informal: you make your own toast on the Aga (which can be a
somewhat leisurely process) and help yourself to home-made marmalade and jam.

🍴 Using organic produce from the pub's own kitchen garden (from which the surplus is
often for sale), not cheap but consistently good food from the lunch and evening menus
might include welsh cheese ploughman's, cream of garden pea soup, tartare of local
smoked salmon, pork and leek sausages with mash, confit of duck leg with apple and
thyme sauce, or hake fillet with capers, with puddings like vanilla crème brûlée or eton
mess; they also offer set meals with two or three courses starting at £15.90 for a two-
course lunch. *Starters/Snacks: £5.00 to £9.50. Main Courses: £8.50 to £19.00. Puddings: £6.00
to £7.00*

Free house ~ Licensees Charles and Edmund Inkin ~ Real ale ~ Bar food (12.30(12 Sun)-2.30,
6.30-9.30(9 Sun); not Mon lunch (exc bank hols)) ~ Restaurant ~ (01874) 620111 ~
Children welcome ~ Dogs allowed in bar and bedrooms ~ Live music Sun night ~ Open 11-11;
11.30-10.30 Sun ~ Bedrooms: £67.50B/£110B

*Recommended by M Fitzpatrick, Rodney and Norma Stubington, Derek Hills, Mrs Philippa Wilson, Paul Goldman,
John and Enid Morris*

GLADESTRY   SO2355   MAP 6

Royal Oak ◖

B4594 W of Kington; HR5 3NR

A thoroughly likeable, welcoming village local on the Offa's Dyke Path

Just below the abruptly steep end of Hergest Ridge, and with new owners since the last edition of the *Guide*, this is an enjoyably unpretentious village pub well liked by locals, farmers and walkers. The simple bar is warmed by an open fire and has beams hung with tankards and lanterns, stripped stone and flagstones, and near the piano hang pictures of the Gladestry football team; there's also a cosy turkey-carpeted lounge, also with an open fire. Chatty groups gather around the tiny bar, where the staff draw Brains Rev James and Hancocks HB from handpump; walking boots are allowed in the main bar only. There's a small, sheltered lawn at the back with picnic-sets and there's a camping field; the bedrooms were being reworked as we went to press. Reports on the new regime please.

🍽 **Very straightforward pubby food includes sandwiches, soup, sausage and chips, lasagne, three-bean chilli, rump steak, puddings and Sunday roasts.** *Starters/Snacks: £3.00 to £4.00. Main Courses: £5.00 to £12.00*

Free house ~ Licensees Brian Hall and Sharon Mallon ~ Real ale ~ Bar food (12-2.30, 7-9.30 (not Sun evening)) ~ (01544) 370669 ~ Children welcome ~ Dogs allowed in bar ~ Open 12-3, 6(7 Sun)-11

Recommended by BOB

GRESFORD   SJ3453   MAP 6

Pant-yr-Ochain 🍽 ♀ ◖

Off A483 on N edge of Wrexham: at roundabout take A5156 (A534) towards Nantwich, then first left towards the Flash; LL12 8TY

Thoughtfully run, gently refined dining pub with rooms, good food all day, very wide range of drinks, pretty lakeside garden

With inventive food, a good choice of real ales, spirits and wines as well as a friendly welcome, the licensees at this 16th-c country house continue to get praise from readers. It has been thoughtfully refurbished inside: the light and airy rooms are stylishly decorated, with a wide range of interesting prints and bric-a-brac on walls and on shelves, and a good mix of individually chosen country furnishings, including comfortable seats for relaxing as well as more upright ones for eating, and there's a recently rebuilt conservatory as well as a good open fire; one area is set out as a library, with floor to ceiling bookshelves. Six real ales on handpump feature Badger Flowers Original and Thwaites Original alongside guests such as Titanic Golden Age and Weetwood Cheshire Cat; they have a good range of decent wines (strong on up-front new world ones), with 24 by the glass, and around 80 malt whiskies. Disabled access is good. The garden overlooks a lake frequented by waterfowl and has benches, mature trees and shrubs.

🍽 **Good food, from a well balanced daily changing menu, and using free-range eggs and chicken, might typically include sandwiches, ploughman's, potato and watercress soup, mushroom soufflé, fried king prawns with garlic butter, smoked salmon quiche, ham and cabbage potato cake with poached egg and cider sauce, shoulder of lamb, fish stew, steak and kidney suet pudding, and mixed grill, with puddings like mango cheesecake with apricot compote or chocolate pot with clotted cream.** *Starters/Snacks: £4.50 to £9.00. Main Courses: £9.95 to £17.95. Puddings: £4.25 to £5.25*

Brunning & Price ~ Licensee Lindsey Douglas ~ Real ale ~ Bar food (12-9.30(9 Sun)) ~ (01978) 853525 ~ Children welcome away from bar till 6pm ~ Open 12-11.30(11 Sun); closed 25, 26 Dec

Recommended by David Johnson, Mr and Mrs J Palmer, Clive Watkin, L and D Webster, Roger and Anne Newbury, Dr Phil Putwain, R T and J C Moggridge

HAY-ON-WYE   SO2242   MAP 6

Blue Boar

Castle Street/Oxford Road; HR3 5DF

Generous home cooking in dual-personality pub – dark cosy medieval bar, light and airy modern dining area

The irregular shape of the bar here gives cosy corners, and its candlelight or shaded table lamps, squared dark ply panelling and handsome fireplace (with a good winter fire) make for a relaxed atmosphere. There are pews, country chairs, and stools at the counter, which has Shepherd Neame Spitfire, Timothy Taylors Landlord, and a beer named for the pub on handpump, a good choice of wines by the glass and whiskies, and interesting bottled ciders including organic ones, and service is good, under a friendly landlady. The long open dining room is light and airy, thanks to big sash windows, fresh cheery décor and bright tablecloths. There's a fire here too, and local artwork for sale, and the long food serving counter does good coffees and teas; piped music. They plan to open bedrooms.

📷 **Enjoyable bar food includes sandwiches, soup, duck breast with orange marmalade, chicken liver parfait with fruit coulis, welsh rarebit, sausages with onion gravy, cod and chips, steak and kidney pie, tuscan bean casserole on couscous, chicken breast wrapped in smoked bacon with brie sauce, lamb shank with minted gravy, bass with basil pesto, and puddings like apple pie or fruit pavlova.** *Starters/Snacks: £4.95 to £7.95. Main Courses: £8.95 to £15.95. Puddings: £4.50*

Free house ~ Licensees John and Lucy Goldsworthy ~ Real ale ~ Bar food (12-2.30, 6-9(9.30 Fri and Sat); all day during school hols and festivals) ~ Restaurant ~ (01497) 820884 ~ Children welcome ~ Dogs welcome ~ Open 9.30am-11pm(11.30 Fri and Sat)

Recommended by Sue Demont, Tim Barrow, Jarrod and Wendy Hopkinson, David Howe

Kilverts

Bullring; HR3 5AG

Friendly and enjoyable bar with decent food and drink

This hotel bar is a very useful place to enjoy a beer and a simple lunch if you're hunting among the second-hand bookshops of this appealing little border town. They've an extensive wine list with several by the glass, as well as Brains Rev James and Wye Valley Butty Bach and Marstons Pedigree on handpump, a decent choice of wines by the glass, several malt whiskies, and good coffees; piped radio, cards, chess, dominoes. Calm and understated, the airy high-beamed bar has some stripped stone walls, *Vanity Fair* caricatures, a couple of standing timbers, candles on well spaced mixed old and new tables, and a pleasant variety of seating. You can sit out at tables in a small front flagstoned courtyard (with outdoor heaters and shelters) or while away the hours by the fountain in a pretty terraced back garden. More reports please.

📷 **Lunchtime snacks and bar food might include soup, ploughman's, sandwiches, steak and kidney pudding, chargrilled rib-eye steak, salmon and crab fishcakes with tomato and herb salsa, and lemon chicken coriander and sesame seed salad.** *Starters/Snacks: £4.25 to £5.95. Main Courses: £7.95 to £12.95. Puddings: £4.50*

Free house ~ Licensee Mrs S. M. Davies ~ Real ale ~ Bar food ~ Restaurant ~ (01497) 821042 ~ Well behaved children welcome in bar until 9pm ~ Open 10am(11.30am Sun)-11pm(11.30pm Sat) ~ Bedrooms: £65S(£70B)/£90S(£100B)

Recommended by Peter Craske, Mike and Mary Carter, MMO, Guy Vowles, Sue Demont, Tim Barrow

---

Real ale to us means beer which has matured naturally in its cask – not pressurised or filtered. We name all real ales stocked. We usually name ales preserved under a light blanket of carbon dioxide too, though purists – pointing out that this stops the natural yeasts developing – would disagree (most people, including us, can't tell the difference!).

Old Black Lion 🍴 🍺 🛏

Lion Street; HR3 5AD

Low-beamed bar with pubby atmosphere, nicely unchanged in feel; good food and drink, pleasant bedrooms

With happy, welcoming staff and enjoyable food, this homely, spotless old inn dates back in part to the 13th c and is right in the heart of town. It has a comfortable low-beamed bar with crimson and yellow walls, nice old pine tables, and an original fireplace. As well as Old Black Lion (which is Wye Valley Butty Bach but with the pub's own label) on handpump, they have a changing Rhymney ale and good value wines; service is polite and briskly efficient. There are tables out behind on a sheltered terrace. Comfortable refurbished bedrooms make this a pleasant place to stay.

🍴 You can eat from either the bar or restaurant menu throughout, with enjoyable food such as soup, lunchtime snacks and sandwiches, soup, starters like roast salmon with horseradish potato salad, or home-cured duck breast, and main courses such as beef wellington, gressingham duck breast on parsnip purée, mushroom and leek crêpes with cheese sauce, steak and kidney pie, and cajun-spiced mushroom and spinach tagliatelle. *Starters/Snacks: £4.95 to £6.25. Main Courses: £8.85 to £18.25. Puddings: £4.65*

Free house ~ Licensee Mrs Leighton ~ Real ale ~ Bar food (12-2.30, 6.30-9.30) ~ Restaurant ~ (01497) 820841 ~ Open 11-11(10.30 Sun); closed 24-26 Dec ~ Bedrooms: £50S(£45B)/£90B

Recommended by Reg Fowle, Helen Rickwood, Richard Marjoram, Steve Harvey, H G Dyke, Richard, Jarrod and Wendy Hopkinson, Sue Demont, Tim Barrow, Neasa Braham, Mrs Philippa Wilson, Guy Vowles

LITTLE HAVEN SM8512 MAP 6

St Brides Inn

St Brides Road – in village itself, not St Brides hamlet further W; SA62 3UN

Cheerful seaside inn with anglo-russian owners, tasty food and a log fire

The russian landlady and english landlord here run this little pub, at the south end of St Bride's Bay on the pembrokeshire coast, with clockwork efficiency. There's a neat stripped-stone bar and linking carpeted dining area, and a good log fire; Marstons Banks and Pedigree on handpump, and several malt whiskies. A curious well in a back corner grotto is thought to be partly Roman; across the road is a sheltered sunny terraced garden. The two bright bedrooms have pine furniture and are en suite; we would welcome reports from readers who stay here.

🍴 Food changes weekly, and along with sandwiches and soup might include beef stroganoff (made to the russian landlady's family recipe), fish pie, curry, rib-eye steak, three-cheese pasta and broccoli bake, specials such as tuna steak, and puddings like apple strudel; they sometimes have russian theme nights. *Starters/Snacks: £3.75 to £5.75. Main Courses: £5.75 to £11.50. Puddings: £2.95 to £4.50*

Marstons ~ Lease Graham Harrison-Jones ~ Real ale ~ Bar food (12-2, 6-9) ~ Restaurant ~ No credit cards ~ (01437) 781266 ~ Children welcome in bar until 7.30pm ~ Dogs allowed in bar ~ Open 12-11; 12.30-11.30 Sat; 11.30-10.30 Sun; closed Mon Nov-May, and first week of Jan ~ Bedrooms: /£55S

Recommended by R and Z Davies, Steve Godfrey, Pat Crabb

LLANARMON DYFFRYN CEIRIOG SJ1532 MAP 6

Hand 🛏

On B4500 from Chirk; LL20 7LD

Comfortable rural hotel in a remote valley; cosy low-beamed bar area, good bedrooms

Well converted from an ancient farmhouse, this inn in the Ceiriog Valley is in rewarding hill-walking country not far from Pistyll Rhaeadr, the highest waterfall in Wales beneath the Berwyn Hills. The black-beamed carpeted bar on the left of the broad-flagstoned entrance hall has a good log fire in its inglenook fireplace, a mixture of chairs and settles, and old prints on its cream walls, with bar stools along the modern bar counter, which has Weetwood Eastgate on handpump, several malt whiskies, and reasonably priced wines by the glass; happy and welcoming staff help towards the warm atmosphere. Round the corner is the largely stripped stone dining room, with a woodburning stove and carpeted floor; TV, games machine, darts, pool and dominoes. This is a peaceful place to stay and they do a good country breakfast; the residents' lounge on the right is comfortable and attractive. There are tables out on a crazy-paved front terrace, with more in the garden, which has flowerbeds around another sheltered terrace. More reports please.

🍴 Besides lunchtime sandwiches and ploughman's, items from a seasonally changing menu might include rib-eye steak with madeira and pink peppercorn sauce, confit of gressingham duck, lasagne, steak and ale pie, a vegetarian dish such as vegetable and nut roast, and grilled trout from a local trout farm in the valley. *Starters/Snacks: £4.50 to £6.00. Main Courses: £7.50 to £14.50. Puddings: £5.00*

Free house ~ Licensees Gaynor and Martin de Luchi ~ Bar food (12-2.15(12.30-2.45 Sun), 6.30-8.45) ~ Restaurant ~ (01691) 600666 ~ Well supervised children welcome ~ Dogs allowed in bar and bedrooms ~ Open 11(12 Sun)-11(12.30 Sat) ~ Bedrooms: £65B/£110B
Recommended by Simon Daws, BOB

LLANBERIS
SH6655 MAP 6

Pen-y-Gwryd £ 🛏

Nant Gwynant; at junction of A498 and A4086, ie across mountains from Llanberis – OS Sheet 115 map reference 660558; LL55 4NT

In the hands of the same family for decades, an illustrious favourite with the mountain fraternity

Full of climbers' mementoes, this family-run mountain inn memorably placed beneath Snowdon and the Glyders has changed remarkably little – one reader noted that everything is probably much as it was on his father's first visit in 1916. It was used as a training base for the 1953 Everest team and their fading signatures can still be made out, scrawled on the ceiling. One snug little room in the homely slate-floored log cabin bar has built-in wall benches and sturdy country chairs to let you gaze at the surrounding mountain landscapes – like precipitous Moel Siabod beyond the lake opposite. A smaller room has a worthy collection of illustrious boots from famous climbs, and a cosy panelled smoke room has more fascinating climbing mementoes and equipment; darts, pool, board games and bar billiards. There's a sociable atmosphere, and alongside Bass on handpump, they've home-made lemonade in summer, mulled wine in winter, and sherry from their own solera in Puerto Santa Maria. Staying here can be quite an experience. The excellent, traditional breakfast is served at 8.30am; they're not generally flexible with this; comfortable but basic bedrooms, dogs £2 a night. The inn has its own chapel (built for the millennium and dedicated by the Archbishop of Wales), sauna and outdoor natural pool.

🍴 The short choice of simple, good-value home-made lunchtime bar food (you order it through a hatch) might include sandwiches, soup, chicken liver pâté, a platter of cold meats, roast lamb, slow-braised pork, fired breast of chicken stuffed with welsh brie and wrapped in prosciutto, cheese and onion tart. and smoked duck and orange salad; puddings such as chocolate pudding or apple and blackberry pie. A gong at 7.30pm signals the prompt start of service in the evening restaurant; they don't hang around – if you're late, you'll miss it, and there's no evening bar food. *Starters/Snacks: £3.50 to £5.95. Main Courses: £6.95 to £7.50*

Free house ~ Licensee Jane Pullee ~ Real ale ~ Bar food (lunchtime only) ~ Restaurant (evening) ~ (01286) 870211 ~ Children welcome ~ Dogs allowed in bar and bedrooms ~ Open 11-11(10.30 Sun); closed all Nov-Dec, and midweek Jan-Feb ~ Bedrooms: £40/£80(£94B)
Recommended by Neil and Angela Huxter, Andrea Rampley, Alec and Joan Laurence, Julian and Janet Dearden, Steve Kirby

LLANDDAROG
SN5016   MAP 6

White Hart 🍺
Just off A48 E of Carmarthen, via B4310; aka Yr Hydd Gwyn; SA32 8NT

Popular thatched pub full of interest and antiques, unusual own-brew beers and good portions of bar food

Cheerfully welcoming and near the National Botanic Garden of Wales, this is a tremendously atmospheric pub dating from 1371, when it was reputedly opened to house builders working on the local church. The rooms are still packed with fascinating details and sundry bits and pieces – 17th-c welsh oak carving, a tall grandfather clock, stained-glass, a collection of hats and riding boots, china, brass and copper on walls and dark beams, antique prints and even a suit of armour. The heavily carved fireside settles by the huge crackling log fire are the best place to sit. But the main attraction today is the range of beers they make using water from their own 300-foot borehole. Named after the family in charge, the small Coles brewery produces ales such as Cwrw Blasus, Golden, Llanddarog, as well as a barley stout, and a lager, and there are usually four available on handpump. There are steps down to the high-raftered dining room, also interestingly furnished. Two minor niggles: the 25p charge for a pint of tap water (unless you're eating) and one couple found they were not allowed to share a sandwich. There are picnic-sets out on a terrace, a children's play area and farmyard; they can put a ramp in place for disabled access. Look out for Zac the macaw and Bendy the galah.

🍴 Using poultry and meat from local farms and fish from Haverfordwest, generous helpings of tasty bar food from the servery include sandwiches, baked potatoes, ploughman's, curries, a range of pies, pizzas, steaks, battered cod, cheese and broccoli bake, with specials such as duck breast in orange and cranberry sauce, lamb shank and whole bass. Starters/Snacks: £4.00 to £6.00. Main Courses: £6.50 to £8.00. Puddings: £4.00 to £6.00

Own brew ~ Licensees Marcus and Cain Coles ~ Real ale ~ Bar food (11.30-2, 6.30-10; 2-2, 7-9.30 Sun) ~ Restaurant ~ (01267) 275395 ~ Children welcome away from bar ~ pen 11.30-3, 6.30-11; 12-3, 7-10.30 Sun; closed 25, 26 Dec

Recommended by Peter Hacker, Richard and Judy Winn, Norma and Noel Thomas, MLR, R J Davies, Tom Evans, Mrs G R Sharman, Dr and Mrs A K Clarke, MDN, B and M Kendall

LLANDUDNO JUNCTION
SH8180   MAP 6

Queens Head 🍴 🍷
Glanwydden; heading towards Llandudno on B5115 from Colwyn Bay, turn left into Llanrhos Road at roundabout as you enter the Penrhyn Bay speed limit; Glanwydden is signposted as the first left turn off this; LL31 9JP

Classy food (all day at weekends) prepared with considerable care in comfortably modern dining pub; some interesting drinks too

'Simply superb', 'consistently high standards' and 'hard to fault' are three readers' endorsements of the food at this very well run dining pub, and its village location is much enjoyed too. Despite the emphasis on eating, locals do pop in for a drink, and you'll find three beers like Greate Orme Best, Tetleys Cask Bitter and Weetwood Old Dog on handpump, as well as decent wines (including some unusual ones and several by the glass), 20 malt whiskies and good coffee. The spaciously comfortable modern lounge bar – partly divided by a white wall of broad arches – has brown plush banquettes and windsor chairs around neat black tables, and there's a little public bar; unobtrusive piped music. There's an outdoor seating area, available for smokers. Northern Snowdonia is in easy reach, and you can rent the pretty stone cottage (which sleeps two) across the road.

🍴 With an emphasis on fresh produce, the well presented and efficiently served dishes typically include soup, open sandwiches, smoked salmon and trout mousse, grilled goats cheese tart with poached pears and walnuts, their own burgers topped with melted cheese and sticky onions, steak and ale pie, haddock in beer batter with chunky chips and home-made tartare sauce, asparagus risotto, seared anglesey king scallops, seafood vol-au-vent, roast belly pork with black pudding and calvados cream sauce, and various steaks; they also have a daily specials board and do all-day Sunday roasts. *Starters/Snacks: £4.35 to £8.95. Main Courses: £8.95 to £17.50. Puddings: £4.50*

Free house ~ Licensees Robert and Sally Cureton ~ Real ale ~ Bar food (12-2, 6-9; 12-9 Sat, Sun) ~ Restaurant ~ (01492) 546570 ~ Children over 7 in evening ~ Open 12-3, 6-11; 12-11 Sat, Sun; closes 10.30pm Sun in winter

Recommended by KC, Matt Anderson, Joan E Hilditch, Margaret and Jeff Graham, Heather McQuillan, GLD, Mike and Mary Carter, Dave Webster, Sue Holland, Revd D Glover

LLANELIAN-YN-RHOS   SH8676   MAP 6
White Lion
Signed off A5830 (shown as B5383 on some maps) and B5381, S of Colwyn Bay; LL29 8YA

Pretty pub with friendly service, generous food, pleasantly traditional bar and roomy dining area

Run by helpful staff, this picturesque old village pub is tucked away at a crossing of narrow lanes in quiet hilly countryside above Colwyn Bay. It has two distinct parts, each with its own personality, linked by a broad flight of steps. Up at the top is a neat and very spacious dining area, while down at the other end is a traditional old bar, with antique high-backed settles angling snugly around a big fireplace, and flagstones by the counter where they serve Marstons Burton and Pedigree and a guest such as Jennings Mountain Man; on the left, another dining area has jugs hanging from the beams, and teapots above the window. Prompt service, good wine list with several by the glass and malt whiskies; piped music. Outside, an attractive courtyard between the pub and the church has sheltered tables (it's also used for parking). More reports please.

🍴 A wide choice of good, generously served food includes sandwiches, ciabattas and hot baguettes, soup, mussels poached in garlic, traditional roasts, sausages and mash, fish stew, chicken curry, stuffed roasted pepper filled with marinated mediterranean vegetables, together with specials such as steak and kidney pie, roast welsh lamb shoulder, fillet steak with stilton and smoked bacon sauce, or tuna steak marinated in chilli and ginger; they also have a children's menu. *Starters/Snacks: £2.25 to £5.95. Main Courses: £6.95 to £14.95. Puddings: £2.95 to £4.25*

Free house ~ Licensee Simon Cole ~ Real ale ~ Bar food (12-2, 6-9) ~ Restaurant ~ (01492) 515807 ~ Children welcome ~ Live jazz every Tues evening, bluegrass Weds ~ Open 12-3.30, 6-11.30(midnight Sat); 12-4, 6-11 Sun; closed Mon

Recommended by Michael and Jenny Back

LLANFERRES   SJ1860   MAP 6
Druid
A494 Mold—Ruthin; CH7 5SN

17th-c inn with beams, antique settles and a log fire in the bar; wonderful views

This cosy, rambling whitewashed inn beneath the eastern side of the Clwydian Hills is in super territory for walks, with the summit of Moel Famau and Offa's Dyke Path not far away. You can enjoy the views from tables outside at the front and from the broad bay window in the civilised, smallish plush lounge. The hills are also in sight from the bigger beamed and characterful back bar, with its two handsome antique oak settles as well as a pleasant mix of more modern furnishings. There's a quarry-tiled area by the log fire, and a three-legged cat, Chu. Marstons Burton and a guest from breweries such as Hook Norton or Jennings are on handpump, and the pub stocks more than 30 malt whiskies. A games room has darts and pool, along with board games; piped music, TV.

If you know a pub's ever open all day, please tell us.

⚏ **A wide range of food (which you can eat in the bar or restaurant) might feature soup, filled baps, steak and ale pie, whole bass stuffed with coriander butter, grilled leg of lamb, sirloin steak with mushroom sauce, fillet of fresh salmon wrapped in smoked bacon, and mushrooms stuffed with stilton, with a few daily specials including fresh fish.** *Starters/Snacks: £3.95 to £5.95. Main Courses: £8.95 to £16.95. Puddings: £2.95 to £4.25*

Union Pub Company ~ Lease James Dolan ~ Real ale ~ Bar food (12-3, 6-9; 12-9.30 Sat; 12-9 Sun) ~ (01352) 810225 ~ Children welcome ~ Dogs allowed in bar and bedrooms ~ Open 12-3, 5.30-11; 12-12 Sat, Sun ~ Bedrooms: £48S/£70S

Recommended by KC, Gordon and Margaret Ormonroyd, Marcus Mann

LLANFRYNACH
SO0725   MAP 6

White Swan ♀

Village signposted from B4558, off A40 E of Brecon – take second turn to village, which is also signed to pub; LD3 7BZ

Revamped, cosily mellow country dining pub with a pretty terrace

There's an enjoyably tranquil atmosphere at this upmarket dining pub in the Brecon Beacons National Park. The original part of the beamed bar has stripped stone and flagstones, with sturdy oak tables and nice carver chairs in a polished country-kitchen style, a woodburning stove, and leather sofas and armchairs in groups around low tables; it opens into an apricot-walled high-ceilinged extension, light and airy, with bare boards and different sets of chairs around each table. On handpump are Hancocks HB and Rhymney Bitter; good wines and coffees; piped music. The charming secluded back terrace has stone and wood tables with a good choice of sun or shade, and is attractively divided into sections by low plantings and climbing shrubs. The pub is well placed for hefty hikes up the main Brecon Beacons summits, or for undemanding saunters along the towpath of the Monmouthshire and Brecon Canal.

⚏ **The good food is very much the centre of attention, with changing lunch menus and à la carte evening fare; at lunchtimes there is a short choice of items like braised shank of welsh mountain lamb, lasagne or chicken curry; evening food might include starters like seared scallops with cajun spices or venison meatballs in a compote of plum tomatoes with beetroot and potato gnocchi, and main courses like daube of venison, fillets of bass stuffed with asparagus spears and wrapped in pancetta, and breast of free-range guinea fowl stuffed with bacon, apple, onion and thyme, with delicious puddings like raspberry and white chocolate cheesecake or baked bramley apple pie.** *Starters/Snacks: £4.95 to £6.95. Main Courses: £8.95 to £14.95. Puddings: £5.25*

Free house ~ Licensee Richard Griffiths ~ Real ale ~ Bar food (12-2(2.30 Sun), 7-9(8 Sun)) ~ Restaurant ~ (01874) 665276 ~ Children welcome (not Sat evening) ~ Open 12-3, 6.30-11(10.30 Sun); closed Mon except bank hols, and first week of Jan

Recommended by Robert Ager, Mr and Mrs R B Berry, Mike and Mary Carter, Norman and Sarah Keeping, Michael and Maggie Betton, Mrs Margo Finlay, Jörg Kasprowski

LLANGOLLEN
SJ2142   MAP 6

Corn Mill ⚏ ♀ ◼

Dee Lane, very narrow lane off Castle Street (A539) just S of bridge; nearby parking can be tricky, may be best to use public park on Parade Street/East Street and walk; LL20 8PN

A strong all-rounder, with personable young staff, super food all day, good beers, and a fascinating riverside building

In addition to the well liked food, this imaginatively restored mill has a great range of drinks, with six real ales from brewers such as Boddingtons, Caledonian Deuchars, Coach House, Conwy, Facers and Plassey, around 50 malt whiskies and a decent wine choice. The position is really special, jutting over the River Dee rushing through its rocky bed; you look across the river to the steam trains puffing away at the nearby station and maybe a horse-drawn barge on the Llangollen Canal. An area with decking and teak tables and chairs is perfect for taking in the view. Quite a bit of the mill machinery remains – most obviously the great water wheel, still turning – but the place has been interestingly refitted with pale pine flooring on stout beams, a striking open stairway with gleaming timber and tensioned steel rails, and mainly stripped stone walls. A lively bustling chatty feel greets you, with quick service from plenty of pleasant young staff, good-sized dining tables, big rugs, nicely chosen pictures (many to do with water) and lots of pot plants. One of the two serving bars, away from the water, has a much more local feel, with pews on dark slate flagstones, daily papers, and regulars on the bar stools. The pub can get busy, so it might be worth booking if you're planning to eat.

🍴 **Good food – served all day – from a daily changing menu could include sandwiches, ploughman's, soup, tempura tiger prawns, caerphilly and leek tartlet, smoked haddock and mozzarella rarebit, lamb koftas with pitta bread and mint raita, whole trout, free-range chicken breast with black pudding mash, and braised shoulder of lamb, with puddings like passion fruit cheesecake with summer fruit coulis or rich sticky toffee pudding.** *Starters/Snacks: £5.00 to £10.00. Main Courses: £8.00 to £15.00. Puddings: £5.00 to £5.50*

Brunning & Price ~ Licensee Andrew Barker ~ Real ale ~ Bar food (12-9.30(9 Sun)) ~ (01978) 869555 ~ Children welcome ~ Open 12-11(10.30 Sun)

Recommended by Malcolm Pellatt, Bruce and Sharon Eden, Mr and Mrs J Palmer, Mike and Mary Carter, Richard and Karen Holt, Kevin Jeavons, Alison Turner, Gerry and Rosemary Dobson, Dr Kevan Tucker, John McDonald, Ann Bond, A Darroch Harkness, Alan and Eve Harding, Phil and Jane Hodson, Meg and Colin Hamilton

MOLD

SJ2465   MAP 6

Glasfryn 🍴 🍷 🍺

N of the centre on Raikes Lane (parallel to the A5119), just past the well signposted Theatr Clwyd; CH7 6LR

Open-plan bistro-style pub with inventive, upmarket food available all day, nice décor, wide drinks choice

Just across the road from Theatr Clwyd, this Brunning & Price pub continues to be liked for its food, attractive layout and fine range of drinks. Although it's unassuming from outside, it is a really buzzing place run with considerable verve by enthusiastic and friendly staff. Open-plan rooms have both spaciousness and nice quiet corners, with an informal and attractive mix of country furnishings, and interesting decorations. Besides a good variety of wines by the glass, local apple juice and around 100 whiskies, they've seven beers on handpump, with Caledonian Deuchars IPA, Thwaites Original and Timothy Taylors Landlord, alongside swiftly changing guests like Sharps Doom Bar and Thwaites Wainwrights. Sturdy timber tables on a big terrace give superb views to the Clwydian Hills – idyllic on a warm summer's evening.

🍴 **From a daily changing menu, the full choice of good, well prepared food (not cheap) is available all day and might include items like sandwiches, deep-fried bass with fennel and orange salad, pressed ham and lancashire cheese with pineapple chutney, grilled asparagus with pine nut and lemon vinaigrette, grilled sardines with roasted vegetables, gnocchi with roasted vegetables and parmesan, minced beef and onion pie, crab and avocado salad, twice-cooked duck breast with stir-fried hoi sin vegetables and rice, deep-fried haddock in beer batter with chips and mushy peas, and puddings like lime and ginger cheesecake or summer fruit pudding with clotted cream.** *Starters/Snacks: £4.25 to £6.75. Main Courses: £8.95 to £14.95. Puddings: £5.00 to £6.25*

Brunning & Price ~ Licensee James Meakin ~ Real ale ~ Bar food (12-9.30(9 Sun)) ~ (01352) 750500 ~ Young children welcome except in evening ~ Dogs allowed in bar ~ Open 11.30-11; 12-10.30 Sun; closed 25-26 Dec

Recommended by R T and J C Moggridge, Dr Phil Putwain, Tom and Jill Jones, Keith and Sue Ward, KC, Clive Watkin, Mr and Mrs J Palmer, Gordon and Margaret Ormondroyd

---

Pubs staying open all afternoon at least one day a week are listed
at the back of the book.

MONKNASH   SS9270   MAP 6

Plough & Harrow 🍺

Signposted Marcross, Broughton off B4265 St Brides Major—Llantwit Major – turn left at end of Water Street; OS Sheet 170 map reference 920706; CF71 7QQ

Marvellously evocative old building full of history and character, with a good choice of real ales

There's a fine choice of up to eight real ales on handpump or tapped from the cask in this wonderfully ancient and unchanged place that originates as part of a monastic grange, the walls and dovecote of which stand close by: the choice might include Bass, Otley O1, Worthington Best Bitter and Wye Valley Hereford Pale Ale alongside guests such as Crouch Vale Brewers Gold, Nelsons Pieces of Eight and Shardlow Reverend Etons. They also have local farm cider, welsh and malt whiskies; helpful service from knowledgeable staff. Built with massively thick stone walls, the dimly lit unspoilt main bar used to be the scriptures room and mortuary. The heavily black-beamed ceiling has ancient ham hooks, an intriguing arched doorway to the back, and a comfortably informal mix of furnishings that includes three fine stripped pine settles on the broad flagstones. There's a log fire in a huge fireplace with a side bread oven large enough to feed a village. The room on the left has lots of Wick Rugby Club memorabilia (it's their club room); daily papers, piped music, darts and TV (for sporting events only). It can get crowded at weekends, when it's popular with families (they do children's helpings). There are picnic-sets in the front garden (with a covered area available to smokers), which has a boules pitch, and they hold barbecues out here in summer. Dogs are welcome in the bar – but not while food is being served. In a peaceful spot not far from the coast near Nash Point, it's an enjoyable walk from here down to the sea, where you can pick up a fine stretch of the coastal path along the top of remarkable candy-striped cliffs full of blow holes and fissures. More reports please.

🍴 Written up on blackboards, the reasonably priced daily changing lunchtime bar food could include sandwiches, leek and stilton bake, sausages and mash, moussaka and welsh faggots; children's menu; more expensive evening food could feature soup, haddock with welsh rarebit crust, and beef medallions with green pepper sauce. *Starters/Snacks: £4.50 to £7.95. Main Courses: £7.95 to £9.50. Puddings: £1.20 to £3.95*

Free house ~ Licensee Gareth Davies ~ Real ale ~ Bar food (12-2.30, 6-9; all day Sat) ~ Restaurant ~ (01656) 890209 ~ Well behaved children welcome in bar until 8pm ~ Dogs allowed in bar ~ Live music Sat evening ~ Open 12-11(10.30 Sun)
Recommended by Blaise Vyner, Gwyn and Anne Wake

OLD RADNOR   SO2459   MAP 6

Harp 🍴 🛏

Village signposted off A44 Kington—New Radnor in Walton; LD8 2RH

Delightfully placed pub with cosy cottagey bar and comfortable bedrooms; tasty food served by caring staff

This is a welcoming place to eat, stay or just enjoy a drink in the atmospherically old-fashioned bar or outside at tables on the grassy area beneath a sycamore tree looking across to the high massif of Radnor Forest. In the evening and at weekends chatty locals gather in the public bar, which has high-backed settles, an antique reader's chair and other elderly chairs around a log fire; board games. The snug slate-floored lounge has a handsome curved antique settle and another log fire in a fine inglenook, and there are lots of local books and guides for residents. They have two changing real ales, from brewers such as Shepherd Neame, Three Tuns and Wye Valley, Dunkerton's farm cider, local apple juice, and a beer and cider festival in June; several malt whiskies; friendly, helpful service. They don't allow large dogs in the bedrooms, which are generally much enjoyed by readers. The impressive church is worth a look for its interesting early organ case (Britain's oldest), fine rood screen and ancient font. Note they don't open weekday lunchtimes.

⑪ Featuring vegetables and rhubarb from the publicans' own garden, well liked bar food typically includes sandwiches (Saturday lunchtime only), broccoli and shropshire blue soup, parma ham with rocket and mango, welsh black rump steak with hand-cut chips and roasted seasonal vegetables, seared parmesan-crusted salmon fillet with pesto mash, gressingham duck breast in redcurrant and madeira jus, and spinach and ricotta cannelloni, with specials like local game casserole, organic lamb chops with butter bean bake or roasted hake in tarragon butter; puddings such as chocolate brownie or apple and pear crumble. *Starters/Snacks: £3.95 to £5.50. Main Courses: £7.95 to £15.00. Puddings: £4.50 to £5.50*

Free house ~ Licensees David and Jenny Ellison ~ Real ale ~ Bar food ~ Restaurant ~ (01544) 350655 ~ Children welcome ~ Dogs allowed in bar ~ Open 6-11; 12-3, 6-11 Sat, Sun; closed weekday lunchtimes, all day Mon (exc bank hols) ~ Bedrooms: £40B/£64B

Recommended by the Didler, MLR, Trevor and Janet Cooper-Tydeman, Reg Fowle, Helen Rickwood, Mike and Eleanor Anderson, Steven and Victoria James

PORTH DINLLAEN   SH2741   MAP 6

Ty Coch
Beach car park signposted from Morfa Nefyn, then 15-min walk; LL53 6DB

Idyllic location right on the beach, far from the roads; simple fresh lunches

The coastal position of this unspoilt place is really special: you can arrive at low tide along a beach backed by low grassy hills and sand-cliffs, with gulls and curlews for company (otherwise you can walk across via the golf course). The pub is said to have been used by 17th-c smugglers and pirates, and the walls and beams are hung every inch with pewter, riding lights, navigation lamps, lanterns, small fishing nets, old miners' and railway lamps, copper utensils, an ale-yard, and lots of RNLI photographs and memorabilia; there are ships in bottles, a working barometer, a Caernarfon grandfather clock, and simple furnishings. An open coal fire burns at one end of the bar; occasional piped music. There are tables outside. Although there's no real ale here, there's a range of bottled beers. More reports please.

⑪ From a short menu, simple lunchtime bar food includes sandwiches, baked potatoes, mussels in garlic butter, pies, warm melted brie with chutney topping, ham or beef salad, and local crab and mussels. *Starters/Snacks: £2.50 to £6.50. Main Courses: £6.50 to £10.50. Puddings: £3.95*

Free house ~ Licensee Mrs Brione Webley ~ Bar food (12-2.30) ~ (01758) 720498 ~ Children welcome ~ Dogs welcome ~ Live music twice weekly in July and Aug ~ Open 11-11(11-3 daily, 6-11 Fri, Sat, Easter to spring bank hol); 11-4 Sun; open during day in Christmas week; Sat and Sun 12-4 only in winter

Recommended by Dr Kevan Tucker, Steff Clegg

PORTHGAIN   SM8132   MAP 6

Sloop
Off A487 St Davids—Fishguard; SA62 5BN

Thoroughly nautical pub in wonderful coastal setting, fresh fish in season, efficient service even at busy times

Right next to a particularly dramatic section of the Pembrokeshire Coast Path, this friendly tavern snuggles in a cove wedged tightly between headlands, giving outstanding cliff walks in either direction – eastwards towards Trevine or southwestwards to Abereiddy. Inside it has seafaring memorabilia in many forms: the walls of the plank-ceilinged bar are hung with lobster pots and fishing nets, ships' clocks and lanterns, and even relics from wrecks along this stretch of the shoreline. Down a step, another room leads round to a decent-sized eating area, with simple wooden chairs and tables, cushioned wall seats, and a freezer with ice-creams for children. On handpump are Brains Rev James, Felinfoel Double Dragon and Greene King IPA, and wine by the glass in three different sized glasses. Rather than having a number for food service, many of the tables are named after a wrecked ship. There's a well segregated games room (used mainly by children) which has a couple of games machines, TV, juke box, pool and darts. At the height of summer they may extend food serving times. Tables on the terrace overlook the harbour, with outdoor heaters for cooler weather. They don't have bedrooms but let a cottage in the village.

🍴 Well prepared bar food often includes fresh fish they catch themselves (they run their own fishing business) such as crab, lobster, scallops and mackerel according to season. The menu might also feature lunchtime sandwiches, soup, welsh black rib-eye steak or sirloin steak, burgers made from organic mince, sausages and mash, and specials like roast coin of lamb or roasted butternut squash and celery risotto; they also do breakfasts. *Starters/Snacks: £5.00 to £8.00. Main Courses: £6.00 to £18.00. Puddings: £3.50 to £5.00*

Free house ~ Licensee Matthew Blakiston ~ Real ale ~ Bar food (9.30-11, 12-2.30, 6-9.30) ~ Restaurant ~ (01348) 831449 ~ Children welcome ~ Open 9.30am-11pm(midnight Sat)

Recommended by Peter and Anne Hollindale, Steve Godfrey, Andy and Alice Jordan, Mr and Mrs A H Young, Ewan and Moira McCall, Simon Watkins, Herbert and Susan Verity, John and Enid Morris, Blaise Vyner, Norma and Noel Thomas, Jeff Davies, MDN, Tom and Ruth Rees

RAGLAN
SO3609 MAP 6

Clytha Arms

Clytha, off Abergavenny road – former A40, now declassified; NP7 9BW

Beautifully placed in parkland, a relaxing spot for enjoying good food and beer; comfortable bedrooms

Readers savour the position of this civilised white house with its setting on the edge of Clytha Park. With long heated verandahs and diamond-paned windows, it's comfortable, light and airy, with scrubbed wood floors, pine settles, big faux fur cushions on the window seats, a good mix of old country furniture and a couple of warming fires. Run by charming licensees, it's the sort of relaxed place where everyone feels welcome, from locals who've walked here for a pint, to diners in the contemporary linen-set restaurant. An impressive choice of drinks includes well kept Evans and Evans Best Bitter, Felinfoel Double Dragon and Rhymney Bitter, three swiftly changing guest beers from brewers such as Brains, Shepherd Neame and Tring, an extensive wine list with about a dozen or so by the glass, over 20 malt whiskies, about three farm ciders and maybe their own perry. They have occasional cider and beer festivals; darts, shove-ha'penny, boules, bar billiards, draughts, large-screen TV for rugby matches, and board games. The pub has its own english setter and collie. Don't miss the murals in the lavatories (one reader felt the loos could still benefit from sprucing up). Service can be slow at busy times. The bedrooms are comfortable, with good welsh breakfasts.

🍴 Usually very enjoyable bar food includes sandwiches, faggots and peas, venison and wild mushroom pudding, smoked haddock fishcakes, welsh black rump steak, and rabbit and guinea fowl pie; the tapas is much liked by readers, and there's a beer and cheese festival at the August bank holiday weekend. The restaurant menu is pricier and more elaborate, with set menus at £19.50 for two courses. *Starters/Snacks: £3.80 to £7.90. Main Courses: £8.50 to £12.50. Puddings: £6.50*

Free house ~ Licensees Andrew and Beverley Canning ~ Real ale ~ Bar food (12.30-2.15, 7-9.30; not Sun evening or Mon lunch) ~ Restaurant ~ (01873) 840206 ~ Children welcome ~ Dogs allowed in bar and bedrooms ~ Open 12-12(10.30 Sun); closed Mon lunchtime; 3.30-6 Mon-Thurs ~ Bedrooms: £60B/£80B

Recommended by Peter Dearing, Paul J Robinshaw, R T and J C Moggridge, Simon Fidler, John Bromley, June Whitworth, M J Daly, Pete Baker, the Didler, Roy Hoing, Guy Vowles, Dr W J M Gissane, Colin McKerrow, William Goodhart

---

If you stay overnight in an inn or hotel, they are allowed to serve you an alcoholic drink at any hour of the day or night.

RED WHARF BAY

SH5281 MAP 6

Ship ♀ ◀

Village signposted off B5025 N of Pentraeth; LL75 8RJ

Nicely old-fashioned inside, with good drinks, sweeping coastal views from benches outside

This cottagey whitewashed 16th-c pub on Anglesey's north coast looks straight on to a huge bay fringed by dunes and headlands, and often dotted with yachts – at low tide it becomes a vast expanse of sands. It's cosily old-fashioned inside, with lots of nautical bric-a-brac in big rooms on each side of the busy stone-built bar counter, both with long cushioned varnished pews built around the walls, glossily varnished cast-iron-framed tables and roaring fires; piped Classic FM (in lounge only). Adnams, Black Sheep, Brains, Tetleys and a guest such as Caledonian Deuchars on handpump, nearly 50 malt whiskies, and a wider choice of wines than is usual for the area (with about ten by the glass). If you want to run a tab they'll ask to keep your credit card behind the bar in a locked numbered box (to which you are given the key). On fine days there are plenty of takers for tables outside that get terrific views.

⑪ **Using food sourced in Anglesey, the bar menu (not cheap) typically includes soup, lunchtime sandwiches, ploughman's, smoked scallops with black pudding and chilli crème fraîche, melon topped with strawberries and vodka dressing, chargrilled pork cutlet with cider sauce, free-range chicken fillet with wild mushroom sauce, roast vegetable lasagne, and chargrilled rib-eye of welsh beef, with puddings like bara brith bread and butter pudding or knickerbocker glory; children's menu.** *Starters/Snacks: £3.95 to £7.95. Main Courses: £7.95 to £14.95. Puddings: £4.25 to £4.95*

Free house ~ Licensee Neil Kenneally ~ Real ale ~ Bar food (12-2.30, 6-9(9.30 Sat); 12-9 Sun) ~ Restaurant ~ (01248) 852568 ~ Children welcome until 9.30 (under 14 in lounge and old cellar rooms) ~ Open 11-11

Recommended by Gordon and Margaret Ormonroyd, John McDonald, Ann Bond, Mike and Mary Carter, Glenwys and Alan Lawrence, Bob and Val Collman, Dr Kevan Tucker, Piotr Chodzko-Zajko

RHYD-Y-MEIRCH

SO2907 MAP 6

Goose & Cuckoo ◀

Upper Llanover signposted up narrow track off A4042 S of Abergavenny; after 0.5 mile take first left, then keep on up (watch for hand-written Goose signs at the forks); NP7 9ER

Remote single-room pub looking over a picturesque valley just inside the Brecon Beacons National Park, good drinks range

Nicely out of the way, this unspoilt, simple little place has a charmingly rural position high above the Usk. It is essentially one small rustically furnished room with a woodburner in an arched stone fireplace. A small picture-window extension makes the most of the view down the valley. They have Brains Rev James, Breconshire Welsh Pale Ale, and a couple of guests on handpump, as well as more than 80 whiskies; daily papers, cribbage, darts and board games. A variety of rather ad hoc picnic-sets is out on the gravel below. The licensees keep sheep, geese and chickens, and may have honey for sale.

⑪ **The choice of simple food includes filled rolls, bean soup, turkey and ham pie, steak and kidney pie and liver and bacon casserole.** *Starters/Snacks: £2.50 to £3.50. Main Courses: £7.00 to £9.50. Puddings: £3.00*

Free house ~ Licensees Michael and Carol Langley ~ Real ale ~ Bar food (12-2.30, 7-9; not Sun evening) ~ Restaurant ~ No credit cards ~ (01873) 880277 ~ Children welcome ~ Dogs allowed in bar ~ Open 11.30-3, 7-11; 11.30-11 Sat; 12-10.30 Sun; closed Mon except bank hols ~ Bedrooms: £30S/£60S

Recommended by MLR, John and Helen Rushton, Reg Fowle, Helen Rickwood, Guy Vowles, Ruth Owens

ROSEBUSH   SN0729   MAP 6

Tafarn Sinc

B4329 Haverfordwest—Cardigan; SA66 7QU

Unique 19th-c curio, a slice of social and industrial history

Laden with character, this is one of the most eccentric pub buildings in all Wales. A maroon-painted corrugated iron shed, it was built in 1876 as a very basic hotel for a halt for a long-defunct railway serving quarries beneath the Preseli Hills. The halt itself has been more or less re-created, even down to life-size dummy passengers waiting out on the platform; the sizeable garden is periodically enlivened by the sounds of steam trains chuffing through – actually broadcast from a replica signal box. Though not exactly elegant, inside is really interesting, almost a museum of local history, with sawdust on the floor and an appealingly buoyant feel, and you may well hear Welsh spoken here. The bar has plank panelling, an informal mix of chairs and pews, woodburners, and Cwrw Tafarn Sinc (brewed specially for the pub), and a weekly changing guest such as Brains Rev James on handpump; piped music, darts, games machine, board games and TV.

🍴 **Basic food includes home-made faggots with mushy peas, vegetable lasagne, lamb burgers, steaks and puddings.** *Starters/Snacks: £2.90 to £4.50. Main Courses: £8.90 to £14.90. Puddings: £2.60 to £3.90*

Free house ~ Licensee Brian Llewelyn ~ Real ale ~ Bar food ~ Restaurant ~ (01437) 532214 ~ Children welcome ~ Open 12-11(midnight Sat, Sun); closed Mon except bank hols
Recommended by the Didler, Paul Goldman, Herbert and Susan Verity, Peter and Anne Hollindale, John and Enid Morris, Jeff Davies, Tom Evans, Mark Flynn

SHIRENEWTON   ST4894   MAP 6

Carpenters Arms

Mynydd-bach; B4235 Chepstow—Usk, about 0.5 mile N; NP16 6BU

Pleasantly unsophisticated former smithy, with nicely timeless décor

There's an enjoyably pubby feel to this friendly former country smithy, which in summer has attractive hanging baskets. Inside are an array of chamber-pots, an attractive Victorian tiled fireplace, and a collection of chromolithographs of antique royal occasions. One of the unusual interconnecting rooms still has blacksmith's bellows hanging from the planked ceiling. Furnishings run the gamut too, from one very high-backed ancient settle to pews, kitchen chairs, a nice elm table, several sewing-machine trestle tables and so forth; darts, board games and piped pop music. On handpump are Bass, Fullers London Pride and Shepherd Neame Spitfire and an occasional seasonal guest. There are tables outside at the front.

🍴 **Straightforward bar food, written up on blackboards, takes in a wide choice, including sandwiches, soup and filled baked potatoes, pies, steaks and a mixed grill; inexpensive senior citizens' specials on weekdays.** *Starters/Snacks: £3.50 to £4.50. Main Courses: £7.95 to £15.50. Puddings: £3.25*

Punch ~ Lease Gary and Sandra Hayes ~ Real ale ~ Bar food (12-2.30, 6.30-9.30; Sun 12-8; not Mon) ~ No credit cards ~ (01291) 641231 ~ Children welcome ~ Dogs allowed in bar ~ Open 12-3, 5.30-12; 12 noon-midnight Sat, Sun; 12-3.30, 5.30-12(10.30 Sun) in winter
Recommended by Dr and Mrs A K Clarke, Donna and Roger, Steve Bailey, Mrs D W Privett

---

Looking for a pub with a really special garden, or in lovely countryside,
or with an outstanding view, or right by the water? They are listed
separately, at the back of the book.

SKENFRITH   SO4520   MAP 6

Bell ⏹ 🍴 ♀ 🛏

Just off B4521, NE of Abergavenny and N of Monmouth; NP7 8UH

Elegant but relaxed, generally much praised for classy though pricy food and excellent accommodation

Getting good reports for food this year, this is a relaxed but smart country inn just over the road from the substantial ruins of Skenfrith Castle and overlooking the River Monnow. The big back bare-boards dining area is very neat, light and airy, with dark country-kitchen chairs and rush-seat dining chairs, church candles and flowers on the dark tables, canary walls and a cream ceiling, and brocaded curtains on sturdy big-ring rails. The flagstoned bar on the left has a rather similar décor, with old local and school photographs, a couple of pews plus tables and café chairs; St Austell Tribute and Timothy Taylors Landlord as well as Broome Farm cider on handpump from an attractive bleached oak bar counter; board games. They have good wines by the glass and half-bottle, and make good coffee. The lounge bar on the right, opening into the dining area, has a nice Jacobean-style carved settle and a housekeeper's chair by a log fire in the big fireplace. There are good solid round picnic-sets as well as the usual rectangular ones out on the terrace, with steps up to a sloping lawn; it's a quiet spot. The bedrooms are comfortable, with thoughtful touches.

🍴 **Using named local suppliers of carefully chosen fresh ingredients and own-grown vegetables, soft fruit and herbs (from their kitchen garden, which they hope will be fully organic by early 2009, and which guests are welcome to look around), the menus might include filled baguettes and focaccias, cream of fennel soup, herefordshire asparagus with soft poached egg and hollandaise sauce, seared fillet of salmon with basil pesto, confit of duck leg, galette of wild mushroom, globe artichoke and garden spinach, and puddings such as dark chocolate and hazelnut brownie or summer fruit pudding with lemon balm ice-cream.** *Starters/Snacks: £4.75 to £9.50. Main Courses: £14.00 to £21.00. Puddings: £6.45*

Free house ~ Licensees William and Janet Hutchings ~ Real ale ~ Bar food ~ (01600) 750235 ~ Children under 9 welcome in restaurant until 7pm ~ Dogs allowed in bar and bedrooms ~ Open 11-11(10 Sun); closed all day Mon in winter ~ Bedrooms: £95B/£105B

Recommended by Mrs A J Evans, Dr C C S Wilson, Guy Vowles, David and Sue Smith, Michael and Jenny Back, William Goodhart, Mr and Mrs R S Ashford, Tom and Ruth Rees, Kevin Jeavons, Alison Turner, Denys Gueroult

ST HILARY   STO173   MAP 6

Bush

Village signposted from A48 E of Cowbridge; CF71 7DP

Cosily old-fashioned village pub, low beams and settles; good food served by helpful staff

In a pretty village not far from Cardiff, this ancient-feeling thatched pub gets a nice mix of locals and visitors and has a welcoming log fire. Comfortable in a quietly stylish way, it has stripped old stone walls, and farmhouse tables and chairs in the low-beamed carpeted lounge bar, while the other bar is pubbier with old settles and pews on aged flagstones. Greene King Abbot, Hancocks HB and a guest or two from a brewery such as Rhymney on handpump or tapped from the cask; TV, cribbage, dominoes and subdued piped music. There are tables and chairs in front, and more in the back garden; reasonable disabled access.

🍴 **The well presented bar food might include lunchtime baguettes and ploughman's, soup, sausages with mash and a pie of the day; also available in the bar except on Sunday, the restaurant menu changes weekly, with starters such as thai fishcake or roasted field mushroom with chargrilled asparagus and parma ham, and main courses such as chargrilled rib-eye of beef, seared fillet of salmon with caramelised bacon salad, creamy chicken with roasted vine tomatoes and penne pasta, and lamb shank. The Sunday lunch, with very good vegetables, is well liked.** *Starters/Snacks: £3.95 to £6.95. Main Courses: £7.95 to £14.95. Puddings: £3.95*

Punch ~ Lease Phil Thomas ~ Real ale ~ Bar food (12-2.30(3 Sun), 6.30-9.30; not Sun evening) ~ Restaurant ~ (01446) 772745 ~ Children welcome ~ Dogs allowed in bar ~ Open 12-11
Recommended by Donna and Roger, Jeremy King

TAL-Y-CAFN   SH7871   MAP 6

Tal-y-Cafn Hotel
A470 Conway—Llanwrst; LL28 5RR

Useful for northern Snowdonia, family-friendly and with efficient staff and sensibly priced bar food

This comfortable and attractive roadside inn stands in scenic surroundings in the Conwy valley and close to Bodnant Garden. Off its entrance lobby are the dining area, the snug and the wood-panelled main bar, with terracotta walls and captains chairs around the low tables on its turkey carpet, and settles round an enormous inglenook fireplace; piped music, TV, games machine, bar billards, children's games and board games. Served by air pressure by efficient staff, Greene King IPA and Speckled Hen and a guest like Bass. You can also sit out in the spacious hedged garden, which has rustic tables and seats by a rose border. It's very popular with families, and there's a large play area. The refurbished bedrooms have wireless internet access. More reports please.

🍴 **Good straightforward bar food includes sandwiches and toasted ciabattas, ploughman's, soup, smoked duck, fishcakes, a roast of the day, steak and mushroom pie, sausages and mash, steaks, haddock and chips, and puddings like cheesecake or bread and butter pudding; they also do a lunchtime set menu (not Sunday) for smaller appetites, with scaled-down courses, at £8.50 for two courses or £9.95 for three; children's menu.**
Starters/Snacks: £3.75 to £5.75. Main Courses: £8.95 to £15.95. Puddings: £4.50

Punch ~ Lease Richard and Anna Scott ~ Bar food (12-9(8 Sun)) ~ Restaurant ~ (01492) 650203 ~ Children welcome ~ Dogs allowed in bedrooms ~ Open 12-12(10.30 Sun); 12-3, 5.30-11 in winter ~ Bedrooms: £39.50S/£69.50S
Recommended by KC, Roger and Cynthia Calrow

TY'N-Y-GROES   SH7773   MAP 6

Groes
B5106 N of village; LL32 8TN
WALES DINING PUB OF THE YEAR

Excelling consistently for food and accommodation, a thoroughly welcoming hotel and bar in northern Snowdonia

Sometimes on Sundays you might be greeted by a harpist at this ancient, neatly kept and hospitable place. Past the hot stove in the entrance area, the rambling, low-beamed and thick-walled rooms are nicely decorated with antique settles and an old sofa, old clocks, portraits, hats and tins hanging from the walls, and fresh flowers. A fine antique fireback is built into one wall, perhaps originally from the formidable fireplace in the back bar, which houses a collection of stone cats as well as cheerful winter log fires. There is also an airy and verdant conservatory. As well as an ale from the family's own Great Orme brewery a couple of miles away, they have Marstons Burton and Tetleys on handpump, and several bottled Great Orme beers too; piped music. The spotless and well equipped bedroom suites (some have terraces or balconies) have gorgeous views, and in summer it's a pleasure to sit outside in the pretty back garden with its flower-filled hayracks; there are more seats on the flower-decked roadside. They also rent out a well appointed wooden cabin, idyllically placed nearby, as well as a cottage in the historic centre of Conwy.

Pubs in outstandingly attractive surroundings are listed at the back of the book.

🍽 Using lamb and salmon from the Conwy Valley, and game birds from local shoots, and the hotel's own bread and home-grown herbs, well presented dishes might include soup, sandwiches, sausages and mash, gammon and egg, pumpkin and ricotta ravioli, poached salmon with hollandaise sauce and steaks, with daily specials such as game casserole; puddings could feature as white chocolate panna cotta or sticky toffee pudding. *Starters/Snacks: £4.50 to £12.25. Main Courses: £8.95 to £19.50. Puddings: £5.25*

Free house ~ Licensee Dawn Humphreys ~ Real ale ~ Bar food ~ Restaurant ~ (01492) 650545 ~ Children welcome until 7pm ~ Dogs allowed in bedrooms ~ Open 12-3, 6-11, 12-11 Sat, Sun ~ Bedrooms: £79B/£95B

Recommended by Steve and Sarah Eardley, Margaret and Jeff Graham, Mike and Mary Carter, Rodney and Norma Stubington, Neil Whitehead, Victoria Anderson, David Glynne-Jones, Richard and Mary Bailey, Joan E Hilditch, Carol and Phil Byng, Denys Gueroult, Di and Mike Gillam, Clive Watkin, Phil and Jane Hodson, Simon Daws, Neil and Angela Huxter, Dr and Mrs P Truelove

USK   SO3700 MAP 6

Nags Head 🍽 ♀
The Square; NP15 1BH

Spotlessly kept by the same family for many years, traditional in style, as warm a reception as could be hoped for, with good food and drinks

The Key family, who have now been landlords here for over 40 years, generate praise from readers from one year to the next: 'a smashing pub' and 'standards never drop, warm welcome, lovely atmosphere, our favourite pub' are typical comments. With a friendly chatty atmosphere, the beautifully kept traditional main bar has lots of well polished tables and chairs packed under its beams (some with farming tools), lanterns or horsebrasses and harness attached, as well as leatherette wall benches, and various sets of sporting prints and local pictures – look out for the original deeds to the pub. Tucked away at the front is an intimate little corner with some african masks, while on the other side of the room a passageway leads to a new dining area converted from the old coffee bar; piped music. There may be prints for sale, and perhaps a knot of sociable locals. They do several wines by the glass, along with four ales on handpump – from Brains Bitter, Bread of Heaven, Rev James or SA and Buckleys Best. The centre of Usk is full of pretty hanging baskets and flowers in summer, and the church is well worth a look.

🍽 Popular, generously served and reasonably priced food includes soup, grilled sardines, frog legs in hot provençale sauce, rabbit pie, steak pie, chicken in red wine, and vegetable pancake, with specials such as brace of boned quail with stuffing and sauce or poached salmon. You can book tables, some of which may be candlelit at night; nice proper linen napkins. *Starters/Snacks: £4.00 to £6.00. Main Courses: £7.50 to £15.00. Puddings: £3.75 to £4.50*

Free house ~ Licensee the Key family ~ Real ale ~ Bar food (12-2, 5.30-9.30) ~ Restaurant ~ (01291) 672820 ~ Children welcome ~ Dogs welcome ~ Open 10.30-3, 5.30-11; 11-3, 6-10.30 Sun

Recommended by David Howe, Dr and Mrs C W Thomas, Reg Fowle, Helen Rickwood, Mike and Mary Carter, Eryl and Keith Dykes, Andrew and Sian Williams, John and Helen Rushton, Sue and Ken Le Prevost, Dr C C S Wilson, Andy and Jill Kassube, Graham Cooper, Mick and CarolCordell, Roger and Anne Newbury, Michael and Maggie Betton

---

A very few pubs try to make you leave a credit card at the bar, as a sort of deposit if you order food. They are not entitled to do this. The credit card firms and banks which issue them warn you not to let them out of your sight. If someone behind the counter used your card fraudulently, the card company or bank could in theory hold you liable, because of your negligence in letting a stranger hang on to your card. Suggest instead that if they feel the need for security, they 'swipe' your card and give it back to you. And do name and shame the pub to us.

LUCKY DIP

Besides the fully inspected pubs, you might like to try these Lucky Dips recommended to us and described by readers (if you do, please send us reports: feedback@thegoodpubguide.co.uk).

ANGLESEY

MENAI BRIDGE [SH5572]
Bridge Inn LL59 5DT [bridge roundabout, Telford Rd (A5/A545); aka Tafarn y Bont]: Spotless and attractive, with wood floors and pine mum in evidence, bay windows, four well kept english ales (may offer tasters), some emphasis on food side, with rather close-set tables in back dining room and bright conservatory; small two-level back terrace, more seating out in front *(Gordon and Margaret Ormondroyd, Mark, Amanda, Luke and Jake Sheard)*
Gazelle LL59 5PD [Glyngarth; A545, half way towards Beaumaris]: Hotel and restaurant rather than pub, in outstanding waterside situation looking across to Snowdonia, lively main bar, smaller rooms off, enjoyable food inc fresh fish, Robinsons real ale; children welcome, steep and aromatic mediterranean garden behind, good bedrooms *(Dave Webster, Sue Holland, Mark, Amanda, Luke and Jake Sheard, LYM)*
RHOSCOLYN [SH2675]
White Eagle LL65 2NJ [off B4545 S of Holyhead]: Reopened 2007 after major refurbishment, splendid remote setting with panoramic views towards Snowdonia from dining area, good food (all day in summer), relaxed upmarket feel, well kept real ale; children welcome, good large garden, lane down to beach, open all day in summer *(Pat and Tony Hinkins)*

CLWYD

BODFARI [SJ0970]
Downing Arms LL16 4DW [A541]: Enjoyable food inc wide choice of fish, Marstons-related ales, friendly service, teapot collection in restaurant; handy for Offa's Dyke Path *(Dave Braisted)*
CARROG [SJ1143]
Grouse LL21 9AT [B5436, signed off A5 Llangollen—Corwen]: Small unpretentious pub with superb views over River Dee and beyond from bay window and balcony, Lees real ales, food all day from sandwiches up, friendly young staff, local pictures, pool in games room; piped music, narrow turn into car park; wheelchair access (side door a bit narrow), tables in pretty walled garden (covered terrace for smokers), handy for Llangollen steam railway, bedrooms *(Edward Leetham, Michael and Jenny Back, Ann and Tony Bennett-Hughes)*
COEDWAY [SJ3414]
☆ *Old Hand & Diamond* SY5 9AR [B4393 W of Shrewsbury]: Charming old pub, beams, panelling and stripped stone in carpeted bar, welcoming landlord and friendly staff, enjoyable competitively priced food from

familiar favourites to interesting specials and vegetarian dishes, succulent local lamb and game, a local real ale, nice wine, light and airy restaurant with local pictures; tables under cocktail parasols on side terrace, lots of climbing roses and hanging baskets, attractive beamed bedrooms *(Jennifer Banks, Louise Gibbons)*
DENBIGH [SJ0566]
Plough LL16 3TF [Bridge St]: Comfortable and welcoming, with good value generous home-made food *(John and Mhegs Hudson)*
GLYN CEIRIOG [SJ2037]
Glyn Valley LL20 7EU: Comfortable lounge bar with blazing fire, interesting local steam tramway memorabilia in dining room, bargain pubby food, Bass, good service *(Richard and Jean Green)*
GWERNYMYNYDD [SJ2162]
Rainbow CH7 5LG [Ruthin Rd (A494)]: Popular for enjoyable food inc some enterprising dishes, meal deals before 7, warm welcome, no piped music *(KC)*
GWYTHERIN [SH8761]
Lion LL22 8UU [B5384 W of Denbigh]: Isolated small village pub sympathetically reworked inside – warmly contemporary, with welcoming enthusiastic licensees, good enterprising pub food and locally popular small restaurant area with log fire, another in attractive main bar, good wines by the glass, two real ales; garden seating planned, nice walks, five good bedrooms, cl wkdy lunchtimes and Mon *(David Johnson, Catherine and Richard Griffin)*
HALKYN [SJ2070]
Blue Bell CH8 8DL [Rhosesmor Rd (B5123 S)]: Good changing farm ciders and perries (often their own cider too), a good value beer brewed just for them in Flint and particularly well kept changing ales, wknd lunches from light dishes to substantial meals using local supplies, warm welcome, real fires, no piped music – live Thurs/Fri, jazz Sun lunchtime; fine spot on Halkyn Mountain, remarkable views in clear weather, cl wkdy lunchtimes, open all day wknds *(anon)*
HIGHER KINNERTON [SJ3261]
Royal Oak CH4 9BE [Kinnerton Lane, off A55/A5104 SW of Chester; also signed off A483]: Ancient picturesque coaching inn with good choice of interesting food in dining area (obliging landlord helps adapt menu for choosy children), decent wines, well kept Timothy Taylors, prompt friendly service, lots of small pictures, log fires, settles and cosy armchairs, low oak beams hung with jugs, teapots, copper kettles and chamber-pots, interesting collection of soda syphons; tables in small garden *(Mark, Amanda, Luke and Jake Sheard)*

LLAN-Y-PWLL [SJ3651]

Gredington Arms LL13 9SD [Holt Rd]:
Recently refurbished, with well kept Hydes,
good value food inc good Sun lunch,
reasonably priced wines, smiling landlady
and ever-working landlord; garden bar and
outside tables with good views
(Jack Pridding)

LLANARMON-YN-IAL [SJ1856]

Raven CH7 4QE [B5431 NW of Wrexham]:
18th-c beamed country local with well kept
local Facers ales, two woodburners, food in
bar and restaurant; seats outside, attractive
village, unspoilt countryside, bedrooms *(LYM,
Edward Leetham)*

LLANASA [SJ1081]

Red Lion CH8 9NE: Friendly two-bar pub in
the hills above Prestatyn, well kept Websters
Yorkshire and two mainstream guest beers,
good value generous food from sandwiches
up, log fire, pool room; walkers welcome
(Brian and Anna Marsden)

LLANDEGLA [SJ1952]

Crown LL11 3AD [Ruthin Rd (A525)]: Quickly
served good value usual food in comfortable
compact bar with welcoming staff and
locals, Lees real ale, good set of Hogarth
prints, popular restaurant; large pub dog; on
Offa's Dyke Path *(KC)*

Plough LL11 3AB [Ruthin Rd]: Cosy civilised
dining pub, wide choice of enjoyable food all
day inc notable fish pie and two-for-one
bargains, efficient staff, Robinsons, large
dining room; unobtrusive piped music;
nr Offa's Dyke Path *(KC)*

LLANGOLLEN [SJ2044]

Abbey Grange LL20 8DD [A542 N]: More
hotel than pub, but welcoming, in beautiful
spot with superb views nr Valle Crucis Abbey;
family bar (all day, at least in summer) with
moderately priced food from good bacon
sandwiches up, Banks's ales, evening
restaurant; picnic-sets outside, comfortable
bedrooms *(Dave Braisted)*

Bridge End LL20 8RY [Mill St; A539 N of
bridge]: Good value food inc outstanding
ploughman's, well kept Robinsons; facing
river *(Chris Evans)*

LLOC [SJ1476]

Rock CH8 8RD [St Asaph Rd (A5151)]: Nicely
refurbished, popular for interesting choice of
generous fresh food in dining room or cosy
bar with good log fire *(KC)*

MAESHAFN [SJ2060]

Miners Arms CH7 5LR [off A494 SW of Mold]:
Small cheerful relaxed local, well kept
Theakstons and a guest beer, good value
simple pub food in bar and dining room,
theatre and jazz memorabilia; walkers
welcome *(Tony Goff)*

MOLD [SJ2364]

Bryn Awel CH7 1BL [A541 Denbigh Rd nr
Bailey Hill]: Hillside modern hotel with
picture-window country views in comfortable
good-sized dining area, welcoming attentive
service, good value food inc thai dishes,
cheerful bustling carpeted lounge bar; may
be piped music; neat bedrooms *(KC)*

We Three Loggerheads CH7 5LH [Ruthin Rd
(A494, 3 miles towards Ruthin)]:
Comfortable two-level bar, warm and
friendly, with tasty and generous if not
cheap food, well kept Wells & Youngs;
piped music; side terrace overlooking
river, open all day at least in summer
*(John and Mhegs Hudson, Mrs Maricar Jagger,
LYM)*

OVERTON [SJ3741]

White Horse LL13 0DT [High St]: Good
refurbishment under new licensees, small
choice of enjoyable pubby food, two real
ales, exemplary lavatories; children welcome
(Deb and John Arthur)

OVERTON BRIDGE [SJ3542]

☆ *Cross Foxes* LL13 0DR [A539 W of Overton,
nr Erbistock]: Appealingly modernised
waterside dining pub with friendly staff,
good value food all day, linked but distinct
areas with lots of pictures and variously
sized tables, big candles at night, good log
fires, Banks's, Marstons and guest beers,
splendid range of wines by the glass and of
spirits, good coffees; children welcome, dogs
allowed in bar, crazy-paved terrace above
lawn to River Dee, play area, open all day
(Andrew Walker, Mr and Mrs J Palmer, LYM)

PENYFFORDD [SJ3062]

Millstone CH4 0JE [Hawarden Rd]:
Contemporary largely brown interior for
Victorian building, friendly accommodating
staff, decent promptly served food inc good
value children's meals, emphasis on wines
and premium lagers (not real ales); pleasant
decking outside *(Mark, Amanda, Luke and
Jake Sheard)*

PONTBLYDDYN [SJ2761]

New Inn CH7 4HR [Corwen Rd (A5104, just
S of A541 3 miles SE of Mold)]: Interesting
consistently good food in unassuming
building's pleasant upstairs dining room,
good service; piped music *(KC)*

RHYDYMWYN [SJ2166]

Antelope CH7 5HE [Denbigh Rd (A541)]:
Pleasant bar and attractive restaurant, good
choice of satisfying food; piped music *(KC)*

ST ASAPH [SJ0374]

Bod Erw LL17 0LA [The Roe]: Dining pub
with wide choice inc daily-changing evening
menu, help-yourself salad bar, pleasant spot
(KC)

ST GEORGE [SH9775]

Kinmel Arms LL22 9BP [off A547 or B5381
SE of Abergele]: Dining pub tucked away in
attractive village, interesting 17th-c former
posting inn with several neat and tidy
refurbished rooms, nice mix of tables and
chairs, rugs on stripped wood, wide range of
affordable modern food from lunchtime
baguettes and dutch-style open sandwiches
up, friendly staff, changing real ales, good
choice of wines by the glass, conservatory;
good contemporary bedrooms, cl Mon
(Keith and Sue Ward)

WREXHAM [SJ3350]

Horse & Jockey LL11 1BD [Hope St]: Busy
19th-c thatched local, five small linked low-

beamed rooms with lots of potential around central servery, Greene King Abbot and Old Speckled Hen and Tetleys, reasonably priced pubby food 9-4 (Sat 10-3, not Sun) from sandwiches and baked potatoes up, back dining area; can be a bit noisy – two TVs, piped music – and has in past been rather rough; open all day *(Roger and Anne Newbury)*

DYFED

ABERYSTWYTH [SN6777]

Yr Hen Orsaf SY23 1LN [Alexandra Rd]: High-ceilinged Wetherspoons in concourse of Cambrian Railways station, their usual food and drink bargains, efficient service, several different areas, platform view; terrace tables by the buffer stops, open all day from breakfast *(B and M Kendall, Reg Fowle, Helen Rickwood)*

AMROTH [SN1607]

Amroth Arms SA67 8NG: Neat bar with good chatty atmosphere, Cambrian or Felinfoel Double Dragon, friendly staff, charity books and videos, pool area, good value dining room; sea-view pavement tables *(Reg Fowle, Helen Rickwood)*

ANGLE [SM8703]

☆ *Old Point House* SA71 5AS [signed off B4320 in village, along rough rough waterside track; East Angle Bay]: Dating from 14th c, unspoilt, comfortable and in idyllic spot overlooking Milford Haven (getting there inc drive over beach is part of the pleasure), with friendly down-to-earth atmosphere, good simple food (almost all fresh local fish), Felinfoel Double Dragon, cheap soft drinks, flagstoned bar with open fire, small lounge bar, lots of charm and character, run by local lifeboat coxswain – many photographs and charts; home-made chutneys and sauces for charity, three pub labradors; plenty of tables and ancient slate seats out by the shore *(Reg Fowle, Helen Rickwood, Richard Pitcher)*

BOSHERSTON [SR9694]

St Govans Country Inn SA71 5DN [off B4319 S of Pembroke]: Big modernised open-plan bar, cheery and simple, with several changing real ales, good climbing photographs and murals of local beauty spots, log fire in large stone fireplace, dominoes, board games, pool (winter only), cheap unpretentious food; piped music, TV, games machine; children welcome, picnic-sets on front terrace, good value bedrooms (car park if you stay), handy for water-lily lakes, beach and cliffy coast *(Ian and Anne Read, LYM)*

BROAD HAVEN [SM8614]

☆ *Druidstone Hotel* SA62 3NE [N of village on coast rd, bear left for about 1.5 miles then follow sign left to Druidstone Haven – inn a sharp left turn after another 0.5 mile; OS Sheet 157 map ref 862168, marked as Druidston Villa]: Cheerfully informal, the family's former country house in a grand

spot above the sea, individualistic and relaxed, ruled out of main entries by its club licence (you can't go for just a drink, must book to eat or stay there); terrific views, inventive cooking with fresh often organic ingredients, helpful efficient service, folksy cellar bar with local real ale tapped from the cask, good wines, country wines and other drinks, ceilidhs and folk events, chummy dogs (dogs welcomed), all sorts of sporting activities from boules to sand-yachting; attractive high-walled garden, spacious homely bedrooms, even an eco-friendly chalet, cl Nov and Jan, restaurant cl Sun evening *(Mark Flynn, Michael Quine, Colin Moore, Adam, LYM, John and Enid Morris, Pauline and Derek Hodgkiss)*

CAPEL BANGOR [SN6580]

Tynllidiart Arms SY23 3LR [A44]: Quaint roadside cottage with woodburner in big stripped-stone bare-boards bar, has its own tiny brewery (in what used to be the gents') with four well kept ales inc a Stout, enterprising food from open kitchen in large two-floor dining area, friendly young staff, nice atmosphere; well behaved children and dogs allowed, small smart terrace *(Mike and Mary Carter, Viv and Glenn Fisher)*

CAREW [SN0403]

☆ *Carew Inn* SA70 8SL [A4075, just off A477]: Wide choice of enjoyable food, well kept Brains Rev James and a guest beer, friendly staff, unpretentious old-fashioned furnishings in small linked beamed rooms with open fires and interesting prints, cosy upstairs dining room, traditional games; very busy in summer, piped music, live Thurs and summer Sun; children and dogs welcome, back garden overlooking spectacular castle ruins, outdoor heaters and summer marquee, good play area, more tables out in front, open all day wknds and summer *(the Didler, Bob and Angela Brooks, Colin Moore, LYM, Pat Crabb)*

CWM GWAUN [SN0333]

☆ *Dyffryn Arms* SA65 9SE [Cwm Gwaun and Pontfaen signed off B4313 E of Fishguard]: Classic rural timewarp, virtually the social centre for this lush green valley, very relaxed, basic and idiosyncratic, with much-loved veteran landlady (her farming family have run it since 1840, and she's been in charge for well over one-third of that time); 1920s front parlour with plain deal furniture inc rocking chair and draughts boards inlaid into tables, coal fire, Bass, Carlsberg Burton or Tetleys served by jug through a sliding hatch, low prices, World War I prints and posters, darts; pretty countryside, open more or less all day (may close if no customers) *(Giles and Annie Francis, the Didler, Richard Pitcher, Herbert and Susan Verity, Colin Moore, LYM)*

CWMANN [SN6143]

Tafarn Jem SA48 8HF [S on A482]: Old drovers' pub, oasis in something of a pub desert, decent food and beer *(Roger Berry)*

FELINDRE FARCHOG [SN0939]
☆ **Olde Salutation** SA41 3UY [A487 Newport—Cardigan]: Well extended pub with good value bar food from toasties and baguettes to local beef and seasonal sea trout, Brains Rev James, Felinfoel Double Dragon and a guest beer, good wines by the glass, genial landlord and friendly staff, stylish conservatory restaurant (Thurs-Sat); disabled access and facilities, comfortable bedroom extension, good breakfast, fishing and good walks by nearby River Nevern (*Paul A Moore, D S and J M Jackson, Colin Moore, Steve Godfrey, Blaise Vyner*)

FISHGUARD [SM9537]
☆ **Fishguard Arms** SA65 9HJ [Main St (A487)]: Tiny front bar with changing real ales served by jug at unusually high counter, warmly friendly staff, open fire, rugby photographs, traditional games in back room; open all day Sun, cl Mon, also perhaps lunchtime Tues and Sat (*the Didler, Blaise Vyner, LYM*)
Royal Oak SA65 9HA [Market Sq, Upper Town]: Dark beams, stripped stone and panelling, big picture-window dining extension, pictures commemorating defeat here of bizarre french raid in 1797, Brains and changing guest beers from bar counter carved with welsh dragon, good value fresh generous food, woodburner; bar billiards, games machine; pleasant terrace, open all day (*the Didler, BB, Simon Watkins*)

GWBERT [SN1649]
Gwbert Hotel SA43 1PP [B4548]: Bargain pubby food from sandwiches up in seaside hotel's recently updated comfortably modern bar and sea-view bistro, a real ale, efficient friendly service, great estuary views; tables out on decking, 16 bedrooms (*Colin Moore*)

HAVERFORDWEST [SM9515]
☆ **Georges** SA61 1NH [Market St]: A one-off, mixing long narrow celtic-theme bar with eclectibles shop and small coffee bar/teashop area, relaxed and idiosyncratic atmosphere underlined by fancy mirrors, glistening crystals and dangly hangings, clogs, aromatherapy and much more for sale; Brains SA or Rev James and a guest beer, good value wines esp New World, quick cheerful service even when busy, larger upstairs restaurant (must book), interesting home-made food using good meat, their own fresh veg and good fish and vegetarian ranges; no dogs; lovely walled garden, open 10.30-5.30, all day Sat, cl Sun (*Steve Godfrey, Richard and Judy Winn, Richard Bowen*)

JEFFREYSTON [SN0806]
Jeffreyston Inn SA68 0RE: Good local atmosphere, friendly staff, Brains Dark, modern open-plan seating area; some live jazz, sports TV; good walks nearby (*Reg Fowle, Helen Rickwood*)

LAMPETER [SN5748]
Black Lion Royal SA48 7BG [High St]: Old-fashioned coaching inn with ample good value food, pleasant helpful staff, public bar beyond coach entry arch; 15 comfortable bedrooms, some sharing bath (*Patrick and Daphne Darley*)

LITTLE HAVEN [SM8512]
☆ **Castle** SA62 3UF: Good value unpretentious pub well placed by green looking over sandy bay (lovely sunsets), hearty helpings of good inexpensive food inc local fish (best to book for meals), efficient cheerful service even when busy, good choice of wines by the glass, Brains, bare-boards bar and carpeted dining area with big oak tables, beams, some stripped stone, castle prints, pool in back area; children welcome, front picnic-sets, two good sea-view bedrooms, open all day from 9.30 (*John Rees, Mark Flynn, Mr and Mrs A H Young, Alan Sutton, Adam, Paul Goldman, Pat Crabb*)
☆ **Swan** SA62 3UL [Point Rd]: Attractive seaside pub reopened 2007 after long closure and major refurbishment, up-to-date bar with leather settees and comfortable alcove seating on new wood laminate floor, window tables overlooking sandy bay, fires each end, Brains and another real ale, upstairs dining room; sports TV (*LYM, Ewan and Moira McCall, Chris and Angela Buckell*)

LLANDDAROG [SN5016]
☆ **Butchers Arms** SA32 8NS: Ancient heavily black-beamed local with three smallish eating areas rambling off small central bar, cheerily welcoming atmosphere, charming friendly service, generous reasonably priced home cooking from sandwiches through hearty country and welsh dishes to nice puddings (menu willingly adapted for children), Felinfoel Best and Double Dragon tapped from the cask, good wines by the glass, conventional pub furniture, fairylights and candles in bottles, open woodburner in biggish fireplace; piped music; tables outside, delightful window boxes, cl Mon (*Tom Evans, Bill and Lynne Boon, BB*)

LLANDEILO [SN6226]
☆ **Angel** SA19 6EN [Rhosmaen St]: Young chef/landlord doing reasonably priced home-made food using fresh produce from baguettes, well filled pitta breads and lunchtime bargain specials to wide range of fish, special Thurs evening buffet, imaginative dishes in comfortable back bistro with thriving civilised atmosphere, attractive open-plan U-shaped bar, friendly helpful young staff, Brains and local ales; tables outside, cl Sun (*Guy and Carol Austin Potter, John Rees*)
☆ **Cottage** SA19 6SD [Pentrefelin (A40 towards Carmarthen – brown sign from Llandeilo)]: Large smart open-plan beamed dining pub, comfortable and welcoming, with huge log fire and lots of horsey prints, plates and brasses, generous good value food from baguettes to good local fish, welsh black beef and delicious puddings, Brains and guest beers, decent house wines, quick thoughtful service, well appointed back dining room; piped music (*Tom Evans, Angus and Rosemary Campbell*)

LLANDOVERY [SN7634]
Red Lion SA20 0AA [Market Sq]: One basic welcoming room with no bar, changing ales tapped from the cask, jovial landlord; restricted opening – may be just Sat, and Fri evening *(BB, the Didler)*

LLANEGWAD [SN5321]
☆ *Halfway* SA32 7NL [A40 Llandeilo— Carmarthen]: Smart popular dining pub (worth booking in season, esp at wknds), imaginative elegantly presented food, good wine choice, nice décor, second upstairs dining area with views; has been cl Sun evening and Mon *(R and Z Davies)*

LLANRHYSTUD [SN5369]
Black Lion SY23 5DG [A487]: Pleasantly refurbished, with well kept Brains and guest ales, good value food (very popular wknds), efficient helpful staff *(Dom Bradshaw, Helen Castle)*

LLANYCHAER [SM9835]
Bridge End SA65 9TB [Bridge St (B4313 SE of Fishguard)]: Former watermill in attractive hamlet, friendly enthusiastic staff, good choice of food from lunchtime snacks to evening meals inc popular Sun lunch, one or two real ales *(Colin Moore)*

NARBERTH [SN1114]
Kirkland SA67 7BU [St James St]: Welcoming old-style local, settles, low stools and bric-a-brac in tiled bar, friendly long-serving landlady, three well kept Felinfoel ales, comfortable lounge bar with pool; some live music; pleasant garden *(Steven and Victoria James)*

NEWCHAPEL [SN2239]
Fynnone Arms SA37 0EH [B4332]: Under new management, recently reopened after tasteful refurbishment, reasonably priced food using local produce, a well kept real ale, spacious beamed bar and restaurant area *(Colin Moore)*

NEWPORT [SN0539]
☆ *Golden Lion* SA42 0SY [East St (A487)]: Nicely refurbished pub with friendly new chef/landlord and landlady, tasty well priced food inc local veg and welsh black beef, several well kept real ales, good local atmosphere in cosy series of linked rooms, some distinctive old settles, games bar with pool; children welcome, good disabled access and facilities, quiet garden behind, good value comfortable bedrooms, big breakfast *(Steve Godfrey, Norman and Sarah Keeping, Kevin Murphy, Ellie O'Mahoney, LYM)*
☆ *Royal Oak* SA42 0TA [West St (A487)]: Bustling and well run sizeable pub with friendly helpful landlady and staff, good generous food inc lunchtime light dishes, local lamb and lots of authentic curries, Tues OAP lunch, Greene King and guest beers, children welcome in lounge with eating areas, separate stone and slate bar with pool and games, upstairs dining room; some tables outside, easy walk to beach and coast path *(Colin Moore, John and Enid Morris, Blaise Vyner)*

PEMBROKE DOCK [SM9603]
Flying Boat SA72 6JL [Queen St]: Unpretentious pub with quickly changing well kept ales (huge pump clip collection), friendly landlord and customers, lots of flying boat pictures *(Dave Braisted)*
Shipwright SA72 6JX [Front St]: Good atmosphere, enjoyable food, plenty of changing real ales; overlooks estuary, five mins from Ireland ferry terminal *(D and M T Ayres-Regan)*

PEMBROKE FERRY [SM9704]
☆ *Ferry Inn* SA72 6UD [below A477 toll bridge]: Former sailors' haunt by the Cleddau estuary, lots of seafaring pictures and memorabilia, open fire and sea views, Bass, Felinfoel Double Dragon and a guest beer under light blanket pressure, some menu emphasis on fish; games machine, unobtrusive piped music; children welcome, dogs allowed in bar, tables on terrace *(Brian McBurnie, Steve and Liz Tilley, LYM)*

PENRHIWLLAN [SN3641]
Penrhiwllan Inn SA44 5NG: Reworked as contemporary dining pub using traditional materials well, good choice of enjoyable food, good value wines, eating areas on different levels off quarry tiled and flagstoned bar, nice furnishings old and new; back verandah with good views *(Chris Wall)*

PORTHGAIN [SM8132]
Shed SA62 5BN: In what looks to be a seaside former boat shed, not a pub but does sell beer and is well worth knowing for good fresh fish in upstairs evening bistro (not winter Sun-Weds), daytime tearoom *(Simon Watkins, MDN)*

ROBESTON WATHEN [SN0915]
Bridge Inn SA67 8EJ [just off A40 – B4314 towards Narberth]: Cottagey and comfortable, with enjoyable local food inc tempting puddings, good choice of wines by the glass, real ale, friendly attentive staff, large eating area; children welcome *(Victoria Moorhouse)*

SAUNDERSFOOT [SN1304]
☆ *Royal Oak* SA69 9HA [Wogan Terrace (B4316)]: Splendid position by harbour, friendly service, several well kept changing ales in comfortable carpeted lounge bar and small public bar, generous popular food (not Sun evening) in dining area – go for the fresh local fish when they have it; piped music, TV; children welcome, tables out on heated terrace making the most of the view, open all day till late *(Steve Godfrey, LYM, the Didler, Mrs Sheila Pearley, Reg Fowle, Helen Rickwood)*
Wisemans Bridge Inn SA69 9AU: Welcoming beach pub with welcoming efficient service, enjoyable honest food inc good fish choice, new dining area, sea views; separate bar with sports TV *(Reg Fowle, Helen Rickwood)*

SOLVA [SM8024]
☆ *Cambrian* SA62 6UU [Lower Solva; off A487 Haverfordwest—St Davids]: Attractive neatly kept open-plan dining pub with enjoyable food all day inc popular Sun lunch, well kept

ales such as Brains Revd James, courteous efficient service, log fires; piped music; children welcome now (new management since 2006), nice spot nr harbour and art and crafts shops (Adam, Simon Watkins, Steve Godfrey, Philip Lane)

Harbour Inn SA62 6UT [Main St]: Three-bar beamed pub coping patiently with the holiday family crowds, wide choice of reasonably priced food from quickly served sandwiches up, Brains beers, lots of local pictures, pool in separate bar; piped music; plenty of tables on suntrap terrace, open all day (Herbert and Susan Verity, Edward Leetham, Norma and Noel Thomas)

ST DAVID'S [SM7525]

☆ **Farmers Arms** SA62 6RF [Goat St]: Bustling old-fashioned low-ceilinged pub by cathedral gate, cheerful and unpretentiously pubby, mainly drinking on the left and eating on the right, central servery with well kept Brains Rev James, generous tasty good value food from baguettes and ploughman's with local cheeses to steaks and Sun lunch, lively friendly young staff, chatty landlord and locals, pool room; they may try to keep your credit card while you eat, TV for rugby; cathedral view from large tables on big back suntrap terrace, and lack of car park means no tour bus groups, open all day (Andy and Alice Jordan, Reg Fowle, Helen Rickwood, Paul Goldman, Tim and Mark Allen, R and Z Davies)

Grove SA62 6SB [High St]: Plain comfortable friendly bars with own side entrance behind hotel and restaurant, good value generous food, well kept Brains Rev James and local farm cider, log fires; piped music, quiz night; good parking, garden tables, bedrooms, open all day (Peter and Anne Hollindale)

STACKPOLE [SR9896]

☆ **Stackpole Inn** SA71 5DF [off B4319 S of Pembroke]: Friendly new licensees here in L-shaped dining pub on four levels, enjoyable food inc imaginative dishes and plenty of local produce, Brains Rev James, Felinfoel Best and Greene King Abbot, quick cheerful service, neat uncluttered décor with light oak furnishings and ash beams in low ceilings, shove-ha'penny and dominoes; piped music; children welcome, disabled access and facilities, attractive garden, good woodland and coastal walks in the Stackpole estate, four-bedroom annexe (Angus and Rosemary Campbell, LYM, Mark Farrington, Reg Fowle, Helen Rickwood, Brian McBurnie, Pat Crabb)

TEMPLETON [SN1111]

Boars Head SA67 8SD [A478]: Spotless recently refurbished pub with large new dining area, friendly staff, comfortable atmosphere (leather seating as well as wooden tables and chairs), Marstons and a guest beer, pool, juke box in separate part; terrace tables (Reg Fowle, Helen Rickwood)

TENBY [SN1300]

Hope & Anchor SA70 7AX [Julian St]: Pleasant pub nr seafront, friendly staff,

generous well presented food (all day at least in summer) from sandwiches to fresh crab and fish, three or four changing ales, coal fire, upstairs family dining room, terrace tables, open all day (Richard Pitcher)

Imperial SA70 7HR [The Paragon]: Substantial hotel on cliffs, good value bar food from sandwiches and baked potatoes to good fish and chips (lunch stops 1.45), decent beer range, superb view of Caldy Island from bar and particularly terrace; comfortable bedrooms (Paul Goldman)

Plantagenet House SA70 7BX [Quay Hill]: Good atmosphere in well renovated early medieval building, stripped stonework, tile and board floors, log fire (marvellous old chimney), friendly staff, downstairs bar, good upstairs restaurant with cane furniture, candles on tables, Flowers IPA; piped music, fine Victorian lavatories; open all day in season, adjacent Tudor Merchant's House (NT) well worth visiting then; has been cl lunchtime out of season (Reg Fowle, Helen Rickwood)

GLAMORGAN

ABERDULAIS [SS7799]

Dulais Rock SA10 8EY [A4109; car park shared with Aberdulais Falls (NT)]: Prettily placed ancient former mill doing well under new owners, good value food all day with smarter evening menu, two or three good beers, bar with antique wood and leather, lighter plusher dining lounge; children welcome, three bedrooms (Michael and Alison Sandy)

BISHOPSTON [SS5789]

☆ **Joiners Arms** SA3 3EJ [Bishopston Rd, just off B4436 SW of Swansea]: Thriving local brewing its own good value Swansea ales, usually three of these and four well kept changing guest beers, decent wines, good value generous simple food from paninis to succulent steaks, friendly young staff, unpretentious quarry-tiled bar with massive solid fuel stove, comfortable lounge, local paintings; big-screen TV for rugby; children welcome, open all day (LYM, Susan and Nigel Brookes, Michael and Alison Sandy)

BLACK PILL [SS6190]

Woodman SA3 5AS [Mumbles Rd (A4067 Swansea—Mumbles)]: Attractive old seafront dining pub, well divided inside, with good value food all day from sandwiches and baguettes to fresh local fish, Courage Directors and guests such as Adnams and Greene King, good choice of wines by the glass in two sizes, good service (though can get very busy), hundreds of wine bottles above panelled dado, airy restaurant and conservatory; car park across busy rd; children welcome in some areas, next to beautiful Clyne Gardens (great rhododendrons in May) (Anne Morris)

BRIDGEND [SS9082]

Ty-Risha CF32 9SN [Pen-y-Cae, handy for M4 junction 36]: Big neatly kept rambling dining pub, Brains ales and well priced food; garden picnic-sets *(Michael and Alison Sandy)*

CARDIFF [ST1776]

Black Pig CF11 9HW [Sophia Cl; aka Y Mochyn Du]: Enjoyable food, well kept Brains and guest beers, good atmosphere, interesting décor; terrace tables, open all day *(the Didler)*

☆ *Cayo Arms* CF11 9LL [Cathedral Rd]: Helpful young staff, well kept Tomos Watkins ales with a guest beer, good value food all day from ciabattas to full meals inc Sun lunch, daily papers, pubby front bar with comfortable side area in Edwardian style, more modern back dining area; piped music, big-screen TV in one part, very busy wknds; tables out in front, more in yard behind (with parking), good value bedrooms, open all day *(the Didler, Dr and Mrs A K Clarke, Bruce Bird)*

Vulcan CF24 2FH [Adam St]: Largely untouched Victorian local surrounded by redevelopment, well kept Brains, good value lunches (not Sun) in sedate lounge with some original features inc ornate fireplace, maritime pictures in lively public bar with darts, dominoes, cards and juke box; open all day, cl Sun pm *(the Didler)*

COITY [SS9281]

Six Bells CF35 6BH [Heol West Plas]: Recently well upgraded, expanding good value menu inc good pies, puddings and popular Sun lunch, friendly staff; tables out by road opp 12th-c castle *(R C Vincent)*

DINAS POWIS [ST1571]

Star CF64 4DE [Station Rd]: Attractively refurbished village pub with bargain pubby food, smart efficient service, Brains ale, heavy beams, stripped stone and panelling, modernised restaurant; children welcome *(Tom Evans, LYM, Sarah and Peter Gooderham)*

GROES-FAEN [ST0781]

Dynevor Arms CF72 8NS [handy for M4 junction 34 via A4119]: Quick food and bar service even though busy, friendly staff, Adnams Broadside, Bass, Hancocks HB and St Austell Proper Job, lots of whisky-water jugs and plates; quiet piped music, silent games machine *(Jeremy King)*

KENFIG [SS8081]

☆ *Prince of Wales* CF33 4PR [2.2 miles from M4 junction 37; A4229 towards Porthcawl, then right when dual carriageway narrows on bend, signed Maudlam and Kenfig]: Interesting ancient local with historic sand dunes, plenty of individuality, well kept Bass and a guest beer tapped from the cask, good choice of malt whiskies and decent wines, enjoyable straightforward food, log fire in chatty panelled room off main bar (which has another), lots of wreck pictures, stripped stone, traditional games, small upstairs dining room for summer and busy wknds; may have big-screen TV for special sports events; children and (in non-carpet areas) dogs welcome, handy for nature-

reserve walks (awash with orchids in Jun) *(John and Joan Nash, the Didler, Phil and Sally Gorton, LYM)*

LISVANE [ST1883]

Ty Mawr Arms CF14 0UF [from B4562 on E edge turn N into Church Rd, bear left into Llwyn y Pia Rd, keep on along Graig Rd]: Large neatly kept country pub with good choice of popular food from baguettes and baked potatoes to steaks, well kept Brains and guest ales, decent wines by the glass, teas and coffees, friendly service, great views over Cardiff from spacious bay-windowed dining area off traditional bar with big log fire; disabled access with help to main bar area, large attractive garden with good play area *(LYM, Chris and Angela Buckell)*

LLANGENNITH [SS4291]

Kings Head SA3 1HX: Attractive old stone-built pub with impressive choice of food from hearty snacks to thai dishes and fresh local fish, Felinfoel, Hancocks HB and Wadworths 6X, good wine selection, friendly staff; large terrace, good walks, not far from great surfing beach *(Tony Lewis)*

LLANTWIT FADRE [ST0784]

Crown CF38 2HL [A473]: Friendly family local with leather sofas and local artwork in lounge, roomy bar, well kept ales, fresh honest food, some entertainment; children and dogs welcome, attractive terrace *(anon)*

MAWDLAM [SS8081]

Angel CF33 4PG [nr M4 junction 37]: Friendly staff, good choice of enjoyable sensibly priced food inc good pies *(Mr and Mrs H J Stephens)*

MISKIN [ST0480]

Miskin Arms CF72 8JQ [handy for M4 junction 34, via A4119 and B4264]: Recently extended unpretentious pub with well kept changing ales such as Brains and Everards, young staff, popular food in bar and restaurant; children and dogs welcome *(Colin Moore)*

NEATH [SS7598]

Crown & Sceptre SA10 8AP [Main Rd, Cadoxton]: Large open-plan roadside pub with Bass and Tomos Watkin ales, reasonably priced food, stables restaurant *(Tony and Wendy Hobden)*

NELSON [ST1095]

Hollybush CF46 6HB [High St]: Recently well refurbished, with good simple food inc welsh black beef, good friendly service, two real ales *(Norman Lewis)*

OGMORE [SS8876]

☆ *Pelican* CF32 0QP: Nice spot above ruined castle, attractive rambling revamp with plenty of beamery and bare boards, good choice of well kept ales, enjoyable food from enterprising big rolls to interesting main dishes, good cheerful service, welcoming open fire; they may try to keep your credit card while you eat; rather grand smokers' hut; tables on side terrace, quite handy for the beaches, open all day *(Martin Jeeves, Phil and Sally Gorton, LYM)*

OLDWALLS [SS4891]
Greyhound SA3 1HA: Good value generous food with two-for-one wkdy bargains, busy but spacious beamed and dark-panelled 1970s-style plush lounge bar and restaurant, four real ales, good coffee inc decaf, decent wine, roaring coal fires, friendly staff, back bar with display cases; big tree-shaded garden with terrace picnic-sets, play area and good views *(Peter Meister)*

PONTYPRIDD [ST0790]
Bunch of Grapes CF37 4DA [off A4054; Ynysangharad Rd]: Friendly and spotless, with reasonably priced food (not Sun evening) from sandwiches up, steaks can be good, rewarding children's choice, smart efficient staff, Bass, Hereford PA and changing ales, interesting imported bottled beers, reasonably priced wines, log fire, bare boards and simple décor, small easy-chair lounge, large dining area opening into grape-vine conservatory, public bar with pool and games machine; two back terraces (one no smoking), open all day *(Valerie Baker, Chris Evans)*

PORTHCAWL [SS8176]
Salthouse on the Square CF36 3BW [The Square]: Recently opened bar/restaurant, enjoyable food, good service and atmosphere, bay views; back terrace *(anon)*

REYNOLDSTON [SS4889]
King Arthur SA3 1AD [Higher Green, off A4118]: Cheerful pub/hotel with timbered main bar and hall, back family summer dining area (games room with pool in winter), popular food from lunchtime baguettes to Sun roasts, Bass, Felinfoel and Tomos Watkins, friendly helpful staff, country-house bric-a-brac and log fire; lively local atmosphere evenings, piped music; tables out on green, play area, open all day, bedrooms *(Eric and Mary Barrett, Tony Lewis, LYM)*

ST FAGANS [ST1277]
Plymouth Arms CF5 6DU: Stately Victorian pub, now a rambling Vintage Inn with log fires, panelling and local prints in bustling linked areas, good range of generous food all day, Marstons Pedigree and St Austell Tribute, decent wines by the glass; lots of tables on extensive back lawn, water-bowls outside for dogs, handy for Museum of Welsh Life *(Michael and Alison Sandy)*

SWANSEA [SS6492]
Bay View SA1 3UL [Oystermouth Rd]: Light and airy, with leather sofas, open fire, enjoyable thai food, good service, Flowers Original *(John and Helen Rushton)*
Brunswick SA1 4HS [Duke St]: Large rambling local with lots of artwork and prints for sale, bargain popular food, Courage Directors, Theakstons XB and a local guest beer, friendly helpful landlord, some live music; sports TV not too obtrusive *(Michael and Alison Sandy)*
Kings Head SA5 9EL [Llangyfelach Rd, Treboeth; B4489; M4, J56]: Enjoyable

generous standard food, changing ales such as Bass, Marstons Pedigree, Rhymney or Wells & Youngs, pleasant dining end, part down steps *(Michael and Alison Sandy)*

GWENT

ABERGAVENNY [SO2914]
Hen & Chickens NP7 5EG [Flannel St]: Relaxed traditional local, wholesome cheap lunchtime food (not Sun), friendly efficient staff, well kept Brains from bar unusually set against street windows, mugs of tea and coffee, interesting side areas with some nice stripped masonry, popular darts, cards and dominoes, Sun jazz; TV, very busy on market day; terrace tables *(Reg Fowle, Helen Rickwood, the Didler, Pete Baker)*

BLAENAVON [SO2508]
Queen Victoria NP4 9BD [Prince St]: Basic friendly Valleys pub, light and airy, friendly helpful staff, well kept Rhymney ales, fresh sandwiches and one or two simple hot dishes, quiet lounge, darts (and TV) in bar; cl Weds, opens 3 other wkdys *(Pete Baker)*

CAERLEON [ST3490]
Bell NP18 1QQ [Bulmore Rd; off B4236, S of bridge]: Cottagey pub with thriving atmosphere in single bar (basic and smarter ends), good value bar food inc interesting welsh and breton dishes (not Weds-Sun evening when there is a more restauranty menu instead, nor Sun-Tues lunchtime), three or four well kept ales such as Rhymney, good Weds folk night and other events; garden tables *(Pete Baker)*

CALDICOT [ST4888]
Castle NP26 4HW [Church Rd]: Attractive and well run open-plan pub with popular food inc Tues/Thurs OAP lunch, well kept changing real ales; by drive of historic castle, garden with play area, covered terrace and smokers' shelter *(Tim and Ann Newell)*

GILWERN [SO2414]
Beaufort Arms NP7 0AR [Main Rd]: Friendly pub, not a food place, with Flowers and usually a guest beer *(Reg Fowle, Helen Rickwood)*

GOVILON [SO2713]
Cordell Country Inn NP7 9NY [B4246 S]: Unpretentious and neatly kept 70s-feel pub with interesting pictures, friendly staff, Felinfoel Double Dragon, food inc bargain Sun lunch in bar eating area and downstairs dining room; handy for Big Pit *(Reg Fowle, Helen Rickwood)*

GROSMONT [SO4024]
Angel NP7 8EP: Tomos Watkins ales, farm ciders and good value straightforward bar food in friendly 17th-c village local owned by village co-operative, pool room with darts; a couple of tables and boules behind, seats out by ancient market cross on attractive steep single street in sight of castle *(BB, Reg Fowle, Helen Rickwood, R T and J C Moggridge)*

LLANDENNY [SO4103]
☆ *Raglan Arms* NP15 1DL: Good fresh food inc some rather unusual dishes cooked to order, leisurely atmosphere, good wines, serious coffee, Wye Valley Butty Bach, friendly young staff, big pine tables and a couple of leather sofas in linked dining rooms leading through to conservatory, big log fire in flagstoned bar's handsome stone fireplace, simple pastel paintwork giving slight scandinavian feel, neat separate public bar with pool and wide-screen TV; garden tables, has been cl Tues in Jan-Mar (BB, LM)

LLANDEWI SKIRRID [SO3421]
☆ *Walnut Tree* NP7 8AW [B4521]: Reopened as appealing eating place much as it used to be under the Taruschios (much of the same staff), with fireside seats and small tables in little flagstoned bar as well as airy informal main dining room; veteran top-notch chef in charge of excellent cooking from delicious breads through interesting fresh vegetarian dishes to classic game, good wines, pleasantly relaxed and individual service; children welcome, cl Sun/Mon (Joyce and Maurice Cottrell, LYM)

LLANGATTOCK LINGOED [SO3620]
☆ *Hunters Moon* NP7 8RR [off B4521 just E of Llanvetherine]: Attractive tucked-away pub dating from 13th c, beams, dark stripped stone and flagstones, friendly locals, well kept Felinfoel and Rhymney, separate dining room (food usually Fri-Sun); children welcome, tables out on deck and in charming dell with ducks, comfortable bedrooms, glorious country on Offa's Dyke walk, cl Mon/Tues (Reg Fowle, Helen Rickwood, LYM)

LLANMARTIN [ST3989]
Old Barn NP18 2EB [handy for M4 junction 24 via A48/B4245]: Welcoming barn conversion, light and airy, with Bass, Butcombe and Worthington, decent wines, reasonably priced pub food inc puddings cabinet, steps down to further back dining wing; terrace and big play area, bedrooms (Dr and Mrs C W Thomas)

LLANTHONY [SO2827]
Half Moon NP7 7NN: Well worn in country local with flagstoned bar and carpeted lounge, character landlord, Bullmastiff beers inc power-packed Son-of-a-Bitch, basic food, log fire, darts; piped music; big back paddock (on the pony treks), gorgeous views from nice back garden, simple bedrooms, clean and comfortable, unspoilt valley with great walks, has been cl Tues lunchtime, other lunchtimes out of season (though usually open wknds then) (MLR)
☆ *Priory Hotel* NP7 7NN [aka Abbey Hotel, Llanthony Priory; off A465, back rd Llanvihangel Crucorney—Hay]: Magical setting for plain bar in dim-lit vaulted flagstoned crypt of graceful ruined Norman abbey, lovely in summer, with lawns around and the peaceful border hills beyond; real ales such as Greene King Ruddles County, summer farm cider, good coffee, simple lunchtime bar food (can be long queue on fine summer days, but number system then works well), evening restaurant; no dogs or children, occasional live music; bedrooms in restored parts of abbey walls, open all day Sat and summer Sun, cl winter Mon-Thurs and Sun evening, great walks all around (Reg Fowle, Helen Rickwood, MLR, the Didler, LYM, Steve Harvey, Jenny and Brian Seller)

LLANTILIO CROSSENNY [SO3815]
Hogs Head NP7 8TA [Treadam, just W off B4233]: Pub opened in converted barn as farm diversification, enjoyable food and real ale, assorted wooden tables and seats (some coloured), woodburner, bare brickwork and rafters, some live music; disabled access (Reg Fowle, Helen Rickwood)

LLANTRISANT FAWR [ST3997]
☆ *Greyhound* NP15 1LE [off A449 nr Usk]: Prettily set 17th-c country inn with relaxed homely feel in three linked beamed rooms of varying sizes, steps between two, nice mix of furnishings and rustic decorations, friendly helpful staff, consistently good home cooking at sensible prices, good sandwiches, two or more well kept ales, decent wines by the glass, log fires, colourful prints in pleasant grey-panelled dining room; attractive garden with big fountain, hill views, adjoining pine shop, good bedrooms in small attached motel (Colin Moore, BB)

MAMHILAD [SO3003]
Star NP4 0JF: Cosy local with banquettes and panelling, friendly service, enjoyable pubby food from sandwiches up, coal fire in one bar, woodburner in another; garden picnic-sets, not far from canal (Irene and Derek Flewin)

MONMOUTH [SO5012]
Kings Head NP25 3DY [Agincourt Sq]: Wetherspoons in former substantial coaching inn, plenty of seating with extensive central family area, quick value-minded food all day, lots of books inc interesting ones – but also several TVs and games machines (B M Eldridge, Reg Fowle, Helen Rickwood, Jestyn Phillips)
Robin Hood NP25 3EQ [Monnow St]: Ancient pub with good home cooking, well kept Bass, friendly service; tables outside with play area (Dr D J and Mrs S C Walker, B M Eldridge)
Three Horseshoes NP25 5AD [Drybridge St]: Neatly kept riverside pub with enjoyable bargain food in comfortable dining area, friendly service, well kept Hancocks, more choice of lagers and wines; small modern sports bar with several TVs (Reg Fowle, Helen Rickwood)

NEWPORT [ST3087]
Engineers NP20 4BS [Albert Terrace, Baneswell]: Well kept Hancocks HB in unashamed local, small character public bar with shove-ha'penny and railway pictures and memorabilia, wknd live music in lounge (Pete Baker)

Olde Murenger House NP20 1GA [High St]: Fine 16th-c building with ancient dark woodwork, bargain Sam Smiths – shame about the flashing games machine; open all day *(Jennifer Banks, the Didler)*

PANDY [SO3322]

Pandy Inn NP7 8DR [A465 Abergavenny—Hereford]: Welcoming old slate-built family pub with increasing emphasis on good reasonably priced bar food inc good value Sun lunch, attentive service, well kept Wye Valley ales, comfortable modern settles, 3D Brecons maps; adjacent walkers' bunkhouse *(Reg Fowle, Helen Rickwood)*

PANTYGELLI [SO3017]

Crown NP7 7HR [Old Hereford Rd, N of Abergavenny]: Pretty stone-built pub below Black Mountains, welcoming inside, with nice old furnishings and dark wood, affable family service, well kept Rhymney Best, Stowford Press farm cider, good wine choice, interesting and enjoyable lunchtime food inc good plate of welsh cheeses, more extensive evening menu, Sun roasts, plenty of local produce; attractive terrace *(Reg Fowle, Helen Rickwood, R T and J C Moggridge)*

PONTLLANFRAITH [ST1794]

Halfway House NP12 2HT [Upper Gellingroes]: Good traditional pub, enjoyable food and drink, good service; garden tables *(Chris Williams)*

ST ARVANS [ST5196]

Piercefield NP16 6EJ: Modern décor and setting in roomy comfortable country-style dining pub, Brains ales, good choice of generous enjoyable food at sensible prices, friendly efficient staff; handy for walkers and Chepstow races *(Mike and Mary Carter, Reg Fowle, Helen Rickwood)*

TINTERN [SO5300]

Anchor NP16 6TE: Smart pub right by abbey, reasonably priced usual food, local perry and cider alongside original medieval cider press in main bar, two well kept real ales, plush banquettes, lots of pictures, large restaurant and separate carvery; daytime teahouse, spacious lawn with pets corner, comfortable bedrooms *(B M Eldridge, Phil and Jane Hodson)*

Rose & Crown NP16 6SE: Welcoming unpretentious inn opp riverside Abbey, low-priced generous pubby food, well kept Greene King Abbot, nice open fire, restaurant, live music some wknds; dogs welcome *(Reg Fowle, Helen Rickwood, Robert Turnham)*

TRELLECK GRANGE [SO5001]

Fountain NP16 6QW [minor rd Tintern—Llanishen, SE of village]: Particularly welcoming cheerful landlord, wide range of good value food from good sandwiches to some interesting dishes, popular Sun lunch, well kept ales, good value house wines, decent malt whiskies, roomy beamed and flagstoned interior with open fire, darts and comfortable dining room; may be nostalgic piped pop music; children allowed away from bar, small sheltered garden with summer kids' bar, peaceful spot on back country road, bedrooms, camping available; may be cl wkdy lunchtimes *(Sara Fulton, Roger Baker, BB)*

USK [SO3700]

Cross Keys NP15 1BG [Bridge St]: Small friendly two-bar pub dating from 14th c, popular food from baguettes and baked potatoes to restaurant dishes, two well kept ales, oak beams, interesting Last Supper tapestry, log fire in handsome fireplace, lots of brass and copper; back terrace, comfortable bedrooms, good breakfast *(Neil and Anita Christopher)*

GWYNEDD

ABERGYNOLWYN [SH6706]

Railway LL36 9YW [Tywyn—Talyllyn pass]: Flower-decked 16th-c two-bar village pub in lovely setting (plenty of customers from the splendid Talyllyn railway), friendly staff, enjoyable straightforward food from sandwiches up, three well kept changing ales, big inglenook fire in welcoming lounge, small dining room; nice outside seating but close to the road, good walks *(Mike and Mary Carter)*

ABERSOCH [SH3128]

St Tudwals LL53 7DS: Robinsons pub with well kept beer and good value meals *(Noel Grundy)*

BALA [SH9235]

White Lion Royal LL23 7AE [High St]: Timbered coaching inn, character beamed bar with settles and inglenook fireplace, leather settees and armchairs in lounge, Bass, Marstons and local beer, good whisky choice, varied well presented food in bars and restaurant, good sandwiches, friendly staff; comfortable bedrooms *(anon)*

BARMOUTH [SH6115]

Last LL42 1EL [Church St]: 15th-c harbourside local behind modern front with low beams, flagstones, nautical bric-a-brac and harbour mural, little waterfall down back bar's natural rock wall, wide choice of simple well presented food, friendly staff, real ale; lovely flowers outside, roadside tables overlooking harbour and bay *(Mike and Mary Carter)*

BETWS-Y-COED [SH7657]

Swallow Falls LL24 0DW [A5 W]: Comfortable bar in hotel/hostel/camping complex, good friendly service, enjoyable bistro meals, pretty décor *(Paula Nichols)*

☆ *Ty Gwyn* LL24 0SG [A5 just S of bridge to village]: Restaurant with rooms rather than pub (you must eat or stay overnight to be served alcohol – disqualifying it from our main entries), but pubby feel in beamed lounge bar with ancient cooking range, easy chairs, antiques, silver, cut glass, old prints and interesting bric-a-brac, really good interesting meals (they do sandwiches too), real ales such as Adnams, Brains Rev James and Greene King Old Speckled Hen, friendly professional service; piped music;

children welcome (high chair and toys), cl Mon–Weds in Jan *(LYM, Mr and Mrs P J Fisk, Revd D Glover, Chris and Jeanne Downing)*

BRYNCRUG [SH6003]

Peniarth Arms LL36 9PH: Well run friendly open-plan pub, lots of big tables, emphasis on decent reasonably priced food, Greene King Abbot; children very welcome *(Brian and Anna Marsden)*

CAPEL CURIG [SH7257]

☆ *Bryn Tyrch* LL24 0EL [A5 E]: Super Snowdonia setting, relaxed bar with easy chairs round low tables, coal fire, pool in plainer hikers' bar, three Great Orme ales and a guest, quite a few malt whiskies, bar food (all day wknds) with good vegetarian choice; children and dogs welcome, steep side garden, bedrooms, open all day, cl most of Jan *(DC, John and Helen Rushton, Anthony Smith, LYM, Trudie Hudson)*

CONWY [SH7877]

☆ *Castle Hotel* LL32 8DB [High St]: Thriving sympathetically refurbished public bar in interesting old building, plenty of well spaced tables, good substantial food all day from sandwiches to interesting dishes here and in restaurant, three Conwy ales, decent wines, good informed service; own car parks (which helps here), 29 bedrooms with own bathrooms *(David Glynne-Jones, Dave Webster, Sue Holland, Keith and Sue Ward)*

GLANDWYFACH [SH4843]

☆ *Goat* LL51 9LJ [A487 Porthmadog—Pen-y-groes]: Within the thick slate walls it's comfortable and much renovated, with friendly helpful family service, good fresh food at reasonable prices, real ale, warm atmosphere, restaurant; disabled access, garden tables, bedrooms *(Deb and John Arthur, J Roy Smylie, Noel Grundy, Brian and Diane Mugford)*

LLANDUDNO [SH7782]

☆ *Kings Head* LL30 2NB [Old Rd, behind tram stn]: Rambling and pretty, much extended around 16th-c flagstoned core, wide range of generous food from good steak sandwiches to restaurant meals (busy at night, so get there early), well kept Greene King and a guest beer, good range of wines by the glass, friendly open-plan service, huge log fire, brightly open-plan but with interesting corners and comfortable traditional furnishings, old local tramway photographs, smart back dining room up a few steps; children welcome, seats on front terrace overlooking quaint Victorian cable tramway's station, open all day in summer *(John and Helen Rushton, LYM)*

LLANENGAN [SH2826]

Sun LL53 7LG: Friendly and cosy Robinsons pub in small village nr spectacular sandy Hell's Mouth beach, three real ales, enjoyable family food, reasonable prices; large partly covered terrace and garden (very popular with children) with outdoor summer bar and pool table, bedrooms *(Noel Grundy)*

LLANUWCHLLYN [SH8730]

☆ *Eagles* LL23 7UB [aka Eryrod; A494/B4403]: Good reasonably priced food from sandwiches to traditional and more enterprising dishes (bilingual menu), helpful and courteous young staff, thriving atmosphere in small front bar and plush back lounge, neat décor with beams and some stripped stone, back picture-window view of mountains with Lake Bala in distance, Theakstons Best, limited wine list, strong coffee, no music; disabled access, picnic-sets under cocktail parasols on flower-filled back terrace, cl lunchtime Mon–Weds *(Michael and Jenny Back, Mike and Mary Carter, Jacquie Jones)*

LLANYSTUMDWY [SH4738]

Tafarn y Plu LL52 0SH: Thoroughly welsh beamed two-bar pub opp Lloyd George's boyhood home and museum, real ales such as Conwy, Felinfoel or Evan Evans, welsh lager, farm ciders, wines, spirits and liqueurs too, enjoyable food from sandwiches to juicy lamb steaks most days, warmly welcoming licensees and chatty locals, log fire, panelled partitions, traditional rustic décor, small restaurant; large peaceful garden *(Gwilym Prydderch)*

MORFA NEFYN [SH2939]

Bryncynan LL53 6AA [A497/B4412 SE]: Modernised pub concentrating (particularly in summer) on reasonably priced popular food, three real ales such as Greene King Old Speckled Hen and Wadworths 6X, quick friendly service even when busy with family groups, quiet in winter with good log fire in the partly tiled bar, restaurant; electronic table game; children welcome, rustic seats outside, has been cl Sun *(Deb and John Arthur, LYM)*

PENMAENPOOL [SH6918]

☆ *George III* LL40 1YD [just off A493, nr Dolgellau]: Attractive inn well known for knowing for lovely views over Mawddach estuary from civilised partly panelled upstairs bar opening into cosy inglenook lounge; beamed and flagstoned downstairs bar for peak times, usual bar food (may be limited to soup and sandwiches or baguettes some lunchtimes, and they may not let you run a tab), real ales such as Evan Evans and Greene King Ruddles County, restaurant; dogs welcome, sheltered terrace, good bedrooms inc some in quiet and interesting conversion of former station on disused line now a walkway, open all day *(Andrew Marshall, Brian and Anna Marsden, Mike and Mary Carter, B and M Kendall, LYM)*

PORTHMADOG [SH5639]

Royal Sportsman LL49 9HB [High St]: Extensively refurbished early Victorian hotel with enjoyable food using local produce inc interesting snacks in popular bar and comfortable coffee lounge with leather armchairs and sofas, more elaborate restaurant meals, good friendly staff, well kept changing ales inc local Purple Moose, log fire; dogs very welcome (the house sheepdog is Gelert), pretty terrace, 28 bedrooms *(anon)*

Spooners LL49 9NF [Harbour Station]: Particularly well kept Marstons Bitter and Pedigree and quickly changing unusual guest beers, bargain wines, good value pub lunches inc good filled baguettes, Thurs-Sat evening meals, popular Sun lunch, railway memorabilia, overflow into station buffet; children welcome, tables out on steam railway platform, open all day *(Mike and Mary Carter)*

ROWEN [SH7571]

Ty Gwyn LL32 8YU [off B5106 S of Conwy]: Friendly and pretty traditional country local in charming village, good basic food 5-9, afternoon light snacks too, Lees real ale, pleasant service; garden tables, cheap bedrooms, good walking country, open all day *(Julian and Janet Dearden)*

TALYLLYN [SH7210]

☆ **Tynycornel** LL36 9AJ [B4405, off A487 S of Dolgellau]: Hotel rather than pub, but worth knowing for its enjoyable bar lunches and great setting below mountains, with picture windows overlooking attractive lake; polite service, comfortable sofas and armchairs, central log fire, nice pictures, extended restaurants and conservatory; keg beer; children welcome, prettily planted side courtyard, open all day, boat hire for fishermen, good bedrooms *(Jacquie Jones, LYM, B and M Kendall, Joy Poustie, Robin and Ann Taylor)*

TREFRIW [SH7863]

Old Ship LL27 0JH: Particularly well kept Marstons and related beers, perhaps a guest such as Conwy, friendly staff, enjoyable generous pubby food from baguettes up, warm woodburner, cheerful local atmosphere *(Martin Cawley, Jan Bertenshaw, Julian and Janet Dearden, Ian Clarke)*

TUDWEILIOG [SH2336]

☆ **Lion** LL53 8ND [Nefyn Rd (B4417), Lleyn Peninsula]: Cheerfully busy village inn with wide choice of enjoyable sensibly priced food in bar and family dining conservatory (small helpings for children, who have a pretty free rein here), quick friendly service, interesting real ales well described by helpful landlord, dozens of malt whiskies, decent wines, games in lively public bar; pleasant front garden, good value bedrooms, great breakfast *(LYM, Noel Grundy, David and Angela George)*

POWYS

BERRIEW [SJ1800]

Lion SY21 8PQ [B4390; village signed off A483 Welshpool—Newtown]: Black and white beamed inn in attractive riverside village (with lively sculpture gallery), old-fashioned inglenook public bar and partly stripped stone lounge bar with open fire, home-made food (not Sun evening) here or in restaurant from sandwiches to good fresh fish choice, helpful service, Banks's and

Marstons real ales, decent house wines, dominoes and cribbage; quiet piped music; children and dogs welcome, bedrooms, open all day *(Jeremy King, LYM, Dave Cuthbert, John and Helen Rushton)*

BLEDDFA [SO2068]

Hundred House LD7 1PA [A488 Knighton—Penybont]: Small relaxed lounge with log fire in huge stone fireplace, L-shaped main bar with attractively flagstoned lower games area, cosy dining room with another vast fireplace, two or three real ales, prompt friendly service, bar food from sandwiches to steaks; bikers welcome, tables in peaceful garden dropping steeply behind to small stream, lovely countryside *(BB, Guy Vowles)*

BRECON [SO0727]

Three Horseshoes LD3 7SN [Groesfford, off A40 E]: Charming small flagstoned bar with log fire, good food, friendly attentive service, well kept Wye Valley and Tetleys, good coffee, neat adjoining restaurant area; children welcome, covered tables outside with partial view of Brecon Beacons *(Gavin Robinson)*

BUILTH WELLS [SO0451]

Lion LD2 3DT [Broad St]: Well kept and tasteful hotel lounge bar with good friendly service, wide range of good value simple lunchtime bar food, well kept Greene King Abbot; comfortable traditional bedrooms *(A and B D Craig, Alan and Eve Harding)*

CARNO [SN9696]

Aleppo Merchant SY17 5LL [A470 Newtown—Machynlleth]: Fair-priced popular food from good sandwiches to steaks (open for breakfast too), helpful staff, Boddingtons and Marstons Pedigree, plushly modernised stripped stone bar, peaceful lounge on right with open fire, restaurant (well behaved children allowed here), back extension with big-screen TV in games room; piped music; disabled access, steps up to tables in attractively enlarged garden, bedrooms, nice countryside *(LYM, Michael and Jenny Back)*

CLYRO [SO2143]

Baskerville Arms HR3 5RZ: Unusual old-fashioned panelled bar area, long and comfortable, with assorted metalwork, small log fire one end, bigger one up stone steps the other, enjoyable reasonably priced bar food inc Sun roasts, friendly welcome, Wye Valley ales, separate restaurant; TV; picnic-sets under cocktail parasols in pleasant garden, fine walking area, good bedrooms *(Reg Fowle, Helen Rickwood)*

CRICKHOWELL [SO1919]

☆ **Nantyffin Cider Mill** NP8 1LP [A40/A479 NW]: In converted barn on attractive stretch of the River Usk, with focus on food (has been good, but no reports since new owners in early 2008), three real ales inc Wye Valley, dining room in raftered barn with cider press, bar with warm grey stonework and woodburner in fine broad fireplace; children and dogs have been welcome, disabled access, cl Mon and winter Sun evening *(LYM)*

☆ *White Hart* NP8 1DL [Brecon Rd (A40 W)]: Stripped stone, beams and flagstones, good value food from lunchtime sandwiches up inc several welsh specialities, Brains ales and a guest beer, friendly staff, bar with end eating area, sizeable restaurant, pub games; may be piped music; children in eating areas, some tables outside, open all day Sat *(Mike and Mary Carter, LYM, David and Sheila Pearcey)*

CWMDU [SO1823]

☆ *Farmers Arms* NP8 1RU [A479 NW of Crickhowell]: Friendly 18th-c country local, popular with walkers, with good welcoming service, hearty home cooking inc good local lamb, beef and cheeses, well kept Brains ales, decent wines by the glass, unpretentious partly flagstoned bar with attractive prints, stove in big stone fireplace, plush restaurant; TV; children welcome, tables in garden, comfortable bedrooms with good breakfast, campsite nearby *(BB, Jenny and Brian Seller, Mike and Mary Carter, J A Ellis)*

DEFYNNOG [SN9228]

Lion LD3 8SB [aka Tafarn y Llew; A4067]: New licensees doing well in traditional pub with four small rooms, cottagey décor, good chatty atmosphere, well kept real ale, generous straightforward food, warm fires *(LYM, Mrs Margo Finlay, Jörg Kasprowski)*

DERWENLAS [SN7299]

☆ *Black Lion* SY20 8TN [A487 just S of Machynlleth]: Cosy 16th-c country pub, good range of enjoyable sensibly priced food, friendly staff cope well at busy times, real ale, decent wines, heavy black beams, thick walls and black timbering, attractive pictures and lion models, tartan carpet over big slate flagstones, great log fire; piped music; garden up behind with play area and steps up into woods, bedrooms *(Mike and Mary Carter, BB)*

ERWOOD [SO0943]

Wheelwrights Arms LD2 3EQ: Wide choice of good value food inc impressive vegetarian range in quiet homely back dining room *(John and Jan Elliott)*

GLASBURY [SO1839]

Harp HR3 5NR [B4350 towards Hay, just N of A438]: Freshened up under friendly new owners (she does the food), good value pubby food inc proper pies, welcoming log-fire lounge with eating area, real ales, airy games bar, picture windows over garden sloping to River Wye; terrace tables, river-view bedrooms *(Reg Fowle, Helen Rickwood, LYM)*

HAY-ON-WYE [SO2039]

☆ *Hollybush* HR3 5PS [B4350 SW]: Old country inn opened up into big single space with areas off, log fire one end, bar the other with Breconshire, Spinning Dog and a guest beer, appealing locally sourced food all day inc inexpensive dishes, comfortable sofas, antipodean landlady, interesting and unusual feel (one reader suggests a cross between Camden Town and aussie walkabout-style

backpackers' roost); some live music; garden with peacocks, bedrooms, camp site by River Wye, open all day from 8 *(MLR, Reg Fowle, Helen Rickwood)*

☆ *Three Tuns* HR3 5DB [Broad St]: Reopened 2007 after careful fire damage restoration, up-to-date food, three real ales inc Wye Valley, sturdy basic furniture on slate floors, blackened beams, some stripped masonry, inglenook woodburners, ancient stairs restored to upper raftered restaurant served by new kitchen; tables out on good covered back terrace *(MLR)*

Wheatsheaf HR3 5AA [Lion St]: Beamed pub with bric-a-brac in nooks and crannies, well kept real ale, attractively priced decent home-made food, cheerful staff, settee and end woodburner, pink-walled dining area with light wood furniture and some stripped masonry, pool room *(Reg Fowle, Helen Rickwood)*

HOWEY [SO0558]

Laughing Dog LD1 5PT: Two-bar pub with friendly new landlady and chef/landlord doing good value fresh local food (not Sun evening or Mon), Woods, Wye Valley and a guest beer, shelf of guide books, games room with darts and pool, carpeted restaurant; children and dogs allowed, terrace tables, open all day Fri-Sun, cl Mon lunchtime *(Pip Woolf, Norman Jones)*

KNIGHTON [SO2872]

Horse & Jockey LD7 1AE [Wylcwm Pl]: Several cosy areas, one with log fire, good traditional and innovative food at attractive prices in bar and adjoining restaurant, prompt service, real ales such as Greene King Old Speckled Hen; tables in pleasant courtyard, handy for Offa's Dyke *(Tim and Mark Allen, Alan and Eve Harding)*

LLANAFAN FAWR [SN9655]

Red Lion LD2 3PN [B4358 SW of Llandrindod Wells]: Attractive ancient timber-framed pub in interesting small village, beams, stripped stone and flagstones, welcoming entertaining landlord, friendly efficient staff, good fresh food using local produce, Felinfoel ale, simple furnishings; roadside tables, lovely nearby churchyard *(MLR, John Joseph Smith)*

LLANDRINDOD WELLS [SO0561]

Llanerch LD1 6BG [High St/Waterloo Rd; pub signed from station]: Cheerful rambling 16th-c inn, good welcoming service, enjoyable reasonably priced food, well kept ales such as Felinfoel, old-fashioned main bar with big inglenook fireplace and more up-to-date lounges off, games room with pool; piped music, big-screen sports TV; children welcome, pleasant terrace and garden with play area, 12 bedrooms, open all day *(LYM, Alan and Eve Harding)*

LLANFIHANGEL-NANT-MELAN [SO1958]

☆ *Red Lion* LD8 2TN [A44 10 miles W of Kington]: Civilised stripped-stone 16th-c roadside dining pub with friendly landlord and good obliging service, good food using carefully detailed local supplies from sandwiches up in roomy main area beyond standing timbers on right, smaller room with small pews around tables, changing real ale such as Woods Parish, nice wine choice, back bar with pool; front sun porch (traffic noise), comfortable simple chalet bedrooms, handy for Radnor Forest walks, nr impressive waterfall, has been cl Tues evening *(J A Ellis, BB, MLR)*

LLANGEDWYN [SJ1924]

☆ *Green Inn* SY10 9JW [B4396 E of village]: Ancient country dining pub with various snug alcoves, nooks and crannies, good mix of furnishings inc oak settles and pretty fabrics, blazing log fire, helpful friendly staff, Tetleys and guest beers such as Cottage Golden Arrow, wide range of enjoyable food from baguettes up; children and dogs welcome, attractive garden over road running down towards River Tanat (fishing permits available), open all day wknds, cl Tues *(Michael and Jenny Back, LYM)*

LLANGENNY [SO2417]

Dragons Head NP8 1HD: Chatty two-room bar in pretty valley setting, friendly efficient staff, quickly changing real ales such as Brains Rev James, local farm cider, reasonably priced wines, wide choice of good value home-made food from sandwiches to welsh black beef, low beams, big woodburner, pews, housekeeper's chairs and a high-backed settle among other seats, two attractive dining areas; picnic-sets on heated terrace and over road by stream, nearby campsite, cl wkdy lunchtimes *(Eryl and Keith Dykes, LYM, Owen Barden)*

LLANGYNIDR [SO1519]

☆ *Coach & Horses* NP8 1LS [Cwm Crawnon Rd (B4558 W of Crickhowell)]: Tidy and roomy flower-decked dining pub with good value bar food from ciabattas up, real ales, comfortable banquettes and stripped stone, nice big log fire, large attractive restaurant; no dogs; picnic-sets across road in safely fenced pretty sloping garden by lock of Newport & Brecon Canal, lovely setting and walks, open all day *(Blaise Vyner, LYM, Mike and Mary Carter)*

LLANGYNOG [SJ0526]

New Inn SY10 0EX [B4391 S of Bala]: Comfortable neatly kept pub/hotel with several linked areas, helpful service, wide choice of bargain generous food from crusty baguettes up, Flowers and perhaps an interesting guest beer, restaurant; disabled access, bedrooms *(Michael and Jenny Back)*

LLANWRTYD WELLS [SN8746]

Neuadd Arms LD5 4RB [The Square]: Wide choice of home-made food inc tasty puddings, local real ale and guest beers, log fire, local pictures, separate small tiled public bar still with old service bells, pleasant restaurant; lots of outdoor events, some rather outré; tables out on front terrace, decent bedrooms, engaging very small town – good walking area *(BB, C J Fletcher)*

LLYSWEN [SO1337]

☆ *Griffin* LD3 0UR [A470, village centre]: Attractive country pub with sensible choice of enjoyable food from good home-baked open sandwiches up, Greene King Abbot, limited but good value wines by the glass, great coffee, attentive welcoming staff, fine log fire in easy-going cosy bar; piped music; children welcome in eating areas, tables out by road, comfortable bedrooms *(Les Baldwin, Bruce and Sharon Eden, LYM)*

MACHYNLLETH [SH7400]

White Lion SY20 8DN [Heol Pentrerhedyn; A489, nr clock tower and junction with A487]: Comfortably worn in and old-fashioned country-town bar with big bay window seats overlooking main street, inglenook log fire, end eating area with enjoyable usual food all day from sandwiches to roasts, Banks's Bitter and Mild and a guest beer, decent wines by the glass, brisk cheerful service even on busy Weds market day; piped music, games machine; children welcome, pretty views from picnic-sets in attractive back garden, some tables out by road too, neat stripped pine bedrooms *(Brian and Anna Marsden, BB)*

☆ *Wynnstay Arms* SY20 8AE [Maengwyn St]: Civilised market-town hotel, softly lit and welcoming, with good sandwiches and interesting hot food in busy and pubby little bare-boards annexe bar, Brains and Greene King, interesting choice of wines by the glass, comfortable and relaxed hotel lounge and good restaurant; courtyard tables, good value bedrooms *(Peter and Anne Hollindale, Andrew Marshall, Dr Ian S Morley, Mike and Mary Carter, Joy Poustie, J and F Gowers, A and B D Craig)*

MALLWYD [SH8612]

Brigands SY20 9HJ: Attractive and welcoming stone-built Tudor-style hotel with big sofas and woodburner in spick and span central bar, cosy snug, dining rooms either side, friendly helpful staff, reasonably priced food from sandwiches up inc good local beef and lamb, good real ales and wine choice; neat extensive lawns with play area, nice bedrooms, lovely views, sea trout fishing on River Dovey *(Sara Fulton, Roger Baker)*

MONTGOMERY [SO2296]

☆ *Dragon* SY15 6PA [Market Sq]: Tall timbered 17th-c hotel with attractive prints and china in pleasant beamed bar, charming service, good reasonably priced food using local produce, good wines and coffee, well kept Woods Special and guest beer, board games, restaurant (not always open); unobtrusive piped music, jazz most Weds; comfortable well equipped bedrooms and swimming pool, quiet little town below ruined Norman castle, open all day *(Tony and Dot Mariner, LYM, Dave Cuthbert, Frank Willy, Alan and Eve Harding)*

NEW RADNOR [SO2160]

Radnor Arms LD8 2SP [Broad St]: Unpretentious two-bar village pub with bargain home cooking, wider evening choice and popular Sun carvery, well kept changing ales such as Cottage, choice of ciders, cheerful efficient staff, dining area; TV in public bar; garden tables, bedrooms, open all day Sat *(MLR, Alan and Eve Harding)*

PAINSCASTLE [SO1646]

☆ *Roast Ox* LD2 3JL [off A470 Brecon—Builth Wells; former Maesllwch Arms]: Reopened after careful restoration, beams, flagstones, stripped stone, appropriate simple furnishings and some rustic bric-a-brac, well kept ales such as Black Country and Hook Norton Old Hooky tapped from the cask, farm cider, decent roasts as well as other enjoyable hearty food, flexible licensees; picnic-sets outside, attractive hill country, ten simple comfortable bedrooms *(LYM, Reg Fowle, Helen Rickwood)*

PENTRE BACH [SN9032]

☆ *Shoemakers Arms* LD3 8UB [off A40 in Sennybridge]: Simple pleasantly furnished country pub in the middle of nowhere, good home-made bar lunches and small restaurant Sun lunchtime and Weds-Sat evenings, helpful cheerful staff, changing real ales such as Thwaites; garden picnic-sets, good walks, open all day Sun, cl Mon/Tues lunchtime *(S J C Chappell)*

RHAYADER [SN9768]

Crown LD6 5BT [North St]: Rambling 17th-c timbered inn with good helpings of sensible food from snacks to steaks, well kept Brains ales, reasonable prices, friendly helpful service, nice nooks and crannies in comfortable beamed bar, interesting photographs; disabled access, small garden behind, open all day (cl Sun afternoon) *(MLR)*

TALYBONT-ON-USK [SO1122]

☆ *Star* LD3 7YX [B4558]: Fine choice of changing real ales in relaxed and unpretentious stone-built local, pubby home-made food from good cheap filled rolls to some tasty main dishes, friendly attentive service, good log fire in fine inglenook with bread oven, farm cider, three bustling plain rooms off central servery inc brightly lit games area, lots of beermats, bank notes and coins on beams, monthly band night; dogs and children welcome, picnic-sets in sizeable tree-ringed garden below Monmouth & Brecon Canal, bedrooms, open all day Sat and summer *(LYM, Pete Baker, the Didler, Jackie Givens, Paul J Robinshaw)*

Usk LD3 7JE: Compact comfortable bar, good reasonably priced food here and in restaurant, Hancocks HB and a guest beer, helpful friendly staff, log fire, panelling and sporting prints; good value well equipped bedrooms *(Drs J and J Parker)*

Post Office address codings confusingly give the impression that some pubs are in Gwent or Powys, Wales when they're really in Gloucestershire or Shropshire (which is where we list them).

Channel Islands

There are sea views galore to be had from main entries on the Channel Islands. The Old Court House in St Aubin faces across an idyllic little harbour towards St Helier, Les Fontaines in St John is in a pretty spot with terrace views to the north, and for shelter while you enjoy the scenery you can head to the glazed conservatory of the interesting Old Smugglers in St Brelade (four real ales). The family-friendly Old Portelet Inn, also in St Brelade, gives views across Jersey's most southerly bay, and La Pulente in St Ouens Bay takes in Jersey's longest beach. The Old Court House is doing particularly well these days – though children are welcome here it tends to be a more grown-up option than many places on the Islands, as does the gently stylish Fleur du Jardin on Guernsey, which is still unbeatable, both for dining and as a charming place to stay. Once again it's the Channel Islands Dining Pub of the Year. This year we're glad to see the ancient Moulin de Lecq at Grève de Lecq on fine form and back among the main entries, after quite a break. One matter for mild regret is that so many island pubs rely on mainland breweries for their beer; we found relatively few stocking either of the local brews, Jersey (confusingly they also brew Guernsey Bitter) and Randalls.

GRÈVE DE LECQ   MAP 1
Moulin de Lecq
Le Mont De La Greve De Lecq; JE3 2DT

Cheerful family friendly old mill in lovely location with pubby food and four real ales

Outside this aged black-shuttered water mill you'll find a massive restored water wheel with its formidable dark wood gears located on the other side of a thick stone wall inside the bar – it's almost worth a visit in itself. During their occupation of the Island the Germans commandeered it to generate power for their searchlights. The pub is in a quiet spot, with a stream trickling past, lots of picnic-sets with umbrellas outside on a terrace, and a good children's adventure playground. The road past here leads down to pleasant walks on one of the only north-coast beaches, and to surrounding forests. Inside, the bar is fairly traditional, with plush-cushioned black wooden seats against white-painted or stone walls, dark wood beams and a good log fire in a stone fireplace. Chatty friendly staff serve four changing beers from brewers such as Ringwood and Skinners on handpump, and a farm cider. Up a narrow flight of stairs there's a popular games room with the old grain-hopper and grinding-wheel box, a fruit machine, pool, juke box and board games; piped music.

🍴 **Bar food might include sandwiches, salads including a warm thai salad, soup, spicy chicken wings, battered cod, scampi, spaghetti bolognaise, vegetable curry, lasagne, steaks, and puddings such as mississippi mud pie and Baileys cheesecake.** *Starters/Snacks:* £2.95 to £6.95. Main Courses: £6.95 to £14.95. Puddings: £2.95

Free house ~ Licensee Kenneth Jenkins ~ Real ale ~ Bar food (12-2, 6-9) ~ Restaurant ~ (01534) 482818 ~ Children welcome ~ Dogs allowed in bar ~ Open 11-11

Recommended by George Atkinson, Chris and Jeanne Downing

KING'S MILLS   MAP 1

Fleur du Jardin 🍴 🍷 🛏

King's Mills Road; GY5 7JT

CHANNEL ISLANDS DINING PUB OF THE YEAR

Lovely country hotel in attractive grounds with stylish interior and thoughtfully sourced and prepared food

You'll be hard pushed to find a more charming place to stay on the Island than this well appointed old hotel. It's peacefully set in good-sized gardens, with tables among colourful borders, shrubs, bright hanging baskets and flower barrels. Its relaxing rooms, with low beams, thick granite walls and a good log fire in the public bar (popular with locals), are stylishly decorated with individual country furnishings. Fullers London Pride, Greene King IPA and Worthington are well kept on handpump, alongside a good wine list (with around 15 by the glass) and a local cider. Service is friendly and efficient; piped music. They have a large car park and there is a swimming pool for residents. Contrary to what you might think, its name derives from a breed of guernsey cow!

🍴 The chef takes great care in sourcing ingredients, which include locally raised pork and beef and of course local seafood. Dishes might include soup of the day, smoked salmon with lemon and dill, home-smoked duck, calves liver with minted pea purée, fish and chips, mushroom, pea and mascarpone risotto, seared tuna niçoise salad, braised lamb shank with rosemary jus, confit duck with pak choi and noodles and fried scallops with smoked bacon. *Starters/Snacks: £4.95 to £6.50. Main Courses: £8.95 to £16.95. Puddings: £4.50*

Free house ~ Licensee Amanda Walker ~ Real ale ~ Bar food ~ Restaurant ~ (01481) 257996 ~ Children welcome ~ Dogs welcome ~ Open 10.30-11.45; 12-10.45 Sun ~ Bedrooms: £69B/£138B

Recommended by Gordon Neighbour, Stephen R Holman, Steve Whalley, Bob and Angela Brooks

ROZEL   MAP 1

Rozel

La Vallee De Rozel; JE3 6AJ

Traditional tucked-away pub with reasonably priced food inc fresh fish in restaurant, nice hillside garden

Just out of sight of the sea, at the edge of a charming little fishing village, this friendly place has a very pleasant steeply terraced and partly covered hillside garden. Inside, the counter (with Bass, Courage Directors and Ringwood under light blanket pressure) and tables in the traditional-feeling and cosy little dark-beamed back bar are stripped to their original light wood finish, and there are dark plush wall seats and stools, with an open granite fireplace and old prints and local pictures on cream walls. Leading off is a carpeted area with flowers on big solid square tables. Piped music, TV, juke box, darts, pool, cribbage and dominoes in the games room. The upstairs restaurant has a relaxed rustic french atmosphere

🍴 Fairly priced bar food served in generous helpings might include vegetable tart, steak and kidney pie, tempura cod and chips, fish platter, and puddings such as sticky toffee pudding and chocolate and black pepper mousse. *Starters/Snacks: £2.95 to £6.50. Main Courses: £6.95 to £17.95. Puddings: £4.10*

Free house ~ Licensee Trevor Amy ~ Real ale ~ Bar food ~ Restaurant (not Sun evening) ~ (01534) 869801 ~ Children welcome ~ Dogs allowed in bar ~ Open 11-11

Recommended by Tom and Ruth Rees, BOB, Michael Butler

> People named as recommenders after the main entries have told us that the pub should be included. But they have not written the report – we have, after anonymous on-the-spot inspection.

ST AUBIN   MAP 1

Old Court House Inn 🛏

Harbour Boulevard; JE3 8AB

Fabulous harbour views from some rooms and deck, traditional bar, food from pubby snacks to restaurant dishes, inc lots of fresh fish; a nice place to stay

Tables out on the decking in front of this very popular 15th-c hotel have glorious views over the tranquil harbour, and on past St Aubin's fort right across the bay to St Helier – the restaurant shares the same views. Feeling huddled low to protect itself from stormy sea weather, the pubby downstairs bar has cushioned wooden seats built against its stripped granite walls, low black beams, joists in a white ceiling, a turkey carpet, and an open fire. A dimly lantern-lit inner room has an illuminated rather brackish-looking deep well, and beyond that is the spacious cellar room (open in summer). The Westward Bar is elegantly constructed from the actual gig of a schooner and offers a restauranty menu with prices to match. The front rooms here were once the home of a wealthy merchant, whose cellars stored privateers' plunder alongside more legitimate cargo, and the upstairs restaurant still shows signs of its time as a courtroom. Two or three beers on handpump might be Bass, Courage and Marstons Pedigree; piped music, TV and board games. It can be difficult to find parking near the hotel.

🍴 **Bar food includes soup, ciabattas, and starters such as chicken liver parfait with apple and cranberry chutney, mussels and tempura prawns with peanut and bean sprout salad, and main courses such as vegetable lasagne, lasagne, sausage and mash, fish and chips, fruits de mer cocktail, plaice, bass and grilled dover sole.** *Starters/Snacks: £6.50 to £7.50. Main Courses: £12.95 to £21.00. Puddings: £4.50*

Free house ~ Licensee Jonty Sharp ~ Real ale ~ Bar food (12.30-2.30, 7-10.30) ~ Restaurant ~ (01534) 746433 ~ Children welcome ~ Open 11-11.30 ~ Bedrooms: £60B/£120B

Recommended by Chris and Jeanne Downing, Michael Butler, Michael Dandy

ST BRELADE   MAP 1

Old Portelet Inn

Portelet Bay; JE3 8AJ

Family-friendly place with generous pubby food (something virtually all day), and good views; can be very busy

Families feel particularly welcome and relaxed at this well run 17th-c farmhouse. There's a supervised indoor play area (half an hour 60p), another one outside, board games in the wooden-floored loft bar, and even summer entertainments; also a games machine, pool and piped music. There are picnic-sets on the partly covered flower-bower terrace by a wishing well, and seats in the sizeable landscaped garden, with lots of scented stocks and other flowers, and it's just a short walk down a long flight of granite steps to the beach – the pub is well placed to give views across Portelet (Jersey's most southerly bay). The low-beamed downstairs bar has a stone counter (with Bass and a guest such as Courage Directors kept under light blanket pressure, and a dozen wines by the glass), a huge open fire, gas lamps, old pictures, etched glass panels from France and a nice mixture of old wooden chairs on bare oak boards and quarry tiles. This room opens into the big timber-ceilinged barn restaurant, with standing timbers and plenty of highchairs; disabled and baby-changing facilities. It can get very busy (they do take coaches), but does have its quiet moments too.

🍴 **From a short snack menu, generous helpings of food, quickly served by neatly dressed attentive staff, include sandwiches, soup, chilli, scampi, mackerel, steak and kidney pudding, roast chicken, beef balti, and puddings such as passion cake and apple pie.** *Starters/Snacks: £3.50 to £5.25. Main Courses: £6.25 to £10.25. Puddings: £3.95*

Randalls ~ Manager Anthony Mulligan ~ Real ale ~ Bar food (12-9(8 Sun)) ~ (01534) 741899 ~ Children welcome ~ Dogs allowed in bar ~ Open 10(11 Sun)-11

Recommended by George Atkinson, Michael Dandy, Stephen R Holman, Michael Butler, Jo Lilley, Simon Calvert

Old Smugglers
Ouaisne Bay; OS map reference 595476; JE3 8AW

Happy unassuming place with four real ales, beer festivals and traditional food; families welcome

Every year they host two real ale and cider festivals at this nicely straightforward old free house.The rest of the time you will find well kept Bass, Ringwood Best, Skinners Betty Stogs and a guest such as Greene King Abbot on handpump, as well as a farm cider. The welcoming bar here, developed just before the war from old fishermen's cottages, has thick walls, low black beams, log fires in a large fireplace and cosy black built-in settles. Children are welcomed with colouring pads and crayons, and they've a TV, sensibly placed darts, cribbage and dominoes. A glassed porch, running the width of the building, takes in interesting views over one of the island's many defence towers.

🍴 As well as their speciality portuguese kebabs, bar food includes, soup, spicy chicken wings, burgers, lunchtime baguettes, salads, spare ribs, chicken curry, fusili with provençale sauce, lamb shank with redcurrant wine jus, battered haddock or cod, king prawns and steaks. *Starters/Snacks: £2.95 to £4.95. Main Courses: £5.95 to £13.95. Puddings: £2.95 to £3.95*

Free house ~ Licensee Andrew Walker ~ Real ale ~ Bar food (12-2, 6-9) ~ Restaurant ~ (01534) 741510 ~ Children welcome ~ Dogs welcome ~ Open 11-11

Recommended by Michael Dandy, BOB

ST HELIER   MAP 1

Town House
New Street; JE2 3RA

Big lively locals pub with simple food, sports bar

With some emphasis on its sports bar, this spacious 1930s pub is popular with an island crowd, particularly local office workers, and they host local events, such as salsa classes. Its two main bars are divided by heavy glass and brass doors. The sports bar on the left has three giant TV screens, darts, pool and a juke box. To the right, the lounge area has parquet flooring, some attractive panelling and upholstered armchairs at low round glass tables. Well kept Jersey Jimmys Special on handpump, and sound house wines; piped music.

🍴 Bar food includes soup, sandwiches, chicken liver pate, prawns in filo, beef and ale pie, fish and chips, chicken curry, mushroom risotto and burgers. *Starters/Snacks: £2.95. Main Courses: £6.95 to £9.80. Puddings: £2.50*

Jersey ~ Manager Graham Warren ~ Real ale ~ Bar food ~ Restaurant ~ (01534) 615000 ~ Children welcome ~ Dogs welcome ~ Live music Sun ~ Open 11-11

Recommended by BOB

ST JOHN   MAP 1

Les Fontaines
Le Grand Mourier, Route du Nord; JE3 4AJ

Nicely traditional public bar, bigger family area, decent food, views from terrace, play area

There seems to be plenty of room for everyone at this big converted farmhouse. You'll find the cheery bustle of happy dining families in one area, and locals, perhaps communing in the true Jersey patois, in the well hidden public bar. As you go in, look out for a worn, unmarked door at the side of the building, or as you go down the main entry lobby towards the bigger main bar go through the tiny narrow door on your right. These entrances take you into the best part, the public bar, which has very heavy beams in the low dark ochre ceiling, massively thick irregular red granite walls, cushioned settles on the quarry-tiled floor and antique prints. The big granite-columned fireplace with a log fire warming its unusual inglenook seats may date back to the 16th c, and still sports its old smoking chains and side oven. The quarry tiled main bar is in marked contrast, with plenty of wheelback chairs around neat dark tables, and a spiral staircase leading up to a wooden gallery under the high pine-raftered plank ceiling. Beers might include Bass and Wells & Youngs Bombardier; piped music and board games. A bonus for families is Pirate Pete's, a play area for children. The pub is in a pretty spot on the north coast, with good views from seats on a terrace.

🍽 **Bar food includes sandwiches, soup, ploughman's, battered cod and cumberland sausage, and specials such as crispy duck, grilled fresh mackerel, baked lamb shank with mash, scallops fried with garlic and herbs, lamb chops glazed with balsamic vinegar, and puddings such as treacle sponge.** *Starters/Snacks: £3.85 to £5.85. Main Courses: £8.75 to £15.00. Puddings: £3.75*

Randalls ~ Manager Hazel O'Gorman ~ Real ale ~ Bar food (12-2.15, 6-9) ~ (01534) 862707 ~ Children welcome ~ Dogs allowed in bar ~ Open 11.30-11

Recommended by Michael Butler

ST OUENS BAY

MAP 1

La Pulente

Start of Five Mile Road; OS map reference 562488; JE3 8HG

Lovely sea views, enjoyable food, friendly atmosphere

Seats outside on the terrace at this bustling seaside pub have marvellous views across the endless extent of Jersey's longest beach – the sunset here is particularly stunning. Inside, the comfortably carpeted lounge (with ragged walls and scrubbed wood tables) and the conservatory share the same sweeping views. Friendly staff serve well kept Bass by handpump; piped music. There's also a beer garden.

🍽 **Traditional bar food includes sandwiches, soup, baked potatoes, ploughman's, crab claws, salmon fishcakes, battered cod, steak and ale pie, thai chicken curry, swordfish steak niçoise, 8oz sirloin and daily specials such as local plaice, monkfish and king prawn kebab, roast duck breast and grilled lemon sole or bream.** *Starters/Snacks: £3.50 to £6.00. Main Courses: £7.50 to £13.00. Puddings: £3.50*

Randalls ~ Manager Julia Wallace ~ Real ale ~ Bar food (12-2.15, 6-9(8.30 Sun); not Sun evening in winter) ~ Restaurant ~ (01534) 744487 ~ Children welcome ~ Open 11-11

Recommended by Jo Lilley, Simon Calvert, Michael Dandy

LUCKY DIP

Besides the fully inspected pubs, you might like to try these Lucky Dips recommended to us and described by readers (if you do, please send us reports: feedback@thegoodpubguide.co.uk).

GUERNSEY

ST ANDREW
Last Post [nr Little Chapel]: Neatly kept and pleasant, with reasonably priced pubby food, Randalls beer *(Gordon Neighbour)*

TORTEVAL
☆ *Imperial* GY8 0PS [Pleinmont (coast rd, nr Pleinmont Point)]: Good choice of enjoyable meals inc good fresh mussels and traditional Guernsey bean jar in dining room which like the neat and tidy bar has a great sea view over Rocquaine Bay, Randalls beers; suntrap garden, bedrooms in hotel part separate from the pub, handy for good beach *(Gordon Neighbour)*

JERSEY

GOREY
Castle Green JE3 6DR [Rte de la Côte; steep climb to castle, above]: French-run dining pub above village, enjoyable fresh local food, good choice of wines by the glass, cosy inside; steps up to deck with superb bay views *(Tom and Ruth Rees)*
Moorings JE3 6EW [Gorey Pier]: Hotel's small front bar leading to bistro-style eating area, Jersey Special and Theakstons, good seafood choice; harbour-view tables outside, 15 bedrooms, many with sea view *(Michael Dandy)*

Village Pub JE3 9EP [Main Rd, Gorey Common]: Friendly and comfortably refurbished, light and cheerful, sizeable carpeted bar and adjacent restaurant, good value straightforward food (not Sun) all day inc good fresh fish, Flowers and Jersey Special, open all day from breakfast *(Michael Dandy)*

ST HELIER

Cock & Bottle JE2 4WG [Halkett Pl]: Small cosy continental-feel pub, lively but smart, with lots of woodwork, bars upstairs (with zinc-topped counter) and downstairs, well kept Jersey Special, good value lunchtime bar food from sandwiches up, fast friendly service; picturesque outside with lots of hanging baskets, tables out on distinguished old tree-lined square *(Michael Dandy)*

Lamplighter [Mulcaster St]: Interesting façade including only Union Flag visible during Nazi occupation, small and friendly inside, with heavy timbers, rough panelling and scrubbed pine tables, well kept Marstons and Wells & Youngs Bitter and Bombardier, bargain simple food; sports TV; open all day *(Reg Fowle, Helen Rickwood, Michael Butler, LYM)*

ST PETER

Victoria JE3 7EG [Vallée de St Pierre]: Much-modernised old building with good value pubby food servery in café-like lounge bar, attentive staff, pool; attractive terrace, NT valley of lush meadows *(Darren Le Poidevin)*

'Children welcome' means the pub says it lets children inside without any special restriction. If it allows them in, but to restricted areas such as an eating area or family room, we specify this. Places with separate restaurants often let children use them, hotels usually let them into public areas such as lounges. Some pubs impose an evening time limit – let us know if you find one earlier than 9pm.

Overseas Lucky Dip

Overseas Lucky Dip

We're always interested to hear of good bars and pubs overseas – preferably really good examples of bars that visitors would find memorable, rather than transplanted 'British pubs'. A star marks places we would be confident would deserve a main entry.

AUSTRALIA

SYDNEY
Australian [100 Cumberland St, The Rocks]: Substantial 1913 modernist Federation-style building, sturdily furnished two-level bar, a dozen beers on tap and over a hundred bottled beers, lots of wines by the glass (and a good 'bottle shop' or off licence specialising in fine wines), bar food inc unusual pizzas and kangaroo pie; roof-terrace views of opera house and Sydney Harbour Bridge, wicker chairs for terrace tables, bedrooms sharing bathrooms *(Dr and Mrs M E Wilson, Mike and Mary Carter)*

AUSTRIA

SEEFELD
Wildmoosalm [on plateau above – steep walk, short bus ride, or summer horse-drawn carriage]: Picturesquely tyrolean family-run bar, three rustic rooms full of striking stuffed birds of prey and animals, walls festooned with football shirts, fresh flowers, good beer, enjoyable food esp the apfelstrudel, jolly atmosphere, may be miniature fountain of free spirits; in summer the terrace is great *(Susan and John Douglas, Ian Phillips)*

BARBADOS

SPEIGHTSTOWN
Fishermans [Queen St]: Traditional beachside rum shop on west coast, sea-view verandah, delicious bargain bajan food from hot counter, cold local Banks beer (not to be confused with Banks's), warm welcome, idyllic spot; may be limbo dancing Weds *(James and Helen Read)*

BELGIUM

ANTWERP
Elfde Gebod [Torfbrug/Blauwmoezelstr]: Large ivy-clad café behind cathedral, the '11th Commandment', surreal mix of religious statues and art; good beer range inc Trappist Westmalle from altar-like bar, good choice of traditional belgian food inc mussels with frites, classic beef stew and good steaks, overflow upper gallery; piped classical music, can get busy – worth the wait *(C J Fletcher, Mark and Ruth Brock)*
Grote Witt Arend [17 Reyndersstraat]: Elegant historic café with several rooms and large courtyard with piped classical music, good beer choice, decent reasonably priced food from lasagne to ostrich steaks *(C J Fletcher)*
Kumulator [Kleine Markt]: Basic bar with over 500 beers, either off the shelf or from the cellar, even old english bottled beers very rare in the UK (eg Courage Russian Stout) or virtually unobtainable (eg Bass Kings Ale), also remarkable belgian and other continental ones, helpful knowledgeable staff and customers *(C J Fletcher)*
Paters Vaetje [1 Blaumoezelstraat]: Compact high-ceilinged café-bar in 17th-c building by cathedral, interesting old interior with marble-top tables on quarry tiles, carved wood counter, old beer advertisements, good beer list with four on tap and over 100 by the bottle, friendly helpful staff, some hot snacks, small eating area in panelled back gallery up steep spiral stairs; enterprising piped music, lavatories clean though not for the shy; tables outside ideal for the carillon concerts *(C J Fletcher, Brian and Anita Randall, Mark and Ruth Brock)*
Trein Dertraagheid [Lane Noord Str]: Quirky and friendly railway-theme backstreet bar with integral first-class dining carriage, Flemish-speaking staff speak little English (and not French) *(C J Fletcher)*

BRUGES
Brugs Beertje [Kemelstraat, off Steenstr nr cathedral]: Unspoilt backstreet local known as the Beer Academy, serving 350 of the country's bottled beers, most of them strong ones, in each beer's distinctive glass, as well as five on tap; vibrant atmosphere, especially in the two basic front rooms, table menus, helpful English-speaking staff (and customers), good basic bar food; open from 4, cl Weds, very popular with tourists *(Joe Green, the Didler, Pete Baker)*
Cambrinus [Philipstockstraat, NE corner of Markt]: Over 400 beers in civilised long narrow café/bar with huge helpings of good food from sandwiches to full meals at sensible prices, efficient staff, relaxed atmosphere *(Joe Green, Donna and Roger, Andrea and Guy Bradley)*
Civière d'Or [Markt 33]: Smart split-level café/restaurant behind crenellated façade, dark panelling, relaxed atmosphere, plenty of beers on tap inc Maes and Grimbergen, good coffee and wines, generous local food from flemish stew and tasty waffles to lobsters from live tank – a civilised if pricy escape from the touristy market and the other day-tripping brits (the only blot on this delightful town with its polite locals

speaking perfect English); heated and covered tables outside (the Didler, George Atkinson)

Craenenburg [Markt]: Large bar with own little turret, Leffe, Hoegaarden and Jupiter brought to table by efficient long-serving staff from splendid back counter, good coffee, cakes and good value waffles, pasta and salads, daily papers, leather and light wood panelling, stained-glass medallions in big picture windows looking over square; pavement tables (the Didler)

☆ **Garre** [1 de Garre – tiny alley between Markt and Burg, off Breidelstraat]: Attractive, welcoming and airy bar in 16th-c beamed and timbered building, stripped brickwork, no smoking gallery up steep stairs, elegant and civilised but very relaxed and unstuffy, well over 100 mainly local beers inc five Trappists and its own terrific strong draught beer (each well served in its own glass with cheese nibbles), good coffees and sandwiches too, sensible prices, knowledgeable helpful staff; unobtrusive piped classical music, smoking allowed, no standing if tables are full – get there early; children welcome (N R White, Mark and Ruth Brock, Mrs Frances Pennell, Andrea and Guy Bradley, Joe Green, the Didler)

Vlissinghe [Blekersstraat]: Panelled café away from the tourist centre, dating from 1515, old paintings and tables (legend that Rubens painted a coin on one to avoid paying), unspoilt relaxed atmosphere, friendly staff, small choice of beers and snacks; piped music; some garden seating with boules, cl Sun pm, Mon/Tues (N R White, Joe Green, the Didler, Mark and Ruth Brock)

BRUSSELS

Bécasse [11 rue de Tabora]: Unpromising corridor opens into rather genteel brown café with ranks of tables on tiled floor, ornate highly polished scrolled brass lamps showing its dark panelling and beams well, unblended Lambic (both white and sweet, young and old) served at the table in traditional grey stone pitchers, also local fruit-flavoured Gueuze and other belgian beers such as Kwak served in its distinctive glass like a mini yard of ale, good cheap food such as croques monsieur or croustades made with beer and asparagus, exemplary lavatories – down steps that seem steeper as time wears on; open all day (Joe Green, the Didler)

Bon Vieux Temps [rue Marché aux Herbes 12]: Classy L-shaped brown café down white-tiled passage, dating from 1695, beautifully carved dark panelling, stained-glass, several unspoiled nooks and crannies, old tables inlaid with delft tiles, eccentrically shaped stove in huge fireplace, friendly landlady and helpful staff, wide range of classic beers such as Duvel, Grimbergen Blonde and Brune, Leffe, Orval; can get very smoky (the Didler, Joe Green)

Brasseurs [De La Grand Place]: City's first brew pub, long and narrow, with three of their beers and good bottled choice,

enjoyable food, friendly service, brewing equipment visible (the Didler)

Delirium [4A Impasse de la Fidelite]: Basement bar with over 2,000 beers inc all current belgian ones, sausages and cheese, cheery young atmosphere, good music; open all day (the Didler)

Imaige de Nostre-Dame [Impasse des Cadeaux, off rue du Marché aux Herbes]: Dark, relaxed and intriguing locals' bar tucked down alleyway nr Grand Place, through elaborate stone arch topped by weathered statue; two rough and ready rooms with bags of character, wide range of belgian beers, barman chatty at least in French, ancient beams, stained-glass, long church settle and old tables on tiled floor, interesting fireplace; outside lavatories; open all day (Joe Green, the Didler)

Mort Subite [R Montagne aux Herbes Potagères; off Grand Place via ornate Galeries St Hubert]: Under same family since 1928, long highly traditional fin de siècle room divided by two rows of pillars into nave with double rows of small polished tables and side aisles with single row, huge mirrors on all sides, leather seats, brisk uniformed polyglot waiters and waitresses bustling from lovely mirrored serving counter on dais on right; lots of belgian beers inc their own speciality Kriek and other fruit beers brewed nearby (served by the bucket if you want), good straightforward food inc big omelettes, croques monsieur or madame, local specialities such as brawn and rice tart, no piped music (Joe Green)

GHENT

Velootje [2 Kalversteeg, off Oudburg; no sign, go through old cloth curtain by woodpile]: Eccentric shadowed candle- and lamp-lit bar/bicycle repair shop so full of junk it's reminiscent of Krook's shop in Bleak House, landlord absolutely in character, roaring log fire, good range of bottled beers (don't expect a glass); piped music, usually classical; usually opens 7ish (the Didler)

Waterhuis aan de Bierkan [9 Groentenmarkt]: Cosy old candlelit beamed bar, well over 100 beers inc 14 on tap and a bargain beer of the month, great atmosphere; riverside terrace (the Didler)

OSTEND

Café Botteltje [Louisa Straat]: Over 400 beers and dozens of gins in big L-shaped bar, soft lighting and dark wood, usual pubby food, friendly efficient staff (Dennis Jones)

CANARY ISLANDS

FATAGA

Albaricoque [calle Nestor Alamo 4-6; Grand Canary]: Friendly pub in small mountain village of tiny cobbled streets, good beers from long wooden bar, interesting décor, singing canaries; thatched sunshades on pretty terrace overlooking canyon (Adrian and Dawn Collinge)

CUBA

HAVANA

Hotel Nacional: Hotel built 1930 as casino in flamboyant Spanish Colonial style, its terrace just the place for a cuba libre or mojito, Bar of Fame cocktail bar with hundreds of former customers from Winston Churchill to Nat King Cole, Yuri Gagarin to the Manic Street Preachers, pictured in floor-to-ceiling paintings in decade order, amazing range of cigars in all sorts of sizes, pubby food in another bar downstairs; bedrooms, open 24 hrs *(David Crook)*

Taberna de la Muralla [Calle San Ignacio/Calle Muralla, Plaza Vieja]: Unique brewpub with good Clara, Negro and Oscura on tap (in iced gallon dispenser if you want), enjoyable food from outdoor grill; covered terrace and nice tables outside *(David Crook)*

CZECH REPUBLIC

PRAGUE

Café Montmartre [Retezova 7]: Tucked nicely away in quiet street parallel to Karlova (between new town square and Charles Bridge), shabby-chic and convivial café-bar with the odd easy chair and sofa as well as bentwood tables and chairs, attractive décor and few if any brits, good drinks hot and cold inc the usual beers from long bar, friendly laid-back staff and customers – some food, but primarily a place where people spin out a drink or a coffee for hours of chat; may be live music *(BB)*

Cerneho Vola [Loretanske Namesti 1]: Up steps above castle, untouristy, friendly and jolly, with beams, leaded lights, long dark benches or small stand-up entrance bar, good Kozel Pale and Dark 12 black beer, and Velkopopovicky Korel lager, local snacks; can get very busy, cl 9 *(Jo Lilley, Simon Calvert, the Didler)*

Fleku [Kremencova 11, Nove Mesto]: Brewing its own strong tasty black Flekovsky Dark 13 since 1843 (some say 1499); helpful waiters will try to sell you a schnapps with it – say Ne firmly; huge, with benches and big refectory tables in two big dark-beamed rooms – tourists on right with ten-piece oompah band, more local on left (music here too), also courtyard after courtyard; good basic promptly served food – sausages, pork, goulash with dumplings; open early morning to late night, can be very busy and noisy with tourists *(the Didler)*

Medvidku [Na Perstyne 5, Stare Mesto]: Superb old building in red light district, namesake bears etched in stone over entry, lots of copper in left bar, bigger right room more for eating, Budvar Budweiser on tap *(the Didler)*

Novomestsky Pivovar [Vodickova 20, Nove Mesto]: Fine brewpub opened 1994 in unlikely spot off shopping arcade, rambling series of basement rooms (some no smoking) with interesting old copper brewing equipment, lots of substantial bric-a-brac and old posters, their own unfiltered Novomestsky light and dark beers, good promptly served cheap food esp goulash – at busy times you have to eat too; open all day *(the Didler)*

Pivovarsky Dum [Lipova 15]: Brewpub with big windows showing fermentation room and brewing equipment, neat modern green décor and woodwork, interesting range inc wheat, banana, cherry and even coffee and champagne beers as well as classic lager, served by the gallon stick with its own tap if you wish, low prices, good choice of english-style food, friendly service; open all day *(the Didler)*

☆ *Zlateho Tygra* [Husova 17, Stare Mesto]: 13th-c cellars with superb Pilsner Urquell 12 and eponymous Golden Tiger served by white-coated waiters; sometimes a queue of locals even before 3pm opening, and no standing allowed, but worth the wait (don't be put off by Reserved signs as the seats, mainly long wooden benches, aren't usually being used till later – and they do make tourists feel welcome) *(the Didler)*

ESTONIA

TALLINN

Hell Hunt [Pikk 39]: Dim-lit, with huge range of good reasonably priced beers and lagers, quick efficient service, cheap interesting hearty food, wooden tables and bare boards *(Jane and Alan Bush)*

FRANCE

DINAN

Bistro d'en Bas [20 rue Haute Voie]: Thriving chatty pub atmosphere, character mustachioed landlord and hard-working landlady, tartines (simple toasts), frequent jazz trio; cl Sun lunchtime and Mon *(Phil and Sally Gorton)*

PARIS

Palette [43 rue Seine]: Charming Left Bank retro bar, walls of its two interestingly original 1902 rooms crammed with paintings, very popular with art-world people, kind service, very good wines by the glass, good value light meals; nice pavement terrace, cl Sun *(BB)*

IRELAND (NORTHERN)

BELFAST

☆ *Crown* [Gt Victoria St, opp Europa Hotel]: Recently restored ornate 19th-c National Trust gin palace well worth sampling, benefiting greatly now from the smoking ban; lively and bustling, with pillared entrance, opulent tiles outside and in, elaborately coloured windows, dark brown curlicued ceiling, handsome mirrors, gleaming intricately carved woodwork, lots of individual snug booths with little doors and bells for waiter service, gas lighting, mosaic tiled floor, pricy Whitewater real ale from imposing granite-top counter with colourful tiled facing, good lunchtime meals till 5 upstairs inc oysters; can be incredibly noisy, very wide range of customers (can take their toll on the downstairs gents'), and shame about the TV; open all day *(Roy and Lindsey Fentiman, Darren Le Poidevin, BB)*

DROMORE

Halfway House [off A1 towards Banbridge; Co Down]: Appealing country pub, busy restaurant with wide menu inc local produce from sea and land *(Colin McIlwain)*

HILLSBOROUGH

Plough [The Square; Co Down]: Popular pub with pleasant staff and enjoyable interesting food, upstairs restaurant *(Jennifer Hurst)*

SAINTFIELD

White Horse [Main St; Co Down]: Attractive renovated village pub, wide range of real ales, hearty food inc good Sun roast *(Colin McIlwain)*

IRELAND (REPUBLIC)

DUBLIN

Brazen Head [Lower Bridge St]: Charming bar, said to be oldest here, maze of dimly lit cosy unspoilt rooms off attractive red and white tiled passage, with old beams, mirrors, old settles inc one given by Thin Lizzy's Phil Lynnot, interesting memorabilia and local-hero pictures, open fires; lunchtime bar food from filled cobs to carvery, evening restaurant, well served Guinness; peaceful front smokers' cobbled courtyard, sheltered and covered, good traditional music each night, main bar very busy Sun lunchtime with music too *(Janet and Peter Race)*

Temple Bar [Temple Bar]: Rambling multi-levelled, many-roomed tourist pub on cobbled street corner, quick friendly service even on lively wknd nights, spirits bottles packed to the ceiling, lots of old Guinness advertisements, good live music from 4pm; tables out in big yard *(Bruce and Penny Wilkie, Terry Buckland)*

GALWAY

Garavans [46 William St]: Quiet old-fashioned traditional pub *(Dr Martin Owton)*

Garveys [Eyre Sq]: High-ceilinged town pub with panelling and bare boards, pubby food from sandwiches up; TV, piped music *(Michael Dandy)*

Huntsman [164 College Rd]: Contemporary two-room bar and adjacent bistro, enjoyable traditional and up-to-date food, good atmosphere, friendly service; bedrooms *(Michael Dandy)*

Kings Head [15 High St]: Long central bar in sizeable town pub, good food choice from grilled sandwiches up, coffee and pastries too, upstairs overflow *(Michael Dandy)*

Lohrans [Upper Salthill]: Modern seaview pub with mixed contemporary furnishings, pubby and other food from sandwiches up, friendly service; seats outside *(Michael Dandy)*

Skeff [Eyre Sq]: Two-bar pub with linked areas and alcoves, simple food; pavement tables by nice square *(Michael Dandy)*

Taaffes [Shop St]: L-shaped music bar with lots of performer photographs, basic snacks; tables outside *(Michael Dandy)*

Tis Neactain [2 Quay St]: Nicely old-fashioned, two small rooms and some booths, interesting food choice from lunchtime sandwiches up, traditional music; lots of seats outside *(Michael Dandy)*

SKERRIES

Pierhouse [Harbour Rd; Co Dublin]: Convivial and roomy, with bar and restaurant food inc lunchtime carvery, picture-window sea views – just the place for a reflective Guinness; 11 bedrooms *(Janet and Peter Race)*

WESTPORT

West Bar [Bridge St; Co Mayo]: Refurbished pub with mix of tables around central servery, interesting old local photographs, food from sandwiches to oysters and steak; TV; back courtyard *(Michael Dandy)*

ISLE OF MAN

LAXEY [SC4382]

Shore [Old Laxey Hill]: Pubby atmosphere, friendly staff, Bosuns Bitter, good value quarter-litres of wine, lovely streamside seating area *(Dr J Barrie Jones)*

PEEL [SC2484]

Creek [Station Pl/North Quay]: Pleasantly refurbished saloon bar in lovely setting on the ancient quayside opp splendid Manannan heritage centre, friendly helpful staff and welcoming relaxed atmosphere, wide choice of sensibly priced food all day inc fish, crab and lobsters fresh from the boats, good local kippers and several unusual dishes, well kept local Okells and guest beers, etched mirrors and mainly old woodwork; plain public bar with TVs; wheelchair access, tables outside, self-catering flats *(JHBS, David and Sue Smith, Paul Humphreys)*

PORT ERIN [SC2069]

Bay [Shore Rd]: Three rooms with bare boards and good furniture, good fresh food (not Tues), up to half a dozen reasonably priced well kept local Bushys beer (brewery owner lives above the bar), guest beers too, wide wine choice, friendly service, lovely spot overlooking sandy beach and across to Bradda Head, live music Fri; flexible opening times *(Derek and Sylvia Stephenson, Andrew Stephenson, Dr J Barrie Jones)*

MADEIRA

FUNCHAL

Prince Albert [off Avenida do Infante, nr Savoy Hotel]: Victorian-style dark panelling, wicker chairs and cast-iron-framed tables on tiled floor, old-fashioned curved bar, lots of advertising mirrors and imperial prints, good value food from snacks to Sun roasts, a dozen unusual if pricy British bottled beers as well as local lagers and keg Kilkenny and

John Smiths, ex-pat owners, darts, books for sale; several screens for SkyTV sports, piped local and 60s music, quiz nights; open all day *(Kevin Thorpe)*

NEW ZEALAND
ARROWTOWN
New Orleans [27 Buckingham St]: Was only hotel here in its 1860s gold rush days, eight real ales, enjoyable food, good choice of wines by the glass, blazing log fire; upstairs back terrace, bedrooms, open all day from breakfast on *(Ian Phillips)*
AUCKLAND
Loaded Hog [204 Quay St]: Vast popular bare-boards brewpub, friendly and lively, part of a chain of this name, in excellent spot overlooking yacht basin, central bar open to street, balcony, its own Hog and other cold beers such as Macs and Speights in chilled glasses, good quick food inc prime burgers, good cheerful service, wide choice of wine by the glass – all cheaper than UK; children welcome (may be free face painting) *(Ian Phillips)*
CHRISTCHURCH
Bard on the Avon [Gloucester St]: Traditional english pub with hearty food all day inc good home-made steak and kidney pie, UK and local beers, live music Thurs-Sun; big-screen sports TV *(Ross Balaam)*
Oxford on the Avon [Colombo St, opp Victoria Park]: Busy bar and cafeteria, huge range of excellent value generous straightforward food from breakfast on inc lovely lamb from upstairs restaurant's good value buffet, Macs, Speights and Steinlager local beers, decent wine by the glass, helpful young staff, quite a pub-like atmosphere; heated tables under weeping willows by the river *(Ian Phillips)*
QUEENSTOWN
Speights Old Ale House [Stanley St]: Copper dome and stone fireplace, high bar stools, good friendly service, full Speights beer range on tap (the sort of place you might have problems remembering leaving), massive helpings of enjoyable food such as liver and bacon with their own bread, no smoking; piped music may be loud, SkyTV; old tractor seats for massive chunky tables outside *(Ian Phillips)*
ROTORUA
Pig & Whistle [Tutanekai/Haupapa St; North Island]: Former police station with appropriate memorabilia, rare example of 1940s architecture, Kilkenny, Macs and Speights beers on tap, lots of wines, good value generous simple meals and all-day snacks; piped music, live wknds; children welcome, large covered heated terrace *(Ian Phillips)*

SWITZERLAND
LES PACCOTS
Lac des Joncs [Rte des Joncs 371]: Cardinal beer on tap, particularly good coffee, enjoyable food inc fondues and trout; snowbound in winter, lovely lake in summer, terrace tables, bedrooms *(Ian Phillips)*

USA
NEW YORK
Back Room [102 Norfolk St, nr Delancey St; look for Lower East Side Toy Co. sign, go down through railings and keep on through unpromising yard]: Interesting speakeasy-feel hideout, rather trendy, with big mirrors and other Victorian and 1920s trappings, drinks in cups rather than glasses (supposedly as in Prohibition days), well reproduced music; the lucky few may see the 'back back room' here, an Art Nouveau treasure-house; cl Sun/Mon *(BB)*
Bemelmans Bar [Carlyle Hotel, 35 E 76th St/Madison Ave]: Delightful whimsical panoramic mural of dressed-up animals in Central Park through the seasons, by Ludwig Bemelmans (the *Madeline* books), proper old-school barmen who still make classic cocktails the right way (increasingly rare in NY despite this being the spiritual home of the cocktail), unobtrusive pianist *(BB)*
King Cole Bar [St Regis Hotel, 2 E 55th St]: Smooth civilised hotel bar, lots of polished dark wood and luxurious perimeter seating, very dimly lit so as to showcase splendid Maxfield Parrish mural of Old King Cole behind long bar, good cocktails and nibbles (the bloody mary may have been born here and still goes strong) *(BB)*
Minetta Tavern [113 Macdougal St, Greenwich Village]: Retro narrow tiled-floor 1930s bar with stools along counter, opening into back panelled dining area with italian food and italian landscape murals, good range of spirits, lots of nostalgic photographs and clippings recalling customers such as e e cummings, Ezra Pound and Lillian Hellman *(BB)*
White Horse [567 Hudson/W 11th St, West Village]: Classic unsmart bare-boards bar built 1880, where Dylan Thomas famously drank his last beer, with pictures of him and other habitués inc Jack Kerouac (*Village Voice* born here), good burgers *(BB)*
Whites [Winecellar Entry]: Low-beamed alehouse said to be town's oldest, very popular esp when there's live music, Hoegaarden, Smithwicks and Guinness on tap *(Darren Le Poidevin)*
McHughs [Queens Sq]: Extensively restored and extended (dates from 1711), with eclectic design in several linked rooms, comfortable leather chairs and settles around marble-top tables, friendly staff, local Whitewater Ale and Porter *(Darren Le Poidevin)*
Morning Star [Pottingers Entry]: Former coaching inn with large island bar, settles, mahogany stools at high tables, snug and side rooms, enjoyable food from enterprising burgers to fresh fish and steaks (even crocodile ones) *(Darren Le Poidevin)*

Special Interest Lists

PUBS WITH GOOD GARDENS

The pubs listed here have bigger or more beautiful gardens, grounds or terraces than are usual for their areas. Note that in a town or city this might be very much more modest than the sort of garden that would deserve a listing in the countryside.

BEDFORDSHIRE
Bletsoe, Falcon
Bolnhurst, Plough
Milton Bryan, Red Lion
Northill, Crown
Old Warden, Hare & Hounds
Riseley, Fox & Hounds

BERKSHIRE
Aldworth, Bell
Ashmore Green, Sun in the Wood
Frilsham, Pot Kiln
Holyport, Belgian Arms
Hurst, Green Man
Inkpen, Crown & Garter
Shinfield, Magpie & Parrot
White Waltham, Beehive
Winterbourne, Winterbourne Arms

BUCKINGHAMSHIRE
Bennett End, Three Horseshoes
Bovingdon Green, Royal Oak
Denham, Swan
Fingest, Chequers
Grove, Grove Lock
Hawridge Common, Full Moon
Hedgerley, White Horse
Lacey Green, Pink & Lily
Oving, Black Boy
Skirmett, Frog

CAMBRIDGESHIRE
Elton, Black Horse
Fowlmere, Chequers
Heydon, King William IV
Madingley, Three Horseshoes

CHESHIRE
Aldford, Grosvenor Arms
Bunbury, Dysart Arms
Haughton Moss, Nags Head
Macclesfield, Sutton Hall Hotel
Marbury, Swan

CORNWALL
Lostwithiel, Globe
St Kew, St Kew Inn
Tresco, New Inn

CUMBRIA
Bassenthwaite Lake, Pheasant
Bouth, White Hart
Ravenstonedale, Black Swan
Staveley, Eagle & Child

DERBYSHIRE
Hathersage, Plough
Melbourne, John Thompson
Woolley Moor, White Horse

DEVON
Avonwick, Turtley Corn Mill
Clayhidon, Merry Harriers
Clyst Hydon, Five Bells
Exeter, Imperial
Exminster, Turf Hotel
Haytor Vale, Rock
Newton Ferrers, Dolphin
Postbridge, Warren House
Poundsgate, Tavistock Inn
Sidbury, Hare & Hounds
Sidford, Blue Ball
Stokenham, Church House
Torbryan, Old Church House

DORSET
Chideock, George
Marshwood, Bottle
Nettlecombe, Marquis of Lorne
Osmington Mills, Smugglers
Plush, Brace of Pheasants
Shave Cross, Shave Cross Inn
Shroton, Cricketers

ESSEX
Fyfield, Queens Head
Great Henny, Henny Swan
Hastingwood, Rainbow & Dove
Margaretting Tye, White Hart
Mill Green, Viper
Peldon, Rose
Stock, Hoop

GLOUCESTERSHIRE
Blaisdon, Red Hart
Cheltenham, Royal Oak
Ewen, Wild Duck
Great Rissington, Lamb
Hinton Dyrham, Bull
Kilkenny, Kilkeney Inn
Nailsworth, Egypt Mill
Nether Westcote, Westcote Inn
North Nibley, New Inn
Northleach, Wheatsheaf
Upper Oddington, Horse & Groom

HAMPSHIRE
Bramdean, Fox
Bransgore, Three Tuns
Dundridge, Hampshire Bowman
Exton, Shoe
Houghton, Boot
Ovington, Bush
Steep, Harrow
Tichborne, Tichborne Arms

HEREFORDSHIRE
Aymestrey, Riverside Inn
Hoarwithy, New Harp
Sellack, Lough Pool
Ullingswick, Three Crowns
Woolhope, Butchers Arms

HERTFORDSHIRE
Ashwell, Three Tuns
Chapmore End, Woodman
Potters Crouch, Holly Bush
Preston, Red Lion

Sarratt, Cock
Willian, Fox

ISLE OF WIGHT
Hulverstone, Sun
Niton, Buddle
Shorwell, Crown

KENT
Biddenden, Three Chimneys
Bough Beech, Wheatsheaf
Boyden Gate, Gate Inn
Brookland, Woolpack
Groombridge, Crown
Newnham, George
Selling, Rose & Crown
Stowting, Tiger
Toys Hill, Fox & Hounds
Ulcombe, Pepper Box

LANCASHIRE
Whitewell, Inn at Whitewell

LEICESTERSHIRE AND RUTLAND
Barrowden, Exeter Arms
Exton, Fox & Hounds
Lyddington, Old White Hart
Peggs Green, New Inn
Stathern, Red Lion

LINCOLNSHIRE
Billingborough, Fortescue Arms
Coningsby, Lea Gate Inn
Lincoln, Victoria
Stamford, George of Stamford

NORFOLK
Brancaster Staithe, Jolly Sailors
Burnham Market, Hoste Arms
Burnham Thorpe, Lord Nelson
Itteringham, Walpole Arms
Ringstead, Gin Trap
Snettisham, Rose & Crown
Stow Bardolph, Hare Arms
Woodbastwick, Fur & Feather

NORTHAMPTONSHIRE
Bulwick, Queens Head
East Haddon, Red Lion
Farthingstone, Kings Arms
Slipton, Samuel Pepys
Wadenhoe, Kings Head

NORTHUMBRIA
Anick, Rat
Blanchland, Lord Crewe Arms
Diptonmill, Dipton Mill Inn
Greta Bridge, Morritt Arms
Haydon Bridge, General Havelock
Newburn, Keelman
Weldon Bridge, Anglers Arms

NOTTINGHAMSHIRE
Caunton, Caunton Beck
Colston Bassett, Martins Arms
Winthorpe, Lord Nelson

OXFORDSHIRE
Aston Tirrold, Chequers
Bloxham, Joiners Arms
Clifton, Duke of Cumberlands Head
Fyfield, White Hart
Highmoor, Rising Sun
Hook Norton, Gate Hangs High
Stanton St John, Star
Swerford, Masons Arms
Tadpole Bridge, Trout

SHROPSHIRE
Bishop's Castle, Castle Hotel, Three Tuns
Chetwynd Aston, Fox
Much Wenlock, Talbot

SOMERSET
Chiselborough, Cat Head
Croscombe, George
Litton, Kings Arms
Monksilver, Notley Arms
Shepton Montague, Montague Inn

STAFFORDSHIRE
Salt, Holly Bush
Stourton, Fox
Wrinehill, Hand & Trumpet

SUFFOLK
Hoxne, Swan
Lavenham, Angel
Laxfield, Kings Head
Long Melford, Black Lion
Newbourne, Fox
Rede, Plough
Rougham, Ravenwood Hall
Stoke-by-Nayland, Crown
Tuddenham, Fountain
Walberswick, Anchor, Bell
Waldringfield, Maybush
Westleton, Crown

SURREY
Charleshill, Donkey
Coldharbour, Plough
Compton, Withies
Eashing, Stag
Elstead, Mill at Elstead
Forest Green, Parrot
Leigh, Seven Stars
Lingfield, Hare & Hounds
Newdigate, Surrey Oaks
Thursley, Three Horseshoes
West End, Inn at West End
West Horsley, Barley Mow
Worplesdon, Jolly Farmer

SUSSEX
Alfriston, George
Balls Cross, Stag
Berwick, Cricketers Arms
Blackboys, Blackboys Inn
Byworth, Black Horse
Coolham, George & Dragon
Elsted, Three Horseshoes
Eridge Station, Huntsman
Ewhurst Green, White Dog
Fittleworth, Swan

Fletching, Griffin
Oving, Gribble Inn
Ringmer, Cock
Rye, Ypres Castle
Sidlesham, Crab & Lobster
Wineham, Royal Oak

WARWICKSHIRE
Ilmington, Howard Arms
Preston Bagot, Crabmill

WILTSHIRE
Brinkworth, Three Crowns
Chicksgrove, Compasses
Ebbesbourne Wake, Horseshoe
Horton, Bridge Inn
Kilmington, Red Lion
Lacock, George, Rising Sun
Norton, Vine Tree
Seend, Barge
Whitley, Pear Tree

WORCESTERSHIRE
Bretforton, Fleece
Eldersfield, Butchers Arms
Hanley Swan, Swan

YORKSHIRE
East Witton, Blue Lion
Egton Bridge, Horseshoe
Halifax, Shibden Mill
Heath, Kings Arms
South Dalton, Pipe & Glass
Sutton upon Derwent, St Vincent Arms

LONDON
Central London, Cross Keys
East London, Prospect of Whitby
North London, Spaniards Inn
South London, Crown & Greyhound,
    Founders Arms, Old Jail, Victoria
West London, Colton Arms, Dove,
    Windsor Castle

SCOTLAND
Badachro, Badachro Inn
Edinburgh, Starbank
Gairloch, Old Inn
Gatehouse of Fleet, Masonic Arms
Kilmahog, Lade
Kirkcudbright, Selkirk Arms
Meikleour, Meikleour Hotel
Thornhill, Lion & Unicorn

WALES
Colwyn Bay, Pen-y-Bryn
Crickhowell, Bear
Gresford, Pant-yr-Ochain
Llanfrynach, White Swan
Llangollen, Corn Mill
Mold, Glasfryn
Old Radnor, Harp
Raglan, Clytha Arms
Rosebush, Tafarn Sinc
Skenfrith, Bell
St Hilary, Bush
Ty'n-y-groes, Groes

CHANNEL ISLANDS
King's Mills, Fleur du Jardin
Rozel, Rozel

WATERSIDE PUBS
*The pubs listed here are right beside the sea,
a sizeable river, canal, lake or loch that
contributes significantly to their attraction.*

BEDFORDSHIRE
Bletsoe, Falcon

BUCKINGHAMSHIRE
Grove, Grove Lock

CAMBRIDGESHIRE
Peterborough, Charters
Sutton Gault, Anchor

CHESHIRE
Chester, Old Harkers Arms
Wrenbury, Dusty Miller

CORNWALL
Bodinnick, Old Ferry
Malpas, Heron
Mousehole, Ship
Mylor Bridge, Pandora
Polkerris, Rashleigh
Polperro, Blue Peter
Port Isaac, Port Gaverne Inn
Porthleven, Ship
Porthtowan, Blue
Tresco, New Inn

CUMBRIA
Staveley, Eagle & Child
Ulverston, Bay Horse

DERBYSHIRE
Hathersage, Plough

DEVON
Beesands, Cricket
Culmstock, Culm Valley
Exminster, Turf Hotel
Newton Ferrers, Dolphin
Noss Mayo, Ship
Torcross, Start Bay
Tuckenhay, Maltsters Arms

ESSEX
Burnham-on-Crouch, White Harte
Fyfield, Queens Head
Great Henny, Henny Swan

GLOUCESTERSHIRE
Ashleworth Quay, Boat

HAMPSHIRE
Exton, Shoe
Houghton, Boot
Ovington, Bush
Portsmouth, Old Customs House
Wherwell, Mayfly
Winchester, Willow Tree

HEREFORDSHIRE
Aymestrey, Riverside Inn

ISLE OF WIGHT
Bembridge, Crab & Lobster
Cowes, Folly
Seaview, Seaview Hotel
Ventnor, Spyglass

KENT
Oare, Shipwrights Arms

LANCASHIRE
Manchester, Dukes 92
Whitewell, Inn at Whitewell

NORFOLK
Brancaster Staithe, White Horse

NORTHAMPTONSHIRE
Wadenhoe, Kings Head

NORTHUMBRIA
Haydon Bridge, General Havelock
Newcastle upon Tyne, Cluny
Newton-by-the-Sea, Ship

OXFORDSHIRE
Godstow, Trout
Tadpole Bridge, Trout

SHROPSHIRE
Shrewsbury, Armoury

SOMERSET
Churchill, Crown
Portishead, Windmill

SUFFOLK
Aldeburgh, Cross Keys
Chelmondiston, Butt & Oyster
Nayland, Anchor
Southwold, Harbour Inn
Waldringfield, Maybush

SURREY
Eashing, Stag
Elstead, Mill at Elstead

SUSSEX
Bosham, Anchor Bleu

WILTSHIRE
Horton, Bridge Inn
Seend, Barge

WORCESTERSHIRE
Knightwick, Talbot

YORKSHIRE
Whitby, Duke of York

LONDON
East London, Grapes, Prospect of Whitby
South London, Cutty Sark, Founders Arms
West London, Bulls Head, Dove

SCOTLAND
Aboyne, Boat
Badachro, Badachro Inn
Edinburgh, Starbank
Elie, Ship
Gairloch, Old Inn
Isle of Whithorn, Steam Packet
Plockton, Plockton Hotel
Port Charlotte, Port Charlotte Hotel
Shieldaig, Tigh an Eilean Hotel
Stein, Stein Inn

WALES
Aberaeron, Harbourmaster
Abercych, Nags Head
Aberdovey, Penhelig Arms
Abergorlech, Black Lion
Cresswell Quay, Cresselly Arms
Llangollen, Corn Mill
Porth Dinllaen, Ty Coch
Red Wharf Bay, Ship
Skenfrith, Bell

CHANNEL ISLANDS
St Aubin, Old Court House Inn
St Ouens Bay, La Pulente

PUBS IN ATTRACTIVE SURROUNDINGS

These pubs are in unusually attractive or interesting places – lovely countryside, charming villages, occasionally notable town surroundings. Waterside pubs are listed again here only if their other surroundings are special, too.

BEDFORDSHIRE
Old Warden, Hare & Hounds

BERKSHIRE
Aldworth, Bell
Frilsham, Pot Kiln

BUCKINGHAMSHIRE
Bovingdon Green, Royal Oak
Hawridge Common, Full Moon
Skirmett, Frog
Turville, Bull & Butcher

CAMBRIDGESHIRE
Elton, Black Horse
Reach, Dyke's End

CHESHIRE
Barthomley, White Lion
Bunbury, Dysart Arms
Marbury, Swan
Willington, Boot

CORNWALL
Altarnun, Rising Sun
Blisland, Blisland Inn
Helston, Halzephron
Polperro, Blue Peter
Ruan Lanihorne, Kings Head
St Kew, St Kew Inn
Tresco, New Inn
Zennor, Tinners Arms

CUMBRIA
Askham, Punch Bowl
Bassenthwaite Lake, Pheasant
Bouth, White Hart
Broughton Mills, Blacksmiths Arms
Cartmel, Kings Arms
Chapel Stile, Wainwrights
Crosthwaite, Punch Bowl
Elterwater, Britannia
Hawkshead, Drunken Duck, Kings Arms
Hesket Newmarket, Old Crown
Ings, Watermill
Langdale, Old Dungeon Ghyll
Levens, Strickland Arms
Little Langdale, Three Shires
Loweswater, Kirkstile Inn
Mungrisdale, Mill Inn
Santon Bridge, Bridge Inn
Seathwaite, Newfield Inn
Stonethwaite, Langstrath
Threlkeld, Horse & Farrier
Ulverston, Bay Horse

DERBYSHIRE
Alderwasley, Bear
Brassington, Olde Gate
Foolow, Bulls Head
Hathersage, Plough, Scotsmans Pack
Hayfield, Lantern Pike
Kirk Ireton, Barley Mow
Ladybower Reservoir, Yorkshire Bridge
Litton, Red Lion
Monsal Head, Monsal Head Hotel
Over Haddon, Lathkil
Sheldon, Cock & Pullet
Woolley Moor, White Horse

DEVON
Blackawton, Normandy Arms
Branscombe, Fountain Head
Buckland Monachorum, Drake Manor
Culmstock, Culm Valley
Exminster, Turf Hotel
Haytor Vale, Rock
Holne, Church House
Horndon, Elephants Nest
Iddesleigh, Duke of York
Kingston, Dolphin
Meavy, Royal Oak
Molland, London
Peter Tavy, Peter Tavy Inn
Postbridge, Warren House
Rattery, Church House
Sandy Park, Sandy Park Inn
Widecombe, Rugglestone

DORSET
Marshwood, Bottle
Nettlecombe, Marquis of Lorne
Osmington Mills, Smugglers
Pamphill, Vine
Plush, Brace of Pheasants
Powerstock, Three Horseshoes
Worth Matravers, Square & Compass

ESSEX
Mill Green, Viper

GLOUCESTERSHIRE
Ashleworth Quay, Boat
Bisley, Bear
Bledington, Kings Head
Chedworth, Seven Tuns
Chipping Campden, Eight Bells
Coates, Tunnel House
Great Rissington, Lamb
Guiting Power, Hollow Bottom
Nailsworth, Weighbridge
Newland, Ostrich
North Nibley, New Inn
Northleach, Wheatsheaf
Sapperton, Bell

HAMPSHIRE
Crawley, Fox & Hounds
East Tytherley, Star
Fritham, Royal Oak
Hawkley, Hawkley Inn
Lymington, Kings Head
Ovington, Bush
Tichborne, Tichborne Arms

HEREFORDSHIRE
Aymestrey, Riverside Inn
Bringsty Common, Live & Let Live
Dorstone, Pandy
Hoarwithy, New Harp
Sellack, Lough Pool
Titley, Stagg
Walterstone, Carpenters Arms
Woolhope, Butchers Arms

HERTFORDSHIRE
Aldbury, Greyhound
Frithsden, Alford Arms
Sarratt, Cock

ISLE OF WIGHT
Hulverstone, Sun

KENT
Brookland, Woolpack
Groombridge, Crown
Newnham, George
Selling, Rose & Crown
Stowting, Tiger
Toys Hill, Fox & Hounds

LANCASHIRE
Bury, Lord Raglan
Denshaw, Rams Head
Tunstall, Lunesdale Arms
Uppermill, Church Inn
Whitewell, Inn at Whitewell

LEICESTERSHIRE AND RUTLAND
Barrowden, Exeter Arms
Exton, Fox & Hounds
Upper Hambleton, Finches Arms

LINCOLNSHIRE
Dry Doddington, Wheatsheaf

NORFOLK
Blakeney, White Horse
Blickling, Buckinghamshire Arms

Brancaster Staithe, Jolly Sailors
Burnham Market, Hoste Arms
Thornham, Lifeboat
Woodbastwick, Fur & Feather

NORTHUMBRIA
Barrasford, Barrasford Arms
Blanchland, Lord Crewe Arms
Diptonmill, Dipton Mill Inn
Great Whittington, Queens Head
Haltwhistle, Milecastle Inn
Langley on Tyne, Carts Bog Inn
Newton-by-the-Sea, Ship
Romaldkirk, Rose & Crown
Stannersburn, Pheasant
Wark, Battlesteads

NOTTINGHAMSHIRE
Halam, Waggon & Horses
Laxton, Dovecote

OXFORDSHIRE
Checkendon, Black Horse
Coleshill, Radnor Arms
Great Tew, Falkland Arms
Hailey, King William IV
Langford, Bell
Oxford, Turf Tavern
Swinbrook, Swan

SHROPSHIRE
Cardington, Royal Oak
Picklescott, Bottle & Glass

SOMERSET
Appley, Globe
Batcombe, Three Horseshoes
Blagdon, New Inn
Cranmore, Strode Arms
Luxborough, Royal Oak
Simonsbath, Exmoor Forest Inn
Tarr, Tarr Farm
Triscombe, Blue Ball
Wells, City Arms

STAFFORDSHIRE
Alstonefield, George
Stourton, Fox

SUFFOLK
Lavenham, Angel
Newbourne, Fox
Snape, Plough & Sail
Walberswick, Bell

SURREY
Cobham, Cricketers
Englefield Green, Fox & Hounds
Esher, Marneys
Forest Green, Parrot
Lingfield, Hare & Hounds

SUSSEX
Alfriston, George
Burpham, George & Dragon
Chilgrove, Royal Oak
Ditchling, Bull
Fletching, Griffin

Rye, Mermaid, Ypres Castle
Sidlesham, Crab & Lobster
Wineham, Royal Oak

WILTSHIRE
Axford, Red Lion
Castle Combe, Castle Inn
Donhead St Andrew, Forester
East Knoyle, Fox & Hounds
Ebbesbourne Wake, Horseshoe
Lacock, Rising Sun
Newton Tony, Malet Arms
Stourton, Spread Eagle

WORCESTERSHIRE
Eldersfield, Butchers Arms
Hanley Swan, Swan
Kidderminster, King & Castle
Knightwick, Talbot
Pensax, Bell

YORKSHIRE
Beck Hole, Birch Hall
Blakey Ridge, Lion
Bradfield, Strines Inn
Chapel le Dale, Hill Inn
Coxwold, Fauconberg Arms
Cray, White Lion
Downholme, Bolton Arms
East Witton, Blue Lion
Grinton, Bridge Inn
Halifax, Shibden Mill
Heath, Kings Arms
Langthwaite, Charles Bathurst
Lastingham, Blacksmiths Arms
Linton in Craven, Fountaine
Litton, Queens Arms
Lund, Wellington
Osmotherley, Golden Lion
Ripley, Boars Head
Robin Hood's Bay, Laurel
Roecliffe, Crown
Shelley, Three Acres
South Dalton, Pipe & Glass
Thornton Watlass, Buck
Wath in Nidderdale, Sportsmans Arms
Widdop, Pack Horse

LONDON
Central London, Olde Mitre
North London, Spaniards Inn
South London, Crown & Greyhound

SCOTLAND
Applecross, Applecross Inn
Gairloch, Old Inn
Kilberry, Kilberry Inn
Kilmahog, Lade
Kirk Yetholm, Border
Meikleour, Meikleour Hotel
Stein, Stein Inn

WALES
Abergorlech, Black Lion
Llanarmon Dyffryn Ceiriog, Hand
Llanberis, Pen-y-Gwryd
Old Radnor, Harp
Porth Dinllaen, Ty Coch

Red Wharf Bay, Ship
Rhyd-y-Meirch, Goose & Cuckoo

CHANNEL ISLANDS
St Brelade, Old Portelet Inn, Old Smugglers
St John, Les Fontaines

PUBS WITH GOOD VIEWS

*These pubs are listed for their particularly
good views, either from inside or from a
garden or terrace. Waterside pubs are listed
again here only if their view is exceptional in
its own right – not just a straightforward sea
view, for example.*

BUCKINGHAMSHIRE
Oving, Black Boy

CHESHIRE
Burwardsley, Pheasant
Langley, Hanging Gate
Willington, Boot

CORNWALL
Falmouth, 5 Degrees West
Ruan Lanihorne, Kings Head

CUMBRIA
Cartmel Fell, Masons Arms
Hawkshead, Drunken Duck
Langdale, Old Dungeon Ghyll
Loweswater, Kirkstile Inn
Mungrisdale, Mill Inn
Stonethwaite, Langstrath
Threlkeld, Horse & Farrier
Ulverston, Bay Horse

DERBYSHIRE
Alderwasley, Bear
Foolow, Bulls Head
Monsal Head, Monsal Head Hotel
Over Haddon, Lathkil

DEVON
Brixham, Maritime
Newton Ferrers, Dolphin
Portgate, Harris Arms
Postbridge, Warren House
Sidbury, Hare & Hounds

DORSET
Worth Matravers, Square & Compass

GLOUCESTERSHIRE
Cranham, Black Horse
Kilkenny, Kilkeney Inn
Sheepscombe, Butchers Arms
Woodchester, Ram

ISLE OF WIGHT
Bembridge, Crab & Lobster
Hulverstone, Sun
Niton, Buddle
Ventnor, Spyglass

KENT
Bodsham, Timber Batts
Tunbridge Wells, Beacon
Ulcombe, Pepper Box

LANCASHIRE
Bury, Lord Raglan
Uppermill, Church Inn

NORFOLK
Blickling, Buckinghamshire Arms
Brancaster Staithe, White Horse

NORTHUMBRIA
Anick, Rat
Barrasford, Barrasford Arms
Seahouses, Olde Ship

OXFORDSHIRE
Hailey, King William IV
Swerford, Masons Arms

SOMERSET
Portishead, Windmill
Shepton Montague, Montague Inn
Tarr, Tarr Farm

SUSSEX
Byworth, Black Horse
Elsted, Three Horseshoes
Fletching, Griffin
Icklesham, Queens Head
Rye, Ypres Castle

WILTSHIRE
Axford, Red Lion
Box, Quarrymans Arms
Donhead St Andrew, Forester
East Knoyle, Fox & Hounds
Lacock, Rising Sun
Semington, Lamb
Upper Chute, Cross Keys

WORCESTERSHIRE
Malvern, Nags Head
Pensax, Bell

YORKSHIRE
Blakey Ridge, Lion
Bradfield, Strines Inn
Downholme, Bolton Arms
Hartshead, Gray Ox
Kirkham, Stone Trough
Langthwaite, Charles Bathurst
Litton, Queens Arms
Shelley, Three Acres
Whitby, Duke of York

LONDON
South London, Founders Arms

SCOTLAND
Applecross, Applecross Inn
Badachro, Badachro Inn
Edinburgh, Starbank
Kilberry, Kilberry Inn
Port Charlotte, Port Charlotte Hotel
Shieldaig, Tigh an Eilean Hotel

Stein, Stein Inn
Weem, Ailean Chraggan

WALES
Aberdovey, Penhelig Arms
Colwyn Bay, Pen-y-Bryn
Llanberis, Pen-y-Gwryd
Llanferres, Druid
Llangollen, Corn Mill
Mold, Glasfryn
Old Radnor, Harp
Porth Dinllaen, Ty Coch
Rhyd-y-Meirch, Goose & Cuckoo
Ty'n-y-groes, Groes

CHANNEL ISLANDS
St Aubin, Old Court House Inn

PUBS IN INTERESTING BUILDINGS

*Pubs and inns are listed here for the particular
interest of their building – something really
out of the ordinary to look at, or occasionally
a building that has an outstandingly
interesting historical background.*

BUCKINGHAMSHIRE
Aylesbury, Kings Head
Forty Green, Royal Standard of England

DERBYSHIRE
Kirk Ireton, Barley Mow

DEVON
Dartmouth, Cherub
Rattery, Church House

HEREFORDSHIRE
Bringsty Common, Live & Let Live

LANCASHIRE
Liverpool, Philharmonic Dining Rooms

LINCOLNSHIRE
Stamford, George of Stamford

NORTHUMBRIA
Blanchland, Lord Crewe Arms
Newcastle upon Tyne, Crown Posada

NOTTINGHAMSHIRE
Nottingham, Olde Trip to Jerusalem

OXFORDSHIRE
Banbury, Reindeer
Fyfield, White Hart

SOMERSET
Norton St Philip, George

SUFFOLK
Laxfield, Kings Head

SURREY
Elstead, Mill at Elstead

SUSSEX
Rye, Mermaid

WILTSHIRE
Salisbury, Haunch of Venison

WORCESTERSHIRE
Bretforton, Fleece

YORKSHIRE
Hull, Olde White Harte

LONDON
Central London, Black Friar, Cittie of Yorke,
  Red Lion (SW1)
South London, George

SCOTLAND
Edinburgh, Café Royal, Guildford Arms

PUBS THAT BREW THEIR OWN BEER

*The pubs listed here brew their own beer on
the premises; many others not listed here
have beers brewed for them specially,
sometimes an individual recipe (but by a
separate brewer). We mention these in the
text.*

CAMBRIDGESHIRE
Peterborough, Brewery Tap

CUMBRIA
Cockermouth, Bitter End
Hawkshead, Drunken Duck
Hesket Newmarket, Old Crown
Ings, Watermill
Loweswater, Kirkstile Inn

DERBYSHIRE
Ashover, Old Poets Corner
Derby, Brunswick
Melbourne, John Thompson

DEVON
Branscombe, Fountain Head

HAMPSHIRE
Cheriton, Flower Pots

HEREFORDSHIRE
Hereford, Victory

KENT
Penshurst, Rock

LANCASHIRE
Bury, Lord Raglan
Manchester, Marble Arch
Uppermill, Church Inn
Wheelton, Dressers Arms

LEICESTERSHIRE AND RUTLAND
Barrowden, Exeter Arms
Oakham, Grainstore

LINCOLNSHIRE
South Witham, Blue Cow

NORFOLK
Binham, Chequers

NORTHUMBRIA
Diptonmill, Dipton Mill Inn
Newburn, Keelman

NOTTINGHAMSHIRE
Caythorpe, Black Horse
Nottingham, Fellows Morton & Clayton

SHROPSHIRE
Bishop's Castle, Six Bells, Three Tuns

STAFFORDSHIRE
Burton upon Trent, Burton Bridge Inn

SUFFOLK
Earl Soham, Victoria
South Elmham, St Peters Brewery

SURREY
Coldharbour, Plough

SUSSEX
Oving, Gribble Inn

WARWICKSHIRE
Netherton, Old Swan
Sedgley, Beacon

WORCESTERSHIRE
Knightwick, Talbot

YORKSHIRE
Cropton, New Inn
Goose Eye, Turkey
Linthwaite, Sair
Litton, Queens Arms
Sheffield, Fat Cat

SCOTLAND
Houston, Fox & Hounds
Kilmahog, Lade
Pitlochry, Moulin

WALES
Abercych, Nags Head
Llanddarog, White Hart

FOOD SERVED ALL DAY

We list here all the pubs that have told us they plan to serve food all day, even if it's only one day of the week. The individual entries for the pubs themselves show the actual details.

BEDFORDSHIRE
Bletsoe, Falcon
Northill, Crown

BERKSHIRE
Cookham Dean, Chequers
White Waltham, Beehive

BUCKINGHAMSHIRE
Dorney, Pineapple

Forty Green, Royal Standard of England
Grove, Grove Lock
Wooburn Common, Chequers

CAMBRIDGESHIRE
Elton, Black Horse
Peterborough, Brewery Tap

CHESHIRE
Aldford, Grosvenor Arms
Aston, Bhurtpore
Bunbury, Dysart Arms
Burleydam, Combermere Arms
Chester, Mill, Old Harkers Arms
Haughton Moss, Nags Head
Mobberley, Roebuck
Peover Heath, Dog
Plumley, Smoker
Prestbury, Legh Arms
Tarporley, Rising Sun
Willington, Boot

CORNWALL
Falmouth, 5 Degrees West
Mitchell, Plume of Feathers
Porthtowan, Blue
Watergate Bay, Beach Hut
Widemouth, Bay View

CUMBRIA
Cartmel Fell, Masons Arms
Elterwater, Britannia
Ings, Watermill
Keswick, Dog & Gun
Levens, Strickland Arms
Seathwaite, Newfield Inn

DERBYSHIRE
Alderwasley, Bear
Beeley, Devonshire Arms
Fenny Bentley, Coach & Horses
Hathersage, Plough
Hayfield, Lantern Pike, Royal
Litton, Red Lion
Monsal Head, Monsal Head Hotel
Monyash, Bulls Head

DEVON
Cockwood, Anchor
Drewsteignton, Drewe Arms
Exeter, Imperial
Iddesleigh, Duke of York
Nomansland, Mount Pleasant
Noss Mayo, Ship
Sidford, Blue Ball

DORSET
Langton Herring, Elm Tree
Osmington Mills, Smugglers

ESSEX
Fyfield, Queens Head
Paglesham, Punchbowl
Youngs End, Green Dragon

GLOUCESTERSHIRE
Almondsbury, Bowl
Brimpsfield, Golden Heart

Broad Campden, Bakers Arms
Cheltenham, Royal Oak
Dursley, Old Spot
Ewen, Wild Duck
Ford, Plough
Great Rissington, Lamb
Guiting Power, Hollow Bottom
Nailsworth, Weighbridge
Sheepscombe, Butchers Arms

HAMPSHIRE
Southsea, Wine Vaults

HEREFORDSHIRE
St Owen's Cross, New Inn

HERTFORDSHIRE
Ashwell, Three Tuns
Royston, Old Bull

ISLE OF WIGHT
Arreton, White Lion
Cowes, Folly
Hulverstone, Sun
Ningwood, Horse & Groom
Niton, Buddle
Shorwell, Crown

KENT
Bough Beech, Wheatsheaf
Brookland, Woolpack
Hollingbourne, Windmill
Langton Green, Hare
Shipbourne, Chaser
Stowting, Tiger
Tunbridge Wells, Beacon

LANCASHIRE
Bispham Green, Eagle & Child
Broughton, Plough at Eaves
Bury, Lord Raglan
Great Mitton, Three Fishes
Liverpool, Philharmonic Dining Rooms
Longridge, Derby Arms
Manchester, Marble Arch
Mellor, Devonshire Arms
Ribchester, White Bull
Waddington, Lower Buck
Wheatley Lane, Old Sparrow Hawk
Wheelton, Dressers Arms
Yealand Conyers, New Inn

LEICESTERSHIRE AND RUTLAND
Ab Kettleby, Sugar Loaf
Newton Burgoland, Belper Arms
Upper Hambleton, Finches Arms
Woodhouse Eaves, Wheatsheaf

LINCOLNSHIRE
South Witham, Blue Cow
Stamford, George of Stamford

NORFOLK
Blakeney, Kings Arms
Brancaster Staithe, Jolly Sailors
Larling, Angel
Morston, Anchor

NORTHAMPTONSHIRE
Oundle, Ship

NORTHUMBRIA
Carterway Heads, Manor House Inn
Great Whittington, Queens Head
Greta Bridge, Morritt Arms
New York, Shiremoor Farm
Newburn, Keelman
Stannington, Ridley Arms
Weldon Bridge, Anglers Arms

NOTTINGHAMSHIRE
Nottingham, Bell, Olde Trip to Jerusalem

OXFORDSHIRE
Godstow, Trout

SHROPSHIRE
Chetwynd Aston, Fox

SOMERSET
Oake, Royal Oak
Stanton Wick, Carpenters Arms
Wells, City Arms

STAFFORDSHIRE
Lichfield, Boat

SUFFOLK
Chelmondiston, Butt & Oyster
Newbourne, Fox
Snape, Plough & Sail
Stoke-by-Nayland, Crown
Waldringfield, Maybush

SURREY
Cobham, Cricketers
Worplesdon, Jolly Farmer

SUSSEX
Arlington, Old Oak
Horsham, Black Jug
Icklesham, Queens Head
Ringmer, Cock
Rye, Ypres Castle
Wilmington, Giants Rest

WILTSHIRE
Seend, Barge
Stourton, Spread Eagle

YORKSHIRE
Beck Hole, Birch Hall
Blakey Ridge, Lion
Elslack, Tempest Arms
Goose Eye, Turkey
Grinton, Bridge Inn
Ledsham, Chequers
Linton in Craven, Fountaine
Long Preston, Maypole

LONDON
Central London, Albert, Argyll Arms,
      Black Friar, Coopers Arms, Harp
South London, Crown & Greyhound,
      Cutty Sark, Fire Station, Victoria

WALES
Llandudno Junction, Queens Head
Monknash, Plough & Harrow
Shirenewton, Carpenters Arms
Tal-y-Cafn, Tal-y-Cafn Hotel

CHANNEL ISLANDS
St Brelade, Old Portelet Inn

PUBS CLOSE TO MOTORWAY JUNCTIONS

*The number at the start of each line is the
number of the junction. Detailed directions
are given in the main entry for each pub. In
this section, to help you find the pubs quickly
before you're past the junction, we give the
name of the chapter where you'll find the text.*

M1
13: Woburn, Birch (Beds) 3.5 miles
16: Nether Heyford, Olde Sun (Northants)
    1.8 miles
18: Crick, Red Lion (Northants) 1 mile;
    Kilsby, George (Northants) 2.6 miles

M3
3: West End, Inn at West End (Surrey)
    2.4 miles
5: Rotherwick, Falcon (Hants) 4 miles
9: Winchester, Willow Tree (Hants) 1 mile;
    Easton, Chestnut Horse (Hants)
    3.6 miles
10: Winchester, Black Boy (Hants) 1 mile

M4
7: Dorney, Pineapple (Bucks) 2.4 miles
9: Holyport, Belgian Arms (Berks) 1.5
    miles; Bray, Hinds Head (Berks) 1.75
    miles; Bray, Crown (Berks) 1.75 miles
11: Shinfield, Magpie & Parrot (Berks)
    2.6 miles
13: Winterbourne, Winterbourne Arms
    (Berks) 3.7 miles
15: Badbury, Bakers Arms (Wilts) 1 mile
17: Kington Langley, Hit or Miss (Wilts)
    2.1 miles; Norton, Vine Tree (Wilts)
    4 miles
18: Hinton Dyrham, Bull (Gloucs) 2.4 miles

M5
4: Holy Cross, Bell & Cross (Worcs) 4 miles
7: Kempsey, Walter de Cantelupe (Worcs)
    3.75 miles; Bredon, Fox & Hounds
    (Worcs) 4.5 miles
16: Almondsbury, Bowl (Gloucs) 1.25 miles
19: Portishead, Windmill (Somerset)
    3.7 miles; Clapton-in-Gordano, Black
    Horse (Somerset) 4 miles
26: Clayhidon, Merry Harriers (Devon)
    3.1 miles
30: Topsham, Bridge Inn (Devon)
    2.25 miles; Woodbury Salterton,
    Diggers Rest (Devon) 3.5 miles

M6
4: Shustoke, Griffin (Warwicks) 5 miles
T6: Lichfield, Boat (Staffs) 3.8 miles
16: Barthomley, White Lion (Cheshire)
    1 mile
19: Plumley, Smoker (Cheshire) 2.5 miles
32: Goosnargh, Horns (Lancs) 2.9 miles
33: Bay Horse, Bay Horse (Lancs) 1.2 miles
35: Yealand Conyers, New Inn (Lancs)
    3 miles
36: Levens, Strickland Arms (Cumbria)
    4 miles
40: Yanwath, Gate Inn (Cumbria) 2.25 miles;
    Askham, Punch Bowl (Cumbria)
    4.5 miles

M9
3: Linlithgow, Four Marys (Scotland)
    2 miles

M11
7: Hastingwood, Rainbow & Dove (Essex)
    0.25 miles
8: Birchanger, Three Willows (Essex)
    0.8 miles
9: Hinxton, Red Lion (Cambs) 2 miles
10: Thriplow, Green Man (Cambs) 3 miles

M20
8: Hollingbourne, Windmill (Kent) 1 mile
11: Stowting, Tiger (Kent) 3.7 miles

M25
4: South London, Bo-Peep (London)
    1.7 miles
10: Cobham, Plough (Surrey) 3.2 miles;
    Cobham, Cricketers (Surrey) 3.75 miles
16: Denham, Swan (Bucks) 0.75 miles
18: Chenies, Red Lion (Bucks) 2 miles;
    Flaunden, Bricklayers Arms (Herts)
    4 miles
21A: Potters Crouch, Holly Bush (Herts)
    2.3 miles

M27
1: Fritham, Royal Oak (Hants) 4 miles

M40
2: Hedgerley, White Horse (Bucks)
    2.4 miles; Forty Green, Royal Standard
    of England (Bucks) 3.5 miles
6: Lewknor, Olde Leathern Bottel (Oxon)
    0.5 miles; Kingston Blount, Cherry Tree
    (Oxon) 1.9 miles; Cuxham, Half Moon
    (Oxon) 4 miles
12: Gaydon, Malt Shovel (Warwicks)
    0.9 miles

M48
1: Littleton-upon-Severn, White Hart
    (Gloucs) 3.5 miles

M50
1: Baughton, Jockey (Worcs) 4 miles
3: Upton Bishop, Moody Cow (Herefs)
    2 miles

M53
3: Barnston, Fox & Hounds (Lancs) 3 miles

M55
1: Broughton, Plough at Eaves (Lancs)
3.25 miles

M61
8: Wheelton, Dressers Arms (Lancs)
2.1 miles

M62
22: Denshaw, Rams Head (Lancs) 2 miles
25: Hartshead, Gray Ox (Yorks) 3.5 miles

M65
13: Fence, Fence Gate (Lancs) 2.6 miles

M66
1: Bury, Lord Raglan (Lancs) 2 miles

Report Forms

Please report to us: you can use the cut-out forms on the following pages, the card in the middle of the book, or just plain paper – whichever's easiest for you, or you can email us at **feedback@thegoodpubguide.co.uk**. We need to know what you think of the pubs in this edition. We need to know about other pubs worthy of inclusion. We need to know about ones that should not be included. And we need to know that vital factor – how good the landlord or landlady is.

The atmosphere and character of the pub are the most important features – why it would, or would not, appeal to strangers, so please try to describe what is special about it. In particular, we can't consider including a pub in the Lucky Dip section unless we know something about what it looks like inside, so that we can describe it to other readers. And obviously with existing entries, we need to know about any changes in décor and furnishings, too. But the bar food and the drink are also important – please tell us about them.

If the food is really quite outstanding, tick the FOOD AWARD box on the form, and tell us about the special quality that makes it stand out – the more detail, the better. And if you have stayed there, tell us about the standard of accommodation – whether it was comfortable, pleasant, good value for money. Again, if the pub or inn is worth special attention as a place to stay, tick the PLACE-TO-STAY AWARD box.

If you're in a position to gauge a pub's suitability or otherwise for **disabled people**, do please tell us about that.

Please try to gauge whether a pub should be a main entry, or is best as a Lucky Dip (and tick the relevant box). In general, main entries need qualities that would make it worth other readers' while to travel some distance to them; Lucky Dips are the pubs that are worth knowing about if you are nearby. But if a pub is an entirely new recommendation, the Lucky Dip may be the best place for it to start its career in the *Guide* – to encourage other readers to report on it.

The more detail you can put into your description of a Lucky Dip pub that's only scantily described in the current edition (or not in at all), the better. A description of its character and even furnishings is a tremendous boon.

It helps enormously if you can give the full address for any new pub – one not yet a main entry, or without a full address in the Lucky Dip sections. In a town, we need the street name; in the country, if it's hard to find, we need directions. Even better for us is the post code. If we can't find out a pub's post code, we no longer include it in the *Guide* – and the Post Office directories we use will not yet have caught up with new pubs, or ones which have changed their names. With any pub, it always helps to let us know about prices of food (and bedrooms, if there are any), and about any lunchtimes or evenings when food is not served. We'd also like to have your views on drinks quality – beer, wine, cider and so forth, even coffee and tea; and do let us know about bedrooms.

If you know that a Lucky Dip pub is open all day (or even late into the afternoon), please tell us – preferably saying which days.

When you go to a pub, don't tell them you're a reporter for the *Good Pub Guide*; we do make clear that all inspections are anonymous, and if you declare yourself as a reporter you risk getting special treatment – for better or for worse!

Sometimes pubs are dropped from the main entries simply because very few readers have written to us about them – and of course there's a risk that people may not write if they find the pub exactly as described in the entry. You can use the forms at the front of the batch of report forms just to list pubs you've been to, found as described, and can recommend.

When you write to The Good Pub Guide, FREEPOST TN1569, WADHURST, East Sussex TN5 7BR, you don't need a stamp in the UK. We'll gladly send you more forms (free) if you wish.

Though we try to answer all letters, please understand if there's a delay (particularly in summer, our busiest period). We now edit and inspect throughout the year, so reports are valuable at any time. Obviously it's most useful of all if you write soon after a pub visit, while everything's fresh in your mind, rather than storing things up for a later batch.

We'll assume we can print your name or initials as a recommender unless you tell us otherwise.

I have been to the following pubs in *The Good Pub Guide 2009* in the last few months, found them as described, and confirm that they deserve continued inclusion:

Continued overleaf

PLEASE GIVE YOUR NAME AND ADDRESS ON THE BACK OF THIS FORM

Pubs visited continued...

By returning this form, you consent to the collection, recording and use of the information you submit, by The Random House Group Ltd. Any personal details which you provide from which we can identify you are held and processed in accordance with the Data Protection Act 1998 and will not be passed on to any third parties.

The Random House Group Ltd may wish to send you further information on their associated products. Please tick box if you do not wish to receive any such information.

Your own name and address *(block capitals please)*

Postcode

In returning this form I confirm my agreement that the information I provide may be used by The Random House Group Ltd, its assignees and/or licensees in any media or medium whatsoever.

Please return to
The Good Pub Guide,
FREEPOST TN1569,
WADHURST,
East Sussex
TN5 7BR

IF YOU PREFER, YOU CAN SEND US REPORTS
BY EMAIL:
feedback@thegoodpubguide.co.uk